1973 BRITANNICA BOOK OF THE YEAR

ENCYCLOPÆDIA BRITANNICA, INC.

WILLIAM BENTON, Publisher

Chicago, Toronto, London, Geneva, Sydney, Tokyo, Manila, Johannesburg, Seoul

Library of Congress Catalog Number: 38–12082
International Standard Book Number: 0–85229–282–1

BRITANNICA BOOK OF THE YEAR

(Trademark Reg. U.S. Pat. Off.)
Printed in U.S.A.

THE UNIVERSITY OF CHICAGO

The Britannica Book of the Year is published with the editorial advice of the faculties of The University of Chicago

Contents

Editorial Staff

Editor in Chief: MICHEL SILVA
Administrative Editor/Yearbooks: NELLIE L. GIFFORD
Editors: DAPHNE DAUME; J. E. DAVIS, London
Classification Advisers: A. G. Armstrong, Morton D. Bogdonoff, M.D., Jess Cook, Jr., Miroslav Kriz, John Kerr Rose, Harvey Sherman
Copy Editors: Judy Booth, David Calhoun, Vanessa Clarke, Ray Dennerstein, R. M. Goodwin, Mary Alice Molloy, Dorothy M. Partington, Judy Fagelston
Consulting Editor: Jacques Havet, Paris
Latin America Editor: César A. Ramos, Mexico City
Art Director: Will Gallagher
Associate Art Director: Cynthia Peterson
Picture Staff: James Sween, Senior Editor; Barbara Forlenza; Elisabeth West, Eve French, London
Layout Artist: Mark Cowans
Art Staff: Martina Daker, Miguel Rodriguez
Geography Editor: Frank J. Sutley
Assistant Geography Editor: Olga A. Titelbaum
Geography Staff: William A. Cleveland, Supervisor; Suzanne Holstein, William Johnson, Gerald E. Keefe, Charlene R. Neidlinger, Marino P. PeBenito, Joseph R. Sturgis. Copy Correspondent: Naomi Gralnek
Editorial Production Manager: J. Thomas Beatty
Production Coordinator: Lorene Lawson
Assistant Coordinators: Barbara W. Cleary, Ruth Passin
Staff: John Atkinson, Necia Brown, Charles Cegielski, Rama Deva, Gerald M. Fisher, Barbara Wescott Hurd, Marilyn Klein, Lawrence Kowalski, Lila H. Morrow, Richard O'Connor, Susan Recknagel, Julian Ronning, Madolynn Scheel, Linda G. H. Schmidt, Elliott Major Singer, Carol Kalata Smith, Cheryl M. Trobiani, Valerie Walker, Penne L. Weber, Anita K. Wolff
Copy Control: Felicité Buhl, Supervisor; Mary K. Finley, Recorder; Shirley Richardson; Barbara Chandler, Pat Woodgate, London
Index Staff: Frances E. Latham, Supervisor; Virginia Palmer, Assistant Supervisor; Gladys Berman, Grace R. Lord, Rosalba Rueda
Editorial Assignments: Barbara Deloney, Allena McCorvey
Editorial Assistant: Sara jo Schwartz
Executive Vice-President Editorial, Encyclopædia Britannica, Inc.: HOWARD L. GOODKIND

I think, therefore I am

PHOTOGRAPHS BY STAN WAYMAN

I think, therefore I am. *Cogito ergo sum*—the phrase the world identifies with the great 17th-century philosopher René Descartes. What a simple yet eloquent reason for existence!

A great deal of discussion and argument surrounded Descartes in his time and in the centuries since. He modified his first great published work for fear he would suffer the fate of Galileo at the hands of the papacy. Historians, philosophers, thinkers—whoever—have had centuries to argue over Descartes, whose latinized name has given the adjective Cartesian to the language.

As publisher of *Britannica Book of the Year* nothing would please me more than to know that within this 1973 edition of the yearbook was a body of thought over which people would argue for centuries to come. I am speaking of the feature section of this edition, which deals provocatively with the subject of behaviour and behaviourism, delving into the questions of how rapidly developing technology has affected and will affect our behaviour. *Cogito ergo sum*—the ideas put forth by the authors of the five articles that make up this year's feature section (totaling 40,000 words) stirred lively arguments among the editors of *Britannica*—Do they or do they not contain ideas for history? Will they be an important part of our future? Those of us involved in the discussions want to share our own special excitement with you so that you will participate in it—over the new ideas of today's frontier of scholarship.

The yearbook feature section, as it has evolved through the years, deals with the events and ideas that present themselves with the urgency of current history. Unlike the scholars who have the time to bring calm certainty to the pages of the *Encyclopædia Britannica* itself, the independent minds that come together in the yearbook feature section must struggle to see the future through the fire and smoke of the present. The authors have given their highly independent interpretations to urgent problems of the '70s: human consequences arising from technology—man's own tools reacting on man. T George Harris, editor in chief of *Psychology Today,* postulates the challenge of a new time in his article, "Era of Conscious Action." Peter F. Drucker, the famed critic of management, and an author and educator, writes about the "Rise of the Knowledge Worker." Clare Boothe Luce describes the plight of women in her brilliant article, "Woman: A Technological Castaway." Industrialist Donald N. Frey writes about the necessity for controlling technology in his article, "Technology Control; A New Level of Choice."

The fifth and final article, by James V. McConnell, professor of psychology at the University of Michigan and a well-known behaviourist, deals with behaviour modification, a subject of raging controversy within the social science community. McConnell argues that devices for behaviour modification offer the first, best chance for man to control his own destiny. But several of *Britannica*'s editors find in McConnell too easy an acceptance of the ideas of Harvard's B. F. Skinner. Several had comments not only on McConnell but on others of the group as well. Philosopher Mortimer J. Adler had this to say, and I feel he is worth quoting at length:

> McConnell's factual description of the case of Meatball McClannahan is interesting and instructive; and it would be interesting and instructive without any of the superstructure of so-called behavioristic theory or any of the claims that McConnell makes for it, none of which is supported by the case at hand. The case illustrates what is involved in breaking a bad habit and replacing it with a good habit. This is a problem that moralists have dealt with from the beginning of Western thought. Good habits are virtues and bad habits are vices, and the moral problem is how to form the one and eliminate the other. Aristotle dealt with this subject at some length in his "Ethics." He was concerned with intemperance as a bad habit, and he offers some suggestions about how to break such bad habits. He knew, for example, that only by restraining one's self from acting in accordance with a bad habit, and in addition, making the effort to act in a manner contrary to the bad habit, could the bad habit be broken and a good one be formed to replace it. He didn't think this was easy to do; and he never supposed that anyone could do it just by willing it. No one was ever fool enough to say that. He did know that rewards and punishments had some effect upon the formation of habits, and favored rewards in certain cases, and punishments, in others. The generalization that the carrot is better than the stick was not a discovery of B. F. Skinner. It was known for centuries; but no one ever said that it was always better than the stick in dealing with human beings, because no one knows that to be true. For some individuals, the stick is better; for others the carrot. Which is better depends upon a great many factors in the individual's temperament and experience.

For the authors, the irony is that technology raises more questions than it answers; indeed, it forces individuals and societies to behave differently—to make choices in the matter of living that once were left to habit, tradition, accident, or Providence.

Charles Van Doren, another of our editors, commented on the article by the gifted Clare Boothe Luce as well. "I am apparently that rare human being," wrote Van Doren, "a man who unqualifiedly approves of Woman's Lib. I'm sure there are some Woman's Libbers who are unpleasant in one way or another. I also know a lot of unpleasant, angry, aggressive, impossible men. I'm more interested in woman's revolutionary crusade. I'm all for it. I really mean all for it. The subjugation of women may have made some kind of sense—at least for the men—five thousand years ago. For the past two centuries it hasn't made much sense, and today it makes no sense at all. Mrs. Luce gives the reasons for that statement much better than I could."

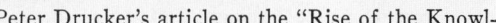

Peter Drucker's article on the "Rise of the Knowledge Worker" raised hackles among many of my friends in education. The chairman of *Britannica*'s Board of Editors and my colleague of 50 years, Robert M. Hutchins, responded to the Drucker piece in this way:

> Drucker defines the knowledge worker as the educated man or woman whose labour involves the use of bookish information. The first example offered is startling. It is the cashier in a cafeteria. Her work is said to require "education—systematic mental training—instead of exposure to experience." My limited observation of cashiers in cafeterias leads me to suspect that their work requires nothing but the ability to see and to count. The object of industry is to get along without people, and this is true even in service industries. There are no waiters in cafeterias, no laundresses in laundromats, and no elevator operators in elevators. No occupation is immune from technological change. Hence knowledge of how to do things—Drucker seems to depreciate any other kind—has an insubstantial, ephemeral quality suggesting that such knowledge is best acquired on the job, when the need for the knowledge is evident and where the most recent knowledge is available. It is false to suppose that because we are living in a highly technical age everybody has to be technically trained in school. The mass of the work force may require *for its work* less technical skill rather than more. We should use education and knowledge not as a means to prosperity and power of the individual and the state but as the process by which we may realize our potential as human beings and as self-governing citizens of a democracy.

So the discussions went at the editorial forum that is *Encyclopædia Britannica:* An open debate, as it were, on the ideas, predictions, and theories of the present and the future presented in the 1973 yearbook feature section. Descartes, as I pointed out, modified his published work—and therefore diluted its immediate impact—out of fear. Other great thinkers, philosophers, and writers have suffered at the hands of people and organizations—long before Descartes and many times since. There are still places in the world where the free expression of ideas is a perilous venture. But there came a time in the history of people when we began to understand the worth of new ideas, of thinking, of designing new worlds, of listening to those who would tell us what our own future should or would be like.

The idea that man should have the right to freedom of speech, freedom of the press, and freedom of religion had its greatest expression in the American experience: the Bill of Rights. The bulwark of democracy has been free expression of ideas and free public education. As owner of perhaps the largest book publishing concern in the world, I seek to preserve those rights, not only for myself but for all people, to see that new ideas are given a chance to breathe, to see that they get the opportunity to stand the test of exposure and time.

You as readers, as owners of *Encyclopædia Britannica* and of the *Book of the Year,* which comes to you each year, are just as duty-bound to acquire knowledge—knowledge of what is past, knowledge of what is the present, and knowledge of the future. Being aware—the key to conducting our lives—involves learning, the acquisition of knowledge, and exposing ourselves to ideas on the frontiers of scholarship and learning. That is the only way a people, a civilization, can be sure of preserving the rights and privileges it has. Only an informed people can act intelligently to make the correct choices technology is now laying before them. When we are able, when we do choose for ourselves correctly, then no government can in the long run abridge, erode, or take away the freedoms we love but often take too much for granted.

Read not only the ideas presented in the feature section of this yearbook, but examine the events of 1972 that are carefully reported to you by our editors and correspondents from all over the world. Let the events, the ideas, and the experiences of the world on the pages of the yearbook stir your mind, let them inform you and help you to greater understanding of yourself and the peoples of all the world.

Wm Benton

"Britannica Book of the Year" feature article authors (top to bottom): T George Harris, Peter F. Drucker, Clare Boothe Luce, Donald N. Frey, and James V. McConnell.

PHOTOGRAPHS BY (FROM TOP): "PSYCHOLOGY TODAY"; FLAG FOTOGRAFF; ALMA MCGOLDRICK; MICHEL SILVA; UNIVERSITY OF MICHIGAN NEWS SERVICE

ERA OF CONSCIOUS ACTION

by T George Harris

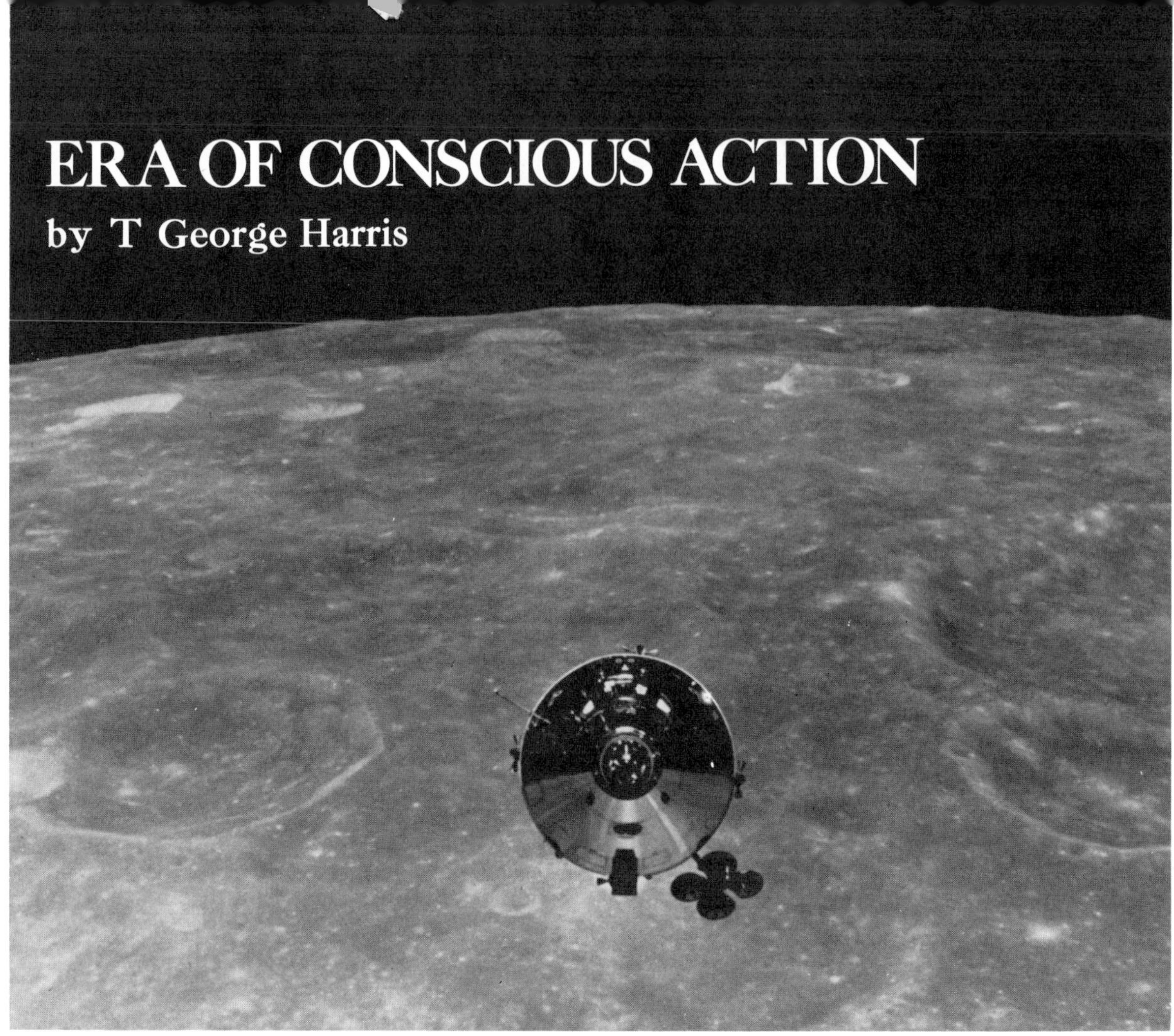

COURTESY, NASA

The industrial world, East and West, came into 1973, and moved toward the final turn of the 20th century, with its first serious reservations about industrialism itself. Air pollution and the environment provided a way of talking about specific fears, but the uncertainty was deeper and more general.

Caution dominated the thoughts of U.S. voters, regardless of party ties, in the 1972 presidential race. In the major financial centres, brokers who usually find an explanation for every up or down in the stock market went through seizures of head scratching. Governments and corporations showed uncommon confusion—not just conflict—over their future budgets, programs, and products. The habits of the postwar world, many found, did not quite fit the times.

Much of the doubt focused on America's advanced economy. "The United States is disintegrating," wrote Yonosuke Nagai in an article published by many of the world's newspapers in May 1972. Nagai had been warning of U.S. troubles for two years, but now his analysis struck a convincing chord with editors and political scientists.

As Japan's leading expert on American affairs, Nagai pointed to sharp conflicts beyond the recent years of race riots, student protest, radical demands, generational war over drug use, bombings, bitter liberation movements—and, more ominously, to the reactive rage stirred by these disorders. The bonds that hold a society together, he argued, are now being replaced by pressures that tear it apart.

Nagai did not contend that such troubles are unique to the U.S. He identified divisive forces that are characteristic of industrial society's new stage. TV, the computer, and other communications technologies short-circuit traditional social networks without building new ones; they heighten conflict more than understanding; they build expectations faster than growth can meet them. Large technological systems, even superhighways and cars, affect so many people as to raise conflicts of interest that existing private and public decision machinery is not prepared to handle.

Even the tidy fabric of Japanese society is beginning to unravel with affluence, Nagai pointed out, and his analysis suggests that disintegration is a worldwide trend.

Decision Replaces Tradition. Many other social scientists view the relative peace of 1972 as anything but permanent. Their probes into the human condition generally point at a fundamental change in the relationship between man and his environment. The rise of massive technology through the physical sciences has suddenly shifted the balance of power between man and the rest of nature.

Man won; he achieved his ancient ambition to hold complete dominion over nature. He thereby gained the power—and thus the necessity—to make conscious de-

---

T George Harris is editor in chief of Psychology Today *magazine.*

cisions in matters once left to chance, nature, tradition, habit, Providence, or his own unconscious.

The consequences are basic. With his new tools, man has the power to foul the biggest river, defoliate the forest, and smother the fields with asphalt. With pharmacology he gains the chemical means to upset nature's delicate balances in plant and animal life, as well as drugs for control of health and for manipulation of mental outlook. He invents his own physical and social world, internal and external.

Routine use of such implements brings unexpected results. For instance, modern medicine has reduced the death rate enough to set off the population explosion that now forces each nation to search for means to avoid overloading its piece of planet.

Though this threat has been talked about for several years, it became serious business by late 1972. In one of the year's widely debated documents, *The Limits to Growth,* a group of the world's leading scientists and businessmen soberly confronted the new situation. (*See* ENVIRONMENT.) It inverts assumptions that have been true since the Industrial Revolution. After philosopher Adam Smith showed how nations create new wealth for more people by expanding their productive power, both entrepreneurial and Communist societies based all policy on a simple belief in the benefits of unlimited economic expansion.

But crude growthmanship now has a question mark over it. In *The Transformation,* California's George B. Leonard showed that if electrical power consumption continued to rise at the present rate, generators would by 2069 throw off enough extra heat to make the U.S. landscape simmer.

Tools of Identity. Such technological power shifts the emphasis away from technology itself toward questions about the behaviour of the men who use it. When individual and collective action have a constant and perhaps final impact upon everyone, then the need to understand the causes of human behaviour becomes urgent. It is no surprise that psychology, anthropology, and the other behaviour disciplines have lately become the core of liberal education in the U.S. By 1977 almost a third of all U.S. university students will be taking degrees in the social sciences. For them the proper business of mankind is now the study of man.

The environmental debate, however, only highlights the more pervasive change that unsettles most societies. In every part of life, men and women must make more and more conscious choices in matters that were once accepted as given.

In politics, government must now use its fiscal and monetary instruments to control the level of economic activity in the society; on the macro level, at least, such deliberate intervention repeals what were once called laws of supply and demand. And in the international monetary system the creation of new central bank credits—Special Drawing Rights, or "paper gold"—has provided the community of nations with instruments to hold down, or at least delay, the trade wars that traditionally let loose the poison of nationalism.

In business, managers must now supervise the design of entire new product systems, create distribution networks, and study consumer behaviour in entirely new markets within a few months; rather than spend their lives learning to follow the rules of a traditional industry, they must consciously invent the next business, or lose out.

Even in private life, the identity crisis has become the typical ailment of educated affluents—precisely because they must choose among the many roles and identities that are available to them. Harvard psychoanalyst Erik Erikson has shown that while the identity crisis is acute among teen-agers, this ultimate decision about the self continues to burden men on through middle age.

Before exploring the outcome of such forced decisions, private as well as public, it is useful to consider the overall result. As the 18th century was called the Age of Reason, the late 20th century opens the Era of Conscious Action. It might be called the age of consciousness—because of the effort to look deeper into men's motives—but the phenomenon runs well beyond intellectual limits into the everyday world where people work for a living.

In this 1973 *Britannica Book of the Year,* four very independent minds join me in an effort to define the era of conscious action and its meaning to the individual. Taken as a whole, their thought provides the first systematic report on the distinctive pressures now building up:

- Peter F. Drucker describes the "Rise of the Knowledge Worker," the new majority in the work force and in U.S. politics. Rather than rely on skill, as workers have for 7,000 years, knowledge labourers learn their jobs through formal education. This new work situation strains all our working institutions and changes the meaning and nature of knowledge—into a form of energy and wealth.

Result: Instead of following their fathers, or standard apprentice routes, young workers now consciously select areas of knowledge in school, then make choices among many jobs all through life. Rather than treat work as an evil necessary for survival, millions more search for fulfilling jobs to answer the existential question: What am I doing here?

- Clare Boothe Luce, a liberated woman before the movement started, uses her acid pen on men. Their mechanization of domestic duties—through prepackaged food, home appliances, diaper services, etc., etc.—has destroyed the worth of the role once fulfilled by women. With the population explosion even motherhood has lost its social support. Now, to find their identity as worthwhile individuals, Luce insists, women must and will force their way into the decisive roles long reserved for men only.

Result: Luce's argument, backed up by her thorough study of recent psychological research on women, provides a major example of technology's impact upon human behaviour, in this case on the majority sex. After 1956 women filled three out of every five new jobs in the U.S. work force, often as white collar menials. So the new feminist movement devotes its energy, as well as its agony, to the conscious search for a redefinition of the person who happens to be born female.

- Donald N. Frey, sophisticated executive in technology companies, defines the need for government regulation of technology. Now that the car population

ENRICO NATALI—RAPHO GUILLUMETTE

"The nuclear family . . . too fragile to hold its own against the giant institutions"?

overloads the air's absorbing capacity, government must set antipollution standards for all cars. Now that computers can keep personal data on everybody, the question of privacy becomes a civil rights issue. Wherever the private decisions intrude upon public interest, the politics of technology brings on complex bargaining about cost, feasibility, and trade-offs.

Result: Large-scale technology forces the society into higher levels of conscious action. Private decisions become public. Decisions about subsystems have to be considered in the context of the larger systems to be affected.

• James V. McConnell, behaviour-modification psychologist, cuts through the terrifying doubts raised by the newest brand of technology—that deliberately designed to manipulate human behaviour. In "Feedback, Fat, and Freedom" he uses the research on an everyday problem—overeating—to argue that the traditional idea of freedom has always left most people functioning as unconscious slaves, controlled against their wishes by others and by their own pretentions about free will. Only if they accept the limits on their freedom, he points out, can they design their own environment to make it reward them for what they want to do.

Result: The technological threat to human dignity raises fundamental new questions about the nature of freedom and control. But by humble analysis of his own behaviour, making himself conscious of the forces that manipulate him, man gains his first, best chance to control his own destiny.

In this body of articles, the demands of the '70s come into useful focus. Decades of more or less accidental actions, of economic development within 19th-century institutions, have brought the industrial world into a time burdened with decisions. The present lack of confidence does not indicate a failure of nerves that once were reliable; it shows a reasonable uncertainty on the part of men and women who sense, however vaguely, that the demands upon them are of a different character from those known before. If each generation must sew its own seam, this new one has just now got hold of the cloth.

Gone are the Savage '60s, with their bombs and apocalyptic panic, but neither the causes of those protests nor the demands they made upon the future have gone up in smoke. In the wake of that vivid period, its meaning comes much clearer. Its self-righteous criticisms of existing society made no sense unless there was an implicit belief that things could be better. And the long tolerance of disorder, often calculated violence, can be explained only if a large body of opinion shared at least part of this belief.

So the period of protest made visible a new set of personal and public aspirations. They are, by comparison with the past, remarkably ambitious, even gaudy. It's as if some idiot had raised the ante on what it takes to be a full person, or a decent society, and the rest of the culture adopted the agenda as normal without noticing the change.

Bloodshed over Schools. Even the aspirations that seem to be traditional have changed their character, often by being extended to a much larger portion of the population. Education, for instance, has long been talked about as the touchstone for mobility in a democratic society. But until recently most students went to college to confirm the social status of the family. Except for a few lower-class mobiles, boys who went to college before World War II could properly settle for a gentleman's C. The daughters of wealth and class went off to join the sororities and find, in class-bound institutions, suitable husbands to perpetuate the family role. Only the drudges, and a few interested in professional scholarship, took seriously to the business of learning.

Today's assumption is that everybody goes to college to learn. The campus protest of the '60s began as a demand for improved education that relates the classroom to the rest of life. Its later phases concentrated on the central role of the university as the critical institution in a knowledge-based economy. The protest died in the '70s only when the majority of students sensed that public anger would, if demonstrations continued, lead not to reform of higher education but to the shutdown of many campuses.

Basic student faith in the university continued high throughout the campus struggles. Sociologist Jeffrey K. Hadden of the University of Virginia discovered, in a national survey of 1969's college seniors, that while many were protective of radical leaders—then attacking university administrators—an overwhelming student majority still had an uncompromising commitment to their local campus. More recently, the Carnegie Commission's massive study of higher education, led by economist Clark Kerr, largely confirms the belief that access to knowledge is now a universal need. Otherwise, most of the civil disorders of the last 20 years would not have been related, directly or indirectly, to schools.

Black Light. The aspirations of black Americans have constantly set the pattern for the dominant whites. In their fight to break out of institutionalized racism, they have forced a conscious reexamination of public schools, business practices, the welfare state, IQ tests, manners, family relations, higher education, and the political parties themselves. If the U.S. survives as a vital influence in the world, perhaps once again as a promising model, its major debt will be to its black citizens. By proving which institutions have become moribund—something a society seldom learns until too late—they destroyed the complacency of a fat nation and got the repair work started.

The self-criticism came down to hard specifics by 1972. In *Setting National Priorities,* the Brookings Institution did a scathing review of the failures in governmental programs. Columbia University sociologist Amitai Etzioni followed up by comparing the program-making process with the rain dances done by witch doctors, the shamans in primitive tribes. Shamanistic politicians, he explained, chant about social problems, dance around building alphabet agencies and keep talking about the work being done—but seldom get around to showing progress or failure on the social problem. Such criticism pushed social scientists, under the leadership of the Russell Sage Foundation, into the first nationwide campaign to develop precise ways to evaluate the effectiveness of any program. If they cannot find measurable benefits from a program, many agreed, it has to be considered shamanistic.

To Cherish Differences. The black movement's more specific impact has to do with the tendency of most cultures to standardize around one life-style. In the process of acculturization, the individual who does not fit the mold learns to act, dress, think, and look like the approved model—in the U.S. like the white Anglo-Saxon male. Recent research shows that European immigrants maintained more of their previous culture than they knew, and often migrated together to the suburbs, but the acculturization ideal made such behaviour suspect.

This conformity route was not open to black Americans; nor did they, after 300 years in the country, care to mimic the techniques of later arrivals. They chose instead to affirm their distinctive ethnic background—black is beautiful—and demand that its merit be recognized. While militant leaders were often attacked as advocates of racial separatism, the outcome was very different: By the early '70s, the U.S. seemed likely to be not only the first large society to break out of a black-white caste system but one of the few to exalt diversity. Instead of demanding conformity around a stereotype, some Americans have begun to cherish the differences they find in one another.

In the changing atmosphere, other ethnics took pride in their unique heritages. The University of California's Charles W. Thomas, father of black psychology, treated the affirmation of ethnicity as a mental-health model and urged young Anglos to discover pride in their whiteness so as to respect the essential pride of black and brown people.

The American Indian, long demeaned by sympathy rather than given respect, began to emerge through the work of anthropologist Carlos Castaneda and novelist Frank Waters, author of *The Man Who Killed the Deer.* If each ethnic group has a distinctive insight, something to teach all others, the Indian's contribution is clear: His art and ritual, now much admired by the young, provide a reverent connection with the ground and nature that the original settler knew for generations before whites and blacks arrived.

PAUL SEQUEIRA

"The identity crisis . . . acute among teen-agers . . . continues to burden men through middle age."

Wholistic Individualism. The diversity ideal took root in the new feminist movement. Like turn-of-the-century feminists, the early leaders constantly compared themselves with men and seemed, as one said, bent upon turning woman into a second-rate male. Some catching up was in order. Psychologist Matina Horner, now president of Radcliffe College, produced experimental proof that women graduate students, brainwashed against beating men, score lower on tests taken in the presence of males than in the company of women. The University of Michigan's Teresa Levitin proved in 1972 that women holding the same jobs as men get paid an average of $3,458 less a year. Mae C. King probed the double jeopardy of the black woman, and Howard University's Joyce A. Ladner showed that her deprivation includes an isolation that makes her more naïve than white women. But as the search for woman's identity moved on, sociologist Alice S. Rossi (Goucher College, Baltimore, Md.) and others became less concerned with comparisons than with the distinctive quality of the feminists.

Beyond that stage, another prospect stands out in the research literature and in everyday work. The roles into which society locks people at birth—by sex, race, class, and nation—deny or minimize the more important qualities of each individual. But if the stigmatizing labels are inverted—for instance, if blackness and femininity prove to be unique assets—then they become no more than attributes of a rich personality. Only by this route will racism, sexism, and snobbery be rooted out—so that they do not corrupt democracy and limit personal potential. Among the new aspirations there is now an almost religious drive toward what can be called wholistic individualism.

Turned-On Family. Few subjects have inspired more handwringing than the supposed decline of the family, the basic social unit. In the U.S., Harvard Business School M.B.A. Robert Rimmer has preached, through popular novels such as *Proposition 31,* that the nuclear family of husband, wife, and children is too fragile to hold its own against the giant institutions on all sides. Rimmer's books suggest larger families, including group marriages made up of several adults and all their children. Along with newspaper stories about swinger institutes such as Sandstone community near Los Angeles, the "Rimmerites" have contributed to public fear that the family is falling apart and wild substitutes are taking over.

The evidence, however, points the other way. The limited research available on group marriages indicates that they are much less stable than monogamy. If it takes two substantial people to make the traditional marriage work, it takes at least three saints to make a group marriage viable. They tend to break up, researchers find, not only over jealousy but over the mundane aggravations about who washes dishes, steals toothbrushes, or selects the food. Anthropologist Margaret Mead, whose field studies produced the classic *Coming of Age in Samoa,* treats the group marriage movement as silly. Among the hundreds of primitive cultures that have been studied, Mead says, no such family arrangements have been found to survive.

But the nuclear family, researchers find, is flourishing. Though the divorce rate turned up sharply in the early '70s, the change was less dramatic than might have been expected with the decline in social sanctions against divorce. The parent-child bond became, if anything, stronger. Black scholars report that the ghetto family, once analyzed in federal documents as a disaster, turns out to be remarkably effective in protecting its members.

The principal change is in the expectations of family life. Members assume that they ought to love each other, understand one another, or at least get their hostilities up front. Anyone who has read Victorian novels knows that such expectations are a historical oddity; in the West, at least, few mothers and almost no fathers of the past dreamed of the emotional luxuries now considered normal. The man was the breadwinner; the woman considered sex a marital duty. Today a wife considers herself a failure unless she can be an orgasmic playmate, intellectual companion, and growth partner, as well as an emotionally independent person—a cross between Madame Pompadour and Madame Curie.

Encounter Wave. The sensitivity now expected in the family has its counterpart in the encounter movement that has spread through companies, schools, and churches. Founded by MIT psychologist Kurt Lewin, the National Training Laboratories used the postwar years to train hundreds of leaders in techniques that help a few people share their innermost feelings with each other. By the end of the '60s, NTL could claim that more than half the presidents of the 500 largest U.S. corporations had exposed themselves to group experience. In churches, almost every denomination fostered group encounters as a form of fellowship; wealthy supporters of evangelist Billy Graham, organized as the Laymen's Institute, split into two bitter camps, one side favouring encounter and the other calling it the work of Satan. California's Esalen Institute, testing more daring techniques ("Tell your mate the three things that could most jeopardize your marriage"), became the founding model for dozens of "growth centres" in the major cities of the U.S. and Europe.

Carl Rogers, best known of the movement's psychologists, announced in the early '70s that group activity had come of age. Companies and public agencies began to drop formal group sessions; a few emotionally disturbed participants had to be hospitalized and if employees felt themselves forced to go into groups, the experience was an invasion of privacy. But by then the openness ethic had seeped into the lives of millions and reappeared in many new forms. The U.S. Navy, busy with Adm. Elmo Zumwalt's reforms, decided late in 1972 to put many of its officers into Leadership Effectiveness Training, a program adapted from Rogers' encounter techniques.

University of Chicago psychologist Morton A. Lieberman recently provided the first rigorous data on what happens to people in encounter groups. While a compelling majority come away feeling like better people, and most continue to think so for six months or more, only a few change their behaviour enough for their family and friends to notice the difference. In his late-1972 report, Lieberman concluded that though groups do not transform the individual, they do provide an experience that many people find lacking in other settings.

Whether viewed as cause or symptom, the remarkable spread of the group ethic tells of another hidden aspiration. Among the educated and mobile middle class, where most relationships tend to be brief and bureaucratic, there is an active search for emotional depth and candour.

Search for Soul. The encounter group also serves, Lieberman's research suggests, as a secular stand-in for the revival and the confessional. It is one of many social indications that the religious impulse has broken out of its confinement in church. In fact, social scientists began in 1972 to probe a wide range of phenomena that suggest a fundamental change in attitudes toward behaviour that is, by traditional scientific standards, irrational or religious.

Priest-sociologist Andrew Greeley uses national surveys for a devastating attack upon the academic assumption that traditional churches are in the decline. Working out of Chicago's National Opinion Research Center, Greeley compares the average citizen's knowledge and involvement in politics, supposedly a vital activity today, with similar measures of religious knowledge and involvement. For instance, only 5 out of 100 American families contribute to a party or candidate, but 40 out of each 100 contribute to religious bodies, and 3% tithe. The result is a convincing, often funny, stack of data suggesting that the church is at least as vital a force as the political party, maybe much more so.

But Greeley's purpose is more serious. His controversial book *Unsecular Man* argues that modern theologians since Dietrich Bonhoeffer have been speaking for themselves, not for the populace, in contending that a "new man" has now emerged who can live without a personal tie to God. Such talk, he believes, is but another intellectual fad. Like the scientific culture of the last couple of centuries, Greeley argues, it glosses over the mystical or superstitious beliefs by which the majority of human beings have always lived. If he is right, witchcraft never died; it went underground.

Such an approach makes 20th-century man something

of a fraud. In spite of all the rhetoric about revolutions in politics, sex, technology, clothes, morality, and everything else, Greeley's evidence suggests, the average family man acts and believes, and prays, pretty much in the casual way his daddy did. Along with a few other social scientists, Greeley insists that the rate of social change up to now, at least in fundamental beliefs, has been wildly overstated by the press, on TV, from the pulpit, and in the writings of most scholars.

But Catholicism's leading researcher does recognize that "something is different," and in this narrow range he admits differences that are profound. For the educated majority, aware of the myths and life-styles of many cultures, living among giant institutions rather than in church-dominated culture, it is hard to accept consciously any body of explanations, religious or scientific, that try to give coherence to the chaos of experience.

Threatened Immortality. Others have been dealing more effectively with the problem of cultural chaos. This generation of adults and students, says anthropologist Mead, is the only one that will ever go through a specific cultural crisis brought on by the sudden rise of communications technology. Most individuals of the past have lived entirely within the behaviour and belief systems of a single culture, and at most have known of only one or two more. But now all cultural alternatives, past and present, primitive and technological, suddenly have come into visible reach. In the student protest of the '60s, for instance, radicals in Chicago and Tokyo and Bonn identified with each other to form a common ideology and life-style, rather than merely to accept or reject the manner of their fathers.

Taking up from there, Yale psychoanalyst Robert Jay Lifton shows the profound effect of modern technology upon the belief systems that help men and women to get up in the morning—by giving them the notion that they are in some sense immortal. It has taken a quarter of a century, Lifton argues, for the concentration-camp gassings and the nuclear bombings to undercut the customary modes by which men cling to immortality. Here is how he sums up the change:

If, as scientists and businessmen and revolutionaries assume, a man's works survive him and give his life meaning, then the prospect of nuclear annihilation undercuts this hope. If, as romantic poets of the past and nature freaks of today assume, man gains immortality by being a part of immutable nature, the bomb can wipe out all of evolution's products. If, as close families tend to hope, there is some permanence in being a part of an ancestral chain, or an unfolding nation, then permanence is totally threatened. Even the life-after-death notion gets shaken a bit by the prospect of a nuclear wipeout. What is left is the fifth mode of immortality, Lifton will argue in his next book, *The Broken Connection,* that comes to man through ecstatic or mystical connection with the timeless world.

Both Greeley and Lifton are fascinated by the rise of Yogis, Zen Buddhists, Jesus People, Satanists, meditators, witches, and other pop-culture religious cults. Many humanistic psychologists have gone into transpersonal psychology, with its emphasis on the suprapersonal or mystical experiences. Such activities tend to support Lifton's view that the technological threats to the sense of immortality have driven many to search for other ways to glimpse a sense of permanence.

"Death Is Hot." Small wonder that morbid subjects have come into the limelight. Studies of death and dying have become one of the fastest growing new areas of social research, in part because both scholars and their audiences are fascinated by this once-suppressed topic. "Death is a hot subject now," says UCLA psychologist Edwin Shneidman, editor of the new scholarly journal *Life-Threatening Behavior.* In Boston, psychiatrist Avery Weisman and others work with hundreds of terminal patients to find out how some manage to find serenity in a sense of "appropriate death." In Czechoslovakia and now in Maryland, medical researcher Stanislav Grof uses LSD to give the dying practice in confronting nonexistence.

The diminished sense of certainty comes through most clearly among the street people, the hippies in America's drug culture. And it is here that the Jesus movement, the fundamentalist sects of new Christians, is making its heaviest impact. University of Nevada's James T. Richardson heads a team of researchers who have been working with the largest nationwide group of "Jesus Freaks." In his 1971 and 1972 interviews with dozens of converts, Richardson found that most had come out of the drug-user world. Having rejected marijuana and "speed" highs, many now go in for glossolalia, the speaking in tongues, as an altered state of consciousness.

The works of C. G. Jung are now being reexamined and used to build models for research into the unconscious. A disciple of Sigmund Freud, Jung broke away on grounds that Freud's emphasis on sexuality kept psychoanalysis from respecting the wisdom of the unconscious. Freudians interpret dreams largely as sexual fantasies, but Jungians search dreams for universal myths, archetypes, and fairy tales that represent man's deepest insight into daily reality. Recent LSD research, they contend, has uncovered the kind of unconscious that Jung knew was there, and they confidently affirm the mystical as inherent to man.

As usual, the youth underground embraced Jung before their elders got serious about him. The Jungian revival goes along with the pop culture's fascination for casting the *I Ching,* playing with astrological futures, and reading Tarot cards.

Natural Creativity. Implicit in such preoccupations is a rejection of the rigorous materialism that has been the distinctive feature of Western thought since Descartes. One reason for the turn is that physiological researchers, including those in advanced brain research, now have instruments precise enough to measure physical reactions that cannot be explained by mechanistic theories of man. In the Soviet Union as in the U.S., reports Stanley Krippner of Maimonides Medical Center in New York, many a serious scientist is beginning to look earnestly into the brain waves of transcendental meditators, into extrasensory perception (ESP), and into other subjects that were once outside the pale. The Menninger Clinic in Topeka has become a clearinghouse for such work.

This trend received its biggest boost late in 1972 with

the publication of *The Natural Mind* by Harvard M.D. Andrew Weil. One of the first researchers to do controlled experiments on the behavioural effects of marijuana and psychedelic drugs, Weil found that the chemistry of drugs affected behaviour less than the subject's expectations. By following up this discovery in psychiatric work with addicts, Weil became convinced that nobody becomes dependent upon drugs unless he has excessive faith in chemistry—which science teaches. More important, Weil argues that the human mind has a natural need, as basic as hunger and the sex drive, to spend part of its time in dreams, fantasies, ecstasy, or other altered states of consciousness. While drugs, including alcohol, help many to get there quicker, Weil believes, in the long run the reliance upon such materialistic gadgets inhibits the individual's discovery that he, not the drug, controls the entry into an altered state. Weil seriously suggests that normal waking consciousness allows rational thought, but that creative thought comes when people free themselves into daydreams, fantasies, and other altered states.

Beyond Affluence. In seeking to cure drug users, Weil became impressed by the fact that many give up drugs when they go into meditation, but few meditators go back the other way into drugs. He speculated, therefore, that the religious experience of meditation is more natural and fulfills the mind's need better. Such a position, taken by a solid researcher with excellent medical credentials, encouraged the culture's new mood of cognitive promiscuity. Roll-your-own liturgies, especially in marriage, and a wide array of half-serious occult practices suggest that strictly scientific explanations no longer satisfy.

If Victorian science and established religion once made an honest lady out of the supernatural, she is now slipping out into the street again. Social critics such as Harvard's David Riesman, co-author of *The Lonely Crowd,* now worry deeply about the cult of the personal, the exaltation of irrationality, and the tendency to find truth in emotion. Theologians such as Martin E. Marty of *The Christian Century* consider the prospect of a new reformation and compare the present with Martin Luther's day. The comparison is not without substance. In daily life as in psychological research, there is a groping for a new definition of what is a person, the fully human animal. Such affirmations cannot come within the logic of a culture, which begins with the existing definition of personality; historically, such redefinitions come with a surge of irrationality that breaks the previous forms, including the religious ones, and like Luther's Reformation they tend to be dangerous, dark, and bloody.

Conscious Control. Abraham Maslow, the humanistic psychologist, used a brilliant research mind to insist that researchers go beyond the mechanistic models of man. Once a person fulfills the animal needs for food and other survival supplies, he can turn toward the distinctly human concerns, for personal fulfillment. Maslow said that these concerns cannot be explained by the mechanistic model; they involve peak experiences of emotion and creative moments. Often inspired by Maslow's works, a generation of thinkers is now at work on these ambitious possibilities.

The need for coherent thought and research is urgent. By gaining conscious control of economic ups and downs, as well as temporary control of international monetary shifts that in the past brought on world depression, the industrial world has given itself unprecedented prosperity. With the spread of affluence, millions have gained relative freedom from grinding economic pressures; in this sense, they have begun to test out societies that can best be described as mass aristocracies. And like the aristocrats of old, they have begun to explore the limits of the sensuous, the peculiarities of new belief systems, and the possibilities for greater control over the environment that affects them. They are redefining themselves and searching for myths to give meaning to the effort.

History provides no models for the management of a mass aristocracy. With the dignity of economic security and higher education now widely diffused, authority has lost its ancient thumbscrews—notably the threat of hunger and a monopoly on knowledge and violence—for forcing compliance with the decisions of a ruling elite. Even in the military, crude orders are giving way to attempts to manipulate compliance. And in the private governance of corporations, both the employee and the public now have a much stronger voice. The rise of conditions of equality is the providential fact of history as Alexis de Tocqueville warned long ago, and the chief danger of the truly egalitarian society is that it becomes immersed in the petty decisions of the many rather than reaching for the few noble decisions demanded of any age.

The new world seems strange in part because of the loss of rigid hierarchies. Throughout most of history, man's everyday experience taught him that he has a boss who has a boss on up to the ultimate—perhaps the monotheist Jehovah of the Hebraic-Christian tradition. Today's more egalitarian experience does not even condition the ordinary citizen to feel the guilt that comes with the sense that omnipresent authorities judge each individual's every act. Right or wrong, the mass aristocracy throws each man and woman back upon the most painful question of life, that of meaning. The existential philosophers now dominate the popular culture precisely because they ask what is the meaning of existence.

Managed Fantasy. The desire for greater control of this strange-seeming environment finds expression in self-modification techniques developed in the '70s. Psychological tools once used for testing—for measuring personality traits—sometimes can be turned around so that they change the behaviour that they measure. Harvard's David McClelland spent most of the '60s at the head of a worldwide research project on achievement motivation. His primary instrument was the TAT, the Thematic Apperception Test, by which psychologists study the individual's fantasies and make reasonably precise measurements of three motives—achievement, power, and affiliation. McClelland and his students used variations of the need-for-achievement index not only to identify individual differences but to explain the rise and fall of ancient civilizations and to predict which nations are now apt to decline or become more powerful.

But in order to use the same device to change behaviour,

not just predict it, McClelland had to make his subjects conscious of why they score high or low. In India he recruited two groups of small businessmen, one only as a control to compare with the experimental group. For ten days he and others trained the experimental group how to manipulate their fantasies so as to think in terms of practical achievements. It worked. Within the next two years the experimental group outdid the control group by a substantial margin: they started four times as many businesses, invested twice as much new capital, and created twice as many new jobs.

McClelland's achievement training is now used in U.S. ghettos, in several urban schools, and increasingly in foreign countries. In concurrent work he found that power motivation, very different from achievement motivation, can lead in frustration to heavy drinking. By 1972 his followers were teaching alcoholics to manipulate their power fantasies so as to become less dependent on the bottle.

Pigeons in Utopia. Such work—conscious manipulation of motives that once were unconscious—is still in its crude stage. Greater precision can be achieved in what is called biofeedback. At Rockefeller University in New York, psychologist Neal E. Miller and others have developed techniques for measuring almost all of the bodily functions that once were thought to be autonomic, out of reach of conscious control. Miller's early research, though now being challenged by others, suggests that man can somehow control almost any such function if he can see or hear an indicator that tells what is going on. The implications of this finding are almost unlimited. If a patient with an erratic heart can watch an indicator of its beat, for instance, he may be able to steady it down and reduce the risk of heart failure. Yogi meditators can control their brain-wave frequencies. In Texas a growing cult of religionists has now been founded on manipulation of the brain's alpha waves. While such peculiar responses suggest the emotion that arises with the possibility of gaining control over unconscious functions, biofeedback development has to be understood in the larger context of man's attempt to redefine his relationship to his environment.

The major new movement in psychology bases itself on B. F. Skinner's 45 years of stern research. Author of the utopian novel *Walden Two,* Skinner is perhaps most noted for a trick he played years ago to prove how well his behaviour-modification techniques work: he taught pigeons to play Ping-Pong. In his learning theory he shows that any organism's behaviour can be shaped if any approximation of the desired behaviour gets reinforced—roughly, that means rewarded—almost instantly. His main invention is the concept of "operant behaviour," by which he means any action taken to affect the environment so that it rewards the active organism. Man's most creative moment, then, comes when he arranges his physical or social environment to make it reward him for what he wants to do.

Positive Responsibility. Skinner started a basic political argument, and drew attacks from U.S. Vice-Pres. Spiro Agnew and others, with his 1971 book *Beyond Freedom and Dignity.* The book called for a total redesign of the culture under behaviour modification discipline. His call to action would not have started a long fight but for the fact that he heads a movement of several hundred Skinnerians—now the strict Jesuits of psychology—who are using behaviour modification technique in schools, hospitals, corporations, prisons, and many other institutions, as well as increasingly in everyday life. No matter how the argument goes, it is now clear that more and more individuals and groups will use such techniques to gain increasing control over their own behaviour and, at times, over that of others. Man is now deeply involved in deliberate efforts to invent himself as he wishes to be.

F. B. GRUNZWEIG—PHOTO RESEARCHERS

Will man "let this earth become a garbage pit or make it a new Eden"?

The policy question ahead was previewed by the U.S. commission that studied the effects of violent TV programs on the behaviour of children. The State University of New York's Robert M. Liebert, head of experimental work for the commission, offers substantial evidence that violent television programs cause children to be more aggressive. Beyond the commission's work, Liebert and his associates did several experiments to show that television can be used to encourage prosocial behaviour. For instance, children can be taught not to fear the dentist. With this evidence, Liebert confronted broadcasters and advertisers with demands that they deliberately write—and test—their programs and ads to produce a gentle society. Here, in his argument, comes the binding issue that arises in each instance of such manipulation: In any activity that influences the behaviour of others, the person or institution wielding influence must accept responsibility for the consequences of that activity.

Failure of Collective Decision. The new aspirations for control—over the environment, the self, and even the myths by which individuals find meaning in life—match the new demands brought on by technology and social change. But as Nagai's warning suggests, the era of conscious action strains the fabric of industrial society and leaves the outcome, even survival, very much in doubt.

Especially among the groups most threatened by the pressures—the less educated workers of what sociologists call the lower middle class—the cautions and fears of the early '70s are already measurable in tangible specifics.

Social science researchers find, for instance, that U.S. citizens have high hopes for themselves as individuals but do not have much hope for their country's future. This split first came to light in *The Hopes and Fears of the American People,* a survey published by Washington's Potomac Associates. The apparent paradox partly indicates declining faith in government; in its general disenchantment with large institutions, the recent college generation has given up America's depression-born faith in federal pills for all ills. As the distrust deepens, it includes serious doubt about the capacity of the traditional decision-making machinery to deal with today's problems. By late 1972 the Institute for Social Research in Michigan found that while three out of four Americans think they are doing well in their personal lives, only one in every six is sure that the quality of national life is getting any better.

The Vietnam war rubbed all the doubts raw, and the pathetic figure of Army Lieut. William L. Calley marked a fundamental split in belief about the relationship between the individual and society's decision-making machinery. The ever larger body of educated people hold a personal view of moral responsibility and believe that even in war a man must decide between right and wrong action; they therefore tend to feel Calley should have been tried—as he was—for his command role in the My Lai massacre.

But blue-collar workers deeply resent the Calley trial. Psychologist Herbert C. Kelman of Battelle Memorial Institute found out why: Accustomed to a place below the decision level in most institutions, the have-less assume a traditional contract with constituted authority. They do what they are told and expect to be honoured for it, or at least protected. In their view, the brass broke the contract to fink on Calley—and on them.

Authoritarianism's Debt to Threat. Such hidden agonies shaped the politics of 1972. In a respectful study of Alabama Gov. George Wallace's followers in many states, Harvard's Thomas F. Pettigrew found racism, but beyond it a deeper sense of what he called "relative deprivation"—the feeling that people like themselves were somehow getting a raw deal. In Boston, sociologist Gary Marx turned up substantial public sentiment for a return to vigilante action. The University of Michigan's Stanley Seashore focused on worker alienation—lack of fulfillment on the job—as the primary source of political and social alienation. The "blue-collar blues," he found, are not limited to blue-collar workers.

More ominously, the protests of the '60s and the threatening doubts of the '70s scared many into security-minded search for rigid authority. In studies of the rise of authoritarianism, Stephen M. Sales at Carnegie-Mellon University found that any environmental threat makes individuals suppress independent judgment in favour of misleading authority. The lust for authority can warp an entire culture. The depression of the '30s, for instance, brought on much more punitive sentences for crimes such as rape, a sharp rise in membership in authoritarian churches, even a pop-culture switch from family comic strips to brutal superheroes. The symptoms of authoritarianism, Sales reports, are now building up again. In France, sociologist Edgar Morin traced an outburst of anti-Semitic rumours in Orleans—Jewish boutique owners were, folks said, kidnapping girls into white slavery—and thus found in a modern city a sense of medieval horror.

In nostalgia and in a rising romanticism over nature, many revealed their distrust of the man-made city. The reaction is not entirely irrational, for the city has hidden impact upon the human organism. The University of Texas' David C. Glass, in a well-controlled study to be published early in 1973, showed the effects on children of growing up in noise-polluted New York apartments over urban superhighways. After three years, the street noise reduced their capacity to discriminate between spoken syllables, and then began to reduce their performance on school tests. In Japan, Osaka University psychologists finished their third national study of early menstruation in girls—once a function of hot climate, later of better nutrition. Girls are now reaching puberty in their 12th year, and the average age declines another seven months every ten years. Why? Because, the Japanese data indicate, TV and other rich stimuli of the city put pressure on the child's body.

In dozens of peculiar ways, people begin to feel nudged around by their own artifacts, to lose control at the time when control is most needed. The characteristic mental diseases of the new era point directly to the sense of helplessness. The *Wall Street Journal* reported a national epidemic of psychological depression cases; the report made sense when the University of Pennsylvania's Martin E. P. Seligman showed that depression is often a form of learned helplessness—a conditioned conviction that nothing the patient does changes his fate. Dozens of researchers around the world, using a test developed by the psychologist Julian B. Rotter, found a rising incidence of people who feel that external forces, not their internal decisions, control their destiny. In B. F. Skinner's terms, the critical question has to do with whether a person's behaviour is "operant"—does it make any difference?

* * *

The future is now embedded in the present. Approaching the three-quarter-century mark, the industrial world comes nervously, doubtfully into confrontation with startling new demands for responsible choice. The wisdom of the past often offers perverse guidelines. Even in the biblical story of the Tower of Babel, as in most of Western mythology, the city is Satan's home and man suffers punishment for the audacity of daring to build his own environment. But most people of the industrial world now live in urban areas where the rivers are superhighways, the mountains are skyscrapers, and the entire firmament is designed by man's own hand. He has now come to a Second Genesis, and for all his fears he has no choice but to make choices once left to nature, habit, tradition, or his god. Depending upon the quality of his knowledge and his courage, he will let this earth become a garbage pit or make it a new Eden.

RISE OF THE KNOWLEDGE WORKER

by Peter F. Drucker

BURK UZZLE—MAGNUM

This year or next, the American worker reaches the end of an epoch that has lasted more than 7,000 years. Since the dawn of Western civilization, most work has been based on skills that a worker learned on the job. Only the professional classes—for centuries mainly doctors, ministers, lawyers, and teachers—went to school to acquire formal knowledge needed in their work. The Industrial Revolution added engineers to the professional list and expanded the number of technical jobs, but for millions it demanded only a shift in skills. Then, in the last few decades, every industrial nation began to witness the rise of the knowledge worker, the educated man or woman whose labour involves the use of bookish information. The United States, with Japan and Western Europe close behind, will soon cross the line into the new epoch; by 1975, 40-odd million knowledge workers will hold more than half the jobs in our economy.

This fundamental change in the nature of work strains all our economic and social institutions and accounts for much of our political turmoil. We face a discontinuity, a break in historical trend lines, that can be compared to the situation our remote ancestors faced after they learned to irrigate land in the Mediterranean Basin for intensive farming. With this technological advance, they turned toward specialization of labour. Like ourselves, they were about to build a new human environment and could sense only a fraction of the changes ahead.

This first great human revolution took place because our forebears applied specialized skill to work and production. Skill supplied the tools to make average people without towering genius capable of advancing from generation to generation by systematic apprenticeship. The discovery of skill made possible the economic performance necessary to support the cultural variety that we call civilization.

The worker's level of skill determined his position in society and his relationship to its institutions. These skill-based forms of social organization became quite stable. By the year 2000 B.C. or so, the irrigation civilizations of the Eastern Mediterranean had developed every one of the basic social, political, and economic institutions, every occupation, and most of the tools man had at his disposal until 200 years ago.

Now we are adding the third dimension to ordinary work. On top of muscle and skill, workers are applying knowledge to their productive activity. Knowledge is not a substitute for skill, but skill alone won't do it anymore. As any coal miner knows, the skill jobs are being wiped out while the knowledge jobs are being multiplied. There are now more computer programmers than steelworkers. Every now and then writers and politicians stir up panic over the prospect that automated tools are taking over most jobs for which men and women get paid. What actually happens, of course, is that machines move into many skill jobs while new entrants into the work force, especially students and women, go after the ever larger number of knowledge jobs.

The work situation now changes the meaning and nature of knowledge as well as our attitudes toward it. Knowledge and work until very recent times were separate and rarely touched each other. Knowledge was prized for its intrinsic beauty and praised as conducive to wisdom. Work, based on experience, was practical, aimed at extrinsic rewards, and considered inherently drab.

Knowledge as Energy. Modern academics tend to be reactionary when confronted with the changing role of knowledge. For most university intellectuals, knowledge is still something in a book, not a factor in production. But as long as it is in a book it is only information, if not mere data. Only when a man applies the information to doing something does it become knowledge. Knowledge, like electricity or money, is a form of energy that exists

---

Peter F. Drucker is the foremost management consultant in the U.S., and author of the classic Practice of Management *and* The Age of Discontinuity. *He is Marie Rankin Clarke professor of social science at Claremont Graduate School, Claremont, Calif.* Dr. Drucker has adapted portions of this article from *The Age of Discontinuity,* copyright 1968, 1969 by Peter F. Drucker and published by Harper & Row, New York, N.Y.

only when it does work. The emergence of the knowledge society is not, in other words, part of "intellectual" history. It is, rather, part of the history of technology, which recounts how man puts tools to work.

The second technological revolution—this second basic change in the nature of work—will have an impact that the application and organization of skill never had: it will have a direct impact upon men's minds. Previously the useful arts had only to do with how man works, plays, eats, and fights. How and what he thinks, how he sees the world and himself in it, his beliefs and values—these were outside the sphere of work. With the application of knowledge to work, however, application and cognition, matter and the mind, tool and purpose, knowledge and control have come together for better or for worse. Knowledge work connects the universe of doing and that of knowing.

It is uncommonly appropriate to explore that connection in the current yearbook of the *Encyclopædia Britannica,* the information storehouse kept in the homes of many busy families. As some of you know, I have spent my life on the problems of human organizations, and in *The Age of Discontinuity,* published four years ago by Harper & Row, I concentrated on the specific ways in which the knowledge economy disconnects us from our past. Since then many of the trends have become more pronounced, and I have come to see them more precisely. So this is a welcome opportunity to test ideas on people who are acutely aware of the knowledge component in work because they deal with it every day, in school if not yet on the job.

The Educated Economy. The substitution of knowledge for manual skill as the productive resource in work is completely changing our society. In technologically advanced countries a large number of people who once worked with their hands are shifting over to work that they do with their minds, almost without direct contact with materials and tools. New nations compress the timetable that has been followed by U.S. labour. In 1900, 18 out of every 20 Americans earned their living by working with their hands, 10 of those 18 as farmers. By 1956 more than half the work force had put on white collars. By 1965 only 5 out of 20—in a vastly larger work force—did manual work, and only one worked on a farm. Most of the rest earned their living primarily with knowledge, concepts, or ideas, with things learned in school rather than at the workbench. (Not all such work is associated with advanced technology; the cashier in a cafeteria is also a knowledge worker. But her work requires education—systematic mental training—instead of exposure to experience.)

On the eve of World War II, the men on the assembly line, the semiskilled machine operators, were the centre of the work force. Today the centre is the knowledge worker. The 1960 census showed that "professional, managerial and technical people," clearly knowledge workers, were the largest single work group. When the majority of the civilian labour force belongs to the knowledge ranks, sometime in 1975, the textbook will have replaced the black lunch box as the symbol of the working man.

As a result of this shift there is a radical change in the position of the manual worker. Neither his job security nor his income deteriorates. But he tends to be seen as economically nonproductive and socially marginal, a hardhat like Archie Bunker to be joked about on television, and his demands are no longer compelling. In his stead, the employed middle class is becoming the new majority. The industrial worker, the most direct beneficiary of the last 70 years of industrial development, suddenly sees his status and function threatened. He is beginning to think and act like a member of a militant minority. This implies that industrial relations are going to become increasingly bitter.

Political Turbulence. A new power group has taken over the centre of our political stage; the professional, technical, and managerial middle class—young, affluent, used to great job security, and highly educated. They will soon displace the old power blocs such as labour, the farm bloc, Big Business in the old-fashioned sense. In the first stage of this shift in power centres, industrial nations have entered on a period of political turbulence unlike anything we have known for at least a generation. The issues are new and unfamiliar ones, concerned less with the allocations of economic benefits than with basic values—moral, aesthetic, philosophical—and with access to better education.

Though we think that we are accustomed to momentous economic changes, our economy has for the last 50 years been in a period of almost unparalleled continuity. True, the economic expansion of the last 25 years has been very fast. But it has been carried largely by industries that were big businesses before World War I. Technologically, the revolutionary changes that the Sunday supplements talk about have been but the fulfillment of promises bequeathed to us by our Victorian and Edwardian grandparents—in steel, electricity, the car, the telephone, pharmaceuticals, the airplane. There are, of course, hundreds of new products: TV sets, jet planes, antibiotics, electrical appliances. But in terms of economic structure, the load is still being carried by the same industries and largely by the same technologies that were in place in 1914. The one major new addition is plastics.

While we have been busy finishing the great 19th-century economic edifice, the foundations have shifted under our feet. The changes in the work force have brought basic changes in the economy. In the past 20 years we have created a brand new form of capital, a brand new resource, namely knowledge. From an economy of goods—which America had as recently as World War II—we have changed into a knowledge economy. By the late 1970s, the knowledge sector, concerned with ideas and information rather than goods and services, will account for one-half of total national product. Formal education, either in schools and colleges or in continuing education, accounts for 12% of our gross national product.

The computer symbolizes the change but directly accounts for only a small part of it. Until a few years ago, when IBM got production up to a thousand a month, computers had made almost no direct impact. Yet without the computer we would not have understood that information, like electricity, is a form of energy.

The computer has become a basic tool in banking, retail trade, hotel management, airline passenger service, government welfare and health programs, monetary management, the planning functions of sizable companies, and physical and social science research. Its capacity to make decisions has often been overrated; it is but one tool for a work force that will soon devote most of its labour to the acquisition and manipulation of information.

Rigidities in Crafts and Taxes. These new information activities represent a qualitative shift rather than merely a quantitative shift. They are different in their structure, in their knowledge foundations, and in their sociology. They represent, therefore, not just a stepping up of the rate of change. They represent a discontinuity fully as great as that of the industries that came into being between the 1860s and 1914. They imply that the modern megalopolis will evolve a character very different from the industrial cities of the past.

The college campus rather than the factory chimney is likely to be the distinctive feature of megalopolis, the college student rather than the proletarian its central political fact. In most medium-sized cities, the local student body is now larger than the biggest factory's work force. In the San Francisco Bay area, the University of California's 28,500-student enrollment is nearly twice the size of the entire membership of Harry Bridges' longshoremen's union.

Student-based political organizations began to make their power felt in the late 1960s, though the special issue of the Vietnam war obscured the inevitability of their appearance. Youth gained visibility enough to expand its own power base by lowering the voting age to 18. Student political workers defeated the incumbent U.S. president, Lyndon B. Johnson, in the 1968 New Hampshire Democratic primary; by 1972 student-style organizations had matured somewhat, formed alliances with the women's movement and black groups, and planned well enough to nominate Sen. George McGovern as the majority party's presidential candidate. Such organizations still lack sophistication, being more gifted at protest than at taking responsibility, but they provide test models for knowledge-worker political action. The politics of the future in the U.S. will depend upon which party comes to represent the real values, not necessarily the public rhetoric, of the educated urbanites.

The knowledge industries are not additions; they are innovations. They are not just a belated service facilitating more basic workings of the economy; knowledge has become the primary industry, the one that supplies the essential and central resource for production. The economic history of the last hundred years in the developed countries can be summed up as "from agriculture to knowledge." Where the farmer was the backbone of any economy a century or two ago—in numbers but also in the importance and value of what was produced—knowledge is now the main cost, the main investment, and the main product of the advanced economy, and the livelihood of the largest group in the population.

In a period of rapid change in which new activities emerge as the new dynamic forces, government policy must above all not prevent or inhibit the mobility of productive resources. Men and capital, the two mobile resources of any economy, must be able to move into the most productive allocation. But the developed countries are organized to prevent mobility of people as well as to penalize mobility of capital. The greatest obstacle is the craft organization of work, with its jurisdictions, which prohibit the learning of new skills and forbid access to skilled jobs by outsiders who did not grow up in the union family. Skill, to be productive today, has to be based on systematic knowledge; the craft is obsolete.

Equally important, today's U.S. tax laws put a tremendous premium on capital retention in the existing big and old businesses. This means that more and more capital is inaccessible to the newcomer, to the small and growing business and the independent innovator. The government is going to have to develop policies to overcome these obstacles to mobility; but these new policies will produce even greater changes in the economy.

Big labour and many of today's big business organizations grew together out of production lines based on 19th-century technology. Their mutual concern for regularity and for security now puts them in conflict with the values of the emergent majority. It is no surprise that AFL-CIO Pres. George Meany felt that the Democratic Party could not accommodate both himself and Sen. George McGovern's followers. Mobile, affluent young workers and managers, some of whom are able to start their own companies, make neither loyal organization men nor faithful union members. They have already begun to attack such established rigidities as those in the craft lines of unions, most notably in the entertainment industry, and have shown a strong interest in reform of tax laws that lead to further concentration of capital in existing organizations.

Overrated Science. In the early '30s, anthropologist Bronislaw Malinowski and the first urbanologist, Lewis Mumford, began to insist that you cannot understand a culture unless you understand its tools. Their argument was then quite radical. Generations of historians had noted the invention of the steam engine and the cotton gin, but as gentlemen-scholars they had paid little more than lip service to technology's place in culture. They kept the world of thought separate from the world of work. This tradition has resisted change, though it now has a few dents in it. For instance, Canadian Marshall McLuhan's book *Understanding Media* provides one clear insight into communications technology; he saw that television as a medium had an impact entirely separate from the content of the programs it carried.

Edwin Denison of Rutgers and Fritz Machlup of Princeton provided, several years ago, the patient research that charts the growth of our new knowledge industries. By suggesting a marriage between labour and thought, their research invites a reexamination of our standard assumptions about the roles served by the specialized fields of knowledge. In particular, it is time to bury the shibboleth that says the scientist produces most of the impetus for change.

Ecology, Personality, Gestalt. Knowledge as a resource is not confined to science. The new economy is not

BRUCE ROBERTS—RAPHO GUILLUMETTE

"There is a radical change in the position of the manual worker . . ."—suddenly he sees "his status and function threatened."

based on science alone, but on new knowledge in its entirety. The development of the computer was founded on symbolic logic, and received its greatest impetus from a theoretical mathematician, the late John von Neumann, not from engineers or physicists. The perception of knowledge "systems," which is absolutely essential to the information industries, is derived from the concept of configuration, which first turned up before World War I in the "ecology" of the biologist, the "personality" of the psychologist, the "Gestalt" of the German students of sense perception, and the "culture" of the anthropologists.

To be sure, scientists have moved toward the centre of the political, military, and economic stage. But so have practically all the other knowledge people; geologists, geographers and mathematicians, economists and linguists, psychologists, anthropologists, and marketing men are all busy consulting with governments, with industry, with the foreign aid program, and so on. Few areas of learning are not in demand by the organizations of our pluralist society.

This is something new, something that sets the new economic activities sharply apart from those of the first half of this century. The technology of the 20th century embraces and feeds off the entire array of human knowledges, the physical sciences as well as the humanities. Indeed, in these new technologies, there is no distinction between the two.

The scientifically trained man again is expected to become a humanist; otherwise he will lack the knowledge and perception needed to make his science effective. And the humanist is expected to acquire an understanding of science or else his humanities will be irrelevant and ineffectual. Above all, the people concerned with the economy, whether as politicians, businessmen, or researchers, must be able to move with ease through all areas of knowledge. With knowledge in its entirety the central resource, technology—tools and the organization of work—finally becomes an integral part of culture, rather than something that is unworthy of a cultured person.

Back to School. The knowledge worker differs from his predecessor, the semiskilled assembly-line worker, not just in the resource he manipulates and applies. His preparation for work is different as well. He must go to school.

As a result, the role of education has changed. By 1900 technology had advanced so far that literacy had become a social need in the industrial countries. A hundred years earlier literacy was essentially a luxury; only a handful of people needed to know how to read and write. But by 1965 those without a substantial degree of formal education, more advanced than anything that had been available even to the most educated 200 years earlier, were actually becoming unemployable.

Education is now making apprenticeship obsolete. The man or woman who once acquired skill now uses a knowledge foundation to learn how to learn. He can then acquire new and different skills as he needs them. Unlike apprenticeship, which prepares for one specific craft and teaches the use of one specific set of tools for one specific purpose, a knowledge foundation enables people to unlearn and relearn.

The most important thing the schools have to teach is not specific skills but a universal skill—that of using knowledge and its systematic acquisition as the foundation for performance, skill, and achievement.

American workers have learned this lesson with a vengeance. They have demanded, and helped to build, a vast educational system inside industry. Few companies of respectable size have failed to develop formal classrooms, and most have set up tuition-grant programs for employees who want outside college courses. The further an employee went in school, the more schooling he demands on the job; he invests his own time in expanding his knowledge. Columbia University's Jacob Mincer has measured the nation's gross annual investment in further education of men and women on the job. By the late '50s, he found, the annual outlay on the college-bred worker had matched, or passed, the national expenditure each year on the next crop still on campus.

A black aerospace technician in Los Angeles recently put it all together this way: "In this business, you have to look upon education as a permanent profession."

The Civil Right to Learn. When knowledge becomes necessary for the individual to participate fully in the society, to work, then education moves into the centre of power politics. A hundred and fifty years ago education was still a privilege, a class luxury rather like horse racing. Around 1850 it first became an opportunity that the educational systems in the developed countries increasingly made available to the gifted and ambitious among the poor. It provided limited mobility between social classes. Within the last 20 or 30 years, access to education became a right.

Access to education is clearly as important today as any of the protections written into the Bill of Rights, for to be denied it is to be consigned to a submachine caste. Indeed, when the U.S. Supreme Court outlawed "separate but equal" classrooms for the American Negro and ordered integration of our public schools in 1954, it clearly affirmed that the right of access to education was solemnly embedded in the U.S. Constitution.

In the race riots of the '50s, black American children claimed their right to this essential dignity by walking to school through mobs of raging whites. The quality of education was becoming, for the first time, not only the hottest political issue but the one most likely to trigger violence. The era of student riots, the political reaction against them, the busing issue in the 1972 presidential campaign, and the many local fights over school finance and control—all these struggles raise different issues about education and the role of the school, but each draws its fervour from public realization that knowledge has become the society's chief resource.

So education, the way knowledge is acquired, is rapidly becoming the centre of spending and investment in the industrially developed society. Total U.S. expenditures on formal education began in the mid-1960s to exceed the defense budget by a substantial amount. About one-third of the U.S. population is now in school. Schoolteachers make up the largest single occupational group. In the struggle for position and power, education tends to replace money and rank as the index of status.

Since the rise of the knowledge worker coincides with the demand of American minorities for full citizenship, the schools at all levels have become the kindling point for racial strife. But improved education is not enough. As this analysis of the changed relationship between knowledge and wealth would suggest, any question about educational improvement also raises questions of economic development. The urban ghettos will not be given their opportunity merely by improved teaching in the public schools.

The black American represents the world's preindustrial people in industrial society. He represents also the most acute problem of colonialism, that is, of a growing inequality between the white and the nonwhite peoples of the world. There are many causes for the increasing disparity, among them the fact that white industrial nations have mechanized farming so that the colonial nations cannot compete—as the black sharecropper cannot compete with the mechanized cotton picker and so must move to the city. But whatever the local reasons, it is clear that this cleavage will be overcome. Either the poor will become richer or the rich will not long remain rich.

LENTON—BLACK STAR

Education is making apprenticeship obsolete—"those without a substantial degree of formal education" are "becoming unemployable."

In recognition of this fact of life, many of our domestic and foreign programs have assumed that the purpose of policy must be simply to make the poor wealthy. But this approach leaves out the critical step: We must learn that the task is to make the poor productive. Any other policy leads to cruel exploitation.

To develop the resources of any community, large or small, requires a balanced investment in the improvement of both talent and tools, of human-capital and plant-capital. To move from preindustrial skills into the knowledge economy, black Americans need an overall program that coordinates economic development with relevant education, as several black leaders have insisted. Yet, we still give hopeful teen-agers vocational training in skills that are obsolete in the economy of the present, let alone the immediate future.

One reason for this failure comes from the isolation of education as if it were unrelated to working life. Education has become too important to be left to the educators. In modern society everybody has a right to consider himself an expert on schools, for everybody during his formative years spends more waking hours in school than in any other institution. School increasingly controls access to careers, opportunities, and advancement.

Public awareness of this power has brought on years

of angry criticism of the schools at all levels. It is not that the schools are suddenly doing a poor job—the school has always done a terribly poor job. But because the value of education to the individual and the society has expanded so greatly, we cannot tolerate such poor performance.

Production in Education. Throughout history, teachers have given themselves an alibi by considering eight or nine out of each ten students either dumb or lazy. And as long as nothing much hinged on performance and success in school, this outcasting habit was accepted. It no longer can be. Today we expect of the school that the great majority of students really learn something—a novel, indeed unprecedented, public demand. We are also concerned with productivity in education, with getting the most learning out of each teacher-hour. Now that education is our single largest national expense, its performance matters a great deal.

Today's curriculum focuses on a small and narrow sector of a human being, the purely verbal; it is still based on the expectation that the great bulk of what one learns is learned outside of school, in "the school of experience." But for the knowledge worker, the interface between learning and experience becomes much more intricate.

The schools are going to be held accountable for performance in specific terms. They are beginning to adopt the general principle of no rejects—to guarantee a basic minimum accomplishment to each child. They are going to become less labour-intensive, to improve productivity by applying more tools to education. They will diversify the curriculum and expand it, to enable each student to acquire excellence in the area for which his talents and abilities fit him the best, rather than transmitting only the scribe's skills. They will become integrated into the community, rather than set apart. And, finally, school at all levels is going to become a continuing part of life, not something done only between 8 A.M. and 4 P.M. on weekdays and only to children and teen-agers.

The Seven-Year Career Itch. The standard arguments about today's jobs follow a line of economic or technological determinism. Everybody has to be highly trained, this argument says, because the implacable march of technology made it that way. Curiously, it happened the other way around. The knowledge worker came before knowledge work; the chicken did come before the egg. For reasons we will discuss below, millions of Americans have been going to school longer and longer, and once there they have refused to accept traditional jobs. Knowledge jobs have had to be created primarily because most people expect and demand such work. This process gained its own dynamic and thus transformed the character of work.

The educational level of the average entrant into the labour force has been going upward steadily. But the extension of the years spent in school is itself only an effect, not a cause. It is the result of a long development that drastically changed working life expectancy in the developed countries. Prior to 1850 there was no country where average life expectancy greatly exceeded 33 or 35 years, which limited the average working life to 20 years. Today, even with our later age of entrance into the work force, the working life-span in the advanced countries is more than twice that of a century ago.

This expansion of working life-span means that the average individual's talents and education now get put to use twice as long as in the past. In effect, we have more than doubled our active inventory of educated talent—our human capital. We have also more than doubled the lifetime earning potential of the individual. Here is the biggest increase ever recorded in what economists call the stock of capital, and the greatest advance ever recorded in the individual's economic resources.

Extending the working life-span has altered the balance between the productive and the dependent members of the population. Not only do people remain self-supporting until a much later age; more important, they stay producers so much longer that, even with a somewhat larger family, the number of dependents per producer has gone down sharply.

One main cause of the lengthened working life-span was undoubtedly the shift from farming as the major occupation; farm work ages one quickly, and in traditional agriculture disabling accidents occur far more frequently than in even the most dangerous industrial jobs.

But the shift from labourer to machine operator was hardly less important. The navvies who built the American railroads with pick and shovel rarely lasted more than five years or so before they were disabled by accident, liquor, syphilis, or plain backbreaking toil. But with scientific management, the most physically destructive tasks have been eliminated from industrial work.

A longer working life-span, in turn, has led almost everywhere to a substantial extension of the years spent in school. It can be argued that this represents a common faith in education as one of the highest human values. It can also be argued that extending the years of schooling is just rational economic behaviour; there is no doubt that earnings rise with education, and the added annual income now gets multiplied by twice as many years.

There is a third explanation of this sharp increase in years of schooling: people just cannot stand a working life of 50 years. The New Biologists, or ethnologists, could very well argue that evolution has left both women and men genetically unprepared for so many years in the same kind of work. They therefore use school not as something desirable of itself, not to advance economically, but merely to postpone the day of entrance into the labour force while keeping the youngsters off the street.

This third kind of explanation gains support from the career crisis that now troubles so many professionals, managers, and other workers in industrial societies. Psychologist Lee Stockford at the California Institute of Technology has studied this phenomenon for 20 years among thousands of men and women in large organizations. Stockford's data show that more than eight out of ten men go into a period of despair within about 18 months of their 36th birthday, before or after, and a similar percentage of working women hit the same kind of crisis when they are five years older, about 41. Psychologist Warren Bennis speaks of this phenomenon as a "destination crisis," because the victim becomes depressed about his or her working role, about success or being useful.

Japanese psychologists have recently begun to explore the crisis symptoms among their hardworking business managers—who seem to suffer most at age 42. But regardless of such cultural differences, this disease often leads to physical illness, breakdowns, family troubles. The seven-year itch turns out to be a career ailment, though it may produce sexual symptoms, and the best cure turns out to be a decided career change into work more suitable to the individual's talents—often made possible by a return to study. We have only begun to work on the desperate need for second careers for engineers, military officers, priests, teachers, and just about everybody else.

All three of the theories above certainly contribute to the trend toward more and more schooling. In the employed work force of 80 million Americans, the average education is that of a college freshman. In all the advanced countries, man has chosen to take a substantial part of the increased wealth made possible by extended working life in the form of extended schooling.

This habit forces each economy to create jobs that apply knowledge to work. The person who has longer schooling has different expectations: of higher pay, of a "career" rather than a "job," and of work in which one uses his mind rather than his hands. Long years of schooling make a person unfit for anything but knowledge work.

It is amazing that the U.S. economy has been able so far to satisfy the job demands of most people with long years of schooling. Had we not created knowledge jobs, we would have today an unemployed and unemployable intellectual proletariat the like of which the world has never seen. India's angry, underused college graduates give us only a hint of the problem the U.S. would have faced.

But we still do not know much about managing the knowledge worker and making him productive. As a result of the change in supply, we now have to create genuine knowledge jobs; it is the only way to make highly schooled people productive. That the knowledge worker came first and knowledge work followed—that, indeed, knowledge work is still largely to come—is a historical accident. From now on we can expect increasing emphasis on work based on knowledge. We can expect that we will develop a true knowledge economy, as we have already developed the work force for it.

Mobicentrics in Multiverse Organizations. Knowledge opportunities and occupations exist primarily in large organizations. It is the emergence of these organizations—business enterprise, government agency, large university, research laboratory, hospital—that has created the job opportunities for the knowledge worker. The modern agency or corporation, when flexible enough to function well, resembles a multiversity managed by a faculty of lawyers, writers, social scientists, artists, engineers, mathematicians, chemists, and humanists.

Modern organization frees the individual to move out of the narrow and tightly restricted environment of tribe, village, and small town. It creates the opportunities for educated people to put knowledge to work and to get paid for it. But these benefits impose on the individual the burden of decision. They impose on him the responsibility for deciding what he wants to be and what he wants to become. As his education has made him conscious of the forces that influence his behaviour, so the working organization constantly confronts him with alternative futures in which his behaviour will influence his environment. He can change, not once but frequently, his life-style, income, location, character of work—in fact, he can select one of several possible identities. The real pressures, if he understands them, are not toward the plodding conformity of the organization man but toward multiple identities of the mobicentric, the person whose life centres upon doing a new job quickly and moving on to the next before the excitement of learning cools off.

Every major task of the developed societies is being carried out in and through an organized and managed institution. Business enterprise was only the first of those and therefore became the prototype by historical accident. But while it has a specific function—producing and distributing economic goods and services—it is neither the exception nor unique. Large-scale organization is the rule, though rigid organizations of any size cannot adapt. Many societies are built by a pyramiding of family units, but ours is characterized by pluralist organizations that we use for different tasks.

It is the organization that is today our most visible environment. "Community" is found increasingly in the organization, especially the one in which the individual earns his livelihood and through which he gains access to function, achievement, and social status. A friend in Manhattan looks upon the organizational skyscrapers—from the Seagram Building to the CBS Building to Equitable Life—as vertical county seats separated by rivers of traffic. The American knowledge worker, unlike his Japanese counterpart, moves with relative ease from one organization to the next. The difference is more apparent than real; a change in companies, for instance, can at times be a way of staying in a narrow specialty. In either society, the knowledge organization can best be understood as a university where the faculty constantly regroups its diverse talents toward new goals. In fact, corporations have considerably more flexibility than university departments and are less hostile to internal renovation.

The knowledge opportunities of yesterday were available largely for independent professionals working on their own. Today's knowledge opportunities are offered largely to people working within an organization, as members of a team or by themselves. The knowledge worker is not the successor to the free professional of 1750 or 1900. He is the successor to the employee of yesterday, the manual worker, skilled or unskilled. Yet he is not proletarian. He is paid for applying his knowledge, exercising his judgment, and taking responsible leadership, and he tends to see himself as a professional of the traditional sort. There is, then, conflict between the knowledge worker's view of himself as a professional and the social reality in which he is the upgraded and well-paid successor to the skilled worker of yesterday. This conflict makes the management of knowledge workers an increasingly difficult task and one that is ever more crucial to the performance and achievement of the knowledge society.

Organization and Authority. We took our present concept of organization from the military, and so it is a rank-focused structure. Since this structure does not work in the high-technology and high-knowledge businesses, thousands of experiments have been set up to test alternatives. Douglas McGregor, the late MIT psychologist, argued 20 years ago that we must change from the theory-x organization—the vertical structure with many layers reporting upward in clear chains of command—toward the theory-y organization with only two or three layers, all in close touch with a wide top layer. As McGregor predicted, there has been a strong shift in this direction, if only because knowledge, like decision, can no longer be monopolized by a few people. In an effort to encourage workers in many knowledge specialties to collaborate more openly, perhaps by heightening their sense of each other's humanity, literally thousands of group encounters have been held for people in working organizations. But this fad has passed its peak as more and more managers realize that the required encounter is an invasion of personal privacy. What remains from such efforts, however, is recognition that at all levels knowledge work calls for team-style task forces of the sort most commonly found among top executives.

We talk today increasingly about the "free form" organization as alone appropriate to knowledge work—in business as well as in the military, the university, and government service. This is an organization in which discipline shifts to the individual. The controlling factor is not rank but task, and as the task changes the responsibility for decision shifts from one worker to the next.

You do need the authority of decisions. There has to be somebody who finally can say "yes" or "no," after which the matter rests and debate ceases. You do need an orderly process for ongoing work. But ideas do not observe these channels; if they do, they die. What we see emerging are, essentially, very complex structures, the analogy to which is not mechanical, as it has been in the traditional organization, but biological. There is no biological organism that has one axis. Biological organizations have at least two and usually many more. We are moving away from the single-axis organization where a few people at the top have all the decision-making power and all the knowledge while the rest stay at their machines; we are moving toward an organization in which the bulk of the people are paid for knowledge input and, above all, for innovation input. This change in structure follows the configurational thought, mentioned earlier, that was associated with the development of the computer.

But we are moving into this new epoch with dangerously little understanding of its requirements. We know that the success of any organization on a task depends upon the proper blend of knowledge workers—upon their specific information-competence to do that specific task. Projects that seem the same as those already done, or natural complements to them, may turn out to be so different as to bring disaster. The Columbia Broadcasting System thought of itself as expert in the television industry, but it lost millions trying to make and sell TV sets. Its competence turned out to be a particular form of information processing. RCA thought of itself as a general information processor, but could not succeed in the computer business.

Our accountants have tried to develop a bookkeeping system that measures the value of knowledge. Such accounting concepts would be decidedly different from the traditional ones based on the productivity of capital equipment of known cost that competes within a well-known industry. The effort to improve the books has so far been a total failure. At best, the accountants can compute the assumed value of a company from its record of prior earnings—in effect, they capitalize the future earnings that are anticipated—but these futuristic guesses often turn out to be wildly wrong. The previous information-competence of a working organization provides little assurance that the same organization will be able to handle new products and new markets in the constantly changing society. In short, we try to weigh the value of knowledge on scales that are still too crude to be more than marginally useful.

We have known for years how to measure productivity in the skilled worker. But we still cannot answer what constitutes productivity in the knowledge worker. Traditional measures such as the number of pieces turned out per hour or per dollar of wage are quite irrelevant if applied to the knowledge worker. Productivity in this respect is primarily a matter of quality, but we cannot even define it yet. So the knowledge worker must be able to plan for himself. Since no outside manager can determine, as in manual work, the "one best way" to perform a task, the burden of decision becomes more and more individualistic.

If future decisions are to have any connection with results, we must gain much greater precision in the measurement of talent and information-competence. What we do know, however, is that to make the knowledge workers more productive will require drastic changes in job structure, careers, and organizations. Jobs must be shaped around the man or the woman, not the other way around, and the environment must invite constant renewal of the person through systematic study. On the deeper level of the intangibles, it is also abundantly clear that the knowledge worker cannot be productive unless he finds out who he is, what kind of work he does best, and how he can tap the creative resources that he can never fully understand.

Socialized Capital and Knowledge Jobs. Every economy has three dimensions. There is the dimension of goods and services, their production, distribution, and consumption. It is the here and now of the economy. The second dimension deals with the formation and investment of capital; it is concerned with the allocation of resources to the future. Finally, in every economy there is the dimension of jobs, of what human beings work at.

Throughout most of our history, most people have had very little choice in any of these three dimensions; there were no mass large-scale markets in goods and services, in capital, or in jobs. The mass-market level in goods and services was not reached anywhere in the world until about 200 years ago, with the "commercial revolution" of the early 18th century in England and the Low Countries.

A sufficient supply of capital to permit mass choice was even longer in coming. As late as the early '30s, when I was a young investment banker in London, it was axiomatic that no more than one out of every three or four hundred people had enough savings to invest in anything but those time-honoured financial necessities, life insurance and the home mortgage. And all economic theory assumed essentially that jobs were scarcer than available labour supply, that one worked at what was available.

The proportion of shareowners in the U.S. now stands at 80% or higher, with most of them holding ownership in the economy through such new financial intermediaries as pension funds or investment trusts. We have not "nationalized" capital in the U.S., but we are "socializing" it. Financial ownership of the means of production is now distributed roughly in the same degree of equality—or inequality—in which consumption of goods and services was distributed in the early '20s in the first great "mass consumption" boom. Since the millions of new shareholders leave their stocks under institutional control, they do not exercise the power of owners. They simply benefit as investors from the profits of industry; they have a second income beyond the earnings in their labour.

Perhaps more important, though less visible, is the emergence of the mass market in careers for educated knowledge workers. The supply of men and women with advanced education has increased almost 20-fold since 1920. But the supply of job and career opportunities for them has increased even faster. During the '60s the career choices for knowledge people seemed to be practically limitless, and the economic resurgence of 1972 restored demand. Today, no matter how unequally educational opportunities are distributed, the majority of the young have access to a college education and, with it, access to mobility and meaningful career choice.

So we have mass markets and mass choice in: goods and services; investment for the future; and jobs.

This is a real revolution in the life of the individual. No longer is this a society of predetermined occupations. It is now possible to make one's living, and a good living at that, doing almost anything one wants to do and applying almost any knowledge. What was once a labour market where people sold themselves into jobs is now the opposite, a job market where organizations sell themselves to the prospective worker.

Most of mankind through the ages has had no choice at all. Son followed father. There was always some mobility, up and down, but it was the exception. A century ago even the educated man could make a living only in a few narrowly circumscribed "professions": clergyman, physician, lawyer, and teacher, plus—the one newcomer—civil servant. Engineers came in at the end of the 19th century.

Of course there are still limits—not only of ability but of wealth, of the accident of location, and certainly of race. But on the whole we are rapidly moving from a society in which careers and occupations were determined largely by the accident of birth into one in which we take conscious choice for granted.

The problem today is not the lack of choice but the abundance thereof.

Suddenly there are career choices; the great majority only yesterday had their careers determined from birth on. Suddenly there are decisions on the direction and purpose of knowledge. Suddenly we have to decide where and how to invest our savings—what developments in the economy we want to back. And of course we are constantly choosing from the huge range of goods and services offered us.

The society of organizations demands of the individual decisions regarding himself. At first sight, the decision may appear only to concern career and livelihood: "What shall I do?" But actually it contains a demand that the individual take responsibility for society and its institutions. "What cause do I want to serve?" is implied. And underlying this question is the demand that the individual take responsibility for himself. "What shall I do with myself?" rather than "What shall I do?" is really being asked of the young by the multitude of choices around them. The range of choice forces the individual to ask of himself: "Who am I?" "What do I want to be?" and "What do I want to put into life and what do I want to get out of it?"

"The computer has become a basic tool."

LEONARD FREED—MAGNUM

WOMAN: A TECHNOLOGICAL CASTAWAY

by Clare Boothe Luce

After a lifetime of casting about in the depths of female psychology, Sigmund Freud made this anguished entry in his diary: "What do women want, My God what *do* they want?"

The feminist answer is: "By God, they want Freedom!" They want to be free, as men are free, to fulfill their own potentials and to seek their own identities. They want political, economic, and social equality with men. And this equality, the feminists contend, is being denied them by overt and covert masculine coercion.

The feminists would seem to have their work cut out. Male supremacy is the most obvious and massive fact of our society.

All our social institutions that exercise power, generate wealth, create the law, form the minds, and guide the actions and opinions of society are male dominated.

The government, military, judiciary, labour unions, churches, universities, communications and advertising media, the banking, production, insurance, and transport systems, and all the significant professions (law, science, medicine, engineering, architecture) are male oriented. Men make all the crucial decisions for society.

In all our great institutions, whether public or private, there are not a hundred women who occupy high policy-making positions. The sporadic appearance of women in so-called top-level appointive political jobs is still largely female tokenism.

Of America's 80 million adult women, only 30 million are gainfully employed. Although women 20 and over now account for one-third of the labour force, the vast majority are working in menial, sex-typed, or dead-end jobs. Women are the "domestics" of the Male Establishment.

Equality of Monogamous Marriage. The only institution in which women appear in equal numbers with men is our institution of monogamous marriage (80% of all adult women are or have been married). Legally, marriage is the most male-dominated institution of all. It is the only institution in which women are expected to work without receiving any stipulated wages and with no fixed working hours. A woman who enters marriage penniless (as most women do) becomes totally dependent on her husband for bed, board, clothing, and whatever monies she may need for running his house and caring for their children. He can give her as much or as little as he chooses. She has no legal claim to any part of his property or income. He is legally responsible for her current debts, but he can also legally disavow future responsibility whenever he finds it too onerous.

If the marriage ends in divorce, the wife must go to work to support herself, or she must depend either on her ex-husband's charity or on the charity of the courts. This charitable handout is called alimony. Permanent alimony is awarded in only 2% of all divorces, and the average alimony award is less than 30% of the ex-husband's wages. In awarding child support, the majority of judges generally expect able-bodied women to go to work and to assume half the cost of supporting their children. The economic problem divorce presents to women with children is told in these statistics: The median income of white men 14 and over in 1971 was \$7,237; of black men, \$4,274; of white women, \$2,448; of black women, \$2,145. (College-educated women earn less than Negro men with eight years of education.) One out of three marriages, nevertheless, ends in divorce. The rate would certainly be higher if women were not faced with the economic problems suggested by the above statistics.

A recent government study of marriage, made on a nationwide basis, shows that only 3 out of 20 women profess to be happily married. Seven out of 20 "get along" but fight a lot. Ten out of 20 confess to being unhappy but stick to their mates for "practical reasons." Men come unstuck more easily than women. More than half the divorces granted are instigated by husbands. Husbands instigate the overwhelming number of divorces involving wives over 40. Many marriages end in the husband's desertion of the wife. Desertion, the "poor man's divorce," does not show up in the statistics.

The average woman who leaves marriage leaves it as poor as she entered it, a good deal older, and far less able to find employment with wages above the poverty level. About 40% of all families with a female head are below the poverty level. In every marriage there are two marriages, his and hers. His is better.

It's a man's world, no two ways about it.

The second obvious fact about our society is that, married or unmarried, this is the way most women seem to like it. The married, however, like it better. Given a (pollster's) choice between the unpaid and increasingly insecure job of "married woman" and any of the other jobs that the Male Establishment offers, women opt overwhelmingly for the job of homemaker. Hands down they prefer the gratifications of motherhood, the privileges of wifehood, and the status conferred by society on the title Mrs. to the condition of the unmarried woman working in a man's world.

But married or unmarried, happy or miserable, the vast majority of women accept their unequal social status. And when they are not indifferent to the efforts of the organized and activist feminists to achieve sex equality, they are openly hostile to them. A recent survey showed that more women than men accept the stereotype view of Women's Liberationists as sexually frustrated, hysteri-

---

Clare Boothe Luce is the world-famous author, playwright, journalist, and ardent feminist of many years' standing.

cal, and unfeminine creatures who, if not "old bags," are probably lesbians.

The fight of any group, class, or minority for equality in a democratic society must be waged in many ways and at many levels. But if it is to be made "within the system," it has to be energetically fought at the ballot box and in the courts.

Forty-seven Years in Committee. Women have had the vote for half a century. Unlike the blacks or Chicanos, women are *not* a political minority. They represent 51% of the electorate. They are a political majority that is treated as a minority. If women, as a class, were to demand legal equality, vote-hungry politicians (a tautological phrase) could not afford to deny it. Women, as a class, have made no such demand.

A case in point is the history of the Equal Rights Amendment. In 1923 a group of militant suffragettes, elated by their success in securing the basic right of every freeborn citizen—the vote—presented a bill to Congress to make women first-class citizens in the eyes of the Constitution.

The language of the Equal Rights Amendment bill was simple: "Equality of Rights under the law shall not be denied or abridged in the U.S. or by any state on account of sex." The bill was sent to the House Judiciary Committee where it remained bottled up for 47 years. The rationale of the Congress, totally dominated by males, was that while passage of the bill would give women the same legal rights as men, it would also result in their losing a handful of legal "privileges." One of these privileges was exemption from military service. The main objection made to it, however, was that it might relieve husbands of their legal responsibility for child support. The masculine view of fatherhood is a pretty dim one.

For almost half a century women voters did not exert enough pressure on the Congress even to have the bill debated on the floor. Many women's clubs and organizations refused to support it. (This was par for the feminist course: in 1912, a decade before women's suffrage was passed, the General Federation of Women's Clubs refused to endorse votes for women.)

The Equal Rights Amendment bill was finally passed on March 22, 1972. But it now requires the ratification of 38 states, 22 of which had ratified it as of November 1972. If the same consideration (or lack of consideration) is given to it by the states as it has received from the Congress, and if women voters continue to remain indifferent to its passage, it could be two or three decades before the Constitution recognizes women as first-class citizens.

All surveys show that the majority of married women prefer to leave political questions—even those adversely affecting their own personal rights—in the hands of their husbands. It would seem that most women are intellectually, as well as economically, dependent on men.

The temptation is to leave the feminist question right there. It's a free society, and its female citizens have the right to pursue life, liberty, and happiness in any way they choose.

If they prefer the feminine gratifications and privileges of marriage to the rights enjoyed by men, if they don't feel themselves to be an oppressed class, well, whose business is it but theirs?

PER DALSGARD—CAMERA PRESS/PICTORIAL PARADE

DENNIS BRACK—BLACK STAR

"The Male Establishment never lets women forget that they are . . . sex objects . . . and domestic servants."

Nevertheless, the widespread indifference of women to their own unequal status in a so-called free society calls for some rational explanation.

The antifeminist point of view was never more clearly expressed than in an editorial in the *New York Herald* of Sept. 12, 1852.

The editor (probably the great James Gordon Bennett), commenting on a women's suffrage meeting in Syracuse, N.Y., wrote:

> How did woman first become subject to man, as she now is all over the world? By her nature, her sex, just as the negro is and always will be to the end of time, inferior to the white race and, therefore, doomed to subjection; but she is happier than she would be in any other condition, just because it is the law of her nature.

The antifeminist today, as well as yesterday, holds

that the physiological and psychological differences between the sexes determine the roles they play—and prefer to play—as well as their condition in society. These differences are genetically and biologically ordained. Each sex possesses a "true nature." Woman's true nature is submissive, passive, dependent, and emotional. (Other adjectives often added are patient, nurturant, faithful, uncreative, and self-sacrificing.) She is born with a "feminine mentality." The true nature of man is dominant, active, independent. He is born with a "masculine mentality." To boil this proposition down to simple language, woman thinks with her womb, man thinks with his penis. Their different "mentalities," so to speak, actually *exude* from their genital organs. (Freud and the God of Adam and Eve in the Garden are in absolute accord on the proposition that anatomy is destiny. It is the ancient and traditional proposition of Judeo-Christian civilization.)

So, say the antifeminists, there really *is* no masculine discrimination or coercion against women after all. Women—at least "real women"—know what they are and what they really want. They want men to dominate them. And, give a little here or take a little there—*maybe* equal wages for equal work, for example—women want to be unequal.

The standard (though not yet traditional) position of the Women's Liberationists is that, while woman's reproductive system differs from man's, there are no other natural differences between them. (Pause, for male chauvinists to say *vive la difference.*)

Some Women's Liberationists posit a sort of prehistoric, Amazonian matriarchy in which women were once not only the natural equals of men but may have been their superiors. They also posit a time when man, more or less consciously, decided to put down and get on top of this naturally free woman, and to subjugate and exploit and enslave her for his own pleasure and profit. This he was able to do because her repeated pregnancies made her physically vulnerable. He then decreed that her physical vulnerability was evidence of her psychological inferiority.

Why, Women's Liberationists ask, if woman was indeed born to be submissive, did man find it necessary to use brute force to put—and keep—her down? (A very good question, really. Freud in his struggle to answer it came up with a melancholy solution: Woman is, by nature, masochistic; man is, by nature, sadistic. She enjoys physical suffering; he enjoys inflicting it. Altogether a dim view of both natures.) After centuries of physical violence, man finally hit upon the use of the carrot, as well as the stick, as the way to reconcile woman to her condition of servitude. He denied her all her rights but gave her certain privileges. Using the techniques that today are known as Pavlovianism and brainwashing, he finally domesticated her.

The Shackles of Her Mind. What man now calls woman's natural feminine mentality is the unnatural slave mentality he forced on her, just as he forced it on the blacks. He made her the "house nigger." (Many Women's Liberationists see women as "nigger.") In the end, man dropped the shackles from woman's body only because he had succeeded in fastening them on her mind. This, according to the Women's Liberationists, he finally did only very recently. Man did not grant woman the vote until he was reasonably certain that her slave mentality had become second nature and that she would not act to bring about her own emancipation.

But he is still taking no chances. Uppity wives are divorced and replaced by more submissive—and usually younger—ones. Uppity female employees, who insist on equal wages for equal work or who organize to protest discrimination, are eased out or fired. Only submissive employees are permitted to survive in the male chauvinist world. Pretty employees who are willing to submit to the casting couch (which, according to Women's Liberationists, is now standard office equipment) are given small privileges, small pay raises, and (sometimes) small promotions. Uppity professional women are ridiculed. (They are called pushy, aggressive, mannish, unfeminine, sexually frustrated, etc.) Altogether, the Male Establishment never lets women forget that they are all but valueless to society except as sex objects (submissive vaginas and fruitful wombs) and as devoted domestic servants (at home or at work) of their superior menfolks. Male chauvinism is the great self-serving masculine put-down of woman—the violation and despoliation of her true nature.

Insofar as both arguments rest on the theory that each sex has a true nature that determines its *social* behaviour, *roles,* and *status,* both arguments rest on a theory that cannot be proved.

Humans are never to be found living in nature—the only place where their "natural" behaviour might be studied. Male and female, they are always found living in society. In the many historical and anthropological societies in which they have lived, they have displayed an astounding variety of behaviour patterns and played an amazing diversity of roles.

Copulation, pregnancy, and childbirth are not social roles. They are biological functions. (The only *role* that cannot be divorced from the sexual function is the role of professional prostitute—male or female—whence it is called the oldest *profession.*)

While whole psychologies have been written about the desire of one sex to possess the genital organs of the other (womb envy, penis envy), each sex is inescapably stuck with its own biological functions and cannot transfer them to the other. But roles (the parts people choose or are given to play in life) are both assignable and transferable. Generally, they are assigned—or reassigned—according to the preferences or prejudices of those who dominate the society. Sometimes a social emergency, great or small, causes a sudden reassignment of roles. War comes, and Rosie the housemaid becomes Rosie the riveter. Mother falls ill and father takes care of the baby and does the housework. Both riveting and child care are assignable and reassignable roles. The assignment of roles to the sexes is often wholly arbitrary. Once a role is assigned, however, the tendency is to give the assignment the force of natural law, either directly or *à deuxième main.* Riveting is "naturally" man's work. But Rosie is doing this "unnatural" work only because it is "natural" for woman to back up her fighting man. Woman, "by nature," is supportive of masculine efforts.

In American pioneer days, it was "natural" for the pioneer wife to drive mule teams and covered wagons over uncharted deserts and mountains, and when necessary to shoot Indians. A few decades later, Pres. Grover Cleveland announced that "woman is too frail to conduct an automobile." The driving role was not "natural" to women because handling machinery, as every man knows, is not "natural" to women.

Today society accepts woman in the role of family chauffeur since it is "natural" for her to do the family shopping and take the kids to school. But her subservient role as wife requires her to relinquish her driver's role to her husband when he and she are in the car—especially when they are with another couple. What is at stake is his masculine ego, involved in the traditional assumption—belied by all insurance statistics—that any man is "by nature" a better driver than any woman.

In history women have played, at one time or another, every role that man has ever played, from absolute monarch to coal miner, from warrior to garbage collector. (She has, albeit rarely, played the "big brain" role. The only person to receive the Nobel Prize twice for science was Marie Curie. Her daughter, who was trained to be a scientist, also received it.)

There is, however, one consistent historical pattern that runs through the role of role assignment. Men are the role assigners, and they assign roles with a very sharp eye to their own interests and prejudices.

Prestigious and profitable roles are invariably assigned by men to men. Nonprestigious and unprofitable roles are assigned to women. Men are assigned the teaching role of teaching men, and *not* teaching women, to assume prestigious and profitable roles. The assignments come first; the law of nature bit comes after. Superior work is man's work because man is naturally superior; woman is naturally inferior, so woman's work (whatever the assignment) is therefore inferior. The method of assigning roles is self-validating.

In the United States, our industrialized, capitalistic society has witnessed the most extraordinary reassignment of "feminine roles" to men (and vice versa) that has ever occurred in human history.

For centuries, in Judeo-Christian society, "woman's work" was the entire preparation of food, the production of household utensils, garments, and necessities (soap, medicines, candles, etc.), the care of farm animals, and, to a large extent, work in the fields (agriculture). These and a host of other roles (together with mothering a vast brood of children) were "woman's" work. Weaving was, perhaps, woman's most prestigious work (whence, even today, women are sometimes referred to as the distaff side). Woman was the first *industrialist.*

Today all the weaving, almost all the preparation and production of food, and the manufacture of all household equipment and utensils are "man's work." Man is now the weaver, baker, butcher, candlestick maker, pot-and-pan manufacturer of society. There is almost no productive domestic task, once traditional and "natural" to woman, that man has not taken over. Even that most "natural" of all feminine tasks, washing the baby's diapers, has become man's work. The president of Tidy Diddie Diaper Service is a man, not a woman. So are the heads of the companies that make tampons for menstruating women.

It would be nice to think that man took over all this woman's work—and these "feminine roles"—to relieve overburdened housewives. The truth, of course, is that he took it over because he saw ways to make it profitable. (Profiting from work is "natural" to man. Unprofitable work is "natural" to women.)

In the United States two vast national emergencies have forced men to reassign many of their profitable industrial roles to women. During World Wars I and II, women were permitted to fill an amazing variety of roles that men had considered them "naturally" too weak, too sensitive, or too stupid to fill. Women filled many of them so well that, when the boys came home, many employers let the women go only because the law required them to do so. (The women were often better, more reliable, and definitely cheaper workers.)

A Role in Decline. The impact of technology and science on woman's world—the home—has been psychologically devastating to her precisely because it has divested her of so many traditional feminine roles that, however onerous, had given not only her personal life its meaning but traditional marriage its *economic* reason for existence.

Today, woman's traditional housewife's and child-rearing roles are in a rapid state of occupational decline.

Jeanne Binstock, a sociologist at the University of Massachusetts at Boston, points out that "mother care," which was once an 18-hour-a-day chore, has now been reduced to a four-hour service. Diaper services, convenience foods, wash-and-wear clothing, new children's medicines have saved Mom hours of child care and concern. An amazing battery of automated household equipment and precooked or convenience foods has reduced the housewife's role to a point where more than half of what she does today is gratuitous make-work. (The time that American women spend in window-shopping is a scandal to many Europeans.) The married woman has long since ceased to be a producer of goods. She has become, par excellence, a *consumer.*

With a life expectancy of $73\frac{1}{2}$ years, a 20-year-old woman with two children can count on about 20 years free from necessary child care and housework.

The question that the Male Establishment must now answer is: What does man now expect woman to *do* with this free time that his technology has given her, and what status is he willing to confer on her for doing whatever it is that he thinks she should be doing?

Man has insisted on making all the crucial decisions for woman. He is now faced with making the most crucial decision he has ever been asked to make about her—and himself. Her future happiness, and his, and the welfare of society depend on his answer. How does he see the "role of woman" in today's world, which is *not* yesterday's world?

To come to the nitty-gritty, what does he think about

FREDA LEINWAND—MAGNUM

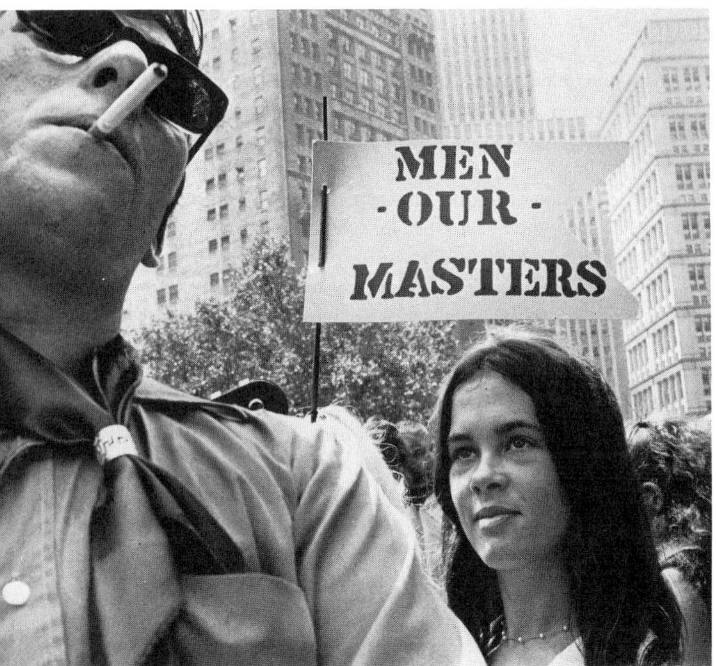

"It's a man's world . . . this is the way most women seem to like it."

the importance of her motherhood role in our overpopulated world?

Throughout most of human history the world was underpopulated. Man's broad back and woman's wide pelvis were the prime tools of human progress. Without plenty of muscles and plentiful wombs, civilization could not have been created. Man placed a high value on motherhood. The "mother of many" was given great status in man's society—so great, indeed, that birth control, abortion, infanticide, and child abandonment were, until most recent times, almost universally considered feminine crimes against nature and were severely punished.

For millenniums the image of the Madonna and Child (male) was Christianity's most revered image. Man esteemed woman—and consequently woman esteemed herself—as the necessary and glorious procreative function of society. Her greatest function was childbearing, her greatest *role* was child care.

Most of her privileges and gratifications, private and public, stemmed from fulfilling her biological function and playing her child-caring role. What human dignity and "superiority" she enjoyed, even in the eyes of her husband, stemmed from being the mother of *his* children. The childless wife was disesteemed. The spinster was an object of pity or ridicule.

The persistence of this attitude of woman herself toward the status that motherhood conferred is exemplified in a *Washington Star* interview (Aug. 8, 1972) with Eunice Kennedy Shriver, wife of Sargent Shriver and mother of 5 of Rose Kennedy's 28 grandchildren.

According to the interviewer, "Mrs. Shriver considers Motherhood the noblest profession" (the best of all feminine careers). She feels that while "Women's Lib has been good on job-discrimination and things like that, it's resulted in the down-grading of the whole concept of Motherhood."

It's not Women's Lib, of course, that is downgrading the motherhood profession; it is the awesome and terrible and ever more visible fact of overpopulation—or, rather, the consequences of overpopulation (crime, pollution, crowding, political disorders, famine, disease, the threat of nuclear war, etc.).

Says Binstock, "A reduction in the occupation of 'Mother' is now mandatory . . . we are face to face with the fact that if we *do not take from women their role of mother and replace it with something else,* we will be throttled with the over-production of babies."

Men who have begun to use computers on difficult problems rather than their brains (on the whole, a benign development in human affairs) have sometime since come to the conclusion that woman's natural and traditional *pursuit* of the profession or career of motherhood may be even more dangerous for society than his own traditional pursuit of war. Men have concluded that the uncontrolled fecundity of woman is out. And birth control is in.

Men have given their social approval to the use of the Pill. They are no longer horrified by the prospect of legal abortion, on demand, in all of the states. Mandatory vasectomies are even being proposed for men. There is already much talk in the (male-dominated) press about the possible future need to sterilize women after the birth of a second child. And there goes the only status career men have allowed women. How often in a lifetime she will be *permitted* to give birth, he will determine in the future. At present he expects (society expects) she will limit herself to two children.

Man is doing his bit, together with the Women's Liberationists, to downgrade motherhood. Consequently, he is also downgrading wifehood as a full-time female role. He is increasingly plunking for easy divorce—no-fault divorce—or divorce on demand, his and hers. His traditional resistance to "letting his wife work" is collapsing fast. Today $62\frac{1}{2}\%$ of all women who are working are married women. He is not only permitting his wife to play the dual role of unpaid housekeeper and underpaid wage earner, he is encouraging her to do so.

What man is not doing is to help woman to find, outside the home, roles that will confer on her some of the status that wifehood and motherhood have given her in the past.

What Will She Do? Man is leaving woman emotionally, physically, and economically underemployed. The result of this cruel and appallingly stupid failure in man's relations with woman is that women are having what psychologists call identity crises all over the lot. They don't know who they are or what they are. *They don't know what they are good for anymore. They don't know where they are really needed, or what society expects of them now.* They don't know how to behave.

And they are in the process of making a painful discovery: the only world that ever was really "woman's world" (the world where she was dominant) was the nursery. The nursery was the only place where she was ever really needed—where she was (when the cradle was full) irreplaceable. The only place where *she* was superior and was looked up to, not looked down on.

Where someone was inferior to her. Where she had authority. Where others were deeply dependent on her. Where her love was freely given and freely returned. Where she could be herself. At the core of that ugly phenomenon of 20th-century life called Momism lies woman's fear of her loss of status as mother and her return to the inferior status as wife. Momism is the empty cradle syndrome which so many women are having today.

If woman must now leave the nursery and the career of keeping the cradle full, what will she do, what *can* she do, but, especially, what will man *permit* her to do that will let her esteem herself and cause man to esteem her?

For countless ages women have been *conditioned* to believe that the meaning—the only meaning—of a woman's life is maternity. What is her traditional role as wife worth to her—or to him—if she is not to be the mother of many children? To both of them, perhaps, very little. "If it weren't for the children, I'd get a divorce" is a phrase that passes both masculine and feminine lips with increasing frequency.

Women are not stupid—as men have sometimes observed despite woman's best efforts to seem so. They see quite clearly the only career that seems to await them in the Male Establishment—to become, at best, the "office wife"; at worst, a dead-end sex-typed employee. And all the way down the line—no status. Marriage and two children—or even one—is better.

The stupidest and most inferior human being cannot long endure a life in which he, or she, does not experience some measure of social approval and acceptance, or in which status cannot be achieved no matter how hard he or she tries.

The awareness, conscious or unconscious, of women today that their traditionally full-time roles of wife and mother are in a state of decline, and that no other roles are open to them that promise them the same gratifications, is at the root of most of the restlessness, discontent, and psychological hang-ups they are experiencing. They are literally being driven crazy, not because they don't know what to do with their "free time" but because they think that men don't really give a hoot *what* they do with it, providing what they do doesn't cost men too much money or otherwise inconvenience or distract them.

The time has come when men must care—if not for woman's sake, for man's.

The bright boys—that is to say, men who are smart enough to forget their prejudices against women long enough to feed the Woman Problem into the computers—have already gotten some pretty clear answers on why they had better begin caring. They already have the answer to the overpopulation problem caused by women: birth control (and, fortunately, there is money to be made out of feeding women pills). They are now beginning to get answers on the problem caused by men: the underemployment of women and the discrimination that exists against them in every one of man's institutions. (She has always been his problem. He has always been hers.) Underemployment and discrimination are costing him plenty of money. The wages he refuses to pay her for working he must now fork over in taxes to keep her out of the gutter and on the relief rolls. The billions he spends on giving her an equal education are wasted when she is not permitted to use her education. She is showing a tendency to become an alcoholic (very expensive habit, for the nation). Her bills for psychiatric treatment and residence in mental institutions are mounting; he has the money; he has to pay them. Worst of all, his traditional attitude that he is superior and she inferior seems to be giving her those very identity crises, hang-ups, and neuroses that in his intimate relations with her as wife or lover are now driving *him* crazy. Altogether, his refusal to grant her equality is souring his business life, his home life—and his sex life.

His computers are also telling him that his automated, push-button, technological world, viewed as a vast machine, is quite ready to receive women operators at every level of manipulation. His political system, with its sacred credo of human equality, has always been ready, even though he has never—up to now—been willing. Today nothing stands between the creation of a Male-Female Establishment but man's own prejudice—which, granted, is a tremendous barrier.

It is not, however, impregnable. The sheer pressure of women, in ever increasing numbers, coming (or being driven) into man's world is forcing them to rise in it. Heretofore, status has never been won by women; it has always been granted to them by men.

When women, especially working women, begin to recover from the shock of realizing that the Women's Liberationists are right after all, and that men do view them as primarily sex objects, they will make the old suffragettes look like Girl Scouts on a picnic. His computers are telling him that, for the first time in history, there is a real rallying of the Sisterhood that is being led by working women and their organizations.

They will demand—and they will get—political, legal, and economic equality. They will then have won status.

The equality of the sexes, despite this author's somewhat gloomy reflections, is slowly coming about. It is bound to revolutionize all our institutions—including its most ancient one of marriage. When woman becomes the equal of man, she will get married, and he will get married, and they will stay married for one reason only —love. (There will be a lot more love in the world, because love is possible in the adult world only between equals.)

Meanwhile, the feminist organizations and the Women's Liberationists are bravely and brilliantly trying to prepare their sisters for the heaviest burden that they have so far in history been called on to carry—the burden of their own freedom.

The Equality Revolution is *not* inevitable. The environment includes nuclear weapons and also man's capacity to use them. The massive reduction of the population by nuclear war would once again require wide pelvises to repopulate the earth and broad backs to cart away the ruins of our civilization. Even the deepest-dyed "male chauvinist pig" must prefer the equality of the sexes to this way of reducing women to submissiveness, passivity, and dependence.

TECHNOLOGY CONTROL: A NEW LEVEL OF CHOICE

by Donald N. Frey

Technology has been until recently the genie of our society, the guiding force that ushered us to world leadership, an unprecedented standard of living, and new dimensions of leisure. It was possible to dream that the unrivaled productive capacities of a technological society could overcome the inequities of poverty, hunger, and ignorance and raise an entire nation—perhaps the world—to a level of affluence never before known.

Today that dream is fading, and we face social and individual problems created by technology or related to it: streams and lakes burdened with pollution, urban support systems such as sewerage and electricity straining to meet burgeoning demands, central cities choked with automobiles, a host of large and small frustrations and failures. In the wake of disillusionment, a small but growing antiscience, antitechnology movement is developing in the United States.

The U.S. is not alone in this experience. Both less developed and developed countries are finding the payoff of advanced technology less certain and often less generous than anticipated. Some applications of advanced technology have failed to meet their promise or have proceeded more slowly than anticipated; others are simply not appropriate to solving the kinds of problems to which they are applied. We have indeed found it easier to put a man on the moon than to revitalize an inner city, reduce health care costs, recycle the solid wastes of large cities, or improve law enforcement. It is time to face the question: What has gone wrong? Can we simply say that there is too much technology?

Who Guides the Machine? The relationships between technology and human society have developed great complexity. We are not simply dependent upon technology; rather, we are interdependent with it. The history of technology shows that its development has always been determined as much by social or political objectives as by scientific discoveries and invention. In fact, technology is by definition the personal and political application of science and invention. Let us take a rudimentary example: 90 million cars are registered in the U.S. alone, but this automobile boom could not have come about without a parallel innovation in economics. The credit system underwent substantial revision to permit time payments (the extension of credit) by blue-collar workers. Further, that modern credit system could not function without the computer-based technology that reads and stores financial information and transactions for millions of citizens.

The cause-effect relationship between technological development and social directions is so complex that there is little reason to assume that in technology we are dealing with an out-of-control or uncontrollable Orwellian technical monster—as long as that technical monster can be managed by the precise interventions of the financing system or the less precise options of a consumer market. However, to exercise our control we will be increasingly forced to make difficult choices between alternatives and, in some cases, we will have to accept the penalties of use.

Macro Effects of Technology. Let us first recognize that in recent times, particularly the last two decades of the 20th century, the scale of technology and its effects have been so great as to give rise to large-scale or macro effects. Most of these results are enormously helpful to mankind, but some are bad. To counter large-scale negative effects, large-scale corrective efforts must be made. It is these macro-scale negative results of technology—automotive air pollution, pollution of air and water by central power plants, industrial water and solid-waste pollution, etc.—that we will examine first.

In 1920 there were one million automobiles and trucks in all of the United States. The sink capability of the air to absorb and convert harmful combustion products was then barely tapped. Today the automotive density of Los Angeles and other cities exceeds this, and the volume of automobile combustion products far outruns the sink capability of the air. Thus individual decisions that affect pollution levels (whether or not to drive, how many cars to own) become, cumulatively, decisions that determine whether the entire population can breathe safely.

Also in 1920, the paved modern highway network in and between cities did not exist. Villages were located and cities emerged on other considerations. Today the highway network largely determines where communities start and how they grow. Consequently, if decisions of highway location are made without consideration of present or future community location, they can lead to public outcry, protest, and intervention.

As another example, population expansion compounded by the growth of prepackaged-food use, convenience packaging, newspapers, and wastepaper generally now exceeds the capacity of many urban waste-disposal systems. The individual options available in an affluent society—convenience, appearance, etc.—coupled with the population explosion pose technical problems of a new order of magnitude.

Suboptimization. Another source of human frustration with large technological systems is what systems experts call suboptimization (failure to perceive the relation of optimum smaller systems to the larger whole). The national debate over the supersonic transport considered the cost of the airplane, its economies of operation, and ecological dangers. It did not appear to consider how well

Donald N. Frey is board chairman of Bell & Howell and former executive vice-president of Ford Motor Co.

PAUL SEQUEIRA

"We are dealing with an out-of-control . . . technical monster."

it integrated into a well-balanced transportation system. While the supersonic speed of the SST had obvious advantages for in-the-air travel time, no one seemed to question whether such speed would exacerbate time-change effects on human beings or, if the same investment were made to speed up portal-to-portal air travel time (faster baggage delivery or rapid transit to and from airports in major metropolitan areas), whether the resulting system as a whole would not be even more satisfactory.

The question of noise pollution serves to bring other subsystem questions into a sometimes doubtful light. As with most technological matters, the trade-offs between technological advances and their effects on human beings involve careful weighing of losses, gains, and side effects.

Perhaps the most commonly provocative meeting of human frustration and technological capacity is the large-scale computerization of people-information. For the first time in history it is economically possible to invade our privacy seriously through the acquisition, storage, and dissemination of extensive, often highly personal, information about all people. As long as only the elite had their privacy invaded, the problem was a limited one. They could fight back. But data banks raise privacy of information to the level of a civil right.

Control and Chance: A Problem of Leadership. These macro effects generally cannot be controlled or corrected without governmental regulatory action, because of four related conditions:

1. The systems are so big that only big government can influence them, and
2. Competitive private-sector companies cannot be expected to stop or limit a business that has become harmful on a large scale unless their competitors are so limited, and
3. Competitive private-sector manufacturing or distribution companies cannot be expected to increase product costs or investments unless their competitors are also required to do so, because
4. It has been demonstrated that the individual consumer will not stop using a service or pay a noncompetitive higher price for a product or service just because one company has, for example, achieved lower pollution levels from its product or manufacturing. In fact, there is some evidence that the consumer will not pay a noncompetitive higher price even for a product or company safety difference.

The need for regulatory government processes is based on the mechanics of a free enterprise market that, in effect, penalizes a private-sector company for attempting to correct its share of macro-scale technological damage. The careful balance between the needs of the society and individual freedom can best be maintained by governmental regulation, provided:

1. All individual user sacrifices are uniformly shared, but
2. Limited to those who use a product or system, and
3. We insist on and obtain the minimum economic cost solutions consistent with the time available to correct or reduce the problem.

The first two requirements are self-evident in a democratic society; society as a whole should not be penalized for the practices of a limited number. The third requirement is the most difficult: the first step toward solving a problem is to define it accurately, then to analyze the alternative or corrective steps toward its solution. Yet large-scale social problems, arising from large-scale technology, often become important issues of politics, and the regulatory legislation needed for their solution is often passed under emotional conditions of early debate by narrow interests. This does not allow for minimum economic cost solutions or realistic time periods, nor does it permit adequate study of the problem, its causes, the secondary or related effects of solutions, or the necessary trade-offs.

The only answer to these very human problems of management and regulation must be a long, slow process of public education, communication, and debate; greater cooperation among technologists, industrialists, and government officials who share responsibility for the management of macro systems; and more active, informed participation by media and citizens in making leadership accountable for the quality of its control.

Given the macro-scale effects of modern technology, formerly private decisions have now become public decisions, subject to public debate. This shift places new requirements on industrialists and their technologists, who make and distribute large-scale systems, to learn to deal more effectively and realistically with political processes. And it requires that governmental officials, both executive and legislative, understand and learn to work with the rudiments of large-scale technology, including the principles of trade-offs, time scales necessary for defining problems and finding solutions, the possibilities of side effects or other system relationships, and use of economic analysis for consideration of alternative solutions.

We are entering an era of higher conscious choice in the public arena. Today we must consciously consider the effects of subsystems on larger systems and the unwanted side effects of macro systems. The demands of higher conscious choice are in themselves likely to be frustrating to all concerned and will require more active and informed public discussion and participation. Finally, under the new conditions of higher conscious choice, all who participate in public decision-making will need to know more about human behaviour.

Compared with the slow rate at which human beings change, today's high level of technical capability and technical rates of change give rise to another category of technology-human behaviour problems. These are much more individual or particular in nature and are measured and dealt with on a small scale. Thus we can call them micro-scale technological problems.

Micro Effects of Technology. Our species, and indeed all living species, measure genetic or inherited changes in terms of millions of years. Technology measures change today in terms of years, and the results can all too often violate instinctive, psychological, or physiological human traits. Ample evidence is also emerging that acquired behaviour of the human species is formed at a much earlier age than we had assumed until recently, and that it changes little in a lifetime. This means that acquired habits, likes, and dislikes are changed at best in terms of generations.

In times past, when technology changed little from generation to generation, problems of human habit rarely arose. Today human resistance to the rate of change of which technology is capable poses the greatest threat to the commercial success of new technology. Yet this decisive relationship—of man to change—is often less well recognized than economic factors in planning technological innovations.

Man the User. The simplest examples of small-scale or micro technical problems can be found in products whose design violates the principles of "human engineering." To be accepted, engineering must be based on both habits and some inherited physical and psychological characteristics of human beings. For example, the levers, buttons, or dials or the location of controls on a machine may be hard to read, difficult to locate, or awkward to move. The consumer may not recognize what is wrong, but may feel uncomfortable, perform marginally, or reject the product.

Acquired habits often decide the success or failure of new designs for road signs, typewriter keyboards, automotive controls, newspaper typography, the taste, colour, and packaging of food, etc. More subtle factors, largely related to physiological characteristics, determine how we perceive motion in movies or video tapes (the mind integrates blurred pictures best at a certain rate); how we read microfilm images (easiest by reflected, not transmitted, light, but probably influenced by relative motion between the image and the person); acceptable pitch variations in audio recordings; and a host of other examples. Perhaps the most ordinary instance of trying to match human habits and characteristics with a technical apparatus is the search for a safe and comfortable seat belt.

Failure to appreciate or foresee micro-scale problems is probably the greatest single factor in the waste of research and development funds. The most critical demonstration of this principle at work can be seen in the various attempts around the world to develop low-cost, high-efficiency protein sources in forms that people will accept and eat. The capacity to process and produce high-quality meat substitutes has been developed (technology), but because these substitute products lack all or some of the colour, flavour, shape, and texture of the traditional foods to which people are accustomed, needy—even starving—peoples have by and large rejected them.

Summary. Disillusionment with technology springs from our failure to understand its limits or recognize the role that human managers must play in guiding its development. Technology, far from being a magician's wand to wave over the problems of the world, is a tool, subject to human choices and control. However, to exercise our powers well, we—citizens, scientists, government officials, and all of the producers and consumers of modern goods and services—must learn to assess the capacity of technology and its effects.

The rudiments of technological control include: the ability to define and analyze unwanted effects of technological change; the ability to recognize the interrelationships between subsystems and larger systems; an understanding of the relationship between technology and human behaviour, including the limitations within that relationship; the principle of trade-offs, by which some disadvantages are bartered for highly desired advantages; the use of realistic time scales in attacking problems; and adequate economic analysis in considering alternative solutions.

We are entering an era of higher conscious choice, when population increases coupled with enhanced technical capacities have raised individual and private questions to a level of concern that involves the entire society. As developed and less developed nations experience the same transition, they too will be called upon to acquire new skills in dealing with social/technological developments. The advantages of technological advancement will be realized only to the extent that those involved in planning and controlling that advance recognize and act upon the principles of human/technological interdependence.

FEEDBACK, FAT, AND FREEDOM

by James V. McConnell

PAUL SEQUEIRA

The idea of freedom is a glorious one, an ideal that many people are willing to fight and even die for. But in spite of its patriotic sound, a growing group of behavioural psychologists now argue that—in its usual meaning, at least—"freedom" is an illusion that blinds us to the way the world really is.

These behaviourists insist that most of our actions and beliefs are determined, or controlled without our knowledge, by the people and institutions around us. Real freedom of action is limited, the argument continues, but comes mainly when we consciously manipulate the environment to make it reward us for doing what we want to do.

This view of individual freedom would not matter much if it were only a continuation of the philosophical debate—the free will versus determinism question—that has been going on for centuries. But the situation has changed. Hundreds of psychologists have conducted thousands of experiments to prove that what most people mean by "unlimited freedom" is really "unlimited ignorance" of the laws of cause and effect controlling human behaviour. More important, these psychologists have developed techniques for the deliberate modification of behaviour, and are using their techniques in schools, prisons, hospitals, business, and everyday life. The United States is the centre of behaviour modification work, but psychologists in England, Australia, the Soviet Union, Japan, and other countries are developing their own unique approaches.

With the rapid spread of such techniques, the abstract question about the nature of man's freedom has begun to emerge as a practical issue for individuals and a hot potato for politicians. Much of the controversy focuses on *Beyond Freedom and Dignity,* the new book published in 1971 by Harvard psychologist B. F. Skinner. The book brought to a boil a violent cultural debate that had been simmering between the behaviourists and a group of scholars who call themselves "humanists."

Fear of Manipulation. The humanists are outraged by what they consider Skinner's mechanistic view of man. They accuse Skinner—and all the rest of us who adopt the behavioural standpoint—of wanting to destroy everything that is pure and sacred about the human race, man's soul as well as his dignity. Because behavioural theory holds that our responses are conditioned by experience, the humanists contend that it is a bold effort to rob man of his individuality and strip him of his powers of choice. They believe that the spread of behaviour modification technique leads to ruthless manipulation of people, and they fear that Skinner's program would destroy democracy as we know it.

At first glance, Skinner's ideas about freedom surely are disturbing, dismaying, even frightening. For Skinner, like all behaviourists, sees man as being much more controlled by his body and his environment than most of us are willing to admit. But anyone who takes the trouble to learn what behavioural psychology is all about soon discovers one very important fact: this theory and the techniques based on it offer a better chance of solving many of the world's most pressing problems than does any other theory we now have available.

Indeed, most of the revolutionary advances that have recently been made in the fields of education, psychiatry and mental health, prison reform, and management techniques in business and industry have all come from skillful use of behavioural technology. At the University of California in Los Angeles, for instance, Ivar Lovaas

---

James V. McConnell, well-known behaviour modifier, is professor of psychology at the University of Michigan at Ann Arbor and editor of The Journal of Biological Psychology.

has used behaviour modification to help children break out of self-destructive patterns. In Illinois, Nathan Azrin has solved the incontinence problem for most patients in state hospitals; if you have ever smelled an old people's ward, you know that the men and women who cannot control their bowels make life unbearable for themselves and everyone around. Azrin's method is spreading to other hospital systems wherever psychologists are sensitive to a patient's need to break out of this embarrassing habit. In Kansas, working groups of psychologists and educators are using behaviour modification to bring about radical improvement in the school system. Both in the U.S. and in other countries, programmed learning and other adaptations of Skinnerian theory are providing the major thrust toward better education.

The list of new applications of behaviour modification is almost endless, and in almost every case the results are dramatic enough to ensure that the techniques will spread to many more groups and be used to solve many more problems. So perhaps it is worth anyone's time to find out what the present cultural debate between the behaviourists and their critics, the humanists, is all about.

Behaviour Modification Practice and Prejudice. Before going further, it is important that you know the extent of my commitment to behaviourism. Though it would be silly for me to try to rig the argument unfairly, I am not a detached observer and do not want to be. In my years of laboratory experiments—with rats, people, and even flatworms—I have become increasingly convinced of the truth of the behaviourist view and of the service that it can offer to any society.

Students in my behavioural psychology course at the University of Michigan have turned up a richer variety of behavioural problems and solutions than I would ever have discovered by myself. As soon as each student proves that he understands behavioural theory—by using it to modify some aspect of his own behaviour—my staff and I send him out into the field to work with any one of a wide range of clients. Our clients typically include mental patients, inmates at a nearby prison, school kids who can't read, overweight people, juvenile delinquents and their families, married couples on the verge of divorce, heavy smokers, and even supervisors at a local company whose workers are not meeting production standards. The students' work has given me an almost unlimited faith in the potential of behaviourism, and has reassured me against the fears of the humanists. As I shall explain later, one student provided a classical case study of the fight to control one's own behaviour.

The question of freedom raised by the humanists cannot be brushed aside. What does the average person want these days? The financial security of a good job? A happy home life? An end to war? All those things, perhaps, and many more. But right up at the top of the list would probably be the word "freedom." Some might call it the right to do our own thing, not to be hassled, while others might say they want to run their own business without government sticking in its nose. Most of us, however, want to control our own destiny, without any limits being imposed upon our behaviour.

Those of us who practice behaviourism, however, believe that we have to begin with an understanding of the limits in order to find freedom. Everything you say or do is influenced by three things: (1) the way your body functions, which includes the biological limits imposed by man's evolutionary experience with his environment; (2) your personal experiences with an environment that taught you to act in particular ways; and (3) the environment you find yourself in, which is really a range of specific stimuli to which you react. Since most of us never learn how crucial these three sets of environmental forces are, we are pushed around willy-nilly all our lives without realizing it. When we fail to get the things we want out of life, we blame everyone but ourselves—and yet, to the behaviourist, it is our own ignorance that keeps us from attaining our most cherished goals. Once we discover how to measure the forces that indeed shape our behaviour, then we are at last free to take conscious control of ourselves. The solving of most problems, large and small, public and private, usually boils down to finding out how to change behaviour—your own or that of people around you. The usual discussion of problem-solving begins on a lofty level and deals with a complex matter like air pollution, a practice that prevents anybody from ever getting down to the practical questions about freedom. To avoid this dead-end street, let us work here with a simple case study of a recent student at Michigan. I shall call him "Meatball McClannahan," not to make light of him but to protect his privacy. His painful experience throws light on the fundamental issues raised by any serious effort to modify behaviour.

When this young man first enrolled in my course, he was 19 years old, stood 5 ft. 6 in. tall—and weighed 213 lb. He was miserable. His friends at the college dormitory made him the butt of a thousand jokes; "Meatball" is actually one of the nicer nicknames they called him. Although he was fond of being with people, his social life was almost nonexistent. He had gone to the university's health clinic several times. The doctors there examined him, found nothing physically wrong, and gave him a diet to follow. He fell off the first diet with a resounding crash, so the dietician gave him another. But he could not manage that one either, so he gave up in disgust. His failure in the effort to deal with this urgent personal problem made him doubt his capacity to do anything well. He was drifting, and stumbled into my class largely by accident.

Once he understood behavioural theory, McClannahan reluctantly realized that the obvious test for him, before he should attempt to modify the behaviour of others, would be to shed a few pounds. He made it. With the help of one of my assistants, he eventually designed his own weight-control program, under which he lost 40 lb. in two weeks. He then invented a less rigorous program to get himself down to a lean, normal weight and stay there.

Fat Research. In gaining control of his own weight, McClannahan learned more about freedom and responsibility, as well as about physiology and psychology, than he could have learned from months of reading a textbook and attending my lectures. He had to discover why his body felt hungry all the time, what in his early life had biased him toward fatness, and how his family and friends influenced what he ate. Only when he had measured the three main factors affecting his eating behaviour was he able to bring them under control.

Any such analysis has to begin with the obvious question: Why do people get fat? The quick and dirty answer is that people eat too much or they exercise too little. If you take in more food energy each day than you use up, your body stores the surplus as fat. Individuals differ in the amount of energy they spend, but what counts is the balance between the gross number of calories taken in and the energy expended. At Harvard's School of Public Health, physiologist Jean Mayer has spent years of research knocking down alternative theories—among them the recurrent notion that some kinds of calories don't count. To lose weight, Mayer insists, you must either increase exercise or cut total calories.

But most of us are not athletes, and even a man who earns his daily bread by digging ditches can grow fat if he eats too many rich foods and drinks too much beer. As a product of evolution, Mayer says, man's body is shaped by the centuries when food was scarce and unreliable, and survival demanded far more effort than most of today's jobs. That is why any weight-control program in this affluent, low-sweat environment must almost always involve a reduction in the number of calories that the person consumes.

Three Theories of Obesity. In general, then, people grow fat because they eat too much. But why do they do so? Being overweight certainly does not help them very much. Medical research shows that the more obese you are, the more likely it is that you will suffer heart attacks, high blood pressure, strokes, and a variety of other physical ills. More than this, fat people are badly discriminated against in most modern societies. Any man or woman who is obese has trouble buying good-looking clothes, getting out of chairs, and squeezing into small automobiles. Fat people are less likely to be hired for many jobs than are individuals of normal weight (how many fat airline stewardesses have you seen?). Mayer and another scientist recently made a study of how well overweight adolescents get along in our school systems. Their answer is: Fat kids don't get along well at all. School counselors are much less likely to write letters of recommendation for an overweight student than for one who is not. Faced with two students of equal intelligence and with equally good grades, colleges are more likely to admit a student of normal weight than one who is noticeably obese. Many studies show that fat students suffer various forms of discrimination: they win fewer school offices and honours, get lower grades than lean students of comparable intelligence, and, of course, have fewer dates. With so many pressures to stay slim, it is clearly irrational for anyone to gorge himself.

So why do they do it? Three brilliant researchers have developed three different theories to answer this question, and each backs up his work with careful experiments. One of the roughest scientific battles of 1973

KEN HEYMAN

An experimental psychologist, not a philosopher, B. F. Skinner rouses legitimate rage among serious humanists.

is apt to come out of their effort to resolve, at last, their different interpretations of each other's data. Harvard's Mayer focuses on the startling differences in energy output by different individuals; even in doing the same thing, such as playing tennis, people prone to obesity exert themselves much less than normals. Psychologist Stanley Schachter of Columbia University has demonstrated that fat people and fat rats react to external stimuli, like the sight of food, more than to the actual hungering of their stomachs. But Richard Nisbet at the University of Michigan, formerly a student of Schachter's, thinks that the decisive factor may be the varying number of hungry fat cells in each individual's body.

Whatever the outcome of this scientific battle, all three agree, as do most scientists, that there is a genetic component to body size—that you may inherit from your parents a tendency to weigh too much or too little. Recent research has uncovered surprising information on the physiology of eating behaviour and how this inherited body machinery may control weight, or fail to. Buried away deep in the centre of your brain is a small bundle of nerves called the hypothalamus. Although it is only about the size of your fingertip, your hypothalamus has a large influence on your emotions and your motivations. From laboratory experiments on white rats, and from studies of humans with various types of brain damage, we have recently learned that two tiny sections of the hypothalamus exercise important control over eating behaviour. One of these tiny bundles of nerve cells is called the feeding centre. If we place the tip of a very thin metal needle, an electrode, in the middle of a rat's feeding centre, we can stimulate or excite

VANCOUVER SUN

"Behavioural theory holds that our responses are conditioned by experience."

the nerve cells there by passing a weak electrical current through the needle. Whenever we do so, the rat begins to eat. Even if the rat has just consumed a huge meal, it will start to nibble away on whatever is handy and will continue to eat until we turn off the current. If we keep the stimulation up long enough, we can make the rat grow quite fat. On the other hand, if we surgically remove this feeding centre from the animal's hypothalamus, it will often stop eating altogether—unless we coax it.

Close to the feeding centre in the hypothalamus is another bundle of nerve cells that scientists have named the satiation centre. If we place an electrode in this part of the rat's brain, we can bring the animal close to starvation merely by stimulating this centre electrically each time the rat starts to eat. As soon as the current is turned on, the rat stops eating, no matter how starved it is. On the other hand, if we remove the satiation centre surgically, the rat goes on a nonstop food orgy. It will eat and eat and eat until it gets so fat it can hardly move.

Like a Thermostat. Under normal circumstances, the nerve cells in the feeding centre and the satiation centre act as alarm mechanisms to let the rest of your brain know whether or not you need food. As soon as you have eaten and digested a meal, the sugar molecules in the food are picked up by your bloodstream and are passed along to all the cells in your body. These sugar molecules stimulate or excite the satiation centre cells much as does electrical current from an electrode. These same sugar molecules have a negative or inhibitory effect on the cells in your feeding centre. The higher your blood sugar level, the more the nerves in your feeding centre are repressed or turned off. On the other hand, when you starve yourself for a while, the opposite set of events occurs—the decrease in the number of sugar molecules allows the nerve cells in your feeding centre to become more and more excited. They feed this message back to the rest of your brain, saying, "Eat—eat—eat!" Meanwhile, the decrease in your blood sugar level inhibits or turns off the cells in your satiation centre, so they stop sending feedback signals to the rest of your brain saying you have had enough.

Most of the diet pills on the market today were designed to fool your hypothalamic centres into responding the same way they do when you have just had a big meal. Unfortunately, none of the pills works very well. To begin with, your stomach also lets your brain know whether or not you have had anything to eat lately. As soon as you ingest a large meal, the muscles in the walls of your stomach go to work to press the food down and help digestion. If you eat lunch at 12 noon each day, the muscles soon learn that they must start work at this time, and they begin performing "warm-up exercises" around 11:30 A.M. Since there is nothing much in your stomach at 11:30, the muscles press down on empty air. Your stomach gurgles and growls a bit, and you often feel a sharp burst of pain when these muscles contract. Your brain quite rightly interprets this "feedback" information as meaning that it's time to eat, so you start thinking about food even before it's time to knock off for lunch. A few of the diet pills available today include chemicals that swell up like a balloon when you swallow them, the hope being that your stomach muscles will be fooled into thinking you have eaten a big meal when you really haven't.

Psychology of Fatness. If controlling your eating behaviour were merely a matter of controlling the feedback that your hypothalamic centres and your stomach muscles send to your brain, medical science could probably solve the problem of obesity rather rapidly. For the most part, however, the doctors have failed to do so. At the 1972 summer meeting of those physicians interested in weight problems, the following facts came to light:

By medical standards 20 to 50 million Americans are overweight. They spend about $400 million a year on reducing drugs and treatments, but most of this is money down the drain. The average family physician treats about 120 patients a year for obesity. At the most, five or six of these patients suffer from an inherited condition or from damage to the hypothalamic centres. These people usually benefit from medical treatment. The other 115 patients are physically normal; they eat too much for purely psychological reasons. Only two or three of these people will show any long-term benefits from the usual diets, pills, and medical treatment. As Alvan Feinstein of the Yale Medical School pointed out recently, the success rate of medically oriented weight-loss programs is "terrible, much worse than in cancer." In 95% of these cases, then, fatness is not the result of physiological malfunction. People grow obese not because they have damaged hypothalamic centres but because they have not learned how to control the feedback these centres give them—and because their stomach muscles have been trained to react the wrong way at the wrong times. As we will see later, an individual can gain control over his bodily processes—but first he must learn how his early childhood experiences and his present crop of friends keep him eating enough to stay fat.

Food not only provides our bodies with fuel, it provides comfort to our minds as well. Food has symbolic or emotional values that often far outweigh its physiological importance.

Most psychologists believe that you cannot treat a person for fatness unless you understand the emotional, symbolic value that food has for that person. Freud, the father of psychoanalysis, was fascinated by symbolic meanings that eating has for most of us. During the first year or so of its life, an infant is almost completely dependent upon its mother for all the food that it gets. Freud called this the "oral sucking period" of a child's life, during which a great many of its pleasures come to it through its mouth. If the mother gives the infant love and affection while she is feeding it, the child will make a healthy adjustment. But if the mother is cold and indifferent, Freud believed that the child's oral needs would not be satisfied and its adjustment would be restricted.

Eating as Conditioned Pleasure. Behavioural psychologists agree with psychoanalysts that oral habits are learned early and that the mother is a very important figure in a child's life. But the behaviourist does not stop there; he looks at the situation in terms of the "reward value" that various types of foods—and ways of eating—come to have. For instance, most fat children have fat parents. In many cultures where starvation is a fact of life, there is a strong belief that a fat child is a healthy child. Therefore, even when food is abundant, these parents may force their children to overeat in the mistaken belief that this action makes their offspring healthy. If the parents are fat themselves, they may *without realizing it* encourage their children to eat to make the kids more like themselves.

Anthropologists find that parents in many cultures use food as a reward for good behaviour. When the child does something particularly good, the child is given sweets or an extra dessert as a form of praise. Later, when the child has grown into a teen-ager, he or she may confuse love and affection with eating too much. When things go wrong and the parents are not around to help out, the young person may raid the icebox as a substitute for the absent arms of its mother and father. The more things go wrong, the more the child eats. And the fatter the young person gets, the more society discriminates against it, so the more it seeks out the substitute affection it finds in rich desserts. Putting this kind of young person on a diet is asking for trouble—unless one first tries to find out what the individual's parents are like and what food habits they themselves have.

Let us come back now to Meatball McClannahan. He was born into what sociologists call a lower-class family, that is, a family whose income is fairly low and comes from jobs involving physical labour. Both his father, an assembly-line worker, and his mother were overweight. This fact should not surprise us. In a recent study of 1,660 adults living in New York City, 32% of the lower-class men and 30% of the lower-class women were found to be obese. However, only 16% of the upper-class men and 5% of the upper-class women were overweight. Four times as many upper-class women in this New York group were judged to be thin as were women in the lower class. Three times as many upper-class people were on diets as were people from the so-called lower class. Interestingly enough, the only exception to these findings came with lower-class individuals who were "upwardly mobile," that is, trying to better themselves in life. People moving up the ladder of success tend to take on the attitudes, values, and behaviours of the next-higher socioeconomic class.

My student found he had become fat because his parents had pushed food on him all his life; he stayed fat even in college because the people around him wanted him to stay that way. Meatball couldn't go on a diet and stick to it until he found some way of changing the behaviour of his close friends and associates.

Friendly Persuaders. Neither McClannahan's parents nor his friends were consciously aware of the effect their behaviour had on the amount that he ate. Indeed, when he tried to point this out to them, they all denied any responsibility for his fatness. It was, they said, his problem and not theirs. But to a behavioural psychologist, it is what you actually do, not what you *think* you are doing, that counts. Nature has given us very fine feedback systems—the hypothalamic centres and the stomach muscles—that let us know what effect our eating has on our blood sugar level. But we have no inborn mechanisms that tell us how what we do affects the people around us. We have to learn what the consequences of our actions are. We have to learn to monitor the awesome influence that everything we do has on everyone near us. Not until the last decade or so have psychologists themselves learned enough about the human mind to develop effective ways of teaching us to monitor our own behaviour.

The inexpensive tape recorder is one of the most effective teaching tools ever discovered because it gives us instantaneous feedback about our verbal behaviour. If a psychologist merely takes notes while a husband and wife talk with each other, then gives the couple his own impressions (feedback) on what they said, they often object that he was a biased or prejudiced observer. If the psychologist plays back a recording of their conversation, stopping it to point out the effect that each person has on the other, the couple can hardly dispute the accuracy of the tape machine. Richard B. Stuart, a behaviourist teaching at the University of Michigan, recently reported a clever use of tape recorders in his research on obesity. Stuart was treating a number of women clients who had failed to lose weight even on the most stringent of diets. Suspecting that their husbands might be part of the cause, Stuart gave these women small tape machines to take home with them and asked them to record their dinner-table conversations for a week or two. Stuart then played the tapes back and analyzed the verbal interchanges between man and wife.

According to Stuart, the husbands exercised a profound if subtle influence over what their wives ate. For example, the men were seven times more likely than their wives to talk about food at the table. The husbands were four times more likely to offer food to their overweight wives than vice versa. And the men were 12 times more likely to offer criticism of their wives' eating behaviour than they were to praise it. When given a questionnaire to answer, 90% of these men stated that they wanted to see their wives lose weight. Their actual behaviour toward their wives suggested that many of them wanted just the opposite—without realizing it.

Stuart undertook fairly extensive interviews with 55 husbands of overweight women. His data indicate that many men have rather plausible but largely unconscious reasons for keeping their women fat. Some men find the dinner table a most pleasant social environment; when their wives go on diets and refuse to share good food, that atmosphere is destroyed. Other men use their wives' fatness as a bargaining point in family arguments; if the wife lost weight, one proof of the man's superiority would lose its power. Some men appeared to be afraid that they could not hold onto their wives if the women became too attractive; by keeping the women fat, the men thought they were keeping them faithful. And a small group of husbands apparently had lost any physical desire for their wives some time before; for these men, the wife's obesity explained both the husband's sexual inattentiveness toward her and his need to chase after other (thinner) women.

Not all husbands push calories onto their wives in order to win arguments or to keep them faithful. The point is that some men did—and felt justified by the belief that their wives were "free" to eat or not eat, because they were convinced that fatness is the sole responsibility of the person doing the overeating.

The Cost of Illusion. Student McClannahan, like most of us, wanted freedom to do anything his heart desired. But one of the first things he learned was that this notion of freedom was only a childish desire to violate the laws of cause and effect, and that you pay a heavy price for this delusionary freedom. He had to learn that there were both physical and psychological limits on everything he did, whether he knew about them or not. He couldn't flap his arms like a bird and fly off into the sunset—the law of gravity kept him earthbound whether he believed in that law or not. He couldn't eat all the rich foods he wanted and just pretend they wouldn't make him fat—because his body obeyed biological laws and paid no attention to his illusions. Before he could change his weight, he had to change his mind. He had to accept the fact that the people around him placed psychological limits on what he could and could not do. But he also discovered that once he knew what these restraints were, he had almost complete choice to do what he wanted as long as he took the limits into account and was willing to pay the price for what he got.

Change always costs you something. McClannahan found that giving up his illusions about himself was painful; giving up his old eating habits hurt even more. For to do so, he had to become a great deal more sensitive to the behaviour of the people around him than he ever had been before. Suspecting that his mother was responsible for his fatness in the first place, he began to observe and record the various ways in which she responded to him and to food. He found that, even when he told her he was on a diet, she kept insisting that he "eat something." She prepared glorious gravies and delicious desserts instead of lean meats and green vegetables. She continually passed him dishes at the table, and she fixed him snacks between meals. It seemed to Meatball that the only way she knew of expressing her affection was to cook for him. Before he could change the shape of his own waistline, Meatball had to find better ways for his mother to show him that she loved him. And this meant that he had to change his ways of responding to what she did.

His mother, he found, had coaxed him into overeating when he was a child, so it was her fault that he grew up to be fat. But he soon realized that he was responsible for her continuing to overfeed him after he was old enough to know better. He discovered to his horror that each time she gave him food he thanked her, smiled at her, hugged her, showed her his appreciation. Together, they were doing a superb job of keeping him overweight. To break this vicious circle, he did two things. First, he stopped giving her social rewards whenever she pressed food on him. He simply ignored all of her efforts to get him to eat. Instead, he enlisted her help in his dieting. Whenever she talked about diets, or how slim he would eventually be, or how he ought to get more exercise, he beamed at her and gave her a kiss. Whenever she talked about the joys of eating, he changed the subject. She soon learned the best way to show her love for him was to help him lose weight—and she prepared low calorie meals for him when he was home on weekends. She even gave him an extra $30 to help with his weight-control program at school.

Once McClannahan had his homelife under control, he cast a jaundiced eye on what his roommates were doing to him. His mother had gotten him fat in the first place but, as he suspected, his friends at school were keeping him that way. First, they enjoyed calling him "Meatball." He was great to poke fun at. When he tried to go on a diet, they enjoyed tempting him to break it. They were not conscious of what they were doing, of course, but the result was the same. They sensed that if he lost weight, they would lose a lot of good times. So he had to change the way his roommates responded to him before he could win his battle of the bulge. Using the $30 his mother had given him, he found a very effective way of making it worth his friends' time to help him stay on his diet.

At his teacher's suggestion, the fat student got a very large piece of graph paper that he posted prominently on the back of his door. He explained to his roommates that he was going to weigh in each morning and record the results on the chart. He told them that the graph would give him daily feedback as to how successful he was, and that you could never change yourself without feedback. But he also needed their help because, as they knew, he did not have the discipline to give up food on his own. So he was willing to hire them as his dietary assistants. Every day his graph went down, meaning that he had lost weight, they were to congratulate him in every way they could think of—and he would respond by paying them $2. Every day he did not lose weight, they were to ignore him—but of course they wouldn't get the two bucks for that day either. He now had made it well worth his friends' time and effort to get him to lose weight. They were so happy with the deal that they spontaneously promised to clean up the apartment on their own each day they got the $2. Since McClannahan hated cleaning chores, their response gave him an extra incentive to do well. Even before he started working on the people around him, my student began to make some changes in himself. He asked the school doctor if he could give up food entirely for two weeks. His mother was sure he would die if he starved for a day or so. After the examination, the doctor told him he could easily live six or seven weeks without eating anything at all, so two weeks wouldn't kill him. In fact, it would do him good. The doctor also gave him an attractive diet that he would be able to follow once the two weeks were over.

Then McClannahan started working on his stomach muscles and his hypothalamic centres. They were accustomed to his eating at very regular intervals, and when he missed a meal, they complained in no uncertain terms. So he began to retrain them. For several weeks—while he was studying the behaviour patterns of his mother and his roommates—he ate at very odd times. Sometimes he had only one big meal a day; at other times he ate several small snacks. By the time he was ready to stop eating altogether, his body didn't know quite what to expect—and so it gave him less misery than he had expected. The first three or four days of complete starvation were the worst, but after that he really didn't feel hungry much at all. And, of course, his roommates were there to help him resist food when the hunger pangs were at their worst.

When this student reported on his project in class, he gave his roommates full credit for their assistance, even though they later admitted they had not really believed he would make it. After all, he had tried dieting many times before with little success. They could not imagine that a graph and $2 a day would make any difference. Therefore, their surprise and pleasure were quite genuine as, day after food-free day, Meatball's weight graph dropped and they earned their money. At the end of the two weeks, when he had shed 40 lb., they had a celebration. They took him out to dinner. All he ate was a big salad, but it was the best-tasting food he could remember. Thereafter, using the doctor's diet, he lost another 20 lb. over a two-month period. Since he wanted to exercise more, he started recording the number of push-ups and sit-ups he did daily on his big graph. His mother promised to buy him new clothes if he met his exercise quotas for the two months he was on the doctor's diet. She called him once or twice a week to find out how he was doing and, when he met his goals, took him on a shopping spree. Now 60 lb. lighter with his well-exercised body in new clothes, he earned a new nickname—"Hotdog."

Any theory of behaviour must, to be useful, come down to the average individual and his conduct. The story of Meatball McClannahan, anonymous and fat student at Michigan, lends perspective to current scientific research on an everyday behaviour—in this case, eating—and the issues that are raised by any attempt to modify that behaviour.

ENRICO NATALI—RAPHO GUILLUMETTE

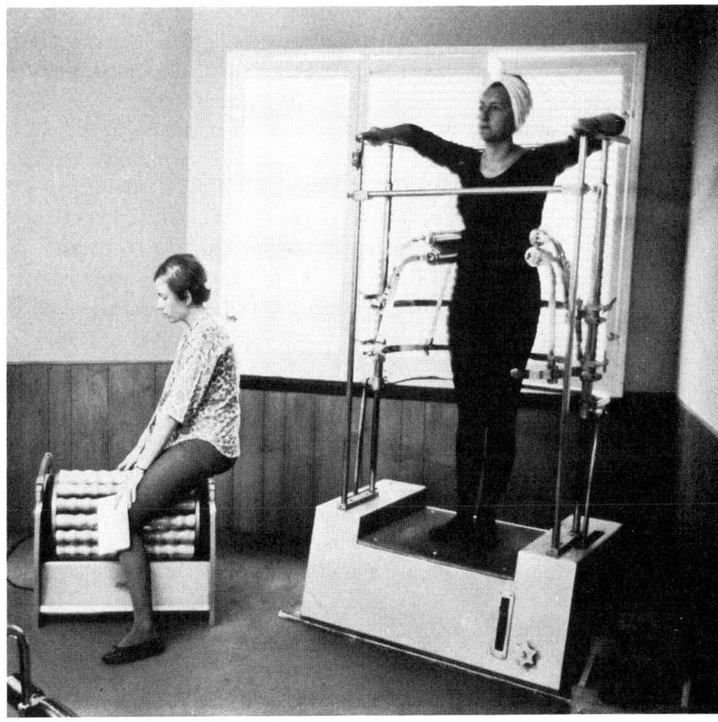

"[Americans] spend about $400 million a year on reducing drugs and treatments . . . most of this is money down the drain."

First and foremost, it is clear that many of us, including the humanists, are prisoners of our own superstitions and ignorance. We think that we have control over everything we do when, in fact, our behaviour is shaped by influences that our cultural traditions hide from us. Most of what we think are our actions are really reactions—reactions to the behaviour patterns of our families, friends, and acquaintances. We cling with emotional fervour to the humanistic notion that we can make of ourselves what we wish merely by willing it; in truth, we cannot make major changes in ourselves without first changing the social environment in which we live.

Second, the student's story suggests that we usually cannot influence the behaviour of people around us unless we are willing to accept responsibility for the consequences of even our smallest actions. Meatball's mother encouraged him to overeat because he continued to reward her for that encouragement. When he wanted to reshape her responses, he first had to alter the small and seemingly insignificant ways in which he responded to her. He had to learn to reward her helping behaviours and not the hindering behaviours that kept him fat. Merely explaining the situation to her—or to his roommates—did no good. For their behaviours were habitual, the product of many years of learning, and they needed his help in changing as much as he needed theirs. In short, he had to retrain them—using things they wanted as rewards—before they could help him retrain himself.

Scientific studies suggest that the most effective way to help someone learn anything new is by a "shaping" technique in which you reward even the smallest step in the right direction and ignore any mistakes or backsliding. From the behaviourist's point of view, one of the very real problems in our society is the widespread belief, even among humanists, that punishment is a more effective tool for changing behaviour than reward. But the opposite is true, as dozens of lab experiments have shown. If you point out a person's mistakes or offer what you think is constructive criticism, the *actual* effect you will typically have is negative. That is, the person will dislike you, reject your comments, and will continue to behave pretty much the same as always. You can sometimes force a person to change—momentarily—by using threats and punishments. But as soon as you turn your back, the person will usually take great glee in working against you. However, if you offer the individual something of value for behaving differently, you not only make changes, you make a friend as well. McClannahan reported in class that, by the time the first two weeks of his starvation were over, he and his roommates were so responsive to each other's needs that they became much closer friends than they ever had been before. Punishment simply would not have achieved the same results.

Many humanists object that rewarding socially acceptable behaviour instead of punishing poor performance is the same thing as bribing people to be good. According to some interpretations of the humanist position, for instance, children owe their parents a certain measure of love and respect no matter what the parents do. The behaviourist sees this as a convenient attempt to violate what we call the Law of TANSTAAFL—that psychological principle that "There Ain't No Such Thing As a Free Lunch." Anyone who has worked with problem children can tell you that most juvenile delinquents have parents who are negative, punishing, and repressive, who attempt to control their child's behaviour with threats and physical abuse instead of using love and encouragement. Sadly enough, families that expect their children to be good for nothing usually wind up with good-for-nothing children. Humanists often talk about man's rights—those things that the world, or Nature, or God should give to man "for free." The behaviourist believes that we must pay for what we get, including the loving responses of the people around us. Our scientific data support the Golden Rule. To our way of thinking, Meatball was merely doing to his mother and his friends what he wanted them to do to him in return.

"We cling . . . to the . . . notion that we can make of ourselves what we wish merely by willing it."

JIM JOWERS—NANCY PALMER PHOTO AGENCY

Another fear often raised concerning the scientific study of human behaviour by Skinner's critics is this: Isn't the new behavioural technology little more than a form of mind control or brainwashing? If governments or big business or the advertising media start using these techniques, won't we be pushed around even more than we are right now? Doesn't behaviourism lead toward dictatorships and the creation of a social climate as frightening as the nightmare world described in George Orwell's novel *Nineteen Eighty-Four*?

Oddly enough, the opposite seems to be true. In Orwell's world, the dictator called Big Brother kept power by torturing or killing anyone who opposed him, not by rewarding his subjects when they behaved properly. Big Brother gave his people no real choice—"obey or die" was his motto. And so his subjects fought and died, because they had no other more effective way of influencing Big Brother's behaviour. The politician who attempts to use rewards instead of punishments finds himself in rather a different world; he must offer worthwhile alternatives to the voters. If they decide against him, then he did not offer them enough of what they wanted or needed. Big Brother pried and snooped into people's private lives to uncover the slightest deviation from his harsh rules; a politician who wants to use behavioural technology must develop effective feedback methods so that his finger is constantly monitoring the pulse of humanity. He must discover what people really desire and make these things available to them, or he is voted out of office. So the voters control him, not the other way around.

Real freedom, then, comes from knowledge—from knowing your own biological and psychological needs, from learning the effects you have on others, from becoming sensitive to how the behaviour of other people actually influences you. But this kind of knowledge always involves the development of finely tuned feedback systems: you come to know your own body when you learn how to listen to its special language, and you best achieve your goals in life by becoming aware of the continuous interplay between you and your social environment. Only by learning the limits on your freedom do you gain control of your destiny. The behaviourist, working within this strict discipline, can claim a hopeful motto: "Ye shall know the truth, and the truth shall make you free."

1972 Chronology of major events

JANUARY

1

Final installment of Kennedy Round tariff reductions went into effect.

2

Saigon military sources said intensive U.S. air raids over North Vietnam, Dec. 26–30, 1971, were not as effective as had been hoped because of bad weather.

3

William R. Tolbert, Jr., was inaugurated as president of Liberia.

Agreement limiting Japanese textile exports to the U.S. was initialed in Washington.

Nonsocialist parties obtained a majority in Finnish parliamentary elections.

U.S. newspaper columnist Jack Anderson continued publication, begun in late 1971, of secret material purporting to show that U.S. policy during the Indo-Pakistani war had been more favourable to Pakistan than was publicly acknowledged.

4

U.S. Food and Drug Administration began a long-range review of the safety and efficacy claims of nonprescription drugs.

5

U.S. Pres. Richard M. Nixon ordered the National Aeronautics and Space Administration (NASA) to begin work on a manned space shuttle.

7

Pres. Nixon and Japanese Prime Minister Eisaku Sato, following two days of talks, the last of Nixon's meetings with world leaders prior to his planned Peking and Moscow visits, announced final terms for the return of Okinawa to Japan on May 15.

Bombs placed in safety deposit boxes in eight major U.S. banks were defused by police after several newspapers received letters giving their locations.

South Vietnamese troops were reported to have moved into northeast Cambodia in the fourth such operation in two months.

8

Bangladesh Pres. Mujibur Rahman was freed from detention in Pakistan; former Pakistani Pres. Agha Muhammad Yahya Kahn was reported to have been placed under house arrest.

9

Mrs. Richard Nixon completed an eight-day tour of West Africa.

"Queen Elizabeth" ocean liner was destroyed by fire in Hong Kong Harbour.

Telephone caller claiming to be millionaire recluse Howard Hughes told reporters that author Clifford Irving's purported biography of him was a fake.

10

U.S. Defense Department announced that a naval task force sent to the Indian Ocean during the Indo-Pakistani war had been withdrawn.

U.S. federal judge ordered the predominantly black schools of Richmond, Va., to merge with predominantly white schools of two suburban counties.

11

Pearce commission arrived in Salisbury, Rhodesia, to test popular acceptability of the November 1971 U.K.-Rhodesian agreement settling Rhodesian independence.

Laotian troops were driven from the Boloven Plateau in southern Laos by North Vietnamese forces.

12

Pres. Joseph Mobutu of Zaire (formerly Congo [Kinshasa]) changed his name to Mobutu Sese Seko as part of an africanization program.

Mujibur Rahman resigned as president of Bangladesh and assumed the post of prime minister; Abu Sayeed Choudhury was sworn in as president under a provisional constitution.

13

Ghanaian Prime Minister Kofi Busia, in London for medical treatment, was deposed in a military coup led by Col. Ignatius Kutu Acheampong.

Egyptian Pres. Anwar as-Sadat explained in a national address that his "year of decision," 1971, had passed without war with Israel because the Indo-Pakistani war had confused the international balance of power.

U.S. officials revealed that an "agreement in principle" on U.S. aid to Israel's defense industry had been signed on Nov. 1, 1971.

Pres. Nixon announced that 70,000 more U.S. troops would be withdrawn from Vietnam within three months, leaving 69,000 by May 1.

14

Formation of a new government in the Yugoslav republic of Croatia was announced in a continuing purge of nationalism begun late in 1971.

Rep. James Scheuer (Dem., N.Y.) was expelled from the U.S.S.R. for "improper activities"; previously he had been detained after visiting Soviet Jews.

15

Margrethe II was proclaimed queen of Denmark following the death of her father, King Frederik IX, the previous day.

Maltese Prime Minister Dom Mintoff canceled his ultimatum ordering all U.K. troops out of Malta that day.

Italian Premier Emilio Colombo and his Cabinet resigned after the Republican Party withdrew its support of the government.

16

Two opposition candidates won congressional seats in Chilean by-elections widely regarded as tests of strength for Pres. Salvador Allende Gossens.

Dallas Cowboys won the National Football League championship by defeating the Miami Dolphins 24–3.

17

New government designed to put Egypt on a war footing was formed by Aziz Sidky, who had replaced Mahmoud Fawzi as prime minister the preceding day.

18

Second session of the 92nd U.S. Congress convened in Washington, D.C.

Egyptian students began a sit-in at Cairo University demanding a more aggressive policy toward Israel.

19

North Vietnamese MiG-21 was shot down over North Vietnam by a U.S. plane, the first such occurrence since March 28, 1970, as the air war over Indochina intensified.

20

Six Persian Gulf countries signed an agreement with Western oil companies compensating them for the devaluation of the U.S. dollar.

Pres. Nixon, in his state of the union address, urged Congress to enact his legislative proposals.

Gaston Eyskens formed a new Cabinet, ending a ten-week government crisis in Belgium.

22

Treaty providing for the entry of the U.K., Denmark, Ireland, and Norway into the European Communities was signed in Brussels.

24

Three officers of the Soviet fishing fleet were charged in an Anchorage, Alaska, court with violating U.S. fishing regulations.

Pres. Nixon submitted to Congress a deficit budget for fiscal 1973.

U.S.S.R. became the first major power to recognize Bangladesh.

Japanese Army Sgt. Shoichi Yokoi was found in the jungles of Guam where he had lived for 28 years since U.S. troops had taken the island in World War II.

25

Pres. Nixon, in a television address, revealed that in October 1971 he had submitted an eight-point plan to end the Vietnam war to the North Vietnamese peace talk delegates in Paris and that secret negotiations over the plan had gone on for some months without results.

U.S. Congress completed action on a bill authorizing foreign aid expenditures of $2,750,000,000 for fiscal 1972.

U.S. Commerce Department announced the U.S. had incurred a $2,047,000,000 trade deficit in 1971, the first since 1888.

Sheikh Sultan ibn Muhammad al-Qasimi became ruler of Sharjah, one of the United Arab Emirates, the day after his brother, Sheikh Khalid, the former ruler, had been killed in an unsuccessful coup.

26

Warsaw Pact party leaders and premiers ended a two-day meeting in Prague, Czech., with a communiqué calling for troop and arms reductions in Europe.

27

Pres. Nixon's economic report to Congress stated that wage and price controls would continue until "reasonable price stability can be maintained."

Soviet Foreign Minister Andrei A. Gromyko, visiting Japan, joined Prime Minister Sato in announcing an agreement to begin negotiations toward a peace treaty within the year.

Pres. Nixon nominated White House assistant Peter G. Peterson to succeed resigning Commerce Secy. Maurice H. Stans.

28

Canadian Prime Minister Pierre Elliott Trudeau reshuffled his Cabinet; John Turner was moved from Justice to Finance and Edgar Benson from Finance to Defense.

30

U.S. Defense Secy. Melvin Laird announced that no men would be drafted before April 1972.

Pakistan withdrew from the Commonwealth of Nations in anticipation of recognition of Bangladesh by the U.K., Australia, and New Zealand.

Thirteen civilians were killed by U.K. troops as violence erupted during an illegal protest march by Roman Catholics in Londonderry, N.Ire.

31

North Vietnamese delegation to the Paris peace talks released a nine-point peace plan said to have been submitted secretly to the U.S. in June 1971.

King Mahendra of Nepal died and was succeeded immediately by his oldest son, Birendra.

FEBRUARY

1

U.K. House of Commons ended an emergency debate on Northern Ireland after the Labour Party forced and lost a vote on its demand that security of Northern Ireland be controlled directly from London.

2

British embassy in Dublin was burned down by a crowd protesting the killing of 13 civilians in Londonderry.

Gold price in London and Zürich passed $49 an ounce, and European central banks intervened in money markets to support the dollar.

4

Britain recognized Bangladesh; Bangladesh announced it would seek Commonwealth membership.

UN Security Council ended a special session in Addis Ababa, Eth., the first held outside New York since 1952; U.K. vetoed a resolution condemning terms of the U.K.-Rhodesian settlement.

Trade agreement announced in Brussels gave the U.S. short term advantage in agricultural trade with the EEC in exchange for U.S. efforts to restrict grain plantings.

Sixth round of the U.S.-Soviet strategic arms limitation talks (SALT) ended in Vienna.

Zambian Pres. Kenneth Kaunda banned the opposition United Progressive Party.

6

Protest march by Roman Catholics was held without violence in Newry, N.Ire., despite government appeals.

7

Pres. Nixon signed a bill authorizing $2,752,000,000 in foreign aid for fiscal 1972.

EEC and Japan signed an agreement permitting Japan to increase cotton-textile exports to the EEC by 12%.

John Marshall succeeded Sir Keith Holyoake as prime minister of New Zealand.

8

Communiqué issued after two days of talks in Calcutta between Indian Prime Minister Indira Gandhi and Bangladesh Prime Minister Mujibur stated that India had agreed to remove its troops from Bangladesh by March 25.

U.S. Court of Appeals granted a stay in the consolidation of the Richmond, Va., public schools with two suburban systems.

9

Pres. Nixon's state of the world message to Congress described 1971 as a year of "a profound change in America's world role."

10

Ras al-Khaimah became the seventh Persian Gulf sheikhdom to join the United Arab Emirates.

11

U.S. and U.S.S.R. signed an agreement establishing a committee of cooperation in matters of public health and medical science.

French Pres. Georges Pompidou and West German Chancellor Willy Brandt, ending their semiannual consultations, agreed in Paris to work toward economic and monetary union within the EEC.

McGraw-Hill publishing company and *Life* magazine announced they had concluded that Clifford Irving's purported biography of Howard Hughes was a fraud and would not publish it.

Greece sent a note to Cypriot Pres. Makarios asking that he acknowledge Greece's special responsibility for Cyprus and urging conciliatory gestures toward Gen. Georgios Grivas, leading exponent of enosis.

U.S. West Coast longshoremen end strike . . . February 21

UPI COMPIX

KEYSTONE

President Nixon and Premier Chou En-lai in Peking . . . February 21

13

XI Winter Olympic Games closed in Sapporo, Jap.; U.S.S.R. led the 35 competing nations with 16 medals.

14

Pres. Nixon liberalized restrictions on U.S. trade with China to the same status given the U.S.S.R.

15

Uruguayan electoral court dismissed voting fraud allegations in connection with Nov. 28, 1971, elections and proclaimed Juan María Bordaberry president-elect.

French Premier Jacques Chaban-Delmas, in a televised interview, denied charges he had evaded paying taxes.

Pres. Nixon named U.S. Deputy Atty. Gen. Richard G. Kleindienst to succeed John Mitchell, who resigned as attorney general to head Nixon's reelection campaign.

France and Israel signed an agreement under which Israel was to be reimbursed for 50 Mirage jets purchased from France but never delivered.

Ecuadorean Pres. José María Velasco Ibarra was deposed in a bloodless coup after he refused to cancel elections scheduled for June.

17

U.K. House of Commons passed by an eight-vote margin a bill adapting British law to EEC regulations.

U.S. ended 29 hours of intensive bombing raids against artillery positions in southern North Vietnam and the demilitarized zone.

Egyptian Pres. Sadat told the National Congress of the Arab Socialist Union that demonstrations by Cairo University students in January had been fomented by Israeli agents.

18

California Supreme Court ruled the death penalty unconstitutional in that state because it inflicted cruel and unusual punishment.

Giulio Andreotti was sworn in as premier of Italy at the head of a one-party government of Christian Democrats.

19

Soviet Defense Minister Marshal Andrei A. Grechko began discussions on new military aid with Egyptian leaders in Cairo as UN mediator Gunnar Jarring opened discussions there on whether he should renew his Middle East peace mission.

Chilean Congress voted overwhelmingly in favour of a series of constitutional amendments that would block government efforts to expropriate private property to achieve economic reforms.

Five U.S. airmen, allegedly captured during intensive bombing raids of February 16–17, were publicly displayed in Hanoi.

21

Pres. Nixon arrived in Peking to begin his week-long visit to China, meeting later in the day with Communist Party Chairman Mao Tse-tung.

Longshoremen returned to work on the U.S. West Coast, ending a strike that had tied up Pacific ports for 135 days.

22

Explosion at an Aldershot, Eng., army base killed seven persons; the Official wing of the Irish Republican Army (IRA) in Dublin claimed responsibility.

Qatar Emir Ahmad ibn Ali ibn Abdullah ath-Thani was overthrown in a bloodless coup by his cousin Sheikh Khalifa ibn Hamad ath-Thani.

Rafael Paasio formed a minority Social Democratic government, ending Finland's four-month government crisis.

Jean-Bédel Bokassa was named president-for-life of the Central African Republic.

23

Eight IRA leaders were arrested in Dublin on order of Irish Prime Minister Jack Lynch.

U.S. Pay Board announced guidelines on the granting of fringe benefits to workers.

Argentina devalued the peso by 9.2% in an effort to ease its economic crisis.

24

North Vietnamese and Viet Cong delegations walked out on the Paris peace talks, which had been resumed after a week's suspension, in protest against U.S. bombing raids over North Vietnam.

U.K. House of Commons passed a bill legalizing Northern Ireland's emergency measures, which had been declared unconstitutional by the Northern Ireland High Court the previous day.

Romania and Hungary signed a new 20-year friendship treaty proclaiming their independence and disregard of the Brezhnev Doctrine.

25

El Salvador National Assembly declared Arturo Armando Molina president-elect; February 20 elections had failed to provide any candidate an absolute majority.

Luna 20, unmanned Soviet probe, returned to earth with samples from the moon's surface.

26

Agreement ending 16 years of civil war in Sudan was reached in Addis Ababa.

27

Communiqué issued in Shanghai by Pres. Nixon and Chinese Premier Chou En-lai at the end of Nixon's China visit indicated agreement on general principles of international relations despite "essential differences."

South Vietnamese forces began their third drive into Cambodia in a month in an effort to block preparations for a suspected Communist offensive.

28

Israeli troops withdrew from southern Lebanon at the end of four days of heavy actions against Palestinian commandos.

British coal miners returned to work, ending a seven-week strike that had crippled industry and forced large-scale power cuts.

Italian Pres. Giovanni Leone dissolved Parliament and set elections for May; Premier Andreotti, who had received a vote of no confidence two days earlier, remained as head of a caretaker government.

29

UN Conference of the Committee on Disarmament began its 1972 session in Geneva.

Columnist Jack Anderson published a memo allegedly written by Dita Beard, lobbyist for the International Telephone and Telegraph Corp., linking settlement of an antitrust action against ITT with a pledge that the company would help finance the Republican national convention.

People's National Party headed by Michael Manley defeated the ruling Jamaica Labour Party of Prime Minister Hugh Shearer in Jamaican general elections.

MARCH

1

Moroccan voters overwhelmingly approved a new constitution proposed by King Hassan II.

2

U.K. Prime Minister Edward Heath told the House of Commons that the use of harsh interrogation methods against detainees in Northern Ireland had been forbidden.

French customs agents in Marseilles seized more than 900 lb. of pure heroin in what was said to be the largest drug seizure ever made.

Two aid agreements were signed in Moscow during a visit by Bangladesh Prime Minister Mujibur.

Holy Synod of the Cypriot Orthodox Church called for the resignation of Archbishop Makarios III as president of Cyprus.

Pioneer 10, unmanned U.S. interplanetary probe, was launched from Cape Kennedy, Fla.

6

Laotian troops called off their month-old offensive in the vicinity of the Plaine des Jarres.

UN Secy.-Gen. Kurt Waldheim arrived in Cape Town to discuss the UN demand that South Africa hand over administration of Namibia (South West Africa) to the UN.

7

U.S. Sen. Edmund Muskie (Dem., Me.) won 48% of the vote in the New Hampshire Democratic presidential primary, followed by Sen. George McGovern (Dem., S.D.) with a surprising 37%; Pres. Nixon won easily in the Republican primary.

9

Pres. Nixon ordered immediate enforcement of tighter security measures for the nation's airlines following an extortion plot and bombing directed against TWA.

10

Cambodian Premier Lon Nol seized power as head of state following the resignation of Cheng Heng, dissolved the National Assembly, and nullified the nearly completed republican constitution.

12

Regional elections in India ended with Prime Minister Gandhi's Ruling Congress Party winning absolute majorities in the legislatures of 14 of 16 states and one of two Union territories.

Pearce commission members arrived in London after spending two months in Rhodesia attempting to determine public opinion regarding the U.K.-Rhodesian agreement of November 1971.

First national black convention, held in Gary, Ind., ended after adopting a political agenda and voting to set up a permanent body to provide leadership for black political and social action.

13

U.K. and China established diplomatic relations at the ambassadorial level after Britain agreed to recognize the government of the People's Republic as the sole legal government of China and Taiwan as a province of China.

U.S. and Chinese ambassadors to France met in Paris in what was regarded as the first of a series of meetings on topics of mutual interest.

Clifford Irving and his wife, Edith, pleaded guilty in federal court to having conspired to defraud McGraw-Hill by selling it a fake autobiography of Howard Hughes.

14

Northern Ireland Unionist Party committee issued a communiqué rejecting virtually all initiatives to end violence; bombings throughout Ulster ended a three-day truce called by the Provisional IRA.

Alabama Gov. George C. Wallace, with 42% of the vote, won the Florida Democratic presidential primary.

15

Jordanian King Husain I proposed the establishment of a federated Arab state to include Jordan and the Israeli-occupied West Bank.

U.S. Congress approved a temporary $20 billion increase in the national debt ceiling to $450 billion through June 30, 1972.

16

Paris peace talks resumed after a three-week interruption.

French Pres. Pompidou announced that France would hold a referendum on the entry of the U.K., Ireland, Norway, and Denmark into the EEC.

17

Pres. Nixon asked Congress for legislation denying the courts power to order busing of elementary school children to achieve racial integration and concentrating federal aid to education in poor districts.

U.S. Price Commission Chairman C. Jackson Grayson, Jr., criticized Agriculture Secy. Earl Butz's encouragement of higher prices for farm products.

19

India and Bangladesh signed a 25-year treaty of friendship and mutual defense in Dacca.

Polish voters elected a single slate of parliamentary candidates in elections described as a vote of confidence in the reform programs of Communist Party First Secy. Edward Gierek.

U.S. aircraft carried out the 100th "protective reaction" strike of the year against North Vietnam.

20

Columnist Jack Anderson began publishing material purporting to show that ITT, in collaboration with the CIA, had attempted to influence the 1970 presidential election in Chile.

21

Greek Prime Minister Georgios Papadopoulos replaced Lieut. Gen. Georgios Zoitakis as regent of Greece.

Chiang Kai-shek was elected to his fifth term as president of Nationalist China by the National Assembly.

U.K. Chancellor of the Exchequer Anthony Barber announced tax cuts amounting to £1,200 million in the fiscal 1972–73 budget.

Chilean Pres. Allende suspended Congress for a week to provide time to negotiate his proposed partial vetoes of antiexpropriation legislation.

22

Sicco Mansholt became president of the EEC Executive Commission, replacing Franco Maria Mal-

Bombed TWA jet in Las Vegas, Nev. . . . March 9

UPI COMPIX

fatti, who resigned to be a candidate for the Italian Parliament.

U.S. Senate completed congressional action on a constitutional amendment to be ratified by the states guaranteeing equal rights for women.

National Commission on Marihuana and Drug Abuse urged the elimination of all criminal penalties in the U.S. for the private use and possession of marijuana.

23

U.S. delegate to the Paris peace talks, William Porter, announced the U.S. was suspending the talks indefinitely.

Pres. Nixon ordered a reorganization of the Pay Board after four of the five labour members announced they would no longer serve.

24

U.K. Prime Minister Heath announced his intention to impose direct rule on Northern Ireland and suspend its Parliament; William Whitelaw, leader of the U.K. House of Commons, was named secretary of state for Northern Ireland.

EEC agricultural ministers agreed on a program to raise farm prices and implement the Mansholt Plan for modernizing agriculture.

25

Agreement to coordinate efforts to control the trade in narcotic drugs was signed by 36 countries in Geneva.

26

U.K. and Malta signed a seven-year defense agreement, ending a nine-month dispute on continued British use of the island's military bases.

27

Northern Ireland Protestants began a two-day general strike to protest the imposition of direct rule by Britain.

Two "Soledad Brothers" were acquitted of slaying a prison guard at California's Soledad Prison in 1970; the third "brother," George Jackson, had been killed at San Quentin prison in 1971.

28

West Bank Arabs voted for ten municipal councils in defiance of calls by Palestinian guerrillas for a boycott.

Polish Sejm elected Henryk Jablonski to succeed Jozef Cyrankiewicz as president.

U.S.S.R. presented a draft treaty outlawing chemical warfare to the UN Disarmament Conference in .Geneva.

SALT resumed in Helsinki, Fin.

Gambian Pres. Sir Dauda Jawara was reelected to a five-year term as his People's Progressive Party won 28 of 32 seats in The Gambia's first parliamentary elections.

29

Jordanian King Husain proposed in a Washington, D.C., interview that joint Jordanian-Israeli administration of Jerusalem be part of a final Middle East peace settlement.

Bolivia ordered the expulsion of 119 Soviet nationals attached to the embassy staff in La Paz.

30

U.K. House of Commons adopted an enabling bill on direct rule for Northern Ireland; the Ulster Parliament was suspended for one year.

North Vietnamese forces opened a major offensive across the demilitarized zone.

Ugandan Pres. Idi Amin ordered the Israeli embassy in Kampala closed, charging Israelis living in Uganda were engaged in antigovernment activities.

Former King Ntare V of Burundi was arrested in Bujumbura after having been returned there by Ugandan authorities.

31

Six outposts near the demilitarized zone were abandoned by South Vietnamese troops as poor weather restricted U.S. air support.

APRIL

2

South Vietnamese forces abandoned the northern half of Quang Tri Province.

3

Catholic women opposing the IRA clashed with women supporting it in Belfast following the funeral of a woman killed in a fight between snipers and U.K. troops.

Yemen (Aden) proposed mutual troop withdrawals from its border with Yemen (San'a') following several border incidents.

Pres. Nixon signed legislation formally devaluing the dollar.

4

U.S. Secy. of State William Rogers announced the formal U.S. recognition of Bangladesh.

Sen. McGovern won 30% of the Wisconsin Democratic presidential primary vote; Gov. Wallace was second with 22% and Sen. Hubert H. Humphrey (Dem., Minn.) third with 21%; Sen. Muskie received 10%.

5

North Vietnamese forces, beginning a new offensive into Binh Long Province, South Vietnam, cut the highway between the city of An Loc and Saigon.

"Harrisburg 7" jury failed to reach a verdict on charges that the defendants conspired to kidnap presidential adviser Henry Kissinger and blow up heating ducts of federal buildings. Two defendants were convicted on minor charges.

6

U.S. planes and naval artillery began heavy, sustained strikes in North Vietnam.

Egypt severed diplomatic relations with Jordan.

Chilean Pres. Allende vetoed a constitutional amendment that would have required congressional approval of expropriations; the Radical Party of the left withdrew from the government in protest.

7

North Vietnamese forces captured Loc Ninh, a district capital of Binh Long Province.

Secy. Whitelaw ordered the release of 73 persons interned or detained on suspicion of terrorism in Northern Ireland and shut down the ship "Maidstone" as a prison.

Reputed Mafia leader Joseph Gallo was slain in New York in what authorities feared was the beginning of a crime syndicate war.

Zanzibar leader Sheikh Abeid Amani Karume, chairman of the Revolutionary Council, was assassinated, allegedly by three Africans and an Arab.

8

Soviet novelist Aleksandr Solzhenitsyn said he was abandoning hope of receiving his 1970 Nobel Prize for Literature in the U.S.S.R.; he canceled a scheduled private ceremony after Soviet officials rejected the visa application of the Swedish Academy officer who was to present the award.

9

U.S.S.R. and Iraq signed a 15-year treaty of friendship and cooperation in Baghdad during a visit by Soviet Premier Aleksei N. Kosygin.

World Health Organization announced a 94% rise in the number of smallpox cases in the world during the first three months of 1972.

10

U.S. B-52s began deep penetration raids into North Vietnam for the first time since November 1967.

Treaty prohibiting the stockpiling of biological weapons was signed by more than 70 nations in ceremonies in Washington, London, and Moscow.

Leftist guerrillas assassinated Gen. Juan Carlos Sánchez, commander of Argentina's II Army Corps, in Rosario; later the body of Oberdan Sallustro, a Fiat company executive kidnapped March 21 by the same group, was found in a suburban Buenos Aires house.

12

Chad resumed diplomatic ties with Libya, broken over alleged Libyan involvement in an abortive 1971 coup.

13

First players' strike in the history of baseball ended in its 13th day, and the delayed opening of the season was scheduled for April 15.

U.S. Senate passed a bill limiting the powers of the president in decisions involving commitment of armed forces to hostile action.

14

South African appeals court overturned the 1971 conviction of the Rev. Gonville Aubrey ffrench-Beytagh, the dean of Johannesburg's Anglican cathedral, on charges of plotting to overthrow the government.

U.S. Justice Department filed an antitrust suit against three commercial television networks charging they monopolized entertainment programming.

Baghdad radio reported clashes with "heavy losses" between Iraq and Iran.

15

Uruguayan Congress declared a one-month "state of internal war" against Tupamaro guerrillas, who had assassinated four persons the day before.

Pres. Nixon ended a two-day visit to Canada by signing, with Prime Minister Trudeau, an agreement on joint U.S.-Canadian efforts to combat pollution of the Great Lakes.

16

U.S. B-52s and Navy fighter-bombers attacked the Hanoi-Haiphong area of North Vietnam.

U.S.S.R. protested damage to four Soviet ships during U.S. bombing of Haiphong Harbour.

Two giant pandas, given to the U.S. by China in return for a pair of musk oxen, arrived at the National Zoo in Washington, D.C.

17

Turkish Prime Minister Nihat Erim resigned; Defense Minister Ferit Melen formed a caretaker government.

18

North Vietnamese tank assault was repulsed in continued fierce fighting around An Loc; shore batteries hit the U.S. destroyer "Buchanan" in the Gulf of Tonkin.

U.K. House of Commons rejected two proposals that British entry into the EEC be submitted for popular approval.

Bangladesh joined the Commonwealth of Nations.

19

North Vietnamese forces overran the district capital of Hoai An in the Central Highlands and cut Route 19 between Qui Nhon and Pleiku.

21

Quebec National Assembly passed emergency legislation ordering an end to the strike begun April 11 by 200,000 government workers, teachers, and hospital personnel.

Zulfikar Ali Bhutto was sworn in as president of Pakistan under the new constitution he had signed the preceding day; martial law was lifted.

22

Drafting of a new constitution was announced in Burma; two days earlier Ne Win had resigned from the Army to become head of Burma's first civilian government in ten years.

23

Christian Democratic Party won 53% of the vote in Baden-Württemberg state elections regarded as a referendum on West German Chancellor Brandt's *Ostpolitik*.

French voters endorsed enlargement of the EEC in very light voting.

25

Sen. McGovern won 52% of the votes in the Massachusetts Democratic presidential preference primary; in Pennsylvania Sen. Humphrey won 35.1%, followed by Gov. Wallace and McGovern, both with 21%.

Edward Short was elected deputy leader of the British Labour Party, replacing Roy Jenkins, who had resigned April 10 in protest over Labour's stand on U.K. membership in the EEC.

26

Pres. Nixon announced his intention to withdraw 20,000 more U.S. troops from Vietnam within two months despite the continuing North Vietnamese offensive.

East and West German state secretaries reached agreement on a treaty regulating traffic between the two states.

27

First session of the Paris peace talks to be held in a month produced no results.

West German Chancellor Brandt's ruling coalition defeated a no confidence motion in the Bundestag by two votes.

Secy. Whitelaw revoked the ban on parades in Northern Ireland and amnestied 283 persons who had been convicted of participating in illegal marches.

U.S. Senate Judiciary Committee approved the nomination of Richard Kleindienst as U.S. attorney general, long delayed because of investigations of Kleindienst's involvement in the ITT affair.

Apollo 16 spacecraft splashed down in the Pacific after a successful mission during which U.S. astronauts John Young and Charles Duke spent a record 71 hours and 2 minutes on the moon.

Sen. Muskie announced he would not campaign actively in any more presidential primaries.

28

Deadlocked vote on the federal budget forced the West German Bundestag to adjourn.

29

Former King Ntare V of Burundi was killed in fighting as supporters attempted to free him from house arrest.

30

Conservative deputies retained control of the Lebanese Parliament at the conclusion of elections held on three consecutive Sundays.

Chinese table tennis team completed a 19-day tour of the U.S.

MAY

1

South Vietnamese forces abandoned Quang Tri city to advancing North Vietnamese troops.

Anastasio Somoza Debayle resigned as president of Nicaragua in accordance with an agreement by which a triumvirate would govern until presidential elections in 1974.

2

Canadian Revenue Minister Herbert Gray issued a policy statement calling for legislation requiring foreign companies to show that any planned take-over of a Canadian business would produce "significant benefit to Canada."

3

Pres. Nixon named U.S. Assistant Atty. Gen. L. Patrick Gray III acting director of the FBI, succeeding J. Edgar Hoover, who died May 2.

Zaire announced it was sending troops to Burundi to help put down continuing civil unrest there.

4

U.S. and South Vietnam called another indefinite suspension of the Paris peace talks.

Israeli Prime Minister Golda Meir began a four-day official visit to Bucharest, Rom.

U.S. ordered more than 50 more fighter-bombers and a sixth aircraft carrier to Vietnam.

6

Indo-Pakistani truce ended two days of fighting in the disputed section of Kashmir.

White House announced that major Japanese and European steel producers had agreed to limit exports to the U.S. for three years.

7

Justin Ahomadegbé succeeded Hubert Maga as head of Dahomey's Presidential Council.

French Finance Minister Valéry Giscard d'Estaing announced that foreign exchange controls would be relaxed, effective the following day.

8

Pres. Nixon announced in a television speech that he had ordered the mining of North Vietnamese ports.

Christian Democratic Party maintained its ruling position by obtaining 38.8% of the vote in two-day Italian parliamentary elections; neofascist parties, with 8.7%, made the strongest gains, while the Communist parties gained only marginally.

Canadian Finance Minister Turner presented to Parliament a deficit budget for 1972–73 that included decreases in corporate taxes to stimulate jobs.

9

Israeli paratroopers recovered a hijacked Belgian jetliner at Lod International Airport; two of four Palestinian hijackers were killed.

U.S. and Brazil signed a treaty regulating the operation of U.S. shrimp boats within the 200-mi. off-shore territorial limit claimed by Brazil.

10

South Vietnamese Pres. Nguyen Van Thieu declared martial law and replaced the military commander in the Central Highlands.

Irish voters overwhelmingly approved entry into the EEC in a national referendum.

11

U.S. Interior Secy. Rogers C. B. Morton announced that he would grant a permit for the trans-Alaska oil pipeline.

U.K. denied charges made May 4 that its planes and warships had attacked Yemen (Aden) in support of an attempt by Arab neighbours to overthrow the Marxist regime.

12

U.S. Environmental Protection Agency refused to delay from 1975 to 1976 the effective date for pollution-emission controls on automobiles.

Two Germanys initialed, in Bonn, an agreement on traffic between their states.

Cambodian military command reported Communist forces had captured four positions in Takeo Province; 11 Cambodian positions had fallen since the loss of Kompong Trach on April 30.

13

South Vietnamese forces began a series of counterattacks in Quang Tri Province and the Central Highlands.

14

Bulent Ecevit was elected chairman of Turkey's Republican People's Party, replacing Ismet Inonu, who after 33 years had resigned May 8 in a dispute over party control.

15

Uruguayan Congress extended the "state of internal war" an additional 45 days.

Gov. Wallace was seriously wounded in an assassination attempt while campaigning at a shopping centre in Laurel, Md.

Queen Elizabeth II and Prince Philip began a state visit to France.

16

U.S. Treasury Secy. John Connally resigned; George P. Shultz was named to succeed him, and Caspar W. Weinberger was to replace Shultz as director of the Office of Management and Budget.

Gov. Wallace easily won the Michigan and Maryland Democratic presidential primaries.

Yugoslav Pres. Tito and Romanian Pres. Nicolae Ceausescu inaugurated the Iron Gate Dam on the Danube, Europe's largest hydroelectric power plant.

17

West German Bundestag ratified, with most Christian Democratic members abstaining, nonaggression treaties with the U.S.S.R. and Poland.

Chiang Ching-kuo, son of Pres. Chiang Kai-shek, was named to succeed C. K. Yen as president of the Executive Yuan (premier) of Taiwan.

U.S. Senate and House conference committee agreed on provisions of an omnibus higher education bill including an antibusing provision.

18

Malagasy Republic Pres. Philibert Tsiranana handed over full

A.F.P. / PICTORIAL PARADE

South Vietnamese forces in Quang Tri . . . May 13

power to the army chief of staff, Gen. Gabriel Ramanantsoa, following a week of violence in Tananarive that grew out of a student protest against French cultural domination.

19

Two bombs exploded at the headquarters of the Axel Springer publishing concern in Hamburg, the latest in a wave of terrorist bombings in West Germany; a bomb exploding in the Pentagon caused considerable damage, but a bomb scare aboard the British liner "Queen Elizabeth II" proved to be a hoax.

Strikes and walkouts protesting the jailing of three union leaders who had urged disobedience of a court order during the Quebec public employees strike ended.

20

Soviet secret police and paratroop units were reported to have quelled rioting in Kaunas, Lithuania, that had followed the funeral of a Roman Catholic youth who had burned himself to death "for political reasons."

21

Michelangelo's "Pietà," in St. Peter's Basilica, Rome, was damaged when Laszlo Toth, a Hungarian-born émigré to Australia, attacked it with a hammer while shouting, "I am Jesus Christ."

Third UN Conference on Trade and Development, in Santiago, Chile, ended after five weeks without taking action on demands of poorer countries for price stabilization and greater market access.

22

Pres. Nixon arrived in Moscow to begin the first official visit of a U.S. president to the U.S.S.R.

Ceylon became the republic of Sri Lanka; Gov.-Gen. William Gopallawa was nominated as president.

Catholic women marched to the Londonderry headquarters of the Official IRA to protest the shooting of an Irish Catholic soldier on leave; terrorist shootings and bombings had increased in Northern Ireland in previous weeks.

23

U.S. Defense Department announced the air war against North Vietnam had been expanded to include new targets.

U.K. Foreign Secy. Sir Alec Douglas-Home told the House of Commons that the Pearce commission had found that the Rhodesian people did not favour the November 1971 agreement on Rhodesian independence; the settlement was being dropped and economic sanctions against Rhodesia were to remain in effect.

25

U.S. Commerce Department announced that economic indicators for April had risen 1.4% and that revised figures for March showed a rise of 1.9%, the biggest increase for any month since March 1971.

North Vietnamese commandos seized control of scattered areas of Kon Tum City.

26

Pres. Nixon and Soviet Communist Party General Secy. Leonid I. Brezhnev signed agreements limiting U.S. and Soviet antiballistic missile systems and offensive missile launchers; agreements signed earlier in Nixon's visit provided for cooperation in technological matters, space exploration, health and environmental affairs, economic differences, and the prevention of accidents at sea.

EEC foreign ministers agreed that the European Commission should participate in most discussions at their fall summit meeting, thus avoiding the threatened resignation of Pres. Mansholt and other Commission members.

U.S. Commerce Department announced the second largest trade deficit in U.S. history, $699.4 million (seasonally adjusted), had been recorded in April.

Organization for Economic Cooperation and Development ended its 11th annual ministerial meeting without reaching agreement on coordination of monetary and trade negotiations.

28

Pres. Nixon expressed his desire for peace in an unprecedented televised address to the Soviet people.

29

Official wing of the IRA announced the suspension of its guerrilla activity in Northern Ireland.

30

Three Japanese gunmen employed by Palestinian guerrillas killed 25 persons and wounded 76 others at Lod International Airport, Israel.

Burundi radio reported that since the April 29 abortive coup at least 50,000 persons had been killed in civil disorders caused by rebels described as planning to exterminate the Tutsi tribe.

31

NATO foreign ministers agreed to begin preparatory talks for a European security conference with the U.S.S.R.

Presidium of the Supreme Soviet ratified the Soviet-West German nonaggression pact.

JUNE

1

Pres. Nixon, returning to Washington from the U.S.S.R. after stops in Iran and Poland, reported to Congress that the trip had laid the basis for a "new relationship" between the U.S. and U.S.S.R.

Andreas Baader, a leader of the West German urban guerrillas believed responsible for recent bombings, was captured with two other members following a gun battle with Frankfurt police.

Iraq nationalized the Western-owned Iraq Petroleum Co.

3

Big Four foreign ministers signed a comprehensive agreement on relations between the divided portions of Berlin.

4

Black militant Angela Davis was acquitted of charges of murder, kidnapping, and conspiracy in a San Jose, Calif., court.

Lon Nol was elected to a full five-year term as president of Cambodia by less than 55% of the vote.

5

New Turkish government of Ferit Melen was installed after winning a vote of confidence in the National Assembly.

6

U.S. Defense Secy. Laird told the House Armed Services Committee that despite recent U.S.-Soviet arms limitation agreements more money would be needed to modernize offensive strategic forces; the previous day Laird had testified that up to $5 billion would be needed to cover the cost of intensified fighting in Vietnam.

U.S. Court of Appeals reversed a lower court order that would have merged the school systems of Richmond, Va., and two suburban counties.

Former U.S. treasury secy. Connally began a month-long tour to discuss international trade and finance and U.S. foreign policy with leaders of 15 countries.

Sen. McGovern won Democratic presidential primary contests in California, New Jersey, New Mexico, and South Dakota, giving him a total of 930 delegate votes.

7

U.S. Supreme Court reversed a 1967 decision by ruling that criminal suspects do not have to have legal counsel present during a police lineup unless they have been formally charged.

North Vietnamese force that had infiltrated Kon Tum on May 25 was driven out by South Vietnamese troops.

8

U.S. Senate approved the nomination of Richard G. Kleindienst as attorney general, ending a four-month dispute over his nomination.

North Vietnamese spokesman in Paris charged that U.S. bombers had deliberately destroyed dams and dikes.

U.S. Congress cleared a higher education bill containing three moderate antibusing provisions.

9

U.S. presidential adviser Henry Kissinger arrived in Tokyo to begin talks with government and business leaders.

10

Flash flood in Rapid City, S.D., killed over 200 persons and caused $120 million in property damage.

Yugoslav Pres. Tito concluded a six-day official visit to Moscow.

11

U.S. Command in Saigon announced that B-52 bombers using laser-guided "smart" bombs had destroyed a major hydroelectric plant in the vicinity of Hanoi.

12

Road to An Loc was opened to civilians; 10,000 refugees trapped for 67 days began to leave the city.

Former commander of the U.S. Air Force in Vietnam, Gen. John D. Lavelle, ret., admitted before the House Armed Services Committee that he had ordered 28 air strikes in violation of regulations barring all but protective reaction strikes over North Vietnam.

13

Israel and Egypt each claimed to have shot down two of the other's planes near the Suez Canal in the first such air battle since the August 1970 cease-fire.

14

U.S. District Court judge ordered the most massive busing program to date to integrate schools in Detroit and 53 suburban districts.

15

U.S.S.R. Pres. Nikolai V. Podgorny arrived in Hanoi; U.S. Air Force announced that bombing raids in the Hanoi area were suspended for the duration of his visit.

Mexican Pres. Luis Echeverría Álvarez, on a tour of the U.S., expressed regret to a joint session of Congress that the U.S. was not applying its "boldness and imagination" in dealing with its enemies to the "simple problems" of its friends.

Ulrike Meinhof, a founder of the Baader-Meinhof urban guerrilla group in West Germany, was arrested in a Hanover suburb.

16

U.S.S.R. imposed stringent controls on the sale of vodka in an intensified drive against heavy drinking.

UN Conference on the Human Environment adjourned after adopting a declaration of 26 international environmental guidelines.

17

Reshuffle of the Cypriot Cabinet by Pres. Makarios the preceding day was hailed by a Greek spokesman as "the outset of the normalization of relations" between the two countries.

Chilean Pres. Allende reshuffled his Cabinet in a move to facilitate new economic policies and deal with growing political opposition.

Five men were seized while apparently trying to install eavesdropping equipment in the Democratic

National Committee headquarters in Washington, D.C.

19

International Federation of Air Line Pilots' Associations declared a 24-hour strike to dramatize demands for more protection against hijacking; most U.S. pilots obeyed court orders enjoining them from striking.

U.S. presidential adviser Kissinger arrived in Peking for talks with Chinese officials.

U.S. Command in Saigon revealed that more than 2,000 U.S. pilots and 150 planes had been transferred from South Vietnam to Thailand.

U.S. Supreme Court refused, in a case brought by baseball player Curt Flood, to remove the immunity of major league baseball from prosecution under the antitrust laws; the court also declared it unconstitutional for the federal government to eavesdrop on domestic radicals without a court warrant.

20

Sen. McGovern won 230 of 248 delegates from New York in the last of the major Democratic presidential primaries.

UN Disarmament Conference resumed meetings in Geneva after a seven-month recess.

21

Israeli armoured force captured five Syrian officers during an attack in southern Lebanon and Israeli planes and artillery struck a suspected guerrilla base in southeastern Lebanon one day after guerrilla attacks across the Israel-Lebanon border had resumed after a four-month lull.

22

Pres. Nixon, at his first press conference in three months, criticized the court-ordered busing of Detroit-area schoolchildren, urged passage of the U.S.-Soviet arms limitation treaties and legislation for new offensive systems, and said he was considering suspending meat import quotas.

23

U.K. Treasury announced it was permitting the pound sterling to float in international money markets for an indefinite period.

Pres. Nixon designated five Eastern states federal disaster areas as Tropical Storm Agnes began to dissipate after causing record flooding.

Communiqué issued at the end of a five-day visit to Poland by Yugoslav Pres. Tito stated that ideological differences were not an obstacle to the successful development of mutual relations between the two countries.

24

West German Chancellor Brandt announced that federal elections would be held in November.

25

French nuclear tests on Mururoa Atoll in the Pacific were reported to have begun despite protests from a number of countries.

26

Centrist coalition government headed by Giulio Andreotti was sworn in by Italian Pres. Leone.

EEC finance ministers agreed to buy dollars if necessary to defend the Smithsonian agreement parities.

White House announced the lifting of meat import quota restrictions in an effort to curb rising food prices.

Truce declared by the Provisional wing of the IRA went into effect in Northern Ireland at midnight; violence had increased since the truce was proposed on June 22.

27

South Vietnamese Senate granted Pres. Thieu authority to rule by decree for six months after opposition senators had walked out.

U.K. committee issued an official report recommending drastic changes in criminal law procedures that would diminish rights of the accused.

Lebanese Prime Minister Saeb Salam and Palestinian guerrilla leader Yasir Arafat agreed to curb commando raids launched against Israel from Lebanon to minimize possible Israeli retaliations against Lebanon.

28

White House named Gen. Frederick C. Weyand commander of U.S. forces in Vietnam, succeeding Gen. Creighton Abrams, who was to become U.S. Army chief of staff.

South Vietnamese troops opened a major drive to recapture Quang Tri Province.

29

U.S. Supreme Court ruled that the death penalty as usually enforced in the U.S. constituted "cruel and unusual punishment" as described in the Eighth Amendment; the court also ruled that journalists could not refuse to divulge to a grand jury the source of information obtained in confidence.

Pres. Nixon told a televised news conference that the Paris peace talks would resume July 13 on the assumption that North Vietnam was prepared to negotiate seriously.

Democratic Party credentials committee ruled that California "winner-take-all" primary was contrary to party rules and that 151 McGovern convention delegates must be apportioned among other candidates.

JULY

1

Pres. Nixon signed a bill extending the federal debt ceiling of $450 billion to October 31, even though he disapproved of the 20% increase in Social Security payments attached to the bill.

John Mitchell resigned as Pres. Nixon's campaign manager after his wife, Martha, announced she would leave him unless he quit politics; he was replaced by Clark MacGregor.

3

Indian Prime Minister Gandhi and Pakistani Pres. Bhutto ended six days of summit talks in Simla by signing an agreement to renounce force in settling their differences, improve relations in the economic and cultural spheres, and hold further negotiations.

4

North and South Korea, in a joint communiqué, announced they had agreed to hold negotiations on reunification.

French Pres. Pompidou and West German Chancellor Brandt ended their semiannual consultations in Bonn without reaching substantive agreement on monetary reform or on the EEC summit meeting planned for October.

5

Jacques Chaban-Delmas resigned as French premier; Pierre Messmer was appointed to form a new government.

6

Kakuei Tanaka took office as prime minister of Japan at a special session of the Diet, succeeding Sato, who had announced his retirement June 17.

Cuban Prime Minister Fidel Castro concluded a two-month tour of Africa and Eastern Europe.

7

South Vietnamese military sources stated that, contrary to earlier Saigon statements, the drive to recapture Quang Tri from the North Vietnamese was stalled.

Canadian Parliament passed emergency legislation ending a seven-week Quebec longshoremen's strike.

Helmut Schmidt was named West German economics and finance minister, replacing Karl Schiller, who resigned in a dispute over foreign exchange policies.

8

Pres. Nixon announced an agreement under which the U.S.S.R. would purchase at least $750 million worth of U.S. grain over a three-year period.

9

Provisional wing of the IRA was ordered to resume its terrorist activities, ending a 13-day truce in Northern Ireland.

10

Philippine government forces launched air and naval attacks against Maoists in Isabela Province; four days earlier the government had moved against bands of Muslim raiders that had been attacking Christian groups in Zamboanga del Sur.

11

Uruguayan government lifted the "state of internal war" against guerrillas that had been in effect since April 15.

First session of the Democratic national convention adjourned at 4:50 A.M. after voting to seat Sen. McGovern's California delegates and refusing to seat 59 Illinois party regulars led by Chicago Mayor Richard J. Daley.

12

Sen. McGovern won the Democratic presidential nomination on the first ballot; earlier in the day the convention adopted the party platform after an 11-hour session.

13

Paris peace talks resumed after ten weeks' suspension.

14

U.S. Sen. Thomas Eagleton of Missouri won the Democratic vice-presidential nomination at about 2 A.M. following a prolonged first-ballot roll call; later in the day Mrs. Jean Westwood was elected chairman of the Democratic National Committee.

15

Pakistani Pres. Bhutto announced that leaders of the Urdu- and Sindhi-speaking communities in Sind Province had reached a compromise resolving the language dispute that had led to riots and the deaths of more than 50 persons.

16

Metropolitan Dimitrios was elected by the Holy Synod of the Eastern Orthodox Church to succeed Athenagoras I, who died July 7, as Ecumenical Patriarch.

17

Finance ministers of present and prospective EEC members agreed on eight long-term objectives for world monetary reform.

UN Secy.-Gen. Waldheim arrived in Moscow to begin his first official visit to the U.S.S.R.

18

Egyptian Pres. Sadat announced he had asked all Soviet military advisers and experts to leave Egypt immediately and had directed that all Soviet bases and equipment be placed under Egyptian control.

U.K. Home Secy. Reginald Maudling resigned because of his past connection with a bankrupt company.

Spanish Chief of State Gen. Francisco Franco published a decree clarifying the Spanish succession; Vice-Pres. Luis Carrero Blanco would become head of government on Franco's death and Prince Juan Carlos, king and chief of state.

19

U.S. presidential adviser Kissinger met privately in Paris with Le

POPPERFOTO / PICTORIAL PARADE

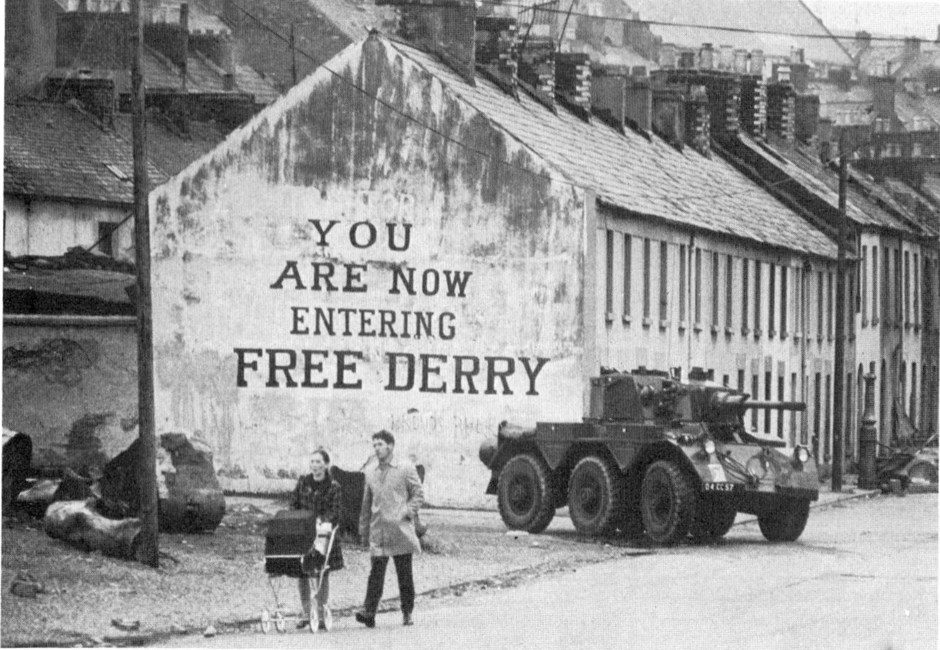

IRA barricades dismantled by British troops . . . July 31

Duc Tho, chief adviser to the North Vietnamese delegation to the Paris peace talks.

AFL-CIO Executive Council voted to remain neutral in the 1972 presidential election, the first time the AFL-CIO had not endorsed the Democratic candidate.

Federal Reserve Bank of New York sold West German and other foreign currencies at declining prices in the first U.S. intervention in foreign exchange markets since the 1971 monetary crisis.

Minority government of Finnish Prime Minister Paasio resigned.

20

U.S. railroads and the United Transportation Union announced a new, complex contract ending a 35-year dispute over featherbedding.

Cabinet of Dutch Prime Minister Barend Biesheuvel resigned after two ministers had left the government in a dispute over the 1973 budget.

21

Twenty-two bombs exploded in 80 minutes in Belfast, killing at least 13 persons and wounding 130; IRA Provisionals claimed responsibility.

22

Pres. Nixon announced that Vice-Pres. Spiro Agnew would be his running mate in the 1972 election.

Former Argentine dictator Juan Perón, nominated for president by the Justicialista Party, said that, for "security reasons," he would not return from Spain to establish residence in accordance with an order by Pres. Alejandro Lanusse.

U.S. planes bombed Hanoi for the first time in a month.

EEC members signed free trade pacts with members of the European Free Trade Association not planning to join the EEC.

23

Libyan Pres. Muammar al-Qaddafi announced that he had proposed the merger of Egypt and Libya and that Egyptian Pres. Sadat had asked for five months in which to study the plan.

24

U.S. Senate adopted an amendment to the foreign military aid bill requiring the withdrawal of U.S. forces from Vietnam provided U.S. prisoners of war were released —and then killed the bill entirely.

Jigme Singye Wangchuk was enthroned as druk gyalpo (king) of Bhutan three days after the death of his father, Jigme Dorji Wangchuk.

Chilean Pres. Allende announced a new economic plan designed to speed national development and combat inflation.

UN Secy.-Gen. Waldheim said he had evidence that the U.S. was deliberately bombing North Vietnamese dikes.

25

Sen. McGovern and Sen. Eagleton, in a joint press conference, revealed that Eagleton had been hospitalized for nervous exhaustion and that McGovern had not known this when Eagleton became his running mate; McGovern insisted Eagleton would remain on the ticket.

U.S. Public Health Service, it was disclosed, conducted a 40-year study of syphilis in which some of the subjects, mostly poor black men, were never treated for syphilis even after penicillin came into general use.

26

Terrorist incidents occurred throughout Argentina on the 20th anniversary of the death of Eva Perón.

Five dockers arrested for illegal picketing were freed by the U.K. National Industrial Relations Court; the arrests had given rise to mounting wildcat strikes and the threat of a general strike by the Trades Union Congress.

27

Egyptian Pres. Sadat rejected the offer of peace talks made the preceding day by Israeli Prime Minister Meir.

Pres. Nixon said at an impromptu press conference that UN Secy.-Gen. Waldheim had been "taken in" by North Vietnamese propaganda when he charged deliberate U.S. bombing of North Vietnamese dikes.

Australia and New Zealand announced the formation of a joint Consultative Committee on Defense Cooperation.

28

Dock workers struck in Great Britain after rejecting proposals to ease unemployment resulting from containerization.

Chinese spokesman confirmed that former defense minister Lin Piao had died in a plane crash in 1971 after attempting to overthrow Mao Tse-tung.

Mexican Pres. Echeverría decreed the expropriation of some 222,000 ha. (about 500,000 ac.) of private estates and distribution of the land to peasants.

29

Pediatrician Benjamin Spock was named as U.S. presidential candidate of the People's Party at its convention in St. Louis, Mo.

31

British troops dismantled barricades barring entry to Catholic and Protestant areas of Belfast and Londonderry and made "selective" searches for suspects and arms in a three-hour, predawn military drive, the biggest ever mounted in Northern Ireland.

EEC ended "compensatory levies" on most imports of agricultural products.

Central African Republic Pres. Bokassa supervised a group of soldiers as they beat 46 inmates of a Bangui prison and said the beatings would continue until theft had been eliminated; four prisoners died.

Sen. McGovern and Sen. Eagleton announced that Eagleton was withdrawing as Democratic vice-presidential candidate because of public debate over his having been hospitalized for psychiatric care.

AUGUST

1

U.K. White Paper proposed the first major reforms in 24 years in the socialized medicine system.

U.S. Commerce Secy. Peterson ended a 13-day visit to the U.S.S.R. and indicated that trade talks between the two countries were stalemated.

2

Libyan Pres. Qaddafi and Egyptian Pres. Sadat agreed to establish a "unified political leadership" for their two countries by Sept. 1, 1973.

Confederation of British Industry and the Trades Union Congress signed an agreement creating independent conciliation machinery for settling labour disputes.

3

U.S. Senate approved overwhelmingly the U.S.-U.S.S.R. treaty limiting antiballistic missile (ABM) sites.

Saigon reported that South Vietnamese troops had retaken Fire Base Bastogne, abandoned a week earlier under intense North Vietnamese attack.

4

Arthur Bremer was found guilty of having shot Gov. Wallace and three other persons on May 15 and sentenced to 63 years in prison.

U.S. Rep. John G. Schmitz (Rep., Calif.) became the presidential candidate of the American Party at its national convention in Louisville, Ky.

5

Explosions shattered oil storage tanks at the terminal of the transalpine pipeline near Trieste, Italy; Palestinian commandos claimed responsibility for the incident.

South Vietnamese Pres. Thieu issued a decree placing new restrictions on the press.

Sargent Shriver was named by Sen. McGovern as his choice for vice-presidential candidate after Sen. Muskie, Sen. Edward M. Kennedy (Dem., Mass.), and several others declined the post.

Ugandan Pres. Amin announced that all Asians with British passports would be expelled from Uganda within three months.

6

Heavy fighting was reported in eastern Cambodia as North Vietnamese troops attacked Kompong Trabek.

Ramsey Clark, former U.S. attorney general, in a recorded interview broadcast over Hanoi radio, described bomb damage to dikes and other civilian installations that he had seen while visiting North Vietnam.

Death toll was reported to have reached 427 in month-old flooding on Luzon Island, Phil.

7

Five-hundredth victim in three years of sectarian violence in Northern Ireland, a Protestant militiaman, was shot down outside his home in Armagh.

U.S. Council on Environmental Quality stated in its third annual report that the nation's air was becoming cleaner but its water more polluted.

8

Foreign ministers of more than 60 nonaligned nations opened a four-day conference in Georgetown, Guyana.

9

U.S. Army announced it was dropping the Cheyenne helicopter program, begun in 1965, because of rising costs and technical problems.

10

U.S. House of Representatives rejected a Senate-approved amendment to the military authorization bill mandating an end to the Vietnam war by October 1.

Eight Czechoslovaks were sentenced to prison for subversion in the latest of a series of trials that had resulted in prison terms for at least 46 persons.

11

UN Secy.-Gen. Waldheim arrived in Peking for high-level talks with Chinese officials.

12

Last U.S. combat troops left South Vietnam; the U.S. Air Force announced its planes had made "probably their heaviest raids ever" over North Vietnam during the preceding 24 hours.

Chinese Communist Party publication accused the U.S.S.R. of complicity in the alleged plot by Lin Piao to assassinate Chairman Mao.

14

U.S. Pay Board announced it would keep its 5.5% guideline for wage increases.

15

U.S. Commerce Department announced that the U.S. balance of payments deficit for the second quarter of 1972 had fallen to $831 million, seasonally adjusted, the lowest since the first quarter of 1969, although the trade deficit increased.

Jewish sources in Moscow stated that the Soviet government had imposed high fees on educated Jews wishing to emigrate to Israel.

U.S. district court lifted an injunction issued in 1970 against construction of the trans-Alaska oil pipeline.

16

King Hassan II of Morocco narrowly escaped assassination when Moroccan Air Force jets strafed the plane in which he was returning to Rabat from France.

U.K. dock workers' union voted to end its 20-day strike despite the protests of militants who said they would not abide by the union's decision.

Pierre Salinger, co-chairman of the Citizens for McGovern Committee, disclosed he had met with North Vietnamese delegates to the Paris peace talks at McGovern's request.

Pres. Nixon vetoed as inflationary a bill appropriating $30.5 billion for the Department of Health, Education, and Welfare in fiscal 1973.

U.K. government offered a £50,000 reward for information leading to the capture of those responsible for the brutal murder of up to 40 Catholics and Protestants in Northern Ireland in the past month.

Arrival of presidential adviser Kissinger in Saigon for talks with South Vietnamese Pres. Thieu set off speculation concerning possible new peace moves; two days earlier Kissinger had held private talks with North Vietnamese delegates to the Paris peace talks.

17

Soviet grain harvest was reported by the Central Statistical Office to be down 15% from a year earlier.

International Court of Justice, in an interim decision, ruled that Iceland could not enforce its newly proclaimed 50-mi. territorial fishing limit.

Israeli Defense Minister Moshe Dayan proposed an interim Israeli-Egyptian truce agreement with the truce line dividing the Sinai Peninsula.

18

Moroccan spokesman announced that Defense Minister Muhammad Oufkir, whose suicide had been announced the preceding day, had been implicated in the assassination plot against King Hassan.

19

Communist forces captured Que Son, a district town in South Vietnam's Quang Nam Province.

21

Chilean Pres. Allende declared a state of emergency in Santiago Province following a 24-hour strike by retailers that resulted in violence.

22

Republican national convention renominated Pres. Nixon as its presidential candidate with one vote going by law to U.S. Rep. Paul N. McCloskey (Rep., Calif.); earlier in the day delegates had adopted the party platform by voice vote and rejected a proposal to increase the representation of populous states at future conventions.

International Olympic Committee, in a move to head off a boycott by African and other black athletes, barred Rhodesia from participating in the forthcoming games.

Deaths of 16 alleged guerrillas during an attempted prison break in southern Argentina triggered demonstrations in several Argentine cities.

U.S. Labor Department announced that the cost of living had risen 0.4%, seasonally adjusted, in July; the price of meat rose 2.8% and was 10.1% higher than a year earlier.

23

U.S. Vice-Pres. Agnew was renominated as the Republican vice-presidential candidate by the party's national convention; several hundred demonstrators were arrested outside the convention hall.

24

U.S. Court of Appeals panel issued an indefinite stay of the massive busing program ordered for the Detroit-area schools.

North Vietnam rejected a South Vietnamese offer to repatriate 600 disabled North Vietnamese prisoners.

25

China used its first Security Council veto to bar Bangladesh from UN membership.

26

XX Olympiad was declared open at ceremonies in Munich, W.Ger.

U.S. General Accounting Office reported that it had found "apparent and possible" violations of the Federal Election Campaign Act, involving up to $350,000, by the (Republican) Finance Committee to Re-elect the President.

28

Pentagon reported that a small Chinese minesweeper had entered Haiphong Harbour, North Vietnam.

UN Special Committee on Colonization approved a Cuban resolution recognizing Puerto Rico's right to independence.

29

U.S. Price Commission refused requests by Ford and General Motors for price increases on 1973 model cars.

White House announced a 12,000-man reduction in U.S. troops in Vietnam that would bring the authorized U.S. troop strength in that country down to 27,000 by December 1.

Sen. McGovern, speaking before the New York Society of Security Analysts, presented his revised program for tax and welfare reform.

Indian and Pakistani officials completed five days of talks in New Delhi with the announcement that guidelines setting a "line of control" in Kashmir had been established.

Typhoon causes flooding in Manila, Phil. . . . August 6

UPI COMPIX

30

France instituted a series of measures to counter the 6% annual rate of inflation.

North and South Korean Red Cross representatives met formally at Pyongyang for the first time.

British Columbia Premier W. A. C. Bennett and his Social Credit Party government were defeated in provincial elections, after 20 years in office, by the New Democratic Party led by David Barrett.

SEPTEMBER

1

Pres. Nixon and Japanese Prime Minister Tanaka ended two days of talks in Hawaii with an agreement designed to reduce the U.S. trade deficit with Japan.

Canadian Prime Minister Trudeau called a general election for October 30.

Raúl Sendic, a founder of the Uruguayan Tupamaros, was captured by police in Montevideo.

Bobby Fischer won the 21st game of his championship match with Boris Spassky of the U.S.S.R., thus becoming the first U.S. world chess champion.

Iceland extended its territorial fishing limit to 50 nautical miles despite a World Court interim judgment to the contrary.

2

Hanoi announced that it planned to release three U.S. prisoners of war, the first to be freed since 1969.

Egyptian spokesman was reported to have confirmed that his country was approaching Western powers seeking military equipment, economic aid, and political backing.

Singapore Prime Minister Lee Kuan Yew's People's Action Party won all 65 seats in Parliament in general elections.

4

First national convention of La Raza Unida, an independent Chicano political party, ended at El Paso, Tex.

Mark Spitz, U.S. champion swimmer from California, became the first person to win seven Olympic gold medals.

Kalevi Sorsa was sworn in as prime minister of Finland at the head of a four-party coalition government.

5

Black September Palestinian terrorists forced their way into the Israeli dormitory in the Olympic Village at Munich, shot two members of the Israeli team and held nine others hostage for several hours before being transported to a Munich airport where the hostages, five terrorists, and one West German policeman died during a shoot-out; the games were postponed for 24 hours.

6

Italian government lifted a ten-day-old freeze on food prices in Rome after the closing of many shops in protest had created a food crisis.

7

Heavy fighting took place as some 1,000 Communist troops attacked the district capital of Tien Phuoc near Da Nang, South Vietnam.

South Korea announced its 37,000 troops remaining in South Vietnam would be withdrawn beginning in December.

UN Disarmament Conference in Geneva adjourned for the year without having made any progress toward a proposed chemical weapons ban.

8

Cambodian troops and civilians looted food shops and clashed with police as food riots in Phnom Penh, brought on by a severe rice shortage, entered their second day.

Sen. McGovern, campaigning in Wisconsin, charged that the sale of U.S. grain to the U.S.S.R. had been made in such a way that it favoured big grain dealers over ordinary farmers.

Israeli planes attacked ten Arab guerrilla bases in Lebanon and Syria in retaliation for the deaths of the 11 Israeli Olympic athletes.

11

New York Times reported that China had contracted to buy $150 million worth of 707 jetliners and related equipment from the U.S. Boeing Co.

Bay Area Rapid Transit (BART), first new mass transit system in the U.S. since 1907, began limited service in the San Francisco Bay area.

U.S. planes destroyed the Long Bien bridge over the Red River in downtown Hanoi.

U.S. Democratic Party, in an amended suit seeking damages for the Watergate break-in, accused Republican campaign finance chairman Stans and three others of conspiracy to commit "political espionage."

Panamanian Assembly voted to reject U.S. payment for use of the Canal Zone, charging it was being "occupied arbitrarily."

14

West Germany and Poland agreed to establish diplomatic relations immediately.

Joint communiqué stated that "significant progress" toward a comprehensive trade agreement had been made during talks between Soviet officials and U.S. presidential adviser Kissinger in Moscow September 11–13.

15

South Vietnamese troops recaptured the devastated provincial capital of Quang Tri.

French Pres. Pompidou, after months of vacillation, issued formal invitations to an EEC summit conference to be held in October; EEC foreign and finance ministers had cleared the way for the conference September 11–12 by agreeing in principle to establish a European monetary fund.

U.S.S.R. and Spain signed a trade agreement, the first between the two countries since the 1936–39 Spanish Civil War.

USDA acknowledged that one of its officials had notified six major grain companies of the Soviet wheat deal 24 hours in advance of the public announcement.

16

North Vietnamese forces began a new offensive in southern Quang Ngai Province.

Spanish police took into custody nine Croatians, three of whom had hijacked an airliner to obtain the release from Sweden of the others; in Sydney, Austr., Croatian terrorists bombed a Yugoslav business, injuring 16 persons.

17

Social Republican Party won all the seats in the upper house of Parliament in Cambodian elections.

18

Tanzanian government said a Ugandan plane had bombed the town of Bukoba near the Tanzania-Uganda border and denied Ugandan charges that the force that invaded Uganda the day before included regular Tanzanian troops; several foreign newsmen and tourists were reported under arrest in Uganda; the first planeload of Asians expelled from Uganda arrived in London.

19

UN General Assembly opened its 27th annual session in New York City; Stanislaw Trepczynski of Poland was elected president.

Progressive Liberal Party of Prime Minister Lynden Pindling won general elections in the Bahamas on a platform of independence from Britain.

Israeli diplomat in the embassy in London was killed by a bomb mailed in a letter; a number of other bombs mailed to Israeli officials in various countries were intercepted before delivery.

20

U.S.S.R. was reported to have accepted in principle the Western position that separate talks on reductions of military forces in Central Europe be held paralleling broader European security talks.

21

Secy. Whitelaw announced that suspected terrorists would no longer be interned in Northern Ireland without trial.

22

U.S. Food and Drug Administration issued stringent rules on the use of hexachlorophene; 39 babies had died in France in August following treatment with excessive amounts of the germicide.

West German Chancellor Brandt lost a vote of confidence in the Bundestag, as planned, to open the way for elections to be held ten months ahead of schedule.

23

Philippine Pres. Ferdinand Marcos declared a state of martial law in order to combat a "Communist rebellion"; the action followed several bombing incidents in Manila and an unsuccessful attempt to assassinate the secretary of defense.

25

Lebanese Prime Minister Salam announced that the Palestinian guerrillas based in southern Lebanon had agreed to abide by government restrictions on their movements.

Norwegian voters rejected entrance of their country into the EEC.

Pres. Nixon, in an address to the opening session of the International Monetary Fund's annual meeting, pledged U.S. support for reform of the international monetary system.

U.S. Commerce Department announced that the U.S. trade deficit for August was the smallest in eight months.

26

U.S. Senate reversed itself and rejected an amendment it had passed two months before that would have cut off funds for the Vietnam war.

Australian Prime Minister William McMahon announced new measures aimed at curbing foreign take-overs of Australian companies.

27

Conference of Northern Ireland political parties at Darlington, Eng., failed to reach any agreement on settlement of the Northern Ireland crisis; four of the province's seven parties boycotted the conference.

Norwegian Prime Minister Trygve Bratteli announced that his Cabinet would resign October 6 as a result of Norway's rejection of entry into the EEC.

28

Three U.S. servicemen released by North Vietnam on September 17 returned to the U.S. aboard a commercial airliner; they were immediately placed under Defense Department escort despite accusations by the antiwar activists who had accompanied them that this was contrary to the terms of their release.

Team Canada won, 6–5, the eighth and decisive game of its ice hockey series with the U.S.S.R. national team.

29

Cambodian government announced that its forces had failed in their attempt to dislodge Communist troops from Angkor.

U.S. Senate Armed Services Committee ended a three-week investigation into charges that Gen. Lavelle had ordered unauthorized bombing of North Vietnam.

China and Japan, in a joint communiqué signed at the end of Japanese Prime Minister Tanaka's official visit to Peking, agreed to end the legal state of war existing between the two countries since 1937 and to establish diplomatic relations; Taiwan broke relations with Japan, describing recognition of China as "a stab in the back."

30

Northern Ireland Protestants marched to Stormont Castle in Belfast to protest worsening violence.

Pres. Nixon signed a congressional resolution supporting the U.S.-U.S.S.R. agreement to freeze offensive nuclear weapons for five years and including a Senate-proposed amendment insisting that numerical missile equality be part of any permanent treaty.

OCTOBER

1

India and Pakistan agreed to a cease-fire following troop clashes on the Kashmir border the preceding day.

3

Belgian small businessmen concluded a two-day strike in protest against government policies alleged to favour large stores.

Pres. Nixon and Soviet Foreign Minister Gromyko signed, in Washington, documents putting into effect the two arms agreements reached in Moscow.

Danish Prime Minister Jens Otto Krag resigned in a surprise announcement made the day following victory in a referendum on Danish entry into the EEC; he was succeeded by Anker Jørgenson, leader of the General Workers Union.

4

U.K. Labour Party annual conference called for renegotiation of the terms of British entry into the EEC.

Soviet Agriculture Minister Vladimir V. Matskevich reported the worst drought in a century had severely curtailed wheat harvests.

Shellfish being harvested in New England were reported by the U.S. Food and Drug Administration to be safe from the "red tide" that had begun contaminating shellfish in New England waters over a month before.

5

U.S. Senate filibuster killed a bill to set up an agency for consumer affairs.

Foreign ministers of Uganda and Tanzania announced in Mogadiscio, Somalia, that they had signed an agreement ending hostilities between their countries.

U.S. F-111 fighter-bombers were returned to combat in Indochina after five days of tests following the mysterious disappearance of one on September 28, the first day the planes had seen war action since 1968.

7

Sir Christopher Soames, U.K. ambassador to France, and Labour MP George Thomson were named Britain's representatives on the European Commission.

Discussions between U.S. officials and Micronesian nationalists in Honolulu were broken off after the Micronesians asked that the talks be broadened to include independence.

9

U.K. Chancellor of the Exchequer Barber announced that the fixed bank rate would be abolished after 270 years as of October 13, and be replaced by a fluctuating rate tied to average discount rates for Treasury bills.

Sudan began withdrawing its troops from the Suez Canal as demanded by Egypt under pressure from the U.S.S.R.

10

Private talks between U.S. presidential adviser Kissinger and Hanoi officials were extended to an unprecedented fourth day in Paris; Sen. McGovern detailed his seven-point program to end the war in a U.S. television address.

Sir John Betjeman was named Britain's new poet laureate.

U.S. Supreme Court upheld a lower court ruling that an Ohio plan to reimburse parents with children in private or parochial schools was unconstitutional.

Canadian government announced that the unemployment rate had reached an 11-year high of 7.1%, seasonally adjusted, in September.

11

French diplomatic mission in Hanoi was severely damaged during a U.S. bombing raid and the French delegate general seriously injured.

New Panamanian constitution was promulgated, Demetrio Lakas was inaugurated as president, and Gen. Omar Torrijos assumed full civil and military powers.

12

Filibuster of Northern liberals killed tough antibusing legislation in the U.S. Senate.

North and South Korean representatives began political talks in Panmunjom.

Chilean Pres. Allende extended martial law to 13 provinces in an effort to cope with an emergency brought on by a truck owners' strike begun October 10.

14

U.S. and U.S.S.R. signed a three-year maritime agreement that established premium rates for U.S. ships carrying Soviet grain purchases.

16

Grand jury subpoenas were served on more than 600 persons throughout the New York City area in a massive probe of organized crime.

17

Treaty regulating traffic between East and West Germany went into effect.

Lars Korvald, leader of the Christian People's Party, was sworn in as prime minister of Norway, ending the government crisis resulting from popular rejection of EEC membership in a September 25 referendum.

South Korean Pres. Park Chung Hee declared martial law, dissolving the National Assembly and suspending all political activities.

Philippine government announced the arrest of at least four persons suspected of taking part in an alleged assassination plot against Pres. Marcos.

Preliminary peace talks between the Laotian government and the Pathet Lao began in Vientiane.

New Cambodian Cabinet headed by Hang Thun Hak was presented to Parliament; Hak succeeded Song Ngok Thanh, who resigned October 14.

18

U.S. and U.S.S.R. signed an agreement on a three-year trade pact; U.S.S.R. waived exit fees for 19 Jewish families in a move apparently timed to coincide with the announcement of the trade pact.

U.S. Congress adjourned after refusing to give Pres. Nixon authority to set a ceiling on spending and overriding his veto of a water pollution bill.

Egyptian Prime Minister Sidky concluded three days of talks with Soviet officials in Moscow that reportedly included the question of continued Soviet aid for Egypt.

20

Pres. Nixon signed the compromise revenue-sharing bill passed by Congress October 13 in ceremonies at Independence Hall, Philadelphia.

New Pakistani constitution was approved at the end of a four-day conference in Rawalpindi; Pres. Bhutto was to become prime minister, heading a cabinet responsible to a federal parliament.

21

Summit conference of present and prospective EEC members in Paris ended with a joint communiqué approving the principle of economic, monetary, and limited political union by 1980.

South Korean Pres. Park Chung Hee declares martial law . . . October 17

UPI COMPIX

22

Oakland Athletics defeated the Cincinnati Reds 3–2 in the seventh and decisive game of the World Series.

Philippine soldiers defeated a major rebel attack in Mindanao.

23

U.S. presidential adviser Kissinger left Saigon following five days of secret talks held amid persistent rumours of an imminent in-place cease-fire in Vietnam.

NATO Council, meeting in Brussels, agreed to begin preparatory talks on November 22 for the proposed European security conference.

Big Four envoys opened new talks in Berlin on their future roles in Berlin and on East and West German applications for UN membership.

24

South Vietnamese Pres. Thieu said, in a nationwide broadcast, that peace terms reportedly worked out between the U.S. and the North Vietnamese and Viet Cong were unacceptable.

"Day of Silence" to protest the socialist programs of Chilean Pres. Allende appeared to have little visible effect as spreading nationwide strikes kept most businesses closed.

Peter Bridge, first newsman to be jailed after the U.S. Supreme Court had ruled in June that journalists could be compelled to answer grand jury questions on criminal matters, was released from Newark, N.J., county jail after being held 21 days for contempt of court.

26

Hanoi radio reported that a nine-point peace plan had been agreed between the U.S. and North Vietnam; in Washington presidential adviser Kissinger told a news conference that peace in Indochina was "at hand"; in Paris North Vietnamese and Viet Cong negotiators demanded the agreement be signed October 31.

Military command in Saigon reported that Communist forces had initiated the largest number of assaults throughout the country in any 24-hour period since the 1968 Tet offensive.

U.K. government, industrial, and union leaders failed to reach agreement on voluntary measures to curb inflation as the price of the pound dropped to a record low of $2.34.

Dahomean Pres. Ahomadegbé and other members of the ruling Presidential Council were deposed in a military coup.

27

U.S. Defense Secy. Laird confirmed a previous report that U.S. bombing of North Vietnam north of the 20th parallel had been halted.

UPI COMPIX

American Indians in front of Bureau of Indian Affairs building they occupied . . . November 8

Secy. Whitelaw announced that local elections in Northern Ireland, scheduled for December 6, would be postponed until 1973.

28

Pres. Nixon approved a bill creating an independent consumer product safety commission; a day earlier he had announced he would pocket veto nine bills that had appropriated or authorized more money than he had requested, including the appropriation for the Departments of Labor and Health, Education, and Welfare.

Egyptian naval commander Rear Adm. Mahmoud Abdel Rahman Fahmy resigned, reportedly in opposition to Pres. Sadat's moves for reconciliation with the U.S.S.R.; two days earlier Gen. Muhammad Sadek had resigned as minister of war and armed forces commander in chief.

Yemen (Aden) and Yemen (San'a') signed an agreement to end their border fighting and merge into one country within a year.

29

West Germany released three Arab guerrillas arrested in connection with the Olympic Games massacre of Israeli athletes as ransom for a hijacked airliner.

30

Liberal Party of Canadian Prime Minister Trudeau lost its substantial majority in Canadian parliamentary elections.

Pres. Nixon signed 60 bills including a Social Security improvement bill, despite earlier rumours of the possibility of a veto.

Widespread strikes broke out in Bolivia in protest against a series of government economic measures including devaluation of the peso.

U.K. government published a Green Paper on Northern Ireland that promised greater political power for the Roman Catholic minority.

31

Six EEC finance ministers adopted a nonbinding program to combat inflation.

NOVEMBER

1

South Vietnamese Pres. Thieu, in a National Day speech, denounced the draft cease-fire agreement as "a surrender of the South Vietnamese people to the Communists."

2

Pres. Nixon, in a nationally televised political address, said a Vietnamese cease-fire would be signed only "when the agreement is right."

Canadian Prime Minister Trudeau announced his intention to remain in power and let the newly elected Parliament determine the fate of his government.

Trades Union Congress rejected U.K. government proposals for voluntary wage and price controls.

Central banks of France and West Germany raised their discount rates to 6.5 and 4%, respectively, in accordance with a nonbinding anti-inflation program adopted by EEC finance ministers in Luxembourg on October 31.

Chilean Pres. Allende named a new Cabinet in which Gen. Carlos Prats González would be interior minister and chief law enforcement official.

3

U.S. military sources disclosed that additional North Vietnamese reinforcements were moving into South Vietnam; a U.S. Defense Department spokesman confirmed the U.S. was increasing shipments of military supplies to South Vietnam.

4

North Vietnamese chief negotiator to the Paris peace talks, Xuan Thuy, indicated willingness for another cease-fire negotiation session provided the U.S. was "serious."

North and South Korea signed an agreement to terms of political and economic cooperation as a step toward eventual reunification.

5

Ismet Inonu led a mass resignation from Turkey's Republican People's Party to protest the party's decision the day before to withdraw from the coalition government of Prime Minister Melen.

Chilean shopkeepers agreed to end their three-week-old strike following a "final offer" by Gen. Prats that included a government promise to consider their demands.

6

U.K. Prime Minister Heath announced a 90-day freeze on wages, prices, rents, and dividends in an effort to curb inflation.

Two Germanys completed negotiations on a "basic treaty" preparing the way for mutual diplomatic relations and eventual UN admission.

7

Pres. Nixon won reelection in a sweep of 49 states, losing only Massachusetts and the District of Columbia to Sen. McGovern; massive ticket splitting meant the Democrats retained control of Congress and took 11 of 18 governorships.

8

Militant American Indians ended their week-long occupation of the Bureau of Indian Affairs headquarters in Washington, D.C., after reaching agreement on their demands for reforms.

Pres. Nixon called for the resignations of all federal department heads, agency directors, and other presidential appointees as he announced plans to revamp the federal executive.

9

Finland formally invited 34 nations to meet in Helsinki on November 22 for exploratory talks for the European security conference.

Israel and Syria clashed with jet fighters, tanks, and artillery for several hours on the Golan Heights in the fiercest fighting in 27 months of "cease-fire."

Big Four announced they would support East and West German applications for UN membership and continue to maintain their rights and responsibilities over Berlin.

Bank of England ordered all banks to turn over 1% of deposits held on November 15 to cut the amount of money in circulation.

10

Letter bombs mailed from India to Jewish companies, organizations, and individuals reached London and Geneva.

U.S. Navy Secy. John W. Warner and Chief of Naval Operations Adm. Elmo R. Zumwalt, Jr., rebuked Navy and Marine Corps leaders for failing to act against racial discrimination in their commands; the day before the Navy reassigned 123 crewmen who had refused to reboard the aircraft carrier "Constellation" until their grievances over discrimination had been resolved.

12

Southern Airways jetliner, its tires shot out by FBI agents, landed in Cuba 29 hours after it was hijacked by three gunmen who had ordered it flown 4,000 mi., with nine stops, and had received $2 million in ransom.

15

Cuba and the U.S. expressed willingness to negotiate an agreement to curb airliner hijackings.

Haitian Pres. Jean-Claude Duvalier dismissed Interior and Defense Minister Luckner Cambronne, considered the strongman of the Haitian regime.

16

Seven NATO nations invited four Soviet bloc nations to meet on Jan. 31, 1973, for exploratory talks on a reduction of military forces in Central Europe.

Two black students were killed on the Baton Rouge, La., campus of Southern University as police attempted to end a student occupation of the administration building.

17

Juan Perón arrived in Buenos Aires from Rome, ending 17 years of exile.

18

Arab League meeting in Kuwait ended without settling the dispute between Jordan and Palestinian guerrillas.

19

West German Chancellor Brandt's coalition government received a resounding vote of confidence in federal elections, obtaining a 48-seat majority in the Bundestag.

Sean MacStiofain, reputed leader of the Provisional wing of the IRA, was arrested in Dublin, Ire., and charged under the Offences Against the State Act.

20

New round of private peace talks between U.S. presidential adviser Kissinger and North Vietnamese chief adviser Le Duc Tho opened in Paris.

21

Foreign ministers of the enlarged EEC announced moves toward closer coordination of policy on the Middle East, Germany, and the European security talks at the end of a two-day conference in The Hague.

SALT II, the second round of the U.S.-U.S.S.R. strategic arms limitation talks, opened in Geneva.

Syrian and Israeli forces fought air, artillery, and tank battles for eight hours on the Israeli-occupied Golan Heights in their most serious clash in two years.

South Korean voters ratified constitutional revisions giving Pres. Park complete power and unlimited tenure in office.

22

Talks intended to prepare for the holding of the European security conference in June 1973 opened in Helsinki.

Belgian coalition government headed by Prime Minister Eyskens resigned after 11 months in office over its inability to resolve linguistic problems.

Widespread strikes in Italy involved three million workers.

U.K. Parliament rejected new immigration laws favouring citizens of EEC countries over those of the Commonwealth in a bill that would have brought U.K. rules in line with the rest of the EEC.

23

Bolivian Pres. Hugo Banzer Suárez imposed a nationwide state of siege, as workers began an antigovernment strike.

24

Finland became the first Western nation to formally recognize East Germany, and the first to establish ties with both Germanys.

UN granted permanent observer status to East Germany based on UNESCO's approval of East German membership in that body on November 21, thus giving East Germany the same status as West Germany.

25

Private peace talks ended in Paris with the announcement that they would resume on December 4.

New Zealand Labour Party, headed by Norman E. Kirk, won an unexpected landslide victory in general elections, ousting the National Party from government after 12 years.

26

Unidentified submarine was reported to have escaped to open seas two weeks after having first been sighted in Sogne Fjord in Norwegian territorial waters.

IMF Committee of 20 opened negotiations in Washington, D.C., on reform of the world monetary system.

27

Canadian Prime Minister Trudeau announced a new Cabinet of 30 ministers including 8 new ministers and 10 with changed portfolios.

Jordanian King Husain confirmed reports his government had thwarted a Libyan-backed Palestinian commando plot to assassinate him earlier in the month.

28

Romanian proposal that rules of procedure for the European security conference disregard military alliances was adopted despite Soviet objections.

Agreement to unite the two Yemens was officially signed in Tripoli, Libya.

Pres. Nixon nominated Elliot L. Richardson to be secretary of defense, Caspar W. Weinberger to succeed Richardson as secretary of health, education, and welfare, and industrialist Roy L. Ash to succeed Weinberger as director of the Office of Management and Budget.

29

Pres. Nixon nominated construction union leader Peter J. Brennan to succeed Secretary of Labor James D. Hodgson.

Netherlands government crisis was precipitated by left-wing gains in general elections, at the expense of the centre-right parties of the coalition Cabinet of Prime Minister Biesheuvel.

30

Indian Foreign Minister Swaran Singh announced in Parliament that India was ready to normalize relations with the U.S. and China.

North Vietnam charged that the U.S. had deadlocked the Paris peace talks by demanding basic changes in the draft agreed to in October.

The bodies of two students killed at Southern University . . . November 16

WIDE WORLD

DECEMBER

1

India and Pakistan exchanged prisoners captured on the western front during the 1971 Indo-Pakistani war.

White House announced Treasury Secy. Shultz would remain in his present post and also assume new duties as a presidential assistant.

2

Irish Dail approved legislation giving the government broad emergency powers to combat terrorism; failure of the bill, which would have caused the dissolution of the government, had been expected until bombs exploding in downtown Dublin the night before killed two persons.

3

Australian Labor Party, headed by Gough Whitlam, received a comfortable majority in national elections, ousting the Liberal-Country Party government after 23 years.

4

Private peace talks between U.S. presidential adviser Kissinger and North Vietnamese Politburo member Tho resumed in Paris.

Honduran military chief Gen. Osvaldo López Arellano seized power for the third time, ousting Pres. Ramón Ernesto Cruz.

5

White House announced that Undersecy. of Commerce James T. Lynn would be nominated secretary of housing and urban development and that Rogers C. B. Morton would continue as interior secretary.

6

Pres. Nixon announced that Agriculture Secy. Butz would continue in office and that textile manufacturer Frederick B. Dent would replace Commerce Secy. Peterson.

7

India and Pakistan announced they had reached agreement on the delineation of a Kashmir truce line.

French government announced emergency anti-inflation measures, including the sale of a 15-year, $1 billion state bond issue to counter the inflationary effects of temporary cuts in the value-added tax.

Imelda Marcos, wife of Philippine Pres. Marcos, was stabbed during a public ceremony near Manila by a man with a long knife who was slain immediately.

California oilman Claude S. Brinegar was named to replace Transportation Secy. Volpe.

8

White House announced Atty. Gen. Kleindienst would remain in office.

9

Robert Strauss was elected chairman of the Democratic National Committee after the resignation of Jean Westwood.

10

Nobel Prizes for 1972 were presented at ceremonies in Stockholm to Sir John Hicks and Kenneth J. Arrow for economics; to Christian B. Anfinsen, Stanford Moore, and William H. Stein for chemistry; to John Bardeen, Leon N. Cooper, and John R. Schrieffer for physics; to Heinrich Böll for literature; and to Gerald M. Edelman and Rodney R. Porter for physiology or medicine; the peace prize was not awarded in 1972.

Liberal-Democratic Party of Japanese Prime Minister Tanaka retained power despite the loss of 15 seats in the lower house in national elections.

North Vietnamese and Viet Cong attacks in South Vietnam declined sharply but U.S. B-52 bombers staged concentrated attacks on the demilitarized zone for the fourth straight day and planned heavy raids in the Saigon area.

Diplomatic sources in Moscow reported that a fire fight in which several Soviet soldiers and civilians were killed had occurred in November on the Sino-Soviet border.

11

UN General Assembly Legal Committee effectively defeated efforts for international legislation to prevent terrorism by approving a resolution sponsored by Arab states calling for exploration of the causes of terrorist acts.

U.S. Sen. Robert J. Dole announced his resignation as Republican national chairman and the choice of UN representative George H. Bush as his successor.

12

South Vietnamese Pres. Thieu proposed that a truce between North and South Vietnam be declared before Christmas and maintained indefinitely while peace talks continued.

"Orange soil" was discovered by Apollo 17 astronauts Eugene Cernan and Harrison H. Schmitt during their second day of exploration on the lunar surface.

13

Private peace talks ended in Paris after ten days amid reports they had broken down over efforts to settle the postwar political status of South Vietnam.

UN General Assembly approved a reduction in the U.S. share of the UN budget from 31.5 to 25% following vigorous U.S. campaigning and over Soviet and Cuban objections.

14

Juan Perón left Argentina for Paraguay and rejected the presidential nomination offered by his party.

White House rejected the cease-fire proposed by South Vietnamese Pres. Thieu, saying the U.S. supported only the position under discussion in Paris.

15

U.S. B-52 bombers concluded the heaviest raid of the war to date, a record 16-mission attack on supply bases in North Vietnam.

U.S. officials announced the U.S. and Chile would start high-level talks December 20 to seek solutions to increasing tensions between the two countries.

Absolute rule ended in Thailand after 13 months with the publication of a new interim constitution.

16

U.S. presidential adviser Kissinger charged at a news conference that private negotiations had stalled because the North Vietnamese reneged on earlier agreements, but acknowledged that South Vietnamese objections to the agreement were serious; the Viet Cong delegation to the regular Paris peace talks released a statement accusing the U.S. of "schemes to revise the contents" of the October peace agreement.

18

White House announced that Pres. Nixon personally ordered the resumption of full-scale bombing and mining of North Vietnam "until such time as a settlement is arrived at."

Nixon administration was reported to have drafted legislation revising television licensing procedures to make local stations accountable for the objectivity of all material they broadcast.

U.S.S.R. economic plan for 1973 was presented to the Supreme Soviet and called for sharp cutbacks in consumer goods production.

20

French Premier Messmer called for National Assembly elections on March 4, 1973, with runoff elections on March 11.

Pope Paul VI, Roman Catholic pontiff, deplored the "sudden renewal of harsh and heavy military operations"; other nations to issue strong official criticism of the renewed U.S. bombing of North Vietnam were Denmark, Finland, Sweden, the Netherlands, China, and the Communist-bloc countries.

Terrorist gunmen killed at least eight persons in Belfast and Londonderry in the bloodiest day of violence in Northern Ireland in several months; the three-year death toll in sectarian violence reached at least 676.

21

Soviet Communist Party General Secy. Brezhnev, in a major speech to world Communist leaders gathered in Moscow to celebrate the 50th anniversary of the U.S.S.R., linked further progress in relations with the U.S. to an end to the Vietnamese war and condemned China for repeated rejection of a nonaggression pact.

EEC and EFTA representatives signed the final documents creating a single European free trade area.

22

White House said Pres. Nixon was "determined" to continue heavy bombing of North Vietnam until it decided to resume negotiations "in a constructive attitude"; Hanoi's largest hospital was reported to have been bombed.

23

Earthquakes destroyed more than half of Managua, Nicaragua, killing 10,000–12,000 persons.

Kuomintang Party of Taiwan Pres. Chiang took most National Assembly seats in the first regular central elections in 23 years.

South Korean Pres. Park was elected to a new six-year term under a new constitution giving him sweeping powers and unlimited tenure.

24

North Vietnamese chief negotiator Xuan Thuy said in a television interview that his government would not resume negotiations with the U.S. as long as bombing north of the 20th Parallel continued.

26

U.S. command in Saigon announced the resumption of bombing of North Vietnam after a 36-hour Christmas pause; a U.S. Defense Department spokesman in Washington said the U.S. had been losing 2–3% of its bombers.

Harry S. Truman, 33rd president of the U.S., died in Kansas City, Mo.

27

Belgium became the first NATO nation to extend full diplomatic recognition to East Germany.

Lester B. Pearson, 1957 Nobel Peace Prize winner and Canadian prime minister from 1963 to 1968, died in Rockcliffe, Ont.

28

U.K. government rejected new demands by Maltese Prime Minister Mintoff that Britain pay a 10% increase in rent for military bases or pull its troops out by March 31, 1973.

North Korean Premier Kim Il Sung was elected president under a new constitution apparently written to provide for coexistence and possible reunification with South Korea.

U.S. command in Saigon announced the heaviest U.S. casualties in nearly two years had been incurred during the previous week: 7 killed, 73 missing, 29 wounded, and, since December 18, 14 B-52 bombers lost.

Egyptian Pres. Sadat, in a broadcast, said he had asked the government to draw up another plan to prepare for war with Israel.

29

Four Arab guerrillas released six hostages taken some 19 hours earlier at the Israeli embassy in Bangkok after securing safe passage out of Thailand.

U.S. State Department confirmed reports that the U.S. had asked Sweden not to send its new ambassador to Washington when the present one left in response to the protest delivered December 23 in which Swedish Prime Minister Olof Palme compared the U.S. bombing of North Vietnam to Nazi massacres in World War II.

30

White House announced that Pres. Nixon had ordered a halt in bombing of North Vietnam above the 20th Parallel and that private peace talks would resume in Paris on January 8.

1972

Advertising

Throughout the industrialized world, the advertising business continued to wrestle with its twin devils of inflation and consumerism. Inflationary pressures and imbalances of trade adversely affected the natural growth of the advertising business in many countries. Agency profits in the U.S. in 1971, measured as a percentage of gross income, were the lowest in ten years, averaging 2.87% against 3.11% in 1970; while Japan, accustomed to an annual growth rate of 17%, had its second lowest year since World War II, with an increase of only 4.1%. U.K. expenditure in 1971 was up by 7% but, with media costs increased by 10%, the actual volume of advertising remained almost unchanged. Nevertheless, this was an improvement for Britain, and the outlook for 1972 was optimistic.

In February 1972 the Council of Europe adopted a resolution advising member states to introduce legislation to prohibit advertising likely to mislead, with particular emphasis on deceptions concerning the physical characteristics of the product, pricing, and the identity or qualification of the producer and supplier. The resolution also recommended the establishment of self-discipline within the advertising industry. The European Association of Advertising Agencies issued a manifesto spelling out the social contribution of advertising, its service to the community, and its essential role in any free enterprise economy.

British advertisers had new problems in 1972. In March the Labour Party published a Green Paper on advertising that was subsequently incorporated in a general policy document endorsed at the annual party conference. This proposed, first, a tax on advertising by permitting only 50% of advertising expenditures to be regarded as business expenses for tax purposes. With corporation taxes already running at about 40%, this would amount to a tax of 20% on general expenditure. The paper also called for the establishment of a National Consumer Authority, financed from the proceeds of the tax, that would supplant the voluntary control system operated by advertisers, agencies, and media. These bodies responded with a formal refutation of the assumptions made in the Green Paper emphasizing the serious consequences such action would have on both the viability of media and consumer prices.

COURTESY, FUJI-PHOTO-FILM (EUROPE) GMBH

More than a little lighthearted humour went into this ad that implores the reader to "Photograph your sunshine in the sunshine." The ad was for Fuji film, and it appeared in the widely read West German magazine "Stern."

Acupuncture:
see Medicine

Aden:
see Yemen, People's Democratic Republic of

The position of advertising was, however, most serious in Sweden, where taxation on advertising, already levied at 6% on daily newspapers and 10% for all other press media, was supplemented in May by a further tax of 10% on all other media including print. Predictably, the Swedish advertising industry recorded a drop in volume through agencies of 9.6%. The ombudsman system whereby the Swedish government maintained control of advertising content was gaining support in Finland and Norway, even though, after 18 months of operation, only 12 of 3,000 complaints received by the ombudsman had sufficient substance to go before the public prosecutor.

The first international consumers' salon was opened in Paris on Nov. 5, 1972, by French Finance Minister Valéry Giscard d'Estaing. Ralph Nader, seeking to extend his influence in Europe in a much publicized tour, participated in discussions previewing the event. Legislation on a variety of subjects including fraudulent advertisements were among the recommendations to come out of the meeting. Earlier in the year, the French advertising world had been rocked by a television "payola" scandal and a Senate investigation into allegations of bribery and corruption involving television officials, public relations men, agencies, and personalities. In Belgium government-owned television was in trouble over "hidden advertising," and all temporary advertising set up to catch the cameras at sports events was forbidden. The Netherlands government announced its intention to impose a levy on radio and television advertising in 1973 to assist the ailing newspaper industry.

The U.S. advertising industry, beset by consumerist and government critics and hampered by a growing number of regulations, began to show signs of restiveness and resentment. Barton A. Cummings, a Compton Advertising executive and chairman of the American Advertising Federation, complained, "We do not need more laws, more regulations, more government bureaus to tell the vast majority of honest businessmen how to conduct themselves in their relations with the American consumer." John H. Crichton, president of the American Association of Advertising Agencies, declared that the Federal Trade Commission (FTC), in various efforts to regulate advertising, had made "serious mistakes" because of "sloppy administration and inferior staff work" and maintained that the agency might be exceeding its legal powers in advocating corrective advertising, in which the advertiser admits to previous deception. Peter W. Allport, president of the Association of National Advertisers, assailed the FTC as a quasi-judicial body acting as judge, prosecutor, and jury. The Federal Communications Commission, looking into the subject of counteradvertising, was advised by a number of experts that many advertisers would quit advertising on television rather than face the possibility that their commercials would bring counterclaims on the air.

Early in 1972, the FTC singled out breakfast cereals —admittedly an industry in which four companies controlled 91% of sales—for a major test of advertising and marketing as antitrust factors. The allegations contained no claim that the cereal companies conspired in the traditional sense, with the result that this seemed to be a pioneering effort to determine whether "market structure" in itself was evidence of illegal monopoly. The FTC charged that the four industry leaders attained a shared-monopoly status by such devices as artificial product differentiation, intensive trademark promotions, brand proliferation, restrictive trade and consumer promotions, restrictive allocation of shelf space in retail outlets, and by using advertising that misled children and adults as to the merits of their products. Later in the year, the FTC issued one of the most extensive orders in its advertising substantiation program. This sought proof for the advertising claims of 16 marketers of cough and cold remedies, ranging from Dristan and Alka-Seltzer Plus cold tablets to Father John's Medicine. The FTC also demanded specific support for advertising claims advanced by air conditioner and electric shaver marketers and decided that Ocean Spray Cranberries must run corrective advertising (one out of every four advertisements) and no longer talk about "food energy" in its Cranberry Juice Cocktail unless it disclosed that it was referring to calories, not vitamins or minerals.

Several advertisers waged successful fights against FTC charges of misrepresentation. Coca-Cola's Hi-C fruit drink was eventually praised by an FTC administrative judge as a "sensible" and "excellent" source of vitamin C for children and said that FTC attorneys had failed to show that the drink's nutritional merits had been misrepresented. The Firestone Tire and Rubber Co. described as "absurd" the FTC ruling that advertising for its Wide Oval tires had falsely implied that the tires were "safe . . . under all conditions of use" and filed an appeal with the U.S. Circuit Court of Appeals. In another action, the FTC was widely criticized for publicizing its charge that a can-stabbing commercial for du Pont's Zerex misrepresented the product's ability to seal automobile radiator leaks and then later discovering that its charges were groundless. The FTC also had to drop a case against Pfizer's Unburn after two years because it failed to prove the advertised claims were conclusively wrong.

The National Advertising Review Board, the industry's new self-regulating group, began to function. Colgate-Palmolive became the first advertiser to agree to change an advertisement following a complaint to the board; it dropped the word "organic" in its Bright Side shampoo commercials. The NARB also upheld a complaint that the American Dairy Association's cartoon ads for milk erroneously implied there was instant energy benefit from drinking milk. Meanwhile, the Dancer-Fitzgerald-Sample advertising agency, which invested at least $60 million in spot television commercials for its clients, advised 40 stations that they would lose its business unless they stopped over-commercialization, the running of more than 16 commercial minutes an hour. Nonetheless, LeRoy Collins, former Florida governor and past president of the National Association of Broadcasters, resigned from the board, saying he doubted the advertising industry was prepared to accept the kind of self-regulating agency it needed.

In August 1972, the advertising industry in Canada, which had led many other nations in the area of self-regulation, published a report on truth in advertising based on an extensive study by a group of theologians. The study recommended that more money be spent

COURTESY, MEDICAL WORLD NEWS

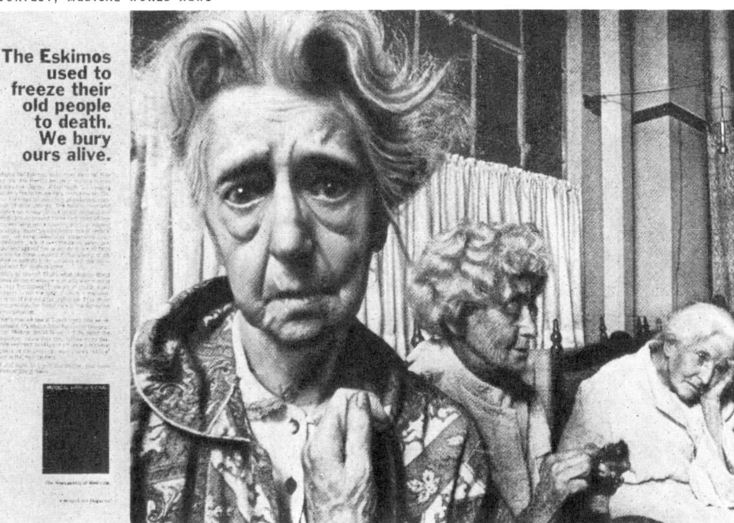

A poignant photograph and a pejorative headline make this ad designed for the magazine "Medical World News" particularly effective. Social awareness was a growing element of print advertising in 1972.

on psychological research into the effects of advertising, that communications courses be offered in more schools, and stress moral norms, and that improvement be made in consumer information programs. The theologians further urged that "truth be the sole basic moral criterion in advertising in Canada" but noted that "truth must be understood analogically. There must be a truth of hyperbole, a truth of symbol . . . , a truth even of implications." The study said that to contemplate restrictive legislation, which some feared Canada would do following the U.S. lead, would reduce advertisers to the use of simple unequivocal statements and make advertising "even more boring than it already is in some cases."

Farther afield, in Brazil measures to curb inflation had resulted in advertising expenditures so low that advertising's rate of growth fell behind that of the general economy. In India government moves to restrict the supply of newsprint to major English language newspapers were challenged in the Supreme Court, where a final decision was still awaited. In Japan the minister of finance recommended a general restructuring of taxation away from personal incomes to corporate incomes, including a flat rate of 10% on advertising expenditures.

Among the advertising agencies, the rush to go public subsided. In the U.S. both Batten, Barton, Durstine & Osborn (BBDO) and Carl Ally postponed their plans to float stock; in Britain both Dorland and Stowe & Bowden reverted to private ownership. Public companies in the U.S. were J. Walter Thompson; Interpublic; Ogilvy & Mather International; Doyle Dane Bernbach; Grey Advertising; Foote, Cone & Belding; Needham, Harper & Steers; Wells, Rich, Greene; Clinton E. Frank; and McCattrey & McCall. In Britain they were Collett, Dickenson, Pearce; Brunning; Geers Gross; and K.M.P. Partnership.

Advertising Age listed the top ten agencies in the world and their billings in 1971 as J. Walter Thompson, $774 million; McCann-Erickson (part of Interpublic Group), $593.9 million; Dentsu Advertising of Japan, $563.3 million; Young & Rubicam, $503.5 million; Ted Bates & Co., $424.8 million; Leo Burnett International, $422.7 million; SSC & B-Lintas International, $361.7 million; BBDO, $331.5 million; Ogilvy & Mather, $296.5 million; and Doyle Dane Bernbach, $280.3 million.

Major agency moves in 1972 might have some effect on this ranking in years to come. The Interpublic Group, whose combined billings of $741 million in

MICHAEL EVANS—THE NEW YORK TIMES

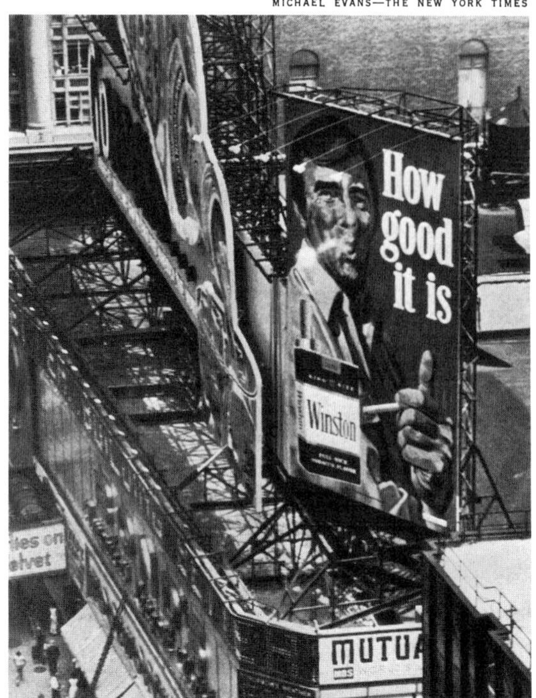

Times Square in New York City is the same again with the return of a smoking billboard (right), one of two put up in 1972. The famous Camel smoker came down in 1966 after 25 years.

1971 included McCann-Erickson's, agreed to purchase the Campbell-Ewald agency, which billed $122 million, including about $80 million for its Chevrolet account. This move made Interpublic the largest agency group in the world; J. Walter Thompson, however, remained the largest company operating under one name. One of the largest Anglo-American agency pacts in history was the merger in October of D'Arcy-MacManus International and Britain's Masius, Wynne-Williams to form the world's seventh largest agency group. In the U.S. Wells, Rich, Greene, started in 1966 and billing nearly $110 million, acquired Gardner Advertising, an agency founded in 1908 and billing $54 million. In France, Intermarco's acquisition by Publicis, the country's second largest agency, meant that two groups, Havas and Publicis, controlled more than 50% of the measured media in France.

Advertising volume in the U.S. in 1972 was expected to reach $22.5 billion, according to an estimate prepared by McCann-Erickson's research department, a recognized authority. This represented a gain of 9.3% over the revised 1971 figure of $20.6 billion. McCann-Erickson also predicted in August that total U.S. advertising in 1973 would surpass $25 billion and that the current boom would mean high growth rates for the industry for the next five years. The U.S. Department of Commerce was even more optimistic. Its publication *U.S. Industrial Outlook* predicted 1972 expenditures of $22.8 billion, including $5.4 billion in newspaper advertising, $3 billion in television, $2.8 billion in direct mail, $1.3 billion in radio, and $1 billion in consumer magazines.

Following a year in which the 100 leading national advertisers reduced their advertising and promotion investments by a slight margin, advertising outlays advanced 6% in 1971, from $4.6 billion to $4.9 billion. Some of this gain, however, was not the result of higher advertising spending but of acquisitions and mergers that made the leading advertisers even bigger. These included Nabisco's acquisition of the J. B. Williams Co., the merger of Plough, Inc. with the Schering Corp., and the purchase by American Cyanamid of Shulton Inc. The biggest advertisers, according to figures compiled by *Advertising Age,* were Procter & Gamble, with an expenditure of $275 million; and Sears, Roebuck, which spent $200 million, some $70 million more than in 1970 and took over second place from General Foods ($160 million). Others in the top ten were General Motors, Warner-Lambert, Bristol-Myers, Colgate-Palmolive, American Home Products, Ford Motor Co., and American Telephone & Telegraph Co.

Some 624 U.S. advertising agencies billed a record $10.5 billion in 1971, $377 million more than in 1970. But with agency profit levels at a ten-year low, agencies continued to cut down on personnel. It developed that the bigger the agency's billings in 1971, the more chance there was of being terminated: the top ten agencies let go 1,443 of the 3,442 employees terminated by the 248 agencies with billings of $5 million or more. At the same time 108 major accounts (those billing $350,000 and over) changed agencies in the first half of 1971. The largest single move was the switch of the $22 million American Motors Corp. account from Wells, Rich, Greene to Cunningham & Walsh.

Advertising expenditures in Canada, which amounted to $1.03 billion in 1970, were expected to total $1.2 billion in 1971. Canadian advertising agencies increased their billings 3.1% to $470,352,117 in 1970 (the latest year for which figures were available), but suffered an 18% decline in profits, which amounted to $7,670,258. The billings went heavily into print, which got 42.5% of the total, and television, which received 36.9%. Peter Hunter, president of McConnell Advertising, declined nomination as president of the Institute of Canadian Advertising, saying that as head of the institute he would have to represent U.S.-owned and U.S.-controlled agencies as well as Canadian agencies. Instead, he wished to oppose the acquisition of Canadian agencies by U.S. companies and to stem the trend of Canadian subsidiaries of U.S. advertisers moving their accounts to the Canadian branches of the agencies handling their U.S. accounts. U.S.-owned agencies had accounted for about 37% of the Canadian industry's total billings in 1970 and their share-of-market was rising at the rate of more than 1% a year.

Other countries could make similar complaints. West Germany spent DM. 10,687,100,000 in measured media in 1971, an increase of 11.9% over 1970. About 20% of this amount was handled by 21 agencies of which only 8 were entirely German. In Australia, Austac, the government-owned advertising agencies council, joined efforts to encourage legislation to counter foreign intrusion into the agency scene. One source claimed that 87% of agency service in Australia was handled by overseas agencies.

In Britain there was a general improvement in 1971 over the poor returns of the previous year, with fewer people handling more business and productivity generally up. There was a 9% drop in the number of people employed by the 272 member agencies of the Institute of Practitioners in Advertising, from 17,200 to 15,600 in 1971. Pre-tax profits as a percentage of turnover fell from 1.9% in 1968 to 1.5% in 1970. The leading advertiser in 1971 was Guinness Brewers, which spent £1,913,000. Of the total U.K. turnover of £552 million, the press received 69.1% or £382 million; television, 25.4% or £140 million; and the other media, 5% or £30 million. The press share included £177 million of trade, technical, financial, and classi-

Aerospace Industry: *see* Astronautics; Defense; Industrial Review; Transportation fied advertising. By comparison, in Japan 35% went to television advertising and 39.37% to newspapers and magazines.

(GEOFFREY DEMPSEY; JARLATH JOHN GRAHAM)

See also Consumer Affairs; Industrial Review; Merchandising; Publishing; Telecommunications; Television and Radio.

Afghanistan

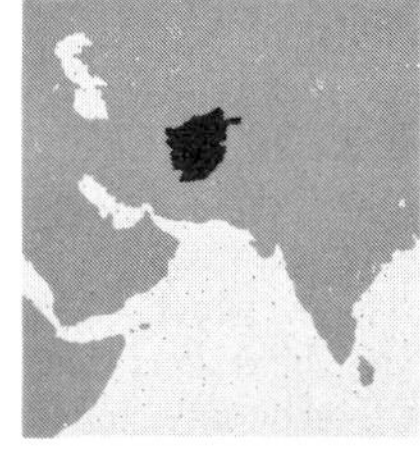

A constitutional monarchy in central Asia, Afghanistan is bordered by the U.S.S.R., China, Pakistan, and Iran. Area: 250,775 sq.mi. (649,508 sq.km.). Pop. (1971 est.): 17,480,280, including (1963 est.) Pashtoon 59%; Tadzhik 29%; Uzbek 5%; Hazara 3%. Cap. and largest city: Kabul (pop., 1971 est., 318,094). Language: Dari Persian and Pashto. Religion: Muslim. King, Mohammad Zahir Shah; prime ministers in 1972, Abdul Zahir until September 25 and Mohammad Shafiq.

Domestic politics in 1972 were overshadowed by economic hardship resulting from the worst drought the country had ever experienced. The lack of rain over large areas in 1971 had decimated the sheep, which constitute the principal source of protein for a meat-eating nation; food crops also suffered severely. The year 1972 brought little relief, and the flow of people into Pakistan and Iran in quest of food continued. Both these countries again responded generously to the government's appeal for external assistance, and later in the year UN agencies gave substantial help. Even so, by the fall the situation in some provinces, particularly Ghor, became desperate. Some 50,000–100,000 people, many of them women and children, faced starvation. At this juncture, the UN Children's Emergency Fund rushed food, medicine, and clothing to the distressed area, and many people who would otherwise have perished were kept alive. The king and his government worked tirelessly to overcome the national emergency, but the country's resources were still limited, communication with many outlying regions was not easy, and effective relief work was handicapped by local traditions of autonomy.

One bright spot was the growing importance of the tourist industry. Foreign travelers naturally followed the excellent roads, constructed mainly with Soviet and U.S. help, that linked the major cities, and were little tempted to go beyond the direct overland route from Europe to India and Nepal, in which Afghanistan was an essential link. Thus they were little affected by the distress in the outlying areas, and the foreign exchange that they brought into the country proved invaluable to the government.

The national preoccupation with economic problems tended to lower the temperature of political life in the capital. Prime Minister Abdul Zahir had been more successful than his predecessor in keeping on good terms with the People's Council and securing the passage of essential legislation. On September 25, however, he tendered his resignation, giving as his reason his inability to overcome unspecified difficulties that had hindered the success of the development program.

In foreign affairs Afghanistan's traditional policy of neutrality was strictly observed, and relations with all its neighbours remained friendly. No attempt was made to take advantage of Pakistan's difficulties, but, at the same time, economic and cultural contacts with India continued. (L. F. RUSHBROOK WILLIAMS)

AFGHANISTAN

Education. (1970–71) Primary, pupils 540,687, teachers 13,117; secondary, pupils 107,609, teachers 4,248; vocational, pupils 5,397, teachers 773; teacher training, students 6,444, teachers 845; higher, students 7,397, teaching staff (1969–70) 881.

Finance. Monetary unit: afghani, with (Sept. 18, 1972) an official rate of 45 afghanis to U.S. $1 (free rate of 110.25 afghanis = £1 sterling) and a free rate of 83 afghanis to U.S. $1 (194 afghanis = £1 sterling). Gold, SDRs, and foreign exchange, central bank: (June 1972) U.S. $51.7 million; (June 1971) U.S. $44,720,000. Budget (1969–70 est.): revenue 6,796,000,000 afghanis; expenditure 7,419,000,000 afghanis (excluding development expenditure financed by foreign aid). Money supply: (March 1972) 7,693,000,000 afghanis; (March 1971) 7,383,000,000 afghanis.

Foreign Trade. (1970–71) Imports U.S. $75.4 million; exports U.S. $85,680,000. Import sources (1970): U.S.S.R. 27%; Japan 18%; India 14%; U.S. 8%; West Germany 7%; Pakistan 6%; Iran 5%. Export destinations (1970): U.S.S.R. 30%; Pakistan 19%; West Germany 13%; U.K. 13%; India 9%. Main exports: fruit and nuts 34%; natural gas 17%; karakul (Persian lamb) skins 12%; cotton 10%; wool 8%.

Transport and Communications. Roads (all-weather; 1970) *c.* 6,700 km. Motor vehicles in use (1969): passenger 30,800; commercial (including buses) 18,200. Air traffic (1970): 115,037,000 passenger-km.; freight 7,987,000 net ton-km. Telephones (Jan. 1969) *c.* 10,000. Radio receivers (Dec. 1968) 248,000.

Agriculture. Production (in 000; metric tons; 1971; 1970 in parentheses): corn *c.* 730 (*c.* 770); wheat (1970) *c.* 2,500, (1969) 2,401; rice (1970) *c.* 415, (1969) 407; barley (1970) 360, (1969) 365; cotton, lint *c.* 29 (*c.* 31); sugar, raw value (1970–71) *c.* 21, (1969–70) *c.* 19; wool, greasy *c.* 31 (*c.* 30). Livestock (in 000; 1970–71): cattle 3,700; sheep *c.* 22,900 (including *c.* 6,000 karakul); horses *c.* 420; asses *c.* 1,360; goats (1969–70) *c.* 3,150; camels (1969–70) 301.

Industry. Production (in 000; metric tons; 1969–70): coal 136; electricity (kw-hr.) 325,000; cement 180; salt (1970) 36; cotton yarn 0.4; cotton fabrics (m.) 49,000.

A starving child lies ignored in a street in Chakhcharan, central Afghanistan, an area that suffered severe food shortages in 1972.

THE NEW YORK TIMES

Africa

The death of Kwame Nkrumah (*see* OBITUARIES), perhaps the most influential African of the 20th century, marked the end of an era. The former president of Ghana died of cancer on April 27, 1972. Having led the first country south of the Sahara to independence from colonial rule in 1957, he continually exhorted Africans to forge a Pan-African union. Energetically and articulately, through his speeches and books, he preached that Africans could only avoid the reimposition of economic, political, and cultural neocolonialism by joining closely together to work for common goals. Only thus could living standards be raised. While most Africans and Ghanaians who were aware of his objectives sympathized with them, many also thought that he was impractical or too far in advance of his time. Most Ghanaians, resenting the excessive demands made upon them in fulfillment of his historic vision, accepted Nkrumah's overthrow in February 1966 with equanimity. His last years were spent in exile in Guinea, where Pres. Sékou Touré shared his perspectives. He was buried, however, in his home town, Nkroful, Ghana.

Those who questioned Nkrumah's views on neocolonialism could point to three of the countries he had criticized as among the faster-growing economies of Africa: the Ivory Coast, Nigeria, and Zaire. And far from being ready for continental union, critics thought that national consolidation had priority.

Burundi. Long-standing tribal animosity came to a climax in Burundi, a small but densely populated state in eastern Africa. Col. Michel Micombero, who had overthrown the monarch, Ntare V, in 1966, and who had ruled as president since then, permitted Ntare to return from exile in March 1972, with assurance for his safety. Arrested shortly thereafter on the charge of involvement in a plot to regain power, the young king was killed when a group of pro-royalists and disaffected Hutu (comprising the majority of the population) attacked the government on April 29. Approximately 20,000 Tutsi, who had traditionally dominated the Hutu even though outnumbered by them, were reported slain.

The government put down the uprising with the aid of troops sent by neighbouring Zaire. During the following weeks the ruling Tutsi (who had been ousted and massacred in neighbouring Rwanda a decade earlier) killed tens of thousands of Hutu in revenge. The government acknowledged at least 50,000 deaths; other estimates ran as high as 200,000. Micombero, a Tutsi, denied that the problem was entirely ethnic, claiming that the Belgians, who had previously ruled Burundi, were trying to divide the country.

Peace in Sudan. By contrast, after more than 16 years, the civil war in the Sudan came to an end with the signing of a pact in Addis Ababa, Eth., in February. For his efforts in persuading the peoples of southern Sudan to agree to the accord, Ethiopia's Emperor Haile Selassie received Sudanese diplomatic support in his own efforts against Eritrean secessionists in his country.

Since 1955, and more especially since 1962, the 12 million Muslim northerners in Sudan had been opposed by the 4 million largely pagan blacks in the south. In the war that continued throughout the years as many as 500,000 may have died. Villages were burned, and tens of thousands of refugees fled to neighbouring lands. Much of the south lay desolate. The accord provided the south with autonomy in dealing with regional matters. The central government would retain control of defense, foreign policy, trade, currency, communications, and transport. English would continue to be a working language in the south along with approximately 80 provincial languages.

Uganda. In Uganda on August 9, Pres. Idi Amin, who had come to power in a coup in January 1971, ordered the expulsion within 90 days of Asians with British, Pakistani, Indian, or other passports. Their numbers, originally reported to be about 50,000, were estimated as approximately 25,000 in October. As in Kenya, which had previously followed the same policy, the Asians were criticized for controlling much of the economy and not merging with African society. Several countries besides Great Britain agreed to accept those with British citizenship, but Kenya and Tanzania barred any of the Asians from entering.

On August 19 President Amin announced that all Asians, even those with Ugandan citizenship (an additional 23,000), would be expelled. This order of the volatile leader was condemned as "racist" by Tanzania's president, Julius Nyerere, who had been a staunch friend of Uganda's ousted president Milton Obote. The order was rescinded a few days later. On September 17 supporters of the exiled Obote invaded Uganda from Tanzania. The battles were brief and ended in Amin's triumph. Earlier in the year Amin had ordered the Israeli military mission, which he had welcomed in 1971, to leave the country. They were accused of meddling in Uganda's affairs. The Israelis, in turn, charged Amin with requesting military aid to drive to the sea through Tanzania, and attributed his change of heart to the promise of Libyan military aid. Amin's praise of Adolf Hitler's extermination policies toward the Jews (as expressed in a telegram to the UN secretary-general) embarrassed many Africans and prompted the suspension of U.S. aid.

Coups and Attempted Coups. By comparison with preceding years there seemed to be more internal governmental stability throughout the continent. Two of the largest nations, Nigeria and Zaire, which had had their "time of troubles" during the 1960s, appeared stable.

Some governments, however, did experience upheavals. On January 13 army officers in Ghana, led by Col. Ignatius K. Acheampong (*see* BIOGRAPHY), seized power from the democratically elected government of Kofi A. Busia. Busia's election in 1969 had marked a milestone in African development, making Ghana the first country in Africa to restore democratic institutions after their loss. Acheampong's promise to restore democratic elections "as soon as circumstances permit" seemed vague. Busia was charged with economic mismanagement. Having devalued the currency by 44% in December 1971, he had not appreciably reduced the foreign debt of more than $1 billion. Acheampong reduced the devaluation, repudiated $94 million of the debt, and declared a ten-year moratorium on repaying several hundred million more dollars.

In Dahomey, which had undergone four coups since 1963, an agreement to rotate the presidency among three men on a two-year basis had previously been arranged. The first transfer of power was peacefully brought about on May 7. On October 26, however, a junta of army officers, led by Maj. Mathieu Kerekou, seized power.

Malagasy (Madagascar) experienced tension during

May when clashes between government troops and protesters led to the deaths of at least 34 persons, the wounding of 400, and the arrest of 400 others. Student demands for educational reforms triggered a mass demonstration and resulted in the resignation on May 18 of Pres. Philibert Tsiranana, who had led the state since independence in 1960. Full powers were turned over to the army chief of staff, Gen. Gabriel Ramanantsoa (*see* BIOGRAPHY).

Morocco, which in 1971 had experienced a bloody but unsuccessful coup, reported on August 18 that Gen. Muhammad Oufkir, minister of defense and King Hassan II's right-hand man, had headed a plot to kill the monarch. Two days earlier Air Force jets had fired on the king's plane, but he was unhurt. Oufkir was declared a suicide on August 17, though he was found with bullet wounds in various parts of his body.

Organization of African Unity and Intra-African Affairs. On June 15, after 11 days of meetings in which representatives of 40 nations participated, the Organization of African Unity (OAU) concluded its ninth annual meeting at Rabat, Morocco. There was general accord. A new secretary-general, 38-year-old Nzo Ekangaki of Cameroon, succeeded Diallo Telli of Guinea, who had held the post for eight years. Criticism of the Western powers was expressed for not doing more to oust the white regimes of southern Africa, for example, and the financial commitment to the guerrillas fighting in southern Africa was raised from $2.6 million to $3.9 million. Spain was urged to conduct a referendum on self-government among the 40,000 nomads of the Spanish Sahara. Israel was criticized on the matter of lands not returned since the war with Egypt in 1967. As an expression of harmony at the meeting, Morocco and Algeria signed documents formally ending their frontier dispute and planning the cooperative development of iron mines in southwestern Algeria.

On August 18 the OAU urged African nations to press for the barring of Rhodesian participation in the Olympic Games, to be held at Munich, W.Ger. As African states began to withdraw from the Games, the International Olympic Committee decided to bar Rhodesia. In another realm of activity an OAU-sponsored fair with 37 African nations participating was held in Nairobi, Kenya. Its aim was to foster intra-African trade.

Intra-African cooperation was manifest in other areas. On September 7 President Nyerere of Tanzania opened a "good neighbour" meeting of 16 east and central African nations, which among other things examined the setting up of a multinational industrial and hydroelectric program. On June 3, at Bamako, Mali, a treaty was signed bringing together seven former French colonies (Dahomey, Ivory Coast, Mali, Mauritania, Niger, Senegal, and Upper Volta) in the Economic Community of West Africa. Guinea and Togo did not sign. The new union was intended to foster regional development. Unlike the former ineffective grouping—the West African Customs Union—which existed from 1959 to 1970, the new body was not to be a customs union. Rifts within the 15-nation, French-speaking Common Organization of Africa, Malagasy, and Mauritius (OCAM), established in 1965, appeared during the year. Zaire withdrew from the organization in April, and Congo did so in September.

African unity on a binational level was evident in Zaire's reconciliation with Congo on August 19, when the two countries reestablished diplomatic relations and planned to cooperate on other levels. Nigeria, reaching out to French-speaking countries, announced a cultural and technical accord with Cameroon on March 27 and economic union with Togo on May 1.

Southern Africa. The most notable development during the year was the negating, after strenuous African opposition, of an accord between Great Britain and Rhodesia signed in November 1971. Negotiations between Great Britain and Rhodesia had continued intermittently since the white-dominated regime of Ian Smith declared its independence from the U.K. in November 1965. The 1971 agreement angered the African majority. In violent demonstrations in the industrial city of Gwelo in mid-January, Rhodesia's Africans indicated to the visiting British commission, headed by Lord Pearce, that they did not approve of the reconciliation. In a month 1,505 were arrested and 14 killed. The recently formed African National Council voiced its emphatic opposition before the Pearce commission, resulting in Britain's formal rejection of the 1971 agreement on May 23. While this constituted an important political victory for the Africans, economic sanctions against Rhodesia seemed largely to have failed.

In South Africa, upon his return from a visit to the United States, Chief Kaiser Matanzima of the Transkei, one of South Africa's three Bantustans (areas reserved for Africans), said that he was inspired with a spirit of nationalism and would refuse the second-class citizenship implied by the Bantustan policy. The next day, August 9, the government's deputy minister for Bantu development stated that there would be no extension of the 13% of the territory reserved for the Africans, though the government would not stand in the way of moves to unite the Bantustans. On June 2 white students in Cape Town protested inequalities in black and white education. They clashed with the police, causing students in other English-language universities to protest and leading the government to ban open-air political meetings in university towns for five weeks.

UN Secretary-General Kurt Waldheim visited

AUTHENTICATED NEWS INTERNATIONAL

Chinese officials watch railway tracks, prelaid on concrete sleepers, or ties, come off the assembly line at the Mangula industrial complex, 185 mi. from Dar es Salaam in Tanzania. The complex was established to service construction of the Tanzam Railway between Tanzania and Zambia.

CAMERAPIX / KEYSTONE

Pres. Jomo Kenyatta of Kenya (in suit) and Emperor Haile Selassie of Ethiopia (in uniform) greet Masai tribal dancers at opening ceremonies of the first all-Africa trade fair in February 1972.

South West Africa in March and was greeted by black demands for self-government for the UN trust territory. On March 8 he said that he believed that the government of South Africa intended to grant self-determination to South West Africa, but others remained skeptical. One tangible result of Waldheim's visit was the acceptance of a UN representative in South West Africa, who arrived in October.

On August 22 the World Council of Churches voted to liquidate its stockholdings in those corporations doing business with white-ruled African countries. On the other hand, Roy Wilkins, executive director of the National Association for the Advancement of Colored People, saw a role for U.S. companies there but only if they worked to improve the lot of the African.

The Portuguese colonies continued to experience African guerrilla fighting. The Portuguese proposal in January to give Angola and Mozambique greater autonomy meant little to the Africans. On February 9 FRELIMO blew up a truck of explosives near the Cabora Bassa Dam. (WALLACE SOKOLSKY)

See also Dependent States; Refugees; articles on the various political units.

ENCYCLOPÆDIA BRITANNICA FILMS. *Africa: Living in Two Worlds* (1970); *Boy of Botswana* (1970); *City Boy of the Ivory Coast* (1970); *A Family of Liberia* (1970); *Two Boys of Ethiopia* (1970); *Youth Builds a Nation in Tanzania* (1970); *Elephant* (1971); *Giraffe* (1971); *Lion* (1971); *Zebra* (1971); *Cheetah* (1972); *Silent Safari* (1972).

Agriculture

Overall, the world's farmers experienced a highly productive year in 1972, with some new records and many near-record achievements. The picture was uneven, however. Portions of Africa, southern South America, Bangladesh, Afghanistan, and apparently wide expanses of the U.S.S.R. and possibly portions of China faced serious crop failures. Large U.S. sales of grain to the U.S.S.R. were among the first fruits of the improved commercial relations between the two countries that followed Pres. Richard Nixon's trip to Moscow.

Despite the Green Revolution, the gap in productivity, as well as in wealth, between the less developed and the developed countries appeared to be widening. Some $100 billion in financial and technical assistance had gone to the less developed countries since World War II, but the results had fallen far short of the hoped-for goals. Late in 1971 the UN Food and Agriculture Organization (FAO) underwent a considerable reorganization, partly to improve its performance in this area. The incumbent director general, A. H. Boerma, was reelected for a four-year term.

NORTH AMERICA

United States. Again blessed with record production, U.S. farmers faced their most severe problems in the areas of rising costs and the increasing scarcity of farm labour. Prices of many farm products were higher because of active demand, and stocks of several major items were reduced despite large crops. Most farm sales were not directly affected by price controls, but farmers claimed that their share of generally higher food prices was largely canceled out by increased taxes, costs (especially of machinery), and wages. In his continuing effort to organize farm labour, César Chávez attempted to follow up his successful grape boycott with a boycott of iceberg lettuce. Sales of so-called organic food (grown without artificial fertilizer) rose, although they still constituted only a small part of the total market. With the number of farms declining, farmers no longer constituted an all-powerful voting bloc. Nevertheless, agricultural issues played a part in the 1972 political campaign, as the Democrats charged the Nixon administration with favouring agribusiness at the expense of the family farm and with giving grain dealers advance notice of sales to the Soviet Union so they could buy large supplies before news of the deal forced prices upward.

Crops. Federal programs and unfavourable weather combined to reduce the 1972 acreage of planted crops to 308 million, down 3% from 1971. Of the total, some 291 million ac. would be harvested, or about 10 million fewer than in the previous year. As of early November the U.S. Department of Agriculture (USDA) total production estimate for 1972 crops stood at 114 (1967 = 100), surpassing the previous record of 112 for 1971, and yields for major crops were indicated at 115, exceeding the 1971 record of 110. Widespread and prolonged wet autumn weather throughout the Midwest and the Southern plains, however, greatly delayed the harvest of feed grains, soybeans, and cotton, probably reducing quantity and quality of those crops, although the extent of the damage had not been ascertained at year's end.

Production of the four feed grains (corn, sorghum, barley, and oats) was indicated at about 198 million tons, 4% below the record production of 1971. Because of the substantial carry-over of corn (maize) from 1971, farmers were encouraged by the government to "set aside" substantial acreage. Corn acreage for harvest was estimated at 57,141,000, compared with 63,819,000 ac. harvested in 1971; the indicated yield rose to 94.5 bu. per ac. from 86.8 bu.; and the preliminary estimate of the crop was 5,400,390,000 bu., second only to the 5,540,253,000 bu. of the previous year. Sorghum for grain, indicated at 895,595,-000 bu., was the largest crop on record. Barley was down 10% to an estimated 418,165,000 bu., while the 730,762,000-bu. oat crop was 17% below 1971. Pasture and range feed conditions were excellent in most areas. The total hay crop of 133,961,000 tons was 2% above the previous year and a new record.

Food-grain production (wheat, rye, and rice) totaled about 52 million tons, 5% below 1971. The wheat crop was 1,558,996,000 bu. from 47,839,000 ac., compared with 1,639,516,000 bu. from 48,453,000 ac. a year earlier. Winter wheat accounted for 1,198,103,000 bu., durum for 73,946,000 bu., and other spring wheats for 286,947,000 bu. The rye crop of 31,315,000 bu. was down 39% from the large crop of 1971, the result of a sharp drop in acreage and some reduction in yield. Rice was estimated at 85,057,000 cwt., with a new record yield of 4,676 lb. per ac.

Oilseed production rose 17% to an indicated 48.3 million tons. Soybeans were planted on some 45,846,000 ac., compared with 42,409,000 ac. harvested in 1971; yield was a record 29.5 bu. per ac.; and the crop was estimated at 1,350,517,000 bu., 15% more than in 1971. Peanut acreage and yield also rose, and a record 3,286,885,000-lb. crop was forecast. Flaxseed production fell to 15.3 million bu., 18% below 1971. At 5.7 million tons, indicated production of cottonseed was 34% above 1971. Cotton lint was estimated at 13,995,100 bales from 13,186,000 ac., compared with 10,473,000 bales from 11,471,000 ac. a year earlier.

The production index for all sugar crops was 136, compared with 122 in 1971. Sugarcane was up 16% to an indicated 28,456,000 tons, while sugar-beet tonnage rose to 28,429,000. Maple syrup output, estimated at 1.1 million gal., was 14% above the preceding year. Production of all tobacco was indicated at 1,733,251,000 lb., compared with 1,707,313,000 lb. in 1971. Flue-cured types fell 5% to 1,010,808,000 lb., but Burley types rose to 563,025,000 lb. from 472,576,000 lb.

Fresh vegetable supplies were slightly larger than a year earlier. Late fall cabbage was especially abundant. Principal vegetable crops for processing were expected to be 6% above 1971 and 15% more than in 1970. The Irish potato crop was forecast at 294,975,000 cwt., compared with 319,354,000 cwt. in 1971, and the fall potato crop was down 7% to an indicated 234,571,000 cwt. The sweet potato crop was estimated at 12,605,000 cwt., 6% higher than in 1971. The dry bean crop rose to 18,338,000 cwt. from 16,168,000 cwt., but dry field peas fell 50% to 1,998,000 cwt. Mushroom production was expected to exceed the previous year's crop of 207 million lb., which had a farm value of $90 million.

The almond crop rose 12% to an estimated 150,000 tons, but other tree nut crops were sharply reduced by spring frosts and other weather troubles. Filberts were down by 10%, pecans by 25%, and California walnuts by 15%. Deciduous fruit crops were forecast at 8.4 million tons, 19% below the 1971 harvest. Only cranberries and nectarines provided larger crops. Apples were forecast at 5,956,100,000 lb., compared with a utilized crop of 6,110,100,000 lb. in 1971. The peach crop was down 13%, and pears totaled 599,100 tons, compared with 701,120 tons a year earlier. Production of California prunes was forecast at 85,000 tons, considerably below the 131,000 tons of 1971. Spring frosts lowered the grape harvest to an estimated 2,674,200 tons from 3,996,720 tons in 1971. Cherry production totaled 247,140 tons, compared with 279,400 tons the year before. Strawberry production was down about 13%, and imports of fresh strawberries, mostly from Mexico, also fell.

Production of citrus fruits in 1972–73 was expected to be some 18% above the previous season. Incomplete estimates indicated an orange crop 30% larger than the 191 million boxes of 1971–72, while lemons were forecast at 32% above the 22 million boxes of a year earlier. Grapefruit was down about 2%, however, and the Florida tangerine, Temple orange, and tangelo crops were smaller than had been anticipated.

Livestock. Output of all livestock and products in 1972 was indicated at an index of 109, compared with 108 in 1971. Cattle numbers on farms and ranches climbed 3% to a new high of 117.9 million head as of the January 1 inventory. Total value rose 16% to a record $24.6 billion, and average value per head was up $24 to $209. High beef prices at retail were a subject of consumer complaint throughout the year, but demand remained strong. The number of cattle in feedlots regularly exceeded year-earlier levels. Choice fat steers in Omaha in July averaged about $38 per hundredweight, about $6 more than a year earlier. In June President Nixon removed quantity restraints on beef imports for the remainder of the year.

The total number of milk cows declined 1% from a year earlier, but replacement heifers held even, at 3,942,000 head, suggesting that the long decline in milk cows might be ending. The milk-feed price ratio continued to be favourable. Milk production during the first eight months of 1972 totaled 82,972,000,000 lb., about 2% more than in the comparable period of 1971. In August the "all milk" price averaged $5.93 per hundredweight, compared with $5.75 a year earlier, while prices paid by dealers in early July for milk used for fluid purposes averaged $7.22 per hundredweight, 11 cents more than in July 1971. As of Aug. 31, 1972, uncommitted inventories under the Commodity Credit Corporation (CCC) dairy support program included 129.7 million lb. of butter and 51.9 million lb. of nonfat dry milk.

Hogs and pigs on farms on June 1, 1972, were estimated at 61.6 million head, 7% less than a year earlier. One of the enigmas of the U.S. livestock economy in 1972 was the slow response of hog producers to very high prices and favourable price-feed ratios. Barrows and gilts averaged $24.60 per hundredweight for the first half of 1972, compared with only $18.45 during 1971, and prices were even higher in September. Because the price of corn was lower, the hog-corn ratio widened to approximately double the average ratio of 1971. Yet June–November farrowing was expected to be 5% below the equivalent period a year earlier.

All sheep and lambs on farms and ranches fell 6% during 1971 to 18,482,000 head on Jan. 1, 1972, continuing the downtrend that began in 1961. Total value fell some $40 million to $424 million. Stock sheep (mostly breeding stock) declined 7% to 15,767,000 head, but lambs on feed for slaughter were 3% more abundant. Shorn wool production was estimated at

Table I. Index Numbers of Volume of Agricultural Production

Average 1952–56 = 100

Region	Total agricultural production			Per capita food production		
	1971*	1970	1948–52	1971*	1970	1948–52
Western Europe	155	147	84	136	130	87
North America	136	124	93	113	103	99
Latin America	159	158	87	102	105	97
Oceania	162	162	89	117	118	102
Far East (excl. China and Japan)	164	161	87	109	110	94
Near East (excl. Israel)	170	163	82	105	105	90
Africa (excl. South Africa)	154	149	85	97	96	94
Eastern Europe and U.S.S.R.	180	177	82	148	147	87
Other developed countries (Japan, South Africa, and Israel)	171	167	81	144	142	87
All above regions† (world)	158	152	87	115	113	93

*Preliminary.
†Excluding China.
Source: Food and Agriculture Organization of the United Nations, *Monthly Bulletin of Agricultural Economics and Statistics*, vol. 21, January 1972, pp. 18–19.

AUTHENTICATED NEWS INTERNATIONAL

Farmer applies a herbicide-laden foam around cotton plants at the Mississippi Delta Experiment Station. Agricultural-foam covers eliminate the danger to the environment from airborne pesticides and still effectively protect crops from weeds, insects, disease, and bad weather.

152.5 million lb., 4% below 1971 and 43% below 1960. Prices to producers in August 1972 averaged 43 cents per pound (greasy basis) for wool and 68 cents for mohair, both more than double a year earlier.

The nation's egg-laying flock averaged some 308 million hens in mid-1972, down 3% from a year earlier. Egg production through April averaged 2% above the comparable period of 1971. Prices to producers fell as a result of large supplies and weak demand. Hatchery production of broiler-type chicks rose 4%, and it was indicated that the total for the year would exceed the 3,168,000,000 head of 1971. Outbreaks of Newcastle disease were especially severe in California, where health officials destroyed some 7.8 million birds. (*See* VETERINARY MEDICINE.) Turkey production was expected to exceed the 128.6 million pullets hatched in 1971.

Commercial honey production was estimated at 106,050,000 lb. from 1,563,000 colonies, compared with 93,982,000 lb. from 1,558,000 colonies in 1971. Prices were uncommonly high. The National Research Council and the USDA sent a committee of experts to South America to study the vicious "African" hybrid honeybees that were migrating north from Brazil. They concluded that no known geographic or climatic barriers would prevent the spread of the bee into North America.

Farm Prices, Costs, Income, and Finances. In August 1972 prices received by U.S. farmers stood at a composite index of 128, compared with 113 a year earlier. The index for all crops was 119, up from 107 in 1971. Only feed grains were below the 1967 base. Livestock and products rose from 117 in August 1971 to 135, with prices of meat animals up sharply from 122 to 151. Cash markets for beef cattle set new 22-year highs in July. Meanwhile, egg contracts in April declined to the lowest level in 12 years. Soviet purchases of wheat after midyear escalated wheat prices by fully one cent per pound, and bakers sought relief from higher costs of flour.

The parity index of production costs paid by farmers for commodities and services, interest, taxes, and wages was 127, compared with 120 a year earlier. The index for feeder livestock was up 17% to 147, but feeds rose only 1%. Farm machinery, interest, taxes, and wage rates all increased during 1972. A total of 4,781,000 workers were employed on farms in October 1972. In April the per-hour wage rate without board or room was $1.84, 4.5% above a year earlier, and the rate per month with house and other allowances was $351, up from $331. Sales of farm machinery rose.

The revised parity ratio, an overall measure of farmers' purchasing power, rose to 101 from 94 a year earlier. Farmers received about 40% of the "all food" market basket, compared with 38% in 1971. In August the index of retail food prices stood at 124.6, while the more inclusive consumer price index was 125.7. Based on the first eight months of the year, cash receipts for farm products in 1972 were projected at more than $57 billion. Nonmoney income and government payments would add $7.9 billion for a gross in excess of $65 billion. Farm production expenses were forecast at about $46.5 billion and farmers' realized net income at approximately $18.8 billion, compared with $16.1 billion a year earlier. In 1971, 253,000 or 8.8% of all farms had sales valued at $40,000 or more, whereas 1,072,000 farms or 37.3% of the total had sales of less than $2,500.

The estimated value of farm assets in 1972 was $335.2 billion, up from $319.1 billion a year earlier; real estate accounted for $223 billion. The national average value of farm real estate per acre rose 8% during the year ended March 1, 1972. Farm debt also continued its long upward trend; mortgage debt rose to $31,353,000,000 from $29,507,000,000 and short-term debt (excluding CCC loans) from $29,738,000,000 to $32,670,000,000. Even the lowest annual interest rates increased to 6.3%.

Trade and Stocks. U.S. farm-product exports in 1971–72 advanced about 4% in value to an all-time high of approximately $8 billion. Most of the increase was accounted for by a 3% rise in prices. In total, farm exports accounted for the output of 65 million ac., or one of every five acres harvested. Soybeans and products set a new export record of about $2 billion. Feed grains, as a group, were in second place. Farm exports to the EEC rose 7% to a record $1.9 billion, and exports to the Comecon countries totaled $300 million, compared with about $170 million in the previous year. Hide exports were curbed in July in an attempt to hold down U.S. shoe prices.

Agricultural imports into the U.S. also increased by 4% in 1971–72, to $6,042,900,000 or three-fourths the value of exports. Led by sugar and beef and veal, supplementary imports rose 7% to $3,950,000,000. Complementary imports declined by 2% to $2,093,000,000; green coffee continued to lead this group with a value of $1,112,000,000. China's exports to the U.S. reached $12 million following suspension of the 22-year embargo; half of the total was hog bristles.

U.S. stocks of agricultural products early in 1972 were sufficiently large so that official restrictions were continued on wheat production and a widespread effort was devoted to obtaining a reduction in feed-grain acreage. In late summer it appeared that the total feed-grain supply for 1972–73 would be an abundant 233 million tons. In July the wheat carry-over as of June 30, 1973, was forecast at about 865 million bu., and the wheat program for 1973 encouraged "set-aside" of acres that would otherwise be planted to wheat. However, the large wheat purchases by the U.S.S.R. would probably reduce existing stocks substantially. (See *Eastern Europe and the U.S.S.R.*, below.)

Legislation and Administration. The Farm Credit Act, passed late in 1971, modernized the existing farm credit laws to meet current and future needs. Among other provisions, it authorized the federal land banks and production credit associations to lend to rural nonfarm residents for housing purposes and allowed the land banks to make loans at up to 85% of appraised value rather than 65%. In an effort to improve rural life, the Rural Development Act of 1972 expanded the basic mission of the USDA to include rural development. For the most part, it expanded existing laws, but it did establish programs dealing with investment, credit, education, technology, and research. The USDA was authorized to share in the cost of controlling agricultural pollution.

Administrative actions relating to pesticide control were of great interest to farmers. (*See* ENVIRONMENT.) An earlier decision not to increase the support price of milk was reversed.

Canada. Contrary to early season indications, the 1972 wheat harvest of about 526 million bu. was only slightly below the 530 million bu. of 1971. With demand for wheat strong and the livestock industry flourishing, it appeared that net farm income would approximate the Can$1.5 billion of 1971. Acreage sown to wheat was 10% above the previous year, but the spring was rather late, the harvest difficult, and yields per acre below average. Canadian wheat exports in 1971–72 were substantially larger than in the previous year, chiefly because of increased exports to the U.S.S.R. and China; also Canadian farmers benefited from the long U.S. West Coast dock strike. One result was that Canada's wheat stocks fell to 18,060,000 metric tons as of July 1, 1972, 18% below a year earlier. Early indications were that limits on 1972–73 exports would relate mostly to handling facilities, rail transportation, and the dock situation. It was expected that wheat acreage would be increased substantially in 1973.

Feed-grain carry-over as of July 1 amounted to about 7 million metric tons; barley carry-over was at record levels despite high exports in 1971–72 and 1970–71. At 10.8 million metric tons, the new barley crop was 17% below the previous year. The record 1971 rapeseed crop of 98.5 million bu. moved into the export market easily in late 1971, but exports slumped early in 1972. Farmers cut back on rapeseed acreage, and the indicated 1972 production was down 37%. Flaxseed acreage was also cut by 22%. With tobacco exports expected to lose Commonwealth preference when the U.K. joined the EEC, the Flue-cured Tobacco Growers Board approved a system guaranteeing 66.5 cents per pound for marketings based on a crop target of 200 million lb. and an incentive fund to encourage exports.

Cattle numbers reached a new high in 1971, and a further increase of 3 to 5% was expected by June 1, 1972. Pork exports, mostly to the U.S., reached the highest level since 1948, although there was a sharp decline later in the year. Total output of red meat was estimated at a record 3,500,000,000 lb. The downward trend in milk production was arrested late in 1971. In May the minister of agriculture announced an increase of 20 cents per hundredweight in the base support level for manufacturing milk in the 1972–73 marketing year.

Canada's long-debated Marketing Agencies Act became law in January 1972. It was designed to permit nationally coordinated marketing agencies to control the production, marketing, price, and promotion of certain commodities moving in interprovince or export trade; products regulated by the Canadian Wheat Board or by the Canadian Dairy Commission were excepted. A small farms development program was announced in December 1971, with a Can$150 million fund that would enable small farmers to use special credit facilities to enlarge their farms to viable size.

LATIN AMERICA

At midyear the Inter-American Development Bank reported that, while the Latin-American economy as a whole continued to grow by about 6.6% in 1971, there had been only slow expansion in food production. According to FAO estimates, total agricultural production rose to an index of 159 (1952–56 = 100) for 1971, compared with 158 for 1970, while food production actually declined, from an index of 166 to 165. Population, meanwhile, increased about 3%, and per capita food production was cut from an index of 105 to 102.

Mexico. Mexico appeared to suffer a slight setback in the 1971–72 crop year. Early high estimates for wheat, corn, and sorghum had to be revised downward at midyear to about 1970–71 levels. Wheat and sorghum imports were increased and corn exports were reduced. The outlook for 1972–73 feed-grain crops was bright, however. Despite heavy rain damage in some areas, the 1971–72 cotton crop was estimated at 1,685,000 bales (480 lb. each), an increase of more than 17% over the previous year. Cotton exports continued to decline, and for the second consecutive year, sugar was Mexico's leading agricultural export. Coffee production rose to 3.3 million bags (60 kg. each), providing an exportable surplus of 1,725,000 bags.

Exports of winter vegetables and fruits to the U.S. continued to draw protests from U.S. producers. Shipments totaled $191 million in 1970–71, nearly double

Table II. Cotton Production of the Principal Producing Countries

In 000 480-lb. bales net

Country	Indicated 1972	1971*	Average 1965–69	Average 1960–64
Argentina	525	410	489	552
Brazil	2,900	3,100	2,730	2,235
China	7,700	7,500	6,740	5,040
Colombia	750	585	479	335
Egypt	2,300	2,300	2,198	2,037
Greece	550	530	407	337
India	5,200	5,900	4,870	4,741
Iran	800	680	623	494
Mexico	1,680	1,710	2,215	2,206
Pakistan	3,500	3,350	2,262	1,656
Peru	380	350	453	632
Spain	170	180	338	427
Sudan	1,000	1,000	937	675
Syria	750	740	694	656
Turkey	2,500	2,400	1,777	1,091
U.S.S.R.	11,100	11,100	9,140	7,370
United States	13,500	10,473	10,589	14,795

*Preliminary.
Source: U.S. Department of Agriculture, Foreign Agricultural Service.

Table III. Orange (including Tangerine) Production in Principal Producing Countries

In 000 boxes

Country	1971*	1970	Average 1960-64
Algeria	14,500	14,000	11,647
Argentina	31,904	39,528	21,540
Brazil	83,019	67,146	27,020
Greece	11,795	13,269	7,646
Israel	33,951	34,360	16,536
Italy	55,616	50,432	30,650
Japan	89,806	94,492	38,314
Mexico	34,959	32,124	23,478
Morocco	25,658	23,709	15,493
South Africa	16,086	15,136	13,939
Spain	68,634	63,136	51,191
Turkey	17,416	16,157	8,522
United States	247,565	248,027	145,937

*Preliminary.
Source: U.S. Department of Agriculture.

WIDE WORLD

A cornfield in Big Flats, N.Y., was ruined in June 1972 by flooding that deposited more than six inches of silt, much of it laden with oil from ruptured fuel storage tanks. Big Flats is near Elmira.

the 1967 level and four times greater than in 1960. Tomatoes accounted for about three-fourths of the value of 1970–71 shipments. In April a study of Mexico's National Foreign Commerce Bank pointed to declining U.S. production of tomatoes and generally refuted charges that increasing exports of these commodities constituted a serious threat to U.S. farmers.

Central America. Production of the main agricultural commodities in Costa Rica, El Salvador, Guatemala, Honduras, and Nicaragua rose in 1971–72. The region's output of cotton was estimated at 1,133,000 bales, nearly a third above 1970–71 and the largest since 1965–66. Yields, averaging 868 lb. per ac., were nearly 20% above a year earlier. A large part of the 1972–73 crop was reported to have been sold before harvest and, in many cases, before planting; prices for the 1971–72 crop averaged 28.5 cents per pound, f.o.b. Pacific ports, and some sales from the 1972–73 crop were reported as high as 37 cents. Sugar production in 1971–72 rose more than 8% to 809,000 metric tons; production in El Salvador increased 25%. Coffee production was up 10% to 6,985,000 bags, but prospects for the 1972–73 crop were dimmed somewhat by an expected 10% decline in El Salvador's harvest and a prolonged dry season in Costa Rica. Guatemala reported success in an intensive spraying program to eliminate a new infestation of the coffee borer.

South America. Brazil's agriculture experienced a good year in 1971–72. The index of total agricultural production was reported by the FAO at 188, compared with 179 a year earlier. The 5% gain in overall production included a sharply increased coffee crop of 23.6 million bags; excluding coffee production, the rise was estimated at 2.6%. The cotton crop was estimated at 3,150,000 bales, second only to the 1968–69 record. Brazil's sugar crop, the largest in South America, rose 4% above 1970–71 to approximately 5,660,000 metric tons. The wheat crop rose 15% to 2 million metric tons, and corn production was up 7% to 14.5 million metric tons.

Exports of farm commodities accounted for more than 75% of Brazil's exports in 1971. To maintain export expansion the government continued to grant liberal incentives, such as tax reductions or forgiveness on export products. Under the ambitious National Integration Program, some 500,000 settlers were to be relocated on farms in the Amazon basin. Another government program, which sparked heated debate, involved the redistribution of large landholdings in Paraiba, Pernambuco, and Ceara.

At midyear the world coffee crop for 1972–73 was forecast at 72,634,000 bags, an increase of 2% over a year earlier, but subsequent reports of severe frosts in Brazil's Paraná State indicated that this might be too high. The world coffee crop in 1971–72 totaled 71,437,000 bags, with South American producers accounting for nearly half of the total. Major controversy developed in the coffee trade during the 1971–72 coffee year (beginning Oct. 1, 1971). By Aug. 1, 1972, green coffee prices in New York had risen to 58 cents a pound from 43 cents a year earlier, setting the stage for a lively session of the International Coffee Council when it met to set export quotas for the 1972–73 coffee year. Consumer nations charged that the price rise had resulted from a unilateral agreement by 13 producer nations to hold exports below quotas, while producer nations claimed the Smithsonian monetary agreement had in effect cut their earnings from coffee by 8%. Agreement was finally reached on an export quota of 49.6 million bags for the 1972–73 trade year; the council then established a first-quarter quota of 13.1 million bags, with no price provisions.

Adverse weather and poor soil conditions reduced Argentina's output of principal crops in 1971–72. Wheat acreage was 25% above a year earlier and production of 5,440,000 metric tons was 20% above the disappointingly small 1970–71 crop of 4,250,000 tons. The corn crop was down 40%. In an attempt to expand beef exports, the government at midyear announced a ban on local beef sales during two out of every three weeks, but strong public reaction forced a return to the alternate-week bans that had been in effect since March 1971. At 1,101,000 metric tons, beef production in the first half of 1972 showed a slight improvement over the same period a year earlier, but 1971 production had been 23% below the 1970 level. Government measures to reduce domestic consumption resulted in a 20% increase in the consumption of poultry meat in 1971, and a further increase was forecast for 1972.

Food shortages and inflation continued to afflict Chile. Wheat production was down by 15% and sugar production by 20%. Continuing drought was reported to have decimated cattle herds. Further, the government and the growing Peasant's Revolutionary Movement disagreed on the size of farms subject to expropriation. Peasants seized properties subject to the expropriation law to prevent their operation by the Agrarian Reform Agency, and in some regions owners of medium and small farms organized brigades to evict the peasants. Agrarian discontent was heightened by the government's failure to implement its land-reform policy by providing adequate credit.

Inflation was also a serious problem in Uruguay, where wheat production declined 3% in 1971–72 and corn production fell 40%. Paraguay's production improved, but a critical shortage of beef continued to jeopardize its foreign exchange position. Agrarian reform continued under Peru's military government, which was reported to have expropriated some 7.5 million ac. The Peruvian government instituted an emergency cattle program designed to take advantage of vegetation resulting from floods in March and April. Although Bolivia's 1971–72 cotton crop exceeded the 1970–71 crop by a third, it was a disappointment to farmers who had increased acreage to 116,000 ac. from 44,000. Colombia's important coffee crop suffered a slight setback in 1971–72. Venezuela's 1971–72 sugar production rose to a new high of 539,000 metric tons, an increase of nearly 25% over a year earlier.

Cuba. Cuba appeared to have abandoned its sugar-harvest goal of 10 million tons per year. Although an output of 9.4 million short tons had been achieved in 1969–70, production in subsequent years had fallen far short of the official target. Several developments indicated an effort to diversify Cuba's agriculture: large-scale irrigation projects; investment in rice plantations; a plan involving 617,500 ac. of citrus plantations; and plans for the expansion of guava and coffee plantations. Sugar production in 1971–72 was estimated at 3.8 million metric tons, but trade sources reported that the 1972–73 outlook was more encouraging.

World sugar production for 1971–72 was estimated at 70,881,000 metric tons, compared with 70,853,000 tons a year earlier. Reduced harvests in Cuba and the U.S.S.R. were offset by gains in South America, Western Europe, Africa, and Oceania. Production in 1971–

World Production and Trade of Principal Grains

In 000 metric tons

	Wheat			Barley			Oats			Rye			Corn (Maize)			Rice		
	Production		Imports— Exports+	Production		Imports— Exports+	Production		Imports— Exports+	Production		Imports— Exports+	Production		Imports— Exports+	Production		Imports— Exports+
	1948–52 average	1971	1968–71 average	1948–52 average	1971	1968–71 average	1948–52 average	1971	1968–71 average	1948–52 average	1971	1968–71 average	1948–52 average	1971	1968–71 average	1948–52 average	1971	1968–71 average
World total	171,647	352,838	−55,584* +46,584*	59,022	151,041	−7,788* +7,950*	61,720	52,611‡	−1,266* +1,174*	36,966	30,900	−545* +579*	39,852	303,856	−27,593* +28,608*	167,349	307,600	−6,816* +6,884*
EUROPE																		
Austria	348	974	−29 +4*	210	1,016	−103	274	284	−37	343	448	−13*	120	721	−78	—	—	−38*
Belgium	525	907	−967† +208*†	244	588	−684† +60*†	483	278	−72† +1*†	221	88	−10† +3*†	3	c.17	−1,261† +356†	—	—	−51† +13*†
Bulgaria	1,776	3,095	−242* +271*	332	1,253	−60*	148	c.95	−1*	240	28‡	—	720	2,518	−41* +224*	37	66‡	−14*
Czechoslovakia	1,493	3,883	−1,210*	1,046	2,850	−153* +34*	961	908	−1*	1,110	611	−94*	316	c.575	−198*	—	—	−76*
Denmark	285	586	−5 +24*	1,708	5,474	−182 +235	922	704	−26 +15	365	150	−21	—	—	−223 +1*	—	—	−7*
Finland	263	443	−27 +60*	201	1,054	−16* +7*	718	1,424	+16*	201	132	−14	—	—	−15	—	—	−16*
France	7,791	15,360	−425 +4,361	1,534	8,950	−2* +3,010	3,392	2,539	+126	573	289	+31	452	8,772	−464 +2,591	46	79	−111 +28
Germany, East	1,243	2,490	−1,494* +9*	593	2,286	−395*	1,188	c.800	−2*	2,516	1,754	−59*	5	14‡	−373*	—	—	−41*
Germany, West	2,669	7,142	−2,135 +828*	1,402	5,774	−1,610 +215	2,523	3,037	−462 +15	3,066	3,029	−73 +80	20	594	−2,545 +46	—	—	−159 +22*
Greece	894	1,905	−42* +72*	211	780	−10* +17*	119	c.110	—	47	9‡	—	225	c.550	−174*	39	75	−3* +7*
Hungary	1,909	3,918	−264* +361*	654	782	−47* +7*	216	c.91	−1*	732	c.180	−3* +25*	2,068	4,674	−26* +109*	40	55	−19* +1*
Ireland	327	c.370	−163	163	c.900	−90 +1*	616	c.200	−9	4	c.1	—	—	—	−123	—	—	−3*
Italy	7,170	10,070	−1,389 +189	258	367	−1,082	495	501	−219	123	55	—	2,306	4,469	−4,486 +7	723	862	−6* +246
Netherlands	324	706	−1,381 +556	201	373	−173 +139	419	199	−86 +74	455	203	−32 +42	26	c.4	−2,339 +372*	—	—	−67 +21*
Norway	58	c.10	−357	109	569	−126 +3*	170	c.275	−7*	2	5‡	−37	—	—	−101	—	—	−6*
Poland	1,833	5,453	−1,317	1,061	2,449	−672* +76*	2,238	3,200	+14*	6,374	7,840	−64* +44*	4	c.13	−271*	—	—	−64
Portugal	499	794	−283	96	84	−28	124	132	—	162	163	—	421	529	−415 +1*	114	164	−27*
Romania	2,778§	5,585	+726‖	412§	665	—	369§	c.150	—	177§	43‡	+3*	2,495§	c.7,762	+371*	35§	65‡	−31‖
Spain	3,625	5,387	−1* +424*	1,909	4,783	−62 +91*	519	577	+27*	482	271	—	520	2,058	−2,172 +3*	280	361	−2* +65
Sweden	677	995	−42 +245	231	2,029	−8 +145*	804	1,867	−1* +202	258	301	−9* +46	—	—	−35	—	—	−12*
Switzerland	260	441	−440	55	170	−414	68	29	−169	34	c.40	−16	6	55‡	−190	—	—	−26*
U.S.S.R.	35,759¶	98,700	−1,075* +5,011*	6,354♀	34,500	+622*	13,005♀	14,600	+8*	17,961♀	12,800	+206*	5,751§	8,600	−355* +245*	202	1,400	−303* +6*
United Kingdom	2,397	4,824	−4,593 +10*	2,061	8,558	−755 +199	2,852	1,371	−16 +40*	52	c.19	−16*	—	—	−3,255 +9*	—	—	−128 +1*
Yugoslavia	2,171	5,604	−39* +2*	323	463	−50* +8*	286	312	−6* +1*	248	134	—	3,078	7,442	−4* +335*	5	32‡	−37*
ASIA																		
Burma	4	c.50	—	—	—	—	—	—	—	—	—	—	30	69‡	+9*	5,481	8,413	+588
Cambodia (Khmer Rep.)	—	—	—	—	—	—	—	—	—	—	—	—	57	121	+61*	1,635	2,732	+138
China	15,913	c.31,000‡	−4,458*	c.12,360	c.19,000‡	+1*	c.1,540	c.2,500	—	—	—	—	c.14,082	c.30,000‡	−20♂ +18*	58,188	c.102,000‡	−19‖ +867‖
India	6,087	23,247	−3,314	2,384	2,865	—	—	—	—	—	—	—	2,165	c.6,500	−25‖	33,383	c.66,000	−345 +15*
Indonesia	—	—	—	—	—	—	—	—	—	—	—	—	1,535¶	2,631	+110‖	9,441	18,778	−756*
Iran	1,879	c.3,000	−268‖ +70*	767	c.850	—	—	—	—	—	—	—	6	c.35	−35‖	c.424	c.1,100	−13‖
Iraq	448	822	−313 +5*	722	432	+52*	—	—	—	—	—	—	14	c.5	−2*	203	207	−1* +1*
Japan	1,375	440	−4,362*	2,020	503	−693*	119	c.60	−82*	6	c.1	−56*	57	c.30	−5,550* +3*	12,736	14,139	−90 +331*
Korea, South	c.139	c.322	−1,297	c.846	c.1,857	−91*	4	—	—	c.36	22‡	—	14	68‡	−113*	c.3,385	5,553	−549*
Lebanon	51	c.45	−291*	25	c.10	−82*	2	c.2♂	—	—	—	—	12	c.1	−79* +1§	—	—	−21*
Malaysia	—	—	−324*	—	—	—	—	—	−6*	—	—	—	8	c.11	−136*	670□	1,788	−333* +4*
Pakistan	c.3,500	6,503	−160* +1*	c.100	c.95	—	—	—	—	—	—	—	384	717	−3*	c.800	2,077	+135*
Philippines	—	—	−531	—	—	—	—	—	−3*	—	—	—	695	2,039	−9*	2,767	5,168	+13*
Syria	761	846	−251* +2*	321	262	−19* +185*	6	c.2	−1*	—	—	—	31	8‡	−3*	13	—	−38*
Thailand	—	—	−50*	—	—	—	—	—	—	—	—	—	31	c.2,075	−2* +1,499*	6,846	13,570	+1,201
Turkey	4,770	13,594	−446 +1*	2,270	4,170	—	326	435	—	500	c.900	—	747	1,060	—	109	241	−6*
Vietnam, South	—	—	—	—	—	−2‖	—	—	—	—	—	—	30	31‡	−62‖	2,395	6,324	−413
AFRICA																		
Algeria	996	c.1,500‡	−559‖	808	c.500‡	−10*	137	c.45‡	+5‖	—	—	—	6	6‡	−6§	—	2‡	−2‖
Egypt	1,111	1,729	−1,372	123	76	—	—	—	—	—	—	—	1,378	2,342	−72	971	2,534	+628
Kenya	101	c.210	+41*	8	c.13	—	5	c.4	—	—	—	—	574◇	c.1,400	−5* +159*	c.6	28	−2* +2*
Morocco	786	2,188	−433 +1‖	1,483	c.2,570	−1‖ +72‖	51	12	+2‖	4	c.2	—	302	350	−2‖ +17‖	8	45	+9*
South Africa	555	1,620	−41*	41§	35	−5*	79§	89	−1* +1*	10	6	−2*	2,629	8,600	−171* +1,639*	c.6	c.2▲	−81 +2*
Tunisia	452	600	−326 +2*	218	140	−32*	14	6▲	—	—	—	—	—	—	−10*	—	—	−1*
NORTH AND CENTRAL AMERICA																		
Canada	13,443	14,253	+9,887	4,245	14,257	+2,096	6,220	5,816	+116	469	629	+154	388	2,746	−537 +4*	—	—	−45*
Mexico	534	1,919	+96	160	c.230	−1‖	47	c.63	−2‖	—	—	—	3,090	c.9,500	−198 +490	173	441	−8* +15*
United States	31,065	44,620	−27 +15,464+	5,843	10,070	−201 +689	18,970	12,712	−23 +90	524	1,294	−17 +53	74,308	140,728	−47* +14,441*+	1,925	3,824	−7* +1,775
SOUTH AMERICA																		
Argentina	5,175	5,200	−131* +1,969	656	553	+139	743	475	+194	526	250	+20*	2,839	9,930	+4,570	137	300	+77*
Bolivia	37	62‡	−36*	39¶	62‡	—	2¶	c.11▲	−1♂	—	—	—	163	c.370‡	—	20	77‡	—
Brazil	498	c.2,056	−2,315*	15	c.26	−42*	9	c.27	−18*	17	c.19	—	5,841	c.14,360	−3* +1,162	2,921	5,130	+118
Chile	928	1,368	−277*	79	114	+7*	80	111‡	+1*	5	13	—	68	258	−164‖	75	67	−10*
Colombia	124	49	−227*	50	112	−28‖	—	—	−8‖	—	—	—	753	950	−6‖ +3‖	248	780	+5*
Peru	146	114	−632	208	150	−12	c.2	c.1	−2*	2	c.1	—	275	578	−4* +1*	191	587	−28*
Uruguay	469	316	+34‖	23	49	+1‖	44	63	—	—	—	—	141	160	—	41	122	+46*
Venezuela	5	c.1	−716*	—	—	—	—	—	−7*	—	—	—	303	c.725	−114*	41	c.240	−4* +34*
OCEANIA																		
Australia	5,161	c.8,380	+7,314	531	2,722	−11* +686	560	1,305	+331	12	c.19	—	126	226	−1* +1*	63	295	−2* +130
New Zealand	139	324	−38*	49	227	—	49	49	—	—	—	—	10	65	−1*	—	—	−5‖

Note: (—) indicates quantity nil or negligible; (c.) indicates provisional or estimated. *1968–70 average. †Belgium-Luxembourg economic union. ‡1970. §Average of 4 years. ‖1968–69 average. ¶Average of 3 years. ♀1950. ♂1968. □Average of 2 years. ◇1948. ▲1966. +Including foreign aid shipments.
Sources: FAO *Production Yearbook 1971*; FAO *Trade Yearbook 1971*; FAO *Monthly Bulletin of Agricultural Economics and Statistics*.

(M. C. MacDONALD)

72 was several million tons below world consumption, and a tight supply situation and higher market prices were expected. The International Sugar Council invited the secretary-general of the UN Commission on Trade and Development to call a conference to negotiate a new sugar agreement; the current International Sugar Agreement would end Dec. 31, 1973.

WESTERN EUROPE

Grain production in Western Europe in 1972 did not quite equal the record of 1971, but supplies of most varieties were at near-record levels. Meats, especially pork and poultry, were also plentiful, and measures to restrain milk output were de-emphasized. Currency instabilities and the forthcoming expansion of the EEC were the subjects of considerable attention.

United Kingdom and Ireland. A late spring and an unusually moist summer reduced wheat production in the U.K. to 4,430,000 metric tons, compared with 4,824,000 tons in 1971. Barley production was also somewhat lower, and total grain production of 13.8 million tons was 7.5% below the preceding year. Prices of wheat and barley grown in the U.K. would be phased up to EEC levels by 1976; until then EEC exporters, mostly French, would have free access to the British cereal market but would receive payments to even out the price difference. It was assumed that once Britain was in the EEC, British farmers would concentrate on beef production.

The 1972 review of guaranteed prices, the last before EEC entry, provided the farming industry with £72 million in additional resources against increased costs of £48 million. Payments for most products were to be increased, some very substantially. Faced with continued low prices for eggs, the Ministry of Agriculture diverted 30,000 cases for overseas disposition in July. After nearly a century of restricting livestock imports to animals for "exhibition or other exceptional purpose," arrangements were made to give priority to those animals most likely to help improve Britain's livestock. All would have to pass stringent veterinary controls.

Wheat production in Ireland fell rather sharply to 288,000 metric tons. Barley, geared more directly to the dominant livestock industry, rose to 950,000 metric tons from 915,000 tons in 1971. The potato crop yielded only 29.3 million cwt. in 1971, compared with 32.4 million cwt. the previous year. Dairying and beef were expected to increase in importance when Ireland entered the EEC. It was hoped that higher EEC prices and expanded markets might lead to a 30–40% increase in the volume of agricultural output by the end of the five-year transition period.

Table IV. Honey Production in Specified Countries

In 000,000 lb.

Country	1970*	Average 1960-64
Argentina	55	47
Australia†	49	41
Austria	11	10
Brazil	15	17
Bulgaria	13	5
Canada	51	35
Chile	12	14
China	37	6
Czechoslovakia	16	9
France	22	32
Germany, West	40	26
Greece	15	13
Guatemala	6	6
Hungary	15	12
Italy	14	15
Japan	16	15
Mexico	66	60
New Zealand	13	12
Poland	19	10
Romania	13	15
Spain	20	20
Turkey	28	20
United Kingdom	9	8
United States	235	253
U.S.S.R.	237	234
Yugoslavia	12	8

*Preliminary.
†Crop year beginning July of previous year.
Source: U.S. Department of Agriculture.

EEC Countries. Currency realignments disrupted the EEC's efforts to maintain common farm prices. Offsetting compensatory levies were imposed following devaluation of the U.S. dollar late in 1971, and in March 1972 it was agreed that guaranteed prices would rise an average of about 6.5%. Negotiations for enlargement of the Community were completed. The U.K., Ireland, Denmark, and Norway signed accession treaties, but Norwegian entry was subsequently rejected by that country's voters. The applicant countries agreed to a basic five-year transition period during which national agricultural policies would be replaced by the mechanisms and regulations of the Common Agricultural Policy, and farm prices would be aligned with the common prices of the EEC. Price alignment was to proceed in six steps, to be completed by the end of 1977.

The EEC approved structural reform measures for agriculture, but they were much less drastic than the proposed Mansholt Plan. Outlays of $162 million a year were to be provided. The measures included consolidation where farms are excessively fragmented, facilitating the retirement of older farmers, education to ease transfer to other occupations, and programs to help modernize farms and to encourage land transfer and farm enlargement.

Production in the six original member countries continued at very abundant levels. France harvested a record 16,042,000 metric tons of wheat, and barley production was 5% larger than in 1971. The corn crop was 8,771,000 metric tons, up from 7,581,000 tons a year earlier. Though many factors seemed to favour French agriculture, one farm was disappearing every 12 minutes and farmers were moving to town at the rate of 2% per year.

West Germany harvested its second largest wheat crop on record. The U.S.S.R. made large purchases of grain late in the year, and West German farmers were reportedly stepping up production in the hope of expanding exports to the U.S.S.R. and Eastern Europe. Italy continued to face social problems resulting from a 40% decline in agricultural employment since the early 1950s. The 1972 wheat crop of 9,455,000 metric tons was slightly below average. An oversupply of citrus was indicated for the next decade, and a search for new markets was under way. After two consecutive record filbert harvests, the 1972 crop was expected to decline 30% to 77,000 short tons (in-shell). A merger of cooperative slaughter plants in the Netherlands created the largest poultry-packing organization in the EEC.

Other Countries. Adherence to the EEC was expected to open new markets for Danish livestock and dairy products. Danish farmers were reported to be putting additional emphasis on economic performance of live hogs and improvement of meat quality. The important Danish barley harvest yielded 5,375,000 metric tons, down slightly from 5,475,000 tons in 1971 but above the 1966–70 average. The oat harvest of 615,000 metric tons was one-third below average, but wheat, at 591,000 metric tons, approximated the above-average harvest of 1971. Norway's rejection of EEC membership was apparently based on refractory fishery problems. In July the country experienced an unusual heat wave with temperatures above 90° F north of the Arctic Circle. Sweden harvested an excellent wheat crop of 1,190,000 metric tons, and other grain crops were also large. Some 500,000 tons of grain were reportedly exported to the U.S.S.R. The Finnish grain crops were slightly larger than in 1971; steps were taken to curb a soft wheat surplus. Switzerland was one of the few countries of Western Europe to produce more milk in 1972, despite a sharp cutback in the number of cows. The price differential between wheat and feed grains in Austria was narrowed to encourage the feeding of domestic wheat to livestock.

Most grain crops in Greece were larger than in the previous year. Greek tobaccos were becoming less competitive in Western Europe; government grants were made for some machinery and equipment, and the indirect export subsidy was continued. The use of fungicides for control of blue mold was given special attention. In Spain the flight from the land continued. The area planted to wheat was reduced in 1972, and the 4,559,000 metric-ton harvest was below that of a year earlier. The barley crop also declined, but 1971–72 sugar output reached a record 1,048,000 tons. The

Table V. Poultry Meat Production in Selected Countries*

In 000,000 lb.

Country	1970†	1969	1968	Average 1955-59
Belgium-Luxembourg	239	222	216	95
France	1,358	1,280	1,199	511
Germany, West	573	508	463	172
Italy	1,380	1,274	1,173	215
Netherlands	679	579	470	96
Total EEC	4,229	3,863	3,554	1,089
Austria	102	94	92	4
Canada	980	895	807	428
Denmark	173	151	142	58
Greece	165	149	113	36
Japan	1,075	741	606	—
Poland	282	273	251	109
Spain	698	655	566	—
United Kingdom	1,257	1,221	1,182	455
United States	10,210	9,728	9,145	5,480

*On ready-to-cook basis (70% of live weight).
†Preliminary.
Source: U.S. Department of Agriculture, Foreign Agricultural Service.

Table VI. Egg Production in Specified Countries

In 000,000

Country	1970*	1969	1968
Argentina	3,000	2,940	2,880
Australia	2,501	2,380	2,328
Belgium-Luxembourg	4,500	3,967	3,424
Brazil	9,636	9,670	9,480
Canada	5,948	5,655	5,436
Czechoslovakia	3,670	3,430	3,270
France	11,200	11,200	10,800
Germany, East	4,445	4,194	4,046
Germany, West	15,375	14,685	14,076
Hungary	3,000	2,640	2,792
Italy	10,600	10,281	9,750
Japan	29,975	27,913	24,694
Mexico	6,570	5,657	5,375
Netherlands	5,500	4,420	4,009
Poland	6,931	6,700	6,315
Romania	3,400	3,315	3,113
U.S.S.R.	40,400	37,190	35,679
United Kingdom†	14,776	14,844	14,916
United States	70,308	69,084	69,276

*Preliminary.
†Year beginning June 1 of year shown.

Table VII. Milk Cows and Milk Production in Specified Countries

	Number of milk cows in 000			Milk production in 000,000 lb.		
Country	1971*	1970	Average 1961-65	1971*	1970	Average 1961-65
Australia	2,600	2,677	3,190	16,113	17,002	15,244
Austria	911	1,085	1,122	7,255	7,326	6,743
Belgium	1,000	1,033	1,024	8,135	8,386	8,664
Canada	2,397	2,471	2,930	17,777	18,386	18,404
Denmark	1,105	1,153	1,428	10,051	10,207	11,713
France	8,968	9,039	9,409	60,746	60,064	54,162
Germany, West	5,489	5,593	5,852	46,661	48,184	45,368
Greece	470	460	434	3,082	2,929	1,159
Ireland	1,690	1,669	1,373	8,132	7,987	6,458
Italy	3,400	3,500	3,448	20,957	20,613	21,872
Japan	1,139	1,060	717	10,626	10,501	5,976
Netherlands	1,890	1,920	1,701	18,466	18,164	15,578
New Zealand	2,995	2,363	2,007	13,521	13,023	12,302
Norway	414	424	568	4,012	3,979	3,666
Sweden	742	746	1,180	6,347	6,512	8,446
Switzerland	869	901	926	7,011	6,909	6,837
United Kingdom	4,515	4,411	4,202	28,074	27,314	24,791
United States	12,347	12,483	16,195	118,640	117,149	125,660

*Preliminary.
Source: U.S. Department of Agriculture, Foreign Agricultural Service.

1971 olive crop was large, and the support program for oilseeds was extended for 1972. Spain became the fourth largest export market for U.S. soybeans. Wheat production fell in Portugal. Efforts were being made to stimulate meat and poultry production.

AFRICA

Agricultural production appeared to move ahead over most of Africa in 1971–72. Good harvests of corn in South Africa, peanuts in Senegal, and cocoa in West Africa contributed to overall growth on the order of 4%, compared with a 3% average in recent years. Gains in South Africa, Nigeria, and Egypt more than offset reduced production in East Africa, where generally unfavourable weather and some political unrest continued to depress crop production. Efforts to improve Africa's access to world markets for agricultural products continued at several levels in 1972. At the African regional meeting of the FAO, held in Gabon in September, 33 countries approved the creation of a commission to promote intra-African trade. Several West African nations reached agreement on the creation of the Economic Community of West Africa. At the same time, the effect of U.K. accession to the EEC left African Commonwealth nations in some doubt as to their trading status in British markets.

North Africa. Agricultural production in Africa's northern tier appeared to sustain or surpass the gains made in 1971. The FAO index of total agricultural production reported improvement throughout the region in 1971, and in 1972 good cereal crops in the Maghreb and Egypt may have offset declining citrus and grape production in Algeria and moderately lower cotton output in Egypt. Morocco's wheat harvest was reported to be a record 2,550,000 metric tons. The 1971–72 olive crop was indicated at a record 350,000 metric tons, and oil output was expected to be almost double that of a year earlier. Sugar production rose 41%. Morocco's 1973–77 development plan gave first priority to agricultural investments. By contrast, Algeria was concentrating on development of industry, and only 15% of new investment in 1970–73 was assigned to agriculture. Efforts were being made to redistribute land owned by absentee landlords and to consolidate small farms into cooperatives. Algerian wheat production was reduced by dry weather, and citrus production declined. The government continued its program of phasing out grape production in conformity with the Muslim ban on alcohol. Tunisia's 1971–72 wheat crop was a record 810,000 metric tons, at least partly attributable to the introduction of high-yielding Mexican varieties. The olive harvest was nearly double that of a year earlier.

The agricultural picture in Egypt appeared to improve in 1971–72. Corn production rose to 2.5 million metric tons from 2,393,000 tons, wheat production was up slightly, rice was 18% above average, and sugar was 11% above 1970–71. Cotton production fell, however; at 2.2 million bales, the 1971–72 harvest was nearly 6% below 1970–71. In March, the minister of agriculture announced that acreage for 1972–73 cotton would be increased to permit a crop of 2.5 million bales. Sudan's cotton crop was reported at 1,150,000 bales, about the same as a year earlier but 22% above the 1965–69 average; nearly 1 million bales were exported. Additional funds were allocated to agriculture under the five-year development plan.

West Africa. Good weather, more efficient farming techniques, generally expanding acreages, and government policies combined to increase production in most West African nations in 1971–72. Senegal's important peanut harvest was reported at 945,000 metric tons, a sharp increase from the 545,000 tons of 1970–71. Nigeria's 1971–72 peanut harvest was a disappointment; production of 880,000 tons was above 1970–71 but still a third less than the 1,360,000 tons harvested in 1969–70. The low production was attributed to the failure of the Northern States Marketing Board to raise producer prices and the fact that prices were announced too late to affect plantings. An increase in producer prices was announced for 1972–73. The West African coffee and rice harvests showed modest gains over a year earlier. Cassava production increased in

Table VIII. Grain Supply and Disappearance in the U.S.S.R.

(000,000 metric tons)

Year beginning July	Area (000,000 ac.)	Yield (metric tons per ac.)	Production*	Imports	Exports	Est. consumption Feed	Est. consumption Total	Est. change in stocks
1963	279	.29	80 (97)	10	4	43	97	−11
1964	288	.37	108 (136)	2	5	48	102	+3
1965	286	.32	91 (110)	9	4	45	99	−3
1966	280	.48	135 (159)	3	5	61	114	+19
1967	274	.42	115 (136)	2	6	66	120	−9
1968	275	.48	131 (157)	1	7	71	125	—
1969	271	.44	119 (149)	1	7	69	123	−10
1970	270	.53	143 (174)	1	7	82	137	—
1971	267	.53	139 (169)	7	5	87	141	—
1972	268	.45	122 (147)	21†	1	89	143	−1

*Storable-grain basis; data in parentheses are "bunker weight" basis.
†Assumes that 5 million tons of the total U.S.S.R. purchases are destined for other countries.
Source: U.S. Department of Agriculture, Foreign Agricultural Service, *Foreign Agriculture* (October 9, 1972).

COURTESY, FAO

Moroccan farmer uses an old-fashioned press to produce olive oil, a traditional staple for thousands of years. Taste preferences were changing, however, and many Mediterranean countries were importing increasing amounts of vegetable oils from the U.S. and Europe.

nearly all the West African nations, and the generally low-yielding cotton crops continued to show gains. Production of sorghum and millet in Nigeria was estimated at 6,785,000 tons. Exports of palm oil, chiefly from Nigeria, Zaire, Dahomey, and Ivory Coast, accounted for only 23% of world trade in 1971; this contrasted with 66% in 1960 and reflected increased domestic requirements, reduced operational efficiency, lack of investment, and production disruptions stemming from civil unrest.

A 6% increase in the 1971–72 West African cocoa crop raised estimated world production to a record 1,552,900 tons, despite an 8% decline in South American production. Generally favourable weather was credited with raising Ghanaian production 16% to 457,000 tons. Nigeria's harvest was reported at 263,000 metric tons, a decline from 323,000 tons a year earlier, but Ivory Coast production was a record 220,000 metric tons. Late 1972 forecasts indicated that world production in the 1972–73 season would be about the same as in 1971–72. World cocoa bean grindings in 1971 exceeded 1.4 million metric tons, with the U.S. accounting for 278,826 tons. With supplies plentiful, prices on the world market declined; the monthly average for African cocoa in New York in 1971 was 26.8 cents per pound, compared with 34.2 cents in 1970. The UN Cocoa Conference continued its efforts to negotiate an International Cocoa Agreement. The Cocoa Producers Alliance of West African nations announced that, if the UN conference failed, it would set up its own cocoa stabilization plan.

The impending entry of the U.K. into the EEC was expected to affect the export positions of West African Commonwealth countries, among them Nigeria, since the U.K. would apply the EEC external tariff against their tropical products while admitting, duty-free, tropical products from the former French, Belgian, and Italian colonies associated with the EEC. At midyear seven of nine French-speaking countries in West Africa signed a treaty establishing the Economic Community of West Africa; Dahomey, Ivory Coast, Mali, Mauritania, Niger, Senegal, and Upper Volta signed the agreement, while Togo reserved its position and Guinea did not attend.

East Africa. Drought reduced many crops in East Africa in 1971–72; cotton, tea, and tobacco were the major exceptions. The important corn crop in Kenya was reported at 1.3 million metric tons, compared with 1.5 million tons in 1970–71; only Zambia and Malawi registered appreciable gains in corn production. The Malagasy Republic reported an 8% increase in rice. Sorghum and millet showed few, if any, gains, and sugar production declined throughout the region with the single exception of the Malagasy Republic. Tanzania's coffee crop was 10% below a year earlier and the Malagasy crop was down 25%. Tea production in East Africa rose to record levels, however, and tobacco production increased throughout the region with the exception of Mozambique.

At 399.2 million lb., Tanzania's sisal production was 10% below 1970–71. World production of hard fibres continued its downward trend, reflecting lower prices and increasing competition from synthetic fibres. World sisal production, estimated at 1,297,100,000 lb., was 3.7% below a year earlier. Abaca was down 9.6% to 183.9 million lb., and henequen totaled an estimated 328 million lb., compared with 335.5 million lb. a year earlier.

Southern Africa. South African agricultural production continued to improve in 1971–72. The Wheat Board estimated the 1971–72 wheat crop at a record 1,515,000 metric tons; a number of factors were responsible, including good weather, heavier plantings of new short-straw varieties, increased acreage, and higher prices. The surplus production would permit South Africa to enter the export market in 1972, but reports indicated that the country did not intend to do so because of the imbalance between domestic and world prices. Favourable growing conditions and a 7% increase in acreage combined to produce a record corn harvest of 10,270,000 metric tons. Together with carry-over stocks, this would provide exportable supplies of about 5.7 million tons, though it was believed that rail facilities were not adequate to permit exports of more than 3 million tons.

Sugar production reached a record 1,865,000 metric tons in 1971–72, more than 50% above the 1962–67 average. A Price Stabilization Fund was established as insurance against drought or depressed world prices. Sheep ranchers continued the voluntary reduction of

Table IX. Centrifugal Sugar Production in Principal Producing Countries

In 000 metric tons, raw value

Country	1971-72	1970-71	Average 1962-63–1966-67
Argentina	991	972	1,021
Australia	2,866	2,589	1,953
Brazil	5,660	5,431	3,897
China	2,268	2,087	1,321
Colombia	793	688	445
Cuba	3,800	5,897	4,783
Czechoslovakia	680	771	996
Denmark	325	291	334
Dominican Republic	1,238	1,098	725
France	3,200	2,695	2,034
Germany, East	517	499	723
Germany, West	2,354	2,054	1,815
India	3,817	4,502	3,318
Indonesia	680	726	613
Iran	630	614	230
Italy	1,255	1,199	1,109
Jamaica	350	396	490
Mauritius	676	621	617
Mexico	2,531	2,476	2,040
Netherlands	827	713	537
Peru	918	903	792
Philippines	1,916	2,059	1,569
South Africa	1,865	1,399	1,206
Spain	1,048	794	518
Taiwan	780	833	899
Turkey	910	643	600
United Kingdom	1,148	985	894
U.S.S.R.	7,877	8,845	8,228
United States	5,292	5,268	4,739
U.S. dependencies*	254	291	837
Yugoslavia	421	385	377
World total	70,881	70,853	59,478

*Puerto Rico and Virgin Islands of the U.S.
Source: U.S. Department of Agriculture, Foreign Agricultural Service.

Table X. Coffee Production (Green) in Principal Producing Countries

In 000 bags, 132.3 lb. each

Country	1972-73*	1971-72	1970-71	Average 1963-64–1967-68
Angola	3,400	3,400	3,300	3,080
Brazil	24,000	23,600	9,750	23,780
Cameroon	1,300	1,250	1,150	994
Colombia	8,000	7,500	7,800	7,920
Costa Rica	1,365	1,330	1,250	1,103
Ecuador	1,000	1,100	1,300	908
El Salvador	2,800	2,600	2,170	2,048
Guatemala	1,800	1,980	1,840	1,798
India	1,450	1,200	1,900	1,187
Indonesia	2,400	2,250	2,350	1,980
Ivory Coast	4,000	4,400	4,000	3,795
Malagasy Republic	1,000	965	1,300	935
Mexico	3,500	3,300	3,200	2,811
Peru	1,030	1,030	990	857
Philippines	865	900	840	709
Tanzania	800	850	950	707
Uganda	2,850	2,850	3,000	2,620
Venezuela	1,100	920	900	789
Zaire	1,350	1,200	1,250	985
Total North America	12,746	12,384	11,742	10,805
Total South America	35,281	34,306	20,872	34,413
Total Africa	19,480	19,667	19,727	16,909
Total Asia and Oceania	5,442	5,080	5,790	4,355
World total	72,949	71,437	58,131	66,484

*Second estimate.
Source: U.S. Department of Agriculture, Foreign Agricultural Service.

flocks that was instituted to combat low world market prices for wool in the 1967–71 period. Wool production fell to 124,000 tons in 1971 from 146,000 tons a year earlier. It was feared that the U.K.'s accession to the EEC would create serious economic difficulties for such export commodities as fresh and canned fruit, corn, wine, sugar, and preserved meat.

Rhodesian farmers continued to switch from tobacco to other crops. Tobacco production in 1972 was estimated at 132 million lb., compared with 233 million lb. in the last year before Rhodesia's unilateral declaration of independence. It had been hoped that the agreement concluded with Britain in late 1971 would lead to revitalization of the tobacco industry, but the settlement collapsed in 1972, and UN trade sanctions against Rhodesia were continued. Even so, it was estimated that between 75 million and 100 million lb. of Rhodesian tobacco continued to be sold on the world market.

Meanwhile, the production of alternative crops rose. The corn harvest was estimated at 1.4 million metric tons in 1971–72, compared with 1.2 million tons a year earlier; wheat, long considered an uneconomic crop, rose to 82,000 metric tons from only 25,000 two years before; and cotton production of 240,000 bales, while about the same as a year earlier, was twice the 1965–69 average. Both sheep and cattle numbers increased. There was a surplus of slaughter stocks, and the Cold Storage Commission, Rhodesia's marketing control organization, ordered a 40% reduction in deliveries to its depots in the May–August period.

EASTERN EUROPE AND THE U.S.S.R.

Emerging grain deficits in the U.S.S.R. placed an unexpected demand on the world agricultural economy. The remainder of this large, diverse area appeared to have had comparatively good conditions in 1972.

Eastern Europe. Despite early season dryness and a wet harvest in some areas, the Eastern European wheat crop of some 29,886,000 metric tons was only 1% below the 1971 record. A large barley crop of 10,776,000 tons reinforced the favourable grain situation, though rye was off by 8% and oats by 10%. Corn, the major feed-grain crop, rose to 23,149,000 tons in 1971 from 20,370,000 tons a year earlier. The upward trend in livestock numbers continued, and meat production in 1971 was generally higher.

The Polish wheat crop was a record 6,105,000 metric tons, 20% more than in 1971 and far above the 1966–70 average. Barley also set a record of 2,942,000 metric tons, but the rye crop was well below 1971 levels. It appeared that concessions to private farmers had paid off and that the planned 2.7% increase in crop production would be surpassed, although the increase in livestock might fall below the planned 6.3%. Czechoslovakia and East Germany presented a mixed picture in 1972. Both countries had above-average wheat harvests, but the rye and barley crops in Czechoslovakia were seriously reduced. Livestock feeding in both countries was improved by imports of oil meals and feed grains. Bulgaria's tobacco crop was record large in 1971; exports increased about 5%.

Wheat and rye production in Yugoslavia declined in 1972, but barley and oats were up slightly. The corn crop in 1971 was a large 5,604,000 metric tons. With 2.1 million milk cows on farms, Yugoslavia made impressive progress in upgrading its herds by importing breeding stock. There was a general boom in livestock; about 800,000 tons of the record 1971 wheat crop were used as animal feed, and some 114 million lb. of beef were exported, mostly baby beef to Italy. Yugoslavia achieved virtual self-sufficiency in poultry meat in 1971. Feed grains and edible oils were large import items, however, and Yugoslavia provided the largest single market for U.S. soybean oil.

The Hungarian wheat harvest of 3,933,000 metric tons was almost exactly the same as the large crop of 1971, despite drought during much of the spring and a wet harvest. The barley crop was substantially larger, but the oats and rye crops declined. A large corn crop of 4,730,000 metric tons was harvested in the autumn of 1971. Corn remained the principal feed grain, although increasing quantities of wheat were used for that purpose. Hog numbers reached an all-time high and poultry numbers continued to rise. New agricultural targets were introduced in Romania. Goals for the 1971–75 period included 43% more cattle, 70% more hogs, 63% more poultry, 12% more sheep, 100% more fresh meat, 59% more canned meat, and 104% more milk and dairy products.

U.S.S.R. The agricultural situation in the Soviet Union appeared to worsen as 1972 got older. As late as December 1971, Soviet spring wheat was being offered in Western Europe at prices below those for U.S. and Canadian spring wheat. A large wheat crop of 81.9 million metric tons had been harvested in 1971; the rye crop was somewhat below the 1966–70 average, but the barley crop was a large 28.6 million metric tons. Even oats, at 12.1 million metric tons, was well above average. There were indications that the highest priority was being given to livestock production, and feed-grain purchases reached unprecedented levels; 3.5 million tons of feed grains were

COURTESY, FOREIGN AGRICULTURE

Modern poultry farms such as this one in Mihailesti, Rom., are capable of producing two million broilers annually. Both Romania and Hungary focused their 1971–75 five-year plans on expanding livestock output.

Table XI. World Cocoa Production in Leading Areas*

In 000 metric tons

Area	Forecast 1972-73	1971-72	1970-71	Average 1962-63–1966-67
North and Central America	91.5	93.2	73.1	82.7
Dominican Republic	38.0	40.0	26.0	32.8
Mexico	30.0	30.0	25.0	21.5
South America	291.1	265.0	286.5	222.2
Brazil	185.0	165.4	182.4	139.3
Ecuador	65.0	60.0	65.0	42.8
Africa	1,121.8	1,153.2	1,092.4	956.1
Ghana	430.0	457.0	392.0	446.8
Nigeria	290.0	263.0	323.0	229.7
Ivory Coast	205.0	220.0	176.3	122.3
Cameroon	112.0	126.0	112.0	83.1
Asia and Oceania	43.2	41.5	41.1	30.0
New Guinea and Papua	30.0	29.0	29.0	18.4
World total	1,547.6	1,552.9	1,493.1	1,291.0

*Crop year, October 1 to September 30.
Source: U.S. Department of Agriculture, Foreign Agricultural Service.

Table XII. Tea Production in Principal Producing Areas

In 000 metric tons

Area	Forecast 1972	1971*	1970	Average 1964–68
World total†	1,151	1,112	1,102	975
Asia	983	962	956	874
Bangladesh‡	20	10	31	28
India	440	433	422	380
Indonesia	50	48	43	41
Japan	94	93	91	83
Sri Lanka (Ceylon)	215	218	212	223
Taiwan	28	27	28	22
U.S.S.R.	70	68	67	54
Africa	139	118	120	79
South America	30	33	26	22

*Preliminary.
†Excluding China.
‡Formerly East Pakistan.
Source: U.S. Department of Agriculture, Foreign Agricultural Service.

purchased from two U.S. companies in November 1971. The 1971 sunflower seed crop was 6% below 1970, but the cotton crop set a new record.

The autumn of 1971 was comparatively dry for planting the winter wheat crop, and winter grain over much of European U.S.S.R. was winter-killed or damaged by exceptionally cold, dry weather. Spring reseeding of some of the damaged area was attempted, and seeding of spring wheat in Siberia was expanded, but spring was late, the summer was uncommonly hot, and autumn came early with millions of tons of wheat yet unharvested. How much of this was attributable to bad weather and how much to inadequate equipment and labour shortages was not clear. In any case, it was estimated that the 1972 grain crop might not total more than 75% of the 1971 harvest. Wheat was indicated at 62.3 million metric tons and rye at 8.3 million tons. Barley, saved by the reseeding operation, rose to 29.9 million metric tons, while oats was down only slightly. Preliminary indications were that the sugar-beet crop might not be much larger than the disappointing crop of 1971. Sunflower seed and other oil crops were probably reduced at least moderately.

Soviet wheat exports to the West were withdrawn in early summer. As early as March there had been indications that the U.S.S.R. might increase grain imports because of winterkill. U.S. Secretary of Agriculture Earl Butz went to Moscow in April, and the Soviet minister of foreign trade continued trade discussions in Washington in May, but these discussions apparently focused on feed grains. Then, in July and August, the U.S.S.R. purchased an unprecedented 11 million-plus tons of wheat from the U.S., as well as several million tons of feed grains and at least one million tons of soybeans. In large part this was a credit transaction; the U.S. agreed to provide the U.S.S.R. with standard short-term CCC financing of up to $500 million outstanding at any one time, repayable in dollars in three equal annual installments after delivery. Interest costs through March 31, 1973, were pegged at $6\frac{1}{8}\%$ on letters of credit issued by U.S. banks and at $7\frac{1}{8}\%$ for foreign bank letters.

Table XIII. Progress in Production of Principal Crops in India Since Independence

Commodity	Preplan average, 1947-48–1950-51	1st 5-yr. plan, 1951-52–1955-56	2nd 5-yr. plan, 1956-57–1960-61	3rd 5-yr. plan, 1961-62–1965-66	3-year average, 1966-67–1968-69	1st 3-yrs. 4th plan 1969-70–1971-72	Percent increase, col. 6 over col. 1
Fibres							
(000 bales of 396.8 lb.)							
Cotton	2,345	3,658	4,542	5,099	5,190	5,437	132
Jute	2,539	3,929	4,441	5,684	4,870	5,435	114
Kenaf	*	853	1,357	1,684	1,133	1,171	37†
Food grains							
(000 metric tons)							
Wheat	6,018	7,901	9,736	11,070	15,528	23,113	284
Rice	21,990	25,038	30,332	35,155	35,937	42,293	92
Coarse grains	16,048	20,198	22,179	23,672	26,011	27,942	74
Total cereals	44,056	53,136	62,246	69,897	77,473	93,348	112
Pulses	8,316	10,044	11,753	11,143	10,289	11,756	41
Total food grains	52,372	63,181	73,999	81,040	87,765	105,104	101
Oilseeds							
(000 metric tons)							
Peanuts	3,306	3,534	4,726	5,125	4,924	5,565	68
Castor	115	113	109	99	116	136	18
Sesame	392	511	400	442	428	506	29
Rape and mustard	777	914	1,086	1,267	1,381	1,876	141
Linseed	412	380	389	419	342	465	13
Total oilseeds	5,000	5,453	6,710	7,353	7,191	8,547	71
Other crops							
(000 metric tons)							
Sugarcane (gur)‡	5,352	5,541	8,107	11,126	10,704	13,159	146
Tea	264	288	316	357	388	414	57
Coffee	20	27	41	48	70	80	300
Potatoes	1,503§	1,857	2,306	3,217	4,160	4,451	196
Tobacco	254	257	292	338	361	354	39

*Not available. †Increase in column 6 over column 2. ‡Raw brown sugar. §Three-year average, 1948-49 through 1950-51.
Source: U.S. Department of Agriculture, Foreign Agricultural Service, D. V. Khosla, "India's Agricultural Production—Twenty-five Years after Independence," *Foreign Agriculture* (August 14, 1972).

The reactions were immediate and widespread. Wheat prices climbed to a nine-year high, and the U.S. dropped its export equalization subsidies. The manner in which the negotiations had been conducted became a political issue in the U.S. Wheat stocks in the U.S. and Canada would be substantially reduced but appeared to be adequate. What was not clear was the degree to which wheat production might be stimulated by the new price levels and whether burdensome world stocks would again be accumulated. Nor was it clear that regular purchasers of U.S. wheat were sufficiently provided for, even at the higher prices, or that transportation and handling systems would be adequate.

In the U.S.S.R. there were indications that the crisis might prod domestic agricultural reforms. The extent to which the grain reduction would require a cutback in the livestock program remained in doubt. So did the question of whether the increased purchases of wheat and feed grains from the West would continue, perhaps (as some hoped) for the next three to five years. Meanwhile, it was reported that Soviet schoolboys had been assigned to dig potatoes and that food was being sought from Eastern Europe.

MIDDLE EAST AND INDIAN SUBCONTINENT

Middle East. Turkey, in some years a wheat exporter, reported a 1972 harvest of 8.5 million metric tons, compared with the record 10.7 million tons of 1971. A record 1971 cotton harvest of 490,000 metric tons provided 305,000 tons for export in 1971–72, up 20% from the previous year. Edible vegetable oil output for 1971–72 fell 6% to an estimated 322,000 tons; an 18% increase in cottonseed and a 12% increase in sunflower seed oil failed to compensate for an "off year" decline in olive oil. Citrus production was up by 11%, and further increases appeared likely for the next several years, the result, in part, of improvements financed by a $25 million World Bank loan. Tobacco production approximated the level of the previous year, but filberts were far below the 1970 record.

Following the announcement in June 1971 that opium poppy cultivation would cease after the 1972 crop, Turkey requested help from the U.S. in planning profitable alternatives. A study team of U.S. experts joined about 50 Turkish experts in conducting surveys and drawing up plans and development programs. Suggestions included seeding with improved strains of wheat, diverting some wheatland to feed grains, trying new oilseed crops, experimenting with forages, increasing irrigation, and starting a commercial livestock industry.

Countries at the eastern end of the Mediterranean experienced good grain harvests. Syria sold 150,000 tons of 1972 durum wheat for export to an unknown destination, its first substantial export of wheat since 1964–65. The 1971–75 development plan envisaged a one-third increase in agricultural production. As part of its program to increase domestic dairy production, Lebanon planned to acquire some 12,000 Holstein-Friesian heifers over a five-year period; the animals would be resold to farmers at two-thirds of cost. Israel harvested a record 280,000 metric tons of wheat; imports in 1972–73 were expected to decline by 35,000 tons to about 245,000 tons. The 1.5 million-ton citrus crop of 1970–71 was also a record, and the 1971–72 crop was nearly as large. About 884,000 tons of citrus were exported in 1970–71.

Iran produced about 4.1 million metric tons of

wheat in 1972, compared with 3,870,000 tons a year earlier; the barley crop showed an even more startling change, rising to 1.2 million metric tons from 800,000. With cotton prices at a high level, a 25% acreage increase in the Caspian region was expected. That, plus increased use of fertilizers and pesticides, gave promise of a bumper crop in 1972–73. The almond harvest was expected to be above average, but severe and widespread fungus infestation destroyed a large fraction of the 1972 pistachio crop. The citrus crop was a record 55,000 tons in 1971, but the dried fruit pack was 14% below 1970.

Afghanistan suffered a severe drought in 1971 and 1972. Deaths from famine and associated health problems were estimated in the tens of thousands. Perhaps half of the livestock had been slaughtered and seed for new plantings was mostly eaten. Relief wheat did arrive, but transportation and distribution systems proved less than adequate.

Indian Subcontinent. Drought, typhoons, and war took their toll in this heavily populated area in 1972. Pakistan harvested a below-average wheat crop of 6.4 million metric tons; acreage declined by 4% to about 14,820,000. Wheat import requirements in 1971–72 were about 650,000 tons. Rice acreage and production in 1972 were a little higher than in 1971, partly because of the expanded use of improved varieties. Vegetable oils were imported in substantial amounts. The 1971–72 cotton crop was revised upward to an all-time record of 3,250,000 bales, and export availabilities were estimated at nearly 1.4 million bales. The maximum agricultural acreage that might be held by any one family was lowered from 500 to 150 irrigated acres and from 1,000 to 300 unirrigated acres. Surplus holdings would be seized without compensation.

A quarter of a century after gaining independence, India continued to pursue the elusive goal of agricultural self-sufficiency. Substantial progress had been made, but distribution remained a problem and civil disturbances relating to land distribution were reported. The government recommended that each family hold not more than 10 to 18 ac. of government-irrigated land and 54 ac. of other land. Wheat production in 1972 rose to some 25.5 million metric tons from 23,247,000 tons in 1971, a result of both favourable weather and larger acreage. For a time it appeared that total food-grain production would surpass the 110.5 million metric tons of 1971 and might even provide 8 million tons for export, but these prospects were ruined by disastrously high temperatures and drought. Instead, increased imports of some foods and financial assistance for the current five-year plan might be needed. A large crop of oilseeds was harvested in 1971–72 for the second consecutive year, although sesame and peanuts were reduced by drought. India neared self-sufficiency in cotton production with an estimated 1971–72 production of 5.6 million bales.

India's sugarcane acreage and production declined in 1971–72 for the second year in succession. Centrifugal sugar production fell by 15% to 3.8 million metric tons. Exports in 1972 were largely restricted to the amounts needed to meet India's quotas in the preferential U.S. and U.K. markets, and rationed distribution through "fair price" shops was reintroduced on January 1. A record tea crop of about 440,000 metric tons was forecast for 1971. The pepper crop for 1971–72 was expected to be 20% above a year earlier. India's jute industry was reported to be facing a variety of problems—a declining world market, growing use of synthetics, and competition from reopened mills in Bangladesh. India arranged to purchase 1.5 million bales of raw jute from Bangladesh. The Planning Commission approved a program to increase India's jute production by 840,000 bales by 1973–74 to a total of 7.5 million bales.

The new country of Bangladesh (created from former East Pakistan late in 1971) comprised a generally productive area, but widespread natural disaster in 1970 and war in 1971 had halted production growth and disrupted channels of distribution. Imports of farm products reached unprecedented levels in 1972, possibly as high as $400 million, and there were reports of food imports piling up at the ports. Agricultural production in 1971–72 was at least 10% below the 1970 level; tea was down 52%; jute, 22%; and rice, 20%. A below-average jute crop was anticipated in 1972–73, partly because of drought. Most of the tea gardens that had provided for exports from Pakistan were now in Bangladesh.

The Ceylonese tea industry faced serious competition from East Africa. The 1971 harvest totaled 217,773 metric tons, but a major drought in March 1972 reduced new-crop production. In August the government approved legislation restricting individual landholdings to 50 ac., but foreign-owned tea and rubber estates were exempted.

FAR EAST

Little firm information was available for large parts of this diverse area, but there were suggestions that, with respect to agriculture, 1972 was not quite so favourable as 1970 and 1971.

The picture in China was uncertain. No goals appeared to have been announced for 1971 (the first year of the fourth five-year plan) or 1972, but there were indications that additional efforts were being made to extend the area planted to crops and to increase productivity through more intensive use of fertilizers, mechanization, capital, water management, and improved varieties of plants. The livestock industry was reported to have had a record year in 1971, with the number of hogs increasing by 11%. Some estimates placed the 1971 grain harvest at 246 million metric tons. According to one source, the 1971 rice crop was an estimated 94 million metric tons, compared with 97,540,000 tons in 1970. Wheat was said to have risen to 24.4 million metric tons in 1972 from 24 million tons a year earlier, and some northern provinces were reportedly self-sufficient in grain. Corn

Table XIV. U.S. Imports of Meat Subject to Meat Import Law*
In 000 lb.

Country of origin	May 1972†	May 1971	Jan.-May 1972†	Jan.-May 1971	Percent change from 1971: May	Percent change from 1971: Jan.-May
Australia	54,691	35,834	219,645	153,472	+53	+43
New Zealand	24,545	14,480	81,047	70,708	+70	+15
Costa Rica	5,082	3,566	32,765	28,164	+43	+16
Mexico	7,418	7,764	34,502	44,787	−4	−23
Nicaragua	3,157	2,506	20,376	16,418	+26	+24
Canada	6,146	6,963	23,130	32,949	−12	−30
Ireland	2,148	3,033	19,875	34,023	−29	−42
Guatemala	1,722	1,001	9,924	7,821	+72	+27
Honduras	1,668	1,149	7,783	7,793	+45	—
Panama	291	70	1,640	1,321	+316	+24
Dominican Republic	920	341	4,841	926	+170	+423
United Kingdom	—	21	37	1,149	—	−97
Haiti	115	51	816	277	−125	+195
Total‡	107,901	76,778	456,382	399,808	+41	+14

*Fresh, frozen, and chilled beef, veal, mutton, and goat meat including rejections. Excludes canned meat and other prepared or preserved meat products.
†Preliminary.
‡May not add due to rounding.
Source: U.S. Department of Agriculture, Foreign Agricultural Service, *Foreign Agriculture* (July 3, 1972).

COURTESY, AUSTRALIAN NEWS AND INFORMATION BUREAU

Australian cattle are driven to terminal from where they will be shipped to the U.K. Australia enjoyed duty-free status for its beef in Britain, but under the Common Market tariff agreement duty was to reach 14% over a four-year period beginning April 1, 1973.

production in 1971 was estimated at 25,340,000 metric tons. Agricultural exports to non-Communist areas, chiefly Hong Kong and Japan, totaled about $1.8 billion in 1970.

Reports in mid-1972 indicated that wheat-growing areas in northern China had been hit by drought, with possible damage to late summer and autumn harvests and to the seeding of winter wheat for harvest in 1973. In any case, China bought rather large amounts of wheat; some 3 million metric tons were purchased from Canada in December 1971 for shipment in 1972, and in June an additional 1.5 million tons were ordered for shipment July 1972 through March 1973. Terms were for 25% down with the balance to be paid in 18 months. Wheat was also purchased from the U.S. and elsewhere.

South Korea's wheat crop declined sharply in 1972, to 243,000 metric tons from 322,000 tons in 1971, although acreage remained about the same. It was anticipated that imports would reach 2 million tons, partly because of a government campaign to encourage wheat consumption. The 1972 barley crop was 2,009,000 metric tons, compared with 1,857,000 tons in 1971, and the 1971 rice crop, at 5,440,000 tons, was slightly above that of 1970. Increased use of meat, fish, milk, and poultry was projected under the third five-year plan (1972–76). Some 264 feeder calves were airlifted from Oklahoma in a project to determine the feasibility of introducing intensive beef feeding on U.S.-style feedlots.

Table XV. Production of Meats in Principal Producing Countries
In 000,000 lb., carcass-meat basis

	Beef and veal			Pork (excluding lard)			Mutton, lamb, and goat meat		
Country	1971*	1970	Average 1961–65	1971*	1970	Average 1961–65	1971*	1970	Average 1961–65
Argentina	4,537	5,754	4,913	414	467	384	307	375	345
Australia	2,309	2,228	1,941	401	384	257	1,819	1,665	1,310
Belgium-Luxembourg	613	595	482	1,032	973	508	3	8	6
Brazil	4,023	3,629	3,095	1,314	1,356	1,030	126	126	106
Canada	1,929	1,903	1,618	1,511	1,328	1,002	19	17	31
Colombia	1,142	1,111	837	165	159	117	4	4	5
Denmark	430	422	357	1,687	1,582	1,466	3	4	3
France	3,556	3,450	3,166	1,945	2,721	2,534	291	267	237
Germany, West	2,998	2,965	2,541	5,271	4,927	3,979	25	23	30
Italy	1,823	1,764	1,388	1,135	1,038	887	101	104	86
Japan	602	574	400	1,658	1,429	649	2	2	6
Mexico	1,401	1,332	1,046	617	575	452	120	123	129
Netherlands	696	719	590	1,659	1,482	923	25	24	18
New Zealand	...	887	601	...	82	94	...	1,233	1,036
Poland	...	1,138	878	...	1,948	1,826	...	57	57
South Africa	1,097	978	998	173	185	115	476	464	282
Spain	...	680	404	...	1,085	608	...	314	267
U.S.S.R.	11,872	11,123	7,142	7,512	7,039	5,872	2,250	2,113	2,226
United Kingdom	2,096	2,087	1,978	2,286	2,087	1,796	506	500	559
United States	22,457	22,272	17,862	14,772	13,434	11,863	555	551	755
Yugoslavia	631	615	529	937	902	844	...	116	117

*Preliminary.
Source: U.S. Department of Agriculture, Foreign Agricultural Service.

Unfavourable weather in 1971 abetted Japan's efforts to cut back its rice production. Official acreage diversion led to an 8% reduction, while spring cold and typhoon damage reduced yields by 7%. The 10.9 million-metric ton crop was 14% below the previous year and some 650,000 tons below the nation's normal rice needs for 1971–72. It appeared that by late 1972 rice carry-over stocks would have fallen to approximately 3 million metric tons from a peak of 7.2 million tons in 1970. Hog slaughter in 1971 rose 17% to a record 13 million head and poultry meat production increased 11% to 539,000 tons. Gross value of agricultural production in 1971 was $12.6 billion; 85% of Japanese farmers received part or most of their income from nonfarm sources.

Increasingly, Japanese interests were involved in agricultural development overseas. A new oil palm venture in Papua New Guinea, would require about $6 million over four years to develop a 5,000-ac. plantation and an oil mill; together with 10,000 ac. of oil palms in associated smallholder blocks, the development could produce more than 20,000 tons of palm oil by 1977. In May 1972 Japanese interests announced plans for a large beef-producing operation, involving the grazing of 100,000 cattle in the Northern Territory of Australia and slaughter and packing facilities in Townsville, Queensland.

In Taiwan agricultural production continued to grow at a rate of about 4.4%; rice, citrus, and sugar all showed substantial increases. The export trade in agricultural products was active, with mushrooms accounting for $16.5 million. Taiwan embarked on a ten-year dairy program designed to increase consumption of domestically produced whole milk from 1.5 lb. per capita in 1971 to 11.8 lb. in 1980.

Hopes for achieving self-sufficiency in rice in the Philippines faded as typhoon damage, civil disturbances, and a virus disease, *tungro,* that attacked the new high-yielding varieties, reduced the 1971–72 crop to 3,360,000 metric tons, 3% below 1970–71. Heavy July and August rains in the major rice bowl in Luzon caused losses of possibly 300,000 metric tons. Rice imports of 800,000 tons, largely from Thailand, were authorized for 1972. Coconut production in 1971 was 31% above the previous year, and sugarcane was a record 23.8 million tons. As part of the Philippines' four-year plan (1972–75), the World Bank approved a loan of $7.5 million to help increase livestock production on small and medium-size farms.

One comprehensive report summarizing ten years of study urged investment of $12 billion in Indochina's Mekong basin over the next 30 years to avert a food and power crisis. Burma, Thailand, and South Vietnam reported improved rice harvests in 1971, with the total crop reaching record levels, but in September 1972 a rice shortage and very high prices caused civil disturbances in Cambodia. Emergency supplies, mostly airlifted by the U.S., were distributed. Malaysia's major crops, rice, rubber, and palm oil, all showed significant increases in 1971; 1972 palm-oil production was affected by below-average rainfall in the first five months of the year. Indonesia's coconut groves were reported to be overstocked with unproductive old trees, and replacement with high-quality seedlings in the near future was said to be imperative.

OCEANIA

Australia. Australian farmers continued to shift from wool and wheat to beef, feed grains, and oilseeds. Agricultural exports in 1970–71 amounted to about

$2.4 billion, or more than half the country's total export earnings. Australia's important export market in the U.K. was expected to decline following Britain's accession to the EEC.

Wheat production in 1971–72 was estimated at 8,644,000 metric tons, 9.5% more than a year earlier. Following a good wheat export year in 1970–71, the Wheat Board had set basic delivery quotas for the 1971–72 crop at 8.9 million tons, compared with 8.3 million tons a year earlier. Exports of wheat declined about 5% in the 11-month period July 1971–May 1972, however. Exports to the U.K. fell sharply, although sales to Egypt, the U.S.S.R., and Japan improved and an A$60 million sale was made to China in the fall. Drought dimmed prospects for the 1972–73 wheat crop. There were also reports that a plague of mice was devastating hundreds of square miles of wheat fields in Queensland.

Australia's feed-grain crops reached a record 5,741,000 metric tons in 1971–72, as farmers diverted land from wheat. Barley production was up 32% and corn production rose to 259,000 tons. Prospects for 1972–73 feed-grain crops were uncertain; drought conditions were expected to reduce barley production by about a third, while cyclones were reported to have ruined the winter rice crop in Queensland. Long a net importer of fats and oils, Australia more than doubled oilseed production in 1971–72 and attained an export surplus for the first time. Cotton was estimated at 175,000 bales in 1971–72, a sharp increase from 87,000 bales a year earlier. Sugar production rose 10% to a record 2,866,000 metric tons.

Production of all meats was estimated at 2.2 million tons in 1971, compared with 1.9 million tons a year earlier; beef production was reported at 1,023,000 tons. Domestic consumption accounted for about 60% of the total. A report by the Queensland Department of Primary Industries projected a doubling of beef supplies available for export by 1976. Exports of meat in 1971–72 were expected to exceed the 1970–71 level of $442 million. The suspension of quota limits on beef imports to the U.S. in effect raised Australia's share of U.S. imports to some 268,000 tons, about 7% more than a year earlier.

Australian wool production continued the decline that had begun in 1969; 1972–73 production was estimated at 1,781,100,000 lb., 7% below 1971–72 and the lowest in five years. World wool production fell 1% overall, with 1972 output (including the 1972–73 season in the Southern Hemisphere) estimated at 5,928,700,000 lb. (greasy basis). There were signs, however, that the long depression in the wool industry might be ending. Demand improved markedly, and the reentry of Japanese buyers into the world market brought a surge of activity to primary markets. By October 1972 prices had risen to 1950–51 levels. Sales by the Australian Wool Commission averaged nearly 70 U.S. cents per pound (greasy basis) in the first week of October, compared with an average of 38 cents for the 1971–72 season, and October 1 stocks held by the commission were reported to be about 70,000 bales, compared with 930,000 bales in December 1971. Heavy production of worsteds in Japan accounted for at least part of the improvement; Japan was reported to have purchased 2.6 million bales of Australian and New Zealand wool, or 37% of the combined output of those two countries.

New Zealand. Agricultural production began to show signs of recovery from the severe drought conditions of 1969–70. Dairy cattle numbers were expected to increase 2% in 1972; milk production was expected to rise 3% and butter production, 4%. Sheep numbers declined 2% in 1971, but hog numbers, which had fallen in 1969 and 1970, rose 7%. Wool production in 1972–73 was expected to reach 715 million lb., compared with 710 million lb. in the preceding year. Farm incomes remained depressed, however, and the New Zealand Federated Farmers sought assistance from the government in the form of a parity-type cost-adjustment scheme using 1964–65 prices as a base for adjusting farm income. The government decided instead to continue its selective assistance and to postpone long-term decisions until the effects of U.K. entry into the EEC became clear.

(JOHN KERR ROSE; HARVEY R. SHERMAN)

See also Alcoholic Beverages; Commercial Policies; Commodities, Primary; Cooperatives; Fisheries; Food; Gardening; Industrial Review; Prices; Tobacco.

ENCYCLOPÆDIA BRITANNICA FILMS. *The Orange Grower* (1967); *The Sheep Rancher* (1967); *Midwest—Heartland of the Nation* (1968); *Produce—From Farm to Market* (1968); *Problems of Conservation—Soil* (1969); *Problems of Conservation—Our Natural Resources* (1970).

Albania

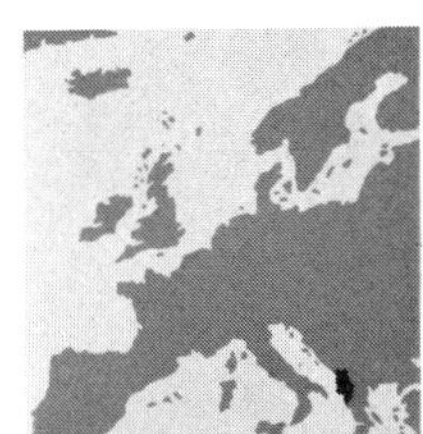

A people's republic in the western Balkan Peninsula, Albania is on the Adriatic Sea, bordered by Greece and Yugoslavia. Area: 11,100 sq.mi. (28,748 sq.km.). Pop. (1971 est.): 2,226,000. Cap. and largest city: Tirana (pop., 1967 est., 169,300). Language: Albanian. Religion: Muslim, Orthodox, Roman Catholic. First secretary of the Albanian (Communist) Party of Labour in 1972, Enver Hoxha; president of the Presidium of the People's Assembly, Haxhi Leshi;

ALBANIA

Education. (1969–70) Primary, pupils 506,683, teachers 17,915; secondary, pupils 22,375, teachers 961; vocational and teacher training, pupils 36,525, teachers 941; higher (including University of Tirana with 12,783 full-time students), students 23,100, teachers 827.

Finance. Monetary unit: new lek, with (Sept. 18, 1972) an official exchange rate of 4.6 leks to U.S. $1 (free rate of 11 leks = £1 sterling). Budget (1969 est.): revenue 4,888,000,000 new leks; expenditure 4,506,000,000 new leks.

Foreign Trade. (1964) Imports U.S. $98 million; exports U.S. $60 million. Import sources: China 63%; Czechoslovakia 10%; Poland 8%; East Germany 5%. Export destinations: China 40%; Czechoslovakia 19%; East Germany 10%; Poland 10%. Main exports: fuels, minerals, and metals (including crude oil, iron ore, chrome ore, and copper) 54%; foodstuffs (including vegetables, wine, and fruit) 21%; tobacco; wool.

Transport and Communications. Roads (motorable; 1960) 3,100 km. Motor vehicles in use (1960 est.): passenger 1,900; commercial (including buses) 3,400. Railways (1969): 205 km.; traffic 220.4 million passenger-km., freight 230 million net ton-km. Shipping (1971): merchant vessels 100 gross tons and over 17; gross tonnage 56,523. Shipping traffic (1969): goods loaded *c.* 1.6 million metric tons; unloaded *c.* 630,000 metric tons. Telephones (Dec. 1963) 10,150. Radio receivers (Dec. 1970) 161,000. Television receivers (Dec. 1969) 2,500.

Agriculture. Production (in 000; metric tons; 1971; 1970 in parentheses): corn *c.* 320 (*c.* 270); wheat (1970) *c.* 145, (1969) *c.* 192; oats (1970) *c.* 15, (1969) *c.* 11; cotton, lint (1970) *c.* 8, (1969) *c.* 8; sugar, raw value (1971–72) *c.* 17, (1970–71) *c.* 17; potatoes *c.* 118 (*c.* 118); wine *c.* 9 (*c.* 8); tobacco *c.* 13 (*c.* 13). Livestock (in 000; Dec. 1970): sheep *c.* 1,600; cattle *c.* 442; pigs *c.* 155; goats (1969) *c.* 1,330; poultry (Oct. 1969) *c.* 1,790.

Industry. Production (in 000; metric tons; 1969): crude oil 1,307; lignite 592; petroleum products 748; chrome ore (oxide content; 1970) 194; iron ore *c.* 400; copper ore (metal content) 6; cement 220; electricity (kw-hr.) 788,000.

Aircraft:
see Defense; Industrial Review; Transportation

Air Forces:
see Defense

chairman of the Council of Ministers (premier), Mehmet Shehu.

"It is not possible to use one imperialism against another," Enver Hoxha had proclaimed at the sixth congress of the Albanian Party of Labour, held in Tirana in November 1971. The only faithful ally of China in Europe, Hoxha then continued his quixotic "two-front struggle" against Soviet and U.S. imperialism and their respective "lackeys." A few months later, his vituperation was suddenly muffled following U.S. Pres. Richard Nixon's visit to Peking. However, *Zeri i Popullit,* the chief Albanian newspaper, wrote in March that "the people of the world do not allow themselves to be deceived by Nixon's olive branch," implying obliquely that the Chinese leaders might have been somewhat too gullible. Soviet propaganda did not miss Tirana's embarrassment, and Albanian-language broadcasts from Moscow argued that Hoxha could not seriously decrease his criticism of the U.S. because this would reduce if not destroy his prestige at home.

Chinese economic aid to Albania since the Soviet-Albanian rupture of 1961 was estimated at more than $125 million. On Dec. 5, 1971, a protocol on the use of unspecified Chinese credit to Albania for 1972 was signed in Tirana by Fang Yi, minister of economic relations with foreign countries, and Kico Ngjela, the Albanian minister of trade.

According to the fifth five-year development plan (1971–75), approved by the party congress in November 1971 and by the National Assembly in December of that year, the gross national product was to increase from 54 to 58% by 1975, as compared with 1970. During the fourth five-year plan (1966–70), the annual rate of increase of Albania's industrial output had risen to 11%; the fifth plan postulated an annual growth of 10.3%.

Replying in the British House of Commons on April 24, 1972, to the question of whether the British government would consider restoring diplomatic relations with Albania, Anthony Royle, parliamentary undersecretary at the Foreign and Commonwealth Affairs Office, said that the matter was being considered. The chief obstacle was the question of compensation arising from the blowing up of two British destroyers in the straits between Corfu and the Albanian coast in October 1946. The International Court of Justice at The Hague had awarded damages of £843,947 to Britain, but the Albanian government had never made payment. (K. M. SMOGORZEWSKI)

Alcoholic Beverages

Beer. World production of beer rose to 658 million hectolitres (hl.) in 1971, an increase of 4.4% over 1970; a similar increase was expected in 1972. European production, accounting for more than half the world total, rose by 4.6% to 360 million hl. Production in the Americas, about one-third of the world total, which increased by only 3.1%, was affected by stagnation and recession in various Latin-American countries, particularly Argentina, Mexico, and Venezuela. Consumption of beer per capita worldwide was 18 litres in 1971; with China and India excluded, it was 32 litres.

The three top beer-producing countries registered the following figures: United States, 150 million hl. (up 4.5%); West Germany, 90 million hl. (up 3.4%); United Kingdom, 57 million hl. (up 3%). Fourth and fifth ranked were the U.S.S.R. (42 million hl.), whose brewing capacity was to be doubled under the current five-year plan, and Japan (31 million hl.).

In most Western countries the largest brewers further increased their share of the market. Thus in the U.S. the leading quartet, Anheuser-Busch Inc. (28.5 million hl. in 1971; up 9.5%), Schlitz (19.6 million hl.; up 10.4%), Pabst (13.8 million hl.; up 12.2%), and Coors (10 million hl.; up 17.1%), increased their combined production by 6.2 million hl., while the rest of the industry achieved an increase of only 300,000 hl.

Production in the European Economic Community in 1971 was 140 million hl., with West Germany providing 65% of the total. Adding production figures for the U.K., Denmark, and Ireland, output of the enlarged EEC would be in the region of 210 million hl., with West Germany's share dropping to about 43%. This loss of absolute predominance would weaken West Germany's ability to insist on "purity" (*i.e.,* the use of natural raw materials only) in the formulation of common EEC standards for the brewing industry. The other EEC members and prospective members rejected the West German purity norm as hindering the introduction of new brewing techniques. The Germans argued that it was the best means of preserving beer's wide popular appeal as a wholesome drink and need not exclude use of the latest techniques. In West Germany, where consumption was about 145 litres per capita per annum, most of the leading brewers stated their intention of keeping to the purity norm even if it should no longer be enforced.

Standards of preparation were not the only bone of contention among EEC brewers. Special problems also arose with regard to the sought-after harmonization of excise duties. Among the original EEC members a beer of about 12% Balling (48° original gravity) strength bore a maximum duty of about $7.50 per hl. (on the average less than $5), as against $30 to $37.50 per hl. in the prospective member countries. The brewery concern with the biggest output in the enlarged EEC would be Bass-Charrington, with about 13 million hl. annually, one of whose plants currently under construction would be the biggest in Europe. Allied Breweries, with about 11 million hl. annually, and Whitbread, with about 8 million hl., would also be among the biggest.

In the technical field, the BREWEX 72 exhibition in London showed evidence of continuing refinement in the automation of practically all main and ancillary brewery operations. (TILMAN SCHMITT)

Spirits. World production and consumption of potable spirits showed further increases in 1971–72, particularly in the bigger and wealthier countries. Many international companies opened new plants in consuming countries, and more local industries sprang up, especially in the production of malt whiskies. Retail prices increased owing to currency devaluations, higher manufacturing and transport costs, and, in some cases, increased fiscal duties. On the whole, however, duties, usually the highest factor in retail price, remained reasonably stable.

Shortages of mature Scotch whiskies developed, partly because of cutbacks in production in the 1960s and partly because of increased demand, growing at the rate of at least 10% per annum. Pure malts increased rapidly in popularity in the U.S. and Europe, further accentuating the shortage for blenders, and premium prices for mature stocks were paid. Nearly 72 million proof gallons were exported in 1971, an increase of 16%, mainly to the U.S. and Europe. Japan continued to be a disappointing market, owing to high domestic production and discriminatory taxation.

Bigger exports of brandies from producing countries caused concern to domestic producers in such countries as South Africa and Australia, and protective tariffs were urged to keep out cheap brandies while still allowing the import of high quality brandies at premium prices. A sales campaign for Californian brandy, with substantial advertising funds, was begun.

British entry into the European Economic Community posed problems for Scotch whisky and gin exporters, particularly with regard to controlled export prices, sole agencies, cereal prices, agricultural levies, and various usages that might conflict with the restrictive practices clauses of the Treaty of Rome. Home prices were generally lower than export prices and, if these were to be equalized to Common Market countries on British entry, it would be hard to deny similar terms to non-EEC buyers, particularly in those countries where some price resistance favouring locally bottled brands imported in bulk was already evident. On the other hand, the possibility of equalization of British fiscal duties with those of other EEC countries was welcomed, as British duties were higher than others. In 1972 France superseded West Germany as the second largest overseas market for Scotch whisky after the U.S. Regulations for a proposed EEC Alcohol Regime were being prepared. It was hoped that it would, inter alia, require all spirits intended for human consumption or for use on the human body to be made only from agricultural products. (J. W. MAHONEY)

Apparent consumption of distilled spirits in the U.S. in 1971 reached a record 381.1 million gal., 3% above 1970. Per capita consumption rose 1.6% to 1.86 gal. Fifty areas of prohibition in 11 states were eliminated in 1971 by local option. In 1972, 15 more states reduced the drinking age to below 21; three lessened or removed bans on serving liquor on election days. Consumer expenditure for alcoholic beverages for 1971 was $24.7 billion, compared with $22.4 billion in 1970. The U.S. federal excise tax on spirits remained at $10.50 per proof gallon. Collections of the tax on alcoholic beverages totaled $5,110,001,000 in fiscal 1972, or 30.3% of all excise taxes collected. U.S. agents seized 2,981 stills producing illicit spirits, 346 less than in 1971.

JEAN LATTES—GAMMA

A potential buyer inspects a selection of France's finest wines in the Palace of Versailles prior to an auction held on June 22, 1972. Increased demand for fine wines has pushed prices to record levels in recent years.

A total of 764,350,925 gal. of distilled spirits were produced in the U.S. in fiscal 1972, 0.67% more than in 1971; this included some not used for beverages. Whiskey production was down 0.74% to 126,273,838 tax gallons; this figure included 31,233,408 gal. of light whiskey distilled at higher than 160 proof, first authorized for production on Jan. 26, 1968, and not offered for sale to the public until July 1, 1972. Total U.S. bottlings rose 4.1% in 1971, to 325,805,447 gal.; whiskey accounted for 192,007,883 gal., or 58.9%. Bourbon whiskey continued as the largest selling spirit in the world, with sales of 84,673,148 gal. Vodka continued its phenomenal increase, jumping 12.6% to 56,475,099 gal. The swing to larger bottles continued; quarts increased 4.7% and half gallons, 21.2%.

Table I. Estimated Consumption of Beer in Selected Countries

In litres* per capita of total population

Country	1968	1969	1970
Belgium†	140	140	140
Germany, West	129.4	135.8	139.17
Czechoslovakia	132.8	135.1	...
Luxembourg	116.1	124.6	126.5
Australia‡	116.8	120.4	123.1
New Zealand	110.4	111.1	114.9
Denmark	94.4	102.2	108.52
United Kingdom	96.5	98.4	100.9
Austria	98.2	99	98.7
Germany, East	86.3	92	95.7
Switzerland	73.7	77.1	...
Canada	71	71.2	73.8
United States	65.2	67.4	70.2
Ireland	85.1	65.3	...
Hungary	51.2	54	58
Sweden	51.8	58.4	57.6
Netherlands	45.4	51.4	57.38
Finland	32.6	52.2	48.8
France	40	40.7	41.3
Venezuela	35	39	...
Spain	32.9	32	38.5
Norway	32.5	34.7	36.76
Bulgaria	27.6	36	...
Colombia	31	...	34
Poland	28.9	30.4	31.4

*One litre = 1.0567 U.S. quarts = 0.8799 imperial quart.
†Including so-called "household beer."
‡Years ending June 30.

Table II. Estimated Consumption of Potable Distilled Spirits in Selected Countries

In litres* of 100% pure spirit per capita of population

Country	1968	1969	1970
Poland	3.3	3.4	3.2
Yugoslavia	2.6	3	...
Germany, West	2.59	2.75	2.97
United States	2.82	2.91	2.87
Spain	2.3	2.5	2.84
Hungary	1.95	2.35	2.65
Sweden	2.55	2.60	2.65
Germany, East	2.2	2.5	2.60
Canada	2.26	2.2	2.41
Romania	—	2.2	2.4
France†	2.2	2.2	2.3
Iceland	1.86	1.92	2.23
Czechoslovakia	1.64	2.20	...
Switzerland	1.8	2.12	...
Netherlands	1.76	1.88	2.04
Luxembourg	1.8	1.1	1.9
Finland	1.4	1.6	1.8
Bulgaria	1.8	...	...
Italy	1.8	2	1.7
Peru	1.7	1.7	...
Norway	1.47	1.48	1.56
Cyprus	2.85	2.60	1.51
Austria	2	1.2	1.50
South Africa	1.07	1.13	1.35
Belgium	1.10	1.08	1.32

†Including alcohol- and wine-based aperitifs and liqueur wines.

Table III. Estimated Consumption of Wine in Selected Countries

In litres* per capita of total population

Country	1968	1969	1970
Portugal	93.2	...	115
Italy	114.2	115.3	114.6
France†	113.0	115	112
Argentina	87.5	...	91.3
Spain	62.1	62.5	61.5
Chile	48.9	...	50
Austria	29.7	31	44.2
Switzerland‡	38.6	40.8	...
Hungary	34.8	38	39
Luxembourg	35.9	32	37
Greece	36.7	35	35
Yugoslavia	26.3	28.3	...
Romania	26.9	25	25
Uruguay	25	25	...
Bulgaria	21.7	...	...
Germany, West	15.3	15.9	16.9
Belgium	11.9	12.1	13.9
Czechoslovakia	15.8	13.2	...
U.S.S.R.	12.0	12.0	...
South Africa	9.1	9.4	9.27
Australia§	7.7	8.2	9.1
Cyprus	11.2	8	8.2
Sweden	5.3	5.8	6.4
Denmark	4.41	5.13	5.91
Poland	5.0	5.6	5.6

†Excluding cider (c. 20 litres per capita annually).
‡Excluding cider (c. 7.8 litres per capita 1968–69).
§Years ending June 30.

Source: Produktschap voor Gedistilleerde Dranken, *Hoeveel alcoholhoudende dranken worden er in de wereld gedronken?*

Total imports of spirits into the U.S., at 102,138,802 tax gallons, were up 12.4% in 1971 and had a value of $568.4 million. Canadian imports amounted to 34,795,117 tax gallons, up 12.1%, and Scotch was 54,300,790 tax gallons, up 11.5%. The percentage of bulk to total whiskey rose from 36.8% to 38.1% for Canadian whiskey and fell from 30% to 28.4% for Scotch. Tequila imports rose 33.3%, to 1,124,575 gal. Total U.S. distilled-spirits exports rose 34.3%, to 5,356,926 gal.; whiskey exports, at 3,861,833 gal., increased 41%.

In Canada public revenue from alcoholic beverage taxes rose 7.7%, to Can$983,903,000 in fiscal 1971. Consumption of spirits climbed 6.24%, to 25,390,000 imperial gallons. Production declined 0.34%, imports fell 1.22%, and exports increased 3.07%.

(JULIUS WILE)

Wine. In 1972 the volume of wine produced throughout the world was estimated at 280 million hl., almost equaling the 1971 total of 284 million hl. Around 78% (220 million hl.) of this figure came from European vineyards and from the Soviet Union (28 million hl.). There was a slight decline in both quantity and quality of harvests because of unfavourable weather during early growth. In most cases corrective processes were able to make good the alcohol deficiencies in European wines.

In France the 1972 harvest, at some 57 million hl., was about 7% down on that of the previous year. The volume and quality of red Bordeaux wines were as good as in 1971 but a slight decline was noted in the white wines. In Burgundy, which benefited from better weather, averages were surpassed everywhere. The volume of the Beaujolais wines was well above average and quality was fresh and fruity. In Champagne the preceding year's harvest was actually doubled, enabling stocks to be replenished.

The Italian harvest was badly hit by a cold, late spring, a bad summer, and an even worse, snowy fall and winter. Around 60 million hl. were produced, a decline of 4 million hl. on the 1971 figure and of 9 million hl. on the 1970 figure. In Sicily, however, the quality was excellent; the sweet moscato grapes were harvested earlier than the rest and survived reasonably well.

The Spanish harvest in 1972 regained its 1969 level at 27 million hl., but the quality was lower. Bad weather affected both the volume and quality of Portuguese wines. The volume of wine produced in West Germany was around 8 million hl., one of the best harvests on record. Quality, however, was inferior, especially in contrast to the previous year.

At an auction of some of the world's rarest vintages, conducted by telephone between London, Paris, and Los Angeles in November, a jeroboam of Chateau Mouton Rothschild 1870, Pauillac Second Grand Cru Classe, fetched a world record price of U.S. $10,953. Both wine and bottle were handmade. (RENÉ PROTIN)

Nature was also rough on U.S. vineyards in 1972. In California some counties along the coast and the upper reaches of the big San Joaquin Valley were hurt in spring by severe frost, in summer by some excessively hot days, and finally by heavy autumn rains. As a result California vineyards produced only 2.3 million tons of grapes in 1972, against 4 million tons in 1971. It was the smallest crop since 1942. In New York, the second most important wine state, a misplaced tropical storm dumped flooding amounts of rain on the vineyards and subsequently nature failed to provide the hot weather necessary to make up for the damage. Instead of matching the 200,000 tons of grapes harvested in 1971, New York vineyards yielded only 110,000 tons.

Possibly because of the comparative smallness of the crop, the grapes brought into California's wineries were widely rated as good and even excellent. Prices paid by California wineries for their grapes established new highs in 1972, averaging roughly one-third above those prevalent the previous year. Wine prices also moved up steadily during the year, affecting the entire range from "jug" wine to the top varietals. Shortages of certain wines developed as the volume of wine sales pushed ahead firmly.

During fiscal 1972 the U.S. wine industry sent 282 million gal. of wine to market, with California supplying 233 million gal. Dessert wine consumption totaled 71 million gal., table wine sales hit 132 million gal., flavoured wines topped 53 million gal., sparkling wines edged the 22 million-gal. mark, and vermouth sales totaled some 5 million gal.

(IRVING H. MARCUS)

Aluminum: *see* Mining

American Literature: *see* Literature

Algeria

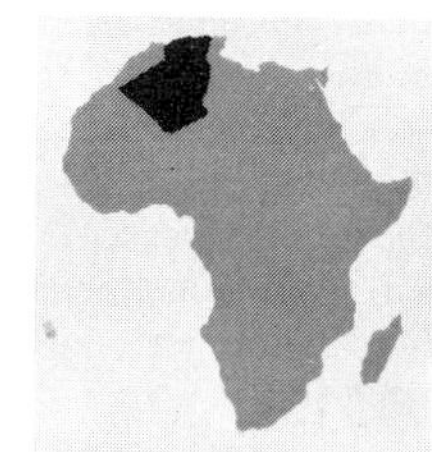

A republic on the north coast of Africa, Algeria is bounded by Morocco, Mauritania, Mali, Niger, Libya, and Tunisia. Area: 896,588 sq.mi. (2,322,164 sq.km.). Pop. (1971 est.): 14,643,700. Cap. and largest city: Algiers (pop., 1970 est., 1,839,000). Language: Arabic, Berber, French. Religion: Muslim. President in 1972, Col. Houari Boumédienne.

As Algeria celebrated in July 1972 the tenth anniversary of its independence, President Boumédienne said that by 1980 the country would have left the ranks of the third world and taken its place among the developed nations. Judging by the progress made in the first three years of the 1970–73 four-year development plan, this was no idle boast. The International Monetary Fund praised the austerity measures that had enabled plan targets to be met; the industrialized nations continued to provide loans and execute contracts for Algeria's industrialization program; and both the settlement of the oil dispute with France and the approval by the United States of imports of Algerian natural gas opened up prospects for greatly increased revenue from hydrocarbons in the rest of the 1970s. Already, in 1972, there was an assured surplus in the balance of trade.

The Saharan oil industry revived in 1972, after curtailment of production during the previous year. Sonatrach, the Algerian state oil corporation controlling 77% of total production, resumed exploration, and the government estimated its oil revenues for the year at not less than $1 billion. With the French taking approximately 12 million tons of crude oil, guaranteed under the 1971 settlement, Sonatrach found no difficulty in marketing the remaining 42 million tons. Heavy demand from Western Europe was supplemented by a new customer for Saharan crude: the U.S.; long-term supply arrangements were concluded with two U.S. companies.

Liquefied natural gas showed promise of being an even greater money-maker than crude oil, with Algeria's overseas sales estimated to reach 50,000,000,000 cu.m. a year by 1977. In addition to existing exports to Britain and contracts for supply to Spain, new delivery agreements were made with Belgium, France, and West Germany. It was, however, to the U.S. that Algeria looked for its major natural gas sales. After considerable debate the U.S. Federal Power Commission granted approval for U.S. firms to receive substantial supplies over a period ranging up to 25 years. To meet the demands for its natural gas, Algeria began work in March on a new pipeline from the gas fields to the existing terminal at Arzew, in western Algeria; in May the pipeline to a new Mediterranean terminal at Skikda, in eastern Algeria, was opened.

Skikda port, its reconstruction completed during the year, became the showplace of the industrialization program and an indication to Algerians that as much attention was being given to the eastern part of the country as was previously given to the Oran-Arzew area in the west. Also in the east, the El Hadjar steelworks, near Annaba, was opened in 1972, and the tractor plant at Constantine was brought into full operation.

Much of the rest of the country remained dependent on agriculture, and the government admitted that as many as half the potential work force of 4.5 million were unemployed or only partly employed. Although 150,000 jobs had been created under the four-year plan, many of these were in construction work and would thus prove temporary. As a palliative to the rural unemployed, the government tried hard to push ahead with the "agricultural revolution" inaugurated in November 1971, under which the larger private landholdings, particularly those belonging to absentee landlords, were to be nationalized and distributed to landless peasants organized into cooperatives. The first title deeds, of land taken over by the state in the Mitidja Plain in central Algeria, were handed over in June, and construction began on the first model village in August, but progress with the "revolution" was slow.

ALGERIA

Education. (1968–69) Primary, pupils 1,585,682, teachers (public only) 36,255; secondary, pupils 130,960, teachers (public only) 5,384; vocational, pupils 40,684, teachers (public only) 2,752; teacher training, students 5,738, teachers (public only) 380; higher (including 2 universities), students 10,681.

Finance. Monetary unit: dinar, with (Sept. 18, 1972) a free rate of 4.55 dinars to U.S. $1 (10.50 dinars = £1 sterling). Gold, SDRs, and foreign exchange, central bank: (June 1972) U.S. $407 million; (June 1971) U.S. $420 million. Budget (1971 est.): revenue 7.5 billion dinars; current expenditure 4.9 billion dinars (four-year development plan was established for 1970–73).

Foreign Trade. (1970) Imports 6,205,000,000 dinars; exports 4,980,000,000 dinars. Import sources: France 42%; West Germany 10%; U.S. 8%; Italy 7%. Export destinations: France 54%; West Germany 13%; U.S.S.R. 5%. Main exports: crude oil 66%; wine 14%.

Transport and Communications. Roads (1970) 75,953 km. Motor vehicles in use (1970): passenger 137,200; commercial (including buses) 106,000. Railways: (1970) 4,100 km.; traffic (1971) 1,097,000,000 passenger-km., freight 1,327,000,000 net ton-km. Air traffic (1970): 514,873,000 passenger-km.; freight 4,137,000 net ton-km. Shipping (1971): merchant vessels 100 gross tons and over 27; gross tonnage 94,838. Shipping traffic (1970): goods loaded 44,261,000 metric tons; unloaded *c.* 3,640,000 metric tons. Telephones (Dec. 1970) 184,000. Radio receivers (Dec. 1969) 700,000. Television receivers (Dec. 1969) *c.* 100,000.

Agriculture. Production (in 000; metric tons; 1970; 1969 in parentheses): wheat *c.* 1,500 (1,326); barley *c.* 500 (466); oats *c.* 45 (44); potatoes 262 (224); dates *c.* 100 (79); figs 66 (24); oranges 487 (470); tomatoes *c.* 85 (*c.* 85); onions *c.* 35 (*c.* 35); tobacco *c.* 5.3 (5); olive oil (1971) *c.* 28, (1970) *c.* 15; wine 869 (871). Livestock (in 000; Nov. 1970): sheep *c.* 8,400; goats *c.* 2,200; cattle *c.* 860; asses (1969) *c.* 310; horses (1969) *c.* 125; camels *c.* 170.

Industry. Production (in 000; metric tons; 1970): crude oil 47,281; natural gas (cu.m.) 2,838,000; electricity (excluding most industrial production; kw-hr.) 1,704,000; iron ore (metal content) 1,546; phosphate rock 492.

CH. SIMONPIETRI—GAMMA

Fidel Castro gets a hand from Pres. Houari Boumédienne as the Cuban leader, en route to the Hassi-Messaoud oil fields in May 1972, attempts to ride a camel.

The process of bringing new life to the sole political organization, the National Liberation Front (FLN), stumbled on amid general political apathy, and President Boumédienne appeared to be under no great pressure to honour his three-year-old promise to reestablish an elected National Assembly. Even the previously vociferous university students were quiet.

In Algeria's relations with its neighbours, all was peace in 1972. President Boumédienne visited Tunis, and Pres. Habib Bourguiba of Tunisia paid his first visit to Algiers. Of greater significance were Boumédienne's two visits to Morocco in June; the border dispute between the two countries was finally buried, and joint exploration of the Tindouf mineral deposits in the border area was agreed upon.

West Germany and Canada were two new partners of Algeria, both politically and economically. Diplomatic relations with West Germany had been restored in December 1971, and Canada appointed its first resident ambassador in Algiers. President Boumédienne was still hesitant to reestablish full diplomatic relations with the U.S., but there were signs of closer understanding in Algeria's willingness to hand back to U.S. airlines the "ransom" money taken to Algiers by hijackers in June and August. On both occasions the hijackers claimed Black Panther connections but, although that organization was still accorded some refuge in Algiers, the government clearly was disillusioned by the activities of the local Panther leaders, especially their attempt after the second hijacking to dictate to their hosts. (PETER KILNER)

Andorra

An independent principality of Europe, Andorra is in the Pyrenees Mountains between Spain and France. Area: 179 sq.mi. (464 sq.km.). Pop. (1972): 21,425. Cap.: Andorra la Vella (Catalan; Andorra la Vieja, Spanish; pop., 1972 parish, 8,534). Language: Catalan, French, Spanish. Religion: predominantly Roman

ANDORRA

Education. (1969–70) Primary, pupils 1,850, teachers 63; secondary, pupils 804, teachers 48.

Finance and Trade. Monetary units: French franc and Spanish peseta. No income tax, death duty, or customs; public treasury is funded by a 3% levy on gasoline and liquor. Exchange and deposit banking is important. Foreign trade (1971): imports from France Fr. 182,182,000 (U.S. $32.8 million), from Spain 1,158,941,000 pesetas (U.S. $16.6 million); exports to France Fr. 5,480,000, (U.S. $1 million), to Spain 44,532,000 pesetas (U.S. $600,000). Tourism (1971) *c.* 2 million visitors.

Communications. Radio receivers (Dec. 1969) 6,000. Television receivers (Dec. 1969) 1,700.

Agriculture. Production: cereals, potatoes, tobacco, wool. Livestock (in 000; 1970): sheep *c.* 25; cattle *c.* 3; horses *c.* 1.

Catholic. Co-princes: the president of the French Republic and the bishop of Urgel, Spain, represented by their *veguers* (provosts) and *batlles* (prosecutors). An elected Council General of 24 members elects the first syndic; in 1972, Francesc Escudé-Ferrero.

Parish elections held on Dec. 14, 1971, under a revised electoral law that extended the franchise to women, all citizens between the ages of 21 and 25, and second-generation Andorrans, resulted in a change in character of the parish councils, as new and younger faces assumed positions in the government. In December 1972, the first syndic and the second syndic completed their terms in office and were replaced by the Council General.

The population census of February 1972 revealed a 4.2% growth to 21,425 inhabitants. Native Andorrans (6,462) continued to constitute a minority while Spaniards, including 3,000 Catalans married and established in Andorra since 1939, numbered 13,035.

The public budget for 1972 was approximately $4 million; expenditure for public security and defense remained at $5. (ROBERT D. HODGSON)

Antarctica

The 12th plenary session of the Scientific Committee on Antarctic Research (SCAR) of the International Council of Scientific Unions (ICSU) was held in Canberra, Austr., Aug. 7–19, 1972. Of the 12 signatory nations to the Antarctic Treaty, 11 were represented along with 6 delegates from affiliated international scientific unions. A highlight of the session was the development of plans, responsibilities, and schedules for the following three emerging interdisciplinary research efforts: International Antarctic Glaciological Project (IAGP), Ross Ice Shelf Project (RISP), and Dry Valley Drilling Project (DVDP).

From October 30 to November 10 the seventh Consultative Meeting of Antarctic Treaty nations took place in Wellington, N.Z. Several nations expressed their concern about emerging interest in exploiting mineral, petroleum, and marine life resources in the Antarctic, and the corresponding lack of provisions for such economic exploitations in the Antarctic Treaty. Similar concern was expressed about inadequate treaty controls over pollution, conservation, tourism, and the preservation of historical monuments.

Four major international research programs were conducted in 1972. Three countries, Japan, New Zealand, and the U.S., joined together in the DVDP, to study the physical, chemical, and biological characteristics of the unique dry valleys, lying 60 mi. W of McMurdo Sound. Preliminary geophysical surveys of the valleys were made in preparation for the drilling, which was to begin in 1973. The IAGP, undertaken jointly by Australia, France, the U.S.S.R., and the U.S., was a continuing ten-year glaciological research program on the vast east Antarctic ice sheet. Its main objective was to determine the ice sheet's history and dimensions, as well as to reconstruct various stages in its evolution and relate these stages to past global climatic variations. The Antarctic ice sheet was estimated to contain 7 million cu.mi. of ice, holding 80% of the world's freshwater supply. Six nations continued to develop plans for the RISP, which included drilling holes through the 1,500-ft.-thick floating shelf in order to study the ice, the underlying waters, and the ocean floor. Argentina, Chile, the U.K., the U.S.S.R., and the U.S. combined scientific and logistic resources in assessing results of the three violent volcanic eruptions that had rocked and reshaped Deception Island since 1967. British and Chilean bases on the island were completely demolished by the eruptions; the surviving Argentine station served as the main logistic base for the international expedition.

The Convention for the Conservation of Antarctic Seals, held in London, February 3–11, bound the treaty nations to curtail and control the harvesting of seals in Antarctic waters, and called on SCAR to evaluate data and provide continuing scientific advice to the treaty powers.

Scientific Programs. Ten of the 12 Antarctic Treaty nations maintained more than 40 stations in Antarctica and nearby islands; Norway and Belgium temporarily closed their stations and operated through the expeditions of other nations. Amundsen-Scott South Pole (U.S.) and Vostok (U.S.S.R.) stations were the only inland bases operating throughout the year. The U.S.S.R. conducted a reconnaissance of the Hobbs Coast and announced its intention of establishing its sixth coastal station on the continent; to be located at Cape Burks, the station was to be named Russkaya. Some of the worst Antarctic winter weather in years was experienced; storms and winds damaged power distribution and utility systems as well as pier facilities at a number of stations.

Argentina. The Argentine Antarctic Institute carried on a broad research program at its seven bases on the Antarctic Peninsula and at one other base on the main continent. Marine mammals, birds, fishes, lichens, and mosses were studied; investigations were also carried out in glaciology, geology, and oceanography. The U.S. icebreaker "Staten Island" cached supplies and equipment on Deception Island for use later by an Argentine glaciological party led by N. H. Fourcade.

Australia. The Australian National Antarctic Research Expedition (ANARE) of more than 100 men enjoyed one of its most productive years in Antarctic research due largely to good flying weather, favourable sea ice conditions, and excellent support from three helicopters and one light aircraft. Activities centred in and near Mawson, Davis, and Casey stations, with resupply again provided by the two ice-strengthened motor vessels "Nella Dan" and "Thala Dan."

Belgium. Though not maintaining bases of its own in Antarctica, Belgium participated with the British and U.S. in the airborne radio-echo sounding of the east Antarctic ice sheet, an effort of the IAGP.

Chile. Studies on marine and terrestrial ecosystems, volcanology, geology, glaciology, meteorology, and oceanography were carried out at several stations along the Antarctic Peninsula, nearby islands, and sur-

Anglican Communion: *see* Religion

Angola: *see* Dependent States

rounding seas. Four Chilean scientists participated with those of three other nations in studying biological and physical changes brought about by the recent volcanic eruptions at Deception Island. I. Vergara and L. Arnaboli proposed a scheme for towing large icebergs from Antarctica to Chile to serve as water sources for irrigating arid lands.

France. The 22nd French Antarctic Expedition was launched to the main base of Dumont d'Urville on the Adélie Coast. The ship "Thala Dan" transported 770 tons of material and 46 members of the expedition; it returned the 13 men who had spent the winter at the station. Heavy sea ice and several blizzards of long duration hampered movement and ship-to-shore operations. The main thrust of research was in the IAGP in joint participation with the U.S. and the U.S.S.R. In preparation for an oversnow tractor-train traverse from Dumont d'Urville to Vostok station, a distance of 1,200 mi., the advance camp, Carrefour, was established 25 mi. inland at an elevation of 2,800 ft. The tractor-train was able to advance approximately 500 mi. before work was halted for the summer.

Japan. For the third consecutive year the icebreaker "Fuji" was trapped in sea ice while trying to resupply Syowa Station, the main Antarctic base for the Japanese Antarctic Research Expedition (JARE). Members of the 13th JARE, along with some light supplies, were airlifted to Syowa Station by helicopters from a point 55 mi. away, where the "Fuji" was beset in ice 6½ ft. thick. After three weeks the "Fuji" freed itself and returned to Tokyo. Thirty members of the winter party returned aboard the "Fuji" along with heavy equipment, construction materials, and fuel originally destined for Syowa. Seven upper atmosphere sounding rockets were launched from Syowa Station to altitudes of 80 mi. to study the aurora, and glaciological studies were undertaken at a remote station 185 mi. SE.

New Zealand. Unusually good weather led to a high level of summer activity at Scott Base and nearby temporary stations. In collaboration with Japanese and U.S. scientists, a geophysical survey of the dry valleys was undertaken in preparation for future deep-drilling operations. A highlight of 1972 was the discovery, for the first time, of marine fossils 200 million years old in north Victoria Land. A wide variety of fossil plants and a thick coal seam were discovered in the southern Transantarctic Mountains.

Norway. Norway had closed its base in Antarctica, but its scientists continued to participate in research programs of other countries. A six-man glaciological party was airlifted by the U.S. to Queen Maud Land, where velocity and gravity measurements were made of the broad Jutulstraumen Glacier.

South Africa. The 13th South African National Antarctic Expedition (SANAE) was the largest ever sent to Antarctica. It consisted of 31 members, 11 of whom participated in the research program in and around the main Sanae Station, situated on western Queen Maud Land. The research ship "RSA" provided ocean transport, which included 25 tons of whale meat and dog food for the 25 Labrador huskies that remained permanently at Sanae.

United Kingdom. The British Antarctic Survey (BAS) conducted a broad range of physical and biological research programs at seven permanent stations on the Antarctic Peninsula and sub-Antarctic islands, as well as at Halley Bay Station, its only base on the continent. Altogether, more than 100 men participated in the BAS program, supported by four ships, two light aircraft, and helicopters. In early February, the "Endurance" ran aground in Marguerite Bay and was laid up for repairs. Heavy snowfall, strong winds, and poor visibility restricted land operations, while unusually light sea ice encouraged oceangoing activities. At Halley Bay Station, glaciological studies were made of the interface between the ice sheet and shelf ice.

U.S.S.R. The 17th Soviet Antarctic Expedition (SAE) comprised more than 100 scientists and technicians working at six permanent stations and several remote sites. A highlight of the expedition was the establishment of an Institute of Polar Medicine at Molodezhnaya Station, the main Soviet research centre in Antarctica. Studies undertaken in the institute were to include microbiology and the physiological and psychological effects on human beings of cold, enforced immobility, living in close proximity to others, and the long polar nights and days. The overall research program continued to emphasize upper atmosphere physics, meteorology, and oceanography. At Bellingshausen Station in the South Shetlands, two species of cereal grains, one previously unknown, were discovered. This marked a new southern limit for flowering plants. Using helicopters and light aircraft, geologists, biologists, and surveyors conducted a two-month exploration of little-known Mac. Robertson Land, an area of about 100,000 sq.mi. They discovered some of the oldest rocks yet uncovered in Antarctica, along with a number of mineral deposits, fossil trees, and imprints of leaves.

United States. The U.S. Antarctic Research Program (USARP) included 200 scientists and technicians from more than 40 universities, government agencies, and industry, supported by more than 1,600 others. Research programs on terrestrial and marine biology, earth sciences, atmospheric sciences, and oceanography were carried out at seven permanent stations, several temporary field sites, and aboard research vessels and icebreakers. The largest single effort, involving 13 participants from Japan, New Zealand, and the U.S., was in a preliminary site survey for the three-year DVDP. Seismicity and resistivity measurements were taken at 28 locations; lake water was analyzed for heavy metal concentration; and soils collected for geophysical, geochemical, and biological properties. A continuing U.K.-U.S. program for measuring the thickness of the Antarctic ice sheet by airborne radio-echo sounding revealed significant under-ice features in east Antarctica. A chain of mountains with peaks up to 9,500 ft. above sea level was discovered in a region of gently undulating lowlands below sea level. The soundings also revealed a new maximum ice sheet thickness of 14,900 ft. in an area 155 mi. NE of Vostok Station.

After 15 years of operation, Byrd Station was closed as a year-round base. Approximately 85% of the new Amundsen-Scott South Pole Station was completed, including the geodesic dome, which covered the station like a giant bubble.

Other Activities. The First Annual Ross Island Games were held at McMurdo Station on June 23–25, 1972, with New Zealand, the U.K., the U.S.S.R., and the U.S. competing in soccer, track, sled races, basketball, volleyball, badminton, bowling, pool, and dart throwing. With the closing of Byrd Station, the traditional New Year's Day football game between scientists and Navy men, which has been played for 11 years, was suspended. In 1972, the scientists won by a score of 13–6; the contest stood at 5 wins for scientists, 4 wins for the Navy, and 3 tie games.

The Antarctic tourist ship "Lindblad Explorer" ran

into uncharted rocks on King George Island during a blizzard on February 11, and was finally freed two weeks later by the West German tug "Arctic." The Chilean Navy transport "Piloto Pardo" provided vital support during the crisis; tourists aboard the ship endured some anxious moments and privations but no injuries. (LAURENCE M. GOULD)

See also Oceanography.

Anthropology

During 1972 anthropology was again characterized by concern with ethical self-evaluation and by new directions in research. The two-year-old controversy over the alleged political involvement of a group of anthropologists in Thailand continued. Anthropological opinion was still divided concerning this particular case and others that presented a similar ethical dilemma. The issues involved, among others, the right of anthropologists to impose restrictions (by moral suasion, censure, licensing, etc.) upon one another, the immorality of secret or war-related research, and the responsibility of anthropologists to protect the people they study from any harmful consequences that might follow the publication of research findings.

Prominent attention was also given to discrimination against women and ethnic minorities, especially in the U.S., and to the past and present relationship between anthropology and colonialism. Accusations that the research of certain anthropologists (particularly those who worked in former British colonies) contributed to the maintenance of colonial rule led to vigorous, if inconclusive, debate. Nevertheless, the possible but inadvertent role of anthropological research in maintaining colonial institutions, and the manner in which such research may have distorted knowledge of small societies under colonial governments, became an issue that would undoubtedly receive continuing attention.

Another focus of debate was the obligation of anthropologists not only to avoid harming the people they study but, where appropriate, to become positive advocates for them. There was growing agreement among anthropologists that they should indeed become advocates, especially when the people they study are relatively powerless against local, national, or international economic or political forces. An example of this concern was provided by the response of Filipino anthropologists to possible commercial exploitation of the Tasaday, a tiny Stone Age tribe discovered in the forests of Mindanao in 1971. Working through PANAMIN (Private Association for National Minorities, Inc.), anthropologists found the Philippine government to be sympathetic to the plight of the Tasaday, who were defenseless against encroaching commercial logging. As a result, Philippine Pres. Ferdinand Marcos set aside the Tasaday homeland as a 46,299-ac. reserve free of outside interference.

Similar humanitarian concerns were reflected in the directions taken by anthropological research. Although anthropologists continued their interest in small, isolated, non-Western societies, a strong emphasis on Western and urban populations was developing. This emphasis—sometimes known as urban anthropology, but actually far broader than that term suggests—focused research on a variety of populations including the urban and rural, migrant labourers, women, the young and the elderly, the ill and the handicapped, as well as all ethnic and racial minorities. Unlike many anthropological studies of the past, this research had a direct problem focus, with social amelioration as a principal goal. It dealt with such problems as the reduction of conflict, the roots of poverty, improvement of medical services, the functions of drugs and sexuality in the youth culture, and the bases of racism.

These changing emphases were exemplified in the controversy over the views put forward by Arthur R. Jensen, Hans Eysenck, William Shockley, and others to the effect that the IQ test scores of U.S. blacks, which average lower than those of white Americans, are the result of inherited intellectual inferiority. (*See* PSYCHOLOGY.) Although somewhat late in their response, perhaps because of their general belief that these issues had been resolved years before, anthropologists entered the arena in 1972 with a collection of papers published by the American Anthropological Association. The papers centred on such matters as the role of culture in producing differences in cognition and competence, conceptual difficulties in the idea of intelligence, the cultural bias inherent in tests of IQ, the inequality of education for even "middle-class" black children, the possible effects of malnutrition, and the pervasive effects of racism on black children's school and test performance.

In a parallel development, linguistics turned increasingly to the study of language in its social context. Much of this research focused on dialectical differences between the English spoken by middle-class white children and the English of poor urban whites and blacks, and the possible relationship of such differences to performance on tests and in academic settings. For example, several studies suggested that black ghetto children utilize, among themselves, a language with a far more complex grammar and vocabulary than the language they use in formal educational testing situations, even when those tests or situations are presented by other blacks. Thus the linguistic deficit shown in school by some black children may arise from the situation and not from any basic linguistic or cognitive deficiency. Linguistic research also reflected a growing interest in universals in language, especially as these universals may illuminate its evolutionary origins. David Premack and Allen and Beatrice Gardner continued their work on the language abilities of chimpanzees, and other research was under way on the possible evolutionary significance of differences in vocal anatomy, development of lateral dominance, and neurophysiological specialization for language.

A largely unrelated research emphasis involved studies of religion, myth, symbolism, and ritual. Research on such matters was reported by anthropologists from many countries, indicating the influence of the French anthropologist Claude Lévi-Strauss. The international impact of his work was illustrated by a volume contributed in his honour which was probably the largest of its kind ever published in anthropology.

An important *Homo erectus* find was reported from the French Pyrenees by Henry and Marie-Antoinette de Lumley. This fossil, with a facial structure similar to that of the well-known skull found at Steinheim, Ger., in 1933, appears to be a precursor to the Neanderthaloids dating from the Mindel-Riss interglacials (some 200,000 years ago) or earlier. This find may join with the Steinheim and Swanscombe, Eng., skulls in clarifying human evolution in Europe prior to the emergence of the classic Neanderthals. Controversy continued over Richard Leakey's discoveries of early man east of Lake Rudolf, Kenya. In

November it was announced that a skull, pieced together from fragments found in volcanic ash some 2.6 million years old, appeared to be much closer to modern man than either the contemporary *Australopithecus* or the later *Homo erectus*.

Debate continued over the relative importance of non-Darwinian evolution, with critical opinion generally running against the importance of random—*i.e.,* nonselective pressure—factors in evolution. At the same time, interest in molecular biology grew, as exemplified by an important controversy concerning the rate and constancy of protein evolution among primates. One theory, based on the assumption of constancy in protein evolution, led to the conclusion that man and the gorilla diverged more than 500 million years ago, an opinion that conflicts with accepted views. This theory had not found general acceptance, even though interest in molecular phylogeny and the so-called evolutionary clock had increased among physical anthropologists. (ROBERT B. EDGERTON)

See also Archaeology.

ENCYCLOPÆDIA BRITANNICA FILMS. *The Egyptologists* (1967).

Archaeology

Eastern Hemisphere. With the lessening of political tensions between the two giant Communist countries and the West, a relatively generous supply of archaeological news was available in 1972 from China and the U.S.S.R. The most spectacular reports concerned the clearance of a Scythian royal tomb in the Ukraine and the remarkable yield from a pair of princely Han dynasty tombs near Chang-sha in central China. In the West a great find of an earlier era was recalled in the British Museum's 50th anniversary exhibition of many of the finest pieces recovered from the tomb of the pharaoh Tutankhamen. The Egyptian government and its Antiquities Service agreed to lend this magnificent collection to the British, perhaps another sign of easing tensions.

The strong stand taken by professional archaeologists against the illicit international trade in antiquities gained more support. Harvard University, the University Museum of Philadelphia, and Chicago's Oriental Institute agreed not to buy, acquire, or accept as gifts any antiquities that lacked a full pedigree and proper export papers issued by the country of origin. At the same time, new and subtle means of laboratory examination revealed that an increasing number of "antiquities" were actually forgeries. Of 66 pieces of pottery vessels and figurines allegedly from Hacilar, Turk., that had found their way into museum or private collections, 48 were proved to be fakes. It was also reported that several U.S. museums had recently paid approximately $25,000 each for forged "Etruscan tomb paintings." Such reports brought wry pleasure to professional archaeologists who knew only too well the destruction caused by illicit diggers supplying the illegal market.

New breakthroughs in methods of laboratory analysis were reported. A study of the carbon-13 and oxygen-18 variations in Greek marbles made possible identification of the quarry sources. A method of assaying age by study of the molecular structure of amino acids in ancient bones reportedly would span the time gap between about 40,000 and 250,000 years ago, for which neither the carbon-14 nor the potassium-argon method yielded accurate results.

Pleistocene Prehistory. At least one "incredibly well-made stone tool" was reported from excavations on the eastern shore of Lake Rudolf, Kenya, in a context dated to 2.6 million years ago. The archaeological context of the pre-Neanderthal skull, found in southern France near Tautavel in the Pyrenees in 1971 and dated at about 200,000 years ago, was reported to be the stone tool industry known as the Tayacian. A new and fully Paleolithic exposure was reported from Christiansfeld in Denmark. Dated to about 75,000 years ago, it was thus far earlier than any other Scandinavian archaeological material yet known. At the large Obirakhmat cave, near Tashkent in Soviet Uzbekistan, deposits were excavated ranging from Mousterian into the Upper Paleolithic.

The Near East. Archaeological work in Egypt was still restricted to urban areas. The Oriental Institute studied recarvings of the reliefs of the temple of Khonsu at Luxor. In Israel an interesting sequence of so-called Middle and Upper Neolithic materials was recovered at Hazorea in the Plain of Esdraelon, and significant exposures were made in 2nd-millennium B.C. and in Philistine levels at Gezer. Yohanan Aharoni of Tel-Aviv University cleared portions of the town plan of ancient Beersheba. In Jerusalem itself, an area adjacent to the Armenian convent was excavated, exposing aristocratic and priestly houses of the early Christian era. According to one tradition, the house of the high priest Caiaphas was in this neighbourhood.

The Jordanian government was said to be encouraging new archaeological activity by qualified foreign teams, but little news of work there was available. News from Lebanon, Syria, and Iraq was also scarce. An early Christian church plan with inscribed mosaic floors was cleared near Apamea, Syria, by a Belgian expedition. In Iraq D. Kirkbride-Helbaek exposed a new and important early village site, Um ed-Dabagh, near Hatra, with reportedly pre-Hassunan (*c.* 6000 B.C.) materials. Along the Saudi Arabian coast Abdullah H. Masri, of the University of Chicago but working for the Saudi government, made significant tests in a number of sites yielding Jemdat Nasr and Ubaid pottery as well as earlier materials.

Jean Perrot's French team contributed to the basic reassessment of earlier French excavations at Susa and Tepe Djaffarabad in Iran. The Royal Ontario Museum clearances on Godin proceeded, but a new site nearby, Seh Gabri, was opened and yielded near-surface levels of the 4th millennium B.C. Similar levels at Godin were covered with a great depth of later materials. Ezat O. Negahban of the University of Teheran opened an important new site with early village materials near Kazvin. Uncovering of a well-preserved Bronze Age centre at Sharh-Sokhta was announced by an Italian-Iranian team. In Soviet Armenia a 14th-century B.C. fortress and cemetery were recovered as the waters of Lake Sevan receded. There were war chariot burials in which the skeletons of all but one individual (the dead chief?) showed broken neck vertebrae. Another important clearance in Armenia was that of a long-occupied (*c.* 2000–750 B.C.) settlement of metalworkers at Metsamor.

Notable progress was made by both Turkish and foreign rescue teams in the Keban Dam salvage area in Turkey. Higher on the Anatolian plateau, where the long-range programs of the University of Ankara at Kanesh-Kultepe and Acemhuyuk continued, Kanesh and its lower town continued to yield cuneiform tablets, architecture, and artifacts of the early 2nd

WIDE WORLD

The 2,000-year-old remains of this Chinese noblewoman, preserved to an extraordinary degree, were found in a charcoal-sealed tomb at Chang-sha. Dating from the Han dynasty, the tomb also contained exquisite textiles, a food-laden banquet table, and 120 clothed wooden figurines.

Antimony:
see Mining

Arab Emirates:
see United Arab Emirates

Arabia:
see Bahrain; Kuwait; Middle East; Oman; Qatar; Saudi Arabia; United Arab Emirates; Yemen, People's Democratic Republic of; Yemen Arab Republic

Arab League:
see Middle East

IRIS C. LOVE

Heads of terra-cotta statuettes unearthed at Cnidus, Turk., by an expedition led by Iris C. Love of Long Island University in New York are evidence that Greek settlements in southwestern Turkey date back to at least 1000 B.C., rather than 340–330 as had been previously supposed.

millennium B.C. Acemhuyuk, dating several centuries later, yielded evidence of the level of culture and of international contacts in early Hittite times.

The Greco-Roman Regions. New light on Aegean prehistory resulted from the work of Jean Deshayes of the University of Paris at Dikili Tash, near Philippi in northern Greece. Below a superficial level with Byzantine and Hellenistic materials, there was a succession of 26 levels with materials referred to as of Early Bronze and Neolithic times. The two were separated by a thick burned horizon. In the former, there was evidence of important linkages with Troy and Anatolia. Another important prehistoric program was resumed at the Franchthi cave in extreme southern Greece by Thomas Jacobsen of Indiana University. Franchthi covers a span from Late Upper Paleolithic times into the range of effective agriculture. For later prehistoric times, the University of Minnesota's Messenia expedition encountered architectural remains from *c.* 1700 B.C. onward and an important record of Mycenaean stratigraphy. Greek archaeologists clearing the volcanic fallout on the island of Thera exposed several groups of well-preserved frescoes of *c.* 1500 B.C.

Two life-size painted marble funerary statues of a young man and woman were found south of Athens. Subsequently, it became clear that the base of the girl's figure fitted an inscribed base, signed by Aristion, already in the Epigraphic Museum of the National Archaeological Museum in Athens. At Halieis, a port midway between Sparta and Athens, Michael Jameson recorded traces of a stadium and a sanctuary dedicated to Apollo, both now awash in the Aegean Sea. The royal Scythian burial of a prince, princess, and infant, found in the Ukraine, included much remarkably fine gold ornament, reputedly the work of Greek craftsmen.

Late Prehistoric and Historic Europe. Two important excavations in Yugoslavia were being carried on with the aid of so-called blocked funds (money owed the U.S. but, by treaty agreement to be used only within the debtor country). The village site of Anza in eastern Macedonia was being worked jointly by Marija Gimbutas of California and Milutin Garasanin of Yugoslavia, while the village site of Divostin, some 50 mi. S of Belgrade, was under excavation by Alan McPherron of Pittsburgh, Pa., and Dragoslav Srejovic of Belgrade. The yields from both sites richly illustrated V. Gordon Childe's observation that the early farmers of Europe "were not slavish imitators" of the peoples of the Near East.

A variety of sites of Saxon and "Dark Ages" times were reported from Britain. Traces of a large hall were exposed at Chalton, Hampshire, and the foundations of a Saxon watermill were cleared at Tamworth, Staffordshire. In Finland underwater efforts yielded much information on an 18th-century Russian warship sunk in a naval battle with Sweden in the harbour of Kotka.

Asia and Africa. What appeared to be a Chinese equivalent of the Tutankhamen find was described in brief reports from Peking. Two tombs, built into a cliff in the Lingshan Mountains south of Peking, contained the bodies of Liu Sheng, Prince Ching of Chung-shan, and his consort. This Han dynasty prince died in 113 B.C.; his body and that of his queen were shrouded in gold-wired jade-plaque suits. There was also a rich supply of mortuary furniture, including items in metal, glass, lacquer, and silk. The Chinese also reported on new work at the Shang dynasty (16th–17th century B.C.) site of Anyang, where a number of inscribed "oracle bones" recorded imperial Shang ceremonies. Wall paintings said to be of exceptionally fine quality were found in a tomb south of Nara in Japan.

From South Africa came claims of very early mining for ocher, from which the appearance of a very early anatomically modern man was inferred. It was still too early to assess the quality of the evidence, however. In his report (*Science*, April 28, 1972) of a survey and test soundings in the Turkana District, Kenya, Lawrence Robbins of Michigan State University described a sequence of Late Stone Age to early modern materials. (ROBERT J. BRAIDWOOD)

Western Hemisphere. Explanation of intracultural variability, the analysis of settlement systems with respect to technological and environmental factors, sampling procedures, and the experimental study of chipped stone technologies constituted major topics of New World archaeological investigation during 1972. Western Hemisphere archaeologists joined their colleagues in expressing concern over the destruction of archaeological sites and monuments, especially as a result of the increasingly commercialized activities of looters. Of particular note was the continuing large-scale theft of monumental sculptures from the Mayan region. Since these sculptures were too large for easy transport, many of them had been illicitly cut into smaller pieces with power tools, often resulting in their complete or near-complete destruction.

Four research laboratories at the University of Utah and a commercial off-campus facility joined to form the Archaeometric Research Group, planned to provide training, research, and contract services involving dating and other types of analysis relevant to archaeology. A wide range of archaeological problems can be investigated through the available techniques, including the study of sedimentary ecology, ceramic analysis, identification of stone remains, and reconstruction of desiccated organic remains. In Florida the Bureau of Historic Sites and Properties began implementing a computerized program for storage and retrieval of archaeological data designed to be compatible with other such systems in the U.S. The potential of such systems was foreshadowed by a technique used by Sylvia Gains of Arizona State University. Excavations under her direction at Hunters Point, Ariz., were directly connected to computer facilities by telephone, permitting immediate verification or modification of aspects of the research design.

Shortages of funds continued to plague archaeological efforts, and increasing use was being made of volunteers working under the direction of trained archaeologists. A widely publicized example was the Koster excavation in southern Illinois, sponsored by Northwestern University, Evanston, which it was hoped would eventually throw light on the development of agriculture in pre-Columbian North America. Threatened several times with closure because of lack of money, the work had been continued in large measure through the enthusiastic volunteer efforts of students, who came to the site from throughout the U.S.

Cultural Ecology. Since basic chronological sequences have been established for most areas in North America, archaeological investigations increasingly focused on relationships between cultural behaviour, as shown in prehistoric remains, and environmental variables. W. James Judge, University of New Mexico, and Jerry Dawson, Southern Methodist University, Dallas, Tex., carried out an analysis based on a reconnaissance of Paleo-Indian settlements in the central Rio Grande Valley, an area encompassing 3,000 sq.mi. Aerial photography combined with field exploration revealed a total of 59 Paleo-Indian settlements, which were identified as components of the Clovis, Folsom, Belen, and Cody cultures. Analysis of environmental variables revealed that a water source appropriate to the needs of large herbivores was a crucial factor in site location, as were drainage for the site itself and proximity to a suitable hunting area. Variations in the relationships between these factors were attributed to the gradually increasing dryness that characterized the postglacial period.

In northwestern Alaska, Douglas D. Anderson, Brown University, Providence, R.I., reported on the results of four years of archaeological survey in the Noatak drainage. A considerable number of unstratified sites were found that provided panoramic views of known caribou migration routes and were believed to represent hunting stations. Such sites were dated to the end of the Paleo-Arctic period (about 6000 B.C.), the Northern Archaic period (3700–3600 B.C.), the Denbigh Flint complex (1500–1200 B.C.), and the recent Eskimo period (A.D. 1500 to the present). It was hypothesized that the gaps in the temporal record reflected fluctuations in caribou population density.

Dean R. Snow of the State University of New York at Albany, reporting on a study of prehistoric adaptation along the Maine coast, refuted the traditional view that the shift from a hunting and fishing subsistence pattern to shellfish collecting, which took place about A.D. 1, was the result of population replacement. Rather, it could be explained by the interplay between cultural, climatologic, and geologic factors associated with the postglacial rise in sea level. A major underwater investigation was conducted by Florida's Bureau of Historic Sites and Properties at the Little Salt Springs site in southern Sarasota County. Human bone, dated by the carbon-14 method at 3270 B.C., was recovered, along with cultural material that had been deposited when the water in the sink was at least 35 ft. below its modern level. Work in progress involved testing the hypothesis that the sink constituted a water source for prehistoric peoples at a time when the climate was significantly drier and the sea level considerably lower than at present.

Mesoamerica. Environmental, technological, and social variables were employed by Richard E. Blanton, Rice University, Houston, Tex., to account for a sequence of settlement systems and demographic patterns revealed by intensive archaeological reconnaissance of the Ixtapalapa Peninsula in the Valley of Mexico. The transition between the Middle and Late Formative periods, dated about 600 B.C., was marked by rapid population growth. The piedmont zone was occupied for the first time, while the lakeshore plain continued to be utilized. Large-scale public architecture began, and communities of markedly different status appeared. Similar changes had been noted in other portions of the Valley of Mexico, and were believed to be related to the introduction of hardier and more productive varieties of maize from the central highlands.

The development of Teotihuacán as an urban centre, beginning in the Terminal Formative period about A.D. 100, was marked by an overall decline in population. Blanton hypothesized that enhanced status differentiation and the concentration of population in a single urban centre tended to exclude rural groups. During the Late Postclassic period, dated A.D. 1200 until the arrival of the Spanish, the number of urban centres increased and the rural population rose once again.

Betty Bell, Southern Illinois University, conducting excavations in a previously unknown region in northeastern Jalisco, uncovered an assemblage related to the shaft-tomb complex characteristic of Nyarit and west-central Jalisco. Horned human figurines, previously known only through the illicit art market, were discovered in an archaeological context for the first time. In another study of a previously little known region, Román Piña Chán, Instituto Nacional de Antropología e Historia, excavated a pyramid and plaza and other remains at Tenango, west of Toluca in the state of Mexico. The materials suggested occupation during the entire Postclassic period, beginning about A.D. 700.

South America. The discovery in the Mucuchíes locality of Mérida, Venezuela, of a cemetery and workshop containing "batwing"-style serpentine artifacts was reported by Erika Wagner and Carlos Schubert, Instituto Venezolano de Investigaciones Científicas, Caracas. Serpentine is not native to the Venezuelan Andes, but it does occur naturally in several Caribbean regions. Thus the finds indicated the importation of raw materials from the Caribbean. Radiocarbon dating and stylistic comparisons placed the find between A.D. 1000 and 1500.

In the adjoining highlands of Colombia, a survey completed by Karen Olsen Bruhns, California State University, San Francisco, provided evidence for a heavy population in the region beginning about A.D. 1000 but gave little indication of earlier occupation. Wesley Hurt, Indiana University Museum, in collaboration with Gonzalo Correal, Instituto Colombiano de Antropología, investigated open terrace sites in the middle Magdalena River valley of Colombia. The terraces yielded chipped stone artifacts, resembling the series from the El Abra rock shelters at Sabana de Bogotá, which had been dated to 10,500 B.C.

Ecological studies continued to be emphasized, with prehistoric methods of cultivation receiving considerable attention. In the lower Cauca-San Jorge region of Colombia, James Parsons, University of California at Berkeley, investigated the relationships between seasonal flooding and the ridged-field agricultural system. In the lowland Venezuelan state of Barinas, Alberta Zucchi, Instituto Venezolano de Investigaciones Científicas, and William M. Denevan, University of Wisconsin, investigated prehispanic ridged fields and their related settlements. Both aerial photographs and field research were employed by Jeffrey Parson, University of Michigan, and colleagues to identify and investigate sunken-field cultivation systems in ten coastal valleys in Peru. This method of cultivation, which represented an enormous expenditure of labour, appeared to have been most significant during the Late Intermediate and Late Horizon periods.

The spread of industrialization was threatening archaeological sites throughout South America, and many emergency salvage programs were under way. In Brazil, Silvia Maranca, Universidade de São Paulo, recorded eight sites in a locality that was being flooded in connection with a hydroelectric power plant at Ilha Solteria. Also in Brazil, Ondemar Ferreira Dias, Instituto de Anqueologia Brasiliera, coordinated a continuing nonemergency investigation of the 1,800-mi.-long São Francisco River valley, designed to connect the archaeologically known areas of Bahia and southern Minas Gerais. Evidence of human utilization was discovered in 17 limestone caves scattered along the entire course of the valley.

(DAVID A. FREDRICKSON)

See also Anthropology.

ENCYCLOPÆDIA BRITANNICA FILMS. *The Egyptologists* (1967).

Architecture

Office buildings and commercial developments in progress or just completed dominated architectural activity in 1972. New sociological and functional ideas were becoming more evident. The trend of company headquarters buildings going up outside city centres continued but at the same time some successful redevelopment projects were completed in downtown areas.

Office Buildings. The Standard Oil Co. of Indiana building, designed by Edward Durell Stone & Associates and Perkins & Will, was topped out at 1,136 ft. in October to become, temporarily, the world's third tallest building. As with the other new skyscrapers, the Chicago building utilized tubular design, a new basic architectural concept. In tubular design the perimeter columns of a building resist the lateral force of wind pressure, thereby permitting more economical construction by eliminating the need for expensive internal bracing.

The twin-towered World Trade Center in New York was, at 1,350 ft., the world's tallest building at the end of 1972, but the Sears Tower in Chicago was scheduled to surpass it during 1973 to reach 1,450 ft. Meanwhile, the owners of the longtime record holder, the 1,250-ft. Empire State Building in New York, announced in October that they were considering an addition to the structure that would make it once again the world's tallest.

The new Toronto-Dominion Centre was completed on a 5½-ac. site south of the new City Hall plaza. The complex was designed by Ludwig Mies van der Rohe (d. 1969), who acted as consultant to two Canadian firms, John B. Parkin Associates and Bregman & Hamann. Mies's hand was certainly apparent in the elegant glass and steel structure, and the centre seemed to represent the final culmination of his search for formal perfection in the glass skyscraper. The Toronto-Dominion Centre comprised two towers, one of 56 and the other of 46 stories, the latter containing the vast single open space pavilion of the Toronto-Dominion banking hall. The windows were of bronze-gray heat-absorbing glass, and the buildings were grouped around an attractive plaza.

Pepsico, Inc., was one of the many large companies to move its headquarters out of expensive, crowded New York City. The new location was a 112-ac. site at Harrison, N.Y., about 30 mi. N of the city. Only 10 ac. of the site were occupied by buildings, the rest being left as a wooded area screening ample parking facilities. The buildings, designed by Edward Durell Stone & Associates, consisted of a series of seven three-story blocks arranged formally around an entrance court. The exterior walls were decorated with patterned precast concrete panels, and the small courts were laid out as sculpture gardens in which works by sculptors such as Henry Moore, Jacques Lipchitz, and Alberto Giacometti were imaginatively set out. In addition, a large stabile by Alexander Calder stood in an open field. The new headquarters enabled the company to house all its divisions in one location.

The new headquarters of Burlington Industries, Inc., a huge textile manufacturing firm, at Greensboro, N.C., occupied the 34-ac. site of a former estate within the bounds of the city. The architects, Odell Associates, designed two separate structures joined by bridges. The six-story tower, which housed executive offices, was constructed with an exposed steel frame and giant X-shaped trusses. Reflected and multiplied by the huge reflective glass walls, the trusses produced a dramatic visual effect. The smaller two-story building contained meeting rooms, offices, and a cafeteria.

The home office of the California Casualty Insurance Group was relocated in San Mateo, Calif., a suburb of San Francisco. The architects, John Carl Warnecke & Associates, chose a formal design of textured reinforced concrete with projecting round towers to house the various services. The site provided enviable views over a golf course in one direction.

Visitors to the Commercial & Industrial Bank, Memphis, Tenn., could enjoy a lush glass-enclosed garden adjacent to the main banking hall. The great wedge-shaped building was designed by Gassner, Nathan, Browne. Offices above the banking hall also looked out onto the garden. All the exterior walls were of concrete poured into place during construction.

A skylit garden was also a feature of the new building for the Equitable Life Assurance Society of the U.S. at St. Louis, Mo. Designed by Hellmuth, Obata & Kassabaum, the 21-story tower was linked to a low-rise commercial centre by a skylit garden. The tower was clad in silver reflective glass to mirror the surrounding cityscape.

The first stage of Brookhollow Plaza in Dallas, Tex., was a 16-story precast concrete office tower designed by Paul Rudolph in conjunction with Harwood K. Smith & Partners. The building, whose components were totally precast except for the floors between stories, was designed to give 16 corner offices

PETER L. GOULD

The world's largest digital clock—50 ft. high—is one of many efforts of architect Melvyn Kaufman to humanize skyscrapers—especially in New York City—with "shock and disruption." Kaufman enlivened the lobby of the office building with neon-lighted corrugated tunnels, a giant fishing lure, and bright boutiques.

per floor instead of the usual four. All structural joints were exposed, a feature which caused the building to be likened to a huge log cabin.

Worcester Center, a new commercial and shopping complex in the old New England town of Worcester, Mass., was designed to reverse the trend toward suburban shopping and to renew and revitalize the city centre. The centre formed part of an extensive redevelopment plan for the city and was designed to provide a community focal point as well as all the facilities and convenience of a suburban plaza. Direct access to the centre from an expressway and ample covered parking facilities were provided. The centrepiece was the Galleria, a two-story shopping arcade reminiscent of the grand 19th-century arcades that had largely disappeared from U.S. cities. The transparent roof of the arcade, 60 ft. high at the centre, consisted of a vaulted skylight of white precast concrete arches, steel ribs, and bronze Plexiglas. Along the 475-ft. length of the arcade were some of the $800,000 worth of works of art selected by Annie Damaz as integral parts of the architectural design. The architects for the Worcester Center were Welton Becket & Associates.

In the U.K. two new buildings for IBM were nearing completion. The first, housing a computer and an assembly plant at Havant, Hampshire, was designed by Ove Arup & Associates. Giant precast concrete cladding gave a massive enclosed feeling to the building. The new office headquarters at Cosham, Hampshire, was a complete contrast. The glass and steel structure designed by Norman Foster Associates seemed to be almost without walls. The open-plan space was delineated by a glass enclosing membrane—a kind of minimal architecture.

In Barcelona, Spain, José Antonio Coderch de Sentmenat was the architect for Edificios Trade, a development comprising four connecting towers with undulating sides sheathed in black glass. In the area connecting the towers were restaurants, a gym, a sauna, and shops on the ground floor, and conference rooms and an auditorium on the mezzanine.

University and College Buildings. Benjamin Thompson & Associates were architects for a new faculty office building and a classroom and administration building for the law school of Harvard University, Cambridge, Mass. The two new buildings were constructed within existing open space to add complexity and interest. The subtle and well-detailed buildings of dark brownish-purple brick were flexibly planned and embodied the best features of the conservative trend followed by many contemporary architects.

New dormitories for Bradford (Mass.) College were designed by architects Campbell, Aldrich & Nulty. They were conceived as domestically scaled residences, each housing ten students and representing a compromise between the traditional vast dormitories and individual apartments. Each house had two single and four double bedrooms with common living room and kitchen and shared bathrooms, and with a study loft at the top level. The roof sections consisted of plywood sheathing glued and nailed to lightweight rafters. This created a stressed skin panel that acted as a diaphragm, transferring its loads to the outside shear walls. The advantages of such a system were that it permitted relatively wide spans unobstructed by beams and columns and allowed greater flexibility in arrangement and appearance. The houses were grouped around an attractively landscaped quadrangle.

Paul Rudolph was the architect for the new Sid W. Richardson Physical Sciences Building for Texas Christian University at Fort Worth. The five-story, $5 million complex was designed to house physical science departments, a computer centre, laboratories, offices, classrooms, and lounges. The building, though very large, managed to retain a human scale through its great richness of form and spatial complexity. Materials used were concrete with smooth brick infill, and the broad overhangs threw dramatic shadow patterns in the strong Texas sun.

The new chemistry building for the Royal Holloway College at Egham, Surrey, Eng., was designed to house the teaching and research departments of a single faculty. The concrete structure was designed by architects Colquhoun & Miller of London to allow for growth and adaptability. Two lecture theatres and a library were also provided within the building.

Civic and Cultural Buildings. Striking among the new civic buildings of 1972 was Finlandia Hall, a concert and congress hall in Helsinki, Fin., designed by Alvar Aalto. The first stage of a long-term development for a new civic centre in the Finnish capital, the building provided a concert hall seating 1,750, a chamber music room seating 350, and conference and restaurant facilities. The structure, of reinforced concrete clad in white marble and gray granite, was notable for its architectural excellence—exciting and monumental but never overpowering.

At the preliminary design stage, plans for the new civic centre for the London Borough of Hillingdon attracted considerable interest. Plans by architects Sir Robert Matthew, Johnson-Marshall & Partners featured a system of hexagonal grids to modulate the interior space.

Another building based on a hexagonal plan was the synagogue for an Israeli Army camp in the Negev Desert. Designed by architects Neumann and Hecker, the structure was composed of piled-up concrete polyhedrons.

In Paris the new Parc des Princes stadium designed by Roger Taillibert opened in June. The stadium, seating 53,000 under cover, was built above the tunnels carrying the expressway around Paris. The structure consisted of a series of prestressed curved concrete arms cantilevered out. It was claimed that the entire full stadium could be emptied in only 20 minutes.

Also in Paris, the new headquarters for the French Communist Party was completed. Designed by Oscar Niemeyer, it consisted of a six-story office block with an undulating glass facade. Situated in an outer section of the city, the building provided offices, conference rooms, an auditorium, dining facilities, a library, and parking space.

Conservation. A notable trend in 1972 was the growing interest in the preservation of old buildings throughout the world. Linked with this was a growing concern with the problem of how to adapt these old buildings to modern uses. In countries where fine old buildings were plentiful many architects seemed to be devoting a large proportion of their time and creative energy to conversions and renovations of all kinds.

In the U.K. the *Architectural Review* devoted its May issue to "New Uses for Old Buildings." Among those featured was the late 18th-century neoclassical saltworks at Arc-et-Senans near Besançon in France, designed by Claude Nicolas Ledoux. The saltworks was converted into a conference and study centre, run by the Fondation Ledoux with the support of organi-

AUTHENTICATED NEWS INTERNATIONAL

Transamerica Corp.'s new 853-ft.-tall pyramid-shaped headquarters stands in San Francisco's financial district, not far from the controversial Bank of America building. San Franciscans objected to the bank building (not shown) because of its dark colour and to the Transamerica structure because of its shape.

zations from all over the world. The centre was opened in 1971 with several short conferences, theatrical productions, and an exhibition entitled "Ledoux et l'architecture visionnaire," and some 20 small apartments were opened in 1972 for the use of research workers.

Many new uses were suggested to solve the problem of unused churches in downtown areas. Thomas Archer's early 18th-century Baroque church of St. John in Smith Square, London, badly bombed in World War II, was restored and converted into a concert hall and cultural centre by architect Marshall Sisson. In Oxford, Eng., the 18th-century church of All Saints in the Turl was being converted into a library for Lincoln College by Robert Potter with the advice of Sir John Summerson.

New uses were found for many other redundant but attractive old buildings. Breweries and malthouses were carefully restored and renovated to become culture centres, and old barns and mills were turned into restaurants, homes, and even a furniture gallery. The Old Brewery at Freshford, Somerset, was being converted into an architects' office by Leonard Manasseh & Partners, and many of the majestic old Victorian water pumping stations to be found throughout Britain were attracting attention as potential homes for museums and other cultural and community features.

In Weston, Mass., architect Lawrence Partridge converted a typical old New England stone barn into a comfortable house. Enough of the old building was retained to give scale and character, and three new sections were added with roofs echoing that of the original barn. A novel house at La Lucila, Buenos Aires, Arg., designed by architects Manteola, Petchersky, Sanchez Gomez, Santos, Solsona and Vinoly of Buenos Aires, featured a sloping roof completely covered with grass, producing a building that certainly blended well into the landscape.

In the U.K. the furore over the redevelopment plans for the historic Covent Garden and Piccadilly areas of London's West End continued to rage. The problem was given a further airing by the *Architectural Review,* which devoted a substantial part of its July issue to an article entitled "Save the Garden."

The American Institute of Architects awarded its Gold Medal for 1972 to Pietro Belluschi. Belluschi, who practiced in Portland, Ore., was well known for his many fine buildings with their imaginative use of wood in the Pacific Northwest. The Royal Institute of British Architects Gold Medal for 1972 was awarded to the U.S. architect Louis I. Kahn *(see* BIOGRAPHY). (SANDRA MILLIKIN)

See also Cities and Urban Affairs; Engineering Projects; Environment; Historic Buildings; Housing; Industrial Review.

ENCYCLOPÆDIA BRITANNICA FILMS. *The Medieval Mind* (1969).

Arctic Regions

The development of oil and gas reserves and the accompanying social and environmental problems dominated the Arctic during 1972. As the year closed there was sufficient progress in resolving most of the major issues involved to predict that the massive oil and gas supplies of northern North America were at last on the verge of being tapped.

After more than two years of delay, the U.S. secretary of the interior on May 11 formally approved the construction of the trans-Alaska crude oil pipeline. In August a U.S. district court judge lifted a 1970 court injunction against building the line. The principal reason given for granting the approval was that the pipeline was in the national interest and would stimulate the development of Alaska. Construction, however, was unlikely to begin until sometime in 1973, and completion of the line was not expected until 1975.

Further legal delays to the construction of the pipeline were caused by court injunctions brought by conservation groups. The U.S. Circuit Court of Appeals announced that it would review the decision of the district court, and the case was expected eventually to be appealed to the U.S. Supreme Court.

In midyear the Alaska legislature approved four bills that provided increased state control over its massive oil industry. The bills were designed to give Alaska an adequate return on its resources and prevent the exploitation, which, the state believed, had characterized earlier efforts at fur, mineral, and fish development. As the year ended, a number of oil companies were challenging the constitutionality of the laws. In March the oil industry had rejected the possibility of state ownership of the multibillion dollar pipeline but offered to offset an expected revenue loss to the Alaska state treasury by advance payments on royalties from eventual North Slope production.

A report issued by a group of independent consultants concluded that the Alaska Railroad could be extended to the North Slope and used to carry oil to an ice-free port for substantially less than the proposed pipeline. The study estimated the railroad would cost $2.8 billion to construct and that five years would be required to build and design it. The Canadian transport minister in July issued a report, "Railway to the Arctic," which examined the technical feasibility of using a railway to move oil over the permafrost region from Prudhoe Bay, Alaska, directly to North American markets. The study suggested that a railway to carry oil at the volumes projected appeared to be technically feasible and would require approximately 360 locomotive units and 11,000 tank cars of 94-ton capacity each in order to move the projected volume of 2 million bbl. of oil a day.

During the year the Canadian government announced that bids were being asked for the construction of the initial phase of the 1,050-mi. Mackenzie Valley highway, which eventually would permit overland travel to the shores of the Arctic Ocean. During the winter of 1972–73 engineers planned to test a cable-operated air-cushioned transporter as a vehicle for ferrying highway traffic over major river crossings. If the tests proved successful, the use of these vehicles as ferries could make the highway operable for all but about five days annually.

The Dome Petroleum Co., one of the major exploration firms, reported to the Canadian National Energy Board during the year that they estimated there were more than 15 trillion cu.ft. of natural gas in the Canadian Arctic and that there was no technological reason why the gas could not be in production within a few years' time. Dome also signed an agreement with three gas-short U.S. pipeline companies in which the firms committed $30 million toward exploration costs in return for having first call on purchasing any gas that Dome may discover.

In February the first oil strike in the Arctic islands

Areas:
see Populations and Areas; *see also the individual country articles*

was announced by Panarctic Oils Ltd. The petroleum was discovered on the Fosheim Peninsula of Ellesmere Island by Panarctic, whose largest single stockholder was the Canadian government. Panarctic held permits covering about 55 million ac. in the Arctic islands and had already made four commercial gas finds in the region.

The Soviet newspaper *Izvestia* reported that natural gas had begun to flow from the remote Medvezhye gas field in Siberia astride the Arctic Circle. The field was reported to have reserves of 50 trillion cu.ft. and was expected to be producing at a rate of 1.3 trillion cu.ft. by 1975. Ultimately, it was expected that Siberian gas would be flowing to Western Europe, and discussions were held late in 1971 regarding the possibility of exporting gas to the U.S. In March it was reported that Soviet oilmen had started an exploratory well on Kolguyev Island in the Arctic Ocean in the hope of tapping the reputed huge petroleum reserves under the continental shelf off the Soviet Union's north coast.

The U.S. government and Alaska reached a settlement in October whereby approximately 79 million ac. of Arctic land were set aside for the federal government for possible use as national parks, forests, and refuge areas. According to the authorities the settlement would "permit the complex and interlocking process of land actions by Alaska natives and the state and federal governments to proceed under the terms of both the 1971 Native Claims Settlement Act and the Statehood Act without needless delay." Meanwhile, Canada established three new national parks north of the 60th parallel: Baffin Park with 8,200 sq.mi., on Cumberland Peninsula, Baffin Island; Kluane Park with 8,500 sq.mi. in the Yukon; and Nahanni Park, 1,800 sq.mi. in the Northwest Territories.

The largest collection of Eskimo art from Canada ever to be shown abroad and the first to be shown in the U.S.S.R. was put on display in the Hermitage Museum in Leningrad, and also in Moscow, as part of the cultural agreement between Canada and the U.S.S.R. The exhibit, which consisted of 403 pieces representing contemporary Eskimo sculpture and the sculpture of Arctic cultures of the past, was also shown in Europe and the U.S.

An international project known as AIDJEX (Arctic Ice Dynamics Joint Experiment), in preparation for several years, continued its effort to understand the forces that control ice movement in the Arctic Ocean. One of the project's goals was to forecast and perhaps control the pack ice sufficiently to permit tankers and ore ships to transport the natural resources from the circumpolar regions. A project with similar goals, sponsored by the Arctic Institute of North America, conducted in January and February the first winter reconnaissance in modern times of the historic "North Water," the large, open-water area that exists during the winter in northern Baffin Bay. An understanding of this region had important commercial implications in view of the large discoveries of gas and oil in the nearby eastern Arctic islands.

Summer surveys at Amchitka Island, Alaska, site of the November 1971 underground nuclear test, convinced biologists that as many as 1,000 sea otters had been killed from the shock waves which pulsed through the Bering Sea. No long-term effects on the seal population were expected, however.

In February it was announced in Geneva that scientists from five circumpolar countries had asked their governments to conclude an agreement to prohibit the hunting of polar bears who live on the pack ice outside territorial waters. As of 1972 the Soviet Union was the only country that had imposed a complete ban on their hunting and exploitation.

The International Ice Patrol reported that the 1972 season was the fourth worst annual period for extreme southerly drift of icebergs on record since the iceberg watch was begun after the loss of the ocean liner "Titanic," in 1912. More than 550 icebergs drifted south of Newfoundland, compared to a normal number of about 80. (KENNETH DE LA BARRE)

Argentina

The federal republic of Argentina, occupying the southeastern section of South America, is bounded by Bolivia, Paraguay, Brazil, Uruguay, Chile, and the Atlantic Ocean. It is the second largest Latin-American country, after Brazil, with an area of 1,072,157 sq.mi. (2,776,888 sq.km.). Pop. (1971 est.): 23,552,000. Cap. and largest city: Buenos Aires (pop., 1970, 2,972,453). Language: Spanish. Religion: mainly Roman Catholic. President in 1972, Lieut. Gen. Alejandro Agustín Lanusse.

Domestic Affairs. An uncertain and violent climate prevailed throughout most of 1972 in Argentina. Oberdán Sallustro, a Fiat executive, was kidnapped by members of the Trotskyite People's Revolutionary Army, who killed him as police arrived at their hideout on April 10; on the same day Gen. Juan Carlos Sánchez, commander of the II Army Corps and a leader of the fight against the guerrillas, was assassinated by machine-gun fire in Rosario. A 48-hour general strike took place in February following a 9.2% devaluation of the Argentine peso, and in June a second general strike was called in support of wage raises and the release of political prisoners. Many students throughout the country demonstrated in sympathy with the strikers. In August, 16 guerrilla prisoners were killed by police, reportedly while trying to escape from the remote Trelew military base. The government was incensed by Chile's refusal to hand back ten other guerrillas, who on August 15 had escaped over the Andes in a stolen jet.

Although former dictator Juan Perón (*see* BIOGRAPHY) failed to meet the government's requirement that presidential candidates for the March 1973 elec-

Rioters in Mendoza wrecked 146 cars in protest over a proposed 110% raise in electricity rates. Three people were killed and hundreds injured or jailed during the April 1972 rioting.

GAMMA

ARGENTINA

Education. (1969) Primary, pupils 3,354,587, teachers 171,759; secondary, pupils 211,537, teachers 31,947; vocational, pupils 519,079, teachers 71,583; teacher training, students 194,190, teachers 25,702; higher (including 38 universities and technical institutes), students 271,496, teaching staff 21,336.

Finance. Monetary unit: peso, with (Sept. 18, 1972) a free rate of 5 pesos to U.S. $1 (12.20 pesos = £1 sterling). Gold, SDRs, and foreign exchange, central bank: (March 1972) U.S. $278 million; (March 1971) U.S. $495 million. Budget (1970 est.): revenue 7,857,000,000 pesos; expenditure 8,450,000,000 pesos. Gross national product: (1969) 79,820,000,000 pesos; (1968) 68,320,000,000 pesos. Money supply: (Feb. 1972) 24,410,000,000 pesos; (Feb. 1971) 17,640,000,000 pesos. Cost of living (Buenos Aires; 1963 = 100): (May 1972) 756; (May 1971) 483.

Foreign Trade. (1971) Imports 8,588,000,000 pesos; exports 7,968,300,000 pesos. Import sources: U.S. 22%; West Germany 12%; Brazil 11%; Japan 8%; Italy 6%; U.K. 6%. Export destinations: Italy 15%; U.S. 9%; Netherlands 9%; Chile 7%; Spain 7%; U.K. 7%; West Germany 7%; Brazil 6%. Main exports: meat 24%; corn 19%.

Transport and Communications. Roads (1970) 201,059 km. Motor vehicles in use (1969): passenger 1,304,300; commercial (including buses) 714,800. Railways: (1969) 39,710 km.; traffic (1971) 12,188,000,000 passenger-km., freight 12,925,000,000 net ton-km. Air traffic (1970): 2,394,925,000 passenger-km.; freight 55,998,000 net ton-km. Shipping (1971): merchant vessels 100 gross tons and over 335; gross tonnage 1,311,874. Telephones (Dec. 1970) 1,748,000. Radio receivers (Dec. 1970) 9 million. Television receivers (Dec. 1970) 3.5 million.

Agriculture. Production (in 000; metric tons; 1971; 1970 in parentheses): wheat 5,200 (4,250); corn 9,930 (9,360); sorghum 4,782 (4,068); barley 553 (367); oats 475 (360); potatoes 1,958 (2,336); sugar, raw value (1971–72) 996, (1970–71) 979; linseed 316 (680); sunflower seed (1970) 1,140, (1969) 876; cotton, lint 84 (145); oranges 1,255 (1,092); apples 424 (445); wine 2,178 (1,836); tobacco 59 (66); beef and veal 2,017 (2,670); cheese 197 (167); wool, greasy *c.* 170 (172); quebracho extract (1969) 118, (1968) 123. Livestock (in 000; June 1971): cattle 49,786; sheep *c.* 43,800; pigs *c.* 4,300; horses (1970) *c.* 3,620; poultry *c.* 55,000.

Industry. Fuel and power (in 000; metric tons; 1971): coal 631; crude oil 21,300; natural gas (cu.m.) 6,448,000; electricity (excluding most industrial production; kw-hr.) 18,734,000. Production (in 000; metric tons; 1971): cement 5,552; crude steel 1,914; cotton yarn 92; passenger cars (including assembly; units) 196; commercial vehicles (including assembly; units) 48.

tion be resident in Argentina by August 25, his personal delegate, Héctor Campora, delivered a ten-point program for national reconstruction drawn up by Perón in Madrid in early October. President Lanusse accepted the program as "a positive contribution" to the solution of the country's problems and at one point appeared ready to accept Perón's return and some accommodation with him. However, on October 17, the anniversary of Perón's rise to power in 1945, his supporters organized demonstrations throughout the country in defiance of a government ban on open-air rallies and demonstrations. Amid a general tightening of security a series of bomb explosions occurred in several cities, causing disruption of rail and road traffic and destroying the top floors of the recently opened Buenos Aires Sheraton Hotel. Earlier, President Lanusse had advanced the date from which electoral campaigning could begin, from November 25 to October 1, and his plans appeared to have at least the tacit support of the armed forces.

In an apparent effort to obtain Perón's backing for the March elections, the government allowed him to return to Argentina after 17 years in exile. On November 17 Perón arrived in his native land and immediately began a series of consultations with the government and his supporters. If his aim was to persuade Lanusse and the military to allow him to run for president, Perón failed, and on December 14 he left the country for Paraguay. The Justicialistas, a Peronista party of long standing, nonetheless nominated him for president, but Perón declined. On December 16 the party, with Perón's blessing, nominated Campora, a move that caused some labour leaders to walk out of the convention.

The government announced in September several constitutional changes, including the election of the president and vice-president by direct popular suffrage, instead of by an electoral college; the reduction of the presidential term from six to four years, with the introduction of the possibility of reelection for a second term; and the extension of regular congressional sessions from five to eight months each year. The Senate was to comprise three senators from each province: two representing the majority party and one the minority. Terms of both senators and deputies were to be for four years, and both could be reelected indefinitely.

Fourteen political parties applied for judicial recognition to present candidates in the elections. Eleven of them were recognized, including the Justicialista Party and the Unión Popular, also a Peronista group.

Armies:
see Defense

Art:
see Architecture; Art Exhibitions; Art Sales; Dance; Literature; Museums and Galleries; Theatre

The Economy. Official preoccupation with the political program to a certain extent made it impossible for the government to face up to the country's most recalcitrant economic problems. For political reasons the government avoided imposing an austerity program, which many commentators believed was the only policy that would put an end to spiraling inflation and monetary instability. From January to September 1972 the cost-of-living index rose by 49.2%, compared with 30.4% in the corresponding 1971 period. The minister of finance, Cayetano Licciardo, resigned on October 8 and was replaced by Jorge Wehbe.

Some improvements were, however, registered in the growth rate of the economy and in the external sector. In January–June 1972 the gross domestic product rose at an annual rate of 4.4% in real terms, compared with 3.6% in the first half of 1971. The improved rate of expansion largely reflected a 9.1% increase in manufacturing output. The output of steel products, tractors, and other industrial goods rose satisfactorily. Agricultural production, however, declined 6.7%, mainly as a result of poor 1972 grain crops.

In the external sector, difficulties persisted: in the first half of 1972 there was an overall deficit on current and capital account of $242 million, compared with $138 million in January–June 1971. International Monetary Fund credits and Special Drawing Rights allocations covered the bulk of the loss, and the net reduction in reserves was limited to $18 million. The gross reserves of the Banco Central stood at $338.7 million at June 30, compared with $566.2 million at the same date in 1971. On May 31 Argentina's public foreign debt falling due in 1972 amounted to $316.7 million, thereby denoting the difficulty authorities would encounter in trying to preserve Argentina's record of meeting all obligations at their due date. In this respect some credit assistance was hoped for from banks in the U.S., Europe, Canada, and Japan.

In September, in a somewhat belated and drastic attempt to improve the country's trade performance, the government announced yet another economic program and severe controls on the opening of letters of credit for exports to Argentina. This was tantamount to a virtual suspension of imports. The government also announced the creation of a commission to formulate a new import policy that would clearly define what constituted permitted imports.

(WILLIAM BELTRÁN)

Art Exhibitions

The ever growing public interest in unusual art exhibitions was evident in London in 1972 when seemingly endless lines formed outside the British Museum to see the "Treasures of Tutankhamun." Originally scheduled to run from April until September, the exhibition was extended until December because of the great interest shown. The 50 items on display were lent by the Egyptian government to mark the 50th anniversary of the discovery of the tomb of the boy king Tutankhamen by the Englishmen Howard Carter and Lord Carnarvon. The priceless collection of ancient Egyptian objects included jewelry, furniture, weapons, and the famous gold and lapis lazuli death mask. The exhibits were individually illuminated in a series of dark rooms designed to recreate something of the atmosphere of the original tomb. Profits from the exhibition were donated to the UNESCO fund for the preservation of the Philae temples on the Nile.

Strong interest in non-Western and ancient art was also evident in the U.S., where many excellent shows were devoted to exotic subjects. The Museum of Fine Arts, Boston, held an exhibition "Ancient Art of the Americas" in the spring. The exhibits were drawn from museums and private collections in New England and included some fine pieces of Olmec art from tropical Mexico. Many items had never before been exhibited or published. Primitive art from New Guinea was shown at the Art Institute of Chicago in an exhibition that included over 200 masks, drums, ornaments, and shields from the Sepik River area.

An exhibition of Chinese calligraphy organized by the Philadelphia Museum of Art was shown at Kansas City, Mo., in the winter and at the Metropolitan Museum of Art in New York in the spring. Examples of scripts covering a period of 2,000 years demonstrated the importance traditionally attached to beauty and vitality of line in Chinese writing. Equally exotic, but closer to home, was the inaugural exhibition "Two Hundred Years of American Indian Art" staged at the Whitney Gallery of Western Art in Cody, Wyo. The show included some 300 objects made by Indians north of the Mexican border between 1700 and 1900.

Paintings by American artists were shown in a number of important exhibitions in 1972. The Amon Carter Museum, Fort Worth, Tex., organized a show devoted to the 19th-century American landscape painter Albert Bierstadt, known for his large and dramatic scenes of the American wilderness. The exhibition was later seen at the Whaling Museum of New Bedford, Mass., the Corcoran Gallery, Washington, D.C., the Whitney Museum of American Art, New York, and the Pennsylvania Academy of Fine Arts, Philadelphia. Eastman Johnson, the 19th-century American painter known for his charming country genre scenes, was the subject of a retrospective exhibition held at the Whitney Museum. The 83 paintings and 24 drawings were later seen in Detroit, Cincinnati, and Milwaukee. Another retrospective was devoted to the work of the American painter of the 1920s Charles Demuth (1883–1935). Organized by the Art Galleries of the University of California at Santa Barbara, the exhibition later traveled throughout the country.

"Worlds of Wonder" was the title of an unusual and entertaining exhibition at the Walters Art Gallery, Baltimore, Md. The exhibition recreated the 17th-century *Wunderkammer*, or chamber of curiosities, and included nearly 340 objects of scientific, naturalistic, or artistic interest, ranging from a stuffed crocodile to pre-Columbian ceramics. Most of the material was drawn from the museum's own resources.

"Caravaggio and His Followers" was a scholarly exhibition held in the winter at the Cleveland (O.) Museum of Art and devoted to this important late 16th-century Italian painter especially known for his dramatic use of light. The show stressed his influence on other artists and works by his followers included some fine canvases by Dutch artists working in Utrecht. While there had been many exhibitions devoted to the great Dutch painters of the 17th century, "Dutch Masterpieces from the 18th Century: Painting and Drawing 1700–1800" was the first major show devoted to 18th-century Dutch art for 25 years. Organized and first shown in Minneapolis, Minn., it later

"The Forest" (left), by Greek artist Pavlos, was an exhibition in Hanover, W.Ger. The forest of fibre glass and paper was complete with the recorded singing of birds. Jean Arp's stainless steel sculpture "Threshold Configuration" (below) was donated to New York's Metropolitan Museum of Art by Arthur and Madeleine Lejwa. Executed from a model after the artist's death, it was the first monumental outdoor work in the museum's 20th-century collection.

KEYSTONE

JACK MANNING—THE NEW YORK TIMES

KEYSTONE

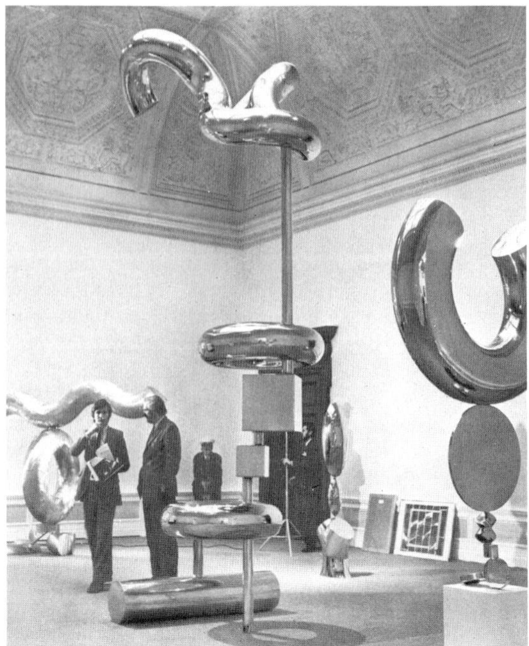

The "British Sculptors '72" exhibition at the Royal Academy of Arts in London surveyed a single aspect of contemporary art. The show presented the work of 24 living British sculptors.

moved to Toledo, O., and Philadelphia. The first of its kind outside the Netherlands, the exhibition consisted of 106 paintings and drawings.

English drawings and watercolours from the Paul Mellon collection were exhibited from April to July at the Pierpont Morgan Library, New York. The 150 items, many of which had never before been exhibited or reproduced, included works by George Stubbs, Richard Wilson, John Constable, and J. M. W. Turner. Drawings were also the medium for an exhibition of stage designs from the collection of the Museo Teatrale alla Scala, Milan, Italy. The show, entitled "La Scala: 400 Years of Stage Design," was made up of watercolours and drawings as well as some costume designs and small model stage sets. Artists represented included the great Italian stage set designers F. G. Bibiena, F. Juvarra, and G. Galliari. The designs were shown first at the National Gallery of Art, Washington, D.C., late in 1971, and in 1972 they traveled to the Detroit Institute of Arts and the University Art Museum at Austin, Tex. Etchings by the Italian 18th-century painters G. B. and G. D. Tiepolo shown at the National Gallery included more than 90 very fine and rare examples of their graphic art.

Early in the spring the New York Cultural Center held the first U.S. museum retrospective for 30 years devoted to the work of the Surrealist painter Giorgio de Chirico. The 150 paintings, drawings, prints, and sculptures covered 60 years of artistic activity. Many of them had never before been shown in the U.S. and most were lent by the artist from his private collection.

An exhibition devoted to the sculpture of Henri Matisse organized by the Museum of Modern Art, New York, was the first show ever to include all 69 known bronzes by the artist. The pieces, dating from 1894 to 1950, were mostly lent by private collectors. The exhibition also included 19 drawings, 4 prints, and a ceramic tile relating to the sculpture. Emphasis was on the growing tendency toward abstraction in the artist's later work. Many of the female figures in the sculptures also appear in paintings by Matisse. The bronzes later traveled to the Walker Art Center, Minneapolis, Minn., and the University Art Museum at Berkeley, Calif. The Solomon R. Guggenheim Museum, New York, organized a centennial exhibition devoted to the Dutch modern painter Piet Mondrian (1872–1944). The exhibition later traveled to Bern, Switz. Also at the Guggenheim in the spring was a show of drawings by the French sculptor Auguste Rodin. The exhibition, previously seen at the National Gallery, included 132 genuine drawings and 27 forgeries, allowing visitors to compare the real with the fake.

In London the Victoria and Albert Museum's exhibition "Victorian Church Art" was the first large-scale show of 19th-century English ecclesiastical art. The exhibition concentrated on church fittings such as chalices, altar frontals, and lecterns. Drawings were also shown. Artists represented included all the major names in 19th-century design: A. W. Pugin, William Butterfield, G. E. Street, G. F. Bodley, J. D. Sedding, and many others.

More Victorian decorative objects were on view at the Royal Academy of Arts in the spring where "Victorian and Edwardian Decorative Art: the Handley-Read Collection" was displayed. The collection was remarkable for the great richness and variety of the furniture, ceramics, paintings, and sculpture included. Objects were placed in settings as close to the original as possible.

The show "Homage to Senefelder" at the Victoria and Albert Museum traced the development of lithography, a technique invented by the playwright Aloys Senefelder (1771–1834). Works from the earliest days of lithography were shown along with works in the medium by contemporary artists. The exhibition was drawn from the fine collection of Felix H. Man.

The Royal Academy of Arts Winter Exhibition, "British Sculptors '72," represented a departure from the tradition of past years. The exhibition showed the work of 24 modern British sculptors and included works by Philip King, Robert Clatworthy, and Bryan Kneale. The common factor uniting the work of the artists included seemed to be an interest in geometric and symbolic form. Working drawings and maquettes for some of the pieces were exhibited concurrently at the Redfern Gallery.

A most enjoyable exhibition at the Tate Gallery was devoted to paintings, drawings, and prints by the English 18th-century artist William Hogarth. The setting was designed to suggest the rooms in which the works would originally have been seen. There were items representing all the phases of Hogarth's varied career.

In the autumn the Tate held an exhibition of works of the great German Romantic artist Caspar David Friedrich, previously little known in England. The exhibition was the first ever held in the U.K. and the largest anywhere. Paintings were lent by many galleries and private collections, including the Dresden Picture Gallery, East Germany, which had the most important collection of Friedrich paintings in the world.

In May the new headquarters of the drawings collection of the Royal Institute of British Architects was opened in London by Queen Elizabeth II. The Heinz Gallery, in Portman Square, was to house over 200,000 architectural drawings. To mark the opening RIBA mounted an exhibition of masterpieces from its collection with 38 drawings from all periods, including works by Inigo Jones, Sir Christopher Wren, Sir John Soane, Sir Edwin Lutyens, and Frank Lloyd Wright.

At the Hayward Gallery, London, an exhibition was devoted to the work of the Dutch architect and designer of the *De Stijl* movement, Gerrit Rietveld. First seen at the Stedelijk Museum, Amsterdam, the exhibition included 75 pieces of furniture and 200 photographs of buildings as well as drawings and models. Especially interesting was the reconstruction of an entire Rietveld room.

Also in London the Council of Europe held its 1972 exhibition devoted to "The Age of Neo-classicism," with sections on painting, sculpture, architecture, and the decorative arts. The exhibition, with its 850-page catalog, was said to have been one of the largest ever held.

English paintings were on view at the Petit Palais in Paris in the spring when the British Council staged an exhibition devoted to English Romantic painting, the first of its kind in Paris since 1938. Over 340 paintings were shown, including 50 items by J. M. W. Turner emphasizing his role as a precursor of French Impressionism.

Perhaps the most remarkable exhibition in Paris was a show at the Orangerie devoted to the little-known 17th-century French painter Georges de la Tour. The show included most of the 30 or so known paintings and copies and engravings of lost works. The pictures were borrowed from collections all over the world and the exhibition was the first, and probably the last, opportunity to study the artist's entire output in one place.

"Architectural Drawings from the Fifteenth to the Nineteenth Century" at the Pavillon de Flore of the Louvre consisted of 80 drawings, mostly by French architects but including works attributed to the Italian Renaissance architects Bramante and Brunelleschi. Many of the drawings were chosen for their value as decorative works of art as well as for their interest as historic documents.

France's many provincial museums were well known for their outstanding exhibitions. Among the most interesting of the year was an exhibition at the Galerie des Beaux-Arts, Bordeaux, of 84 canvases from the Budapest Museum. These included paintings by Raphael, Titian, Goya, El Greco, and Reynolds.

In West Germany the municipal museum of Munich mounted an exhibition entitled "Bavaria—Art and Culture" for visitors to the 1972 Olympics. The centrepiece was the reconstruction in the courtyard of the museum of a Roman villa discovered near Ingolstadt three years earlier.

Another major exhibition in West Germany was "Femininity Around 1900" at the Wallraf-Richartz Museum, Cologne, featuring work by illustrators of the period. Also in Cologne the Kunstverein held a summer show devoted to ancient Chinese bronzes and ceramics, including many rare pieces from the Shang-Yin dynasty (*c.* 1500–*c.* 1027 B.C.). The Städtische Kunsthalle, Bielefeld, showed works by the French sculptor Henri Laurens and the Wiesbaden Museum showed important wood engravings by artists of the Expressionist *Die Brücke* movement.

"Flamboyant Gothic in Austria" was the theme of a summer exhibition at the Carolino Augusteum Museum, Salzburg, Aus. Emphasis was on painting, but some stained glass and illuminated manuscripts were included. In Geneva the Petit Palais was the site of an exhibition "Armand Guillaumin, Gustave Loiseaux et leur temps." Subtitled "Autour de l'Impressionisme," the show was devoted to French art of the period 1880–1930.

Russian museum visitors were treated to an exhibition at the Hermitage, Leningrad, of the French sculptor Antoine Bourdelle that included 50 bronzes and 30 paintings and drawings. The exhibition later moved to the Pushkin Museum in Moscow. In Copenhagen the Nationalmuseet showed an exhibition of sculpture by Canadian Eskimos. It included figures of humans and animals dating from about 800 B.C. that were remarkable for their monumentality of conception. The exhibition was also seen in Paris, Leningrad, London, and Philadelphia, and was expected to return to Ottawa early in 1973. In Genoa, Italy, "An Image for the City" at the Accademia di Belli Arti and Palazzo Reale focused on pictures illustrating modern industrial city life, and included works by F. Léger, F. Picabia, and Andy Warhol.

(SANDRA MILLIKIN)

See also Biography: *O'Keeffe, Georgia;* Museums and Galleries; Photography.

ENCYCLOPÆDIA BRITANNICA FILMS. *Meaning in Modern Painting* (1967); *The Artist at Work—Jacques Lipchitz Master Sculptor* (1968); *Henry Moore—The Sculptor* (1969); *Siqueiros—"El Maestro"* (1969); *Richard Hunt—Sculptor* (1970); *Interpretations* (1970).

Art Sales

The two great London salesrooms held their positions as leaders in the world art market, Sotheby Parke-Bernet with total sales of £43,296,900 and Christie's with £24,539,365. Christie's figure again included prices bid for items that did not reach their reserve prices and were therefore unsold, probably about 10% of the total.

The prospect of the value-added tax being introduced when Britain joined the EEC was a source of great anxiety to the art and antique trade, since at first there seemed no way of avoiding the 10% tax, and it was feared that London would lose its attraction as a tax-free auction centre. However, in July the government decided to use a loophole available in the rules for secondhand goods and to levy the tax only on the dealer's profit or auctioneer's commission, and even then not on sales to foreign clients. This announcement brought little joy to artists in the U.K., however, since their work when first sold would not be covered

This lively T'ang dynasty glazed pottery figure of a polo player was sold in 1972 at Sotheby's in London for £28,000. A similar piece was sold in 1964 for £3,500.

COURTESY, SOTHEBY AND CO., LONDON

CENTRAL PRESS/PICTORIAL PARADE

The sale of this early Gainsborough at Sotheby's in London for £280,000 set a new world auction record for an English painting. Previously, the highest price paid for a Gainsborough was £130,000.

by the rule. Any artist whose gross sales reached £5,000 a year would be liable to the tax.

Impressionist and modern pictures brought the largest total sum. In New York, Parke-Bernet's sold Henri Rousseau's "Paysage Exotique" for $775,000. Some works by old masters also sold for remarkably high figures. A portrait of the duc de Beuvron by Jean-Honoré Fragonard went for £340,000 at Sotheby's, and "The Ponte delle Navi, Verona" by Bernardo Bellotto for £315,000 at Christie's.

Especially interesting to U.S. collectors whose predecessors had bought 18th-century English portraits so lavishly in the 1920s and '30s was the renewed attention paid to the work of Gainsborough, Romney, and Reynolds. A portrait of the Gravenor family by Gainsborough was sold at Sotheby's for £280,000. At Christie's a particularly fine group of the Gower family by George Romney went for £147,000 and a portrait by Sir Joshua Reynolds of the actress Mrs. Abington for £105,000. The highest previous auction price for a Reynolds had been £25,000 in 1965, although H. E. Huntington was believed to have paid Joseph Duveen about £70,000 for one in the 1920s.

Discerning bidders vied for rarities in most fields of art, and prices for the best examples continued to rise steadily. A drawing by Annibale Carracci of "A Boy in the Act of Drinking" sold for £40,000 at Sotheby's and "The Harvest Moon," a tiny oil by Samuel Palmer, for £46,200 at Christie's. An intricately painted and framed 14th-century Italian altarpiece was sold at Christie's for £257,250. A splendid 14th-century Chinese ceramic wine jar went for £220,500 to a dealer from Japan after an expert from Christie's had noticed it serving as an umbrella stand in a house where he had been called to advise on the sale of some continental china. More Japanese buyers than ever before were taking back Oriental art from London.

The market in silver revived somewhat, although some important pieces sold for less than they had a few years before. For instance, a George II Royal Race prize teapot, sold in 1967 for £40,000, went for £38,000 in 1972. However, an early 18th-century American silver punch bowl, made in Boston by John Coney and discovered in a farmhouse on the Scottish border, was sold by Phillips of London for £15,500.

Works of modern art sold by Parke-Bernet's in New York included an elm wood "Reclining Figure" by Henry Moore for $260,000, a painting, "Shade," by Jasper Johns for $60,000, and "Mauve Intersection No. 12 1948" by Mark Rothko for $42,000. Interest in Americana was clearly increasing; "Death of a Gambler," painted by Charles M. Russell in 1904, fetched $100,000.

In Switzerland, Galerie Fischer of Lucerne sold a 14th-century French ivory diptych for SFr. 68,000, a painting, "Madonna and Children," by Vittore Carpaccio for SFr. 140,000, and a drawing by Amedeo Modigliani for SFr. 22,000. In Geneva modern pictures sold by Galerie Motte included "Innondation," signed and dated 1881 by Claude Monet, for SFr. 625,000, "Fenêtre Ouverte" by Pierre Bonnard for SFr. 322,000, and "Paysage (vers 1884)" by Camille Pissarro for SFr. 240,000.

West German art sales included a painting of the "Death of Mary" by the 15th-century Oberrheinischer Meister, sold in Cologne by Kunsthaus Lempertz for DM. 180,000, and "Strand bei Scheveningen" by Jan van Goyen, sold for DM. 270,000. An exquisite Meissen porcelain service of 1723 went for DM. 46,000, and a German silvergilt lidded tankard of 1570 for DM. 13,000.

From the point of view of the small collector, possibilities were increased by the expertise and enterprise of auctioneers. Sales of early photographs were held at Sotheby's, Belgravia, which specialized in the 19th century. The highest price was £4,800 for an album of 32 photographs by Octavius Hill and Robert Adamson, but the lowest was £1. Old and modern etchings were not always highly priced, and small pieces of late 18th- and 19th-century silver were easily obtainable in London for under £10. Even at Sotheby's and Christie's more than two-thirds of the items were sold for under £100, and for other salesrooms the figure would be much smaller. (WILMA LAWS)

Book Sales. Although the U.S. university libraries saw their budgets cut drastically, high-quality items maintained a satisfactory level and there was a buoyant rise in medium and small collectors' pieces. Sotheby's once again had the largest number of sales, nearly 60. For the 1971–72 season, sales of books and manuscripts by Sotheby Parke-Bernet totaled £3,000,500.

At Sotheby's in June 1972, the Chetham's Library of Manchester sold for £62,000 the elephant folio copy of Audubon's *The Birds of America,* to which it had been one of the original subscribers over a century and a half before. A manuscript of John Keats's poem "To Hope" brought £5,800. Bought in below the reserve price of £25,000 in 1971, in one of the endless Philipps sales, Sir Walter Raleigh's autograph notebook (sold in 1935 as an anonymous commonplace book for £3) was presented by Philip and Lionel Robinson to the British Museum to commemorate the centenary of the death of Sir Thomas Philipps.

A further sale of the Boies Penrose library at Sotheby's included such early geographical manuscripts as a 15th-century portolan by Grazioso Benincasa (£5,000) and a late 16th-century map of Guiana (£4,000). Among musical autographs, Erik

Asbestos:
see Mining

Association Football:
see Football

Satie's piano score for *Parade* brought £1,400 and a Debussy *Fête galante* fetched £1,600. The Dickens collection of Comte Alain de Suzannet, sold at Sotheby's, gave the British Museum the opportunity of acquiring, for £12,000, the first 22 pages—the last surviving portion still in private ownership—of a chapter of *Nicholas Nickleby*. Three sets of *The Pickwick Papers* in parts brought £1,700, £1,700, and £1,100, and Dickens' own annotated copy of *Mrs. Gamp* (Boston 1868) reached £3,600.

At Sotheby's in November a first edition of the first complete English Bible, translated by Miles Coverdale, printed in Marburg, and published in 1535, went for £12,000 to New York dealer John Howell. Thirteen copies are recorded in England and ten in the U.S. The cool reception that greeted the charming collection of calligraphica formed in recent years by Mrs. E. F. Hutton of New York showed how resentful the trade could be to the quick disposal of a collection—even when it has been made without any lucrative purpose. The 85 remarkable lots of books and manuscripts brought a mere £30,000.

The French market came to the forefront as the noteworthy collection of the Armenian jeweler R. Esmerian was put on auction in Paris. This rather mixed selection of books was notable for a few gems that had been cleverly picked up during various periods of recession. Among them was the 1499 Rahir *Hypnerotomachia* in a supremely elegant 16th-century binding adorned with gilt tooling and gold powder. It brought Fr. 638,570. Of the same quality were the Major Abbey set of the 1498 Aldine *Aristotles* in six volumes (which at Fr. 163,590—even against the £7,600 in Major Abbey's sale of 1965—still seemed rather cheap) and the Cortlandt Bishop *Herodotus* of 1556, which brought Fr. 149,070.

Modern illustrated books fetched high prices. A sale in Paris in March displayed expensive copies of the finest books illustrated by Chagall, Matisse, and others. Copies of Gogol's *Les âmes mortes,* 2 vol., 1948, illustrated by Chagall, varied from Fr. 39,890 to Fr. 49,790. Matisse's *Jazz,* 1947, brought from Fr. 37,690 to Fr. 57,490 according to condition and additional material. A few days later Jules Renard's *Histoires naturelles,* illustrated by Toulouse-Lautrec, 1899, fetched Fr. 32,740. In West Berlin Goethe's *Faust,* 1927, illustrated by Max Slevogt, sold for DM. 3,000. (PIERRE BERÈS)

Astronautics

Clearly the biggest news in manned space flight for 1972 was the announcement that the U.S. and U.S.S.R. would participate in a joint manned flight in July 1975. But in spite of the joint effort and a new U.S. space shuttle, the U.S. space program in 1972 continued the steady decline that began in the late 1960s. The fiscal year 1973 authorization for the National Aeronautics and Space Administration (NASA) was $3,431,650,000, down from the high of $4,968,000,000 for fiscal 1967. On July 1 rocket pioneer Wernher von Braun retired from NASA and accepted a position with Fairchild Industries, Inc.

The number of U.S. astronauts continued to dwindle. In August astronauts James B. Irwin and Edgar D. Mitchell resigned. Others who left in 1972 included Donald L. Holmquest, Philip K. Chapman, and Anthony W. England. Two former astronauts, still with NASA in other capacities, also left the space agency. Donn F. Eisele began training to become Peace Corps director in Thailand; James A. McDivitt became senior vice-president of the Consumer Power Co. By 1974 the astronaut corps would consist of 14 men, it was estimated. At its peak, in 1967, it had 63 men in training.

Apollo 15 astronauts David R. Scott, James B. Irwin, and Alfred M. Worden were officially reprimanded by NASA when it was disclosed that stamped envelopes they took to the moon were being sold in West Germany for $1,500 apiece. The same astronauts also left a small statue on the moon. Replicas of the statue, "The Fallen Astronaut" by sculptor Paul Van Hoeydonck, were placed on sale in New York for $750, again bringing the astronauts under criticism. Worden and Scott were later removed from astronaut status.

The end of an era came at Kennedy Space Center in Florida on February 1 when the Saturn I-B Launch Complexes 34 and 37 were sold to the highest bidder. The two sites cost $140 million and were sold for $15,051 to a concern that was to demolish them for scrap. Fifteen space shots in the Saturn-Apollo program were launched from the two complexes.

The European Launcher Development Organization (ELDO) announced expenditures in 1972 of $79.3 million. It also announced that Great Britain would continue to make available Blue Streak vehicles as first stages for the Europa series of boosters despite England's withdrawal from the program. Gen. Robert Aubinière, director general of the French Centre National d'Études Spatiales, was named ELDO's new secretary-general. The European Space Research Organization (ESRO) said it would spend $283.6 million on its space projects in the 1972–74 budgetary period.

France increased its space budget for the year, the figure rising from $132 million in 1971 to $150 million in 1972. In the same period, Japan increased its space outlays. Funding rose from $51,332 to $80,000. West

Astronaut John W. Young works at the Descartes landing site during the second extravehicular activity of Apollo 16.

COURTESY, NASA

Germany, however, reduced its financial support to both ELDO and ESRO.

India lost Vikram A. Sarabhai, chairman of its Space Research Organization, who died on Dec. 30, 1971. He was replaced by M. G. K. Menon, former director of the Tata Institute of Fundamental Research in Bombay. On May 10 Menon signed an agreement with the Academy of Sciences of the Soviet Union for the development of cooperation in space between the two countries.

Manned Space Exploration. With U.S. Pres. Richard Nixon's announcement in May 1972 of the joint U.S.-Soviet space effort, NASA revealed details of the mission and of the docking mechanisms being jointly designed by engineers of the two countries. A team of 25 Soviet scientists and engineers met with their U.S. counterparts at the Manned Spacecraft Center in Houston, Tex., on July 6 to discuss technical details.

What resulted was a far cry from the mission originally envisioned. The U.S.S.R. at first had suggested that a U.S. Apollo command module dock with their Salyut space station or, even better, that a Soyuz dock with one of the U.S. Skylab space stations. When U.S. officials explained that Skylab was a one-shot affair, the Soviets began to doubt the American commitment to manned space flight. Later, for technical reasons, the Apollo-Soyuz mission was adopted.

As proposed in 1972, the Soviet Union would launch a Soyuz vehicle into an orbit about 140 mi. above the earth. About 7½ hours later, an Apollo would be launched by a Saturn I-B booster from the Kennedy Space Center. After perhaps 14 orbits it would rendezvous and dock with the Soyuz. The Apollo would have a crew of three; the Soyuz only two men.

Because of the difference in atmospheric pressures within the two craft, a docking airlock module was to be developed. It would permit the Soviet and U.S. crews to visit each other's spacecraft without suffering "the bends." Once docked, the two craft would stay joined for 48 hours. After separation the Apollo would remain in orbit for an additional ten days, performing earth resources experiments. The Soyuz would return to earth within a day or so.

Apollo 16 lifted off on April 16 from the Kennedy Space Center. It headed toward the moon on a voyage that was filled with major and minor problems. However, none of them proved ultimately serious enough to jeopardize either the astronauts or the mission. The crew consisted of John W. Young, commander; Charles M. Duke, Jr., lunar module pilot; and Thomas K. Mattingly, command module pilot.

On the way to the moon a transient electrical signal in the command module's guidance and navigation system occurred after Mattingly had taken a "fix" using the optical navigation subsystem. At first there was some concern in Mission Control over the signal, but later analysis proved that the problem was not serious. As the astronauts were docking with the lunar module, they noticed that paint was flaking off one of the panels covering the craft's reaction control system and it was feared that the sun might heat up the interior of the lunar module. The fears turned out to be groundless because of the favourable angle of the sun.

More serious was a problem that arose after the command and lunar modules had separated while in orbit around the moon. In making a check prior to firing the engine of the service module to circularize the orbit of the craft at an altitude of 72 mi., Mattingly discovered an apparent malfunction in the system that points the engine in the proper direction for firing. The ignition of the engine was postponed while earthbound engineers worked on the problem. For four hours the two craft orbited the moon waiting for instructions from Mission Control at Houston. Finally, the problem was resolved and Young and Duke were cleared for the lunar landing. They landed in the Cayley Plains of the Descartes region on April 20.

During their first excursion from the lunar module on April 21, Young and Duke set up the Apollo Lunar Surface Experiments Package (ALSEP) and collected 42 lb. of rocks and soil samples. In doing so, the two logged 2.6 mi. on their lunar roving vehicle (LRV). The moon surface trip lasted 7 hours and 11 minutes. For the first time, a far-ultraviolet camera/spectrograph was set up to photograph the earth and various galaxies to learn more about the distribution of interplanetary and intergalactic hydrogen.

In deploying the ALSEP, Young inadvertently tangled his foot in the cable of the heat-flow experiment and tore it loose, rendering the instrument useless. Other features of this excursion included the firing of a thumper device 19 times to provide seismic waves for an array of geophones. This experiment indicated that the regolith, or rocky layer, of the lunar surface at that point was about 55.7 to 88.6 ft. deep.

On returning to the lunar module, the two astronauts put their LRV through an engineering test called "the Grand Prix." While Duke photographed him, Young buckled his seat belt and raced the LRV across the moon's surface, making sharp turns, accelerating, and slamming on the brakes. He reached a top speed of 7.2 mph, but later in the mission achieved 10.2 mph, only 0.2 mph less than the vehicle's top speed.

On the second excursion, April 22, which lasted 7 hours and 23 minutes, Young and Duke collected an additional 71 lb. of lunar rocks and soil and put an additional 7.1 mi. on their LRV. They explored the slope of Stone Mountain, about 2.5 mi. to the south, taking photographs and core samples of the soil.

The third and final excursion, on April 23, lasted 5 hours and 40 minutes. During it, the astronauts added another 7.1 mi. to the LRV and gathered an additional 100 lb. of rocks, bringing their total to a record 213 lb. The final journey was spent in exploring North Ray Crater, about three miles north of the lunar module. In addition to the usual rock and soil samples, the two astronauts took several readings of the local magnetic field strength in the area, using a portable magnetometer. Readings as high as 313 gamma were found on the slope of Smoky Mountain, higher by a factor of 100 than either U.S. or Soviet scientists had predicted. Later on April 23 the lunar module lifted off the moon.

While astronauts Young and Duke were exploring the Cayley Plains, Mattingly in the orbiting command module photographed the lunar surface and operated a battery of scientific instruments in the service module.

He made many visual observations for geologists in Houston, including one that raised the possibility of the presence of an active volcano on the moon. In a wall of the Crater Guyot on the far side of the moon he noticed a hole and something that resembled a pool of material that had oozed from it. Mattingly compared it to similar sightings he had made flying over the Hawaiian Islands, the site of numerous volcanoes, active and dead.

When the two astronauts transferred back into the command module, the crew separated the ascent stage, which was to impact the moon for seismometers left by earlier Apollo missions. Something went amiss, however, and the stage went into lunar orbit, where it could remain for years. While they were still in lunar orbit, the Apollo 16 crew released a subsatellite from the service module on April 24. It went into a circular orbit at 61.1 mi. Its instruments were designed to measure the moon's gravitational field and to provide data on the mysterious mascons, believed to be concentrations of dense material lying beneath the lunar surface. However, the subsatellite made only 425 orbits before crashing onto the far side of the moon on May 29.

On April 25, during the return home, Mattingly left the command module and pulled himself through space hand over hand to the service module. From it he retrieved the film magazines from the cameras that had helped map the moon. On April 27 the Apollo 16 command module splashed down about a mile from its recovery ship, the USS "Ticonderoga."

The mission had two unscheduled events. When Duke was describing the effects of cosmic rays penetrating his head, a voice began speaking and singing in Spanish for several minutes, then ceased abruptly. The voice was that of a telephone lineman in Spain who had inadvertently tied into the Apollo communications network in Madrid. The second incident involved Young. Thinking his microphone was off, he complained openly and in colourful language of recurring flatulence he attributed to an orange-flavoured drink spiked with potassium salt to prevent the heart arrhythmia experienced by the Apollo 15 astronauts.

As a result of the Apollo 16 mission, lunar geologists began modifying their theories about Cayley Plains. The abundance of impact breccia or rocks of angular fragments cemented together and a lack of basaltic rocks suggested that the Cayley region was not formed by volcanic flows as had previously been thought. Core samples from the region also seemed to indicate that they contained iron, an element not found in any other lunar samples.

Apollo 17, the final mission in the Apollo series and perhaps man's last opportunity to walk on the moon in the 20th century, was launched from Cape Kennedy on December 7. Thousands lined the beaches and roadsides of Florida to watch the first nighttime launch, a spectacle that was delayed almost three hours because the oxygen tank in the third stage of the Saturn V did not receive an automatic command for pressurization. After lift-off, however, Apollo 17, with Eugene Cernan, Ronald Evans, and Harrison Schmitt aboard, enjoyed a trouble-free flight. On December 11 Cernan and Schmitt, a geologist, landed on the moon in a narrow valley near the southeast rim of the Sea of Serenity, while Evans remained in lunar orbit. During their explorations, both on foot and in a lunar rover, Cernan and Schmitt found orange and red soil, a discovery that scientists believed might indicate volcanic activity on the moon. On December 14, after spending a record amount of time on the lunar surface, Cernan and Schmitt with 249 lb. of rocks and soil rejoined Evans. They orbited the moon, surveying its surface with instruments, and then returned to a successful splashdown in the Pacific on December 19.

On January 18 NASA also announced the names of the nine astronauts assigned to the Skylab flights, scheduled for April 1973. The first mission was to be headed by Charles "Pete" Conrad. He would be accompanied by Joseph P. Kerwin, science pilot, and Paul J. Weitz, pilot. Commander of the second mission was to be Alan L. Bean, with his fellow crewmen to be Owen K. Garriott, science pilot, and Jack R. Lousma, pilot. The final mission was to be headed by Gerald P. Carr, and he would be accompanied by Edward G. Gibson, science pilot, and William R. Pogue, pilot.

COURTESY, NASA

This remarkable composite photograph of the Seattle-Tacoma, Wash., area was taken July 28, 1972, by Earth Resources Technology Satellite-1 from an altitude of nearly 570 mi. Easily recognizable is Puget Sound (black area in upper centre) triangulated by snow-covered Mount Rainier (lower right), the Cascade Mountains (upper right), and the mountain ranges of Olympic National Park (upper left).

On July 26 three astronauts at NASA's Manned Spacecraft Center began a simulated Skylab mission of 56 days' duration. The three were sealed in a duplicate of the Skylab workshop inside an environmental chamber that produced a vacuum similar to that of space. The checkout of Skylab was completed without incident.

For the Soviet Union's space program, 1971 ended on an unhappy note, a sadness and disappointment that could be shared by space enthusiasts everywhere. The three cosmonauts who had successfully docked their Soyuz-11 with the Salyut space station and had lived on the space station had perished from an oxygen failure on reentry June 30, 1971. After that, the orbit of the space station had been adjusted several times in hopes that other cosmonauts would be able to reach it and retrieve experiments left on board. Unfortunately, redesign and testing of a new seal for the hatch of the Soyuz spacecraft descent module took longer than anticipated. It then became necessary for the Coordinating and Computing Centre in Moscow to command the firing of the retrorocket of the Salyut space station, causing it to plunge and burn upon entering the earth's atmosphere on October 11.

Unmanned Satellites. Late in 1971 the Soviet Union again demonstrated its capability of destroying satellites with other satellites. On November 29, Cosmos 459 was launched from Plesetsk by an SS-5 Skean missile. On December 3 Cosmos 462 was launched from Tyuratam by an SS-9 Scarp missile. As it approached the other satellite, Cosmos 462 exploded into 13 pieces, also destroying Cosmos 459.

The event prompted the U.S. Air Force to announce

Major Satellites and Space Probes Launched Oct. 1, 1971–Sept. 30, 1972

Name/country/ launch vehicle/ scientific designation	Launch date, lifetime*	Physical characteristics: Weight (kg.)†	Shape	Diameter (m.)†	Length or height (m.)†	Experiments	Orbital elements: Perigee (km.)†	Apogee (km.)†	Period (min.)	Inclination to Equator (degrees)
Astex/U.S./Thor Agena/ 1971–89A	10/17/71	1,184 (2,610)	Cylinder and rectangular box with 2 panels	1.52 (5)	9.81 (32.2)	Advanced Space Technology Satellite carried two unfurlable solar cell panels	773 (479)	801 (497)	100.5	92.7
Prospero (X-3)/U.K./Black Arrow/1971–93A	10/28/71	658 (1,451)	Polyhedron	0.7 (2.3)	1.12 (3.67)	First scientific satellite launched by U.K. with its own booster	425 (264)	1,444 (895)	106.4	82.0
DSCS-1/U.S./Titan IIIc/ 1971–95A	11/3/71	519 (1,145)	Cylinder	2.74 (9)	3.66 (12)	Communications satellite of U.S. Department of Defense	35,184 (21,814)	36,256 (22,479)	1,435.2	2.7
DSCS-2/U.S./Titan IIIc/ 1971–95B	11/3/71	519 (1,145)	Cylinder	2.74 (9)	3.66 (12)	Communications satellite of U.S. Department of Defense	35,136 (21,784)	36,080 (22,370)	1,438	2.3
Explorer 45/U.S./Scout 1971–96A	11/15/71	51.6 (113.8)	Octagon with five booms	0.73 (2.4)	0.7 (2.3)	First in series of small scientific satellites (SSS)	231 (143)	26,896 (16,676)	467.1	3.6
Molniya 2/U.S.S.R./A IIe/ 1971–100A	11/24/71	1,250 (2,756)	Cylinder with cone and six panels	1.6 (5.25)	4.2 (13.78)	First in a series of improved communications satellites	516 (320)	39,553 (24,523)	712	65.5
Intercosmos 5/U.S.S.R./B I/ 1971–104A	12/2/71	1,070 (2,359)	Ellipsoid	1.2 (3.94)	1.8 (5.91)	International scientific satellite	197 (122)	1,055 (654)	97.2	48.4
Ariel 4/U.K./Scout/ 1971–109A	12/11/71	99.8 (220)	Cylinder with conical end and four panels	0.76 (2.49)	0.91 (2.99)	Scientific satellite	476 (295)	591 (366)	95.2	83.0
Molniya 1/U.S.S.R./A IIe/ 1971–115A	12/19/71	1,000 (2,205)	Cylinder with conical end and six panels	1.6 (5.25)	3.4 (11.15)	Communications satellite	496 (308)	38,928 (24,135)	92.1	65.4
Intelsat 4 (F 3)/U.S./Atlas Centaur/1971–116A	12/20/71	705.7 (1,555.8)	Cylinder	2.41 (7.9)	2.83 (9.3)	Communications satellite	35,750 (22,165)	35,827 (22,213)	1,436.2	0.4
Aureole 1/France-U.S.S.R./‡ 1971–119A	12/27/71	300 (661)	Cylinder	1.5 (4.92)	2 (6.56)	International scientific satellite	400 (248)	2,477 (1,536)	114.6	74.0
Meteor 10/U.S.S.R./A I/ 1971–120A	12/29/71	‡	Cylinder with two panels	1.5 (4.92)	5 (16.4)	Weather satellite	876 (543)	890 (552)	102.7	81.3
Big Bird/U.S./Titan IIIc/ 1972–02A	1/20/72 2/29/72	11,340 (25,000)	Cylinder with conical end	3.63 (11.9)	15.33 (50.3)	Military photoreconnaissance satellite	470 (291)	550 (341)	89.4	97.0
Intelsat 4 (F 4)/U.S./ Atlas Centaur/1972–03A	1/23/72	705.7 (1,555.8)	Cylinder	2.41 (7.9)	2.83 (9.3)	Communications satellite	35,625 (22,088)	35,787 (22,188)	1,432	0.7
Heos 2/ESRO/Delta/ 1972–05A	1/31/72	116.6 (257.1)	Cylinder	2.55 (8.37)	1.3 (4.27)	Scientific satellite	439 (272)	248,160 (153,859)	7,835.4	90.2
Luna 20/U.S.S.R./Proton/ 1972–07A	2/14/72 2/25/72	1,360 (2,998)	Two-stage landing vehicle	4.3 (14.11)	4.3 (14.11)	Soft-landing lunar probe	Landed on moon February 21 and returned to earth February 25			
IMEWS 3/U.S./Titan IIIc/ 1972–010A	3/1/72	816 (1,800)	Cylinder with conical end and four panels	2.44 (8)	6.1 (20)	Missile early warning satellite	35,456 (21,983)	35,648 (22,102)	1,434	0.87
Pioneer 10/U.S./Atlas Centaur/1972–012A	3/2/72	258 (569)	Hexagon with circular dish	1.22 (4)	2.9 (9.5)	Bypass probe to Jupiter	Solar system escape trajectory			
TD-1A/ESRO/Delta/ 1972–014A	3/12/72	468 (1,032)	Rectangular box with two panels	1 (3.28)	2 (6.56)	International scientific satellite	527 (327)	545 (338)	95.3	97.5
Samos/U.S./Titan IIIc/ 1972–016A	3/17/72	‡	Cylinder with conical end	1.52 (5)	7.92 (26)	Military photoreconnaissance satellite	141 (87)	396 (246)	89.9	110.9
Venera 8/U.S.S.R./Proton/ 1972–021A	3/27/72	1,178 (2,597)	Cylindrical body with conical end and spherical soft lander	1.2 (3.94)	3 (9.84)	Scientific probe to Venus	Heliocentric orbit			
Meteor 11/U.S.S.R./A I/ 1972–022A	3/30/72	‡	Cylinder and two panels	1.5 (4.92)	5 (16.4)	Weather satellite	867 (538)	890 (552)	102.5	81.2
Molniya 1/U.S.S.R./A IIe/ 1972–025A	4/4/72	1,000 (2,205)	Cylinder with conical end and six panels	1.6 (5.25)	3.4 (11.15)	Communications satellite	442 (274)	39,911 (24,745)	717.7	65.5
SRET 1/France/A IIe/ 1972–025B	4/4/72	15 (33)	Octagon	0.6 (1.97)	‡	Scientific and technological satellite launched piggyback with Molniya 1	458 (284)	39,250 (24,335)	704.6	65.5
Intercosmos 6/U.S.S.R./B I/ 1972–027A	4/7/72 4/11/72	1,070 (2,359)	Ellipsoid	1.2 (3.94)	1.8 (5.91)	International scientific satellite	197 (122)	334 (207)	90.0	51.8
Prognoz 1/U.S.S.R./‡/ 1972–029A	4/14/72	1,297 (2,859)	‡	1.8 (5.91)	‡	International scientific probe	1,005 (623)	199,667 (123,794)	5,782.1	65.0
Apollo 16/U.S./Saturn V/ 1972–031A	4/16/72 4/27/72	46,782 (103,136)	Cylinder with conical end	3 (9.84)	9 (29.5)	Fifth successful lunar landing mission in the Apollo program	Landed on moon April 20			
Molniya 2/U.S.S.R./A IIe/ 1972–037A	5/19/72	1,238 (2,729)	Cylinder with conical end and six panels	1.4 (4.59)	5 (16.4)	Communications satellite	433 (268)	39,295 (24,363)	4,005	65.3
Intelsat 4(F 5)/U.S./Atlas Centaur/1972–41A	6/13/72	705.7 (1,555.8)	Cylinder	2.41 (7.9)	2.83 (9.3)	Communications satellite	35,777 (22,182)	35,967 (22,300)	1,440.4	0.4
Cosmos 496/U.S.S.R./‡/ 1972–045A	6/26/72 7/2/72	6,500 (14,330)	Two spheres joined to a cylinder	2.2 (7.22)	7.5 (24.61)	Unmanned test of Soyuz spacecraft	176 (109)	253 (157)	88.8	51.6
Prognoz 2/U.S.S.R./‡/ 1972–046A	6/29/72	1,297 (2,859)	‡	1.8 (5.91)	‡	International scientific probe	550 (341)	200,000 (124,000)	5,820	65.0
Intercosmos 7/U.S.S.R./B I/ 1972–047A	6/30/72	1,070 (2,359)	Ellipsoid	1.2 (3.94)	1.8 (5.91)	International scientific satellite	260 (161)	550 (341)	92.7	48.4
Meteor 12/U.S.S.R./A I/ 1972–049A	6/30/72	‡	Cylinder with two panels	1.5 (4.92)	5 (16.4)	Weather satellite	897 (556)	929 (576)	81.2	81.2
Big Bird/U.S./Titan IIIc/ 1972–052A	7/7/72	11,340 (25,000)	Cylinder and cone	3.63 (11.9)	15.33 (50.3)	Military reconnaissance satellite	173 (107)	257 (159)	88.7	96.8
ERTS-1/U.S./Delta/ 1972–058A	7/23/72	891 (1,965)	Annular body with two solar panels	1.52 (5)	3.32 (10.9)	First earth resources technology satellite	898 (557)	916 (568)	103	99.1
Explorer 46/U.S./Scout/ 1972–061A	8/13/72	175 (386)	Cylinder	7 (23)	3.2 (10.5)	Meteoroid technology satellite	509 (316)	813 (504)	98	37.3
Denpa/Japan/Mu-4S/ 1972–064A	8/19/72	82.5 (181.9)	Sphere	0.69 (2.26)	‡	Radio exploration satellite	239 (148)	6,302 (3,907)	157.2	31
Copernicus (OAO-C)/U.S./Atlas Centaur/1972–065A	8/21/72	2,223 (4,900)	Octagon	1.07 (3.5)	3.05 (10)	Orbiting astronomical observatory	735 (456)	744 (461)	99.6	35
Transit/U.S./Scout/ 1972–069A	9/2/72	94 (207)	Dumbbell	‡	7.32 (24)	Navigation satellite of U.S. Navy	743 (461)	838 (520)	100.6	90.1
Explorer 47/U.S./Delta/ 1972–073A	9/21/72	390 (860)	16-sided tube	1.34 (4.4)	1.58 (5.2)	Interplanetary monitoring platform	201,600 (124,992)	235,639 (146,096)	17,702	17.2

*All dates are in universal time (UT).
†English units in parentheses: weight in pounds, dimensions in feet, apogee and perigee in statute miles.
‡Not available.

(MITCHELL R. SHARPE)

a contract to study the problems of developing a similar satellite-destroying capability for the U.S.

Also, as 1971 ended, ESRO agreed to cooperate with the U.S. in the development of an aeronautical satellite on a 50–50 funding basis. Associated with the member nations of ESRO were Australia, Japan, and Canada. The scheme called for satellites to be placed over the Atlantic and Pacific oceans to aid in the communications and navigation of transoceanic aircraft.

Explorer 45, Small Scientific Satellite 1, was launched into an equatorial orbit on November 15 from the San Marcos platform off the coast of Kenya. The NASA satellite carried the first onboard computer that could be reprogrammed from the ground. Made of riveted rather than machined aluminum sections, the satellite was much cheaper than its predecessors. Explorer 45 was instrumented to study the earth's magnetosphere and the interaction of the solar wind with it.

The U.S. began its year in space with the successful launching of an Air Force Big Bird reconnaissance satellite from the Western Test Range on January 20. The 25,000-lb. photographic satellite was placed into a near-polar orbit by a Titan IIIC. NASA launched Intelsat 4 (F 4) from Kennedy Space Center on January 23. The Atlas Centaur placed the satellite into a synchronous orbit over the Pacific Ocean. Its first task was to transmit pictures of the visit of President Nixon to China in May. The final Intelsat 4 was boosted into orbit over the Indian Ocean on June 13.

The largest satellite yet produced by ESRO was launched on March 12 from the U.S. Western Test Range. Weighing 1,040 lb., TD-1A carried seven scientific experiments provided by various European universities. They were designed to measure the forms of energy radiating from stars and galaxies.

March 16 marked the tenth anniversary of the Soviet Union's Cosmos series of satellites. Cosmos 478, launched the day before the anniversary, celebrated the occasion. Approximately 70% of the satellites in the series have been military in nature. On March 30, the U.S.S.R. successfully launched Meteor 11 weather satellite into a near-circular orbit at an altitude of nearly 560 mi., considerably higher than previous satellites in this series.

Another Big Bird multipurpose reconnaissance satellite was launched by the U.S. Air Force on July 7 from Vandenberg Air Force Base. It had the capability of close-look and search-and-find missions. The U.S.S.R., in turn, launched eight military satellites with the same booster on July 20. Labeled Cosmos 504–511, they were either communications or navigation satellites for the Soviet armed forces.

The world's first earth resources satellite was orbited on July 23 when NASA launched ERTS-1. The 1,965-lb. satellite was boosted from the Western Test Range by a new model of the Delta. Data from the sensors of ERTS-1 were to be sent to 300 scientists in 37 countries. These scientists were seeking information in seven different areas: meteorology, marine resources, water resources, agriculture and forestry resources, environment, land use, and mineral and land resources. The data would be provided in the form of photographs made in various wavelengths by seven special sensors in the satellite. Each photograph covered an area 115 mi. square (for a total included area of 13,000 sq.mi.). ERTS-1 was able to transmit 1,316 such pictures per day.

The first pictures from ERTS-1 arrived at Goddard Space Flight Center on July 25. They were of the San Francisco Bay area. The satellite could map the entire nation with only 500 pictures. A high-altitude airplane would require 500,000 such pictures to do the same job.

On August 7 OSO-7 (Orbiting Solar Observatory) reported a violent solar eruption that may have been the greatest ever recorded. In one hour the energy released from the sun was equal to the entire U.S. electric power consumption for 100 million years at the present rate of consumption.

The heaviest and most complex scientific satellite ever launched by the U.S. was orbited from Cape Kennedy on August 21. OAO-C (Orbiting Astronomical Observatory) weighed 4,900 lb. Its main optical device was a 32-in.-diameter mirror in a 10-ft.-long cylinder. The primary objectives of the satellite were to study the interstellar absorption of hydrogen, oxygen, carbon, and silicon and to investigate the ultraviolet radiation from young, hot stars. The satellite was named "Copernicus" in honour of the famous Polish astronomer of the 16th century.

Interplanetary Probes. Mariner 9, which had entered Martian orbit on Nov. 13, 1971, continued to send back a wealth of information about the planet in 1972. Once the dust storm abated in December 1971, extremely high-resolution pictures of the topography of the planet were transmitted by the probe's two cameras. Among the features of interest to geophysical scientists were a rille or chasm in the Tithonius Lacus region that was approximately 2,500 mi. long, 75 mi. wide, and 4 mi. deep (four times deeper than Grand Canyon). It cannot be seen by telescopes on earth because of the angle of the sun. One of the most dramatic pictures was a view of Nix Olympica, a volcanic caldera about 310 mi. in diameter. Pictures of the south pole puzzled geologists because they showed pits and hollows that suggested glaciation or wearing away by ice.

So different were the pictures of Mariner 9 from those of Mariners 6 and 7 that scientists completely revised their concept of Mars. Harold Masursky of the U.S. Geological Survey said, "Our photographs show something very, very different indeed. By seeing much more of the planet, we can see great volcanic piles and because of the crispness of the edges and the lack of craters, we think these are geologically young. The only thing we can keep as a primitive body are the two Martian satellites. Those do look like unevolved bodies, but Mars itself turned out to be even more dynamic than we hoped." Mariner 9 took close-up pictures of Phobos and Deimos, the planet's two satellites, in November 1971.

Other instruments in Mariner 9 sent back equally important data. From an analysis of S-band radio waves defracted by the planetary atmosphere, scientists computed the atmospheric pressure on the planet's surface to range between 3 millibars at the heights and 8.3 millibars at the lowest points. The average surface pressure was about 5.5 millibars (compared with 1,013 millibars at the surface of the earth). Studies in the variation of the acceleration of the probe in its orbit also led scientists to theorize that Mars has a bulge of approximately 0.6 to 1.2 mi. at two places on the equator, one at 110° W and the other at 70° E. The probe's infrared spectrometer indicated that there is about one-thousandth the amount of water vapour in the atmosphere above the Martian south pole as there is in the same region of earth.

The surface temperatures reported by Mariner 9

COURTESY, NASA

Scuba divers assist astronauts selected for the Skylab space program during a test in the neutral buoyancy simulator at Marshall Space Flight Center, Ala. Results from the three manned Skylab missions should provide information on physiological responses to long-term manned space flight.

were generally cooler than those reported by earlier probes. The daytime high at midafternoon in the equatorial regions was about −81° F while temperatures in the polar regions dipped as low as −189° F.

After examining Mariner 9 photographs of the Martian surface, scientists of the Jet Propulsion Laboratory began looking for likely landing sites for the Viking probe, to be soft-landed on Mars in 1975. They also had enough pictures of the planet to produce a map of its surface showing details as small as 3,000 ft. in diameter.

Little information appeared in the Western press on the results of the two Soviet probes of Mars. Mars 2 entered an orbit of the planet on Nov. 27, 1971. It detached a pod which crashed onto the planet's surface, apparently an unsuccessful attempt to soft-land an instrument package. Mars 3 arrived at the planet on Dec. 2, 1971. It also ejected an instrument package that succeeded in reaching the surface. However, it transmitted data for only 20 seconds after touching down.

Among the data later released by the Soviets were: (1) The electron temperature in the vicinity of Mars is several times less than that near earth. (2) Surface temperatures on the planet varied from 55° F at 2 P.M. sun time at a point near 11° S latitude to −135° F at 7 P.M. near a point at 19° N latitude. (3) Material on the surface appears to be dry sand or dust. The dark areas of the planet are also about 10° F warmer than the lighter areas. (4) The northern polar cap exists all year round, unlike the southern cap. (5) Average atmospheric pressure is between 5.5 and 6 millibars, but it varies greatly with altitude. (6) Five microns of precipitated water were reported during the entire experiment, about 1/10 of what had been predicted. Mars 3 ended its mission after only 20 orbits of the planet, while Mars 2 made 362 orbits before its mission was completed.

The Soviet Union also launched a probe to Venus on March 27. Venera 8, weighing 2,596 lb., lifted off from Tyuratam and headed for a four-month voyage to the planet. It arrived on July 22 and soft-landed an instrument package that was "quick frozen" to help it survive the heating by the planet's atmosphere. The package transmitted data for 50 minutes before being destroyed by the combined heat and pressure of the Venusian environment. It reported a daytime temperature of 789° F and an atmospheric pressure of 93 atm. It also reported that sunlight does penetrate the thick atmosphere, which consists of 97% carbon dioxide, 2% nitrogen, and the remainder a mixture of oxygen, water vapour, and ammonia. The rocks at that part of the surface of the planet appeared to be similar to granite.

The first probe to Jupiter, Pioneer 10, was launched on March 2 from Kennedy Space Center. Boosted by a three-stage Atlas Centaur, the spacecraft attained the highest velocity ever reached by a probe, 32,000 mph (with respect to earth). The 569-lb. craft contained 11 scientific experiments to provide new knowledge about Jupiter, the solar system, and the Milky Way. It was the first probe to have electric power furnished by a radioisotopic thermoelectric generator, *i.e.,* an atomic battery. At the distance it would be traveling, solar cells could not provide power.

The 620 million-mi. voyage to Jupiter would take Pioneer 10 through the potentially hazardous belt of asteroids that orbit the sun between Mars and Jupiter. On May 25 Pioneer 10 crossed the orbit of Mars and entered a region of space never before penetrated by a man-made object. By June the probe reported that it had been hit by 41 very small meteoroids. On July 16 it entered the 175 million-mi.-wide asteroid belt, which would require seven months to cross. The probe was scheduled to swing past Jupiter in December 1973.

The moon received an unmanned probe on February 21. Luna 20, launched by the U.S.S.R. from Tyuratam on February 14, soft-landed in the highland region of the Sea of Fertility and the Sea of Crises about 72 mi. north of the landing site of Luna 16. The probe had an improved drill that was remotely controlled by engineers in the Soviet Union by means of television. The drilling required 30 minutes and was believed to have reached a depth of 13 in. At a depth of 5.7 in., the drill head struck extremely hard material, and it took almost seven minutes to remove the core from the hole. The return vehicle lifted off the moon on February 23 with 3.5 oz. of lunar soil and landed in Kazakhstan, U.S.S.R., on February 25.

On April 14 the U.S.S.R. launched a solar probe into earth orbit. Prognoz 1 was launched from Tyuratam into a highly elliptical orbit with a perigee of 623 mi. and an apogee of 123,793 mi. It weighed 2,860 lb. and was instrumented to measure solar corpuscular, gamma, and X radiation as well as the interaction of solar plasma streams with the earth's magnetosphere. Prognoz 2 was launched on June 29. It had an elliptical orbit and instrumentation similar to Prognoz 1. In addition, it had a special instrument developed by French scientists to measure the solar wind.

Space Shuttle and Other Launch Vehicles. In mid-May four U.S. aerospace consortia submitted proposals to NASA for the space shuttle orbiter. North American Rockwell, which had built the Apollo command and service modules as well as the second stage of the Saturn V booster, won the contract in July with a low bid of $2.6 billion. The company would be responsible for the design, development, and production of the shuttle orbiting vehicle and for integration of all elements of the shuttle vehicle. The company's Rocketdyne division had won the contract for the shuttle main engine in 1971.

In April, NASA officially announced that the launching sites for the space shuttle would be Kennedy Space Center and Vandenberg Air Force Base. The former site would be utilized by NASA for its missions, while the latter one would be used by the U.S. Air Force for its military satellites.

Two Soviet scientists, writing in *Aviatsiya i Kosmonavtiki,* stated that the U.S.S.R. was also at work on a space shuttle. Since the Soviet Union launches three times as many spacecraft annually as does the U.S., a Soviet space shuttle would certainly be an economical undertaking for that country.

Despite their poor showing on Dec. 5, 1971, when an explosion in the second stage of the Diamant B booster cost France its Polaire satellite, the French were making plans for a third-generation Diamant booster. It was to consist of the first and second stages of the Diamant B with a new stage to be inserted between them. The new stage would be an adaptation of the second stage of France's MSBS (underwater-launched intermediate-range missile). The new Diamant was expected to be capable of placing a 440-lb. satellite into a circular orbit at an altitude of 186 mi.

In India development continued on that country's SLV-3 launch vehicle. The four-stage booster was to be 69 ft. long and weigh 40,000 lb. The first launch was scheduled for 1974, and the rocket was expected to be able to place a 66-lb. satellite into a circular orbit 250 mi. above the earth.

With the sixth consecutive failure in the Europa launch vehicle program on Nov. 5, 1971, ELDO began openly doubting the future of Europa III. A Europa II vehicle had exploded in flight after a launch from Kourou, French Guiana. An immediate consequence was postponement of the flight scheduled for April 1972 so that an exhaustive investigation could be completed. (MITCHELL R. SHARPE)

See also Astronomy; Defense; Industrial Review; Meteorology; Telecommunications; Television and Radio.

ENCYCLOPÆDIA BRITANNICA FILMS. *Controversy over the Moon* (1971); *Man Looks at the Moon* (1971); *Space Exploration: A Team Effort* (1972).

Astronomy

Instruments and Techniques. Several large new optical telescopes were close to completion at the end of 1972. These included the Soviet Union's giant 6-m. reflector in the Caucasus Mountains, in southern U.S.S.R. near its border with Iran, which was to be the largest optical telescope in the world. Several telescopes of about 3.8-m. aperture were expected to be operating in 1973 or 1974 from sites in North America (Kitt Peak, Arizona), Chile, and Australia, and two large Schmidt telescopes (0.9 m. and 1.2 m.) were soon to begin southern sky surveys from Australia and Chile.

Television equipment was in use by 1972 in many observatories. A group from the Princeton and Hale observatories used an integrating television camera (SEC Vidicon) at the Coudé spectrograph of the 200-in. Hale telescope to observe the spectrum of the quasi-stellar object PHL 957; this object has a visual magnitude of 16.6, and the astronomers were able to record its spectrum in a six-hour exposure with a resolution of 0.75 Å (1 Å = 10^{-7} mm.). The spectrum showed 31 absorption lines between 4270 and 4495 Å, with at least four different redshifts and possibly ten.

The measurement of stellar diameters is a difficult but important task for astrophysics. It has been done by classical double-aperture interferometry (the Michelson interferometer), lunar occultations, and the intensity interferometer of Hanbury Brown and Twiss. Recently, D. Gezari and associates (State University of New York, Stony Brook) devised a new technique, speckle interferometry. This method uses the full aperture of a single large telescope; high-resolution information is extracted from the "speckle" detail observed in stellar images at large telescopes. The speckle pattern is an interference effect in the image produced by random phase and amplitude perturbations impressed upon the incident wave front by atmospheric turbulence and telescope aberrations. Mathematical analysis of this pattern allows the measurement of stellar diameters down to about 0.01 arc-seconds at the 200-in. telescope for objects as faint as the 9th magnitude.

Origin of the Elements. The origin of the chemical elements in the universe remained a major problem. While the ratio of helium to hydrogen is believed to be approximately the same in most kinds of unevolved stars in the Milky Way galaxy, there is a tremendous range among the stars in the ratio of heavy elements to hydrogen. This ratio is usually characterized by the relative abundance of iron to hydrogen, Fe/H. For some of the oldest stars in the galaxy, Fe/H is approximately 10^{-2} of the solar value. Most stars of all ages have Fe/H near the solar value, but some appear to have Fe/H several times larger; these are the super-metal-rich (SMR) stars. It was not yet known whether the galaxy contained

Eclipses, 1973

Jan. 4	Sun, annular (begins 7:45 A.M.*), visible Pacific O., S. America, E. Africa, Atlantic O.
Jan. 18	Moon, penumbral (begins 2:17 P.M.*), visible Greenland, E. Atlantic O., Europe, Africa, Asia, Indian O., Australia, Arctic regions
June 15	Moon, penumbral (begins 2:05 P.M.*), visible S.E. Europe, Africa, S. Atlantic O., Antarctica, Indian O., Asia, Australia
June 30	Sun, total (begins 4:01 A.M.*), visible S. America, Africa, S. Europe, Indian O.
July 15	Moon, penumbral (begins 5:44 A.M.*), visible E. Asia, Australia, Pacific O., N. & S. America, Antarctica
Dec. 9	Moon, partial (begins 6:37 P.M.*), visible W. Asia, Europe, Africa, N. & S. America, Atlantic O.
Dec. 24	Sun, annular (begins 7:02 A.M.*), visible N. & S. America, N.W. Africa, S.W. Europe, Atlantic O.

Equinoxes and Solstices, 1973

March 20	Vernal equinox, 1:13 P.M.*
June 21	Summer solstice, 8:01 A.M.*
Sept. 22	Autumnal equinox, 11:21 P.M.*
Dec. 21	Winter solstice, 7:08 P.M.*

Earth Perihelion and Aphelion, 1973

Jan. 2	Perihelion, 91,321,000 mi. from the sun
July 4	Aphelion, 94,479,000 mi. from the sun

*Eastern Standard Time.

only H and He when it formed and then produced its own heavy elements very early in its lifetime, or whether it inherited some heavy elements from the intergalactic medium out of which it came. J. Silk and R. Siluk (University of California, Berkeley) argued that the intergalactic medium was enriched by quasi-stellar sources ejecting enriched matter into the medium. This matter, they believed, is recycled through successive generations of quasi-stellar sources, progressively enriched to an abundance about 10^{-2} of the solar value, and then accreted by the protogalaxy. The alternative, that the galaxy produced its own heavy elements, would require that the first generation of stars were all massive and evolved rapidly; otherwise, there should be at this time some low-mass stars from this generation, with extremely low abundances (less than 10^{-2} of the solar value).

The real nature of the SMR stars is controversial: are they really overabundant in heavy elements, or is it some feature of their atmospheres that makes the abundances appear high? D. Branch and R. Bell (Hale Observatories and University of Maryland) analyzed high-dispersion spectra of the SMR dwarf star HR 72 and found Fe/H to be about 2.5 times the solar value. However, they also found that 14 other elements are overabundant by approximately the same factor. This suggests that the overabundance may be caused by a reduction in the hydrogen and an increase in the helium content of this star's atmosphere, rather than by an increase in the number of heavy element atoms per gram of stellar matter.

Pulsating Stars. Classical Cepheids are young, massive, pulsating variable stars. Apart from their intrinsic interest as variable stars, they are vitally important as indicators of distance for nearby galaxies; because Cepheids appear to have a tight relation between their periods, colours, and intrinsic luminosities, their distances can be accurately estimated from their observed periods, colours, and *apparent* luminosities. The theory for the pulsation of these variables has become highly developed, but there are some important inconsistencies between their observed properties and the theory.

The mass of a normal Cepheid can be estimated in two ways. (1) An *evolutionary* mass is determined by comparing its estimated intrinsic brightness with the results of stellar evolution theory. (2) Its estimated brightness and surface temperature combined with the results of the pulsation theory lead to a *pulsation* mass. The pulsation masses for galactic Cepheids have come out as much as 40% smaller than the evolutionary masses. The reason for this discrepancy is a serious problem: is it in the observations or the theory? I. Iben and R. Tuggle (Massachusetts Institute of Technology) argued that the problem lies in the observations; either the estimated absolute brightnesses are too dim by about 30% or the temperatures are too high by about 6%. If the former is right, then the whole distance scale for the universe would be stretched by about 15%. K. Fricke and associates (Cambridge, Eng.) pointed out that the theories could be correct, but that uncertainties in the physical and empirical data used to evaluate the evolutionary and pulsation masses may be large enough to account for the discrepancy.

Another way of estimating Cepheid masses is derived from the few Cepheids that appear to pulsate in the fundamental (pulsating as a whole) and first overtone simultaneously. These are called *beat* Cepheids; the ratio of the two periods, together with an observationally determined radius, leads to another mass estimate. E. Schmidt (Steward Observatory) studied the beat Cepheid TU Cas. He found that the beat mass and evolutionary mass agreed well, but the pulsation mass was again lower. This means that either the interpretation of the beat phenomenon in terms of the period ratio is incorrect, or that the model calculations of periods and period ratios are in error. At the year's end the problem remained unresolved.

Clusters of Galaxies. It should be possible to estimate the mass for a cluster of galaxies from its radius and the random velocity of galaxies within it. When this procedure is followed, the resulting mass is many times greater than the total mass of the cluster's constituent galaxies. For example, H. Rood and associates (Wesleyan University, Middletown, Conn.) showed that the random velocity for 102 members of the rich Coma cluster is about 900 km/sec.; to make this cluster gravitationally bound would then require a "missing mass" about seven times the mass of the known cluster members. The alternative is that the cluster is disintegrating very rapidly, and this seems most unlikely. The nature of the missing mass, if it exists at all, is an old problem. Much has been written about it recently, but the answer remained unclear.

There is almost certainly some diffuse matter between the galaxies in the Coma cluster; an extended diffuse region (size about 45 arc-minutes) was detected in the centre of the cluster, at radio, optical, and X-ray wavelengths. However, G. Welch and G. Sastry (Wesleyan University) argued that the mass of matter needed to produce this radiation is far less than the missing mass needed to bind the cluster. On the other hand, H. Gursky and associates (American Science and Engineering) reported that the Uhuru satellite observed X-ray emissions from many rich clusters of galaxies. A. Solinger and W. Tucker (American Science and Engineering) pointed out that this X-ray luminosity correlates strongly with the random velocity of a cluster in the sense that the most luminous clusters have the largest velocity spread. They inferred from this that the clusters are, or were once, gravitationally bound.

More evidence for intergalactic matter in clusters came from an analysis of the properties of 34 simple double radio sources by D. de Young (National Radio Astronomy Observatory, Green Bank, W.Va.). He showed that the mean separation of the two components for those sources not in clusters of galaxies is slightly more than twice the mean separation for sources in clusters, and the mean size-to-separation ratio for sources outside clusters is about 0.6 of the mean of those inside. This difference may be due to the presence of a significant amount of intergalactic gas in clusters of galaxies.

Many astronomers believed that the missing matter may be hot (10^5–10^6 °K) ionized gas. This should emit Lyman-α recombination-line radiation. R. Henry (Naval Research Laboratory, Washington, D.C.) searched for this radiation from the Coma cluster with a rocket-borne detector. He was able to place a low upper limit on the Lyman-α flux, which makes it unlikely that the binding mass is hot ionized gas.

W. Tifft (Steward Observatory) pointed out a remarkable feature of the redshift-magnitude diagram for 70 galaxies in the core of the Coma cluster. The galaxies appear to group about a series of parallel bands, sloping fainter with increasing redshift; the galaxies with higher redshifts are predominantly nonellipticals. Tifft ascribed the presence of the bands to some intrinsic effect which is not understood. The width of the individual bands represents the true random velocity of galaxies in this cluster, which then becomes no more than 220 km/sec. (compared with the usual estimate of about 900 km/sec.). At this velocity the cluster is gravitationally bound, and so there is no missing mass problem. It will be interesting to see whether other apparently unstable clusters show this band structure in their redshift-magnitude diagrams; there was already some evidence that the Virgo cluster may do so.

Observational Cosmology. To compare certain features of cosmological models with observational data about the expanding universe, a homogeneous isotropic model (the Friedmann model) is often used. The parameters for this model are the Hubble constant H_0 (a measure of the present rate of expansion) and the deceleration parameter q_0 (a measure of the rate at which the expansion of the universe is slowing down). The present density of the universe is related to q_0 by $\rho_0 = \frac{3H_0^2 q_0}{4\pi G}$, where ρ_0 is the density and G the gravitational constant. For a closed universe, q_0 is greater than 0.5, while it lies between zero and 0.5 for an open universe. The most promising way of estimating q_0, and hence the nature of the universe, is from the redshift-magnitude diagram, which shows how the apparent velocity of distant galaxies increases for fainter galaxies; this depends on the value of q_0. For this experiment it is necessary to use a particular kind of galaxy, the brightest elliptical in a cluster, because these galaxies all appear to have similar intrinsic luminosities. However, the observed apparent magnitudes of these galaxies must be corrected by a known amount to take into account the fact that their energy curves are shifted to the red by their redshifts; for the most distant galaxies, a correction for evolution may also be necessary, because we see them as they were several billion years ago.

The effects of this evolution are an active area for study; for example, if galaxies were significantly brighter then than they are now, the value of q_0 estimated from the redshift-magnitude diagram would be greater than its true value. A. Sandage and J. Oke (Hale Observatories) and H. Spinrad (University of California, Berkeley) showed that the intrinsic colours and the detailed spectral energy distribution of elliptical galaxies change very little with increasing redshift; this may be evidence that evolutionary effects are negligible. However, B. Tinsley (University of Texas, Dallas) calculated that these galaxies evolve rapidly toward fainter luminosities, despite their negligible evolution in colour. As a result, she claimed that q_0 will be overestimated by about 0.5 from the redshift-magnitude diagram if evolution is ignored. This is obviously an important point, and at the year's end it remained unresolved.

Another problem concerned the validity of a homogeneous model. Since nearby galaxies are distributed inhomogeneously, does an estimate of H_0 (the expansion rate) from nearby galaxies have any relevance to the rate of expansion of the universe as a whole? Sandage and his associates at Hale Observatories studied the velocity fields of 30 local clusters of galaxies and showed that there appears to be no significant local perturbation to the redshift-magnitude diagram; therefore, the local value of H_0 is probably universally valid.

CENTRAL PRESS/PICTORIAL PARADE

Technicians are dwarfed by one of eight radio telescope dishes at Cavendish Laboratory, Cambridge, Eng., that were to be used to study quasars. The eight dishes combined total three miles in diameter. A computer is used to control the complex.

X-ray Astronomy. Major advances in X-ray astronomy included the discovery of extended sources associated with clusters of galaxies (already described above), sources associated with bright stars, and two pulsating sources in eclipsing binaries. H. Gursky (American Science and Engineering) showed that ten bright stars are within the area of positional uncertainty of known X-ray sources, although only two were expected on the basis of chance. This study was prompted by the identification of the source Cyg X-1 with a bright BO supergiant binary star. The X rays are believed to result from accretion of gas from the supergiant onto its nearby compact companion.

The binary nature of the pulsating source Cen X-3 was established by E. Schreier and associates (American Science and Engineering). This object pulsates with a period of 4.8 sec. and is eclipsed by its companion each 2.087 days. The orbital motion of the source produces an observed sinusoidal variation in the 4.8-sec. pulsation period due to the Doppler effect. Although no optical counterpart had been discovered by the end of the year, the nearby eclipsing binary LR Cen (period 2.095 days) provided an interesting red herring for many observers until it became clear that the two periods are significantly different and that the positions of the two objects are entirely too far apart.

The second binary is the source Her X-1. Its X-ray periods are 1.24 sec. (pulsation) and 1.700 days (orbital). Many investigators associated this source with the irregular blue variable HZ Her, detecting both periods at optical wavelengths. This makes HZ Her the second known optical pulsar.

Many astronomers suggested that neutron stars may be associated with X-ray sources. B. Margon and associates (University of California, Berkeley) observed the X-ray spectrum of the source GX 340 + 0. This spectrum is compatible only with a blackbody model. (A blackbody is a body or surface that completely absorbs all radiant energy falling upon it and, as a result, the intensity of the radiation it emits is a particular function of the wavelength.) Its blackbody temperature is about 10^7 °K and it follows from the X-ray flux that its radius is only about 8 km. This source may provide direct evidence for the existence of a neutron star. S. Sofia (University of South Florida) argued that the compact object producing the pulsed X-radiation in the binary system Cen X-3 is unlikely to be a white dwarf or a "black hole" and is probably a neutron star.

Radio Stars. C. Wade and R. Hjellming (National Radio Astronomy Observatory, Green Bank, W.Va.) detected 11-cm.-wavelength radio emissions from the M supergiant Antares in 1971. The radio flux is variable and is associated with the B3 companion rather than with the supergiant itself. The optical spectrum of the B star shows sharp emission lines of iron and silicon, but no hydrogen emission lines. This spectrum is probably related to particle streaming in the environs of the B star. Two other M supergiants, α Ori and π Aur, were detected at radio frequencies.

Wade and Hjellming also detected the eclipsing binaries β Per (Algol) and β Lyr at 2,695 and 8,085 MHz (11-cm. and 3.7-cm. wavelengths). Algol is strongly variable at 2,695 MHz, but there is no clear correlation between the radio variation and the optical light curve. Again, these objects demonstrate evidence of gas motions within the binary system. There are some interesting physical processes yet to be understood in even the best observed double stars.

Mars. Data returned by U.S. and Soviet space probes during the year disclosed that Mars is not the geologically dead planet astronomers had envisioned. Instead, a number of large volcanic mountains were discovered, indicating that the planet has or had a hot interior. The fact that all the volcanoes are on only one side of Mars led astronomers to speculate that the planet is just beginning to heat up.

Other surprising features included what appeared to be dried-up riverbeds and a giant canyon approximately 2,500 mi. long, 75 mi. wide, and 4 mi. deep. Some astronomers believed that the canyon might be the first evidence of continental drift on Mars.

(KENNETH C. FREEMAN)

See also Astronautics.

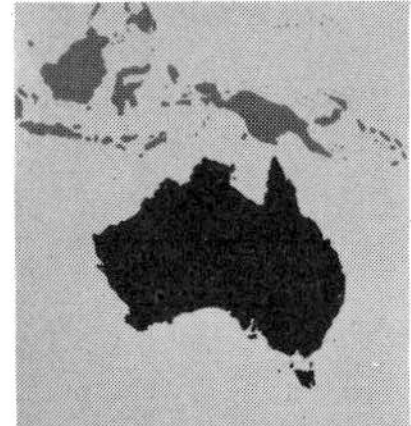

Australia

A federal parliamentary state and a member of the Commonwealth of Nations, Australia occupies the smallest continent and, with the island state of Tasmania, is the sixth largest country in the world. Area: 2,967,909 sq.mi. (7,686,849 sq.km.). Pop. (1972 est.): 12,943,803. Cap.: Canberra (pop., 1971, 141,575). Largest city: Sydney (metro. pop., 1971, 2,717,069). Language: English. Religion: (1966) Church of England 34%; Roman Catholic 26%; Methodist 10%; Presbyterian 9%. Queen, Elizabeth II; governor-general in 1972, Sir Paul Hasluck; prime ministers, William McMahon and, from December 5, Gough Whitlam.

Domestic Affairs. The Australian Labor Party took over the government of Australia for the first time in 23 years in the elections of Dec. 2, 1972. Led by Gough Whitlam (*see* BIOGRAPHY), the ALP obtained 67 seats in the 125-seat House of Representatives to defeat the Liberal-Country Party coalition, which had come to power in 1949. Whitlam assumed office on December 5, following McMahon's resignation.

The ALP victory followed by only a week that of the New Zealand Labour Party under Norman Kirk, and Whitlam was expected to cooperate closely with New Zealand. In foreign policy generally, he promised a "more independent" outlook. On his first day in office he announced the end of the military draft, the freeing of draft offenders, and the immediate opening of talks between the Australian and Chinese ambassadors in Paris aimed at establishing diplomatic relations.

Domestically, Whitlam had tried to focus public opinion on local government reform. He argued that the pattern of Australia's urban and regional development would be distorted unless the federal government provided relief. The ALP also presented an alternative health scheme. ALP proposals involved compulsory contributions of a percentage of annual income to a central fund and the abolition of the large number of private health insurance agencies.

McMahon's public support had dwindled since he unseated John Gorton as prime minister in 1971, but the improved stability of the LCP coalition had encouraged him to issue the call for elections. Within the LCP there had been only one major crisis during the year. The minister for social services, William Wentworth, believed that the government ought to set up a national pension program, while the treasurer, Billy Mackie Snedden, contended that it could not afford the cost of such a reform. Subsequently, Snedden announced that men and women over 65 years of age were to receive pensions without having to satisfy the government that they did not have the means to carry on without them. The pension was to

AUSTRALIA

Education. (1970) Primary, secondary, and vocational, pupils 2,768,233, teachers 120,041; teacher training, students 39,853; higher (at 15 universities only), students 116,778, teaching staff 7,371.

Finance. Monetary unit: Australian dollar, with (Sept. 18, 1972) a free rate of A$0.84 to U.S. $1 (A$2.06 = £1 sterling). Gold, SDRs, and foreign exchange, reserve bank: (June 1972) U.S. $4,396,000,000; (June 1971) U.S. $2,345,000,000. Commonwealth budget (1971–72 est.): revenue A$8,669,000,000; expenditure A$7,969,000,000. Gross national product: (1970–71) A$32,390,000,000; (1969–70) A$29,470,000,000. Money supply: (Feb. 1972) A$5,738,000,000; (Feb. 1971) A$5,419,000,000. Cost of living (1963 = 100): (Jan.–March 1972) 137; (Jan.–March 1971) 128.

Foreign Trade. (1971) Imports A$4,140,100,000; exports A$4,612,900,000. Import sources: U.S. 22%; U.K. 22%; Japan 16%; West Germany 7%. Export destinations: Japan 28%; U.S. 12%; U.K. 10%; New Zealand 5%. Main exports: wool 12%; machinery 11%; wheat 10%; meat 10%; iron ore 9%; nonferrous metals 6%; nonferrous metal ores 5%.

Transport and Communications. Roads (1970) 884,290 km. (including 141,400 km. main roads). Motor vehicles in use (1970): passenger 3,898,500; commercial (including buses) 971,500. Railways: (government; 1970) 40,330 km.; freight traffic (1970–71) 25,190,000,000 net ton-km. Air traffic (1970): 9,268,445,000 passenger-km.; freight 270,008,000 net ton-km. Shipping (1971): merchant vessels 100 gross tons and over 350; gross tonnage 1,105,236. Shipping traffic (1971): goods loaded 112,006,000 metric tons; unloaded 24,074,000 metric tons. Telephones (Jan. 1971) 3,913,000. Radio licenses (Dec. 1971) 2,684,000. Television licenses (Dec. 1971) 2,798,000.

Agriculture. Production (in 000; metric tons; 1971; 1970 in parentheses): wheat *c.* 8,380 (7,988); barley 2,722 (2,472); oats 1,305 (1,651); sorghum 1,266 (762); corn 226 (203); rice 295 (247); potatoes 747 (762); sugar, raw value (1971–72) 2,794, (1970–71) 2,524; apples (1970) 424, (1969) 422; oranges *c.* 275 (*c.* 295); wine *c.* 250 (288); wool, greasy 885 (886); milk *c.* 7,320 (7,790); butter 196 (214); beef and veal *c.* 1,100 (1,040); mutton and lamb *c.* 870 (808). Livestock (in 000; March 1971): sheep 179,137; cattle 24,372; pigs 2,580; horses *c.* 475; chickens *c.* 23,100.

Industry. Fuel and power (in 000; metric tons; 1971): coal 48,990; lignite 23,384; crude oil 14,409; natural gas (cu.m.) 2,222,000; manufactured gas (cu.m.) 4,704,000; electricity (kw-hr.) 59,681,000. Production (in 000; metric tons; 1971): iron ore (65% metal content) 62,010; bauxite 12,540; pig iron 6,127; crude steel 6,744; zinc 259; aluminum 224; copper 120; lead 163; tin 6.3; nickel concentrates (metal content; 1970) 29; sulfuric acid 1,600; cement 4,720; cotton yarn 29; wool yarn 28; gold (troy oz.; 1970) 620; silver (troy oz.) 28,000; passenger cars (including assembly; units) 391; commercial vehicles (including assembly; units) 78. Dwelling units completed (1971) 141,000.

be subject to income tax. At the same time the government appointed a committee to examine and report on financing the proposals.

The government's administration of aborigines was heavily criticized. Aborigines camped in tents outside Parliament House in Canberra to draw attention to their claims for land rights. In Perth an aboriginal "consulate" was set up outside the state Parliament to publicize the aboriginal housing problem, and a similar camp was set up in Adelaide. The federal government subsequently passed an ordinance under which the aborigines were forcibly removed from their camp in Canberra. Legal challenges of the ordinance were successful, the court finding that the ordinance had not been properly promulgated. The aborigines immediately re-camped outside Parliament House, but the government remedied the legislative defect and again ejected them. On the positive side, the government increased expenditure on aboriginal advancement to A$53 million in 1972–73, an increase of 70%.

The LCP gained prestige following its success in selling A$50 million worth of wheat to the Soviet Union and A$60 million worth to China. The ALP had contended that China was deliberately not buying Australian wheat because the Chinese government disapproved of Australia's hostile stand on diplomatic recognition. Another bright spot was the strength of the new season wool sales. There was a 100% clearance, with prices for merino fleece wool 10–20% above the closing rates of the previous season. By October wool prices had reached their highest level in 20 years. (*See* Industrial Review.)

Earlier in the year, Whitlam had faced embarrassment when a draft resister, Barry Johnston, was endorsed in March as the ALP candidate for the Victorian seat of Hotham. The ALP also failed in its campaign to give 18-year-olds a vote in the election. Whitlam received a further rebuff from the economics committee of the ALP when he suggested revaluation of the Australian dollar. The economics committee countered that it did not think that revaluation was appropriate in the current circumstances.

International terrorism affected Australia in 1972. Letter bombs were sent from overseas to the Israeli embassy in Australia, and Croatian extremists were held responsible for explosions in Sydney that destroyed two Yugoslav travel agencies.

A major development in the industrial relations field was the amalgamation of three left-wing labour unions into one organization. The Amalgamated Metalworkers' Union, with around 200,000 members, thus became the country's largest union.

Foreign Affairs. In 1972 Australia began to look more intently at the Indian Ocean following increasing Soviet interest in the area. A foreign affairs committee of the federal Parliament pointed out that the Indian Ocean was of great strategic significance to Australia; more than 60% of Australia's total exports and imports passed over it. In the course of an overseas visit Prime Minister McMahon discussed the security of the Indian Ocean with the U.S. administration and with British ministers. He reported mutual agreement that a careful watch ought to be continued in the area and confirmation that the U.S. and Britain would continue their respective naval presences.

The Australian combat role in South Vietnam had ended in December 1971. By March 1972 the Army and Air Force rear parties that had remained in Vietnam to complete withdrawal arrangements had finished their tasks and returned to Australia. The last commander of the Australian forces in Vietnam, Maj. Gen. Donald Beaumont Dunstan, terminated his appointment on March 6, 1972. On the same day, the Australian Army Assistance Group came into being to provide continuing training and advisory assistance to South Vietnam.

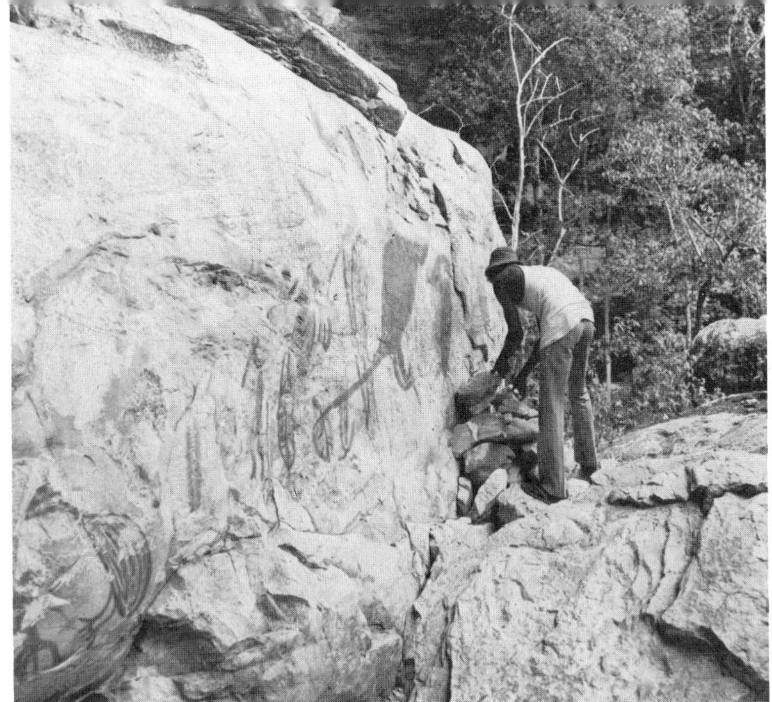

COURTESY, AUSTRALIAN NEWS AND INFORMATION BUREAU

This rock painting, found in the Northern Territory of Australia, marks the secret entrance to one of the most remarkable aboriginal sacred burial sites ever recorded. The only two male elders of the Amurrag tribe with knowledge of the area disclosed the site when they feared they would die without having claimed it as the rightful heritage of their people.

The Australian government opposed French nuclear tests made in the Pacific in June. In a note to the French government, the foreign minister reaffirmed Australia's interest, as a party to the partial nuclear test ban treaty of 1963, in seeing the treaty universally applied and supported.

President Suharto of Indonesia visited Australia in 1972. He had meetings with Foreign Office officials and with members of the Department of Trade and Industry, and spoke to businessmen in both Melbourne and Sydney. The visit was followed by an agreement signed on October 9 finally settling the boundary between Australia and Indonesia in the Timor and Arafura Sea area.

In 1972 Australia helped Papua New Guinea toward self-government. Elections were held between February and March for the third Papua New Guinea House of Assembly. The Australian government decided that this house, which was to run until 1976, would have responsibility for all initiatives on the pace and nature of constitutional development. It was designed to guide the country to internal self-government. On May 18 the minister for external territories, Andrew Peacock, announced that because of the elections Papua New Guinea was in a position in which ministers who were part of an elected executive would formulate and determine policy over a wide range of government activities. Gavera Rea, the new Papua New Guinea minister for labour, endorsed this when he told the UN Trusteeship Council that for the first time the elected government was in a position really to govern the country. A UN mission visited Papua New Guinea to observe the elections and found that the conduct of the administering authority had been comprehensive, thorough, and fair. The leader of the National Coalition, Michael Somare, indicated that the government had plans to intensify political education programs.

Prime Minister McMahon visited Indonesia, Singapore, and Malaysia in mid-1972, wishing to strengthen

Athletics:
see Baseball; Basketball; Bowling and Lawn Bowls; Boxing; Cricket; Cycling; Football; Golf; Hockey; Ice Skating; Rowing; Skiing; Sporting Record; Swimming; Tennis; Track and Field Sports

COURTESY, AUSTRALIAN NEWS AND INFORMATION BUREAU

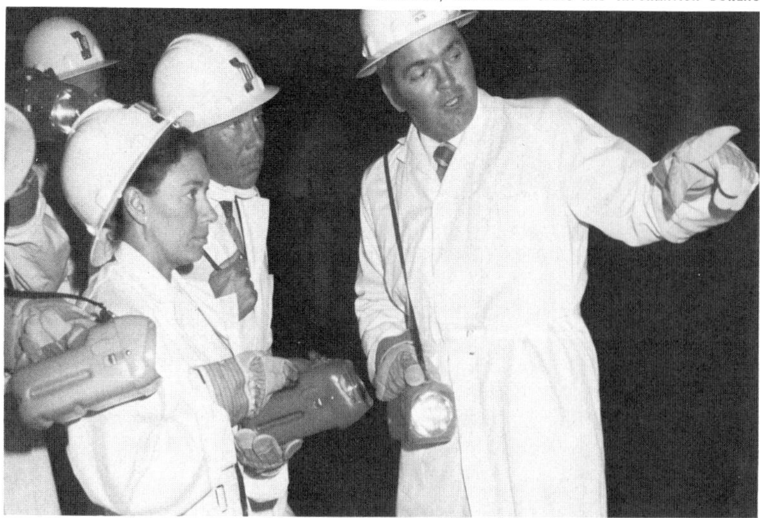

Princess Margaret and Lord Snowdon inspect a nickel mining operation at Kambalda in Western Australia during a visit there in October 1972.

the confidence and goodwill between Australia and those three neighbouring nations. McMahon believed that while U.S. Pres. Richard Nixon's visits to Moscow and Peking had reduced tension between the great powers, many countries in Australia's region were still under internal threat by subversive elements supported from outside, making the prospects for peace and stability in Southeast Asia uncertain.

The Economy. The government faced two major problems in the economic field, unemployment and the question of whether to revalue the Australian dollar. There was a strong case for upvaluing the dollar by at least a modest percentage. Interest rates that were relatively higher in Australia in 1971–72 than in other countries, and talk of currency revaluations, attracted an exceptionally high capital inflow. Overseas reserves rose by A$1,484,000,000. Throughout 1972 there was a flood of capital from abroad, rising overseas interest in taking over Australian companies, and a depressed stock market. Arguing against revaluation, the Bank of New South Wales said that appreciation would cut the incomes of farmers and reduce the profitability of mineral exports.

The government took action on foreign investment in Australia in September. The leader of the Country Party and deputy prime minister, John Douglas Anthony, stated that the only overseas investment wanted was that which developed Australian resources and set up new industries. The government had always had the view that capital inflow was important to develop Australian resources, but the stage had been reached when the volume that was coming in was so great that the LCP could afford to lay down conditions. The conditions were that restrictions would be made on portfolio investment from overseas, that take-overs would be opposed, and that Australians were themselves to be allowed to invest their funds overseas.

The government was not successful in its attempt to reduce unemployment. By September Australia had 2.14% of its work force unemployed, the highest unemployment level since October 1961. The growth rate of the economy in 1971–72 was 3%, the year having been a difficult one from both domestic and international standpoints. The 1972 budget aimed at stimulating the economy without any excessive growth of federal expenditure. Although spending had run ahead fast in the public sector, it was lacking in the private sector. Therefore, the government tried to provide a boost for private sector spending by reducing taxes as much as possible. The LCP had concluded that in recent years the burden of taxation had been inequitably distributed. The government reduced the rate of personal income tax by an average of 10%. In total, the income tax cuts were likely to cost A$432 million in 1972–73.

The largest single item of budget expenditure was payments to the states, including funds to finance state roads and housing programs. Grants to the states increased by A$395 million to A$3,449,000,000. The defense expenditure proposed for 1972 was A$1,323,000,000, A$106 million more than the previous year. Provision was made in the defense vote for the refitting of HMAS "Vendetta" and three destroyers were ordered, with ancillary helicopters, at a total cost of A$355 million. There was a forecast reduction of A$22 million on arms expenditure for the Army, and of A$7 million on maintenance, caused by the withdrawal of the Army component from Vietnam. The estimates provided for a total of A$220 million to be spent on official economic aid to less developed countries, including A$145 million allocated for Papua New Guinea.

To benefit children from low-income and other special-need families, the government introduced legislation to assist with the establishment and running of nonprofit child-care centres. It was envisaged that the centres would care for the children of working parents, giving priority of admission to children in special need, such as those from single-parent families and with sick and incapacitated parents.

There was one major industrial dispute in 1972, a strike that deprived Australians of gasoline. The strike was extremely disruptive, led to the closing down of many other industries, and had a drastic effect on the whole community. (A. R. G. GRIFFITHS)

Austria

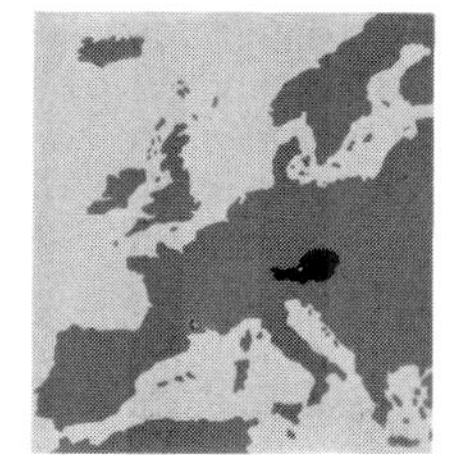

A republic of central Europe, Austria is bounded by West Germany, Czechoslovakia, Hungary, Yugoslavia, Italy, Switzerland, and Liechtenstein. Area: 32,375 sq.mi. (83,850 sq.km.). Pop. (1971): 7,456,403. Cap. and largest city: Vienna (pop., 1971, 1,614,841). Language: German. Religion (1969 est.): Roman Catholic 91%. President in 1972, Franz Jonas; chancellor, Bruno Kreisky.

Addressing the new Parliament in November 1971, following the October general election victory of the Socialist Party of Austria (SPÖ), Chancellor Kreisky had outlined his government's policy for 1971–75. Its central features were a comprehensive modernization program for state and society, the reorganization of the economy to make it "ready for Europe," and further development of the welfare state. The most important condition for the economy's being ready for Europe was achieved by a special relations agreement with the EEC, signed on July 22, 1972, after nearly ten years of discussion and delay. The complexity of Austria's relations with the EEC derived largely from the need to combine economic advantages with the preservation of Austrian neutrality and its other obligations under international law. The kernel of the agreement was a mutual concession of free trade in industrial products, to be phased in gradually over a period of years. The first tariff cut came into force on October 1. In addition, an "agricultural package" provided for certain mutual trade concessions in relation to agricultural produce.

To increase the competitiveness of the steel industry, it was decided in June to form a comprehensive concern employing 68,000 people. This was to consist of the amalgamated firms of United Austrian Iron and Steel Works (VÖEST) and Austrian Alpine Montan Steel Corp., with the refined-steel companies of Böhler Brothers and Schoeller-Bleckmann as subsidiaries.

Developments in the welfare state included introduction of a 42-hour week for all employees, flexible working hours in the public service, a marriage grant of 15,000 schillings, free schoolbooks, the extension of free travel for schoolchildren, and income tax reform. After heated debate and much initial opposition, legislation was passed introducing taxation of the salaries of members of Parliament and state officials. Between February and July there was also violent controversy in Parliament over the placing of the architectural commission for the UN City project. The opposition accused the chancellor of sharp practices, leading to a distinct chilliness in the internal political climate.

AUSTRIA

Education. (1969–70) Primary, pupils 886,990, teachers 39,355; secondary, pupils 157,975, teachers 9,932; vocational, pupils 216,109, teachers 11,936; teacher training, students 3,906, teachers 566; higher (including 6 universities), students 56,290, teaching staff 6,445.

Finance. Monetary unit: schilling, with (Sept. 18, 1972) a par value of 23.3 schillings to U.S. $1 (free rate of 56.42 schillings = £1 sterling). Gold, SDRs, and foreign exchange, central bank: (June 1972) U.S. $2,345,000,000; (June 1971) U.S. $1,759,000,000. Budget (1972 est.): revenue 112,863,000,000 schillings; expenditure 118,803,000,000 schillings. Gross national product: (1971) 415.7 billion schillings; (1970) 373.9 billion schillings. Money supply: (March 1972) 80,620,000,000 schillings; (March 1971) 70.8 billion schillings. Cost of living (1963 = 100): (June 1972) 142; (June 1971) 134.

Foreign Trade. (1971) Imports 104,476,000,000 schillings; exports 78,991,000,000 schillings. Import sources: EEC 56% (West Germany 41%, Italy 7%); Switzerland 7%; U.K. 7%. Export destinations: EEC 39% (West Germany 23%, Italy 9%); Switzerland 11%; U.K. 7%. Main exports: machinery 20%; iron and steel 14%; textile yarns and fabrics 13%; timber 7%; paper and board 6%; chemicals 5%. Tourism (1970): visitors 8,867,000; gross receipts U.S $999 million.

Transport and Communications. Roads (1970) 94,831 km. (including 478 km. expressways). Motor vehicles in use (1970): passenger 1,197,000; commercial 121,000. Railways: state (1970) 5,910 km.; private (1969) 636 km.; traffic (state only; 1971) 6,330,000,000 passenger-km., freight 9,600,000,000 net ton-km. Air traffic (1971): 416.2 million passenger-km.; freight 4,470,000 net ton-km. Telephones (Dec. 1970) 1,427,000. Radio licenses (Dec. 1970) 2,026,000. Television licenses (Dec. 1970) 1,426,000.

Agriculture. Production (in 000; metric tons; 1971; 1970 in parentheses): wheat 974 (810); barley 1,016 (913); rye 448 (363); oats 284 (272); corn 721 (612); potatoes 2,717 (2,704); sugar, raw value (1971–72) 272, (1970–71) 324; apples (1970) 309, (1969) 327; wine 181 (310); meat 454 (450); timber (cu.m.; 1970) 11,800, (1969) 12,000. Livestock (in 000; Dec. 1970): cattle 2,468; sheep 113; pigs 3,445; chickens 12,140.

Industry. Fuel and power (in 000; metric tons; 1971): lignite 3,770; crude oil 2,516; natural gas (cu.m.) 1,892,000; electricity (kw-hr.) 28,748,000 (71% hydroelectric in 1970); manufactured gas (Vienna only; cu.m.) 652,000. Production (in 000; metric tons; 1971): iron ore (30% metal content) 4,171; pig iron 2,848; crude steel 3,961; magnesite (1970) 1,609; aluminum 157; copper 21; lead 11; zinc 16; cement 5,493; paper (1970) 1,017; nitrogenous fertilizers (N content; 1970–71) 219; cotton yarn 21; woven cotton fabric 18; wool yarn 12; rayon fibres (1970) 79.

The sixth session of SALT took place in Vienna from November 1971 to February 1972. In November 1971 President Jonas made a state visit to Italy, the first republican head of state of Austria to do so. This marked the end of the long dispute over the South Tirol, an area of Italy largely populated by Italian citizens of Austrian descent, which had been granted autonomy under a 1970 agreement. U.S. Pres. Richard Nixon's stopover in Salzburg on his way to Moscow in May 1972 was the occasion of clashes between police and demonstrators. As a result of incidents on the Czechoslovak border, where a Czechoslovak exile was allegedly shot and abducted from Austrian territory, Austria lodged a complaint with the Council of Europe in May and a resolution was passed condemning Czechoslovakia.

On Jan. 1, 1972, career diplomat and former foreign minister Kurt Waldheim took up his post as UN secretary-general. Former chancellor Alfons Gorbach, a founder-member of the Austrian People's Party (ÖVP) and a prominent and popular figure in Austrian politics, died in July (*see* OBITUARIES).

Increases in the gross national product of 7.8% in 1970 and 5.2% in 1971 had put Austria among the world's leaders in rate of GNP growth. The economic boom continued unabated in 1972, fueled by capital investment, full employment, increased production, increased private consumption, and new record earnings from tourism, together with domestic peace and stability. At the same time, however, the rate of inflation reached 6%, forcing the government to decide on a drastic policy of price control and restraint. This was particularly necessary since, in view of the favourable economic situation, it had been decided to introduce the value-added tax system on Jan. 1, 1973, and it was feared that this might lead to further price increases. The government decided to launch the most comprehensive exercise in price control ever attempted in Austria. A computer would accumulate 500,000 prices and ascertain the most favourable at any given time, thus providing a basis upon which to issue warnings to producers charging excessively high prices.

In July 1972 the *Kurier*, Austria's highest-circulation daily paper until it was overtaken by the *Kronen-Zeitung*, was put up for sale. To prevent its being acquired by the *Kronen-Zeitung*, a consortium of 200 individuals and businesses was formed to purchase the *Kurier* so that it might continue to function as an independent vehicle of opinion.

(ELFRIEDE DIRNBACHER)

Bahrain

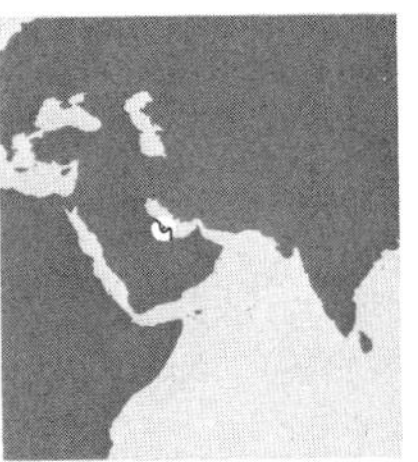

An independent emirate, Bahrain consists of a group of islands in the Persian Gulf, lying between the Qatar Peninsula and Saudi Arabia. Total area: 256 sq.mi. (662 sq.km.). Pop. (1972 est.): 220,000. Cap.: Manama (pop., 1971, 88,785). Language: Arabic (official), Persian. Religion: Muslim. Emir, Isa ibn Sulman al-Khalifah.

In 1972 Bahrain established diplomatic relations with most Arab states and with the principal non-Communist countries. It was announced in January that part of the naval base formerly used by Britain would be leased to the small U.S. Middle East fleet. The pending formation of a constituent council as a first step toward democracy was announced in June by Sheikh Isa. In March the Organization of Petro-

Automobile Industry: *see* Industrial Review; Transportation
Automobile Racing: *see* Motor Sports
Aviation: *see* Defense; Transportation
Bahama Islands: *see* Dependent States

BAHRAIN

Education. (1969–70) Primary, pupils 36,612, teachers 1,547; secondary, pupils 12,144; teachers 728; vocational, pupils 907, teachers 103; higher, students 310, teaching staff 40.

Finance and Trade. Monetary unit: Bahrain dinar, with (Sept. 18, 1972) a free rate of 0.44 dinars to U.S. $1 (1.07 dinars = £1 sterling). Budget (1969 est.): revenue 12,750,000 dinars, expenditure 12,580,000 dinars. Foreign trade (1971): imports 105,005,000 dinars (30% from U.K., 12% from Japan, 12% from U.S., 6% from China, 5% from Netherlands); exports (excluding oil) 28,405,000 dinars (49% to Saudi Arabia, 12% to Kuwait, 6% to Qatar, 5% to Dubai). Main exports: crude oil and petroleum products.

Industry. Production (in 000; metric tons): crude oil (1971) 3,760; petroleum products (1970) 12,322.

leum Exporting Countries chose Bahrain as the site for its dry dock, to be completed by 1975 at an estimated first-stage cost of $60 million. The contract, originally awarded to the British firm Vickers Ltd., was transferred to the Portuguese firm Lisnave when it was revealed that Vickers was supplying three submarines to Israel. (PETER MANSFIELD)

Bangladesh

An independent republic and member of the Commonwealth of Nations, formerly East Pakistan, Bangladesh is bordered by India on the west, north, and east, by Burma in the southeast, and by the Bay of Bengal in the south. Area: 55,126 sq.mi. (142,776 sq.km.). Pop. (1972 est.): 75 million. Cap. and largest city: Dacca (pop., 1971 est., 799,601). Language: Bengali, English. Religion: Muslim 80%, with Hindu, Christian, and Buddhist minorities. Presidents in 1972, Sheikh Mujibur Rahman and, from January 12, Abu Sayeed Choudhury; prime minister from January 12, Sheikh Mujibur Rahman.

The enthusiasm born of independence for the new republic of Bangladesh was tempered in 1972 by the enormous task of reconstruction and rehabilitation. The wholesale destruction of the economy during the nine months of occupation by the Pakistani Army in 1971 had left deep scars across the face of the nation. Sheikh Mujibur Rahman (*see* BIOGRAPHY) returned to take over the reins of government in early January, after his release from a Pakistani jail. The first of approximately 10 million refugees who had fled to India began trickling back, while some 30 million more who had been uprooted from their homes began the search for new homes and a new footing. A threatened famine was averted through massive food aid from the United Nations and India.

Sheikh Mujib, who had been named president while he was still incarcerated in Pakistan, adopted a provisional constitution envisaging a parliamentary system of government, and installed a new Cabinet with Abu Sayeed Choudhury as president and himself as prime minister. A 25-year treaty of friendship and cooperation was signed with India, closely followed by a trade agreement. Mujib announced the nationalization of domestic banks, insurance companies, and jute, textile, and sugar mills and promised his people that within three years his *Sonar Bangla* ("Golden Bengal") would be self-sufficient in food.

That was the picture on March 26, 1972, exactly a year after the Pakistani Army had begun its savage attempt to suppress the independence movement in what was then Pakistan's east wing. But six months later little headway had been made in solving the country's many problems, and discontent was widespread among the people. Sheikh Mujib was still regarded as *Bangabandhu* ("Friend of Bengal") and was by far the most popular leader, but on his return from London, where he had gone for gallbladder

Bihari Muslims beg for food in Dacca. The 1.5 million members of the ethnic minority were persecuted because of suspected leanings toward Pakistan. Widespread famine throughout Bangladesh was averted by massive food shipments from the United Nations and India.

JASON LAURE—RAPHO GUILLUMETTE

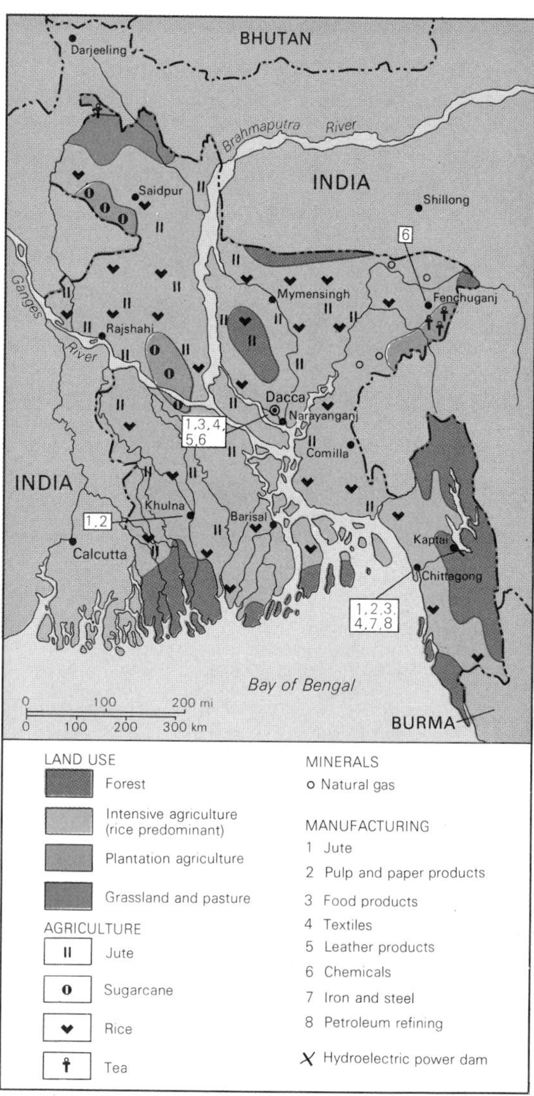

RAGHUBIR SINGH—WOODFIN CAMP

Thousands of Bengalis cheer Sheikh Mujibur Rahman's triumphant return to Dacca following a nine-month ordeal in a Pakistani prison. He returned in January 1972 to assume the reins of government.

treatment, he faced hostile demonstrations for the first time. Mujib was criticized for failure in the distribution of food grains and other essential consumer goods, resulting in skyrocketing prices and runaway inflation. While he himself was looked upon as incorruptible, his Cabinet colleagues and Awami League officials were accused of diverting for their personal financial benefit large quantities of rice and other goods brought in to feed the starving people.

The Bangladesh currency, the taka, officially on a par with the Indian rupee, was worth only half that on the black market. Some of the ills were traced to the smuggling of goods across the Indian border. The trade agreement with India had provided for an exchange of Rs. 250 million of goods by year's end, but nothing substantial had moved through legal channels. Border trade between the two countries was suspended in October, pending establishment of adequate controls. Under the agreement Bangladesh was to exchange jute, newsprint, fertilizers, and fish for Indian consumer goods, drugs and chemicals, and machinery for the reconstruction of roads, bridges, and harbours. Export earnings were understandably low since production of jute and tea, the main foreign-exchange earners, had been disrupted by the civil war.

In some quarters India, hailed as the country's liberator after it crushed Pakistan in the December 1971 war, was being blamed. Many of Bangladesh's difficulties could be attributed to the lack of trained administrators, most of whom were still being held in Pakistan. There was also a minor law-and-order problem. The last Indian soldier had been withdrawn well before the March 25 deadline, and the Bengali freedom fighters were slow in surrendering their arms. Observers reported persecution of the minority Biharis, who had generally sided with the Pakistanis during the civil war.

Politically, there was no alternative to the leadership of the Awami League headed by Mujib, but cracks began to appear in the league itself. A student wing, which had played a major role in preindependence politics, broke away to join the Muzafar Ahmed group of the National Awami Party. The rest of the opposition consisted of the National Awami Party itself, led by nonagenarian Maulana Abdul Hamid Khan Bhashani, who was anti-Moscow and anti-Peking, and three Communist groups. An opposition demand for a new general election was met by the government, and March 1973 was set as the election date. On November 5 the National Assembly approved a new constitution, which came into effect on December 16, the first anniversary of the country's liberation.

The first major country to recognize Bangladesh

BANGLADESH

Education. (1969–70) Primary, pupils *c.* 7,350,000; secondary, pupils *c.* 600,000; vocational, pupils 20,600; primary, secondary, and vocational, teachers (1966–67) 135,539; higher (including 5 universities), students *c.* 83,000.

Finance. Monetary unit: taka, with (Sept. 18, 1972) a free rate of 7.70 taka to U.S $1 (18.87 taka = £1 sterling). Foreign exchange (Aug. 1972 est.) U.S. $170 million. Budget (1972–73 est.): revenue 7,356,000,000 taka; expenditures 2,346,000,000 taka, development 5,010,000,000 taka. Cost of living (Narayangani; 1963 = 100): (Nov. 1971) 150; (Nov. 1970) 130.

Foreign Trade. (Excluding trade with Pakistan; 1970–71) Imports 1,575,200,000 taka; exports 1,251,400,000 taka. Export destinations (jute only): U.K. 14%; Belgium 8%; West Germany 5%; France 5%. Main exports: jute 40%; jute fabrics 36%; jute bags 13%. Trade with Pakistan (1970–71): imports 1,377,617,000 taka; exports 803,756,000 taka.

Transport and Communications. Roads (with improved surface; 1970) 3,940 km. Motor vehicles in use (1969): passenger 22,000; commercial 9,000. Railways (1968–69): 2,820 km.; traffic 3,555,000,000 passenger-km., freight 1,167,000,000 net ton-km. Navigable waterways (1970) *c.* 8,000 km. Radio licenses (March 1969) 531,000.

Agriculture. Production (in 000; metric tons; 1971; 1970 in parentheses): rice 11,144 (12,005); wheat 112 (105); potatoes 863 (865); sweet potatoes 832 (852); jute 1,251 (1,319); tea 31 (30); tobacco 41 (40); bananas 593 (745).

Industry. Production (in 000; metric tons; 1969–70): steel 177; cement 54; jute fabric 589; cotton yarn 48; paper 79.

Balance of Payments: *see* Payments and Reserves, International

Ballet: *see* Dance

was the U.S.S.R., in January. Britain extended recognition in February; Bangladesh was admitted into the Commonwealth in April; and recognition by a total of 86 countries followed. The new republic was denied universal acceptance, however, when China cast its veto in the Security Council in August to block the entry of Bangladesh into the UN. Relations with Pakistan were still strained, but hopes for an eventual settlement were raised when India and Pakistan signed an agreement in Simla in July pledging to work for a durable peace in the subcontinent. Pakistan refused to recognize the new state, and this lack of recognition ruled out any meeting between the leaders of the two countries. One stumbling block was Mujib's steadfast determination to try some of the 93,000 Pakistani prisoners of war being held in India on charges of genocide against his people.

In June Finance Minister Tajuddin Ahmed presented his first budget. Emphasis in reconstruction and development was placed on education and agriculture. Ahmed hoped to secure at least 3,750,000,000 taka (about U.S. $517 million) in foreign assistance and to generate the balance for development from domestic resources. Foreign aid promised or effected was generous—the U.S. $267.5 million, India $236 million, Canada $52 million, Britain $35 million, and West Germany $25 million. UN aid totaled $18.5 million by September 1972. The figure for Soviet aid was not available but was believed to be substantial, and the U.S.S.R. also helped to clear Chittagong Harbour and supplied technicians and material for repairing bridges and communications. Worldwide concern among youth for the welfare of the new nation was manifested in the donation, to Bangladesh relief, of proceeds from the sale of the record of a Bangladesh benefit concert, given in August 1971 in New York City by a number of popular musical groups. Advance sales amounted to some $3 million and the total was expected to reach $20 million.

The finance minister announced that the country was poised to launch its first five-year plan in 1973, though the plan and the budget would hold little meaning if the government failed to arrest inflation (there had been a 70% rise in the wholesale price index between February and September) and restore the infrastructure of transport and communications.

(GOVINDAN UNNY)

Barbados

The parliamentary state of Barbados is a member of the Commonwealth of Nations and occupies the most easterly island in the southern Caribbean Sea. Area: 166 sq.mi. (430 sq.km.). Pop. (1971 est.): 243,700, 90% Negro. Cap. and largest city: Bridgetown (pop., 1970, 8,789). Language: English. Religion: Christian, with Anglicans in the majority. Queen, Elizabeth II; governor-general in 1972, Sir Winston Scott; prime minister, Errol Walton Barrow.

Opening the new session of Parliament in late 1971, the governor-general announced that the government would set guidelines for foreign ownership and participation in the economy in an effort to increase local control over the country's resources. An intensification of economic nationalism in 1972 was foreshadowed by Minister of Home Affairs Rameses Caddle when he imposed tighter controls over work permits for expatriates. There were also reports of

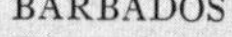
BARBADOS

Education. (1966–67) Primary, pupils 40,712, teachers 1,163; secondary, pupils 25,136, teachers 1,074; vocational, pupils 2,362, teachers 141; teacher training, students 300, teachers 30; higher, students 373, teaching staff 85.

Finance and Trade. Monetary unit: East Caribbean dollar, with (Sept. 18, 1972) a free rate of ECar$1.96 to U.S. $1 (ECar$4.80 = £1 sterling). Budget (1970–71 est.): revenue ECar$90,009,000; expenditure ECar$85,560,000. Foreign trade (1970): imports ECar$235,005,000 (30% from U.K., 21% from U.S., 10% from Canada, 7% from Trinidad and Tobago); exports ECar$78,080,000 (39% to U.K., 19% to U.S.). Main exports: sugar 48%; shellfish 7%; molasses 6%; clothing 6%; rum 5%. Tourism (1969) 138,000 visitors.

Agriculture. Sugar production, raw value (metric tons; 1971–72) *c.* 107,000, (1970–71) *c.* 137,000.

increased bias against the island's small white elite and of increased militancy at the local campus of the University of the West Indies.

Sugar production from the 1971 crop totaled 134,552 tons, and the projected figure for 1972 was 105,000 tons. These two figures were the lowest since 1948; drought and indiscriminate burning of sugarcane were named as the major causes. The minister of agriculture subsequently decided to reduce the compulsory percentage of arable land to be planted in vegetable and food crops from 12 to 5%, with a view to fulfilling Commonwealth Sugar Agreement quotas for 1973 and 1974. In July, Barbados, along with the other three independent countries and eight associated states comprising the Caribbean Free Trade Area (CARIFTA), agreed to seek a group relationship with the enlarged EEC.

Tourism continued to increase its lead over sugar as a foreign exchange earner, with tourist figures for 1971 up nearly 20% over the preceding year. Early reports for 1972 were optimistic, with a high ratio (35%) of repeat visitors. (SHEILA PATTERSON)

Baseball

The first general player strike in organized baseball's 102-year history delayed opening day and shook the sport to its very moorings in 1972. But the season ended on its normal suspenseful note when the underdog Oakland Athletics won the World Series by beating the Cincinnati Reds, 3–2, in the seventh and final game.

The Major League Baseball Players Association, headed by Marvin Miller, the executive director, sought higher pension benefits to offset a 17% boost in the cost of living since adoption of the last schedule of pension payments in 1969. Miller and John Gaherin, the club owners' chief negotiator, were key figures in the negotiations that followed.

The strike started April 1, lasted until April 13, and postponed the opening games from April 5 until April 15. The players asked for $1,072,000 to accommodate the pension hike, including the transfer of $817,000 on reserve in the pension fund plus $255,000 additional from the clubs. They eventually settled for $500,000 in transferred funds. The agreement stipulated that all games delayed as a result of the strike would be canceled, with the players forfeiting their pay for that period. The number of games canceled per team ranged from six to nine, depending on the schedule. Eighty-six games were canceled altogether. While estimates varied, the strike possibly cost the

Banking:
see Money and Banking
Baptists:
see Religion

club owners $5 million in revenue and the players $1 million in pay.

Final attendance figures for 1972 put the National League total at 15,529,395, a decline of 1,795,462. The American League total was 11,445,318, a decline of 423,242.

Once on the field, major league baseball provided an exciting season. Both pennant play-offs went the five-game limit, and the World Series went to the maximum seven games. The final game in all three showdowns was decided by one run. The mustachioed Oakland team, managed by Dick Williams, annexed the American League pennant by ousting Detroit 2–1 in the decisive fifth game. George "Sparky" Anderson's Cincinnati club overturned the defending world champion Pittsburgh Pirates 4–3 in the chaotic ninth inning of the fifth game to take the National League pennant. The Pirates, who had been leading the Reds throughout the game, were bested in the bottom half of the ninth by a Johnny Bench homer, followed by two singles and a wild pitch that scored the winning run.

The U.S. Supreme Court, in a 5–3 decision, extended baseball's exemption from antitrust laws. In an opinion handed down June 19, the court in effect urged Congress to settle the question. The decision was an outgrowth of a suit filed by Curt Flood, who in 1970 challenged baseball's reserve clause, which binds a player to the team with which he originally signs unless that team elects to sell his contract or trade him.

Major league baseball entered the Dallas-Fort Worth area as the Texas Rangers made their debut at Arlington (Tex.) Stadium. Pittsburgh's Roberto Clemente collected his 3,000th hit on September 30 to become the 11th player ever to reach that plateau. Hank Aaron of Atlanta smashed 34 home runs to run his career total to 673. Aaron thus moved within striking distance of Babe Ruth's all-time record 714. Pitcher Steve Carlton of Philadelphia (*see* BIOGRAPHY) turned in a sensational season, winning 27 games for a last-place team that won only 59 in all. He was the top winner in the majors, and was the winning pitcher in 46% of the games won by the Phillies.

Three pitchers accounted for no-hit, no-run games: Burt Hooton and Milt Pappas of the Chicago Cubs and Bill Stoneman of Montreal. Pappas came within one pitch of a perfect game when he walked Larry Stahl of San Diego on a 3–2 pitch with two out in the ninth.

For the eighth straight season, Lou Brock of St. Louis surpassed the 50-mark in stolen bases, tying the record of Ty Cobb. Brock stole 63 in 1972. San Diego's Nate Colbert broke three National League records and tied another on August 1 when he hit five home runs and drove in 13 runs during a double header in Atlanta. Pittsburgh became the first team ever to produce nine players with more than 100 hits apiece in a single season.

The Hall of Fame at Cooperstown, N.Y., boosted its membership by eight: Sandy Koufax, Yogi Berra, Early Wynn, Josh Gibson, Walter "Buck" Leonard, Vernon "Lefty" Gomez, Will Harridge, and Ross Youngs. Gil Hodges, 47-year-old manager of the New York Mets, died of a heart attack on April 2 (*see* OBITUARIES). Yogi Berra was named his successor. A heart attack claimed the life of Jackie Robinson, major league baseball's first black player, on October 24 (*see* OBITUARIES).

WIDE WORLD

Oakland Athletics' Gene Tenace, World Series most valuable player, slams one of the eight hits he made in the series. Above, relief pitcher Rollie Fingers is hugged jubilantly by teammates after the last out in the series.

Major Leagues. The Detroit Tigers won the American League's Eastern Division by one-half game over Boston in the most dramatic of the four divisional races in 1972. The two teams were matched in the final three games of the regular season, and the Tigers captured the first two to clinch Eastern honours. Baltimore and New York also had seriously threatened to win the title until faltering in the last week. Oakland survived the American League Western by putting down a late-season bid by the Chicago White Sox, who lost out by 5½ games after a neck-and-neck struggle with the Athletics almost to the end.

Pittsburgh and Cincinnati grabbed division championships with ease in the National League. The Pirates took the Eastern by 11 games over the Chicago Cubs, and Cincinnati prevailed by 10½ over Houston and Los Angeles in the Western.

The World Series opened in Cincinnati. A record

Table I. Final Major League Standings, 1972

American League
Eastern Division

Club	W.	L.	Pct.	G.B.	Det.	Bos.	Balt.	N.Y.	Clev.	Mil.	Cal.	Chi.	K.C.	Minn.	Oak.	Tex.
Detroit	86	70	.551	—	—	9	8	7	8	10	7	7	7	9	4	10
Boston	85	70	.548	½	5	—	11	9	8	11	8	6	6	4	9	8
Baltimore	80	74	.519	5	10	7	—	7	8	10	6	8	6	6	6	6
New York	79	76	.510	6½	9	9	6	—	11	9	8	5	5	6	3	8
Cleveland	72	84	.462	14	10	7	10	7	—	5	4	4	6	8	2	9
Milwaukee	65	91	.417	21	8	7	5	9	10	—	5	3	5	4	4	5

Western Division

Club	W.	L.	Pct.	G.B.	Oak.	Chi.	Minn.	K.C.	Cal.	Tex.	Balt.	Bos.	Clev.	Det.	Mil.	N.Y.
Oakland	93	62	.600	—	—	7	9	11	10	11	6	3	10	8	8	9
Chicago	87	67	.565	5½	7	—	8	8	11	14	4	6	8	5	9	7
Minnesota	77	77	.500	15½	8	6	—	9	8	11	6	8	4	3	8	6
Kansas City	76	78	.494	16½	7	9	9	—	6	8	6	6	6	5	7	7
California	75	80	.484	18	8	7	7	9	—	10	6	4	8	5	7	4
Texas	54	100	.351	38½	4	4	7	6	7	—	6	4	3	2	7	4

National League
Eastern Division

Club	W.	L.	Pct.	G.B.	Pitt.	Chi.	N.Y.	St.L.	Mon.	Phil.	Atl.	Cin.	Hou.	L.A.	S.D.	S.F.
Pittsburgh	96	59	.619	—	—	12	6	10	12	13	6	4	9	5	10	9
Chicago	85	70	.548	11	3	—	10	10	10	10	7	8	3	8	9	7
New York	83	73	.532	13½	8	8	—	7	12	13	5	4	6	5	7	8
St. Louis	75	81	.481	21½	8	8	9	—	8	7	6	2	8	4	8	7
Montreal	70	86	.449	26½	6	5	6	9	—	10	8	4	4	6	6	6
Philadelphia	59	97	.378	37½	5	7	5	8	6	—	6	2	3	5	6	6

Western Division

Club	W.	L.	Pct.	G.B.	Cin.	Hou.	L.A.	Atl.	S.F.	S.D.	Chi.	Mon.	N.Y.	Phil.	Pitt.	St.L.
Cincinnati	95	59	.617	—	—	11	9	9	10	8	4	8	8	10	8	10
Houston	84	69	.549	10½	6	—	7	7	13	12	9	8	6	9	3	4
Los Angeles	85	70	.548	10½	5	11	—	8	9	13	4	6	7	7	7	8
Atlanta	70	84	.455	25	9	7	7	—	7	6	5	4	7	6	6	6
San Francisco	69	86	.445	26½	5	5	9	11	—	10	5	6	4	6	3	5
San Diego	58	95	.379	36½	10	2	5	11	4	—	3	6	5	6	2	4

Tie—Atlanta 1, Chicago 1.
Source: *The Sporting News*.

ERNEST SISTO—THE NEW YORK TIMES

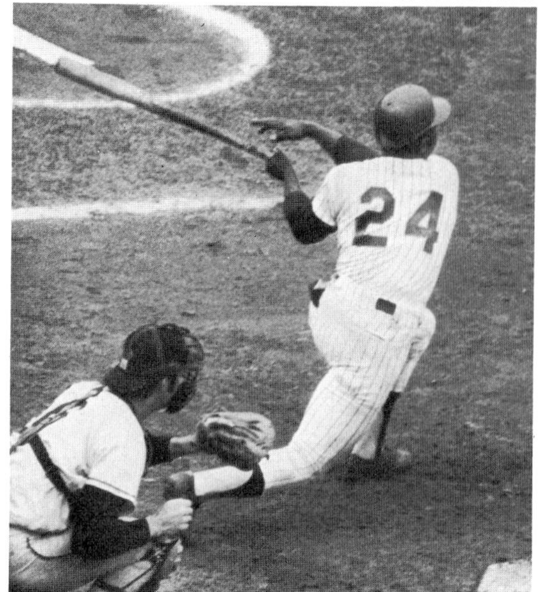

In his first game as a member of the New York Mets on May 14, 1972, 41-year-old Willie Mays hits a game-winning home run that defeated his teammates of 21 years, the San Francisco Giants.

Riverfront Stadium crowd of 52,918 saw Oakland catcher Gene Tenace become the first player in history to hit home runs in each of his first two times at bat in Series competition. The blasts by Tenace propelled the Athletics to victory, 3–2. The starting and winning pitcher for the Athletics was Ken Holtzman, the loser, Gary Nolan.

Oakland won the second game 2–1, when left fielder Joe Rudi, whose third-inning home run developed into the winning run, made a spectacular defensive play in the ninth inning. The Reds' Tony Perez led off the bottom of the ninth with a single off winning pitcher Jim "Catfish" Hunter, who owned a 2–0 lead. Denis Menke then slammed a drive deep to left only to have Rudi respond with a miraculous catch high off the wall. Perez moved to second as reserve first baseman Mike Hegan brilliantly retired Cesar Geronimo by stabbing his ground ball. Pinch-hitter Hal McRae's single wrecked Hunter's shutout, and Rollie Fingers then came on in relief to register the final out. The loser was Ross Grimsley.

The Series then switched to Oakland, where Cincinnati registered its first win, 1–0. Perez, who had singled and moved up on a sacrifice, scored the lone run in the seventh on Geronimo's single. He slipped on the wet turf halfway between third and home but recovered and scored before Oakland's defense was aware he had fallen. A crowd of 49,410 witnessed a stirring pitching duel between the winner, Jack Billingham, and the loser, John "Blue Moon" Odom.

Oakland erased a 2–1 deficit with two runs in the bottom of the ninth to win the fourth game 3–2 and take a commanding lead of three games to one. Singles by Gonzalo Marquez and Tenace launched the rally with one out. Don Mincher singled to tie the score, and Angel Mangual singled to win the game. Marquez, Mincher, and Mangual all appeared in pinch-hitting roles. Superb pitching by Holtzman and Tenace's third series homer in the fifth inning off Reds' starter Don Gullett left the Athletics with a 1–0 lead through seven innings. Holtzman was removed in favour of Vida Blue in the eighth with a runner on third and two out. Blue walked Joe Morgan, who then scored when Bobby Tolan rifled a two-run double to right for a 2–1 Cincinnati lead. That set the stage for the dramatic finish. The winner in relief was Fingers, the loser, Clay Carroll.

The Reds stayed alive by capturing the fifth game 5–4, in another frenzied finish. The contest ended on a double play as Morgan caught a foul pop-up behind first base and then threw home to get pinch-runner Odom, who was attempting to score from third with the tying run. The first pitch of the game resulted in a home run by Pete Rose off Hunter, and it was Rose who also singled in Cincinnati's winning run in the ninth. Tenace tied a Series record by uncorking his fourth home run in the second inning. Grimsley was the winner in relief, and Fingers the loser.

The teams returned to Cincinnati for the sixth game, and the Reds evened things at three games apiece with an 8–1 rout. A five-run outburst in the seventh, keyed by two-run singles by Tolan and Geronimo, climaxed the Cincinnati offensive. Grimsley earned his second straight win in relief, while starter Blue suffered the loss. Johnny Bench homered for Cincinnati in the fourth, and after the Athletics tied it in the fifth the Reds put over what proved to be the winning run in the bottom of the fifth on Dave Concepcion's sacrifice fly. Tolan stole two more bases to run his Series total to five and the Reds' total to 11.

It was Odom for the Athletics and Billingham for the Reds as another record Cincinnati turnout of 56,040 gathered for the final game. For the sixth time in seven games, the margin was one run, and Oakland emerged the victor, 3–2. Hunter gained the pitching victory in relief, aided by Fingers' vital save. Tenace singled home Oakland's first run after a three-base error by center fielder Tolan in the first inning. The Reds tied it at 1–1 in the fifth on McRae's sacrifice fly. Doubles by Tenace and Sal Bando sent across two runs for the Athletics in the sixth, and Oakland was never again headed. Victim of the rally was pitcher Pedro Borbon. Tenace, who drove in 9 of the 16 runs scored by the Athletics, was voted most valuable player of the Series.

Billy Williams of the Cubs won the National League batting title with .333, finished second to Cincinnati's Johnny Bench in runs-batted-in, and third to Bench and San Diego's Nate Colbert in home runs. Bench drove in 125 runs to 122 for Williams and hit 40 homers, to 38 for Colbert and 37 for Williams.

In addition to Philadelphia's Steve Carlton, the National League's 20-game winners included Tom Seaver of the New York Mets, with 21, and the Cubs' Ferguson Jenkins and the Los Angeles Dodgers' Claude Osteen, each of whom won 20. It was the sixth successive 20-game season for Jenkins.

Dick Allen (*see* BIOGRAPHY), the force behind the rejuvenated White Sox in 1972, dominated American League batting figures. He slugged 37 home runs and drove in 113 runs for leadership in both categories. Minnesota's Rod Carew won the batting title with .318, with Allen finishing in a third-place tie at .308.

The American League produced six 20-game winners. Wilbur Wood of the White Sox and Gaylord Perry of Cleveland posted 24 wins apiece, and Detroit's Mickey Lolich had 22. Oakland's Hunter, Baltimore's Jim Palmer, and Chicago's Stan Bahnsen each registered 21.

Atlanta Stadium was the site of the annual All-Star Game, and the National League beat the American League, 4–3, in 10 innings. It was the seventh time the All-Star game took extra innings, and the National League prevailed in all seven. Joe Morgan singled home the winning run in the bottom of the 10th to clinch the pitching verdict for Tug McGraw of the New York Mets. The loser was Baltimore's Dave Mc-

Nally. The National League thus gained its 24th All-Star triumph against 18 losses and 1 tie.

Manager of the year awards went to "Sparky" Anderson of the Reds in the National League and Chuck Tanner of the White Sox in the American. Winners of the Cy Young awards for outstanding pitching were Steve Carlton of the Phillies in the National League and Gaylord Perry of the Cleveland Indians in the American. Most Valuable Player awards went to Johnny Bench in the National League and Dick Allen of the Chicago White Sox in the American; named rookies of the year were pitcher Jon Matlack of the New York Mets for the National League and catcher Carlton Fisk of Boston in the American.

Amateur. Southern California edged Arizona State, 1–0, to win its third straight College World Series at Omaha, Neb. The Trojans, en route to their eighth national title, tallied their lone run in the third on a wild pitch by Jim Crawford. Tim Steele, who had singled and moved to third on a walk and an infield out, scored the clincher. Sophomore Russ McQueen, who picked up three wins and a save in the double elimination tournament, triumphed in the final game when he came on in the fifth inning, pitched his way out of a bases-loaded jam, and restricted Arizona State to one hit and no runs over the last five innings. McQueen pitched 14 innings in the tournament and gave up no runs. (JACK BRICKHOUSE)

Japanese. The Yomiuri Giants of Tokyo captured the 1972 pennant of the Central League for the eighth consecutive year, led by the batting of first baseman Sadaharu Oh and center fielder Isao Shibata and the pitching of Tsuneo Horiuchi, who won 26 games. In the rival Pacific League, the Hankyu Braves of Osaka won the pennant for a second straight year, largely through the batting of center fielder Yutaka Fukumoto and the 20 wins of pitcher Hisashi Yamada.

Tsutomu Wakamatsu of the Yakult Atoms of Tokyo won the Central League batting title with a .329 average, while Sadaharu Oh of the Giants hammered 48 homers to capture home-run honours for the 11th straight year. In the Pacific League, the batting laurels went to Isao Harimoto of the Toei Flyers of Tokyo, who hit .358, while Tokuji Nagaike of the Hankyu Braves hit 41 home runs to lead the league in that category for the second time.

For the eighth straight year the Yomiuri Giants won the World Series of Japan, defeating the Hankyu Braves four games to one. Sadaharu Oh paced the Giants, slamming a home run in the final game, which the Tokyo team won 8–3. (RYUSAKU HASEGAWA)

Basketball

United States. *Collegiate.* The unprecedented collegiate basketball dynasty at the University of California at Los Angeles (UCLA), built largely by seasoned athletes, remained unbroken in 1972. Three sophomores, most notably 18-year-old Bill Walton, named player of the year by the country's coaches, led the Bruins to a 30–0 record and their sixth consecutive National Collegiate Athletic Association (NCAA) championship.

With that achievement, UCLA erased its own record of five straight NCAA championships, ran its tournament winning streak to 32 games, won its eighth title in the past nine years, boosted its record for that period to 251–15, and elicited visions of yet another type of statistical immortality. Coupled with 15 consecutive victories in 1971 after a loss to Notre Dame, UCLA's 1972 performance left the Bruins just 15 wins short of the University of San Francisco's record of 60 straight.

Coach John Wooden directed UCLA to its latest heights by blending sophomores Walton, Keith Wilkes, and Greg Lee with junior Larry Farmer and senior Henry Bibby, who became the Bruins' floor leader as well as their foremost long-range shooter. The result was a team far different from the Bruins of recent years, who had worn down the opposition methodically, even mechanically. But while Wooden always let his teams' talents dictate their styles, it was no secret that he preferred players equipped to run a racehorse offense. The Bruins of 1972 were so equipped. They ranked fourth in the country on offense by averaging 94.6 points a game.

The facet of the game that remained constant at UCLA was defense. Only seven other teams in the nation gave up fewer than the 64.3 points per game averaged by the Bruins' defense.

In a season when the overall quality of college basketball declined, Marquette, Pennsylvania, and North Carolina were considered the prime threats to UCLA. Marquette advanced to the NCAA tournament's Mideast Regional, where it fell to Kentucky 85–69, but its season had really ended a month before, in February. At that time, Jim Chones, a 6-ft. 11-in. junior centre who had led the Warriors to 21 straight wins, signed a $1.5 million contract with the New York Nets of the American Basketball Association (ABA), ending his collegiate career prematurely.

North Carolina, the champion of the 1971 National Invitational Tournament (NIT), destroyed whatever hopes Penn's tall Quakers had 73–59 in the Eastern Regional. The Tar Heels, whose centre, Robert McAdoo, was being courted by both professional leagues, went on to get bumped 79–75 in the semifinals by surprising Florida State. The Seminoles, with two 5-ft. 7-in. guards directing a helter-skelter offense and an effervescent defense, had been given little chance in the tournament, but it was they who wound up in the finals against UCLA.

All the while, the Bruins were mowing down every team that crossed their path. Weber State was first in the tournament, losing 90–58. Long Beach State, with a team built around nomadic athletes, one of whom was at his sixth college, was next, falling 73–56. UCLA's semifinal battle with Louisville ended in a 96–77 victory for the Bruins.

In the final the Bruins defeated Florida State 81–76 in a game that grew close near the finish. An early burst of scoring by Wilkes and the floor play of re-

Major College Champions, 1972

League	Team and location	League record	All games
Eastern (Ivy)	Pennsylvania (Philadelphia)	13-1	25-3
Yankee	Rhode Island (Kingston)	8-2	15-11
Atlantic Coast	North Carolina (Chapel Hill)	9-3	26-5
Southeastern	Kentucky (Lexington)	14-4	21-7
	Tennessee (Knoxville)	14-4	19-6
Southern	Davidson (N.C.)	8-2	19-9
Ohio Valley	Eastern Kentucky (Richmond)	9-5	15-11
Big Ten	Minnesota	11-3	18-7
Mid-American	Toledo (O.)	7-3	18-7
	Ohio (Athens)	7-3	15-11
Big Eight	Kansas State (Manhattan)	12-2	19-9
Missouri Valley	Louisville (Ky.)	12-2	26-5
	Memphis State (Tenn.)	12-2	21-7
Southwest	Texas (Austin)	10-4	19-9
	Southern Methodist (Dallas, Tex.)	10-4	16-11
AAWU (Pacific Eight)	UCLA (Los Angeles, Calif.)	14-0	30-0
Western	Brigham Young (Provo, Utah)	12-2	21-5

WIDE WORLD

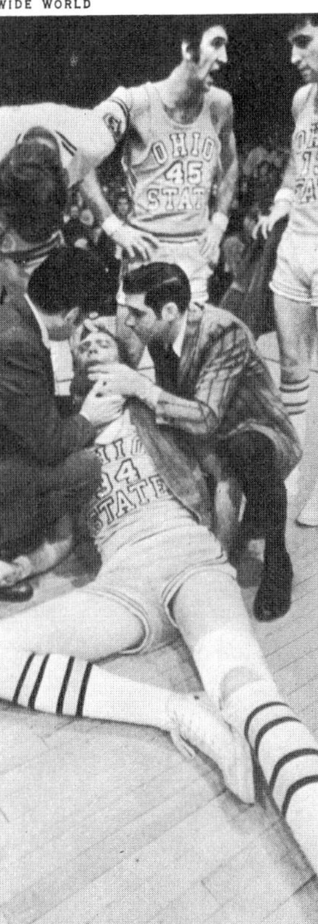

First aid is given to Ohio State centre, Luke Witte, injured in melee that erupted during Big Ten Conference game against Minnesota on Jan. 25, 1972. The fight involved players, coaches, police, and spectators. Two Minnesota players, Ron Behagen and Corky Taylor, were suspended for the remainder of the season.

UPI COMPIX

With an elbow in Jerry Lucas' chest, a protective device on his wrist, and a big grin, Wilt Chamberlain of the Los Angeles Lakers wrests control of the basketball from Lucas of the New York Knickerbockers in an NBA championship game May 7, 1972. The Lakers won the title.

serve guard Tommy Curtis, a resident of Tallahassee, Fla., the home of the Seminoles, gave the Bruins a 50–39 half-time lead. When Walton picked up his fourth foul early in the second half, Florida State fought back, mainly on the long jump shots of Ron King. The Bruins hung on, though, as the 18-year-old Wilkes knocked a pass away, controlled a jump ball, and scored UCLA's final basket to lock up the victory. Although Walton was far from his best in the championship game, he was named the tournament's most valuable player.

Maryland, expected by Coach Lefty Driesell to become "the UCLA of the East," won the 1972 NIT to bring a happy conclusion to a season that had begun with losses to a series of lacklustre teams. The Terrapins humbled Niagara 100–69 in the championship game, as 6-ft. 11-in. Tom McMillen had 19 points and 10 rebounds and 6-ft. 9-in. Len Elmore had 16 points and 15 rebounds. McMillen was named the tournament's most valuable player.

Adolph Rupp, possessor of more victories than any other collegiate coach, was retired by the University of Kentucky at the end of the season. At 70, the school's mandatory retirement age, Rupp had just finished leading the Wildcats to the NCAA tournament for a record 20th time. In his 42 years at Kentucky, Rupp compiled a record of 879-120. His teams won four NCAA championships and one NIT title.

Schools in their first seasons as legitimate basketball powers provided the nation's two top scorers. Dwight Lamar, a junior guard from Southwestern Louisiana, led the country by averaging 36.3 points a game and scoring a total of 1,054 points. Right behind him was Rich Fuqua, another guard, who had a 35.9 average and 1,006 points for Oral Roberts University.

For the second straight year, Greg Starrick of Southern Illinois won the free-throw percentage title, converting 148 of 160 penalty shots for a .925 average. Starrick established an NCAA career record of .909 in his three years at Southern Illinois. The best percentage shooter from the field was Kent Martens of Abilene Christian, who sank 136 of 204 shots for a .667 percentage.

Two UCLA players, Walton and Bibby, were elected to the National Association of Basketball Coaches' All-American team. They were joined by Ed Ratleff of Long Beach State, Tom Riker of South Carolina, and Jim Price of Louisville.

Roanoke (Va.) won the championship in the NCAA's college division, which is limited to smaller schools, by defeating Akron 84–72. Kentucky State defeated Eau Claire (Wis.) 71–62 for the title in the National Association of Intercollegiate Athletics tournament.

Professional. The Los Angeles Lakers, frustrated in seven previous attempts to win a National Basketball Association (NBA) championship since their 1960 move from Minneapolis to the West Coast, finally succeeded in 1972. After establishing a spate of regular-season records, the Lakers swarmed past the last two teams to capture NBA titles—the Milwaukee Bucks and the New York Knickerbockers—to win one of their own.

It was an achievement anticipated since the arrival of Wilt Chamberlain (*see* BIOGRAPHY) in Los Angeles in 1968. A trade with the Philadelphia 76ers teamed the 7-ft. 2-in. centre, who once scored 100 points in a game, with the Lakers' two home-grown stars, Jerry West and Elgin Baylor. Still, the three of them could not bring Los Angeles a championship.

The situation changed in 1971 with the arrival of coach Bill Sharman, who was fresh from winning the American Basketball Association championship with the Utah Stars, and the departure of Baylor, whose crippled knees forced him to retire after 14 years as a professional. Baylor's retirement early in the season eased the way for Sharman to put the faster Jim McMillian, a second-year man from Columbia University, in the starting lineup.

While running away with the Pacific Division, one of the NBA's four leagues, the Lakers set league records for the highest winning percentage (.841) and the most victories in a season (69). Thirty-three of those victories came in a row, breaking the professional sports record of 26 set in 1916 by the New York baseball Giants. The Lakers also established NBA records for the widest victory margin in a game (63 points) and the most games over 100 points (81).

In the play-offs, Los Angeles defeated the Chicago Bulls in four straight games before meeting the defending champion Milwaukee Bucks, who had beaten the Golden State Warriors in five games to reach the semifinals. Milwaukee had 7-ft. 2-in. Kareem Abdul Jabbar, the dominant player in professional basketball, but it was hurt by the uncertain status of Oscar Robertson, a veteran playmaker and shooter, who was forced to the bench frequently by an abdominal muscle pull. Although West, the highest scorer in play-off history with more than 4,000 points, went into a serious slump offensively, his teammates McMillian and Gail Goodrich made up for him. Simultaneously, the 35-year-old Chamberlain out-rebounded the 25-year-old Jabbar and outplayed him on defense. The Lakers won the series four games to two.

New York, which finished second to Boston in the Atlantic Division, advanced to the finals by defeating the Baltimore Bullets and the Boston Celtics. The Knicks began the season with the same lineup with which they won the NBA title in 1970, but a knee injury forced Willis Reed, their star centre, to the sidelines early in the campaign. Jerry Lucas, a 6-ft. 8-in. veteran from Ohio State, took his place and performed commendably.

The Lakers performed as sloppily in their first game against the Knicks as they had in their first game against the Bucks, and the result was the same—they lost. From there, though, they won four straight, including a 116-111 overtime game in which Chamberlain took command after severely spraining his right wrist. The game after that was the last of the season as the Lakers clinched the title 114-100. Chamberlain was named the most valuable player in the play-offs.

Jabbar won the Podolof Cup, symbolic of the league's most valuable player during the regular season, for the second straight year. He gathered 581 points in a poll of NBA players, finishing ahead of West, who was second for the third straight season, and Chamberlain. Sidney Wicks, of the Portland Trail Blazers, was named the NBA's rookie of the year.

Jabbar and West headed the NBA all-star team selected by the players. They were joined by guard Walt Frazier of New York and forwards John Havlicek of Boston and Spencer Haywood of the Seattle SuperSonics.

Jabbar led NBA scorers with a 34.8 average, 3.1 points better than his league-leading average in 1971, and finished second in field goal percentage (.574) and third in rebounding (16.6). Chamberlain won both of those categories, grabbing 19.2 rebounds a game and shooting .649 from the field. Jack Marin of Baltimore led from the free-throw line with .894.

A less pleasing statistic to the owners was the NBA's total attendance of 5,896,052, a drop of 298,554 from 1971. The Cincinnati franchise, which had the league's lowest attendance (147,514), was shifted to Omaha-Kansas City at the end of the season.

Although a record 2,436,826 people attended ABA games during the season, the delay in the decision on merger with the NBA—as well as anemic fan support —proved fatal for two ABA franchises, the Floridians and the Pittsburgh Condors. A new team, the San Diego Conquistadors, was established and the Memphis Pros were renamed the Memphis TAMs under new ownership.

The Indiana Pacers, with the most successful business operation in the ABA, proved to be the league's best team in 1972. Blending big players with small and veterans with rookies, the Pacers defeated the New York Nets four games to two to win their second ABA championship in three years. Outstanding for Indiana were guards Freddie Lewis and Bill Keller.

Artis Gilmore of the Eastern Division champion Kentucky Colonels was named the league's most valuable player and rookie of the year. The 7-ft. 2-in. Gilmore was selected to the ABA all-star team with teammate Dan Issel, Donnie Freeman of the Dallas Chaparrals, and two players from New York, Rick Barry and Bill Melchionni.

Charlie Scott played with Virginia long enough to establish himself as the league's leading scorer, averaging 34.5 points a game to the second-place Barry's 31.4. Glen Combs of Utah shot a league-leading .406 on three-point attempts. (JOHN SCHULIAN)

World Amateur. The final game in the 1972 Olympic basketball competition in Munich, W.Ger., terminated the dominance of the United States in Olympic basketball. After falling behind early in the final against the U.S.S.R., the U.S. fought back to a 50–49 lead with three seconds left. As the Soviets threw the ball into play from the end line, two of the remaining three seconds were played. The referee then stopped the game while he questioned the scorer about a signal that the latter had mistakenly sounded before the last U.S. point. It was then decided that the clock should be reset to three seconds and the game restarted from the end line, but before the clock could be reset the ball was thrown into play. Immediately, the horn sounded and the game was again stopped; at this point most people believed it was all over and that the U.S. had won the gold medal. In due course the referee regained control, the clock was reset to three seconds, and with the score 50–49 the ball was thrown in by the U.S.S.R. for the third time—a perfect pass the full length of the court into the outstretched hands of Aleksandr Belov, who scored the last and winning basket in the final second, to give the U.S.S.R. (51–50) the gold medal.

The 17th European championships for men confirmed that the U.S.S.R. was number one in Europe. In the final game Yugoslavia led the Soviet Union 37–33 at halftime, and the U.S.S.R. had lost Ivan Edeshko and Aleksandr Belov with five fouls each. But in the second half outstanding performances by Modestas Paulauskas and Sergei Belov assured victory for the U.S.S.R., 69–64. (K. K. MITCHELL)

Belgium

A constitutional monarchy on the North Sea coast of Europe, Belgium is bordered by the Netherlands, West Germany, Luxembourg, and France. Area: 11,781 sq.mi. (30,514 sq.km.). Pop. (1971 est.): 9,695,379. Cap.: Brussels (pop., 1971 est., 158,186). Largest city: Antwerp (pop., 1971 est., 222,775). Language: Dutch, French, and German. Religion: predominantly Roman Catholic. King, Baudouin I; prime minister in 1972, Gaston Eyskens.

Seventy-five days after the general election of November 1971, Belgium had a new government on Jan. 21, 1972, again presided over by Gaston Eyskens, who had resigned as a matter of course following the election. Formation of the government had been complicated by the uncompromising attitudes of Flemish leaders reacting to the sharp gains made by the Walloon federalist parties. Nonetheless, the coalition of Social Christians and Socialists was continued. For the first time the Cabinet included ten secretaries of state, posts created by constitutional revisions approved in 1971. The new government announced its intention to implement other constitutional provisions, approved by the previous Parliament.

Friction between the Flemish and French-language communities, supposedly eased by the constitutional revision, resurfaced over the issue of regionalization and led to the government's resignation on November 23, although Eyskens remained in office in a caretaker capacity. Art. 107 of the revised constitution recognized three regions: Brussels, Flanders, and Wallonia, and provided for the delegation of certain powers to local assemblies. Legislation to implement art. 107 required a two-thirds majority in Parliament, which the government parties were unable to muster. Advocates of federalism urged the creation of a regional executive and an elective assembly separate from the national Parliament. Flemish political leaders, concerned over the size of the Brussels region, wanted it limited to the existing agglomeration of 19 communes. The introduction of bilingualism in the small Voer region in eastern Belgium, requested by all Walloon politicians, caused further discord. Walloon political leaders also criticized the way funds for regional economic expansion had been split.

Divergent views emerged, too, on the creation of public companies for regional development, called for in economic planning and decentralization legislation. While one such company would cover the whole

Beekeeping: *see* Agriculture

Beer: *see* Alcoholic Beverages

of Wallonia, there were to be five in Flanders (one for each province) and one for the Brussels agglomeration.

For the first time, cultural matters were debated separately by the Dutch- and French-speaking members of Parliament during meetings of their respective cultural councils. On February 24 all parties, except the Flemish nationalist Volksunie, signed an agreement to prevent discrimination in the application of cultural autonomy.

Inflation was the main economic concern. Overriding objections by the Federation of Belgian Industries, the outgoing minister of economic affairs, Edmond Leburton, imposed further price restrictions on Dec. 28, 1971. Small shopkeepers, also angry over the price freeze as well as the mounting administrative work resulting from introduction of the value-added tax, expressed their discontent by closing down their shops in a mass protest on October 2–3. Nonetheless, prices continued to climb; the retail price index rose during the first nine months at an annual rate of 5.85%.

The 1972 ordinary budget showed a BFr. 6 billion deficit and stood 13.7% above the previous year's budget. A balanced budget was promised for 1973, but total expenditures of BFr. 416 billion represented yet another 13.7% increase. Though the government was pledged not to raise taxes, it allowed public services to boost their prices. At the end of September a crisis threatened between the government and the major oil companies following a unilateral decision by the minister of economic affairs, Henri Simonet, to cut their profit margin on gasoline by BFr. 0.35 per litre while increasing excise duties by BFr. 1 per litre in order to collect an extra BFr. 4.5 billion in taxes. The government sought to cut expenditure on universities by raising tuition fees and limiting the number of foreign students to 5% of the total student body (12.08% in February 1972).

Mixed feelings greeted the announcement by the Socialist Cooperative Movement that it would set up a limited company to run a chain of supermarkets. The Cristalleries du Val-Saint-Lambert glassworks were nationalized after being threatened by closure or a foreign take-over. Four Belgian holdings, among them Brufina (Société de Bruxelles pour la Finance et l'Industrie) and the Lambert group, merged to form the Brussels-Lambert Company for Finance and Industry, with assets valued at BFr. 15,680,000,000.

The setting of traps and snares to catch birds, a favourite pastime for thousands, was finally banned. The decision was hotly contested, particularly by ministers fearing voter reaction. (JAN R. ENGELS)

BELGIUM

Education. (1968–69) Primary, pupils 1,018,334, teachers (1967–68) 47,902; secondary, pupils 309,137, teachers (1967–68) 40,074; vocational, pupils 518,709, teachers (1966–67) 47,956; teacher training, students 19,759, teachers (1967–68) 6,089; higher (4 universities), students 64,779, teaching staff (1967–68) 5,489.

Finance. Monetary unit: Belgian franc, with (Sept. 18, 1972) a par value of BFr. 44.82 to U.S. $1 (free rate of BFr. 107.62 = £1 sterling). Gold, SDRs, and foreign exchange, central bank: (June 1972) U.S. $3,289,000,000; (June 1971) U.S. $2,679,000,000. Budget (1971 est.): revenue BFr. 318,895,000,000; expenditure BFr. 322,401,000,000. Gross national product: (1970) BFr. 1,285,000,000,000; (1969) BFr. 1,152,000,000,000. Money supply: (Dec. 1971) BFr. 464 billion; (Dec. 1970) BFr. 418.6 billion. Cost of living (1963 = 100): (June 1972) 141; (June 1971) 134.

Foreign Trade. (Belgium-Luxembourg economic union; 1971) Imports BFr. 626.8 billion; exports BFr. 603.9 billion. Import sources: EEC 63% (West Germany 25%, France 18%, Netherlands 16%); U.S. 6%; U.K. 6%. Export destinations: EEC 69% (West Germany 25%, France 20%, Netherlands 19%); U.S. 7%. Main exports: iron and steel 15%; machinery 11%; motor vehicles 10%; chemicals 10%; textile yarns and fabrics 8%; nonferrous metals 6%.

Transport and Communications. Roads (1970) 94,000 km. (including 488 km. expressways). Motor vehicles in use (1970): passenger 2,059,600; commercial 226,688. Railways: (1970) 4,165 km.; traffic (1971) 8,365,000,000 passenger-km., freight 7,350,000,000 net ton-km. Air traffic (1971): 2,722,000,000 passenger-km.; freight 211,178,000 net ton-km. Shipping (1971): merchant vessels 100 gross tons and over 244; gross tonnage 1,183,081. Shipping traffic (1971): goods loaded 27,912,000 metric tons; unloaded 61,560,000 metric tons. Navigable inland waterways in regular use (1970) 1,533 km. Telephones (Dec. 1970) 2,036,000. Radio licenses (Dec. 1970) 3,604,000. Television licenses (Dec. 1970) 2,087,000.

Agriculture. Production (in 000; metric tons; 1971; 1970 in parentheses): wheat 907 (735); barley 588 (527); oats 278 (196); rye (1970) 65, (1969) 73; potatoes 1,609 (1,597); apples (1970) 250, (1969) 300; sugar, raw value (1971–72) *c.* 860, (1970–71) *c.* 606; pork *c.* 530 (522); beef and veal *c.* 250 (244); milk *c.* 3,750 (3,749); fish catch (1970) 53, (1969) 59. Livestock (in 000; May 1971): cattle *c.* 2,910; pigs 3,912; sheep *c.* 156; horses *c.* 75; chickens *c.* 43,000.

Industry. Fuel and power (in 000; 1971): coal 10,990 metric tons; manufactured gas 2,974,000 cu.m.; electricity 33,189,000 kw-hr. Production (in 000; metric tons; 1971): pig iron 10,402; crude steel 12,450; copper 328; lead 94; zinc 212; tin 3.9; sulfuric acid 1,988; cement 6,931; cotton yarn 70; cotton fabrics 72; wool yarn 88; woolen fabrics 42; rayon and acetate yarn and fibres 40.

Bhutan

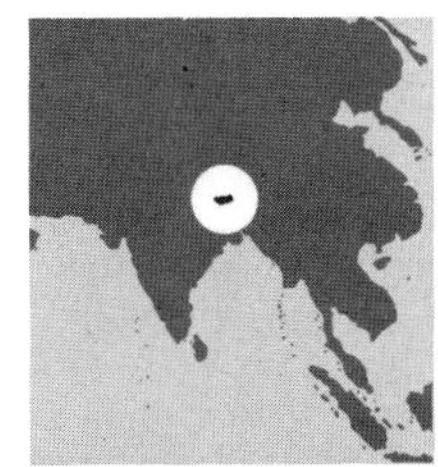

A monarchy situated in the eastern Himalayas, Bhutan is bounded by China, India, and Sikkim. Area: 18,000 sq.mi. (47,000 sq.km.). Pop. (1971 est.): 854,000. Official cap.: Thimphu (pop., approximately 10,000). Administrative cap.: Paro (population total unavailable). Language: Dzongkha (official). Religion: approximately 75% Buddhist, 25% Hindu. Druk gyalpo (king) in 1972, Jigme Dorji Wangchuk until July 21 and, from July 24, Jigme Singye Wangchuk.

King Jigme Dorji Wangchuk (*see* OBITUARIES) died on July 21, 1972, in a Nairobi, Kenya, hospital where he had been receiving treatment for heart disease. He was succeeded by the 17-year-old crown prince, Jigme Singye Wangchuk, who was enthroned on July 24.

A trade agreement was signed with India on January 19, and Bhutan was one of 12 less developed states to which generalized trading preferences were extended by the EEC on June 27. On March 1 the Bank of Bhutan was reorganized as a step in the kingdom's long effort to change from a barter to a money economy. (R. J. M. DENNERSTEIN)

BHUTAN

Education. (1968–69) Primary, pupils 12,601, teachers 275; secondary, pupils 2,559, teachers 141; vocational, pupils 153, teachers 14; teacher training, students 62, teachers 7.

Finance and Trade. Monetary unit: Indian rupee, with (Sept. 18, 1972) a free rate of Rs. 7.65 to U.S. $1 (Rs. 18.71 = £1 sterling). Budget (1968–69) balanced at *c.* Rs. 11 million. Third five-year development plan (1971–76) total expenditure (est.) Rs. 350 million; development aid from India (including aid to Sikkim; 1968–69) Rs. 50 million. About 95% of external trade is with India. Main exports (1963–64): timber Rs. 1,250,000; coal Rs. 220,000.

Benelux:
see Belgium; Luxembourg; Netherlands

Bermuda:
see Dependent States

Beverages, Alcoholic:
see Alcoholic Beverages

Bicycling:
see Cycling

Biochemistry:
see Life Sciences

ACHEAMPONG, IGNATIUS KUTU

After overthrowing Kofi Busia's civilian government on Jan. 13, 1972, Lieut. Col. Ignatius Acheampong became Ghana's new head of state. It was the West African republic's second military coup since independence in 1957. Accusing Busia of mismanaging the country's economy and of allowing malpractices similar to those that grew up under former president Kwame Nkrumah (*see* OBITUARIES), Acheampong set up a National Redemption Council with himself as chairman.

His leadership once established, Acheampong's most dramatic step was to repudiate a substantial part of the heavy burden of international debt inherited from the Nkrumah regime; this was considered by many Ghanaians as a major impediment to economic development. He also adopted a militant attitude toward African questions, supporting the liberation movements in southern Africa and rejecting the diplomatic overtures to South Africa made by Busia. His campaign for voluntary labour in conjunction with a "Feed Yourself" program to avoid importing foodstuffs won immediate popular support. He restored considerable freedom of action to the labour unions and encouraged a freer press. Although he had to deal with an attempted countercoup less than eight months after taking power, Acheampong had little difficulty in surmounting it. A gesture that won him considerable popular support was his assent to a state funeral in Ghana for Nkrumah following the latter's death in exile.

Almost unknown outside the Army before he took power, the 40-year-old "Ike" Acheampong was a studious, rather reserved infantry officer. Born in Kumasi, he joined the Army after school, winning selection for officer training at the Mons Officer Cadet College, Aldershot, Eng., and later at the General Staff College, Ft. Leavenworth, Kansas. After Nkrumah's overthrow in 1966 he served for two years as chairman of the first military regime's Administration Commission in the Western Region. In 1969 he was promoted to take command of the 5th Battalion and later of the 1st Brigade, then spent more than a year abroad as a member of a military tribunal following an army mutiny in Trinidad. (COLIN LEGUM)

AGNEW, SPIRO THEODORE

The most remarkable phenomenon in U.S. politics in recent years was the modeling and remodeling of political figures. No one on the U.S. political scene epitomized the phenomenon more than Vice-Pres. Spiro T. Agnew. In Pres. Richard M. Nixon's first term, Agnew played the tough antagonist, the unrelenting, unyielding voice of the predominantly conservative wing of the Republican Party and the man who led the grass roots struggle to win over normally Democratic blue-collar voters. His attacks on the liberal establishment were unvarnished. He took on the "eastern liberal press establishment" and it took his verbal attacks lying down. Known during this period of his vice-presidential career as a man with a vocabulary, Agnew attacked elitists with erudite, if pedantic, phrases, the most remembered of which probably was "effete corps of impudent snobs."

He did his job well. Then as the 1972 presidential election neared, there was talk of a "dump Agnew" movement generated by the liberal wing of the Republican Party and apparently pressure that did not go unheeded in the Oval Office at the White House. There were, after all, other equally formidable vice-presidential candidates in the wings, not the least of whom was former treasury secretary John Connally. But a different Spiro Agnew emerged and the dump Agnew talk simply died out for want of any further serious sponsorship.

He campaigned assiduously for the Republican ticket in 1972, but gone were the strident, hard-hitting attacks on liberal sacred cows. A new Agnew was in the making and when he accepted the vice-presidential nomination in Miami and later in an election victory speech, he spoke in statesmanlike terms, softly, but firmly.

As the vice-president to a lame-duck president, Agnew would emerge as a strong contender for the top spot on the Republican national ticket in 1976. And the new Agnew seemed far more of a presidential figure as the new year began than he did in the rough-and-tumble earlier days in office.

Agnew's rise in politics was surprising and quick. He was born in Baltimore, Md., on Nov. 9, 1918, and the only elective offices he had ever held before becoming governor of the state were that of Parent-Teacher Association president and Baltimore County executive. In 1968, the selection of Agnew as Nixon's running mate was a national surprise that caught everyone off guard. (PHILIP KOPPER)

ELLIOTT ERWITT—MAGNUM

Spiro Agnew

ALLEN, DICK

"A problem child of gigantic proportions" for several years and several teams, Richard Anthony Allen settled down to play serious baseball in Chicago in 1972 and, as a sign of his new seriousness, changed his nickname from Richie to a more adult Dick. His efforts as a slugging first baseman nearly made division champions of the White Sox and won him a landslide victory in the sportswriters' most valuable player award balloting.

Allen's career began auspiciously enough; he was named National League rookie of the year when he broke in with the Philadelphia Phillies. Then followed "seven years of mounting unpleasantness," according to one report. "He missed planes and buses but he never missed a drink." The Phillies traded him to the St. Louis Cardinals, who in turn unloaded him on the Los Angeles Dodgers. Having played for three teams in as many years, "baseball's bad boy" was traded to the American League's White Sox, managed by long-time acquaintance Chuck Tanner.

"I thought 'what are they trying to do to me?' But I found a home in Chicago," he said. "It was a blessing in disguise and I'm glad I came." Still, his selection as most valuable player was leavened in advance by the White Sox' defeat for the Western Division title by the Oakland A's who went on to win the World Series. The team had made extraordinary progress though. Three seasons earlier the White Sox chalked up the worst record in the major leagues, along with the lowest attendance. In 1972 only the Detroit Tigers enjoyed a busier gate.

Part of the renewed popular appeal was Allen's powerful bat. A former teammate said, "There were times when we wondered if his line drives would hit that building over there (an exhibition hall at spring training camp) and turn it around." Allen led the league with 37 homers and 113 runs batted in. He missed the triple crown batting honours with a still laudable .308 average. But he was tops in the eyes of fans. When he came up to bat on Dick Allen Night, he got a standing ovation as the stadium organist played "Jesus Christ Superstar." To join the ranks of MVP winners like Lefty Grove, Jimmy Foxx, Lou Gehrig, and Joe DiMaggio, the 30-year-old native of Wampum, Pa., won 21 of the 24 first-place votes. (PHILIP KOPPER)

JOYCELYNE BENZAKIN

Salvador Allende Gossens

ALLENDE GOSSENS, SALVADOR

Entering the third year of his term and nearing his 65th birthday, Salvador Allende Gossens of Chile presided uneasily over a nation caught up in turmoil and discontent. The avowedly Marxist economic policies followed by Allende since his narrow election victory in 1970 had frightened away foreign investment and discouraged private business, and these difficulties were compounded by a falling market and low world prices for copper. A lifelong Socialist, Allende found himself caught between the united opposition of the right, centre, and liberal left, which controlled the Congress, and his more radical followers, who wanted a totally Marxist state.

Allende faced a major crisis late in 1972 when a truckers' strike, brought on by his attempt to set up a state transport system, ballooned into a paralyzing nationwide shutdown that included professionals and businessmen. When the strike was finally settled, Allende began a trip that took him to Mexico, the UN in New York (where he delivered a stinging attack on the U.S.), the U.S.S.R., and Cuba, seeking support and aid. Abroad he faced legal action by the Kennecott Copper Corp. to recover compensation for its nationalized properties, while at home the 1973 congressional elections threatened to reduce further the effectiveness of his leftist coalition government.

Allende was born July 26, 1908, in Santiago. His studies won him degrees in both medicine and law, but he soon turned to politics. He lost three efforts to win the Chilean presidency but established himself as leader of the Socialists and eventually as president of the Senate. In September 1970 he again ran for the presidency on a platform of agrarian reform and nationalization of basic industries and won with 36.7% of the popular vote.

Allende's most popular move as president was his expropriation of the U.S.-owned copper companies. His policy of agrarian reform often encouraged illegal land seizures by peasants, which had the effect of reducing agricultural production. A price freeze and a large increase in wages instituted by his government caused many small businesses to shut down. (JEREMIAH A. O'LEARY)

ANDERSON, JACK NORTHMAN

Jack Anderson, the muckraking newspaper columnist who worked in the late Drew Pearson's shadow for more than two decades, finally came into his own in 1972 with a series of sensational stories. One of them won him a Pulitzer Prize; another led to a humiliating apology to Sen. Thomas F. Eagleton of Missouri.

Anderson's first major story broke on Dec. 30, 1971, when he began publication of top-secret government reports showing that, contrary to its publicly proclaimed neutrality, the Nixon administration had had a strong anti-Indian bias during the 1971 Indo-Pakistani war over Bangladesh. The story won Anderson the 1972 Pulitzer Prize for national reporting.

In his second story, first published February 29, Anderson reported that the Justice Department made a favourable settlement of an antitrust suit pending against the International Telephone and Telegraph Corp. at about the same time ITT pledged $400,000 to the Republican national convention, then set to be held in San Diego, Calif. That exposé, based in part on a secret memo allegedly written by ITT lobbyist Dita Beard, endangered the confirmation as U.S. attorney general of Richard G. Kleindienst, whom Anderson charged with involvement in the case, and prompted a Senate investigation. Anderson devoted his March 21 and 22 columns to documents purporting to show that ITT, in collusion with the CIA, had tried to stop the 1970 election of leftist Pres. Salvador Allende of Chile.

With three big stories to his credit, Anderson had achieved a considerable reputation by mid-1972. Then on July 27 he reported that Senator Eagleton (*q.v.*), who was fighting to remain the Democratic vice-presidential candidate, had been arrested several times for reckless and drunken driving. Anderson's source, whom he identified as "a former high official from Missouri," turned out to be Washington attorney William True Davis, who had lost a Senate primary election to Eagleton in 1968. On August 1 Anderson issued a public apology: "There is no question in my mind that the senator is not guilty of these . . . charges."

Jack Northman Anderson was born in Long Beach, Calif., on Oct. 19, 1922. He worked as a foreign correspondent in China and, after his discharge from the Army in 1947, was hired by Drew Pearson to help gather material for the "Washington Merry-Go-Round" column. Anderson inherited the column when Pearson died in 1969.

(RICHARD L. WORSNOP)

ANDREOTTI, GIULIO

The final breakup of the centre-left coalition government, which under several premiers had ruled Italy for nearly ten years, gave Christian Democrat Giulio Andreotti the chance to prove his ability when fears of extremist violence were challenging the democratic principles of the republican constitution. On Feb. 5, 1972, Andreotti was asked by newly elected Italian Pres. Giovanni Leone (*q.v.*) to form a one-party Christian Democratic government to carry the country to an unavoidable general election. This he did, while succeeding in reaffirming the principles of law and order.

After the elections, held on May 7–8, it became clear that a centre coalition government was a possibility and Andreotti was again asked to form a government. On June 26 he announced his Cabinet, composed of Christian Democrats, Social Democrats, and Liberals, and with the outside support of the Republican Party. His program's main points were economic stabilization, greater respect for law and order, and cooperation in solving international problems.

Born in Rome on Jan. 14, 1919, Andreotti took a degree in law and wrote for the Catholic press, acting as editor of the university weekly magazine *Azione Fucina*. In 1942 he was appointed president of the Italian Catholic University Federation, an office he held until 1945 when he started his political career. He also edited the newspaper *Il Popolo* during its clandestine period. National delegate of the Young Christian Democrats, he was elected to the Constituent Assembly, and in the 1948 election was returned to the Chamber of Deputies for the region of Lazio. He was undersecretary (1947–53) to Alcide De Gasperi (premier, 1945–53), under whose guidance he was responsible for liaison between the government and Parliament.

Andreotti also interested himself in questions concerning sports, the cinema industry, and the theatre, and was the author of various books on historical, political, and social subjects. He held various Cabinet posts in several governments. He also became chairman of the Christian Democratic parliamentary group in the Chamber of Deputies.

(FABIO GALVANO)

ARANDA, GABRIEL

On Sept. 12, 1972, Gabriel Aranda was unknown to the general public in France. The next day he sprang into a blaze of nationwide publicity and in little more than a week the "Archangel Gabriel" had achieved a celebrity rivaling that of Brigitte Bardot or the president of the republic.

A somewhat incongruous folk hero, this self-effacing, plumpish, balding former ministry official and journalist had taken upon himself the task of "cleansing the royal stables." He set about his crusade by leaking to the press contents of the large number of documents that he had photocopied in the course of his duties as assistant to the minister of public works in Jacques Chaban-Delmas' government. These, he claimed, proved misuse of influence, undercover maneuvers, compromising activities, and other scandals. As a result one Gaullist deputy, accused of corruption, had to resign, while others trembled, protested, or offered explanations.

Required to explain his possession of the documents, Aranda fled, suddenly reappearing several days later to hand the documents over to the *juge d'instruction* (examining magistrate) appointed to look into the affair; no action was taken against him. Although a month later the public prosecutor stated that only in two cases had Aranda's revelations justified further inquiries, Aranda himself declared that he was satisfied that his activity had been a useful public service.

Aranda claimed to be a staunch Gaullist, intent on weeding out corrupt elements in the party. His own account of his campaign, published in book form (*L'État piégé*) in December, painted a picture that offered little comfort to the regime at a time when opinion polls showed the opposition to be gaining ground.

Born in 1938 to parents in modest circumstances, Aranda was apprenticed to a pastry cook at the age of 14. In 1957 he obtained a mathematics degree through night school and after military service became a financial journalist. During 1965–69 he was personal assistant to Albin Chalandon, director of a private bank. When Chalandon became minister of public works in 1971, Aranda rejoined him as his aide.

(PIERRE VIANSSON-PONTÉ)

AUDEN, W(YSTAN) H(UGH)

With England's poet laureateship *sede vacante*, W. H. Auden was proposed as one who would fill it handsomely. The 65-year-old poet quickly made clear his total disinterest and the honour eventually fell to Sir John Betjeman (*q.v.*). Nevertheless, during the year Auden at last put an end to his long "exile" from England, deserting his home in New York City's East Village on grounds that U.S. cities and the Lower East Side were too perilous to the survival of older people. He had settled in the U.S. in 1939 and acquired citizenship in 1946. He accepted an invitation from Oxford Cathedral Chapter to return to "spend my second childhood where I spent my first" in the university city and establish residence at Christ Church.

One reason Auden gave for his decision to settle in Oxford was the fact that he now felt himself too old to live alone during the winter and preferred the alternative of community life. The college authorities expressed the hope that his presence would itself be an inspiration and a source of creativity. That his own creative springs still bubbled Auden proved with the publication in September of a new collection, *Epistle to a Godson and Other Poems*. One of the poems noted that

> if at Cambridge
> the tuning's a wee bit sharp, then
> at Oxford it may well be flat.

His own presence at the latter might do much to improve the pitch.

Born Feb. 21, 1907, in York, Eng., the son of a physician, Auden established his public reputation as a poet during the 1930s with numerous collections (including *Poems* and *Look, Stranger!*). During this period, from which also date the poetic plays (notably *The Ascent of F.6*) written in collaboration with Christopher Isherwood, he was deeply influenced by the thinking of Freud and Marx. In the 1940s, however, his work began to evidence a new, Christian awareness—the transition being marked by *New Year Letter* (1941; U.S. title, *The Double Man*). His later poems were increasingly personal in tone. Auden received numerous awards and honours, including the King George Gold Medal for Poetry (1937) and a Pulitzer Prize (1948), and was generally recognized as one of the most versatile and intellectually challenging poets of the 20th century. (DAVID HATELY)

BENTON, WILLIAM

In April 1972, in London, publisher William Benton was formally installed as vice-president of the National Book League, the only U.S. citizen to be vice-president of the prestigious organization. Elected as a member of the Connecticut delegation to the Democratic national convention in June, he served on the party's platform committee in Washington, D.C., and attended the July convention in Miami, Fla. In September the University of Connecticut, which he had served as trustee for 15 years, dedicated the William Benton Museum of Art, the university's new art gallery. In November Benton was designated a Chubb fellow by his alma mater, Yale, and spent a full week on campus, lecturing and talking with students. In a similar capacity later in the year he addressed students at the Lyndon B. Johnson School of Public Affairs at the University of Texas at Austin and was a guest of the former U.S. president and his wife at the LBJ ranch.

The William Benton Foundation, of which he was president and chairman, continued to provide major support to innovative research and experimentation in mass communications. A grant to Connecticut Public Television made possible live broadcasts of state legislative sessions. Other grants went to the National Citizens Committee for Broadcasting and to the National Media Council, which, with support from several foundations, was formed in 1972 to monitor the fairness and accuracy of U.S. news media, both electronic and print. In addition, the foundation provided support for the Aspen Institute for Humanistic Studies to examine public aspects of the mass media.

Born in Minneapolis, Minn., on April 1, 1900, Benton was graduated from Yale in 1921. He and Chester Bowles founded the advertising agency of Benton and Bowles in 1929. Benton became vice-president of the University of Chicago in 1937. In 1943, in partnership with the university, Benton became owner and publisher of *Encyclopædia Britannica* and chairman of its board. He was named U.S. assistant secretary of state by Pres. Harry S. Truman in 1945 and served until 1947. During that time he was instrumental in developing the first U.S. peacetime worldwide information and education program to complement U.S. foreign policy. Among the projects begun under his direction at the State Department were the Voice of America, the United States information offices, and enabling legislation for U.S. participation in the United Nations Educational, Scientific and Cultural Organization (UNESCO).

Appointed to the U.S. Senate as a Democrat in 1949, Benton was elected to a two-year term in 1950. He was the first senator on either side of the aisle to take on Sen. Joseph R. McCarthy both on and off the floor of the Senate. When McCarthy's Communist witchhunt at the State Department was in full swing, it was Benton who introduced a resolution in the Senate calling for the expulsion of the Wisconsin Republican. The resolution was never acted upon by the Senate, and Benton was not reelected in the 1952 Eisenhower landslide. (The Senate later voted to censure McCarthy.)

Benton traveled widely and wrote extensively. He is the subject of a biography, *The Lives of William Benton,* by Sidney Hyman, published in 1969 by the University of Chicago Press. (NELLIE L. GIFFORD)

GAMMA

Jack Anderson

BERLINGUER, ENRICO

For three years, while Italian Communist Party leader Luigi Longo was incapacitated by illness, Enrico Berlinguer had been the real party power. The party congress formally recognized his tutelage by electing him secretary-general on March 17, 1972, giving Longo the newly created role of party president. The decision could not have been delayed. Italian Pres. Giovanni Leone (*q.v.*) had called a general election for May 7–8 and the party needed to clear all internal matters before facing the electorate.

It was a difficult campaign, permeated by the struggle against the advancing popularity of the right-wing, neofascist Italian Social Movement, and made even more delicate by the continuous accusations the two parties were hurling at each other of plotting to overthrow the democratic system in Italy. Berlinguer countered these accusations by asserting that his party would cooperate in a centre-left coalition with the more progressive wing of the Christian Democrats. In the elections, the Communist vote increased only marginally compared with the previous election, and his cooperation was not sought by the Christian Democrats.

Berlinguer was born in Sassari, Sardinia, on May 25, 1922. From 1937 on he was in contact with antifascist groups, and in 1943 he became a member of the Communist Party. He was jailed for a few months following antifascist demonstrations in Sassari early in 1944 and, at the end of that year, was called to Rome as a member of the National Secretariat of the Young Communists' Movement. From 1947 to 1956 he was secretary-general of the Young Communists' Federation. In 1945 he had also become a member of the party's Central Committee, and in 1948 a member of the executive. After a series of posts within the party, both in Rome and in Sardinia, he became secretary for the region of Lazio. He was returned to the Chamber of Deputies on May 19, 1968. In 1969 he became vice-secretary of the Italian Communist Party, a post that he held until his election as secretary-general. (FABIO GALVANO)

BETJEMAN, SIR JOHN

Insofar as the English poet laureate is the nation's poet (his traditional duty is to celebrate royal and patriotic occasions in verse), the choice, announced in October 1972, of Sir John Betjeman to succeed Cecil Day-Lewis (*see* OBITUARIES) in the office was singularly appropriate. Betjeman was truly popular in the sense of being widely read; more than 100,000 copies of the first edition (1958) of his *Collected Poems* were sold.

The laureateship also carries a suggestion of accolade, a recognition of preeminence. On this score the appointment was somewhat less justifiable, for few critics would place Betjeman in the very first rank of living English poets. He was a poet of the particular, writing about a village in Cornwall, a street in North London or Oxford, a specific provincial railway station. Master of sudden, often self-deprecatory humour, he also displayed a settled melancholy reminiscent of Thomas Hardy. Much of his appeal was through nostalgia, although he rarely extended his readers' imaginative range. Although he was sometimes dismissed as a poet for the elderly, Betjeman's sense of immanence, of the existential importance of things and places, put him—theologically, at any rate—in line with modern thought which refuses to make a distinction between spiritual and material. His poetry was essentially personal, human, and endearing.

Born in London in 1906, Betjeman, an only child, was educated at Marlborough and at Magdalen College, Oxford (the long autobiographical poem, *Summoned by Bells,* 1960, describes this first phase of his life). Unwilling to enter his father's business, he turned to writing and broadcasting, achieving distinction not only as a poet but as an authority on English, especially Victorian, architecture. *Ghastly Good Taste* (1933; new ed., 1970) appeared in the same year as his first book of poems, *Mount Zion,* and was followed by a regular output of architectural and guide books, one of the latest of which was *Victorian and Edwardian London* (1969). Sir John was knighted in 1969. (STEPHANIE MULLINS)

BHUTTO, ZULFIKAR ALI

In the chaos that followed the secession of Pakistan's east wing as the new republic of Bangladesh, Zulfikar Ali Bhutto emerged as his country's leader. One of his first acts upon replacing the discredited Yahya Khan as president on Dec. 20, 1971, was to release the imprisoned leader of Bangladesh, Sheikh Mujibur Rahman (*q.v.*). He did not officially recognize the new republic, but succeeded in partially restoring relations with India. His early achievements were to rescue his country from the trauma of defeat at the hands of the Indian Army and—at least partially—to salvage its shattered economy. He also showed considerable skill and daring in preventing the threatened further fragmentation of Pakistan into several small states.

Bhutto was born on Jan. 5, 1928, into a wealthy landowning family in the desert province of Sind, where his family had lived for 350 years. Unlike his father, Sir Shah Nawaz Bhutto, a former prime minister of Junagadh State, Zulfikar Ali became a rebel against the establishment. He graduated from the University of California at Berkeley and Oxford University before becoming a barrister at the Middle Temple in London. On his return, he supported the Muslim League and quickly rose to become minister of commerce in Pakistan's military regime in 1958. As foreign secretary (1963–66) he played a conspicuous role in establishing close relations with China, but became disillusioned with the military regime and resigned in 1966 to form his own Pakistan People's Party (PPP). He was imprisoned for a time in 1968. In the 1970 elections he led the PPP to a sweeping victory in West Pakistan.

Suave, elegant, and highly sophisticated, Bhutto proved to be a skillful diplomat and a magnetic orator. His own life-style remained that of a wealthy aristocrat, despite his growing commitment to socialism. On becoming president he appealed for time to achieve the reforms he believed were necessary to restore democracy to Pakistan, to modernize its institutions, and to distribute wealth more fairly. But most of his reforms had to wait while he struggled with the divisive problems left in the wake of the disastrous war with the Bengalis and Indians in Bangladesh. (COLIN LEGUM)

BIRENDRA BIR BIKRAM SHAH DEVA, KING

A much-traveled old Etonian, expert parachutist, and impressionistic painter, Birendra Bir Bikram Shah Deva ascended the throne of Nepal on Jan. 31, 1972, after the death of his father, King Mahendra (*see* OBITUARIES). From Mahendra the new monarch inherited a deep-rooted belief in the kingdom's partyless Panchayat (legislative) system because he felt it was "patterned on the basic structure, tenets, and attitude" of his people. However, the system was challenged soon after his reign began by a wide section of Nepalese society demanding democratic and social reforms that the new king's father had promised for over a decade but had never implemented. King Birendra, although not averse to changes in the system to suit modern times, sensed a threat to the monarchy itself and dealt summarily with the politicians and students actively involved. (*See* NEPAL.)

King Birendra was born on Dec. 28, 1945, at the royal palace in Katmandu. He lost his mother at the age of five and came under the direct influence of his father, then crown prince, during the hectic days of the Rana regime. Birendra had his early education at Darjeeling, India, and went to Eton College in England in August 1959. He spent almost five years at Eton, taking time off during this period to join his father on his tours of the United Kingdom in 1960 and Europe in 1961. The prince was an observer at the nonaligned nations' conference in Belgrade in 1961 when his father led the Nepalese delegation.

After leaving Eton in June 1964 Birendra toured the Soviet Union and Iran before returning to Nepal. In October of the same year he acted for the first time as chairman of the Regency Council when his father was touring Egypt. To acquaint himself with life in various parts of the country, he traveled incognito throughout the kingdom in 1965–66. He also traveled extensively in Asia, Africa, Europe, and the Americas, spending some months as a student at Tokyo University. In 1967 he went to Harvard University to study economics and political science. (GOVINDAN UNNY)

Tony Boyle
WIDE WORLD

BOYLE, W. A. ("TONY")

A colourful and brutal chapter in U.S. labour history ended in 1972 when W. A. ("Tony") Boyle was unseated as president of the 200,000-member United Mine Workers by reform candidate Arnold Miller, a partly disabled miner from the West Virginia coal country. Boyle had taken over the union presidency in 1963 as the handpicked successor of John L. Lewis, the fiery Welshman who had built the UMW into one of the most powerful and dynamic of U.S. unions. He left it in disarray, amid charges that he and his clique had used the union for their own purposes rather than for the betterment of its members.

In March the $50,000-a-year union president had been convicted on 13 counts of conspiracy and corrupt political campaign practices, including the surreptitious donation of $49,250 in union funds to various political candidates between 1967 and 1969. He was sentenced in June to serve two concurrent five-year terms in prison and fined $130,000. But this case was only one heat in the field day of Justice Department actions against the union leadership.

In 1969 Boyle had been challenged for the UMW presidency by Joseph A. Yablonski, who pledged to clean up corruption in the union. Boyle won by a 2 to 1 margin, but the campaign was so rife with improprieties that a federal judge in May 1972 ordered the Labor Department to oversee a new election in December. Less than a month after the 1969 election, Yablonski, his wife, and daughter had been found murdered in their Clarksville, Pa., home. At the murder trial, in May 1972, the FBI produced evidence allegedly linking the murders to the UMW hierarchy.

A lesser bit of chicanery involved a suit brought by retired miners and miners' widows. They charged—and the court confirmed—that union pension funds were deposited in non-interest-bearing accounts at a Washington, D.C., bank largely owned by the union.

The 1972 election was perhaps the most closely supervised in U.S. labour history, with Labor Department personnel overseeing the printing, casting, and counting of the ballots. When the votes were finally tabulated, on December 16, Miller had received 70,373 to Boyle's 56,334, and shortly thereafter Boyle resigned. Miller's group, the Miners for Democracy, hoped—in the words of *Business Week*—to "democratize the union . . . and bring an end to nepotism in the UMW hierarchy. And they would probably be more militant on safety in the mines." They might even move the union's headquarters from Washington to the mine fields.

Boyle was born in Bald Butte, Mont., on Dec. 1, 1904. He joined the union hierarchy in 1948 as assistant to the international president. (PHILIP KOPPER)

Marlon Brando

RENE CHATEAU—GAMMA

BRANDO, MARLON

The man with the magic mumble, Marlon Brando proved that Hollywood was not dead in 1972. He played the title role in *The Godfather,* a record-breaking film that made previous cinematic ventures seem like rummage sales. It grossed $42,988,000 in its first 31 weeks, and promised to earn three times that amount in the long run. But the brutal, blood-bathed adaptation of Mario Puzo's best-selling novel was significant not only for the treasure troves that 15 million Americans surrendered at box offices. Brando gave an extraordinary por-

UPI COMPIX

Avery Brundage

trayal of a soft-voiced, wheezy Mafia chief who cuddled cats and played hide-and-seek with his grandson. (Notably, the word Mafia was never used because of objections from Italian-American groups.)

The film was partly a nostalgic '40s adventure and partly a parable. "Don Corleone is just any ordinary American business magnate who is trying to do the best he can for the group he represents and for his family," Brando said. When his henchmen prepare a rival for summary execution they tell him "'Just business. Nothing personal.' When I read that, McNamara, Johnson and Rusk flashed before my eyes."

Brando wanted the part and director Francis Ford Coppola wanted him for it, but the actor's temperamental foibles had cost producers money before, and Paramount moneymen pushed George C. Scott, Sir Laurence Olivier, and even trial lawyer Melvin Belli. So the actor quietly suggested a screen test—unheard-of for a star of his stature. When it was done, the producers could not recognize the man who had gained fame as the urban-earthy Stanley Kowalski in *A Streetcar Named Desire,* slick Sky Masterson in the musical *Guys and Dolls,* the illiterate revolutionary in *Viva Zapata!,* and the savvy vengeance-seeker in *One-Eyed Jacks.*

Born in Omaha, Neb., April 3, 1924, and raised in Evanston, Ill., Marlon Brando, Jr., went to New York when he was 19. He appeared on Broadway and in the film *The Men* before setting the movie world on its heels in 1952 with his Method performance in *Streetcar.* In 1954 Brando won an Oscar for his portrayal of Terry Malloy, the pigeon-keeping longshoreman in *On the Waterfront.* His latest film, Bernardo Bertolucci's sexually explicit *Last Tango in Paris,* created a sensation at its pre-release showing at the 1972 New York Film Festival.

Reportedly a private man, Brando did not like interviews. It was known that he had been married twice and missed *The Godfather*'s premiere because of litigation over the custody of a teen-age son. He spent much time on a Pacific island that he owned, and he planned to open a research centre there to study such environmentally oriented matters as solar energy and marine food harvesting. Brando did not consciously study his craft or even watch his own performances. "You don't learn to be effective from film but from life." "Acting is the guy who returns from some out of town wingding with some bimbo and tells his wife 'Oh, I had a terrible time.'" (PHILIP KOPPER)

BRANDT, WILLY

The outcome of the West German federal elections on Nov. 19, 1972, was a great personal triumph for Willy Brandt, who on December 14 was confirmed as chancellor of the Federal Republic for a second term. For the first time the Social Democratic Party (SPD)—whose main campaign slogan had been "Willy Brandt must stay chancellor"—emerged as the strongest party in the Bundestag.

The election result was also an unmistakable endorsement of Brandt's *Ostpolitik.* In May the Bundestag had ratified the treaties with the U.S.S.R. and Poland that accepted the geographic status quo in Europe, leaving the way open for effective implementation of the four-power agreement on Berlin, and—of potentially greater significance—for a European conference on security and cooperation. Just prior to the elections Brandt's government had concluded a general relations treaty with East Germany, the first to be negotiated between the two German states, and this was signed in East Berlin on December 21.

Although better relations with Eastern Europe had always been a cornerstone of Brandt's foreign policy, he had done more than any other statesman to break down French objections to an enlargement of the EEC, especially with regard to British entry, which was to become effective on Jan. 1, 1973.

Born Herbert Ernst Karl Frahm in Lübeck on Dec. 18, 1913, Brandt changed his name on fleeing to Norway in 1933 when his activities as a young Social Democrat brought him to the attention of the Gestapo. In Norway, and in Sweden following the German invasion of Norway, he earned his living as a journalist. After the war he returned to Germany as a Norwegian citizen but took up German nationality again and in 1949 was elected to the Bundestag. From 1957 to 1966, when he became foreign minister and vice-chancellor in the SPD-Christian Democratic Union grand coalition, he was governing mayor of West Berlin. He became chairman of the SPD in 1964 and suffered two defeats as a candidate for the chancellorship in 1961 and 1965 before achieving success in 1969. In 1971 Brandt was awarded the Nobel Peace Prize. (NORMAN CROSSLAND)

BRIDGE, PETER J.

To be ordered to jail without a single newsman present to record the event was the height of indignity for Peter Bridge, a reporter who knew all too well what it was to have an exclusive story. In May 1972 Bridge had reported exclusively that one of the commissioners of the Newark, N.J., Housing Authority had been offered $10,000 to vote for an unidentified man's choice for executive director of the Authority. Bridge's report led to a grand jury investigation and he was called to testify. He answered more than 50 questions but refused to answer five others about the alleged extortionist's identity, information not contained in his story. Bridge claimed a journalist's right to immunity under the First Amendment of the U.S. Constitution and under the New Jersey "shield law" that protects newsmen from prosecution for material they report.

On July 7 Bridge was held in contempt of court. In its finding, the court cited a ruling handed down only eight days before by the U.S. Supreme Court that denied reporters any special protection when asked to testify on criminal matters. Bridge was disappointed that the press had not responded to his predicament. "I seriously wondered," he said later, "if I wanted to continue in a profession that was too fat and lazy to defend itself against a dangerous attack." After a series of appeals failed, Bridge went to jail on October 4 and was released just prior to the disbanding of the grand jury at the end of October.

Reporters, meanwhile, visited Bridge constantly during his incarceration; he had received as many as 1,000 letters of support and several job offers (his paper, the *Newark Evening News,* had folded on August 31), and various groups had raised at least $4,000 for his legal defense. "This is a funny society," Bridge said. "It does put a premium on being recognized and I'm going to jump on board now and ride." He spent the rest of the year telling his story and spreading his message at banquets and symposia throughout the U.S.

Bridge, 36, graduated from Syracuse (N.Y.) University in 1960. He had been a reporter with the *Evening News* for more than 11 years when it folded. His third child, a daughter, was born six days after his release from jail. (NELLIE L. GIFFORD)

BRUNDAGE, AVERY

Avery Brundage was the Zeus of the modern Olympic Games—or the Nero. For two decades he presided over the International Olympic Committee (IOC), a post he relinquished in 1972 after the most controversial and tragic Olympic Games in history. The 1972 Olympics were torn by arguments over eligibility rules and biased referees—and punctuated by mass murder. (*See* SPORTING RECORD: *Special Report.*)

As a tireless devotee of the ideals of amateur sport, Brundage, in his career with the Olympics, was used to such controversy. Over the years harangues over the amateur or professional status of competitors confused and often outraged the public. Before the 1972 Winter Games at Sapporo, Jap., Brundage and the IOC disqualified Austrian skiing ace Karl Schranz because, like most European superstars, he promoted ski equipment.

Schranz remained a scapegoat and went home to a hero's welcome. Other Europeans who endorsed athletic gear were permitted to compete, while Soviet athletes (who are subsidized royally) and American collegians (who get athletic scholarships worth thousands of dollars) entered the lists without so much as a wink from the committee. Such devotion to amateurism might be noble, but in this day and age it was unrealistic and was especially deplorable because of the inconsistency with which the code of amateurism was honoured.

Brundage was born in Detroit on Sept. 28, 1887, and was amateur all-around champion of America in 1914, 1916, and 1918. A wealthy industrialist and art collector, Brundage over the years had amassed a $50 million collection of Oriental art, which he donated to the city of San Francisco. He was succeeded as IOC president by 58-year-old Irishman Lord Killanin. (PHILLIP KOPPER)

BUNKER, ARCHIE

Archie Bunker was born a middle-aged, bigoted failure on a Tuesday night in January 1971. By May he was the most popular television character in America, and in 1972 he chalked up one vice-presidential vote at the Democratic national convention. Every

UPI COMPIX

Steve Carlton

Saturday night Archie and his "All in the Family" clan trooped into more living rooms than any other TV show.

A shipping clerk and moonlighting cab driver, Archie was a loser, a ragged individualist. If he were real he would be frustrated, but in fantasy he was the incredibly indefatigable loudmouth, a victim constantly claiming victory. He was antiblack, anti-Semitic, anti-Catholic, and anti-Puerto Rican. Only his absurdly simplistic world view enabled him to be a king in his own tawdry castle. Yet there was a perverse Everyman quality about him, a littler-than-life element that was highly comic.

Norman Lear and Bud Yorkin adapted "All in the Family" from a highly successful British series, "Till Death Us Do Part." The British series was tougher, and the leading character, created by Johnny Speight, was less sympathetic, but even so, "All in the Family" came as a shock to U.S. viewers. As played by Carroll O'Connor (whose own antiracist credentials were impeccable), Archie was forever telling his wife, Edith (Jean Stapleton), to "stifle yourself" and unsuccessfully trying to stifle his freeloading "Polack meathead" son-in-law. Shattering taboos, he threw "Hebe" and "jungle bunny" around like suds in a detergent commercial.

Not everyone was enchanted. The Anti-Defamation League, *Ebony* magazine, and Laura Z. (*Gentleman's Agreement*) Hobson all said he glorified bigotry. Despite the debunkers, the program won six Emmy Awards in 1972 and spawned a new look in situation comedies. The first spin-off was "Maude," another Lear-Yorkin creation, featuring Archie's knee-jerk liberal cousin-in-law. "Sanford and Son," also based on a British series, introduced a black junkman and con artist. "Bridget Loves Bernie" tried to update *Abie's Irish Rose*.

The common denominator of these shows was their rejection of the conventional Madison Avenue see-no-evil attitude. Archie coped with blockbusting, unemployment, and hypocritical puritanism. Edith coped with the menopause. Maude, pregnant at 47, considered abortion. Observers might legitimately be nervous, but the end result could be a new maturity for what had been a poly-unsophisticated medium. (PHILIP KOPPER)

CARLTON, STEVE

"I don't give a damn if he never pitches another ball for the Cardinals."

So said St. Louis Cardinal owner August Busch in 1970 about Stephen Norman Carlton, a pitcher who was holding out for more money. Carlton did pitch another year for the Cardinals but then in 1972 was traded to Philadelphia. There he made baseball history. Pitching for the last-place Phillies, he won 27 games—the most victories ever achieved in one season by a pitcher for a cellar-dwelling team. Carlton's win total accounted for 46% of Philadelphia's victories and tied Sandy Koufax's record for most wins in a season by a southpaw. He led the National League in complete games with 30 and in strikeouts with 310. At the season's end he was the unanimous choice for the National League's Cy Young Award.

Carlton attributed much of his success to a ten-page letter he received from a man in Tucson, Ariz., in August 1970. That letter and later ones from the same man gave him a new positive outlook and "made me realize that man is the only animal who puts limitations on himself," Carlton said. Before receiving the letter Carlton had a 6–18 record for the year; after it he won 75% of his games.

Carlton was born Dec. 22, 1944, in Miami, Fla. He pitched in high school and junior college and then was signed by the Cardinals in 1965. After a year in the minor leagues he was brought up to St. Louis in 1966.

Carlton's major league career was immediately successful. He pitched in his first World Series in 1967 and in 1968 made the National League All-Star team. In 1967, 1968, and 1969 he won 14, 13, and 17 games, respectively, while turning in an earned run average of under three each season.

But 1970 was a disaster for the tall left-hander. Because of his holdout status, which prompted the remark from Busch, he missed three weeks of spring training. Although he was 4–1 after receiving the letter from Arizona, he finished the year with a 10–19 record. Carlton then came back in 1971 to have his first 20-win year, but Busch, remembering the holdout, traded him before the 1972 season to Philadelphia for Rick Wise. (KIM EISLER)

CARR, ROBERT

Two unexpected switches of British Cabinet posts brought new opportunities for Robert Carr in 1972. Seemingly typecast as the Heath government's principal labour relations expert, Carr became leader of the House of Commons in April after William Whitelaw (*q.v.*) took over in Northern Ireland. Three months later Carr moved to the Home Office when Reginald Maudling resigned as home secretary because of his involvement in an inquiry into the affairs of a former business associate, architect John Poulson.

RALPH CRANE, LIFE MAGAZINE © 1972 TIME INC.

Wilt Chamberlain

For Carr this move meant exchanging one kind of tumultuous controversy for another. At the Department of Employment he had been responsible for steering the new Industrial Relations Act through Parliament in 1971, and was at the centre of the controversy over its enforcement that led to widespread industrial unrest and the imprisonment of five docker pickets for contempt of court. He moved to the Home Office in time to take charge of the resettlement in Britain of Asians driven out of Uganda by Pres. Idi Amin. At the same time he was confronted by an outbreak of prison unrest. His handling of these widely differing issues confirmed his reputation for coolness, reasonableness, and moderation, and added to it a new air of authority which so impressed the Conservatives' annual party conference in October that he was being talked of as a possible future contender for the party leadership.

Born on Nov. 11, 1916, Carr had an enduring interest in industrial relations, grounded in his experience in a metal-manufacturing business founded by his great-grandfather. After taking a degree in metallurgy at Cambridge University, he served his apprenticeship on the foundry floor, and for four years during World War II worked as a shift foreman. Entering Parliament in 1950, he took a large part in the shaping of Conservative industrial and trade-union policy, and was the principal author of the Conservative Party document *Fair Deal at Work*. This led to the Industrial Relations Act, which Carr insisted was not directed against trade unions but provided the legislative framework for ensuring a fair deal for both workers and management. (HARFORD THOMAS)

CARRERO BLANCO, LUIS

In 1972 Gen. Francisco Franco Bahamonde took a further step toward orderly transfer of political power in Spain after his own death or retirement. He had already selected Prince Juan Carlos de Borbón y Borbón to assume the vacant throne of Spain and to succeed him as chief of state. On July 18 a law was enacted formalizing Franco's wish that the position of premier, which Franco also held, would pass automatically to the vice-premier. Adm. Luis Carrero Blanco, an experienced politician and trusted friend of Franco, had been vice-premier since 1967. A scholarly man who had written authoritatively on naval matters, he had achieved political stature in the Cortes, the Spanish Parliament, as an apologist of the regime.

Luis Carrero was born in 1903; he became a naval cadet at 15. After serving in the Moroccan war during 1924–26, he attended Naval War School in Madrid, where in 1935 he was appointed professor of naval war studies. When the Civil War began in 1936 he went into hiding, emerging a year later as a Franco supporter. In August 1939 he was made operations chief of the Naval High Command. He joined the government shortly afterward as undersecretary in the premier's office, and earned his reputation as the power behind the throne of the Franco regime. Well connected politically (it was said that the rise of the technocrats of Opus Dei in Spanish politics was largely due to his intervention), he remained aloof nevertheless from political factions, a practice that allowed him to emerge as Franco's choice of successor in the office of premier.

As vice-premier, Carrero was responsible for governing the country in the absence or sickness of General Franco, who was 80 in 1972. The new legislation signified that unless he retired before the general, or fell from favour, Carrero would become interim premier. He would then be the man most likely to be confirmed as premier by Prince Juan Carlos. (RALPH DEANE)

CHAMBERLAIN, WILTON NORMAN

"The elder statesman of basketball" (according to the *New York Times*), "Wilt the Stilt" Chamberlain dribbled, tossed, tipped, and rebounded the Los Angeles Lakers to their first championship in 1972. Winning the title was no fluke; the team won 69 games in the regular season to set a National Basketball Association record that included an unprecedented 33-game winning streak. The team's not-so-secret weapon was the combination of guard Jerry West and 7-ft. 2-in. Wilt, who, despite painfully chipped hand bones, belied his reputation as a court giant whose talents shriveled in the clutch. "For a long time, fans of mine had to put up with people saying Wilt couldn't win the big ones," he said. "Now maybe they'll have a chance to walk in peace, like I do."

"Throughout his career he has always been the villain," one Stilt-watcher wrote, a simple bully overpowering smaller players. Nonetheless, he was vastly popular—the recipient of 300 fan letters a day and four times the league's most valuable player—because of his unequaled ability, lapses notwithstanding. By the time he sparked the Lakers to championship victory over the New York Knicks his résumé included an enviable .649 field goal percentage and an average of more than 19 rebounds a game. By February 1972 he had scored a total of 30,000 points in his career, including 100 in a single game.

A man of several facets, Chamberlain spoke four languages, played exhibition volleyball, and once considered facing heavyweight boxer Muhammad Ali in the ring. He also became something of an architecture patron by virtue of commissioning a $1.5 million home that featured a four-story living room and a 72-sq.ft. bed beneath a mirrored ceiling that slid away to reveal the sky.

Born on Aug. 21, 1936, in Philadelphia, Chamberlain was as destined for basketball as Noah's dove was for reconnaissance duty off Ararat. He was 6 ft. 9 in. when he entered junior high school. After three years of college he joined the Harlem Globetrotters, then moved to the San Francisco Warriors in 1959, and returned to his hometown to hoop the Philadelphia 76ers to the NBA title in the 1966–67 season. He was traded to the Lakers in the summer of 1968 in a deal comparable to sending "the Jolly Green Giant to Heinz for a soup recipe and two vats of pickles." (PHILIP KOPPER)

CHAPLIN, CHARLES SPENCER

After 20 years of estrangement from the U.S., Charlie Chaplin returned to Hollywood in April 1972 to receive a special award from the Academy of Motion Picture Arts and Sciences. It was a belated accolade to one of motion pictures' most famous pioneers, now generally recognized as the greatest single figure to emerge in the cinema's first three-quarters of a century.

Chaplin had left the U.S. in 1952, and surrendered his reentry permit (he had never become a U.S. citizen) when advised that it would be questioned by the U.S. Department of Justice. Before then he had been pressed by the government for back taxes and hounded—like many lesser men in that heyday of Sen. Joseph McCarthy's anti-Communist crusade—with charges of "subversion." He was then a youthful 63, still creatively active. In 1947 he had made his modern Bluebeard story, *Monsieur Verdoux*. Following his exile he released one of his most charming later films, *Limelight* (1952). He was to make two more films in Britain: *A King in New York* (1957) and *A Countess from Hong Kong* (1966). But clearly America had been the fertile soil his creativity needed.

He returned an old and evidently frail man of 83. Generally he walked only with assistance, and when he spoke it was briefly and simply, to say that he was "very moved" to be fêted and to see the great audience at the award ceremonies delight in films—*The Kid* and *The Pilgrim*—he had made a half-century before. Then he retired once more to his retreat at Vevey, Switz.

Born in London on April 16, 1889, the child of a wastrel music hall singer and a mother afflicted with mental illness, he was raised in the institutions and mean streets of a still Dickensian London. He found work in the music halls, went to the U.S., and was engaged by Mack Sennett. In his second film he began the process of building and refining the character that was to make him famous—the little tramp Everyman. He moved from company to company and finally became his own producer. Having turned out some 70 short and medium-length films in seven years, he then worked slowly and with intense care on his classic feature films: *A Woman of Paris* (1923), which he directed, but in which he did not appear; *The Gold Rush* (1925); *The Circus* (1928); *City Lights* (1931); *Modern Times* (1936); and *The Great Dictator* (1940). (DAVID ROBINSON)

UPI COMPIX

Charlie Chaplin

CHIANG CHING-KUO

Taiwan (Nationalist China) saw the U.S., its best friend and principal big power backer, suddenly turn away from it in 1972 in the direction of Communist China. In an apparent but meaningless effort to boost morale, Taiwan's 84-year-old Chiang Kai-shek named his son, Chiang Ching-kuo, premier on May 26, less than a week after Generalissimo Chiang took office for a fifth term as president. The appointment was taken as merely setting the stage for the succession of the son.

Born in Chekiang Province on March 18, 1910, Chiang was not, as some presumed, the generalissimo's son by the famous Madame Chiang Kai-shek, née Soong Mei-ling. He was born of Chiang Kai-shek's first wife, from whom he was later divorced; she was killed in a Japanese bombing raid in 1939. Chiang, 17 when his father remarried, participated in radical student activities in Shanghai and Peking. In 1925 he went to Moscow for higher studies. While there he held alternate membership in the Communist Party, leaned toward Trotskyism, and was put to work on a collective farm. He also married a Soviet woman.

Returning to China in 1937 after 12 years in the Soviet Union, Chiang renounced his past affiliations and progressively identified himself with his father's strident anti-Communism. As a regional administrator during the Sino-Japanese War, he became known as the "Iron Commissioner." Subsequently, he held numerous posts in the Nationalist government, chiefly connected with military and internal security affairs. For a long period he was in charge of Taiwan's secret police. He also organized and led the Youth Corps. In 1969 he was named deputy premier and chairman of important economic planning committees. Perhaps because he lived under the shadow of his father for 35 years, ever since his return from the Soviet Union, Chiang displayed a retiring disposition. A diabetic, he was often seriously ill although in 1972 he was reported to be very fit. (T. J. S. GEORGE)

CHISHOLM, SHIRLEY

"Fighting Shirley Chisholm," as she liked to be called, fought her way to the U.S. Congress in 1968 to become the first black woman ever to win a seat there. Her seat was hardly warm before she broke precedent as a freshman congressman by refusing her assignments to House subcommittees dealing with forestry and family farms on the grounds that they offered small opportunity for her to serve her Brooklyn constituency, which is mainly an urban slum. "I guess all the gentlemen know about Brooklyn is that a tree grew there," she caustically remarked. She won that bout, and in 1972 served on the House Education and Labor Committee, where her experience and abilities were more appropriate to the legislative task.

Although she vociferously championed the poor and attacked discrimination and the Vietnam war, she rejected the labels of socialist, racist, feminist, and pacifist.

In 1971 she entered the race for the Democratic Party's presidential nomination despite criticism that her candidacy would fragment the already troubled reform bloc within the party. She had no illusions about her chances, but did accomplish her aim of forcing the party to take seriously a representative of two groups—women and blacks—that were seldom given even lip service in the search for presidential candidates. "I am, was, and always will be a catalyst for change," she wrote, and went back to her congressional battles.

Born in Brooklyn on Nov. 30, 1924, Shirley Anita St. Hill lived with her maternal grandmother on a farm in Barbados from the age of 3 to 11.

Returning to her parents in Brooklyn, she went to Brooklyn College and graduated cum laude. After earning an M.A. in education from Columbia University, she began teaching and later became director of a day nursery. She entered politics in 1964, winning election to the New York State Assembly. In 1949 she married Conrad Chisholm, a New York City government official who helped her campaign. (PAT TUCKER)

DENNIS BRACK—BLACK STAR

Shirley Chisholm

CHRISTO

Christo, who claimed fame as an artist by wrapping things up, spread his wings—and his materials—in 1972. After spending months of effort and $700,000 of other people's money, he hung a 400-ft.-high curtain across Rifle Gap, a quarter-mile-wide pass in the Colorado Rockies. Dyed bright orange, it was very pretty against the blue sky. People admired it, and the wind wafted it for about 24 hours before ripping it apart. "That the curtain no longer exists only makes it more interesting," Christo said.

Born Christo Javacheff in Bulgaria on June 13, 1935, Christo fled to the West in 1956. In Paris in 1962 he blocked the rue Visconti with 204 oil drums to earn his credentials as one of the *nouveaux réalistes.* Two years later he went to the U.S. where he started wrapping things in a small way (notably a motorcycle and a nude) before graduating to the Chicago Museum of Contemporary Art, which he covered with tarpaulin. In 1969 he enveloped about a mile of the Australian coastline in plastic. Inspired by memories of Paris, he hoped to stack up 2.5 million oil drums—when he could find the wherewithal, the barrels, and the room.

UPI COMPIX

Christo

The Rifle Gap project was his most ambitious to date. In 1971 he hired engineers and contractors, answered ecologists who thought the giant shadow of his curtain would harm the flora and fauna, and persuaded state authorities to let him hang his fabric across one of the roads bisecting the valley (after posting a $50,000 bond guaranteeing he would take it down afterward). The financial, physical, and personnel problems were almost as enormous as the curtain, which had 60 mi. of seams. The 1971 effort failed, though the economy of Rifle (pop. 2,300) enjoyed a miniboom. A year later, Christo succeeded.

"We call Christo's huge projects art because we have no other choice," said the magazine *Art in America.* "The Valley Curtain, instead of being a device to deliver or delay the spectacle, *is* the spectacle." A Rifle Gap workman told *The New Yorker*'s man that he too had come to grasp the whole thing. "Trouble is, after you explain what it is, then you're *really* in deep water. . . . Now I've got so I just tell 'em it's to feed my wife and kids." (PHILIP KOPPER)

CLARK, RAMSEY

When former U.S. attorney general Ramsey Clark visited North Vietnam in July–August 1972, administration apologists, notably John N. Mitchell, Clark's successor as attorney general, lambasted him for accepting a Communist invitation to tour the bomb-beleaguered country. Calling him "naïve" and "a dupe," Mitchell and others accused Clark of traitorous conduct because his voice was heard over Radio Hanoi.

"I have to live with myself," was Clark's reply, as he reported to Americans the civilian damage and destruction wrought by U.S. bombing. "Whole villages had been wiped off the earth," he declared. "There was no conceivable military significance. . . . There are only people." As for the implications of treason, Clark acknowledged that he had been interviewed by newsmen and that his remarks could have been recorded, but denied that he had ever taped any comments for broadcast.

Clark's candid report on the effects of U.S. bombing was disturbing—the more so because of his eminence and credibility among the American people. The son of Tom Clark, Pres. Harry Truman's attorney general and Supreme Court justice emeritus, Ramsey Clark was born in Dallas, Tex., Dec. 18, 1927. After serving in the Marines and taking a law degree at the University of Chicago, he entered private law practice, then joined the Justice Department in 1961 during the Kennedy administration. President Johnson named him the nation's 66th attorney general in 1967.

After leaving government in 1969, Clark returned to private—if quite visible—practice. He traveled to Moscow in 1972 to "lobby" against repression of Soviet Jews; in 1971 he represented antiwar veterans who were arrested after demonstrating in Washington, D.C. A humanist and a frequent critic of recent war policies, Clark was appalled by what he encountered in Vietnam. "We have to end this killing, and we have to understand what we have done. The only way to do that is to see what we have done. If we're afraid to see that, we'll do it again." (PHILIP KOPPER)

COLES, ROBERT

Often called the most influential living U.S. psychiatrist, Robert Coles gained renown for his determination—and ability—to shatter the stereotypes that help keep down the poor and helpless. His weapons were his empathy, his tape recorder and camera, and his eloquence. With them he exposed the cold statistics of poverty and prejudice as the personal affronts to individual human liberty that they are.

By 1972, Coles had won a fistful of awards for his hundreds of articles and 15 books. Of the four books published in 1972, two—*Migrants, Sharecroppers, Mountaineers* and *The South Goes North*—were volumes 2 and 3 of *Children of Crisis,* his continuing study of slums and backwaters from the deep South to Alaska. The other two were a children's book, *Saving Face,* and *Farewell to the South*.

Born in Milton, Mass., on Oct. 12, 1929, to a Yorkshireman who became a U.S. engineer and a farm girl from Iowa, Coles grew up in a comfortable home where music, books, and conversation were an integral part of everyday life. He graduated from the Boston Latin School and Harvard University, then studied medicine at Columbia University. There his teachers, noting his reluctance to give pain for however therapeutic a reason, steered him toward psychiatry.

After specializing in psychiatry, Coles feared that the usual psychiatric practice would keep him too much in the realm of the mind and too far from the neighbourhood and society and therefore turned his attention to social issues. He sought to learn about groups of people, not by relying on surveys but by spending his time with them. He once rode a black ghetto school bus for a year, and in 1972 was living in New Mexico in order to experience at first hand Chicano and Indian family life in the Southwest for volume 4 of his study.

Often consulted by congressional leaders of both parties, Coles played a key role in such projects as launching the hunger crusade of 1967 and rescuing migrant worker programs from annihilation at the hands of Congress and the Office of Management and Budget. (PAT TUCKER)

COSELL, HOWARD

With a delivery that had all the resonance of a clogged Dristan bottle, sportscaster Howard Cosell talked "Monday Night Football" to the top of the television ratings in 1972. While one critic said Cosell made "the world of fun and games sound like the Nürnberg trials," his commentary addicted 25 million viewers to the heady ritual of weekly "legalized violence."

The fall series featured the best camera work and technical production of televised sports. Although Cosell was the narrative star, plain-speaking Frank Gifford provided the play-by-play and former backfield ace Don Meredith a drawling analysis of instant replays. Cosell's nasal snarl punctuated the proceedings with polysyllabic barbs, staccato observations, and ad-libbed virtuoso summaries. His long suit was brutal candour, for, as a fan's banner proclaimed at one game, he would "tell it like it is," the devil take both hindmost and the butterfingered.

An occasional stand-in for talk show hosts, guest performer on situation comedies, cameo character (playing himself) in Woody Allen movies, and the unlikely recipient of 12 honorary college degrees in 1972, Cosell had his own free-wheeling radio interview program and did 22 sports spots a week. He was also a featured and controversial reporter at the Olympic Games in Munich, where he took the occasion to say of the International Olympic Committee czar: "There was a time for Avery Brundage . . . that of William of Orange." When two U.S. sprinters were scrubbed because a coach told them to report for a qualifying heat at the wrong time, Cosell mercilessly cross-examined the hapless coach on camera. One observer said Cosell "seems to think of himself as a crusading district attorney."

In fact he was a lawyer. Born in Winston-Salem, N.C., on March 25, 1920, and raised in Brooklyn, N.Y., Cosell earned honours at New York University and its law school. Business did not boom for the private attorney and, as a spin-off of one of his nonlegal activities, he became the unpaid moderator of a Little League baseball radio program on Saturday mornings in 1953: A few years later he forsook the bar completely. Cosell had been the first newsman to consistently call boxer Cassius Clay by his chosen name, Muhammad Ali. Ali now said, "We're both No. 1 in our fields." Not one to take a verbal back seat even to a champ, Cosell said, "I'm It and everyone of you knows it." (PHILIP KOPPER)

UPI COMPIX

Howard Cosell

DAVIS, ANGELA YVONNE

Black militant Angela Davis won two notable court victories in 1972. In June she was acquitted of charges of kidnapping, murder, and conspiracy in connection with a 1970 shoot-out at the Marin County (Calif.) courthouse. In October the U.S. Supreme Court let stand a lower court ruling that she could not constitutionally be fired from the faculty of UCLA because she was a member of the Communist Party.

In the four months between these court decisions, she traveled widely. Shortly after her acquittal in the first case, she undertook a three-week tour of the U.S. to raise money to defray her $250,000 legal expenses. She then visited the Soviet Union, where she received a heroine's welcome, and other Eastern European countries. Neal Ascherson of the London *Observer* wrote of a speech she delivered in Prague: "She talked . . . like those old Communists of blazing conviction who are now so rare in Europe. She left her audience a long way behind." But Czechoslovak journalists who had taken part in the "Prague spring" of 1968 deprecated her uncritical support of the Soviet role in their country.

Her criminal trial, which began on Feb. 28, 1972, stirred interest all over the world. The prosecuting attorney suggested that romantic passion for "Soledad Brother" George Jackson, who was killed in San Quentin prison in 1971, had driven her to plot the Marin County affair in an attempt to free him, but she dismissed the suggestion as male chauvinism. The chief argument of her lawyer was that there was insufficient evidence for a case against her. On June 4 a jury of 11 whites and one Mexican-American found her not guilty.

Angela Davis was born Jan. 26, 1944, in Birmingham, Ala., and was graduated magna cum laude from Brandeis University in 1965. After studying philosophy from 1965 to 1967 at the Johann Wolfgang von Goethe Institute in Frankfurt, W.Ger., she enrolled at the University of California at San Diego, where she earned her M.A. in 1968. Hired to teach at UCLA in the spring of 1969, Miss Davis was dismissed the following September because of her Communist Party membership. Later reinstated through court action, she was dismissed a second time in June 1970. (RICHARD L. WORSNOP)

DEVANEY, ROBERT

Bob Devaney tried to accomplish in 1972 what no college football coach ever had before: to lead a team to top national standing three years in a row. He failed and the

University of Nebraska Cornhuskers barely finished in the top ten. But in the post-season, glory returned as Devaney choreographed a spectacular 40–6 rout over Notre Dame in the Orange Bowl. He switched his superstar and Heisman Trophy winner Johnny Rodgers from flanker to "I back" and watched him score four touchdowns (and pass for a fifth) to break by five points the previous Orange Bowl record, set in 1953. Even the Notre Dame players described the performance as "fantastic, unbelievable, incredible."

For Devaney the poor finish in the regular season was a clay capstone to a sterling coaching career, because the 1972 season was his last. Before the season opened, his teams had posted a rare .819 win average with an aggregate record of 127 wins, 28 defeats, and 6 ties. This made Devaney the winningest of living college coaches. It also won him the plaudits of the nation's top fan, Pres. Richard Nixon, who called the 1971 Cornhuskers "the greatest team in college football history."

Though never voted coach of the year, Devaney won seven Big Eight titles in ten years. His teams won 23 consecutive games and once went 32 contests without a defeat. Born in Saginaw, Mich., on April 13, 1915, and an end while attending Michigan's little Alma College, Devaney started his coaching career at Big Beaver (Mich.) High School, running up a 52–9–0 record there and at several other secondary schools before joining the fabled Duffy Daugherty at Michigan State. He became head coach at the University of Wyoming in 1957. When he arrived at Nebraska five years later to revive its flagging football fortunes, a sportswriter coined a jingle to help the fans at least pronounce his name correctly: "Get off your fanny and help Devaney." (PHILIP KOPPER)

DIMITRIOS I

On July 16, 1972, in Istanbul, the Holy Synod of the Eastern Orthodox Church elected Metropolitan Dimitrios as the church's 269th Ecumenical Patriarch. Dimitrios I succeeded Patriarch Athenagoras I (Aristoklis M. Spyrou), who died on July 7 (*see* OBITUARIES).

The Turkish government, which considered the Orthodox Patriarchate to be an institution subject to Turkish laws, asked the 15-member Holy Synod to present a list of "at least three" candidates for examination before proceeding to its choice of a successor. The Holy Synod submitted the names of all 15 metropolitans, evidently to dispense at the outset with objections the Turkish authorities might have to any of them. The Turkish prime minister, Ferit Melen, deleted three names from the list, including that of Metropolitan Meliton, the Holy Synod's dean and metropolitan of Khalkidhiki, who allegedly adopted an "anti-Turkish" stand by supporting the union of Cyprus with Greece. As a result of this veto, Metropolitan Dimitrios received 12 of the 15 votes. The ballots were cast into a silver urn, then read one by one. When the simple majority of eight was reached, the dean of the Synod gave the traditional cry of *Axios!* ("He is worthy!"). The new patriarch pledged himself to follow the "bright, straight path" to Christian reunion laid down by his predecessor and said that the links with the Roman Catholic Church would be strengthened and promoted.

Dimitrios Papadopoulos was born in Istanbul in 1914. After studies at the French lycée at Galatasaray, he entered the Holy Trinity School of Theology on the island of Heybeli (Khalki) in the Sea of Marmara. He was ordained priest in 1942, served for a few years as parish administrator in northern Greece, and was later appointed chaplain to the small Greek community in Teheran, Iran. He was consecrated bishop in 1964 and on Feb. 15, 1972, was appointed metropolitan of Imroz (Imbros) and Bozcaada (Tenedos), two Greek-populated islands ceded by Greece to Turkey under the Treaty of Lausanne in 1923.

(K. M. SMOGORZEWSKI)

DONALDSON, SIR JOHN FRANCIS

A British judge who dispensed with robes and wig and cut out the rotund formalities of judicial address, preferring to be called only "Sir," might have attracted public attention for that alone. Sir John Donaldson did make a markedly favourable impression by the informality of his approach when he took over as first president of the National Industrial Relations Court (NIRC), established by the Industrial Relations Act, 1971, to administer a new code of labour-relations law. More than any other judge, he made himself approachable, arguing that his aim was always to seek an agreed solution to disputes.

Yet in his first year as president of the new court, Sir John found himself at the centre of a violent controversy when he had to deal with defiance of the court's rulings by a number of militant trade unionists. The act provided that "blacking" (forbidding and preventing) of certain work by trade unionists might constitute an unfair industrial practice. After a long wrangle between dock workers and Midland Cold Storage Ltd., which was operating a container-packing plant, the court ordered docker pickets to stop "blacking" lorries (trucks) going to the company's East London depot. On July 21, 1972, five dockers who ignored this order were sent to prison for contempt of court.

Sir John pinned the decision on the maintenance of the rule of law. "It is a very simple issue," he said, "but vastly important, for our whole way of life is based upon acceptance of the rule of law." However, the NIRC's credibility suffered when the official solicitor, a somewhat arcane figure in the British legal system, secured the release of the five men, thereby averting a threat of nationwide sympathy strikes and so extricating the government from an awkward predicament.

Born on Oct. 6, 1920, Donaldson was the youngest High Court judge when appointed to the bench in 1966. He had made a reputation in commercial law, without much publicity. As a lawyer often concerned with industrial affairs, he had investigated at first hand the working conditions of miners in the coal pit, seamen on board ship, and railwaymen on the locomotive footplate.

(HARFORD THOMAS)

EAGLETON, THOMAS FRANCIS

The nomination of U.S. Sen. Thomas F. Eagleton as the running mate of Sen. George S. McGovern on the 1972 national Democratic ticket became an instant bona fide historical footnote when the young Missourian belatedly announced that he had been treated several years before in the psychiatric section of St. Louis' prestigious Barnes Hospital and at the Mayo Clinic in Rochester, Minn., for nervous exhaustion and depression. The therapy included electric shock treatments. McGovern stood "1,000%" behind Eagleton for about one week after the disclosure, then dropped him from the ticket in favour of Sargent Shriver.

During the interim, Washington columnist Jack Anderson also joined the historical footnote club, but not with honour. Anderson, on the word of a "most reliable" source, published a report that Eagleton had been arrested for drunken driving. After Eagleton was dropped from the ticket, the spurious drunken-driving charges were laid to rest, along with some of Anderson's credibility.

In his first term in the Senate, Eagleton had shown himself to be a thoughtful and hard-working legislator in the tradition of such Missouri senators as Harry S. Truman, Thomas Hennings, Stuart Symington, and Thomas Hart Benton. Eagleton steadfastly opposed the war in Vietnam; contributed substantially to halting the colossal overproduction of amphetamines in the U.S.; and was the only senator in recent memory to kill a wasteful defense item from an appropriation bill in a Senate floor fight (a new main battle tank called the MBT-70, on which about $2 billion had been spent without one tank being produced in eight years). He was chairman of the Senate Committee on the District of Columbia, spearheading long-sought home rule for the District; vice-chairman of the Air and Water Pollution Subcommittee, from which all national legislation on pollution emanates; and chairman of the Senate's Subcommittee on Aging.

Eagleton was born in St. Louis on Sept. 4, 1929, and was graduated cum laude from both Amherst College and Harvard Law School. He was elected St. Louis circuit attorney in 1956; attorney general of Missouri in 1960; and lieutenant governor of Missouri in 1964. He was elected to the U.S. Senate in 1968.

EHRLICHMAN, JOHN DANIEL

Suspicious of the bureaucracy inherited from the Democrats and even of its own Cabinet appointees, the Nixon administration had gradually increased the size and power of the White House staff. John Ehrlichman was a major beneficiary as well as a proponent of the change. Counsel to the president for most of 1969, he rose to presidential assistant for domestic affairs when Arthur Burns became chairman of the Federal Reserve Board early the following year. In June 1970, when Nixon created the Domestic Council as a counterpart to the National Security Council for foreign and defense affairs, Ehrlichman was named executive director.

Ehrlichman did not become the "home-front Kissinger" many expected and for a while shared policy-making power with Attorney General John Mitchell. Mitchell's resignation in 1972 increased Ehrlichman's standing, but he was, nonetheless, exercising extraordinary influence all along. The final filter for all domestic ideas and programmatic proposals making their way to the president, he was the top contact man with the Cabinet secretaries, and the generalist who sifted and analyzed much of the raw material directed to the president. He rapidly won a reputation as the broadest-gauged, most open-minded member of the president's inner circle. He was also regarded as the fairest. While compromising the conflicting positions of lesser administration lights, he "leaves no more blood around on the floor than he can help," according to one participant.

Rumours of an Ehrlichman appointment as attorney general followed Nixon's re-election in 1972, but were soon stanched. Instead, Ehrlichman yielded administrative direction of the Domestic Council to an aide to concentrate on issues of peculiar or long-range concern to the president. One of these was formulation of an administration approach to the energy crisis.

Ehrlichman was born in Tacoma, Wash., on March 20, 1925. He graduated from the University of California at Los Angeles and took a law degree at Stanford (Calif.) University. He specialized in zoning cases for his Seattle, Wash., law firm until moving into politics as the Nixon advance man who charted the logistics of the 50,000-mi. 1968 presidential campaign. (JESS COOK, JR.)

EVERT, CHRIS

"If Billie Jean [King] is the queen, Chris [Evert] is undeniably the magnetic, crowd-pleasing princess," a *Newsweek* writer declared. Once known as "Little Miss Poker Face," the Florida teen-ager became the darling of international tennis in 1972.

In February she beat Mrs. King to avenge her semifinal loss in the U.S. Open the year before and win a Fort Lauderdale tournament. In July she met Evonne Goolagong in the semifinals at Wimbledon and lost a close match to Australia's 1971 Wimbledon champion, but then bounced back to beat Miss Goolagong when the world tournament circuit reached Ohio. The spectacle of the flamboyant Goolagong against Evert, whose concentration was as taut as gut strings, promised to be an annual draw for years to come. "A jazz drummer playing against a metronome," one sportswriter described it.

Chris Evert's rise to tennis fame coincided with a distaff movement in the professional tennis world known as "Women's Lob," its goal being to give women players equal status (and prize money) with men. Asked her views, the future pro said "I haven't given much thought to the structure of women's tennis. I'm still in high school." When she turned professional, on her 18th birthday (December 21), she retained her affiliation with the U.S. Lawn Tennis Association, although the Women's International Federation tour might be more lucrative. She wanted a chance to win the U.S. and Wimbledon championships, she said, and there was a possibility that WIF players might be barred from those events.

Christine Marie Evert was ranked third among U.S. women (behind Mrs. King and Nancy Richey Gunter). She started playing at the age of five when her father, a tennis professional, stuck a racket in her hand. Since then she had collected approximately 250 trophies, while the rest of the family has garnered about 100 more. Her father Jim Evert, a former national indoor champion, reached the quarterfinals in the U.S. Open at Forest Hills in 1941. Chris's brother Drew in 1972 was ranked third in Florida; younger sister Jeanne was first-ranked among national junior girls; and youngest brother John was ninth-ranked in Florida at the age of ten. (PHILIP KOPPER)

FAURE, EDGAR JEAN

Edgar Faure's reappearance in the forefront of the French political scene in 1972 was unexpected. He was known to be on bad terms with Pres. Georges Pompidou, who had dismissed him from the government in June 1969; he had been increasingly critical of the regime and its policies, in the name of a passionate, if belated, fidelity to Charles de Gaulle; and he was seen as wavering between the majority and the opposition. But when the Messmer government was formed in July 1972, Faure was appointed to the highly sensitive post of minister of state for labour and social affairs, with the task of presenting a new "social contract" to the electorate in anticipation of the 1973 general election. Regarded as a possible champion of conciliation between the Gaullists and the non-Communist left, he made it clear

UPI COMPIX

John D. Ehrlichman

MCNEELY—MAGNUM

Thomas Eagleton

Bobby Fischer

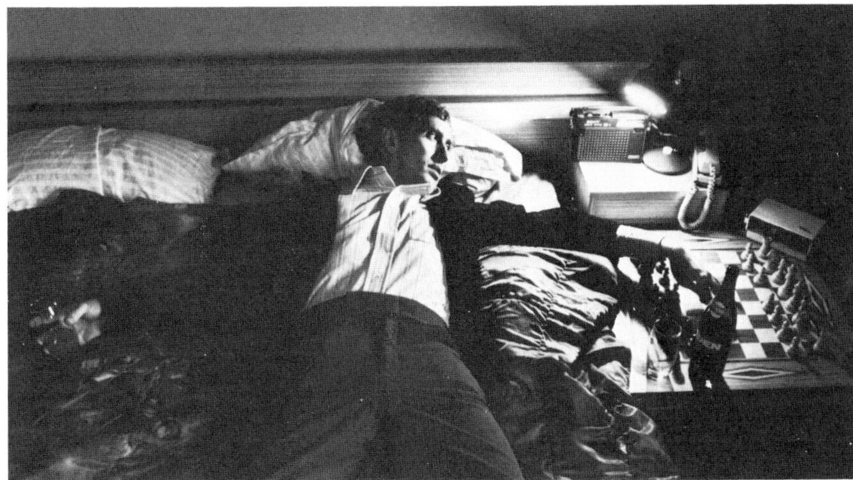

HARRY BENSON, LIFE MAGAZINE © 1972 TIME INC.

that he envisaged some form of cooperation on important social issues.

It was not the first comeback in this durable and able politician's long career. Elected deputy in 1946, he had risen to become premier for six weeks in 1952 and for a year in 1955. Then came the collapse of the Fourth Republic and de Gaulle's rise to power in 1958. Although at first firmly excluded by de Gaulle, from 1962 Faure was given delicate and important missions abroad and in 1966 was made minister of agriculture. Appointed minister of education after the student rebellion in May–June 1968, he transformed the university system within a year.

De Gaulle's resignation in 1969 meant a second downfall for Faure, whose reforms were not approved by Pompidou. This time there were fewer years in the wilderness. Nevertheless, if, as seemed probable, Faure meant to stand for the presidency in 1976, he would have to force the pace.

Born Aug. 18, 1908, at Béziers, the son of a military doctor, Faure, a brilliant scholar, became a barrister and, in 1962, professor of law at Dijon University. He was also the author of several books, mainly on historical topics. (PIERRE VIANSSON-PONTÉ)

FISCHER, BOBBY

Bobby Fischer officially became the world champion chess player Sept. 1, 1972. For years he had bragged he was titlist in everything but name; he proved his boast in Iceland when champion Boris Spassky of the U.S.S.R. conceded the 21st game of their 24-game match. (*See* CHESS.) This marked the challenger's seventh win against three defeats (including one forfeit) and 11 ties for a final score of $12\frac{1}{2}$ to $8\frac{1}{2}$ (players get $\frac{1}{2}$ point for a draw, 1 point for a win).

More surprising than Fischer's comfortable margin was the fact that the competition occurred at all. For months Fischer wrangled with the International Chess Federation (FIDE) over the terms of the match. Days before it was to begin he balked at playing for a share of the $125,000 purse, richest in the history of formal chess competition, until a British financier volunteered to double the prize money.

In the United States the championship match liberated chess from the musty dens of old men and pipe-smoking intellectuals. "Almost overnight," an observer wrote, Fischer "has singlehandedly turned the sedate and ancient game . . . into a national craze of the first rank." For months stores could not keep sets in stock. The bad-mannered kid from Brooklyn—probably the strongest player in history—did more for the game in two months than all the others who had quietly pushed 16 pieces around 64 squares for over three millennia.

Robert James Fischer was born in Chicago on March 9, 1943. Several years later his mother took him and his sister to

MARILYN SILVERSTONE—MAGNUM

Indira Gandhi

live in Brooklyn. He started playing chess at the age of 6 and at 13 became the youngest national junior champion. In 1958, when he was 14, he won the first of his five U.S. championships; at the age of 15 he became the youngest international grand master in history. He also earned a reputation for being an enfant terrible, and for a time withdrew from competition.

(PHILIP KOPPER)

GANDHI, INDIRA PRIYADARSHINI

Indian Prime Minister Indira Gandhi's task in 1972 was to consolidate the gains of the previous year's decisive encounter with Pakistan and to make the national mood of self-assertion serve her larger objectives. Her Congress Party won 14 of 16 states and one of two territories in regional elections. But Mrs. Gandhi did careful homework both in selecting candidates and in campaigning. She traveled 16,000 mi. and addressed 185 meetings in February–March. After the elections she installed chief ministers of her choice in most states, and further strengthened her hold on the party.

In March she visited Bangladesh, where she signed a treaty of friendship and co-operation with Sheikh Mujibur Rahman (*q.v.*). Toward Pakistan she pursued a policy of deliberate speed and cautious accommodation, making it clear to Pakistan and to domestic critics that India did not intend to keep territories taken in combat. Her invitation to Pres. Zulfikar Ali Bhutto (*q.v.*) led to a meeting between the two at Simla and to an agreement (July 2) by which the two countries pledged themselves to bilateralism in settling differences.

Earlier in the year Pres. Varahagiri V. Giri conferred upon Mrs. Gandhi the country's highest honour, the Bharat Ratna. In June she was the principal speaker at the UN Conference on the Human Environment at Stockholm. While welcoming the worldwide concern for ecology, she hoped that it would not divert attention from support to the efforts of less developed countries to

WIDE WORLD

Isaac Hayes

overcome poverty, which, she said, was one of the greatest pollutants. At home she appointed a national committee on environment.

Indira Gandhi was born in Allahabad on Nov. 19, 1917, the only child of Jawaharlal Nehru, India's first prime minister. Her formal education was intermittent because of the family's involvement in the struggle for independence from Great Britain. In 1942 she married Feroze Gandhi (d. 1960), and both were imprisoned soon afterward. She was elected president of the Indian National Congress in 1959. On her father's death in 1964 she joined Lal Bahadur Shastri's Cabinet as minister for information and broadcasting and then became prime minister in 1966. (H. Y. SHARADA PRASAD)

GERSTENBERG, RICHARD CHARLES

"Old Gerstenberg, the bookkeeper," became board chairman and chief executive officer of General Motors on Dec. 6, 1971. Amiable and self-effacing enough to style himself a bookkeeper when he was in fact executive vice-president in charge of financial matters for the world's largest industrial corporation, Richard Gerstenberg was nonetheless a company man. He was one of several groomed through 39 years of service in accordance with GM's tradition of always having several excellent choices for its top jobs.

The selection of an executive officer with an exclusively financial background, rather than one from engineering or management ranks like Gerstenberg's predecessor, James M. Roche, was seen as an indication of what GM expected the business climate to be in the years before Gerstenberg's mandatory retirement in 1974. As one analyst saw it, "the board [of directors] clearly signaled its consideration that costs, prices, profits, and productivity are, for the time being at least, more vital to GM's good health than styling, sales, and engineering." Recognized as one of the company's chief diplomats, Gerstenberg had spent much of his career justifying GM prices and price increases, first before the Office of Price Administration during World War II and, in recent years, before numerous congressional committees. He was seen as the man most likely to get the most for GM from negotiations with an administration attempting to enforce economic controls.

To increase GM's net profits in a tight economy, Gerstenberg would have to come to grips with one factor that blotched the company's books, the 6% rate of absenteeism plaguing mass production operations throughout the U.S. Gerstenberg was also regarded as more than willing to take up "the cudgel on behalf of minority hiring" and career opportunities.

Born in Little Falls, N.Y., on Nov. 24, 1909, Gerstenberg worked his way through the University of Michigan, receiving a degree in business administration in 1931, the heart of the depression. He could get only labourer's work until a friend landed him a timekeeper's position at GM's Frigidaire plant in Dayton, O., in 1932. His pay was $125 a month; in 1972 he was earning an estimated $800,000 in salary and bonuses.

(PHILIP KOPPER)

GRAY, L(OUIS) PATRICK, III

L. Patrick Gray III followed "the toughest act in Washington" in 1972. The first new principal in half a century to take centre stage at the FBI, he was named to succeed J. Edgar Hoover as the agency's acting director. During his first six months he performed with all the discipline, tact, flair, and finesse that might be expected of a submarine officer who turned attorney and made it to high presidential circles. Yet it remained to be seen whether he would get the job permanently.

Hoover died on May 2 at the age of 77, his power unchallenged but his capability in some doubt. On May 3 Pres. Richard Nixon told Gray to vacate his assistant attorney general's office for the east end of Justice Department headquarters. Within weeks he made long overdue policy changes, ranging from the cancellation of Hoover's finicky rules to substantive matters. G-men, he said, could wear coloured shirts, grow their hair longer, sport neat beards, and even make creative critical suggestions within the bureau. Women agents were hired for the first time, and recruiting among ethnic minorities was stepped up. Gray told reporters that the FBI would spend less time snooping into political dissidents' affairs and more energy fighting organized crime. He also started easing out some of Hoover's entrenched old guard—quietly at first, later to some public clamour, which was startling in itself. He was quick to take full responsibility when his agents were criticized for shooting the tires of a skyjacked airliner as it was about to take off.

Gray was widely applauded for many of these actions, but his nomination as permanent director, if and when it came, would almost certainly meet stiff opposition. The reason: cronyism. Gray had met Nixon at a Washington party in 1947, became his confidant, campaigned for him in 1960 and '68, and was named a sub-Cabinet officer in the Department of Health, Education, and Welfare in 1969. He moved to Justice as head of the Civil Division, and his appointment as deputy attorney general was pending when Hoover died. These considerations, critics said, made him too "political" to maintain the total, nonpartisan independence of the agency Hoover had built.

Gray was born in St. Louis, Mo., July 18, 1916. He worked his way through Rice University, Houston, Tex., and was appointed to the Naval Academy. He served on submarines during World War II and the Korean War. The Navy sent him to law school, and he counseled both the Joint Chiefs of Staff and the secretary of defense before resigning his commission and entering private practice in 1960. (PHILIP KOPPER)

HAYES, ISAAC

Superstar Isaac Hayes, a self-styled "Black Moses," was a double presence in the galaxies of show business. A composer, he had "written" 200 songs, among them several hits of the first magnitude; a performer of musical rituals, he could pack the Hollywood Bowl, Lincoln Center, and Boston Garden.

Born in a tin shack in Covington, Tenn., on Aug. 20, 1942, and raised by sharecropping grandparents who taught him to chop cotton and sing gospel, the bearded baritone with the shaved head now lived in Memphis amid the long-sought luxury that only four "platinums"—records that sold $2 million wholesale—and personal appearance fees of $15,000 can support. When he appeared in concert, he was escorted on stage by four armed bodyguards while a woman performed an "African dance of adoration" before taking his cape. Wearing black tights, fur cuffs, a leather vest, and gold chains, he would sing six or seven songs in two hours, strew souvenir medallions among the crowd, and vanish. "The rite," as one critic put it, "is over."

Hayes began singing in choir lofts when he was five, according to one account, and formed his first music group as a teen-ager. "Sir Isaac and the Doo-Dads" toured the South playing one-night stands in moonshine joints and small towns. Teamed with lyricist David Porter, he ad-libbed his compositions for Stax Records, humming a melody into one tape recorder, then the rhythm into another. An arranger combined the two—Hayes reportedly did not read or write music himself. His style was eclectic, a combination of cool blues, hot soul, hard rock, white pop, and old black gospel.

Perhaps his most widely heralded composition was the Oscar-winning theme song of the movie *Shaft*. The score for the movie won three Grammys. Among his biggest hit albums were "Presenting Isaac Hayes," "Hot Buttered Soul," and "Black Moses." His most notable single was "By the Time I Get to Phoenix," a Glen Campbell ballad he stretched into a 19-minute exegesis. Hayes didn't just sing the song, he introduced it with "a rap"—a prefatory narration accompanied by an orchestral B♭ 11 chord. He developed this trademark playing nightclubs and bars; his rapping gave the audience time to quiet down and allow this master of black musical expression to explain the white man's song in terms of black experience. (PHILIP KOPPER)

HEATH, EDWARD RICHARD GEORGE

When Edward Heath became prime minister of the United Kingdom in June 1970, he promised the country "a quiet revolution." The most far-reaching component in Heath's revolutionary program was to bring Britain into the EEC, and during 1972 the necessary legislation for this was put through Parliament with a determination his critics found ruthless. But Europeanism was one of Heath's most consistent characteristics (he had won the Charlemagne Prize for services to the unity of Europe in 1963, after Britain's first application for entry into the EEC had been frustrated by France's veto), and by the time negotiations for Britain's accession to the Community had been completed, Heath was establishing himself as a dominant European figure. He came away from the summit meeting of prime ministers of the Nine in October 1972 not only with a commitment to the completion of European union by 1980 but also with important concessions to the British point of view.

Another key element in his political philosophy was his faith in a free market economy, in which equal opportunities and fair working and living conditions for all would create the conditions for "one nation." His efforts to break with the economic interventionist policies of his Labour predecessors were largely frustrated, however, by the need to assist industries in serious difficulties —such as Clyde shipbuilding—and at the midpoint in his government's term of office, he had to cope with wage inflation, bitter labour disputes, and a million unemployed. Although his reputation as a European thus was offset by disappointments at home, his control of the Conservative Party nevertheless seemed secure.

Born at Broadstairs, Kent, on July 9, 1916, Heath, the son of a carpenter and builder, obtained a scholarship to Oxford University. Typical of the new-style Conservative of middle-class background with none of the advantages of birth or wealth, he entered Parliament in 1950. In 1955 he became Conservative chief whip and in 1965 was elected leader of the party. A bachelor, he was regarded as a somewhat aloof person, although he was a remarkably successful yachtsman and an enthusiastic musician. When *The Guardian*'s reviewer called two new biographies of him published in 1972 "more enigma variations," this fairly reflected the public view of a prime minister who had won respect rather than affection. (HARFORD THOMAS)

HESBURGH, THEODORE MARTIN

An outspoken opponent of racial injustice, a member of the U.S. Commission on Civil Rights since its inception in 1958 and its chairman since 1969, and president of the University of Notre Dame, the Rev. Theodore M. Hesburgh in November 1972 became the first appointed official to be removed by Pres. Richard M. Nixon as he prepared for a second term in office. After some confusion over whether Hesburgh's resignation from the civil rights body had been voluntary, the White House conceded that it had asked him to leave.

Hesburgh's rift with the White House was attributed to the commission's irrepressible criticism of federal policies that, in its view, set back the progress of race relations in exchange for the popular support of the white majority. The commission had been particularly critical of the practices of the Federal Housing Administration and of the president's position against busing to achieve racial integration of schools. In September the Roman Catholic priest became the first recipient of the Reinhold Niebuhr Award, established by New York City's Union Theological Seminary in memory of the renowned Protestant theologian, who had died in 1971. In accepting the award, Hesburgh made his views explicit: "There is no legitimate excuse for our politicians to foreclose educational opportunities for generations of deprived blacks because it would be popular with the white majority. No one has the right any more to play games with human life in America."

As an educator, Hesburgh was equally forceful. Appointed Notre Dame's 16th president in 1952, he developed the Roman Catholic school from an all-male football factory into one of the country's outstanding universities and, in the fall of 1972, opened it to coeducation. He eased the clergy out of control in favour of laymen and gave students a greater voice in university affairs. He also appointed Protestants, Jews, and blacks to the staff.

Born in Syracuse, N.Y., on May 25, 1917, the son of a glass company official, Hesburgh was educated at Notre Dame and Gregorian University in Rome. He entered

UPI COMPIX

Theodore Hesburgh

KEYSTONE

Edward Heath

the Congregation of the Holy Cross in 1934 and was ordained a priest in 1943, after which he resumed his studies at Catholic University, Washington, D.C., joining the Notre Dame faculty in 1945.

(NELLIE L. GIFFORD)

HULL, ROBERT MARVIN, JR.

Tagged the "most celebrated player in contemporary professional hockey" as early as 1966, in 1972 Bobby Hull signed a contract for more money, probably, than any athlete in history. He received a down payment of $1 million on a $2,750,000 contract to cover his services as player and coach for ten years.

The event was remarkable not just for the number of dollars involved. It marked the explosive popularity of professional hockey and the sudden respectability of the World Hockey Association, fledgling rival of the established National Hockey League. Hull's signing was a major coup for the WHA, one made possible by the peculiar economics of professional sports. Franchises were available in the NHL for $6 million. Savvy promoters sold the first ten WHA franchises for a very modest $25,000 apiece. Consequently, the new teams could all afford to chip into a common purse to seduce the superstar away from the NHL and onto their circuit as sparkplug of the Winnipeg Jets.

While Hull's prowess might freeze the WHA players on the ice, his spectacular performance was certain to make them toasty warm all the way to the bank each time his name packed a rink. A flashy player, he was the speediest sport's fastest skater; he had been clocked at 29.2 mph and could slap a puck goalward at 118 mph, more than four times his skating speed. Hull's speed was undoubtedly a factor in his fabulous scoring ability. In the 1968–69 season he scored 58 goals to set a new NHL mark. His career total was 604 goals in 15 seasons, only 182 less than the league record achieved by Detroit Red Wing Gordie Howe in 25 seasons.

Hull was born on Jan. 3, 1939, in Pointe Anne, Ont. He began skating before he was three, and ten years later began playing for a boys' team supported by the Chicago Black Hawks. He made his professional debut with the Black Hawks at 18, scoring twice in his first game. The team he joined occupied the basement; after the "Golden Jet" took over the left-wing position the Hawks became a regular play-off competitor. Named most valuable player two years in succession and Canada's athlete of the year, Hull had a reputation for being an exceptionally friendly, approachable star off the ice. (PHILIP KOPPER)

IRVING, CLIFFORD MICHAEL

Parodying its own annual feature, *Time* magazine dubbed its Feb. 21, 1972, cover portrait "Con Man of the Year." The subject was Clifford Irving, an expatriate minor novelist whose fiction-as-nonfiction biography of multimillionaire recluse Howard Hughes became a front-page sensation.

The first news stories broke when the respected publishing house of McGraw-Hill announced a major coup—after years in seclusion Hughes had at last consented to publication of his autobiography. Next, Hughes held his first press conference in decades (by telephone) to say that the book was a fake. Gradually the story unfolded, revealing such tantalizing tidbits as a forged passport, secret Swiss bank accounts, and beautiful mystery women. But when all was told, nothing was left but a baroque fraud perpetrated by a hack writer.

UPI COMPIX

Bobby Hull

CAMERA PRESS/PICTORIAL PARADE

Henryk Jablonski

KEYSTONE

Roy Jenkins

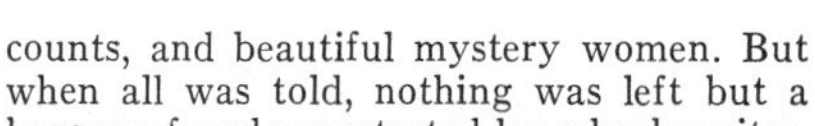

Irving was born in New York City, Nov. 5, 1930. He went to Cornell and, after a varied career that included four wives and seven mildly successful books, eventually settled on the Spanish island of Ibiza. A magazine report on the eccentric Hughes gave Irving his idea. Collaborating with researcher Richard Suskind, he forged some letters purporting to show that Hughes was ready to talk at last. When McGraw-Hill asked for a contract, Irving flew to Mexico and returned with a signed letter of agreement that satisfied the publisher, although it later developed that he had spent his time with Baroness Nina van Pallandt, a nightclub singer.

Plagiarizing the purloined memoirs of a disgruntled Hughes aide and using previously published material about the millionaire, Irving and Suskind created a convincing corpus of "tape transcripts" and a bright autobiography. The checks the publisher intended for "H. R. Hughes," totaling $650,000, were given to Irving's wife, Edith. In disguise and using a forged passport, she deposited the money in a bank in Zürich, Switz., waited for the checks to clear, and then transferred the cash to another Swiss bank.

But if to the public the story seemed a real-life James Bond, it was somewhat more serious to McGraw-Hill, to *Life* magazine, which had subsidiary rights, and to the Swiss and U.S. authorities, who called it felony. Edith was fined $10,000, served a short jail sentence, and was then extradited to Switzerland to face charges of fraud and forgery. Irving was fined the same amount and sentenced to two and a half years' imprisonment. To help pay the fine he dashed off a book about his book. Once in jail, he proved to be a model prisoner; his prison job was to teach creative writing. (PHILIP KOPPER)

JABLONSKI, HENRYK

The election on March 28, 1972, of Henryk Jablonski, a former professor of history, as chairman of the Polish Council of State—second in the country's Communist hierarchy and nominal president of the republic—was a delayed sequel to the workers' revolt of December 1970. Jablonski's predecessor and friend, Jozef Cyrankiewicz, became a scapegoat for the events that had brought about the fall of former party leader Wladyslaw Gomulka.

Jablonski was born into a worker's family on Dec. 27, 1909, at Waliszewo, in the Lowicz district. Graduate of the humanities department of the University of Warsaw, he obtained a doctorate in historical sciences in 1934. He joined the Polish Socialist Party in 1931. During World War II he served in the Polish Army, escaping to France where he joined the Polish Highland Brigade, one of the units of the new Polish Army reformed on French soil. As part of a British-French-Polish expeditionary force, the Highland Brigade landed in northern Norway in mid-April 1940 and fought the Germans successfully at Narvik, but had to be re-embarked at the beginning of May.

After the French surrender, Jablonski remained in unoccupied France at Grenoble, where he was able to continue his historical research. He returned to Poland in 1945, became a member of the provisional Home National Council, was elected as a Socialist to the Sejm (parliament) in January 1947, and was returned in every subsequent election. Siding with Cyrankiewicz in 1948, when the latter supported the merger of the Polish Socialist Party and the Polish Workers' Party, he was elected a member of the Central Committee of the Polish United Workers' Party. On Dec. 20, 1970, he was elected alternate member of the party's Politburo, becoming a full member of that body on Dec. 11, 1971.

From 1945 Jablonski was professor of modern history, first at the Academy of Political Sciences and, from 1946, at the University of Warsaw. In 1956 he was elected a member of the Polish Academy of Sciences, and until 1965 he served as its scientific secretary. In December 1965 he was appointed minister of higher education, and in November 1966, when his ministry was united with that of public instruction, he became head of the combined administration. (K. M. SMOGORZEWSKI)

JOHN EBSTEL

The library at Phillips Exeter Academy, Exeter, N.H., designed by Louis Kahn

JOAN RUGGLES

JENKINS, ROY HARRIS

The most notable political casualty in the British Labour Party's internal feuding over Britain's entry into the EEC was Roy Jenkins, successively minister of aviation, home secretary, and chancellor of the Exchequer in the Wilson governments of 1964–70 and deputy leader of the Labour Party in opposition. Jenkins was a fervent and consistent advocate of joining the EEC. At a time when his party was turning against Europe he was awarded, in March 1972, the Charlemagne Prize for services to European unity. In April he resigned his post as deputy leader because he could not support the shadow cabinet's decision to press for a referendum on entry into Europe. He complained that the party had changed its ground and was now opposing EEC membership on principle rather than merely challenging the terms. In November his efforts to further Britain's entry into the EEC received additional recognition with the award of the Robert Schuman Prize. At the end of the year, in an outspoken letter to Prime Minister Edward Heath, Jenkins urged the British government to condemn publicly U.S. bombing of North Vietnam.

Jenkins, born Nov. 11, 1920, at Abersychan, Wales, entered Parliament in 1948. He could claim family roots in the Labour movement; his father had been a miners' union official, an MP, and parliamentary private secretary to Clement Attlee, Labour prime minister from 1945 to 1951. But he had gone to Oxford University with the help of scholarships, and came to be regarded in the party as an intellectual. At one time he considered giving up politics for writing, but within a year of the formation of the 1964 Wilson administration he joined the Cabinet as home secretary, gaining a reputation as a reformist in that office before moving to the Treasury in 1967.

His intellectual and perhaps rather mandarin approach to politics offended many on the militant left wing of the Labour Party. In 1970 he was elected deputy leader by a convincing majority of 133 to 67 over left-winger Michael Foot, but his position weakened steadily, and in November 1971 he was reelected by a reduced margin of 140 to 126. (HARFORD THOMAS)

JOSEPH, SIR KEITH SINJOHN

In Britain's "quiet revolution," proclaimed by Edward Heath in 1970, the responsibility for the social services was given to Sir Keith Joseph, a second-generation baronet who inherited his title from his father, a former lord mayor of London. Elected to Parliament in 1956, Joseph had been at the Ministry of Housing and Local Government. In opposition (1964–70), he was Conservative spokesman for the social services and then "shadow" minister for trade. Long experience in the family construction and building firm of Bovis would have fitted him for the Board of Trade, but his interests and a lively social conscience equally fitted him to take his place in the Heath Cabinet as secretary of state for health and social security.

His faith in the free market economy made some of his views on the social services controversial, particularly his ideas of how they should be paid for. He believed in self-help within a civilized capitalist economy, based on competitive free enterprise and underpinned by humane provisions for the unfortunate. In practice, some of his ideas, such as payment for medical drugs graded according to their cost, raised so many objections that he did not pursue them. He was, however, able to establish a new administrative structure for the National Health Service and to switch attention and resources to neglected areas, notably the care of the old, the mentally ill, and the long-term sick. He pressed on with a big hospital-building program and introduced improved pensions. In his concern to relieve family poverty, he worked with the chancellor of the Exchequer, Anthony Barber, in devising a new form of taxation that provided grants for those with substandard incomes. In December he announced a new family-planning policy under which advice and contraceptives would be freely available.

Joseph was born on Jan. 17, 1918. Credited with one of the best intellects in the government, he took a first-class degree in law at Oxford, becoming a fellow of All Souls, and was given his first Cabinet post at the age of 44. (HARFORD THOMAS)

KAHN, LOUIS

Light was a passion of Louis Kahn, for whom 1972 was a year of triumph in 71 years of life and architecture. "Light," said Kahn, "is the giver of all presences. . . . Material is that which casts a shadow, and the shadow belongs to light." Nearing completion as the year drew to an end was a 1,000-ac. building complex in Dacca, begun as the eastern capital of Pakistan and, surviving the explosive birth of Bangladesh, ending up as the capital of a new country.

Completed during the year were a library at Phillips Exeter Academy; the Kimbell Art Museum in Fort Worth, Tex.; and Temple Beth-El in Chappaqua, N.Y. Kudos added to Kahn's long list of honours included the Gold Medal for architecture from the Royal Institute of British Architects and the Creative Arts Medal for architecture from Brandeis University. But Kahn himself transcended the medals and awards and the materials that shaped his structures. He was a form-giver, an artist-architect, recognized for his original rethinking of the design process, his thoughtful assembling of interior spaces.

He was the first U.S. architect to break with the glass-and-steel box buildings of the International Style pioneered by Walter Gropius and the Bauhaus School and later copied ad nauseam in places like the Avenue of the Americas in New York City. His massive structures flaunt the structural sources of their strength. Examples: the characteristic unfinished concrete surface of the stairwell of the Yale Art Gallery completed in 1953; the fortress-like, almost medieval look of the Salk Institute in La Jolla, Calif.; the Indian Institute of Management at Ahmedabad; and the Erdman dormitory at Bryn Mawr (Pa.) College.

Kahn was born Feb. 20, 1901, on the Estonian island of Saaremaa, the son of a sergeant in the Imperial Army of Czar

CENTRAL PRESS/PICTORIAL PARADE

Henry Kissinger

Nicholas I of Russia who was also a stained-glass craftsman. The family moved to Philadelphia in 1905. The younger Kahn became a U.S. citizen in 1915, and Philadelphia remained his home. As an adolescent and before, Kahn showed promise in both drawing and piano, but a high school architecture course struck deep into his being. He rejected art scholarships and enrolled in the University of Pennsylvania architecture school, earning his way by playing the piano and organ accompaniment to silent movies.

In 1947 Kahn went to Yale University for a week as a visiting critic. The students refused to let him go and he became the school's chief design critic. He was resident architect at the American Academy in Rome in 1950, then returned to Yale as professor of architecture until 1957, when he transferred to the University of Pennsylvania. He never received a commission from the city of Philadelphia nor did he ever design a home for himself. He lived in a modest brick row house and worked in a shabby, sun-filled loft, assisted by younger architects.

(PAT TUCKER)

KIM IL SUNG

The historic July 4, 1972, joint statement by North and South Korea on peaceful reunification was, to North Korea's enduring premier, Kim Il Sung, a vindication of Korean genius. Both Koreas claimed full credit for the initiative, but the North claimed it more loudly and, because of its unabashed personality cult, Kim appeared to be the font of wisdom that had made it all possible. His position as the "shining sun of Korea" was part of the continuing scenario Kim had been directing in his country ever since its government became Communist in 1945. In what was believed to be a campaign to make himself an independent power centre of world Communism, he was critical of both Soviet revisionism and Chinese dogmatism.

Kim was born Kim Song Chu near Pyongyang on April 15, 1912. He adopted the name of an anti-Japanese guerrilla hero as part of his official posture as the warrior-patriot father of Korean nationalism. Spending his early years in Manchuria, he founded the Korean Independence Alliance and was imprisoned for a year for anti-Japanese activities. When war broke out in Europe, Kim was believed to have gone to Moscow. When he returned to Korea in 1945, he was a captain in the Soviet Red Army and was decorated by Stalin for his services.

The Soviets chose him as their man for Korea. By 1946 he was head of North Korea's first central government, the Interim People's Committee. Consolidation of power followed rapidly. He obtained control of the reformed Communist Party, proclaimed the Democratic People's Republic of Korea in September 1948, assimilated independent groups into the central political organization which in 1949 was renamed the Korean Workers' Party, and periodically purged "unreliable elements." His resort to political methods to extend his authority to South Korea came unstuck, and in 1950 he tried military force. U.S. intervention frustrated that bid. Confirmed in office by successive party conferences, he was secretary-general of the party, member of the Political Committee, premier, and supreme commander of the armed forces. On Dec. 28, 1972, he was named president and head of state by the National Assembly.

(T. J. S. GEORGE)

KIRK, NORMAN ERIC

Following a landslide victory in the general election which gave his Labour Party 56 out of the 87 seats in the House of Representatives, Norman E. Kirk on Dec. 8, 1972, became at 49 New Zealand's youngest prime minister in 50 years. Kirk's success was expected to bring considerable change to the New Zealand political scene. Labour supporters awaited the abolition of wage controls, stricter price regulations, recognition of China, withdrawal of military training teams from South Vietnam, and, after consultation with allies, a pulling out from the New Zealand-Australian force in Singapore and Malaysia.

Regional development, tax relief, and social services expansion were high on the government's list of priorities. Kirk made it clear that were the U.K. to restrict the immigration of New Zealanders, as seemed probable because of Britain's new EEC role, he would consider reciprocal action. The prime minister showed considerable concern for environmental problems; in particular, he reaffirmed that if France continued its nuclear tests in the Pacific he would send a frigate into the area manned by a volunteer force and with a Cabinet minister aboard.

The 280-lb. cabinetmaker's son who was now to apply these relatively abrasive policies was little known outside New Zealand, although he had led his party for 7 of its 12 years in the political wilderness and had traveled widely in the U.S., Asia, and Europe. He had joined the party at 20 in 1943 and ten years later was elected mayor of the South Island borough of Kaiapoi. In 1957 he won the seat of Lyttleton in the House of Representatives, holding the seat with majorities in the 1960 and 1963 elections. He was first elected to the Labour Party National Executive in 1959 as divisional representative for Canterbury. He became vice-president in 1963 and president in 1964. In 1965 he was elected leader of the Parliamentary Labour Party. He retained the Lyttleton seat in the general election of 1966 and won the Sydenham seat in 1969.

Kirk was born at Waimate, Canterbury, N.Z., on Jan. 6, 1923. His formal education ended in primary school and before entering Parliament he was an apprentice fitter and turner, and later a foreman with the Railways Department.

(R. J. M. DENNERSTEIN)

KISSINGER, HENRY ALFRED

Henry Kissinger, assistant for national security affairs to U.S. Pres. Richard Nixon, secret peace negotiator, secret advance man to Peking, *Time* magazine's man of the year (with President Nixon), and sometime bon vivant, became in 1972 the nearly successful (again with President Nixon) architect of U.S.-Vietnam peace.

Early in 1972, President Nixon revealed that Kissinger had traveled to Paris fully a dozen times in 30 months to negotiate secretly with the North Vietnamese. Weeks later, the U.S. chief executive made his historic visit to China, with the man whose clandestine trips had prepared the meeting at his side. In the spring, Kissinger escorted the president to Moscow. By fall he was back in Paris in one-to-one negotiations with Le Duc Tho, a ranking official of the North Vietnamese negotiating team. Kissinger's announcement, on October 26, that "peace is at hand," culminated those negotiations.

Suspicion that the pronouncement—made less than two weeks before the U.S. elections—was politically motivated gained weight following a subsequent Kissinger visit to Saigon, when it became clear that the bilateral pact between the U.S. and Hanoi did not have the support of South Vietnamese Pres. Nguyen Van Thieu. Peace talks were stalemated and in mid-December intensive bombing north of the 20th parallel was resumed by order of President Nixon. North Vietnamese air defense tactics had changed, however, and U.S. B-52 losses soared amid confusing and conflicting reports from both sides.

Public frustration and political recrimination centred on the highly visible negotiator, sparking rumours that Kissinger had fallen from executive grace. The most likely benefactor of such a downfall, speculation continued, would be former treasury secretary John Connally. Yet by year's end Nixon had ordered the bombing stopped; negotiations had been scheduled to resume; and it seemed likely that Kissinger would not only survive the crisis but might yet participate in a successful peace settlement.

Kissinger was born in Fürth, Ger., on May 27, 1923, and became a U.S. citizen after fleeing Nazi Germany with his family in 1938. Prior to his appointment to the White House post in December 1968, he was a professor of government at Harvard University.

(PHILIP KOPPER)

KLEINDIENST, RICHARD

An Arizona conservative with blue-ribbon Republican Party credentials, Richard Kleindienst was nominated by Pres. Richard Nixon to succeed John Mitchell as U.S. attorney general when the latter resigned to direct Nixon's reelection campaign. Despite grumbling among liberals, confirmation of the appointment by the U.S. Senate seemed almost routine in February, until columnist Jack Anderson (*q.v.*) published a "personal and confidential" memo by a Washington, D.C., lobbyist to her boss at International Telephone and Telegraph (ITT). The memo said that Mitchell "is definitely helping us" settle an antitrust suit brought by the U.S. Department of Justice against ITT, and mentioned that the corporation had a "$400 thousand commitment" to help defray costs for the Republican national convention. Subsequent evidence suggested that the quid pro quo had been arranged by Kleindienst when he was deputy attorney general.

At this point Kleindienst was acting attorney general, and he asked Sen. James Eastland, the conservative chairman of the Senate's Judiciary Committee, to reopen the hearings so that he could tell his side of the story and clear himself. The renewed hearings went on for 22 days, longer than any Cabinet confirmation hearings in history. In late April the committee, which had unanimously endorsed him earlier, voted 11 to 4 in Kleindienst's favour, effectively exonerating him. The Senate then confirmed the appointment 64–19. Kleindienst was one of the comparatively few major officials retained in office in Nixon's post-election overhaul of the administration.

Born Aug. 5, 1923, on land his grandfather had homesteaded near Winslow, Ariz., Kleindienst fought in the Italian campaign during World War II and was discharged from the Army as a lieutenant in 1946. Attending Harvard University on the GI Bill, he graduated magna cum laude in 1947. He took a law degree at Harvard in 1950 and then returned to Arizona to practice law. He served in the state legislature, was a Republican national committeeman, and unsuccessfully ran for governor.

In the Department of Justice, Kleindienst was said to be articulate and aggressive. He directed a crackdown on drug smuggling from Mexico and favoured "carefully controlled" wiretapping to gather information in national security and organized crime cases. (PHILIP KOPPER)

KORBUT, OLGA

Probably no other competitor in the 1972 Munich Olympic Games delighted onlookers, including millions of television viewers, more than the diminutive Soviet gymnast Olga Korbut. Performing her exercises with grace, precision, and, above all, charm, the 17-year-old girl from Grodno, Belorussia, justified the faith of her coach, Renald Knysh, by carrying off two gold medals and a shared silver medal.

Born on May 16, 1955, Olga was always annoyed at being the shortest in her class at school, but she determinedly offset her lack of inches by running faster than the rest of her classmates—boys as well as girls. Her pace and power prompted someone to suggest she try her hand at gymnastics, and, together with her sister, she joined the local gymnastic school, where Elena Volchetskaya, a medalist in the 1964 Olympics, was her first tutor. After a year Olga, then 11, began blossoming into a first-rate gymnast and Knysh, the school's head, decided to coach her personally. She progressed so well that after four years Knysh sought and received special permission for his protégée to compete in the Soviet national championships, competitors in which must normally have reached the age of 16. Olga backed her coach's judgment by placing fifth.

She trained assiduously and practiced new exercises, including a back somersault on the beam, and her proficiency was such that she was selected as a reserve for the world championships in Ljubljana, Yugos., in 1970. She was hit by injury the following year but managed a fourth place in the Peoples Games. In 1972, before the Olympics, she finished third in the Soviet national championships to Liudmila Tourischeva and Tamara Lazakovitch, who both won medals in Munich, but then turned the tables on her colleagues to win the U.S.S.R. Cup. At the Olympics she won gold medals in the floor exercises and balance beam, a silver jointly with Erika Zuchold of East Germany in the uneven parallel bars, and helped the Soviet Union to the gold in the team event. It was an outstanding performance for one so young and so small—she stood 5 ft. 1 in. and weighed just 84 lb.

After the Olympics Olga suffered an injury to her spine during a trip to Denmark. At the year's end she was recuperating at a spa in the Caucasus.

(TREVOR WILLIAMSON)

LAVELLE, JOHN DANIEL

In the spring of 1972, Gen. John D. Lavelle, commander of U.S. air forces in South Vietnam, lost one of his four stars and was quietly retired from the service. Then the Senate learned that Lavelle had been waging his own private war, ordering at least 28 air strikes over North Vietnam in direct violation of standing orders. He had covered up his actions by filing false reports to the Pentagon, which in turn had covered up the reason he was fired. The case raised two alarming possibilities: that Lavelle's insubordination might have upset delicate peace negotiations; and that military brass who command vast armaments can take affairs into their own hands, despite the long-standing U.S. tradition of civilian control.

At the time of Lavelle's initiatives, U.S. air strikes over North Vietnam had been halted, but under the so-called "protective reaction" policy, U.S. fighter-bombers escorting unarmed reconnaissance planes could attack North Vietnamese defenses if they were fired on first or were pinpointed by North Vietnamese radar. Under Lavelle's command there was a suspicious increase in "protective reaction" strikes. In fact, his planes attacked without provocation. Then the Pentagon was told they had been fired on first. Meanwhile, at the Paris peace talks, U.S. negotiators argued that North Vietnam was breaking the informal "understanding" between Hanoi and Washington by firing on unarmed overflights. With more justification, as it turned out, Hanoi in turn accused the U.S. of breaking its "understanding" not to bomb the North.

Lavelle's private policy was revealed when Lonnie Franks, an intelligence sergeant, wrote to Sen. Harold Hughes, a member of the Armed Services Committee, who informed the Pentagon. Lavelle was offered a two-grade demotion and reassignment or quiet retirement with a $27,000 annual pension and the loss of one star, the option he chose. Later summoned before congressional committees, he defended his actions and implied that Gen. Creighton W. Abrams, then U.S. commander in Vietnam, knew what was going on. The evidence was contradictory, however, and after some delay Abrams was exonerated and confirmed as army chief of staff.

Born in Cleveland, O., Sept. 9, 1916, Lavelle took a science degree at John Carroll University in Cleveland in 1938 and was commissioned in the Army Air Corps two years later. Before his Vietnam command, he directed the hush-hush Defense Communications Planning Group.

(PHILIP KOPPER)

LEE, HAROLD B.

The century-old Tabernacle building in Salt Lake City, Utah, was packed as members of the Church of Jesus Christ of Latter-day Saints gathered for the 142nd semiannual conference in early October 1972. The highlight of the proceedings took place on October 6, when Harold B. Lee was confirmed —or "sustained"—as the 11th prophet and president of the more than three million-member church.

The procedures that placed him in office were almost automatic. As president and senior member of the Council of the Twelve Apostles, which becomes the highest governing body of the church on the death of the first president, Lee had been named to the position by his fellow council members in July, following the death of Joseph Fielding Smith. Formal acceptance of the council's action by the 7,000 leaders of the priesthood at the October conference was unanimous.

Even before he was sustained by the priesthood, the new first president was carrying out the duties of his office. In August he traveled to Mexico to participate in the first area general conference ever held for Mexico and Central America. The following month he made a three-week swing through Great Britain, Switzerland, Italy, West Germany, Greece, and Israel to visit church communities.

Lee faced the problem—a pleasant one, he noted—of a mushrooming membership that required suitable responses in the areas of leadership development, building construction, and membership indoctrination. He also faced a sensitive issue in the church's attitude toward blacks of African descent. There were an estimated 2,000 such members. They were accepted for membership, admitted to all church buildings, and allowed to perform certain temple work, but were barred from the priesthood, a status open to other male Latter-day Saints (though not to women). The prohibition applied only to dark-skinned persons of African Negro lineage and was based on the belief that the African Negro is descended from Cain and bears his curse. Change could come only through a revelation from God to the church's president.

Lee, the new first president, had spent most of his life in the service of his church. He was a member of the Council of the Twelve Apostles for over 30 years. Born March 28, 1889, in Clifton, Ida., Lee attended Albion State Normal College (later merged with Idaho State University) and the University of Utah. In 1937 he became managing director for the newly formed church-wide welfare programs.

(BERNARD S. KATZ)

LEEK, SYBIL

One of the world's better-known witches in 1972, Sybil Leek had journeyed from England to the U.S. some years earlier to publicize a book she had written about her antique shop. But that was not what the newsmen asked her about. As one reporter said, "Authors are a dime a dozen, but gee, a witch!"

Mrs. Leek, who traced her lineage back to the early 12th century, was a practitioner of the Old Religion, a pre-Christian occult worship. For many nonpractitioners, occultism suggests the secret arts of satanic witchcraft, including Black Magic—described by Mrs. Leek as a debased art rather than a religion. Her kind of occultism "simply seeks knowledge beyond the range of ordinary perceptions." As a "white," or benevolent, witch, she accepted certain tenets of faith based on a Supreme Being.

"Witches," she said, "have always been good at getting a bad press." But with interest in the occult on the rise, Sybil Leek, for one, was giving witches a reasonably good one. Now a resident of the U.S., she continued to turn out books, give lectures, and appear on radio and TV.

Her most popular book, *Diary of a Witch* (1968), provided a glimpse of her life, though in some ways the book concealed more than it revealed. The reader learns that she married a concert pianist at the age of 16 and was widowed at 18, but there is nothing about the man's name or background or about a subsequent marriage, which produced two sons. At 48 she was considered to be "practically a millionaire" (perhaps something of an exaggeration). At various times she had engaged in record making, dress designing, numismatics, and public relations, and for a time she wrote an astrology column for a women's magazine. In October 1972 she was in St. Louis, Mo., to determine the feasibility of starting a business in the downtown Gaslight Square area.

She gained initial fame in England when she appeared in a TV film on witchcraft. She was born Sybil Falk in Staffordshire, Eng., and, shortly after her first husband died, was initiated as a full-fledged witch at a coven held in France, near Nice. For a time she lived with gypsies in the New Forest, later opening her first antique shop in Somerset. (BERNARD S. KATZ)

LEONE, GIOVANNI

The election of Giovanni Leone as sixth president of the Italian republic, on Dec. 24, 1971, was interpreted as a triumph for compromise after the direct choices of the main political parties had failed to obtain the necessary two-thirds majority. A few weeks afterward, Leone was faced with a government crisis brought on by the resignation of Prime Minister Emilio Colombo. After many unsuccessful attempts to restore a firm basis to the political life of the country, he invited Giulio Andreotti (*q.v.*) to form a caretaker government and dissolved Parliament so that a general election could take place on May 7. During the year President Leone received several foreign heads of state and of government and paid a state visit to the Vatican. (*See* ITALY; VATICAN CITY STATE.)

Leone was born in Naples on Nov. 3, 1908. A brilliant law student, he graduated from the University of Naples at the age of 21 and the following year took a second degree in political and social sciences. For many years he followed an academic career that took him from Camerino to Messina, to Bari, to Naples, and finally to Rome in 1956. He was chairman of the Italian group of the "Association Internationale de Droit Penale," and published various law books, some of which became standard works in Italian judicial literature.

In 1944 Leone became a member of the Christian Democratic Party, and the following year was elected secretary of the Naples branch. In 1946 he was elected to the Constituent Assembly and was one of the main authors of the constitution. Returned to the Chamber of Deputies in 1948, he was elected vice-president of the Chamber of Deputies in 1950. In 1955 he became president, replacing Giovanni Gronchi, who became president of the republic. In June 1963 he was asked to form a caretaker government to carry the budget through Parliament. In 1967 Pres. Giuseppe Saragat made him a lifetime senator, and the following year, after the resignation of the prime minister, Aldo Moro, he formed a second caretaker government, which lasted five months. (FABIO GALVANO)

CHESTER HIGGINS—RAPHO GUILLUMETTE

George McGovern

P. MICHAEL O'SULLIVAN

Sean MacStiofain

McGOVERN, GEORGE STANLEY

George S. McGovern led himself to an overwhelming defeat in the U.S. presidential election on Nov. 7, 1972. To the end the liberal Democrat maintained a small, devoted following, but on election day only Massachusetts and the District of Columbia remained in the Democratic column as the South Dakota senator had the unhappy distinction of losing even his home state. McGovern was not only too "extremist" for erstwhile Dixiecrats, he was too liberal for traditionally middle-of-the-road voters, who rejected his candidacy almost as decisively as they had rejected Barry Goldwater's diametrically opposite platform eight years earlier.

First and foremost, McGovern was an antiwar candidate and public opinion polls had reported widespread opposition to the Vietnam war. But McGovern's pledge to withdraw U.S. forces within 90 days of inauguration day and "plead" for the release of U.S. prisoners of war disturbed chauvinistic citizens of a nation that had not "lost" a war since its founding. McGovern's economic and social proposals, especially his hastily devised welfare plan, further alienated middle-class voters. He later admitted the figures in his first plan had been faulty, but the Republicans continued to belabour it and, when he introduced new proposals, they were lost amid the rhetoric.

A modest, softspoken man with a colourless, professorial manner, McGovern had one asset that compensated for his lack of dramatic appeal—his reputation for plain honesty and moral courage. But that dissolved during his handling of the affair of Thomas Eagleton (*q.v.*). When it was revealed that his vice-presidential choice had been treated for mental illness, McGovern first stood by him and then, a week later, dumped him with what many people considered all the misguided pragmatic calculation of any old-time hack politician.

McGovern was born in Avon, S.D., on July 19, 1922, the son of a country minister. After distinguished service as a World War II bomber pilot, he graduated from Dakota Wesleyan University and earned a doctorate at Northwestern University, Evanston, Ill. He taught history and political science at Dakota Wesleyan and then as executive secretary reorganized the moribund state Democratic Party. After serving two terms in the U.S. House of Representatives, he became a special assistant to Pres. John F. Kennedy, was elected to the Senate in 1962, and reelected in 1968.

When McGovern announced his presidential candidacy early in 1971—nearly a year before any major opponent—the press and party regulars ignored him. His strong showing in the New Hampshire primary undermined Sen. Edmund S. Muskie's favoured position and his victory in the Wisconsin primary effectively put the Maine senator out of the running. McGovern's nomination was all but assured when he defeated former vice-president Hubert H. Humphrey in the June California primary. (PHILIP KOPPER)

MacSTIOFAIN, SEAN

On Nov. 25, 1972, a Dublin court convicted Sean MacStiofain of being a member of the Irish Republican Army (IRA), an illegal organization. MacStiofain was reputedly chief of staff of the Provisional wing of the IRA that was conducting the terror campaign in Northern Ireland and his arrest on

November 19 heralded a firmer anti-IRA line by the government of the Republic of Ireland. After his arrest MacStiofain began a hunger strike. Following the trial, he was moved from prison to a Dublin hospital (where armed sympathizers, some disguised as priests, unsuccessfully tried to free him), then to a military hospital at Curragh, County Kildare.

John Edward Drayton Stephenson (he adopted the Gaelic form of his name in the late 1940s) was born in Leytonstone, Essex, Eng., on Feb. 17, 1928, of parents born in England, and was baptized a Protestant. He left school at 14, did his national service in the Royal Air Force after World War II, and in 1950, after holding various jobs, started a small building firm in north London with a partner, marrying the same year. He became increasingly involved with Irish organizations and after his building business collapsed in 1951 became an IRA activist. In 1953 he was arrested and charged with stealing munitions from a school cadet armoury. With two other men he was sentenced to eight years' imprisonment and served six years.

After his release in 1959 he moved to Ireland to live for the first time in what he regarded as his homeland. Already a fluent Gaelic speaker, he worked for a Gaelic-language organization. At this time the Republican movement, embracing Sinn Fein (the political wing) and the IRA, was showing signs of internal division because of the limited success of the 1956–62 border campaign. When the campaign ended, left-wing and pacifist ideals began to dominate the movement. This did not suit MacStiofain, whose dream was for a Gaelic-speaking, Catholic Ireland untainted by Marxism and won, if necessary, by the gun.

The 1969 riots in Belfast, N.Ire., were an open invitation to the Republican movement to bring the gun back into politics. The Provisional, more militant wing of the movement was established in January 1970, with MacStiofain as chief of staff.

(BRUCE ARNOLD)

MANLEY, MICHAEL

After his People's National Party won general elections in Jamaica on Feb. 29, 1972, Michael Manley took office on March 2 as prime minister of the Caribbean island nation.

A passionate advocate of democracy and an anti-Communist, Manley faced severe problems in his country, including a high unemployment rate and a limited number of jobs in sugar, mining, and tourism. Demands by some in the country for increased black power caused concern, but Manley believed that he could alleviate the situation by working for an equitable distribution of goods and ownership.

A former Royal Canadian Air Force pilot in World War II and a postwar graduate of the London School of Economics, Manley was born Dec. 10, 1923, in Kingston. His late father, Norman W. Manley, was one of Jamaica's national heroes and served as prime minister from 1959 to 1962.

Like his father, Manley became closely allied with the labour union movement in Jamaica, which was primarily connected with the bauxite and sugar industries. For a time he worked as a free-lance journalist for the British Broadcasting Corporation and as co-editor of the newspaper *Public Opinion* in Jamaica.

He was associated with the National Workers' Union in a successful strike of bauxite workers against Aluminum Co. of Canada (Alcan) in 1953. This action for the first time in Jamaica produced wage scales based on ability to pay. This success led to Manley's appointment as organizer for the sugar workers in the NWU, and in 1955 he became first vice-president of the union. He was also elected president of the Caribbean Bauxite and Mine Workers Union and in 20 years of labour work became recognized as one of the most skilled union negotiators in the English-speaking world.

Manley entered elective politics in 1967 when he was elected to Parliament for the Central Kingston constituency. He became leader of the opposition at a time when the People's National Party, founded by his father, had lost two general elections. Manley's victory in 1972 led to the first smooth transition of leadership from one party to another in the history of the new Caribbean nations.

(JEREMIAH A. O'LEARY)

MARCHAIS, GEORGES

Georges Marchais's election as secretary-general of the French Communist Party at its 20th congress in December 1972 was a foregone conclusion: he had been the party's de facto leader for the past three years, during which time the nominal secretary-general, Waldeck Rochet, had been seriously ill. (Rochet was elected honorary president of the party. His illness had by 1972 incapacitated him totally.)

The formalization of Marchais's leadership came six months after he had signed an agreement with the French Socialist Party led by François Mitterrand (*q.v.*) and with the left-wing Radicals on a "common government program." The pact had only one precedent: in 1935 the same parties had combined and in the following year's election had come to power as the Popular Front. Now Marchais was speculating on a similar result, and the possibility seemed less remote than at any time since Charles de Gaulle's return to power in 1958.

The Communists claimed more members than any other French political party, and opinion polls published in December showed that the new union could expect some 45% of the votes in the 1973 election; the Gaullists and their partners could expect 38%. Nevertheless, the "common government program" was radical enough to scare off middle-of-the-road voters, and Marchais was at pains to stress the Communists' devotion to democracy. "We are not the party of the raised fist," he declared at the congress. "We are the party of the hand stretched out toward the French people."

Somewhat forbidding in appearance, Marchais was described by Alain Peyrefitte, the Gaullist secretary-general, as "not the sort of man you'd stop to give a lift to." With increasingly frequent public appearances, however, his coldness and lack of humour showed signs of softening.

Born June 7, 1920, at La Hoguette, Calvados, Marchais was a mechanic by trade. During World War II he worked in Germany under the compulsory labour system and did not join the Communist Party until 1947. By 1959, despite some resentment among party veterans, he had become a member of the Central Committee and a candidate member of the Politburo, and in February 1970 he became deputy secretary-general.

(PIERRE VIANSSON-PONTÉ)

MARGRETHE II

"To be queen is a richer experience than I have ever dreamed of," said Queen Margrethe II of Denmark at the first press conference ever to be given by a reigning monarch of the 1,000-year-old kingdom. Facing more than 100 journalists assembled at Fredensborg, the royal summer palace, in November 1972, with her consort, Prince Henrik, at her side, she answered—or skillfully parried—in Danish, English, and

GAMMA

Margrethe II

Swedish, questions on such diverse topics as the future of the monarchy, home rule for Greenland, abortion, and women's liberation.

Queen Margrethe II (the first Margrethe was queen of Denmark, Norway, and Sweden from 1387 to 1412) succeeded to the throne on Jan. 14, 1972, on the death of her father, King Frederik IX (*see* OBITUARIES). Born April 16, 1940, she was baptized Margrethe Alexandrine Thorhildur Ingrid. After attending school in Copenhagen, she continued her studies at the universities of Copenhagen, Århus in Jutland, Cambridge, the London School of Economics, and the Sorbonne. In 1953, following a change in the Danish constitution to permit female succession to the throne, Margrethe, the king's eldest daughter, assumed the title of "throne heiress" (*i.e.,* crown princess, although that title, in Denmark, denotes the wife of a male heir to the throne). As such, from her 18th birthday she regularly took part in meetings of the Council of State in preparation for her future regal duties.

On June 10, 1967, she married Count Henri de Laborde de Monpezat, a French diplomat, who afterward took the title of Prince Henrik. Their first child, Crown Prince Frederik, was born on May 26, 1968, and a second son, Prince Joachim, on June 7, 1969. A popular figure from her childhood days during the German occupation of Denmark in World War II, when she was called "Princess Sunshine," the new queen, highly educated, charming, and with a ready wit, seemed well equipped to occupy the secure place in the affections of the Danish people that her father had held during his 25-year reign.

(STENER AARSDAL)

MEINHOF, ULRIKE

Co-leader of the Baader-Meinhof gang of West German urban guerrillas, Ulrike Meinhof was arrested in an apartment near Hanover Airport on June 15, 1972. Andreas Baader had been seized after a gun battle with police two weeks earlier, and he, Meinhof, and others of the group's hard core faced charges of murder, arson, and bank robbery.

The gang's activities began in April 1968, when fire broke out in two Frankfurt stores. Within 48 hours three young men and a woman were arrested on suspicion of arson. All members of the extra-parliamentary opposition, they had started the fires as a demonstration against what they felt to be an ultramaterialistic society and its indifference to the victims of the war in Vietnam. One of the four was Andreas Baader. All were sentenced to three years' imprisonment but, in accordance with West German practice, were set free until the verdicts became legally binding. Baader went underground in West Berlin. There he met Ulrike Meinhof, and discovered that their political views were as good as identical.

Meinhof was born Oct. 7, 1934, in Oldenburg, but spent her childhood in Jena, where her father was head of the civic museum. At the university, where she was a brilliant student and an active protester against what she held to be a cynical, cruel, fragmented society, she met the man who later published the left-wing monthly *Konkret*. Eventually they married and had two children, but were subsequently divorced. Meinhof was editor of the magazine for a time, and she and her husband were prominent in the literary establishment.

Meinhof then turned her back on bourgeois life and went to West Berlin. When Baader was arrested there, she helped to free him when he was allowed out of prison, under guard, to visit a library. Later the two of them, with other members of the gang, went to the Middle East for training in guerrilla warfare. They admitted responsibility for several explosions in West Germany in the early months of 1972, when they were operating under the name of Red Army Faction, or RAF. The gang's strategy was based on the belief that, since capitalist society could not be brought down by revolution, the most effective alternative would be an urban guerrilla movement on South American lines. (NORMAN CROSSLAND)

MELEN, FERIT

As reward for inspiring confidence in the military leadership of his country, Ferit Melen was appointed prime minister of Turkey by Pres. Cevdet Sunay on April 17, 1972. As minister of defense Melen had earlier acted as liaison between the civilian administration headed by Nihat Erim and the military commanders who had installed it in power on March 26, 1971, after ousting the democratically elected government of Suleyman Demirel.

Melen had once before benefited from a military intervention in politics. He first held office as minister of finance in Ismet Inonu's coalition governments between 1962 and 1965, the troubled period between the military coup of May 27, 1960, and the elections that brought the Justice Party to power in October 1965. Melen was then a leading member of Inonu's Republican People's Party (RPP), the party established by Kemal Ataturk, founder of the Turkish republic, as the instrument of the country's westernization.

Born in Van in 1906, Melen became a finance official and by 1944, at age 38, had risen to the key position of director general of revenue in the Ministry of Finance. In May 1950 he was elected RPP deputy for his home town in the country's first freely contested elections.

In addition to his public service background, Melen had another asset in the eyes of the military commanders. This was his staunch anti-Communism, a common sentiment for a citizen of the small eastern Anatolian fortress town of Van, occupied by the Russians in World War I, and still claimed by Armenian nationalists. In 1967 Melen's anti-Communist feelings led him and 47 of his colleagues to resign from the RPP, which had veered to the left under a new secretary-general (Bulent Ecevit), and to form the small Reliance Party. The new party declared itself the true heir of Ataturk's nationalist tradition.

(ANDREW MANGO)

MESSMER, PIERRE

To the surprise of many observers, Pierre Messmer emerged from relative obscurity in July 1972 to become France's premier, leader of the parliamentary majority, and second in command of the Fifth Republic. Few had noticed how this trusted lieutenant of Charles de Gaulle had unobtrusively come to stand in the same relationship to Pres. Georges Pompidou, de Gaulle's successor. With opinion polls increasingly favouring the opposition left-wing alliance, many doubted whether the somewhat colourless Messmer was the right man to undertake the daunting task of leading the Gaullists into the March 1973 elections.

Born March 20, 1916, at Vincennes, Messmer took a doctorate in law at the University of Paris and also graduated at the National School of Oriental Languages. In 1940 he rallied to de Gaulle, fought as a Free French company commander at the siege of Bir Hakeim in Libya, and was parachuted into Tongking and captured by Ho Chi Minh's troops in 1945. From 1946 he served in the French colonial administration, first in Indochina, then in Africa, where he was successively governor of Mauritania and of the Ivory Coast. After a period at the Ministry of Overseas France, where he was involved in the first steps toward decolonization initiated by the Socialist minister Gaston Defferre, he became high commissioner for Cameroun, then, successively, for French Equatorial Africa and French West Africa.

In spite of this outstanding career, de Gaulle's 1960 appointment of Messmer as minister of defense, immediately after the abortive "generals' putsch" in Algiers, was unexpected. He remained at that post through crises and reshuffles until 1969, when he followed de Gaulle into retirement. He was one of the last visitors to Colombey shortly before the general's death.

Founder of Présence et Action du Gaullisme, the association uniting the most faithful of de Gaulle's "companions," he was always ready to give lessons in Gaullist orthodoxy to the general's successors. However, realism and political sense soon overcame his bitterness and suspicion of the new order. He returned to the government in February 1971 as unobtrusively as he had left it, as minister for overseas *départements* and territories. (PIERRE VIANSSON-PONTÉ)

MINNELLI, LIZA

Once known as Judy Garland's daughter, Liza Minnelli in 1972 again persuasively demonstrated her own spectacular talents as a singer and considerable ability as an actress. She was outstanding in *Cabaret,* the screen adaptation of Harold Prince's Broadway hit, based on Christopher Isherwood's Berlin tales. The film, co-starring Joel Grey as a leering nightclub emcee, was set in the soul-withering atmosphere of Berlin in the early 1930s. Liza played Sally Bowles, a tawdry, fame-seeking chanteuse, to the quick of her green-painted nails. She seemed assured of an Academy Award nomination for her performance and was also likely to be in the running for an Emmy award after her electrifying television special, "Liza with a Z."

Born in Hollywood, Calif., March 12, 1946, Liza grew up in a show business en-

CAMERA PRESS/PICTORIAL PARADE

Pierre Messmer

vironment. Not only was her mother a star but her father, Vincente Minnelli, directed such outstanding movie musicals as *An American in Paris* and *Gigi.* Her godmother, *Eloise* author Kay Thompson, said, "Liza was always show business. The basic quality has been there since she said her first 'goo.' " When she was 2½, Liza had a toddle-on part in one of her mother's movies. At 7 she danced on New York's Palace Theater stage while Judy sang. At 14 she herself starred for the first time in a Scarsdale (N.Y.) High School production of *The Diary of Anne Frank.*

Fed up with education at 17—her mother's frenetic life, frequent emotional crises, and roller-coaster fortune had shunted Liza to 20 schools—she quit the Sorbonne for New York. There, in 1963, she landed a featured role in an off-Broadway revival of *Best Foot Forward* and won one of *Theater World's* "Promising Personalities" awards.

At 19 she became the youngest Tony Award winner for the title role in *Flora, The Red Menace,* a short-lived and swiftly forgotten charade about U.S. leftists in the 1930s. Her screen debut was with Albert Finney in *Charlie Bubbles.* Then came an Academy Award nomination as kookey Pookie Adams, the hapless antiheroine in *The Sterile Cuckoo,* a role that assured her peerless stature as performer of "the happy trauma." Meanwhile, she was becoming a veteran stand-up singer on the nightclub circuit. There audiences often begged for traces of Judy Garland, but when they requested "Over the Rainbow," Liza would say, "It's been sung." (PHILIP KOPPER)

MITCHELL, MARTHA

The most gregarious and outspoken Cabinet wife in recent memory, Martha Mitchell was muzzled briefly in the spring of 1972 in an incident as bizarre as the event that prompted it, the "Watergate Caper," an attempt to bug the headquarters of the Democratic National Committee in the Watergate Office Building in Washington, D.C. The matter soon became a cause célèbre as the press, with the *Washington Post* in the forefront, worked diligently to unearth facts and implications of the Watergate scandal, which were soon leading in many directions. Though the Watergate affair had no apparent effect on the presidential election, it appeared possible that some people close to the president authorized and financed the criminal incursion at the Watergate as well as other acts of political sabotage.

BURT GLINN—MAGNUM

Liza Minnelli

UPI COMPIX

Martha Mitchell

Shortly after the break-in an enterprising reporter called Mrs. Mitchell, an ardent believer in the telephone. Asked for a comment on the Watergate matter, Mrs. Mitchell later recalled replying, "Politics is a dirty business," only to have a bodyguard terminate the conversation and jerk the phone from the wall. Then, she later reported, several bodyguards held her down while someone gave her a sedative injection. She said she had been held incommunicado for 24 hours.

Mrs. Mitchell made public an ultimatum issued to her husband, former attorney general John N. Mitchell, shortly after the alleged bodyguard incident: give up either politics or her. Mitchell made his choice and resigned as Pres. Richard Nixon's campaign manager. The Mitchells then took up residence in a New York City apartment.

Born in Pine Bluff, Ark., Sept. 2, 1918, Mrs. Mitchell was remembered in a high school yearbook by a still timely ditty: "I love its gentle warble,/ I love its gentle flow,/ I love to wind my tongue up,/ and I love to let it go." (PHILIP KOPPER)

MITTERRAND, FRANÇOIS MAURICE

In 1965 François Mitterrand had stood against Charles de Gaulle as the sole candidate of the Socialist and Communist left for the French presidency. He collected over seven million votes and forced de Gaulle to a second ballot. On June 27, 1972, he again threw down the gauntlet, this time against the less formidable Pres. Georges Pompidou, when he announced agreement between his Parti Socialiste Français and the Parti Communiste Français, led by Georges Marchais (*q.v.*), on a common policy platform to fight the spring 1973 legislative elections. Should the united left be successful, Mitterrand would undoubtedly be its presidential candidate in 1976. The agreement, ratified by the respective party congresses in July, was regarded as the most significant event for the French left since the Socialist Congress at Tours in 1920, when the left wing of the Socialists had seceded to form the Communist Party. With public opinion late in 1972 veering strongly in favour of social reforms after 14 years of Gaullist rule, Mitterrand's challenge was not to be ignored.

Mitterrand was born on Oct. 26, 1916, at Jarnac, Charente, France. The son of a stationmaster, he became the youngest minister of the Fourth Republic in the Socialist government of Paul Ramadier in 1947, having been elected deputy for Nièvre the previous year. He subsequently served in 11 short-lived governments.

During World War II Mitterrand escaped from a German prison camp, but before becoming a leader of one of the principal resistance movements, he spent several months working for the Vichy government and was awarded a medal for loyalty to the Pétain régime. This fact, and his sudden change of attitude toward the Algerian secessionists in 1957, from bellicose hostility to firm support, fed the fire of opponents' accusations that his political convictions were shallow. But Mitterrand had twice proved himself the strongest and most effective leader of the French Socialists, and he was one of the very few to have opposed de Gaulle consistently from 1958 onward.

(PIERRE VIANSSON-PONTÉ)

MOBUTU SESE SEKO

During 1972 President Mobutu of Zaire continued his campaign to promote "the authentic African personality" of his people. Following the changing of the country's name from Congo to Zaire in October 1971, foreign place and personal names were africanized and Mobutu changed his own Christian names, Joseph-Désiré, back to his earlier tribal names, Sese Seko ("daring and unconquerable warrior"—his full appellation being Mobutu Sese Seko Kuku Ngbendu Wa Za Banga). Although he had been brought up in the Catholic faith and remained a staunch Christian, his "authenticity" campaign led to a confrontation with Joseph-Albert Cardinal Malula (who left the country for a time) and almost ruptured diplomatic relations with the Vatican before the conflict was resolved.

Mobutu was born Oct. 14, 1930, at Lisala in the Équateur Province of the Belgian Congo, into a colonialist society that was felt by the local inhabitants to be strongly discriminatory and that left a sharp imprint on him and his fellow countrymen. After seven years in the Belgian-officered Force Publique, he had the unusual privilege of a year at a Belgian university, where he studied social sciences. On his return he became a journalist and joined Patrice Lumumba's Mouvement National Congolais. At independence in 1960 he became defense secretary in Lumumba's government, then chief of staff of the Congolese Army. Five years later he staged a coup from which he emerged as the most powerful figure in the country.

Although only 35 when he seized power, Mobutu showed a remarkable capacity for tough, often ruthless leadership. He turned his once disorderly and ill-trained army into a modern, well-disciplined force, created his own ruling party, the Mouvement Populaire de la Révolution, and embarked on a series of radical reforms that included nationalizing Union Minière, the Belgian mining corporation that once controlled most of the great copper and cobalt wealth of the Katanga region. Nevertheless, he succeeded in maintaining a cooperative relationship with Belgium. His foreign policies were essentially Western-oriented, notwithstanding the nationalist ardour that prompted his call for "authenticity." (COLIN LEGUM)

MOLINA BARRAZA, ARTURO ARMANDO

In an election that triggered a bloody and abortive coup by rebel military forces, Col. Arturo Armando Molina Barraza of El Salvador was chosen president of Central America's smallest republic on Feb. 25, 1972. Molina, a career soldier, was in the United States when the fighting broke out in San Salvador, but forces loyal to outgoing Pres. Fidel Sánchez Hernández acted in concert with the Air Force to defeat the rebels. Order was restored, and Molina, who had been secretary to Sánchez, was inaugurated for a five-year term on July 1.

Before the presidential campaign, Molina was almost unknown outside of government and military circles. But Sánchez, El Salvador's strong man, supported him for the presidency as candidate of the National Conciliation Party. No candidate received a clear majority in the February election, and Molina, the front-runner by 10,000 votes, was declared elected by Congress. The runner-up, José Napoleón Duarte, candidate of the left-of-centre National Opposition Union, charged that the election was a fraud. Duarte was arrested during the uprising that followed the election.

Born in San Salvador on June 18, 1927, Molina graduated first in his class at the Salvadoran Military Academy. He became an artillery officer and studied at the Mexican Superior War College and the Infantry School in Spain. He served for several years on the board of the Salvador Railway Co. and on the port authority for Acajutla. His rise to prominence began in 1969 when Sánchez made him his private secretary.

Molina described himself as a "Central Americanist." He was anti-Communist and

J.-P. LAFFONT—GAMMA

Richard M. Nixon

dedicated to settling the differences between El Salvador and Honduras, which still faced many unsolved problems resulting from their armed conflict of 1969.

(JEREMIAH A. O'LEARY)

NIXON, RICHARD MILHOUS

In the last year of his first term as U.S. president Richard Nixon could point to some notable accomplishments—and to two notable failures. He visited Moscow and signed the first U.S.-U.S.S.R. agreement to limit nuclear arms proliferation. He became the first U.S. president to visit China and in doing so symbolically exorcised 20 years of binational phobia. And in November he was reelected by a margin that compared to the landslide victories of Franklin D. Roosevelt and Lyndon B. Johnson. But the domestic economy, though improving, refused to conform to his appointees' rosy predictions and he had not yet succeeded in ending the war in Vietnam.

In fact, when cease-fire negotiations conducted by Henry Kissinger (*q.v.*) broke down, Nixon escalated the air war over North Vietnam, mercilessly pounding the capital, Hanoi, and the port city of Haiphong with the most devastating aerial bombardment in history. On December 30 the White House announced that Kissinger would return to negotiations in Paris on Jan. 8, 1973, and that bombing north of the 20th parallel would be halted indefinitely. There was speculation that the announcement was as much a response to resounding cries of outrage at home and abroad as it was to any overtures from North Vietnam.

In the election Nixon faced, or rather ignored, the hapless George McGovern (*q.v.*). He struck a statesmanlike pose, barely appearing on the hustings and sending instead cohorts of "surrogate candidates," such as his Cabinet members, aides, wife, and daughters. Despite this and credible charges of campaign espionage, including the Watergate bugging incident, Nixon's popular vote margin was 23%; he won 60% of the votes, barely one percentage point less than Johnson in 1964, and overwhelmed McGovern in 49 states. The dimensions of the victory were belied by the absence of Nixon's coattails, however. Ticket-splitting was epidemic as Democrats ran successfully for the majority of state offices and for seats in both congressional houses.

The most outstanding events of Nixon's year took place in Peking and Moscow. His talks with Chairman Mao Tse-tung and Premier Chou En-lai produced little more solid than future people-to-people exchanges and a trade agreement, but long-term ramifications were as important as they were ineffable. As André Malraux said, it would take half a century to understand what had occurred in a week. The Moscow visit had more concrete results, including a treaty limiting antiballistic-missile systems, an executive agreement limiting offensive nuclear weapons, and pacts calling for cooperation in health and scientific research, trade, space exploration, environmental protection, and maritime navigation.

Born in Yorba Linda, Calif., on Jan. 9, 1913, Nixon was graduated from Whittier College and Duke University Law School. After serving in the Navy during World War II, he was elected a U.S. representative from California in 1946, a senator four years later, and vice-president in 1952. He was defeated by John F. Kennedy in the 1960 presidential election but returned in 1968 to defeat Hubert H. Humphrey.

(PHILIP KOPPER)

O'KEEFFE, GEORGIA

Still filled with "unjaded joy," Georgia O'Keeffe at 85 continued to create the paintings that brought delight to the millions who knew and loved her work. Andrew Wyeth was the only U.S. artist who could draw more people to an exhibit. Three major retrospective exhibits in New York, Chicago, and San Francisco, embracing the whole of her creative life until then, had brought O'Keeffe's gifts to new and old admirers across the country in 1970–71.

Her painting was the only part of her life O'Keeffe was willing to share with the world. Calling herself a creature of solitude, she rarely left her New Mexico retreats—a summer home at Ghost Ranch, 50 mi. N of Santa Fe, where she rose each dawn to walk the arroyos, and a nine-room winter house in the tiny village of Abiquiu (pop. about 300). But she had not always lived as a loner.

Born in Sun Prairie, Wis., on Nov. 15, 1887, she studied art in Chicago and New York, gave up painting to teach, and then took up art again, this time in black and white.

In late 1915 a friend, strictly against instructions, showed some of her drawings to that moody genius of photography Alfred Stieglitz, who promptly exhibited them. O'Keeffe marched to Stieglitz' place in a rage to demand their removal and found a friendship that culminated in marriage in 1924. Stieglitz loved people, and their home became the lively centre of a spirited avant-garde movement.

O'Keeffe's first visit to New Mexico in 1929 convinced her that this was her true home, and she moved there after Stieglitz died in 1946. For a time she traveled widely, but by 1972 she left only when her work demanded it.

O'Keeffe hallmarks were lean, clean line; clear, vivid colour; a combination of sweep and precision, mystery and starkness. Each canvas had an almost hallucinatory quality. Although her paintings had the enchantment of Surrealism, they were of particular things and places. She concentrated in turn on Jimsonweed, desert roses, bones bleached white by the desert sun, clouds, and rocks. The world showered O'Keeffe with honours, the latest being the Edward MacDowell Medal for outstanding contribution to the arts.

(PAT TUCKER)

PAPP, JOSEPH

From New York's Central Park and the Public Theatre in the East Village, producer Joseph Papp made the transition to Broadway in 1972, and in the process garnered critical acclaim and awards. Identified for 18 years with New York's free "Shakespeare in the Park" summer program, in December 1971 Papp had opened his first play on Broadway, the John Guare and Mel Shapiro updated version of Shakespeare's *Two Gentlemen of Verona*. The musical had proved highly successful in its Central Park presentation and continued its hit career in 1972 at the St. James Theatre. Papp's second production, *Sticks and Bones*, the David Rabe play about a returning Vietnam veteran, opened on Broadway in March after a successful run at the Public Theatre.

In April the League of New York Theatres gave a Tony for best musical to *Gents* and one for best play to *Sticks*. Later, the New York Drama Critics Circle named *Gents* as the best musical and Jason Miller's *That Championship Season* as the best play of the year. The latter was another Papp production, which had opened early in the year at his Public Theatre and by September had gone to Broadway. By November Papp chalked up another play on Broadway when

PHILIPPE—GAMMA

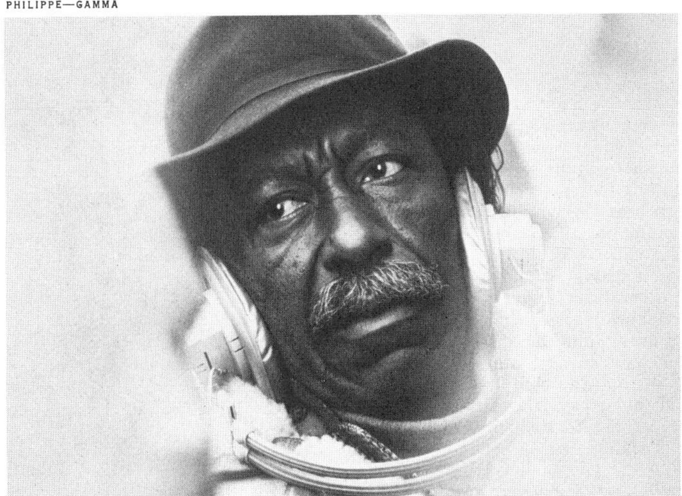

Gordon Parks

Much Ado About Nothing opened after an enthusiastic reception during the summer in Central Park.

If the awards and recognition gladdened Papp's heart, they also helped to focus attention on his long-standing efforts to provide playwrights with a stage and audience. Off-Broadway, he noted, still seemed to be the only place where producers could take a chance on young directors and writers. With Central Park and the year-round Public Theatre at his disposal, Papp could put on plays of varying scope. His Mobile Theatre, another offshoot of the Shakespeare program, took plays to the people throughout New York's boroughs. Early in 1972 the Rockefeller Foundation gave him a grant to explore the possibility of establishing an agency that would tour professional companies throughout the U.S.

Born Joseph Papirofsky on June 22, 1921, in Brooklyn, N.Y., Papp served in the Navy in 1942–46, where he helped produce shows that toured the Pacific area on board an aircraft carrier. He began his association with the Central Park program in 1954.

(BERNARD S. KATZ)

PARKS, GORDON

Photographer, composer, writer, and successful film director, Gordon Parks won the NAACP's 1972 Spingarn Medal that goes annually to a preeminent American of African descent. It was only the latest of a number of awards for Parks, who had been honoured by the Philadelphia Museum of Art, the University of Missouri School of Journalism, and the National Conference of Christians and Jews. A restless, extraordinarily creative man, Parks recently had concentrated on motion-picture direction. He directed the low-budget box-office smash *Shaft,* one of the earliest and best made in the sudden new wave of adventure films featuring sex, violence, and—notably—black heroes as titanic detectives or legendary crooks. These films appealed largely to black urban audiences and revived the fortunes of movie houses long since languishing in cities from which affluent white residents had fled.

These filmed fantasies appeared to be the modern black equivalent of the James Cagney or Humphrey Bogart crime epics that won the adulation of mass white audiences in decades past, and they certainly borrowed from superwhite James Bond's brand of bed-and-blood heroics. But they dismayed many black leaders, who said they glorified antiheroes, "superdudes" such as killers and dope dealers. Parks replied, "It's ridiculous to imply that blacks don't know the difference between truth and fantasy and therefore will be influenced by these films in an unhealthy way. I knew a black preacher in Chicago, and I remember people who wanted to kill their white bosses coming to prayer meeting, and being calmed down by the preacher. These movies are serving the same therapeutic function." Said the noted black actor James Earl Jones, "If they're going to put the damper on John Shaft, let them put it on John Wayne, too, and they'll find out that there are a lot of people who need those fantasies." (The ghetto epic that caused the most furious outcry, *Super Fly*, directed by Parks's son, Gordon Parks, Jr., grossed $11 million in two months as city audiences packed movie houses to cheer the adventurous exploits of a cocaine dealer who in the end out-cons crooked white cops.)

The elder Parks earned fame first as a *Life* photographer for his picture essays on human topics ranging from ghetto life to Spanish bullfighting. Unlike many visual artists, he also emerged as an accomplished writer with the publication of *The Learning Tree,* an autobiographical novel about a black youth in a small Kansas town. The book became a movie, which Parks directed and for which he created the musical score. It was his first attempt at moviemaking. He also wrote an undisguised autobiography, *A Choice of Weapons*.

Born in Fort Scott, Kan., Nov. 30, 1912, Parks emerged from a violent youth. He supported himself with a variety of odd jobs, including playing piano in a brothel, did a stint with the Civilian Conservation Corps, and drifted to Harlem with a jazz band that featured his compositions. He later wrote serious modern music, including several concertos. He studied photography and worked for the Farm Security Administration, later for the Office of War Information and Standard Oil Co. of New Jersey before joining *Life* in 1948.

(PHILIP KOPPER)

PERÓN, JUAN DOMINGO

Once the all-powerful dictator of Argentina and for 17 years an exile, Juan Perón returned to his native land in 1972. As the leader of a large and powerful political grouping, he was in a position to play a kingmaking role in his country's convoluted politics. His decision as to whether to be a candidate for the presidency or to endorse another loomed as a vital factor in the March 1973 elections, when the South American country he once governed was scheduled to return to democratic rule after six years of military control.

The Peronista movement had never died out in Argentina, and in 1972 it prepared to return as an active—and legal—political force. On January 24 the neo-Peronistas (now called Justicialistas) were recognized by a federal judge in Buenos Aires as a legal political organization, and on April 7 the last legal obstacle to Perón's return was removed when a 1955 treason charge against him was dismissed. The Justicialistas proclaimed him as their presidential candidate in June.

It was not to be that simple, however. Subsequently, Pres. Alejandro Lanusse decreed that all candidates must be in Argentina by August 25. On July 22 Perón announced that he would not return for "security reasons." He later changed his mind, however, and returned to Argentina on November 17, stating that his wish was for the military government to "call free, pure elections without conditions or proscriptions."

On Perón's arrival the government instituted strict security precautions, but at no time during his stay did Perón encourage mass demonstrations or uprisings and only scattered incidents occurred. After 28 days of consultations with the government and his supporters, he left Argentina on December 14 for a visit to Paraguay, en route to his home in Madrid. At year's end, the Peronistas appeared to be uniting around the candidacy of Héctor Campora, who had been Péron's longtime personal representative in Argentina.

Perón was born Oct. 8, 1895, in Buenos Aires Province. Elected president in 1946, he set out on a revolutionary program of nationalization, industrialization, and social welfare. Basing his rule on the support of the proletariat and catering to anti-U.S. feeling, he—with his second wife, Eva—ruled Argentina absolutely until his overthrow by the military. He fled to Paraguay in 1955 and eventually settled in Spain.

(JEREMIAH A. O'LEARY)

PETERS, MARY ELIZABETH

After years of training Mary Peters reached the pinnacle of her long athletic career when she mounted the rostrum in Munich in September 1972 to receive the Olympic gold medal for the women's pentathlon. She scored a world record 4,801 points in the five events (100-m. hurdles, shot put, high jump, long jump, 200 m.), beating West Germany's Heide Rosendahl, eight years her junior, by 10 points. The success of this cheerful, outgoing secretary from Belfast, N.Ire., was just reward for complete dedication to her chosen sport. Seven times winner of the British pentathlon title, she trained regularly in the Belfast gymnasium of her coach and employer, Buster McShane, and used the winter indoor competitions early in 1972 to sharpen up her sprinting and improve her weak event, the high jump. A switch to the "flop" style brought an improvement from her normal best of 5 ft. 5 in. to a potential 6 ft., and she was within a quarter of an inch of that height during the Olympics.

Born in Liverpool on July 6, 1939, Mary Peters went to Portadown College in County Armagh and first appeared on the major athletics scene when she was selected for the Northern Ireland team in the 1958 Commonwealth Games at Cardiff, Wales. From then on she competed in many top tournaments and in 1962 came under the wing of McShane. Two years later she went to Tokyo with the British team for the XVIII Olympic Games as captain of the women's team and finished fourth in the pentathlon. In 1968, with several local successes behind her, she went to Mexico but finished only ninth in the pentathlon. This poor showing steeled her resolve to beat the world's best, and in the 1970 Commonwealth Games at Edinburgh, Scot., she collected gold medals in the shot put and pentathlon. She then decided to pass over domestic and European competitions in 1971 and focus all her attention and training on winning the gold at Munich. She was helped in this aim by being awarded a Winston Churchill travel scholarship that took her away from troubled Ulster and enabled her to train in the sunshine and peace of California. On her return she took part in the Highland Games in Scotland, winning both the shot put and the pentathlon and setting a British record of 4,630 points in the latter.

(TREVOR WILLIAMSON)

POMPIDOU, GEORGES

After nearly three years of comparative calm since taking the French helm, Pres. Georges Pompidou in 1972 began to encounter rough patches. His first serious reversal came in April, when he held a referendum on the enlargement of the EEC. He had hoped to get the nation to underwrite his European policy and at the same time enhance his personal prestige and pave the way for the 1973 legislative elections. Although two out of three of those who voted were in favour, the 40% rate of abstention robbed the result of any real satisfaction.

After this partial failure, a number of cases of corruption involving government deputies came to light. These led Pompidou in July to replace Premier Jacques Chaban-Delmas with Pierre Messmer (*q.v.*), an orthodox Gaullist, at the head of a reshuffled government. But worse was yet to come. In September Gabriel Aranda (*q.v.*) burst upon the scene with "136 documents involving 48 persons," goading Pompidou to an unusual show of anger in his biannual press conference on September 21.

The EEC "summit" meeting, held in Paris in October, also had disappointing results for Pompidou: the choice of Paris as the seat of the EEC's political secretariat was rejected, and the introduction of monetary union was postponed. Toward year's end there was speculation as to how far Pompidou would open the government to the left should the Socialist-Communist alliance fulfill the promise of opinion polls and win the 1973 elections.

In the realm of personal diplomacy, Pompidou received several heads of state and government and visited others in their own countries. He made two trips to Africa and while in Upper Volta in November announced the cancellation of a Fr. 1 billion debt owed to France by its former African colonies.

Pompidou was born on July 5, 1911, at Montboudif in the Cantal. A teacher of literature from 1935 until 1944, he became director of Charles de Gaulle's Cabinet during the transition between the Fourth and Fifth Republics and, in 1962, premier. Following the student disturbances of May 1968 he was dismissed, but the following year he was elected president after de Gaulle's resignation.

(PIERRE VIANSSON-PONTÉ)

POTTER, PHILIP ALFORD

A representative of the third world—a black born on the island of Dominica in the West Indies—became the third general secretary of the World Council of Churches in 1972. The Rev. Philip Alford Potter was elected to succeed Eugene Carson Blake in the group's top executive post at a meeting of the council's Central Committee in Utrecht, Neth., on August 16. The organization he would guide was composed of more than 260 Anglican, Orthodox, and Protestant churches in 90 countries and territories, representing a total membership of 400 million Christians.

CAMERA PRESS / PICTORIAL PARADE

Philip A. Potter

CENTRAL PRESS / PICTORIAL PARADE

André Previn

Potter, a Methodist, was no stranger to the World Council. In 1948 he attended the first assembly of the council as a youth delegate. Before being named general secretary, he was chairman of Program Unit I on Faith and Witness and director of the Commission on World Mission and Evangelism. A strong believer in the unity of the church, Potter associated that unity with a unity of mankind. Such a unity is not to be achieved by abstract concepts. As a religious activist, Potter saw the gospel of Jesus Christ as having political implications: the church cannot function without taking cognizance of the struggle for justice and playing its part in that struggle.

He noted that power in the World Council still resided with the West rather than the third world countries, and as general secretary he would undoubtedly press for changes of emphasis that would include taking greater note of the newly independent nations. He saw an urgent need to translate the word of God into social deeds and viewed the ecumenical movement as having forced the churches to the point of action. At the same time, he pointed out that "We need to consider anew what it means to be the people of God in the world today . . . to rethink the universality of the church."

Potter was born in Roseau, the capital of Dominica, on Aug. 19, 1921. He received his bachelor of divinity degree from London University in 1948 and his master of theology in 1954. He was the pastor of a Methodist church in Haiti from 1950 to 1954, secretary of the World Council of Churches' youth department from 1954 to 1960, and served as field secretary for Africa and the West Indies for the British Methodist Missionary Society from 1960 to 1967.

(BERNARD S. KATZ)

PREVIN, ANDRÉ GEORGE

With an indefinitely prolonged contract with the London Symphony Orchestra (LSO) in 1972, André Previn had shaken off his earlier image of a Hollywood whiz-kid and firmly established himself as one of the foremost conductors on the international musical scene. He had done so partly through television appearances where he used his relaxed, informal manner to expound to the man in the street the mysteries, or otherwise, of serious music. In 1972 he was invited to organize South Bank Summer Music in London, and took a leading part in this miniature festival as player and conductor.

Previn had conducted the LSO for the first time in 1965 and three years later had become its principal conductor, initially for a three-year period. Having undertaken several U.S. and European tours with the orchestra, and still continuing to play the piano and make numerous classical and jazz recordings, in 1971 he launched "André Previn's Music Night" for BBC television; a second series was given in 1972. Also in 1972, to mark the centenary of the birth of composer Ralph Vaughan Williams, he completed his integral recording of Vaughan Williams' symphonies, and at Sir William Walton's 70th birthday concert at Festival Hall, London, he conducted Walton's *Belshazzar's Feast*.

Previn was born April 6, 1929, in Berlin; he and his family emigrated to California in 1939. He had already written incidental music for radio shows when pianist José Iturbi suggested to Metro-Goldwyn-Mayer that the 16-year-old Previn might help with the arrangement and orchestration of film scores. Of the 35 cinema scores he wrote, four (*Gigi, Porgy and Bess, Irma la Douce,* and *My Fair Lady*) received Oscars; those of which he was proudest were *Elmer Gantry, Two for the See-Saw, Irma la Douce,* and *Bad Day at Black Rock*. In 1960 he decided almost overnight that he wanted to change his life completely and devote his time to classical music. After learning his craft with various provincial orchestras he became musical director of the Houston Symphony Orchestra (1967–69). A U.S. citizen, Previn married actress Mia Farrow in 1970.

(ALAN BLYTH)

RAHMAN, MUJIBUR

In January 1972 Sheikh Mujibur Rahman—known to his people as "Mujib"—became the first president of Bangladesh (formerly East Pakistan), the new republic established on the Indian subcontinent after the defeat of the Pakistani Army by the supporters of

Mujib's Awami League and the Indian Army. He came to the president's office from imprisonment in Pakistan, the latest of many incarcerations he had endured during his political career.

Mujib's essentially moderate policies came under severe strain during his first year in office when he was faced with the grim problems of the aftermath of war, including a serious economic crisis, widespread unemployment, and the corrupt practices of his own government. He also was committed to conducting war crimes trials against Pakistani soldiers and administrators as well as local collaborators, although by the end of the year no date for such trials had been set. The strains of office had clearly begun to affect Mujib's health, already impaired by his prison experiences.

Mujib was born in 1920 in Tongipara in the district of Faridpur, to a family of middle-class landowners. He graduated in 1942 at the University of Calcutta and continued with law studies at the University of Dacca. He founded the East Pakistan Students' League, which later played a major and often violent role in the challenge that finally led to the breakdown of military rule in Pakistan. For these activities he was expelled from the university and served his first term of imprisonment.

His formal political career began when he became secretary of the Awami League in the early 1950s. In 1954 he was elected to the East Pakistan Assembly. Although he served briefly as a minister, his main preoccupation was as a party organizer of the Awami League, whose objective was autonomy for East Pakistan. When Pres. Muhammad Ayub Khan took power in Pakistan in 1958, he at once imprisoned Mujibur, who refused to buy his release by pledging not to engage in politics for five years. When finally released, he continued to make "seditious speeches" which earned him further terms in prison. The clamour for his release precipitated mob violence that effectively undermined Ayub Khan's authority in East Pakistan. (COLIN LEGUM)

RAMANANTSOA, GABRIEL

In October 1972 Gen. Gabriel Ramanantsoa won an overwhelming majority in a national referendum to become the Malagasy Republic's second president. He succeeded the island republic's first president and "father of the nation," Philibert Tsiranana, whom he had helped to overthrow in a military take-over in May.

The 66-year-old new president, elected for a five-year term, was essentially a conservative who acted reluctantly against Tsiranana, and then only because the country was moving toward a state of anarchy. Militant students and workers, backed by radical politicians and parties, were staging massive demonstrations that could not be brought under control by the ailing Tsiranana's discredited regime.

Although Ramanantsoa came to power with the support of militant radicals, his background and training were not very different from those of the man he replaced. Born in 1906, he was a leading member of the elite Merina, the hill people of Indonesian origin who had traditionally dominated the coastal peoples of the island of Madagascar.

Trained at the famed French military academy of St. Cyr, he fought with distinction in World War II and in the French colonial war in Indochina before associating himself with the Malagasy nationalists' own struggle. As the first Malagasy army chief after independence he displayed a strong dislike for political involvement, but his aloofness, soft-spoken prudence, and natural authority recommended him to both radicals and conservatives at a time of crisis.

After taking office, President Ramanantsoa showed himself ready to change the quality of Malagasy's relations with France without weakening their close ties. He acted decisively to change the direction of Malagasy's policies by resuming the broken diplomatic relations with the United States, by entering into relations with the Soviet Union, by drawing closer to the radical circles of the Organization of African Unity, and by reversing his predecessor's policy of developing economic and diplomatic relations with South Africa. At home, however, civil disturbances recurred in December; Ramanantsoa blamed them on "certain foreign elements." (COLIN LEGUM)

REID, JIMMY

When a committee of shop stewards took over the running of the old John Brown shipyard at Clydebank on Clydeside in the summer of 1971, Scotland provided a practical demonstration of the philosophy of workers' control. The effective leader of the group was a 39-year-old Glasgow-born trade unionist, Jimmy Reid, who had devoted his life to working-class politics. As far as Reid was concerned, the occupation of the shipyard was something more than an improvised act of desperation, though it started as that. It was the expression of a deeply felt belief, and a protest against the injustice of an economic system that left men without jobs. With the collaboration of the liquidator who had been sent in to close the shipyard, the work-in was effective in keeping it open for 12 months until the Marathon oil rig construction corporation of Texas took over with new contracts.

During this time Reid made a reputation for himself, not only by his professional knowledge and competence in helping to manage the yard, but also by his highly articulate exposition of his views. "Man's inalienable right to work" was his theme. The students of Glasgow University elected him their rector in October 1971, and in his rectorial address in May 1972 he expounded his philosophy with great oratorical skill as well as passion. "A rat race is for rats," he told the students. "We are not rats, we are human beings. Reject these attitudes." Talking of the alienation of the worker from society and attacking profit as the sole criterion of success, he proclaimed that politics is about people, not power, and that society should be geared to social need.

Reid's first job was in a stockbroker's office, and it was said that this was what outraged his sense of social justice. He then took an apprenticeship in marine engineering, but in 1966 became full-time secretary of the Scottish Communist Party. He returned to shipyard work in 1969 in order to earn more money for his family. (HARFORD THOMAS)

RICHARDSON, ELLIOT

In World War II a Boston draftboard rejected Elliot Richardson for poor vision. But he wangled his way into uniform as a litter bearer, leading a battlefield medical team serving the unit that suffered the highest casualty rate in the Normandy invasion. He was dubbed "Lucky" for his frequent narrow escapes, and "Fearless Fosdick" for his outstanding bravery and jut-jawed profile. He was awarded two Purple Hearts and a Bronze Star for valour. This proof positive of a talent for tenacious daring could only stand the erstwhile reject in good stead as 1972 ended, for on November 28 Pres. Richard Nixon named Richardson, then secretary of health, education, and welfare

WIDE WORLD

Guillermo Rodríguez Lara

(HEW), to be secretary of defense, succeeding Melvin R. Laird.

Richardson enjoyed the reputation of a supremely competent administrator who earned the devoted respect of subordinates. It remained to be seen whether he could conquer the Defense Department as he had less militant agencies. A reserved, aristocratic man, he was widely regarded as the most liberal, distinguished, and able member of Nixon's second Cabinet. Richardson was reported to have sought the job of secretary of state, but he acquiesced to Nixon's wishes, telling a news conference that the president "made me an offer I could not refuse."

Richardson was born on July 20, 1920, in Boston, the family domain since his ancestors were numbered among its first colonists. He was graduated cum laude from Harvard and after the war he returned to its law school where he edited the *Harvard Law Review*. He served as law clerk to Judge Learned Hand and Supreme Court Justice Felix Frankfurter before entering private practice. As assistant secretary of HEW during the Eisenhower administration he wrote the National Defense Education Act and was acting head of the department for a time. He returned to Massachusetts as U.S. attorney and prosecuted Bernard Goldfine, chief figure in a scandal involving Sherman Adams, Eisenhower's presidential assistant. Richardson was elected lieutenant governor of Massachusetts in 1964 and state attorney general in 1966. Nixon named him undersecretary of state in 1969 and HEW secretary in 1970. (PHILIP KOPPER)

RODRÍGUEZ LARA, GUILLERMO

As leader of a bloodless coup d'etat that sent aged Pres. José María Velasco Ibarra into exile, Brig. Gen. Guillermo Rodríguez Lara became the president of Ecuador on Feb. 15, 1972. He said he took control with reluctance because of the eccentricity of the Velasco government, but many believed a major reason was the widespread fear that former Guayaquil mayor Assad Bucaram, an unpredictable populist, would win the presidential election that was to have taken place in June 1972. The six million people of Ecuador accepted the change with little stir and Rodríguez and his military regime ruled thereafter in a climate of rare domestic tranquillity and with no announced intention of returning to electoral processes.

The new Ecuadorean government was best characterized as nationalist and the 48-year-old Rodríguez himself defied any label of right, left, or centre. He let it be known he did not fancy the widespread social and economic changes wrought by the military regime in neighbouring Peru. His government hinted it favoured eventual restoration of relations with Fidel Castro's Cuba.

His major preoccupations were the issue of sovereignty over 200 mi. of Pacific Ocean waters off Ecuador's coast and the financial arrangements to be worked out with Texaco, Inc., and the Gulf Oil Corp. on the rich new oil fields the U.S. companies had opened in Ecuador. The territorial waters issue got hotter every fishing season (December–March) as U.S. and other foreign flag tuna boats continued to be seized by Ecuadorean gunboats for fishing without a license in what Washington regarded as international waters. The oil fields, which were expected to net Ecuador at least $70 million a year, caused problems because the Rodríguez government felt the concessions, granted by the previous regime, were overly generous.

Born in the small Andean town of Pujilí, in Cotopaxi Province, Rodríguez was a little-known staff officer in the Army until he seized power. Most of his career had been spent in staff assignments or in military schools, including the U.S. Command and Staff College, the School of the Americas in the Canal Zone, and the Colombian Military Academy. (JEREMIAH A. O'LEARY)

ROTHSCHILD, LORD

Head of the banking family of Rothschilds in Britain, Lord Rothschild, the third baron, deserted banking for science, became a Cambridge don, and went into big business as a scientific adviser. In 1970, when still designated as a Labour peer, he took a newly created key job in Edward Heath's Conservative administration as head of the Central Policy Review Staff in the Cabinet Office—an organization that quickly became known as Heath's "think tank." Its controversial recommendations on government research policy were embodied in a July 1972 White Paper, "Framework for Government Research and Development."

The CPRS was set up to provide expert, independent evaluation of some of the larger, long-term policy issues that might either overlap the responsibility of a number of departments or escape the attention of ministers too busy with the problems of the moment. Of the many subjects referred to Rothschild's "think tank" for strategy review, the one that touched off an explosive controversy was the allocation of government funds for research.

Rothschild's group argued that applied research and development must be done on a customer-contractor basis. This was taken to imply that government departments should spend a greater part of their research funds on precisely commissioned contracts, and that the semiautonomous research councils for agriculture, medicine, and the natural environment should have correspondingly less money and less freedom. The ensuing controversy touched on such issues as the need to maintain a totally independent approach to research, the elitist habits of the scientific establishment, the practicability or desirability of closely specified commissioned research, and the need for the government to control its research resources more carefully.

Temperamentally, Lord Rothschild (born Oct. 31, 1910) was well able to cope with this debate. He knew of research from his own university work on spermatozoa, which won him membership in the Royal Society. He had shown nerve and daring in secret work on the dismantling of bombs during World War II, for which he was awarded the George Medal, and he had had experience with customer-oriented research as research director of Royal Dutch/Shell. (HARFORD THOMAS)

RYLE, SIR MARTIN

Sir Martin Ryle was made Britain's astronomer royal in June 1972. Such recognition took into account not only his preeminence as an astronomer but also his pioneer role in radio astronomy. After spending World War II in radar research designing vital radar equipment, Ryle returned to Cambridge University to start work on radio astronomy at sites on the outskirts of the town. The first radio astronomical observations at Cambridge were made in 1946. By 1953 Ryle's department had acquired the world's first radio telescope, more than an acre in total surface area. As opposed to the huge single dish radio telescope built under the direction of Sir Bernard Lovell at Jodrell Bank, Ryle pioneered the use of groups of small radio dishes. On a site west of Cambridge, a one-mile radio telescope was completed in 1964. Employing a disused stretch of railroad track over a conveniently flat site at Lord's Bridge, near Cambridge, a 5-km. radio telescope was completed in 1972, giving performance equivalent to that of a steerable dish 5 km. in diameter. It was said that this required the most accurately surveyed 5-km. line in the world.

Ryle's development of radio exploration of the universe vastly extended the range of observations into depths of space beyond the reach of optical telescopes, and yielded a series of important new discoveries. Radio sources with huge outputs of energy named quasars were identified in 1962 at distances of 1,500,000,000 light-years. Stars of immense density named pulsars were located in 1967. The Cambridge radio telescopes were being used in the mapping of the galaxies, for the study of interstellar gas, and for the investigation of exploding stars.

Ryle was born on Sept. 27, 1918, the son of a medical professor. Director of the Mullard Radio Astronomy Observatory, Cambridge, from 1958 and professor of radio astronomy at Cambridge from 1959, he was knighted in 1966; he received the Royal Society's Hughes Medal (1954), the Royal Astronomical Society's Gold Medal (1964), and the U.S. National Academy of Sciences' Henry Draper Medal (1965). His appointment to the honorific post of astronomer royal was unprecedented in that the title had traditionally been awarded to the director of the Royal Greenwich Observatory. (HARFORD THOMAS)

SCHENK, ARD

The first man in 60 years to win all four distances in the same world ice speed skating championships was Ard Schenk of the Netherlands. He achieved this feat at Oslo, Nor., in February 1972. Less than two weeks earlier he earned three gold medals in the Winter Olympic Games at Sapporo, Jap. The "Flying Dutchman," as Schenk was inevitably dubbed, was the individual hero of the Winter Olympics, the kind of hero readily associated with romantic fiction—a blond, disarmingly handsome, 6-ft. 3-in. bachelor who had earned his first wages as a farm boy, later to become an articulate, witty speaker as well as a physically impressive figure.

Born on Sept. 16, 1944, at Anna Paulowna, a tiny Dutch village north of Amsterdam, Schenk made his first world championship appearance in 1964 at Helsinki, Fin., finishing seventh overall. Each subsequent year, except in 1969, he never placed lower than third, and in 1972 won the world overall title for the third successive time, a feat never bettered and accomplished by only two other men since the first championship in 1893. After a modest Olympic debut at Innsbruck, Aus., in 1964, Schenk took a silver medal for the 1,500 m. in the 1968 Olympics at Grenoble, France. In 1972 he became the third male skater to win three events, the 1,500 m., 5,000 m., and 10,000 m., in one Olympic meeting.

At the beginning of 1972 he held five of the six major world records, ranking as the fastest man over all the internationally recognized distances except the 500 m. In all, by the end of 1972 he had broken world records on 14 occasions—four times over 3,000 m., three times each in the 1,000 m. and 1,500 m., and twice each for the 5,000 m. and 10,000 m. After consistent success over middle and long distances, Schenk's remarkable versatility was underlined when he tied for first place in the 500-m. sprint in the 1972 world championship. A powerful, gracefully smooth stride and shrewd line-hugging technique made him master in a sport from which he refuted any suggestion of retirement. (HOWARD BASS)

SCHMIDT, HELMUT H. W.

One of West Germany's most able and colourful politicians, Helmut Schmidt was a key figure in Chancellor Willy Brandt's post-election Cabinet, sworn in on Dec. 15, 1972. Although the Ministries of Finance and Economics, which had been combined under Karl Schiller (whom Schmidt had succeeded in July), were again separated, it was clear that Schmidt, as finance minister, would remain the Federal Republic's economic "overlord." In that capacity, following Schiller's resignation, he bore the brunt of the opposition's election campaign criticism that the government was responsible for a 6%-plus rate of inflation over the last year. He favoured a fairer distribution of wealth, but was by no means on the left of the Social Democratic Party (SPD).

Schmidt was born on Dec. 23, 1918, in Hamburg, the son of a grammar school teacher. After passing his university entrance examination, he was called up by the Army. During World War II he served with an armoured division on the Eastern front and later in Western Europe, ending the war as a lieutenant. Afterward he studied economics in Hamburg, and subsequently joined the department of economics and transport in the city administration. He was elected to the Bundestag in 1953.

In 1961 he gave up his seat and returned to Hamburg as senator for internal affairs. Four years later he was back in the Bundestag, and he served as leader of the SPD parliamentary party during the period of the "grand coalition" with the Christian Democrats, 1966–69. As defense minister in Willy Brandt's government, from 1969, he advocated a strong Western defensive alliance and insisted that the Luftwaffe must continue to be armed with nuclear weapons carriers.

Schmidt was a brilliant speaker—undoubtedly a match for the chairman of the Christian Social Union, Franz Josef Strauss—and staged some memorable performances in the Bundestag. He was ambitious, but he made no challenge for the leadership of the party and gave the appearance of complete loyalty to the chancellor. He was, however, regarded as Brandt's natural successor. (NORMAN CROSSLAND)

SCHMITZ, JOHN GEORGE

In the 1968 U.S. presidential election, George Wallace (*q.v.*) of Alabama, candidate of a loose confederation of right-wing state organizations known as the American Independent Party, had won 13.5% of the popular vote, 46 electoral votes, and for a time threatened to throw a deadlocked contest into the House of Representatives. But in 1972 the (renamed) American Party was a Wallacite group without Wallace. Its candidate, former California congressman John Schmitz, polled about 1.4% of the 77,684,082 votes cast.

Schmitz campaigned on a platform advocating more restrictive immigration laws, strong law and order measures, and voluntary school prayer. He opposed women's liberation, school busing to achieve integration, and aid to Israel. His own summing up of the party's platform was succinct: "Those who work should live better than those who won't, and don't go to war unless you intend to win." Both Schmitz and his running mate, Thomas J. Anderson, were members of the far-right John Birch Society.

Early in 1971 Wallace had rejected a third-party candidacy and entered the race for the Democratic nomination. He was campaigning in Maryland on May 15, 1972, when a would-be assassin shot him. He survived, but remained partially paralyzed. When the American Party convened in Louisville, Ky., in August, the 1,900 delegates were determined to again make Wallace their candidate. Only after his own voice, piped in via telephone hookup from his hospital bed, convinced them he could not run, did they nominate Schmitz.

Schmitz was born in Milwaukee, Wis., on Aug. 12, 1930, graduated from Marquette University in Milwaukee in 1952, and served for eight years as a Marine Corps pilot. He held the reserve rank of lieutenant colonel. For several years he taught anti-Communism at the leadership school at El Toro (Calif.) Marine Corps Air Station. In 1964 he was elected as a Republican to the California State Senate, and in 1970 won a special election to an unexpired term to represent California's 35th congressional district. He was reelected in November 1970 with 68% of the vote, a larger majority than any other candidate for the House in that year. In June 1972 the Republicans failed to renominate him, and he did not run for Congress again. Before his term expired, Schmitz registered as a member of the American Party, making him the first American Party member to sit in Congress. (PAT TUCKER)

SHRIVER, (ROBERT) SARGENT, JR.

Sargent Shriver, Jr., was the Democratic vice-presidential candidate in 1972, following Sen. Thomas F. Eagleton's withdrawal from the Democratic ticket. After six others had declined the number two spot, George McGovern asked Shriver to run. Campaigning was not new to the personable and outgoing Shriver; he had worked for his brother-in-law, John F. Kennedy, in 1960. Nor was he any stranger to politics. He had been the first head of the Peace Corps, created by the Kennedy administration. Pres. Lyndon B. Johnson had appointed him director of the fledgling Office of Economic Opportunity and, later, ambassador to France. But as a Kennedy-by-marriage, his chance to run for national elective office had always been preempted by someone else in the family. He did test the Maryland gubernatorial waters in 1970 but found them uncomfortable.

Born of an old Maryland family in Westminster, Nov. 9, 1915, Shriver did well at an elite boys' preparatory school. When the family fortune disappeared in the 1929 crash, he won a scholarship to Yale, where he was editor of the *Yale Daily News* and graduated cum laude in 1938. At law school he and Kingman Brewster, who later became Yale's president, organized an isolationist America First group. He graduated from Yale Law School in 1941 and entered the Navy, serving on battleships and submarines before being mustered out at war's end with the rank of lieutenant commander.

After the war he tried his hand at journalism as an assistant editor of *Newsweek*. A friend's father asked him to edit the memoirs of an aviator son who was killed in World War II. The diaries proved unpublishable, but the father, Joseph P. Kennedy, Sr., offered Shriver a job at Chicago's Merchandise Mart, then the world's largest privately owned office building. In 1953 Shriver married Eunice Kennedy. The couple, who went on to have five children, set up housekeeping in Chicago, where Shriver became president of the Board of Education, which oversees the second largest school system in the nation.

Labouring under an in-law's shadow, "Sarge" repeatedly proved himself as an unusually energetic, visionary, and, many said, brilliant administrator. He was known as a supremely engaging man, once "the best salesman in Washington." Possessed of a gifted common touch, he was nonetheless elegant enough to cause the French government to suggest that he remain as ambassador after the 1968 U.S. elections. He stayed in Paris for two years under the Nixon administration. After the Democratic defeat in the November 1972 election, Shriver returned to his $125,000-a-year law practice. (PHILIP KOPPER)

CAMERA PRESS/PICTORIAL PARADE

Ian Smith

KEN REGAN—CAMERA 5

Sargent Shriver

SIDKY, AZIZ

Aziz Sidky became prime minister of Egypt on Jan. 16, 1972, succeeding Mahmoud Fawzi, who had held office since Pres. Gamal Abd-an-Nasser's death in September 1970. Fawzi had resigned to make way for a younger man "who could undertake the responsibility for unceasing and demanding work in the coming stage," said Pres. Anwar as-Sadat. The new government was described as a Cabinet of confrontation (with Israel), but the emphasis was on strengthening the home front. It included a number of young Western-trained technocrats, although the key ministries of War, Industry, Economy, and Information remained under the same deputy prime ministers as before.

Sidky enjoyed good relations with the Soviets and compared the terms of Communist aid favourably with aid from Western countries. The failure of his mission to Moscow in July, which it was hoped would secure deliveries of advanced Soviet weapons, followed by President Sadat's expulsion of the Soviet advisers from Egypt, appeared to discredit his views, although Soviet economic aid to Egypt continued. However, when he revisited Moscow in October a Soviet-Egyptian rapprochement ensued, marked by the replacement of Egyptian war minister Muhammad Ahmed Sadek by the pro-Soviet Gen. Ahmed Ismael.

Sidky was born on July 1, 1920. An engineering graduate of Cairo University with a doctorate in economic planning from Harvard University, he became a university teacher. Shortly after the revolution that deposed the Egyptian monarchy, he was appointed a technical adviser to the prime minister's office. He later served as a full-time member of the services board until 1956, when President Nasser brought him into the government as minister of industry to supervise the Soviet-financed industrialization program. In 1957 Sidky launched a five-year industrialization plan, which was later merged into the general five-year development plan for 1961–65. Promoted deputy prime minister for industry and mineral resources and minister of minerals and petroleum in 1964, he earned the reputation of an all-out economic expansionist. In November 1970 he became deputy prime minister for production and trade. (PETER MANSFIELD)

SMITH, IAN DOUGLAS

Rhodesian Prime Minister Ian Smith almost settled the long-standing dispute between Rhodesia and Britain in 1972. The agreement he had negotiated late in 1971 would have given legality to the colony's unilateral declaration of independence (UDI) of Nov. 11, 1965. It foundered, however, when a commission headed by Lord Pearce reported that the country's African majority overwhelmingly objected to it. (*See* RHODESIA.)

Smith had promised his Rhodesian Front supporters (almost all whites) that UDI would be no more than "an eight days' wonder" before being accepted as an accomplished fact. But, led by Britain, the UN committed itself to mandatory economic sanctions as a means of isolating Rhodesia within the world community. Although the sanctions did not destroy Rhodesia's econ-

RAYMOND DEPARDON—GAMMA

Mark Spitz

omy, they did succeed in putting it under siege conditions and in keeping the rebel republic diplomatically isolated.

Mainly because of these pressures, in November 1971 Smith agreed with British negotiators to terms whereby the eventual right to majority rule in Rhodesia would be constitutionally guaranteed. For Smith this concession represented a crucial reversal of his policies, since the main object of his act of rebellion against the British crown had been to ensure that the African majority of almost five million would never be allowed to dominate the small white minority of about 250,000.

Ian Smith was born April 8, 1919, at Selukwe, Southern Rhodesia, the son of a Scottish settler. He entered politics in 1948 as a member of the Rhodesia Liberal Party. When the Federation of Rhodesia and Nyasaland (Malawi) was set up in 1953, he joined the ruling United Federal Party, becoming government chief whip in 1958. He resigned from the government in 1961 to join the newly founded Rhodesian Front, which demanded independence and white supremacy. The new party won a majority in 1962 and, following dissolution of the federation in 1963, Smith succeeded Winston Field as prime minister of Southern Rhodesia in April 1964. (COLIN LEGUM)

SMITH, STANLEY ROGER

In an age when sports heroes were becoming increasingly flamboyant and unpredictable, Stan Smith became a hero to middle America with his consistent, gentlemanly, and disciplined display of tennis skills. His techniques led him to victory in 1972 in the Wimbledon singles and to triumphs in the Davis Cup finals in Romania. With a placid personality and a booming serve that earned him the nickname "Steamer," Smith displayed a different type of championship image. "Success," he said, "is living for Christ and what he taught," and he devoted much of his energy off the courts to Big Brothers, a group that spends time with fatherless children. Called as "emotional as a sphinx" on and off the tennis court, the 25-year-old Smith provided an interesting contrast to his most constant antagonist during the year, the fiery and controversial Romanian Ilie Nastase.

Smith was born in Pasadena, Calif., where his father was a college athletic coach. An excellent basketball and tennis player for Pasadena High School, he had to make a choice between the two sports. Tennis prevailed, and he headed for the University of Southern California on a tennis scholarship.

Smith captured his first major championship in 1969 at the U.S. Lawn Tennis Association indoor singles tournament. He won the U.S. Open in 1971 by beating a Czechoslovakian, Jan Kodes. Later in that year Smith lost to John Newcombe of Australia in the Wimbledon finals but then came back to lead the U.S. to its fourth consecutive Davis Cup win.

Because Newcombe, as a contract professional, was not eligible in 1972 at Wimbledon, the road was cleared for Smith to become the first U.S. Wimbledon champion since 1963. Smith, who had already won the U.S. indoor championships, won the final match against Nastase in a titanic struggle, and in a rare emotional gesture hurled his racket high into the air to acknowledge the victory. In October the Romanians, led by Nastase, mounted their most serious attempt to take the Davis Cup into a Communist country for the first time. However, Smith won both his singles matches and teamed with Erik Van Dillen to win the doubles, leading the U.S. to its fifth straight Davis Cup win. (KIM EISLER)

SOAMES, SIR (ARTHUR) CHRISTOPHER (JOHN)

No more traditionally English figure could have been selected as one of the two British members of the Commission of the EEC than Sir Christopher Soames, the British ambassador to France, who was to quit Paris for Brussels when Britain became a member of the EEC on Jan. 1, 1973. Son-in-law of Winston Churchill, a former Conservative minister of agriculture, and an English farmer in his own right, Soames was, nevertheless, a convinced and ardent European who had played a crucial diplomatic role in the final stages of the negotiations for British EEC entry.

It was the misfortune of losing his seat in Parliament in 1966—he had been an MP since 1950—that had cast Soames for this role, for he was then free to take up the invitation of the Labour prime minister, Harold Wilson, to become ambassador to France in 1968. Wilson was then preparing to make Britain's third application for EEC entry. For this to succeed it was essential to dispel the suspicions of the French and to win the support of their government.

Soames was the man who more than anyone else brought this about. He was well suited for the part. He had been military attaché in Paris after World War II, and spoke fluent French. He was a bon viveur, and the British embassy parties were said to be the best in Paris. But Soames was also an accomplished politician and had been Churchill's parliamentary private secretary. He understood the intricacies of agricultural policy and, beginning in 1961, had shared with Edward Heath the first negotiations for entry, vetoed by French Pres. Charles de Gaulle in 1963. Thus, in the final stages of negotiation, Soames was able to impress the French with the seriousness of the Heath government's intentions, and he helped to bring about a close understanding between Heath and French Pres. Georges Pompidou.

After the completion of the entry negotiations in 1971, Soames, born Oct. 12, 1920, was young enough to contemplate a return to parliamentary politics and, no doubt, to the Conservative Cabinet. However, he preferred to accept nomination as a commissioner in Brussels. (HARFORD THOMAS)

SOMOZA DEBAYLE, ANASTASIO

Unable to succeed himself as president under the Nicaraguan constitution, Gen. Anastasio Somoza stepped down from the presidency on May 1, 1972, and turned over the nominal leadership of the country to a triumvirate that would act as president until he could be reelected in 1974. Where the power really lay became clear in the aftermath of the earthquake that, in the early hours of December 23, leveled much of the capital city of Managua and killed some 10,000–12,000 of its inhabitants. Somoza, who had retained command of the Guardia Nacional, took charge of the stricken city, and also of the massive aid sent to Nicaragua, principally by the U.S.

Somoza's actions were only natural in the country that he had run like a private estate. Nonetheless, he had always been sensitive to charges of dictatorship, and in 1971 he and his Nationalist Liberation Party had devised the accord with the opposition Conservatives whereby the letter of the constitution could be observed. Somoza would leave the presidency, a constitutional assembly would be elected to serve as the legislature for 2½ years, and the triumvirate would act as executive until the 1974 election. His retention of the Guardia command had been a form of insurance that the agreement would be kept.

Actually, Somoza and his family not only ran Nicaragua, they owned a large part of it. Somoza's personal holdings included ranch lands, farms, a steamship line, newspapers, various manufacturing concerns, and an airline, LANICA. The airline, actually one jet and a few propeller-driven planes, accounted for a visit to Nicaragua during the year by the enigmatic U.S. industrialist Howard Hughes. In July it was learned that Hughes had acquired a 25% interest in LANICA and that the airline had obtained two Convair jets, reportedly as the first move to upgrade Nicaraguan tourism—to the financial benefit of both Hughes and Somoza. Hughes was still in Managua when the earthquake struck, but he left immediately for London.

Somoza was born Dec. 5, 1925, in the homeland his family dominated from 1936 when his tough father, Gen. Anastasio Somoza García, seized power. When the old general was assassinated in 1956, his two sons, Luis and "Tachito" ("Little Anastasio"), continued the dynasty. (JEREMIAH A. O'LEARY)

SPITZ, MARK

"Mark the Shark was going about his predatory business. Day after day a fresh group of victims would solemnly walk the length of the pool deck to the starting blocks. . . . In however long it would take to swim the prescribed distance faster than anybody had before, all would be over." Thus did the magazine *Sports Illustrated* summarize the unprecedented performance of Mark Spitz at the 1972 Olympic Games in Munich.

Competing in seven events, Spitz won gold medals and set world records in all of them. He thus became the first athlete to win more than five gold medals in one Olympiad, the Italian fencer Nedo Nadi having won five in 1920. Spitz won the 200-m. butterfly in 2 min. 0.7 sec.; the 200-m. freestyle in 1 min. 52.78 sec.; the 100-m. butterfly in 54.27 sec.; and the 100-m. freestyle in 51.22 sec. He also competed in the victorious record-setting 400-m. freestyle relay, the 800-m. freestyle relay, and the 400-m. medley, in which he raced the butterfly leg.

The performance of Spitz was all the more remarkable since it marked a stunning comeback in Olympic competition and the laying of a ghost that had haunted him for four years. Spitz had claimed that he would win six gold medals in the Mexico City Olympics of 1968 but came away with firsts only in two relays.

Spitz was born Feb. 10, 1950, in Modesto, Calif., and started splashing in the Pacific off Honolulu when he was two. His father urged him on as a swimmer, seeing to it that he was well coached from the time he was eight and the family had returned to California. "Swimming isn't everything, winning is," said the elder Spitz, a steel company executive. "I never said to him, 'You're second, that's great.' I told him . . . 'I care for world records.' "

By the time Spitz was ten he was training 90 minutes a day, seven days a week. He qualified for the U.S. Amateur Athletic Union (AAU) competition when he was 14 and took four gold medals the following year in Tel Aviv's Maccabiah Games. He won five gold medals at the 1967 Pan-American Games. After his disappointment in the Olympic Games in 1968 he entered Indiana University, where he was coached by Jim (Doc) Counsilman, a tutor of champion teams. In 1969 he took six gold medals at Tel Aviv. In 1972 he won the AAU's Sullivan Award as the outstanding amateur athlete of 1971. After his Olympic success Spitz, who had planned to attend dental school, was deluged with offers for personal appearances and endorsements and signed a contract to endorse the products of a razor company. (PHILIP KOPPER)

STEINEM, GLORIA

Gloria Steinem was a living refutation of the comfortable theory that women's protest was the whine of sour grapes. Trim, mod, attractive, and successful, she was one of the best known and most effective champions of women in the U.S. in 1972, and a willing wailing wall for any woman suffering from sex discrimination—politically, socially, or financially.

A journalist by profession, Steinem was editor of the new feminist magazine *Ms. Ms.* began as an insert in a December 1971 issue of *New York* magazine. Regular publication started in July 1972. The editors saw *Ms.* not primarily as a "movement" journal but as a medium covering a new phase of human development, of vital interest to everyone who wanted to understand the times. By mid-October 1972 *Ms.* had 200,000 subscribers at $9 a year and was selling close to 300,000 copies at $1 each on the newsstands—a phenomenal record for a new magazine.

Steinem was born in Toledo, O., on March 25, 1936, the second daughter of an itinerant antique dealer and his wife, Ruth, a former newspaperwoman. Her grandmother, Pauline Steinem, an early suffragette, was one of two U.S. delegates to the 1908 meeting of the International Council of Women. Following her parents' divorce, when Gloria was 11, she lived with her mother in a depressing East Toledo slum, where she learned to sleep curled up to discourage the rats from biting her toes. Her mother sold her house to send Gloria to Smith College, where she earned a degree in government, magna cum laude, and a fellowship for postgraduate study in India.

Back in New York, Gloria worked her way up as a free-lance writer. Research for one story included infiltrating the Playboy Club as a bunny. In 1968 she got her own column in *New York* magazine. In search of material for the column, she attended a meeting of a women's liberation group called the Redstockings in November 1968 and never looked back. She became a leader in the National Organization for Women and in 1971 helped form the National Women's Political Caucus. Much in demand as a lecturer, she became familiar to additional millions through TV coverage of the Democratic national convention, where she was an active supporter of Sen. George McGovern. (PAT TUCKER)

STOCKHAUSEN, KARLHEINZ

Master of the new music and of new technical means for its realization, in 1972 West German composer Karlheinz Stockhausen was more concerned with performance than with composition and during the year he was much in the foreground of the international musical scene. Apart from playing, conducting, or directing concerts in West Germany, Switzerland, England, and Italy, his most important performances were that of his *Hymnen* (electronic music with instruments) with the Berlin Philharmonic Orchestra in May, the two intensive series of concerts given during the Munich Olympics and at the Shiraz Festival of the Arts in Iran (of which he was the controversial central attraction), the new work *Alphabet for Liège*—a "process-plan" for numerous audiovisual performers in different rooms with mobile public, premiered at the Belgian Radio building in Liège on September 23—and the world premiere of the complete version of one of his most imposing scores, *Momente* (spatial music), on December 8 in Cologne, W.Ger.

Stockhausen was born Aug. 22, 1928, at Mödrath, near Cologne. From 1947 to 1951 he studied school music and piano at the Cologne Musikhochschule, earning his living by playing the piano in bars, conducting amateur operatics, and improvising accompaniments for a conjurer. He spent 1952 in Paris where he visited Olivier Messiaen's analysis classes and made friends with Pierre Boulez. In 1953 he returned to Cologne as "permanent collaborator" of the then newly established Cologne Studio for Electronic Music at the West German Radio. He became the studio's artistic director in 1963.

From 1953 to 1956 Stockhausen studied phonetics and communications research with Werner Meyer-Eppler at Bonn University. From 1957 he held annual lectures or seminars at the Darmstadt Courses for New Music, and from 1958 gave concert and lecture tours throughout the world. During 1963–68 he ran the Cologne Course for New Music and in 1964 founded a small group of musicians that subsequently gave hundreds of performances of his live-electronic and "intuitive" compositions. In 1971 he was appointed professor of composition at the Cologne Musikhochschule. (TIM SOUSTER)

STONE, I(SIDOR) F(EINSTEIN)

I. F. Stone stopped being an anachronism on the first day of 1972 and the United States might be the worse for it. For 19 years I. F. Stone's weekly newsletter of fact and opinion prickled mendacious or incompetent government officials more sharply than three networks, the ubiquitous wire services, and all the establishment dailies combined. Izzy wrote, edited, and proofed the copy, and his wife, Esther, handled business affairs of the little paper—the "journalistic equivalent of the old-fashioned Jewish momma-and-poppa grocery store"—that began with 5,300 subscriptions at $5 each and was grossing $100,000 by 1968.

Henry Steele Commager called Stone "a modern Tom Paine"; Einstein, Bertrand Russell, and Eleanor Roosevelt were among

JOAN NEARY, LIFE MAGAZINE © 1972 TIME INC.

I. F. Stone

his charter subscribers. *Ramparts* magazine lauded him for having "taken upon himself the painful role of watchdog in a time when most of his colleagues bark rarely and bite not at all." When *I. F. Stone's Weekly* was ten years old, he said, "I am, I suppose, an anachronism. In this age of corporation men, I am an individual capitalist . . . a wholly independent newspaperman . . . beholden to no one but my good readers." His journal was a bellwether of celebrated causes, and he had a way of blasting conservatives with words. Ronald Reagan was "the TV Tarzan of Republican politicos"; Billy Graham "spiritual backscratcher of the pious rich." Richard Nixon, in his view, was "indecisive, weak, and tricky, with neither the statesman's vision nor the politician's finesse." Stone's prose may not have been as finely rifled as H. L. Mencken's during the days of the Bull Moose, but his scattershot phrasing was deadly against birds of mid-century politics.

Born in Philadelphia on Dec. 24, 1907, and raised in New Jersey, Isidor Feinstein Stone first became a pamphleteer as a high school sophomore when he published a five-cent monthly. He was reporting for established newspapers before he left high school, then entered the University of Pennsylvania while working ten hours a day on the *Philadelphia Inquirer* copy desk. He dropped undergraduate philosophy studies to pursue newspapering and the fringes of politics, went to Washington as correspondent for *The Nation* in 1938, and later wrote for several short-lived New York papers, notably *PM* and the *New York Daily Compass*, which folded in 1952.

Over the years he wrote ten books and collected several prizes, among them *(MORE)* journalism review's first A. J. Liebling Award for "unrelenting investigation," and some honorary degrees. Stone gave up his weekly to carry on as a contributing editor of the *New York Review of Books* because "the compulsion to cover the universe in four pages has become too heavy a burden." Still he had not lost his humane and sympathetic view of the world. "I tell people to take the long view," John Neary reported him as saying in *Life* magazine. "Remember that when Moses came down from Mount Sinai, the race had advanced far enough by then that it was not necessary to have a commandment about cannibalism." (PHILIP KOPPER)

STONE, W(ILLIAM) CLEMENT

Pres. Richard Nixon, said Chicago multimillionaire W. Clement Stone, had "Positive Mental Attitude," Stone's formula for success. PMA notwithstanding, Stone (by his own accounting) gave over $1 million to Nixon's 1972 campaign, making him by far the GOP's largest contributor. It was believed that Stone wanted an ambassadorship, perhaps to Britain's Court of St. James's.

PMA, combined with hard work and personal sacrifice, had brought Stone a long way. The stocky multimillionaire with slicked-down black hair, pencil-thin moustache, and a penchant for polka-dotted bow ties ruled a vast business empire from the Chicago home office of his Combined Insurance Co. of America. He began life as the son of an impoverished gambler. At 6 he sold newspapers to help his widowed mother, and at 13 he owned his own newsstand. He devoured Horatio Alger stories, finding *Robert Cloverdale's Struggle* particularly inspiring.

He started selling insurance in his late teens, and when he was 20 invested his $100 savings in his own insurance agency. By 1939 he had acquired the management contract of the American Casualty Co. of Dallas, Tex. The following year he organized the Combined Mutual Casualty Co. in Chicago and, through adroit mergers, acquisitions, and investments, systematically built it into a far-flung organization that made him one of the world's richest men. His 1972 holdings were estimated at about $400 million.

Stone acknowledged that his main inspiration came from the Bible, the writings of Émile Coué (who in the 1920s urged his followers to repeat, "Every day in every way I'm becoming better and better"), and the Rev. Norman Vincent Peale. He collaborated with Napoleon Hill in writing *Success Through a Positive Mental Attitude* (1960) and with Norma Lee Browning on *The Other Side of the Mind* (1964). He himself wrote *The Success System That Never Fails* (1962). PMA was drummed into all his executives and salesmen, and some of his many charities were devoted to introducing PMA to convicts and other unfortunates. A political conservative, Stone contributed over $500,000 to Nixon's 1968 campaign and in 1970 gave over $800,000 to some 50 GOP candidates.

Born in Chicago on May 4, 1902, Stone was largely self-educated, though he got a diploma from a night course at the YMCA Central High School in Chicago and took some classes at the Detroit College of Law and Northwestern University.

(WILLIAM MADER)

STRONG, MAURICE FREDERICK

According to one biographer, Maurice F. Strong was "a contemporary anomaly: a good man who finishes first." The self-made Canadian who organized the UN Conference on the Human Environment held in Stockholm in June 1972 was an environmentalist in the best sense of the word. What set him apart from the faddists was his extraordinarily broad, utterly realistic viewpoint, coupled with inexhaustible energy and enormous practical intelligence.

Before taking the UN job, Strong told a reporter, "I became increasingly aware of the importance of interdependence on earth, and that—not merely pollution—is at the heart of the environment issue: the necessity of conducting ourselves on this planet in a way that corresponds with the realities of the physical world. To survive we simply must have better standards of collaborative behavior. Rugged individualism is passé. . . . The environmental issue is more a matter of political and social management than anything else: You can't go on forever with four competing service stations at every crossroads and a deficiency in hospital beds."

Strong himself was a rugged competitor. Born in Oak Lake, Man. (pop. 400), April 29, 1929, he remembered his father, with rags wrapped around his feet, chopping wood at −40° F. He left home at 13, stowed away on a Great Lakes freighter, then worked on ships bound for Alaska and back. After returning home to finish school, he became, at 15, an apprentice fur trader for the Hudson's Bay Company, learning Eskimo and studying economics and geology during the long Arctic nights. Within two years he organized a mining company. Excited by an old newspaper article about the birth of the UN, he went to New York where he filled water glasses, sharpened pencils, and vowed to return as an official.

Years later he did just that, but first he made a small fortune and became president of the Power Corporation of Canada, a giant holding company. In 1966 he took a $163,000 salary cut to reorganize Canada's foreign aid program and later, for Prime Minister Pierre Trudeau, he planned the organization of an internal development agency. He was slated to head that agency when U Thant persuaded Trudeau to lend Strong to the UN.

(PHILIP KOPPER)

TANAKA, KAKUEI

The stocky, robust politician who in 1972 took charge of Japan's first major effort in independent postwar diplomacy was a self-made millionaire and career politician with virtually no experience in international affairs. But this was not the only unusual aspect of Kakuei Tanaka, who became prime minister of Japan on July 5. Not only was he the country's youngest prime minister since World War II but he was also its first "non-establishment" one, in that he was not a graduate of Tokyo University. In fact, he was not even a high-school graduate. But during his first few months in office, he acted swiftly and decisively. One of his outstanding achievements was establishing relations with China without humiliating Japan or jeopardizing its ties with the U.S.

Tanaka's emergence as prime minister after 15 years in various Cabinet posts marked a new turn in Japanese history. With its economic might and growing political power, Japan was moving from its postwar subservience to the U.S. to a more independent stance. But even before his first meeting with U.S. Pres. Richard Nixon in Hawaii in September Tanaka stressed that close ties with the U.S. would remain a cornerstone of Japanese foreign policy. He also made it clear that he would concentrate considerable effort on internal reforms.

Tanaka was born May 4, 1918, in Niigata Prefecture, the son of a poor farmer. At an early age he moved to Tokyo, where an uncle financed his elementary education. He was drafted into the Army in 1938 and sent to Manchuria, but returned home and was discharged a few months later because of acute pneumonia. After World War II, Tanaka took over his uncle's tiny construction business. Through clever land speculation and business sense, he rapidly turned himself into a millionaire builder. He also joined the Liberal-Democratic Party and established himself as an outstanding political organizer. When the party began losing its appeal in urban areas because of its conservatism, the politically moderate Tanaka quickly shored up its vote-getting potential. He also gathered a following among the party's younger members. His work paid off in 1972, when his well-organized backers, the popular demand for a change, and his own political cunning gained him the office of prime minister. These factors also figured in the Liberal-Democratic victory in the December election, although the margin of success was not as great as Tanaka had hoped.

(WILLIAM MADER)

THOMSON, GEORGE

One of the two British nominees to the enlarged Commission of the EEC was George Thomson, a Labour member of Parliament who had led the negotiations for Britain's entry initiated by the Labour prime minister, Harold Wilson. After the general election defeat of 1970 the Labour Party turned against EEC membership, but Thomson, one of the party's most steadfast pro-Marketeers, remained convinced that membership was still a vital British interest.

When the terms negotiated by Geoffrey Rippon were condemned by Wilson and other Labour leaders, Thomson said openly that in his view they were acceptable and the kind of terms a Labour government would have negotiated. During the debates of 1971 he argued that Britain would be doomed to a second-class existence if it did not join Europe. He was one of the Labour MPs who voted with the Conservative government in a number of crucial debates on Europe, and after voting against his party he resigned from the shadow cabinet (in which since 1970 he had been in charge of defense) in June 1972. But he insisted that after a lifetime working in the Labour Party he would remain a party member.

A Scot from Dundee, Thomson was born on Jan. 16, 1921. After working for some years as editor of the Socialist paper *Forward,* he was elected MP for Dundee East in 1952, and had therefore been 20 years in Parliament when he accepted his new post in Brussels. He was a minister in the Wilson governments from 1964 to 1970, most of the time at the Foreign Office or the Commonwealth Relations Office. Apart from his interests in Europe, he was involved in Middle East affairs, and in 1965 was the first British minister to visit Egypt since the Suez crisis. When at the Commonwealth Relations Office he headed abortive negotiations with Ian Smith of Rhodesia. Then in 1969 he was put in charge of the British team preparing the ground for the EEC negotiations that were taken over by the Heath government in 1970.

(HARFORD THOMAS)

TOLBERT, WILLIAM RICHARD, JR.

The scholarly churchman William Richard Tolbert, who had become provisional president of Liberia on July 23, 1971, on the death of the assertive and flamboyant William Tubman, was inaugurated as his country's 19th president on Jan. 3, 1972. From the moment of taking provisional office Tolbert showed himself capable of decisive action. In order to reduce the price of rice, in a country where most people were earning as little as $100 annually, he took the rice monopoly away from a company owned in part by the late president's son Shad Tubman (who was also Tolbert's son-in-law); he dismissed an undersecretary of state, two unpopular security chiefs, and his minister of planning and economic affairs for corruption and inefficiency; he set up a commission to reorganize the civil service; he agreed on the reciprocal establishment of embassies with the U.S.S.R.; and in November 1972 invited a delegation of U.S. black bankers and businessmen to Liberia, and offered dual citizenship to those black U.S. citizens who "wished to formalize their historic ties with Africa in general, and with Liberia in particular."

For 20 out of the 28 years of Tubman's marathon rule Tolbert had served as the country's vice-president, a position to which he was first elected in 1951 at the age of 38. A quiet, unostentatious, and patient politician who had formerly directed much of his own activity into the affairs of the Baptist Church, he was president of the Liberian Baptist Missionary and Educational Convention, Inc., and of the Baptist World Alliance (1965–70). In the latter role he achieved international prominence in the ecumenical movement.

Tolbert was born in Bensonville, Liberia, on May 13, 1913, of a prominent family of early settlers. He took his degree in 1934 in Liberia College (forerunner of the university). In 1952 the university conferred on him a doctorate in civil law. After graduating, he worked as a typist in the Liberian Treasury, then worked his way up to higher government posts. Entering politics in the early 1940s, he was elected to the House of Representatives for his home county, Montserrado, in 1943. Eight years later he was chosen by Tubman to be his running mate as vice-president. (COLIN LEGUM)

TREPCZYNSKI, STANISLAW

His name was hardly a household word, even among diplomats, but in September 1972 the 27th UN General Assembly ensured that Stanislaw Trepczynski of Poland would be known in chancelleries around the world.

On September 19 he was unanimously chosen president of the General Assembly's 1972–73 session, the second Communist official to be granted that honour (the first was Corneliu Manescu, foreign minister of Romania, in 1967). Trepczynski was a recent entrant into foreign affairs, having spent most of his adult life in labour and administrative affairs of the Polish Communist Party. He joined the party in 1945 and, through his aggressive loyalty, political acumen, and ruthlessness, rose rapidly to the upper echelons. Within a few years his skills and loyalty brought him to the attention of Edward Gierek, then party secretary in Poland's industrial Western Region.

For years, one of Trepczynski's prime tasks was to see that industrial workers maintained "proper discipline," that the party's interests—in terms of production and ideology—were not betrayed. If he felt that former party boss Wladyslaw Gomulka was insensitive toward rising consumer demands, Trepczynski did not betray it, at least not in public. In the last days of Gomulka, he held the important executive position of chief of the Central Committee's secretariat. In effect, his job was to make sure that the top leadership's decisions were carried out.

When Gomulka fell, as the result of the "food riots" of December 1970, Gierek emerged as the party leader. Shortly afterward Trepczynski was named deputy foreign minister and was suddenly plunged into the world of international affairs. Totally unknown abroad, he again appeared to be chiefly responsible for ensuring that Polish policy was carried out effectively, yet with proper ideological content. In a sense, Warsaw's putting him forward for the General Assembly presidency was a reward for his efforts.

Thus marked as a "post-Gomulka Pole," Trepczynski had the hallmarks of a typical Communist apparatchik—superb self-control and surface impassivity. He was also noted for his vast capacity for work—another sign of the successful apparatchik—and he smoothly absorbed the mountains of UN documents that spew forth during an assembly session. He was practical and careful enough not to allow ideology to openly influence his actions as assembly president.

Born in Lodz, in central Poland, on April 7, 1924, Trepczynski attended the University of Lodz. During the Nazi occupation, he went underground, studied languages to pass the time, and learned to speak English, French, German, and Russian with varying degrees of fluency. (WILLIAM MADER)

TRUDEAU, PIERRE ELLIOTT

By the end of 1972, Pierre Elliott Trudeau had all he could do just to hang onto his job. His Liberal Party emerged from general elections on October 30 with only 109 of the 264 seats in the House of Commons, and the Canadian prime minister would have to submit to the will of Parliament if his government was to continue. For a man who had maintained a virtual rule of personality for four years, this would be hard to take.

Trudeau's personality dominated the election, although in direct contrast to the way it had four years before, when his flamboyance had won him broad support for his call for a "Just Society" for all Canadians. In 1972 Trudeau waged a cool, aloof campaign, dismissing as "moaners" opponents who decried the lack of action against persistent unemployment and inflation. The one achievement of the "Just Society," the Official Languages Act, which made French the equal of English in all government business, had not been the step toward national unity he had claimed. None of the parties made bilingualism an election issue, but the bill's passage had strengthened Trudeau's appeal in Quebec and was often seen elsewhere as the work of a Frenchman taking care of his own.

Trudeau was also no longer seen as the unconventional personality and unorthodox politician who had inspired the "Trudeaumania" of four years before. The "swinger" of those days had become a family man, having ended his 51 years of bachelorhood in 1971. His haughty disregard of Parliament, common enough during his premiership, had been seen again in his call for elections before Parliament acted on two bills to curb foreign take-overs of Canadian companies, legislation many Canadians regarded as vital to the preservation of their nationalism in the face of U.S. encroachment. Efforts to relieve the long-strained relations with the U.S. also had not been made. A pledge to clean up the Great Lakes was signed during an April visit to Ottawa by U.S. Pres. Richard Nixon, but negotiations on trade difficulties never got under way.

Trudeau was born on Oct. 18, 1919, in Montreal. In 1965, in his first try for public office, he was elected to the House of Commons from a prosperous Montreal suburb. Three years later he defeated six others to become leader of the Liberal Party and went on to victory in general elections. (RICHARD L. WORSNOP)

UNGAR, GEORGES

Having learned to engineer formidable control over his environment, man turned to ways to engineer the human race itself. In 1972 Georges Ungar, research scientist and professor of pharmacology at Baylor College of Medicine in Houston, Tex., was breaking new and controversial ground in his chosen part of this awesome and dangerous new adventure: the chemical coding of memory.

In 1968 Ungar had published the revolutionary results of his experiments with transferring the memories of rodents. He trained rats to fear the dark, made an extract of their brain tissue, and injected it into the abdomens of untrained mice, which normally prefer the dark. He found that, contrary to accepted belief that what an individual learns can be transmitted only by teaching or example, many of the injected mice began to shun the dark. While others were attempting to confirm his results, Ungar sought to define the mechanism of transfer, which he concluded was an amino acid complex. By 1971 he had identified one particular peptide, a sequence of 15 amino acids, which he named scotophobin, from the Greek words for "fear" and "dark." One of his colleagues synthesized scotophobin accurately enough, for it caused mice to avoid the blackout boxes in their cages. The result of Ungar's work on four other "memory molecules" was expected in 1973.

The possibilities for both good and evil opened up by Ungar's work were staggering, ranging from the chance to ameliorate mental retardation or senility with simple injections to wild Orwellian fantasies of administering college educations by hypodermic, or brainwashing populations with precision. Ungar pointed out, however, that the effects of his injections were temporary; he saw as the main significance of his work the insight it could bring to study of the brain.

Ungar was also the co-discoverer of the antihistamine and oral antidiabetic drugs. A citizen of the Western world, he was born in 1906 in Budapest, Hung., where his father, a French architect, was working. He was educated and later taught in France, did research and lectured in England during World War II, and taught in Montreal and then in Chicago, where he became a U.S. citizen in 1954. After directing pharmaceutical research in New York and California for a number of years, he settled at Baylor in 1963. (PAT TUCKER)

VILLELLA, EDWARD JOSEPH

Edward Villella upheld his reputation in 1972 as one of the world's greatest dancers. His incredible leaps and ability to appear suspended in air were put to magnificent use in productions of *The Prodigal Son,* the "Rubies" section of *Jewels,* and *Le Corsaire* pas de deux. He extended the range of his artistry, however, in Jerome Robbins' controversial ballet *Watermill.* It was an important new role for him, requiring intense concentration and control rather than technical virtuosity.

Villella was born on Oct. 1, 1936, in the New York City borough of Queens. Knocked unconscious by a baseball at the age of ten, Villella was kept off the diamond and sandlots by his mother, who sent him to ballet classes with his sister. A few months later he was awarded a scholarship to the School of American Ballet, where he studied for several years. He quit dancing to enter the Rhodes School in Manhattan and later attended the New York Maritime College, where he returned to the baseball diamond and became a campus welterweight boxing champion. He also resumed his ballet study. He received a B.S. in marine transportation in 1959, two years after he had joined the prestigious New York City Ballet. He became a principal dancer in 1960.

Acclaimed as one of the world's most powerful and exciting dancers, Villella was always much in demand. Besides his regular performances with the New York City Ballet in 1972, he appeared as guest artist with regional companies throughout the U.S., performed on television and at concerts, gave lecture-demonstrations, and acted and danced in New York City Center revivals

MARTHA SWOPE

Edward Villella

of *Brigadoon*. In 1962 a cheering audience at Moscow's Bolshoi Theatre had accorded him the honour of an encore, unprecedented in the New York City Ballet and quite rare at the Bolshoi.

In 1972 he also became artistic director of the semiprofessional New Jersey Ballet Company and hoped to lift it to professional status and to expand its schools.

Villella showed that a dancer could become a financial success, and his powerful, dynamic performances helped dispel the American myth that male ballet dancers are effeminate. Villella felt deeply that nothing could equal dancing for total control and total awareness of what the human body could do. (BARBARA W. CLEARY)

VIREN, LASSE

Two years' hard training gave Lasse Viren, a 23-year-old Finnish policeman, two gold medals at the 1972 Olympic Games in Munich. He won the 10,000-m. race on September 3 in the world record time of 27 min. 38.4 sec. and a week later the 5,000 m. in the Olympic record time of 13 min. 26.4 sec.

These and other successes gave Finland back its pre-World War II dominance in middle- and long-distance running and recalled the feats of Paavo Nurmi and other giants of the 1920s and 1930s. When Viren and his teammate Pekka Vasala (1,500-m. gold medalist at Munich) returned to Helsinki, they were welcomed as national heroes and personally congratulated by Pres. Urho Kekkonen—once a champion athlete himself.

Both Viren and his trainer Rolf Haikkola had expected good results in 1971, but when Viren finished only seventh in the 5,000 m. in that year's European championships they decided to intensify training. From October 1971 they carried through an exacting program that made no concessions to the rigours of the Finnish winter.

On July 25, 1972, Viren won a 5,000-m. race at the Helsinki Olympic Stadium in 13 min. 19 sec.—a national record and the third best time ever returned. And four days after his Olympic 5,000-m. victory he set a new world record for the distance in Helsinki in the time of 13 min. 16.4 sec., beating the Australian Ron Clarke's six-year-old record by one-fifth of a second. Viren's record was short-lived, however, as on September 20, at Heysel, Belg., Belgian runner Emiel Puttemans clocked 13 min. 13 sec.

According to Haikkola, Viren's training program demanded "lashing himself, a strong will, scientific research, and first-class skill as a runner." New Zealander Arthur Lydiard, who in the 1960s spent a few years in Finland as a coach, laid the foundation of the Finnish training system, but Haikkola worked out a special program with Viren that was "partly Paavo Nurmi, partly Percy Cerutty [Herb Elliott's trainer], and partly Lydiard." A beautiful stylist, Viren had superb physical and mental control as was shown when, after falling during the 10,000 m. in Munich, he recovered himself and went on to beat the world's best.

(CARL FREDRIK SANDELIN)

WALLACE, GEORGE CORLEY

Once a one-issue Southern politician who had parlayed his appeal to blue-collar Americans into 13.5% of the popular vote in the 1968 presidential election, Gov. George Wallace of Alabama left his American Independent Party in 1972 to seek the Democratic presidential nomination. That effort ended on May 15, in a shopping centre in the Washington, D.C., suburb of Laurel, Md., when Wallace, campaigning for primary votes, was shot and seriously wounded by a drifter named Arthur Bremer. Bremer's diary revealed that he had previously stalked another target: Pres. Richard M. Nixon.

Wallace was left paralyzed from the waist down, a disability doctors believed would be permanent. Nonetheless, he made an appearance at the Democratic national convention, where 377 delegates were pledged to him, and he remained an influence in U.S. politics. Asked about his plans, he told reporters, "I do not rule . . . out" a future candidacy.

Wallace, then Democratic governor of Alabama, emerged on the national scene in 1963, when he "stood in the schoolhouse door" to prevent federal officials from enrolling a black student in the previously segregated University of Alabama. An outspoken segregationist, he was a presidential candidate for the first time in 1964. He did well in three primaries before withdrawing in favour of conservative GOP nominee Barry Goldwater.

In 1968 Wallace, with former air force general Curtis LeMay as his running mate, was the formal candidate of the American Independent Party, which was formed to support his bid for the presidency. By 1972 he was no longer appealing exclusively to segregationists but had emerged as the spokesman for rank-and-file voters who opposed ever increasing taxes and Topsy-like bureaucracies. Observers spoke of a "new populism," although in his primary campaigns Wallace still leaned heavily on opposition to busing to achieve racial integration.

Wallace was born Aug. 25, 1919, in Clio, Ala., and received a law degree from the University of Alabama. He became governor in 1963 and, barred from a second term by state law, stood aside for his wife, Lurleen, who was elected by an overwhelming plurality. She died of cancer in May 1968. Wallace, who remarried in January 1971, was elected governor again in 1970.

(PHILIP KOPPER)

WHITELAW, WILLIAM STEPHEN IAN

When the Stormont government of the United Kingdom's troubled Ulster province was displaced by direct rule from Westminster in March 1972, William Whitelaw was chosen to be secretary of state for Northern Ireland. He seemed to have the patience, tact, and courage that would be needed to reconcile the warring Protestants and Catholics of Ulster. Reasonable, good tempered, and relaxed—charming, yet shrewd—Whitelaw had the reputation of being one of the most skillful of conciliators in British politics. Much of his life as a member of Parliament since 1955 had been spent in the invisible business of party management, culminating for him in the leadership of the House of Commons in the Heath government of 1970. He had become one of Prime Minister Edward Heath's closest and most influential confidants.

On assuming his duties in Northern Ireland, he described his new job as "a most terrifying, difficult, and awesome task." He worked tirelessly, but the progress he made in breaking down the prejudices of centuries was slow and uncertain. "It really is time to start talking and stop shooting," he said in June, yet the IRA cease-fire of June 26 lasted only until July 9.

The concessions he made to the Catholic community, such as the release of low-risk internees, exasperated the Protestant extremists, and when he placated Protestant feeling by clearing the barricades from the Catholic "no go" areas, the IRA Provisionals renewed and intensified the violence. With great persistence Whitelaw pressed for all parties to join in talks, but when these were held in September the Social Democratic and Labour Party refused to attend, and his attempt to steer a reasonable, fair course earned him the hostility of hard-liners in his own party.

Whitelaw, born on June 28, 1918, came from a Scottish landed and army family and had some of the characteristics of a Tory squire—a successful farmer enjoying country recreations, a burly, bluff, John Bull figure, and a courageous soldier who won the Military Cross in Normandy.

(HARFORD THOMAS)

WHITLAM, (EDWARD) GOUGH

On Dec. 5, 1972, Gough Whitlam was sworn in as Australia's first Labor prime minister since 1949, following a 3.5% swing to the Australian Labor Party in the general election of December 2. From his father, who had been crown solicitor from 1936 to 1948 and had helped draft the UN Universal Declaration of Human Rights, Whitlam had inherited a humanitarian passion for international justice. Radical changes were expected from a foreign ministry that was to be directly under his control. His tours of Papua New Guinea had already forced the long-ruling Liberal-Country Party to accept self-government for the dependency in 1973, and his 1971 visit to Peking had thrown the ruling coalition's foreign policy into confusion.

At his first press conference as prime minister, Whitlam expressed the desire for "an Australia which will be less militarily oriented and not open to suggestions of racism." Changes to be made included transfer of recognition from Taiwan to Peking; reduction of Australia's role in the South East Asia Treaty Organization to observer status; a revision of the five-power defense agreement with New Zealand, Britain, Malaysia, and Singapore; unequivocal support for UN resolutions against apartheid; and withdrawal of Australia's remaining 140 military advisers from Vietnam. At the press conference he announced an end to conscription and the release of jailed draft resisters. Whitlam's first major foreign policy challenge was to stop French nuclear tests in the Pacific, initially by seeking an injunction at the International Court of Justice. He was expected to visit Peking, Jakarta, and Tokyo in 1973. In internal matters the government would no longer be inhibited by states' rights from dealing with education, health, land costs, and transport.

Gough Whitlam was born in Kew, Victoria, on July 11, 1916. He was a good classics scholar, was admitted to the bar in 1947, and became a queen's counsel in 1962. He was a member of the House of Representatives for the New South Wales seat of Werriwa from 1952 and deputy leader of the ALP from 1960. His most significant party triumph came in 1970 when he secured replacement of the vote-losing management of the Victoria branch of the party, curbed the power of its socialist-left leadership, and went on to revive the party after 15 years of dissension and defeatism.
(R. J. M. DENNERSTEIN)

YEH CHIEN-YING

One of the most prestigious "old marshals" of Chinese Communism, Yeh Chien-ying became the de facto defense minister of China soon after the apparent death of Lin Piao, Chairman Mao Tse-tung's heir apparent. There was some question of Yeh's tenure when his formal appointment as defense minister failed to materialize, either on Aug. 1, 1972, People's Liberation Army Day, or on October 1, China's National Day. Nevertheless, Marshal Yeh appeared to be top man in the Chinese Army, functioning as both spokesman and representative for it. He ranked third in the party hierarchy after Mao and Chou En-lai, and continued to hold the post of vice-chairman of the Central Committee's Military Affairs Commission.

Born in 1899 in the province of Kwangtung, Yeh joined the Yunnan Military Institute when he was 20, and then worked briefly as a magistrate. It was Sun Yat-sen's Nationalist movement that attracted him to politics. In 1924 he was in the Whampoa Military Academy, where he joined the Communist Party. For two years he actively participated in various military campaigns, commanding units of the Nationalist Revolutionary Army. In 1927 he fled to Hong Kong, where he cared for a sick comrade, Chou En-lai. A year later he was in Moscow studying military tactics and also during this period spent a full year studying drama and the training of actors. After his return to China in 1930, while actively engaged in the development of the Red Army, Yeh took a leading role in organizing Communist dramatic troupes.

Yeh drafted the military plan for the famous Long March of 1934–35, the retreat of the Communists to northwest China. During the Sino-Japanese War he achieved outstanding success in infiltrating the ranks of the Nationalist Chinese Army of Chiang Kai-shek. After the Communist victory over the Nationalists, he headed the Military Control Commission for Peking and simultaneously was mayor of Peking. He became marshal in 1955, member of the party Presidium in 1956, and member of the Politburo in 1969. In the post-Lin Piao military hierarchy Yeh was one of the few officers who had past connections with the Soviet Union.
(T. J. S. GEORGE)

YOKOI, SHOICHI

For 28 years Sgt. Shoichi Yokoi was believed to be dead, killed along with thousands of other Imperial Japanese soldiers who had sworn to die defending Guam rather than surrender the largest of the Mariana group to the Allies. But early in 1972 he was found very much alive on the tiny Pacific island, one of a handful of unrelenting World War II troops who still survived.

Following the month-long battle for Guam in 1944 and Japan's ultimate surrender the following year, Yokoi and nine companions eked out a living in the jungle interior of the 209-sq.mi. island. Separating from the others to afford a greater chance for survival, he maintained contact with two of them until one day he found that they had died. For eight years Yokoi was alone, an Oriental Robinson Crusoe who inhabited a subterranean cave lit with coconut-oil lamps. A tailor in peacetime, he made clothes from bark and lived on what the jungle provided: mangoes, nuts, shellfish, rats. From airborne leaflets he had learned that peace had come, but he stayed in hiding until he was finally caught by two native fishermen as he tended his fish trap.

Flown back to a vastly changed Japan, he was given a hero's welcome. It did not include an audience with the emperor, who had been considered divine when the 25-year-old Yokoi left home for the service in the summer of 1940. He did visit the Imperial Palace, however, and left a message: "Your Majesties, I have returned home. I deeply regret that I could not serve you well."

His back pay came to $129 and he was due an annual pension of $432, but this was handsomely augmented by $80,000 in contributions and by gifts that flowed in, along with numerous marriage proposals. Still, "I'm ashamed," the 57-year-old ex-soldier said. "We Japanese soldiers were told to prefer death to the disgrace of getting captured alive." Many were still taking that option. Later in the year, on the remote Philippine island of Lubang, Pfc. Kinshichi Kozuka was killed while raiding a village for food. His companion, Lieut. Hiro Onoda, escaped back into the jungle. The search party sent to find him included his former commanding officer, who went to countermand the order never to surrender.

But Yokoi's private war was over. He visited his family tombstone, which bore his name, and wept when he learned of his mother's death years earlier. By year's end he had married Mihoko Hatashin, and the couple had settled in Yokoi's old hometown of Nagoya.
(PHILIP KOPPER)

YOUNG, ANDREW J., JR.

The election of the Rev. Andrew J. Young, Jr. (Dem., Ga.), as the first black U.S. representative from the South since Reconstruction was as much an individual success as it was a reflection of the continued emergence of black political strength in the South. Young, who first gained prominence as a Southern Christian Leadership Conference (SCLC) aide of the Rev. Martin Luther King, Jr., had run for Congress in 1970 and lost to incumbent Fletcher Thompson (who in turn lost a Senate bid in 1972 to Sam Nunn). In 1972 Young was one of some 400 black candidates for state and local offices in old Confederate territory. "Far more ran than won," the *Washington Post* summarized. "But more won this time than two years ago." Their greater success seemed the aggregate result of similar conditions and strategies in many localities rather than the product of a cohesive nationwide movement.

Young typified his peers in some respects. "I'm not concentrating on national goals or national problems," he told columnist Joseph Kraft during the campaign. "I want to concentrate on the special problems of this city. I believe we can create here in Atlanta [heart of Georgia's 5th congressional district] a school system that is integrated and offers quality education. When we do that other cities are going to follow. I see myself in the Congress getting federal funds for Atlanta so we can work . . . on the problems we do not know how to solve nationally." This sentiment was symptomatic of a negative consensus that had been noticed around the country since the popular decline of the Lyndon Johnson administration: public disillusionment with the panacea of centralized action.

Young was born March 12, 1932, in New Orleans, La. He attended Dillard University, then transferred to Howard, the nation's preeminent black educational institution, where he graduated in 1951. He received a theological degree at Hartford Seminary four years later and was ordained in the Congregational Church. For two years he served a parish in Thomasville, Ga., and then joined the National Council of Churches as associate director of its youth division. In 1961 he became executive secretary of the SCLC, the organization through which King coalesced national concern for civil rights and equal opportunity in the U.S.
(PHILIP KOPPER)

ZAID IBN SULTAN AN-NAHAYAN

On Dec. 2, 1971, Sheikh Zaid, ruler of Abu Dhabi, was elected president of the newly formed United Arab Emirates by the heads of the six Trucial States that then comprised the union—Abu Dhabi, Ajman, Dubai, Fujairah, Sharjah, and Umm al-Qaiwain (Ras al-Khaimah, the seventh Trucial State, joined in 1972). With the help of the immense oil wealth of his tiny state and his own forceful personality, Zaid had already established himself as a figure of political importance in the Arab world.

Sheikh Zaid was born in 1918. In 1946 his elder brother Shakhbut, who had become ruler of Abu Dhabi in 1928, appointed him *wali* (governor) of al-Ain in the Buraimi region of the interior. With few resources he did what was possible to develop the oasis. In 1954–55 during the dispute over Buraimi between Saudi Arabia and Britain, which was the protecting power in the Trucial Coast, it was alleged that the Saudis attempted to bribe Zaid with offers that included a guarantee of his personal status, £30 million in cash, and 50% of future oil profits if he prevented the British company, Petroleum Concessions Ltd., from operating in Abu Dhabi and allowed the U.S. company, Aramco, to do so. Zaid refused the bribe; it was said he had promised his mother to respect his brother's life and rule. However, when Abu Dhabi's oil revenues began to increase rapidly in the 1960s and his eccentric and suspicious-minded brother refused to allocate funds for development, Zaid was persuaded, with British encouragement, to overthrow Shakhbut and establish himself as ruler. He at once embarked on an extensive program of development; a new port and airport, roads, schools, and hospitals were all speedily built. Abu Dhabi's first five-year development plan was launched in 1968.

The huge increase in spending would have caused serious problems if it had not been matched by the rise in oil revenues, which reached about $337.5 million in 1971 and were substantially higher in 1972, giving Abu Dhabi probably the highest per capita income in the world. Sheikh Zaid made substantial loans and gifts to various Arab states and individuals and to further the Arab cause, but the dominant position he gained for Abu Dhabi in the Trucial Coast caused some resentment among other rulers in the area.
(PETER MANSFIELD)

See also Nobel Prizes.

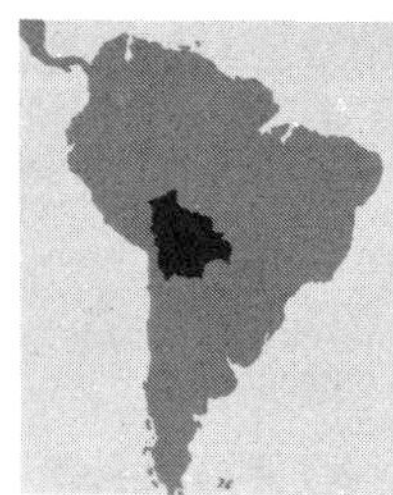

Bolivia

A landlocked republic in central South America, Bolivia is bordered by Brazil, Paraguay, Argentina, Chile, and Peru. Area: 424,162 sq.mi. (1,098,581 sq.km.). Pop. (1971 est.): 5,062,500, of whom more than 50% were Indian. Language: Spanish (official). Religion: Roman Catholic. Judicial cap.: Sucre (pop., 1971 est., 69,800). Administrative capital and largest city: La Paz (pop., 1971 est., 850,000). President in 1972, Col. Hugo Banzer Suárez.

Events in 1972 gave grounds for cautious optimism over Bolivia's future, although devaluation of the peso late in the year led to strikes and the declaration of a state of siege. There were fears at the beginning of the year that nothing had changed after President Banzer reshuffled his Cabinet, late in 1971, and ousted the man who had been instrumental in bringing him to power—Col. Andrés Selich. Colonel Selich was sent to Paraguay as ambassador but was later recalled and ordered to retire from the Army after being accused of plotting to overthrow the president. There followed a purge of the supporters of Selich and of former president Gen. Juan José Torres Gonzales within the armed forces, and President Banzer was consequently able to establish himself in a strong position with the Army.

The Army's ally, the Nationalist Popular Front (FPN), was less united. The traditional cleavages in the Nationalist Revolutionary Movement (MNR) manifested themselves once more at the party's conference in April. Former president Hernán Siles Zuazo, whose wing of the MNR supported Torres and had participated in the People's Assembly in 1971, was expelled as vice-president of the MNR and was replaced by Guillermo Bedregal. Siles later revealed that his successor had written to him offering support at the time of Banzer's coup in August 1971. The revelation succeeded in alienating the Army, the Bolivian Socialist Falange (FSB), and sections of the MNR from Bedregal, and he went into exile.

As was to be expected of two parties that had been sworn enemies up until 1971, the FSB and MNR frequently sniped at one another within the FPN coalition. This culminated in September in resignations from the Cabinet on both sides. Notwithstanding this, President Banzer appeared to have found a new and workable formula for Bolivian politics.

Problems for the regime arose after President Banzer's October 27 devaluation of the peso from approximately 12 to 20 to the U.S. dollar, an action government supporters claimed was forced by the International Monetary Fund. Although devaluation was accompanied by the establishment of family bonuses, most of this additional income was offset by price rises. Labour unrest began almost immediately, and in November workers in La Paz called a protest strike. Claiming that the strike was part of a conspiracy to overthrow his government, Banzer declared a state of siege, which remained in effect even after the strikers returned to work and wage negotiations were begun.

In handling the economy, Banzer emphasized projects that would build the nation's productive capacity and continued diversification in order to boost exports. The U.S. Agency for International Development granted loans totaling $14 million, and the U.S.S.R. provided finance for a tin-volatilization plant at Potosí to convert low-grade ore into high-grade tin. A bismuth smelter was planned at Telamayo. In the longer term and of potentially greater importance to Bolivia's future export performance was the beginning of iron-ore shipments from the Mutún deposits in August, although financing had yet to be arranged for further development. In April a gas pipeline between Santa Cruz and Yacuiba was opened, bringing an estimated annual income of $13 million.

The government made a conscious effort to gain the confidence of foreign investors. The International Metal Processing Corp. (IMPC) was paid $1,450,000 in compensation for the nationalization of its installations by Torres, and the U.S. Steel Corp. was to receive $13.4 million in compensation for the nationalization of the Matilde zinc mine. A hydrocarbons law passed in March indicated that the government sought foreign investment from private sources as well as governments.

(JEREMY WILLOUGHBY)

BOLIVIA

Education. (1969) Primary, pupils 663,829, teachers 24,832; secondary, pupils 61,787, teachers 3,798; vocational, pupils 9,692, teachers 1,382; teacher training, students 4,765, teachers 245; higher (including 8 universities), students 27,352, teaching staff 2,727.

Finance. Monetary unit: peso boliviano, with (Sept. 18, 1972) a free rate of 11.88 pesos to U.S. $1 (29.07 pesos = £1 sterling). Gold, SDRs, and foreign exchange, central bank: (June 1972) U.S. $53.4 million; (June 1971) U.S. $39 million. Budget (1969 rev. est.) balanced at 1,265,300,000 pesos. Gross national product: (1969) 10,822,000,000 pesos; (1968) 9,939,000,000 pesos. Money supply: (March 1972) 1,769,400,000 pesos; (March 1971) 1,449,500,000 pesos. Cost of living (La Paz; 1963 = 100): (July 1971) 158; (July 1970) 152.

Foreign Trade. (1971) Imports U.S. $171,283,000; exports U.S. $212,253,000. Import sources: U.S. 31%; Japan 16%; Argentina 10%; U.K. 5%. Export destinations: U.K. 46%; U.S. 28%; Japan 6%; Argentina 6%. Main exports (1970): tin 39%; antimony 12%; tungsten 7%; zinc 5%.

Transport and Communications. Roads (1971) 25,637 km. Motor vehicles in use (1970): passenger *c.* 19,200; commercial (including buses) *c.* 28,800. Railways: (1971) 3,588 km.; traffic (1969) 256 million passenger-km., freight (1968) 316 million net ton-km. Air traffic (1970): 108,970,000 passenger-km.; freight 1,730,000 net ton-km. Telephones (Jan. 1970) 38,000. Radio receivers (Dec. 1968) 1,350,000.

Agriculture. Production (in 000; metric tons; 1970; 1969 in parentheses): corn 283 (289); wheat 53 (45); barley 62 (61); potatoes 655 (627); cassava 221 (213); oranges 65 (57); sugar, raw value (1971–72) 93, (1970–71) 134; rubber (exports) *c.* 3 (*c.* 3). Livestock (in 000; Oct. 1970): sheep *c.* 6,850; cattle *c.* 2,400; pigs *c.* 950; horses *c.* 300; asses *c.* 660; goats *c.* 2,500; llamas *c.* 1,500.

Industry. Production (in 000; metric tons; 1970): cement 80; crude oil 1,123; electricity (kw-hr.) 731,000 (82% hydroelectric); gold (troy oz.) 51; other metal ores and concentrates (exports; metal content) tin 28, lead 26, antimony 12, zinc 47, tungsten (oxide content) 2.4, copper 8.8, silver 0.19.

Botswana

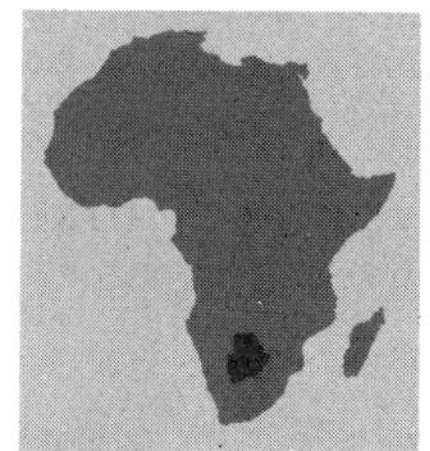

A landlocked republic of southern Africa, Botswana, a member of the Commonwealth of Nations, is bounded by South Africa, South West Africa, and Rhodesia. Area: 220,000 sq.mi. (570,000 sq.km.). Pop. (1971 est.): 667,000, almost 99% African. Capital: Gaborone (pop., 1971 est., 14,467). Largest city: Serowe (pop., 1969 est., 34,186). Language: English (official) and Tswana. Religion: Christian 60%; animist. President in 1972, Sir Seretse Khama.

Biological Sciences: *see* Life Sciences

Biophysics: *see* Life Sciences

Birth Statistics: *see* Vital Statistics

Boating: *see* Motor Sports; Rowing; Sailing

Bonds: *see* Savings and Investment; Stock Exchanges

Books: *see* Art Sales; Literature; Publishing

Botany: *see* Life Sciences

BOTSWANA

Education. (1969) Primary, pupils 82,214, teachers 2,037; secondary, pupils 3,049, teachers 157; vocational, pupils 876; teacher training, students 303, teachers 26.

Finance and Trade. Monetary unit: South African rand, with (Sept. 18, 1972) a free rate of R 0.80 to U.S. $1 (R 1.95 = £1 sterling). Budget (1969–70 est.): revenue R 21,404,000; expenditure R 20,394,000. Foreign trade (1969): imports R 30,833,000 (65% from South Africa in 1966); exports R 13,060,000 (18% to South Africa in 1966). Main exports (1967): meat 42%; hides and skins 18%; meat extract 14%; other meat products 11%; live cattle 5%.

Agriculture. Production (in 000; metric tons; 1971; 1970 in parentheses): sorghum 73 (8); corn 17 (5). Livestock (in 000; 1970–71): cattle *c.* 1,400; sheep 396; goats 1,055; poultry 268.

With its remarkable economic development reflected in the 1972–73 budget, balanced (at R 23.5 million) for the first time without British aid, Botswana gained proportionately in political importance within southern Africa during 1972. On the economic front more than 40 separate agreements (including one for a DM. 222 million credit) were completed with West German, U.S., and other interests in the Shashi copper-nickel project. Economic cooperation with South Africa continued, although the devaluation of the rand led to an escalation in development costs. This was exacerbated by the Shashi project, which gathered momentum despite the strike of 400 workers protesting against job preference being given to South Africans.

Sir Seretse Khama officially opened the Orapa diamond mine on May 26; it was estimated that production would represent one-third of the diamond output of all southern Africa and provide Botswana with a revenue exceeding R 8 million annually. Although heavy rains brought widespread flooding and damage during January, major road construction continued, supported by British, Swedish, and International Development Association funds.

President Khama opened the year with a major government reshuffle. Under an agreement with his native country, T. A. Aguda of Nigeria was sworn in as Botswana's chief justice in February.

(MOLLY MORTIMER)

Bowling and Lawn Bowls

The Fédération Internationale des Quilleurs (FIQ), the world governing organization of bowling, celebrated its 20th anniversary in 1972. The additions of Bermuda, Indonesia, and Taiwan during the year increased the number of member countries to 48. In those 48 countries there were more than 10 million registered bowlers. The growth of tenpins was strongest in Japan and other Far Eastern countries, and it was estimated that by the end of 1972 there would be as many bowling lanes in Japan alone as in the entire United States.

In 1972 the national eliminations for the World Cup, the leading amateur singles tournament, were run in 35 different countries, with international finals in Hong Kong. About 250,000 bowlers participated in the national eliminations, and the national winners were invited to Hong Kong. All 35 finalists, together with the defending champion of the previous year, Klaus Müller, a bricklayer of West Berlin, bowled 24 qualifying games. Then, the 20 top bowlers, led by R. Dalkin (U.S.), 4,774, R. M. Reyes (Phil.), 4,733, and S. Mackie (Austr.), 4,672, proceeded to bowl a one-game match-play round robin against one another. For each game won, 20 bonus points were given, plus 5 bonus points for each game over 200 pins. After those 19 games the top eight bowlers were qualified for the quarterfinals. Those eight were topped by Dalkin, 4,209 (including 290 bonus points), Mackie, 4,026 (270), and Müller, 4,023 (305). These eight quarterfinalists then proceeded to bowl another match-play round robin with the same point system. The four best bowlers qualified for semifinals; they were Dalkin, 1,538 (120), Reyes, 1,485 (110), Corona of Mexico, 1,415 (110), and Müller, 1,407 (120).

Müller thus had a chance to win this respected tournament for a second straight year. The four semifinalists continued to bowl match-play round robin, this time, however, carrying forward their scores from the quarterfinals. After the three semifinal matches there were only two bowlers left for the grand final of three games to be bowled. The scores after the semifinals were: Dalkin, 2,143 (145), Corona, 2,115 (180), Reyes, 2,075 (115), and Müller 2,050 (170). In the final three-game series the 21-year-old Dalkin, an engineering student from Atlanta, Ga., triumphed over Corona with a total of 542 against 524. Dalkin was the third American to win the tournament.

The annual invitational Tournament of the Americas drew participants from 20 North and Latin-American countries. The winners of the various events were: teams of four, U.S., 3,690; mixed doubles, U.S., 2,401; women's doubles, U.S., 3,398; men's doubles, Mexico, 3,606; women's singles, Livesay, U.S., 2,957; men's singles, Alfredo Boyd, Panama, 3,111; women's all events, Adela de Cardoze, Panama, 7,061; men's all events, Boyd, 7,411; champion division, women, Lorrie Koch, U.S., 1,717, and men, Larry Turner, U.S., 1,707.

(YRJÖ SARAHETE)

United States. Nelson Burton, Jr., appeared to be headed for his second bowler-of-the-year honour in three years with just a handful of tournaments remaining in the 1972 schedule. In late summer Burton captured his third Professional Bowlers Association (PBA) tournament championship of the year, at Waukegan, Ill., and increased his lifetime total of PBA titles to ten. Earlier in 1972 the 30-year-old St. Louis, Mo., bowler finished first in PBA meets in Miami, Fla., and Milwaukee, Wis. The number two man in the standings was 1971 bowler-of-the-year Don Johnson of Akron, O.

Neither Burton nor Johnson were serious contenders in the year's richest tournament, the $125,000 Firestone Tournament of Champions, in Akron. Mike Durbin of nearby Chagrin Falls, O., a former tour regular who had won just $310 in three prior meets in 1972, was the Firestone winner. Durbin placed third in the 48-game qualifying test, but this qualified him for the five-man nationally televised final round. There he totaled a spectacular 775 while scoring three consecutive victories, including a 258–187 triumph over Tim Harahan, Canoga Park, Calif., in the title game. Durbin won $25,000 and Harahan, $14,000.

In the 69th annual American Bowling Congress (ABC) tournament, in Long Beach, Calif., Teata Semiz of River Edge, N.J., was the only double winner, capturing the Classic Division (for professionals) singles title with 754 and the nine-game all-events crown with 1,994. Other Classic Division champions included: doubles, Carmen Salvino, Chicago, and Barry Asher, Costa Mesa, Calif., 1,366; team, Basch

Advertising, New York City, 3,099. In the Regular Division the winners were: singles, Bill Pointer, Pontiac, Mich., 739; doubles, Jerry Nutt and Bill Stanfield, Grand Rapids, Mich., 1,350; team, Hamm's Beer, Minneapolis, Minn., 3,101. Bill Beach of Sharon, Pa., won the Masters Tournament, also held at Long Beach.

The highest three-game score in the 53-year history of the Women's International Bowling Congress (WIBC) tournament was rolled in the 1972 event in Kansas City, Mo., when Mrs. D. D. Jacobson, Playa Del Rey, Calif., bowled 737 to win the Open Division singles title. The former record was 712, by Marie Clemensen, Chicago, in 1934, and by Betty Remmick, Denver, Colo., in 1965. The same Mrs. Remmick teamed with Judy Roberts of Denver to bowl 1,247 and win the Open doubles championship at Kansas City. Mrs. Mildred Martorella, Rochester, N.Y., had a nine-game total of 1,877 to take the all-events championship, and the Open Division team title was won by Angeltown Creations, Placentia, Calif., with 2,838. Division One winners in the tournament included: team, Donson Inc., Alsip, Ill., 2,707; singles, Shirley Frank, Woodside, N.Y., 657; doubles, Evelyn Porter and Billie Caldwell, Chicago, 1,215; all-events, Janice Denning, Wilmington, Del., 1,827. In the Queens Tournament at the WIBC site, Dotty Fothergill, North Attleboro, Mass., gained first prize by defeating Maureen Harris, Madison, Wis., in the final four-game match, 890–841.

In the National Duckpin Tournament held at Willow Bowl, Richmond, Va., the winners in men's competition were: team, Guida's Dairy, New Britain, Conn., 2,070; doubles, Charles Creamer and W. M. Jenkins, Richmond, 915; singles, Wally Adams, Cheshire, Conn., and Irvin Wagner, Mt. Airy, Md., each 468; all-events, James Garton, Hagerstown, Md., 1,292. Women's champions included: team, Ports Sport Shop, Baltimore, Md., 1,902; doubles, Terry Vaccaor and Dorothy Czajka, Glastonbury, Conn., 798; singles, Barbara Brown, Richmond, 461; all-events, Cathy Sanders, Baltimore, 1,203. Winners in the mixed events were: team, Swineford Florist, Richmond, 1,946; doubles, Mary Orme and Robert Marchone, Washington, D.C., 830.

(JOHN J. ARCHIBALD)

Lawn Bowls. The second World Bowling Championships were staged at Beach House Park, Worthing, Eng., from June 5 to June 17, 1972. Unlike the Australian Bowling Association in 1966, the English Bowling Association (EBA) was unable to find an overall sponsor for the championships and so the £55,000 budget had to be generated within the English game. Gate receipts, contributions from the constituent counties of the EBA, advertising rights, souvenir and program sales, etc., eventually raised more than this sum and left the association with a small surplus.

Tournament play reached higher levels than in Australia in 1966, especially among the participants from countries not generally considered leaders in the game. Nevertheless, the main titles were distributed without major surprises. Scotland won the Leonard Team Trophy, its bowlers scoring 8 points out of a possible 16 from the four individual events. South Africa and the United States each scored seven, Hong Kong and Wales six each, and England four. Scotland's victory in the event was not confirmed until the last round of matches on the final day, an example of the closeness of competition. Yet this would not have happened except that an interpretation of the laws of the game cost Scotland a match in the triples and, in consequence, the silver medal in that event. With the match against Fiji apparently won, the Scottish skip forfeited his last bowl, the head was broken, and the score cards were signed. Then an umpire ordered the end to be replayed, and Fiji won. This ruling clearly contravened Law X (3a) of the International Bowling Board but, to general surprise, the IBB failed to have the decision changed.

Individual events winners were: fours, Norman King, Cliff Stroud, Ted Hayward, Peter Line, Eng.; triples, Clive Forrester, Bill Miller, Dick Folkins, U.S.; pairs, Cecilio Delgado, Eric Liddell, Hong Kong; singles, Maldwyn Evans (Wales). David Bryant of England, the 1966 singles winner, finished sixth. However, Bryant two months later won the English singles championship for the fourth time, thus equaling Percy Baker's record.

After the world championships, changes in laws were introduced, including the controversial one concerning the delivery or nondelivery of the last bowl of each end. The minimum depth of ditches was reduced to two inches, while a new maximum was created by the New Zealand women's association: 16 in. instead of 14 in. as the height of a hemline measured from the green. The reformers claimed that women were failing to take up the game because they were not allowed to wear short dresses. Indoor bowls continued to thrive in Britain, and in Australia the comparatively new indoor green in Melbourne was to be supplemented by another. (C. M. JONES)

Boxing

Joe Frazier (U.S.) remained world heavyweight boxing champion in 1972, and his long-awaited return fight for the title against Muhammad Ali did not materialize. Frazier twice defended the title, knocking out U.S. challengers Terry Daniels in four rounds and Ron Stander in four rounds. Ali was more active, scoring victories on points over Mac Foster (U.S.) in Tokyo and George Chuvalo (Can.) in Vancouver. He also knocked out U.S. opponents Jerry Quarry at Las Vegas, Nev., Al "Blue" Lewis in Dublin, Ire., and Bob Foster, the world light-heavyweight champion, at Stateline, Nev. And he stopped an old rival, Floyd Patterson, in New York. America's other heavyweight world contender, former Olympic champion George Foreman, retained his undefeated professional record, bringing his total of victories to 38. His five victims, all knocked out in two rounds, included Clarence Boone, Murphy Goodwin, Ted Gullick, Miguel Angel Paez, and Terry Sorrells.

Despite his knockout defeat by Ali, Bob Foster remained supreme in the light-heavyweight division, successfully defending the World Boxing Council (WBC) championship four times: he beat Brian Burden (U.S.) in 3 rounds, Vicente Rondon (Venez.) in 2, Mike Quarry (U.S.) in 4, and Chris Finnegan (Eng.) in 14. Foster's victory over Rondon cleared up a dispute in this division, as the World Boxing Association (WBA) had recognized Rondon as champion.

Carlos Monzon (Arg.) continued to dominate the world middleweights and traveled to Europe three times to defend his title successfully by beating Denny Moyer (U.S.) in 5 rounds in Rome, Jean-Claude Bouttier (France) in 12 in Paris, and Tom Bogs (Den.) in 5 in Copenhagen. Koichi Wajima (Jap.) retained the junior middleweight championship, beating

UPI COMPIX

World middleweight champion Carlos Monzon scores a knockdown against challenger Tom Bogs in the fifth round of their title bout in Copenhagen, Aug. 19, 1972. Monzon retained his title on a technical knockout.

Domenico Tiberia (Italy) in one round and Matt Donovan (Trinidad) in three.

José Napoles (Mex.) remained welterweight champion with knockout wins against Ralph Charles (Eng.) in London and Adolph Pruitt (U.S.) at Monterrey. The junior welterweight crown continued to be shared: Bruno Arcari (Italy) successfully defended the WBC version against João Henrique (Braz.) with a 12th-round knockout and against Everaldo Costa Azevedo (Arg.) with a win on points. The WBA-recognized championship, however, changed hands twice: after Alfonso Frazer (Pan.) had taken the title from Nicolino Loche (Arg.) with a win on points in Panama City, he lost it to Antonio Cervantes (Colom.) by a knockout in ten rounds.

The world lightweight championship continued to be in dispute. Roberto Duran (Pan.) took the WBA title from Ken Buchanan (Scot.) with a 13-round win in New York. Considerable argument and confusion arose after Mando Ramos (U.S.) received a disputed decision over Pedro Carrasco (Spain) in Madrid in a contest for the vacant WBC version of this title. Later, Chango Carmona (Mex.) stopped Ramos in eight rounds in Los Angeles, and the WBC title was finally settled when Rodolfo Gonzalez (U.S.) was accepted as champion.

Ricardo Arredondo (Mex.) retained the WBC junior lightweight championship with knockout wins against William Martinez (Nic.) in 5 rounds in Mexico City and Susumu Okabe (Jap.) in 12 rounds in Tokyo. Ben Villaflor (Phil.) captured the WBA junior lightweight title with a decision over defending champion Alfredo Marcano (Venez.) in Honolulu. Villaflor later retained the title when held to a draw by Victor Echegaray (Arg.), also in Honolulu.

Two new world featherweight champions were crowned. After retaining the WBA version with a seventh-round knockout against Raul Martinez Mora (Mex.), Antonio Gomez (Venez.) lost the title on points to Ernesto Marcel (Pan.). The WBC championship was taken over by Clemente Sanchez (Mex.) with a third-round knockout win against Kuniaki Shibata (Jap.) in Tokyo.

The world bantamweight championship changed hands twice. After successfully defending it by stopping Jesus Pimental (Mex.) in 11 rounds in Los Angeles, Ruben Olivares (Mex.) was knocked out in eight rounds by Rafael Herrera (Mex.) in Mexico City. But Herrera lost the title a few months later when outpointed by Enrique Pinder (Pan.).

Masao Ohba (Jap.) retained the WBA flyweight championship, defeating Susumu Hanagata (Jap.) on points and knocking out Orlando Amores (Pan.) in five rounds. Both fights took place in Tokyo. The

Boxing Champions

As of Dec. 31, 1972

Division	World	Europe	Commonwealth	Britain
Heavyweight	Joe Frazier, U.S.	Joe Bugner, Eng.	Danny McAlinden, N.Ire.	Danny McAlinden, N.Ire.
Light heavyweight	Bob Foster, U.S.	Rudiger Schmidtke, W.Ger.	Chris Finnegan, Eng.	Chris Finnegan, Eng.
Middleweight	Carlos Monzon, Arg.	Vacant	Tony Mundine, Austr.	Bunny Sterling, Eng.
Junior middleweight	Koichi Wajima, Jap.	Carlos Duran, Italy	Charkey Ramon, Austr.	...
Welterweight	José Napoles, Mex.	Roger Menetrey, France	Vacant	Bobby Arthur, Eng.
Junior welterweight	Bruno Arcari, Italy Antonio Cervantes, Colom.*	Cemal Kamaçi, Turkey	Joe Tetteh, Ghana	...
Lightweight	Rodolfo Gonzalez, U.S. Roberto Duran, Pan.*	Antonio Puddu, Italy	Percy Hayles, Jam.	Jim Watt, Scot.
Junior lightweight	Ricardo Arredondo, Mex. Ben Villaflor, Phil.*	Lothar Abend, W.Ger.	...	...
Featherweight	José Legra, Spain Ernesto Marcel, Pan.*	José Legra, Spain	Bobby Dunne, Austr.	Tommy Glencross, Scot.
Bantamweight	Enrique Pinder, Pan.	Augustin Senin, Spain	Paul Ferreri, Austr.	Vacant
Flyweight	Venice Borkorso, Thai. Masao Ohba, Jap.*	Fritz Chervet, Switz.	Henry Nissen, Austr.	John McCluskey, Scot.

*Recognized as champion only by the World Boxing Association.

UPI COMPIX

Heavyweight champion Joe Frazier decks Terry Daniels in a title fight in New Orleans, La., Jan. 15, 1972. Frazier was declared the winner after a TKO in the fourth round and kept his crown.

WBC flyweight title changed hands when Venice Borkorso (Thai.) stopped Betulio Gonzalez (Venez.) in ten rounds in Bangkok.

In Europe many new champions were crowned. The heavyweight title twice changed hands. Jurgen Blin (W.Ger.) took it from José Urtain (Spain) with a win on points, but lost it to former titleholder Joe Bugner (Eng.) when knocked out in eight rounds.

Chris Finnegan (Eng.) won the light-heavyweight championship from Conny Velensek (W.Ger.) and successfully defended it against Jan Lubbers (Neth.) with an eighth-round knockout, but later lost it to Rudiger Schmidtke (W.Ger.), the referee stopping the fight after 12 rounds.

Jean-Claude Bouttier (France) retained the middleweight title, knocking out Bunny Sterling (Eng.) in 14 rounds in Paris, but near the end of the year this title was declared vacant by the European Boxing Union when the champion declared he was more interested in making another bid for the world title than in defending his European crown. Roger Menetrey (France) retained the welterweight crown, knocking out Robert Gallois (France) in six rounds in Paris and Jørgen Hansen (Den.) in ten rounds in Copenhagen. For a listing of the Olympic winners, *see* SPORTING RECORD: *Special Report*. (FRANK BUTLER)

Brazil

A federal republic in eastern and central South America, Brazil is bounded by the Atlantic Ocean and all the countries of South America except Ecuador and Chile. Area: 3,286,470 sq.mi. (8,511,965 sq.km.). Pop. (1972 est.): 98,854,300. Principal cities (pop., 1970): Brasília (cap.) 272,002; Rio de Janeiro 4,252,-009; São Paulo 5,186,752. Language: Portuguese. Religion: Roman Catholic 93%. President in 1972, Gen. Emílio Garrastazú Médici.

The Economy. Two events that could have profound influences on Brazil's economic future were reported in 1972. Development began in the north on eight million acres of trees that produce the material from which cellulose is made, with the certain promise, because of shortages everywhere else, that Brazil could become the world's major source of cellulose. The trees require eight years to mature.

In mountains 300 mi. inland from the port of São Luís, core samples of iron ore were assayed purer than any found in modern times. Only the construction of a road from the mountains to the port city remained to give Brazil what could amount to a corner on iron.

These promising economic developments were coupled with continuation of 1971's phenomenal growth rate of 11.3%, reported to be the highest ever attained in Brazil and one of the highest in the world. But even though promising economic developments and apparent political and social calm were the predominant facts of Brazil in 1972, the country was not without the spectre of high inflation. In addition, there was some question of how many of Brazil's 98 million people were realizing any benefits from the economic growth. The *Wall Street Journal* reported that the booming economy might not have had any impact on well over half the country's citizens. According to reports published by the Economic Research Institute of the University of São Paulo, the cost of living rose 9.1% from January to June 1972. It had risen 13.6% in the first half of the previous year, 30% in 1967, and 45% in 1966.

The industrial sector grew the most in 1972. Exports reached an equivalent value of $2,850,000,000 in 1971, $1.7 billion in the first six months of 1972, and were expected to reach $3.5 billion by the end of 1972. Exports now included automobiles (there were 13 automobile-manufacturing plants in São Paulo alone), with a total 1971 production of 515,000 cars and trucks; sugar (200,000 metric tons sold to the U.S.S.R. in 1972); meats ($100 million sold to the U.S.); concentrated frozen citrus juices and fresh fruit (total production of fruit estimated at 58.3 million boxes, of which 35 million were processed for juice, mostly for export); and a variety of other products including steel, shoes, rubber products, and, of course, coffee and cotton.

In other economic terms, production burgeoned and employment was on the upswing, with Brazil having closer to full employment than any other country in Latin America. Agricultural production increased at a slow rate of 2.6% in 1971, but was expected to be much higher in 1972. Coffee remained the largest item in Brazil's exports, but the 1972 total was expected to be lower than in 1971 because of heavy frosts in July.

Domestic Affairs. The strong executive regime established after the 1964 revolution—under the provisions of the 1967 constitution as amended in 1969 and the special emergency laws known as Institutional Acts—appeared consolidated. The federal Congress continued to go about its business of discussing and approving the legislative measures either proposed or backed by the administration. In May it passed constitutional amendment number one, proposed by the president. This amendment provided for the indirect election of state governors and vice-governors. The constitution already provided for the indirect election of the nation's president and vice-president.

Many opposition political leaders were alleged to have been harassed or placed under police surveillance during the year. The authorities continued to impose censorship of news and publications by indirect pressure or outright prohibition, although certain influential newspapers were allowed to criticize freely the arbitrary arrest of citizens.

The dreaded "Death Squad" whose bloody actions appalled the nation in previous years, seemed to have been disbanded. At the end of 1971 eight police officers were said to have been fired under accusation of corruption, participation in drug traffic, and membership in the Squad, a secret society originally established to avenge the slaying of a state policeman. Others were reported to have been arrested, tried, and sentenced to jail terms.

In his message to Congress when it reopened on March 31 for its eighth session, President Médici stressed the urgent need to adopt effective measures to stimulate economic development. These were to include a 15% increase in exports, the reduction of the national budget deficit, and similar measures to reduce the rate of inflation, estimated at 20% in 1971. In his talk to the nation the same day, commemorating the revolution's eighth anniversary, the president declared that everything had changed in the last eight years. The country, he said, had matured.

BRAZIL

Education. Primary (1968), pupils 11,943,506, teachers 423,145; secondary (1969), pupils 2,689,442, teachers 176,625; vocational (1969), pupils 602,016, teachers 51,312; teacher training (1969), students 337,917, teachers 37,336; higher (incl. 48 universities; 1969), students 346,824, teaching staff 39,188.

Finance. Monetary unit: cruzeiro, with (Sept. 18, 1972) a free rate of 6 cruzeiros to U.S. $1 (14.74 cruzeiros = £1 sterling). Gold, SDRs, and foreign exchange, official: (March 1972) U.S. $1,951,000,000; (March 1971) U.S. $1,202,000,000. Budget (1971 est.): revenue 22,309,000,000 cruzeiros; expenditure 26,739,000,000 cruzeiros. Gross national product: (1969) 131,883,000,000 cruzeiros; (1968) 98,957,-000,000 cruzeiros. Money supply: (Nov. 1971) 46,-766,000,000 cruzeiros; (Nov. 1970) 33,975,000,000 cruzeiros. Cost of living (São Paulo; 1963 = 100): (Dec. 1971) 1,360; (Dec. 1970) 1,127.

Foreign Trade. Imports (1971) 18.1 billion cruzeiros; exports 14,152,000,000 cruzeiros. Import sources (1970): U.S. 32%; West Germany 13%; Japan 6%; Argentina 6%; U.K. 6%. Export destinations: U.S. 25%; West Germany 9%; Italy 7%; Argentina 7%; Netherlands 6%; U.K. 5%. Main exports: coffee 21%; raw cotton 5%.

Transport and Communications. Roads (1970) 1,030,800 km. (including *c.* 64,000 km. main roads). Motor vehicles in use (1969): passenger 2,002,600; commercial (including buses) 656,100. Railways (1969): 32,015 km.; traffic 13,338,999,000 passenger-km., freight 25,207,000,000 net ton-km. Air traffic (1971): 4,983,000,000 passenger-km.; freight 189,-666,000 net ton-km. Shipping (1971): merchant vessels 100 gross tons and over 420; gross tonnage 1,730,-877. Shipping traffic (1970): goods loaded 39,970,000 metric tons; unloaded 28,073,000 metric tons. Telephones (Dec. 1970) 2,001,000. Radio receivers (Dec. 1970) 5.7 million. Television receivers (Dec. 1969) 6.5 million.

Agriculture. Production (in 000; metric tons; 1971; 1970 in parentheses): corn *c.* 14,360 (14,216); rice 5,130 (7,553); cassava (1970) 29,464, (1969) 30,-074; sweet potatoes (1970) 2,134, (1969) 2,173; wheat *c.* 2,200 (1,657); cotton, lint 499 (672); coffee 1,665 (755); cocoa (1970–71) 187, (1969–70) 211; bananas (1970) *c.* 6,396, (1969) *c.* 6,023; oranges (1970) 3,344, (1969) 3,126; tobacco *c.* 255 (244); peanuts *c.* 850 (928); sugar, raw value (1971–72) *c.* 5,500, (1970–71) *c.* 5,431; dry beans *c.* 2,430 (2,211); soybeans *c.* 2,218 (1,509); beef and veal *c.* 1,900 (*c.* 1,900); rubber *c.* 24 (25); timber (cu.m.; 1970) 169,800, (1969) 165,600; fish catch (1969) 493, (1968) 495. Livestock (in 000; Dec. 1970): cattle *c.* 97,300; horses *c.* 9,050; pigs 66,374; sheep 24,727; goats 14,700; chickens *c.* 297,000.

Industry. Fuel and power (in 000; metric tons; 1971): crude oil 8,467; coal 2,498; natural gas (cu.m.) 1,177,000; electricity (kw-hr.; 1970) 45,460,000 (88% hydroelectric in 1970). Production (in 000; metric tons; 1971): pig iron 4,738; crude steel 5,998; iron ore (metal content; 1970) 20,400; bauxite (1969) 362; manganese ore (metal content; 1969) 885; gold (troy oz.; 1970) 200; cement 9,660; asbestos (1968) 345; wood pulp (1970) 741; paper (1970) 1,081; passenger cars (including assembly; units) 363; commercial vehicles (including assembly; units) 152.

President Médici also insisted that it was imperative to avoid disturbing the nation with the discussion of the presidential succession, which he declared to be premature. The presidential elections were scheduled for 1974, and, according to Médici, only in the second half of 1973 should the question be publicly debated.

At the end of 1971 the president submitted to Congress his first national development plan for the period of 1972–74. He declared that his government intended to take appropriate measures to assure the country's economy an 8–10% annual growth. The plan included recommended measures for the national integration of the less developed areas of the northeast and the Amazon River valley. The national income must be increased, he declared, so as to afford the equivalent of at least a $500 yearly income per capita. Per capita income in 1972 was estimated at $400.

Under a previously adopted national integration plan, $430 million was to be devoted to the economic and social development of the drought-ridden northeastern states and the Amazon area during 1971–74. The plan included the opening of vast areas of the Amazon valley by the construction of an extensive system of highways, including two main roads: the trans-Amazon (3,000 mi. connecting the Atlantic seaboard with the Peruvian boundary) and the Cuiabá–Santarém (connecting the interior western state of Mato Grosso with the city of Santarém, on the southern bank of the Amazon River). In mid-1972 it was announced that 775 mi. of the trans-Amazon road had been completed and would be inaugurated by President Médici as part of the 150th independence anniversary. The paving of the road connecting Brasília with Belém, at the mouth of the Amazon, continued and was expected to be finished in 1973.

Together with the road construction plan, a vast program of land redistribution was adopted. The program called for the expenditure of approximately $760 million to finance the purchasing and expropriation of privately owned land (of more than 2,200 ac.) to be redistributed among small farmers, mostly from the northeastern states.

As a consequence, in part, of the road-building program in the Amazon valley and the opening of previously undeveloped areas in the jungle, clashes were reported to have occurred between workers and prospectors on one hand and Indian tribes on the other. The government, through the National Indian Foundation (FUNAI), adopted measures to protect the Indians from violence and to assist them in other ways. New Indian reservations were created.

The seventh Inter-American Indian Congress, held in August under the sponsorship of the Organization of American States at Brasília, adopted a declaration recommending measures for the social integration of the Indians of the Americas and respect for their tribal institutions. The Indian population of Brazil was estimated at 180,000.

During 1972 the nation commemorated the 150th anniversary of its independence with an elaborate program including a huge industrial exposition (Brazil-Export 72) staged in the city of São Paulo (September 5–14). As part of the commemoration in April the body of the first emperor, Dom Pedro I—who headed the independence movement and first declared the nation's independence from Portugal on Sept. 7, 1822—was brought to Brazil from Lisbon where it had lain since 1834. After being exhibited to the people throughout the nation, the body was interred in a

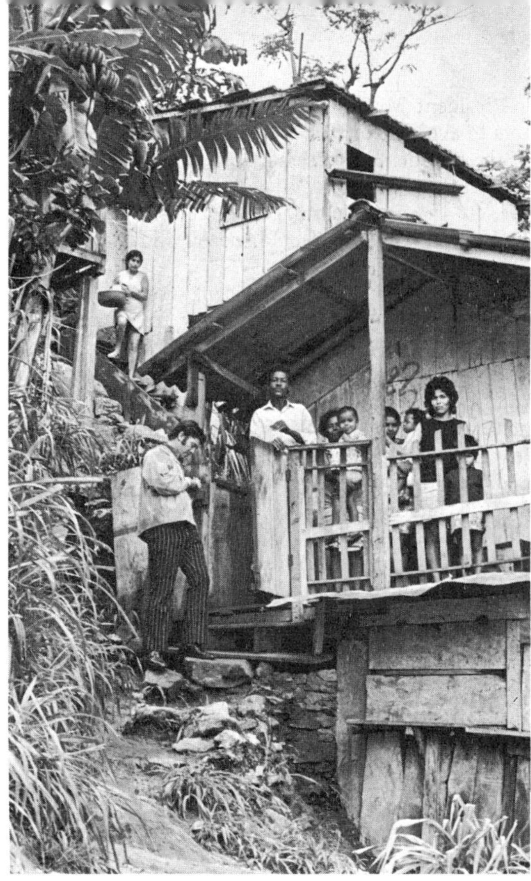

WIDE WORLD

Members of a slum family in a shantytown near Rio de Janeiro express their feelings about slum life to a reporter (left). The Brazilian government has pledged replacement of such slums—called favelas—with decent housing by 1976.

monument at Ipiranga, near the city of São Paulo, where independence was first publicly declared.

Foreign Affairs. In December 1971 President Médici visited the United States at the invitation of Pres. Richard Nixon. The two leaders exchanged views on questions of mutual interest. The meeting, it was reported, was conducted on a footing of equality.

The decision of the Brazilian government to extend the nation's territorial waters to 200 mi. off the coast (presidential decree-law of March 25, 1970, implemented on June 1, 1971) was maintained. Although the decision was received with misgivings abroad, several governments entered into negotiations with Brazil for the right to fish, particularly for shrimp, within the outer 100 mi. of the claim. The countries included Spain, France, Surinam, Trinidad and Tobago, and the U.S. A draft agreement between Brazil and the U.S. was announced in March. The agreement, to expire on Jan. 1, 1974, was subject to revision after one year. Signed at Brasília on May 9, it provided that no more than 325 vessels of U.S. registration could fish for shrimp in Brazilian-claimed waters in any one year. The U.S. was also to pay Brazil $200,000 annually for using the waters. The value of the shrimp catch was estimated at $30 million a year, about 90% taken by U.S. vessels. (RAUL D'ECA)

Bulgaria

A people's republic of Europe, Bulgaria is situated on the eastern Balkan Peninsula along the Black Sea, bordered by Romania, Yugoslavia, Greece, and Turkey. Area: 42,823 sq.mi. (110,912 sq.km.). Pop. (1971 est.): 8,565,000. Cap. and largest city: Sofia (pop., 1970, 994,000). Language: chiefly Bulgarian. First secretary of the Bulgarian Communist Party in 1972 and chairman of the Council of State, Todor Zhivkov; chairman of the Council of Ministers (premier), Stanko Todorov.

Todor Zhivkov began his 19th year as head of the Bulgarian Communist Party in February 1972. Though only 62, he was the dean of party leaders in the Soviet bloc countries of Eastern Europe. Of the 11 members of the Politburo, 4 were over 70 and one over 80; this gerontocracy was no doubt partly responsible for the manifest gap between official ideology and Bulgaria's younger generation.

Economically Bulgaria continued to progress in spite of the fact that 75% of its foreign trade was transacted with Comecon countries (more than half with the U.S.S.R. alone). These countries were supplying 100% of Bulgaria's hard coal, coke, copper, aluminum, sulfur, and potash fertilizers. In addition 85% of crude petroleum and pig iron, 80% of iron ore, cotton, phosphorous fertilizers, timber, and paper, as well as 60% of rolled steel and cellulose, were coming from the same area. Industrial production was expanding, but agriculture, though employing only 40% of the working population, still produced 55% of Bulgaria's exports.

The timid attempt of 1967 to give some autonomy to industrial enterprises had produced no real changes, and the national economy continued to be centrally planned and directed. It was significant, however, that at the seventh congress of Bulgarian Trade Unions, held in Sofia in March, Kostadin Gyaurov, chairman of the general council, criticized this superfluous centralization; he also insisted that the unions should assume the defense of working class interests.

In June the archbishop of Canterbury, Arthur

BULGARIA

Education. (1969–70) Primary, pupils 1,064,200, teachers 48,140; secondary, pupils 102,795, teachers 6,242; vocational, pupils 274,836, teachers 17,045; teacher training, students 157, teachers 6; higher (including Sofia University with 13,036 students in 1968), students 95,706, teaching staff 7,191.

Finance. Monetary unit: lev, with an official exchange rate of 1.08 leva to U.S. $1 (2.63 leva = £1 sterling) and a tourist rate of 1.85 leva to U.S. $1 (4.50 leva = £1 sterling). Budget (1972 est.): revenue 6,526,000,000 leva; expenditure 6,514,000,000 leva.

Foreign Trade. (1970) Imports 2,142,300,000 leva; exports U.S. $2,344,500,000. Main import sources: U.S.S.R. 52%; East Germany 9%; Czechoslovakia 5%. Main export destinations: U.S.S.R. 54%; East Germany 9%. Main exports: machinery 29%; tobacco and cigarettes 13%; metals 7%; wines and spirits 6%; clothing 6%.

Transport and Communications. State roads (1970) 36,143 km. (including 2,384 km. main roads). Motor vehicles in use: passenger (1969) *c.* 17,000; commercial (1961) *c.* 20,000. Railways: (1970) 4,196 km.; traffic (1971) 6,223,000,000 passenger-km., freight 14,918,000,000 net ton-km. Air traffic (1970): 305,060,000 passenger-km.; freight 5,560,000 net ton-km. Shipping (1971): merchant vessels 100 gross tons and over 148; gross tonnage 703,878. Telephones (Dec. 1970) 473,000. Radio licenses (Dec. 1970) 2,291,000. Television licenses (Dec. 1970) 1,028,000.

Agriculture. Production (in 000; metric tons; 1971; 1970 in parentheses): wheat 3,095 (3,032); corn 2,518 (2,375); barley 1,253 (1,167); sunflower seed (1970) 407, (1969) 543; dry beans *c.* 88 (69); tomatoes 721 (685); grapes 1,059 (1,040); apples 344 (363); tobacco *c.* 125 (122); meat 335 (320). Livestock (in 000; Jan. 1971): sheep 9,768; cattle 1,279; goats 335; pigs 2,369; horses 169; asses 305; poultry 33,706.

Industry. Fuel and power (in 000; metric tons; 1971): lignite 26,602; coal 389; crude oil 305; electricity (kw-hr.) 21,017,000. Production (in 000; metric tons; 1971): iron ore (32% metal content) 3,001; manganese ore (metal content; 1970) 10; copper concentrates (metal content) 37; lead concentrates (metal content) 90; pig iron 1,375; crude steel 1,947; copper (1970) 38; lead (1970) 99; zinc (1970) 76; cement 3,880; sulfuric acid 514; soda ash (1970) 300; cotton yarn 75; cotton fabrics (m.) 326,000; wool yarn 25; woolen fabrics (m.) 27,000.

Michael Ramsey, paid a five-day visit to Bulgaria. He was cordially received by Patriarch Maxim, who in July 1971 had been elected head of the Bulgarian Orthodox Church. According to official statistics, 85% of the population had belonged to the Orthodox faith in 1946. By 1962 their number had allegedly fallen to 27%, and no later figures had been published.

Zhivkov and Todorov paid a state visit to Prague, Czech., in March. In April they received, in Sofia, Erich Honecker, first secretary of the East German Communist Party, and Willi Stoph, the East German minister president. A Bulgarian military delegation led by the minister of defense, Gen. Dobri Dzhurov, visited East Berlin in May. In September, in Varna, the Bulgarian leaders met Nicolae Ceausescu, general secretary of the Romanian Communist Party, and Ion Gheorghe Maurer, the Romanian premier. It was decided at this meeting that the two countries would cooperate in building a hydroelectric complex on the lower Danube between Cioara and Belene. Bulgarian-Yugoslav relations, always difficult, improved somewhat. Probably under Soviet advice, the Bulgarian media stopped attacking "revisionist" Yugoslavia and claiming that the Macedonians were a part of the Bulgarian nation.

On April 27 Georgi Traikov, secretary-general of the Agrarian Union, ceased to be president of the National Assembly; instead he was elected chairman of the national council of the Fatherland Front and first deputy chairman of the Council of State. Vladimir Bonev became president of the National Assembly. Ivan Bashev, who had died in December 1971, was succeeded as foreign minister by Peter Mladenov.

(K. M. SMOGORZEWSKI)

Burma

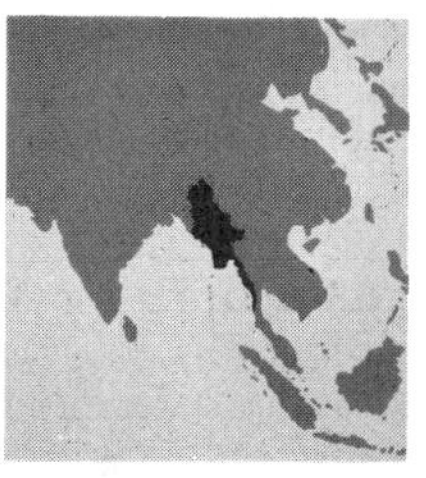

A republic of Southeast Asia, Burma is on the Indochinese Peninsula, bordered by Bangladesh, India, Tibet, China, Laos, and Thailand. Area: 261,789 sq.mi. (678,034 sq.km.). Pop. (1970 est.): 27.6 million. Cap. and largest city: Rangoon (metro. pop., 1971 est., 1,844,000). Language: Burmese. Religion (1970): Buddhist 85%. Chairman of the Revolutionary Council and prime minister in 1972, Ne Win.

Burma's slow progress toward socialism was marked by two important steps in 1972—on April 20 Gen. Ne Win and his Revolutionary Council colleagues shed their military ranks, and on April 22 the first draft of a socialist constitution was introduced. Before its official proclamation, scheduled for 1974, the constitution was to be "carried" to the people by trained cadres of the Burma Socialist Program Party (BSPP). It envisaged a socialist democratic republic with an elected unicameral People's Congress. A one-party system was proposed under which only BSPP members would be elected to the congress. The 16-chapter, 210-article document provoked widespread interest, especially among minority groups such as the Mons, Arakanese, and Chins. To placate these rebellious elements, Ne Win accepted the creation of three separate states within the Socialist Union of Burma.

The "demilitarization" of the council gave a civilian tinge to the government after ten years of continuous military rule. It also helped, as a Cabinet spokesman explained, to draw the "lines of responsibilities for the military and civilians." Ne Win also instituted changes in the old administrative system, which he described as "colonial and bureaucratic." He abolished the Central Secretariat and made each ministry directly responsible for its affairs and reduced the number of ministries from 25 to 20.

In the face of deepening economic stagnation, a National Economic Committee was set up under the leadership of Deputy Prime Minister San Yu to examine socialist economic plans and projects and to assist and supervise their possible implementation. Revolutionary Council members toured the countryside exhorting farmers to produce more food grains and other agricultural products. Milled rice production for 1971–72 was estimated at 2,152,215 tons, of which 1,050,000 tons were earmarked for domestic consumption and the rest for export. A land reform bill worked out by the agricultural ministry limited landholdings to 50 ac. per family. Those owning more were allowed to pass on the excess to parents or to children under 18. The government could take over excess land on payment of compensation.

Development projects commissioned during the year included a 70,000-ton-capacity urea fertilizer plant, built at a cost of 132 million kyats, at Kyunchaung, central Burma. A vigorous program of mineral exploitation was undertaken to increase output, which had suffered as a result of rebel insurgency. Aid to rehabilitate mines was provided by West Germany, the U.S.S.R., Canada, and the UN. Japanese assistance was pledged for the construction of two new thermal power stations with a total capacity of

BURMA

Education. (1969–70) Primary, pupils 3,328,000, teachers 65,326; secondary, pupils 692,290, teachers 21,814; vocational, pupils 4,080, teachers 393; teacher training, students 3,245, teachers 255; higher (including 2 universities), students 45,876, teaching staff 2,310.

Finance. Monetary unit: kyat, with (Sept. 18, 1972) a par value of 5.35 kyats to U.S. $1 (free rate of 12.90 kyats = £1 sterling). Gold, SDRs, and foreign exchange, official: (June 1972) U.S. $56.7 million; (June 1971) U.S. $69.8 million. Budget (1971–72 est.): revenue 8,962,000,000 kyats; expenditure 9,633,000,000 kyats. Gross national product: (1966–67) 8,586,000,000 kyats; (1965–66) 8,282,000,000 kyats. Money supply: (Dec. 1969) 2,501,000,000 kyats; (Dec. 1968) 2,351,000,000 kyats.

Foreign Trade. (1971) Imports 446.3 million kyats; exports 591.9 million kyats. Import sources (1970): Japan 26%; India 13%; U.K. 9%; West Germany 8%; U.S. 6%. Export destinations (1970): Sri Lanka 14%; Singapore 9%; India 8%; U.K. 8%; Japan 7%; Indonesia 7%; Hong Kong 6%; Malaysia 6%. Main exports: rice 49%; teak 23%; oilcakes 7%.

Transport and Communications. Roads (1970) *c.* 25,000 km. (including 13,174 km. all-weather). Motor vehicles in use (1970): passenger 29,800; commercial (including buses) 31,000. Railways (1970): 3,100 km.; traffic 2,360,000,000 passenger-km., freight 755 million net ton-km. Air traffic (1970): 141,159,000 passenger-km.; freight 2,379,000 net ton-km. Shipping (1971): merchant vessels 100 gross tons and over 38; gross tonnage 54,617. Telephones (Dec. 1970) 26,000. Radio licenses (Dec. 1970) 400,000.

Agriculture. Production (in 000; metric tons; 1971; 1970 in parentheses): rice 8,413 (8,162); rubber (exports) *c.* 7 (*c.* 7); sesame *c.* 102 (102): peanuts *c.* 520 (520); dry beans *c.* 140 (*c.* 140); cotton, lint *c.* 15 (15); jute *c.* 41 (27); tobacco 41 (61); sugar, raw value (1971–72) *c.* 243, (1970–71) *c.* 238; timber (cu.m.; 1970) 15,600, (1969) 15,300. Livestock (in 000; March 1971): cattle *c.* 6,800; buffalo (1970) *c.* 1,450; pigs *c.* 1,340; goats (1970) *c.* 750; sheep *c.* 185; chickens *c.* 13,500.

Industry. Production (in 000; metric tons; 1970): cement 156; crude oil 752; electricity (excluding most industrial production; kw-hr.; 1971) 474,000; lead concentrates (metal content) 4.1; zinc concentrates (metal content) 3.7; tin concentrates (metal content) 0.3.

Bridge:
see Contract Bridge

Bridges:
see Engineering Projects

British Commonwealth:
see Commonwealth of Nations; *articles on the various member states*

British Honduras:
see Dependent States

Broadcasting:
see Telecommunications; Television and Radio

Brunei:
see Dependent States

Buddhism:
see Religion

Budgets, National:
see Government Finance

Building and Construction Industry:
see Engineering Projects; Housing; Industrial Review

589,000 kw. in Kyunchaung and Myanaung by the end of 1973. Japan also gave credits amounting to 80 million kyats for the importation of Japanese commodities during 1972–73. An economic delegation headed by Finance Minister U Lwin visited China in June–July and discussed economic cooperation with Peking officials, but there was no indication that any agreement had been reached.

The relaxation of entry rules helped to increase tourist traffic. The kyat was pegged at 5.3 to the U.S. dollar in December 1971, but the black market rate remained at 15 to the dollar. Foreign exchange reserves declined to a new low of U.S. $52.1 million.

Ne Win released more than 150 political detainees in two batches during 1972, apparently to show that he was not unduly perturbed over the continuing insurgent movements. Former prime minister U Nu was still reported to be in Thailand, but his efforts to foment right-wing reaction were no longer considered a threat. The Karen National Union Party (KNUP) rebels suffered a blow when their leader, Saw Kyaw Mya Than, died of a heart attack in April in the Pegu Yoma region. (GOVINDAN UNNY)

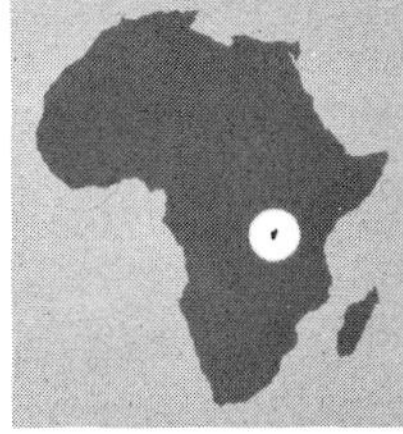

Burundi

A republic of eastern Africa, Burundi is bordered by Zaire, Rwanda, and Tanzania. Area: 10,759 sq.mi. (27,865 sq.km.). Pop. (1971 est.) 3,615,000, mainly Hutu, Tutsi, and Twa. Cap. and largest city: Bujumbura (pop., 1970 est., 110,000). Language: Kirundi and French. Religion (1964): Roman Catholic 51%; Protestant 4%; animist 45%. President in 1972, Michel Micombero; prime minister from July 15, Albin Nyamoya.

Hutu refugees rest in Zaire after fleeing their homes in Burundi, where reprisals were being taken by members of the ruling Tutsi tribe. Tribal conflict following an attempted coup in April decimated the country's population.

WIDE WORLD

Tribal massacres and a refugee exodus to neighbouring countries decimated Burundi's population in 1972. Sombre developments began with the arrival of exiled King Ntare V in Uganda from West Germany on March 21. Interviewed by Burundi officials in the presence of Uganda's president, Gen. Idi Amin, he was promised safe conduct and amnesty, with written confirmation from President Micombero. On his arrival in Burundi, March 30, Ntare was taken by the Army to an undisclosed destination, and on March 31 an official broadcast announced his arrest for trying to invade the country with mercenaries, a statement refuted by Uganda on April 4. Further radio statements called for government support, and on April 29 the government was dismissed by presidential decree. On April 30 an official broadcast stated that an attempted coup of April 29 had been averted but the king had been killed while his supporters were attempting to rescue him from the palace at Gitega. President Micombero later disclosed that Ntare had been tried and executed the night of the attack. A new military government under presidential control was established and public assembly prohibited.

At first, confusion reigned over whether the uprising was monarchist or Maoist; it was later officially accepted as far-leftist, as Burundi had long been a centre of Chinese infiltration. But the rising was clearly the result of repression of the Hutu (who made up over 80% of the total population) by the dominant Tutsi and was planned and started with the simultaneous slaughter of Tutsi in Bujumbura, the Bururi region in the south, and Gitega in the centre. With aid from Zaire and Tanzania the rebellion was largely crushed within two weeks, but reprisals by the Tutsi, often against the best-educated Hutu, continued throughout May, and the double genocide was reckoned at anything from 50,000 to 200,000. At least 500,000 people were rendered homeless, and thousands of refugees entered Tanzania, Rwanda, and Zaire.

On May 28 President Micombero broadcast that "calm reigned" following the execution of the original rebel leaders. An official announcement on May 30 stated that the 31-day tragedy, allegedly an attempt to exterminate the Tutsi by "criminal men aided by foreign mercenaries," was over. On July 15 a new 14-member government was named; the appointment of Albin Nyamoya as prime minister, secretary-general of the governing political party, and minister of the interior represented a shift to the left; this was emphasized when a Chinese technical mission arrived in late summer. Hutu representation in the Cabinet was reduced from five (out of the previous ten ministers) to four.

Many observers feared that the retaliation against educated Hutu would set the country back many years. The economic situation appeared disastrous, since coffee, the main export, responsible for 80% of foreign earnings, came from the ravaged south and food crops lay neglected. With no railway and only 50 mi. paved out of 3,000 mi. of road, recovery could only be slow. Not able to support itself, Burundi continued to rely heavily upon foreign aid, mainly from Belgium but supplemented by West Germany, France, and international agencies. (MOLLY MORTIMER)

BURUNDI

Education. (1969–70) Primary, pupils 182,444, teachers 4,877; secondary, pupils 3,701, teachers 328; vocational, pupils 2,264, teachers 230; teacher training, students 2,892, teachers 214; higher (including University of Bujumbura), students 397, teaching staff 90.

Finance. Monetary unit: Burundi franc, with (Sept. 18, 1972) a par value of BurFr. 87.50 to U.S. $1 (free official rate of BurFr. 228 = £1 sterling). Gold, SDRs, and foreign exchange, central bank: (June 1972) U.S. $19,050,000; (June 1971) U.S. $14,390,000. Budget (1971 est.) balanced at BurFr. 2,121,000,000.

Foreign Trade. (1971) Imports BurFr. 2,618,000,000; exports BurFr. 1,622,000,000. Import sources (1968): Belgium-Luxembourg 26%; Japan 12%; West Germany 12%; U.S. 7%; Iran 6%; France 5%; U.K. 5%. Export destinations (1968): U.S. 72%; Belgium 11%. Main exports: coffee 80%; cotton 10%.

Agriculture. Production (in 000; metric tons; 1970; 1969 in parentheses): corn *c.* 200 (237): cassava 1,577 (1,024); sweet potatoes 1,082 (874); sorghum *c.* 123 (51); dry beans 349 (311); dry peas 34 (20); coffee (1971) 24, (1970) 22. Livestock (in 000; Dec. 1970): cattle 683; sheep *c.* 240; goats (1969) *c.* 470.

Cambodia

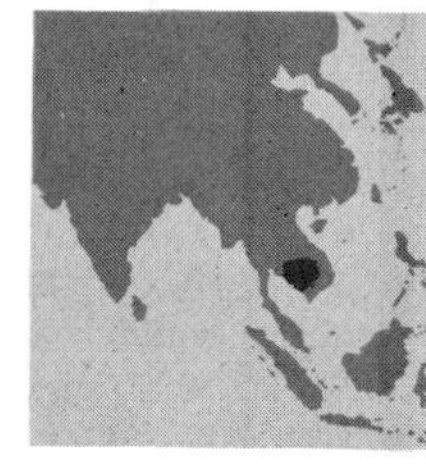

A republic of Southeast Asia, Cambodia (officially known as the Khmer Republic) is the southwest part of the Indochinese Peninsula. Area: 69,898 sq.mi. (181,035 sq.km.). Pop. (1971 est.): 6,968,200, including (1962 est.) Khmer 93%; Vietnamese 4%; Chinese 3%. Cap.: Phnom Penh (pop., 1971 est., 479,300). Language: Khmer (official) and French. Religion: Buddhist. Chiefs of state in 1972, Cheng Heng until March 10, then Gen. Lon Nol (also president from March 14); premiers, Gen. Lon Nol until March 18, Son Ngoc Thanh from March 18 until October 14, and, from October 14, Hang Thun Hak.

Sudden leadership changes at the top and a string of highly controversial elections held the spotlight in Cambodia for most of 1972, but it was the war itself that dominated everything for the third year in succession. So hopeless was the military situation and so flimsy the country's own internal cohesion that the real achievement of the year appeared to be the survival of the Lon Nol government.

The year dawned with rumours that Lon Nol would order a drastic reshuffle of his Cabinet; these had replaced earlier rumours that the government faced imminent collapse. A movement erupted among students in Phnom Penh for the removal of Sisowath Sirik Matak, the "premier delegate" who had been in virtual control since Lon Nol's paralytic stroke the previous year.

On March 10 Chief of State Cheng Heng announced that he was stepping down and handing over his post to Lon Nol. The announcement coincided with Lon Nol's return to Phnom Penh from a five-week rest cure in Kompong Som (formerly Sihanoukville). Two days later Lon Nol dissolved the government.

A period of confusion followed. Four days after he became chief of state, Lon Nol swore himself in as president. Simultaneously, he said he would also be premier. All this was in addition to his position as commander in chief. Sirik Matak remained in office as deputy premier. It appeared that Lon Nol was making desperate efforts to contain student opposition to his trusted aide. But widespread feeling that Sirik Matak would find a key position in the new system kept the agitation going, with some military and Buddhist circles joining the students.

On March 16 Sirik Matak publicly announced his withdrawal from political life, and Lon Nol found himself president of a country without a government. After six days of governmental vacuum, the political chaos ended on March 20 with the announcement of an 18-man Cabinet. Lon Nol became the president of the Cabinet, and the premier was Son Ngoc Thanh,

CAMBODIA

Education. (1968–69) Primary, pupils 1,024,456, teachers 21,371; secondary, pupils 104,227, teachers (1967–68) 3,886; vocational (1967–68), pupils 5,787, teachers 464; teacher training, students 1,769, teachers (1966–67) 104; higher (including 9 universities), students 11,094, teaching staff 1,200.

Finance. Monetary unit: riel, with (June 30, 1972) a free rate of 186.26 riels to U.S. $1 (455 riels = £1 sterling). Budget (1970 est.) balanced at 9,820,000,000 riels.

Foreign Trade. (1970) Imports U.S. $76.7 million; exports U.S. $63.1 million. Import sources (1969): Japan 27%; France 24%; U.S. 11%; China 9%; Singapore 7%. Export destinations (1968): France 23%; South Vietnam 17%; Hong Kong 11%; China 10%; Singapore 8%. Main exports: rice 70%; rubber 22%.

Transport and Communications. Roads (1970) *c.* 11,000 km. Motor vehicles in use (1970): passenger 27,500; commercial (including buses) 11,200. Railways: (1971) 649 km.; traffic (1970) 109 million passenger-km., freight 83 million net ton-km. Air traffic (1970): 30.8 million passenger-km.; freight 516,000 net ton-km. Inland waterway (Mekong River; 1970) *c.* 1,400 km. Telephones (Jan. 1971) 8,000. Radio receivers (Dec. 1968) 1 million. Television receivers (Dec. 1969) 50,000.

Agriculture. Production (in 000; metric tons; 1971; 1970 in parentheses): rice 2,732 (3,814); corn 121 (137); rubber *c.* 35 (13); bananas (1969) 141, (1968) 136; dry beans (1970) *c.* 37, (1969) 37; jute *c.* 8 (8). Livestock (in 000; Dec. 1970): cattle *c.* 2,460; buffalo *c.* 900; pigs *c.* 1,250.

WIDE WORLD

Cambodian soldier fires into a bunker where North Vietnamese soldiers and Viet Cong guerrillas were entrenched during a battle near the ancient temple of Angkor Wat early in 1972.

officially called first minister and minister of foreign affairs. Thanh, 64, was a veteran nationalist leader with a militant following, but he was suspected by students and intellectuals of being too close to the United States undercover establishment.

Lon Nol's attempts to legitimize the political organization of his country continued. On April 30 a referendum was held to approve a newly drafted republican constitution. Official spokesmen said that 97.45% of the electorate had voted in favour and that the new constitution would come into force on May 12. This was followed by another election on June 4 to choose the country's president. Opposing Lon Nol were In Tam, a former minister and popular leader, and Keo An, dean of the law faculty of Phnom Penh University. Lon Nol obtained 55% of the votes, In Tam 26%, and Keo An 19%. Both the losing candidates alleged "gross irregularities" in the election. Lon Nol was officially sworn in on July 3. Elections for the lower house of the National Assembly took place on September 3, and to the upper house on September 17. A month before the lower house elections In Tam's Democratic Party and Sirik Matak's Republican Party withdrew from the race, alleging unconstitutional ground rules and gerrymandering which all but guaranteed a government victory. This left only the pro-government Socio-Republican Party and a dummy organization called the People's Party, both organized by Lon Nol's influential younger brother, Col. Lon Non. The Socio-Republican Party won all 26 lower house seats. All 40 upper house seats also went to government candidates. Popular apathy toward the elections and alienation from government were obvious.

The elections focused attention on the disunity among Cambodia's top leaders. An unsuccessful assassination attempt on Premier Son Ngoc Thanh in August was also attributed to internal disunity, rather than to Communist terrorism. On October 14 Son Ngoc Thanh resigned. Lon Nol appointed Hang Thun Hak, secretary-general of the Socio-Republican Party, to form a new government. Hang Thun Hak's Cabinet included Col. Lon Non.

The Communists were holding their own on the

Business Review: *see* Economy, World

Butter: *see* Agriculture

UPI COMPIX

A Cambodian father transports his daughter away from the perils of combat near Phnom Penh. The fighting between Cambodian and North Vietnamese troops occurred on the outskirts of the Cambodian capital city. The six-week struggle ended in January 1972.

military front. As government troops were locked in what one Army spokesman called "a battle in which the Khmer Republic has all to lose and nothing to win," Communist forces held effective control of much of the countryside. Six of the seven highways linking Phnom Penh with the provinces remained cut for most of the year. These included the "rice road" from Battambang in the northwest; by September, rice was selling in the capital at prices 500% higher than at the beginning of the war. Revealing light was thrown on the scarcity of essential items as well as on the calibre and morale of government troops when bands of uniformed soldiers joined civilians in ransacking the central market in Phnom Penh in early September. The looting lasted a whole day, but the government did not intervene.

The Communists seemed able to mount major offensives at will, including rocket attacks on Phnom Penh. Repeated attempts by the Cambodian Army to launch counteroffensives and eject the guerrillas from their strongholds either ended in routs or were stalled. In August government spokesmen said that the guerrillas were using tanks for the first time in Cambodia. In September the government announced that one entire battalion of up to 400 men was missing after the abandonment of rear garrisons along the main highway from Phnom Penh to Saigon.

There was apparently no lack of military aid from outside. The U.S. was reportedly sending in supplies at the rate of 5,000 tons a month, half of them ammunition. Also, some 50,000 Cambodian troops were said to have received training in South Vietnam, Thailand, the U.S., Indonesia, Malaysia, and elsewhere by mid-1972. The total strength of the Cambodian armed forces was placed officially at 200,000, while government sources reported the presence in Cambodia of 50,000 North Vietnamese troops and 15,000 to 20,000 Khmer Rouge fighters.

Unconfirmed reports during the year spoke of Prince Sihanouk losing his grip over his exile government in Peking. But in August he won a major diplomatic victory when the conference of nonaligned nations, meeting at Georgetown, Guyana, voted to accord membership to the exile government as the rightful government of Cambodia, the Phnom Penh regime being ousted. This produced fears in Phnom Penh that China would now lead a campaign in the UN to get the Lon Nol government expelled and the Sihanouk government admitted in its place. As Sihanouk kept himself in the news by traveling to Eastern Europe and North America, the Cambodian government issued an official declaration in September calling him a false neutralist and describing as wishful thinking any hopes he might have of returning to power in Phnom Penh. (T. J. S. GEORGE)

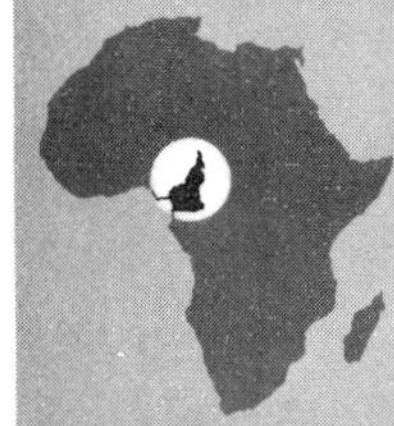

Cameroon

A republic of west equatorial Africa on the Gulf of Guinea, Cameroon borders on Nigeria, Chad, the Central African Republic, the Congo, Gabon, and Equatorial Guinea. Area: 179,557 sq.mi. (465,054 sq.km.). Pop. (1970 est.): 5,836,000. Cap.: Yaoundé (pop., 1970 est., 178,000). Largest city: Douala (pop., 1970 est., 250,000). Language: English and French (official), Bantu, Sudanic. Religion: mainly animist; some Christian and Muslim. President in 1972, Ahmadou Ahidjo.

On May 6, 1972, President Ahidjo announced to the National Assembly in Yaoundé that the people of Cameroon were to be consulted by means of a referendum on the immediate establishment of a unitary state, to be called the United Republic of Cameroon, with a single National Assembly of 120 members. Previously there had been separate administrations in East and West Cameroon as well as a federal administration in Yaoundé. Ahidjo added that the official status of the French language in the East and of English in the West would be formally guaranteed.

The referendum, in which about three million people were entitled to vote, was held May 21. According to official figures, 98.5% of the electorate voted, 99.97% of these for creation of a unitary state.

The first Cabinet of the newly constituted United Republic of Cameroon was announced on July 3. The new government comprised 24 ministers and 4 deputy ministers, including 8 English-speakers from the former West Cameroon. Major portfolios went to Charles Onana Awana (finance), Vincent Efon (foreign affairs), and Simon Achidi Achu (justice).

Cameroonian foreign policy was characterized by a certain coolness toward the French-speaking African bloc, together with diplomatic rapprochement with the countries of the East. Thus, in pursuing the integration of the two former federated states, President Ahidjo was a somewhat halfhearted partner in the Francophone Common Organization of Africa, Malagasy, and Mauritius (OCAM). Cameroon Airlines came into service late in 1971.

While maintaining a steadfastly conservative policy at home, President Ahidjo followed a far more radical line abroad. In February Cameroon and Guinea jointly introduced a motion on Rhodesia and Namibia (South West Africa) for discussion by the Council of Ministers of the Organization of African Unity. Moreover, in September Cameroon and North Vietnam agreed to establish diplomatic relations at the embassy level. (PHILIPPE DECRAENE)

CAMEROON

Education. (1969–70) Primary, pupils 888,435, teachers (including preprimary) 18,972; secondary, pupils 48,131, teachers 1,964; vocational, pupils 15,782, teachers 913; teacher training, students 2,030, teaching staff 210.

Finance. Monetary unit: CFA franc, with (Sept. 18, 1972) a parity of CFA Fr. 50 to the French franc and CFA Fr. 255.79 to U.S. $1 (free rate of CFA Fr. 612.37 = £1 sterling). Federal budget (1971–72 est.) balanced at CFA Fr. 45.3 billion.

Foreign Trade. (1970) Imports CFA Fr. 67,160,000,000; exports CFA Fr. 62,780,000,000. Import sources: France 50%; West Germany 8%; U.S. 8%. Export destinations: France 31%; Netherlands 23%; West Germany 12%; U.S. 10%. Main exports: cocoa 24%; coffee 23%; aluminum 9%; cotton 8%; timber 7%.

Transport and Communications. Roads (1970) 25,516 km. (including 2,000 km. with improved surface). Motor vehicles in use (1970): passenger 32,400; commercial (including buses) *c.* 32,000. Railways: (1969) 839 km.; traffic (1970) 219 million passenger-km., freight 271 million net ton-km. Telephones (Jan. 1970) 6,000. Radio receivers (Dec. 1969) *c.* 210,000.

Agriculture. Production (in 000; metric tons; 1971; 1970 in parentheses): corn *c.* 355 (c. 348); sweet potatoes (1970) 328, (1969) 234; cassava (1970) 930, (1969) 902; coffee (1970) *c.* 88, (1969) 82; cocoa (1970–71) 115, (1969–70) 110; bananas (1970) *c.* 125, (1969) *c.* 120; peanuts 195 (*c.* 190); rubber (exports) 12 (11); cotton, lint *c.* 18 (*c.* 15); millet and sorghum (1970) *c.* 385, (1969) 376; palm oil 56 (54); palm kernels 47 (45); timber (cu.m.; 1969) *c.* 7,100, (1968) *c.* 7,100. Livestock (in 000; Dec. 1970): cattle *c.* 2,100; pigs 350; sheep *c.* 1,150; goats *c.* 2,100; chickens *c.* 8,700.

Industry. Production: aluminum (1971) 51,000 metric tons; gold (1969) 200 troy oz.

Canada

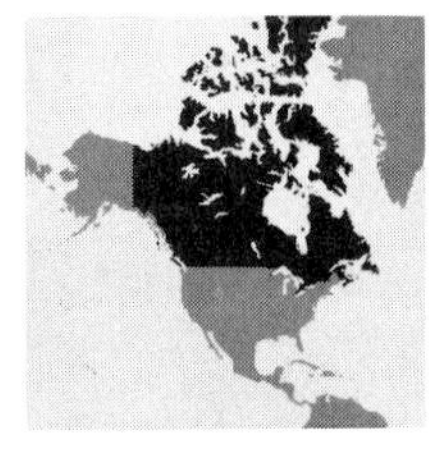

Canada is a federal parliamentary state and member of the Commonwealth of Nations covering North America north of conterminous United States and east of Alaska. Area: 3,851,809 sq.mi. (9,976,185 sq.km.). Pop. (1972 est.): 21,830,000, including (1961) British 43.8%; French 30.4%; other European 22.6%; Indian and Eskimo 1.2%. Cap.: Ottawa (pop., 1971, 302,341). Largest city: Montreal (pop., 1971, 1,214,352). Language (mother tongue, 1971): English 60.1%; French 26.9%; others 13%. Religion (1961): Roman Catholic 45.7%; Protestant 47.7%. Queen, Elizabeth II; governor-general in 1972, D. Roland Michener; prime minister, Pierre Elliott Trudeau.

Canadians went to the polls on Oct. 30, 1972, and withdrew a substantial amount of the strong mandate they had given the Liberal government of Pierre Elliott Trudeau four years before. Some interpreted the fall in Liberal strength as a reaction against the government's efforts to extend French language rights across Canada; most observers put the blame on the government's apparent inability to deal with the twin economic problems of unemployment and inflation.

Party strength after the election reflected the persistent regional divisions of Canada, a result that challenged efforts toward national unity. In addition, the fact that the Liberals emerged holding onto only two seats more than the Conservatives held in the House of Commons indicated that Canada was reentering a time of minority governments, which had come to an end with the 1968 Trudeau victory. Many Canadians felt that this reappearance meant an unpromising political environment in which to deal with Canada's economic problems and the resolution of its commercial difficulties with the U.S.

Trudeau called the election on September 1, at the dissolution of the fourth session of the 28th Parliament. No large issues appeared in the two-month campaign and "Trudeaumania," the personal appeal that had been characteristic of Trudeau's previous campaign, was noticeably absent. Instead, Trudeau campaigned on the record on his government, dwelling on its efforts to satisfy linguistic and regional aspirations through a flexible federal system. The Conservatives did not choose to debate this theme but concentrated on economic issues. Robert L. Stanfield, the party's leader from Nova Scotia, urged immediate personal income tax cuts in order to stimulate the economy and stated his readiness to impose wage and price controls to cope with inflation. He was critical of the government's broadening of unemployment insurance benefits, which he said had called into question the will to work in Canada. David Lewis, leader of the smaller New Democratic Party, seized on an effective issue early in the campaign when he criticized large corporations for not paying their fair share of taxes. The Social Credit Party, tirelessly led by Réal Caouette, attempted to reach voters across Canada by emphasizing income and job security and improved welfare benefits.

PETER BREGG—CANADIAN PRESS

Prime Minister Pierre Trudeau campaigns in Ontario prior to the October election. His Liberal Party suffered a stunning upset and faced a virtual standoff with the Conservatives in Parliament.

Provincial premiers also entered the fray, most notably in Ontario, where William Davis placed his powerful organization behind Stanfield. The three New Democratic premiers in the West actively supported the Lewis campaign. In general the parties held fewer mass rallies and spent more time in meeting smaller groups than in most previous campaigns. Eligible voters numbered 12.9 million, about 20% of whom

CANADA

Education. (1969–70) Primary, pupils 3,841,040, teachers (including preprimary) 163,513; secondary, pupils 1,505,571, teachers 100,791; vocational (excluding Quebec), pupils 246,502; higher (including 64 universities), students 562,648, teaching staff (university only) 21,840.

Finance. Monetary unit: Canadian dollar, with (Sept. 18, 1972) a free rate of Can$0.98 to U.S. $1 (Can$2.40 = £1 sterling). Gold, SDRs, and foreign exchange, official: (June 1972) U.S. $5,891,000,000; (June 1971) U.S. $4,347,000,000. Budget (1970–71, est.): revenue Can$12,803,000,000; expenditure Can$13,182,000,000. Gross national product: (1971) Can$92,130,000,000; (1970) Can$84,470,000,000. Money supply: (May 1972) Can$20,190,000,000; (May 1971) Can$15.2 billion. Cost of living (1963 = 100): (June 1972) 135; (June 1971) 129.

Foreign Trade. (1971) Imports Can$15,603,000,000; exports Can$18,449,000,000. Import sources: U.S. 70%; EEC 6%; U.K. 5%; Japan 5%. Export destinations: U.S. 68%; U.K. 8%; EEC 6%. Main exports: motor vehicles 24%; machinery 11%; metal ores 8%; nonferrous metals 8%; timber 7%; newsprint 6%; wheat 5%; wood pulp 5%; crude oil 5%.

Transport and Communications. Roads. (1970) 810,144 km. (including 2,759 km. expressways). Motor vehicles in use (1970): passenger 6,602,200; commercial (including buses) 1,736,000. Railways (1970): 72,808 km.; traffic 3,657,000,000 passenger-km., freight 160,750,000,000 net ton-km. Air traffic (1970): 15,397,238,000 passenger-km.; freight 432,009,000 net ton-km. Shipping (1971): merchant vessels 100 gross tons and over 1,228; gross tonnage 2,366,175. Shipping traffic (1971): goods loaded 94,082,000 metric tons; unloaded 54,762,000 metric tons. Telephones (Dec. 1970) 9,751,000. Radio receivers (Dec. 1970) 15,890,000. Television receivers (Dec. 1968) 6.1 million.

Agriculture. Production (in 000; metric tons; 1971; 1970 in parentheses): wheat 14,253 (9,023); barley 14,257 (9,051); oats 5,816 (5,673); rye 629 (570); corn 2,746 (2,564); potatoes 2,484 (2,511); rapeseed 2,234 (1,637); linseed 652 (1,243); tobacco *c.* 100 (101); butter 134 (153); cheese (1970) 111, (1969) 112; beef and veal *c.* 918 (899); pork *c.* 690 (608); timber (cu.m.; 1969) 121,800, (1968) 111,900; fish catch (1970) 1,377, (1969) 1,405. Livestock (in 000; Dec. 1970): cattle 12,225; sheep 670; horses (June) 328; pigs 7,703; chickens (June) 92,517.

Industry. Labour force (June 1972) 8,868,000. Unemployment: (May 1972) 6.3%; (May 1971) 6.3%. Index of industrial production (1963 = 100): (1971) 154; (1970) 150. Fuel and power (in 000; metric tons; 1971): coal 14,392; lignite 3,079; crude oil 66,370; natural gas (cu.m.) 77,510,000; electricity (kw-hr.) 215,028,000 (77% hydroelectric in 1970). Metal and mineral production (in 000; metric tons; 1971): iron ore (shipments; 55% metal content) 43,282; crude steel 11,040; copper ore (metal content) 653; nickel ore (metal content; 1970) 279; zinc ore (metal content) 1,267; lead ore (metal content) 394; aluminum (1970) 962; asbestos (1970) 1,500; gold (troy oz.) 2,209; silver (troy oz.) 46,000; uranium oxide (1970) 3.6. Other industrial production (in 000; metric tons; 1971): wood pulp 15,842; newsprint 7,528; sulfuric acid 2,517; synthetic rubber 198; passenger cars (units) 1,096; commercial vehicles (units) 280. Dwelling units completed (1971) 201,230.

EDWARD COWAN—THE NEW YORK TIMES

This partially built pellet plant at Sept-Îsles in Quebec is indicative of the economic growth in the north shore area of the St. Lawrence Seaway, a contrast to the rest of the province.

were young people between the ages of 18 and 21 enfranchised for the first time. In the polling, ballots were cast by 74% of the eligible voters and by almost 1.5 million more people than in 1968.

When the election results became final the Liberals had lost 46 seats since 1968 to hold 109 in the 264-seat House of Commons. Their main strength was in Quebec, where they won 56 seats. In the Atlantic provinces they picked up three seats from the Conservatives, to win ten in all. Ontario was a disappointment, for the party's standing there was cut from 64 to 36 seats. The West was even more disappointing; in the four provinces the 25 seats held since 1968 were reduced to 7. In Alberta the Liberals failed to elect a single member and in British Columbia they dropped from 16 to 4 seats, 2 held by senior Cabinet ministers. Four members of the Trudeau Cabinet were defeated: in Quebec, Jean-Luc Pepin, minister of industry, trade, and commerce, lost a close race; Martin O'Connell, minister of labour, lost a Toronto riding; and in Alberta, H. A. "Bud" Olson, the minister of agriculture, and Patrick Mahoney, minister of state assisting in the Department of Finance, lost their seats. The Liberal share of the popular vote was 38.3%, 7% less than in 1968.

The Conservative's 107 seats were filled by 22 members from the Atlantic provinces, 40 from Ontario (a gain of 16), 2 from Quebec, and 43 from the Western provinces. Conservatives won all 19 seats in Alberta and 8 in British Columbia, where they had been shut out in 1968. The results from Quebec provided the only flaw in what was a substantial electoral gain. There a former Liberal provincial minister, Claude Wagner, had been persuaded to lead the Quebec Conservatives; he managed to win his seat and only one other. Across Canada the Conservatives won 35% of the popular vote, a 4% gain.

The New Democratic Party increased its standing by nine seats to take 31 ridings. Its popular vote came to 17.8%, a slight gain over 1968. The party made inroads in urban areas in Ontario and British Columbia but failed to win a seat in either the Maritimes or Quebec. Nonetheless, with the two major parties virtually balanced, the New Democrats would cast the deciding votes on any legislative program. The Social Credit Party's share of the popular vote was only 7% across Canada but it rose to 24% in Quebec, where it elected all 15 of its members. The separatist party, the Parti Québécois, did not contest seats in Quebec. The new Parliament would also have two independents, one of them Lucien Lamoureux, the speaker of the previous House; five women, four more than the previous one; and the youngest member in its history, 20-year-old Sean O'Sullivan, elected from a Hamilton, Ont., riding.

The decline in Liberal support outside Quebec did not show that English Canada did not care to cooperate with Quebec, as separatist leader René Lévesque claimed. Almost half the seats in predominantly English-speaking Toronto went to Liberals, and other Ontario centres regarded as bulwarks of the English-Canadian viewpoint supported Liberal candidates. The Conservatives, and especially their leader, had played down racial or linguistic issues in their campaign. Fundamentally, Stanfield agreed with the Trudeau approach to make bilingualism an official reality in Canada although he questioned the manner in which the policy was being implemented in the public service. The election results, however, did indicate a criticism of Trudeau's policies on the economic front. There was no question of the prime minister's commitment to national unity but his approach to the plight of the unemployed and the underprivileged was seen to be that of a detached and even callous wealthy man.

At a press conference on November 2 Trudeau indicated that he and his ministers would remain in office in order to meet the new Parliament and test its sentiment. In taking this stand he was following sound constitutional practice that makes the will of Parliament, not popular support, the ultimate arbiter of a government's fate. While minority government posed many problems, it also possessed advantages. A minority administration would more likely be responsive to currents of opinion in Parliament and in the country, and Trudeau would have to give continuous attention to the will of Parliament in implementing his policies, a difficult task for a prime minister who had often shown impatience with Parliament's slow and cumbersome procedures. Parliament was to be recalled on Jan. 4, 1973.

Domestic Affairs. The Trudeau Cabinet was reconstituted on January 28 when ten ministers were given new offices. Edgar Benson, author of the massive tax reforms passed in 1971, moved from Finance to National Defence (and ultimately left active politics at the dissolution of Parliament). John Turner, who had been minister of justice, succeeded Benson; Donald Macdonald left National Defence and went to the Department of Energy, Mines, and Resources; Otto Lang was given the Justice portfolio and the responsibility of watching over the operations of the Canadian Wheat Board. At the end of the parliamentary session two Cabinet members, Arthur Laing and Jean-Pierre Côté, resigned to go to the Senate, together with J. J. Greene, the former energy minister, who had retired from the government earlier in the year. A former senior member of the Trudeau Cabinet, Paul Hellyer, who resigned from the Liberal government in 1969, joined the Conservatives in July and retained his seat in the October election.

The third session of Canada's 28th Parliament, which had opened on Oct. 8, 1970, and was formally prorogued on Feb. 16, 1972, was the first for 30 years to spill over three calendar years. The latter part of the session had been occupied with consideration of the 743-page tax reform measure and the 150 amendments to it. One of the most complex measures to come before Parliament in years, the bill was approved by the Commons, 182–83, on Dec. 17, 1971, and by the Senate four days later, to take effect at the beginning of 1972. It provided tax cuts of 7% for corporations and 3% for individuals, introduced the principle of taxes on capital gains, and made innumerable changes in allowances and exemptions. A farm-products marketing bill was passed on December 31 after an all-night sitting of the Commons. It created a Canada-wide farm marketing council with national agencies for particular commodities and had been bitterly opposed by rural members because it seemed to introduce the principle that the agencies could dictate farm output.

The fourth session opened on February 17. Of the 29 items mentioned in the speech from the throne, less than 10 had been approved when the session ended on September 1. Major measures left in the air were an election expenses act, a bill to set up a screening agency to review foreign take-overs of Canadian business, a new competition policy for business, legislation about wiretapping, and an amendment to the labour code permitting the process of technological change to be a subject for negotiation between management and labour. Another prized piece of legislation, the Family Income Security Plan, was not approved through a technicality in the House's procedure on July 7. The measure would have abolished universal family allowances and replaced them by higher payments for children of needy parents. The opposition claimed that the task of confirming the incomes of those seeking payments and administering the payments would have led to a bureaucratic nightmare.

Parliament had to take up the problem of two dock strikes during the summer. The first, at three St. Lawrence River ports where longshoremen refused to carry out new working arrangements, ended after almost eight weeks on July 7 when Parliament ordered the men back to work and outlawed strikes, slowdowns, or lockouts at the affected ports. The second strike, which closed six British Columbia ports for most of August, was ended by the passage of a bill sending longshoremen and their employers back to the bargaining table. The measure took less than seven hours to clear both houses on September 1, after which Parliament was dissolved.

After the election, on November 27, Trudeau introduced eight new Cabinet members in a reshuffle that he said showed the Canadian people "we did understand their message in the election." He cited as an example the choice of Donald C. Jamieson as minister of regional expansion, replacing the controversial Jean Marchand.

The year was uneventful in the field of federal-provincial relations. The equalization payments program, by which the federal government transferred funds to the "have-not" provinces in order to bring their public services up to a standard roughly comparable with other provinces, was extended for another five years after it expired on March 31. The program represented a transfer of over $1 billion in a year, or about 20% of the conditional and unconditional grants made by the federal government to the provinces. At a conference of provincial premiers held at Halifax, Nova Scotia, August 3–4, Quebec's desire for more fiscal independence in the federation found a large measure of support. A special meeting held before the main sessions to allow the premiers of the five Atlantic provinces (including Quebec on this occasion) to take up the critical question of the sharing of revenues from offshore oil and gas royalties failed to reach agreement on a specific stand for negotiations with Ottawa.

There were two changes in provincial administrations in 1972. In Newfoundland an election held on Oct. 28, 1971, led to a confused result that was not settled until mid-January when a judicial inquiry awarded the election to the Conservatives. Premier Joseph Smallwood and his Liberal government resigned, ending over 22 years in office. The new premier, Frank Moores, called a second election for March 24 and obtained his desired working majority when 33 Conservatives were elected in the 42-seat House. In February Edward Roberts, 31, who had been Smallwood's minister of health, was chosen the new Liberal leader.

In British Columbia 72-year-old W. A. C. Bennett, who had presided over a Social Credit administration for just over 20 years, was defeated in a startling upset in a provincial election on August 30. The Bennett government, although very successful in developing the economy of the Pacific province, had made many enemies during its long career, especially among organized labour, physicians, and teachers. The New Democratic Party, which Bennett had previously kept at bay, increased its standing from 12 to 38 seats in the 55-seat legislature. Bennett held onto his own seat, but 11 of his 15 Cabinet members were defeated. The new premier, David Barrett, 41, who had led the New Democrats for only two years, took office on September 15.

Lester Pearson, prime minister of Canada from 1963 to 1968 and winner of the 1967 Nobel Peace Prize, died on December 27 (*see* OBITUARIES).

Foreign Affairs. To attempt to deal with the trade difficulties caused by the economic measures imposed in the U.S. in August 1971, Trudeau and U.S. Pres. Richard Nixon exchanged visits. In Washington on Dec. 6, 1971, Trudeau was assured that the U.S. did not desire a continuing surplus in its overall trade with Canada. Later, on April 13, President and Mrs. Nixon, accompanied by Secretary of State William Rogers, began a three-day visit to Ottawa. Addressing Parliament, Nixon frankly admitted that difficult problems existed between the two countries but felt that they would yield to patient negotiation that recognized each country's interests. Private talks between the two leaders were expected to lead to a resumption of the trade discussions regarding modifications of the automotive agreement of 1965 and other problems. But as the year passed it seemed clear that both countries were unwilling to enter into serious negotiations until after their respective national elections.

Before leaving Ottawa Nixon signed the Great Lakes Water Quality Agreement, designed to improve the quality of water in the Great Lakes, particularly in Lakes Erie and Ontario. The agreement provided for the construction and upgrading of municipal sewage treatment facilities in all communities bordering on the Great Lakes. Although the agreement was not a binding treaty and did not set out sums to be spent, Canadian expenditures on the project were expected to reach $250 million, with U.S. expenditures rising as high as $2 billion. Standards for water quality were laid down and the International Joint Commission, founded in 1909 to deal with common boundary-waters problems, was asked to assume research and monitoring functions under the plan.

On May 2 a statement of policy regarding foreign investment was issued. Known as the Gray report after its principal author, Herb Gray, the minister of national revenue, it proposed legislation to create a board that would review the purchase of Canadian

UPI COMPIX

Picketers march on April 11, 1972, during public service strike affecting 200,000 government workers, teachers, and hospital personnel in Quebec Province.

companies by foreign concerns, approving only those investments and take-overs that were seen to be of significant benefit for Canada. The legislation failed to win approval in 1972 and was laid aside for reintroduction later.

Canada expressed serious reservations in 1972 about the proposed U.S. trans-Alaska pipeline, which Canada saw as a threat to the environment of the North and as part of a route that involved the risk of oil spillage along the British Columbia coast. A spill at Cherry Point, Wash., on June 4 and a U.S. Coast Guard report indicating that an annual spillage of 140,000 barrels was possible added to Canadian apprehensions. Canada urged the study of an alternative route down the Mackenzie Valley but an official U.S. report in early May rejected this route and recommended that the pipeline project go forward.

There was considerable activity in Canadian-Chinese relations during 1972. Mitchell Sharp, the secretary of state for external affairs, led a delegation of 600 Canadians to Peking in August to participate in events associated with a Canadian trade fair. The fair earned Canada $25 million worth of sales in nickel, potash, aluminum, electrical machinery, and animal breeding stock. For the year it was expected that Canadian sales to China would total over $250 million, mostly for wheat. Premier Chou En-lai, meeting with Sharp, confirmed that China would continue to buy Canadian wheat as long as the price was competitive and thanked Canada for its lead in the movement in recent years to recognize China and for its support of China's bid for UN membership in 1971. A cultural agreement covering exchanges of students and physicians as well as exhibitions and sports groups was also signed in Peking. Later, in October, it was announced that a direct air link between Canada and China would be set up early in 1973.

The Chinese also carried their wares to the Canadian National Exhibition in Toronto, putting on the largest foreign exhibit in the history of the fair. They were seeking to improve exports to Canada, which amounted to only $24 million in 1971. The Chinese visitors invariably found their way to Gravenhurst, Ont., birthplace of Norman Bethune, the Canadian surgeon revered for his association with the Chinese Communist armies in their struggle with the Japanese.

Canada met the crisis created by Uganda's decision to expel about 25,000 Asians holding British passports by offering to admit those who wished to settle in Canada and could meet the country's immigration requirements. Since these were based on qualifications embodying education, occupation, linguistic skills, and adaptability to Canadian life, and since most of the Asians were shopkeepers, businessmen, lawyers, and teachers, it was not expected that many difficulties would arise.

At the end of March, 56 Bomarc B nuclear missiles at the Canadian NORAD (North American Air Defense Command) bases at North Bay, Ont., and La Macaza, Que., became nonoperational. With the threat of bomber attack on North America reduced, the Canadian government had decided to phase them out.

Canada won the "world hockey championship" on September 28 with a narrow victory in Moscow over the Soviet team. Eight games were played in the series, four in each country; Canada won four, the U.S.S.R. three, and one was tied.

The Economy. While unemployment was disturbingly high in 1972, other indicators revealed a strong Canadian economy. At midyear the gross national product topped $102 billion, exceeding $100 billion for the first time and showing an annual growth in real output of 6%. Commodity trade was healthy, with improvement in the U.S. economy assisting Canadian exports. For the first nine months of 1972, exports came to $14,140,000,000, a gain of 8.4% over the same period in 1971, while imports rose by 19.8% to $13,540,000,000. Canadian automobiles moved to the U.S. under the provisions of the 1965 auto agreement, while forest products, newsprint, iron ore, and oil found good markets in North America and elsewhere abroad. Wheat exports, with large sales recorded to the Soviet Union and China, were also strong.

The labour force continued to grow at a rate higher than in any other nation in the Western world, a reality that underlay all the discussions on employment. The economy provided more jobs each year but its growth could not keep pace with the increase in young people seeking employment. In September the unemployment rate reached 7.1% of the labour force on a seasonally adjusted basis, the highest rate over ten years. Prices also began to show an upward movement in 1972. The consumer price index (1961 = 100) moved from 134.9 in October 1971 to 142 in October 1972, a gain of 5.3%.

The budget for 1972 was presented to the House of Commons on May 8 by Finance Minister Turner. Sizable tax cuts were provided for the manufacturing and processing industries and additional financial support was given to the aged and the disabled. There were no reductions for the average taxpayer on personal income, since Turner regarded such reductions as inflationary. His concern, he stated, was to encourage private enterprise to bring down prices, to renew equipment, and to create much-needed employment. The budget thus gave decided concessions to labour-intensive industries. The freeze on old-age pensions was removed and arrangements were outlined by which payments would be tied to annual increases in the cost of living. The federal government's expenditures for fiscal 1972–73 were estimated at $16,120,000,000 and revenues at $15,670,000,000, leaving a deficit of $450 million. (D. M. L. FARR)

ENCYCLOPÆDIA BRITANNICA FILMS. *The Legend of the Magic Knives* (1970).

Central African Republic

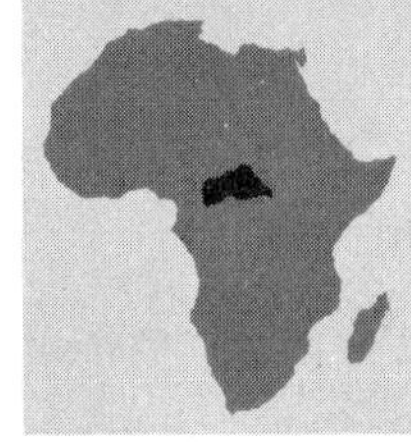

The landlocked Central African Republic is bounded by Chad, Sudan, Congo, Zaire, and Cameroon. Area: 240,377 sq.mi. (622,577 sq.km.). Pop. (1971 est.): 1,637,000. Cap. and largest city: Bangui (pop., 1968, 298,579). Language: French (official). Religion: mainly animist. President and premier in 1972, Jean-Bédel Bokassa.

A congress of the country's sole political party, the Movement for Social Evolution in Black Africa (MESAN), held in Bangui on Feb. 22, 1972, proclaimed Jean-Bédel Bokassa president for life. Bokassa's often authoritarian and unpredictable behaviour during the year presented a striking analogy with his Ugandan counterpart, Gen. Idi Amin.

During the summer President Bokassa decided to conduct an all-out crusade against crime, particularly theft, and personally supervised the beating of convicted thieves with wooden batons. The seriously injured survivors were then exhibited to the population, together with the mangled bodies of those who had died. A decree published by the government prescribed the following penalties for theft: the authorities would slice off a thief's ear for the first offense, the other ear for a second offense, and his right hand for a third; for a fourth offense he would be publicly executed. The savagery of the campaign was the more extraordinary in that a few weeks previously Bokassa had decided to release all those detained in prison.

The beatings at Bangui prison provoked strong protests from UN Secretary-General Kurt Waldheim and from the International League for the Rights of Man. President Bokassa replied by heaping insults on Waldheim in a speech given on the 12th anniversary of his country's independence at Bangui in August, accusing him of meddling in problems that did not concern him while failing to solve those that did. The League received similarly short shrift. President Bokassa congratulated himself on his ability to solve his own problems and concluded his speech by rejoicing in the excellent relations between his country and those represented by the assembled diplomats, particularly France. After a period of tension in 1971–72, Bokassa had indeed pursued a policy of rapprochement with France, and in June he was received by senior members of the French government in Paris.

Despite his increasingly unpredictable behaviour, it was nonetheless true that Bokassa was one of the few African heads of state who could safely leave his country for a period of weeks or even months. However, frequent Cabinet reshuffles—there were major changes in January and May 1972—doubtless served to remind his colleagues of the fragility of their positions. (PHILIPPE DECRAENE)

A.F.P./PICTORIAL PARADE

Prisoners wounded in a crackdown on thievery in the Central African Republic are displayed in Bangui. Pres. Jean-Bédel Bokassa announced rather medieval punishment for thieves: first offense, loss of an ear; second, the other ear; third, the right hand; and fourth, public execution.

CENTRAL AFRICAN REPUBLIC

Education. (1969–70) Primary, pupils 170,048, teachers 2,757; secondary, pupils 7,231, teachers 359; vocational, pupils 1,202; teachers 130; teacher training, students 249, teachers 25. The University of Bangui was founded in 1970.

Finance. Monetary unit: CFA franc, with (Sept. 18, 1972) a parity of CFA Fr. 50 to the French franc and CFA Fr. 255.79 to U.S. $1 (free rate of CFA Fr. 612.37 = £1 sterling). Budget (1971 est.) balanced at CFA Fr. 12,539,000,000.

Foreign Trade. (1970) Imports CFA Fr. 9,492,-000,000; exports CFA Fr. 8,494,000,000. Import sources: France 58%; West Germany 8%; U.S. 6%. Export destinations: France 50%; Israel 14%; Belgium 13%. Main exports: diamonds 41%; cotton 22%; coffee 22%.

Agriculture. Production (in 000; metric tons; 1970; 1969 in parentheses): cassava *c.* 1,000 (*c.* 1,000); peanuts *c.* 85 (75); sweet potatoes *c.* 47 (47); bananas *c.* 170 (*c.* 170); coffee *c.* 9 (11); cotton, lint 20 (22). Livestock (in 000; 1970–71): cattle *c.* 480; pigs *c.* 56; sheep *c.* 65; goats *c.* 525; chickens *c.* 1,-100.

Industry. Diamond production (1970) 494,000 metric carats.

Ceylon (Sri Lanka)

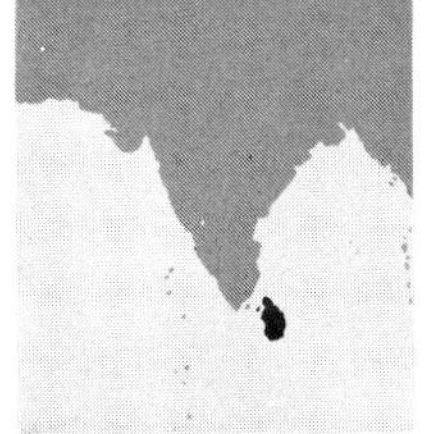

An Asian republic and member of the Commonwealth of Nations, Sri Lanka occupies an island off the southeast coast of peninsular India. Area: 25,332 sq.mi. (65,610 sq.km.). Pop. (1971): 12,711,143, including Sinhalese about 72%; Tamil 21%; Moors 7%. Cap. and largest city: Colombo (pop., 1971, 562,162). Language: Sinhalese (official), Tamil, English. Religion (1971): Buddhist 67%; Hindu 18%; Christian 7%; Muslim 7%. Queen until May 22, 1972, Elizabeth II; governor-general and, from May 22, president, William Gopallawa; prime minister, Mrs. Sirimavo Bandaranaike.

The main event of 1972 was the completion by the Constituent Assembly of the new constitution and its proclamation on May 22, on which day the Republic of Sri Lanka came into being (Sri Lanka is the Sinhalese name for Ceylon). The legislature was to be a unicameral National State Assembly—the Senate having been abolished in September 1971—designated as the supreme instrument of the state, exercising the legislative, executive, and judicial powers "of the People." Sinhalese became the official language, with provision for the use of Tamil in specified cases.

The constitution included a section on "Principles of State Policy" which set a goal of establishing a socialist democracy. A section titled "Fundamental Rights and Freedoms" included freedom of thought and expression, but freedom of the press was not specifically mentioned. The Buddhist religion was to be given "the foremost place." A Constitutional Court with limited powers was established. Provision was

Central America: *see* Inter-American Affairs; *articles on the various countries*

made for the proclamation of a state of emergency when necessary.

No general election was held. The constitution provided that sitting members of the old House of Representatives could keep their seats for a further five years, so the 1972 government (barring an early dissolution) could remain in power for seven years. The normal duration of the National Assembly was to be six years.

There was no repetition of the insurgency of the previous year. About 5,000 of the 15,000 interned were still in detention camps undergoing "rehabilitation," though further releases were expected. Some of the "hard core" were being tried by a special court with summary procedures, while a few insurgents were still holding out in jungle country.

The economy of Sri Lanka showed little improvement. It appeared that the subsidizing of food, particularly rice, and the advanced welfare measures introduced since independence had been more than the economy could bear. In November 1971 Finance Minister N. M. Perera tried to modify the subsidizing of rice, flour, and sugar in his budget proposals, but failed to obtain government approval. He warned Parliament that this would mean continued unemployment (over half a million in 1972). The government attempted to prevent the outflow of money by stricter exchange controls and to reduce the share of foreign interests, mainly British, in the country's trade, though special concessions were made to foreign investors. Henceforth companies trading in Sri Lanka had to be incorporated in the island. A capital levy on companies and individuals was imposed. Power was vested in the state to take over estates and businesses and to obtain a controlling interest in export and agency firms. A ceiling on personal incomes and salaries was proposed amounting to CRs. 2,000 a month after deduction of income tax, wealth tax, and compulsory savings. The acreage of land that a man and his wife could own was limited to 50. All imports and the production and distribution of rice were strictly controlled and in many cases were taken over by the state. The prime minister announced an ambitious five-year plan that was designed to stabilize Sri Lanka's shaky economy.

In June Mrs. Bandaranaike paid a ten-day official visit to China, where she was warmly welcomed. The Soviet Union made strong efforts to retain its influence, though the official section of the Communist Party in the government ran into trouble when it raised objections to certain features of the court set up to try insurgents. (SIDNEY A. PAKEMAN)

CEYLON (SRI LANKA)

Education. (1969–70) Primary, pupils 2,298,200; secondary, pupils 342,300; vocational, pupils (state only) 7,565; primary, secondary, and vocational, teachers 94,113; teacher training, students 5,800, teachers (1967–68) 438; higher, students 14,400, teaching staff (1966–67) 1,064.

Finance. Monetary unit: Ceylonese rupee, with (Sept. 18, 1972) a free rate of CRs. 6.37 to U.S. $1 (par value of CRs. 15.60 = £1 sterling). Gold, SDRs, and foreign exchange, official: (June 1972) U.S. $64 million; (June 1971) U.S. $53 million. Budget (1970–71 est.): revenue CRs. 2,878,000,000; expenditure CRs. 3,089,000,000. Gross national product: (1970) CRs. 12,633,000,000; (1969) CRs. 11,661,000,000. Money supply: (Feb. 1972) CRs. 2,067,000,000; (Feb. 1971) CRs. 1,955,000,000. Cost of living (Colombo; 1963 = 100): (June 1972) 139; (June 1971) 130.

Foreign Trade. (1971): Imports CRs. 1,986,000,000; exports CRs. 1,947,000,000. Import sources (1970): U.K. 14%; China 12%; India 10%; Japan 8%; West Germany 6%; U.S. 6%. Export destinations (1970): U.K. 23%; China 13%; U.S. 7%. Main exports: tea 59%; rubber 16%; coconut products 14%.

Transport and Communications. Roads (1971) 21,496 km. Motor vehicles in use (1971): passenger 88,250; commercial 33,700. Railways: (1970) 1,500 km.; traffic (1969–70) 2,920,000,000 passenger-km., freight 366 million net ton-km. Air traffic (1971): 112,050,000 passenger-km.; freight 2,330,000 net ton-km. Telephones (Dec. 1970) 60,000. Radio receivers (Dec. 1969) 500,000.

Agriculture. Production (in 000; metric tons; 1971; 1970 in parentheses): rice 1,397 (1,616); cassava (1970) 354, (1969) 403; sweet potatoes (1970) 72, (1969) 66; onions (1970) 37, (1969) 35; tea *c.* 218 (212); rubber *c.* 141 (*c.* 159); copra *c.* 195 (183). Livestock (in 000; June 1971): cattle *c.* 1,600; buffalo *c.* 720; sheep *c.* 25; goats *c.* 560; pigs *c.* 110; chickens *c.* 6,900.

Industry. Production (in 000; metric tons; 1970): cement 326; graphite (1969) 11; electricity (kw-hr.) 816,000.

Chad

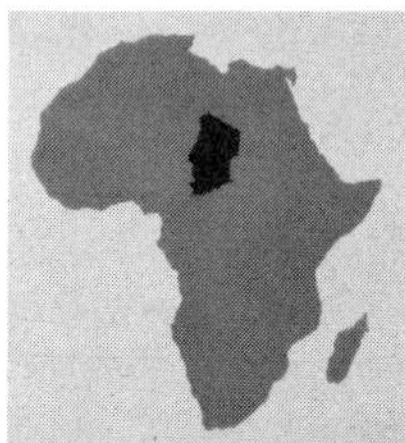

A landlocked republic of central Africa, Chad is bounded by Libya, the Sudan, the Central African Republic, Cameroon, Nigeria, and Niger. Area: 495,752 sq.mi. (1,284,000 sq.km.). Pop. (1972 est.): 3,791,000, including Saras, other Africans, and Arabs. Cap. and largest city: Fort-Lamy (pop., 1972 est., 166,600). Language: French (official). Religion (1964): Muslim 41%; animist 30%; Christian 29%. President and premier in 1972, François Tombalbaye.

On Sept. 1, 1972, French military intervention in Chad officially ended when Gen. Édouard Cortadellas, French military representative and commander in chief of the Franco-Chadian forces, left the country and was not replaced. Col. Félix Malloum, chief of staff of the Chad National Army, took command of the security forces and the Army. In theory, the Chadian army now stood alone against a rebellion that it had managed so far to contain but not entirely to quell; in practice, however, some 2,500 French personnel remained in Chad. In the three years of intervention about 50 French soldiers and more than 3,000 Chadians had lost their lives, and the cost of French military aid was estimated at over Fr. 40 million.

The internal situation seemed to have improved somewhat in January, and French Pres. Georges Pompidou's visit passed without incident. However, in February there were violent clashes between government and rebel forces in the east, and in June a strong rebel force was intercepted close to the capital. Government forces were least in control of the situa-

CHAD

Education. (1969–70) Primary, pupils 162,333, teachers (public only; 1968–69) 2,542; secondary, pupils 8,504, teachers 313; vocational, pupils 903, teachers 73; teacher training, students, 504, teachers 33.

Finance. Monetary unit: CFA franc, with (Sept. 18, 1972) a parity of CFA Fr. 50 to the French franc and CFA Fr. 255.79 to U.S. $1 (free rate of CFA Fr. 612.37 = £1 sterling). Budget (1970 est.): revenue CFA Fr. 11.8 billion; expenditure CFA Fr. 13.5 billion. Cost of living (Fort-Lamy; 1963 = 100): (Feb. 1972) 155; (Feb. 1971) 146.

Foreign Trade. (1970) Imports CFA Fr. 17,216,000,000; exports CFA Fr. 7,715,000,000. Import sources: France 39%; Nigeria 9%; Congo 9%. Export destinations: France 73%; Zaire 10%; Congo 5%. Main export cotton 71%.

tion in the north near the Libyan border, where dissident Toubou factions were receiving diplomatic and military aid from Libya via the Chad National Liberation Front (Frolinat). Indeed, the rebellion seemed to depend for its survival upon that one outside source of aid, and in April President Tombalbaye declared that the government's main aim must be to cut off the "plotters" from their "accomplices."

As the political situation continued to smolder, President Tombalbaye's position became increasingly isolated. Numerous arrests at Fort-Lamy in August included several ministers and ex-ministers. Security measures were further increased, and an action committee was set up to try suspects, who would have no right of appeal against its decisions. A number of French journalists and technical aides were expelled from the country during the course of the year.

In February, President Tombalbaye resigned as president of the Common Organization of Africa, Malagasy, and Mauritius (OCAM), and Chad's relations with other members of the organization deteriorated thereafter. (PHILIPPE DECRAENE)

Chemistry

Physical and Inorganic. *Trace Element Analyses by Atomic Fluorescence Spectroscopy.* Research groups at the University of Florida and Imperial College, London, made notable breakthroughs during the year in the development of atomic fluorescence spectroscopy for the analysis of elements. The method was an extension of atomic absorption spectroscopy, already widely accepted as the main laboratory method in the trace analysis of elements.

In atomic absorption spectroscopy it was necessary to create the atomic line spectra of each element for detection by a separate hollow cathode lamp and to measure the signal attenuation at the centre of the absorption line by using separate monochromators and photodetectors for each element. In atomic fluorescence spectroscopy the detector was placed at right angles to the flame with the source of excitation, and hence a continuous source of illumination could be used for all elements. In common with atomic absorption spectroscopy, atomic fluorescence spectroscopy provided absolute specificity of response, but the new method also offered much greater sensitivity. The intensity of the fluorescence signal was not only proportional to the density of the atomic population for low densities but also proportional to the line intensity of the source. Since the measurement involved an absolute fluorescence signal, instead of a small difference in relatively large signals, electronic signal amplification and integration could be applied. Sensitivities in the range 10^{-1} to 10^{-3} ppm were obtained.

The most recent atomic fluorescence spectrometer used six hollow cathode lamps switched in rapid sequence to simulate fluorescence in a single air-acetylene or nitrous oxide-acetylene flame. The signals were collected by an efficient light-gathering system and stored in a series of integrators prior to simultaneous discharge of the integrated signals in each channel on a printout. With this system monochromators were replaced by simple cutoff filters to isolate the analytical signals, thereby considerably reducing the size of the instrument. Samples could be handled rapidly, and applications included trace metal analyses in natural waters, oils, soil extracts, and alloys.

Heaviest Natural Isotope, Plutonium-244. Toward the end of 1971 research workers at the University of California, working at Los Alamos, N.M., in collaboration with scientists of the General Electric Co., isolated the isotope plutonium-244 from a sample of bastnasite (cerium-bearing) ore. The isotope was the heaviest element found in nature, although it had previously been created artificially in a particle accelerator. Approximately 85 kg. of the ore yielded 8×10^{-15} g. of plutonium-244, which was identified by mass spectrometry.

The discovery of the isotope explained the occurrence in meteorites of trace quantities of the rare gas xenon, which would not have resulted from nuclear reactions in the early history of the solar system. It was postulated that long after the meteorites had cooled the xenon arose from the spontaneous nuclear fission of plutonium-244, which had a half-life of 8×10^7 years.

Surface Structure and Surface Chemistry. Considerable attention was focused during 1972 on the unprecedented increase in knowledge of the physical chemical properties of surfaces, brought about by: (1) the development of semiconductor devices with large surface-to-volume ratios that required a better understanding of the structural and electrical properties of clean (gas-free) surfaces, (2) the availability of ultrahigh vacuum ($< 10^{-8}$ torr) technology as a result of the space exploration programs, and (3) the exploitation of recent experimental techniques for studying surfaces on an atomic scale.

Foremost among the experimental techniques were field-ion microscopy (FIM) and low-energy electron diffraction (LEED). The former method allowed individual atoms in different crystal planes to be distinguished. By creating a large electric field ($\sim 10^9$ v./cm.) at a small crystal tip, scientists ionized helium atoms that were incident on the tip. The positive ions were then radially repelled from the surface and accelerated onto a fluorescent screen, where a greatly magnified image of the crystal tip was displayed. The intensity of the image on any part of the screen was proportional to the number of incident helium atoms. Since the concentration of helium ions produced at each crystal surface depended upon the unique atomic and electron densities in the different surface planes, the various crystal surfaces and atomic positions of the end of the tip could be distinguished by studying the intensity contrast of the fluorescent screen.

The LEED method was even more widely applied to study surface structures. To obtain diffraction from surface atoms, the incident wave of electrons had to satisfy the condition $\lambda \leq d$ where λ is the wavelength of the incident beam and d is the interatomic distance in the surface. In addition, the incident beam had largely to back-diffract from the surface so that the scattered beam reflected the properties of the surface atoms and not those of the bulk solid. Low-energy electrons fulfilled these conditions. In the LEED experiment monochromatic electrons were backscattered from one face of a single crystal, and those that were elastically scattered, which conserve energy on scattering, revealed the diffraction information. These electrons were impinged on a fluorescent screen that displayed the diffraction pattern. The technique was particularly suitable for studying the rearrangement of surface atoms as a function of temperature or exposure to added gases. The results of these studies, mostly involving high-density, low-index (high-sym-

Cheese: *see* Agriculture

Chemical Industry: *see* Industrial Review

metry) crystal faces of monatomic or diatomic solids, revealed that the crystal surfaces which appeared smooth to the naked eye were heterogeneous on a microscopic or submicroscopic scale. (J. A. KERR)

Organic. E. J. Corey of Harvard University published a comprehensive account of progress made in the computer-assisted analysis of complex synthetic problems. The aim of this continuing study is to provide a means of systematic analysis of possible synthetic routes to complex molecules, where these routes are not obvious by analogy with previous syntheses. The object of the synthesis, the target molecule, is taken as the starting point, and the molecular changes which can possibly give rise to that product are then considered. The converse of the chemical reaction is the computer transform, which, operating on the target structure, defines a number of precursors, the most useful of which are simpler or more readily accessible. This procedure eventually generates a synthetic tree, leading ultimately to known starting materials. The examination of the problem thus proceeds in the reverse direction of the chemical synthesis.

The power of the computer program, named LHASA (for Logic and Heuristics Applied to Synthetic Analysis), lies in its ability to present the problem by the drawing of conventional structural formulas on an electrostatic tablet, with continuous communication between operator and machine, while all possible routes for elaborating the carbon skeleton and introducing functional groups are rapidly surveyed. Furthermore, the classification and organization of basic chemical data required by the computer program proved beneficial in advancing the general understanding of the principles of chemical synthesis.

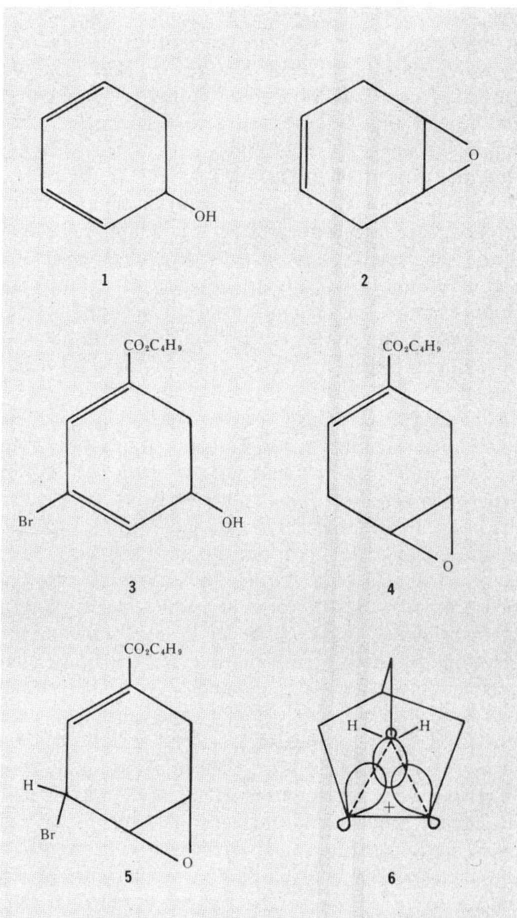

On a more mundane level, two improved syntheses of tetra-substituted alkenes were reported. Compounds containing an active methylene group, such as ethyl cyanoacetate, were converted into alkenes by refluxing (boiling for some time, with the vapour evolved being condensed and returned to the reaction flask) with a slight excess of thionyl chloride:

$$2RCH_2X \rightarrow R(X)C = C(X)R$$

Tetraalkyl ethylenes were shown to be obtainable from nitroparaffins, the sodium salts of which couple on treatment with bromine:

$$R_2CNO_2^- + Br_2 \rightarrow Br^- + R_2C(Br)NO_2:$$
$$R_2C(Br)NO_2 + R_2CNO_2^- \rightarrow (R_2CNO_2)_2.$$

Conversion of dinitroalkane to alkene was achieved with sodium sulfide under the influence of light in a radical-ion chain reaction. The preparation of "benzene hydrate" and some of its derivatives from epoxycyclohexenes was described. The parent molecule, **1,** was obtained by treatment of the epoxide **2** with methyl-lithium. The bromoester **3** was prepared by allylic bromination of the epoxide **4,** one of the resulting position isomers **5** yielding **3** on treatment with potassium *tert*butoxide.

G. A. Olah of Case Western Reserve University, Cleveland, O., added photoelectron spectroscopy to the array of techniques used for the investigation of positively charged organic ions (carbocations). Of particular interest is the discovery that the carbon 1s electron energy is quite sensitive to the degree of positive charge on the atom. (The pair of 1s electrons are lowest in energy in the carbon atom, and are not directly involved in the bonding.) The photoelectron spectrum of the *tert*butyl ion $(CH_3)_3C^+$ showed two peaks with a separation of about 3.9 eV, and intensities in the ratio 1:3, corresponding to the tertiary carbon atom and the methyl carbon atoms, respectively. In the norbornyl cation two distinguishable peaks were also found, but they were separated by only 1.7 eV and had intensities in the ratio 2:7. Clearly, the overall unit charge was divided equally between two atoms, in accordance with the "nonclassical" structure **6.**

Olah also suggested a refinement of the nomenclature relating to carbocations. The term carbonium ion, he said, should be reserved for four- and five-coordinate species of the "nonclassical" type, such as CH_5^+, while the "classical" three-coordinate ions of the type R_3C^+ should be renamed carbenium ions.

A reexamination of the hydration of simple alkenes showed that the reaction was susceptible to general acid catalysis and thus proceeds by direct formation of a carbenium ion without the intervention of a π complex:

$$>C = C< + H^+ \rightarrow \overset{\diagdown}{\underset{\diagup}{C^+}} - \overset{\diagup}{\underset{\diagdown}{C}} - H, \text{ not } \begin{matrix} H^+ \\ \uparrow \\ >C = C< \end{matrix}$$

Proof was also obtained that the active species in the reaction of alkenes with hypochlorous acid is the protonated acid H_2OCl^+.

Molten tetra-n-pentylammonium halides were found to decompose entirely to tripentylamine and n-pentyl halide at 180° C in a vacuum. The rate of decomposition measured was in the order of $Cl^- > Br^- > I^-$ and was considered to represent the relative intrinsic nucleophilic activity of the halide ions uninfluenced by solvation. (J. C. YOUNG)

See also Industrial Review; Life Sciences; Physics.

Chess

The most important event of the year, possibly the most important chess event of the century, was the match for the world championship, July–September 1972, between the titleholder, Boris Spassky of the U.S.S.R., and his challenger, Bobby Fischer (*see* BIOGRAPHY) of the U.S. After innumerable difficulties as to location and conditions, the match started at Reykjavik, Ice., on July 11. Fischer lost the first game and defaulted the second, but thereafter outplayed his adversary to such an extent that he was leading by three points when only half the match had been played. Spassky put up a brave resistance in the second half of the match but could not prevent his opponent from scoring a decisive victory by $12\frac{1}{2}$–$8\frac{1}{2}$. Fischer was the first native-born American to win the world title.

CAMERA PRESS/PICTORIAL PARADE

Boris Spassky (left) and Bobby Fischer during the famous and controversial world championship chess match in Reykjavik, Iceland, in 1972.

Queen's Gambit Declined (sixth game of the World Championship match played at Reykjavik in July 1972)

White	Black	White	Black
R. Fischer	B. Spassky	R. Fischer	B. Spassky
1 P—QB4	P—K3	22 P—K5	R—Kt1
2 Kt—KB3	P—Q4	23 B—B4	K—R1
3 P—Q4	Kt—KB3	24 Q—KR3	Kt—B1(f)
4 Kt—B3	B—K2	25 P—QKt3	P—QR4
5 B—Kt5	O—O	26 P—B5	P×P
6 P—K3	P—KR3	27 R×P	Kt—R2
7 B—R4	P—QKt3(a)	28 R(B1)—B1(g)	Q—Q1
8 P×P	Kt×P	29 Q—Kt3	R—K2
9 B×B	Q×B	30 P—KR4	R(Kt1)—Kt2
10 Kt×Kt	P×Kt	31 P—K6	R(Kt2)—B2
11 R—B1	B—K3	32 Q—K5	Q—K1
12 Q—R4	P—QB4	33 P—R4	Q—Q1
13 Q—R3	R—QB1	34 R(B1)—B2	Q—K1
14 B—Kt5(b)	P—R3	35 R(B2)—B3	Q—Q1
15 P×P	P×P	36 B—Q3	Q—K1
16 O—O	R—R2(c)	37 Q—K4(h)	Kt—B3(i)
17 B—K2	Kt—Q2(d)	38 R×Kt	P×R
18 Kt—Q4	Q—B1	39 R×P	K—Kt1
19 Kt×B	P×Kt	40 B—B4	K—R1
20 P—K4(e)	P—Q5	41 Q—B4	resigns(j)
21 P—KB4	Q—K2		

(a) The Tartakower variation, which has been much favoured by Spassky in the past. This game shows up its weaknesses. (b) Played so as to hinder the development of Black's queen-side pieces. (c) Better than this artificial move is Geller's suggestion 16 . . ., Q—Kt2. (d) Here Petrosian has suggested 17 . . ., P—B5; 18 Q×Q, R×Q; 19 Kt—Q4, Kt—B3. (e) A very strong move after which Black is always struggling. (f) White has a strong attack after 24 . . ., R×P; 25 B×P, Kt—Kt3; 26P—B5. (g) And not 28 R—B7, on account of 28 . . ., Kt—Kt4. (h) Threatening R—B7. (i) Or 37 . . ., R×KP; 38 R—K5! (j) After 41 . . ., K—Kt1 Fischer intended to play 42 Q×RP.

Ruy Lopez (tenth game of the World Championship match played at Reykjavik, August 1972)

White	Black	White	Black
R. Fischer	B. Spassky	R. Fischer	B. Spassky
1 P—K4	P—K4	29 QR—Q1	R—K2(e)
2 Kt—KB3	Kt—QB3	30 B×Pch	R×B
3 B—Kt5	P—QR3	31 Q×Rch	Q×Q
4 B—R4	Kt—B3	32 Kt×Q	B×P(f)
5 O—O	B—K2	33 R×B	K×Kt
6 R—K1	P—QKt4	34 R—Q7ch	K—B3
7 B—Kt3	P—Q3	35 R—Kt7	R—R8ch(g)
8 P—B3	O—O	36 K—R2	B—Q3ch
9 P—KR3	Kt—Kt1(a)	37 P—Kt3	P—Kt5
10 P—Q4	QKt—Q2	38 K—Kt2	P—R4
11 QKt—Q2	B—Kt2	39 R—Kt6	R—Q8
12 B—B2	R—K1	40 K—B3	K—B2(h)
13 P—QKt4	B—KB1	41 K—K2	R—Q4
14 P—QR4	Kt—Kt3	42 P—B4	P—Kt3
15 P—R5	QKt—Q2	43 P—Kt4	P×P
16 B—Kt2	Q—Kt1(b)	44 P×P	P—Kt4
17 R—Kt1	P—B4	45 P—B5	B—K4
18 KtP×P	QP×P	46 R—Kt5	K—B3
19 P×KP	QKt×P	47 R(K4)×P	B—Q5
20 Kt×Kt	Q×Kt	48 R—Kt6ch	K—K4
21 P—QB4	Q—B5	49 K—B3(i)	R—Q1
22 B×Kt	Q×B	50 R—Kt8	R—Q2
23 P×P	KR—Q1(c)	51 R(Kt4)—Kt7	R—Q3
24Q—B1	Q—QB6	52 R—Kt6	R—Q2
25 Kt—B3	Q×P(d)	53 R—Kt6	K—Q4
26 B—Kt3	P×P	54 R×P	B—K4
27 Q—KB4	R—Q2	55 P—B6	K—Q5(j)
28 Kt—K5	Q—B2	56 R—Kt1	resigns

(a) The idea of this Breyer System is to regroup the queen-side pieces, bringing the knight to Q2 and the bishop to QKt2. (b) Placing the queen in line with his KP, after he has played an eventual P—QB4. (c) If 23 . . ., QR—Q1; 24 Q—B1, Q—QB6; 25 B—R4, Q×RP; 26 P×P, Q×B; 27 P×B, and White wins. (d) Better than this decentralization of the queen was P×P followed after R×P by B—R3. (e) And not 29 . . ., R×R; on account of the mating continuation 30 B×Pch, K—R1; 31 Kt—Kt6ch, P×Kt; 32Q—R4. (f) Or 32 . . ., K×Kt; 33 R—Q7ch, with a straightforward win for White. (g) Rather better was 35 . . ., P—Kt5. (h) And here he should have played P—Kt4. (i) Threatening mate by R—K6. (j) Neither 55 . . ., K—K3; 56 R—K8ch, nor 55 . . ., R—KB2; 56 R—Q8ch, K—K3; 57 R—K8ch, is of any avail for Black.

In August 1971 a new record for the number of moves in a game was set when Ristoja (Fin.) and Nykopp (Swed.) played a game of 300 moves in the Finnish open championship at Tampere. Two Soviet players, Alla Kushnir and Nana Alexandria, qualified for the final of the candidates' matches to decide who would challenge the woman world champion, Nona Gaprindashvili (U.S.S.R.). Later Kushnir beat Alexandria, and was herself beaten by Gaprindashvili in May 1972 by $8\frac{1}{2}$–$7\frac{1}{2}$. Spassky showed he was not in good form by only tieing with H. Ree (Neth.) for first place in the Canadian open championship at Vancouver, B.C., in September 1971. The U.S.S.R. championship was won by V. Savon at Leningrad with one round to spare. There was a tie for first place at the Rubinstein Memorial Tournament at Polanica Zdroj, Pol., between H. Pfleger (W.Ger.), and M. Spiridonov (Bulg.). S. Gligoric (Yugos.) won first prize at the German open international championship in Berlin.

Henrique Mecking, a young Brazilian player, was an easy first at the Kostic Memorial Tournament at Vrsac, Yugos. Argentina became Pan-American team champions at the first Pan-American Team Tournament at San Miguel de Tucumán, Arg. At 17, Irina Levitina became the youngest player ever to win the Soviet women's championship, at Sochi in November. The Yugoslav grand master L. Ljubojevic and O. Panno (Arg.) tied for first place at Palma de Mallorca, Spain. A powerfully contested tournament, in which every one of the 18 players was a grand master, was played in Moscow in November and December 1971 as a memorial to Alexander Alekhine. A. Karpov and L. Stein (both U.S.S.R.) tied for first place.

Early in 1972 it was announced that the sixth world correspondence championship had been won by H. Rittner (E.Ger.). There was a tie for the annual Hastings (Eng.) Premier Tournament between V. Korchnoi and Karpov (both U.S.S.R.). The European Junior Championship at Groningen, Neth., was won by Gyula Sax (Hung.). The Hungarian grand master L. Portisch was an easy first at the Hoogoven International Tournament in the Netherlands. The ninth Capablanca Memorial Tournament, at Cienfuegos,

Cuba, was won by A. Lein (U.S.S.R.). Bent Larsen (Den.) scored his first real success after his disastrous defeat at the hands of Fischer the previous year by winning first prize in the Teesside (Eng.), Grandmaster Tournament in April and May. With Fischer absent, the U.S. championship in New York City ended in a triple tie between R. Byrne, L. Kavalek, and S. Reshevsky.

The Clare Benedict International Team Tournament, played at Vienna in May, was won by West Germany. The IBM International Tournament in Amsterdam was won by L. Polugaievsky (U.S.S.R.). The Hungarian A. Adorjan won first prize at Varna and Portisch scored yet another success at the international tournament at Las Palmas in the Canary Islands. At Ohrid, Yugos., the U.S.S.R. beat Yugoslavia. Mecking won the South American Zonal Tournament at São Paulo, Braz., and M. Cuellar (Colombia) won the Central American Zonal at Bogotá. A European zonal tournament at Caorle, Italy, ended in a tie between B. Ivkov and Ljubojevic (both Yugos.). The U.S.S.R. won the World Students Team Championship at Graz in Austria. The British championship at Brighton was won by B. Eley. The U.S.S.R. retained the world team championships for both men and women, at the Skopje (Yugos.) Olympiad.

(HARRY GOLOMBEK)

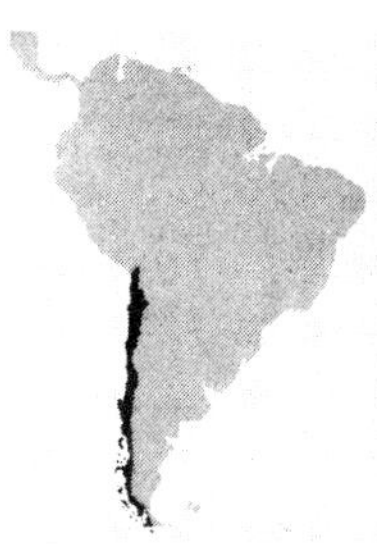

Chile

A republic extending along the southern Pacific coast of South America, Chile has an area of 292,257 sq.mi. (756,945 sq.km.), not including its Antarctic claim. It is bounded by Argentina, Bolivia, and Peru. Pop. (1970): 8,834,820. Cap. and largest city: Santiago (metro. pop., 1970, 2,757,659). Language: Spanish. Religion: predominantly Roman Catholic. President in 1972, Salvador Allende Gossens.

During the two years since a Marxist coalition won the presidency for Allende by a margin of less than 2% with under 37% of the votes cast, Chile encountered severe economic reverses accompanied by inflation, food shortages, and nationwide unrest. Allende had set out to change the economic, social, and political structure of Chile along socialist lines, but the results of his policies were often disastrous as he encountered widespread resistance. The coalition of opposition parties, including the conservative National Party, the left-of-centre Christian Democrats, and much of the Radical Party, controlled both houses of the Chilean Congress. The result was an executive branch at perpetual odds with the legislative bodies, with the armed forces adopting a hands-off policy until and unless the Constitution was violated. Allende abided by the Constitution, but this restraint, coupled with his lifelong Marxist principles, created a situation that prevented either total reform or total adherence to the former social and economic structure.

Most Chileans applauded Allende's expropriation of the foreign-owned (primarily U.S.) copper companies, but the nation in 1972 found that it could no longer rely on copper as its primary cash earner. Among the reasons for the decline of copper were falling prices and production, and the reluctance of world buyers to purchase Chilean copper because the expropriated U.S. firms received no compensation.

Marxist management of the economy also used up the nation's money reserves, which declined from $400 million in 1970 to a minus $70 million in 1972, and raised the inflation rate to a conservatively estimated 35% per year. Allende's government printed millions in new paper escudos that had nothing to back them up, and the value of the national currency plummeted while the money supply increased 100% in each of the previous two years. It appeared that one of Allende's major mistakes in his first months in office was to freeze prices and raise wages up to 45%, while at the same time ordering production to soar. This drove many small businessmen to close their doors.

Food became scarcer and more expensive during the year, and Chile faced the prospect of importing as much as $400 million of it a year. Chilean farmers fell behind consumer demand, mainly because of agrarian reform laws and illegal seizure of farmlands by peasants.

A series of events that culminated in a nationwide crisis began on October 11 when truck owners and drivers throughout Chile went on strike in protest against a government plan to set up a state-run transport system in southern Chile. The truckers said that the plan would lead to complete nationalization of the industry, and they were soon joined in the strike by

CHILE

Education. (1969) Primary, pupils 1,980,815, teachers (public only) 35,588; secondary, pupils 178,887, teachers (1968) 10,242; vocational, pupils 85,987, teachers (1967) 7,398; teacher training, students 2,895; higher (including 8 universities), students 73,025, teaching staff (1965) 8,835.

Finance. Monetary unit: escudo, with (Sept. 18, 1972) a multiple exchange rate system varying from a trade rate of 20 escudos to U.S. $1 (49 escudos = £1 sterling) to a tourist rate of 85 escudos to U.S. $1 (208 escudos = £1 sterling). Gold, SDRs, and foreign exchange, central bank: (Jan. 1972) U.S. $194.6 million; (Jan. 1971) U.S. $345.3 million. Budget (1970 rev. est.): revenue 17,938,000,000 escudos; expenditure 23,832,000,000 escudos. Gross national product: (1970) 90,320,000,000 escudos; (1969) 61,457,000,000 escudos. Money supply: (March 1972) 24,995,000,000 escudos; (March 1970) 13,264,000,000 escudos. Cost of living (Santiago; 1963 = 100): (March 1972) 899; (March 1971) 671.

Foreign Trade. (1970) Imports U.S. $1,005,000,000; exports U.S. $1,246,900,000. Import sources: U.S. 33%; West Germany 10%; Argentina 10%; U.K. 5%. Export destinations: West Germany 20%; Japan 17%; U.S. 13%; U.K. 12%; Italy 8%; France 6%; Argentina 6%. Main exports: copper 73%; iron ore 6%.

Transport and Communications. Roads (1970) 70,549 km. Motor vehicles in use (1970): passenger *c.* 220,000; commercial *c.* 70,000. Railways (1970): state 8,218 km.; other 2,552 km.; traffic (principal railways only) 2,388,000,000 passenger-km., freight 2,533,000,000 net ton-km. Air traffic (1971): 1,112,500,000 passenger-km.; freight 47,393,000 net ton-km. Shipping (1971): merchant vessels 100 gross tons and over 135; gross tonnage 387,810. Telephones (Dec. 1970) 357,000. Radio receivers (Dec. 1970) 1.4 million. Television receivers (Dec. 1970) 500,000.

Agriculture. Production (in 000; metric tons; 1971; 1970 in parentheses): wheat 1,368 (1,307); barley 114 (97); oats (1970) 111, (1969) 95; corn 258 (239); potatoes 836 (684); rapeseed *c.* 64 (70); dry beans 68 (66); onions (1970) *c.* 133, (1969) *c.* 80; sugar, raw value (1971–72) 169, (1970–71) 193; apples (1970) *c.* 65, (1969) *c.* 70; wine *c.* 803 (*c.* 628); beef and veal *c.* 170 (*c.* 170); wool, greasy *c.* 26 (*c.* 26); timber (cu.m.; 1969) 6,900, (1968) 7,100; fish catch (1970) 1,161, (1969) 1,078. Livestock (in 000; 1970–71): cattle *c.* 2,980; sheep *c.* 6,800; pigs *c.* 1,150; horses *c.* 450.

Industry. Production (in 000; metric tons; 1971): crude oil 1,652; coal (1970) 1,382; electricity (kw-hr.; 1970) 7,550,000; iron ore (metal content; 1970) 6,940; pig iron 500; crude steel (ingots) 607; copper (1970) 461; nitrate of soda (1970) 674; manganese ore (metal content; 1970) 11; iodine (1970) 2.2; molybdenum (metal content; 1970) 5.7; silver (troy oz.; 1970) 2,450; gold (troy oz.; 1970) 52; woven cotton fabrics (m.; 1970) 110,000; fish meal (1970) 197.

Child Welfare:
see Education; Social Services

shopkeepers, physicians, dentists, and other business and professional men. Faced with a deteriorating situation that included growing shortages of food and fuel and the imposition of martial law in some areas, all 15 members of Chile's Cabinet resigned on October 31 in order to give Allende a free hand in seeking ways to end the conflict. On November 2 Allende named a new Cabinet, which included three high-ranking military officers; the Army throughout the strike had refused right-wing entreaties to stage a military coup.

The new interior minister, Gen. Carlos Prats Gonzalez, announced in a nationwide broadcast on November 5 that the strikers must return to work the next day or face "severe action." He promised that specific professional grievances would be dealt with. Leaders of the walkout ordered their supporters to return to work, and on November 6 the strike, which had cost Chile approximately $150 million, ended.

A major reason for the settlement of the strike was the commitment by the opposing groups to wait for the forthcoming national elections and abide by their result. The Chilean electorate in March 1973 was to vote on the entire Chamber of Deputies and about half of the Senate. Allende's Unidad Popular coalition of Marxists and Socialists controlled neither house in 1972, and all political indicators were that they would be fortunate to obtain 28% of the vote in 1973. Thus, the prospect was that the opposition parties would have a stronger grip on Congress than in 1972 and that the Allende regime would stand repudiated. Allende would also continue to face the threat from his own extremist followers, who were impatient with his attempts to rule as a Marxist within the framework of democracy and who fomented much unrest during the year. (JEREMIAH A. O'LEARY)

China

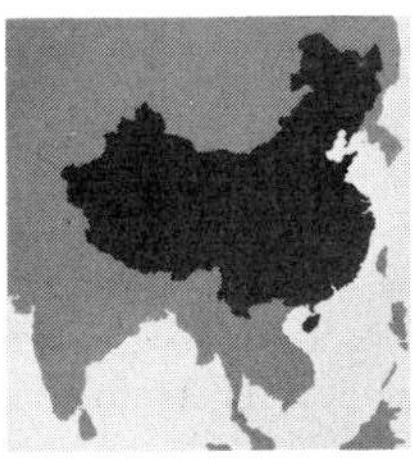

The most populous country in the world and the third largest in area, China is bounded by the U.S.S.R., Mongolia, North Korea, North Vietnam, Laos, Burma, India, Bhutan, Sikkim, Nepal, Pakistan, and Afghanistan. From 1949 the country has been divided into the People's Republic of China (Communist) on the mainland and on Hainan and other islands, and the Republic of China (Nationalist) on Taiwan (see TAIWAN). Area: 3,691,-500 sq.mi. (9,561,000 sq.km.), including Tibet but excluding Taiwan. Pop. of the People's Republic (1971 est.): 787,176,000. Cap.: Peking (metro. pop., 1970 est., 7.6 million). Largest city: Shanghai (metro. pop., 1970 est., 10.8 million). Language: Chinese (varieties of the Mandarin dialect). Chairman of the Communist Party in 1972, Mao Tse-tung; premier, Chou En-lai.

In February 1972, U.S. Pres. Richard Nixon made a historic visit to China to seek normalization of Sino-U.S. relations. He came at the invitation of Premier Chou En-lai and with the approval or acquiescence of Chairman Mao. The visit was concurrent with the open attack on the radical left and the high command of the People's Liberation Army that followed the mysterious disappearance of Defense Minister Lin Piao, formerly Mao's close comrade-in-arms and heir designate. These constituted the most significant events of the year, signifying a major shift from a doctrinaire to a pragmatic approach in internal affairs and foreign policies. Because of continuous tensions on the long Sino-Soviet borders, the internal leadership struggle, and massive problems of reconstruction and modernization, China sought rapprochement with the West while at the same time relaxing its rigid regimentation and control over the people. This reflected Chou's ascending power and influence in the Communist Party and government, and a receding of Mao's ideology and leadership.

While the collective leadership of the Central Committee of the party was seriously weakened by the purge of Lin Piao and his close associates, the reorganization and restaffing of the administrative structure under Chou entered its final phase. During the year the unwieldy State Council, composed of 40 ministries, 11 commissions, and 21 special agencies, was reduced to 17 ministries, 3 commissions, and 15 special agencies. Li Hsien-nien, Premier Chou's right-hand man, continued as first deputy premier. After the death of Ch'en Yi (longtime foreign minister), Chi P'eng-fei, a senior vice-minister, became minister of foreign affairs.

Following the disappearance of Lin Piao in 1971, Yeh Chien-ying (*see* BIOGRAPHY), an old and close associate of Chou and vice-chairman of the Military Affairs Commission of the party, returned to the limelight in charge of the Ministry of Defense. In the wake of the downfall of Lin Piao and several top military commanders, steps were taken to lessen the influence of the military in civil affairs.

Internal Politics. Although the political crisis and turmoil brought about by the Cultural Revolution of the mid- and late 1960s was officially concluded with the convocation of the ninth Communist Party Congress in 1969, factional struggle for political preeminence in the party and government continued during 1972. The task of rebuilding both remained far from complete.

In the 26 provinces and 3 special municipalities, the tripartite Revolutionary Committees (the Army, the party, and the Red Guards), which had been created as supervisory and administrative organs during the Cultural Revolution, became dominated by military leaders. When all the 29 party committees were finally established in August 1971, two-thirds of the 29 first-secretary posts were filled by military men. As military representatives thus assumed leadership in provincial party and administrative organs, the Army under Lin Piao emerged as the dominant force in China. Its overbearing presence in national policy eventually aroused opposition from the Mao-Chou civilian hierarchy. To wrest political and administrative power from the military leaders, the civilian hierarchy began to attack Lin and other top military officers. In particular, Lin was accused of opposing Mao's revolutionary line and policy and of plotting against Mao himself. Following the purge of Lin and his associates in mid-1971, the removal of their supporters and the winning of the loyalty of all regional military commanders became an urgent issue in the civilian control over the military.

The disappearance of Lin, his wife (Yeh Chun, also a Politburo member), and several high-ranking military officers, presumably in a plane crash in Mongolia in September 1971, was first confirmed in a secret party document of Jan. 13, 1972. It did not appear in the press until July. During the summer Mao chose to break the official silence by mentioning Lin's conspiracy and unsuccessful attempt to flee to Moscow to Prime Minister Sirimavo Bandaranaike of Sri Lanka

WIDE WORLD

U.S. Pres. Richard Nixon (left) and Chairman Mao Tse-tung shake hands at the moment of their historic first meeting on Feb. 21, 1972.

(Ceylon) and French Foreign Minister Maurice Schumann. On July 28 authorities in Peking formally sealed Lin's fate by acknowledging for the first time that Lin was among those killed in the plane crash after an abortive coup against Mao.

Concurrently with the attack on leaders of the military and civilians of the extreme left, a campaign was begun to rehabilitate veteran senior officials and technicians who had been ousted from their positions in the party, government, and institutions. Many senior officials were either permitted to return to their original jobs or given new positions, and a number of prominent victims reappeared in public. Meanwhile, the adjustment in foreign policy and political attitudes was apparently extended to the daily life of the people. For instance, a number of books that had been banned during the Cultural Revolution were released for sale, and the publication of comics, previously condemned as bourgeois, also received official approval. The learning of foreign languages was encouraged again, and English-language courses were introduced in the curricula of some primary schools. Examinations, formerly denounced as reactionary, were restored in the educational system. As a means of encouraging peasant initiative and production, material incentive schemes, which had been criticized as capitalistic during the Cultural Revolution, were reintroduced to compensate diligence and productivity.

Foreign Relations. Internal developments in 1972 did not affect China's diplomatic offensive to end its international isolation by stressing peaceful coexistence and conventional diplomatic ties with as many nations as possible. Diplomatic initiatives were undertaken with three immediate purposes in view: to establish relations with all the major industrial powers; to bid for leadership in the so-called third world of less developed nations; and to weaken and isolate the Chinese Nationalist government in Taiwan.

The most important event of the year in China's foreign affairs was the summit conference between Chou En-lai and President Nixon, and this was followed by negotiations between Chou and Prime Minister Kakuei Tanaka (*see* BIOGRAPHY) of Japan. The results of these summit meetings and the talks between President Nixon and Soviet leader Leonid Brezhnev in Moscow and between Nixon and Tanaka in Hawaii created a four-way balance of power in the Pacific with the United States in the centre of the new relationship and a reshaping of alignments throughout the world.

The diplomatic offensive gathered momentum in 1972 with several heads of government paying state visits; with more than two dozen delegations led by Cabinet ministers arriving for diplomatic, trade, and economic negotiations; and with numerous foreign visitors passing through Peking, including many citizens of countries that had no diplomatic relations with China. In addition, more than a dozen Chinese military, economic, trade, and technical missions were sent to some 15 countries in various parts of the world, and Chinese table-tennis players and other athletic teams visited approximately 50 countries around the globe.

Since the admission of China to the UN in late October 1971, replacing Nationalist China, the number of countries that had established or reopened diplomatic relations with Peking rose from 54 to over 80 by late 1972. About two dozen of these nations entered diplomatic relations with Peking following President Nixon's announcement of July 1971 concerning his journey to Peking, and over half of them extended recognition during 1972. Of the European countries only Spain did not recognize China. After being represented for more than two decades by chargés d'affaires, the United Kingdom and China agreed in March to exchange ambassadors. To strengthen Sino-British relations British Foreign Secretary Sir Alec Douglas-Home visited Peking toward the end of October.

Sino-U.S. Relations. To pave the way for a fruitful summit meeting in Peking, President Nixon had adopted a series of measures relaxing trade restrictions with China in 1971. On Feb. 14, 1972, just one week prior to his arrival in China, a further relaxation was announced, putting China on the same trade footing with the U.S. as the Soviet Union. In his foreign policy report to the Congress on February 9, Nixon outlined the principles that would guide him in his summit talks and stressed the importance of seeking good relations between the two countries "for the sake of our two peoples and the people of the world."

On February 21 Nixon, accompanied by U.S. Secretary of State William Rogers and Henry Kissinger, arrived in Peking. When the president arrived at the Peking airport he received a rather subdued welcome from Chinese officials, and people were kept away from the airport. However, shortly after his arrival and before the official banquet in the evening, Nixon made his first official call on Chairman Mao at his residence. Then the interview was widely and enthusiastically publicized in China, and the Chinese people became fully aware of the importance which their leaders attached to the Nixon visit.

During his five days in Peking, Nixon held lengthy discussions with Premier Chou on problems confronting the two countries in their search for peaceful solutions. The talks continued in Hangchow and Shanghai on February 26 and 27. On February 27, the day before Nixon left China, he and Chou reached agreement on a joint communiqué issued in Shanghai.

From the communiqué it could be surmised that views were frankly exchanged on such important issues as the Indochina war, Taiwan, and relations with

South Korea, Japan, and South Asia, but no fundamental disagreements were resolved. The most difficult question in normalizing relations was the U.S. diplomatic tie with Nationalist China in Taiwan. From the separate statements in the communiqué it became clear that the U.S. no longer challenged Peking's firm one-China position. The U.S., however, reaffirmed its interest in a peaceful settlement of the Taiwan question, and promised to withdraw U.S. forces and military installations from Taiwan as tensions in the area diminished. While the U.S. gave no indication of any intention to withdraw its recognition from Nationalist China and abrogate the 1954 mutual-defense treaty with Taiwan, Peking refrained from specific demands on the subject. Furthermore, at the summit talks Nixon seemed to have convinced Chou that the U.S. had no aggressive designs on China, while Chou tacitly agreed that Peking would not use force to "liberate" Taiwan.

Although fundamental differences between the two powers persisted, both governments desired to co-operate in areas that were mutually beneficial. To further broaden the understanding between the two peoples, agreement was reached on taking the following steps: (1) maintenance of official contacts by periodic ambassadorial meetings and by sending a senior U.S. representative to Peking from time to time; (2) development of bilateral trade; and (3) development of scientific, cultural, athletic, and journalistic exchanges. At Nixon's suggestion, Chou invited two U.S. senators, Mike Mansfield and Hugh Scott, to visit China. Accompanied by their wives and aides, the senators took an extensive tour of China from April 18 to May 3, and discussed the Indochina question and other matters with Chou and other officials. House leaders Hale Boggs and Gerald Ford and their wives also visited China from June 26 to July 5. In the meantime, ambassadorial contacts in Paris and at the UN were established.

The two senators' presence in Peking coincided with an announcement that China and North Vietnam had just concluded a supplementary military and economic aid agreement for 1972. Peking expressed deep concern over the U.S. bombing of North Vietnam's rail and highway links with China and the mining or blockade of North Vietnamese ports. Obviously seeking China's support in the efforts to end the Vietnam war, Kissinger visited Peking on June 19–23 for the fourth time within a year and held secret talks with Chou En-lai. Although the official statement on the meeting was confined to cultural measures and made no mention of the Vietnam war, events confirmed that Peking did not wish to risk direct military confrontation with the U.S. in Vietnam.

The program of cultural exchange began with the arrival of a Chinese table-tennis team in April for a series of matches in the U.S. A stream of U.S. professors, scientists, journalists, artists, and physicians visited China during the year. In September, contacts between the two countries were stepped up with the tour of the U.S. by a group of Chinese newspaper editors and with the extended visit to China by members of the American Society of Newspaper Editors. To return a visit by individual U.S. physicians, a group of Chinese doctors arrived in New York in mid-October for a one-month tour of medical schools and research centres in the United States.

Indicating improved trade relations, dozens of U.S. business representatives attended the Canton trade fair in April for the first time and concluded their first direct business deals. Subsequently, the Boeing Co. was granted an export license to sell ten 707 jetliners to China for $125 million, and in September the U.S. Department of Agriculture confirmed a private sale of 15 million bu. of wheat to China. On October 27, President Nixon announced the sale of 300,000 tons of corn valued at $18 million to Peking. These transactions represented the first direct trade between the two countries in two decades. The ban on travel to China by U.S. ships and planes was also eased.

Sino-Japanese Relations. The Nixon-Chou summit talks hastened the Japanese decision to take independent action to establish diplomatic relations with China. Peking and Tokyo had maintained important trade and extensive cultural dealings, but because Japan had signed an advantageous peace treaty with Nationalist China in 1952, the Japanese government had remained friendly with the Nationalists. Prior to the announcement of his retirement in June, Prime Minister Eisaku Sato repeatedly offered to go to Peking to seek a rapprochement, but the overtures were spurned. Premier Chou made it abundantly clear that his government would not deal with Sato, and insisted on three stiff conditions for establishing diplomatic relations between China and Japan: recognition of Peking as the sole legitimate government of all China; affirmation of the status of Taiwan as an integral part of China; and abrogation of the Japan-Nationalist China peace treaty.

With Sato's retirement, Peking moved quickly to initiate the process of normalizing Sino-Japanese relations. On July 7, the day after Tanaka was sworn in

CHINA

Education. Primary, pupils (1959–60) 90 million, teachers (1964) *c.* 2.6 million; secondary (1958–59), pupils 8,520,000; vocational (1958–59), pupils 850,000; teacher training, students (1958–59) 620,000; higher (1962–63), students 820,000.

Finance. Monetary unit: jen min piao or people's bank dollar, also called the yuan, with (Sept. 18, 1972) an official exchange rate of 2.25 yuan to U.S. $1 (5.44 yuan = £1 sterling). Budget (1960 est.; latest published) balanced at 70,020,000,000 yuan. Latest five-year plan began in 1971. Gross domestic product (1970 est.) U.S. $130 billion.

Foreign Trade. (1970) Imports *c.* U.S. $2.2 billion; exports *c.* U.S. $2,010,000,000. Import sources: Japan *c.* 25%; West Germany *c.* 7%; Canada *c.* 6%. Export destinations: Hong Kong *c.* 23%; Japan *c.* 13%; Singapore *c.* 6%. Main exports: textiles and clothing, metal ores, meat products, hides and skins, tungsten.

Transport and Communications. Roads (1970) *c.* 800,000 km. (including *c.* 300,000 km. all-weather). Motor vehicles in use (1969): passenger *c.* 60,000; commercial *c.* 400,000. Railways: (1970) *c.* 35,000 km.; traffic (1959) 45,670,000,000 passenger-km., freight 265,260,000,000 net ton-km. Air traffic (1960): 63,882,000 passenger-km.; freight 1,967,000 net ton-km. Inland waterways (including Yangtze River; 1970) *c.* 160,000 km. Shipping (1970): merchant vessels 100 gross tons and over 265; gross tonnage 1,022,256. Telephones (1951) 255,000. Radio receivers (Dec. 1965) *c.* 11.5 million. Television receivers (Dec. 1969) *c.* 300,000.

Agriculture. Production (in 000; metric tons; 1970; 1969 in parentheses): rice *c.* 102,000 (*c.* 95,000); corn *c.* 30,000 (*c.* 26,000); wheat *c.* 31,000 (*c.* 28,500); barley *c.* 19,000 (*c.* 17,500); potatoes *c.* 35,000 (*c.* 31,000); soybeans (1971) *c.* 11,500, (1970) *c.* 11,430; peanuts *c.* 2,650 (*c.* 2,350); cotton, lint *c.* 1,518 (*c.* 1,518); jute *c.* 500 (*c.* 500); rapeseed *c.* 990 (*c.* 940); sugar, raw value (1971–72) *c.* 4,030, (1970–71) *c.* 3,900; tobacco *c.* 785 (*c.* 776); tea *c.* 172 (*c.* 169); pears *c.* 900 (*c.* 850); oranges *c.* 700 (*c.* 670); timber (cu.m.; 1970) 171,000, (1969) 167,000; fish catch (1960) 5,800, (1959) 5,020. Livestock (in 000; 1970–71): cattle *c.* 63,150; sheep *c.* 71,000; pigs *c.* 270,000; goats *c.* 57,500; buffalo *c.* 29,500; horses *c.* 7,400; asses *c.* 11,600.

Industry. Fuel and power (in 000; metric tons; 1971): coal (including lignite) *c.* 325,000; coke (1970) 18,000; crude oil 25,500; electricity (kw-hr.; 1960) *c.* 58,500,000. Production (in 000; metric tons; 1971): iron ore (metal content) 27,000; pig iron 22,000; crude steel (1971) 21,000; lead (1970) *c.* 100; copper (1970) *c.* 100; aluminum (1970) *c.* 130; tungsten concentrates (oxide content; 1970) *c.* 10; cement *c.* 10,000; salt (1970) *c.* 16,000; sulfuric acid (1966) *c.* 2,500; chemical fertilizers 17,000; cotton yarn (1968) 1,453; cotton fabrics (m.; 1970) 7,500,000.

as prime minister, Premier Chou indicated his willingness to open talks on the establishment of diplomatic relations. The new Japanese government expressed its willingness to accept the first two conditions but found it difficult to abrogate the peace treaty with Nationalist China before entering into negotiations with Peking. Peking indicated a flexible attitude by ceasing its denunciations of the U.S.-Japanese security treaty and U.S. bases in Japan. At a press conference on July 19, Tanaka said that he was prepared to negotiate a new Sino-Japanese relationship. In a formal statement welcoming Tanaka's announcement, Chou omitted mention of his third condition for opening negotiations. On August 7, three weeks before the Tanaka-Nixon summit in Hawaii, Tanaka declared that he would go to Peking to seek diplomatic relations with China.

Accompanied by approximately 70 officials and many newsmen, Tanaka arrived in Peking on September 25. After some hard bargaining the two premiers reached agreements on the basic issues, and then Tanaka was granted an audience with Chairman Mao on the evening of September 27, implying Mao's approval of the negotiations. On September 29, Chou and Tanaka signed a joint communiqué immediately establishing diplomatic relations between the two countries. The communiqué fully incorporated Chou's first two conditions for entering the diplomatic relationship but made no reference to the peace treaty with the Nationalists. The two countries agreed to exchange ambassadors as soon as possible.

Sino-Soviet Relations. The unsettled Sino-Soviet border problems, the conflict with the Soviet Union over ideology and leadership in the Communist and third world countries, as well as fear of a Soviet attempt to contain and isolate China were believed to be the external factors that prompted Peking to move toward conciliation with the U.S. and Japan. Although the U.S.S.R. took no public position against the U.S.-Chinese rapprochement, the Soviet press railed at Peking for "plotting with Imperialists." In an important address to the Trade Union Congress in Moscow on March 20, Soviet leader Leonid Brezhnev expressed the hope that forthcoming U.S.-Soviet talks would help strengthen world peace and stated that the Soviet Union had made specific proposals to China on navigation and the settlement of border issues.

Negotiations on Sino-Soviet border issues resumed in Moscow in late March, while separate talks on the navigation of border rivers also took place in the Soviet capital. Tensions between the two Communist giants began to ease, and in June a new Sino-Soviet trade agreement was concluded. During the second week of July, however, the chief Soviet negotiators left for Moscow for consultation and did not return to Peking until mid-October. Early in August the Soviet government newspaper *Izvestia* attacked a new Chinese atlas which claimed for China approximately 600,000 sq.mi. of Soviet territory acquired originally from China under the tsarist regimes. This was a clear indication that the border negotiation had become deadlocked again, and the exchange of charges and accusations intensified thereafter.

Early in September there were press reports on the movement of additional Soviet troops toward the frontier with China. On October 1 the Chinese People's Republic celebrated its 23rd anniversary with a denunciation of Soviet schemes to encircle China as more deceitful and dangerous than old-line imperialism. The first fighting along the border since 1969 broke out in late November. According to a Soviet report a force of Chinese crossed the Soviet frontier into Kazakhstan about November 25 and killed five Soviet soldiers and several shepherds. The Soviets reportedly captured a Chinese prisoner, whom Peking later disowned and called a "bandit." (HUNG-TI CHU)

See also Propaganda; Taiwan.

ENCYCLOPÆDIA BRITANNICA FILMS. *China: A Portrait of the Land* (1967); *China's Industrial Revolution* (1967); *China's Villages in Change* (1967).

The highly political dance drama "Red Detachment of Women" was seen by Pres. Richard Nixon and Mrs. Nixon during the president's unprecedented China visit in 1972.

WIDE WORLD

Cities and Urban Affairs

National governments in all parts of the world, as well as the United Nations, showed great concern for urban problems in 1972. A main topic of discussion at the UN's June Conference on the Human Environment in Stockholm was the planning and management of human settlements for environmental quality. The future health and well-being of humanity, it was pointed out, depended on the ability of urban governments to reduce and eliminate such problems as slums, pollution, congestion, noise, unemployment, poverty, the inability to dispose of wastes, shortages of water and energy, and biological and general health hazards.

A number of changes at national and international levels were necessary, it was generally acknowledged, if urban degradation was to be halted. One of the major causes of the urban crisis was the overriding importance given by governments at all levels to economic development, too often at the expense of social needs and environmental values. That this one-sided attitude was undergoing change was evidenced by the emphasis on noneconomic targets set for the UN's Second Development Decade and by the recommendations that came out of the Stockholm conference with regard to governmental policies and actions concerning improved living conditions in human settlements of all sizes.

Political Consensus and Citizen Participation. A major factor in the success of any urban policy was the degree of political consensus involved. As political consensus could best be obtained by involving citizens in public affairs, increased participation in urban decision-making was being encouraged. Traditional methods of keeping citizens informed about local affairs continued to be used, but urban officials and administrators were also initiating new opportunities for broadening communication with citizens, such as providing times at which citizens could present complaints and suggestions, holding discussion and information meetings in neighbourhoods, undertaking demand surveys and public opinion polls, and appointing ombudsmen to protect citizens from the results of bureaucratic behaviour and unfair treatment.

In the Netherlands some urban governments granted powers to representatives of nonpolitical associations, such as youth councils, to draft policy recommendations on issues relevant to their sphere of interest and to settle disputes arising among groups within their area of concern. In other countries, autonomy had been granted to submunicipal units, or neighbourhood governments, in the planning and maintenance of roads, recreational facilities, cultural amenities, and other local matters. Urban governments were also establishing service centres or neighbourhood city halls to provide focal points for information and help for people who would not attempt to solicit these at a far-off city hall or at the various city departments.

Again, city governments were providing funds, facilities, and technical assistance to stimulate the formation of functional councils to deal with, for example, youth activities, sports programs, care of the aged, etc. They also were giving support to citizen and neighbourhood groups interested in improving local social and environmental conditions as well as to special community work projects, experiments in new forms of living, and the like. The less developed countries particularly were seeing the need for community development officers to promote civic education and encourage self-help projects.

One way in which local administrators and representatives were attempting to bridge the gap between themselves and their citizens was through the use of local radio and television facilities. Through improved technology, particularly the development of cable broadcasting, it was anticipated that there could be far-reaching effects on local government and citizen participation in decision-making. Cable television held particularly high promise for minority interests within an urban area and for widespread neighbourhood programming. Once two-way channels were available, further possibilities for the use of cable television would arise. The use of two-way channels could permit direct questioning of local officers and representatives, instant referenda on priorities and policies, and instant communication with special interest groups or individual neighbourhoods. Administrative efficiency and economy could result from the use of cable television for employment services, in-service training programs for municipal personnel, and public surveillance of property. (*See* TELECOMMUNICATIONS: *Special Report.*)

Environmental Protection and Improvement. During 1972 research into the causes of the various kinds of pollution that plague urban areas continued. While many problems of environmental pollution required national and international action, there were, nevertheless, steps that could be taken by local governments to lessen adverse effects on the urban environment.

To curb air pollution, local governments could:

Adopt higher standards for emission than those prescribed in national or state legislation, as permitted by law;

Make permits for new or expanded industrial building dependent on meeting clean air requirements and, where such procedures were in existence, improve their control and supervision, if necessary by attracting expert personnel;

Establish systems for monitoring air pollution and provide for the possibility of forbidding industrial emissions entirely under adverse weather conditions;

Encourage the use of low sulfur- and lead-content fuels, if possible by tax incentives;

Forbid open burning;

Equip municipal buildings and installations with natural gas instead of coal and oil burners;

Encourage the use of public transportation rather than private automobiles by closing city centres to traffic;

Equip municipal vehicles and public buses with antipollution devices.

Measures to curb the discharge of harmful effluents into municipal sewage systems and public waters might include:

Taxing industries in accordance with the quantities of waste they discharge;

Imposing standards for maximum permissible levels of pollution;

Making the construction or expansion of industrial plants conditional upon approval of a water quality compliance plan;

Banning the sale or use of such pollutants as phosphate-based detergents or certain pesticides.

In order to reduce the amounts of waste that urban areas must dispose of, city governments could:

Set an example by purchasing products that were recycled or biodegradable;

Operate collection centres for glass and plastics;

If permitted by state or national law, ban the sale of nonreturnable containers or tax packaging materials in general.

Local noise abatement proposals could include:

Slowing down and diverting traffic from busy streets;

Closing off streets in order to create islands of silence;

Prohibiting the playing of portable radios and record players in some or all public places;

Setting an example by purchasing equipment incorporating noise control features.

BARTON SILVERMAN/THE NEW YORK TIMES

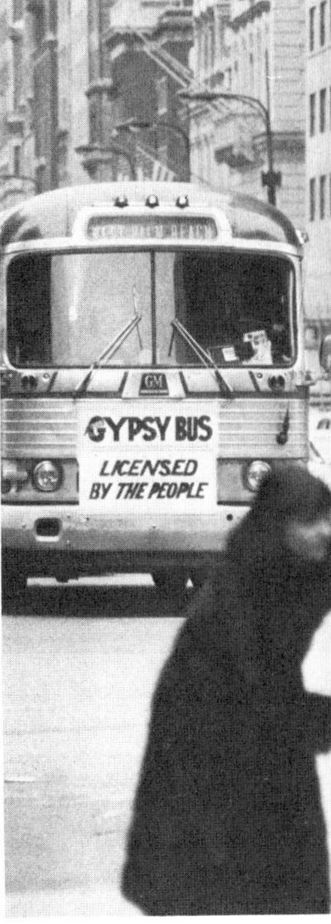

New York taxi drivers dramatized their opposition to proposed licensing of gypsy cabs by chartering a gypsy bus, shown above on Fifth Avenue on Feb. 17, 1972.

Christian Church (Disciples of Christ): *see* Religion

Christianity: *see* Religion

Christian Science: *see* Religion

Chromium: *see* Mining

Churches of Christ: *see* Religion

Church Membership: *see* Religion

Church of England: *see* Religion

Church of Scotland: *see* Religion

Cigars and Cigarettes: *see* Tobacco

Cinema: *see* Motion Pictures

Circuses: *see* Fairs and Shows

WIDE WORLD

Wisely or not, New York City may spend millions obliterating subway graffiti that in the scene at right might be mistaken for a creative outburst of a pop artist.

National Associations of Local Government. During the year, national associations of local authorities in many countries continued to provide a variety of advisory and technical services to their members and to defend the interests of local authorities collectively vis-à-vis central government departments and agencies. Particularly in Western Europe, where most national associations were established between 1890 and 1925, the associations had the respect of both their members and the central governments for their efforts in promoting municipal interests. In most other countries, especially those independent in 1955 or later, these associations had not yet reached their full potential.

Most national associations derived the major part of their income from membership fees, which usually were supplemented with subsidies from state and central governments, donations, sales of publications, and fees for services performed. The associations in Trinidad and Tobago and in the Dominican Republic were financed entirely by the central government, a method that might well limit the kinds of activities an association could carry out. The most common of these activities were advisory, primarily the giving of legal advice in general or on particular laws and ordinances. Associations may also draw up model laws and ordinances which members can adopt in toto or adapt to their particular needs. Associations in Denmark and the Netherlands helped share the expenses of a local government's lawsuit when it involved an issue of importance to all members. Advice was also given on technical and financial aspects of urban affairs.

While pursuing their interests vis-à-vis central governments, local government associations kept watch on legislation affecting local affairs, monitored activities of ministries and other agencies that might affect local authorities, drew up draft legislation or gave advice on proposed laws and regulations, ensured that local government was represented on central and state government commissions and committees, and in other ways brought to the attention of the central authorities matters of interest to their members. Finally, the associations provided a variety of cooperative services that brought savings to their members and helped standardize local government practices and procedures.

The national associations often had close links with special-purpose bodies which, in many instances, they had been instrumental in establishing. The Finnish Association of Cities, for example, appointed some of the members of the governing bodies of the Municipal Pension Institute and the Finnish Hospital Federation. In the U.K. local government associations had helped establish and were financing such organizations as the Local Authorities Mutual Investment Trust, the Local Authority Management Services and Computer Committee, the Local Government Information Office, and the Local Government Training Board. The German local government associations created the Joint Municipal Centre for Administrative Efficiency in Cologne; the Dutch Union established the Institute of Public Administration, whose courses for local government personnel were officially recognized by the central government. Israel's Union of Local Authorities was a shareholder in the municipal bank and a sewerage company.

National associations did not always have the strength their supporters might wish, often because of lack of funds, a universal complaint of local governments. Moreover, in many countries local government did not have the support it required. There were signs, however, that central governments, especially in the world's most urbanized areas, were coming to a realization of the role that local government could play in national development. This, in turn, could lead to increased national support of local government associations.

Population Growth and Distribution. Degeneration of urban environment was often linked to the lack of national policies on population growth and distribution. Cities could increase urban services and initiate environmental improvements, but these would meet with only limited success if the migration to cities continued at the rate of past decades. When it was considered that the world population in the year 2000 was expected to reach 7,000,000,000, three-quarters of whom would live in the less developed countries with 45% of their populations in urban areas, and one-quarter in developed countries where 80% would be city dwellers, it was clear that action at national levels was necessary. Many countries launched birth control programs, with only limited success; even less effective were efforts to guide the distribution of population by programs aimed at improving conditions in rural areas or at providing inducements to counter the appeal of urban areas.

One country that attempted a policy of population dispersal was Israel. In 1948, when the number of immigrants to the country threatened to be larger than the existing population, the national government was faced with the possibility of the development of enormous squatter settlements on the outskirts of cities along the western coast, with all the social and environmental consequences such a development would entail. Moreover, there was the necessity of settling sparsely populated regions in order to overcome regional imbalance of development, to exploit natural resources in desert areas, and to establish the missing level in the governmental structure, the medium and small town. The theory behind the plans for development towns in Israel was that there be a "central place" that would dominate its rural hinterland and serve as a regional centre. In practice, this met with mixed success. The small size of the country and its good road system meant that rural areas were already within easy reach of urban areas. Also, much of the rural area had already reached a higher degree of development than could be offered by the new towns. It became apparent that the new towns would not become commercial and service centres, and a strong drive to attract industry meant that many became single-industry towns, with all the hazards this entailed for economic stability. Future implementation of the population dispersal policy in Israel, therefore, will undergo modification, with fewer new towns being built, but of a larger size.

Romania, too, had a government policy of limiting the size of urban areas, initiated at a time when the country was 40% agricultural. An overall survey indicating natural regions, soils, forests, lines of communication, and areas of settlement was developed to serve as the basis for industrialization plans and for limiting the growth of urban centres. In other countries new towns had been developed for a variety of reasons other than population dispersal. In the U.S.S.R., for example, new cities were being built in Siberia to provide industrial centres near sources of raw materials. A number of new cities were being developed in Poland to provide a good geographic distribution of industrial workers outside the traditionally industrialized zones. Ciudad Guayana was built by the Venezuelan government both to provide an alternative to the cities of Caracas and Maracaibo for migrants from rural areas and to develop a growth zone based on industries other than the country's chief one, petroleum. Choosing a site for the new capital of Brazil, Brasília, was the first step in a policy of opening the undeveloped interior of that country.

In Western Europe new towns continued to be built for several reasons. They were meant to encourage people to leave densely populated metropolitan areas, as in the case of those situated outside London, to halt the economic decline of a region, as in the new towns in the north of England, or to restructure mining and industrial zones. English new towns were built primarily outside established urban regions with open space between them and the old cities. On the other hand, in the regions surrounding Stockholm, Copenhagen, and Helsinki, and in the western part of the Netherlands, new towns were continuations of central cities, connected with them by transportation networks. Other new towns being built in England and France were to be completely self-contained. (IULA)

A novel variation in new town planning was a major element in one of the most ambitious approaches to urban renewal envisioned in the U.S., a plan for the social and physical revitalization of most of the Hartford, Conn., area over a 20-year period. The program called for a "new town in town" consisting of the complete renewal of the northern, predominantly black half of the city to update housing, schools, job opportunities, health care, and social services. It also called for subsidized low- and moderate-income housing on 300-ac. "new neighbourhoods" throughout 28 suburban jurisdictions and an entirely new community of 20,000 in an outlying region. The venture was the brainchild of the Hartford business community and was being carried forward by a group called Greater Hartford Process. The entire project was so utopian in character that it was easily viewed with skepticism, but its very massiveness was being hailed by its promoters, who were already pledging funds and securing land for it, as the reason it might succeed where less ambitious efforts had failed. (X.)

During 1972 the Commission on Population Growth and the American Future issued its report, *Population and the American Future,* which included a chapter on "Population Distribution" focusing on trends and problems of metropolitan growth. The report noted that metropolitan population in the U.S. increased by 26 million during the 1960s, one-third from territorial expansion of the metropolitan areas and two-thirds from population increases within the 1960 boundaries. Of the total increase, the excess of births over deaths (natural increase) accounted for about three-fourths and net migration both from within the U.S. and from abroad accounted for the remainder. As reported by the census of 1970, 69% of the population was concentrated in metropolitan areas.

The report indicated that by the year 2000 about 85% of the population of the U.S. would be resident in metropolitan areas (from 71% in 1970 by the commission's definition). Natural increase would be the main source of the growth. If the two-child family became the norm, metropolitan population would increase by 40 million without any migration; with migration it would total 225 million, an addition of 81 million in little more than one human generation. If the three-child family were the norm, metropolitan population, with migration, would number 273 million, an increase of 129 million above the 1970 figure.

In 1970 over 40% of the U.S. population was living in metropolitan areas of one million or more; by 2000, 60% would be living in such areas, which would have increased in number from 29 in 1970 to between 44–50. The report also called attention to the emergence of the urban region—"a continuous zone of metropolitan areas and intervening counties within which one is never far from a city." In 1920 ten such regions contained over one-third of the total population; by 1970 about three-fourths of the population lived in about 19 urban regions; by 2000, it was estimated, urban regions would embrace one-sixth of the land area in the continental U.S. and contain five-sixths of its population.

To deal with this metropolitan prospect the commis-

World's 25 Most Populous Cities

		City proper		Metropolitan	
Rank	City and country	Most recent population	Year	Most recent population	Year
1	Tokyo, Japan	8,818,216	1972 estimate	22,082,044	1970 census
2	New York, U.S.	7,895,563	1970 census	11,575,740	1970 census
3	Shanghai, China	...	...	10,800,000*	1970 estimate
4	Peking, China	...	...	7,600,000*	1970 estimate
5	London, U.K.	—	—	7,392,995†	1971 census
6	Moscow, U.S.S.R.	6,942,000	1970 census	7,061,000	1970 census
7	Greater Bombay, India	—	—	5,970,575	1971 census
8	Seoul, South Korea	5,536,377	1970 census	—	—
9	São Paulo, Brazil	5,186,752	1970 census	8,062,130	1970 census
10	Cairo, Egypt	5,139,000	1971 estimate	6,255,000	1970 estimate
11	Jakarta, Indonesia	4,576,009	1971 census	...	...
12	Tientsin, China	...	...	4,300,000*	1970 estimate
13	Rio de Janeiro, Brazil	4,252,009	1970 census	7,094,211	1970 census
14	Delhi, India	—	—	3,647,023	1971 census
15	Teheran, Iran	3,639,000	1971 estimate	...	...
16	Leningrad, U.S.S.R.	3,513,000	1970 census	3,950,000	1970 census
17	Chicago, U.S.	3,366,957	1971 estimate	6,978,733	1970 census
18	Madrid, Spain	3,197,336	1971 estimate	...	...
19	Calcutta, India	3,148,746	1971 census	7,031,382	1971 census
20	Buenos Aires, Argentina	2,972,453	1970 census	8,352,900	1970 census
21	Osaka, Japan	2,907,831	1972 estimate	14,886,005	1970 census
22	Mexico City, Mexico	2,902,969	1970 census	8,589,631	1970 census
23	Los Angeles, U.S.	2,840,000	1972 estimate	7,085,380	1972 estimate
24	Rome, Italy	2,799,836	1971 census	...	...
25	Bogotá, Colombia	2,680,100	1972 estimate	2,818,300	1972 estimate

*Municipality. †Greater London.
Berlin, both sectors combined 1971 population 3,182,706, is excluded due to the political as well as physical division of the city.

DICK SRODA/THE NEW YORK TIMES

This scene in the Woodlawn area of Chicago was typical of inner cities throughout the U.S.: children playing with the backdrop of an abandoned building earlier ravaged by fire.

sion proposed a dual strategy "of attenuating and simultaneously better accommodating current trends." It proposed that: (1) The federal government develop a set of national population distribution guidelines to serve as a framework for regional, state, and local plans and development. (2) Regional, state, and metropolitan-wide governmental authorities take the initiative, in cooperation with local governments, to conduct needed comprehensive planning and action programs to achieve a higher quality of urban development. (3) The process of population movement be eased and guided in order to improve access to opportunities now restricted by physical remoteness, immobility, and inadequate skills, information, and experience. (4) Action be taken to increase freedom in choice of residential location through the elimination of current patterns of racial and economic segregation and their attendant injustices.

Hope for the Urban Future? The commission's report raised such questions as whether, with an ever increasing metropolitan population, the already chronic problems of the cities would worsen, and whether there were any indications that the U.S. was seriously attempting to deal with these problems. The year 1971–72 continued to be one of crises in urban affairs in the U.S., and financial problems continued to constitute a major element in these crises. A number of significant developments, however, pointed if not to a quick solution of urban problems, at least to a more frontal attack upon them. But the beginning of hopeful indications could not be confused with the stark reality of the problems.

For the 1971 fiscal year, as reported by the U.S. Bureau of the Census, U.S. municipalities spent $39.1 billion, $1.7 billion in excess of total revenues of $37.4 billion. Total expenditures increased by 14.4% over fiscal 1970, while total revenues increased by about the same percentage, 14.3%. The gap between expenditures and revenues increased by $200 million, or 13.3%. Taxes imposed by the cities yielded $15.1 billion, about half of all general city revenues. Property taxes remained the predominant source, accounting for $10 billion, or two-thirds of the tax yield. State governments provided $7.4 billion to municipalities, and additional moneys from the federal government and from other local governments (mostly counties) raised the total revenues from all intergovernmental sources to $9.7 billion, or over one-fourth of total revenue from all sources. Total intergovernmental revenue increased by 22.7% over fiscal 1970, intergovernmental revenue from state governments increased by 19.9% and from the federal government by 39.2%. Thus, intergovernmental sources provided 25.9% of all revenue in fiscal 1971, as compared with 24.2% in fiscal 1970.

Although the federal government substantially increased its revenue contributions to municipal governments, the cities were still in financial trouble. The revenue sharing legislation proposed by the administration was passed by the Congress in October in considerably modified form. Under its provisions $5.3 billion would be distributed by the federal government to states and municipalities during the first year effective Jan. 1, 1972, with increased amounts distributed in each of the following four years. One-third of the funds were to be allocated to state governments and two-thirds to local governments. The legislation as passed also provided $2.5 billion annually for "social services," less money for such programs than had previously been authorized. The revenue sharing money might enable cities to eliminate the gaps between revenues and expenditures, but it was not likely to have much effect in improving municipal public services. The legislation, however, represented a significant step forward in principle and, as such, pointed the way to possible future resolution of city financial distress.

Although it was still predominantly true that U.S. cities, which were creatures of state government, possessed neither the legal authority nor sources of revenue with which to deal with their problems, a trend toward "home rule," endowing municipalities with broader legal authority, was evident. Home rule provisions were embodied in the state constitutions of Illinois and New Mexico. In Florida home rule was granted to all counties, although not to cities. Colorado provisions for home rule were extended to cover municipalities with populations under 2,000, and limited home rule was provided in Indiana by permitting municipalities to have powers not expressly forbidden by the constitution or general statutes. The Missouri and Wyoming legislatures put home rule amendments to the voters for approval. In Alabama the Constitutional Commission recommended that cities and counties be given home rule. In Iowa a home rule bill was debated but not adopted. Several additional states took other actions to remove municipalities from previous state constraints, demonstrating a trend toward modernization of local government.

The trend toward the creation of mechanisms to deal with metropolitan-wide and regional problems also continued. A number of legislatures authorized the establishment of planning districts, clearinghouses for federal aid, water districts, rapid transit systems, and regional airports. Multistate compacts continued to be effected for sharing of facilities; a compilation made in 1970 by the Council of State Governments listed 160 such compacts and 31 proposals for others. Moreover, the federal government was also becoming party to multistate compacts. Congress expanded the authority of the Delaware and Susquehanna River Basin Compact commissions by making their decisions binding on federal agencies. Twelve mechanisms had been developed from the three federal statutes passed in 1965 authorizing cooperation between groupings of states and the federal government in dealing with problems that transcend state boundaries; seven of these were aimed at economic development and five involved water resources.

New arrangements for intergovernmental cooperation continued to proliferate. In 1972 there were, for example, about 650 multijurisdictional planning bodies covering both urban and rural areas. In addition, special districts continued to be created to perform functions that cut across local governmental lines. The number of local government units would continue to increase until some form of general purpose unit, such as a metropolitan government unit, was adopted. It was sobering to recognize that public services in the U.S. were provided by more than 80,000 separate governments—and that this number was still increasing.

The burgeoning programs of federal grants-in-aid created a need for regional coordination of activities. Especially significant in this respect were the requirements of the "A-95" review contained in Section 204 of the Demonstration Cities and Metropolitan Development Act of 1966. This called for applications by local government for specific grants-in-aid to be reviewed by "any areawide agency which is designated to perform metropolitan or regional planning for the area within which the assistance is to be used." Such review bodies were operating in almost all metropolitan areas in 1972. Grants subject to review included those for airport and highway planning and construction, water and sewerage facilities, outdoor recreation, hospitals, law enforcement facilities, community action programs, and dozens of other programs.

Notable achievements resulted from this required review process. The Miami Valley Regional Planning Council in the Dayton, O., metropolitan area was successful in getting the agreement of a number of local governments on a plan allocating the development of low- and moderate-income housing. The Metropolitan Washington (D.C.) Council of Governments drew up a model fair housing ordinance adopted by a number of its local governments.

The obvious need for restoring adequate and attractive mass transit facilities for intrametropolitan circulation of people, together with increasing public pressure, led state legislatures to face up to the problem during 1971–72. Fifteen states had created transportation departments and a number actively undertook the improvement of mass transit by increased planning activities and funding arrangements.

Residential construction increased to 2.1 million units in 1971, a fourth of which were for low- and moderate-income families. The official national goal of providing every U.S. family with "a decent home and a suitable environment" was far from being met, however, and patterns of residential segregation in urban areas were not diminishing appreciably. Elements of progress included the creation of state housing finance agencies designed to encourage private enterprise construction by facilitating and assisting in financing; the direct provision by some states of low- and moderate-income housing, usually in cooperation with federal programs; the adoption of legislation permitting and facilitating the use of factory-built housing and dealing with mobile homes, access to housing, and more enlightened building codes. What might become a significant step forward in desegregation occurred in Chicago, where a federal district court judge issued orders designed to extend public housing beyond the borders of the city's black-occupied areas.

Public school education remained the most expensive public service in most cities. Since it was financed mainly by local property taxes, which had soared to unprecedented highs, public resistance to increased educational expenditures mounted. Meanwhile, public schools throughout the nation, and especially in the inner cities, failed to provide children with basic skills, salable skills, or civic skills. Some hope was to be found, however, in the several court decisions holding dependence on the local property taxes for school financing unconstitutional because it made quality schooling dependent on wealth. Such decisions were handed down by the California Supreme Court, a New

The use of his playground as a dump during a Toronto trash collectors' strike in April 1972 evidently does not concern a young boy shown happily mashing a bag of garbage.

JULIEN LEBOURDAIS—NANCY PALMER

Jersey state court, and federal courts in Texas and Minnesota; other court challenges were pending. A number of states were studying alternative methods of school financing and some increased state financial assistance to the schools.

A number of other developments merited attention as representing steps toward resolution of the plight of the cities. The New York state legislature approved a constitutional provision which, if confirmed by the voters, would enable the state to stimulate private enterprise efforts toward urban renewal, especially in the inner city, by using the credit and resources of the state to back such activities. Several states arranged for state training of local law enforcement officers under federal grants (the Safe Streets Act) to help professionalize police and other law enforcement agencies. These actions had been precipitated by riots in recent years and by the increasingly perplexing problems of dealing with urban violence. Some states were also considering further activity in matters of consumer protection, drug abuse, and the rising frictions in public employee-government relations. Finally, efforts were under way in a number of states to improve the calibre of personnel and increase the efficiency of operations; increased salary scales and greater utilization of the computer were helpful in achieving these objectives.

Unrelieved Elements of the Urban Crisis. Although these developments gave some basis for hope in the urban future, they did not in any way alleviate the serious components of the current urban crisis. Frustration, alienation, and hostility of underprivileged minority groups by all indications remained unchanged. Although gains in income and education during the 1960s were reported in the 1970 census, it was doubtful that the gains kept pace with the rising expectations of the poor, disproportionately members of minorities. Countering these improvements in socioeconomic status were the persistence of high minority group unemployment, especially among youths under 25, the continued high segregation indexes of minorities in central cities, the deteriorating neighbourhoods and poor housing, the relatively high incidence, albeit a decreasing one, of poverty, and the continued poor quality of inner city public school education. Although there was no "hot summer" in 1972, there were other indications that minority group hostility was not diminished and that violence continued to be one means of expressing that hostility.

The FBI reported during the year that 126 law enforcement officers were killed by felonious criminal action in 1971. This constituted a 26% increase over 1970, when 100 law enforcement officers were killed in the line of duty. Over the ten-year period 1962–71, 722 officers were slain, an average of 72 per year. The 1971 record was, then, 75% above the ten-year average. Indicative of the mounting hostility to law enforcement officers as symbols of "the establishment" was the increased number of killings through "ambush." In 1962–66 there were 12 such murders; in 1967–71 there were 49. Similarly, the number of officers killed attempting to make arrests for reasons other than burglaries or robberies in progress rose from 64 to 116, for "traffic stops" from 10 to 39, and for "civil disorders" from 2 to 8. The total number of killings of officers rose from 270 during the first five-year period to 452 during the second. Of the 126 police murder cases in 1971, 115 were "cleared" with the arrest of 174 offenders, 42% of whom were white and 58% black. Over the ten-year period, when 96% of the police murders were "cleared," 52% of the offenders were white and 48% black. Early reports for 1972 indicated that, at least in New York City, the number of policemen killed declined but the number of attacks on them increased. The facts left little doubt that the killing of law enforcement officers was at least one indicator of the mounting alienation and hostility of minority groups.

Over the 1966–71 five-year period, when the U.S. population rose by 5% and the number of persons between 15 and 24 increased by 18%, the "Index Crimes" of the FBI increased in absolute number by 83%. Crimes of violence (murder, forcible rape, robbery, and aggravated assault) rose by 90% and the rate for such crimes by 80%. Crimes against property (burglary, larceny $50 and over in value, and auto theft) increased by 82% and the rate for such crimes by 73%. During 1971 the total number of Index Crimes rose by 7.4%, violent crimes by 10.5% and property crimes by 6.9%. During the first six months of 1972 Crime Index offenses increased by 1% over the same period in 1971, the smallest increase since the FBI began its quarterly releases in 1960. But there was considerable variation among the specific categories: forcible rape, for example, increased by 14%, aggravated assault by 6%, and murder by 1%, while robbery decreased by 4%. Arrests for narcotic drug violations in 1971 were at a level 11% above that for 1970. During the 1966–71 period such arrests increased by 469%.

It was to be borne in mind that these crime rates were based only on crimes known to the police. Surveys of the population indicated that only about half the crimes actually committed become known to the police. Moreover, the number of known crimes might vary with changes in police enforcement policy and action. Rough as the statistics were, however, they did indicate the serious nature of the social and economic pathology that afflicted the U.S.

Another symptom of social malaise was afforded by the incidence and character of civil disorders and, as an index of minority group unrest, race-related civil disorders. Data collected and analyzed by the Lemberg Center for the Study of Violence at Brandeis University identified 578 civil disorders in the five summers of 1967–71 as race-related. The peak year for such events was 1967, with 176; the summer of 1968 was also relatively long and hot with 158 race-related civil disorders. Since those years there had been a steady decline to the low of 46 in the summer

No doubt the Royal Borough of Kensington and Chelsea in London was first to develop a technological answer to the question of where dogs can make their toilets with a modicum of dignity.

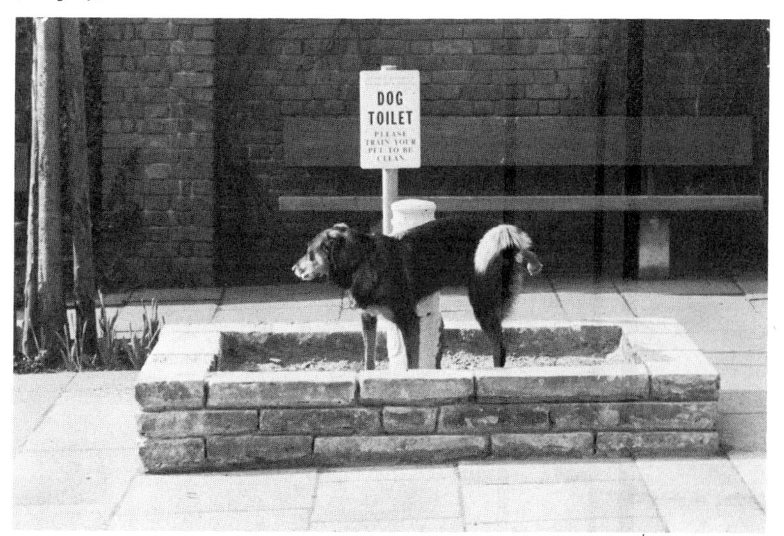

LONDON DAILY EXPRESS/PICTORIAL PARADE

of 1971. In 1967 race-related disorders constituted 69% of all civil disorders; but in 1968 they constituted only 21%. This sharp decrease was not so much the result of the decrease in the number of race-related incidents as it was the result of the dramatic increase in all disorders from 259 in 1967 to 724 in 1968. In 1969 the total number of civil disorders rose to 835 and then decreased to 240 by 1971. Race-related disorders diminished to 11% by 1970 and then rose to 19% in 1971. The largest proportion of race-related disorders consistently occurred in the larger cities, those with more than 250,000 persons, from a low of 27% in 1967 to a high of 48% in 1971.

The Lemberg Center analysis also revealed that these disorders became less serious over the five-year period. In 1967, 70% of the race-related disorders were characterized by one or more "extreme acts" (arson, fire-bombing, looting, sniping, or fire-setting); by 1971 only 27% of the disorders involved such acts. Thus, the "long, hot summer" seemed to be phasing out. But this did not mean that alienation or hostility among minorities was diminishing. There was evidence that civil disorders were diffusing to other parts of the year and that other channels of expressing hostility were being found in, for example, the killing of law enforcement officers or increased bloc political activity. John P. Spiegel, director of the Lemberg Center, had aptly summarized the situation in his statement, "As long as our underlying social conflicts continue at their current high level of intensity, the symbols of public authority may continue to be marked for attack. Violence in one form or another is likely to persist." (PHILIP M. HAUSER)

See also Architecture; Crime; Environment; Historic Buildings; Housing; Law; Police; Transportation.

ENCYCLOPÆDIA BRITANNICA FILMS. *The Northeast—Headquarters for a Nation* (1967); *Operation Bootstrap* (1968); *Problems of Conservation—Air* (1968); *The House of Man, Part II—Our Crowded Environment* (1969); *Manuel from Puerto Rico* (1969); *The South: Roots of the Urban Crisis* (1969); *Chicano from the Southwest* (1970); *The Garbage Explosion* (1970); *The Industrial City* (1970); *Linda and Billy Ray from Appalachia* (1970); *The Rise of the American City* (1970); *What Is a Community?* (1970); *Jesse from Mississippi* (1971); *Noise—Polluting the Environment* (1971); *Turn off Pollution* (1971).

Colombia

A republic in northwestern South America, Colombia is bordered by Panama, Venezuela, Brazil, Peru, and Ecuador and has coasts on both the Caribbean Sea and the Pacific Ocean. Area: 439,735 sq.mi. (1,138,914 sq.km.). Pop. (1972 est.): 22,490,500. Cap. and largest city: Bogotá (pop., 1972 est., 2,680,100). Language: Spanish. Religion: Roman Catholic (91%). President in 1972, Misael Pastrana Borrero.

The most important political event of 1972 was the April departmental and municipal elections, in which the Liberals (who decisively headed the poll) and Conservatives not only regained control of all the departmental assemblies, many of which had been in the hands of the Alianza Nacional Popular (supporters of ex-president Gustavo Rojas Pinilla), but also won majorities on a large number of the municipal councils.

The Liberal Party remained divided into two groups—a conservative wing led by ex-president Alberto Lleras Camargo and his former foreign minister, Julio Turbay Ayala; and a progressive wing led by ex-president Carlos Lleras Restrepo together with his former foreign minister, Alfonso López Michelsen. During the second half of 1972, efforts were made to unite the party, and it seemed likely that the progressives would be responsible for organizing the 1973 party convention, at which a candidate would be chosen for the 1974 presidential elections.

The improved political situation was matched by a good recovery from the economic setbacks of 1971. The recovery began in the last quarter of 1971, due to a combination of firmer coffee prices, a steady rise in minor exports, and a greatly increased flow of foreign capital. At the end of 1971 the net international reserves of the Banco de la República reached a record $170.4 million. This encouraging trend continued into 1972.

As a result of a successful meeting of the Credit Consultative Group in Paris at the end of February, Colombia expected to receive foreign assistance totaling approximately $500 million during 1972. The director of the Departamento Nacional de Planeación, Roberto Arenas Bonilla, indicated that in 1972 Colombia would receive untied loans totaling $370 million from the World Bank, the Inter-American Development Bank, and the U.S. Agency for International Development. He stressed that Colombian policy was to obtain long-term loans at favourable interest rates to ensure that the nation's payments on its external debt did not grow excessively. The government stressed, however, that if its export program

COLOMBIA

Education. (1968) Primary, pupils 2,733,432, teachers 100,629; secondary, pupils 407,966, teachers 39,056; vocational, pupils 191,573, teachers 22,328; teacher training, students 54,527, teachers 5,441; higher (including 32 universities), students 61,359, teaching staff 10,147.

Finance. Monetary unit: peso, with (Sept. 18, 1972) a free rate of 22 pesos to U.S. $1 (54 pesos = £1 sterling). Gold, SDRs, and foreign exchange, central bank: (June 1972) U.S. $214 million; (June 1971) U.S. $165 million. Budget (1970 est.): revenue 11,030,800,000 pesos; expenditure 12,132,500,000 pesos. Gross domestic product: (1970) 130,590,000,000 pesos; (1969) 110,950,000,000 pesos. Money supply: (June 1970) 19,640,000,000 pesos; (June 1969) 15,737,000,000 pesos. Cost of living (Bogotá; 1963 = 100): (March 1972) 233; (March 1971) 207.

Foreign Trade. (1970) Imports 15,543,000,000 pesos; exports 11,351,000,000 pesos. Import sources: U.S. 48%; West Germany 8%; Japan 6%; Spain 5%. Export destinations: U.S. 36%; West Germany 14%; Netherlands 5%; Spain 5%. Main exports: coffee 61%; crude oil 5%.

Transport and Communications. Roads (1967) *c.* 45,000 km. (including 7,200 km. with improved surface). Motor vehicles in use (1969): passenger *c.* 150,500; commercial (including buses) *c.* 135,000. Railways (1970): 3,509 km.; traffic 235 million passenger-km., freight 1,172,000,000 net ton-km. Air traffic (1971): 1,701,000,000 passenger-km.; freight 64,275,000 net ton-km. Shipping (1971): merchant vessels 100 gross tons and over 50; gross tonnage 208,837. Telephones (Dec. 1970) 809,000. Radio receivers (Dec. 1970) 2,217,000. Television receivers (Dec. 1970) 800,000.

Agriculture. Production (in 000; metric tons; 1971; 1970 in parentheses): corn 950 (800); rice 780 (753); wheat 49 (50); barley 112 (90); potatoes 1,084 (900); cassava (1970) 1,200, (1969) 950; coffee 520 (570); bananas (1970) 780, (1969) 780; cotton, lint 111 (128); cane sugar, raw value (1971–72) *c.* 813, (1970–71) *c.* 744; sugar, panela (1971–72) *c.* 730, (1970–71) 700; tobacco 47 (45). Livestock (in 000; Dec. 1970): cattle 21,082; sheep 1,700; pigs *c.* 3,850; goats 928; horses *c.* 1,100; poultry 38,188.

Industry. Production (in 000; metric tons; 1971): crude oil 11,127; natural gas (cu.m.; 1970) 1,472,000; coal (1970) 3,000; electricity (kw-hr.; 1970) 8,750,000; crude steel (ingots) 248; gold (troy oz.) *c.* 175; salt (1970) 469; cement 2,827.

Civil Rights:
see Race Relations

Clothing:
see Fashion and Dress; Furs

Coal:
see Fuel and Power; Mining

Cobalt:
see Mining

Cocoa (Cacao):
see Agriculture

Coffee:
see Agriculture

Coinage:
see Philately and Numismatics

Colleges:
see Education

was successful the need for such loans would diminish; under its latest four-year export plan Colombia aspired to increase the value of minor exports to $617 million, which together with coffee and petroleum would bring the total value of exports to more than $1 billion by 1975.

In mid-1972 the minister of finance, in a review of the economy, stated that there were signs of recovery in all sectors and that the prevailing confidence of investors and business would be an important factor in sustaining progress. Inflation was moderate in 1972. The Fundación para el Desarrollo y la Educación Superior forecast that the value of the U.S. dollar on the exchange certificate market would rise from 21.95 pesos on June 30 to 22.99 pesos on Dec. 31, 1972. With government plans to increase agricultural productivity, the rise in the consumer price index was expected to be somewhat less than the 14.7% recorded in 1971.

The economic growth rate in 1971 was estimated at 5.5%, compared with 6.8% in 1970. The reduction was attributed to the fall in coffee prices in the first nine months of the year together with the unusually prolonged rainy season which hampered agricultural production.

Following the acquittal of six men and two women who admitted massacring 16 Cuiba Indians in 1967, the bishops of Colombia in July 1972 denounced the "tremendous injustice" suffered by the jungle Indians, whose lands were coveted by white and half-caste settlers. The accused had contended that Indian-hunting was a centuries-old tradition that had never been regarded as a crime. One local news correspondent recalled that some 20 years earlier a Swiss traveler in the region was still able to buy five Indian skins "well-salted and ready for tanning." The government announced its intention to seek a retrial.

(R. B. LEWRY)

Commercial Policies

The world trading system was seriously unsettled on Aug. 16, 1971, when the United States temporarily suspended the full convertibility of the dollar, imposed a 10% surcharge on imports, and took a series of other measures, such as the introduction of the job development tax credit, which openly discriminated against foreign suppliers of capital equipment to the U.S. market. The persistent deficit in the U.S. balance of payments, long regarded with serious concern by U.S. trading partners as being the main cause of the repeated international monetary crises, had reached a point where drastic action became inevitable. The U.S. position was that such drastic actions were necessary to jolt the Europeans and the Japanese into a more attentive mood and to make them more responsive to U.S. pleadings for economic and financial cooperation.

The U.S. action triggered five months of anxious consultations in capitals and international monetary and trade policy organizations. During these months some of the deeper divergencies of interests between the larger trading partners came out into the open more clearly. The U.S. made sweeping trade demands of the EEC, among them that the EEC should stockpile 10% of its grain crop for two years so that the U.S. could sell more; that the EEC's new system for taxing tobacco should be amended so as not to damage U.S. exports; that the EEC should abolish the preferences on citrus fruits that it was giving to Mediterranean countries; and that the EEC should halt the negotiations with its prospective new members and with other Western European countries for industrial free-trade agreements until some sort of compensation formula for the U.S. and other nations had been worked out. From the Japanese, apart from the adjustment of the undervalued yen, the U.S. demanded curbs on the growing rate of exports flooding its market, and improved access for, and a substantial increase of, its own exports to the Japanese market. For weeks the danger of a world trade war, possibly to be waged with surcharges, retaliatory tariff increases, quotas, and embargoes, loomed; uncertainties in the monetary field and embittered negotiating positions were evident.

The Smithsonian Agreement. The atmosphere of crisis was relieved on Dec. 18, 1971, with the conclusion of the Smithsonian agreement. The dollar was officially devalued; other currencies were juggled up or down into a new pattern of temporarily fixed rates; and the range within which exchange rates would be allowed to move was widened. But there was no agreement on the conditions that would govern future changes in parities, on the conditions that would make one reserve asset convertible into another, or on measures for the creation of new reserve assets. The proper role of gold and the reform of the international monetary system over the longer term were left to the future. Following the agreement the U.S. import surcharge was removed, as well as the tax credit discrimination against foreign capital equipment.

The agreement and the relief it brought from the anxiety of floating rates set the stage for quieter and longer-term thinking on the adjustment of future international relations in matters of trade, investment, and development aid. There was then general awareness, however, that the international readjustment process must be revamped so that trade measures would play a more active role in redressing international disequilibrium.

Foremost among the basic changes that were affecting international trade relations were the redeployment of economic strength among the EEC, the U.S., and Japan; the growing importance of the process of regional integration, especially in Europe; and the economic emergence and claims to assistance of less developed countries. The difficulty of reconciling the requirements of new interests with the rules and institutions of the postwar trade system had, for a time, appeared to be out of hand. Confrontation and retaliation, rather than consultation and conciliation, tended to predominate in the settlement of trade problems and differences.

Bilateral Negotiations. The bilateral consultations involving the U.S., the EEC, and Japan, which had started before the Smithsonian agreement, continued into 1972. By February they bore fruit and joint statements were issued by Japan and the U.S. and by the EEC and the U.S. on international economic relations. These were communicated to the contracting parties to the General Agreement on Tariffs and Trade (GATT) in February, inviting them to associate themselves with the declarations. The statements amounted to a decision by the three leading traders to open multilateral negotiations in 1973 on the basis of mutual advantage with overall reciprocity and covering agricultural as well as industrial trade. Most other developed countries promptly associated themselves with these sentiments and intentions.

Colonies:
see Dependent States

Comecon:
see Soviet Bloc Economies

Commerce:
see Commercial Policies; Economy, World; Merchandising; Trade, International

Both statements recognized the need for proceeding with a comprehensive review of international economic relations with a view to negotiating improvements in the light of structural changes that had taken place in recent years. The review was to cover all elements of trade, including measures that impeded or distorted agricultural, raw material, and industrial trade. Both declarations reaffirmed support for greater liberalization of world trade and called for future multilateral and comprehensive negotiations within the framework of GATT. In the meantime the settlement of particular trade problems should take place within GATT. Only on the question of the use of international commodity agreements did the U.S. and the EEC have divergent views, the latter in favour of making use of such devices in appropriate cases and the former considering such agreements not to offer a useful approach.

These bilateral statements each made reference to the importance of giving attention to the trade interests of the third world. In general the less developed countries welcomed this new initiative but said that they would reserve their positions until they could get a clearer view of their own roles and expectations. They were also concerned over the possible erosion of the tariff advantage laboriously acquired in the past year under the so-called Generalized System of Preferences for less developed countries. They made it clear that their association with the proposed multilateral negotiations was conditional on their acceptance of the details as regards the manner in which they would be allowed to participate.

In July bilateral talks took place in Tokyo between the U.S. and Japan. These were followed a month later by a summit meeting, during which U.S. Pres. Richard Nixon and Prime Minister Kakuei Tanaka pledged joint efforts to bring trade between the two countries into better balance and the Japanese government announced a plan to purchase more than $1 billion of U.S. goods and services to help ease the pressure on the dollar.

UNCTAD. Against a background of sustained, if groping, discussions concerning international monetary reform and prospects of multilateral trade negotiations, actively supported by industrialized countries, the third session of the United Nations Conference on Trade and Development (UNCTAD) convened in April at Santiago, Chile. In general the developed countries' concern over preparation for action in the monetary and trade field dampened their readiness to respond to the requests put forward by the less developed countries. Nevertheless, a number of sweeping resolutions were passed. Apart from the unanimous agreement on special measures for the least developed countries, it was claimed as a matter of major importance that the less developed countries should be allowed to participate effectively in the decision-making process for reforming the monetary system.

On multilateral trade negotiations, Resolution 82(III), adopted without dissent, stipulated that they should be governed by certain principles formulated by less developed countries. These included: the less developed countries shall not suffer, directly or indirectly, adverse or prejudicial effects as a result of these negotiations, but on the contrary shall be provided with additional benefits; any adverse effects to the preferential advantages enjoyed by less developed countries must be compensated for by the developed countries; better access to and a large share of the markets of developed countries shall be provided for the products of less developed countries; all concessions exchanged by developed countries shall be extended to less developed countries, but concessions exchanged among the latter shall not be extended to the developed countries; concessions agreed upon in the negotiations in favour of less developed countries should be made available to them immediately; and all less developed countries should be entitled and enabled to participate in the negotiations at all stages. The resolution also provided that special techniques and ground rules should be established for the participation of less developed countries so that special attention would be given to their interests and that substantive assistance should be given them by the secretariats of UNCTAD and GATT during the various stages of the negotiations.

When the Trade and Development Board of UNCTAD met in October 1972 to review the implementation of the Santiago resolutions, it drafted a further resolution on multilateral trade negotiations. However, because the U.S. strongly objected to it as constituting an infringement on the responsibilities of GATT, and because other countries also denied it support, the draft resolution was withdrawn. It was replaced by a statement by the chairman of the board which simply reiterated the substance of the Santiago resolution on multilateral trade negotiations, stressing the less developed countries' need for technical assistance and advice.

The U.S. detailed its policy in regard to pending negotiations in a report published in August by Pres. Richard Nixon's Council of Economic Advisers. The report emphasized the direct link between negotiations on trade reform and those on monetary reform and spelled out the principles underlying the U.S. negotiating position, namely, that a trade agreement should be comprehensive and should cover agricultural as well as industrial trade, and include all forms of trade barriers, tariff as well as nontariff. The desired result should be a system that places maximum reliance on market-directed trade. The real cost of any social programs, such as agricultural income support measures, should be borne by the country implementing them and should not be passed on to its trading partners. Finally, a trading system must be equipped with safeguards that would give economically sensitive industries in participating countries sufficient time to adjust to shifts in patterns of production and trade.

The Rey Report. In September the long-awaited "Rey Report," prepared by a special high-level group of the Organization for Economic Cooperation and Development (OECD), was published. The group was chaired by Jean Rey, former president of the Commission of the European Economic Community, and its report was expected to play an influential role in the preparation of guidelines for future trade negotiations.

Broadly, the report called for reform of the world monetary system but, while there was a consensus that the system should be the servant, not master, of the international economic fabric, views were widely divergent as to the scope of reform and on the relationship between trade measures and the monetary mechanism in the adjustment process. The report advocated greater liberalization of world trade through such means as the elimination of quantitative restrictions and voluntary export restraints, and also stressed the need to improve such existing institutions as the GATT, the International Monetary Fund, and the

OECD. It contained no unanimous agreement on the major issues concerning agriculture and regional policies. A U.S. proposal for the complete elimination of industrial tariffs over a ten-year period was considered, as were less radical approaches, but dissent within the group prevented the report from reflecting any decided preference.

European Economic Integration. Meantime, European integration made an important breakthrough. On January 22 Britain, Denmark, Ireland, and Norway signed treaties in Brussels opening the way for their membership in the EEC as of Jan. 1, 1973. By October, following a negative popular vote on its accession, Norway dropped out of the group. With this change, the prospective enlarged EEC would have nine members. On July 22 Austria, Iceland, Portugal, Sweden, and Switzerland signed free-trade agreements with the EEC.

Because both accession to the EEC and the undertaking of free-trade obligations affected a country's international obligations under the General Agreement on Tariffs and Trade, the new agreements would have to be examined by the contracting parties to GATT. This work was begun in March 1972 with a view to the renegotiation of tariff bindings under GATT. In some ways these so-called renegotiations could be considered as a starting point for the broader trade negotiations to come.

East-West Trade. The enlargement of the EEC was not the only change occurring in the pattern of world trade. On the other side of the world the momentous efforts at reconciliation with China opened new vistas of trade in a possibly not-too-distant future.

Of more immediate significance to East-West trade relations was a detailed trade agreement between the U.S. and the Soviet Union. By its terms the U.S. would grant most-favoured-nation treatment to Soviet imports, and there would be an estimated threefold increase of trade between the two countries, which would reach approximately $1.5 billion in three years. The U.S. Congress was expected to ratify the agreement early in 1973. The implications of U.S. trade suddenly expanding to include the East were not expected to go unnoticed in the struggle for a new pattern of trade relations.

GATT Conference. In an atmosphere of hopeful expectancy the 28th session of the contracting parties to GATT opened in November to place on record officially their collective intention to begin multilateral negotiations in 1973. Apparently the member countries of GATT had gained sufficient confidence to announce a timetable and to outline the coverage of the future negotiations.

The final summing up of the conference, which was approved by all the contracting parties with the exception of four less developed countries, brought the trading world one step closer to the realization of the grand scheme. It noted that a number of contracting parties, accounting for a substantial proportion of world trade, reaffirmed their intention to initiate and actively support multilateral trade negotiations in 1973 within the framework of GATT, subject to such internal authorization as might be required. The parties agreed that the negotiations should cover both industrial and agricultural goods, including tropical products, and should take particular account of the need to find solutions to the problems of less developed countries. They also agreed to reexamine the adequacy of the multilateral safeguard system, welcomed the participation of other interested nations in the preparatory work for the negotiations, and expressed the hope that the negotiations could be concluded in 1975. The GATT countries reaffirmed their belief that the objectives of expansion and ever greater liberalization of world trade and improvement in the standards of living of people throughout the world could best be achieved by coordinated efforts to solve in an equitable way the trade problems of both the developed and the less developed countries.

The conference also agreed that the multilateral negotiations should aim at securing additional benefits for the international trade of the less developed countries so as to achieve a substantial increase in their foreign exchange earnings, diversification of their exports, and an acceleration of the rate of growth of their trade. Representatives of less developed countries, both contracting parties to GATT and some noncontracting parties, stated their interest in these trade negotiations and their interest in participating in their preparation.

It was further agreed that a preparatory committee, with open membership, would be set up to develop methods and procedures. The committee's report would be examined at a ministerial meeting in September 1973. At that time, the negotiations themselves were expected to start, under guidelines to be provided by a new Trade Negotiations Committee.

(CONSTANT CHUNG-TSE SHIH)

See also Agriculture; Commodities, Primary; Development, Economic; Trade, International.

Commodities, Primary

Trends in World Production. Combined world production of agricultural, fishery, and forest products in 1971 maintained its long-term annual increase of nearly 3%. However, as indicated by UN Food and Agriculture Organization (FAO) estimates (*see* Table I), an increase of more than 3% in agricultural products was offset by smaller rates of growth in output of fishery and forest products. The long-term rapid increase in fishery production slowed down substantially to a gain of about 2%, while forest production rose by about 1%.

Despite the rise of more than 3% in agricultural production, 1971—the first year of the UN Second Development Decade—was disappointing for the less developed countries. World agricultural production maintained its relatively favourable trend in relation to population growth only because of substantial increases in the developed countries. In the less developed nations during 1971, agricultural production rose by only 1–2%, well below the goal of a 4% annual growth rate during the 1970s and contrasting sharply with the 6% gain in the developed countries. Based on preliminary data, world agricultural output in 1972 remained at the 1971 level with no change in the developed regions and no acceleration in the 1971 rate of increase in the less developed countries. It appeared that unless agricultural progress in the less developed nations showed a much more dynamic rise during the next few years, the goals of the UN Second Development Decade would not be realized.

Strong demand and growing tightness in supplies of fishery products occurred in 1971, with landings estimated at 62 million metric tons, slightly below 1970. The most significant change occurred in Latin America, where landings were down by 11%. Global production value rose markedly, as prices of many items reached record levels. Net gains by producers, however, were often not proportionate owing to a rapid rise in production costs.

Because of a standstill in pulpwood output, world production of roundwood grew more slowly in 1971 than in previous years. Output of logs for plywood and sawn wood manufacture rose, mainly because of growing demand for these products in North America. Indonesia accounted for a large share of the rise in roundwood production in less developed countries. The lowest figure occurred in Western Europe, where output fell by 3%. Production of industrial roundwood remained heavily concentrated in the industrialized regions, which in 1971 accounted for approximately 90% of the world total.

Among other primary commodities—excluding agricultural, fishery, and forest products—production of crude petroleum, cement, tin, aluminum, and natural rubber continued to rise in 1971. (*See* Table II.) Aluminum and natural rubber were plagued with excess supplies and sluggish demand, which depressed prices. Competing synthetic rubber continued to meet the bulk of the world's new rubber requirements. Lead and zinc production, after rising for several years, declined sharply as a sharp rise in producers' operating costs led to the shutdown of some mines and smelters. Copper output, after moving up noticeably for several years, also leveled off in 1971 in response to weaker demand, rising supplies, and strikes.

Prices and Terms of Trade. Trends in primary commodity prices during recent years are shown in Table III. Although there was considerable variation among the various products, declines exceeded rises in 1971. Prices of cocoa beans, coffee, copper, copra, lead, rice, rubber, tin, tobacco, and wool showed the largest declines. Rises were particularly noticeable for butter, hides, jute, and sugar. In 1972, with the marked exception of copper, copra, and natural rubber, prices of commodities generally moved higher as demand improved in the face of tightening supplies. Particularly noteworthy were the rises in prices of beef, butter, cocoa beans, coffee, cotton, hides, jute, peanuts, petroleum, rice, sugar, and wool. Wheat prices, reflecting poor crops in the U.S.S.R. and other producing countries, also rose sharply after mid-1972.

The value of world exports of agricultural, fishery, and forest products combined rose about 5% in 1971, less than half the gain made during 1970. Agricultural trade, after spurting 14% in 1970, increased 6% in 1971, close to its longer term rate of growth. The value of trade in fishery and forest products also gained, but by less than in 1970.

In 1970, the expansion of world agricultural exports was shared, although unequally, by both developed and less developed countries. However, in 1971 there was an absolute decline in agricultural exports from the less developed countries whereas agricultural exports from the developed countries rose 11%. In Africa the value of exports fell 8% compared with a large increase in 1970; in Latin America, a decrease of 3% contrasted sharply with the strong expansion in 1970 and the longer term rate of growth.

Products suffering losses in export value in 1971 were largely those of importance in the export trade of the less developed countries, such as coffee, cocoa beans, rubber, oil cakes, and meal. Less developed countries also earned less from exports of some temperate-zone products, particularly wine, wheat, hides, skins, and wool. However, food and feed products, mainly of temperate-zone origin, again resulted in most of the expansion in agricultural export earnings. Since prices of agricultural products of major export interest to the less developed countries were depressed and those of manufactured products rose significantly, real purchasing power of the agricultural export earnings of less developed countries undoubtedly declined in 1971.

World exports of fishery products continued upward in value in 1971—despite a drop in shipments and a weakening of fish meal and fish oil markets—largely because of sharp rises in prices of fishery products for human consumption. In terms of value, shipments of fresh, frozen, and canned fish products from one developed country to another continued to lead in importance. As in other recent years, the less developed countries dominated the export trade in crustacean products, fresh and frozen shrimp in particular, while Peru, Chile, and Angola shared a large part of world markets for fish meal and fish oil with Norway, South Africa, and Iceland.

As usual, the U.S., Japan, and Western European countries in 1971 imported the major part of the fishery supplies in world trade. Japan's imports followed their remarkable climb of recent years, their value approaching that of the country's fishery exports.

Less developed countries increased their exports of forest products at a much higher rate than imports. The value index for exports reached 452 (1957–59 average = 100) in 1971, while the index for imports was 252. The developed countries were not similarly successful with their relative expansion of exports, as their growth of exports and imports was almost equal.

Commodity Policies. *National Policies.* The large purchases of grain by the Soviet Union in 1972 apparently indicated a major shift in that country's policy toward its consumers. In previous years of short crop production the Soviets cut back consumption rather than import the full amount needed to cover the deficit in domestic supplies. But in 1972 import purchases of grain may have surpassed the decline in that country's grain production. This suggested that a higher priority than ever before was being placed upon meeting consumer needs and expectations and upon obtaining feed to achieve targets for the expanded output of livestock products. These targets called for meat production, which rose from 10.7 million to 12.3 million metric tons during 1966–70, to reach 16 million tons by 1975.

Years of previous production declines in the U.S.S.R. generally meant smaller supplies and less choice in food stores, presumably because it was more important to use foreign exchange for purposes other than food imports. However, the Soviet people in 1972 expected a more dependable supply of better foods.

On Aug. 15, 1972, India celebrated 25 years of independence. During this period the nation achieved important increases in its agricultural production. During the early 1950s Indian leaders and visiting specialists recognized that the country must bring its agriculture up to date in order to produce enough food to meet the needs of the rapidly expanding population. Thereupon, the Indian government, assisted by the U.S. Agency for International Development, the Ford and Rockefeller foundations, international agencies, and many individual nations, instituted an intensive agricultural development program which provided the necessary methods and policies to begin a transition to a modern and more productive agriculture.

Especially large increases among food crops in India during the period of independence included food

Table I. Indexes of World Production* of Agricultural, Fishery, and Forest Products

1961–65 average=100

Item	1967	1968	1969	1970	1971†
Total production	112	116	117	120	123
Agriculture	112	116	117	120	124
Fisheries	122	127	130	137	140
Forestry	108	110	112	114	116
Population	108	110	113	115	117
Per capita production	104	105	103	104	105
Agriculture	104	105	104	104	106
Fisheries	113	115	116	119	119
Forestry	99	99	99	99	98

*Excluding China.
†Preliminary.
Source: Food and Agriculture Organization of the United Nations, *The State of Food and Agriculture* (1972).

Table II. Indexes of World Production of Certain Raw Materials

1963 average=100

Raw material	1967	1968	1969	1970	1971
Coal*	105	105	106	109	109
Crude petroleum	135	147	158	174	183
Cement	128	138	145	152	160
Pig iron†	130	139	150	156	154
Crude steel	129	137	148	153	149
Copper (smelter)‡	102	118	128	135	133
Zinc‡§	119	133	144	140	132
Lead‡§	110	114	128	131	124
Tin‖	121	128	124	124	127
Aluminum‡§	145	155	175	189	199
Natural rubber	118	125	137	138	143

*Including coal equivalent of brown coal and lignite.
†Including ferroalloys.
‡Excluding the U.S.S.R., East Germany, and North Korea.
§Excluding Czechoslovakia and Romania.
‖Excluding the U.S.S.R. and Eastern Europe.
Source: United Nations, *Monthly Bulletin of Statistics* (November 1972).

grains, with a rise of 101%; sugar (in terms of brown sugar), 146%; and potatoes, 196%. These and other increases were attributed largely to expansion in the area under irrigation, increased use of chemical fertilizers and pesticides, greater use of high-yielding varieties of seeds, and some improvement in farm credit and marketing facilities.

On Jan. 1, 1973, the U.K., Ireland, and Denmark would join West Germany, France, Italy, the Netherlands, Belgium, and Luxembourg in an enlarged European Economic Community (EEC). Although the new members were scheduled to apply most of the provisions of the EEC's Common Agricultural Policy (CAP) by Feb. 1, 1973, the arrangements for doing so had not been worked out by late 1972. One problem was when and how to introduce export rebates for British distillers for spirits, particularly whiskey, made from EEC-grown grains. The relationship between British cane sugar refineries and EEC beet sugar producers also remained unsolved. It was hoped that a compromise acceptable to all EEC members would be reached before February 1. Pork, eggs, and poultry presented a problem since compensatory amounts for them were fixed according to the amount of cereal grains that went into their production. Denmark, which had an important export market to preserve in Britain, wanted the compensatory amounts as high as possible because its grain feeding costs were higher. Britain, of course, wanted them low.

To encourage production of crops in demand at home and abroad, the U.S. Department of Agriculture on December 11 announced a 1973 feed-grain program directed toward putting about 12 million ac. idle in 1972 back into crops. Total feed-grain land expected to be taken from production in 1973 was about 25 million ac., compared with 37 million ac. in 1972. Under the plan, corn plantings could increase between 5 million and 6 million ac. from the 66.8 million in 1972. Similarly, soybean plantings could increase to a total of about 52 million ac. from 46.4 million in 1972.

International Policies. The International Sugar Council met in London November 15–17 to determine the initial export quotas for 1973 under the International Sugar Agreement and to make arrangements for a new International Sugar Agreement. Export quotas under the agreement were inoperative in 1972 since the world price of sugar exceeded the limit under which the quotas would go into effect. Likewise, yearly supply commitments—under which each importing member of the International Sugar Agreement had the option of purchasing from each of its traditional export members at the "supply commitment price" (6.95 cents per pound, f.o.b. Caribbean ports in bulk)—were also inoperative during most of 1972.

The council estimated net import requirements of sugar in the world free market during 1973 at about 10.3 million metric tons. It was thought that, over the year as a whole, total sugar supplies would be sufficient to meet these requirements. Nevertheless, the council decided not to allocate initial export quotas for 1973 or to fix any other limitations on exports. Also, the council was informed that a UN Sugar Conference would open in Geneva on May 7, 1973, to negotiate a new International Sugar Agreement. It would come into force on Jan. 1, 1974, when the current pact expired.

Members of the Intergovernmental Council of Copper Exporting Countries (CIPEC) in late 1972 voted support to Chile in that country's difficulties with the Kennecott Copper Corp., the largest U.S. copper producer. The latter, which owned the huge El Teniente copper mine in Chile before it was nationalized, attempted to secure reimbursement in various world courts for its uninsured equity in this mine and other properties appropriated by the Chilean government. CIPEC denounced Kennecott's action as "economic aggression" and pledged to cease all dealings with the company. CIPEC members (Chile, Zaire, Zambia, and Peru), which exported about 50% of the world's copper, also planned to boycott any markets that developed as a result of Kennecott's legal actions. Observers doubted, however, that such action would have pronounced effect on the copper market. The CIPEC countries had considerable need for foreign currencies and could not afford a boycott for any sustained length of time. Previous attempts at solidarity by CIPEC members had been unsuccessful. (*See* LAW.)

Table III. Changes in International Prices of Selected Major Commodities

Commodity, unit, country of origin, and market	Wholesale price in U.S. dollars 1964	1969	1970	1971	July 1972
Beef (100 lb.) U.S. (N.Y.)	28.70	38.93	41.32	42.51	50.82
Butter (100 lb.) New Zealand (London)	42.38	32.14	33.49	46.88	57.80
Cocoa (100 lb.) Ghana (N.Y.)	23.43	45.68	34.17	26.77	32.28
Coffee (100 lb.) Brazil (N.Y.)	47.36	40.35	53.94	45.17	53.66
Copper (100 lb.) U.K. (London)	43.84	66.51	64.17	49.02	46.90
Copra (100 lb.) Philippines (London)	8.79	9.23	10.13	8.53	6.25
Cotton (100 lb.) Egypt (Liverpool)	48.96	63.20	62.60	61.72	65.66
Hides (100 lb.) U.S. (Chicago)	10.40	14.60	12.90	14.50	29.30
Jute (short ton) Bangladesh (N.Y.)	346.00	356.00	332.00	346.00	356.00
Lead (100 lb.) U.K. (London)	12.69	13.14	13.78	11.46	13.77
Newsprint (short ton) Canada (Quebec)	116.60	128.20	131.90	134.80	140.50
Peanuts (100 lb.) Nigeria (London)	8.03	9.02	9.54	9.10	11.70*
Petroleum (bbl.) Venezuela (La Cruz)	2.80	2.80	2.80	2.80	3.21
Rice (100 lb.) Thailand (Bangkok)	6.23	8.48	6.51	5.86	6.22
Rubber (100 lb.) Malaysia (Singapore)	22.26	22.81	18.47	15.09	14.70
Sugar (100 lb.) Caribbean (N.Y. for exp.)	5.89	3.38	3.76	4.52	5.60
Tea (100 lb.) Ceylon-India (N.Y.)	53.00	42.60	45.80	48.70	51.00
Tin (100 lb.) Malaysia (Penang)	151.80	153.40	163.00	154.70	165.60
Tobacco (100 lb.) U.S. (U.S.)	57.30	69.33	80.61	73.23	77.57
Wheat (bu.) Canada (Fort William)	1.91	1.76	1.71	1.75	1.73
Wool (100 lb.) Australia (Sydney)	60.40	49.50	40.50	33.50	49.50†
Zinc (100 lb.) U.K. (London)	14.88	12.98	13.40	13.98	16.48

*April 1972.
†June 1972.
Source: International Monetary Fund, *International Financial Statistics*.

The International Tin Council (ITC), at its October 3–8 meeting in Jakarta, decided not to impose export controls on producing members of the International Tin Agreement. Instead, the ITC voted to give added financial support to the buffer stock manager in hopes of halting the decline in prices. However, increased production, along with nearly full ITC warehouses, forced the buffer stock manager to stop his support of tin prices. Prices began to slip again before the decline was arrested by currency developments. Since prices in late 1972 were too low for producing members of the ITC, the imposition of export controls in early 1973 seemed likely.

At a UN Cocoa Conference held from September 11 to October 20 in Geneva, 53 of the 55 nations in attendance adopted, without reservation, the text of an International Cocoa Agreement. The U.S., which accounted for about 20 to 25% of world cocoa imports, and West Germany, with 10 to 12% of imports, were the dissenters. The agreement provided for export quotas and a buffer stock to regulate prices within a range of 23 to 32 cents per pound. It was open for signature through Jan. 15, 1973, and was scheduled to become effective when ratified by nations accounting for 70% of cocoa imports and 80% of production.

For the first time in more than nine years, producing members of the International Coffee Agreement (ICA) in late 1972 were free to sell as much as they could. Although ICA export quotas totaling nearly 13.1 million bags (132.3 lb. each) were in effect for October–December 1972, the International Coffee Organization (ICO), which administered the ICA, on December 11 suspended all export restrictions. This action was taken because the 62 member countries of the ICA (21 consumers and 41 producers), after more than a week of negotiations in London, had failed to agree on export quotas for the remaining nine months (January–September) of the 1972–73 coffee year.

Having second thoughts about selling in a completely free market, several producers met on December 12 and adopted an "informal" export quota of approximately 11.2 million bags for January–March 1973 for the 41 producing members of the ICA. If the ICA composite price based on the four-coffee group rose above 55.50 cents per pound for 15 consecutive market days, the January–March quota was to be upped by 1.1 million bags.

It remained to be seen how successful the coffee producers would be in this unilateral action. Favouring the producers was the fact that the estimated 1972–73 world exportable coffee output of 53.6 million bags was about the level of the anticipated demand. Also, the world coffee surplus had dwindled to about 30 million bags, of which about 20 million were in Brazil and were low in quality. In addition, the next crop in Brazil was expected to be small. On the other hand, some producers might be forced to sell to acquire needed foreign exchange. (NORMAN R. URQUHART)

See also Agriculture; Commercial Policies; Development, Economic; Food; Mining; Payments and Reserves, International; Trade, International.

Commonwealth of Nations

Full members of the Commonwealth at the end of 1972 included: United Kingdom, Australia, Bangladesh, Barbados, Botswana, Canada, Ceylon (Sri Lanka), Cyprus, Fiji, The Gambia, Ghana, Guyana, India, Jamaica, Kenya, Lesotho, Malawi, Malaysia, Malta, Mauritius, New Zealand, Nigeria, Sierra Leone, Singapore, Swaziland, Tanzania, Tonga, Trinidad and Tobago, Uganda, Western Samoa, and Zambia.

Between Feb. 8 and March 26, 1972, Queen Elizabeth II, accompanied by Prince Philip and Princess Anne, made an extensive tour of the Commonwealth nations in the Indian Ocean, Malaysia, Singapore, and Kenya. The royal tour pointed up the fact that the Commonwealth represented one-quarter of the world's population, and that seven out of ten of its citizens were Asians. This Asian dimension proved increasingly significant as Chinese pressures grew during 1972, and as the armed conflict of two Commonwealth nations, India and Pakistan, in December 1971, led to Pakistan's withdrawal from the Commonwealth in January 1972 and the recognition and acceptance by the Commonwealth in April of the breakaway state of Bangladesh.

Africa. Uganda's military dictator, Gen. Idi Amin, threatened a second intra-Commonwealth war. After economic crisis and increasing political unrest, he ordered the expulsion, first, of a large Israeli mission and, then, of all Asians holding British passports. He was finally faced with an invasion force from Tanzania, which he claimed was inspired by British and Israeli collusion to reestablish Milton Obote, the president Amin had deposed the previous January. Amin's forces, supported by a late-arriving contingent of Libyans, repulsed the force of 1,000 pro-Obote Ugandan exiles and his Air Force bombed several Tanzanian towns before a peace plan was accepted by both countries. The imminent breakup of the East African Community thus seemed averted. In December Amin nationalized all British companies in Uganda and set in motion an exodus of British personnel.

At the ninth meeting of the Organization of African Unity in Rabat, Morocco, African Commonwealth countries supported directives aimed at strengthening guerrilla movements against white supremacist southern Africa but refused to implement resolutions calling on them to set up official armies. Zambia, although rent by economic deterioration and tribal dissension that resulted in its becoming a virtual dictatorship in February 1972, continued to harbour guerrilla groups, which, the OAU commission admitted, had organized opposition that led to the rejection of the settlement of the Rhodesian question proposed late in 1971. Malawi, however, maintained close relations with South Africa, whose president paid a state visit there in March.

Parts of Commonwealth Africa continued to serve as arenas for Peking-Moscow rivalry. Tanzania, shocked by the assassination of Zanzibar's Communist dictator and the murder of the Iringa Region commissioner, enforced a severe preventive detention act while accepting a continuing Chinese presence in the form of a MiG squadron to protect the Tanzam Railway. The 7,000-km. Trans-African highway from Kenya to Nigeria, with only 500 km. to complete, received a British feasibility acceptance survey in 1971; the estimated cost of $2,500,000 was to be borne by a Western consortium.

There were no signs of return to democracy in black Africa. In addition to the events in Uganda, Ghana moved into the military dictatorship group. In January Col. Ignatius Acheampong's coup replaced Kofi Busia's attempt at civil democracy. Nigeria showed no signs of the promised return to civilian rule, but many of economic prosperity. In September a foreign-backed attempt to sow dissension in the

Common Market: *see* Commercial Policies; European Unity

Army and plunge the nation into a fresh crisis was reported to have been foiled.

Far East. Following the breakup of Pakistan, India signed a treaty of friendship with the new state of Bangladesh on March 19, while Pres. Zulfikar Ali Bhutto (*see* BIOGRAPHY) of the defeated western wing and Indian Prime Minister Indira Gandhi agreed in July to withdraw all troops from their mutual borders. The future of Kashmir and the fate of 90,000 prisoners of war held by India and 1,500,000 Biharis of Bangladesh who had supported Pakistan were to be discussed in further negotiations. At the other end of the subcontinent, Ceylon, becoming the Republic of Sri Lanka on May 22, ended rebellion and moved cautiously to the right.

India's offensive intervention in East Pakistan, which followed its treaty of friendship with the U.S.S.R., highlighted Soviet expansion in the Indian Ocean and seemed to stress the potential importance of the Southeast Asia Treaty Organization. SEATO's Canberra meeting in June concentrated on counter-subversion, and the organization, in conjunction with the nations that inaugurated a five-power treaty in November 1971, continued to provide some security for the independence of Southeast Asian Commonwealth countries and the South Pacific, with Britain providing both naval and air patrols. The Integrated Air Defence System held its first combined exercises to protect Malaysia and Singapore early in 1972.

The second meeting of the South Pacific Forum in February 1972 explored immigration and communications and set up a permanent bureau in Fiji, where the third meeting took place in September. New Zealand, which contributed 16% of the budget and 15% of the staff of the South Pacific Commission, gave the highest total of aid relative to population in the world. Further contributions were made to the new forum and to the Colombo Plan. New Zealand hosted the seventh consultative meeting of Antarctic Treaty nations in November and opposed the attempt in January of a U.S. syndicate to occupy Minerva reef, claimed by Tonga.

Canada and the Caribbean. Canada's preoccupation lay with Northern Territory developments and its U.S. relationship, particularly after Pres. Richard Nixon's 1972 visit, which resulted in an agreement to reopen trade negotiations and plans for cleaning up the Great Lakes and for Alaskan oil links. Nevertheless, Canada maintained interest in the Caribbean Commonwealth, mainly via the Caribbean Free Trade Area (CARIFTA); immigration became a lively issue when population figures showed that West Indians outnumbered Italians in Toronto.

Militant Black Power movements harassed West Indian governments, as Trinidad succumbed to another state of emergency following racial and industrial strife. Despite the November 1971 Grenada agreement outlining the formation of a new nation to incorporate Guyana, Dominica, Grenada, St. Kitts-Nevis, St. Lucia, and St. Vincent, political integration remained far off (St. Lucia and Grenada withdrew almost immediately). Economic ties grew through the Common Services Agreement, Regional Secretariat, and Caribbean Development Bank, but Commonwealth edges were blurred as some members sought association with other regional organizations. Guyana received considerable U.S. aid and achieved, in April, a $26,000,000 trade deal with China, yet kept its third world image by hosting the fourth conference of nonaligned nations in August.

Communications: *see* Telecommunications; Television and Radio

The Mediterranean. In Malta, Prime Minister Dom Mintoff unilaterally abrogated the 1964 defense agreement, pressing for and eventually obtaining in March 1972 increased aid from Britain and NATO powers. Malta agreed to bar Warsaw Pact nations from its ports. In Cyprus intercommunal talks remained deadlocked.

Economic Affairs. Commonwealth economic life continued under the uncertain shadow of the EEC, to which Britain signed the Treaty of Accession on Jan. 22, 1972. Though the status quo was to remain until 1975, relationships among the various trade groups remained uneasy. The Commonwealth Development Corporation's 1972 report showed a record year, with 28 new projects at £29,000,000, bringing total investment commitment to £190,000,000 on 210 projects. Total British aid, official and private, to less developed countries, overwhelmingly to the Commonwealth, passed the 1% GNP target. The total intra-Commonwealth flow in 1970 rose from £268,000,000 to £335,000,000, of which Britain was the largest donor. Over half went to Asian countries. U.K. trade with Africa and the more developed Commonwealth nations increased dramatically in 1971, to more than double the increase to EEC countries. Trade with Nigeria grew at a startling rate, from £78,000,000 to £140,000,000 (1969–71).

Commonwealth conferences held in 1972 included that of finance ministers in London in September; the Youth Conference (over half the Commonwealth's 865,000,000 inhabitants were under 25); and many educational, technical, and scientific meetings. The smooth operation of some 300 specialized organizations bore out the secretary-general's new concept of the Commonwealth as "functional."

(MOLLY MORTIMER)

See also articles on the various political units.

Communist Movement

In December 1972 many Communists throughout the world joined their Soviet colleagues in celebrating the 50th anniversary of the U.S.S.R.'s conversion from Soviet Russia to a multinational Union of Soviet Socialist Republics. This conversion was extolled throughout the year as the "Leninist solution" to the Soviet nationalities question—to the joint problems of reconciling nationalism with an international movement and internal national diversity with centralized direction from Moscow. There was irony in these assertions, however, since it was clear that divisive elements of "bourgeois nationalism" remained strong within several Communist countries and that differences in national outlook between the various Communist parties still lay at the root of some of the most serious difficulties confronting the international movement.

Sino-Soviet Relations. Primary among these difficulties in 1972 remained the conflict between China and the Soviet Union, which together contained about two-thirds of the world's Communists. Over the years, and especially since the 1968 crisis in Czechoslovakia, the Soviet leaders had insisted that relations between Communist parties and states must be based on the Leninist principles of "proletarian internationalism." In the Soviet view, the principles of noninterference and "peaceful coexistence" formed a suitable basis for relations between states with different social systems, but not for relations between fraternal socialist states.

Nevertheless, in March Soviet party leader Leonid I. Brezhnev announced his willingness to proceed with China on the basis of "peaceful coexistence" if differences could be settled in no other manner.

This concession undoubtedly reflected Soviet recognition that the Chinese challenge was moving from ideological combat to national competition. Despite some improvement in formal state relations and an increase in trade, however, Brezhnev's overture did not seem to have paid off, either in terms of restoring the unity of the Communist movement or in terms of getting China to accept his proposals for a nonaggression pact. Relations between the two parties continued to be strained, and by late summer the mutual polemics had resumed. In late November five Soviet soldiers were killed in a brief border conflict.

Brezhnev's offer came just a month after U.S. Pres. Richard Nixon visited Peking and was probably stimulated by concern that the Sino-U.S. summit meeting was aimed against the Soviet Union. In addition, Brezhnev presumably sought to demonstrate to Moscow's critics within the movement that the fault for the continued rift lay with the Maoists. However, the circumstances of President Nixon's visit to Moscow in May tended to counteract Brezhnev's efforts. Only two weeks before he was scheduled to arrive, Nixon made the decision to mine the harbours of North Vietnam, thereby forcing the North Vietnamese to depend on land routes from China for their strategic supplies. The Soviet leaders had to choose between their desire for top-level discussions with the U.S. president on a variety of important questions and national pride and their obligations to their Vietnamese ally. The demotion of Politburo member Petr Shelest from his post as Ukrainian party first secretary on the eve of Nixon's arrival may have indicated that a faction within the Soviet leadership strongly opposed the decision to go ahead with the talks. The whole situation added grist to the Chinese propaganda mills concerning the Soviets' desire for collusion with their fellow superpower, although the Chinese were willing to come to an agreement on the transshipment of Soviet supplies to Vietnam.

The Chinese seemed particularly concerned that the Soviet Union would reach an agreement with the U.S. on the stabilization of Europe, since such an agreement would allow the Soviet leaders to concentrate their attention on China and would free additional troops for service on the Chinese border. Accordingly, the Chinese had sought to encourage the independence of the Communist states of Eastern Europe and had supported the development of the EEC as a source of resistance to both U.S. and Soviet imperialism. Despite these efforts, the July meeting of the heads of government of the Comecon nations in Moscow and the subsequent informal meeting of party leaders in the Crimea gave indications that the Soviet Union was making progress in getting its Eastern European allies to work more closely with one another. Not only did the Comecon nations agree on new measures for industrial and scientific cooperation, but there were signs that the recalcitrant Romanians and nonaligned Yugoslavs were establishing a somewhat closer relationship to Moscow.

The main focus of Chinese propaganda, however, was the third world, as was clearly evident in China's first year of activities at the UN and in its rapidly expanding economic and military aid program to a variety of Asian, African, and even a few Latin-American countries. To help stave off Maoist influence in radical Arab circles, the Soviet Communist Party backed the one legal Communist Party in the Arab world, the Lebanese, in playing host in January to the largest conference of Arab Communists and associated parties ever assembled. In the spring the U.S.S.R. stepped up its aid to Syria and formally established party relations with the Syrian Baathists. While Pres. Nikolai V. Podgorny was entertained in Turkey, Premier Aleksei N. Kosygin flew to Baghdad in April to sign a 15-year treaty of friendship and cooperation with Iraq. Soviet aid to the Palestinian guerrillas was also increased. All this meant that Egyptian Pres. Anwar as-Sadat's decision in July to expel all Soviet military advisers, though a definite setback, was not the disaster for Soviet policy it would have been a few years earlier.

Communism in Europe. One of the dominant themes in the domestic policies of the ruling Communist parties of Europe in 1972 was the effort to gain increased popular support through reforms, which usually included major improvements in living standards and in the production of consumer goods. A second major theme was the need to be on guard against the subversive influence of "bourgeois ideology," including excessive reformism and nationalism.

The Soviet Party encountered a number of difficulties in carrying out these policies. It was a disastrous year for agriculture, and the need to purchase large amounts of grain abroad inevitably damaged the party's plans to improve the standard of living. The party's efforts at ideological consolidation were reflected in the nationwide preparations for a general party purge and in a series of decrees aimed at instilling greater party-mindedness among intellectuals. Nevertheless, there were a number of manifestations of ideological dissent and anti-Russian nationalism, the most dramatic of which occurred in Lithuania and involved cases of self-immolation and rioting.

The dangers of "bourgeois nationalism" were even more evident in "revisionist" Yugoslavia. Riots in Croatia, sparked by charges of economic discrimination against Croatia and the traditional antagonism between Croats and Serbs, had led to a decision to overhaul the Croatian Party leadership in December 1971. In January a group of Croatian intellectuals were arrested on charges of plotting secession, and it was announced that more than 700 Croatians had been expelled or had resigned from the party. Efforts were made to respond to the real economic grievances of the Croatians, but the terrorist activities of Croatian *ustakhi* abroad and an attempt by a group of them to infiltrate into Yugoslavia kept the situation tense. As part of his reemphasis on the guiding role of the party, President Tito indicated he was considering an overhaul of the economic reform that had allowed some Yugoslavs to become multimillionaires.

A somewhat different face of nationalism was revealed in Hungary, where rioting by young Hungarians occurred on their national day in March. The riots were apparently directed less against the relatively liberal policies of Janos Kadar than against Hungary's dependence on the Soviet Union. Only a few days later Premier Jeno Fock stated that there were some "major difficulties" in his country's economic relations with the U.S.S.R., an unusual step that evoked remarks about "bourgeois nationalism" from both the U.S.S.R. and the superloyal Czechoslovaks. A similar type of nationalism had been openly exhibited in Romania for several years and had provided Romanian party leader Nicolae Ceausescu with

PANA-INDIA/KEYSTONE

Indian Communists participate in May Day celebration at Ramlila grounds in Delhi. Rough translation of banner is "long live unity."

Membership of the Major Communist Parties of the World*

Countries with a membership of 2,000 or more persons

Country	Membership
Albania	87,000†
Argentina	60,000
Australia	3,900
Austria	25,000
Belgium	12,500
Bolivia‡	2,800
Brazil‡	13,000
Bulgaria	700,000†
Burma‡	§
Canada	2,000
Chile	90,000
China	17,000,000†
Colombia	11,000
Cuba	125,000†
Cyprus	13,000
Czechoslovakia	1,200,000
Denmark	5,000
Finland	47,000†
France	275,000
Germany, East	1,909,800†
Germany, West	39,400
Greece‡	28,000
Guadeloupe	2,000
Hungary	693,000†
India	162,000
Iraq‡	2,000
Israel	2,000
Italy	1,521,000
Japan	300,000
Korea, North	1,600,000†
Laos	13,000
Malaysia‡	2,000
Mexico	5,000
Mongolia	58,000†
Nepal‡	10,000
Netherlands	10,000
Norway	2,250
Paraguay‡	4,500
Peru	3,200
Poland	2,270,000†
Portugal‡	2,000
Romania	2,175,000†
Spain‡	5,000
Sri Lanka (Ceylon)	4,000
Sudan	7,500
Sweden	17,000
Switzerland	3,500
Syria‡	3,000
U.S.S.R.	14,455,000†
United Kingdom	29,000
U.S.	§
Uruguay	20,000
Venezuela	8,000
Vietnam, North	1,100,000†
Vietnam, South‡	§
Yugoslavia	1,049,000†

*Estimated from figures available December 1971.
†Official claim.
‡Communist Party illegal.
§No estimate available.
Source: U.S. Department of State, Bureau of Intelligence and Research, "World Strength of the Communist Party Organizations" (May 1972).

a considerable degree of popular support, despite his regime's rather harsh internal economic and cultural policies. Economic pressures seemed to be forcing Ceausescu into a somewhat closer relationship with Moscow and Comecon, but his continued independence from Soviet control was demonstrated on several occasions. In February it was reported that the general in charge of the Bucharest military garrison had been shot as a Soviet spy, and in May Ceausescu played host to Prime Minister Golda Meir, although the U.S.S.R. had broken relations with Israel.

In July the Romanian party conference decided to shift economic priorities from heavy industry to consumer goods and to institute broad reforms directed at providing more housing, higher wages, better pensions, and a shorter work week. These measures were similar to those already taken by the Polish Communist Party in response to the riots of December 1970. Earlier in the year the East Germans announced their intention to carry out a $2.5 billion program designed to accomplish similar ends.

The behaviour of the Czechoslovak party leadership indicated that, unlike some of their neighbouring parties, they had been unable to gain a significant degree of national support. Numerous arrests of liberal Communists and other supporters of the 1968 reform movement occurred in early 1972, and a series of subversion trials began in July. Although party chief Gustav Husak personally justified these trials as a defense of Marxism-Leninism, condemnations were voiced by several Western Communist parties, including the two largest, the French and Italian. The decision of the Italian Communists to attack the trials was to be expected, given their generally independent and liberal stance. At the Italian Party's 13th congress in March, which elected Enrico Berlinguer (*see* BIOGRAPHY) as secretary-general in place of the ailing Luigi Longo, their independent position in regard to the Sino-Soviet dispute was reasserted. In the case of the staunchly pro-Soviet French party, the protest against the Prague trials was evidently inspired by the need to reassure the French electorate and the Socialist Party, with whom the Communists finally managed to hammer out a joint program in June.

Communism in Asia. In the summer, official Chinese sources confirmed rumours that Chairman Mao Tse-tung's former heir apparent, Defense Minister Lin Piao, had been killed the previous September in an air crash in Mongolia while attempting to escape to the Soviet Union following an abortive coup d'etat. It was also asserted that the plotters had direct contact with the Soviet military. Whatever the truth of these allegations, which the Soviets termed "absurd inventions," the internal policy of the Chinese Communists, like their foreign policy, moved further away from the orientation it had taken during the Cultural Revolution. A number of officials who had been purged were rehabilitated. The activities of the Red Guards were strictly limited, examinations in the schools were resumed, and much attention was focused on economic production, including the production of more consumer goods.

China's diplomatic initiatives evoked varying responses from the other Asian Communist parties. The North Korean Communists, while carefully maintaining their friendly ties with Moscow, refused to join in condemning the Chinese activities. Like the Chinese, they began to break out of their self-imposed isolation. Premier Kim Il Sung pressed forward with negotiations with the South Koreans aimed, ultimately, at finding a formula for peaceful reunification. Steps were taken toward normalization of relations with Japan, and interest was shown in establishing at least some contact with the U.S.

The North Vietnamese Communists maintained a stony silence about President Nixon's trips. Both Chou En-lai and President Podgorny traveled to Hanoi after Nixon's visits to their respective countries, but they apparently encountered a rather cold reception. In August the North Vietnamese indicated their bitterness in an editorial that accused those Communists favouring "peaceful coexistence" of betraying the revolutionary struggle. The strongly nationalist Japanese Communist Party was far more outspoken than the Vietnamese could afford to be in denouncing the Nixon trip to Peking as a sellout.

Communism in Latin America. The Soviet policy of "peaceful coexistence" with even repressively anti-Communist governments and the moderate, nonviolent orientation of the orthodox pro-Moscow Communist parties continued to annoy and frustrate the more radical revolutionary groups throughout Latin America. Nowhere was this conflict of views more evident than in Chile, where the Communists were among the more conservative members of the governing Popular Unity coalition of Pres. Salvador Allende. Faced with a deepening economic crisis and growing restiveness among the people, the Communists urged their coalition partners to proceed more cautiously with the nationalization of industry and to make overtures to the opposition Christian Democrats. They also urged stricter controls on the ultra-radical Movement of the Revolutionary Left (MIR).

Another frustration for the more violent Latin-American revolutionaries was the less radical image presented by both the Chinese and the Cuban Communists. In late 1971, when Cuban Prime Minister Fidel Castro visited Chile, he strongly urged the MIR to support the Allende government, and during 1972 Castro's main preoccupation continued to be the solution of his island's economic difficulties. Obviously bothered by the potential implications for Cuba of President Nixon's trip to Moscow, the Cuban leader in May began a two-month tour of Africa, Eastern Europe, and the U.S.S.R., where he was awarded the Order of Lenin. This was the first time since the fall of Nikita Khrushchev that Castro had been to Moscow. Probably as a result of his visit, Cuba was accepted as a full member of Comecon in July.

(DAVID L. WILLIAMS)

See also China; Czechoslovakia; Defense; Intelligence Operations; Soviet Bloc Economies; and articles on the various countries.

ENCYCLOPÆDIA BRITANNICA FILMS. *China: A Portrait of the Land* (1967); *China's Industrial Revolution* (1967); *China's Villages in Change* (1967).

Computers

Highlights in the computer industry during 1972 included the introduction of new bipolar technology, the installation of a computerized fault-location system in automobiles to help mechanics pinpoint trouble spots, and a declaration by the U.S. Department of Justice that IBM should be broken up into several smaller companies.

New Technology. Researchers at Thomson-CSF in France found a holographic technique, using barium titanate doped with iron, that indicated the possibility of a computer memory storing one trillion bits or more in a volume of only about 100 cc. A similar technique had previously been developed by RCA Corp. in the United States, using lithium niobate.

Fairchild Camera and Instrument Corp. unveiled a 1,024-bit bipolar random-access memory in a single integrated circuit (IC) roughly 0.150 in. square. This memory is not to be confused with those of similar size and capacity but made with metal oxide semiconductor (MOS) technology. The latter, introduced earlier, had become almost standard products in 1972. Bipolar technology, which utilized the bipolar junction transistor as the principal element in an IC, offers a much greater speed potential than does MOS, and the arrays are easier to use than the MOS arrays, but until the Fairchild breakthrough only MOS had succeeded in putting as many as 1,000 bits in one IC. Meanwhile, MOS designers were hard at work on 2,048- and 4,096-bit arrays; several preliminary versions of these designs were announced during the year.

MOS technology was also used in a complete eight-bit processor in a single IC measuring 0.250 in. by 0.280 in. The circuit, enormous by IC standards, contained more than 7,000 transistors. The processor was one of 11 ICs, most of them of nearly conventional size, used in a new version of a computer built by Four-Phase Systems, Inc., of Cupertino, Calif. The computer, called System IV/70, had been introduced in 1970 for use in scientific and laboratory work, where binary representation of data is satisfactory. To expand into business data processing, Four-Phase needed a decimal arithmetic capability as well; combining this with the earlier binary arithmetic in a single processor resulted in the huge package, which its designers unofficially dubbed "Superchip."

In February IBM Corp. unveiled an operating semiconductor memory system using charge-coupled devices (CCD). Although strictly an experimental assembly, it was the first use of CCD technology outside the laboratory and in a potential working machine environment. Charge-coupled devices store data at densities perhaps ten times as great as those of conventional semiconductor arrays and are easier and cheaper to build because they require no internal connections.

New Applications. Volkswagenwerk AG, West Germany's biggest automobile maker, began introducing a computerized fault-location system to help mechanics pinpoint problems in malfunctioning cars. Using test circuits installed in new models of VW cars, the system carries out up to 88 tests, automatically or semiautomatically, and prints out the results. Two West German firms—Siemens AG and Hartmann and Braun—were chosen to build the computerized diagnostic stands, installation of which began in more than 4,000 Volkswagen service shops in West Germany and overseas.

Meanwhile, in France, the government began thinking about a computerized safety system to be installed directly in cars. The system would take over the function of the driver's judgment, monitoring environmental factors such as outside temperature and humidity and limiting acceleration, top speed, and suddenness of braking to fit road conditions. Furthermore, it would evaluate the driver's physical condition by comparing his driving movements against a standard, and would shut off the engine if it detected drunkenness or extreme fatigue.

A group of physicians at the University of Alabama developed a new fetal monitoring system for use in hospital obstetrical wards that provides almost instant indication of failure in such critical functions as fetal heart rate, uterine activity pressure, and contraction rate. It uses a commercially available fetal monitoring unit, a small computer, and a network of electrodes; but unlike conventional electronic systems it need not be watched constantly—it prints out a warning within ten seconds of its detection of an abnormality. Also, the printer need not be in the labour room but can be, for example, at the nurse's station down the hall.

Courts of law began to use computers for indexing, docketing, and information-gathering. This made possible the obtaining of complete arrest records through the Federal Bureau of Investigation in a matter of hours, and of summaries in minutes, compared with the days required by mail requests. Eventually, such computer systems might be extended to scheduling of cases, legal research, and even jury selection.

The U.S. Department of Health, Education, and Welfare began formulating plans to place computer terminals in drugstores throughout the nation, linking them to doctors' offices and data banks containing prescriptions and health information for the entire population. The terminals would link more than 50,000 pharmacies that are expected to dispense 2,000,000,000 prescriptions per year by 1975, and also cope with increasingly comprehensive health insurance programs.

Business Events. The Univac division of Sperry Rand Corp. acquired 500 new customers, who had installed about 1,000 RCA computers worth perhaps $1 billion and who had been left stranded when RCA abruptly dropped out of the general-purpose computer business in 1971. To serve these customers, Univac

TASS / SOVFOTO

Photograph shows a computer assembly plant at Yerevan in the Soviet Union. Increased production of third-generation computers was part of a five-year plan and a long-term project to computerize the entire Soviet economy.

AUTHENTICATED NEWS INTERNATIONAL

Testing a plastic assembly containing dozens of fibre optic channels can be completed in minutes on the IBM 1800 computer being demonstrated above.

also hired 2,500 former RCA employees. Later, Digital Equipment Corp. bought RCA's former ferrite-core memory system manufacturing operation and began making its own memory systems for its computers instead of buying them from outside manufacturers.

The Arpanet, the experimental coast-to-coast network of computers put together by the Advanced Research Projects Agency (ARPA) of the U.S. Department of Defense, became largely operational. It linked about two dozen government and university computer centres from New England to southern California with high-speed telephone lines and special communications miniprocessors that connected the local large-scale computers to the telephone lines. ARPA continued to manage the network but was actively looking for a way to turn it over to another government or private agency, perhaps one created especially for the task.

BART, the Bay Area Rapid Transit surface and subway system serving San Francisco and the surrounding area, became operational over 27 mi. of its eventual 75-mi. length in September, carrying its first paying customers. It was supposed to be the world's first fully automatic train system, but as it opened trains were still unable to operate at full speed because of malfunctions in the controlling computer. Later, the system suffered its first accident as a train rolled through a station and hit a barricade; five persons were hurt.

T. Vincent Learson, board chairman of IBM, announced that he would retire at the end of 1972, having reached his 60th birthday. During his tenure as chairman, Learson was credited with giving IBM a stiffer competitive stance in the computer industry—which it already dominated with about two-thirds of the industry's total dollar volume. An example of the new stance occurred in the early spring of 1972 when IBM was faced with increasing competition from independent manufacturers of core and semiconductor memories, who were adding to or replacing the IBM-supplied memories on the computers of many IBM customers, at lower prices. Although IBM could grumble about this, it could do little within the restraints of the antitrust laws as long as the add-on or replacement was within the maximum memory capacity specified by IBM for the particular computer model. But in some cases the capacity had been enhanced beyond IBM's specifications; IBM announced that it would not service such machines because the enhancement entailed internal modifications to the computers.

One of the independents, Advanced Memory Systems, Inc. (AMS), and its marketing agent, Itel Corp., sued IBM on the grounds that the changes were minor and that the withholding of service effectively denied AMS a substantial part of its market. AMS won; the court decreed that IBM would have to service those parts of the computers that were not affected by the enhancement and that the enhancement would have to be so installed that it could be effectively deactivated by flicking a switch.

The U.S. Department of Justice in October called for the breaking up of IBM into "several discrete, separate, independent and competitively balanced entities." IBM denied that it dominated the computer industry to the extent described by the government and stated that its share of the market was declining every year.

Control Data Corp. and National Cash Register Co. announced a plan to cooperate on a program to "expand each company's future role" in the general-purpose computer industry. Essentially, Control Data would continue to make large-scale scientific computer systems, while National Cash Register would concentrate on smaller systems for business data processing. The two companies formed a joint subsidiary to manufacture certain peripheral equipment to be used by both.

The six major Japanese computer companies began a major realignment in which they would join forces to make the most of each other's strengths and overcome their weaknesses. The first overt move in this realignment was an announcement that two of the six companies, Hitachi and Fujitsu, would jointly develop their next generation of computers.

New Products. Univac announced its new model 9700, which it hoped would replace many old IBM 1400-series computers, a line of medium-size machines dating back to the late 1950s and early 1960s. The 1400 series was so popular that many newer computers were emulating them—that is, running 1400-series programs unmodified. The 9700 incorporated the capability of emulating the 1400-series machines much more flexibly than before, taking another step toward what might eventually become basically incompatible lines of computers from various manufacturers that can nevertheless run one another's programs through emulation.

After six years of development, Texas Instruments, Inc., disclosed some details about its giant Advanced Scientific Computer. A multiprocessor, it consists of three processors, eight memories, and a full complement of input/output equipment. From a single processor three 32-bit operands can be transferred to or from the memory in 60 nanoseconds (billionths of a second); this rate of activity can be maintained from several arithmetic units and input/output devices simultaneously.

IBM announced three new models in its System 370 line of computers during 1972. In August came the large-scale models 158 and 168, and in October the small model 125. All three were built with metal oxide semiconductor memories, IBM's first use of this technology in a computer main memory, and all three had "virtual storage." Virtual storage is a combination of hardware and software that permits a programmer to ignore the physical capacity of the computer's memory; what spills over is kept on a disk or drum and retrieved automatically as needed. Virtual storage, like semiconductor memory, was not new in 1972, but its use by IBM in three models seemed to herald its wide acceptance after limited use in some machines by several other companies. And hard on the heels of IBM's announcement came news that two researchers at the University of Massachusetts succeeded in installing virtual storage in a minicomputer.

Iomec, Inc., brought out a flexible magnetic disk storage system intended to offer disk-drive performance at digital tape cassette prices. It used a flexible magnetic disk in a cartridge that could be plugged into a mechanical drive in somewhat the same way that a tape cassette is inserted into a tape unit, but could write 2,000 records of 128 characters each in nine seconds, as compared with three to six minutes required for the same job with a cassette. Memorex Corp. also introduced a flexible disk drive; and the reloadable control store in the latest IBM computers used a similar device to load new control sequences.

(WALLACE B. RILEY)

Confederation of Arab Republics: *see* Egypt; Libya; Syria

Congo, Democratic Republic of the: *see* Zaire

Congo, People's Republic of the

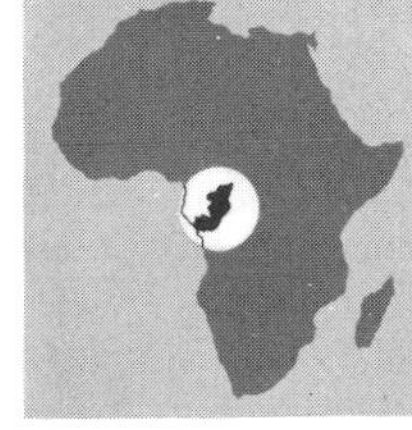

A people's republic of equatorial Africa, the Congo is bounded by Gabon, Cameroon, the Central African Republic, Zaire, Angola, and the Atlantic Ocean. Area: 132,000 sq.mi. (342,000 sq.km.). Pop. (1970): 1,089,300, mainly Bantu. Cap. and largest city: Brazzaville (pop., 1970, 175,000). Language: French (official) and Bantu dialects. Religion: mainly animist, with a Christian minority. President in 1972, Maj. Marien Ngouabi.

During 1972 the Congo continued to go through a period of considerable political confusion, and it was hard to say exactly who was to the left of whom in the country's sole political party, the Congolese Workers' Party (PCT). A predilection for the use of Marxist phraseology by both President Ngouabi and his opponents did little to promote a clear understanding of often apparently incongruous events.

In February the authorities announced the failure of an attempted coup, and a large number of public figures were arrested. The detainees included former premier Ambroise Noumazalay and former chief of state Alfred Raoul, who had been dismissed as vice-president in the purge of December 1971. Also arrested was the former first secretary of the PCT's political bureau, Claude-Ernest Ndalla.

President Ngouabi's opponents accused him of having set a trap for them, of having, as it were, engineered a scheme whereby they would be provoked to an attempted coup so that the president could crush it in his own good time. Ngouabi and his allies denied this, their own version of the events tending to support the theory of a threat to state security.

In March Ngouabi was received by French Pres. Georges Pompidou in Paris, where he sought to justify his position. He also gave a public assurance that whatever the severity of the penalties imposed, none of the alleged conspirators would be executed.

On March 25 death sentences were passed on 13 of the defendants, including Ambroise Noumazalay. Later in the day, however, all 13 sentences were commuted to life imprisonment by presidential decree. Ndalla was sentenced to life imprisonment and Raoul to ten years. The latter's release in April seemed as inexplicable as his arrest.

In this political state of siege, the death of former president Fulbert Youlou on May 5 in Madrid, Spain, where he had been granted political asylum, passed almost unnoticed by his compatriots. (*See* OBITUARIES.)

In September, for reasons that remained obscure, the Brazzaville authorities decided to break with the Common Organization of Africa, Malagasy, and Mauritius (OCAM) and gave notice of the Congo's withdrawal from the organization. At the same time, a cooperation agreement with France was abrogated, and the Congolese authorities demanded the renegotiation of all agreements made between France and the Congo at the time of the latter's accession to international sovereignty. (PHILIPPE DECRAENE)

CONGO, PEOPLE'S REPUBLIC OF THE

Education. (1969–70) Primary, pupils 228,578, teachers 3,787; secondary, pupils 25,228, teachers 672; vocational, pupils 2,594, teachers 317; teacher training, students 583, teachers 34; higher, students 1,786, teaching staff 103.

Finance. Monetary unit: CFA franc, with (Sept. 18, 1972) a parity of CFA Fr. 50 to the French franc and CFA Fr. 255.79 to U.S. $1 (free rate of CFA Fr. 612.37 = £1 sterling). Budget (1970 est.) balanced at CFA Fr. 18.1 billion.

Foreign Trade. (1970) Imports CFA Fr. 16,640,-000,000; exports CFA Fr. 8,560,000,000. Import sources (1968): France 58%; West Germany 10%; U.S. 5%. Export destinations (1968): West Germany 25%; Netherlands 19%; Belgium-Luxembourg 14%; France 12%; Israel 6%; South Africa 6%. Main exports: timber 53%; diamonds 9%.

Transport and Communications. Roads (1970) *c.* 11,000 km. (including 243 km. with improved surface). Motor vehicles in use (1968): passenger 7,200; commercial 5,600. Railways: (1970) 795 km.; traffic (1971) 146 million passenger-km., freight 534 million net ton-km. Air traffic (1970): 72,734,000 passenger-km.; freight 6,530,000 net ton-km. Telephones (Dec. 1970) 10,000. Radio receivers (Dec. 1970) 65,000. Television receivers (Dec. 1970) 1,800.

Agriculture. Production (in 000; metric tons; 1970; 1969 in parentheses): cassava *c.* 450 (*c.* 450); coffee *c.* 2 (1.8); peanuts *c.* 20 (20); sugar, raw value (1971–72) *c.* 122, (1970–71) *c.* 98; palm kernels *c.* 3.8 (2.8); palm oil *c.* 5.7 (5.7). Livestock (in 000; 1970–71): sheep *c.* 60; cattle *c.* 38; pigs *c.* 38.

Consumer Affairs

Substantial advances both in governmental activities to protect the consumer and in the continuing growth of the organized consumer movement were made in 1972. National governments proposed or enacted a large volume of consumer-oriented legislation, and tended to increase or expand the executive or administrative agencies charged with protecting the consumer. On the international level there were important developments in the programs of the intergovernmental organizations on behalf of the consumer. Membership in consumer associations and in the International Organization of Consumers Unions (IOCU) continued to grow, with a corresponding increase in the level and range of their activities. This broadening of interests took two main directions: environmental protection and the economic betterment of the less developed countries, both of which emerged clearly as trends at the 1972 World Consumer Conference convened in Stockholm in August by the IOCU. In consequence, the consumer movement strengthened its links with the activities of the UN, and in particular with its Second Development Decade and its Conference on the Human Environment, where in June the IOCU was one of the few nongovernment organizations of the many hundreds present to be invited to address a plenary session.

WIDE WORLD

Consumer affairs official Virginia Knauer in a New York speech announced new clothing label regulations effective in July 1972 aimed at alleviating confusion over how certain fabrics should be laundered properly.

Legislation. New laws and regulations to protect the consumer covered a wide front and, although most of the legal action occurred in the North Atlantic countries, a growing proportion happened in the less developed regions. National governments engaged in a broad range of consumer-based actions: Canada published guidelines governing the radio and television advertising of children's vitamin products, imposed regulations controlling the importation and sale of children's car seats and harnesses, and announced a program to help low-income debtors; Ireland introduced unit pricing in July for a range of foodstuffs; France introduced a bill to regulate door-to-door sales; Nigeria placed legal checks on misleading and injurious advertising of food and drugs; Sweden proposed a bill giving the state power to control increases

Congregational Churches: *see* Religion

Conservation: *see* Environment

Construction Industry: *see* Engineering Projects; Housing; Industrial Review in prices that particularly affected the consumer; and Yugoslavia introduced legislation to ensure the proper description of goods offered for sale.

In the U.K. a bill to introduce unit pricing had its first reading in March. The Department of Trade and Industry also studied possible new measures to provide greater protection for consumers and to answer their grievances as part of a general review of consumer-based reforms.

A number of governments also proposed, introduced, or expanded the existing scope of state agencies to protect the consumer interest. The West German government proposed to extend the Federal Cartel Office to cover both competition in trade and consumer protection, and the Social Democratic Party called for a number of measures including the creation of a body of consumer representatives and the introduction of an "ombudsman" on the Swedish model. In Sweden plans were completed to merge the Consumer Council, the National Institute for Consumer Affairs, and the Labeling Board into a newly established Directorate for Consumer Affairs, a "superagency" that would come into effect on Jan. 1, 1973. This change did not affect the consumer ombudsman and the quasi-judicial Marketing Court. Following Sweden's lead in pioneering the ombudsman principle, the Norwegian Storting approved a law establishing a similar official and a Marketing Council. The Irish National Prices Commission called in June for the establishment of three consultative councils responsible for investigating complaints and advising on policy matters of consumer concern.

Jamaica established a ministerial post in 1972 with a portfolio that specifically included consumer protection. The British government made a similar ministerial appointment on November 5, when Sir Geoffrey Howe was named minister of trade and consumer affairs within the Department of Trade and Industry. A group of Conservative MPs had included such a recommendation in a report issued in September that had also called for the setting up of arbitration services and consumer advice centres; seven such centres were opened or announced in the United Kingdom in 1971 by local authorities operating with the cooperation of the independent British Consumers' Association.

In the U.S. it was announced that by midyear no fewer than 45 states, Puerto Rico, the Virgin Islands, 53 cities, and 18 counties had established some form of specifically designated consumer office. At the federal level, Congress passed only one piece of major consumer legislation; a number of bills, including one to create an independent federal consumer agency with wide powers, did not survive the 92nd Congress, allegedly for lack of White House support (*see* below).

Intergovernmental Organizations. Concern for the consumer at the national level in 1972 was paralleled by the activities of a number of intergovernmental organizations. The Codex Alimentarius Commission of the UN's Food and Agriculture Organization (FAO) and World Health Organization (WHO), concerned with the drawing up of international food standards, pressed its work in 1972 into such fields as processed meat products, processed fruit and vegetables, meat hygiene, infant foods, food additives, dietary foods, the date marking of foods, and advertising of foods for infants. IOCU papers drawing attention to the world consumer view on topics relating to its work were contributed to the special Committee of the Economic and Social Council on Review and Appraisal of the Second Development Decade, to UNICEF, to the UN Industrial Development Organization (UNIDO), and to the Council of Europe. At the 89th session (May–July) of its Executive Board, UNESCO invited IOCU to take up "information and consultative relations" with it.

In February the Committee of Ministers of the Council of Europe adopted a resolution calling on the Council's 17 member governments to protect consumers against advertising likely to mislead them directly or indirectly. The governments were asked to introduce legislation containing penalties severe enough to act as a deterrent. In May the Consultative Assembly unanimously adopted a further resolution on consumer protection policy and called for common principles of consumer protection and assistance to be defined and written into a "European Consumers Charter." Other activities of the Council of Europe included the work of an expert committee on consumer consultation and participation in decision-making bodies, consumer education programs, and consumer information through the mass media; the Committee for Legal Cooperation looked into legislation on controlling door-to-door sales, judicial systems for legal protection of consumers, proper contract terms, and the liability of producers.

In July the Committee on Consumer Policy of the Organization for Economic Cooperation and Development (OECD) had its mandate extended for five years. (It had been created in 1969 on a provisional basis.) In the same month the committee published its reports on labeling and on comparative testing of consumer products. In September the committee published its report on present consumer policy in member countries, a comprehensive study based on a two-year overall review.

In the European Community, the EEC appropriated an additional BFr. 10 million for its work in the consumer protection field, and publicly recognized the need in the enlarged Community for "a comprehensive coherent consumer policy," and for "a powerful central organization to protect consumers." The EEC Commission had previously collaborated in this field with the Consumers Contact Committee, which became unable to operate effectively and was dissolved early in 1972. The Commission subsequently agreed to enter into direct relations for consumer representation with the European Bureau of Consumers Unions. In its first report on competition, the Commission examined the advantages of the Common Market for consumers. It revealed that in the 14 years since the founding of the EEC, consumer spending had increased 96% in real terms and that private spending had changed considerably.

In the field of standardization, the International Organization for Standardization (ISO) published its first batch of standards under its new procedure describing them as "international standards" instead of "recommendations" intended to be used as the basis for national standards. The ISO claimed that both consumer organizations and multinational companies were pressing for more international agreements on technical questions. It therefore was engaged during 1972 in the formulation of standards in a large number of consumer areas, from blankets to slide projectors. Consumer organizations participated, through IOCU, in discussions on international shoe-sizing, informative labeling, the care labeling of textiles, clothing sizes, and comparative product testing.

Consumer Movement. The consumer movement achieved substantial advances in 1972 in growth and credibility and in the range of its activities. The number of consumer organizations grew, chiefly through the emergence of new groups in the less developed regions, particularly in Asia. The IOCU admitted 17 new member organizations during the year, representing such countries as the Philippines, Lebanon, Malaysia, Fiji, India, and Nigeria. The established organizations all experienced steady, and in some areas dramatic, growth. For example, the number of subscribers to *Que Choisir?* ("What to Choose?"), published by the French Union Fédérale des Consommateurs, rose from 42,250 to over 100,000; the Dutch Consumentenbond had an increase in membership of 40,000 over the previous figure of 290,000; the Danish Statens Husholdningsråd issued 931,000 of its publications, 200,000 more than the previous year; and the Consumers Union of the U.S. saw the circulation of its monthly *Consumer Reports* rise by 166,000 to nearly 2,250,000 by the end of 1972. New consumer publications included *Handyman Which?*, a quarterly stablemate to the British Consumers' Association's *Money Which?*, and *Que Choisir? Budget*, a quarterly introduced by the Union Fédérale des Consommateurs in September.

An important means of publicizing these activities and recruiting new members that gained rapidly in favour was the holding of "consumer weeks." These programs typically included exhibitions, displays and demonstrations, talks and discussion sessions, film, slide and photographic exhibits, and training courses on practical consumer subjects such as money management, health, and housing. Countries where consumer weeks were held in 1972 included Canada, the U.S., Spain, the Philippines, Malaysia, and India. Bombay was to have been the scene of a major international consumer seminar organized by IOCU during the last week of 1971. The outbreak of hostilities in the Indian subcontinent forced the last-minute postponement of this conference, but in March Bombay again made consumer news by becoming the location of the first All-India Conference on Consumer Protection.

Other examples of the broadening of activities by consumer organizations were Consumentenbond's introduction of a special service to deal with members' questions; the setting up by the U.K. Consumers' Association of an Advice Centre Servicing Unit to provide the materials and expertise needed to run the consumer advice centres being introduced by local authorities; the opening of consumer recycling centres in Canada and other countries; and the setting up of two ancillary organizations by the U.S. Consumers Union, a Consumer Interests Foundation to explore in depth some of the more pressing consumer problems and the expansion of the CU Washington, D.C., office to undertake consumer advocacy activities. Substantial progress also occurred in the development of testing projects carried out jointly by two or more organizations of different countries.

(JOHN CALASCIONE)

Consumerism in the U.S. Because consumerism was in many ways more a concept than an identifiable political special interest, no reliable yardstick existed to measure what had been achieved and what remained uncompleted. In practice, consumerism tended to go beyond such obvious concerns as the products and product information offered in the marketplace to embrace issues ranging from social values

UPI COMPIX

A girl's nightgown is aflame in a demonstration of inadequacies of standards set by existing U.S. legislation. The blaze was set by a single match during House of Representatives Commerce Subcommittee hearings on consumer safety legislation.

to the protection of the environment. In an effort to understand and respond, one company (Swift & Co.) arrived at the definition: "The desire by people for proper representation, full participation, complete and truthful information, and the opportunity to use this information to make decisions." A less precise but relevant definition devised by a U.S. Commerce Department advisory committee, the National Business Council for Consumer Affairs, said consumerism should be thought of as "the growing framework of expectations with which the consumer views the business establishment."

Whatever its definition, consumerism fell short of its legislative hopes in the closing session of the 92nd Congress, but the tempo of activity on consumer issues quickened at other levels of government and business, producing an array of laws, regulations, and operational reforms in industry that showed that the phenomenon continued to spread. Of the three major bills before Congress, only the Consumer Product Safety Act reached the White House and became law, but at the federal regulatory agencies, progress was made on issues related to product safety actions under existing laws and on proposals for more informative labels and advertising.

The consumer movement encountered its most persistent resistance in those cases where it sought more participation in the decision-making process. Legislation calling for the creation of a special government agency to represent consumer interests in proceedings before regulatory agencies and courts had been regarded as a priority legislative goal for 1972. The bill had been approved by the House of Representatives in 1971 but became enmeshed in a Senate filibuster in 1972 and had to be abandoned. Likewise, at the Federal Communications Commission (FCC) there was little to show for the variety of petitions seeking a right of access to radio and television airwaves for "counteradvertising" messages. Nonetheless, there was a proliferation of additional state, county, and city laws and actions on selling practices, no-fault insurance, and landlord-tenant relationships, and there was an obvious pattern in ombudsman-like recourse programs set up by associations and companies to deal with consumer ideas and complaints.

Federal Legislation. The Consumer Product Safety Act, approved by Congress and signed by Pres. Richard Nixon on October 28, was characterized by consumer leaders as landmark protection legislation comparable to the automobile safety law of 1966. It was the outgrowth of more than two years of studies by the National Commission on Product Safety. The new law created an independent five-member commission with authority to establish mandatory standards to guard against "unreasonable" hazards in an all-inclusive list of household items other than foods, drugs, and cosmetics and to ban the sale of items that could not be made "reasonably" safe. A unique provision of the law permitted persons who failed to get satisfaction from the commission to obtain court orders requiring the commission to make a determination. While existing regulatory arrangements for automobiles and for foods, drugs, and cosmetics were left untouched, the authority to administer several existing product safety laws was transferred to the new commission; among the laws affected were the Hazardous Substances Act, previously in the hands of the Food and Drug Administration (FDA), and the Flammable Fabrics Act, originally administered by the Department of Commerce.

Two other bills that were identified as consumer laws were passed during 1972. The Drug Listing Act, signed into law August 16, provided the FDA with authority to secure a listing of every company marketing drugs and the identity of the drugs each marketed. The Motor Vehicle Information and Cost Savings Act, which became law October 20, authorized the secretary of transportation to establish cost-effective bumper performance standards for new cars manufactured in or imported into the U.S., to conduct studies of crash-worthiness, damage susceptibility, and ease of diagnosis and repair among various car makes and models, to assist states in developing automotive diagnostic centres, and to outlaw tampering with vehicle odometers.

Consumer affairs advocates succeeded in resisting some unwelcome legislation, notably a bill passed by the House calling for the reimbursement of businesses for losses incurred after the Department of Health, Education, and Welfare had banned the use of cyclamates as a sweetener in foods and drugs, and a bill exempting soft drink bottlers from provisions of the antitrust laws that restrict exclusive territory contracts.

Two major bills that had high priority among consumer advocates but were lost in 1972 were one that would have established a council of consumer advisers in the executive branch, provided for an independent Consumer Protection Agency, and authorized a program of grants to support consumer activities at the state and local level; and another that would have prohibited the use of misleading warranties and given the Federal Trade Commission a variety of additional powers, including authority to seek court orders to stop suspected deceptive advertisements before the completion of hearings, power to seek cash restitution for consumers who had been cheated, and power to eliminate unfair and deceptive practices through industrywide rules rather than through individual lawsuits. Other consumer-oriented bills that were lost included one dealing with abuses that arise from computerized billing, a truth-in-advertising bill requiring advertisers to provide to consumers, on request, the data supporting their claims, legislation establishing federal standards for no-fault automobile insurance, which was opposed by President Nixon, and a proposal, strongly opposed by businesses, that would permit plaintiffs to bring class action lawsuits in federal courts on behalf of themselves and all other persons similarly deceived or injured.

Regulatory Agencies. Against the background of slow congressional action, federal regulatory agencies were maintaining a brisk pace in the enforcement of existing laws. Enforcement actions by the FDA under the Hazardous Substances Act and the Poison Prevention Packaging Act resulted in the requiring of "childproof" closures on a variety of products ranging from aspirin to furniture polish to prescription drugs, a ban on explosive fireworks, and intensified action against unsafe toys. The number of inspectors assigned to food plant cleanliness was doubled under a program designed to ensure that every plant was inspected no less than once every two years. The antibacterial agent hexachlorophene was among the food and cosmetic ingredients restricted during the year. Other additives being questioned included Red 2, a colouring used in foods and cosmetics, and the sweetening agent saccharine.

After more than three years of preparation, in July the Department of Commerce put into effect a regulation setting flammability standards for children's sleepwear sizes 1 through 6X. Substandard garments could continue to be sold for one year provided they carried a label stating they had not met flammability standards.

The number of automobiles recalled under federal safety programs since 1968 passed the 30 million mark, with 240 recalls totaling 7 million cars during the first nine months of 1972. New regulations required more sophisticated seat belt and bumper systems and at least four times during the year car owners received warnings of suspected safety defects at early stages of the investigation, in contrast to the former practice of providing notice only after all evidence was in.

Consumer protection advocates found themselves in a heated dispute with broadcasters and other business groups as they pressed the FCC to advertise against products and product claims. The commission reiterated its view that advertising came under the "fairness" requirements of the Communications Act only when it went beyond a product claim to argue one side of a controversy of public importance and held in a test case that antipollution claims for one gasoline constituted an affirmative product claim rather than discussion of a public issue. The counteradvertising dispute assumed broader implications after the Federal Trade Commission (FTC) intervened in support of consumer advocates, prompting sharp criticism from administration leaders.

This support was one of several moves by the FTC to help consumers get better values. It adopted rules requiring the posting of octane ratings on gasoline pumps and care labels on textile garments, restricted the use of negative option methods in mail order selling, and gave purchasers a three-day opportunity to back out of sales contracts written by door-to-door salesmen. In order to make product comparison commercials more meaningful, the FTC negotiated an agreement eliminating television network policies that prevented advertisers from identifying "Brand X." The commission reached the tentative conclusion that at least one third of the performance claims in ads for such products as automobiles, air conditioners, dentifrices, and cold remedies could not be supported adequately and launched an enforcement campaign by issuing complaints charging lack of substantiation against three marketers of air conditioners and two auto manufacturers.

The precise nature of the FTC's authority to act on behalf of consumers received considerable attention. In practice the agency's power to act in the public interest against unfair corporate practices had been used to protect the consuming public as well as businesses. The proposed warranty/FTC improvement bill would have stated this authority more precisely, but it died in committee. However, in March the Supreme Court ruled unanimously that the FTC had the authority to take on cases involving "public values beyond simply those enshrined in the letter" of the antitrust laws, even though it turned aside as having been improperly presented the case under consideration, one involving practices of the Sperry & Hutchinson trading stamp company. Soon afterward, in dismissing a complaint against advertising for a sunburn remedy, Unburn, the FTC attached an opinion by Chairman Miles Kirkpatrick that the commission saw the fairness concept as a source of consumer protection opportunities.

The FTC's enforcement program featured new cases on such issues as deceptive nutritional claims (Amstar Corp.), gasoline performance claims (Sun Oil Co.), health protection claims (Warner-Lambert's Lysol), and television demonstrations (American Home Products Corp.). In cases involving leading marketers on analgesics and breakfast cereals, the commission raised product differentiation issues that reflected a merging of its antitrust and deceptive practices work. According to the FTC, both marketers were able to get "monopoly" prices by using intensive advertising to convince consumers that distinctive therapeutic and nutritional benefits existed when, in fact, no substantial agreement among experts was found. In a third set of cases the FTC charged that exclusive territory agreements in the hearing aid business enabled dealers to charge an average of $350 for instruments wholesaling for about $100.

The FTC had yet to make a final decision upholding tough penalties in cases initiated with widespread publicity in 1970 and 1971. Although the corrective advertising concept was bitterly attacked by advertising industry leaders as unfair and vindictive, the FTC continued to defend it as a remedy that would remove misconceptions planted by false advertising, deprive the offender of ill-gotten gains, and be far more effective than a cease and desist order. Various degrees of "corrective" and "clarifying" ads were secured under negotiated settlements with advertisers, including the marketers of Ocean Spray Cranberry Juice Cocktail and the Sugar Association. But by the end of 1972, the FTC had yet to impose corrective advertising requirements on an advertiser who resisted and insisted on a full hearing.

In a move to provide a firm basis for closer supervision of advertising claims for nonprescription drugs, the FDA began an intensive review of the entire proprietary drug business. It also tentatively adopted regulations providing for nutritional labeling of foods and committed itself to a program that was supposed to provide more precise names and ingredient information for food products.

State and Local Actions. States, counties, and cities increased their consumer protection roles in many ways. By midyear new consumer offices had been established by five states, nine counties, and eight cities. At least eight states, counties, and cities took steps to prohibit misleading advertising practices, require proof of advertising claims made, or require additional disclosure of special conditions. Three local government units were added to the list of those requiring unit pricing and three mandated open dating of perishables. Other new local-level regulations dealt with visibility in bacon packaging and the labeling of frozen meats. Multilevel pyramid distribution systems and mobile home construction standards and park operations became new sectors of concern.

Nongovernmental Activities. Although business organizations resisted consumer bills and regulatory proposals, associations and individual companies displayed increased interest in developing their own programs related to consumer complaints and the certification of quality service. Among the industries praised for their innovations by Virginia Knauer, special presidential assistant for consumer affairs, were the auto repair industry, home builders, and furniture manufacturers. In the auto industry, American Motors wooed approval by offering all-inclusive warranties, and Ford offered improved warranties on repairs. A trend toward ingredient disclosures for cosmetics developed after two chains—Giant Foods in Washington, D.C., and Osco Drugs in Chicago—announced they would print ingredient information on their private brand health and beauty products. When an estimated 100,000 letters deluged the FCC with complaints about children's television programs, the National Association of Broadcasters amended its codes to reduce the number of commercials, and three leading makers of vitamins agreed to stop advertising on children's programs.

A number of organizations provided leadership for business on consumer-related issues. The Commerce Department's National Business Council on Consumer Affairs, consisting of more than 100 top executives appointed by President Nixon, issued several policy advisories urging, among other things, increased involvement by top personnel to make sure that advertising and other company activities conformed to the public interest. A self-regulation program initiated by the advertising industry, the National Advertising Review Board, reported it received about 300 "cases" in its first year, and had resolved about half of them. The Council of Better Business Bureaus, reorganized during 1971, offered a number of new programs, including a system of arbitration to provide assurance that persons who felt they were cheated would have an opportunity to get restitution.

The Consumer Federation of America, representing about 200 groups with a membership of 35 million, continued to be the spokesman for consumer interests on legislative matters, but much of the active promotion of consumer issues originated with individuals and centres dedicated to the public interest, like those organized by Ralph Nader. Organizationally the most noticeable change during 1972 was at Consumers Union, where new leadership moved beyond the traditional role of collecting and publishing test data by creating an office in Washington, D.C., to take an active part in consumer litigation, and by creating a

UPI COMPIX

At a press conference following publication of a book on congressional operations, Ralph Nader warned of "terrible consequences" resulting from a massive shift of power from Congress to the White House.

UPI COMPIX

This experimental safety car, developed by Fairchild Industries for the U.S. government, has a front bumper that automatically extends 12 in. at speeds over 30 mph to provide extra cushioning in the event of a high-speed crash.

research institute to provide technical support for other consumer groups involved in litigation. The Nader organization reported it recruited over 900 persons and would spend approximately $250,000 for the massive report on Congress that it began to issue late in 1972. At the same time, Nader's affiliates continued to maintain active programs in such areas as tax reform, health, advertising, and auto safety. Nader released reports on the mental health complex, the First National Bank of California, and E. I. du Pont de Nemours and Co. His lawsuits included an unsuccessful effort to reopen an antitrust settlement negotiated with International Telephone and Telegraph by the Justice Department.

Consumer organizations explored the effectiveness of the advertising industry's self-regulation program by submitting test cases, and several reported disappointing results. Other consumer groups pressed for television time, both paid and free. One group denied an opportunity to buy time to oppose the Vietnam war asked the Supreme Court to determine whether broadcasters should be allowed to refuse to sell time for discussion of public issues. Through a West Coast affiliate the Stern Community Law Firm, which planned the drive for counteradvertising, offered several countering ads for print as well as broadcast. (STANLEY E. COHEN)

See also Advertising; Merchandising.

Contract Bridge

The return to contract bridge of the Italian Blue Team clearly left the game in the hands of Italy and the Precision Club bid in 1972. The Blue Team had held the world championship from 1957 until 1969, when it had retired from play.

The Precision Club bid, as it was being used in 1972, formed the basis for several intricate bidding systems. Most of them permitted an opening demand bid of one club to indicate a big hand of 16 or more high-card points, without regard for distribution. The partner answered with one diamond if he had less than eight points, or made a positive response based on his card distribution if he held more than eight points. This was followed by various complicated step responses that were intended to give the declarer a precise knowledge of the partner's hand.

The attraction of the new system proved irresistible to two of the Italian pairs—Pietro Forquet and Benito Garozzo, and Walter Avarelli and Giorgio Belladonna. In the big money spectacular at Las Vegas, Nev., in December 1971 against the reigning world champion Dallas Aces, these two pairs played their newly adopted system with considerable success while the third Italian pair—Massimo D'Alelio and Camillo Pabis Ticci—relied on their better-tried methods; but they, too, were soon converted. In June all three pairs played Precision when they returned to international competition representing Italy in the fourth Bridge Olympiad at Miami Beach, Fla. Thirty-nine countries competed and, as in the European Championships in Athens, Italy won both the Open and the Women's Championship.

In the Open Series all 39 teams met in a round robin, which meant a grueling schedule of three matches a day for 13 consecutive days. The top four teams were to contest the semifinal and final rounds. Italy and the Dallas Aces, representing the United States, were assured of their semifinal places some time before the end; the remaining two places were not decided until almost the last deal of the last match, when Canada and France came through. In the semifinal round Italy and the Aces won comprehensively against France and Canada, respectively. In the final, Italy beat the Aces no less convincingly than it had in December, six months earlier. The Olympiad final produced no hand quite so spectacular as the classic deal that occurred during the Las Vegas match (*see* box).

In the Women's Championships the United States, with what it regarded as its best team ever, proved to be no match for the Italian ladies and was, in fact, edged out of second place by South Africa, runner-up for a second successive time.

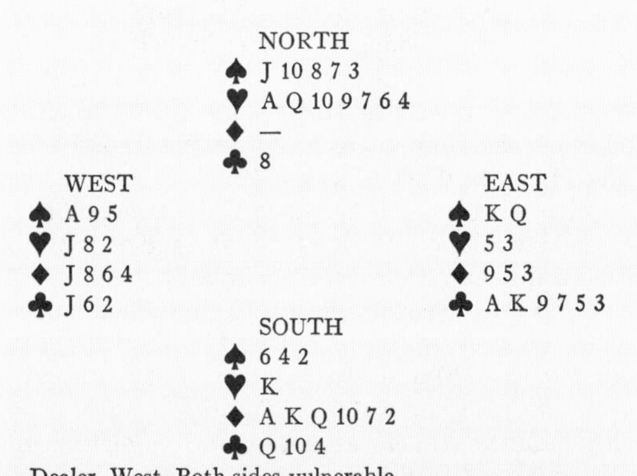

NORTH
♠ J 10 8 7 3
♥ A Q 10 9 7 6 4
♦ —
♣ 8

WEST
♠ A 9 5
♥ J 8 2
♦ J 8 6 4
♣ J 6 2

EAST
♠ K Q
♥ 5 3
♦ 9 5 3
♣ A K 9 7 5 3

SOUTH
♠ 6 4 2
♥ K
♦ A K Q 10 7 2
♣ Q 10 4

Dealer, West. Both sides vulnerable.

In the closed room the Italians Belladonna and Avarelli, playing North and South, reached four hearts after an auction in which only hearts and diamonds were bid. East led the king of clubs and West played the two. East then played the king of spades followed by the queen, and, still holding the lead, could do no more. Declarer made ten tricks.

In the open room Bobby Wolff, for the Dallas Aces, opened as North with four hearts, the final contract. East—Garozzo—also opened with a club honour and continued with the king and queen of spades. But on the second spade Forquet reasoned as follows: if my partner had thought we had a second club trick he would have taken it before playing the second spade. If he had three or four spades headed by the king-queen he would have led a low spade at trick 3. His spade play, therefore, is consistent only with his holding of king-queen-jack or king-queen. Forquet overtook the second spade with his ace and returned a third spade to defeat the contract.

The two years prior to 1972 had been marked by the emergence of a new professional in contract bridge, as manifested in the performance of the Dallas Aces, who won the world championship in both 1970 and 1971. There were, however, signs of discontent within the Aces organization; one of the members, Billy Eisenberg, had left the team in 1971 as a result of "personality differences" with its controller, Ira G. Corn, Jr., a Texas millionnaire-industrialist. In both the Las Vegas match and the Olympiad Eisenberg's place was taken by a new recruit, Paul Soloway. There were possibilities that other members of the team might leave the Aces, which might create a problem when 1973's world championship took place in South America. The Aces qualified by virtue of their status as defending champions. But whether the qualification resided in the organization known as the "Dallas Aces" or in the individual players might give rise to future dissension.

Nor were the Olympiads entirely free of political considerations. The tournament regulations had provided for the fact that teams might decline to play against other teams for reasons beyond their control. In pursuance of this condition neither Lebanon nor Morocco played their matches against Israel. Israel was awarded an arbitrary score of 12 out of 20 for each of these matches and their opponents, nil. With two days to play before the conclusion of the round robin there developed a distinct possibility that Israel might fail to qualify for the semifinal because it lacked the opportunity to score a maximum 40 points in these matches or, conversely, that it might qualify by virtue of the 24 points it had been accorded without playing. It seemed likely that rules would be introduced to prevent the recurrence of such a dubious situation.

(HAROLD FRANKLIN)

Cooperatives

During 1972 further progress was made in consolidating the structural changes proposed by the cooperative movements in Denmark, West Germany, the Netherlands, and Switzerland. Leaders of consumer cooperatives in the EEC, Denmark, and the United Kingdom discussed the feasibility of joint purchasing of food and nonfood items in the enlarged EEC at a meeting held in Copenhagen in August.

A resolution concerning the promotion of the cooperative movement during the United Nations Second Development Decade was approved by the UN Economic and Social Council (Ecosoc) in May. The UN Conference on Trade and Development, held April–May in Santiago, Chile, adopted a resolution on the important role of cooperatives in economic development. Similar recognition was given by the Food and Agriculture Organization of the UN (FAO), which set up an independent cooperative unit.

The International Cooperative Alliance. In May 1972 the first Open World Conference on the Role of Agricultural Cooperatives, organized by the ICA in collaboration with the FAO, the International Labour Organization, and the International Federation of Agricultural Producers, was held in Rome. Addeke H. Boerma, director general of the FAO, opened the conference with an address on the role of agricultural cooperatives in economic and social development. Pope Paul VI, receiving the representatives to the conference in special audience, spoke on agricultural cooperation in the service of development.

The 25th congress of the ICA took place in Warsaw, Poland, in October. One of the main themes was "Multinational Corporations and the International Cooperative Movement: Financial and Managerial Imperatives." The paper presented by the ICA stated that the distinguishing feature of the multinational firm was its facility for production in more than one country, taking ultimate decision-making out of the country of operation; hence multinationals were, to a large extent, removed from the influence of governments, of trade unions, and of consumers. The economic power of multinationals endangered labour standards, job security, the established systems of collective bargaining, and work participation. They eroded national sovereignty over economic and social policies, distorted international trade, and exploited the interests of less developed countries. The cooperative movement faced a great responsibility in helping to combat these abuses through political influence and, more directly, through the countervailing force of its own economic potential.

"Technical Assistance for Cooperatives in Developing Countries" was the theme of the other paper presented to the congress, outlining the aid being given by cooperative movements in developed countries. In the discussion the importance of additional resources from national aid agencies and the UN and its agencies was stressed. It was also recognized that better expertise was needed in the less developed countries for the formulation of projects, and that cooperative education and training had to be relevant to the requirements of those countries. The congress unanimously adopted an emergency resolution calling on the cooperative movements of the developed countries to give aid to cooperatives in the new nation of Bangladesh.

A conference jointly organized by the International Committee of Workers' Productive and Artisanal Cooperative Societies and the UN Industrial Development Organization (UNIDO), held prior to the congress, discussed industrial cooperatives in the economic and social development of less developed countries.

A paper dealing with savings and finance in cooperative housing was the main theme discussed at the ICA housing conference. At the annual meeting of the International Cooperative Housing Development Association, a report was received on a plan for long-term technical assistance in cooperative housing development, to be carried out in collaboration with the government of Bangladesh and CARE. The needs of the cooperative movement of Bangladesh were discussed at a seminar organized by the ICA Regional Office and Educational Centre for South East Asia in collaboration with the Bangladesh cooperative union, held in Dacca in June. The seminar identified areas for the development of the cooperative movement and made a number of recommendations relating to all aspects of cooperative activity.

Progress in cooperative insurance was reported at the conference of the International Cooperative Insurance Committee. Seventy-two organizations in 27 countries were affiliated to the committee. The Insurance Development Bureau, together with the Reinsurance Bureau, continued to survey the possibilities for cooperative insurance in various countries. A scholarship fund to be used for training insurance personnel from less developed countries was established.

INTER-COOP, representing wholesale and retail interests, reported a membership of 31 in 20 countries at its annual meeting. Further attention had been given to the enlargement of joint purchases in the food and nonfood sectors. The International Cooperative Petroleum Association, at its annual meeting, reported sales amounting to over $10 million in 1971–72. A lubricating-oil blending plant was currently being built by the ICPA for the national oil company of Burma. A seminar on research by developed countries relating to cooperatives in less developed countries, jointly organized by the ICA and the Polish Cooperative Research Institute, was held in Warsaw in June.

Membership and Trade. At the end of 1972, the number of cooperative federations in membership with the ICA totaled 161 in 62 countries. The latest available statistics showed an increase in the number of cooperative societies in membership with the ICA from 560,532 in 1969 to 564,398 in 1970. Membership within these societies rose from 268 million to 281 million during the same period. The largest membership was reported from India (61.3 million), followed by the U.S.S.R. (59.6 million) and the U.S. (45 million). Of the total membership, the greatest proportion was in consumer societies (42.57%), followed by the credit societies (29.57%), agricultural societies (16.34%), miscellaneous societies (6.14%), building and housing societies (2.58%), workers' productive and artisanal societies (2.24%), and fisheries societies (0.56%).

A joint organization to promote the export of Scandinavian furniture to the U.S. was established by Nordisk Andelseksport, representing the interests of Scandinavian cooperative wholesale societies, and U.S. cooperators. During 1972 UNICOOP Japan promoted the export of produce from agricultural and fishermen's cooperatives in Japan to Australia and Scandinavia. (LOTTE KENT)

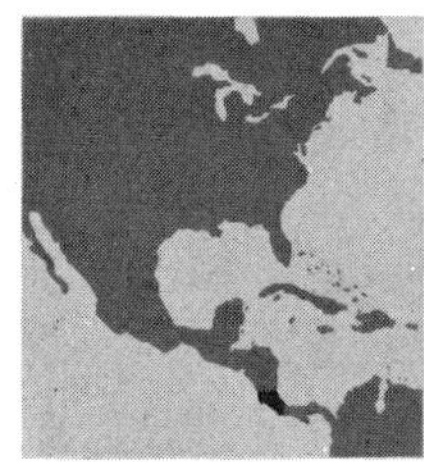

Costa Rica

A Central American republic, Costa Rica lies between Nicaragua and Panama and has coastlines on the Caribbean Sea and the Pacific Ocean. Area: 19,652 sq.mi. (50,898 sq.km.). Pop. (1972 est.): 1,832,081, including white and mestizo 97.6%. Cap. and largest city: San José (pop., 1972 est., 217,772). Language: Spanish. Religion: predominantly Roman Catholic. President in 1972, José Figueres Ferrer.

Among the more important developments of 1972 was the granting of loans by the West German government and the World Bank for important infrastructure projects. The loan from West Germany was to be used for development of the important port of Limón on the Atlantic coast. Improvements to its facilities had been under consideration for some time, but the West German funds provided the necessary impetus to put these plans into operation. The World Bank loan of U.S. $24 million, directed toward Costa Rica's electric power and telecommunications program, was the largest the country received during the year.

Following negotiations between the government, the Instituto Costarricense de Electricidad, the U.S.S.R., the World Bank, and the Aluminum Co. of America, it was agreed to undertake feasibility studies on the establishment of a hydroelectric plant and an aluminum smelter. This represented the first concrete step toward development of the nation's bauxite resources. The interest of the Soviet Union was one of the results of a drive by President Figueres to widen the market for Costa Rican products. Commercial agreements with the U.S.S.R., Bulgaria, and Romania were signed during the year, and embassies were established by the U.S.S.R. and Czechoslovakia.

State intervention in the affairs of the British-owned Northern Railway Co. was precipitated when its employees struck for higher pay. The company felt it was unable to meet union demands without an increase in freight rates, a move it could not make without prior government approval. The government took steps to maintain service, the lack of which was seriously affecting the export trade. An agreement was subsequently initiated between the company and the government on the payment of compensation, and a final settlement was expected early in 1973.

In an effort to control the growing balance of payments deficit, the government had introduced a multiple exchange rate system in 1971. The trade position continued to deteriorate, however, reaching about U.S. $100 million, compared with $80 million in 1970. In February the number of imports from outside Central America qualifying for preferential treatment was reduced, and in August the free market rate of exchange was applied to nonessential imports from the region for the first time. The government also introduced new taxes on dividends and interest remitted abroad, on consumption, and on income.

Shortly after the August change in the exchange rate, trade between Costa Rica, Guatemala, El Salvador, and Nicaragua was suspended for approximately six weeks. Detailed negotiations between the five Central American countries led to an agreement, scheduled to run until February 1974, under which the August free market rate of 8.60 colones to the U.S. dollar was retained for nonessential imports while es-

COSTA RICA

Education. (1968–69) Primary, pupils 322,683, teachers 11,287; secondary, pupils 55,732, teachers 2,404; vocational, pupils 6,524, teachers 315; higher, students 11,449, teaching staff (universities only) 678.

Finance. Monetary unit: colón, with (Sept. 18, 1972) an official rate of 6.62 colones to U.S. $1 (free rate of 16.27 colones = £1 sterling) and a free rate of 8.60 colones to U.S. $1 (21.04 colones = £1 sterling). Gold, SDRs, and foreign exchange, central bank: (June 1972) U.S. $36,280,000; (June 1971) U.S. $14,470,-000. Budget (1970 est.): revenue 1,071,329,000 colones; expenditure 974,837,000 colones. Gross national product: (1970) 6,124,000,000 colones; (1969) 5,546,000,000 colones. Money supply: (Feb. 1972) 1,344,500,000 colones; (Feb. 1971) 1,046,900,000 colones. Cost of living (San José; 1963 = 100): (May 1972) 123; (May, 1971) 119.

Foreign Trade. (1971) Imports 2,317,700,000 colones; exports 1,535,800,000 colones. Import sources: U.S. 33%; Japan 11%; Guatemala 8%; West Germany 8%; Nicaragua 8%; El Salvador 6%; U.K. 5%. Export destinations: U.S. 41%; West Germany 9%; Guatemala 7%; Nicaragua 7%; Netherlands 5%; El Salvador 5%. Main exports: bananas 32%; coffee 26%.

Transport and Communications. Roads (1970) 18,742 km. (including *c.* 3,250 km. all-weather and 665 km. of Pan-American Highway). Motor vehicles in use (1970): passenger 39,300; commercial (including buses) 27,100. Railways (1970): 735 km.; traffic *c.* 55 million passenger-km., freight *c.* 18 million net ton-km. Air traffic (1971): 197 million passenger-km.; freight 12,260,000 net ton-km. Telephones (Jan. 1971) 61,000. Radio receivers (Dec. 1970) 125,000. Television receivers (Dec. 1970) *c.* 100,000.

Agriculture. Production (in 000; metric tons; 1971; 1970 in parentheses): coffee *c.* 100 (97); bananas (1970) 1,100, (1969) 967; sugar, raw value (1971–72) 214, (1970–71) 200; dry beans *c.* 14 (13); cocoa (1970–71) 9.1, (1969–70) 8; palm oil (1970) 13, (1969) 12. Livestock (in 000; 1970–71): cattle 1,-513; horses *c.* 110; pigs *c.* 185.

Industry. Electricity production (1970) 1,028,000,-000 kw-hr. (91% hydroelectric).

Copper: *see* Mining
Corn: *see* Agriculture
Cosmetics: *see* Fashion and Dress

sential imports continued at the official rate of 6.62 colones. At the same time, some Costa Rican prices were lowered in terms of the dollar by application of the free market rate to certain exports. Further talks on the restructuring of the Central American Common Market were scheduled. (ROBERT STENT)

Cricket

Two major tours took place in 1972, New Zealand visiting West Indies for the first time, and Australia visiting England. In addition, to replace a South African tour of Australia canceled due to political pressures, a Rest of the World team was hastily assembled under G. S. Sobers and beat Australia 2–1, with two draws.

Australia v. Rest of the World. Though several leading players were not invited and others could not accept, some spectacular cricket was played by Sobers' team. His own 254 at Melbourne was rated the best innings ever seen in Australia. Others who batted well were R. B. Kanhai (West Indies), H. M. Ackerman (South Africa), Zahir Abbas (Pakistan), and S. M. Gavaskar (India). The leading bowlers were the South African-Scotsman A. W. Greig and slow bowlers Intikhab Alam (Pakistan) and B. S. Bedi (India); F. M. Engineer (India) kept wicket.

The features of Australia's batting were the success of the Chappell brothers, I. M., the captain, making four centuries, two in one match, and G. S., who scored two centuries. In addition, K. D. Walters and K. R. Stackpole each made two centuries. The progress of D. K. Lillee as a genuinely fast bowler resulted in an analysis of 8 for 29 in the second test and 24 wickets in the series.

The first test at Brisbane was drawn: Australia made 389 for 4 declared (Stackpole 132, I. Chappell 145) and 220 for 3 declared (I. Chappell 106); Rest of the World 285 for 4 declared (Ackerman 112, Kanhai 101) and 108 for 4. Australia won the second test at Perth by an innings and 11 runs: Australia 349 (Walters 125); Rest of the World 59 (Lillee 8 for 29) and 279 (Kanhai 118). Rest of the World won the third test at Melbourne by 96 runs: Rest of the World 184 (Greig 66, Lillee 5 for 48) and 514 (Sobers 254, Zahir 86); Australia 285 (G. Chappell 115 not out) and 317 (Walters 127). The fourth match at Sydney was drawn: Australia 312 (Stackpole 104, R. W. Marsh not out 77) and 546 (G. Chappell not out 197, I. Chappell 119, Stackpole 95); Rest of the World 277 (Intikhab not out 73, Greig 70, R. A. L. Massie 7 for 76) and 173 for 5 (Ackerman 87, Gavaskar not out 68). The fifth test match at Adelaide was won by Rest of the World by 9 wickets: Australia 311 (J. Benaud 99, G. Chappell 85, Greig 6 for 30) and 201 (I. Chappell not out 111); Rest of the World 367 (R. G. Pollock 136, Zahir 73) and 146 for 1 (Ackerman not out 79).

West Indies v. New Zealand. New Zealand under G. T. Dowling drew all five tests in a series characterized by dull batting, especially by the visitors, who also drew all their other first-class matches. Unfortunately, Dowling had to return home injured, and B. E. Congdon succeeded him. New Zealand's outstanding batsman was G. M. Turner, who played for Worcestershire in England. He made two double centuries and a 95, and with T. W. Jarvis set a New Zealand record of 387 for the first wicket at Georgetown. Congdon, with two centuries and an 82, and 13 wickets, rose

CENTRAL PRESS/PICTORIAL PARADE

England's batsman Barry Wood survives an appeal for leg-before-wicket off R. A. L. Massie (arms raised) in the first innings of the fifth and final test against Australia. The match, which Australia won, took place at the Oval in London on Oct. 10, 1972.

splendidly to his responsibilities, and M. G. Burgess and B. F. Hastings each made one century. New Zealand's leading bowler was B. R. Taylor (fast medium) who took 7 for 70 in the third test and 27 wickets in all. Slow left-hander H. J. Howarth bowled tirelessly for his 14 wickets. The best feature of the series was New Zealand's brilliant fielding.

Sobers returned from Australia to captain West Indies once more. He took 10 wickets, and his century in the third test saved his side from almost certain defeat when he and C. A. L. Davis added 254 for the 6th wicket. R. C. Fredericks played one big innings, and two new batsmen made splendid debuts. In the first test, L. Rowe made 214 and 100 not out, and in the last two tests A. Kallicharran made 100 not out and 101. Sobers' chief bowling supporters were V. A. Holder (fast) 12 wickets and Inshan Ali (slow left) 9, including 5 for 59 in the fifth test.

The first draw was at Kingston: West Indies 508 for 4 declared (Fredericks 163, Rowe 214) and 218 for 3 declared (Rowe not out 100); New Zealand 386 (Turner not out 223, K. J. Wadsworth 78) and 236 for 6 (Burgess 101). The second draw was at Port of Spain, Trinidad: New Zealand 348 (Congdon not out 166) and 288 for 3 declared (Turner 95, Congdon 82); West Indies 341 (Davis 90, Fredericks 69) and 121 for 5. The third draw was at Bridgetown, Barbados: West Indies 133 (Taylor 7 for 70) and 564 for 8 (Davis 183, Sobers 142); New Zealand 422 (Congdon 126, Hastings 105). The fourth draw was at Georgetown, Guyana: West Indies 365 for 7 declared (Kallicharran 100 not out) and 86 for no wicket; New Zealand 543 for 3 declared (Turner 259, Jarvis 182). The final draw was at Port of Spain: West Indies 368 (Kallicharran 101, Fredericks 60) and 194 (Taylor 5 for 41); New Zealand 162 (Inshan Ali 5 for 59) and 253 for 7 (Congdon 58, Turner 50).

England v. Australia. An Australian team under I. M. Chappell drew a thrilling series with England, each side winning two matches. This was a fair result because, though England suffered cruelly from injuries, their best batsman, G. Boycott, being available for only two tests, opening bowler G. G. Arnold for three, and the captain, R. Illingworth, spraining an ankle when his offbreaks might have won the fifth

Cotton: *see* Agriculture; Industrial Review

Council for Mutual Economic Assistance: *see* Soviet Bloc Economies

Council of Europe: *see* European Unity

Credit and Debt: *see* Government Finance; Money and Banking; Payments and Reserves, International test, Australia provided most of the best individual performances. G. Chappell made two centuries, and Stackpole, I. Chappell, and R. Edwards one each. Stackpole invariably gave Australia an aggressive start, while G. Chappell was the highest class batsman on either side. Wicketkeeper Marsh played the most spectacular innings of the rubber, 91 in two hours at Old Trafford. Lillee and Massie were a remarkable pair of opening bowlers. Lillee set an Australian record with 31 wickets, and Massie achieved the phenomenal feat of taking 16 wickets in the Lord's test.

For England, fast bowler J. A. Snow took 24 wickets, and D. L. Underwood (slow-medium left) 16, including 10 on a poor pitch at Headingley. England's leading batsmen failed against Lillee's pace and Massie's swing. No one made a century, though B. W. Luckhurst (96) and A. P. E. Knott (92) came near. Most of the runs came from the middle-order batsmen, Greig, B. L. D'Oliveira, and Knott.

England won the first test in cold, dreary weather at Old Trafford, Manchester, by 89 runs: England 249 (Greig 57) and 234 (Greig 62, Lillee 6 for 66); Australia 142 (Stackpole 53) and 252 (Stackpole 67, Marsh 91). Australia won the second test at Lord's, London, by 8 wickets: England 272 (Greig 54, Massie 8 for 84) and 116 (Massie 8 for 53); Australia 308 (G. Chappell 131, I. Chappell 56, Marsh 50, Snow 5 for 57) and 81 for 2 (Stackpole 57 not out). The third test at Trent Bridge, Nottingham, was drawn: Australia 315 (Stackpole 114, D. J. Colley 54, Snow 5 for 92) and 324 for 4 declared (Edwards not out 170, G. Chappell 72, I. Chappell 50); England 189 and 290 for 4 (Luckhurst 96, D'Oliveira not out 50). England won the fourth test at Headingley, Leeds, by 9 wickets: Australia 146 and 136 (Underwood 6 for 45); England 263 (Illingworth 57, A. A. Mallett 5 for 114) and 21 for 1. Australia won the fifth test at the Oval, London, by 5 wickets: England 284 (Knott 92, P. H. Parfitt 51, Lillee 5 for 58) and 356 (B. Wood 90, Knott 63, Lillee 5 for 123); Australia 399 (I. Chappell 118, G. Chappell 113, Edwards 79) and 242 for 5 (Stackpole 79).

One-Day Internationals. After the test series, the sides played three one-day internationals—the shape of things to come? England won the first at Old Trafford by six wickets, Australia the second at Lord's by five wickets, and England the deciding contest at Edgbaston, Birmingham, by 2 wickets. England's outstanding batsman was D. L. Amiss, the only century-maker on either side, and K. W. R. Fletcher was a worthy runner-up. For Australia Stackpole continued his consistently good form, aggregating 150 in three innings, and the Chappell brothers were not far behind. Arnold had the best bowling performance, 4 for 27 at Edgbaston.

County and National Cricket. The English county championship, reduced from 24 to 20 matches, was won by Warwickshire, thanks to the skill of four West Indian test players, Kanhai, Kallicharran, L. R. Gibbs, and D. L. Murray, to fine batting by M. J. K. Smith and Amiss, and to good fast bowling by N. M. McVicker, D. J. Brown, and R. G. D. Willis in support of Gibbs' offspinners. Kent finished with a rush in August to place second ahead of Gloucestershire, which, due to splendid all-round cricket by the South African M. J. Procter, had looked like possible champions. But their chance was spoiled by an injury to Procter in mid-August. In a wonderfully contested Gillette Cup final between Lancashire and Warwickshire, Lancashire won for the third consecutive year after a superb 126 by the West Indian C. H. Lloyd. Kent just beat Leicestershire by one point for the Players' League title, but Leicestershire, in compensation, won a new one-day competition for the Benson and Hedges Cup, beating Yorkshire easily. The leading batsmen in county cricket were Kanhai and M. J. Khan (Pakistan), the best Englishmen being Boycott and Fletcher. Two Englishmen just missed taking 100 wickets, T. W. Cartwright (Somerset) and B. Stead (Nottinghamshire) each taking 98. Five distinguished cricketers retired at the end of 1972, the West Indian R. E. Marshall (Hampshire), J. S. E. Price and W. E. Russell (Middlesex), D. A. Allen (Gloucestershire), and D. J. Shepherd (Glamorgan). (REX ALSTON)

Crime

Acts of political terrorism dominated 1972, highlighted by the savage Palestinian commando killing of hostage Israeli athletes at the Munich Olympics (*see* SPORTING RECORD: *Special Report*) and the slaying of 28 persons at Tel Aviv's Lod Airport by Japanese ultra-leftists. On Halloween night in Belfast, N.Ire., two children were killed when a bomb exploded near the pub where they were begging. Deaths of such innocents in the struggle between Protestant and Catholic extremists rose steadily and even reached into England, where seven persons were killed in an explosion set by the Official wing of the Irish Republican Army at Aldershot Army Base. Such political acts were so widespread that they masked reports that 40 brutal murders in July and many others throughout the year were laid to a "gang of psychopaths." In Uruguay and Argentina robbery and kidnapping by urban guerrillas went on amid clashes with government forces. A bomb attack on a Yugoslav travel agency in Sydney, Austr., by Croatian partisans injured 16 bystanders. In Tanzania, Sheikh Abeid Amani Karume, chairman of the Revolutionary Council of Zanzibar, was assassinated, while playing cards, by three black Africans and an Arab. (*See* articles on individual countries.) In the U.S. at a May 15 rally in Laurel, Md., Alabama Gov. George C. Wallace (*see* BIOGRAPHY) was paralyzed by shots fired by Arthur Bremer, whose diary revealed he had also stalked Pres. Richard Nixon.

In September, at the opening of the UN General Assembly in New York, the U.S. asked for an early international conference to act on terrorism. A draft convention providing for the prosecution or extradition of terrorists was opposed by Arab countries with strong support from African states and China. The International Criminal Police Organization (Interpol), at its annual General Assembly held in Frankfurt, W.Ger., discussed terrorism and sought ways for more effective cooperation among national police forces to combat the problem without violating the organization's political neutrality. (*See* POLICE.)

Trends in Crime and Criminology. Aerial hijackings continued at an alarming rate. In the first nine months of 1972, 25 airliners from 13 countries were hijacked, 26 attempts were frustrated, 140 passengers and crew members were killed, and 97 were wounded. Political motivations of certain hijackers, like the young Vietnamese student who was killed trying to hijack a Pan American 747 jet to Hanoi, made them martyrs in the eyes of some people. Even less "idealistic" hijackers were viewed with sympathy. The U.S. Marine who hijacked a jet from California to Rome in 1969 had a $7\frac{1}{2}$-year prison sentence in Italy reduced

UPI COMPIX

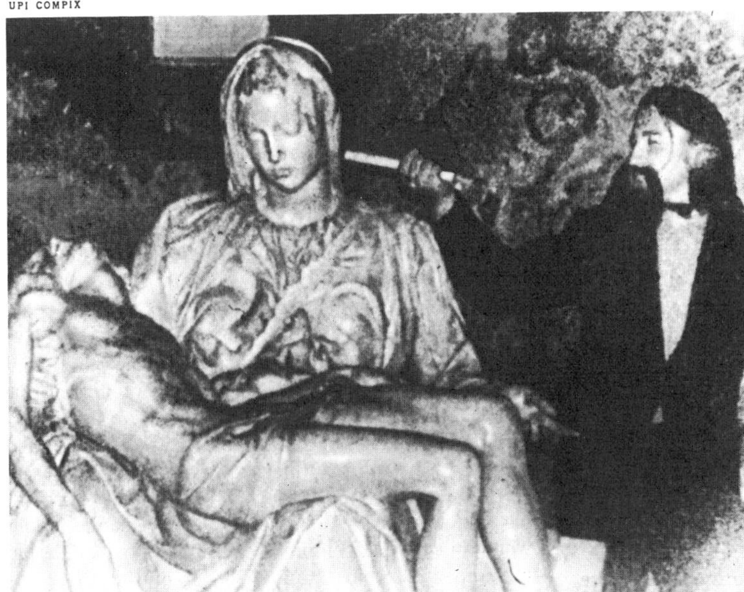

Left, Laszlo Toth wields hammer in attack on Michelangelo's famed "Pietà" in St. Peter's Basilica in Rome. Damage was extensive, as indicated in close-up study above: the left arm is broken off and the hand shattered, and the nose and an eye are chipped.

to 2½ years and was being hailed as somewhat of a folk hero. "D. B. Cooper," the only known name for the hijacker who parachuted over Oregon wilderness with a $200,000 ransom in November 1971, was lauded in songs, posters, and other items of pop culture; he also had several less successful imitators.

Crime was said to have become a major problem affecting tourism in many African nations. Following a 30% increase in crime in Nairobi in 1971, the Kenyan Parliament instituted the death penalty for certain types of armed robbery. In Nigeria military firing squads publicly executed numbers of armed robbers. Soldiers in Uganda were authorized to shoot *kondos* (robbers) on sight. Pres. Jean-Bédel Bokassa of the Central African Republic personally supervised the beating of prisoners at Bangui and said the beatings would continue until theft was eliminated. Nations outside Africa moved toward the abolition of capital punishment. A landmark decision of the U.S. Supreme Court affecting over 600 people convicted of capital crimes effectively placed the U.S. among some 40 countries to have abolished capital punishment altogether or retained it only for exceptional crimes or in exceptional circumstances. (*See* LAW.)

Art objects were the targets of several major thefts or acts of vandalism. In Montreal thieves stole 18 paintings and 39 art objects, valued at more than $2 million, from the Museum of Fine Arts. A Rembrandt, two Gauguins, and a Picasso, valued at more than $1 million, were taken from the Worcester (Mass.) Art Museum. Religious objects from New Mexico's Spanish colonial past continued to disappear, as they had for the preceding two years. In Rome, Michelangelo's "Pietà," one of the world's most celebrated sculptures, was damaged in a hammer attack by a deranged man. (*See* VATICAN CITY STATE.) Art thefts in churches, museums, and private collections throughout Italy caused an outcry for better protection of that country's cultural heritage.

The U.K. experienced a wave of muggings, usually by teen-age gangs. The first gun battle between police and robbers in London's history occurred in December; one would-be bank robber was killed and a policeman, another robber, and a bystander were wounded. In the first six months of 1972 robberies increased by 18%, rape by 50%, and other crimes of violence by more than 10%.

A wave of violent crime in West Germany, dramatized by a long and intensive hunt for a gang of anarchists, the Baader-Meinhof group, stirred wide debate. (*See* BIOGRAPHY: *Meinhof, Ulrike.*) Police authorities attributed at least four deaths—two policemen shot down in the streets and two alleged gang members—to the activities of the gang, whose leaders were caught in June. The furore over the gang and other crime led to calls for law and order from conservative groups, while police chiefs in Frankfurt and Munich instituted special sharpshooting courses for their patrolmen.

Crime was a major issue in the 1972 U.S. presidential campaign. While the Federal Bureau of Investigation—whose director since 1924, J. Edgar Hoover (*see* OBITUARIES), was succeeded by L. Patrick Gray (*see* BIOGRAPHY)—reported that the crime rate rose more slowly in 1971 (up 7% over 1970) than it had at any time since 1965, the statistics indicated that the slowdown resulted from decreased growth rates for crimes against property, not for crimes of violence. These trends were confirmed in the FBI Uniform Crime Reports for the first half of 1972: the overall crime rate had increased by 1% over the same period in 1971, but forcible rape offenses rose 14% while robberies and auto thefts each declined 4%. Violent crime rose 11% in suburban areas and 8% in rural areas. In a Gallup poll nearly six out of every ten women interviewed said they were afraid to go out alone at night.

The growth rate of violent crime gave renewed impetus to the development of crime victim compensation programs. Alaska joined six other U.S. states in offering compensation to innocent victims of violent crime, while support was sought in Congress for a measure designed to establish a federal program. Worldwide progress in this area was reviewed at the third International Conference of Crime Victim Compensation Programs held in September in Toronto. A U.S. Department of Commerce study calculated the annual losses sustained from property crime by U.S. businesses to be at least $16 billion. The study suggested that businessmen start to view crime as a component of the cost of doing business and stressed the need for more positive prevention measures, which were estimated to have cost $3.3 billion in 1969.

Controversy associated with the control of pornog-

Bloodstained baggage is sorted at Lod Airport, near Tel Aviv, Israel, where Japanese terrorists, hired by Palestinian guerrillas, machine-gunned to death 28 people and injured 72 on May 30, 1972.

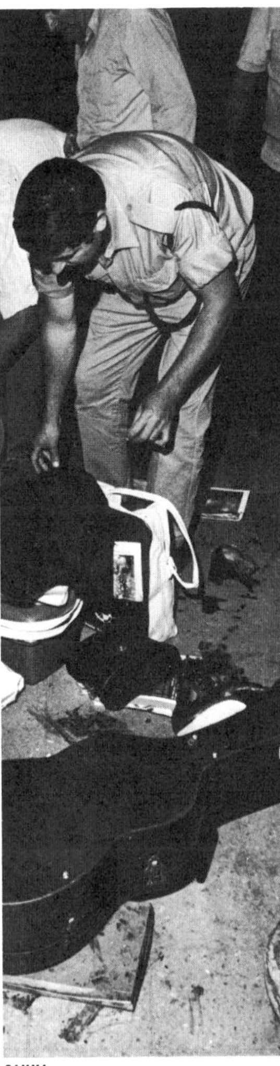

GAMMA

raphy continued. Danish authorities ordered the closing of live sex shows and "flesh film" theatres, reportedly to cut the flow of capital to underworld figures. In the U.K. a report by a private group headed by Lord Longford concluded that the country needed tougher laws against obscenity. (*See* PUBLISHING.)

A sensational anti-Mafia drive in New York City in October resulted in the issuing of subpoenas to more than 650 people including about 100 police, detectives, businessmen, and a judge. A shabby trailer in a Brooklyn junkyard, said to have been a Mafia summit headquarters, had been "bugged" and filmed for six months. A report by Italy's anti-Mafia commission, released after a nine-year inquiry, contained virtually nothing that was not already known.

The increasing international manifestation of many forms of criminal behaviour was being reflected in criminal justice research studies. The Max Planck Institute in West Germany began an international comparative study of procedures for the reopening of criminal cases; researchers at the Cambridge Institute of Criminology in England and the School of Criminal Justice at Albany, N.Y., opened a comparative study of rape in London and New York; the Battelle Law and Justice Study Center in Seattle, Wash., moved toward completion of a review of the administration of victim compensation programs; and researchers based at Northwestern University, Evanston, Ill., began looking at official responses to public order offenses in several cities. The results of completed studies formed the subject matter of the conference of the American Society of Criminology held in November in Caracas, Venez. (DUNCAN CHAPPELL)

Notable Crimes and Criminal Trials. The year's most bizarre murder case ended in Britain on June 29 when Graham Frederick Young was sentenced to life imprisonment for the murder and attempted murder by poisoning of his colleagues at work. In 1962 Young had poisoned his father, his sister, and a school friend. He was released on probation from a hospital for the criminally insane on Feb. 2, 1971. In his second group of "experiments" Young added antimony or thallium to his fellow workers' tea and coffee and kept a diary of their painful deterioration. The suspicion of the police was only aroused after a pathologist had read Agatha Christie's *The Pale Horse,* in which thallium is used and its symptoms described.

On December 6 the longest trial ever held at the Central Criminal Court, London, ended with sentences of ten years apiece on four members of the anarchist "Angry Brigade," responsible for a series of explosions, some at the homes of Cabinet ministers.

Abdul Malik (alias Michael X), former London-based Black Power leader wanted in Britain on charges of robbery and assault, was sentenced to death by hanging in Trinidad in August. He was found guilty of murdering Joseph Skerritt, a hairdresser, whom he had beheaded and buried in his garden; the body of the daughter of a former British MP was also found in the garden.

Major Crime Rates in Selected Countries, 1970
(per 100,000 population)

Category	United States	United Kingdom*	Sweden	West Germany	Poland	Israel	Thailand†	Japan
Murder, homicide	7.1	0.6	11.3	0.9	1.5	5.2	30.7	1.9
Sex and moral offenses	52.9	18.5	36.3	10.8	5.9	76.6	10.9	17.7
Robbery	40.9	...	18.2	5.8	303.8	6.2	21.8	2.6
Burglary	127.8	144.2	1,304.4	...	167.8	1,125.5	...	...
Fraud, forgery, embezzlement	55.6	25.2	839.5	93.4	16.2	144.3	11.6	72.1
Theft	335.0	352.2	3,396.0	267.6	197.2	2,318.2	86.2	1,005.0

*Convictions. †1969.
Source: country statistics.

On August 4, 1972, in the Chicago suburb of Barrington Hills, gunmen murdered retired insurance executive Paul M. Corbett, his wife, and two other members of the family. A few weeks later three members of the Stephen Hawtree family were found slain in their Monee, Ill., home. On October 15, police announced the arrest of eight men for these and two other brutal killings of whites in the Chicago area. Initially, the police claimed to have linked all the slayings with the De Mau Mau, a group formed originally by black soldiers in Vietnam, but the credibility of this connection was later called into question. In Sicily three masked men burst into a party at the villa of retired physician Vincenzo Loddo. When Loddo resisted being robbed, the bandits opened fire, killing his wife, his elder brother, and a nephew, and wounding Loddo. Within 24 hours bandits in Palermo kidnapped Luciano Cassina, son of one of the city's wealthiest businessmen, holding a crowd at bay with pistols. On St. Croix in the Virgin Islands on September 6, eight persons who apparently panicked during a robbery were gunned down. Five persons were arrested after a massive manhunt throughout the resort island.

Bombings continued to present a serious crime problem in North America. On January 26, a fire bomb thrown into the New York City offices of Sol Hurok, promoter of cultural exchanges between the Soviet Union and the U.S., resulted in the death of one woman and injuries to 13 other persons. Also in January letters sent to the news media, purportedly by a group called Movement in Amerika, advised that time bombs had been placed in safe-deposit boxes in nine specified banks—three in New York City, three in Chicago, and three in San Francisco. Some of the bombs had been planted as long as seven months earlier; one placed in a San Francisco bank had exploded in September 1971, but the incident had not been publicized. In Montreal on the night of September 1, Molotov cocktails thrown into the stairway near the entrance to a crowded second-floor dance hall killed 36 persons and injured 54 others. Police issued a coroner's warrant for three men who had been ejected from the club and allegedly returned to throw fire bombs into the stairway.

Warfare among some of New York City's organized crime "families" resulted in numerous slayings in 1972. Joseph (Crazy Joe) Gallo was killed and his bodyguard was wounded on April 7 by four gunmen in a restaurant where he was celebrating his birthday. Following the murder Joseph Luparelli, an associate of the acting head of the Joseph A. Colombo family, turned himself in to the FBI and reportedly admitted involvement in the assassination. In recent years, Gallo had feuded with Colombo, who was critically wounded during an Italian-American rally in June 1971. Eight other gangland-type slayings had occurred in the New York area by July 16, when the body of Thomas Eboli, alias Tommy Ryan, who had shared the leadership of the powerful Vito Genovese family with Gerardo Catena, was found in a residential section of Brooklyn.

In France on March 2 customs officials seized the biggest haul of illicit heroin ever discovered—935 lb., with a market value approaching $200 million—concealed in the cement lining of an extensively remodeled yacht. Two weeks later French police arrested Joseph Césari and at his secret laboratory at Aubagne seized 264 lb. of heroin. Césari, reputedly one of the best illegal chemists in the world and a leader of the Corsican underworld that ran the drug trade, was found hanged in a Marseilles prison on March 23. Another clandestine French laboratory was discovered and 33 lb. of heroin seized in July. In October, Auguste-Joseph Ricord, a Corsican believed to be the head of a worldwide heroin trafficking organization, lost an 18-month battle against extradition to the U.S. from Paraguay. He was returned to New York to face charges of masterminding the shipment of 97.5 lb. of heroin seized by U.S. agents in October 1970. Louis Cirillo, alleged to have been supplying one-sixth of the heroin consumed each year in the U.S., was sentenced to 25 years in prison in May. Despite increased enforcement efforts, however, a study of worldwide drug trafficking released in August by the U.S. State Department noted that only a small fraction of the total illegal flow of heroin was being curtailed. (*See* DRUGS AND NARCOTICS.)

Within a two-day period in February alarmed citizens overwhelmed police in virtually all major Italian cities with complaints of gangsterism, housebreaking, shoplifting, car thievery, and mugging. During the spring parliamentary election campaign the neofascists charged that law and order had decayed under parliamentary democracy. The Italian government countered with statistics showing that killings per 100,000 inhabitants had decreased from 4.9 in 1930 to 2.1 in 1970 and that robberies and kidnappings declined from 6 to 5.7. Burglaries and other thefts, however, rose from 459 per 100,000 persons in 1930 to 999 in 1970. On March 14, 1972, left-wing millionaire publisher Giangiacomo Feltrinelli, 45, was killed in an explosion as he was apparently preparing to dynamite a high-tension power line pylon near Milan. Ten days earlier police sources had stated that special protection was being given to 15 politicians and businessmen believed to be designated as targets for terrorist action by an underground network linked with Feltrinelli. On May 17, Luigi Calabresi, deputy chief of the political section of the Milan police force and one of those investigating Feltrinelli's death, was assassinated. Calabresi's leading role in the investigation of extremist groups believed responsible for terrorism had made him one of Italy's most hated policemen.

One of the more sensational swindles in recent U.S. memory was concluded in a New York federal court in March when author Clifford Irving (*see* BIOGRAPHY), his wife Edith, and researcher Richard Suskind pleaded guilty to charges of grand larceny and conspiracy to obtain more than $750,000 from the McGraw-Hill publishing house for a bogus autobiography of industrialist Howard Hughes. Mrs. Irving also faced Swiss charges for her use of a doctored passport and the name H. R. Hughes to open a Swiss bank account for the money. (*See* PUBLISHING.)

In a case that became a presidential campaign issue, seven men, including two former White House aides, were indicted on charges of conducting electronic surveillance and stealing and photographing documents belonging to the Democratic National Committee. Five of the men had been seized by police inside the Democratic headquarters in the Watergate apartment and office complex in Washington, D.C., on June 17. In other court actions during the year, black activist Angela Davis was found innocent of kidnapping, murder, and conspiracy charges stemming from a bloody shootout at the Marin County (Calif.) courthouse in August 1970; charges against State's Attorney Edward V. Hanrahan and 13 others were dropped in Chicago after a judge's ruling that the prosecution had failed to prove any conspiracy to block prosecution of the policemen who staged a raid in which two Black Panther Party leaders were killed; Paul E. Gilly was found guilty of the December 1969 murders of United Mine Workers insurgent Joseph A. Yablonski, his wife and daughter, and cases against six others remained in various stages of court action; and W. A. Boyle (*see* BIOGRAPHY), who had defeated Yablonski for the union presidency, was convicted on March 31 of making illegal political contributions with union funds.

In London in May, Sami Patel, former London manager of the Central Bank of India, and two others received prison sentences for attempting to defraud the bank of about £1 million. Peter Jackson, described as "junior director" of the biggest British banknote forgery gang in history, was jailed for ten years in April. The gang had forged £5 notes to the value of more than £250,000 that were still turning up at banks at the rate of £200 a week at the end of 1972. On Jan. 21, 1972, a grand jury in New York indicted 71 persons charged with stealing luxury cars to order.

Among objects of note stolen during the year were a first folio of Shakespeare's plays valued at £10,000 from the library of Manchester University; the sword of King Robert the Bruce, from the home of the Earl of Elgin in Dunfermline, Scot.; a 26-ft.-high model of the Soviet Vostok spacecraft in which Yuri Gagarin had made man's first space flight in 1961, along with samples of moon dust valued at over $20 million,

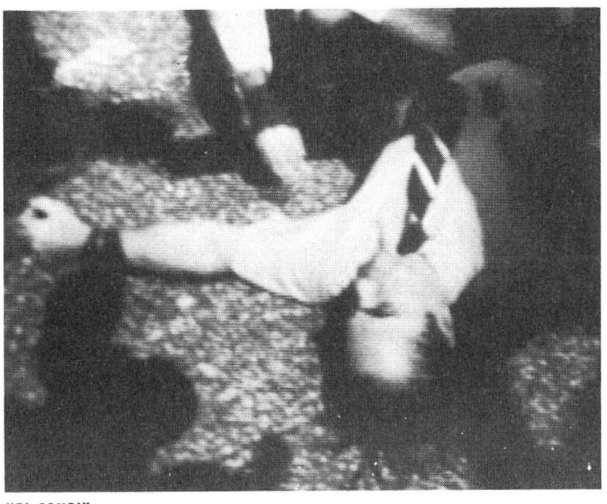

UPI COMPIX

Frames from a CBS news film show the attempted assassination of George Wallace in Laurel, Md., on May 15, 1972. A man who later was identified as Arthur Bremer fires shots (top) at close range, critically wounding Wallace (bottom). Bremer was convicted of the crime and sentenced to 63 years in prison.

which vanished en route from Moscow to a Soviet exhibition in Rättvik, Swed.; and an estimated $1 million–$5 million in loot ransacked from the safe-deposit boxes of New York's fashionable Pierre Hotel on January 2 by well-dressed gunmen who arrived by limousine.

(R. J. M. DENNERSTEIN; VIRGIL W. PETERSON)

See also Museums and Galleries.

Cuba

The socialist republic of Cuba occupies the largest island in the Greater Antilles of the West Indies. Area: 42,827 sq.mi. (110,922 sq.km.), including several thousand small islands and cays. Pop. (1971 est.): 8,657,160, including (1953) white 72.8%; mestizo 14.5%; Negro 12.4%. Cap. and largest city: Havana (pop., 1970, 942,348). Language: Spanish. Religion: predominantly Roman Catholic. President in 1972, Osvaldo Dorticós Torrado; prime minister, Fidel Castro.

Cuba was politically stable and made some economic progress in 1972. Prime Minister Castro remained firmly in power; he strengthened his position during the year by expanding mass organizations that supported the government, such as the neighbourhood Committees for the Defense of the Revolution, youth bodies, and labour unions, rather than operating through the Communist Party or the Cabinet. Official efforts were made to strengthen the labour union organization, the Central de Trabajadores de Cuba.

From May to early July, Castro paid official visits to several African and Eastern European countries; the tour culminated in a visit to the Soviet Union, June 26–July 6, his first there since 1964. During his stay in Moscow he requested and obtained increased economic and financial aid; in return, however, the Soviet government was allowed a greater say in the planning of Cuban economic policy. In April the two countries signed a new trade-and-payments agreement, to remain in force until 1975. It established that the U.S.S.R. would continue to supply Cuba with crude oil and its derivatives, with rolled and pig iron, sawn timber, foodstuffs, and other essential goods; and would purchase at least 80% of Cuba's annual sugar production. In addition, Soviet technical assistance was to be provided for the improvement of ports, for manufacturing sugarcane cutters, for increasing nickel and electricity output, and for training personnel to manage industrial plants. On July 11 Cuba became a full member of the Council for Mutual Economic Assistance (Comecon) and consequently could expect to receive increased economic aid from other Eastern European countries. All these events demonstrated that relations with the Soviet bloc had become very close; they had improved progressively since Castro expressed support for the Soviet invasion of Czechoslovakia in August 1968. Soviet aid to Cuba in 1972 was estimated at $600 million, excluding military assistance; and at the end of 1971 the total Cuban debt to the Soviet Union was estimated at $5.7 billion, including the purchase of sugar at below world market prices.

Cuba had some success in strengthening ties with other Latin-American countries during the year. Relations with Chile became closer as a result of Castro's state visit there in November and December 1971. An important trade agreement was signed with Mexico, and relations with that country improved; they had become cool during the late 1960s following accusations and counteraccusations of espionage. On July 8 diplomatic relations were established with Peru.

The government persisted in its efforts to promote trade with other Western countries. A four-year trade-and-payments pact was signed with Spain in December 1971, following long and difficult negotiations, principally over debts on past commercial transactions and compensation for Spanish property expropriated in Cuba. Trade with Japan and Italy increased during the year, and a British bank provided a loan of £3 million for the purchase of goods from the U.K.

The U.S. continued to apply the trade embargo it had enforced since the early 1960s. Despite this, there was a limited resumption of official communications. A small U.S. delegation attended an oceanographic conference in Havana in June. The airlift of refugees to Miami, Fla., was resumed for a few days in the spring and again in December. Following the spectacular hijacking of a Southern Airways jetliner with 31 passengers and crew aboard to Havana in November (*see* TRANSPORTATION), the Cuban government announced that it planned to put the hijackers on trial and offered to negotiate an antihijacking agreement with the U.S. Negotiations opened in late November, with the Swiss ambassador to Havana acting as intermediary.

There were indications of an all-round improvement in the economy. Thanks largely to increased Soviet pressure, the formulation of economic policy became more pragmatic; no new large-scale schemes were announced, and plans were concentrated on diversifying the economy so as to reduce its dependence on sugar. The 1972 sugar crop amounted to only 4.1 million tons, compared with 5.9 million tons in 1971, but its harvesting was carried out by a reduced labour force and with greater mechanization; the cane-firing

CUBA

Education. (1969–70) Primary, pupils 1,427,607, teachers 52,008; secondary, pupils 174,700, teachers 13,409; vocational, pupils 60,332, teachers 4,780; teacher training, students 31,619, teachers 1,543; higher (including 3 universities), students 30,708, teaching staff 4,335.

Finance. Monetary unit: peso, with (Sept. 18, 1972) an official rate of 0.92 peso to U.S. $1 (free rate of 2.20 pesos = £1 sterling). Budget (1966) balanced at 2,718,000,000 pesos.

Foreign Trade. (1970) Imports 1.3 billion pesos; exports 1,043,000,000 pesos. Import sources (1968 est.): U.S.S.R. 61%; China 7%; France 6%. Export destinations (1968 est.): U.S.S.R. 44%; China 9%; Spain 6%; Czechoslovakia 6%; East Germany 5%. Main export (1966) sugar products 85%.

Transport and Communications. Roads (1970) *c.* 13,000 km. (including *c.* 1,200 km. of the Central Highway). Motor vehicles in use (1969): passenger *c.* 71,000; commercial (including buses) *c.* 31,000. Railways (1971) *c.* 14,490 km. (including *c.* 9,440 km. plantation). Air traffic (1970): 502,206,000 passenger-km.; freight 11,710,000 net ton-km. Shipping (1971): merchant vessels 100 gross tons and over 264; gross tonnage 384,885. Telephones (Dec. 1970) 269,000. Radio receivers (Dec. 1970) 1,330,000. Television receivers (Dec. 1968) *c.* 575,000.

Agriculture. Production (in 000; metric tons; 1971; 1970 in parentheses): rice *c.* 452 (450); corn *c.* 115 (*c.* 115); cassava *c.* 220 (*c.* 220); sweet potatoes (1969) *c.* 240, (1968) *c.* 233; sugar, raw value (1971–72) *c.* 4,000, (1970–71) *c.* 5,924; coffee 28 (*c.* 28); oranges (1970) *c.* 140, (1969) 130; tobacco *c.* 40 (*c.* 40). Livestock (in 000; 1970–71): cattle *c.* 7,000; pigs *c.* 1,460; sheep *c.* 290; goats *c.* 83.

Industry. Production (in 000; metric tons; 1969): crude oil 91; petroleum products *c.* 5,300; electricity (kw-hr.; 1968) 4,700,000; chrome ore (oxide content; 1967) *c.* 11; manganese ore (metal content; 1968) 20; nickel ore (metal content; 1968) 37.

Crops:
see Agriculture

method, which was used successfully in 1971 on an experimental basis, was employed once again. Official statistics established that there had been significant rises in industrial production and productivity; there was some evidence of improved living standards, with a greater variety of consumer goods available, and an increase in food rations.

Events during the year underscored the fact that the improvement of education was the Castro government's greatest achievement since coming to power in 1959. A record number of schools were under construction. It was reported in September that a total of 2.4 million persons were enrolled in schools and universities, of whom 74.5% were in primary schools, 10.5% in secondary schools, 13.8% in specialized courses for adults, and 1.3% in universities. Nevertheless, there was a decline in the number of children between the ages of 13 and 16 attending school. Teaching was interrupted by the mobilization of labour for harvesting the sugar crop; many U.S. students traveled to Cuba to help. (ROBIN CHAPMAN)

Cycling

The Rhine River in 1972 marked the frontier between amateur and professional cycling. To the east, Berlin, Warsaw, and Prague were the key cities of the amateur "Peace Race" marathon, and Munich was the site of the Olympic Games. Westward, Paris staged the finish of the 59th Tour de France, and Marseilles organized the world professional track championships. Of these contests only the Olympics drew worldwide entries, the "Peace Race" being mainly a prestige clash between the U.S.S.R. and neighbouring nations and the professional events remaining the usual big business affair of West Europeans.

Although Belgian amateur riders had a poor season, their professional compatriots again dominated the commercial scene with Eddy Merckx adding to his impressive list of victories. Deriving a quarter of an estimated annual income of $625,000 from his Italian sponsors, Merckx was under an obligation to ride the three-week-long Tour of Italy (May 20–June 11) as well as the Tour de France three weeks later. The Belgian star accordingly made a more cautious start to the season than usual but still won the 180-mi. Milan–San Remo race for the fifth time on March 19. A month later on his home roads he was first in both "weekend Ardennais" classics, Flèche Wallonne and Liège–Bastogne–Liège.

An unexpected challenge to Merckx in the Tour of Italy came from José Manuel Fuente (who earlier had won his own country's stage race, the Tour of Spain) but the Belgian won the 2,500-mi. race by 5 minutes. Fuente did not ride the Tour de France, but another Spaniard, Luís Ocana, took his place as Merckx's chief opponent. Ocana might have beaten Merckx in the 1971 tour but for a serious mountain fall. After threatening Merckx for 1,000 mi., Ocana crashed again, though less seriously, and then caught bronchitis and was forced to retire. Merckx rode through comfortably to score his fourth successive tour win 10 min. 41 sec. ahead of Felice Gimondi (Italy), who just edged out the 36-year-old French hero, Raymond Poulidor.

Next on Merckx's list of priorities was the defense of his world road championship title at Gap, France (August 6), but he finished fourth. The winner was Marino Basso (Italy), a "roadman-sprinter" who usually was prominent only in one-day races but had heralded a more versatile season by winning the Tour of Sardinia (February 27–March 2). Other important stage-race winners were: Paris–Nice, Poulidor; Tour of Belgium, Roger Swerts (Belg.); Tour of Luxembourg, Roger Rosiers (Belg.); Tour of Switzerland, Louis Pfenninger (Switz.); Dauphiné Libéré, Ocana. One-day early-season classics and winners were: Paris–Roubaix, Roger de Vlaeminck (Belg.); Tour of Flanders, Eric Leman (Belg.); Amstel Gold Race, Neth., Walter Planckaert (Belg.); Grand Prix of Frankfurt, W.Ger., Gilbert Belonne (France). End-of-season stage-race winners were: Paris–Tours, N. Van Tyghem (Belg.); Tour of Lombardy, Merckx; Grand Prix des Nations time trial, Swerts (Belg.); Tour de la Nouvelle France, Canada, Guido Reybroeck (Belg.); and the amateur Tour de l'Avenir, F. Den Hertog (Neth.). In October Merckx set a new world record by cycling 49.409 km. in one hour.

Hugh Porter (U.K.) was the most impressive winner of the professional track championships at Marseilles (July 29–August 2), taking the 5,000-m. pursuit for the third time. Other titles and winners were: 1,000-m. sprint, Robert Van Lancker (Belg.) and 100-km. motor-paced, Theo Verschueren (Belg.). Because it was an Olympic year there were no amateur titles at stake except the 50-km. motor-paced, won for the second year in succession by Horst Gnas (W.Ger.).

The women's world championships were contested at the same meetings, and although the Soviets again dominated, a new threat came from the United States whose 17-year-old Sheila Young was third in the sprint; the gold medal went to Galina Ermolaeva for the sixth time, while Tamara Garkushina scored her fourth success in the 3,000-m. pursuit; on the Gap road circuit the 37½-mi. race produced a home champion in Geneviève Gambillon (France).

With the Olympic Games at Munich the goal of road and track riders, early 1972 amateur events were keenly contested. While many West European roadmen chose the 1,500-mi. Tour of Britain (May 29–June 10) to build up their stamina, the East Europeans were at grips over a similar distance on the Warsaw–Prague–Berlin triangle. This "Peace Race" was a bitterly fought affair; the outcome was in doubt until the last minute. Final victory went to Vlastimil Moravec (Czech.) by two seconds over Wladislaw Neljubin (U.S.S.R.), but in the coveted team-race section the positions were reversed with the U.S.S.R. taking the honours. There was also a close finish to the "Milk Race" Tour of Britain in which Hennie Kuiper (Neth.) snatched victory in the final sprint from Marcel Duchemin (France). (For Olympic results, *see* SPORTING RECORD: *Special Report.*)

(JOHN B. WADLEY)

A.F.P./PICTORIAL PARADE

Cyclists led by Willy Teirlinck enter Paris in the final stage of the Tour de France on July 23, 1972. Overall winner for the fourth successive year was Belgium's Eddy Merckx.

Cyprus

An island republic and a member of the Commonwealth of Nations, Cyprus is in the eastern Mediterranean. Area: 3,572 sq.mi. (9,251 sq.km.). Pop. (1971 est.): 639,000, including Greeks 77%; Turks 18%. Cap. and largest city: Nicosia (metro. pop., 1971 est., 117,000). Language: Greek and Turkish. Religion: Greek Orthodox 77%; Muslim 18.3%. President in 1972, Archbishop Makarios III.

After the fourth round of talks between the Greek and Turkish Cypriots ended in deadlock in September

Currency:
see Money and Banking
Cybernetics:
see Computers

1971, the governments of Cyprus, Greece, and Turkey had agreed to a proposal by then UN Secretary-General U Thant that his representative on the island, Bibiano Osorio-Tafall, should participate in the next round of intercommunal negotiations. It was also decided that two constitutional experts, from Greece and Turkey, should be present to advise the Greek and Turkish Cypriot negotiators. Hopes that this initiative would soon resolve the difficulties separating the two communities were frustrated early in 1972, however, as a result of disagreements between Cyprus and the Greek and Turkish governments, and the opening of the expanded talks was delayed until the summer.

In the last quarter of 1971, the activities of Greek Cypriot opponents of the president had given rise to fears of a right-wing coup. In January 1972 a quantity of arms purchased by the government from Czechoslovakia was landed clandestinely in Cyprus. At that time there was a renewal of tension between the two communities—a Greek Cypriot was shot dead in Nicosia by a Turkish Cypriot on January 10—and the news that the president had acquired armaments threatened to increase intercommunal discord further. In February Greece and Turkey, the two foreign powers most interested in a peaceful resolution of the Cyprus problem, insisted that President Makarios hand over the arms to the UN peace-keeping force. Since Makarios was unwilling to do this, the Greek and Turkish governments held up the opening of intercommunal talks. The Turks were satisfied when Makarios gave effective custody of the weapons to the UN force in March, but the president's relations with Greece were not eased until May.

The Czechoslovak arms affair precipitated a crisis in relations between Greece and Cyprus. In a strongly worded note sent to President Makarios on February 11, the Greek regime recommended that he reform his administration, which it regarded as left wing and anti-Greek, and establish a government of "national unity." Mass demonstrations in February testified to Makarios' popularity among many Greek Cypriots, and Gen. Georgios Grivas, his principal political opponent, refused to endorse the Greek note.

The president was compelled to accede to some of the Greek demands in order to maintain his authority, however. From early March three Cypriot bishops sought to bring about his resignation on the ground that it was unsuitable for him, as an archbishop, to hold government office, and on March 3 he was urged by Parliament to normalize relations with Greece. Makarios had discussions with General Grivas in March and also negotiated with other opposition leaders, but they refused to join his government. The foreign minister, Spyros Kyprianou, resigned on May 5, allegedly on the insistence of the Greek regime. On June 16 the Cabinet was reshuffled; seven of the eight ministers appointed were new to the government. This appeared to satisfy Greece. Subsequently the president's position grew more secure.

The expanded intercommunal talks finally began on June 8, and the briefing stage was completed in September. Although the atmosphere prevailing at these meetings was described as "friendly," the Cyprus government remained opposed in principle to the concession of a wide measure of autonomy to the Turkish Cypriots. On July 17 the president declared that a solution based upon a form of cantonization or federation was unacceptable, since this would presage a division of the island between Greece and Turkey. (LESLIE COLLINS)

CYPRUS

Education. (Excluding Turkish-Cypriot schools; 1969–70) Primary, pupils 71,236, teachers 2,279; secondary, pupils 35,003, teachers 1,569; vocational, pupils 4,218, teachers 279; higher, students 580, teaching staff 48.

Finance. Monetary unit: pound, with (Sept. 18, 1972) a par value of C£0.38 to U.S. $1 (free rate of C£0.93 = £1 sterling). Budget (1970 est.): revenue C£31,210,000; expenditure C£27,753,000. Gold, SDRs, and foreign exchange, monetary authorities: (June 1972) U.S. $304 million; (June 1971) U.S. $229.2 million.

Foreign Trade. (1971) Imports C£107,970,000; exports C£47,630,000. Import sources: U.K. 29%; Italy 10%; West Germany 7%; Greece 6%; U.S. 6%; France 5%. Export destinations: U.K. 41%; West Germany 12%; U.S.S.R. 5%. Main exports: citrus fruit 26%; copper 13%; potatoes 10%.

Transport and Communications. Roads (1970) 8,134 km. Motor vehicles in use (1970): passenger 55,500; commercial (including buses) 13,700. Air traffic (1971): 188 million passenger-km.; freight 2,855,000 net ton-km. Shipping (1971): merchant vessels 100 gross tons and over 277; gross tonnage 1,498,-114. Telephones (Dec. 1970) 46,000. Radio licenses (Dec. 1970) 167,000. Television licenses (Dec. 1970) 49,000.

Agriculture. Production (in 000; metric tons; 1971; 1970 in parentheses): wheat 90 (43); grapes 184 (183); potatoes *c.* 200 (208); oranges (1970) 99, (1969) 107; grapefruit (1970) 46, (1969) 44; olives 15 (8). Livestock (in 000; 1970–71): sheep 435; cattle 42; pigs 115; goats 360.

Industry. Production (in 000; metric tons; 1969): asbestos 22; copper ore (exports; metal content) 19; chromium ore (oxide content) 11; cement (1971) 308; electricity (excluding most industrial production; kw-hr.; 1971) 562,000.

Czechoslovakia

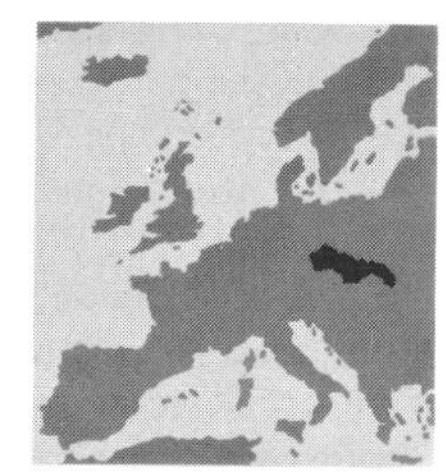

A federal socialist republic of central Europe, Czechoslovakia lies between Poland, the U.S.S.R., Hungary, Austria, and Germany. Area: 49,373 sq.mi. (127,876 sq.km.), including Slovakia 18,924 sq.mi. Pop. (1972 est.): 14,435,613 (Slovakia 4,580,667), including (1970 est.) Czech 65%; Slovak 29%. Cap. and largest city: Prague (pop., 1972 est., 1,083,717). Language: Czech and Slovak (official). General secretary of the Communist Party of Czechoslovakia in 1972, Gustav Husak; president, Ludvik Svoboda; premier, Lubomir Strougal.

The slow grind of "normalization" continued to claim its victims in Czechoslovakia during 1972. Although Husak held with some justification that no one was being tried for supporting Alexander Dubcek in 1968, but only for "acts committed against the state" since the Soviet invasion in the summer of that year, his balancing act was not easy. The Soviet Union was reluctant to jeopardize its plans for a European security conference, but political dissidents in Czechoslovakia had to be curbed if stability in Eastern Europe was to be maintained.

Early in February the journalist Jiri Lederer was sentenced to two years' imprisonment for writing articles critical of the Polish Communist regime. By March, it was reported, more than 200 dissidents had been jailed, including former members of the party's Central Committee, well-known journalists, and the prominent Marxist ideologist Karel Kosik, as well as former student leaders and representatives of the "New Left." In March the Czechoslovak Journalists' Centre announced that 40% of Czechoslovak journalists (*i.e.*, more than 1,200 individuals) had been dismissed from the profession since the Soviet invasion because they had rejected "the fundamental postulates of socialism." The Czech chess master Ludek Pachman, held in jail for 18 months in 1969–70 for protesting against the Soviet occupation, was rearrested in January 1972 but then released in May on grounds of poor health; he was allowed to emigrate to the West on November 28. However, 46 others went on trial in Prague and Brno in July. On August 1, Milan Huebl, former rector of the Communist Party college and Husak's friend, received a sentence of six and a half years on charges of subversion.

Intellectual conformity was also enforced by administrative means. For example, the avant-garde "Theatre Beyond the Gate" (*Divadlo za brancou*) was closed down under safety and fire regulations, and publishing enterprises were instructed to submit the names of their readers and editors for approval. Early in June the Congress of the Czech Writers' Union confirmed that the regime had no intention of allowing a return to the intellectual freedom of 1968.

In April the Central Committee of the Czechoslovak Communist Party issued a long report on the role of religion, which denied the possibility that religion could in any way function as a "progressive" force. The document accused the Roman Catholic Church of trying to use the relaxation of political control under Dubcek to achieve the reintroduction of monastic orders, dissolved in 1950. Czechoslovakia had not followed the policy of coexistence with the Catholic Church pursued by most of the other Eastern European countries. There were no official contacts with the Holy See, and the ten million Catholics in Czechoslovakia were virtually leaderless since no bishops or apostolic administrators were being appointed. On October 27 a British clergyman, the Rev. David Hathaway of the Pentecostal Church, was sentenced to two years' imprisonment; he had been arrested at the border four months previously with a cargo of contraband Bibles and other Christian literature.

The Husak regime tried hard to compensate for the absence of political freedom by offering a greater measure of consumer satisfaction. The primary goal of the 1971–75 five-year plan was reflected in the shop windows and restaurants of Czechoslovakia's main cities. On the other hand, the psychological effects of the Soviet invasion persisted, and the regime found it difficult to persuade workers to do more than the absolute minimum. Too many experts had been removed for political reasons, many enterprises lagged behind their plan targets, and the return to centralized planning forced the planners back on political slogans as a means of increasing productivity. The eighth Congress of Czechoslovak Trade Unions, in June, rejected as revisionist and counterrevolutionary "right-wing theories about the unions' independence of the Party's leading role." Even so, more homes were being built, automobiles could be delivered almost at once, and production levels in agriculture were being raised.

Despite this minor consumer boom, the regime succeeded in keeping inflation at a reasonable level; in the first nine months of 1972 both incomes and turnover in consumer goods rose by 6%. This increase in consumption was largely covered by imports, and it was officially admitted that Czechoslovakia's adverse trade balance with the "capitalist" West had tripled from 309 million koruny in 1965 to more than 1 billion koruny in 1971. Although Czechoslovakia's trade balance with its Comecon partners showed a credit balance approximately equal to the deficit in trade with the West, short-term credits, dating from the crisis years 1968 and 1969, were being repaid to Comecon's International Bank for Economic Cooperation in Moscow.

The relative success of Husak's policies was reflected in the maneuvers staged by the Warsaw Pact in Czechoslovakia in September under the code name Shield 72. Troops from the U.S.S.R. Poland, Hungary, East Germany, and, of course, Czechoslovakia participated in the exercise. Husak's speech at the concluding ceremonies stressed yet another aspect of "normalization"—Czechoslovakia's readiness to go on negotiating with Bonn about the abrogation of the 1938 Munich agreement. (OTTO PICK)

CZECHOSLOVAKIA

Education. (1969–70) Primary, pupils 2,002,053, teachers 98,640; secondary, pupils 107,383, teachers 6,782; vocational, pupils 274,178, teachers 15,013; teacher training, students 8,496, teachers 423; higher (including 18 universities), students 133,524, teaching staff 16,856.

Finance. Monetary unit: koruna, with an official exchange rate of 6.63 koruny to U.S. $1 (free rate of 16.10 koruny = £1 sterling) and a tourist rate of 15 koruny to U.S. $1 (free rate of 36.02 koruny = £1 sterling). Budget (1970 est.): revenue 205,860,000,000 koruny; expenditure 194,313,000,000 koruny.

Foreign Trade. (1971) Imports 28,870,000,000 koruny; exports 30,090,000,000 koruny. Import sources: U.S.S.R. 34%; East Germany 12%; Poland 7%; West Germany 6%; Hungary 5%. Export destinations: U.S.S.R. 32%; East Germany 11%; Poland 8%; Hungary 6%; West Germany 6%. Main exports (1969): machinery 36%; motor vehicles 10%; iron and steel 9%; chemicals 5%.

Transport and Communications. Roads (1970) 145,923 km. Motor vehicles in use (1970): passenger 766,452; commercial 198,588. Railways (1970): 13,308 km. (including 2,510 km. electrified); traffic 17,298,000,000 passenger-km., freight (1971) 63,465,000,000 net ton-km. Air traffic (1971): 904.8 million passenger-km.; freight 15,651,000 net ton-km. Shipping (1971): merchant vessels 100 gross tons and over 12; gross tonnage 82,731. Telephones (Dec. 1970) 2,003,000. Radio licenses (Dec. 1970) 3,858,000. Television licenses (Dec. 1970) 3,091,000.

Agriculture. Production (in 000; metric tons; 1971; 1970 in parentheses): wheat 3,883 (3,174); barley 2,850 (2,280); oats 908 (776); rye 611 (454); corn c. 575 (513); potatoes 4,506 (4,793); sugar, raw value (1971–72) c. 674, (1970–71) c. 763; beef and veal c. 370 (362); pork c. 590 (586). Livestock (in 000; Jan. 1971): cattle 4,288; pigs 5,530; sheep 981; chickens 37,570.

Industry. Index of industrial production (1963 = 100): (1971) 166; (1970) 156. Production (in 000; metric tons; 1971): coal 28,807; brown coal 84,791; electricity (kw-hr.) 47,179,000; iron ore (30% metal content) 1,608; pig iron 8,074; steel 12,065; cement 7,955; sulfuric acid 1,163; nitrogenous fertilizers (N content; 1970) 352; phosphate fertilizers (1970) 313; cotton yarn 119; cotton fabrics (m.) 552,000; woolen fabrics (m.) 54,000; rayon and acetate yarn and fibres 70; nylon, etc., yarn and fibres 35; passenger cars (units) 149; commercial vehicles (units) 52. Dwellings completed (1971) 79,000.

Dahomey

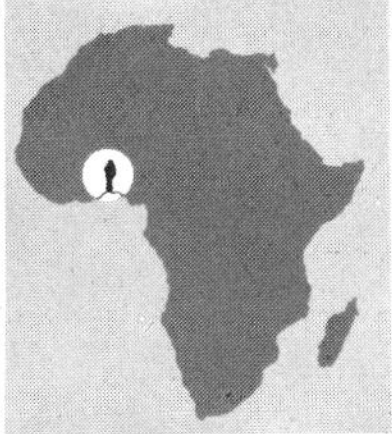

A republic of West Africa, Dahomey is located north of the Gulf of Guinea and is bounded by Togo, Upper Volta, Niger, and Nigeria. Area: 43,483 sq.mi. (112,620 sq.km.). Pop. (1971 est.): 2,792,000, mainly Dahomean and allied tribes. Cap.: Porto-Novo (pop., 1971 est., 90,000). Largest city: Cotonou (pop., 1971 est., 152,000). Language: French and local dialects. Religion: animist, with Christian and Muslim minorities. Chairmen of the Presidential Council in 1972, Hubert Maga and, from May 7 until October 26,

DAHOMEY

Education. (1968–69) Primary, pupils 148,625, teachers 3,565; secondary, pupils 14,918, teachers 634; vocational, pupils 717, teachers 102; teacher training, students 137, teachers 20; higher, students 174, teaching staff 18.

Finance. Monetary unit: CFA franc, with (Sept. 18, 1972) a parity of CFA Fr. 50 to the French franc and CFA Fr. 255.79 to U.S. $1 (free rate of CFA Fr. 612.37 = £1 sterling). Budget (1971 est.): receipts CFA Fr. 10.4 billion; expenditure CFA Fr. 11.8 billion.

Foreign Trade. (1971) Imports CFA Fr. 21.2 billion; exports CFA Fr. 11,650,000,000. Import sources (1969): France 39%; Netherlands 7%; U.S. 6%; West Germany 5%. Export destinations (1969): France 36%; Nigeria 13%; Netherlands 13%; U.S. 10%; West Germany 8%. Main exports: palm products 34%; cocoa 24%; cotton 19%.

Agriculture. Production (in 000; metric tons; 1971; 1970 in parentheses): corn 216 (216); cassava (1970) 736, (1969) 681; sweet potatoes (1970) 605, (1969) 599; millet and sorghum 68 (60); peanuts 65 (57); cottonseed 26 (18); palm oil 47 (45); palm kernels 80 (94); cocoa (exports) 19 (7); coffee 2.5 (1.3). Livestock (in 000; 1970–71): cattle *c.* 590; sheep *c.* 580; pigs *c.* 370.

Justin Timotin Ahomadegbé; president from October 26, Maj. Mathieu Kerekou.

Dahomey's civilian Presidential Council, established in April 1970, was overthrown Oct. 26, 1972, in the fifth military coup since independence. President Ahomadegbé, who on May 7 had succeeded Hubert Maga in accordance with the council's plan of two-year terms, was surrounded in his palace by troops under the leadership of Maj. Mathieu Kerekou, deputy chief of the armed forces. Immediately after the coup Major Kerekou was named president and defense minister. The border with Togo was closed and telecommunications with Paris were suspended.

There had already been signs of instability earlier in the year. On February 23 President Maga announced that a group of army mutineers had attempted to overthrow the government and that Army Chief of Staff Col. Paul-Émile de Souza had been slightly wounded in the incident. Subsequent arrests included Lieut. Col. Maurice Kouandété, deputy secretary-general for defense and a leader of two previous coups in 1967 and 1969, and seven other soldiers.

The defendants refused to cooperate with the court, and for procedural reasons Dahomean lawyers refused to defend them. Thus, it was not until May that the alleged conspirators were brought to trial and sentenced by a military court, against whose decisions there was no appeal. The proceedings consisted largely of the reading of statements said to have been made by the defendants before a commission of inquiry. On May 16 the court passed death sentences on Kouandété (later commuted), two captains, and a sergeant major, as well as two soldiers in absentia. One life sentence and several shorter prison terms were also imposed. (PHILIPPE DECRAENE)

Dance

Certainly the most impressive, most highly publicized dance event of 1972 was the New York City Ballet's Stravinsky Festival, presented at the New York State Theater. Creatively unparalleled in the sheer volume of production, it consisted of some 30 ballets (20 choreographed especially for the occasion and thus classified as world premieres) all set to Stravinsky scores. The festival was conceived by Lincoln Kirstein, general director of the New York City Ballet, and by George Balanchine, the troupe's artistic director and a lifelong collaborator and friend of Stravinsky, who had died the year before. New Balanchine ballets to Stravinsky music included *Violin Concerto* (the most highly praised new work of the entire festival), *Symphony in Three Movements, Duo Concertant,* and a short movement from a sonata that Stravinsky had composed 70 years before (two years before Balanchine was born). Among the great Balanchine-Stravinsky collaborations from the past seen at the festival were *Apollo, Orpheus,* and *Agon.* New creations by Jerome Robbins included *Dumbarton Oaks, Circus Polka,* and *Scherzo Fantastique,* in addition to a revival of *The Cage,* set to nonballet music. Balanchine and Robbins together created *Pulcinella* (with scenery and costumes by Eugene Berman) and even performed in it. Todd Bolender, John Taras, and John Clifford were other choreographers who contributed to this Stravinsky Festival. Many productions were reproduced for the troupe's annual July season at the Saratoga Performing Arts Festival.

The New York City Ballet also presented the world premiere of Robbins' *Watermill,* a ceremony rather than a ballet, to music of Teiji Ito. All ingredients were co-equal in a total-theatre expression, with Edward Villella (*see* BIOGRAPHY), acting instead of dancing, as the focal point. Other novelties included a presentation of Michel Fokine's *Chopiniana* (the original, and still the European title for *Les Sylphides*), staged by Alexandra Danilova and performed in practice costumes. Late in 1972, the troupe made an extensive tour abroad, including performances in the U.S.S.R. and Poland.

The American Ballet Theatre enjoyed successful national tours, and performed extensive engagements at both the New York City Center (winter) and the New York State Theater (summer) and at the John F. Kennedy Center for the Performing Arts in Washington, D.C., where it was the official dance company. Eliot Feld not only brought to the American Ballet Theatre some ballets he had choreographed for his short-lived American Ballet Company but also created *A Soldier's Tale* (*L'Histoire du Soldat*) and *Excentrique,* both to music of Stravinsky. Another novelty was *Some Times,* a Dennis Nahat ballet to a commissioned score by Claus Ogerman. Peter Van Dyk's *Unfinished Symphony* (Schubert) and *Grand Pas Classique* (Gsovsky-Auber, restaged by Oleg Briansky) were given their U.S. premieres. Revivals included Anton Dolin's showpiece for a quartet of men, *Variations for Four* (Marguerite Keogh), David Lichine's *Helen of Troy* (Offenbach), and Fokine's *Le Spectre de la Rose* (von Weber), remounted especially for Paolo Bortoluzzi, formerly a star with Maurice Béjart's Ballet of the 20th Century and a new American Ballet principal. Carla Fracci (from Italy) and Natalia Makarova (from the Soviet Union) continued to head the roster of the troupe's most popular ballerinas, along with the American Cynthia Gregory, who received ovations for her new interpretation of *Giselle,* along with her ever popular *Swan Lake* and performances in modern ballets.

The City Center Joffrey Ballet played a total of 12 weeks (half in the spring and half in the fall) at its home theatre. New works included *Double Exposure* (based very loosely on Oscar Wilde's *The Picture of Dorian Gray*), choreographed by Joe Layton to a score made up of music of Scriabin and electronic sounds by Henri Pousseur; *Chabriesque*

Dairy Products: *see* Agriculture
Dams: *see* Engineering Projects

(Chabrier), choreographed by the company's resident choreographer, Gerald Arpino; and Arpino's *Sacred Grove on Mount Tamalpais* (Alan Raph).

During the year the interracial company headed by Alvin Ailey was made a constituent of the New York City Center of Music and Drama as the Alvin Ailey City Center Dance Theater. Works performed included the new *Lark Ascending* (Ailey-Ralph Vaughan Williams) and *A Song for You* (Ailey-popular) and a revival of *Kinetic Molpai* (Shawn-Jess Meeker), the famous dance for an all-male ensemble of nine by Ted Shawn (*see* OBITUARIES). The City Center of Music and Drama presented its American Dance Marathon '72, produced by Charles Reinhart, involving the talents of 18 companies and 2 soloists drawn from all over the U.S. for a long run at the ANTA Theater. A workshop project involving the Martha Graham Dance Company was instituted and, following a year of illness, Miss Graham assumed direction of the junior group in a repertory of her own creations. A glimpse of ballet in China was afforded by a movie, *The Red Detachment of Women.*

U.S. troupes not centered in New York and producing new works in their home cities and on tour were the Boston Ballet, the Pennsylvania Ballet, the Cincinnati Ballet, and the National Ballet (Washington, D.C.). The Harkness Ballet continued to focus upon touring, both in Europe and in America. Modern dance, including avant-garde activities, was represented by many troupes both large and small, among them Utah's Repertory Dance Theater, the Juilliard Dance Company, the companies of Alwin Nikolais and Murray Louis, the Dance Theater Workshop, Merce Cunningham, James Cunningham, Lar Lubovitch, Louis Falco, and Don Redlich.

Of particular importance to dance research was the project to save the dance collection of the New York Public Library, the most extensive dance archives in the world, from closing because of lack of funds (the library's theatre and music collections faced similar fates). A gala produced by Donald Saddler and enlisting the contributed talents of world-renowned dance stars, held at the City Center to see if $60,000 could be raised, realized more than $100,000 in an evening. (WALTER TERRY)

In Britain the Royal Ballet, moving toward a repertory relating its classical background with more contemporary forms, took Glen Tetley's *Field Figures* (Stockhausen), previously mounted by the touring group, into the Covent Garden repertory. In the summer of 1972 Tetley created a work specially for the larger company—*Laborintus* (Berio) for eight dancers including Lynn Seymour and Rudolf Nureyev. Kenneth MacMillan created a new work, *Triad* (Prokofiev). Revivals included Robbins' *Afternoon of a Faun* (Debussy), Ninette de Valois's *Checkmate* (Bliss), and John Cranko's *Poème de l'extase* (Scriabin). The Royal Ballet's smaller company (now called the New Group) revived two works of Herbert Ross, *Caprichos* (Bartok) and *The Maids* (Milhaud), and Hans van Manen's *Grosse Fuge* (Beethoven). New creations included Joe Layton's *O.W.* (Walton), MacMillan's *Ballade* (Fauré), and Frederick Ashton's *Siesta* (Walton).

London Festival Ballet put on a new production by Beryl Grey of *Swan Lake* (Tchaikovsky). Works new to the company's repertory were Ulf Gadd's *Ebb and Flow* (Telemann), Walter Gore's *Dansscape* (Hindemith), and Dennis Nahat's *Mendelssohn Symphony* (Mendelssohn).

Ballet Rambert added to its repertory with new works from Tetley, *Rag Dances* (Hymas), and Norman Morrice, *Solo* (Downes). The main part of the company's work in 1971–72 was the development of programs for thrust stages. These programs, called "Dance of New Dimensions," were first given at London's Young Vic arena theatre; most notable among them were: Christopher Bruce's *For those who die as cattle* (no music), Morrice's *Ladies, Ladies!* (Hymas), and Joseph Scoglio's *Stop-over* (Takemitsu). Later, John Chesworth created a work for the thrust stage at the Crucible Theatre, Sheffield—*Pattern for an Escalator* (Jonathan Harvey instrumental score, George Newson electronic score). Ballet Rambert had now developed a Dance Unit for four dancers who toured the provinces.

London Contemporary Dance Theatre had given several seasons at The Place in London as well as increasing its provincial and overseas touring. Five new works added to the best of the existing repertory early in 1972 were Richard Alston's *Cold* (Adam), Barry Moreland's *Kontakion* (Renaissance and medieval music), Noemi Lapzeson's *One Was the Other* (Finnissy), Anna Sokolow's *Scenes from the Music of Charles Ives,* and Xenia Hribar's *Some Dream* (Vivaldi-Albinoni). During a summer season two full-length multimedia works were given: Remy Charlip's *Dance* and Richard Alston's *Combines.* Later Alston established his own group, Strider, for which he created *Tiger Balm* (Lockwood), *Thunder* (various singers interpreting "Stormy Weather"), and *Routine Couple* (a comedy record of George Burns and Gracie Allen).

Britain's two principal regional companies, Scottish Theatre Ballet (formerly Western Theatre Ballet) and Northern Dance Theatre, had become firmly established and their respective repertories were considerably strengthened. The Scottish company put on a full-length work by its director, Peter Darrell, *The Tales of Hoffmann* (Offenbach). Shorter creations included Ashley Killar's *Arriving Bellevue Sunday . . .* (Janacek), Stuart Hopps's *An Clò Mor* (traditional Gaelic songs), and there was a revival of Andrée Howard's *La Fête Étrange* (Fauré). A new development in the work of this company was a late-night experimental program, "Tangents."

Northern Dance Theatre added five new works to the repertory: Jonathan Thrope's *Quartet* (Beethoven); Laverne Meyer's *Valse Triste* (Sibelius) and

Jorge Donn (centre) dances the title role of the legendary Russian dancer Nijinsky in the Ballet of the 20th Century's production "Nijinsky, Clown of God," created by Maurice Béjart.

AGIP/PICTORIAL PARADE

KEYSTONE

The scene above is from the opera-ballet "Le Rossignol," presented as a tribute to Sergei Diaghilev and Igor Stravinsky by Le Ballet Théâtre Contemporain in Paris.

Schubert Variations; Suzanne Hywel's *Threequarter Profile* (Martin); and Simon Mottram's *Tchaikovsky Suite.*

London saw a continual stream of visiting companies during 1971–72 including the French Ballet Théâtre Contemporain and Ballet of the 20th Century from Brussels in Maurice Béjart's *Nijinsky, Clown of God,* both of which also appeared in the U.S. The Netherlands Dance Theatre toured the U.S. and Australia featuring Tetley's nude ballet, *Mutations.* New works in 1972 included Louis Falco's *Huescape* (Pierre Henry) and *Journal* (Alcantara's sound collage), Tetley's *Small Parades* (Varèse), and Frans Vervenne's *Pudding and Yesterday* (Supersister pop group). The Dutch National Ballet mounted a production of *The Sleeping Beauty* (Tchaikovsky), and put on several new works, including Rudi van Dantzig's *Painted Birds* (Castiglioni and Bach) and *Après-Visage* (Berio), Ethery Pagava's *La Cage* (Penderecki and Serocki), Hans van Manen's *Twilight* (John Cage), and Toer van Schayk's *Past Imperfect* (Ligeti).

West Germany now had 25 ballet companies attached to the various opera houses. The company that had achieved greatest international importance was the Stuttgart Ballet, which not only had great success in the U.S. but also on a tour of the U.S.S.R. Cranko's *Initials R.B.M.E.* (Brahms) was the principal addition to the main company, while the smaller offshoot, the Noverre Ballet, mounted Jan Stripling's *Voices from the Past* (Crumb), Jiri Kylian's *Incantations* (Jolivet), and Cranko's *Into the Cool* (Getz). The Ballet of Frankfurt State Theatre also had many successes thanks to the work of its ballet director and principal choreographer, John Neumeier, whose most recent creation was *Pictures I, II, III* (Scriabin, various composers, Mussorgsky). Most of the works for the Hamburg State Opera Ballet were revivals of works by Balanchine.

In France, the Paris Opéra Ballet returned to the Opéra but the main part of its work consisted of classical revivals. Modern work in France was mainly given by Le Ballet Théâtre Contemporain, now headquartered in Paris and Angers. The Royal Danish Ballet revived its Bournonville repertory, and put on Flemming Flindt's *Nutcracker* (Tchaikovsky) and *Triumph of Death* (Koppel). (PETER WILLIAMS)

See also Music; Theatre.

Deaths:
see Vital Statistics; *see also biographies of prominent persons who died in 1972, listed under* Obituaries

Debts, National:
see Government Finance

Defense

The May 1972 Moscow summit meeting between U.S. Pres. Richard Nixon and Soviet leaders marked U.S. recognition of the Soviet Union as an equal superpower. Thus the real importance of the first agreement on limiting strategic arms, signed on May 26, was political rather than strategic, embodying mutual Soviet-U.S. acceptance that nuclear war had ceased to be a reasonable option for either. The agreement would allow both to curb the rising costs of strategic weapons by freezing existing weapons at or near their current levels, although neither country would be able to reduce significantly its spending on strategic weapons research, development, and procurement.

There were actually four separate agreements: a formal treaty for an indefinite period, with a review every five years, limiting antiballistic missile (ABM) systems; an interim agreement on the limitation of offensive strategic missiles for the next five years; a protocol defining the effects of these limitations on submarine-launched ballistic missiles (SLBMs); and a memorandum of interpretations and understandings initialed at the strategic arms limitation talks (SALT) in Helsinki, Fin., where the agreements had been worked out by representatives of the two countries. The complexity of each document helped explain why the talks had taken two and a half years and emphasized the impossibility of measuring the superpower strategic balance by any single quantitative standard.

Nevertheless, the main effects of SALT I were clear. The U.S. and U.S.S.R. were each allowed to have two ABM "deployment areas," one centred on its capital (like the Soviets' 64 launchers for Galosh missiles around Moscow) and the other defending part of its intercontinental ballistic missile (ICBM) force (as with the U.S. ABM site near Grand Forks, N.D., scheduled to become operational by late 1974). Each deployment area was to have a radius of up to 150 km. (94 mi.), with a centre point at least 1,300 km. (810 mi.) from that of the other area, and could contain up to 100 ABM launchers, able to fire only one ABM missile and warhead. To prevent any expansion of these deployment areas, radars capable of guiding ABMs were restricted.

There were no qualitative limitations on ABMs, so both sides could replace existing ABMs with more advanced types, within the ceiling of 100. Thus the U.S.S.R. could expand its Moscow defense to 100 launchers, replace the Galosh missiles with more advanced models (which seemed likely), and construct a new ABM defense for one of its ICBM fields (an option it might well decline to exercise). Conversely, the U.S. would probably complete the Grand Forks ABM site and experiment with the development of the Hardsite ABM using less vulnerable radars, but forgo the option of a second deployment to protect Washington, D.C. Here, as elsewhere, SALT I seemed concerned less with the esoteric forms of regulating the strategic arms race envisaged by academic strategists than with the need to translate the desire for political accord into a codification of the strategic status quo, while permitting sufficient research and development to allow each side to feel confident the other was not acquiring some significant technical advantage.

The freeze on strategic missiles, although more ambiguous, was clearly intended to fulfill the same objectives. It froze ICBM and SLBM launchers at the number that were operational or under construction on May 26 (for SLBMs) and July 1 (for ICBMs). Except for the very large Soviet SS-9s, frozen at 309, missiles and submarine launchers could be modernized or replaced at will, while ICBM launchers deployed before 1964 or on older submarines could be exchanged for an equal number of SLBM launchers. The probable resultant balance would be 1,054 U.S. ICBMs against 1,618 for the U.S.S.R. The U.S. could replace 54 Titan ICBMs with the same number of new SLBMs, probably the underwater long-range missile system (ULMS) being developed for the Trident submarine. The U.S.S.R. could replace its 210 SS-7 and SS-8 ICBMs and 66 SLBMs in diesel-powered submarines with SLBMs in nuclear-powered submarines. The overall limits were 656 SLBMs in 41 submarines (which could be raised to 710 SLBMs in 44 submarines) for the U.S. and 950 SLBMs and 62 modern submarines for the U.S.S.R.

Arguments about the relative advantage either side might gain were largely irrelevant to the broader fact that neither could utilize such an advantage. Moreover, as Henry Kissinger, the president's special adviser on national security affairs, emphasized, in the absence of SALT I the Soviets, at their current rate of building, would have obtained, by 1977, about 1,200 SLBMs and nearly 2,800 ICBMs while the U.S. remained fixed at 656 SLBMs. Strategic bombers, where the U.S. had a considerable advantage of 455 to 140 for the U.S.S.R., were excluded from the agreement. The U.S. lead in multiple independently targeted reentry vehicles (MIRVs) was also large, giving the total U.S. strategic forces the ability to deliver about 4,300 warheads on 3,550 separate targets. The U.S.S.R. appeared to have deployed multiple reentry vehicles (MRVs) on SS-9 and SS-11 ICBMs, enabling it to attack an estimated 2,090 targets. SALT's significance lay in the tacit Soviet acceptance of the view that mutual assured deterrence was possible at relatively low force levels, probably lower than those already existing, even if one side's surprise attack were to be highly successful.

Negotiations toward a second agreement, SALT II, were started in late 1972 with a view toward exploring further limitations on strategic arms and securing some reduction in forward-based systems (FBS) for delivering tactical warheads. Success on FBS reduction seemed less probable, since it was linked to talks on mutual and balanced force reductions in Europe. It was also less important. To the Western Europeans, U.S. forward-based systems in Europe were a source of stability because they guaranteed that the U.S. deterrent would operate if Europe was attacked. Politically, a reduction in U.S. FBS without a cutback in the 700 Soviet medium-range ballistic missiles (MRBMs) and intermediate-range ballistic missiles (IRBMs) able to hit Western Europe from Eastern Europe would suggest that détente between the superpowers was being achieved at the expense of their allies.

In a larger sense, the Moscow summit codified the relationship between the two superpowers and between the superpowers and Europe, although much remained to be worked out. On the other side of the world, the earlier Peking summit marked U.S. recognition of China as at least a regional great power and, barring unforeseen circumstances, U.S. military involvement in Southeast Asia was drawing to a close. President Nixon and Kissinger appeared to be thinking in terms of a new balance of power, in which the

WIDE WORLD

Under an ornate chandelier in the Kremlin's Vladimir Hall, U.S. Pres. Richard Nixon and General Secretary of the Soviet Communist Party Leonid I. Brezhnev sign the strategic arms limitation agreement on May 26, 1972.

post–World War II bipolar world dominated by the U.S. and the Soviet Union was replaced by a pentagonal balance formed by the U.S., the Soviet Union, Europe, China, and Japan. Whether such a world would be more or less stable—and whether such a world view was even realistic, given the continued military preponderance of the two superpowers—were matters of intensive analysis and heated debate at year's end.

DISARMAMENT

SALT I seemed to be a major step forward in arms control, while the biological warfare convention opened for signature in April was hailed as the first disarmament measure since 1945. Nevertheless, there was increasing skepticism that either SALT or the Geneva conference of the Committee on Disarmament could achieve disarmament or arms control in any meaningful sense. This view was supported by a critical examination of the effects of SALT I on armaments (as distinguished from its political significance), the lack of effective limitations on biological or chemical warfare, the absence of any progress toward a comprehensive nuclear test ban treaty, and the probable failure of the 1969 nuclear nonproliferation treaty to inhibit proliferation.

SALT I would save the U.S. an estimated $11 billion on ABMs, but against this had to be set the costs of the new advanced manned bomber (B-1) and the Trident submarine carrying ULMS, expected to total $25 billion. Secretary of Defense Melvin Laird had made their development a precondition for Department of Defense agreement to SALT I. Both were expected to come into service in 1978–79 after the SALT I freeze, and so represented a form of insurance against its failure. Spending on strategic forces would still account for $19 billion of the projected $83.4 billion defense budget requested by the Nixon administration for fiscal 1973. The strategic force budget included provision for converting 31 Polaris submarines to Poseidon missiles; replacing earlier Minuteman ICBMs with Minuteman IIIs, carrying MIRVs; 10 Trident submarines; and an unknown number of B-1s.

A comprehensive nuclear test ban agreement offered the only possibility of a qualitative restraint on the superpower arms race that could complement the minimal quantitative limits of SALT I. U.S. Senate hearings had shown that the obstacles to a comprehensive test ban were political rather than technical.

Table I. Comparison of Strategic Forces After SALT I Agreement

Weapons systems	Max. range (mi.)	Warheads* No.	Warheads* Yield	Max. speed† (Mach)	Bomb load† (lb.)	Deployment First	Deployment Number (July 1972)	Deployment Launch vehicles‡ (submarines)
UNITED STATES								
ICBMs§								
Titan II	7,200	1	5–10 mt.	—	—	1962	54	—
Minuteman I	7,500	1	1 mt.	—	—	1962	300	—
Minuteman II	8,000	1	1–2 mt.	—	—	1966	500	—
Minuteman III	8,000	3‖	200 kt.	—	—	1970	200	—
Total							1,054	
SALT I allowance							1,054	
SLBMs§								
Polaris A-2	1,750	1	800 kt.	—	—	1962	128	8 nuclear
Polaris A-3	2,880	1 or 3¶	1 mt. or 200 kt.	—	—	1964	368	23 nuclear
Poseidon	2,880	10‖	50 kt.	—	—	1971	160	10 nuclear
Total							656	41 nuclear
SALT I allowance							656 or 710♀	41 nuclear or 44 nuclear♀
Strategic bombers								
B-52 D-F	11,500	—	—	0.95	60,000	1956	172	—
B-52 G/H	12,500	—	—	0.95	75,000	1959	283	—
		(Total megatonnage 15,500δ)						
Forward-based systems								
Sergeant (SRBM)	85	1	kt. range	—	—	1962	500	—
Pershing (SRBM)	450	1	kt. range	—	—	1962	250	—
Medium-range bombers□								
F-B-111A	3,800	—	—	2.5	37,500	1969	76	—
F-111AE	3,800	—	—	2.5	25,000	1967	75	—
A-7D	3,400	—	—	0.4	15,000	1968	◇	—
F-4	2,300	—	—	2.4	16,000	1962	475	—
U.S.S.R.								
ICBMs§								
SS-7	6,900	1	5 mt.	—	—	1961	210 (SS-7 and SS-8)	—
SS-8	6,900	1	5 mt.	—	—	1963		
SS-9	7,500	1 or 3¶ or as FOBS	20–25 mt. or 4–5 mt.	—	—	1965	290	—
SS-11	6,500	1 or 3?¶	1–2 mt. or 200 kt.	—	—	1966	970	—
SS-13	5,000	1	1 mt.	—	—	1968	60	—
Total							1,530	
SALT I allowance							1,618	
SLBMs§								
SS-N-4	350		mt. range	—	—	1961	36	12 diesel
SS-N-5	750		mt. range	—	—	1964	30	10 diesel
SS-N-6	1,750		mt. range	—	—	1969	494	39 nuclear
Total							560	61
SALT I allowance							950	62 nuclear
Strategic bombers								
Tu-95	7,800	—	—	0.78	40,000	1956	100	—
Mya-4	6,050	—	—	0.87	20,000	1956	40	—
		(Total megatonnage 3,600δ)						
Forward-based systems								
SS-1b (SRBM)	50		kt. range	—	—	1957	300 (SS-1b, SS-1c, SS-12)	—
SS-1c (SRBM)	185		kt. range	—	—	1965		
SS-12 (SRBM)	500		kt. range	—	—	1969		
SS-4 (MRBM)	1,200	1	1 mt.	—	—	1959	500	—
SS-5 (IRBM)	2,300	1	1 mt.	—	—	1961	100	—
SS-N-3 (Long-range cruise missile)	450		kt. range	—	—	1962	432▲	—

Note: kt. = kiloton(s); mt. = megaton(s).
*For missiles only.
†For manned bombers only.
‡For submarine-launched ballistic missiles (SLBMs) only.
§Covered by SALT I agreements.
‖Multiple independently targeted reentry vehicle (MIRV).
¶Multiple reentry vehicle (MRV).
♀If the 54 Titan missiles are replaced by SLBMs.
δEquivalent megatonnage (MTE), obtained by computing the two-thirds power of the yield, for U.S. strategic bombers is 7,900 and for Soviet strategic bombers, 1,700.
□Long-range nuclear capable strike aircraft.
◇Land- and sea-based.
▲100 on land, 292 in submarines, 40 in surface ships.

Both the U.S. and the U.S.S.R. could detect virtually all tests down to ten kilotons (half the size of the Poseidon missile warheads) with their own verification systems, and these could be developed to detect most tests in the five–ten kiloton range. Militarily effective cheating on a unilaterally verified test ban would be virtually impossible, since a series of tests were necessary to develop a reliable new warhead, and concealment through decoupling (muffling the seismic signal of a test by carrying it out in an underground cavern) was not possible for a test series. So, as Canada and Sweden had long argued, the nominal gap between the U.S. demand for seven on-site inspections per year as against the U.S.S.R.'s offer of three inspections was meaningless. The Nixon administration's view was that, while it would reexamine the U.S. position, the Soviet refusal to discuss a comprehensive test ban seriously made progress unlikely.

But if a comprehensive test ban was unlikely, the prospects for success of the nuclear nonproliferation treaty were even worse. India, which refused to sign the treaty, was openly developing a nuclear capability directed against China. The withholding of U.S. nuclear fuel supplies, the treaty's only real sanction, had been ensured by a trilateral safeguards agreement whereby the International Atomic Energy Agency (IAEA) would verify that such materials were not diverted for use in weapons. India was free, however, to divert its own fissionable materials to weapons purposes, and its acceptance of trilateral safeguards outside the treaty suggested that it felt assured of supplies, either of its own manufacture or from the U.S.S.R. Japan was still officially adhering to the principle that it would not manufacture nuclear weapons or allow them to be stationed on its territory (now including Okinawa) under normal circumstances. Unofficial discussions suggested an increasing willingness on Japan's part to consider acquisition of the technology for nuclear weapons and the necessary delivery systems by the end of the decade. Israel continued to reject the nonproliferation treaty while leaving its own nuclear status unclear. Various authoritative studies confirmed that Israel could develop nuclear weapons within a few months, if it did not already possess them.

Even the biological warfare convention, opened for signature in April 1972, was less promising than it appeared. Adherents undertook not to use biological weapons and to destroy their existing stocks by Jan. 10, 1973, but there was no verification and all complaints of violations had to go through the Security Council, where the big powers could exercise the veto. The U.S. did turn over its Pine Bluff, Ark., biological warfare complex to the Department of Health, Education, and Welfare for nonmilitary use and continued to destroy its stocks of biological and chemical weapons, but there was no progress toward U.S. ratification of the 1925 Geneva protocol forbidding the first use of poison gas.

Despite its ambiguities, especially with regard to riot-control gases and herbicides, the 1925 protocol seemed likely to remain the chief instrument of restraint on chemical warfare. The Committee on Disarmament was insisting that any new convention should include the destruction of stockpiles of chemical weapons and the means of producing them, but intensive studies seemed to confirm the impossibility of verifying compliance. However, the committee appeared to have seized on chemical and biological warfare as the only area left for it to discuss, since all the other important matters were under negotiation between the superpowers and their allies, in SALT and in the multilateral preparatory talks looking toward a European security conference. (See *NATO,* below.)

UNITED STATES

The last year of President Nixon's first term of office saw the achievement of the basic defense policy objectives set by the president and Henry Kissinger, although a negotiated peace in Vietnam still eluded them. (See *Southeast and East Asia,* below.) Most U.S. forces were withdrawn from Vietnam, and the resources saved (on paper, $7.5 billion for fiscal 1972) were being used to preserve the strategic deterrent and to finance the switch from a conscript to an all-volunteer army, while preserving the capability to defend, and therefore deter an attack on, Japan and Western Europe. The unsuccessful Democratic presidential candidate, Sen. George McGovern, had pledged that he would reduce the defense budget by about $30 billion, although many observers doubted that cuts of this order could have been made without a potentially destabilizing abandonment of U.S. interests, especially in Western Europe.

Total U.S. forces in South Vietnam fell from 151,000 to a residual force of 24,000 by December; all ground combat units were withdrawn, and the remaining support troops, mostly the 15,800 men of the 7th Air Force, were expected to follow. In part, this reflected a reshuffling of forces within Indochina, since U.S. forces in Thailand had increased to about 50,000. Thus in June seven fighter-bomber squadrons, totaling some 120 aircraft and 4,000 men, were transferred from Da Nang in South Vietnam to Thailand, but these forces were scheduled to be withdrawn, as were the 20,000 troops in South Korea.

The ending of the draft in June 1973 seemed to have been accepted by Congress, which approved a raise in basic military pay rates to $332 per month in January 1973, compared with $288 in 1972 and $83 in 1964. Some 65% of the fiscal 1973 defense budget was earmarked for personnel costs. By mid-1973 the armed forces would total 2,336,000 men (as against 2,391,000 in July 1972), the lowest figure since 1950 and one requiring reductions, in 1972, of 20,000 men by the Army and 13,000 by the Air Force. Navy strength remained virtually unchanged.

These cuts meant that the fiscal 1973 obligational authority of $83.4 billion ($76.5 billion of which was likely to be spent) would provide fewer effective divisions. In 1972 the total remained at 12, comprising 3 armoured, 1 air-cavalry, 4 mechanized infantry, and 2 infantry divisions, 1 airborne and 1 air-portable division, plus 2 independent infantry brigades, 1 independent airborne brigade, and 5 armoured cavalry regiments. The major overseas deployment area once more became West Germany, where the 7th Army comprised four divisions (two armoured and two mechanized infantry), plus two armoured cavalry regiments and one mechanized brigade. At the normal strength of about 16,000 men per infantry division, these forces would total some 72,000 men, but support forces brought the total to 190,000. They could be reinforced in a crisis by the Strategic Reserve, although, of its theoretical six divisions, only one was considered to be effective. An additional dual-based infantry division was earmarked for the 7th Army, with its heavy equipment stored in West Germany. As the Army ran down toward its zero-draft goal of 11 divisions, withdrawals from Southeast Asia would account for the necessary reductions, while the forces in Western Europe and the U.S. were brought up to strength.

Of the three services, the Army was experiencing the most difficulty with the change to an all-volunteer service. Severe morale problems were reported, evidenced by a doubling of the rate of "fragging" (grenade attacks on officers by their own men). Voluntary enlistment for the combat branches had risen from 300 to 3,000 men per month, however, as against the 5,000 needed, and further increases were expected. Civilians were replacing military personnel in some nonmilitary functions as part of the move to offer incentives similar to those provided by civilian employers. The experimental Tricap (triple-capable) division continued to prove its effectiveness in an antitank role, using a platoon formation of three Scout and five Cobra helicopters armed with the TOW antitank missile.

The Navy was also experiencing morale problems. Adm. Elmo Zumwalt, chief of naval operations, had introduced a number of measures designed to make the service more attractive and less restrictive, but they were not always fully implemented by the more tradition-minded naval establishment. Some cases of sabotage aboard ship were reported. In November the aircraft carrier "Constellation" was forced to return to port from maneuvers at sea when more than a hundred seamen, most of them black, staged a protest meeting in the ship's main mess hall and accused the officers of "calculated racism." In order to avoid possible violence, 137 men were put ashore at North Island in San Diego Bay. Subsequently, 129 of them refused to obey orders to return to the ship and held a sitdown demonstration at dockside. Later the carrier "Kitty Hawk" returned to the U.S. after racial troubles erupted on board while the ship was on station in the Vietnam war zone. Admiral Zumwalt publicly reprimanded his subordinates and insisted that racist practices be eliminated. An investigation into the racial problems of the Pacific fleet was held by the House Armed Services Committee.

The Navy increased its share of the defense budget, reflecting the need to replace obsolescent World War II vessels and the relative success of sea-based air-

Colours of the last U.S. combat unit in Vietnam are rolled up in deactivation ceremony at Da Nang on Aug. 12, 1972. The unit was the 3rd Battalion, 21st Infantry.

UPI COMPIX

power in South Vietnam, especially in providing rapid reinforcements at an acceptable political cost. Increasing emphasis was being placed on SLBMs, whose mobility and concealment made them invulnerable to a surprise attack. The replacement program, due for completion by 1980, envisaged a navy of 15 attack carriers and 4 antisubmarine warfare (ASW) carriers; 3 nuclear hunter-killer submarines (SSNs) to be built each year; and amphibious lift for 1⅔ Marine divisions, plus support vessels.

Significantly, the Navy's major projects all received congressional approval. The SSN-688 class was approved, as were the ULMS I, to be fitted to submarines carrying Poseidon missiles, and the ULMS II, for which the Trident-class submarines would be built. Construction of a nuclear-powered aircraft carrier, the CVN-70, to replace the two carriers due to retire by 1973, was finally authorized for fiscal 1974. Despite major problems with cost overruns, work on the F-14A fighter and the 30 DD-963 destroyers proceeded, at an estimated cost of $734.8 million and $612.1 million, respectively. To lessen the cost premium of 40% on sea-based airpower, it was proposed to substitute sea-control ships for some carriers; these ships, which cost about $100 million, carried 20 aircraft or helicopters. Naval personnel totaled 588,000; almost 602,000 were authorized for fiscal 1973. The core of the fleet remained its 14 attack carriers, including the nuclear-powered "Enterprise." Despite intensive research, the Navy still lacked an effective medium-range ship-to-ship missile and missile gunboats comparable to those developed by the U.S.S.R.

The Marine Corps remained at its authorized 1972 level of 198,000, organized in three divisions of 19,000 men, with organic air support from a total of 550 aircraft. Increasing use was being made of vertical envelopment techniques utilizing helicopters. Of the three divisions, two were stationed in the U.S. and one in the Pacific.

The Air Force was anxious to preserve the triad of U.S. deterrent forces—bombers, ICBMs, and SLBMs—since this gave the USAF two out of the three systems. Despite the doubts expressed about its ability to survive even a very limited Soviet first strike, procurement of the B-1 strategic bomber was accelerated, with $444 million allocated in fiscal 1973. In part, the B-1 was envisaged as a general-purpose heavy bomber to replace the aging B-52s, about half of which were assigned to duty in Southeast Asia. The increased emphasis on air support from secure U.S. bases in South Vietnam exemplified a long-term development, aimed at enabling the U.S. to support its allies while avoiding commitments that could escalate.

USAF personnel in the general purpose forces outside of the United States consisted of 120,000 in the Pacific (including 15,800 in South Vietnam in July 1972) and 50,000 in the U.S. Air Force, Europe. In addition, the Military Airlift Command had 90,000 men. The original order for 120 C-5A Galaxy transports at $3 million–$4 million each had been reduced to 81 at $4.9 million each, of which 79 would be in service by mid-1973. The controversial F-111 fighter-bomber returned to combat in Vietnam, but it continued to be plagued by unexplained losses.

As U.S. ground involvement in Vietnam was ending, the armed forces became involved in a major dispute, centring on charges that Gen. John Lavelle (*see* BIOGRAPHY) had authorized raids on North Vietnam in violation of orders that U.S. aircraft could attack only in response to hostile North Vietnamese action. Lieut. Delbert Terrill and others charged that General Lavelle had planned raids in advance and then cited nonexistent North Vietnamese attacks as justification. A House inquiry revealed that General Lavelle had accepted a demotion to the rank of three-star general and retirement after military authorities substantiated the charges. General Lavelle's suggestion that the then U.S. commander in Vietnam, Gen. Creighton Abrams, was aware of his action led to a delay in Senate confirmation of Abrams' appointment as Army chief of staff, but this was eventually approved. The new vice-chief of staff for the Army was Maj. Gen. Alexander M. Haig, Jr., the president's military adviser, who was promoted over the heads of 243 more senior officers.

At the same time, the hostility to the U.S. military establishment generated by the Vietnam war seemed to be diminishing, as U.S. combat casualties fell and draft calls decreased. The results of the presidential election suggested that the trend toward neo-isolationism, in the sense of a preoccupation with U.S. internal interests at the expense of its interests abroad, had slowed, at least temporarily.

U.S.S.R.

U.S. acceptance of the Soviet Union as a political and military equal reflected the fact that in almost every field of military activity the U.S.S.R. had achieved quantitative, if not qualitative, superiority. The primary Soviet objectives seemed to be strategic parity in modern ICBMs and SLBMs, continued modernization of its antiaircraft defenses, completion of the buildup of forces on the Sino-Soviet border without weakening those in Europe, and the expansion of Soviet political influence through a naval presence and military advisers. Estimating the costs of these objectives in dollar terms reflecting the allocation of real resources presented major difficulties, especially since Soviet manpower costs were drastically lower than those of the U.S. Assuming that Soviet manpower costs amounted to 30 to 35% of the total defense budget, as against 52% for the U.S. (including the National Guard), revised estimates of total Soviet defense spending, including reserves, would be $84 billion in 1971 and $91 billion in 1972, about 5–10% higher than U.S. spending and roughly constant at 11% of the gross national product (GNP).

In addition to its long-range strategic capability, the U.S.S.R. possessed the capacity to destroy Western Europe with 600 IRBMs east of the Urals, plus a further 100 SS-11 ICBMs sited within those missile fields. The Air Defense Command had a dual task: it provided a much more effective defense against attack by nuclear bombers than the U.S. possessed and also supplied air cover for Soviet land forces—hence the greater emphasis on interceptors than in NATO forces. The extensive surface-to-air missile network comprised 10,000 launchers at about 1,600 sites. Half the force was composed of SA-2 missiles with a slant range of 25 mi., effective between 1,000 and 80,000 ft., but these were being supplanted by the SA-5, with a slant range of 50 mi., which was usable against air-to-surface missiles. Low-level protection was provided by the SA-3 and its replacement, the SA-6, plus modern antiaircraft guns. The Tactical Air Force had 4,300 combat aircraft, and the Air Transport Force, 1,700 aircraft plus 1,750 helicopters.

The Army remained at a nominal 105 motorized rifle and 51 tank divisions with two million men, but there was increasing debate in the West as to how many effective 10,000-man divisions the U.S.S.R. could field. The Soviet Army seemed to maintain more forces with fewer men than NATO. The answer to this paradox probably lay in Soviet planning for two different types of warfare: a blitzkrieg campaign against Western Europe and an extended campaign against China. Thus in Central and Eastern Europe the Soviets maintained 31 divisions: 20 (10 tank) in East Germany; 2 tank divisions in Poland; 4 divisions (2 tank) in Hungary; and 5 divisions (2 tank) in Czechoslovakia. A further 29 divisions, probably in the same proportion of half tank and half mechanized infantry, could be mobilized within a month from the nominal 60 divisions in European U.S.S.R. Since a short (90-day) campaign would defeat NATO unless tactical nuclear weapons were used, the Soviet Union needed only half as many supporting forces as NATO. In the Sino-Soviet border area Soviet forces had risen to 44 divisions, about half at combat strength and half at the second degree of combat readiness (not requiring major reinforcement in time of war). The same balance was maintained in the 21 divisions in the southern U.S.S.R. There were also eight divisions at the third degree of readiness (requiring major reinforcement in time of war) in the central U.S.S.R.

Army equipment continued to reflect World War II experience, emphasizing medium-cost weapons and quantitative superiority so the Army could absorb heavy losses and still maintain a rapid pace of advance. The T-54/55 medium tank was being replaced by the T-62, comparable to the West German Leopard widely used in NATO. Most Soviet tanks were equipped for amphibious crossing and many for night fighting. A large proportion of artillery was self-propelled. Some 900 surface-to-surface missiles were distributed among the divisions, notably the Frog (10–45 mi. range, depending on the warhead), Scud A (50 mi.), Scud B (185 mi.), and Scaleboard (500 mi.).

The 475,000-man Navy continued to extend the range of its ASW activities in conjunction with the shore-based naval air force. Additional coverage would be provided by the two 33,000-ton aircraft carriers expected to enter service in 1973–74. All surface vessels also performed a political role by demonstrating Soviet power and support for friendly governments. Some capability for making this support forcible was being developed; the strength of the naval infantry (marines) was raised to 14,000 men, equipped with T-54/55 tanks, although its main role was still to conduct amphibious operations in support of the Army. Other examples of a dual-purpose ASW force able to exercise political influence were the first 10,000-ton Kara-class cruiser, the two Kresta II- and four Kresta I-class cruisers, and the four Kynda-class cruisers, all fitted with SS-N-3 long-range (300 mi.) surface-to-surface missiles, surface-to-air missiles, and extensive ASW systems. Like the Moscow-class ASW helicopter carriers, these vessels were probably the result of decisions taken around 1958–61, given that it takes about ten years to design and build a Soviet warship.

The accompanying destroyers fell into three main groups: 34 built in the 1960s; 17 Kotlin-class destroyers (1955–57), comparable to immediate post-1945 destroyers; and 40 Skory-class destroyers similar to the wartime U.S. Fletcher class. That the Soviet Navy suffered from a post-World War II bulge of largely obsolescent vessels similar to the West's was evident from the 17 Sverdlov-class gun cruisers, 104 Riga- and Kola-class escorts, and 210 diesel submarines. The latter were being replaced by nuclear-powered attack submarines. Nevertheless, the general conclusion remained that the West had overreacted to the Soviet discovery of the political capabilities of sea power and was investing heavily to counter what was primarily a political threat.

NATO

The preparatory discussions on a European security conference, which opened Nov. 22, 1972, in Helsinki between 32 European countries plus the U.S. and Canada, took place in the context of a military balance continuing to shift against Western Europe. This shift explained the increased emphasis in Western Europe on the need for a continuing U.S. presence at about the current level of four divisions, acting as a deterrent to Soviet aggression and able to offer a limited conventional defense before resorting to tactical nuclear weapons.

Politically, the Helsinki meeting confirmed that the initial Soviet objective of convening a single European security conference legitimizing Soviet control over Eastern Europe was unlikely to be attained. Western insistence on a conference on security and cooperation in Europe, involving all NATO and Warsaw Pact members, had created what were, de facto, the bloc to bloc discussions the Soviets had tried to avoid. It also linked progress in the security conference to the separate exploratory discussions on mutual and balanced force reductions (MBFR) between NATO and Warsaw Pact powers, scheduled for January 1973. This meant the Soviets would be unable to avoid detailed public scrutiny of their unwillingness to discuss meaningful reductions in their forces on the asymmetrical basis necessary to achieve a true balance of forces in Europe.

Even if it was attained, MBFR seemed unlikely to resolve the contradiction between the desire to reduce defense spending, evident in the U.S., West Germany, and Italy, and the desire to obtain increased security in terms of a longer time before nuclear response. Any large-scale reduction in NATO forces seemed likely to lower the threshold of nuclear response drastically, since the forces available would become inadequate to offer any defense at some points on the central front. Simple quantitative comparisons were misleading—for example, matching NATO's 6,000 main battle tanks plus a superiority in antitank weapons against the Pact's 16,000 less powerful tanks —but attempts to take account of these factors in assessing relative force capabilities ran into the expected difficulty of trying to assess different, and often noncomparable, capabilities. Moreover, the already large gap between NATO and Pact reinforcement capabilities would be increased in any situation where NATO needed more troops, since in a crisis NATO governments might hesitate to bring in reinforcements because they feared escalation. So the difficulties of deciding what constituted force reductions that were balanced so as not to lessen the security of either side seemed insurmountable, making it likely that any agreed cuts would amount to not more than 10% of the simple quantitative totals.

Including French forces, there were 700,000 NATO troops in northern and central Europe against one million for the Pact, with, respectively, 2,064 tactical aircraft against 4,200. NATO had some 7,000 nuclear warheads, deliverable by about 2,250 launch vehicles, while the Pact had about 3,500 larger warheads with more delivery systems per warhead. Esti-

WIDE WORLD

Smoke billows from two bombs exploding on North Vietnamese positions in Quang Tri City on Aug. 10, 1972. The air war was stepped up against North Vietnam during U.S. troop withdrawal and afterward.

mates of NATO's reinforcement capability varied, but it was certainly less than the Pact's 29 divisions (290,000 men) in a month. Only in naval power was NATO stronger, and even here the balance had been shifting, since Pact naval forces would be operating under increasingly powerful land-based air cover. Political pressures for cuts in defense spending were evident among NATO members, given the superpower détente and a belief that, if deterrence ultimately depended on the U.S. nuclear guarantee, unilateral conventional force reductions did not matter. They were exemplified by the decision of the Danish government to proceed with its December 1971 defense reform bill, which would virtually halve the armed forces.

Norway's September referendum rejecting entry into the enlarged EEC could increase the political problems in defending NATO's northern flank. The Soviet maneuvers of 1968 (North) and 1970 (Ocean) had prepared the Soviet forces for an occupation of Norway to prevent the Navy from being bottled up in Murmansk. NATO replied with the Strong Express maneuvers of Sept. 14–21, 1972, involving 65,000 men, 350 ships, and 700 aircraft, which made two landings in Norway. NATO's earlier exercise, Dawn Patrol (May 2–14), dealt with a simulated threat to the southern flank in Greece.

UNITED KINGDOM

The February 1972 Defence White Paper was very much a limited progress report, reflecting the continued reduction in Britain's military presence overseas, as well as an increasing perception of a politically usable Soviet threat to Western Europe and the consequent European need to demonstrate to the U.S. that Western Europe was bearing its share of the mutual defense burden. This, together with the demands of an increasing military presence in Northern Ireland, resulted in a defense budget of £2,858 million ($6.9 billion), representing 5% of GNP, compared with 3.1% for France, 2.8% for West Germany, and 7.3% for the U.S. Surprisingly, there was no provision for building a fifth Polaris submarine or for upgrading the Polaris missiles in the four that now constituted Britain's only deterrent force. Talks on nuclear cooperation with France continued, but there seemed little prospect of a joint Franco-British nuclear force.

There were only seven overseas bases left with a British presence. The March 26, 1972, agreement with Malta gave the U.K. and its NATO allies exclusive use of the dockyard facilities for a £12,750,000 down payment, an additional £3.5 million on Jan. 1, 1973, and further payments of £14 million yearly. Elsewhere in the Mediterranean one infantry battalion was with the UN peace-keeping force in Cyprus, another was in the Sovereign Base area, and one battalion was in Gibraltar. Singapore had an infantry battalion group as part of the Australian-New Zealand-U.K. force, and there was one Gurkha brigade in Brunei. Hong Kong absorbed two British and three Gurkha infantry battalions, mostly in internal security duties, while a solitary infantry company remained in British Honduras. The British Army of the Rhine (BAOR) was thus able to reach its full authorized strength of 54,900. Of these, about 3,000 troops were on detachment to Northern Ireland at any one time.

Britain's commitment in Northern Ireland was fast threatening its ability to reinforce its troops in West Germany. An increasing number of troops were being tied down in Northern Ireland, often with only six months between operational tours. The Strategic Reserve, comprising the 3rd Division's three air-portable brigades, two parachute battalions of the U.K. Mobile Force, and the Special Air Service Regiment, was the main reinforcement for the BAOR. Withdrawals to meet commitments in Northern Ireland had reached the brigade level by mid-1972, when the number of troops in Northern Ireland rose to 21,000, compared with 6,000 in 1969. The Army's Operation Motorman on July 31, reestablishing governmental authority in the so-called no-go areas of Londonderry, was relatively successful, but there seemed little hope of either a political or a military solution to a situation that was increasingly involving the traditionally apolitical British Army in politics. Brig. Gen. Frank Kitson, who had commanded the 39th Brigade in Ulster, was criticized for his book *Low Intensity Operations,* in which he emphasized that all antisubversion operations were political and involved extensive intelligence gathering. (*See* UNITED KINGDOM.)

Both the Navy and the Royal Air Force continued their long-delayed modernization programs. Orders were placed for a 7th Type 42 destroyer and an 11th nuclear-powered attack submarine. Including ships in reserve or undergoing refit or conversion, the Navy had 6 nuclear- and 24 diesel-powered submarines, 1 attack carrier, 3 commando carriers, 2 assault ships, 2 missile cruisers with the Seacat surface-to-air missile, 9 destroyers with the Seaslug II and Seacat surface-to-air missiles, 3 other destroyers, 33 general purpose frigates, and 24 ASW frigates, 3 of which were retired in 1972. Provision of air cover when the aging attack carrier became obsolete continued to pose a problem. The main alternative seemed to be land-based air cover, effective for up to 500 mi. with the longer-range Phantoms and in-flight refueling, supplemented by through-deck cruisers carrying 12–18 Harrier vertical/short take-off and landing (V/STOL) fighter-bombers.

In view of exercises showing the vulnerability of U.K. bases to conventionally armed Soviet stand-off bombs, the RAF decided to retain 100 Lightnings after 1975 instead of replacing them with Phantoms in the air defense role, for which the Anglo-French Jaguar would also be available. The Phantom was becoming the RAF's main aircraft. The last Hunter fighter squadron and two out of six squadrons of Canberra reconnaissance bombers were retired, as were all six Shackleton maritime patrol squadrons. About 50 Vulcans were retained as medium bombers, supplemented by three squadrons of Buccaneers and some 50 Harriers for close support.

FRANCE

French defense spending rose sharply in 1972, from $5.2 billion to $6,240,000,000, although the shifting exchange rate exaggerated the increase. The bulk of the money continued to go to the nuclear deterrent forces. Two of the five ballistic missile submarines with MSBS underwater-to-surface missiles were operational, as were all 18 SSBS IRBMs. The Pluton, a 15-kiloton tactical missile mounted on an AMX-30 tank chassis, was due to become operational in 1973–74. It was to have been stationed on West German territory under French control, but the West Germans wanted a two-key system giving them a veto over its use, so Pluton might have to be stationed in Alsace-Lorraine. The French had spent some $12 billion over ten years on nuclear weapons, and there were suggestions that within five years France might withdraw its two mechanized divisions from West Germany as an economy measure. The series of tests of nuclear warheads for the SLBMs and the Pluton system, conducted by the French in the Pacific in 1972 despite diplomatic protests, indicated significant progress in improving the yield-to-weight ratio. Peru, a large purchaser of French arms supplies, had threatened to break off diplomatic relations because of the tests, but did nothing.

Although the French Army was now 50% professional, it still relied on 12-month compulsory national service. Only its five mechanized divisions could be considered as effective in a European war. However, the Army air arm had been modernized with 450 Bell and Alouette helicopters plus 50 SA-330 Puma helicopters. In addition, 170 Gazelle SA-341 helicopters had been ordered, at a rate of 30 per year. About 2,000 French troops were still in Chad fighting the Chad National Liberation Front (Frolinat), which had suffered an estimated 2,900 casualties to about 100 French. Some 300 French troops were in the Malagasy Republic, two battalions were in the French Territory of the Afars and Issas, and a like number were in the Pacific territories.

The Navy's 15-year modernization program envisaged the introduction of nuclear-powered hunter-killer submarines to protect the ballistic missile submarines, a task the 19 diesel attack submarines could not carry out effectively. Instead of the Jaguar aircraft, at $5 million each, the Navy preferred the cheaper A-4 Skyhawk to replace the three squadrons of Etendard IV-Ms and IV-Ps and two squadrons of Crusaders on the two attack carriers. The carriers, together with the helicopter carrier and the helicopter cruiser, were to be replaced by vessels similar to the U.S. sea-control ship and the U.K. through-deck cruiser—ships designed to provide limited defense against attack from enemy aircraft, ships, or submarines, especially those using long-range antiship missiles like the Soviet Shaddock, which required midcourse guidance and was vulnerable to air attack. France was building 14 mine-carriers of the Avisio-70 class as coastal protection vessels; they displaced 1,150 tons and were armed with sextuple rocket launchers, 2 ASW torpedo launchers, and Exocet antiaircraft missiles. Of the 17 destroyers, 4 had been fitted with the Tartar surface-to-air missile while 6 were fitted for ASW, 4 for aircraft direction, and 3 for command.

The Air Force remained oriented toward protecting the 36 Mirage IV-A bombers of the strategic forces and their 12 tankers. The Air Defense Command had three squadrons of Mirage III interceptors; its 30 Vatour II all-weather interceptors were scheduled for replacement by the Mirage F1, supplementing three squadrons of the Super-Mystère B-2 interceptors. The Tactical Air Force, providing support primarily for the five mechanized divisions of the *force de manoeuvre,* had been standardized around various marks of the Mirage III; eight squadrons were equipped with the Mirage III-E fighter-bombers.

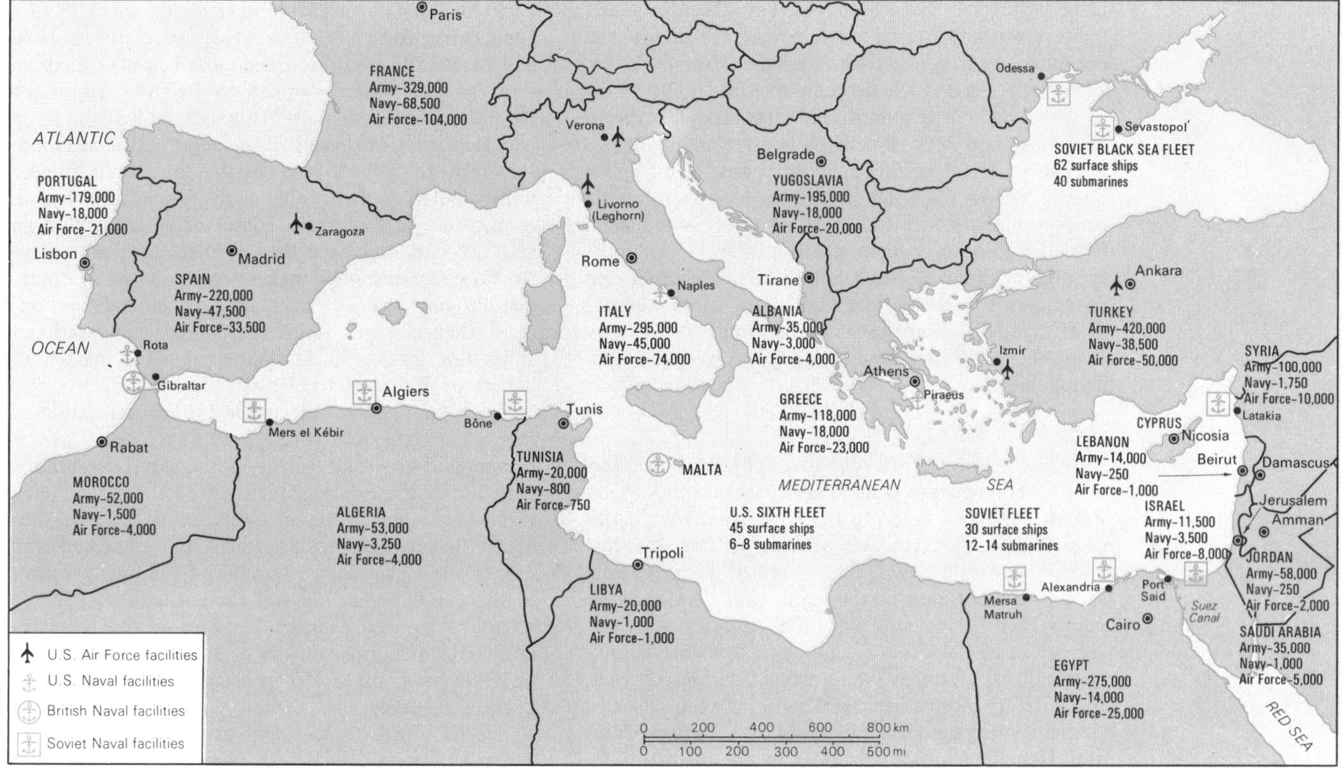

TASS / SOVFOTO

Soviet soldiers man a rocket launcher with chemical warfare capabilities during training exercises. NATO officials put the chemical warfare capability of the Soviet military well above that of NATO forces.

Reconnaissance was provided by three squadrons of Mirage III-Rs and III-RDs. The only other front-line equipment consisted of the Mystère IVA fighter-bombers, organized into two squadrons. France retained the largest paramilitary forces within NATO, with a 58,000-strong gendarmerie and 15,000 men in the Compagnies Republicaines de Securité under the Ministry of the Interior.

Under Pres. Georges Pompidou, French defense policy continued to be characterized by an emphasis on the interests of France on its own, rather than as part of NATO. France refused to participate in the MBFR negotiations scheduled for January 1973 on the ground that, if they were successful, they would reduce Western Europe's security and, if they failed, they would encourage unilateral U.S. troop withdrawals. French arms sales continued to be high; 50 Panhard AML armoured cars, valued at $2.5 million, were sold to Ireland; an unknown number of motor torpedo boats to Greece and Turkey; 21 Mirage F1 fighters worth $261 million to Spain, which took an option on a further 18; Gazelle helicopters to Yugoslavia; SA-330 Puma helicopters to Abu Dhabi; tanks to Lebanon; 44 Panhard AML armoured cars to Malaysia; and 300 Astazou 16 G aircraft engines to Argentina. An interesting innovation was the first joint French sale of the Otomat surface-to-surface missile produced jointly with Italy, part of a developing trend toward European cooperation in military technology. France continued to assist South Africa in producing 36 Mirage F1 interceptors and an unknown number of Mirage III fighters under license, but failed to persuade the Swiss government to buy the Mirage Milan fighter-bomber.

WEST GERMANY

The prospect of MBFR, long sought by the West German government as a complement to Chancellor Willy Brandt's *Ostpolitik,* led to the realization that, paradoxically, West Germany's position as the strongest military power in NATO might create strains with its European allies even as the major objectives of *Ostpolitik* were being achieved. The treaties with the U.S.S.R. and Poland, recognizing the existing boundaries of East Germany, were ratified during the year, and a treaty normalizing relations between the two German states was signed in December. Defense Minister Helmut Schmidt's transfer to the finance portfolio in July pointed up the changes in West German defense policy brought about by the Nixon Doctrine of encouraging self-help among U.S. allies and the consequent need to bring NATO strategy into line with its members' capabilities.

For West Germany this meant accepting the problems of fighting a forward battle with a 15-month conscript army. The call-up was increased from 195,000 to 240,000 per year, and there was a slight drop in the shortage of NCOs to 19,500. The number of conscientious objectors rose from 20,000 in 1970 to 28,000 in 1971, and the final figure for 1972 was expected to reach 40,000. The real problem was less the number of conscientious objectors than the provisions allowing them to appeal for exemption after entering the services, thereby immobilizing large numbers of troops. Complaints about conditions of service came more from the officers and NCOs, who had fared badly in comparison with their civilian counterparts because the rapid expansion of the Bundeswehr in the late 1950s had created promotion bottlenecks. Personnel problems were clearly going to be the new defense minister's major priority, since the 1971–72 Defense White Paper had set the main strategic guidelines.

The defense budget for 1972 totaled DM. 24,219,000,000, or about $7,568,000,000 allowing for changes in the exchange rate. This represented an increase of $564 million over the previous year in terms of constant dollars, but at 3% of GNP it was still low compared with East Germany's 6%. The Army was being reorganized to fight a mobile defensive battle, using a europeanized version of the Bell AH-1G Huey Cobra helicopter with TOW antitank missiles. The new antitank units would resemble the U.S. Tricap platoons. In keeping with the decision to put all ground combat forces under the control of theatre commanders, they would cooperate with regiments of 108 Leopard tanks, under the direction of a corps headquarters.

The 1970 White Paper target of 13 armoured brigades was reached. Armament included 2,200 Leopard 40-ton medium tanks with 105-mm. guns, leaving only 1,050 of the 47-ton M-48A2 Pattons with 90-mm. guns, dating from 1955. The highly successful Leopard had practically become the standard NATO medium tank, and had been supplied to Belgium, Italy, the Netherlands, and Norway. Although the British 53-ton Chieftain embodied the U.K. doctrine that it was more important to have the best possible tank, even if fewer were available, their talks with West Germany on cooperation in building a successor to the Chieftain and Leopard suggested they were coming around to the West German view that it was better to have more qualitatively inferior tanks, given a combat environment where the tank would face increasing operational difficulties, and anything approaching the mass tank battles of World War II was impossible.

This thinking was reflected in the reorganization of the command structure. Three territorial commandants were established—Schleswig-Holstein, the North, and the South—and each of the six military regions was placed under a territorial defense command. Besides the medium tanks, these had received 235 of the new Marder armoured fighting vehicles. Artillery was being adapted for antitank use. There were 12 armoured infantry, 3 motorized rifle, 2 mountain, and 3 airborne brigades of 3,000–4,000 men each in 12 divisions of 15,500 men each, the same size as in the U.S. Army.

The Air Force replacement program had been settled at 175 two-seater RF-4E Phantom fighter-bomber reconnaissance aircraft, costing $265 million. Four heavy reconnaissance squadrons with 60 Phantoms were already in service, and two wings per year would be introduced as the old Starfighters were phased out. There were still 122 F-104Gs in seven fighter-bomber squadrons and 105 F-104Gs in seven fighter-bomber/interceptor squadrons. The 168 G-9F Fiats in eight light ground-attack squadrons were to be replaced by the new West German Alpha jet costing $1.1 million each. The emphasis on fighter-bombers primarily intended for a nuclear strike role reflected the late 1950s doctrine of an almost immediate resort to tactical nuclear weapons in case of attack in Europe, whereas NATO now wanted to delay their use long enough for a major attack to be identified. To bring the West German forces more into line with NATO doctrine, an attempt was being made to improve West Germany's capability for air defense.

The Navy was receiving increasing attention. The 1971–72 Defense White Paper had stressed the growth of Soviet naval power; the Soviet forward submarine patrol line now stretched from the northwest coast of Norway to the Faeroes. However, West Germany could not acquire the long-range destroyer escorts it needed to meet its increased responsibilities in the North Sea and the Baltic unless the Paris Agreements of 1954, limiting the size of ships it could build, were abrogated. Currently, the Navy was the poor relation of the services, with 36,000 men to the Army's 327,000 and the Air Force's 104,000. West Germany had only 6 coastal submarines, 11 destroyers, 6 fast frigates, and 13 fast combat support ships, plus 40 fast patrol boats, none with antiship missiles. The Naval Air Command had only 60 F-104G fighter-bombers and 2 maritime reconnaissance squadrons with 15 BR-1150 Atlantic aircraft; its S-58 antisubmarine helicopters were being replaced by 22 SH-3D Sea King Mk 41s. All three services were extremely uncertain about the utility of their reserves or their ability to recall them in time to be of use.

CHINA

The deaths of Marshal Lin Piao and several other high military officials in a plane crash in Mongolia in September 1971 were officially confirmed in 1972. Whether the dead men had been planning a military coup, as Chairman Mao Tse-tung alleged, was uncertain. Although the military influence in the national party structure, the revolutionary committees, and the central government had become virtually unchallengeable, it was difficult to distinguish between military and party roles. It seemed probable, however, that Lin Piao and his supporters, worried by the Soviet military buildup on China's borders, wanted better relations with the U.S.S.R. rather than with the U.S., especially given China's minimal nuclear capability and vulnerability to a limited Soviet conventional attack. Mao Tse-tung and Premier Chou En-lai apparently calculated that Chinese and Soviet differences over Southeast Asia and the Chinese territory lost to the tsars in the 19th century were irreconcilable, though they would not necessarily lead to military conflict beyond occasional border clashes, such as the one reported in late 1972. In contrast, Kissinger's secret exploratory visits established what President Nixon implicitly confirmed during and after his visit to Peking: the U.S. had no fundamental conflicts with China and saw China as a counterweight to Soviet influence in Southeast Asia.

The new U.S. view of China's role, partially shared by the Chinese, was that of a regional great power, with a sphere of influence corresponding to the historic Chinese zone of suzerainty and extendable as far as China's limited conventional forces, allied with local Communist parties, could take it. The U.S. appeared to have renounced any long-term interest in whether Southeast Asian governments were Communist or not, and indicated that the future of Taiwan was to be determined by negotiations. This removed the basis of the 25-year-old conflict between the U.S. and China and, indeed, the U.S. might well guarantee the Chinese nuclear deterrent against a Soviet attack while China acquired an assured second strike capability (probably by 1980).

Three nuclear tests in the 20–200-kiloton range were conducted during the year, bringing the total since 1964 to 14. About 15–20 IRBMs with a range of 1,500–2,500 mi., comparable to the U.S. Thor IRBM of the late 1950s, appeared to have been deployed. Whether they used liquid, storable liquid, or solid fuel was uncertain, but their ability to reach Moscow and most parts of Asia seemed likely to deter a preemptive Soviet strike. Medium-range weapons included 20–30 MRBMs deployed in northeastern China; the Tu-16 bomber with a 1,600-mi. radius of action, and some 200 nuclear-capable F-9 fighters. The SALT I agreement further strengthened the credibility of the Chinese deterrent, since the Soviet ABMs around Moscow had been anti-Chinese, and the absence of any thin area defense in the U.S.S.R. and the U.S. indicated that neither superpower believed it could prevent unacceptable damage from the lesser nuclear powers.

At the opposite end of the spectrum, the People's Liberation Army remained essentially a World War I army, able to offer a limited conventional defense against invasion or to conduct guerrilla operations. Its manpower increased from 110 to 120 infantry divisions, supported by 3 cavalry and 2 airborne divisions. Heavy support was limited to five armoured divisions, equipped with Chinese-produced versions of the Soviet T-59 medium tank, T-62 light and T-60 amphibious tanks, and various armoured personnel carriers. All these were designed in the mid-1950s, but in sufficient quantities they could provide a serious obstacle to a conventional attack. The 20 artillery divisions were similarly equipped with Soviet weapons or Chinese copies. Air support was provided by 1,700 MiG-15 and MiG-17 fighter-bombers; 1,000 MiG-19 and 75 MiG-21 fighters; and 200 F-9 twin-jet fighters designed and built in China. The Navy remained confined to a coastal defense role, although a nuclear-powered attack submarine armed with conventional torpedoes was reportedly being built.

All three services were integrated under the commanders of the 11 military regions. Excluding artillery, there were 40 divisions in the north and northeast, 25 in the east and southeast, 20 in south-central China, 15 in midwest China, and 30 in the west and southwest. The rapprochement with the U.S. appeared to have enabled China to shift its forces toward the Soviet border. There were 15,000–20,000 construction troops in Laos and North Vietnam. The agreement to give military aid to North Vietnam was renewed in June 1972, and the 1961 mutual defense treaty with North Korea remained in force, but aid to Pakistan seemed to have ended with that country's defeat in the December 1971 Indo-Pakistani war. Estimates of China's defense expenditure ranged from $10 billion to $16 billion; since most PLA troops were

Soldiers at the Royal School of Artillery, Larkhill, Eng., demonstrate an advanced 105-mm. artillery piece that fires a 35-lb. shell at a maximum range of more than ten miles.

CENTRAL PRESS/PICTORIAL PARADE

self-supporting, it seemed unlikely that the defense burden was excessive.

INDIA AND PAKISTAN

The Simla agreement, signed by India and Pakistan on July 3, 1972, and later ratified by both countries, appeared to have settled the partition of former British India after 25 years of dispute. East Pakistan's replacement by independent Bangladesh was accepted. Both sides agreed to withdraw their forces to the international boundaries existing prior to the December 1971 war. In Jammu and Kashmir the Dec. 17, 1971, cease-fire line was accepted by both sides as a de facto boundary, and the exact demarcation of the line was completed in December. India agreed to repatriate the 3,000 Pakistanis captured in the west, but 91,000 captured in the east were still being held. In December Pakistan released more than 600 Indian POWs in a unilateral goodwill gesture.

Total casualties in the 1971 war were estimated at 3,300 killed and 8,600 wounded for India, against 6,000 killed and 13,000 wounded for Pakistan, plus 5,400 killed and 4,700 wounded in fighting against the guerrillas in Bangladesh. Estimates of matériel losses varied so sharply that the only meaningful comparison was between the two sides in July 1972 as against July 1971. Both air forces had incurred the greatest proportionate losses; Pakistan claimed to

Table II.—Approximate Strengths of Regular Armed Forces of the World

Country	Military personnel in 000s			Warships				Total ships listed	Aircraft		Defense expenditure as % of GNP
	Army	Navy	Air force	Aircraft carriers	Submarines*	Cruisers	Destroyers/ frigates		Bombers†	Fighters	
I. NATO											
Belgium	66.0	4.2	20.0	—	—	—	—	—	80 FB	24	2.3
Canada	34.0	14.0	36.0	—	4	—	22	26	50 FB	66	1.8
Denmark	27.0	6.6	9.8	—	6	—	6	12	48 FB	48	2.4
France‡	328.0	79.0	105.0	3	19 + 1 SSBN (FBMS)	3	46	72	225 FB, 36 SB 30 B	150	3.1
Germany, West	327.0	36.0	104.0	—	6	—	17	23	398 FB	60	2.8
Greece	118.0	18.0	21.0	—	2	—	12	14	108 FB	54	3.3
Italy	306.6	44.5	76.5	—	9	3	16	28	135 FB	100	2.6
Netherlands	80.0	20.0	22.2	—	6	2	18	26	90 FB	36	2.9
Norway	18.0	8.6	9.4	—	15	—	5	20	80 FB	16	3.1
Portugal	179.0	18.0	21.0	—	4	—	11	15	60 FB	20	6.3
Turkey	360.0	39.0	50.0	—	10	—	10	20	146 FB	36	3.3
United Kingdom§	180.5	84.6	111.0	4	24, 6 N 4 FBMS	2	74	114	110 FB, 130 B	150	4.7
United States§	1,059.0	602.0	730.0	16	35, 56 N 41 FBMS	9	218	343	1,400 FB, 540 SB	1,240	7.3
II. OTHER EUROPEAN											
Albania	28.0	3.0	4.0	—	4	—	—	4	—	72	...
Austria	40.0	—	3.0	—	—	—	—	—	39 FB	—	1.0
Finland	34.0	2.5	3.0	—	—	—	3	3	—	47	1.4
Spain§	220.0	47.5	33.5	1	4	1	23	29	191 FB	13	1.8
Sweden	48.2	12.1	12.1	—	22	—	13	35	150 FB	390	3.7
Switzerland	17.5	—	10.0	—	—	—	—	—	195 FB	100	1.9
Yugoslavia	190.0	18.0	20.0	—	5	—	1	6	180 FB	132	4.7
III. WARSAW PACT											
Bulgaria	117.0	7.0	22.0	—	2	—	—	2	66 FB	144	...
Czechoslovakia	145.0	—	40.0	—	—	—	—	—	168 FB	252	5.8
Germany, East	90.0	16.0	25.0	—	—	—	2	2	—	303	5.9
Hungary	90.0	0.5	12.5	—	—	—	—	—	—	108	3.5
Poland	200.0	19.0	55.0	—	5	—	4	9	144 FB, 48 B	450	5.2
Romania	150.0	8.0	21.0	—	—	—	—	—	—	200	3.5
U.S.S.R.	2,000.0‖	475.0	550.0	—	210, 34 N 29 FBMS 20 BMS, 51 SSM	24	207	575	2,000 FB, 1,150 B 140 SB	5,500	11.0
IV. FAR EAST AND OCEANIA											
Australia	47.7	17.4	22.8	1	4	—	13	18	60 FB, 12 B	—	2.9
Burma	135.0	6.0	7.0	—	—	—	1	1	21 FB	—	2.9
Cambodia	200.0	1.5	3.8	—	—	—	—	—	—	—	...
China‖	2,500.0	160.0	220.0	—	32	—	13	45	500 FB, 400 B	1,500	10.0‖
India	840.0	28.0	92.0	1	4	2	19	26	280 FB, 45 B	210	3.4
Indonesia§	250.0	34.0	33.0	—	12	—	30	42	32 B	27	2.2
Japan	180.0	39.0	41.0	—	11	—	40	51	230 FB	160	0.7
Korea, North	360.0	13.0	30.0	—	3	—	—	3	408 FB, 70 B	110	24.9
Korea, South§	593.0	16.7	25.0	—	—	—	10	10	128 FB	97	5.1
Laos	72.0	—	1.8	—	—	—	—	—	—	—	11.0
Malaysia	43.0	3.5	4.0	—	—	—	2	2	16 FB	—	4.3
New Zealand	5.5	2.9	4.2	—	—	—	4	4	24 FB	—	1.7
Pakistan	278.0	10.0	17.0	—	3	—	6	9	180 FB, 24 B	15	4.2
Philippines	16.0	6.0	9.0	—	—	—	1	1	20 FB	40	1.8
Taiwan	385.0	35.0	80.0	—	—	—	29	29	80 FB	145	9.8
Vietnam, North	500.0	3.2	10.0	—	—	—	—	—	8 B	210	21.5
Vietnam, South§	423.0	39.0	41.0	—	—	—	7	7	100 FB	20	12.0
V. MIDDLE EAST, AFRICA, AND LATIN AMERICA											
Algeria	53.0	3.2	4.0	—	—	—	—	—	105 FB, 30 B	30	2.1
Argentina	85.0	33.0	17.0	1	4	3	12	20	63 FB	30	2.3
Brazil	120.0	43.0	35.0	1	3	2	11	17	15 FB	—	2.5
Chile	24.0	15.0	8.5	—	2	3	8	13	—	29	...
Colombia	50.0	7.2	6.0	—	—	—	7	7	—	24	1.2
Cuba	90.0	6.0	12.0	—	—	—	4	4	20 FB	165	6.1
Egypt	285.0	15.0	25.0	—	12	—	5	17	320 FB, 28 B	220	21.7
Ethiopia	40.9	1.4	2.2	—	—	—	—	—	21 FB, 4 B	16	1.4
Iran	160.0	9.0	22.0	—	—	—	7	7	150 FB	—	8.5
Iraq	90.0	2.0	9.8	—	—	—	—	—	80 FB, 9 B	100	6.5
Israel¶	61.5/275.0	4.5/5.0	11.0/20.0	—	2	—	1	3	292 FB, 10 B	9	23.9
Jordan	65.0	—	4.0	—	—	—	—	—	35 FB	15	11.3
Mexico	54.0	13.2	6.0	—	—	—	9	9	12 FB	—	0.7
Nigeria	262.0	5.0	7.0	—	—	—	3	3	12 FB, 6 B	—	1.9
Peru	39.0	8.0	7.0	—	4	2	7	13	20 B	30	...
S. Africa	32.3	4.2	8.0	—	3	—	6	9	95 FB, 23 B	37	2.4
Syria	100.0	1.7	10.0	—	—	—	—	—	120 FB	90	9.8
Zaire	49.0	—	0.8	—	—	—	—	—	—	15	2.0

Note: Data exclude paramilitary, security, and irregular forces. Naval data exclude vessels of less than 100 tons standard displacement.
*Nuclear hunter-killers (N), fleet ballistic missile submarines (FBMS), ballistic missile submarines, short-range (BMS), long-range cruise missile submarines (SSM).
†Medium and heavy bombers (B), fighter-bombers (FB), and strategic bombers (SB).
‡French forces were withdrawn from NATO in 1966, but France remains a member of NATO.
§Includes Marine Corps.
‖Approximate.
¶Second figure is fully mobilized strength.
Sources: International Institute for Strategic Studies, 18 Adam Street, London, *The Military Balance, 1971–72*, *Strategic Survey 1970–71*.

have shot down 24 Mirages in the west and 28 Indian Air Force planes in the east while losing 72 aircraft itself, but both sides had received replacements from their allies. Pakistan had about 24 B-57B light bombers against 32 a year earlier; 24 Mirage III-E fighter-bombers against 32; 36 multipurpose Sabre F-86s against 112; 48 MiG-19 fighter-bombers against 80; 12 F-104A fighters; and a mixed reconnaissance squadron. The greatest quantitative losses had been in the older F-86s and MiG-19s, but the Mirages were qualitatively more important. India had lost fewer aircraft out of a larger force. It had left 4 light-bomber Canberra squadrons, due for retirement; 6 fighter-bomber squadrons of Soviet Su-7s; and 2 fighter-bomber squadrons with the Indian-designed and built HF-24 Marut 1-A, which seemed to have been kept clear of combat because of its uncertain performance and the damage to India's prestige if any were lost. The eight squadrons of MiG-21s produced under license in India seemed to have been maintained at 120. Some 24 French-built Mystère IV fighter-bombers were reported as lost, though two squadrons were still maintained at reduced strength. Losses of Hunter F-6 fighter-bombers and Gnat light fighters were also reported. Clearly, India had tried to risk only its older aircraft.

Naval losses were also high, though for the most part they involved obsolete ex-British vessels. India sank the destroyer "Khaibar," damaged the destroyer "Shah Jehan," and sank two minesweepers in the battle of December 4, while losing the frigate "Khukri" to a Pakistani submarine on December 9. The obsolete Sea Hawk aircraft on the 16,000-ton attack carrier "Vikrant" had performed well in the war, but they were being replaced with Sea King helicopters. India's modern navy comprised four ex-Soviet F-class submarines, five ex-Soviet Petya-class destroyer escorts, eight frigates, and six Osa-class missile patrol boats. Obsolete vessels included two carriers and three destroyers. Pakistan had only three modern submarines and two fast frigates, plus one training cruiser and four elderly destroyer escorts.

Militarily, the December 1971 war had confirmed two lessons. First, whichever side could gain air superiority and use this to destroy enemy strongpoints and armour would win a quick victory, especially if, as in East Pakistan, the defenders were politically unable to withdraw to the best available positions. This suggested that NATO's strategy of flexible response would be extremely difficult to implement without an early recourse to nuclear weapons. Second, wars between those few third world countries with sophisticated armed forces were likely to end before the superpowers could make their influence felt, unless they intervened directly. Thus the U.S. decision to sail the "Enterprise" into the Bay of Bengal during the war had no effect on India. The suggestion here was that any future Middle East conflict could only be influenced decisively against Israel by a Soviet intervention, which the U.S. could quickly counterbalance. Ironically, given the diminishing U.S. involvement overseas, these conclusions were to its advantage, suggesting that the U.S.S.R. would find itself equally unable to control its allies.

The Soviet Union continued to support India's arms buildup, although the main threat now seemed to come from internal disorder. India's 840,000-strong Army could probably defeat any neighbour except China. It included two armoured divisions with 300 Vijayanta medium tanks (38 tons, 105-mm. gun), 450 T-54/55 tanks (36 tons, 100-mm. gun), 200 Centurion Mk 5/7 tanks (52 tons, 105-mm. gun), plus 250 obsolete Shermans, 150 Pt-76s, and 140 AMX-13 light tanks. The 13 infantry divisions were of the World War II pattern, with limited numbers of armoured personnel carriers and about 3,000 guns, mostly the old 25 pounder. New guns included the Model 56 105-mm. pack howitzer and about 350 100-mm. and 140 130-mm. guns, plus the SS-11 and Entac antitank guided weapons. The defense budget for 1972–73 totaled $1,-817,000,000, a negligible increase over the previous year. The war was estimated to have cost some $200 million.

WIDE WORLD

Chinese soldiers near Peking simulate bayonet combat. China's Army was made up entirely of volunteers. There was no shortage of volunteers, Chinese officials said.

With only former West Pakistan left to defend, Pakistan's new president, Zulfikar Ali Bhutto, could presumably deter any Indian invasion. The 1972–73 defense budget of $405.5 million provided for an army of ten infantry divisions and two armoured divisions, the latter equipped with 400 medium tanks and 200 light tanks. The infantry divisions, like those of India, relied on the 25-lb. gun and antitank weapons. The total strength of the armed forces was 278,-000.

MIDDLE EAST

The increasing strains on Egypt's alliance with the U.S.S.R. culminated in Pres. Anwar as-Sadat's July 18 decision to terminate the missions of Soviet military advisers and experts in Egypt, and to man all military equipment and installations built after June 1967 with Egyptian personnel. This meant the withdrawal of most of the Soviet Union's ten squadrons of MiG-21Js, Su-11s, and Tu-16s, plus all of the few MiG-23s flying air combat patrols over the Suez Canal zone. The 8,000 Soviets manning the 65 supporting SA-2 and Sa-S surface-to-air missile sites and the 6,000 operating Soviet air and naval facilities in Egypt were also withdrawn. Some of the 6,000 Soviet instructors and advisers were expected to remain.

Unless startling advances had been made, it seemed unlikely that the Egyptians could maintain the sophisticated Soviet equipment, even if the necessary supplies were forthcoming from the U.S.S.R. With conventional war between Egypt and Israel seemingly ruled out, and with Israeli reprisals against guerrilla raids from Lebanon and Syria becoming increasingly effective, the Palestinians returned to aerial piracy and other terrorist tactics, most notably in the massacre of 11 Israeli athletes at the Olympic Games in Munich, W.Ger. (*See* SPORTING RECORD: *Special Report*.) This change in tactics hardened Israel's resolve not to surrender the gains it had made in the 1967 Six-Day War. Israel was also encouraged by President Nixon's reelection, with its promise of four more years of U.S. diplomatic support and military aid.

Militarily, the balance between Israel and the Arabs had undergone a qualitative change in Israel's favour. The U.S. continued to supply Israel with equipment to restore the balance upset by a Soviet military intervention that had failed either to modernize the Egyptian Army or to provide it with air cover. Quantitatively, the Arabs remained far superior. At $1,-510,000,000, Egypt's defense budget for 1972–73 remained about constant at 22% of GNP. This provided an army of 285,000, with three armoured, three mechanized infantry, and five infantry divisions. Equipment levels remained relatively unchanged. The main tanks were 1,500 T-54/55s (36 tons, 100-mm. gun), 400 T-34s (35 tons, 85-mm. gun), plus 100 PT-76 light tanks (14 tons, 76-mm. gun) and 50 JS-3 heavy tanks (46 tons, 122-mm. gun) dating from 1945. There were also ten of the latest T-62 tanks (37 tons, 115-mm. gun), introduced into the Soviet Army in 1965, which were presumably intended to form the nucleus of an elite Egyptian armoured group, now unlikely to materialize. The mechanized infantry divisions were plentifully provided with armoured personnel carriers of varying types. The reduction to three mechanized infantry divisions from four the previous year suggested that considerable difficulty was being encountered in training Egyptian troops for armoured warfare. If this was the case, it seemed unlikely that the modern T-62 would replace the T-54/55.

Artillery support remained at 16 brigades with 1,500 152-mm., 130-mm., and 122-mm. guns and howitzers, 40 siege howitzers (203 mm.), and about 150 self-propelled SS-152 and SS-100 guns. Antitank arms included 100-mm. and 85-mm. guns and the Snapper antitank guided weapon. Whether the Egyptians would be able to retain or operate the Frog-3 and 7 or the Samlet short-range surface-to-surface missile was doubtful, as was their ability to maintain the antiaircraft guns protecting the surface-to-air missile network. The Air Force, with 25,000 men, had increased little; 150 of its 568 combat aircraft were in storage. The first-line core continued to be 220 MiG-21 Fishbed interceptors and 120 Su-7 Fitter fighter-bombers, backed up by 200 MiG-17 fighter-bombers, 200 MiG, Yak, and L-29 trainers, plus 28 obsolete Il-28 and Tu-16 medium bombers. Considerable airlift capability was offered by 180 Mi-1, Mi-4, Mi-6, and Mi-8 helicopters and 60 Il-14 and 20 An-12 military transports.

With the ending of the civil war in the Sudan, the Tu-16 bombers and MiG-21 fighters supporting the government there had been withdrawn. Nevertheless, Egypt remained unable to contemplate an opposed crossing of the Suez Canal or a renewal of the 1970 war of attrition that had cost 10,000–15,000 casualties (equivalent to a division). In October, in what was apparently a conciliatory move toward the Soviets, President Sadat removed Gen. Muhammad Sadek as minister of war and replaced him with Gen. Ahmed Ismail. General Sadek had led the army group that opposed growing Soviet control over Egyptian policy and criticized Soviet refusal to give Egypt the MiG-23s it considered necessary to strike into Israel.

Strategically, Israel's position had improved dramatically. In case of war, it could now expect to hold the Bar Lev line with limited forces while using the Golan Heights as a jumping-off point to destroy the Syrian Army, reversing the 1967 strategy of annihilating the Egyptian Army and inflicting a limited defeat on Syria. With a 1972–73 defense budget of $1,247,-000,000, Israel had managed to reduce its defense expenditure from the 1971–72 record 26.5% of GNP to 23.9%. The Army retained its two-tier structure of 15,500 regulars and 50,000 conscripts (12,000 women) in peacetime, which could be raised to 275,-000 on mobilization. These would provide ten armoured, nine mechanized, five infantry, five parachute, and three artillery brigades. Tank strength remained largely unchanged, with 450 M-48s (48 tons, 105-mm. gun) and 950 Centurions (52 tons, 105-mm. gun), 200 of which were of a more modern French pattern known as the Ben Gurion.

Artillery support remained concentrated around 352 105- and 155-mm. guns, plus 900 mortars (120-mm. and 160-mm.) on AMX chassis. New antitank weapons included the Cobra and the weapons-carrier-mounted SS-10/11 missile. The 280-mi.-range Jericho surface-to-surface missile was in production but not deployed. The Air Force of 10,000 regulars and 1,000 conscripts (20,000 on mobilization) was standardizing around three types of aircraft: the Phantom, the Skyhawk fighter-bomber, and the Mirage III-C fighter-bomber interceptor. Israel was also developing its own version of the Mirage, with Israeli engines; France finally agreed to pay Israel compensation for the 50 Mirage fighters ordered but not delivered after the Six-Day War. Additional deliveries of Phantoms and Skyhawks were anticipated, leaving the 27 older Mystère IV-A fighter-bombers in reserve and the 30 Ouragan fighter-bombers for training. Airlift was provided by 12 Super Frelon, 10 CH-53C, 30 AB-205, and 20 Alouette helicopters. The Israeli Navy of 3,500 regulars and 1,000 conscripts (5,000 on mobilization) was confined to a coastal defense role. Its 2 submarines, 12 fast patrol boats with Gabriel surface-to-surface missiles, and 4 motor torpedo boats would be adequate for defense against the small Egyptian Navy, which consisted, effectively, of 12 submarines, 4 destroyers, and 12 Osa- and 6 Komar-class patrol boats with the Styx surface-to-surface missile.

Syria was receiving increased Soviet military aid, similar to that formerly granted to Egypt, for an air defense network, but the Syrian forces seemed equally unlikely to be able to absorb such sophisticated equipment. Their shortage of trained personnel was evident in the Air Force, which was forced to store some of its 100 MiG-21 interceptors and 30 Su-7 fighter-bombers, though the 80 older MiG-17 day fighter/ground-attack planes were operational. The Army of 100,000 comprised two armoured, one mechanized, and two infantry divisions, with 900 T-54/55 and 270 T-34 medium tanks. Although this represented an increase of one armoured division, the combat efficiency of the Army remained doubtful, especially after Jordan's defeat of an attempted Syrian intervention in 1971. The defense budget for 1972 was $206,452,000, an increase of $30 million, keeping defense spending in the neighbourhood of 10–12% of GNP.

Jordan's defense budget had dropped to about the same percentage of GNP; the budget for 1971 was estimated at $90.4 million. Jordanian forces were still limited to one armoured, one mechanized, and one infantry division, with 190 M-47 and M-48 medium tanks and 140 Centurions. The Air Force had only 35 ground attack Hunters and 15 U.S.-supplied F-104A interceptors. Libya was emerging as a significant air power; 45 of the 110 Mirage IIIs ordered from France were delivered and one squadron was operational although 6 were reported to have been crashed by Egyptians assisting the Libyans. In November it was reported that France had lifted its five-year-old embargo on the shipment of arms to the Middle East. This would permit continued arms shipments to Libya even if the merger of Libya and Egypt should materialize.

SOUTHEAST AND EAST ASIA

A truce in Vietnam seemed within reach during the latter part of 1972, but the year ended without any agreement having been achieved. After a period of extended secret negotiations in Paris and Saigon, Kissinger announced late in October that "peace is at hand" and indicated that only a few details remained to be ironed out. The draft agreement was said to include a cease-fire in place throughout Indochina; release of all U.S. POWs; an agreed timetable for the withdrawal of all U.S. forces; mixed control commissions to oversee the cease-fire, plus an international control commission, possibly composed of Canada, Hungary, Indonesia, and Poland; and mixed political commissions to work out new political arrangements.

Signing of the agreement was delayed, however, despite repeated insistence by North Vietnam that it be concluded immediately, and a further round of negotiations in Paris failed to produce results. South Vietnamese Pres. Nguyen Van Thieu was said to have stiffened his resistance to certain provisions. On December 16 Kissinger, in announcing the failure of the negotiations, admitted Thieu's intransigence but placed the major blame on North Vietnam which, he said, had made additional and unacceptable demands. Similar charges against the U.S. were made by the North Vietnamese.

On December 18 President Nixon ordered a resumption of full-scale bombing of the North and the mining of North Vietnamese harbours, which had been suspended for some two and a half months while negotiations were in progress. The aerial strikes that followed were the most intensive of the war and reportedly caused widespread destruction in the North, especially in the Hanoi-Haiphong area. At the same time, U.S. B-52s, previously only used south of the 20th parallel, encountered the most effective antiaircraft system in Southeast Asia; the U.S. admitted the loss of 32 planes, including some 15 of the B-52s, although North Vietnamese claims were higher. On December 30 President Nixon suddenly called a halt to the bombing north of the 20th parallel and announced that negotiations would resume on January 8. At year's end, it was unclear whether North Vietnam had signaled some concession or whether the cause lay in rising domestic and overseas criticism of the renewed bombing and the heavy U.S. losses.

The opening of negotiations in the fall had followed a period of intense fighting in the South, beginning with the North Vietnamese offensive in March. Coming as it did in a U.S. election year, the offensive was reminiscent of the Tet offensive of 1968, which had dramatized to the U.S. public the fact that the war was not being won and had forced Pres. Lyndon Johnson to decide not to seek reelection. The 1972 offensive failed to have comparable political effects, however. President Nixon was elected by an overwhelming majority against an opponent who had come to prominence on the peace issue and promised during the campaign that, if elected, he would pull all U.S. troops out of Vietnam within 90 days. Nixon's decision to mine Haiphong harbour, announced only a short time before his scheduled visit to Moscow, produced none of the adverse international or domestic reactions that had been feared, and it succeeded in severely cutting the flow of military supplies to North Vietnam at a time when they were being consumed rapidly. Similarly, the massive increase in the U.S. bombing of North Vietnam and the Ho Chi Minh Trail from bases in Thailand and Laos further reduced enemy supplies while arousing comparatively little domestic criticism since almost no American lives were lost. By the time of the election, only the 500-plus U.S. prisoners of war being held in North Vietnam remained a major U.S. domestic issue.

In the broader context of the Indochina war, however, North Vietnam's strategy made sense as an attempt to bring as much of South Vietnam under their political control as possible and to inflict proportionately greater damage on the South Vietnamese Army before a cease-fire, leaving the North Vietnamese and the National Liberation Front in a better position to take over South Vietnam at some future time, probably in about two years. In these objectives the North appeared to have succeeded. In the bitter fighting to recapture Quang Tri and prevent the fall of An Loc, Kon Tum, and Hue, the South Vietnamese Army suffered severe damage to 6 of its 12 divisions, including the elite Ranger groups, and lost many of its best officers and men. By drawing government troops away from the countryside, the North Vietnamese and the NLF were able to move back to the Mekong Delta and to gain control of most of the five northernmost provinces in military Region I in the north, giving them the ability to seize control of the Vietnamese coast as far south as Quang Ngai.

Casualties were estimated at 100,000 killed and 300,000 wounded for the Communists, as against 36,000 killed and 90,000 wounded for the South Vietnamese. As of December 1972, total U.S. casualties were an estimated 45,916 killed and 303,555 wounded; in addition, the U.S. had spent $136 billion in military aid and $5 billion in economic aid. South Vietnam had lost 184,727 killed, and between 500,000 and 600,000 had been wounded. North Vietnam had lost some one million men and, given a similar three to one ratio of wounded to killed, three million had been wounded. This meant that, out of 45 million Vietnamese, 1 in 35 had been killed and 1 in 15 wounded. There were estimated to be 1.1 million refugees in South Vietnam. These figures suggested that peace might come partly through mutual exhaustion.

Militarily, the balance still favoured the North, with its army of 500,000 organized into 15 infantry divisions of 12,000 men, plus 2 training and 1 artillery divisions. Artillery was plentiful. The two armoured regiments had some 20 T-34 heavy and 175 T-54 medium tanks; the 100 P-76 light tanks, less well handled in the 1972 campaign, had been exposed to antitank fire and air strikes. Army deployment was estimated at 200,000 troops in South Vietnam (about eight or ten infantry divisions plus support), 63,000 in Laos, and 40,000 in Cambodia. The Air Force, which was part of the air defense system, had 60 MiG-21F/

PF interceptors carrying Atoll air-to-air missiles and 30 MiG-19 and 130 MiG-15/17 interceptors.

Against these forces, South Vietnam could field an army of 410,000, comprising 11 infantry and 1 airborne divisions, all below strength. Each division was about half the size of a North Vietnamese division. The six independent armoured cavalry regiments, each 2,000 strong, were equipped with M-47 and M-48 medium tanks and M-24, M-41, and AMX-13 light tanks, all of limited utility in South Vietnam, as both sides had discovered. The Air Force, which reflected the inevitably slow pace of vietnamization, had about 20 F-5 tactical fighters, 100 A-37 Skyhawk fighter-bombers, and 465 UH-1 and 15 CH-47 helicopters, plus 60 obsolescent Skyraider fighter-bombers. Despite U.S. attempts to ship large quantities of equipment to South Vietnam before a cease-fire, it seemed doubtful whether the South Vietnamese could absorb this new material in time for it to be of value, especially since the South would be extremely vulnerable without U.S. air cover.

The U.S. disengagement from Southeast Asia was paralleled by Japan's rising economic and political involvement. This was symbolized by Prime Minister Kakuei Tanaka's September visit to Peking where he formally opened diplomatic relations between Japan and China, thus ending a conflict that had lasted since 1931. Japanese defense spending totaled $2.6 billion; this represented a drop from 0.8 to 0.7% of GNP, reflecting a continued feeling of security. The Air Force had only 160 modern F-104J Starfighter interceptors, 16 RF-86F Phantom reconnaissance jets, and 14 RF-4EJ reconnaissance Phantoms built under license. Its mainstay remained 230 aging F-86F Sabres, to be replaced by Phantoms. The Base Air Defense Ground Environment system was equally small, with only 24 control and warning units and 100 Nike-Hercules surface-to-air missile launchers. The Army of 180,000 was adequate for self-defense. The one helicopter brigade had 220 helicopters. The Navy continued to grow, with 11 submarines, 27 destroyers, 12 destroyer escorts, and 20 submarine chasers.

North and South Korea moved toward a cautious and surprising rapprochement in 1972, based on virtual military parity. With U.S. logistic and air support, the South was able to defend against attack north of Seoul (only 30 mi. S of the border). The return of the 2 infantry divisions from South Vietnam would bring South Korean forces to 560,000 men in 19 infantry divisions, plus 10 divisions in cadre, 1 marine corps division of 33,000, and 2 armoured brigades with M-24 light tanks. North Korea, with less than half the South's manpower, was unlikely to be able to match its effective strength. It had an army of 360,000 in 20 infantry divisions and 2 armoured divisions, equipped with 750 T-34 and T-54 medium tanks and PT-76 tanks. North Korea, with 100 MiG-21 fighter-bombers, was superior in the air. Neither navy was significant, except for the North's six Komar- and five Osa-class fast patrol boats with the Styx surface-to-surface missile and 50 motor torpedo boats.

The Danish Air Force and Army accepted about 20 young women each, including this passel of Danes charging the camera with automatic weapons. Denmark was the first NATO member to accept women for military service on an equal status with men.

SCANDIA PHOTOPRESS/KEYSTONE

SOUTH OF THE SAHARA

Black Rhodesians rejected the proposed settlement of Britain's dispute with Rhodesian Prime Minister Ian Smith in 1972, and the country's status remained uncertain. (*See* RHODESIA.) Together with the Portuguese territories, Rhodesia was becoming increasingly dependent on South African support. For its part, the South African government seemed willing and able to commit its defense forces more openly than before, particularly if Chinese-supported guerrillas from Zambia and Tanzania continued to infiltrate Rhodesia and the Portuguese territories near the Cabora Bassa Dam project. Further escalation seemed likely; to an increasing degree, the guerrillas were using land mines in hit-and-run raids that could be prevented only by preemptive strikes on their Tanzanian and Zambian bases.

The three white regimes were in a good military position for such ventures. South Africa remained by far the strongest military power in southern Africa. Its 1972–73 military budget of $448.3 million had actually decreased as a percentage of GNP to 2.4%. This provided a small regular army of 10,000 men, armed with Centurion and Comet medium tanks, AML-60, AML-90, and M-3 armoured cars, and Saracen armoured personnel carriers. The 80,000-strong citizen force provided trained reserves, supplemented by 75,000 commandos organized and trained as a home guard. The front-line air force was to be standardized around the French Mirage III fighter produced under license; 16 Mirage III-CZs were to carry the R-530 air-to-air missile, also domestically produced. Ground support would be provided by the Italian MB-326 Impala armed trainers being built in South Africa, 75 of which were completed. The helicopter force, which would be extremely effective against guerrillas, included 60 Alouette IIs and IIIs, 16 Super Frelons, and 16 SA-330 Pumas, with 14 more on order. Operation of the 9 Canberra and 14 Buccaneer Mk-50 light bombers was hampered by age and possible future U.K. restrictions on providing spare parts, but they represented a significant force by African standards. The Navy served mainly as a counter to the Soviet presence in the Indian Ocean.

Rhodesia's minimal defense forces nevertheless sufficed to patrol its borders. There were only 3,500 regulars, supported by a 10,000-strong territorial force reserve and 8,000 active and 35,000 reserve paramilitary police, three quarters of whom were drawn from the white population. The Air Force was adequate for counterinsurgency duties, though the planes were extremely old: 10 Canberra B-2 bombers, 12 Hunter FGA-9s, and 11 Vampire fighter/ground-attack planes, plus 12 T-52 Jet Provost reconnaissance/light-attack aircraft. Spares for these could probably be obtained through international arms dealers, but they would still pose a problem. Rhodesia also had 12 Alouette III helicopters. The defense budget for 1970–71 was estimated at $25 million, representing 1.8% of GNP, and it was believed that this remained approximately the same in 1971–72.

In contrast, Portugal's estimated 1972 defense spending of $459.4 million represented 6.3% of GNP. This was by no means as intolerable a burden as was often suggested, however, since the percentage had dropped steadily from 7.4% in 1968. The Portuguese Army of 179,000 men was organized in 2 tank, 7 cavalry, and 35 infantry regiments; there were 2 half-strength divisions in Portugal and 25 infantry regiments and supporting forces overseas. Equipment included M-47 and M-4 medium tanks, M-41 light tanks, Humber Mk IV and EBR-75 armoured cars, AML-60 scout cars, and FV-1609 and M-16 half-track armoured personnel carriers, plus 105-mm. and 140-mm. howitzers, all adequate for antiguerrilla operations. Including locally enlisted forces, there were 55,000 men in Angola, 60,000 in Mozambique, and 27,000 in Portuguese Guinea.

The supporting Air Force was a heterogeneous collection of 150 elderly aircraft, including two light bomber squadrons with World War II B-26 Invaders and PV-2s, one squadron of F-84G Sabre fighter-bombers and one of F-86F fighters, two light-strike squadrons of G-91s (one stationed in Guinea), plus 6 counterinsurgency (COIN) flights of T-6 armed trainers. There were about 85 Alouette II/III and SA-330 Puma helicopters. Nonetheless, these forces seemed able to prevent the COREMO and FRELIMO guerrillas from disrupting development of the territories' resources. Claims as to territory controlled were meaningless since much of it was largely uninhabited, especially in the areas away from the coast.

Elsewhere in Africa, the long civil war in the Sudan came to an end. Uganda was invaded briefly by a force from Tanzania; Tanzanian villages were bombed in reprisal, but the Tanzanian government claimed the invaders were Ugandan exiles, supporters of deposed Pres. Milton Obote, who hoped to take advantage of the confusion attendant on Pres. Idi Amin's expulsion of Commonwealth Asians. (*See* UGANDA.)

(ROBERT J. RANGER)

See also Astronautics.

Denmark

A constitutional monarchy of north central Europe lying between the North and Baltic seas, Denmark includes the Jutland Peninsula and 100 inhabited islands in the Kattegat and Skagerrak straits. Area (excluding Faeroe Islands): 16,629 sq.mi. (43,069 sq.km.). Pop. (1972 est.): 4,994,335. Cap. and largest city: Copenhagen (pop., 1971 est., 805,331). Language: Danish. Religion: predominantly Lutheran. King to Jan. 14, 1972, Frederik IX; queen from January 14, Margrethe II; prime ministers in 1972, Jens Otto Krag until October 3 and, from October 4, Anker Henrik Jørgensen.

Prime Minister Krag signed the treaty of accession in Brussels by which Denmark would become a member of the EEC as of Jan. 1, 1973. The signing occurred just a week after the death of King Frederik on Jan. 14, 1972. He was succeeded by his eldest daughter, Margrethe (*see* BIOGRAPHY; OBITUARIES).

For constitutional reasons, the treaty had to be ratified by a referendum, which took place on October 2. The result was a substantial majority in favour of joining. Almost 90% of Denmark's registered electors took part in the referendum, 1,995,932 of them voting in favour of entry and 1,124,106 against. Greenland, however, responded with an unequivocal "no." In the Folketing (parliament), the EEC bill had been passed in December 1971.

The referendum was preceded by a vociferous and somewhat emotional campaign in which there was considerable exaggeration on both sides. The People's Movement Against the Common Market prophesied, among other disasters, loss of sovereignty, the reduction of Denmark to the status of a satellite state, and a take-over of the economy by huge multinational corporations. In addition to other, more idealistic, arguments the pro-marketeers concentrated on the sad state of the Danish economy, predicting a further increase in Denmark's massive foreign debt with consequent devaluation of the krone, leading to mass unemployment, increased taxation, price freezes, credit

DENMARK

Education. (1969–70) Primary, pupils 534,000; secondary, pupils 215,890; primary and secondary (1968–69), teachers 43,537; vocational, pupils 171,629; higher (including 4 universities), students 70,062, teaching staff (1968–69) 8,956.

Finance. Monetary unit: Danish krone, with (Sept. 18, 1972) a par value of 6.98 kroner to U.S. $1 (free rate of 16.85 kroner = £1 sterling). Gold, SDRs, and foreign exchange, central bank: (June 1972) U.S. $721 million; (June 1971) U.S. $398.1 million. Budget (1971–72 est.): revenue 40,097,000,000 kroner; expenditure 36,812,000,000 kroner. Gross domestic product: (1970) 115,920,000,000 kroner; (1969) 104,-940,000,000 kroner. Money supply: (March 1972) 32,410,000,000 kroner; (March 1971) 27,160,000,000 kroner. Cost of living (1964 = 100): (May 1972) 163; (May 1971) 154.

Foreign Trade. (1971) Imports 34,193,000,000 kroner; exports 27.3 billion kroner. Import sources: EEC 32% (West Germany 18%); Sweden 17%; U.K. 13%; U.S. 8%. Export destinations: EEC 22% (West Germany 12%); U.K. 19%; Sweden 16%; U.S. 8%; Norway 7%. Main exports: machinery 21%; meat and meat products 18% (including bacon 6%); chemicals 6%; dairy products 6%.

Transport and Communications. Roads (1969) 61,500 km. (188 km. expressways in 1971). Motor vehicles in use (1970): passenger 1,076,900; commercial 247,400. Railways: state (1970) 2,352 km.; private (1969) 538 km.; traffic (state only; 1971) 3,637,000,-000 passenger-km., freight 1,760,000,000 net ton-km. Air traffic (including Danish part of international operations of Scandinavian Airlines System; 1970): 1,616,368,000 passenger-km.; freight 71,304,000 net ton-km. Shipping (1971): merchant vessels 100 gross tons and over 1,264; gross tonnage 3,520,021. Shipping traffic (1970): goods loaded 6,774,000 metric tons; unloaded 31,522,000 metric tons. Telephones (including Faeroe Islands; Dec. 1970) 1.7 million. Radio licenses (Dec. 1970) 1,597,000. Television licenses (Dec. 1970) 1,311,000.

Agriculture. Production (in 000; metric tons; 1971; 1970 in parentheses): wheat 586 (512); barley 5,474 (4,813); oats 704 (631); rye 150 (134); potatoes 750 (1,033); sugar, raw value (1971–72) 325, (1970–71) 291; apples (1970) 121, (1969) 126; butter 124 (131); cheese 120 (112); pork *c.* 760 (738); beef and veal *c.* 210 (221); fish catch (1970) 1,226, (1969) 1,275. Livestock (in 000; July 1971): pigs 8,626; cattle 2,766; sheep 57; horses *c.* 40; chickens *c.* 18,300.

Industry. Production (in 000; metric tons; 1971): pig iron 203; crude steel 470; cement 2,730; nitrogenous fertilizers (1970–71) 74; phosphate fertilizers (1970–71) 95; manufactured gas (cu.m.) 386,000; electricity (net; excluding most industrial production; kw-hr.) 17,198,000. Merchant vessels launched (100 gross tons and over; 1971) 805,600 gross tons.

squeezes, and a host of other evils, all of which could be avoided only by joining the EEC.

It seemed undeniable that, in the short term, Danish agriculture would prosper as a result of entry, although economists differed as to the extent of the probable improvement and the cost to the consumer in terms of increased prices. Certainly it seemed reasonable to argue that if a new market was being established to include both Europe's largest agricultural exporter and its largest importer of foodstuffs, it would be very much in Denmark's interests to get in on it. At any rate, a large majority of both electorate and Folketing clearly believed in the benefits to be derived from membership. It remained only for Denmark's political, industrial, and agricultural leaders to realize some if not all of those advantages.

A referendum in Norway a week earlier had resulted in a resounding "no" to the EEC. Sweden also remained outside. Thus, in the context of traditional Scandinavian cooperation, Denmark would be a kind of "Nordic ambassador to the EEC." It was felt that Denmark had a duty to try to form a "Scandinavian bridgehead in Europe."

The surge of optimism in Denmark that followed the referendum had its roots in the economic situation. For a decade Denmark had had a more or less continuous balance of payments deficit, and over the years a massive net foreign debt of some 20 billion kroner had accumulated. The positive decision on entry into the EEC meant that the following year's deficit could be projected at a "mere" 1 billion kroner, as against an estimated 3 billion–4 billion kroner if Denmark had remained outside the enlarged Community. Notwithstanding the expected improvement, a strict economic and fiscal policy remained a necessity. To this end, the government had already introduced measures aimed at curbing state expenditure.

Workers' participation in the ownership and management of industry remained a central issue in Danish politics, and plans for the introduction of economic democracy were the subject of continued debate. A labour organization put forward a plan whereby wage-earners would contribute to a central fund to be used to buy shares in companies. Others suggested a more direct method based on individual companies, on the ground that workers would be more interested in their own firms than in a remote centralized fund. Economic democracy was expected to be a major issue in the wage negotiations scheduled to take place the following spring, and the Social Democratic Party was expected to introduce one or more bills to hasten its realization.

Thus, once again, economic and fiscal problems were central issues in Danish political life, the optimistic majority believing that entry into Europe would bring immense economic advantages while the pessimistic few maintained that any such advantages had been swallowed up already. Many of these problems were mentioned by the prime minister when he delivered the government's policy speech at the opening session of the new Folketing the day after the referendum. He thanked the Danish people for having voted so clearly, and then announced to a stunned assembly that after a quarter of a century in public life he intended to become a private citizen again. Having achieved a great personal triumph in Denmark's unequivocal "yes" to Europe, Jens Otto Krag resigned.

The Social Democratic Party executive supported his choice of a successor: 50-year-old Anker Jørgensen, former chairman of the General Workers' Union, Denmark's largest trade union, a man with no previous ministerial experience. The Social Democratic minority government that Jørgensen now commanded had a working majority of one by virtue of the support of the Socialist People's Party—the only party in the Folketing to have voted unanimously against entry into the EEC. Faced with Denmark's grave economic problems, a difficult round of labour negotiations in the spring, and all the practical problems of entry into the EEC, the new prime minister clearly had a difficult task ahead. (STENER AARSDAL)

Dependent States

At the annual UN debate on colonialism in October 1972, the Hungarian delegate stated that since the 1960 "Declaration on the Granting of Independence to Colonial Countries and Peoples" about 60 million people had been "liberated from the yoke of colonialism." Of these, 48 million had lived under British rule and 8 million under Belgian rule. Britain had granted independence to 741 million people before the UN declaration had been passed. Two chief groups of territories remained to be liberated: Portuguese Africa, Namibia (South West Africa), and Rhodesia, with a total of 19 million inhabitants, and 35 other territories, mainly scattered islands, with a population totaling about 16 million.

The British dependent territories continued to move toward self-government and viability, though an increasing tendency to choose the middle path of association rather than full independence was evident—for example, in Niue, allied to New Zealand, and in the Seychelles, where Chief Minister James Mancham won two elections on an anti-independence platform. There were further attempts at unification in the Caribbean, especially welcome since a proliferation of tiny states could create Commonwealth problems unless special status such as Nauru's were to be widely extended. Grenada, St. Vincent, and St. Lucia entered into a new agreement for unity that was to come into effect in August, following local elections. After talks between British and Bahamian representatives, held in London in December, it was announced that the Bahamas would become independent in July 1973. British Honduras' final step to independence was still hampered by Guatemala's territorial claims and the threat of Latin-American sanctions against the British military presence. In February Guatemala signed an agreement with Argentina by which Argentina supported Guatemala's claim to British Honduras and Guatemala supported Argentina's claim to the Falkland Islands.

Under a 1971 agreement with Argentina, Britain, though opening up communications between the Falkland Islands and the mainland, had reiterated that no change could be made without the consent of the islanders. A similar proposed sovereignty "umbrella" agreement over Gibraltar showed no signs of being accepted by the people of Gibraltar. June elections put Joshua Hassan's Gibraltar Labour Party in power, but this had no effect on the sovereignty issue. Spain continued its blockade.

Africa. *French Africa.* France continued to maintain its hold on the territory of Afars and Issas (French Somaliland). Djibouti was built up to take over some of Aden's functions, while the claims of Ethiopia and Somalia to the territory remained dead-

Dentistry:
see Medicine

locked. In October an opposition delegation led by two former vice-presidents of the council, Ahmed Dini and Hassan Gouled, visited Paris and delivered a memorandum to Pres. Georges Pompidou protesting against what they claimed was a government of vested interests that refused to hear their complaints and stifled democratic liberties.

South Africa. With a mandate from the UN Security Council, Secretary-General Kurt Waldheim visited South Africa on March 6 and held talks with Prime Minister B. J. Vorster on the promotion of self-determination and independence for Namibia. After a month-long tour of the region by Waldheim's special representative, former Swiss diplomat Alfred Escher, a compromise agreement on Namibia's fate was announced in mid-November; however, Escher denied the agreement. According to Vorster's plan, beginning in January 1973 the South African government was to establish a multiracial advisory council presided over by Vorster himself. The council would be composed of regional leaders chosen roughly on the basis of the existing land divisions, perpetuating the homelands system. There appeared to be just enough agreement between the Vorster regime and the UN to persuade black African governments to allow efforts to continue, and Waldheim, in December, urged further talks. Nevertheless, questions of a definite timetable for Namibian autonomy, safeguards for minorities, a test of acceptibility of the proposed federal constitutional status, the restoration of legislative powers to Windhoek, and the rate at which discriminatory legislation was to be repealed all remained unanswered.

A conference arranged by the South West African People's Organization (SWAPO) on Namibia was held in Brussels, in May. Delegates from more than 40 governments attended. The conference concluded that South Africa's rule over Namibia was made possible by the collusion of Western multinational companies, which were appropriating the country's fish, base minerals, diamonds, and uranium. The Organization of African Unity (OAU) was asked to boycott such companies, and an appeal was made to the EEC to avoid negotiations and deals with the South African government. In February the West German government withdrew financial support from a German consortium exploring for uranium in Namibia.

After a series of strikes by Ovambo migrant workers protesting against the contract labour system, which resulted in the deaths of a number of Ovambos in clashes with police, the government offered some concessions. These were considered quite inadequate by the South African Institute of Race Relations, however. As a result of the unrest, Ovamboland (containing almost 50% of Namibia's population and the bulk of the best grazing ground) was promised, as of 1973, a status similar to that of the Transkei, involving internal self-government and its own high court. The consolidation of two other homelands, the Kaokaland and the Namaland, took place in April and May, respectively.

Portuguese Africa. On May 1, 1972, the Portuguese National Assembly approved an organic law designating the provinces of Angola and Mozambique as autonomous states. They were to elect their own governing bodies, draft their own budgets, and collect their own taxes, and would have powers of legislation over all internal affairs. Diplomatic relations with foreign powers, the appointment of diplomatic representatives and of governors of states, and responsibility for defense remained the prerogative of the Portuguese government, which also retained a supervisory authority over the administration and economy of the states. On November 14 the UN General Assembly voted 98 to 6, with 8 abstentions, to condemn Portugal's policy in Africa and to call for negotiations toward independence of the Portuguese territories. Britain, the U.S., Portugal, Spain, Brazil, and South Africa voted against the resolution.

Activities by the Mozambique Liberation Front (FRELIMO) increased markedly in the Tete district during the year. In September the rebels claimed to have opened a new front in the huge Manica-Sofala district, bordering Rhodesia. Although the guerrillas met with little success in the immediate vicinity of the Cabora Bassa Dam, many roads were mined and the railway between Beira and Moatize, which carried most of the supplies for the dam, was sabotaged. In spite of these disruptions, work on the dam was not seriously impeded, and some elements within FRELIMO claimed that they did not wish to see the dam destroyed. Although they hoped to make its construction as costly to the Portuguese as they could, they looked forward to the day when the dam would become the property of the African people. In the meantime, guerrilla activities were having an adverse effect on Malawi's tourist earnings and on sugar supplies, since the road connecting Malawi with Rhodesia ran through the Tete district.

"Africanization" in Mozambique continued, at least up to junior officer level (40% of the troops were black). Perhaps following the U.S. experiment in Vietnam, Gen. Antonio Spinola, the governor and commander in chief, was rapidly establishing a large number of *aldeamentos,* fortified hamlets into which many of the rural people were herded for their own "protection" and to deprive the guerrillas of indigenous support.

In March representatives of a number of church and action groups urged the World Council of Churches to press certain companies to leave Angola and Namibia. They also called for opposition to the Cunene River scheme in Angola, financed largely by Portugal and South Africa, because of its military and political implications. In August the WCC resolved that it would withdraw its funds invested in companies that traded with the Portuguese territories in Africa, South Africa, and Rhodesia.

Spanish Africa. Although Spain agreed to a referendum permitting Spanish Sahara to decide its own future, no agreement was reached concerning the number of nomadic peoples claiming citizenship. Spain said there were about 76,000, while Morocco put the figure nearer 250,000. The March summit of Algeria, Morocco, and Mauritania to discuss the future of the area was suddenly postponed and, simultaneously, riots in the capital of El Aaiún petered out. Settlement became increasingly urgent to Morocco during 1972, since the Bu Craa phosphates (with reserves of 1,000,000,000 tons, estimated to be the world's largest) became operational and exports already equaled those of Morocco.

Caribbean. Yet another call for an East Caribbean federation was made in June by 14 leading West Indians. In July initiatives by the Caribbean Free Trade Area (CARIFTA) and other Caribbean economic organizations toward giving the East Caribbean Common Market (the associated states and Montserrat) association with the EEC were reported. Later it was announced that negotiations along this line for all

AUTHENTICATED NEWS INTERNATIONAL

Having voted in the 1972 election, these natives of Papua New Guinea load ballot boxes onto helicopters bound for a central counting location. The voters were choosing a House of Assembly that would lead the country to self-government and possible full independence from Australia over the following four years.

Commonwealth Caribbean countries would be conducted under cover of CARIFTA.

Moves toward greater political independence intensified in the Commonwealth Caribbean. "Absolute and final separation" from St. Kitts-Nevis was the aim of Ronald Webster, whose People's Progressive Party in July won six out of the seven elective seats in the new Anguilla Council. In October Premier Eric Gairy of Grenada led a two-party delegation to London to discuss arrangements for a constitutional conference in May 1973. Earlier, Antigua's premier, George Walter, had said that his ruling Progressive Labour Movement would campaign for complete independence in the 1976 general election.

The three Windward Islands, Grenada, St. Lucia, and St. Vincent, agreed on steps toward unification. St. Vincent's first elections since statehood resulted in a six–six tie between the former ruling party, Milton Cato's St. Vincent Labour Party, and the opposition People's Political Party, led by Ebenezer Joshua. James Mitchell, the former Labour minister, won the Independent seat and, after some negotiation with the PPP, became premier. Soufrière volcano, dormant since 1902, went into mild eruption for several months, causing considerable disruption and a loss of breeding stock and planting time.

The political scene in Bermuda remained unchanged as a result of the general election, won by the ruling United Bermuda Party with 30 seats to the opposition Progressive Labour Party's 10. In the Bahamas' general election in September, Premier Lynden Pindling won a landslide victory (30 out of a possible 38 seats) on the independence issue.

Like their British neighbours, the islands of the French Antilles (Martinique [340,000] and Guadeloupe [328,600]) were characterized by overpopulation, unemployment, and underdevelopment, but they had been integral parts of France since 1946, and their inhabitants continued to have total freedom of movement between their homes and the metropolitan area. In contrast to British migration arrangements, moreover, the French government from the early 1960s had embarked on a policy of encouraging labour migration from the islands with a view to easing the growing unemployment there and helping to meet the labour shortage in France. The number of West Indians in France in 1972 was estimated at around 200,000.

Despite its expanding bauxite industry, Dutch-speaking Surinam continued to suffer from high unemployment, a high birthrate, and lack of agricultural diversification. In the absence of restrictions on migration, the Netherlands had attracted about 57,000 Surinamese migrants in search of jobs and, in the case of older people, the more generous metropolitan welfare and pension schemes. In July a member of the European Commission assured the Dutch Caribbean territories that the aid they received from EEC development funds would not be reduced by the enlargement of the Community.

Persian Gulf. With the accession of Ras al Khaimah to the United Arab Emirates on Feb. 11, 1972, British protection of the former Trucial States officially came to an end. A degree of British military presence in the Gulf area was maintained through secondment of personnel to the local forces.

Indian Ocean. *French Dependencies.* Legislative elections in the Comoro Islands on December 3 resulted in gains for the two parties favouring total independence: the Rassemblement Démocratique du Peuple Comorien (RDPC) and the Union Démocratique Comorien (UDC). On Réunion a new Socialist Party was formed, distinct from that of metropolitan France. Its aims were greater autonomy through an assembly elected by proportional, universal suffrage of all those over 18.

British Dependencies. Queen Elizabeth II, accompanied by Prince Philip and Princess Anne, visited the Seychelles March 20 during an extensive tour of Southeast Asia. The queen opened the new international airport on Mahé, which had been built by the U.K. government at a cost of £5 million. (*See* LABOUR UNIONS.)

Australian Dependencies. An official report on the Cocos (Keeling) Islands, ceded to Australia by Britain in 1955, described conditions in the territory as "neo-feudal." John Clunies Ross, head of the family that had retained ownership of the islands since 1827, regarded himself as absolute sovereign over the inhabitants, whom he restricted from leaving and paid as little as A$2 a week. Clunies Ross expected the Australian government either to buy him out (with an eight-figure sum) or to leave the islands to independence under his rule.

Pacific. *British Pacific Territories.* Despite its exclusion from EEC arrangements, Hong Kong's phenomenal economic expansion continued unabated. The volume of trade increased by 14% in 1971, and the labour force reached almost one million. Two new industrial townships were completed in the New Territories despite the fact that the lease was due to expire in 1997.

In the Solomons a committee on constitutional reform considered establishment of a full legislative council and a second house with the right to vote for self-government. Some critics of swift change cited the economic cost of independence. Unless Bougainville achieved its aim of joining the Solomons, economic viability did not appear possible, despite current Commonwealth Development Corporation investment and British aid.

After 80 years, the Gilbert and Ellice Islands Council separated from the Western Pacific High Commission in January, and the first governor was sworn in as resident commissioner. The copra price fell disastrously, but aid for fishing via a U.S. tuna company and a British "sea school" at Betio gave hope for the economic future. Although Ocean Island with its still-rich phosphate deposits was officially included in the colony, this was vigorously disputed by its Banaban people, who were mainly living on Rabat (Fiji).

French Pacific Territories. Movements toward independence in the Pacific were regarded with suspicion by French authorities, already angry over Australian and New Zealand actions against France's nuclear tests. Without consulting Britain, the then minister of overseas territories, Pierre Messmer, stated in May that there would be no independence for the Anglo-French condominium of New Hebrides. There were indications of French hope that Britain would relinquish its claims in the islands. Messmer made similar statements against political autonomy in New Caledonia, while the July election in Tahiti, creating 44 new communes and decentralizing power, was seen by local autonomists as a means of dividing opposition.

Australian External Territories. Papua New Guinea, although geographically between Southeast Asia and the Pacific, faced problems more akin to those of emergent Africa. The March 1972 elections returned a Pangu-Pati coalition under Michael Somare pledged to full self-government in 1973 (to which the Australian government agreed in October), despite the hostility of highland people and the total incomprehension of many remote tribes. Intertribal warfare marred the early months of the government, which was engaged in setting up a committee to decide on a constitution, a committee of inquiry on land, and settlement of a border dispute with Queensland. The 1879 sea line marking Queensland's territorial border ran within 200 yd. of the Papuan coast and encompassed traditional fishing grounds, but islands on the Queensland side preferred the benefits of Australian citizenship and services.

Although the government, in its 1973 development plan, indicated pressure for "localization" and refusal of any double citizenship for Europeans, the country remained heavily dependent on Australia. Over half of the 1971–72 budget of nearly A$200 million was provided by Australia, which also provided half the trade of Papua New Guinea, though Japan's share rose to second place in 1971. The government continued to block the secession of Bougainville, naturally part of the Solomon Islands; the A$400 million copper investment there was expected to double government revenue by 1980.

U.S. Territories. After protracted negotiations with the administering power, the Micronesian Congress Joint Committee came to agreement over the political future of the Caroline and Marshall Islands. The Marianas, nearer to American Guam, opted for separate and closer association with the U.S. The main points discussed included ultimate sovereignty; the form of future association (Micronesian leaders refused the Puerto Rican form of commonwealth status, preferring a freer form of association with a unilateral right of secession); and the balancing of U.S. strategic requirements with Micronesian economic needs. With the return of the Southern Ryukyu Islands (Okinawa) to Japan on May 15, Micronesia became increasingly important to the North Pacific strategy of defense and for nuclear experimentation. In return for exclusive rights and rentals, the U.S. agreed to continue its support, which was over $60 million in 1972.

Indian Protected State. There were minor political rumblings in the tiny Indian-protected Himalayan state of Sikkim in 1972. In June the chogyal (king) assumed all executive powers, previously held by the "sidlon" (chief executive), I. S. Chopra, an Indian national. To placate the Indians, he later dismissed Kazi Lhendup Dorji Khangsarpa, a known critic of the Indo-Sikkim treaty, from the post of executive councillor.

Economic Aid. British aid to its associated states and dependencies in 1972 amounted to roughly £22 million. Aid of £1.8 million was granted to the Falkland Islands for airport development, and £5 million was granted to Gibraltar for housing development. Aid to the Seychelles in 1970–71 through the Commonwealth Development Corporation was £1,679,000. CDC was one of the chief investors in the new Reef Hotel on Mahé, providing management, technical, sales promotion, and staff training services.

(KENNETH INGHAM; MOLLY MORTIMER; SHEILA PATTERSON; GOVINDAN UNNY)

See also Africa; Portugal; South Africa; United Nations.

ANTARCTIC, THE

Claims on the continent of Antarctica and all islands south of 60° S remain in status quo according to the Antarctic Treaty, to which 16 nations are signatory. Formal claims within the treaty area include the following: Australian Antarctic Territory, the mainland portion of French Southern and Antarctic Lands (Terre Adélie), Ross Dependency claimed by New Zealand, Queen Maud Land and Peter I Island claimed by Norway, and British Antarctic Territory, of which some parts are claimed by Argentina and Chile. No claims have been recognized as final under international law.

AUSTRALIA

CHRISTMAS ISLAND

Christmas Island, an external territory, is situated in the Indian Ocean 875 mi. NW of Australia. Area: 52 sq.mi. (135 sq.km.). Pop. (1971): 2,691. Cap.: The Settlement (pop., 1968 est., 1,500).

COCOS (KEELING) ISLANDS

Cocos (Keeling) Islands is an external territory located in the Indian Ocean 2,290 mi. W of Darwin, Austr. Area: 5.5 sq.mi. (14 sq.km.). Pop. (1971): 618.

NEW GUINEA

New Guinea, a trust territory administered with the Territory of Papua, consists of the northeastern part of the island of New Guinea, the Bismarck Archipelago, and several other nearby islands. Area: 92,160 sq.mi. (238,693 sq.km.). Pop. (1971 est.): 1,795,602. Cap.: Port Moresby, Papua (pop., 1971, 66,244).

Education. (1969) Primary, pupils 149,026, teachers 4,736; secondary, pupils 10,672, teachers 501; vocational, pupils 2,870, teachers 190; teacher training, students 1,230, teachers 142.

Finance and Trade. Monetary unit: Australian dollar, with (Sept. 18, 1972) a free rate of A$0.84 to U.S. $1 (A$2.06 = £1 sterling). Budget: *see* Papua. Foreign trade: *see* Papua.

Transport. Shipping (1971): merchant vessels 100 gross tons and over 49; gross tonnage 24,779.

Agriculture. Production (in 000; metric tons; 1970; 1969 in parentheses): copra *c.* 112 (120); cocoa (1970–71) 26, (1969–70) 25; coffee *c.* 29 (*c.* 25); timber (including Papua; cu.m.; 1969) 4,100, (1968) 4,000. Livestock (in 000; June 1969): cattle 61; pigs 5; horses 1; poultry 173.

Industry. Production (in 000; troy oz.; 1969–70): gold 26; silver 18.

NORFOLK ISLAND

Norfolk Island, an external territory, is located in the Pacific Ocean 1,035 mi. NE of Sydney, Austr. Area: 14 sq.mi. (36 sq.km.). Pop. (1971): 1,683. Cap. (de facto): Kingston.

PAPUA

Consisting of the southeastern part of the island of New Guinea and several offshore island groups, Papua, an external territory, is governed in an administrative union with the Trust Territory of New Guinea. Area: 86,103 sq.mi. (223,006 sq. km.). Pop. (1971 est.): 671,384. Cap.: Port Moresby (pop., 1971, 66,244).

Education. (1969) Primary, pupils 64,368, teachers 2,059; secondary, pupils 5,597, teachers 297; vocational, pupils 1,281, teachers 98; teacher training, students 464, teachers 62; higher (University of Papua and New Guinea), students 1,201, teaching staff 154.

Finance and Trade. Monetary unit: Australian dollar. Budget (including New Guinea; 1970–71): revenue A$135,791,000 (including A$71,420,000 grant by Australian government); expenditure A$135,822,000. Foreign trade (including New Guinea; 1969–70): imports A$214,161,000; exports A$93,746,000. Import sources: Australia 53%; Japan 12%; U.S. 10%; U.K. 6%. Export destinations: Australia 44%; U.K. 16%; U.S. 12%; Japan 9%; West Germany 8%; Netherlands 5%. Main exports: coffee 22%; cocoa 17%; copra 14%; coconut oil 6%.

Dependent States

Agriculture. Production (in 000; metric tons; 1971; 1970 in parentheses): copra *c.* 17 (*c.* 16); rubber (exports) *c.* 5.3 (6.5). Livestock (in 000; June 1969): cattle 13; pigs 1; poultry 118.

DENMARK

FAEROE ISLANDS

The Faeroes, an integral part of the Danish realm, are a self-governing group of islands in the North Atlantic about 360 mi. W of Norway. Area: 540 sq.mi. (1,399 sq.km.). Pop. (1972 est.): 38,731. Cap.: Thorshavn (pop., 1970 est., 10,726).

Education. (1970–71) Primary, pupils 5,539; secondary, pupils 1,564; primary and secondary, teachers (1966–67) 299; vocational, pupils 1,131, teachers (1966–67) 88; teacher training, students 94, teachers (1966–67) 12; higher, students 39.

Finance and Trade. Monetary unit: Danish krone, with (Sept. 18, 1972) a par value of 6.98 kroner to U.S. $1 (free rate of 16.85 kroner = £1 sterling). Foreign trade (1970): imports 228,-368,000 kroner; exports 251,016,000 kroner. Import sources: Denmark 74%; U.K. 7%; Norway 7%; Sweden 5%. Export destinations: Denmark 24%; Italy 13%; U.S. 12%; West Germany 12%; Portugal 7%; Spain 7%. Main exports fish and products 92% (including fish meal 8%).

Transport. Shipping (1971): merchant vessels 100 gross tons and over 125; gross tonnage 40,-626.

Agriculture and Industry. Fish catch (metric tons; 1970) 208,000, (1969) 176,000. Livestock (in 000; June 1971): sheep *c.* 70; cattle *c.* 3. Electricity production (1970–71): 71 million kw-hr. (84% hydroelectric in 1969–70).

GREENLAND

An integral part of the Danish realm, Greenland, the largest island in the world, lies mostly within the Arctic Circle. Area: 840,000 sq.mi. (2,175,600 sq.km.), 84% of which is covered by icecap. Pop. (1970): 46,531. Cap.: Godthaab (pop., 1970, 7,478).

Education. (1968–69) Primary, secondary, and vocational, pupils 9,816, teachers 570; teacher training, students 44, teachers (1967–68) 3.

Finance and Trade. Monetary unit: Danish krone. Foreign trade (1970): imports 396,299,-000 kroner (94% from Denmark, 6% from U.K.); exports 104,960,000 kroner (81% to Denmark, 13% to U.S.). Main exports: fish and products 79%; fur skins 7%; cryolite 7%.

Agriculture. Fish catch (metric tons; 1970) 38,000, (1969) 39,000. Livestock (in 000; Nov. 1970): sheep 45; reindeer *c.* 4.

Industry. Production (in 000; metric tons; 1970): coal 18; cryolite (1968) 67; electricity (kw-hr.) 75,600.

FRANCE

AFARS AND ISSAS

The self-governing overseas territory of Afars and Issas is located on the Gulf of Aden between Ethiopia and Somalia. Area: 8,900 sq.mi. (23,000 sq.km.). Pop. (1971 est.): 97,000. Cap.: Djibouti.

Education. (1969–70) Primary, pupils 7,639, teachers 259; secondary, pupils 887, teachers 45; vocational, pupils 219, teachers 15; teacher training, students 14, teachers 9.

Finance. Monetary unit: Djibouti franc, with (Sept. 18, 1972) a par value of DjFr. 197.47 to U.S. $1 and DjFr. 38.60 to 1 French franc (free rate of DjFr. 468 = £1 sterling). Budget (1971 est.) balanced at DjFr. 2,487,000,000.

Foreign Trade. (1968) Imports DjFr. 8,195,-000,000; exports DjFr. 817 million. Import sources (1967): Iran 24%; France 18%; U.K. 12%; Ethiopia 7%. Export destinations (1966): France 66%; Yemen (Aden) 5%. There is a transit trade through Djibouti for Ethiopia, which fell following the closure of the Suez Canal. Main exports: hides, cattle, coffee.

Transport. Ships entered (1969) vessels totaling 5,142,000 net registered tons. Shipping traffic (1969): goods loaded 113,000 metric tons, unloaded 832,000 metric tons.

COMORO ISLANDS

The self-governing overseas territory of the Comoro Islands is in the Indian Ocean approximately midway between the northern tip of Madagascar and the mainland of Africa. Area: 863 sq.mi. (2,235 sq.km.). Pop. (1970 est.): 271,-000. Cap.: Moroni, Grande Comore (pop., 1970 est., 14,000).

Education. (1969–70) Primary, pupils 13,776, teachers 235; secondary, pupils 1,102, teachers 60.

Finance and Trade. Monetary unit: CFA franc, with (Sept. 18, 1972) a parity of CFA Fr. 50 to the French franc and CFA Fr. 255.79 to U.S. $1 (free rate of CFA Fr. 612.37 = £1 sterling). Budget (1970 est.) balanced at CFA Fr. 1,349,000,000. Foreign trade (1969): imports CFA Fr. 2,092,000,000; exports CFA Fr. 577.9 million. Import sources (1965): France 47%; Malagasy Republic 17%; Cambodia 10%; Thailand 7%; Argentina 6%. Export destinations (1965): France 47%; U.S. 26%; Malagasy Republic 6%. Main exports (1968): essential oils 42%; vanilla 35%; copra 17%.

FRENCH GUIANA

French Guiana is an overseas *département* situated between Brazil and Surinam on the northeast coast of South America. Area: 34,750 sq.mi. (90,-000 sq.km.). Pop. (1972 est.): 50,400. Cap.: Cayenne (pop., 1967, 19,668).

Education. (1969–70) Primary, pupils 7,962, teachers 262; secondary, pupils 2,030, teachers 96; vocational, pupils 895, teachers 42.

Finance and Trade. Monetary unit: local franc, at par with the French (metropolitan) franc (Fr. 5.12 = U.S. $1; free rate of Fr. 12.24 = £1 sterling). (*See* FRANCE.) Budget (1970 rev. est.) balanced at Fr. 100.2 million. Foreign trade (1970): imports Fr. 252,038,000 (69% from France, 11% from U.S.); exports Fr. 23,811,000 (78% to U.S., 7% to France, 6% to Martinique). Main exports: shrimps 71%; timber 7%.

FRENCH POLYNESIA

An overseas territory, the islands of French Polynesia are scattered over a large area of the south central Pacific Ocean. Area: 1,261 sq.mi. (3,265 sq.km.). Pop. (1971): 119,168. Cap.: Papeete, Tahiti (pop., 1971, 25,342).

Education. (1969–70) Primary, pupils 28,300, teachers 952; secondary, pupils 4,839, teachers 281; vocational, pupils 847, teachers 69; teacher training, students 69, teachers 4.

Finance. Monetary unit: CFP franc, with (Sept. 18, 1972) a parity of CFP Fr. 18.18 to the French franc and CFP Fr. 93 to U.S. $1 (free rate of CFP Fr. 222.68 = £1 sterling). Budget (1971) balanced at CFP Fr. 3,112,000,-000.

Foreign Trade. (1970) Imports CFP Fr. 13,-642,000,000 (56% from France, 18% from U.S. in 1969); exports CFP Fr. 1,840,000,000 (81% to France, 7% to Italy in 1969). Main exports (1969): coconut oil 19%; vanilla 5%. Tourism: visitors (1970) 48,803; gross receipts (1967) U.S. $4.7 million.

GUADELOUPE

The overseas *département* of Guadeloupe, together with its dependencies, is in the eastern Caribbean between Antigua to the north and Dominica to the south. Area: 687 sq.mi. (1,780 sq.km.). Pop. (1971 est.): 332,000. Cap.: Basse-Terre (pop., 1967, 15,458).

Education. (1969–70) Primary, pupils 69,419, teachers (including preprimary) 2,229; secondary, pupils 21,715; vocational, pupils 3,805; secondary and vocational, teachers 1,230; teacher training, students 234, teachers 10; higher, students 376, teaching staff (1968–69) 8.

Finance and Trade. Monetary unit: local franc, at par with the French (metropolitan) franc. Budget (1970 est.) balanced at Fr. 421 million. Foreign trade (1970): imports Fr. 709,-370,000 (73% from France, 6% from U.S.); exports Fr. 208,997,000 (68% to France, 24% to U.S.). Main exports: sugar 59%; bananas 27%; rum 8%.

MARTINIQUE

The Caribbean island of Martinique, an overseas *département,* lies 24 mi. N of St. Lucia and about 30 mi. SE of Dominica. Area: 431 sq.mi. (1,116 sq.km.). Pop. (1972 est.): 341,800. Cap.: Fort-de-France (pop., 1967, 99,051).

Education. (1969–70) Primary, pupils 68,-437, teachers (including preprimary) 2,799; secondary, pupils 30,313; vocational, pupils 1,740; secondary and vocational, teachers 1,656; teacher training, students 127, teaching staff 6; higher, students, 1,673, teaching staff (1966–67) 21.

Finance and Trade. Monetary unit: local franc, at par with the French (metropolitan) franc. Budget (1970 est.) balanced at Fr. 328 million. Foreign trade (1970): imports Fr. 810,-608,000 (73% from France, 6% from U.S.); exports Fr. 166,827,000 (90% to France). Main exports: bananas 50%; rum 16%; fruit conserves 11%; sugar 8%.

NEW CALEDONIA

The overseas territory of New Caledonia, together with its dependencies, is in the South Pacific 750 mi. E of Australia. Area: 7,366 sq.mi. (19,079 sq.km.). Pop. (1972 est.): 121,073. Cap.: Nouméa (pop., 1972 est., 55,000).

Education. (1970) Primary, pupils 24,676, teachers 940; secondary, pupils 3,745, teachers 251; vocational, pupils 1,346, teachers 127; teacher training, students 41, teachers 26; higher, students 85, teaching staff 13.

Finance. Monetary unit: CFP franc. Budget (1971 est.) balanced at CFP Fr. 8,696,000,000.

Foreign Trade. (1970) Imports CFP Fr. 23,-271,000,000; exports CFP Fr. 19,362,000,000. Import sources: France 64%; Australia 17%; West Germany 7%. Export destinations: Japan 54%; France 40%. Main exports: nickel 40%; ferronickel 38%; nickel castings 20%.

Industry. Production (in 000; metric tons; 1970): nickel ore (metal content) 138; iron ore (metal content; 1968) 95; electricity (kw-hr.) 729,000.

RÉUNION

The overseas *département* of Réunion is located in the Indian Ocean about 450 mi. E of Madagascar and 110 mi. SW of Mauritius. Area: 970 sq.mi. (2,512 sq.km.). Pop. (1972 est.): 462,-400. Cap.: Saint-Denis (pop., 1971 est., 85,444).

Education. (1969–70) Primary, pupils 96,-639, teachers (including preprimary) 3,366; secondary, pupils 27,098; vocational, pupils 2,117; secondary and vocational, teachers 1,257; teacher training, students 317, teachers 19; higher, students 639, teaching staff (1966–67) 26.

Finance and Trade. Monetary unit: CFA franc. Budget (1970) balanced at CFA Fr. 11,-448,000,000 (including French aid of CFA Fr. 1,889,000,000). Foreign trade (1970): imports CFA Fr. 44.7 billion (62% from France, 12% from Malagasy Republic); exports CFA Fr. 14.1 billion (75% to France, 20% to Italy). Main export sugar 89%.

SAINT PIERRE AND MIQUELON

The self-governing overseas territory of Saint Pierre and Miquelon is located about 15 mi. off the south coast of Newfoundland. Area: 93 sq.mi. (242 sq.km.). Pop. (1972 est.): 5,650. Cap.: Saint Pierre, Saint Pierre.

Education. (1969–70) Primary, pupils 880, teachers 38; secondary, pupils 283, teachers 32; vocational, pupils 83, teachers 13.

Finance. Monetary unit: CFA franc. Budget (1970 est.) balanced at CFA Fr. 763 million.

Foreign Trade. (1971) Imports CFA Fr. 3,-117,000,000; exports CFA Fr. 1,381,000,000 (including ship's stores CFA Fr. 668 million). Import sources: Canada 57%; France 32%. Export destinations (excluding ship's stores): Canada 60%; U.S. 32%; France 8%. Main exports (excluding ship's stores, 82% of which were petroleum products): livestock 59%; fresh fish 34%.

WALLIS AND FUTUNA

Wallis and Futuna, an overseas territory, lies in the South Pacific west of Western Samoa. Area: 98 sq.mi. (255 sq.km.). Pop. (1971 est.): 9,000. Cap.: Matautu, Uvea (pop., 1969, 566).

INDIA

SIKKIM

This protected kingdom is bordered by China, Bhutan, India, and Nepal. Area: 2,744 sq.mi. (7,107 sq.km.). Pop. (1972 est.): 202,000. Cap.: Gangtok (pop., 1968 est., 9,000).

Education. (1970) Primary and secondary, pupils c. 20,000.
Finance and Trade. Monetary unit: Indian rupee, with (Sept. 18, 1972) a free rate of Rs. 7.65 to U.S. $1 (Rs. 18.71 = £1 sterling). Budget (1970 est.) revenue c. Rs. 20 million. Third five-year development plan (1966–71) Rs. 90 million, all financed by India; development aid from India (including aid to Bhutan; 1968–69) Rs. 50 million. Foreign trade mainly with India. Main exports (1960): cardamom, oranges, potatoes, apples.

NETHERLANDS

NETHERLANDS ANTILLES

The Netherlands Antilles, a self-governing integral part of the Netherlands realm, consists of an island group near the Venezuelan coast and another group to the north near St. Kitts-Nevis-Anguilla. Area: 385 sq.mi. (996 sq.km.). Pop. (1971 est.): 229,261. Cap.: Willemstad, Curaçao (pop., 1960, 43,547).
Education. (1968–69) Primary, pupils 43,193, teachers (1967–68) 1,270; secondary, pupils 10,415, teachers (1967–68) 412; vocational, pupils 5,317, teachers (1967–68) 153; teacher training (1966–67), students 311.
Finance. Monetary unit: Netherlands Antilles guilder or florin, with (Sept. 18, 1972) a parity of 0.52 Netherlands Antilles guilder to the Netherlands guilder and 1.69 Netherlands Antilles guilder to U.S. $1 (free rate of 4.30 Netherlands Antilles guilders = £1 sterling). Budget (central; 1968 est.): revenue 69,252,000 Netherlands Antilles guilders; expenditure 69,206,000 Netherlands Antilles guilders. Cost of living (Curaçao; 1963 = 100): (Feb. 1972) 118; (Feb. 1971) 113.
Foreign Trade. (Curaçao and Aruba; 1970) Imports 1,492,343,000 Netherlands Antilles guilders; exports 1,273,967,000 Netherlands Antilles guilders. Import sources: Venezuela 61%; U.S. 12%; Netherlands 5%. Export destinations: U.S. 52%; Canada 9%; Puerto Rico 5%. Main export petroleum products 94% (from crude oil imports, accounting for 64% of imports).
Transport and Communications. Roads (1968) 1,183 km. (Curaçao 541 km.; Aruba 380 km.; Bonaire 209 km.; St. Maarten 53 km.). Motor vehicles in use: passenger (1969) 33,400; commercial (1968) 3,700. Shipping traffic (1969): goods loaded c. 39.3 million metric tons, unloaded c. 44,930,000 metric tons. Telephones (Dec. 1970) 28,000. Radio receivers (Dec. 1970) 115,000. Television receivers (Dec. 1970) 32,000.
Industry. Production (in 000; metric tons; 1970): petroleum products 46,031; phosphate rock (exports) 109; electricity (kw-hr.; 1969) 1,256,000.

SURINAM

A self-governing integral part of the Netherlands realm, Surinam is on the northern coast of South America bounded by French Guiana, Brazil, and Guyana. Area: 70,060 sq.mi. (181,455 sq.km.). Pop. (1971): 384,900. Cap.: Paramaribo (pop., 1971, 102,300).
Education. (1964–65) Primary, pupils 71,397, teachers 2,052; secondary, pupils 10,252, teachers 463; vocational, pupils 1,430, teachers 78; teacher training, students 1,583, teachers 150; higher, students 667, teaching staff 74.
Finance. Monetary unit: Surinam guilder or florin, with (Sept. 18, 1972) a parity of 0.52 Surinam guilder to the Netherlands guilder and 1.69 Surinam guilder to U.S. $1 (free rate of 4.30 Surinam guilders = £1 sterling). Budget (1971 est.): revenue 176.5 million Surinam guilders; expenditure 200.2 million Surinam guilders.
Foreign Trade. (1970) Imports 217 million Surinam guilders; exports 256 million Surinam guilders. Import sources: U.S. 42%; Netherlands 19%; U.K. 9%; Japan 9%; West Germany 7%. Export destinations: U.S. 39%; West Germany 15%; Netherlands 11%; Norway 8%; Italy 8%. Main exports (1968): bauxite and alumina 70%; aluminum 16%; rice 5%.
Transport and Communications. Roads (main; 1970) 1,335 km. Motor vehicles in use (1970): passenger 16,200; commercial 3,500. Railways (1970) 86 km. Shipping traffic (1969): goods loaded c. 4,650,000 metric tons, unloaded c. 850,000 metric tons. Telephones (Dec. 1969) 9,900. Radio receivers (Dec. 1970) 92,000. Television receivers (Dec. 1970) 28,000.
Agriculture. Production (in 000; metric tons; 1970; 1969 in parentheses): rice c. 122 (113); oranges c. 12 (c. 12); grapefruit c. 6 (c. 5); sugar, raw value (1970–71) c. 17, (1968–69) c. 17; coffee c. 0.2 (c. 0.4); bananas c. 25 (c. 25). Livestock (in 000; January 1971): cattle c. 45; goats c. 5; sheep c. 3; pigs c. 11.
Industry. Production (in 000; metric tons; 1970): bauxite 6,011; aluminum 55; gold (troy oz.; 1969) 2.4; electricity (kw-hr.; 1969) 1,242,000 (72% hydroelectric in 1968).

NEW ZEALAND

COOK ISLANDS

The self-governing territory of the Cook Islands consists of several islands in the southern Pacific Ocean scattered over an area of about 850,000 sq.mi. Area: 93 sq.mi. (241 sq.km.). Pop. (1971): 21,317. Seat of government: Rarotonga Island (pop., 1971, 11,437).
Education. (1969) Primary, pupils 5,870, teachers 310; secondary, pupils 959, teachers 69; teacher training, students 27, teachers 7.
Finance and Trade. Monetary unit: New Zealand dollar, with (Sept. 18, 1972) a free rate of NZ$0.84 to U.S. $1 (NZ$2.05 = £1 sterling). Budget (1968–69 actual): revenue NZ$1,559,000 (excluding grant-in-aid of NZ$2,062,000); expenditure NZ$3,619,000. Foreign trade (1970): imports NZ$5,495,000 (68% from New Zealand, 8% from U.K., 6% from Australia in 1967); exports NZ$2,668,000 (99% to New Zealand in 1967). Main exports (1967): fruit juice 51%; clothing 22%; citrus fruit 9%; copra 6%.

NIUE ISLAND

The territory of Niue Island is situated in the Pacific Ocean about 1,500 mi. NE of New Zealand. Area: 100 sq.mi. (259 sq.km.). Pop. (1971 est.): 4,901.
Education. (1969) Primary, pupils 1,308, teachers 69; secondary, pupils 525, teachers 29; vocational, pupils 19, teachers 5; teacher training, students 5.
Finance and Trade. Monetary unit: New Zealand dollar. Budget (1970–71): revenue NZ$1,037,000 (excluding grant-in-aid of NZ$972,000); expenditure NZ$2,103,000. Foreign trade (1970): imports NZ$748,000; exports NZ$177,000. Bulk of trade is with New Zealand. Main exports: passion fruit 20%; honey 9%; copra 5%.

TOKELAU ISLANDS

The territory of Tokelau Islands lies in the South Pacific about 700 mi. N of Niue Island and 2,100 mi. NE of New Zealand. Area: 4 sq.mi. (10 sq. km.). Pop. (1971 est.): 1,655.

NORWAY

JAN MAYEN

The island of Jan Mayen, a Norwegian dependency, lies within the Arctic Circle between Greenland and northern Norway. Area: 144 sq.mi. (373 sq.km.). Pop. (1972 est.): 36.

SVALBARD

A group of islands and a Norwegian dependency, Svalbard is located within the Arctic Circle to the north of Norway. Area: 23,957 sq.mi. (62,050 sq.km.). Pop. (1971 est.): 2,822.

PORTUGAL

ANGOLA

The overseas province of Angola is located on the southwestern coast of Africa, bordered by Zaire, Zambia, and South West Africa. Area: 481,350 sq.mi. (1,246,700 sq.km.). Pop. (1970): 5,673,046. Cap.: Luanda (pop., 1970, 475,328).
Education. (1968) Primary, pupils 333,767, teachers 7,434; secondary, pupils 30,384, teachers 1,726; vocational, pupils 14,530, teachers 1,102; teacher training, students 1,147, teachers 108; higher, students 1,252, teaching staff 176.
Finance and Trade. Monetary unit: Angola escudo, at par with the Portuguese escudo (27.25 escudos = U.S. $1), with (Sept. 18, 1972) a free rate of 65.57 escudos to £1 sterling. Budget (1970 est.) balanced at 6,836,000,000 escudos. Foreign trade (1971): imports 12,128,000,000 escudos; exports 11,788,000,000 escudos. Import sources: Portugal 32%; West Germany 11%; U.S. 11%; U.K. 9%; Japan 6%; France 5%. Export destinations: Portugal 31%; U.S. 20%; Japan 10%; Netherlands 7%; Canada 5%. Main exports: coffee 34%; crude oil 15%; diamonds 13%; iron ore 10%; cotton 6%.
Transport and Communications. Roads (1970) 72,291 km. Motor vehicles in use (1970): passenger 78,000; commercial (including buses) 29,400. Railways: (1969) 3,159 km.; traffic (1970) 204 million passenger-km., freight 5,230,000,000 net ton-km. Ships entered (1970) vessels totaling 8,712,000 net registered tons. Shipping traffic (1971): goods loaded 12,074,000 metric tons, unloaded 1,748,000 metric tons. Telephones (Dec. 1969) 25,000. Radio receivers (Dec. 1970) 95,000.
Agriculture. Production (in 000; metric tons; 1971; 1970 in parentheses): corn c. 500 (456); dry beans c. 65 (c. 66); sugar, raw value (1971–72) c. 70, (1970–71) 73; coffee c. 210 (204); cotton, lint c. 33 (30); sisal c. 53 (68); palm oil (1970) c. 38, (1969) c. 38; palm kernels (exports; 1970) c. 14, (1969) 12; fish catch (1970) 368, (1969) 419. Livestock (in 000; Dec. 1970): sheep 171; goats 821; cattle 2,727; pigs 332.
Industry. Production (in 000; metric tons; 1971): crude oil 5,830; cement (1970) 446; iron ore (60–65% metal content) 6,160; manganese ore (1970) 23; diamonds (metric carats; 1970) 2,396; salt (1970) 88; fish meal (1970) 67; electricity (kw-hr.; 1970) 644,000.

CAPE VERDE ISLANDS

The Cape Verde Islands, an overseas province, form an archipelago in the eastern Atlantic Ocean about 380 mi. off the coast of Senegal. Area: 1,557 sq.mi. (4,033 sq.km.). Pop. (1970): 272,071. Cap.: Praia, São Tigao (pop., 1970, 21,494).
Education. (1968–69) Primary, pupils 26,990, teachers 589; secondary, pupils 2,793, teachers 149; vocational, pupils 395, teachers 23.
Finance and Trade. Monetary unit: Cape Verde escudo, at par with the Portuguese escudo. Budget (1969 est.): revenue 303 million escudos; expenditure 276 million escudos. Foreign trade (1970): imports 469,418,000 escudos (57% from Portugal, 16% from Angola); exports 47,731,000 escudos (69% to Portugal, 13% to U.S.). Main exports: fish products 24%; bananas 21%; fish 13%.
Transport. Ships entered (1970) vessels totaling 7,815,000 net registered tons. Shipping traffic (1969): goods loaded 48,000 metric tons, unloaded c. 536,000 metric tons.

MACAU

The overseas province of Macau is situated on the mainland coast of China 40 mi. W of Hong Kong. Area: 6 sq.mi. (16 sq.km.). Pop. (1971 est.): 321,000.
Education. (1967–68) Primary, pupils 28,308, teachers 900; secondary, pupils 7,119, teachers 491; vocational, pupils 1,660, teachers 93; teacher training, students 57, teachers 20.
Finance and Trade. Monetary unit: patacá, with a par value of 1 patacá to 4.75 escudos and 5.74 patacás to U.S. $1 (free rate of 14.05 patacás = £1 sterling). Budget (1970 est.) balanced at 62,579,000 patacás. Foreign trade (1971): imports 2,124,000,000 escudos; exports 1,383,000,000 escudos. Import sources: Hong Kong 65%; China 27%. Export destinations: West Germany 17%; Angola 13%; France 12%; Portugal 11%; U.S. 7%; Mozambique 5%. Main exports: textiles 64%; chemicals 7%; animal products 7%.
Transport. Shipping traffic (1970): goods loaded 60,000 metric tons, unloaded 289,000 metric tons.

MOZAMBIQUE

Mozambique, on the southeastern African coast, is an overseas province bounded by Tanzania, Malawi, Zambia, Rhodesia, South Africa, and Swaziland. Area: 303,073 sq.mi. (784,961 sq. km.). Pop. (1970): 8,233,834. Cap.: Lourenço Marques (pop., 1970, 354,684).
Education. (1967) Primary, pupils 485,045, teachers 6,274; secondary (1966), pupils 10,092, teachers 697; vocational, pupils 15,346, teachers 836; teacher training, students 1,061, teachers 104; higher, students 904, teaching staff 192.

Finance and Trade. Monetary unit: Mozambique escudo, at par with the Portuguese escudo. Budget (1970 est.): revenue 6,452,000,000 escudos; expenditure 6,451,000,000 escudos. Foreign trade (1970): imports 9,302,000,000 escudos; exports 4,497,000,000 escudos. Import sources: Portugal 27%; South Africa 15%; U.S. 10%; U.K. 8%; West Germany 8%; Japan 6%. Export destinations: Portugal 38%; South Africa 10%; U.S. 9%; U.K. 5%; Angola 5%. Main exports: textiles 21%; cashew nuts 19%; sugar 12%; copra 5%; tea 5%.

Transport and Communications. Roads (1970) 37,106 km. Motor vehicles in use (1969): passenger 70,700; commercial (including buses) 16,400. Railways: (1969) 3,876 km.; traffic (1970) 274 million passenger-km., freight (1969) 2,758,000,000 net ton-km. Ships entered (1969) vessels totaling 15,390,000 net registered tons. Shipping traffic (1970): goods loaded 9,829,000 metric tons, unloaded 4,041,000 metric tons. Telephones (Dec. 1970) 27,000. Radio receivers (Dec. 1970) 90,000.

Agriculture. Production (in 000; metric tons; 1971; 1970 in parentheses): cotton, lint *c.* 40 (46); sisal *c.* 29 (*c.* 29); sugar, raw value (1971–72) *c.* 300, (1970–71) 284; copra (exports) *c.* 62 (*c.* 60); bananas *c.* 25 (*c.* 25); tea 16 (17). Livestock (in 000; Dec. 1970): cattle *c.* 2,100; sheep *c.* 220; goats *c.* 860; pigs *c.* 250.

Industry. Production (in 000; metric tons; 1970): petroleum products 701; cement 385; electricity (kw-hr.) 558,000.

PORTUGUESE GUINEA

The African overseas province of Portuguese Guinea has an Atlantic coastline on the west and borders Senegal on the north and Guinea on the east and south. Area: 13,948 sq.mi. (36,125 sq.km.). Pop. (1971 est.): 563,000. Cap.: Bissau (pop., 1970, 62,101).

Education. (1966–67) Primary, pupils 17,805, teachers 497; secondary, pupils 446, teachers 21; vocational, pupils 652, teachers 34.

Finance and Trade. Monetary unit: Guinea escudo, at par with the Portuguese escudo. Budget (1969 est.): revenue 452 million escudos; expenditure 392 million escudos. Foreign trade (1971): imports 879,172,000 escudos (53% from Portugal, 11% from Italy, 7% from U.K., 5% from Japan); exports 57,189,000 escudos (77% to Portugal, 10% to West Germany, 7% to Cape Verde Islands). Main exports: peanuts 43%; coconuts 32%; peanut husks 5%.

Agriculture. Production (in 000; metric tons; 1971; 1970 in parentheses): peanuts *c.* 65 (*c.* 65); rice *c.* 35 (35); palm kernels (exports) *c.* 12 (*c.* 8); palm oil *c.* 8 (*c.* 8). Livestock (in 000; 1970–71): cattle *c.* 270; pigs *c.* 150; sheep *c.* 65; goats *c.* 175.

PORTUGUESE TIMOR

Portuguese Timor, an overseas province consisting of the eastern portion of the island of Timor, is located about 300 mi. N of Australia. Area: 5,763 sq.mi. (14,925 sq.km.). Pop. (1971 est.): 614,000. Cap.: Dili (pop., 1970, 29,312).

Education. (1968–69) Primary, pupils 27,299, teachers 541; secondary, pupils 477, teachers 23; vocational, pupils 476, teachers 22; teacher training, students 114, teachers 8.

Finance and Trade. Monetary unit: Timor escudo, at par with the Portuguese escudo. Budget (1969 est.): revenue 136 million escudos; expenditure 170 million escudos. Foreign trade (1971): imports 203,280,000 escudos; exports 121,132,000 escudos. Import sources: Portugal 26%; Singapore 13%; Australia 13%; Macau 12%; Mozambique 10%; Japan 10%; U.K. 5%. Export destinations: Belgium-Luxembourg 25%; Denmark 16%; Netherlands 16%; U.S. 11%; Singapore 9%; Portugal 8%; West Germany 8%. Main exports: coffee 85%; copra 6%.

Agriculture. Production (in 000; metric tons; 1970; 1969 in parentheses): corn *c.* 18 (16); rice *c.* 15 (13); sweet potatoes *c.* 7 (*c.* 7); copra *c.* 2.4 (2.5); coffee *c.* 5 (5). Livestock (in 000; 1970): cattle 71; sheep 43; goats 217; pigs 224; buffaloes 127; horses 114.

SÃO TOMÉ AND PRÍNCIPE

The overseas province of São Tomé and Príncipe Islands lies in the Gulf of Guinea off the west coast of Africa. Area: 372 sq.mi. (964 sq.km.). Pop. (1970): 73,811. Cap.: São Tomé (pop., 1970, 7,710).

Education. (1968–69) Primary, pupils 8,281, teachers 280; secondary, pupils 997, teachers 58; vocational, pupils 127, teachers 19.

Finance and Trade. Monetary unit: Guinea escudo, at par with the Portuguese escudo. Budget (1969–70 est.): revenue 209 million escudos; expenditure 172 million escudos. Foreign trade (1970): imports 260,522,000 escudos (51% from Portugal, 23% from Angola, 5% from Netherlands, 5% from West Germany); exports 237,440,000 escudos (34% to Portugal, 32% to Netherlands, 12% to West Germany, 7% to Denmark, 5% to U.S.). Main exports: cocoa 80%; copra 11%.

Agriculture. Production (in 000; metric tons; 1970; 1969 in parentheses): copra 4.5 (5.2); bananas 2 (2); cocoa (1970–71) 10, (1969–70) 10; palm kernels (exports) *c.* 3 (2.6); palm oil *c.* 1 (0.9). Livestock (in 000; Dec. 1970): cattle *c.* 3; sheep *c.* 2; pigs *c.* 3; goats *c.* 1.

SOUTH WEST AFRICA (NAMIBIA)

South West Africa has been a UN territory since 1966, when the General Assembly terminated South Africa's mandate over the country, renamed Namibia by the UN. South Africa considers the UN resolution illegal and has stated that it is determined to continue its jurisdiction over the area. Area: 318,261 sq.mi. (824,296 sq.km.). Pop. (1970): 746,328. National cap.: Windhoek (pop., 1970, 61,260). Summer cap.: Swakopmund (pop., 1960, 4,701).

Education. (1970) Primary and secondary, pupils 129,927, teachers 3,790.

Finance and Trade. Monetary unit: South African rand, with (Sept. 18, 1972) a free rate of R 0.80 to U.S. $1 (R 1.95 = £1 sterling). Budget (1969–70): revenue R 53,818,000; expenditure R 54,476,000. Foreign trade included in the South African customs union. Main exports: diamonds and other minerals (1969) R 139 million; karakul pelts (1967) R 14.5 million.

Agriculture. Production (in 000; metric tons; 1971; 1970 in parentheses): corn *c.* 12 (*c.* 12); millet *c.* 13 (*c.* 13); butter *c.* 2 (*c.* 2); beef and veal *c.* 64 (*c.* 62); fish catch (1970) 717, (1969) 820. Livestock (in 000; 1969–70): cattle *c.* 2,500; sheep *c.* 4,000; goats *c.* 1,700; horses *c.* 36; asses *c.* 56.

Industry. Production (in 000; metric tons; 1970): lead ore (metal content) 70; zinc ore (metal content; 1969) *c.* 70; copper ore (1966) 37; tin concentrates (metal content) 0.7; silver (troy oz.; 1969) 1,273; diamonds (metric carats) 2,200; electricity (kw-hr.; 1963) 188,000.

SPAIN

SPANISH SAHARA

Spanish Sahara is a province in northwest Africa, bordered by Morocco, Algeria, Mauritania, and the Atlantic Ocean. Area: 102,703 sq.mi. (266,000 sq.km.). Pop. (1970): 76,425. Cap.: El Aaiún (pop., 1970, 24,519).

Education. (1969–70) Primary, pupils 2,988, teachers 69; secondary, pupils 1,079, teachers 63.

Finance and Trade. Monetary unit: Spanish peseta, with (Sept. 18, 1972) a par value of 64.47 pesetas to U.S. $1 (free rate of 155.32 pesetas = £1 sterling). Budget (1969 est.) balanced at 250 million pesetas. Foreign trade (1969): imports 387,410,000 pesetas; exports negligible.

Agriculture and Industry. Livestock (in 000; 1970–71): camels 61; goats 162; sheep 21. Electricity production (1969) 5,120,000 kw-hr. Phosphate production began in 1972.

UNITED KINGDOM

ANTIGUA

The associated state of Antigua, with its dependencies Barbuda and Redonda, lies in the eastern Caribbean approximately 40 mi. N of Guadeloupe. Area: 171 sq.mi. (412 sq.km.). Pop. (1970): 70,000. Cap.: Saint John's (pop., 1960, 21,396).

Education. Primary and secondary, pupils (1966–67) 17,027, teachers (1963–64) 470; higher (1963–64), students 50, teachers 3.

Finance and Trade. Monetary unit: East Caribbean dollar (ECar$1.96 = U.S. $1; ECar $4.80 = 1£ sterling). Budget (1971 est.) balanced at ECar$27,608,004. Foreign trade (1967): imports ECar$39,094,190 (29% from U.S., 23% from U.K., 10% from Trinidad and Tobago); exports ECar$4,968,599 (21% to Canada, 9% to U.S., 5% to U.K., 5% to Puerto Rico). Main export petroleum products 85%. Tourism (1970) 65,000 visitors.

BAHAMAS

The self-governing colony of the Bahamas comprises a 90,000-sq.mi. archipelago that extends for over 600 mi. ESE of Florida. Area: 5,382 sq.mi. (13,939 sq.km.). Pop. (1971 est.): 181,000. Cap.: Nassau, New Providence (pop., 1970, 3,233).

Education. (1969–70) Primary, pupils 35,169, teachers 1,542; secondary, pupils 16,236, teachers 499; vocational, pupils 399, teachers 40; teacher training, students 113, teachers 18; higher, students 252, teaching staff 40.

Finance and Trade. Monetary unit: Bahamian dollar, with (Sept. 18, 1972) a free rate of B$0.98 to U.S. $1 (B$2.38 = £1 sterling). Budget (1971 est.): revenue B$107.2 million; expenditure B$106.5 million. Foreign trade (1971): imports B$515,586,000 (32% from U.S., 8% from U.K.); exports B$264,944,000 (75% to U.S., 9% to Puerto Rico, 7% to Canada). Main exports: petroleum products 83%; pharmaceuticals 6%; cement 5%. Tourism (1970): visitors 1,298,300; gross receipts U.S. $221 million.

Transport and Communications. Shipping (1971): merchant vessels 100 gross tons and over 145; gross tonnage 357,845. Telephones (Dec. 1970) 44,000. Radio receivers (Dec. 1969) 125,000. Television receivers (Dec. 1964) *c.* 4,500.

BERMUDA

The colony of Bermuda lies in the western Atlantic about 570 mi. E of Cape Hatteras, North Carolina. Area: 20 sq.mi. (53 sq.km.). Pop. (1971 est.): 52,610. Cap.: Hamilton, Great Bermuda (pop., 1970, 2,060).

Education. (1968–69) Primary, pupils 8,137, teachers 330; secondary, pupils 3,712, teachers 247; vocational, pupils 495, teachers 45.

Finance and Trade. Monetary unit: Bermuda dollar, with (Sept. 18, 1972) a par value equal to the U.S. dollar (free rate of Ber$2.45 = £1 sterling). Budget (1971–72 est.): revenue Ber$35,657,000; expenditure Ber$32,969,000. Foreign trade (1971): imports Ber$108,478,000 (excluding Ber$79,306,000 for free-port area); exports Ber$91,575,000. Import sources: U.S. 45%; U.K. 22%; Canada 12%. Export destinations (drugs and medicines only): U.K. 25%; Australia 19%; Netherlands 16%; France 12%; Japan 7%. Main exports drugs and medicines 82%. Tourism (1970): visitors 388,914; gross receipts U.S. $72.8 million.

Transport and Communications. Shipping (1971): merchant vessels 100 gross tons and over 47; gross tonnage 814,017. Telephones (Dec. 1970) 30,000. Radio receivers (Dec. 1970) 38,000. Television receivers (Dec. 1970) 17,000.

BRITISH HONDURAS

British Honduras, a self-governing colony, is situated on the Caribbean coast of Central America, bounded on the north and northwest by Mexico and by Guatemala on the remainder of the west and south. Area: 8,866 sq.mi. (22,963 sq.km.). Pop. (1970): 119,934. Cap.: Belmopan (pop., 1970, 274).

Education. (1969–70) Primary, pupils 31,080, teachers 1,212; secondary, pupils 3,629, teachers 230; vocational (1968–69), pupils 44; teacher training, students 80, teachers 6; higher, students 89, teaching staff 14.

Finance and Trade. Monetary unit: British Honduras dollar, with (Sept. 18, 1972) a free rate of BH$1.63 = U.S. $1 (BH$4 = £1 sterling). Budget (1970 est.): revenue BH$26,460,000 (including U.K. development grants of BH$9.9 million); expenditure BH$26,483,000. Foreign trade (1968): imports BH$44,200,780; exports BH$25,194,350. Import sources: U.S. 33%; U.K. 29%; Jamaica 7%; Netherlands 6%. Export destinations: U.K. 32%; U.S. 29%; Mexico 16%; Canada 15%. Main exports: sugar 39%; oranges and products 10%; grapefruit and products 6%.

BRITISH INDIAN OCEAN TERRITORY

Located in the western Indian Ocean, this colony consists of the Chagos Archipelago and the islands of Aldabra, Desroches, and Farquhar. Area: 85 sq.mi. (221 sq.km.). Pop. (1972 est.): 350. Administrative headquarters: Victoria, Seychelles.

BRITISH SOLOMON ISLANDS

British Solomon Islands is a protectorate in the southwestern Pacific east of the island of New Guinea. Area: 10,983 sq.mi. (28,446 sq.km.). Pop. (1972 est.): 173,510. Cap.: Honiara, Guadalcanal (pop., 1971 est., 13,350).

Education. (1970) Primary, pupils 21,270, teachers 885; secondary, pupils 1,042, teachers 64; vocational, pupils 248, teachers 23; teacher training, students 110, teachers 11.

Finance and Trade. Monetary unit: Australian dollar. Budget (1971 est.) balanced at A$11,-117,000 (including development aid of A$4,608,-000). Foreign trade (1970): imports A$10,020,-000 (45% from Australia, 16% from U.K., 10% from U.S., 7% from Japan); exports A$7,047,000 (53% to Japan, 14% to Australia, 11% to Norway, 10% to Netherlands, 8% to West Germany). Main exports: copra 53%; timber 40%.

BRITISH VIRGIN ISLANDS

The colony of the British Virgin Islands is located in the Caribbean to the east of the U.S. Virgin Islands. Area: 59 sq.mi. (153 sq.km.). Pop. (1970): 10,298. Cap.: Road Town, Tortola (pop., 1970, 2,183).

Education. (1970–71) Primary, pupils 1,718; secondary, pupils 865; primary and secondary, teachers 139.

Finance and Trade. Monetary unit: U.S. dollar (free rate at Sept. 18, 1972, of U.S. $2.45 = £1 sterling). Budget (1970 est.): revenue U.S. $6,352,000; expenditure U.S. $6,785,000. Foreign trade (1970): imports U.S. $10,224,000 (51% from U.S., Puerto Rico, and U.S. Virgin Islands, 23% from U.K.); exports U.S. $65,328 (94% to U.S. Virgin Islands). Main exports: fish 40%; motor vehicles (reexport) 21%; sheep 6%; bananas 5%.

BRUNEI

Brunei, a protected sultanate, is located on the north coast of the island of Borneo, surrounded on its landward side by the Malaysian state of Sarawak. Area: 2,226 sq.mi. (5,765 sq.km.). Pop. (1971): 136,256. Cap.: Bandar Seri Begawan (pop., 1971, 36,574).

Education. (1969–70) Primary, pupils 27,580, teachers 1,203; secondary, pupils 16,587, teachers 655; vocational, pupils 79, teachers 8; teacher training, students 541, teachers 31.

Finance and Trade. Monetary unit: Brunei dollar, with (Sept. 18, 1972) a free rate of Br $2.77 to U.S. $1 (Br$6.78 = £1 sterling). Budget (1971 est.): revenue Br$173,552,000; expenditure Br$161,019,000. Foreign trade (1970): imports Br$265,122,000; exports Br$292,063,-000. Import sources: U.S. 20%; U.K. 18%; Singapore 17%; Japan 15%; Malaysia 6%. Export destination Malaysia (Sarawak) 98%. Main export crude oil 95%.

Agriculture. Production (in 000; metric tons; 1971; 1970 in parentheses): rice *c.* 8 (*c.* 8); rubber (exports) *c.* 0.3 (0.3). Livestock (in 000; Dec. 1970): cattle 3; pigs *c.* 13; goats 1.

Industry. Production (1970): crude oil 6,685,-000 metric tons; natural gas 224 million cu.m.

CAYMAN ISLANDS

The colony of the Cayman Islands lies in the Caribbean about 170 mi. NW of Jamaica. Area: 100 sq.mi. (259 sq.km.). Pop. (1971 est.): 11,-300. Cap.: George Town, Grand Cayman (pop., 1970, 3,975).

Education. (Public only; 1969–70) Primary, pupils 1,203, teachers 39; secondary, pupils 551, teachers 30.

Finance and Trade. Monetary unit: Jamaican dollar, with (Sept. 18, 1972) a free rate of Jam $0.82 to U.S. $1 (Jam$2 = £1 sterling). Budget (1970 rev. est.): revenue Jam$1,594,800; expenditure Jam$1,777,000. Foreign trade (1970): imports Jam$7,767,000; exports Jam$9,276. Main exports: turtle shell, turtle meat. Tourism: visitors (1970) 22,888; gross receipts (1969) *c.* Jam$2.4 million.

Transport. Shipping (1971): merchant vessels 100 gross tons and over 39; gross tonnage 26,643.

DOMINICA

The associated state of Dominica lies in the Caribbean between Guadeloupe to the north and Martinique to the south. Area: 289 sq.mi. (750 sq.km.). Pop. (1972 est.): 71,793. Cap.: Roseau (pop., 1970, 9,949).

Education. (1969–70) Primary, pupils 19,812, teachers (1963–64) 459; secondary, pupils 1,-507, teachers 89; vocational, pupils 70, teachers 4.

Finance and Trade. Monetary unit: East Caribbean dollar. Budget (1971 est.) balanced at ECar$21,727,000. Foreign trade (1969): imports ECar$24,712,700 (33% from U.K., 15% from U.S., 11% from Trinidad and Tobago, 10% from Canada, 6% from the Netherlands, 5% from West Germany); exports ECar$14,147,700 (84% to U.K.). Main exports: bananas 73%; essential oils 6%; fruit juices 5%.

FALKLAND ISLANDS

The colony of the Falkland Islands and Dependencies is situated in the South Atlantic about 500 mi. NE of Cape Horn. Area: 6,150 sq.mi. (15,930 sq.km.). Pop. (1971 est.): 2,042. Cap.: Stanley (pop., 1971 est., 1,083).

Education. (1970) Primary and secondary, pupils 383, teachers 37.

Finance and Trade. Monetary unit: Falkland Island pound, at par with the pound sterling. Budgets: (colony; 1971–72 est.) revenue FI£430,700, expenditure FI£483,000; (dependencies; 1969–70) balanced at FI£17,000 (including U.K. grant of FI£5,000). Foreign trade: (colony; 1969) imports FI£509,000, exports FI£909,000 (mainly wool); (dependencies; 1968) imports FI£133,000, exports nil.

GIBRALTAR

Gibraltar, a self-governing colony, is a small peninsula that juts into the Mediterranean from southwestern Spain. Area: 2.25 sq.mi. (5.80 sq.km.). Pop. (1971 est.): 28,694.

Education. (1969–70) Primary, pupils 3,239, teachers 153; secondary, pupils 1,780, teachers 104; vocational, pupils 33, teachers 11.

Finance and Trade. Monetary unit: Gibraltar pound, at par with the pound sterling. Budget (1970 est.): revenue Gib£4,180,000; expenditure Gib£3,934,000. Foreign trade (1971): imports Gib£9.5 million (49% from U.K., 21% from EEC); exports Gib£1.2 million (31% to EEC, 16% to U.K.). Tourism (1970) 141,000 visitors.

Transport. Shipping (1971): merchant vessels 100 gross tons and over 12; gross tonnage 27,413. Ships entered (1970) vessels totaling 10,172,000 net registered tons. Shipping traffic (1970): goods loaded 4,000 metric tons, unloaded 255,000 metric tons.

GILBERT AND ELLICE ISLANDS

The Gilbert and Ellice Islands colony is scattered over an area of more than two million sq.mi. in the western Pacific Ocean. Area: 283 sq.mi. (734 sq.km.). Pop. (1971 est.): 58,000. Seat of government: Tarawa Atoll (pop., 1968, 12,642).

Education. (1970) Primary, pupils 14,570, teachers 546; secondary, pupils 622, teachers 44; vocational, pupils 337, teachers 16; teacher training, students 112, teachers 16.

Finance and Trade. Monetary unit: Australian dollar. Budget (1970 est.): revenue A$4,-356,000; expenditure A$3,329,000. Foreign trade: imports (1970) A$3,917,000 (60% from Australia, 11% from U.K. in 1968); exports (1969) A$7,306,000 (63% to Australia, 24% to New Zealand, 12% to U.K. in 1968). Main exports (1968): phosphates 84%; copra 14%.

GRENADA

Grenada, a West Indian associated state, includes the island of Grenada and its dependency, the southern Grenadines. Area: 133 sq.mi. (344 sq.km.). Pop. (1971 est.): 96,000. Cap.: Saint George's (pop., 1969 est., 8,644).

Education. (1968–69) Primary, pupils 29,194, teachers (1966–67) 690; secondary, pupils 2,703, teachers (1966–67) 119; vocational (1966–67), pupils 432, teachers 9; teacher training, students 64, teachers (1966–67) 11.

Finance and Trade. Monetary unit: East Caribbean dollar. Budget (1971 est.) balanced at ECar$35,613,000. Foreign trade (1968): imports ECar$26,346,000; exports ECar$9,962,000. Import sources: U.K. 33%; U.S. 10%; Canada 10%; Netherlands 5%. Export destinations: U.K. 64%; West Germany 10%; Netherlands 9%; U.S. 5%. Main exports: bananas 40%; cocoa 21%; nutmegs 25%; mace 7%.

GUERNSEY

Located 30 mi. W of Normandy, France, Guernsey, together with its small island dependencies, is a crown dependency. Area: 30 sq.mi. (78 sq.km.). Pop. (1971): 53,734. Cap.: St. Peter Port (pop., 1971, 16,303).

Education. Primary and secondary, pupils (1970) 8,927.

Finance and Trade. Monetary unit: pound sterling. Budget (1970): revenue £7,723,000 (including £196,000 for Alderney); expenditure £5,549,000 (including £130,000 for Alderney). Foreign trade included with United Kingdom. Main exports: tomatoes, flowers, stone. Tourism (1970) 239,000 visitors.

HONG KONG

The colony of Hong Kong lies on the southeastern coast of China about 40 mi. E of Macau and 80 mi. SE of Canton. Area: 400 sq.mi. (1,036 sq.km.). Pop. (1971): 3,948,179. Cap.: Victoria (pop., 1971, 520,932).

Education. (1969–70) Primary, pupils 746,-429, teachers 22,444; secondary, pupils 241,234; vocational, pupils 13,383; secondary and vocational, teachers 9,952; higher, students 19,874, teaching staff 1,992.

Finance. Monetary unit: Hong Kong dollar, with (Sept. 18, 1972) a par value of HK$5.65 = U.S. $1 (free rate of HK$13.90 = £1 sterling). Budget (1971–72 est.): revenue HK$3,118,000,-000; expenditure HK$2,862,000,000.

Foreign Trade. (1971) Imports HK$20,256,-000,000 (24% from Japan, 16% from China, 13% from U.S., 8% from U.K., 5% from Taiwan); exports HK$17,164,000,000 (35% to U.S., 12% to U.K., 7% to West Germany, 7% to Japan). Main exports: clothing 32%; electrical equipment 9%; textile yarns and fabrics 8%; toys 6%. Tourism (1970): visitors 927,260; gross receipts HK$1,774,000,000.

Transport and Communications. Roads (1970) 975 km. Motor vehicles in use (1970): passenger 97,100; commercial (including buses) 29,200. Railways (1969) 35 km. Shipping (1971): merchant vessels 100 gross tons and over 108; gross tonnage 572,243. Ships entered (1970) vessels totaling 27,512,000 net registered tons. Shipping traffic (1971): goods loaded 3,-206,000 metric tons, unloaded 11,653,000 metric tons. Telephones (Dec. 1970) 583,000. Radio receivers (Dec. 1970) 694,000. Television receivers (Dec. 1969) 158,000.

ISLE OF MAN

The Isle of Man, a crown dependency, lies in the Irish Sea approximately 35 mi. from both Northern Ireland and the coast of northwestern England. Area: 221 sq.mi. (572 sq.km.). Pop. (1971): 56,289. Cap.: Douglas (pop., 1971, 20,-389).

Education. (1970–71) Primary, pupils 4,739; secondary and vocational, pupils 3,641.

Finance and Trade. Monetary unit: pound sterling. Budget (1971–72 est.): revenue £12,-784,000; expenditure £12,411,000. Foreign trade included with United Kingdom. Main exports: fish products, metal ores, tweeds. Tourism (1971) 465,000 visitors.

JERSEY

The island of Jersey, a crown dependency, is located about 20 mi. W of Normandy, France. Area: 45 sq.mi. (117 sq.km.). Pop. (1971): 72,-629. Cap.: St. Helier (pop., 1971, 28,135).

Education. (1970–71) Primary, pupils 5,460; secondary, pupils 3,245.

Finance and Trade. Monetary unit: Jersey pound, at par with the pound sterling. Budget

(1970): revenue £17,062,000; expenditure £15,950,000. Foreign trade included with United Kingdom. Main exports: potatoes, tomatoes. Tourism (1970) passengers arrived by sea 254,000, by air 565,000.

MONTSERRAT

The colony of Montserrat is located in the Caribbean between Antigua, 27 mi. NE, and Guadeloupe, 40 mi. SE. Area: 40 sq.mi. (102 sq.km.). Pop. (1971 est.): 13,076. Cap.: Plymouth (pop., 1971 est., 1,400).

Education. (1969–70) Primary, pupils 2,641, teachers 100; secondary, pupils 222, teachers 18; vocational, pupils 12, teachers 1; teacher training, students 12, teachers 3.

Finance and Trade. Monetary unit: East Caribbean dollar. Budget (1970 est.): revenue ECar$4,061,000; expenditure ECar$4,008,000. Foreign trade (1968): imports ECar$7,731,000; exports ECar$242,000. Main exports fruit and vegetables 18%.

PITCAIRN ISLAND

The colony of Pitcairn Island is in the central South Pacific, 3,200 mi. NE of New Zealand and 1,350 mi. SE of Tahiti. Area: 1.75 sq.mi. (4.53 sq.km.). Pop. (1972): 85. Cap. (de facto): Adamstown.

ST. HELENA

The colony of St. Helena, including its dependencies of Ascension and Tristan de Cunha islands, is located in the Atlantic off the southwestern coast of Africa. Area: 119 sq.mi. (308 sq.km.). Pop. (1971 est.): 6,562. Cap.: Jamestown (pop., 1969 est., 1,600).

Education. (1968–69) Primary, pupils 773, teachers 36; secondary and teacher training, pupils 334, teachers 31.

Finance and Trade. Monetary unit: pound sterling. Budget (1971 est.): revenue £688,500; expenditure £727,000. Foreign trade (1970): imports £472,000 (61% from U.K., 28% from South Africa in 1968); exports £200 (73% to U.K., 20% to South Africa in 1968).

ST. KITTS-NEVIS-ANGUILLA

This associated state consists of the islands of St. Kitts and Nevis; Anguilla was under direct British administration. Area: 135 sq.mi. (350 sq. km.). Pop. (1970): 64,000. Cap.: Basseterre, St. Kitts (pop., 1970, 13,055).

Education. (Including Anguilla; 1969–70) Primary, pupils 12,786, teachers 392; secondary, pupils 3,178, teachers 125; vocational, pupils 1,250, teachers 15.

Finance and Trade. Monetary unit: East Caribbean dollar. Budget (including Anguilla; 1971 est.): revenue ECar$13,174,000; expenditure ECar$15,475,000. Foreign trade (including Anguilla; 1969): imports ECar$19,304,000 (28% from U.K., 14% from Canada, 14% from U.S., 10% from Trinidad and Tobago, 5% from Barbados); exports ECar$8,621,000 (76% to U.K., 10% to Canada). Main exports: (St. Kitts-Nevis) sugar and preparations 88%; (Anguilla) postage stamps, salt.

ST. LUCIA

The Caribbean island of St. Lucia, an associated state, lies 24 mi. S of Martinique and 21 mi. NE of St. Vincent. Area: 238 sq.mi. (616 sq.km.). Pop. (1971 est.): 103,000. Cap.: Castries (pop., 1964 est., 5,100).

Education. (1969–70) Primary and secondary, pupils 25,571, teachers 854; teacher training, students 90, teachers 12.

Finance and Trade. Monetary unit: East Caribbean dollar. Budget (1971 est.): revenue ECar$18,345,000; expenditure ECar$18,546,000. Foreign trade (1969): imports ECar$41,468,000 (31% from U.K., 14% from U.S., 12% from Trinidad and Tobago, 11% from Canada, 6% from Netherlands Antilles, 5% from Barbados in 1968); exports ECar$11,170,000 (82% to U.K., 7% to Barbados in 1968). Main exports (1968): bananas 82%; copra 11%; coconut oil 5%. Tourism (1970): visitors 70,400; gross receipts (1969) ECar$7.2 million.

ST. VINCENT

St. Vincent, including the northern Grenadines, is an associated state in the eastern Caribbean about 100 mi. W of Barbados. Area: 150 sq.mi. (389 sq.km.). Pop. (1971 est.): 90,000. Cap.: Kingstown (pop., 1969 est., 4,994).

Education. (1969–70) Primary, pupils 36,089, teachers 843; secondary, pupils 3,004, teachers (1968–69) 92; vocational, pupils 225, teachers 3; teacher training, students 288, teachers 25.

Finance and Trade. Monetary unit: East Caribbean dollar. Budget (1971 est.) balanced at ECar$25,047,000. Foreign trade (1969): imports ECar$24,651,000 (31% from U.K., 16% from Trinidad and Tobago, 12% from Canada, 11% from U.S. in 1967); exports ECar$7,371,000 (57% to U.K., 14% to Trinidad and Tobago, 9% to U.S. in 1967). Main exports: bananas 55%; arrowroot 14%.

SEYCHELLES

The colony of Seychelles consists of a group of about 80 islands scattered over 400,000 sq.mi. in the western Indian Ocean northeast of Madagascar. Area: 107 sq.mi. (278 sq.km.). Pop. (1972 est.): 54,000. Cap.: Victoria, Mahé (pop., 1972 est., 14,000).

Education. (1970) Primary, pupils 9,224, teachers 381; secondary, pupils 2,131, teachers 106; vocational, pupils 228, teachers 14; higher, students 87, teaching staff 7.

Finance and Trade. Monetary unit: Seychelles rupee, with (Sept. 18, 1972) a free rate of SRs. 5.45 to U.S. $1 (SRs. 13.33 = £1 sterling). Budget (1970 est.): revenue SRs. 37,599,000 (including overseas loans and grant-in-aid of SRs. 15,573,000); expenditure SRs. 25,466,000. Foreign trade (1970): imports SRs. 55,924,000; exports SRs. 10,164,000. Import sources: U.K. 43%; Kenya 8%; Netherlands 7%; South Africa 6%. Export destinations: India 50%; U.S. 30%; U.S.S.R. 7%; U.K. 5%; Mauritius 5%. Main exports: copra 50%; cinnamon bark 36%.

TURKS AND CAICOS ISLANDS

The colony of the Turks and Caicos Islands is situated in the Atlantic southeast of the Bahamas. Area: 166 sq.mi. (430 sq.km.). Pop. (1971 est.): 6,000. Seat of government: Grand Turk Island (pop., 1970, 2,330).

Education. (1968) Primary, pupils 1,527, teachers 82; secondary, pupils 165, teachers 10.

Finance and Trade. Monetary unit: Jamaican dollar. Ordinary budget (1969 actual): revenue Jam$1,363,000; expenditure Jam$1,367,000. Foreign trade (1969): imports Jam$993,000; exports Jam$216,000. Main exports: crayfish 96%; salt 4%.

UNITED KINGDOM and FRANCE

NEW HEBRIDES

The British-French condominium of the New Hebrides is located in the southwestern Pacific about 500 mi. W of Fiji and 250 mi. NE of New Caledonia. Area: 5,700 sq.mi. (14,800 sq.km.). Pop. (1972 est.): 86,000. Cap.: Vila (pop., 1972 est., 8,500).

Education. (1970) Primary, pupils 18,250, teachers 778; secondary, pupils 541, teachers 50; vocational, pupils 143, teachers 12; teacher training, students 100, teachers 9.

Finance. Monetary units: Australian dollar and New Hebridean franc, with a free rate (Sept. 18, 1972) of NHFr. 81 = U.S. $1 (NHFr. 198.1 = £1 sterling). Condominium budget (1970 est.) balanced at A$4,021,000. British administration budget (1970–71 est.) balanced at A$2,107,000. French administration budget (1970 est.) balanced at A$4,718,000.

Foreign Trade. (1971) Imports A$18,142,000; exports A$12,849,000. Import sources: Australia 39%; France 16%; Japan 12%; U.K. 7%. Export destinations: U.S. 37%; France 34%; Japan 18%; New Caledonia 7%. Main exports: fish 51%; copra 33%.

Agriculture. Copra production (metric tons; 1971) *c.* 40,000, (1970) 31,000.

UNITED STATES

AMERICAN SAMOA

Located to the east of Western Samoa in the South Pacific, the unincorporated territory of American Samoa is approximately 1,600 mi. NE of the northern tip of New Zealand. Area: 77 sq.mi. (200 sq.km.). Pop. (1970): 27,159. Cap.: Pago Pago (pop., 1970, 2,451).

Education. (1969–70) Primary, pupils 7,957, teachers 356; secondary and vocational, pupils 2,122, teachers 119.

Finance and Trade. Monetary unit: U.S. dollar. Budget (1970 est.) revenue $14,446,000 (including U.S. grant $9,423,000). Foreign trade (1970): imports $15,713,000 (91% from U.S.); exports $36,735,000 (96% to U.S.). Main exports: canned tuna 90%; pet food 5%.

CANAL ZONE

The Canal Zone is administered by the U.S. under treaty with Panama and consists of a 10-mi.-wide strip on the Isthmus of Panama through which the Panama Canal runs. Area (land only): 362 sq.mi. (964 sq.km.). Pop. (1970): 44,198. Administrative headquarters: Balboa Heights (pop., 1970, 232).

Education. (1968–69) Primary, pupils 8,693, teachers 358; secondary and vocational, pupils 5,709, teachers 265; higher, students 1,190, teaching staff 70.

Finance. Monetary unit: U.S. dollar (Panamanian balboa is also used). Budgets: (Canal Zone government; 1970) revenue $43,695,000, expenditure $43,768,000; (Panama Canal Company; 1970) revenue $175,096,000, expenditure $173,989,000.

Traffic. (1970–71) Total number of oceangoing vessels passing through the canal 14,020; total cargo tonnage 118,626,906; tolls collected U.S. $97,380,000. Nationality and number of commercial vessels using the canal: Liberian 1,587; British 1,558; Japanese 1,462; U.S. 1,368; Norwegian 1,202; West German 1,069; Panamanian 948; Greek 629; Netherlands 494; Swedish 479; Danish 454.

GUAM

Guam, an organized unincorporated territory, is located in the Pacific Ocean about 6,000 mi. SW of San Francisco and 1,500 mi. E of Manila. Area: 209 sq.mi. (541 sq.km.). Pop. (1970): 84,996. Cap.: Agana (pop., 1970, 2,119).

Education. (1969) Primary (including preprimary), pupils 17,618, teachers 650; secondary, pupils 9,607, teachers 491; higher, students 2,215, teaching staff 100.

Finance and Trade. Monetary unit: U.S. dollar. Budget (1968 est.): revenue $36,241,000 (including U.S. grants $3,989,000); expenditure $38,984,000. Foreign trade (U.S. trade only): imports (1969) $45,539,000; exports (1970) $6,686,000. Tourism (1970) *c.* 50,000 visitors.

Agriculture and Industry. Main crops: corn, sweet potatoes, lemons, cassava. Industrial production (1969): stone 593,000 metric tons; electricity 698 million kw-hr.

PUERTO RICO

Puerto Rico, a self-governing associated commonwealth, lies about 885 mi. SE of the Florida coast. Area: 3,421 sq.mi. (8,860 sq.km.). Pop. (1972 est.): 2,824,700. Cap.: San Juan (pop., 1972 est., 471,558).

Education. (1969–70) Primary (including preprimary), pupils 481,700, teachers 14,960; secondary and vocational, pupils 261,850, teachers 9,580; higher (including 3 universities), students 56,681, teaching staff *c.* 3,500.

Finance. Monetary unit: U.S. dollar. Budget (1969–70): revenue $1,210,000,000; expenditure $1,081,000,000. Gross domestic product: (1970–71) $5,464,000,000; (1969–70) $4,857,000,000. Cost of living (1963 = 100): (May 1972) 132; (May 1971) 127.

Foreign Trade. (1969–70) Imports $2,681,000,000 (77% from U.S.); exports $1,680,000,000 (93% to U.S.). Main exports (1968–69): clothing 21%; petroleum products 9%; chemicals 9%; electrical machinery and equipment 8%; cigars 6%; shellfish 5%; sugar 5%. Tourism (1970): visitors 1,088,000; gross receipts U.S. $223 million.

Transport and Communications. Roads (motorable; 1970) 7,356 km. Motor vehicles in use (1970): passenger 499,800; commercial (including buses) 102,600. Telephones (Dec. 1970) 306,000. Radio receivers (Dec. 1969) 1,625,000. Television receivers (Dec. 1969) 410,000.

Agriculture. Production (in 000; metric tons; 1970; 1969 in parentheses): bananas 114 (113); sweet potatoes 21 (23); coffee (1971) *c.* 10, (1970) 15; sugar, raw value (1971–72) *c.* 259, (1970–71) *c.* 291; tobacco *c.* 2.9 (3.6); pineapples 57 (49); oranges 29 (33); grapefruit 10 (9); milk *c.* 400 (*c.* 385). Livestock (in 000; Jan. 1971): cattle 530; pigs 196; chickens 4,311.

Industry. Production (in 000; metric tons; 1971): cement 1,792; sand and gravel (1969) 8,557; stone (1969) 6,337; electricity (kw-hr.) 9,156,000.

TRUST TERRITORY OF THE PACIFIC ISLANDS

The Trust Territory islands, numbering more than 2,000, are scattered over 3 million sq.mi. in the Pacific Ocean from 450 mi. E of the Philippines to just west of the International Date Line. Area: 717 sq.mi. (1,857 sq.km.). Pop. (1971 est.): 107,054. Seat of government: Saipan Island (pop., 1971 est., 10,458).

Education. (1969–70) Primary, pupils 28,360, teachers 1,210; secondary, pupils 5,186, teachers 260; vocational, pupils 68, teachers 7; teacher training (1968–69), students 971, teachers 55.

Finance and Trade. Monetary unit: U.S. dollar. Budget (1971 est.): revenue $62,916,000 (including U.S. grant $59,295,000); expenditure $51,391,000. Foreign trade (1971): imports $26.1 million (50% from U.S., 28% from Japan in 1968); exports $3 million (57% to Japan). Main exports: copra 55%; fish 30%; meat, fruit, and vegetables 8%.

Agriculture. Production (in 000; metric tons; 1970; 1969 in parentheses): copra *c.* 13 (13); bananas *c.* 2 (*c.* 2). Livestock (in 000; June 1971): cattle 9; pigs 19; goats 5; poultry 154.

VIRGIN ISLANDS

The Virgin Islands of the United States is an organized unincorporated territory located about 40 mi. E of Puerto Rico. Area: 133 sq.mi. (344 sq.km.). Pop. (1970): 62,468. Cap.: Charlotte Amalie, St. Thomas (pop., 1970, 12,220).

Education. (1969–70) Primary (including preprimary), pupils 12,800, teachers 500; secondary and vocational, pupils 4,800, teachers 330; higher, students 1,425, teaching staff 40.

Finance and Trade. Monetary unit: U.S. dollar. Budget (1970 actual): revenue $105,903,000; expenditure $94,757,000. Foreign trade (1970): imports $410,615,000 (41% from U.S.); exports $262,168,000 (93% to U.S.). Main exports: petroleum products, watches, rum, fish. Tourism (1968–69): visitors *c.* 1.1 million; gross receipts *c.* $100 million.

Industry. Production (1969): stone 373,000 metric tons; electricity 387.5 million kw-hr.

Development, Economic

In contrast to the earlier emphasis on economic growth in the less developed countries, greater attention was being paid in 1972 to the "newer" development problems, among them population growth, poverty, malnutrition, unemployment, income distribution, education, urbanization, and environmental deterioration. In a sense, this marked a merging of the problems of the developed and less developed nations. For example, in *The Limits to Growth,* a study sponsored by the Club of Rome (an informal international association of citizens concerned with global problems), population, agricultural production, industrialization, environmental pollution, and the consumption of nonrenewable resources were measured and projected on a worldwide scale. The study concluded that if growth of these factors was not halted, there would be a general collapse of the earth's life-support systems.

Basic agreement on the need for action in these areas emerged at the 114-nation UN Conference on the Human Environment, held in Stockholm in June, but there was also evidence of a divergence in emphases. The poorer countries were less concerned with the environmental end products of industrialization, such as air pollution, and tended to define environmental quality in broader terms. Thus India and Libya proposed that an international fund be set up to help improve housing and other aspects of "residential environment" in the third world nations. (*See* ENVIRONMENT.)

Clearly the less developed nations were demanding a greater voice in decisions affecting them, and nowhere was this more evident than in the area of international finance. The less developed countries had not contributed to the recurring monetary crises that culminated in the 1971 devaluation of the U.S. dollar, but they were affected by the breakdown of the existing international monetary system and were eager to play an influential role in the shaping of a new one. Hitherto, international monetary matters had been decided largely by the Group of Ten major industrial nations. In 1972, after considerable international negotiation, it was decided to establish a new committee of the Board of Governors of the International Monetary Fund, to be known as the Committee on Reform of the International Monetary System and Related Issues or, more informally, as the Group of Twenty. All members of the Fund, including the less developed countries, would have a voice in choosing the committee membership. Along similar lines, early in September the executive directors of the Fund published a study that considered, among other matters, the position and interest of the less developed countries in the working of the international monetary system and the possibilities for increasing the flow of resources for development purposes within the framework of a reformed system. (*See* PAYMENTS AND RESERVES, INTERNATIONAL.)

Part of the impetus toward increased participation of the less developed countries in deliberations on the monetary system came from the third meeting of the UN Conference on Trade and Development (UNCTAD), held in Santiago, Chile, in April–May 1972. There was agreement within UNCTAD III that the less developed countries had a right to a larger voice in the determination of international monetary policy, and the conference also called on the Fund to study ways of using its Special Drawing Rights (SDRs or "paper gold") to assist development. Perhaps even more important was the clear recognition by UNCTAD III of the special needs of the least developed nations. The UN General Assembly had identified these as Afghanistan, Botswana, Bhutan, Burundi, Chad, Dahomey, Ethiopia, Guinea, Haiti, Laos, Lesotho, Malawi, Maldives, Mali, Nepal, Niger, Rwanda, Sikkim, Somalia, Sudan, Tanzania, Uganda, Upper Volta, Western Samoa, and Yemen (San'a'). UNCTAD III adopted a detailed resolution spelling out measures needed to assist these countries in a number of fields, including trade, shipping, financial aid, and technical assistance.

Growth. In 1971 the combined gross domestic product (GDP) of the less developed countries grew at a rate of 6.9%, substantially higher than the average for the decade of the 1960s and above the 6.5% reached in 1970. (*See* Table I.) This relatively favourable performance was also reflected in a rise in the growth of per capita income, even though population expanded in 1971 at a somewhat higher rate than in 1970. As always, the overall figures disguised important regional variations. Africa and south Asia were considerably below the average, while the Middle East was much above it. Brazil was an example of outstanding progress and reached a per capita income of over $400.

Thus, although the efforts to achieve a slowdown in population growth rates had not shown significant results in the less developed world as a whole, the efforts of past years to increase output capacity were reaping substantial benefits. As in previous years, the less developed countries as a group grew more rapidly in 1971 than the developed countries as a group.

The low-income countries did not do as well in increasing output in the critically important agricultural sector, however. Although the need to improve agricultural production was generally recognized as having a very high priority, in 1971, when world agricultural production was estimated to have increased by 4% (compared with a 2% gain in 1970), the less developed countries gained only 2 to 3%, allowing for no increase in per capita agricultural output. In Latin America the increase was well below the rate of population growth.

Ironically, though the need for increased food production was much greater in the low-income countries than in those with high incomes, the richer countries were expanding agricultural production more rapidly. Furthermore, this was being achieved despite the continuing steep decline in the agricultural population. Agriculture in the developed countries was becoming a capital-intensive rather than a labour-intensive industry, with larger outputs stemming from progress in the application of technology to agriculture, new varieties of cereals and other crops, and greater application of fertilizer and other purchased inputs. Thus the much-heralded Green Revolution in the third world had been overtaken by a more widespread, more rapid, and more secure Green Revolution in the developed countries, an experience that typified the problems of trying to reduce the inequalities between rich and poor countries. Moreover, the Green Revolution in the less developed countries had given rise to serious social and economic problems, including unemployment and greater inequality of income. In the developed countries the resulting social and economic disturbances were much less drastic, and the countries concerned were able to cope with them much more effectively.

Foreign Trade. International trade fared relatively poorly in 1971. World trade volume grew at a rate of 5½%, considerably lower than the average rate of increase for the 1960s. Foreign trade prices continued to advance, however—by about 5½% measured in U.S. dollars. The principal reason for the slower growth of world trade in 1971 was the cyclical slowdown of economic activity in continental Europe and Japan. The higher prices reflected primarily the pervasiveness and intensity of inflationary forces in the main industrial countries.

For the less developed countries, 1971 was marked by generally weaker gains in export volume and by sagging average prices for primary products other than petroleum. (*See* Table II.) With the prices of their imports (mostly the exports of the industrialized countries) continuing to rise, the purchasing power of these countries' export earnings apparently suffered

Table I. Selected Economic Indicators for Less Developed and Industrialized Countries, Regional Summary

Region	Average annual real rates of growth (%)						Shares in GNP (%)	
	Total GDP	Agricultural production	Manufacturing production	Population	GDP per capita	Total gross investment	Gross investment	Savings
Less developed countries*								
1961–66	5.1	2.4	8.3	2.5	2.6	6.7	18.4	15.8
1970	6.5	2.5	7.6	2.5	3.9	7.5	19.7	16.6
1971†	6.9	3.1	...	2.6	4.2	...	...	...
Africa								
1961–66	4.4	2.1	9.7	2.5	1.9	5.9	16.2	12.7
1970	7.4	0.6	8.3	2.6	4.7	14.8	19.9	16.2
1971†	4.6	4.1	...	2.7	1.8	...	...	...
Southern Europe								
1961–66	7.1	4.1	11.6	1.4	5.6	11.1	24.2	20.9
1970	6.2	0.7	6.0	1.5	4.6	8.3	24.0	20.8
1971†	7.1	8.1	...	1.5	5.5	...	...	...
East Asia								
1961–66	5.6	3.8	9.4	2.7	2.8	12.6	15.2	11.0
1970	6.8	4.3	10.2	2.7	3.9	7.4	19.4	15.4
1971†	7.1	3.9	...	2.8	4.2	...	...	...
Middle East								
1961–66	7.3	4.6	9.8	3.0	4.2	7.9	19.3	14.2
1970	8.0	—4.3	8.9	3.1	4.7	7.3	21.6	14.4
1971†	10.2	—0.1	...	3.1	7.0	...	...	...
South Asia								
1961–66	3.3	0.6	8.0	2.4	0.9	3.6	16.3	13.3
1970	5.0	4.1	7.4	2.4	2.6	4.3	14.5	12.4
1971†	4.8	1.8	...	2.4	2.4	...	...	...
Western Hemisphere								
1961–66	5.1	3.2	6.0	3.0	2.0	4.0	18.6	17.8
1970	7.0	1.7	8.0	3.1	3.8	6.8	20.3	18.1
1971†	8.2	1.7	...	3.1	5.0	...	...	...
Industrialized countries‡								
1961–66	5.3	1.9	6.3	1.2	4.0	6.6	21.6	22.1
1970	2.6	0.5	3.9	1.1	1.5	2.1	22.3	22.9
1971†	4.0	6.2	...	1.0	2.9	...	...	...

*Less developed countries (75 countries and territories covering approximately 96% of GDP of all less developed areas with market economies): Africa—Algeria, Angola, Cameroon, Egypt, Ethiopia, Gabon, Ghana, Ivory Coast, Kenya, Libya, Malagasy Republic, Malawi, Mali, Mauritius, Morocco, Niger, Nigeria, Rhodesia, Senegal, Sudan, Tanzania, Togo, Tunisia, Uganda, Upper Volta, Zaire, Zambia (coverage 91%); south Asia—Bangladesh, Burma, India, Pakistan, Sri Lanka (coverage 100%); east Asia—Hong Kong, Indonesia, Korea, Malaysia, Philippines, Singapore, Taiwan, Thailand, Vietnam (coverage 98%); southern Europe—Cyprus, Greece, Portugal, Spain, Turkey, Yugoslavia (coverage 100%); Western Hemisphere—Argentina, Bolivia, Brazil, Chile, Colombia, Costa Rica, Dominican Republic, Ecuador, El Salvador, Guatemala, Guyana, Haiti, Honduras, Jamaica, Mexico, Nicaragua, Panama, Paraguay, Peru, Trinidad and Tobago, Uruguay, Venezuela (coverage 99%); Middle East—Iran, Iraq, Israel, Jordan, Lebanon, Syria (coverage 78%).

†Preliminary.

‡Industrialized countries: Australia, Austria, Belgium, Canada, Denmark, Finland, France, Germany, Iceland, Ireland, Italy, Japan, Luxembourg, Netherlands, New Zealand, Norway, South Africa, Sweden, Switzerland, United Kingdom, United States.

Source: World Bank.

Table II. Trade Balance of Less Developed Countries

In U.S. $000,000,000

Item	1966	1967	1968	1969	1970	1971*
Less developed countries						
Exports (f.o.b.)	42.0	43.8	47.3	53.7	60.3	67.1
Imports (c.i.f.)	48.2	49.7	53.8	59.7	67.8	75.6
Trade balance	—6.2	—5.9	—6.5	—6.0	—7.5	—8.5
Excluding less developed countries of southern Europe†						
Exports (f.o.b.)	38.0	39.4	43.2	48.4	54.1	60.0
Imports (c.i.f.)	40.1	41.6	45.2	49.7	55.7	63.2
Trade balance	—2.1	—2.2	—2.0	—1.3	—1.6	—3.2
Excluding southern Europe and major petroleum exporters‡						
Exports (f.o.b.)	29.4	29.8	32.5	37.1	41.6	44.4§
Imports (c.i.f.)	35.7	36.9	39.8	43.9	49.7	55.5§
Trade balance	—6.3	—7.1	—7.3	—6.8	—8.1	—11.1

*Preliminary.

†Greece, Portugal, Spain, Turkey, Yugoslavia.

‡Iran, Iraq, Kuwait, Libya, Saudi Arabia, Venezuela.

§Estimate for Saudi Arabia based on first quarter data. Estimate for Libya based on data for first three quarters.

Source: International Monetary Fund, *International Financial Statistics*.

Table III. Total Official and Other Flows of Long-Term Financial Resources (Net)* from DAC Countries to Less Developed Countries and Multilateral Agencies by Country

In U.S. $000,000

Country	Official flows				Other flows				Total flows			
	1968	1969	1970	1971	1968	1969	1970*	1971*	1968	1969	1970†	1971
Australia	160	175	202	202	46	57	179	187	206	232	381	38
Austria	23	15	19	10	51	66	77	83	74	81	96	93
Belgium	88	116	120	143	155	141	189	157	243	257	309	300
Canada	175	245	346	342	133	119	280	418	308	364	626	766
Denmark	29	54	59	74	54	97	27	64	83	151	86	138
France	853	955	1,006	1,107	867	755	863	549	1,720	1,710	1,869	1,659
Germany, West	557	579	599	734	1,106	1,449	888	1,181	1,663	2,028	1,487	1,915
Italy	146	130	147	173	404	718	535	689	550	848	682	862
Japan	356	436	458	511	693	827	1,366	1,630	1,049	1,263	1,824	2,141
Netherlands	123	143	196	216	153	226	261	374	276	369	457	590
Norway	27	30	37	42	32	45	30	23	59	75	67	65
Portugal	27	58	39	52	21	40	30	57	48	98	69	109
Sweden	71	121	117	159	58	91	112	84	129	212	229	243
Switzerland	24	29	30	28	215	90	107	192	239	119	137	220
United Kingdom	415	431	447	561	346	715	832	1,009	761	1,146	1,279	1,570
United States	3,242	3,092	3,050	3,324	2,775	1,733	3,204	3,721	6,017	4,825	6,254	7,045
Total	6,316	6,610	6,873	7,679	7,109	7,169	8,978	10,417	13,425	13,779	15,851	18,096

*Net of loan repayments and private capital repatriation.

†Including grants by voluntary agencies.

Source: OECD, *Development Assistance Committee*.

Table IV. Average Terms of Official Development Assistance Loan Commitments

Country	Average maturity (years)		Average interest rate (%)	
	1970	1971	1970	1971
Total DAC countries	30.2	28.6*	2.8	2.7*
United States	37.4	34.8*	2.6	2.9*
United Kingdom	28.6	24.0*	1.7	1.1*
France	16.7	...	3.8	...
Germany, West	27.6	29.6	2.9	2.0
Italy	13.1	13.1	4.9	3.1
Japan	21.4	22.1	3.7	3.5

*Provisional.

Source: OECD, Development Assistance Committee.

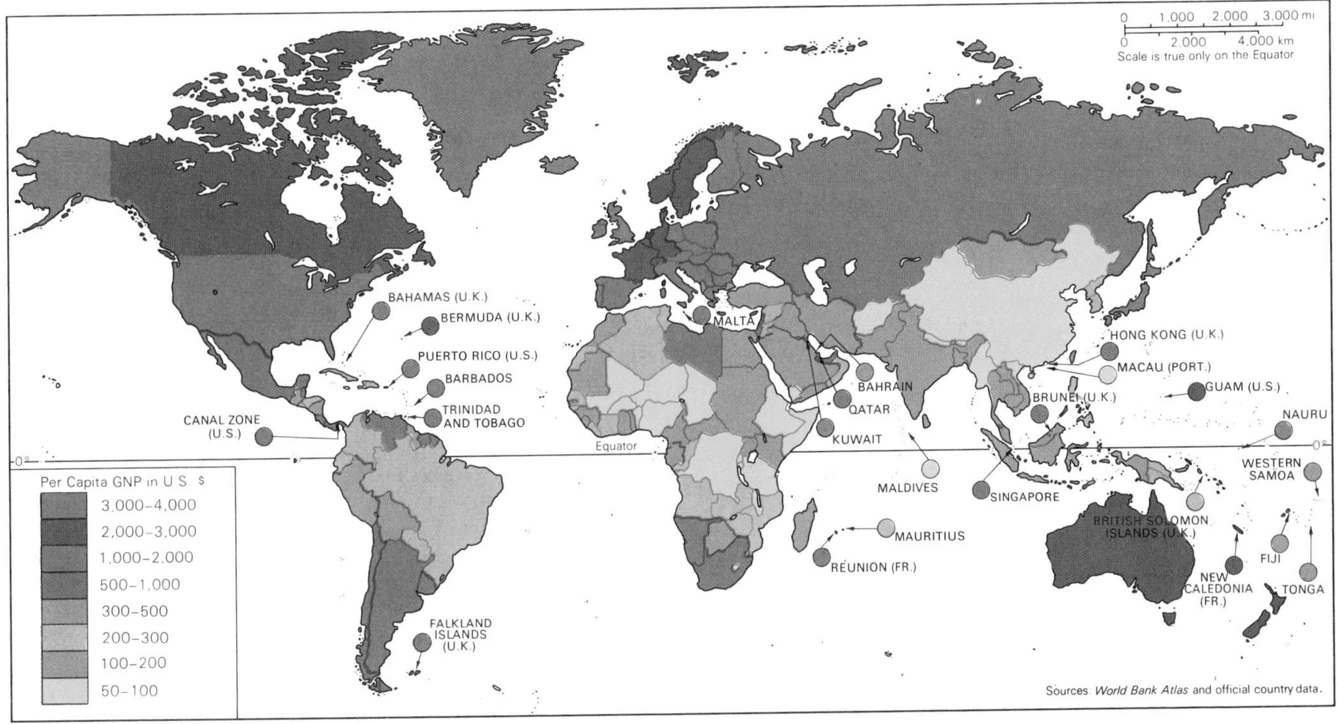

a net decline. It was expected that their trade balance might deteriorate further in 1972 as a result of the 1971 and 1972 realignments of currencies among the industrialized nations. For the first time in many years, the rate of growth of imports did not parallel the corresponding changes in exports. Instead, imports in 1971 were exceptionally high.

The less developed countries' need to increase exports was greater than ever; more exports were needed to help deal with the problems of external debt accumulation and debt servicing and to encourage higher levels of output and investment. But when, as was the case in 1971, business conditions slacken in the developed countries but remain strong in the less developed countries, the export markets of the less developed countries weaken while their demand for imports remains strong. The situation was exacerbated by the inflation in the industrialized countries, which raised the prices of imports even further. (*See* TRADE, INTERNATIONAL.)

Domestic Savings. As indicated in Table I, domestic savings financed over 85% of total investment in the less developed countries. This meant that, on average, over 16% of the gross national product (GNP equals GDP plus net factor payments on foreign investments) had been saved despite the low per capita income. From this viewpoint, the savings efforts of the low-income countries were much more impressive than the comparable efforts of the industrialized countries, where 22–23% of GNP was saved but per capita income was much higher. These savings efforts, combined with the inflow of foreign resources, enabled the less developed countries to maintain gross investment rates that exceed their savings rates. Nevertheless, investment rates, on average, were still higher in the industrialized countries, a fact that helped explain the continuing very wide differences in per capita income between the two groups of countries. The marked difference in population rates was another key factor. If the less developed countries could achieve a significant decline in population growth coupled with an increase in investment, the inequalities of income among the world's countries could be sharply reduced.

Given the widespread and growing unemployment in the less developed countries, the question arose how best to utilize the limited savings and foreign inflows to achieve the best combination of increased productive capacity and improved employment conditions. The pressures of necessity were causing a basic reexamination of long-held assumptions about savings, investment, employment, and growth. Progress was being made, but more savings were hard to achieve. Increasing attention was being paid to ways of using savings more effectively in light of available resources of manpower and capital.

Table V. External Public Debt Outstanding and Debt Service Payments for Less Developed Countries*

In U.S. $000,000

Year	Total	Africa	East Asia†	Middle East‡	South Asia	Southern Europe§	Western Hemisphere‖
Debt outstanding, Dec. 31							
1967	48,303	8,181	5,290	3,678	11,295	5,116	14,743
1968	54,315	9,019	6,295	4,364	12,666	5,601	16,369
1969	60,174	9,688	7,776	5,018	13,654	6,368	17,671
1970—Total	66,699	10,694	9,195	5,733	14,742	6,963	19,372
—Disbursed	50,618	7,626	6,738	3,909	11,848	5,166	15,332
—Undisbursed	16,081	3,068	2,457	1,824	2,894	1,798	4,041
Service payments during							
1967	4,012	461	259	230	561	443	2,058
1968	4,525	596	286	334	595	503	2,211
1969	4,997	682	387	452	689	542	2,246
1970	5,890	788	614	479	746	702	2,560

Note: Items may not add to totals due to rounding.

*Includes the following countries: Africa—Botswana, Burundi, Cameroon, Central African Republic, Chad, Dahomey, Egypt, Ethiopia, Gabon, Ghana, Guinea, Ivory Coast, Kenya, Lesotho, Liberia, Malagasy Republic, Malawi, Mali, Mauritania, Mauritius, Morocco, Niger, Nigeria, Rhodesia, Rwanda, Senegal, Sierra Leone, Somalia, Sudan, Swaziland, Tanzania, Togo, Tunisia, Uganda, Upper Volta, Zaire, Zambia, plus the East African Community; east Asia—Indonesia, Malaysia, Philippines, South Korea, Singapore, Taiwan, Thailand; Middle East—Iran, Iraq, Israel, Jordan, Syria; south Asia—Afghanistan, India, Pakistan (incl. Bangladesh), Sri Lanka; southern Europe—Cyprus, Greece, Malta, Spain, Turkey, Yugoslavia; Western Hemisphere—Argentina, Bolivia, Brazil, Chile, Colombia, Costa Rica, Dominican Republic, Ecuador, El Salvador, Guatemala, Guyana, Honduras, Jamaica, Mexico, Nicaragua, Panama, Paraguay, Peru, Trinidad and Tobago, Uruguay, Venezuela.

†Does not include publicly guaranteed private debt of the Philippines estimated at $600 million in 1970.

‡Does not include undisbursed portion of the debt of Israel.

§Does not include nonguaranteed debt of the "social sector" of Yugoslavia contracted after March 31, 1966.

‖Debt outstanding of Brazil includes some nonguaranteed debt of the private sector to suppliers and excludes the undisbursed portion of suppliers' credits and of bilateral official loans except for those owed to the U.S. government. It excludes financial credits that are mostly to the private sector.

Source: World Bank.

As might be expected, the differences in the savings/investment picture in the less developed world were great. The poorest countries and regions presented a far different picture from those less developed countries with higher incomes, *e.g.,* in Latin America and southern Europe, which came much closer to the average found in the industrialized countries.

External Sources of Finance. In 1971 there was a marked increase in the total net flows of long-term financial resources to the less developed countries and the multilateral agencies from the member countries of the Development Assistance Committee (DAC) of the Organization for Economic Cooperation and Development (OECD). (*See* Table III.) However, the total of about $18 billion was still below the UN target of 1% of the GNP of the industrialized countries.

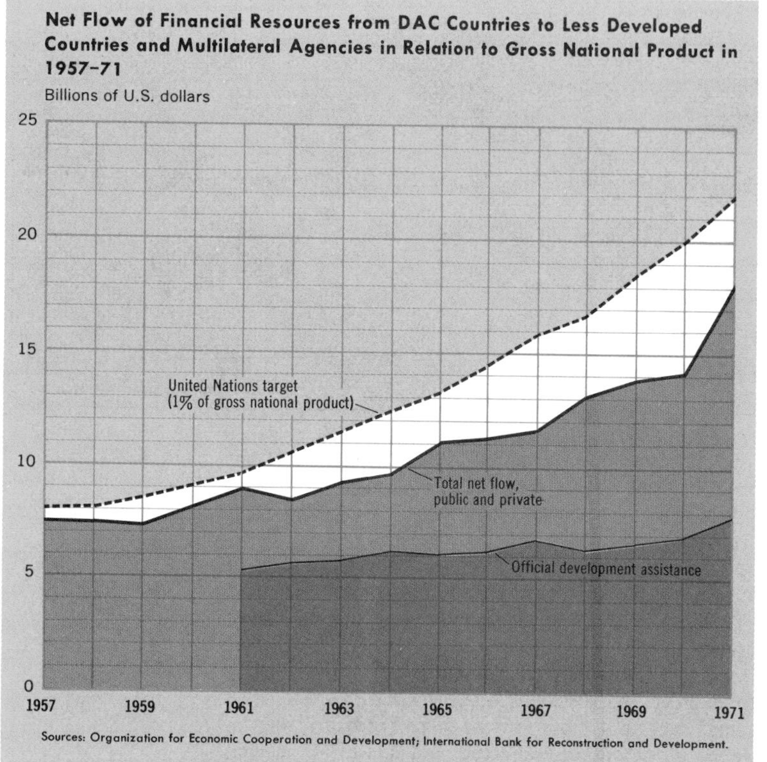

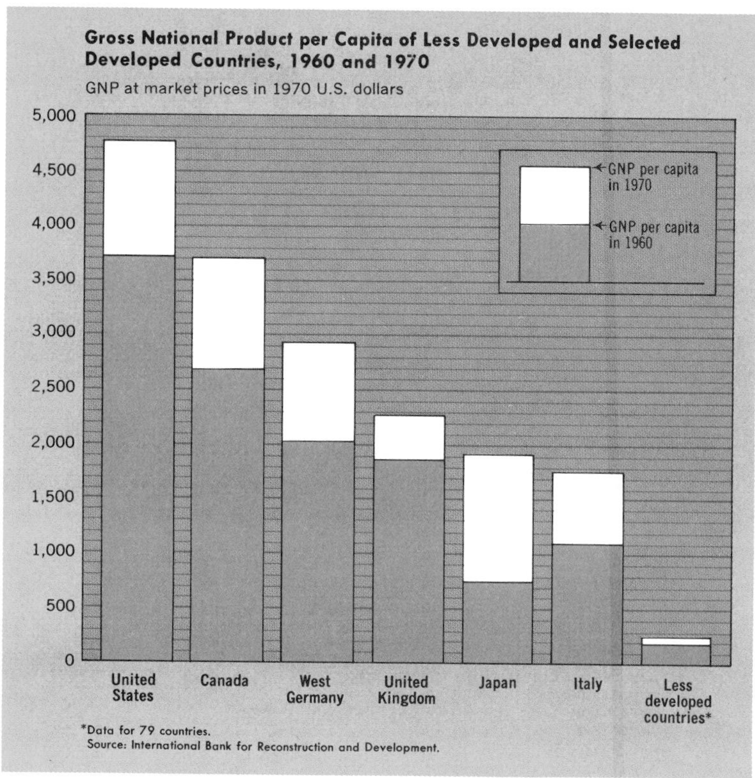

As in the past, the U.S. was the largest single source, providing over $7 billion. This figure was of particular interest because the U.S. was experiencing intense external financial difficulties. Long-term capital flows, however, reflect commitments made in previous years and do not react quickly to changes in current conditions unless governments intervene to suspend or interrupt them. The U.S. government took no such steps in 1971; indeed, U.S. flows during that year were estimated to have been more than $700 million above the 1970 level. Japan was the second largest supplier of capital to the less developed countries; its net capital exports were well below those of the U.S., but above the levels of West Germany, France, and the United Kingdom, the other leading suppliers. Australia and Canada contributed smaller but still notable amounts.

Official Development Assistance. Official development assistance rose markedly during 1971 as compared with 1970 and 1969. The U.S. and West Germany accounted for most of the increase. The U.S. provided about 40% of the total. France was second, followed by Japan and the United Kingdom. Total official assistance in 1971 represented less than 0.43% of the GNP of the donor countries.

The average maturity of official loan commitments declined in 1971 as compared with 1970, though it was still above the 28.1-year average of 1969. (*See* Table IV.) Average interest rates also fell somewhat. The sharp differences in terms among donor countries could be seen in the average lengths of maturity—as short as 13.1 years for Italy and as long as 34.8 years for the U.S. Differences in interest rates were also evident, with U.S. rates rising and others declining. Most of France's official assistance was on a grant basis.

There was evidence of increasing U.S. reluctance to provide development assistance, and it was clear that other resources would need to be developed. A hopeful trend was the increasing importance of the multilateral agencies, particularly the World Bank Group (the World Bank, the International Development Association [IDA], and the International Finance Corporation). During their fiscal year ended June 30, 1972, the World Bank and IDA approved loans totaling nearly $3 billion, and lending operations for the Group as a whole had expanded 136% over the 1964–68 average. However, the implementation of about $320 million of loans extended by IDA awaited action by the U.S.

Other Flows. Also important in the development picture are flows of private capital and of official funds that do not qualify as development assistance; *e.g.,* official export credits. Private flows include direct investment and private export credits. Increasingly important were direct private investments in securities of multilateral agencies, such as bonds issued by the World Bank, the Inter-American Development Bank, and the Asian Development Bank. As seen in Table III, such flows rose markedly in 1971, exceeding the figure for official development assistance by about $2.5 billion, and accounted for a very large proportion of the increase in total flows in 1971 as compared with 1970. The largest increases in this category were in flows from the U.S., West Germany, and Japan.

In many respects increased private flows are welcome, but they can increase external debt burden excessively. Private borrowing may be done on onerous terms because official development assistance is inadequate. In this connection, the increased participation by less developed countries in international capital markets is noteworthy. Borrowing for development in 1971 reached a new high of nearly $2.3 billion, an increase of 40% above the level of 1970. About 80% of this total ($1.8 billion) represented marketings by international institutions; the remainder was borrowings by the less developed countries themselves. The multinational institutions can borrow at lower interest rates than are available to the less developed countries and can pass this advantage along in the loans they make. However, even these rates are "hard" for poor countries.

External Public Debt. The external public indebtedness of the less developed countries continued to rise. As of the end of 1970, it was estimated at about $66.7 billion, of which about $16 billion was still undisbursed. The $66.7 billion represented more than a 10% increase over the previous year. (*See* Table V.)

Western Hemisphere nations owed the largest single bloc of external debt, probably more than $20 billion by mid-1972. Service payments on this debt exceeded $2.5 billion. South Asia was next, but its service payments were much lower because more of the debt was incurred on "developmental" terms. Nations owing the largest sums were Argentina, Brazil, Chile, Colombia, India, Indonesia, Iran, Israel, Mexico, Pakistan (combining the figures for Pakistan and Bangladesh), South Korea, Spain, Turkey, and Yugoslavia.

Debt service payments increased about 10% per year in the 1960s, partly because of stiffer terms on borrowing and partly because some of the major debtor countries like Indonesia undertook multilateral debt negotiations in the latter part of the decade. In 1970 service payments rose even more sharply—almost twice the recent average—and the increase in private and other capital flows could well point to an acceleration of the already onerous problems of external debt servicing. During the year debt negotiations took place with Chile, Egypt, Ghana, India, Pakistan, and Yugoslavia. (IRVING S. FRIEDMAN)

See also Agriculture; Commodities, Primary; Industrial Review; Inter-American Affairs; Investment, International.

Disasters

The loss of life and property in disasters during 1972 included the following. (*See also* METEOROLOGY.)

AVIATION

Jan. 7 Ibiza I. off Valencia, Spain. Spanish Iberia Airlines Caravelle commercial passenger jet en route from Valencia to the Mediterranean island of Ibiza crashed into a mist-covered rocky peak as it made an approach to the Ibiza Airport; all 104 persons aboard were killed instantly.
Jan. 21 Northern Colombia. Colombian Satena Airlines DC-3 crashed and burned in the Andes Mountains killing 35 persons.
Jan. 21 Bogotá, Colombia. Colombian Airlines turboprop failed to gain altitude after taking off in a rainstorm, fell to the ground, and brought death to 20 persons.
Jan. 26 Northwestern Czechoslovakia. Yugoslav Airlines DC-9 jetliner en route from Stockholm to Belgrade exploded in mid-air and plunged into a snow-covered mountain slope; 27 of the 28 persons aboard perished, a stewardess survived the 31,000-ft. drop.
March 14 Near Kalba, United Arab Emirates. Danish Sterling Airways Super-Caravelle jet on a charter vacation flight returning from Ceylon to Copenhagen crashed in an attempted landing in torrential rain at Dubai Airport; all 112 persons aboard the plane died.
March 19 Near Aden, People's Democratic Republic of Yemen. Yugoslav Airlines DC-9 chartered by Egyptian Airways smashed into the side of Shamsan Mountain killing all 30 persons aboard.
April 18 Addis Ababa, Eth. East African Airways VC-10 en route from Nairobi to London and taking off from its first stop at Addis Ababa hurtled from the end of the runway into a farmhouse; of the 107 aboard (many of them British children on vacation) 41 persons were killed and about 40 others injured.
May 5 Palermo, Sicily. Alitalia DC-8 jetliner en route from Rome encountered bad weather as it neared Punta Raisi Airport and slammed into a 2,250-ft. mountainside; all 117 persons aboard perished.
May 18 Kharkov, Ukraine. Soviet Aeroflot Antonov-10 turboprop went down near Kharkov taking the lives of 108 persons.
May 21 Lobito, Angola. Angola Airlines twin-engine turboprop plunged into the sea in an attempted landing at the fog-bound Lobito Airport; 20 of the 23 persons on board were killed.
June 14 New Delhi, India. Japan Air Lines DC-8 jetliner on a flight from Tokyo to London crashed in flames moments after getting clearance to land at Palam International Airport; 83 of the 89 persons aboard the plane were killed as were 2 others on the ground.
June 15 Pleiku, S.Viet. British Cathay Pacific Airlines Convair 880 jetliner on a scheduled flight from Bangkok to Hong Kong broke up at high altitude and went down in the Central Highlands killing all 81 persons aboard.
June 18 London, Eng. British European Airways Trident-1 aircraft went into a stall and plunged to the ground shortly after taking off in rainy weather from Heathrow Airport; all 118 crewmen and passengers perished in Britain's worst air disaster to date.
July 29 Villavicencio, Colombia. Midair collision between two Colombian Avianca Airlines planes ended in tangled wreckage deep in the Las Palomas Mountains and the deaths of 37 persons.
Aug. 14 Königs Wusterhausen, E.Ger. East German state airline (Interflug) Soviet-built Ilyushin-62 on a charter flight to a Black Sea resort crashed at Königs Wusterhausen moments after takeoff from Schönefeld Airport in East Berlin; all 156 persons aboard were killed.
Aug. 27 Southeastern Venezuela. Linea Aeropostal Venezolana DC-3 twin-engine plane flying between Canaima and Ciudad Bolívar suffered engine failure and went down in deep jungle; all 24 persons aboard perished.
Aug. 28 Papua New Guinea. Royal Australian Air Force Caribou transport plane carrying a group of Papua New Guinea army school cadets plunged into the thickly jungled slopes of Mt. Kulama; 24 persons were killed, 5 cadets were rescued.
Sept. 13 Dhulikhel, Nepal. Royal Nepalese DC-3 on a training flight came in low between two rocky heights, struck one, spun into a high-tension cable, and exploded; all 31 servicemen (including 27 student paratroopers) aboard were killed.
Sept. 24 Sacramento, Calif. Eighteen-year-old U.S. surplus F-86 Sabrejet, converted for use in air shows, failed in a takeoff attempt, bounced across a road hitting three cars, and smashed into an ice cream parlour; 22 persons (12 children and 10 parents) died in the flaming ice cream parlour, 16 others were injured; the inexperienced pilot survived.
Oct. 3 Sochi, U.S.S.R. Soviet Aeroflot Ilyushin-18 airliner exploded moments after takeoff from the Black Sea resort city of Sochi bringing death to all 100 persons aboard the aircraft.
Oct. 13 Krasnaya Polyana, U.S.S.R. Chartered by Intourist, a Soviet Aeroflot Ilyushin-62 passenger jet en route from Paris crashed and exploded as it attempted to land in rain and fog at Moscow's Sheremetyevo International Airport; a reported 176 persons perished in what was to date the world's worst disaster in the history of commercial aviation.
Oct. 13 Near San Fernando, Chile. Uruguayan Air Force F-27 turboprop transporting members and relatives of Uruguay's Old Christians rugby team from Montevideo to Santiago went down high in the Andes Mountains; 21 persons died in the crash, 8 others perished later in an avalanche; 16 surviving team members were rescued after 70 days.
Oct. 21 Athens, Greece. Greek Olympic Airways plane on a flight from the island of Corfu in a heavy rainstorm undershot the Athens Airport and plunged into the sea; 37 persons died, 16 others were rescued.
Oct. 30 Bari, Italy. Aero Trasporti Italiani domestic airliner crashed en route from Naples to Taranto killing all 27 persons on board.
Nov. 28 Moscow, U.S.S.R. Japan Air Lines DC-8 jet en route from Copenhagen to Tokyo burst into flames and fell to the ground moments after taking off from Sheremetyevo International Airport; 66 of the 76 persons aboard the plane were reportedly killed.
Dec. 3 Santa Cruz de Tenerife, Canary Is. Spanish Convair 990-A Coronado chartered from the Spantax Airlines by a group of predominantly German tourists fell from a height of about 500 ft. as it left the runway at Las Rodeos Airport en

UPI COMPIX

Autos were strewn over railroad tracks in downtown Rapid City, S.D., by rampaging waters of a disastrous flash flood that struck the Black Hills area on June 10, 1972. The official death toll was 235.

Diamonds: *see* Mining

UPI COMPIX

Firemen work to extricate passengers trapped in the twisted wreckage of two Illinois Central trains that collided on Oct. 30, 1972, killing 45 persons and injuring more than 320. The single-deck coach, at left, rammed the double-deck train, at right, which was backing into a commuter station on Chicago's South Side. It was the worst train disaster in Chicago's history.

route to Munich; all 155 passengers and crewmen died.
Dec. 8 Chicago, Ill. United Air Lines Boeing 737 flying from Washington into Midway Airport failed in an attempt to pull up from its landing pattern and plowed into a cluster of houses; 45 persons (including 2 in a destroyed home) perished in the inferno.
Dec. 23 Oslo, Nor. Norwegian Braathens S.A.F.E. Fokker Fellowship airliner flying through rain and fog crashed in a forest near the outskirts of the city bringing death to 39 of the 45 persons aboard.
Dec. 29 Florida Everglades. U.S. Eastern Airlines $19 million L-1011 TriStar superjet came in too low on its approach to the Miami International Airport and pancaked into the swampy terrain of the Everglades strewing wreckage over a 1,520-ft. area; 101 persons aboard the 350,000-lb. jumbo aircraft died, most of the 75 survivors received injuries.

FIRES AND EXPLOSIONS

Jan. 16 Tyrone, Pa. Electrical overload in zero degree weather caused a fire that leveled the Pennsylvania House Hotel and brought death to 12 persons, 33 others were injured.
Feb. 24 São Paulo, Braz. Starting on the mezzanine floor of the Pirani Department Store, a fire quickly spread upward through the 29-story building, which also housed offices, forcing thousands of workers and shoppers to jump from windows; at least 16 persons died, more than 400 others were injured.
March 6 Barcelona, Spain. Early dawn explosion, supposedly attributed to a gas leak, caused the collapse of a ten-story apartment building and killed 18 persons.
March 30 Rio de Janeiro, Braz. Fire and explosions in Brazil's largest oil refinery claimed the lives of 21 persons, 48 others were severely injured.
May 6 Springfield, Ill. The Carver Convalescent Home, cited for numerous public health violations, was the scene of an early morning fire that brought death to 10 elderly patients.
May 13 Osaka, Jap. Patrons of the Play Town cabaret atop a seven-story department store were cut off from escape when a discarded cigarette started a fire on the third floor; 117 persons died of asphyxiation or injuries received in jumping or falling to the ground, at least 37 others were hurt.
July 2 Seoul, S.Kor. In refueling a lamp a child mistakenly used gasoline in place of kerosene and set fire to a farm home in which 13 children died, 7 others were hospitalized.
Sept. 23 Rhodes, Greece. Started by an electrical short-circuit, a fire swept through the plastic decorations of the two-story Oscar Club, a tourist restaurant; 31 of the 80 persons trapped on the upper floor perished, 16 other visitors were hurt.
Oct. 29 Barcelona, Spain. Reportedly caused by a gas leak, an explosion reduced a four-story apartment building to rubble and buried the occupants beneath tons of debris; at least 12 persons were dead or missing, 21 others received injuries.
Nov. 21 Singapore. Robinson's Department Store, a landmark institution of colonial days, was destroyed by a fire that killed at least 12 persons trapped in two elevators; damage was thought to run as high as $5 million.
Nov. 30 Rome, Italy. Explosion and fire in an illegal fireworks factory caused the deaths of 15 persons and injured 65 others.
Dec. 2 Seoul, S.Kor. Fire raced through Citizens Hall gutting the city's largest theatre building; caused by faulty stage lights the inferno brought death to 51 persons and injured 76 others.
Dec. 15 Weirton, W.Va. A natural-gas leak was believed to have touched off a series of violent explosions in a new coking plant at the Weirton Steel Co.; twisted falling girders and chunks of cement caused the deaths of some of the 19 workmen killed, 10 others were injured in the blasts.

MARINE

Jan. 1 Off Qais I. Qatari ship "Al-Rayyan" foundered in a heavy storm and sank in the Persian Gulf; at least 40 persons drowned, 2 others were rescued.
Jan. 1 Off Lower California. Dutch freighter "Dordrecht" with 35 hands aboard was flooded in rough seas; 20 crewmen were rescued by the Liberian-registered freighter "Golar Arrow," 15 others were presumed dead.
Jan. 3 Persian Gulf. A launch bearing 160 falcons and a cargo of hunting equipment belonging to the ruler of Qatar sank beneath the waves and drowned 80 persons, 2 others survived.
Jan. 9 W of Vancouver I., B.C. "Dona Anita," 7,840-ton freighter of Somali Republic registry, fighting hurricane-force winds, went down when water flooded the engine room; all 42 crewmen aboard were lost and presumed dead.
Feb. 1 Gulf of Mexico. U.S. 572-ft. tanker "V. A. Fogg," on a trip from Freeport to Houston, Tex., disappeared in 90-ft.-deep water about 32 mi. S of Freeport; all 39 men aboard were presumed drowned.
May 4 Canea, Crete. Small fishing boat carrying a group of high-school girls on an outing overturned in a sudden squall; 21 girls drowned, 6 others and the boat's captain were rescued.
May 11 Montevideo, Uruguay. Early-dawn collision at the channel entrance of the Río de la Plata between the British cargo ship "Royston Grange" and the "Tien Chee," a Liberian-registered tanker, caused the dumping of the broken tanker's 20,000 tons of crude oil which ignited and burned both vessels as they wallowed in the fog-enshrouded waters; all 74 persons aboard the "Royston Grange" and 10 others from the "Tien Chee" perished, 32 men were saved.
June 28 Bombay, India. Explosion aboard a Greek-owned tanker, the 17,103-ton "Tarsos," undergoing repairs at dockside killed at least 22 persons and injured 30 others.
Aug. 21 Off Cape Agulhas, S.Af. Collision of the 43,339-ton tanker "Texanita" with the 48,320-ton tanker "Oswego Guardian," both of Liberian registry, caused explosions that brought death to 47 of the 50-man crew of the "Texanita."
Nov. 8 Brunswick, Ga. Seabound freighter, the 11,000-ton "African Neptune," smashed into the mile-long Sidney Lanier drawbridge and sent cars and people tumbling from the crumpling structure into the Brunswick River; divers recovered the bodies of 10 persons.
Dec. 25 Gulf of Alaska. Ships and planes searched stormy seas for traces of the Liberian-registered 13,000-ton freighter "Pacrover" in response to a signal of distress; the colliery ship en route from Vancouver, B.C., to Japan was presumed to have gone down with the loss of the 30-man Korean crew.

MINING AND TUNNELING

Jan. 31 South Africa. A fire in the West Driefontein gold mine, the world's richest, reportedly brought death to at least 13 African miners.
May 2 Kellogg, Ida. Flash fire of unknown origin raced through the Sunshine Silver Mine spewing flames, smoke, and

carbon monoxide fumes throughout miles of corridors between the 3,100- and 3,700-ft. levels and blocking hoist exits used by the miners working below the 4,600-ft. level; 108 miners quickly escaped from upper levels, 2 miners trapped in the lower levels were found alive seven days later but 91 others had perished.
June 6 Wankie, Rhodesia. Violent explosion in the no. 2 shaft of the Wankie Colliery tore down walls of rock and coal and blew twisted machinery and a cable car up the shaft and out into the open air; of the 426 men in the mine 422 were entrapped and died, 5 others killed on the surface brought the death toll to 427.
July 31 Ipswich, Queensland, Austr. To prevent further explosions at a nearby explosion-ridden and fire-ravaged colliery, bulldozers sealed the mine entrance entombing 17 miners and rescue workers who had perished in the fires.
Nov. 6 Ishikari, Hokkaido, Jap. Methane gas explosion in the Ishikari coal mine killed 31 miners.

MISCELLANEOUS

July 10 Chandka Forest, India. Thirsty, heat-crazed elephants were reported to have run rampant through five nearby villages destroying crops and huts and trampling to death at least 24 persons.
Sept. 16 Naga City, Phil. An 18-ft.-wide wooden bridge gave way beneath the weight of hundreds of pilgrims observing a religious festival; 72 persons, mostly women and children, died as they plunged into the rocks and water below.
Nov. 21 Trujillo, Peru. Cakes made from cake flour containing a strong insecticide first killed 5 children in a family, more cake served later to mourners of the earlier victims caused another 6 persons to die for a final toll of 11 family members.
Dec. 20 Rio de Janeiro, Braz. About 2,500 sq.yd. of concrete roof collapsed upon the heads of shoppers and workers in the newly opened Ideal Supermarket; at least 16 persons died.

NATURAL

Jan. 4 Buenos Aires, Arg. Scorching ten-day heat wave with a steady temperature of 100° F settled over the capital city and resulted in a death toll of 100 from dehydration, traffic accidents, and drownings.
Jan. 4 Philippines. Typhoon Kit left an official death toll of 67, although 200 was considered a more realistic figure.
Jan. 26 San Josecito, Colombia. Triggered by heavy rains a landslide killed an estimated 70 villagers.
Feb. 4 Istanbul, Turk. A two-week wave of snowstorms and subfreezing temperatures brought death to at least 30 persons.
Feb. 10 Iran. Two weeks of heavy blizzards and freezing temperatures with up to 26 ft. of snow resulted in avalanches, stranded cars, and collapsing roofs that took the lives of at least 60 persons.
Feb. 26 Buffalo Creek, W.Va. Collapse of a dam built of coal refuse impounding a pond used for wastes from a coal preparation plant released millions of gallons of water and sludge to wreak havoc in the narrow valley below; 118 persons died, 4,000 others were homeless.
March 14 Peru. Flooding from a month-long deluge of rain brought death to at least 40 persons and left another 200,000 homeless in 41 cities and villages.
March 26 Herat Prov., Afg. Floods in the province were reported to have claimed 118 lives.
April 2 Mymensingh District, Bangladesh. Tornado with winds of 160 mph struck the area and killed at least 200 persons, leaving another 25,000 homeless.
April 10 Southern Iran. Devastating earthquake centring on the village of Ghir in Fars Province caused great destruction over an area that included some 60 towns and villages; an estimated 4,000 persons died, thousands of others were injured.
April 29 Mymensingh District, Bangladesh. The second tornado in less than a month lashed the district killing more than 200 persons; crop and property damage was extensive.
May 3 Mexico City, Mex. Violent thunderstorms caused flash floods that swept rocks, mud, and tree trunks from the hills and onto the city; 37 persons died, at least 70 others were injured, and some 100,000 left homeless.
May 14 New Braunfels, Tex. Two-inch rainfall along the Guadalupe River brought the river over its banks to reach 9 ft. above flood stage; 17 persons drowned in the swirling waters.
June 9–10 Rapid City, S.D. Cloudburst in the Black Hills triggered runoff floods that roared down Rapid Creek swelling it to a width of 400 ft., inundating the city and surrounding countryside, tearing out bridges, roads, railroad tracks, disrupting communications lines, and washing out the earthen dam holding back the waters of Canyon Lake; the death toll climbed to 235, with 500 homes destroyed and damage totaling about $100 million.
June 15–25 Caribbean-Eastern U.S. Spawned off the Yucatan coast a tropical depression grew into Hurricane Agnes, moved on to Cuba and the Florida Keys before slapping into central Florida and the panhandle; losing intensity and again labeled a tropical depression, it moved inland to deluge the Carolinas; regaining velocity and reclassified, Tropical Storm Agnes struck the eastern seaboard with deadly torrents of rain that flooded the six-state area of Virginia, West Virginia, Pennsylvania, Maryland, New Jersey, and New York; the final death toll (including Cuba and Florida) stood at 134; 128,000 homes and businesses were destroyed with total damage estimated at more than $60 billion.
June 18 Hong Kong. Three days of torrential rain started hundreds of tons of boulders and mud rampaging over the British crown colony; at least 100 persons died in the slides, 69 others were missing and 1,000 homeless.
June 25 Sylhet District, Bangladesh. Devastating floods destroyed hundreds of homes and about 80,000 ac. of crops; at least 50 persons were reported dead.
July 5 Oimawashi, Jap. Rescue workers attempting to find a family buried in a previous landslide set off a second slide that pushed a local train into a river; 80 persons buried in the debris were presumed dead.
Aug. 6 Philippines. Month-long floods brought on by incessant rains devastated Luzon Island causing shortages of food, medicine, and fuel, and threatening outbreaks of cholera: the death toll reached 427 as the waters began to recede.
Aug. 19 Bihar, India. Prolonged drought reportedly resulted in starvation conditions in the state that cost the lives of at least 250 persons.
Aug. 19–20 South Korea. Two-day deluge poured 17.8 in. of rain on Seoul and lesser amounts on the provinces of Kyonggi and Kangwon; flooding and landslides killed 467 persons, at least 100 others were missing, about 400 injured, with 326,000 homeless; property damage (including 54,000 homes destroyed or damaged) was estimated at $17 million.
Sept. 14 South Korea. Second round of rains and floods in Korea in less than a month inundated the southern part of the peninsula bringing death to 101 persons with 29 others missing and 59 injured.
Sept. 16 Japan. Typhoon Helen slammed out of the Pacific onto Honshu Island, killing at least 50 persons, destroying 400 houses, and damaging or sinking 75 ships.
Oct. 21 Srinagar, Kashmir. Strong winds accompanying a severe snowstorm surged through 12,500-ft.-high Rajdhan Pass 43 mi. N of the city and hurled 75 mountain porters down the mountainside where 50 of them perished.
Nov. 13 Northern Europe. High winds and torrential rains hit the Netherlands, Belgium, West Germany, and the British Isles, leaving at least 25 dead.
Nov. 14 Midwestern and Northeastern U.S. Storms from the West battered the Great Lakes with heavy rain, churning waves, and snow in some areas before passing through New England and out to sea; at least 24 deaths were recorded.
Dec. 5 Philippines. Tropical Storm Theresa slashed the Philippines with relentless force before fading out over the China Sea; at least 169 persons died, 2,500 were left homeless.
Dec. 23 Managua, Nicaragua. Earthquakes, with the strongest tremor registering 6.25 on the Richter scale, leveled the capital city; an estimated 10,000–12,000 persons were believed dead, 15,000 others were injured, and over 300,000 left homeless.

RAILROAD

Jan. 16 Larissa, Greece. Head-on collision between an international express and a freight train killed 15 persons and injured at least 60 others.
March 31 Potgietersrus, S.Af. Nine-coach passenger train en route through the northern Transvaal jumped the tracks as it passed over a small bridge; 38 persons died and another 174 were injured.
June 4 Jessore, Bangladesh. Crowded passenger train running at full speed was misdirected as it entered the station and crunched into a stopped train killing at least 76 persons, more than 500 others were injured.
June 16 Vierzy, France. Partial collapse of the Vierzy railway tunnel caused the derailment of a six-coach Paris–Laon train when it piled into the heaps of debris; about an hour later a Laon–Paris express entered the opposite end of the tunnel at 60 mph and smashed into the first jack-knifed train; at least 107 persons were killed and about 90 others injured in the worst French rail accident to date.
July 21 Lebrija, Spain. The 14-coach Madrid–Cádiz holiday express with 500 passengers collided head-on with a four-coach local that had apparently run a red signal light a few miles down the track; 76 of the 200 persons riding the local were killed, 103 others injured.
Aug. 6 Liaquatpur, Pak. Passenger train bound for Karachi from Rawalpindi plowed into the rear of a freight train standing at the Liaquatpur station and killed 57 passengers, more than 100 others were injured.
Sept. 29 Malmesbury, S.Af. Seven coaches of the Cape Town–Bitterfontein train jumped the tracks in rounding a curve and threw three cars and the locomotive over a steep embankment; 48 persons died, more than 150 others were injured.
Oct. 5 Saltillo, Mex. Speeding downhill, a 22-coach passenger train carrying pilgrims returning from a religious fiesta at the Shrine of St. Francis in Catorce swerved off the tracks, overturned, and caught fire; 208 persons perished in the wreckage, almost 700 others were injured.
Oct. 30 Chicago, Ill. Illinois Central morning rush-hour commuter train rammed into the rear of a new double-decker coach of another IC commuter as the new train backed into an overshot station stop; 45 persons died, at least 320 others received injuries.
Oct. 30 Karl-Marx-Stadt, E.Ger. Two East German passenger trains collided killing 25 persons and injuring 70 others.
Oct. 31 Eskisehir, Turk. Konya–Istanbul passenger train sped head-on into a track-repair train and burst into flames killing at least 30 persons, with dozens of others severely injured.
Dec. 10 Venchan, Bulg. Sofia–Tolbukhin passenger train slammed into a stationary freight and killed 26 passengers.

LONDON DAILY EXPRESS/PICTORIAL PARADE

The liner "Queen Elizabeth," transporter of the very rich on Atlantic crossings and a valiant lady to U.S. troops in World War II, encounters death by fire in Hong Kong Harbour in January 1972, 32 years after her maiden voyage.

TRAFFIC

Jan. 21 Bogotá, Colombia. Collision between a bus and a tanker truck 45 mi. E of the city killed 20 of the 37 passengers aboard the bus.

Feb. 5 Mahasu, India. A bus lurched off the road and into a Himalayan mountain gorge killing 19 persons.

Feb. 18 Kafr Saad, Egypt. Port Said–Cairo bus blew a front tire, careened into a rock wall, then plunged into the Tefiki irrigation canal; most of the 77 persons who died were students.

March 4 Minab, Iran. In attempting to ford the Kae River a bus was swept away by the strong current; 32 persons drowned, 37 others were rescued.

March 19 Carsamba, Turk. A passenger bus collided head-on with a minibus and killed 17 persons, 15 others were injured.

May 13 Taipei, Taiwan. Transporting a group of schoolgirls, a bus veered off the roadway into a ravine and killed 14 persons.

May 13 Bean Station, Tenn. A double-decker Knoxville–New York Greyhound bus, behind schedule and speeding along in the early dawn on a wet U.S. 11W, a winding two-lane highway, whipped into a tractor-trailer outfit and was split in half killing 14 persons (including the drivers of both vehicles) and injuring 15.

May 15 Minia, Egypt. On its way to a monastery with a group of Christian pilgrims a bus skidded from the road and fell into the Nile River where more than 50 persons drowned.

June 11 Shady Nook, La. Wheat-laden semitrailer truck ripped into the rear of a pickup truck as the small vehicle turned off the highway on its way to a swimming hole with a load of children; the young woman driver and 11 of the 13 children were killed.

July 10 Ayacucho, Peru. Passenger-filled truck toppled into a ravine and took the lives of 15 persons.

Aug. 4 South Iran. Collision of a bus and a truck reportedly killed 18 persons and injured 23 others.

Aug. 27 Northern Ecuador. A crowded bus went over an embankment and into a 150-ft. ravine killing 19 persons, 5 others were seriously injured.

Sept. 8 Crete, Greece. En route to a religious ceremony a passenger bus left the road and dropped over a 150-ft. cliff in southeastern Crete; 21 pilgrims died and 28 others were injured.

Sept. 21 Pernik, Bulg. Transport bus carrying a team of Czechoslovak parachutists to the Warsaw Pact parachute jumping championship was hit by a train at a grade crossing; 11 team members were killed.

Sept. 30 Saraburi Prov., Thailand. Failing in an attempt to pass another vehicle, a truck rammed head-on into a bus and killed 20 passengers, 15 others were hospitalized.

Oct. 6 Kericho, Kenya. A crowded bus racing through the night careened off the road and into a flooded ditch taking the lives of at least 25 persons, 63 others were hurt.

Oct. 23 Belo Horizonte, Braz. Collision between a coal truck and a bus killed 12 persons and injured at least 25 others.

Nov. 4 Greytown, S.Af. An open truck filled with riders veered off the road and rolled down a slope killing 18 of the occupants, 4 others were seriously injured.

Dec. 12 Slogoimo, Indonesia. Toppling off the road a bus caught fire and burned as 45 riders perished, 13 others received injuries.

Dec. 26 Near Glorieta, N.M. A bus transporting a Baptist Church youth group from Austin, Tex., to the Vadito ski resort in New Mexico collided with a cattle trailer which jackknifed across the road when the truck clipped the rail of an extremely narrow bridge as the two vehicles attempted to squeeze past one another; 19 passengers were killed.

Disciples of Christ: *see* Religion

Divorce: *see* Vital Statistics

Docks: *see* Transportation

Dominican Republic

Covering the eastern two-thirds of the Caribbean island of Hispaniola, the Dominican Republic is separated from Haiti, which occupies the western third, by a rugged mountain range. Area: 18,658 sq.mi. (48,323 sq.km.). Pop. (1972 est.): 4,304,873, including (1960) mulatto 73%; white 16%; Negro 11%. Cap. and largest city: Santo Domingo (pop., 1972 est., 768,887). Language: Spanish. Religion: Roman Catholic. President in 1972, Joaquín Balaguer.

President Balaguer proclaimed 1972 "Community Development Year," and announced that governmental expenditures would total $300.9 million, compared with $264.3 million for 1971. Education, health and social security, agriculture, and transport received the largest budget allocations: $54.6 million, $40.7 million, $28.3 million, and $29.5 million, respectively. Of the total budget, $275.6 million came from internal sources and the remainder was covered by credits from the U.S. Agency for International Development, the World Bank, and the Inter-American Development Bank.

Political events early in the year focused on far-reaching tax and agrarian reform legislation proposed by Balaguer in February and enacted by the government in early March. Comprising a package of 14 bills, they involved the transfer of responsibility to the Agrarian Reform Institute for exhausted and rice-producing land, the reclamation of state lands fallen into private hands, the prohibition of sharecropping

DOMINICAN REPUBLIC

Education. (1969–70) Primary, pupils 726,398, teachers (including preprimary) 12,584; secondary, pupils 97,501, teachers 4,183; vocational, pupils 4,636, teachers 231; teacher training, students, 570, teachers 58; higher, students 18,817, teaching staff 1,319.

Finance. Monetary unit: peso, at parity with the U.S. dollar, with (Sept. 18, 1972) a free rate of 2.45 pesos to £1 sterling. Gold, SDRs, and foreign exchange, central bank: (June 1972) U.S. $31.7 million; (June 1971) U.S. $28.3 million. Budget (1970 est.): revenue 267.1 million pesos; expenditure 262.9 million pesos. Gross national product: (1968) 1,169,200,000 pesos; (1967) 1,084,400,000 pesos. Money supply: (March 1972) 186.4 million pesos; (March 1971) 161.9 million pesos. Cost of living (Santo Domingo; 1963 = 100): (June 1972) 114; (June 1971) 107.

Foreign Trade. (1971) Imports 311.1 million pesos; exports 243 million pesos. Import sources (1970): U.S. 56%; Japan 13%; Canada 8%; West Germany 6%. Export destination (1970) U.S. 84%. Main exports: sugar 57%; coffee 10%; tobacco 8%; bauxite 7%; cocoa 6%.

Transport and Communications. Roads (1970) *c.* 6,250 km. Motor vehicles in use (1970): passenger 39,300; commercial (including buses) 21,600. Railways (sugar estates only; 1970) *c.* 1,400 km. Telephones (Jan. 1971) 47,000. Radio receivers (Dec. 1970) 164,000. Television receivers (Dec. 1970) *c.* 100,000.

Agriculture. Production (in 000; metric tons; 1971; 1970 in parentheses): rice *c.* 210 (210); corn *c.* 45 (45); sweet potatoes (1970) *c.* 107, (1969) 86; cassava (1970) *c.* 107, (1969) 86; dry beans *c.* 32 (25); peanuts *c.* 83 (75); sugar, raw value (1971–72) *c.* 1,238, (1970–71) *c.* 1,131; oranges *c.* 58 (*c.* 58); bananas (1970) *c.* 275, (1969) *c.* 267; coffee 37 (40); tobacco *c.* 24 (22). Livestock (in 000; June 1971): cattle *c.* 1,150; sheep *c.* 85; pigs *c.* 1,360; horses *c.* 170; chickens *c.* 7,300.

Industry. Production (in 000; metric tons; 1970): bauxite 1,086; cement 493; electricity (kw-hr.; 1969) 855,000.

contracts, and the definition of *latifundios* (large landed estates that benefit from favourable taxes and a legal system that encourages peonage) with the aim of their eventual elimination. By midyear, the proposal that caused most concern was the rice lands law, which provided that all publicly irrigated land used for rice cultivation be turned over to the government's Agrarian Reform Institute. Parcels of less than 80 ac. were exempt, so that the measure affected major landowners who had been using public irrigation facilities to maximize their own profits.

Early economic projections indicated that 1972 would be the fourth consecutive year of above average economic growth. A sharp increase in world market sugar prices in late 1971 improved economic prospects for 1972 with sugar exports projected to earn $150 million. The additional foreign exchange reserves available from increased sugar exports at higher prices strengthened the foreign and domestic investment climate.

Investment opportunities were greatest in the field of tourism. The Dominican government sought to dispose of its three 100- and 250-room hotels in Santo Domingo city. Investors were also sought to finance the development of beach properties and to purchase urban subdivisions.

Mining operations in 1972 were considerably expanded under a new Dominican law that levied a flat 40% tax on mining projects and an 18% tax on profits. Government inducements to invest were given to promoters in the form of exemptions from import duties on mine equipment and freedom to move all clear dividend earnings out of the country. New York & Honduras Rosario Mining, a U.S. company, took up a concession to dig an open-pit gold and silver mine. At least $20 million was expected to be invested in the mine, with estimated annual production put at 225,000 oz. of gold and 1.5 million oz. of silver.

The $50 million per year improvement in the import market continued in 1972, and sales showed expansion in the capital goods and raw materials categories. The movement toward the establishment of industries that can provide goods now imported was demonstrated by the construction of about 15 factories, mostly of relatively small size, on the outskirts of Santo Domingo. (GUSTAVO A. ANTONINI)

Drugs and Narcotics

The 1972 profile of "the war on drugs" came into focus with the publication, on August 16, of the *World Opium Survey 1972,* a joint undertaking of the U.S. Department of State, the Central Intelligence Agency, the Bureau of Narcotics and Dangerous Drugs, the Bureau of Customs, and the Department of the Treasury. It noted that, despite intensified enforcement efforts, "the rising level of seizures still represents only a small fraction of the illicit flow. The international heroin market almost certainly continues to have adequate supplies to meet the demand in consuming countries."

The latest available figures on the legal production of opium, as reported to the International Narcotics Control Board, showed that in 1970 world production decreased slightly to 1,157 tons (1,219 tons in 1969). During the same period world needs reached a new peak of 1,367 tons, and stocks fell to 826 tons, the lowest level in 11 years. Iran increased its production from 8 tons in 1969 to 78 tons. Production in Turkey fell from 117 tons to 51, reflecting the government's policy of replacing the opium poppy with other cash crops. Production in India fell slightly from 868 tons to 794 tons, but in the U.S.S.R. it rose from 217 to 227 tons. Some 1,214 tons of opium went into the manufacture of 177 tons of morphine, the bulk of which (89.2%) was converted into codeine.

However, an assessment of the available information by the U.S. and other governments indicated that at least 1,000 tons of illicit opium were produced in 1971. A minimum of 700 tons was produced in the hill region of Burma, Thailand, and Laos—the so-called Golden Triangle, which constituted the largest single area of opium production. At least another 220 tons were produced illicitly in India, Pakistan, and Afghanistan. Illicit Turkish production was estimated at a minimum of 35 tons, Mexico produced from 10 to 20 tons, and another 20 to 50 tons were estimated to come from Eastern Europe. Persistent reports of expanded poppy cultivation in the highlands of Latin America suggested that production in that area was rising.

The fundamental reason for increased production and markets could be summarized in one word: money. Illustrations of profit opportunities abounded. The *World Opium Survey* stated that operations of French traffickers indicated that the acquisition of 100 kg. (1 kg. = 2.2 lb.) of heroin represented an initial investment of between $120,000 and $300,000. In 1960 the price of one kilogram of heroin delivered to a U.S. buyer by a French trafficking group was about $4,000. By early 1972 the delivery price of one kilogram had risen to approximately $10,000. The initial investment of $120,000–$300,000, therefore, should have yielded the traffickers a gross of some $1 million, one-half to three-fourths of which was net profit. With such a profit margin, it seemed unlikely that rising prices of heroin production—caused by the attempts to outlaw production in Turkey, for example—would significantly affect the market, since traffickers could afford to absorb the additional costs.

Strategy and Tactics. There was general agreement that illicit use of drugs was growing throughout the world. Reports from countries as disparate as India, Egypt, and Switzerland indicated an alarming rise in drug abuse, particularly among the young. Only

continued on page 249

LYNN PELHAM, LIFE MAGAZINE © TIME INC.

Former FBI agent James Cusack, a Tampa, Fla., attorney, poses by a billboard advertising a drug abuse program he devised. Tipsters were given code names to preserve anonymity. Rewards up to $500 were available for information leading to conviction.

Drama:
see Motion Pictures; Theatre

Dress:
see Fashion and Dress; Furs

MARIJUANA IN PERSPECTIVE

By Harry Nelson

"Marihuana's relative potential for harm to the vast majority of individual users and its actual impact on society does not justify a social policy designed to seek out and firmly punish those who use it."

The words are not those of *Ramparts* or *Rolling Stone,* but of the National Commission on Marihuana and Drug Abuse, a conservatively oriented panel named by the U.S. Congress and Pres. Richard Nixon. During the 1960s pot had become a focus of heated controversy, viewed by some as an irreversible step toward the perdition of hard drugs, particularly heroin, and touted by others as an instrument of social liberation. But by March 1972, when the commission published its recommendations, some perspective was beginning to emerge. Thirty-five years after Congress outlawed marijuana in the U.S., the American attitude toward it appeared to be changing.

What had happened was that intensive scientific, social, and legal scrutiny aimed at eliciting fact rather than emotion had demonstrated that much of the thought about marijuana embedded in laws and public opinion was mythical. While simple "yes or no" answers were not yet possible, it was clear that the U.S. not only needed but was on the verge of a major change in national policy. A large segment of society was beginning to realize that the across-the-board punitive approach was a failure and, in fact, might be causing great harm to youth.

As regards marijuana's effect on health, it was also clear that most of the fears that had permeated American thinking for at least 40 years were either false or unproven. Neither the National Commission nor most scientists believed that marijuana was totally innocuous; researchers who were familiar with its varied actions and the importance of dosage, setting, and the psychological makeup of the user were well aware of the drug's potential for harm. But the scientific evidence to date simply did not support the once dominant concept of marijuana as a "killer weed" that causes madness and violence and leads to heroin addiction and crime. On the contrary, the current evidence indicated that marijuana, as it is typically used in the U.S., is not a serious health hazard or a major cause of crimes against persons.

The Drug. Marijuana comes from the leaves, stems, and seeds of the plant *Cannabis sativa,* an annual that grows widely throughout the world but most luxuriantly in warm climates. The principal active ingredient responsible for the drug's psychic effects is delta-9-tetrahydrocannabinol or THC, a substance that can now be synthesized.

Besides marijuana, two other widely used THC-containing drugs come from the *Cannabis* plant. They are hashish or charas, which is made from the resin produced by the plant's flowers, and ganja, a less powerful preparation made by crushing the leaves that grow near the flowers. Of the three, marijuana is the weakest in THC content. The marijuana commonly used in the U.S. seldom contains more than 1% THC and usually less. Hashish used in India averages 4 to 5% and may reach 12%. Ganja contains about 3%.

It has been estimated that the typical pot user in the U.S. smokes one or two cigarettes twice a week. A single cigarette yields 5 to 20 mg. of THC. Even heavy American users seldom receive more than 50 mg. per day. This compares with 200 to 400 mg. for hashish users in the Far East, and helps explain why most U.S. researchers are skeptical about the significance to Americans of reports from other countries linking hashish with psychosis.

Alcohol is the U.S.'s major drug abuse problem, with more than nine million known alcoholics. Next to alcohol, marijuana is the most widely abused psychoactive drug. Its toxicity is considerably less than that of alcohol, however, and marijuana has not so far shown itself to be as devastating to the body as alcohol. Animal experiments indicate it would be necessary to smoke 800 marijuana cigarettes within a few hours to obtain a lethal dose. Using, as an index of safety, the ratio between a single lethal dose and the amount necessary to achieve a medically effective result, marijuana has been calculated to be a thousand times safer than barbiturates and five thousand times safer than alcohol.

At one time *Cannabis* extracts were as commonly used for medical purposes in the U.S. as aspirin is today. Medicinal use began to fall off around the end of the 19th century—partly because of the introduction of the more easily administered opiates. There is no evidence that marijuana causes cancer, birth defects, or chromosome damage. A few scattered reports have claimed mild liver dysfunction, but other researchers have failed to confirm these findings. The 1972 report on "Marihuana and Health" prepared by the U.S. Department of Health, Education, and Welfare states that, with the exception of an occasional allergic reaction, a survey of world scientific literature reveals "little evidence at this time that light to moderate use of cannabis has deleterious physical effects."

The health outlook for long-term, heavy users of marijuana may not be as benign. In an effort to find out, the National Institute of Mental Health was supporting intensive medical, neurological, and psychiatric studies of heavy hashish users in Greece and of ganja users in Jamaica. As of 1972, the studies had failed to reveal any significant health differences between the subjects and their nonuser countrymen. These conclusions were preliminary, however, and the long-term effects of marijuana were still largely unknown. Eventually, valid health reasons for avoiding marijuana and related drugs may be found, just as research provided ample evidence that tobacco and alcohol can be harmful at dosages not uncommonly used in the U.S.

One of the chief areas of concern involves undesirable effects on the brain, as reflected by changes in personality and behaviour. Is marijuana, for example, responsible for the "dropping out" phenomenon among youth? Some researchers believe that loss of motivation and will to "make it" in a competitive world can be traced to marijuana. This view is related to the long-held popular association between the drug and indolence. It is often supported by references to similar behaviour observed in the Near and Far East, where hashish is widely used, although the greater potency of hashish and the differences in nutrition and general health status of the populations involved make such comparisons questionable.

No one disputes that marijuana can produce such psychiatric reactions as depression and panic, especially in inexperienced users, but they disappear as soon as the drug wears off. One problem in determining the true mental effect of marijuana, experts say, is the difficulty in measuring the importance of pre-existing borderline mental conditions that may be triggered into an overt stage by the drug. Another is that many marijuana users also take other psychoactive substances. In 1971 a widely publicized British study reported evidence of cerebral atrophy in a group of ten young men who had been smoking marijuana heavily for from 3 to 11 years. Other authorities challenged the accuracy of the test used (air encephalography, a special kind of brain X ray) but, perhaps more significantly, the subjects were all using other drugs, including amphetamines and LSD,

Harry Nelson is the medical writer of the Los Angeles Times.

making it difficult to trace the damage (if any) to marijuana alone. Summing up, the "Marihuana and Health" report stated: "At present evidence that marihuana is a sufficient or contributory cause of chronic psychosis is weak and rests primarily on temporal association."

It should be pointed out that new findings could change that conclusion at any time. A great deal remains to be learned about the various steps whereby the body metabolizes THC and eliminates it. For example, a recent British study with mice revealed that a particular metabolite of THC bound itself so closely to brain tissue that it could not be isolated. Metabolic breakdown products of THC, which are known to remain in the body as long as a week, may be responsible for a phenomenon called reverse tolerance. Unlike users of heroin and other narcotics, regular users of marijuana require less, not more, of the drug to produce the desired result as time goes by. This is believed to be due to the cumulative effect of some of the long-lasting metabolites. What other effects they may have is unknown, although it has been proved to the satisfaction of practically all authorities that marijuana, unlike narcotics, produces no physical dependence. Whether it produces psychological dependence is debatable, but the majority of experts believe that it does.

It is, of course, the mental effects of marijuana—the euphoria, relaxation, dream-like state, and enhancement of the senses—that constitute its chief attractions. But to a degree seen in few other drugs, marijuana's effects depend on the setting in which it is taken. Anticipation and pleasant surroundings seem to be as important as the pharmacologic effect on the brain. Studies have shown that regular marijuana users often cannot tell the difference between a real marijuana cigarette and one made of inert material, presumably because they expected certain sensations and their expectations were met. On the other hand, working-class Jamaicans, who regularly use ganja as a work break, reportedly never experience its psychedelic effects.

The importance of the social setting has been studied extensively by psychologist Charles Tart of the University of California at Davis. Tart believes that many of the adverse reactions reported by scientists studying marijuana are due more to the circumstances of the experiment than to the drug itself. The psychological effects of impersonal "scientific" settings, the uncertainty about the nature of the drug being taken, and the subject's lack of control over the dosage he receives are sufficient to nullify the validity of any observation the researcher may make, according to Tart. A drug of known quality, taken in surroundings that are aesthetically pleasing to the user and in amounts that the user controls, may yield entirely different results. This is not to say that chemistry plays no role. A fair comparison can be made with alcohol; as every drinker knows, the degree of inebriation depends on some combination of dosage, social setting, and the drinker's mental and physical condition.

Surveys support the observation that the search for pleasure and recreation is the basic motivation for marijuana use. At the same time, many nonusers link the drug with hedonism and sexual promiscuity and consider marijuana to be the breast milk for a counterculture in direct conflict with the moral, political, and social principles of American society. It is precisely for that reason that marijuana has become a kind of symbol of protest for youths revolting against political beliefs and social mores that they see as crass, narrow, and hypocritical.

The Users. Marijuana is primarily a young person's drug. According to a careful survey conducted by the National Commission, it has been tried one or more times by 24 million Americans, most of them under 25. A government estimate places the number expected to try it by 1976 at 30 million to 50 million. This is not the whole story, however. The commission's comprehensive survey also indicated that, while 24 million have tried it, 16 million no longer use it. If marijuana truly is destined to become the new social drug, why have so many quit?

The principal reason for stopping, former users report, is loss of interest. The second most important reason is concern over marijuana's legal status. From the standpoint of the majority of the population, for whom marijuana has little or no appeal, this tendency to quit is a hopeful sign. Furthermore, it has been reported that 61% of all youth and 73% of those who have never used marijuana would not try it under any circumstances.

Nevertheless, eight million people are still gambling with the law, risking their freedom for the sake of experiencing the forbidden drug. Presumably these are the ones who should concern us, since the 16 million who express disenchantment may well be the sort of people who are not greatly attracted to marijuana in the first place. Sociologists have identified a list of traits that they claim can be used to identify potential users with almost 100% accuracy. The variable traits are sex, religiousness, political liberalism, and cigarette smoking. In a study of college students, sociologist B. D. Johnson of Brooklyn (N.Y.) College found that of all nonreligious, politically liberal males who smoke cigarettes daily, 97% had tried marijuana and 62% used it at least once a week. Of all religious, politically conservative, nonsmoking women, only 4% had ever tried marijuana and not one used it once a week or oftener.

Use of alcohol by a young person who also smokes cigarettes is a strong indication that he or she is likely to try marijuana and other dangerous drugs. In fact, a far better case can be made to show that alcohol and tobacco lead to marijuana and other illegal drugs than can be brought to support the commonly held—and largely discredited—belief that marijuana leads to heroin. A scientific report issued in 1972 by the World Health Organization points out that while most heroin users have taken marijuana, the great majority of marijuana users never proceed to the morphine-like drugs. It appears likely, the report says

U.S. customs agents weigh 347 lb. of marijuana sniffed out by a trained dog aboard a Colombian freighter in Houston, Tex., on May 4, 1972. A growing trend for law enforcement agencies was to ignore users and go after suppliers.

UPI COMPIX

KEN REGAN—CAMERA 5

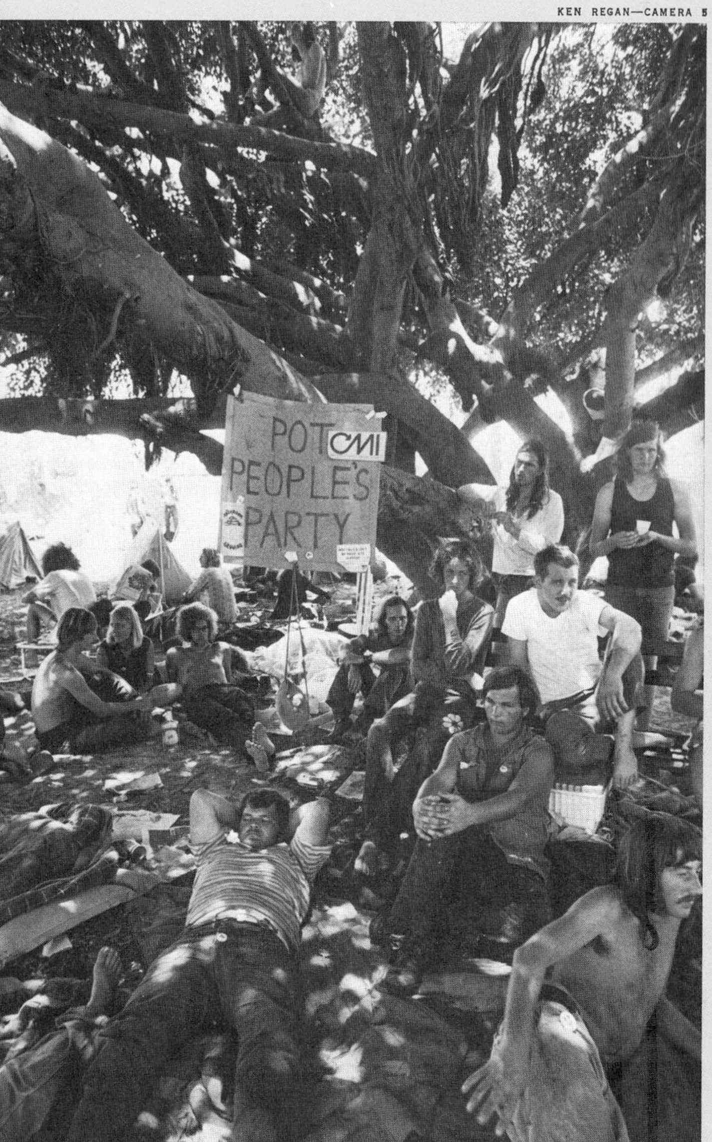

"Pot People's Party" gathers in Miami Beach, Fla., during the Democratic national convention in July 1972. Later in the year, conservative William F. Buckley, Jr., endorsed decriminalization of marijuana in his "National Review."

that sociocultural and personal factors largely determine whether an individual will progress from marijuana to other drugs. A similar view was held by the National Commission.

But any realistic attempt to resolve the drug problem must grapple with the fact that, even though marijuana has little attraction for the majority of the population, millions of persons are so attracted. Furthermore, the latter group consists predominantly of young people, including a very large percentage of those now in colleges and universities. In view of the phenomenal increase in users that has occurred in spite of stringent laws, the question arises whether strict legal punishment is the answer.

The Law. The National Commission's 1972 report created a stir across the country because of its recommendation that laws regarding personal use of marijuana be softened. In a report to Congress and the president, the commission favoured complete decriminalization of private possession of small amounts and recommended that public possession of more than one ounce or distribution in public of small amounts be subject only to a $100 fine, provided the purpose was not to make a profit. A majority of the Canadian Government Commission of Inquiry into the Non-Medical Use of Drugs made similar recommendations to decriminalize marijuana in Canada. At the same time, the National Commission declared its support for continuing efforts by educators and others to discourage use of the drug and its support of stiff laws to control the supply. Outright legalization was ruled out because the commission felt it would "institutionalize availability of a drug which has uncertain long-term effects."

"In its response to concern about marihuana use," the commission reported:

> [the public] failed to take into account *scientifically* validated findings concerning the true properties of marihuana; did not distinguish between the dangerous street criminal, often an addict, and the young person who used marihuana as a social facilitator; and expressed its frustration with the protests and antics of contemporary youthful life styles without distinguishing between social cause and social behavior.
>
> For a time, the harsh penalties for possession and use of marihuana, frequently meted out across the country, served as a means, both actual as well as symbolic, by which the authority of (adult) society could assert itself over sometimes ungrateful and often unconventional youth. In short, (adult) society was going to have the last word. It was not long, however, before the picture in the puzzle began to emerge and society found itself with a rather serious dilemma: how to uphold the image of law and order without imprisoning tens of thousands of youth from the mainstream of middle and upper-middle class America.

More than 200,000 persons are arrested each year on marijuana charges, most of them for possession of small amounts. The typical arrestee is a young white male blue-collar worker or student who has never before had contact with the police. In 50% of the cases involving adults and 70% involving juveniles, the case was terminated before trial.

In responding to the commission's report, some lawmen alleged that allowing use of marijuana in private while using the full force of the law to run down suppliers would create a "schizophrenic legal situation." In practice, however, the policy in many jurisdictions was for officers to ignore the private use of pot and concentrate on bigger game. In 1970 federal law was changed to allow the court to place first offenders in possession cases on probation rather than entering a judgment of guilt. Defendants 21 or under could have all mention of the incident erased from the record.

On the state level, every legislature had made some change in its marijuana laws since 1969, with the trend being toward reduced penalties and a more marked distinction between possession and sale. The movement was not in a straight line, however. A handful of states still classified marijuana as a narcotic (pharmacologically it is a hallucinogen) and considered even simple possession to be a felony. In Texas all marijuana offenders were subject to punishment by life imprisonment. In March 1972 the Michigan Supreme Court declared unconstitutional the state's law allowing up to ten years in prison for the first offense in marijuana possession cases. A new law making possession a misdemeanour went into effect on April 1 and, as a result, almost 100 people in prison for marijuana offenses were released. In California a nonprofit counterculture organization called the California Marijuana Initiative succeeded in placing on the November ballot an initiative that would remove penalties for personal use and allow cultivation, manufacture, and transportation of the crop, provided it was for personal use. The measure was rejected by the voters, however, and, in the meantime, the California legislature killed two measures that would have reduced possession from a felony to a misdemeanour.

Some measure of the difficulty in changing long-established views about marijuana, even when advocated by conservative forces, was provided at the summer meeting of the American Medical Association. The AMA's Council on Mental Health and Committee on Alcoholism and Drug Abuse recommended that possession of marijuana for personal use and transfer of "insignificant" amounts should not be considered a criminal act. Before the AMA House of Delegates had the opportunity to act on the recommendation, publicity on the impending action drew a rain of protests from around the country. Bowing to pressure, the delegates passed a compromise proposal recommending that possession be considered at most a misdemeanour. But it should be noted that even the compromise was a relaxation of the AMA's former stand.

The move to decriminalize marijuana was not a black and white issue, with liberals in favour and conservatives against. The National Commission itself was created largely through the efforts of Rep. Edward Koch (Dem., N.Y.), a liberal, but its composition was predominantly nonliberal. Its executive director was a former counsel for the Bureau of Narcotics and Dangerous Drugs, one of the federal agencies responsible for controlling marijuana in the U.S. and long noted for its hard-line stand. When the recommendations for decriminalization were announced in March, they were applauded not only by several counterculture groups but also by conservative columnist William F. Buckley, Jr., who called existing antimarijuana laws "excruciatingly anachronistic."

The widespread popular belief that marijuana is a "killer weed" leading to violence and addiction seemed to be shared to some degree by many of the nation's legal prosecutors. Forty percent of district attorneys said they believed marijuana led to aggressive acts, and 75% believed it was a stepping-stone to hard-drug use. The majority, however, agreed that existing laws do nothing to deter use in persons under 30, and nearly two-fifths believed a parking-ticket type of arrangement for possession would deter as much as or more than the threat of incarceration. A similar survey of judges, probation officers, and court physicians revealed that most believed the criminalization approach was inappropriate. Very few approved of imprisonment of users.

Society, like the district attorneys, appeared to be split into different camps. One segment urged even stricter laws and enforcement; another group urged removal of all legal bars to private use; and a middle group seemed to be leaning toward relaxation of legal restrictions. The status of eventual legalization probably depended on how far this moderate group would eventually lean and how large its membership would become. This, in turn, depended on two important considerations. One was the outcome of the ongoing studies to learn whether chronic use of marijuana in moderate amounts results in serious harm to health. The second consideration was whether pot was here to stay or whether it was a fad that would gradually fade away.

The old fear that marijuana causes crime and violence was countered by more careful analyses of the physiological effects of the drug and the statistics purporting to show that marijuana leads to crime. As of 1972 there was no evidence that marijuana catalyzes violent or aggressive acts by releasing inhibitions or destroying willpower. Although marijuana has been found to reduce inhibitions in some persons, it does not appear to enhance existing aggressiveness to any noticeable degree. On the contrary, the evidence indicated that marijuana decreases the inclination toward physical activity.

Recent studies show that the seemingly significant statistical correlation between marijuana and lawbreaking depends not on the chemical effects of the drug but on the fact that many marijuana users are part of a drug-using subculture that tends to be lax about obeying the law. Some behavioural scientists believe that a less punitive attitude toward the private use of marijuana might help defuse the disaffection with society felt by a large segment of young people. To the extent that this served to bring these young people back into the mainstream, it might—in this view—weaken the link between marijuana and lawbreaking rather than strengthening it.

In its analysis of the role of marijuana in the youth society, the National Commission concluded that the key to understanding

> lies in the changes which have taken place in society within recent years and the effects these changes have had on succeeding generations of youth. The increased use of marihuana is only one of those effects. . . .
>
> When the issue of marihuana use is placed in this context of society's larger concerns, marihuana does not emerge as a major issue or threat to the social order. . . .
>
> . . . it is unlikely that marihuana will affect the future strength, stability or vitality of our social and political institutions. The fundamental principles and values upon which society rests are far too enduring to go up in the smoke of a marihuana cigarette.

continued from page 245

the U.S.S.R. (where alcoholism was admittedly a major concern) claimed to have no drug problem. Reliable statistics were difficult to come by, however, and much of the evidence was based on clinical impressions, indirect evidence from administrative and other nonmedical sources, and on the testimony of addicts themselves.

There was less agreement on the etiology of drug addiction and on the measures needed to deal with the individual user. Insofar as the maintenance and propagation of the drug habit depended on the availability of drugs, however, there was logic in the effort to deal with the problem by cracking down on traffickers and cutting off supplies. National and international authorities continued to be unrelenting in this respect. This was clear from the report of the International Narcotics Control Board on its work in 1971. It called for a "renewed attack on the illicit channels of distribution, concentration of, and effective control over, licit production of raw materials and suppression of such production where it is illicit or uncontrolled." Interpol was more active than ever in countering international drug transactions, while many governments redoubled their police and enforcement efforts to eliminate illicit trafficking within their own territories.

In the U.S., Pres. Richard Nixon labeled the drug abuse problem "America's public enemy number one" and requested $729 million to finance the administration's antinarcotics program in fiscal 1973—$135 million more than in fiscal 1972 and a 1,000% increase over fiscal 1969. While federal support of treatment programs and research—primarily to develop an effective antagonist to heroin—would be increased, indications were that the major share of federal funding would continue to be directed toward law-enforcement activities.

Typical of the administration's thrust was the Office for Drug Abuse Law Enforcement (DALE), created by executive order of the president on Jan. 28, 1972, as a part of the law-enforcement campaign against street pushers and narcotics distributors. DALE "task forces" operated in 34 target cities through investigation-prosecution teams that included 250 to 350 federal investigators, some 106 attorneys and assistant U.S. attorneys, and more than 1,000 state and local police officers. Thirty-eight special grand juries had been impaneled to consider indictments. According to the *World Opium Survey,* DALE had made more than 1,000 arrests and identified some 3,000 pushers. It operated the Heroin Hot Line (800-368-5363), whereby citizens could report information regarding alleged narcotics law violators in strict confidence and toll free. Five thousand Hot Line calls had been classed as "valuable."

Domestic heroin seizures by the Bureau of Narcotics and Dangerous Drugs (BNDD) and the U.S. Bureau of Customs increased from 1,161 lb. in fiscal 1971 to 1,626 lb. in fiscal 1972. Total seizures almost doubled in the 12-month period: from 241,663 lb. to 472,640 lb. The street value of the seizures also doubled: from $1,063,000,000 to $2,132,000,000. In addition to narcotics, the BNDD seized 207,094,393 dosage units of hallucinogens, depressants, and stimulants in fiscal 1972, more than 14 times the 14,366,-666 dosage units taken in fiscal 1971. Arrests rose from 12,947 to 16,144.

Public concerns relating to the drug problem in 1972 centred largely on the burglaries, robberies, muggings, and murders that, in the public mind, had become commonplace happenings in urban life. How much of this was drug related could not be satisfactorily estimated under any current system of data collection. To the general public, however, the proliferation of crimes of violence had a direct relationship to the spread of heroin addiction. This belief was behind the growing trend within the federal government to revert to harsher penalties within the criminal justice system.

In 1970 the Comprehensive Drug Abuse Prevention and Control Act became law. The statute did away with mandatory minimum penalties for drug offenders and reduced the penalties for possession. Simultaneously, penalties for trafficking were doubled. The statute was widely praised as a progressive and humanitarian approach to law enforcement, because it offered hope to the addict for rehabilitation while providing more stringent penalties against the drug pusher. By October 1972 the administration had indicated, in a statement by the attorney general, that it planned to draft legislation that would return federal law to the pre-1970 situation. Such a reversion to harsh criminal penalties for drug addiction, per se, was opposed by the scientific and health community and those persons working in the "helping professions." Their point of view was expressed in a *New York Times* editorial of Aug. 18, 1972, published following release of the *World Opium Survey:*

> It can now be taken for granted that the maximum that can be achieved through enforcement activity, diplomatic pressure or the like is the possibility of restricting the supply in ways that will . . . create so many difficulties for addicts that more will become interested in trying to enter methadone maintenance or other treatment programs.
>
> . . . The longer range hope for a solution to this devastating problem will have to come from other types of attack. The research on . . . narcotics antagonists . . . needs to be pushed even more intensively. So does research on the psychological, physiological and sociological roots of addiction.

Treatment and Research. In a climate at times approaching desperation, methadone maintenance treatment programs for heroin addiction continued to proliferate in 1972. Even though the controversial aspects of treating one addiction (heroin) by prescribing another addictive drug (methadone) had not been solved, methadone continued to be the drug of choice in the vast majority of treatment programs, usually for lack of anything better. Faced with a demand for treatment far in excess of available resources, most methadone programs had long waiting lists, and few had the resources to provide individual therapy. An unknown number of young persons were being addicted to methadone (at times without a history of heroin addiction), and methadone itself had become an illicit street-market drug. In an effort to stem this trend, the U.S. Food and Drug Administration, in December, issued strict new regulations governing the use of methadone. Nevertheless, proponents of methadone maintenance could point to the successful rehabilitation of some heroin addicts, at least on a short-term basis. To a small, pioneering extent, some employers, industries, and trade unions were beginning to provide jobs for addicts as long as they continued as active participants in methadone maintenance programs.

Clearly, federal funding in drug abuse programs was heavily weighted toward solving the problem of heroin addiction. However, continuing concern for persons who abuse other dangerous drugs resulted in $31.3 million in new federal grants to provide treatment and rehabilitation services in communities throughout the U.S. Administered by the National Institute of Mental Health, the grants were designed to support development of diversified approaches required to reach all ages and types of drug users. Of major potential significance were nine "initiation and development" grants awarded to individual communities to "develop reliable estimates of the extent of the local drug problem and assess the needs for treatment and rehabilitation programs."

The most obvious result of the treatment dilemma was an increase in activity in research laboratories. Heading the list was the search for an effective, long-lasting chemical antagonist to heroin. The Special Action Office for Drug Abuse Prevention of the Executive Office of the President and the National Institute of Mental Health jointly awarded more than $2 million in contracts for work on a series of narcotic antagonists, including cyclazocine.

Abuse of marijuana and heroin received the most attention, but many other drugs were abused. Heroin was not the major drug of abuse, either in the U.S. or, to judge by the reports, in most other countries. Excluding marijuana (*see* Special Report), drugs of abuse included the hallucinogens (primarily LSD), the stimulants (primarily amphetamines), the depressants (primarily barbiturates), and volatile substances (primarily glue). The number one drug of abuse by an overwhelming margin was alcohol.

Reasons for Drug Abuse. In May 1972, the Engineer Strategic Studies Group, U.S. Department of the Army, published a two-volume *Profile of Drug Abuse in the United States*. Among its findings were that drug abuse had only become extensive in the U.S. in the past five years, but it was increasing at a growing rate and showed no signs of leveling off. "The drug culture is considered primarily a youth culture," the report said; few drug users were over 30 and most young people who had used drugs discontinued them when they reached their late 20s. This pattern might not continue, however, since so many more young people were using drugs than had been the case a few years earlier. "What was once a youthful experiment has become, for many, a life style they may be reluctant to change."

Clearly, before any effective solution to the drug problem could be found, the roots of the problem would have to be identified and understood. They were related to the reasons why young people found drug abuse so inviting. Basic reasons for drug abuse were complex, and most people, when asked why they used drugs, gave symptoms of reasons rather than reasons themselves. If, for example, they said, "Because it's fun," this was no answer to the basic question: "Why is it considered fun?"

Wherever studies had been undertaken, the findings had a similar ring. In Spain it was found that "the use of drugs among young men [appeared] to be due to a desire to satisfy a subjective appetite or need, such as curiosity, companionship or a temporary escape from the daily routine." Schoolchildren in the Leeds area of England seemed to be in search of "kicks." Among adolescents in Chile the motivations were said to be curiosity, fanned by the mass media and later by a craving for repeated psychotomimetic experiences. The Philippine youth was described as "increasingly eager for new experiences." Drug abuse among young people in Egypt was "found to be associated with exposure to influence of a drug-taking person." In England it was suggested that the back-

Penalties for Simple Possession of Marijuana

Alabama
2–10 years and/or $20,000

Alaska
0–1 year and/or $1,000 or rehabilitation treatment by state for 1 year

Arizona
0–1 year in county jail and/or $1,000 or 1–10 years

Arkansas
0–1 year and/or $250

California
County jail for up to 1 year or 1–10 years

Colorado
Under ½ oz., 0–1 year and/or $500; over ½ oz., 2–15 years and/or $10,000

Connecticut
0–1 year and/or $1,000 or up to 3 years in custody of commissioner

Delaware
0–2 years and/or $500

Florida
Less than 5 g., 0–1 year and/or $1,000; more than 5 g., 0–2 years and/or $1,000

Georgia
Under 1 oz., 0–1 year and/or $1,000; over 1 oz., 0–2 years and/or $2,000

Hawaii
0–5 years

Idaho
0–6 months and/or $300

Illinois
Less than 2.5 g., 0–1 year and/or $1,500; over 2.5 g., 2–10 years and/or $5,000

Indiana
Less than 25 g. or 5 g. hashish, 0–6 months and/or $25–$100; over these amounts, 30 days to a year and/or $500

Iowa
0–6 months and/or $1,000

Kansas
0–1 year

Kentucky
0–1 year mental health facility

Louisiana
0–1 year and/or $500

Maine
0–11 months and/or $1,000

Maryland
0–1 year and/or $1,000

Massachusetts
0–3½ years in prison, or 0–2½ years in jail and/or $1,000

Michigan
0–10 years and/or $5,000

Minnesota
Under 1.5 oz., 0–1 year and/or $1,000; over 1.5 oz., 0–3 years and/or $3,000

Mississippi
0–4 years and/or $2,000

Missouri
Under 35 g. or 5 g. hashish, 0–1 year and/or $1,000; over these amounts, 0–5 years and/or $1,000

Montana
Up to 60 g. or 1 g. of hashish, 0–1 year and/or $1,000; over these amounts, 0–5 years

Nebraska
Less than 1 lb., 7 days in county jail to be held separately and/or $500; over 1 lb., 0–6 months in county jail or 1 year in prison and/or $500

Nevada
If under 21 and less than 1 oz., 0–1 year and/or $1,000 and/or suspension of driver's license; if over 1 oz., 1–6 years and/or $2,000

New Hampshire
Less than 1 lb., 0–1 year and/or $500; over 1 lb., 0–5 years and/or $2,000

ground to regular drug usage could be traced back to childhood and to difficulties in individual and social adjustment.

A consensus of most drug experts and drug users identified pressures to accept or resist drug abuse as follows: peer pressure, orientation of society toward drugs, individual psychology, social situation, special meanings, and the stress and frustration of the individual as related to the complex society. There was no consensus as to which cause was most important, but a general agreement that all of them were interrelated. Many youngsters who felt helpless to accommodate to or change an unacceptable world consciously chose to alter their own. As one youngster stated it, "Since you cannot alter the world or determine the direction in which it will go, you must alter your state of consciousness and perception. All that is important is one's subjective state. That's where you can create a new reality."

Basically, it could be concluded from observation and questioning over the preceding five years that the decision to use drugs is based on attitude and emotions of the moment and is not rational; that there is no single reason for drug abuse, but rather many interrelated reasons; and that deciding to use drugs is not a one-time decision, but is made on many occasions throughout life.

Trends and Alternatives. Since the overriding trend was for drug abuse to continue to increase, the goal of eliminating it appeared to be unobtainable within the foreseeable future. What might be attainable was toleration and control of drug abuse within limits, while providing attractive and acceptable alternatives. This could be a reasonable goal. The U.S. population and its officials already tolerated some nine million known alcoholics; 37,000 deaths annually from direct or indirect effects of alcohol; and some 300,000 deaths each year from tobacco-related problems. Extremes in punitive laws and extremes in permissiveness had both proved ineffective in responding to the drug problem. Central to the entire situation was the need to arrive at a uniform and humane policy that clearly separated the use of drugs, per se, from criminal activities relating to drugs.

Many thoughtful social critics focused attention on the dearth of opportunities in the modern world for experiences that provide high adventure, involvement, creativity, open and direct communication with others, or the sense of accomplishment and personal potency that comes from being able to control or change one's environment. To stimulate exploration of a creative experiment in drug prevention, the National Institute of Mental Health in the spring of 1972 launched a project called Alternative Pursuits for America's Third Century. In the simplest terms, an alternative may be viewed as something that either is, or generates, a natural "turn-on" or "high"—an exhilarating or emotional experience. Through participation by individuals in several hundred communities, the initial Alternative Pursuits project developed a way, and provided materials and techniques, to involve small voluntary groups in a creative search for alternatives and, most important, helped them implement projects.

Participants in the initial Alternatives project agreed that it showed sufficient potential to warrant further exploration.

There was extensive subjective evidence indicating that activities through which young people are given an opportunity for creative accomplishment and growth, instead of boredom and frustration, can provide a setting in which drugs simply have no place. A new direction for the future could be to develop and support additional alternative "pursuits" projects, permitting evaluation of the hypothesis that increasing the positive options open to youth will have some effect in lessening the abuse of drugs.

(STANLEY F. YOLLES; ROY GOULDING)

Economics

Economists were more modest in their pretensions in 1972 than they had tended to be during the 1960s. "The Underdevelopment of Economics" was the title of E. H. Phelps Brown's presidential address to the British Royal Economic Society, in which he compared the larger economic tasks to be performed with the more limited achievements of recent years. Sensitivity to outside charges of social irrelevance permeated the professional literature. Relatively more emphasis was placed on distribution and less on production; relatively more on equity and less on efficiency. Ecology was mentioned in professional discourse as frequently as technology, and with more approval. Economic growth, viewed during the 1960s as the key to solving such problems as poverty and urban decay, took a back seat to the economics of environmental preservation. Technological progress was viewed with skepticism. No-growth economics sometimes echoed the bliss of John Stuart Mill's stationary state.

Joan Robinson of Cambridge University spoke in the Ely lecture on "The Second Crisis of Economic Theory" (*American Economic Review,* May 1972). The first crisis, which came to a head during the depression of the 1930s, centred on the failure of economic theory to explain the determinants of the quantity of employment and output, and was met with the publication in 1936 of John Maynard Keynes's *General Theory of Employment, Interest and Money.* The second, current crisis arose from the failure of economists to explain satisfactorily how the quality or content of employment and output is determined.

Robinson seemed to say that economic theory is too much the handmaiden of the capitalist system to give honest answers to pressing problems. She cited air and water pollution as by-products of the pursuit of private profit. Divergencies between social and private costs have long been featured in welfare economics, but they have been treated as exceptions to the rule. Robinson saw the exception as the rule and the rule as the exception. The content or quality of production also reflects the way in which income is distributed between wages and profits, since the poor consume different products than the rich. The so-called marginal productivity theory of income distribution does not give any real answer to who gets how much and why.

James Tobin's presidential address to the American Economic Association on "Inflation and Unemployment" reflected the continuing preoccupation of economists with these issues, and especially with the presumed trade-off between inflation and unemployment (*American Economic Review,* March 1972). Early Nixon economic policy presupposed that a small increase in unemployment would stop price inflation, but inflation continued along with unemployment. Like most economists, Tobin viewed inflation as involving a much lower social cost than unemployment, and he saw no virtue in a relatively high rate of unemployment associated with zero inflation.

Penalties for Simple Possession of Marijuana

New Jersey
Under 25 g. or 5 g. hashish, 0–6 months; over 25 g., 0–5 years and/or $15,000

New Mexico
0–1 year in county jail and/or $1,000

New York
Less than 25 cigarettes or ¼ oz., up to 1 year; 25–99 cigarettes or ¼–1 oz., 1–7 years; over 100 cigarettes or over 1 oz., 1–15 years

North Carolina
Less than 1 g., misdemeanour with fine or imprisonment left to court; over 1 g., 0–5 years and/or $1,000

North Dakota
0–1 year and/or $500

Ohio
0–1 year and/or $1,000

Oklahoma
0–1 year

Oregon
0–1 year in county jail and/or $5,000 or 0–10 years in prison and/or $5,000

Pennsylvania
2–5 years of separate or solitary confinement and/or $2,000

Rhode Island
0–10 years and $5,000

South Carolina
Under 1 oz. or 10 g. of hashish, 0–3 months and/or $100; over these amounts, 0–6 months and/or $1,000

South Dakota
Less than 1 oz., 0–1 year in county jail and/or $500; over 1 oz., 0–5 years and/or $5,000

Tennessee
Commitment to a state-operated drug treatment facility or community mental health centre or, at the discretion of the court, up to 11 months, 29 days and/or $1,000

Texas
2 years to life

Utah
0–6 months and/or $299

Vermont
0–6 months and/or $500

Virginia
0–12 months and/or $1,000

Washington
Less than 40 g., 30 days; over 40 g., 0–5 years and/or $10,000

West Virginia
90 days–6 months and/or $1,000

Wisconsin
0–1 year in county jail and/or $500

Wyoming
0–6 months and/or $1,000

District of Columbia
0–1 year and/or $100–$1,000

Source: U.S. Department of Justice, Bureau of Narcotics and Dangerous Drugs. Data compiled by the National Organization for the Reform of Marijuana Laws.

Earthquakes: *see* Disasters; Seismology

Eastern Orthodox Churches: *see* Religion

Ecology: *see* Environment; Life Sciences

A 1972 symposium on monetary theory attempted to uncover the basic disagreements between the theories of Keynes and those of Milton Friedman (*Journal of Political Economy,* September/October 1972). In 1970 and 1971 Friedman had specified for the first time the transmission mechanism by which, in his theory, changes in the quantity of money influence national income and output. In Keynes's theory the transmission mechanism had always been clear: an increase in money lowers the interest rate, which in turn increases investment, which via a multiplier increases national income. Out of the larger income, the expenditure on consumption increases.

Friedman indicated that the transmission mechanism in his theory was analogous to that of Keynes except that it involved "a far wider range of assets and interest rates." Friedman assumed prices to be generally flexible, and he correctly attributed to Keynes an assumption of inflexible prices and wages. Friedman praised Keynes for using a theoretical model appropriate "in its simplicity and its concentration on a few key magnitudes." Friedman found, however, that Keynes's theory is wrong because it does not isolate the right key factors and is contradicted by empirical evidence. Contrary to Keynes, Friedman found that changes in governmental expenditures and taxation have no significant effect on output.

Through more than a hundred pages of discussion, Friedman and his fellow professionals failed to reach agreement or to specify the basis of disagreement. The symposium illustrated once again the grave difficulties economists have in resolving controversies. In an issue of profound significance for both economic theory and policy, the difficulty appeared to arise because the two schools, the Keynesians and the Friedman monetarists, were using their theories as arguments for their respective policies without acknowledging the point.

Pres. Richard Nixon's new economic policy of August 1971 stimulated discussion of whether direct price and wage controls would be temporary or permanent tools of economic policy. A symposium in the *Review of Economics and Statistics* (August 1972) addressed itself to this issue. According to one view, price and wage freezes serve primarily to dispel inflationary psychology. A second view held that some form of price and wage restraint must become a permanent feature of national economic policy. A commitment to low unemployment and low inflation appears to be a political necessity in democratic societies, but the concentration of private economic power in big business and big unions, widespread dissatisfaction with existing relative shares in personal income distribution, and increased welfare and social security payments, as well as higher wages and salaries, all contribute to inflationary pressure that can only be managed by direct controls.

(DUDLEY DILLARD)

See also Nobel Prizes.

Economy, World

Output, employment, and incomes throughout the industrial world—the U.S., Western Europe, Japan, and Canada—expanded strongly in 1972, following the slowdown in the rate of growth during the previous two years. The upswing was, however, marked by a strengthening of inflation, particularly in Europe. Even in the U.S., where less than full utilization of resources until late in 1972 and short-term productivity gains, reinforced by controls on prices and wages, helped to hold down inflation, the rate of price increases was still well above the average of the 1960s. Not too surprisingly, the upswing, amid signals for restraint, led toward year-end efforts to apply brakes to the economies.

The Upswing. As 1972 began, the economies of the industrial world were sluggish. The U.S., following a 0.5% decline during 1970 in its output of goods and services—the so-called gross national product (GNP) —had moved ahead in 1971 at a real growth rate of only 2.7%. Western Europe and Japan had experienced mild recessionary tendencies in 1971 that continued into early 1972. But as the year ended, the industrial world outside the Soviet Union found itself in full upswing (*see* Table I). The U.S., which accounts for almost one half of world output, had a 6.3% rise in real output. Other industrial countries thus received a powerful stimulus—a stimulus that particularly helped Japan which had in 1972 the highest figure for economic growth, 8.5%. Canada, like the U.S., recorded a 6% expansion. West Germany, Italy, and the U.K. showed increases of the order of 3%; France had the steadiest record of growth, at somewhat over 5%. For the seven major countries, gross national product as a whole increased by 5.8%—a rate even higher than the average for the 1960–70 decade.

Toward the year's end, industrial output, another key measure of economic activity, accelerated particularly rapidly in the U.S., but increased its pace also in Western Europe (*see* Chart 1). In the U.S., it stood in December 10% above a year earlier. The advance was broadly based, with particularly strong gains in the output of business equipment and consumer durable goods, especially automobiles.

The rise in employment lagged behind the expansion of output, as is normal because productivity tends to increase in the early phase of a cyclical upswing. In many countries, labour forces—swollen by demographic factors and by the rising participation of women—grew faster than opportunities for employment, which in turn gave rise to more unemployment. In the U.S., unemployment fell, overall, from 6% of the labour force in December 1971 to 5.2% a year later, a rate that was quite a distance from the so-called full employment level of 4%. But the jobless rate among married men was down to 2.4%. In the U.K., unemployment also fell but remained high. In continental Europe, the unemployment trend was generally upward. In Canada and Italy, the situation worsened. Almost everywhere, faster growth of output made only a small dent in the number of unemployed.

The upswing was helped by the natural resilience of the economies and strengthened by a rebound of business confidence following the Smithsonian compromise on exchange rates that governments had reached in December 1971. Everywhere, however, there was intense monetary and fiscal stimulation. In the view of the *Economic Outlook,* published by the Organization for Economic Cooperation and Development (OECD) in December 1972, the U.S. followed "possibly the most expansionary policy" on the fiscal side. The U.K. also had a strongly expansionary budget. In France and West Germany, the budgets were only moderately stimulative.

As in earlier periods of recovery from recession, personal expenditures for consumption and housing played a preponderant role, stimulated by cuts in income taxes (the U.S. in 1971, Canada and the U.K. in 1972) and a vast expansion of social security payments (the U.S. in 1972). In the U.S., retail sales, paced by automobile buying, rose strongly; the demand for new automobiles during the year was the highest in history. The housing boom also displayed extraordinary strength; purchases of new one-family homes climbed to record levels during the closing months.

Business investment in plant and equipment rose only in the later stages of the upswing. In the U.S., business expenditures on plant and equipment during the first three quarters ran 8.2% above the average for the comparable period of 1971, a rate of growth a bit more than 2% below the intended increase in these expenditures reported in the U.S. Commerce Department's survey at the beginning of 1972. Thus, capital expenditures did not take on the aspect of a spending boom. Even at current prices, capital outlays by manufacturing industries in the third quarter of 1972 were less than in late 1969 and 1970 and not much higher than in late 1966 and early 1967. Growth in total outlays was attributable primarily to nonmanufacturing industries, particularly public utilities and communications.

Private investment in Western Europe was slow to rise due to relatively low profit margins. Because of sharp rises in wages, capital expenditures were directed mainly toward reducing manpower requirements rather than increasing capacity, especially in Europe. In Italy, business investment showed little rise. In Japan, a major stimulus came from government investment.

For Italy, the Netherlands, and several other smaller trade-dependent European countries, the prime factor behind the growth of output was an increase in exports. Export-led growth was, however, less in evidence in Switzerland and Austria, whose economies were running at full capacity.

Table I. Growth of Real Gross National Product

Country	Annual percent changes 1959–70	1971	1972
Japan	11.3	6.7	8.5
United States	4.2	2.7	6.3
Canada	4.8	5.5	6.0
France	5.8	5.1	5.5
West Germany	5.3	2.8	3.3
United Kingdom	3.1	1.4	3.3
Italy	5.8	1.1	3.0
Seven major countries	5.3	3.3	5.8
Spain	6.7	4.6	7.0
Austria	4.9	5.2	5.5
Denmark	5.1	3.6	4.5
Finland	5.5	2.3	4.5
Switzerland	4.8	3.9	4.5
Norway	4.9	5.0	4.3
Ireland	4.1	2.8	2.8
Sweden	4.6	0.3	2.0
All industrial countries	5.3	3.4	5.5
Of which:			
Europe	5.1	3.2	4.0

Source: Adapted from OECD, *Economic Outlook* (December 1972).

Table II. Price Trends in Industrial Countries*

Country	Annual percent increases 1959–70	1971	1972
United States	2.4	4.7	3.0
Canada	2.6	3.3	4.5
Japan	4.7	4.8	5.8
France	4.4	5.0	5.5
Italy	3.9	6.9	6.0
West Germany	3.1	7.6	6.5
United Kingdom	3.6	9.0	6.8
Major countries	3.1	5.3	4.3

*As measured by deflators of gross national product.
Source: Adapted from OECD, *Economic Outlook* (December 1972).

In the world business cycle, the U.S. economy, having begun its upswing as far back as November 1970, was well ahead of Japan and West Germany, the second and the third largest industrial countries (not counting the Soviet Union), which emerged from the business slowdown only in early 1972. True, these divergences in cyclical positions—rising demand in the U.S., which in turn increased demand for imported consumer goods, industrial materials, and equipment, and sluggish demand in the rest of the industrial world, which held down demand for U.S. exports—contributed to the weakening of the U.S. merchandise trade balance in 1972. The trade deficit reached $6.4 billion, the highest ever recorded. It remained obstinately high, even bearing in mind that there was bound to be a substantial time lag before the devaluation of the dollar produced a positive response in the nation's exports and imports. With business recovery in Western Europe and Japan, demand for U.S. exports tended to strengthen.

The advance of the U.S. in the world's business cycle helped the long-term capital account of the U.S. balance of payments. As industrial profits in the U.S. rose—by 15% after taxes for 1972 as a whole—while the profit performance in Western Europe and Japan remained rather mediocre, marked changes occurred in the flow of long-term investment funds: outflows of dollars from the U.S. for direct investments abroad, which had risen sharply in 1970 and 1971, fell noticeably in 1972; at the same time, inflows of foreign funds for direct investment in the U.S., which had been negative during 1971, rose, and foreign purchases of U.S. corporate stocks picked up on a sizable scale.

Signals for Restraint. Given the momentum of expansion, reinforced during much of the year by strong monetary and fiscal stimulation, the economies were, as 1972 ended, approaching full capacity utilization in most industrial countries, except Japan and Italy. In the U.S., unemployment among married men was down to 2.4%, as already noted. Delivery schedules lengthened as did the list of materials reported to be in short supply (for example, zinc, electric motors, lumber, bearings). Most importantly, because of the relatively slow pace of capital outlays in manufacturing industries mentioned earlier, a number of industries in the U.S. were at or close to capacity operating limits. In the fall of 1972, the automotive, rubber, and paper industries were operating at above 90% of capacity while the nonferrous metals, textiles, and food and beverage industries were closing in on this level. With controls on prices and profit margins—limited to a company's average in the best two of its last three fiscal years—businesses faced considerable uncertainty with regard to their ability to raise prices to cover the higher costs of additional output. Ironically, this effect of controls ran directly counter to the intent of controls.

Another visible signal for restraint was the rise in prices (*see* Table II and Chart 2). In the U.S., for reasons already mentioned, the rate of increase of the general price level—the so-called GNP deflator—was kept to 3% in 1972; although this was a notable improvement from the 4.7% in 1971, the average for the decade ended 1970 was much less: 2.4%. The consumer price index rose by 3.3%. Food prices, which had been exempt from controls in 1971, were a special cause for concern, which led in June 1972 to the imposition of controls on prices for unprocessed farm products "after the first sale" and to the lifting of import quotas on meat. But controls merely suppress inflation. The very sharp rise in agricultural prices in the closing months of 1972 exemplified the inherent vulnerability of the price structure in the U.S. economy as well as worldwide.

In several Western European countries, consumer prices rose in 1972 twice as fast as the annual averages during the decade ended 1970. The greatest rise was in the U.K., followed by France and West Germany. The peak of price increases had already been reached by mid-1971, but while the pace slowed in the second half of 1971 and the first half of 1972, it greatly accelerated in the second half of 1972. Meat shortages, increases in "administered" prices of food, electricity, gas, and transportation, the passing-on of earlier above-average increases in unit labour costs, and the relaxation of price controls were special contributing factors; but the basic factor was the relapse into inflation. Japan recorded a consumer price rise that was not far from the long-term average; but the pace accelerated in the closing months of 1972. Canada also had a relatively good experience in 1972, with some weakening toward the end.

The rise in wage costs was particularly rapid during 1972 in the U.K., West Germany, and Italy (Table III shows at a glance where countries stood relative to one another). In Canada, the rise in wage costs slowed somewhat. The U.S. had the best performance, which, toward the year's end, displayed the following salient features: Productivity in the private nonfarm sector rose during the third quarter at an annual rate of 6.3%—more than double the postwar average. Meanwhile, compensation per man-hour increased at a 5.9% annual rate, well below the average of the previous four years. With productivity rising faster than compensation, unit labour costs inched downward for the second consecutive quarter, the first declines since 1965. In 1969 and 1970, when the rate of price inflation was at a peak, unit labour costs were rising at close to 7% annually. The real spendable weekly wage of the average production worker, which had not improved at all between 1965 and 1970, rose sharply. This lesson that workers did better in regard to real take-home pay during a period of wage restraint than in the preceding years of high wage settlements would not, it was hoped, be lost for 1973; but many more major claims were to be put forward than in 1972, including those of automobile workers.

Money depreciated still further (*see* Table IV). In the U.S., the average rate of depreciation of the dollar—down to a 3.2% pace from 4.3% in 1971—was an improvement, but was still uncomfortable. At the rate of depreciation pertaining in 1972, the dollar would lose one half of its buying power in 22 years; with a 4% rate, the halving would occur in 17 years; and with a 5% rate, the process would take only 14 years. In Europe, generally, rates of depreciation of buying power outstripped the already high pace of earlier years.

The reduced pace of price-cost increases in the U.S. relative to other industrial countries made the U.S. foreign trade position better than it otherwise would have been. The devaluation of the dollar also improved the price-competitive position of American goods. True, the effective 11% depreciation of the dollar (as weighted by trade) stemming from the Smithsonian agreement was, at the close of 1972, somewhat eroded by the floating of the British pound. But the 1971 exchange rate realignment was accompanied by sizable increases in export prices of manufactures throughout the entire industrial world outside the U.S.; U.S. export prices rose more slowly. In appraising these trends, illustrated in Chart 2, it should, of course, be remembered that international competition tends to curb the ability of exporters to raise prices even when domestic costs and prices rise; exporters often absorb exchange rate increases in order to maintain established markets. Nevertheless, the profitability of export sales was greatly affected by changes in exchange rates, which gradually influenced the direction of trade.

To have corrected the overvaluation of the dollar was not enough. What was also needed was reasonably free access to markets and the removal of handicaps for U.S. exporters stemming from differences in tax systems, and in the availability and cost of export credit. However, even if access to markets abroad were widened and, hopefully, freed meaningfully, much would still depend on the determination and ability of the U.S. to safeguard the degree of export-import price competitiveness it had regained. The edge that the U.S. had in its international economic position presupposed that it would not dissipate the result of the devaluation through renewed inflation at a pace in excess of other industrial countries.

Applying Brakes. The concern about inflation in the U.S. and the actual outbreak of inflation in Western Europe raised awkward and explosive problems for governments. For this happened at a time when unemployment remained at levels regarded as politically and socially unacceptable. In Europe, a striking feature was the fact that prices rose almost everywhere at more or less the same rates, despite considerable differences among countries in the degree of demand pressure and of monetary and fiscal stimulation.

Governments thus faced the necessity to hold down or even to restrict aggregate demand while maintaining acceptably high employment. Toward the year's end, the U.S. administration endeavoured to restrain federal spending through a shock therapy: a rigid ceiling on expenditures. Having been denied a freeze or near-

Table III. Industrial Countries Ranked by Price-Cost Performance

Item	Percent change in: 1972*	1971	1970
Consumer prices			
United States	3.3	4.3	5.8
Japan	4.5	6.1	7.8
Canada	4.8	2.9	3.3
Italy	4.9	4.8	4.9
West Germany	5.7	5.1	3.8
France	5.8	5.6	5.5
United Kingdom	7.2	9.4	6.4
Hourly earnings in manufacturing			
Canada	7.9	7.5	5.4
United States	8.3	1.3	0.5
Italy	8.9	13.6	21.5
West Germany	9.7	13.7	12.7
France	11.0	11.1	10.4
United Kingdom	11.2	11.4	12.6
Japan	13.8	13.7	17.6
Output per man-hour in manufacturing			
Japan	8.2	6.0	16.3
France	7.5	5.9	6.5
United States	6.6	—	−4.8
Canada	6.0	4.0	−0.3
West Germany	5.2	4.5	3.0
Italy	1.3	−3.3	6.7
United Kingdom	—	−0.2	1.2
Wage costs per unit of output in manufacturing			
United States	2.4	2.6	6.0
Canada	2.6	3.2	6.1
France	2.8	3.8	4.2
Japan	3.5	8.1	4.2
United Kingdom	3.7	7.7	11.1
West Germany	4.4	7.9	13.0
Italy	4.7	13.3	13.7

*1972 to date, compared with the same period of 1971.
Source: Adapted from national sources and from OECD, *Economic Outlook* (December 1972).

freeze on federal spending, President Nixon attempted to impound funds already appropriated in an effort to keep actual disbursements in the 1972–73 fiscal year as close to $250 billion as possible and thus obviate tax increases. The administration was ready to accept new spending initiatives but sought to prune old programs. The Federal Reserve showed no disposition to accommodate an acceleration of inflation. Late in 1972 monetary policy appeared to move toward a mid-course correction, with the general trend of interest rates upward. But, judging from the authorities' moral suasion to hold down interest rates and from congressional views and attitudes, any tightening of money and credit appeared technically ticklish and politically unwelcome.

While in the U.S. the expansion of money supply was fast—12% (average for the year relative to 1971)—it was unusually rapid in several European countries—27% in the U.K., 20% in France, and 16% in West Germany (on broad definitions). In Canada and Japan, money supply also increased—16 and 22%, respectively. In the closing months of the year, most countries, with the notable exceptions of Italy and Japan, introduced or tightened monetary restrictions. In fiscal policy, the emphasis in West Germany, after the December elections, was on income tax increases rather than on holding down government expenditures. In France, where cuts in indirect taxation were announced in December as one means of holding down price increases, the loss of revenue was to be made up by issuance of a large government loan, with amortization and interest payments tied to the European monetary unit used in the EEC, based on gold at the $35 per ounce price; the second purpose of the loan was to help mop up funds that otherwise would be spent on the purchase of consumer goods.

Table IV. Depreciation of Money

Country	Indexes of value of money (1961=100) 1966	1971	Annual rates of depreciation (percent) '61–'71*	'70–'71	'71–'72†
Industrial countries					
United States	92	74	3.0	4.3	3.2
Greece	89	80	2.2	2.2	3.8
Japan	74	56	5.6	5.4	4.3
Canada	90	75	2.8	3.6	4.6
Luxembourg	87	74	2.9	3.2	4.8
Italy	79	66	4.0	3.4	4.9
Belgium	85	72	3.3	3.4	5.1
West Germany	86	74	2.9	2.8	5.4
Sweden	80	64	4.4	4.5	5.7
Austria	84	70	3.6	3.7	5.7
France	83	65	4.2	4.7	5.8
South Africa	88	73	3.1	3.8	5.8
Finland	76	59	5.1	4.9	5.8
Australia	91	76	2.7	3.6	5.9
Denmark	76	55	5.7	6.0	6.0
Switzerland	83	69	3.7	3.7	6.1
Norway	81	62	4.7	5.2	6.6
New Zealand	87	64	4.4	6.0	7.0
United Kingdom	84	64	4.4	5.4	7.2
Spain	68	52	6.4	5.2	7.6
Iceland	56	32	10.7	10.6	8.0
Ireland	81	59	5.1	6.1	8.0
Netherlands	80	63	4.6	4.9	8.1
Portugal	85	59	5.2	7.1	11.1
Yugoslavia	47	29	11.5	8.8	13.6
Less developed countries					
Singapore	94	88	1.2	1.2	1.5
Indonesia	1	‡	56.6	33.2	2.8
Venezuela	94	86	1.5	1.7	3.0
Thailand	91	81	2.1	2.2	3.4
Morocco	85	78	2.4	1.6	3.8
Nigeria	83	61	4.9	6.2	3.8
Costa Rica	92	79	2.3	3.0	3.9
Mexico	89	76	2.7	3.2	4.5
Jamaica	91	67	3.9	5.9	4.6
Taiwan	94	77	2.6	4.0	4.9
Pakistan	83	68	3.8	3.8	5.5
Iran	94	83	1.8	2.2	5.9
India	69	55	5.8	5.8	6.0
Ecuador	83	63	4.5	5.3	6.9
Philippines	76	51	6.6	7.8	7.1
Peru	62	40	8.8	8.5	7.2
Paraguay	75	69	3.6	1.7	8.4
South Korea	48	28	12.0	10.2	9.5
Israel	70	55	5.7	4.6	11.7
Colombia	51	35	10.1	7.4	12.0
Turkey	81	49	6.8	9.3	14.6
Brazil	9	3	29.6	19.0	15.6
South Vietnam	47	13	18.5	22.5	19.6
Chile	26	8	21.9	20.3	28.7
Argentina	30	12	18.9	16.5	36.1

Note: Depreciation of money is measured by rates of decline in the domestic purchasing power of national currencies (as computed from reciprocals of official cost-of-living or consumer price indexes), not by rates of price inflation. For example, a rate of inflation of 100% is equivalent to a 50% rate of depreciation of buying power of money.
*Compounded annually.
†Based on average monthly data available for 1972 compared with corresponding period of 1971.
‡Less than one.
Source: First National City Bank, New York, N.Y.

Restraints on private credit and fiscal discipline as the main ways in which to reduce inflation came, however, to be regarded as inadvisable under the year's circumstances. In this view, markets could not be counted on to check the upward course of prices and wages, even when aggregate demand for goods and services was held back or entered a decline in the course of business recession. The way out was sought in a multipolicy attack on inflation—supplementing monetary and fiscal controls on aggregate demand with controls on prices and incomes (wages, salaries, dividends, rents, and other incomes). The measures of price and incomes controls adopted in the U.S. in August 1971 came to be imitated in the hope that they might, at least, damp expectations of continuing price increases and provide a breathing space.

In the U.K., after extensive but unsuccessful efforts to win approval from business and labour for a voluntary agreement on parallel restraints on pay and price increases, the government in November imposed a general freeze on prices and incomes (wages, rents, and dividends) for 90 days, with an option to extend it for another 60 days. The freeze was introduced to allow time to work out legislation in the light of "agreed objectives of economic management" that could accelerate economic growth to a stated target of 5%. Previously, incomes and price policies relied on government efforts to gradually bring down the level of wage settlements, and on voluntary price restraint exercised by nationalized industries and some 200 of the largest enterprises. The U.K. had practiced incomes policy in the 1960s, but the experiment was a failure. Among the reasons were the failure to grant price and incomes administrators the authority necessary to deal comprehensively with decisions of businesses to raise prices and with major wage negotiations (they could deal only with cases referred to them by the government); lack of substantive power (administrators had merely the power of postponement); acceptance of rather indefinite productivity promises as the basis for wage increases; and the overambitious objective implied by the norms that were set of complete price stability—a target unattainable in practical reality.

The U.S. controls on pay and prices, introduced in November 1971 under Phase Two of the Economic Stabilization Program, were more realistic and, perhaps for this reason, more successful than the earlier British experience. They were more realistic because their objective was more nearly achievable—a 5.5% increase in wages in the face of an official target of a 2–3% rise in consumer prices. Despite the sharp increase in food prices, which were not covered by the controls programs as enacted in 1971, price inflation was brought down perceptibly. On the whole, of course, not only controls but also the cyclical position of the U.S. economy, and the special factors noted earlier in this article, helped to reduce the pace of price-wage inflation.

The principal changes during 1972 consisted of removing controls from small enterprises with 60 or less employees (May) and from workers earning less than $2.75 an hour (August); extending controls to unprocessed farm products after the first sale, coupled with the suspension of import quotas for meat (June); and reimposing controls on 62,000 lumber companies (July). The controls were to expire in April 1973, unless the legislative authority for the program was extended.

CHART 1.

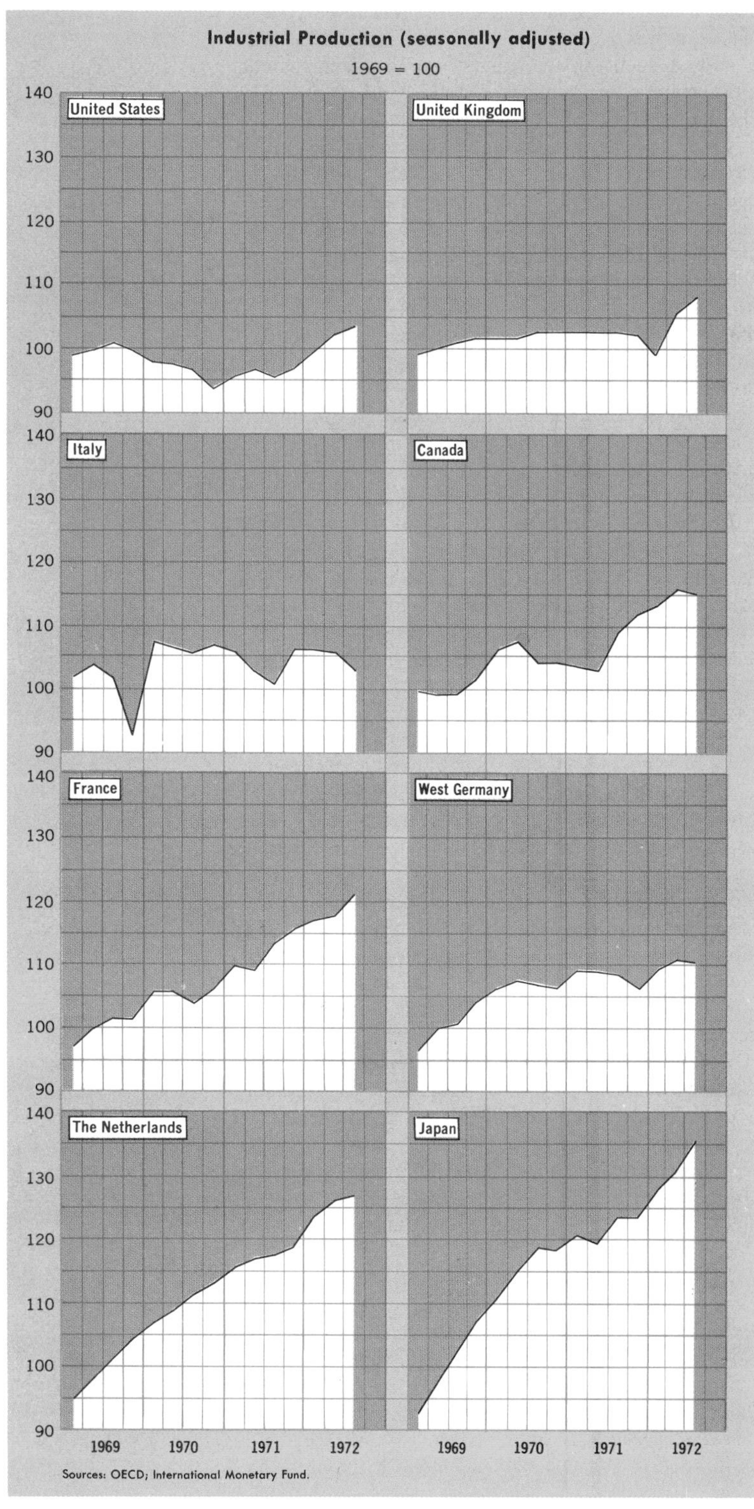

Sources: OECD; International Monetary Fund.

Several continental European countries, without instituting comprehensive controls as the U.S. had done, had recourse to price-wage surveillance and reporting or intensified existing procedures. In France, where price controls had been loosened substantially in March 1972, the government decided in August to freeze public service charges and to extend the duration of price agreements; and in December, it recommended to employers and unions that they limit increases in wages and salaries to 6% during 1973. The Netherlands in November reintroduced price controls that had been lifted the year before. Italy (and, in November, France) provided partial relief by practically exempting food from indirect taxation and cutting taxes on textiles, etc. But, by the year's end, West Germany had imposed no controls. In Canada, the surveillance and reporting of important price developments expired in mid-1972.

Since the days of Diocletian, no government has succeeded in controlling prices save for very short periods. The U.S. or British governments, having turned somersaults in that they ended up by imposing price and incomes controls they had previously deprecated, remained philosophically committed to a return to primary reliance on free markets. Embracing price and incomes controls was not exactly a love match for a Republican administration and a Conservative government, but a marriage of convenience. It was recognized that, with the passage of time, controls would become increasingly irritating, ineffective, and a greater source of inefficiency. But to turn the clock back or, perhaps, return to voluntary guidelines of the sort the U.S. had in the Kennedy and Johnson administrations was regarded as an invitation to relapse into the combination of strong inflationary pressures and weak controls that set off the inflation in 1965–66.

Economic freedom requires monetary and fiscal discipline. In the worldwide inflationary environment, and amid deep-seated political and social pressures, free-market economies were on the defensive throughout the entire industrial world.

A new development in 1972 was the effort of the nine EEC countries, announced in October, to achieve simultaneous and mutually supportive action to reduce the rate of price increases. The main stress was placed on monetary restraint. Fiscal policy was also referred to amply, but it was, in effect, relieved of its duty in stemming price inflation—not too surprisingly since governments authorized for themselves an increase in spending that corresponded to the nominal growth rate of gross national product. Price surveillance was emphasized strongly; but earlier proposals to cut tariffs for the first half of 1973 as a means of exerting pressure on domestic prices fell through. In the declaration of intent, it was stated that by 1974 the growth rate in money supply would be reduced to that of the real gross national product plus the so-called standard price rise of about 4% considered "inevitable."

By and large, people seemed eager to distribute more income among themselves, and to enjoy shorter working hours, longer vacations, and larger pensions, as if they could consume or use otherwise more than they produced. Demands for even more were increasingly insistent as if trees could grow beyond a certain height. In this atmosphere, it appeared unrealistic to count on a marked decline in the rate of inflation in most industrial countries. For one thing, governments could console their people by pointing out that the performance of other nations was equally bad. And for another, the greater permissiveness with regard to exchange-rate changes meant that it became easier than in the past for governments to deal with adverse balance of payments repercussions of domestic inflation.

Trends in the Primary Producing Countries. Resumption of a faster rate of economic expansion in the industrial world helped strengthen output in the primary producing countries of Asia, Africa, and South America. These countries had in 1970–71 felt the effects of the recessionary slowdown in the U.S., Europe, and Japan; and the speedup in economic activity in 1972 brought about an increase in output of raw materials.

Prices of primary producers' export commodities rose substantially in 1972. The steadiest increase was in prices of foodstuffs, notably wheat, coffee, cocoa, and sugar; while prices of base metals remained relatively stable, those of rubber, wool, and hides increased markedly. Petroleum prices received another boost. Shortages of supplies also pushed up prices for certain commodities, most spectacularly wheat, in the aftermath of the partial failure of the harvest in the Soviet Union.

The rise in the output of commodities and in their prices resulted in increased export earnings of primary producing countries. Several of the more developed nations, notably Australia and South Africa, added substantially to their monetary reserves. But among the less developed countries, strong reserve gains were confined to the oil-producing nations of the Middle East and Africa; these countries, as a group, almost tripled their reserves in the space of only three years.

Throughout the primary producing world, rises in output and in export prices of commodities were accompanied by pressures on domestic price levels. These pressures were in part transmitted from the industrial world through the increases in import prices of finished goods; but, in large part, they were also the outcome of purely domestic forces of inflation. The currencies continued to lose buying power at rapid rates (*see* Table IV).

A Disappointing Year for the U.S.S.R. The year 1972 was a difficult one for the Soviet Union. It had a miserable harvest, officially the consequence of deadly frosts in winter, the worst summer drought in a century, and forest fires. But there was awareness outside the Soviet Union, and reportedly in the country itself—where half of the labour force was still tied to agriculture—that even a good harvest was not as good as it might be if Soviet agriculture were better organized and more efficient. On the collectivized land there was too little mechanization, too little skill in using available machinery, and too little incentive to work as hard as on the peasants' own private smallholdings.

To make good the harvest shortfall, the U.S.S.R. purchased 400 million bu. of U.S. wheat, representing one-fourth of the 1972 U.S. crop. To increase the animal protein component of the national diet, the Soviet Union also bought or was expected to buy some 250–275 million bu. of U.S. corn and 40 million bu. of U.S. soybeans. These purchases forced up the prices of wheat and feed grains in the world market and thus contributed to the rise in food prices for Americans as well as for people in countries that depend on imported wheat. Thus, U.S. consumers, and,

continued on page 259

CHART 2.

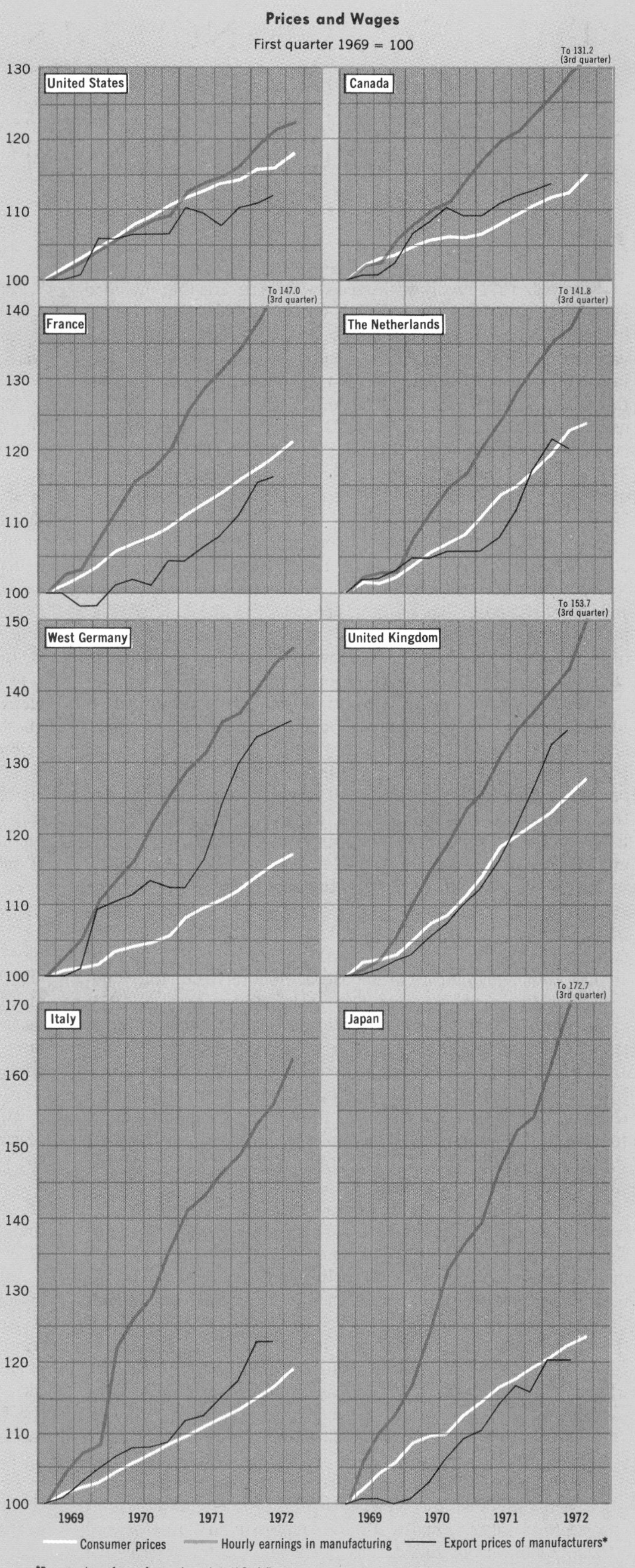

*Export prices of manufactured goods in U.S. dollar terms.
Sources: OECD; International Monetary Fund; National Institute for Economic and Social Research.

THE UNITED KINGDOM'S ENTRY INTO THE EUROPEAN ECONOMIC COMMUNITY

The year 1972 finally witnessed—after a decade that included several sterling crises, two French vetoes (the first one coming in 1963), and extensive debate on the advantages and disadvantages of U.K. accession—the entry of the United Kingdom into the European Economic Community. Effective Jan. 1, 1973, the U.K., together with Ireland and Denmark, joined the six nations—Belgium, France, West Germany, Italy, the Netherlands, and Luxembourg—that had created the Community in 1957. The enlargement of the Common Market gave it new dimensions politically as well as economically. (*See* EUROPEAN UNITY: *Special Report.*)

The Terms. After the formal opening of negotiations on June 30, 1970, it took the Six and the U.K. a year and a half to come to terms on the treaty of accession. The treaty was signed on Jan. 22, 1972, after having been approved by the U.K. Parliament on Oct. 28, 1971, by a substantial margin in both the House of Commons (356 votes to 244, with 69 Labour MPs voting with the majority) and the House of Lords.

Britain accepted the basic principles on which the Common Market is run and the common policies by which these principles are put into practice. The negotiations centred around temporary exceptions to these principles and the transitional periods before full application of the common policies. No transitional periods were provided for Britain's accession to the EEC's two ancillary groups, the European Coal and Steel Community and Euratom.

The EEC is a customs union that provides for free trade among members and, in its relationships with nonmember countries, for a common external tariff on industrial goods and a system of variable levies on agricultural imports. Britain is to abolish completely tariffs on industrial imports from the Community in five equal steps of 20% each between April 1, 1973, and July 1, 1977, and to move toward the common external tariff in four steps, beginning with a 40% cut on Jan. 1, 1974, and ending on July 1, 1977, with the last of three 20% steps. The tariff adjustments will be sizable since Britain presently charges an arithmetic average duty of 10.2% on imports coming from outside the sterling area but only 1.2% on goods originating within the sterling area; the arithmetic average duty under the Community's common external tariff is 7.6%.

The transitional period for agricultural imports is to be five years, with the U.K. making its sixth and last move toward the Community's price levels at the end of 1977. Under the Community's common agricultural policy, market prices for the main farm products are maintained with regard to imports through variable levies and with regard to domestic products through support programs. Prices in the six Common Market countries in 1972 were considerably higher than in Britain, which will, therefore, incur sizable increases in the cost of food.

Fisheries are a major exception to the five-year rule, since the Community's principle of free access to the waters of other member states will not be applied for at least ten years. Special rules were provided for New Zealand's butter and the Commonwealth's sugar. Finally, Britain accepted an "orderly and gradual rundown" of the sterling balances; and the progressive alignment of "the external characteristics" of sterling to those of other Community currencies.

Economic Significance. For Britain, the entry into the Community of the Six opened new markets for industrial goods. Britain's entry, however, implied long-term evolution rather than sudden change: the Six already were Britain's largest trading partner.

Another concrete benefit to Britain was the broadening scope for the financial activities of the City of London. Also, a vital consideration for Britain was the expected EEC help in restructuring its less developed regions, such as Wales and Scotland. To finance development in the U.K., as well as in less developed parts of other Common Market countries, the Community set up in 1972 a regional development fund.

The U.K. expected that membership would help reinvigorate its economy after many years of balance of payments difficulties, a disappointing record of industrial investments, and a low rate of economic growth. While it is not possible to attribute Britain's relatively weak economic performance—2.8% annual rate of growth between 1958 and 1971—entirely to its absence from the EEC, its accession was justified by the government on the ground that it would help the nation achieve a record comparable to that of the Six, which for the same period worked out to 5.8%. Britain's accelerated growth would, it was hoped, enable it to meet the balance of payments costs of its membership—its contribution to the Community's budget and the effects of agricultural integration on British food prices resulting from Britain's acceptance of the EEC agricultural policy.

For the Six, Britain's accession represented the most important event in the process of European integration since 1957. The enlarged Community—totaling over 250 million people—accounts for two-fifths of world trade, compared with one-eighth for the U.S. Thus, it finds itself in a position to develop an identity of its own with greater authority than heretofore. In fact, its development as a regional group will tend to confer upon it a single bargaining power in international monetary and trade negotiations with other economic powers—the Soviet Union, China, Japan, and the U.S.

The Enlarged Community and the U.S. In Washington, official support of Britain's decision to join the EEC lacked the fervour that had been displayed in 1961 and 1967, the years of Britain's two previous attempts to get into the Community. In 1972 the U.S. was concerned about the Community's rejection of an American suggestion for a phased elimination of all industrial tariffs among developed countries and about the Common Market's actual or planned arrangements for preferential treatment of Mediterranean and African countries. But it was in the field of agricultural trade that the U.S. pressure was greatest for reviewing the Common Market's arrangements; evidently, the U.S. would also be pressed to review some of its own agricultural arrangements. Other issues revolved around the fundamental differences of viewpoints between Europe and the U.S. regarding international monetary reform, as summed up elsewhere in the *Book of the Year*.

Toward the year's end the Community, as well as the U.S., reiterated its intent to maintain a constructive dialogue regarding the progressive liberalization of tariffs and nontariff barriers to trade on a comprehensive basis during the multilateral negotiations in 1973 for a more equitable and open world economic order.

continued from page 257
indeed, consumers in all countries importing food, such as the U.K., in effect, subsidized the backwardness and inefficiency of Soviet agriculture and of its economic organization.

Industry, the privileged sector of the Soviet economy, also had a poor year. Economic growth was lower, and productivity improved less, than stipulated in the five-year plan (1971–76). Output of consumer goods, which only recently was given priority over heavy industry, was cut back. Premier Aleksei N. Kosygin revealed that the Soviet Union's long-standing economic difficulties had been barely touched by the reform program of the mid-1960s that called for "market socialism." He strongly urged the importance of what the Soviets call "intensification"—a drive for intensifying growth based on new management methods and scientific and technological advances in industry. The renewed Soviet interest in importing capital goods and technology from the U.S. and Japan, on top of its established trade relationships with Western Europe, was thus linked to the performance of its domestic economy.

Enter China. The sudden reappearance on the world's diplomatic stage of a country with a population of 800 million and, potentially, an industrial and military superpower was a momentous event in 1972. Official Chinese news bulletins drew attention to the further increase in industrial output, an increase that, judging from newspaper reports, was accompanied by many difficulties. The country experienced critical shortages of equipment and essential raw materials; and policies aimed at regional self-sufficiency and decentralization gave rise to bottlenecks. Costs were high and productivity low. To modernize agriculture and industry, China wanted trade with the U.S. and Japan. While China avoided long-term borrowing as a matter of policy, preferring to scale down imports to the amounts of foreign exchange available from export earnings, its increased participation in international trade appeared, at the close of 1972, as a new fact of international economic life.

(MIROSLAV A. KRIZ)

See also Economics; Employment, Wages, and Hours; Income, National; Industrial Review; Labour Unions; Payments and Reserves, International; Prices; Profits; Savings and Investment; Trade, International.

Ecuador

A republic on the west coast of South America, Ecuador is bounded by Colombia, Peru, and the Pacific Ocean. Area: 109,483 sq.mi. (283,561 sq.km.), including the Galapagos Islands (3,075 sq.mi.). Pop. (1972 est.): 6,598,300. Cap.: Quito (pop., 1972 est., 575,116). Largest city: Guayaquil (pop., 1972 est., 879,016). Language: Spanish, but Indians speak Quechuan and Jivaroan. Religion: mainly Roman Catholic. Presidents in 1972, José María Velasco Ibarra and, from February 16, Brig. Gen. Guillermo Rodríguez Lara.

On Feb. 15, 1972, José María Velasco Ibarra, five times president of Ecuador, was deposed—for the fourth time in his career—by the armed forces. A new government, described as "nationalist and revolutionary," was proclaimed by the commanders-in-chief of the Army, Navy, and Air Force, and Brig. Gen. Guillermo Rodríguez Lara (*see* BIOGRAPHY) was appointed president. The general elections scheduled for June 4 were canceled. The new Cabinet included two civilians, in charge of finance and foreign affairs.

The new government's program aimed at a basic reorganization of economic, social, and administrative structures, to include raising the standard of living, streamlining the public service, improving education, developing natural resources, reestablishing the "principle of authority," increasing respect for human rights, and fulfilling international commitments. President Rodríguez also stated that he would revise foreign oil contracts "if necessary," defend Ecuador's claim to a 200-mi. territorial waters limit, and permit absolute freedom of expression for news media. On the question of agrarian reform, he said that those with legitimate rights who worked the land had no cause for alarm and that it was government policy to guarantee legally acquired property. Plans for tackling the large unfinanced deficit inherited from the previous administration included an austerity program involving a revision of basic taxes, tight control of public expenditure, extreme caution in the handling of public credit, and the channeling of bank loans toward diversification and development in agriculture.

In August Ecuador became an oil-exporting country when the Lago Agrio–Esmeraldas pipeline went into operation with an initial output of 150,000 bbl. a day, to be increased later to 250,000 bbl. a day. It was hoped that the pipeline's capacity would eventually be raised to 400,000 bbl. a day. It was announced that 94 oil wells had been drilled in the Oriente region

ECUADOR

Education. (1968–69) Primary, pupils 928,687, teachers 24,426; secondary, pupils 105,362, teachers 8,147; vocational, pupils 50,998, teachers 3,300; teacher training, students 17,254, teachers 987; higher (including 10 universities), students (1969–70) 33,562, teaching staff (1968–69) 2,256.

Finance. Monetary unit: sucre, with (Sept. 18, 1972) an official rate of 25 sucres to U.S. $1 (free rate of 62.44 sucres = £1 sterling). Gold, SDRs, and foreign exchange, central bank: (June 1972) U.S. $93.2 million; (June 1971) U.S. $64.8 million. Budget (excluding development budget; 1970 est.): revenue 5,142,000,000 sucres; expenditure 5,061,000,000 sucres. National income: (1970) 29.7 billion sucres; (1969) 25.9 billion sucres. Money supply: (May 1972) 5,915,000,000 sucres; (May 1971) 5,351,000,000 sucres. Cost of living (Quito; 1965 = 100): (May 1972) 144; (May 1971) 135.

Foreign Trade. (1971) Imports U.S. $303 million; exports U.S. $237.8 million. Import sources (1970): U.S. 42%; Japan 10%; West Germany 9%; Colombia 7%; U.K. 6%. Export destinations (1970): U.S. 36%; Japan 25%; West Germany 10%. Main exports: bananas 51%; coffee 15%; cocoa 11%.

Transport and Communications: Roads (1970) 17,200 km. Motor vehicles in use (1970): passenger 39,600; commercial (including buses) 51,200. Railways (1970): 990 km.; traffic 85 million passenger-km., freight 56 million net ton-km. Air traffic (1970): 255,323,000 passenger-km.; freight 10,687,000 net ton-km. Telephones (Dec. 1970) 130,000. Radio receivers (Dec. 1970) 1.7 million. Television receivers (Dec. 1970) 150,000.

Agriculture. Production (in 000; metric tons; 1971; 1970 in parentheses): corn *c.* 230 (221); barley *c.* 110 (107); potatoes *c.* 350 (*c.* 370); rice *c.* 150 (184); cassava (1970) *c.* 410, (1969) *c.* 400; dry beans *c.* 30 (*c.* 30); bananas (1970) *c.* 3,000, (1969) *c.* 2,800; coffee *c.* 72 (*c.* 78); cocoa (1971–72) 55, (1970–71) 60; oranges (1970) *c.* 195, (1969) 196; sugar, raw value (1971–72) *c.* 313, (1970–71) *c.* 293; cotton, lint *c.* 13 (*c.* 4). Livestock (in 000; 1970–71); cattle *c.* 2,500; sheep *c.* 1,900; pigs *c.* 1,360; horses *c.* 250; chickens *c.* 5,450.

Industry. Production (in 000; metric tons; 1970): petroleum products 1,175; crude oil (1971) 174; electricity (kw-hr.) 949,000; cement 458; gold (troy oz.) 8.5; silver (troy oz.) 71.

in 1967–71, with an additional 64 expected in 1972. The Texaco-Gulf consortium estimated that its daily output would reach 250,000 bbl. a day by 1973, rising to 325,000 bbl. a day by 1974. Total exportable production, including Texaco-Gulf, was expected to exceed 400,000 bbl. a day by 1976.

Shortly after taking office, the new government canceled a contract granted to Marubeni Iida of Japan for the construction of a $50 million state oil refinery at Puerto Balao (near Esmeraldas) on the ground that it had been signed "without due consideration," and new bids were asked for. Foreign-owned oil companies were requested to sign new contracts with the government by the end of 1972. Additionally, the government reserved the right to transport up to 50% of the oil exports. It was decided that a tanker fleet should be organized by a new company, the Flota Petrolera Nacional (Transnave). Despite uncertainty as to government intentions, most of the oil companies announced increased investments for 1972.

Other sectors of the economy showed encouraging signs in the early part of 1972. The net international monetary reserves of the Banco Central rose from $17.4 million at the end of 1971 to $21.4 million on April 30; with the addition of a $40 million loan from a U.S. bank, the total rose to $66.1 million on May 26. The economic improvement stemmed also from a significant reduction in the trade deficit, from $19 million in the first quarter of 1971 to $15 million in the same period of 1972.

Petroleum developments apart, there seemed to be good possibilities for diversifying the economy away from bananas, coffee, and cocoa, which in 1971 had accounted for more than 75% of total export exchange. Fish products replaced sugar as Ecuador's fourth main export commodity in 1971, the principal types being shrimp, lobster, and especially tuna. The value of fish exports rose spectacularly from $7 million in 1970 to $15 million in 1971, and it was estimated that the development of marine resources could produce additional exchange earnings of up to $30 million a year from tuna alone. There were also promising developments in vegetable oils, particularly cottonseed and African palm, and the emergence of nontraditional export commodities such as tea, mushrooms, and abaca suggested that Ecuador had by no means reached the limits of its agricultural diversification potential. Moreover, a meeting of the International Atomic Energy Agency concluded that uranium deposits in the Loja area could become as important as petroleum. (R. B. LEWRY)

Education

About 650 million people in the world were in some form of institutionalized education in 1972. In the remaining years of the 20th century the number of people of school and university age would, it was predicted, increase by more than 1,000,000,000, representing an average annual increase of 36 million potential pupils and students. Despite doubts in the early 1960s of matching the educational explosion with an adequate supply of teachers, there were indications that the current demand for teachers was being met.

Global estimates of growth, however, ought not to conceal the fact that in the less developed countries, most of them African, progress was much less than satisfactory. Although the world rate of illiteracy was continuing to decline—to an estimated 33% in 1972—absolute numbers were still increasing simply because of the enormous population growth. There were some 40 million adult illiterates in Latin America, 50 million in the Arab states, 140 million in Africa, and more than 500 million in Asia. It was expected that the illiteracy rate would continue to decline to about 29% in 1980, but this would still leave 820 million adult illiterates in the world.

World spending on education was estimated at about $200 billion in 1972. The proportion of national budgets allocated to education averaged 16%, although the number of big spenders (over 20% of national budgets on education) had gone down compared with the mid-1960s. The average worldwide public spending on education was increasing more rapidly than the average worldwide gross national product (GNP). Again, however, there were substantial differences between regions. There was also continued evidence of serious waste in the less developed countries through high dropout rates at the primary stage.

As a result of a study of these and other statistics conducted for UNESCO and described as the most comprehensive of its kind, a special international committee on the development of education recommended that universal primary education become a top educational priority in the 1970s. The commission warned, however, that efforts to combat illiteracy would have to move outside the realm of formal education toward "more immediate, more practical, more massive, and also more lively nontraditional educational patterns."

In the more developed countries the chief concern of governments about education was with its steeply escalating cost. This was manifest in the Netherlands, for example, where the government expressed its determination to contain the rising cost of education, which reached the level of 7.5% of its GNP in 1972. Sweden, however, spent 8.5% of GNP in 1972, and, understandably, the government vigorously tried to contain educational expenditures. All the developed countries were anxious to get better value for their money in higher education. It was there that costs escalated most during the 1960s—the period of the great "pupil explosion." In the U.K. the annual percentage increase in expenditure during the 1960s on schools was 8.5%; on universities it was 15%. Ways of improving higher education and especially of applying selective entrance policies were much in evidence. Attempts to better balance educational expenditures between national and local governments were also being made. The local school board in the U.S. or the canton or half-canton in Switzerland, for example, was found inadequate to cope with the burden of education. In addition, the trend toward comprehensive secondary education, initiated on a large scale in Sweden in the late 1950s and largely modeled on the U.S. example, continued in most countries on a seemingly inexorable course. There also was evidence of a sharply increased enthusiasm for providing nursery education, notably in those countries where it had been underprovided in the past, like Sweden, West Germany, and Great Britain.

Nursery and Primary Education. In Great Britain, by either custom or law, over the past century children had started to school at age five, which was a year or two younger than in most countries in Europe. There had, nonetheless, been a long-standing demand for nursery schools starting at age three, partly from middle-class parents but also increasingly from working-class areas, where it was realized that preschool education confers considerable advantages on children.

Ecumenical Movement:
see Religion

This view was dramatically confirmed in June 1972 with the publication of a report titled *From Birth to Seven*. The report was based on a study undertaken by the National Children's Bureau of 17,000 children born in one week in March 1958 and charting their progress to the seventh birthday. It showed that the difference in educational standard—measured by reading age—among the children of unskilled families compared with professional families was on the average two years. The gap between the least advantaged children growing up in large families and with bad housing compared with the most advantaged professional-class children was as much as four years. The disadvantages even extended to physical development; the difference in height between children of unskilled families and professional families at the age of seven averaged 1.3 in.

Subsequently, the British secretary of state for education and science, Margaret Thatcher, announced that there would be increased investment in nursery education. A White Paper published December 6 stated that current expenditure on the under-fives in England and Wales would rise from about £42 million in 1971–72 to £65 million in 1976–77.

Another inquiry that had far-reaching effects in Britain emerged from an experiment comparable to the compensatory education programs in the U.S. The study of five "educational priority areas" in four big cities—London, Liverpool, Birmingham, and Dundee—and in a run-down area of the county of Yorkshire (West Riding) highlighted, as *From Birth to Seven* had done, the significance of the preschool years. Perhaps its most important finding was the value of a new type of teacher, the peripatetic "educational visitor" who had in one area visited parents and their children in the preschool years. In other words, parental involvement—for that matter parental education—was essential to the success of any compensatory program.

In Sweden children started to school at age seven, and there had long been strong parental opposition to starting any younger. But it was clear by mid-1972 that a move to get the statutory age reduced was well under way and was influenced, more than in Britain, by pedagogical researchers. Official figures suggested that by the fall of 1972 nearly half of six-year-olds in Sweden were attending school and that within three to four years most children were likely to be in school by the age of five. In Sweden, unlike Britain, fees were charged for nursery schooling. In the Netherlands, on the other hand, where nursery schooling was well developed, fees for four- and five-year-olds attending schools were actually removed, and instead a means-tested fees program was introduced in secondary schools, together with higher fees and a loan system for higher education (see *Higher Education*, below).

In the U.S. an estimated 40% of all children aged 3–5 received some type of formal education in the fall of 1971, an increase of 15% over 1964. Although a considerable portion of this steady growth could be attributed to efforts to provide early educational opportunities for underprivileged youngsters, enrollments remained highest (47%) among children of white-collar workers.

U.S. schools admitted 35.9 million students at the elementary level (and 15.5 million at the high-school level) in the fall of 1972. Just how long the school year would run was in doubt in some financially hard-pressed cities. Detroit had enough funds in view to operate for 117 days, 63 days short of the mandated year. Philadelphia, after carrying on a summer program in students' homes, faced the possibility of a curtailed calendar. Los Angeles contemplated a cutback in days or the holding of double sessions if additional funds were not found, and Chicago warned of extra-long holiday periods. The problem generally was one of education budgets caught between rising costs and voter resistance to proposed tax levies and bond issues. Salaries in particular sent budgets soaring; the average teacher's pay has jumped from $5,500 to over $9,000 a year in ten years.

Strikes marred the opening of the new school year in more districts than in 1971, but tended to affect smaller districts. Philadelphia was the only major city in which teachers refused to report for several weeks. Both the American Federation of Teachers and the National Education Association were turning more toward political action than walkouts, seeking the election of candidates favourable to their goals, which included increased federal funding in the face of local and state fiscal problems. The two teacher organizations leaned toward the presidential candidacy of Sen. George S. McGovern, though the NEA remained officially neutral. Pres. Richard M. Nixon's veto of the Health, Education, and Welfare appropriations bill, which included $4.1 billion for public schooling, brought forth a charge of "callous disregard" for schools from the NEA. It was the third straight year of presidential vetoes of HEW appropriations, but this time two months after the veto Congress enacted similar legislation with an added measure giving the president authority to cut the authorized amount by $1.2 million (13%). Even with these potential cuts the appropriation was far above the level requested by Nixon and on October 27 he once again vetoed the bill.

Although no clear solution to U.S. school fiscal problems surfaced, the year witnessed a definite turning to state financing of education as the thrust of the immediate future. The governor of Michigan proposed that a state income tax should produce the necessary revenue. The governor of New Jersey advocated a combination of income tax and statewide property tax. Officials in other states studied a variety of means to replace reliance on the local property tax as the principal source of school funds. But the decisive factor in the search for state revenues for education was a 1971 decision of the California Supreme Court. It held that children in poorer districts were entitled to as good an education as children in more affluent ones. Other cases moving through the courts, including a key one brought against the schools of San Antonio, Tex., appeared certain to strengthen the principle. Side by side with the effort to cut costs were new programs and other needs that seemed essential to schoolmen. In New York City a stepped-up bilingual curriculum was designed to aid the 250,000 Puerto Rican youngsters in the city schools. In Massachusetts a new state law required instruction by a bilingual teacher when a certain number of Spanish-speaking youngsters were enrolled. On the federal level a "Right to Read" program was launched with the awarding of $4 million to 68 school districts.

Federal aid was promised, too, to parochial schools, predominantly Roman Catholic, by President Nixon, to sustain them in a time of financial crisis. Senator McGovern espoused a similar view. The principal avenue for aid appeared to be legislation granting tax credits to parents for a portion of private and church-related school tuition. Several bills were introduced in Congress to grant credits up to several hundred dol-

WASHINGTON EVENING STAR-NEWS

Julie Nixon Eisenhower presents the 1972 National Teacher of the Year award to James M. Rogers, Jr., of Durham, N.C., in a ceremony at the White House on April 24, 1972. Also in the photograph are (from left) Elliott Richardson, secretary of health, education, and welfare, A. Craig Phillips, North Carolina superintendent of public instruction, and Warren E. Preece, general editor of "Encyclopædia Britannica." The award is sponsored by "Encyclopædia Britannica," the "Ladies' Home Journal," and the Council of Chief State School Officers.

lars per child. Deepening financial problems were forcing the closing of Catholic schools at an estimated rate of one a day in 1972. In March the Census Bureau reported that enrollment in Roman Catholic schools, both elementary and secondary, had declined 30% between 1967 and 1971, a decline of 1.7 million students. The National Association of Laity noted that in 1970–71 only 36.9% of Catholic children attended church schools. An October ruling in which, without explanation, the U.S. Supreme Court held unconstitutional an Ohio law calling for payments of $90 to parents for each parochial school child would ultimately affect seven other states with similar laws and two states considering them.

The Canadian provinces continued to experience imbalances in regional funding under the dual educational structure that entitled public and Roman Catholic school boards to municipal and industrial taxes according to the religious identity or choice of the taxpayer. In 1970, in a move to level such differences, Ontario had established a complex system of weighting factors by which funds for each of the province's school districts would be established. Simultaneously, the Ontario Ministry of Education established ceilings on educational expenditures. By 1972 most school boards were operating within their limits with relative ease, and despite the anxiety of many teachers and parents, the plan was working with no change in pupil/teacher ratios or reductions in special services. In 1972 the Ontario government ordered a freeze on construction of new schools and the Manitoba legislature turned down proposals to study further financial aid to private and parochial schools.

Desegregation. Public opposition to "forced busing" reached a new high in the U.S. in 1972. In March a Gallup Poll reported that 69% of those polled opposed compulsory busing to achieve school desegregation and 20% favoured it. That same month Florida voters, in the first statewide referendum on busing, rejected the idea by an even higher percentage. The intensity of feeling became evident when, in the spring, a group of women from Pontiac, Mich., marched to Washington in protest, gathering adherents along the way, and a motorcade from Richmond, Va., snarled traffic in the capital city. Some politicians were surprised by the antibusing fervour. They had not anticipated it as a major campaign issue. President Nixon took up the cudgel against large-scale busing, decried court decisions that decreed massive transporting of students, and urged Congress to put a stop to it by constitutional amendment if necessary. Congress responded by enacting one of two restrictions the president wanted passed. This, a provision of the Higher Education Amendments Act, prohibited implementation of court-ordered busing, pending appeal, until Jan. 1, 1974. A second measure that would have required judges to consider alternative methods for achieving desegregation before resorting to busing passed the House, but was dropped after a filibuster by liberal senators could not be broken.

Contributing to the aroused passions were court decisions affecting Detroit and Richmond, Va., schools. In both cases black city schools would have to exchange students with white suburban schools to break the walls of segregation. The Richmond verdict was reversed in 1972, but both cases were appealed to the Supreme Court. Opposition to the Detroit decision, which affected the city and 53 suburban communities, was particularly strong; all school-board members supporting the plan were voted out of office. Meanwhile, a desegregation case involving Denver schools moved into the Supreme Court and would provide the first ruling affecting a city that never had a dual school system.

On the state level, too, school districts faced challenges over segregation. The Buffalo, N.Y., school board defied an order from the state education commissioner to submit a busing plan to achieve integration. Illinois districts were chastised by state officials for noncompliance with a desegregation ruling and were ordered to submit desegregation plans within 90 days.

In 1971–72 Boston lost $14 million in state aid for failing to comply with a 1965 state law, the first of its type, which required that no school enrollment be more than 50% nonwhite, the penalty being loss of state funds to the district. The Boston school committee tried to compromise with the state board of education, arguing that no viable method was available for achieving integration. The board cited a study purporting to show that the redrawing of district lines plus small-scale busing would produce the desired results, but the committee rejected this approach in the face of community hostility. Later, a Superior Court judge ordered the release of $54 million in aid being withheld from Boston for 1972–73 and provided a timetable for the city and state to resolve their impasse.

The Boston school system was also charged with violating the 1964 Civil Rights Act in the first action taken by the Department of Health, Education, and Welfare against a major school district outside the South. At issue was $12 million–$15 million in federal funds. While avoiding charges of deliberate school segregation, HEW officials claimed segregation resulted from committee policy, the effects of which the committee should have foreseen and prevented.

Secondary Education. It was Sweden, the first European country to "go comprehensive" on the lines of the U.S. high school, that recorded the most dramatic progress in secondary education in 1972. Following the establishment of the nine-year compulsory comprehensive school (for ages 7–16) Sweden had developed a further "comprehensive" three-year tier, called the upper secondary school. By the fall of 1972 it was clear that well over 80% of Swedish children were staying in school up to the age of 17 or 18—an unheard-of proportion in European countries. It became increasingly clear, too, that schools that catered to a very wide range of ability presented problems of curriculum and teaching method that needed radical solution. Part of the answer seemed to lie in turning much of the secondary school curriculum (at least for ages 13–16) over to "project work" where children spent much of the time in discovering knowledge for themselves. Further, it was necessary to step up the in-service training of teachers. The wide ability range also caused difficulties in giving final gradings to students. A minimum final grade of 2.3 out of a possible 5 was required for entry to higher education; for medical schools it was as high as 4.8. The fact that so many of wide ability were remaining in school meant that many more failed to achieve qualifying grades.

The other countries of Scandinavia, whose secondary education systems had been modeled to some extent on that of Sweden, also recorded achievements. Denmark made nine years of schooling compulsory, although the majority of children already remained in school that long. In Norway, following a law passed in 1969 making nine years of schooling compulsory, the 1971–72 school year was the first in which the age for leaving school was 16. In Finland by the fall of 1972 the nine-year comprehensive school was established in one region and would eventually be established throughout the country.

In Britain the policy of the Conservative government elected in 1970, which, unlike its Labour predecessor, did not encourage comprehensive schools, began to manifest itself. It was doubtful if by the end of 1972 more than 25–30% of secondary school children were in genuine comprehensive schools. It was hardly possible, therefore, to draw any firm conclusions about the educational merits of these schools, although such evidence as there was suggested that they did not compare at all unfavourably with the previous system of a grammar school or gymnasium for a selected group at age 11 and a general secondary education for the remaining 70–75% of children.

Standards of literacy among those leaving school, however, gave rise to concern, and in the summer Mrs. Thatcher set up a committee of inquiry into the teaching of reading. A survey published in March 1972 showed that reading standards were static if not actually declining, compared with 1964. Despite a good deal of hostility from the Conservative rank and file and from the teaching profession—notably in Scotland—Mrs. Thatcher stuck to her resolve to raise the age for leaving school to 16 in the fall of 1972.

In July the heads of the 11 West German Länder (states) and the federal government agreed on an overall plan by which educational development in the Länder could proceed more or less in step. It emerged that the general intention of most of the Länder was to make the tenth year compulsory; that is, set the age for leaving school at 16. The more conservative Bavarians, the last to raise the compulsory age from 14 to 15 two years previously, were evidently disinclined to see it raised further.

In Israel a reform proposed as long ago as 1958 that would create a form of middle school for ages 12 to 15 continued to cause controversy. There was also persistent controversy about inequalities that seemed to favour Jews of European and American extraction. Many educationalists were also anxious to do more to integrate the Arabs into the Israeli state and to encourage more teaching of Arabic and put less insistence on Arab children learning Hebrew.

Some of the virtues of having specialist education for a few children were displayed by East Germany and to a lesser extent the Soviet Union, through their remarkable successes in the Olympic Games at Munich in August–September. The East Germans, in particular, had established special sports schools. Following the Olympic Games, in several countries—notably in Britain—the demand went up for the introduction of such schools.

In Italy, unhappily, the state of secondary education—and primary and higher as well—continued to draw severe criticism. The situation was so acute that in the fall of 1972 both the president and the minister of education, Oscar Luigi Scalfaro, published messages to the nation's schoolchildren openly recognizing the many defects of the system but calling on pupils to do all they could to cooperate and exercise a sense of responsibility. In Ireland, too, although small rural schools were amalgamated and a few "community" schools established in 1972, progress was far from remarkable. Critics maintained that the highly centralized and rather rigid nature of Irish educational administration was largely to blame. Criticism was sharpened when publication in September of the national education appropriation accounts for 1970–71 showed that a considerable proportion of sums granted for specific purposes was returned unspent.

WIDE WORLD

Lesson One
We Are Chairman Mao's Red Guards
I
Chairman Mao, Chairman Mao!
sun in our hearts.
ommander.
Guards.
commander

Veneration of Mao Tse-tung is evident in this English-language class in a Peking secondary school. Poems about Chairman Mao and the Red Guards are used as study material for first-year classes.

In Australia educational provision in general was subject to severe criticism, despite the fact that the federal government increased its education budget by some 20%. Critics complained that an absurdly small proportion of children of semiskilled and unskilled workers ever got beyond the secondary school stage. Much of the blame was put on the fact that each state administered its own education system, and that there were wide differences between them.

In Canada Ontario's previously experimental ungraded secondary school system became universal in September 1972. Each student was to concentrate his studies in one of four major subject areas—science, pure and applied; communications, including languages; social and environmental studies, including law; and the arts—and would receive a high school certificate upon completion of an established number of credit hours in his major concentration and minimum requirements in the other three areas. A free correspondence school that would make it possible to gain a high school certificate equivalent by mail was also in operation in Ontario with an enrollment of 50,000 in 1972.

In the U.S. on May 15 the Supreme Court ruled that a Wisconsin law requiring school attendance until age 16 violated the constitutional rights of the Amish religious sect. The Amish believed secondary education taught worldly values at odds with their simple way of life. The ruling, the first in which the court exempted a religious group from compulsory school attendance laws, was broad enough to apply to other states with similar laws but could not be automatically applied to other groups or sects.

Higher Education. If there was an all-pervading theme to European higher education in 1972, it was that of the numerus clausus, the principle of restricted entry to higher education. It was traditional to allow all who qualified free and open access to the university. It had been obvious that this policy could not go on unchecked, and in 1972 the restraints were firmly applied. In West Germany the numerus clausus was actually put to the legal test. In July the Federal Constitutional Court in Karlsruhe decided that a numerus clausus as a temporary measure was permissible and that it did not involve a deliberate violation of the law that "all Germans have the right to choose . . . their trade or profession . . . and their place of training." The court, however, rejected the two cases before it as being based on arbitrary procedures and charged the Länder legislatures with the duty of making decisions about the kind of criteria that ought to be applied for university admission. Unfortunately, proposed federal legislation to reform admissions policy became a political issue and was not passed.

In Sweden, policy on the containment took a rather different form. In the 1960s the university student population had increased fivefold, and costs eightfold (at current prices). It was announced in 1972 that the number of full-time students currently in higher education—150,000—would be increased to no more than 170,000 by the 1980s and that higher education would be made "comprehensive" and in effect integrated within a regional university system. Courses would have to be career-oriented from the start and built up on a modular system—rather as they were in the U.S.

In Britain, both main political parties favoured development of higher education along "binary" lines, that is, with universities on the one hand and the polytechnics and other institutions like colleges of education on the other. Supporters of the binary system argued that the nonuniversity side offered a more flexible and indeed radical alternative to the university; critics contended that the nonuniversity side was cheaper, and that this was a shabby virtue. The December White Paper announced a new nonuniversity two-year diploma course of higher education. Britain's most interesting and unusual departure in higher education—the Open University—continued to flourish. (This involved university-level study by correspondence, the use of television and other audiovisual aids, and short courses.) It was announced that 17,000 new students would begin their studies in January 1973, making the total enrollment 42,000. It was also announced during the year that as an experiment 500 students between the ages of 18–21 (at present the lower age limit was 21) would be recruited.

By 1972 the pressure for university places within the arts and social sciences was no longer so great as to leave many science and technology places unfilled. In Israel, however, the manpower planning authority announced that there was a chronic shortage of scientists and engineers and stricter control of university entry was, therefore, applied chiefly to the arts, humanities, and law. The same trend was evident in Hungary where there were five applicants for every place in the arts faculty in Budapest University. It was in the Netherlands that the most draconian measures had to be introduced. University fees were trebled (even so, they were very much less than the economic cost), and courses were reduced from seven years to four. A means-tested loans scheme was also introduced. These measures were not altogether surprising: some 20% of the current university population had been there for nine or more years and there was, moreover, a 40% dropout rate. There was also evidence in many countries in 1972 that it was growing difficult for quite highly qualified chemists and chemical engineers to get jobs fresh from the university and that elsewhere, in Japan and Nigeria, for example, there was acute concern over higher education's failure to match the real needs of industry and commerce.

Debate about the need to improve teacher training was endemic in Western Europe. In Britain, a radical set of proposals known as the James report (the chairman of the government-appointed committee was Lord James) argued that would-be teachers should either get a university degree or a "diploma in higher education" after two years of work at a college of education, followed in either case by two years of professional training and a third "cycle" of in-service training consisting of one term's sabbatical training in every seven years. The Joxe report in France argued that teacher training should be widened so as to break down barriers between specialities and to introduce more techniques such as team teaching. Reactions from teachers' unions to both reports were, on balance, hostile. Some of the James report's proposals were accepted in the December White Paper, however.

Financial problems predominated at many U.S. colleges and universities during 1972, affecting even some state-supported institutions in need of larger appropriations by their legislatures to meet rising costs. For large numbers of private colleges the gap between income and costs widened because of decreased enrollments as 300,000 places went unfilled, more than double the number of a year earlier. Yet enrollment was up in most state institutions, particularly in community colleges, and degree credit enrollment at all U.S. colleges and universities reached 9 million, up from 8.5 million in 1971. Two large institutions, New York University and Boston's Northeastern University, admitted publicly their dire financial straits because of decreased enrollments. Compared with the 1950s, when half of the U.S. college population attended private institutions, in 1972 70% were enrolled in public institutions, which charged less because they received tax subsidies. Most private-college administrators favoured some sort of adjustment, either through the raising of state tuitions or through a

Education versus Defense Expenditures of Selected Countries, 1971

As percent of national budget expenditures

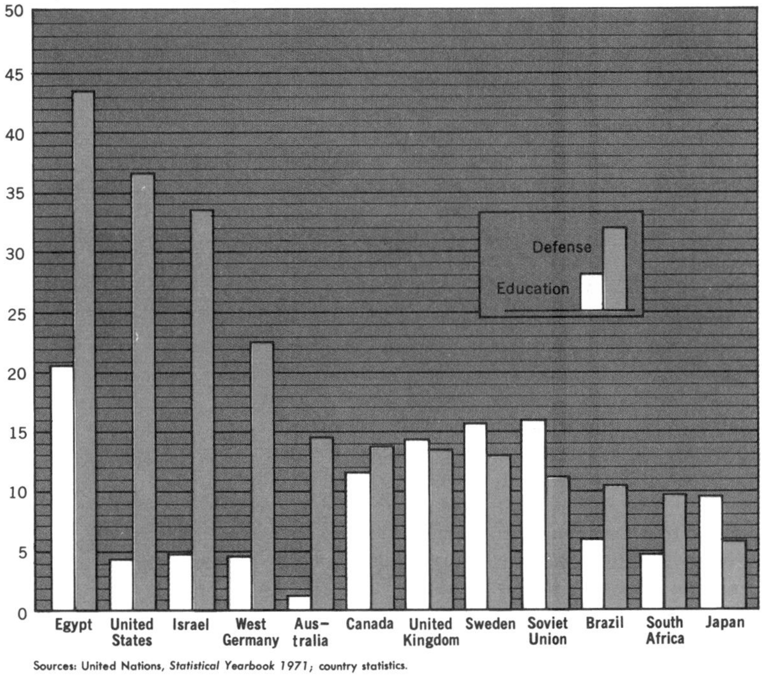

Sources: United Nations, *Statistical Yearbook 1971*; country statistics.

voucher system, with the state covering the basic cost of a student's education at the college of his choice.

A handful of private colleges pulled themselves out of the deficit pattern by starting the 1972–73 year with balanced budgets. Tighter management procedures and the lopping off of some courses and staff members accounted for much of this financial improvement. Much of this anticipated a midyear report of the Carnegie Commission on Higher Education, which called for a 20% reduction in campus costs by the end of the decade. The commission expressed the opinion that half of the saving could be effected by shortening the time a student spent in college, the other half by a variety of ways that included larger teaching loads, more off-campus study, higher student-faculty ratios, minimum effective size for campuses and departments, management training for personnel, and consortiums.

Experiments aimed at cutting the time required for a degree took differing forms. The State University of New York set up a three-year program for high-school graduates, as well as a four-year program for high-school juniors. Several private colleges began three-year degree programs and Dartmouth and Colgate began year-round calendars offering the option of completing four years' work in three years' time. Off-campus study expanded as colleges sought more opportunities to develop urban semesters, work-study programs, overseas study, and community-agency and employer cooperation. Movement of students from one campus to another was one more strong trend, whether under the name of regionalism or consortium arrangement. Behind this development was the fact that duplication of courses, specialized libraries, and small-enrollment programs were an expense that most colleges and universities could ill afford. Another way of reducing costs while increasing student options was the external-degree program, under which individuals worked closely with an adviser but did much of their studying off-campus. Experiments in this approach to learning continued in New York and California, while Rutgers University and three other academic centres began testing Britain's Open University concept.

Meanwhile, the University Without Walls issued its first annual report. After one year of operation, in 20 institutions, UWW programs that were designed as "a distinct alternative" to customary undergraduate programs had 3,000 enrollees, many of whom probably would not have continued their education otherwise. A somewhat similar development, begun in the 1971–72 academic year, was the Vermont Regional Community College, a noncampus, community-based instructional system that covered much of the state.

Apart from the rallies, sit-ins, and teach-ins on a number of campuses in April–May to protest renewed U.S. bombing of North Vietnam, violence and disruptive protests were limited mainly to black campuses in the U.S. in 1972. These culminated in the shooting deaths on November 16 of two students at Southern University in Baton Rouge, La., during an attempt by police to dislodge students occupying the administration building. The disturbances at Southern had begun in October with a week of demonstrations by students demanding the resignation of the university's president, G. Leon Netterville, improved food and housing, and greater say in university decisions. Similar demands had produced disturbances at Southern's New Orleans campus, which ended November 9 when the campus head resigned; at Grambling College, New Orleans, where 24 students were arrested November

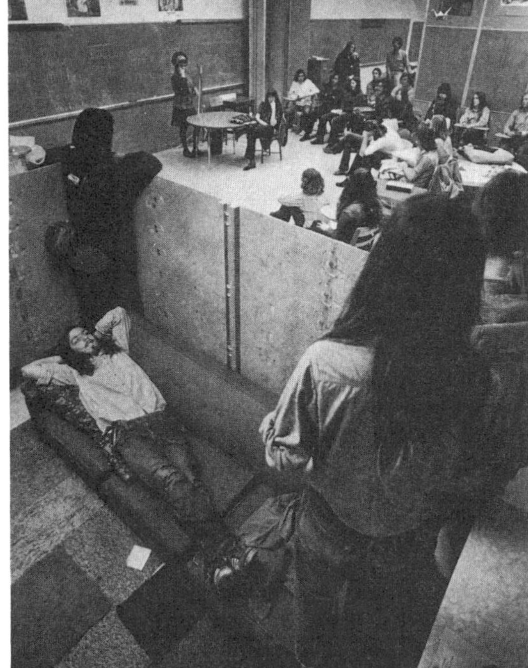

CHRISTOPHER SPRINGMANN

Community High, one of six alternative high schools housed within the six-block-square complex of Berkeley (Calif.) High School, offers its diversely motivated students a rich fare of unusual courses, ranging from karate to transcendental meditation.

2; and at Morris College, Sumter, S.C., where students demanded the resignation of the newly inaugurated president. In general, black or predominantly black colleges in Southern states had been established as alternatives to black attendance at white schools, had never been adequately financed, and had been run by aging administrators who attempted to keep students and faculty in line with blatant disregard for civil liberties or academic freedom. The students and some faculty members seemed to be using the methods of social protest they had employed successfully in the civil rights movement to obtain reforms in their colleges.

In other parts of the world campus unrest took a myriad of forms. At Cairo University Egyptian students staged sit-ins in January as part of a series of demonstrations demanding a more aggressive policy toward Israel. Pres. Anwar as-Sadat charged February 17 that the disturbances had been fomented by Israeli agents. Several weeks of violence growing out of a student protest against French cultural domination led to the virtual resignation of Malagasy Republic Pres. Philibert Tsiranana in May. On June 6 South Africa announced a one-month ban on student rallies after several weeks of student activities protesting apartheid. At the University of Toronto in March students occupied university buildings in a challenge to the university senate's ruling restricting first-year students and the public from use of a new library. In Madrid in January violent clashes between students and police, who had been stationed on the University of Madrid campus since January 1969, followed the suspension of nearly all 4,000 medical students for refusing to end their seven-week strike against curriculum changes. The police were withdrawn from the campus later in the year.

A general strike organized by students to protest the plight of the Bihari minority in postwar Bangladesh disrupted business and closed all schools in Karachi, Pakistan, on February 7. The law and arts faculties of Tunis University were closed from February to mid-April following demonstrations against the regime of Tunisian Pres. Habib Bourguiba. Hungarian officials confirmed that a student demonstration had occurred in Budapest March 15 in connection with a rally staged to commemorate the 124th anniversary of Hungarian independence. This was believed to be the first such demonstration since the 1956 revolt. And in an unprecedented action, students at Stirling University, Scotland, shouted obscenities at Queen Elizabeth II as she visited the university, apparently in protest against the cost of the visit.

There was greater response to women's demands on U.S. campuses, although the pressure was not uniform and took differing forms where felt. In some places the focus was on admission of more women and additional courses relating to women, but most commonly the aim was for increased numbers of women teachers, higher positions for them, and pay equal to that of men in similar positions. Dartmouth College opened its doors to women in the fall, and two women were nominated for the first time to the U.S. Naval Academy. Congress supported the feminist movement by prohibiting, through the Higher Education Amendments Act of 1972, sex discrimination in all schools and educational programs receiving federal monies.

Faculty unionization took on new dimensions as the American Association of University Professors voted overwhelmingly to pursue collective bargaining aggressively. Faculty members were now more receptive to joining collective-bargaining units. One reason was staff cutbacks at colleges in attempts to reduce costs; another was administration retaliation against politically active faculty. Of the several cases of the latter during the year, the most celebrated was the dismissal of H. Bruce Franklin of Stanford University for allegedly encouraging students to riot, apparently the first discharge of a tenured professor by Stanford in 70 years. Elsewhere, untenured faculty took their fight to the courts when their contracts were not renewed, but no clear-cut decisions were reached.

As Ph.D.s continued to experience difficulty in finding employment commensurate with their training, some U.S. graduate schools scaled down their doctoral programs. The popularity of medical and law programs increased, however, as a record 106,000 students took the Law School Admissions Test (one-third were accepted), and an estimated 35,000 competed for 13,000 places in medical schools.

An omnibus higher-education bill, authorizing an estimated $18.5 billion over three years, became law after a lengthy struggle between two factions: those favouring grants directly to colleges, and those supporting direct aid to students. Provisions for both were included in the complicated law. Designed to assist low- and middle-income students, it established a level of aid according to family income and then tied grants, loans, and work-study earnings together to make up an aid package for each qualifying student. Problems in interpreting the new rules governing the guaranteed loan program left large numbers of students without needed funds for the fall term. As a result, President Nixon gained congressional approval for postponing the new guidelines until March 1973.

Attired properly for dueling, A. M. Woodruff, president of the University of Hartford, Conn., and Eric V. Litsky, chairman of the Student Association, have at one another with custard pies at two paces. In comic contrast to most campus confrontations, the event was part of "Insanity Day" held on Nov. 13, 1972.

UPI COMPIX

Only $595.3 million was appropriated by Congress for the higher education programs of the U.S. Office of Education for the 1973 fiscal year. The unusually low sum was in line with the administration's request that only programs requiring funding before spring be included; supplemental funds were expected when the new Congress convened in January 1973.

In Canada the Ontario budget, announced in March, called for a 4.5% increase in spending, with funds to be raised, among other means, by nearly doubling the student tuition for post-secondary education. By April 15 a number of students were reported planning to continue their educations elsewhere. The provincial government postponed plans to cancel awarding of cash prizes to secondary school students with high grades, which it believed would have saved nearly $1 million.

Administration. In several countries in Western Europe there were signs of radical change in local administration of education. In England and Wales a law was passed in October that had the effect of reducing the number of local education committees from 164 to 101. In Northern Ireland the eight local education committees were abolished and replaced by five "Area Education Boards." Proposals were also made for reducing the number of education committees in Scotland. In every case the motives were chiefly to increase the size of education authorities to close to 200,000.

In Sweden (which had as many as 2,000 education committees 20 years before) local education authorities were to be reduced to 280 by 1974, the minimum population to be 10,000. In Switzerland, where the 25 cantons and half-cantons had always tended to go their own way in education, there was a marked trend toward centralization. In Yugoslavia, on the other hand, the legislation adopted in 1971 proceeded apace; this provided for the handling of education entirely by the various republics in accordance with the "self-management" trend in Yugoslav social policy.

International Developments. Much discussion in Western Europe centred on Britain's forthcoming entry to the EEC. There was no specific reference to education in the Treaty of Rome, although it called for mutual recognition of diplomas in all of the participating countries. It was only too clear, however, that hardly any progress had been made among the original six members toward mutual recognition. It was noted, too, that the part of the Treaty of Rome that allowed the free movement of workers did not apply to those in public employment, including, of course, teachers.

There were signs among the teachers' organizations, however, of growing international cooperation. At the annual meeting of the World Confederation of Organizations of the Teaching Profession (WCOTP) held in London in August, a committee was set up with the object of protecting the mutual interest of teachers' unions in the EEC countries. There were signs, too, that the cold war was gently melting between the

World Education

Most recent official data

Country	1st level (primary) Students (full-time)	Teachers (full-time)	Total schools	General 2nd level (secondary) Students (full-time)	Teachers (full-time)	Total schools	Vocational 2nd level Students (full-time)	Teachers (full-time)	Total schools	3rd level (higher) Students (full-time)	Teachers (full-time)	Total schools	Literacy % of population	Over age
Afghanistan	572,932	14,651	3,332	127,162	5,282	685	11,576	811	37	9,190	1,039	17	8.	15
Albania	555,300	18,944	1,374	32,867	7,157	46	50,072	1,205	85	25,500	926	5	71.	9
Algeria	1,888,353	43,656	6,241	190,248	7,837	409	58,473	3,650	256	16,900	...	26	67.	9
Angola	384,884	8,714	4,000	35,916	2,142	160	17,086	1,375	87	1,757	213	5	30.	...
Argentina	3,671,451	198,610	25,311	404,668	58,120	1,647	602,869	80,037	2,517	51,870	8,857	704	91.5	15
Australia	1,795,116	63,400	8,528	924,615	49,400	2,570*	180,000	...	230	175,000	...	210	...	...
Austria	609,262	...	4,110	516,483	24,439	1,922	81,621	7,199	495	70,971	8,476	34	99.	15
Bahrain	39,957	1,611	84	12,661	657	34	1,233	107	4	312	33	2	47.	10
Bhutan	4,357	249	69	4,564	187	19	321	36	2	...	—	—	5.	...
Bolivia	748,506	27,046	8,887	86,365	4,116	383	8,114	1,060	80	37,692	3,026	16	39.8	15
Botswana	78,447	2,407	288	4,740	250	13	1,226	139	12	66	19	2	32.9	10
Brazil	12,294,343	435,881	145,479	3,053,255	208,312	8,707	1,030,331	100,240	6,072	425,478	42,968	586	68.	10
Bulgaria	1,045,004	50,089	3,898	103,884	6,514	285	291,358	17,839	576	105,235	8,193	48	91.4	8
Burma	3,328,000	65,326	16,599	692,290	21,814	1,673	7,611	783	32	78,245	4,912	25	68.3	8
Burundi	182,664	4,892	970	3,969	397	18	4,200	457	30	470	67	2	10.	...
Cambodia (Khmer Republic)	484,088	18,444	1,450	96,401	2,560	103	6,516	288	83	7,349	303	35	54.1	10
Canada	4,029,517	265,036†	16,207†	1,755,135	...	...	212,420	5,533	371	483,241	38,041	401	95.	14
Chile	1,980,906	35,588‡	7,302	178,887	7,374‡	461	92,014	6,571‡	276	52,937	...	8	83.6	14
Colombia	3,282,387	93,980	31,901	688,746	21,511	2,457	103,745	3,963	358	109,639	5,304	45	78.5	15
Congo	244,160	3,793	895	30,371	697	56	3,969	344	36	1,788	117	4	...	...
Costa Rica	356,171	12,109	2,530	78,224	...	121	7,679	462	19	17,366	1,275	5	84.74	15
Cuba	1,759,167	65,189	15,369	201,810	15,966	478	55,111	6,344	143	30,386	...	4	...	...
Cyprus§	66,027	2,271	564	40,339	1,747	76	4,640	324	10	810	78	6	80.7	7
Czechoslovakia	1,939,590	97,204	10,747	112,676	7,095	340	212,668	16,241	661	102,251	16,030	37	99.6	15
Denmark	548,300	33,700	2,700	227,600	15,700	...	100,000	3,000	120	78,000	7,800	100	100.	10
Dominican Republic	808,836	14,957	5,298	117,547	4,486	885	4,060	230	16	20,183	1,098	10	64.5	15
Ecuador	975,480	25,137	7,472	194,682	14,421	720	...	...	...	33,562	2,298	15	69.4	15
Egypt	3,740,595	96,693	8,418	1,146,474	41,038	1,705	300,213	15,689	317	192,605	9,886	106	26.3	14
Ethiopia	513,981	10,403	1,844	88,861	3,399	84	7,204	508	74	6,225‖	533‖	24‖	10.	10
Fiji	126,331	3,911	627	18,094	720	73	1,530	151	25	754	90	1	81.	14
Finland	386,230	17,319	4,507	407,978	14,999	1,150	101,713¶	5,784	747	59,769¶	6,267¶	24	100.	15
France	4,853,725	212,388	61,500	3,643,034	295,203	7,502	867,546	2,928♀	3,419	781,596	...	...	100.	7
French Guiana	11,108	348	54	3,520	146	7	925	68	4	...	—	—	74.3	14
Gabon	105,601	2,435	678	9,387	693	41	2,120	202	18	1,221	...	...	20.	13
Gambia, The	17,463	684	94	3,338	253	22	301	32	3	...	—	—	10.	...
Germany, East	2,649,727	144,573†	6,742	57,278	...	295	428,650	14,924	1,070	110,991	...	54	100.	15
Germany, West	6,711,992	208,896	25,176	2,258,457	104,796	4,611	1,907,936	36,502	5,892	709,434	43,548	3,699	99.9	15
Greece	919,067	29,011	9,097	458,771	14,277	900	85,322	450♂	348	97,130	3,458	49	82.2	10
Haiti	275,192	6,778	1,909	23,047	1,286	75	5,892	383	26	1,313	226	11	26.7	15
Honduras	376,966	10,437	4,143	33,392	2,516	110	1,202	140	9	2,883	...	5	45.	15
Hong Kong	739,944	22,172	1,293	235,750	9,096□	290	15,156	...	31	14,571	1,422	16	80.9	10
Hungary	1,115,993	63,125	5,480	122,988	7,196	332	110,303	6,246	215	53,821	9,791	74	98.2	10
Iceland	27,727	1,153	199	18,753	974	138	13,940	266	105	2,701	162	2	100.	15
India	39,033,000	994,513	398,951	32,647,000	1,129,620	114,567	231,000	16,548	2,593	856,000	72,715	2,933	33.31	15
Indonesia	13,219,490	338,077	68,047	1,411,402	85,024	5,657	540,337	49,575	2,928	117,974	8,998	40	39.	15
Iran	3,230,776	75,641	26,024	1,400,213	34,360	4,918	68,127	2,238	331	97,338	3,639	105	22.8	15
Iraq	1,193,236	54,187	5,978	311,821	13,674	966	7,818	570	25	42,930	1,318	39	38.	14
Ireland	526,765	16,499	4,163	201,128	...	893	3,754	...	83	26,218	...	67	100.	15
Israel	517,860	23,540	1,880	72,658	...	334	66,223	...	339	65,207	...	...	90.7°	13
Italy	4,891,454	228,998	38,083	2,840,087	247,521	11,068	983,302	84,860	4,162	678,845	9,437	77	91.6	7
Ivory Coast	507,514	11,273	2,367	66,133	2,990	115	4,288	448	24	5,621	189	15	20.	...
Japan	9,595,021	374,871	24,540	8,523,287	429,181	15,631	1,583,867	120,675	1,428	1,791,514	97,208	947	100.	15
Jordan▲	318,667	8,046	1,731	101,698	4,480	710	3,046	178	16	5,170	233	15	43.5	15
Kenya	1,427,589	41,479	6,123	126,855	5,881	783	9,958	622	36	6,398	690	4	60.	16
Korea, South	5,775,880	105,672	6,197	2,055,871	51,424	2,269	382,933	13,767	555	190,885	10,784	133	85.3	13
Kuwait	77,945	3,942	136	72,768	5,479	114	3,302	720	6	2,593	189	1	47.6	10
Laos	246,400	6,845	3,281	9,519	410	32	4,686	380	33	1,131	87	4	34.3	15
Lesotho	175,336	3,928	1,087	12,446	633	92	623	57	18	692	104	1	58.37	15
Liberia	120,245	3,384	889	15,494	918	195	1,277	66	5	1,109	164	3	23.6	5
Libya	418,859	15,291	1,581	54,337	4,112	255	9,186	894	29	6,291	357	2	30.	6
Luxembourg	35,737	1,637	498	10,149	610	19	6,676	...	36	318	89¶	2	99.	7
Malagasy Republic	1,004,445	14,881	6,055	107,781	5,181	535	9,213	759	126	226	50	1	39.	...
Malaysia	1,760,839	55,504	6,324	656,368	24,731	1,126	16,115	685	71	20,673	1,666	26	...	...
Mali	218,416	6,265	873	2,823	197	10	4,358	281	24	628	107	4	2.2	15
Mexico	9,248,290	201,453	46,010	1,219,792	80,331	4,530	364,550	29,191	1,107	247,637	17,103	374	76.2	9
Mozambique	496,381	6,607	4,095	17,831	1,150	91	2,754	292	25	1,145	213	9	...	...
Netherlands	1,536,437	55,354	9,035	598,740	39,772¶	1,621	407,484	38,100¶	1,998	177,753	17,200¶	366	100.	7
New Caledonia	26,103	1,098	1,035	3,830	253	146	1,398	180	79	84	46	3	80.2	15
New Zealand	517,537	18,791	2,593	186,743	9,932	386	1,882	859	8	31,231	2,642	20	100.	15
Nicaragua	309,697	8,071	2,143	52,193	1,979	222	2,432	129	9	9,381	216	5	58.4	...
Niger	94,509	2,488	743	6,366	365	23	1,426	181	11	95	10	1	5.8	6
Nigeria	3,515,827	103,152	14,902	310,054	14,118	1,155	45,423	2,608	226	15,444	1,549	14	25.	15
Norway	386,496	18,239	2,991	253,060	17,729	912	57,310	5,405	598	49,757	5,442	108	100.	15
Panama	287,565	10,004	1,971	56,531	3,042	75	30,062	1,392	131	15,074	823	2	79.35	10
Papua New Guinea	224,663	6,664	1,515	20,667	909	66	7,037	499	84	...	...	3	...	...
Paraguay	444,894	15,304	2,587	55,797	5,793	560	3,069	948	44	7,224	618	2	68.7	15
Peru	2,562,695	64,004	20,034	547,316	21,863	1,451	127,207	6,333	414	41,633	2,175	124	61.1	15
Philippines	6,700,367	221,856	38,776	1,505,830	46,083	3,478	88,169	1,915	652	638,768	27,303	705	72.	10
Poland	5,257,000	211,500	26,126	401,300	17,500	858	1,710,700	63,600	9,726	209,800	31,900	85	95.7	7
Portugal	992,446	29,554	17,018	290,969	17,018	1,602	155,239	9,907	407	49,461	2,726	68	66.5	15
Qatar	17,511	899	89	4,396	284	7	507	85	4	—	—	—	...	...
Rhodesia	756,289	18,965	3,711	57,323	3,026	188	6,107	339	33	2,105	306	7	28.62	16
Romania	2,886,855	133,842	14,928	261,749	13,679	572	366,635	19,892	949	106,302	13,166	49	100.	8
Saudi Arabia	432,622	18,176	1,850	68,993	4,053	335	13,570	1,005	62	14,305	977	42	...	...
Senegal	255,493	5,608	1,319	42,228	1,468	138	9,568	459	26	3,376	205	3	6.	14
Sierra Leone	154,898	5,011	1,023	29,058	1,364	81	1,739	189	13	1,116	384	2	7.7	10
Somalia	51,384	1,665	295	5,947	286	21	736	63	5	964	58	3	15.	...
South Africa	3,801,219	86,275	13,661	486,651	21,255	1,337	64,203	2,818	253	85,579	12,313	64	...	...
Soviet Union	49,418,000	...	201,920	4,301,500	...	4,191	...	...	...	4,548,300	...	800	99.7	...
Spain	4,749,483	139,207	135,699	1,517,265	37,626	2,846	409,961	26,489	1,007	216,542	15,380	49	94.3	15
Sudan	610,798	12,986	3,352	190,749	9,020	1,210	2,983	251	23	11,833	1,002	12	19.4	10
Sweden	658,521	42,000	4,039	577,566□	40,500□	800□	...	...	...	137,295	...	62	99.	15
Syria	813,225	22,249	5,069	242,917	11,108	954	3,566	433	20	33,027	545	3	44.	...
Taiwan	2,456,615	60,576	2,331	1,038,458	40,715	766	199,833	8,212	168	222,505	11,471	96	80.58	15
Thailand	5,776,667	181,845	29,272	583,695	24,609	1,647	150,296	10,759	311	59,571	5,693	25	70.8	10
Togo	257,885	4,271	983	24,595	778	72	2,712	228	16	880	...	1	10.5	...
Turkey	5,100,410	147,932	39,589	1,239,467	27,304	2,721	162,542	9,744	518	166,958	5,987	75	52.15	15
Uganda	709,708	21,074	2,720	46,483	2,067	118	6,728	519	46	3,767	483	4	20.	...
United Kingdom	5,955,884	222,221	28,688	3,682,774	213,088	6,818	313,164	52,293	937	354,897	45,295	246	100.	...
United States	36,700,000	1,308,000	81,249	15,150,000□	1,051,000□	30,482□	...	...	...	8,390,000	617,000	2,556	99.	14
Upper Volta	105,706	2,379	603	9,145	439	38	1,917	124	14	194	30	1	10.5	...
Venezuela	1,769,680	45,160	10,509	320,942	13,721	665	187,531	8,970	455	80,741	7,680	12	84.4	10
Vietnam, South	2,910,872	54,721	8,377	840,953	25,132	1,078	22,018	1,028	60	68,649	1,570	14	80.	...
Yemen (Aden)	134,522	4,316	872	16,631	769	81	891	102	12	110	13	1	10.5	...
Yugoslavia	2,835,658	119,613	13,994	186,298	10,259	422	501,574	15,400	1,428	240,000	15,950	247	84.8	10
Zaire	3,088,011	69,999	4,756	185,370	2,516	646	67,864	3,232	557	12,363	1,386	32	15.	15

Note: Third level may include individual faculties within a university. *Includes 1,316 combined primary-secondary schools.
†Primary and secondary combined. ‡Public only. §Greek schools only. ‖Includes teacher training at both 2nd and 3rd levels.
¶Includes part-time. ♀Teacher training only. Vocational teachers included with 2nd general teachers.
♂Excludes teachers in the lower vocational schools. □General and vocational combined.
°Jewish population only. ▲Data, except literacy, refer to East Bank of Jordan only.

WCOTP and the Communist-dominated teachers' international—the Fédération Internationale des Syndicale de l'Enseignement. Despite this trend, however, teachers' internationals remained unhappily divided, just as teachers' unions were in most countries in the West.

The biennial Didacta—the European educational materials fair—was held in 1972 in Hanover, W.Ger. It attracted some 800 firms specializing in educational materials or books, notably from West Germany and Great Britain. The emphasis was chiefly on scientific equipment and teaching aids, with advanced audio-visual aids particularly in evidence.

Visiting Harvard University on the 25th anniversary of the Marshall Plan, which had provided West Germany alone with $1.5 billion for economic recovery after World War II, West German Chancellor Willy Brandt announced his country would donate DM. 150 million over the next 15 years for the establishment and operation of a U.S.-run foundation specializing in the study of European problems. Brandt commented that "Europeans and Americans can still learn a lot from each other."

(TUDOR DAVID; KENNETH G. GEHRET)

See also Libraries; Medicine; Motion Pictures; Museums and Galleries; Police; Race Relations.

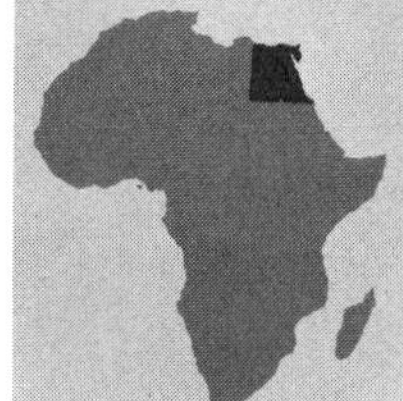

Egypt

A republic of northeast Africa, Egypt is bounded by Israel, Sudan, Libya, the Mediterranean Sea, and the Red Sea. Area: 386,900 sq.mi. (1,002,000 sq.km.). Pop. (1971 est.): 34,076,000. Cap. and largest city: Cairo (pop., 1971 est., 5,139,000). Language: Arabic. Religion: Muslim 93%; Christian 7%. President in 1972, Anwar as-Sadat; prime ministers, Mahmoud Fawzi and, from January 16, Aziz Sidky.

In 1972 Egypt's relations with the Soviet Union underwent an important change. The country also continued to suffer the difficulties of pursuing a "no peace, no war" policy with Israel. As the year opened President Sadat explained that he had not made 1971 a "year of decision" in the conflict with Israel as he had promised because at the crucial moment the Indian-Pakistani conflict had diverted the attention of the world, and especially of the Soviet Union, from the Middle East. Egyptian student dissatisfaction with the situation gave rise to serious rioting on January 24 and 25. Signs of anti-Soviet feeling appeared among the militant students, who demanded more genuine preparations for war, military training for students, and an increased share of the economic burden by the rich.

On January 16 Sadat replaced the 72-year-old Mahmoud Fawzi, who had been prime minister since Oct. 20, 1970, with Aziz Sidky (*see* BIOGRAPHY), one of the architects of Egypt's industrialization program. Sidky formed a 32-member government which he described as a "Cabinet of confrontation" and included in it several young technocrats with degrees from Western universities. However, the key ministries of interior, economy, information, and war (temporarily) remained in the same hands. The foreign minister, Mahmoud Riad, regarded as a hard-liner on conflict with Israel, was replaced by a former ambassador to Moscow, Murad Ghaleb, and Sayid Marei, a former minister of agriculture, became first secretary of the Arab Socialist Union (ASU). To assist the war effort one of the new government's first actions was to announce a 10% cut in investments for 1971–72 and various reductions of government expenditure. Increases in the price of gasoline and car import duties and the banning of various luxuries followed on February 2.

President Sadat visited the Soviet Union on February 2–4 and again April 27–29. Although he described his second visit as a "huge success," there were already several signs of Soviet-Egyptian tension. The second visit was cut short, and full-scale talks between the Soviet and Egyptian leaders lasted only five hours. On May 14–18 the Soviet defense minister, Andrei A. Grechko, visited Egypt, and the Cairo press reported a new arms deal.

On May 14 President Sadat publicly rejected a proposal put forward in a memorandum by a group of prominent Egyptians, including two former key members of the Revolution Command Council, Abdul Latif al-Baghdadi and Kamal ad-Din Husain, for the formation of a new National Union to replace the ASU. The memorandum also included criticisms of the Soviet Union which President Sadat rejected in strong terms. However, signs increased during the summer that the Egyptian regime's relations with the Soviet Union were moving toward a crisis. A series of articles by Muhammad Hassanein Heikal, *al-Ahram* editor and President Sadat's confidant, pointed out that while

EGYPT

Education. (1969–70) Primary, pupils 3,618,750, teachers 97,268; secondary, pupils 1,087,035, teachers 41,949; vocational, pupils 245,862, teachers 12,491; teacher training, students 25,075, teachers 2,673; higher (including 6 universities), 197,055, teaching staff 11,316.

Finance. Monetary unit: Egyptian pound, with (Sept. 18, 1972) a nominal par value of E£0.43 to U.S. $1 (free rate of E£1.06 = £1 sterling) and a tourist rate of E£0.70 to U.S. $1 (E£1.70 = £1 sterling). Gold, SDRs, and foreign exchange, central bank: (May 1972) U.S. $173 million; (May 1971) U.S. $145 million. Budget (1971–72 est.): revenue E£1,920 million; expenditure E£1,692.3 million. Gross national product: (1969–70) E£2,927 million; (1968–69) E£2,649 million. Money supply: (March 1972) E£834.6 million; (March 1971) E£770.3 million. Cost of living (Cairo; 1963 = 100): (Dec. 1971) 151; (Dec. 1970) 148.

Foreign Trade. (1971) Imports E£387.1 million; exports E£343 million. Import sources (1970): U.S.S.R. 12%; India 8%; West Germany 8%; France 7%; Italy 7%; U.S. 6%; East Germany 5%. Export destinations (1970): U.S.S.R. 37%; East Germany 6%; India 6%; Czechoslovakia 5%. Main exports (1970): cotton 45%; cotton yarn 11%; rice 10%; cotton fabrics 5%; crude oil 5%.

Transport and Communications. Roads (1970) *c.* 50,000 km. (including *c.* 22,000 km. with improved surface). Motor vehicles in use (1970): passenger 130,700; commercial (including buses) 30,100. Railways: (1969) 4,510 km.; traffic (1969–70) 6,529,000,000 passenger-km., freight 3,333,000,000 net ton-km. Air traffic (1971): 955.9 million passenger-km.; freight 18,081,000 net ton-km. Shipping (1971): merchant vessels 100 gross tons and over 127; gross tonnage 241,429. Telephones (Dec. 1968) *c.* 365,000. Radio licenses (Dec. 1970) 4.4 million. Television licenses (Dec. 1970) 475,000.

Agriculture. Production (in 000; metric tons; 1971; 1970 in parentheses): corn 2,342 (2,393); wheat 1,729 (1,516); barley 76 (83); sorghum 854 (874); potatoes 451 (522); rice 2,534 (2,605); sugar, raw value (1971–72) *c.* 535, (1970–71) *c.* 515; tomatoes (1970) 1,533, (1969) 1,548; onions (1970) 456, (1969) 587; dry broad beans 296 (277); dates 340 (*c.* 355); oranges 809 (*c.* 680); lemons 74 (*c.* 70); bananas (1970) *c.* 90, (1969) 91; grapes 122 (109); cotton, lint 536 (509); cheese *c.* 190 (*c.* 185). Livestock (in 000; 1970–71): cattle *c.* 2,120; sheep *c.* 2,033; goats *c.* 1,150; buffalo *c.* 2,100; asses *c.* 1,330; camels *c.* 130; chickens *c.* 24,800.

Industry. Production (in 000; metric tons; 1970): iron ore (metal content) 227; crude oil (1971) 14,706; cement (1971) 3,883; phosphate rock 699; salt 446; asbestos (1968) 2.6; cotton yarn 164; cotton fabrics 101; electricity (kw-hr.; 1969) 7,134,000.

Eggs:
see Agriculture

Israel, the U.S., and the U.S.S.R. all benefited from the "no peace, no war" situation, Egypt only suffered.

The basis of the Soviet-Egyptian difficulties was the Soviet delay in providing Egypt with advanced offensive weapons, and the consequent strong anti-Soviet feeling among Egyptian officers. President Sadat later declared that the Soviets had repeatedly promised to supply the weapons to Egypt but had failed to do so. On July 13 he sent Sidky to Moscow for what appeared to be a final effort to persuade the Soviets to fulfill Egypt's requirements, but the visit, although planned to last three to five days, was cut short after one day. On July 18 Sadat announced the withdrawal of Soviet military advisers and personnel from Egypt. Western sources estimated these as including 4,000 advisers with units of the Egyptian armed forces, 12,000 Soviet soldiers manning missile sites and other Soviet equipment, and 200 pilots with ground crews for MiG-21s and 23s. By the end of July diplomatic sources reported that approximately 15,000 Soviet personnel and 25,000 dependents had left and about 2,000 remained.

Egypt attempted to avoid the appearance of a complete breach with the Soviets, and *al-Ahram* reported that a letter from Soviet Communist Party leader Leonid I. Brezhnev might lead to a summit meeting. But Sadat later told the Peoples' Assembly that the letter was unacceptable in its tone and contents, and criticism of the Soviet Union in the Cairo press grew more open. The replacement on September 8 of Foreign Minister Ghaleb, one of the architects of Soviet-Egyptian relations, by Muhammad Hassan az-Zayyat increased the impression of a reorientation of Egyptian policy. Increased Soviet arms supplies to Syria aroused expectations that the Soviets were aiming to cut their losses in Egypt in order to concentrate on Syria and Iraq. But the Soviets retained great economic interests in Egypt, where they were assisting in the rural electrification program, the extension of the Helwan iron and steel complex, and other major projects. They also had an interest in retaining their naval facilities. At the same time, Egypt remained dependent on Soviet spare parts for its weapons. Thus, motives for a rapprochement existed, and in October, after a surprise visit to Moscow by the Egyptian deputy premier for information, Muhammad Abdul Kader Hatem, Sidky himself again visited Moscow for talks. Soon after his return and following reports of an attempted army coup against Sadat, War Minister Muhammad Ahmed Sadek was relieved of his post and replaced by Gen. Ahmed Ismael, chief of Egypt's intelligence service.

Egypt's expulsion of the Soviets was favoured by Libya, its partner along with Syria in the tripartite Arab union. President Sadat had several meetings with the Libyan leader Col. Muammar al-Qaddafi during the year, and on August 2 they announced jointly in Benghazi that the two countries would form a complete merger by September 1973.

There were several signs that President Sadat was adopting a more traditional Islamic policy than had his predecessor, Nasser. In March he visited Saudi Arabia, Kuwait, and Sudan (which was also loosening its ties with the Soviet Union) to strengthen his relations with those countries. On April 25 he made an unprecedented attack on the Jews, whom he described as "mean, traitorous and treacherous" people who had rightly been evicted from Arabia by the Prophet. Relations with Pres. Gaafar Nimeiry's regime in the Sudan, however, deteriorated later in the year as, following a settlement of its southern problem, Sudan sought Western aid and renewed diplomatic relations with the U.S.

If President Sadat hoped his break with the Soviet Union would cause a change in U.S. Middle East policy, he was disappointed and his criticisms of U.S. support for Israel remained undiminished. On the other hand, Egypt launched a diplomatic campaign in Western Europe and approached several Western countries, including Britain, to buy arms. The campaign received a setback from the massacre of Israeli athletes by Arab terrorists at the Olympic Games in Munich, which especially affected Egypt's recently renewed relations with West Germany.

The government's policies met with unprecedented criticism during a debate in the People's Assembly in December, after a special parliamentary commission had commented adversely on Sidky's report to the Assembly (November 27) to the effect that the "program of national preparation for the war" had been completed. Later in December Heikal was the object of a violent press campaign, in which he was accused of sabotaging the nation's morale.

(PETER MANSFIELD)

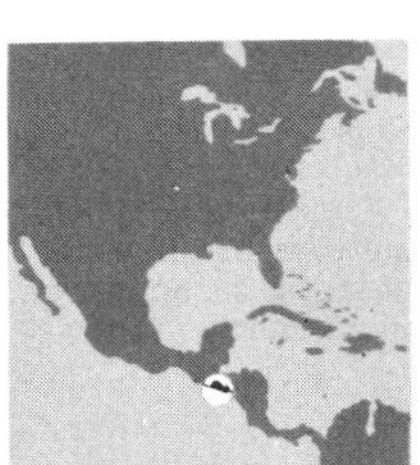

El Salvador

A republic on the Pacific coast of Central America and the smallest country on the isthmus, El Salvador is bounded on the west by Guatemala and on the north and east by Honduras. Area: 8,098 sq.mi. (21,975 sq.km.). Pop. (1972 est.): 3,649,197. Cap. and largest city: San Salvador (pop., 1972 est., 387,489). Language: Spanish. Religion: Roman Catholic. Presidents in 1972, Col. Fidel Sánchez Hernández and, from July 1, Col. Arturo Armando Molina.

Presidential politics dominated events in El Salva-

EL SALVADOR

Education. (1969–70) Primary, pupils 516,875, teachers 13,491; secondary, pupils 57,533; vocational, pupils 27,250; secondary and vocational, teachers 3,430; higher, students 8,151, teaching staff 537.

Finance. Monetary unit: colón, with (Sept. 18, 1972) a par value of 2.50 colones to U.S. $1 (free rate of 6.21 colones = £1 sterling). Gold, SDRs, and foreign exchange, central bank: (June 1972) U.S. $84.1 million; (June 1971) U.S. $79.2 million. Budget (1970 est.): revenue 241,320,000 colones; expenditure 239,650,000 colones. Gross national product: (1970) 2,519,000,000 colones; (1969) 2,362,000,000 colones. Money supply: (April 1972) 351.4 million colones; (April 1971) 323.1 million colones. Cost of living (1963 = 100): (March 1972) 108; (March 1971) 109.

Foreign Trade. (1971) Imports 623.6 million colones; exports 570.7 million colones. Import sources (1970): U.S. 30%; Guatemala 19%; Japan 10%; West Germany 8%; Costa Rica 5%; Netherlands 5%. Export destinations (1970): West Germany 25%; U.S. 21%; Guatemala 17%; Japan 11%; Costa Rica 9%; Nicaragua 6%. Main exports: coffee 41%; cotton 13%.

Transport and Communications. Roads (1970) 8,641 km. (including 307 km. of Pan-American Highway). Motor vehicles in use (1970): passenger 35,100; commercial (including buses) 18,500. Railways (1970) 623 km. Telephones (Jan. 1971) 39,000. Radio receivers (Dec. 1970) 405,000. Television receivers (Dec. 1970) 92,000.

Agriculture. Production (in 000; metric tons; 1971; 1970 in parentheses): rice *c.* 45 (44); corn *c.* 375 (363); sorghum 156 (147); coffee *c.* 144 (134); sugar, raw value (1971–72) *c.* 198, (1970–71) 149; cotton, lint *c.* 64 (55). Livestock (in 000; 1970–71): cattle 1,492; pigs 419; horses *c.* 65; poultry *c.* 7,900.

Industry. Production (in 000; metric tons; 1970): cement 167; cotton yarn 3.7; electricity (kw-hr.; 1971) 735,500,000.

Eire:
see Ireland

Electrical Industries:
see Fuel and Power; Industrial Review

Electronics:
see Computers

WIDE WORLD

Dazed children mingle with Red Cross rescue workers in the rubble of a San Salvador orphanage bombed accidentally by a military plane during an attempted coup on March 25, 1972. High winds diverted the bomb that struck the orphanage from its intended target.

dor in 1972. Col. Fidel Sánchez Hernández, president since 1967, was constitutionally banned from succeeding himself, and four candidates vied for his office. Col. Arturo Armando Molina, formerly private secretary to President Sánchez, represented the incumbent and moderate right-of-centre National Conciliation Party. The major opposition party, the left-of-centre Christian Democrats, joined with two other parties to nominate a former mayor of San Salvador, José Napoleón Duarte.

Only little more than one-half of the registered voters went to the polls on February 20. Molina received the largest number of votes, winning over his nearest opponent, Duarte, by 10,000. Duarte branded the election a fraud. However, because Molina failed to gain a plurality as required by the constitution, the decision on who was to be the new president rested with the Sánchez-controlled National Assembly. That body met on February 25 and proclaimed Molina the next president. The ruling National Conciliation Party won handily in congressional and municipal elections on March 12, securing 38 of the 52 seats in Congress and 206 of the 261 municipal mayoralties.

The post-elections atmosphere was tense. Early on March 25, rebel army troops marched on San Salvador, seized control of the nation's communications network, sealed the country's borders, and took President Sánchez and his daughter into custody. On the afternoon of the same day, loyal army troops, supported by the Air Force, advanced successfully against the rebels, who surrendered early that evening. The president and his daughter were released unharmed. This abortive coup resulted in more than 100 military and civilian deaths and left some 200 wounded. Some of those accused of participating in or encouraging the rebellion either were jailed or went into exile. Immediately after the uprising, President Sánchez proclaimed a curfew, martial law, and a state of siege. This last action remained in effect until June 3.

President Molina began his five-year term on July 1. His first major action occurred July 19 when he ordered troops to occupy and close the National University in a move to purge left-wing influences in the school. A number of faculty were expelled, and the foreign professors among them were asked to leave the country. Some native-born faculty chose to go into exile. (ALLEN D. BUSHONG)

Employment, Wages, and Hours

Inflation continued to be a matter of serious concern during 1972. The blame for rising prices was often put on trade union demands for higher wages: it was argued that because wages are the most important part of manufacturers' costs these costs need to be stabilized if prices are not to be raised, and so the policy is to "freeze" wages by law. But recent studies showed that the problem was not as simple as this; in particular, government tax policy may be one of the major causes of wage-price inflation. Table I shows how, in every industrial market economy over the period 1955–57 to 1967–69, taxes rose quite sharply as a proportion of the national income, on average from 26.7 to 33.4%, the average rise thus being 6.7 percentage points. Social security contributions and taxes on personal incomes rose, as did taxes on expenditure. All these taxes affect the wage earner: the first two make a direct difference between gross-of-tax earnings and net-of-tax take-home pay; the last affects what can be bought with the paycheck. By contrast, taxes on corporations fell in nearly all countries, the average fall being one-half of a percentage point. Thus, the rising burden of taxation was borne by households.

Government tax revenues can be used for two purposes: to pay for public consumption, such as municipal services or social security, or to pay for investment (either directly by the government or indirectly through subsidies). Because economic growth depends on investment that adds to the productive capacity of the economy, governments had for a long time been trying to promote more investment. A lot of investment is paid for out of profits and, therefore, taxes on the profits of corporations had, at the very least, not been increased, while extra tax concessions were often given to private investment. In the interests of the balance of payments, governments also tried to promote exports, and this again meant that private consumption had to be held back, so that productive capacity could be devoted to exporting. As Table II shows, in most countries the long-run growth of both private and public consumption was slightly below the growth rate of national income, while the rates of growth of investment and exports were, respectively, more than one-third and two-thirds higher than the rate of growth of national income.

Thus taxes had been used to restrain increases in consumption and to stimulate investment or exports. The way in which such a tax policy may affect rates of increase in standards of living is shown in Table III. In the United Kingdom from 1956 to 1968 the rate of growth of money incomes before tax increased slightly, but higher rates of price inflation meant that the rate of growth of real pretax incomes remained roughly constant. But, because of the rising incidence of income taxes and social security contributions, the rates of growth of real take-home pay fell steadily from an annual rate of 2.1% in the period 1956–60 to 0.5% in the period 1964–68. The years 1968–70 then saw a "wage explosion," which raised the rate of growth of money wages to an annual average rate of 10%, overcoming the problem of the rising incidence of taxation. In the United States, between the first and second half of the 1960s, this tax effect was even more marked.

If it is generally the case that taxes are being

used to restrain rises in standards of living, then the recent international phenomena of high wage demands supported by strikes appeared not so much the fault of trade unions as of a grass-roots reaction to, and revolt against, government fiscal policies. The appropriate remedy would thus seem to require a reduction in the incidence of taxation, rather than a simple freeze on wages.

Employment and Unemployment. In 1970 the growth of employment, particularly in manufacturing, tended to slow down (*see* Table IV). This produced differing changes in unemployment in various countries. In the U.S. and Canada, where manufacturing employment actually declined, the rise in unemployment was quite sharp; in European countries, on the other hand, manufacturing employment continued to rise and rates of unemployment tended to fall.

Third World Economies. In many of the third world countries for which there were data, unemployment recorded large increases because of rapid rates of population growth, which averaged a little over 2% as against 1% in the more developed countries. An exception was Zambia, where an increase in construction activity led to a marked fall in recorded unemployment (*see* Table V). Tanzania also enjoyed rapid increases in manufacturing employment, mostly in publicly owned industries that had substantial increases in exports. Other countries with rapid manufacturing growth and falling unemployment were Greece, Guyana, and Singapore.

In Greece shortages of skilled workers and a consequent high rate of labour turnover as firms competed for labour were beginning to have an adverse effect on industrial expansion and to raise wage levels. This was an ironic development because in past years Greece had "exported" much of its skilled labour to Western Europe; efforts were now being made to induce the emigrants to return. Singapore's policy of expanding the shipbuilding and repair industry was proving very successful: output expanded by one-third in 1971 and over 25,000 workers were now employed in this industry. The rest of the economy was expanding rapidly, and in February 1972 the government established a National Wages Council to advise on wage structures and wage increases, a sign of the need to cope with growing shortages of labour.

Chile had a dramatic change in the incidence of unemployment as the Marxist government of Pres. Salvador Allende expanded production and employment, especially in the construction sector, in an effort to improve the lot of the working class. Recorded unemployment in Santiago fell from over 8% of the labour force in 1970 to under 4% by the end of 1971. Industrial production rose by 11% and gross national product by about 8½%. In 1972 increasing shortages of foreign exchange hampered further growth and late in the year strikes and work stoppages, undertaken largely by middle class workers fearing sweeping nationalization of their businesses, crippled the economy for nearly a month.

Although the general level of employment rose by 2.8% in India in 1970, partly because of the successful expansion of agriculture, unemployment continued to rise rapidly and Indira Gandhi's government began a crash program of rural development. This was likely to be part of a more comprehensive fifth five-year plan promoting employment formulated in response to Mrs. Gandhi's declared policy of improving economic equality rather than economic growth. In Sri Lanka (Ceylon) there was little expansion in manufacturing output in 1970 and 1971, partly because of a lack of investment and partly because of balance of payments difficulties. Unemployment, therefore, continued to increase, and remained very high.

Table I. Taxes Paid Out of Income as a Percent of Gross National Product

Country	Total taxes as % of GNP 1967–69†	Total taxes as % of GNP 1955–57†	% Changes 1955–57 to 1967–69*: Total taxes	Social security contribution	Income tax	Tax on corporations	Tax on expenditure
Austria‡	36.3	30.2	6.1	2.1	1.8	−0.2	2.3
Belgium	33.0	24.2	8.8	3.7	1.7	0.5	2.9
Canada‡	30.0	23.8	6.2	1.5	2.9	−0.7	2.5
Denmark	34.1	24.2	9.9	0.5	4.6	−0.4	5.2
France	37.0	32.9	4.1	3.5	1.5	−0.2	−0.7
Germany, West	35.1	32.4	2.7	1.9	2.0	−0.7	−0.5
Italy	30.3	24.7	5.6	3.7	1.6	0.2	0.1
Ireland‡	27.7	22.3	5.4	1.1	2.1	0	2.1
Netherlands	37.8	28.5	9.3	7.6	2.4	−1.0	0.3
Norway	38.7	30.1	8.6	6.1	2.2	−1.5	1.8
Sweden‡	40.7	28.3	12.4	4.8	5.0	−1.8	4.3
Switzerland	23.1	18.6	4.5	1.1	2.0	0.8	0.6
United Kingdom	34.2	28.0	6.2	1.9	3.8	−1.9	2.5
United States	30.0	25.4	4.6	2.4	2.0	−0.6	0.7
Unweighted average	33.4	26.7	6.7	3.0	2.5	−0.5	1.7

*May not add exactly because of rounding.
†Annual average of these years.
‡To 1966–68.
Source: Organization for Economic Cooperation and Development, *Expenditure Trends in OECD Countries 1960–1980* (1972).

The decline in both tourism and construction in Malta led to a large increase in unemployment in 1971 to about 6½% of the labour force. The situation was further threatened by the possible withdrawal of British military forces, but a settlement was achieved. The government now planned for economic development with increasing employment and was trying to promote emigration to Europe as a partial solution.

Industrial Market Economies. In the more developed economies the slowing down in the rate of growth of employment in 1970 continued into 1971

Table II. Ratios of Growth Rates of Expenditures to Growth Rate of GNP: 1955–69

Country	Private consumption	Public consumption	Investment	Exports
Austria	1.05	0.69	1.20	1.78
Belgium	0.84	1.37	1.34	1.76
Canada*	1.02	0.65	0.85	1.52
Denmark	0.91	1.10	1.78	1.51
France†	0.99	0.58	1.56	1.48
Germany, West‡	1.02	0.85	0.92	1.98
Italy	0.99	0.74	0.98	2.54
Ireland†	0.89	0.92	2.41	1.78
Japan	0.84	0.55	1.50	1.35
Netherlands	1.09	0.48	1.39	1.71
Norway	0.88	1.28	0.96	1.83
Sweden*	0.86	1.06	1.37	1.48
Switzerland	1.02	0.99	1.52	1.59
United Kingdom	0.92	0.62	1.86	1.24
United States	1.01	1.06	0.87	1.49
Unweighted average	0.96	0.86	1.37	1.67

*1955–68.
†1959–69.
‡1960–69.
Source: Organization for Economic Cooperation and Development, *Expenditure Trends in OECD Countries 1960–1980* (1972).

Table III. Effect of Prices and Taxes on Take-home-pay Annual Rates of Growth

In Percent

Period	Pretax money income	Pretax real income	Post-tax real income
United Kingdom: (manual workers)			
1956–60	5.0	2.9	2.1
1960–64	5.5	2.2	1.3
1964–68	6.6	2.5	0.5
1968–70	10.0	3.6	1.3
United States:			
1961–65	3.4	1.9	2.3
1966–70	4.7	0.8	−0.3

Note: The difference between the first and second columns shows the effect of rising prices; the difference between the second and third columns shows the effect of the changing incidence of taxes and of social security contributions paid by the employee.
Source: D. Jackson, H. A. Turner, and F. Wilkinson, *Do Trade Unions Cause Inflation?* (Cambridge, 1972).

and 1972; in both of these years manufacturing employment fell on the average by over half a percent (*see* Table VI). Correspondingly, there were large rises in unemployment. This was the result of continuing policies of economic restraint in the unsuccessful efforts to reduce the rate of price inflation through conventional monetary and fiscal policies. Increasingly, therefore, governments were searching for new ways to contain inflation without the socially disruptive effects of rapidly growing unemployment.

In the U.S. unemployment fell somewhat in 1972 after rising by over one-fifth in 1971. The turnaround in economic activity resulting from the tax reduction of December 1971 and the easing of monetary policy was clearly visible in the figures for manufacturing employment, which showed a decline for 1971 and an increase for 1972. There was still a considerable amount of unused capacity in the economy, so that these favourable trends were likely to continue for some time. Following in the wake of its large neighbour, Canada showed similar trends in employment and unemployment: after a steep rise in unemployment in 1970, monetary and fiscal policies were used to promote a faster rate of economic growth and by mid-1972 manufacturing employment had begun to expand and unemployment to contract.

In the U.K. there were sharp falls in manufacturing employment as the "shake-out" of the labour force continued; this represented manufacturers' attempts to reduce labour costs per unit of output. Unemployment rose by one-third in 1971 and in January 1972 reached the one million mark. But the rate of increase in unemployment slowed as the government's economic policies began to take effect.

In France, too, the rate of growth of unemployment slowed in 1972 after a sharp rise in 1971, but manufacturing employment changed only a little. It had been forecast that the French labour force would rise by 0.9% a year between 1970–75, but there was expected to be a considerable fall in agricultural employment, and these workers would have to be provided with jobs elsewhere in the economy. In West Germany there was a sharp rise in unemployment in 1971 and again in 1972 as the decline in manufacturing employment became relatively large. This was caused by policies designed to restrain the growth in demand and, together with the appreciation of the mark, had marked effects on other smaller European economies. In both Belgium and the Netherlands unemployment rose suddenly: by the second quarter of 1972 it was twice as high in the Netherlands as it had been in the

Table IV. Employment, Unemployment, and Population

Changes for 1970 over 1969 (%)

Country	Employment General	Employment Manufacturing	Numbers unemployed	Population
Third world				
Chile	...	−0.1	20.3	2.2
India	2.8	...	16.3	2.5
Korea, South	2.5	2.3	−5.3	2.8
Philippines	0.6*	0	...	3.0
Puerto Rico	2.0	−1.7	10.6	0.4
Sierra Leone	−0.4	−15.8	4.4	1.2†
Taiwan	2.5	−12.5	−7.1	1.7
Tanzania	1.9	9.4	...	2.6
Turkey	4.1*	4.5	...	2.5
Zambia	5.5	6.7	−33.1	3.1
Average	2.4	−0.8	0.9	2.2
Industrial market				
Australia	3.4	2.3	−6.6	2.0
Austria	1.4	3.2	−13.0	0.3
Belgium	1.7	4.5	−16.4	0.3
Canada	1.3	−2.0	29.6	1.5
France	1.2*	1.7	17.5	0.9
Germany, West	1.3	4.1	−17.0	1.2
Italy	0.5	3.4	−7.2	0.9
Japan	1.1	2.5	3.5	1.2
Netherlands	1.4	—	−12.3	1.2
Norway	2.9	3.2	−19.9	0.8
Sweden	1.8	0.6	−19.2	0.9
United Kingdom	−0.7	−0.1	6.4	0.3
United States	0.9	−4.0	44.0	1.1
Average	1.4	1.6	−0.8	1.0
Centrally planned				
Bulgaria	2.4	0.8	...	0.7
Czechoslovakia	1.7	0.9	...	0.4
Germany, East	1.2	−0.3	...	−0.1
Hungary	1.2	0.4	...	0.4
Poland	1.7	1.7	27.3	0.8
Romania	3.0	4.3	...	1.2
Yugoslavia	3.9	4.0	−3.3	0.8
U.S.S.R.	1.7	1.7	...	0.9
Average	2.1	1.7	12.0	0.6

*Nonagricultural sector.
†1968 to 1969.
Sources: International Labour Office, *Year Book of Labour Statistics* (1971) and *Bulletin of Labour Statistics* (third quarter 1972); United Nations, *Monthly Bulletin of Statistics* (October 1972).

Table V. Unemployment: Third World

Changes over previous year (%)

Country	1971	1970
Burma	17.8	4.9
Chile	−20.0	20.3
Cyprus	1.4	4.1
Ghana	11.5	10.0
Greece	−37.8	−26.8
Guatemala	0	−9.6
Guyana	−22.2*	−19.1
India	23.5	16.3
Korea, South	2.5	−5.3
Malaysia	−7.2	20.6
Malta	36.2	3.4
Mauritius	44.4†	47.0
Morocco	...	15.3
Nigeria	6.7	10.7
Puerto Rico	10.6	10.6
Sierra Leone	−15.6	4.4
Singapore	−25.1	−14.7
Sri Lanka (Ceylon)	10.2	24.5
Surinam	−57.3	8.7
Trinidad	0*	−3.3
Zambia	1.0	−33.3
Average	−1.0	4.2

*June 1971. †April 1971.
Source: United Nations, *Monthly Bulletin of Statistics* (October 1972).

Table VI. Employment and Unemployment in Manufacturing: Industrial Market Economies

Changes over previous year (%)

Country	Employment 1972*	Employment 1971	Unemployment 1972*	Unemployment 1971
Canada	1.7	−1.0	−2.0	11.5
United States	1.6	−3.9	−0.8	22.1
Japan	−3.0	−0.2	8.0	11.4
Austria	2.2	6.1	−1.8	−10.2
Belgium	1.1†	−3.2	26.5	0
France	0.4	0.5	16.4	28.6
Germany, West	−2.3	−0.8	44.2	26.2
Ireland	−2.0†	−0.5	20.0	0
Italy	−1.0	2.1	10.2	−0.5
Netherlands	—	−1.9	108.9	34.8
Sweden	−1.4	−0.9	2.2	50.0
United Kingdom	−4.8	−3.4	15.2	32.7
Average	−0.7	−0.6	20.6	17.2

*Second quarter 1972 over second quarter 1971.
†First quarter 1972 over first quarter 1971.
Source: Organization for Economic Cooperation and Development, *Main Economic Indicators* (October 1972).

Table VII. Output, Employment, Wages, and Prices: Centrally Planned Economies

Change in 1971 over 1970 (%)

Country	Manufacturing production	Manufacturing employment	Average earnings in manufacturing	Consumer prices
Bulgaria	8.7*	1.5	3.2	...
Czechoslovakia	16.5	0*	3.6	−0.3
Hungary	8.6	0	3.7	2.0
Poland	8.3	3.2	5.5	2.2
Romania	10.5†	5.9	...	...
U.S.S.R.	7.9	1.5‡	7.1§	...
Yugoslavia	9.8	5.0	21.8	15.3

*Industrial sector.
†Industrial production: first three quarters 1971 over first three quarters 1970.
‡Estimated by applying productivity growth of 6.5% to output growth.
§All sectors.
Sources: United Nations, *Monthly Bulletin of Statistics* (October 1972); *Economist* Intelligence Unit *Quarterly Reports* on individual countries.

JOHN ROBATON—CAMERA 5

Jobless people line up to collect their unemployment checks early in 1972. The rate of unemployment in the U.S. was dropping late in the year.

second quarter of the previous year. Italy, too, had a similar, though less marked pattern of fluctuations in employment.

Because of the restrictive policies used to improve the balance of payments in Sweden, employment in manufacturing fell and unemployment increased sharply in 1971. In the autumn of 1972 the government announced special measures involving public spending, investment incentives, and retraining, all aimed at reducing unemployment.

In Japan unemployment rose again in 1972, with a continuing fall in manufacturing employment. The economy experienced its longest postwar recession, a slowing down from its usually rapid rate of growth.

Centrally Planned Economies. The growth of manufacturing production and employment in the centrally planned economies was rapid during 1971 (*see* Table VII). In the U.S.S.R. money incomes tended to outrun the supply of goods, but the increase in earnings was part of the new emphasis on the production of consumer goods and foodstuffs. In Czechoslovakia manufacturing production rose very steeply, largely because of improvements in labour productivity, while the success of the rigorous policy of controlling prices was evident in the slight decline in consumer prices. In Hungary there was no change in manufacturing employment but output rose considerably and prices rose by 2%. The economy was experiencing considerable shortages of labour and the government raised the wages of the lower-paid workers. There was a 5½% rise in money wages in Poland as part of a new social policy of raising living standards; prices rose by only 2.2% and so increases in real incomes were assured. The main problem now was to increase the output of consumer goods to match the rise in the purchasing power of wages: much of this demand was being met by imports of consumer goods.

In Romania manufacturing employment continued to rise rapidly and expanded by nearly 6% in the year, as investment and output continued at high rates. Bulgaria's economic expansion was considerably assisted by investment from the U.S.S.R. Price inflation became an even more serious problem in Yugoslavia: the dinar was devalued at the beginning of 1971 and again at the end of the year, pushing up costs; investment increased rapidly, pushing up demand. The government tried through various measures to reduce these pressures on the economy but average earnings rose during the year at twice the planned rate.

Wages. *Industrial Market Economies.* It was to be hoped that the movement of wages and prices shown in Table VIII was a pointer to the future: on the average there was a slight fall in the rates of growth of both wages and prices as more countries took stronger direct measures to slow down rates of inflation. In the U.S., Pres. Richard Nixon's policy of directly controlling pay and prices, which began with a 90-day freeze in August 1971 and continued under Phase Two with a Pay Board and a Price Commission applying standards of 5½% for pay rises and 2½% for price increases, caused a noticeable drop in the rate of price inflation from nearly 6% in 1969–70 to nearly 4% in 1970–71 and to 3% from the second quarter of 1971 to the second quarter of 1972. However, the rate of wage increase rose slightly and real wages advanced quite sharply, particularly when the freeze ended. The real test of the policy would come in 1973, when many wage contracts were to be renegotiated. Price inflation in Canada continued to be high, reflecting the pressure of rising wages; the government had little success in influencing wage settlements and the Prices and Incomes Commission's attempt to moderate inflation was unlikely to succeed.

In Europe it appeared that the rate of wage increase might be slackening off slightly, but not the rate of price inflation, so that increases in real wages tended to be lower than previously. In France the rates of both price and wage inflation remained high in 1971 and 1972. The government attempted to reduce price increases by not raising public prices in return for price restraint from the private sector.

In West Germany wage increases moderated slightly in 1971 and 1972 largely because of the beneficial internal effects of the appreciation of the mark, which reduced import prices and so raised the standard of living. Price increases persisted, however, partly as a delayed reaction to the rapid wage increases of 1970 and 1971 and partly because a number of publicly controlled prices were raised.

In the first half of 1971 the Dutch government tried to enforce direct limitations on wage and price increases, but in the second half of the year these policies were ended and wages began to rise faster than formerly.

The rate of price inflation in Italy accelerated and it was expected that wage increases would probably follow suit. Although there were calls for an incomes policy, the trade unions were not willing to accept a wage policy and the civil service was not equipped to police the necessary price controls. In Norway government policy reduced the rate of price inflation only slightly but had a more marked impact on the rate of wage increase. The recession in Sweden, together with a direct freeze on prices, led to a slight reduction in the rate of price inflation, but wages rose very sharply in 1972 because of continuing wage demands from the trade unions.

In the U.K. the rate of price inflation declined considerably as a result of the Confederation of British Industries' policy of voluntary price restraint, but the rate of wage increase remained high. At the end of September 1972 the government started talks with the trade unions and the employers to try to obtain a voluntary policy on pay and prices. These talks broke down at the beginning of November and the prime minister announced a 90-day wage and price freeze.

Table VIII. Money and Real Wages in Manufacturing and Consumer Prices: Industrial Market Economies

Changes over previous year (%)

Country	Money wages 1972*	Money wages 1971	Real wages 1972*	Real wages 1971	Prices 1972*	Prices 1971
Canada	7.1	8.4	3.1	5.1	3.9	3.2
United States	6.9	5.8	3.8	1.8	3.0	3.9
Japan	15.4	13.7	10.3	7.7	4.6	5.5
Austria	10.1	13.6	3.8	8.5	6.0	4.7
Belgium	11.9	12.2	6.4	8.0	5.3	3.9
Denmark	14.6†	15.1	7.7†	8.6	6.4†	6.0
France	10.9	11.2	4.8	4.8	5.8	6.1
Germany, West	9.3	11.0	3.5	5.8	5.6	5.0
Ireland	13.5†	16.4	3.9†	6.8	9.2†	9.0
Italy	8.9	13.4	3.5	8.4	5.3	4.7
Netherlands	12.6	11.7	4.3	3.7	8.0	7.8
Norway	9.5†	12.4	3.2†	5.6	6.2†	6.4
Sweden	17.7	7.7	10.7	0.3	6.3	7.4
Switzerland	8.4	9.8	2.3	2.5	6.0	7.1
United Kingdom	11.7	11.4	5.3	1.6	6.1	9.6
Average	11.2	11.6	5.1	5.3	5.8	6.0

*Second quarter 1972 over second quarter 1971.
†First quarter 1972 over first quarter 1971.
Source: Organization for Economic Cooperation and Development, *Main Economic Indicators* (October 1972).

Table IX. Money and Real Wages in Manufacturing and Consumer Prices: Third World

Changes over previous year (%)

Country	Money wages 1971	Money wages 1970	Real wages 1971	Real wages 1970	Prices 1971	Prices 1970
Barbados	8.2	18.3	0.7	9.7	7.5	7.8
Chile	42.2	44.2	18.4	9.0	20.1	32.3
El Salvador	2.1	2.2	1.8	−0.7	0.3	2.9
Greece	8.8	5.9	5.6	2.7	3.0	3.1
Guatemala	0	0	0.5	−2.3	−0.5	2.4
Korea, South	20.0	25.6	4.2	8.7	15.2	15.6
Malawi	5.0	2.0	−2.9	−6.9	8.1	9.5
Philippines	14.0	13.2	−2.9	7.3	17.4	5.5
Puerto Rico	6.8	6.7	2.4	3.2	4.3	3.4
Sri Lanka (Ceylon)	2.2	8.3	−0.5	2.3	2.7	5.9
Average	10.9	12.6	2.7	3.3	7.8	8.8

Sources: United Nations, *Monthly Bulletin of Statistics* (October 1972); International Labour Office, *Bulletin of Labour Statistics* (third quarter 1972).

Table X. Weekly Hours of Work in Manufacturing

Country	1971	1970	Absolute change
Industrial countries			
Austria	37.0	37.4	−0.4
Canada	39.7	39.7	0
Finland	38.5	38.3	0.2
France	44.5	44.8	−0.3
Germany, West	43.0	43.8	−0.8
Ireland	42.3	42.7	−0.4
Japan	42.6	43.3	−0.7
Netherlands	43.8	44.2	−0.4
Norway	34.8	35.3	−0.5
Switzerland	44.6	44.7	−0.1
United Kingdom	43.6	44.9	−1.3
United States	39.9	39.8	0.1
Czechoslovakia	43.7	43.7	0
U.S.S.R.	40.4	40.5	−0.1
Average	41.3	41.7	−0.3
Third world			
El Salvador	47.5	48.0	−0.5
Greece	44.1	44.6	−0.5
Guatemala	46.3	45.9	0.4
Korea, South	54.4	54.0	0.4
Puerto Rico	37.2	36.6	0.6
Average	45.9	45.8	0.1

Source: United Nations, *Monthly Bulletin of Statistics* (October 1972).

The Japanese recession reduced the rates of wage and price inflation. Profits had fallen sharply and manufacturers were not willing to grant the large increases in wages that were common in the late 1960s.

Third World Economies. The growth rates of money wages in manufacturing in the sample of third world economies covered in Table IX continued to be quite high. In Chile the rate of increase in money wages was maintained while the rate of price increase was held down by the government. Workers enjoyed a very large increase in their standards of living as part of a deliberate government policy to redistribute income to the wage-earners. This expansion of working-class purchasing power was meant to stimulate industrial and agricultural production of consumer goods, and in 1971 the share of wages and salaries in national income rose from 50 to 59%. In 1972, however, inflation erased most gains and brought on economic controls.

A higher rate of increase in money wages in Greece, combined with continued moderate price rises, meant a fairly sharp rise in the rate of growth of real wages. The government introduced a law permitting the formation of strictly nonpolitical trade unions and recognizing the right to strike in limited cases. In October 1971 the minimum wage was raised, and this extra impact on wages continued into 1972.

In the Philippines the rate of price inflation increased more than threefold in 1971, partly because storm damage in 1970–71 reduced the rice harvest, and there was a sharp fall in real wages. The price index for Sri Lanka (Ceylon) probably understated the true rate of inflation, but there was some slowing down in that rate and wages increased very little in 1971.

Hours. Partly because of the continuing decline in economic activity and partly because of negotiated reductions in the working week, hours worked in manufacturing in most industrial countries declined from an average of 41.7 hours per week in 1970 to 41.3 in 1971 (*see* Table X). In most of the third world economies weekly hours of work were considerably above those prevailing in the industrial countries, showing another dimension in the difference of living standards between poor and rich nations. (D. A. S. JACKSON)

See also Economics; Economy, World; Income, National; Industrial Review; Prices.

ENCYCLOPÆDIA BRITANNICA FILMS. *The Industrial Revolution—Beginning in the United States* (1968); *The Rise of Labor* (1968); *The Industrial Worker* (1969); *The Rise of Big Business* (1970); *The Progressive Era* (1971).

Engineering Projects

Bridges. *Suspension Bridges.* Work on the bridge over the Kanmon Straits between Honshu, the largest of the Japanese islands, and Kyushu, the southernmost of the major islands, was completed in 1972. With its centre span of 2,336 ft. it was the largest suspension bridge in Asia. In the United States the Dent Bridge over the Clearwater River in Idaho came into service; a smaller construction with a span of only 1,050 ft., its cables, like those of the Japanese bridge, were prefabricated. Work was under way on the six-lane Bosporus Bridge over the Bosporus in Turkey. The main span was to be 3,524 ft. long.

Cable-Stayed Bridges. In the U.K. the Erskine Bridge, on the Clyde west of Glasgow, opened to traffic. This bridge, 4,326 ft. long, had a 1,000-ft.-long cable-stayed main span. The slender pylons, made up of steel concrete-filled caissons, each supported a single cable anchored to the deck, which was an orthotropic plate 101 ft. wide carried on a streamlined caisson girder.

In Australia, work resumed on the West Gate Bridge on the Lower Yarra River at Melbourne. Work had stopped following an accident in October 1970 that killed 35 people. The reinforced-concrete floor in the original design was replaced by a lighter orthotropic floor, and the number of provisional piles needed for the work was increased.

In Calcutta a cable-stayed bridge freeing a span of 1,500 ft. was planned to cross the Hooghly River. The bidding for the project produced a confrontation between the partisans of welded caissons and of riveted caissons. Those favouring the second form of construction pointed to accidents that had occurred on welded structures.

Cable-stayed structures made their appearance in the U.S. The first experiment, the John O'Connell Memorial Bridge above the port of Sitka in Alaska, made a somewhat timid beginning with a main span only 450 ft. long, the main advantage of cable-staying being that it permitted extremely wide spans.

Other Metal Bridges. In the U.S., Fremont Bridge, under construction in Portland, Ore., with an opening of 1,255 ft. between the supports, was designed to be the largest metal arch in the world. Work was held up by the discovery of wide gaps that opened up at the deck and arch junctures.

A three-mile-long bridge across the Mississippi between Crittenden County, Ark., and Memphis, Tenn., opened to traffic. Two bowstrings of 900-ft. span each provided nearly 60 ft. of clearance above the deepest navigable water.

The U.S. continued to build large trellis-girder bridges such as that over the Thames River between New London and Groton, Conn. ($1\frac{1}{4}$ mi. long with a main span of 540 ft.), and the Grandad Creek Bridge in Idaho with a centre span of 504 ft.

Prestressed Concrete Bridges. In the Netherlands, on the Waal near Tiel, a bridge approximately 4,500 ft. long was under construction. The main viaduct had a centre span 876 ft. long consisting of two 330-ft. cantilevers supported by cables and linked by an independent span 210 ft. long in light concrete. Two caisson girders with a constant depth of 11 ft. carried a platform 101 ft. wide. The cables, in prestressed concrete, were constructed of prefabricated rectangular sections 17 ft. long, assembled by means of joints concreted in place. The tensioning of these cables ensured compression of the prefabricated sections and staying of the deck.

In West Germany, on the Main near Frankfurt, work concluded on a 486-ft.-span prestressed bridge. The deck, formed of a caisson girder nearly 9 ft. in depth, carried two roadways 30 ft. wide and separated by a railway. The cables consisted of a cluster of prestressing bars in a steel tube injected with a liquid cement after tensioning. They were not prestressed as in the case of the Waal bridge, as the injected product was not compressed and served solely to protect the steel. Both techniques seemed to provide satisfactory solutions to the problems of cable corrosion.

The bridge over the Urado Bay at Kochi, Jap., was completed. With a centre span of 754.6 ft. it topped the previous world record set by the Bendorf Bridge at Koblenz, W.Ger. The caisson girder supporting the deck varied in height from 13 to 41 ft.

In France, the Bonhomme Bridge, on the Blavet, was a strut-supported structure. The spans, measured between the points of attachment of struts and deck, were 200 ft., 460 ft., and 200 ft., with a maximum 600 ft. at the base of the struts. To span such distances girders of varying depth were generally used. However, at Mannheim, W.Ger., the bridge over the Neckar (length about 2,400 ft., main span 340 ft.) used caisson girders of a constant height, for aesthetic reasons.

During the year accidents involving loss of life occurred in West Germany, Britain, and the U.S. when falsework supporting bridges under construction collapsed. In Britain the Construction Industry Research and Information Association, with government support, was conducting research with a view to establishing standards for falsework design.

(ROBERT CHAUSSIN)

Buildings. There was an increasing tendency in 1972 for builders and developers when planning new construction to be concerned with more than just the engineering and architectural features of buildings. In many parts of the world, economic and social conditions continued to shape new approaches to the building process. Involved in this process were planners, engineers, contractors, architects, and many types of scientists who were applying their special knowledge to the design, location, and construction of buildings.

The high cost of construction created by widespread inflation, the extensive need for housing for low-income families, high densities of population in urban areas, and environmental concerns such as resource conservation and pollution were the problems the interdisciplinary teams sought to solve. These teams increasingly used computers and systems analysis to obtain certain desired social objectives and to reduce overall building costs.

The residential needs of families and single people in urban areas resulted in the construction of condominiums and apartment buildings with a diversity of designs. Many garden apartments, town houses, and low-rise apartments were planned in conjunction with recreation and community facilities. With the continuing rise in construction costs, there was broader acceptance of modular, or factory-built, housing and also of mobile-home living.

The building of low-cost housing, as well as other types, was frequently tied in with efforts to rehabilitate downtown areas or to cope with transportation and congestion problems. The rehabilitation of downtown areas involved the construction of large office and apartment buildings and the demolition of older structures to make way for recreational areas, parking lots, and pedestrian malls. While much building took place without appropriate study and application of knowledge, there was, nevertheless, increasing attention to what may be called the research approach to the building process.

While research and imaginative approaches to community planning and residential buildings were producing some revolutionary ideas for the future, research and technical advances were having an effect on the rather routine construction of residential buildings. For example, southeast of Paris, a new community of curved buildings was nearing completion in

TURNERS (PHOTOGRAPHY) LTD.

A steel-mesh walkway between two 542-ft.-high towers spans the Bosporus in the first stages of a Turkish government-financed suspension bridge scheduled for completion in October 1973.

1972. This new development, called La Grande Borne, was designed to contain 3,700 dwelling units in buildings three and five stories tall. The buildings were made of precast concrete panels standardized to one size and finished with colourful mosaics. Located on a 90-ac. triangular site, the community had 40 units per acre and contained only one point of entrance or exit. In Urbino, a small Italian mountain town, a low-cost housing project, La Pineta, was designed to take advantage of the setting and involve the economies of low-cost construction. It contained two kinds of housing, low-rise buildings located alongside the road from Palino which had ground-floor porches providing an excellent view of the valley below, and high-rises designed to fit the steep contours of the hillside. The heights of the buildings varied from two to nine stories because the roadside roof level was kept constant. Access to all apartments was from the roof so that one took an elevator down rather than up.

Another effort to introduce economies could be seen in the Oriental Masonic Gardens housing project in New Haven, Conn. In this project modular housing units, factory-assembled with plumbing, wiring, and finishes, were transported 250 mi. to the New Haven site for installation. Paul Rudolph, the developer, then stacked the units in clusters and arranged them to provide maximum privacy and to avoid the boxlike uniformity common in suburban developments.

While economies may not be introduced by the design of structures, more acceptable living conditions can be made possible. One such effort by Charles Hilgenhurst was reported as being designed to provide more livable row housing. Given the limitations of a small lot of 9,000 sq.ft., he designed one with a patio in the centre. The house was divided into two parts, the part facing the street containing a private office, a two-car garage, and upstairs, a sundeck open to the sky but screened from the street and from neighbours. The back part of the house contained the living room, kitchen, and dining room on the main floor with three bedrooms upstairs.

Projects on the drawing boards were illustrated by two plans for innovative cities. One plan envisioned a "tetrahedral" city, consisting of an open truss structure that could house 300,000 families, or 1 million people, with each family living in a terrace apartment. The apartments were conceived as traylike receptacles, in which occupants would be able to "plug in" their trailers, houseboats, or other "mobile environment controls." According to the design, the open truss structure could be either floated in coastal waters or placed in an inland area.

The Triton City proposal was similar but would accommodate fewer people than the "tetrahedral" city. Designed to be located in waters adjacent to a large metropolitan area, it envisaged two kinds of floating neighbourhoods. One would consist of from four to six rafts each holding 1,000 people. The other would be

Major World Dams Under Construction in 1972*

Name of dam	River	Country	Type†	Height (ft.)	Length of crest (ft.)	Volume content (000 cu.yd.)	Gross capacity of reservoir (000 ac-ft.)
Auburn	American (N. Fork)	U.S.	A	685	4,150	6,000	2,300
Ayvacik	Yesil	Turkey	A	551	1,715	1,464	689
Balimela	Sileru	India	E	230	15,200	29,627	3,097
Beas	Beas-Indus	India	E	440	6,400	44,200	6,600
Cabora Bassa	Zambezi	Mozambique‡	A	550	994	589	129,389
Carters Lake	Coosawattee	U.S.	E	450	2,050	14,300	475
Charvakskaya	Chirchik	U.S.S.R.	ER	551	2,499	24,975	1,620
Chirkeyskaya	Sulak	U.S.S.R.	A	764	1,109	1,602	2,252
Chivor	Bata	Colombia	R	771	984	14,400	660
Cochiti	Rio Grande	U.S.	E	251	28,200	41,100	513
Emosson	Barberine	Switzerland	A	590	1,821	1,400	182
Gran Suarna	Navia	Spain	A	499	1,150	882	567
Idikki	Periyar	India	MA	561	1,201	609	1,182
Ilha Solteira	Paraná	Brazil	EG	262	20,300	32,838	17,172
Inguri	Inguri	U.S.S.R.	A	892	2,198	4,967	891
Jayakwadi	Godavari	India	E	120	32,493	15,409	2,110
Jocassee	Keowee	U.S.	E	437	1,950	11,600	1,160
Kapchagay	Ili	U.S.S.R.	E	164	7,741	10,338	22,761
Keban	Euphrates	Turkey	RG	679	3,598	19,600	25,110
Khantaika	Khantaika	U.S.S.R.	ER	213	21,058	2,452	16,743
Kölnbrein	Malta	Austria	A	607	1,814	1,804	130
Las Portas	Camba	Spain	G	498	1,587	977	609
Libby	Kootenai	U.S.	G	446	2,240	4,200	5,850
Marimbondo	Grande	Brazil	EG	295	11,970	24,328	5,184
Melones, New§	Stanislaus	U.S.	ER	625	1,600	15,970	2,400
Mratinje	Piva	Yugoslavia	A	722	853	1,019	689
Nader Shah	Marun	Iran	R	574	1,050	9,940	1,313
Nurek	Vakhsh	U.S.S.R.	E	1,017	2,390	70,806	8,424
Patia I	Patia	Colombia	R	755	1,540	26,000	11,200
Reza, Shah Kabir	Karun	Iran	A	656	1,246	1,786	2,350
Sayano-Shushenskaya	Yenisei	U.S.S.R.	A	774	3,503	11,916	25,353
Tachien	Tachia	Taiwan	A	591	853	562	188
Tarbela	Indus	Pakistan	ER	470	9,000	186,000	11,100
Toktogul	Naryn	U.S.S.R.	A	705	1,352	3,480	15,800
Ust-Ilim	Angara	U.S.S.R.	EG	344	11,695	17,090	48,100
Zeyskaya	Zeya	U.S.S.R.	G	371	2,312	10,456	55,080
MAJOR WORLD DAMS COMPLETED IN 1971 AND 1972*							
Almendra	Tormes	Spain	AG	649	1,860	2,844	2,147
Castaic	Castaic	U.S.	E	340	5,200	44,000	183
Don Pedro, New§	Tuolumne	U.S.	ER	585	1,900	16,760	2,030
Dworshak	Clearwater (N. Fork)	U.S.	G	717	3,287	6,500	3,453
Gokcekaya	Sakarya	Turkey	A	518	1,529	850	737
Kanev	Dnepr	U.S.S.R.	E	82	52,950	49,520	2,125
Krasnoyarsk	Yenisei	U.S.S.R.	G	407	3,493	5,685	59,425
Mica	Columbia	Canada	R	800	2,600	42,000	20,000
Missi Falls, Control, South	Churchill	Canada	ER	90	6,500	1,400	30,000‖
Saratov	Volga	U.S.S.R.	E	131	4,130	19,034	10,854
Talbingo	Tumut	Australia	R	530	2,300	18,500	747

*Having a height exceeding 492 ft. (150 m.); or having a total volume content exceeding 20 million cu.yd. (15 million cu.m.); or forming a reservoir exceeding 12 million ac-ft. capacity.

†Type of dam: E=earth; R=rockfill; A=arch; G=gravity; MA=multiple arch.

‡Mozambique is a Portuguese possession.

§Replacement of present dam.

‖Reservoir formed by several dikes and natural lake.

a crystal-shaped tetrahedral platform for 3,500 to 6,500 people. Three to six of these components would make up a new town rather than an addition to a town and would accommodate facilities for community services and functions. (CARTER C. OSTERBIND)

Dams. In Spain, the Almendra arch dam (height 649 ft., crest length 1,860 ft.) on the Tormes River, and the Contrera concrete gravity dam (height 422 ft.) on the Cabriel River were finished in 1971. The Odivelas multiple-arch and earth dam (height 361 ft.) on the Odivelas River was completed in 1972. The Las Portas gravity dam (height 498 ft., crest length 1,587 ft.) on the Camba River, the Arenos rockfill dam (height 344.5 ft., crest length 1,427 ft.) on the Mijares River, and the Albarelos arch dam (height 312 ft., crest length 984 ft.) on the Avia River were under construction.

The Kölnbrein arch dam, on the Malta River (height 607 ft., crest length 1,814 ft., volume 1,804,-000 cu.yd., storage 162,600 ac-ft.), became the highest dam in Austria. The Breitenau earthfill dam on the Steyr River (height 459 ft., width at base 1,968 ft., crest length 1,968 ft., volume 16,350,000 cu.yd.), was in the early stages of construction. The dam, a part of the Malln multipurpose pumped-storage project, was to have a core of impervious material and would be planted with trees and bushes on the downstream face to give it a natural appearance to blend with surrounding slopes.

In Yugoslavia, the Glaznja concrete gravity dam, on the Lipovicka Reka, was completed in 1971 (height 262 ft., volume 193,584 cu.yd., storage 17,886 ac-ft.), while three dams were under construction: on the Piva River, the Mratinje double-curvature arch dam (height 722 ft., volume 1,019,000 cu.yd., storage 689,000 ac-ft.); on the Uvac River, the Sjenica rockfill dam (height 361 ft., storage 154,472 ac-ft.); on the Ibar River, the Gazivode rockfill dam (height 354 ft., storage 300,813 ac-ft.).

In the Soviet Union, the Toktogul arch dam on the Naryn River (height 705 ft., volume 3,480,000 cu.yd.) was designed to withstand seismic shocks up to force 10 on the 12-point Mercalli scale, and to resist transverse earthquake shocks and damage from rock falling from the canyon slopes. The completed structure would impound a 15,800,000 ac-ft. reservoir that would help to irrigate more than one million acres. Construction continued on the 1,017-ft.-high Nurek earthfill dam on the Vakhsh River. The reservoir was filled in the fall of 1972 when 8,424,000 ac-ft. of water were drained from the Vakhsh. Also under construction was the Andizhan concrete gravity dam on the Karadarya, in central Asia's earthquake country (height 328 ft., crest length 3,280 ft., volume 5 million cu.yd., storage 1.6 million ac-ft.). The dam had a "high seismic proofness," able to withstand earthquakes up to force 9 on the Mercalli scale. It was to consist of 35 sections joined with seams of rustless steel, rubber, and other materials, allowing for some vertical movement.

In India, construction on the Idikki multiple-arch dam, which would be the highest of its kind in Asia, continued. The earthcore, gravel-shell Beas Dam on the Beas River was to be built in five stages: the most difficult was the first, which involved the construction of the right abutment, where about 150,000 cu.yd. of unsound rock affected by cracks had to be removed. Special treatment was necessary to seal plastic seams in the core and key trench areas. The Nam Ngum concrete gravity dam on the Mekong River in Laos was inaugurated in January 1972 (height 247 ft., volume 458,000 cu.yd., storage 5,715,500 ac-ft.).

In Japan, the Shintoyone double-curvature arch dam on the Ohnyu River was completed late in 1972 (height 382 ft., volume 478,728 cu.yd., storage 32,500 ac-ft.). The dam, divided into 21 blocks, created a multipurpose reservoir for pumped storage and flood control. In the Philippines, construction started on the Nueva Ecija earthfill dam on the Upper Pampanga River (height 351 ft., crest length 1,968 ft., volume 15,696,000 cu.yd.).

The 57-year-old Ryan concrete gravity dam on the Missouri River in the U.S. was tied to bedrock with prestressed single-tendon anchors, the largest in the nation. The Dworshak concrete gravity dam on the Clearwater River was completed late in 1972. Construction continued on the Auburn arch dam on the American River (height 685 ft., volume 6 million cu.yd.) and also on the Lower Teton earth and rockfill dam on the Teton River in eastern Idaho (height 305 ft., length 3,050 ft., volume 9.5 million cu.yd.).

In Canada, the rockfill Mica Dam on the Columbia River (height 800 ft., storage capacity 12 million ac-ft.) was completed. The dam had a near-vertical central impervious till core and was scheduled to start impounding water in April 1973. The Manic 3 earthfill dam on the Manicouagan River (height 350 ft.) was under construction. To seal the foundation, two thin concrete cutoff walls were sunk to 430 ft. In Peru, the Kichuas arch-gravity dam on the Mantaro (height 262 ft., storage 14,600 ac-ft.), built in a narrow gorge, was completed. (ALDO MARCELLO)

Roads. France completed several important projects during 1972, including 20 mi. of the Orange-Perpignan Highway 9; the Aix-en-Provence-to-Marseilles highway; 20 mi. of the A8 expressway between Cannet-des-Maures and Puget-sur Argens; the first section of the St. Nazaire–Nantes highway; and a 10-mi. section of the A9 expressway between Nîmes and Remoulins.

Italy completed the 110-mi. expressway between Genoa and Livorno and opened the first Sicilian expressway, a link between Catania and Messina. A 20-mi. section of the 235-mi. A14 freeway was opened to traffic in May. The new section ran between Foggia and Canosa.

In East Germany the 11 mi. of the Leipzig-Dresden expressway linking Grimma and Leisnig opened to traffic. A 12-mi. section of the same expressway was added later in the year. The more recent section ran from Döbeln to Deutschborn, linking up with the Eisenach–Dresden expressway.

In Great Britain, the building of new expressways slowed down, with only 62 mi. opened to traffic in 1972. However, this included the following important additions to the still-growing network: 7 mi. of the M56 near Sale and Altrincham and another 3 mi. between Preston Brook and Clifton Road, near Runcorn; the 10-mi. Mid-Wirral expressway; $12\frac{1}{2}$ mi. of the M4 (London–South Wales) expressway at St. Quintin and Lydiard Tregoze, Wiltshire; and 12 mi. of the southern extension of the M6 expressway, including the junction with the M1 at Catthorpe in Leicestershire.

The U.S. Federal Highway Administration announced that by the end of 1971 more than 32,392 mi. of the 42,500-mi. Interstate Highway System had been completed, with 4,115 mi. still under construction. In December 1971 Toronto opened Canada's largest intersection. Its 29 mi. of two-lane pavements

ARNOLD ODERMATT

This metal monster is a tunnel borer, one of two being used for a highway tunnel project in Switzerland. The hydraulically powered excavator arms are capable of carving out a tunnel profile 9 m. (about 30 ft.) high.

served the 12-lane Macdonald-Cartier Freeway and the 10-lane Highway 27.

In a massive engineering program, carried out largely by the Army, Brazil continued building the huge highway network intended to make it the communications hub of South America. The most impressive part of the network, the controversial trans-Amazon highway, was opposed by conservationists. Objections centred on the wastefulness of building a road across a continent that already had an easily navigable river—the Amazon—running in the same direction, but the determination of the military, which considered the project as a vital part of plans to open up the Amazon area and as having both an economic and a strategic purpose, could not be shaken. The highway would link with Peru and Bolivia, thus ensuring a direct road connection from the Atlantic to the Pacific.

Bolivia completed a 177-mi. road complex running to Villa Tunari in the country's interior. Part of the complex, the 90-mi. branch from Cochabamba to Villa Tunari, rose to 12,000 ft. above sea level. In Panama, work began on the 9-mi. stretch of road from Canita to the Bayano River; this was the first section of the Darien part of the Pan-American Highway.

Egypt brought into use the 193-mi.-long Pyramids–Bahria Oasis road; Ethiopia completed the 80-mi. stretch between Nazeret and Awash in April and announced plans for resurfacing the 91-mi. road between Agaro and Jimma. The road from Nova Lisboa to Alto-Uama, Balombo, and Lobito in Angola, the Conakry Freeway in Guinea, and the Warri–Benin road in Nigeria were also completed. In Malawi the Lilongwe–Zomba road and the Lake Malawi shore road were opened to traffic.

By the end of 1971, road construction projects in Afghanistan had increased the country's mileage to about 9,500 mi., of which about 4,000 mi. could be used by vehicles other than jeeps and trucks. India announced a total addition of about 3,000 mi. of pavement, the largest expansion of its road system since independence in 1947.

In 1972 Japan published plans for a 4,722-mi. network of toll expressways, of which 1,243 mi. were already under construction. Indonesia, too, was expanding its road network. In 1968 it allocated $13 million out of its budget for road construction projects. This increased each year, rising in 1971 to $73 million. By the end of 1971, Indonesia's total road mileage was 51,250 mi., of which 7,500 mi. had asphalt surfacing. It was announced that the Asian Highway Network, a project started in 1960, in 1972 comprised 40,937 mi., of which 24,062 mi. were classified as primary routes. When completed, the network would link major towns and cities in 15 South Asian countries. (R. S. MILLARD)

Tunnels. Work continued at Hamburg, W.Ger., on the construction of the Elbe Tunnel. Eight precast concrete tunnel sections, submerged and joined end-to-end on the river bed, completed the 1,057-m. underwater stretch. Two of the world's largest semimechanical shields were used to drive the approach tunnels, which were 11 m. in diameter. The project, costing an estimated $140 million, was scheduled for completion in 1974.

In Madrid, an 8-m.-diameter tunneling machine was supplied by a U.S. firm for boring a 5,182-m.-long section of the new subway. In Italy, realignment of the Rome–Florence trunk railway would require the tunneling of an 11-m.-diameter bore.

With the 2,111-m.-high pass through the St. Gotthard in Switzerland closed for five or six months of the year because of severe storms, high winds, and snowdrifts, work started on an alternative route for key travel between northern and southern Europe: a new $80 million St. Gotthard Tunnel, 16.4 km. long from portal to portal. Contractors made slow progress because of bad rock, large ground pressures, and floods, and by the end of 1972 the job was a year behind schedule. It was hoped to have the bore open to traffic in 1978, when it would be the world's longest vehicular tunnel.

In the U.K., London's new Fleet Underground Line between Stanmore and the Strand, estimated to cost $129,850,000, was expected to open in 1977. An experimental tunnel eventually to be incorporated in the new Fleet Line was driven in water-bearing gravel using a Bentonite shield. Experiments indicated that gravel sizes up to 0.20 or 0.23 m. in diameter could be handled successfully through the shield, which should reduce dependence upon the use of compressed air for tunneling in noncohesive water-bearing soils.

Work proceeded at Liverpool on the construction of a 4,023-m. stretch of railway tunnel required for a loop with five stations to interconnect the existing surface electric railways. The tunnel was driven through bunter sandstone containing water and therefore very abrasive. Most of the station excavation would be in clay, with the running tunnel in bunter sandstone. A machine was developed from road headers used in mining to excavate in these conditions. The tunnel, 5 m. in diameter, was expected to cost about $18 million, including the stations, and to open in 1975.

Work began on the driving of the pilot tunnel (4 m. in diameter) for the second crossing under the River Thames at Dartford, prior to the driving of the 10-m.-diameter two-lane main tunnel. The pilot tunnel would be used for an extensive program of chemical grouting and soil stabilization in clay and gravel. Completion of the project, expected to cost in excess of $36,750,000, was scheduled for 1976.

Work began on the construction of the first 11 mi. of subway in Washington, D.C. Difficult ground conditions made it necessary to use a 6.4-m.-diameter hand shield. Subsidence problems were solved by creating a grout curtain wall around the tunnel. Shotcrete was used and a special study undertaken to see how this material behaved under load. The opening date for the first section was scheduled for late 1974.

Work began in 1971 in Australia on a $54 million subway loop for Melbourne. Cut and cover methods were used for the construction of underpasses prior to the main tunneling. Boring for the 5.5-m.-diameter running tunnels was expected to begin in 1973, and the project (four tunnels and three underground stations) was scheduled for completion in 1976–77.

A tunneling machine 20 m. in overall length and operated by laser control, the first to be built under license in Australia, was used to drive the 5.5-m.-diameter, 8,047-m.-long tunnel for the Potts Hill Water Scheme in Sydney.

International tunneling interest centred on the construction of the world's longest railway tunnel, to be completed in 1980. Two consortia of contractors were appointed to drive the 27,000-m. underwater section of the 51,000-m.-long Seikan Railway Tunnel to link the Japanese islands of Honshu and Hokkaido. The difficult combination of igneous and sedimentary rocks contained water in fissures under very high pressure. Exploratory work, estimated to cost $655 million, had begun in 1963. (DAVID A. HARRIES)

ENCYCLOPÆDIA BRITANNICA FILMS. *Holland: Hold Back the Sea* (1967); *The Mississippi System: Waterway of Commerce* (1970).

Environment

For environmentalists 1972 was highlighted by the United Nations Conference on the Human Environment, which took place in Stockholm in June. The two-week gathering of 1,200 politicians and officials from 114 nations provided the opportunity for a major discussion of a wide range of problems and also facilitated the drawing up of plans and agreements for international cooperation in pollution control. Among major nations, only the Soviets stayed away—not through lack of interest but because of a dispute over the seating of East Germany. The participating countries reported on marine pollution, wildlife conservation, resource depletion, pesticides, industrial and domestic wastes, land reclamation, the architectural heritage, urban decay, general issues of economic and technical changes, and the involvement of the public in environmental policy making.

The contrasting and often apparently competing interests of rich and poor countries formed a persistent theme among the speakers. Specific resolutions for continued worldwide discussion and cooperation through a new UN Environmental Agency, a detailed Action Plan, and a complex Declaration on the Human Environment were important in themselves, but they also typified the growing opportunities for international and intercontinental activity in the field. In seven main recommendations submitted by the conference to the UN General Assembly, member governments were invited to:

1. Promote a convention to restrict dumping of harmful substances in the world's oceans.
2. Minimize the release of notably dangerous pollutants, such as the heavy metals and organochlorine compounds.
3. Organize worldwide monitoring of atmospheric, marine, terrestrial, and human health hazards.
4. Promote "genetic banks" to safeguard the existence of all species of animals and plants.
5. Halt all commercial whale catching for ten years.
6. Set up an international exchange service for information on the environment.
7. Increase emphasis on population control.

In particular, there was increasing awareness that effective pollution control depended on widely adopted standards. The protection of oceans from indiscriminate dumping and oil pollution was a classic example. A more subtle case was that of industries operating in international markets whose viability would be severely prejudiced by the need to conform to higher standards than those of their foreign competitors. International cooperation was also sought in the exchange of techniques for environmental protection. Agreements were negotiated to provide improved information for monitoring of air and water pollution and for the scientific comparison of other common problems. As more nations established their own central agencies and environmental research institutions, the opportunities for technical cooperation were correspondingly multiplied.

In addition to the Stockholm conference, 1972 saw the publication of many substantial books and studies with a worldwide emphasis. A controversial report titled *The Limits to Growth* described studies undertaken by a team of scientists from the Massachusetts Institute of Technology, led by Dennis L. Meadows and sponsored by an international group of industrialists and scientists known as the Club of Rome. Another was the special edition of the British magazine *The Ecologist,* which set out a "Blueprint for Survival" with the support of 33 eminent British scientists. A third publication, *Only One Earth,* written unofficially for the UN conference by Barbara Ward and René Dubos, presented a somewhat more conservative view.

While these documents centred on global problems, global forecasts, and ecological imbalance, the problems immediately affecting the largest number of people were those of the cities. In her Stockholm address, India's prime minister, Indira Gandhi, pointed out that, in her view, the most pressing environmental problems were those of the millions of people living on the pavements of Calcutta and Bombay. While tightly packed settlements of squatters mushroomed almost overnight around such cities as Lima, Peru, the wealthier residents of European and North American cities were seeking more space and a better environment in the countryside, leaving behind them in the inner areas an unhealthy mixture of poor housing, poor residents, and a decline in the number of manual jobs.

STUDIES AND RESEARCH

The Limits to Growth was based on work done by systems analysts using mathematical formulas and computer processing to describe the complex relationships between such factors as population growth, per capita industrial output, food consumption, natural resources, and pollution. By making a variety of assumptions about rates of growth, consumption, and production, the authors illustrated a corresponding variety of outcomes in worldwide terms. They concluded that existing trends would lead to catastrophic scarcities and severe pollution levels within 130 years, but that "global equilibrium" could be achieved by implementing a set of policies designed to maximize stability of capital investment and population size and promote a carefully balanced relationship between the two.

The Ecologist's "Blueprint for Survival," published in January, brought together facts and arguments about resources and pollution, concentrating in particular on British problems. It called for a stable society in which there would be: (1) minimum disruption of ecological processes; (2) maximum conser-

England: *see* United Kingdom
English Literature: *see* Literature
Entertainment: *see* Dance; Fairs and Shows; Motion Pictures; Music; Television and Radio; Theatre
Entomology: *see* Life Sciences

vation of materials and energy; (3) a population in which recruitment would equal loss; and (4) a social system in which the individual could enjoy rather than feel restricted by the first three conditions. The authors, all professionally engaged in the study of environmental problems, envisaged the replacement of conurbations by decentralized settlements that would be as self-sufficient and self-regulating as possible, developing, for example—in the long term—their own arrangements for food production and waste disposal.

News of less glamorous but in many respects more fundamental research was issued in a report completed for the UN Economic Commission for Europe by the Centre for Environmental Studies, London, reviewing investigations into urban and regional planning problems in 13 countries. The report showed an equal interest in the processes of urbanization, regional growth, and urban obsolescence and in the administrative policies and planning techniques devised to cope with them. Studies of population movements in predominantly rural and peripheral regions were carried out in Cyprus, Finland, Ireland, and Norway, and research into the administrative and political aspects of planning was undertaken in Sweden, the U.S., Finland, France, and Britain. Studies of this kind were increasingly concerned with political processes and public involvement.

Studies of the urban environment published in 1972 included an important examination of residents' attitudes to public housing in England and two research projects relating to the landscape in and around cities. The attitude survey was carried out by the U.K. Department of the Environment. The investigators concluded that two-thirds of households without young children were happy to live above ground level, even in high-rise buildings, but families with young children disliked living above ground level, especially because it inhibited children's play. A yet unpublished work indicated that residents preferred bright, colourful buildings with plenty of greenery and disliked gray, drab buildings and large blocks with an "institutional" appearance. Sadatoshi Tabata of Tokyo University had studied the effects of urban growth on open land around Tokyo over the past 40 years: in 1932, 61% of the urban area consisted of greenery, but by 1969 this had been reduced to 29%. He also showed that the incidence of respiratory diseases was proportional to population density and inversely proportional to the amount of open land. He concluded that to improve the city's environment it would be necessary to maintain 25% open space or a per capita allocation of at least 25 sq.m.

During 1972 the Organization for Economic Cooperation and Development (OECD) initiated an ambitious three-year study of air pollution in conjunction with ten member countries. The work would be concerned with the degree to which sulfur and strong acids in the atmosphere originated locally or were transmitted considerable distances. Concentrations of these pollutants would be measured daily by 80 ground stations in the ten states and by aircraft at various altitudes. The results would be coordinated by the Norwegian Institute for Air Pollution at Kjeller, near Oslo, and evaluated by a committee from the countries concerned, together with representatives from the European Economic Community (EEC) and the World Meteorological Organization.

A 469-page report on radiation levels issued by a special committee of the U.S. National Academy of Sciences–National Research Council gave no immediate cause for alarm. It indicated, however, that the guidelines set up by the federal government might be too lenient and pointed out that artificial additions to the natural radiation level would need constant monitoring.

THE URBAN ENVIRONMENT

In a statement to the Stockholm conference, the International Union of Local Authorities emphasized that environmental problems were concentrated in the large cities. They claimed that, to cope with current trends of urbanization, the equivalent of twice the existing number of cities would have to be constructed within the next 30 years. The quality of these developments was therefore of the utmost importance. Unfortunately, the pace of change in many less developed countries was such that the requisite standards were not being achieved. It was estimated that by 1980 Accra and Dakar would have to house one million people, representing 8.5% and 22% of Ghana's and Senegal's respective populations, whereas by that time industry would be able to provide only 5% of all employment. A not untypical illustration of the hardship involved was a building worker employed in Medellín, Colombia, who traveled for nearly eight hours each day on foot and by bus from his rural home where the rest of his family was trying to scratch a living off the land.

One of London's chief planning officers, David Eversley, warned of the mounting dangers of urban decay and the development of an "urban underclass" in the inner parts of older British cities. He pointed to unsupported families, the old, the unskilled, and those with problems of chronic illness or disability or a prison record as the categories of poor citizens who tended to be concentrated in areas of rapid decline. These people could not compete for better housing and services, nor could they find local jobs. The British government had a continuing urban aid program for such areas, and the secretary of state for the environment had announced six experimental studies of needy towns.

The Greater London Council announced in September that it would delay part of its £2,000 million urban expressway program: the construction of considerable stretches of its proposed system, including a section through fashionable Hampstead, was to be put back by 20 years. There was also concern about traffic conditions in Paris, and about the means being adopted to ameliorate them. Over 7,000 new parking places were being provided each year, and a new inner ring road would be completed by the end of 1972, but residents were unhappy about the cost and disruption involved. France's development plan for 1971–75 contained proposals for better public transport, possibly including minibuses and collective taxis.

In Paris three tall office buildings being constructed at the Défense across the Seine from Neuilly became visible to the west of the Arc de Triomphe and in a direct line with the view from the Champs-Élysées, thus interrupting the famous perspective. This apparently unforeseen intrusion resulted in high-level discussions during the late summer, and it was thought that the towers would be lowered by official decree. However, in early October it was announced that the cost (some Fr. 400 million in compensation) was too high and that the government would adhere to its original approval of the scheme.

In Tokyo the most critical environmental problem was the recurrent photochemical smog, caused principally by nitrogen oxides from motor-vehicle exhausts. The city was again seriously affected in May, and the number of people suffering from the effects of smog in 1972 might well exceed the figure of 48,000 for the previous year. The metropolitan government increased its efforts to counter pollution of all kinds. Loans were made available to induce firms to install pollution-control devices, and over $1 million was to be spent on research into the smog problem. Tokyo's 1972 budget for environmental improvement was 40% more than that in 1971, as compared with an increase of 15% for roads. In addition to atmospheric pollution, the prosperous Japanese economy raised formidable problems of waste disposal, with 35 million tons of garbage, including such cumbersome items as discarded television sets, to be disposed of annually.

Air pollution, together with vibrations from heavy traffic and a nearby underground railway, was causing alarming decay of the 1,900-year-old Colosseum in Rome. Traffic in Bern, Switz., was to be reduced after a six-month experiment during which motor vehicles were banned from most of the historic town centre. In England the principal experiment in this field was a government-subsidized "pedestrianization" scheme in Leeds, where special small buses were used for travel between parking lots and shops. The outcome of these and other measures was likely to be discussed during the Council of Europe's Architectural Heritage Year 1975. (*See* HISTORIC BUILDINGS.)

(DAVID L. SMITH)

NATURAL ENVIRONMENT

At Stockholm Maurice F. Strong (*see* BIOGRAPHY), secretary-general to the UN conference, declared that by the year 2000 world food supplies would have to be doubled to feed the predicted population of 7,000,000,000 people. In the less developed countries, the pressures on land resources were forcing crop farming into regions of low rainfall, harsh climate, steep topography, or poor soil. Inevitable consequences were loss of natural plant cover, wind and water erosion, disturbance of the hydrologic cycle, and the silting up of rivers, irrigation channels, and reservoirs. In arid zones deserts were expanding, and the southern edge of the Sahara was advancing over grazing grounds at a rate of $1\frac{1}{2}$ mi. yearly.

Governments, said Strong, should incorporate environmental considerations into all agricultural developments. Research into basic needs must be followed up by legislation, education, and financial measures to put recommendations into practice. Major problems were soil degradation, long-term pollution by persistent pesticides, and overintensification of agriculture. In the more developed countries, the mechanization and concentration of food raising had led to an exodus of country dwellers to the towns, with resultant social problems. Political as well as scientific measures were essential to protect the biosphere, the thin layer of matter enveloping the earth upon which all life depends. International cooperation was essential, since natural and economic forces take little heed of man-made frontiers.

On the conference's home ground, the Swedish Forest Industry's Foundation for Water and Air Protection announced an antipollution research program costing 24 million kronor per year, to be directed mainly toward the problems of effluent disposal at the country's enormous pulp and paper mills, which were discharging vast quantities of chemical waste into rivers feeding the almost landlocked Baltic Sea. This theme was followed up by the other countries bordering the Baltic, especially Finland and the U.S.S.R., which also operated huge chemical pulp mills. Pollutants dumped into this almost tideless sea dispersed very slowly, and oil dumped at the northern end might take 20 years to reach the southern exit. Norway took strong measures to regulate the discharge of industrial wastes along its Atlantic seaboard, the home of its economically vital fishing industry; the use of mercury was terminated in all Norwegian pulp and paper mills.

At Stockholm a number of biologists from various countries used the word "ecocide" to describe the deliberate destruction of effective human environments in the course of warfare. They claimed that U.S. strategy in Vietnam was being directed against crops rather than people. Herbicides that killed off all plant life were being reinforced by giant plows deliberately employed to scrape off irreplaceable topsoil. It was further asserted that U.S. attacks on the Red River dike system close to Tonkin were aimed at creating disastrous floods to disrupt the vital rice crop. The U.S. denied that it was deliberately bombing the dikes, though witnesses claimed to have seen bomb damage far from military targets.

During April there were reports of similar military attacks on the environment by the Portuguese authorities in Mozambique. The Mozambique Liberation Front guerrillas, active in the north, were sustained by crops of corn, cassava, beans, peanuts, and bananas, cultivated in small jungle clearings. The clearings were easily located from the air, and it was thus possible to eliminate the crops by aerial spraying of defoliants, though only at a very high cost.

Land Conservation. Throughout the Stockholm conference, the Brazilian government came under strong international pressure to conserve its enormous tropical rain forests. The reasoning behind this was not entirely disinterested. Brazil held roughly one-sixth of the world's forest area, some 600 million ha. out of a world total of 3,712,000,000 ha. Tropical forests are particularly effective in fixing the carbon element of atmospheric carbon dioxide in solid form, and the loss of large forest areas could lead to an ever increasing and harmful level of carbon dioxide in the world's atmosphere. Brazil, however, regarded the problem as an internal matter. Under pressure of ever increasing population, migrant settlers were moving into the forest, felling and burning tall timber trees, and cultivating the clearings, enriched with wood ash, for two or three seasons only. As they moved on to make new clearings, the land was taken over by cattle ranchers. The resultant grazing and trampling permanently damaged the land, as once-porous, water-absorbent forest soil became hard and water-resistant.

South American forest policies attracted further international attention in October at the seventh World Forestry Congress of the UN Food and Agriculture Organization, held in Buenos Aires, Arg. The congress reviewed the consequences of agricultural reforms on the management of forests and the maintenance of economic wood-using industries. Delegates visited Argentina's impressive plantations of newly introduced fast-growing timber trees, notably species of *Eucalyptus* from Australia, pines from the southern U.S., and hybrid poplars originating in Europe.

Also in October, the American Forestry Association convened a National Tree Planting Conference in

continued on page 284

D. GORTON—THE NEW YORK TIMES

Evening-rush-hour traffic heads west on the Santa Monica Freeway from downtown Los Angeles into a smoggy sunset. Despite improved air cleanliness statistics cited by officials, many environmental and citizens' groups were demanding more stringent antipollution efforts.

SPECIAL REPORT

THE KOUPREY: ONE MORE INEXCUSABLE LOSS TO MAN

By Jon Tinker

The wildlife of today," said King George VI, "is not ours to dispose of as we please. We have to account for it to those who come after." Pres. John F. Kennedy put it differently: "We must expand the concept of conservation to meet the imperious problems of the new age. We must recover the relationship between man and nature." But does this relationship have any relevance in a technological, urban age? Is it not mere sentimentalism to wonder whether our children's children will grow up to ask: "What *was* a rhino?" Why set up a nature reserve for the hairy-nosed wombat when a billion people do not have enough to eat, when the great cities of Latin America and Asia are ringed by squalid slums, when malaria and leprosy still stalk the globe, when wars and rumours of war daily bring fear to half the homes of mankind?

At best, wildlife conservation seems to many people a sentimental hankering after a bygone pastoral life, a romantic attachment to the days when men were men and buffalo still roamed the Great Plains. At worst, giving money to save the fur seal or to protect the white rhino seems to demonstrate a callous indifference to human suffering. Nevertheless, although such attitudes may still prevail, today the conservation of wild animals and plants must be regarded as a matter of global good housekeeping. Far from being sentimental, it is only hard realism to retain living resources that mankind may one day desperately need.

The Kouprey: War Casualty. To the outsider, the conservationist often does seem to have an odd set of priorities. Consider, for example, his perverse behaviour toward the end of 1970. While the rest of the world was debating the rights and wrongs of the U.S. thrust into Cambodia, wildlife conservationists were worrying over the fate of the kouprey, a rare Indochinese wild cow, which this sudden shift in the war zone had probably driven into extinction.

The kouprey is such a shy animal, grazing in open glades and retreating into the thick forest if disturbed, that it was only discovered by scientists just before World War II. It has been dodging Japanese, French, Viet Minh, U.S., and Viet Cong bullets ever since. A large blackish-brown beast, the bull kouprey stands over six feet tall at the shoulders, with prominent white legs and a chestnut face pattern. It was probably once distributed throughout Indochina, but by 1964 the total was down to 200, concentrated in three kouprey reserves specially established by Prince Norodom Sihanouk near the Vietnam border. Sihanouk gave the kouprey full legal protection, but he also armed the frontier villages of Cambodia, and unauthorized kouprey-hunting was widespread.

In 1968 the National Academy of Sciences in Washington, D.C., was concerned enough about the fate of the kouprey to send out a special expedition, in the hope of capturing some and establishing a breeding herd in captivity. They found four, but the animals died of an allergic reaction to the tranquilizing drugs used to sedate them. Since then, there have been no confirmed sightings. Two of the three sanctuaries were occupied by the Viet Cong, whose favourite food is said to be beef; the third sanctuary was the scene of prolonged fighting in late 1970. Even if a few scared kouprey do still survive deep in the Indochina forests, they are unlikely ever to meet up and breed. Barring a miracle, another wild species has gone to join the dodo in total extinction.

To most people, in comparison with the bloodshed and misery of the Vietnam war, the loss of the kouprey is totally insignificant. But by the year 2000 we may be regretting an easy dismissal of the Cambodian wild cow. For the kouprey represents an inexcusable loss of genetic material, which could have played a key role in Asian agriculture. It is thought to have been one of the wild ancestors of the humped zebu cattle of India, and cross-breeding between the kouprey and zebu could have helped to improve this and other domestic strains.

Over the next few decades, bioengineering is likely to be as vital and as fast growing a scientific field as electronics has been in the past two. Geneticists are probably within a few years of being able to manipulate chromosomes in a test tube in order to accentuate desired characteristics, of being able to cross one species with another at will and produce fertile offspring. The animals grazing in our fields in 1990 may well contain the bloodlines of half a dozen of today's wild or domestic species. If we are to grow enough food for a world population that—even at the most optimistic forecast—will continue to increase until well into the next century, we shall need new and improved crops and domestic animals. The "miracle rice" whose yields have recently had such a dramatic effect on Far Eastern food supplies is merely the beginning. But tomorrow's bioengineers will be as dependent on genes for their raw material as today's engineers are on the chemical elements. To have thrown away the kouprey will seem as big a crime as it would today to abandon titanium, the key element in the high-temperature steels of the aerospace age.

Ecological Mismanagement. Agricultural man is remarkably conservative. We are still content with the same animals and plants that the Babylonians domesticated, despite all evidence of their inefficiency. Consider the history of livestock farming in Africa, a depressing tale of ecological mismanagement that has parallels in many parts of the world.

Cattle are not indigenous to Africa, but there are now more cows there than in Europe. Compared with the sleek cattle of England or Denmark, they are hopelessly nonproductive. A complex community of wild herbivores has been steadily exterminated in favour of a European cow that is totally unsuited to the climate and the food. After two centuries of cattle farming in Africa, yields are still low compared with wild game. A mixed antelope community on marginal scrub can produce four times as much meat per square mile as cows on neighbouring well-managed grassland. The quality of the meat, too, is strongly in the wild game's favour: the dressed carcasses of domestic African cattle contain up to 30% fat and only 50% lean meat, while the carcasses of game of similar weight contain less than 5% fat and as much as 80% lean. The reason is simple: the wild game are adapted to the local environment, and the European cattle are not.

The supreme illogicality of farming the wrong species in the wrong places appeared in the great tsetse-fly campaigns of East Africa, an attempt to exterminate the disease of sleeping sickness. Wild game are not bothered by the flies, and the disease gives them the equivalent of a slight cold, but the alien cattle can tolerate neither. So animals that did *not* object to being bitten were slaughtered in order to introduce those that *did.* Millions of pounds of international aid were spent in Rhodesia and elsewhere in East Africa to create a habitat for cows that are incapable of producing a quarter as much meat as the species they have replaced. Local wildlife, in the meantime, is confined to ever smaller game reserves. Europeans tend to make fun of

---

Jon Tinker is environment consultant to the New Scientist *and former editor of* Wildlife and the Countryside.

PAUL SEQUEIRA

Child visiting Chicago's Lincoln Park Zoo studies the symbol used by zoos throughout the U.S. to emphasize species in danger of becoming extinct in their natural homes.

the way Indians allow cows to eat crops and wander through the city streets. Western man's devotion to cattle has been far more absurd.

In Africa the tide is at last turning. First, there is game ranching, where mixed communities of wild game are confined in enclosures many miles square. Cattle will only eat the soft, sweet herbage, but a dozen species of antelope and other game are together able to graze all the grasses as well as browse the shrubs and low trees, utilizing a wide variety of vegetation without destroying it. By carefully controlled shooting, killing exactly the right numbers of each sex and each species, a high crop of meat can be taken every year and the community kept in perfect balance with the habitat.

Eventually, truly wild game stocks may be replaced by fully domesticated strains, mixed herds of half a dozen species of antelope plus zebra and wildebeeste, all improved breeds carefully suited to the local habitat. Already some wild species are being domesticated and farmed like cattle. The eland, largest of the African antelopes, has been successfully tamed and bred in captivity, and is being used in Kenya and South Africa for both milk and meat production. It can withstand poor water supplies and extremes of heat much better than the cow, so it is far better suited to arid scrubland. Thomson's gazelle, a much smaller antelope that is among East Africa's most familiar mammals, has also been domesticated. Eventually, perhaps by crossing several existing species, it should prove possible to breed special strains of antelope that are well suited physiologically to the African environment—and that give ten times the meat yield of the cattle being reared there now.

There are hundreds of varieties of large herbivorous animals in different parts of the world. The animal breeder of the future will regard them all as potential raw material. He will not be confined, as we are today, to the goat, sheep, pig, and cow. But he will not be able to breed from species that have become extinct.

In different parts of the world, a surprising variety of animals are being considered for domestication. Manatees, large freshwater sea cows, have been used to keep navigation channels free from waterweed, but they could also be reared in ponds for meat. Hippos—especially, perhaps, the pygmy hippo of West Africa—might provide a meat crop from the fringes of huge African reservoirs like Kariba and Volta. Saiga antelopes, on the verge of extinction in Soviet Asia 50 years ago, now provide 6,000 tons of meat a year from Kazakhstan, where cattle cannot cope with the steep hills and sandstorms. New Zealand exports some U.S. $4 million of venison a year, shot from red deer that were originally introduced from Scotland. African eland provide milk in the Ukraine. Musk ox are being domesticated for their wool in Canada. Turtles in Malaya and the Caribbean are being farmed for their eggs and shells. It is impossible to forecast what animals the bioengineers of the 21st century will use as their raw genetic material to fashion new breeds for meat, wool, skins, or other products. We can only preserve for them as much variety as possible.

Plant Conservation. Mammal and bird conservation has always tended to receive the most attention from wildlife enthusiasts, with plants coming a long way behind. But it should not be forgotten that the loss of the 20,000 plant species now facing extinction could be far more serious than that of the threatened animals.

As vegetarians are always ready to explain, the conversion of plant protein into animal tissue must involve an energy loss; it takes around ten tons of grass to produce one ton of meat. The process is only worthwhile because man cannot digest grass himself. The pressures of human population are likely to force many countries to concentrate increasingly on vegetable food, and, as is the case with animals, new species will have to be cultivated. In the future, agricultural research will probably concentrate less on making existing crops grow where conditions for them are not suitable. Instead, the bioengineer will search for plants that grow fast in each environment and that contain a high proportion of protein. These he will try to improve, so as to make the protein digestible by man.

Already, agricultural breeding stations are cooperating with wildlife conservationists in preserving wild species that are closely related to existing food plants, for only from wild or primitive strains can new genes be introduced. Like Simenon's Inspector Maigret, the plant geneticist always directs his attention to the close relatives of the subject under investigation. Tomatoes, for example, originally came from Mexico in the 16th century: the Italians called them *pomi d'oro* or golden apples. Subsequent breeding has changed the colour to red, as well as removing most of the flavour and (more importantly, perhaps) nearly all the vitamin C. In the hope of coming up with high-yield strains that retain the size of modern tomatoes but that recapture the taste and nutritional value of their wild ancestors, plant breeders have gone back to the high Andes for the tiny yellow fruits that the conquistadores knew. Fortunately, these have not been exterminated in the meantime.

Many other wild plants, though, have already disappeared. We cannot say that any particular one among those currently threatened with extinction should be saved because it will one day prove of use to man, but among 20,000 it is a matter of statistical certainty that there will be hundreds of potential new foods, fodder plants, timbers, garden flowers, or drugs. Can we easily consign these plants to the botanical history books? Do we think synthetics will supply *all* our future needs? Forecasting the future is a perilous business, but most scientists are agreed that the heat produced by all forms of energy production is a severe long-term problem for mankind. The manufacture of man-made substitutes for natural products requires large amounts of energy, and it is at least possible that in the 21st century we shall want to return to plants, which derive their energy from the sun.

The need for plant conservation is nowhere more obvious than when we consider medicinal drugs. A large proportion of our drugs originally derived from plants, although many are now manufactured in the laboratory. The pharmaceutical industry still spends millions of dollars a year trying to locate new plant-based drugs, not least by picking the brains of traditional witch doctors and herbalists from India to Latin America. Recent drugs isolated from plants include a tumour-suppressive agent from the rosy periwinkle in the West Indies, reserpine from the Indian snakeroot, and a new snail-killing compound from the African soapwort, which may allow control of the spreading snail-borne disease bilharziasis.

As is the case with food plants, the standard trick of the drug-hunters is to search among the close relatives of a plant that contains promising pharmacological properties. The Maigret approach, for instance, was employed by the U.S. Department of Agriculture in the 1950s, as they examined agaves, yuccas, and yams from deserts and jungles all over the world in the hope of finding a better plant source for cortisone, a major therapy against rheumatoid arthritis. And although today cortisone comes mainly from cattle bile, it has in the past been manufactured from sisal leaves and vines. Examining close relatives may allow doctors to avoid dangerous side effects of some drugs. For instance, the heart stimulant digitalis, derived from the common English foxglove, has only a narrow gap between the effective and the fatal dose; if he takes too much, a patient will die. But the very similar drug digoxin, which is extracted from the Spanish foxglove, has a far larger safety margin. We do not know if there are any foxgloves in danger of extinction, but it would be a pity to let them go without making sure they do not offer the heart specialist an even better tool.

One of the main groups of plant-based drugs is the alkaloids, complex molecules that often have medicinal properties. Only 2% of the planet's estimated two million wild-flower species have ever been screened for alkaloids, and from them about a thousand different plant alkaloids have been isolated. On that basis it seems likely that among the wild flowers currently threatened with extinction, there are around 50,000 new alkaloids to be identified. Can medicine afford to dismiss them all?

The appalling improvidence of letting potentially useful plants vanish each year has at last begun to receive official recognition. The Food and Agriculture Organization of the UN already has a detailed program for collecting and preserving primitive strains and races of existing food plants, and it is hoped that this will soon be extended to potential new crops. Here again the Maigret principle will be to the fore, and the search will be concentrated in continents where cultivation has not developed far among indigenous peoples. Is there, for example, an Australian yam that might enable this vital tropical crop to be extended to more marginal land in Africa? The possibility is by no means remote, for the aborigines have never practiced agriculture and so have not developed local species of edible plants.

continued from page 281

New Orleans, La., to launch a campaign for planting 75 million ac. during the "Environmental Seventies." William E. Towell, executive vice-president, declared that plantings could be increased on 5 million ac. of national forest lands, besides 70 million ac. of private lands that lay idle. With trees spaced six to eight feet apart, over 60,000,000,000 seedlings would be needed. The association reaffirmed its belief in "balanced forest-use," with due consideration given to timber production on a sustained-yield basis, water conservation, wildlife preservation, public recreation, and forage for livestock.

In September an international conference, attended by 700 delegates from 100 countries, met at Yellowstone National Park, Wyoming, to celebrate the centenary of America's first wilderness reserves. Despite its vast extent of more than two million acres, set aside by Congress "as a public park or leisuring ground for the benefit and enjoyment of the people," Yellowstone Park suffered serious problems of overcrowding when visitors poured in during the summer season. Every year 800,000 cars traversed its fine macadam roads, on their way to parking places well equipped with restaurants and souvenir shops. While elk, moose, and bison fled from the influx, grizzly and black bears would hang around campsites, scavenging for food from garbage bins. The conservationists' main problem, a worldwide one, was how to attract people to a natural environment without, in the process, ruining the wilderness they had come to enjoy.

In a critical review of African national parks, now totaling 150, Jeremy Swift found that their financial returns exceeded those from agricultural production on comparable land, since they attracted foreign tourists eager to see elephants, giraffes, lions, and antelopes in natural surroundings. All the parks had been established by European administrations in colonial times but, despite demands by African farmers for new land, the countries found it profitable to maintain the parks and to check poaching.

D. P. Ackerman of the South African Department of Forestry outlined proposals for new wilderness areas to be demarcated on state forest lands. The objectives were scientific (to preserve natural ecosystems), scenic, and recreational. Management would involve minimum interference with nature, though wildlife would be conserved and the soil protected. All powered vehicles would be excluded, though horses would be allowed, and to prevent overuse visitors would only be admitted by permit. Over 600,000 ac. of land, mainly on mountain rainwater catchments, were being considered for demarcation.

Water Conservation. In the Near East a confused political situation surrounded construction of the enormous dam across the Euphrates at Tabqa (Tabaqah) in the north Syrian desert. The project, scheduled for completion in 1974, was planned to irrigate 1.6 million ac. of land, besides generating 800 Mw. of electricity. Syria depended on Turkey to the north for the sustained flow of the river, which had an annual flow of 25,000,000,000 cu.m. at the frontier. The Turks, meanwhile, planned to use 10,000,000,000 cu.m. for their own irrigation schemes. If this loss was added to Syria's planned net abstraction of some 8,000,000,000 cu.m., only 7,000,000,000 cu.m. would flow onward into Iraq, compared with the current 27,000,000,000 cu.m. Faced with this loss, the Iraqi government began construction of a new canal from the Tharthar depression to divert supplies of floodwater from the Tigris River into the lower Euphrates.

In England and Wales new legislation was passed creating regional water authorities for each major river basin. The boards would control water supplies, land drainage, recreational use of waterways, and sewage disposal, replacing a hodgepodge of smaller statutory bodies with limited powers. The new regional boards would be supervised by a National Water Council. At the 1972 meeting of the British Association, concern was expressed over the condition of Britain's inland waters. Heavy annual nitrate and phosphate fertilization programs inevitably led to seepage of these nutrients into lakes and rivers where they stimulated the growth of algae and water plants, but there was no simple means of removing them from the nutrient cycle.

Northern Ireland became the first part of the U.K. to introduce overall control of water resources. Its Water Act, 1972, gave comprehensive powers over water supplies to the ministries of Development and Agriculture. The purity of Lough Neagh, Ireland's largest inland reserve which could supply 30 million gal. of fresh water a day to Belfast, was already threatened by excess phosphorus from domestic and industrial sources.

Following the Oslo Convention for the Prevention of Marine Pollution by Dumping (see *National Policies,* below), Norway, whose economy depended largely on fish, proposed a conference on the prevention of pollution in the Arctic. This would bring in the circumpolar countries of the U.S., Canada, Denmark (by virtue of its possession of Greenland), and the U.S.S.R. In the cold polar seas, organic substances readily broken down elsewhere were liable to persist indefinitely. Oil from northern fields, such as that in Alaska, or from offshore drilling was considered a major threat. Persistent insecticides such as DDT were also carried into polar waters by ocean currents, and traces could already be found in most Arctic organisms.

Studies of the seabed by the research vessel "Glomar Challenger" threw fresh light on the development of the world's oceans. The Mediterranean, for example, appeared to have been isolated from the Atlantic at various times, since beds of salt, deposited when the sea dried out because evaporation exceeded inflow, were discovered below the present-day sea floor. The project was being carried out for the U.S. National Science Foundation by the Scripps Institute of Oceanography, La Jolla, Calif. Traces of oil encountered during the deep-sea drilling attracted the attention of leading petroleum companies. (*See* OCEANOGRAPHY.) (HERBERT L. EDLIN)

Wildlife. In January 1972 the International Union for the Conservation of Nature and Natural Resources (IUCN) made a special plea for support for the International Convention on the Import, Export, and Transit of Wildlife, for more control of trade in species with decreasing populations, and for a virtual ban on trade in species threatened with extinction. IUCN and the World Wildlife Fund urged that trade in wild creatures for use as pets be restricted to those existing in sufficient abundance in the wild state, likely to make suitable pets, and unlikely to be a health risk to the importing country or to become a pest if they should escape from captivity.

In the U.K. the report of the Advisory Committee on the Animals (Restriction of Importation) Act, 1964, showed that in 1971 only 63 mammals belonging to endangered species were imported under license. Of these, 42 were wallabies from New Zealand, where they had been introduced and where some species were pests. The committee recommended that tortoise importation be limited to April, May, and June to reduce winter mortality. It also drew attention to the need to restrict importation of animal products as well as living animals. Both the U.K. and the U.S. put an embargo on importation of wool of the vicuña, a South American mammal of the camel family, gravely depleted in numbers.

During 1972 the Ecuador National Park Service eliminated feral goats from Barrington Island in the Galápagos to permit recovery of vegetation needed by the giant tortoises. On Abingdon Island, in the same group, the giant tortoise *Testudo elephantopus abingdonii,* believed to be extinct, was rediscovered.

According to a survey completed at the end of March by Norman Myers, the leopard had maintained its numbers in East Africa but the cheetah was increasingly endangered. In the eastern deserts of Iran, however, the cheetah was reported to be holding its own.

The International Council for Bird Preservation celebrated its 50th anniversary. It was founded in 1922 in London under the leadership of T. Gilbert Pearson, himself a founder and then president of the U.S. National Audubon Society, with the help of Jean Delacour of France. In June R. B. Clark and J. P. Croxall of the Research Unit for the Rehabilitation of Oiled Seabirds at the University of Newcastle upon Tyne, Eng., published new and simpler methods of cleaning oiled birds.

In June the International Whaling Commission, meeting in London, failed to accept the ten-year moratorium on whaling recommended by the Stockholm conference. Instead, it substituted an individual quota for each whale species for the previously used blue-whale unit, and agreed to the appointment of international observers on all whaling ships. There were believed to be only 100 blue whales left, and their survival was considered unlikely; the humpback whale had been reduced to the point of extinction, and the finback, slaughtered by the thousands in the early 1960s, was fast disappearing from Antarctic waters, which now yielded only 2,500 annually. On June 29 the British secretary of state for the environment, Peter Walker, speaking at the annual general meeting of the Fauna Preservation Society, noted the society's recommendation that Great Britain prohibit the importation of products of all baleen whales, thus following the lead of the U.S. where importation of all whale products had been banned.

During April the first tiger census started in India; previous assessments had been based merely on state estimates. To help identify individual tigers, a new glass "tiger-tracer," on which details of pug marks could be drawn in the field, was being used. In Sri Lanka (Ceylon) total protection was given to all marine turtles with their nests and eggs; the palm civet and other animals were added to the protected list. In January, Canada banned commercial sealing in the Gulf of St. Lawrence and, in agreement with Norway, reduced the kill of harp seals in international waters off Labrador from 245,000 to 150,000 annually.

Hugh Cott completed his fourth survey of the Nile crocodile below Murchison Falls in Uganda. He reported a steady fall in numbers since 1967, due partly to poaching but also to disturbance of nesting crocodiles by motorboats. In South Australia a 22-sq.mi. sheep station was purchased for the National Parks

Workmen in Rio de Janeiro gather tons of fish killed by pollution resulting from Brazil's rapid industrialization.

UPI COMPIX

UPI COMPIX

Mountains of glass bottles at the Glass Container Corp.'s Dayville, Conn., reclamation centre were recycled for use in "glassphalting," replacing the gravel and stone mix commonly used in asphalt. The product had its initial test in a parking lot in Windsor, Conn.

Commission by the Chicago Zoological Society, with a grant from the Forest Park (Ill.) Foundation, to protect a population of 2,000 hairy-nosed wombats, *Lasiorhinus latifrons*. In Queensland a national park was created to protect the entire known population of another hairy-nosed wombat, *L. barnardi*. (*See* Special Report.) (C. L. BOYLE)

NATIONAL POLICIES

In February a new agreement known as the Oslo Convention for the Prevention of Marine Pollution by Dumping was signed by members of the North-East Atlantic Fisheries Commission. Designed to prevent pollution by dumping from ships and aircraft in the area, it divided waste materials into three categories. The first consisted of a blacklist of materials not to be dumped at all: mercury and cadmium compounds, chlorinated hydrocarbons, and nonperishable plastics and other synthetic materials that might float or remain in suspension. The second and third categories could be deposited only by permission of the national authority: these included most "heavy" metals, cyanides, fluorides, and pesticides, other toxic substances, and chemicals likely to persist in food chains. In November, 79 countries signed an international convention prohibiting the dumping of oil, mercury and cadmium compounds, and highly radioactive wastes into the oceans. Dumping of certain other dangerous substances, including pesticides, could be done only with government permission, and the convention called for care in the disposal of a third group, which included scrap metal. The convention was to come into force in 1973 following ratification.

At a meeting in Paris, government delegates from Algeria, Belgium, Spain, France, Italy, Libya, Morocco, Monaco, Norway, the Netherlands, West Germany, Great Britain, and Tunisia agreed to cooperate in a scheme to check oil pollution. The western Mediterranean was to be divided into eight zones, each to be the responsibility of the nearest and most directly affected bordering state. The participating states would require their sea captains to report all oil spillages and would inform and assist each other in a general antipollution campaign.

A program put forward by the West German government at the end of 1971 was designed to provide for long-term environmental planning; to enforce the principle that the polluter pays for the damage he causes; to adapt technology to meet new environmental standards; and to promote better information and education and more effective international cooperation. In the first three years the program was expected to cost about DM. 38 billion, 50% of which was to be provided by federal, regional, and local authorities and 50% by industry.

In the U.K. the Deposit of Poisonous Wastes Act, 1972, was hurriedly passed in March following the discovery of cyanide waste on open ground near Coventry. The act defined an environmental hazard as "waste deposited so as to subject persons or animals to material risk of death, injury, or impairment of health, or so as to threaten the pollution of the water supply." The creation of such a hazard was punishable by much heavier penalties than under previous legislation: up to £400 and/or up to six months' imprisonment on summary conviction, and heavier penalties on indictment.

In the U.S.S.R. a special resolution authorized the spending of about 1 billion rubles over three years to build purification plants for more than 400 industrial complexes and 15 cities. From 1980, towns in the Volga and Ural basins would be allowed to discharge only purified water into the rivers.

Following protests from conservationists in neighbouring countries, Belgium's minister of agriculture announced that the practice of netting wild birds was to be outlawed. Under a system of licensing, 20 million birds were said to have been captured every year. Italy was now the only EEC country where the practice was still permitted. (DAVID L. SMITH)

In the first quarter of 1972, the U.S. appeared to be on the verge of zero population growth (ZPG), one of the major goals of the environmental movement. (*See* VITAL STATISTICS.)

However, the Commission on Population Growth and the American Future dampened optimistic interpretation of the demographic trend. In reporting on its two-year study, the commission noted that before the U.S. population could be stable, the ZPG rate would have to hold for 60 years or more. The U.S. population was expected to rise by 50 million before the year 2000, and the percentage of the population living in metropolitan concentrations would increase from 70 to 85. The astonishing mobility of the American people would place an enormous burden on government, society, and the environment (nearly 40 million Americans, one in five, changed homes each year). Finally, the report noted that staggering increases in resource consumption, energy demands, and public service requirements multiplied the environmental effects of each American. These and other observations were mostly overlooked, however, in the controversy that followed the commission's strongly worded recommendation that women be given an unrestricted right to abortion.

The dilemma of the automobile continued. The automakers still doubted that they could meet the 1975 deadline of a 90% reduction in pollutant emissions as required under the 1970 Clean Air Act, but the U.S. Environmental Protection Agency (EPA) denied an industry request for a one-year extension. A National Academy of Sciences study said the deadline could be met, provided that the public absorbed a $200 per car cost, along with increased operating expenses and lower engine efficiency. A study for the Office of Science and Technology showed that the cost of pollution control could be offset by sacrifices in nonessential conveniences and styling frills. In the fall Ford was forced to withdraw several thousand 1973 models because overzealous employees had made unauthorized repairs on the pollution-control devices of test models.

In early May the Department of the Interior gave permission for construction of the trans-Alaska pipeline between oil operations around Prudhoe Bay on the Arctic Ocean and Valdez, an ice-free port on the southern Alaska coast. After a two-year delay forced by court action, Interior had produced a thorough impact statement as required by the National Environmental Protection Act (NEPA). This statement contained disturbing data; for example, if the pipe were ruptured, 64,000 bbl. of oil would spill out before pumps could be stopped and cutoff valves closed. Officials pointed to the country's overriding need for fuel, but the decision was appealed by environmentalist groups.

In a decision that caused some alarm among environmentalists, the U.S. Supreme Court ruled that the conservationist Sierra Club did not have standing to sue Walt Disney Productions over plans for a massive recreational development in Mineral King Valley, adjacent to the Sequoia National Park in California. The court said that henceforth parties to such suits would have to show that they personally would be affected by the action they sought to stop. It was too early to tell whether the ruling would obstruct future suits, because the court clearly gave the Sierra Club an opportunity to reopen the attack. The organization simply named several members as persons whose enjoyment of the wilderness would be directly infringed by the Disney plan.

A decision with far-reaching implications was handed down by the California Supreme Court which ruled that state and local governments must provide environmental impact statements before they approve building construction plans, just as federal agencies were required to do under NEPA. Mrs. Andrea Mead Lawrence, former Olympic gold-medal skier, had filed suit to stop construction of a tall apartment building in an area of the High Sierras where single cabins were the existing form of development. Even though the new project would rise on private land, the suit contended that the public environment would be degraded and the court agreed. Hundreds of impact statements were ordered, and some cities stopped issuing building permits.

Congress took several important actions during the year. The Environmental Pesticide Control Act gave intra- as well as interstate jurisdiction over pesticide sales to EPA (which had virtually banned DDT earlier in the year), required registration of all selling points, set up a system for classifying pesticides for public handling and use, and streamlined cancellation proceedings when a product was found to be harmful. One apparent loophole in the law was the requirement that manufacturers be fully reimbursed for banned products. Environmentalists complained that this would encourage both manufacturers and the government to allow possibly dangerous shortcuts in testing new products.

Congress also passed a strong noise control bill that empowered EPA to set decibel levels for all noise sources. The loophole in this law was assignment of the Federal Aviation Agency, which was primarily interested in promoting air transportation, to administer the guidelines for aircraft noise.

Pres. Richard Nixon vetoed the 1972 water quality act because of its $24.6 billion price tag, but Congress overrode the veto, giving the nation a new approach for cleaning its waterways. The act provided new matching funds for municipal waste-treatment plants and prescribed strict standards for the regulation of industrial and municipal discharges.

After six years of hearings, Congress created an Office of Technology Assessment to study and advise on the economic, social, and environmental effects of all scientific and technological legislation. An ocean dumping bill gave EPA authority to review all permits for disposal of radioactive, chemical, and numerous other kinds of wastes at sea, and the Coastal Zone Management Act established a national land-use policy to protect the shoreline, estuaries, and wetlands. Another law protected whales, dolphins, porpoises, sea otters, and polar bears within U.S. territorial limits.

The states were also active. New Mexico and Pennsylvania passed constitutional amendments guaranteeing environmental quality as a public right, and a number of states established EPA-type agencies or departments. At least 27 states were considering new transportation regulations that would reduce air pollution from motor vehicles. Perhaps the area of greatest activity was that of noise pollution, with at least three states passing laws aimed at snowmobiles. At least seven states required impact statements similar to those called for under NEPA. Florida set up a planning agency to designate and then issue guidelines for land development in "areas of critical concern." Despite well-financed opposition, California voters approved a proposition designed to protect the state's coastline. And Colorado voters cut off state funds for development of an area near Denver for the 1976 Winter Olympic Games, chiefly on the ground that it would cause environmental damage.

(RICHARD SALTONSTALL, JR.)

See also **Cities and Urban Affairs; Life Sciences.**

ENCYCLOPÆDIA BRITANNICA FILMS. *Water for Living Things* (1967); *The Everglades: Conserving a Balanced Community* (1968); *Problems of Conservation—Air* (1968); *The House of Man, Part II—Our Crowded Environment* (1969); *Problems of Conservation—Forest and Range* (1969); *Problems of Conservation—Minerals* (1969); *Problems of Conservation—Water* (1969); *The Garbage Explosion* (1970); *Problems of Conservation—Our Natural Resources* (1970); *Problems of Conservation—Soil* (1970); *Problems of Conservation—Wildlife* (1970); *A Field Becomes a Town* (1970); *The Aging of Lakes* (1971); *Noise—Polluting the Environment* (1971); *Turn off Pollution* (1971); *Poison Plants* (1972); *The Great Lakes* (1972); *The Environment: Everything Around Us* (1972); *Buffalo: An Ecological Success Story* (1972).

Equatorial Guinea

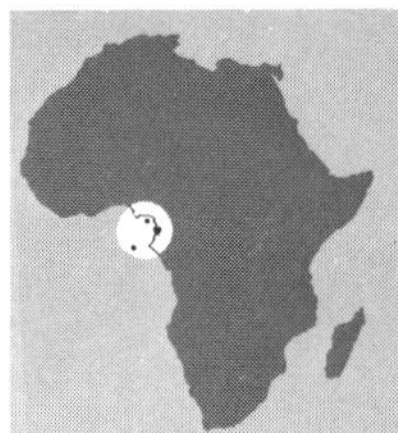

The African republic of Equatorial Guinea consists of Río Muni, which is bordered by Cameroon on the north, Gabon on the east and south, and the Atlantic Ocean on the west; and the offshore islands of Fernando Po and Annobón. Area: 10,830 sq.mi. (28,-050 sq.km.). Pop. (1971 est.): 289,000. Cap. and largest city: Santa Isabel, on Fernando Po (pop., 1965 est., 37,152). Language: Spanish. President in 1972, Francisco Macías Nguema.

Francisco Macías Nguema was appointed president for life at the second National Congress of Equatorial Guinea's Party of National Unity on July 14, 1972. On April 11 Interior Minister Angel Masie Natutumde announced that Equatorial Guinea was arranging to recruit 15,000 Nigerians to work on the Fernando Po cocoa plantations, following a new labour agreement

Epidemics: *see* Medicine

Episcopal Church: *see* Religion

EQUATORIAL GUINEA
Education. (1966–67) Primary, pupils 38,395, teachers 504; secondary, pupils 2,343, teachers 40; teacher training, students 130, teachers 28.
Finance and Trade. Monetary unit: peseta Guineana, at par with the Spanish peseta, with (Sept. 18, 1972) a free rate of 63.50 pesetas to U.S. $1 (155 pesetas = £1 sterling). Budget (1969–70 est.): revenue 712.5 million pesetas; expenditure 1,139,000,000 pesetas. Foreign trade (1966): imports 1,278,000,000 pesetas (58% from Spain in 1965); exports 1,817,000,000 pesetas (97% to Spain in 1965). Main exports (1965): cocoa 44%; coffee 21%; timber 19%.
Agriculture. Production (in 000; metric tons; 1971; 1970 in parentheses): coffee *c.* 7.2 (*c.* 7.2); cocoa (1971–72) 24, (1970–71) 23; palm kernels (exports) *c.* 2 (*c.* 2); palm oil *c.* 4 (*c.* 4). Livestock (in 000; 1970–71): sheep *c.* 29; cattle *c.* 3; pigs *c.* 6; goats *c.* 7; chickens *c.* 78.

providing better pay and conditions signed between the two governments in December 1971; 20,000 Nigerians had returned to Nigeria after completing contracts under the old terms (denounced in Lagos as near slavery), and it was feared that the cocoa crop might be adversely affected by their loss.

In August Gabon occupied the two disputed Atlantic islands of Mbanie and Cocotiers after Gabonese fishermen had allegedly been attacked by an armed force from Equatorial Guinea. President Nguema on September 12 demanded UN intervention to oust the Gabonese "invaders." (R. J. M. DENNERSTEIN)

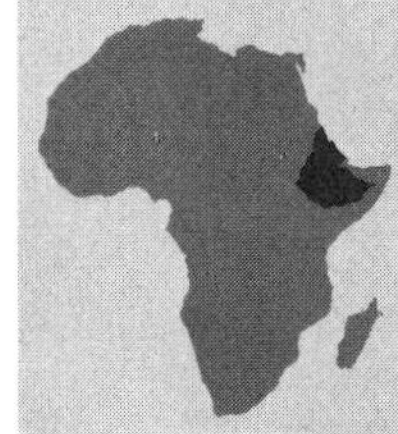

Ethiopia

A constitutional monarchy of northeastern Africa, Ethiopia is bordered by Somalia, Afars and Issas, Kenya, Sudan, and the Red Sea. Area: 471,800 sq.mi. (1,221,900 sq.km.). Pop. (1972 est.): 25,564,000. Cap. and largest city: Addis Ababa (pop., 1972 est., 958,700). Language: Amharic (official) and English. Religion: mainly Ethiopian Orthodox (Coptic), with Muslim and animist minorities. Emperor, Haile Selassie I; prime minister in 1972, Aklilu Habte-Wolde.

Haile Selassie's 80th birthday in July 1972 was observed with three days of national celebration. The much-traveled emperor continued his energetic program of personal diplomacy with visits to Sudan, Egypt, Sierra Leone, Nigeria, Kenya, Liberia, Morocco, Britain, France, and Yugoslavia. He received visits from UN Secretary-General Kurt Waldheim, the prince and princess of Spain, Pres. Zulfikar Ali Bhutto of Pakistan, Pres. Varahagiri Venkata Giri of India, and Pres. Mobutu Sese Seko of Zaire. The emperor, who received the UN Peace Medal during the secretary-general's visit, played a key role in the improvement of Senegal-Guinea relations and in the solution of the problems between northern and southern Sudan.

The emperor's active personal diplomacy brought significant results. After his 1971 visit to China, the Chinese promised Ethiopia a long-term loan of about Eth$210 million, and China entered the Ethiopian coffee market with an initial purchase worth Eth$5 million. British aid rose to an annual level of more than Eth$4 million, and an agreement was reached to permit through flights of Ethiopian Airlines to London, beginning in February 1973. Italy signed an Eth$95 million loan agreement; Japan was to provide Eth$27 million for textile development and airport improvement; and Canada lent Eth$3.2 million for mineral prospecting in the Omo Valley. A significant chapter in bilateral relations was recorded in the July agreement with Sudan, which defined the common frontier and initiated joint action on transport links and problems related to the agricultural development area in the Setit plains.

The economy continued to suffer from an unfavourable balance of trade, still characterized by heavy dependence on U.S. coffee imports. Devaluation of the U.S. dollar aggravated the situation. Mineral exploration financed by the UN Development Program confirmed the existence of large geothermal power sources in the Afar Plain along the Red Sea.

The "minimum package" program of assistance to peasant farmers, launched in 1971, showed progress. There was generally more emphasis on rural development, including an expanding feeder road program and the construction of rural primary schools. In urban areas an active program of road development for Addis Ababa was launched, and a project for the improvement of water and sewerage facilities was to be initiated with financing from the World Bank. Asmara secured a large new reservoir at Mai Nefai, and in Dire Dawa the two parts of the town were finally united by a bridge over the Laga Dechatu River.

Industrial developments included the inauguration of an Eth$15 million tire factory in Addis Ababa and a cotton gin in Gondar for processing raw cotton from the lowlands at Setit Humera. Agriculture was expected to benefit from the rapidly developing livestock program being supported by an Eth$10.3 million loan from the International Development Association. (G. C. LAST)

ETHIOPIA
Education. (1969–70) Primary, pupils 590,445, teachers 11,964; secondary, pupils 105,652, teachers 3,971; vocational, pupils 6,168, teachers 508; teacher training, students 2,623, teachers 131; higher, students 5,831, teaching staff 503.
Finance. Monetary unit: Ethiopian dollar, with (Sept. 18, 1972) a par value of Eth$2.30 to U.S. $1 (free rate of Eth$5.59 = £1 sterling). Gold, SDRs, and foreign exchange, central bank: (June 1972) U.S. $72.5 million; (June 1971) U.S. $68.8 million. Budget (1971–72 est.): revenue Eth$714.9 million; expenditure Eth$732.9 million. Money supply: (June 1972) Eth$415.5 million; (June 1971) Eth$423.1 million. Cost of living (Addis Ababa; 1963 = 100): (June 1972) 134; (June 1971) 150.
Foreign Trade. (1971) Imports Eth$472.2 million; exports Eth$314 million. Import sources: Italy 16%; Japan 15%; West Germany 11%; U.K. 9%; U.S. 9%; Iran 7%. Export destinations: U.S. 44%; West Germany 8%; Saudi Arabia 6%; Afars and Issas 6%; Italy 5%. Main exports: coffee 56%; oilseeds 10%; hides and skins 8%; cereals 7%.
Transport and Communications. Roads (1971) *c.* 23,400 km. (including 8,170 km. all-weather). Motor vehicles in use (1970): passenger 36,750; commercial 10,000. Railways (1970): 1,088 km.; traffic (including traffic of the Afars and Issas portion of Djibouti-Addis Ababa line; 1967) 82 million passenger-km., freight 216 million net ton-km. Air traffic (1971): 367.6 million passenger-km.; freight 16,708,000 net ton-km. Telephones (Dec. 1970) 46,000. Radio receivers (Dec. 1970) 160,000. Television receivers (Dec. 1969) 8,000.
Agriculture. Production (in 000; metric tons; 1971; 1970 in parentheses): millet, sorghum, and teff *c.* 2,680 (2,630); barley *c.* 1,550 (*c.* 1,525); wheat *c.* 860 (*c.* 840); corn 960 (*c.* 950); linseed *c.* 66 (*c.* 60); sugar, raw value (1971–72) *c.* 91, (1970–71) *c.* 82; chick-peas *c.* 189 (*c.* 185); dry peas *c.* 130 (*c.* 127); dry broad beans *c.* 143 (*c.* 138); lentils *c.* 109 (*c.* 107); sweet potatoes *c.* 254 (253); potatoes *c.* 163 (*c.* 162); coffee *c.* 215 (*c.* 205). Livestock (in 000; 1970–71): cattle *c.* 26,330; sheep *c.* 12,800; goats *c.* 11,320; horses *c.* 1,415; mules *c.* 1,440; asses *c.* 3,900; camels *c.* 990; poultry *c.* 46,800.
Industry. Production (in 000; metric tons; 1968–69): cement 166; cotton yarn 5; cotton fabrics (sq.m.; 1966–67) 58,000; electricity (kw-hr.) 455,000.

Espionage: *see* Intelligence Operations
European Economic Community: *see* Commercial Policies; European Unity
European Free Trade Association: *see* Commercial Policies; European Unity

European Unity

Despite various setbacks, 1972 was, on balance, a year of progress toward greater unity in Europe. This was especially true for the Common Market or European Economic Community (EEC) and the two ancillary Communities, those for Coal and Steel and for Atomic Energy. The year began on a high note, a ceremony on January 22 in the Palais d'Egmont in Brussels celebrating the pledged accession to the Treaty of Rome of four new members, Britain, Ireland, Denmark, and Norway. More than 60 signatures were affixed to the treaty of accession and various annexes and protocols. The action was to result, officially on Jan. 1, 1973, in bringing together into a common trading and economic area a population of more than a quarter of a billion, more than a quarter of the world's imports and exports, and a gross national product second only to the U.S. (*See* Special Report.)

A second, though not quite so high, point came in October when the first summit conference of the expanded market nations met in Paris to pledge commitment to the formation of a "European union" by 1980. By the time the meeting took place Norway was no longer participating; its voters had rejected EEC membership in a September referendum.

Toward an Enlarged EEC. Having been formally signed, the treaty of accession required ratification by the ten states. The process was complicated by the decision in certain states that ratification must be accomplished by popular referendum rather than by representative parliamentary means—or that a referendum should supplement parliamentary action. Considerable publicity attended the first of these referenda, that held by Pres. Georges Pompidou of France on April 23. Charges that Pompidou hoped that the inevitable affirmative vote would be regarded as an endorsement of his leadership were not without some merit. Although the treaty was safely ratified, only a little more than half of the French voters went to the polls and of those, two-thirds voted for the expansion of the EEC and one-third voted against it.

The idea of a referendum was also seized upon by the Labourite foes of British membership in the EEC and complicated the British effort to ratify the treaty. The British enabling legislation was introduced in Parliament on January 26 and in mid-February Prime Minister Edward Heath was able to secure parliamentary acceptance in principle on the second reading by a majority of eight votes. He owed this scant majority entirely to the small Liberal Party whose five affirmative votes turned in the victory. It was at this point that Labour's leader, Harold Wilson, insisted that Britain submit the legislation to a popular decision. Since opinion polls had on occasion rejected British membership in the EEC by as much as 70%, a popular decision might well have been in the negative and prevented Britain's accession.

Advocacy of a referendum proved to be bad tactics for the Labour opposition because it caused certain leading party members, notably Roy Jenkins (*see* BIOGRAPHY), to give up their posts in the shadow cabinet and announce their future adherence to the bill. Prime Minister Heath eventually won his victory, although by a very narrow margin, in July.

Elsewhere, among the six original EEC states there appeared to be no doubt of parliamentary ratification; the three other applicant states, however, had provided for referenda. The one held in Ireland on May 10 secured a surprising affirmative majority of 83% of those voting. In the Norwegian two-day vote, completed on September 25, a majority of 53.9% to 46.1% voted against membership. The anti-Market coalition consisted of conservative nationalists, pan-Scandinavians, left-wing unionists, farmers, fishermen, environmentalists, and young radicals, all of whom had reasons, though often contradictory, for opposing membership. Although the vote was not binding on the Storting, it led to the resignation of the government of Trygve Bratteli and the formation of an anti-Market, three-party cabinet, whose first job became the negotiation of a separate free-trade agreement with the EEC. Fears that the Norwegian vote would influence Danes to follow suit in a binding referendum were allayed the following week when a record voter turnout chose the EEC by nearly 2–1.

The major elements in the year's EEC record were the continuing difficulties besetting moves toward monetary union. The monetary crisis of 1971 largely brought to naught what seemed to have been promising earlier steps toward such a union. Another beginning was made after the settlement at Washington, D.C., in December 1971, the Smithsonian agreement, in which subscribing nations agreed that national currency fluctuations might move up or down from established parity by a somewhat more generous total of $4\frac{1}{2}$%. In April the six original and four prospective EEC members agreed that currency fluctuations among themselves should not total more than half of the allowable maximum, that is, $2\frac{1}{4}$%, and that even this discretion should gradually be narrowed until their currencies enjoyed fixed parity.

By June, however, even this modest effort had been seriously undermined by Britain's decision to allow the pound to seek its own level and by the demands of Italy and Denmark for more flexible arrangements. Some EEC states, especially France, continued to insist upon the development of closer monetary ties within the EEC, while others, notably West Germany, were equally insistent that efforts to harmonize monetary policy would not succeed unless EEC states were willing to submit to a more supranational discipline.

What the West Germans were talking about was, of course, the nub of the matter. Monetary union could not succeed until there was a greater degree of economic union. But efforts toward that end would be greatly hampered by the considerable variation that existed within the various national economies, their productivity, and the degree of economic discipline they were willing or able to impose. There was great difference, for example, between the extent of industrialization (and attendant economic and social policies) of West Germany and Ireland; and Italy acknowledged more than once that it was at a disadvantage in economic competition among the Six and was fearful that the disadvantage would be aggravated in a larger union.

Italy's ambivalent attitude and the doubts that it could or would play by the rules were emphasized when the president of the EEC Commission, Franco Malfatti, resigned to run for a seat in the Italian Parliament. Italy's EEC partners, obviously nettled by this apparently cavalier attitude, thereupon rejected the candidacy of an Italian replacement and elected instead Sicco Mansholt, the Dutch father of EEC's common agricultural policy. Mansholt made himself felt during his brief tenancy by insisting, amid

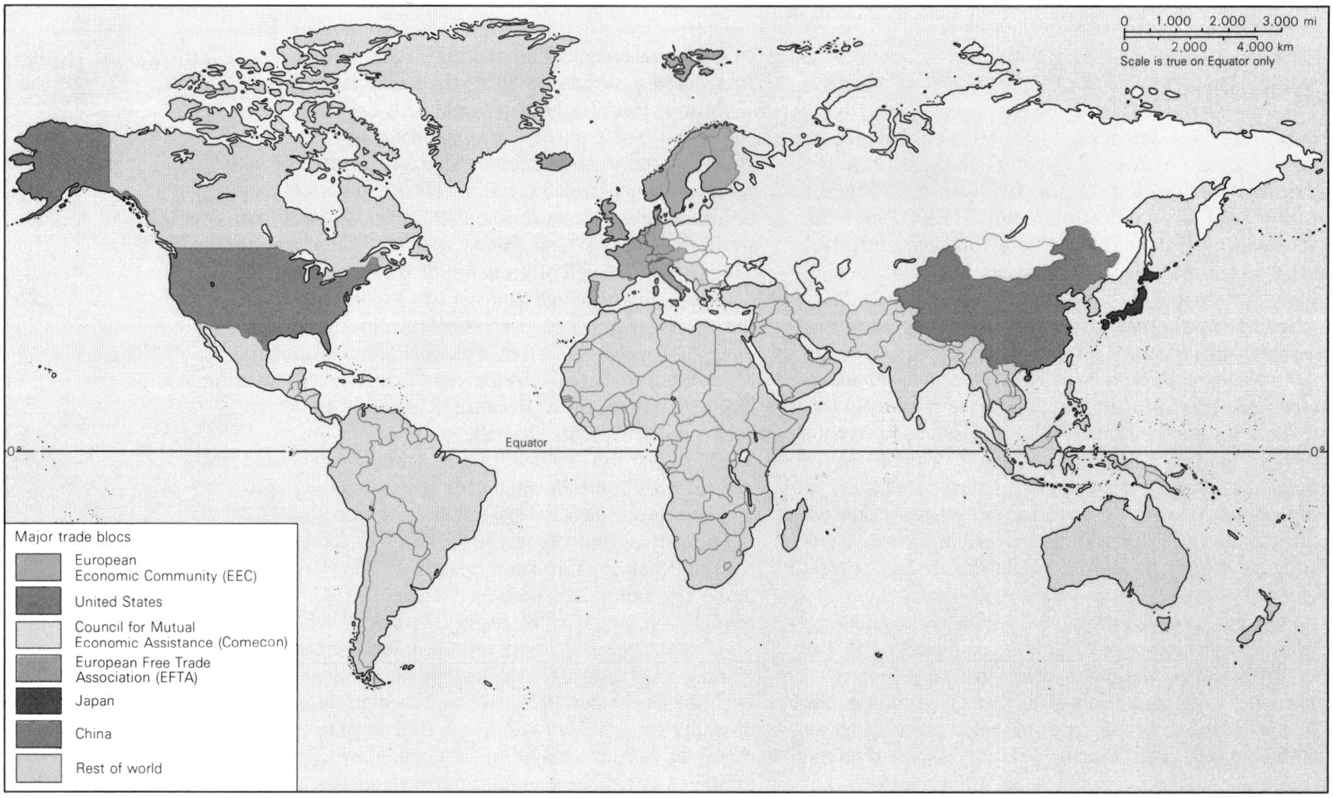

0 1,000 2,000 3,000 mi
0 2,000 4,000 km
Scale is true on Equator only
Equator
Major trade blocs
European Economic Community (EEC)
United States
Council for Mutual Economic Assistance (Comecon)
European Free Trade Association (EFTA)
Japan
China
Rest of world

Value of Foreign Trade
Billions of U.S. dollars
300
250
200
150
100
50
0
EEC
U.S.
Comecon
EFTA
Japan
China
Rest of World
Major trade blocs

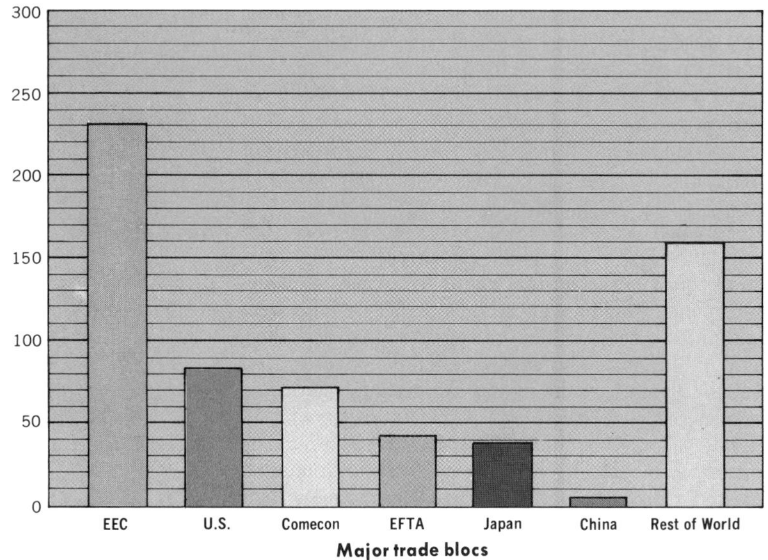

hints that he would resign, that he and the Commission be party to all political discussions.

The summit conference had been proposed by President Pompidou in August 1971 as a means of forging a common monetary policy with which to face the U.S. in the major conference of trading nations scheduled to begin in 1973 under the auspices of the General Agreement on Tariffs and Trade (GATT). That it would be held at all was in doubt most of 1972. It was only after the September meeting of EEC foreign and finance ministers in Rome and Frascati, Italy, had reached a limited monetary agreement that Pompidou issued the invitations. The September agreement provided a fund of $1.4 billion in credits to be used to support members' currencies on exchange markets. It was little more than promise to extend multilaterally what had existed bilaterally, but it meant that a document of some substance could be signed at the summit and that more difficult monetary issues could be postponed until after national elections were held in West Germany in November and in France by the spring of 1973.

The opening session of the two-day summit set April 1, 1973, as the date for establishing the fund, and set up a timetable for moving into a more critical second stage in the development of the fund—a program of intense economic cooperation aimed at moving the economies of the Nine into one cycle—by ordering studies on the mechanisms of such a move. Most remarkable about the discussions was Pompidou's relaxation in attitude toward the U.S. The second day saw the Nine pledging themselves to unity by 1980 and setting commitments to provide reports on what such a union should mean by the end of 1975. The French-proposed, undefined goal of "irreversible monetary and economic union" was a compromise between the strong demands of the Netherlands for a specific commitment to a pan-European government and the resistance of others to any precise promises to convert what remained essentially a customs union into a single parliamentary state.

Somewhat vague discussion also occurred during the year about the creation of a political secretariat, presumably the administrative nucleus of an eventual harmonized foreign policy. The idea quickly sparked contention; France was at first adamant that the secretariat's offices be located in Paris rather than in Brussels, but was outpointed on this issue at the summit meeting.

Meanwhile, a solid, if not spectacular, advance in one of the supranational EEC powers was registered on July 14 when the seven-man EEC court at Luxembourg (the European Court) upheld the EEC Commission in assessing fines of more than $50,000 against each of ten European chemical companies. The deci-

continued on page 293

THE EUROPEAN COMMUNITY—A NEW WORLD FORCE?

By Roy Jenkins

The past 20 years have been a period of remarkable achievement for Europe. The new Community has overcome both the disillusion of French opposition to British inclusion in 1963 and 1967 and the British hesitancy—which appeared at times to border on disdain—of the early postwar years. British governments then, although they made an important contribution to European economic recovery, also made the political mistake of seeing their relationship with the countries of Western Europe as akin to that of the United States with continental Europe. In the 1960s, the two French vetoes not only imposed a further decade of delay on British entry, they also devalued the force of the European idea and caused a weakening ideological split within the existing Community. The visions of the future that emanated from the founders of the European idea, and the inspiration that seized those who met at the proselytizing Hague conference in 1948, were not related solely to arrangements among an exclusive group of powers. They offered a new prospect of learning from the bitterness and destruction of the war years, a new prospect of transcending the restrictions of national sovereignty.

When these objectives had been set, they could not be limited to only six countries without undermining their own basis. It was not possible to proclaim that national sovereignty was outdated and yet to refuse to let more than six nations escape from its confines. It could not be claimed that Europe could solve its own problems only on a European basis and yet insist that European countries anxious to join should not be allowed to make a full contribution.

The achievements of the past two decades have in essence been twofold. They have laid to rest the old Franco-German quarrel that so damaged Europe and the world for at least a century. It is a mark of the completeness of this achievement that the world now accepts it as though it could hardly be otherwise, as though little had needed to be done, and forgets how much has in fact been accomplished. In addition, Europe has been made rich. Not only has recovery been complete but standards of material achievement and expectation, widely spread throughout the several nations, have exceeded all previous bounds. The Common Market has brought a high degree of common material prosperity. And with that wealth has come a greater sense of security, from both external and internal threats.

The new Europe has not yet matched its wealth by its inspiration or by its influence in the world. In part this has been because Europe has been too inward-looking. In part, too, it has been because of the preeminent position of the United States. The countries of Western Europe, both inside and outside the Community, have grown used to being a somewhat ill-coordinated group of junior partners within the Western Alliance. But, with the massive suddenness that has always been a characteristic of the development of its civilization, America has run itself up against overcommitment and overstrain. This is true militarily, monetarily, politically.

The Rt. Hon. Roy Jenkins is a member of Parliament and former Chancellor of the Exchequer of the United Kingdom.

Europe and the Third World. The new European Community must be prepared to fill at least part of the gap. The greatest challenge to its future security is not primarily a military one. It is whether Western Europe, now emerging as the richest and most powerful trading bloc, can make the rest of the world, and particularly that part of it where poverty is still so grinding as to make a mockery of human existence, feel that European success is the ally and not the enemy of its advance.

The amount of Community and bilateral aid must not only be increased substantially but must also be fairly distributed throughout the less developed world. There has been an understandable but regrettable tendency for disproportionate amounts of aid from the Six to go to the former French colonies in Africa; the enlarged Community will be able to redress this balance by an expanded program in Asia, as well as by a redirection of aid in Africa into agriculture, and specifically into aid for subsistence farmers.

The new Europe must also devote itself quite consciously and deliberately to speak and vote on behalf of the poor majority when the rich nations fix terms of international trade, or commodity agreements, or monetary and reserve arrangements such as Special Drawing Rights. If European unity can be made an accepted force not only for European but for world progress, then the Community will indeed be fulfilling a new leadership role. But if it is indifferent to this challenge, then as the remaining decades of the 20th century wear on, Europeans will find themselves living anxiously on an insecure pinnacle of wealth, surrounded by an increasingly menacing and embittered majority of the world.

In world trade and aid, in international investment and monetary arrangements, a united Europe can and, almost certainly, will grow into a new world force *directly*. But it can also become an immensely powerful agent in a different sense—by force of example; it may produce significant *demonstration effects*. Different European nations have at different times in the last 2,000 years been a force in both senses all over the world—whether in North America and Australasia, or in most of today's poor countries in Asia, Africa, and Latin America.

This has produced a long-bubbling controversy—reminiscent in some ways of the growth versus amenity argument—about whether the people of the third world have benefited from European invasion and infusion. This controversy is as sterile for the practical planner as it is stimulating to the political philosopher. The fact is that vast changes have taken place in these countries —and while political institutions imposed by the force of the controlling colonial power have frequently withered or collapsed, much of the colonial legacy has remained, not just in the shape of language or culture but, equally significantly, in administrative structure and economic organization.

The European Example. The new Europe will not create political institutions directly in the grand old colonial manner—a formal federation here, an unnatural upper house there. In the development of political institutions—and ideas—in the rest of the world the force of Europe will now be exerted by example. Exactly how beneficial this force will be, and on what criteria one determines the benefits, will be matters for interminable speculation about detail for some and a deep-rooted set of convictions about the principles for many. The fact remains that the force of the European Community already exists and will grow; the new Europe must contain and channel it; and the rest of the world will have to come to terms with it.

The new Community also has a huge potential for exerting these twin pressures of direct influence and force of example in industrial and commercial life. Many within the Community have already taken a leading part in spreading the message that an increase in the output of goods is not the same as an improvement in the amenity of life. The time will soon come for this message and this concern to be supplemented by practical proposals not merely for eradicating the black spots of pollution or price rings but also for enabling individual workers and consumers to express their views in the much wider and grayer areas of choice and "trade-off"—between new cars and old city centres, or between more advanced colour television systems and the strains of long hours of unsatisfying, repetitive work for which money is the only compensation.

For the individual company, this will entail both a concept and a scale of planned industrial democracy that will be quite new to most enterprises, trade unions, and workers both inside and outside Europe. On the political level, it will entail a determination by politicians and administrators to design a new structure of incentives and controls to reflect the needs of the individuals in a manner of which the market economy in its previous and present forms has so far been incapable. European institutions will provide the direct mechanisms to make these changes within the new Community. Habit is at least as powerful a force in industry as in human nature in general. But a lead can be given that changes the whole range of private and public industrialists' attitudes about their raison d'être and the forces that they must take into account in their decisions; and business executives are no longer concerned only with profitability. If action within Europe produces such a change, which would be substantial although gradual, then it would be extraordinary if the effects of this change in an economy as crucial as the European Community were not felt throughout most of the world, so close are the links of multinational ownership and international trade, business custom, and practice as well as criteria for investment, price, and wage decisions.

Europe and the Superpowers. During the 1960s, as the cold war was coming to an end, many believed that Europe had become a backwater in international affairs. Their attention was focused on the struggle in Vietnam, which, it was felt, would determine the pattern of development for much of Asia and Africa. For 20 years world politics had been dominated by the conflict between the two superpowers and their rival ideologies. In Europe the division at the end of World War II into spheres of interest looked likely to endure for the foreseeable future. In Asia and Africa the position was the more interesting for its seeming instability. The influence and military strength of the main European countries and of the former European colonial empires was small compared with that of the U.S.S.R. and the U.S.

Today there are signs that the world of the two superpowers is fading fast. Their military dominance remains almost as great, but the emergence to great-power status of China may not allow this bipolar dominance to continue. And both superpowers are feeling the strain of massive military expenditure. The strategic arms limitation agreement appears to be motivated by a genuine desire to limit the increase in spending on nuclear weapons; and a European security conference could lead to reductions in conventional forces in Europe. There is certainly strong pressure in the U.S. for such a reduction, and it would be surprising if there were no similar, if more hidden, pressure in Moscow, accentuated by tension on the Chinese border.

Soviet leaders also seem to be growing more concerned about increasing the standard of living of their people and moving some way in the direction of what Westerners in the 1950s and early 1960s called the "consumer society." The continued presence of Aleksei N. Kosygin as Soviet premier may be construed as evidence of this objective, which conflicts with the familiar strong-arm pressures for increased military spending. The battle in the Kremlin between the supporters of more light, consumer-based industry and the usually united heavy capital goods and heavy military expenditure camp is far from over, but the battle is being fought over very different ground from the days when Georgi M. Malenkov promised to enlarge consumer industries and became a notable casualty of Nikita Khrushchev's ascendancy.

It is already clear that the relations between Europe and both superpowers have entered a new phase. The weakening of the U.S. economic position, partly but not wholly because of the burden of Vietnam, has inevitably had an impact on political relationships. Europe is much less dependent on American goodwill and is in an increasingly strong position to bargain on such issues as trade and monetary reform where there is both a visible and a significant conflict of interest. Growing U.S. demand for greater European self-sufficiency in defense is bound to lead to further changes in the relationship when large-scale withdrawals take place. Relations are friendly and must remain so, but they are approaching a basis of more equal partnership.

East-West Détente. The rise of Chinese power is not the only cause of the changing Soviet attitude toward Europe. The West German *Ostpolitik* has done much to bury the bogey of German "revanchism." Soviet actions are always difficult to predict, but almost five years have passed since the invasion of Czechoslovakia, and there are signs of renewed liberalization in Eastern Europe. It may be that Eastern European countries will grow away from the Soviet Union in much the same way as Western Europe has ceased to rely economically on U.S. support, and with this goes a growing political independence as these countries switch a growing proportion of their trade to the Community, and to West Germany in particular, which is geographically and historically their natural source of supply for sophisticated industrial products.

On the Western European side as well, moves toward a political détente have a strong economic rationale. Industry in the Community is feeling the effects of Japanese competition both in the U.S. market and throughout the less developed world. Japanese electrical exports have already gained a significant slice of the European market, and Japan is at last seen as a serious threat by European car manufacturers. In these circumstances it is natural for Western European countries to seek to increase their exports to Eastern Europe, which—in some ways despite, in other ways because of, its rapid development since World War II—still hungers for foreign capital and consumer goods. And if people and ideas as well as machine tools can flow between the two halves of Europe, there is no reason why the political barrier through Central Europe should be immovable; it is already far from impenetrable.

The Community has developed what may most accurately be called a common external *front* in some foreign policy areas—for example, the Middle East and, recently, Vietnam. There is, however, an important internal precondition for the achievement of a genuinely common and comprehensive external *policy*. A successful foreign policy contains a very full measure of attitude and style; ministers and administrators have to rely far more on persuasion and public relations than is either necessary or advisable in economic or social policy. The main Western European foreign ministries, and the British and French in particular, have over many years developed their own established attitudes and their own well-turned styles. If the new Europe is to create a common foreign policy that amounts to more than a hopeful declaration of intent, then it is essential that national institutions as well as aspirations grow together into one Community whole.

The new Europe will never challenge the political and economic structure of the U.S., the U.S.S.R., or China by military force. But it provides the prospect of a unit strong enough both economically and politically to attack the problems of world injustice on a world scale rather than merely creating a cosy and contented society within its own walls. Nostalgia for an idyllic pastoral society has always appealed in troubled times, but the roseate hue of this prospect holds no more for the future than does a dying sunset. The new Europe will rank with what will soon be three other great powers. None of these has built a system that successfully combines economic and social justice with freedom of action and expression for the individual. Europe has a long way to go before it achieves this. But its attempt to do so can be the major new contribution to world leadership by example in the next decade.

continued from page 290

sion interpreted a common pricing policy as a "concerted practice," outlawed by the Treaty of Rome. The Commission also placed on the court's calendar a case against a U.S. metal-packaging company, apparently the first occasion for invoking a treaty provision against market domination by a single company.

EFTA and the EEC. With two of the member states of the European Free Trade Association now ensconced within the framework of the Treaty of Rome and a third approaching and then rejecting association, the remaining EFTA states (Austria, Switzerland, Portugal, Sweden, Finland, and Iceland) gave serious consideration to their future posture. Primary importance, therefore, was assigned to negotiations with the EEC Commission, which began in December 1971, on ways to preserve the existing free-trade arrangements of surviving EFTA states with those former EFTA members that were going behind the EEC tariff wall, and even to extend such arrangements to the whole of the EEC membership, at least respecting industrial goods. As a result treaties were signed in Brussels on July 22 establishing a free-trade area for the 16 nations involved, effectively merging the EEC and EFTA into a single trading bloc to be established with the formal enlargement of the EEC in 1973. The agreements provided for mutual reductions of tariffs on industrial goods by 20% each year until 1977, and permitted longer transition periods for products, notably paper, fish, and certain agricultural commodities, for which free trade could seriously affect local economies.

These arrangements inspired protests on the part of the U.S., which regarded special trade arrangements by GATT members as contrary to GATT policy. The anticipated GATT conference might, therefore, bring these arrangements up for review and possible modification. Meanwhile, it appeared that the Stockholm Convention of 1959, which brought EFTA into being, would continue to provide a formal legal framework for the surviving EFTA states, and that its provisions would continue, as far as was practicable, to control commercial relations among the members.

Council of Europe. One of the oldest European bodies (created in 1949) and also the largest (17 members), the Council of Europe continued its role as an intergovernmental agency providing the machinery for cooperative European action on many fronts. Among the many matters that concerned the Council's Committee of Ministers during the first months of the year were the creation of a European youth foundation, harmonization of national legislation to protect the health of workers, standardization of the concepts of domicile and residence in European law, and the project to protect Venice from the inroads of the sea.

The Council's one rather significant operating responsibility was that for the enforcement machinery of the European Convention on Human Rights. Nine cases claiming violation of rights, involving six different states as plaintiffs or defendants, had been presented in January. One of these was an appeal of Ireland against Britain charging violations of human rights in Northern Ireland prisons.

(ARNOLD J. ZURCHER)

See also Commercial Policies; Defense; Payments and Reserves, International; Taxation; Trade, International; and articles on the various countries.

Fairs and Shows

Revenues and attendance at most of the world's public and trade fairs continued to rise in 1972. Revenues increased nearly 22%, compared with an average increase of 12% in 1971, while attendance gained an estimated 3% over the previous year. More than 1,100,000,000 persons attended the world's 14,400 public fairs and shows. An estimated 2,100,000,000 people visited over 17,000 amusement parks, and another 1,800,000,000 people flocked to some 58,000 stadiums, arenas, and auditoriums, and other entertainment facilities. Registered buyers at nearly 1,000 commercial trade fairs numbered an unprecedented 46 million.

Spokane, Wash., received official sanction from the Bureau International des Expositions, Paris, to hold the only world's fair scheduled for 1974. With a population of 170,000, it would be the smallest city ever to play host to such an event. The fair, to be called Expo 74, was to be based on an environmental and outdoor recreation theme. It would be located on two islands in the Spokane River that were currently being used as industrial sites, and at year's end the city received a federal grant of $1,749,689 for land-site acquisition. After spending $3.4 million in promotional efforts, Philadelphia abandoned its plans to hold a U.S. bicentennial exposition in 1976. Instead, regional celebrations were planned, with funds to be distributed by the federal government to bicentennial commissions in each state. Accounts for the New York World's Fair, 1964–65, were finally closed in 1972. It was reported that 62.4 cents had been returned on each bondholder's dollar. The money was not distributed, however, and a court ruled that it should be given to New York City for educational purposes.

ISTVAN BARA—CAMERA PRESS/PICTORIAL PARADE

A symbolically fitting sculpture is displayed at the International Viticulture and Wine Producing Exhibition held in August 1972 in Budapest, Hung.

Evangelical Churches: *see* Religion

Exchange Rates: *see* Payments and Reserves, International

Exhibitions: *see* Art Exhibitions; Fairs and Shows; Museums and Galleries; Photography

Expeditions, Scientific: *see* Antarctica; Arctic Regions; Mountaineering; Oceanography; Speleology

Faeroe Islands: *see* Dependent States

International Trade Fairs. An estimated 1,000 commercial trade fairs were held in 78 countries in 1972. Attendance at these fairs was largely restricted to accredited trade buyers, although such major events as the Milan (Italy) Samples Fair, the International Trade Fair at Plovdiv, Bulg., and the International Trade Fair at Marseilles, France, catered to both buyers and the general public. The U.S. Department of Commerce sponsored U.S. exhibitor participation at more than 200 fairs in addition to its fixed-base trade centres. An increasing number of pollution-control exhibitions were held, including the Pollution Control Exhibition and Congress at Vienna, the Environmental Pollution Control Exhibition at London, the International Air and Water Pollution Control and Noise Abatement Exhibition at Jönköping, Swed., and the International Water Usage and Effluent Treatment Exhibition at Amsterdam.

Fairs. The majority of the world's annual public fairs reported record gross income and attendance.

Selected Major National and International Fairs, 1972

Country and date	Event and place	Attendance
Algeria		
Aug. 25–Sept. 10	International Trade Fair, Algiers	1,650,000
Australia		
Sept. 21–30	Royal Melbourne Show, Melbourne	810,000
March 24–April 4	Royal Easter Show, Sydney	1,095,000
Austria		
March 5–12	International Spring Trade Fair, Vienna	680,000
Sept. 1–10	International Agricultural Fair, Wels	1,300,000
Belgium		
Jan. 12–23	International Motorcycle and Cycle Show, Brussels	750,000
Brazil		
July 14–23	National Machinery Trade Fair, São Paulo	410,000
Bulgaria		
Aug. 24–Sept. 3	International Trade Fair, Plovdiv	470,000
Canada		
Aug. 16–Sept. 4	Canadian National Exhibition, Toronto	3,561,000
July 6–15	Calgary (Alta.) Exhibition and Stampede	908,035
Aug. 17–Sept. 4	Pacific National Exhibition, Vancouver, B.C.	1,192,737
Sept. 8–16	London (Ont.) Western Fair	428,674
Egypt		
March 2–23	International Fair, Cairo	760,000
France		
May 6–15	International Fair of Bordeaux	500,000
Aug. 28–Sept. 10	International Motor Exhibition, Paris	1,000,000
Sept. 7–18	European Samples Fair, Strasbourg	700,000
Germany, East		
Sept. 3–10	International Trade Fair, Leipzig	840,000
Germany, West		
April 8–16	International Light Industries Fair, Munich	356,000
Greece		
Aug. 28–Sept. 18	International Trade Fair of Thessaloniki	1,550,000
Hungary		
May 19–29	International Fair, Budapest	1,120,000
India		
Nov. 3–Dec. 17	Asian International Trade Fair, New Delhi	210,000
Iraq		
Oct. 1–21	Baghdad Fair	750,000
Israel		
Nov. 10–20	Modern Homes Exhibition, Tel Aviv-Yafo	400,000
Italy		
April 24–May 8	International Arts and Crafts Fair, Florence	600,000
May 27–June 11	Fair of Rome	1,320,000
Libya		
March 1–20	International Fair, Tripoli	600,000
Scotland		
Oct. 4–21	Modern Homes Exhibition, Glasgow	300,000
South Africa		
March 21–April 3	Rand Easter Show, Johannesburg	700,000
Spain		
May 6–16	International Samples Fair, Valencia	450,000
July 1–12	International Trade Fair, Bilbao	670,000
Switzerland		
Sept. 9–24	Comptoir-Suisse National Fair, Lausanne	1,000,000
April 15–25	Swiss Industries Fair, Basel	1,040,000
Syria		
Aug. 25–Sept. 20	International Fair, Damascus	1,280,000
Turkey		
Aug. 20–Sept. 20	International Fair, Izmir	1,270,000
U.S.S.R.		
Sept. 20–Oct. 1	Sport and Tourist Equipment Exhibition, Kiev	270,000
August–September	International Agricultural Equipment Exhibition, Moscow	700,000
United States		
Jan. 28–Feb. 6	Southwest Exposition and Fat Stock Show, Fort Worth, Tex.	510,000
Feb. 26–March 5	International Auto Show, New York City	500,000
Aug. 11–20	Illinois State Fair, Springfield	553,839
Aug. 3–12	Great Allentown (Pa.) Fair	693,493
Aug. 11–20	Wisconsin State Fair, West Allis	900,082
Aug. 25–Sept. 10	Michigan State Fair, Detroit	670,000
Aug. 24–Sept. 4	Ohio State Fair, Columbus	2,209,993
Oct. 7–22	State Fair of Texas, Dallas	3,122,501
Yugoslavia		
May 12–22	International Agricultural Fair, Novi Sad	550,000

Source: Frederick P. Pittera, *Fairs of the World* (1972).

Front gate admissions were raised more than 40% in an effort to cover higher labour and materials costs. At the same time, an increasing number of fairs were featuring free grandstand shows in an effort to boost attendance. North American fairs spent more than $23 million for grandstand attractions. Fairs with fixed-base facilities were attempting to use their buildings and grounds on a year-round schedule by attracting such events as trade shows and industrial expositions, conventions, and sports.

Over 150 million people jammed an estimated 4,000 state, county, provincial, and district fairs in the U.S. and Canada. The State Fair of Texas at Dallas and the Canadian National Exhibition at Toronto continued to maintain their lead among North American fairs with attendance records of over three million visitors each. The average run of U.S. and Canadian fairs was from 3 to 5 days for county and district agricultural fairs and from 9 to 14 days for state and provincial fairs. European and most Asian and South American agricultural fairs generally operated for longer periods. Some U.S. fairs sought and received federal sanction for trade fair status, permitting foreign exhibitors to participate under a duty-free concession.

Industrial Shows. Exhibit space sales at industrial shows slipped marginally in 1972, reflecting the cancellation of a number of small shows. Meanwhile, the trend toward consolidation continued, and large shows became even larger. Prices for exhibit space remained on a par with 1968 prices, while attendance was as much as 30% above that year. Worldwide, some $15 billion was appropriated for new construction of exhibit and convention facilities in 1972. New York's long-discussed convention and exposition centre was finally launched during the year when a contract was let to an architectural firm. The proposed centre, scheduled for completion on July 4, 1976, would cost $100 million and would provide 750,000 sq.ft. of exhibit space.

Amusement Parks. Gross income from kiddielands, amusement and theme parks, aquariums, zoos, and roadside tourist attractions throughout the world was estimated at over $4.5 billion. Approximately 2,100 facilities in North America attracted 455 million visitors, who collectively spent over $1 billion. Average per capita spending at U.S. and Canadian parks was $2.75; in Europe each visitor spent slightly less; while Asian and South American facilities accounted for approximately $1.05 per capita. More than one thousand new parks opened in 1972. HemisFair Plaza, San Antonio, Tex., and Man and His World at Montreal were still suffering huge deficits. On the other hand, Walt Disney World at Orlando, Fla., announced a $50 million expansion program as attendance for the first year exceeded ten million.

Carnivals, Rodeos, and Circuses. An estimated 1,925 mobile carnivals, nearly 1,200 major independent operators, and a score of smaller units appeared at fairs and festivals in 1972 in over 80 countries. Revenues rose 11% over 1971, and most operators experienced their best season on record. The midway section at the Canadian National Exhibition grossed $2 million, an all-time record for a single event other than a world's fair. At the same time, most major U.S. and Canadian carnivals had been forced to bid for choice fairs and dates, and the percentage of the gross going to fair managements reached as much as 50%.

The International Rodeo Association won a long-fought victory during the year when an Ohio state code prohibiting the use of the flank strap on rodeo animals was ruled unconstitutional. Over 2,600 independent rodeo organizations toured some 48 U.S. states and 5 Canadian provinces in 1972, and prize money totaled a record $5 million. Rodeos failed to capture European audiences, however. Only nine European countries held rodeo shows, and most U.S. rodeos that toured European cities lost money.

Approximately 665 circuses toured the world in 1972. Most indoor shows reported better-than-usual results, with revenues averaging 15% above the previous year. Outdoor or tented circuses experienced slightly lower attendance and revenue as the cost of setup and production in big tops continued to spiral. Most circuses were becoming more like theatrical productions, with the result that greater use was made of independent circus act bookings. North America's 55 circuses performed for generally packed houses during the year. The Moscow State Circus returned to the U.S. for the third time since 1964. Ringland's Circus of Great Britain was forced to cancel its engagement in Liverpool, Eng., when hundreds of youths rampaging through the circus site smashed caravan windows, stoned tethered animals, and attempted to lower the big top. The fifth International Circus Congress met in late September at Amsterdam. Several hundred circus operators attended a symposium on the further development of the circus as a family entertainment medium.

Livestock and Horse Shows. Most of the world's 24,000 livestock shows drew capacity crowds in 1972, and stock entries reached record levels. Market sales of breed stock were the highest in history. A number of major livestock events were held in Great Britain, which boasted the oldest shows on record—the Smithfield Show, London, the 124th British Royal Show at Trumpington near Cambridge, and the 133rd Royal Highland Show at Ingliston, near Edinburgh, Scot. The International Livestock Exposition at Chicago observed its 72nd year.

Over 17,500 horse shows were held throughout the world during the year; 4,500 of them took place in the U.S. and Canada, including some 900 sponsored by the American Horse Shows Association. Many U.S. horse shows had been canceled in 1971 as a result of the severe outbreak of Venezuelan equine encephalomyelitis (VEE) in Mexico and Texas, and participation by foreign entries was substantially limited in 1972 as stricter health regulations were imposed on animal imports. (*See* VETERINARY MEDICINE.) Appaloosa and Quarter Horse shows continued to gain in popularity. (FREDERICK P. PITTERA)

ENCYCLOPÆDIA BRITANNICA FILMS. *Circus: Serrina Becomes an Acrobat* (1972).

Fashion and Dress

Fashion did an about-face in 1972, ushering in a new era of classicism. Leaving behind the costumes and gimmicks of past seasons, clothes returned to a more traditional mode of "comfort and ease first," conformable to Establishment views of wearability. The French fashion world labeled this new trend *le chic anglais,* and the Paris ready-to-wear group borrowed an English word for their best-selling autumn garment, a shortened, back-flaring coat, worn over trousers, that became *le riding coat.* If all this failed to inspire dramatic headlines, it certainly started the cash registers ringing once more. In all the top fashion capitals, the thinning ranks of couture designers played for safety first. Words such as style and elegance were reinstated, and the images of two recently departed greats, Chanel in 1971 and Balenciaga in March 1972 (*see* OBITUARIES), hovered over the fashion scene.

Hemlines were stabilized just above the knee. Thus freed from the tyranny of an erratic hemline that had turned out disastrously for the fashion industry, women searched for something more feminine than the ubiquitous pantsuit. Although still very much a basic, pants were worn with softer tops, blousons, and shirtlike or cardigan styles shirred at the waist or loosely belted. This type of outfit offered many possibilities for the still prevailing layered fad, launched in Paris the previous year by Emanuel Ungaro.

Couture designers played down the aggressiveness of the 1940s, revived in 1971 by Yves Saint Laurent. They softened shoulders and rounded lapels, but kept the idea of the separate jacket, pairing it off with a low-pleated, printed dress. The perennial spring navy and white combination was seen everywhere, especially in flannel, and the nautical influence was made explicit by the widespread use of sailor collars. Woolen materials also appeared in two-colour reversible effects, extensively used for coats with the newly dropped shoulder seam, as well as the raglan and deep, batwing armhole. Silks were printed in colourful floral, geometric, or—very popular—ceramic patterns. Flounces took over from pleating for after-five wear, appearing at the necklines, sleeves, and hemlines of silk crepe dresses with slender busts, cinched waists, and even, occasionally, fitted hips. Memories of the 1950s began to stir the fashion world; there was more than a hint of Hollywood and of Rita Hayworth in plunging necklines, strapless tops, and bare backs with halter necks.

In London the "vamp" look was developed by Mary Quant and Ossie Clark, while the English designer Jean Muir, a specialist in feminine curves and softly draped jersey dresses, made a name for herself in Paris. Following in the footsteps of his compatriot Kenzo, who had captured fashion headlines in Paris a few seasons before, another Japanese, Issey Miyake, made a good start in London with designs and materials based on Japanese tradition but with a contemporary feeling. His models were equally well received in New York and Paris.

A few whiffs of the 1940s remained in the development of shoe styles. Soles became thicker and thicker, first in wedge and then in platform shape, while heels rose to 4 and 4½ in. or more, but remained heavy. In the summer clumsy wartime clogs, in shades of green, red, yellow, blue, or pink, were popular with the young crowd. Girls matched the clogs to their skintight pants, worn with very full smocks or loose, short-sleeved white surplices, both with square necklines and with yokes, frequently in two-colour gingham checks or thick lace. With bad weather continuing through the summer, it was not unusual to see these light, flowing tops worn over wool turtleneck sweaters. Paris shop windows showed their spring displays in harmonies of Matisse-inspired pink and green, until all-white took over later on. For summer, hemlines surged upward to mid-thigh and above, reestablishing the mini dress for the junior market. The little girl look also reappeared, with short puffed sleeves and sash or bow belts.

"Kooky" and "kitsch" summer clothes were also evident in London. Here again it was the smock, worn over a striped or printed T-shirt and topping jeans

Falkland Islands: *see* Dependent States
Farming: *see* Agriculture

A.F.P./PICTORIAL PARADE

COURTESY, SAINT LAURENT RIVE GAUCHE

COURTESY, SAINT LAURENT RIVE GAUCHE

The 1972 Chanel collection included a beige shantung suit (top) with a short, fitted jacket and knee-length straight skirt. Yves Saint Laurent's Rive Gauche collection featured a camel-hair smock coat (centre) worn over a pleated tweed skirt and ribbed cardigan; and pleated baggy trousers (bottom), short suede jacket, and a rolled collar pullover.

rolled up to uncover multicoloured striped socks and the inevitable bright clogs. As in Paris, the whole outfit was adorned with a mass of pins, brooches, and beads. Jeans, of course, were patched, frayed, and faded to comply with the still prevailing "poor look." Even at Deauville, the previously rather conservative Normandy resort, faded jeans, usually topped with a tricolour striped pullover, were a basic. An alternative was the cuffed faded denim shirt worn over a pair of striped trousers. Jazzy St. Tropez went one better by adding metal studs to jeans for sparkle and as conversation pieces. Studding became quite an art, being used to form naïve flowers, stars, figures, names, and telephone numbers. Alongside the skintight jeans, the oversize blouson, the tank tops, the stripes, the gingham checks, and the clogs, however, the summer picture did include an occasional romantic touch. Immaculate white blouses with puffed and even leg-of-mutton sleeves, eyelet embroidery, and lace insets were used to create quite a different fashion mood.

In New York the Chinese influence, first evident in the fall of 1971 after Pres. Richard Nixon announced his visit to Peking, continued unabated. Replicas of the Chinese worker's blue cotton uniform appeared in the shops, while Chinese styles were reflected in most of the top designers' collections. Bill Blass, Donald Brooks, and Oscar de la Renta were foremost in developing this new fad in glittering silks, with golden buckles and frog closings. As the birthplace of jeans, the U.S. offered every type including second-hand ones dipped in Javel. The young continued the fad for "individualizing" jeans, utilizing not only studs but embroidery and appliqué as well. But *le chic anglais* was developed in New York too, with gray flannel trousers, camel-hair coats, and multicoloured sweaters. From the 1950s came a broad selection of big tops with dolman sleeves on short cropped jackets, full swirling coats, and the inevitable platform shoes.

It was sweaters that really showed the designers' imagination during 1972, and the response was enthusiastic. The persistent fad for the layered look, the chilly summer, and the classic fall styles all called for an extra sweater to brighten up the picture. The extra loose and extra long ones, gaily striped in bright Scandinavian designs, were worn with skintight trousers; the close-fitting ones with high, ribbed waistbands, such as Sonia Rykiel designed in Paris, went with straight, wide, flannel pants. After Kenzo launched wide, square-armholed kimono sleeves on sweaters, even tank-top models developed winged-shoulder effects. Necklines ranged from a high turtleneck to a V, square, or round shape cut to show the shirt collar of the blouse worn underneath. Twin sets—another '50s favourite—were important. Both cardigans and pullovers appeared in a tremendous variety of jacquard designs done in pure wool, mohair, angora, and cashmere.

In the fall there was a concerted feeling among designers that women were tired of pants, and that it was time for dresses and skirts to make a comeback. To reinstate the dress successfully it was necessary to avoid the finished-off look. With pants the look could be changed easily by switching tops, shifting from boots to platform shoes, or adding a bulky blouson or cape. But with a dress the look was definite, and many women thought it less young and less modern. Suggestions for avoiding this included shirt dresses worn unbuttoned over pants or skirts. But after battling so hard for the right to wear pants at the office, women were not ready to give them up, even if a dress did present an amusing alternative. Pants remained a refuge for warmth and practicality. Evening wear was a different matter, however. Women began looking to dresses for a new sophistication, and there was a great revival of the all-black evening look, with deep, soft armholes, plunging necklines, black fox trimming, and black draped turbans.

To avoid a "backward look," designers in London and Paris emphasized accessories and makeup to complete the total look. For daytime Jean Muir showed neat little stitched pull-on hats, and in Paris the same type of hat was adopted to finish off *le chic anglais.* Costume jewelry became more delicate and less folkloric. Ivory and wood were used for bracelets. Mobile jewels were part of the Chinese influence.

Whether British or Chinese inspired, the 1972 fashion direction was toward a more traditional silhouette with a revived taste for quality and discreetness. The aim was no longer to dazzle but rather to charm with a form of elegance really discernible only to the knowledgeable eye. As Mary Quant said: "It's alright to look rich again after everything has looked as poor and worn-out as possible."

Cosmetics and Hair Styles. In keeping with current environmental preoccupations, fresh air, fresh water, and natural products became constant leitmotivs in 1972. There was much emphasis on the quality and safety of beauty products. Estée Lauder produced a range of products utilizing a milk base: a "Pure Milk Creme Wash," a "Pure Milk Freshener," an "Iced Milk Mask," and a "Pure Milk Moisturizing Lotion," followed by a "Pure Milk Body Creme" and a "Pure Milk Hand Emulsion." Lipsticks were made to moisten and protect lips. Helena Rubinstein's "Lip Dew" came out in "Tomato" and "Carrot" to harmonize with spring's acid tones, and Charles of the Ritz produced "Sapporo," a luscious poppy red. With Indian pink back in fashion, blue-tinted reds, like Revlon's "Pretty Vivid Pink," reappeared.

The focus was on eyes even more than on lips. With spring fashion pointing to grass green for clothes, green was used for eye shadow. At least four tones were needed to acquire the desired shaded, halo effect. Eyeliner was back, always in harmony with the eye shadow—all in mother-of-pearl as in Charles Revson's "Lotus Petal Look" for "'Ultima' II," or iridescent as at Orlane. Guerlain's "Rainbow" makeup included waterproof eyeliner. Colours were eggplant, beige, deep blue, gray, bronze green, and black.

With fall's more discreet colours—camel-hair beige and black for after dark—makeup was used to avoid possible drabness and add sophistication when needed. Mary Quant and Biba both recommended dark colours, with dark green predominating for eye shadow and nail polish. Elizabeth Arden's "Darling Look" consisted of plum shading on eyelids and cranberry or "Darling Pink" on lips, set off by a powder like a pinkish mother-of-pearl cloud.

A natural look predominated in hair styles. With a shorter cut, well-brushed, glossy hair became most important. Heads were rounded, sometimes with a frothy fringe brushed on the bias, as in Alexandre's "hop" line. A round cut was also favoured by Carita, but with smooth hair tucked in at the ends and an off-centre part. Curls were only for special evening occasions. Carita named her line "Les Divines" in memory of the old-time Hollywood stars. The Hollywood influence was also apparent in hair colours—the favourites included ash blond, chestnut, and auburn.

(THELMA SWEETINBURGH)

AQUASCUTUM LTD.

The Glen Urquhart check in this suit, introduced for the fall season of 1972, made its debut over 100 years ago. The bold bow tie obviously came back, as did boldly striped shirts.

Men's Fashions. The 1972 menswear shows produced many national variations on the theme of renewed elegance, first noted the year before. Lively and colourful styles were shown at IMBEX 72 in London, subdued black and whites and grays at the International Men's Fashion Week in Cologne and the Dutch Menswear Fair in Amsterdam. The individualism of the Italians was apparent at SAMIA and Mode Selezionne in Turin, the flair of the French at SEHM in Paris, and the classic conservatism of the British at the MAB Exhibition in Harrogate.

Most countries agreed on one fabric and one colour, however. The fabric was a soft, milled flannel, usually wool or worsted but sometimes wool blended with a man-made fibre. The colour was gray. The traditional white or silver-gray chalk stripes on the gray flannel suit were missing, however, replaced by coloured stripes in blue, brown, mustard, or wine. Sometimes the stripes were broken and often they were set from seven-eighths to one inch apart instead of the conventional one-fourth inch. Single-breasted styles continued to be more popular than double-breasted.

The bow tie, long a favourite among individualists in the older age groups, became a top fashion accessory for the younger man. Traditional ties continued to be wide, though not as wide as previously. Designs tended to revert to the classic and conservative, and the big, bold designs lost some of their former popularity. A return to classic styling was also seen in knitwear, the Fair Isle and cable stitch patterns being two examples. Square neck pullovers and slipovers provided alternatives to the V-neck. The polo neck was less fashionable.

Shirts were less colourful. It appeared that white would make a comeback, but the new fashion was for white backgrounds rather than all-white shirts. Black and gray stripes on white and gray backgrounds were also in evidence.

Sports trousers for the younger man were much wider at the bottom, almost to the widths of the Oxford bags of the 1920s, and carried very deep cuffs. The ready-to-wear clothing manufacturers continued to set the pace in men's fashion, but there was a resurgence in custom tailoring. (STANLEY H. COSTIN)

See also Furs.

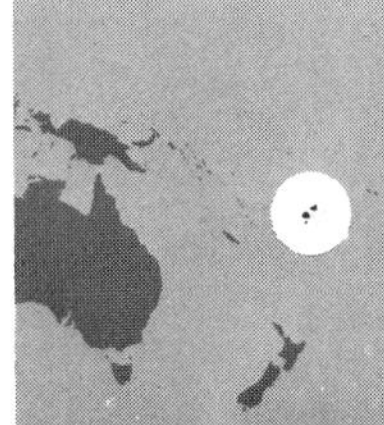

Fiji

An independent parliamentary state and member of the Commonwealth of Nations, Fiji is an island group in the South Pacific Ocean, about 2,000 mi. E of Australia and 3,200 mi. S of Hawaii. Area: 7,055 sq.mi. (18,274 sq.km.), with two major islands, Viti Levu (4,011 sq.mi.) and Vanua Levu (2,137 sq.mi.), and several hundred smaller islands. Pop. (1971 est.): 535,357. Cap. and largest city: Suva (pop., 1971 est., 63,172). Language: English, Fijian, and Hindi. Religion: Christian and Hindu. Queen, Elizabeth II; governor-general in 1972, Sir Robert Foster; prime minister, Ratu Sir Kamisese Mara.

In a quiet general election Ratu Sir Kamisese Mara and his Alliance Party retained office, winning 33 of 52 seats in the new House of Representatives. The National Federation won the remaining 19. Alliance claimed that its policy of multiracial harmony had triumphed.

The government agreed to pay the Colonial Sugar Refining Co. of Australia F$10 million for the assets of South Pacific Sugar Mills Ltd., to be taken over in 1973. The sole right to manufacture sugar would be given to the Fiji Sugar Corporation Ltd., in which the government would have the majority of shares and nominate the board of directors in consultation with the parliamentary opposition. The future of this vital industry depended on obtaining associate membership or a trading agreement with the EEC after expiration of the Commonwealth Sugar Agreement in 1974. The government decided to open a diplomatic mission in Brussels in early 1973. (MARY BOYD)

FIJI

Education. (1970) Primary, pupils 121,374, teachers 3,717; secondary, pupils 16,207, teachers 598; vocational, pupils 1,413, teachers 92; teacher training, students 702, teaching staff 34; higher (University of the South Pacific; 1969), students 430, teaching staff 52.

Finance and Trade. Monetary unit: Fiji dollar, with (Sept. 18, 1972) a free rate of F$0.86 to U.S. $1 (F$2.10 = £1 sterling). Budget (1971 est.): revenue F$44,004,000; expenditure F$45,054,000. Foreign trade (1970): imports F$90,502,000; exports F$62,307,000. Import sources: Australia 24%; U.K. 17%; Japan 15%; New Zealand 12%. Export destinations: U.K. 31%; U.S. 16%; Canada 12%; Australia 9%; New Zealand 7%. Main exports: sugar 66%; coconut products 12%; gold 7%. Tourism (1970): visitors 110,000; gross receipts U.S. $28 million.

Transport and Communications. Roads (1970) c. 2,400 km. Railways (private only; 1970) 644 km. Shipping (1971): merchant vessels 100 gross tons and over 21; gross tonnage 6,380. Ships entered (1970) vessels totaling 2,167,000 net registered tons; goods loaded (1971) 618,000 metric tons, unloaded 641,000 metric tons. Telephones (Dec. 1970) 17,000. Radio licenses (Dec. 1970) 50,000.

Agriculture. Production (in 000; metric tons; 1970; 1969 in parentheses): sweet potatoes c. 16 (c. 15); cassava c. 86 (c. 86); sugar, raw value (1971–72) c. 333, (1970–71) 361; copra 28 (34); bananas (exports) 3 (3). Livestock (in 000; Sept. 1971): cattle c. 130; pigs c. 27; horses c. 27.

Industry. Production (in 000; 1970): cement (metric tons) 60; gold (troy oz; 1969) 92; electricity (kw-hr.) 158,000.

Feed Grains: *see* Agriculture

Field Hockey: *see* Hockey

Finance, International: *see* Development, Economic; Economy, World; Money and Banking; Payments and Reserves, International

Finland

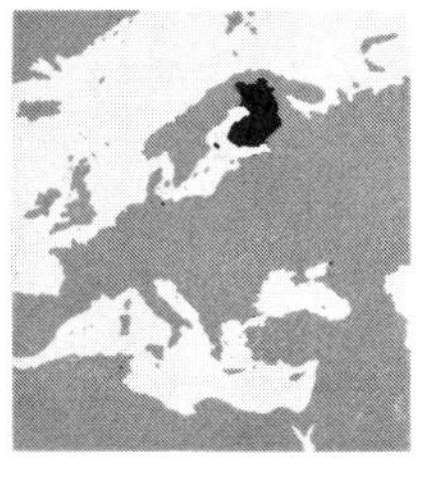

The republic of Finland is bordered on the north by Norway, on the west by Sweden and the Gulf of Bothnia, on the south by the Gulf of Finland, and on the east by the U.S.S.R. Area: 130,128 sq.mi. (337,032 sq.km.). Pop. (1971 est.): 4,633,985. Cap. and largest city: Helsinki (pop., 1971 est., 519,902). Language: Finnish, Swedish. Religion (1970): Lutheran 92.5%. President in 1972, Urho Kaleva Kekkonen; prime ministers, Teuvo Aura to February 23, Rafael Paasio to July 19, and, from September 4, Kalevi Sorsa.

Premature general elections on Jan. 2–3, 1972, did not help to solve the political difficulties that, on Oct. 29, 1971, had led to the resignation of Ahti Karjalainen's four-party coalition. The nonsocialist majority in Parliament was reduced from 113–87 to 107–93, but the slight change did not pave the way for an easy solution of the nation's economic and farming policy. The Social Democratic Party confirmed its position as the largest political group, increasing its seats in Parliament from 52 to 55. Other results (with previous representations following) were: People's Democratic League 37 (36); Centre Party 35 (36); Conservatives 34 (37); Rural Party 18 (18); Swedish Party 10 (12); Liberal Party 7 (8); and Christian League 4 (1).

General elections had originally been due for 1974, when President Kekkonen's third six-year period as head of state was to expire. His decision to hold elections in 1972 was aimed mainly at easing the deadlocked political situation, but it was also felt that two decisive political elections within 1974 would have an unsettling effect on the general atmosphere, especially if political instability prevailed. A caretaker Cabinet headed by Helsinki's mayor, Teuvo Aura, was in power for four months until Feb. 23, 1972, when Kekkonen appointed a Social Democratic minority government under party chairman Rafael Paasio—the only political solution left after other efforts had failed.

An important one-year wage agreement was reached at the end of March between the Finnish Employers' Confederation (STK) and the Confederation of Finnish Trade Unions (SAK). It was approved by the SAK board by the Social Democratic majority of 14 to the People's Democratic League's 8 votes—the latter had demanded increases higher than the agreement's average of more than 7%. A series of unofficial strikes, arranged by the Communists, had troubled especially the metal industry during the winter months.

Paasio's minority Cabinet resigned on July 19, both because of difficulties in carrying out its economic policy and because the Cabinet and Kekkonen felt that a free trade agreement between Finland and the European Economic Community should be approved by a majority government. On July 22 at Brussels, Finland initialed an agreement with the EEC. The text stated that customs duties on industrial goods would progressively be abolished during a four-and-a-half year period, whereas the abolition of duties affecting Finland's important paper exports would cover 11 years. Talks were opened in the fall with Comecon, concerning technical cooperation, including the exchange of statistics and information on standardization, traffic, and monetary policy.

The second political Cabinet of the year, similar to Karjalainen's four-party coalition, was formed on September 4. The new prime minister was the Social Democratic Party secretary, Kalevi Sorsa, 42, who had been foreign minister in Paasio's Cabinet. Besides seven Social Democrats, the Cabinet included five representatives of the Centre Party, two of the Swedish Party, one of the Liberal Party, and one nonpolitical minister.

On September 6 the government initialed for ratification an agreement between Finland and East Germany on diplomatic relations, once again announcing its intention to give equal treatment to the two Germanys. Official recognition was extended to both East and West Germany on November 24, although there was no indication as to when representatives would be exchanged. Between March 28 and May 26, U.S. and Soviet delegates met in Helsinki to work out the first agreement on strategic arms limitation. In late November representatives of 32 European countries, the U.S., and Canada assembled in Helsinki for talks in preparation for a European security conference, expected to begin some time in 1973.

President Kekkonen met twice in 1972 with Soviet leaders to discuss a wide range of bilateral and international questions. As a result of these talks an agreement was signed facilitating the sale of Finland's surplus grain and butter to the Soviet Union. On December 14, Kekkonen announced that he would not run for reelection.

In the field of sport Finland once again won recognition as a nation of long-distance runners when Lasse Viren (*see* BIOGRAPHY) won gold medals for the 5,000-m. and 10,000-m. races at the Olympic Games at Munich, W.Ger. (CARL FREDRIK SANDELIN)

FINLAND

Education. (1969–70) Primary, pupils 393,942, teachers (full-time) 17,752; secondary, pupils 396,067, teachers 21,110; vocational, pupils 99,808, teachers 9,841; teacher training, students 1,660, teachers 391; higher (including 9 universities), students 58,444, teaching staff 5,695.

Finance. Monetary unit: markka, with (Sept. 18, 1972) a par value of 4.10 markkaa to U.S. $1 (free rate of 10.11 markkaa = £1 sterling). Gold, SDRs, and foreign exchange, central bank: (June 1972) U.S. $735.3 million; (June 1971) U.S. $462.3 million. Budget (1972 est.) balanced at 12,683,000,000 markkaa. Gross national product: (1970) 42,850,000,000 markkaa; (1969) 38,420,000,000 markkaa. Money supply: (April 1972) 4,581,000,000 markkaa; (April 1971) 3,817,000,000 markkaa. Cost of living (1963 = 100): (June 1972) 165; (June 1971) 154.

Foreign Trade. (1971) Imports 11,739,000,000 markkaa; exports 9,897,000,000 markkaa. Import sources: Sweden 17%; West Germany 16%; U.S.S.R. 14%; U.K. 14%; U.S. 5%. Export destinations: U.K. 19%; Sweden 16%; U.S.S.R. 11%; West Germany 10%; U.S. 5%. Main exports: paper 29%; timber 16%; wood pulp 10%.

Transport and Communications. Roads (1971) 72,666 km. (including 121 km. expressways). Motor vehicles in use (1971): passenger 752,915; commercial 118,895. Railways (1970): 5,870 km.; traffic 2,156,000,000 passenger-km., freight (1971) 5,759,000,000 net ton-km. Air traffic (1971): 754.9 million passenger-km.; freight 26,093,000 net ton-km. Navigable inland waterways (1970) 6,674 km. Shipping (1971): merchant vessels 100 gross tons and over 390; gross tonnage 1,470,825. Telephones (Dec. 1970) 1,181,000. Radio licenses (Dec. 1970) 1,759,000. Television licenses (Dec. 1970) 1,036,000.

Agriculture. Production (in 000; metric tons; 1971; 1970 in parentheses): wheat 443 (409); rye 132 (131); barley 1,054 (933); oats 1,424 (1,330); potatoes 803 (1,136); sugar, raw value (1971–72) 65, (1970–71) 60; butter *c.* 91 (87); timber (cu.m.; 1970) 45,000, (1969) 44,200; fish catch (1969) 87, (1968) 93. Livestock (in 000; June 1971): cattle 1,865; sheep 175; pigs 1,129; horses 73; chickens 8,410.

Industry. Production (in 000; metric tons; 1971): iron ore (66% metal content) 744; pig iron 1,030; crude steel 1,042; copper 32; cement 1,811; plywood (cu.m.; 1970) 701; cellulose (1970) 4,187; mechanical wood pulp (1970) 1,960; chemical wood pulp (1970) 4,511; newsprint 1,364; other paper and board (1970) 2,955; electricity (kw-hr.) 23,454,000; manufactured gas (cu.m.) 51,000.

LONDON DAILY EXPRESS/ PICTORIAL PARADE

A profound and dramatic protest against liberal abortion laws is held in Helsinki. Fifty protesters participated, each carrying an infant's coffin to represent the number of fetuses legally aborted in one day.

Fisheries

Disputes over territorial fishing limits dominated events in 1972. For some years South American nations had been claiming exclusive fishing rights up to 200 mi. The U.S. shrimp fleet had been harassed when it failed to observe these limits, but the effect was limited. In 1972, however, the fever began to spread, with Iceland claiming a 50-mi. limit that virtually encompassed its continental shelf, Senegal claiming 110 mi., and several other nations carefully observing with an eye toward possible moves of their own. The root cause of these moves lay in the greatly increased mobility of the world's big fishing fleets. No area was safe from the far-ranging European vessels, seeking new fishing grounds as old ones became depleted. Alarm over decreasing stocks was mounting, and control of catches was accepted as an eventual necessity.

It was the nature of the control that was at issue. Wide-ranging nations such as the U.S.S.R., West and East Germany, the U.K., Poland, and Spain supported the concept of international control by quota, based on past catches and favouring those nations whose own fish resources were inadequate for their needs. Nations having well-stocked continental shelves wanted to conserve what was on their doorstep. Iceland, with an economy 80% dependent on home-caught fish, was a prime example. It ignored an interim ruling by the International Court of Justice permitting foreign trawlers to fish Icelandic waters. It could equally well ignore any ruling of the UN Law of the Sea Conference, scheduled for Stockholm in 1973. In the fall of 1972, British and West German trawlers entering Iceland's 50-mi. limit were threatened by armed patrol boats. (*See* ICELAND.) If

Fires: *see* Disasters; Insurance

Table I. World Fisheries, 1970*

Country	Catch in 000 metric tons	Value in U.S. $000
Peru	12,612.8	187,210
Japan	9,308.5	2,357,672†
U.S.S.R.	7,252.2	...
Norway	2,980.2	196,770
United States	2,714.3	496,861‡
India	1,745.9	341,333
Thailand	1,595.1	218,619
South Africa	1,519.4	...
Spain	1,496.6	378,013
Canada	1,377.5	186,434
Indonesia	1,249.0	...
Denmark	1,226.5	113,993
Chile	1,161.0	27,386§
United Kingdom	1,099.0	187,961
Philippines	989.8	433,926
Korea, South	933.6	210,556
France	775.2	286,665
Iceland	733.8	...
Taiwan	613.0	178,860
Germany, West	612.9	106,234
Vietnam, South	577.4	122,238‖
Brazil†	493.0	98,195
Poland	469.3	...
Portugal†	457.0	74,037
Burma	432.4	87,470
Pakistan	420.0	238,299
Italy	403.4	231,653
Angola	368.4	8,387
Malaysia	364.9	93,891
Mexico†	353.2	75,264
Germany, East	321.8	...
Netherlands	300.7	77,545
Sweden	293.7	46,516
Morocco	256.0	17,587
Argentina	214.8	20,232
Faeroe Islands	207.8	...
Tanzania	195.0	15,702
Senegal	189.2	32,181
Ghana	187.1	35,271
Turkey	178.0†	...
Nigeria	155.8	...
Uganda	129.0	19,460

Some double counting may occur.
China, North Korea, and North Vietnam are all estimated to have a catch of more than 300,000 tons a year.
*Excludes whaling.
†1969. ‡1968. §1967. ‖1966.
Source: United Nations Food and Agriculture Organization, *Yearbook of Fishery Statistics*, vol. 30.

the limit was enforced, the U.K.'s distant-water catch could be cut by 40%.

If countries continued to claim territorial limits as they saw fit, the effect on world fishing economics could be disastrous. Billions of dollars had been invested in fleets dependent on fishing grounds that could be closed at short notice. Under the circumstances, it was not surprising that the building of big distant-water trawlers by the North Atlantic nations was restrained. Norway had already stopped building big herring purse seiners and restricted the tonnage of new trawlers. West Germany's industry was at low ebb, although some replacement tonnage was commissioned. The U.K. did order 18 big stern trawlers, reflecting confidence after a profitable year.

Another exception was Iceland. Confident of its limits claim, it was reportedly placing orders for a number of big stern trawlers, presumably to harvest a bigger share of the cod, haddock, and plaice that Iceland was so successfully selling to the U.S. The annual catch in 1971 was 500,000 tons of bottom fish. Greenland ordered the first of 16 or 20 stern trawlers of 750 tons, raising fears that it too planned to extend its limits.

Table II. Whaling: 1970-71 Season

Area and country	Fin whale	Humpback whale	Sei whale	Sperm whale	Others	Percentage assigned under quota agreement*
	Number of whales caught					
Antarctic: pelagic (open sea)						
Japan	1,607	...	4,137	192	...	55
Norway	...	...	...	...	...	9
U.S.S.R.	1,283	...	2,016	2,863	...	36
Total	2,890	...	6,153	3,055	...	...
Outside the Antarctic†	2,055	15	5,194	22,740	301	...

*Antarctic only.
†1969–70.
Source: Committee for Whaling Statistics, *International Whaling Statistics*.

In the Southern Hemisphere the mood was one of expansion, founded on the knowledge that fish and shellfish stocks were, in many cases, underexploited. Investment continued in the Pacific, as well as in India and Pakistan where major industries began to be involved. Big U.S. corporations seeking to diversify showed an understandable interest in fish and shrimp farming. The 1971 U.S. catch decreased, with the exception of tuna, and no great investment in trawling tonnage was apparent in 1972. Peru was heavily hit by a shortage of anchoveta, the result of El Niño, the ocean current that periodically disturbs the fish-laden Humboldt Current.

New, tougher whaling quotas were established to divert effort to the less profitable but more plentiful types. The U.S. ban on the import of whale products may well have been the beginning of the end for whaling, although it may have come too late to save some species from extinction. (H. S. NOEL)

See also Environment.

Food

Supplies. Food supplies for the world's growing population in 1971–72 increased somewhat over those of a year earlier, with a 4% growth in food production in 1971 and further gains reported throughout the first half of 1972. The United Nations Food and Agriculture Organization (FAO) estimated food production at an index of 161 (1952–56 = 100), compared with 154 in 1970. Further indications of improvement were seen in early 1972 reports of a record harvest of 240 million metric tons of grain in China, not included in the FAO's estimates.

While reports of food gains in 1971–72 were encouraging, their effect was reduced by rapid population growth. The FAO estimated that world population in 1971 increased more than 2%, a factor that effectively reduced gains in per capita food supplies to only about 1.7% over 1970. Even this modest gain, which reflected a worldwide food-population balance, was further depressed when regional disparities in food production and population growth were considered. On a per capita basis, all of the gains in food production in 1971 were made in the developed regions of the world—those nations lying largely in the Northern Hemisphere, plus Oceania and some scattered exceptions. In the so-called less developed regions, comprising mainly Latin America, Africa, and the Middle and Far East, per capita food production declined from an index of 107 in 1970 to 106. Furthermore, these gross estimates considered only the availability of food supplies. Distribution failures, as well as political and economic disruptions, continued to inconvenience, if not threaten, the lives of people in several regions in 1972. With fair regularity throughout most of 1972, reports of food shortages, famine, and even starvation assaulted the senses of generally well-fed people in the developed nations.

A critical food shortage in the new nation of Bangladesh early in 1972 was relieved to some extent by shipments of food grains from India, the U.S., and the UN. Following two rainless years in the central and western provinces of Afghanistan, widespread

KEYSTONE

Muslim farmers tearfully pray for an end to the severe drought that caused the loss of seven million tons of crops in India.

famine and starvation of an untold number of people were reported; one official estimated that half the country's sheep had been slaughtered. Flooding caused by Typhoon Rita resulted in food riots on Luzon Island in the Philippines in July. A prolonged drought in 13 of India's 21 states delayed the sowing of new crops in July, resulting in deaths from malnutrition-related diseases. A sharp debate in India's Parliament was followed by the government's announcement of relief measures, which included distribution from its 10 million-ton stock of wheat to check rising prices.

At the request of UN Secretary-General Kurt Waldheim, the U.S. agreed in July to donate $4,450,000 in food and aid to refugees of the civil war in Sudan. Early in September, Premier Lon Nol of Cambodia appealed to the U.S. to airlift rice supplies into Phnom Penh to alleviate a critical food shortage resulting from military operations, which was causing food riots and the looting of food stores. In South America, Uruguay, Chile, and Argentina enforced intermittent and highly unpopular bans on the sale and consumption of beef, mainly to increase supplies for export. Although rationing was not officially in force in Chile, food shortages produced de facto rationing, and Pres. Salvador Allende's "Message to the People," in early October, announced an "economic politics of wartime," which carried a strong hint of food rationing. In the Soviet Union poor weather reduced the wheat and potato harvests, creating bread shortages and exhortations to consumers to economize; it also accounted for unprecedented purchases of wheat and feed grains from the U.S.

Production. The 4% gain in food production reported by the FAO for 1971 could be credited, in large measure, to the output of an estimated 1,313,700,000 metric tons of food grains, a 7% gain over 1970. Most of the increase, which amounted to 104.1 million tons, was reported from the developed regions, where production rose 88.8 million tons from a year earlier. Grain production in North America rose 60.9 million tons above the 215.1 million tons produced in 1970, and production in Western Europe increased 19.5 million tons.

Among the less developed regions, increases in grain production in 1971 were far more modest. Latin America's grain crops rose 1.5 million metric tons above the 70.1 million tons reported in 1970; in the Middle Eastern countries, a 3.7 million-ton increase pushed grain production to 43 million tons; a 6.1 million-ton increase reported for African countries raised grain production to 55.7 million tons; and among countries in the Far East grain production fell about 1 million tons from 1970, to 251.7 million tons.

World sugar production in 1971 was reported at 74.6 million metric tons, about equal to a year earlier; a gain of about 2.1 million metric tons in the developed regions (mainly Western Europe) was offset by an almost equal decline in the less developed regions, particularly Latin America. Production of root crops—potatoes, sweet potatoes, yams, and cassava—declined to an estimated 536.9 million metric tons, approximately 13.4 million tons less than in 1970 and accounted for by reduced production in Eastern and Western Europe; slight gains were reported for Latin America and Africa. Production of 112 million metric tons of oilseeds in 1971 was 3% more than a year earlier.

World production of all meats totaled an estimated 100.5 million metric tons in 1971, an increase of 3% over a year earlier. About two-thirds of this production was accounted for by countries in the developed regions, where production rose 5% above 1970; in the less developed regions, slight increases in meat production in the Far East and in Africa were offset by a decline of nearly 6% in Latin America. Three-fourths of the total world production of 403.5 million metric tons of milk was produced in the developed countries in 1971. World milk production increased less than 1% in 1971 from a year earlier.

Indications of further improvements in food production were reported as a result of near-record harvests in Canada and the U.S. in 1972, though heavy rains late in the year were expected to reduce the U.S. crop. Generally good production in the northern portions of South America offset continued reverses in Chile and Argentina. Production of grains and other food crops in Western Europe in 1972 appeared to be near the record levels achieved a year earlier. Large wheat and feed-grain harvests in Eastern European countries in 1972 were offset by a sharp reduction in

Floods:
see Disasters; Engineering Projects

the U.S.S.R., where adverse weather reduced harvests by as much as 25% from a year earlier, requiring heavy imports from the U.S.

In Africa food production in 1972 continued to improve throughout much of the continent; overall growth of about 4% exceeded gains of previous years, as improved crops in Egypt, Nigeria, and South Africa offset generally poor harvests in the East African nations. Countries in the Middle East and the Indian subcontinent experienced generally favourable conditions in 1972, although production in Pakistan declined and a continuing severe drought in Afghanistan produced famine conditions. Elsewhere in the Orient, rice production declined in Japan, the Philippines, and Cambodia. Australia's 1971–72 wheat crop was nearly 10% above a year earlier.

Consumption, Expenditures, and Prices. Food consumption in the U.S. in 1972 was expected to decline slightly from the record levels of 1971, largely as a result of a slight reduction in red meat supplies and an indicated reduction in the availability of fresh fruits. Consumption of all foods in 1972 was reported by the U.S. Department of Agriculture (USDA) on a preliminary basis at an index of 103 (1967 = 100), compared with 103.5 in 1971. The 1972 index exceeded that of every year since 1960, with the exception of 1971.

Consumption of red meat in the U.S. in 1972 was expected to decline 1% from the 191.8 lb. per person record reported for 1971; pork consumption in 1972 was expected to decline 5 lb. from the 73 lb. per capita used in 1971; and further declines of 3 and 9%, respectively, were expected in per capita consumption of lamb and veal. Offsetting reduced per capita consumption of red meats, a new high was expected for use of chicken and turkey in 1972; rates of consumption in the first half of the year indicated that per-person consumption of chicken would increase 4% above the 41.4 lb. for 1971, and consumption of turkey would increase 5% above 8.5 lb. for 1971.

Per-person use of eggs in the U.S. in 1972 was indicated at 1% less than the 322 reported for 1971. A slight increase was expected to raise per capita consumption of fish in 1972 to about 11.3 lb. Fluid milk consumption in 1972 was indicated at 2% less than the 259 lb. per capita of 1971, while cheese consumption, reflecting a sharp increase in production, was expected to increase 5% above the 12.2 lb. per capita used in 1971. Per capita use of fats and oils in 1972 was expected to about equal the 52 lb. reported for 1971; consumption of butter was expected to decline 4% below the 5.1 lb. used in 1971, while the use of margarine would increase 1%, to an average of 11.1 lb. per person.

There were indications that per capita consumption of fresh and processed fruits in 1972 would decline 2 and 3%, respectively, from 1971 levels; generally poor conditions for deciduous fruit production were credited. Consumption of commercial fresh vegetables was expected to reach an all-time low in 1972; per capita use was indicated at 2% less than the 98.7 lb. reported in 1971. However, it appeared that the use of processed vegetables would increase, with canned vegetables expected to remain at the 51.2 lb. per capita reported for 1971 and frozen vegetables increasing 3% above the 9.7 lb. used in 1971. Per capita consumption of potatoes was expected to decline about 2% from the 121 lb. reported for 1971.

The USDA's midyear preliminary estimate of total food expenditures by U.S. consumers in 1972 was $123 billion, about 5% more than the $117.3 billion spent in 1971. Spending for food in the second quarter rose 2.2% above the first quarter, the most rapid pace in two years, but the USDA noted that the increase in food expenditures was far less than the 8% rise in total personal consumption expenditures that had taken place in the previous year. For the first half of 1972, expenditures for all food were estimated at 15.7% of disposable personal income, compared with 15.8% for 1971 and 20% for 1960.

Retail food prices in the U.S. at midyear 1972 were reported by the Department of Labor at an index of 122.6 (1967 = 100), an increase of 3.5% from a year earlier. The increase in food prices compared with a 3.2% increase in the retail prices for all goods and services, and a 3% increase for all items other than food. By mid-1972 the Department of Agriculture's report of retail food prices indicated increases from a year earlier of 9.1% for meat; 1.8% for sugar, fruits, vegetables, and dairy products; 2.1% for fats and oils; and 0.5% for cereal and bakery products. No change was reported in the retail price of poultry, and the retail price of eggs was reported to be 5.1% below mid-1971.

Increases in retail food prices in 1972 fueled lively debate throughout most of the year among a wide range of spokesmen for consumers and retailers, as well as politicians and public officials, almost all of whom, at one point or another, blamed farmers, retailers, public officials, and even a lack of understanding on the part of consumers. Early in the debate, two major retail food chains took full-page advertisements urging housewives to buy meat substitutes, serve meatless meals, and forgo purchases of red meats until retail prices fell. This untypical advice was sharply criticized by the American National Cattlemen's Association, several farm-state representatives, and Secretary of Agriculture Earl Butz. Secretary Butz's statement in March that higher meat prices were "the best way to insure a good supply of the better cuts of beef that I prefer" was in turn criticized by Price Commission Chairman C. Jackson Grayson, Jr., as "damaging to the stabilization program."

By early June reports that foodstore chains were

Angered by soaring food prices, residents of Stockholm stage a protest march on Feb. 26, 1972.

WIDE WORLD

contemplating new price increases coincided with further action by the Price Commission, which included recommendations to the Cost of Living Council to extend controls to raw agricultural products and to abandon meat import quotas. On June 26 U.S. Pres. Richard Nixon ordered the removal of restrictions on meat imports for the balance of the year; although the action permitted increased shipments of beef and lamb to the U.S., officials acknowledged that it might not have a very immediate effect on retail meat prices, because of both the time lag involved in importing additional supplies and the fact that most imported meat was of such a grade as to make it only marginally competitive with domestic production. Nixon also stated that he intended to monitor the food price situation very closely and that he would take further measures as they appeared necessary and appropriate.

As the summer wore on without discernible slackening in food price increases, the debate resumed its vigour. Early in September, Cost of Living Council Director Donald Rumsfeld, citing August data that revealed a 37-cent margin between the carcass price of beef and retail prices, sent a telegram to approximately 100 leading food retailers telling them retail beef prices were still too high and notifying them he had ordered the Internal Revenue Service to monitor their profit margins.

Early in September the government announced that it would not allow the request of the baking industry to increase by one cent per loaf the price of bread. The Price Commission, in its denial, cited stabilization rules that did not permit increases when profit margins of the companies involved exceeded certain historical levels. By late September few if any signs convinced consumers that the retail price spiral was abating. A report by the USDA was interpreted to show that food processors and retailers had widened the gap between farmers' and consumers' prices of beef to a record margin in August, thus failing to pass along to consumers recent declines in cattle prices. The USDA also reported that shortages of fresh produce, resulting from Tropical Storm Agnes, caused sharp increases in summer farm prices for fruits and vegetables; it was only the second time in 35 years that August produce prices had not fallen below those for June.

Discontent with rising food prices in 1972 was not limited to the U.S. Consumers in almost every European as well as some non-Western countries found it more and more difficult to accept higher prices of meat and produce, as inflation rates of 8% in the Netherlands, 6.3% in the U.K., 5.4% in France, 5.1% in West Germany, and 4.5% in Japan reduced purchasing power. In August retail prices of beef in Paris were reported to be 40% more than a year earlier. Protesting a 17% increase in food prices attributed to a new farm policy, Swedish housewives in February organized a widespread boycott, with beef and milk as first targets. Late in August many retail food outlets closed in protest against a government order freezing food prices in Rome. The decree, a reaction to a 6% increase in food prices over a three-month period, was conceived as a 60-day experiment preliminary to a nationwide policy regulating both prices and wages.

Assistance. Food assistance programs in the U.S. reached a total of nearly 15 million Americans in May 1972, according to a report by the USDA. Of this number, 11.8 million persons in low-income families participated in the Food Stamp Program, a new record for participation and 1,366,000 more than a year earlier. An additional 3,125,000 family members received benefits from the Food Distribution Program, a decline from 3,735,405 a year earlier. Participation in the National School Lunch Program was reported to be 24,474,000 children, compared with 24,526,733 a year earlier; of the schoolchildren eating lunch prepared at schools receiving federal assistance under the program, 8,118,000 received free or reduced-price lunches, an increase from 7,215,129 a year earlier.

Total federal cost of all food programs in the year ended June 30, 1972, was $3,267,000,000, an increase of nearly 18% over a year earlier. Of this amount, federal costs of food stamps valued at about $5 billion was $1,803,000,000, an increase from $1,522,000,000 a year earlier. Food distribution programs in fiscal 1972 cost the federal government about $619 million, a decline from $634 million; in 1971 food distribution under this program included 231.6 million lb. of beef and pork; 127.8 million lb. of poultry; 466.2 million lb. of dairy products; 316.7 million lb. of fruits; 231.2 million lb. of vegetables; and 778 million lb. of cereal products, for a total of 2,412,500,000 lb. of food, or 1.1% of total U.S. food consumption. Child nutrition programs, which included the National School Lunch Program and the School Breakfast Program, along with special food and milk programs, totaled $845 million in federal costs, compared with $635 million a year earlier.

The USDA's administration of all these programs was criticized by various consumer groups as well as by a congressional committee. A report by the Select Committee on Nutrition and Human Needs of the U.S. Senate in June, reacting to information that the department would be returning about $400 million to the U.S. Treasury out of funds appropriated for the Food Stamp Program, charged that policies of the department "have resulted in funds going unused in every food assistance program." The report also charged that the department had pursued policies limiting participation in the programs beyond the intent of the Congress.

The administration of the Food Stamp Program came in for sharp criticism in late 1971 and early 1972 when the USDA proposed new regulations that, in effect, would have made an additional 1.7 million persons eligible for benefits, while reducing benefits for 2 million and eliminating altogether the eligibility of 60,000 to 75,000 other recipients, most of them elderly citizens. After protests from many senators and governors, Secretary of Agriculture Butz announced on January 16 that he had ordered actions to preserve the eligibility of participants in the program, while at the same time conforming to the government's overall income strategy by establishing uniform national eligibility standards, ensuring every family sufficient assistance to provide nutritionally adequate diets costing no more than 30% of the recipient's income and free food stamps to those with the least income.

The World Food Program, a joint enterprise of the UN and the FAO, reported that pledges made for the 1973–74 program represented an increase over a year earlier. Canada pledged $34 million; Denmark, $23 million; the Netherlands, $16 million; Sweden, $14 million; and Norway, $8.2 million. All of these were substantial increases over a year earlier. The report noted that the U.S., which until the end of 1972 had contributed up to half of the food commodities used in the program, had reduced its overall percentage commitment to 40% of the program's $300 million goal; even so, the U.S. 1973–74 pledge was nearly 9% more than its 1971–72 contribution of $125 million.

Manufacturing and Marketing. Profit margins of U.S. food manufacturers and processors in 1971 were reported by the USDA to be slightly higher than a year earlier. Profits as a percentage of the combined sales of dairy processors, bakeries, and meat-packers were reported at 2.4%, an increase from 2.3% a year earlier. Profit margins of dairy processors and bakeries were 2.3% of sales, compared with 2.1% for dairy processors and 1.9% for bakeries in 1970; meat-packers' profits were estimated at 1.3%, compared with 0.9% in 1970. By mid-1972 scattered reports of earnings of large food manufacturers indicated record earnings, in particular from diversified sectors that included a wide variety of nonfood enterprises. One midyear report indicated a varied outlook among more than 5,000 food manufacturers, but margins were controlled by Price Commission rules that limited gross profits to an average of their highest two out of the previous three fiscal years. A report of first-quarter earnings by 45 of the largest food manufacturers indicated an increase of 12% in sales over a year earlier, and profits showed a 4% improvement.

Diversification continued, in most cases, to widen profit margins, although the nation's largest food manufacturer disclosed in January that it had lost $83 million over a three-year period, mostly on a fast-food chain it had acquired in 1968. A report to the Congress by the General Accounting Office in April estimated that "serious potential or actual food adulteration" existed in 1,000 of 4,550 food manufacturing plants in 21 states, and that unsanitary conditions existed in an additional 800 plants. The estimate was based on a sample of 97 plants, and findings included the presence of rodent excreta and other foreign matter, improper use of pesticides, and use of unsanitary equipment.

The Federal Trade Commission (FTC) brought a suit against four of the largest manufacturers of ready-to-eat breakfast cereals early in the year. The four companies, which shared 90% of the industry with annual sales of $650 million, were charged with violating the section of the Federal Trade Commission Act prohibiting unfair and deceptive trade practices, including the restraint of competition. The FTC complained that the market structure of the industry had resulted in the maintenance of a noncompetitive market in which the companies had achieved a shared monopoly. The FTC proposed breaking up the alleged monopoly in the industry by ordering divestiture of some facilities to allow new and competitive industries to enter the market. In August the Department of Agriculture ordered that nitrates and nitrites used in cured meats, such as bacon, ham, and frankfurters, be listed on the retail package beginning early in 1973. (*See* below.)

Profits of retail food stores in the U.S. declined in 1971. A report by the USDA indicated that profit ratios—after federal income taxes—of 15 of the largest retail chains declined to 0.9% of sales in 1971 from 1.1% a year earlier. Food retailers were affected throughout much of the year by a severe price war, which began with a policy of price discounting and moved to the scrapping of retail promotion "frills" such as trading stamps and games. (*See* MERCHANDISING.)

One industry report indicated that net earnings for food retailers in fiscal 1972 fell to an all-time low of 0.82% of sales, a 5% decline from a year earlier and 37% less than in 1966. At the same time, food retailers' payroll expenses rose to an all-time high of 11.4%, an increase of 5% from 1971.

In the U.K. controversy developed over the introduction of the hypermarket, by most common definition a retail store with at least 25,000 sq.ft. of selling area, as opposed to the supermarket, with around 10,000 sq.ft. A report, *Superstores in the 70s,* proposed the introduction of such stores in Britain for the benefit of consumers. By mid-1971, West Germany had 368 hypermarkets, France had 128, and Belgium had 34. As of 1972 there was only one in the U.K., largely because of difficulties they would pose to planning authorities and the present state of British retailing, both of which were said to be oriented to the development of town centres. Because of automobile parking requirements, a hypermarket needed to be located outside of town and thus its introduction threatened efforts by local authorities to develop town centres and to preserve the environment of the countryside. By early 1972 introduction of fast-food retail outlets in Australia was proceeding at a rapid pace. Providing the impetus was the record of one U.S. chain (Kentucky Fried Chicken), which over a three-year period had come to dominate the market with almost 100 retail outlets. (HARVEY R. SHERMAN)

Processing and Technology. Food technologists were increasingly preoccupied with various environmental problems. These included the effect of nurture on the composition and nutritional quality of vegetable and animal products and its bearing on human health; disposal of food processing wastes and by-products; contamination of the environment by foodstuffs packagings; and the effect of air, water, and soil contamination by industrial and agrochemicals on the quality and safety of foodstuffs.

In view of nitrate accumulations in some vegetables, further attention was given to the problem of excessive treatment of some vegetable crops with nitrate-containing fertilizers. Such vegetables may be hazardous when used for infant feeding, and nitrates may cause excessive tinplate corrosion in canned foods. Some plants and marine organisms accumulate high concentrations of toxic metals or radionucleotides which are present in only minute amounts in the environment. In this connection Japanese scientists discovered that the comfrey plant has an outstanding capacity to absorb cadmium from the soil, and so it was proposed that it might be used to cleanse soil of this metal. A Japanese fisheries experiment station introduced robot buoys anchored offshore to transmit early warnings of marine pollution.

A considerable quantity of poultry in Britain was condemned because of a "musty" taint in the meat. This resulted from the use of wood shavings treated with a chlorophenol preservative since it was established that certain fungi convert chlorophenols into chloroanisoles, which have a strong musty odour at concentrations of four parts per billion. U.S. space scientists estimated that about 50% of the methane present in the upper atmosphere was attributable to the belching of ruminants, and Scottish scientists established that 6–10% of the food energy of such animals is converted to methane, representing a loss amounting to £90 million a year in Britain alone. It was found that long-chain fatty acids or a trace of chloroform included in the feed substantially reduced methane production.

The USDA and the British Agricultural Research Council instituted research programs into the effect of feeding regimens on the nutritional value of meat, especially the ratio of fat to lean and the composition of the fat. Australian workers succeeded in modifying the composition of milk fat and also the body fat of cattle and sheep by feeding protected polyunsaturated fats. Commercial production of this feed was subsequently licensed.

Many food manufacturers faced high, nonrecoverable operating costs in the treatment of wastes as a result of legislation introduced in various countries to protect rivers and oceans from pollution. However, some notable advances were made in turning such wastes to profit or at least to recovering the cost of treatment. A Norwegian organization found that a by-product (lignosulfonate) of the papermaking industry could be used to recover valuable proteins and fats from meat factory effluents. The need to reduce the quantity of waste water in the peeling of various vegetables and fruits led to the development of a new dry-peeling technique that reduced waste to a minimum and helped retain some nutrients.

A Swedish company developed a process for the fermentation of starch processing wastes resulting in the production of valuable single-cell protein for feed use. Many other processes were developed for the fermentation of food wastes, utilizing fungi, yeasts, and bacteria. A British company developed such a process using fungi for the fermentation of many types of carbohydrate wastes and established an organization to assist processors internationally. Great strides were made in the technical applications of ultrafiltration and reverse osmosis, especially for recovering protein and lactose in the treatment of cheese whey. Several cheese factories in the U.S., Europe, and New Zealand introduced this method of treatment.

Widespread contamination of the environment with polychlorinated biphenyls (PCBs), used in electrical heating equipment, caused much contamination of foodstuffs in many countries and led to the condemnation of eggs and poultry in the U.S. Environmental pollution from food packaging materials led to angry demonstrations in a number of countries; both Britain and the U.S. allocated funds for research on biodegradability. Progress was made in the development of edible films and coatings, especially in the U.S. and Japan.

The formation of traces of potentially cancer-producing compounds (nitrosamines) from nitrates and nitrites used in the curing of meat and fish products received much attention. Both the U.S. and British governments established monitoring facilities to ascertain the levels present in retail samples, but preliminary reports were reassuring. A British research institute developed and patented an improved curing process requiring less nitrite.

The effect of global pollution on the quality and safety of food and water supplies was the subject of international conferences in Berlin and Stockholm. Worldwide monitoring of the oceans and food supplies was instituted for mercury, lead, cadmium, PCBs, and other organochlorine compounds, of which about 75,000 tons were dumped annually into the Atlantic Ocean. In the U.S. substantial quantities of tuna, swordfish, and cheese were condemned because of contamination. The enormous rains of Tropical Storm Agnes in June diluted the salt content of Chesapeake Bay to such an extent that thousands of oysters, clams, and crabs were killed. In September a "red tide," an infestation of poisonous algae, struck the New England coast. Bans on the harvesting of clams, scallops, and mussels were instituted by the affected states. By the year's end these had been gradually lifted.

FLETCHER DRAKE

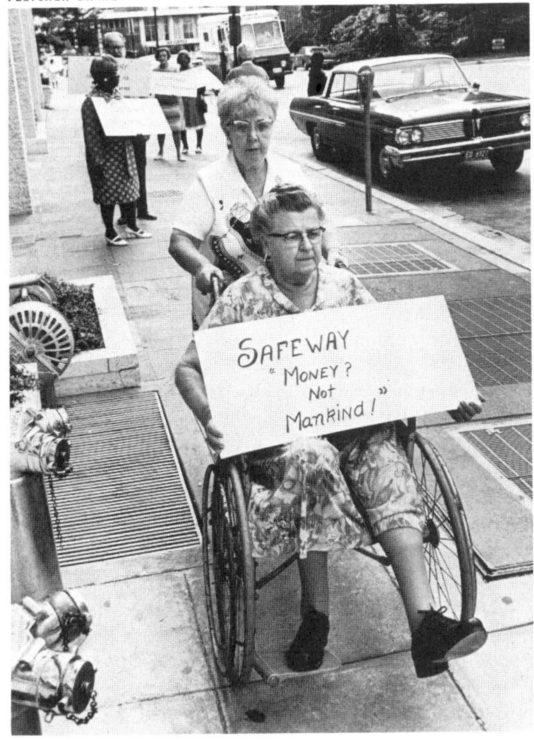

Older citizens protest the closing of a neighbourhood grocery store in Silver Spring, Md., in September 1972.

The need for more protein in many parts of the world continued to receive widespread attention. An enzymatic hydrolysate of fish protein to supplement cereals was developed in Chile; a French government institute and a Swedish company developed completely new processes for the isolation of rapeseed protein; the International Rice Research Institute reported progress in the development of rice strains of improved protein content and quality; the preparation of blue cheese from soy protein was reported from Hong Kong; U.S. workers made simulated potato chips from soy protein and synthetic potato flavour; and protein isolates from linseed, alfalfa leaf, defatted Mexican cashew-nut meal, and African locust bean were developed.

Food Industry. Three United Kingdom milk processing and dairy product groups representing almost the entire milk and milk products supplies of the British Isles uniquely coordinated their research facilities in one company. Labour shortages in many countries accelerated the adoption of long-life milk distributed through supermarkets. Indian scientists succeeded in developing a satisfactory quick-ripening cheddar cheese using buffalo's milk.

A British company installed in Spain one of Europe's largest automated animal and poultry by-products complexes, capable of processing 1,000 tons of raw material a week. Another British company established a large intensive poultry project in Chile. Hungarian scientists developed a novel process, using a high-frequency magnetic field, for extracting fatty substances from animal protein without denaturation.

South African scientists reported on a new process for the economical production of glucose or corn syrups directly from unpurified starch. Bulgarian workers developed a new enzymatic process for the production of glucose from starch. A Japanese company reported upon an improved enzymatic technique for the production of maltose and its hydrogenation to maltitol, a new noncaloric sweetener. A French firm completed the installation of a starch-glucose and by-products plant in the Philippines with a daily capacity of 100 tons. Much original research was undertaken in Iran to improve the yields and harvesting of sugar beets in view of the growing importance of this commodity.

Automation. Many novel developments in speeding up production and economizing on labour costs were reported. Typical ones included a new system in Puerto Rico for harvesting coffee beans. It involved collecting the beans in low-cost plastic netting and required only 20 man-days per 15-ac. plantation, compared with 66 man-days for the previous method. Much effort was put into the development of completely automated production to satisfy the large and growing demand for pizzas in Western countries. The preparation of shelled hard-boiled eggs was automated by a U.S. company. A French process for the continuous heat-processing of canned foods was claimed to give better process control and to eliminate the risk of recontamination.

A novel instrument for assessing the efficacy of sterilization during the processing of canned foods resulted from British government-sponsored research. Workers at the USDA succeeded in applying the principle of nuclear magnetic resonance to the detection of insects within the kernels of stored grain.

Legislation and New Products. The British government announced reviews of various regulations concerning food additives with a view to coordinating them with corresponding regulations of the EEC countries. New labeling regulations came into force in Britain, and comprehensive proposals were made for a system of open-date marking of prepacked foods. In the U.K. the Lead in Food Regulations were tightened to restrict further the lead content of infant foods, and in Canada manufacturers agreed voluntarily to restrict the salt content of baby foods.

A U.S. company introduced sliced precooked bacon requiring only a 90-second heating in a toaster. A new type of beefsteak was introduced in which the less tender parts of beef, after deboning and the removal of fat, are sliced into paper-thin flakes that are molded into strip steaks. Another U.S. innovation was the introduction of instant rice that reconstituted with hot water. Other developments included imitation cheddar and blue cheese from a wheat-flour base, an egg-white substitute from lactalbumin, a cold water-soluble agar, and nutlike products from soybeans. The Japanese in collaboration with the Australians introduced a smoked cuttlefish cheese. The Bulgarians developed a dried yogurt containing active yogurt bacteria. (H. B. HAWLEY)

See also Agriculture; Commodities, Primary; Fisheries; Prices.

ENCYCLOPÆDIA BRITANNICA FILMS. *Produce—From Farm to Market* (1968).

Football

Association Football (Soccer). World Cup qualifying matches, the Olympic Games (*see* SPORTING RECORD: *Special Report*), and continental competitions provided most of the soccer highlights in 1972. The problem of violence, on and off the field, was ever present.

The World Cup, with the finals in 1974 to be held in Munich, W.Ger., barely got off the ground during 1972; but the South Americans, led by Uruguay, proposed that the Fédération Internationale de Football Association (FIFA) should rule that Great Britain must be represented in the competition as one country and not under four separate flags (England, Scotland, Wales, and Northern Ireland). The motion was withdrawn from the FIFA conference, but such a proposal might well be repeated.

The violence of fans was perhaps highlighted by the ugly outbursts in Barcelona, Spain, at the European Cup-Winners' Cup final. These prodded the Union of European Football Associations (UEFA) to propose that in all future finals spectators be separated from the playing field by a wire fence seven feet high. A second-round European Cup match in West Germany also caused trouble: the first leg between Borussia Mönchengladbach and Inter-Milan in October 1971 was declared void because a can thrown onto the field struck the Italian centre forward Roberto Boninsegna. Borussia had won the game 7–1 but could only manage a goalless draw in the replayed leg in Berlin and, having lost 2–4 in Milan, was eliminated from the competition. The Greek team, Panionios, was banned from the UEFA Cup after two of its players attacked the referee at a game in Hungary with Ferencvaros.

In England the Football League introduced a system of penalty points for the 1972–73 season; fouls were graded from 1 to 4 points; when a player had collected 12 points he would automatically be banned for two games. Ejection from a game would mean an automatic three-game suspension.

European Championship. West Germany took the European championship for the first time by defeating the U.S.S.R. in the final at the Heysel Stadium in Brussels on June 18. The Germans won clearly and convincingly 3–0, with Gerd Müller scoring twice and Herbert Wimmer getting the other. Inspired in midfield by Günter Netzer and Wimmer, and by their captain, Franz Beckenbauer, operating in front of the back four, the Germans produced a sparkling display of football to render ineffective the dogged Soviet rearguard action. When the Soviets did move forward to take the pressure off their goalkeeper, Evgeni Rudakov, the wily Beckenbauer and Netzer pumped long passes through to expose the defense. The Soviet goalkeeper turned in a magnificent performance, producing saves that seemed impossible. The Soviet captain, Murtaz Khurtsilava, did his best to keep the Germans at bay, organizing the defense well, but even his efforts—including a couple of searing drives late in the game—could not prevent West Germany from winning.

In its semifinal West Germany had a closer contest against Belgium in Antwerp, but the deadly finishing of Müller tipped the scales: he headed two goals from precision passes by Netzer. Sepp Maier, tending goal for the West Germans, was beaten once by a snap shot from Odilon Polleunis, but despite a fierce offensive in the second half the Belgians could not tie the score. In the other semifinal, in Brussels, the U.S.S.R. beat Hungary with a goal by A. Konkov.

European Cup. Ajax of Amsterdam became one of only four teams to win the European Cup in consecutive seasons when they defeated Inter-Milan (who had performed the feat in 1964 and 1965) 2–0 on their native Dutch soil in Rotterdam (the other two clubs to have performed the feat were Real Madrid of Spain and Benfica of Portugal). This second victory by Ajax meant that the trophy went to the Netherlands for the third consecutive time, Feyenoord having won it in 1970 in Milan. The 1972 final was a personal triumph for Johan Cruyff, who scored both goals: the first was a fine shot just after the start of the second half and the second a smart header when he leapt higher than the Italian defense to head the ball wide of Ivano Bordon, the Inter-Milan goalkeeper.

The Italians, long regarded as one of the best defensive teams in Europe, found more than their match in the enterprising Dutchmen who attacked almost continuously. True, the Italians lost Mario Giubertoni but the substitute Mario Bertini was an experienced player. Strangely, the Inter-Milan forwards, who included the Brazilian Jair Da Costa and the Italian internationals Sandro Mazzola and Boninsegna, had all too little influence on the game and never made a sustained threat to Ajax's supremacy. Inter-Milan, which had almost been eliminated from the competition in the second round in Mönchengladbach before the tie was replayed (*see* above), only reached the final by beating Glasgow Celtic 5–4 on penalties in the semifinal, whereas Ajax did not lose a match in the competition.

Inter-Continental Cup. The reputation of this competition, which pits the winners of the European Cup against those of the South American Cup, for bruising, brawling games prompted Ajax, which triumphed in Europe, to opt out of the 1971 event. Its place, on UEFA's recommendation, was taken by Panathinaikos of Athens, the defeated finalists. The Greek team met Nacional of Uruguay.

The first game was played in Athens in mid-December 1971 and was marred by an accident to the Greek club's right back, Gianis Tomaras. He broke a leg after a tackle by Julie Morales, who was sent out of the game after an hour's play with the score at 1–1. The Uruguayans' goal was scored by veteran Luis Artime, an Argentine international who equalized the goal scored by Panagiotis Filakouris. Artime clinched the trophy for the South Americans when he scored once in each half of a tough tackling return match in Montevideo. This game was refereed by Scotsman Bill Mullan, who never allowed it to get out of hand. Mimi Domazos scored a consolation effort for the Greeks in the final seconds, but by then the game was lost for Panathinaikos, which had no answer to the skills of Luis Cubilla and his colleagues of Nacional.

European Cup-Winners' Cup. The final of this tournament in Camp Nou Stadium, Barcelona, Spain, on May 24, 1972, was spoiled by the behaviour of the Glasgow Rangers fans, who invaded the playing field and battled with the local police in a near riot when the Scottish team beat Moscow Dynamo 3–2. The incidents, during which about 200 police made baton charges, occurred when the Rangers' supporters wanted to join in the celebration of their team's success in their third final of the competition (Rangers had been defeated in finals in earlier years by Fiorentina, Italy, and Bayern Munich, West Germany). The fans rained bottles and cans onto the field during the "battle." The sequel was a number of arrests and a two-year ban from European competition imposed by UEFA on the Rangers. The ban was reduced on appeal to one year. Despite protests from the Soviets, UEFA allowed the Glasgow team to retain the trophy, although the Dynamo authorities claimed that their men were intimidated and that the final should be replayed.

The game itself belonged to the Rangers; Colin Stein, their centre forward, gave them a 1–0 lead after 23 minutes, and Willie Johnston added a second goal 5 minutes before half time, when the Soviet rearguard failed to cut out the danger from David Smith's centre. The Dynamo defense was hesitant and allowed Johnston to score again shortly after the beginning of the second half when the winger thundered in another shot. The Soviets then staged a fierce rally and scored a goal by Valery Eschtrekov. They added a second by Aleksandr Machovikov a few minutes from the end of the game, but by then it was too late. Thus, the Rangers brought the trophy back to Britain for the third year in succession, following Chelsea and Manchester City.

UEFA Cup. Tottenham Hotspur maintained England's run of success in the UEFA Cup tournament by beating their compatriots, the Wolverhampton Wanderers, in the two-legged final during the first part of May. Though it was a new competition, the UEFA Cup was in effect a continuation of the old European Fairs' Cup, and so Tottenham followed Leeds, Arsenal, and Newcastle as winners. Tottenham won the first leg of the final at Wolverhampton on May 3 with two goals from centre forward Martin Chivers, and though Wolverhampton skipper Jim McCalliog scored a goal, the Wanderers could not close the gap.

When the return match was played in London a fortnight later, approximately 54,000 spectators crowded into White Hart Lane to see a fine game. Wolverhampton, being a goal down after the first game, had to adopt an attacking policy, and the Spurs realized that they could not "sit on" such a narrow margin; so the game lived up to expectations. Alan Mullery gave the Spurs the lead with a splendid header, and though the Wolves never gave up they managed only once to break through the home defense in which goalkeeper Pat Jennings (Northern Ireland) and Mike England (Wales) were outstanding. Their

Alan Clarke's goal wins the Football Association Cup for Leeds United, beating Arsenal 1–0 in the finals at Wembley Stadium, London, on May 6, 1972.

POPPERFOTO/PICTORIAL PARADE

goal from David Wagstaffe, the speedy left winger, was a splendid one but did not affect the final result.

British Isles Championship. England just sneaked in to finish first in this tournament, defeating Scotland in a bruising battle 1–0 with a first-half goal by Alan Ball of Arsenal, at Hampden Park, Glasgow, on May 27. The game was so liberally bespattered with fouls that it was almost universally condemned. Three players were booked by the referee.

On the same day at Wrexham, Wales and Northern Ireland battled out a goalless draw to leave the Welsh at the bottom of the standings, not having scored in their three matches. The game was a particular disappointment to the Irish, as they had already registered a shock win over England at Wembley, London, in the first Irish victory over England in 15 years. The margin of victory was a single goal scored by Terry Neill, Northern Ireland's player-manager. The reshuffled England team could not get through the Irish defense, though Emlyn Hughes (Liverpool) did smack a shot onto the top of the goal frame.

The following night Scotland slipped in ahead of Wales at Hampden Park, also by a single goal that was created by the Leeds pair Billy Bremner and Peter Lorimer. Bremner, the Scottish captain, provided the vital pass for Lorimer.

The opening games in the series, on May 20, had seen England completely crush a disjointed Wales 3–0 at Ninian Park, Cardiff, and Scotland beat Northern Ireland at Hampden Park. At Cardiff, goals by Hughes and the Manchester City pair, Rodney Marsh and Colin Bell, told part of the story as England pummeled the Welsh defense for almost the whole of a one-sided match. The Irish gave notice of their effective play when they fell to the Scots 2–0 only in the last four minutes when it seemed they would emerge with a more than creditable draw. Then Denis Law of Manchester United, back on the Scottish side after a successful recall against Peru the previous month, whipped home a cross from Lorimer, who had come on as a substitute and who himself added a second goal. (TREVOR WILLIAMSON)

Rugby. *Rugby Union.* The 1971–72 period included no long major international tour, but there were many shorter ones. There were also several innovations, notably by England, which became the first national team to tour Japan and the first to play against nonwhite teams in South Africa.

England toured the Far East in September and October 1971 and played three matches in Japan, one in Hong Kong, one in Singapore, and one in Ceylon. England finished with the impressive record of played 7, won 7, points for 228, points against 52, but was hard pressed in both international matches against Japan before winning 27–19 in Osaka and 6–3 (two penalty goals to one penalty goal) in Tokyo. The Japanese tackling was particularly impressive.

A team representing Canada toured Wales, playing 5 matches, winning 2 and losing 3 with a points record of 66 for and 141 against. In their two most difficult matches the Canadians were beaten 38–10 at Swansea by Wales B and 56–10 at Cardiff by "a Welsh 15" which included six full international players.

In November 1971 Australia undertook the first tour of France they had ever made independently of a visit to the British Isles. Two international matches were played, the Australians winning 13–11 at Toulouse, and France winning 18–9 in Paris. The Australians' final record was played 8, won 4, lost 4, points for 110, points against 101.

In another innovation a team of Coloured (racially mixed) players representing the South African Rugby Federation toured England in December 1971, playing six games in southeast England. They were matched mainly against minor counties and ended with a record of played 6, won 2, drawn 1, lost 3, points for 57, points against 107.

The home international championship was spoiled by the refusal of both Scotland and Wales to undertake their matches against Ireland in Dublin because of political unrest in Ireland. This was particularly unfortunate for the Irish, who showed, in beating France 14–9 in Paris and beating England 16–12 at Twickenham, that they had a team with a good chance of winning the championship. Wales, too, possessed another potential championship-winning team, as they displayed in beating England 12–3 at Twickenham, Scotland 35–12 at Cardiff, and France 20–6, also at Cardiff. Scotland made a grand start, defeating France 20–9 in Edinburgh, but lost heavily to Wales before ending their season with a convincing victory 23–9 over England in Edinburgh. France had a generally poor season except for their startling victory by 37–12 over England in Paris—the largest number of points ever scored against England in one match. For England it was the worst home international season in history. Never before had they lost all four matches in one season. As some consolation for the Irish, who had lost both their home games with the refusal of the Welsh and Scots to play in Dublin, France agreed to play an extra game in Dublin at the end of the season. This resulted in a win for Ireland, 24–14. In Ireland's game against England, Tom Kiernan, the Irish fullback and captain, became the first man from any of the four home countries ever to play in 50 international matches. Barry John, the Welsh standoff half, scored 35 points for Wales in the season. This was a new Welsh record, and John achieved it in only three matches. He retired from rugby at the end of the season.

Following their unsuccessful home season, England astonished the rugby world with its play in South Africa in May and June 1972. Captained by John Pullin, England not only remained unbeaten on the tour but defeated South Africa 18–9 in Johannesburg in the only test match. Their final record was played 7, won 6, drawn 1, points for 166, points against 58. In the course of their tour England defeated a Coloured team 11–6 in Cape Town and an African team 36–3 in Port Elizabeth. This was the first time a white touring team had ever competed against nonwhite players in South Africa. England was the first team since 1891 to return unbeaten from a tour of South Africa.

France achieved a similar record during their tour of Australia in May and June. The French played nine matches, winning eight of them and drawing one, with a points record of 254 for and 134 against. Captained by Walter Spanghero, of Narbonne, they played two test matches against Australia, drawing the first 14–14 in Sydney and winning the second 16–15 in Brisbane. The Australians, following this defeat by France, set off for a tour of New Zealand, where they played three more test matches and lost all three. The New Zealanders won 29–6 in Wellington, 30–17 in Christchurch, and 38–3 in Auckland.

There was an increase in competition rugby in both England and Wales. In England, for instance, the Rugby Football Union organized the country's first national club knockout competition. This met with snags. Some players, for example, had to play hard matches on the Saturday and Sunday of the same weekend, and the final between Gloucester and Moseley at Twickenham was spoiled by injuries and by Moseley's having a player sent off the field by the referee. This was the first time a player had been sent off in a big match at Twickenham since 1925. But it was generally agreed that the competition had been worthwhile, it having brought money to the clubs involved and having stimulated interest among many of the smaller clubs. Gloucester beat Moseley in the final 17–6 in front of a crowd of 15,000.

Rugby League. The outstanding event of the 1971–72 period was New Zealand's achievement of winning a test series in England for the first time. On their tour of England in the autumn of 1971 they won the first test match 18–13 at Salford and clinched the series by winning the second 17–14 at Castleford. In the Great Britain *v.* France series the British won in France for the first time in four years. The match was played in Toulouse, and the score was 10–9. In the return match the French forwards were disappointingly weak, and Great Britain won 45–10.

(DAVID FROST)

U.S. Football. The Miami Dolphins won the championship of professional football by defeating the Washington Redskins 14–7 in the Super Bowl on Jan. 14, 1973, at Los Angeles. The Dolphins won 17 straight games to become the first undefeated Super Bowl winner. Southern California was the top-ranked college team.

College. The University of Southern California raced past Oklahoma and Nebraska and other pretenders to the 1972 national collegiate championship on the legs of a stumpy sophomore running back named Anthony (A. D.) Davis. Number one in every poll in the country, the Trojans concluded their season by demolishing ninth-ranked Ohio State 42–17 in the Rose Bowl as Davis gained 157 yd. and fullback Sam Cunningham scored four touchdowns. It was the 12th victory without a defeat for USC, which won its third national title in 11 years.

Along the way in 1972, Coach John McKay's Trojans won the Pacific Eight championship and beat a respectable Notre Dame team 45–23, Davis scoring six touchdowns. The conference championship was assured when they defeated UCLA 24–7.

UCLA, meanwhile, had begun its season with a 20–17 upset of the Nebraska Cornhuskers, who were seeking their third consecutive national championship. Nebraska finished as the fourth-ranked team in the country and the second-place team in the Big Eight. Oklahoma, which defeated the Cornhuskers and lost only to Colorado, finished first in the Big Eight and second in the Associated Press's national rankings. The Sooners' strength showed in their 14–0 Sugar Bowl victory over tenth-ranked Penn State. Nebraska, meanwhile, drubbed Notre Dame 40–6 in the Orange Bowl. Texas moved up to third in the national standings by defeating seventh-ranked Alabama 17–13 in the Cotton Bowl. Auburn had little trouble proving itself worthy of a fifth-place ranking nationally, beating Colorado 24–3 in the Gator Bowl.

Freshman football players returned to varsities across the country after a 21-year absence, more than a few of them making a considerable impact. Fans became aware of their presence when, in Ohio State's second game of the season, 18-year-old Archie Griffin ran for a school record of 239 yd. against North Carolina. Throughout the season, offense proved the place where freshmen showed their chief assets. At North Carolina State, quarterback Dave Buckey found a target in his twin brother Don, an end. Tinker Owens, the 17-year-old brother of 1969 Heisman Trophy winner Steve Owens, caught key passes in Oklahoma's victories over Nebraska and Penn State.

WIDE WORLD

High stepping into the end zone, University of Southern California's star running back Anthony Davis scores against USC's Rose Bowl opponent, Ohio State, on New Year's Day, 1973. USC crushed Ohio State 42 to 17.

While the freshmen were making reputations, collegiate football's proven stars were living up to theirs. Johnny Rodgers, Nebraska's 5-ft. 9-in. running back, wide receiver, and kick returner, won the Heisman Trophy as the outstanding player of the year. Rodgers was selected over teammate Rich Glover, who won the Outland Trophy as best collegiate lineman, and Greg Pruitt, a running back from Oklahoma.

Rodgers established a collegiate record by gaining 5,586 yd. on runs, pass receptions, and kick and punt returns. The smallest running back in the country at a major college, 5-ft. 5-in. Howard Stevens of Louisville led the large schools in all-purpose running, averaging 213.2 yd. a game rushing, receiving, and returning kicks. Pete Van Valkenburg, a senior tailback from Brigham Young, averaged 138.6 yd. a game to lead the nation in rushing.

College football's top passer was Don Strock of Virginia Tech, who completed 53% of his attempts for 3,243 yd. and 18 touchdowns during the season. Although Tony Adams of Utah State had to content himself with being the second leading passer, he established a National Collegiate Athletic Association (NCAA) single-game record by throwing for 561 yd. in a 44–16 rout of Utah.

Oklahoma was the country's best rushing team for the second straight year, averaging 368.8 yd. a game, but Arizona State had by far the best total offense. The Sun Devils amassed an average of 516.5 yd. and 46.6 points for their 11-game regular season.

College football attendance reached an all-time high for the 19th consecutive season. National Collegiate Sports Services reported that 30,828,802 persons attended games, an increase of 1.23% over 1971. The rise was attributed to a 5.28% growth in attendance for the 11 major conferences.

Penn State, an independent power, compiled a 10–1

regular-season record, losing only to Tennessee, to win the Lambert Trophy, symbolic of supremacy in the East. Quarterback John Hufnagel and running back Johnny Cappelletti, only the third Nittany Lion in history to gain 1,000 yd. rushing, led Penn State. Dartmouth won its fourth Ivy League championship in a row to establish a record. But second-place Yale gained more national attention because of its superior senior running back, Dick Jauron. Yale overcame a 17–0 deficit to defeat Harvard 28–17 in the 89th meeting between the two schools.

In the East's other major traditional contest, the 73rd Army-Navy game, Army commandeered a 23–15 victory when Scott Beaty ran a blocked field-goal attempt 84 yd. for a touchdown. Massachusetts became the champion of the Yankee Conference for the second consecutive year.

Alabama triumphed in its first ten games of the season, hungering all the while to overcome USC in the race for the national championship. Then the Crimson Tide met Auburn. Bill Newton blocked two Alabama punts, and teammate David Langner ran both back for touchdowns to give the Tigers a 17–16 victory. Alabama's consolation prize was the Southeastern Conference championship. Quarterbacks Bert Jones of Louisiana State and Gary Huff of Florida State were the most heralded players in the South.

In the Atlantic Coast Conference, North Carolina won its second straight title with a 6–0 league record. The Tar Heels were 10–1 overall. East Carolina triumphed in the Southern Conference, and Tennessee Tech prevailed in the Ohio Valley Conference.

Though its national stature had diminished in recent years, the Big Ten produced two teams worthy of national ranking, Michigan and Ohio State. They shared the conference championship with 7–1 records, but Ohio State traveled to the Rose Bowl on the strength of its 14–11 upset of the Wolverines. The Buckeyes were the first team to score two touchdowns against Michigan all season.

The Big Eight continued its reign as the country's glamour conference. It sent five teams—Oklahoma, Nebraska, Colorado, Missouri, and Iowa State—to post-season bowl games. Oklahoma and Nebraska, the only two to win in the bowls, again decided the conference championship on Thanksgiving Day, with the Sooners avenging their 1971 loss by winning 17–14.

Arkansas was supposed to run away with the Southwest Conference, but it was Texas that did it. The Longhorns, powered by the running of sophomore Roosevelt Leaks, won their fifth consecutive league title by three games, the biggest margin in conference history.

Professional. Before they ever reached the Super Bowl, the Miami Dolphins assured themselves a place in the National Football League (NFL) record book by racing to 14 regular-season victories without a defeat. Not since 1942 had the NFL had an unbeaten team, when the Chicago Bears accomplished the feat in 11 games. The Bears also went undefeated in 1934 with a 13-game schedule. Although the 1948 Cleveland Browns won 14 straight regular-season games and one play-off contest, they did it in the old All America Conference.

No professional team ever displayed as potent a running attack as did Miami. The Eastern Division champions of the American Conference amassed 2,952 yd. rushing for an NFL record, and they were the first team in history to have two running backs, Larry Csonka and Eugene ("Mercury") Morris, gain more than 1,000 yd. apiece in one season. Larry Little, a 6-ft. 3-in., 265-lb. guard, cleared the way for them repeatedly and, beyond that, provided protection for Earl Morrall, Miami's 38-year-old quarterback. Morrall took over the job when Bob Griese, all-NFL at the position in 1971, suffered a broken leg in the fifth game of the season.

Miami lost the previous Super Bowl to the Dallas Cowboys 24–3, and Coach Don Shula got the Dolphins back for a second try with victories over the Cleveland Browns 20–14 and the Pittsburgh Steelers 21–17 in the American Conference play-offs. The Browns led Miami 14–13 late in their game until Morrall's passing set up a touchdown by running back Jim Kiick. Against Pittsburgh, Griese, recovered from his mid-season injury, took over at quarterback in the second half and watched Kiick score the two touchdowns that gave Miami the conference championship.

By defeating Dallas for the National Conference title, the Washington Redskins became a champion for the first time in almost 30 years. Curt Knight put the Redskins in the Super Bowl and made sure the Cowboys, last year's champions, would not get there by kicking a record four field goals in the 26–3 victory. Knight, who endured a mid-season slump, booted three field goals a week earlier when Washington defeated the Green Bay Packers 16–3.

Victory justified the means George Allen took to build the Redskins in his two years as head coach. Eschewing rookies—only one made the team in 1972—he sought veterans, and he wheeled and dealed to get them. Allen devoted most of his efforts to building a defense around tackle Diron Talbert, end Ron McDole, linebackers Jack Pardee and Chris Hanburger, cornerback Pat Fischer, and safety Roosevelt Taylor.

Washington's offense revolved around Larry Brown, the NFL's premier runner in a year that featured outstanding running backs. Aided by the blocking of Charlie Harraway, his partner in the backfield, Brown gained 1,216 yd. in the Redskins' first 12 games and then sat out the last 2, both of which Washington lost. Injuries continued to haunt Redskin quarterback Sonny Jurgensen, so Billy Kilmer once again inherited his job.

Pittsburgh had to wait 40 years for a team of

NFL Final Standings and Play-offs, 1972

AMERICAN CONFERENCE			
Eastern Division	W	L	T
Miami	14	0	0
New York Jets	7	7	0
Baltimore	5	9	0
Buffalo	4	9	1
New England	3	11	0
Central Division			
Pittsburgh	11	3	0
*Cleveland	10	4	0
Cincinnati	8	6	0
Houston	1	13	0
Western Division			
Oakland	10	3	1
Kansas City	8	6	0
Denver	5	9	0
San Diego	4	9	1
NATIONAL CONFERENCE			
Eastern Division			
Washington	11	3	0
*Dallas	10	4	0
New York Giants	8	6	0
St. Louis	4	9	1
Philadelphia	2	11	1
Central Division			
Green Bay	10	4	0
Detroit	8	5	1
Minnesota	7	7	0
Chicago	4	9	1
Western Division			
San Francisco	8	5	1
Atlanta	7	7	0
Los Angeles	6	7	1
New Orleans	2	11	1

*Fourth qualifier for play-offs.

Play-offs

American semifinals
Miami 20, Cleveland 14
Pittsburgh 13, Oakland 7

National semifinals
Dallas 30, San Francisco 28
Washington 16, Green Bay 3

American finals
Miami 21, Pittsburgh 17

National finals
Washington 26, Dallas 3

Super Bowl
Miami 14, Washington 7

In the fourth quarter of the American Conference championship game, Pittsburgh Steeler quarterback Terry Bradshaw is dumped in a blitz by charging Miami Dolphin players (in light uniforms). The Dolphins won 21–17.

WIDE WORLD

championship status. The American Conference's Central Division title was the first ever won by the Steelers. Their patient owner, 71-year-old racehorse owner Art Rooney, saw the bad times turn good with the arrival of Franco Harris, a rookie running back from Penn State. Harris rushed for more than 100 yd. in six straight games to tie an NFL record. The Steelers' 11–3 finish put them one game ahead of Cleveland, whose second-place record got it into the play-offs as a wild-card team.

Controversy surrounded Pittsburgh's 13–7 play-off victory over the Oakland Raiders, champions of the American Conference's Western Division. Officials ruled that a pass thrown to John Fuqua of Pittsburgh with five seconds left in the game bounced off Fuqua and then was touched by Oakland safety Jack Tatum before Harris plucked it out of the air and ran 42 yd. for the winning score. Had Tatum not touched the ball, the play would have been voided, for no two receivers on the same team can touch a pass consecutively. Television instant replay showed the official decision to be correct.

In the Super Bowl Miami maintained its perfect record by defeating Washington 14–7. Griese passed 28 yd. to Howard Twilley and Kiick plunged 1 yd. for the two Miami touchdowns. Washington tallied when Mike Bass recovered a midair "fumble" by Garo Yepremian after a blocked field-goal attempt and ran 49 yd. One Miami touchdown was called back, a 47-yd. pass from Griese to Paul Warfield.

In all, ten ballcarriers achieved the previously rare 1,000-yd. mark in 1972. O. J. Simpson of the Buffalo Bills took advantage of Larry Brown's two-game absence to capture the ground-gaining title with 1,251 yd. Brown finished second. After him, in order, came: Ron Johnson of the New York Giants (1,182); Csonka of Miami (1,117); Marv Hubbard of Oakland (1,100); Harris of Pittsburgh (1,055); Calvin Hill of Dallas (1,036); Mike Garrett of the San Diego Chargers (1,031); John Brockington of Green Bay (1,027); and Morris of Miami (1,000).

The running backs' rush to daylight brought emphasis back to offense in the NFL. The lag in offense was reflected by the fact that 111 fewer touchdowns had been scored in the NFL in 1971 than in 1969. To rectify that, NFL officials adjusted the position of the inbounds markers, called hash marks. In past seasons, they sat 20 yd. from each sideline. They were moved in slightly more than three additional yards to give offensive units more operating room. As a result NFL teams scored 324 more points in 1972 than they did in 1971.

Johnny Unitas played quarterback for the Baltimore Colts for the last time in the game that gave Miami its NFL victory record. Unitas, who had passed for nearly 23 mi. in his career, left open the possibility that he would play for another team. The 39-year-old star vowed he would never play for the Colts again because he thought he had been benched unfairly in mid-season.

U.S. Pres. Richard Nixon requested Pete Rozelle, the NFL commissioner, to lift the local television blackout policy from play-off games if tickets were sold out 48 hours ahead of time. Rozelle refused, bringing a promise from the Nixon administration that the league's antitrust exemption statute would be scrutinized in the future. As was noted, however, there was no antitrust exemption statute relating to football.

NFL attendance continued to climb. A record 10.8 million fans watched the 182 regular-season games, compared with 10.3 million fans in 1971.

WIDE WORLD

Washington Redskins' Charley Taylor catches a perfect pass from quarterback Billy Kilmer and gallops into the end zone for his second touchdown of the National Conference championship game against the Dallas Cowboys, who were overwhelmed 26 to 3.

Canadian Football. Guided by Chuck Ealey, a rookie quarterback from the U.S. overlooked by every team in the NFL, the Hamilton Tiger-Cats, five times champions between 1953 and 1967, regained possession of the Grey Cup, the Canadian Football League's top prize. Ealey passed to Garney Henley, voted the league's most outstanding player, to set up the 26-yd. field goal by rookie Ian Sunter that defeated the Saskatchewan Roughriders 13–10 for the title.

Americans played vital roles for the Tiger-Cats. Coach Jerry Williams came to Hamilton from the Philadelphia Eagles, and the Tiger-Cats' defense was built around Angelo Mosca, a 285-lb. tackle from Notre Dame. But the key to the championship season was Ealey, who did not become a starter until Hamilton's third game. Although he was never beaten in 30 games in high school and in 35 at the University of Toledo, he was not among the 442 players selected in the NFL's 1972 talent draft. Critics said the fact that Ealey is a black quarterback made him unwanted. (JOHN SCHULIAN)

France

A republic of Western Europe and head of the French Community, France is bounded by the English Channel, Belgium, Luxembourg, West Germany, Switzerland, Italy, the Mediterranean Sea, Monaco, Spain, Andorra, and the Atlantic Ocean. Area: 210,038 sq.mi. (543,998 sq.km.), including Corsica. Pop. (1972 est.): 51,487,400. Cap. and largest city: Paris (pop., 1972 est., 2,461,000). Language: French. President in 1972, Georges Pompidou; premiers, Jacques Chaban-Delmas and, from July 5, Pierre Messmer.

In 1972 the battle lines were drawn in preparation for the general election scheduled for March 1973, when the ruling majority would for the first time face a united opposition from the left. Moreover, the centre had regrouped to form the Reform Movement, which hoped to pick up a fair number of seats from the Gaullist Union des Démocrates pour la République (UDR), whose image had taken something of a beating during the year as a result of a succession of

Foreign Aid: *see* Development, Economic

Foreign Exchange: *see* Payments and Reserves, International

Foreign Investments: *see* Investment, International

Forests: *see* Environment; Timber

Formosa: *see* Taiwan

financial scandals, including a tax avoidance scandal involving Premier Jacques Chaban-Delmas. Chaban-Delmas was later replaced by Pierre Messmer (*see* BIOGRAPHY), an orthodox Gaullist, and a major government reshuffle took place aimed at improving the majority's chances in the forthcoming elections. On September 5 Alain Peyrefitte was elected secretary-general of the UDR, replacing René Tomasini.

Domestic Affairs. Electoral considerations were reflected in the press conference given by President Pompidou (*see* BIOGRAPHY) on September 21, most of which was devoted to home affairs. Both in length (1¾ hours) and in tone it bore little resemblance to the previous six press conferences of Pompidou's presidency. Where earlier ones had maintained a balance between the central themes of domestic and foreign affairs, more than half of the seventh was devoted to internal problems and scandals, in particular the "Aranda affair," which flared up early in September.

Gabriel Aranda (*see* BIOGRAPHY), former press adviser to Albin Chalandon, minister of public works under Chaban-Delmas, had threatened to disclose photocopies of a large number of compromising documents, amassed during his time at the ministry, implicating many prominent figures connected with the administration in various planning and development scandals. As the contents of the documents were systematically leaked to the press, particularly the formidable satirical journal *Le Canard enchaîné*, the affair took on the proportions of a major political scandal. The documents were finally handed over to a magistrate, who, while he found nothing justifying immediate action by the public prosecutor, nevertheless recommended the thorough investigation of a number of incidents. In his press conference the president criticized Aranda's methods but stressed that corruption must be ruthlessly eliminated wherever it was found.

The president also gave his first explanation for the replacement of Chaban-Delmas in July, saying that a premier should not remain in office for as long as the president and that he had never intended to keep Chaban-Delmas until the elections "for no one can act if he already knows the date of his demise." Asked what he would do if a left-wing coalition won a majority in the National Assembly, Pompidou replied that he would form a government whichever side won. If it was subsequently voted down by the National Assembly, he could dissolve the assembly and appeal to the citizens of France. He made it clear that whatever the outcome of the elections he had no intention of inviting either the Socialist leader François Mitterrand (*see* BIOGRAPHY) or the Communist leader Georges Marchais (*see* BIOGRAPHY) to take part in the government.

The tone of the press conference came as a surprise to the listeners. Instead of his usual measured, courteous approach, the president allowed anger to show. For the first time he descended into the political arena and counterattacked in all directions. In doing so, he set himself up as the sole guardian of the country's institutions and the sole exponent of official policy. The reasons for this apparent loss of innocence might have been the increasing difficulty of the president's position. Having himself been reelected on a wave of reaction against the chaos of 1968, he found himself faced with a united opposition and an imminent parliamentary election at a time when his party was in considerable disarray and his own image not a little bruised by the humiliating results of the April referendum.

The referendum, held on April 23 to ratify the enlargement of the EEC, had singularly failed to bring the president the increase in prestige he had expected. The Socialists had advised their supporters to abstain, while the Communists counseled outright opposition. Less than 16 million of the country's almost 30 million registered electors submitted valid votes and 5 million of those were against the proposal. An additional 2 million submitted blank or spoiled ballot papers. The massive rate of abstention of nearly 40%—the highest for more than a century and twice as high as in any previous referendum—clearly represented a definite political gesture rather than mere indolence on the part of the electorate. While the president could console himself that the "yeses" amounted to nearly 70% of the votes cast, the fact remained that they represented little more than 35% of the total electorate. The overall effect was to weaken Pompidou's position just when he was expecting his authority to be enhanced by a massive vote of approval. Nevertheless,

FRANCE

Education. (1969–70) Primary, pupils 5,019,-837, teachers (full time) 220,295; secondary, pupils 3,121,810; vocational, pupils 953,609; secondary and vocational, teachers (full-time only) 248,934; teacher training, students 31,228, teachers (full time only) 2,309; higher (including 23 universities), students 615,326, teaching staff 31,-039.

Finance. Monetary unit: franc, with (Sept. 18, 1972) a par value of Fr. 5.12 to U.S. $1 (free rate of Fr. 12.24 = £1 sterling) for the commercial rate and a free "financial" rate of Fr. 5 to U.S. $1 (Fr. 11.92 = £1 sterling). Gold, SDRs, and foreign exchange, official: (June 1972) U.S. $8,941,000,000; (June 1971) U.S. $5,655,000,-000. Budget (1971 est): revenue Fr. 175,102,-000,000; expenditure Fr. 171,883,000,000. Gross national product: (1970) Fr. 735 billion; (1969) Fr. 731.5 billion. Money supply: (May 1972) Fr. 260,540,000,000; (May 1971) Fr. 235,140,000,-000. Cost of living (1963 = 100): (June 1972) 145; (June 1971) 138.

Foreign Trade. (1971) Imports Fr. 118 billion; exports Fr. 113,970,000,000. Import sources: EEC 50% (West Germany 22%, Belgium-Luxembourg 11%, Italy 10%, Netherlands 6%); U.S. 8%; U.K. 5%. Export destinations: EEC 49% (West Germany 21%, Belgium-Luxembourg 11%, Italy 11%, Netherlands 6%); U.S. 5%; Switzerland 5%; U.K. 5%. Main exports: machinery 25%; motor vehicles 16%; textiles 11%; iron and steel 10%; chemicals 10%. Tourism (1970): visitors 13.7 million; gross receipts U.S. $1,322,000,000.

Transport and Communications. Roads (1971) 789,000 km. (including 1,715 km. expressways). Motor vehicles in use (1971): passenger 13,130,000; commercial 1,795,000. Railways: (1970) 36,019 km.; traffic (1971) 41,033,000,000 passenger-km., freight 67,028,-000,000 net ton-km. Air traffic (1970): 13,587,-039,000 passenger-km.; freight 557,780,000 net ton-km. Navigable inland waterways in regular use (1970) 7,433 km.; freight traffic 14,183,000,-000 ton-km. Shipping (1971): merchant vessels 100 gross tons and over 1,399; gross tonnage 7,011,476. Telephones (Dec. 1970) 8,774,000. Radio licenses (Dec. 1969) 15,796,000. Television licenses (Dec. 1969) 10,121,000.

Agriculture. Production (in 000; metric tons; 1971; 1970 in parentheses): wheat 15,360 (12,-921); rye 289 (302); barley 8,950 (8,126); oats 2,539 (2,070); corn 8,772 (7,592); potatoes 9,333 (8,904); rice 79 (101); rapeseed 621 (567); tomatoes (1970) 565, (1969) 507; onions (1970) 198, (1969) 196; apples 2,886 (4,036); pears 526 (531); flax fibre 53 (40); sugar, raw value (1971–72) *c.* 3,918, (1970–71) 2,694; wine 6,133 (7,437); tobacco 43 (46); beef and veal *c.* 1,690 (1,624); pork *c.* 1,450 (1,303); milk 32,575 (31,820); butter *c.* 515 (506); cheese *c.* 810 (792); fish catch (1970) 775, (1969) 770. Livestock (in 000; Oct. 1970): cattle 21,621; sheep 10,239; pigs 11,572; horses 672; poultry *c.* 186,000.

Industry. Index of production (1963 = 100): (1971) 160; (1970) 152. Fuel and power (in 000; 1971): coal (metric tons) 33,004; electricity (kw-hr.) 147,790,000; natural gas (cu.m.) 7,149,000; manufactured gas (cu.m.; 1970) 7,258,000. Production (in 000; metric tons; 1971): iron ore (32% metal content) 55,872; bauxite 3,115; pig iron 18,345; crude steel 22,-858; aluminum 479; lead 133; zinc 218; cement 28,947; cotton yarn 281; cotton fabrics 221; wool yarn 166; wool fabrics 72; rayon filament yarn 53; rayon staple fibre 79; nylon filament yarn 97; nylon staple fibre 116; sulfuric acid 3,924; petroleum products (1970) 90,588; nitrogenous fertilizer (1970–71) 1,423; phosphate fertilizer (1970–71) 1,819; potash fertilizer (1970–71) 1,389; passenger cars (units) 2,694; commercial vehicles (units) 342. Merchant shipping launched (100 gross tons and over; 1971) 1,111,600 gross tons.

in terms of votes cast, France had ratified the treaty of enlargement and Pompidou could press on with his efforts toward the construction of the new Europe.

The New Government. The resignation of the government and the replacement of Premier Chaban-Delmas by Pierre Messmer in July marked the end of a period in which the premier's relations with the ruling majority had become increasingly strained and his personal image and authority had been severely shaken by a series of financial scandals. These culminated in a tax avoidance scandal early in 1972 when Chaban-Delmas' income tax returns were published in *Le Canard enchaîné* with details of how he had contrived, quite legally, to pay no tax whatever from 1966 to 1970. Moreover, the premier had also come under heavy fire in the spring for the state of affairs that had been allowed to develop within the French radio and television network (ORTF). After revelations of illicit advertising and financial mismanagement, the ORTF had been extensively reformed and reorganized and both the director general and the chairman of the board of governors dismissed. (*See* TELEVISION AND RADIO.)

After a long period of silence, and despite a vote of confidence in favour of Chaban-Delmas on May 24, President Pompidou finally made the decision to replace him on July 5. The following day, Pierre Messmer, minister of defense under Charles de Gaulle from 1961 to 1969, was appointed premier and a major government reshuffle took place.

The composition of the new government reflected a double aim: to secure a balance between the various currents of opinion within the ruling coalition and particularly the UDR and to achieve the best possible conditions for the electoral battle the following spring. Apart from the appointment of an orthodox Gaullist as premier, salient features of the reorganization included the entry into the government of a former premier, Edgar Faure (UDR; *see* BIOGRAPHY), and the creation of a superministry combining supply, housing, and regional planning for Olivier Guichard (UDR), a close confidant of the president. Along with Faure there were three other new members of the government: Jean Charbonnel (UDR, industrial and scientific development), Jean Foyer (UDR, public health), and Hubert Germain (UDR, posts and telecommunications). Eight ministers, including Guichard, changed portfolios.

On October 3 Messmer made his first statement to the National Assembly, where he faced the task of winning the support of the house. Almost the whole of his speech was devoted to domestic problems, leaving foreign affairs to the president. Where Chaban-Delmas had been content to announce the creation of a "new society" without elaborating on the details, Messmer took up the same theme but announced a number of definite proposals aimed at favouring the least privileged sectors and creating a "just and more humane society." The new government's policy seemed to be one of pursuing necessary reforms within the framework of a stricter Gaullist orthodoxy. Messmer promised an increase in the minimum wage and an amnesty for farmers and shopkeepers imprisoned for acts of violence or demonstrations. An ombudsman would be appointed to mediate between the public and the administration. In December sizable cuts were announced in the value-added tax, and a major state loan program was begun in an effort to compensate for the lost revenue and to curb inflation. Other anti-inflationary measures included stiffer controls on bank credit.

KEYSTONE

This immense Cross of Lorraine, a memorial to Charles de Gaulle, French president and patriot, stands at Colombey-les-Deux-Églises. The dedication ceremonies were held June 18, 1972.

The Socialist-Communist Alliance. An event of major importance for the French left occurred on June 27 when an agreement laying down a "common government program" was signed by Georges Marchais and François Mitterrand. The agreement was ratified by the respective party congresses a fortnight later. The agreement, which included the partial or total nationalization of certain industries and an undertaking to abide by the processes of democratic elections, would allow the left to go into the election battle better armed than ever before and was regarded by many observers as the most significant event for the French left since the split at the socialist congress at Tours in 1920. Certainly the ruling majority could ill afford to ignore the threat of a new Popular Front government implied in the alliance.

Industrial Relations. The labour unions, like the opposition, continued to demand a minimum monthly wage of Fr. 1,000, a 40-hour week, and retirement at age 60. A number of one-day strikes took place during the summer and fall. In August, after talks with union and management leaders, Premier Messmer proposed a system of economic participation aimed at "improving capitalism socially without destroying it." However, the pronouncement failed to impress the labour movement and further stoppages took place, culminating in an "action week" late in October.

The only really violent confrontation occurred in February when a young worker dismissed from the Renault car works was shot and killed by a factory guard during a demonstration outside the factory gates. This led to a protest by 30,000 people in which violence broke out between police and demonstrators. The factory guard gave himself up and was charged with murder.

Social Issues. Two matters in the forefront of public discussion during the year were abortion and capital punishment. Addressing a Gaullist women's rally in November, Premier Messmer hinted that liberalization of the 52-year-old abortion law would be a matter for the next Parliament.

After death sentences were imposed on June 29 on Claude Buffet for the murder in September 1971 of a prison guard and a nurse and on Roger Bontems (who with Buffet had held the two victims hostage) for complicity in the murders, there was speculation—in view of strong public feeling against a reprieve—as

MARIE-LAURE DE DECKER—GAMMA

Premier Pierre Messmer replaced Jacques Chaban-Delmas, who resigned under pressure in July 1972.

to whether President Pompidou would exercise his right of granting clemency, as he had in every other case since he became president. He did not do so, and Buffet and Bontems were guillotined on November 28, the first persons to be so executed in France since 1969.

On June 12 Mme Nicole de Hauteclocque, UDR deputy and councillor for the 15th *arrondissement,* was elected president of the Council of Paris. She became the first woman to hold the capital's highest office.

Foreign Affairs. President Pompidou's main concern in 1972 was the enlargement of the EEC, a project culminating in the "European summit" held in Paris in October. In preparation for the summit Pompidou had several important meetings with heads of state of member and applicant countries. In Paris in February Pompidou and Chancellor Willy Brandt of West Germany agreed upon a resumption of efforts to bring about a European economic and monetary union. This was followed by talks between Pompidou and U.K. Prime Minister Edward Heath in Britain. Another meeting between Pompidou and Brandt took place in Bonn in July, but no definite conclusions were reached on the position of European currencies with regard to the dollar. Later in July Pompidou visited Italy. A third meeting with Chancellor Brandt during the Munich Olympics helped to iron out certain remaining differences, and the meetings in Rome and Frascati, Italy, in September of the foreign and finance ministers of the member and applicant states paved the way for the October summit meeting in Paris.

The two-day summit conference, on October 19–20, established a European monetary fund and pledged a "European union" among the six original EEC countries and the three new members by 1980. (*See* EUROPEAN UNITY.)

In the context of the enlargement of the EEC an official visit to France in May by Queen Elizabeth II and Prince Philip was an important event. The royal couple were received at the Elysée Palace for the second time since Queen Elizabeth's accession to the British throne, an exception to the British rule that a head of state never makes more than one official visit to a non-Commonwealth country (Elizabeth and Philip had been received by Pres. and Mme René Coty in 1957).

While the EEC summit meeting was taking place in Paris, the initial agreement for the construction of the Channel railway tunnel was signed in London and Paris. Excavation was to begin in August 1973.

During the summer French nuclear tests in the Pacific brought strong criticism from a number of countries, including a public protest by the governor of South Australia, himself a former nuclear scientist. France, however, ignored the outcry and completed the series of tests. Unconfirmed reports of a further series planned for 1973 led to renewed protest in the fall, and New Zealand was taking steps at the UN to mobilize international support for a comprehensive ban on tests.

Without sacrificing any of his major diplomatic voyages, President Pompidou also visited a number of France's smaller European neighbours, including the Netherlands, Belgium, and Luxembourg. He also received in Paris Queen Juliana of the Netherlands and the head of the Swiss diplomatic service. Visits to France by Soviet Foreign Minister Andrei Gromyko and Defense Minister Andrei Grechko, Emperor Haile Selassie of Ethiopia, Pres. Habib Bourguiba of Tunisia, King Hassan of Morocco, and Polish First Secretary Edward Gierek allowed France to strengthen links with a number of countries, while Maurice Schumann became the first Western foreign minister to visit Peking since the Cultural Revolution of 1966.

Africa remained a constant preoccupation and France continued to maintain close ties with former colonies. In January Pompidou visited Niger and Chad and in November Togo and Upper Volta, where he announced the cancellation of Fr. 1 billion of debts owed to France by its former African territories. A visit to Dahomey was canceled after a military coup in October. (JEAN KNECHT)

French-Canadian Literature:
see Literature

French Community:
see Dependent States; *articles on the various member states*

French Guiana:
see Dependent States

French Literature:
see Literature

Friends, Religious Society of:
see Religion

Frozen Foods:
see Food

Fruit:
see Agriculture

Fuel and Power

Developments in the field of fuel and power during 1972 made it clear that the United States was undergoing a fundamental change from a position of abundant, cheap energy to one of more expensive energy associated with supply problems. Thus, imports as a percentage of total oil consumption continued to rise, despite the fact that Texas allowed oil wells in that state to produce without any limitation for the first time since 1948. The search for new reserves of oil and gas carried well drilling to record depths. In January a well in west Texas was bottomed at a depth of 28,500 ft., exceeding the previous record depth set in 1970 by 2,900 ft. Only 22 days later another well in western Oklahoma equaled that depth and in March bottomed at a new record of 30,050 ft. Neither of these wells produced from their record depths, but in May a new record producing depth was set by a well, also in western Oklahoma, which yielded commercial quantities of gas from a depth of 24,500 ft.

The electric power supply in the U.S. was again critical during the periods of peak demand in summer heat waves. Although no widespread power shortages such as those of 1970 were experienced, a July heat wave caused voltage reductions in New York City and Michigan and the situation was precarious in several other localities until cooler weather arrived.

In late summer a gasoline supply shortage suddenly developed, the result of a surge in demand at the same time that the crude oil supply was tight and refineries were already operating at the effective limit of 90% of theoretical capacity. An apparent contribution to the high demand level was the sharply reduced mileage performance of 1972 automobiles, which were equipped with emission-control devices in compliance with new air pollution regulations. Although some gasoline marketers were forced to close their pumps, no motorists were deprived of gasoline. It was, however, a new peacetime experience for the U.S., and gasoline prices in most parts of the country rose by several cents a gallon.

The situation in natural gas continued to worsen, as pipelines and distributing companies instituted "curtailments" which limited or stopped the attachment of new customers and reduced deliveries to some large industrial users. In an effort to improve the supply of gas over the longer term, the U.S. Federal Power Commission (FPC) in August adopted a new policy that permitted producers to commit new gas reserves to pipelines at any price that could be demonstrated to be in the public interest, subject to certain limitations on future price increases for existing gas commitments.

Other governmental actions both helped and hindered efforts to improve the energy supply situation. In June U.S. Pres. Richard Nixon signed a law permitting the Atomic Energy Commission (AEC) to issue temporary operating licenses for nuclear power plants under certain conditions, even though a full-term license was in the process of environmental review. In January a court decision suspended a scheduled government sale of oil and gas leases in the offshore waters of the Gulf of Mexico on the grounds that under the National Environmental Protection Act a review of the environmental impact of the resulting oil and gas operations was required. This was the first application of the act to this kind of governmental action. The environmental review was duly made, and the lease sale was held in September.

The controversial pumped storage project at Storm King Mountain on the Hudson River to supply electricity to New York City, first approved by the FPC in 1965 and subject to litigation by environmentalist opposition ever since, cleared the last federal legal barrier when the U.S. Supreme Court approved it in June. Litigation at the state level continued, however, and the project remained in doubt. In May the AEC abandoned its attempt to store solidified high-level radioactive wastes in an abandoned salt mine in Kansas. The move had been strongly criticized as not offering a sufficient guarantee that radioactivity would not be released to the environment. As a substitute, the AEC turned to aboveground storage of the wastes, despite the fact that this method had been criticized in a 1966 report by the National Academy of Sciences.

In January it was announced that the Tennessee Valley Authority and a private utility would jointly build the first commercial breeder reactor in the U.S. Using liquid sodium metal as the coolant, it would produce more nuclear fuel than it consumed and would open the way to use of the abundant supplies of otherwise unusable uranium-238. The plant was to be located 25 mi. W of Knoxville, Tenn., and have a generating capacity of 300,000–500,000 kw. Costing between $300 million and $400 million, it would be the most expensive power plant ever built.

In September a contract was signed to build the world's first offshore nuclear power plant. To be finished in 1980, the facility was to be located a few miles off the coast opposite Atlantic City, N.J. It would float on a barge in 45 ft. of water and would be protected by a massive breakwater designed to resist the strongest hurricanes.

In Canada Prime Minister Pierre Trudeau dedicated the hydroelectric project at Churchill Falls, Nfd., in June. Only 2 of the scheduled 11 turbines were installed at the time, but when it was completed, sometime before 1976, the total capacity of 5.2 million kw. would make it the largest single hydroelectric power site in North America.

Further significant discoveries of oil and gas at remote sites in Canada continued to be made during the year. The second and third discoveries of gas occurred at Sable Island, a 20-mi.-long sandbar in the Atlantic 110 mi. SE of Nova Scotia. Although the discoveries were not themselves commercial, they greatly strengthened the prospects that further exploration would eventually lead to commercial production in this new area. Discoveries of both gas and oil at even more remote sites continued to be made in the Canadian Arctic in the fourth year of intensive exploration of that region.

The continuing exploration of the North Sea also made news, with large oil and gas discoveries in almost all the national sectors announced throughout the year. Several large, new oil fields were discovered in both the British and Norwegian sectors. Denmark became the second country to produce North Sea oil with the first commercial shipment in the country's history from the Dan field in its sector. One of the oil discoveries in the British sector recorded a potential flow of 28,000 bbl. a day, the largest yet reported for the North Sea and large even by Middle East standards.

The energy news from Great Britain was not all happy, however. January 9 marked the beginning of a coal miners' strike that lasted 47 days. Although total coal stocks at electric power plants constituted an eight-week supply, the stocks were unevenly distributed. Within three weeks the Central Electricity Generating Board was forced to cut voltage levels. By February 9 several power plants had shut down and others were operating at only partial capacity. A state of emergency was declared. The use of electricity for advertising and most outdoor lighting was banned. Despite the fact that it was the height of the heating season, electric heating of stores, offices, restaurants, and theatres was also banned. In order to conserve remaining coal stocks a system of rotating power cutoffs was instituted, with different areas being cut off from power in turn for periods as long as 12 hours. By the time the strike ended the British power system was on the verge of total shutdown, for almost three-quarters of the total generating capacity was coal-fired. The experience was a dramatic reminder to the country of the full significance of its new-found oil and gas.

In the ongoing struggle between the international oil companies and the oil-producing countries of the Middle East, the companies continued to give ground in 1972. In January the oil companies reached agreement with six Persian Gulf countries whereby the posted price of crude oil (on which taxes and royalties are based) was increased by 8.49% to offset the producing countries' revenue losses caused by devaluation of the dollar. The agreement also provided for further automatic changes to reflect any subsequent change in the value of the dollar. A similar agreement was reached in May between Libya and its foreign oil companies. In March it was announced that the oil company operating in Saudi Arabia had agreed to a 20% government ownership. This was the first success in the oil countries' announced campaign to obtain first 20% and ultimately 51% "participation" in all the oil companies operating within their boundaries.

The year's most serious conflict between producing countries and companies took place in Iraq. Because of a severe drop in tanker rates caused by temporary overcapacity, it became cheaper to move crude oil from the Persian Gulf to Europe by tanker around the Cape of Good Hope than to ship it to the eastern Mediterranean via pipeline. As a result the pipeline from Iraq was operating at only 65% of capacity, and production in that country was correspondingly reduced. In May Iraq issued an ultimatum to the oil companies, demanding that they restore oil exports to "maximum capacity." Just as the major company moved to comply, the government suddenly nationalized it. The following day Syria nationalized the pipeline from Iraq. The Iraqis immediately moved to market their own oil, but ran into serious difficulties because of possible threatened legal actions by the oil company against buyers. (BRUCE C. NETSCHERT)

COAL

World hard coal production in 1971, at an estimated 2,190,300,000 metric tons, was 7 million tons greater than in 1970. A work stoppage in the U.S. in 1971 accounted for a loss of more than 60 million metric tons. Japan's imports from Australia and Canada grew. Reductions in production in Western Europe amounted to 1%, but Eastern Europe's output (including the Soviet Union) increased 2.66%. China, with a level of 390 million metric tons, a gain of 30 million tons, maintained the position of the world's third largest producer.

With the world's energy requirements expected to double those of 1970 by the mid-1980s, coal was expected to remain a major primary source of energy. The three major producing countries, the Soviet Union, U.S., and China, estimated that their annual coal production would exceed 1,000,000,000 tons well before the end of the century.

U.S.S.R. In 1971 hard coal production totaled 485 million metric tons, a gain of 2.3% over 1970; 167 million tons were of the coking variety. Lignite production was 155 million tons, an increase of 5.1%. Over a quarter of the output came from open-pit operations. New facilities were brought into operation, and expansion of raw coal production to 720 million metric tons (412 million cleaned coal) by 1980 was planned. Almost 28 million tons of coal were exported, chiefly to Eastern European countries. Plans to develop Siberian coking coal reserves to satisfy some of the future needs of the Japanese steel industry were discussed in 1972.

United States. Demand for bituminous coal in 1972 was expected to exceed 1943's record consumption of 593.8 million short tons. In 1971, 553 million short tons of bituminous coal and lignite were produced, 8.3% short of 1970's 603 million short tons. A decline in domestic demand in 1971 was offset by increased consumption by the electric power utilities, which accounted for 64.9% of total national coal consumption. Demand from the electric power sector was expected to rise by over 6% yearly through 1977.

The predicted shortage of gas led to further research into the gasification of coal. Concern over pollution led to increased research into reducing the sulfur content of coal and its combustion products. The environmental disadvantages of open-pit mining operations, accounting for about half of U.S. coal production, received attention.

Exports in 1971 dropped 20% below the 1970 record. Reduced amounts to Japan and Europe accounted for most of the decline. Anthracite production, at 8.7 million tons, was down 11% from 1970.

European Economic Community (EEC). The five EEC coal-producing nations suffered further reductions in output in 1971, the Community-wide decline averaging 3.66%. Belgium produced 10.9 million metric tons, 402,000 tons less than in 1970. France showed a decrease of 4,350,000 to 33 million tons, and Italy fell by 242,000 tons, a loss of 18%. The Netherlands, planning to phase out production by 1975, suffered a 16.2% reduction to 3.6 million tons. West German production fell only 8.4% to 110,795,000 metric tons. Hard coal production in the EEC was again expected to fall in 1972. The number of miners declined in 1971 by 4.8% to 255,000.

United Kingdom. A seven-week miners' strike in the first two months of 1972, the first national strike since 1926, together with a preceding ten-week overtime ban, accounted for a production loss of 25.5 million long tons. Consequently, the National Coal Board (NCB) ended the financial year 1971–72 with a deficit, after interest repayments, of £157 million. NCB deep-mined output was 109.2 million long tons during the 1971–72 financial year, with an additional 9.9 million long tons from open-pit operations. There were also 1.2 million tons produced by licensed deep mines and open pits. Only three NCB collieries were closed, the lowest number in any year since nationalization of the industry. There was a marked reduction in fatalities, and the fatal accident rate, 0.1 per 100,000 manshifts worked, was the lowest on record. Output per manshift in underground mines dropped by 4.9% to 2.095 long tons.

Exports, at 2.1 million long tons, dropped nearly 1 million tons. Solid fuel imports in 1971–72 were about 5.5 million long tons.

Recovery from the strike was more rapid than expected. The long-term prospects for the industry were thought to be good provided industrial relations and consumer confidence could be restored.

Poland. In 1971 the coal industry continued to flourish; 145.5 million metric tons of hard coal were produced, an increase of 5.4 million over 1970. Production of lignite approached 35 million tons. Increased output was achieved by further mechanization and reduction in manpower. One new mine and development work at existing mines increased the annual production capacity by 8.4 million tons of hard coal. Poland was second only to the U.S. in coal exports, with 30.3 million tons in 1971, an increase of 1.5 million tons over 1970.

India. In the 1971–72 fiscal year coal production dropped to 69 million metric tons, compared with 71.9 million tons in 1970–71. The industry was beset with financial and technical problems. Competition from other fuels and transport deficiencies again caused stocks at mines to rise. Nationalization of 214 coking coal mines to conserve coking coal reserves and to increase output to meet the needs of the expanding steel industry was announced in October. Output for 1973–74 was planned to reach 90 million tons, a target unlikely to be achieved. Exports to Bangladesh, on which negotiations were begun in 1971, were expected to reach two million tons a year.

Japan. During 1971 output dropped by 6.3 million tons to 33.4 million metric tons of hard coal. Due to high production costs, adverse working conditions, and poor quality coal it remained cheaper to import. However, imports fell by 3.2 million to 46.9 million metric tons. Imports from the U.S. dropped by 26.7% to 18,490,000 metric tons, while Australia, Japan's second largest supplier, showed a modest increase with a record 16,590,000 metric tons. Canada registered a sharp increase to 6.8 million metric tons, nearly double the figure for 1970.

Australia. In 1971 exports reached a record 20,463,000 long tons, although production of black coal fell for the first time since 1959 to 48 million long tons, a decline of 800,000 long tons. The reversal in the trend of increasing yearly production was attributed to work stoppages during the third quarter and a reduction in the working week. Queensland's increase of 885,000 long tons was not enough to counteract the fall of 1,313,000 long tons in New South Wales. Production of brown coal in Victoria totaled 23 million long tons. Exports of bituminous coal to Japan were 16.8 million long tons; the bulk of the remainder went to European destinations.

Africa. Of an estimated output of 64 million metric tons of coal in Africa in 1971, 58.7 million were produced by South Africa and 3.1 million tons by Rhodesia. Production in 1972 was expected to be severely reduced by a methane explosion at the No. 2 Wankie Colliery in June 1972, which involved considerable loss of life. South African bituminous coal production in 1972 rose sharply by 7.4% to 56.8 million metric tons, allowing additions to coal stocks which had been drawn on in 1970. The South African coal industry confidently expected to join in the expanding world trade in high-quality coking and steam coals, and to this end new rail links and a new deepwater port facility were under construction at Richard's Bay, Natal. However, concern over the actual amount of workable reserves was expressed.

South America. Coal production during 1971, at 8.4 million metric tons, a gain of 100,000 tons over 1970, accounted for only 0.4% of the world total. This slow, but steady, increase in production still fell considerably below the continent's requirements. Colombia was the largest producer, with 3.7 million tons; Brazil produced 2.4 million tons, and Chile 1.5 million tons.

Canada. In Canada, where coal production had doubled since 1969, a total of 19.3 million short tons of all types of coal was produced in 1971. This figure represented an increase of 16.4% over 1970 and exceeded the previous record set in 1951 of 19.1 million short tons.

Canada's exports reached a record 7.8 million short tons, an impressive increase compared with the 1.4 million short tons exported in 1969. Exports to Japan accounted for over 7.4 million short tons, a staggering increase nearly doubling the 1970 figure. By the mid-1970s exports were expected to reach 14 million short tons a year.

Contracts to provide 200 million short tons of coking coal to Japan over the next 15 years assured a bright future for the industry, with coal production forecast to reach 30 million short tons a year by 1975.

(R. J. FOWELL)

ELECTRICITY

In 1972 the rate of increase in electricity production continued to slow down, a trend already noticeable in 1971, despite the steady growth in consumption of electricity by domestic and commercial users. Nuclear power achieved competitiveness with fuel oil, but was not likely to replace it for several years. When fast-breeder reactors were perfected, one ton of uranium would supply more power than 650,000 tons of oil, and it was therefore not surprising that leading oil companies showed interest in the building of such devices.

Nuclear Electric Power. In May 1972 world production of nuclear electricity passed 500 billion kw-hr., the U.K. leading the field with 43.7% of the total. Some 53% of this production came from gas-graphite reactors, but the days of these were numbered, production having been abandoned in favour of the light-water reactors, both pressurized-water (PWR) and boiling-water (BWR) reactors. No visible progress was made in solving the problem of producing the quantities of enriched uranium that such stations required, and European producers had to buy supplies from the U.S., which still had excess capacity. The feasibility of establishing facilities in Europe for the enrichment of uranium was studied. France, with a factory at Pierrelatte, supported gas diffusion, the only technique so far applied. It, however, required massive investment, adequate production facilities costing about $1 billion, and would consume great quantities of electricity. The U.K., West Germany, and the Netherlands combined to perfect the centrifuge technique, which needed smaller facilities.

At the beginning of 1972, 23 nuclear power stations (10,041 Mw.) were in service in the U.S., with an additional 106 stations (97,-349 Mw.) under construction or on order; the combined total was about twice the capacity of the rest of the world. For these all to be fully operational by the end of the decade, the U.S. nuclear industry would need to overcome legal, administrative, and juridical chaos, and attacks from those persons and groups opposed to the development of nuclear power stations. (*See* INDUSTRIAL REVIEW: *Nuclear Industry*.) In 1971 there were no authorizations for the inauguration of new nuclear stations in the U.S. However, legislation introduced in 1972 allowed the Atomic Energy Commission (AEC) to issue temporary authorizations for bringing stations into service where local demands for electricity were urgent, and 15 new stations were expected to be so covered.

As a consequence of opposition by environmentalists, consideration was given to using offshore floating stations. The Public Service Co. of New Jersey announced that suitable sites had been selected for two such stations, but the consequent furore made it clear that offshore sites too would present environmental problems. However, despite the setbacks, the development of nuclear power in the U.S. did not appear to be threatened. Orders for nuclear reactors for 1972 were expected to reach 35 units (40,000 Mw.), compared with 23 units (23,370 Mw.) in 1971. The Commonwealth Edison Co. and the Tennessee Valley Authority (TVA) set up the Breeder Reactor Corp. to build the first large-scale demonstration breeder reactor in the U.S. with government finance providing $100 million and the rest of the money coming from the electricity companies and the plant manufacturers.

In the U.K. studies were made on replacing the carbon gas used in advanced gas-cooled reactors (AGRs) with helium in an attempt to reduce oxidization. The British government deferred until 1974 a decision on an intermediate reactor. Possibilities under consideration included an improved AGR, a high-temperature reactor (HTR), a heavy-water reactor of the SCHWR or the Canadian CANDU type, or a light-water reactor (BWR or PWR). The Wylfa station in North Wales, inaugurated in May, was at the year's end the most powerful station in service anywhere in the world.

In other developments West Germany, the Netherlands, and Belgium combined to set up a 300-Mw. fast-breeder station at an estimated cost of $460 million. The Euro-HKG Company, a consortium of West German, French, Italian, and British producers, was formed in December 1971 to collaborate on the development of high-temperature reactors. The government of Hesse, W.Ger., announced that no more stations would be authorized to use Rhine waters for cooling. The last of France's natural uranium-gas-graphite reactors, Bugey I (540 Mw.), was linked to the grid in April 1972. The stations at Würgassen (BWR, 670 Mw.) and Stade (PWR, 640 Mw.) in West Germany commenced production at the beginning of the year. Spain's nuclear capacity reached 1,093 Mw. when the Franco-Spanish station at Vandellos was linked to the grid in May. Spain had five more nuclear power stations on order. Sweden's first nuclear power station, a 440-Mw. BWR at Oskarshamm, was also inaugurated in May.

In Switzerland, growing public hostility delayed the movement toward nuclear power necessitated by the exhaustion of hydroelectric resources. The situation was complicated by a ruling that the cooling capacity of the Rhine had been exhausted. Refrigeration towers might have provided a solution, but their use was vetoed on aesthetic grounds. Switzerland accordingly signed two agreements with France to provide for 30% Swiss participation in the Fessenheim I and Bugey II stations and a 30% right to the electricity produced.

In the Soviet Union, the third section of the Novo-Voronedz station (PWR, 440 Mw.) went into service in June, and construction of the Shevchenko reactor was completed. Bulgaria began to build its first nuclear station, near Kozlodin, capacity 880 Mw., from equipment supplied entirely by the Soviet Union.

The Gentilly nuclear station in Canada reached maximum capacity (250 Mw.), and the third sector of the Pickering station, capacity 540 Mw., was brought into operation in May. Canada's nuclear program was delayed by the failure of the heavy water factory at Glace Bay, and it seemed that supplies of heavy water would have to be obtained from other countries.

In Japan, at the beginning of 1972, there were 4 nuclear power stations in service and 12 more under construction. Like the U.S., Japan was investigating offshore nuclear power stations.

Thermoelectricity. Conventional thermal stations still provided for most of the increased electricity consumption, with oil continuing to advance at the expense of coal. The TVA's Cumberland power station in the U.S., with 1,350 Mw. of capacity and the largest of its kind in the world, was inaugurated in July. Several other units of 700–800-Mw. capacity were brought into service. In the Soviet Union plans for a 1,200-Mw. capacity unit were completed, and three new coal-fired stations, total capacity 7,100 Mw., were brought into service in the Donets basin. In France the second group of the La Maxe station, near Metz, went into operation at the beginning of the year; the station was entirely automatic with a staff of six. No new stations were ordered by the British Central Electricity Generating Board (CEGB) in 1972.

In Australia, work began on extending the Vales power station in New South Wales. The capacity of the station was to be increased from 875 Mw. to 2,195 Mw., and completion was scheduled for 1978.

Hydroelectricity. The less developed countries still had natural resources to exploit, while the industrialized countries concentrated on pumped storage equipment. Ten conventional hydroelectric groups, total capacity 500 Mw., and seven reversible generator-motor pumping groups, total capacity 1,500 Mw., became operative in the U.S.

In Canada, the Churchill Falls project, in Labrador, started to supply electricity. When fully in operation, the station would have a capacity of 5,225 Mw. and a mean annual output of 34.5 billion kw-hr. Bids were invited for the underground station at Mica on the Columbia River, and work started on the 10,000-Mw. James Bay project in Quebec Province and on the Nelson River scheme at Long Spruce, Man.

In Europe, the French hydroelectric power station at Strasbourg (mean annual output, 747 million kw-hr.), the last of the eight stations on the Rhine, was inaugurated in September. Greece started construction of a hydroelectric project on the Polyphiton River in western Macedonia. In the U.K., the CEGB planned construction of an underground pumped storage plant, capacity 1,440 Mw., at Dinorwic, North Wales.

In Zambia, the inauguration of the fourth 150-Mw. group completed the first stage of the project to harness Kafue Gorge, on the Kafue River (a tributary of the Zambezi).

Installed Capacity and Production of Electric Power in Selected Countries, Jan. 1, 1971

Political division	Hydroelectric power: Operating plants: Installed capacity (000 kw.)	Hydroelectric power: Operating plants: Production (000,000 kw-hr.)	Total electric power: Installed capacity (000 kw.)	Total electric power: Production (000,000 kw-hr.)
World	...	...	...	4,901,100
Afghanistan*	212	306	230	325
Algeria†	340*	576	639*	1,704
Angola	211	386‡	312	644
Argentina*	609	1,341	6,318	19,879
Australia*	3,592†	9,045†	12,263†	53,826
Austria	5,467	21,240	7,976	30,036
Belgium	66†	246†	6,769§	30,523‖
Bolivia*	171	601	252	731
Brazil	8,829	39,863	11,233	45,460
Bulgaria	816†	2,152†	4,117	19,513
Burma	193	418	258	629
Cambodia†	—	—	63‡♀	132.7
Cameroon	152	1,145	179	1,170
Canada	28,299	156,285	42,826§	203,702‖
Central African Republic†	7¶	42	10¶	46
Chile	1,067	4,307	2,143	7,550
Colombia	1,164‡	6,058*	2,250*	8,750
Costa Rica	182	940	244	1,028
Cuba	—	81†‡	1,400‡	4,266*
Czechoslovakia	1,542	3,670	10,808	45,163
Denmark	9†	24†	4,775	18,864
Ecuador	106	405	304	949
Egypt*	1,920†	4,002†	3,848	7,134
El Salvador	108†	473†	204	671
Ethiopia	91*†	240*	292¶	455*
Finland	2,093*	9,434	4,683*	22,562
France	15,219	56,612	38,809§	140,708‖
Germany, East	690‡	1,251	12,669§	67,650‖
Germany, West	4,779	17,758	50,833§	237,209‖
Ghana	512†‡	2,882†	631‡	2,920
Greece	1,041†	2,630†	2,395*	8,427*
Guatemala	43†‡	181*†	177*	589‡
Honduras	31*†	204*†	92*	310
Hungary	20†	88†	2,733	14,537
Iceland	244†	1,413†	354□	1,470◇
India	6,458	24,551	16,429§	59,975‖
Indonesia*†	310	1,169	667	1,871
Iran	462*†	1,336*†	1,313*†	7,044
Ireland†	219*	594*	1,410*	5,817
Israel♀	—	—	1,226†	6,838
Italy	14,962	41,300	33,252§□	117,423‖◇
Jamaica	16†	113*†	257‡	1,550
Japan	20,044	—	68,311§□	—
Kenya†	68	316	153	512
Korea, South	329†	1,217†	2,556	9,780
Lebanon†	246*	877	426*	1,230
Liberia	38	242	224	502
Libya†♀	—	—	140	426
Luxembourg	932†	887†	1,157	2,148
Malaysia:				
Malaya	293‡	1,202	866	3,347
Sabah♀	—	—	35	90
Sarawak♀	—	—	45	108
Mexico	3,326†	14,992	7,414□	28,608
Morocco	300†	1,333†	466	1,935
Netherlands♀	—	—	10,560§	40,859‖
New Zealand†	2,971	11,266	3,793□	13,706◇
Nicaragua	57†	267†	170	550†
Nigeria	29†‡	1,365†	805	1,550
Norway	12,783	57,261	12,910	57,606
Pakistan†	666*	2,913*	2,398	6,886*
Panama	15*†	80*†	249	859*
Paraguay	...	117*†	110*	220
Peru	934‡	3,168δ	1,672‡	5,324
Philippines*	547†	1,763†	2,036	8,213
Poland	771†	1,887†	13,891	64,531
Portugal	1,556	5,794	2,186	7,379
Rhodesia	705†	5,247†	1,192	6,410
Romania	1,200	2,773	7,346	35,088
Singapore†♀	—	—	644	2,205
South Africa	...	...	...	48,680
Spain	10,592	27,430	17,900§	55,901‖
Sri Lanka (Ceylon)	195	723	281	816
Sweden	10,862	41,538	15,307§	60,645‖
Switzerland	9,120‡	29,330	9,880*§	33,173‖
Syria	—	—	333	947
Taiwan	901†	2,846†	2,851	13,554
Tanzania†	41¶	...	72¶	396
Thailand*	451†	1,046	1,044	3,728
Tunisia	28*†	40†	257	794
Turkey	723	3,028	2,292	8,616
Uganda	150*†	727*†	161δ	734†
U.S.S.R.	31,368	124,377	166,150§	740,400‖
United Kingdom	2,158	5,666	66,975§	248,588‖
United States	55,752	250,612	360,355§□	1,638,010‖◇
Uruguay	225†δ	1,141†‡	470δ	1,944δ
Venezuela	...	2,748‡	3,210	12,631
Vietnam, South†	163δ	—	513*	1,134
Yugoslavia	3,327	14,741	6,406	26,024
Zaire	—	2,847*	—	3,194
Zambia	180	...	364	949

1969. †Public sector only. ‡1968. §Includes nuclear (in 000 kw.): Belgium 11; Canada 240; France 1,771; Germany, East 75*; Germany, West 958; India 420; Italy 642; Japan 1,336; Netherlands 54; Spain 153; Sweden 10; Switzerland 350*; U.S.S.R. est. 1,150‡; U.K. 4,813; U.S. 6,493. ‖Includes nuclear (in 000,000 kw-hr.): Belgium 57; Canada 969; France 5,147; Germany, East 425*; Germany, West 6,030; India 2,348; Italy 3,176; Japan 4,581; Netherlands 368; Spain 923; Sweden 56; Switzerland 523*; U.S.S.R. 2,500‡; U.K. 25,428; U.S. 21,801. ¶1966. ♀Thermal only. δ1967. □Includes geothermal (in 000 kw.): Iceland 2.6; Italy 402; Japan 31; Mexico 4; New Zealand 192; U.S. 84. ◇Includes geothermal (in 000,000 kw-hr.): Iceland 12; Italy 2,725; Japan 243; New Zealand 1,185; U.S. 525.

Source: United Nations. (FRANK H. SKELDING)

The first group of Tumut 3, the last and largest of the Snowy Mountains schemes in New South Wales, went into operation in Australia, and Tasmania's Hydro Electric Commission undertook a project, to include an underground power station, on the Gordon River.

The Brazilian government approved construction of a station at Salto de Santiago with an eventual capacity of 1,160 Mw. The Itauba plant on the Rio Jaciu in the south would have a capacity of 500 Mw. A consortium of Brazilian, West German, and French firms was formed to build the 1,400-Mw.-capacity Merimbondo station on the Rio Grande.

The first two groups of the Nurek power station in the Soviet republic of Tadzhikistan were brought into service. When completed, the station would have a capacity of 2,700 Mw. (LUCIEN CHALMEY)

GAS

Natural gas demand in the U.S. continued to diminish reserves in 1972. The situation, however, brought action aimed at assuring adequate future supply. Federal regulators allowed higher returns on newer discoveries hoping that this would provide greater incentive toward future gas exploration and production. The courts continued to iron out litigation affecting at least 39 trillion cubic feet (Tcf) of gas and perhaps as much as 327 Tcf in Alaska.

Users in the U.S. once again tapped one Tcf more gas yearly. They were expected to require as much additional gas each year for the next two decades. To meet the increasing demand the U.S. had an estimated 278.8 Tcf of proved reserves, including 31 Tcf in Alaska, plus any proved reserves off the shore of Louisiana opened up by federal government lease sales.

New discoveries off the shore of southern Alaska were said to rival earlier untapped deposits on the state's North Slope. Geological surveys and bottom samplings were being made by the federal government along the Atlantic outer continental shelf north of Cape Hatteras. Public Service Co. of Indiana and Westinghouse Electric began tests to convert high-sulfur coal into nearly pollution-free synthetic gas to fuel a power plant. A group of 11 companies planned to help finance the Continental Oil Co. and the British and Scottish gas councils to perform tests to raise coal gas to natural gas standards. People's Gas Co. announced a $50 million plant near Chicago to convert petroleum liquids into substitute natural gas. Lone Star Gas drilled a record 30,050 ft. deep in Texas earth in search of gas.

Louisiana and Texas provided 64.9% of the nation's gas reserves and 71.7% of its production; by adding Arkansas, New Mexico, and Oklahoma, 90.7% of gas reserves and 92.1% of production were accounted for. Of the net annual production, which continued to be about 22 Tcf, approximately two-thirds was handled in interstate markets. The U.S. Federal Power Commission (FPC) moved to divert more gas earmarked for within a state to the interstate market by allowing higher charges by producers.

Under leadership of the Independent Natural Gas Association of America, industry also recognized that steps must be taken to remedy the gas supply squeeze. Specifically, INGAA recommended immediate development of a price structure taking into account the true value of gas in relation to alternate fuels; a statutory time frame for the conclusion of regulatory processes and procedures; sanctity of contract gas prices within current regulatory jurisdiction; streamlining of price, facilities, and service jurisdiction; accommodation with Canada on gas; resolution of Arctic gas transportation problems; orderly, flexible, accelerated, and timely policy for federal leasing of lands; expediting the importation of liquefied natural gas; and a practical and timely approach to environment laws.

Toward similar goals of cutting red tape, the U.S. Price Commission allowed regulatory agencies to set price increases under its watchful eye. The FPC moved to allow higher price ceilings for new gas contracts. The U.S. Supreme Court upheld the FPC's right to allocate in times of scarcity gas supplies between industrial and home users.

Questions were raised as to methods of accounting for exploration expenses. Efforts by the FPC to stimulate exploration by allowing regulated monopolies and near monopolies to set higher prices in situations of public convenience and necessity ran into stiff opposition from purists among regulatory experts and from the U.S. Congress. Some indicated that pricing difficulties stemmed from a tendency of the FPC to favour the gas industry rather than its consumers. The FPC finally allowed the new regulatory step as an option on new gas under a number of specified conditions, including agreement by all contracting parties.

The FPC during the year allowed the importation of liquefied natural gas (LNG) under circumstances it believed fair in the U.S. domestic market. While several companies lined up to import LNG from Algeria and Australia—1,000,000,000 cu.ft. daily for 25 years from Algeria alone—the FPC ran into difficulty nationally and internationally in its attempts to list a fair price for the imported LNG. Algeria complained about the price, and applicant companies fretted over FPC stipulations: price ceilings, separate billing requirements for imported gas, and possible changes left open for FPC to make later. The threat of litigation lingered over the LNG situation. The fact that the U.S. Supreme Court in 1972 forced El Paso Natural Gas to divest itself of the holdings acquired in a 1957 merger with Pacific Northwest Pipeline Corp., after 15 years of litigation, further dampened the outlook.

Canadian proved reserves climbed 2.1 Tcf in 1971 to 55.5 Tcf, and annual production stood at 2 Tcf. Reserves were estimated to be 50 Tcf for the next 25 years, with two-thirds to be used at home and one-third earmarked for export. Discoveries in the Canadian Arctic were to be added later, with 10 Tcf already earmarked for export to the Wisconsin-Michigan area over two decades beginning in the mid-1970s. Current exports to the U.S. increased in 1971 for the 12th consecutive year, almost reaching 1 Tcf. (JOSEPH J. ACCARDO)

The British part of the North Sea continental shelf, particularly off the Scottish coast and the Orkneys and Shetlands, was one of the busiest exploration areas in the world in 1972 as major international oil companies continued their highly successful search next door to one of the world's major markets for fuel. While the main emphasis of the search was on oil, gas—either associated with oil or on its own—was also discovered in significant quantities. In the Frigg field, straddling the median line between British and Norwegian waters, the gas was not associated with oil and the field was thought to be the second biggest so far discovered in the North Sea. (The largest, Leman Bank, began production in 1968.)

At the height of the 1972 exploration season, 15 offshore drilling platforms (still in short supply internationally) were at work in the North Sea. Throughout the year preliminary exploration was carried out over a wide area of virgin territory. Besides the North Sea, attention focused on parts of the Irish Sea, the Western Approaches, and the Bristol and English channels. In addition, there was considerable exploration activity onshore in various parts of the U.K.

In fiscal 1971–72 total gas sales in the

Electric Power Production of Selected Countries, 1970
By source

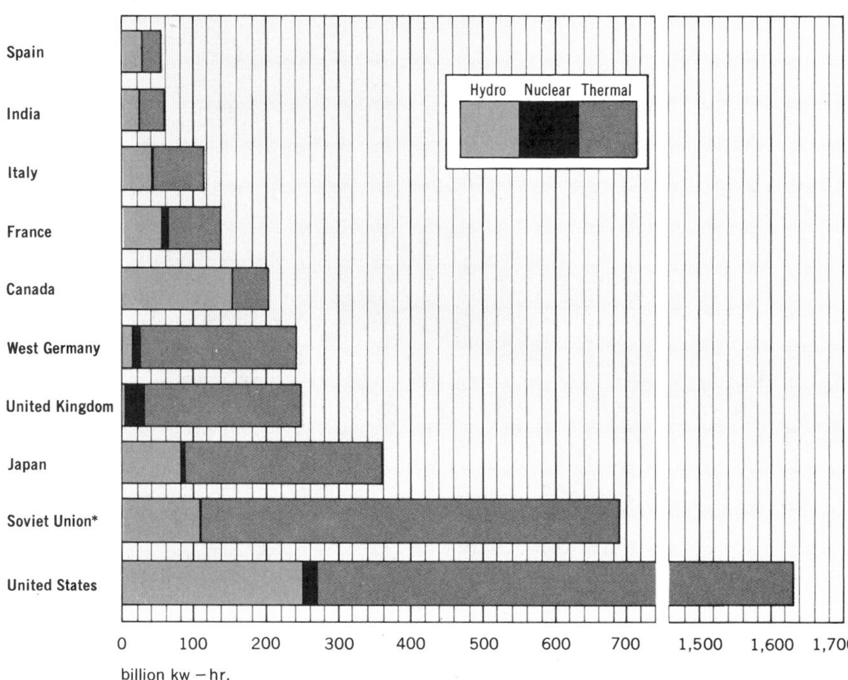

*1969

Sources: United Nations, *Statistical Yearbook 1971*; United Nations, *World Energy Supplies 1966–1969*.

U.K. were 8,040,000,000 therms, 30% over the previous year. Almost 90% of the total was natural gas (against 70% of the much smaller total in 1970–71). The gas sales boom continued throughout 1972, helped no doubt by the reaction to the previous winter's coal strike and electricity power cuts. The national program of converting appliances to burn natural instead of manufactured gas passed the halfway mark, and by the end of the year about 7½ million customers, out of a total of 13½ million, were using the new gas. The program was expected to be virtually completed by 1977.

The massive engineering works to exploit North Sea gas also continued. The mileage of large-diameter pipeline laid in 1971–72 dropped compared with previous years, as the system length neared the 2,500-mi. target for the mid-1970s, but more work was done on compressor stations placed at strategic points on the network to boost gas pressure and help keep the pipelines running at nearer their maximum capacity.

At the northern end of the national transmission system, Europe's first natural gas liquefaction plant, at Glenmavis, Scot., was commissioned during the year. North Sea gas from the pipeline was liquefied and stored in a giant, insulated tank holding the equivalent of 1,000,000,000 cu.ft. of gas. When gas demand reached a peak, the liquid was evaporated and gas fed back into the pipeline to boost supplies for northern Britain. A similar but bigger plant was under construction at Partington, Eng., and design work started on one for South Wales.

As a second way of meeting winter peaks in natural gas demand, the economics and operation of a substitute natural gas plant began to be studied in the U.K. during the year with the adaptation of part of Portsmouth gasworks. The gas, produced from a fraction of oil, was fully compatible and interchangeable with natural gas: customers could not tell the difference. The Portsmouth experiment aroused interest in the United States, where Britain was building a thriving export market for its gas manufacturing technology. Plants ordered in the past two years by U.S. gas utilities and based on developments pioneered in the U.K. would have a capacity equal to the entire output of the British gas industry in 1971. The plants, using various petroleum products as raw materials, were designed to make a substitute natural gas to help supplement falling natural gas reserves in the U.S.

In the Netherlands, where, as in the U.S., gas accounted for about one-third of all fuel used, gas sales continued to expand rapidly in 1972 following the 38.5% rise in 1971. The 1972 increase was expected to be 33%, with sales, including exports, reaching 58,000,000,000 cu.m. During the year future output of the giant Groningen field was reassessed. The yearly level expected to be reached by the later 1970s was put at 82,500,000,000 cu.m., against the previous estimate of more than 100,000,000,000 cu.m. a year. Exports of Dutch gas to West Germany were expected to reach 14,000,000,000 cu.m. by 1975; to Belgium, 11,000,000,000; to France, 9,000,000,000; to Italy, 6,000,000,000; and to Switzerland, 500 million. By 1980 total exports should reach 50,000,000,000 cu.m.

The European gas export business grew more complex in 1972 as a result of an agreement signed by the Netherlands, Italy, France, and the U.S.S.R. The main agreement, signed in principle in 1971, involved the last two countries—with France taking approximately 2,500,000,000 cu.m. of Soviet gas annually over a 20-year period. To avoid costly pipelining, however, Italy agreed to take the Soviet gas—through a pipeline being laid as part of a 1969 Italo-Soviet deal—and to cede to France equivalent quantities of Dutch gas. The Soviets also did new business with West Germany during the year. The amount of gas under an earlier contract would be increased from 3,000,000,000 cu.m. to 7,000,000,000 by the end of the decade. The U.S.S.R. would thus become West Germany's largest foreign supplier.

In Australia the natural gas business was also booming, but there indigenous resources were being tapped. Commercial usage during the year ended June 30, 1972, was 92,801,000,000 cu.ft., compared with 69,275,000,000 in 1970–71. (M. BERNARD SMITH)

PETROLEUM

The year was again marked by discussions between members of the national oil industries and those from the Organization of Petroleum Exporting Countries (OPEC). Initially these centred on the impact upon tax reference prices of the de facto devaluation of the U.S. dollar in August 1971. OPEC claimed an increase in prices of 11.7%, but the principal oil companies contended that the provisions of the Teheran and Tripoli five-year agreements of January and April 1971 covered the situation. A compromise was reached at Geneva on Jan. 20, 1972, and an 8.49% increase was granted.

The continuing negotiations on the issue of participation by the producing countries were more crucial. These were conducted in accordance with Resolution No. 139 passed at the 25th OPEC conference in Beirut, Leb., in September 1971, with the Saudi Arabian oil minister, Ahmad Zaki al-Yamani, acting on behalf of OPEC. He negotiated with a representative committee of the companies concerned to secure an initial 20% participation, eventually to rise to 51% of the estimated book value of the assets. The companies at first resisted participation, but later accepted it, securing more favourable terms for those assets to be disposed of, better safeguards for assets to be retained, and a better return for the oil that they would have to make available to the national oil companies of the countries concerned.

Iraq nationalized the northern concessions of the Iraq Petroleum Co. (IPC), and Nadim Pachachi, secretary-general of OPEC, and Jean Danner, director of the Compagnie Française des Pétroles (CFP), were appointed arbitrators between the Iraq government and IPC. The shah of Iran announced in London on June 24 that he had settled with the consortium of oil companies in Iran for a separate agreement, outside the participation mandate agreed upon by OPEC. The main provisions of the agreement consisted of an investment program to double production by 1980, the handing over of the Abadan refinery, an equal participation venture for oil exploration and development in Lurestan, and the delivery of crude oil for marketing at an "advantageous price."

Middle East production continued important, providing almost one-third of the world's total consumption, with reserves approaching nearly 60%. Outside the Middle East, interest centred on the North Sea. A string of discoveries during 1972 confirmed the area as a major source with estimated recoverable reserves of 7 billion bbl. Suggestions were made that the area should fall within the sphere of EEC energy policy, but national policies seemed to run counter to such proposals and the rejection by Norway of EEC membership made it less realizable in the near future. In the U.S., where import restrictions were further eased, the projected shortage of energy caused considerable concern. On the North Slope of Alaska activity was suspended pending the outcome of appeals by conservationists against proposals to authorize the construction of the pipeline. In the U.S.S.R. discussions took place with U.S. and Japanese interests on opening up the oil and gas fields of Siberia for commercial production and constructing the necessary pipelines to the coastal terminals.

The growth rate for petroleum products declined during 1971 and the first six months of 1972. The earnings and profits of the oil industry fell at the same time, while the need for funds for increased investment rose. In 1971 a group of companies representing 75% of the industry was reported to have spent $12.9 billion on capital expenditure. The proposed legislation respecting motor vehicle exhaust emission and other antipollution measures in most countries taxed the ingenuity of petroleum chemists and motor manufacturers throughout the year.

Reserves. At the beginning of 1972 the total world proved and probable oil reserves increased to 641,800,000,000 bbl., compared with 620,700,000,000 bbl. for the previous year. This was enough for 33 years at current rates of consumption and discovery. The Western Hemisphere share was 87,200,000,000 bbl., remaining at 13.4% of the total, and that of the Eastern Hemisphere, 554,600,000,000 bbl., also unchanged at 86.6%. The Middle East accounted for the largest share of the world reserves, 366,800,000,000 bbl., increased to 57.6%, while the U.S.S.R., Eastern Europe, and China decreased to 15.4%, and the U.S. to 6.8%.

Production. During 1971 world crude oil production increased by 5.6% to 50,370,000 bbl. a day. The increase in 1970 had been 9.6%. The Middle East dominated production with an increased share of 32.4%, 16,156,000 bbl. a day, with considerable increases from Saudi Arabia, 4.5 million bbl., 13.5%, and 4,540,000 bbl., 16.5%, from Iran. The U.S. produced 9,530,000 bbl. a day, 19.1% of the world total, a drop of 1.1% from 1970. Venezuelan production was 3,610,000 bbl. a day in 1971, 7.5% of the total and a 4% decrease from 1970. During 1971 Nigeria continued its spectacular increase, production being 1,525,000 bbl. a day, a 40.2% increase over 1970.

World crude oil production totaled 49,678,000 bbl. a day during January–June 1972, an increase of 1.9% over the corresponding period of 1971. The Middle East accounted for 17,266,000 bbl. a day, an increase of 7.6%, and the Soviet Union produced 8,138,000 bbl. a day, up 5.4%.

Consumption. World consumption of petroleum in 1971 was 48,770,000 bbl. a day, an increase of 5.4% over 1970. Japanese demand fell from 17.7% of the world total in 1970 to 10.5% in 1971 to 4,440,000 bbl. a day, 9%, in 1972. The U.S. remained the largest single consuming nation, 14,780,000 bbl. a day in 1971, a 3% increase over 1970 and 30% of the world total. Western European consumption in 1971 was 13,180,000 bbl. a day, an increase of 4.2% over 1970 and 27% of the world total. Approximately 86% of European imports came from the Middle East and North Africa. Japan took 83% of its requirements from the Middle East. Two-thirds of Caribbean exports went to the U.S. Analyzing consumption by sectors of industry, in the U.S. transport consumed the most oil followed by domestic and commercial usage and manufacturing. In Western Europe the three sectors were about the same in their requirements, but in Japan manufacturing took most, followed by transport and domestic and commercial usage.

Refining. World refining capacity in 1971 was 55.6 million bbl. a day, an increase of 9% over 1970. The capacity of the Western Hemisphere was 20,930,000, Western Europe 15,850,000, the Middle East 2,370,000, and the U.S.S.R., Eastern Europe, and China 8,720,000 bbl. a day. The U.S. accounted for 23.7% of the world total and Japan for 6.8%. In Western Europe, Italy had the largest share at 6.2%, while the region as a whole had 28.5%.

Transportation. The world tanker fleet at the beginning of 1972 totaled 175.3 million tons deadweight (dw.), a sizable increase of 19.6% over 1970. Of this tonnage almost one-third was owned by the oil companies, nearly two-thirds were in private ownership, and the rest were government owned. Nearly a quarter of the tonnage was made up by vessels of 205,000 tons dw. and over.

Petrochemicals. The 1971–72 period remained difficult for the petrochemical industry. Continuing lower profits, rising costs, and slackening economic activity caused companies everywhere to be cautious, retrenching capital expenditure. In Italy the publication of the National Chemical Plan aroused much controversy over control policies and investment and the roles of the companies that dominated the industry.

(R. W. FERRIER)

See also Engineering Projects; Industrial Review; Mining; Transportation.

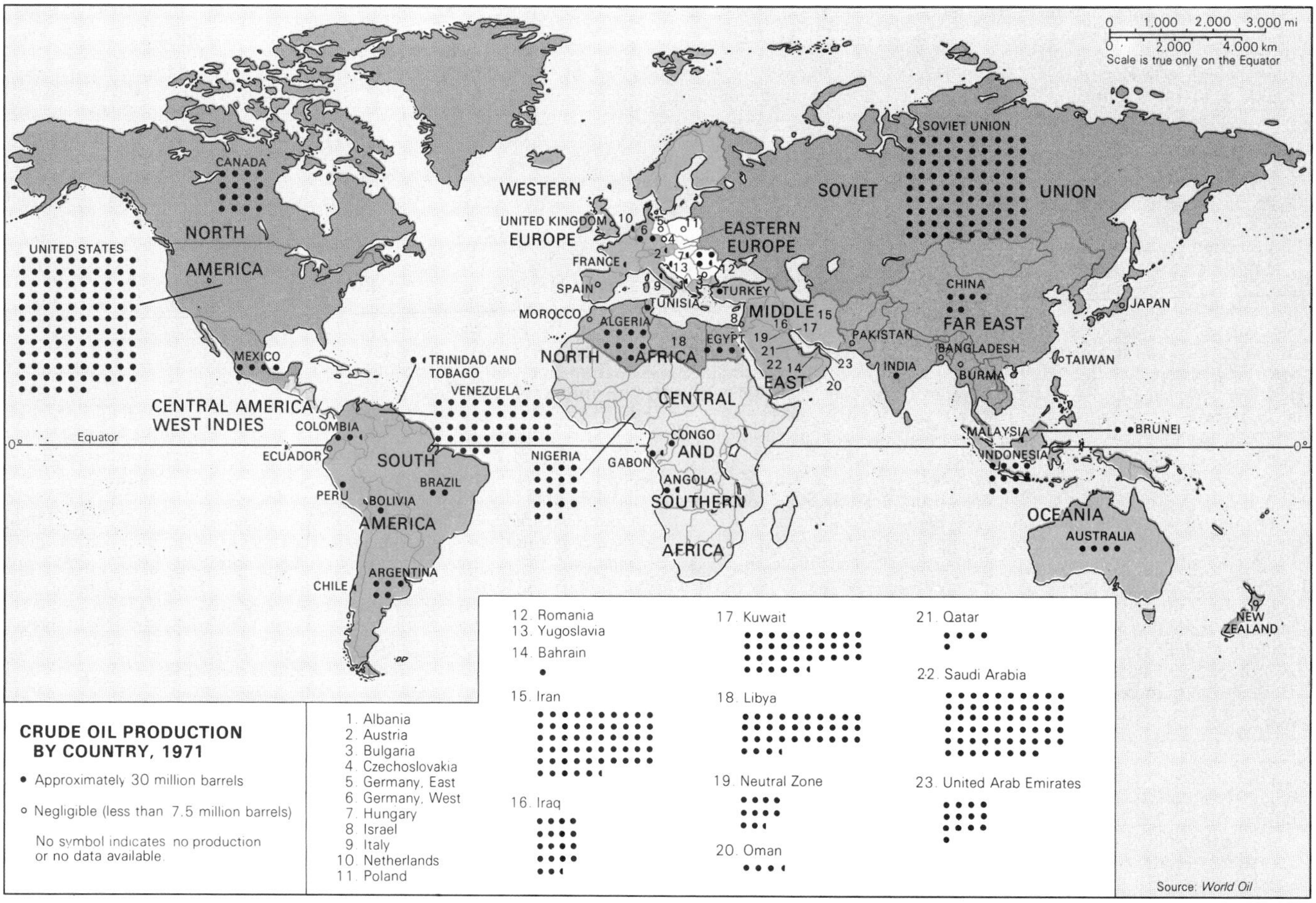

CRUDE OIL PRODUCTION BY COUNTRY, 1971

- ● Approximately 30 million barrels
- ○ Negligible (less than 7.5 million barrels)

No symbol indicates no production or no data available.

1. Albania
2. Austria
3. Bulgaria
4. Czechoslovakia
5. Germany, East
6. Germany, West
7. Hungary
8. Israel
9. Italy
10. Netherlands
11. Poland
12. Romania
13. Yugoslavia
14. Bahrain
15. Iran
16. Iraq
17. Kuwait
18. Libya
19. Neutral Zone
20. Oman
21. Qatar
22. Saudi Arabia
23. United Arab Emirates

Source: *World Oil*

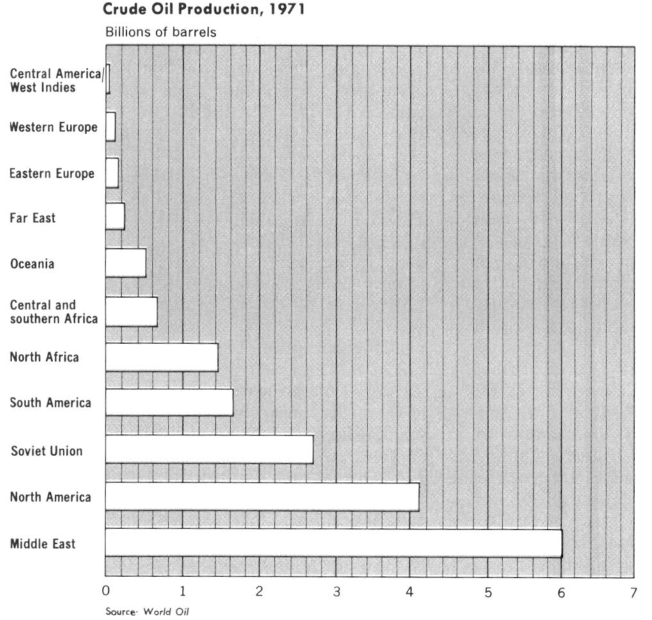

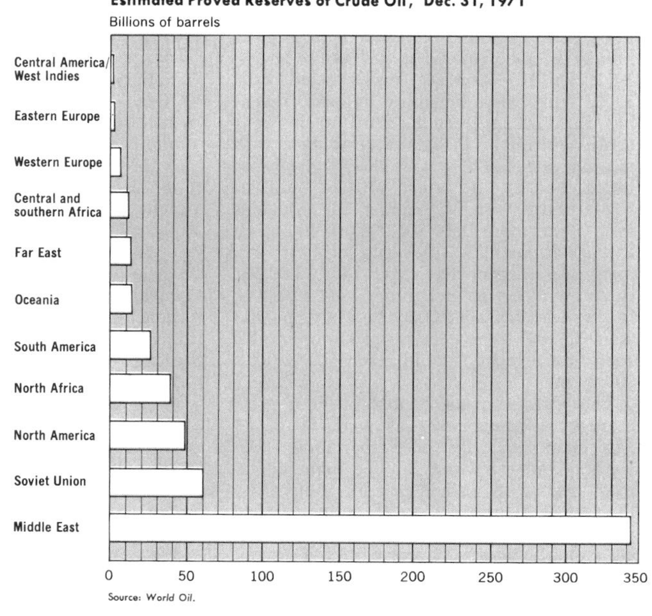

Furs

The U.S. retail fur business staged a comeback in 1972, following the severe depression of the previous year. Although no official statistics were available at year's end, unofficial estimates placed retail fur sales at least 10% above 1971. The uncertainty over coat lengths dissipated, and women returned to their furriers with greater confidence. Customers appeared to endorse the new length of an inch below the knee, while the versatile three-quarter length gained in popularity.

Antifur campaigns by humane and conservationist-oriented organizations were muted, while the fur industry mounted its first coordinated promotion effort —through the Fur Conservation Institute of America —to emphasize its almost total dependence on furs from animals specifically bred for that purpose. Significantly, producers of fake furs had a difficult year.

But while retail sales improved, the industry continued to contract. Few young people were entering a business that held little hope of real expansion. The manufacturing segment of the industry shrank by more than 20% during the year, mainly as a result of retirements. The skin-dealing area also experienced a sharp reduction as merchants, once the crown princes of the fur industry, saw their capital dwindling.

Fewer mink were produced in 1972. According to Ivar Thome of the International Fur Trade Federation, world mink production declined by one million pelts to 15.8 million. Production fell 15% in the U.S., 10% in Canada, 10% in Denmark, and 6% in Norway. Most other countries remained stable, and only Sweden showed a slight increase. The decline was far less than had occurred in the previous year, however, and it was expected that the trend would level out and perhaps turn upward. Prices for mink (as well as for most other furs) rose 30% and more in 1972. This reflected strong buying by European furriers, who were enjoying a price advantage following devaluation of the U.S. dollar. Europeans, principally West Germans and Italians, also dominated the spring and fall sales of Alaska sealskins, which had once gone exclusively to the New York fur trade. U.S. consumer demand for the item was improving, however, and prices were well above the depressed levels of 1971.

The U.S. Department of Agriculture's Crop Reporting Board estimated the number of mink ranches in the U.S. at 1,615 at the beginning of 1972, 27% below a year earlier. The number of female mink was down 15% to 858,000, and 1972 U.S. production was estimated at 2.9 million pelts, compared with 3.3 million in the preceding year. In addition to the standard dark and the many mutation minks in various colours, a new mutation was developed that resembled Russian sable far more closely than any other mink. With sable pelts bringing many times the price of mink, this had long been an aim of mink geneticists. Only about 1,500 "Samink" were raised in 1972, but an expansion program was launched on the basis of the pelt's initial reception.

Production of other ranched furs either held steady or increased. Karakul (persian lamb) production levels were maintained in the principal producing countries—the U.S.S.R., South and South West Africa, and Afghanistan. Through breeding techniques, the African group had changed its karakul from a curly fur to a flat broadtail type that, according to

CHRISTIAN DIOR-FOURRURE

The 1972–73 winter fur collection of Christian Dior includes these two coats made from the pelts of coypus, South American aquatic rodents whose fur is usually called nutria. The darker coat is brown and has a Russian marmot collar. The lighter coat has a collar of badger fur.

the producers, reflected consumer demand. There was also a resurgence of demand for fox, the darling of the 1920s and '30s. Although production on ranches in North America was insignificant, the output in Europe had become important, with Finland, Norway, and Poland all showing strong increases. This, again, reflected price advances amounting to 30% or more early in the year. An estimated 525,000 blue fox were produced in 1972, compared with 455,000 the year before.

One positive accomplishment during the year involved cooperation among the mink-breeding associations of the U.S., Canada, and Scandinavia. Traditional rivals, they were persuaded by adversity to seek a common ground for promotion of their product. The result was an organization called Mink International. Each partner contributed to its budget on the basis of two cents per pelt, and this was used for an advertising campaign promoting mink in general. Each partner retained the right to promote its own trademark independently. At year's end discussions were being held concerning an additional two-cents-per-pelt assessment to be used for a special program to bolster the U.S. fur market. (SANDY PARKER)

See also Fashion and Dress.

Gabon

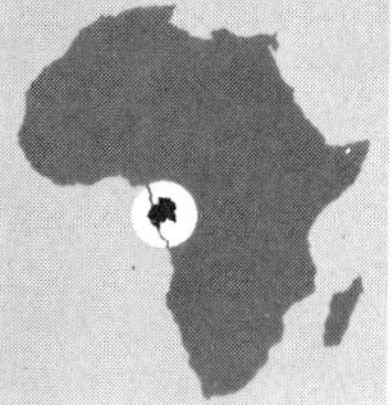

A republic of western equatorial Africa, Gabon is bounded by Río Muni, Cameroon, the Congo, and the Atlantic Ocean. Area: 103,346 sq.mi. (267,667 sq.km.). Pop. (1970): 950,009. Cap. and largest city: Libreville (pop., 1970, 105,080). Language: French and Bantu dialects. Religion: traditional tribal beliefs; Christian minority. President in 1972, Albert Bernard Bongo.

Domestic affairs proceeded smoothly in 1972, a major event being the release of former foreign minister and opposition leader Jean-Hilaire Aubame, imprisoned after the abortive coup put down by the

GABON

Education. (1969–70) Primary, pupils 94,914, teachers 2,208; secondary, pupils 6,846, teachers 322; vocational, pupils 1,273, teachers 156; teacher training, students 136, teachers (1968–69) 22; higher, students 58.

Finance. Monetary unit: CFA franc, with (Sept. 18, 1972) a parity of CFA Fr. 50 to the French franc (CFA Fr. 255.79 = U.S. $1; free rate of CFA Fr. 612.37 = £1 sterling). Budget (1971 est.) balanced at CFA Fr. 16.7 billion.

Foreign Trade. (1970) Imports CFA Fr. 22,230,-000,000; exports CFA Fr. 33,610,000,000. Import sources: France 59%; West Germany 10%; U.S. 10%. Export destinations: France 41%; Netherlands Antilles 11%; West Germany 8%; U.S. 5%. Main exports: crude oil 41%; timber 27%; manganese 10%; uranium 4%.

Transport and Communications. Roads (1971) 6,047 km. Motor vehicles in use (1970): passenger 7,100; commercial 5,800. Railways (1970) 372 km. Telephones (Dec. 1970) 7,000. Radio receivers (Dec. 1970) 62,000. Television receivers (Dec. 1970) 1,200.

Agriculture. Production (in 000; metric tons; 1971; 1970 in parentheses): corn *c.* 2 (*c.* 2); coffee *c.* 0.9 (*c.* 0.9); cocoa (1971–72) 5, (1970–71) 5; bananas *c.* 10 (*c.* 10); timber (cu.m.; 1969) 2,900, (1968) 2,700. Livestock (in 000; 1970–71): cattle *c.* 4; pigs *c.* 5; sheep *c.* 54; goats *c.* 60.

Industry. Production (in 000; metric tons): crude oil (1971) 5,780; manganese ore (metal content; 1970) 729; electricity (kw-hr.; 1970) 98,000.

French in 1964. Despite his declared commitment to a liberal economy, President Bongo decided in June that all private companies should hand over 10% of their shares to the government.

Ties were strengthened with most members of the Common Organization of Africa, Malagasy, and Mauritius (OCAM), particularly Senegal and the Ivory Coast. Relations with Equatorial Guinea, however, deteriorated steadily. A dispute over a number of offshore islands, exacerbated by Gabon's decision to extend its territorial waters to 100 mi., led to serious clashes and appeals to the UN by both sides. Ostensibly a purely territorial matter, there were deeper political and economic reasons for the dispute: first, the contested area was particularly rich in petroleum; second, it seemed that Guinean territory was being used for training Gabonese opponents of President Bongo's regime. However, due to the conciliatory efforts of Zaire and the Congo, the two countries later agreed to seek a peaceful settlement.

In September the government announced the discovery that, according to experts, a vast deposit of uranium in the hollow of a rock basin had begun acting as a natural nuclear reactor about 1,700,000,000 years ago. (PHILIPPE DECRAENE)

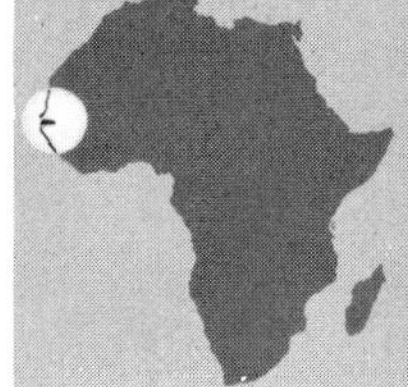

Gambia, The

A small republic and member of the Commonwealth of Nations, The Gambia extends from the Atlantic Ocean along the lower Gambia River in West Africa, and is surrounded by Senegal. Area: 4,467 sq.mi. (11,569 sq.km.). Pop. (1971 est.): 374,770, including (1963) Malinke 40.8%; Fulani 13.5%; Wolof 12.9%; Diola 7%; Soninke 6.8%; non-Africans 1.9%. Cap. and largest city: Bathurst (pop., 1971 est., 36,570). Language: English (official). Religion: predominantly Muslim. President in 1972, Sir Dauda Jawara.

President Jawara and his People's Progressive Party won a resounding victory in the March 1972 elections, retaining 28 out of 32 seats (though winning only 63% of the popular vote) and maintaining The Gambia's enviable record of tolerance and fair elections in contrast to other African states. In a speech on development President Jawara emphasized the importance of agricultural diversification. The Gambia was the first Commonwealth African country (followed by Mauritius) to seek a trade association with the EEC similar to that of the 18 African countries that signed the Yaoundé Convention in 1969. This was because of its dependence on peanuts and close association with Senegal, the major peanut producer of the existing 18 associates.

GAMBIA, THE

Education. (1969–70) Primary, pupils 17,140, teachers 690; secondary, pupils 5,178, teachers 228; vocational, pupils 141, teachers 11; teacher training, students 149, teachers 12.

Finance and Trade. Monetary unit: dalasi, with (Sept. 18, 1972) a free rate of 2.04 dalasis to U.S. $1 (par value of 5 dalasis = £1 sterling). Budget (1971–72 est.): revenue 20,050,000 dalasis; expenditure 20,730,000 dalasis. Foreign trade (1971): imports 49,860,000 dalasis; exports 27,680,000 dalasis. Import sources (1970 est.): U.K. 42%; Japan 23%; Senegal 6%; France 5%. Export destinations (1970 est.): U.K. 43%; Portugal 24%; Switzerland 11%; West Germany 10%; France 5%. Main exports peanuts and products 93%.

Tourism continued to develop as a major industry, with numbers rising from 2,700 in 1971 to 8,000 in 1972. A £5 million project to develop Yundum as an international airport was begun, as was a £2 million port extension at Bathurst, where 299 ships, including cruise vessels, called during 1971. The budget, introduced on June 22, included higher taxes on luxury articles and entertainment. (MOLLY MORTIMER)

Gardening

Hope of curing American elm trees infected with Dutch elm disease came closer to reality in 1972. Benomyl, a systemic fungicide, had been found in 1969 to be effective in saving diseased young elm trees, but was not readily taken up from the soil by mature trees. Plant pathologists Winand K. Hock and Lawrence R. Schreiber and technician Donald E. Wuertz of the U.S. Department of Agriculture (USDA) Agricultural Research Service's Shade Tree and Ornamental Plants Laboratory, Delaware, O., found a way to make benomyl more soluble in water and, in cooperation with plant pathologist Eugene B. Himelick, associated with the Illinois Natural History Survey, Urbana, developed a pressure technique to inject solutions into trees. It was expected to take two to four years to put the method into general use. Many factors needed assessment, including whether trees needed more than a single treatment, what concentration of benomyl would work best, and how the fungicide would affect a mature tree over a period of time.

Experiments by W. J. Carpenter and J. M. Kuderks at Michigan State University indicated that citric-flavoured soft drinks, when diluted with equal volumes of water, were comparable to several commercially available flower preservatives in nearly doubling the vase life of roses. The sugar in these drinks provided energy, the acidity was sufficient to retard bacterial growth, and citric acid permitted metabolism of flower tissues. Diet drinks were not effective because they lacked sugar.

A new type of seed-propagated geranium, the midi-geranium or semidwarf, was developed at Pennsylvania State University and by commercial plant breeders. In 1965 three dwarf geraniums had resulted from a breeding project at Penn State. These were crossed with tall varieties and the resulting F_1 hybrids were all intermediate in size. Continued crossing resulted in midi-geraniums, believed to combine the best characteristics of the tall and dwarf parents.

The USDA released 23 collections of Impatiens, flowering herb annuals, to commercial nurserymen and plant breeders. These plants were collected in 1970 by Harold F. Winters and J. J. Higgins in the highlands of New Guinea and Java and represented a wealth of genetic characters not seen previously in commercial varieties grown in the U.S. Lilies, rhododendrons, junipers, and birches were among the 290 plant collections gathered by John R. Creech, USDA plant explorer, in the first botanical exploration of Siberia since the 1930s. Many of these collections would be used to expand the range of adaption of ornamental plants in the U.S.

Air pollution injury to vegetation increased across the U.S. Citing an example of the mounting problem, Russell J. Seibert, director of Longwood Gardens, near Kennett Square, Pa., said "we have not been able to grow or fruit a papaya (*Carica papaya*) in the usual 14 months since 1965, and now we can't find one that will survive, much less mature even in five years." Seibert noted, however, that some newer cultivars of poinsettia, chrysanthemum, and petunias were resistant to air pollution injury, probably because their breeding and selection were taking place in areas where air pollutants were on the increase.

Diana, a unique new cultivar of rose of Sharon, *Hibiscus syriacus*, was developed at the U.S. National Arboretum by research horticulturist Donald R. Egolf. The pure-white, heavy-textured blooms remained fully open, even in hot weather, and during cooler weather, the plant produced a display of flowers far greater than that of any other cultivar. Since Diana was a triploid, little or no seed was produced. In eight years, Diana developed into a dense, upright shrub. The plant was expected to thrive in the greater part of the U.S. and southern Canada.

Three hybrid teas won 1973 All-America rose selection awards: Electron, bright rose-pink; Gypsy, orange-red; and Medallion, apricot-pink. Electron, hybridized by Sam McGredy IV, of Portadown, N.Ire., already had won nine awards in Europe under the name of Mullard Jubilee. Gypsy was hybridized by O. L. Weeks; Medallion was the result of a cross made ten years before by William Warriner. In honour of the first lady, a dark-red, velvety floribunda rose was named Pat Nixon by C. W. Stuart & Co., Newark, N.Y. The rose was created by Mme Louise Meilland, wife of the late Francis Meilland, who hybridized the Peace Rose, probably one of the most famous of all modern roses. (TOM STEVENSON)

In Britain, the Royal National Rose Society's President's International Trophy for the best new seedling rose was won by Topsi, a floribunda raised by M. Tantau, of West Germany. The bloom is semidouble, a glowing orange-scarlet with 12 petals per flower. The Henry Edland Memorial Medal for the most fragrant rose on trial went to Mala Rubinstein, a hybrid tea raised by A. Dickson & Sons Ltd., N.Ire.

The most spectacular event in Europe was the Floriade, held in Amsterdam from April to September. Gardening and recreational exhibits staged in 175 ac. of parks and 259,200 sq.ft. of greenhouses attracted 4.5 million people. In the flower arrangement contest, 26 nations competed for a world cup. The largest Garden Centre Congress ever assembled was held in Paris; 220 delegates represented at least ten European countries.

A British seed firm raised a lupine that flowered at 24 in., an *Antirrhinum* that was resistant to all known rust strains, and a double-flowered form of *Eschscholtzia* that did not close up when the sun went in. Marigolds were being grown on an increasing scale in Europe to provide a long season of bloom during the summer months. A new variety raised by crossing the African and French types was to be released in Britain. Called Sunrise, it was an F_1 hybrid with red-throated, golden-yellow petals. To meet the demand for a rapid means of increasing the stocks of narcissus, a Dutch technique of dissecting out and rooting the scales was being perfected in Britain. By this means, a hundredfold increase from one bulb was possible. In the Netherlands, the 1971 edition of the *Classified List and International Register of Tulip Names* was published by the Royal General Bulbgrowers' Society. Some 150 new varieties registered since the 1969 edition were included and some 400 varieties considered to be extinct were omitted.

Compounds that influence and control the growth of plants were obviously going to be used increasingly in the future. Bayers in West Germany had a compound that, when applied to green crotons just prior to the marketing stage, turned the leaves bright scarlet. Other plants were stopped with another chemical and produced a circle of shoots with one spray, and yet another chemical produced growth from the axils of the leaves all the way up the stem. AAgrunol Ltd. of Groningen, Neth., introduced a chemical that would bring carnations cut in bud into full flower without any loss of quality or vase life.

(J. G. SCOTT MARSHALL)

See also Agriculture; Life Sciences.

ENCYCLOPÆDIA BRITANNICA FILMS. *Gardens for Everyone* (1967).

Geography

The environment, social concerns, international events, and advanced technology characterized geography in the United States in 1972. Essentially all are interrelated, part of the relationship having been demonstrated by the first Earth Resources Technology Satellite (ERTS-1) being launched into a near-polar orbit about 560 mi. above the earth. For geographers ERTS-1 presented an unparalleled opportunity to study a variety of regional growth and change characteristics such as crop production, urban growth and development, and the nature and extent of pollution. In addition, the satellite was expected to provide opportunities for amassing regional data for resource development inventories on a scale never before possible.

Because geographers themselves spend a great deal of time interpreting maps and aerial photographs, an abundance of trained people to process the ERTS-1 data was available. Tremendous advances in computer cartography were expected to assist considerably in mapping the massive data from the satellite. Not only would crude printouts be available quickly but these could also be translated effectively into a variety of readable thematic maps.

The Commission on College Geography of the Asso-

Garment Industry:
see Fashion and Dress; Furs

Gas Industry:
see Fuel and Power

Genetics:
see Life Sciences; Medicine

GARY SETTLE—THE NEW YORK TIMES

On Dana Butte in the heart of Grand Canyon National Park, Arizona, explorer-cartographer Bradford Washburn and an associate use a laser beam to make measurements for a map of the area. Use of the laser would result in the most precise map ever made of the magnificent canyon.

ciation of American Geographers (AAG) produced a number of resource papers on environmental themes—air pollution, perception of environment, man and nature, man and environment, permafrost—and was at work on a comprehensive compendium of resource essays by environmental specialists. These seminal essays were to review the state of the art, cite pertinent literature, and suggest appropriate research themes and problems. The authors were expected to address such topics as biogeochemical cycles and energy flows, climatic modification, man's impact on stream regimen and quality, deforestation, human impact on animals, accelerated soil erosion, the environmental impact of urbanization, food production problems, energy crises, and recreation and land use.

The National Geographic Society (NGS) enhanced its long and continuing interest in ecology and environmental problems with the publication of *Great American Deserts,* a book portraying the fragile balance of nature in those regions. A recent article in *National Geographic* on mercury perils provided a classic example of chemical pollutants in a chemical-filled age, while a recent film emphasized the conflict between man and wildlife on Africa's Serengeti Plain.

The urban environment was the special focus of a research project sponsored by the AAG. The first phase asked about progress in meeting needs in such national urban public policy arenas as employment and poverty, land use and transportation, recreation and open space, and modification of the physical environment. Urban geographers were working to prepare more than 20 studies of U.S. metropolitan areas and also an atlas of urban America.

Antipode: A Radical Journal of Geography, founded in 1970, continued to flourish with articles, reports, and statements on such social issues as American poverty, epistemology and social engineering, advocacy planning, access to public services, and social geography. Planned were special issues on ecology, urban problems, and the status of women in geography.

Considerable progress toward bringing minority groups into the mainstream of U.S. geography was evident in 1972. The AAG Commission on Geography and Afro-America reported the participation of more than 60 blacks in its graduate fellowship programs, and several hundred secondary school and college teachers from black institutions attended its workshops and leadership conferences. Two geographical journals featured black America in special issues: "Contributions to an Understanding of Black America," *Economic Geography* (January 1972), and "Geographic Aspects of Black America," *The Southeastern Geographer* (November 1971).

The AAG also received a National Science Foundation grant to conduct research on black enclaves in the suburbs of large metropolitan areas. These towns were to be studied as ports of entry to the suburbs, as sites for enhanced economic opportunities, as alternative residential areas, and as models for truly integrated suburban communities in the future.

Almost 2,500 geographers from 74 countries convened at the University of Montreal for the 22nd International Geographical Congress in August 1972. Moscow was named host of the next full meeting of the congress, scheduled for 1976.

(SALVATORE J. NATOLI)

See also Antarctica; Oceanography.

ENCYCLOPÆDIA BRITANNICA FILMS. *If You Could See the Earth* (1967); *Earth: Man's Home* (1970).

Geology

More than 700 scientists gathered in Houston, Tex., in January 1972 for the third Lunar Science Conference to review the findings of Apollos 11, 12, 14, and 15. One of the obvious outcomes of these missions was the clear demonstration that geologic methods can be applied to the moon. They showed that the moon is heterogeneously layered, with a crust, mantle, and core. The ages of rocks collected on Apollos 11, 12, 14, and 15 ranged between 3.1 and 4.1 billion years. However, the lunar soil presented the enigma of appearing to be even older, 4.6 billion years.

In April, during the 71 hours spent on the moon by Apollo 16, astronauts John Young and Charles Duke steered their lunar rover to a variety of features characteristic of the Descartes highlands. Their rock collection surpassed in size and variety the samples collected on previous missions. Perhaps the most interesting rock type consisted of white anorthosite (a plagioclase feldspar rock). It appears to have been formed by the crushing of older and more primitive crustal rocks. Perhaps the moon at one time melted to a great depth, allowing the low-density plagioclase to float to the surface.

Harvard-trained geologist Harrison Schmitt became the 12th man and the first geologist to set foot on the moon when, together with Eugene Cernan, he landed at the Taurus-Littrow site, on the southeastern rim of the Sea of Serenity, during the Apollo 17 mission in December. The geology of this area was the most complex of any Apollo landing site. During three separate, seven-hour excursions outside the lunar lander, using the roving vehicle, Cernan and Schmitt collected even more samples than the Apollo 16 crew. Their most exciting find was orange-coloured soil. All other materials previously seen on the moon had been gray or black. This orange soil appeared to represent the last stages of volcanism that could have occurred relatively recently in the moon's history. Seismic studies, aided by the detonation of explosive charges, revised earlier estimates of the thickness of the lunar crust from an apparent thickness of 36 mi. to only 15 mi.

Mariner 9. Remarkable insight into the geology of the planet Mars began when Mariner 9 was successfully inserted into orbit around the planet in November 1971. It arrived during a dust storm that obscured the surface features of the planet when viewed by television. During the third week, however, the atmosphere began to clear, revealing details of the surface over the next several months.

Though earlier studies of the Martian surface in the Mariner 4, 6, and 7 missions seemed to depict a heavily cratered surface similar to the moon, Mariner 9 revealed that Mars has features quite unlike anything seen on either the moon or the earth. Mars is an active planet on which fracturing, collapse, huge volcanic cones, and other features of internal origin are seen. For instance, Nix Olympica is a volcanic cone at least four miles high, much higher than any comparable volcanic cone on the earth. A branching set of huge chasms about 2,500 mi. long and 75 mi. wide dwarfs any canyons on the earth. It seems unlikely that these chasms could have formed by erosion; instead, they probably formed along lines of weakness and collapse of the planet's crust.

Crustal Resources. Geologists from more than 90 countries throughout the world participated in the 24th International Geological Congress in Montreal during the last two weeks in August. With more than 1,200 papers delivered, the topics covered were, as usual, quite diverse. However, an increasingly important theme in geology was sounded by the first scientific plenary session of the congress, which was devoted to "Geology and the Quality of Life." In the session an international group of earth scientists expressed concern about conflicting needs for vast amounts of nonrenewable mineral and energy resources and for the avoidance of environmental degradation.

In the U.S. a similar concern was expressed in the keynote address, delivered by the director of the U.S. Geological Survey, V. E. McKelvey, to more than 4,000 geologists attending the annual meeting of the American Association of Petroleum Geologists and the Society of Economic Paleontologists and Mineralogists in Denver, Colo., in April 1972. McKelvey noted that "in the next 28 years we will create a 'second America' in the very real sense that we will mine, pump, manufacture, and build as much by the year 2000 as we did in all previous American history."

In underlining some of the problems that will challenge earth scientists during the coming decades, McKelvey pointed to increased population, urbanization, and road construction, and burgeoning demands for fuel minerals, water, and underground space. He also stressed that natural geologic hazards will become increasingly important. Annually, the actual and potential losses from earthquakes, landslides, and possibly volcanoes in the U.S. were estimated by the Survey to average several tens to several hundreds of lives, and hundreds of millions to billions of dollars in direct and indirect costs. According to McKelvey, the problem of earthquakes—particularly in the western U.S.—had become more acute as the pressure of increasing population was forcing urban expansion into areas highly susceptible to severe earthquake damage.

Energy Crisis. One of the most actively debated topics among geologists during the year was undoubtedly energy and the "energy crisis." Early in 1972, the U.S. Bureau of Mines estimated that the energy consumed in the U.S. during 1971 was 6.9×10^{16} BTUs, which was more than a third of the world's consumption. This figure was 2.3% greater than in 1970. Energy consumption in the U.S. had doubled since 1950. Most of that increased demand was met by increased domestic production of oil and natural gas and by increased imports of crude oil. As an example, the desire for clean energy increased the demand for natural gas in 1971 by 3.2% over the 1970 figure. In April the annual growth of demand for petroleum through 1975 was projected to be 5% for the U.S. and 7.5% in the rest of the Western world. Furthermore, estimates of future electricity demand in the U.S. suggested that demand would double every ten years for the rest of the century.

The consensus of speakers at meetings of the American Association of Petroleum Geologists appeared to be that the demands for increased oil and gas could only be met by higher costs and with policies that would immediately stimulate exploration and development. They further stated that there are very few discovered but undeveloped oil reserves in the U.S. except on the North Slope of Alaska. Responding to the concern of the geologists, U.S. Pres. Richard M. Nixon sent a special message to the U.S. Congress in March, in which, among other goals for research funded by the federal government, he included "Providing new sources of energy without pollution." In line with that policy it was announced in November that the budget of the U.S. Geological Survey had been increased from $130,979,000 in 1972 to $150,450,000 in fiscal 1973. Out of this, $4,478,000 was to be spent on offshore geologic investigations stressing oil and gas potential and $2,530,000 (up from $1,826,000) on geothermal investigations.

Considerable interest was focused on geothermal resources, the natural heat of the earth, during the year. Natural steam piped from the ground had been used to generate electricity at Larderello, Italy, since 1904. Exploration for geothermal resources by private industry and government agencies was being carried out in Ethiopia, Greece, Mexico, India, and the western U.S. Three types of resources were being investigated—steam, hot water, and hot rock. The only operational commercial geothermal source in the U.S., the Geysers steam field north of San Francisco,

KEYSTONE

Chinese geologists scale a sheer slope in the Kunlun Mountains, where rich mineral deposits were discovered.

reached an installed capacity of 180 Mw., and plans were announced to add 110 Mw. of generating capacity every year for several years. Although substantial technical problems remained, it appeared that world geothermal resources are considerable and may provide more than 100,000 Mw. of generating capacity by the year 2000. (W. A. ELDERS)

See also Antarctica; Astronautics; Fuel and Power; Mining; Oceanography; Seismology; Speleology.

ENCYCLOPÆDIA BRITANNICA FILMS. *How Solid Is Rock?* (1968); *Reflections on Time* (1969); *Heartbeat of a Volcano* (1970); *How Level Is Sea Level?* (1970); *Controversy over the Moon* (1971); *Earthquakes—Lesson of a Disaster* (1971); *Geyser Valley* (1972); *Ecology of a Hot Spring* (1972).

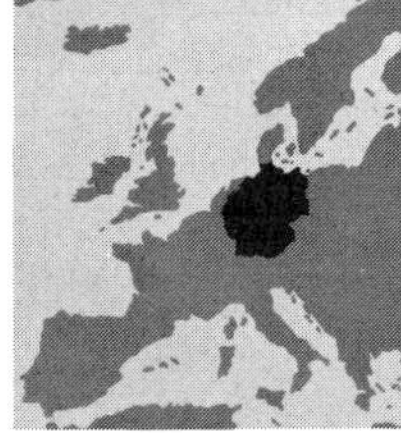

Germany

A country of central Europe, Germany was partitioned after World War II into the Federal Republic of Germany (Bundesrepublik Deutschland; West Germany) and the German Democratic Republic (Deutsche Demokratische Republik; East Germany), with a special provisional regime for Berlin. Germany is bordered by Denmark, the Netherlands, Belgium, Luxembourg, France, Switzerland, Austria, Czechoslovakia, and Poland and the North and Baltic seas.

Federal Republic of Germany. Area: 95,979 sq. mi. (248,587 sq.km.). Pop. (1971 est.): 61,280,600. Provisional cap.: Bonn (pop., 1971 est., 277,135). Largest city: Hamburg (pop., 1971 est., 1,788,599). (West Berlin, which is an enclave within East Germany, had a population of 2,097,840 in 1971.) Language: German. Religion (1970): Protestant 49%; Roman Catholic 44.6%; Jewish 0.05%. President in 1972, Gustav Heinemann; chancellor, Willy Brandt.

By giving Chancellor Willy Brandt (*see* BIOGRAPHY) and his *Ostpolitik* an overwhelming vote of confidence in the federal election of Nov. 19, 1972, the majority of West Germans finally showed that they were willing to accept the consequences of their defeat in World War II. In a record turnout of 91.2%, the coalition of the Sozialdemokratische Partei Deutschlands (Social Democratic Party, or SPD) and the Freie Demokratische Partei (Free Democratic Party, or FDP) gained a majority of 46 seats in the 496-seat Bundestag. The SPD took 45.9% (42.7% in 1969) of the vote and 230 seats (224), the FDP a remarkable 8.4% (5.8%) and 41 seats (30). The opposition Christlich-Demokratische Union (Christian Democratic Union, or CDU) and its Bavarian sister party, the Christlich-Soziale Union (Christian Social Union, or CSU), obtained 44.8% (46.1%) and 225 seats (242). The Communists took 0.3% (0.6%) and remained without representation. In all, extremists gained less than 1% of the vote.

Domestic Affairs. An attempt to elect opposition leader Rainer Barzel as chancellor had been made (and had failed by two votes) on April 27, after Willy Brandt's majority had been reduced to two by the defection of SPD deputy Herbert Hupka in February and of FDP deputy Wilhelm Helms in April. The subsequent defection of Günther Müller from the SPD to the CSU effectively paralyzed the work of the Bundestag.

It was this deadlock that made a federal election inevitable. However, the constitution, designed to promote political stability, made midterm elections difficult to arrange. The only course open to the chancellor was to ask the Bundestag for a vote of confidence and, in the event he did not achieve it, to dissolve Parliament and hold elections within 60 days, as provided for in the constitution. On September 22 the Bundestag rejected Brandt's motion for a vote of confidence by 248 to 233; members of the government abstained to ensure failure, and he was able to go ahead with the election.

The SPD and, to a large extent, the FDP placed the emphasis of their election campaign on the policy of détente, embodied in the treaties with the U.S.S.R. and Poland, ratified earlier in the year, and the comprehensive treaty with East Germany, signature of which was being held in abeyance pending the outcome of the election. The main issue of the CDU-CSU's campaign was economic stability. They blamed the government for causing the inflation that had raised the cost of living by more than 6% during the year.

The Bundestag had voted to ratify the treaties with the U.S.S.R. and Poland on May 17, with the opposition abstaining. Barzel and the CDU would have supported ratification, but were prevented from doing so by the chairman of the CSU, Franz Josef Strauss, whose distaste for the *Ostpolitik* was marked. The

GERMANY: Federal Republic

Education. (1969–70) Primary, pupils 6,098,425, teachers 232,022; secondary, pupils 2,194,802, teachers 143,725; vocational, pupils 2,086,194, teachers 109,863; higher (including 38 universities), students 440,647, teaching staff (1968–69) 36,438.

Finance. Monetary unit: Deutsche Mark, with (Sept. 18, 1972) a par value of DM. 3.22 to U.S. $1 (free rate of DM. 7.82 = £1 sterling). Gold, SDRs, and foreign exchange, central bank: (June 1972) U.S. $21,584,000,000; (June, 1971) U.S. $15,698,000,000). Budget (federal; 1971 est.): revenue DM. 96,240,000,000; expenditure DM. 100,125,000,000. Gross national product: (1971) DM. 756.1 billion; (1970) DM. 682.8 billion. Money supply: (June 1972) DM. 120.8 billion; (June 1971) DM. 105 billion. Cost of living (1963 = 100): (June 1972) 133; (June 1971) 127.

Foreign Trade. (1971) Imports DM. 119,630,000,000; exports DM. 135,910,000,000. Import sources: EEC 47% (France 13%, Netherlands 13%, Italy 11%, Belgium-Luxembourg 10%); U.S. 10%. Export destinations: EEC 40% (France 12%, Netherlands 11%, Belgium-Luxembourg 9%, Italy 8%); U.S. 10%; Switzerland 6%; Austria 5%. Main exports: machinery 31%; motor vehicles 15%; chemicals 12%; iron and steel 7%; textile yarns and fabrics 5%.

Transport and Communications. Roads (1971) 417,000 km. (including 4,829 km. autobahns). Motor vehicles in use (1971): passenger 15,476,000; commercial 1,191,000. Railways: (1970) federal 29,479 km. (including 8,590 km. electrified), private 3,644 km.; traffic (1971) 38,810,000,000 passenger-km., freight 65,411,000,000 net ton-km. Air traffic (1971): 8,609,000,000 passenger-km.; freight 573,793,000 net ton-km. Navigable inland waterways in regular use (1970) 4,371 km.; freight traffic 48,813,000,000 ton-km. Shipping (1971): merchant vessels 100 gross tons and over 2,826; gross tonnage 8,678,584. Telephones (Dec. 1970) 13,835,000. Radio licenses (Dec. 1970) 19,622,000. Television licenses (Dec. 1970) 16,750,000.

Agriculture. Production (in 000; metric tons; 1971; 1970 in parentheses): wheat 7,142 (5,662); rye 3,029 (2,663); barley 5,774 (4,754); oats 3,037 (2,484); potatoes 15,174 (16,247); apples 1,955 (1,763); sugar, raw value (1971–72) 2,345, (1970–71) 2,056; wine 527 (879); milk *c.* 21,016 (21,893); butter 462 (505); cheese *c.* 500 (493); beef and veal 1,232 (1,292); pork 2,373 (2,186); fish catch (1970) 613, (1969) 652. Livestock (in 000; Dec. 1970): cattle 14,025; pigs 20,969; sheep 843; horses used in agriculture 253; chickens 98,601.

Industry. Index of production (1963 = 100): (1971) 157; (1970) 154. Unemployment: (1971) 0.8%; (1970) 0.7%. Fuel and power (in 000; metric tons; 1971): coal 110,794; lignite 104,477; crude oil 7,420; coke (1970) 39,914; electricity (kw-hr.) 259,629,000; natural gas (cu.m.) 15,360,000; manufactured gas (cu.m.) 18,860,000. Production (in 000; metric tons; 1971): iron ore (32% metal content) 5,019; pig iron 30,224; crude steel 40,348; aluminum 703; copper 400; lead 280; zinc 262; cement 40,544; sulfuric acid 4,382; cotton yarn 221; woven cotton fabrics 179; wool yarn 85; rayon, etc., filament yarn 75; rayon, etc., staple fibres 106; nylon, etc., filament yarn 335; nylon, etc., fibres 269; nitrogenous fertilizer (1970–71) 1,131; potash fertilizer (1970–71) 1,185; phosphate fertilizer (1970–71) 913; synthetic rubber 335; plastics and resins 4,775; passenger cars (units) 3,698; commercial vehicles (units) 277. Merchant vessels launched (100 gross tons and over; 1971) 1,650,000 gross tons. New dwelling units completed (1971) 554,000.

CDU's misgivings about the treaties had been largely dispelled by an all-party declaration stating that "the treaties do not prejudice a settlement for Germany under a peace treaty and do not create a legal basis for existing borders." Strauss's success in overruling Barzel was a mark of the Bavarian's power within the opposition. The new Bundestag met on December 13, and Brandt was confirmed as chancellor the next day. The treaty with East Germany was signed December 21.

In July the economics and finance minister, Karl Schiller, resigned from the government over the Cabinet's decision to introduce a form of exchange control, designed to stop the flow of speculative money into the country. Eventually, he also resigned from the SPD, which he felt was moving too far to the left. His post was filled by the former defense minister, Helmut Schmidt (*see* BIOGRAPHY).

Points of conflict likely to arise within the ruling coalition in its new four-year term included the degree of worker participation in management, tax increases, the level of public expenditure, and ambitious SPD plans for the redistribution of wealth. The FDP clearly acted as a brake on socialism. In December there was a reshuffling of Cabinet responsibilities. Among the more important changes, the Ministry of Economics and Finance was split into a Finance Ministry under Schmidt and a smaller Economics Ministry under Hans Friderichs. Horst Ehmke was given charge of a new Ministry for Research and Technology, which took over research planning and coordination from the Ministry of Education and Science. The Interior Ministry's environmental responsibilities were expanded.

The Olympic Games in Munich were overshadowed by tragedy. On September 5 eight Arab guerrillas, members of the Black September organization, forced their way into the quarters of the Israeli team in the Olympic Village, killed two Israelis, and took nine hostage. In exchange for the hostages, the guerrillas demanded the release of 200 Arab prisoners in Israel and free passage from West Germany. After prolonged negotiations, the West German authorities concluded that the only solution was to attempt to free the hostages by force. In the late evening the guerrillas and the hostages were flown in helicopters to the military airport of Fürstenfeldbruck, near Munich, where they were ostensibly to board an aircraft bound for Egypt. In fact, police marksmen had been posted at the airport to shoot the guerrillas as they boarded the plane. During the gun battle that followed, all the hostages and five of the guerrillas were killed and three guerrillas were captured. The Israelis had all been killed by the guerrillas, several of them when a hand grenade was tossed into one of the helicopters. (*See* SPORTING RECORD: *Special Report*.)

An inquiry into the tragedy, conducted by the federal government, the Bavarian government, and the Munich police, came to the conclusion that it was unavoidable. Before the Games started, Israeli officials had inspected arrangements at the Olympic Village and had not expressed any dissatisfaction with the security measures. In a subsequent inquiry, however, the Israeli government did express dissatisfaction with West German security. On October 29 the West German government released the three captured guerrillas after two other Black Septembrists had hijacked a Lufthansa Boeing 727 on its way from Damascus, Syria, to Frankfurt and threatened to blow it up, with the crew and passengers, if their demands were not met. The hijacked plane circled over Zagreb, Yugos., while the three prisoners, who had been awaiting trial, were taken from separate prisons and flown to Zagreb in a Hawker Siddley 125 Executive jet. The guerrillas were taken aboard the Boeing, which then flew to Tripoli, Libya, where the passengers and crew were released and the Arabs welcomed as "heroes of the Munich operation."

SIMONPIETRI—GAMMA

At Friedrichstrasse Station between East and West Berlin, a mother and daughter embrace for the first time in six years, when West Berliners were permitted to cross the border for one week beginning March 29, 1972.

In June, after a hunt that lasted almost two years, police managed to track down the hard core of the Baader-Meinhof group of urban guerrillas, including the ringleaders who gave the group its name, Andreas Baader, aged 29, a former political columnist, and Ulrike Meinhof (*see* BIOGRAPHY), aged 37. The self-declared aim of the group was to overthrow the existing system of West German society. Its members had been compared to the Tupamaros of Uruguay, the Palestinian guerrillas, and the Irish Republican Army. Several members of the Baader-Meinhof group faced charges of murder, arson, and bank robbery.

It was announced in October that the West German author Heinrich Böll had been awarded the Nobel Prize for Literature. (*See* NOBEL PRIZES.)

Foreign Affairs. The ratification of the treaties with the U.S.S.R. meant that the four-power agreement on Berlin could come into effect. (See *West Berlin*, below.) The Soviets had insisted that the treaties must be approved first. The Berlin agreement, signed on June 3, made provision for visits by West Berliners to East Berlin and East Germany, and for facilitating transport between West Germany and West Berlin. The Soviet government accepted as a fact of life the ties that had grown up between West Germany and West Berlin over the years, although the agreement made it clear that West Berlin was not a part of West Germany. After the signing ceremony, the Soviet foreign minister, Andrei Gromyko, paid a brief visit to Bonn.

The first treaty to be concluded between the two German states was ratified in October. It regulated transport between East and West Germany, other than air transport, almost in accordance with normal international standards. The principal difference was that there was still no completely free movement of people between the two states.

The comprehensive treaty normalizing relations

German Literature: *see* Literature

D.P.A./PICTORIAL PARADE

East German soldiers are applauded by officials in the reviewing stand during the 1972 May Day parade. Among the officials is 78-year-old Walter Ulbricht (13th from left, front row), chief of state of the German Democratic Republic.

between the two states was initialed in Bonn on November 8 and signed in East Berlin on December 21. At first Chancellor Brandt had planned to sign the treaty in person, together with the East German minister president, Willi Stoph, but early in December the two governments announced that the formal ceremonies would be carried out by the two official negotiators, Egon Bahr of West Germany and his East German counterpart, Michael Kohl. There was speculation that East Germany wished to avoid another enthusiastic popular reception such as Brandt had received during his 1970 visit to Erfurt.

The treaty established formal relations between the two states, but not full diplomatic relations. Each would be represented in the other capital by a permanent representative with the title of minister plenipotentiary. East Germany did not share the West German view that though there were two German states there was only one German nation, but the parties agreed to disagree on this question. The treaty called for the development of neighbourly relations on a basis of equality, while the "national question" of eventual unification was left open. The signing of the treaty cleared the way for entry of the two German states into the UN. (See *German Democratic Republic,* below.)

Foreign Minister Walter Scheel visited Peking in October and signed an agreement establishing diplomatic relations between West Germany and China. Bonn had shown some hesitation in taking this step, evidently for fear of offending the Soviet Union.

Diplomatic relations with Lebanon and Egypt were resumed after a break of seven years, but stricter control of Arabs in West Germany following the Munich tragedy caused friction between Bonn and the Arab world. Many Arabs suspected of having contacts with terrorist organizations were ordered to leave the country, and many were refused entry. Relations with Israel reached a low ebb following the release of the three Munich terrorists; unofficial Israeli sources accused the West German government of having planned the release in order to escape the embarrassment and probable violence that would have resulted from their trial. (NORMAN CROSSLAND)

West Berlin. The final protocol of the four-power agreement on West Berlin was signed on June 3, 1972, in the former Allied Control Council Building in West Berlin. According to Klaus Schütz, West Berlin's governing mayor, the agreement ended the "era of crisis within and concerning our city." The Berlin agreement recognized the links between West Berlin and West Germany and provided for unimpeded traffic of persons and goods.

When the basic treaty between East and West Germany was initialed on November 8, the two governments sent separate notes to the four powers confirming that the treaty in no way affected the powers' rights and responsibilities and the related quadripartite agreements, decisions, and practices. Between them, the four-power agreement and the treaty provided the three requirements stipulated by the West Berlin Senate: continuation of the quadripartite arrangements; consideration of the terms of the West German constitution; and inclusion of West Berlin in West German agreements.

Another evidence of the changed climate in relations between West Berlin and East Germany was the initialing on July 19 of an agreement to move the Berlin Wall back to the Potsdamer Platz in order to remove an obstruction to traffic. The agreement gave West Berlin about 21 ac. of land in return for a payment of DM. 31 million.

German Democratic Republic. Area: 41,768 sq. mi. (108,178 sq.km.). Pop. (1971): 17,040,926. Cap. and largest city: East Berlin (pop., 1971, 1,084,866).

GERMANY: Democratic Republic

Education. (1969–70) Primary, pupils 2,485,367; secondary, pupils 51,923; primary and secondary, teachers 134,000; vocational, pupils 582,380; teacher training, students 25,233; vocational and teacher training, teachers 20,115; higher (including 7 universities), students 91,947, teaching staff (1966–67) 14,200.

Finance. Monetary unit: Mark of Deutschen Demokratischen Republik, with (Sept. 18, 1972) an official exchange rate of M. 2.05 to U.S. $1 (M. 5.30 = £1 sterling) and a commercial rate (Valuta Mark) of VM. 3.15 to U.S. $1 (VM. 8.34 = £1 sterling). Budget (1970): revenue M. 70,582,000,000; expenditure M. 69,890,000,000. Net material product (at 1967 prices): (1971) M. 113.6 billion; (1970) M. 108.7 billion.

Foreign Trade. (1971) Imports VM. 20,830,500,000; exports VM. 21,320,500,000. Import sources: U.S.S.R. 38%; Czechoslovakia 10%; West Germany 9%; Poland 6%; Hungary 5%. Export destinations: U.S.S.R. 38%; Czechoslovakia 9%; Poland 9%; West Germany 8%; Hungary 6%. Main exports (1970): machinery 38%; transport equipment 11%; chemicals; lignite; textiles.

Transport and Communications. Roads (1971) *c.* 160,000 km. (45,620 km. main roads, including 1,464 km. autobahns). Motor vehicles in use (1971): passenger 1,268,000; commercial 198,000. Railways (1971): 14,525 km. (including 1,370 km. electrified); traffic 18,406,000,000 passenger-km., freight 43,650,000,000 net ton-km. Air traffic (1969): 842.7 million passenger-km.; freight 23,319,000 net ton-km. Navigable inland waterways in regular use (1971) 2,100 km.; freight traffic (1970) 2,358,000,000 ton-km. Shipping (1971): merchant vessels 100 gross tons and over 430; gross tonnage 1,016,205. Telephones (Dec. 1970) 2,089,000. Radio licenses (Dec. 1970) 5,985,000. Television licenses (Dec. 1970) 4,499,000.

Agriculture. Production (in 000; metric tons; 1971; 1970 in parentheses): potatoes 9,412 (13,054); wheat 2,490 (2,132); rye 1,754 (1,483); barley 2,286 (1,926); oats *c.* 800 (558); sugar, raw value (1971–72) *c.* 538, (1970–71) *c.* 490; rapeseed *c.* 210 (180). Livestock (in 000; Dec. 1971): cattle 5,293; sheep 1,607; pigs 9,995; horses used in agriculture 106; poultry 43,343.

Industry. Index of production (1963 = 100): (1971) 160; (1970) 153. Production (in 000; metric tons; 1971): lignite 258,100; coal (1970) 1,049; petroleum products (1970) 11,377; manufactured gas (cu.m.) 4,480,000; electricity (kw-hr.) 69,431,000; iron ore (metal content; 1970) 104; pig iron 2,027; crude steel 5,351; cement (1970) 7,987; potash (1970–71) 614; sulfuric acid 1,076; synthetic rubber (1970) 118; cotton yarn (1970) 69; rayon filaments and fibres (1970) 163; passenger cars (units; 1970) 127; commercial vehicles (units; 1970) 27.

Language: German. Religion (1950): Protestant 81.3%; Roman Catholic 11%. First secretary of the Socialist Unity (Communist) Party (SED) in 1972, Erich Honecker; chief of state, Walter Ulbricht; minister president (premier), Willi Stoph.

A middle-aged woman crossing from East to West Germany to visit her sick father on Oct. 19, 1972, opened a new chapter in the history of divided post-World War II Germany. She was the first East German to take advantage of the new traffic treaty between East and West Germany. The first formal agreement between the two German governments and the first fruit of the ratification by the Bundestag of Chancellor Brandt's treaties with the U.S.S.R. and Poland, it meant the end of travel restrictions that had kept thousands of families divided for 24 years. The treaty, finally approved by the People's Chamber of the East German Parliament on October 16, came into force at midnight on October 18. It settled technical details of traffic by road, rail, and water but made no mention of air traffic. Citizens of West Germany might visit relatives and friends in the East for a total of 30 days a year, and there was provision for business and tourist visits over and above this quota. East German citizens, for their part, might make several visits to West Germany each year, instead of only one as before, and East Germans other than pensioners might visit West Germany on compassionate grounds.

The treaty between East and West Germany, signed on December 21, represented a striking change in East Germany's approach to relations with West Germany. A statement issued by the Council of Ministers described the treaty as fully reflecting the foreign policy of establishing peaceful coexistence between East Germany and the capitalist countries. In an exchange of letters, the two governments said they would keep each other informed about the date of applying for UN membership. On November 9, a day after the treaty was initialed, the U.S., Britain, France, and the U.S.S.R. released a declaration agreed on November 5 that enabled the two states to take this step without impairing the four powers' rights and responsibilities in Germany. Practical improvements contained in the treaty covered postal services and telecommunications, travel regulations, noncommercial exchange of goods, reunion of families, opening of more border crossing points, travel in the border areas, and the possibility for West German journalists to work in the East (their East German colleagues had enjoyed such facilities in West Germany for several years).

In the second half of the year several non-Communist countries took steps to initiate or fully develop diplomatic relations with East Germany. On August 14 Switzerland agreed to exchange trade missions authorized to carry out certain consular functions; they included the issuance of visas, the legalization of documents, and the giving of legal aid and assistance in safeguarding the interests of citizens. India granted full diplomatic recognition to East Germany on October 8, and the two countries agreed to raise their diplomatic representations to embassy level (India had established a consulate general in August 1970). Finland recognized both East and West Germany on November 24. Generally speaking, it became clear as the year went on that the movement toward recognition of East Germany was gathering momentum.

A three-day visit to Romania by an East German government delegation led by Erich Honecker, first secretary of the SED, and Willi Stoph in the first half of May resulted in the conclusion of a new treaty of friendship, mutual assistance, and cooperation. The treaty was given a markedly friendly reception in the Romanian press, which devoted considerable space to the event. A communiqué issued at the conclusion of an official visit by Prime Minister Fidel Castro, June 12–21, stated that Cuba and East Germany intended to broaden their bilateral consultations.

Following Honecker's visit to Moscow, April 4–10, it was stated that "practical measures for the improved planning of cooperation between the U.S.S.R. and the German Democratic Republic on a long-term basis" would have to be taken. There was no indication that agreement had yet been reached on the long-term planning of raw material supplies up to 1985, as had been hinted by Hungarian Premier Jeno Fock on his return to Budapest from Moscow in March.

Speaking at a ceremony to commemorate the 23rd anniversary of the establishment of the East German state on October 9, Stoph reported a 9.3% increase in retail sales of industrial products in the first nine months of the year, as well as a substantial increase in the GNP. However, he also criticized industrial plants, particularly those producing consumer goods, for failing to meet their planned commitments.

An event unique in the history of East Germany occurred on March 9 when members of the People's Chamber voted against proposed legislation; 14 members opposed a measure permitting free abortion and 8 abstained. (S. E. SCHATTMANN)

Ghana

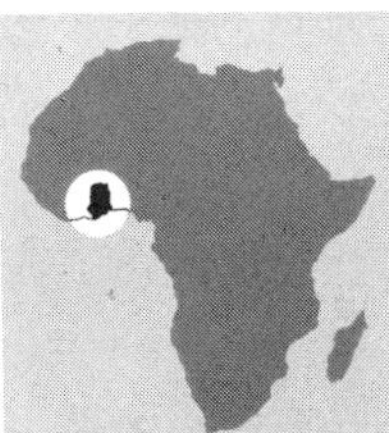

A republic of West Africa and member of the Commonwealth of Nations, Ghana is on the Gulf of Guinea and is bordered by Ivory Coast, Upper Volta, and Togo. Area: 92,100 sq.mi. (238,500 sq.km.). Pop. (1970): 8,559,313. Cap. and largest city: Accra (pop., 1970, 564,194). Language: English (official); local Sudanic dialects. Religion (1960): Christian 43%; Muslim 12%; animist 38%. President to Jan. 13, 1972, Edward Akufo-Addo; prime minister to January 13, Kofi Busia; chairman of the National Redemption Council from January 13, Col. Ignatius Kutu Acheampong.

A tumultuous year for Ghana began with the Jan. 13, 1972, coup led by Col. Ignatius Acheampong (*see* BIOGRAPHY). Underlying causes of the coup included forced retirement of senior army officers and cuts in the Army's budget, alienation of the civil servants over dismissals, and brushes with the trade unions and judiciary; but the precipitating factor was Prime Minister Busia's 44% devaluation of the cedi, bringing huge rises in the cost of living.

The new regime established a 12-man National Redemption Council, chaired by Col. Acheampong and tribally balanced (four Akans, four Ewes, two Gas, and two Northerners). A National Security Council was set up, also chaired by the colonel. Political activities were banned; the act prohibiting a one-party state was repealed; and press freedom was restricted. Assets of the Busia regime were frozen, and a commission was established to investigate them and government contracts. Many supporters of that regime remained in preventive detention.

In April Col. Acheampong became commander in chief of all armed forces. Local government was decreed in the form of 37 district councils and 270 subordinate local councils. Trade-union activity was curtailed by the minister of labour who announced that strikes, demonstrations, and the formation of new labour movements would be regarded as a challenge to authority. An abortive July 1972 coup, said to have been inspired by Busia with foreign aid, led to the retroactive Subversion 1972 Decree imposing the death penalty for ten offenses, mainly concerned with overthrowing the government but including robbery, smuggling timber, diamonds, or gold, stealing cocoa, diamonds, gold, telephone cables and wires, and wilfully damaging public property.

The emotions generated by the death in April of Kwame Nkrumah (*see* OBITUARIES), the architect of Ghana's independence and its first president, after six years of exile in Guinea and Romania, led the NRC to model itself after Nkrumah's radical pan-African image. The regime adopted a leftward "nonaligned" policy, opposing dialogue with South Africa and sending an increased number of missions to Communist countries. Relations with Guinea, broken after the 1966 coup and strained by dispute over the return of Nkrumah's body for burial in Ghana, were reestablished.

Acheampong still faced the economic problems that had led to Busia's downfall: the nation's huge external debts, largely incurred by Nkrumah, and a catastrophic drop in cocoa prices. His solution was to proclaim an economic "unilateral declaration of independence." He revalued the cedi by 42% in February. In canceling £36.3 million due to four British firms, he announced that he could not recognize any debt settlements concluded after 1966 unless the creditor could prove their validity. He was willing to accept arbitration, but even those debts established as technically viable and untainted by corruption could only be honoured after a ten-year moratorium and over a 50-year repayment period. The government would "respond" to any reprisals taken against debt repudiation.

Internally, Col. Acheampong put Ghana's economy on something like a war footing, cutting out all but essential imports and establishing an Operation Feed Yourself with a crash agricultural program. Five industrial projects abandoned after Nkrumah's downfall were resuscitated, including the Soviet prefabricated concrete project in Accra and the Chinese pencil project in Kumasi. Severe controls over foreign-dominated interests were promised, and in December the government assumed 55% participation in all the country's mining enterprises. (MOLLY MORTIMER)

GHANA

Education. (1968–69) Primary, pupils 1,281,003, teachers 50,563; secondary, pupils 183,535; vocational, pupils 8,932, teachers 510; teacher training, students 18,728, teachers 1,275; higher (including 3 universities), students 5,699, teaching staff 681.

Finance. Monetary unit: new cedi, with (Sept. 18, 1972) a par value of 1.28 cedi to U.S. $1 (free rate of 3.14 cedis = £1 sterling). Gold, SDRs, and foreign exchange, official: (June 1972) U.S. $86.6 million; (June 1971) U.S. $65.8 million. Budget (1972–73 est.) balanced at 329 million cedis; development expenditure 98.8 million cedis. Gross domestic product: (1970) 2,571,000,000 cedis; (1969) 2,328,000,000 cedis. Money supply: (May 1972) 367.3 million cedis; (May 1971) 279.6 million cedis. Cost of living (Accra; 1963 = 100): (Jan. 1972) 205; (Jan. 1971) 173.

Foreign Trade. (1970) Imports 419,050,000 cedis; exports 466,820,000 cedis. Import sources: U.K. 24%; U.S. 18%; West Germany 11%; Japan 6%. Export destinations: U.K. 23%; U.S. 18%; West Germany 10%; Netherlands 9%; U.S.S.R. 9%; Japan 6%; Yugoslavia 6%. Main exports: cocoa 64%; timber 8%; gold 7%; cocoa butter 6%.

Transport and Communications. Roads (1970) *c.* 31,000 km. Motor vehicles in use (1970): passenger 36,500; commercial (including buses) 27,000. Railways (1970): 953 km.; traffic 543 million passenger-km., freight 311 million net ton-km. Air traffic (1971): 147,370,000 passenger-km.; freight 3,189,000 net ton-km. Shipping (1971): merchant vessels 100 gross tons and over 73; gross tonnage 165,748. Telephones (Dec. 1970) 64,000. Radio receivers (Dec. 1970) 703,000. Television receivers (Dec. 1970) 16,000.

Agriculture. Production (in 000; metric tons; 1971; 1970 in parentheses): corn *c.* 430 (442); cassava (1970) 1,596, (1969) 1,320; sweet potatoes (1970) 1,617, (1969) 1,305; millet and sorghum 292 (179); rice *c.* 70 (69); peanuts *c.* 70 (60); cocoa (exports; 1971–72) 411, (1970–71) 396; timber (cu.m.; 1969) 9,200, (1968) 8,700; fish catch (1970) 187, (1969) 163. Livestock (in 000; 1970–71): cattle 599; sheep 1,177; pigs *c.* 340; goats *c.* 775.

Industry. Production (in 000; 1970): gold (troy oz.) 710; diamonds (metric carats) 2,550; manganese ore (metal content; metric tons) 191; bauxite (metric tons; 1971) 329; electricity (kw-hr.; 1971) 2,943,000.

Gibraltar:
see Dependent States

Glass Manufacture:
see Industrial Review

Gold:
see Mining; Payments and Reserves, International

Golf

The transcending skills of Jack Nicklaus was the dominant theme in golf during 1972. His attempt to achieve the grand slam of professional golf (Masters, U.S. Open, British Open, PGA) was of compelling interest until Lee Trevino broke the spell in the British Open, but failure had no adverse effect on Nicklaus. He set a new record for official prize money won in the United States with $320,542, surpassing his record total of the previous year ($244,490), and in so doing won seven tournaments. Considering that he played in many fewer events than his nearest rivals, this was an extraordinary mark of his supremacy. Trevino finished second in earnings with $214,805.

Early in the year Nicklaus said that he thought the grand slam was possible, especially as the four championships were on courses that suited his game. When he opened with a 68 in the Masters at Augusta, Ga., a score that proved to be the lowest of the tournament, he took a grip that seemed unlikely to be loosened. Although he was not at his commanding best, Nicklaus won by three strokes from Bruce Crampton, Bobby Mitchell, and Tom Weiskopf, and for the first time in years the final round looked drawn.

The plot was similar at Pebble Beach, Calif., for the U.S. Open. After the second round Nicklaus was never out of the lead. The great course, with its numerous challenging shots, especially on the ocean holes, and small fast greens, took a terrible toll of many distinguished players. Scores in the high 70s and above were frequent, and on the last day, when a strong wind arose, the only player to equal par was Jim Simons, then an amateur. Trevino, ill only a few days earlier, made a brave attempt to retain his title and Arnold Palmer, summoning some of his greatest golf, was in contention until the last few holes, but in the end Crampton's unshakable steadiness took him into second place. Nicklaus, who almost holed a majestic one-iron shot into the teeth of the wind at the 17th, cruised safely home by three strokes.

When the scene shifted to Muirfield, Scot., for the British Open, the golf world was alight with expectation. Nicklaus prepared with ruthless care, but for three rounds, until his cause was almost lost, could not command his finest golf. As in 1966, when Nicklaus won his first British title, control, not length, was the essence. Nicklaus was criticized for playing too defensively, but the truth was that he hit far too many indifferent strokes into the greens, and none of his scores came easily.

With a round to go Nicklaus trailed Trevino by six

shots and Tony Jacklin by five, and he knew that only a monumental performance could give him any chance of victory. Trevino had taken the lead from Jacklin with a fantastic finish to his third round. In the last five holes he sank two long putts, a badly hit bunker shot, and a chip.

On the last afternoon Nicklaus came within a fraction of the greatest last round in Open history; at one point he had regained the six strokes and actually was leading; he played the round in 66, having missed five putts between 5 and 12 ft. When Nicklaus finished, Trevino and Jacklin were at the 17th hole, each needing two pars to win. The par-five 17th then produced one of the largest swings of fortune in modern golf: Trevino drove into a bunker and was in back of the green in four, while Jacklin was 15 ft. from the hole in three. Trevino, looking like a condemned man, chipped hurriedly, almost carelessly, but the ball vanished into the hole. Jacklin needed three putts from 15 ft. and a solid par four at the last hole gave Trevino the championship. Nicklaus' dream was destroyed, and Ben Hogan remained the only man to have won three of the four titles in the same year.

The Professional Golfers Association of America (PGA) championship at Oakland Hills, Mich., was an anticlimax for Nicklaus and Trevino. A great third round of 67 took Gary Player into the lead from Billy Casper, but with a few holes to play the next day he was one behind Jim Jamieson, who had finished among the top ten in the Masters. If ever one stroke won a championship, Player's nine-iron, 150-yd. blind shot over trees and a lake on the 16th hole was it. The stroke placed him 4 ft. from the cup, and he holed for a birdie. Later, Player won the first prize of $50,000 in the World Series of Golf at Akron, O.

Nicklaus closed out the year in convincing fashion, winning the Walt Disney World Open in Florida by nine strokes. Gay Brewer, the Canadian Open champion, came close to winning the largest prize of the year in Britain when, together with Peter Oosterhuis, he finished a stroke behind Bob Charles in the John Player Classic at Turnberry, Ayrshire, Scot. Victory was worth £15,000 to Charles who, the next week, won the Dunlop Masters, while Brewer in Tokyo beat David Graham of Australia in a sudden death play-off for the $300,000 Pacific Masters.

While Graham was making his mark in Japan, two other young Australians were doing so in Europe. Graham Marsh won the German and Swiss opens, and Jack Newton the Dutch Open and the Benson and Hedges Festival in England. Peter Thomson won the Wills tournament in Scotland and the Qantas Australian Open in Adelaide, 21 years after his first victory in that championship. Bruce Devlin had one of his most successful years, and, together with Bruce Crampton, made Australia a powerful force in golf.

The World Cup was played at Royal Melbourne in November. Australia, represented by Crampton and Bill Dunk, challenged until the last three holes, but the final issue lay between Taiwan and Japan. Hsieh Min-nan, who won the individual title, and Lu Liang-huan finished strongly to gain Taiwan its first victory and beat the Japanese, T. Kono and T. Murakami, by two strokes over 54 holes; one day's play was canceled through rain. South Africa gained third place, one stroke ahead of the United States and Australia.

In amateur golf the United States was successful in the three biennial contests. In Buenos Aires in the world team championships, strong finishes enabled the U.S. men to overtake and beat Australia by five strokes to retain the Eisenhower Trophy, while the women finished four strokes ahead of France in the contest for the Espirito Santo Trophy. In the Curtis Cup match at Western Gailes in Scotland the U.S. women led the U.K. 5–3 on the first day and would have been hard pressed to win had Beth Barry and Hollis Stacy not halved their foursome the next morning after being four down and six to play. The day's honours were shared, and the U.S. won 10–8. Michelle Walker of Britain was the outstanding player of the match, the only one undefeated. Later she retained her British amateur title.

UPI COMPIX

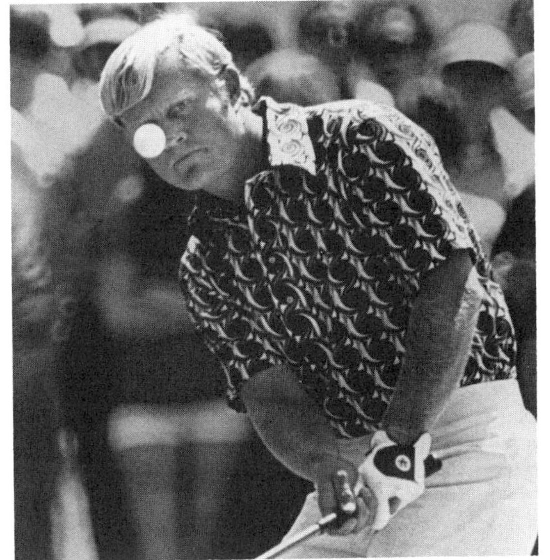

His eye firmly planted on the ball—or possibly vice versa—Jack Nicklaus, golf's record money winner in 1972, chips to the sixth green in the opening round of the Masters. He scored a 68 for the round and won the tournament by a comfortable three strokes.

Women's professional golf in the U.S. offered record prize money of approximately $900,000. Susie Berning won the U.S. Women's Open, beating Pam Barnett by one stroke. Winners of other tournaments included Kathy Whitworth, Jane Blalock, Kathy Ahern, and Carol Mann. The Ladies PGA disqualified Jane Blalock from the Bluegrass tournament in May, allegedly for improving the lie of her ball, and suspended her from competition for one year. Miss Blalock filed a $5 million antitrust suit against the LPGA, and in June a federal district court allowed her to continue in competition pending settlement of the suit. (P. A. WARD-THOMAS)

Government Finance

The financial activities of local governments are essentially restricted to revenue raising to meet the costs of public services. National governments are expected to focus their attention on a more complex set of goals, many of which are not encountered by subnational governments or by the private sector. At the national level, expenditure, borrowing, and tax programs must be arranged to provide: (1) the desired allocation of resources between private and public consumption; (2) an acceptable distribution of after-tax income; (3) a climate that encourages reasonable economic growth; and (4) stable prices and full employment. In 1972 national governments were confronted with frequent adjustments of budget and financial policies to deal with all of these goals.

United States. The economic recovery of 1971, following the 1970 recession, was not as vigorous as had been previously expected, and the unemployment rate remained at the unsatisfactory high level of 6.1%

in December 1971, just a month prior to the release of the fiscal year 1973 federal budget. The standard means of fighting unemployment is an expansionary fiscal and monetary policy. However, the administration of Pres. Richard Nixon was reluctant to pursue such a policy in 1971 because of the persistence of inflation. The far-reaching new economic policy, announced by President Nixon on Aug. 15, 1971, had attacked the inflation problem with direct controls on wages, prices, and rents. The new economic policy also included a number of tax cuts mostly designed to stimulate business investment, but the immediate stimulus provided by the cuts was offset by a number of reductions in government spending.

In January 1972 the administration decided that monetary and fiscal policy could be allowed to exert a more expansionary thrust than had seemed prudent when inflation was not under control. Thus, in the federal budget for fiscal 1973 the administration proposed a more expansive policy by way of a speedup in federal spending in the first half of calendar year 1972, followed in fiscal 1973 by continued though declining stimulus.

The expansionary fiscal policy was to be reduced as the year progressed because economic growth was strong in the fourth quarter of 1971, and the administration projected even more rapid growth (9.4%) accompanied by a significant reduction in unemployment for 1972. The proposed program for fiscal stimulus was reflected in the budget projection of a $38.8 billion deficit in fiscal 1972 and a $25.5 billion deficit in fiscal 1973. The official full-employment budget, a measure of budget stimulus, was expected to move from a surplus of $4.9 billion in fiscal 1971 to a deficit of $8.1 billion in fiscal 1972 to an approximate balance in fiscal 1973.

The actual budget deficit is often a misleading indicator of fiscal policy because it fails to distinguish between the effect of the budget on the economy and the effect of the economy on the budget. The full-employment budget, on the other hand, is designed to distinguish between discretionary changes in the budget resulting from congressional action or administration policy changes and passive changes in the budget that are induced by cyclical movements in income and tax receipts. The full-employment budget is an estimate of budget posture that would exist at a hypothetical level of full employment. If the economy were actually at full employment, there would be no essential difference between the full-employment budget and the actual budget.

The full-employment budget showed that much of the real impact of the spending speedup would spill over into the second half of calendar year 1972. Defense purchases did increase significantly in the second quarter of 1972, but a significant portion of the planned increase in spending in the first half of the year was merely an accounting technique to reduce budget outlays in fiscal 1973. Even on a budget basis the Nixon administration's planned fiscal stimulus in the first half of 1972 was not realized. The budget deficit for fiscal 1972 was $15.8 billion less than the $38.8 billion projected in January 1972, and the deficit in the official full-employment budget was $4.5 billion less than projected.

Summary of the U.S. Federal Budget

In $000,000,000

Item	Fiscal year ending June 30 1971 actual	1972 actual	1973 estimate*
Budget receipts	188.4	208.6	223.0
Budget outlays	211.4	231.6	250.0
Actual deficit (—)	—23.0	—23.0	—27.0
Full employment surplus or deficit (—)	4.9	—3.6	—3.0

*Source: Mid-Session Review of the 1973 Budget released by the Office of Management and Budget on June 5, 1972.

A number of factors combined to produce these large forecast errors. Nearly half of the $5 billion error in the expenditure estimate was attributable to a delay in the enactment of federal revenue sharing. Federal government receipts were about $10.8 billion higher than expected, and perhaps nearly half of this error was due to overwithholding of personal income taxes relative to liabilities. The overwithholding of personal taxes resulted from the failure of taxpayers to adjust their declared exemptions for withholding purposes, as expected, when the Department of the Treasury adopted a new withholding schedule in January 1972. By the end of 1972 it appeared that significant overwithholding had continued throughout the entire year. There was some concern that the budget would be too stimulative in the spring of 1973 because many taxpayers would have very favourable personal tax settlements at that time due to overwithholding in 1972.

For fiscal year 1973 the January budget proposed outlays of $246.3 billion. New legislation and supplemental budget requests by the administration raised the official request to $250 billion by June 1972. As the year progressed it became evident that legislation would be enacted that would raise spending by $6 billion to $8 billion above the $250 billion estimate. The Nixon administration requested legislation providing an absolute ceiling of $250 billion on outlays in fiscal 1973, but no such ceiling was enacted. News reports indicated that Congress was not willing to grant the president the authority to select spending cuts at his discretion, and a compromise bill limiting the president's power to make such cuts was not acceptable to the White House. Administration spokesmen then announced plans to limit spending to $250 billion by "impounding" appropriated funds where necessary. Although earlier administrations had impounded such funds, the constitutional authority for this practice was a matter of considerable controversy. The controversy entered a new phase when the administration announced that it would not spend a considerable portion of the funds recently appropriated by Congress over President Nixon's veto for water pollution control. The city of New York and other interested parties indicated that they would challenge the president's action in the courts. Authorities doubted, however, that the issue would be resolved in the courts in time to affect outlays in fiscal 1973.

The categories of federal spending that had grown most rapidly in preceding years were transfer payments, including Social Security and Medicare, and grants to state and local governments. Transfer payments were increasing greatly in 1972 even before a 20% Social Security benefit increase went into effect in October. The rapid growth in federal grants was accelerated in the fourth quarter of 1972 by the first payments to state and local governments under the newly enacted general revenue sharing program.

In October 1972 Congress enacted landmark legislation providing for federal revenue sharing with state and local governments. Unlike earlier categorical grants this new grant program placed few strings on the disposition of the funds. Thus, there were few, if any, restrictions on the kind of capital expenditures that might be made with revenue sharing funds. As for the use of revenue sharing for operation and maintenance, the law provided considerable latitude within the broad categories of local spending activities such as: public safety (including police and fire protection); environmental protection (including sewerage, sanitation, and pollution abatement); public transportation; health; recreation; social services for the poor and aged; and financial administration and libraries.

Over a five-year period federal outlays for general revenue sharing were expected to total more than $30 billion, with the cost of the first full year about $5.3 billion. Under a complex distributional formula more than 38,000 government units were to share the funds, with state governments receiving one-third and local governments about two-thirds. When the revenue sharing bill was first proposed, state and local governments were hard pressed for funds. Later the financial needs of state and local governments became somewhat questionable because these governments, as a unit, were experiencing significant budget surpluses prior to the first general revenue sharing payments in December 1972.

West Germany. Fiscal policy in West Germany swung toward an expansionary stance late in 1971. Weak private demand caused the federal government to release blocked appropriations for road building projects in the fourth quarter of 1971. The Annual Economic Report submitted by the government to the Bundestag in January 1972 foresaw a continued need for government action to support aggregate demand. Accordingly, authorities planned to implement the supplementary budgets of the federal government and the state (*Länder*) governments, which amounted to about DM. 4 billion. Expenditures under these contingency budgets were to be concentrated in investment projects and to be financed by the release of the countercyclical funds the governments had deposited in frozen accounts at the Bundesbank. In addition, the government decided to repay in the summer of 1972 the DM. 5.9 billion temporary income tax surcharge collected in 1970–71. This was nine months in advance of the legal deadline for such repayment. Finally, DM. 1 billion was to be made available in low interest loans to small enterprises, and DM. 1,250,000,000 of health insurance contributions by retirees was to be repaid. Implementation of all these proposals would have totaled about 1.6% of GNP.

As 1972 progressed, however, economic activity proved to be more buoyant than had been expected. This resulted in part from the revival in business confidence after the conclusion of the Smithsonian realignment of international currencies in December 1971, but a considerable role was played by the larger than anticipated rise in public expenditures. This increase was particularly strong in the first quarter of 1972 and resulted in part from a change in revenue sharing arrangements in favour of the state and communal governments. As it became increasingly clear that the recovery of private demand was becoming broader, the federal government decided not to activate the supplementary budgets and, in addition, to hold expenditures below budgeted levels. This decision was facilitated by the fact that the government's 1972 expenditure proposals were not formally approved until the end of the year, thus forcing agencies to operate with expenditure ceilings about 10% below budget proposals.

Because of the November 1972 federal elections, no budget proposals were put forward for 1973. However, because of the continued high rate of inflation, the government announced before the election that revenues in excess of estimates should be used to reduce borrowings; that increases in budget expenditures at all levels of government should be held to a rate equal to the nominal rise in GNP in 1973; and that no new jobs should be created in the public sector. On the whole, budget proposals for 1973 were expected to be characterized by the government's stabilization efforts.

United Kingdom. Fiscal policy in the U.K. in 1972, as in 1971, was mainly directed toward reducing unemployment. Price pressures continued to be high, with price increases accelerating even in the face of growing unemployment and lagging demand. However, the authorities decided that any lowering of the pressure of aggregate demand would be counterproductive both in the fight against inflation and in regard to the government's aim to improve the long-run investment climate in Britain by eliminating the stop-go policies that had characterized the 1960s. The budget for 1972–73, presented in March 1972, was accordingly expansionary. The chancellor of the Exchequer stated that the budget was intended to start the necessary revitalization of U.K. industry called for by Great Britain's impending entry into the European Economic Community; to raise the rate of real economic growth in the 1970s to twice that achieved in the 1960s; and to assure that all sectors of the economy participated in the growth in prosperity.

For the short term, the assessment was that economic activity would slow down rather than grow in the absence of stimulative measures, and so the budget was designed to provide a stimulus to demand sufficient to raise output in the first half of 1973 by 2% over what it would have been otherwise. In order to achieve this, personal exemptions from income tax were increased substantially and purchase tax rates were lowered. Also, free depreciation on all new investment in plant and machinery was introduced throughout the country, which meant that depreciation allowances could go up to 100% in the first year not only for regional development projects as before but also for all investments. These measures, together with earlier moves designed to accelerate public expenditure programs, were estimated to add about 3% to economic growth in 1972–73 as compared with 1971–72—probably the largest stimulus provided by the budget of any year in the previous decade.

In the framework of longer-term tax reforms, the budget spelled out details of the reform plans announced in 1971. These included a change in the corporation tax aimed at reducing fiscal discrimination against distributed profits by adoption of the "imputation" system operative in France and West Germany. Under this system a uniform tax rate is applied to all taxable profits, distributed or retained, with part of the tax on distributed earnings treated as revenues held in escrow against the tax liabilities of stockholders on dividends. Further, the value-added tax, to be introduced in April 1973, was provisionally fixed at a 10% rate, but the government was to have the power to vary the introductory rate up or down by 2½%. After that, existing rates could be varied up to 20% depending upon the economic situation. Food, except for a few items, and fuels and passenger fares were exempt from the tax as were all new construction and a large part of the service sector.

The chancellor stated in his budget message that

in order to help remove the uncertainties caused for industry by previous stop-go policies he would be prepared to alter the exchange rate of the pound sterling if the balance of payments circumstances so dictated rather than interrupt the government's expansionary program. As events proved, this was the option chosen as sterling began to float against other currencies in the summer of 1972.

Although demand and output clearly began to expand from the second quarter of 1972, unemployment remained high in the U.K. Despite the indicated large productivity increases, prices rose even faster. Not wishing to halt the pace of the current expansion, the government imposed a wage and price freeze in November 1972, allowing fiscal policy to remain on an expansionary course but tightening monetary policy considerably. Fiscal measures taken since the introduction of the 1972–73 budget were related entirely to the longer-term reform program on the tax side, but expenditure programs for 1973 seemed likely to show a rapid rate of increase.

Japan. The Japanese recession touched bottom around the turn of the year, after which economic activity continued to strengthen. Fiscal policy played a major role in the economic turnaround, particularly at the beginning of the year. In the first half of fiscal 1971 (April–September) public programs had already been speeded up. But in October, when uncertainties about the international financial climate worsened an already depressed business situation, a supplementary budget designed to raise GNP by 2% in the six months to the end of fiscal 1971 was introduced.

The fiscal 1972 budget continued this expansionary trend, with expenditures budgeted to rise by 18.6% over the (revised) fiscal 1971 levels. Expenditures for capital projects were budgeted to rise by 13.4%, and the Fiscal Investment and Loan Program (FILP) was to be increased by 12% over the already heavily increased 1971 estimates. In addition to the tax cuts authorized in the supplementary budget of October 1971, small reductions in personal income taxes were proposed for fiscal 1972 as well as some reductions designed to stimulate residential construction.

During the year the economic recovery continued to gather strength. But business investment demand remained weak, and the rate of economic activity proved insufficient to make significant inroads into the amount of unutilized resources. Consequently, there also was no noticeable reduction in Japan's external balance of payments surplus. This situation prompted the government in October 1972 to take a series of measures aimed at broadening the recovery and at reducing the foreign balance. The domestic measures included a large supplementary budget, which was approved by the Diet on November 13. It provided for an increase in central government expenditures of about 650 billion yen and in that for local governments of about 300 billion yen, or about 1% of GNP. In addition, new expenditures under FILP were to be expanded by about 500 billion yen. The additional expenditures brought total appropriations for fiscal 1972 to almost 30% above the fiscal 1971 level.

Canada. Canadian budgetary policy in 1971–72 continued to provide broad support for the economic recovery that started toward the end of 1970. The May 1972 federal budget followed a series of six official and minibudgets starting in 1970 that had aimed mainly at reducing the continuing high rate of unemployment. The May budget included new measures for faster depreciation of the cost of new investment in machinery and equipment in manufacturing or processing industries, and a broadening of depletion allowances in mineral resource industries to include processors. Starting in January 1973, the ceiling rate on corporate taxes applying to manufacturing or processing profits was to be reduced from 49 to 40%.

The new budget also contained various measures that would raise consumption demand but were aimed at reducing certain social inequities. They included tying old-age security and veterans' pension payments to the cost-of-living index; increasing special tax exemptions for old or infirm persons; and introducing a special tax exemption for full-time trainees and students. Following the budget proposals, expenditure and revenues both appeared to have expanded faster than projected. While the fiscal stimulus emanating from federal government actions was not much different in 1972 than in 1971, policies pursued by provincial governments probably increased the overall stimulus.

(HELLA B. JUNZ; WILLIAM J. BEEMAN)

See also Economics; Economy, World; Payments and Reserves, International; Taxation.

Greece

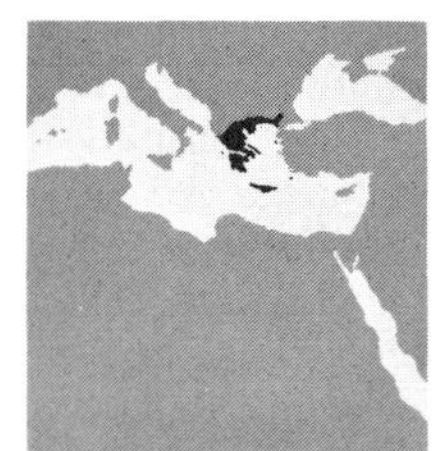

A constitutional monarchy of Europe, Greece occupies the southern part of the Balkan Peninsula. Area: 50,944 sq.mi. (131,944 sq.km.), of which the mainland accounts for 41,277 sq.mi. Pop. (1971): 8,768,640. Cap. and largest city: Athens (pop., 1971, 867,023). Language: Greek. Religion: Orthodox. King, Constantine II, in exile since Dec. 14, 1967; regents in 1972, Gen. Georgios Zoitakis and, from March 21, Georgios Papadopoulos; prime minister, Georgios Papadopoulos.

Two significant events of 1972 implied that Prime Minister Papadopoulos, while keeping all options open, might be setting the stage for the abolition of the monarchy and the proclamation of a presidential republic with himself as chief executive. On March 21 Papadopoulos dismissed General Zoitakis, who had been regent since the abortive royal countercoup of Dec. 13, 1967, and took over the post himself. He continued as prime minister and also retained the portfolios of defense, foreign affairs, and government policy and planning. On July 31 a major reshuffle regrouped Papadopoulos' original 12 junta partners within the government. Some of them, including his brother Konstantinos, joined the policy-making 18-man Cabinet; the others were undersecretaries. After the reshuffle, the government consisted of 23 civilian members and 19 who had a military background. A decree abolishing the monarchy, signed by all the ministers, would be in the nature of a second coup d'etat.

One fact was clear: the establishment born out of the five-year-long dictatorship—the officers, big business, shipowners, and opportunists—was digging in its heels against application of the 1968 constitution. The constitution allowed for the reinstatement of King Constantine and possibly the ruling hierarchy preceding the current establishment and thus posed the possibility of retribution as well as the overthrow of the dictatorship. Only if the "man at the top" was one of them could the new establishment trust him to evolve politically since, in case there was trouble, he would be sharing their destiny. King Constantine would not. Papadopoulos seemed to be orienting him-

Great Britain:
see United Kingdom

self in this direction. In an address to the people on April 21, marking the coup's fifth anniversary, he declared that there was no hard-and-fast formula of government for all countries and all peoples.

What evidently encouraged Papadopoulos to hold fast against pressures for further substantial steps toward democratic rule was the open support his regime received from U.S. Pres. Richard Nixon's administration, culminating in the Washington "leakage" (January 22) that Greece had agreed in principle to home-port naval facilities for a U.S. carrier task group in the general area of Athens-Piraeus. This involved the stationing of one aircraft carrier and its auxiliary vessels and of six destroyers. They would have a complement of 6,600 officers and crew. Some 3,100 U.S. navy dependents would settle in the Athens area. The disclosure angered the regime's opponents, who saw the move as an additional U.S. commitment to the status quo. By mid-September, U.S. Destroyer Squadron 12 had taken up home-port stations at Phaleron Bay, off Athens, and over a thousand U.S. dependents had arrived and had been granted extraterritorial rights.

U.S. gestures toward the regime included a visit by Secretary of State William P. Rogers (July 4–5). This was soon followed by visits from many Western European Cabinet-rank ministers, virtually ending the boycott imposed after the 1967 coup. The visitors included a French and a West German foreign undersecretary (September 25), as well as Lord Carrington, the British secretary of state for defense (September 6). They served to underline how economic, trade, and defense considerations could override political and ideological objections. Greek initiatives in foreign relations included an agreement with Peking (June 5) for an exchange of ambassadors (leading to a break in relations with Taiwan), as well as exchanges of visits with Arab, African, and Eastern European government leaders to make up for the scarcity of significant Western contacts.

The Cyprus issue flared up once again when the Greek regime, having concluded that the Cypriot president, Archbishop Makarios III, was the only obstacle to a settlement with Turkey, tried to remove him from the scene, using some heavy-handed diplomacy on the occasion of secret delivery of a Czechoslovak arms shipment to Cyprus. (*See* CYPRUS.)

Peace and order were maintained within Greece, but at a price. Martial law was restricted to the areas of Athens-Piraeus and Salonika, but the violation of individual liberties safeguarded by the constitution continued to be a daily occurrence. Arbitrary arrests and detentions continued on a large scale. Two periodical publications unfriendly to the regime were discontinued as a result of intimidation by the military police. Administrative exile was reimposed on eight prominent Greeks, including John Pesmazoglu, former deputy governor of the Bank of Greece. This served as an additional deterrent to opposition, as two cultural organizations—the Society for the Study of Greek Problems (of which Pesmazoglu was president) and the Greek-European Youth Movement—attempted to press for greater intellectual freedom.

There were bomb explosions—all without casualties—but these diminished as special military tribunals administered harsh sentences to those charged with violating the laws on explosives. Opposition activity shrank as former politicians realized that to issue statements critical of the regime produced little more than sympathy abroad. Despite academic declarations of concert and agreement, the pre-coup bourgeois parties remained hopelessly romantic. The Communists (although deeply divided) were lying low at the behest of the Eastern bloc, which was convinced that the Greek regime, one way or another, was working for its long-term benefit.

The Greek economy was riding on the wave of European economic prosperity. The gross national product was growing at an annual rate of 7.5%. High liquidity was reflected by enormous bank deposits, nonproductive foreign loans, and, rather absurdly, rapidly increasing foreign exchange reserves that included convertible, and therefore immediately exportable, deposits.

The import of foreign capital was notable for the absence of substantial development investments. In November 1971 Aristotle Onassis had decided to back

WIDE WORLD

Eight Greek men accused of plotting to kidnap John F. Kennedy, Jr., and of planning bank robberies to finance a guerrilla group dedicated to the overthrow of the Greek dictatorship appear in court as their trial begins in Athens on Aug. 3, 1972.

GREECE

Education. (1968–69) Primary, pupils 960,812, teachers 28,192; secondary, pupils 402,994, teachers 12,429; vocational, pupils 95,432; higher (including 4 universities), students 74,962, teaching staff 2,365.

Finance. Monetary unit: drachma, with (Sept. 18, 1972) a par value of 30 drachmas to U.S. $1 (free rate of 73.15 drachmas = £1 sterling). Gold, SDRs, and foreign exchange, central bank: (June 1972) U.S. $698.9 million; (June 1971) U.S. $296 million. Budget (1972 est.): revenue 72.1 billion drachmas; expenditure 65.1 billion drachmas. National income: (1970) 266.3 billion drachmas; (1969) 242 billion drachmas. Money supply: (March 1972) 58,680,000,000 drachmas; (March 1971) 50,650,000,000 drachmas. Cost of living (1963 = 100): (June 1972) 127; (June 1971) 123.

Foreign Trade. (1971) Imports 62,944,000,000 drachmas; exports 19,888,000,000 drachmas. Import sources: EEC 43% (West Germany 19%, Italy 9%, France 7%); Japan 10%; U.K. 7%; U.S. 7%. Export destinations: EEC 48% (West Germany 20%, France 9%, Italy 9%, Netherlands 6%); U.S. 9%; Yugoslavia 5%. Main exports: tobacco 13%; cotton 8%; chemicals 7%; aluminum 7%; fresh fruit 6%; dried fruit 6%; textiles 6%. Tourism (1970): visitors 1,407,500; gross receipts U.S. $194 million.

Transport and Communications. Roads (1971) 35,306 km. (including 11 km. expressways). Motor vehicles in use (1971): passenger 262,981; commercial 117,636. Railways (1970): 2,571 km.; traffic 1,531,000,000 passenger-km., freight 688 million net ton-km. Air traffic (1971): 2,342,700,000 passenger-km.; freight 36,107,000 net ton-km. Shipping (1971): merchant vessels 100 gross tons and over 2,056; gross tonnage 13,065,930. Telephones (Dec. 1970) 1,045,000. Radio receivers (Dec. 1969) 1,184,000. Television receivers (Dec. 1969) 86,000.

Agriculture. Production (in 000; metric tons; 1971; 1970 in parentheses): wheat 1,905 (1,930); barley 780 (718); oats *c.* 110 (106); corn *c.* 550 (481); potatoes 628 (*c.* 590); rice 75 (81); tomatoes (1970) 920, (1969) 822; oranges (1970) 452, (1969) *c.* 510; lemons (1970) 920, (1969) 118; sugar, raw value (1971–72) *c.* 155, (1970–71) *c.* 188; cotton, lint 108 (110); olive oil *c.* 201 (*c.* 190); wine *c.* 485 (483); raisins *c.* 150 (168); currants and sultanas (1970) 168, (1969) 186; figs (1970) *c.* 130, (1969) *c.* 130; tobacco 72 (79). Livestock (in 000; Dec. 1970): sheep *c.* 7,650; cattle *c.* 985; goats *c.* 4,100; pigs *c.* 380; horses *c.* 250; asses *c.* 355; chickens *c.* 24,500.

Industry. Production (in 000; metric tons; 1971): lignite 10,887; electricity (excluding most industrial production; kw-hr.) 10,609,000; petroleum products (1970) 4,950; bauxite 2,833; magnesite (1970) 718; cement 5,546; cotton yarn 45.

out of the oil refinery contract awarded to him, and this was followed by an international competition. Lucrative refinery contracts were awarded to two other Greek shipowners who maintained close contacts with the regime, but, unlike Onassis, they were not required to carry out onerous parallel investments. The only major contract was a £13 million concession to Austria's Steyr-Daimler-Puch concern for the production of trucks and tractors in Greece. The regime's handling of the national economy was underlined by the fact that two former members of the junta were holding ministerial jobs in the Ministry of National Economy. By the end of 1972, the new five-year plan (1973–77) had not yet been drafted. Instead, the regime's brain trust had produced a 15-year plan to increase per capita income from $1,125 to $2,625—according to experts, an 800-page exercise in wishful thinking. (MARIO MODIANO)

Guatemala

A republic of Central America, Guatemala is bounded by Mexico, British Honduras, Honduras, El Salvador, the Caribbean Sea, and the Pacific Ocean. Area: 42,042 sq.mi. (108,889 sq.km.). Pop. (1972 est.): 5,603,840. Cap. and largest city: Guatemala City (pop., 1972 est., 819,440). Language: Spanish, with some Indian dialects. Religion: predominantly Roman Catholic. President in 1972, Carlos Manuel Arana Osorio.

Early in March 1972 the newspaper *El Gráfico* reported that the previous year had been characterized by "a paroxysm of violence unprecedented in the history of Guatemala." The press had officially listed approximately 1,000 violent deaths (including those of 15 mayors and 3 deputies), 171 kidnappings, and 174 missing persons. In June and July 1972, after a lull, renewed attacks by members of the left-wing Fuerzas Armadas Rebeldes (FAR) resulted in the deaths of a number of prominent members of the ruling right-wing National Liberation Movement (MLN), including that of the vice-president of the Congress, Olivero Castañeda Paíz.

The ever present guerrilla problem aside, the government of President Arana was absorbed in formulating and executing an economic and development plan as the year began. When Guatemalan troop concentration on the border with British Honduras (Belize) was reported, British troops were sent to the colony, ostensibly for routine exercises. Guatemala had a long-standing territorial claim on Belize, and talks had been going on between the British and Guatemalan governments on the future status of the colony, which sought full independence. These talks were subsequently broken off amid Guatemalan protests.

The ending of the preferential treatment of exchange remittances to other Central American countries by the Banco Central de Costa Rica on June 16 thrust the Central American Common Market (CACM) once again to the forefront of Guatemalan politics. Further restrictive measures were enacted in August when the Costa Ricans decided to apply the free market rate of exchange to regional imports, and in early September trade between Costa Rica and Guatemala, El Salvador, and Nicaragua was suspended for approximately six weeks. Detailed negotiations then followed, and as a result an agreement was signed which introduced certain exchange rate adjustments to help rectify Costa Rica's trade deficit.

Other significant developments during the year included the delay experienced by the Eximbal nickel project; the purchase by the government of a controlling interest (96%) in Empresa Electrica de Guatemala; the discovery by Resources International of Canada of a petroleum deposit in the Las Tortigas Valley (Alta Verapaz); the serious damage caused to crops in certain areas by drought; and the revisions made to the country's banking legislation.

The Eximbal project was concerned with the exploitation of nickel deposits near Lake Izabal, and involved a total investment of approximately $250 million over 40 years. Negotiations between the government and the company were concluded in 1971, but there was little progress because of the difficulty of raising the necessary funds. In the second half of 1972 the exploratory drilling conducted by Resources International discovered a petroleum deposit in the Las Tortigas Valley. (ROBERT STENT)

GUATEMALA

Education. (1969–70) Primary, pupils 489,565, teachers 13,662; secondary, pupils 41,292, teachers 4,583; vocational, pupils 11,784, teachers 1,380; teacher training, students 7,569, teachers 1,008; higher (including 4 universities), students 14,151, teaching staff 771.

Finance. Monetary unit: quetzal, at par with the U.S. dollar (free rate, at Sept. 18, 1972, of 2.45 quetzales to £1 sterling). Gold, SDRs, and foreign exchange, central bank: (June 1972) U.S. $100.6 million; (June 1971) U.S. $95.4 million. Budget (1972 est.) balanced at 250.9 million quetzales. Gross national product: (1970) 1,786,000,000 quetzales; (1969) 1,645,000,000 quetzales. Money supply: (May 1972) 195.3 million quetzales; (May 1971) 169.2 million quetzales. Cost of living (Guatemala City; 1963 = 100): (May 1972) 108; (May 1971) 106.

Foreign Trade. (1971) Imports 296.5 million quetzales; exports 290.1 million quetzales. Import sources (1970): U.S. 35%; El Salvador 14%; Japan 10%; West Germany 10%. Export destinations (1970): U.S. 28%; El Salvador 13%; West Germany 11%; Honduras 10%; Costa Rica 7%; Japan 7%; Nicaragua 5%. Main exports: coffee 34%; cotton 9%; bananas 6%.

Transport and Communications. Roads (1970) c. 12,000 km. (including 1,095 km. highways). Motor vehicles in use (1970): passenger 42,600; commercial (including buses) 24,400. Railways (1970): c. 800 km.; freight traffic 106 million net ton-km. Air traffic (1970): 104,090,000 passenger-km.; freight 6,820,000 net ton-km. Telephones (Jan. 1971) 49,000. Radio receivers (Dec. 1968) 559,000. Television receivers (Dec. 1970) 72,000.

Agriculture. Production (in 000; metric tons; 1971; 1970 in parentheses): corn 751 (719); cotton, lint 52 (57); cane sugar, raw value (1971–72) 192, (1970–71) 198; sugar, panela (1971–72) c. 45, (1970–71) c. 45; dry beans 63 (63); coffee 129 (147); bananas (1970) c. 80, (1969) c. 80. Livestock (in 000; March 1971): cattle c. 1,450; sheep c. 510; pigs c. 800; poultry c. 9,700.

Industry. Production (in 000; metric tons; 1970): cement 251; petroleum products 724; lead ore (metal content) 1.1; zinc ore (metal content; 1969) 0.9; electricity (kw-hr.; 1968) 589,000.

Greek Orthodox Church: *see* Religion

Greenland: *see* Dependent States

Gross National Product: *see* Economy, World; Income, National

Guiana: *see* Dependent States; Guyana

Guided Missiles: *see* Defense

Guinea

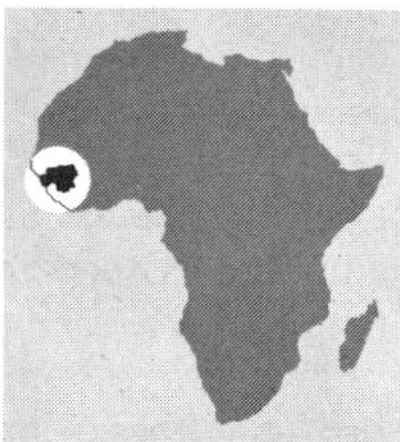

A republic on the west coast of Africa, Guinea is bounded by Portuguese Guinea, Senegal, Mali, Ivory Coast, Liberia, and Sierra Leone. Area: 94,925 sq.mi. (245,856 sq. km.). Pop. (1971 est.): 4,010,000. Cap. and largest city: Conakry (pop., 1967 est., 197,267). Language: French (official). Religion: mostly Muslim. President in 1972, Sékou Touré; premier from April, Louis Lansana Beavogui.

GUINEA
Education. (1968–69) Primary, pupils 167,340, teachers (1965–66) 3,990; secondary, pupils 33,448; teachers (1965–66) 567; vocational, pupils 5,334, teachers (1965–66) 261; teacher training, students 2,954, teachers (1965–66) 52; higher, students 942, teaching staff (1965–66) 95.
Finance. Monetary unit: Guinea franc, with an official rate (Sept. 18, 1972) of GFr. 227.36 to U.S. $1 (free rate of GFr. 556.35 = £1 sterling). Budget (1970–71 est.) balanced at GFr. 22.9 billion.
Foreign Trade. (1968–69) Imports GFr. 16.1 billion; exports GFr. 14.1 billion. Import sources (1964): U.S. 22%; U.S.S.R. 12%; China 10%. Export destinations (1964): France 16%; U.S. 11%; Cameroon 10%; Poland 8%. Main exports (1962): aluminum 60%; bananas 10%; palm products 7%; coffee 6%; iron ore 6%.

On Nov. 22, 1972, Guinea observed the second anniversary of the attempted invasion by Guinean exiles and Portuguese troops in 1970. The uncertainty that followed the abortive invasion and the plots and conspiracies of 1971 continued to weigh heavily upon Guinean daily life. In April 1972 it was announced that the National Assembly had "ratified" verdicts passed by local revolutionary courts in the mass trial of "fifth-column agents" that had begun in July 1971, but the penalties inflicted were not disclosed.

In April a new post of premier was created and conferred upon Louis Lansana Beavogui, a close confidant of the president. However, it seemed likely that Touré would continue to wield unrestricted power through the intermediary of his new premier.

After several years of crisis and dispute a reconciliation was achieved with Senegal. However, the collapse of the Organization of Senegal River States seemed irreversible, as Senegal, Mali, and Mauritania had already regrouped without Guinea to form a new Organization for the Development of the Senegal River (OMVFS). Attempts at reconciliation between Guinea and the Ivory Coast by Ivory Coast Pres. Félix Houphouët-Boigny broke down when Touré demanded the immediate return of Guinean exiles.

Guinea and Ghana were at loggerheads for some time following the death of former Ghanaian dictator Kwame Nkrumah (*see* OBITUARIES). The Guineans, who had granted asylum to Nkrumah and conferred upon him the co-presidency of their country, refused to return his body for burial in Ghana unless his reputation was rehabilitated and his followers reinstated. However, after lengthy negotiations Nkrumah's body was returned to Ghana for solemn burial at his native village. The two countries later agreed to resume diplomatic relations, broken off after Nkrumah's overthrow in 1966. (PHILIPPE DECRAENE)

Guyana

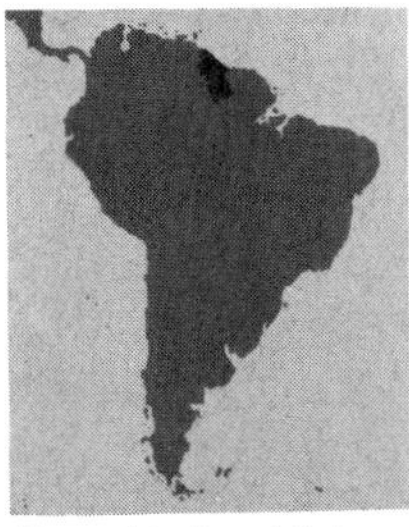

A republic and member of the Commonwealth of Nations, Guyana is situated between Venezuela, Brazil, and Surinam on the Atlantic Ocean. Area: 83,000 sq.mi. (215,000 sq.km.). Pop. (1970): 714,233, including (1970) East Indian 51%; African 30.7%; mixed 11.4%; Amerindian 4.4%. Cap. and largest city: Georgetown (pop., 1970, 66,070). Language: English (official). Religion: Protestant, Hindu, Roman Catholic. President in 1972, Arthur Chung; prime minister, Forbes Burnham.

GUYANA
Education. (1968–69) Primary, pupils 130,836, teachers 4,402; secondary, pupils 50,407, teachers 1,821; vocational, pupils 1,938, teachers 130; teacher training, students 733, teachers 49; higher, students 816, teaching staff 110.
Finance. Monetary unit: Guyanan dollar, with (Sept. 18, 1972) a free rate of Guy$2.13 to U.S. $1 (Guy$5.21 = £1 sterling). Budget (1971 est.): revenue Guy$146.8 million; expenditure Guy$130.6 million.
Foreign Trade. Imports (1971) Guy$265.2 million; exports (1970) Guy$267,976,000. Import sources (1970): U.K. 31%; U.S. 23%; Trinidad and Tobago 12%; Canada 9%. Export destinations: U.S. 29%; U.K. 19%; Canada 18%; Trinidad and Tobago 8%; Norway 8%. Main exports: bauxite 34%; sugar 27%; alumina 17%; rice 7%.
Agriculture. Production (in 000; metric tons; 1971; 1970 in parentheses): rice 136 (222); sugar, raw value (1971–72) 396, (1970–71) 375; cassava (1970) *c.* 12, (1969) *c.* 12; oranges *c.* 10 (8). Livestock (in 000; 1970–71): cattle 258; sheep 99; pigs 82.
Industry. Production (in 000; 1970): electricity (kw-hr.) 323,000; bauxite (metric tons; 1969) 4,306; diamonds (metric carats) 61.

For the Guyanese, 1972 began with assurance that the year's Guy$225 million budget would inflict no increase in taxes and would allow relief at certain levels. Spending was concentrated mainly on agriculture, education, and cooperatives, and plans were afoot to enter the shrimping industry.

The state-owned Guyana Bauxite Co. Ltd. (GUYBAU), formerly the Canadian-owned Demerara Bauxite Company (DEMBA), reported a profit, after tax, of Guy$7.4 million between July 15 and Dec. 31, 1971. It found new customers in China and the Soviet Union.

The number of cooperatives was increasing as well as their deposits, share capital, and other assets. Foreign observers maintained, however, that the number of cooperative failures was fairly high, if not discouraging, because of inexperience and irregular practices. On July 31 the prime minister obtained the resignation of all 15 Cabinet ministers and reallocated ministries after allegations of misuse of office by party members holding ministerial and cooperative posts. The new 18-member Cabinet, announced on August 2, contained 14 of the previous Cabinet ministers and 3 new ministers for housing, economic development, and finance.

At the People's National Congress annual convention in April, Prime Minister Burnham told members of plans for nationalizing vital sectors of the economy, including the remaining foreign-owned (U.S.) bauxite plant. The Commonwealth Development Corporation timber holdings, the sole foreign timber holdings in the country, were acquired by the government.

In August Guyana was host to a conference of nonaligned countries. Viet Cong and Royal Cambodian delegates were recognized, despite walkouts by 3 of the 64 states represented. Also represented were guerrilla movements from other third-world countries.

Burnham's power remained unshaken, despite grave charges of corruption against two ministers. There were more defections from Cheddi Jagan's People's Progressive Party, while many opposition groupings either lost ground or dwindled away completely. Burnham enhanced his Caribbean prestige at the August meeting of the Commonwealth Caribbean countries by backing the inclusion of non-Commonwealth members and upholding the resolution for the speedy formation of a Caribbean Economic Community.

(RANDOLPH RAWLINS)

Guinea, Portuguese: *see* Dependent States

Gynecology and Obstetrics: *see* Medicine

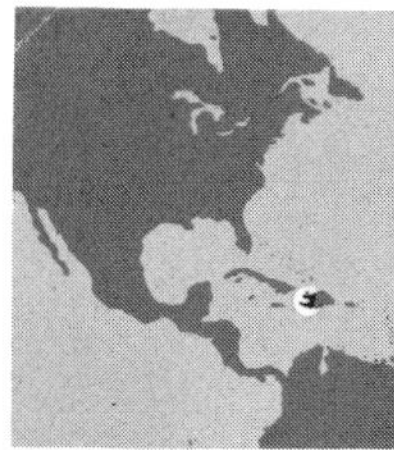

Haiti

The Republic of Haiti occupies the western one-third of the Caribbean island of Hispaniola, which it shares with the Dominican Republic. Area: 10,714 sq.mi. (27,750 sq.km.). Pop. (1971): 4,243,926, of whom 95% are Negro. Cap. and largest city: Port-au-Prince (pop., 1971, 419,947). Language: French (official) and Creole. Religion: Roman Catholic; Voodooism practiced in rural areas. President in 1972, Jean-Claude Duvalier.

The presidency of Jean-Claude Duvalier was strengthened by the dismissal in November 1972 of two of his father's most notorious henchmen—Rosalie Adolphe, mayor of Port-au-Prince and former commandant of Fort Dimanche, the country's chief political prison, and Luckner Cambronne, minister of the interior and defense, who, with Simone Duvalier, the widow of the former president, had effectively run Haiti since his death. Cambronne held monopolies in many sectors of the economy, his schemes including the Hemo Caribbean Co., which made profits exporting the blood and corpses of undernourished Haitians to U.S. hospitals. He was replaced by a new favourite of Mme Duvalier, Roger Lafontant, and flew into exile on November 26. In March plans had been announced to reform the constitution, with proposals to create a national assembly and to establish the office of prime minister, for which Cambronne had been the leading contender. Meanwhile, Jean-Claude Duvalier toured the country to build up popular support for the regime, trying to help the U.S. improve the image of "Duvalierism" for purposes of regional stability.

By September it had become apparent that the U.S. was seeking improved relations with Haiti. A top-level mission from Haiti visited Washington in March to seek bilateral economic aid, but it was politely rebuffed. Nevertheless, in January the U.S. Department of State announced that it had licensed the Miami concern Aerotrade to sell arms to Haiti, and several Haitian Air Force officers were sent to the U.S. for training during the year. In August an eight-man team of U.S. military experts visited Port-au-Prince to assess the needs of the Haitian armed forces, and the resumption of full official military aid, which had been cut off since 1963, was discussed. A request for military assistance valued at $10 million was rejected, and the U.S. made it plain that any aid was conditional upon its being used for legitimate defense purposes only and not to build up the Volontaires de la Sécurité Nationale and Tontons Macoutes militia.

U.S. private investors showed renewed interest in Haiti. In January Honolulu-based Wendel-Phillips Oil was granted a 35-year concession for the exploration and development of crude petroleum deposits on the continental shelf, on islands, and inland; the company undertook to invest $20.5 million. Du Pont Caribbean announced plans in March to develop the island of Tortuga as a tourist centre, but these plans subsequently foundered.

There were indications of an all-round improvement in the economy, particularly between January and June. The Organization of American States (OAS) in April reported an upswing in agricultural and industrial production in 1971, and that the tourist boom had continued. In May the state planning board, CONADEP, forecast an annual growth rate of 7.7% between 1972 and 1976; over the same period coffee exports were expected to increase by 70% to 490,000 bags a year and sugar shipments by 60% to 59,000 bags. A yearly rise in industrial output of 12% was also foreseen. In March the second generator of the Péligré hydroelectric plant was inaugurated; a third turbine was to be opened in 1973, by which time it was considered that sufficient power would be available to sustain industrial expansion.

(ROBIN CHAPMAN)

HAITI

Education. (1968–69) Primary, pupils 291,000, teachers 6,700; secondary, pupils 27,600, teachers 1,700; vocational, pupils 6,400, teachers 400; teacher training, students 230, teachers 60; higher (University of Haiti; 1966–67), students 1,527, teaching staff 209.

Finance. Monetary unit: gourde, with (Sept. 18, 1972) a par value of 5 gourdes to U.S. $1 (free rate of 12.23 gourdes = £1 sterling). Gold, SDRs, and foreign exchange, central bank: (June 1972) U.S. $15.1 million; (June 1971) U.S. $7.8 million. Budget (1971–72 est.) balanced at 148 million gourdes. Cost of living (Port-au-Prince; 1963 = 100): (March 1972) 132; (March 1971) 130.

Foreign Trade. Imports (1971) 283.2 million gourdes; exports 231.1 million gourdes. Import sources (1970 est.): U.S. 52%; Japan 9%; Canada 7%; Italy 6%; France 5%. Export destinations (1970 est.): U.S. 65%; France 9%; Italy 7%; Belgium-Luxembourg 6%. Main exports: coffee 43%; bauxite 14%; sugar 8%.

Transport and Communications. Roads (1970) *c.* 4,000 km. (including *c.* 350 km. with improved surface). Motor vehicles in use (1970): passenger 11,600; commercial 1,400. Telephones (Jan. 1969) *c.* 4,450. Radio receivers (Dec. 1970) 83,000. Television receivers (Dec. 1970) 11,000.

Agriculture. Production (in 000; metric tons; 1971; 1970 in parentheses): coffee 25 (28); sugar, raw value (1971–72) *c.* 70, (1970–71) *c.* 68; bananas (1970) 212, (1969) 212; sisal 27 (27). Livestock (in 000; 1970–71): pigs *c.* 1,800; cattle *c.* 960; goats *c.* 1,390; sheep *c.* 81.

Industry. Production (in 000; metric tons; 1970): cement 65; bauxite (exports) 673; electricity (excluding most industrial production; kw-hr.) 88,000.

Harbours: *see* Transportation

Harness Racing: *see* Horse Racing

Hay: *see* Agriculture

Health: *see* Medicine

Heart Disease: *see* Medicine

Hebrew Literature: *see* Literature

Highways: *see* Engineering Projects; Transportation

Hinduism: *see* Religion

Historical Studies: *see* Literature

Historic Buildings

Under the aegis of the General Conference of UNESCO in 1970, drafts of a Convention and of a Recommendation for the Protection of the Cultural and Natural Heritage of Mankind were prepared in 1972. During April a committee of governmental experts from 60 member states of UNESCO examined and amended the drafts for submission to the October–November session of the General Conference. The U.S. delegation underlined the interest of its government in preservation and suggested that the concept of a "world heritage," mentioned by Pres. Richard Nixon in a speech to Congress in February 1971, be incorporated; this suggestion was adopted. The convention also foresaw the establishment of a world heritage committee and fund.

The change of government in Italy delayed adoption of the bill to finance the preservation of Venice. The newly elected government announced that the bill would be given first priority, however, and it was subsequently submitted to Parliament. Meanwhile studies begun on the Venetian lagoon continued. In November it was announced that emergency braces were being put on the Leaning Tower of Pisa, and in 1973 a competition would be opened for a plan to consolidate the soil under the structure.

Studies of problems involved in preserving the 9th-century Buddhist monument of Borobudur in Indonesia during 1972 included an investigation of sealants for waterproofing, cements to repair sculptured stone, and refinement of designs for the new foundations. The total cost was estimated at $7,750,000.

The government of Pakistan also carried out a series of studies on the problem of preserving the 5,000-year-old site of Mohenjo Daro in the Indus Valley. This site, the largest known urban centre of that period, was first discovered in 1922. Excavations since then had revealed many features of the ancient civilization, including the use of a still undeciphered pictographic script. The development of irrigation agriculture in the area had contributed to the deterioration of Mohenjo Daro by the introduction of salts into the brickwork. Government experts proposed to construct a ring of 14 tube wells to lower the water table by 20 ft. Eventually other wells would be drilled in successive rings so that the water table could be lowered sufficiently to permit archaeological excavations in still unknown levels. Total cost of the project was estimated at $8 million.

The intensification of the conflict in Southeast Asia continued to menace the site of Angkor Wat, Cambodia. Since 1970 Bernard Groslier of the École Française d'Extrême-Orient had been permitted by occupying Communist forces to continue work on the restoration of the monuments, but he and the workmen were expelled in early 1972. In an attempt to ensure the safety of the monuments in combat areas, the government applied to have the monuments in Angkor Park and Roluos, a refuge, and two other monumental sites placed on the International Register of Cultural Property under Special Protection.

In South Vietnam fears were also expressed about the safety of the Citadel of Hue. The 150-year-old structure once had more than 100 buildings within it, but many were destroyed during the post-World War II conflicts. In addition, holes were blown in the surrounding walls and additional damage was done during the 1968 Tet offensive. Many pieces from the museum were packed and shipped away after Quang Tri fell to North Vietnamese units in May 1972.

Many countries, especially the industrially developed ones, plagued by pollution, urban expansion, and the automobile, were increasingly concerned and attentive to the condition of the urban environment. (*See* ENVIRONMENT.) In San Francisco a study carried out on the effects of urban redevelopment programs (replacement of older, lower buildings by high-rise buildings) showed that, instead of leading to increased income for the city, the changes contributed to a growing deficit. This was partially caused by loss of residents, who moved to the suburbs, and by increased amenity costs, which were greater than the income derived from the change. These changes also accelerated the deterioration of marginal property and contributed to the anomie of the population. The authors noted that the redevelopment projects had also helped to destroy the "image" of San Francisco and to erode the tourist industry, the city's biggest source of revenue.

In Boston high-rise construction about Scollay Square and Haymarket left 17th- and 18th-century buildings surviving as tiny anachronisms against smooth-flanked curtain-walled buildings. In Washington, D.C., it was reported that the secretaries of transportation and the interior had agreed that the only feasible route for a proposed link between two freeways would have to take land from the grounds of the Lincoln Memorial and the Tidal Basin. For fiscal 1972 the Department of the Interior awarded over $5 million in grants-in-aid for historic preservation to the National Trust, 45 different states, and the District of Columbia.

In the U.K. another of several projects proposed for London's Piccadilly Circus was heavily criticized. Although retaining the famous Fountain of Eros, the plan, like the earlier ones, proposed the construction of massive reinforced-concrete structures and emphasized rapid circulation of motor vehicles. Soho, in the immediate neighbourhood and containing many early Georgian houses, would be affected by the new plans, as it was a working class area where a village-like social structure had developed. Worries were also expressed about changes taking place along Regent Street (first built by John Nash and radically rebuilt in 1927), leading from Oxford Circus to Piccadilly Circus; the facades lining it still presented one of the most elegant frontages of the city.

Preservationists sounded the alarm about changes proposed for the city of Bath. The city was architecturally unique in England since it was built largely during a single period, the Georgian (with Palladian styles predominating), and had a pattern of carefully laid out streets opening on a succession of vistas. The scale of its buildings had also been carefully planned relative to the landscape. Associated with the homes of the aristocracy and the wealthy were buildings housing the workshops of artisans, shops, and homes of tradesmen. Many of these, classified as substandard, were being demolished. In addition, the City Council had decided to approve a four-lane highway across the city and through a new tunnel to be built under the Georgian area. The proposed plan extensively modified the original project prepared by C. D. Buchanan in 1965 by requiring the destruction of many buildings of historical interest and changes in the appearance of the river frontage. Thus, in Janu-

UPI COMPIX

UPI COMPIX

Having survived years of use by citizens of Rome and centuries of tourists, the famed Colosseum in Rome faced its gravest peril from automobile exhaust fumes, traffic vibrations, air pollution, and weeds. The famous structure was partially closed in September 1972. Italy lacked sufficient funds for complete restoration. Californian Thomas Merrick (above) offered to buy the Colosseum for $1 million.

A.F.P./PICTORIAL PARADE

Efforts to restore the home of the painter Vincent van Gogh in Cuesmes, Belg., were begun in 1972. Some 150,000 French francs were being sought for the project.

ary 1972 the Bath Preservation Trust declared that "until confidence in the standards of the taste of the city authorities has been restored, and until a greater respect for the scale and general style of the city becomes evident, the trustees feel that it will be essential to challenge the needs for demolition of every building, great or small, forming part of the city's heritage."

In Paris high-rise structures, once limited to the Défense area northwest of the city, were being built in many sections. The most prominent was the Tower of Montparnasse in the south. In addition, new high-rise structures were also going up along the Seine. One of the city's landmarks, the iron footbridge known as the Pont-des-Arts, erected in 1804 (the oldest iron bridge in France), which linked the Institut de France to the Louvre, was to be destroyed to make way for an expressway. A Committee to Save Paris was established, its latest project being an attempt to preserve three handsome 19th-century town houses on the southern margins of the Parc Monceau.

In Rome one of the wettest summers on record weakened the foundations of a number of monuments. The Palatine, the Forum, and the Arch of Titus were closed to visitors. Large pieces fell from exposed portions of the Colosseum and it too was closed off. (In September a U.S. multimillionaire offered to buy it, planning to restore and reopen it to the public for an entrance fee.) The problem of vandalism also plagued the city. Statues that had lined the Appian Way for nearly 2,000 years were being defaced or stolen.

In the spring of 1972 new regulations were adopted by the Kyoto City Council to ensure a protective zone around the principal monuments, such as the Imperial Palace and major temples. In addition, the historic quarter surrounding the Kiyomizu temple was identified and zoned, and construction was to be controlled. This action followed by more than two years an international symposium on the preservation of the historic cities of Kyoto and Nara, threatened by residential and industrial development, organized by the Japanese National Commission for UNESCO.

The Council of Europe organized a new Committee of Monuments and Sites, which met for the first time during November–December 1971 to prepare for the "European Architectural Heritage Year 1975." Activities planned included congresses, seminars, competitions, festivals, and radio and television programs.

Nearly 500 delegates from 36 countries were present at the third General Assembly of the International Council of Monuments and Sites (ICOMOS), held in Budapest, Hung., in June 1972. Piero Gazzola and Raymond Lemaire were reelected president and secretary-general, respectively. Work on the Coach House (Les Communs) of the Hôtel St. Aignan, Paris, was completed during the year. The third floor was strengthened to permit the installation of a "compactus" system of filing for the UNESCO-ICOMOS international documentation centre, and the organization began a campaign to raise funds to begin operations. Simultaneously, the City of Paris began restoring and adapting the principal buildings of the Hôtel St. Aignan to serve as the city archive.

(HIROSHI DAIFUKU)

See also Architecture; Museums and Galleries.

Hockey

Professional Ice Hockey. The National Hockey League might never be the same again. For years it had been the only big-time hockey league, but in 1972 the new World Hockey Association pirated several of its biggest stars, notably Bobby Hull (*see* BIOGRAPHY), with big money and long-term contracts.

Then a confident Team Canada—made up of players recruited from NHL teams—barely squeaked by the Soviet Union's national team in a widely heralded series that brought a team of Canadian professionals and the Soviet team together for the first time. Four games were played in Canada and four in Moscow. The two teams proved to be practically even. The Canadians won four games, lost three, and tied one. They won the last one on September 28 in Moscow when Paul Henderson of the Toronto Maple Leafs scored a goal in the last minute for a 6–5 win.

The challenge of the World Hockey Association cost the NHL such outstanding players as Hull, who abandoned the Chicago Black Hawks for the Winnipeg Jets in exchange for a ten-year contract worth about $2,750,000. Hull was followed into the WHA by such stars as Derek Sanderson, who left the Boston Bruins for the Philadelphia Blazers, and Gerald Cheevers, who left Boston for the Cleveland Crusaders. Goalkeeper Bernard Parent quit the Toronto Maple Leafs for the Blazers.

A court order obtained by the Black Hawks prevented Hull from playing for Winnipeg in the early part of the 1972–73 season, but the WHA began play in October with 12 teams. The teams were split evenly into two divisions, Eastern and Western. Cleveland, the Quebec Nordiques, New England Whalers, New York Raiders, Ottawa Nationals, and Philadelphia

NHL Final Standings, 1971–72

	Won	Lost	Tied	Goals	Goals against	Pts.
EAST DIVISION						
Boston Bruins	54	13	11	330	204	119
New York Rangers	48	17	13	317	192	109
Montreal Canadiens	46	16	16	307	205	108
Toronto Maple Leafs	33	31	14	209	208	80
Detroit Red Wings	33	35	10	261	262	76
Buffalo Sabres	16	43	19	203	289	51
Vancouver Canucks	20	50	8	203	297	48
WEST DIVISION						
Chicago Black Hawks	46	17	15	256	166	107
Minnesota North Stars	37	29	12	212	191	86
St. Louis Blues	28	39	11	208	247	67
Pittsburgh Penguins	26	38	14	220	258	66
Philadelphia Flyers	26	38	14	200	236	66
California Seals	21	39	18	216	288	60
Los Angeles Kings	20	49	9	206	305	49

made up the Eastern section. Winnipeg, the Los Angeles Sharks, Alberta Oilers, Houston Aeros, Minnesota Fighting Saints, and Chicago Cougars comprised the West. On November 8 a federal district court issued a temporary injunction restraining the NHL from using its reserve clause to prevent players from jumping to the WHA. Hull and other former NHL players were then allowed to compete.

The NHL began the 1972–73 season with 2 new teams to raise the total to 16. The New York Islanders joined the East Division, and the Atlanta Flames became new members of the West.

In 1971–72 competition the Boston Bruins won their second Stanley Cup in three years. Boston eliminated Toronto and St. Louis in preliminary series before defeating the New York Rangers four games to two in the final. New York had qualified for the final by disposing of Montreal and Chicago in earlier rounds.

Bobby Orr, the innovative Boston defenseman, continued his dominance of the individual awards. For the third successive year he won the Hart Memorial Trophy as the most valuable player in the NHL, and for the fifth year in a row he was awarded the James Norris Memorial Trophy as the league's best defenseman. Phil Esposito, Boston's rangy centre, accumulated 133 points and won the Art Ross Trophy for the second straight season as the game's leading scorer. Jean Ratelle, a centre for New York, received the Lady Byng Trophy as the player best combining skill with sportsmanlike conduct. Montreal's goalkeeper Ken Dryden was selected as the NHL's rookie of the year, while Tony Esposito and Gary Smith of Chicago combined to win the Vezina Trophy as the goalkeepers whose team allowed the fewest number of points.

In the minor professional associations, the Dallas Black Hawks beat the Tulsa Oilers for the championship of the Central League, and the Nova Scotia Voyageurs defeated the Baltimore Clippers for supremacy in the American League. The Denver Spurs won the Western League title in a final series against the Portland Buckaroos. (R. H. BEDDOES)

Amateur Ice Hockey. Twenty nations competed in the 39th world amateur ice hockey championship in 1972, the first time that a separate tournament was held during an Olympic season instead of deciding Olympic and world titles concurrently. Six teams as usual competed in Group A, all playing each opponent twice, in Prague, Czech., on April 7–22. The Czechoslovakians became champions for the first time since 1949, effectively thwarting Soviet efforts to gain a tenth successive win. The outcome hinged on what proved to be two classic matches between the two clearly outstanding teams. In the first, the U.S.S.R. fought back from a 2-goal deficit to force a 3–3 draw, but the Czechoslovakians won the crucial second encounter 3–2. The Czechoslovakians, also retaining their European title, won all their games against the other four teams. The only other nation to take a point from the U.S.S.R. was Sweden, which finished third above Finland and West Germany. As in the previous year, Aleksandr Maltsev, the Soviet centre, was top scorer with 22 points—10 goals and 12 assists. Jiri Holecek of Czechoslovakia was the most successful goalkeeper. For the third year, Canada declined to compete.

Poland edged out the U.S. to head a seven-team Group B at Bucharest, Rom., on March 24–April 2. This earned the Poles promotion to Group A in 1973, displacing 1972's last-place Switzerland. Below the U.S. were East Germany, Romania, Japan, Yugoslavia, and Norway. The leading Group B scorer was Leszke Tokarz of Poland, with 8 goals and 5 assists in six games. Austria won promotion from Group C, at Miercurea Ciuc, Rom., on March 3–12, with Italy the runner-up. Hungary and Belgium finished third and fourth, equal on points but with better goal average than fifth-placed China, which was competing for the first time. The bottom two teams were the Netherlands and Denmark. The joint top scorers in Group C were T. Havran (Hung.) and J. Puschnig (Aus.), each with 9 points.

(For results of the Olympic Games, *see* SPORTING RECORD: *Special Report*.) (HOWARD BASS)

Field Hockey. All of the 16 countries entering the field hockey tournament at the 1972 Olympic Games stepped up their training during the year. International match programs were expanded, and tours and practice matches arranged to bring the teams to their peak for the start of the competition on August 27. The most ambitious single project in Great Britain's program was a tour of India at the end of 1971. Although the U.K. failed to win any of the four tests played, the results were close. Between March and June 1972, Great Britain played six international matches, of which four were won, one drawn, and one lost.

After an easy opening match at the Olympics, in which they defeated Mexico 6–0, Great Britain suffered two sharp reverses, losing 5–0 to India and 2–1 to New Zealand. The British team finished third in their pool, which meant playing off with Australia, Malaysia, and Spain for fifth to eighth places; Great Britain defeated Spain but lost the last match of all to Australia in extra time and so finished sixth.

West Germany, which dropped only one point in nine matches, finished first in the Olympic tournament and thoroughly deserved the gold medal. The best drilled and most mobile team in the field, the West Germans were led by such skillful players as Wolfgang Baumgart, Horst Droese, and Uli Vos. Second-place Pakistan lacked a little of the speed and precision that had made them Olympic champions in Mexico in 1968. They lost to West Germany in the final by a penalty corner goal to nil. Afterward the Pakistan team delayed the medal ceremony for 20 minutes while their supporters demonstrated excitedly in front of the main stand, protesting against Pakistan's defeat, and then

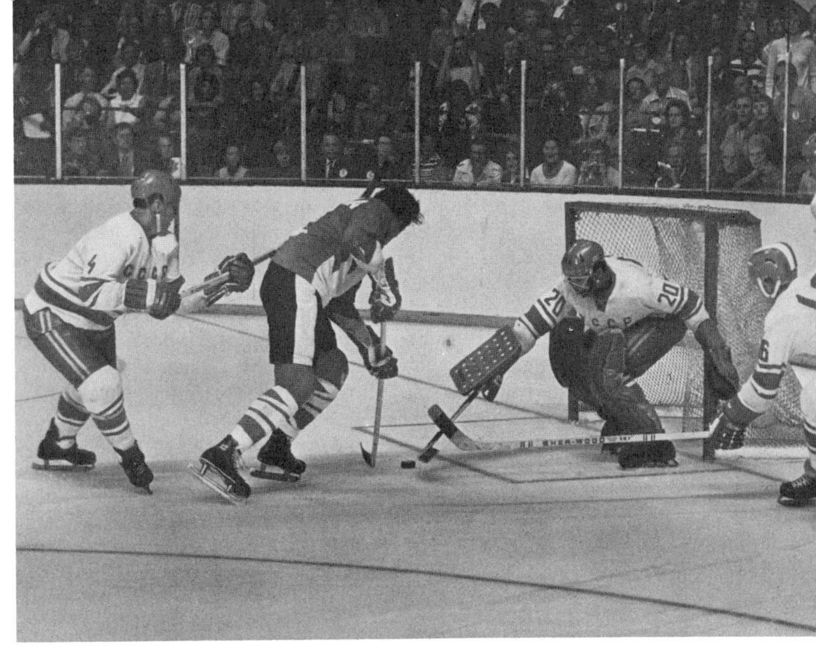

TOP, PETER BREGG—CANADIAN PRESS
ABOVE, FRANK LENNON—TORONTO STAR

Phil Esposito (top) scores on Soviet goalie Vladislav Tretiak in the second game of the series between Team Canada and the Soviet Union's national hockey team. Paul Henderson (above) expresses the jubilation felt by thousands of Canadian hockey fans after his dramatic series-winning goal in the final game with only 34 seconds to play.

accepted their medals with such bad grace that they were subsequently suspended by the International Olympic Committee from future Olympic competition and by the International Hockey Federation from all international hockey for a period to be determined.

India, which won the bronze medal for third place for the second straight Olympics, combined skill and style in graceful rhythm as did no other team in the tournament but was not the devastating force of old. The Indian forwards, especially Ashok Kumar at inside left and Ganesh at outside right, had moments of brilliance but also suffered occasional lapses. (For additional information on the Olympic Games, *see* SPORTING RECORD: *Special Report.*)

In non-Olympic competition England was unbeaten in the British Isles, winning the games against Ireland and Scotland and playing a goalless draw with Wales, which had a good season. Besides drawing with England, Wales defeated Czechoslovakia and Kenya and drew with Scotland. Wiltshire won the English county championship in March for the fourth time in six years, defeating Northumberland in the final 4–2. In April, Hounslow became first winners of the National Club Championship of England, sponsored by the tobacco firm Benson and Hedges; in the final Hounslow defeated the Eastern Counties champion, the Norwich Grasshoppers, 3–0. Hounslow went on to defeat the cup winners of Northern Ireland (Queen's University, Belfast), Scotland (Stepps), and Wales (Northop Hall) in a tournament played on the Isle of Man in May.

In September, a new off-side rule was introduced by the reconstituted International Hockey Rules Board, which had become a satellite of the International Hockey Federation instead of a British organization, as it had been from its foundation in 1900 until the end of 1971. The change in the rule reduced the number of opponents required to determine whether a player is off side or not from three to two. The board hoped that the change would help to lift the game out of the defensive rut into which it had sunk by giving forwards greater freedom and thus increasing the number of goals scored.

In women's hockey the series of "home" internationals was restricted by the decision of England and Wales to withdraw from their matches against Ireland that were to have been played in Dublin and Limerick, respectively. "Ladies' Day" at Wembley (March 11), the day of the All-England Women's Hockey Association, saw England suffer one of its rare defeats at the hands of Scotland, which won 2–1. Scotland drew with Ireland 0–0, and England beat Wales 2–0. But the England team won their medals back a few weeks later when they defeated the Netherlands.

(R. L. HOLLANDS)

Seconds after defeating the New York Rangers 3–0 and clinching the Stanley Cup on May 11, 1972, Boston Bruins teammates rush to congratulate jubilant Bruins goalie Gerry Cheevers.

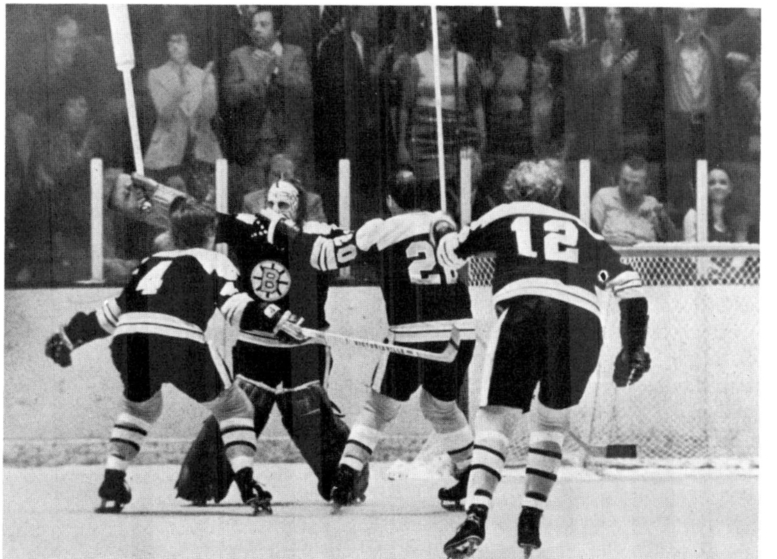

WIDE WORLD

Honduras

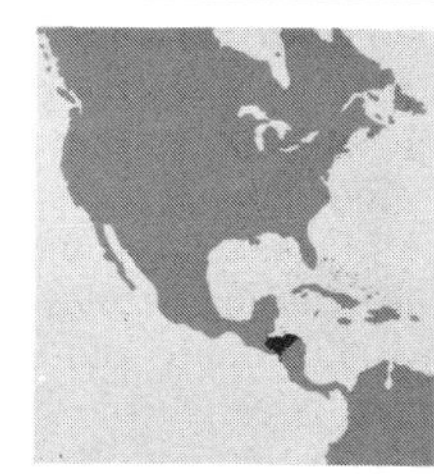

A republic of Central America, Honduras is bounded by Nicaragua, El Salvador, Guatemala, the Caribbean Sea, and the Pacific Ocean. Area: 43,277 sq.mi. (112,088 sq.km.). Pop. (1972 est.): 2,756,200, including 90% mestizo. Cap. and largest city: Tegucigalpa (pop., 1972 est., 365,366). Language: Spanish; some Indian dialects. Religion: Roman Catholic. Presidents in 1972, Ramón Ernesto Cruz and, from December 4, Gen. Oswaldo López Arellano.

President Cruz, 68, and a leading lawyer, was overthrown by the Army in a bloodless coup on December 3, while General López attended a World Amateur baseball series in Managua, Nicaragua. Cruz was simply locked inside his home and his wife and children sent to the U.S. General López, commander of the armed forces who helped overthrow the government in 1963 and had been president until Cruz's inauguration, announced he would serve the five years left of Cruz's term.

HONDURAS

Education. (1968–69) Primary, pupils 376,966, teachers 10,437; secondary, pupils 25,365; vocational, pupils 4,923; teacher training, students 4,506; secondary, vocational, and teacher training, teachers 2,689; higher, students 3,459.

Finance. Monetary unit: lempira, with (Sept. 18, 1972) a par value of 2 lempiras to U.S. $1 (free rate of 4.89 lempiras = £1 sterling). Gold, SDRs, and foreign exchange, central bank: (June 1972) U.S. $28,340,000; (June 1971) U.S. $26.3 million. Budget (1970 est.) balanced at 225.2 million lempiras. National income: (1971) 1,443,800,000 lempiras; (1970) 1,360,400,000 lempiras. Money supply: (Dec. 1971) 174,530,000 lempiras; (Dec. 1970) 165.5 million lempiras). Cost of living (Tegucigalpa; 1966 = 100): (June 1972) 117; (June 1971) 108.

Foreign Trade. (1971) Imports 387.8 million lempiras; exports 375.1 million lempiras. Import sources (1970): U.S. 41%; Guatemala 13%; El Salvador 7%; Japan 8%; Nicaragua 6%; Costa Rica 6%; Venezuela 5%; West Germany 5%. Export destinations (1970): U.S. 54%; West Germany 11%; Italy 5%. Main exports: bananas 51%; coffee 12%; timber 10%.

Transport and Communications. Roads (1969) 5,185 km. (including 153 km. of Pan-American Highway). Motor vehicles in use (1970): passenger 18,800; commercial (including buses) 16,900. Railways (1970) 1,012 km. Air traffic (1970): 163,755,000 passenger-km.; freight 3,870,000 net ton-km. Shipping (1971): merchant vessels 100 gross tons and over 54; gross tonnage 69,683. Telephones (Jan. 1971) 14,000. Radio receivers (Dec. 1970) 147,000. Television receivers (Dec. 1970) 22,000.

Agriculture. Production (in 000; metric tons; 1971; 1970 in parentheses): corn *c.* 283 (*c.* 346); coffee *c.* 36 (*c.* 34); sorghum *c.* 50 (*c.* 50); sugar, raw value (1971–72) *c.* 118, (1970–71) 113; dry beans *c.* 65 (64); bananas (1970) *c.* 1,400, (1969) 1,280; cotton, lint *c.* 3 (3); beef and veal *c.* 48 (*c.* 48). Livestock (in 000; 1970–71): cattle *c.* 1,600; pigs *c.* 820; chickens *c.* 7,000.

Industry. Production (in 000; metric tons; 1970): silver 0.11; gold (troy oz.) 2.5; lead ore (metal content; exports; 1969) 6.7; zinc ore (metal content; exports; 1969) 8.4; electricity (kw-hr.) 310,000.

Cruz held office for 18 months and was the nation's first popularly elected president since 1932. Internal political disputes had surfaced early in the year between the incumbent National Party and the opposition Liberal Party. But observers felt the coup stemmed from impatience with Cruz's legalistic "nit-picking" that threatened Honduras' position in attempting to enter the Central American Common Market. Cruz, who had been General López' candidate in the 1971 presidential election, had been a member of the International Court of Justice. But after 18 months of Cruz's "paper-shuffling," López, and obviously his followers, felt the country had stood still.

On June 12 the U.S. Senate, by a vote of 74–0, ratified a treaty recognizing Honduras' sovereignty over the Swan Islands. The ratification ended several years of active negotiations during which representatives of the governments of Honduras and the U.S. signed a treaty in San Pedro Sula, Honduras, on Nov. 22, 1971. The Swan Islands, which lie 98 mi. off Honduras' north coast, had not been occupied until the U.S. did so in 1863. The treaty allowed the U.S. to continue to operate and maintain a weather station and telecommunications and air navigation facilities.

Efforts continued to settle differences resulting from the open conflict between Honduras and El Salvador in 1969. On February 23, President Cruz offered to settle border differences directly with El Salvador. In September, the two foreign ministers met in Guatemala in a further effort toward resolving the differences between their nations.

Resolution of the rift between Honduras and El Salvador was vital to the recovery of the area's regional economic body, the Central American Common Market (CACM). Prospects for an early settlement received a setback on August 26 when Honduras and Nicaragua signed a bilateral trade agreement, an action counter to the rules for CACM members. Both nations viewed the action as necessary in light of what they saw as the irregular situation in CACM and the need for less favoured members to defend their interests. (ALLEN D. BUSHONG)

Horse Racing

Thoroughbred Racing. *U.S.* The highlight of Thoroughbred racing in the U.S. in 1972 was the complete domination of the two-year-old filly division by La Prévoyante and of the two-year-old colt division by Secretariat. Although La Prévoyante (Buckpasser-Arctic Dancer, by Neartic), a homebred Canadian owned by Jean-Louis Levesque, was undefeated in 12 starts to equal the record established by J. R. Keene's Colin in 1907, Secretariat edged the filly for horse of the year honours. Secretariat won with more verve, in faster times, and in what appeared to be a division with tougher competition.

Secretariat (Bold Ruler-Somethingroyal, by Princequillo), owned and bred by the Virginia-based Meadow Stable of Christopher T. Chenery (which provided the 1971 two-year-old colt champion in Riva Ridge), won the Laurel Futurity at Laurel, Md., the same day La Prévoyante annexed the Selima at the same track. Each carried 122 lb. on a sloppy track. Secretariat, charging from far behind in characteristic fashion under jockey Ron Turcotte, won by eight lengths in 1 min. 42.8 sec. for $1\frac{1}{16}$ mi. La Prévoyante, ridden by regular jockey John O. LeBlanc, scored by 14 lengths in 1 min. 46.4 sec. for the same distance.

Secretariat failed to finish first only once, in his initial race. He slammed into the gate at the start, encountered additional trouble, and although closing strongly could finish no better than fourth. He won the prestigious one-mile Champagne Stakes by two lengths in 1 min. 35 sec. but was disqualified for bearing in on runner-up Stop the Music. Secretariat also captured the Sanford, Hopeful, Futurity, and Garden State stakes for an overall record of seven victories and one second in nine starts and earnings of $456,404.

Dividing her competition between Canada and the U.S., La Prévoyante won most of her races by wide margins. She triumphed over turf and against males in Canada and won such U.S. stakes as the Matron, Frizette, and Gardenia while amassing winnings of $417,109.

Other champions crowned in the annual poll conducted by the Thoroughbred Racing Associations, the *Daily Racing Form,* and the National Turf Writers Association were: Key to the Mint, three-year-old colt; Susan's Girl, three-year-old filly; Typecast, older mare; Autobiography, older horse; Cougar II, grass horse; and Chou Croute, sprinter. Mrs. John Tweedy, who managed the Meadow Stable for her ailing father, was voted the most outstanding owner. Other honours went to jockey Braulio Baeza, apprentice jockey Thomas Wallis, and trainer Lucien Laurin (Secretariat and Riva Ridge).

Key to the Mint (Graustark-Key Bridge, by Princequillo), owned and bred in Virginia by the Rokeby Stable of Paul Mellon, finished a poor fourth to Riva Ridge in the Belmont Stakes and then reeled off consecutive victories in the Brooklyn, Whitney, Travers, and Woodward stakes. In all except the Travers he faced older horses. His most important triumph came in the Woodward, in which he defeated his three-year-old filly stablemate Summer Guest by $1\frac{1}{4}$ lengths. Autobiography was third and Riva Ridge fourth.

Riva Ridge became the early leader in the three-year-old colt division by sandwiching easy victories in the Kentucky Derby and Belmont Stakes with a shocking loss to Bee Bee Bee in the Preakness Stakes, raced over a sloppy track (Riva Ridge was fourth, Key to the Mint third). Riva Ridge next took the Hollywood Derby but failed in his final four races of the season.

Of all the divisions, competition was keenest among the three-year-old fillies. Fred W. Hooper's much-traveled Florida homebred Susan's Girl (Quadrangle-Quaze, by Quibu) made 13 appearances, all in stakes, while racing in California, the Middle West, and the East. She opened her campaign by winning the Pasadena Stakes at Santa Anita on January 30 and closed it September 9 at Belmont Park by downing older fillies and mares in the Beldame. Her other victories included the Kentucky Oaks, Acorn, and Gazelle, and she never finished worse than third while compiling a 9–2–2 record. A close competitor for the divisional honours was Rokeby Stable's Summer Guest, whose victories included the Black Eyed Susan, Coaching Club American Oaks, Monmouth Oaks, and the 2-mi. Alabama. She was second in the Beldame.

Sigmund Sommer's Kentucky-bred Autobiography, a four-year-old son of Sky High II-King's Story, by Bold Ruler, was voted best in the lacklustre older division primarily because of a 15-length decision in the 2 mi. Jockey Club Gold Cup at Aqueduct. Mary F. Jones's Cougar II and John M. Schiff's Droll Role, other leaders in the division, were primarily successful in turf races.

Hogs: *see* Agriculture
Holland: *see* Netherlands
Honduras, British: *see* Dependent States
Hong Kong: *see* Dependent States

Winning by a narrow margin over Droll Role as best grass horse, the Chilean-bred Cougar II (Tale of Two Cities-Cindy Lou, by Madara) won four stakes, three of them on turf and all in California. He was shipped east to compete in the International but was not raced because of a soft course, and Droll Role won the event.

Early in the season jockey Willie Shoemaker broke Eddie Arcaro's career record of 554 stakes victories when he guided Royal Owl home first in the San Jacinto Stakes at Santa Anita. Keeneland set highs in two categories at its annual summer sales when 324 yearlings fetched $12,020,700 for an average of $37,-101. Prices at Saratoga declined slightly from the previous year's record figures, as 210 yearlings were auctioned for a gross of $6,075,300 and an average of $28,930. (JOSEPH C. AGRELLA)

Canada. In both 1970 and 1971 a young daughter of Canada's greatest Thoroughbred, Northern Dancer, was recognized as the country's horse of the year. In 1972 a two-year-old filly from a full sister to Northern Dancer claimed the Canadian title and launched a powerful bid for North American championship honours. La Prévoyante, bred and raced by Jean-Louis Levesque of Montreal, was undefeated and never extended in her first ten starts.

Best of the country's two-year-old males was Bo-Teek Farm's Zaca Spirit, by Up Spirits, who won the Summer Stakes at Fort Erie and the Coronation Futurity at Woodbine. Stafford Farm's Good Port, a son of Amber Morn, improved sharply toward the end of the season, winning the important Cup and Saucer Stakes.

All-time Canadian records for wagering and attendance were set on Queen's Plate day at Woodbine in June. Green Hills Farm's Victoria Song, by Victoria Park, scored an upset victory in the Plate, the major event of the racing year and the first race in Canada's Triple Crown for three-year-olds. Reaching for the second jewel, the Prince of Wales Stakes at Fort Erie, Victoria Song was edged by Windfields Farm's turf specialist, Presidial, a son of English Derby winner Psidium. With Victoria Song sidelined by injury, Presidial was heavily favoured in the final event of the series, the Breeders' Stakes at Woodbine, but he finished as runner-up to Nice Dancer, a late-developing Northern Dancer colt. Nice Dancer also won the Manitoba Derby and the Achievement Stakes for owners T. A. Morton and the Harlequin Ranches. In the three-year-old filly division, C. J. Jackson's Happy Victory, by New Providence, won the prestigious Canadian Oaks and two other stakes.

Riva Ridge (centre) is en route to winning the 98th Kentucky Derby at Churchill Downs on May 6, 1972. At left is No Le Hace, 3¼ lengths back, and at right is Hold Your Peace, 6¾ lengths back.

WIDE WORLD

Sandy Hawley won the Canadian riding championship for the fourth consecutive year. In the final weeks of the season he moved into first place among all North American jockeys in number of wins. (ERIC A. ASTROM)

Europe and Australia. In 1971–72 National Hunt racing suffered little interruption from fog or frost and consequently maintained its growth in popularity. No great steeplechaser or hurdler made his way to the front, but The Dikler became a steeplechasing favourite with displays that included a victory from Spanish Steps and Titus Oates in the King George VI Steeplechase at Kempton in December 1971. The hurdler Bula showed all his brilliance to win the Champion Hurdle at Cheltenham. Leap Frog won the Massey Ferguson Gold Cup; Bighorn, the Hennessy Gold Cup; and Grey Sombrero, the Whitbread Gold Cup. The Schweppes Gold Trophy hurdle race was won by Good Review from Ireland, and Glencaraig Lady, an Irish mare, took the Cheltenham Gold Cup. Stan Mellor rode his 1,000th winner—a National Hunt record—in his last season as a jockey.

In flat racing in England, 1972 promised much but turned out to be a rather disappointing season of confused form and of frustration from the effects of the equine virus which ran insidiously through so many training quarters. Crowned Prince, the best two-year-old of 1971, was found to have a soft palate and had to be withdrawn from racing; and the "race of the century" between the two best horses in training in Europe, four-year-olds Mill Reef and Brigadier Gerard, did not take place. Mill Reef, after winning the Prix Ganay and Coronation Cup at Epsom, caught the virus and then fractured a foreleg in training and had to be retired without the chance of taking his revenge on Brigadier Gerard for his sole defeat, in the 1971 Guineas. Brigadier Gerard stamped himself as one of the greatest 1–1¼ mi. horses ever bred in England. In all, he won 17 out of 18 races in his three-year racing career, losing only in his 16th race to Roberto in the £40,000 Benson and Hedges Gold Cup run over 1 5/16 mi. at York in record time. He won just under £250,-000 in stakes money, and was retired to stud at Newmarket.

In England the Two Thousand Guineas was won by High Top from Roberto; the Thousand Guineas by Waterloo. Lester Piggott equaled S. Donoghue's record of six Derby winners when he just got Roberto home ahead of Rheingold. Roberto, trained in Ireland by Vincent O'Brien, flopped in the Irish Derby, which was won by Steel Pulse from Scottish Rifle. The Epsom Oaks was won by Ginevra, trained by H. R. Price. The St. Leger went to Boucher, well handled by Piggott in riding his seventh St. Leger winner.

The luckless Rock Roi lost the Ascot Gold Cup on disqualification for the second time, on this occasion to Erimo Hawk, but had the satisfaction of being the first English horse to win the French equivalent, the Prix du Cadran, from another English horse, Parnell. The three-year-old Deep Diver and the four-year-old

Irish filly Abergwaun were perhaps the best sprinters. The two-year-old picture was far from clear: Rapid River, winner of the Gimcrack Stakes, was fast, and the filly Jacinth won the Cheveley Park Stakes at Newmarket convincingly, but perhaps the colt Lunchtime was the pick of the juveniles after his victory in the Dewhurst Stakes.

Of the French classics, the equivalent of the Two Thousand and One Thousand Guineas were won by Riverman and Mata Hari, respectively; the Prix du Jockey Club (Derby) by Hard to Beat from Sancy and Flair Path; the Prix de Diane (Oaks) by Rescousse from Prodice and Paysanne; and the Prix Royal Oak (St. Leger) by Pleben. Pleben had won the Grand Prix de Paris, Riverman the Prix Jean Prat and the Prix d'Ispahan, and Rheingold the Grand Prix de Saint-Cloud from Arlequino and Hard to Beat. Queen Elizabeth II's filly Example won the Prix Jean de Chaudenay at Saint-Cloud. The Prix de l'Arc de Triomphe was won by the filly San San (who had dead-heated with Paysanne in the Prix Vermeille) from Rescousse and Homeric. The crack French two-year-old colts were reckoned to be Filiberto and Zapoteco, winners of the Prix Morny and Prix de la Salamandre, respectively, but they lost to Satingo in the Grand Criterium in October.

The Italian Derby was won by Gay-Lussac. The West German Derby, in Hamburg, was won by Tarim from Experte and Prince Ippi, the time of 2 min. 40.2 sec. breaking the 1936 record by more than 11 sec. The Norwegian Derby, in Oslo, went to the French-bred filly Abaris.

In Australia the A$100,000 Melbourne Cup was won by the Tasmanian outsider Piping Lane from the New Zealand mare Magnifique. For the first time the race was run over a metric distance, 3,200 m.

(R. M. GOODWIN)

Harness Racing. The four-year-old pacer Albatross and the three-year-old trotter Super Bowl set new standards for world harness racing in 1972, and also led a parade of top stars of the sport in North America into early retirement to the breeding ranks. Leaving the racing wars at the season's end, along with Albatross and Super Bowl, were such outstanding performers as the three-year-old pacing champion Strike Out, Albatross' four-year-old archrival Nansemond, the four-year-old trotting king Speedy Crown, the former juvenile pacing world record holder Entrepreneur, and the free-for-all trotting stars Dayan and Fresh Yankee, the latter retiring as the richest money-winning harness horse in North American history with earnings of $1,294,252.

New champions appeared on the scene even before the older ones departed, the brightest being the two-year-old pacing colt Ricci Reenie Time, who paced the fastest mile in history by a juvenile, 1 min. 56.2 sec., at Lexington, Ky. The major laurels, however, belonged to Albatross and Super Bowl, two of the most successful performers in the sport's history. Each was named best of the year at his gait, and Albatross outpolled the young trotting champion in balloting by the nation's harness writers to become harness horse of the year for the second straight season.

Clinching those honours for Albatross was a mile in 1 min. 54.6 sec., the fastest race mile in 166 years of harness racing history, at Chicago's Sportsman's Park in July, and another world record effort, 1 min. 55.6 sec.—the fastest mile race ever on a half-mile track—at Delaware, O., in September. Trainer Stanley Dancer drove on both occasions. During the year Albatross won 20 of 26 starts, finished second four times, and was third once, winning $459,921. He retired to Hanover Shoe Farms and stallion duty at season's end with a lifetime record of 59 victories, 8 seconds, and 3 thirds in 71 starts, and career earnings of $1,201,470.

His trotting counterpart (and stablemate in the Stanley Dancer stable), Super Bowl, joined Albatross in the Hanover Shoe Farms stallion band in Pennsylvania at the end of the year. Before his retirement Super Bowl also wrote new chapters in harness racing's record books. The big, strapping colt by Star's Pride out of the Rodney mare Pillow Talk won 18 straight races, including the $119,000 Hambletonian, $100,000 Colonial, $93,097 Yonkers Futurity, and $56,210 Kentucky Futurity. In capturing the Hambletonian he trotted the fastest mile in history by a three-year-old, 1 min. 56.4 sec., and his 1972 earnings of $441,711 represented an all-time record for a single season by a trotter. On 12 occasions he trotted miles in two minutes or faster, also a single season mark for trotters. In November in the $50,000 Pacific Trot at Hollywood Park, he moved out of the three-year-old division to challenge the best older trotters in the world, including the great Une de Mai of France and Dayan and Flower Child of the U.S., and defeated them in a front-racing wire-to-wire victory with a 1 min. 57.4 sec. mile.

The half-mile track at Delaware, O., produced world marks by a three-year-old pacing colt (Strike Out, 1 min. 56.6 sec.); a three-year-old pacing filly (Bret's Pet, 1 min. 57.8 sec.); a two-year-old pacing colt (J. R. Skipper, 1 min. 58.8 sec.); and a three-year-old trotting colt (Songcan, 1 min. 58.6 sec.). The mile by Bret's Pet was the fastest ever on a half-mile track by a female Standardbred, regardless of age, and J. R. Skipper's mile equaled the world mark set in 1969 by Columbia George.

The three-year-old pacing division produced two outstanding performers in Strike Out and Silent Majority. Both paced in identical record times—1 min. 56.6 sec.—with Strike Out setting his record over Delaware's half-mile track in the $104,916 Little Brown Jug and Silent Majority getting his over the mile track at Lexington, Ky. Silent Majority earned more money—$304,179 to $298,436—and defeated Strike Out six times in nine meetings over two seasons, but Strike Out was named three-year-old of the year by the nation's harness writers. Neither colt was fastest in the division. That honour went to Hilarious Way with a mile in 1 min. 55.4 sec.

Speedy Crown, syndicated for $1 million and retired in late summer, finished up as the most successful older trotter in the sport. The four-year-old, named trotter of the year in 1971, won the $125,000 International, the $150,000 Challenge Match Race (against Une de Mai of France and Fresh Yankee of Canada), and the $92,505 Realization, all at Roosevelt Raceway, and retired to Lana Lobell Farm with seasonal earnings of $354,128.

As usual, Hervé Filion of Quebec was the world's leading driver during the year. During 1972 he became the first driver to win more than $2 million in purses in a single season, and the first North American to win 4,000 victories. His 605 victories shattered his 1971 single-season world record of 543.

(STANLEY F. BERGSTEIN)

The New Zealand Cup of 1971–72 for $30,000 over 2 mi. was won by True Averil from Radiant Globe and Intrepid in 4 min. 11 sec. Bay Foyle won the New Zealand Free For All for pacers. Tony Bear took the trotters' FFA; Bachelor Star the New Zealand Pacers' Derby; and Precocious the $10,000 Dominion Trotting Handicap.

Top horse of 1972 in Australia was Welcome Advice, winner of the three feature cup races in Sydney and the Inter-Dominion Championship in Brisbane for a total of $70,685. Nicotine Prince led the three-year-olds with $24,447, and the leading two-year-old was Paleface Adios, earning $18,200.

In France the Criterium for three-year-olds at the end of 1971 had a prize of $61,200 and was won by the filly Clissa. The great mare Une de Mai started the season with a $40,000 win at Cagnes-sur-Mer, won the Prix de Bourgogne of $32,600 in Paris, and then took the $62,000 Prix de France. Une de Mai won several more races of $30,000 and upward to become the richest trotting mare in history, with earnings approaching $2 million. The $145,000 Prix d'Amérique was again won by Tidalium Pélo in record time, 3 min. 21.4 sec. over 2,600 m.

In Italy the $32,000 Premio Tor di Valle in Rome went to Barbablu. In Sweden Big Elma won more than $60,000, including the $10,000 Swedish Championship, with Lyon second. The Scandinavian Trotting Championship held in Stockholm was won by Lyon in a record time of 2 min. 4 sec. over 2,600 m. with Big Elma second.

In England the best aged pacer appeared to be Saunders Pearl, later shipped to the U.S. The National Pacing Derby at Chasewater went to Eastwood Playboy, the Trotting Derby to Broadway, and the Corbie Wood Derby to Forrest Lad. (NOEL SIMPSON)

Housing

While the sheer size of the housing stock in relation to the demand for homes remained the primary concern of less developed countries, social aspects of housing, such as slum clearance and overcrowding, were the major concerns in most developed nations. Before discussing these concerns some numerical assessment of recent international developments must be attempted.

The new Thamesmead apartment complex in South London was designed to be a model city of social and architectural balance. The structures are on a 1,450-ac. site in Abbey Wood.

FOX PHOTOS/PICTORIAL PARADE

Volume of New Housing. Statistical comparisons between widely varying countries with different attitudes toward housing remained a difficult (and sometimes misleading) task. A major problem was the lack of direct comparability due to differences in definition. International comparisons thus must remain an inexact exercise. Using UN data, Table I summarizes the progress made in house building in the first part of 1972 in those countries for which recent information was available.

Though the period over which the average monthly figures for 1972 were calculated was shorter than a full year and therefore more likely to produce error, it seemed that more countries among those listed built, on average, a smaller number of dwellings per month in 1972 than in either 1970 or 1971. Whereas 1971 appeared to be a year of stagnation in housing construction, 1972 gave every indication of being a year in which the volume of new dwelling production actually fell in a large number of countries. Denmark, Finland, West Germany, Italy, South Korea, Portugal, South Africa, Spain, Sweden, Tunisia, the United Kingdom, and Yugoslavia all showed a reduction in average monthly housing construction in the early months of 1972 as compared with the two preceding years. The percentage decline in average monthly housing construction over 1971 in some of the countries was great. For example, West Germany completed an average of 45% fewer dwellings per month in the early part of 1972 as against 1971. In Italy, the decline was 44%, in Finland 39%, in Yugoslavia 34%, and in South Korea 25%.

Those countries that in the first part of 1972 showed an increase in monthly average construction figures over 1971 included Canada, East Germany, Japan, Morocco, New Zealand, Puerto Rico, Turkey, and the U.S. But, on the whole, the increases were less dramatic than the decreases, the largest increase over 1971 figures being 22% in East Germany. Other countries showed a fluctuation in the early part of 1972 between the construction rates for the previous two years. Thus, the Netherlands showed in 1972 an increase over the 1970 construction rate but a slight fall from 1971, as was also the case in Switzerland. In Norway and Poland, on the other hand, the 1972 construction figure dropped from the 1970 rate but increased over 1971.

Such figures as these only show "construction performance" within a country over time. They do not allow one to compare the performance in housing construction between countries. Though such measures are, indeed, difficult to obtain, one simple but crude technique is to calculate the average monthly house construction figure as a percentage of the total population of the country. This is a crude measure since population totals do not necessarily represent "housing needs." It does, though, give some indication of the relative impact of a house building program. Table II shows, for the same countries, the monthly average house construction figures for the early months of 1972, expressed as a percentage of the population of the country at mid-1971.

Social Concerns. In those countries where a desperate shortage of housing to meet the basic accommodation needs of great sectors of the population no longer existed, attention in 1972 continued to focus on problems of the quality, cost, financing, and location of housing. In most of the developed countries, the previous year showed a continuing concern with those aspects of housing considered unsuitable and unjustifiable in a time of increasing affluence. The problem differed in the various countries, as did the steps taken to solve it. Britain's major concerns were substandard housing in many large urban centres and the rapidly escalating cost of housing. In France the large stock of aging and deteriorating housing presented its own difficulties, while in Czechoslovakia there was an imbalance between dwelling and household sizes to tackle. East and West Germany and the Netherlands still faced the losses caused by war damage, and U.S. authorities had to cope with the housing imbalances resulting from racial ghettoization.

Against these different backgrounds, however, there emerged some common issues. Basic to all of them was the growing sophistication of the consumer of housing, who was expressing more precise and demanding needs. The "solutions" adopted in the 1950s and 1960s no longer seemed appropriate in the 1970s. For example, the replacement of slums with high-rise apartment buildings, a common practice in recent years, was under attack. Research in the U.S., Britain, France, and Scandinavia showed a widespread reaction against living in such buildings. This concern was found to be rooted in the unsuitable environment they provided for families and their rapid deterioration. Buildings that only two decades ago had been shining examples of the vigorous drive to remove slum conditions from large cities had themselves become the slums of the 1970s. Whether this was an inherent feature of the form of such dwellings or resulted from an inability of the people who lived in them to adapt to a different form of living was not fully understood, but research continued into the matter in many European countries and in the U.S.

Another problem was the changing nature of the demand for housing. Pressure for housing continued to grow in the large urban centres, often paralleled by depopulation and reduced demand in many rural areas. Such a situation occurred acutely in southern Italy, France, Britain, and the U.S., and in each case it pointed to the necessity of examining housing policies in parallel with employment policies. So long as employment continued to be concentrated in large urban areas, the demand for housing would grow there; increasingly, this demand could not be met because of land shortage and escalating costs.

Even the solutions specially adopted to meet this problem seemed to bring their own difficulties at times. In Britain the decentralization of employment and the growth of the New Towns led to an absolute decline in the population of London (and other large cities), but to the surprise of many this did not result in reduced demand for London housing. Indeed, the pressure on housing in the city continued to grow at an alarming rate. This was mainly due, as was also the case in France and Scandinavia, to increased "household fission." Large extended families were breaking down rapidly and new households formed more rapidly. Young couples were no longer content to stay in the parental home and wanted to establish a home of their own in a separate dwelling. The implication of this situation was the need wherever possible to convert existing large dwellings into a greater number of smaller accommodation units.

Another emerging issue in many countries was the recognition of the housing demands of "special need" groups. At the 31st World Congress of the International Federation for Housing and Planning, held in the U.K. in June 1972, delegates from France and the Netherlands noted the rapid formation of such special need groups as elderly households, immigrant workers, young workers, students, single persons, and the physically handicapped. The housing needs of all these groups frequently were not met by standard housing policies, and new and separate policies would have to be adopted.

PRESSENS BILB AB

A scene in the slums of East St. Louis, Ill., where some 15,000 living quarters stand empty and derelict. The U.S. government has classified the city as "blighted."

Perhaps the most important "social" aspect of housing to have emerged as a policy priority in most developed countries was the problem of providing enough housing of sufficiently high quality for all who needed it at prices they could afford. There was a growing recognition that the operation of free market forces was both inadequate and inefficient as a means of providing and allocating housing. Thus, government-subsidized housing became a necessity.

The financial arrangements adopted to subsidize housing varied considerably among different countries. In France the Habitations à Loyer Modéré (HLM) was established as an organization to coordinate and

Table I. Dwelling Construction in Early 1972, Compared with 1970 and 1971

Country	Monthly average (early 1972)	Monthly average 1970	Monthly average 1971	New* or total†	Type of measure
Canada	17,489	14,652	16,769	New	Buildings completed
Denmark	3,881	4,188	4,181	New	Buildings completed
Finland	2,570	4,145	4,206	Total	Buildings completed
Germany, East	7,750	6,340	6,342	Total	Buildings completed
Germany, West	25,372	39,838	46,200	Total	Buildings completed
Italy	16,106	31,437	28,771	Total	Buildings completed
Japan	139,733	123,713	121,980	Total	Buildings completed
Korea, South	4,825	6,009	6,393	Total	Building permits granted
Morocco	1,324	1,178	...	Total	Building permits granted
Netherlands	11,374	9,774	11,462	New	Buildings completed
New Zealand	2,217	1,972	...	New	Buildings completed
Norway	3,220	3,267	3,200	Total	Buildings completed
Poland	11,400	16,181	11,000	Total	Buildings completed
Portugal	1,980	2,266	...	Total	Buildings completed
Puerto Rico	2,184	...	2,066	New	Building permits granted
South Africa	1,035	1,144	1,265	New	Private buildings completed
Spain	15,041	15,441	15,922	Total	Buildings completed with state aid
Sweden	8,298	9,154	8,932	New	Buildings completed
Switzerland	2,120	1,858	2,257	New	Buildings completed
Tunisia	543	644	555	New	Building permits granted
Turkey	13,281	12,911	12,529	Total	Building permits granted
U.K.	28,174	30,189	30,290	New	Buildings completed
U.S.	196,100	122,200	173,700	New	Buildings started
Yugoslavia	1,965	3,432	2,995	Total	Buildings completed

*New dwellings only.
†New dwellings plus conversions, extensions, etc.

Horticulture:
see Gardening

Hospitals:
see Medicine

Table II. Average Monthly House Construction in Early 1972 as a Percentage of the Mid-1971 Population

Country	1972 average monthly construction as % of 1971 population	Country	1972 average monthly construction as % of 1971 population
Canada	0.080	Poland	0.034
Denmark	0.078	Portugal*	0.022
Finland	0.055	Puerto Rico	0.079
Germany, East	0.048	South Africa†	0.005
Germany, West	0.042	Spain	0.044
Italy	0.029	Sweden	0.102
Japan	0.130	Switzerland	0.033
Korea, South	0.015	Tunisia*	0.010
Morocco	0.008	Turkey	0.037
Netherlands	0.086	U.K.	0.051
New Zealand	0.078	U.S.	0.095
Norway	0.082	Yugoslavia	0.010

*Mid-1970 population figure used.
†Because of the racial split in South Africa, and the fact that the construction figure relates only to private building, the situation is unclear.

effect the subsidization of housing construction. The most extensive such organization in Europe, HLM made use of low-interest loans from a special fund to account for approximately 40% of the annual dwelling completions in France. An entirely separate means of providing subsidized housing was that adopted in Scandinavia, where about 30% of all housing fell into what was known as the "voluntary" sector. This comprised the housing cooperatives, associations, and societies established by groups of tenants or trade unions which by common action and lower interest rates were able to provide housing at less than market costs. At opposite extremes in the subsidized housing field were Britain and West Germany. In the former, most subsidized housing was provided by local government authorities for renting—at rents often heavily subsidized by central government. In West Germany, on the other hand, public aid for housing almost exclusively consisted of subsidies and tax concessions to private house builders.

If there was a common theme to the general outlook on subsidized housing, it was the recent but growing feeling in many countries (not least in the U.S. and Britain) that it was both inefficient and inequitable to subsidize the "bricks and mortar" of housing—by paying subsidies in various forms to the builders of housing—and that there should be a shift to subsidizing the occupants of housing. This philosophy perhaps gained its firmest expression in new legislation in Britain to set fair rents for all dwellings and then to pay rent rebates to those families who could not afford to pay the fair rent. Similar views were also expressed in the U.S. by officials in the Department of Housing and Urban Development.

(JOHN EDWARDS)

See also Architecture; Cities and Urban Affairs; Economy, World; Environment; Industrial Review; Money and Banking.

ENCYCLOPÆDIA BRITANNICA FILMS. *Equality Under Law—The California Fair Housing Cases* (1969); *The House of Man, Part II—Our Crowded Environment* (1969).

Hungary

A people's republic of central Europe, Hungary is bordered by Czechoslovakia, the U.S.S.R., Romania, Yugoslavia, and Austria. Area: 35,919 sq.mi. (93,030 sq.km.). Pop. (1972): 10,374,000, including (1970) Hungarian 95.8%; German 2.1%. Cap. and largest city: Budapest (pop., 1972 est., 2,038,000). Language (1970): Magyar 95.8%. Religion (1956): Roman Catholic 67%; Protestant 27.3%; Orthodox 2.5%; Jewish 1.5%. First secretary of the Hungarian Socialist Workers' (Communist) Party in 1972, Janos Kadar; president of the Presidential Council (chief of state), Pal Losonczi; president of the Council of Ministers (premier), Jeno Fock.

On May 26, 1972, Janos Kadar received a telegram from Leonid I. Brezhnev, general secretary of the Soviet Communist Party, congratulating him on his 60th birthday and announcing that he had been awarded the Order of Lenin. The message was received with relief in Budapest because it ended—at least temporarily—a tension in Hungarian-Soviet relations.

At the beginning of February, *Pravda*, the Soviet Communist Party newspaper, had criticized the functioning of the Hungarian New Economic Mechanism. Sensing trouble, Kadar left for Moscow on February 11 and remained there until the 14th, discussing with Brezhnev "questions of specialization and cooperation in production between the two countries and joint participation in the carrying out of the comprehensive program of socialist economic integration." On March 27 and 28 Premier Fock discussed the same questions with Brezhnev and Soviet Premier Aleksei N. Kosygin. Back in Budapest, Fock spoke with remarkable frankness of "minor and major difficulties" in implementing the current five-year plan and complained that he had been unable to get assurances from

HUNGARY

Education. (1969–70) Primary, pupils 1,177,887, teachers 62,834; secondary, pupils 124,220, teachers 7,291; vocational, pupils 330,332, teachers 14,510; higher (including 16 universities), students 53,237, teaching staff 9,413.

Finance. Monetary unit: forint, with (Sept. 18, 1972) an official exchange rate of 10.81 forints to U.S. $1 (28.18 forints = £1 sterling) and a tourist rate of 27.63 forints to U.S. $1 (68.40 forints = £1 sterling). Budget (1972 est.): revenue 212.6 billion forints; expenditure 215.8 billion forints. National income (net material product): (1971) 298.8 billion forints; (1970) 272.4 billion forints.

Foreign Trade. (1971) Imports 35,098,000,000 forints; exports 29,355,000,000 forints. Import sources: U.S.S.R. 34%; East Germany 11%; Czechoslovakia 8%; West Germany 6%; Poland 5%. Export destinations: U.S.S.R. 35%; East Germany 10%; Czechoslovakia 8%; Poland 7%; Italy 6%; West Germany 5%. Main exports: machinery 21%; chemicals; motor vehicles; iron and steel; livestock and meat; fruit and vegetables; textiles and footwear.

Transport and Communications. Roads (1971) 109,351 km. (including 157 km. expressways). Motor vehicles in use (1971): passenger 294,000; commercial 98,000. Railways (1971): 8,663 km.; traffic 13,637,000,000 passenger-km., freight 19,612,000,000 net ton-km. Air traffic (1970): 334,321,000 passenger-km.; freight 6,466,000 net ton-km. Telephones (Dec. 1970) 824,000. Radio licenses (Dec. 1970) 2,530,000. Television licenses (Dec. 1970) 1,769,000.

Agriculture. Production (in 000; metric tons; 1971; 1970 in parentheses): corn 4,674 (4,013); wheat 3,918 (2,722); rye c. 180 (157); barley 782 (552); potatoes 1,488 (1,430); sugar, raw value (1971–72) 262, (1970–71) 252; tomatoes (1970) 293, (1969) 400; sunflower seed 149 (95); dry peas c. 115 (109); apples c. 700 (661); wine c. 438 (438); tobacco c. 26 (18); beef and veal c. 180 (184); pork c. 400 (316). Livestock (in 000; March 1971): cattle 1,917; pigs 7,510; sheep 2,657; horses 219; chickens 66,148.

Industry. Index of production (1963 = 100): (1971) 151; (1970) 144. Production (in 000; metric tons; 1971): coal 3,941; lignite 23,485; crude oil 1,955; natural gas (cu.m.) 3,714,000; electricity (kw-hr.) 14,990,000; iron ore (25% metal content) 688; pig iron 1,986; crude steel 3,110; bauxite 2,090; cement 2,711; sulfuric acid (1970) 485; nitrogenous fertilizers (nitrogen content; 1970–71) 381; cotton yarn 56; wool yarn 15; commercial vehicles (units) 10.3.

Soviet comrades about the quantities of raw materials they intended to make available to Hungary over the next 10 to 15 years. Subsequently, some adjustments in the plan were made by the Hungarian Central Committee. That these met with Soviet approval was indicated in a communiqué, issued December 2 following a five-day visit by Brezhnev to Budapest, in which it was stated that the Hungarian and Soviet leaders shared "an entire identity of views on all matters."

Over 40% of Hungary's national income stemmed from foreign trade, the most dynamically developing sector of its national economy. This development contributed not only to the acceleration of domestic industrial production but also to a substantial improvement in home market supplies. For two successive years the country's foreign trade balance had deteriorated considerably, however, and the Soviet leadership had been obviously disturbed by the Hungarian consumer boom.

In April the National Assembly adopted a series of amendments to the 1949 constitution prepared by a special committee under the chairmanship of Gyula Kallai, president of the Patriotic People's Front. The original intention had been to give the country a completely new constitution declaring Hungary a "socialist state." However, Kadar told the Assembly that the party Central Committee believed the time was not yet ripe. Obviously taking into account Moscow's ideological susceptibilities, he admitted that there were a number of negative features in Hungary's "society of socialism in the making." Novelist Jozsef Darvas, president of the Association of Hungarian Writers, welcomed the guarantee of freedom for creative scientific and artistic work that was one of the amendments to the constitution. Richard Horvath, a Catholic priest and member of the drafting committee, said that the revised constitution reflected "a deep humanism."

On October 12 a preliminary financial agreement was initialed in Washington by Carl Salans, a juridical adviser of the U.S. Department of State, and Janos Fekete, vice-president of the National Bank of Hungary. The bank offered $20 million in settlement of Hungary's unpaid prewar debts and in compensation for U.S. property nationalized by Hungary. In return, the U.S. government was to advise Congress to extend to Hungary the most-favoured-nation treatment already accorded to Poland, Yugoslavia, and the U.S.S.R.

A meeting of some 30 of Europe's mayors gathered in Budapest on September 26 for a three-day celebration of the capital's centenary.

(K. M. SMOGORZEWSKI)

Iceland

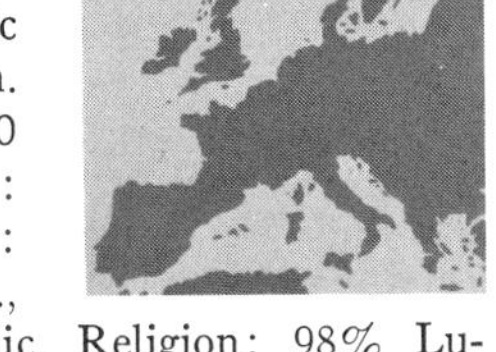

Iceland is an island republic in the North Atlantic Ocean. Area: 39,768 sq.mi. (103,000 sq.km.). Pop. (1971 est.): 207,174. Cap. and largest city: Reykjavik (pop., 1971 est., 82,892). Language: Icelandic. Religion: 98% Lutheran. President in 1972, Kristjan Eldjarn; prime minister, Olafur Johannesson.

On Sept. 1, 1972, the extension of Iceland's fisheries limit from 12 to 50 mi. off the nation's coast went into effect, provoking strong protests from other nations, particularly Britain and West Germany. (*See* FISHERIES.) Iceland claimed that the extension was needed to combat overfishing and that it needed a larger share of the catches in order to strengthen its economy. The protesting nations, however, claimed that the extension violated international law. The Icelandic government refused to recognize the jurisdiction of the International Court at The Hague in the matter and disregarded an interim court ruling favouring the protesters. The latter, meanwhile, continued to disregard the new limit. Agreements were reached with Belgium and the Faeroe Islands, but negotiations with the major protesters met with no initial success and the fall of 1972 saw a revival of the 1958 "cod war" with confrontations between foreign and Ice-

WIDE WORLD

Cutters remove skin of a whale in preparation for processing at an Icelandic factory.

ICELAND

Education. (1968–69) Primary, pupils 27,356, teachers 1,319; secondary, pupils 15,675, teachers 1,229; vocational, pupils *c.* 5,000, teachers 548; teacher training, students 909, teachers *c.* 97; higher (at Reykjavik University), students 1,302, teaching staff 150.

Finance. Monetary unit: króna, with (Sept. 18, 1972) a par value of 88 krónur to U.S. $1 (free rate of 213.05 krónur = £1 sterling). Gold, SDRs, and foreign exchange, central bank: (June 1972) U.S. $64.7 million; (June 1971) U.S. $61.2 million. Budget (1970 est.): revenue 8,396,000,000 krónur; expenditure 8,187,000,000 krónur. Gross national product: (1970) 42,160,000,000 krónur; (1969) 33.7 billion krónur. Money supply: (April 1972) 6,782,000,000 krónur; (April 1971) 5,476,000,000 krónur. Cost of living (Reykjavik; 1963 = 100): (May 1972) 274; (May 1971) 249.

Foreign Trade. (1971) Imports 18,446,000,000 krónur; exports 13,175,000,000 krónur. Import sources: West Germany 16%; U.K. 14%; U.S. 10%; Denmark 10%; U.S.S.R. 7%; Netherlands 6%; Sweden 6%; Norway 5%. Export destinations: U.S. 37%; U.K. 13%; U.S.S.R. 8%; Denmark 7%; Portugal 6%; West Germany 6%. Main exports: fish and products 84%; aluminum 8%.

Transport and Communications. Roads (1971) 11,137 km. Motor vehicles in use (1971): passenger 46,737; commercial 5,706. There are no railways. Air traffic (1971): 1,829,500,000 passenger-km.; freight 19,998,000 net ton-km. Shipping (1971): merchant vessels 100 gross tons and over 288; gross tonnage 125,912. Telephones (Dec. 1970) 71,000. Radio licenses (Dec. 1970) 62,000. Television licenses (Dec. 1970) 38,000.

Agriculture. Production (in 000; metric tons; 1970; 1969 in parentheses): potatoes 5 (4); hay 289 (310); milk 117 (112); mutton and lamb 12 (13); fish catch 734 (689). Livestock (in 000; Dec. 1970): cattle 53; sheep 736; horses 33; poultry 135.

Industry. Production (in 000): electricity (public supply only; kw-hr.; 1971) 1,592,000; aluminum (metric tons; 1970) 38.

Hovercraft: *see* Transportation

Hurricanes: *see* Disasters; Meteorology

Hydroelectric Power: *see* Engineering Projects; Fuel and Power

Ice Hockey: *see* Hockey

landic vessels in the disputed area. Talks between Britain and Iceland collapsed late in November.

The World Chess Championship in Reykjavik, in which Bobby Fischer (*see* BIOGRAPHY) of the U.S. overwhelmed Boris Spassky of the U.S.S.R., attracted unprecedented worldwide interest. (*See* CHESS.) Also in Reykjavik, the second International Art Festival drew many international celebrities.

Work began on bridging the rivers of Skeidharársandur in southern Iceland to form the last link in a ring road around the country. Frequent glacier bursts had kept the gap open, but it was hoped to close it by 1974. UN experts working on tourist projects were concerned with extending the short tourist season.

Reelected as sole candidate, Kristjan Eldjarn began his second four-year term as president on August 1. In December the central bank announced a 10.7% devaluation of the króna, from 87.20 to about 99 krónur to U.S. $1. (VALDIMAR KRISTINSSON)

Ice Skating

The addition of artificial rinks to winter sports mountain resorts, particularly in North America and the European Alps, continued in 1972. The sport grew notably in Canada, where skaters were believed to number more than 200,000; of these, more than 40,000 were registered with 614 figure-skating clubs. With indoor rinks available in most of the 31 member nations of the International Skating Union, few of the world's current leading figure skaters had ever performed on natural ice. The popularity of speed skating in the Netherlands was underlined by the building of a ninth artificially frozen outdoor rink there.

Only three weeks after the Winter Olympic Games (*see* SPORTING RECORD: *Special Report*), 103 skaters from 18 countries contested the world ice figure and dance skating championships at Calgary, Alta., on March 7–11. Ondrej Nepela (Czech.) comfortably retained the men's title with a freestyle performance that was methodical, efficient, and undramatic, including cleanly landed triple Salchow and triple loop jumps. Sergei Chetverukhin, the Soviet runner-up, excelled with two high double axels in rapid succession, outpointing the champion in free-skating. He got two sixes for artistic impression but was too far behind in the compulsory figures to catch Nepela. Another Soviet skater, Vladimir Kovalev, was third. The competition overall produced the best general jumping standard for several years.

Finland's Leo Linkovesi speeds on his way to a sensational 500 m. in 38 sec. flat for a new world speed skating record. The event was held in January 1972 at Davos, Switz.

KEYSTONE

Beatrix Schuba (Aus.) held her women's crown with conservative free-skating that proved adequate after she had gained a 130-point lead in the figures. Ranking with Cecilia Colledge and Jeannette Altwegg as the best at figures the world had seen, she afterward announced her retirement from amateur competition. The freestyle duel for second place between Karen Magnussen of Canada and Janet Lynn (U.S.) was an eye feast so smoothly artistic that it could almost be forgotten they were balanced on steel strips three-sixteenths of an inch wide. Spurred on by her home supporters, Miss Magnussen emerged the better all-rounder but Miss Lynn, ultimately third, was the top freestyle scorer, including two sixes.

The Soviet Union again kept the pairs and the ice dance titles. Aleksei Ulanov and Irina Rodnina of Moscow became the sixth couple to win the pairs championship for a fourth time. Their freestyle was short of their best, but three blatant timing errors were understandable results of reaction from Miss Rodnina's earlier training fall, and just before going on the ice she complained of double vision. Their brilliant double twist and overhead lifts were thus the more creditable, and they again defeated their Leningrad rivals, Andrei Suraikin and Ludmila Smirnova. A superb thrown axel by the Americans Ken Shelley and Jo Jo Starbuck probably gained them third place.

The ice dance event provided the keenest competition of the meeting, between the defending Soviet husband and wife, Aleksandr Gorshkov and Ludmila Pakhomova, and West Germany's new European champions, brother and sister Erich and Angelika Buch. Scoring a six, the Soviets split the judges 5–4 in their favour, with third place going to James Sladky and Judy Schwomeyer of the U.S. The solo events of these championships were the last to be held using the traditional six compulsory figures, new rules henceforth requiring each competitor to skate only three.

Ard Schenk of the Netherlands (*see* BIOGRAPHY) enjoyed the rare distinction of winning all four distances (500 m., 1,500 m., 5,000 m., and 10,000 m.) to retain the men's world speed skating title in Oslo, Nor., on February 19–20. Roar Grønvold, overall runner-up for Norway, shared first place with Schenk in the 500 m. Schenk's Netherlands team colleague, Jan Bols, finished third in the four races.

Dutch supremacy was also confirmed in the women's world speed championship, at Heerenveen, Neth., on March 4–5. Atje Keulen-Deelstra, first in both 1,000 m. and 1,500 m., narrowly outpointed her compatriot Stien Baas-Kaiser, the 3,000-m. winner. The U.S. skater Dianne Holum won the 500 m. and finished third overall. Separate world sprint championships for men and women were won by Leo Linkovesi (Fin.) and Monika Pflug (W.Ger.) at Eskilstuna, Swed., on February 26–27.

New world records during the year were set over four men's and two women's distances: 38 sec. for the 500 m. was clocked three times, by Erhard Keller (W.Ger.), Linkovesi, and Hasse Börjes (Swed.). Keller also lowered the 1,000 m. to 1 min. 18.5 sec., and Schenk completed his outstanding season with new marks of 4 min. 8.3 sec. in the 3,000 m. and 7 min. 9.8 sec. in the 5,000 m. Anne Henning (U.S.) lowered the women's 500 m. to 42.5 sec. and the 1,000 m. to 1 min. 27.3 sec. (HOWARD BASS)

Income, National

The world economy achieved a growth rate in 1971 broadly similar to that achieved in 1970. Preliminary estimates made by the United Nations in the "World Economic Survey, 1971" suggested that world gross domestic product (GDP) rose in real terms by 4.2% in 1971 as compared with 3.9% in 1970, both well below the longer term annual growth rate for GDP of 5.3% between 1961 and 1970. Experience varied between different countries and groups of countries, as Table I shows.

The industrial countries, as a group, achieved an increase in growth rate and were led by the U.S., which began to come out of the deep recession of 1970. However, in most countries in the group of other developed areas growth rates declined. UN estimates for the less developed countries as a whole, including those not listed in Table I, suggested that the growth rate in 1971 was about 5.4%, as compared with 5.8% in 1970, and an average annual rate of 5.1% for 1961–70. For the first time in more than a decade China published data on economic growth. The data showed a 10% growth for 1971 in the "combined production of industry and agriculture" (that is, excluding all services, and thus not comparable with data from other countries).

Estimates published by the Organization for Economic Cooperation and Development in *Economic Outlook* (December 1972), and shown in Table I, suggested a general increase in growth rate for the developed countries in 1972. While the OECD estimates were based on the latest available evidence, they should be regarded as provisional, although similar estimates published in 1971 proved to be reasonably reliable in most cases. The OECD secretariat forecasts for 1973 suggested continued acceleration in growth for this group of countries. These changes reflected expansionary policies and improved business confidence following the Smithsonian agreement on currency exchange rates in December 1971, and the subsequent floating of the pound sterling in June 1972. This continued rapid growth represented a taking up of the slack that existed in many industrial countries in 1970–71.

Comparisons between Eastern European and other countries were difficult because the former excluded from national income accounts certain "unproductive services," such as public administration and personal and professional services. If such items were included, the growth rates in the centrally planned economies would probably be somewhat lower than the ones recorded. The section of Table I that records their performance shows that experience varied widely. The average growth rate for the group as a whole declined in 1971, largely because of the decline in the growth rate of the U.S.S.R.

Recent trends of expenditure on GDP are analyzed for a number of countries in Table II. Such figures were not always completely comparable because of differences in national accounting practices, but they did serve to show major differences. In some cases, too, the original national accounts included a statistical discrepancy between the total and the sum of its components; the items shown, therefore, do not add up to 100%. Particular caution was necessary in comparing 1972 figures because some countries had begun to adopt a new system of national accounts (SNA) based on definitions recommended by the UN; many countries, however, were still using the former SNA.

Associated with this conversion were changes in the presentation of summary national accounts in UN publications, which had led in 1972 to the replacement of the usual analysis of expenditure shares in gross national product (GNP) with a table analyzing shares of gross domestic product. GDP excludes and GNP includes net factor income from abroad (payments such as dividends and interest arising in one country that are paid to residents of another country). The international surplus, as shown in Table II, was thus the difference between exports of goods and services and imports of goods and services as a share of total GDP.

Table III shows the latest available figures for levels of national income, considered on both a total and a per capita basis, in more than 70 countries. The concept of national income is designed to measure the output of the national economy at the cost of producing that output, less the value of the deprecia-

Table I. Growth of Real Gross Domestic Product, 1961–72

Country	Percentage real increase			
	Average 1961–70	1970 over 1969	1971 over 1970	1972* over 1971
Industrial countries				
Austria	4 7	7.1	5.2	5½
Belgium	4.9	6.1	3.7	4½
Canada	5.0	3.2	5.5	6
Denmark	4.9	3.1	3.6	4½
France	5.8	5.9	5.1	5½
Germany, West	4.8	5.7	2.8	3¼
Italy	5.5	5.3	1.1	3
Japan	11.1	10.5	6.7	8½
Luxembourg	3.4	3.5	2	...
Netherlands	5.2	6.0	4.7	3½
Norway	4.8	3.6	5.0	4¼
Sweden	4.4	4.6	0.3	2
Switzerland	4.3	4.2	3.9	4½
United Kingdom	2.7	2.0	1.4	3¼
United States	4.0	−0.7	2.7	6¼
Other developed areas				
Australia†	5.2	5.8	4.3	3¼
Finland	5.4	7.8	2.3	4½
Greece	7.4	7.6	...	...
Iceland	4.8	5.3	...	...
Ireland	3.9	1.5	2.8	2¾
New Zealand‡	3.9	4.0	3.5	4½
Portugal	6.5	8.7	5.1	...
South Africa§	5.8	4.8	3.6	...
Spain	7.6	6.8	4.6	7
Turkey	6.2	4.9	7.8	...
Centrally planned economies‖				
Albania	7.5	6.0	...	...
Bulgaria	7.7	7.0	9.4	...
Czechoslovakia	4.4	5.3	4.7	...
Germany, East	4.3	5.6	4.5	...
Hungary	5.5	5.0	6.9	...
Poland	6.1	5.2	7.5	...
Romania	8.4	7.1	12.5	...
U.S.S.R.	7.1	9.0	5.6	...
Yugoslavia	6.9	6.7	8.5	...
Less developed areas				
Brazil	5.5	9.5	11.3	...
Cyprus	5.5	3.8	12.1	...
Ecuador	5.2	9.6	14.0	...
Guatemala	5.6	5.7	5.7	...
Honduras	5.2	3.9	6.1	...
India‡	3.6	5.4	...	...
Iran‡	8.7	11.1	8.6	...
Kenya	6.5¶	7.0	6.0	...
Korea, South	9.8	10.1	10.8	...
Malawi	4.4¶	2.0	10.1	...
Malta	5.8	9.0	1.3	...
Mexico	7.1	6.9	3.7	...
Nicaragua	6.7	5.0	5.7	...
Pakistan†	4.6	6.4	−2.3	...
Uganda	4.8	1.5	1.7	...
Venezuela	5.4	4.4	4.4	...

*Except for Australia and New Zealand, the figures for 1972 are estimates based on incomplete data published in OECD, *Economic Outlook* (December 1972).
†Financial year ending June 30.
‡Financial year ending March 31 (for Iran, March 20).
§Includes Namibia (South West Africa).
‖Growth of material product. *See* text for discussion of comparability with other figures.
¶1964 to 1970 only.
Sources: Official publications of the United Nations, the Organization for Economic Cooperation and Development, and the International Monetary Fund; other national sources.

tion of the capital stock for the year being considered. The table includes all countries that had a national income of $1 billion or more in 1963. The national figures at current prices have been converted to U.S. dollars at current exchange rates. Thus, the figures as given in Table III are affected by changes in the price level and do not indicate the growth of real per capita income.

Two important qualifications have to be made about the use of this procedure. First, the use of current exchange rates determined for foreign trade and payments purposes may not adequately reflect differences in the purchasing power of the various national currencies. Furthermore, devaluations and revaluations will distort the figures as between different years. For 1971 the exchange rates used are those in force at the end of the year, that is, after the Smithsonian agreement. Second, the figures in national currencies are themselves estimated in a variety of ways, and there are differences in the definitions used among various countries. In particular the figures for 1971 are affected by the as yet incomplete changeover to the new system of national accounts described above.

Bearing these difficulties in mind, one may draw some tentative conclusions from the data presented. About four-fifths of the aggregate income of the listed countries is accounted for by the 15 industrial countries, while the 51 less developed countries represent 10–15% of the total. The dominating size of the U.S. economy in relation to all other non-Communist countries is shown in the table; it is roughly four times the size of the next largest, Japan, and four to five times the size of West Germany. It is likely, however, that a more sophisticated analysis allowing for differences in the internal purchasing power of national

Table II. Disposal of Gross Domestic Product in Percent

Country	Year	Public consumption	Private consumption	Change in inventory	Gross fixed capital formation	International surplus
Industrial countries						
Austria	1969	14.9	57.3	2.3	24.7	0.8
	1970	14.6	55.8	3.1	26.2	0.2
	1971	14.6	56.0	1.0	28.6	−0.2
Belgium	1969	14.0	63.0	1.9	21.0	0.1
	1970	14.0	60.4	1.3	22.1	2.3
	1971	14.4	60.5	1.1	22.4	1.5
Canada	1969	17.6	58.4	1.8	21.4	0.2
	1970	19.0	57.4	0.2	21.0	2.6
	1971	19.5	56.8	1.5	21.4	1.6
Germany, West	1969	15.7	55.3	2.2	24.2	2.5
	1970	15.8	54.1	1.8	26.5	1.8
	1971	17.0	54.2	0.6	26.7	1.5
Italy	1969	13.3	63.5	0.9	20.7	1.6
	1970	12.7	64.4	1.6	21.2	0.1
	1971	14.3	64.3	0.4	20.0	1.1
Netherlands	1969	15.9	57.4	2.4	24.5	−0.2
	1970	16.2	57.5	2.3	25.5	−1.5
	1971	16.9	56.7	1.3	25.4	−0.4
Norway	1969	16.4	55.7	0.6	24.6	2.8
	1970	15.7	54.5	3.1	27.2	−0.5
	1971	16.0	54.6	1.8	29.3	−1.6
Sweden	1969	20.9	56.2	1.3	22.0	−0.4
	1970	21.2	54.6	2.9	21.8	−0.6
	1971	22.8	54.0	1.0	21.1	1.0
Switzerland	1969	11.9	58.7	27.0		2.5
	1970	11.8	59.2	29.8		−0.8
	1971	11.7	58.7	30.0		−0.5
United Kingdom	1969	17.5	63.2	0.8	18.1	0.4
	1970	17.8	62.7	0.8	18.0	0.7
	1971	18.4	62.5	0.0	17.8	1.3
United States*	1969	22.7*	62.8	0.8*	14.1*	−0.4
	1970	22.7*	63.6	0.3*	13.7*	−0.3
	1971	22.4*	63.6	0.2*	14.3*	−0.6
Other developed areas						
Australia	1968–69	12.5	59.5	2.5	26.8	−1.4
	1969–70	12.4	58.9	1.7	26.6	0.0
	1970–71	12.9	58.5	1.3	26.6	−0.1
Finland	1969	15.9	53.8	5.9	23.5	0.9
	1970	15.8	52.6	7.2	25.6	−1.4
	1971	16.6	51.8	7.4	26.2	−2.0
Ireland	1969	13.3	70.0	2.6	23.1	−8.9
	1970	14.3	69.5	2.1	22.1	−8.1
	1971	14.9	68.3	1.3	23.0	−7.5
Malta	1969	16.7	78.0	2.0	31.1	−27.6
	1970	19.5	78.2	3.0	29.2	−29.7
	1971	20.2	76.2	3.4	26.8	−26.6
Portugal	1969	13.1	74.1	0.4	16.8	−4.4
	1970	14.1	75.8	−0.2	17.0	−6.6
	1971	13.8	75.4	0.9	16.8	−6.9
South Africa (including Namibia)	1969	11.5	61.0	2.8	23.3	1.2
	1970	12.1	62.2	4.1	25.4	−3.2
	1971	13.2	62.5	3.0	26.5	−3.9
Spain	1969	10.6	68.2	2.0	21.8	−2.6
	1970	11.0	67.2	1.8	21.[illegible]	−1.2
	1971	11.2	66.9	1.7	19.6	0.6
Less developed areas						
Costa Rica	1969	13.6	65.5	5.9	20.4	−5.4
	1970	13.9	68.8	2.1	22.2	−7.0
	1971	14.6	67.6	3.6	23.6	−9.5
Cyprus	1969	11.7	72.5	1.7	22.3	−8.2
	1970	11.9	74.2	0.9	24.4	−11.3
	1971	12.1	72.7	1.4	23.2	−9.3
El Salvador	1969	10.5	78.1	1.3	11.5	−2.6
	1970	10.8	75.4	1.8	12.0	−0.5
	1971	10.9	76.7	2.4	12.8	−3.7
Fiji	1969	12.2	66.4	2.5	22.5	−3.9
	1970	12.9	64.2	2.5	21.7	−3.1
	1971	12.9	66.6	2.7	25.1	−8.9
Guatemala	1969	7.8	80.4	−2.1	13.5	0.4
	1970	7.9	78.4	0.3	12.5	0.8
	1971	7.2	79.8	0.9	13.2	−1.2
Honduras	1969	11.0	72.2	1.1	18.9	−3.2
	1970	11.6	73.4	2.8	19.4	−7.2
	1971	11.8	73.5	−1.5	18.3	−2.1
Kenya	1969	16.5	63.2	1.6	18.0	0.7
	1970	16.3	63.6	2.3	19.5	−1.7
	1971	16.7	63.3	3.6	22.4	−5.9
Korea, South	1969	11.0	72.8	3.3	27.1	−12.6
	1970	11.1	72.9	2.4	25.7	−10.3
	1971	11.5	74.2	2.7	23.4	−11.4
Malawi	1969	15.7	78.7	−0.4	20.0	−14.0
	1970	15.5	77.9	2.2	17.9	−13.5
	1971	13.5	79.4	1.9	16.3	−11.0
Mexico	1969	7.7	73.8		19.4	−0.9
	1970	7.8	74.7		19.6	−2.1
	1971	8.1	74.6		18.6	−1.3
Morocco	1969	14.5	74.2	−1.3	13.8	−0.6
	1970	14.7	74.1	−0.6	15.3	−4.1
	1971	14.5	73.1	0.5	14.0	−2.7
Nicaragua	1969	10.8	71.5	2.1	17.9	−2.3
	1970	10.4	72.7	2.1	16.8	−2.0
	1971	9.8	73.8	2.0	16.4	−2.1
Panama	1969	12.5	65.0	2.3	21.2	−1.1
	1970	14.3	62.6	1.9	24.4	−3.3
	1971	14.3	62.5	1.8	25.8	−4.4
Tanzania	1969	11.9	71.0	1.1	14.5	−0.5
	1970	13.1	69.5	2.1	19.8	−4.4
	1971	13.8	66.5	3.0	24.1	−7.4
Venezuela	1969	13.9	54.5	1.5	24.5	5.6
	1970	14.8	55.5	1.8	22.8	5.1
	1971	15.8	53.7	0.9	23.5	6.0

*Fixed capital formation and change in inventory are for private sector only. Public sector fixed investment and inventory building are included in public consumption.
Sources: UN, OECD, and IMF publications; official national sources and research institute estimates.

Table III. National Income and Income per Capita

Country	National income in U.S. $000,000,000 1971	National income per capita in U.S. $ 1958	1963	1971
Industrial countries				
Austria	13.3	590	830	1,785
Belgium	25.2	935	1,190	2,590
Canada	69.7	1,505*	1,600*	3,230
Denmark	13.9	890*	1,335*	2,795
France	136.1	855	1,320	2,655
Germany, West	180.0	790	1,255	2,935
Italy	88.1	495	795	1,630
Japan	206.6	290	575	1,975
Luxembourg	0.6†	1,075*	1,340	1,970†
Netherlands	31.8	695*	995*	2,415
Norway	9.9	870*	1,205*	2,550
Sweden	29.3	1,250	1,800	3,615
Switzerland	21.3	1,195	1,675	3,375
United Kingdom	114.3	1,015	1,305	2,055
United States	855.7	2,115*	2,560*	4,135
Other developed areas				
Australia‡	29.3§	1,125*	1,470*	2,345§
Finland	9.0	725	1,130	1,915
Greece	7.5§	325	455	855§
Iceland	0.3§	965	1,270	1,560§
Ireland	3.8	465	655	1,270
New Zealand‖	5.2§	1,170	1,505	1,845§
Portugal	6.1	215*	300*	670
South Africa¶	14.5	315*	400*	635
Spain	33.2	305	450	975
Turkey	8.3	180	225	235
Less developed areas				
Africa				
Algeria	2.2♀	235	195	...
Egypt‡	5.7†	110*	140	175†
Ghana	1.6♂	140	190	200♂
Kenya	1.6	70*	85*	135
Libya	2.3†	110	360	1,250*
Morocco	3.6	160	165	235
Nigeria‖	4.1□	50	65	70□
Rhodesia	1.2§	175	185	235§
Sudan‡	1.4◊	80	90	95◊
Tanzania	1.1	50*	60*	85
Tunisia	1.0§	160*	195*	190§
Uganda	1.0	60	65	95
Zaire	1.4§	70*	120*	65
Zambia	1.2§	110	135	290§
Caribbean and Latin America				
Argentina	16.8†	490	485	735†
Brazil	27.2§	140	225	285§
Chile	5.9§	330*	260*	670§
Colombia	5.5§	190	225	260§
Costa Rica	0.7	295	315	370
Ecuador	1.5	155	160	235
El Salvador	0.9	205	215	255
Guatemala	1.7	235	265	310
Honduras	0.7	175*	185*	245
Jamaica	1.0	315	375	550
Mexico	32.4	270	350	640
Nicaragua	0.8	225	265	405
Peru	4.3§	165	200	305§
Puerto Rico‡	4.3§	540	830	1,580§
Uruguay	2.1§	540	535	710§
Venezuela	9.7	630*	605*	900
Asia, East and Southeast				
Burma▲	1.8♂	55	60	65♂
Hong Kong	1.3♀	245	380	...
India‖	42.1†	65*	80	80†
Indonesia	8.2§	80	75	65§
Iran‖	9.2§	145	185	310§
Korea, South	7.0	125	130	220
Malaysia	3.0†	195	225	290†
Pakistan‡	15.0†	60	80	120†
Philippines	5.1§	195	220	135§
Singapore	2.3	420	480	1,080
Sri Lanka (Ceylon)	1.8§	120*	130	145§
Taiwan	4.3§	90	150	305§
Thailand	5.1†	80*	100*	155†
Vietnam, South	2.8♂	90*	80*	155♂
Middle East				
Iraq	2.3†	160	190	255†
Israel	4.3§	630	840	1,470§
Jordan	0.6§	140	190	240§
Kuwait‖	2.2†	1,825*	3,430*	3,335†
Lebanon	1.4§	210	380	485§
Saudi Arabia‡	2.5♂	125*	225	330♂
Syria	1.5§	155	165	235§

*Data not strictly comparable with later years.
†1969.
‡Financial year beginning July 1.
§1970.
‖Financial year beginning April 1 (for Iran, March 21).
¶Including Namibia (South West Africa) throughout, and also Botswana, Lesotho, and Swaziland for 1958 and 1963.
♀1963.
♂1968.
□1966.
◊1967.
▲Financial year ending September 30.
Sources: Publications of UN, OECD, and IMF; official national sources.

currencies would show a somewhat different picture. The available evidence for Western Europe in relation to the U.S. is based on data for the 1950s. The complex changes that took place after that time suggest that such a study was needed for a more recent year. It seemed likely that the real output of some Western European countries was relatively higher than that suggested by the 1971 figures in the table.

(M. F. FULLER)

See also Economy, World.

India

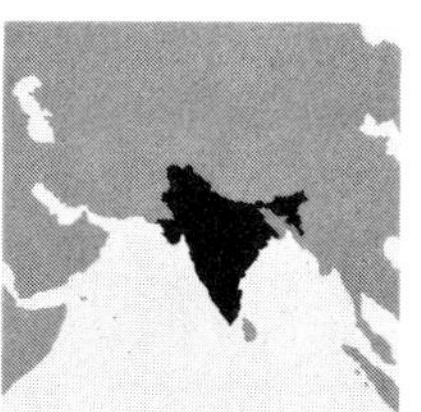

A federal republic of southern Asia and a member of the Commonwealth of Nations, India is situated on a peninsula extending into the Indian Ocean with the Arabian Sea to the west and the Bay of Bengal to the east. Area: 1,261,810 sq.mi. (3,268,090 sq.km.), including the Pakistani-controlled section of Jammu and Kashmir. Pop. (1971): 547,949,809; Indo-Aryans and Dravidians are dominant, with Mongoloid, Negroid, and Australoid admixtures. Cap.: New Delhi (pop., 1971, 301,801). Largest cities: Calcutta (metro. pop., 1971, 7,031,382) and Greater Bombay (metro. pop., 1971, 5,970,575). Language: Hindi and English (official). Religion (1971): Hindu 82.7%; Muslim 11.2%; Christian 2.6%; Sikh 1.9%; Buddhist 0.7%; others 0.9%. President in 1972, Varahagiri Venkata Giri; prime minister, Mrs. Indira Gandhi.

India completed 25 years of independence at the end of 1972. The mood of exultation generated by the military victory over Pakistan changed into one of anxiety because of growing economic difficulties.

Foreign Affairs. The first major event of the year was a brief halt in Delhi by Sheikh Mujibur Rahman (*see* BIOGRAPHY), president of Bangladesh, on his way to Dacca from London on being released by Pakistan. He made a longer visit to Calcutta in February. All Indian troops stationed in Bangladesh were withdrawn by March 12. The return to Bangladesh of ten million refugees who had sought shelter in India was organized with remarkable speed and efficiency.

Population of Administrative Units of India

Unit	Population
States	
Andhra Pradesh	43,502,708
Assam	14,625,152
Bihar	56,353,369
Gujarat	26,697,475
Hariana	10,036,808
Himachal Pradesh	3,460,434
Jammu and Kashmir	4,616,632
Kerala	21,347,375
Madhya Pradesh	41,654,119
Maharashtra	50,412,235
Manipur	1,072,753
Meghalaya	1,011,699
Mysore	29,299,014
Nagaland	516,449
Orissa	21,944,615
Punjab	13,551,060
Rajasthan	25,765,806
Tamil Nadu	41,199,168
Tripura	1,556,342
Uttar Pradesh	88,341,144
West Bengal	44,312,011
Union Territories	
Andaman and Nicobar Islands	115,133
Arunachal Pradesh	467,511
Chandigarh	257,251
Dadra and Nagar Haveli	74,170
Delhi	4,065,698
Goa, Daman, Diu	857,771
Laccadive, Minicoy, and Amindivi Islands	31,810
Mizoram	332,390
Pondicherry	471,707
Total	547,949,809

Source: *Census of India: Paper 1 of 1972: Final Population.*

India gave Bangladesh Rs. 200 million in cash and 900,000 metric tons of grain and also assisted in the rebuilding of roads and railways. Mrs. Indira Gandhi (*see* BIOGRAPHY) visited Dacca in March, and the two countries signed a 25-year treaty of friendship and cooperation. Soon afterward, joint commissions for irrigation and power were formed. But the envisaged bilateral trade had not developed by the end of the year. On the whole, India adopted a low profile toward Bangladesh, but opposition groups there still spoke of Indian designs of domination.

After allowing Pakistani Pres. Zulfikar Ali Bhutto (*see* BIOGRAPHY) time to consolidate his position, Mrs. Gandhi sent D. P. Dhar to Pakistan to settle the agenda for a meeting of heads of government. The two met at Simla, India, from June 28 to July 3. Belying forecasts of a breakdown, an agreement was signed by which both countries pledged themselves to peaceful and bilateral solution of their differences. India offered to restore to Pakistan 5,140 sq.mi. of territory won in fighting, in return for 69 sq.mi. to be returned by Pakistan. Both sides agreed to respect the line of control that existed on Dec. 17, 1971, when the cease-fire came into force. Other difficult questions, such as the release of prisoners and the status of Kashmir, were left to future discussions.

Parliament and political parties generally endorsed the agreement, with the exception of the Jan Sangh. But the Simla spirit seemed to evaporate rapidly. Pakistan's recognition of Bangladesh, which President Bhutto had hinted at, did not materialize. India continued to maintain that its Pakistani prisoners of war (about 91,000) could not be released without agreement with Bangladesh, since they had surrendered in Bangladesh to an Indo-Bangladesh joint command. With Pakistan withholding recognition and China vetoing Bangladesh's admission to the UN, the deadlock remained unresolved. Even the expected withdrawal of troops by India and Pakistan did not take place until mid-December, when military negotiators finally agreed on the line of control. The two countries did agree to exchange civilians captured during the war. Pakistan announced that it would repatriate 10,000 Bengalis and in November it released some 600 Indian POWs.

The Indo-Soviet treaty of 1971 and the breakup of Pakistan seemed to harden China's attitude toward India. The improved relations between China and the United States added to Indian apprehensions. Relations with the U.S. continued to be under strain, which was not eased by the visit of John B. Connally, Jr., former U.S. secretary of the treasury, in July, and U.S. economic assistance remained suspended. In September Shankar Dayal Sharma, president of the Congress Party, accused the U.S. Central Intelligence Agency of fomenting trouble in India. After the re-election of U.S. Pres. Richard Nixon, Mrs. Gandhi expressed the hope that Indo-U.S. relations would be strengthened. Nixon responded in kind. On November 30 Foreign Minister Swaran Singh, speaking to Parliament, made exceptionally conciliatory statements regarding both the U.S. and China.

In other political actions India raised to ambassadorial level its diplomatic representation in North Vietnam and East Germany. The Soviet Union's continued delineation of the disputed Indo-Chinese border on official Soviet maps in such a manner as to support Chinese claims led to angry protests in the Delhi Parliament in May. External Affairs Minister Swaran Singh attempted to defend the U.S.S.R.'s stance by saying that the Kremlin had given an oral assurance that no political significance attached to the maps. In September, D. P. Dhar visited Moscow to make the final arrangements for Indo-Soviet economic cooperation as defined in the 1971 friendship treaty.

Although in August the government refused to accept any of the Ugandan Asians expelled by Pres. Idi Amin of Uganda, this decision was reversed in September, and the government then agreed to accept temporarily U.K. passport holders who preferred to go to India in the first instance. Those who accepted would not lose the right to continue on to the U.K.

The British Broadcasting Corporation, whose Delhi office was closed because of its refusal to stop screenings of Louis Malle's films on India, agreed in February to conform to Indian conditions including precensorship. It was then allowed to appoint one British staff man to its Delhi office.

Domestic Affairs. Manipur, Meghalaya, and Tripura became full states, and Mizoram was constituted into a union territory in 1972. The North East Frontier Agency also became a union territory and was renamed Arunachal Pradesh. Elections to state assemblies were held in March throughout the country except in Kerala, Nagaland, Orissa, Tamil Nadu, and Uttar Pradesh. The Congress Party won a majority in all the states and territories except Goa, Manipur, and Meghalaya. Its victory was particularly impressive in West Bengal. Many states elected new

INDIA

Education. (1965–66) Primary, pupils 49,499,000, teachers 1,393,930; secondary, pupils 7,022,394, teachers 342,350; vocational, pupils 450,101, teachers 31,220; teacher training, students 177,607, teachers 13,460; higher (including 62 universities), students 1,054,273, teaching staff (1963–64) 80,247.

Finance. Monetary unit: rupee, with (Sept. 18, 1972) a free rate of Rs. 7.65 to U.S. $1 (Rs. 18.71 = £1 sterling). Gold, SDRs, and foreign exchange, official: (June 1972) U.S. $1,170,000,000; (June 1971) U.S. $1,050,000,000. Budget (1971–72 est.): revenue Rs. 35,620,000,000; expenditure Rs. 35,870,000,000. National income: (1969–70) Rs. 346.6 billion; (1968–69) Rs. 311.6 billion. Money supply: (June 1972) Rs. 84,780,000,000; (June 1971) Rs. 74,580,000,000. Cost of living (1963 = 100): (May 1972) 180; (May 1971) 169.

Foreign Trade. (1971–72) Imports Rs. 18,120,000,000; exports Rs. 15,635,000,000. Import sources: U.S. 25%; U.K. 13%; Japan 10%; Iran 7%; West Germany 7%; Canada 7%; U.S.S.R. 5%. Export destinations: U.S. 17%; U.S.S.R. 13%; Japan 12%; U.K. 11%. Main exports: jute manufactures 17%; tea 10%; iron ore 7%; cotton fabrics 6%; leather 6%.

Transport and Communications. Roads (1971) 983,000 km. (including 24,000 km. main roads). Motor vehicles in use (1971): passenger 619,800; commercial 333,300. Railways: (1969) 60,023 km.; traffic (state only; 1970–71) 113,080,000,000 passenger-km., freight 119,860,000,000 net ton-km. Air traffic (1971): 3,612,000,000 passenger-km.; freight 125,978,000 net ton-km. Shipping (1971): merchant vessels 100 gross tons and over 397; gross tonnage 2,478,031. Telephones (Dec. 1970) 1,175,000. Radio licenses (Dec. 1970) 11,837,000. Television licenses (Dec. 1970) 25,000.

Agriculture. Production (in 000; metric tons; 1971; 1970 in parentheses): wheat 23,247 (20,093); rice *c.* 66,000 (63,672); barley 2,865 (2,716); corn *c.* 6,500 (7,413); millet *c.* 8,500 (12,074); sorghum *c.* 7,800 (8,188); potatoes 4,640 (3,913); cassava 5,216 (5,214); tea *c.* 433 (422); chick-peas 5,247 (5,546); bananas (1970) *c.* 3,300, (1969) 3,105; sugar, raw value (1971–72) *c.* 3,365, (1970–71) 4,098; tobacco 350 (338); rapeseed and mustard seed 1,963 (1,564); linseed 455 (469); peanuts 5,712 (6,065); cotton, lint 1,127 (954); jute 1,028 (883). Livestock (in 000; 1970–71): cattle *c.* 176,600; sheep *c.* 42,800; pigs *c.* 4,780; buffalo *c.* 54,500; goats *c.* 68,000; poultry *c.* 117,000.

Industry. Production (in 000; metric tons; 1971): coal 69,109; iron ore (61% metal content) 33,720; pig iron 6,906; crude steel 6,034; electricity (excluding most industrial production; kw-hr.) 58,918,000; aluminum 176; cement 14,932; cotton yarn 884; woven cotton fabrics (m.; 1970) 7,849,000; petroleum products (1970) 16,649; sulfuric acid 1,001; caustic soda 374; gold (troy oz.; 1970) 105; manganese ore (metal content; 1970) 644.

chief ministers: S. C. Sinha in Assam, Kedar Pandey in Bihar, G. Oza in Gujarat, P. C. Sethi in Madhya Pradesh, D. Devaraj Urs in Mysore, G. Zail Singh in Punjab, and S. S. Ray in West Bengal. S. Mir Qasim, who became Kashmir chief minister after the death of G. M. Sadiq the previous December, continued in office, as did the Congress Party chief ministers of Andhra Pradesh, Hariana, Himachal Pradesh, Maharashtra, and Rajasthan. A political crisis in Orissa forced the Biswanath Das ministry to resign, and the Congress Party formed a government in June under Mrs. Nandini Satpathy. In October the Dravida Munnetra Kazhagam, the ruling party in Tamil Nadu, split into two.

The princely order was finally abolished January 1 after the adoption and signing of the Constitution (26th Amendment) Bill in December 1971. Some transitional allowances were promised to the former rulers in lieu of the privy purses that were withdrawn. Four more bills to amend the constitution were adopted subsequently, creating the union territories of Mizoram and Arunachal Pradesh (27th amendment), abolishing special service conditions of officers of the old Indian Civil Service (28th), protecting Kerala land reforms (29th), and facilitating certain kinds of appeals to the Supreme Court (30th).

Mrs. Gandhi reorganized her Cabinet in July, appointing D. P. Dhar as minister of planning and T. A. Pai as minister of railways, transferring C. Subramaniam to industrial development, and dropping Moinul Haq Chowdhury and K. Hanumanthaiya. Earlier, Nurul Hasan was appointed minister of education.

The Congress Party directed its governments to carry out land reforms urgently. Andhra Pradesh, Gujarat, and Jammu and Kashmir led the way in adopting legislation for enforcing a ceiling on landholdings and redistributing surplus land among landless labourers. The work of providing house sites to landless labourers also made progress. A ministerial committee was working on proposals to determine ceilings on urban property. The Supreme Court struck down, as a restriction on freedom of speech, an order of the union government limiting the size of newspapers to ten pages.

A six-year project to save the tiger was drawn up. Parliament adopted a bill to protect wildlife and another to curb the export of antiquities and art treasures. Notable persons who died during the year included D. Sanjivayya, president of the Congress Party, Sant Fateh Singh, militant Sikh leader, and Charu Mazumdar, leader of the pro-Maoist Marxist-Leninist Communist Party. An unusual event was the surrender of several hundred dacoits (criminals in roving gangs) of the ravines of Madhya Pradesh. They renounced violence under the influence of followers of Mohandas Gandhi.

The Economy. If 1971 was the year of Bangladesh, 1972 was the year of spiraling prices. Among factors contributing to inflation were lower farm and factory production in 1971–72, power shortages, increased public expenditure due to refugee relief, military operations, drought relief, and wage increases to government employees, and the late arrival and erratic behaviour of the 1972 monsoon, which adversely affected summer crops. The wholesale price index on October 14 was 10.1% higher than 12 months earlier. The index for grains was 16.3% higher, and that for sugar 35.9% higher. Money supply in the hands of the public had increased 10.9% over the same period.

ROBERT TRUMBULL—THE NEW YORK TIMES

In mountain villages such as this one in the wild and little-known Arunachal Pradesh, accelerated education and development programs were helping these primitive tribes "leapfrog" centuries.

In October the government announced measures to achieve distribution of essential supplies through fair price shops, to take over the wholesale grain trade, and to absorb the money supply.

The union government's budget for 1972–73, presented on March 16, placed revenue at Rs. 44,760,000,000 (including Rs. 1,330,000,000 from new taxation), expenditure at Rs. 41,240,000,000, capital receipts at Rs. 20,950,000,000, and capital expenditure at Rs. 26,890,000,000, leaving an uncovered deficit of Rs. 2,420,000,000. Preliminary proposals for the fifth five-year plan set the objectives for achievement during 1974–79 as attainment of 5.5% average annual growth and self-reliance through a public outlay of Rs. 355,950,000,000.

In January Mrs. Gandhi instructed the Finance Ministry and planning commission to redirect economic development plans on the assumption of lower foreign aid. In May the foreign trade minister, L. N. Mishra, visited Moscow to sign a protocol likely to make the Soviet Union India's largest single trading partner. In a policy statement in February the foreign trade secretary, H. Lal, voiced India's fears that British entry to the EEC would place severe restrictions on Indian exports. In May India renewed its application for a trade agreement with the EEC before Jan. 1, 1973.

Mrs. Gandhi opened India's "Asia '72" trade fair on November 3 in New Delhi. Forty-six nations participated, but the U.S. was not among them. India was particularly eager to become a major seller of military armaments. Exports of such equipment had already reached Nepal, Malaysia, Kenya, Egypt, and other states in the Middle East, and had brought in about $10 million in 1972.

Major projects to go into production during the year were the country's second nuclear power station (near Kota), a fast-breeder reactor at Trombay, and the first unit of the Soviet-aided steel plant at Bokaro. The first Indian-built frigate, "Nilgiri," was commissioned by the Indian Navy. The government took over the Indian Iron and Steel Co., the entire domestic trade in raw jute under a newly formed Jute Corp. of India, 46 textile mills, and the British-incorporated

Indian Copper Corp. Under a formula for "progressive indianization," drawn up by the Ministry of Industrial Development in February, foreign companies were to be allowed to expand only if they agreed to increase Indian equity participation in proportion to their growth. (H. Y. SHARADA PRASAD)

See also Bangladesh; Pakistan.

Indonesia

A republic of Southeast Asia, Indonesia consists of the major islands of Sumatra, Java, Kalimantan (Indonesian Borneo), Celebes, and Irian Barat (West New Guinea) and approximately 3,000 smaller islands and islets. Area: 782,658 sq.mi. (2,027,087 sq.km.). Pop. (1971): 119,232,499. Cap. and largest city: Jakarta (pop., 1971, 4,576,009). Language: Bahasa Indonesian (official); Javanese; Sundanese; Madurese. Religion: mainly Muslim; some Christian, Buddhist, and Hindu. President and prime minister in 1972, General Suharto.

The constitutional development of Indonesia progressed significantly in 1972. For the first time since the 1945 proclamation of independence, a People's Consultative Congress (MPR) was sworn in as a prelude to the election of a president and vice-president in accordance with the constitution. In foreign affairs, partly as a reaction to the disengagement of the United States from Southeast Asia and a concomitant U.S. rapprochement with China, Indonesia moved to strengthen relations with its immediate neighbours, in particular Australia, Malaysia, New Zealand, and the Philippines, and also with Japan.

Domestic Affairs. Ironically, for a year that ended on a note of political stability, 1972 opened harshly with the eruption of what was popularly called the "mini-affair." The issue developed when Mrs. Tien Suharto, the wife of President Suharto, launched a plan to build a $25 million Disneyland-style "Indonesia-in-Miniature" to attract tourists and to strengthen national unity through a display of the country's richly diverse cultural heritage. Relatively little notice was taken of the project, which was to be financed and managed privately, until Mrs. Suharto addressed a governors' conference and suggested that each of the country's 26 provinces set aside part of their budget for it. Several senior army officers and their wives emerged as the plan's co-sponsors, and rumours spread that pressure was being brought to bear on private firms to make "voluntary contributions."

The "mini-affair" mushroomed into a political crisis as the press, intellectuals, and students denounced the scheme as a wasteful expenditure, reminiscent of the grandiose plans of the former Sukarno era. Suharto, visibly upset by the public outcry, rushed to his wife's defense and accused her critics of exploiting the issue in order to undermine the government. The uproar over so minor an issue, it was widely believed, reflected misgivings over the dominant role of the Army in public affairs. As for the president, he was said to have been embarrassed by his wife's involvement in the affair. Both the government and the opposition appeared surprised by the tension that the affair generated and both sides retreated. The project was submitted to Parliament for a feasibility study and, for all practical purposes, was dropped.

For all sides in the controversy—the president, the Army, and the general public—the "mini-affair" in retrospect appeared to have had a salutary effect on the political scene. It helped clarify the power relationships between the quasi-military government and its critics among the educated classes. With its collapse, a new climate of stability emerged. The critics appeared satisfied that they had been heard and taken into account in the formation of government policy, and the government was relieved that the criticism was not simply "opposition for opposition's sake" but the work of a "loyal opposition."

In the new atmosphere, political events moved smoothly for the remainder of the year, and on October 1, on the seventh anniversary of the abortive coup of the Indonesian Communist Party (PKI), the 920-member MPR, formed under the constitution, was sworn in for the first time. To be convened once every five years, the MPR was empowered to elect the nation's president and vice-president and determine "the broad lines of the policy of the state." In March 1973, the MPR was scheduled to elect a new chief of state, and Suharto, who appeared to have a genuinely popular base in the country, was expected to be reelected to a five-year term by acclamation. The vice-presidency, however, was expected to be contested. Since 1956, when Muhammad Hatta resigned the vice-presidency in protest against Sukarno's chaotic rule, the office had been vacant.

In other landmark developments during the year, Indonesia adopted a new system of standardized spelling, which was expected to save newspapers alone five tons of paper daily and to bring the language into closer conformity with Malay, the official language of Malaysia and the dominant language of the region. And for the first time an Indonesian president ad-

INDONESIA

Education. Primary (1969–70), pupils 12,802,415, teachers 323,218; secondary (1968–69), pupils 1,121,181, teachers 81,620; vocational (1968–69), pupils 358,833, teachers 35,462; teacher training (1968–69), students 130,361, teachers 12,385; higher (1967–68), students 192,416, teaching staff 21,309.

Finance. Monetary unit: rupiah, with (Sept. 18, 1972) an official rate of 415 rupiah to U.S. $1 (free rate of 1,016 rupiah = £1 sterling). Budget (total; 1972–73) balanced at 751.6 billion rupiah. Gross domestic product: (1970) 3,196,200,000,000 rupiah; (1969) 2,593,900,000,000 rupiah. Money supply: (Dec. 1971) 312,550,000,000 rupiah; (Dec. 1970) 241,060,000,000 rupiah. Cost of living (Jakarta; 1963 = 100): (June 1972) 73,089; (June 1971) 70,350.

Foreign Trade. (1971) Imports U.S. $1,082,200,000; exports U.S. $1,242,300,000. Import sources (1970 est.): Japan 30%; U.S. 25%; West Germany 9%; Philippines 5%. Export destinations: Japan 50%; U.S. 16%; West Germany 8%. Main exports: petroleum and products 45%; rubber 16%.

Transport and Communications. Roads (1971) 84,382 km. Motor vehicles in use (1971): passenger 256,988; commercial 112,877. Railways: (1969) 7,282 km.; traffic (1968) 3,884,000,000 passenger-km., freight 655 million net ton-km. Air traffic (1971): 1,007,300,000 passenger-km.; freight 18,636,000 net ton-km. Shipping (1971): merchant vessels 100 gross tons and over 501; gross tonnage 618,805. Telephones (Dec. 1970) 201,000. Radio receivers (Dec. 1970) 13,796,000. Television receivers (Dec. 1970) 90,000.

Agriculture. Production (in 000; metric tons; 1971; 1970 in parentheses): rice 18,778 (17,894); corn 2,631 (2,888); cassava (1970) 10,451, (1969) 11,034; sweet potatoes (1970) 3,029, (1969) 3,021; sugar, raw value (1971–72) *c.* 850, (1970–71) 742; tea 70 (64); copra *c.* 730 (*c.* 694); soybeans *c.* 391 (488); palm oil (estates only) *c.* 225 (215); peanuts 467 (488); coffee *c.* 180 (185); tobacco *c.* 92 (87); rubber *c.* 830 (811); fish catch (1970) 1,249, (1969) 1,214. Livestock (in 000; Dec. 1970): cattle *c.* 7,200; pigs *c.* 2,630; sheep *c.* 3,750; horses *c.* 610; buffaloes *c.* 2,700; goats *c.* 7,000; chickens c. 66,500.

Industry. Production (in 000; metric tons; 1971): crude oil 43,788; coal 173; tin concentrates (metal content) 20; bauxite (1970) 1,229; electricity (excluding most industrial production; kw-hr.; 1969) 1,871,000.

dressed himself publicly to the drug problem, which he said "threatened the future welfare of our nation." Drug usage rose dramatically among Indonesian youth, and authorities feared that with the drying up of the market among U.S. troops in Vietnam the traffickers in narcotics would seek to dispose of their stocks in Indonesia.

The Economy. The economy continued to display marked improvement, regaining the momentum lost during the troubled Sukarno period. Under Suharto's stewardship, the rate of inflation decreased from 650% in 1966 to 2.5% in 1972; developmental expenditure rose during that period at an appreciable rate; and the mobilization of domestic funds through savings increased dramatically, doubling between 1971 and 1972 to a record 110 billion rupiah ($1 = 415 rupiah).

The implementation of the country's first five-year plan (1969–74) also moved satisfactorily. Not only did rice production increase annually under the plan but the fixed targets were surpassed. The spurt in agriculture, however, had potential political consequences. In 1972 Suharto expressed concern that the market price of rice would drop if output of the crop continued to rise. This, he said, "will result in a fall of the income of the greater part of the Indonesian population" and thereby defeat the plan's strategy to promote economic development "from below." Accordingly, the rice target for 1973–74 was trimmed from 15.4 million to 14.8 million tons.

The economy also received a tremendous lift from the mining sector. During the year, Indonesian oil production exceeded 1.3 million bbl. daily, and the oil industry earned almost $1 billion in foreign exchange—a record. In addition, progress was registered in bringing copper, nickel, iron sand, and granite mines into production.

In a surprising development, forestry in 1972 emerged as the country's third largest export after oil and rubber. More than 10 million cu.m., or four times the plan target, were cut, earning nearly $200 million in foreign exchange. The economy's rapid recovery, especially the increasing prosperity in rural areas, became one of Suharto's principal sources of political strength.

Foreign Relations. During his era of power Sukarno had sought to leapfrog Indonesia into the status of a major power by placing it into what he termed an "axis" relationship with China. Suharto, however, dismantled the "Jakarta-Peking axis" and sought to make the same jump by cultivating Japan as a unique source of massive Asian economic, technical, and military assistance. In 1972 this policy was clearly in evidence.

In the aftermath of U.S. Pres. Richard Nixon's journey to China and North Vietnam's March offensive, Suharto flew to Japan to confer "unofficially" on the East Asian situation. *Angkatan Bersendjata,* the official army newspaper which mirrors Suharto's views, linked the visit directly to the Sino-American détente and developments in Vietnam. "Recent international developments," an editorial said, "have compelled [Japan and Indonesia] to review the nature of their relationship and whether it cannot be intensified in keeping with new challenges." Significantly, perhaps, during his Tokyo sojourn in May, Suharto conferred not only with Prime Minister Eisaku Sato but also with the man who later emerged as Sato's successor, Kakuei Tanaka. At the conclusion of the talks, Japan extended a new loan of $200 million to Indonesia in return for guaranteed shipment of 50 million tons of Indonesian oil over a ten-year period. As a result of the agreement, Japan, already Indonesia's major trading partner, became Indonesia's principal foreign aid donor.

Suharto also worked to strengthen ties with Indonesia's immediate neighbours. He paid state visits to Australia, New Zealand, and the Philippines, and the Indonesian armed forces carried out joint military exercises with Australia, Malaysia, and the Philippines. The increasing emphasis on improving military cooperation with neighbouring powers reflected growing uneasiness over the outcome of the Vietnam conflict and what Indonesia interpreted as the continuing U.S. withdrawal from Southeast Asia. A trade agreement with Australia was signed in November.

The changing situation in the region led Indonesia to make its first moves to improve relations with China. Relations with China had been suspended (but not severed) in 1966 following Indonesian charges that Peking was involved in the attempted Communist coup in 1965. "Whether these relations will thaw or remain as they are now," Suharto said on August 16 on the eve of Indonesian independence day, "depends on their attitude toward us." The following day, in New York, at the invitation of the Indonesian delegation, the Chinese chief delegate, Huang Hua, attended an Indonesian independence day reception at the United Nations headquarters.

On October 1, at the invitation of the Chinese, the Indonesian chief delegate to the UN, Anwar Sani, attended a Chinese diplomatic reception at the UN. In Jakarta Foreign Minister Adam Malik derided speculations that Japan would serve as an intermediary in the unfreezing of Sino-Indonesian relations. A major condition for the resumption of normal relations was Jakarta's insistence that China abandon its propaganda attacks on the "fascist military Suharto regime" and withdraw its diplomatic, political, and financial support of a remnant PKI faction that operated out of Peking. As the year drew to a close, Foreign Minister Malik had entered into correspondence with Chinese Premier Chou En-lai, and in October he announced that Indonesia was actively seeking a "normalization" in relations with Peking.

(ARNOLD C. BRACKMAN)

Industrial Review

Industrial activity could not entirely recover during 1971 from the recession that began a year earlier in the United States. Following a long period of relatively fast growth of the order of 6–7% a year in the 1960s, world manufacturing output (excluding the centrally planned economies) rose only 2% in 1970 and at an even somewhat lower rate in 1971.

As in 1970, the depressed economic climate in the industrial countries was responsible for this slow progress. Their manufacturing activity rose only 1½%, whereas that of the less industrialized countries increased by 7½%. After a decline of 5% in 1970, output in the United States continued to stagnate, while production in Western Europe rose by less than 3%, half the rate achieved a year earlier. The small gain in Western Europe was due mainly to the virtual stagnation in West Germany and the United Kingdom, and recession in Italy. These slowed down the growth in some of the smaller European countries. Even in Japan, the growth of manufacturing activity declined from 16% in 1970 to 4½% in 1971. The centrally planned economies of the Soviet Union and Eastern Europe maintained their growth rate of the previous year, raising it from 8½ to 9%.

There were signs of improvement toward the end of 1971, followed by a more marked upswing in the first half of 1972; it seemed likely that production would rise quickly in 1972, reaching or perhaps exceeding the average growth rate of the 1960s. The recovery in North America coincided with faster progress in those European countries that were the laggards in 1971 and with continued expansion elsewhere. The industrial advance was expected to continue well into 1973.

In the U.S. the marginal decline of manufacturing in 1971 from the already depressed level of a year earlier was due to a 7% fall in the output of equipment; production of consumer goods rose by 5%. This reflected the weakness of business investment and the rise of private consumption. Public expenditure on goods and services was, in real terms, marginally below the 1970 level. Residential investment was the most vigorous element in the economy. To some extent the higher private consumption was due to spending on automobiles. Toward the end of the year expansionary monetary and fiscal policy, the resumption of building stock inventories after some decline earlier in 1971, and increased government expenditure (mainly on defense and agricultural support) stimulated the revival.

Canadian industry resumed its growth after the decline in 1970, though at a modest rate. Private housing and consumer durables were the fastest growing components of industrial demand.

By Japanese standards that nation's industry was in a serious recession, one that lasted for almost two years. The slowdown was originally caused by a cyclical downturn in industrial investment and deceleration in building stock inventories. It was then aggravated by domestic and external developments, such as a consumer boycott of colour television sets, the weakening of domestic demand for automobiles, and U.S. Pres. Richard Nixon's "economic package" of Aug. 15, 1971. This was followed by an agreement to limit exports of noncotton textiles to the U.S. and the flotation and revaluation of the yen. Lack of business confidence and the general uncertainty following the U.S. measures were other contributory factors. Policy measures could do little to mitigate the effects of all this before early 1972, when activity gained momentum again.

Manufacturing output in the U.K. showed practically no change. Budgetary measures helped to stimulate demand for consumer goods, but the modest increase in those industries was offset by declines elsewhere, such as metals, certain categories of engineering, paper, and printing. Although private house building and exports rose relatively fast, investment in public housing and in private industries fell significantly. Worsening industrial relations and rapidly rising wage rates were further disturbing factors leading to the weakening of the competitive advantage gained by the devaluation of the pound in 1967. The consumer boom generated by government measures started to raise industrial activity during 1972, although the miners' strike and the consequent energy shortages hampered production in the first quarter of the year.

After a buoyant start in the early months of 1971, West German industrial production slowed down during the year and actually declined in the second half of the year. The metalworkers' strike in the Stuttgart area directly involved about 350,000 workers and caused widespread shutdowns elsewhere, mainly in the automobile industry, which faced a general falling off in demand both at home and from abroad. This eventually forced both Volkswagen and Opel, the two leading producers, to stop production for a week in their major plants early in 1972. The floating of the mark gave foreign competitors a currency advantage, and this seriously affected West German industry, which had passed the U.S. to become the largest exporter of manufactured goods. Especially unfavourably affected were the capital goods producers. There was some marginal improvement in the early months of 1972.

France was the only larger European country that succeeded in maintaining a fast rate of growth throughout. French industry had become so closely linked with the West German and Italian markets that it could not entirely escape the adverse conditions in those countries, but lively domestic con-

Table I. Index Numbers of World Production, Employment, and Productivity in Manufacturing Industries
1963 = 100

Area	Relative importance		Production			Employment			Productivity*		
	1963	1971	1969	1970	1971	1969	1970	1971	1969	1970	1971
World†	1,000	1,000	149	152	155	...	...	...	...	...	...
Industrial countries	876	864	149	151	153	...	...	...	...	...	...
Less industrialized countries	124	136	149	159	171	...	...	...	...	...	...
North America‡	480	430	145	139	139	...	...	...	...	...	...
Canada	28	28	147	146	149	118	116	115	125	126	130
United States	452	402	146	139	138	119	114	110	123	122	125
Latin America§	49	56	151	163	176	...	...	...	...	...	...
Mexico	8	10	172	188	...	...	...	...	...	...	...
Asia‖	88	133	197	223	235	...	...	...	...	...	...
India	16	14	129	135	139	...	...	...	...	...	...
Japan	55	98	227	264	276	117	120	121	194	220	228
Pakistan	3	3	176	181	...	...	...	...	...	...	...
Europe¶	350	346	141	149	153	...	...	...	...	...	...
Austria	7	7	142	154	164	97	101	104	146	152	158
Belgium	11	11	137	144	150	...	...	...	...	...	...
Denmark	6	6	152	157	...	107	110	107	142	143	...
Finland	4	4	150	166	165	107	...	...	140	...	...
France	51	53	143	154	163	98	100	100	146	154	163
Germany, West	89	91	147	156	158	103	107	106	143	146	149
Greece	2	3	168	152	204	112	117	125	150	130	163
Ireland	1	1	148	152	159	114	116	114	130	131	139
Italy	36	34	140	151	146	104	107	110	135	141	133
Netherlands	12	13	153	166	172	98	100	99	156	166	174
Norway	4	4	136	143	148	107	110	...	127	130	...
Portugal	2	2	164	173	168	...	...	...	...	...	...
Spain	12	14	194	210	221	120	...	...	162	...	...
Sweden	14	14	146	158	161	97	99	96	151	160	168
Switzerland	10	9	132	142	146	95	95	93	139	149	157
United Kingdom	73	61	126	127	127	100	100	97	126	127	131
Yugoslavia	13	16	159	174	191	114	119	127	139	146	150
Rest of the world♀	33	35	...	...	...	...	...	...	...	...	...
Australia	14	13	136	140	143	117	119	120	116	118	119
South Africa	5	5	151	159	163	146	155	161	103	103	101
Centrally planned economiesδ	...	...	164	178	194	...	...	...	...	...	...

*This is 100 times the production index divided by the employment index, giving a rough indication of changes in output per person employed.
†Excluding Albania, Bulgaria, China, Czechoslovakia, East Germany, Hungary, Mongolia, North Korea, North Vietnam, Poland, Romania, and the U.S.S.R.
‡Canada and the United States.
§South and Central America (including Mexico) and the Caribbean islands.
‖Asian Middle East and East and Southeast Asia, including Japan.
¶Excluding Albania, Bulgaria, Czechoslovakia, East Germany, Hungary, Poland, Romania, and the U.S.S.R.
♀Africa, the Middle East, and Oceania.
δThese are not included in the above world total and consist of Albania, Bulgaria, Czechoslovakia, East Germany, Hungary, Poland, Romania, and the U.S.S.R.
Sources: UN *Monthly Bulletin of Statistics;* U.K. National Institute of Economic and Social Research, *Economic Review.*

Table II. Industrial Production in the U.S.S.R. and Eastern Europe
1963=100

Country	1969	1970	1971
Bulgaria	199	218	238
Czechoslovakia	144	156	165*
Germany, East	144	153	160
Hungary	135	144	151
Poland	163	177	192
Romania	201	229	253*
U.S.S.R.	162	175	189

*Provisional.
Source: UN *Monthly Bulletin of Statistics.*

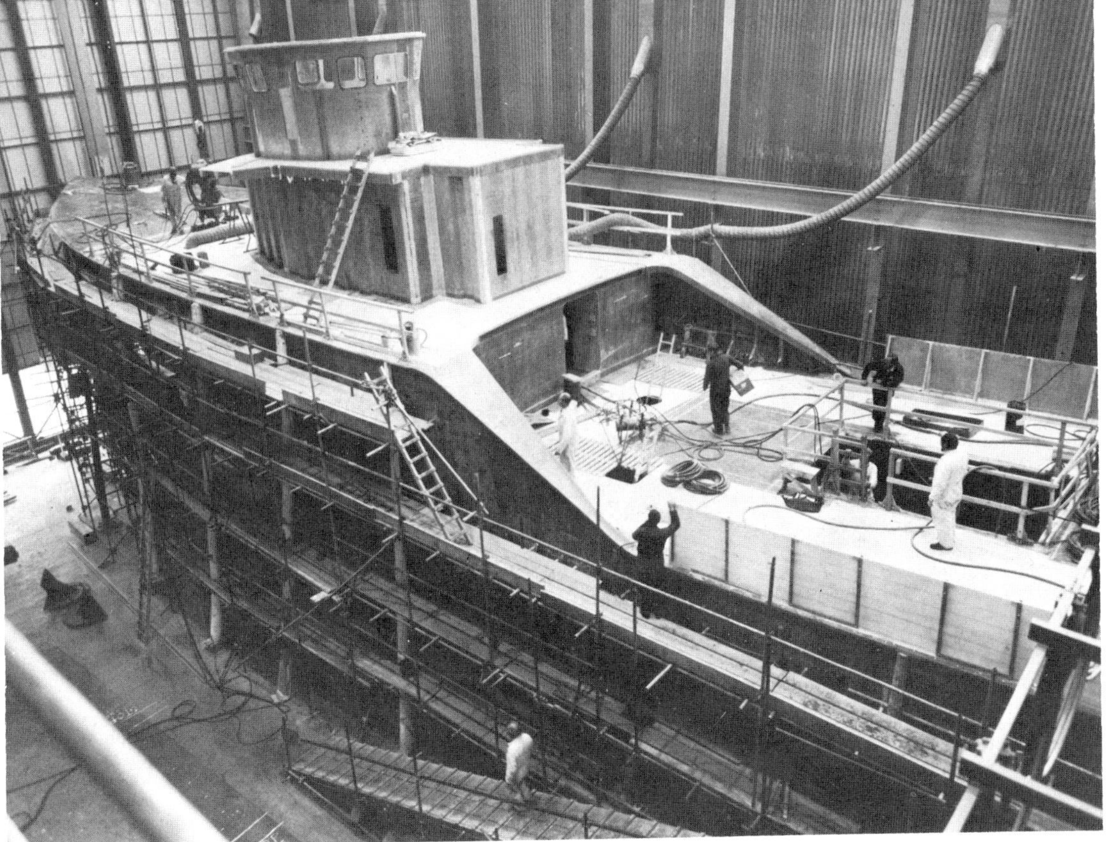

FOX PHOTOS/PICTORIAL PARADE

The HMS "Wilton," the world's largest glass-reinforced plastic ship, is under construction at Southampton, Eng. The 153-ft. Royal Navy minesweeper required 100,000 sq.yd. of fibre glass for construction.

sumption as well as increased investment activity helped to overcome those difficulties. Private investment rose appreciably in 1971, whereas public investment, although increasing too, lagged behind the target of the economic plan. Increased public spending on housing programs, civil engineering projects, and accelerated investment in the nationalized industries aimed at maintaining the rapid advance in the capital goods sector, and with a continued high level of consumption French manufacturing was expected to remain one of the fastest growing industries in Europe.

Italian industry was in a serious recession in 1971, and output fell by about 3%. In some sectors the decline was more severe, for example, the building and allied industries fell by 6%. Favourable currency realignment, massive sums pumped into public investment, and a general upturn of demand were expected to enable Italian industry to progress modestly during 1972.

Although considerable industrial gains were achieved in some of the moderately industrialized smaller European countries—such as Ireland, Yugoslavia, and especially Greece—the bulk of these nations suffered from the stagnation of their larger neighbours. Thus, the Belgian, Dutch, Swiss, and Austrian industries all registered lower growth rates in 1971 than in 1970, although the advance was still rapid in Austria. General stagnation in Sweden affected the Scandinavian countries. Output actually fell marginally in Finland and more markedly in Portugal. Spanish manufacturing output, which rose by about 10% in the two preceding years, also slowed down to a growth of 5% in 1971. Similarly depressed was production outside the industrial belt: although manufacturing activity continued to expand in India, Australia, and South Africa, the progress in 1971 lagged behind that in earlier years.

Industrial output in the U.S.S.R. rose in 1971 at the same rate, 8%, as in the previous year. In Eastern Europe, Romania remained the fastest growing country, although its 14% increase in 1970 was reduced to $10\frac{1}{2}\%$ in 1971. The Polish and Bulgarian industries continued their expansion at previous high rates; Hungary continued its rate of advance in 1971, while East Germany and Czechoslovakia slowed down.

Productivity rose rather fast in the major countries, with the exception of Italy. Rapidly rising wages caused managers to make their plants more efficient and led to labour-saving investments, resulting in a significant increase in output per hour worked in manufacturing. (G. F. RAY)

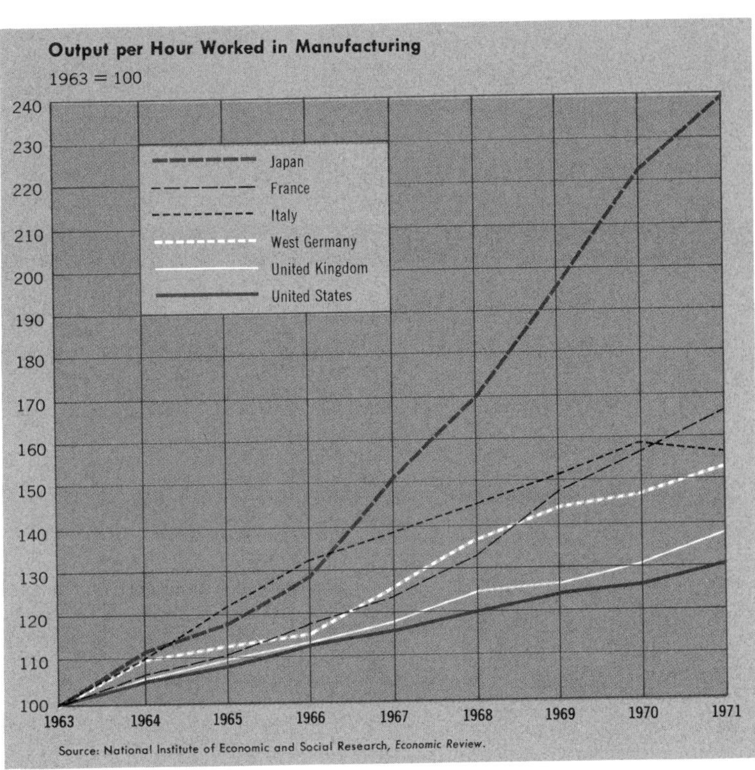

AEROSPACE

In 1972 the aerospace industry in the West began to expand, halting the severe decline that had occurred during 1970–71 as a result of the general economic climate and the slowdown of the Vietnam war. The main emphasis in Europe was on production of new civil aircraft, but there were reassuring signs that space programs in both the U.S. and Europe were beginning to revive after the shock of the Apollo program cutback.

Collaboration, a significant feature of the European aerospace industry since the late 1960s, was further intensified, with previously uncommitted airframe and engine manufacturers joining forces both inside and outside the European Economic Community on a variety of civil and military projects. There were also signs that this form of cooperation would extend to North America in the not-too-distant future.

Concorde, the Anglo-French supersonic transport, made by British Aircraft Corp. (BAC) and Aérospatiale France, received its first firm orders—totaling nine—from British and French airlines. Because of cost and environmental considerations U.S. airlines held off from placing orders. Britain's prototype of the Concorde flew a 40,000-mi., ten-nation sales promotion tour in June. In October the European airbus, the A-300B, made its first flight. This aircraft was a collaborative effort among airframe manufacturers in five Western European countries (France, Netherlands, Spain, U.K., West Germany) and was powered by turbofans made in the U.S.

Some of the other collaborative projects under way included: Europlane, a projected quiet, short takeoff and landing (QTOL) aircraft with up to 180 seats, which was being designed by Messerschmitt-Bölkow-Blohm (MBB) of West Germany, BAC, SAAB (Sweden), and Casa (Spain); Sepecat, the joint company formed by BAC and Dassault-Breguet (France), which was well into production with the Jaguar strike-trainer aircraft; Panavia (BAC, MBB, and Aeritalia of Italy), which was due to begin final assembly of the first of seven prototype MRCAs (multirole combat aircraft) in December; and Turbo-Union, a three-nation company (Rolls-Royce, Motoren-Turbinen-Union of West Germany, and Fiat of Italy), formed to develop and manufacture engines for multinational aircraft.

Following the crash of the first prototype VFW 614 (made by the Dutch-West German company VFW-Fokker) in February, modifications were made to the controls and rear fuselage. The second and third prototypes were then successfully test-flown, and production was expected to resume in early 1974. The Jetstream and Islander aircraft, products of two British companies that had been in financial difficulties in previous years, were confirmed during the year as best sellers under their new managements, Scottish Aviation and Fairey Britten-Norman. In fact the British aerospace industry as a whole did considerably better in terms of sales and exports in 1972 than in the previous two years.

One of the most important decisions affecting the U.S. industry was made on July 26 when NASA picked North American Rockwell as prime contractor for the space shuttle program, thus ending months of fierce competition for the award between that company, Grumman, Lockheed, and McDonnell-Douglas. It was estimated that between 6,000 and 10,000 firms would share the subcontract work, which would constitute 53% of the total project. Powered by three liquid-fueled rocket engines made by NAR Rocketdyne Division, the shuttle would carry up to 65,000 lb. of cargo into earth orbit and land in conventional aircraft fashion. The initial contract, valued at $540 million, was the biggest single dollar item in the U.S. space budget, and with the final Apollo mission completed in December the industry was in the process of changing to what became known as the post-Apollo phase. Apart from the shuttle, preeminence was given to unmanned spacecraft to investigate distant planets, communications satellites, and earth resource satellites. The latter two represented the tip of the iceberg for commercial exploitation of space flight as opposed to the national and military usage that had formerly been the backbone of the industry.

KEYSTONE

Europe's entry into the airbus "derby" made its first appearance on a Toulouse, France, airfield in October 1972. Built to compete with U.S. jumbo jets—the DC-10 and the L-1011—the A-300B was the product of an industrial consortium consisting of the major aircraft companies of France, West Germany, the Netherlands, Spain, and the U.K.

For the first time since 1968 military spending in the U.S. showed an increase, with most of the money being allocated for development of the Air Force NAR B-1 advanced manned strategic aircraft and the Navy undersea long-range missile system. Among new developments to reach the post-prototype stage was the Grumman F-14, while the McDonnell-Douglas F-15 first flew in July. Evaluation of the two close air support aircraft for the Air Force began in October—the competitors being the Northrop YA-9A and the Fairchild YA-10A. The Navy ordered 13 Lockheed S-3A Viking antisubmarine aircraft, worth $121 million, in May.

In September the U.S. Congress approved the expenditure of $127 million for the first four of six Boeing 747s, which were to be used to set up the Advanced Airborne National Command Post. This completed a cycle begun with the Boeing KC-135 aerial tanker, later developed into the civil 707. With the 747 the situation was reversed, a highly successful civil design finding a military role. Because the airlines had increasing load factors during the year the commercial aircraft market leveled off from its decline in the previous two years, in terms of both sales and manpower requirements. Deliveries of the rival trijets, the DC-10 and L-1011 TriStar, went ahead as planned, but there was a further hardening of the market in favour of quieter, cleaner aircraft and short takeoff projects, although no new civil aircraft of these types made a first appearance.

In the largest commercial transaction between the U.S. and China since the end of World War II, the Boeing Co. signed an agreement to sell 10 Boeing 707s and related equipment to Peking for about $150 million. The deal climaxed five months of negotiations, and China was expected to take possession of the jets almost immediately.

(JOHN BENTLEY)

AUTOMOBILES

Traditional patterns of evolution in the automobile industry receded still further into history during 1972. Spending for styling changes as a stimulus to sales continued to decline because a still higher proportion of the total resources available for product development and retooling had to be used to comply with the new safety standards and emission requirements imposed by government agencies. Increases in mechanical complexity, structural weight, and manufacturing cost were unwelcome results. Although the United States continued to set the pace, similar trends were followed in almost every country where cars and trucks were made in large numbers. Worldwide interest was also expressed in conferences and displays concerned with solving the problems of urban transportation, of which Transpo 72, staged at Dulles International Airport (near Washington, D.C.), was the outstanding example.

The continued refusal of the U.S. Environmental Protection Agency to delay the enforcement of new and extremely stringent emission regulations beyond 1975 intensified the research for catalysts and other devices both in the U.S. and in Europe. The development of alternatives to the piston engine was also stepped up, and in August Richard C. Gerstenberg, board chairman of General Motors Corp., announced that progress with the Wankel rotary engine had reached a point where "a commitment will be made for limited manufacturing facilities and tools." He considered that the introduction of the engine as an option for the Chevrolet Vega might be made in about two years. Later reports by GM were even more optimistic. Concurrently, Ford Motor Co. disclosed that it had reached an agreement with N. V. Philips Co. of Eindhoven, Neth., and U.S. Philips Corp. of New York to exploit the Stirling engine, in which combustion is continuous instead of intermittent. The development of the Wankel and other new automobile power plants smaller than the engines in general use for many years was looked upon by U.S. automobile manufacturers as an economic trade-off between the substantially cheaper production costs of such new engines and the anticipated higher costs of manufacturing safer automobiles according to increasingly stringent government specifications.

A more immediate problem for car makers was to find methods for reducing the emission of oxides of nitrogen, which had been added to the list of restricted pollutants by a U.S. regulation that became effective at the start of the 1973 model year (fall 1972). Manufacturers found it necessary to recirculate a controlled proportion of the exhaust gases back into the air/fuel mixture entering the engine; this procedure cut back the formation of oxides of nitrogen during the combustion process by reducing peak flame temperatures. Other automatic devices had to be added in order to preserve reasonable "driveability" and assure proper ignition.

There was greater public appeal in the new energy-absorbing bumpers, which (by law) were required to enable 1973-model cars to survive a frontal barrier impact at 5 mph (or a rear-end impact at 2½ mph) without damage to lamps, cooling system, steering, brakes, or other essential parts. Several methods evolved for meeting this requirement, all involving some degree of clearance to allow the bumper to retract, on impact, without striking the adjacent sheet metal. In the Delco "Enersorber" system, used on a number of models by GM and American Motors, the massive front bumper was backed by hydraulic pistons, which permitted a travel of several inches on impact; compressed nitrogen gas was used to return the bumper to its normal location.

GM's program for 1973 included a number of new models ranging from the luxury class to a "hatchback" coupe for the Chevrolet Nova, with a swing-up rear door. The Omega was introduced as an important addition to the Oldsmobile line, selling in the "compact" class. Pontiac announced a new intermediate-sized sports model.

The full-sized Fords were changed extensively for 1973 with a new grill, impact-absorbing bumpers, and a new instrument panel. Power front disc brakes were standardized on all full-sized models. Among a number of new engineering features, Chrysler announced that all models would be equipped with steel beams within the side doors (beginning Jan. 1, 1973) to give increased protection against side impacts. Induction-hardened exhaust-valve seats, a new choke control responsive to ambient temperature, and a coolant reserve system (preventing water loss) were other Chrysler innovations.

Statistics available for the first eight months of 1972 showed a slight drop in U.S. automobile production, compared with the equivalent period in 1971, but a substantial increase in the production of commercial vehicles (1,780,000 against 1,530,000). Comparable Canadian production figures reflected a slight increase in cars and a 12% gain in commercial vehicles. In making these comparisons it must be noted that 1971 production figures were high in both Canada and the U.S.

Varying results were reported from the main European manufacturing countries for the first half of 1972. The United Kingdom, France, and Italy all showed substantial gains in automobile production, varying from 9 to 13%, compared with the first half of 1971; Sweden showed only a small gain, and West Germany a small decrease. Opel's share of the new cars registered in West Germany during the first half of 1972 exceeded Volkswagen's share for the first time (262,447 against 241,030). In the U.K., cutbacks in the purchase tax (*see* TAXATION) and the removal of credit restrictions resulted in the biggest expansion of car sales in Europe.

With the exception of France and Sweden, the production of commercial vehicles decreased slightly in European countries during the first half of 1972. The U.K. maintained its lead as the major European exporter of commercial vehicles, and the British motor industry expected to benefit from the progressive reduction in EEC truck tariffs (currently 22%) that would follow Britain's entry into the EEC.

European statutory requirements with regard to safety in car design and pollutants in exhaust gases, while by no means negligible, did not increase in numbers or severity at the tempo reached in the U.S. Some success was achieved in standardizing the legal measures enacted in EEC countries (soon to include the United Kingdom, Denmark, and Ireland), and countries outside the Community tended to fall into line. The outstanding exception was Sweden, which continued to be strongly influenced by U.S. policies.

Small cars weighing less than 1,800 lb., with engine displacements of between 0.9 and 1.8 litres (55 and 110 cu.in.), continued to account for a high proportion of the total sales in most European markets and posed technical problems that differed in many respects from those that applied to the larger U.S. vehicles. Quick steering response, directional stability, and effective brakes—all directed toward avoidance of accidents—took precedence in Europe over attempts to make passengers immune from collision damage. The experimental safety vehicles (ESVs) built by Daimler Benz, BMW, Volkswagen, Volvo (and also Toyota and Datsun of Japan) were all larger cars of a size commercially less important in Europe and Japan than the small automobile. However, Fiat, with a domestic market in which the percentage sale of very small cars remained exceptionally high, developed an interesting safety version of its little 500 model and found that the weight was increased by 46% and the estimated cost by 40%.

Of the relatively small number of new European cars introduced during 1972, two important low-priced examples were the Renault 5 and the Peugeot 104; each had four-cylinder, one-litre engines and front-wheel drive. The Renault had a two-door sedan body with a tailgate; the Peugeot was a more conventional four-door sedan. A novel Renault feature was the use of fibreglass plastic moldings to shield the front and rear sheet metal, in place of conventional bumpers. Immunity from damage up to impact speeds of 7 kph (4.35 mph) was claimed. Peugeot developed an extremely compact transverse engine and transmission unit for its 104 in which aluminum alloy die-castings were used extensively.

In the larger two-litre car class, GM's two subsidiaries—the West German Opel and British Vauxhall—announced new Rekord and Victor models early in the year; they had certain resemblances but did not reflect the close coordination of model policy and design that Ford established between its British and German products. Ford's principal move was to replace the top-of-the-line Zodiac and Taunus models with a new Granada/Consul series having slightly smaller overall dimensions but adequate seating space. Later in the year, Opel offered a 2.1-litre diesel engine (primarily designed for a van) as an option for the Rekord passenger car, the first challenge to Mercedes-Benz in this field. There were two important announcements by Mercedes-Benz—a new high-performance, six-cylinder engine with twin overhead camshafts and a new "S-class" line to replace its big-car range; size and weight were both increased. Audi introduced a new front-drive Model 80 in August with a novel stabilized steering system claimed to aid the driver to maintain control in the event of a tire blowout. Volkswagen in the fall announced changes to the Beetle 1303, of which the most important were a curved windshield and padded instrument panel.

Jaguar's V-12 engine, previously available only in the E-type sports car, made its predicted debut in the XJ sedan model in July. Station wagons were added to the Hillman Avenger line by Chrysler and to the Morris Marina by British Leyland. The latter corporation also introduced new six-cylinder versions of its 1800 series of medium-sized, front-drive cars, with the engine located transversely. Lotus announced a new high-performance, low-emission, four-cylinder engine, with four valves per cylinder, for use in a Jensen-Healey sports car as well as in its own model line. Borg-Warner introduced an entirely new four-speed automatic transmission expressly designed for small cars with engines of one to two litres displacement and manufactured in the firm's British

Table III. Production and Exports of Motor Vehicles by the Principal Producing Countries
In 000 units

Country	1969		1970		1971	
	Passenger cars	Commercial vehicles	Passenger cars	Commercial vehicles	Passenger cars	Commercial vehicles
Production						
United States	8,224.3	1,980.7	6,550.2	1,733.4	8,583.7	2,088.0
Japan	2,611.5	2,062.8	3,178.7	2,110.4	3,717.9	2,092.9
Germany, West	3,312.5	292.0	3,527.9	314.4	3,696.8	285.9
France	2,168.5	290.6	2,458.0	292.0	2,694.0	316.3
United Kingdom	1,717.0	465.7	1,641.0	457.5	1,741.9	456.2
Italy	1,477.4	185.6	1,719.7	134.5	1.701.1	116.0
Canada	1,035.4	314.4	937.2	250.2	1,096.1	276.0
Australia	371.1	80.7	391.9	81.8	391.2	78.9
Sweden	242.9	27.8	279.0	31.2	287.4	29.7
U.S.S.R.	293.6	550.7	344.0	572.0	518.0	612.0
Other countries*	1,830.0		1,412.3	520.7	1,604.9	559.1
World total	29,535.2		22,439.9	6,498.1	26,033.0	6,911.0
Exports						
Germany, West	1,875.1	164.3	1,934.5	177.7	2,155.9	163.2
United Kingdom	771.6	181.2	690.3	172.3	721.1	194.7
France	787.5	56.6	1,061.3	65.9	1,148.6	65.4
Italy	594.6	35.5	632.1	38.9	640.2	40.3
United States	333.4	103.5	285.0	92.7	386.6	99.1
Sweden	141.8	18.8	186.5	24.0	212.5	23.4
Japan	560.4	297.6	788.9	306.1	1,299.4	479.7
Canada	714.5	409.7	733.2	430.9	822.3	390.7

*A reliable breakdown between cars and commercial vehicles was not available for "Other countries" until 1970.

Source: British Society of Motor Manufacturers and Traders, *The Motor Industry of Great Britain*.

plants. Production of a three-speed version of the new mechanism began in midyear at the Borg-Warner plant in Japan.

During the first half of 1972, automobile production in Japan increased by 10% (a relatively low figure), and commercial vehicle production showed little change; in each case the comparison was related to the first half of 1971. In order to compensate for the much-reduced growth rate of domestic sales, a phenomenal increase in export sales was achieved in 1971, an effort that was continued in 1972. A main attack in Europe was made in Switzerland, traditionally an important market for West German vehicles. In the U.K., some success resulted from marketing the Datsun Cherry and Toyota Carina in the low-priced area.

One of the most interesting of the new Japanese cars introduced during the year was the Honda Civic, a small two-door, hatchback sedan with a modern overhead camshaft, four-cylinder engine arranged transversely and driving the front wheels. Aluminum die-castings were used for the cylinder block and head. This size of car, with an overall length of 134 in., was more practical than the diminutive minicars, which had declined in popularity in Japan and were not well-suited to export markets.

Japanese cars had sufficient impact in the Australian market to prompt a decision to raise tariffs on imported vehicle components unless at least 85% of the completed vehicle was made in Australia, beginning in 1975. In September, Nissan responded by announcing that it would build new plants for manufacturing engines and for assembling vehicles in Australia at a probable cost of $A100 million. This was a challenge for GM-Holden, Ford, Chrysler, and British Leyland in a market that remained almost static in 1972. (MAURICE PLATT)

BUILDING AND CONSTRUCTION

Expenditures for new construction in the United States during 1972 were estimated at $122 billion, compared with the previous record outlay of $109 billion in 1971. This represented an annual increase of almost 12% compared with the previous year's gain of 16%. It appeared, however, that the rate of inflation would not be as great in 1972 as in the previous year and that the real increase in construction would compare favourably with that in 1971.

The primary factor contributing to the record dollar outlay in 1971 was the housing boom. In that year 2,050,000 private units were started, accounting for expenditures of $34 billion and representing 66% of the gain in outlays for all new construction. The housing boom continued into 1972, and it appeared that the number of residential starts would be 290,000 greater than in 1971, bringing the total to 2,340,000 units. Contributing to the continuation of the boom in 1972 was the ready availability of financing for new home construction. While the major part of the new home construction was made up of single-family units, a large volume of multiunit structures was being built to meet the need for low-rent housing.

Mobile home shipments in 1970–72 totaled about 20% of all housing starts in the U.S. The rapid growth of the mobile home industry was due to a number of factors, including the relatively low price of the homes and the increasing availability of funds from financial institutions to finance their purchase. While the prices of conventional homes were increasing rapidly, the mobile home cost per square foot remained relatively stable in 1971 and 1972.

The expected 12% gain in expenditures for new construction was due primarily to private rather than to public building. The outlays for public construction in 1972 were expected to be at about the same level as in 1971 when they were $29.8 billion. While, as noted, the greatest gain in the private sector was due to the increase in residential building, a gain of 5% was expected in nonresidential construction. Inflation continued as a deterrent to industrial construction in 1972; outlays declined 19% from the low level attained in 1971 when they had amounted to only $5.4 billion. However, spending for commercial buildings rose 20%, and it appeared that it would equal the $13.9 billion of 1971.

In June 1972, the U.S. Department of Commerce composite construction cost index was 138 (1967 = 100), an increase of 2.2% over the December 1971 figure of 135. This was, however, a more favourable situation than the 5.6% increase during the first six months of 1971. It appeared that the wage-price freeze in August 1971, which continued during Phase One of Pres. Richard Nixon's new economic program, had some dampening effect on price increases, but the continued boom in residential construction was exerting new pressures on prices during 1972—especially the prices of softwood lumber, selected hardwood lumber, and plywood.

In Canada the gross national product increased at a rate of about 6% in 1972. Contributing importantly to this growth was a housing boom that began in 1971 and continued into 1972. In the U.K. the output of the construction industry had declined in 1969 and 1970, but in 1971 this trend was stopped and a slight upturn occurred. The outlook for 1972 was better, and the expectation was that the industry as a whole would grow as a result of private residential building. In Japan building construction declined largely as a result of the downturn in investment in manufacturing and other industrial building.

Industrial investment in France was expected to rise about 5% in 1972 over the previous year. To continue the real growth in the economy the government made plans for increases in public spending. Housing and civil engineering projects received the biggest boosts in funds. In West Germany in 1972 the economy was recovering from the recession of 1971, during which industrial and manufacturing investments had declined and the construction industry had slumped. (CARTER C. OSTERBIND)

CHEMICALS

After several lacklustre years, chemical industries in developed countries throughout the world indicated a return to earlier growth rates during the first three quarters of 1972. The U.S. industry, traditionally the leading barometer of chemical activity, registered sharp gains during the first part of 1972. Shipments of chemicals and allied products, according to the U.S. Department of Commerce, amounted to $52,170,000,000 in 1971, 6% higher than the $49,253,000,000 shipped in 1970. During the first five months of 1972, chemical shipments (seasonally adjusted) were $23,120,000,000, 9% higher than the $21,164,000,000 worth of shipments recorded for the same period in 1971. The Federal Reserve Index of Chemical Production, which averaged 126.4 (1967 = 100) in 1971, climbed steadily during the first six months of 1972, reaching 139.5 in June.

Better demand for chemical products permitted higher plant operating rates, which in turn helped stabilize or improve chemical prices somewhat. The U.S. Department of Labor's *Index of Wholesale Prices for Chemicals and Allied Products* averaged 102.2 (1967 = 100) in 1970 and then rose to 104.2 in 1971. Although it dipped slightly in the first quarter of 1972, it started to increase slightly in the second quarter, reaching 104.3 in June.

A more favourable economic climate indicated a high level of capital investment for new plant and equipment by the U.S. chemical industry. The U.S. Department of Commerce reported that capital expenditures by the chemical industry in 1970 and 1971 were $3,440,000,000 in each year. In the March 1972 *Survey of Current Business,* chemical investment in 1972 was forecast to drop marginally to $3,430,000,000. But indications were that companies were raising their sights as business improved and that 1972 might prove a record year.

At the end of the third quarter of 1972, the U.S. chemical industry was looking to a mixture of promises and problems for 1973 and beyond. Among the problems it had to face were tighter controls on emissions from chemical plants and more rigid control over the manufacture and sale of chemical products. The new regulations were expected to increase significantly the cost of doing business. The much-discussed energy crisis would have a severe impact on chemical production. The industry was the largest single user of electricity in the U.S., accounting for approximately 30% of all the electricity generated. It also depended upon natural gas, particularly on the Gulf Coast, both as a raw material (to make methanol, ammonia, hydrogen, acetylene, and carbon black) and as a fuel. Natural gas liquids were the principal raw materials used to make ethylene, the important chemical building block. Projections indicated that the cost of energy would triple along the Gulf Coast through the 1970s. This would mean higher costs and perhaps even some curtailment for chemical operations.

On the bright side of the chemical ledger were a number of entries. Many of the environmental and energy problems, for example, were ones that the chemical industry appeared technologically equipped to solve. Although the situation on automotive emissions remained cloudy through the first three quarters of 1972, it appeared that a catalytic muffler would be required on 1975 model cars. The device, installed in the exhaust system of the car, would catalytically convert unburned hydrocarbons and carbon monoxide into carbon dioxide and water. For 1976 models, restrictions on nitrogen oxide emissions from new cars would require either an improved catalytic muffler or an extra one. A number of chemical companies had spent years in development of suitable catalysts for the task. The leading candidates for the 1975 models appeared to be supported noble metals (metals resistant to high-temperature oxidation). For example, small amounts of platinum deposited on the surface of a refractory material showed considerable promise.

Many of the problems in the energy area also seemed to lend themselves to solution by chemical means. Included were the reduction of sulfur dioxide emissions from stack gases; production of SNG (substitute natural gas) from either petroleum liquids or coal; harnessing of solar energy for large-scale electricity generation; the development of a practical breeder reactor (in which more fissionable fuel is produced than is consumed); and demonstration of the scientific practicality of generating electricity from nuclear fusion (as in the H-bomb) rather than nuclear fission (as in the atomic bomb).

For the U.S. a better rapport with the Soviet Union in international affairs seemed to offer opportunities for increased trade as well. In 1971 the U.S. exported only $40 million worth of chemicals to the U.S.S.R. By contrast, in that same year, U.S. chemical exports to Canada amounted to $600 million. Indirectly, an agreement on grain reached during 1972 was expected to help U.S. chemical companies. The Soviets agreed to buy $750 million worth of U.S. grain over a three-year period. Producing that much grain in the U.S., it was estimated, would require $100 million in the form of fertilizer and pesticides.

In the fall of 1972, the Organization for Economic Cooperation and Development presented a broad picture of the non-Communist world's chemical industry in *Chemical Industry—1970/1971*. The agency pointed out that precise comparisons between countries cannot be made because of differences in definitions and methods of accounting. The report did, however, permit an approximate comparison. It showed that world chemical sales in industrialized countries were $109,390,000,000 in 1970, 6% higher than 1969 sales of $103,240,000,000. The U.S. industry was the largest with $49,-253,000,000 in sales in 1970. However, that represented only a 1.2% increase over the preceding year. European member countries combined posted sales of $45.1 billion in 1970, a 10% increase over 1969. Japan's chemical sales rose 12.8% in 1970 to $12.9 billion, while Canada's sales increased less than 1% in 1970 to $2,050,000,000.

(DONALD P. BURKE)

ELECTRICAL

The growth rate of demand for electricity slowed down in many countries in 1971–72, and manufacturers of electrical plant and apparatus regarded trading prospects for 1973 with little optimism. Although provisional world trade figures indicated a recovery in domestic electrical appliance sales, more manufacturers of industrial electrical equipment reported that they were working below capacity.

In 1971 the U.S., the world's largest exporter of electrical equipment and apparatus, accounted for 21.2% of the total electrical exports by non-Communist countries. West Germany was second with 18.5%, followed by Japan with 17.2% and Britain, 8.8%. Over the previous four years the U.S. share of the total value of electrical exports had been falling and the Japanese share rising rapidly. West German and British shares had remained fairly static.

West Germany faced a minor economic recession with cutbacks in both capital and consumer spending coupled with a high rate of inflation. The output of its electrical industry in 1971 was 5.7% higher than in 1970, but the 1970 output had been 17.6% over that of 1969. Although many companies had reported healthy order books in the first half of 1972, the orders received were mainly from domestic customers and there was some pessimism over the immediate outlook for exports. In Britain too the majority of companies reported that their 1972 export orders were either static or down. However, British manufacturers were more optimistic than their West German counterparts about future prospects.

The U.S. electrical and electronic manufacturing industry was expected to grow at the low rate of 7.5 to 8% a year over the next decade, according to a report by the Institute of Electrical and Electronic Engineers. The report said that U.S. government spending in domestic areas would probably not offset the decreases in military and space spending until at least 1980. Engineering employment in the industry would increase at a rate of not more than 2% a year, and probably the most effective approach for broadening U.S. technical employment opportunities would be to develop maximum trade among nations.

Forecasting the future pattern of international trading activities at the end of 1972 was hazardous because of the unpredictable effects of the widening of the EEC. Also important was the growing public concern with environmental issues. This led, among other things, to a delay in the construction of power stations.

Because of the high atmospheric pollution associated with large coal- and oil-fired power stations, the first of a number of combined steam-gas cycle stations was ordered in the U.S. late in 1971. These stations, with their higher efficiency, required less fuel and less cooling water than the traditional type, but their design was such that larger numbers of generators that were much smaller than those previously produced were required. For transmission systems, compact metal-clad switchgear, less obtrusive and noisy than the conventional air-blast breaker, rapidly became the preferred standard design. Technical changes and the modifications in world trading patterns created by the enlargement of the EEC made it difficult for heavy power plant manufacturers in the U.S. to formulate their future expansion policies with any degree of confidence.

The electrical manufacturing industry in Europe faced additional problems. British manufacturers, who over the past few years had been successfully increasing their exports to EEC countries at the expense of their historical markets, did not expect EEC membership to make any further expansion easy. Prior to Britain's joining the EEC on Jan. 1, 1973, British electrical companies began buying their way into Europe by purchasing majority holdings in continental companies. EEC countries invested in Britain to a somewhat lesser extent, but all these activities were at a fairly low level and no large multinational groupings emerged despite encouragement by governments on both sides of the English Channel. In Britain and France considerable streamlining of the electrical industry had taken place over the past few years, and it had become obvious that the establishment of one or two pan-European companies was essential in order to compete in world markets on equal terms with the U.S. giants such as General Electric and Westinghouse.

In June 1972 a stockholders' meeting of the Italian Industrie Riunite Elettrodomestici (IRE) ratified an agreement between Philips of the Netherlands and Giovanni Borghi of Italy, under which complete control of Italy's largest refrigerator manufacturer was ceded to the Dutch. Italy's other chief manufacturer of electric household appliances, Zanussi of Pordenone, having faced financial difficulties and labour troubles, was completely reorganized, with West Germany's Allgemeine Elektricitäts Gesellschaft (AEG) securing 25% of the shares. In the meantime, Westinghouse, among others, was active in acquiring manufacturing facilities in Europe, and few observers doubted that within the next year or two a new pattern of international trade in the electrical industry would emerge from the commercial agreements made with or by European companies.

The recent feverish activity in the commercial areas of the electrical industry was emphasized by a notable lack of information on technical developments. Reduced research budgets and increased reluctance to disclose data on innovations in view of the increasingly competitive world markets were to blame. However, the Soviets disclosed plans to put a prototype superconducting cable into operation in 1975. Superconducting cables operate at extremely low temperatures at which the resistance of the wires to the flow of electric current virtually disappears. A 12-m. (39.4 ft.) length of an experimental cable designed to carry 10,000 amp., cooled by liquid helium, was tested in Moscow. By 1990, the Soviets believed that superconducting cables would be used both to carry power from very large nuclear stations to urban areas and to store energy at night to meet peak demands during the day by tapping electric currents circulating in loss-free coils.

(T. C. J. COGLE)

GLASS

Glass industries throughout the world reported increased activity in 1972. Rising standards of living meant growing demand for window glass, automobile windshields, and glass containers. In the U.K., United Glass Ltd., having completed its $2.6 million program at Alloa, Scot., announced a further investment of $6.2 million in glass-container production. The U.S. Corning Glass Works attributed its improved performance to greater plant efficiency and faster translation of development projects to the marketplace.

Pilkington Brothers Ltd. planned a $1.2 million plant in the U.K. to manufacture solar-control glass with highly reflective surfaces, the fastest growing market for flat glass. Pilkington was to develop the first float-glass plant in Australia, together with Australian Consolidated Industries. Moss Glasværk, Norway, announced a $5 million extension to its glass-container plant, and the Yugoslav glassworks at Paracin and Pancevo in Serbia reported major reconstruction work to improve output of containers and rolled glass.

Environmental matters continued to receive attention, ranging from the utilization of raw materials and fuel to the disposal of products. The basic raw materials of glass—sand, sodium carbonate, and limestone—are among the most commonly found on the earth's surface, but fuel presented a different problem. The glass industry was dependent on gas and oil; experiments in using electricity were made, but, although conventional oil- or gas-fired furnaces were frequently boosted by electricity, electric melting was still rare. Although cleaner and conducive to better working conditions, it was more expensive, and effective utilization of electricity would require radical alterations in furnace design. Investigations into the reclamation of used glass (cullet) continued. Large-scale experiments in the use of cullet as a road-surfacing material were carried out in the U.S., and in the U.K. cullet-utilization projects were discussed with a number of research establishments.

Glass manufacturers became involved in developing equipment for atmospheric control. Pittsburgh Plate Glass was working on a glass-fibre "agglomerator" for filtering out undesirable particles from automobile-exhaust systems. Glass-ceramic rotary heat exchangers for gas turbine engines, developed by Corning, made more economical use of fuel, resulting in lower levels of unburned hydrocarbons and carbon monoxide.

In France, Boussois Souchon Neuvesel gained control of Glaverbel, the largest glass company in Belgium. This meant that BSN controlled about 65% of the European production of building glass. BSN also reported considerable success in the container market, having meshed its food and beverage industry and its glass interests.

To protect a prestige industry, the Belgian government nationalized Cristalleries du Val Saint-Lambert. The company had run into serious financial difficulties and control might have gone overseas. Owens-Illinois, Inc., increased its holding in United Glass Ltd., becoming an equal partner with the Distillers Company Ltd.

Libby-Owens-Ford Co. developed a glass coating for the windows of the Mariner 9 spacecraft that was resistant to moisture and harmful chemicals in the atmosphere and protected the cameras from infrared rays. (CYRIL WEEDEN)

IRON AND STEEL

World steel production was estimated to have risen in 1972 to 628 million metric tons, about 8% more than 1971. This increase represented a resumption of the annual upward trend in output, which had taken place every year since World War II until 1971, when output fell below the previous year's level. World trade in steel during the year was, on the other hand, at about the same rate as in 1971, approximately 90 million metric gross product tons.

The year 1972 marked a turning point in the world steel market, with the emergence from a period of depression that had persisted since the latter part of 1970. The year opened with demand at a low ebb in most of the major steel-producing and consuming countries in the non-Communist world. This was mainly a consequence of the continuing effects of the various deflationary measures that had been introduced in 1970 in many countries, but it was exacerbated by the reduction of stocks of steel by consumers throughout 1971. As the year progressed, signs of an upturn in demand began to appear, although the timing and extent of the improvement varied substantially from country to country. By the end of 1972 the outlook was more encouraging.

Price levels both in domestic and international markets in 1972 remained at an unsatisfactory level both from the point of view of generating adequate funds for reinvestment and also for meeting the increasing costs of raw materials and labour. The continuing poor level of prices was in part due to market pressures in a situation where capacity exceeded demand, but it was also influenced by national policies of price restraint in, for example, the U.S. and U.K.

Because of the excess capacity throughout the world, producers in the traditional steelmaking countries noted with some anxiety the growth of capacity in the developing countries, which in some cases had been suppliers of raw materials. While understanding the natural desire of these countries both to upgrade their exports from raw materials to semifinished and finished steel products, and to aim at self-sufficiency in steel, the traditional producers had become increasingly conscious of the dangers of excessive capacity.

In the difficult international steel market situation that prevailed throughout the year, an important development was the voluntary restraint of exports to the U.S. undertaken by Japanese and European steel producers, and the voluntary restraint of exports to Europe by Japanese producers. There were further developments during the year in the field of international trade policy which affected steel. The final reduction in the Kennedy Round program of tariff cuts took place on January 1 in many countries. This marked the completion of a series of reductions that had done much to reduce tariff barriers among the principal steel-producing and trading countries, and to bring about a measure of harmonization of tariff rates. Further important changes in tariff relationships were in prospect, however, with the enlargement of the EEC by the membership of Denmark, Ireland, and the U.K. as of Jan. 1, 1973.

Steel production in the U.S. in 1972 was estimated at 120 million tons, 10% above the output in the previous year. Demand for steel in the U.S. recovered early in the year, largely as a result of the growth in expenditure on durable consumer goods, particularly automobiles. Stocks of steel in consumers' hands also stabilized, with a decrease in the first half of the year being balanced by some rebuilding in the second half.

Capital expenditure on investment projects in the U.S. steel industry was about 7% down from the 1971 level. Imports of steel for 1972 were estimated to have been slightly less than the 1971 record level, reflecting the voluntary restraint of deliveries to the U.S. market by Japanese and European steel producers.

Japanese steel output in 1972 was estimated at 93 million tons, 5% above the previous year. This increase marked the recovery of the Japanese domestic economy from a period of stagnation that had persisted since the latter part of 1970. The recovery itself was based on growth in public investment and housing, and increased spending on durable consumer goods. The profitability of the Japanese steel industry continued to suffer from a combination of increasing production costs and a relatively poor level of prices. Investment in new plants was, however, maintained at the same rate as in the previous year.

Steel output in the European Coal and Steel Community was estimated at 110 million tons, nearly 6% above the output in 1971. The recovery in demand in the Community started early in the year with an upturn in general economic conditions. The principal impetus behind the recovery was the increased spending on consumer durables; in the steel-intensive capital goods sector, improvement in demand was not generally apparent even by the end of the year. The general financial situation of the Community steel industries was unsatisfactory in spite of domestic price increases during the year. Investment in capital projects was lower than the previous year's figures in West Germany, Belgium, and the Netherlands, but in France and Italy there were substantial increases over 1971 investment.

Production of steel in the U.K. was estimated at 25 million tons, about the same as in 1971. The British economy began to expand during the first half of the year, prin-

Table IV. World Production of Pig Iron and Blast Furnace Ferroalloys
In 000 metric tons

Country	1967	1968	1969	1970	1971
World	351,630	˙376,320	407,420	426,030	423,060
U.S.	78,910	80,540	86,620	83,320	74,120
U.S.S.R.	74,810	78,790	81,630	85,930	89,300
Japan	40,090	46,400	58,150	68,050	72,250
Germany, West	27,270	30,310	33,760	33,630	29,990
United Kingdom	15,400	16,700	16,650	17,670	12,170
France	15,710	16,450	18,210	19,220	18,350
China*	15,000	15,500	16,000	16,000	19,000
Belgium	8,900	10,370	11,210	10,840	10,390
Italy	7,310	7,840	7,780	8,330	8,540
Canada	6,310	7,600	6,770	8,280	7,820
India	6,890	7,290	7,190*	6,900	6,670
Czechoslovakia	6,820	6,920	7,040	7,620	8,070
Poland	6,330	6,640	7,030	7,300	7,500
Australia†	4,970	5,290	5,800	6,150	6,130
Luxembourg†	3,960	4,310	4,870	4,810	4,590
South Africa	3,470	3,830	3,930	3,930	4,010
Brazil†	2,960	3,350	3,700	4,200	4,740
Romania	2,460	2,990	3,490	4,210	4,380
Netherlands†	2,590	2,820	3,460	3,590	3,760
Spain†	2,680	2,780	3,330	4,160	4,830
Sweden	2,360	2,490	2,500	2,610	2,570
Austria†	2,140	2,470	2,820	2,960	2,850
Germany, East	2,530	2,330	2,100	2,000	2,030
Korea, North*	1,800	1,800	1,800	2,200	2,300
Hungary	1,670	1,650	1,760	1,840	1,990
Mexico†	1,290	1,600	1,700	1,660	1,690
Yugoslavia†	1,180	1,200	1,200	1,270	1,510
Bulgaria	1,240	1,080	1,120	1,200	1,330
Finland	1,040	1,140	1,230	1,210	1,010
Norway	640	670	680	680	630

*Estimated.
†Pig iron only.
Source: British Steel Corporation.

Table V. World Production of Crude Steel
In 000 metric tons

Country	1967	1968	1969	1970	1971	1972 Year to date	1972 No. of months	1972 Annual rate	Percent change 1972-71
World	496,010	528,440	571,620	593,610	580,200	...	...	610,950	...
U.S.*	115,410	119,260	127,980	119,140	109,270	79,130	8	118,700	+ 8.6
U.S.S.R.	102,240	106,530	110,290	115,820	120,640	41,500	4	124,500	+ 3.2
Japan	62,150	66,890	82,170	93,320	88,560	61,680	8	92,520	+ 4.5
Germany, West	36,740	41,160	45,320	45,040	40,310	28,712	8	43,068	+ 6.8
U.K.	24,280	26,280	26,850	28,320	24,180	18,438	9	24,584	+ 1.7
France	19,660	20,410	22,510	23,770	22,860	15,642	8	23,463	+ 2.7
Italy	15,890	16,960	16,430	17,260	17,450	13,029	8	19,543	+12.0
China†	14,000	15,000	16,000	18,000	21,000	...	...	22,000†	+ 4.8
Belgium	9,710	11,570	12,840	12,610	12,440	9,404	8	14,106	+13.4
Poland	10,410	11,010	11,290	11,790	12,690	4,487	4	13,460	+ 6.1
Czechoslovakia	10,000	10,560	10,820	11,480	12,070	5,367	5	12,880	+ 6.7
Canada	8,800	10,210	9,350	11,200	12,050	5,120	5	12,290	+ 2.0
India	6,330	6,510	6,500	6,230	5,830	...	...	6,200†	+ 6.3
Australia	6,290	6,470	6,690	6,820	6,740	3,047	6	6,090	− 9.6
Sweden	4,770	5,090	5,330	5,480	5,270	2,759	6	5,520	+ 4.7
Spain	4,510	4,920	5,990	7,390	7,780	4,550	6	9,100	+16.8
Luxembourg	4,480	4,830	5,520	5,460	5,240	3,618	8	5,427	+ 3.6
Romania	4,090	4,750	5,540	6,520	6,800	...	...	6,900†	+ 1.5
Brazil	3,670	4,440	4,900	5,390	6,000	1,506	3	6,020	+ 0.3
Germany, East	4,650	4,700	5,140	5,050	5,750	910	2	5,460	− 5.0
South Africa	3,700	4,050	4,620	4,750	4,740	2,162	5	5,190	+ 9.5
Netherlands	3,400	3,710	4,710	5,030	5,080	3,684	8	5,526	+ 8.8
Austria	3,020	3,470	3,930	4,080	3,960	1,987	6	3,970	+ 0.3
Mexico	3,040	3,260	3,420	3,830	3,820	1,043	3	4,170	+ 9.2
Hungary	2,740	2,900	3,030	3,120	3,110	1,380	5	3,310	+ 6.4
Yugoslavia	1,830	2,000	2,220	2,230	2,580	1,279	6	2,560	− 0.8
Argentina	1,330	1,550	1,650	1,830	1,910	959	6	1,920	+ 0.5
Bulgaria	1,240	1,460	1,510	1,800	1,950	895	5	2,150	+10.3

*Excludes production of independent foundries.
†Estimated.
Sources: British Steel Corporation; International Iron and Steel Institute.

cipally because of increased consumer expenditures, but the effects of this on total steel demand were offset by a continuing depressed situation in investment expenditure. Steel stocks were depleted in the first half of the year, although at a lower rate than in the second half of 1971. The situation improved toward the end of 1972 with total demand rising and stocks stabilizing.

Production in the Soviet Union and Eastern Europe continued to increase. In the U.S.S.R. output in 1972 was estimated at 125 million tons, 3% more than in the previous year. In the countries of Eastern Europe production increased in most areas, East Germany being an exception.

(LESLIE C. BATEMAN)

MACHINERY AND MACHINE TOOLS

World production of machinery and machine tools recovered in 1972 after a dismal record in 1971. Machine-tool builders in 1971 had been particularly hard hit by the depressed economies in Europe and Japan and the economic problems faced by U.S. industries. As 1972 began most U.S. machine-tool manufacturers expressed very guarded optimism. However, as the year progressed conditions improved and by the start of the fourth quarter of 1972 orders had exceeded $100 million in seven of the last eight months. In all of 1971, the highest monthly orders had totaled $91.6 million.

The International Machine Tool Show, sponsored by the National Machine Tool Builders and held in Chicago from October 5 to 15, allowed countries other than the U.S. to show machines for the first time. About one-third of the floor space was made up of displays from other countries. After viewing the displays it became evident that the U.S. was finding it more difficult to compete with the conventional equipment built by Japan and European countries. Their machine tools could be purchased for about two-thirds of the U.S. price.

In the more sophisticated types of machines, however, the U.S. remained strong. The show also indicated that increasing competition for the U.S. was coming from Japan, Eastern Europe, and Italy, instead of West Germany, where price differentials were not a factor. Another trend that was evident was toward simpler numerical control (NC). Prior to 1972, many manufacturers had projected a greater demand for manufacturing systems that would link minicomputers on the machine tools to larger computers in order to control their entire system. Later, however, buyers became reluctant to purchase the total plan but were moving toward the use of minicomputers to control one or more machine tools.

The most significant new market for U.S. machinery and machine-tool manufacturers was the U.S.S.R. A trade delegation of more than 100 Soviets attended the Chicago tool show, and there was much optimism that many large orders would result from the visit. Manufacturers hoped to sell the Soviets equipment for automotive plants and machinery to make consumer items. The prospects of such sales were expected to depend upon the relaxation of the U.S. government's former restrictions on exportation of these types of machines.

Soviet builders of machine tools were very active in achieving greater output of NC tools and transfer machines to meet the nation's demands. They planned to increase their production 89% in a 12-month period, and in 1974 expected to have tools for sale at the Chicago tool show.

The design of all types of equipment placed greater emphasis on noise control. In the U.S. the first national action was taken to set limits on the decibel levels that a worker could withstand for specified periods of time. The Occupational Safety and Health Act set these standards, and manufacturers would continually be faced with finding methods to produce equipment to meet regulations that would undoubtedly be tightened. The main problem confronting engineers was the establishment of uniform standards so that they would not have to design to meet different state and municipal government regulations.

The global emphasis on environmental problems was a boon to manufacturers of machinery that controls air and water pollution. In the U.S., costs for this type of equipment amounted to about 37% of the capital expenditure budget in the paper production industry, and in the steel industry it was estimated that 20% of the capital expenditures in 1972 were for pollution control equipment.

(ORLAND B. KILLIN)

NUCLEAR INDUSTRY

Outside the U.K., the nuclear industry continued active, particularly in the U.S. where the environmental controversy over nuclear power slowly made both the industry and the government more responsive to the public interest. The chairman of the U.S. Atomic Energy Commission (AEC), James R. Schlesinger, implemented major changes in the operational and regulatory sides of the AEC with a change of priorities giving more emphasis to programs involving the environment and safety of nuclear energy. Important procedural changes were instituted in the granting of construction permits and operating licenses. Main issues were the emergency core cooling system (ECCS), the release of radioactive effluents, and the environmental effects of the heat dissipated to water sources.

The ECCS was a safety system forcing water into the uranium core of the reactor in any emergency that resulted in loss of coolant. Critics contended that the ECCS had never been satisfactorily proven and that the AEC limit of radioactive releases was too high. The U.S. also planned to prohibit the discharge of all effluents into inland water systems, yet it was not certain that waste heat was an effluent.

Despite the problems, utilities decided that there were no adequate alternatives to nuclear power. Only one of the 25 stations ordered in 1971 was canceled, due to licensing delays, and lead times in ordering stations were increased. By the end of the year more than 30 were on order, 8 of them with Westinghouse Electric Corp., which also gained one order in Sweden and two in Spain. Two of the U.S. orders were for the barge-mounted offshore units for the Public Service Electric and Gas Co. of New Jersey. In Europe, Westinghouse finally established itself in France. General Electric (GE) gained an order for the first Mexican reactor. GE's latest reactor design, BWR/6, claimed to be safer and cheaper, had a good initial response. GE also consolidated its effort in Europe. Gulf General Atomic Co. received further orders for a high temperature, gas-cooled reactor (HTGR) and drew closer to Europe through a joint fuel effort with NUKEM in West Germany, an agreement with Brown Boveri (Mannheim, W.-Ger.) for the construction of HTGRs in West Germany, and negotiations with the French for the introduction of the HTGR in France. Combustion Engineering entered into a joint engineering effort with Siemens (West Germany).

The AEC accepted a proposal from Commonwealth Edison and the Tennessee Valley Authority (TVA) to construct a prototype fast-breeder reactor on the TVA's electricity system. Bids were received from GE, Westinghouse, and Atomics International. The AEC, shifting its policy on uranium enrichment, gave 21 private firms access to its technology and held discussions with Japan, Canada, Australia, and the European Economic Community (EEC) on the joint construction of a gas-diffusion enrichment plant. The expected development of the ultracentrifuge enrichment process brought future uranium enrichment needs into question, and the sale of the AEC's uranium stockpile to Japan was considered.

In Switzerland, West Germany, and Japan, delays in nuclear power programs resulted from public action. In Europe, the overuse of rivers for cooling water discharged from power stations was feared. By midyear, Kraftwerk Union (KWU), the joint Siemens and AEG-Telefunken nuclear construction company, had only one unit on order, compared with seven in 1971. The situation did not help the West German Babcock and Wilcox company in its attempts to get into the market. In France, Framatome/Creusot-Loire, Westinghouse's French licensee, won the first four light-water reactor nuclear station orders. Westinghouse was to participate in two companies, one for the construction of nuclear components and the other for the manufacture of fuel. The French government, wanting a second group as a plant supplier, considered both the CGE group and Babcock-Atlantique or a possible association of the two.

In the U.K., where no nuclear orders had been given in two years, the government decided to continue support for the national breeder reactor program for the future needs of electricity and to keep open all other options. No large nuclear plant had been ordered for delivery before 1974 and perhaps only five nuclear stations by 1980. The government indicated that one design and construction company was sufficient, and the industry was left to sort out balanced participation by itself.

Spain ordered six 900-Mw. units, all from Westinghouse, and began to set up a manufacturing company with foreign minority holdings and a similar company for fuel manufacture. Japan, having slowed down on ordering nuclear stations but not on building those already ordered, looked seriously at ECCS and at other safety and environmental issues. Attempts were made to participate in an enrichment plant project with either the U.S. or France. Japan's nuclear ship, NS "Mutsu," was working by the end of the year. Sweden had one commercial station in operation and eight more under construction or ordered. Italy decided to order a fifth nuclear unit, despite the time schedule for the fourth unit having slipped badly. The Italian state utility, ENEL, joined in the French and West German fast-breeder program. Finland ordered a second Soviet reactor. Canada, although successful in commissioning three of the four units, all of the unique Canadian CANDU reactor design, at the Pickering plant, was still plagued with difficulties regarding heavy water supply.

Euratom continued to survive, with no decision on its future. The European Nuclear Energy Agency, the most successful of the international nuclear organizations, accepted the membership of Japan and changed its name to the Nuclear Energy Agency.

(RICHARD W. KOVAN)

See also FUEL AND POWER.

PAINTS AND VARNISHES

With pollution remaining a worldwide preoccupation in 1972, the U.S. paint industry faced the likelihood of tighter restrictions on the use of toxic heavy metals, especially lead and mercury, in paint manufacture. Pollution consciousness stimulated interest in water-based and powder coatings, and water-based electropaints were being used throughout the world to prime automobile bodies. Plastic powder coatings, offered by a growing number of British and European paint makers, were adopted more slowly, and there was some discussion as to whether a dry powder could be called a paint. Coil coating, also known as prefinishing, attracted international interest. Steel-aluminum sheet, coated at the mill and subsequently cut and formed, was widely used for building cladding in the U.S.; the British Steel Corp. installed a second production line for wide sheeting in Wales.

In the U.S. sales for 1971, estimated at 874 million gal. and valued at $2,830,000,000, were divided almost equally between building paints and industrial finishes. Profits were estimated at 7.3% of net worth, or 2.8% as a margin on sales. The industry had experienced little growth since 1965. Sales of electropaints at about $20 million were one bright spot, and there was also growth in powder coatings and radiation-curable materials. Japanese production was growing at about 5% a year, compared with 10% in the recent past; total output for 1971 was estimated at 1,411,800 tons.

Most British paint manufacturers looked back on 1971 with some satisfaction. After several difficult years of rising costs, unmatched by higher selling prices, the industry enjoyed the best margins since 1966. Output per employee rose by 9% while employment in the industry fell 5%. Sales, at £207 million, were about 7.5% higher in volume than in 1970. British paint makers thus faced the challenge of entering the EEC in much better shape than had seemed likely earlier. U.K. output represented about 15% of the Western European total. The EEC countries accounted for 68%; West Germany led with 30%, followed by France with 20% and Italy with 11%. The total output of Western Europe closely matched that of the U.S.

Sweden used more paint per capita than any other country in Western Europe in 1971. West Germany was second, followed by France, Belgium, the Netherlands, and the U.K. On the continent profitability was greatest in industrial and automotive paints, whereas British manufacturers found the decorative market more rewarding.

(LIONEL BILEFIELD)

PAPER AND PULP

World production of paper and paperboard amounted to approximately 131 million metric tons in 1971, an increase of only about 1.3% over 1970. This was one of the smallest increases in recent years, reflecting a slowing of economic growth in North America, Europe, and Japan. Taken together, these areas accounted for over 90% of world production and consumption of paper and paperboard and more than three-quarters of the international trade in pulp and paper products.

Total world production of all pulp and paper products rose 1.5% in 1971, compared with the average rate of about 5% annually in recent years.

Growth was slow in the U.S., the largest producer. There were moderate increases in Finland, West Germany, France, and the U.S.S.R., while output in Canada, the world's second largest producer, actually declined. This was also true of a number of the other major producing nations, including Japan, Sweden, Norway, Britain, and Italy.

Manufacturing and other costs continued to increase in most regions. In addition, large investments in water and air pollution control devices were necessary. There was also a substantial surplus of manufacturing capacity for some of the major products, such as newsprint and chemical wood pulp, and this tended to keep prices at depressed levels. The result was that earnings generally suffered substantial declines, in some instances to levels well below those necessary to attract new investment.

The economic upturn that occurred in 1972, notably in North America, brought stronger demand and improved business conditions. However, expansion of pulp and paper manufacturing facilities in the next two or three years was expected to be at rates below those of the previous decade. For example, in Canada total capacity for manufacturing wood pulp was expected to increase at an average annual rate of 3.3% in 1971–74, compared with an annual rate of 5.3% during the previous ten years. The pattern was similar in the U.S., where growth in pulp-manufacturing capacity in 1971–74 was forecast at 2.4% annually, well below the rate of the preceding decade. Profits from pulp and paper manufacture would have to increase considerably before growth rates could be expected to return to their previous levels.

Of the total paper and paperboard consumed throughout the world, some three-quarters was made from virgin fibre. The balance came from waste paper and other materials that had been recycled. These proportions had not changed very much in recent years, but interest in recycling was increasing. In some countries of Western Europe, such as West Germany and Britain, waste paper provided more than 40% of the fibre required for paper and paperboard production. In Scandinavia and North America, where forest resources were more plentiful and most pulp and paper mills were located closer to forests than to large urban centres where substantial quantities of waste paper were available, the proportion was much smaller. The proportion of secondary fibre to virgin fibre in the U.S. was only about 20%, but it was expected to rise as techniques for collecting, transporting, and using waste paper as a raw material were improved.

The U.S. led the world in per capita consumption with some 565 lb. in 1971. Other major consumers, all accounting for more than 250 lb. per capita, were Canada, most of the Western European nations, and Japan. Citizens of the U.S.S.R. used an average of 60 lb. each. Consumption was sharply lower in some of the less developed countries; *e.g.*, an estimated 11 lb. in China and 4 lb. in India.

(GORDON MINNES)

PETROLEUM PRODUCTS

In 1972 the international petroleum industry felt the first full impact of environmental and governmental factors that were expected to strongly influence both the production and consumption of petroleum products for years to come.

Demand for gasoline and fuel oils in the U.S. rose sharply, a development not fully anticipated by industry analysts. This resulted mainly from new rules designed to reduce air pollution but also stemmed from the immediate shortage of natural gas and a lagging nuclear power program. At the same time, the U.S. reached a peak in domestic oil production that was not expected to be exceeded in the near future. With no increases in the price of crude oil in prospect, independent producers and oil companies were not able to justify large expenditures of cash for sustained exploration and development of new oil reserves.

The principal new prospect for reserves in the Gulf of Mexico off Louisiana was closed to initial exploration when a lease sale planned for December 1971 was postponed by court action until September. As demand for crude oil mounted, the industry resorted to foreign sources as imports rose to nearly 25%.

For natural gas the outlook on price improvement was brighter. Although all natural gas sold in interstate commerce was rigidly controlled in price by the U.S. Federal Power Commission (FPC), the current shortage boosted prices paid for gas that did not cross state lines. This competition for new supply, plus a gradual realization that continued low prices had aggravated the shortage, prompted the FPC to begin relaxing some price controls on newly found gas.

The prospect for better prices had the expected result of reviving exploration for natural gas. For the year, the number of exploratory wells was expected to jump by nearly 40%, the greatest spurt in many years. This strong upturn in exploration resulted in some new supplies. But because it takes years to find, develop, and pipeline natural gas to market, the full effect of 1972 activity was not expected to be felt much before 1975.

Meanwhile, the supply of natural gas in the U.S. continued to fall further behind total demand. In advance of the winter of 1972–73 a total of 15 major long-distance gas pipeline companies announced curtailment programs. Altogether, they planned to cut back a total of more than one trillion cubic feet of gas from their customers. This amounted to nearly 10% of their total 1970 deliveries. Most of this curtailment was to affect industrial consumers and electric power companies, which paid a much lower price for their gas than did commercial and residential users. Most of them were able to substitute oil or coal for the gas they would not get.

But problems were also arising in the coal industry. New environmental laws greatly lowered the permissible sulfur content of all fuels, unless that sulfur was removed before being released to the atmosphere as sulfur dioxide. At the end of 1972 there was no economical method for removing sulfur from coal, and the same was true of methods for taking sulfur dioxide out of stack gases where coal high in sulfur content was burned.

The effect of the natural gas and coal shortages was that consumers turned to their only alternative, liquid fuel oil. Much of the heavy fuel oil manufactured in the U.S. and imported from Venezuela and other countries had more sulfur than the law allowed. Unlike coal, however, heavy fuel oil can be desulfurized economically or blended with low-sulfur stocks. Several giant plants were installed in Venezuela and in the Bahamas and other Caribbean islands to provide this admissible fuel, and reserves of low-sulfur crude oil from throughout the world were being sought to make more fuel oil that would not require treatment.

Even heavy residual fuel oil, however, fell somewhat short of total demand in 1972. Suppliers therefore resorted to lighter distillate fuels, similar to the furnace oils sold to homeowners. This large unexpected increase in both heavy and light fuel oils was expected to challenge the industry's ingenuity to meet needs in the winter of 1972–73. Both industry and government believed that all needs would be met, even those superimposed by the shortages in gas and the restrictions laid down on coal.

Because of the new environmental standards applied to 1972 model cars, drivers burned up roughly 20% more gasoline for every mile they drove. The oil industry expected that this mileage factor would continue to boost gasoline demand as post-1970 models increased in the total car population.

In 1972 refiners learned more about the kind of gasoline they would have to produce when the Clean Air Act passed by the U.S. Congress became fully effective in 1975. Producers were preparing to remove the last vestiges of lead and to otherwise tailor their gasoline to meet the requirements of the cars that would hit the roads in late 1974. One thing was certain. To manufacture the new gasoline would require more crude oil, thus piling one more demand factor on the nation's oil requirements.

One mounting concern at the close of 1972 was the lagging program for building new refineries in the U.S. The combined problems of finding capital, estimating exactly what specifications of gasoline would be needed, and obtaining permits for new sites delayed new building to the extent that a shortage in producing capacity for petroleum products would be a potential threat by the mid-1970s. (GEORGE WEBER)

PLASTICS

Despite real commercial barriers, world use of plastics in 1972 expanded by a further 10%. The year 1971 had been a watershed year for the world's plastics industry, when it finally came to terms with the realization that its growth would not automatically continue at the previous headlong rate. With profit margins slashed in a period of inflation, economic slowdown, and consequent overcapacity, plans for the future would have to be rethought.

A more mature industry found 1972 a better year. Inflation remained a problem almost everywhere, but economic activity picked up sharply in the U.S. and, to a lesser extent, in Western Europe (except for Italy and the U.K.). Plastics consumption rose as a result. Cautiously and more selectively, the big chemical companies again thought of investment, although they were determined to avoid overcapacity this time.

U.S. plastics materials output grew by about 15%, from 9.3 million metric tons in 1971 to some 10,750,000 tons in 1972. The comparable estimates for Western Europe were 11,750,000 tons in 1971 and 13 million tons in 1972, representing a growth rate of 12%. West Germany recovered from the doldrums of 1971 to produce almost 5 million tons. The best growth performance in Europe was again provided by France, which may have supplanted Italy as Europe's second largest producer (after West Germany); both countries were close to the 2 million-ton mark. The U.K. experienced a small improvement from virtually zero growth in 1971, when 1,450,000 tons were produced, but output was not much above 1.5 million tons.

In Japan, the world's second largest plastics materials producer, output appeared to have remained at a near-static level of around 5 million tons for several years. In the early 1960s, Japan's plastics industry had experienced an unparalleled expansion. Lower exports, on which the industry depended heavily, were a major factor in the slowdown, and there was also a general recession in Japan. The closing months of 1972 indicated more encouraging prospects for 1973.

Overall, world plastics output in 1972 was assessed at 34 million tons, compared with 31 million tons in 1971. This included production of 3.5 million tons in the Communist countries in 1971 (U.S.S.R., 2 million tons) and of 4 million tons in 1972 (U.S.S.R., 2.4 million tons).

It was expected that growth would continue to be greatest among the "commodity" thermoplastics; polyolefins (polythene, both low and high density, and polypropylene); polyvinyl chloride (PVC) and vinyl copolymers; and polystyrene and styrene copolymers, including ABS. These materials accounted for two-thirds of world plastics output. Specialized, higher-priced "engineering" plastics continued to be profitable, however, and research into new polymers was concentrated in this area. Three new materials of above-average interest emerged from the preliminary laboratory stage during 1972 for wider commercial assessment: polychloral (du Pont), with notably good nonflammable characteristics; polyethersulfone (ICI), which performed well at high temperatures; and ethylene/tetrafluoroethylene (ETFE) copolymers (Montedison), which possessed a good combination of mechanical, electrical, and chemical resistance properties over a wide temperature range. Activity also continued in the development, processing, and application of more sophisticated forms of familiar materials, such as fibre-reinforced composites and structural foams.

Pipe, particularly in the U.S., and furniture were especially active markets during the year. Packaging formed the largest single market for plastics, about a quarter of the total, and the industry was therefore closely involved in questions of pollution. In areas as diverse as Japan, the Netherlands, Scandinavia, and the U.S., attempts were made to find commercial applications for developments arising from work on additives to render polymers degradable by the action of ultraviolet light or by biological action, such as that done by Gerald Scott at the University of Aston, Birmingham (U.K.). Products concerned included containers and agricultural mulch.

Attention was also paid to recycling of plastics waste. Thermoplastics, by definition, were excellent candidates for such consideration. Reuse of thermoplastic scrap in the plant was normal practice, but collection of litter and sorting of consumer waste once the plastics products left the factory remained a problem. Some aspects of the environmental movement positively favoured increased use of plastics; for example, the continuing move toward improved automobile safety standards and heightened consciousness of the value of sound insulation in everyday life.

On the machinery and processing side, there was a slowing of the drive toward even larger products and—in keeping with the general search for cost efficiency—more attention toward rethinking the smaller end of the market in terms of machine efficiency and possibilities for automation. Nevertheless, some very large items attracted attention, including one-piece thermoformed PVC swimming pools from West Germany and the HMS "Wilton," the largest glass-reinforced plastic vessel ever built and the first to join the Royal Navy. (ROBIN C. PENFOLD)

PRINTING

The printing industry was depressed in the first part of 1972. In Britain more than 200 printers closed down, and several important companies closed in West Germany. However, investment began to pick up in midyear, when the largest printing machinery and equipment show ever held, Drupa, took place at Düsseldorf, W.Ger. About half the 1,100 exhibitors were German, with the largest foreign participation coming from the U.S., Italy, and Britain.

Drupa provided little real technological news—not surprisingly, since it followed so closely on Ipex, the international printing machinery show held in London the year before. However, substantial orders were placed, including many for the new Roland-Miehle offset machines. The Roland 800 series offered automated ink control and a speed of 10,000 sheets an hour on multicolour machines, with a new delivery system that could handle a considerable variety of papers and boards. Small-format offset machines, an answer to the challenge of instant photocopiers, were introduced by Schnellpressenfabrik Heidelberg of West Germany, the world's largest printing-machine manufacturer.

The two largest rotogravure presses ever built were delivered to the West German publishers Bauer and Grüner & Jahr. The 250-cm.- and 280-cm.-wide presses, from MAN and Albert, respectively, were widely thought to be the last of the giants, however, since the trend in gravure was toward standardized multipurpose, medium-size machines. Drastic worldwide increases in postal charges led subscriber magazines and mail-order catalog firms to search for lightweight printing papers that would carry the strong colour gravure offers. Dow Chemical announced experiments with magnesium etching for newspaper production by gravure. Electronic gravure cylinder engraving direct from colour copy was introduced by Dr.-ing. Rudolf Hell.

Andreotti of Italy, in cooperation with Giori of Switzerland and König & Bauer of West Germany, installed multicolour printing presses for postage stamps at Harrison & Sons in Britain. The same manufacturers also introduced an in-line extrusion coater for linking to rotogravure packaging presses. Transfer printing by rotogravure onto paperbacked heat-pressure transferable materials became popular in a number of countries for textile printing and for applying full-colour pictures to such items as plastic containers.

James Halley, in Britain, introduced numerical control for speeding up reprints. In Italy, Cerutti designed a computer-controlled press operation to permit predetermination of a production run, and similar systems were offered by Rockwell's Goss division and by Harris-Intertype in the U.S. Wifag, in Switzerland, pioneered remote ink control on rotary presses, which was applied to the press systems from MAN, Albert, and König & Bauer.

The success of British web offset machines in Japan led several European manufacturers, including MAN, König & Bauer, and Wifag, to conclude agreements for local construction of their own presses. The trend in web offset was toward small- and medium-size presses. Baker Perkins satellite presses, made also in Japan by Tokyo Kikai, achieved impressive sales in North America. The Cottrell Marinoni M-1000 remained a best seller, but sales of Albert presses in smaller formats and of West Germany's Saphir, Zirkon, and Ultraset 72 compact web offset presses also rose steeply. The three largest West German rotary press makers announced their entry into the compact web offset press field. Several new business-form presses were introduced, Schriber, in the U.S., claiming to be among the first to have presses of this type used for quality full colour.

Letterpress remained in the doldrums, although newspapers continued to favour the process. Grace Letterflex in the U.S. and BASF Nyloprint in West Germany announced a production rate of 60 plates an hour. The Japanese Asahi Chemical photopolymer plate found new adherents in New Zealand, Australia, the U.S., and Europe, although most printers continued to find photopolymer letterpress plates too expensive or too slow.

Electronic colour scanners were put on serial production to meet rising demand; enlarging and reducing scanners from Crosfield Electronics and Dr.-ing. Rudolf Hell were being installed at a rate of 20 a month. Extra-fast colour scanning from Linoscan produced four separations simultaneously. The Dainippon Screen scanner was offered outside Japan for the first time, and Dr.-ing. Rudolf Hell demonstrated screening by laser on an electronic colour scanner.

New colour preproofing methods were introduced by du Pont (Cromalin), Remak of Australia (Transfer Process), and Process Shizai in Japan. In phototypesetting, Klett in West Germany installed the first Magnaset 226 from Britain. Scotland's *Daily Record* and *Sunday Mail* introduced complete photosetting on a Linotron 505C system, thus becoming the world's largest daily newspaper to be printed by photoset web offset. In the U.S., RCA discontinued its activities in phototypesetting. Photon was installing its high-speed 700 CRT system, based on Alphanumeric's system and used earlier by IBM, at a rate of two a week.

Several European printer-publishers, including Esselte in Sweden, ordered the West German Digiset to photoset not only on film or paper but also on microfilm or microfiche. A Swedish automobile manufacturer estimated that direct microfiche photosetting would save him at least $50,000 a year in catalog production and mailing costs. Electronic picture generation for direct insertion into photoset columns or pages was demonstrated on the Digiset. Compact computer-assisted phototypesetting machines became cheaper, with U.S. machines offering the best bargains. (W. PINCUS JASPERT)

SHIPBUILDING

Few orders for new ships of over 10,000 tons deadweight (dw.) were placed in the first half of 1972, and in some countries, notably West Germany, no orders were placed with the larger shipyards. Despite this, world shipbuilding was in a healthier state than it had been for five years. During that period Japan's share of world output totaled 50.2% in terms of deadweight tons, followed by Sweden (8.18%), West Germany (6.93%), and the U.K. (5.45%).

At mid-1972, 1,941 steamships and motor vessels were under construction, totaling a record 24,199,485 gross registered tons (grt). This did not include vessels building in the U.S.S.R. and China, or ships of less than 100 grt. The reduction in the demand for new ships, plus high tonnage figures for vessels already completed, caused a drop in the total world order book (ships building and to be built) to 80,639,552 grt. Even Japan suffered a reduction in the total tonnage on order. Japan continued to head the shipbuilding countries with a total order book of 34,470,616 grt, followed by Sweden (6,832,296 grt), Spain (4,818,743 grt), France (4,254,502 grt), the U.K. (4,221,207 grt), and West Germany (4,112,642 grt).

Ship orders fell during the first half of 1972 but began to pick up later, with gains in the tanker groups both above and below 150,000 tons dw. Orders fell in the ore-bulk-oil and dry-bulk groups, and the dry-cargo section faltered. Tanker orders at the end of the year stood at a little above 120 million tons dw. Liberia had the highest tonnage of tankers of more than 150,000 tons dw. on order, followed by Japan and the U.K. Liberian flag tankers numbered 45, totaling 2,546,430 tons dw., whereas Japan's 157 tankers had an aggregate of 2,067,000 tons dw. The most important unit of the world's mercantile fleet remained the conventional dry-cargo vessel. More than 580 such vessels, totaling 4,590,465 tons dw., were completed in 1971. The total dry-cargo fleet built between 1967 and 1971, including cargo liners, general purpose tramp-type vessels, and specialized carriers (but not container ships), had a deadweight tonnage of 19,313,116.

In 1971, 39 full container ships were completed, totaling 810,250 tons dw. West German shipyards, which built mainly for export, had a clear lead in this type of vessel. The U.S. and Japan built mainly for domestic use. The value of the container fleet built since 1967 amounted to $1,250,000,000, and the fleet represented a lifting capacity in excess of 120,000 containers. Most of the vessels involved were capable of 21 to 23 knots, but several container ships were delivered with service speeds exceeding 26 knots. The Overseas Container Line and Associated Container Transportation Ltd. had third-generation vessels with a speed of 27 knots, built by West German yards, coming into service.

Interest in liquefied natural gas (LNG) carriers was growing. By the end of 1971 orders were held for 33 larger vessels with an estimated value of $800 million. Large LNG carriers in the 120,000- to 125,000-cu.m. range cost about $62.5 million. Japan had a considerable lead in the building of carriers for liquefied petroleum gas, but Italy and France led in building carriers for LNG. In the U.S. two yards were capable of building the complex LNG vessel at a price only about 10% higher than that quoted in Europe.

Passenger ships continued to provide a flourishing business for certain yards. A large number of passenger/car ferries were building in Japan, and Finnish, Danish, Italian, Yugoslavian, Swedish, and Norwegian yards had several orders on their books.

(W. D. EWART)

TEXTILES AND FIBRES

Textile Industry. More mills closed down or amalgamated in the U.K. in 1972, and there was more unemployment. Consumption of yarns and fabrics did not keep pace with fibre production. Prices of some raw materials were depressed but improved later in the year, and production was maintained at satisfactory levels. The jute industry was severely hit by the ban on exports from Bangladesh. Exports of yarns and finished goods were disappointing. The volume of textile imports into the U.K. was a sore point with manufacturers, and many wondered about the impact of entry into the Common Market on an already badly hit industry.

Despite almost chaotic economic conditions, scientific and technical developments were distinctly encouraging. Machine improvements provided higher speeds and greater efficiencies in spinning, winding, weaving, textile printing, dyeing, and finishing techniques. A new stereomicroscope enabled technicians to study a section of a fibre or fabric sample in close detail, using zoom control, and to view in three dimensions at the same time. Other innovations included a device for use on draw-twisters, an electronic system for continuous measurement of knitted fabrics, an electronic double-jersey machine, a braiding machine with new yarn feeds and self-lubricating tension control for faster operation, warp-knitting and raschel machines with a new thread feed system, and a new V-bed machine for garment knitting. More accurate assessment of dimensional stability of fabrics became possible. Open-end spinning systems received attention, and a new blender could open, clean, and blend all fibres at up to 4,000 lb. an hour. Dyeing times for textured polyester yarns were drastically reduced.

Compelled by a need to economize and to streamline activities, British research organizations made staffing cuts and devoted more time to sponsored projects. The Shirley Institute received a £20,000 U.S. contract to develop new methods for producing novel colour effects on fabrics. Progress was noted in the range and variety of nonwoven fabrics, made from fibre-punching techniques, thermoplastic binder fibres, mechanical interlacing operations, and stitch-bonding methods. Product ranges widened appreciably.

In the Netherlands, an air-jet loom capable of 400 picks per minute was announced after ten years' research. However, more than 6,000 jobs were lost when production of nylon and polyester filament was cut back 20%. Swiss technical contributions included improved versions of spinning and weaving machinery, precision testing equipment, a control system for high-production cards, and a new method for pretreatment of cellulosic fibres. Improved spinning and weaving accessories achieved success. A rapid-dyeing machine was introduced in Belgium.

In France, where exports had risen considerably in recent years, there was a tendency toward more company mergers and amalgamations. Textile production in West Germany remained fairly high. One firm brought out a new toe-to-top machine for handling all deniers and types of synthetic fabrics. Another introduced a system for treating yarn hanks for deep-pile and high-bulk tufted carpets. The Romanian government formulated plans for the output of filament and staple polyester. Hungary engaged in a five-year plan for reorganizing weaving capacity.

The U.S. had its production and consumption problems. A considerable sum was spent on new machines and reequipment projects. Improvements were made in conventional processing methods, with significant progress in instrument technology, such as twist counters, wrap reels, hardness testers, yarn and cloth examining machines, tension measuring units, speed monitoring systems, friction measuring meters, laser thread counters, automatic control of continuous bleaching, drafting systems, yarn cutters for winding frames, yarn evenness testers, soiling testers, strength testers, and moisture testers. Further progress was made in computerized machine monitoring, and in handling and packaging methods.

(ALFRED DAWBER)

Natural Fibres. *Cotton.* Following the steady upward trend in prices over the two previous years, growers were encouraged to increase their operations during the 1971–72 season. Acreage expanded significantly, and record yields were obtained in many areas. Not only was the huge gap between production and consumption closed but about one million bales were added to carry-over stocks in mid-1972.

An additional two million ac. in world cotton plantings brought output to a record 56 million bales, an increase of 4.5 million bales over the previous season. Adverse growing conditions in the U.S. again prevented a real recovery in yields and production there, but a record output was grown in the U.S.S.R. Elsewhere, output increased by 18% in such areas as Brazil, India, Pakistan, and Turkey. World supplies during the season rose from 73 million bales to 75 million bales.

Price levels fluctuated widely as a result of variations in the availability of supplies. The Liverpool index of average values rose from below 33½ cents per pound to a peak of over 40 cents in the first six months of the season. Subsequently there was an even larger decline, bringing the average cost down to 31½ cents by mid-September.

Prospects for increased supplies during 1972–73 were encouraging. In the U.S. the area planted was about 12% higher than in the previous season, and output of more than 13.5 million bales was anticipated, compared with less than 10.5 million bales in 1971–72. Reports from other countries indicated an overall rise in plantings, especially in Central America and the Middle East.

World consumption in 1971–72 increased by nearly one million bales, establishing a new record. The most buoyancy was seen in the Soviet bloc, where two consecutive record crops in the U.S.S.R. had provided abundant supplies. In Asia aggregate cotton use continued to expand, but at a slower rate. Consumption in the U.S. was maintained by a rising demand for textiles generally and the strong fashion appeal of certain cotton fabrics.

In Western Europe the manufacturing situation improved, with consumption rates in West Germany, France, and Italy all higher than a year earlier. Demand prospects for 1972–73 remained promising; supplies were expected to increase further, and overall demand for textiles was likely to expand. The competitiveness of cotton compared with the man-made fibres remained crucial, but the price factor that favoured synthetics early in 1972 was reversed later in the year.

(ARTHUR TATTERSALL)

Silk. Overbuying by the silk-consuming countries at the Canton Trade Fair in 1970, coupled with some temporary decline in demand outside Japan, resulted in a surplus of stocks that took longer to liquidate than had been anticipated. It was not until April 1972 that stocks had disappeared and manufacturers found themselves looking for spot goods—and found merchants without a bale to spare. In the U.K. many restocking purchases were in progress when the pound was floated in June, entailing a cost increase of some 8%. To this was added, in August, a price rise of 2% imposed by China on all markets.

World demand remained high, largely as a result of continued buoyancy in the Japanese domestic market. Consumption in Japan was estimated at 27,000 tons for 1972–73, as against 26,000 tons for 1971–72—a 4% increase. Prices in Japan rose from 7,000 yen per kilogram in January 1972 to 8,600 yen by the end of August, partly because of fears—first expressed at the Canton Trade Fair in April—that China would not have sufficient silk to supply both Japan and the West. At the end of 1971 the Japanese government had granted the Raw Silk Corp. a monopoly in order to control imports "when necessary," but this proved ineffective. Prices were further inflated by forecasts of a frost that did, in fact, occur in early June, reducing the spring crop by as much as 9%. By August the Raw Silk Corp. had released all its stocks purchased in previous years, and the authorities no longer had any instrument through which to control the upward price spiral.

The continued good prices favoured Japanese sericulture, but there was an awareness of the threat of a flood of silk imports in the future should China fail to find customers for its production elsewhere. Japan, therefore, welcomed the Chinese initiative toward creating funds for the promotion of silk in Europe. U.S. consumption of raw silk had dropped drastically since 1965, although signs of a revival were apparent, and the danger persisted that an overall decline in silk consumption outside Japan might make that country the target of heavy sales pressure from the Chinese. On the other hand, European demand remained good, and the promotion effort proposed by Peking should help to increase volume. Meanwhile, China harvested a bumper cocoon crop in the spring of 1972, and was taking energetic and successful steps to augment production.

(PETER W. GADDUM)

Wool. There was a distinct improvement in the world wool situation early in 1972, but it was feared that excessive price rises later in the year might prove damaging in the long run. In 1971, the second successive year of declining consumption, the weight of virgin wool consumed was estimated by the International Wool Secretariat at 1,530,839 metric tons, 3% lower than in 1970 and 5% lower than in 1969. This caused world wool prices to fall to extremely damaging levels. Uneconomic production entailed debt and bankruptcy for individual growers and also led to a reduction in sheep numbers, with consequently lower production in the 1972–73 season. In Australia the latest available estimates indicated a fall of 9% in production compared with the previous season, and world wool output, at 1,510,000 metric tons, was down by 2%. Estimated production for 1972–73 was 7% below the 1968–69 record.

Declining production, together with a rise in consumption, led to a reversal of the downward price trend by the end of 1971. In January 1972 wool prices began to rise steadily, and this tendency continued with only brief setbacks until the first full-scale auctions of the 1972–73 season were held in Australia in the latter half of August. Within two or three weeks the rise accelerated, and by October prices were the highest recorded since the boom of 1951 during the Korean War. The speed of the September-October price rise was, in fact, considerably sharper than that experienced in 1951, reflecting a realization that an actual wool shortage might develop, at least in the short term.

The increase in consumption was not as great as the price rise might suggest, however. In the first half of 1972 consumption in nine leading countries was about 6% higher than in the corresponding, very depressed, period of 1971. The mere fact that the balance had turned from one of surplus wool production and stocks to one of shortage was enough to cause the excessive price rises. The average for 64s-count merino wool was 133 pence per kilogram in September 1972, compared with 74 pence in December 1971, and price gains in October at times added another 20 to 30%. Crossbred prices rose similarly; the quotation for 50s-count wool was 50 pence per kilogram in December 1971 and 102 pence in September 1972, with sharp rises continuing. Such extreme price changes were not considered helpful to wool's position vis-à-vis man-made fibres. Statistics indicated that, prior to the price boom, wool had been gaining favour with consumers. (H. M. F. MALLETT)

Man-Made Fibres. In 1972 world overproduction of man-made fibres escalated, and this situation, combined with restrictions on Japanese imports into the U.S. market, caused the price structure of polyester fibres to sustain a serious collapse. As nylon prices had already tended to be unprofitable for several years, this was a blow to the man-made-fibre producers. As the year advanced, however, two forces began to have a favourable influence on world markets: a general broadening in demand following the textile depression of 1971, and the decision of some of the major producers in several countries, including the U.K. and Japan, to curtail their total output. These trends resulted in a general hardening in nylon prices, followed later in the year by a much firmer trend in polyester prices.

Part of the problem of trading in these fibres arose from a formerly very brisk demand for jersey fabrics in false-twist polyester fibre, followed by a sharp downward trend. While there was some recovery in this market, the level of activity did not reach that of 1971, when, contrary to the general state of textile activity, it had attained record levels. Similarly, the demand for jersey fabrics in acrylic fibres had settled down to a lower average level than was attained in the 1970–71 period. While cellulosic fibre in staple form continued to make steady progress, with particular stress on the advanced types such as the high-wet-modulus qualities, it appeared that the scrapping of machinery for the production of continuous viscose fibres had been overdone on an international scale. This resulted in some shortage of filament rayon yarns. Increased prices were introduced to offset the higher production costs, particularly those resulting from more expensive raw cellulose, and leading producers in several countries were able to obtain better margins in selling filament rayon than they had found possible for a number of years. As so frequently happens in the textile industry, shortages of fibres appeared to create a strengthening of demand.

Technically, one of the most important advances in nylon was the successful introduction of additives to the polymer to defeat or reduce the problem of static electricity. It seemed likely that within the next few years there would be a steady swing to antistatic nylon, with its higher absorbency and comfort factor. In unconventional methods of fabric structure there was notable progress with the British heterofil nylon, which had an outer casing of nylon that had a lower melting point than that in the core, enabling structures to be made by simple heat treatment. These fabrics found their way into such varied applications as matting to prevent trucks from sinking in muddy ground during road construction and slipcovers for upholstery. There was a particularly strong demand in most countries for carpet fibres, and both the modified rayons and acrylic and nylon fibres continued to make headway. Bulked continuous filament nylon for tufting increased in popularity, and there were many innovations in the patterning of tufted carpets.

(P. M. ROWE)

See also: Advertising; Alcoholic Beverages; Cooperatives; Economy, World; Employment, Wages, and Hours; Fisheries; Food; Fuel and Power; Housing; Labour Unions; Merchandising; Metallurgy; Mining; Prices; Rubber; Television and Radio; Timber; Tobacco; Tourism; Toys and Games; Trade, International.

Insurance

Sales of private insurance rose to more than $130 billion in 1972. The U.S. maintained its sizable lead, accounting for approximately 60% of the total market. No other nation had more than 10%, but Japan was rapidly approaching that figure. West Germany was third, with the U.K., France, Canada, Italy, Australia, the Netherlands, Sweden, and Switzerland following. The ratio of premium (sales) volume to national income grew rapidly in most countries, rising to more than 8% in the U.S. and exceeding 6% in Australia, Canada, New Zealand, and the Netherlands; only a few of the less developed nations were below 2%. On a per capita premium basis, however, there were still wide disparities, ranging from more than $330 per year in the U.S. to less than $6 per year in Brazil, Mexico, India, Pakistan, and the Philippines.

Life Insurance. The value of life insurance in force continued to grow faster than national income in almost all countries. Measured in these terms, the world leaders were Canada, the U.S., New Zealand, Sweden, Japan, Australia, the Netherlands, and the U.K. Growth rates of premiums were somewhat lower in many countries, however, largely because of monetary depreciation, expanding social insurance systems, and increasing competition from alternative forms of savings. Group insurance, mostly sold through employers, was the fastest growing sector of life insurance. Sales of term policies emphasizing protection were increasing more rapidly than contracts that featured savings, such as endowments and whole life insurance.

Total life insurance in force in the U.S. exceeded $1.5 trillion, held by more than 145 million persons and averaging about $26,000 per insured family. As of mid-1972, assets of U.S. life insurance companies totaled $230 billion, nearly three-fourths of which represented investments in bonds and mortgages. Total income of U.S. life insurers amounted to more than $55 billion, comprising 75% premium income (approximately one-half from life insurance, one-third from health insurance, and one-tenth from annuities) and 25% investment and other income.

Almost 300 U.S. life insurers had affiliated mutual funds in 1972, and more than 100 offered variable annuities. Several insurers were beginning to sell "variable life insurance," in which the face value of the contract changes with an equity index, but large-scale marketing awaited decisions on regulation by the Securities and Exchange Commission. Another new contract, called "split life insurance," combined an individual annuity with term insurance written at rates significantly lower than the cost of separate term life insurance contracts.

Record new business was written by British life offices in 1971. New policies written during the year amounted to £13,000 million, or 19% more than in 1970. All the companies maintained a solid base of traditional whole life and endowment insurance, but the proportion of pension business varied widely. The same was true of term or temporary insurance in the form of "family income" provisions, mortgage protection, large policies in connection with gifts between living persons, and the equity-linked plans. Actuarial valuation of the life funds disclosed high surpluses and resulted in higher reversionary bonus distributions and special bonuses payable at the time of claim. Insurance in force at the end of 1971 amounted to £58,600 million. Funds held by the companies for the discharge of these obligations totaled £13,600 million.

Health insurance was an area of great controversy in 1972, especially in the U.S. where health care costs, variously estimated, ranged from $60 billion to $75 billion a year. More than $25 billion of this was underwritten by private insuring organizations, with life insurance companies writing a major portion. Expansion of the seven-year-old federal Medicare program continued, but efforts to enlarge this program into a system of national health insurance were still in the discussion stage. (*See* MEDICINE.)

Property and Liability Insurance. Floods resulting from Hurricane Agnes caused several billion dollars in damages in the eastern U.S. in June 1972; preliminary insured losses amounted to about $60 million, largely in the state of Pennsylvania. In an effort to encourage participation in the National Flood Insurance Program, subsidized rates were reduced by about 40% in many areas. In August the Federal Housing Administration began to require flood insurance in connection with its housing loans in flood-prone areas.

The 1972 results for automobile insurance appeared promising, as many U.S. insurers continued to register the underwriting profit gains that had appeared in 1971 for the first time in half a decade. Major interest centred around "no-fault" legislation, under which the traditional tort liability is largely replaced by payment to the insured for economic losses, regardless of liability, up to specified limits. The results of no-fault plans in Puerto Rico and Massachusetts appeared to be favourable. Florida, Connecticut, and New Jersey passed similar legislation, while Oregon and Delaware adopted plans using the no-fault idea on a partial optional basis.

The Federal Crime Insurance Program, designed to make crime insurance more readily available in high-crime areas, was moving slowly. As of 1972 the program, which was sponsored by the U.S. Department of Housing and Urban Development and written through private insurance companies, was in effect in the District of Columbia and ten states (Connecticut, Illinois, Maryland, Massachusetts, Missouri, New York, Ohio, Pennsylvania, Rhode Island, and Tennessee). In August rates for both residential and commercial properties were cut up to 50%.

For the first time since 1967, member companies of the British Insurance Association (BIA) produced an underwriting profit in 1971 on worldwide fire, accident, and automobile business. The profit was minimal—£12.4 million or 0.6% of premiums—but it was significant to insurers when set against the £30 million loss experienced in 1970. A breakdown of the figures showed a £42.2 million profit on fire and accident business, offset by a loss of £29.8 million on automobile premiums. The worldwide premium income total was £2,104 million (against £1,810 million in 1970), of which £1,294 million related to fire and accident and £810 million to automobile insurance.

Fire and accident business written in the U.K. by BIA companies in 1971 produced premiums of £481 million and an underwriting profit of £40.6 million, while U.K. automobile premiums of £296 million recorded a loss of £25.5 million. Underwriting results in the U.S. market were better than they had been for many years, with an overall profit of £7.9 million.

Improved underwriting was also announced by

Information Science and Technology: *see* Computers

Lloyd's underwriters, with an overall profit for the 1967–69 account of £52.1 million, the highest in Lloyd's nearly 300-year history. This represented 7.5% of the premium income of £693.7 million, which included a sizable marine account.

Inflation remained the major problem affecting insurance underwriting. Its effects were worldwide and particularly severe in those classes of insurance where claims settlements are often delayed for several years. In the U.K., for example, compensation awards for some personal injury claims under automobile and employers' liability policies were in the £45,000–£50,000 bracket, against a comparable assessment of £20,000 or less at the time of the accident. Automobile premiums also had to take the strain of increased repair costs.

Payments for crime losses by British companies rose 3% in 1971 to £21.3 million. Household losses were up 10%, to £7.7 million, but losses in the industrial and commercial sector registered a 10% decline. Payment for money losses rose 25%, largely as a result of some sizable bullion robberies. In the general liability and miscellaneous sector, insurers made a determined attempt to improve their profitability through a policy of rate increases, resurveys, and insistence on higher security standards. An increase in white-collar crime rendered the fidelity guarantee business much less profitable than formerly.

British fire insurers incurred substantial liabilities for property damage in Northern Ireland. The law provided for compensation to be made from public funds in certain circumstances; some such payments were made in 1971, but there remained many doubtful cases for which insurers needed to set up additional reserves. U.K. fire damage in 1971 was estimated at £128.7 million but, because of the unusual situation in Northern Ireland, this was not strictly comparable with the £110.9 million total for 1970.

(DAVID L. BICKELHAUPT; PERCY STEBBINGS)

See also Cooperatives; Disasters; Industrial Review; Social Services.

Intelligence Operations

Referring to the "inevitable and increasing tension" in a democracy between the need for a wide diffusion of information and the need to keep some matters secret for the safety of the state and the efficiency of government, a British Home Office committee, in a four-volume report published in September 1972, said that the very wide terminology of Section 2 of the 1911 Official Secrets Act "obscures the important distinction between espionage and leakage." The committee recommended that the section be replaced by an Official Information Act. (*See* PUBLISHING.)

A Newark, N.J., federal grand jury in November 1971 indicted Roger Xavier Delouette and Col. Paul Fournier (real name Claude Ferrer), a senior member of the French External Documentation and Counter-Espionage Service (SDECE), on charges related to heroin smuggling. Later in the month Col. Roger Barberot, a former SDECE official, said in an interview broadcast from Radio Luxembourg that an SDECE agent had planted the heroin so that the U.S. Central Intelligence Agency would discover it and Fournier—whom his U.S. colleagues allegedly detested—would be caught and dismissed. The plotters, according to Barberot, were members of SDECE who had escaped the purge that had been going on for a year under the orders of SDECE's new head, Col. Alexandre de Marenches. Barberot went further when he accused Col. Jacques Beaumont (Bertrand), a former deputy director of SDECE, of being "guilty of high treason." Beaumont replied on November 22 at a press conference by saying that he would sue Barberot for slander.

UPI COMPIX

David Bingham and his wife, Maureen, whose bingo losses and taste for new clothes drove her husband to sell British defense secrets to the Soviets. Bingham, a submarine warfare expert in the British Royal Navy, began serving a 21-year prison term in March 1972.

John Ingersoll, director of the U.S. Bureau of Narcotics and Dangerous Drugs, said in Paris on Jan. 17, 1972, that 23 people, of whom 21 were French nationals, had been arrested and indicted for conspiring to smuggle drugs. Both Ingersoll and Jacques Solier, head of the French Central Office for the Repression of Traffic in Drugs, refused to make any comment on the "Delouette affair," making every effort to convince the assembled press of the complete harmony between U.S. and French authorities.

It was announced in Paris, on November 1, that Jean Rochet, 51, the outspoken head of the French DST (Internal Security Service) from 1967, was appointed *préfet* (governor) of the Meurthe-et-Moselle *département*. He had been at odds with the French Ministry of Foreign Affairs since he had said on television in 1971 that half the members of the East European diplomatic missions in Paris were engaged in espionage.

Rochet had also found himself at the centre of a libel action brought against him by a Polish Jew, Leopold Trepper, whom he had accused of collaborating with the Gestapo. Trepper was the leader of the famous wartime Soviet espionage ring code-named *Rote Kapelle* (Red Orchestra). Based in Paris and known as Gilbert Otto, Trepper had warned Joseph Stalin in May 1941 that Germany would soon attack the Soviet Union. In November 1942 he was caught by the Germans, escaped after nine months, and then hid in Paris until the liberation, when he was flown to Moscow. Instead of being given a hero's reception Trepper found himself in the Lubianka prison. He was not released until 1955, and only in 1957 was he able to return to Poland. He wished to go to Israel, but the Polish authorities, probably under Soviet pressure, refused him an exit visa. Apparently the Soviets feared that Trepper could still be a security risk and tell the West too much about the Soviet secret service. In the meantime a new "official history" of the Red Orchestra was being prepared in Moscow.

Enrico Berlinguer, new first secretary of the Italian Communist Party, declared shortly before the May 1972 general elections that the activities of foreign secret services in Italy had lately been intensified. At the same time foreign correspondents in Rome had been supplied with photographic copies of the most recent U.S. Defense Intelligence Agency manual allegedly instructing their agents as follows: "The Department of Defense has a manifold interest in acquiring information on both civil and military intelligence, counter-intelligence, security and subversive organizations of foreign nations, to include not only those of an enemy or potential adversary, but also those of allies. . . ."

William Vassall (48), who had served 10 years of his 18-year sentence for spying for the Soviets at the Royal Navy Portland base in Dorset, Eng., was released on parole on Oct. 24, 1972. Sub-Lieut. David James Bingham, a 31-year-old British Royal Navy officer, was sentenced on March 13, at Winchester, to 21 years for selling secrets "almost beyond price" to the Soviet Union. Later in March his wife, Maureen (35), who apparently had incited her husband and made the initial contact in order to get money, was charged with having committed an act preparatory to a spying offense. She was sentenced to two and a half years' imprisonment on November 15. In April Leonard Michael Hinchliffe (39), an assistant administrative officer of the Foreign and Commonwealth Office, was sent to prison for ten years for passing secret documents and codes to a Soviet agent named Andrei while attached to the British embassy in Khartoum, Sudan, in 1970.

The London *Daily Telegraph* on August 24 expressed the belief that Col. Rudolf Abel, Soviet master spy who died in Moscow in November 1971, was the son of Henry Fisher, a friend of Lenin who had left St. Petersburg (Leningrad) in 1891 and settled in England. Fisher returned to Russia after the Bolshevik Revolution, taking back with him his son of 17; this would explain Abel's faultless English.

Late in the year Israeli authorities arrested more than 30 persons who were alleged to be part of a Syrian espionage and sabotage ring, the largest such organization ever uncovered in Israel. Among those arrested were six Jews, including the son of one of the Communist members of the Knesset.

In February Valery Ivanovich Markelov, a Soviet employee of the UN Secretariat, was indicted for trying to obtain for the U.S.S.R. secret plans concerning the Grumman F-14A fighter plane. Bolivia in March asked the Soviet embassy in La Paz to withdraw 119 members of its staff for aiding leftist Bolivian guerrillas. In August the U.S. sentenced Air Force Sgt. Walter Perkins to three years in prison for attempting to smuggle top-secret national defense documents to Soviet agents in Mexico City.

(K. M. SMOGORZEWSKI)

Inter-American Affairs

The lack of any new U.S. initiative in 1972 toward Latin America to enhance relationships or make new policies reinforced the growing belief among observers that the administration of Pres. Richard M. Nixon did not consider Latin America important to the U.S. Yet Nixon was unwilling to relinquish the U.S. role as "Colossus of the North," and threats to this position continued to be dealt with by traditional means.

U.S. relations with Paraguay were strained when Paraguay at first refused to extradite a Frenchman, Auguste-Joseph Ricord (*see* CRIME), whom the U.S. authorities suspected of heading a gigantic international heroin smuggling operation. In response, the U.S. Senate threatened to cut off aid to Paraguay, and a Senate committee revised an earlier recommendation of a House committee to give Paraguay a sugar quota. Ricord was finally extradited.

U.S. relations with Chile and Peru did not improve, and no aid was forthcoming to those countries. President Nixon and his former treasury secretary, John Connally, Jr. (who visited several Latin-American countries in June), both hinted that those countries that did not pay prompt, adequate, and effective compensation for the nationalization of U.S. property would not receive further aid. A Treasury spokesman also emphasized that Congress was unlikely to approve further massive capital deposits for the Inter-American Development Bank unless prompt compensation was paid. The first high-level talks in two years between Chilean and U.S. representatives were held in Washington in December, with nationalization believed to be high on the list of subjects.

In the case of Chile the nationalized concerns took their own action. A U.S. copper corporation, Kennecott, was allowed by a Dutch court to seize a freighter containing 1,250 tons of copper from Chile, bound for France, which Kennecott claimed as part compensation for the nationalization of their Chilean enterprises in 1971. The copper was eventually unloaded at Le Havre. In late November a French court permitted payment to Chile but ordered that country to place an equal amount of money in escrow pending final settlement of the issue. (*See* LAW.)

Chile was also in conflict with one of its neighbours—Argentina. In August a group of guerrillas escaped from prison in Argentina, hijacked an airplane, flew to Chile, and asked for political asylum. Initially, Chilean Pres. Salvador Allende Gossens (*see* BIOGRAPHY) handed the guerrillas over to the courts to decide whether Argentina's demand for extradition should be granted, but it was later discovered that a group of prisoners who had helped the guerrillas escape had been shot. Allende then decided not to return the guerrillas.

Nixon's increasing preoccupation with Vietnam, the Middle East, and relations with the Soviet Union and China caused many Latin Americans to argue that if the U.S. could make new approaches to its cold-war rivals, Latin Americans should do the same with Cuba. Peru started the ball rolling by establishing diplomatic relations with Cuba in July. Previously, Peru had submitted a proposal to the Organization of American States (OAS) to permit individual nations to resume bilateral relations with Cuba at whatever level seemed appropriate, but this move was defeated by 13 votes to 7, with 3 abstentions. The seven affirmative votes were cast by Peru, Chile, Mexico, Panama, Ecuador, Jamaica, and Trinidad and Tobago; the abstainers were Argentina, Barbados, and Venezuela. In December Barbados, Jamaica, Trinidad and Tobago, and non-OAS member Guyana established relations with Cuba. There was little evidence that Cuba wanted to rejoin the OAS; on July 11 it was granted full membership in the Soviet bloc's Council for Mutual Economic Assistance (Comecon). This had the effect of spreading the responsibility for aid to Cuba among all Comecon members rather than just the Soviet Union. The U.S.S.R. showed continued

ROBERT TROSTLE—KEYSTONE

Chilean Pres. Salvador Allende waves at crowds lining streets of Mexico City during a tumultuous welcoming parade on his arrival for an official state visit in November 1972. Standing beside Allende is Luis Echeverría, president of Mexico. In the wake of crippling strikes and civil disturbances in Chile, Allende made a 21,000-mi. tour of Mexico, the U.S., Moscow, and Cuba seeking foreign aid and support.

interest in other parts of Latin America, particularly in Chile, as did China. The U.S. continued to insist that any rapprochement with Cuba was impossible under present circumstances, but some limited contacts did occur. Late in the year negotiations looking toward a possible antihijacking agreement were begun, with the Swiss ambassador in Havana acting as intermediary.

The United Kingdom made a concerted effort to intensify contacts with Latin America. The U.K. minister of state for foreign affairs, Joseph Godber, visited Argentina, Brazil, Chile, and Peru, and two seminars held in London were attended by representatives from Latin America.

Inter-American Organizations. The most newsworthy of the inter-American organizations in 1972 was the Inter-American Development Bank, which held its 13th annual meeting in Quito, Ecuador, in May. At this meeting it was agreed: first, that terms for the granting of "soft" (easy-term) loans from the Fund for Special Operations would be further eased, the length of term for each loan would be extended, interest would be 2%, and the period of grace would be extended to between seven and ten years; second, that greater emphasis was to be placed on granting loans involving two or more Latin-American countries in order to spur economic integration; and third, that the wealthier countries of Latin America were to take up future bond issues of the bank.

After heated debate over the admission of Canada and further extensions of membership, Canada was finally admitted as the 24th member of the development bank. The Latin-American countries insisted on retaining at least 55% of the bank's voting shares. Canada's $300 million entrance contribution entitled it to 6% of the shares; thus the only alternative, which was finally agreed on, was to reduce the U.S. share from 42 to 36%. The U.S., however, stated that it would not have its share reduced below 35% (and so lose its veto rights).

Very little emerged from the OAS General Assembly, which met in Washington, D.C., April 11–21. One of the main problems was that the timing of the meeting clashed with the third United Nations Conference on Trade and Development (UNCTAD), which was being held in Santiago, Chile, and which many preferred to attend. The division over attendance was roughly between Brazil and Hispanic America. The Spanish speakers believed that UNCTAD was the more important, and they hoped to use it as a medium for pushing their claims as less developed nations. Brazil, however, saw itself not as a less developed nation but as a nation emerging from that stage, and the OAS therefore took priority. The Assembly did agree to send an OAS observer to British Honduras to check on British forces stationed there.

Regional and Subregional Integration. The nations of Latin America showed little inclination to act in concert within their own organizations. The Comisión Especial de Coordinación Latinoamericana (CECLA) failed to agree on a joint position for the "Group of 77" meeting in Lima on whether less developed nations should take joint action outside the IMF to solve international monetary problems. At the meeting Mexico proved obstructionist and seemed careful not to offend the U.S.

There were no signs that the members of the Central American Common Market (CACM—El Salvador, Honduras, Nicaragua, Guatemala, and Costa Rica) were any nearer reaching agreement on the continuation and future progress of the organization, although at the beginning of the year there had seemed to be grounds for cautious optimism. In December 1971 the five economics ministers of the CACM member countries met at San José, Costa Rica, and agreed on the immediate initiation of bilateral negotiations between Honduras and three other members, Nicaragua, Guatemala, and Costa Rica. It was hoped that in this way trade between Honduras and the three others could be promoted as a first step toward the reintegration of the former, which in 1971 had imposed tariff barriers on imports from other CACM members. During the previous October, settlement had been reached on the regulation of trade between El Salvador and the other three countries. In this way it was hoped that the common market of four would evolve and that when political circumstances permitted it would be possible to merge again into one market of five. Relations between El Salvador and Honduras, which fought an armed conflict in 1969, seemed to have eased and in June 1972 the foreign ministers of those countries met for the first time since 1969, in Santo Domingo.

Costa Rica remained worried about the trade imbalance with the other four CACM member countries. In June the other members expressed concern over new trade regulations proposed by Costa Rica under which it would pay for its imports on a six-monthly basis, abolishing the preferential three-monthly term it had accorded its partners in the CACM. Furthermore, at the end of August the executive board of the Banco Central de Costa Rica decided to apply the free-market rate of exchange to nonessential imports from Central America, rather than use the former preferential rate. Shortly afterward, Guatemala, El Salvador, and Nicaragua suspended their trade with Costa Rica. Trade was resumed six weeks later, when an agreement was signed in San José which was scheduled to extend until February 1974. The agreement provided for an effective devaluation of the colón (Costa Rica's currency), with about three-quarters of Costa Rican imports being paid for at a free market rate of 8.60 colones to the dollar and the rest at the official rate of 6.62 to the dollar. For exports the proportion was halfway between free and official rates. In return Costa Rica promised to pay promptly for imports from other CACM countries.

In spite of these efforts the future development of the CACM remained in doubt, especially while the disagreement between El Salvador and Honduras continued. The agreement at San José did, at least, go some way toward easing the economic problems confronting Costa Rica and left the door open for a similar solution to the economic difficulties of some of the other members.

The Latin American Free Trade Association (LAFTA) showed no more enthusiasm to regain its initial dynamism. At its 11th annual conference, held in December 1971, the contracting parties granted concessions on 137 products, of which 113 related to new items. Argentina granted the largest number of concessions with a total of 84, of which 72 referred to new products. Six protocols were signed relating to industrial agreements on chemicals and petrochemicals. Industrial agreements were signed on refrigeration, air-conditioning equipment, and electrical domestic appliances by Argentina and Brazil. Agreements on the photographic industry were signed in January by Argentina, Brazil, Mexico, and Uruguay.

The Andean Group remained the more dynamic subgroup of LAFTA. Toward the end of 1971 the Andean Group Commission reached agreement on Decision No. 40, by which taxation in an Andean Group member country was to be incurred once only, in the country in which the taxable profit was generated. In June the foreign ministers of the Andean Group member countries met in Lima and agreed that satisfactory progress had been made in the three years since the group's foundation. They also stated that the principal objective was to intensify efforts toward more rapid regional integration and that these economic objectives could be pursued despite differences in political objectives.

The dominant issue of the year was the long-awaited application from Venezuela to join the Andean Group. The formal application came early in the year, and negotiations on the terms of admission began in Lima in March. Since 1969 Venezuela had strengthened its links with Colombia, Ecuador, Peru, Bolivia, and Chile on a bilateral basis and had been bringing some of its external tariffs into line with the Andean pact regulations. However, the attitude of the group to foreign investment as embodied in Decision No. 24, which restricted foreign investment, had always been a stumbling block. Private industrial groups in Venezuela felt threatened by the competition from within the Andean Group because of the high cost structure of some of Venezuela's traditional industries. Other groups, however, felt that a potential market of 65 million people would stimulate some of Venezuela's newer industries and help break the dependence on oil.

Negotiations were probably made more difficult by the underlying tension between Venezuela and Colombia over the undrawn frontier in the oil-rich Gulf of Venezuela. Also in dispute was the unauthorized migration of Colombians into Venezuela.

Progress in the other subgroup of LAFTA, the Río de la Plata Basin Group (Argentina, Brazil, Bolivia, Paraguay, and Uruguay), was slow. Brazil refused to agree to a decision made by the other Río de la Plata Basin countries to set up a $100 million fund for economic integration. The Brazilian government objected to the principle that Argentina and Brazil should contribute the most toward the fund but would only have equal rights with the three smaller nations in the group's resources.

Bilateral Relations. Pres. Alejandro Lanusse of Argentina met with Brazilian Pres. Emílio Médici in Brasília in March. Although the general atmosphere of the talks was described by some observers as "chilly," the two leaders signed a joint communiqué that emphasized their agreements. They concurred that world trade arrangements should be made more favourable to poor nations and that their two countries should cooperate in improving transportation and communications over their common borders and should also work to encourage tourism.

The communiqué avoided mentioning matters that were in dispute between the two nations. Those included Argentina's desire to have Brazil consult with it before proceeding with two huge hydroelectric projects on the Paraná River.

Brazil and Bolivia in April signed agreements that provided increased Brazilian aid to its neighbour. Brazil agreed to advance $5 million to Bolivia for road-building equipment, to contribute $1 million to a regional development plan in Bolivia's tropical lowlands, and to purchase Bolivian crude oil from fields near Santa Cruz for two years beginning in July.

(JEREMY WILLOUGHBY)

ENCYCLOPÆDIA BRITANNICA FILMS. *Siqueiros: "El Maestro" (March of Humanity in Latin America)* (1969).

International Organizations

The following table shows the membership of the world's sovereign states in various international organizations in 1972. The growing realization that political and economic problems transcended international boundaries led to a proliferation of international organizations after World War II. Of these, the UN and its specialized agencies (some of which, such as the ILO and the UPU, antedated the war) aimed at least theoretically at universality. The World Bank, originally established to provide help to war-devastated nations, turned more and more in succeeding years toward concentration on the problems of economic development. Organizations with more restricted membership included regional political groupings (OAS, OAU), military alliances (NATO, the Warsaw Pact), and organizations with a primarily economic orientation (EEC, Comecon). Such groupings as the Colombo Plan were chiefly vehicles for channeling aid from the developed to the less developed countries.

International Bank for Reconstruction and Development: *see* Development, Economic
International Criminal Police Organization: *see* Police
International Law: *see* Law
International Monetary Fund: *see* Payments and Reserves, International

Membership in International Organizations, December 1972

Country	UN 1	FAO 2	IMCO 3	IAEA 4	ICAO 5	ILO 6	IBRD 7	IDA 8	IFC 9	IMF 10	ITU 11	UNESCO 12	UPU 13	WHO 14	WMO 15	GATT 16	CE 17	AL 18	OAS 19	WEU 20	OCAS 21	C-Plan 22	Comecon 23	Euratom 24	ECSC 25	EEC 26	EFTA 27	IDB 28	LAFTA 29	OECD 30	ANZUS 31	CENTO 32	NATO 33	SEATO 34	WTO 35	Antarctic treaty 36	OAU 37	SPC 38
Afghanistan	●	●		●	●	●	●	●	●	●	●	●	●	●	●							●																
Albania	●			●							●	●	●	●	●																						●	
Algeria	●	●	●	●	●	●	●	●		●	●	●	●	●	●			●																			●	
Argentina	●	●	●	●	●	●	●	●	●	●	●	●	●	●	●	●			●									●	●							●		
Australia	●	●	●	●	●	●	●	●	●	●	●	●	●	●	●	●						●								●	●			●		●		●
Austria	●	●		●	●	●	●	●	●	●	●	●	●	●	●	●	●										●			●								
Bahrain	●	●			●					●				●				●																				
Bangladesh				●		●	●	●		●		●		●		●						●																
Barbados	●	●	●		●	●				●	●	●	●	●	●	●			●									●										
Belgium	●	●	●	●	●	●	●	●	●	●	●	●	●	●	●	●	●			●				●	●	●				●			●			●		
Belorussia	●			●		●					●	●	●	●	●																							
Bhutan	●												●									●																
Bolivia	●	●		●	●	●	●	●	●	●	●	●	●	●	●				●									●	●									
Botswana	●	●					●	●		●	●		●		●																						●	
Brazil	●	●	●	●	●	●	●	●	●	●	●	●	●	●	●	●			●									●	●									
Bulgaria	●	●	●	●	●	●					●	●	●	●	●								●												●			
Burma	●	●	●	●	●	●	●	●	●	●	●	●	●	●	●	●						●																
Burundi	●	●			●	●	●	●		●	●	●	●	●	●	●																					●	
Cambodia	●	●	●	●	●	●	●	●		●	●	●	●	●	●							●																
Cameroon	●	●	●	●	●	●	●	●		●	●	●	●	●	●	●																					●	
Canada	●	●	●	●	●	●	●	●	●	●	●	●	●	●	●	●						●						●		●			●					
Central African Rep.	●	●			●	●	●	●		●	●	●	●	●	●	●																					●	
Chad	●	●			●	●	●	●		●	●	●	●	●	●	●																					●	
Chile	●	●		●	●	●	●	●	●	●	●	●	●	●	●	●			●									●	●							●		
China	●		●		●	●	●	●	●	●	●	●	●	●	●																							
Colombia	●	●		●	●	●	●	●	●	●	●	●	●	●	●				●									●	●									
Congo (Brazzaville)	●	●			●	●	●	●		●	●	●	●	●	●	●																					●	
Costa Rica	●	●		●	●	●	●	●	●	●	●	●	●	●	●				●		●							●										
Cuba	●	●	●	●	●	●					●	●	●	●	●	●							●															
Cyprus	●	●		●	●	●	●	●	●	●	●	●	●	●	●	●	●																					
Czechoslovakia	●	●	●	●	●	●					●	●	●	●	●	●							●												●	●		
Dahomey	●	●			●	●	●	●		●	●	●	●	●	●	●																					●	
Denmark	●	●	●	●	●	●	●	●	●	●	●	●	●	●	●	●	●										●			●			●			●		
Dominican Rep.	●	●	●	●	●	●	●	●	●	●	●	●	●	●	●	●			●									●										
Ecuador	●	●	●	●	●	●	●	●	●	●	●	●	●	●	●				●									●	●									
Egypt	●	●	●	●	●	●	●	●	●	●	●	●	●	●	●	●		●																			●	
El Salvador	●	●		●	●	●	●	●	●	●	●	●	●	●	●				●		●							●										
Equatorial Guinea	●						●			●	●		●																									
Ethiopia	●	●		●	●	●	●	●	●	●	●	●	●	●	●																						●	
Fiji	●	●					●			●	●		●																									●
Finland	●	●	●	●	●	●	●	●	●	●	●	●	●	●	●	●														●								
France	●	●	●	●	●	●	●	●	●	●	●	●	●	●	●	●	●			●				●	●	●				●			●	●		●		●
Gabon	●	●		●	●	●	●	●	●	●	●	●	●	●	●	●																					●	
Gambia, The	●	●					●	●		●				●		●																					●	
Germany, East																							●												●			
Germany, West		●	●	●	●	●	●	●	●	●	●	●	●	●	●	●	●			●				●	●	●				●			●					
Ghana	●	●	●	●	●	●	●	●	●	●	●	●	●	●	●	●																					●	
Greece	●	●	●	●	●	●	●	●	●	●	●	●	●	●	●	●														●			●					
Guatemala	●	●		●	●	●	●	●	●	●	●	●	●	●	●				●		●							●										
Guinea	●	●			●	●	●	●		●	●	●	●	●	●																						●	
Guyana	●	●			●	●	●	●	●	●	●	●	●	●	●	●																						
Haiti	●	●	●	●	●	●	●	●	●	●	●	●	●	●	●	●			●									●										
Honduras	●	●	●		●	●	●	●	●	●	●	●	●	●	●				●		●							●										
Hungary	●	●	●	●	●	●					●	●	●	●	●								●												●			
Iceland	●	●	●	●	●	●	●	●	●	●	●	●	●	●	●	●	●										●			●			●					
India	●	●	●	●	●	●	●	●	●	●	●	●	●	●	●	●						●																
Indonesia	●	●	●	●	●	●	●	●	●	●	●	●	●	●	●	●						●																
Iran	●	●	●	●	●	●	●	●	●	●	●	●	●	●	●							●										●						
Iraq	●	●		●	●	●	●	●	●	●	●	●	●	●	●			●																				
Ireland	●	●	●	●	●	●	●	●	●	●	●	●	●	●	●	●	●													●								
Israel	●	●	●	●	●	●	●	●	●	●	●	●	●	●	●	●																						
Italy	●	●	●	●	●	●	●	●	●	●	●	●	●	●	●	●	●			●				●	●	●				●			●					
Ivory Coast	●	●	●	●	●	●	●	●	●	●	●	●	●	●	●	●																					●	
Jamaica	●	●		●	●	●	●		●	●	●	●	●	●	●	●			●									●										
Japan	●	●	●	●	●	●	●	●	●	●	●	●	●	●	●	●						●								●						●		
Jordan	●	●		●	●	●	●	●	●	●	●	●	●	●	●			●																				
Kenya	●	●		●	●	●	●	●	●	●	●	●	●	●	●	●																					●	
Korea, South		●	●	●	●		●	●	●	●	●	●	●	●	●	●						●																
Kuwait	●	●	●	●	●	●	●	●	●	●	●	●	●	●	●	●		●																				
Laos	●	●			●	●	●	●		●	●	●	●	●	●							●																
Lebanon	●	●	●	●	●	●	●	●	●	●	●	●	●	●	●			●																				
Lesotho	●	●					●	●		●	●	●	●	●																							●	
Liberia	●	●	●	●	●	●	●	●	●	●	●	●	●	●																							●	
Libya	●	●	●	●	●	●	●	●	●	●	●	●	●	●	●			●																			●	
Liechtenstein				●							●		●																									
Luxembourg	●	●		●	●	●	●	●	●	●	●	●	●	●	●	●	●			●				●	●	●				●			●					
Malagasy Rep.	●	●	●	●	●	●	●	●	●	●	●	●	●	●	●	●																					●	
Malawi	●	●			●	●	●	●	●	●	●	●	●	●	●	●																					●	
Malaysia	●	●		●	●	●	●	●	●	●	●	●	●	●	●	●						●																
Maldives	●	●	●								●		●	●								●																

Continued, with key, on page 376

Membership in International Organizations, December 1972

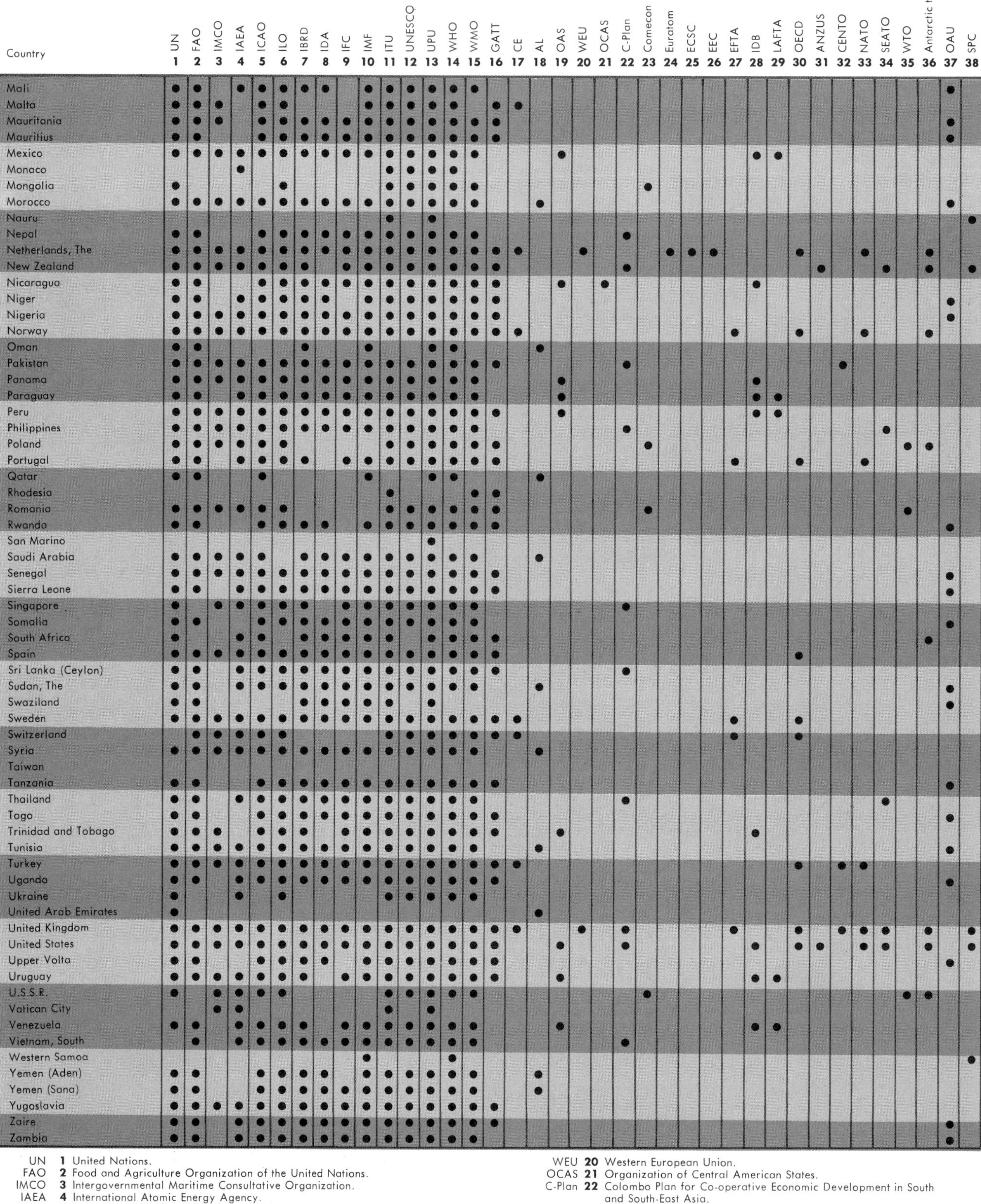

Country	UN 1	FAO 2	IMCO 3	IAEA 4	ICAO 5	ILO 6	IBRD 7	IDA 8	IFC 9	IMF 10	ITU 11	UNESCO 12	UPU 13	WHO 14	WMO 15	GATT 16	CE 17	AL 18	OAS 19	WEU 20	OCAS 21	C-Plan 22	Comecon 23	Euratom 24	ECSC 25	EEC 26	EFTA 27	IDB 28	LAFTA 29	OECD 30	ANZUS 31	CENTO 32	NATO 33	SEATO 34	WTO 35	Antarctic treaty 36	OAU 37	SPC 38
Mali	●	●		●	●	●	●	●		●	●	●	●	●	●																						●	
Malta	●	●	●		●	●				●	●	●	●	●		●	●																					
Mauritania	●	●	●		●	●	●	●	●	●	●	●	●	●	●	●																					●	
Mauritius	●	●			●	●	●	●	●	●	●	●	●	●	●	●																					●	
Mexico	●	●	●	●	●	●	●	●	●	●	●	●	●	●	●				●									●	●									
Monaco				●							●	●	●	●																								
Mongolia	●					●					●	●	●	●	●								●															
Morocco	●	●	●	●	●	●	●	●	●	●	●	●	●	●	●			●																			●	
Nauru											●		●																									●
Nepal	●	●			●	●	●	●	●	●	●	●	●	●	●							●																
Netherlands, The	●	●	●	●	●	●	●	●	●	●	●	●	●	●	●	●	●			●				●	●	●				●			●			●		
New Zealand	●	●	●	●	●	●	●		●	●	●	●	●	●	●	●						●									●			●		●		●
Nicaragua	●	●			●	●	●	●	●	●	●	●	●	●	●	●			●		●							●										
Niger	●	●		●	●	●	●	●		●	●	●	●	●	●	●																					●	
Nigeria	●	●	●	●	●	●	●	●	●	●	●	●	●	●	●	●																					●	
Norway	●	●	●	●	●	●	●	●	●	●	●	●	●	●	●	●	●										●			●			●			●		
Oman	●	●					●			●			●	●				●																				
Pakistan	●	●	●	●	●	●	●	●	●	●	●	●	●	●	●	●						●										●						
Panama	●	●	●	●	●	●	●	●	●	●	●	●	●	●	●				●									●										
Paraguay	●	●		●	●	●	●	●	●	●	●	●	●	●	●				●									●	●									
Peru	●	●	●	●	●	●	●	●	●	●	●	●	●	●	●	●			●									●	●									
Philippines	●	●	●	●	●	●	●	●	●	●	●	●	●	●	●							●												●				
Poland	●	●	●	●	●	●					●	●	●	●	●	●							●												●	●		
Portugal	●	●		●	●	●	●		●	●	●	●	●	●	●	●											●			●			●					
Qatar	●	●			●					●			●	●				●																				
Rhodesia											●				●	●																						
Romania	●	●	●	●	●	●					●	●	●	●	●	●							●												●			
Rwanda	●	●			●	●	●	●		●	●	●	●	●	●	●																					●	
San Marino													●																									
Saudi Arabia	●	●	●	●	●		●	●	●	●	●	●	●	●	●			●																				
Senegal	●	●	●	●	●	●	●	●	●	●	●	●	●	●	●	●																					●	
Sierra Leone	●	●		●	●	●	●	●	●	●	●	●	●	●	●	●																					●	
Singapore	●		●	●	●	●	●		●	●	●	●	●	●	●							●																
Somalia	●	●			●	●	●	●	●	●	●	●	●	●	●																						●	
South Africa	●			●	●		●	●	●	●	●		●	●	●	●																				●		
Spain	●	●	●	●	●	●	●	●	●	●	●	●	●	●	●	●														●								
Sri Lanka (Ceylon)	●	●		●	●	●	●	●	●	●	●	●	●	●	●	●						●																
Sudan, The	●	●		●	●	●	●	●	●	●	●	●	●	●	●			●																			●	
Swaziland	●	●					●	●	●	●	●		●																								●	
Sweden	●	●	●	●	●	●	●	●	●	●	●	●	●	●	●	●	●										●			●								
Switzerland		●	●	●	●	●					●	●	●	●	●	●	●										●			●								
Syria	●	●	●	●	●	●	●	●	●	●	●	●	●	●	●			●																				
Taiwan																																						
Tanzania	●	●			●	●	●	●	●	●	●	●	●	●	●	●																					●	
Thailand	●	●		●	●	●	●	●	●	●	●	●	●	●	●							●												●				
Togo	●	●			●	●	●	●	●	●	●	●	●	●	●	●																					●	
Trinidad and Tobago	●	●	●		●	●	●		●	●	●	●	●	●	●	●			●									●									●	
Tunisia	●	●	●	●	●	●	●	●	●	●	●	●	●	●	●			●																			●	
Turkey	●	●	●	●	●	●	●	●	●	●	●	●	●	●	●	●	●													●		●	●					
Uganda	●	●		●	●	●	●	●	●	●	●	●	●	●	●	●																					●	
Ukraine	●			●		●					●	●	●	●	●																							
United Arab Emirates	●																	●																				
United Kingdom	●	●	●	●	●	●	●	●	●	●	●	●	●	●	●	●	●			●		●					●			●		●	●	●		●		●
United States	●	●	●	●	●	●	●	●	●	●	●	●	●	●	●	●			●			●						●		●	●		●	●		●		●
Upper Volta	●	●			●	●	●	●		●	●	●	●	●	●	●																					●	
Uruguay	●	●	●	●	●	●	●		●	●	●	●	●	●	●	●			●									●	●									
U.S.S.R.	●		●	●	●	●					●	●	●	●	●								●												●	●		
Vatican City			●	●							●		●																									
Venezuela	●	●		●	●	●	●		●	●	●	●	●	●	●				●									●	●									
Vietnam, South		●		●	●	●	●	●	●	●	●	●	●	●	●							●																
Western Samoa										●				●																								●
Yemen (Aden)	●	●			●	●	●	●		●	●	●	●	●	●			●																				
Yemen (Sana)	●	●			●	●	●	●	●	●	●	●	●	●	●			●																				
Yugoslavia	●	●	●	●	●	●	●	●	●	●	●	●	●	●	●	●																						
Zaire	●	●		●	●	●	●	●	●	●	●	●	●	●	●	●																					●	
Zambia	●	●		●	●	●	●	●	●	●	●	●	●	●	●																						●	

UN **1** United Nations.
FAO **2** Food and Agriculture Organization of the United Nations.
IMCO **3** Intergovernmental Maritime Consultative Organization.
IAEA **4** International Atomic Energy Agency.
ICAO **5** International Civil Aviation Organization.
ILO **6** International Labour Organization.
IBRD **7** International Bank for Reconstruction and Development.
IDA **8** International Development Association.
IFC **9** International Finance Corporation.
IMF **10** International Monetary Fund.
ITU **11** International Telecommunication Union.
UNESCO **12** United Nations Educational, Scientific, and Cultural Organization.
UPU **13** Universal Postal Union.
WHO **14** World Health Organization.
WMO **15** World Meteorological Organization.
GATT **16** General Agreement on Tariffs and Trade.
CE **17** Council of Europe.
AL **18** Arab League.
OAS **19** Organization of American States.
WEU **20** Western European Union.
OCAS **21** Organization of Central American States.
C-Plan **22** Colombo Plan for Co-operative Economic Development in South and South-East Asia.
Comecon **23** Council for Mutual Economic Assistance.
Euratom **24** European Atomic Energy Community.
ECSC **25** European Coal and Steel Community.
EEC **26** European Economic Community.
EFTA **27** European Free Trade Association.
IDB **28** Inter-American Development Bank.
LAFTA **29** Latin American Free Trade Association.
OECD **30** Organization for Economic Cooperation and Development.
ANZUS **31** Security treaty between Australia, New Zealand, and the United States.
CENTO **32** Central Treaty Organization.
NATO **33** North Atlantic Treaty Organization.
SEATO **34** Southeast Asia Treaty Organization.
WTO **35** Warsaw Treaty Organization.
36 Antarctic Treaty.
OAU **37** Organization of African Unity.
SPC **38** South Pacific Commission.

Investment, International

The value of investment abroad by the main lending countries (the industrial nations of Europe, North America, and Japan) was about $16 billion in 1971. This represented a small increase over the previous year. Direct investment (the purchase of productive assets) amounted to $12.5 billion, which was $1.1 billion higher than 1970. Portfolio investment (the purchase of foreign securities) is made up of many sales and many purchases, and the net value of sales minus purchases is recorded in each country. This type of investment is sensitive to differences in interest rates between countries and to expectations of changes in exchange rates. Changed conditions in 1971 reduced portfolio investment below its 1970 level. The years 1971 and 1972 were notable for the number of countries that were imposing restrictions on capital flows, especially the U.S., Japan, and the Netherlands.

United States. Foreign investment by U.S. residents and corporations continued to be restrained in 1971 and 1972 by the Foreign Direct Investment Program, the Interest Equalization Tax, and the Voluntary Credit Restraint Program. The effect of most of these measures was to confine increases in investment to within expressed guidelines or to exempted categories. Total U.S. foreign investment in 1971 was about $500 million higher than in 1970, a relatively low annual increase compared with recent years (*see* Table I). This investment brought the total value of U.S. foreign assets to more than $107 billion at the end of 1971 (*see* Table IV). One-third of the direct investments (fixed productive assets, such as factories and mines) were in Western Europe, and 28% were in Canada. More than half the portfolio investments (ownership of foreign government and corporation securities) were in Canada; Western Europe and Canada together accounted for nearly two-thirds of the stock of U.S. foreign assets.

Table I. U.S. Investment Abroad

In $000,000

Item	1967	1968	1969	1970	1971	1972*
Direct investment						
New funds	3,137	3,209	3,254	4,403	4,765	2,932
Reinvested profits	1,598	2,175	2,604	2,948	3,116	...
Total	4,735	5,384	5,858	7,351	7,881	...
Portfolio investment	1,292	1,133	1,484	943	909	1,474
Total	6,027	6,517	7,342	8,294	8,790	...

*Seasonally adjusted; at annual rate.
Source: U.S. Department of Commerce, *Survey of Current Business.*

Table II. Foreign Investment in U.S.

In $000,000

Inflow of funds	1967	1968	1969	1970	1971	1972*
Direct investment	258	319	832	969	−67	−28
Portfolio investment	1,016	4,389	3,112	2,190	2,282	4,014
Total	1,274	4,708	3,944	3,159	2,215	3,986
Total earnings†	1,764	2,231	3,686	4,143	3,059	3,064

*First half of year, seasonally adjusted, at annual rate.
†Excluding undistributed profits.
Source: U.S. Department of Commerce, *Survey of Current Business.*

Table III. U.K. Investment Abroad

In £000,000

Item	1960	1968	1969	1970	1971	1972*
Direct investment†						
New funds	165	133	226	203	258	...
Reinvested profits	85	277	321	305	277	...
Total	250	410	547	508	535	540
Portfolio investment‡	−37	236	34	102	67	450
Oil and miscellaneous	109	81	96	144	123	120
Total	322	727	677	754	725	1,110

*Estimate based on first half of year.
†Excluding oil and, in 1960, insurance.
‡Net disinvestment in 1960.
Sources: *U.K. Balance of Payments, 1972; Economic Trends.*

Table IV. U.S. Foreign Assets, Investment, and Earnings by Region, 1971

In $000,000

Area	Value of assets at end of year			Investment during year			Earnings		
	Direct	Portfolio	Total	Direct*	Portfolio	Total*	Direct*	Portfolio	Total*
Canada	24,030	11,983	36,013	226	279	505	1,000	873	1,873
Latin America	15,763	1,288	17,051	668	40	708	1,124	517	1,641
Western Europe	27,621	3,340	30,961	2,082	−46	2,036	1,658	470	2,128
Japan	1,818	847	2,665	211	126	337	151	267	418
Other countries	12,450	2,239	14,689	1,035	234	1,269	2,920	321	3,241
International organizations and unallocated	4,319	1,977	6,296	543	276	819	433	108	541
Total	86,001	21,673	107,675	4,765	909	5,674	7,286	2,556	9,842

*Excluding reinvested profits (*see* Table I).
Source: U.S. Department of Commerce, *Survey of Current Business.*

Table V. U.S. Investment Earnings

In $000,000

Item	1967	1968	1969	1970	1971	1972*
Direct investment						
Repatriated profits	4,517	4,973	5,658	6,026	7,286	7,190
Reinvested profits†	1,516	2,049	2,316	2,707	2,910	...
Total	6,033	7,022	7,974	8,733	10,196	...
Portfolio investment						
Total income	1,717	1,949	2,267	2,597	2,556	2,624
Total earnings	7,750	8,971	10,241	11,330	12,752	...

*Seasonally adjusted; at annual rate.
†Excluding interest but before deducting foreign withholding taxes.
Source: U.S. Department of Commerce, *Survey of Current Business.*

Direct investment by U.S. corporations in 1971 was more than $500 million higher than in 1970. The larger part of this was accounted for by the outflow of new funds; reinvested profits increased by only $170 million. This increased outflow was partly brought about by expectations of exchange rate changes. The flow of new investment capital to Western Europe increased by almost 10% to $2.1 billion (*see* Table IV). The major change occurred in investment in Canada, which fell from $915 million in 1970 to $226 million in 1971 as a result of reduced capital flows by the automobile and petroleum industries. The increase in direct investment in 1971 was concentrated in the petroleum industry, which increased by $400 million to $1.9 billion in 1971, thus accounting for 40% of U.S. foreign direct investment.

U.S. portfolio investment in 1971 was at much the same level as in the previous year, but within this total there were some changes in detail. Purchases of newly issued foreign corporation stocks fell from $145 million in 1970 to only $14 million in 1971; but, whereas on balance in 1970 U.S. residents had sold $77 million of existing foreign corporation stock, in 1971 their purchases were equal to their sales.

During 1972 U.S. foreign investment was running at a lower rate than in 1971. As confidence was restored in the dollar, outflows that had resulted from exchange rate considerations came to an end. Marked reductions in direct investment in Europe and Latin

Table VI. U.K. Investment Earnings

In £000,000

Item	1960	1968	1969	1970	1971	1972*
Direct investment†						
Repatriated profits	173	291	329	376	417	...
Reinvested profits	85	277	321	305	277	...
Total	258	568	650	681	694	740
Portfolio investment	125	164	161	171	167	162
Oil and miscellaneous	286	375	525	515	559	608
Total earnings	669	1,107	1,336	1,367	1,420	1,510

*Estimate based on first half of year.
†Excluding oil and, in 1960, insurance.
Sources: *U.K. Balance of Payments, 1972; Economic Trends.*

Investment:
see Investment, International; Savings and Investment; Stock Exchanges

America took place, but investment in Asia and Africa increased. Portfolio investment was at a higher rate than in 1971 due largely to some very large placings of Canadian provincial bonds on the U.S. market.

Earnings on U.S. foreign investments increased by $1.4 billion in 1971 over the 1970 level to $12.8 billion (*see* Table V). About 80% of the earnings were from direct investments, which also accounted for all of the increase between 1970 and 1971; earnings on portfolio investments were marginally lower in 1971 than in the previous year. Earnings on European direct investments were about $300 million higher at $1.7 billion, and earnings from Asia and Africa increased by $600 million to $2.7 billion. Earnings in the first half of 1972 were at a level similar to that of the corresponding period of 1971, with higher earnings from Asia and Africa offsetting lower receipts from Latin America.

Foreign investment in the U.S. fell sharply in 1971 as foreign corporations actually reduced their U.S. assets (*see* Table II). Portfolio investment was maintained in 1971 and increased sharply in the first half of 1972.

Exchange rate considerations were at the heart of the reduction in direct investments in 1971. As confidence in the dollar revived there were signs during 1972 that foreign funds were returning.

United Kingdom. Investment abroad by U.K. residents and companies in 1971 declined slightly below the level of 1970, but there was a large increase in the first half of 1972 which was concentrated in portfolio investment (*see* Table III). Direct investment increased by about £30 million in 1971 to £535 million. Most of this increase was accounted for by increased investment in existing overseas subsidiaries, but several British companies made acquisitions abroad. As Table VII shows, the growth in the flow of investment was shared between sterling area and nonsterling area countries.

U.K. portfolio investment fell to modest levels in 1971 due largely to net selling of investments in other sterling area countries amounting to £61 million. Portfolio investment in countries outside the sterling areas increased from £85 million in 1970 to £128 million in 1971. A very large increase took place in the first half of 1972 mainly because of investment by U.K. financial institutions in the U.S. and the EEC and also because of renewed investment in the sterling area.

Earnings on U.K. foreign investments rose little in 1971 (*see* Table VI). The bulk of the increase was accounted for by higher oil earnings following the price increases arranged by the Organization of Petroleum Exporting Countries. Early data for 1972 suggested a higher level of earnings for both direct investment and for the oil and miscellaneous category.

In 1971 for the first time foreign investment in the U.K. exceeded British investment abroad (Table IX). Foreign investment in the U.K. in 1971 was distributed approximately equally among the direct, portfolio, and the oil and miscellaneous categories. The major change in 1971 occurred in the large increase in foreign purchases of U.K. securities and bonds, particularly in the U.K. public sector. Foreign purchases of U.K. government stock and loans to U.K. nationalized industries amounted to £180 million in 1971, compared with an annual average of only £20 million during the previous decade. This high rate of foreign portfolio investment in the U.K. was encouraged by exchange rate considerations and by an expected decline in the high yields on U.K. shares, thus giving a capital gain to the investors. These conditions, which prevailed strongly in the first half of 1971, no longer applied in 1972 and the flow of capital was reduced to a more usual rate.

Other Industrial Countries. Data on foreign investment by, and in, other industrial countries is given in Table VIII.

Belgium. Direct foreign investment by Belgian companies, which had increased sharply in 1970 from negligible amounts in 1969, increased further in 1971; steel and oil companies were particularly responsible for the increased outflow. Belgian portfolio investment also increased in 1971 largely due to subscriptions to various issues by international organizations. At the same time, foreign investment in Belgium, both direct and portfolio, increased (the latter due mainly to foreign purchases of shares in Belgian oil companies). The overall net outflow of capital was thus reduced from $160 million to $35 million.

Table VII. U.K. Direct Investment and Earnings: by Region*

In £000,000

Area	Investment 1968	1969	1970	1971	Earnings 1968	1969	1970	1971
North America	114	89	178	...	135	136	141	...
Latin America	17	21	13	...	34	33	32	...
EEC	73	105	71	...	65	83	93	...
EFTA	19	14	21	...	13	17	22	...
Others	10	7	12	...	35	37	37	...
Total nonsterling area	233	236	295	306	282	306	325	336
Total sterling area	177	313	213	229	286	344	356	358
Total	410	549	508	535	568	650	681	694
Of which less developed countries (included above)	91	147	134	145	170	193	200	210

*Excluding oil companies.
Sources: *U.K. Trade and Industry Journal; U.K. Balance of Payments, 1972.*

Table VIII. Other OECD Countries' International Investment, 1970–71

In $000,000

Country	1970 Direct	1970 Portfolio	1970 Total	1971 Direct	1971 Portfolio	1971 Total
Belgium						
Outflow	155	315	470	170	440	610
Inflow	320	−10	310	430	145	575
Net	−165	325	160	−260	295	35
Canada						
Outflow	235	−60	175	...	−195	...
Inflow	725	550	1,275	...	190	...
Net	−490	−610	−1,100	−590	−385	−975
France						
Outflow	...	...	500	...	...	500
Inflow	...	...	1,500	...	...	1,300
Net	...	...	−1,000	...	...	−800
West Germany						
Outflow	675	545	1,220	705	−160	545
Inflow	420	360	780	975	605	1,580
Net	255	185	440	−270	−765	−1,035
Italy						
Outflow	120	415	535	245	370	615
Inflow	725	420	1,145	760	485	1,245
Net	−605	−5	−610	−515	−115	−630
Japan						
Outflow	...	...	2,000	...	...	2,300
Inflow	100	300	400	100	1,100	1,200
Net	...	...	1,600	...	...	1,100
Netherlands						
Outflow	520	250	770	475	430	905
Inflow	540	675	1,215	610	770	1,380
Net	−20	−425	−445	−135	−340	−475

Sources: Annual reports of International Monetary Fund, Bank for International Settlements, and national banks.

Table IX. Foreign Investment in U.K.

In £000,000

Item	1960	1968	1969	1970	1971	1972*
Direct investment†						
New funds	68	98	187	168	185	...
Reinvested profits	67	176	132	171	175	...
Total	135	274	319	339	360	270
Portfolio investment	42	50	136	74	370	180
Oil and miscellaneous	55	259	218	317	372	340
Total	232	583	673	730	1,102	790

*Estimate based on first half of year.
†Excluding oil and, in 1960, insurance.
Sources: *U.K. Balance of Payments, 1972; Economic Trends.*

Canada. The net inflow of foreign capital into Canada fell from $1.1 billion in 1970 to less than $1 billion in 1971; this compared with a net inflow of $2.2 billion in 1969. The main factor in this change was the reduction in the inflow of foreign portfolio investment. The central bank policy of easy credit removed the interest rate differential between the Canadian and foreign money markets, thus reducing considerably the incentive to borrow abroad. The net new issue of foreign currency bonds by Canadian provinces, municipalities, and business corporations fell from $1.4 billion in 1969 to $720 million in 1970 and to only $430 million in 1971.

West Germany. In 1969 West German investment abroad had exceeded foreign investment in West Germany by $2.6 billion. This net outflow of capital was reduced to $440 million in 1970, and in 1971 the balance swung the other way and West Germany became a net importer of long-term capital to the value of more than $1 billion. Foreign investors who had been selling West German securities in 1969 began increasing their holdings in mid-1970, and these purchases increased in 1971. Foreign purchases of fixed-interest West German securities doubled in 1971 to about $450 million, while purchases of shares and investment fund units remained more or less unchanged at $130 million. By contrast, West German investors reduced their holdings of foreign securities by $160 million, the main factor being net sales of foreign Deutsche Mark bonds to the value of $300 million.

West German direct investment abroad had increased sharply during 1967–70 but showed only a modest increase in 1971. On the other hand, foreign direct investment in West Germany increased to almost $1 billion, more than double the average rate in the three previous years but equal to the rate in 1965–67.

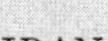

Italy. Italian investment abroad increased slightly in 1971 to $615 million. The main change was a doubling in direct investment from $120 million to $245 million. This figure was made up of new investments of $400 million and disinvestments of $155 million. A large increase was recorded in investment in oil exploration and prospecting, which accounted for $142 million, double the 1970 figure. There was also considerable investment by Italian banks and firms in foreign banking and financial companies, especially in Luxembourg and Switzerland.

Japan. The gross outflow of capital from Japan increased from $2 billion in 1970 to $2.3 billion in 1971; at the same time, the inflow of foreign capital increased sharply from $400 million to $1.2 billion in 1971. This inflow mainly reflected foreign investment in Japanese securities, which in the first half of 1971 alone amounted to almost $1 billion. During the year the large overall balance of payments surplus was causing Japan considerable embarrassment, and various measures were taken to encourage capital outflows and discourage inflows. They included free authorization for residents to purchase securities and real estate and to undertake direct investment abroad, yen loans to the World Bank by the Bank of Japan; and tight controls on the issuing of bonds abroad by residents to raise funds for domestic purposes.

Netherlands. Marked changes in the pattern of direct investment took place in the Netherlands in 1971. Dutch investment abroad fell, but foreign investment in the Netherlands increased. Through 1969 direct investment had traditionally resulted in a net outflow, but in 1971 there was a net inflow of $135 million. The outflow of portfolio investment increased sharply in 1971, much of the increase being due to higher purchases by the Netherlands of U.S. securities; also important was the purchase of Japanese stocks and Swiss bonds. (A. G. ARMSTRONG)

See also Development, Economic; Payments and Reserves, International; Trade, International.

Iran

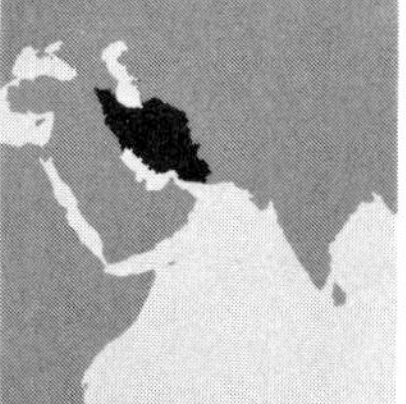

A constitutional monarchy of western Asia, Iran is bounded by the U.S.S.R., Afghanistan, Pakistan, Iraq, and Turkey and the Caspian Sea, the Arabian Sea, and the Persian Gulf. Area: 635,932 sq.mi. (1,647,064 sq.km.). Pop. (1971 est.): 30,151,275. Cap. and largest city: Teheran (pop., 1971 est., 3,639,000). Language: Farsi Persian. Religion: (1966) Muslim 96%; Christian, Jewish, and Zoroastrian minorities. Shah-in-shah, Mohammed Reza Pahlavi Aryamehr; prime minister in 1972, Emir Abbas Hoveida.

Iran entered 1972 in a mood of well-founded confidence. The solid foundation of popular approval on which the monarchy rested had been increasingly demonstrated during the preceding 12 months, not only by the angry reaction of peasants' and workers' organizations to student unrest in Teheran and elsewhere but also by the outcome of the 1971 general elections, which resulted in an overwhelming victory for the New Iran Party, on which Prime Minister

IRAN

Education. (1969–70) Primary, pupils 2,916,266, teachers 89,320; secondary, pupils 897,443, teachers 25,890; vocational, pupils 23,335, teachers 2,165; teacher training, students 9,275, teachers 505; higher (including 8 universities), students 67,268, teaching staff 6,103.

Finance. Monetary unit: rial, with (Sept. 18, 1972) a par value of 75.75 rials to U.S. $1 (free rate of 185.80 rials = £1 sterling). Gold, SDRs, and foreign exchange, central bank: (June 1972) U.S. $811 million; (June 1971) U.S. $313 million. Budget (1971–72) balanced at 481 billion rials. Gross domestic product: (1970–71) 852.1 billion rials; (1969–70) 772.5 billion rials. Money supply: (June 1972) 182,570,000,000 rials; (June 1971) 136,890,000,000 rials. Cost of living (1963 = 100): (June 1972) 128; (June 1971) 121.

Foreign Trade. (1971) Imports 141,750,000,000 rials; exports 200,120,000,000 rials. Import sources (1971–72): West Germany 19%; U.S. 14%; Japan 13%; U.K. 11%; U.S.S.R. 7%; Italy 5%; France 5%. Export destinations (1970 est.): Japan 38%; West Germany 9%; U.K. 7%; Netherlands 6%. Main export crude oil 87%.

Transport and Communications. Roads (1971) 42,703 km. Motor vehicles in use (1971): passenger 285,000; commercial (including buses) 96,300. Railways (1970): 3,480 km.; traffic 1,800,000,000 passenger-km., freight 2,758,000,000 net ton-km. Air traffic (1970): 683,810,000 passenger-km.; freight 9,634,000 net ton-km. Shipping (1971): merchant vessels 100 gross tons and over 77; gross tonnage 131,667. Telephones (Jan. 1971) 307,000. Radio receivers (Dec. 1968) 2.5 million. Television receivers (Dec. 1969) 250,000.

Agriculture. Production (in 000; metric tons; 1971; 1970 in parentheses): wheat *c.* 3,000 (*c.* 3,800); barley *c.* 850 (880); rice *c.* 1,100 (1,046); sugar, raw value (1971–72) *c.* 646, (1970–71) *c.* 620; dates *c.* 280 (*c.* 310); grapes *c.* 500 (*c.* 500); raisins *c.* 60 (*c.* 60); tea *c.* 21 (20); tobacco *c.* 20 (17); cotton, lint *c.* 140 (160). Livestock (in 000; Oct. 1970): cattle *c.* 5,100; sheep *c.* 35,500; goats *c.* 12,500; horses (March) *c.* 380; asses (March) *c.* 2,000; chickens *c.* 30,500.

Industry. Production (in 000; metric tons; 1970–71): cement 2,577; coal 323; crude oil (1971) 227,752; lead concentrates (metal content) *c.* 23; chrome ore (oxide content) *c.* 145; electricity (kw-hr.) 7,044,000.

Hoveida's government was based. The party won 230 of the 268 seats in the Majlis (Chamber of Deputies) and 28 seats of the 30 that made up the elected half of the Senate. The new Cabinet showed few changes, perhaps the most important being the appointment of Abbas Ali Khalatbari as foreign minister. Khalatbari had been secretary-general of the Central Treaty Organization (CENTO) from 1962 to 1967. In 1972 it was again Iran's turn to nominate for this post, to which another career diplomat, Nassir Assar, previously deputy prime minister, was appointed.

Throughout 1972 the social and economic advances that were the main program of the New Iran Party made steady progress. The extreme nationalist Pan-Iranian Party had lost so much ground that it did not even attempt to contest the elections; and throughout the year its influence declined further. Secret trials of political opponents of the regime continued. Early in the year at least 20 people accused of guerrilla activities, ranging from the murder of policemen to belonging to Communist underground movements, were executed by firing squad. Many others were thought to be held (and some tortured) by the Savak (secret police). The procedure of the courts was criticized for the vagueness of the charges, the absence of witnesses, the paucity of legal advice available to accused persons, and the methods used by the Savak to obtain its information.

In April, the country was saddened by a terrible earthquake disaster in the southern part of Fars province. Known casualties numbered over 6,000, of whom more than 4,000 were dead. Offers of help and medical supplies came from many countries, especially from Iran's partners in the Regional Cooperation for Development (RCD) project, Turkey and Pakistan.

In the field of international affairs, Iran continued to hold a key position in the politics of the Middle Eastern area, the shah's influence being exercised on the side of moderation. Iran was encouraged in its attitude of pursuing friendly relations and fostering economic progress throughout the Middle East by the success of the detente between the U.S. and the Soviet Union and between the U.S. and China. In May, U.S. Pres. Richard Nixon made a brief visit to Teheran and held frank discussions with the shah and his prime minister on the range of their common interests in the Middle East, the Persian Gulf, and Southeast Asia. In October, the shah paid a ten-day visit to Moscow.

An Iranian flees from the village of Ghir in southern Iran, which was devastated by an earthquake in April 1972.

WIDE WORLD

Throughout the year the Iranian government continued to be active in the affairs of CENTO. The 19th meeting of the Council of Ministers was held in London in June, attended by representatives of the U.S., Iran, Turkey, and, for the first time since 1966, Pakistan. The principal emphasis was laid not only on common defense problems but also on economic and cultural exchanges and on the improvement of the lines of communication between Turkey, Iran, and Pakistan. The extension of the new Turkey–Iran railway link between Istanbul and Teheran through Bam and Zahedan to Quetta in Pakistan was actively considered, as was the improvement of the trunk roads linking the three RCD countries. The Scientific Coordination Board, which controlled joint research projects and arranged technical training, opened its headquarters in Teheran.

On October 5, Iran National Airlines signed a letter of intent to purchase two Concorde supersonic airliners valued at £46 million and took an option on a third. Iran was also interested in purchasing arms from Britain, in particular the Rapier ground-to-air missile. The purchase of 580 U.S. helicopters, valued at $750 million, was reported in December.

(L. F. RUSHBROOK WILLIAMS)

Iraq

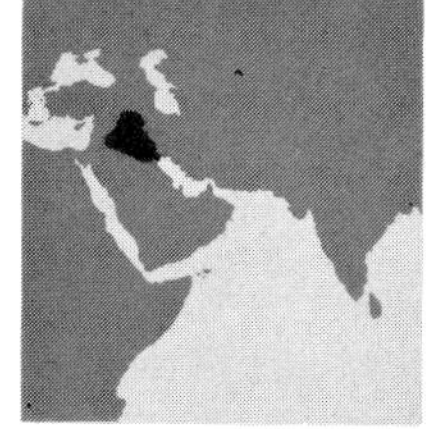

A republic of western Asia, Iraq is bounded by Turkey, Iran, Kuwait, Saudi Arabia, Jordan, Syria, and the Persian Gulf. Area: 168,927 sq.mi. (437,522 sq.km.). Pop. (1972 est.): 10,074,169, including Arabs, Kurds, Turks, Assyrians, Iranians, and others. Cap. and largest city: Baghdad (pop., 1970 est., 2,183,760). Language: Arabic. Religion: mainly Muslim, some Christian. President in 1972, Gen. Ahmad Hassan al-Bakr.

In 1972 Iraq's Baathist regime took some tentative steps toward reducing its isolation within the Arab world and greatly strengthened its ties with the Soviet Union. Its relations with Iran remained bad, and there was a danger of renewed trouble with the Kurdish minority. The economic situation was seriously affected by a dispute with the Iraq Petroleum Co. (IPC).

A preparatory visit to the Soviet Union by Saddam Husain at-Takriti, vice-chairman of the Revolutionary Command Council and a key member of the regime, prepared the way for a visit to Iraq in April of Soviet Premier Aleksei N. Kosygin. On April 9 a 15-year Soviet-Iraqi treaty of friendship and cooperation was signed. The 14-clause treaty, closely resembling the Soviet-Egyptian treaty of 1971, spoke of the "permanent, unbreakable friendship" between the two countries. It stipulated that neither would join any alliance directed against the other and that they would hold consultations immediately if either was threatened. During his stay in Iraq, Kosygin inaugurated the export of oil from the North Rumaylah field of southern Iraq which was claimed by the IPC but was being developed with Soviet assistance. It was forecast that exports from North Rumaylah would rise from 5 million tons in 1972 to 18 million tons in 1974 and 70 million tons sometime thereafter.

The Soviet Union's decision to place greater emphasis on its relations with Iraq was partly motivated by its difficulties in Egypt and was calculated to strengthen Iraq's position in the Persian Gulf area and vis-à-vis Iran. In the government reshuffle of May 14, two prominent Iraqi Communists, members of the party's Central Committee, were included in the new Cabinet. This was seen as a response to Soviet wishes.

Soviet support was especially important to Iraq in its deepening dispute with the IPC. Talks between the Iraqi government and IPC were held in early 1972 on the basis of Iraq's demand for $240 million in back payments of revenues and for a 20% participation in the company. Iraq claimed that IPC was holding back production in the northern oil fields to put pressure on the government, but the company maintained this was due to the high cost of transport from the north. Talks broke down on May 17 when Iraq issued a 14-day ultimatum, and on June 1 the president announced the nationalization of all the company's assets in Iraq, estimated at around $350 million. Iraq offered to make a separate agreement with the French state-owned Compagnie Française des Pétroles, which had a 23.75% share in IPC, in recognition of the French government's attitude toward the Arab-Israeli question, and an agreement was reached in Paris on June 18 for France to buy Kirkuk oil.

Despite IPC's threats of legal action Iraq had some success in securing crude oil sales contracts from Greece, Spain, Italy, and Turkey, which President Bakr visited on his return from Moscow in September. Both OPEC and OAPEC (the Organizations of Petroleum and of Arab Petroleum Exporting Countries) expressed support for the act of nationalization, and OAPEC provided a loan of around $135 million to help Iraq with its budgetary difficulties due to the fall in oil revenues. The government made plans to reduce imports by 50 million dinars. The economy was greatly assisted by the first surplus in the grain harvest for 15 years.

Despite Egyptian accusations of official Iraqi implication in assassination attempts on Iraqi exiles in Cairo some rapprochement between Egypt and Iraq took place during 1972. Two pro-Egyptian Iraqis were included in the new government in May, although President Bakr's proposal that Iraq should join the Libyan-Syrian-Egyptian union aroused little response in Cairo. The quarrel with Iran continued to smolder, with frequent border incidents and Iranian charges of mistreatment of Iranians living in Iraq.

The Kurdish problem, which the regime hoped had been settled by the March 11, 1970, agreement, continued to cause concern. The second anniversary of the agreement was celebrated throughout Iraq, and on April 6 Kurdish was declared an official language equal to Arabic in the northern provinces. But the Kurds were reportedly discontented with progress toward full implementation of the terms of the agreement, and the Kurdish Democratic Party blamed government security agents for an attempt on the life of its leader, Mustafa al-Barzani, on July 15. There were reports that the Kurdish nationalists were considering resuming hostilities. (PETER MANSFIELD)

IRAQ

Education. (1969–70) Primary, pupils 1,040,968, teachers 48,290; secondary, pupils 302,611, teachers 10,114; vocational, students 9,994, teachers 1,022; teacher training, students 3,625, teachers 198; higher (including 5 universities), students 36,736, teaching staff (1968–69) 1,879.

Finance. Monetary unit: Iraqi dinar, with (Sept. 18, 1972) a par value of 0.33 dinar to U.S. $1 (free rate of 0.81 dinar = £1 sterling). Gold, SDRs, and foreign exchange, central bank: (June 1972) U.S. $678.7 million; (June 1971) U.S. $608.4 million. Budget (1970–71 est.) balanced at 373 million dinars. Gross national product: (1969) 961.9 million dinars; (1968) 897.3 million dinars. Money supply: (April 1972) 235.1 million dinars; (April 1971) 217.2 million dinars. Cost of living (Baghdad; 1963 = 100): (June 1972) 124; (June 1971) 125.

Foreign Trade. (1971) Imports 247.9 million dinars; exports 549.4 million dinars. Import sources (1970): U.K. 12%; U.S.S.R. 11%; France 6%; Belgium-Luxembourg 5%. Export destinations (1970): Italy 29%; France 15%; Netherlands 7%; Greece 5%. Main export crude oil 96%.

Transport and Communications. Roads (1970) 18,605 km. Motor vehicles in use (1971): passenger 71,850; commercial 33,687. Railways: (1969) 2,352 km.; traffic (1970–71) 374 million passenger-km., freight 1,462,000,000 net ton-km. Air traffic (1971): 249,770,000 passenger-km.; freight 2,164,000 net ton-km. Telephones (Jan. 1971) 120,000. Radio receivers (Dec. 1970) 1.7 million. Television receivers (Dec. 1970) 350,000.

Agriculture. Production (in 000; metric tons; 1971; 1970 in parentheses): wheat 822 (1,236); barley 432 (691); rice 207 (180); dry broad beans *c.* 12 (*c.* 18); dates *c.* 330 (*c.* 330); sesame *c.* 8 (13); linseed *c.* 8 (14); tobacco *c.* 10 (16); cotton, lint *c.* 15 (14). Livestock (in 000; 1970–71): sheep *c.* 14,000; cattle *c.* 1,920; goats *c.* 2,500; buffalo *c.* 290; camels *c.* 220; horses *c.* 127; asses *c.* 580.

Industry. Production (in 000; metric tons): crude oil (1971) 83,787; cement (1969) 1,381; electricity (excluding most industrial production; kw-hr.; 1970) 2,115,000.

Ireland

Separated from Great Britain by the North Channel, the Irish Sea, and St. George's Channel, the Republic of Ireland shares its island with Northern Ireland to the northeast. Area: 27,136 sq.mi. (70,282 sq.km.), or 83% of the island. Pop. (1971): 2,978,248. Cap. and largest city: Dublin (pop., 1971, 567,866). Language: English (80%) and Gaelic. Religion: predominantly Roman Catholic (95%). President in 1972, Eamon de Valera; prime minister, John Lynch.

The treaty of accession to the EEC was signed in Brussels by Prime Minister Lynch and the minister for foreign affairs, Patrick J. Hillery, on Jan. 22, 1972. Overwhelming national endorsement was given to the government in its moves toward EEC membership in a referendum on May 10, when the people voted 5 to 1 in favour. Membership was to become effective as of Jan. 1, 1973.

Strengthened by the public support expressed in the May referendum and by a landslide victory in the Mid-Cork by-election early in August, Prime Minister Lynch adopted through the year an increasingly tough attitude toward the Provisional Irish Republican Army (IRA) and its political wing, Sinn Fein. At the end of May two IRA leaders were arrested, but prosecutions brought against them were unsuccessful. Also in May special courts were set up to deal with IRA offenses. Nevertheless, Lynch's attitude on the steadily worsening Northern Ireland situation remained ambivalent. The burning down of the British embassy in Dublin, to protest the killing of 13 people in Londonderry on January 30, demonstrated the strength of public feeling. Ireland's envoy to London was recalled at that time, and the already strained relations between the two countries were at their lowest point. But the mood was not sustained, nor were earlier pressures by the government for greater involvement in Northern Ireland affairs.

The introduction of direct rule in Northern Ireland

KEYSTONE

After hoisting the Irish tricolour, this angry mob, protesting Bloody Sunday in Londonderry, burned the British embassy in Dublin to the ground on Feb. 2, 1972.

was welcomed by the Dublin government, but subsequent meetings between Lynch and British Prime Minister Edward Heath, held in Munich, W.Ger., in September and in Paris after the EEC summit meeting in October, achieved little beyond keeping both leaders mutually informed. The intention of the Northern Ireland authorities to hold a referendum on the partition issue was opposed by the Dublin government and both opposition parties in the Dail, whose attitude was that the only justifiable referendum was one covering both North and South. The Dublin government cautiously welcomed the British government's Green Paper in October, which stated that any new administrative structure in the North should be accepted by the republic.

There was growing criticism during the year that the republic's desire for unity was insincere, that the government's expressed wish to be involved more closely in the solution of the Northern Ireland crisis was only motivated by internal political considerations, and that the proof of this was to be found in the limited actions taken to modify constitutional and social circumstances that blocked closer North-South relations. To refute such criticism, the government announced a referendum that included provision for the deletion from the constitution of art. 44, which bestowed a special position on the Roman Catholic Church. This was held on December 7, when 85% of those voting (50% of the electorate) supported the change. No changes were proposed in other articles dealing with territorial claims to Northern Ireland; the position of Gaelic as the official language; or laws on divorce and contraception.

The arrest on November 19 of Sean MacStiofain (*see* BIOGRAPHY), chief of staff of the Provisionals, marked a new phase in the government's efforts to curb IRA activities. MacStiofain's arrest followed an interview he had given to the Irish national broadcasting service (RTE), as a result of which the entire RTE governing board was dismissed and replaced under provisions prohibiting the broadcasting of material likely to promote illegal activities. The government then introduced a bill to enable conviction of suspected IRA members on the sole testimony of a senior police officer. This was passed by the Dail in the wake of bomb explosions in Dublin that undoubtedly influenced voting, and was enacted on December 3. Further arrests followed, including those of Rory O'Brady, president of the Provisional Sinn Fein, in Dublin on December 29 and of Martin McGuiness, chief of the Provisional IRA in Derry, and his deputy Joseph McCallion, in County Donegal on December 30.

The economy continued to be seriously threatened by inflation. Food prices increased by over 12% and the cost of living generally by 10%. There were more than 11,000 layoffs during the year. Tourism was also severely hit, both by inflation and by the worsening Northern Ireland situation.

The Irish government successfully pressed for an investigation by the European Commission on Human Rights into charges of British brutality in Northern Ireland. The commission accepted five of the seven charges brought against Britain at Strasbourg.

There were internal difficulties in the two main opposition parties, Fine Gael and Labour. Liam Cosgrave, leader of Fine Gael, the second largest party in the state, successfully withstood intraparty challenges. Within the Labour Party the spokesman on Northern Ireland affairs, Conor Cruise O'Brien, was strongly criticized for his view that talk of unity with Northern Ireland at this time was "futile and mischievous." (BRUCE ARNOLD)

See also United Kingdom.

IRELAND

Education. (1968–69) Primary, pupils 521,546, teachers (1967–68) 15,941; secondary, pupils 138,703, teachers (1967–68) 8,592; vocational (1967–68), pupils 83,206, teachers 5,595; higher, students *c.* 25,660, teaching staff (1967–68) *c.* 1,370.

Finance. Monetary unit: Irish pound, at par with the pound sterling, with a free rate (Sept. 18, 1972) of U.S. $2.45 = £1. Gold, SDRs, and foreign exchange, official: (June 1972) U.S. $1,001,000,000; (June 1971) U.S. $770 million. Budget (1971–72 est.) balanced at £551 million. Gross national product: (1970) £1,710 million; (1969) £1,550 million. Money supply: (May 1972) £418.9 million; (May 1971) £436.2 million. Cost of living (1963 = 100): (May 1972) 169; (May 1971) 157.

Foreign Trade. (1971) Imports £754.5 million; exports £541.1 million. Import sources: U.K. 49%; U.S. 9%; West Germany 7%. Export destinations: U.K. 66%; U.S. 11%. Main exports: meat 16%; livestock 13% (cattle 11%); textiles and clothing 10%; dairy produce 7%; machinery 5%. Tourism (1970): visitors 1,825,000; gross receipts U.S. $186 million.

Transport and Communications. Roads (1971) 87,202 km. Motor vehicles in use (1970): passenger 393,500; commercial (including buses) 52,800. Railways: (1970) 2,189 km.; traffic (1971) 575 million passenger-km., freight 521 million net ton-km. Air traffic (1971): 1,812,000,000 passenger-km.; freight 66,270,000 net ton-km. Shipping (1971): merchant vessels 100 gross tons and over 90; gross tonnage 174,459. Telephones (Dec. 1970) 307,000. Radio licenses (Dec. 1970) 630,000. Television licenses (Dec. 1970) 506,000.

Agriculture. Production (in 000; metric tons; 1971; 1970 in parentheses): potatoes 1,330 (1,468); oats *c.* 200 (210); barley *c.* 900 (782); wheat *c.* 370 (381); sugar, raw value (1971–72) *c.* 181, (1970–71) *c.* 150; cow's milk *c.* 3,700 (3,634); butter *c.* 78 (75); cheese *c.* 30 (*c.* 30); beef and veal *c.* 340 (337); pork *c.* 147 (144); fish catch (1970) 81, (1969) 68. Livestock (in 000; June 1971): cattle 6,142; sheep 4,167; pigs 1,309; horses *c.* 124; chickens *c.* 9,500.

Industry. Index of production (1963 = 100): (1971) 160; (1970) 151. Production (in 000; metric tons; 1971): coal 90; cement 1,500; electricity (excluding most industrial production; kw-hr.) 6,105,000; manufactured gas (cu.m.) 209,000; beer (hl.; 1969–70) 3,751; wool fabrics (sq.m.) 6,000; rayon, etc., fabrics (sq.m.) 6,800.

Israel

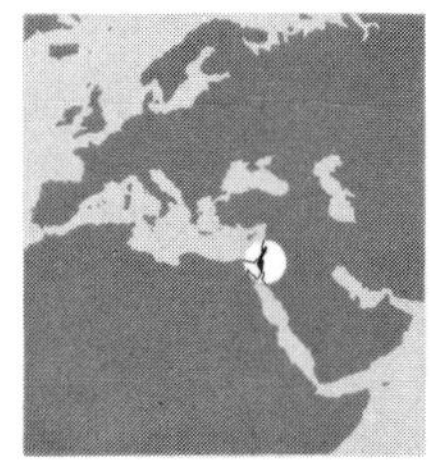

A republic of the Middle East, Israel is bounded by Lebanon, Syria, Jordan, Egypt, and the Mediterranean Sea. Area (not including territory occupied in the June 1967 war): 7,992 sq.mi. (20,700 sq.km.). Pop. (1971 est.): 3,066,000. Cap.: Jerusalem (pop., 1970 est., 291,700). Largest city: Tel Aviv-Yafo (pop., 1970 est., 384,000). Language: Hebrew and Arabic. Religion: predominantly Jewish. President in 1972, Schneor Zalman Shazar; prime minister, Mrs. Golda Meir.

In 1972 Israel began a long process of self-questioning, as a new, largely native-born, generation erupted into the political life of the country. The initial impetus of this potentially revolutionary self-questioning did not come from opposition to the government or from the impatient younger generation but from elements within the ruling establishment. It received its most articulate and perceptive formulation in the thoughts of the then director general of the prime minister's office, Ya'acov Herzog, who died on March 8 after a long illness.

Herzog had sown a seed, and in 1972 Israel took a hard look at itself and its prospects. Nor was this introspection confined purely to Israeli affairs; it embraced also the ideology of the founding fathers, the essence of Zionism, and became suddenly linked to the question of the general election in 1973 and to the ultimate succession to the prime ministership when—and if—Mrs. Meir decided to step down. Out of the tumult of voices, two—those of Prime Minister Meir and Defense Minister Moshe Dayan—stood out from the rest. On the whole, Mrs. Meir was content with things as they were. At least during the first months of 1972, she argued that Israel had never been in a better position and that there were no compelling reasons for seeking any change or taking any political initiative that might alter the balance of power. She had established the best of relations with the United States administration of Pres. Richard Nixon, and Israel enjoyed a maximum of U.S. military and diplomatic assistance. Superficially, Defense Minister Dayan appeared to say the same thing as Mrs. Meir—that the status quo was the best possible strategic position that Israel could attain. But he believed that this state of affairs could be preserved only by the most intensive policy initiatives at home and abroad. Dayan welcomed the Soviet-U.S. détente and understood it to mean "nonintervention and nonconfrontation of the two superpowers in the Arab-Israeli conflict, rejection of an enforced settlement, continuation of the cease-fire, and resumption of negotiations by political means and not by arms."

Dayan acknowledged that the peace terms on which Israel would agree would not be acceptable to the Arab leaders, and the Arab terms for a peace would not be acceptable to Israel. As a consequence of these opposing attitudes he believed that Israel might have to stay on its existing borders for the next 10 or 15 years before conditions for a real peace might arise. Israel had therefore to think ahead and revise its military and political outlook so that it would be as effective in 1980 and 1985 as it was in 1972.

Nor was the defense minister talking only in abstract terms. He had effectively demonstrated that his liberal policy in relation to the occupied territories, the West Bank (of the Jordan River), the Gaza Strip, and the Golan Heights, was producing results. The occupied territories enjoyed an economic boom of unprecedented dimension; 50,000 Arabs from Gaza and the West Bank traveled daily across the so-called Green Line to work in Israel. Guerrilla and terrorist resistance inside the occupied territories and in Israel itself had virtually come to an end; 153,000 Arabs from outside Israel visited friends and relatives in the occupied territories and in Israel during the summer of 1972 and stayed as long as three months. The Jordan River bridges were open to trade and to Arab individuals with virtually no restrictions.

Even the festering sore of the Gaza Strip refugees had been tackled with marked success (despite the October resignation of the mayor of Gaza, Rashad Shawa, in protest against supplying water and sanitary services to the Shati refugee camp), and as the year advanced acts of terror and sabotage in the Gaza area became comparatively rare. The proposals of Jordan's King Husain for the creation of a semi-autonomous Palestinian state within a Jordanian federal monarchy were received with no great joy by the Palestinians, with hostility by the Arab governments and the Palestine Liberation Organization, and with distinct coolness by the Israeli government.

This reflected a realistic evaluation by the Israelis that Husain was not in a position to make a separate peace with Israel on acceptable terms. In fact, the most energetic discussion about a future Palestinian state or entity was carried on by the Israelis rather than by the Palestinians. It had been initiated by the former secretary-general of the Labour Party, Liova Eliav, who had introduced into his election campaign a sustained argument for the establishment of a Palestinian state on the West Bank. But he encountered much bitter hostility from many of his former colleagues, who shared Mrs. Meir's view that the only Palestinian state possible was one based on Jordan.

On the whole, Mrs. Meir could have been right during the first months of the year: things had never been better for Israel. But then the political climate suddenly and drastically changed. The government's relations with the labour unions grew progressively worse. Labour resentment at what seemed a widening gap between rich and poor was satisfied only by extreme demands which were encouraged by the militant and powerful general secretary of the Labour Federation, Itzhak Ben-Aharon. Labour's anger was further fed by a spate of economic scandals involving Cabinet ministers and officials. They were subsequently absolved from responsibility by public inquiry, but the investigation left behind unanswered questions and a suspicious public.

But all this was largely overshadowed by a series of attacks carried out by an offshoot of the Palestinian Al Fatah guerrillas, calling itself the Black September group. The first attack involved hijacking a Belgian Sabena airliner on May 9 and holding it for ransom at Israel's Lod International Airport. The Palestinians demanded the release of a large number of their fellows held in Israel on charges of terrorism, murder, and subversion. However, Israeli forces freed the airliner and passengers. One passenger died as a result of wounds received, and two of the four hijackers were killed.

This attack was followed on May 30 by another at Lod Airport carried out by three Japanese acting on behalf of a Palestinian terrorist group, which re-

Ireland, Northern:
see United Kingdom

Iron and Steel:
see Industrial Review; Mining

Islam:
see Religion

STARPHOT/PICTORIAL PARADE

Israeli infantry, reinforced by armoured troops, enter Lebanon in search of Palestinian guerrilla bases. The massive raid, in retaliation for the Olympic massacre, was made on Sept. 16–17, 1972.

sulted in 28 dead and many wounded. Among the dead was Israel's foremost physicist, Aharon Katzir (*see* OBITUARIES) of the Weizmann Institute. The airport massacre was followed by the killing of a total of 11 members of Israel's Olympic team at Munich, W.Ger., on September 5 (*see* SPORTING RECORD: *Special Report*), the shooting of an Israeli diplomat in Brussels on September 11, and the killing of another in London. And on October 28 came a daring coup by the Palestinians in the form of yet another hijacking which freed the three surviving Munich terrorists held in West German jails. On December 28 four terrorists held six hostages in the Israeli embassy in Bangkok, Thailand, for 19 hours before Thai officials negotiated their release.

The impact on Israeli thinking of these Palestinian operations was far-reaching. Apart from the expected review of Israel's security services, which, on the whole, had not been found wanting, the Palestinian "successes" gave a new impetus to the country's consideration of its relations with its own Arabs and its Arab neighbours. For it raised a question that had not previously been apparent. At a time when Israel's military domination of the whole area was generally accepted, Israel found it necessary to consider on what terms it could overcome this new type of Palestinian terrorism.

While the attacks presented no real threat to the security of Israel, they began to have an indirect impact that seemed to belie the confident assurance of Israel's foreign minister, Abba Eban, in May, that "the Middle East is no longer one of the world's trouble centres." Israel's international position at the end of 1972—as distinct from its military power—was weaker than at any time since the Six-Day War of June 1967. Its mission in Uganda had been expelled by Pres. Idi Amin under the influence of Libya's Col. Muammar al-Qaddafi, and its overall link with African states had noticeably weakened. These African ties had been for many years one of the principal pillars of Israeli diplomacy.

Another such pillar was also considerably shaken by Israeli reaction to the freeing of the three accused killers of the Olympic athletes following the October hijack threat. A significant aspect of this was the West German response to Israeli criticism, for it gave voice to a gathering mood in Europe, if not elsewhere, that the Middle East conflict should not be allowed to poison relations among European countries and involve them beyond their national interests. A similar reaction was noted in the cool response of the United States to Israeli urging that it should not proceed with its massive trade agreement with the Soviet Union until the U.S.S.R. modified its restrictions on Jews seeking to leave the Soviet Union for Israel. (For a further discussion of this situation, *see* Special Report.)

Thus the final months of 1972 erased much of Israel's earlier complacency, and this was reflected in the popular desire for change at the helm of state. By October Defense Minister Dayan had established a three-to-one lead in opinion polls over his nearest rival, Deputy Prime Minister Yigal Allon. But party machines being what they were in Israel, the public did not always have the last word. The Labour Party machine, supported by Mrs. Meir, was clearly seeking an alternative leader who could displace General Dayan in popular esteem or, more likely, in the party caucus. The general's fate was already a dominant theme in Israel in 1972. (JON KIMCHE)

ISRAEL

Education. (1969–70) Primary, pupils 456,079, teachers 26,547; secondary, pupils 72,130; vocational, pupils 58,469; teacher training, students 3,929; secondary, vocational, and teacher training, teachers 12,657; higher (including 4 universities), students 49,076, teaching staff (universities only) *c.* 4,650.

Finance. Monetary unit: Israeli pound, with (Sept. 18, 1972) a par value of I£4.20 to U.S. $1 (free rate of I£10.29 = £1 sterling). Gold, SDRs, and foreign exchange, central bank: (June 1972) U.S. $1,079,900,000; (June 1971) U.S. $538.2 million. Budget (1970–71 est.): revenue I£6,108 million; expenditure I£7,906 million. Gross national product: (1970) I£18,454 million; (1969) I£15.883 million. Money supply: (March 1972) I£4,751 million; (March 1971) I£3,586 million. Cost of living (1963 = 100): (June 1972) 171; (June 1971) 152.

Foreign Trade. (1971) Imports I£6,798.8 million; exports I£3,599.5 million. Import sources: U.S. 24%; U.K. 15%; West Germany 13%; Italy 5%; France 5%. Export destinations: U.S. 19%; U.K. 10%; West Germany 9%; Netherlands 6%; Japan 5%; Hong Kong 5%; France 5%; Belgium-Luxembourg 5%. Main exports: diamonds 32%; citrus fruit 16%; textiles and clothing 12%; chemicals 8%; fruit preparations 5%.

Transport and Communications. Roads (1970) 9,307 km. Motor vehicles in use (1971): passenger 174,400; commercial 75,300. Railways (1971): 795 km.; traffic 371 million passenger-km., freight 419 million net ton-km. Air traffic (1971): 3,026,300,000 passenger-km.; freight 111,978,000 net ton-km. Shipping (1971): merchant vessels 100 gross tons and over 102; gross tonnage 645,585. Telephones (Dec. 1970) 521,000. Radio licenses (Dec. 1968) 627,000. Television licenses (Dec. 1969) 210,000.

Agriculture. Production (in 000; metric tons; 1971; 1970 in parentheses): wheat 195 (125); sorghum 21 (11); potatoes *c.* 130 (137); oranges (1970) 938, (1969) 878; grapefruit (1970) 284, (1969) 263; grapes *c.* 75 (61); sugar (1971–72) 32, (1970–71) 29; tomatoes (1970) 159, (1969) 175; olives (1970) 7, (1969) *c.* 28; bananas (1970) 61, (1969) 53; cotton, lint *c.* 37 (35); fish catch (170) 25, (1969) 22. Livestock (in 000; Dec. 1970): cattle 251; sheep 188; goats 31; chickens *c.* 10,900.

Industry. Index of production (1963 = 100): (1971) 228; (1970) 203. Production (in 000; metric tons; 1971): cement 1,395; electricity (kw-hr.) 7,646,000; salt (1970) 66; potash (oxide content; 1970–71) 530. New dwelling units completed (1971) 38,000.

SPECIAL REPORT

ISRAEL'S NEW CITIZENS

By Ernest Krausz

Israel's acceptance of more than one million Jewish immigrants in less than 25 years has created for both the state and its new citizens problems of integration and assimilation probably more intense and more numerous than ever before experienced in any nation's history. The Jewish population of what is now Israel increased from 24,000 to 2,561,400 between 1882 and 1970. When the state of Israel was established in 1948, there were only 650,000 Jews then within Israel's borders.

It is not simply the demographic proportions that loom large in creating these problems, although the colossal tasks of building sufficient accommodations and providing basic services are alone quite daunting. The economic and military situations are also of considerable importance and closely allied to the demographic question, and both are double-edged: more people demand more jobs but also create them; security considerations are a strain on the country but are at the same time conducive to greater unity and the acceptance of austere conditions. But the most complex aspect of the rise of this new nation must be understood from a sociological angle. The waves of immigrants have had varied origins with grossly divergent occupational, educational, religious, and cultural backgrounds and standards. In terms of an integrative process this inevitably leads to difficulties of social adjustment and to unequal rates of social mobility and political and educational advancement. The conditions pertaining during the particular periods when the various groups arrived adds one more complicating factor, which makes comparisons difficult.

The Six-Day War of June 1967 may be regarded as an immigration watershed; the prewar influx was dominated by so-called "Oriental" Jews from North Africa and the Middle East, the postwar one by Jews from the West and the Soviet Union. Although in the late 1940s and 1950s European Jews, particularly the remnants of the Nazi Holocaust, continued to swell the ranks of the original Zionist settlers, the bulk of new immigrants came from Iraq, Yemen, Egypt, Syria, Algeria, Morocco, and Tunisia. By 1970 the Oriental Jews were in a majority, representing 48% of the total Jewish population, as against 44% of European and American origin and 8% second-generation Israeli.

"Two Nations." In recent years a good deal of attention has been focussed on the persisting disparity in the economic standards, educational achievements, and political roles of the Oriental and European population groups—an ethnic differentiation that seems paradoxical and antithetical to the religious and ideological basis of the Jewish state. In 1968 and 1969 the tensions created by the aftermath of the Six-Day War still served to conceal these disparities. But in the relative calm and relaxation of 1971 and 1972 the frustrations felt by Oriental Jews came to the surface (as they had in riots in 1959). There were frequent newspaper and radio reports about demonstrations by "Black Panthers"—a militant group composed mainly of young Oriental Jews—which culminated in demonstrations outside the opening session of the World Zionist Congress in Jerusalem in January

En route to Israel from the U.S.S.R., a Jewish family, Simeon and Riva Shimshilashvili and their son Isaac, peer from a sealed coach of the Chopin Express as it arrives in Vienna. Some 30,000 Soviet Jews immigrated to Israel during 1972.

1972. Quite a number of the older Oriental Jews and those who are more moderate side with the militants on many counts. Some go so far as to claim that the European Jews not only prevent the equalization of opportunities but are also intent on the cultural genocide of Orientals. On this point many European Jews argue that the closing of the gap and the equalization of opportunities is prevented by the disadvantageous cultural backgrounds of the Oriental Jews.

Narrowing the Gap. While there are some indications that the differences in attainments and standards of the two major ethnic groups are being pared down, the whole exercise in comparisons rests on some oversimplified assumptions. For example, each of the two groups is in fact culturally somewhat heterogeneous and there are also within each some variations in socioeconomic background. Thus, most of the Egyptian Jews and a substantial proportion of the Iraqi Jews have a high socioeconomic and educational background, unlike the vast majority of the other Orientals. Similarly, sections of the Romanian and other East European Jewish groups have much lower cultural and socioeconomic standards than European Jews in general. Nevertheless, because of the significant overall differences between the two major ethnic groups, especially in socioeconomic status, it does not unduly distort reality to contrast Europeans and Orientals. There are also signs that many of the sociocultural characteristics of the two groups persist in the first Israeli-born generation. As the generations pass, a great deal of fusion will, of course, take place between the various groups. To discern such signs of fusion one would have to deal with the forces leading to the integration of the European and Oriental groups. This would inevitably produce a complex picture taking into account such factors as settlement patterns, which so far have on the whole induced segregation; trends in intermarriage between the two groups, which have tended to promote integration; as well as other important factors such as religion and the Army. There are some simpler indicators, however, which can show whether the gap between the two groups is being at all narrowed. They are economic standards, social welfare and housing, education, and political roles.

These indicators emanate from official statistics, which provide a plethora of figures pointing to a much improved situation for Oriental Jews. Thus, overcrowded accommodations are no longer a large-scale problem. The density of four or more persons per room declined from 18.5% of the population in 1961 to just over 5% in 1970. Many nonluxury durable goods, such as refrigerators and washing machines, are owned by the vast majority of Oriental Jews, and the number among them who own television sets has also risen very substantially. In purely basic material terms, the gap is certainly being bridged.

Ernest Krausz is reader in sociology at the City University, London, and, during 1972–73, professor at Bar-Ilan University, Israel; he is the author of Sociology in Britain *and* Ethnic Minorities in Britain.

In the educational sphere the advances made have been more spectacular, although the statistical figures hide the real improvement. Many of the more radically dissatisfied Oriental Jews point to the fact that, although they represent more than half the Jewish population of Israel, only some 15% of university students come from their midst, and also that they are severely underrepresented in the higher occupational categories, such as the professions. Considering, however, that the parents of these Oriental Jews had a very poor record in education and literacy, the modest improvement made by their children as far as more advanced education is concerned, and the very substantial improvement in completely eliminating illiteracy and in extending considerably the number of years of schooling during the 1961–70 period, are signs of real progress.

Even in political leadership there has been some improvement. In the first Knesset (Israel's parliament) in 1949 there were 8 Jewish members of Oriental origin; in the sixth Knesset in 1965 there were 19—still well below what might be expected on the basis of electoral strength. In local government, however, a combination of factors had produced a tremendous increase in representatives of Oriental origin—from 13% in 1950 to nearly 45% in the late 1960s. Furthermore, many of these Oriental representatives have increasingly been playing leading roles at the local level.

But much of this quantitative improvement, discernible from the kind of figures quoted above, will appear far less imposing if the qualitative aspect of the situation is considered. For figures regarding density per room do not reveal anything about the standards of housing in question or the type of areas inhabited by the Oriental Jews. Similarly, figures about the extension of education provide no indication as to the type and quality of schools frequented by the Oriental groups. And doubts are raised about a political system in which ability to command votes is rewarded with political leadership at the less important local level, such leadership becoming dependent on the more powerful and important central political machinery which is still largely controlled by those originating from European groups.

Relative Deprivation. In absolute terms, therefore, the Oriental Jews have experienced improved conditions; in relative terms, however, larger proportions of the Orientals are still deprived. This has become further highlighted since the Six-Day War by the provisions made for the new immigrants who have come from the West and from the Soviet Union. Special tax concessions, the allocation of housing and mortgages, and the opening of occupational opportunities, particularly in the professions, are among the signs that immigrants with a European background are given extra inducements to settle in Israel. This latest influx of immigrants has been much smaller than the mass immigration of two decades ago. Since 1967 only 35,000 American Jews have arrived, of whom some 20% have already left the country. During 1971 and the first half of 1972 about 31,000 Soviet Jews arrived in Israel, bringing the total to approximately 32,000 for the period early-1970 to mid-1972.

The American and Soviet Jews, as well as those from other countries such as Britain and Argentina, are much better qualified than the Oriental Jews were on their arrival. It is known, for instance, that 68% of all immigrants from the Soviet Union are professionals and/or college graduates. It is this factor and the fact that Israel is now a relatively prosperous country suffering from lack of workers rather than, as at the time of the Oriental influx, from mass unemployment that has prompted the government, and has enabled it, to offer inducements to the more recent immigrants. The resentments against the privileges granted the newcomers easily become myths about free houses and free cars given especially to Soviet Jews. At a more sophisticated level the charge is made that the established elite, composed in the main of the early Russian Jewish pioneers or their immediate offspring, are showing perhaps a natural bias.

The Privileged Citizens. An objective assessment of Israel's record concerning Jewish immigrants from any part of the world would undoubtedly show that its primary aim has always been to receive all Jews with open arms—quite naturally, since this is the raison d'être of the state. There have been, however, special considerations given to Soviet Jews. Even the Citizenship Law

Chancing the disapproval of government officials in the Soviet Republic of Georgia, a man and a young boy pray in a synagogue in the city of Tbilisi, which is also known as Tiflis.

STERN / BLACK STAR

was amended (1971) in their favour, so as to make possible the granting of Israeli citizenship to Jews outside Israel in those cases where they desired to emigrate but were being prevented from doing so by the authorities in the countries which they wished to leave. This must be seen, however, from the particular perspective of the plight of the three million Jews (Jewish estimate) in the Soviet Union. Their willingness to fit into the Communist system and the readiness of the majority of them to assimilate themselves into Soviet society were thwarted by the continued anti-Semitic atmosphere in the Soviet Union and particularly by the last years of Stalinist rule when they were subjected to open and vicious attack. The complete alignment of the Soviet Union with the Arabs and the Israeli victory in 1967 despite that alignment proved traumatic events for both Israel and Soviet Jews.

The most significant outcome of those events for Soviet Jews was the resurgence of their identification with the Jewish people in general and with Israel in particular. The extent of this resurgence may be gauged from the large number of applications for exit visas. This number has been rising fairly steeply with about 14,000 made in the first two months of 1972, and the backlog of applications has been variously estimated at between 70,000 and 100,000. Considering the dangers and difficulties with which such moves are fraught, this is no mean achievement. Viewed in this context, of a dangerous struggle for Jewish self-determination, the privileged position accorded by Israel to Jews from the Soviet Union can easily be understood.

Yet despite the euphoria at the arrival of the first planeloads of Jews from behind the Soviet iron curtain, and despite the hopes for the future, strains in the absorption process have appeared. The old settlers and their children and the immigrants of the pre-1967 days have been showing some resentment. Many of the Oriental Jews still remain in the slums into which they were put in the 1950s. Their temporary housing, although perhaps better than that in their former lands, has become permanent. It is not surprising, therefore, that they resent the new apartment buildings going up in their midst and designated for other special immigrants. Another group to complain are the young sabras (Israeli-born), who, having served in the military for three years, return to get married but find there is little housing available. (About one-quarter of the housing to be completed in 1972 was earmarked for Soviet immigrants.)

The special treatment given to Soviet Jews has not obviated their own pains at being absorbed into a new society. The Georgian Jew, who has been a small tradesman and who is a deeply religious man, naturally feels frustrated when given a factory job in an irreligious neighbourhood. The professional man from Riga or Leningrad has to adjust to new techniques and new standards in his work. And all share in what may be described as "culture shock," for Soviet society, not putting a premium on individual initiative and beset by secretiveness, is very different from the enterprising and open spirit of Israeli society.

For Israel's bureaucracy, the problems of tackling the difficulties posed by immigrants are not unnaturally great. The financial situation seems the least worrying; not only has the United States Senate voted $85 million to help resettle Soviet Jews in Israel, but world Jewry is generously rallying to the cause once again. The really crucial problems are that no advance information of impending arrivals is available, which hampers planning; the immigration is in no way controlled by Israel, and the occupational cross-section of immigrants thus may vary greatly from month to month, creating employment problems; and inadequate knowledge of the nature of Israeli society among Soviet Jews often results in unrealistic conceptions and expectations.

Problems of immigrant absorption, like problems of security, have become a way of life for Israel. They are being tackled vigorously by the Ministry of Immigrant Absorption and the Jewish Agency (acting for the World Zionist Organization), whose efforts will in part be reflected in the future by the measure of prosperity and social integration achieved by an Israeli nation recuperating from 2,000 years in exile.

Italy

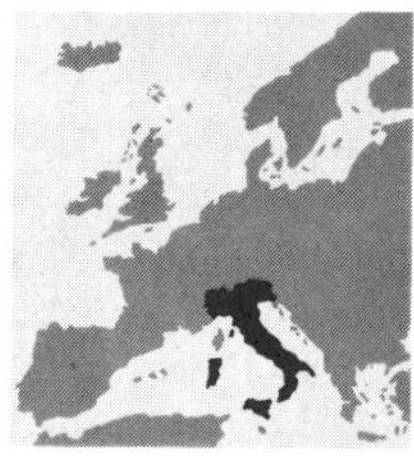

A republic of southern Europe, Italy occupies the Apennine Peninsula, Sicily, Sardinia, and a number of smaller islands. On the north it borders France, Switzerland, Austria, and Yugoslavia. Area: 116,313 sq.mi. (301,250 sq.km.). Pop. (1971): 54,025,211. Cap. and largest city: Rome (pop., 1971, 2,799,836). Language: Italian. Religion: predominantly Roman Catholic. President in 1972, Giovanni Leone; premiers, Emilio Colombo until January 15 and, from February 17, Giulio Andreotti.

Domestic Affairs. A new course for Italian politics was set in 1972. General elections were called one year ahead of time, in the hope of resolving the unstable pattern of successive centre-left coalition governments that had ruled the country for the previous ten years. This proved the first major test for newly elected Pres. Giovanni Leone (*see* BIOGRAPHY), a former premier chosen on Dec. 24, 1971, to succeed Pres. Giuseppe Saragat, whose seven-year term had expired. President Leone's first act was to reject the resignation tendered by Premier Colombo, a customary constitutional practice after the election of a new president. But on January 15, following the announcement by the Republican Party that it would no longer take part in the existing coalition (together with Christian Democrats, Socialists, and Social Democrats), Colombo was forced to resign in earnest.

President Leone again offered him the chance to form a new coalition capable of taking the country through the general elections required to clarify the political situation. The reasons for his resignation, mainly disagreements on social and economic policy, on the relationship with the Communist Party, and on a possible referendum to revoke the recently passed law on divorce, again made it impossible for him to reach an agreement with all the coalition parties. On February 5 Christian Democrat Giulio Andreotti (*see* BIOGRAPHY) was asked by President Leone to undertake the difficult task. On February 17 Andreotti announced the formation of a Christian Democratic government, but a few days later he failed to obtain a vote of confidence from the Senate. On February 28 President Leone dissolved Parliament, announcing general elections for May 7–8. The Andreotti government was to act as a caretaker government until that date.

The political campaign was fierce and was not without episodes of violence, especially between the supporters of the two main extremist parties, the Communists and the neofascist Italian Social Movement (MSI), which had joined forces with the Monarchists. The results of the election were far less dramatic than expected. The Christian Democrats suffered a slight loss (from 39.1% of the votes in 1968 to 38.8%), while the Communists gained marginally (from 26.9 to 27.2%). The most dramatic change saw the neofascist and monarchic vote increase from 5.8 to 8.7%. Of the coalition parties, the Republicans had a net gain (from 2 to 2.9%) while the Socialists (9.6%) and the Social Democrats (5.1%) more or less maintained their positions. Liberal strength fell from 5.8 to 3.9%.

Various forms of coalition were examined, and on June 4 Andreotti was asked by President Leone to

KEYSTONE

Members of the Italian Divorce League protest at the Vatican over papal refusal to sanction divorce.

form a new government. On June 26 he announced his Cabinet, formed with the support of a centre coalition in which, for the first time in the history of the republic, the Liberals had an active part, together with Christian Democrats and Social Democrats. The Republicans, although absent from the Cabinet, promised their support. Economic stabilization, greater respect for law and order (called for especially after the murder in Milan of police chief Luigi Calabresi, who had been involved in cases of political terrorism), and a marked interest in international problems were the main aims expressed by Premier Andreotti. Parliament duly granted its vote of confidence.

On April 1 the new regional setup, as envisaged by the constitution and approved by Parliament in 1970, came into effect. Described as "the biggest piece of institutional engineering since the formation of Italy in 1861," it gave the 15 ordinary regions independent powers with regard to public works, medical welfare, agriculture, transport, and other aspects of community life. Their organization was similar to that in the five regions that, for ethnic, economic, or historical reasons, already had a special regional statute.

In March the centenary of the death of Giuseppe Mazzini, one of the greatest Italian patriots in the Risorgimento, was commemorated. The first European university was established in Florence; it was to begin operations in 1973 and would be financed by the EEC.

Foreign Affairs. The successive governments of Colombo and Andreotti both emphasized the importance of widening the frontiers of the EEC and striving for the success of a greater Europe. Colombo also stressed the importance of an economic and monetary union, which would ensure greater security for the member nations. Later Giuseppe Medici, foreign minister in the Andreotti Cabinet, stressed the necessity for political integration and for the unification of economic policies.

Italy played a leading part in the solution, on March 26, of the Maltese crisis, which arose from the request of Malta's prime minister, Dom Mintoff, for greater financial contributions in exchange for renewal of the contract for NATO bases on the island.

A sad chapter in Italy's relations with Libya was added by the Tripoli government's decision to remove the Christian cemetery in the capital, containing the remains of over 20,000 Italian soldiers, allegedly because of "urban improvements." A unit of the Italian Navy brought the remains to Bari, where they were buried in the local military mausoleum.

Diplomatic activity included talks between President Leone and Norwegian Prime Minister Trygve Bratteli, UN Secretary-General Kurt Waldheim, Austrian Chancellor Bruno Kreisky, Pres. Léopold Sédar Senghor of Senegal, French Pres. Georges Pompidou, and British Prime Minister Edward Heath. Leone also paid a state visit to Pope Paul VI on September 22, his first to what was technically a foreign country.

The Economy. Industrial unrest and consequent loss of production, inflation, and political uncertainty combined to worsen a situation that had already shown clear signs of stress in 1971. The encouraging uptrend in the last part of that year did not continue, and Bank of Italy governor Guido Carli indicated that many firms faced bankruptcy because they lacked a market capable of absorbing their products. Even a great increase in public expenditure did not yield the expected results; productivity failed to increase and the gap between prices and incomes widened. Industrial production in the first six months of the year rose by only 2% over the corresponding period of 1971. The mining industry was particularly unsatisfactory, with a reduction in output of 0.7%, whereas manufacturing went ahead by 2.4% and the power industry by 6.8%. Demand for automobiles, usually a good guide to the Italian economy, showed signs of weakness; the increase in registrations over the first six months was

ITALY

Education. (1969–70) Primary, pupils 4,728,075, teachers 216,877; secondary, pupils 2,488,105, teachers 206,971; vocational, pupils 917,337, teachers 78,664; teacher training, students 234,832, teachers 18,488; higher (42 universities; 1970–71), students 678,845, teaching staff (1968–69) 31,908.

Finance. Monetary unit: lira, with (Sept. 18, 1972) a par value of 581.50 lire to U.S. $1 (free rate of 1,423 lire = £1 sterling). Gold, SDRs, and foreign exchange, official: (June 1972) U.S. $6,081,000,000; (June 1971) U.S. $5,761,000,000. Budget (1972 est.): revenue 13,318,900,000,000 lire; expenditure 15,695,700,000,000 lire. Gross national product: (1970) 57,937,000,000,000 lire; (1969) 51,758,000,000,000 lire. Money supply: (May 1972) 36,844,000,000,000 lire; (May 1971) 31,654,000,000,000 lire. Cost of living (1963 = 100): (June 1972) 141; (June 1971) 134.

Foreign Trade. (1971) Imports 9,894,000,000,000 lire; exports 9,359,000,000,000 lire. Import sources: EEC 42% (West Germany 20%, France 14%); U.S. 9%. Export destinations: EEC 45% (West Germany 23%, France 14%, Netherlands 5%); U.S. 10%; Switzerland 5%. Main exports: machinery 23%; textiles 11%; clothing 8%; chemicals 7%; motor vehicles 7%; petroleum products 6%. Tourism (1970): visitors 12,718,700; gross receipts U.S. $1,639,000,000.

Transport and Communications. Roads (1971) 287,474 km. (including 4,323 km. expressways). Motor vehicles in use (1971): passenger 11,350,000; commercial 935,000. Railways: (1970) state 16,073 km., private 4,016 km.; traffic (1971) 33,943,000,000 passenger-km., freight 17,226,000,000 net ton-km. Air traffic (1971): 9,502,000,000 passenger-km.; freight 323,870,000 net ton-km. Shipping (1971): merchant vessels 100 gross tons and over 1,690; gross tonnage 8,138,521. Telephones (Dec. 1970) 9,369,000. Radio licenses (Dec. 1970) 11,702,000. Television licenses (Dec. 1970) 9,717,000.

Agriculture. Production (in 000; metric tons; 1971; 1970 in parentheses): wheat 10,070 (9,689); corn 4,475 (4,729); barley 367 (315); oats 501 (486); potatoes 3,268 (3,668); rice 862 (850); dry broad beans 349 (369); onions (1970) 481, (1969) 468; sugar, raw value (1971–72) *c.* 1,247, (1970–71) 1,202; tomatoes (1970) 3,618, (1969) 3,670; wine 6,427 (6,887); olives *c.* 2,550 (2,124); oranges 1,820 (1,601); lemons 734 (798); apples 1,698 (2,062); pears 1,706 (1,906); peaches (1970) 1,128, (1969) 883; figs 176 (198); tobacco 79 (78); cheese *c.* 465 (*c.* 460); beef and veal *c.* 540 (550); pork *c.* 370 (354). Livestock (in 000; Jan. 1971): cattle 8,721; sheep 7,968; pigs 8,980; goats 1,019; horses, mules, and asses 708; poultry *c.* 110,000.

Industry. Index of production (1963 = 100): (1971) 146; (1970) 150. Unemployment: (1971) 3.1%; (1970) 3.1%. Fuel and power (in 000; metric tons; 1971): lignite 1,325; coal 257; crude oil 1,294; natural gas (cu.m.) 13,371,000; manufactured gas (cu.m.) 2,920,000; electricity (kw-hr.) *c.* 126,000,000. Production (in 000; metric tons; 1971): iron ore (50% metal content) 683; pig iron 8,726; crude steel 17,429; aluminum 117; zinc 144; lead 48; cement 31,730; cotton yarn 155; rayon, etc., filament yarn 83; rayon, etc., staple fibre 100; nylon, etc., filament yarn 126; nylon, etc., fibres 174; nitrogenous fertilizers (1970–71) 956; sulfuric acid 3,102; petroleum products (1970) 109,387; passenger cars (units) 1,702; commercial vehicles (units) 116.

only 2.63% higher than in the corresponding period of 1971. Imports, particularly, were affected, and this was taken as a symptom of a contracting market. Prices had soared by 5% in the 12 months ended in May, and a new escalation in food prices was registered by August, leading Andreotti to encourage greater control by local authorities.

Foreign trade reflected the reduced demand on the home market. In the first half of the year exports increased by 17.9% and imports only by 8.8%, the trade balance for the period January to June showing a deficit of 134 billion lire, compared with a deficit of 498 billion lire in 1971. A greater drain of capital abroad, however, contributed to worsen the balance of payments, which showed a clear deficit in the first few months of the year as opposed to an encouraging surplus in the same period of 1971. Rumours of a possible 4% devaluation of the lira were repeatedly denied by the Treasury.

Details of a new five-year plan (1971–75) were announced in February. It foresaw an increase in national income of 5.7% per year in real terms, slightly less than the 6% achieved with the previous plan. Its aims were full employment, socioeconomic leveling between the depressed areas of the South and the rest of the country, and maintenance of a dynamic balance between internal and international prices.

(FABIO GALVANO)

Ivory Coast

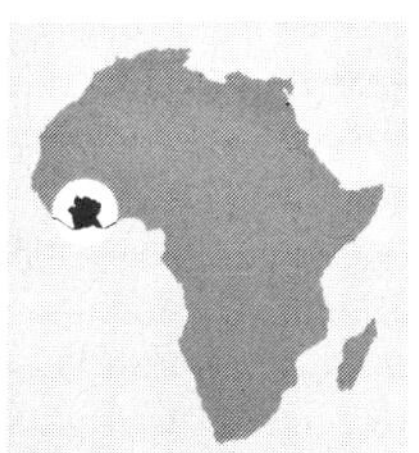

A republic on the Gulf of Guinea, West Africa, the Ivory Coast is bounded by Liberia, Guinea, Mali, Upper Volta, and Ghana. Area: 123,483 sq.mi. (319,822 sq.km.). Pop. (1971 est.): 4,420,000, including about 15,000 Europeans. Cap. and largest city: Abidjan (pop., 1963 est., 285,000). Language: French and local dialects. Religion: animist 65%; Muslim 23%; Christian 12%. President and premier in 1972, Félix Houphouët-Boigny.

IVORY COAST

Education. (1969–70) Primary, pupils 464,817, teachers 10,094; secondary, pupils 53,267, teachers 1,910; vocational, pupils 4,794, teachers 402; teacher training, pupils 1,615, teachers 95; higher, students (1968–69) 2,943.

Finance. Monetary unit: CFA franc, with (Sept. 18, 1972) a parity of CFA Fr. 50 to the French franc (CFA Fr. 255.79 = U.S. $1; free rate of CFA Fr. 612.37 = £1 sterling). Gold, SDRs, and foreign exchange, central bank: (May 1972) U.S. $92.1 million; (May 1971) U.S. $90.2 million. Budget (1971 est.) balanced at CFA Fr. 62.7 billion. Money supply: (March 1972) CFA Fr. 100,950,000,000; (March 1971) CFA Fr. 89,840,000,000.

Foreign Trade. (1971) Imports CFA Fr. 110,840,000,000; exports CFA Fr. 126,560,000,000. Import sources: France 47%; Italy 7%; U.S. 7%; West Germany 7%; Netherlands 5%. Export destinations: France 33%; U.S. 17%; Netherlands 9%; West Germany 9%; Italy 8%. Main exports: coffee 33%; timber 20%; cocoa 17%.

Agriculture. Production (in 000; metric tons; 1971; 1970 in parentheses): corn 280 (231); sweet potatoes (1970) 1,572, (1969) 1,541; cassava (1970) 540, (1969) 532; rice *c.* 350 (316); millet *c.* 42 (37); peanuts *c.* 43 (43); coffee *c.* 249 (*c.* 240); cocoa (1971–72) 200, (1970–71) 180; bananas (1970) 179, (1969) 172; cotton, lint 15 (13); timber (cu.m.; 1969) 9,000, (1968) 8,900. Livestock (in 000; 1970–71): cattle *c.* 400; pigs *c.* 168; sheep *c.* 850; goats *c.* 770; poultry *c.* 8,000.

Broadly based diplomacy abroad and austerity at home remained salient features of government policy in 1972. President Houphouët-Boigny's spectacular reconciliation with Pres. Léopold Sédar Senghor of Senegal in December 1971 was an event of major significance for French-speaking Africa in general and for the Economic Community of West Africa in particular. On July 24 Houphouët-Boigny visited Guinea in an attempt to hasten Pres. Sékou Touré's return to the French-speaking African fold. However, the discussions broke down when Touré demanded the immediate return of Guinean political exiles in the Ivory Coast.

In February the arrest of several senior officials for financial malpractice was announced but later denied. Meanwhile, an austerity program considerably curbed the hitherto somewhat extravagant life-style of many senior public servants.

The austerity measures, though explained more than sufficiently by the sharp fall in world cocoa prices, caused exaggerated alarm abroad. This was apparently reinforced by a World Bank report that seemed to cast doubt upon the strength of the Ivory Coast economy. Like most of his countrymen, President Houphouët-Boigny seemed inclined to view any unfavourable comment on the limits of his country's economic growth potential as the work of forces with a grudge against him.

Nevertheless, the Ivory Coast remained the most prosperous of all West African states, with a balanced budget and a continuing surplus in the balance of trade. Agricultural production soared as efforts at diversification increased.

(PHILIPPE DECRAENE)

Jamaica

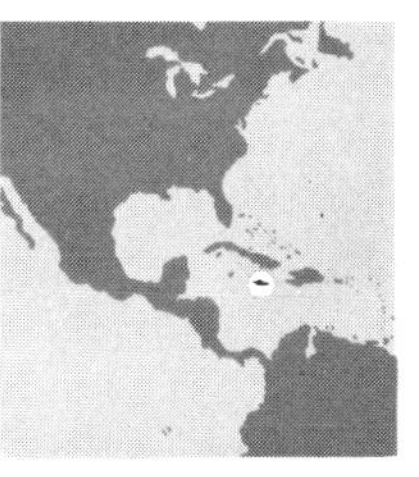

A parliamentary state within the Commonwealth of Nations, Jamaica is an island in the Caribbean Sea about 90 mi. S of Cuba. Area: 4,244 sq.mi. (10,991 sq.km.). Pop. (1971 est.): 1,911,420, predominantly Negro, but including Europeans, Chinese, Indians, and persons of mixed race. Cap. and largest city: Kingston (pop., 1971 est., 144,058). Language: English. Religion: Christian, with Anglicans and Baptists in the majority. Queen, Elizabeth II; governor-general in 1971, Sir Clifford Campbell; prime ministers, Hugh

JAMAICA

Education. (1968–69) Primary, pupils 353,997, teachers (including preprimary) 7,087; secondary, pupils 40,641, teachers 1,787; vocational, pupils 4,127, teachers 239; teacher training, students 321, teachers 7; higher (1967–68), students 2,234.

Finance. Monetary unit: Jamaican dollar, with (Sept. 18, 1972) a free rate of Jam$0.82 to U.S. $1 (par value of Jam$2 = £1 sterling). Budget (1971–72 est.): revenue Jam$301.3 million; expenditure Jam $297.5 million.

Foreign Trade. (1970) Imports Jam$435,220,000; exports Jam$283,090,000. Import sources: U.S. 43%; U.K. 19%; Canada 9%. Export destinations: U.S. 53%; U.K. 15%; Canada 8%; Norway 8%. Main exports: alumina 39%; bauxite 27%; sugar 11%.

Agriculture. Production (in 000; metric tons; 1970; 1969 in parentheses): sweet potatoes *c.* 150 (*c.* 150); cassava *c.* 10 (*c.* 10); sugar, raw value (1971–72) *c.* 390, (1970–71) 385; bananas *c.* 145 (*c.* 155); oranges *c.* 87 (*c.* 85); grapefruit *c.* 19 (*c.* 21); copra *c.* 18 (16). Livestock (in 000; 1970–71): cattle *c.* 270; goats *c.* 380; pigs *c.* 190; sheep *c.* 13.

Industry. Production (in 000; metric tons; 1970): bauxite 12,010; cement 457; gypsum (1968) 260; petroleum products 1,698; electricity (kw-hr.) 1,550,000.

Italian Literature:
see Literature

Lawson Shearer and, from March 2, Michael Manley.

The general election of Feb. 29, 1972, resulted in a landslide victory for the People's National Party headed by the charismatic Michael Manley (*see* BIOGRAPHY), son of Norman Manley, the party's founder. The PNP had been in opposition throughout Jamaica's ten years of independence. Two of the major election issues were alleged widespread corruption and the denial of the right to vote to people under 23. The new government set up a commission of inquiry to investigate the award of contracts and expenditure on public projects since 1962, and a law was passed lowering the voting age to 18.

The new government declared that it meant to practice the "politics of participation." Committees and working groups on a variety of subjects were established in an effort to involve as wide a cross-section of the public as possible. Censorship of literature coming into the country was eased, confiscated passports were returned, and freedom of comment was encouraged. Coincidentally, it was announced that a new daily paper would begin publication in June 1973.

The election was interpreted as a mandate for change. A five-year program to wipe out illiteracy was begun. The performance of the agricultural sector continued to be a matter of concern, and it was proposed that the more than 40 commodity organizations in existence should participate in a farmers' union. Extensions planned for Kingston's port facilities would make it the major transshipment centre for the Caribbean. (GLORIA C. CUMPER)

Japan

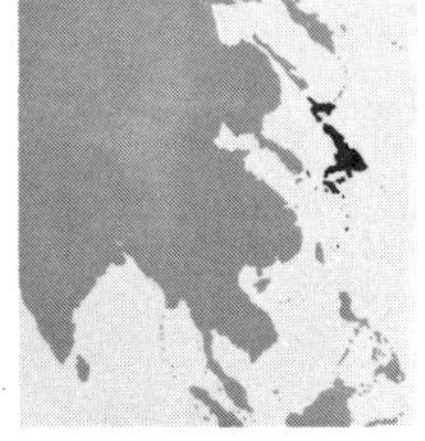

A constitutional monarchy in the northwestern Pacific Ocean, Japan is an archipelago composed of four major islands (Hokkaido, Honshu, Kyushu, and Shikoku) and minor adjacent islands. Area: 143,818 sq.mi. (372,488 sq.km.). Pop. (1972 est.): 106,251,000. Cap. and largest city: Tokyo (pop., 1972 est., 8,818,216). Language: Japanese. Religion: primarily Shinto and Buddhist; Christian 0.5%. Emperor, Hirohito; prime ministers in 1972, Eisaku Sato until July 5 and, from July 6, Kakuei Tanaka.

BARRY SHLACHTER—NANCY PALMER PHOTO AGENCY

Kakuei Tanaka became prime minister of Japan in July 1972.

Domestic Affairs. On February 2, nine days after he had emerged from 28 years of hiding in the Guam jungles and 31 years after he left his homeland, former Imperial Army sergeant Shoichi Yokoi (*see* BIOGRAPHY) returned to Japan. Three decades of spectacular changes astounded him. Fully recovered from World War II, Japan boasted the second largest gross national product (GNP) in the non-Communist world. But the costs of growth were high: inflation, a business cycle which in 1972 produced a sharp recession, and the worrisome problem of pollution.

Japan's spectacular growth as a world economic power was recognized in December 1971, when the exchange rate of the yen was altered upward for the first time in 100 years. In a general agreement governing world currencies, Japan accepted the highest revaluation rate (16.88%) among the advanced industrial nations. The rate moved from 360 to 308 yen = $1. Japan's GNP for fiscal 1971 (April 1, 1971–March 31, 1972), according to the Economic Planning Agency, reached 60,911,300,000,000 yen ($182.4 billion). In terms of per capita national income, Japan ranked 13th in the world at $1,840.

Despite currency revaluation and determined government efforts to cut back exports, Japan's overall balance of payments surplus continued to increase. By the end of September, the country's gold and foreign exchange reserves, as reported by the Finance Ministry, stood at $16.5 billion. Meanwhile, Japanese and U.S. business leaders had been meeting to reduce the most critical trade imbalance, that between the U.S. and Japan. After a three-day meeting in June in Tokyo, a joint statement was issued in which the parties promised a cooperative study "to redress the current trade payments imbalance and chart the most desirable form of economic interchange to be attained by 1975 and 1980."

Despite trade surpluses, Japan's growth rate had slowed markedly during fiscal 1971. The GNP registered a real gain of only 5.7% (a sharp drop from 1970, which recorded a 9.5% gain in real terms). The gap between nominal and real growth was, of course, accounted for by price inflation. The Office of the Prime Minister reported that the national consumer price index for January–June 1972 stood at an index of 109.5 (1970 = 100). On this scale, in July Tokyo's consumer price index reached 111.3.

On January 12 the government formally approved an expansive 11,470,472,000,000 yen budget for fiscal 1972, representing an increase in expenditures of 21.8% over 1971. Emphasis was placed on stimulating the laggard economy in the face of the persistent recession and widespread impact of yen revaluation, as well as on improving the quality of life. The government hoped that this large budget would push the real GNP growth rate up to 7.7% for fiscal 1972.

After the 1971 midyear elections for the (upper) House of Councillors, party representation in the Diet was as follows: (lower) House of Representatives: Liberal-Democrats (LDP) 300, Japan Socialists (JSP) 90, Komeito (KMT) 47, Democratic Socialists (DSP) 32, Japan Communists (JCP) 14, independents 3, vacancies 5 (total, 491); House of Councillors: LDP 136, JSP 66, KMT 23, DSP 13, JCP 10, independents (including Niin Club) 4 (total, 252). Despite the sizable majorities held by the ruling LDP, the popular support of Prime Minister Sato had disastrously declined to 18% of those polled in a survey (October 1971) by the private Japan Research Center.

In April Sato admitted that he felt "deeply responsible" for a series of controversial irregularities connected with negotiations on Okinawa's reversion to Japan and revealed in Japan's "secret documents" case. On June 17 Sato announced that he planned to retire as president of the LDP (and therefore as prime minister), after a record seven years and eight months of service as the nation's head of government. The announcement came shortly before an emotionally charged press conference, where Sato in a fit of anger expelled news reporters.

Japan's new prime minister was chosen in effect on July 5, when Kakuei Tanaka (*see* BIOGRAPHY) defeated Foreign Minister Takeo Fukuda for the LDP presidency in a second, runoff ballot. Eligible voters were 429 LDP Diet members—295 in the lower and 134 in the upper house—and 47 local delegates, one from each of the 47 prefectures. On July 6 the Diet formally elected Tanaka, and later that day he was attested by Emperor Hirohito as the 40th prime minister of Japan. Tanaka promptly formed a new Cabinet with Masayoshi Ohira in the post of foreign minister, a significant appointment in view of Tanaka's promise to normalize Japan's China relations. Takeo Miki, a powerful LDP faction leader, became state minister without portfolio, while Yasuhiro Nakasone took the critical position of minister of international trade and industry.

The LDP's consolidation under Tanaka came none too soon for the party, for there were signs of political disaffection at the local level. Despite Sato's triumph in obtaining the reversion of Okinawa to Japanese control, on June 25 incumbent governor Chobyo Yara defeated an LDP candidate to be reelected chief executive of the Ryukyu government. The fourth Socialist candidate to be elected governor (the other three were in Tokyo, Kyoto, and Osaka), Yara represented the Okinawans' aversion to control by the national government, born out of memories of totalitarian rule before the war and neglect of the island's welfare under U.S. administration. In Japan's prefectural assembly election, leftist parties increased their strength and acquired a majority of 23 seats. On July 3 the LDP suffered another blow with the election of Yawara Hata as governor of Saitama prefecture. Hata, who was supported by the JSP, DSP, and JCP, ended 27 years of conservative rule in Saitama.

The December 10 elections for the House of Representatives also proved disappointing to the LDP. Its total number of seats fell from 297 just before the election to 271—still a majority but much less than had been hoped for—although its popular vote declined only slightly, from 47.6% in the 1969 election to 46.9%. The JCP, with 38 seats, made the greatest gain. The JSP also improved its position, capturing 118 seats, while the KMT and DSP declined to 29 and 19, respectively. Five independents were elected.

On February 3 Japan opened the 11th Winter Olympic Games in Sapporo, Hokkaido. It was the first winter Olympics held in Asia, and the government spent about $450 million on it. Not only were new stadiums, ski slopes, and jump platforms built, but also new express highways, housing facilities, and the first subway in Japan constructed north of Tokyo. For a discussion of the Olympics, *see* SPORTING RECORD: *Special Report*.

Meanwhile, the Japanese, like residents of all advanced nations, were beginning to pay the price for the rapid growth of the 1960s. According to a survey conducted in urban areas by the General Council of Trade Unions (Sohyo), 70% of all workers responding were dissatisfied with their housing situation. The average age of a worker who bought a home increased from 30 (in 1960) to 37.7 (in 1972); the average cost of a house was 3.5 times the average worker's annual income. Respondents complained about high rents, poor equipment, narrow lots, lack of playgrounds for children, long commuting time (53.1 minutes one way for workers in the Tokyo-Kawasaki-Yokohama district), traffic accidents, and industrial pollution.

LONDON DAILY EXPRESS/PICTORIAL PARADE

Three Japanese youths, claiming to be victims of industrial pollution in their homeland, bring their message to the UN-sponsored world Conference on the Human Environment in Stockholm in June 1972.

In a landmark case decided on July 24, the Tsu district court ruled that six firms of a petrochemical complex in Yokkaichi (near Nagoya) were jointly responsible for polluting the air and ordered them to pay 88 million yen in damages to 12 victims and their relatives. The case involved some of Japan's most famous firms, including the Mitsubishi conglomerate, and was only one of four pollution trials in Japan. The other three dealt with cadmium poisoning (*itai-itai*) disease in Toyama prefecture, mercury pollution in Niigata prefecture, and another mercury poisoning (Minamata disease) in Kumamoto prefecture.

Such cases served to highlight Prime Minister Tanaka's bold plan to renovate the islands of Japan through systematic social and economic schemes,

JAPAN

Education. (1969–70) Primary, pupils 9,403,193, teachers 362,986; secondary, pupils 7,399,361; vocational, pupils 1,833,786; secondary and vocational, teachers 438,700; higher (including 120 universities), students 1,631,319, teaching staff *c.* 145,600.

Finance. Monetary unit: yen, with (Sept. 18, 1972) a par value of 308 yen to U.S. $1 (free rate of 736 yen = £1 sterling). Gold, SDRs, and foreign exchange, official: (June 1972) U.S. $15.3 billion; (June 1971) U.S. $7,156,000,000. Budget (1971–72) balanced at 9,414,000,000,000 yen. Gross national product: (1971) 78,960,000,000,000 yen; (1970) 70,985,000,000,000 yen. Money supply: (May 1972) 27,418,000,000,000 yen; (May 1971) 22,500,000,000,000 yen. Cost of living (1963 = 100): (June 1972) 160; (June 1971) 153.

Foreign Trade. (1971) Imports 6,908,900,000,000 yen; exports 8,396,500,000,000 yen. Import sources: U.S. 25%; Australia 9%; Iran 7%; Canada 5%. Export destinations: U.S. 32%; Liberia 4%. Main exports: machinery 22% (including telecommunications 7%); iron and steel 15%; motor vehicles 13%; textile yarns and fabrics 9%; ships 8%; chemicals 6%.

Transport and Communications. Roads (1971) 1,022,936 km. (including 1,099 km. expressways). Motor vehicles in use (1971): passenger 10,572,000; commercial 9,280,000. Railways: (1969) 28,007 km.; traffic (1971) 287,500,000,000 passenger-km., freight 62,476,000,000 net ton-km. Air traffic (1971): 10,430,000,000 passenger-km.; freight 479,660,000 net ton-km. Shipping (1971): merchant vessels 100 gross tons and over 8,851; gross tonnage 30,509,280. Telephones (Jan. 1971) 26,233,000. Radio receivers (Dec. 1968) 25,742,000. Television receivers (Dec. 1970) 22,658,000.

Agriculture. Production (in 000; metric tons; 1971; 1970 in parentheses): rice 14,139 (16,479); wheat 440 (474); barley 503 (573); sweet potatoes 2,041 (2,564); potatoes 3,156 (3,611); tea *c.* 93 (91); onions (1970) 1,587, (1969) 1,723; apples *c.* 1,050 (1,021); oranges (1970) 2,814, (1969) 2,392; tobacco *c.* 150 (150); pork *c.* 670 (648); timber (cu.m.; 1970) 50,000, (1969) 50,500; fish catch (1970) 9,308, (1969) 8,613; whale and sperm oil (1969–70) 76, (1968–69) 73. Livestock (in 000; Feb. 1971): cattle 3,615; sheep 26; pigs 6,904; goats 160; horses 125; chickens 172,226.

Industry. Index of production (1963 ≒ 100): (1971) 270; (1970) 258. Fuel and power (in 000; metric tons; 1971): coal 33,431; crude oil 751; natural gas (cu.m.) 2,700,000; manufactured gas (cu.m.; 1970) 3,179,000; electricity (kw-hr.) 379,120,000. Production (in 000; metric tons; 1971): iron ore (55% metal content) 1,422; pig iron 74,634; crude steel 88,558; petroleum products (1970) 162,984; cement 59,463; cotton yarn 534; woven cotton fabrics (sq.m.) 2,482,000; rayon, etc., filament yarn 121; rayon, etc., staple fibres 377; nylon, etc., filament yarn 539; nylon, etc., fibres 628; sulfuric acid 6,658; cameras (units) 5,342; radio receivers (units) 28,092; television receivers (units) 13,231; passenger cars (units) 3,715; commercial vehicles (units) 2,105; motorcycles (units) 3,401. Merchant vessels launched (100 gross tons and over; 1971) 11,992,000 gross tons. New dwelling units started (1971) 1,464,000.

which became the central issue in the new Cabinet's domestic policies. A book written by Tanaka prior to assuming office, entitled *Nihon Retto Kaizo Ron* ("Remodeling the Japanese Islands"), sold hundreds of thousands of copies. Opposition spokesmen argued that Tanaka's plan for decentralization of industry from the crowded Pacific coastal zone would result simply in spreading pollution throughout Japan.

Foreign Affairs. Japanese questioning of the price of economic growth was projected onto the international scene at the UN Conference on the Human Environment, which met in Stockholm in June. Buichi Oishi, director general of the Environment Agency, speaking on June 6 at a plenary session, reported that the Japanese people were seriously reconsidering for whom and for what purpose economic development had been pursued. He stated that the Japanese government would strongly support the Declaration on the Human Environment. Japanese, he added, would be especially interested in a ban on the use of weapons of mass destruction including nuclear arms. Japan was prepared to contribute 10% of the UN Environment Fund if other developed nations would also make substantial contributions.

On the other hand, Japanese officials on June 9 reacted strongly to a proposal for a total ten-year ban on commercial whaling pushed through the conference. One of two nations voting against the U.S.-sponsored resolution, Japan sought formulation of whaling policies "based on scientific grounds" in a later meeting of the International Whaling Commission held June 26–30. With the U.S.S.R., Japan successfully opposed the ban at the IWC.

Japan's postwar "special" relationship with the U.S. was subtly changing, as the "fateful triangle" of China-Japan-U.S. reasserted itself. Following two days of talks between Prime Minister Sato and U.S. Pres. Richard Nixon at San Clemente, Calif., on January 7 the two leaders agreed that Okinawa should revert to Japanese administration on May 15. Their joint statement recognized the U.S. intention to "confirm upon reversion that the assurances of the United States government concerning nuclear weapons on Okinawa have been fully carried out." Sato regarded the return of nuclear-free Okinawa as the climax of his career.

President Nixon's journey to Peking on February 21 had a major impact on millions of Japanese who watched on TV the historic arrival in China. The visit was a shock to Sato and his government. The general effect on the Japanese people was that the statures of Nixon, Mao Tse-tung, and Chou En-lai were enlarged and that of Sato was diminished.

A drum-beating and chanting Buddhist priest halts a U.S. military truck near Yokohama Harbour in demonstrations on Nov. 8, 1972, involving 6,000 persons protesting the use of the port for shipping combat vehicles. Behind the priest are Japanese riot police.

WIDE WORLD

The Sato government was embarrassed on March 27 when two Socialist members of the Diet charged that Japan had committed itself to shoulder the $4 million which the U.S. agreed to pay Okinawan landowners for damage done during military occupation. On April 4 metropolitan police arrested a 41-year-old woman secretary in the Foreign Ministry who allegedly had leaked "secret documents" about Japan-U.S. negotiations to a *Mainichi Shimbun* reporter.

The long-postponed visit to Japan by the U.S. presidential adviser Henry Kissinger took place in June. At a press conference held in Tokyo on June 12, Kissinger said, "Japan should take care of its conventional defense, and there will be no American pressure to expand its military role in other parts of Asia," then revealed that President Nixon had invited Emperor Hirohito to visit the U.S. "at an appropriate time." Court officials revealed that the 71-year-old emperor would travel to the U.S. during 1973.

After his election Tanaka prepared to visit China. On August 12 a Japan Air Lines DC8-62 and an All-Nippon Airways 727-200 completed survey flights to Shanghai, and were thus the first Japanese commercial aircraft to land at a mainland China airport since World War II. In late August, Foreign Minister Ohira told the Diet that the Japan-Republic of China (Taiwan) peace treaty would lose effect as "a natural consequence" of the normalization of Japan-mainland China relations. Government leaders expressed the hope, however, that relations with Taiwan in investment, trade, and other fields, including culture and sports, might be maintained.

On his return from summit talks with President Nixon held on August 31–September 1 in Hawaii, Tanaka reaffirmed the intention of the two governments to maintain the Japan-U.S. bond. The prime minister and the president recognized the importance of Nixon's visits to Peking and to Moscow, and shared the hope that the forthcoming visit to Peking by Tanaka would further serve to relax tension in Asia. On September 14, after careful consultation with 300 LDP members of the Diet, a consensus to approve Tanaka's China visit was achieved.

On September 25, millions of Japanese watched on television the arrival of the first Japanese prime minister in office to visit mainland China since World War II. Within hours Tanaka and Chou En-lai agreed in principle to establish diplomatic relations after four decades of separation. Prime Minister Tanaka agreed to a delicate wording concerning Japan's war guilt: "The Japanese side is keenly aware of Japan's responsibility for causing enormous damages in the past to the Chinese people through war and deeply reproaches itself." In turn, China, "in the interest of the friendship between the peoples of China and Japan," renounced any demand for indemnities. Other major points included: (1) recognition of the government of mainland China "as the sole legal government of China"; (2) reaffirmation by Peking that Taiwan is "an inalienable part" of the territory of China (Japan "fully understands and respects this stand"); (3) restoration of diplomatic relations as of September 29; and (4) a declaration of intention to exchange ambassadors as soon as possible.

In many other ways, Japan's diplomacy in 1972 showed signs of moving "from dependence to independence," of maintaining close ties with the U.S.

but also of striking out on separate paths of foreign relations. On January 27 in Tokyo, the foreign ministers of Japan and of the U.S.S.R. agreed that the two nations would begin to study the conditions prerequisite to the conclusion of a peace treaty. (A joint declaration reestablishing diplomatic relations had been signed in 1956.) Soviet Foreign Minister Andrei A. Gromyko stated that the U.S.S.R. was anxious to have Japan participate in the exploration of continental shelf oil resources in northern Sakhalin, coking coal development in Yakutsk, and exploitation of resources in the Tyumen oil fields. The Soviet delegation significantly made no mention of preconditions related to the so-called northern territories dispute with Japan. Speaking to this issue, Prime Minister Sato stated on January 31 in the Diet that Japan would continue its territorial claims over two southern Kuril islands, Kunashiri and Etorofu.

Japan signed its first private trade agreement with North Korea on January 23. The five-year pact, designed to expand annual trade volume to approximately 160 billion yen by 1976, was signed in North Korea. In early August, however, Justice Minister Yuichi Kori rejected Tokyo Gov. Ryokichi Minobe's request for entry permits for a 12-man North Korean mission invited to Tokyo. When Minobe pressed the government, Foreign Minister Ohira informed the governor that visits from North Korea would be limited temporarily to the fields of culture, education, technology, and sports. In September in Seoul, Japan and South Korea wound up a two-day ministerial conference with a joint communiqué in which Japan pledged 52.4 billion yen in aid for 1972.

Two Japanese terrorists were killed after participation in a wholesale massacre at Israel's Lod International Airport on May 30. They were Yasuyuki Yasuda, 25, a student at Kyoto University, and Takeshi Okudaira, 26, a former Kyoto student. Kozo Okamoto, 24, a former student at Kagoshima University, the lone survivor, was immediately placed in custody in Israel for his part in the shoot-out which left 28 dead and more than 70 injured. All had been affiliated with the Red Army faction of the radical movement. Returning from Tel Aviv to Tokyo on June 5, special envoy Kenji Fukunaga reported that Israeli leaders as well as the Israeli people had been impressed by the prompt action taken by the Japanese government. Appropriate compensation was paid through the Japanese Red Cross to the families of those killed and to those injured in the shooting. Additional funds were conveyed to the Israeli Red Shield of David, as Fukunaga delivered an official apology to the Israeli government. (ARDATH W. BURKS)

Jordan

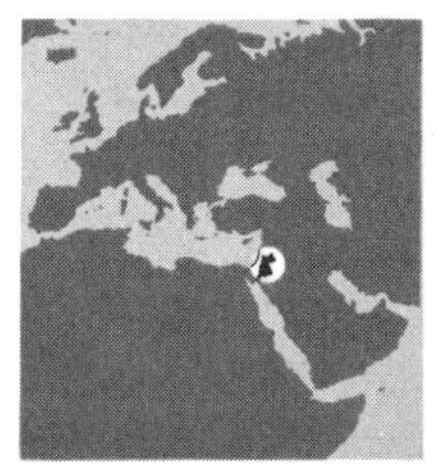

A constitutional monarchy in southwest Asia, Jordan is bounded north by Syria, northeast by Iraq, east and south by Saudi Arabia, and west by Israel. Area (including territory occupied by Israel in the June 1967 war): 37,737 sq.mi. (97,740 sq.km.). Pop. (1971 est.): 2,383,000. Cap. and largest city: Amman (pop., 1970 est., 570,000). Language: Arabic. Religion (1961) Muslim 94%; Christian 6%. King, Husain I; prime minister in 1972, Ahmed al-Lawzi.

In 1972 the regime of King Husain appeared fairly self-confident despite its isolated position within the Arab world. The king insisted repeatedly that Jordan would not become involved in another war with Israel (although in a September speech he hinted otherwise), but he denied Jordan's intention to negotiate a separate peace with Israel. The Jordan government had some success in strengthening its ties with the moderate Palestinian leadership in the Israeli-occupied territories, and in August a 45-man delegation from Gaza led by the Israeli-appointed mayor, Rashad Shawa, visited Amman. But the Palestinian resistance leaders remained relentlessly hostile. In late January Yasir Arafat, head of the Palestine Liberation Organization, said there could be no more negotiations with the Jordanian authorities. On March 15 Husain announced his plan for a federal state to include the East and West banks of Jordan and to be known as the United Arab Kingdom. It would have two capitals, Amman and Jerusalem, and a governor-general with a peoples' council in each region. Amman would be the federal capital, and the country would have a single army. On March 26 the king traveled to the United States to explain his plan and to undergo medical treatment.

Arab reaction to the plan was almost universally hostile, and it was denounced as treachery by Palestinian organizations. The king made it clear that his plan depended on Israeli withdrawal from territories occupied in 1967, but said that Jerusalem should remain the capital of Israel as well as of the West Bank region. Egypt broke diplomatic relations with Jordan over the plan on April 6.

Elections to the Jordanian National Union (established in September 1971) began on August 30, and it was announced that the West and East banks would each have 120 elected members with another 120 ap-

JORDAN

Education. (1969–70) Primary, pupils 259,388, teachers 6,433; secondary, pupils 85,289, teachers 3,757; vocational, pupils 2,801, teachers 171; higher (including University of Jordan), students 4,463, teaching staff 368.

Finance. Monetary unit: Jordanian dinar, with (Sept. 18, 1972) a par value of 0.357 dinar to U.S. $1 (free rate of 0.870 dinar = £1 sterling). Gold, SDRs, and foreign exchange, central bank: (June 1972) U.S. $223.9 million; (June 1971) U.S. $225.4 million. Budget (1972 est.) balanced at 124.8 million dinars. Gross national product: (1969) 231.5 million dinars; (1968) 197.3 million dinars. Money supply: (June 1972) 110,520,000 dinars; (June 1971) 109,830,000 dinars. Cost of living (Amman; 1967 = 100): (June 1972) 126; (June 1971) 120.

Foreign Trade. (1971) Imports 76,630,000 dinars; exports 11,440,000 dinars. Import sources: U.S. 20%; U.K. 9%; Lebanon 7%; Japan 6%; West Germany 6%; Saudi Arabia 6%; Egypt 5%. Export destinations: Saudi Arabia 13%; Syria 13%; Kuwait 12%; Lebanon 8%; India 8%; Iraq 7%. Main exports: phosphates 19%; tomatoes 10%; oranges 7%; cement 5%.

Transport and Communications. Roads (1971) 5,693 km. Motor vehicles in use (1971): passenger 16,270; commercial 6,300. Railways (1968) 366 km. Air traffic (1971): 185,070,000 passenger-km.; freight 2,713,000 net ton-km. Telephones (Dec. 1970) 31,000. Radio receivers (Dec. 1970) 150,000. Television receivers (Dec. 1969) 25,000.

Agriculture. Production (in 000; metric tons; 1971; 1970 in parentheses): wheat 168 (54); barley 26 (5); lentils *c.* 22 (5); onions (1970) 3, (1969) 2; tomatoes (1970) 137, (1969) 150; olives *c.* 25 (10); oranges (1970) 50, (1969) 27; lemons (1970) 14, (1969) *c.* 10; tobacco *c.* 2 (1.2). Livestock (in 000; 1970–71): cattle 32; goats 349; sheep 664; camels 10; asses 44; chickens *c.* 2,000.

Industry. Production (in 000; metric tons; 1970): phosphate 913; cement (1971) 419; electricity (kw-hr.) 165,000.

Japanese Literature: *see* Literature
Jazz: *see* Music
Jehovah's Witnesses: *see* Religion
Jewish Literature: *see* Literature

pointed by the king, one of whose objectives was to counter any plans to set up a Palestinian state outside his jurisdiction. When Pres. Anwar as-Sadat of Egypt proposed in September the setting up of a Palestinian government-in-exile, Jordan promptly rejected the idea.

Jordan failed in its consistent attempts to persuade Kuwait and Libya to resume aid, which was only being maintained by Saudi Arabia. The U.S. increased its aid to Jordan, but the economic situation remained precarious and on May 10 the Jordanian dinar was devalued by 8.5%. Although Iraq resumed its commercial relations with Jordan, broken off in July 1971, Syria maintained its closed border with Jordan until December 1, then reopened it for reasons of economic and political self-interest at a time of tension with Israel. On August 22 Jordan had closed the Syria-Saudi Arabia route through its territory.

A Libyan-inspired coup aiming to kill the king and Crown Prince Hassan was reportedly foiled on November 6. Following the arrest of about 300 officers and civilians, a Palestinian air force pilot, Talal al-Khatib, strafed the king as he was entering his helicopter. Husain was hit in the thigh and spent some time in a military hospital; Khatib was shot. On July 8 King Husain's father, ex-King Talal, died in a psychiatric clinic in Istanbul, aged 61 (*see* OBITUARIES). On December 21 Husain divorced his British-born wife, Princess Muna, and five days later married a 24-year-old Jordanian, Alia Toukan, who became queen.

(PETER MANSFIELD)

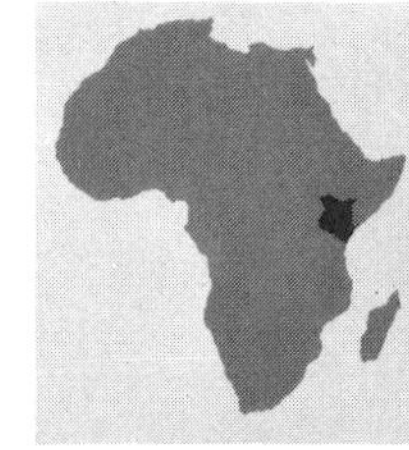

Kenya

A republic and a member of the Commonwealth of Nations, Kenya is bordered on the north by Sudan and Ethiopia, east by Somalia, south by Tanzania, and west by Uganda. Area: 224,960 sq.mi. (582,646 sq.km.), including 5,172 sq.mi. of inland water. Pop. (1972 est.): 12,068,000, including (1969) African 98.1%; Asian 1.5%. Cap. and largest city: Nairobi (pop., 1969 est., 509,000). Language: English and Swahili. Religion (1962): Christian 57.8%; Muslim 3.8%. President in 1972, Jomo Kenyatta.

Economics dominated Kenyan affairs in the early months of 1972. Credit restrictions had been imposed late in 1971 and on December 1 the minister of finance and economic planning, Mwai Kibaki, had announced that foreign exchange would not be made available for the purchase of commodities that could be produced in Kenya. This was followed in January 1972 by a total ban on some imports and further restrictions upon others, and by an exhortation to local manufacturers to produce more goods both to help the country's finances and to provide greater employment opportunities. Industrialists were also urged to seek new markets in Ethiopia, Zambia, and Somalia. By the middle of the year concern was beginning to be felt at the prospect of a serious decline in exports to Uganda and Tanzania because of exchange controls introduced among the three countries.

Early in the year assistance in the shape of a grant of some $1,350,000 spread over five years came from the Swedish government and the Swedish International Development Authority to support the Special Rural Development Program in South Nyanaza. A UN Development Program mission also visited Kenya to investigate causes of unemployment and to suggest methods of overcoming it, particularly by encouraging projects in rural areas, where populations were falling. To support such projects the government spent some $50 million on roads each year.

In February the Organization of African Unity's first continental trade fair opened in Nairobi. Thirty-seven member states were represented and Kenya contributed over $300,000, almost three-quarters of the total cost of the fair, in the hope that Nairobi's advantages as a centre of international trade and communications would be recognized. The occasion provided President Kenyatta with an opportunity to urge businessmen to overcome the obstacles of language and currency in order to expand the continent's trade. A few days earlier the minister for commerce and industry, James Osogo, together with representatives from Tanzania and Uganda, began talks in Nairobi with members of the EEC in the hope of getting better terms for East African exports.

Acknowledging the impartiality of the Pearce Commission Report, which had sounded out majority opinion on proposed constitutional changes in Rhodesia, Foreign Minister Njoroge Mungai urged the British government in May to hold a conference with representatives of all the people of Rhodesia in order to achieve majority rule. President Kenyatta celebrated Kenya's ninth anniversary of internal self-government on June 1 by defying a warning not to attend a rally in Nairobi because of plots to assassinate him. The crowd responded with a vocal demonstration of loyalty and Kenyatta addressed them on proposed changes in school curricula aimed at preparing young people for more employment requiring skill. On August 11 at the Egerton Agricultural College, Nakuru, the brother of a man mistaken for an assassin was beaten

KENYA

Education. (1970–71) Primary, pupils 1,427,589, teachers 41,479; secondary, pupils 126,855, teachers 5,881; vocational, pupils 2,136, teachers 143; teacher training, students 8,017, teachers 575; higher (at University of Nairobi), students 1,226.

Finance. Monetary unit: Kenyan shilling, with (Sept. 18, 1972) a par value of KShs. 7.14 to U.S. $1 (free rate of KShs. 17.51 = £1 sterling). Gold, SDRs, and foreign exchange (June 1971) U.S. $189.1 million. Budget (1970–71 est.): revenue KShs. 1,874,500,000; expenditure KShs. 1,625,800,000. Gross national product: (1969) KShs. 10,228,000,000; (1968) KShs. 9,-456,000,000. Cost of living (Nairobi; 1963 = 100): (June 1972) 124; (June 1971) 115.

Foreign Trade. (Excluding trade with Tanzania and Uganda; 1971) Imports KShs. 3,682,000,000; exports KShs. 1,567,000,000. Import sources: U.K. 31%; Japan 11%; U.S. 9%; West Germany 9%; Iran 5%. Export destinations: U.K. 20%; West Germany 9%; U.S. 7%; Zambia 7%. Main exports: coffee 25%; tea 15%; petroleum products 11%; meat 5%.

Transport and Communications. Roads (1971) 44,932 km. Motor vehicles in use (1970): passenger 58,000; commercial 52,700. Railways: (1970) *c.* 2,300 km. (operated under East African Railways Corp., serving Kenya, mainland Tanzania, and Uganda with a total of 5,897 km.); traffic (total East African; 1966) 4,529,000,000 passenger-km., freight (1970) 3,941,000,000 net ton-km. Air traffic (East African Airways Corp., including Tanzania and Uganda; 1971): 863.5 million passenger-km.; freight 31,346,000 ton-km. Telephones (Dec. 1970) 77,000. Radio receivers (Dec. 1969) 500,000. Television receivers (Dec. 1970) 16,000.

Agriculture. Production (in 000; metric tons; 1971; 1970 in parentheses): corn *c.* 1,400 (*c.* 1,500); wheat *c.* 210 (205); coffee 60 (59); tea 38 (41); sugar, raw value *c.* 147 (141); sisal *c.* 50 (48); cotton, lint *c.* 5 (5); fish catch (1970) 34, (1969) 32. Livestock (in 000; 1969–70): cattle 10,190; sheep *c.* 3,700; pigs 70; goats *c.* 4,000; camels 516; chickens 13,586.

Industry. Production (in 000; metric tons; 1970): salt 39; soda ash 158; gold (troy oz.; 1969) 18; cement 792; electricity (excluding most industrial production; kw-hr.; 1971) 556,000.

Journalism:
see Publishing
Judaism:
see Israel; Religion
Kashmir:
see India; Pakistan
Khmer Republic:
see Cambodia

to death by a crowd that had come to hear Kenyatta.

Following Pres. Idi Amin's expulsion of the Asian community from Uganda in August, Kenya increased its border patrols to stop infiltration by Asian refugees. Loyal non-African Kenyans were assured that Kenya would not follow Amin's example, although the gradual take-over of business activity by Africans would continue. (KENNETH INGHAM)

Korea

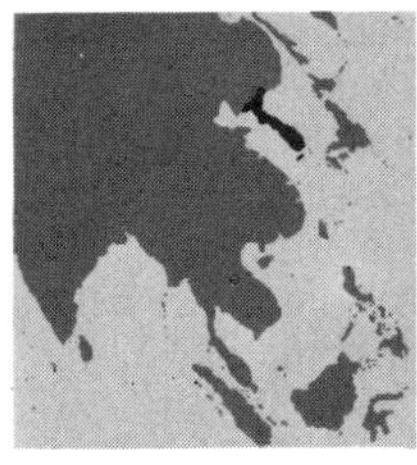

A country of eastern Asia, Korea is bounded by China, the Sea of Japan, the Korea Strait, and the Yellow Sea. It is divided into two parts at the 38th parallel.

The impossible became possible in Korea in 1972. On July 4, after a quarter century of the most hostile confrontation across the 38th parallel, the South and North Korean governments issued a joint statement revealing that secret negotiations between them had been going on for several months and that agreement had been reached on a wide range of concrete measures to achieve reunification and peace. The agreement stipulated that: the two sides would not slander or defame each other or undertake armed provocations but would take positive measures to prevent inadvertent military incidents; personnel exchanges would be undertaken in various fields; both sides would cooperate positively for the early success of the Red Cross talks (aimed at reuniting families separated by the Korean War); and a direct telephone line would be installed between Seoul and Pyongyang. To implement the new plans, the two sides agreed to establish a South-North Coordinating Committee.

The agreement was signed by the men who had held secret negotiations in the two capitals from at least May—the director of the South Korean Central Intelligence Agency, Lee Hu Rak, and the director of North Korea's Organization and Guidance Department, Kim Yong Ju, the younger brother of North Korean leader Kim Il Sung (*see* BIOGRAPHY). The idea of South and North Korean leaders thrashing out an agreement for eventual peace struck the world as sensational. However, the euphoria seemed to subside immediately after the dramatic joint declaration. South Korean leaders asked their people to continue to be vigilant against Communist machinations; praising or supporting the Communist regime of the North remained a punishable offense. Three days after the joint declaration the South Korean defense minister told senior military commanders to strengthen the defense posture and upgrade combat capabilities because "though a dialogue is open after 27 years of confrontation, it is dangerous to look for hasty results or to engage in a sentimental argument for unification." The South Korean ambassador in Washington said that any premature attempts by friendly nations to improve relations with North Korea at this moment would weaken the position of South Korea and hamper the new agreement for reunification. Pres. Park Chung Hee himself warned South Koreans against possible infiltration of Communist thought into their society in the course of reconciliation with the North.

UPI COMPIX

Hundreds of South Korean high-school girls hold cardboard cards forming a portrait of South Korea's Pres. Park Chung Hee during an Armed Forces Day parade on Oct. 1, 1972.

In the first week of October North Korea came charging back. In an unusually bitter attack, the official Central News Agency accused President Park of being a traitor and a running dog of U.S. and Japanese imperialists. It said: "If the South Korean reactionaries depart from the road of treachery and return to the position of true Koreans, we will not ask about their past but discuss and settle the domestic issue of the nation with them."

KOREA: Republic

Education. (1969–70) Primary, pupils 5,622,816, teachers 96,358; secondary, pupils 1,441,700, teachers 36,653; vocational, students 259,601, teachers 8,425; higher (including 27 universities), students 186,675, teaching staff 9,417.

Finance. Monetary unit: won, with a free rate (Sept. 18, 1972) of 400 won to U.S. $1 (977 won = £1 sterling). Gold, SDRs, and foreign exchange, central bank: (June 1972) U.S. $597.1 million; (June 1971) U.S. $568.9 million. Budget (1971 est.): revenue 510.7 billion won; expenditure 523.2 billion won. Gross national expenditure: (1970) 2,545,900,000,000 won; (1969) 2,047,100,000,000 won. Money supply: (May 1972) 365.7 billion won; (May 1971) 315.7 billion won. Cost of living (1963 = 100): (June 1972) 314; (June 1971) 280.

Foreign Trade. (1971) Imports 827 billion won; exports 368,770,000,000 won. Import sources: Japan 39%; U.S. 28%. Export destinations: U.S. 50%; Japan 25%. Main exports (1969): clothing 26%; plywood 13%; textile yarns and fabrics 11%; electrical machinery and equipment 6%; fish and products 5%.

Transport and Communications. Roads (1970) *c.* 34,000 km. (including 428 km. expressways). Motor vehicles in use (1970): passenger 60,700; commercial (including buses) 64,700. Railways: (1970) 5,448 km.; traffic (1971) 8,246,000,000 passenger-km., freight 8,473,000,000 net ton-km. Air traffic (1970): 445,150,000 passenger-km.; freight 6.9 million net ton-km. Shipping (1971): merchant vessels 100 gross tons and over 337; gross tonnage 940,000. Telephones (Dec. 1970) 659,000. Radio receivers (Dec. 1970) 4,012,000. Television licenses (Dec. 1970) 418,000.

Agriculture. Production (in 000; metric tons; 1971; 1970 in parentheses): rice 5,553 (5,476); wheat *c.* 322 (357); potatoes *c.* 600 (605); barley *c.* 1,857 (1,974); sweet potatoes (1970) 2,136, (1969) 2,123; soybeans *c.* 230 (232); tobacco *c.* 72 (56); fish catch (1970) 934, (1969) 979. Livestock (in 000; Dec. 1970): cattle 1,242; pigs 1,400; goats *c.* 98; chickens *c.* 24,000.

Industry. Production (in 000; metric tons; 1971): coal 12,786; iron ore (50% metal content) 442; steel 472; cement 6,871; tungsten concentrate (oxide content; 1970) 2.8; kaolin (1970) 195; fluorite (1970) 48; limestone (1970) 9,104; gold (troy oz.; 1970) 44; silver (troy oz.; 1970) 846; electricity (excluding most industrial production; kw-hr.) 10,539,000.

KOREA: Democratic People's Republic

Education. (1970–71) Primary, secondary, and vocational, pupils *c.* 3 million, teachers *c.* 100,000; higher, students 214,000, teaching staff (1964–65) 9,013.

Finance and Trade. Monetary unit: won, with (Sept. 18, 1972) an official exchange rate of 1.11 won to U.S. $1 and an effective nominal rate of 2.52 won to U.S. $1 (6.17 won = £1 sterling). Budget (1971 est.) balanced at 7,277,000,000 won. Foreign trade (excluding trade with China; 1966): imports *c.* U.S. $126.5 million (68% from U.S.S.R., 6% from France); exports *c.* U.S. $148,742,000 (62% to U.S.S.R., 15% to Japan, 7% to Czechoslovakia). Main exports (1964): metals 50%; minerals 12%; farm produce 11%.

Agriculture. Production (in 000; metric tons; 1971; 1970 in parentheses): rice *c.* 2,500 (*c.* 2,500); corn *c.* 1,800 (*c.* 1,800); barley *c.* 275 (*c.* 275); potatoes *c.* 1,000 (*c.* 1,000); fish catch (1964) 770, (1963) 640. Livestock (in 000; Dec. 1970): cattle *c.* 740; pigs *c.* 1,370; sheep *c.* 192; goats *c.* 173.

Industry. Production (in 000; metric tons; 1970): coal *c.* 24,000; iron ore (metal content; 1969) *c.* 3,750; pig iron 2,359; steel (1969) *c.* 2,000; lead 25; zinc (1969) *c.* 60; magnesite (1969) 1,250; cement (1969) *c.* 2,798; electricity (kw-hr.; 1965) 13,300,000.

The Red Cross talks made only limited progress. Although timetables were worked out at a snail's pace, some scheduled meetings were canceled. Finally the official conference opened in Pyongyang on August 30, with a second round in Seoul on September 13. Visiting delegates from either side were received with popular enthusiasm in the other. The talks ended without any agreement, following a South Korean complaint that the Northern delegation was injecting politics into what was essentially a humanitarian issue. On November 4, however, leaders of the two nations signed an agreement to establish joint machinery to promote reunification.

Republic of Korea (South Korea). Area: 38,022 sq.mi. (98,477 sq.km.). Pop. (1972 est.): 33,167,144. Cap. and largest city: Seoul (pop., 1970, 5,536,337). Language: Korean. Religion: Buddhist; Confucian; Tonghak (Chondokyo). President in 1972, Gen. Park Chung Hee; prime minister, Kim Chong Pil.

The state of emergency declared in December 1971 continued into 1972 although the reason given for the proclamation—the imminence of an armed invasion from the North—appeared to have lost its validity following the agreement by the two Koreas to renounce force in the settlement of their differences. The opposition New Democratic Party asked Park to "give up the dictatorial system" and show the people that the accord with the North was not intended to prolong his rule.

But in fact Park went in the opposite direction and on October 17 suddenly declared martial law, suspended the constitution, banned all political activity, and dissolved the one-house National Assembly. He said he would propose revisions to the constitution by October 27 and call for a national referendum one month later. He added that by the end of the year "at the latest" he would restore constitutional rule.

There was no clear-cut explanation for the decision to impose martial law. Park said that the measure was intended to reform the national structure to better meet a critical moment when the nation sought territorial unification. Significantly, he also said that "we must guard ourselves against the possibility that the interests of third or small countries might be sacrificed for the relaxation of tension between big powers." This raised speculation as to whether the Park government was anticipating problems of insecurity in the wake of the U.S.-China and Japan-China détentes and the prospects of a Vietnam peace settlement. It had, however, received an assurance from the U.S. that the 43,000 U.S. troops in South Korea would not be pulled out immediately.

The chairman of the ruling Democratic Republican Party had said in July that Park would not seek reelection when his current term expired in 1975. The party, he said, had "absolutely no plans" to change the existing constitution under which no man might serve as president for more than three consecutive terms. The constitution which Park subsequently announced provided for a new government body, the National Conference for Unification, which "shall be the depository of the national sovereignty." It would elect the president as well as the National Assembly, whose powers were drastically reduced. The president's powers were vastly increased: his term was raised from four years to six with no mention of the number of terms he could have. He also was empowered to exercise sole jurisdiction "in the whole range of state affairs" whenever "the national security or the public safety and order is seriously threatened or anticipated to be threatened." The November referendum approved the constitution.

Democratic People's Republic of Korea (North Korea). Area: 46,800 sq.mi. (121,200 sq.km.). Pop. (1971 est.): 14,281,000. Cap.: Pyongyang (metro. pop., 1967 est., 1,364,000). Language: Korean. Religion: Buddhist; Confucian; Tonghak (Chondokyo). Secretary-general of the Korean Workers' (Communist) Party and chairman of the Council of Ministers (premier) in 1972, Marshal Kim Il Sung; presidents, Choi Yong Kun and, from December 28, Marshal Kim Il Sung.

North Korea actively extended to foreign affairs the principle of strict self-reliance and independence in a bid to build up international support for its policies, especially on the questions of reunification and the UN role in Korea. During 1972 several independent journalists—U.S. and Japanese among them—were allowed to go to Pyongyang and interview Kim Il Sung. In April about 100 people from 30 countries were invited to a conference organized by the North Korean Academy of Social Science. Representatives from Communist countries were conspicuously absent.

Following the July 4 declaration with the South, Pyongyang tried hard to project the idea that the initiative for the proposed détente had emanated from the North—just as the South claimed the initiative as its own. In September Kim Il Sung reiterated proposals put forward on April 12, 1971, for a confederation of the South and the North which would keep their separate political systems intact while they worked for reunification. On December 28 North Korea adopted a new constitution apparently aimed at achieving coexistence and reunification with the South. A significant change from the old charter was a statement that Pyongyang is the capital of North Korea; previously, Seoul had been declared the capital of all Korea with Pyongyang only a temporary headquarters until reunification. At the same time, Kim Il Sung was elected president and retained his title of premier.

(T. J. S. GEORGE)

Kuwait

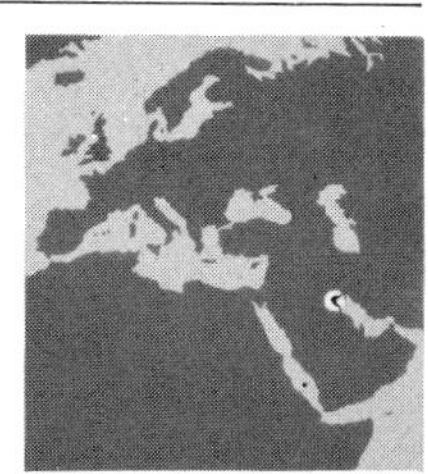

An independent emirate, Kuwait is on the northwestern coast of the Persian Gulf between Iraq and Saudi Arabia. Area: 6,880 sq.mi. (17,818 sq.km.). Pop. (1972 est.): 815,000. Cap.: Kuwait (pop., 1970, 80,008). Largest city: Hawalli (pop., 1970, 106,507). Language: Arabic. Religion (1970): Muslim 94.7%; Christian 4.6%. Emir in 1972, Sheikh Sabah as-Salim as-Sabah; prime minister, Crown Prince Sheikh Jabir al-Ahmad al-Jabir as-Sabah.

In 1972 Kuwait enjoyed a big increase in oil revenues, which were expected to rise by 54% to 512.5 million dinars ($1,558,000,000) in fiscal 1972–73, compared with 332.7 million dinars ($1,011,000,000) in 1971–72. However, a U.S. firm of consultants was reported to have estimated that oil reserves were much less than had previously been forecast and that they would be exhausted in 12 years at the current rate of increase in production. Although a later government report was more optimistic, a government decision was made to keep production below three million barrels a day.

KUWAIT

Education. (1969–70) Primary, pupils 54,418, teachers 2,789; secondary, pupils 56,705, teachers 3,900; vocational, pupils 1,733, teachers 309; teacher training, students 2,547, teachers 405; higher, students 1,713, teaching staff 158.

Finance. Monetary unit: Kuwaiti dinar, with (Sept. 18, 1972) a par value of 0.329 dinars to U.S. $1 (free rate of 0.803 dinars = £1 sterling). Gold and foreign exchange, official: (June 1972) U.S. $359.9 million; (June 1971) U.S. $196.5 million. Budget (1971–72 est.) balanced at 359.6 million dinars. Money supply: (June 1972) 140.4 million dinars; (June 1971) 106.6 million dinars.

Foreign Trade. (1971) Imports 242.3 million dinars; exports 860.3 million dinars. Import sources (1970): Japan 15%; U.S. 13%; U.K. 12%; West Germany 8%; Italy 5%; France 5%. Export destinations (1970): U.K. 21%; Japan 17%; Italy 13%; Netherlands 13%; France 10%; Belgium-Luxembourg 5%. Main exports (1970) petroleum and products 95%.

Industry. Crude oil production (1971) 147,019,000 metric tons.

In 1972 the Kuwait Fund for Arab Economic Development provided loans for Jordan and Sudan, but the Kuwait government, with support from the National Assembly, continued to withhold the aid to Jordan agreed upon after the 1967 Arab-Israeli war in disapproval of Jordan's treatment of the Palestinian guerrillas. In contrast, Kuwait gave Syria $29 million, following a visit to Kuwait of the Syrian president; after Iraq and Syria's nationalization of the Iraq Petroleum Co., Kuwait contributed 25% of the Organization of Arab Petroleum Exporting Countries $150 million loan to those two countries.

(PETER MANSFIELD)

Labour Unions

Faced with inflationary price movements and consequent balance of payments difficulties, governments in 1972 continued to express concern over the growing power of unions and their ability to impose high wage settlements. At the same time, unions, conscious of the power they derived from relatively high levels of employment and the complexity and interdependence of an increasingly technological society, resisted government encroachments into what they considered the preserve of unions and employers. Governments usually got their way initially, but they were unable to resolve the fundamental issues. (*See* Special Report.)

Industrialized Countries. Britain in 1972 provided a classic case of such a situation. When the year began, the British Industrial Relations Act, 1971, was not fully in force, and some industrial disputes escaped its effect. The most important of these, the miners' strike, nonetheless involved a confrontation between union and government. In the late summer of 1971, the National Union of Mineworkers had submitted a claim for wage increases of up to 47%. This was rejected by the National Coal Board, a strike vote was held, and 59% of the miners voted in favour of a strike that started on January 9. The strike was characterized by determined, large-scale picketing beyond the precincts of mines. Coal suppliers were prevented from moving coal, and large-scale coal users, such as power stations, were prevented by picketing from obtaining coal supplies. Transport workers on the railways and roads supported the miners and many refused to cross picket lines. The result was that the economic effects of the strike began to be felt relatively early. Power supplies to both industrial and domestic consumers were cut. A state of emergency came into force, and the government set up a court of inquiry. The court's recommendations formed the basis of a settlement with the government that gave miners wage increases ranging up to 32%. The strike lasted seven weeks and some 1.6 million workers were laid off as a result.

The end of the miners' strike coincided with the complete implementation of the Industrial Relations Act, and the government attempted to take full advantage of it. The first serious attempt to apply the act came during a railway work-to-rule in April over a wage claim. There was severe disruption of railway traffic, and on April 19 the National Industrial Relations Court (NIRC) imposed a 14-day cooling-off period. The cooling-off period ended on May 8 without an agreement, so the government successfully applied to the NIRC for a compulsory ballot of all railwaymen, in the belief that the unions were not representative of the ordinary workers. The result, announced on May 31, showed that 90% of the eligible workers had voted and, of those, 85% were in favour of continuing industrial action. A settlement was eventually reached on June 12, in which the unions obtained concessions that had previously been refused.

While the railway dispute was in progress, the Industrial Relations Act was being applied against the dockers and the Transport and General Workers' Union (TGWU), which organized them. On March 21 Heaton's Transport, a firm operating at Liverpool docks, complained to the NIRC that the dockers were "blacking" its trucks, refusing to unload them in a dispute over the handling of containerized cargo and that this was an unfair industrial practice under the act. The court agreed.

The Trades Union Congress had advised its members to blacklist the institutions set up under the act, so the TGWU refused to attend the NIRC hearings and was eventually fined £55,000 with a threat of sequestration of its funds. The dockers also ignored the NIRC, but the court ruled that the union was re-

continued on page 401

UPI COMPIX

The driver of a truck loaded with coal beats off striking English coal miners in Dover attempting to stop the delivery of coal from other parts of England. The incident occurred Jan. 17, 1972.

SPECIAL REPORT

THE CRISIS IN COLLECTIVE BARGAINING

By Victor L. Allen

Collective bargaining was in crisis in 1972. After decades of tough and sometimes bloody struggle, the labour movement would not relinquish it lightly. Yet many voices were heard claiming that collective bargaining had not only failed to provide industrial peace and equity but was rapidly bringing on economic chaos.

The crisis had many roots. Some lay in the very success of the unions themselves, some in the delicately balanced interrelationships within modern industrial societies, some in governments' post-Keynesian assumption of the burden of regulating the economy. Under the classical concept of collective bargaining, representatives of management and labour bargain over the conditions of work. It entails the existence of labour unions and their recognition by employers, either singly or on an industry-wide basis. Against the economic power of the employers, the workers ultimately pit their ability to withhold their labour, so the strike, or the right to strike, has evolved as an inherent part of the collective bargaining process.

The criticisms of collective bargaining have been based on its failure in recent years to be accepted as an alternative to strike action and its inability, in consequence, to act as a medium for settling wage disputes in an inflationary situation. Strikes have become harsher in their impact because they now have repercussion effects far beyond their prime target. A strike of steelworkers can cause men to be laid off in the auto industry; a strike of workers in a components firm can cause the auto industry itself to close down. A dockers' strike can upset a country's balance of payments—apart from preventing a Toyota from entering an American garage. A railroad strike can dislocate an entire economy. The issue is more sharply defined in the case of public employees. There the management may be a local authority or state legislature and the victim may be a vital social service.

Yet, as labour leaders point out, there is considerable justification for the retention and protection of the right to strike. Employers have not been slow to take advantage where the right to strike has not existed. Frequently the comparatively poorly paid workers in public and private employment have suffered. Increasingly, in both Great Britain and the United States, a solution to the dilemma has been sought in government action.

Growth of Collective Bargaining. Collective bargaining developed over different periods in the U.S. and Great Britain, and different forms have emerged. In Britain there were examples of it in the late 19th century. It received a stimulus from the recommendations of the Whitley Committee on industrial relations in 1917, but its main period of growth occurred after the general strike of 1926. By World War II it was an established means of regulating industrial relations. In the U.S. it developed much later. By and large, U.S. employers were slower to recognize unions than their British counterparts, and it was not until after the passage of the Norris-La Guardia Act and the Wagner Act in the early 1930s that real progress was possible. These acts gave unions legal protection to organize industries and a legal framework within which to establish negotiating procedures.

In Britain the law played virtually no part, so that collective bargaining was essentially voluntary, while in the U.S., particularly after passage of the Taft-Hartley Act of 1947, a form of voluntary bargaining took place within a relatively complex legal framework. Largely because of the model suggested by the Whitley Committee, and because of the particular historic context, collective bargaining in Britain was centralized and industry-wide. In the U.S. a localized system was established first, and the movement toward industry-wide bargaining was slow.

Collective bargaining was a sacred cow in the 1950s. In both Britain and the U.S. it was generally regarded as the only viable method of regulating labour relations consistent with social democracy, and it was advocated with missionary zeal wherever those countries had influence. Then, in the 1960s, criticism began to emerge. The governments of both countries were confronted by problems of inflation, unemployment, and foreign balances. First in Britain, then in the U.S., free collective bargaining came to be regarded more and more as an obstacle to the solution of those problems.

The attempts by the Labour government after 1964 to regulate incomes through legislation acted as a catalyst for the reconsideration of collective bargaining in Britain. The discussion continued unbroken through the proceedings of the Royal Commission on Trade Unions and Employers' Associations (1965–68) and the legislative attempts to control unofficial strikes that crystallized in 1971 as the Industrial Relations Act. Whereas in Britain discussion largely followed government initiative, in the U.S. it followed crises but preceded practical government action. In both countries academic specialists and politicians, concerned about the rising incidence of strikes, the proliferation of "intolerable" strikes in the public and private sectors, and the size and extent of wage demands, made suggestions for "revamping" collective bargaining. The third annual Collective Bargaining Forum held in New York in 1971 by the Institute of Collective Bargaining and Group Relations was dominated by its perception of the crisis. Even George Meany, president of the AFL-CIO and the foremost and longest-lived advocate of collective bargaining, acknowledged some defects and was seeking an alternative to strike action.

Unions versus Governments. The discussions were about procedures but the crisis was one of industrial relations, and the power of the unions was at the root of it. Insofar as the crisis produced a confrontation, it was between unions and governments. This was a universal issue. There was no country in the world where labour unions existed without government control of some kind. Everywhere there was a framework of legislation within which industrial relations had to be conducted. This legislation usually related to the right of workers to act collectively, to the categories of workers who could exercise the right, to the manner in which collective action could be practiced, the methods, including strike action, that could be employed, and the circumstances under which they could or could not be tolerated.

A necessary condition for the establishment of collective bargaining is, of course, the existence and recognition of trade unions. In the case of public employment in the U.S., this condition was satisfied only recently. As of 1972, relatively strong unions existed in various areas of government service and were able to engage in nationally significant industrial action, even though no formalized procedures for bargaining collectively existed. Many government employees, particularly at the state and local levels, had no legal right to strike. However, there had been a sharp increase in the number of illegal strikes. In an analysis of 63 strikes and strike threats by state and local government employees in 20 states between July 1965 and December

---

Victor L. Allen, Reader in Industrial Relations at the University of Leeds, is author of several books on trade unions and a regular contributor to the Britannica Book of the Year.

1969, it was found that the number of strikes increased by 100% compared with the previous 27-month period. There was also a significant increase in the duration of strikes. In most of the states such strikes were explicitly prohibited by law. (James E. Young and Betty L. Brewer, "Strikes by State and Local Employees," *Industrial Relations,* University of California, vol. 1969–70, pp. 356–361.)

There was widespread opposition by state and local government bodies to establishing genuine forms of collective bargaining with their employees. Of the 20 states in the sample, 12 did not permit public employees to organize or engage in bargaining, 3 allowed employees to present their grievances but did not require employers to take any notice, and one recognized the right of state employees to bargain but omitted mention of other public employees. Only four states had positive legislation. Furthermore, the issue of illegal strikes was intensified by the federal government's efforts to control public expenditure as a means of countering inflation. Labour costs are the most significant variable cost in public expenditure, so the salaries of government workers were under pressure. A big question for the U.S. government, then, was how to cope with the growing strength of public-sector unionism while preserving some control over the collective activities of public servants.

Collective bargaining in Britain was founded at a time when unions were relatively weak. During the 1930s, a period of high unemployment, tight commodity markets, and consequent downward pressure on wages, the unions found that centralized bargaining procedures, by retarding this pressure, worked to their advantage. After 1945, however, economic conditions tended to transfer negotiating strength to the workers themselves. By bringing pressure on employers, small groups of workers could achieve quicker results than were obtainable through formal procedures. British industrial relations thus came to be characterized by increasing industrial action outside the procedural provisions for settling disputes. It was estimated that 95% of all strikes in Britain were in infringement of agreements.

"Intolerable" Strikes. The problems of public service employment in the U.S. and of "unofficial" collective action in Britain raise the common issue of government regulation of unionism. The situations in both countries possess closer similarities, however. The "intolerable" strikes that give rise to government concern in the U.S. occur in the private as well as the public sector. The long dock strikes on the East and West coasts in 1971 and 1972 are a case in point. These strikes were conducted by unions in accordance with procedural agreements with employers. But the fact that they arose out of disputes that were not resolved within the collective bargaining machinery indicates that the machinery is defective—just as surely as if it had been bypassed, as in Britain. Collective bargaining, moreover, had not had a moderating effect on wage demands in the U.S., so the U.S. government, as much as the British, was preoccupied with the need to alter the institutional means of wage determination so as to hold back the level of wages.

Britain had its own public sector issue. British unions in public employment developed within a framework of collective bargaining. The Whitley report was concerned about removing unrest in private industry, but its recommendations were taken up and applied first by the civil service unions. Government at the national and local levels preceded most private employers in recognizing and encouraging trade unionism. The greatest stimulus to unionism in government employment, however, was

A strike of British coal miners caused factories like this Jaguar assembly line at Coventry to be deserted because of government orders limiting use of coal-generated power. Such action idled at least 1.6 million workers. The strike ended on Feb. 28, 1972.

LONDON DAILY EXPRESS/PICTORIAL PARADE

the post-World War II inflation, together with government efforts to control it by reducing public expenditure. Public employees were a vulnerable first target, and this created industrial militancy. The unions took the initiative in challenging government incomes policies, and some engaged in bitter struggles with governments. Thus the problem of union power among public employees was also acute in Britain, but for different reasons.

Throughout the whole spectrum of industrial relations, a number of interrelated issues had arisen in both countries because of the growth of union power. Government responses and policies in Britain were following—in a sense copying—those of the U.S. It is instructive, therefore, to study the U.S. situation first.

Arbitration or Bargaining? The pressure of the growing public employment unions in the U.S., combined with the effect of illegal strikes, was forcing government bodies at all levels to consider instituting collective bargaining machinery. The first question was: What form should this take? Given the government view that public servants cannot be treated like employees generally because of their close involvement in government or the security nature of their employment, the private sector model, including the right to strike, was unsuitable. The alternative was a closed system of bargaining that did not leave the option to strike—in other words, some form of compulsory arbitration. At the same time, the private sector model was itself under attack for its failure to prevent "intolerable" strikes. Debate at the federal level about the private sector model was intense, and it was there that changes were likely to occur first.

The government's main concern was to prevent or control strikes in the transportation industry, where some of the most bitter disputes had occurred. The railroads and airlines were covered by the Railway Labor Act of 1926, while most of the remaining transportation industries were under the Taft-Hartley Act of 1947. Under the terms of the Railway Labor Act, a step-by-step delaying procedure regulated the actions of employers and unions from the initial notice to alter the terms of an agreement to the report of an emergency board. After the report stage there was a status quo period of 30 days, followed by the right to strike or lock out. The National Mediation Board administered the act. Between 1950 and 1970 the board disposed of 3,984 cases, 94 of which required the final step of establishing an emergency board. In all, the president appointed 71 emergency boards to investigate and report on railroad and airline disputes.

The reports rarely provided the bases for quick settlements. It was argued that the machinery encouraged both parties to hold out until the government intervened, and that they did not use the machinery in good faith. In a statement before a U.S. House subcommittee on July 28, 1971, Secretary of Labor James D. Hodgson stated that "the Railway Labor Act . . . has been increasingly unsatisfactory. . . . The machinery of the act has failed time and time again, and the pace of the failures is accelerating. Only strong individually applied measures by the chief executive and Congress have averted major rail disruption. . . . The national trauma which accompanies each such crisis, even though a strike is averted, has caused disruption, bitterness, and public disenchantment with the act's collective bargaining system . . ."

Under the terms of the Taft-Hartley Act, the president may appoint a board of inquiry when he believes that an actual or threatened strike or lockout might endanger "the nation's health or safety." After the board of inquiry has reported, the president may direct the attorney general to petition a federal district court to impose an 80-day cooling-off period, during which the board of inquiry makes a second investigation and the employees vote on the employer's last offer. Government intervention is more difficult here than under the Railway Labor Act, but it occurs because, when agreement cannot be reached, the president has no alternative other than to ask Congress for special legislation. It so happens that during 1947–70 all the cases where strikes or lockouts continued after the cooling-off period involved transportation industries. As Pres. Richard Nixon emphasized in a message to Congress in February 1970, it was in those industries that "the emergency procedures of present laws—the Railway Labor Act of 1926 and the Taft-Hartley Act of 1947—have most frequently failed."

As the government saw it, the defects in the system stemmed from the restrictions that the acts placed on the president's discretion. Accordingly, early in 1970 President Nixon proposed an Emergency Public Interest Protection Bill that would have modified both the acts insofar as they concerned the transportation industries. The Taft-Hartley Act was to be amended to give the president a choice of three options: he could extend the cooling-off period by up to 30 days; require partial operation of the industry; or require each party to submit one or two final offers encompassing all the issues in dispute, which would be the subject of a mandatory five-day bargaining period. Under the third option, if no agreement was reached at the end of the five-day period, a Final Offer Selection Board would choose one offer, and that would comprise the collective bargaining agreement under which the parties would operate. Various amendments to the Railway Labor Act were suggested.

The presidential proposals were attacked by the AFL-CIO as a means of introducing compulsory arbitration into the transportation industries. Some employers were also opposed to them. The bill was submitted to Congress twice, but its progress was frustrated by opposition groups and it was withdrawn in July 1972.

Labour and the Law. While the inadequacies of existing legislation were causing concern in the U.S., a rough copy of the Taft-Hartley Act was being introduced in Britain. The British Industrial Relations Act became law in August 1971 and fully operative in February 1972. It provided a new legal framework for British industrial relations. The act was very lengthy and detailed, but its emergency provisions can be stated briefly. It established a National Industrial Relations Court with the status and powers of a High Court. Any party to a labour dispute—indeed, any employer or worker—could submit complaints within the terms of the act. A list of unfair industrial practices was contained in the act, and anyone who believed he was being subjected to one had the right to complain to the court. The government could go to the court to impose a 60-day cooling-off period or to enforce compulsory votes to test opinions during disputes.

The British trade-union movement, which had successfully persuaded Harold Wilson's Labour government to withdraw restrictive provisions from its proposed legislation, was unequivocally opposed to the act from its inception. After it became law, the Trades Union Congress (TUC) advocated and largely practiced a policy of noncooperation with the agencies established under it. By and large, trade unions did not register under the act, as they were required to do in order to benefit from its provisions. Unions that did register were disaffiliated from the TUC. There was disagreement between the unions that insisted on giving no recognition to the act at all and those who wished to use it to defend themselves but not to initiate issues under it. Following the September 1972 TUC annual conference, the situation was that unions might not register but could appear before the National Industrial Relations Court to protect their interests. There was no real sign that trade-union opposition was weakening, and the future of the act was in doubt.

The real question that the act posed, however, was whether the issues raised by an increasingly intransigent trade unionism can be satisfactorily dealt with by legal measures. In the U.S. the contention was that collective bargaining within the framework provided by the Taft-Hartley Act had limitations that in some cases amounted to failures. In Britain the contention was that free collective bargaining had failed. In both cases "failure" referred to a growing strike phenomenon that the existing means have been unable to prevent. In both cases, too, the issue was being tackled through legal methods. In the U.S. additional legal devices had been sought, while in Britain new ones had been introduced.

Collective action in general and strike action in particular are endemic to situations where there are free labour markets—that is, where many people have to sell their labour in order to subsist and a much smaller number buy it for purposes of production. Historical evidence shows that collective action will occur as long as these conditions exist. Labour unionism belongs to all free market economies. It has disappeared—temporarily—only under oppressive laws such as those in Nazi Germany and Fascist Italy. Labour laws in general have influenced the shape of unionism but have never dominated it. They have helped to institutionalize the conflict between employers and employees, but they have never treated that conflict's basic causes. More than this, laws have had relatively little effect on the propensity to strike. Strikes have occurred in defiance of all but the most oppressive legal and institutional barriers. They were common in Spain where free unionism is a criminal offense; they grew in intensity in Britain during two world wars when they were illegal; they occurred with increasing frequency in Sweden and West Germany, which until recently had been hailed as models of industrial peace.

It is in this historical context that discussions about compulsory arbitration in the U.S. and legal action to prevent unofficial strikes in Britain must be seen. The discussions were given point by the 1972 dock strikes in both countries. The question "could the government have forced the 15,000 longshoremen on the West Coast to end their strike?" cannot automatically be answered in the affirmative. The longshoremen, after exhausting the president's powers under the Taft-Hartley Act, resumed their strike. Would this determination have been overridden by compulsory arbitration?

An understanding of such situations has to take account of the limitations on governments seeking redress against collective refusals to obey laws. In general, compulsory arbitration can only work if such a method is voluntarily accepted by the parties. Democratic governments cannot take punitive action against thousands of workers without bringing themselves into disrepute. Moreover, the ethic of solidarity, which lies at the basis of labour unionism, makes it likely that a dispute will spread rather than contract when punitive action is taken against a group of workers, no matter how small.

This point was illustrated when five British dockers were imprisoned in July 1972 for acting in contempt of the National Industrial Relations Court. A London-based container firm had obtained an order from the court restraining the dockers from picketing its premises. The dockers disregarded the order and were committed to prison on Friday, July 21. By the evening of that day, 26,000 dockers were on strike in support of the imprisoned men. Sympathetic strikes spread, so that by Monday, July 24, no national newspapers were being printed in London and many industrial workers, public transport workers, and coal miners were either striking or preparing to strike. On Wednesday, July 26, the General Council of the TUC voted to call a one-day general strike for the following Monday. All of this happened even though sympathetic strikes were illegal under the Industrial Relations Act. No action under the act was taken against the sympathetic strikers. On the evening of the TUC decision the court ordered the release of the dockers, whereupon the strikes were ended and the general strike did not materialize.

Although different industrial relations situations and forms of collective bargaining exist throughout the world, the lesson of the British dockers' incident has universal implications. It is that, whatever the solution might be, the law has a limited role to play in the settlement of industrial disputes. But the lesson is hard to learn. Once the law is used to intrude into the direct day-to-day relationship between employers and unions, later defects in the system always seem to be attributed to too little law rather than too much.

continued from page 397

sponsible for their actions. This ruling was reversed by the Court of Appeal and restored by the House of Lords.

Container firms in several ports were blacked, but the centre of action was London. A case against the picketing of its trucks was made by the Midland Cold Storage Co., and on July 5 seven London dockers were summoned to appear before the NIRC. They refused to attend, and on Friday, July 21, five of them were imprisoned for contempt of court. British trade unions had threatened strike action if any of their members were imprisoned under the act. As soon as the news of the arrests was known, dockers throughout the country went on strike, followed by many others in sympathy. On July 26 the General Council of the TUC voted 18 to 7 to call a one-day general strike for the following Monday. The NIRC ordered the release of the dockers the same evening. By the next day most of the sympathetic strikes were ended, and the general strike did not materialize.

Opposition to the Industrial Relations Act continued, however. About 100,000 workers in the Coventry area, mostly concerned with the automobile industry, went on strike against the act on August 14. The TUC reaffirmed its opposition at its annual meeting in September and suspended 32 unions that had registered under the act and had failed to revoke their registration. Early in November the NIRC fined the Amalgamated Union of Engineering Workers £5,000 for contempt of court in another case arising from the act. The union executive refused to pay the fine.

In the U.S. 1971 had been marked by major strikes in the transportation industry, some of which carried over into 1972. On the railways, working-rule alterations resulting from technological changes had caused perpetual difficulties and many strikes. One dispute between the 240,000-member United Transportation Union and the railroad companies, involving the companies' demand that firemen be eliminated from diesel freight locomotives, had started in 1937. It was settled on July 20, 1972, with an agreement that all engineer vacancies were to be filled from among the 18,000 firemen on freight trains.

Dock strikes on the East and West coasts carried over into 1972. The West Coast Longshoremen resumed their strike on January 17 after unanimously rejecting the employer's last offer. On January 21 Pres. Richard Nixon asked Congress to establish a three-member arbitration board whose decisions on all issues in the strike would be legally binding on the parties for at least 18 months. On the Atlantic seaboard the shipping companies agreed in January to a three-year contract with the International Longshoremen's Association, raising the basic hourly rate from $4.60 to $6.10. Other demands were settled on a port-by-port basis. The West Coast strike, the longest port strike in U.S. history, ended on February 19.

On Dec. 22, 1971, President Nixon had signed into law a bill allowing him to impose controls on the economy for an additional year, until April 30, 1973. The bill contained guidelines for the Pay Board, which had been responsible in 1971 for the wage-price-rent freeze. The Pay Board had agreed in November 1971 to set a pay maximum of 5.5% for annual wage and benefit increases in 1972. The labour members of the board had voted against this, and as time went on they became increasingly dissatisfied with the board's decisions. On March 22 three labour members, led by the AFL-CIO president, George Meany, resigned.

POPPERFOTO / PICTORIAL PARADE

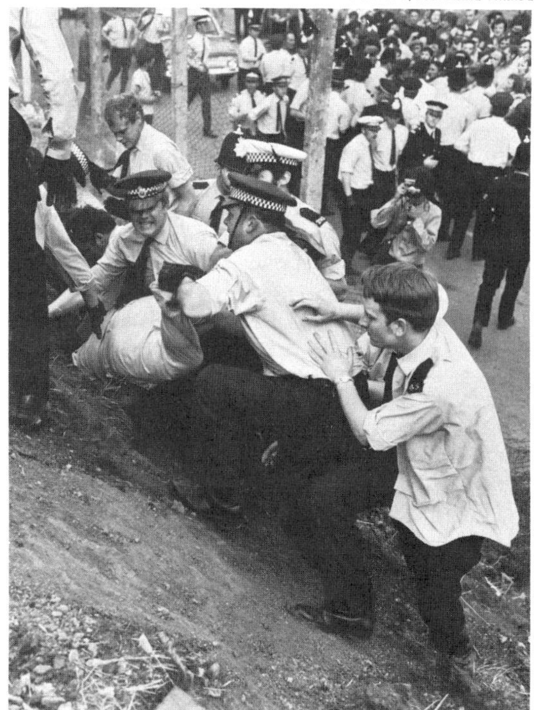

British police wrestle a Lincolnshire longshoreman to the ground at Neap House wharf during dockers' strike in August 1972.

Despite this apparent break with the administration, Meany withheld the usual AFL-CIO support from the Democratic presidential candidate, Sen. George McGovern, whom Meany considered to be too radical on a number of issues. Labour votes contributed to President Nixon's overwhelming electoral victory, and in late November the president announced that the next secretary of labour would be Peter Brennan of New York, a construction workers' union official. Brennan was the first union man to head the Department of Labor since Martin Durkin of the plumbers' union took the job for a few months in 1953, then decided a union leader could wield more influence outside than inside the government and resigned.

There was a relatively light collective bargaining schedule in 1972, but local strikes against General Motors aroused considerable interest. Early in the year, United Automobile Workers members struck the GM plant at Lordstown, O. The Lordstown assembly line was said to be the fastest and most modern in the world, and the workers, most of them young, claimed that the company had instituted a speedup and that the work force had been reduced and extra work given to those who remained. The strike, which lasted for 22 days, came after a long period of unrest punctuated by alleged acts of sabotage. It was followed by a 172-day strike (the longest in GM's history) at the Norwood, O., plant, in which similar issues were involved. The militance of the young workers and their dissatisfaction with what they considered to be boring and repetitious jobs were widely interpreted as presaging a new outlook on the part of labour, in which conditions of work would overshadow the bread-and-butter issues that had preoccupied an earlier generation.

The powerful and autocratic United Mine Workers encountered difficulties during the year. A federal district judge found the UMW, a bank it largely owned, and two individuals guilty of misusing union pension funds, and ordered payment of $11.5 million in damages. The union president, W. A. (Tony) Boyle (*see* BIOGRAPHY), was sentenced to five years in prison and fined $130,000 for making illegal political contributions with union funds. Boyle's 1969 reelection to the union presidency after a violence-ridden campaign was overturned, and a new election was held in December under strict supervision of the Department of Labor. Arnold Miller, the insurgents' candidate, won by a decisive margin, and Boyle resigned on December 19.

The perennial strike problem in Spain continued. In March 1972, in the state-owned Bazan shipyards in El Ferrol, police opened fire on workers demonstrating against the imposition of an agreement signed by the government-controlled unions. Two workers were killed and 36 seriously injured. Subsequently, 20 workers were arrested, the shipyards were closed, and, following a Cabinet decision, 4,000 Bazan workers were declared subject to military law. On March 21 marines were drafted into all departments of the shipyard. In neighbouring Portugal, Daniel Cabrito, general secretary of the Lisbon district of the Bank Employees' Union, was arrested on June 30, 1971, for signing a letter to the International Labour Organization complaining about the composition of the workers' delegation to the ILO. On Feb. 10, 1972, Cabrito was sentenced to two years' imprisonment and 15 years' loss of political rights. Four other trade unionists tried with Cabrito were also sent to prison. The governing body of the ILO complained to the Portuguese government in April.

The "spring wage offensive" in Japan began with the country in recession. The joint Spring Offensive Committee, organized by Sohyo and Churitsuroren, determined the rate of wages sought and the industrial union chosen to make the "key" bargain that other unions would adopt. The committee published its intentions in a wage White Paper on Dec. 15, 1971. Domei, the second largest national labour organization, presented its demands separately.

The joint Spring Offensive Committee, representing 168 national unions with 8.2 million members, began its activities at the end of February. There was a quick voluntary settlement in the iron and steel industry, and the climax was reached with general strikes on the railways on April 27 and 28. By the end of June a 15% increase in wages had been obtained. This was a slightly lower percentage than that obtained in 1971, though it was higher in absolute terms.

In Japan industrial disputes were usually brief and often sectional because of the fragmented nature of Japanese trade unions. The only truly national industrial union was Kaiin, the All Japan Seamen's Union, an affiliate of Domei, which negotiated with only two employers. Kaiin presented a wage demand that was refused at the time of the spring offensive, and on April 14 it called a strike that lasted until July 12, the longest in the history of Japanese shipping. The final settlement was considerably above the average obtained in the spring offensive. The union expended $7.5 million in strike pay. The loss to shipowners was reputed to be about $129.9 million.

Strikes in the EEC, particularly in France and Italy, were frequent but of short duration and of a token character. There was a week-long strike of about 40,000 Belgian bank employees over salaries in June. In the settlement the employees obtained an 8.5% increase, compared with the 12% they had demanded. Also in June the French Confédération Générale du Travail (CGT) called a 24-hour general strike in support of a higher minimum wage and retirement at 60 years. There were many token strikes in Italy during the year. The 210,000 railwaymen, for instance, staged a 24-hour strike on August 3, demanding higher wages and an improvement in the railway system. The government agreed that the railways were understaffed and railwaymen overworked, but insisted that the railwaymen's claims could not be met because of the economic situation. Negotiations between the Italian chemical workers' unions and the chemical employers ended successfully in October. A significant result of the negotiations was the establishment of a single pay scale for both factory and office workers. In July a federation was formed by the Communist Italian General Confederation of Labour, with 3.4 million members, the Catholic Italian Confederation of Workers Unions, with 2.2 million members, and the non-Communist secular Italian Union of Labour, with 1.5 million members.

At the end of 1971 a new law on workers' participation in industry was passed in West Germany. It established a conciliation bureau, staffed on a basis of parity between employers and workers. It also guaranteed trade-union officials access to factories and obliged employers to provide fuller information than before on finances, investment programs, and plans for automation. The new law did not affect the steel and mining industries.

Unions were increasingly concerned with the issue of multinational companies. Trade-union representatives from some of the biggest European-based multinational companies met in Brussels in February in order to exchange information. The situation of Nestlé, the world's largest food-processing company, was the subject of a three-day conference in May in Geneva. Delegates from 14 countries in Europe, Africa, Asia, North America, and Australia discussed labour union rights, workers' participation in decision-making at all levels, and wage discrimination. A conference was also held in West Germany in October to discuss conditions at the Oetker food and drink company, which employed 23,000 workers in 150 firms throughout the world. Joint action by the chemical workers' unions in the Netherlands, West Germany, and Belgium forced the multinational AKZO chemical company to withdraw planned closures of three plants—in Breda, Neth., Wuppertal, W.Ger., and Ghent, Belg.—and to cancel its plans to dismiss more than 6,000 workers. The workers in Breda occupied the plant for four days.

A movement started early in the year culminated in the creation of a Council of Nordic Trade Unions, comprising the national federations of Denmark, Finland, Norway, and Sweden and the central organizations of nonmanual workers in Finland and Sweden. The new council, representing 4.7 million members, held its first meeting in June.

Despite the antagonism between unions and the government in Britain, consultations took place intermittently during the summer between the TUC, the Confederation of British Industry, and the government over controlling inflation. The discussions collapsed early in November, largely over the issue of price control, and on November 7 Prime Minister Edward Heath announced a statutory 90-day freeze of wages and prices.

Less Developed Countries. A strike broke out among 6,000 Ovambo workers in Namibia (South West Africa) in December 1971 against the contract labour system, which applied to all migrant workers in the South African gold mines. Contracts ran for about 18 months, after which the workers were forced to return to their tribal homes. The basic wage amounted to about $13.50 a month. There was a tight disciplinary code, infringements of which were often regarded as criminal cases. The police took repressive action, and the South African government introduced a new Law and Order Proclamation. By April more than 200 Namibians had been arrested and detained, including the strike leaders. It was alleged that between Dec. 15, 1971, and Jan. 31, 1972, 7 Africans had been killed in Windhoek, 4 in Okahandja, 10 in Tsumeb, and over 50 in Ovamboland, while many people were missing and unaccounted for. Some concessions were made to the strikers, but the basic features of the contract system were retained. There were reports in September that the strike was continuing and that production was being maintained with imported labour.

In February the Indonesian trade-union federation, Sarbumusi, urged the government to restore the rights of workers laid down in the 1945 constitution. Sarbumusi complained that the Department of Manpower was approving the dismissal and suspension of workers and was siding with employers, while the government was restricting the activities of the unions. In August the International Transport Workers' Federation protested to the Indonesian government about its plans to compel transport workers to join a state-organized body called Kopri.

In the British-controlled Seychelles Islands, the General Workers' Union called a strike of 1,800 workers on April 1 over a wage demand. The police reacted by using tear gas and batons. In the second week, 4,000 workers from the private sector joined the strikers. The government set up an arbitration tribunal that awarded wage increases of between 30 and 35%. Twenty-five of the strike leaders were arrested and two were sent to prison.

In Cyprus management reacted to a strike of bank employees in April by locking out their staffs. Greek and Turkish workers joined together in the strike and were given financial support by international and foreign union organizations. The imposition of martial law in the Philippines on September 23 involved a ban on strikes and demonstrations and resulted in the arrest of a number of trade-union leaders. Strikes continued to be banned in Nigeria. In Turkey the martial law imposed on 11 major cities in 1970, under which no trade union could call a strike without prior permission, was eased in October. (V. L. ALLEN)

See also **Employment, Wages, and Hours; Race Relations.**

ENCYCLOPÆDIA BRITANNICA FILMS. *The Rise of Labor* (1968); *The Industrial Worker* (1969); *The Rise of Big Business* (1970); *The Progressive Era* (1971).

Laos

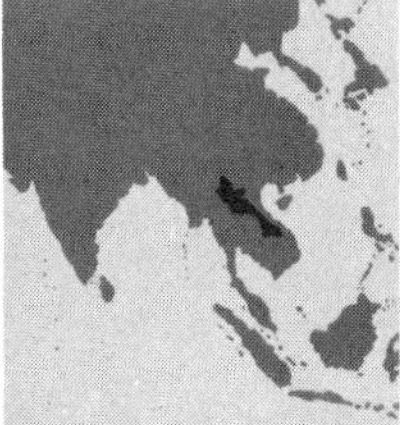

A constitutional monarchy of Southeast Asia, Laos is bounded by China, North and South Vietnam, Cambodia, Thailand, and Burma. Area: 91,400 sq.mi. (236,800 sq.km.). Pop. (1971 est.): 3,033,000. Administrative cap. and largest city: Vientiane (pop., 1968 est., 140,000). Royal cap.: Luang Prabang (pop., 1968 est., 25,000). Language: Lao (official); French and English. Religion: Buddhist; tribal. King, Savang Vatthana; premier in 1972, Prince Souvanna Phouma.

In the context of the U.S. rapprochement with China and the prospect of an end to the Vietnam war, royalist Laos in 1972 came closer than ever to military defeat and began discussions with the Neo Lao Hak Sat (Laotian Patriotic Front, or LPF), the political wing of the pro-Communist Pathet Lao. The annual major offensive of the North Vietnamese and Pathet Lao, which had begun unusually early in December 1971, gave them control of both the Plaine des Jarres in northern Laos and the Boloven Plateau in the south by early January; during similar occupations in 1970 and 1971 the Communists had withdrawn in the summer months, but on this occasion the already decimated government forces failed to launch a successful offensive in either sector, and by August it was estimated that only one-third of the country remained under government control.

The Meo tribesmen of Gen. Vang Pao, who had originally formed a major part of the U.S. Central Intelligence Agency's operations in Laos, had been reduced from about 38,000 in 1968 to fewer than 3,000 by March 1972 and were being replaced by Thai "volunteers," also controlled by the CIA. On January 14 Prince Souvanna Phouma, premier of the Vientiane government, stated that Thai strength in Laos had risen to about 15 battalions and was expected to increase by another 5 or 6 by the month's end. Following a February report of the U.S. Senate Foreign Relations Committee which had stated that Laos was "closer to falling now than at any time in the past nine years" and that its preservation depended only on "the restrictions which the North Vietnamese . . . imposed on themselves," it was revealed that the U.S. had undertaken to finance and organize a 25-battalion expeditionary force of Thais to Laos at an estimated annual cost of $100 million.

The North Vietnamese, Pathet Lao, and left-wing neutralist offensive in the northern provinces began on Dec. 18, 1971, and was the biggest of the war, employing 15,000 men, tanks, 130-mm. field guns with a range of over 20 mi., and an antiaircraft regiment. It overran the Plaine des Jarres within four days and caused several Thai battalions to flee back to Thailand. On January 11–13 the Communists gained control of a range of hills overlooking Long Cheng, the main headquarters of Gen. Vang Pao's Meo force. While intermittent battles raged for command of the hills around the base, neutralist forces of Col. Deuane Sispaseuth managed to cut Highway 13, the only road between Vientiane and Luang Prabang, capturing the towns of Sala Phou Khoun (January 21) and Muong Kassy (February 2). However, government forces succeeded in recapturing Muong Kassy on February 13 and reopened the highway on May 1.

Some North Vietnamese forces were transferred to the aid of an offensive that began in South Vietnam on March 30, resulting in a considerable decline in military activity in Laos. About 7,000 Communist troops remained on the Plaine des Jarres, but the shelling of Long Cheng ended on March 31. Several government attempts to retake the plain failed.

In the southern provinces a simultaneous Pathet Lao offensive had begun in December 1971 on the Boloven Plateau. Saravane was evacuated by government troops on December 6, and on December 12 the strategic town of Thateng fell, followed by Pak Song on Jan. 3, 1972. Ban Nhik, the last government outpost on the plateau, was abandoned on January 11. Ten days later Communist forces had advanced to within 14 mi. of Pakse, the second largest town in Laos. Its surrounding villages having been captured, the town was able to receive supplies only via Highway 10, which ran westward to Thailand.

On the political front Prince Souphanouvong, half brother of Souvanna Phouma and president of the LPF, continued to insist on an end to U.S. bombing and a cease-fire as preconditions for peace talks with the government. On July 15 Souphanouvong's representative, Prince Souk Vongsak, arrived in Vientiane to resume discussions that had been broken off in August 1971. Souphanouvong rejected a cease-fire based on separation of the military and political aspects of the conflict. This had been proposed by Souvanna Phouma, who was reported as saying that the U.S. bombing would continue until all North Vietnamese had left Laos. Despite these differences, on October 17 in Vientiane negotiations continued between Gen. Phoun Sipraseuth of the LPF Central Committee and government delegates led by Interior Minister Pheng Phongsavan. They agreed to adopt the LPF five-point peace plan of March 6, 1970, as a basis for discussions.

In general elections held on January 2 only 20 of the 60 National Assembly deputies were returned, and several members of the powerful Sananikone and Champassak families lost their seats. The results reflected growing war weariness and dissatisfaction with alleged widespread corruption. On May 22 the right-wing Group for the Protection of the Constitution demanded that the premier submit to a National Assembly vote of confidence; this he refused to do. On July 10 Souvanna Phouma reshuffled his Cabinet, but King Savang Vatthana refused to approve the changes without a vote of confidence in the government. On July 20 the U.S. embassy was reported to have informed the president of the National Assembly, Phoui Sananikone, a right-wing candidate for the premiership, that Washington considered any change of government at that time singularly inopportune.

On July 21 Souvanna Phouma dropped his proposed ministerial changes. Demands for his resignation proved fruitless, and his position was strengthened by support from the U.S., the Army, and from a newly formed Union of Laotian Parliamentarians for Peace, which advocated "sincere negotiations" with the LPF. At year's end the peace talks in Vientiane centred on conflicting royalist and LPF proposals for establishing a government of national unity.

(R. J. M. DENNERSTEIN)

LAOS

Education. (1969–70) Primary, pupils 216,577, teachers 5,813; secondary, pupils 8,486, teachers 374; vocational, pupils 1,625, teachers 181; teacher training, students 2,994, teachers 190; higher, students 559, teaching staff 26.

Finance. Monetary unit: kip, with (Oct. 16, 1972) an official exchange rate of 605 kips to U.S. $1 and a free rate of 845 kips to U.S. $1 (2,000 kips = £1 sterling). Budget (1972–73 est.): revenue (excluding foreign aid) 8,308,000,000 kips; expenditure 22,808,000,000 kips (including military expenditure of 10.1 billion kips).

Foreign Trade. (1971) Imports (excluding gold) 19,740,000,000 kips; exports (excluding reexports of gold) 795 million kips. Import sources (1969): Thailand 26%; Japan 21%; U.S. 17%; France 8%; Singapore 6%. Export destinations (1969): Singapore and Malaysia 54%; Thailand 37%; South Vietnam 7%. Main exports: tin 49%; timber 48%.

Transport. Roads (1971) 7,231 km. (including 2,489 km. all-weather). Motor vehicles in use (1970): passenger 10,969; commercial (including buses) 1,892. Air traffic (1970): 26,190,000 passenger-km.; freight 728,000 net ton-km. Telephones (Dec. 1970) 2,000. Radio licenses (Dec. 1970) 50,000.

Agriculture. Production (in 000; metric tons; 1971; 1970 in parentheses): rice *c.* 900 (916); corn *c.* 25 (25); coffee *c.* 3.5 (3.2); tobacco *c.* 4 (3.8). Livestock (in 000; 1970–71): cattle *c.* 435; buffalo *c.* 940; pigs *c.* 1,150; chickens *c.* 12,000.

Industry. Production (in 000; 1971): tin concentrates (metric tons) 1.6; electricity (excluding most industrial production; kw-hr.) 16,128.

Latin America: *see* Inter-American Affairs; *articles on the various countries*

Latin-American Literature: *see* Literature

Latter-day Saints: *see* Religion

Law

Court Decisions and Related Developments. Lawsuits involving the issues of abortion, cartels, confiscation, consumers, and labour relations crowded the calendars of courts throughout the world in 1972.

Abortion and Prenatal Rights. The Supreme Court of Victoria, Austr., and the federal Supreme Court of West Germany ruled that a child could seek damages for injuries caused to it before birth by the negligent behaviour of other individuals. Both cases involved automobile accidents in which the negligence of a driver resulted in injuries to a child still in its mother's womb.

While these decisions reached the same result as cases that had been decided earlier in the U.S., they were seen by some legal authorities as having a possible effect on continuing debates, legislative activity, and court rulings involving abortion. The implication was that anyone, including a physician, might be held responsible for civil damages sought on behalf of an unborn child injured in an attempted abortion. Similarly, the mother or father who had authorized the abortion also might be held liable for such injuries in a civil damages suit. Even where the abortion was successful the possibility of damages being recovered under this theory would not be precluded, because in all cases the unborn child must necessarily be represented by someone else in the lawsuit and this representation would be possible even if the child were killed. In most cases, including those under discussion from Australia and West Germany, however, representation had been made by one of the parents and it was generally believed that a parent who had consented to an abortion would be estopped from suing on behalf of the child whose birth was aborted. Others probably would not have "standing to sue" in most countries.

In Yugoslavia the Novi Sad District Court sentenced an author to three years of "rigorous imprisonment" for publishing an article titled "Everyday Abortion." The court found that the article was "nationally and racially disruptive." In a ruling that many believed had connotations relating to abortion, the U.S. Supreme Court struck down a Massachusetts statute permitting married persons to obtain contraceptives but prohibiting distribution of contraceptives to single persons. The statute, said the court, violated the equal protection clause of the U.S. Constitution.

Court decisions involving abortion undoubtedly stimulated or were reflected in legislative proposals or action on this subject around the world. An Islamic conference, organized by the International Planned Parenthood Federation, was said to have surprised its hosts by coming down strongly against abortion and sterilization on religious grounds. The conference decided that Muslims might lawfully use "safe and legitimate" contraceptive devices but that religious law prohibited abortion and sterilization. East Germany and West Germany proposed new abortion laws and some German newspapers thought that each state was trying to outdo the other. The West German law, however, permitted abortion only where the circumstances of the mother's health made such a procedure desirable. The East German law contained no such limitation; it provided that a pregnancy might be terminated "on demand" up to the end of the third month, and after that if the mother's life was in danger. In the U.S. the New York State Assembly voted 79–68 to repeal its "abortion-on-demand" law. Gov. Nelson Rockefeller vetoed the bill, and the state remained one of the easiest places in the world to obtain a legal abortion.

Cartels and Trade Secrets. Legal scholars were excited by four decisions in 1972 in the area of cartels and trade secrets—two from the European Economic Community (EEC), one from West Germany, and one from Great Britain. In some respects the opinion from West Germany thrust in a direction different from that of the EEC decisions. The Berlin Kammergericht, in the so-called Mannesmann Case, decided that a restrictive practice otherwise contrary to the West German Cartel Act was valid and legal if it affected only exports to foreign markets and did not have even an indirect effect on the home market. The EEC, on the other hand, in the so-called Dyestuffs Case, decided that concerted actions to increase prices by chemical manufacturers who were not residents of the EEC were violations of the law and subject to fine. The EEC held that it had jurisdiction over external activities and events that produced effects within the EEC.

In another interesting judicial development, the EEC ordered the Continental Can Co. of the U.S. to divest itself of certain acquired and developed EEC companies. Continental Can was appealing the decision to the European Court of Justice.

In an important trade secrets case, *Norwich Pharmacal Co.* v. *Commissioners for Customs & Excise,* a U.K. court held that the owner of a drug patent was entitled to learn from the commissioner of customs and excise the names and addresses of individuals who were supposedly importing a drug alleged to infringe upon the patent of the owner. This "discovery" technique, long denied by the British courts, was considered to be a great step forward in the protection of the owners of English patents, trademarks, copyrights, and trade secrets.

Confiscation. Resolution 1803, enacted in 1962 by the UN General Assembly as a declaration of world law on confiscation, provided that "nationalization, expropriation, or requisitioning shall be based on grounds of public utility or the national interest" and that "in such cases, the owner shall be paid appropriate compensation." Pursuant to this law, in July 1971 Chile confiscated the El Teniente Mining Co. The owner of El Teniente was Kennecott Copper Corp. of the U.S., and it sought in Chile "appropriate

Despite his full-page plea published in the "New York Times" on Jan. 30, 1972, publisher Ralph Ginzburg began serving a three-year prison sentence on February 17. (He was paroled on October 11.) He had been convicted in 1963 of using the mails for disseminating allegedly obscene promotional material for his now defunct "Eros" magazine and had fought his conviction for nearly ten years.

WIDE WORLD

UPI COMPIX

Angela Davis is kissed by friend Victoria Machado after Davis was found innocent of conspiracy, kidnapping, and murder by an all-white jury in San Jose, Calif. The sensational trial ended on June 4, 1972. It was the result of a 1970 shoot-out at the Marin County (Calif.) courthouse in which a judge and three others were killed.

compensation" for the mine. The book value of the mine was said by Kennecott to be $365,000,000 and this figure was not seriously disputed by the Chilean government. But the government proceeded to deduct $220,000,000 for what it termed "prior years reevaluation" and subsequently Pres. Salvador Allende decreed that Kennecott owed his government $410,000,000 in excess profits tax, retroactive to the year 1955. Kennecott responded that the mine had not even earned that much money since 1955, but the Chilean government ruled against this contention, ordered the mine confiscated, and levied a deficiency against Kennecott. Kennecott immediately announced that it rejected the decision of the Chilean government and that it would pursue its rights in the various courts throughout the world.

"Kennecott's Private War"—as it was described by *The Economist*—fascinated international lawyers during 1972 and resulted in a number of judicial decisions that clarified and fortified the UN resolution. Starting in the U.S., Kennecott obtained a favourable ruling in the federal courts that permitted it to attach Chilean assets in the U.S. to be applied to its claim. These assets, however, were not sufficient to pay Kennecott's claim, and it continued its effort to collect compensation for the mine by resorting to legal procedures to seize copper being exported by the Chilean government. This effort was markedly successful in France and the Netherlands and occasioned statements of great outrage from President Allende. The French Tribunal de Grande Instance held, importantly, that it had jurisdiction to hear the Kennecott versus Chile case with respect to copper shipped from Chile to France, and it reaffirmed a principle of French law and the UN resolution to the effect that it would not recognize the acts of nationalization by foreign governments if no just compensation had been paid to the initial owners. A similar decision was handed down in Rotterdam. Both cases were being appealed.

If Kennecott won these appeals, its private war against Chile would be won. Even if it lost the appeals—and most legal scholars predicted otherwise—its tactics already had had a profound impact. For example, the four major copper-producing nations of the world—Chile, Peru, Zambia, and Zaire—called a high-level conference to strike back against the French court order in favour of Kennecott. The conference produced a statement of "solidarity and defense" against seizure of copper shipments. A subsequent conference of ministers was called, to be held in Santiago, Chile, to decide on specific counter actions to be taken. Additionally President Allende appeared before the UN to argue his cause.

Consumers. Judicial opinions reflected the worldwide popular concern over consumer protection and credit. The U.S. Supreme Court added a constitutional dimension to consumerism in *Fuentes* v. *Shevin,* a case that would have an important effect on consumer relations. This case involved the repossession of personal property that had been sold to a buyer (Fuentes) on a secured credit basis. The agreement of sale provided that the buyer was to make specified installment payments to satisfy her obligation for the price and that the seller could repossess the goods if these payments were not made. The buyer made several payments but refused to pay further, alleging that the goods were defective. She argued that she was entitled to deduct the sum of the defects from the price. The seller, nevertheless, obtained a writ of replevin (repossession) from a Florida court upon the posting of a bond, and this writ enabled him to retake the goods, pending the decision of the court as to the merits of the dispute. The buyer contended that this procedure violated her constitutional rights, since it had the effect of denying her the right to use her property prior to a decision on the merits of the controversy.

The Florida courts ruled against this contention, but the U.S. Supreme Court sustained the contention of the buyer. It held that any taking of property without the debtor being given an opportunity to be heard on the validity of the underlying claim was a violation of the due process clause of the U.S. Constitution. In writing the decision for the court, Justice Potter Stewart ruled on several matters that had been debated in legal circles: (1) The kind of property taken was not important. It had been argued that the states could not constitutionally provide remedies for creditors that would enable them to seize a debtor's wages without an opportunity to be heard but that they could provide similar remedies that might reach less important property, such as phonographic equipment and the like. Justice Stewart said there was no basis in the Constitution for such a distinction. (2) The posting of a bond by the creditor was not critical. It had been suggested that a repossession from a debtor was not significantly dangerous or harmful to him if the creditor was required to post a bond as a condition to such repossession that would reimburse the debtor for any loss that might be suffered by the latter should the merits of the case ultimately be resolved in his favour. Justice Stewart held that the Constitution did not make this kind of differentiation. (3) The contractual authorization for the taking was not valid unless the debtor made it knowingly, voluntarily, and intelligently. It had been asserted that the debtor, in any case, could waive his right to possession of goods pending a hearing on the merits and that a waiver could be effectuated in advance by appropriate contractual language. Justice Stewart did not deny these contentions but held that any waiver of the right to be heard would be valid only if made voluntarily, intelligently, and knowingly. He found that Mrs. Fuentes had not waived her rights under this standard.

As a result of the Fuentes case, the provisional remedies—that is, the remedies that creditors could use prior to judgment against their debtors—were largely thought to be unconstitutional in the U.S. The various states embarked on feverish legislative activity to redraft them so as to meet the new constitutional standards.

In other countries urgent consumer cases also occupied the attention of the courts. In West Germany, for example, two cases that could have weighty repercussions were decided. In one the federal Supreme Court held that "superlative" advertising could be a violation of the unfair competition law. The case was interesting to the legal community because of the holding of the court that minor puffing could rise to the level of "superlative" advertising. Specifically, the case involved an advertisement concerning a razor that was said to be "bought more than any other in the world." The statement was technically true, but the German court held it to be a "superlative" one and hence a violation of the law of unfair competition because there was on the German market a razor that exceeded it in sales. To many West Germans the decision portended a crackdown on advertising generally.

In another West German case the consumer fared less well. The federal Supreme Court held that a consumer had no action against a customs official who approved for importation wine that subsequently was found to be defective. The consumer was personally injured by the bad wine.

In the U.K. the efficacy of disclaimer clauses in contracts—that is, clauses that exonerate one party, usually the seller or the one who provides a service, from liability if the goods or service are defective—had been under heavy judicial attack. The attack was fortified in 1972 by legislation by Parliament invalidating clauses in parking-lot contracts that exonerate the parking lot from liability for damage to cars incurred while in the lot.

In France fairly common decisions against house-to-house sellers were declared into legislative law through a new "doorstep-sales act." Under this act, doorstep salesmen had to have a special identity card; all sales had to be in writing and the written form had to contain a tear-off renunciation form; no payment could be required until five days after the sale and then only if the renunciation form had not been received by the seller. Under this law, every buyer had five days to "repent" his purchase and repentance was always possible before any of the price had been paid.

Labour Relations. Two interesting labour law cases were decided in Ireland. The first involved a decision that a trade union infringed a member's constitutional right of free association in its refusal to consent to his transfer to another trade union. The second also involved the Irish constitution, specifically its guarantee that all human persons shall be held equal before the law. Trade union members picketed to force an employer to dismiss a bar waitress solely on the ground that she was a woman. The Irish High Court held that this picketing could be enjoined as a violation of the equal protection clause of the constitution.

In West Germany trade unions alleged that a person being detained pending criminal proceedings was "unemployed" within the meaning of the social security law and thus entitled to benefits. The federal Social Security Court ruled to the contrary.

In Austria a lawyer successfully attacked a legal aid system that he alleged compelled him to do legal work for indigents without a fee. The Austrian court held that the allegations, if proved, were admissible protests under the Austrian constitution and the laws propounded by the Council of Europe.

The U.S. Supreme Court had the occasion to determine the meaning of the term "employee" as used in the National Labor Relations Act. Under the amended act, mandatory subjects of collective bargaining included pensions and insurance benefits of "employees." The court determined that the word "employee" as used in the act was to be taken in its ordinary meaning, that is, someone who works for another for hire, and that the term, accordingly, excluded retirees. The effect of the decision was to deny former, now retired employees the right to collectively bargain for modifications of pension rights.

(WILLIAM D. HAWKLAND)

International Law. *Organizations.* Apart from antitrust cases discussed above, the main developments within the EEC were a new draft directive on harmonization of company law, providing for the introduction of supervisory boards on the German model, the fresh draft directive on the supply of services by the legal profession, and the ratification by all six original member states of the 1968 convention on the recognition and enforcement of judgments (a sort of EEC "full faith and credit" provision), which was to go into effect on Jan. 1, 1973. In addition, agreement was reached in Luxembourg on the draft for a European Patent Convention, to be wider than the EEC itself, which would create a special "European patent" valid in all member countries but would not in itself preclude the continued existence of national patents. The new patent would be based on a prima facie test of obviousness and would be operated from a proposed European Patent Office in Munich (where the Max-Planck-Institut for industrial property was already established). The draft would be discussed further and approved at a diplomatic conference in 1973.

At the UN the General Assembly, in its December 1971 session, approved for submission to member states for ratification an amendment to the UN Charter to double the number of members of the Economic and Social Council to 54. Fourteen would come from Africa, 11 from Asia, 10 from Latin America, 6 from Eastern Europe, and 13 from Western Europe and elsewhere.

The International Court of Justice experienced a slight resurgence in activity, which came just in time to preserve its morale. It delivered judgment in the case presented to it in 1971 appealing a decision of the International Civil Aviation Organization Council, in spite of the applicant state's (India's) request to drop it. The court held that ICAO was entitled to consider the propriety of India's ban on overflight of Indian territory by Pakistani planes. It also received two more cases: a request by the Committee on Applications for Review of Administrative Tribunal Judgments for an advisory opinion on an administrative issue; and a double action by both the U.K. and West Germany against Iceland arising out of the latter's unilateral extension of its exclusive fishery limits to 50 mi. offshore, an action in which the court issued an interim injunction to Iceland, which the latter disregarded.

World economic organization made little progress at UNCTAD III, the meeting of the UN Conference on Trade and Development held in Santiago, Chile, but the General Agreement on Tariffs and Trade (GATT) did approve a protocol to permit 16 less developed countries to introduce mutual tariff concessions inter se without the obligation to extend most-

continued on page 410

UPI COMPIX

Deputy Attorney General Richard Kleindienst was nominated by Pres. Richard Nixon on Feb. 15, 1972, to replace Attorney General John Mitchell, who had resigned to become Nixon's campaign manager. Kleindienst was to occupy the same post in Nixon's second administration.

SPECIAL REPORT

DO WE NEED A BILL OF RIGHTS FOR CHILDREN?

By Lisa Aversa Richette

Only recently has the justice system modified its traditional view of children as a special class of citizens with few, if any, constitutional rights. In this respect, U.S. democratic processes have not differed radically from notions held by ancient and medieval societies that regarded children as the chattels of parents or other adults or, if they were of the pauper class, as state wards. Until the passage of the juvenile court acts at the beginning of the 20th century, children accused of crimes were subjected to the same procedures and penalties as adults. This paradox—that children were rightless pawns to be moved about at will by the state but with full adult responsibility for antisocial behaviour that threatened the state—still persists as an underlying reality, although attacks by lawyers, social workers, and citizens have resulted in a widespread movement for change in the juvenile justice system.

The State as Parent. The doctrine used by courts to legitimate state intervention in the lives of children is summed up in the Latin phrase *parens patriae,* a term first used by the Pennsylvania Supreme Court in 1839 and taken up by the Illinois Supreme Court in 1882 in the case of *In re: Ferrier* (103 Illinois 367), where, for the first time, it was used to justify the removal of a child from home and its commitment to an institution. *Parens patriae,* meaning that the state is the ultimate parent and hence can deal with the child at will, proved, as the U.S. Supreme Court was to state almost a century later, "to be a great help to those who sought to rationalize the exclusion of juveniles from the constitutional scheme, but its meaning is murky and its historical credentials are of dubious relevance" (*In re: Gault,* 387 U.S. 1, 1967).

During the 18th and 19th centuries, homeless, poor, disturbed, neglected, and orphan children were committed to workhouses and asylums where they mingled with other community outcasts. The establishment in 1824 of the New York House of Refuge provided separate shelter for such children, and some of the more blatant indignities were softened, although the basic system of herding them into low-cost, dehumanizing institutions was to persist into the latter half of the 20th century. Not until early 1972 did Massachusetts take the lead in abolishing all "correctional" institutions for children and providing, in the place of jails, community-based facilities such as group homes and therapeutic communities.

Throughout the 19th century, no fundamental challenge was posed to the right of the state to intervene in the child's life, and no theoretical principles grounded in legal right were asserted to ensure Eighth Amendment protections against "cruel and unusual punishments" to children or to afford them due process of law. The establishment in 1899 in Cook County, Ill., of the juvenile court system and its rapid expansion to all states in the next decade were heralded as ushering in a "new era for the child." Actually, the juvenile court movement congealed *parens patriae* into a monolithic dogma. Because the juvenile court acts spoke in terms of the salvation of children, courts consistently ruled that their procedures and methods should not be scrutinized carefully, if at all.

Despite the ambitious rhetoric of the juvenile court laws and the idealism of juvenile court judges, the facilities available for mending children's lives were largely limited to latter-day versions of the 19th-century shelters and jails. Often punishment cells, termed "strip cells" as late as 1972, were the preferred tools of rehabilitation. Children were regimented, sent off to rural settings far from their communities and families, their heads often shaven, their bodies clad in drab uniforms, to be stigmatized psychically for life and to suffer permanent alienation, under the indifferent eyes of the community and the highest courts alike.

During the 1950s social and personal dislocations in American family life resulted in a rise in juvenile alienation. The difficulties encountered in Northern ghettos by black emigrants in search of social justice and better living opportunities produced another new source of concern for the already overworked, inadequate juvenile justice system. Faced with mounting public pressure for the control of unruly children, juvenile courts responded by mass procedures that resulted in detention centres where children slept on floors or four to a single cell, "quickie" hearings, and rubber stamp commitments of a long-term nature for even trivial offenses seen as part of an incipient pattern of delinquency. Graphic documentation of the realities of the juvenile justice system are found in Howard James's *Children in Trouble* (1970), in my own work *The Throwaway Children* (1970), and, most authoritatively, in the 1967 report of the President's Commission on Law Enforcement and the Administration of Justice.

The Courts and the Community. The total lack of constitutional procedures, coupled with scandalous conditions in children's institutions throughout the country, finally compelled the Supreme Court to pry open the closed doors of juvenile courts in the historic *Gault* decision of 1967. For the first time in U.S. legal history, children were declared to be persons within the Fourteenth Amendment and entitled to due process of law. *Gault* guaranteed juveniles accused of delinquent behaviour the right to a day in court with notice of the charges, the right to counsel, the right to confront and to cross-examine their accusers, and the right to remain silent. The majority opinion of the 8–1 court, written by Justice Abe Fortas, seemingly set aside *parens patriae* by stating that "the Fourteenth Amendment and the Bill of Rights are not for adults alone."

Presaging *Gault,* the Supreme Court had declared a year earlier that one advantage always held by the state against older children, the right to try them as adults if they were charged with serious crime, could not be exercised unless the state gave the child a full due process hearing on the issue of whether or not he was to be certified to an adult court (*Kent* v. *United States,* 383 U.S. 541, 1966). In at least one state, Texas, the *Gault* case was circumvented by the practice of detaining children until their 17th birthday, then charging them as adults for offenses committed while they were of an age where transfer to an adult court could not have occurred under state law. In *Whitaker* v. *State* (467 S.W. 2nd, 264, 1971), a 16-year-old boy was charged with rape, interrogated by juvenile authorities, and, after being warned of his privilege against self-incrimination, confessed after being in police custody for over 12 hours without being permitted to call his only relative. He was then detained for two months and indicted as an adult after he became 17. At his trial his "confession" was admitted as evidence, and he received a sentence of 50 years in the state penitentiary.

In the wake of *Gault,* several crosscurrents were apparent in the development of juvenile rights. Legislatures rewrote juvenile codes to include *Gault* rights, but deep-seated public apathy and the resistance of the "child savers" had not extended reform beyond label changing. To deny Gault-type hearings to children not accused of specific crimes, new categories were devised with

---

Lisa Aversa Richette, a judge in the Court of Common Pleas, Philadelphia, and author of The Throwaway Children, *is presently working on a second book about the civil rights of children.*

amusing acronyms: PINS, CINS, or MINS (persons, children, or minors in need of supervision).

What the due process rights of these children shall be when they are charged with violations of court orders made after "informal hearings" is an undetermined question. Many towns and cities have no formal system for providing counsel for children, a class that is by definition almost totally indigent. Juvenile court judges accustomed to a paternalistic role have not extended *Gault* but have awaited further word from the Supreme Court.

Except for granting children First Amendment freedom of speech rights in schools as long as the health, safety, and welfare of other pupils are not in jeopardy (*Tinker* v. *Des Moines Independent School District,* 393 U.S. 508, 1969) and for establishing the principle that a delinquency adjudication may result only after the reasonable doubt test used in adult courts has been met (*In re: Winship,* 397 U.S. 358, 1971), the Supreme Court has been unwilling to orchestrate the legal rights of children more fully. In line with Chief Justice Warren Burger's dissent in *Winship,* the court ruled in *McKeiver* v. *Pennsylvania* (403 U.S. 528, 1971) that jury trials for juveniles are not part of their due process rights. The court expressed faith in the underlying *parens patriae* concepts of the juvenile court, despite the belief of many legal scholars and critics that it is a failed experiment.

Child Victims. The narrow *Gault* brush left unretouched the dreary area of neglected, dependent, and abused children. Since their status as victims is in no way analogous to adult criminal situations, the protections extended in *Gault* to children charged with crime cannot be considered to have included them. Here the juvenile court can effectively cling to the label of a civil proceeding in which there is no possibility of punishment, and its role of child saviour seems less vulnerable to attack than in the delinquency situation.

Wyman v. *James* (400 U.S. 309, 1971), dealing with the legal rights of welfare recipients, may serve as an indicator of how the current Supreme Court would view a challenge to the juvenile court's powers over alleged dependent, abused, and neglected children. *Wyman* upholds the right of welfare visitors to "inspect" recipients' homes without a search and seizure warrant. The court's ruling relied heavily on a belief that the government's interest in dependent children is of such a benevolent and humane nature that it overcomes all constitutional objections. It seems likely that the court will sanction the policy of imposing "help" against the will of children and parents who are without lawyers and knowledge of the court procedures. Thus, emotionally ill and retarded children without family means of securing proper therapy will continue to be warehoused and "placed" in facilities that range from mediocre to deplorable. U.S. television viewers were shocked in 1972 by a documentary on Willowbrook, a facility maintained by the state of New York for the mentally retarded, where naked and desperate children were penned into facilities reeking of urine and excrement.

The rights of children involved in private custody disputes between parents are also undefined. In *Magaziner* v. *Montemuro* (1972), the U.S. Court of Appeals for the 3rd Circuit refused to order a state court to permit a lawyer, chosen by three teen-age children, to appear on their behalf during lengthy and bitter litigation over their custody.

The availability to children of the constitutional protections given to adults in arrest and interrogation procedures remains questionable. No Supreme Court ruling exists to guide juvenile aid officers, intake personnel, and other persons involved with the child before he comes to court. Arrests without warrants remain a widespread practice, and interrogation of children without the assistance and counsel of parents or lawyers forms the basis of "confessions" and statements. In the *Miranda* decision, the Supreme Court had held that a suspect must be apprised of his constitutional rights before interrogation, but whether or not a child may voluntarily and intelligently waive those rights is a perplexing issue not faced by the legal system. Law journal editors tested students in the top track of a local high school system

BRUCE DAVIDSON—MAGNUM

In 1967, for the first time in U.S. legal history, children were declared to be persons within the Fourteenth Amendment and entitled to due process of law.

and found that 75% of those interviewed did not understand their constitutional rights. Considering the fear and anxiety of children detained under custodial interrogation, and the less than top-track performances of most children found to be "delinquent," it seems unlikely that the waiver of constitutional rights is legal under the prevailing law.

The right to bail, another fundamental right of U.S. citizens, is also at best an uncertain hope for children detained before a full hearing. Only one state, Arkansas, guarantees bail for children; the other states either deny the right or are silent. Although *Gault* focused only on the rights of children during the court hearing on guilt or innocence, its language upholding constitutional rights for children was compelling enough to persuade a Kentucky court to declare a state law denying bail to children unconstitutional (*Payne* v. *Baker,* #148392, 194, Jefferson Circuit Court). In the absence of a national policy enunciated by the Supreme Court, local courts, when challenged in an individual case, will release the child without bail or resolve the problem by ordering a speedy trial.

The final and perhaps most important part of the juvenile court proceeding, the disposition or sentence phase, has not been permeated by a *Gault* approach. Often the court bases its decision on psychiatric and social reports that are not available to the child's counsel and cannot be refuted. Hearsay statements by probation officers, teachers, and neighbours also help to determine the court's final order.

The child's right to substantive due process, to the rehabilitation that has been promised him, presents perhaps the greatest legal problem of all. Whether the Supreme Court will continue to refrain from interfering with state juvenile court systems—a posture it advocated in the *McKeiver* decision—or whether it will assert that the right to treatment is a fundamental guarantee remained a disquieting question. In the case of *In re: Savoy* (Nos. 70-4803, 70-4714, D.C. Juv. Court, Oct. 13, 1970), a judge found that a detention centre was totally inadequate and ordered a new one built within two years. In light of recent federal district court decisions concerning prison conditions and prisoners' rights, lawyers may succeed in removing children from the most visible and shocking facilities. But the individual child's right to a proper diagnosis and treatment program may remain an unfulfilled promise.

As long as the civil-criminal label game is played and sanctions are placed against children in the name of rehabilitation, little fundamental change will occur. The Supreme Court refused to consider the case of a 17-year-old girl sentenced to four years at the Connecticut State Farm for Women because she was "in manifest danger of falling into habits of vice" (*Mattielo* v. *Connecticut,* 154 Conn. 737, petition for certiorari dismissed, 1969), and the Burger court's decision to limit juvenile rights to *Gault* seemed to indicate that the search for juvenile justice would be a continuing one for the '70s.

OLIPHANT, THE DENVER POST 1972 © THE LOS ANGELES TIMES SYNDICATE

"Eight to four—that's guilty enough, by golly! Thirty years!"
The cartoon is a jibe at the U.S. Supreme Court's decision holding that juries in state criminal cases no longer need to reach unanimous verdicts. The court held that "heavy majority" verdicts were sufficient for conviction.

continued from page 407

favoured-nation treatment to other members, covering some 300 items and in derogation of GATT rules. At the same time, the EEC system of generalized preferences was working successfully, and in a number of cases the concessions were closed as particular countries used up their permitted quotas.

Regional economic communities were agreed upon for the Caribbean, through transformation of the existing CARIFTA (Caribbean Free Trade Area), and for West Africa, in the outline Treaty of Bamako (to be supplemented by a further detailed treaty) between seven francophone states. In addition, the first summit meeting of the Chad Basin Commission (set up in 1964) was held at Fort-Lamy, at which it was agreed to set up a development fund and two specialized agencies. Comecon for the second time extended itself beyond Europe by accepting a Cuban application for membership.

The Nordic Council, which had taken an important institutional step in 1971 with the institution of a Council of Ministers, followed that with the creation of a permanent Secretariat for Nordic Cooperation. This was to be subordinate to the Council of Ministers but staffed by independent officials.

International Conventions. Among the large number of international conventions, those that were particularly noteworthy included the UN Convention on International Liability for Damage Caused by Objects Launched into Outer Space (London, Moscow, and Washington; March 29, 1972), the UN Convention on the Prohibition of the Development, Production, and Stockpiling of Bacteriological (Biological) and Toxin Weapons and on their Destruction (London, Moscow, and Washington; April 10, 1972), and the UN Declaration on the Rights of Mentally Retarded Persons (Dec. 20, 1971). The Council of Europe established conventions on State Immunity, on the Place of Payment of Money Liabilities, on the Calculation of Time Limits, on the Establishment of a Scheme of Registration of Wills (Basel; May 16, 1972), and on the Transfer of Proceedings in Criminal Matters (Strasbourg; May 15, 1972). The Benelux Convention on the Unification of the Rights of Customs Duties was established within the Benelux Customs Area (Luxembourg; May 29, 1972). The convention on the manufacture, import, and export of copyrighted music tapes was signed in Geneva. A protocol to the 1961 UN Single Convention on Narcotic Drugs extended the powers of the International Narcotics Control Board (Geneva; March 25, 1972).

Also of importance was the entry into force of the 1964 Hague conventions on a Uniform Law on the Contract for the International Sale of Goods (Corporeal Movables) and on the formation of contracts. These took effect in August 1972 after ratification by six states.

Human Rights. The European Commission on Human Rights, having in June 1971 upheld the complaints of three persons who had been imprisoned under the Belgian vagrancy laws, delivered a further judgment on March 10, 1972, refusing to award them damages for unlawful detention. One of the rare interstate cases under the convention was the one brought by the Republic of Ireland against the U.K. arising out of the troubles in Northern Ireland; the case was still before the European Commission, which had held it to be admissible.

The Sea. Following recent trends, an ever increasing segment of international law was being devoted to maritime affairs. This was to have culminated in a major UN conference on the law of the sea in Geneva in 1973, but a postponement until 1974 seemed increasingly likely.

Questions of maritime boundaries seaward continued to cause concern. The tendency to push out to 12 mi., either for territorial waters (as by France and Kenya) or for fishery limits (as proposed by West Germany and the Netherlands), continued. But of greater concern were the more excessive claims, such as Gabon's extension of territorial waters to 100 mi., the extension of fishery limits by French Guiana to 80 mi. and by Iceland to 50 mi., and a threat by Norway that it might have to do the same if no international agreement on fishery conservation could be reached.

A new development was the claim made by Indonesia, Singapore, and Malaysia of a right to impose "sound dues" on passage through the Strait of Malacca and the institution of a survey as a preparatory step to doing so. Similarly, Ecuador issued a decree imposing on all cargo ships using its territorial waters "navigation dues" to pay for lighthouses and other navigational aids.

The main developments as regards fishery protection were the coming into force at the end of 1971 of the Southeast Atlantic Fisheries Convention and the institution of a partial ban on salmon fishing off Greenland, particularly by Danish fishermen, following strong diplomatic pressure, a Danish-U.S. agreement, and a resolution of the Northwest Atlantic Fisheries Commission. One of the few positive recommendations to emerge from the UN Conference on the Human Environment at Stockholm was a resolution to increase protection of whales, but a consequent U.S. proposal for a ten-year moratorium on whaling was rejected in the International Whaling Commission. Instead, the quota system was maintained, but at a reduced rate. Japan, the Soviet Union, and Norway also signed an agreement to limit whaling in Antarctic waters to nonreproductive whales only.

There was little activity relating to the seabed apart from the coming into force in May 1972 of the Treaty on the Prohibition of the Emplacement of Nuclear Weapons and Other Weapons of Mass Destruction on the Seabed and Ocean Floor and in the Subsoil Thereof (February 1971), after ratification by the three depository powers. Otherwise the UN Seabed Committee continued to prepare for the Geneva conference.

As was natural in the year of the UN Conference

on the Human Environment, greater emphasis was placed on pollution problems. This included the coming into force of the Canadian Arctic Waters Pollution Act and an agreement between Canada and the U.S. (Ottawa, April 15, 1972) on prevention of pollution of the Great Lakes. Iran and the U.S.S.R. were also discussing an agreement on pollution of the Caspian Sea. The Convention on Civil Liability During Carriage of Nuclear Material by Sea was signed in Brussels on Dec. 17, 1971, and the following day the Inter-Governmental Maritime Consultative Organization (IMCO) Convention on Civil Liability for Oil Pollution Damage was signed, also in Brussels, to amend the 1969 convention. Questions of navigation control in congested seaways continued to be discussed and tentative first steps toward some form of sea traffic control were taken when the U.K., France, and Belgium agreed on a procedure for reporting oil spillage in the Strait of Dover and the U.K. and France did the same for the English Channel. The dumping of waste at sea aroused strong protest and resulted in the Oslo Convention to control such dumping in the North Sea and the signing by 57 nations of a convention on ocean pollution.

Family Law. One of the growing areas in law reform, particularly in Europe, was family law. Major changes were under way in both Catholic and Protestant countries. The most dramatic of these were being worked out in Sweden where, following a report early in the year proposing changes in social security arrangements to emphasize the equality of husband and wife, the first interim report of the Family Law Reform Committee recommended, as expected, the virtual equivalence of marriage and cohabitation.

In Italy, where the battle against the new divorce law by means of a popular referendum was interrupted by new elections, the basic principles of family law were reformulated to emphasize the equal status of husband and wife. A total revision of Part II of the Swiss Civil Code, on family law, began with the enactment of a new article 321 on adoption. This was followed by the appointment of a committee to study the law applicable to children, particularly the equal treatment of illegitimate and legitimate children. In France, where equality of husband and wife was introduced in 1971, a new act gave illegitimate children equal rights.

Administrative Law. New Zealand's successful introduction of an Administrative Court into its legal structure was followed by the report of the Kerr Committee on Administrative Review recommending the same for Australia. The first Australian ombudsman was instituted in Western Australia. In Switzerland the city of Zürich's ombudsman issued his first report; and the British government announced its intention to introduce a separate ombudsman system for local government and another for the hospital services. Even the French premier, after a well-developed campaign by a small number of influential lawyers, announced the intention to introduce an ombudsman under the influence of the Quebec Protecteur du Citoyen, but apparently more on the British pattern of channeling complaints through members of Parliament. On the other hand, the Mauritius experiment seemed to have failed when the first ombudsman returned to his native Sweden complaining of too much governmental interference.

(NEVILLE MARCH HUNNINGS)

See also Cities and Urban Affairs; Crime; Environment; Police; Race Relations.

ENCYCLOPÆDIA BRITANNICA FILMS. *Equality Under Law—The Lost Generation of Prince Edward County* (1967); *Freedom to Speak (N.Y. v. Feiner)* (1967); *Equality Under Law—California Fair Housing Cases* (1969); *Free Press vs. Fair Trial by Jury—The Sheppard Case* (1969); *The Schempp Case—Bible Reading in Public Schools* (1969).

Lebanon

A republic of the Middle East, Lebanon is bounded by Syria, Israel, and the Mediterranean Sea. Area: 3,950 sq.mi. (10,230 sq.km.). Pop. (1970 est.): 2,126,325. Cap. and largest city: Beirut (pop., 1970 est., 475,000). Language: Arabic. Religion: Christian majority with strong Muslim minority. President in 1972, Suleiman Franjieh; prime minister, Saeb Salam.

In 1972 Lebanon's economic prosperity was endangered by clashes with Israel that became increasingly severe throughout the year. Israeli incursions into southern Lebanon in January and February in retaliation for isolated Palestinian guerrilla attacks from Lebanese territory caused Lebanese right-wing politicians to criticize strongly the November 1969 Cairo agreement between the guerrillas and the Lebanese Army. However, the Palestine Liberation Organization (PLO) made efforts to conciliate the Army and the government maintained that it stood by the Cairo agreement. Following the massacre of passengers at Tel Aviv's Lod Airport on May 30, which the Israelis claimed had been planned in Lebanon—an allegation that the Lebanese authorities strongly de-

LEBANON

Education. (1968–69) Primary, pupils 425,840; secondary, pupils 129,960; primary and secondary, teachers 29,974; vocational, pupils 2,103; teacher training, students 2,661, teachers 416; higher (including 4 universities), students 33,587, teaching staff 1,697.

Finance. Monetary unit: Lebanese pound, with a free rate (Sept. 18, 1972) of L£3 to U.S. $1 (L£7.31 = £1 sterling). Gold, SDRs, and foreign exchange, central bank: (June 1972) U.S. $592.9 million; (June 1971) U.S. $420.9 million. Budget (1971 est.) balanced at L£774 million. Gross national product: (1970) L£4,866 million; (1969) L£4,565 million. Money supply: (April 1972) L£2,059 million; (April 1971) L£1,789 million. Cost of living (Beirut; 1966 = 100): (April 1972) 114; (April 1971) 111.

Foreign Trade. (1970) Imports L£1,826 million; exports L£602 million; transit trade L£1,533 million. Import sources: Switzerland 12%; U.K. 11%; U.S. 10%; France 9%; West Germany 9%; Italy 7%; Iraq 5%. Export destinations: Saudi Arabia 16%; Kuwait 10%; Syria 6%; Jordan 5%; Iraq 5%; Libya 5%. Main exports: fruit and vegetables 13%; precious stones and metals 10%; machinery 10%; textiles and clothing 8%; transport equipment 7%; chemicals 6%; livestock and meat 5%. Tourism (1970): visitors 1,210,200; gross receipts U.S. $132 million.

Transport and Communications. Roads (1971) 7,400 km. Motor vehicles in use (1971): passenger 146,300; commercial 15,600. Railways: (1970) 335 km.; traffic (1971) 7.2 million passenger-km., freight 26.8 million net ton-km. Air traffic (1971): 1,028,400,000 passenger-km.; freight 199,132,000 net ton-km. Shipping (1971): vessels 100 gross tons and over 65; gross tonnage 127,325. Telephones (Jan. 1971) 192,000. Radio receivers (Dec. 1970) 600,000. Television receivers (Dec. 1970) 260,000.

Agriculture. Production (in 000; metric tons; 1971; 1970 in parentheses): wheat *c.* 45 (*c.* 50); tomatoes (1970) *c.* 75, (1969) 70; grapes *c.* 82 (*c.* 80); olives *c.* 40 (*c.* 20); figs *c.* 13 (*c.* 13); bananas (1970) *c.* 30, (1969) 29; oranges (1970) *c.* 205, (1969) 162; lemons (1970) *c.* 85, (1969) 65; apples *c.* 100 (90); tobacco *c.* 7.3 (*c.* 7.3). Livestock (in 000; 1970–71): cattle *c.* 84; goats *c.* 318; sheep *c.* 218; poultry *c.* 17,800.

Industry. Production (in 000; metric tons; 1971): cement 1,499; petroleum products (1970) 1,904; electricity (excluding most industrial production; kw-hr.) 1,366,000.

Lawn Bowls:
see Bowling and Lawn Bowls

Lawn Tennis:
see Tennis

Lead:
see Mining

JACQUES HAILLOT—GAMMA

The body of a Palestinian guerrilla is carried during the funeral of 18 guerrillas killed by Israeli troops in reprisal for the murder of 11 Israeli Olympic athletes on Sept. 5, 1972.

nied—an exceptionally heavy Israeli attack caused approximately 40 deaths among guerrillas and Lebanese civilians. The guerrillas evacuated the border areas, and the PLO agreed to freeze its activities and discipline its members although some extremist groups repudiated the agreement.

After the murder by guerrillas of 11 Israeli Olympic team members at Munich, W.Ger., on September 5, the Israelis launched an even more powerful attack at brigade strength on September 8 and followed it up on September 16 by bombarding refugee camps in southern Lebanon which it claimed were sheltering guerrilla bases. (*See* SPORTING RECORD: *Special Report*.) However, Lebanese fears that Israel planned a permanent occupation of part of southern Lebanon were not fulfilled. A veto by the United States in the UN Security Council prevented condemnation of Israel's action.

During the year a series of sabotage and assassination attacks were directed mainly against Palestinian and pro-Palestinian targets. In November a form of martial law was declared after leftist groups called for strikes and demonstrations to protest the killing of two striking workmen by police.

Parliamentary elections held in three stages in the second half of April led to the re-election of many traditional political leaders but also to a certain success for a mixed left-wing group led by the socialist Druze politician Kamal Jumblatt. The prime minister, Saeb Salam, resigned early in May but was asked to form the new government, which he did on May 27. Only two of his outgoing ministers held posts in the new government, which, in contrast to the previous extraparliamentary "technocrat" government, was formed almost entirely from inside parliament.

Despite a real expansion in all sectors of the services-dominated economy, including banking, tourism, building, light industry, and fruit growing, the government was seriously concerned with inflation and took steps, with only limited success, to hold down the rise in prices. An additional worry was that the nationalization by Iraq and Syria of the Iraq Petroleum Co. might lead to a loss in oil transit revenues.

(PETER MANSFIELD)

Lesotho

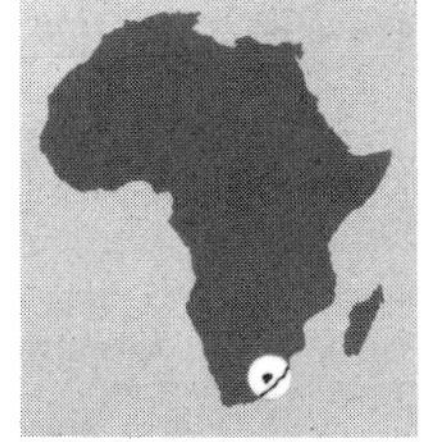

A constitutional monarchy of southern Africa and a member of the Commonwealth of Nations, Lesotho is completely surrounded by South Africa. Area: 11,720 sq.mi. (30,355 sq.km.). Pop. (1972 est.): 1,081,000. Cap. and largest city: Maseru (pop., 1972 est., 18,800). Language: English and Sesotho (official). Religion: about 80% Christian. Chief of state in 1972, Paramount Chief Moshoeshoe II; prime minister, Chief Leabua Jonathan.

The April 1972 congress of the Basuto National Party (BNP) confirmed Chief Jonathan's leadership and his policy of conciliation with Ntsu Mokhehle's opposition Basutoland Congress Party (BCP). Two leading members of the BNP, suspected of subversion, were expelled: Thomas Mofolo, president of the Senate, and Assistant Minister J. Mokotoso. In June Chief Jonathan began a campaign to establish a coalition government to include BCP members. Though Lesotho's survival continued to depend upon South Africa's goodwill, the prime minister's move led to the postponement of dialogue with the republic.

The budget estimates for 1972–73 indicated a large increase in revenue, allowing a reduction in British assistance. Most of the additional money came from Lesotho's share in the South Africa Customs Union pool, which accounted for 52% of total revenue of R 11.6 million. Expenditure was estimated at R 12.3 million. Rio Tinto Zinc continued to survey the possibility of establishing a diamond mine at Letseng. It was hoped that this enterprise might permit some of the 200,000 Basuto workers in South Africa to return home, though their remittances constituted the most important single export item. (MOLLY MORTIMER)

LESOTHO

Education. (1968) Primary, pupils 179,386, teachers (1967) 3,065; secondary, pupils 4,141, teachers (1967) 152; vocational, pupils 511, teachers (1967) 44; teacher training, students 675, teachers (1967) 47; higher (University of Botswana, Lesotho, and Swaziland), students (1969) 388, teaching staff (1967) 60.

Finance and Trade. Monetary unit: South African rand, with (Sept. 18, 1972) a free rate of R 0.80 to U.S. $1 (par value of R 1.95 = £1 sterling). Budget (1971–72 est.): revenue R 10.3 million; expenditure R 11.3 million. Foreign trade (1970): imports R 22,876,000; exports R 3,716,000. Main exports: wheat 25%; diamonds 18%; wool 15%; mohair 11%. Most trade is with South Africa.

Agriculture. Production (in 000; metric tons; 1971; 1970 in parentheses): corn *c.* 80 (*c.* 40); wheat *c.* 70 (*c.* 60); sorghum *c.* 60 (30); wool *c.* 2.2 (2.2); meat 24 (24). Livestock (in 000; Sept. 1971): cattle *c.* 410; goats *c.* 940; sheep *c.* 2,100.

Liberia

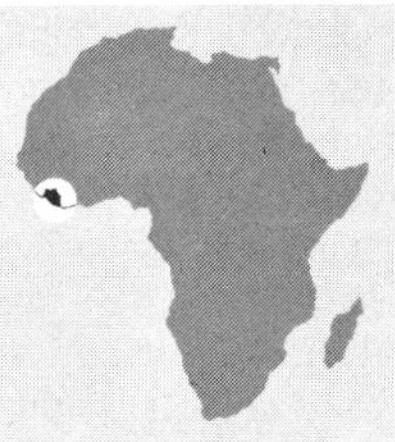

A republic on the west coast of Africa, Liberia is bordered by Sierra Leone, Guinea, and Ivory Coast. Area: 43,000 sq.mi. (111,400 sq.km.). Pop. (1971 est.): 1,571,477. Cap. and largest city: Monrovia (pop., 1970 est., 150,000). Language: English (official) and tribal dialects. Religion: mainly animist. President in 1972, William R. Tolbert, Jr.

President Tolbert (*see* BIOGRAPHY), who succeeded the late William V. S. Tubman in July 1971, was formally inaugurated as Liberia's chief executive on Jan. 3, 1972, in Monrovia. Among the foreign dignitaries attending the ceremony was Mrs. Richard M. Nixon, wife of the U.S. president. In his inaugural address, Tolbert said: "We reaffirm our friendship with the United States, with whom we share the pursuit of liberty, dignity, order and justice." His administration, he added, would be characterized by "an accent on youth and speed, and on competence and effectiveness."

One week after his inauguration, Tolbert announced a sweeping reorganization of the Liberian government. In the major Cabinet changes, Rochefort L. Weeks replaced Joseph Randolph Grimes as secretary of state; the president's brother, Stephen Tolbert, succeeded J. Milton Weeks as secretary of the treasury; and Clarence L. Simpson became attorney general, taking over from J. A. A. Pierce.

In mid-May, Tolbert traveled to neighbouring Guinea to attend funeral services for Kwame Nkrumah, deposed former president of Ghana, who had died in Romania in April. Tolbert delivered the eulogy. On June 10, Liberia announced that it and the Soviet Union intended to open embassies in each other's capitals within a matter of weeks.

Responding to popular resentment against foreign control of Liberia's economy, the government notified foreign corporations that it wanted to renegotiate existing long-term leases, some of which extend to the 21st century. In a statement issued in July, Tolbert said: "Liberia has not always derived its fair share of profits realized from these concessions in return for offering liberal incentives, the most stable political climate in Africa, a complete absence of exchange control, and other benefits."

A ten-year-long mapping project jointly carried out by the U.S. Geological Survey and the new Liberian Geological Survey was completed in mid-1972, giving Liberia the most complete mapping coverage of any African nation. V. E. McKelvey, director of the U.S. Geological Survey, explained that the project was significant primarily because it would help Liberia utilize its resources effectively. (RICHARD L. WORSNOP)

LIBERIA

Education. (1970–71) Primary, pupils 120,245, teachers 3,384; secondary, pupils 15,493, teachers 918; vocational, pupils 887, teachers 66; teacher training, pupils 390, teachers 32; higher, students 1,109, teaching staff 164.

Finance. Monetary unit: Liberian dollar, at par with the U.S. dollar and with a free rate (Sept. 18, 1972) of L$2.45 to £1 sterling. Budget (total; 1970 est.) balanced at L$65.2 million.

Foreign Trade. (1969) Imports L$114.6 million; exports L$195.9 million. Import sources: U.S. 34%; West Germany 14%; Japan 9%; U.K. 8%; Sweden 5%. Export destinations: U.S. 28%; West Germany 23%; Netherlands 10%; Italy 9%; Belgium-Luxembourg 7%; Japan 6%; France 5%; U.K. 6%. Main exports: iron ore 70%; rubber 16%; diamonds 5%.

Transport and Communications. Roads (1970) *c.* 3,700 km. Motor vehicles in use (1970): passenger 14,800; commercial (including buses) 8,400. Railways (1970) 493 km. Shipping (1971): merchant vessels 100 gross tons and over 2,060 (mostly owned by U.S. and other foreign interests); gross tonnage 38,552,240. Telephones (Jan. 1970) 6,000. Radio receivers (Dec. 1970) 155,000. Television receivers (Dec. 1970) 6,500.

Agriculture. Production (in 000; metric tons; 1970; 1969 in parentheses): rice *c.* 153 (*c.* 153); cassava *c.* 370 (*c.* 370); rubber (exports) 76 (67); palm kernels (exports) *c.* 14 (12); cocoa (1971–72) 1.8, (1970–71) 1.8; coffee *c.* 5.1 (*c.* 4.5). Livestock (in 000; August 1971): cattle *c.* 30; pigs *c.* 83; sheep *c.* 156; goats *c.* 140.

Industry. Production (in 000; 1970): iron ore (metal content; metric tons) 15,388; diamonds (exports; metric carats) 826; electricity (kw-hr.) 502,000.

Libraries

UNESCO's International Book Year 1972 greatly stimulated the production, use, and appreciation of books and libraries in many countries, and IBY committees were set up in 57 countries to promote economic development through reading. A "Charter of the Book" was published by UNESCO, and special IBY activities were reported from some 110 member states. In celebration of the IBY, the General Council of the International Federation of Library Associations (IFLA) met in Budapest, Hung., in late August. UNESCO's Department of Documentation, Libraries and Archives promoted the establishment of national information and documentation systems in less developed countries; pilot projects were already under way in Morocco and Bulgaria, financed by the UN Development Program. UNDP assistance also made it possible to found a school of librarianship in Jamaica for the English-speaking countries of the Caribbean. In cooperation with UNESCO and the IFLA, the European Conference on the International Exchange of Publications was held in Vienna in April 1972 to encourage governments to facilitate the free international exchange of publications.

The International Standard Book Number (ISBN) for numbering of books by publishers was widely adopted. At the meeting of the International Standards Organization Technical Committee 46, Documentation, at Scheveningen, Neth., in September further progress was made with the introduction of the International Standard Serials Number for the identification of periodical publications, and of the International Standard Record Number for records, tapes, and cassettes.

In Sweden a new computerized library and information system, LIBRIS, was introduced at the new University of Linköping. At the University of Nice, France, the various services of the library were automated and a catalog of periodicals produced by computer was in use. In East and West Germany further efforts were made toward cooperation between libraries of all kinds to form "networks."

In the U.K. a conference was convened by the Library Association of delegates from 21 countries outside the U.K. to found a Commonwealth Library Association. A constitution was drawn up, and in 1972 the Commonwealth Foundation established grants of £29,500 to support its first three years and of £1,000 to do the initial work. Library services in London were improved by the opening of the St. Pancras Library as the new reference library for the Borough of Camden, in the same building as the Shaw Theatre, and by the opening at the College of Librarianship, Aberystwyth, Wales, of the first library in Britain built for a school of librarianship. In the field of school libraries, a new multimedia trend, started in 1970 with the publication by the Library Association of *School Library Resource Centres: Recommended Standards for Policy and Provision,* was augmented in 1972 by a supplement on nonbook materials.

With the passing of the Local Government Act 1972, which reduced the number of local authorities in the U.K. from 350 to 80, many public municipal and county libraries faced amalgamation and reorganization. The question of the right to lend books to the public was again widely discussed, following the announcement by the paymaster general that the British government would consider amending the Copyright Act to restrict the right to lend books. Meanwhile, the method established in Norway for rewarding authors through the Norwegian Cultural Fund became a model.

In the U.S. the National Library of Medicine was sued for alleged copyright infringement in connection with photocopying, and a congressional committee was working on a bill to revise portions of copyright law; the American Library Association tried to safeguard the right to photocopy for interlibrary loan and the right of "fair use" for library users. The ALA, as active as ever, organized special activities for the IBY, including a "Black Caucus" project for cultural exchanges between the U.S. and Africa.

Many new library buildings were opened, notably the National Library of Macedonia at Skopje, Yugos., rebuilt after destruction by an earthquake in 1963, and an exemplary public library at Miskolc, Hung., based on the plan of the City Library of Göteborg, Swed. In West Germany most of the bookstock of the Staatsbibliothek Preussischer Kulturbesitz was moved from Marburg into the new building in West Berlin designed by Hans Scharoun. Work on the foundation of a third building for the Library of Congress in Washington, D.C., was completed; the building, designed by Ludwig Mies van der Rohe, was scheduled for completion by 1975. (ANTHONY THOMPSON)

ENCYCLOPÆDIA BRITANNICA FILMS. *Library of Congress* (1969).

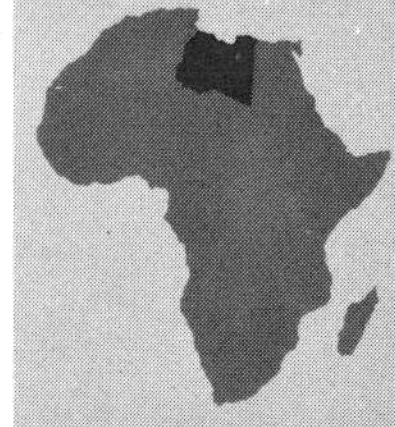

Libya

A socialist republic on the north coast of Africa, Libya is bounded by Egypt, Sudan, Tunisia, Algeria, Niger, and Chad. Area: 675,000 sq.mi. (1,749,000 sq.km.). Pop. (1971 est.): 2,010,000. Cap. and largest city: Tripoli (pop., 1970 est., 264,000). Language: Arabic. Religion: predominantly Muslim. Leader of the Revolutionary Command Council in 1972 and prime minister until July, Col. Muammar al-Qaddafi; prime minister from July, Maj. Abdul Salam Jalloud.

Libya's 18-man Cabinet took a new shape in July 1972 when civilians were appointed to all but the office of prime minister and the key positions of defense and interior. These remained in the hands of army officers of the Revolutionary Command Council. Colonel Qaddafi withdrew as prime minister and appointed Army Maj. Abdul Salam Jalloud as his successor.

Colonel Qaddafi again urged union with Egypt, although such a move was by no means popular. Union was promised within the year by Pres. Anwar as-Sadat of Egypt, after a three-day meeting with Qaddafi in Tobruk and Bengasi in late July and early August. The combination of Libya's wealth and Egypt's industrial and military strength had much to recommend it, especially in view of Qaddafi's avowed intention of deeper involvement in the Arab struggle against Israel. The unification of the military command would significantly affect the balance of arms in the area, since Libya had arms contracts with Western powers, notably with France for 110 Mirage fighters, of which about half had been delivered. The move was seen as a sign that Sadat required an alternative to dependence upon Soviet assistance, and in Libya he possibly hoped to find a more cooperative partner.

Relations with other Arab states were often poor, especially with Jordan and other surviving monarchies. Diplomatic ties were severed with the revolutionary regime in Iraq in April, after Iraq had signed a treaty with the U.S.S.R. Since Syria, Egypt, and Libya were supposedly linked in the Confederation of Arab Republics, Syria could only have been offended by an explosive Qaddafi speech on July 24, in which he claimed that Libya was alone in working to drive Israel from the occupied territories. On several occasions Qaddafi made clear his wish to intervene in international and guerrilla conflict, despite the distance of his country from the trouble centres and the state of Libya's military competence. He claimed to be supporting guerrilla organizations in the U.S., and to be supplying arms to the Irish Republican Army. Later he afforded heroes' burials in Tripoli to the five Arabs shot while implementing the Munich Olympic kidnappings, and his response to the developments in the internal position in Uganda in September was to dispatch a force of 400 troops by air to assist Pres. Idi Amin. This move was in line with Qaddafi's policy of strengthening the Muslim President Amin, especially in his removal of Israeli influence in Uganda.

Britain's relations with Libya were poor throughout 1972, following the nationalization of British Petroleum in December 1971. The Anglo-Libyan defense treaty was finally broken off on January 25, and an open demonstration of hostility broke out in August when the British embassy in Tripoli was attacked.

LIBYA

Education. (1969–70) Primary, pupils 310,846, teachers 11,122; secondary, pupils 44,612, teachers 3,250; vocational, pupils 1,457, teachers 220; teacher training, students 4,710, teachers 556; higher (at University of Libya; 1966–67), students 2,215, teaching staff 252.

Finance. Monetary unit: Libyan dinar, with (Sept. 18, 1972) a par value of 0.329 dinar to U.S. $1 (free rate of 0.803 dinar = £1 sterling). Gold and foreign exchange, central bank: (June 1972) U.S. $3,141,-900,000; (June 1971) U.S. $2,324,400,000. Budget (1971–72 est.) balanced at 201 million dinars. Gross national product: (1969) 1,043,000,000 dinars; (1968) 908.7 million dinars. Money supply: (May 1972) 386,010,000 dinars; (May 1971) 269,760,000 dinars. Cost of living (Tripoli; 1964 = 100): (March 1972) 140; (March 1971) 143.

Foreign Trade. (1971) Imports 250 million dinars; exports 960 million dinars. Import sources: U.K. 10%; Italy 23%; West Germany 9%; France 9%; U.S. 7%; Japan 6%. Export destinations: Italy 24%; West Germany 18%; U.K. 16%; France 12%; U.S. 6%; Netherlands 6%. Main export crude oil 99.9%.

Transport and Communications. Roads (with improved surface; 1970) *c.* 5,200 km. (including 1,822 km. coast road). Motor vehicles in use (1970): passenger 100,100; commercial (including buses) 45,400. Railways (1970) 165 km. Air traffic (1970): 172,-851,000 passenger-km.; freight 1,551,000 net ton-km. Ships entered (1970) vessels totaling 4,381,000 net registered tons; goods loaded (1970) 161,133,000 metric tons, unloaded 2.6 million metric tons. Telephones (Dec. 1970) 41,000. Radio licenses (Dec. 1970) 85,-000. Television licenses (Dec. 1970) 1,000.

Agriculture. Production (in 000; metric tons; 1971; 1970 in parentheses): wheat *c.* 70 (21); barley 32 (53); olives *c.* 105 (71); dates *c.* 50 (49). Livestock (in 000; 1970–71): goats *c.* 1,200; sheep 2,284; cattle 109; camels *c.* 160; asses *c.* 96.

Industry. Production (in 000; metric tons; 1970): salt 11; crude oil (1971) 132,506; electricity (Tripolitania; excluding most industrial production; kw-hr.) 426,000.

Life Insurance:
see Insurance

The attack was a reaction to Britain's reported extradition from Gibraltar of Moroccan Air Force officers, who had fled by helicopter after a second attempted coup. Qaddafi made no secret of his antipathy toward King Hassan and his regime in Morocco.

In 1971 Libya fell from fifth to seventh place in the world league of oil producers in terms of tonnage. The loss of British Petroleum production and a policy of conservation rather than of production made it unlikely that output for 1972 would top the 133 million metric tons in 1971, when petroleum provided 99.7% of exports by value. The oil companies operated under a threat of further nationalization, while the Libyan government remained in a very favourable position. (J. A. ALLAN)

Liechtenstein

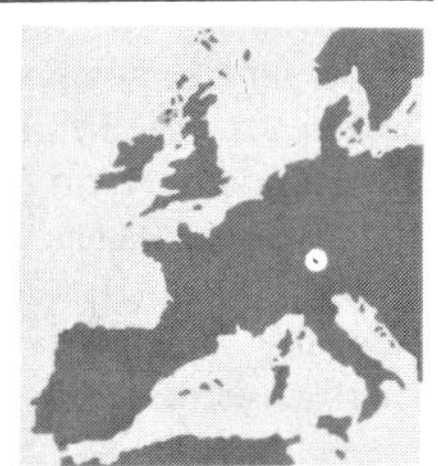

A constitutional monarchy between Switzerland and Austria, Liechtenstein is united with Switzerland by a customs and monetary union. Area: 62 sq.mi. (160 sq.km.). Pop. (1972 est.): 23,000. Cap. and largest city: Vaduz (pop., 1972 est., 4,200). Language: German. Religion (1970) Roman Catholic 90.1%. Sovereign prince, Francis Joseph II; chief of government in 1972, Alfred Hilbe.

The Landtag (parliament) in May 1972 unanimously approved an amendment to the constitution increasing the size of the Landtag from 15 to 21 members and requiring all political parties, in order to qualify for representation, to receive a minimum of 8% of the total votes cast in the entire principality. The amendment was defeated—by 70 votes—in a national referendum on July 2. The last such referendum, on women's suffrage, had been defeated by a similar margin in 1971, leaving Liechtenstein the only European state in which women could not vote.

On July 22, 1972, the present and future members of the EEC signed a free industrial trade pact with the five members of the European Free Trade Association (including Switzerland) not seeking EEC membership. Although not an EFTA state, Liechtenstein, as a consequence of its customs union with Switzerland, became a member of the pact. (ROBERT D. HODGSON)

LIECHTENSTEIN
Education. (1969–70) Primary, pupils 2,356, teachers 82; secondary, pupils 850, teachers 76.
Finance and Trade. Monetary unit: Swiss franc, with (Sept. 18, 1972) a par value of SFr. 3.84 to U.S. $1 (free rate of SFr. 9.27 = £1 sterling). Budget (1971 est.): revenue SFr. 54,091,000; expenditure SFr. 43,227,000. Exports (industrial; 1970) SFr. 333 million. Export destinations (1969): Switzerland 35%; West Germany; U.K.; Austria. Main exports: light manufactures (screws, needles); corn, vegetables, fruit, wine, livestock products. Tourism: visitors (1970) 73,600; gross receipts (1969) *c.* SFr. 16 million.
Agriculture. Livestock (in 000; April 1971): cattle *c.* 7; sheep *c.* 1; pigs *c.* 7; chickens *c.* 42.

Life Sciences

Never since the early days of Darwinism had biological matters been the object of so much public attention as in 1972, the year of the United Nations Conference on the Human Environment. "Ecology" entered the popular vocabulary much as "evolution" had done a century earlier. An important shift in emphasis took place toward concern with the fact that the survival of any community is closely dependent upon its complexity and that any human activity that substitutes uniformity for complexity is a threat to survival. (*See* ENVIRONMENT.)

Science likewise depends upon its own complexity and is threatened by any policies that restrict its scope. Such a threat came from the worldwide economic situation that necessitated stricter public accountability for expenditure on science and emphasis on "useful" as opposed to "academic" research. Yet the outstanding advances recorded in the following sections are in some ways less important than the developments in the infrastructure of techniques, facts, and ideas, largely of merely academic interest, upon which they are based.

Examples are numerous. A new technique for staining chromosomes in 1967 and for hybridizing mouse and human cells in 1971 attracted little attention except among specialists, but by 1972 their application to the mapping of human chromosomes and identification of gene loci had inaugurated what was described as perhaps the most significant development in human biology for decades. A conference on photobiology brought together botanists and zoologists linked by the fact that chloroplasts and retinal rods are related through their common ancestry among the flagellates. The retinal pigment rhodopsin was also found in bacteria. The common basis of plant and animal life was further emphasized by the demonstration of action-potentials in plants and of cyclic AMP (adenosine monophosphate) as an agent in the production of plant hormones.

Studies of the actin-myosin mechanism were no longer confined to muscles but were applied to amoeboid and flagellate movements, nuclear and cell division, and movements along nerve axons and in fibrils of slime molds. Among the slime molds, amoebulas of diverse origins assemble into aggregates with differentiated regions comparable to metazoan bodies. This is brought about by a chemical pheromone now shown to be cyclic AMP and this was shown to be produced, not continuously, as previously thought, but in bursts, a discharge from one cell evoking answering discharges from its neighbours. This type of cell com-

UPI COMPIX

Nobel laureate William Shockley is confronted in his Stanford University classroom by students, some in Ku Klux Klan sheets, angered over Shockley's public statements of his belief that blacks may be intellectually inferior on genetic grounds. Shockley is a physicist.

munication had not been discovered in other organisms but, if found to be at all general, could have important bearings in embryology, physiology, etc., including perhaps current work in which dissociated mouse brain cells were found to reassemble into organized aggregates showing the particular characters of the brain regions from which they were derived.

Conservation and molecular biology continued to provide the dominant interests and to have the major influence in determining the directions of research. Almost equally influential were the problems of immunology, no longer primarily a medical concern but entering into almost every aspect of cell activity, especially those dependent upon the cell membrane, such as the mutual interactions of cells, reactions to hormones and drugs, behaviour of nerve cells, and the formation of cyclic AMP. Spectacular advances were made in studies of the brain, particularly in the roles of specific nucleic acids and proteins in its activities and in the distinctive functions of the left and right sides of the cerebral cortex. These considerably widened ideas concerning the normal and pathological functioning of the human brain and the nature and evolution of mammalian intelligence. Important discoveries of early hominid remains also encouraged activity in this field, reported in a new *Journal of Human Evolution.* The European Molecular Biology Organization, now supported by 13 nations, was at last housed permanently in Heidelberg, W.Ger. Meanwhile, news concerning such hitherto unorthodox matters as acupuncture, scotophobin (*see* BIOGRAPHY: *Ungar, Georges*), the effects of noise on plant growth, reactions of migratory birds to the earth's magnetic field and of migratory fish to very weak electric fields served as a reminder that traditional ideas about the ways living things live were perhaps not as complete as was customarily believed. (HAROLD SANDON)

BOTANY

Information accumulated in recent years on the ultrastructure of phloem tissue and the dynamics of food transportation led to further additions to the dozen or so extant theories of the mechanism of translocation within this complex tissue system of higher plants. The "slime bodies" described by earlier microscopists were shown to comprise arrays of protein molecules (P-protein, or microfibrillar material) arranged in parallel strands. The callose material seen blocking the sieve tube pores in many preparations (suggesting to some that the pores were blocked in vivo) was found, in fact, to be formed very rapidly on cutting the plant. Callose was thus seen as an efficient sealing mechanism preventing major sap loss after mechanical injury. Experiments in which radioactive tracers were injected into individual cells in living phloem tissue of *Heracleum* showed that while sucrose and potassium ions traveled in both directions from the point of injection, the former appeared to be transported in discrete pulses. A bimodal theory of phloem translocation was put forward in which both the pulse- and mass-flow systems depended on a peristaltic type movement of the P-protein strands, with the sieve plates acting as pumps rather than barriers. However, other workers continued to argue in favour of the mass-flow theory which requires the sieve tube pores to be free of both callose and excessive P-protein.

The first report of a structure similar to a pollen tube in pteridosperm fossils was made in 1972. Previously it was not known whether the pteridosperms (which were gymnospermous plants with fernlike leaves and cycadlike wood anatomy) produced motile male gametes, as cycads do, or pollen tubes, as do the gymnosperms and angiosperms. A species of *Callospermarion*-type ovule dating from the Paleozoic Era contained pollen that could be assigned to the genus *Vesicaspora.* Some of these pollen grains possessed outgrowths identified as branched pollen tubes somewhat similar to those found in the Araucariaceae and Taxodiaceae. The finding was not conclusive evidence that fertilization was achieved by siphonogamy; the tubes might have had a haustorial function.

Studies on a species of higher plant, *Tidestromia oblongifolia,* which carries out most of its growth in the hot season in Death Valley, Calif., one of the hottest and most arid climates of the world, produced some remarkable findings. The plants showed maximum rates of transpiration and photosynthesis at midday when the temperature of the leaves reached 40°–50° C (104°–122° F). Most other species in similar environments tend to reduce water loss and photosynthesis. Further experiments showed that carbon dioxide uptake by *T. oblongifolia* at 20° C (68° F) was only 25–30% of that at 45° C (113° F). The thermal endurance of the plant was linked to the biochemical processing of the carbon compounds via its C_4 dicarboxylic acid pathway, but its method of stabilizing enzymes normally denatured at temperatures far below 45° C remained unknown.

An extensive series of measurements on the microclimate and physical characteristics of fields of corn (*Zea mays*) led to the development of a computer model for simulating the soil/plant interface. The model was based on energy conservation, balancing that received from the sun against that dissipated through evaporation and transpiration (40–90%), heating of the air (10–60%), heating of the soil (5–10%), and photosynthesis (1–5%). The extreme changes in light and wind distribution and in leaf area that occur from the soil to the top of the plants could be predicted with some accuracy.

Two noteworthy experiments using the giant unicellular alga *Acetabularia* were reported during 1972. Soviet workers described the first successful reassembly of a plant cell after separating the nucleus, cytoplasm, and cell wall. The cytoplasm was first centrifuged out of the recipient stalks, donor cytoplasm was then injected, and the cell fragments tested for survival. Finally, isolated nuclei were injected into surviving stalks and the reassembled cells were followed through the reproductive phase. About 75% of cells survived but only about 15% made reproductive caps. Survival rates were drastically reduced if the stalk or cytoplasm was kept in the dark prior to surgery, or if the recipient stalk was stored after removal of its own cytoplasm.

In the second set of experiments, West German investigators noted that different species of *Acetabularia* showed different electrophoretic patterns of their insoluble chloroplast membrane protein, carried out interspecific nucleus implantation, and then followed the protein patterns of the hybrid cells. After about six weeks, all chloroplasts of the hybrids showed the electrophoretic patterns characteristic of the species that donated the nucleus. This result was somewhat surprising in view of some earlier (though circumstantial) evidence that these proteins might be coded for by chloroplast rather than nuclear material. It was still possible, however, that the implantation resulted only in a minor alteration to the chloroplast proteins. (C. L. F. WOODCOCK)

MARINE BIOLOGY

During 1972 there was a review on in situ marine biological studies carried out by conventional diving, remote monitoring, and saturation diving from underwater habitats. These included responses of fish to traps and nets, general behaviour of fish and other organisms, and the biology of coral reefs. Notable German work in the Red Sea applied ethological methods to make in situ studies of reef fishes, including *Siphamia,* which shelters among the spines of sea urchins. Model urchins with many spines were visually selected in preference to models with few or no spines. Other work showed how an inhibitory mucoprotein on the surface of anemone fishes on reefs permits them to avoid the effects of nematocyst discharge from the host tentacles.

Ecological studies considered the sandy subtidal sediments of the continental shelf. Oxygenated water and food is driven by surface wave action through these sediments, which are part of the earth's largest filter system. In 100,000 sq.km. (38,600 sq.mi.) of West Atlantic shelf the pump exchanges 1,300 cu.km. (45,909,000 cu.ft.) of water annually. Primary production studies showed that marine phytoplankton in Indian Ocean waters, as in fresh waters, normally liberate a substantial proportion of photosynthetic products into the sea. This may be up to 20% of the total carbon fixed and may play a significant role in energy transfer in the ecosystem. The seaweed zone off eastern Canada was shown to be most dense down to 20–30 m. (66–98 ft.), with intertidal seaweeds comprising less than 10% of the biomass in unit area. Estimated algal biomass over a whole bay was calculated as 1.38 kg. per sq.m. fresh weight, giving 912 kg-cal. per sq.m.

Off the northwest coast of Spain similar studies showed annual productivity of *Laminaria ochroleuca* and *Sacchoriza polyschides* to be 1.7 and 3.9 kg. per sq.m., respectively. Highest values occurred where current surge was high and wave action moderate, the value for *S. polyschides* being the highest reported for naturally occurring seaweeds. Energy budget calculations for *Sagitta elegans* in St. Margaret Bay, Nova Scotia, gave uptake values of 0.7–1.1% of the total energy produced by copepods. These were very low figures since *S. elegans* was reputedly the most important copepod predator in the area.

The extreme diversity of species in the deep sea had previously been argued to be the result of long-term stability of the environment, which permitted each deposit-feeding benthic species to occupy an increasingly narrow niche based on increasingly specialized feeding habits. Recent work claimed that many deep benthic species are generalized feeders and suggested that high diversity is achieved through predictable disturbance by the selective action of cropping species. This would reduce competitive exclusion in benthic forms and permit coexistence of many species sharing the same resources. Pollution studies on the polychaete *Nereis diversicolor* showed that copper-tolerant forms may survive where mining pollution occurs and that copper tolerance may be genetically controlled.

Behavioural studies on the midge *Clunio marinus,* which lays its eggs low on the shore, showed that emergence times are correlated with the occurrence of low tide at a particular time of day. Emergence and development, therefore, are controlled by a physiological "clock" of semilunar periodicity. Other behavioural studies suggested that oysters maintain their populations in the James River off Chesapeake Bay on the Virginia coast, where they might be expected to show net loss from the estuary, because the pelagic larvae swim up on the flooding tide, probably in response to increased salinity, and remain on the bottom during ebb. The supposedly neotenous pelagic bivalve *Planktomya henseni* was shown never to exhibit breeding characteristics. It is probably the larva of a Leptonacean, but the link between the larva and an adult could not be established without further research.

A second specimen of *Stygiomedusa fabulosa,* a viviparous bathypelagic medusa, was found at 1,300 m. (4,264 ft.) in the Bay of Biscay, and a new species of Ascothoracic barnacle (*Weltneria hessleri*) was found unusually deep, at 1,000 m. (3,280 ft.), off Bermuda. A study of the Spirorbinae, a group of tube worms of some importance in ship fouling, demonstrated the evolutionary importance of their mode of egg incubation. Northern and Southern hemisphere forms brood eggs in the tube, but this method is less common in warmer seas where anoxia is perhaps a risk. In tropical seas opercular brooding predominates and presumably acts as a barrier contributing to the evolutionary divergence of the two forms.

Another study proposed convergent evolution of form and function in cephalopods and fishes caused by physical demands of marine environments and by dynamic interactions between the two groups from the Paleozoic, when each acquired locomotory methods permitting increase in size. Despite the fact that many sturgeons were well known to breed in freshwater but spend most of their lives in the sea, little was known of their physiology of salt and water balance. *Acipenser medirostris* and *A. transmontanus* on the Oregon coast were now shown to have slower salt regulation than other euryhaline teleosts. Reexamination of electrophoretic variations suggested that some previous genetic inferences concerning the possibility of two races of North Atlantic eel were statistically unjustified. Increased use of fish for culture and biological screening in relation to pollution prompted emphasis to be placed on developing a fish pathology and hematology.

Interesting historical investigations of skeletal material buried from rich herring catches in Bohuslän Province, Swed., between 1747 and 1809 indicated that the fish could not have been Norwegian winter herring but were probably another race of North Sea herring. This contradicted the hypothesis put forward on several occasions that when herrings were present in great numbers in the Bohuslän area they were absent from the west coast of Norway, and vice versa.

(ERNEST NAYLOR)

See also Oceanography.

MOLECULAR BIOLOGY

In 1970 H. M. Temin and D. Baltimore established independently that viral RNA can serve as a template for the production of DNA, and discovered the enzyme that catalyzes that flow of genetic information, a DNA polymerase now known as reverse transcriptase. Because most viruses known to cause cancer had an RNA core, work based on the discovery affected many disciplines, destroying the barriers that distinguished them. By 1972 the biophysicist and the geneticist could both insist that the same study belonged to the purview of each, stressing the new dimensions it added to the old definition of his discipline. Thus, the efforts of the past 20 years to establish molecular disciplines had to be abandoned.

COURTESY, AUSTRALIAN NEWS AND INFORMATION BUREAU

Artist has reconstructed amphibians (left) from footprints (above) that are 100 million years older than any previously discovered. The prints were found embedded in sandstone in eastern Victoria, Austr.

Biochemistry. The flowering in man's understanding of the intricacies of the chemical bases of life continued in 1972, as could be seen by considering the simple substance oxygen. Since the time of Louis Pasteur it was known that oxygen, at ambient concentrations, is toxic to certain organisms, called obligate anaerobes, while being essential for the survival of others. With the advent of hyperbaric chambers, it became apparent that oxygen, at concentrations higher than ambient, is toxic to all organisms. This exposed the fact that most living things that easily tolerate oxygen possess adequate defenses against its potential toxicity. Early attempts to explain the toxicity of oxygen revolved primarily around hydrogen peroxide, which is generated when oxygen accepts electrons and was known to be the product of a number of biological oxidations, and around the observation that the enzyme catalase, which converts hydrogen peroxide into water plus oxygen, is widely distributed among oxygen-tolerant organisms and missing from obligate anaerobes.

By 1972, however, it was established that hydrogen peroxide is only one of the aspects of oxygen toxicity. The univalent reduction of oxygen was shown to occur during a number of biological oxidation reactions and to result in the generation of a reactive free radical of oxygen called the superoxide anion. The superoxide radical, well known to radiation chemists but previously a stranger to biochemists, would be even more damaging to a living cell than would hydrogen peroxide and one would expect the existence of some defensive mechanism. A defense, in the form of an enzyme that catalyzes the conversion of the superoxide radicals into oxygen and hydrogen peroxide, was indeed discovered and called superoxide dismutase. It is present in all of the oxygen-utilizing organisms surveyed and absent in a dozen species of obligate anaerobes. It thus appeared likely that superoxide radical is an agent of the toxicity of oxygen and that superoxide dismutase is an important element in the defense against oxygen toxicity. Supporting this concept was the isolation of a mutant of an oxygen-tolerant microorganism (*Escherichia coli*) that possessed a defective superoxide dismutase and had a concomitant defect in its ability to tolerate oxygen.

Superoxide dismutase had been studied for over 30 years and described as a "cuprein" on the basis of its copper content and visible colour by numerous scientists unaware of its catalytic capability. It was not until it was isolated independently from red blood cells on the basis of its catalytic activity that its identity as a "cuprein" was appreciated. In the cytosol of eukaryotic (nucleated) cells superoxide dismutase contains copper and zinc and is blue-green in colour.

When superoxide dismutase from bacteria that grow in air was isolated, it proved to be a strikingly different reddish protein containing manganese in place of copper and zinc and having a molecular weight, amino acid composition, and stability unrelated to those of the previously studied eukaryotic enzyme. The catalytic properties of these two enzymes are, however, very similar. It appeared likely that both enzymes were evolved independently by the progenitors of present-day eukaryotes and prokaryotes in response to the threat of atmospheric oxygen.

Aerobic eukaryotes contain intracellular organelles, the mitochondria, which are primarily concerned with oxidative reactions that generate a large fraction of the cell's energy. Mitochondria contain DNA and the machinery for synthesizing a limited number of proteins strikingly similar to their counterparts in bacteria and at the same time very different from those in the rest of the eukaryotic cell. These facts support the theory that mitochondria originated as prokaryotes that entered into an endocellular symbiotic relationship with a protoeukaryote. The study of superoxide dismutase provided unexpected reinforcement for this theory when the enzyme isolated from liver mitochondria was found to be a reddish protein containing manganese and totally unlike the blue-green enzyme isolated from liver cytosol.

In another development promising important future findings, R. T. Schimke and his co-workers at Stanford (Calif.) University used the specificity of the antigen-antibody reaction to show that polypeptide chains begin to fold into the native configuration while their biosynthesis is still in progress and while they are still associated with the messenger RNA and ribosomes that are carrying it out. Their results also permitted the isolation and identification of the polysome synthesizing a specific protein, that for ovalbumin, the predominant protein in the white of hen's eggs. Hen's oviduct was chosen for these studies because fully 60% of the protein it synthesizes during ovulation is ovalbumin, but the results were of general interest and importance because they showed it was possible to select from a complex mixture those polysomes engaged in the synthesis of a specific protein and to study the RNA message for that protein. (IRWIN FRIDOVICH)

Biophysics. Investigations of DNA replication in 1972 were most intensive in the associated area of infection and neoplastic transformation of mammalian cells by DNA and RNA viruses. Experimental difficulties were encountered because the process of virus replication is involved in the transmission of the RNA virion, but replication is not the same as neoplastic transformation. Nevertheless, rapid progress was made and it was hoped that the relationship of RNA viruses to human disease would soon be known.

Temin reported new experiments on the reversal of information flow in chick embryo cells and R. Gallo at the National Cancer Institute reported on similar experiments in normal human blood lymphocytes stimulated by phytohemagglutinin. Purified DNA polymerases from chick embryo cells or unstimulated lymphocytes, like all normal DNA polymerases, did not accept exogenous natural RNAs as templates, but transformed chick embryos and stimulated lymphocytes contained RNAase-sensitive DNA polymerases (reverse transcriptases) that synthesized RNA-DNA hybrid molecules from natural RNAs. Baltimore found that the polymerase activity of reverse transcriptase cannot be separated from its complementary action as a "hybridase" that attacks RNA-DNA hybrids. His results suggested that this is a novel DNA polymerase, since no known DNA polymerase associates with an RNAase. Baltimore and his group also showed, by measuring the densities of the product molecules at different times of synthesis, that reverse transcriptase from avian myeloblastosis requires a small RNA primer molecule to initiate synthesis of single-stranded DNA on the larger template RNA molecule.

One of the first properties noticed for reverse transcriptase was its lack of template specificity, unlike the usual fastidious enzymes for RNA replication in RNA bacteriophage. This knowledge made possible the synthesis of radioactively labeled DNAs complementary to specific messenger RNAs. Both Baltimore's group and that of Sol Spiegelman at Columbia University used reverse transcriptase from avian myeloblastosis virus to synthesize DNA complementary to globin messenger RNA obtained from rabbit or from human red blood cells. The reaction is very similar to that of normal DNA replication, requiring the same four deoxyribonucleoside triphosphates and suitable concentrations of magnesium ions. The process was expected to be eminently useful because it could produce probes for genes and gene products in normal cells.

Reverse transcription also seemed to occur in some normal cells, providing for gene amplification during differentiation. This involvement of reverse transcriptase was suggested by M. Crippa and G. P. Tocchini-Valentini of the Laboratory of Cell Biology, Rome, who found that gene amplification in *Xenopus* oocytes was inhibited by a derivative of rifamycin, which also inhibits the reverse transcriptase of tumour viruses.

The test for malignant transformation of cells was to put them into the living animal, which was later examined for the formation of tumours. This test was tedious and other possibilities were under study. For example, it was known that specific glycolipids in cell membranes are diminished in transformed cells; unfortunately the enzymatic step affected and the amount of glycolipids remaining apparently vary with different cell types. Nor is cell coat thickness a satisfactory indicator because it differs about as much in transformed as in untransformed cells. Some hope might come from the work of H. Rubin and his colleagues at the University of California, who showed that the mechanism that regulates the rate of uptake of the sugar 2-deoxyglucose is affected by transformation.

Working with the simian DNA virus SV40, J. E. Darnell and his group at Columbia found that the virus-specific RNAs isolated from the nuclei of transformed cells are much longer than a single transcript of one complete SV40 DNA molecule. By hybridizing the nuclear RNA both to pure SV40 DNA and to DNA obtained from untransformed cells, R. Wall and Darnell obtained evidence that these RNAs are not simply multiple copies of the SV40 genomes, but are transcripts of both viral and cell DNA. The question remained, however, where transcription of RNA begins, at a cellular promoter site or a site within the SV40 DNA?

A recent finding by C. R. Merril, M. R. Geier, and J. C. Petricciani of the National Institutes of Health, if confirmed, would augment and revise thinking on the processes of infection and integration of tumour viruses. Merril and his co-workers used genetically defective fibroblasts incapable of metabolizing the sugar galactose, and infected these cells with bacterial viruses that carried the appropriate genes to correct this deficiency. They found that these infected cells metabolized galactose, and in addition, that phage-specific RNA was produced by these cells and persisted at the same level for 40 days of culture. Although the phage gene might be preserved within mammalian cells by any of a variety of methods, these results indicated a much greater biochemical similarity between divergent species than had been previously supposed, with a greater potential for cross-contamination and for interference in normal genetic controls by exogenous genetic material.

(H. E. KUBITSCHEK)

Genetics. Temin's theory of reverse transcription blossomed into a potent concept not only for RNA tumour virology and the cancer problem, but also for molecular genetics. Advances made in 1972 indicated that reverse transcriptase activity may be involved in gene amplification. These included labeling DNA with the base analogue bromodeoxyuridine and examining the amplified gene products for base substitutions that this analogue is known to produce. None were found. Also, it was discovered that the drug rifampicin, a known inhibitor of RNA polymerase and also of reverse transcriptase, inhibits gene amplification. Together these results suggested that gene amplification could be mediated by reverse transcriptase: an RNA transcript of the ribosomal genes would be made, which in turn would serve as a template for reverse transcriptase to synthesize numerous DNA copies of the ribosomal genes.

During the year, two important reports supported Temin's original proposal that reverse transcriptase is necessary for establishing the RNA tumour virus in the DNA environment of the cell. In the first, Gallo and his co-workers studied the effects of three classes of derivatives of the drug rifamycin SV on two tumour viruses: Class A was shown to be a strong inhibitor for DNA-dependent RNA polymerase but a weak inhibitor of reverse transcriptase activity; Class B was found to be an intermediate inhibitor for both enzyme activities; Class C was found to be a weak inhibitor for the RNA polymerase reaction but a strong inhibitor for reverse transcriptase activity, both in vitro and in vivo. When vesicular stomatitis virus, a lytic, not an oncogenic, virus containing the RNA polymerase but not reverse transcriptase, was treated in the same way, the rifamycin derivative had no effect on the activity of this virus nor on the activity of the RNA polymerase enzyme.

In the second study, M. Hill and J. Hillova, at the Institute Gustave-Roussy, Villejuif, France, provided evidence that a double-stranded DNA copy of the RNA tumour virus persists in the transformed cells. DNA was extracted from rat cells transformed by a strain of Rous sarcoma virus and from hamster cells transformed by a temperature-sensitive mutant of this virus. The DNA was purified by centrifugation in a cesium chloride gradient. By exposing cultures of chick embryo fibroblasts to the DNAs they found that cells exposed only to intact DNA from transformed cells are themselves transformed and produce virus. They further showed that the viruses produced belong to the same antigenic subgroup as the original strains and that the temperature-sensitive mutation was maintained.

Another important development involving RNA tumour viruses and reverse transcriptase originated from an earlier report by D. Moore and co-workers at the Institute for Medical Research, Camden, N.J., that viruslike particles in human milk samples are similar in morphology to mouse mammary virus. Spiegelman further explored this relationship and found that the viruslike particles in human milk contained reverse transcriptase and a single-stranded RNA molecule with a sedimentation value of 70s. This molecule was found to be homologous in base sequence to mouse mammary tumour virus RNA. These results strongly favour the earlier suggestion that human mammary tumour is a virus disease.

The replicon model of F. Jacob (Pasteur Institute, Paris) and S. Brenner (Cambridge) proposed that DNA replicates as an entity that contains information to control its own replication. Temperature-sensitive mutants of bacteria had been obtained that are defective in initiating DNA replication at a high or nonpermissive temperature, where the mutation is phenotypically expressed. The vitality of the replicon model was again confirmed when it was shown that another cell duplicating unit could integrate into the temperature-sensitive replicon and direct replication of the complex at the nonpermissive temperature, a process called integrative suppression. Nishimura, Caro, Berg, and Hirota (Oak Ridge, University of Connecticut, and Pasteur Institute) demonstrated this effect by infecting the temperature-sensitive cells of *E. coli* with an F-factor, an autonomous replicon distinct from the chromosomal replicon. Lindhal and Hirota (Pasteur Institute) and Jacob (College of France) reported a similar effect when this temperature-sensitive mutant was infected with the phage P2, which is capable of replicating at the nonpermissive temperature.

It had been known for some time that DNA polymerases can continue replication but that to start it they need an oligonucleotide primer that pairs with the template to be copied. Researchers at Stanford found that rifampicin blocked conversion of single-strand DNA circles of phage M13 to the double-stranded form. Since chloramphenicol, a protein inhibitor, did not interfere with this conversion, it was concluded that rifampicin was not simply blocking subsequent protein synthesis off the RNA template. Continuing their work they found that RNA synthesis was necessary for conversion of the single-stranded DNA forms to the double-stranded form of the phage. In another study K. G. Lark of the University of Utah found that rifampicin will block DNA replication when it is added up to ten minutes before DNA synthesis is to start, again suggesting that RNA synthesis is necessary for starting DNA synthesis. In a revealing study, Sugino and Okazaki at Osaka University found that newly made DNA fragments are heavier in density than would be expected if they were composed of DNA alone. When these fragments are treated with alkali or ribonuclease, treatments that degrade RNA but not DNA, they show the characteristic density of single-stranded DNA. This was direct evidence that RNA precursors are attached to newly replicated DNA.

A further extension of ideas on organization of the chromosome in higher forms was presented by Cambridge's Francis Crick in his attempt to account for the seemingly excessive amount of DNA found in these chromosomes. He viewed the basic unit of the chromosome, the chromatid, as consisting of a single DNA molecule with alternating regions of denatured or globular DNA and paired, double-stranded DNA. The latter would be present in lesser amounts and serve to code for proteins; the former, unpaired regions do serve as recognition sites for regulatory molecules, such as DNA and proteins.

(JAMES C. COPELAND)

See also Medicine.

ZOOLOGY

Advances in the study of animal growth were reported in fishes, cockleshells, and coral. G. Pannella studied the growth banks in the otoliths of three species of bony fishes collected along the Atlantic coast of North America. Otoliths are inorganic concretions present in the inner ear and important in equilibrium and sound detection. Seasonal bands had long been known to be present, but Panella was able to conclude that daily bands can also be recognized under the microscope. He found two types of bands, fast-growing and slow-growing. Since there were approximately 360 such bands during each of the first three to four years of life, he concluded that each band was deposited in one day. In another study, J. W. Evans found that the only way he could adequately explain the smallest growth increments of cockleshells (*Clinocardium nuttalli*) was to conclude that growth stops during exposure of the animal at low tide. There was excellent correlation between the widths of the smallest detectable growth bands and the interval between low tides. Finally, studies by D. W. Knutson, R. W. Buddemeier, and S. V. Smith with coral in the reefs of atolls used for nuclear tests disclosed an additional aspect of growth rings. Bands rich in radioactivity had been laid down in the years in which nuclear tests had taken place but no radioactivity was detectable in the coral bands deposited during years in which tests had not occurred. The results supported the conclusion that the bands are laid down annually and are thus excellent indications of annual growth of the coral. All three studies also provided information bearing on the validity of techniques widely used to determine organ growth.

A number of fascinating structural or functional adaptations were reported. For example, Q. Bone found that the skin of a marine fish, *Ruvettus pretio-*

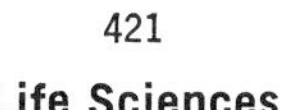

AUTHENTICATED NEWS INTERNATIONAL

The radio equipment on this penguin's back transmits data on the bird's cardiovascular adjustments during exercise to University of Washington scientists studying the blood chemistry and circulation of Antarctic birds and their possible relevance to human heart disease.

sus, has important structural characteristics that aid in swimming. This bottom fish's sharp ctenoid scales, resulting in its name of "scour fish," constitute an elaborate girder system, holding subdermal spaces connected to the surface by pores. The spaces are normally filled with sea water, which is expelled when the fish swims, imparting momentum. Buoyancy is increased by the presence of large amounts of oil in the tissues, not unique to this fish. Although the exact habits of the fish are unknown, it was concluded that its relatively anterior centre of buoyancy permits it to rest near the bottom and seize small fishes from below. J. N. Layne described a situation of tail "autotomy" (hitherto known mainly in reptiles and amphibians) in the Florida mouse, *Peromyscus floridanus*. He found that the absence of fibres in the dermis of the skin of the distal portion of the tail produces a zone of weak anchorage of the skin to the vertebrae and the tail breaks easily when it is seized and slips off the vertebrae. The situation could not be regarded as true autotomy, as in lizards where there is a voluntary loss of part of the tail. It was concluded that this ability, limited to the Florida mouse, evolved as an antipredator device.

The role of panting in temperature regulation by desert lizards was the subject of a report by E. C. Crawford, Jr., who worked with the chuckawalla, *Sauromalus obesus*. He fitted thermocouples to both brain and cloaca, cooled the lizards to 15° C (59° F), and then transferred them to a 45° C (113° F) incubator. Panting began at a brain temperature of 39° C and resulted in the brain maintaining a temperature about 3° C below the ambient temperature, whereas the deep body temperature (cloacal) was only about 1° C below ambient. Thus he demonstrated that panting affects the brain more than the body as a whole, and that panting does play some role in keeping the brain slightly below the environmental temperature, which may be of importance for desert life.

Water balance regulation in amphibians was the subject of an important report by V. H. Shoemaker and others, who studied an Argentine frog, *Phyllomedusa sauvagii*, which dwells in semiarid regions and must conserve water. They found that this frog excretes uric acid in the form of a semisolid product, thereby avoiding the loss of large amounts of water in the urine usual for amphibians. This report, plus earlier work on this and another species, showed that previous concepts that adult frogs excrete only urea had to be revised.

Freezing resistance in polar fishes was further explained by work of A. R. Hargens who showed that these fishes have much higher plasma protein concentrations than other polar animals. Earlier work had shown that serum glycoproteins, which contain carbohydrate, may be the active agents inhibiting ice crystal growth in Antarctic fishes.

Among the interesting findings in the field of animal communication was a study by C. D. Hopkins on the production and perception of electrical discharges in electric fish in Guyana. In one species, *Sternopygus macrurus*, he found the first known case of significant differences between the sexes in electric organ discharge. He also found that males modify their electrical discharges by "rises" and "interruptions" in the presence of females. F. H. Pough found in tests of six species of salamanders that one, the Eastern red-spotted newt (*Notophthalmus viridescens*), emitted secretions that are toxic to leeches. He concluded that the newt's skin glands must secrete something responsible for driving off the leeches, and that this protection evolved because the adults of this species have a longer aquatic period than the adults of nonresistant species.

Description of new animals continued to be an important part of zoology. R. R. Hessler and co-workers discovered a giant amphipod at a depth of 5,304 m. (17,397 ft.) in the eastern North Pacific Ocean. Amphipods are crustaceans with usually a laterally compressed body. The new animal was 11 in. (28.2 cm.) long, twice as long as the largest previously known amphipod. It was discovered in photographs taken by a deep-sea camera above a bait can on the sea bottom. It was probably a member of the family

Lysianassidae and appeared to be a versatile omnivore and scavenger, spending most of its time on the bottom, but occasionally swimming up to the lighted (photic) zone. (RONALD R. NOVALES)

Entomology. At the 14th International Congress of Entomology, held in Canberra, Austr., in August 1972, a major recurrent theme was the need to protect man's hard-pressed resources against attack by insects, mites, and ticks, but without adding to the burden of global pollution. In the keynote address, E. F. Knipling of the U.S. Department of Agriculture stressed the need to apply many approaches to insect control, separately or in combination, according to circumstances; A. W. A. Brown of the World Health Organization pointed out that the number of species known to be resistant to pesticides had risen 10% to 250 since the previous congress in 1970; and speakers such as S. Prahan of New Delhi, India, drew attention to large numbers of natural enemies of pests that had proved more vulnerable to insecticides than the pests themselves—with the result that many pests had become more serious since the organic insecticides had been introduced. Hopeful progress in new methods of control, was, however, described by many speakers.

G. B. Staal of the Zoecon Corp. in California discussed synthetic compounds that mimic the growth-regulating hormones of insects. Such compounds could be used as contact insecticides; they interfered with embryonic, juvenile, or adult development, or with fecundity; some were as active as the insecticides currently in use, were biodegradable, highly selective, and of negligible toxicity to nontarget organisms. J. P. Tette, also of Zoecon, spoke of the use of synthetic pheromones—volatile chemicals that serve as behaviour signals to insects—to confuse or trap pest species. In one area, continuous release of sex attractant of the cabbage looper moth had resulted in the habituation of the males to this stimulus so that they were then unable to find and mate with the females; a formulation that was even more attractive than the natural female attractant of the red-banded leaf roller had been used to trap so many males that the species had ceased to be an economic pest.

It was pointed out that optimum control was not necessarily maximum control, especially where genetic control was attempted. H. Laven of Johannes Gutenberg University, Mainz, W.Ger., described an experiment carried out with J. Cousserans and G. Guille of Montpellier University, France, in which the mosquito *Culex pipiens* was successfully controlled by releasing males that carried a chromosome translocation. This caused 50% sterility in offspring into a local population, which then greatly declined. As long as carriers remained, the reduced productivity of the species kept the population at tolerable levels.

B. Hölldobler of the Zoologisches Institut, Frankfurt am Main, W.Ger., described recent work on communication among ants. Scouts of *Camponotus socius* used a "waggle" display, reminiscent of the waggle dance of bees, which excited their nest mates to follow a pheromone trail laid down by the scouts. Hölldobler also pointed out that one pheromone in a harvester ant could act as a recruitment and following substance at low concentration but as an alarm pheromone at high concentration. J. A. A. Renwick of the Boyce Thompson Institute for Plant Research, Inc., Yonkers, N.Y., explained how different species of bark beetles had as aggregating pheromones mixtures of a number of common compounds, but with proportional differences that accounted for species integrity.

H. Maldonado and J. C. Barros-Pita of the Instituto Venezolano de Investigaciones Científicas, Caracas, Venez., described research into the learning patterns of a praying mantis. The insect could be trained not to strike at a moving object, and could be habituated to cinematographic projections of moving birds so that defensive behaviour was no longer elicited. Both kinds of learning improved as trials were repeated, provided the trials were separated by sufficient time during which a change of protein content of the brain could be shown to have taken place.

P. S. Callahan of the U.S. Department of Agriculture pointed out that insects were sensitive to infrared radiation and that the construction of the cuticle of insects allowed it to act as a solid-state transducer able to convert infrared radiation into electric signals. He suggested that sensilla were able to act as piezoelectric transducers (responding to bending) or thermoelectric transducers (responding to changes in temperature). The scanning electron microscope revealed that insects appeared to have dielectric array antennae, capable of selecting infrared signals directionally. It was also possible that some chemical senses, especially regarding very low concentrations of molecules such as sex attractants, were the result of sensitivity to the characteristic resonant frequencies of the molecules in the infrared spectrum, since this would account for both the fine structure of the sensilla and the speed of reaction of the insect to such stimuli.

D. Norris of the University of Wisconsin described a remarkable relationship between the bark beetle *Xyloborus* and a symbiotic bacterium. The beetles breed by producing fertilized, diploid females and parthenogenetic, haploid males. The stimulus to the nucleus of an egg to begin developing parthenogenetically is provided by the bacteria; if they are totally excluded from the insect and its diet, no males are produced.

K. Schurr of Bowling Green (O.) State University pointed out that a properly designed sewerage lagoon system produces quantities of filamentous algae and water plants, together with an associated fauna, much of it insectan. Harvesting and recycling this biomass provided a particularly nutritious supplement to animal feed and improved the function of the sewerage system. (PETER W. MILES)

Ornithology. In a fascinating paper, C. H. Fry discussed "cooperative breeding" in a colony of red-throated bee-eaters on the northern savannas of Nigeria. Adult birds of both sexes and all ages (but particularly one-year-old males) helped breeding pairs with the excavation of the nest, with incubation, and by collecting food for the nestlings. There could be up to three helpers at each nest. The pairs themselves mated for life, and the bonds formed between the breeding pair and their helpers could last from one season to the next.

By aqualunging below the Antarctic ice at Cape Crozier, ornithologists studied the diving behaviour of emperor penguins. Previously the greatest depth ever recorded for a bird was 60 m. (197 ft.) by a common loon. Emperors were recorded as deep as 265 m. (869 ft.), and one stayed submerged for more than 18 minutes.

In the first detailed report on the white-throated rail, the last of the "flightless" birds of the western Indian Ocean (a group of species that formerly included the dodo), M. J. Penny and A. W. Diamond estimated 1,000 birds on Middle Island of the Aldabra atoll, and additional birds on smaller islands in the north of the atoll. They were conspicuously absent from Grande Terre Island where there were feral cats.

A detailed study of wood pigeons (not street pigeons, but the species that in the country is so shy) in central London by Stanley Cramp showed that the town birds have a much longer nesting season than their country cousins. Also, they were much more successful in rearing their young to the fledgling stage due to the scarcity of enemies in inner London, particularly egg-thieves. The London birds were at an advantage because bread was in ample supply.

A proposal to flood the main breeding ground of the pink-footed goose in central Iceland demanded an up-to-date assessment of its importance. This one small area held approximately 75% of the entire Greenland/Iceland population—the one that wintered in Britain. If the area were flooded to the designed level, over eight nests in ten would be lost and the vegetated area remaining could not provide sufficient food to raise more than a small proportion of the goslings.

The black swan of Australia and New Zealand, though widespread and abundant, was only beginning to receive intensive study. The populations moved from summer-molting refuges and feeding grounds in lakes and estuaries to less permanent swamps where they bred, mainly in winter. Nesting success, however, was very dependent on the availability of food during the breeding season. The social behaviour of the species was unusual for a swan in that the pair-bond between male and female was weak.

Calculations from fossil material indicated that *Archaeopteryx* was poorly adapted for landing on the ground, flew poorly, and was incapable of hovering. The probable body weight of the bird was still in dispute, but may have been 200–250 grams by analogy with living arboreal birds of similar wingspan.

Man and Birds by R. K. Murton (1971) was a very useful and stimulating digest of the biology of those birds that could be considered pests. The various species were dealt with under broad habitat headings: the rook under farmland, the bullfinch under horticulture, the oyster catcher under fisheries, and so on. Many species pose real problems but ornithologists need to know much more of their ecology before they can make well-based practical decisions. Books published in 1972 included an important new field guide covering the birds of the western Palaearctic (Europe, North Africa, and the Middle East) by H. Heinzel, R. S. R. Fitter, and John Parslow. C. W. Mackworth-Praed and C. H. B. Grant completed their *African Handbook of Birds,* which in six volumes published over 20 years was one of the most monumental avifaunas in the history of ornithology; *Birds of West Central and Central Africa* revealed the same detail and synthesis of fact that readers had come to expect from earlier volumes. R. E. Moreau's *Palearctic-African Bird Migration Systems* concerned the movements of Eurasian species into Africa from Greenland to the Bering Strait and from the Mediterranean to Arctic Siberia. Changes in the ecology since the last glaciation were outlined, as were the circumstances and dangers of the migrants' journeys. The author's guess at the number of birds involved was 5,000,000,000 land birds. (JEFFERY BOSWALL)

ENCYCLOPÆDIA BRITANNICA FILMS. *Chromosomes of Man* (1967); *Life Story of a Social Insect: The Ant* (1967); *Looking at Mammals* (1967); *Monarch Butterfly Story* (2nd ed., 1967); *Photosynthesis* (2nd ed., 1967); *Water for Living Things* (1967); *Insect Parasitism—The Alder Woodwasp and Its Enemies* (1968); *The Ears and Hearing* (2nd ed., 1969); *Muscle: Chemistry of Contraction* (1969); *Muscle: Dynamics of Contraction* (1969); *Muscle: Electrical Activity of Contraction* (1969); *The Origin of Life—Chemical Evolution* (1969); *Radioisotopes: Tools of Discovery* (1969); *Theories on the Origin of Life* (1969); *Succession on Lava* (1970); *The Nerve Impulse* (1971); *Seed Dispersal* (3rd ed., 1971); *Investigating Hibernation* (1972); *A Bird of Prey: The Red Tailed Hawk* (1972).

Literature

The 1972 Nobel Prize for Literature was awarded to the West German novelist, playwright, and short-story writer Heinrich Böll, who was cited for his contribution to "a renewal of German literature" following World War II. (*See* NOBEL PRIZES.)

AMERICAN

Fiction. American fiction in 1972 was marked by considerable quantity and less than considerable quality. As always, the commercial markets were well supplied by productions of those authors whose names seemed ubiquitous on the best-seller lists. Harold Robbins at least changed his strategies a bit in *The Betsy* (published December 1971), a lengthy chronicle of the life and loves of (of all things) an automobile. While on the surface this might have appeared to be Robbins' bid for serious consideration, it turned out to be just another in the long line of sex and sensation books that had made him one of the wealthiest writers of the century. Michael Crichton added to his earnings from *The Andromeda Strain* with *The Terminal Man,* a story of space-age electronic brain control, and, although he did not make the best-seller lists, the indefatigable Frank Yerby added to his previous 24 novels *The Girl from Storyville,* a heavily sex-laden tale about the life of a prostitute in the 19th-century brothel district of New Orleans. John O'Hara returned, posthumously, with *The Ewings,* a long and tedious examination of family wealth and decay set in the Midwestern United States of World War I.

The year did, however, see some works of excellence published, and perhaps even a few of real brilliance. Moreover, some new names appeared that would bear close watching in the future. And there seemed to be some signs that American fiction of the 1970s might move in some directions noticeably different from the eclectic experimentation that characterized so much of it in the previous decade. In the best of the year's work there was a strong sense of convention, of attention to form and precision of style, and, in the broadest range of the term, to history.

Easily the finest of the year's work dealing overtly and consciously with the expansion and contraction of time was Eudora Welty's *The Optimist's Daughter.* In part, it was what one had come to expect from Miss Welty: a clear yet flexible style, sensitivity to human values, and great feeling for place. But in tracing the effects on Laurel Hand of the death of her father and her confrontation, in his dying days, with his second wife, Miss Welty pursued her examination of the conflict between the privileged graces of the old order and the rough energies of the new further and with more precision than in any of her previous books. Long regarded as a major Southern writer, Miss Welty showed once and for all that she was in fact a writer of subtle yet significant regional distinctions. But most importantly, Miss Welty never equivocates, never backs off from the problem posed by conflict between opposing attitudes toward life that are both

Liquors, Alcoholic: *see* Alcoholic Beverages

COURTESY, HARPER & ROW

Roger Kahn's book about the old Brooklyn Dodgers, "The Boys of Summer," was published in 1972.

appealing and distasteful in nearly equal portions. *The Optimist's Daughter* alone would suffice to place Eudora Welty among the major American novelists of the 20th century.

A concern for place, an eye for the simple yet revealing detail, and an unerring ability to arrest a character at that moment of transition between something passing and something yet to be born were all found also in the work of Larry McMurtry, particularly in his spare, almost bleak first two novels, *Horseman, Pass By* and *The Last Picture Show.* But, with the publication of his fourth novel, he showed himself to be a brilliant creator of intense and highly personal fiction. In *All My Friends Are Going to be Strangers,* we follow the author-surrogate, Danny Deck, as he moves from Texas to California and back to Texas, through a brief marriage and a fitful affair as he struggles to accommodate himself to the growing realization that the desolate images of the Southwestern landscape are, in fact, reflections of a desolation of purpose within himself.

Just as Welty and McMurtry kept their eyes hard on certain aspects of American realism, so Philip Roth and Ishmael Reed were receptive to the mythic and fantastic dimensions of the contemporary American experience. Roth's *The Breast* and Reed's *Mumbo Jumbo,* though vastly different in manner, both celebrated the human condition by placing experience in a realm at once grotesque yet believable.

After the frequent pretensions and allegorical posturings of *Portnoy's Complaint,* Roth's slim tale of a professor of comparative literature who, through an " 'endocrinopathic catastrophe,' and/or 'a hermaphroditic explosion of chromosomes,' " becomes an enormous female breast appears as a taut and compelling fictional tour de force. David Kepesh's condition is clearly impossible; but he comes, after his various crises, to affirm the essential urge to partake of life in whatever ways are left him (and there are only a few, all grotesque). Ultimately, Kepesh's condition and his telling about it bring to mind not only Swift, Gogol, and Kafka but all those writers who understood the difference between reality and fiction and showed, by inventing fictions, that reality is our daily bread and what sustains us in the end.

Ishmael Reed's third novel, *Mumbo Jumbo,* would also plead for a place of eminence among the year's work. His first two novels, *The Free-Lance Pallbearers* and *Yellow Back Radio Broke-Down,* showed Reed's connections with the leading black humorists yet indicated he had a new ingredient to offer. *Mumbo Jumbo* brought that ingredient, a rich and complex private mythology, to the fore and the mixture (of black humour and classical allusion) was what made this novel so singular an experience. *Mumbo Jumbo* has an incredible plot that defies summary, and a richness of verbal style that resists comparative analysis. The narrative, carried on by several narrators, takes place in the 1920s when an epidemic of a disease called "Jes Grew" has broken out. A black hero-figure of complex mythic origins emerges to rescue his people from the disease. The book would certainly, in time, locate Reed at the forefront of black American writers.

Of the many first novels published during the year, one stood out as marking the start of what was sure to be an important career for its young author. *Three Wogs,* by Alexander Theroux, treats contemporary English prejudice as it operated, in turn, on a Chinese, an Indian, and a black. Three separate narratives were brilliantly joined by a style that contained the richest word-hoard of any American writer in some years. Comparisons would be made with Joyce, but they would be gratuitous, for Theroux has a voice of his own.

Harry Crews added another to his growing list of distinguished novels with an incredible little satire about a man who eats a car (Ford Maverick) as a public performance. *Car* carried to its absurd conclusion the unnatural U.S. obsession with the machine. Crews's art was at its best here and though the narrative fell down limply at the end, there was enough else in this little novel to warrant naming it the best of Crews's five novels to date.

Among a number, one excellent "feminist" novel deserved note. Cynthia Buchanan's *Maiden* related the sometimes grim, sometimes riotous experiences of Fortune Dundy as she, at age 30, struggles to overcome her virginal state by joining a Los Angeles swinging singles club. Both the style and the subject called up a comparison with Joan Didion's *Play It as It Lays* and Sylvia Plath's *The Bell Jar,* but Buchanan's command of narrative directness and her strong sense of story made this the premier novel of that fortuitous trilogy. Buchanan's satire was both sharp and better placed for her adherence to a conventional narrative structure than either Didion's or Plath's.

Other novels of note published during the year included the second ventures of Mike Mewshaw, whose *Waking Slow* was a sensitive treatment of the search for maturity of a young GI recently back from Vietnam, and of John Seelye, whose *The Kid* used the sound and sense of his earlier version of Huckleberry Finn to provide a memorable satire on things Western and American in the late 19th century. D. Keith Mano added to his youthful yet impressive work with *The Proselytizer* and Brock Brower revived his name, fleetingly yet hauntingly remembered from *Debris,* with *The Late Great Creature.* And a writer who should have reaped considerable success (but did not) from his first work appeared with a novel that could easily be placed alongside those treated above at some length. In *End Zone,* Don DeLillo homed in on a small Southwestern college where football was equated with war, war seen as a native-soil substitute for the one the U.S. was presently engaged in, and in the process commented shrewdly and excitingly on the thin vagaries of a peoples' propensity for violence.

Also deserving mention were a collection of short stories by Joyce Carol Oates, *Marriages and Infidelities,* and a fine novel of the Vietnam war, *The Lionheads,* by Josiah Bunting. (HARRY T. ANTRIM)

History, Biography, and Belles Lettres. The late Bill Lawrence of the *New York Times* and ABC News could never be faulted for lack of candour. His posthumously published memoirs, *Six Presidents, Too Many Wars,* presents vintage Lawrence from his first major assignment to cover the General Motors strike of 1936–37 to the administrations of Roosevelt through Nixon, with interspersed commentaries on stints in the Soviet Union, Korea, and elsewhere. What one relished in a book like this was flavour more than fact. Lawrence, for instance, corroborates Arthur Krock's anecdote that Averell Harriman contributed equally to the campaigns of Roosevelt and Willkie, just in case. He further describes the hodgepodge of the sincere and the absurd in the Henry Wallace foray for the presidency. He admits how grossly he (and others) underestimated both the vote-getting prowess and occasional statesmanship of Harry Truman. He dwells on the indecisiveness that cost Adlai Stevenson the chance to be appointed Kennedy's secretary of state. He underlines Eisenhower's general contempt for politicians and his particular disdain for Joseph McCarthy but he adds that Eisenhower was saved from being overpowered by McCarthy because McCarthy's hubris led him to his own undoing.

Lawrence's chapters on Kennedy are the best examples of presidential portraiture in the book, perhaps because Lawrence knew Kennedy long before Kennedy became president. Lawrence reveals his genuine affection for Kennedy's ability and wit, and provides numerous examples of Kennedy's propensity to leak news to Lawrence simply because he knew that Lawrence would be judicious about revealing it. But Lawrence's dislike for Richard Nixon and his estimate of him as an opportunist and political climber are tacit behind the coolness of his prose on the Nixon years. How Lawrence maintained his contacts in Washington at the highest levels without becoming anyone's crony remained a tribute to the man's personal independence.

O Jerusalem! was a sequel by Larry Collins and Dominique LaPierre to their deservedly successful *Is Paris Burning?* and *Or I'll Dress You in Mourning.* The subject of the new book is the war between Arabs and Zionists before and after the partition of Palestine in the late 1940s. The authors are hard-pressed to find one leader among the Arabs who acted with real patriotism, except Abdul Khader Husseini; otherwise the Arabs suffered from mutual suspicion, conflicting ambitions, and an inability to subordinate ego and self-interest to necessity. The Zionists, on the contrary, concentrated on organization, singleness of purpose, and the relentless pursuit of arms by purchase, bribery, coercion, subterfuge, and other tactics that, according to the authors, were prefigured by pressures in the United Nations to create a Jewish state in the first place. The one myth that was forever laid to rest in *O Jerusalem!* is that the Palestinians were urged by the Zionists to remain rather than abandon their homes when hostilities began.

A good sequel to *O Jerusalem!* was Georgie Anne Geyer's *The New 100 Years War.* In the heap of polemics, propaganda, and travel literature about the Middle East, it has been difficult in the U.S. to find evenhanded reportage. The strength of Geyer's chapters was that she was (amazingly) not prejudiced for or against either side. Proceeding existentially, she ticks off Arab faults and with equal candour notes how the Israelis exploited these vulnerabilities to their own advantage and justification. Two things raised Geyer's book out of the ordinary among books on the Middle East. The first was that she was not unaware of what desperation can do to a population such as the Palestinians over a period of time, and the second was that she saw how the politics and verve of the third world were the real forces to reckon with in the Middle East. For her the rest was mythology.

Unlike *Days of Life and Death and Escape to the Moon,* William Saroyan's *Places Where I've Done Time* did not make his personal past significant to anyone else's personal present but simply opted for reminiscence. They were readable reminiscences, to be sure, but they were ultimately too private to be memorable. Saroyan's prose style kept the narrative alive, but the effect was not unlike what a person feels after he has read a newspaper. When you're finished, you're finished. Compared with Saroyan's journalese, Janet Flanner's *Paris Was Yesterday* and Wendell Berry's *A Continuous Harmony* showed what good writing on solid subjects can be. One came away from both of these books with increased respect for how the American language can be written.

More notable belles lettres included *New Directions 24* (including poems by Pagliarani, James Purdy, and an interesting young American named Daniel Halpern, as well as a good short story by Yumiko Kurahashi); Daniel Hoffman's *Poe Poe Poe Poe Poe Poe Poe,* good critical prose by a man whose talent as a poet is matched by his critical sensibility; Stephen Birmingham's *The Late John Marquand;* Mike Weaver's *William Carlos Williams: The American Background,* which contained excerpts from Thomas Ward's *Passaic,* a poem of the 19th century that "forms an interesting comparison with the general organization of Williams' *Paterson*"; and Thomas R. Edwards' *Imagination and Power: A Study of Poetry on Public Themes.*

Turning to pure Americana, what made Roger Kahn's *The Boys of Summer* not merely interesting but interesting as literature was that it transcended baseball without ever denying or falsifying it. The subject was the Brooklyn Dodgers of the early 1950s as

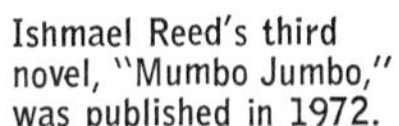
Ishmael Reed's third novel, "Mumbo Jumbo," was published in 1972.

CARLA REED

Alexander Theroux published "Three Wogs" in 1972.

followed by the then young Kahn and seen again almost 20 years later as he sought out, position by position, the team in its diaspora. The book was not merely reportage or memoir but a testimony to things past as present and things present as past.

Poetry. Why John Berryman titled his last book *Delusions, Etc.* was difficult to explain. Some of his most touching and lucid poems were here, and they assumed a deeper lucidity against the background of his suicide and the fact that *Delusions, Etc.* was a posthumous volume. The poems of spiritual anguish that concluded Berryman's previous *Love & Fame* were in full flower in the new book, and the pith of the lines was just as rich: "Surely their spiritual life is not what it might be?/Surely they are half-full of it?/Tell them to leave me damned well alone with my insights." There are superb elegies to Beethoven and Dylan Thomas as well as a poignant lyric entitled "He Resigns."

If the test of poetry is that it remains always capable of transcending the present, Louis Simpson's *Adventures of the Letter I* contained two poems that met that challenge justly. There were other good poems in this first book of Simpson's since his *Selected Poems* appeared some years back, but "American Dreams" and "Doubting" were outstanding.

Ned O'Gorman's new book, *The Flag the Hawk Flies,* was really a repetition of his earlier books. The religious imagery and orientation were tuned up a degree or two but the poems were weakened rather than strengthened by that. In the itemized imagery of "Color" and "Ten Poems of a Misanthrope" the result was simply prolixity. Even though there were better poems, like "The Drunken Organ Repairman" and "A Philosophy" in this book, the entire corpus reminded one of Robert Penn Warren's axiom that the purer the poetry, the greater the risk of mediocrity. These poems were close to that kind of purity.

Philip Levine's *They Feed They Lion* was too often a West Coast reincarnation of East Coast provincialism; the good poems were constantly striving to overcome the tendency. Not so the poems in Stephen Dobyns' *Concurring Beasts.* Here was a natural and undiluted talent; Dobyns' prose poems were reminiscent of Baudelaire's *Spleen* but with an American accent.

David Wagoner's selections from Theodore Roethke's notebooks in *Straw for the Fire* were quite possibly the cream of Roethke's talent. Not since Winfield Townley Scott's *A Dirty Hand* had there been such an unignorable book. Not only were there the germinal images that did or did not evolve into poems but there were pungent prose entries that were a feast in themselves: "The flower's by-its-selfness"; "If I feel good, I can't think"; "Those Catholic pictures always scared the living Jesus out of me."

New books by younger poets included James Tate's *Absences* and Mary Oliver's *The River Styx, Ohio, and Other Poems.* Tate's talent was undoubtedly true, but the charm of the poems evaporated with rereadings. Mary Oliver's poems, on the other hand, not only passed the rereading test but invited it. There was no turgidity, no sense of inspissation, no false feeling. She took Philip Booth's advice and found Eden in her own backyard.

Of all the books published in 1972, Archibald MacLeish's *The Human Season: Selected Poems, 1926–1972* was an event by itself. MacLeish's critical sensibility permitted him to select the very cream of his work from almost a 50-year period for this single volume. There was not a weak page in the book.

(SAMUEL HAZO)

CANADIAN

English Language. There was a significant change in English Canadian literature in 1972, with many plays by new dramatists. *A Collection of Canadian Plays* included Stewart Boston's *Counsellor Extraordinary,* which examines the careers of Francis Bacon and his master, the earl of Essex. *Wu-feng,* by Munro Scott, dealt with a legendary Formosan folk hero. *Love Mouse* and *Meyer's Room,* by Sheldon Rosen, were both witty fantasies. Michael Cook's *Colour the Flesh the Colour of Dust* describes a moving experience set in the early days of Newfoundland. *Exit Muttering,* by Donald Jack, mirrored a humorous marital situation. *Creeps,* by David Freeman, was a witty and compassionate study of cerebral palsy victims living in a shelter workshop.

Canadian poetry was characteristically personal. George Johnston's *Happy Enough: Poems 1935–1972* was a compilation based on *The Cruising Auk* (1959) and *Home Free* (1966), along with 32 new poems. Johnston's sly humour and deft characterization distinguished his observations on man and nature. *Lies,* by John Newlove, were personal, peaceful poems that demonstrated his maturity. Gwendolyn MacEwen's book of new poems, *The Armies of the Moon,* expressed the war within the individual, with a wide variety of metaphors. *The Best Name of Silence,* by David Helwig, was his first book of poetry in three years. It was mature, sensitive, and richer than his earlier poems. In *The Energy of Slaves,* Leonard Cohen revealed himself as a continuing writer of intense and powerful poems. *Four Parts Sand* was a selection of recent works of four leading concrete poets, each introducing his own work—alphabeings by Earle Birney, poemdrawings by Judith Copithorne and Andrew Suknaski, and typescapes by Bill Bissett.

The Narrative Voice: Short Stories and Reflections by Canadian Authors, edited by John Metcalfe, provided an orientation to present-day Canadian short-story writing and essays. It included the work of established writers as well as of two newcomers, Clarke Blaise and Shirley Faessler.

By dedicating *Norman* to ". . . the strangers in

Kanada," Gwendolyn MacEwen established the thread that was to run through her first book of stories. Imaginative and bizarre, with a quality of timelessness, her tales explore myth and reality in Canada's past and present. Jacques Ferron's *Tales from the Uncertain Country* employed fables, legends, and myths in striking fashion to deal with his wide range of characters. *Pandora,* by Sylvia Fraser, portrayed childhood as a time of both beauty and love, as well as of confusion, pain, and hatred, through the eyes of her seven-year old heroine, Pandora Gothic. Margaret Atwood's work *Surfacing* portrayed a powerful, frightening, and lonely journey inward, surfacing through childhood memories and present relationships, teetering on madness as the author dealt with all the brutalities inflicted on the main character, a young woman in search of her past. John Metcalf, in *Going Down Slow,* presented clear-cut characters, sharp, fast-paced prose, and realistically defined settings in his novel about David Appleby, a teacher, who battles the educational establishment. In *The Manticore* Robertson Davies continued his descriptions of his favourite characters as they struggle to find themselves.

Mike: Memoirs, Vol. 1, 1897–1948 of Lester B. Pearson recorded the formative years of the man who became prime minister and a Nobel Peace Prize winner (*see* OBITUARIES). James M. Minifie, distinguished political commentator, recorded in *Homesteader* his family's pioneer days in Saskatchewan, where the bankers were remorseless. *The Girls,* by Rebecca Sisler, described the achievements and personal life-styles of Frances Loring and Florence Wyle, whose sculpture studio was a focus for art activities in Toronto from 1913 to 1968. Combining historical and political interest, in *Letters to Limbo* Sir Robert L. Borden, prime minister of Canada from 1911 to 1920, gave some of his views on events during the latter years of his life.

James Eayrs's most recent work, *In Defence of Canada, Peacemaking and Deterrence,* was a history of Canada's defense and foreign policy from the closing years of World War II to 1950. With critical, careful judgment, he wrote in a scholarly, witty, and very readable style. Donald Creighton's *Towards the Discovery of Canada* was a collection of important essays by Canada's most widely known present-day historian.

In other works on political themes, Pierre Vallières, whose earlier work had been an emotional defense of violence and terrorism, displayed a new commitment to the parliamentary process and the Parti Québecois in his latest work, *Choose!,* and W. Blair Neatby's *The Politics of Chaos* explained how the economic depression in Canada caused the rise of new radical parties and their leaders. George Woodcock, in *The Rejection of Politics and Other Essays,* revealed his own development as one of Canada's chief literary critics and writers. James Woodford's description of Canada's northern resources policy in *The Violated Vision* combined criticism of industrial exploitation with suggestions for alternative action. In *A Whale for the Killing,* Farley Mowat channeled his anger at a Newfoundland village's sport into a powerful plea to preserve the species.

Canadian art from the 1930s was surveyed by Paul Duval in *Four Decades: The Canadian Group of Painters and Their Contemporaries.* He outlined the work of numerous individual artists, with emphasis on the contribution of the group as a whole to Canadian development. William Withrow, director of the Art Gallery of Ontario, examined the work of two dozen Canadians in *Contemporary Canadian Painting.* Limiting discussion meant omitting some noteworthy artists, but allowed study of the individuals concerned. Helen J. Dow, in *The Art of Alex Colville,* dealt with this important Canadian artist and his work.

(H. C. CAMPBELL)

French Language. The impression that there was nothing exciting about the literature that tended more and more to be called "québécoise" rather than "French-Canadian" was dispelled by the number of important works published in 1972. Most remarkable about this list were new works by well-known writers. Among the novelists were Jacques Ferron, with two novels, *La Chaise du maréchal ferrant* and *Le Saint-Elias;* Jacques Godbout, with *D'Amour P.Q.;* André Langevin, with *L'Élan d'Amérique;* Gabrielle Roy, with *Cet Été qui chantait;* Jean-Jules Richard, with *Louis Riel Exovide;* Marie-Claire Blais, with *Le Loup;* and Yvette Naubert, with *Les Pierrefendre.* Few of these new books were likely to add much to their authors' fame. Among the new and younger writers Victor-Lévy Beaulieu produced two novels, *Les Grands-pères* and *Un Rêve québécois,* Gilbert La Rocque had *Après la boue,* Jacques Garneau published an interesting book, *Memoire de l'Oeil,* and Claude Robitaille provided an excellent first book of short stories, *Rachel-du Hasard.*

The best poetry published was found in the complete works of the well-known poets Fernand Ouellette, Gilles Hénault, Rina Lasnier, and Gustave Lamarche. In addition, Pierre Trottier published *Sainte-Mémoire;* Suzanne Paradis, *Il y eut un matin;* Paul Chamberland, *Éclats de la pierre noire d'où rejaillit ma vie;* Félix A. Savard, *Le Bouscueil;* and Gemma Tremblay, *Souffles du midi.*

One novelty in the literature "québécoise" was the growing number of plays being published. In 1972 Michel Tremblay published a musical, *Demain matin Montréal m'attend,* which was very successful on the stage, and *En pièces détachées.* Marcel Dubé published *L'Echéance du vendredi, Paradis perdu,* and *Entre midi et soir,* which was regarded as excellent. A newcomer, Dominique de Pasquale, provided *On n'est pas sorti du bois.*

The literary studies published during the year included Odette Condemine's remarkable critical study of the poetry of Crémazie in the collection *Présence* and Roger LeMoyne's *L'Amérique et les poètes français de la Renaissance.* Antonine Maillet, whose novel of the year before, *La Sagouine,* had been very successful, provided *Rabelais et les traditions populaires en Acadie.* The Montreal University Press published the best letters of Elisabeth Bégon, *Lettres au cher fils,* and Placide Gaboury titled the first of a series of essays *L'Homme inchangé.* (ADRIEN THERIO)

DANISH

Failures and outsiders featured in the year's Danish fiction. Hans Lyngby Jepsen's *Din omgang* was the story of an artist turned alcoholic, written with sensitivity and some humour. The obsessed outsider was the essence of Frank Jæger's tragicomical tales *Provinser.* In one, a lonely Dane spends his war years in Helsingør watching a house in Swedish Hälsingborg across the Sound through a telescope, not realizing that what he sees is being put on for the benefit of him and others like him. The voyeur theme emerged again in Leif Panduro's *Vinduerne* (1971), where a lonely teacher, pursued by a neurotic girl pupil, watches an apartment opposite his own and is led to witness a woman killing her separated husband. It looks like self-defense, but has she arranged it? Yet another harmless voyeur appeared in Poul Ørum's detective novel *Syndebuk*. Here, as in *Den stjålne ild* (1971), Ørum showed his skill at depicting the provincial scene. More provincial life was to be found in Ole Sarvig's *Glem ikke,* a basically serious "burlesque" about a Dane who has lived in Tenerife most of his life and returns to provincial Denmark to find a girl with whom he has fallen in love.

Bent Nielsen's *Du skal skyde din hund* was an interesting and unusual novel about the clash of cultures resulting from the modernization of Greenland, the story being told through the thoughts of the main characters.

Klaus Rifbjerg turned to the banal in *Lena Jørgensen, Klintevej 4, 2650 Hvidovre,* the story of an ordinary woman from the Copenhagen suburbs. The everyday life of young people was also the theme of the main story of his collection *Den syende jomfru.*

In a class of its own was Christian Elling's *Aftenspil* (1971), memoirs and aphorisms expressed through the medium of a diary account of the years 1967 and 1968. A man of great culture, Elling wrote in polished Danish on a host of subjects and people. In stark contrast was the second volume of Elsa Gress's memoirs, *Fuglefri og fremmed* (1971), telling of the author's life in the 1930s and 1940s—lively, concise, at times controversial, but never dull. Anders Bodelsen wrote memoirs as unrelated essays in *Pigerne på broen,* whose title piece was a fantasy on Edvard Munch's famous painting of girls on a bridge.

Johannes Wulff's *Udvalgte digte. Vi som er hinanden* contained poems written between 1928 and 1970 and emphasized originality and ethical awareness. A poet's own selection of his work, from 1953 to 1971, was Jørgen Gustava Brandt's *Upraktiske digte. Udvalg.*

(W. GLYN JONES)

ENGLISH

Prose. Will the ghosts of Bloomsbury never be laid? Certainly they stalked as confidently as ever in 1972, this hugely intelligent, self-regarding group of Edwardian iconoclasts—an opposition party finally transformed into apostles of the current literary establishment, and perhaps now more influential than they were in their own time. This year it was Virginia Woolf's nephew, art historian Quentin Bell, son of Clive and Vanessa, who managed to corner most of the attention with an excellent two-volume study of his sainted aunt, *Virginia Woolf: A Biography.* There were also two volumes, edited by Denys Sutton, of *The Letters of Roger Fry* (a friend and biographical subject of Virginia Woolf, and a more influential arbiter of taste than Clive Bell); a volume of *Recollections of Virginia Woolf* by her contemporaries, including such surviving Bloomsbury acolytes as Stephen Spender and Christopher Isherwood; and, a little to one side as always, a posthumous collection of stories (*The Life to Come*) by E. M. Forster. In 1973 would follow the collected letters of Mrs. Woolf and some of her previously uncollected stories (*Mrs. Dalloway's Party*). Then perhaps the Bells would be ready for development, and Duncan Grant, to say nothing of the second Bloomsbury generation. . . .

No doubt the attention still claimed by the Bloomsbury group might be explained partly as nostalgia for their world and its privileged circumstances, partly as a retreat from contemporary problems of a civilization "in metamorphosis," as George Steiner put it in 1971. John Bayley, in a review of Quentin Bell's second volume, suggested that their legacy had been more widespread in English society than was generally believed: "Their righteous intolerance, their contempt for privacy and decorum, and their pensioned irresponsibility (though the pensioner is now the state) may be seen in our day to have become part of a wider and more democratic privilege."

That sentence suggests where Bloomsbury would have stood in the Great Pornography Debate, which also occupied much time and space during the year—though the reception of the Longford report itself was oddly muffled. Raymond Williams, reviewing the report alongside a collection of essays, *The Case Against Pornography,* edited by David Holbrook, thought that readers coming to the subject by way of this round of the argument might conclude there was no case against pornography and no case for it, either.

Meanwhile, hardliners both for and against literary censorship could find ammunition in the scoop achieved in mid-September by the *Times Literary Supplement* (*TLS*), which published a hitherto unknown introduction by George Orwell to his *Animal Farm,* describing the unofficial censorship (for the *raison d'état* of alliance with Stalin) that prevented the novel's publication by people as politically dissimilar as Victor Gollancz and T. S. Eliot. For example: "A genuinely unfashionable opinion is almost never given a fair hearing [in Britain] either in the popular press or in the highbrow periodicals," and, "If liberty means anything at all it means the right to tell people what they do not want to hear."

Fiction. The flight from naturalism and linear narrative continued. John Berger's *G* (for which he received the year's Booker Prize), for example, was an elaborate fictional mosaic patterned with historical allusion, philosophical speculation, and authorial comment on the method of his project: the result was a work of great resonance, connecting many areas of modern consciousness, and it was narrated—as Frank Kermode observed—in a tone of "extraordinary authority." Aidan Higgins' *Balcony of Europe* was a more "old-fashioned" sort of experimental novel, allusive and finely sensuous in its effects, that presented an Irish artist's late love affair through a collection of scenes arranged and seen as might be a collection of paintings. Another Irish anatomist of the heart and kindred organs, Edna O'Brien, brought out a short novel, *Night,* that read as a sort of appendix to Molly Bloom's monologue in *Ulysses* and seemed to be a further diversion of this author's real talent into a slack and derivative kind of impressionism: "steam of consciousness," someone would call it before long.

The Needle's Eye, on the contrary, showed Margaret Drabble working away at a sort of heightened naturalism. The novel's epigraph was Yeats's "the fascination of what's difficult," though it pointed mainly toward the moral difficulties attending its middle-class heroine's attempt to live, in a "bad" district of London, a life that did not exploit anyone. The *TLS* reviewer, despite some reservations, found it "a very ambitious, marvellously written, morally admirable book." P. J. Kavanagh's second novel, *A Happy Man,* shared some of its aspirations: "To write a novel of affirmation," wrote Norman Shrapnel in his *Guardian* review, "a confirmed statement of belief in life is so suspect these days, so against the grain of the times, as to run the risk of seeming irritatingly perverse." Against all these odds Kavanagh managed to make his hero, an American refugee doggedly glad to be alive in still rural England, a credible spokesman for the life force.

Not that joy was unconfined. The central figure in David Storey's *Pasmore* was a man driven by breakdown into total withdrawal from his loved and loving family. Both character and author speculate on this condition in a somewhat baffled and self-indulgent way —and more than one reviewer ended up shifting his sympathies, against the author's intentions, to the abandoned family. Samuel Beckett's *The Lost Ones* was a parable (60-odd pages, this time!) of beings trapped, in a neo-Dantean purgatory, on the mill of an obsessive cycle of endeavour and lethargy. Its appearance in the same week as C. P. Snow's *The Malcontents* presented something like the gamut of serious modern fiction: the intense refinement of Beckett's language and perception contrasting sharply with Snow's narrative amble and worldly wise psychologizing (here he was having a second go at the motives and mores of the revolutionary young).

The year brought new work from several writers who had been silent for some time. From David Garnett there was a lurid Gothic epic, *The Sons of the Falcon*—"a kind of Border Ballad transferred to the mountains of Transcaucasia in the sixties of the last century," one reviewer thought: "fierce, scarlet, unforgettable stuff." James Hanley published *Another World,* a rather disappointing novel by this Welsh writer much admired in the 1930s. Gabriel Fielding's set of rather dandified short stories, *New Queens for Old,* did not suggest a way forward for the author of *The Birthday King* and the Greenbloom novels.

There were important posthumous publications of work by older contemporaries of David Garnett. *The Life to Come* consisted largely of hitherto unpublished short stories by E. M. Forster, one of them written as late as 1957–58. Several of them were, like his novel *Maurice,* on a homosexual theme. "There is nothing here," the reviewer decided, "to contradict the statement that his ability to write fiction died with *A Passage to India.*" The stories did, however, suggest that the reason he dried up was that he felt he had to write about homosexual love and knew that society would not let him. " 'Only connect' was an injunction that Forster found insuperably difficult," the reviewer concluded. There appeared, for the first time in England, *The First Lady Chatterley* as well as—for the first time in English—D. H. Lawrence's second version of his last novel, called for this edition *John Thomas and Lady Jane.*

On the publication of V. V. Nabokov's *Glory* there was a general and slightly incredulous lament that the end of the master's rich store of youthful novels had been reached. But not, of course, the end of his influence. Martin Green even detected it—though misplaced, or misapplied—in some of Doris Lessing's short stories collected in *The Story of a Non-Marrying Man* (the best of which, thought the same reviewer, showed an excellence as "Socialist realism at a high level of complexity"). There were also collections of short stories from several other masters and mistresses of that form: Nadine Gordimer's *Livingstone's Companions,* William Trevor's *The Ballroom of Romance,* and Elizabeth Taylor's *The Devastating Boys* were among the best of them. It was a good year for high-grade thrillers, with Patricia Highsmith (*A Dog's Ransom*) and Eric Ambler (*The Levanter*) at the top of their form; Len Deighton (*Close-Up*) slightly below his; and Frederick Forsyth matching the success of his *The Day of the Jackal* with a brilliant (and thought-provoking) documentary narrative about a hunt for a Nazi war criminal, *The Odessa File.*

One of the more remarkable fictional oddities of the year was Elizabeth Jenkins' *Dr. Gully*—an account of a famous Victorian scandal, the Charles Bravo case —in which, so Miss Jenkins shyly confessed, much of the detailed description was supplied direct by the book's central character in automatic writing. Very interesting much of it was, too.

Biography, History, Criticism. Two of the finest biographies of the year studied a disparate pair of eminent Victorians. Cecil Woodham-Smith, one of the best historians at large outside the groves of academe, produced the first volume (to 1861) of *Queen Victoria: Her Life and Times.* Some reviewers thought its appearance so hard on the heels of Lady Longford's large volume (*Victoria RI*) a sort of diseconomy, given the shortage of good biographers and the plenitude of neglected subjects. But it was valued for presenting its subject in a wider historical context than earlier studies had attempted. The eminence of the subject of Yvonne Kapp's biography-in-progress (the two-decker was becoming common form again) had been established only retrospectively, so to say: "It was hardly to be expected that she would become a public figure in her own right," said Eric Hobsbawm in his *Listener* review of volume one of Miss Kapp's *Eleanor Marx,* "but this is just what has happened." The author's sympathetic, scholarly study of this touching and vivid actor in the desperate tragicomedy of Marx's domestic life might turn out to be one of the biographies of the decade. An even more bizarre Victorian domestic arrangement was revealed in the book that Derek Hudson worked up from the diaries of Arthur Munby, barrister, minor poet, clerk for the Ecclesiastical Commissioners, and connoisseur of braw working-class girls; *Munby: Man of Two Worlds* was a mine of inside information on Victorian attitudes toward sex and class.

Malcolm Muggeridge launched his autobiographical *Chronicles of Wasted Time* with a volume (*The Green Stick*) that took his difficult pursuit of happiness over the institutional hurdles of the British liberal-left

COURTESY, HOGARTH PRESS

Art historian Quentin Bell, author of a two-volume biography of his aunt Virginia Woolf, published in 1972.

Establishment (notably C. P. Scott's *Manchester Guardian*) and well into the 1930s. *A Chapter of Accidents,* an episode in the life of Goronwy Rees that was dominated by his friendship with Guy Burgess, also had some interesting things to say about the more insidious aspects of the Cambridge-Bloomsbury legacy.

Two generations younger than these, Teresa Hayter in *Hayter of the Bourgeoisie* and Tariq Ali in *The Coming British Revolution* each offered lively reflections on their youngish lives and the neo-Marxist conclusions drawn from them. The middle, though hardly the meat, of a British generational sandwich was provided in *Trust an Englishman* by John Knowler, an apologist for the squad of anxious pragmatists who grew up during World War II to become (in Irving Howe's phrase) "the generation that did not show up."

From the political front row there was yet another installment of Harold Macmillan's memoirs, without which no publishing year would seem complete: *Pointing the Way* covered events of 1959 to 1961, stretching roughly from his own African "Wind of Change" speech up to the election of Pres. John F. Kennedy. There were collections of speeches by Roy Jenkins (*What Matters Now*) and by Enoch Powell (*Still to Decide*) that indicated likely battlegrounds of the 1970s. Of the several postmortems on Harold Wilson's government, conducted by various old hands, the most significant were Richard Crossman's *Inside View* and Lord Wigg's memoir, *George Wigg.* The press, however, fell most avidly on *Inside Number Ten,* a chatty and pugnacious self-defense by Wilson's personal and private secretary, Marcia Williams, who—like Crossman—attacked the civil service as frequently obstructionist during Labour's term of office. *The Cecil King Diary 1965–70,* a totally indiscreet record of ruling-class gossip, also caused much fluttering in political dovecotes. Robert Rhodes James's *Ambitions and Realities* was a Conservative historian's useful early

KEYSTONE

Sir John Betjeman was appointed poet laureate of Great Britain in 1972.

attempt at a more fundamental analysis of the politics of this period.

Two considerable studies of powers behind earlier thrones were A. J. P. Taylor's avowed apologia for a "beloved friend," *Beaverbrook,* and Christopher Sykes's *Nancy: The Life of Lady Astor.* A rather different aspect of the preoccupation with the problems of power was shown in a rash of translations and reprints of works of P. A. Kropotkin and other anarchist thinkers. These and other fashionable interests found an echo in a work of longer historical range, Christopher Hill's *The World Turned Upside Down,* which treated seriously what had often been regarded as merely the lunatic fringe of the English Revolution—those anarchical leveling sects (the Ranters, Diggers, Seekers) whose names suggest so many latter-day pop groups. Richard Cobb's *Reactions to the French Revolution* provided another absorbing parade of those "individual people he has released [from the French] into our streets, our minds, our eyes, even our noses," as Gwyn Williams put it.

As a counterbalance to the continuing interest of the best academic historians in social and political history there appeared during the year the first signs of something like a wave of commercially inspired works of "costume history"—of which the series of "Kings and Queens of England" biographies, edited by Antonia Fraser, might be taken as typical. A more interesting book of a kind that few academics would now dare undertake was Paul Johnson's boldly opinionated one-volume history of the English, *The Offshore Islanders;* and Jonathan Gathorne-Hardy produced a lively piece of commercially viable social history in *The Rise and Fall of the British Nanny.* Irish history remained a going concern for English publishers: there were readable works by Robert Kee (*The Green Flag,* a history of Irish nationalism) and Terence de Vere White (*The Anglo-Irish*). Useful for its commentary on Ulster's desperate situation was *States of Ireland,* a personal and political history by Conor Cruise O'Brien, whose earlier book of 1972, *The Suspecting Glance,* urged self-criticism on the no-longer-new left and more concern with "what man is actually like."

Once again there was a thinnish crop of literary criticism. Perhaps the best thing in this field was Christopher Ricks's excellent study, *Tennyson.* F. R. Leavis' lectures, *Nor Shall My Sword,* strayed even further than usual from literature into the realm of broad cultural criticism, but neither it nor Richard Hoggart's Reith lectures, *Only Connect,* was among its author's most significant work. The arguments of the scientists were more urgent. The Club of Rome's report, *The Limits to Growth,* was widely and ardently debated as was *The Doomsday Syndrome,* a quick polemical reply by the optimistic editor of *Nature,* John Maddox. Some of the protagonists in this debate should have been directed to P. B. Medawar's lucid and toughly argued essays on the nature of scientific activity, *The Hope of Progress,* which showed the author once more to be, as Alex Comfort said, "one of the obligatory sources for people who write about science." Another absorbing scientific study for the serious common reader (a classification that Medawar might not allow) was the story, edited by Muriel Gardiner, of one of Freud's most famous cases, *The Wolf-Man and Sigmund Freud.*

Finally, a monument by which 1972 would be remembered in the English-speaking world: the publication of the first third (A to G) of the *Supplement to the Oxford English Dictionary,* already becoming known as the Sexy Supplement for its high assay of four-letter words. (W. L. WEBB)

Poetry. Following the growing trend of recent years, collections of poetry by both established and unestablished poets flowed from the literary presses, ranging from Michael Horovitz' *The Wolverhampton Wanderer,* a book-length poem exuberantly celebrating the public interest in football in terms of pop culture, and Kathleen Raine's *The Lost Country,* deploring the lack of values of contemporary society, to the pyrotechnics of Adrian Mitchell's *Ride the Nightmare.* Despite the immense variety, however, the results, with but few exceptions, were rather unimaginative and dull.

Scores of new poets were introduced, but if many of them produced technically accomplished work, they were surprisingly unadventurous and reluctant to tackle anything resembling a major theme. Most of these young poets appeared to be subdued or depressed, overburdened by their domestic situations in hostile suburban environments. It was true that in *Footsteps on Snow* Anne Beresford attempted to cope with complex problems in a forthright language that here and there struck fire from the stone, and in *The Snowing Globe* Peter Scupham managed occasionally to break out of his domestic concerns to glance at the world outside. On the other hand, *The Holly Queen* by Sally Purcell tended to reflect the author's studious preoccupation with folklore and legends, and *The Crying Embers* by Martin Booth, though making effective use of dream symbols and imagery, was somewhat literary in origin and treatment. Other first collections of interest were *Sounds Before Sleep* by James Aitchison, *Saint David's Day* by Florence Bull, and *The Rain-Giver* by Kevin Crossley-Holland, previously known for his translations.

Easily the most impressive of these first volumes was James Fenton's *Terminal Moraine*—and not only because it was the most audacious in attack and exciting in its employment of diction and ideas. Perhaps the best things were the witty and impudently satirical "Open Letter to Richard Crossman," an ambiguous piece entitled "The Kingfisher's Boxing Gloves," and the Newdigate Prize poem, "Western Furniture," featuring Commodore Perry's trip to Japan in 1850.

Most of the established poets duly added to their production, if not always to their reputations. Among the collected editions were *Selected Poems* by Vernon Scannell, *Collected Poems* by the Australian A. D. Hope, *Collected Poems 1958–70* by George MacBeth, and the posthumous *Collected Poems* of W. R. Rodgers.

In *The Happier Life* Douglas Dunn successfully extended his range beyond the neat and circumstantial observations on northern urban existence to include glimpses of fantasy; in *The Violent West,* Zulfikar Ghose, a Pakistani poet educated in England and at the time of publication lecturing in Texas, transferred his attention and his search for identity to the American scene; Norman Nicholson continued doing his thing in *A Local Habitation,* with its realistic descriptions of everyday life and people in his native Cumberland. As a contrast to Nicholson, R. S. Thomas, in the curiously titled *H'm,* seemed to be turning away from the bleak landscape of the Welsh hill farms and the even bleaker personalities of the farmers to find a meaningful relationship between himself and the world outside. The posthumous *Scorpion,* with its wry humour and acute perception, proved a fitting epitaph for Stevie Smith (d. 1971).

The death of Cecil Day-Lewis (*see* OBITUARIES), and the announcement in October, after much speculation and controversy, that Sir John Betjeman (*see* BIOGRAPHY) had succeeded Day-Lewis as poet laureate, made poetry front page news once again. So also did the return from the U.S. to Oxford of W. H. Auden (*see* BIOGRAPHY), who during the year published *Epistle to a Godson.* (HOWARD SERGEANT)

FRENCH

Fiction. A somewhat neglected genre, the short story, attracted the attention of a number of able writers in 1972. Daniel Boulanger's *La Barque amirale* led *Le Monde's* critic, Pierre-Henri Simon, to describe him as "a master of the genre." In *L'Ombre et la rive* Emmanuel Roblès captured critical moments in the relations between men and women with "stylistic mastery and psychological finesse." Jean Fougère continued to portray, at times almost to caricature, the humbler members of society in *La Belle Femme,* for which he was awarded the French Academy's Grand Prix de la Nouvelle.

The Prix Goncourt went to Jean Carrière, a disciple of Giono and a writer of indisputable talent, for *L'Épervier de Maheux,* a passionate hymn to the high country of the Cévennes. The Prix Fémina went to Roger Grenier's *Ciné-roman,* the story of a group of life's failures and their unsuccessful attempt to reestablish a provincial cinema.

A number of journalists produced competent novels, rich in professional experiences and romantic encounters: Gabriel Barrault's *La Foire aux crabes,* Max Gallo's *Le Cortège des vainqueurs,* and Olivier Todd's *L'Année du crabe* were all potential contenders for literary awards. Nevertheless, the Prix Renaudot was carried off by an outsider—British journalist, photographer, and theatrical producer Christopher Frank, with *La Nuit Américaine,* a tale of love lost and found in a world of brittle sophistication. The Prix Interallié went to yet another journalist, Georges Walter, for his modern fairy tale, *Des Vols de Vanessa.*

Other, less flamboyant novels of equally high quality included Pierre Boudot's *Les Sept Danses du tétras,* a Bernanos-style struggle between good and evil. Michel Huriet's *La Fiancée du roi* described a mystical love between an Italian nun and a Japanese, while Louis Fafournoux' *L'Abbaye du grand vent* was a Proustian study of life in a Benedictine monastery. In *Agnès ou le bonheur des signes* Jean Plumyène adopted the manner of the *Heptaméron* to recall the events of 1968. *Le Marin de Lesbos,* a novel with a strong Greek flavour by Clément Lépidis, won the Prix du Roman Populiste. With *Les Soldats de bois* Bernard Matignon joined the ranks of young writers who chose occupied France as the background for their characters' trials and tribulations. These also included Patrick Modiano, who received the French Academy's Grand Prix du Roman for *Les Boulevards de ceinture,* the story of the hero's search for an apparently unworthy father.

An Auvergnat raciness permeated Jean Anglade's three latest novels. *Un Front de marbre,* centring on intrigues around a war memorial, was irresistibly comic. The Algerian writer Rachid Boudjedra's *L'Insolation* was a somewhat confused, semiautobiographical account of a psychiatric case, while two new novels by Andrée Chedid, a writer of Egyptian origin honoured as a poet with the Aigle d'Or, were widely appreciated, particularly *La Cité fertile.* Nicole Avril's *Les Gens de Misar,* a work of great evocative power set in a mysterious, isolated village in a far-off land,

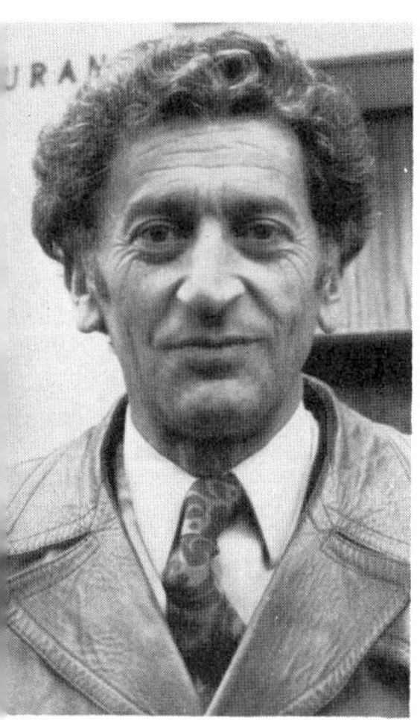

WIDE WORLD

French journalist Georges Walter (top) was awarded the 1972 Prix Interallié for his book "Des Vols de Vanessa." The Prix Goncourt was awarded to Jean Carrière (bottom), author of "L'Épervier de Maheux."

was compared to the works of such disparate authors as Kafka and Pierre Benoit. A real masterpiece was Simone Schwarz-Bart's *Pluie et vent sur Télumée miracle,* a hymn of exaltation going to the very heart of life on Guadeloupe. In a quite different style, *La Part des choses* by Benoite Groult described a group of upper-class travelers in the East. The Prix Médicis went to dramatist, short-story writer, and teacher of philosophy Maurice Clavel for *Le Tiers des étoiles,* which presented a debauched world of *cinéastes* and *artistes* in which God was to be attained through sexuality, although there was rather more sex than God in this somewhat unbalanced work.

Among those who had become the classical writers of their own time, the laurels went once again to J.-P. Hervé-Bazin for *Cri de la chouette,* re-creating the unforgettable virago of *Vipère au poing.* In *Les Oreilles de jungle* Pierre Boulle satirized the Americans in Vietnam while Bernard Clavel's *Le Seigneur du fleuve* provided a poignant evocation of the last voyage of a Rhône boatman. The year's longest success was Robert Merle's *Malevil,* which dealt with the problems of survival after a nuclear attack. The reign of the classical novel continued to be maintained by Jean Dutourd (*Le Printemps de la vie*), Michel de St. Pierre (*L'Accusée*), and Henri Troyat (*La Pierre, la feuille et les ciseaux*).

Among the adherents of the *nouveau roman,* Daniel Apruz threw himself joyfully into the task of pillorying the inconveniences of modern life, while Alphonse Boudard provided a humorous if, at times, somewhat inaccessible picture of life in a hospital. Nathalie Sarraute's *Vous les entendez* found its inspiration in the generation gap and provoked a wide variation of response from the critics. A newcomer to the genre was Anne Rolland-Jacquet, whose *Aria da capo* seemed to centre on the awaiting of a new love, while death was the dominant theme of her *A capella.*

Nonfiction. A sparkling array of new works appeared during 1972. The French Academy's Grand Prix de Littérature was awarded to Jean-Louis Curtis for his already considerable contribution to French literature. During the year Curtis also published a further work, *La Chine m'inquiète,* a series of pastiches of striking reality and delicate humour inspired by such figures as de Gaulle, Proust, Malraux, and Aragon. In a more serious vein Jacques Duron's *Valeurs* was an erudite, high-minded, and finely written treatment of such figures as Joan of Arc, Mozart, Valéry, and, above all, Santayana. *Figaro ou la vie de Beaumarchais,* a successful work by the duc de Castries, a new academician, clarified many obscure points while at the same time providing a gripping account of its hero's adventures. Henri Guillemin brought his usual passion and erudition to *La Liaison Musset-Sand,* describing the Venetian period of the liaison and launching into a furious diatribe against George Sand. J.-N. Marque devoted an important study to *Léon Daudet,* a pamphleteer of genius driven by a consuming patriotism. *L'Homme que fut Blaise Cendrars* by A. T'Serstevens was "not a study of the works but the story of a life in its human reality" in which the author did not hesitate to substantially demythologize his hero. J. L. de Vilallonga's *Gold Gotha* was a well-deserved success with lively, colourful sketches of contemporary figures from King Umberto of Italy to Aristotle Onassis.

Histoire de la France, produced under the direction of Georges Duby, was the first large-scale work of its kind since that of Ernest Lavisse (d. 1922), retaining an overall unity despite the large number of contributors. In addition to the simple chronology of events, the work, by historians trained in modern methods of historical inquiry, probed "the archaeology of daily existence, the anthropology of the past." Unfortunately, however, history up to the 14th century was compressed into a single volume, while the second brought the story up to 1852 and the third to modern times.

Other historians confined their attention to the city of Paris. In *Paris et ses fantômes* André Rigaud traced the Latin origins of modern nomenclatures, bringing out truth through humorous evocation of legend. Georges Pillement's *Paris en fête* spanned six centuries of public events, from victory celebrations and royal marriages to riots and public executions, while Jacques Levron's *Paris se souvient* concentrated on the buildings once inhabited by famous people, concealing a wealth of erudition in a witty and entertaining style.

J.-F. Chiappe devoted a passionate and compelling study to *Georges Cadoudal,* whose republican hatreds he shared. Three writers who had won their spurs as novelists also turned to history: José Cabanis with *Charles X roi ultra,* which brought him the Prix des Ambassadeurs; Jean-Louis Bory with *La Révolution de juillet 1830,* in which the author gave himself wholeheartedly to the cause of the people; and Armand Lanoux with *Le Coq rouge,* in which blind admiration for the Communards and equally blind hatred for journalist-statesman Louis Adolphe Thiers precluded any possibility of historical objectivity. In a quite different tone, Jean Duché combined attractively disguised erudition and ardent feminism in *Le Premier Sexe.*

La Marée du soir, the final collection of Henry de Montherlant's notebooks, provided reflections on the author's work and on the accident that caused him to lose an eye and eventually hastened the suicide to which he had always been drawn (*see* OBITUARIES). *Ce qui reste de jour,* the latest volume in Julien Green's *Journal,* while not indifferent to external events, was more deeply marked by the inner turmoils of the author and his church. After *Bestiaire sans oubli,* the final volume of his enchanting cycle about the natural world, Maurice Genevoix's *La Mort de près,* a recollection of World War II, was a poignant testimony unmarred by sentimentality.

Michel Robida's *L'Enfant sage des années folles* was a chronicle of a great bourgeois dynasty, a psychological study of a society in eclipse, with a charm analogous to that of the duc de Brissac's *En d'autres temps,* which took the aristocracy as its subject. Maurice Chapelan's *Mémoires d'un voyou* was a delightfully cynical, disrespectful, and erotic little masterpiece based on memories of adolescence. Simone de Beauvoir's *Tout Compte fait,* however, the fifth, monumental, and heavily didactic volume of a ponderously political autobiography, did little for its author's literary reputation. The bulky *Correspondance générale* of Paul Léautaud, spanning 78 years, showed this well-known grumbler and close friend of Valéry to be full of discretion and reserve while expressing the most unexpected literary opinions in a delightful style.

A number of works of a high standard satirized contemporary life. Pierre Daninos' *Le Pyjama* ridiculed the so-called malaise of contemporary society and the modern tendency to weep for the criminal rather than the victim. Paul Sérant's *Lettre à Louis Pauwels sur les gens inquiets* was full of wit and wisdom and a refreshing sharpness, as was Robert Escarpit's *Lettre ouverte au diable,* which, nevertheless, retained a certain optimism. Despite its popularity, *Le nouvel ingénu,* a pastiche of Voltaire's *Candide* by Pierre Gaxotte, failed to reach the author's usual high standard.

In the realm of linguistics, the *Grand Larousse de la langue française* was a remarkable work of etymology, including technical and scientific neologisms as well as archaic words and phrases.

During the year the French Academy lost a number of important writers, including Montherlant, Jules Romains, and Pierre-Henri Simon (*see* OBITUARIES). Pasteur Vallery-Radot was succeeded by Étienne Wolff, and Jean-Jacques Gautier and Jean Cardinal Daniélou were elected to the Academy.

Poetry. Marie Noël's posthumous *Chants des quatre temps* contained poignant, at times macabre, laments, while Philippe Chabaneix's *Musiques d'avant la nuit* was moving and classical in style. Pierre Moussaric's *Chansons du temps présent* immediately captivated the reader, while Pierre Loubière's *Mémoire buissonnière* offered lyricism "with a scent of wild herbs." Maurice Courant's *Soleil de ma mémoire* was marked by severity of style and reminiscences of Valéry, Hélène Parmelin's *De Songe et de silence* by grace and nostalgia, Claire de Soujeole's *Pas dans la rosée* by a delightful freshness, and Micheline Dupray's *L'Herbe est trop douce* by a pleasing harmony. Further from the style of classical prosody were the elliptical, incantatory poems of Marc Alyn's *Infini au delà* and the symbolism of Eugène Guillevic's *Encoches.*

Poètes maudits d'aujourd'hui, a collection of essays by various authors, deplored the indifference of the public toward 12 poets, among them Artaud and de Richaud, of whom 7 took their own lives and all died in penury. In *Trésor de la poésie baroque et précieuse* André Blanchard drew parallels between poets of the 17th century and those of contemporary times. Striking examples of the latter were Robert Mallet's *La Rose et ses remous,* characterized by intelligence and preciosity, and Hervé-Bazin's *A la poursuite d'Iris.* An excellent study of *Pierre Béarn* was provided by Dansel and J. L. Pierris.

The title of "Prince of Poetry" went to a Belgian poet, Maurice Carême, while Patrice de la Tour du Pin received the Société des Poètes Française award and Jean Tardieu the French Academy's Grand Prix de Poésie. (ANNIE BRIERRE)

GERMAN

Literature and literati could still create public controversy. When the participants at the Olympic Games were presented with a new anthology of German literature (*Deutsches Mosaik,* edited by Dieter Hildebrandt and Siegfried Unseld), strong protests were made by the East Germans at some of the passages included. Earlier Heinrich Böll provoked considerable hysteria in the right-wing press by appealing for calm, understanding, and a fair trial for the Baader-Meinhof anarchists (*see* BIOGRAPHY: *Meinhof, Ulrike*). The awarding of the Nobel Prize for Literature to Böll did nothing to rehabilitate him in these quarters.

In the novel "fiction" continued to be distrusted; autobiographical and documentary works predominated. Peter Handke expressed part of the dilemma in his *Wunschloses Unglück,* the story of his mother, who committed suicide in November 1971. Fiction for Handke was an empty ritual, yet every attempt to relate events tends to fictionalize them; the individual uniqueness of his mother threatened to be swamped by the formulas invented for such occasions. Handke seemed to be moving toward more traditional narrative forms; in *Der kurze Brief zum langen Abschied,* published earlier in the year, an account of a journey across America, he felt himself akin to "Green Henry," the hero of a 19th-century novel by Gottfried Keller. Indeed, the strength and attraction of both works was the air of unselfconscious innocence pervading them.

The same might be said of Walter Kempowski's very different *Uns geht's ja noch gold,* an extremely vivid account of the immediate post-World War II years in Rostock. As in his earlier works, Kempowski refused to comment: his narrative was a montage of brief scenes and conversations in which the banality of people's reactions highlights the horror of what happens.

The child's perspective was also to be found in parts of Wolfgang Georg Fischer's *Möblierte Zimmer,* the sequel to his *Wohnungen.* It described the immediate prewar years from the point of view of a well-to-do half-Jewish family in Vienna, which hopes Hitler will "go away," moves temporarily to Yugoslavia, and finally splits up. Unlike Kempowski, Fischer gave his novel historical depth; but here too the strength lay in the period vignettes.

More directly autobiographical works included Erwin Strittmatter's *Die Blaue Nachtigall,* four rather bucolic sketches from his early years, Max Frisch's highly successful *Tagebuch 1966–1971,* and Günter Grass's *Aus dem Tagebuch einer Schnecke.* Both Frisch and Grass introduced fiction into their diaries. But where Frisch emerged as the uncompromising liberal individualist, distrustful of political parties, Grass declared his commitment to the politics of gradual progress, the "snail" of the title.

The documentary novel was represented by Hans Magnus Enzensberger's *Der kurze Sommer der Anarchie,* an investigation of the life and death of Buenaventura Durruti, an anarchist leader in the Spanish Civil War, and Dieter Wellershoff's *Einladung an alle,* the fruits of detailed research into a criminal case of the 1960s, society's persecution of an outsider. The former was the less digested and digestible of the two, a collection of often mutually contradictory documents interspersed with Enzensberger's commentaries.

More conventionally written novels treated the problem of individuality in relation to the collective. Martin Walser's best seller *Die Gallistl'sche Krankheit* analyzed the crisis of the liberal intellectual in terms reminiscent of Hugo von Hofmannsthal's Chandos and Jean-Paul Sartre's *La Nausée;* the solution implied, however, was to reject capitalist individualism and embrace the socialist collective. As usual Walser was strong on the satirical presentation of bourgeois society; his latest work was much more concise, indeed schematic, than his earlier novels. *Abschied von Parler,* by the East German Wolfgang Joho, confronted the West German liberal individualist with the real socialist collective of the German Democratic Republic (GDR, East Germany); somewhat woodenly written, it provided an interesting study of current attitudes in the East. No doubt this particular collective was *not* what Walser had in mind. The narrator of Herbert Heckmann's *Der grosse Knock-out in sieben Runden* took the opposite direction; the individualist who emigrates to America

CAMERA PRESS/PICTORIAL PARADE

West German author Heinrich Böll won the 1972 Nobel Prize for Literature.

becomes the conformist toy factory executive whose features are used on the firm's most successful product, a tumbler doll.

Heckmann's best effects were achieved through the grotesque. This was true also of Herbert Rosendorfer's much more imaginative *Deutsche Suite,* an at times uproariously funny political satire of Bavaria from the 1920s to the present. More unobtrusive was the humour of H. C. Artmann's latest book, *Der aeronautische Sindtbart.* Arno Schmidt's *Die Schule der Atheisten,* on the other hand, a Utopian novel of life in 2014, was strictly for addicts.

Other novels included a revised version of Alfred Andersch's *Die Rote,* the East German Hermann Kant's *Das Impressum,* an entertaining account of life through the Third Reich to the GDR, Stefan Heym's allegory of the GDR, *Der König David Bericht,* Alfred Kolleritsch's impenetrable "seismographic novel" *Die Pfirsichtöter,* and the inevitable, rather pernicious war novels: from the West, Hildegard Gartmann's *Blitzmädchen* and Hans Lebert's *Der Feuerkreis;* from the East, Fritz Hofmann's *Die Erbschaft des Generals.*

The short story was represented in publications by Günter Herburger (*Die Eroberung der Zitadelle*), Gabriele Wohmann (*Gegenangriff*), Alois Brandstetter (*Ausfälle*), Rainer Brambach (*Für sechs Tassen Kaffee*), and Ingeborg Bachmann (*Simultan*). The most impressive collection was Peter Rosei's *Landstriche,* a set of four Kafkaesque allegories.

The most important plays of the year were Franz Xaver Kroetz's *Stallerhof* and Thomas Bernhard's *Der Ignorant und der Wahnsinnige.* The former, part of the new realist tendency in the German theatre, was remarkable for its ability to imply through and beyond the naturalist dialogue and the banal inhumanity of the characters not merely social criticism but a sense of almost metaphysical pity and shame. Bernhard's play too was about inhumanity, the inhumanity of science (a large part consisted of the detailed description of an anatomical dissection) and of culture—the play centred on an opera singer who had become a mere machine for producing coloratura. Bernhard also published *Der Italiener,* a highly disturbing film-text.

Other works for the theatre included Rolf Hochhuth's weak comedy *Die Hebamme* and collections by Otto Jägersberg (*Cosa Nostra*) and Rainer Werner Fassbinder (*Antiteater 2*). Karlhenz Braun and Peter Iden edited an anthology of contemporary short plays, *Neues deutsches Theater,* a useful documentation of current streams.

Important collections of lyric poems included Andreas Okopenko's *Orte wechselnden Unbehagens,* Reiner Kunze's *Zimmerlautstärke, Neue Gedichte* by Peter Huchel, Günter Kunert's *Offener Ausgang,* and Beat Brechbühl's *Der geschlagene Hund pisst an die Säule des Tempels.* In the year of his Nobel Prize, Böll produced his first volume of *Gedichte,* nine poems of some interest and charm if not greatness. The outstanding single work was a long poem of sustained visionary power on death and transfiguration by Heiner Bastian, *Tod im Leben.*

In the realm of popular science C. W. Ceram's *Der erste Amerikaner* was a best seller. The many collections of essays included Alfred Andersch's important *Norden Süden rechts und links,* Wolfgang Beutin's *Invektiven, Inventionen,* Luise Rinser's *Grenzübergänge,* Urs Widmer's *Das Normale und die Sehnsucht,* Rudolf Bayr's *Momente und Reflexe,* and Barbara Frischmuth's *Tage und Jahre.* (J. H. REID)

ITALIAN

Four grand old men of Italian literature returned to poetry in 1972. Riccardo Bacchelli's *La stella del mattino* was perhaps the least successful collection, as the emotions that the poems were intended to describe and the variety of content were not matched by the rather uniform tone. Marino Moretti's *Tre anni e un giorno* expressed a wholehearted acceptance of old age with all its disabilities but also with its greater wisdom and mellowness. Aldo Palazzeschi's *Via dalle cento stelle* was quietly provocative, raising embarrassing questions on religion, art, and morality in a simple matter-of-fact style reminiscent of his early works, often only narrowly avoiding banality. Tommaso Landolfi, whose *Viola di morte* won the Fiuggi Prize, carried into his verse the good taste, restraint, and subdued irony characteristic of his prose.

The return of older writers to poetry was less surprising in light of the gradual dissolution of the literary avant-garde of the 1960s—guilty, despite its left-wing protestations, of accepting both the capitalist conception of books as consumer goods and the now discredited view that social change may be hastened by revolutionary use of language.

Edoardo Sanguineti's *Wirrwarr* and Giorgio Manganelli's *Agli Dei ulteriori* seemed to offer little content or motivation beyond a narcissistic concern with the process of their own writing. It is inevitable and proper that poetry and fiction, whatever their content, also concern the act of writing, as literature is the first protagonist of its own creations. Nevertheless, just as language, which implicitly conveys all the information necessary for its own decoding, does not limit itself to a metalinguistic function but explicitly points to extralinguistic reality, literary experimentation is convincing only when it arises out of nonliterary experience, as in Ferdinando Camon's *La vita eterna,* a cruel and moving book about violence, religion, poverty, and war.

Traditional devices may be given a new lease on life when rooted in real emotion: in *Opus* Franco Cordero used indirect free speech to chart the exciting adventures of a human mind trying to free itself from harmful beliefs; and Carlo Laurenzi adopted the well-known conventions of the historical novel, including the "manuscript," to combine in *Quell'antico amore* the story of the duke of Parma's love for a Florentine gentlewoman with critical essays on the writing of fiction and fragments of his own spiritual autobiography. Linguistic experimentation appeared almost natural in the complex pattern of modern and older Italian and Venetian dialects woven by Neri Pozza in his stories of Renaissance artists, *La putina greca* (a continuation of *Processo per eresia e altre storie,* 1970).

Unfortunately, however, the creative use of old devices was rare. Alfredo Todisco's *Il corpo* added little to the well-worn theme of an older man's love for a young woman, and a sensitive portrait of the gentle Miriam in the first half of Fulvio Tomizza's *La città di Miriam* did not save the second from becoming a tedious catalog of a middle-aged man's banal sexual fantasies. *L'odore del fieno* added new details to Giorgio Bassani's broad fresco of Jewish Ferrara: some pictures, however, look better before the finishing touches are added. Goffredo Parise's first novel, *Il ragazzo morto e le comete,* was reissued after 11 years: those who, according to the author's own blurb, considered it his best novel were probably wrong.

The huge success of *La donna della domenica* indicated the extent of demand for readable and enjoyable stories. The authors, Carlo Fruttero and Franco Lucentini, apparently set out deliberately to write a best-selling thriller, and achieved precisely that. Alberto Arbasino's slangy, with-it account of a love affair between a rich girl and a truck driver, *La bella di Lodi,* aimed at a slightly more sophisticated readership, but the approach was the same: a book written to a well-tried recipe, albeit cooked and served up with above-average skill.

Vittorio Schiraldi's *Baciamo le mani* was evidently not inspired by *The Godfather* and similarities were to be regarded as accidental; however, the two novels had something in common in that both stood to profit from current publicity about the Mafia. To those who remembered the clarity and forcefulness of the first of all the Mafia books, Leonardo Sciascia's *Il giorno della civetta* (1961), Sciascia's latest novel, *Il contesto,* a hazy story of a murder investigation, was a disappointment, as if the author had capitulated to the very forces that, as he said in a postscript to the earlier book, had prevented his telling the whole truth.

The 1972 Strega Prize went to Giuseppe Dessì's *Paese d'ombre,* an undramatic but moving and perceptive novel about social change in Sardinia and a work of undeniable literary merit. Its only flaw was that Dessì seemed to have set out to try to please everyone: conservatives could approve of his adherence to traditional literary and moral values; reformists could find in the book a confirmation of their views; and revolutionaries could note the protagonist's gradual alienation from his working-class background under the corrupting influence of inherited wealth and political power. Saverio Strati's *Noi lazzaroni,* one of the few good novels about the social evil of forced emigration, gave a far more realistic picture of working-class aspirations and frustrations.

In the realm of the essay, Sciascia's *La corda pazza* presented an interesting and critically sharp picture of the achievements and contradictions of Sicilian culture. *Letteratura e ribellione,* by Giulio Cattaneo, was a personal view of the tense relationship between culture and politics, literature and society in Italy since World War II. Carlo Alianello's pamphlet *La conquista del Sud,* on the Piedmontese "colonization" of southern Italy, contained some points worth pondering despite a partisan and superficial outlook. Of particular interest to English-speaking readers was Itala Vivan's fascinating *Caccia alle streghe nell'America puritana,* a detailed investigation of 17th-century witch-hunts in the American colonies based on original and often little-known sources and suggesting some uncomfortable parallels and conclusions to those with an eye for more recent forms of intolerance.

(GIOVANNI CARSANIGA)

JAPANESE

Beginning in the latter half of 1971 an extremely progressive trend appeared in Japanese literature, an attempt to destroy the tradition of the personalized "I novel" (*Shishosetsu*). Politically speaking, this new trend was also marked by a strong leaning toward democracy.

The most representative fictional works of 1972 were *Seinen no Wa* ("The Ring of Youth") by Hiroshi Noma, *Leyte Senki* ("Leyte War Memoirs") by Shohei Ooka, *Shi no Shima* ("The Isle of Death") by Takehiko Fukunaga, and *Shosetsu Watanabe Kazan* by Mimpei Sugiura. *Shi no Shima,* based on the atomic bombing of Hiroshima, was artistically epoch-making. *Leyte Senki,* written in a documentary form, was a uniquely successful attempt to challenge the "limits of modern fiction" by adhering to facts and achieving an effect that was more vivid than what could be wrought by fiction, much as Norman Mailer did in *Armies of the Night.*

In contrast, several excellent books by writers in their 40s appeared: *Tatta Hitori no Hanran* ("Revolt of One") by Saiichi Maruya; *Natsu no Yami* ("Darkness in Summer") by Ken Kaiko; *Haikyosha Julianus* ("Julianus the Apostate") by Kunio Tsuji and, under his pseudonym Morio Kita, *Yoidore Bune* ("A Drunken Boat"); and *Kokoromi no Kishi* ("The Shore of Trial") by Kunio Ogawa. While these differed in theme and content, they could all be said to indicate a new literary trend inaugurated by a generation that came through the war. In other words, they were writing about present-day Japan with experience of war and yet with detachment from it. Together these works marked a turning point in the history of Japanese literature, for they did not reflect the odious influence of the "I novel" but breathed the spirit of new Japanese literature. They were also on the same literary level as many works of modern fiction being produced in the United States and Europe.

Two noteworthy creations by women writers were *Aru Hitori no Onna no Hanashi* ("Story of a Woman") by Chiyo Uno and *Juei* ("Shadow of Leaves") by Ineko Sata. *Juei,* on the theme of the bombing of Nagasaki, was written in a nostalgic and beautiful style yet expressed the author's uncompromising attitude toward atomic bombs. Both authors are writers of long standing, and the two books epitomized their past works.

Sawako Ariyoshi's *Kōkotsu no Hito* ("Person in a Trance") caused a great stir. The book's significance lay not so much in its literary value as in its protest against the neglect of old age. On April 16, 1972, Nobel Prize-winning writer Yasunari Kawabata (*see* OBITUARIES) committed suicide at the age of 72.

(HAJIME SHINODA)

JEWISH

Hebrew. Hebrew literature again demonstrated its vitality. Prevalent political tension did not impede the publication of all genres of fiction and nonfiction. A number of leading authors died during 1972, among them one of the pioneers of the modern Hebrew story, G. Schoffman, and the eminent literary critic B. Kurzweill. There was, however, uninterrupted growth, with younger schools of writing exerting influence. Among these were such novelists as A. B. Yehoshua, with *Bithilat Kayitz 1970,* and D. Shahar, with *Masa le-Ur Kashdim.* Also of interest were the novels *ha-Pardes* by B. Tamuz and A. Megged's *ha-Hayim ha-Ketzarim.* Surrealist in tone were H. Guri's *ha-Sefer ha-Meshuga* and Y. Oren's *Etgarim.* A more classic yet modern vein was evident in the distinguished volume by S. Halkin, *ba-Nehar.*

A study of the development of the Hebrew story from its beginnings was *Sippur ve-Shorsho* by Sh. Wershes. H. Barzel's critical essays were entitled *Shira u-Morasha,* while G. Shaked's *Im Tishohah ai-Paam* evaluated American-Jewish writing. *Maitarim u-Maarahot* contained A. Kariv's disquisitions. A series of critiques of prominent Hebrew authors edited by D. Miron drew attention; included was a volume on Y. H. Brenner introduced by Y. Bakon. Related to this was A. Cohen's *Yetzirato ha-Sifrutit shel Y. H. Brenner.*

Contemporary aspects of Western culture and Israel were the subject of E. Livnes' *Yisrael Umashber ha-Zivilizazia ha-Maaravit.* Israel's Pres. Schneor Zalman Shazar recalled figures of the past in *Orai Dorot.* Illuminating also were some letters, simply entitled *Iggerot,* by Israel's first president, Chaim Weizmann, and first prime minister, David Ben-Gurion. An intriguing volume of memoirs was Y. Bar-Yosef's *Bain Zefat li-Yerushalaim.*

Many volumes of poetry appeared. A. Shlonsky's *Ketavim* represented the work of a poet considered a rebel some decades earlier. Collected by D. Pagis and edited by Y. Cohen was David Fogel's *Kol ha-Shirim.* One of the first "modern" Hebrew poets, Fogel still affected younger writers. E. Zussman, in *Atzai Tamid,* displayed virtuosity, while T. Ribner's *Ain Lehashiv* and Y. Hurwitz' *Narkisim le-Malhut Madmena* spoke the contemporary poetic idiom, as did A. Kovner's rather mystic *Lahakat ha-Katzav.* Not obviously "new" were D. Chomsky's poems, *Avak Huzot.*

Hebrew literature in the U.S. was at a standstill. However, in Israel there did appear a scholarly collection, *Hagut Ivrit be-Amerika.* Partly of a related nature was the bilingual *Sefer Yovel Lichvod Yizhak Kiev.* Seminal articles of a 19th-century Hebrew author were eruditely introduced by the American-born critic E. Spicehandler in *Maamarim maet Yehoshua Heschel Shorr.* Also published was S. Rubinstein's *Rishmai Taiar,* a traveler's notebook.

(GABRIEL PREIL)

Yiddish. The progress of Yiddish literature, whose creators lived on all continents, could not be measured by the number of books published in 1972 but by their intrinsic value, which was considerable. The majority of the new books were printed in Tel Aviv or New York. Women were predominant in poetry: Asya's *Quiver of Boughs* and Beileh Schechter-Gottesman's *Footpaths Between Walls* introduced two newcomers. Zyameh Telesin's *Cries of Memory* and Rachel Baumwoll's *Longed For* symbolized the contributions of Soviet Yiddish poets who had settled recently in Israel. Israel's President Shazar, a historian and essayist when writing in Hebrew, enriched Yiddish verse with two books: *During a Mission* and *For Myself.* Collections of poetry deserving special mention were Rivkah Bassman's *Bright Stones;* Malkah Chefetz-Tuzman's *Leaves Do Not Fall;* Rachel H. Korn's *On the Edge of a Moment;* Joshuah Rivin's *Rainbow of Song;* and Saul Maltz's *With Joy and Song* for younger readers.

In the fields of fiction and drama mention should be made of Alter Katzizneh's posthumously issued scenic reportage *Schwartzbard;* Joseph Luden's novel *Like a Sail in the Storm;* Nahman Rapp's biblical tales *The Beginning;* Levi Papiernikov's *Of Today and the Past;* S. Tenenbaum's *The Last Witness,* a collection of short stories; and M. Tzanin's *Love During Storm,* the fifth volume of a historical novel of Jewish life in Poland. Two posthumous collections ranked high in the field of criticism: Jacob Glatstein's *In the World with Yiddish* and Samuel Niger's *Yiddish Writers of the Twentieth Century.*

Since World War II, Yiddish literature had considered books of reminiscences of great importance. The latest additions to this category were Menukha Alperin's *Under Strange and My Own Skies;* Helen Londinsky's *In the Mirror of Yesterday;* Jonas Turkow's *The End of Illusions,* dealing with the era from the Munich pact to the gas chambers of Auschwitz; and Shlomo Tenzer's *The Story of My Life.* New volumes of collective histories of the annihilated Jewish communities in Eastern Europe were also added to the Yiddish bookshelf. Collective works of a generally historical or linguistic character included the second volume of the *Recordbook for the Research of Yiddish Literature and Press, The Golden Book of the Jewish Settlement in Argentina,* and the third volume of *The Great Dictionary of the Yiddish Language.*

(MOSHE STARKMAN)

LATIN-AMERICAN

Throughout the continent politics seemed to enslave Latin-American literature. Argentine writers, except Jorge Luis Borges and his followers, supported and awaited the return of Juan Perón, while Mexican writers were bitterly divided in regard to Pres. Luis Echeverría's administration. The October issue of Octavio Paz's magazine *Plural* dealt with the situation. The magazine's readers, mostly students and middle-class professionals, demanded that new books be political in content; works of exclusively literary content were regarded suspiciously. In agreement with Cuban postulates, the Uruguayan Mario Benedetti defined the intellectual's mission in Latin America as "the duty to combat the class enemy of the people, returning culture to them and restoring their right to beauty and liberty." Everything seemed to indicate that a "compromise" notion would dominate Latin-American literature in the 1970s.

Writers with established reputations remained active but none could be said to have increased or decreased their prestige. Pablo Neruda published *Geografía infructuosa,* and another Nobelist, Miguel Angel Asturias, published *Viernes de dolores.* Among the Argentines, Julio Cortázar presented two narratives: *El libro de Manuel* and *Prosas del observatorio,* which, despite their dazzling style, could not be compared with *Rayuela* or with any other of his best stories. In *Oro de los tigres* Borges offered another combined volume of verse and prose. It was moving to see him undefeated either by fame or blindness and continuing to write sometimes with passion, always with mastery.

José Bianco broke three decades of silence to present his chronicle of the disintegration of the Argentine bourgeoisie in *La pérdida de un reino.* Marta Lynch analyzed the effects of political struggle on private lives in *El cruce del río.* Eduardo Gudiño Kieffer's *Guía de pecadores* was a roguish pop novel of present-day Buenos Aires. Mastery of colloquial language and an ability to literarily upgrade base materials could be observed in *La Perinola,* a first novel by Julio Sexer. A few days before committing suicide Alejandra Pizarnik published her last poems, *El infierno musical.* Argentine literary criticism, deeply influenced by the structuralists, was represented by several notable works, among them *El fuego de la especie* by Noé Jitrik.

Six years of terrible Bolivian history—from the lynching of Pres. Gualberto Villaroel in 1946 to the take-over by Víctor Paz Estenssoro in 1952—were recalled in *Los muertos indóciles,* a novel by Fernando Medina Ferrada. The vilification of aspects of national life was attacked in verse by Pedro Shimose when he wrote *Quiero escribir pero me sale espuma.*

In Brazil the works of Joâo Guimaraes Rosa were contained in *Ave Palabra,* published posthumously. The ambiguity of his outstanding work, *Grande Sertão: Veredas,* was analyzed by Walnice Nogueira Galvâo (*As Formas do Falso*). Alfredo Bosi published a modern *História Concisa da Literatura Brasileira.* Décio Pignatari surged as the Marshall McLuhan of his country in *Contracommunicaçâo. Colidouescapo,* by Haroldo de Augusto de Campos, was a poem based on *Finnegans Wake* that made for uncertain reading, susceptible to multiple interpretations. Thanks to the bilingual *An Anthology of Twentieth-Century Brazilian Poetry,* compiled by Elizabeth Bishop, excellent Brazilian verse came out of undeserved obscurity.

Colombian letters had yet to recover from the universal success of Gabriel García Márquez, whose *Cien años de soledad* was in its 32nd printing and who published seven interrelated stories under the endless title *La increíble y triste historia de la cándida Eréndira y de su abuela desalmada.* The stories were splendid in context and the magic of the narrative persisted. Two pirate editors published García Márquez' earliest stories under different titles, *Ojos de perro azul* and *El negro que hizo esperar a los ángeles;* neither gave evidence of the great writer to come.

One exception to the rule that envy is the professional ailment of novelists was the 665-page study *García Márquez: historia de un deicidio* by the great Peruvian writer Mario Vargas Llosa. Vargas Llosa's theme was that the novelist creates worlds of words because he refuses to accept reality as it is; each novel constitutes a symbolic assassination of reality. Angel Rama, the notable Uruguayan critic, kept up a running polemic with Vargas Llosa, published in *Marcha* in Montevideo and elsewhere, which maintained that these were archaic ideas that ignored the social perception of the author and his works. Nevertheless, Vargas Llosa's ability to contemplate the novelistic phenomenon from inside gave him the advantage.

Since the publication of his *El siglo de las luces* in 1962, Alejo Carpentier had been expected to produce what would be the epic of the Cuban revolution. While finishing it Carpentier came out with a short novel, *El derecho de asilo,* in which, for the first time, he did not use the baroque prose style but incorporated humoristic elements. The image of Donald Duck in this narration deserved the demolishing analysis of Marxist orientation it received in *Para leer al Pato Donald,* by Ariel Dorfman and Armando Materlant, two Chilean critics. Elsewhere in Cuban writings the novelty in *La huella del pulgar* by Noel Navarro was that it dealt with the building of socialism, not with the usual Cuban theme of the old regime and the revolution. Roberto Fernández Retamar's militant essay about Latin-American culture, *Calibán,* was considered an answer and complement to *Ariel,* the famous 1900 work by José Enrique Rodó. In Retamar's interpretation, the symbol of Latin-American and all third world peoples was not Ariel, but Caliban. A Cuban exile, Severo Sarduy, gained recognition through his work *Cobra,* which he described as "rococo, eccentric, macaronic, extravagant, art nouveau, pornographic, and outrageous."

Ecuador's Jorge Icaza, recognized as a classic writer of the indigenous novel for his *Huasipungo,* returned to print with a powerful trilogy called *Atrapados.*

In Mexico, as "an antidote against the notions of author and the intellectual property, and as a criticism of self and the writer and his masks," Octavio Paz published *Renga,* a collective poem in four languages, written in collaboration with Jacques Roubaud, Edoardo Sanguineti, and Charles Tomlinson. Outstanding Mexican poets of the 1950s with new works were Rosario Castellanos (*Poesía no eres tú,* her complete works to date); Jaime García Terrés (*Todo lo más por decir*); Jaime Sabines (*Maltiempo*); Enrique Gonzáles Rojo (*Para deletrear el infinito*); and Oscar Oliva (*Estado de sitio*). In contrast to the realistic narrative of such writers as Juan García Ponce (*Encuentros*), Sergio Pitol (*El tañido de una flauta*), or Roberto Páramo (*La condición de los héroes*), Hugo Iriart was a healthy anomaly trying to create a sort of *Lord of the Rings* with his novel *Galaor.* Although the best critical works came from Ramón Xirau, José Luis Martínez, Sergio Fernández, and especially from Gabriel Zaid (*Leer poesía*), the best narrative prose came from José Emilio Pacheco in *El principio del placer.*

Two collections of stories by José Luis González gave special brilliance to the literature of Puerto Rico: *La galería* and *Mambrú se fué a la guerra. Figuraciones en el mes de Marzo* by Emilio Díaz Valcárcel deserved equal mention for its humorous and critical vision of the bilingualism and the forced cultural schizophrenia in the island.

In Peru Alfredo Bryce Echenique established himself as the most outstanding post-Vargas Llosa narrator with *Huerto cerrado* (1968) and *Muerte de Sevilla en Madrid.* Mirko Lauer's works *Santa Rosita* and *El péndulo ondulante* were more experimental, halfway between prose and verse. The poems of Blanca Varela in *Valses y otras confesiones* brought forth lucidity and feeling.

Uruguayan rebel poetry showed the unanimous attitude adopted by intellectuals as a result of the crisis in their country. Some excellent works showed that there was still a place for lyricism: *Oidor andante,* by Aída Vitale; *Poemas de amor,* by Idea Vilariño; *Con bigote triste,* by Hugo Achugar. (SALVADOR BARROS)

NORWEGIAN

Min arm Min tarm confirmed septuagenarian Johan Borgen's position as one of Norway's most modern writers and perhaps its most intellectually mature. Through the experiences of a 32-year-old schoolmaster, the novel approached contemporary problems with refreshing humour and sparkling use of idiom and quotation. *Mitt hundeliv* provided an irresistible account of Borgen's relationships with dogs. Another contribution came from his daughter, Ane Borgen, *Evas,* a collection of short stories. Petter Mørk's short stories, *Grått og grønt,* were remarkable for their combination of storytelling, atmosphere, and social involvement.

Stein Mehren's successful first novel, *De utydelige,* dealt with young people torn between contemporary fads and ideologies. More parochial in outlook and less convincing as fiction, Dag Solstad's *Arild Asnes, 1970* described a young socialist writer's conversion to a Maoist-Leninist ideology. Finn Alnæs' *Festningen faller* dealt with the personal responsibilities of military command and Magnar Mikkelsen's documentary, *Masi, Norge,* with hydroelectric development in Finnmark.

The historical novel continued to attract attention. Sissel Lange-Nielsen's central figure in *Fangen på Patmos* was St. John the Apostle, while Kåre Holt's *Farvel til en kvinne* was set in early Viking times with Queen Åsa as a colourful heroine. With *Nikolas,* Ragnhild Magerøy continued a series of novels of medieval Norway, the Nikolas of the title being the Nikolaus Arnesson made famous by Ibsen in *The Pretenders.* Kåre Prytz' *Lenken* centred on the illicit love affair of a young priest of Hamar cathedral, also in medieval times. Marta Schumann's *Jomfru Maria på Sæbostad* portrayed 18th-century town and country cultures, while Knut Hauge's *Tidevatn* dealt with emigration to America from a 19th-century farming community. Upper-class life in mid-19th-century Norway provided the background of Yngvar Hauge's *Fru Julie.*

Nils Johan Rud's *Noveller i utvalg* consisted of 57 short stories selected by the author, while Tarjei Vesaas' posthumous *Huset og fuglen* was a copiously illustrated collection of odds and ends spanning 50 years of creative activity.

Outstanding among many volumes of poetry, Hans Børli's *Kyndelsmesse* had social involvement and premonitions of death as central themes. A sense of time running out also permeated Per Arneberg's *Oktobernetter.* Playful use of language and marked social purpose characterized Ernst Orvil's *Nok sagt.* A selection from 11 earlier volumes by this prolific writer, *Dikt i utvalg,* had appeared in 1971.

Hans Heiberg's *Så stort et hjerte. Henrik Wergeland* drew a lively portrait of an outstanding figure in Norwegian literature, while Finn Thorn's *Arne Garborg og kristendommen* surveyed central aspects of Garborg's work. (TORBJØRN STØVERUD)

SOVIET

The cleavage between the Western view of Soviet literature and official opinion in the Soviet Union widened during 1972. The position occupied by Aleksandr Solzhenitsyn, novelist and Nobel Prize winner, illustrated this cleavage; while the Soviet authorities feared the influence of his works, in the West his novels were best sellers and he was revered as a symbol of the free spirit struggling against the confines of an enclosed society. During 1972 Solzhenitsyn was constantly in the news; openly in the West, secretly in the Soviet Union. Repeated postponement of the Nobel Prize-giving ceremony, and final refusal by the Soviet government to allow it to take place, even in Moscow; an interview with Western journalists in which he described the atmosphere of suspicion and surveillance in which he lived; an outspoken Lenten letter to the patriarch of the Russian Orthodox Church, criticizing its timidity and time-serving; and publication in August of the Nobel lecture he had never been permitted to give created a public image of a man of high principle, courage, and spiritual insight. Translations during the year of *August 1914,* the first part of his epic interpretation of the tragedy of Russian history from 1914 to the 1960s, caused it to be acclaimed as a novel in which could already be seen unfolding the pattern of a work in the great tradition of Russian regenerative art.

Solzhenitsyn's fame saved him from violent persecution: others were less fortunate. Vladimir Bukovski, a leading young liberal writer and journalist who had already spent almost seven years in prisons, labour camps, and undergoing "psychiatric treatment," was sentenced to seven years' imprisonment, with five more in exile, for anti-Soviet propaganda. In May, Iosif (Joseph) Brodsky, widely regarded in the West as the most outstanding young poet writing in Russian, was expelled from the Soviet Union. A defendant in the political trials of the early 1960s, in 1964 he had been convicted of "social parasitism" and sent into exile near the Arctic Circle. He returned to Leningrad in 1966 but his poetry was not officially recognized although he was allowed to work as translator, mainly of the English Metaphysicals.

Since the defection in 1969 of the novelist Anatoli Kuznetsov, few Soviet writers had chosen to leave. Some preferred to risk arrest, imprisonment, detention in a mental hospital, and to work from within to change the regime. For the majority, however, acceptance of the official view of a writer's duty in a Communist society—to educate the new generation in the principles of Soviet Communism and to inspire them with a sense of patriotism, devotion to duty, and civic responsibility—presented no problems. These were the writers who were acclaimed as "loyal servants of the state."

Two of the year's most impressive works of fiction were inspired by the inauguration in 1970, to commemorate the centenary of Lenin's birth, of an All-Union Prize for the best study of the lives and achievements of Soviet workers. The first prize went to Antonina Koptyayeva's *On the Ural River,* an epic

Antonina Koptyayeva won the Soviet All-Union Prize for her novel "On the Ural River," published in 1972.

NOVOSTI PRESS AGENCY

NOVOSTI PRESS AGENCY

"The Choice," a play by Aleksei Arbuzov, was published in 1972.

novel about the revolutionary struggles and final victory of the workers in the Orenburg district in 1917–19. Olga Slavenko's *Horizons*, winner of the second prize, was a series of stories about Soviet steelworkers today. Of novels recalling the "Great Patriotic War," most outstanding were the third volume of Aleksandr Chakovski's *Blockade*, about the heroic defense of Leningrad; *896 Kilometres to Berlin*, sketches written in 1945 by the war correspondent Boris Polevoi; and the Ukrainian novelist D. Vishnevski's *Three Nights*.

Present-day heroism and devotion to duty were the themes of Anatoli Markusha's *No!*, a novel dedicated to his fellow pilots. Ernst Krenkel's continuation of *RAEM Are My Call Signals*, a fictionalized account in diary form of the rescue, against heavy odds, of the icebreaker "Chelyuskin," trapped in the ice in the Soviet Arctic in 1934, was also a story of real-life adventure, showing profound faith in the powers of endurance that enable man to conquer the elements.

Novels about modern life and its problems included Yuri Trifonov's *The Long Goodbye*, developing themes and characters from his earlier stories, and *Exchange* and *Preliminary Results*. The former fighter pilot Vladimir Semenikhov, who first gained fame with *Cosmonauts Live on Earth* (1966), exemplified, in *There Were Once Two Friends*, the need for a man to choose between friendship and duty.

In poetry, too, patriotism was a popular theme. Konstantin Simonov's *Vietnam. Summer 1970*, written after visiting Vietnam as a special correspondent, conveyed the horror, indignation, and pity aroused by the experience. The most impressive poems in the veteran Aleksandr Bezymenski's retrospective collection, *The Law of the Heart*, were tributes to Lenin, written in 1970. In his long, philosophical *Revolt of the Intellect* the Kalmyk poet David Kugultinov used effectively the metres and idiom of his native country's folk epic to denounce with passionate, visionary eloquence the forces at work to bring about the earth's destruction.

Among autobiographies that re-created the atmosphere of the past were Yuri Nagibin's *Byways of My Childhood;* the second volume of *Man and Time*, the memoirs of Marietta Shaginian, the great authority on Lenin's life (the first volume appeared in 1971); and the memoirs of Anastasia Tavetayeva, daughter of I. Tavetayev, an early 20th-century leader of new movements in art and literature, and sister of the poet Maria Tavetayeva, of interest for their inside information on developments in Russian cultural life. Two autobiographical works original in conception and execution were the continuation of Rasul Gamzatov's *My Dagestan*, a deeply personal, poetic account of his native country to which use of native idiom added piquancy; and Vera Ketlinskaya's *Evening. Windows. People*, three reflective essays in which she recalled, incidentally, memories of her life.

(DOROTHY M. PARTINGTON)

SPANISH

In critical circles, in literary journals, and in publishers' manifestos, a pedantic polemic centring on the possible existence or nonexistence of the contemporary Spanish novel was the most strident note of 1972. The controversy's main points of departure were provided by nationalist "international" congresses held in Spain and Spanish-speaking America, programmed colloquies in which new theories were propounded and transformed into instant dogma.

As the argument raged, the rhetorical question "Does a New Spanish Novel exist?" became a kind of publicity slogan for every new novel to come off the presses. Three novels by young writers, all published by Barral Editores (Barcelona), appeared on one fall day: *Las lecciones de Jena* by Félix de Azúa; *Alimento del salto* by Javier Fernández de Castro; and *La espiral* by Javier del Amo. Three principal characteristics were to be found in all three novels: a feigned and *fantaisiste* proletarian background; the use of prosaic language in place of any sensory or evocative use of language; and a tendentious assignment of blame to received spiritual concepts for the disorderly fate of contemporary man. On the basis of these three, at any rate, the answer to the question was bound to be an emphatic and unequivocal "no."

Worth a mountain of fashionable criticism was an edition of *Los solos de Clarín* (Leopoldo Alas). One of the pieces, a brief assessment of Menéndez y Pelayo, a wry eulogy of the most intelligent Spaniard of his century, was a masterpiece of humour, not normally a prominent feature of Spanish criticism.

An important poetical collection was *Poesía*, a wisely nonchronological selection of the verse of Pedro Salinas. The items were chosen by Julio Cortázar not from the point of view of the poet's "evolution" but on the basis of natural "affinities and rhythms and points of contact." Love poems predominated. *Palabra sobre palabra*, presenting the collected verse of Angel González, was characterized by a bitter, original humour under close poetic control. A collection of studies published in Spain by the Argentine Saul Yurkievich, *Fundadores de la nueva poesía latinoamericana*, provided considerable insight into the work of the five principal poets of Hispanic America, from César Vallejo to Octavio Paz—a survey of "approximations" to what Jorge Luis Borges had called "the ritual metaphors of the race."

Translations of foreign works into Spanish reached new heights of production, largely perhaps because native literature remained at a very low ebb. Notable was the achievement of Barral Editores in publishing the first translation in any language of Aleksandr Solzhenitsyn's *August 1914*. The work was expertly translated by José Laín Entralgo and Luis Abollado

Vargas. Laín Entralgo, who had spent many years in the Soviet Union, died a few days before publication in February.

One of the more exotic items of Hispanica to appear in 1972 was a bilingual edition, the first of its kind, of Romanian verse. *Poesía rumana contemporánea,* translated and edited by Darie Novaceanu and J. M. Caballero Bonald, included first translations of many works by Romanian poets from Tristan Tzara, a founder of Dada, to Dumitru Ion, who was born in 1945. (ANTHONY KERRIGAN)

SWEDISH

A threatened economic crisis in publishing curtailed publication of works by new authors in 1972, though established writers were not affected. Ylva Eggehorn consolidated her success as a Christian poet with *Jesus älskar dig,* as did Majken Johansson with *Från Magdala* and Bo Setterlind with *Landet i höjden.* Göran Sonnevi's *Det oavslutade språket* confirmed his intellectual and moral strength in grappling with problems of communication and alienation, while Werner Aspenström's *Under tiden* and Sandro Key-Åberg's *På sin höjd* illuminated the modern predicament in racier idiom. By comparison, the retrospection and poetic form of academician Harry Martinson's *Dikter om mörker och ljus* seemed rather old-fashioned.

Numerous memoirs and biographies included Tora Dahl's autobiographical *Brevet till Leonard,* former prime minister Tage Erlander's memoirs, and Staffan Tjerneld's biography of Alfred Nobel. Poet Jarl Hammarberg-Åkesson described communal family life in *Mina kvinnor min storfamilj,* and author/doctor P. C. Jersild presented episodes from his past in short story form. Märit Paulsen's *Du, människa?* was a blow by blow account of a few days in a woman factory-worker's struggle for human dignity, while Göran Palm's *Ett år på LM* described a year's experience on the shop floor. Lars Norén published *I den underjordiska himlen,* continuing his autobiographical trilogy with pimps, prostitutes, and hair-raising interiors, and two poetry collections, *Viltspeglar* and *Solitära dikter.*

Sune Jonsson's *Minnesskrift över den svenska bonden* combined superb photography with masterly prose commentary on bureaucratic agricultural policies that spelled death to traditional farming communities. Skillful use of the short story form was shown in Margareta Ekström's *Förhållandet till främmande makter,* Sören Fallgård's *Ansikten, hundar och cyklar,* and Lars Norman's *Löken.*

Among new novels, Artur Lundkvist's *Tvivla korsfarare,* about a 12th-century crusade, and Tore Zetterholm's *Vi möts vid Rynge,* about a 19th-century priest who sides with oppressed farmers, were also restatements of contemporary problems, while Ole Söderström's *Dr Eskilson och Sverige* concerned a Swedish editor/politician's Nazi sympathies in the 1930s. In *Berättelsen om Josef,* Per Gunnar Evander described the tragedy of an aging worker who kills his wife in terms of a murder case in which society may have been the real culprit. Kerstin Ekman's *Mörker och blåbärsris* amusingly described eking out a living in northern Sweden, Per Agne Ekelius' *Hemma i Sverige* told of a young couple's efforts to relate to a real world, and Sivar Arnér's *Byta människa* showed an anthropology lecturer, his mistress, and students exploring the need for restructured interpersonal relationships. (KARIN PETHERICK)

See also Libraries; Philosophy; Theatre.

ENCYCLOPÆDIA BRITANNICA FILMS. *Bartleby by Herman Melville* (1969); *Dr. Heidegger's Experiment by Nathaniel Hawthorne* (1969); *The Lady, or the Tiger? by Frank Stockton* (1969); *The Lottery by Shirley Jackson* (1969); *Magic Prison* (1969); *My Old Man by Ernest Hemingway* (1969); *James Dickey: Poet* (1970); *The Deserted Village* (1971); *The Lady of Shalott* (1971); *The Prisoner of Chillon* (1971); *Shaw vs. Shakespeare—Part I: The Character of Caesar; Part II: The Tragedy of Julius Caesar; Part III: Caesar and Cleopatra* (1971); *The Greek Myths* (1972); *Walt Whitman: Poet for a New Age* (1972); *Look in the Answer Book* (1972).

Luxembourg

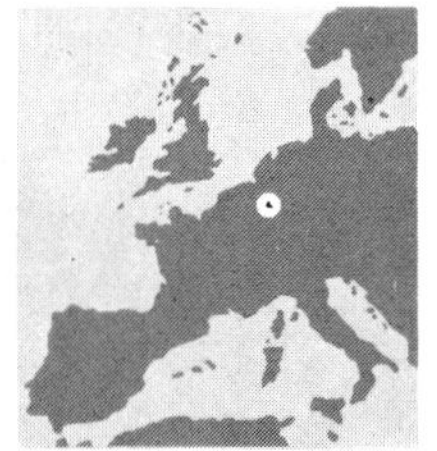

A constitutional monarchy, the Benelux country of Luxembourg is bounded on the east by West Germany, on the south by France, and on the west and north by Belgium. Area: 999 sq.mi. (2,586 sq.km.). Pop. (1972 est.): 342,000. Cap. and largest city: Luxembourg (pop., 1972 est., 78,500). Language: French, German, Luxembourgian. Religion: Roman Catholic 97%. Grand duke, Jean; prime minister in 1972, Pierre Werner.

On Jan. 13, 1972, the Chamber of Deputies approved a constitutional amendment that gave 18-year-olds the right to vote and lowered the age for holding elective office from 25 to 21 years.

Under the general realignment of currencies the Luxembourg franc was pegged at U.S. $0.0223135, a revaluation upward of 11.57%; the three Benelux states also adopted the wider 2.25% band of permissible fluctuations from the new parity. The increase in Luxembourg's gross national product for 1972 was estimated to be 2%, approximately three times that of 1971. Steel production continued to form the basis of the economy, but steel's portion of the GNP decreased from 30 to 25%. Under a national policy of diversification, over $200 million would ultimately be invested by U.S. corporations planning to use Luxembourg as a base from which to sell their products within the EEC.

The royal family made a state visit to the U.K. on June 14–15. Pres. Georges Pompidou and Mme Pompidou of France visited the Grand Duchy on

LUXEMBOURG

Education. (1969–70) Primary, pupils 36,035, teachers 1,758; secondary, pupils 8,689, teachers 629; vocational, pupils 9,347, teachers 690; higher, students 422.

Finance. Monetary unit: Luxembourg franc, at par with the Belgian franc, with (Sept. 18, 1972) a par value of LFr. 44.82 to U.S. $1 (free rate of LFr. 107.62 = £1 sterling). Budget (1972 est.): revenue LFr. 14,335,000,000; expenditure LFr. 14,463,000,000. Gross domestic product: (1970) LFr. 50.3 billion; (1969) LFr. 45 billion. Cost of living (1963 = 100): (June 1972) 136; (June 1971) 129.

Foreign Trade. *See* BELGIUM.

Transport and Communications. Roads (1971) 4,447 km. Motor vehicles in use (1971): passenger 98,813; commercial 12,182. Railways: (1970) 271 km.; traffic (1971) 259 million passenger-km., freight 748 million net ton-km. Air traffic (1970): 77,450,000 passenger-km.; freight 528,000 net ton-km. Telephones (Dec. 1970) 111,000. Radio licenses (Dec. 1970) 157,000. Television licenses (Dec. 1970) 71,000.

Agriculture. Production (in 000; metric tons; 1971; 1970 in parentheses): wheat 39 (28); oats 38 (34); rye 6 (3); barley 53 (44); potatoes 59 (68); wine 12 (24). Livestock (in 000; May 1971): cattle 192; sheep 4; pigs 106; chickens 410.

Industry. Production (in 000; metric tons; 1971): iron ore (30% metal content) 4,507; pig iron 4,588; crude steel 5,241; electricity (kw-hr.) 2,363,000; manufactured gas (cu.m.; 1970) 12,000.

Livestock and Animal Products: *see* Agriculture
Lumber: *see* Timber
Lutherans: *see* Religion
Machinery and Machine Tools: *see* Industrial Review
Madagascar: *see* Malagasy Republic
Magazines: *see* Publishing

May 3–4. Luxembourg recognized Bangladesh on February 11, and agreed to establish diplomatic relations with Albania at a future date. (ROBERT D. HODGSON)

Malagasy Republic

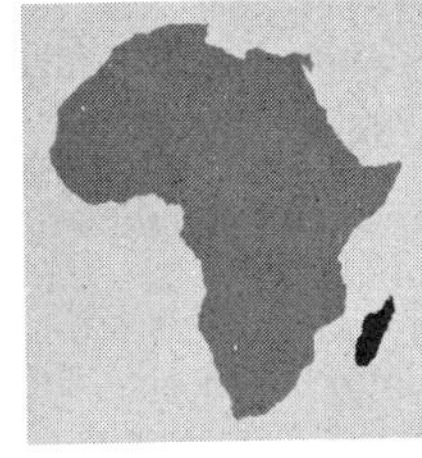

The Malagasy Republic occupies the island of Madagascar and minor adjacent islands in the Indian Ocean off the southeast coast of Africa. Area: 226,442 sq.mi. (586,486 sq. km.). Pop. (1970 est.): 7,423,864. Cap. and largest city: Tananarive (pop., 1971 est., 381,512). Language: French and Malagasy. Religion: Christian (approximately 50%) and traditional tribal beliefs. President until Oct. 8, 1972, Philibert Tsiranana; prime minister from May 18 and head of government from October 12, Gen. Gabriel Ramanantsoa.

While 1972 began auspiciously enough for President Tsiranana, reelected in January with more than 99% of votes cast, it was nonetheless to be the year of his political doom. On October 8, divested of all power, he was forced to retire.

The process began with disturbances at Tananarive medical school, which was promptly closed, provoking a wave of protest that spread to schools and colleges throughout the island. By early May the streets of the capital were the scene of almost constant demonstrations. The government retaliated by closing the schools and colleges and arresting the students' leaders.

The turning point came on May 13 when the security forces, overwhelmed by the turn of events, opened fire on the demonstrators, killing large numbers of them. Two days later the labour unions called a general strike. A curfew and a state of emergency were proclaimed, but the following day a huge crowd surged through the streets of the capital and set fire to the town hall, bringing further reprisals, more deaths, and the resignation of the minister of culture. In desperation Tsiranana gave full powers to Army Chief of Staff Gen. Gabriel Ramanantsoa (*see* BIOGRAPHY), whom he appointed prime minister.

WIDE WORLD

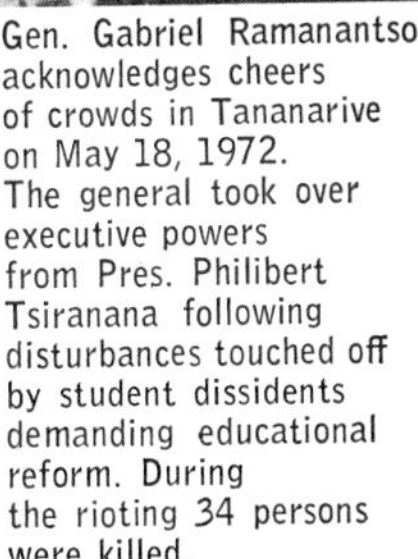

Gen. Gabriel Ramanantsoa acknowledges cheers of crowds in Tananarive on May 18, 1972. The general took over executive powers from Pres. Philibert Tsiranana following disturbances touched off by student dissidents demanding educational reform. During the rioting 34 persons were killed.

Ramanantsoa immediately negotiated a return to work by the unions, formed a new Cabinet with key powers in the hands of the military, and ordered the release of political prisoners, including former vice-president André Resampa. Dissociating itself from the policies of the old regime, the new government broke off diplomatic relations with South Africa, replaced French teaching staff with Malagasys, and established diplomatic relations with the U.S.S.R.—a direct contrast with the obsessive anti-Communism of Tsiranana.

In September extremists of the "Malagasy May"—the Marxist Kim and Zoam movements—made further demands, including the replacement of central government by people's communes, the evacuation of French bases, and the immediate dismissal of Tsiranana, still nominally chief of state. Ramanantsoa replied by proposing a referendum in which he asked the people to give him full powers for a five-year period. Tsiranana's warnings about military dictatorship went unheeded, and on October 8, in the first genuinely free electoral consultation in Malagasy history, Ramanantsoa's proposal was approved by 96% of the votes cast. As the new constitution did not provide for a president, Tsiranana was dismissed.

Ethnic rioting over proposed educational reforms in secondary schools, involving introduction of Malagasy as the sole language of instruction, broke out in Tamatave in mid-December. On December 14 the government declared a state of siege in and near the port city. (PHILIPPE DECRAENE)

MALAGASY REPUBLIC

Education. (1968–69) Primary, pupils 815,307, teachers 12,862; secondary, pupils 94,104, teachers 4,158; vocational, pupils 6,376, teachers 494; teacher training, students 2,627, teachers (1964–65) 118; higher (at University of Madagascar), students 3,429, teaching staff 162.

Finance. Monetary unit: Malagasy franc, at par with the CFA franc, with (Sept. 18, 1972) a parity of MalFr. 50 to the French franc (MalFr. 255.79 = U.S. $1; free rate of MalFr. 612.37 = £1 sterling). Gold, SDRs, and foreign exchange: (June 1972) U.S. $52.1 million; (June 1971) U.S. $44.6 million. Budget (1972 est.) balanced at MalFr. 52.5 billion.

Foreign Trade. (1971) Imports MalFr. 59,270,000,000; exports MalFr. 40,810,000,000. Import sources: France 56%; West Germany 9%; U.S. 5%. Export destinations: France 34%; U.S. 22%; Réunion 8%; Malaysia 7%. Main exports: coffee 26%; vanilla 9%; rice 5%.

Transport and Communications. Roads (1970) 26,937 km. (including 8,513 km. main roads). Motor vehicles in use (1970): passenger *c.* 45,500; commercial (including buses) *c.* 42,300. Railways: (1969) 883 km.; traffic (1971) 200 million passenger-km., freight 246 million net ton-km. Air traffic (1971): 304.4 million passenger-km.; freight 10,719,000 net ton-km. Telephones (Dec. 1970) 27,000. Radio receivers (Dec. 1970) 540,000. Television receivers (Dec. 1970) 3,200.

Agriculture. Production (in 000; metric tons; 1971; 1970 in parentheses): rice 1,901 (1,865); corn 118 (109); cassava (1970) 1,218, (1969) 1,253; sweet potatoes (1970) 350, (1969) 367; potatoes 108 (94); dry beans *c.* 52 (49); bananas (1970) 262, (1969) 257; peanuts 40 (41); sugar, raw value (1971–72) 115, (1970–71) 102; coffee 65 (67); tobacco 5.7 (4.9); sisal 25 (26). Livestock (in 000; Dec. 1970): cattle *c.* 10,000; sheep *c.* 500; pigs *c.* 530; goats *c.* 900; chickens *c.* 11,200.

Malawi

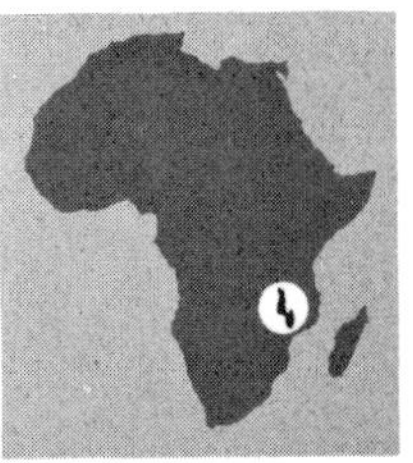

A republic and member of the Commonwealth of Nations in east central Africa, Malawi is bounded by Tanzania, Mozambique, and Zambia. Area: 45,747 sq.mi. (118,484 sq.km.). Pop. (1971 est.): 4,552,000. Cap.: Zomba (pop., 1971 est., 20,000). Largest city: Blantyre (pop., 1971 est., 169,000). Language: English and Nyanja. Religion: predominantly traditional

CENTRAL PRESS/
PICTORIAL PARADE

Following a visit by Pres. J. J. Fouché of South Africa, Pres. H. Kamuzu Banda (above) called on African governments to refrain from criticizing South Africa.

beliefs. President in 1972, Hastings Kamuzu Banda.

In the closing months of 1971 an estimated 3,000 refugees crossed into Malawi from the Tete area of Mozambique, some, at least, to escape the soldiers searching for supporters of the Front for the Liberation of Mozambique (FRELIMO). In December 1971 it was learned that South Africa had offered to sell arms to Malawi for use against FRELIMO guerrillas who might threaten the border region. This was the first known occasion when South African-made arms had been exported.

The United Kingdom granted Malawi 2.3 million kwachas (£1 million) toward construction of an army barracks for the 2nd Battalion Malawi Rifles to be established at Lilongwe, site of the new capital city. Under the agreement Malawi was to buy British military equipment from its own resources. The establishment of a second battalion would effectively double the Army's strength.

In mid-March Pres. J. J. Fouché of South Africa paid the first state visit ever made by a South African president to an independent black African state when he visited Blantyre. Fouché appealed for peaceful coexistence and for cooperation among African states in order to make possible a concerted attack on poverty, ignorance, and disease. On Fouché's departure President Banda called on African governments not to attack South Africa because to do so could only lead to their downfall. Following criticism of Malawi's ties with South Africa voiced by other members of the Organization of African Unity (OAU), Malawi alone failed to send a delegation to attend the 19th session of the OAU, which was held in Rabat, Morocco, in June.

Following President Banda's description of the banned sect of Jehovah's Witnesses (numbering about 20,000) as "devil's witnesses," the youth wing of the ruling Malawi Congress Party was reported to have instituted a purge against the sect's members, who refused to recognize any nonreligious authority.

MALAWI

Education. (1968) Primary, pupils 333,876, teachers 8,564; secondary, pupils 9,283, teachers 508; vocational, pupils 536, teachers 53; teacher training, students 1,085, teachers 119; higher (University of Malawi), students (1969) 980, teaching staff 129.

Finance. Monetary unit: kwacha, with (Sept. 18, 1972) a free rate of 0.82 kwacha to U.S. $1 (par value of 2 kwachas = £1 sterling). Gold, SDRs, and foreign exchange, official: (June 1972) U.S. $34,080,000; (June 1971) U.S. $28,560,000. Budget (1970–71 rev. est.) balanced at 37,120,000 kwachas (total expenditure 86,210,000 kwachas).

Foreign Trade. (1971) Imports 89,853,000 kwachas; exports 59,302,000 kwachas. Import sources: U.K. 28%; Rhodesia 15%; South Africa 10%; Japan 7%; Iran 7%. Export destinations: U.K. 44%; Rhodesia 7%; Zambia 7%; Ireland 5%; South Africa 5%. Main exports: tobacco 37%; tea 20%; peanuts 10%.

Transport and Communications. Roads (1971) 10,721 km. Motor vehicles in use (1971): passenger 10,200; commercial 7,600. Railways: (1970) 465 km.; traffic (1971) 65 million passenger-km., freight 202 million net ton-km. Air traffic (1970): 27,662,000 passenger-km.; freight 427,000 net ton-km. Telephones (Dec. 1970) 13,000. Radio receivers (Dec. 1970) 90,000.

Agriculture. Production (in 000; metric tons; 1971; 1970 in parentheses): corn *c.* 1,100 (*c.* 900); cassava (1970) *c.* 144, (1969) *c.* 143; sweet potatoes (1970) *c.* 45, (1969) *c.* 43; tobacco 22 (19); cotton, lint *c.* 9 (8); peanuts *c.* 180 (*c.* 152); tea 19 (19). Livestock (in 000; 1970–71): cattle 426; sheep 118; goats 636; pigs 143; poultry 8,000.

Industry. Production (1971): electricity (public supply) 144 million kw-hr.; cement 65,000 metric tons.

About 18,000 refugee Witnesses had fled into neighbouring states by December.

While denying any attempt at nationalization, the president announced on Dec. 7, 1971, that the Companies' Act was to be amended to require foreign companies in Malawi to set up subsidiaries with boards of directors responsible either to local stockholders or to the government. In his third Cabinet reshuffle in four months, Banda in June assumed responsibility for the portfolios of agriculture (which made up 90% of Malawi's exports) and natural resources. In the same month the three-year-old ban on miniskirts was somewhat relaxed to help promote tourism. (KENNETH INGHAM)

Malaysia

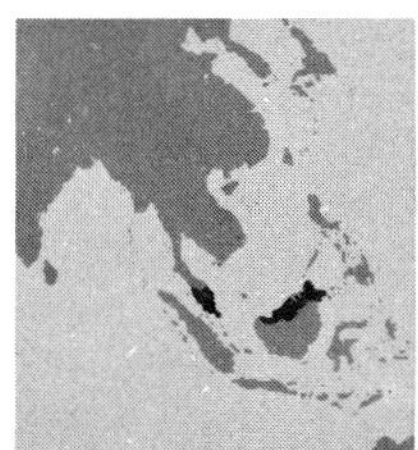

A federation within the Commonwealth of Nations comprising the 11 states of the former Federation of Malaya, Sabah, and Sarawak, Malaysia is a federal constitutional monarchy situated in Southeast Asia at the southern end of the Malay Peninsula (excluding Singapore) and on the northern part of the island of Borneo. Area: 127,316 sq.mi. (329,747 sq.km.). Pop. (1971 est.): 12,324,000. Cap. and largest city: Kuala Lumpur (pop., 1970, 451,810). Official language: Malay. Religion: Malays are Muslim; Indians mainly Hindu; Chinese mainly Buddhist, Confucian, and Taoist. Supreme head of state in 1972, with the title of *yang di-pertuan agong,* Tuanku Abdul Halim Mu'azzam Shah ibni al-Marhum Sultan Badlishah; prime minister, Tun Abdul Razak.

The Alliance Party, a coalition of the United Malays National Organization, the Malaysian Chinese Association, and the Malaysian Indian Congress, which had been in control of Malaysia since independence, formed coalition governments in 1972 at the state level with the Sarawak United People's Party in Sarawak, the Gerakan Rakyat Malaysia Party in Penang, the People's Progressive Party in Perak, and the Partai Islam in Kelantan. With the coalitions, the opposition strength in the 144-member House of Representatives was reduced to 26, made up of Democratic Action Party 9, Sarawak National Party 9, Social Justice Party 4, and independents 4.

Prompted by the need for a peaceful and stable Southeast Asia, free from the pressure and manipulation of power politics, Malaysia called for the neutralization of the region by the superpowers, including China. This concept became one of the main priorities of Malaysia's foreign policy and was endorsed by the foreign ministers of Indonesia, Malaysia, the Philippines, Singapore, and Thailand at a meeting of the Association of Southeast Asian Nations (ASEAN) held in Kuala Lumpur in November 1971. Their declaration called for the recognition of Southeast Asia as a zone of peace, freedom, and neutrality. In association with Indonesia, Malaysia rejected the proposal by the big powers that the Strait of Malacca be internationalized, arguing that the strait was territorial waters shared by the two countries. Malaysia did, however, guarantee the right of "innocent passage" to all ships.

Internally, Communism and subversion, although under control, remained a threat to security. Continuing operations by security forces against infiltrating

Communist guerrillas frustrated their attempts at establishing permanent footholds in the country. In Sarawak, the terrorist activities conducted by the Sarawak Communist Organization were more pronounced, as the Communist underground apparatus geared itself to prepare for armed struggle. In February the government issued a White Paper to highlight this threat. Malaysia and Indonesia signed a joint agreement for better cooperation and more effective control and action against the Communists along their common border in East Malaysia. A similar agreement existed between Malaysia and Thailand, whereby security forces of both sides could enter five miles into each other's territory during anti-Communist operations.

The performance of the economy in 1971 fell short of the average annual 6.5% growth projected under the second five-year plan (1971–75), as a result of which the per capita gross national product rose only marginally from M$1,065 in 1970 to M$1,075 in 1971. However, in spite of the decline in export earnings, Malaysia enjoyed another year of surplus in the overall balance of payments, which rose by M$124 million, compared with a surplus of M$58 million in 1970. If the allocation of Special Drawing Rights for 1971, amounting to M$61 million, was added to the overall surplus, there was an increase of M$185 million in the net external reserves from M$2,589,000,000 at the end of 1970 to M$2,774,000,000 at the end of 1971—sufficient to finance more than eight months of retained imports at the 1971 level. This contributed in no small way to Malaysia's creditworthiness, which enabled it to borrow on better terms in foreign capital markets and helped to encourage foreign investment. Unemployment, although slightly better than in 1970, stood at almost 7.8%.

In February Queen Elizabeth II paid a two-week state visit to Malaysia and was installed as vice-chancellor of the University of Malaya. Prime Minister Tun Abdul Razak made a very successful tour of Eastern Europe and the Soviet Union in October. Malaysia and Indonesia agreed on a joint spelling system for the national language. The Malaysian Airlines System (MAS) was launched as the national flag carrier following the split-up of Malaysia-Singapore Airlines (MSA). A number of letter-bombs addressed to diplomats representing Middle Eastern states in Europe and the U.S. were discovered to have been posted at Kuala Lumpur International Airport in October. (MAHINDER SINGH RANDHAVA)

MALAYSIA

Education. *West Malaysia.* (1969) Primary, pupils 1,369,376, teachers 44,987; secondary, pupils 512,212, teachers 19,726; vocational, pupils 12,632, teachers 407; higher (including 2 universities; 1968), students 13,045, teaching staff 1,160. *East Malaysia:* Sabah. (1969) Primary, pupils 114,322, teachers 4,655; secondary, pupils 29,380, teachers 1,071; vocational, pupils 180, teachers 20; teacher training, students 730, teachers 50. *East Malaysia:* Sarawak. (1970) Primary, pupils 144,007, teachers 4,404; secondary, pupils 35,459, teachers 1,424; vocational, pupils 343, teachers 28; teacher training, students 269, teachers 55; higher, students 430.

Finance. Monetary unit: Malaysian dollar, with (Sept. 18, 1972) a par value of M$2.82 to U.S. $1 (free rate of M$6.78 = £1 sterling). Gold, SDRs, and foreign exchange, official: (June 1971) U.S. $787 million; (June 1970) U.S. $652 million. Budget (1971 est.): revenue M$2,433,000,000; expenditure M$2,463,000,000. Gross national product: (1970) M$11,734,000,000; (1969) M$10,985,000,000. Money supply: (June 1972) M$2,341,000,000; (June 1971) M$2,036,000,000. Cost of living (West Malaysia; 1963 = 100): (June 1972) 109; (June 1971) 106.

Foreign Trade. (1971) Imports M$4,381,000,000; exports M$5,001,000,000. Import sources: Japan 19%; U.K. 15%; Singapore 8%; U.S. 7%; Australia 6%; West Germany 5%; China 5%. Export destinations: Singapore 22%; Japan 18%; U.S. 13%; U.K. 7%. Main exports: rubber 29%; tin 18%; timber 17%; palm oil 8%.

Transport and Communications. Roads (1970) 23,710 km. Motor vehicles in use (1970): passenger 279,400; commercial (including buses) 72,600. Railways (1970): 1,822 km.; traffic (including Singapore) 647 million passenger-km., freight 1,208,000,000 net ton-km. Air traffic (Malaysia-Singapore Airlines; 1971): 1,713,300,000 passenger-km.; freight 33,285,000 net ton-km. Shipping (1971): merchant vessels 100 gross tons and over 94; gross tonnage 85,473. Shipping traffic (1970) goods loaded 23,397,000 metric tons, unloaded 9,593,000 metric tons. Telephones (Jan. 1971) 177,000. Radio licenses (Dec. 1968) 423,000. Television receivers (Dec. 1969) 130,000.

Agriculture. Production (in 000; metric tons; 1971; 1970 in parentheses): rice 1,788 (1,678); rubber 1,325 (1,276); copra *c.* 182 (176); palm oil 762 (646); tea (East Malaysia only) *c.* 3.5 (3.4); bananas (1970) *c.* 355, (1969) *c.* 355; pineapples (1970) 353, (1969) 376; pepper (Sarawak only; 1970) 24, (1969) 29; timber (cu.m.; 1970) 23,400, (1969) 22,300; fish catch (1970) 365, (1969) 372. Livestock (in 000; 1970–71): cattle 362; pigs *c.* 990; goats 359; sheep (West Malaysia only) *c.* 40; buffalo 309; poultry *c.* 29,250.

Industry. Production (in 000; metric tons; 1971): tin concentrates (metal content) 75; bauxite 978; cement (West Malaysia only) 1,096; iron ore (West Malaysia only; 56% metal content) 950; crude oil (Sarawak only) 3,275; gold (troy oz.; 1969) 5.4; electricity (kw-hr.) 3,700,000.

Maldives

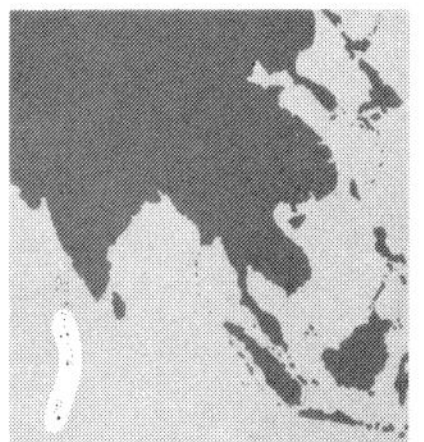

Maldives, a republic in the Indian Ocean consisting of about two thousand small islands, lies southwest of the southern tip of India. Area: 115 sq.mi. (298 sq.km.). Pop. (1970): 114,469. Cap.: Male (pop., 1970, 13,610). Language: Divehi. Religion: Muslim. Sultan, Emir Muhammad Farid Didi; president in 1972, Ibrahim Nasir.

Queen Elizabeth II's visit to Maldives in March 1972, during the royal tour of the Indian Ocean, contributed substantially toward improved relations between the Maldivian government and Britain. Maldives' foreign policy of nonalignment had veered leftward with that of neighbouring Sri Lanka (Ceylon), and weapons and other aid were being supplied to the country by the Soviet Union. Nonetheless, the queen's gesture of friendship and gifts for education and medicine helped ease the delicate relationship between Maldives and the Royal Air Force, which leases a staging post in Addu Atoll on Gan.

The queen officially opened a new radio station on Gan and met the atoll chief, Ahmed Salih Ali Didi. Her visit coincided with a remarkable air-sea rescue when 6 of 13 Maldivian fishermen were saved after 19 days adrift at sea. The RAF continued supplying meteorological information to the entire area, as well as maintaining a link between Great Britain and Hong Kong in the defense of Southeast Asia.

(MOLLY MORTIMER)

MALDIVES

Education. (1970–71) Primary, pupils 648, teachers 29; secondary, pupils 327, teachers 26.

Finance and Trade. Monetary unit: Maldivian rupee, with (Sept. 18, 1972) a nominal free rate of MRs. 6.36 to U.S. $1 (MRs. 15.57 = £1 sterling). Budget (1970) expenditure MRs. 17,289,000. Foreign trade (1970): imports MRs. 11,790,000; exports MRs. 22,986,000. Trade is mainly with Ceylon. Main exports (metric tons): fish 5,200; copra 78; shells 49.

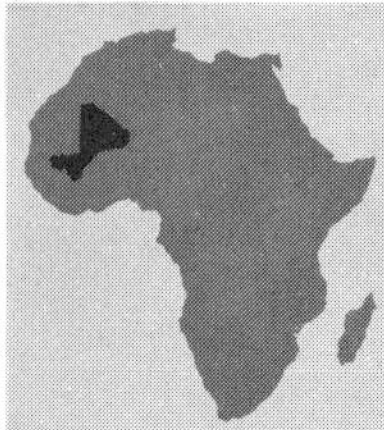

Mali

A republic of West Africa, Mali is bordered by Algeria, Niger, Upper Volta, Ivory Coast, Guinea, Senegal, and Mauritania. Area: 478,822 sq.mi. (1,240,142 sq.km.). Pop. (1971 est.): 5,143,000. Cap. and largest city: Bamako (pop., 1969 est., 189,200). Language: French (official); Hamito-Semitic and various tribal dialects. Religion: Muslim 65%; animist 30%. Head of military government in 1972, Col. Moussa Traoré.

In 1972 Mali's foreign relations were marked by a distinct rapprochement with France and with other states of French-speaking Africa as well as by the continued development of cooperation with the U.S.S.R. French Defense Minister Michel Debré in January paid an official visit to Mali during which he announced an imminent increase in French economic aid. On April 24–28 Col. Moussa Traoré paid an official visit to France. French Pres. Georges Pompidou renewed the promise of increased economic and technical assistance, and the two heads of state discussed the problems caused by the influx of Malian immigrant workers into France. The French secretary of state for foreign affairs visited Mali in September.

A delegation from the U.S.S.R. headed by the Soviet vice-minister of defense was received in Bamako in March, and in September the Malian defense minister paid a visit to Moscow. Both visits concerned the supply of Soviet equipment to the Malian Army and the training of Malian Air Force personnel by Soviet pilots and technicians. In July the Soviet Union offered a loan of $3 million to finance further development of Mali's mining industry.

While there were no overt signs of internal tension during the year, a persistent undercurrent of hostility to the military regime seemed to remain. In June international opinion was alerted about the condition of approximately 50 political prisoners held since the coup of November 1968. It was said that the prisoners had been transferred to the Taoudenni salt mines in the Sahara where four had died and others were in a critical condition. In August, Capt. Yoro Diakité, former vice-president of the Military Committee of National Liberation, was sentenced to forced labour for life for participating in an attempted coup on March 9, 1971. (PHILIPPE DECRAENE)

MALI

Education. (1969–70) Primary, pupils 218,416, teachers 6,265; secondary, pupils 2,823, teachers 233; vocational, pupils 2,889, teachers 281; teacher training, students 1,469, teachers 93; higher, students 392, teaching staff 92.

Finance. Monetary unit: Mali franc, with (Sept. 18, 1972) a par value of MFr. 511.57 to U.S. $1 (free rate of MFr. 1,225 = £1 sterling). Budget (1970 est.) balanced at MFr. 22,651,000,000. Money supply: (March 1972) MFr. 34,240,000,000; (March 1971) MFr. 30,210,000,000.

Foreign Trade. (1971) Imports MFr. 30.5 billion; exports MFr. 19,630,000,000. Import sources (1969): France 39%; U.S.S.R. 10%; Ivory Coast 9%; China 8%; Senegal 8%. Export destinations (1969): Ivory Coast 40%; Ghana 21%; France 16%; Japan 5%. Main exports: cotton 25%; peanuts 18%; fish 6%.

Agriculture. Production (in 000; metric tons; 1971; 1970 in parentheses): millet and sorghum 900 (600); rice 150 (138); corn *c.* 80 (*c.* 80); peanuts *c.* 170 (158); sweet potatoes *c.* 67 (*c.* 67); cassava (1970) *c.* 155, (1969) *c.* 150; cotton, lint *c.* 25 (22); beef and veal *c.* 50 (*c.* 50); mutton and lamb *c.* 34 (*c.* 33). Livestock (in 000; 1970–71): cattle *c.* 5,500; sheep *c.* 5,900; horses 174; asses *c.* 460.

Malta

An island in the Mediterranean Sea, between Sicily and Tunisia, Malta is a parliamentary state and a member of the Commonwealth of Nations. Area: 122 sq.mi. (316 sq.km.), including Malta, Gozo, and Comino. Pop. (1971 est.): 322,070. Cap.: Valletta (pop., 1971 est., 15,401). Largest city: Sliema (pop., 1971 est., 21,887). Language: Maltese and English. Religion: mainly Roman Catholic. Queen, Elizabeth II; governor-general in 1972, Sir Anthony Mamo; prime minister, Dom Mintoff.

A new relationship was established between Malta and the U.K. in 1972. Protracted and hard negotiations between the parties reached a critical stage more than once during the first three months of the year. The archbishop of Malta, NATO Secretary-General Joseph Luns, and the Italian government all intervened during the discussion. Meanwhile, the withdrawal of British forces from the island, begun in January after Dom Mintoff had demanded higher payments in return for continued use of the naval base, proceeded steadily.

Finally, on March 26, an agreement was signed in London superseding the ten-year agreement on defense and financial aid entered into by the preceding Maltese government. Henceforth, the Malta base could only be used for British and NATO defense purposes, and it could not be used against any Arab country. The U.K. government undertook to pay Malta £14 million annually for the next seven years. The Maltese government would also enter into agreements with the Italian, West German, Canadian, and other governments, leading to payment of a further £7 million, part of which would be in the form of grants and part in the form of soft loans. Mintoff's request in December for an additional payment to compensate for the effects of the floating of sterling was rejected

MALTA

Education. (1967–68) Primary, pupils 52,585, teachers 2,494; secondary, pupils 9,946, teachers 791; vocational, pupils 2,359, teachers 215; higher (including Royal University of Malta), students 1,449, teaching staff (1966–67) 172.

Finance. Monetary unit: Maltese pound, with (Sept. 18, 1972) a free rate of M£0.95 to £1 sterling (M£1 = U.S. $2.57). Gold, SDRs, and foreign exchange, official: (June 1972) U.S. $227.4 million; (June 1971) U.S. $186.3 million. Budget (1971–72): revenue M£45,262,000; expenditure M£44,315,000.

Foreign Trade. (1971) Imports M£65,377,000; exports M£18,815,000. Import sources: U.K. 37%; Italy 17%; West Germany 5%; U.S. 5%. Export destinations: U.K. 40%; Italy 8%; West Germany 8%; Belgium-Luxembourg 5%; 10% as ship's stores. Main exports: clothing 29%; textile yarns and fabrics 10%; rubber products 9%; petroleum products 7%. Tourism (1970): visitors 170,900; gross receipts U.S. $23 million.

Transport and Communications. Roads (1969) 1,200 km. Motor vehicles in use (1970): passenger 41,800; commercial (including buses) 11,300. There are no railways. Air traffic (1971): 169,250,000 passenger-km.; freight 2,207,000 net ton-km. Shipping (1971): merchant vessels 100 gross tons and over 23; gross tonnage 34,500. Ships entered (1969) vessels totaling 1,722,000 net registered tons; goods loaded (1970) 50,000 metric tons, unloaded 956,000 metric tons. Telephones (Dec. 1970) 40,000. Radio receivers (Dec. 1968) 89,000. Television licenses (Dec. 1970) 47,000.

by Britain and its NATO allies. In April Mintoff concluded an economic agreement in Peking; the Chinese government was to provide an interest-free loan of £17 million, repayable up to 1994 with commodities exported to China.

Decimal currency was adopted on May 16. Following the U.K. government's decision to allow sterling to float, the Maltese government maintained its policy of steering the Maltese pound away from any automatic parity with foreign currencies under pressure. The budget for 1972–73 was underlined by a new policy of limiting borrowing to the barest minimum and on the softest possible terms. There were increases in charges for electricity, telephone, and postal services and in income tax payable by limited liability companies. (ALBERT GANADO)

Mathematics

Noteworthy advances in analysis, topology, algebra, and algebraic geometry were achieved in 1972. In analysis, progress was made on the Bieberbach conjecture that deals with certain functions of one complex variable. Let $f(z)$ be such a function; assume that it is analytic for $|z| < 1$ and univalent there (never takes the same value twice). Analyticity means that f is given by a power series, and it is a harmless normalization to assume that the series has the form $z + a_2z^2 + \ldots a_nz^n \ldots$. The conjecture that $|a_n|$ can be no larger than n was made by Ludwig Bieberbach in 1916, and he proved it for $n = 2$. The case $n = 3$ was handled by K. Löwner in 1923, and $n = 4$ was settled by Paul Garabedian and Menahem Schiffer in the mid-1950s. There are indications that the problem becomes easier when n is an even number, for in 1968–69 M. Ozawa and Roger Pederson, working independently, skipped $n = 5$ and successfully went on to $n = 6$. In 1972 Pederson and Schiffer filled the gap by proving $|a_5| \leqq 5$.

In topology in 1972 foliations became better understood. A foliation of a topological space is, roughly speaking, a slicing of it into well-behaved pieces, something like shredding a head of lettuce into its leaves. The following had been a basic question. Let S_n be the n-sphere, that is, the set of all points at unit distance from the origin in $(n + 1)$-dimensional Euclidean space. If n is odd, does there exist a foliation of S_n into $(n - 1)$-dimensional pieces? (One assumes n to be odd, since a relatively easy argument shows that there can be no such foliation of an n-sphere for an even n.)

In 1944 G. Reeb had found a foliation of the 3-sphere. The leaves for this foliation look like open discs (interiors of circles) except for a final leaf that is a torus (the topologist's name for a doughnut-shaped space). After 28 more years the general problem was solved when I. Tamura, building on the work of H. Blain Lawson, found a foliation for every odd-dimensional sphere.

The first of two achievements in algebra concerned finite simple groups. A group is an abstract mathematical system with a multiplication satisfying some reasonable assumptions. Groups arise nearly everywhere in mathematics and in the applications of mathematics to the sciences. Groups can be broken down into primordial building blocks which are called simple. All finite simple groups known until 1962 had the property that the number of elements in the group was divisible by 3. Then, Michio Suzuki discovered a family of groups for which divisibility by 3 did not occur. In 1972 John Thompson discovered a proof that the only such groups with this property are the ones found by Suzuki.

The second algebraic discovery answered an old question on division algebras. A division algebra has two operations, written as addition and multiplication, which satisfy all the familiar rules of arithmetic except that multiplication is not assumed to be commutative (the product AB need not equal BA). If multiplication is commutative, the system is called a field. Previously, all known examples of division algebras had been of a type called crossed products, the name coming from the fact that they are obtained by "crossing" a group with a field in a certain way. Every division algebra has a certain dimension that is known to be a square number, and up to dimension 16 it had been proved by Joseph H. M. Wedderburn and Abraham A. Albert that division algebras are necessarily crossed products. But S. A. Amitsur constructed some new division algebras and proved that they were not crossed products. The smallest of his dimensions was 64, and so the status of dimensions 25, 36, and 49 remained uncertain.

In algebraic geometry C. Clemens and P. Griffith gave a counterexample to J. Lüroth's theorem in dimension three. Although the problem is motivated by geometry and studied in a geometric way, it is most simply described in a purely algebraic manner. A field k in which any polynomial equation is solvable is called algebraically closed, and the complex numbers form the most important example. Let L be the field of all rational functions (ratios of polynomials) in n variables with coefficients in k. L is said to be "purely transcendental" over k. Let K be a field lying between k and L. Is K purely transcendental over k? For $n = 1$ the affirmative answer (due to Lüroth) is a century old, and is valid whether or not k is algebraically closed. For $n = 2$, the answer is again "yes" (G. Castelnuovo and Oscar Zariski). But for $n = 3$, the answer is now known to be "no." The field used for this discovery comes from the amazingly simple equation $x^3 + y^3 + z^3 + t^3 = 1$, so that K can be explicitly exhibited by adjoining to k the three variables x,y,z and then the cube root of $1 - x^3 - y^3 - z^3$. It is easy to trap K between k and a purely transcendental field. However, the proof by Clemens and Griffith that K is not itself purely transcendental is quite elaborate and uses much of the sophisticated machinery of today's algebraic geometry.

(IRVING KAPLANSKY)

Mauritania

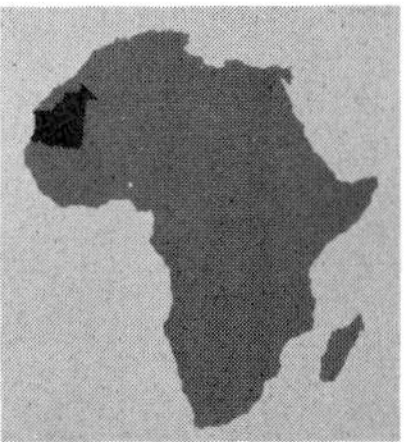

The Islamic Republic of Mauritania is on the Atlantic coast of West Africa, adjoining Spanish Sahara, Algeria, Mali, and Senegal. Area: 398,000 sq.mi. (1,030,700 sq.km.). Pop. (1971 est.): 1.2 million. Cap.: Nouakchott (pop., 1971 est., 35,000). Language: Arabic, French. Religion: Muslim. President in 1972, Mokhtar Ould Daddah.

In 1972 there were confrontations between the Mauritanian government and both the student and the trade union movements. Serious disturbances in the secondary schools in February led to a large number of expulsions and the temporary closing of several schools and colleges. Throughout the year the student movement kept up a constant barrage of protest against the repressive measures taken in the secondary

Manganese: *see* Mining

Manufacturing: *see* Economy, World; Employment, Wages, and Hours; Industrial Review

Marine Biology: *see* Life Sciences

Marriage: *see* Vital Statistics

MAURITANIA
Education. (1969–70) Primary, pupils 28,500, teachers (1965–66) 1,025; secondary, pupils 3,012, teachers (1963–64) 61; vocational (1968–69), pupils 159; teacher training (1968–69), students 294.
Finance. Monetary unit: CFA franc, with (Sept. 18, 1972) a parity of CFA Fr. 50 to the French franc (CFA Fr. 255.79 = U.S. $1; free rate of CFA Fr. 612.37 = £1 sterling). Gold, SDRs, and foreign exchange, central bank: (May 1972) U.S. $5.9 million; (May 1971) U.S. $4.2 million. Budget (1971 est.) balanced at CFA Fr. 9 billion.
Foreign Trade. (1971) Imports CFA Fr. 15,780,-000,000; exports CFA Fr. 25,129,000,000. Import sources: France 41%; U.S. 11%; U.K. 7%; Senegal 6%; West Germany 5%. Export destinations: France 21%; U.K. 16%; Belgium-Luxembourg 13%; West Germany 12%; Italy 11%; Spain 9%; Japan 6%. Main exports: iron ore 83%; fish 7%; copper ore 4%.

schools. In addition a wave of industrial action and demands late in 1971 led the government to take on the official Union des Travailleurs Mauritaniens.

In foreign affairs President Ould Daddah's policy remained resolutely progressive. He received a visit in February from Libya's revolutionary leader Col. Muammar al-Qaddafi, and in June from deposed Prince Norodom Sihanouk of Cambodia. The question of the political future of the Spanish Sahara preoccupied the president, and in this connection he visited Algeria in January and Morocco in September. On November 28 Ould Daddah announced that Mauritania proposed to introduce its own currency and sought a revision of its relationship with the West African Monetary Union. In December two new "superministries" of Finance and Trade and Planning and Development were set up. (PHILIPPE DECRAENE)

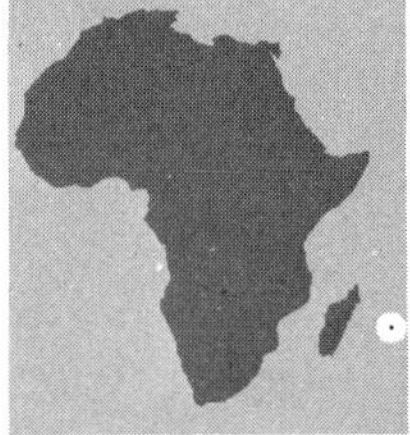

Mauritius

The parliamentary state of Mauritius, a member of the Commonwealth of Nations, lies about 500 mi. E of the Malagasy Republic in the Indian Ocean. Area: 720 sq.mi. (1,865 sq.km.). Pop. (1971 est.): 856,000, including Indian and Pakistani 67%; Creole (mixed French and African) 29%; others 4%. Cap. and largest city: Port Louis (pop., 1971 est., 142,270). Language: English (official). Religion (1962): Hindu 49%; Roman Catholic 32%; Muslim 16%. Queen, Elizabeth II; governor-general in 1972, Sir Leonard Williams (d. December 27; *see* OBITUARIES); prime minister, Sir Seewoosagur Ramgoolam.

The fifth year of independence saw the first visit by a reigning sovereign when Queen Elizabeth II landed on Mauritius during her Indian Ocean tour in March 1972. The prime minister visited Peking in April, establishing diplomatic links at ambassadorial level and obtaining a reported $75 million loan. Despite a commitment not to jeopardize British naval facilities, fueling rights were granted to Soviet ships.

A state of emergency, declared in December 1971 in the wake of strikes protesting a law regulating work stoppages, continued in 1972. The government was increasingly challenged by Paul Berenger's Mouvement Militant Mauricien on social conditions and with demands for a general election (due in 1972 but postponed until 1976). The $125 million 1971–75 development plan remained overshadowed by unemployment, which was estimated at 50,000 in 1971. On June 12 Mauritius became an associate member of the EEC under the Yaoundé Convention.

(MOLLY MORTIMER)

MAURITIUS
Education. (1969–70) Primary, pupils 146,490, teachers (1968–69) 4,253; secondary, pupils 42,444, teachers (1968–69) 1,706; vocational (1968–69), pupils 603, teachers 34; teacher training, students 668, teachers (1968–69) 25; higher (1968–69), students 178, teaching staff 41.
Finance and Trade. Monetary unit: Mauritian rupee, with (Sept. 18, 1972) a free rate of MauRs. 5.45 to U.S. $1 (par value of MauRs. 13.33 = £1 sterling). Budget (total 1970–71 est.) balanced at MauRs. 338.7 million. Foreign trade (1971): imports MauRs. 461.2 million; exports MauRs. 360,615,000. Import sources: U.K. 22%; South Africa 8%; France 7%; U.S. 7%; Japan 7%; Australia 7%; Iran 5%; West Germany 5%. Export destinations: U.K. 55%; Canada 28%; U.S. 6%. Main export sugar 89%. Tourism: visitors (1968) 15,600; gross receipts (1970) U.S. $5 million.
Agriculture. Production (in 000; metric tons): sugar (1971–72) *c.* 610, (1970–71) 576; tea (1971) *c.* 4.1, (1970) 3.5; tobacco (1971) 0.6, (1970) 0.4. Livestock (in 000; April 1971): cattle *c.* 49; pigs *c.* 3; sheep *c.* 3; goats *c.* 68; chickens *c.* 400.

Queen Elizabeth II and Prince Philip during their visit to Mauritius in March 1972.

A.F.P./PICTORIAL PARADE

Medicine

"Change is inevitable. In a progressive country change is constant." Benjamin Disraeli's statement applies to professional disciplines as well as nations. In medicine, which is nothing if not progressive in its search for ways to combat disease and extend life, change is constant, and much that has taken place has been revolutionary in nature. Jenner's discovery of vaccination, deliberate exposure to a mild form of disease in order to trigger the body's defenses against the more virulent variety, was epoch-making. So were the invention of anesthesia, the discovery of penicillin and sulfa drugs, the development of a polio vaccine, and the first organ transplant. Nothing similarly spectacular took place in medicine during 1972, but even without such dramatic developments, medicine was hardly in stasis. Just as the molecules in a bar of apparently inanimate iron are constantly in movement, so are those persons dedicated to the art and science of medicine. As a result, medicine is in a perpetual state of evolution, a process of constant mutation that leaves it ever more able to cope with a changing environment.

This evolution was destined to be incomplete, the challenges that confront medicine infinite. In recent decades, many of the diseases that once afflicted humanity had simply disappeared, proving, once the light of scientific curiosity was focused on them, to be no less mortal than their victims. Modern sanitation and refuse-disposal techniques, in large part the products of medicine's increased understanding of the conditions that contribute to illness, had defeated plague-type diseases that once killed millions. Such childhood diseases as diphtheria, whooping cough, and scarlet fever were becoming medical rarities; some students could go through medical school, internship, and residency and into practice without seeing a case. Tuberculosis was being brought under control. A vaccine for rubella, or German measles, a disease that left thousands of children born after a 1964 epidemic with weak hearts, deafness, and mental retardation, was developed. Its effectiveness was not yet truly known, however, because of the episodic nature of the disease. Whether it was really safe had still to be completely determined.

This did not mean, of course, that medicine had achieved mastery over disease. As old ailments disappeared or became controllable, new ones were "discovered" to take their places. Actually, there was nothing new about many of these discoveries; some of the diseases themselves were as old as man. But medicine had succeeded in identifying and naming these maladies, giving the profession better perspectives for its efforts. Cancer in its myriad forms, heart disease, environmental and industrial ailments, all remained to be better understood and ultimately cured before their places were taken by still newer illnesses—some of them, ironically, of man's own making as he contaminated the air he must breathe and the water he must drink, added chemicals to his foods, or unthinkingly unleashed forces he could not control.

CLINICAL ADVANCES

Medicine is engaged in a constant search to understand illness and spends millions on research to learn more about illness as well as health. Of late, these investments had begun to pay off. Researchers and physicians had developed the vaccines that brought such diseases as measles, polio, and mumps under control, pioneered the techniques of organ transplantation and reconstructive heart surgery, and, through the growing science of molecular biology, unlocked some of the secrets of the cell and learned more about the cellular abnormality called cancer.

It was impossible to predict when a major breakthrough would occur in an area currently under research, or when an accidental discovery—like Fleming's discovery of penicillin—would open up new vistas. Such an event could occur just as easily tomorrow as it could ten years from now. But even without a dramatic landfall, medicine's slow yet steady accumulation of knowledge has led to significant progress in several important areas.

Heart Disease. Heart disease in its various forms was the major killer of Americans, claiming 675,000 lives in 1971 alone. It was the major cause of death of people over 65 years of age, but its effects were hardly restricted to the aged. Of those Americans who died of heart attacks in 1971, at least 176,000 were under 65, victims of what public officials called premature heart disease.

LONDON DAILY EXPRESS/PICTORIAL PARADE

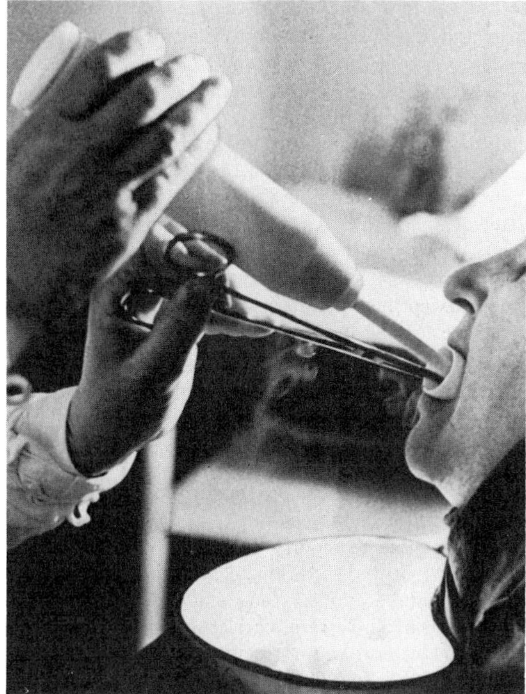

The frozen point of a cryoapplicator, cooled by liquid nitrogen, is used to freeze tonsils prior to their excision. This procedure, used in a Moscow hospital, reduced operating time to a few minutes.

More important, the number of premature deaths was rising. The coronary death rate for men between 25 and 44 had increased from 46 to 52 per 100,000 within two decades. The mortality among men in the 45-to-64-year age bracket climbed from 575 to 598 per 100,000.

The causes for this increase are popularly laid at the door of the American life-style as characterized by a rich diet, heavy cigarette smoking, sedentary living, and a high degree of psychic tension. The public mind conceptualizes certain elements of life-style as leading to heart disease. Lay people tend to connect coronary artery disease with cigarette smoking, increases in blood pressure with increased anxiety, and elevations in cholesterol levels in the blood with high caloric intake.

While no responsible physician would urge a patient to overeat, smoke in excess, if at all, or to eschew exercise and increase psychic tension, it was by no means scientifically clear that indulging in this life-style would specifically cause heart attacks and heart disease or that giving it up for a more austere existence would prevent heart attacks.

Scientists, nevertheless, were studying possible connections between the way Americans live and the pathology of heart disease. The National Heart and Lung Institute planned to spend $1.4 billion over three years to expand its programs for combating heart, blood vessel, lung, and blood diseases. It was also looking into the insidious process that lies at the root of most heart problems—atherosclerosis (an early stage of arteriosclerosis or hardening of the arteries), the gradual accumulation of deposits of fatty substances and fibrous matter on the linings of the body's arteries. How or why these deposits build up was still a mystery, but how they weaken the heart was not. Narrowing the blood vessels and restricting the flow of blood through them, they force the heart to work harder to pump blood to the body. They also interfere with the blood flow to the brain, helping to cause the strokes that kill more than 200,000 Americans each year. In addition, they limit the flow of blood to the heart itself, depriving the heart muscle of oxygen and setting the individual up for the pains of angina pectoris and, ultimately, the infarctions or heart attacks that can cripple and kill.

Atherosclerosis is endemic among Americans. Yellowish streaks of fat can be found in the arteries of children as young as three. Postmortem examinations of young men killed in the Korean War showed that eight out of ten had atherosclerosis; in 10% it was so extensive that it had closed off one or more major arteries.

No one was really sure why some people are more susceptible to atherosclerosis than others, but some are. A long-term survey of people living in the suburb of Framingham, Mass., revealed that some people seem to have a hereditary tendency to produce cholesterol, a blood fat linked with heart disease. Some seemed to produce little or no cholesterol despite diets rich in the saturated fats responsible for it. Others produced copious quantities of cholesterol despite careful dietary habits.

It is possible to modify factors believed to be involved in the predisposition to heart attacks. Reducing one's intake of fatty foods, such as well-marbled meats, and of cholesterol carriers, such as egg yolks, helps. Cholesterol and heart attack rates are lower in countries where the diet contains little fat. Trials of clofibrate, a cholesterol-reducing agent, were under way in the U.S. and the U.K.; the drug could prove a boon to those with abnormally high serum lipid levels.

Other changes in life-style may also help avoid heart disease. Cutting down on cigarette and alcohol consumption is desirable; heavy smokers are twice as likely to have heart attacks as nonsmokers. Weight reduction is definitely indicated. So is exercise. Medical investigations showed that regular exercise, such as jogging, handball, or even just plain walking, can improve cardiac output; it not only greatly reduces the risk of heart attacks in those who have not yet been stricken but helps many who have already had heart attacks back to health.

Even with all this advice, some heart attacks are inevitable. They need not be fatal, however. Care of the coronary victim had improved markedly in recent years; an increasing number of hospitals in the U.S. and Europe had established special coronary care units to assure the monitoring that heart patients need. The use of drugs to control high blood pressure, prevent clotting, and dilate arteries in order to prevent attacks of angina had also expanded.

Meredith Thring of Queen Mary College, London, demonstrates his spoke-wheeled climber. The test model safely transports invalids up and down stairs on its 48 spring-loaded spokes.

KEYSTONE

One of the most promising developments in reducing the number of deaths from heart attack was the increasing number of hospitals equipped with emergency cardiac units designed to maintain life and stabilize the vital life functions of heart attack victims. Many deaths from heart attack occur simply because the victim and emergency treatment are not gotten together quickly enough. Some larger cities even established mobile emergency cardiac units. One of the most important elements of emergency cardiac units is a heart defibrillator, a device that can stabilize a wildly beating heart.

In some quarters, the medical community was advising people of the classic symptoms of the onset of a heart attack and urging those who experienced such symptoms to see to it that they got immediate medical attention, preferably, of course, where there was emergency cardiac equipment.

Surgery also offered increasing help for the victim of heart disease. Heart transplants, once regarded as the ultimate operation, proved to be a function of how much effort a cardiac surgery team believed was suitable in terms of what it could accomplish for the community of patients it served. In terms of the number of heart patients whose lives can really be extended, the monumental effort required for the performance of a heart transplant may not be as worthwhile as other, less radical surgical procedures.

Replacement of diseased mitral valves with spares of Teflon and stainless steel was being done in dozens of hospitals around the world. So was other reconstructive work, including sophisticated vessel reconstruction. Bypass operations, in which the blocked artery is circumvented by some sophisticated plumbing, were also becoming more common. A surgical team at the Cleveland (O.) Clinic had done more than 3,000.

The concept of the bypass operation is simple. Once the blockage is located (usually through an ultrasophisticated X-ray process called cinecoronary arteriography), a piece of vein is sewed into the artery above the obstruction, then fastened to the vessel below it, providing a channel by which blood can bypass any bottleneck. The execution of the operation is somewhat more complex. Surgeons must first obtain the vein, a task generally accomplished by taking a piece of the saphenous vein from the lower leg. Then the vein must be trimmed of its capillaries and the holes sealed, a task demanding nothing if not sewing skill. Once this is done, the operation itself can begin. Surgeons must open the chest, stop the heart, and switch the task of maintaining the patient's circulation over to a heart-lung machine. Then the vein, the size and consistency of a piece of cooked spaghetti, must be sewed into the aorta, bypassing the blockage. Though only careful follow-up would disclose the long-term effect on those who had undergone revascularization, the short-term results were promising. Some of the Cleveland team's earliest patients had lived three years with their new systems. A few had even taken up jogging.

Other aid was also available for heart patients. One example was a balloon assist pump that helps stricken hearts. Inserted into the aorta, the main artery leading from the heart, by means of a catheter, or tube, the balloon is alternately inflated and deflated, augmenting the pumping function of the heart until the damaged muscle heals. In at least one case it was used successfully on a man actually undergoing a myocardial infarction, keeping him alive while doctors performed emergency surgery. Doctors were also experimenting with various types of booster pumps to be inserted into the chest cavity to provide temporary or even permanent assistance to the heart. Powered by air from exterior tanks, these boosters had succeeded in keeping patients alive for periods ranging from a few days to a few weeks. Doctors envisioned a time when such pumps could be inserted and operated until a patient's heart recovered from an attack, then shut off but left in place in case they should be needed in the future.

Pacemakers were also helping heart patients. More than 50,000 Americans had these tiny, battery-powered devices implanted within their chests, sending out regular impulses that kept their hearts beating at the desired rate. As of 1972 most pacemaker patients had to undergo regular surgery to overhaul their monitors and replace the batteries, but even this inconvenience might be eliminated. French doctors and scientists had developed a nuclear-powered pacemaker battery that should last longer than the patient.

Nor was this the only area where doctors and engineers had been working together. Many doctors believed that it might prove more practical to replace badly damaged hearts with artificial pumps than to battle the rejection problems involved in transplantation, and work on such a pump was under way in laboratories in France and the United States. Surgeons had been experimenting with various types of pumps, although none had succeeded in overcoming one of the primary problems involved in developing such a device. Blood tends to coagulate when it comes into contact with a foreign body, and none of the materials yet used had been able to avoid this. Once such a material was found, replacement of the heart would move a significant step closer to reality.

Cancer. Cancer also received an increasing share of medicine's attention during the year. The interest was justified. In the U.S., for example, cancer was, after heart disease, the leading cause of death. In 1972, the disease claimed approximately 330,000 American lives. Its incidence in other countries was also on the rise.

Cancer is not a distinct disease with a single set of symptoms. Rather, it is a spectrum of diseases that includes more than 100 kinds. No two cancers are exactly alike, but all share two common characteristics: rapid, uncontrolled cell growth and a tendency to spread from one part of the body to another. No one really knows what causes cancer. Most researchers agree, however, that the villain is probably a virus, a miniature packet of nucleic acid and protein on the hazily defined border between life and nonlife.

Viruses are unable to reproduce themselves; thus they invade normal cells, take over their genetic equipment, and use it to produce more viruses. Eventually, the infected cells fill with viruses and rupture, releasing the newly formed viruses to attack other cells. Tumour viruses, which as early as 1911 were shown to cause cancerous growths in animals, behave differently, however. Some researchers found that RNA tumour viruses contain certain enzyme activities capable of reversing the normal order of genetic transmission (in which DNA produces RNA), using their RNA (ribonucleic acid) to produce DNA (deoxyribonucleic acid), the double-helix master molecule. In a manner still not understood, this causes the host cell's genetic machinery to order cell division, causing the cancerous growth that is then perpetuated as the cell continues to replicate and divide.

At first the enzyme associated with the tumour virus discovery (known as RNA-directed DNA polymerase, or reverse transcriptase) was believed to be unique to cancer cells. Later, this enzyme was found in normal cells as well as in human and animal embryonic tissue. This discovery strengthened the view of many researchers who believed that cancer is probably an aberration of normal cell growth. It was hypothesized that normal cells manufacture RNA, the messenger molecule, which moves to neighbouring cells in the form of a protovirus, or template, and stimulates the production of a new form of DNA. If this RNA somehow transmits a garbled message, it can cause the production of an altered DNA that orders cells to grow abnormally.

At the National Cancer Institute there was speculation that the seeds of cancer are a part of man's inheritance. According to this theory, cancer is caused by a noninfectious virus that is a part of every living thing. This virus, known as the C-type virus or C particle, is a tiny bit of RNA passed vertically from one generation to another; it may even play a part in normal development by causing the cells of an embryo to grow. According to this hypothesis, the C particle should become inactive as the fetus matures. If it fails to do so, or if it somehow activates later in life, the result is the rapid, undifferentiated cell growth that characterizes cancer.

Though some of their discoveries appeared promising, researchers had yet to isolate a human cancer virus. But this did not mean that such viruses do not exist. Viral antigens or footprints—immunological evidence of the viral presence or, at least, passage—had been found in the bloodstreams of humans with various kinds of cancer. So had other evidence of viral involvement in this deadly disease.

In 1970 an international cooperative research effort demonstrated for the first time the presence of an RNA (ribonucleic acid) virus of the B-particle type in the milk of young women with family histories of breast cancer. A virus of this kind had been known since 1939 to be the causative agent of mouse mam-

X ray shows a permanent pacemaker surgically implanted in a 26-hour-old infant at Chicago's Mt. Sinai Hospital. The baby, believed to be the youngest recipient of a pacemaker, had been born with a congenital block that prevented her heart from beating more than 50 times a minute.

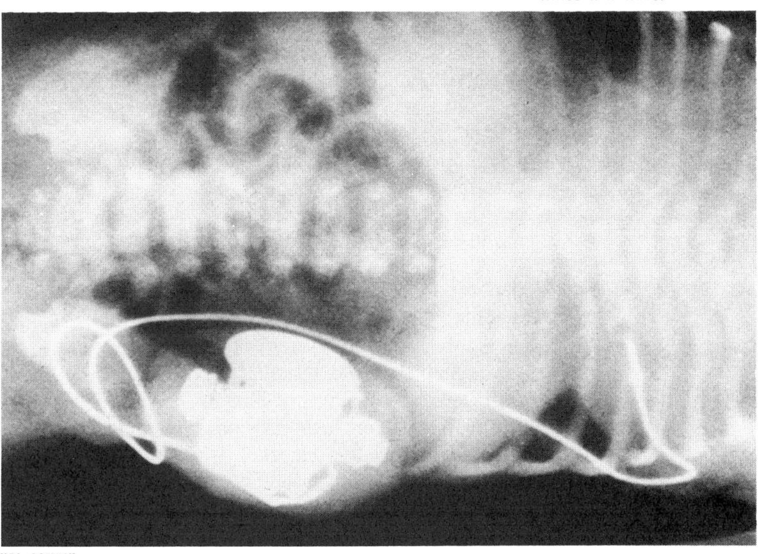

UPI COMPIX

mary tumour. The Parsees, descendants of the Zoroastrians who fled Persia 1,200 years ago and settled in India, provided researchers with an opportunity to study a nearly undiluted ethnic strain whose members had married almost exclusively within their own sect. It was found that nearly 40% of the Parsee women, whom statistics show are three times more likely to develop breast cancers than other Indian women, had the virus-like particles in their milk. The prevalence of such particles is hardly unique to the Parsees, however. At the Institute for Medical Research in Camden, N.J., similar findings resulted from analysis of milk from 166 American women. Of 156 women with no family histories of breast cancer, only 7 showed evidence of the particles in their milk. But six of the ten women whose families had a history of the disease were found to harbour large numbers of the particles.

These findings were given greater significance by the observations of researchers at Columbia University. In a double-blind study conducted at both Camden and Columbia, a 100% correlation was found between human milk virus particle concentrations and the presence of the RNA-directed DNA polymerase associated with animal RNA tumour viruses.

Even stronger evidence of viral involvement was provided by a study at the University of Southern California School of Medicine, Los Angeles. Working in cooperation with the National Cancer Institute, the researchers identified what might, in fact, eventually prove to be a true human cancer virus. Using cells obtained from a child suffering from rhabdomyosarcoma, a rare and generally fatal cancer of the body's voluntary muscles, the researchers tried without success to coax out chemically the viruses they suspected were there. But when they injected a solution made from the malignant cells into unborn kittens, the results were startling. Four of the animals, all from different mothers, developed tumours that proved, on examination, to be almost entirely of human cellular composition. More significant, one of the tumours was found to be shedding C-type viruses at a prodigious rate.

Further work was essential before anyone could say with certainty that the California researchers had succeeded in isolating a true human cancer virus. But once they—or any of the other researchers currently involved in the quest—found this grail, the effect could be enormous. Identification of human cancer viruses could lead to the development of tests for the early detection of cancer and to a broader understanding of the role of viruses in the disease process. Ultimately, this identification could also lead to a means of curing or controlling some forms of the disease.

There were no such magic cures for cancer in 1972, but the prospects for cancer patients had improved greatly. In 1940 only one out of every five patients found to have cancer could expect to survive for five years. By 1972, according to a study undertaken by the National Cancer Institute, one out of three would survive that long. Based on a study of patients diagnosed between 1940 and 1970 in 100 hospitals throughout the U.S., the NCI report offered little encouragement to victims of lung or pancreatic cancers; survival rates for such tumours had increased little, if at all, during the 30 years, while the incidence of the tumours had increased. But the survival rates for other forms of cancer had risen. The three-year survival rate for patients with bladder cancer had increased from 48 to 62%, that for breast cancer from 63 to 72%, and that for cancer of the cervix from 53 to 63%. Also up were the survival rates for patients with cancers of the prostate, larynx, brain, skin, bones, and thyroid. Most striking, however, was the improvement in the survival rates of patients with leukemia, a cancer of the blood-forming tissues that accounted for at least a third of all cancer deaths in children under 15. Until 1949 only 4% of the victims of acute leukemia survived three years; in 1972 at least half of those treated at children's medical centres were alive and free of the disease five years after diagnosis.

These reductions in the mortality rate from cancer were due in large part to better methods of detecting cancer in its earliest stages, when treatment is more likely to succeed. The Pap smear, performed routinely in many doctors' offices and clinics, had led to a drastic drop in the death rate from cervical cancer. Xeroradiography, a photoelectric process that photographs the breast on a selenium plate specially treated to make it sensitive to X rays, offered doctors a similar early warning system for breast cancer. Once the plate is exposed it is inserted into a machine similar to an office copier, which produces a picture of the breast, its internal tissues, and any cancer that might be present. The machine was faster and more accurate than conventional X rays and could make widespread screening for breast cancer practical. As yet, however, it was available at only a few hospitals. Efforts were also under way to determine whether cancers might also make their presence known chemically by releasing chemicals into the bloodstream.

There had also been some significant progress in understanding how tumours, which can grow from pinhead to marble size in little more than a week, achieve their fantastic growth. Researchers at the Harvard Medical School found that solid tumours appear to require the presence of a recently identified protein substance that scientists call tumour angiogenesis factor (TAF). This work, carried on with a variety of solid tumours including those of the brain, showed that tumours must develop their own circulation systems in order to obtain nutrients and carry off wastes. To do this, they release TAF, which is found in fetal but not normal adult cells; the chemical causes tiny blood vessels or capillaries to grow into the cancerous mass. That this growth is essential to the tumour's survival and continued growth was proved by the Harvard researchers' experiments. When TAF's effects were canceled out by isolating the tumours from blood supplies, no capillaries formed and the tumours choked on their own wastes and failed to grow. This finding suggests that a chemical capable of inhibiting TAF production could halt or perhaps prevent tumour growth, and the search for such an agent was under way.

New treatments were also contributing to a reduction in cancer mortality. Surgery remained the treatment of choice for most forms of cancer, but two new approaches were proving valuable.

The older of the two was chemotherapy or drug treatment. Researchers found that various cytotoxic or cell-destroying drugs will slow down or even check certain types of cancer. Some doctors used the drugs in sequence, administering one until the body—and cancer—developed a tolerance to it, then switching to another. Others used the drugs in combination, administering as many as three or four at a time. So far, this approach had been most successful against

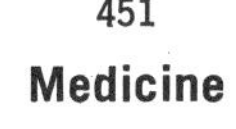

certain types of leukemia and Hodgkin's disease, a cancer of the lymphatic system.

A newer approach involved an immunological technique for stimulating the body's natural defenses against disease. Normally the body mobilizes its internal defense forces against the agents that cause illness, manufacturing antibodies to fight specific bacteria and viruses. Once these enemies have been vanquished, the antibodies, which remember the disease they are supposed to battle, remain in the system, providing the body with immunity against future attacks of the same disease. Thus, a person who has had measles develops a natural resistance to the disease, just as a person deliberately exposed to cowpox develops an immunity to the antigenically similar smallpox.

Triggering the system to fight most diseases is not too difficult; scientists need only isolate the agent that causes the particular disease, develop a weakened variety of the virus or bacillus involved, and inject it into the system. Enabling the body to fight cancer is another matter. For one thing, cancer cells are produced by the body itself. They are not, therefore, readily identifiable by the immunological system as "foreign." For another, cancer frequently deluges the body with a virtual rain of tumour cells and fragments that can overwhelm the immunological system and render it useless. In addition, there was speculation that cancer cells may secrete a substance that actually blocks the effects of the immune system.

To overcome these problems, some researchers were treating cancer cells with a special enzyme that heightens their immunologic visibility, making them easier for the body to recognize. Others were attempting to produce, in the vicinity of the cancer, a reaction called delayed hypersensitivity. In this method, which had been used with skin cancers, substances designed to cause strong allergic reactions were applied to the area around the cancer in the hope that they would cause the body to react not only to the irritant but to the cancer as well. It was far too early to say that this method worked, but several of the patients involved experienced remissions of the disease as a result of the treatment.

A variation on this theme had also been used to treat such deep cancers as cancer of the breast. Five patients who had already undergone breast cancer surgery and were suffering recurrences of the disease were injected with an antituberculosis vaccine (BCG). The injection was made directly into the cancerous lesions. Then, as the cancers showed signs of healing, regular applications of a tuberculin skin cream were substituted for the painful shots. Most people have had active tuberculosis antibodies in their systems at some time in their lives. In the case of the women, the vaccine awoke their bodies' immunological memories, triggering the production of more antibodies. It also appeared to induce an immune response to cancer. All five of the women were alive two years after beginning treatment and were showing varying degrees of improvement.

A physician at Emory University, Atlanta, Ga., tried an even more unusual approach. He inoculated patients with a vaccine made, at least in part, from tissues taken from tumours similar to their own. These injections were followed up by cross-injection of the patients with white blood cells from patients who had presumably been sensitized to the tumour antigens. Only long-term testing would tell whether this approach was effective, but the preliminary results were encouraging. One patient with bowel cancer had been free of the disease for several years; others had shown remissions.

Cancer patients understandably follow the progress of research aimed at curing their disease. Few, however, argue with their doctors when it comes to treatment. The reason for their acquiescence, whether to surgery, chemotherapy, or immunotherapy, is simple: in the majority of cases, there are no alternatives. But where there are, a growing number of cancer patients were questioning the doctor's traditional advice and searching out an alternative approach; women with breast cancer, who once submitted quietly, if unhappily, to the mutilative procedure known as radical mastectomy, were now opting for a simpler operation.

One must sympathize with their search; perhaps no cancer is more feared by women than that of the breast. In 1972 alone, approximately 71,000 American women learned that they had the disease; some 30,000 would die of it. At least 1,000 women a week underwent surgery, which usually involved removal not only of the breast but of the underlying muscle and the lymph glands under the arm, a disfiguring operation that left many feeling "like half a woman."

Many doctors felt that only radical mastectomy offered breast cancer patients a reasonable hope for survival, but this belief was being challenged. On the ground that preservation of the patient's morale is at least as important as saving her life, the challengers turned to an operation called "lumpectomy," re-

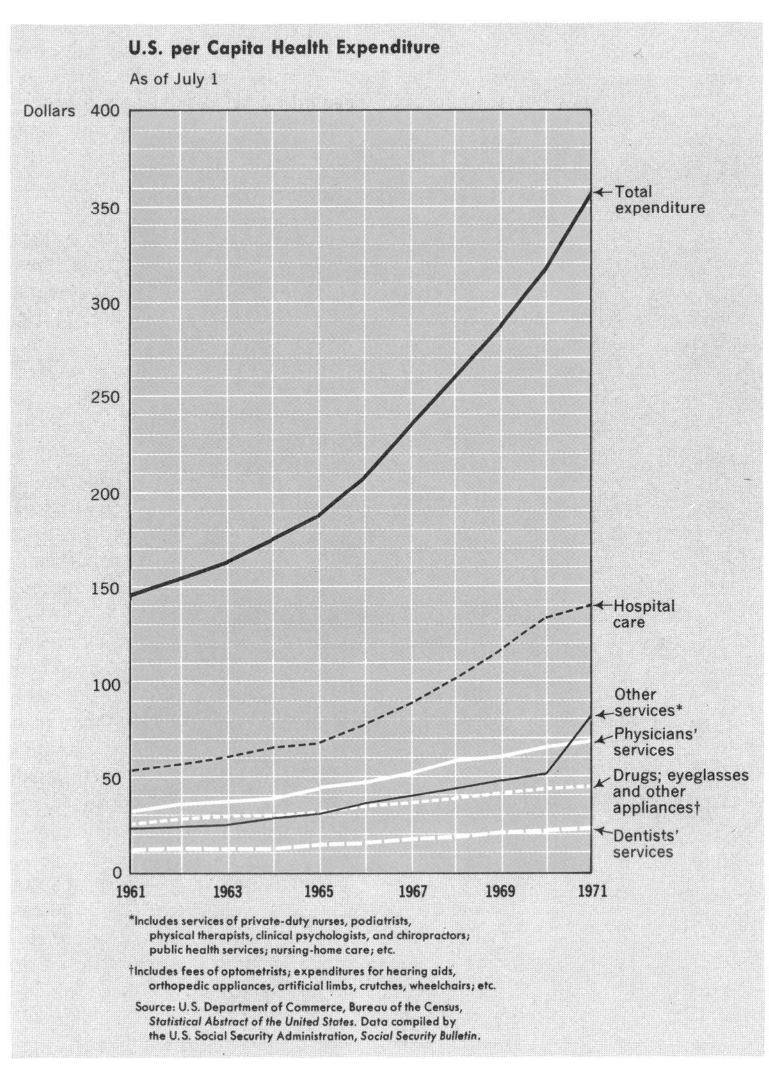

*Includes services of private-duty nurses, podiatrists, physical therapists, clinical psychologists, and chiropractors; public health services; nursing-home care; etc.

†Includes fees of optometrists; expenditures for hearing aids, orthopedic appliances, artificial limbs, crutches, wheelchairs; etc.

Source: U.S. Department of Commerce, Bureau of the Census, *Statistical Abstract of the United States*. Data compiled by the U.S. Social Security Administration, *Social Security Bulletin*.

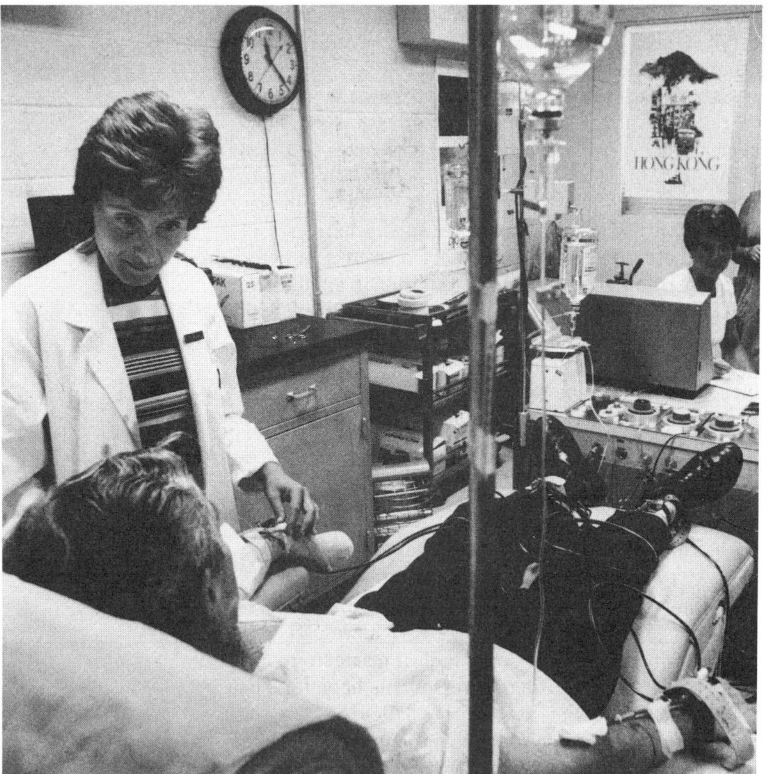
EDWARD HAUSNER—THE NEW YORK TIMES

Lilian Reich treats a cancer patient at the Sloan-Kettering Institute in New York City, where several strategies suggested by basic research were being explored to utilize the body's immunologic defenses in combating cancer.

moval of the cancerous mass alone. Many physicians believed that the operation, which was usually followed up by radiotherapy to prevent the spread of stray cancer cells, should be performed only on early or Stage I cancers. Figures indicated that for some patients, at least, the operation was as good as the more traditional approach. One physician took 81 women who had had radical mastectomies between 1955 and 1965, paired them by age and other factors with an equal number of lumpectomy patients, then compared their survival rates. At the end of five years, 70.4% of the radical mastectomy patients and 71.6% of the lumpectomy patients were still alive.

The less radical approach was likely to make women more willing to face a diagnosis of breast cancer. So would another newly developed technique in which the breast was reconstructed following surgery, using a silicone form. Most of the patients who had undergone this treatment had been so pleased by the success of the initial implant, which gives the wearer a normal appearance in clothes, that they had not bothered with the additional operations necessary to complete the restoration.

No one could even guess where the next discovery would move cancer research. Pres. Richard Nixon had signed legislation authorizing $1.6 billion to be spent on cancer research and detection over a three-year period. This expanded program was to be administered by the National Cancer Institute of the National Institutes of Health. But, although the project had been compared with both the Manhattan and Apollo projects, the analogy was inaccurate. The principles of nuclear fission were understood long before anyone attempted to package a nuclear device; the basic research for space flight had been done long before the Soviets orbited Sputnik to start the space race. All both projects did was utilize already acquired knowledge. In the case of cancer, science had no such knowledge upon which to draw. Thus, to expect that creation of the agency—ambitious and worthwhile as its plans might be—would lead to a cure of the disease was to ignore the realities of both research and government.

The research, of course, was continuing. Efforts were under way to isolate and identify human cancer viruses. Cooperation between the U.S. and the Soviet Union in the form of exchanges of cancer tissues, suspected viruses, and drugs would also help. But a quick cure seemed unlikely. What was likely was the discovery of drugs that would appear to arrest certain types of cancer, lengthy experimentation and study, and, finally, the realization, perhaps five years after tests had begun, that the patients were still alive. At that point, doctors might be ready to announce a cure of sorts. Until then, cancer would remain a source of mystery, misery, and vexation.

Genetics. Heredity has always been a source of pleasure and puzzlement to man. From the earliest times, parents were pleased that their offspring had their eyes, hair, or other features. But their pleasure has always been muted by heredity's balancing feature: offspring inherit bad features as well as good ones. A man's children may inherit his looks; they may also inherit diseases that can shorten or blight their lives.

Ever since he understood this, however vaguely, man has sought for a way to control the inheritance he passes along to his posterity. In recent years, he acquired this power. The remarkable advances in molecular biology after 1950 not only gave man an understanding of the basic processes that shape his life but provided the key to their eventual management. The knowledge was welcome. Man is heir to a host of inherited imperfections, ranging from diabetes to degenerative nerve disease. Each individual carries between five and ten potentially harmful genes in his cells, and these, along with the genes that determine whether a child will have brown hair or blue eyes, are passed along every time conception takes place.

No one really knows how often these genes combine to produce genetic disease. Nature takes care of the worst mistakes in conception; one out of every 130 conceptions ends before the mother even realizes she is pregnant because the defective egg fails to attach itself to the wall of the uterus. Fully 25% of all conceptions fail to reach an age at which they can survive outside the uterus. Of these, at least a third prove, on examination, to have identifiable chromosomal abnormalities. Still, despite this quality-control system, one out of every 100 babies born has some genetic defect.

By 1972 scientists had succeeded in identifying more than 400 such defects, and the list was growing. Some were obvious deformities like mongolism, or Down's syndrome, which occurs once in every 600 births and is caused by the presence of an extra chromosome. Others, which have more subtle symptoms and are less easily spotted, result when defective genes fail to order the production of essential enzymes necessary to trigger or mediate various biochemical reactions. Phenylketonuria (PKU) occurs when the body lacks the enzyme necessary to metabolize the amino acid phenylalanine; as a result, toxins accumulate in the body and eventually cause convulsions and brain damage. Cystic fibrosis, characterized by abnormal secretion of certain glands and respiratory-tract blockage that can lead to death by pneumonia, is the most common inborn error of metabolism; it is believed to be the product of a single defective gene.

Ever since 1856, when an Austrian monk named

Gregor Mendel first began experimenting with pea plants, man has known that the odds of inheriting some genetic characteristics can be figured mathematically. Now, at last, man was using this understanding in an attempt to avoid genetic disease.

One way he was using it was through genetic counseling. In its simplest form, genetic counseling is little more than the old Mendelian numbers game. A genetic counselor, who need not be an M.D., can merely sit down with a couple for an interview and determine whether they or any members of their families suffer from diseases known to be genetic in origin. Since the method of transmission of many such diseases or conditions is known (colour blindness, for example, is carried by females and passed on to their male offspring), the counselor can advise the parents on the odds of their children inheriting such a condition. If both parents carry the trait for sickle-cell anemia, which is recessive, the odds are one in four that each of their children will have the disease; if only one parent carries the trait, he can pass the trait, but not the disease itself, on to his offspring. If the gene that carries the disease is dominant, however, the chances of passing it on are greater. Huntington's chorea is a degenerative nerve disease that strikes its victims at around age 40 and is always fatal. If one parent carries the defective gene, there is a 50% chance that each of his children will inherit it.

In theory, simple genetic counseling enables informed parents to evaluate the risks of hereditary illness and make informed choices about childbearing. In practice, it often fails. Many couples desperately want children and are unwilling to forego parenthood unless they are certain their children will be adversely affected. Such certainties were increasingly obtainable, however. Using a new technique, doctors were able to examine many fetuses before birth and determine, with almost 100% accuracy, whether or not they were carrying lethal legacies.

Amniocentesis, from the Greek *amnion* ("membrane") and *kentesis* ("pricking"), is performed by inserting a long needle through the pregnant mother's abdomen and drawing off a small sample of the amniotic fluid, the liquid in which the developing fetus floats. Fetal skin cells, which slough off into the amniotic fluid during development, are then placed in a nutrient bath, where they continue to grow. By examining these cells microscopically and analyzing them chemically, doctors can detect the presence of many genetic diseases.

Performed between the 13th and 18th weeks of pregnancy, amniocentesis was not without certain risks to both mother and baby. But in cases where family history or other factors raised the suspicion of genetic disease, the benefits more than justified any danger, for the tests were extremely accurate. In one series of tests, mongolism was diagnosed in 10 of 155 high-risk pregnancies; subsequent examination of the fetuses showed that the diagnosis was correct in all cases.

Amniocentesis had been performed on more than 10,000 American women, and a few futurists envisioned a day when all individuals applying for marriage licenses would undergo screening for genetic diseases and all pregnancies would be screened via amniocentesis as a matter of routine. Such a day, if it came at all, was far distant. Doctors had neither the skill nor, given the state of their art, the justification for screening all prospective parents. Nor—considering the cost and the risks, not to mention the social problems, involved—could they consider monitoring all pregnancies. Although genetic engineering, the manufacture of genes to replace those that are defective or missing and their implantation in the developing fetus, might one day be possible, it was still more fiction than science. The only thing doctors could offer a woman who learned through amniocentesis that she was about to have a baby with some serious genetic defect was the opportunity to terminate the pregnancy. Many found such an alternative unacceptable.

But this did not mean that wide-scale genetic screening and counseling were impractical. Quite the contrary. As recent developments showed, doctors could deliver genetic help to large segments of the community. Physicians at the John F. Kennedy Institute at Johns Hopkins University School of Medicine conducted a screening program in the Baltimore-Washington, D.C., area for Tay-Sachs disease, a fatal metabolic disease that occurs almost exclusively among Jews of Eastern European ancestry. The disease meets all the requirements for a genetic screening program: it occurs in a population that is readily and easily identifiable; it can be detected in a carrier state; and, equally important, it can be detected in utero, therefore enabling the monitoring of pregnancies at risk.

To get the program going, doctors met with local rabbis and members of religious organizations, explaining the nature of the disease, its effects, and the

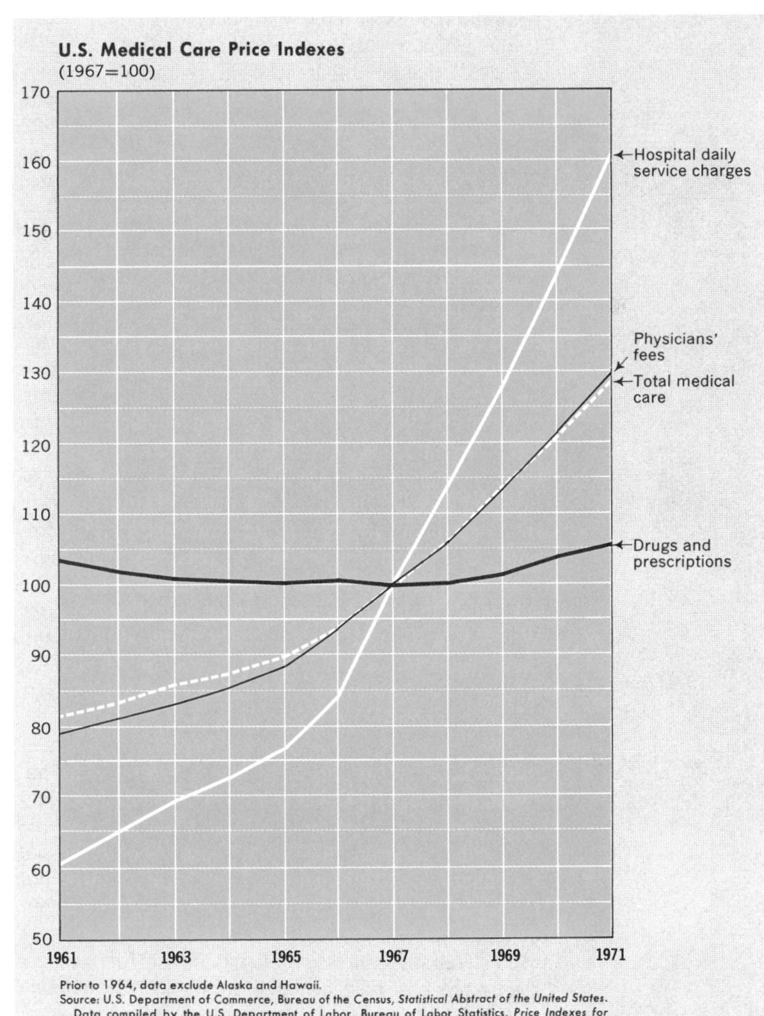

Prior to 1964, data exclude Alaska and Hawaii.
Source: U.S. Department of Commerce, Bureau of the Census, *Statistical Abstract of the United States*. Data compiled by the U.S. Department of Labor, Bureau of Labor Statistics, *Price Indexes for Selected Items and Groups, Annual Averages*.

ways in which it could be prevented. Convinced that the program was for their own benefit, thousands took advantage of it, showing up at screening centres in synagogues and schools to give blood samples for analysis. Couples in which only one prospective parent carried the trait were relieved to know that they ran no risk of transmitting the disease to their offspring. When both were carriers, they were informed that there was one chance in four that any children they might have would be affected. But they were also offered some practical help; future pregnancies could be screened via amniocentesis and the couples given the opportunity to selectively have children unaffected by the disease.

Other programs to detect and prevent genetic illness were also under way. Testing for sickle-cell anemia, 99% of whose U.S. victims are black, was initiated in New York City, where more than 50,000 persons elected to take free, voluntary tests. Those found to carry the trait, which is benign but transmittable, or the disease itself (which is not detectable in utero) could then make informed choices concerning childbearing. Many doctors believed that women who had given birth to mongoloid children should also be offered the opportunity to undergo amniocentesis, and some would like to see the process even more widely used. Older women are far more likely to bear mongoloid children than younger ones, and doctors believed that the incidence of this condition could be cut in half if all pregnant women over 40 were screened and offered the option of therapeutic abortion if the tests showed that a fetus was mongoloid.

Some doctors, however, were afraid that the "new genetics" could be abused. With visions of Orwell's *1984* in their minds, they feared that indiscriminate or compulsory genetics programs could violate rights to privacy or, worse, establish genetic norms that would result in a society with a dangerous intolerance for imperfection. There was some evidence that their fears might be justified. New York City adopted a law requiring that applicants for marriage licenses be screened for sickle-cell anemia. Some officials, who felt the law was unconstitutional because it would require them to determine an applicant's race, refused to obey it. The courts, they thought, were unlikely to insist they do so.

Acupuncture. Of all the clinical developments in 1972, few aroused as much interest, in the U.S. at least, as acupuncture, the ancient Chinese practice of inserting needles into various parts of the body to treat a catalog of ills ranging from arthritis to impotence. Long dismissed in the West as little more than superstitious folklore, acupuncture became the subject of increased scientific interest in Europe after World War II and was currently being studied and used regularly, if not widely, in the Soviet Union, France, West Germany, and Britain. In 1972 it was sparking interest in the U.S. as well.

The reason for this was as much political as scientific. The thaw in the long frozen relationship between the U.S. and China enabled U.S. scientists, doctors, and journalists to visit the mainland for the first time in over 20 years. Those who witnessed acupuncture brought back enthusiastic reports not merely of its use to relieve pain and cure illness but of its increasing application as an anesthetic as well.

Their enthusiasm was understandable for, as they themselves observed, acupuncture works. U.S. doctors watched in amazement as a woman, her pain apparently prevented by a few well-placed needles, underwent removal of a large ovarian cyst. They saw another patient, anesthetized with only a tranquilizing shot of morphine and a single needle in his forearm, endure an operation to remove a lobe of one lung. They returned to the U.S. convinced that Western scientists must study and learn more about acupuncture themselves.

There was much to learn, for little was known about either the whys or the wherefores of acupuncture. Ancient Chinese texts on the subject were more metaphysical than medical. *The Yellow Emperor's Classic of Internal Medicine,* a 2,300-year-old treatise on the art, postulates that the body has 12 more or less vertical channels or "meridians"; along these meridians are 365 points (one for every day in the year) where the insertion of a needle will have a physiological effect. The book maintains that the forces of yang (positive) and yin (negative) flow through the meridians and must be precisely balanced if health is to be maintained. If a patient has too much yin somewhere, the acupuncturist jabs a selected point with a gold yang needle. Modern Chinese acupuncturists had abandoned gold needles for stainless steel ones, which were sterilized and sometimes connected to a battery-powered device, which provides stimulation. They had also increased the number of points to around 800. But they had not succeeded in explaining—at least in scientific terms—how a needle inserted in the corner of the eye can prevent a patient from feeling a pain in his chest or how a needle inserted in the neck can relieve the pain of a migraine headache.

Nor had their Western colleagues done any better. French Air Force doctors measuring the body's electrical emanations observed that the points at which the greatest current can be detected coincide with the acupuncture points and that currents appear to follow the ancient meridians. A few scientists found that the skin at the acupuncture points appears to be thinner than elsewhere on the body. But neither of these observations unraveled the mystery of acupuncture.

An explanation that did seem plausible, at least for acupuncture's anesthetic properties, was one originally proposed in 1965 by Ronald Melzack of McGill University, Montreal, and Patrick Wall of University College, London. Known as the gate theory, it suggests that stimulation of what are known as A-delta fibres in the sensory nerves (as would logically result from the insertion and rotation of a needle) shuts a "gate" in the spinal cord. This would block pain impulses from moving up the cord and into the brain, providing, of course, that the pain originated at a point below the neck.

This theory could explain how needles might prevent patients from feeling pain in the extremities; it does not explain how a needle placed in the toe could prevent a patient from experiencing the pain of abdominal surgery. A new theory put forward by the Chinese themselves might. Physiologists at Shanghai's Academy of Sciences used microelectrodes to measure the body's electrical impulses. As a result of their observations, they hypothesized that pain sensations are channeled and controlled by at least four gates—in the spinal cord, the thalamus, the brain stem, and the cerebral cortex. Thus, they believed, acupuncture needles inserted along strategic pathways leading to these gates would suppress pain messages by somehow closing one or more of the gates and preventing impulses from reaching the brain.

Whatever the explanation, U.S. doctors were becoming increasingly curious about acupuncture. Doctors at New York City's Albert Einstein College of Medicine and the Downstate Medical Center performed operations using acupuncture as an anesthetic with moderate success. In two operations, a skin graft and a tonsilear biopsy, the patients experienced no pain, but in a third, a hernia repair, the patient was so uncomfortable that the doctors switched to a more conventional painkiller midway through the procedure.

The National Institute of General Medical Sciences was planning to underwrite research to determine the scientific basis of acupuncture. Most U.S. doctors agreed that the needles could eventually prove a valuable addition to the physician's armamentarium, particularly as an anesthetic, since acupuncture would avoid many of the problems connected with more commonly used anesthetics. Meanwhile, many physicians were concerned about possible abuse of acupuncture. Their concern was more than theoretical. The current wave of interest had brought to the fore many Chinese-trained acupuncturists who had previously confined their practice to the Chinese community and who were not licensed under state laws. It had also attracted some medical entrepreneurs, who sought to capitalize on the American public's peculiar penchant for medical fads by opening acupuncture clinics where unlicensed practitioners worked under the putative supervision of an accredited physician.

Reaction against both groups was swift. Health officials in New York state closed down a Manhattan acupuncture clinic and ordered unlicensed practitioners in New York City's Chinatown to put down their needles or face legal action. California also attempted to regulate would-be needle-wielders, but without stifling experimentation with acupuncture. The state adopted legislation that specifically allowed unlicensed acupuncturists to practice, under the supervision of a doctor, if the work was being done for the purposes of scientific investigation and not for profit.

PERSISTENT PROBLEMS

Despite the progress and innovation that had taken place in medicine, many health problems persisted. Among the most serious was that of infectious disease. Cholera, a highly contagious disease caused by a microorganism that breeds in the human intestinal tract, was still endemic to some parts of Asia, particularly the Indian subcontinent. In 1970 a pandemic originating in Indonesia in 1935 reached Egypt and the Soviet Black Sea port of Odessa. In 1971 a major epidemic broke out in India among refugees from the fighting in what was then East Pakistan; of 71,386 cases reported on the subcontinent, 51,000 were among those who had fled the war-torn country. The disease, which thrives in areas with contaminated water supplies, was not considered a serious public health threat in Western Europe or North America. Health officials feared, however, that a serious outbreak could erupt in Africa or South America.

Western Europe and the U.S. did experience a brief thrill of fear in 1972 when smallpox, long controlled by vaccination and all but extinct in the world's industrial nations, erupted in Yugoslavia. Believed to have been brought to Serbia by some Muslims who had stopped over in Baghdad, Iraq, on their way back from pilgrimages to Mecca and Medina, the disease spread rapidly, infecting some 200 and killing at least 28 before a massive immunization program brought it under control. The outbreak worried health officials elsewhere in Europe, who were concerned that tourists

CAMERA PRESS/PICTORIAL PARADE

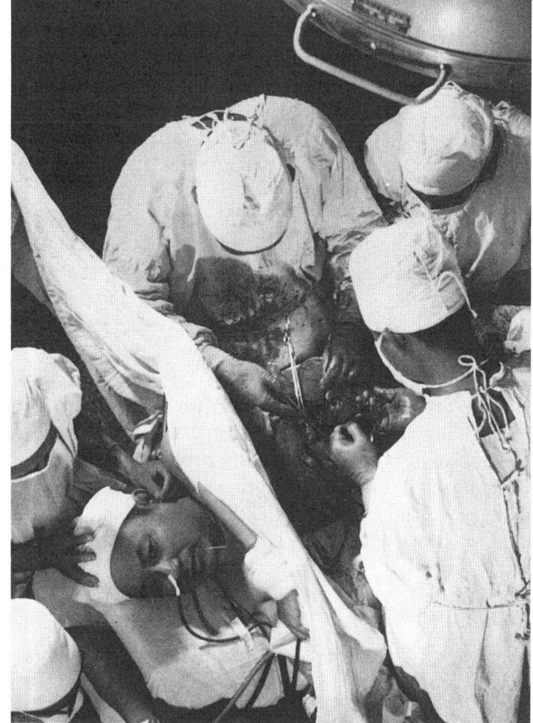

With three needles inserted in his left ear and left forearm, a patient, anesthetized by acupuncture at the No. 3 Teaching Hospital, Peking Medical College, is able to remain fully conscious and cooperate with the physician, who is removing a tumour from his esophagus. Western doctors were undertaking extensive research to explain the mechanism of acupuncture, which has been practiced in China for at least 2,300 years.

returning from Yugoslavia's popular resort areas might bring the disease with them. Authorities in West Germany quarantined more than 600 people known to have come into contact with a Yugoslav worker who contracted the disease. U.S. officials, who no longer required proof of vaccination from Americans returning from most foreign countries, began demanding that travelers coming back from Yugoslavia show an immunization certificate or stay in touch with health agencies for at least two weeks.

The world did appear to get a respite from one disease. Influenza, which had claimed more than 30 million lives in the worldwide 1918 epidemic and more than 200 in the U.S. alone in 1968, seemed to subside in 1972. This temporary armistice might enable scientists to be ready for the next outbreak, which, given the tendency of flu to erupt at ten-year intervals, was predicted for the latter part of the 1970s. Previous attempts to guard against influenza had been largely unsuccessful because the flu virus has an apparently unlimited ability to undergo antigenic changes or mutations; thus the vaccine developed to fight one strain of virus may be of limited value against its progeny. Researchers at the Allergy and Infectious Diseases branch of the National Institutes of Health might have found a way to overcome this obstacle, however. By combining A_2 Hong Kong flu viruses from the 1968 epidemic with chemically altered samples of a 1965 strain, they produced a virus strong enough to induce immunity to the disease but too weak to cause the disease itself. The virus can be grown quickly in culture and, the researchers believed, could be tailored to fight different varieties of the disease. Most important, they thought that, using live but attenuated viruses, they could have the new vaccine perfected in time for the next expected outbreak.

Venereal Diseases. Unfortunately, no such progress was made in the fight against veneral disease, which had reached pandemic proportions and become the major public health problem in the U.S. The incidence of both syphilis and gonorrhea had dropped dramatically in the years following World War II and reached an all-time low during the mid-1950s, but in the 1970s the two diseases were returning—and with a vengeance. According to the U.S. Public Health Service's Center for Disease Control in Atlanta, Ga., 95,997 cases of syphilis and 670,268 cases of gonorrhea were reported during 1971. The figures for 1972 were expected to be even higher.

Venereal disease is undiscriminating; it strikes all segments of society. Bankers and businessmen have it, as do policemen, teachers, and even doctors—and the boy or girl next door. For most of those afflicted are young. At least one out of every five persons with gonorrhea in 1972 was under 20; cases as young as 9 had been reported, and some doctors believed that half the present youth population would contract VD before they turned 25. The reason was obvious: relaxed sexual mores, in large part evolving from widespread use of birth-control pills and other devices, made opportunities for infection inevitable. Spread only by sexual contact, VD passes quickly from one partner to another, and each one can infect every other person with whom he or she has relations.

The irony is that VD is easily curable, at least in its early stages. Penicillin and other antibiotics can clear up primary gonorrhea or syphilis in a matter of a few weeks. Unfortunately, many VD victims fail to seek treatment. The delay is dangerous. Untreated syphilis, which makes its early presence known by a chancre, or open sore, on the genitals or other mucous tissues, eventually goes underground, often leading the uneducated to believe the disease has disappeared. It has not. It has merely passed into a more deadly stage in which the spiral-shaped *Treponema pallidum* that causes the disease goes to work on the brain and spinal cord, where its action can result in blindness, paralysis, insanity, and death. Gonorrhea, though less lethal than syphilis, can spread through the reproductive system and produce sterility. It is also harder to detect, particularly in women, in whom the symptoms may pass unnoticed.

Medical researchers had been trying for years to develop vaccines against both syphilis and gonorrhea. So far, success had eluded them. Until they found such a vaccine, treatment was the answer, and public health officials across the U.S. were working on programs to educate people as to VD's dangers and cures. Their job was not easy. Many state laws prohibited doctors from treating minors without parental permission; because many young people were reluctant to let their parents know they had VD, they often put off treatment until it was too late. Social attitudes also inhibited people in search of treatment for venereal disease. To overcome these obstacles, several states set up free clinics where people could be tested for VD and receive treatment without the embarrassment of going to their own family physicians. California enacted legislation allowing doctors to treat minors for VD without parental permission.

Many felt this two-pronged approach—education and treatment—would eventually bring the venereal disease problem under control.

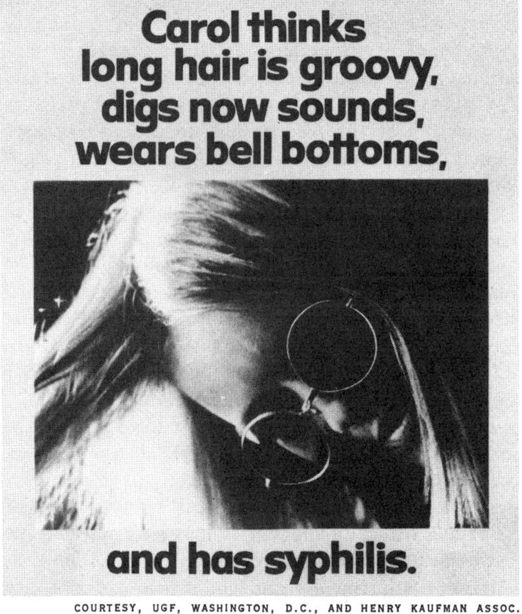

Carol thinks
long hair is groovy,
digs now sounds,
wears bell bottoms,
and has syphilis.

COURTESY, UGF, WASHINGTON, D.C., AND HENRY KAUFMAN ASSOC.

To combat venereal disease, which has reached epidemic proportions in the U.S., health and social organizations launched multimedia educational campaigns, including advertisements in popular magazines, aimed primarily at youth, who suffer the highest incidence of VD.

THE SHAPE OF THINGS TO COME

There was no question that clinical and scientific developments would change the way physicians approach and treat disease. But the breakthroughs that would really revolutionize medicine, particularly in the U.S., were not scientific but organizational. Before the 1970s ended, U.S. medicine was likely to undergo a dramatic mutation. The medicine of the future, it was predicted, would resemble that of today in only one important respect: the emphasis on maintaining health would remain unchanged. The ways in which this goal was sought would be, in Yeats's words, "changed utterly."

The New Doctor. One of these changes was already being reflected in the attitudes of U.S. doctors. Medicine is traditionally a conservative profession and its members are slow to adopt and adapt to the new. But new was the only way to describe the way many doctors were thinking. Interns and residents, who were once to senior staff what initiates were to old-time fraternity men, were now talking back and dreaming, not always in vain, of new, more egalitarian forms of practice. An increasing number of younger doctors no longer aspired to careers in the research laboratory or the plusher specialties; instead, they were looking backward toward the old model of the general practitioner. Few of them wanted to return to the horse-and-buggy medicine of an earlier generation, but a new specialty, known variously as community medicine or family practice and stressing a general and person-oriented approach to medicine, was gaining in popularity.

Such attitudes are interesting. American medicine had already undergone several mutations since Abraham Flexner published his comprehensive—and highly critical—report on medical education in 1910. Flexner's report, which revolutionized medical training (prior to its publication, some medical schools did not even require their students to hold high school degrees), ushered in the era of the general practitioner with his broad, though not always deep, training in the scientific and clinical techniques of his day. For nearly a quarter of a century, this figure dominated American medicine. But in the 1940s, as doctors realized that no physician could possibly be competent in all areas of medicine, a new breed of doctor began to emerge—the specialist, who devoted his practice exclusively to one area of medicine, such as pediatrics, obstetrics, or cardiology, and often subspecialized in an even narrower field. In the late 1950s, the specialist's preeminence was challenged by yet another type of physician—the researcher who eschewed the consulting room for the laboratory, dealing with patients, if at all, only as a method of studying and learning more about their diseases.

In the 1970s medicine appeared to be entering a new phase as doctors, realizing the need for providing better clinical care to more people, sought new forms of practice. None of the new doctors proposed doing away with either the specialist or the research physician; both are essential, possibly indispensable, to the proper functioning of a sound health-care system. But many believed that the day of the old solo practitioner was drawing to an end. Some were forming group practices, joining together with others to establish what amounted to mini-medical centres where various specialists provided a complete range of medical care. A number of doctors were seeking salaried jobs in clinics and hospitals. Others were looking toward the large, prepaid operations like California's Kaiser Plan, which operated its own hospitals and provided complete medical service to its subscribers for a fixed annual fee.

Obviously, some young doctors interested in such alternate forms of practice might work differently from their older colleagues, but the degree of difference is not as great as is popularly believed. Younger physicians seemed more willing to work in shared relationships. Interns were demanding and getting salaries in excess of $10,000 a year and residents as much as $20,000 from administrators more and more willing to pay these amounts. Many younger doctors do not fear government involvement in medicine as much as older physicians might; most see some form of government financing—and, hence, influence—as essential to guaranteeing good health care for all. Younger doctors are indifferent and, in some cases, actually hostile to the U.S. medical establishment. Although the total membership of the American Medical Association had increased, the proportion of eligible physicians joining the organization had, in fact, fallen in recent years.

Some younger physicians genuinely did not feel the AMA spoke for them and therefore they chose not to become members. But the AMA's problem of declining membership was more complex. Conservative and radical right-wing physicians attacked the AMA for being "progressive," for sponsoring even such moderate legislation as its "Medicredit" plan for financing national health care. In 1972, particularly, a large contingent of AMA members put tremendous pressure on the organization over President Nixon's wage-price freeze insofar as it affected health services. The angry physicians wanted the AMA to do more to get government approval for higher physicians' fees. Some of these disappointed physicians were muttering about forming a doctors' union, one that would be responsive to their demands for higher fees for service. Others even banded together to form their own societies or quasi-unions. One such group even became affiliated with a local of the AFL-CIO.

Another AMA problem arose from the proliferation of specialty societies in medicine and their growing preeminence as the sources for continuing medical education. Besides being concerned over its membership problems, the AMA was carefully watching declining attendance at its two traditional annual conventions, which were once not only events of national importance in medical education, but profitable as well. By the late 1970s, the AMA might be an entirely different organization in structure and primary purpose. The first sign of significant change occurred in November 1972, when the AMA dropped nine councils and committees from its organizational structure, cut back on free subscriptions to its journals as a benefit of membership, and scrapped a large advertising campaign. Further cutbacks, including staff reductions and further reductions in the number of councils and committees, were anticipated as the organization moved to trim its budget by $1 million.

Medical schools were already responding to new attitudes by changing their curricula to meet the needs of modern medicine. In some, class hours once devoted to the pure sciences were reduced to permit earlier and more intense exposure to clinical work. Students at the Albert Einstein College of Medicine followed pregnant women through delivery, providing pre- and postnatal care for them and their babies. M.D. candidates at the University of Missouri's new medical school at Kansas City began making hospital rounds on their first day of classes, an experience that shocked many into an awareness of the problems and pressures confronting anyone who wishes to practice medicine.

At least 25 schools had taken steps to speed up the new doctor's debut by lopping up to a year off the traditional four-year program. The move should allow schools to turn out more doctors at less expense and might help combat the doctor shortage facing many areas of the country (though it was not, many believed, a per capita shortage). Postgraduate programs were also changing. Montefiore Hospital in New York City initiated a four-year residency in social medicine; participants involved themselves in such community projects as neighbourhood health clinics, maternal and child health programs, and housing and sanitation plans. Medical schools began instituting courses in sex education after it was realized that physicians in the field were not necessarily knowledgeable enough to deal with the many sexual problems of patients who required attention below the level of psychoanalysis.

Programs were also under way to increase doctors' efficiency and productivity. Recognizing that much of the work that occupies a doctor's time can be handled just as easily by nonprofessionals, several medical schools were developing programs for the training and use of paramedics, highly trained semiprofessionals who can function as physicians' assistants, emergency medical specialists, and the like. Started in 1965 at Duke University, Durham, N.C., paramedic training programs were being offered at some 40 schools around the U.S., and the demand for graduates, who undergo an average of two years' training, was increasing.

One of the most successful of these programs was called Medex. Launched in 1969 at the University of Washington, the program took former armed forces medical corpsmen, already well trained, as well as a number of people from nonmilitary backgrounds, put them through intensive schooling, then paired them with doctors in the Seattle, Wash., area. The Medex took patient histories, helped give physical examinations, sutured minor wounds, applied and removed casts—and, according to the doctors with whom they worked, freed physicians to concentrate on more serious problems. A Colorado program, in which pediatric nurses carried medical care to rural families who might otherwise never see a doctor, screened for disease and passed those needing a physician's attention on to hospitals and clinics, was similarly successful.

A growing number of doctors saw paraprofessionals as key elements in the delivery of medical care. The AMA was on record as favouring the expansion of training programs and the development of licensing programs to assure not only that more paramedics were trained but that those who were trained were properly qualified and regulated. Most U.S. authorities envisioned such paraprofessionals as working only under the direct supervision of a physician. The World Health Organization urged even broader use. Citing the Soviet Union's use of *feldshers,* nondoctors who provide basic medical care in rural areas, WHO suggested that less developed countries might turn to similar expedients to get immediate medical care out to their people.

Automation was also increasingly making its way into medicine. The robot doctor described in Michael Crichton's novel *The Andromeda Strain* was now a reality. Computerized multiphasic screening centres, in which patients pass from station to station while sophisticated machinery analyzes blood and urine samples, performing in minutes tests that would otherwise take hours, were operating in major cities across the country. The centres, which relied on doctors to perform many phases of the examination and to interpret test results, could perform complete annual physicals in an hour. Many believed that, by enabling more people to undergo regular checkups, they would find many more cases of disease that were still easily curable.

The National Health Debate. In terms of gross medical resources, no nation on earth could compare with the U.S. The country had more than 300,000 practicing physicians and more doctors per patient than most industrial nations. It had more medical schools and more hospital beds, although the beds were not well or equitably distributed. It also spent more on health than any other nation. In sheer dollar terms, health had become the second largest industry in the country, turning over an estimated $75 billion a year. In terms of individual outlay, Americans spent $324 per person per year in their attempts—not always successful—to avoid illness.

These investments did not always ensure a high level of health, however. Despite the medical profession's high standards of skill, statistics showed that people in other, less wealthy countries might be healthier. Women in 10 other countries lived longer than U.S. women; men in 17 other nations outlasted U.S. men. Eleven other nations had lower infant mortality rates than the U.S.

The reasons for this gap were obvious. Most of the country's medical resources—hospitals, schools, and doctors—were concentrated in a few large cities. Medical resources in rural areas—and in urban ghettos as well—were few and far between. There were more than 100 rural counties in the U.S. that had no medical facilities at all. Many Americans saw doctors only in the event of serious illness or injury. One out of 50, some 40 million people, never saw a doctor during their lifetimes.

Nor could those with access to doctors always afford to take advantage of their skills and services. From 1960, the costs of health care had climbed by more than 50%, outstripping even the 31% rise in the

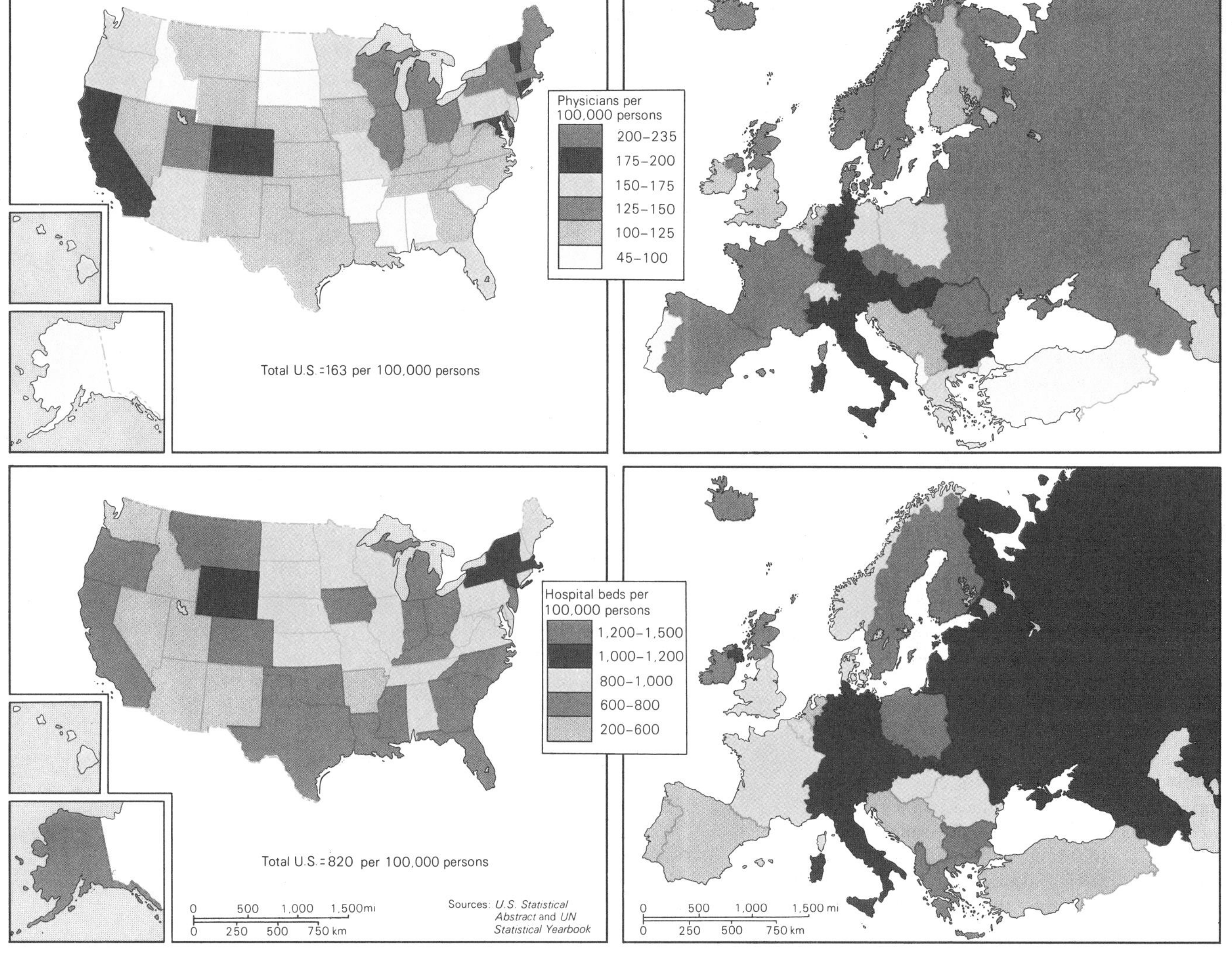

consumer price index. Physicians' fees alone had risen by nearly 60%; hospitalization, which averaged $35 a day in 1962, now costs more than $80.

The effect of these increases had been enormous. A routine surgical procedure like hernia repair could end up costing $1,000 in doctor and hospital bills; charges totaling $1,200 for a routine delivery followed by a four-day stay in a maternity ward were not uncommon. The costs of major, catastrophic illnesses could be astronomical. Hemodialysis, essential to keep a victim of kidney disease alive, could cost $25,000 a year. The expenses of caring for a cancer or cardiac patient were often equally high.

Insurance did not always cover these bills. Though 85% of the U.S. population under 65 carried some sort of health coverage, the protection was frequently flawed. At least 20% had no coverage for hospitalization, 32% had no coverage for in-hospital doctor's bills, half got no benefits for X rays, and 97% had no dental insurance. Even the most generous plans were limited in their benefits, which usually ran out long before catastrophic illnesses were cured. As one insurance man learned to his chagrin, not even a policy that provided $40,000 in benefits could cover his expenses when his son's injury resulted in bills of $6,000 a month.

Concerned about the costs of illness, Americans tried numerous ways to avoid or evade them. Elective surgery was often delayed or postponed until the condition could be covered under emergency plans. Illnesses were tolerated until the victim was eligible for coverage. A few people even moved to nations like Canada, Sweden, and West Germany where medical care was provided under national government plans.

Their exodus was understandable. Ever since Bismarck first initiated a health plan for German workers in 1883, medical care had been an important aspect of the welfare state. Britain adopted a comprehensive national health system in 1948; Sweden had had one since 1955, Norway since 1956. Now, the American public—and, naturally, American politicians—were coming around to the belief that the U.S. must take the first step toward establishing a similar system. Several major pieces of legislation were before Congress, and while action on health was in abeyance during the 1972 election campaign, most government officials expected some movement toward expanded medical care during 1973.

The bills before Congress covered a broad spectrum of approaches and benefits. The AMA, which long opposed any government involvement in medicine, finally recognized the inevitable. Its Medicredit plan would seek to expand health insurance protection by allowing tax benefits for premium payments. A proposal offered by Sen. Jacob Javits (Rep., N.Y.) would gradually expand Medicare to cover the entire population. The American Hospital Association's Ameriplan would create, with federal assistance, some 400 health-care corporations across the country. Each would be responsible for assembling the personnel and facilities to meet health needs in its area, providing services on a prepayment basis to those who could afford them and making them available free to those who could not. Other plans provided for government-financed coverage of catastrophic illness.

But the major contest was not between these bills. It was between the National Health Insurance Partnership Act, put forward by the administration, and the Health Security Act sponsored by Sen. Edward Kennedy (Dem., Mass.), Rep. Martha Griffiths (Dem., Mich.), and a coalition of liberal Democrats and labour leaders. The two bills differed considerably in both benefits and approaches.

The administration plan was based on mandated coverage through the existing insurance industry. Under it, employers would be required to provide their employees with a tax-deductible insurance plan that would include hospitalization and major medical and catastrophic illness coverage with a maximum benefit of $50,000. A separate program would be established for the self-employed, while the government would finance the entire cost of coverage for families of four with incomes below $3,000 a year and pay partial premiums for those with incomes of up to $5,000. While the poor would receive less coverage than others, Medicare recipients would get a break. The government would pick up the entire $1.4 billion bill for the Plan B supplement, which covers doctors' bills.

This plan would also seek to encourage greater efficiency in medicine by setting aside $23 million for grants to groups of doctors willing to establish prepaid practices or health maintenance organizations (HMOs), and would attempt to help medical schools train more doctors by appropriating another $100 million for medical education. The total cost of the administration plan: $3 billion a year in new federal funds, another $2 billion a year in lost tax revenues, and about $6 billion a year from business and industry.

The Kennedy-Griffiths plan was far more comprehensive. Based on a plan originally drafted by the late United Automobile Workers president Walter Reuther, the bill would have the government pay at least 50% and, in some cases, 70% of the cost of nearly all health services, including dental care for children under 15, prescription drugs, and psychiatric treatment. Basically a broadening of the Social Security system, the bill would be financed by a payroll tax on employers, a smaller tax on employees, and general federal revenues. It, too, would seek to encourage the establishment of group practices, allocating $600 million for physicians willing to form HMOs. It would also seek to promote cost control by requiring health-care institutions to negotiate and provide health care within annual budgets and by putting doctors on salary or paying them set fees per patient.

What the bill would not do, however, was reduce the country's total annual outlay for health. The bill's backers put the cost of their plan at around $68 billion, much of it in funds already being spent on health. Administration critics said the bill would cost $77 billion. Even its supporters admitted that its long-term costs would be hard to figure. Both Medicare and Medicaid were costing the government—and the taxpayers—far more than had been expected. The Kennedy-Griffiths bill, which would necessitate the creation of a federal bureaucracy to administer it, seemed equally subject to cost overruns.

The U.S. medical establishment viewed both bills with mixed feelings. A majority of doctors favoured some federal involvement in the financing of health care, but many were suspicious of any system that would give the government control over the way medicine is practiced. A significant number of medical students, interns, and younger physicians claimed that they were willing to work for a salary and to involve the medical consumer in decisions concerning the organization and delivery of health care. But many physicians found anything resembling federal control anathema. "I went into medicine so that I could be my own boss, not to work for the government," said one middle-aged orthopedic surgeon. He spoke for a large number of his colleagues, who feared that any system that made doctors employees of the government would destroy initiative and further erode the already rapidly disappearing doctor-patient relationship.

Those familiar with European health-care systems found that these fears were realistic. Many Swedes were unhappy about their country's health-care setup, which was characterized by long waits for all but emergency care, a lack of personalized treatment, and a complete absence of choice when it came to physicians. Others noted that Swedes paid more taxes than almost any other people to help support their health-care system.

But few believed the U.S. system could long withstand change, and many doctors were moving quickly to assure their influence over any system that might eventually be adopted. Steps had been taken in some areas to include patients on hospital and physician review boards. A couple of states tried to force physicians to keep current with modern medical developments by establishing continuing education requirements for licensure. Doctors and hospital officials in the Phoenix, Ariz., area sought to reduce inefficiency and duplication by combining the management and facilities of six hospitals into a regional medical complex.

A few doctors seemed determined to maintain the status quo and some even spoke darkly of a doctors' revolt if the government attempted to regulate the practice or shape the organization of medicine. Most did not. Medicaid and Medicare, once damned as steps toward "socialized medicine," had become an accepted part of health care in the U.S. It seemed unlikely that a European-style health-care system would be adopted in the U.S. for many years, if at all, but the first move toward removing the economic barriers to health care was generally recognized as a necessity. No one was sure just what form this move would take. Most, however, did expect it to be made in 1973.

(PETER STOLER)

OTHER DEVELOPMENTS

• Progress was made in the management of asthma. A steroid compound, beclomethasone dipropionate, administered as an aerosol, was said to have exceeded all expectations in early tests and did not cause the side effects associated with conventional steroid drugs. The death rate from asthma had fallen since warnings about overuse of self-administered inhalers, but attempts to desensitize asthmatic sufferers to housemite dust, thought to be one of the commonest allergens, were unsuccessful.

• A Harvard study of nearly 4,000 women showed that the risk of developing breast cancer was related to the age at which menopause occurred; the earlier the onset, the lower the incidence. Production of artificial menopause in younger women seemed to delay the onset of breast cancer indefinitely.

• Studies in Australia and the U.S. showed that women taking oral contraceptives had fewer premenstrual and menstrual complaints than those not taking the pill and performed better in examinations and at work. A curious finding was reported from Birmingham, Eng.; a form of jaundice occurring in newborn babies who were breast fed was commoner in those babies whose mothers had previously been taking the pill. No explanation was offered, but it was pointed out that "breast milk jaundice" was first recorded in 1963, shortly after the widespread introduction of the pill.

• Five patients with gallstones at the Mayo Clinic, Rochester, Minn., were treated for up to two years with a naturally occurring bile detergent, chenodeoxycholic acid; the stones diminished in size and, in one patient, dissolved completely. This raised cautious hopes that it might be possible to avoid surgery in the future, but the drug was costly to prepare and might prove toxic.

• The problem of bacterial resistance to antibiotics was highlighted by reports from Mexico of an epidemic of typhoid fever that did not always respond to chloramphenicol, hitherto the mainstay of treatment. However, a new combined antibiotic, co-trimoxazole, was found to be effective in sporadic cases in Britain.

• Criticism of psychosurgery was voiced in Britain and the U.S. in cases where certain areas of the brain were deliberately destroyed to produce more amenable individuals. The treatment was being increasingly used with violent criminals, addicts, homosexuals, and even overactive children. It had been outlawed in 1950 in the Soviet Union, although the practice of confining political dissenters in psychiatric institutions there was growing.

• Among 600 U.S. students, habitual users of marijuana scored lower grades than abstainers, while casual users had higher grades.

• The increasing use of methadone as a substitute for heroin in addicts was criticized on the ground that it replaced one form of dependence with another. From Iran came news of intensive cultivation of a miniature black poppy, the seeds of which contained thebaine, said to be a useful heroin antagonist.

• The British National Child Development Study, involving nearly 17,000 children born in March 1958, reported a 28% increase in late fetal and neonatal mortality among babies of women who continued smoking after the fourth month of pregnancy. Birth weights were lower on average and differences persisted, so that at age seven the children tended to be shorter, smaller, and less intelligent. Possible hope for cigarette smokers came from the demonstration that phenylmethyloxadiazole, used as a cough mixture, prevented thickening and overgrowth of mucous glands in the bronchi when added to cigarettes to which rats were exposed. Another finding from the Child Development Study was that more than half the mothers of children who died of leukemia or Hodgkin's disease had had influenza during pregnancy.

• An environmental hazard that caused increasing concern was lead. High levels found in the blood of workers and people living nearby caused the closure of a large smelting works in Britain; and taxi drivers and individuals residing near new expressways were being carefully monitored. Four workers were poisoned by tetraethyl lead while sealing a tank, and the British government announced that the lead content of gasoline was to be reduced to half its current level over the next three years. The lead content of moss and shellfish was found to be a useful indication of the degree of atmospheric pollution. Mercury in the Greenland ice sheet had doubled in 20 years; this was thought due to man's action in disturbing the earth's crust rather than to industrial processes, a view supported by the fact that there had been no general increase in the amount of mercury in tuna and swordfish in the last century. A working party in Britain found levels in foodstuffs to be below the strict safety limit of one-half part per million set by the U.S.

• DDT and organochloride insecticides were reported responsible for impotence in farmers, fortunately recoverable after about a year. These compounds were deposited in the testes and prostate, but it was also possible that they stimulated production of liver enzymes that destroyed testosterone, the male sex hormone.

• Homosexuals were found to have about one-third the normal level of blood testosterone, but it was not clear whether this was a cause or effect of homosexuality—at least it argued that there was more than a purely psychological explanation, and other studies suggested that the determination of sex drive might be due to the level of testosterone in the blood at birth. Fetal testes were transplanted into a 28-year-old man in Beirut, Lebanon, who had had to give up hormone treatment because of side effects. Six weeks later he was said to be sexually active for the first time.

• Warnings were issued about the possible dangers of hexachlorophene after feeding experiments in rats caused brain damage reminiscent of a rare disease of infants known as spongy degeneration. Hexachlorophene, a chlorinated phenol, had been widely used as an antibacterial agent for over 20 years. For example, it was customarily applied to the skin of newborn babies in liberal quantities; blood concentrations after repeated washing were found to reach two-thirds of the minimum levels in the rat experiments. That it could prove dangerous was tragically shown by the deaths of at least 28 babies in France treated with a talcum powder containing 6% hexachlorophene (considerably higher than the recommended upper limit of 1%); many more were believed to have suffered brain damage.

• An unexpected health hazard was found in some brands of carbonless copying paper used in Japan. These were impregnated with polychlorinated phenyls, which in 1968 caused food poisoning among more than 1,000 Japanese who had eaten contaminated rice. The hands of volunteers using the paper were appreciably tainted, and there was fear that reprocessing of waste paper might lead to its use for wrapping food.

• Also in Japan, a drug widely used for minor gastrointestinal disorders was linked with subacute myeloptic neuropathy (SMON). It was noticed that cases of the disease began to appear after the introduction of clioquinol, a halogenated oxyquinolone. Symptoms of unsteady gait, visual disturbance, and sometimes a green discoloration of the tongue tended to disappear when the drug was stopped—though sometimes there was severe disability and even death —and the incidence of the disease fell after the drug was withdrawn. SMON was rare in other countries where clioquinol was available, but it had been reported from Scandinavia, Australia, and the U.K.

• A London researcher believed that osteoarthritis of the hip was caused by slipping of the femoral head in adolescence as a result of overindulgence in sport. He questioned 250 young people about the attitude of their schools toward sport and found a 24% incidence of tilt deformity of the hip in those who had been educated at schools with an emphasis on games, as opposed to 9% where games were voluntary.

• Indulgence in sauna baths by middle-aged men was found to be accompanied by electrocardiographic (EKG) changes similar to those occurring in coronary artery disease. Sharp increases in heart rate, together with "ischemic" looking tracings, were reminiscent of those found in racing drivers some years earlier using the same technique of telemetry. Tests were also carried out on 45 young professional brass players with similar results; trumpeters produced more marked EKG changes while playing than horn players, while trombonists showed the fewest signs of rhythm disturbances and heart strain.

PAUL SEQUEIRA

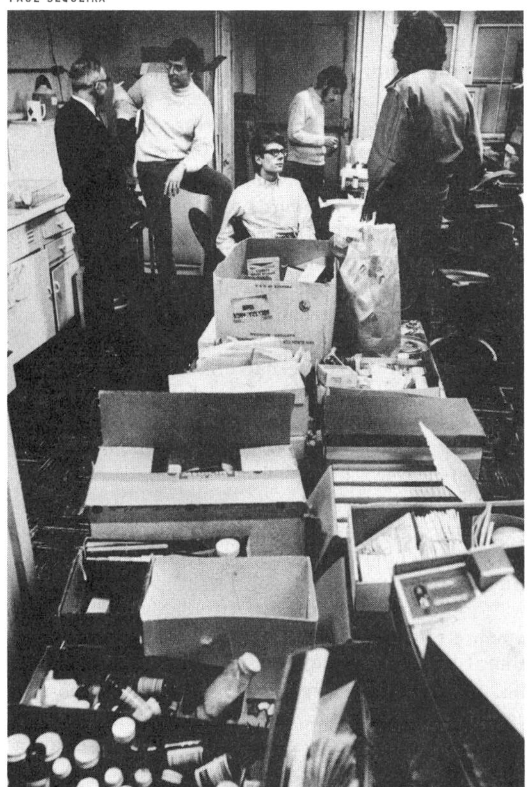

A group of doctors at work in a free neighbourhood clinic in Chicago's Uptown area face a jumbled array of medical supplies, records, and community problems. The growing number of such clinics demonstrated consumer demand for better access to medical care and the desire of many young doctors to return to a more person-oriented practice of medicine.

• A major reorganization of the British National Health Service was heralded by the publication of no less than four government documents containing plans to integrate the health and welfare services. A tripartite structure of local authority, hospital, and general practitioner services was to be closely integrated by means of some 200 area health boards, which would coincide with the new local government areas to come into existence in 1974. The government put its faith in improved management, with members of local communities playing a greater part in health affairs. At the same time, the medical profession saw the need for a new role for doctors in administration and public health as "community physicians." Calls for a better method of dealing with complaints within the health service were recognized by the government's intention to appoint a health service commissioner or ombudsman. A storm of protest led by medical scientists followed the publication of the Rothschild report on the financing of research, which proposed to transfer part of the funds currently allocated to the various research councils to government departments. The report expressed the view that more research should be undertaken on a customer-contractor basis, but critics argued that it was difficult to draw a line between basic and applied research and that dictation by the customer, *i.e.*, government departments, was a threat to the independence of research councils and to university-based research, much of which was financed by the councils. (ALEXANDER PATON)

DENTISTRY

Dental researchers during 1972 reinforced emphasis on the importance of plaque control in the prevention of tooth decay and periodontal disease. Although much remained to be learned about these disorders, scientists had discovered that certain forms of tooth decay and periodontal disease were related to certain types of bacteria found in most mouths. These bacteria attach themselves to the teeth and multiply into increasingly larger bacterial colonies called dental plaque, a colourless, transparent film. Research findings established that once plaque is formed on the teeth, more bacteria lodge in the sticky mass and reproduce. Many of these bacteria also act on sugars to produce acids which then attack the tooth enamel. Researchers were trying to identify the specific types of bacteria that cause this condition; some of those implicated were identified as threadlike, filament-shaped organisms.

To step up the battle against plaque and its fellow-travelers, tooth decay and periodontal disease, the American Dental Association (ADA), in consultation with top experts in the preventive field, began to map a new strategy that leaned heavily on massive health education programs. Although continuing to maintain that brushing after every meal served its purpose of cleansing the teeth, the ADA recommended as another effective means a once-a-day thorough oral cleaning including tooth brushing, the use of dental floss to remove plaque from surface between teeth, the use of a fluoride-containing dentifrice, water spray devices, and the self-application of solutions to search out any areas that still harbour plaque. In addition, the drinking of fluoridated water and the limitation of consumption of sweets, two suggestions long advocated by the dental profession, should also be included in any realistic preventive program. It was stressed that prevention of dental disease required both the supervision of a dentist and the full and informed participation of the patient. The ADA anticipated that increasing numbers of U.S. dentists would incorporate "plaque control" education into their everyday practice.

Fluoridation of water supplies remained the key weapon against tooth decay. A study conducted in Connecticut, the first state to pass a statewide fluoridation law, disclosed that an estimated $100 million in dental care expenses were saved because the water supply had been fluoridated for 22 years. But, a disquieting note was injected during 1972 by the U.S. Environmental Protection Agency, which revealed that a survey of water systems in eight states showed that only half of them were fluoridated at the recommended level. Laxity in surveillance and inadequate training of water system operators were blamed. The agency also found procedures for bacteriological control were inadequate in some water systems.

Another milestone on the road to prevention was the introduction of so-called adhesive sealants aimed at eliminating decay of the pits and fissures of teeth. A number of sealant materials had become commercially available to dentists and, in May 1972, the ADA announced provisional acceptance of one sealant as an agent capable of "restoring or sealing off anatomically deficient regions of the tooth." The ADA cautioned, however, that this acceptance in no way indicated therapeutic or decay-preventing qualities of the sealant. This liquid sealant is brushed or painted on the occlusal surfaces of teeth and the material then hardens to a transparent coating under ultraviolet light. The sealants did not have restorative value for other tooth areas particularly susceptible to decay, for instance, the surfaces between the teeth and at the gum line. One adhesive sealant, however, had been tested for its ability to stop marginal leakage of dental fillings, a major cause of recurrent decay and the necessity to replace old fillings.

Two researchers from the University of California School of Dentistry in San Francisco found that women were smoking more and developing a higher rate of oral cancer. They reported that smokers had a six times greater risk of developing oral cancer than nonsmokers, and that the risk for women was nine times as great. Women, they noted, also had recurrence of cancer of the mouth more frequently than men, probably because of "the greater reluctance on the part of women to reduce or stop smoking."

A cement with which a tiny marine animal fastens its colony permanently to shells, rocks, and the hulls of ships might help dentists set crowns, bridges, and inlays in place quickly and firmly. If the cement can be identified and reproduced chemically it undoubtedly would make a quick-setting material that would work as well in the human mouth as it does in the sea. Currently, a number of metal-based dental adhesives required dry surfaces.

Freeze-dried skin grafts taken from a skin bank might one day accelerate wound healing following periodontal surgery, a Navy dental scientist told the general session of the International Association for Dental Research in March 1972. Clinical findings showed that healing was much more rapid in the surgical sites where the freeze-dried skin was applied than in the control sites without freeze-dried skin. Freeze-dried skin was being used frequently in the treatment of extensive burns.

Researchers at the University of California at Los Angeles discovered that high-pressure chambers used to treat the "bends" in deep-sea divers may be of value in treating patients with a severe, inflammatory, destructive disease of the jawbone called mandibular osteomyelitis. In a test, the patients placed in hyperbaric chambers responded with regeneration of bone and healing of pathologic fractures in the areas of the wasting bone infection. (LOU JOSEPH)

See also Drugs and Narcotics; Life Sciences; Psychology; Social Services; Vital Statistics.

ENCYCLOPÆDIA BRITANNICA FILMS. *Chromosomes of Man* (1967); *The Eyes and Seeing* (1968); *The Work of the Heart* (1968); *Ears and Hearing* (1969); *Muscle: Chemistry of Contraction* (1969); *Muscle: Dynamics of Contraction* (1969); *Radioisotopes: Tools of Discovery* (1969); *Respiration in Man* (1969); *The Nerve Impulse* (1971); *Health (Eye Care Fantasy)* (1972); *Venereal Disease* (1972); *Regulating Body Temperature* (1972); *Health: Toothache of the Clown* (1972).

Merchandising

Inflation was a common problem throughout Europe and North America in 1972. In the United States the pace of inflation slowed somewhat under the influence of Pres. Richard Nixon's wage and price control program, but the man in the street was hard pressed to understand how it really worked and what effect it was having on him. Economists in many quarters warned that a severe price spiral might resume, possibly in 1973. The prices of food—especially meat—continued to rise steeply during much of the year. Consumer anger over this situation, combined with declining profit margins for retail food marketers, was behind what some observers called the great supermarket war. One major chain, the Great Atlantic & Pacific Tea Co. (A & P), which had suffered declining profits for several years, embarked on a nationwide food-discounting operation, accompanied by heavy television and newspaper advertisements. Since food-store chains traditionally operate on small profit margins—usually 1% of gross sales—the A & P's action caused considerable soul-searching in corporate boardrooms, and most competing chains were forced to respond with price cuts of their own.

In addition to price-cutting and converting to discount operations, marketers were treating consumers to "fringes": longer store hours—in some cases 24-hour operation; the dropping of trading stamps in favour of apparent lower prices; and better labeling of packaged foods so that the consumer could more easily compare prices of competitive merchandise of varying weights. The *New York Times* reported in July that Giant Foods, one of the largest U.S. chains, had hired Esther Peterson, the former presidential assistant for consumer affairs, as its consumerism expert and had instituted a program of consumer advisories, culminating in a highly controversial advertisement in the spring in which the public was advised to boycott meat products.

By the end of the year the supermarket battle had become so serious that major U.S. banks were being asked to reconsider their lending policies toward supermarket chains, many of which might need substantial loans to meet the A & P threat. Some estimates indicated that A & P was prepared to wage full-scale war for as long as 18 months, and many major chains would have serious difficulty surviving over that long a period. The banking community was apparently trying to decide at year's end whether to remain aloof.

In the United Kingdom "hypermarkets" (retail stores with at least 25,000 sq.ft. of selling area) were in the news. Carrefour opened Britain's first hypermarket in September at Caerphilly in South Wales. Its 55,000 sq.ft. of space, although small by comparison with some continental markets, still attracted enough customers to jam the roads leading to it for miles, and the managing director offered the local council financial help to improve the public road system around the complex. The store had 26 checkout points and parking for 960 cars. A few miles away, in Cardiff, Tesco made planning application for a 130,000-sq.ft. store. The cooperative movement, fighting to arrest its relative decline in total retail sales, established Coop Superstore Development Agencies for the purpose of building suburban stores that would have up to 100,000 sq.ft. of selling area. The new agencies would coordinate retail societies that could not raise sufficient capital individually. The first stores were planned at Manchester and Birmingham.

Just as the elevator helped to revolutionize department store design in the early part of the century by enabling stores to extend upward, so the development of glideways or moving pavements, capable of carrying fully laden store-trolleys, could have a big effect on hypermarkets. A supermarket in Mansfield, Nottinghamshire, Eng., had a unit installed on these lines. Another technical development with far-reaching implications was the electronic cash register. Some half dozen companies were already manufacturing these units. The registers could be linked to a computer to give an exact record of the stock and cash in each shop and could be keyed into the ordering and distribution pattern. Further into the future, the cash register

COURTESY, AMERICAN EXPRESS CARD DIVISION, R. H. MACY & CO. INC., AND OGILVIE & MATHER

A first for a national department store chain in the U.S. was Macy's invitation in November 1972 for customers at their East and West Coast stores to charge purchases on American Express credit cards. This extension of credit followed a trend set by many smaller retailers and threatened to force other large chain stores to reassess their policies.

could be linked by computer to the customer's bank, and purchases could be debited from his account in one automatic operation.

Paradoxically, as most stores seemed to be growing larger, Japan came up with the technology for miniaturized supermarkets. In part developed by Hitachi Industries, an electronics firm, in conjunction with the OK retail organization, the mini-markets would display only one sample of each item. The customer would insert a magnetically coded card into a slot to purchase the item, which would then be delivered automatically at the checkout point. It was said that only 5,382 sq.ft., half of it stock area, would be required to handle 2,000 items. Four persons in the stockroom and two in the sales area would complete the work force.

American Motors Corp. (AMC) did extremely well in 1972 automobile sales: $30.2 million in its fiscal 1972 year, compared with years of disappointing results and losses. Some observers believed AMC's unique "Buyer Protection Plan" had contributed to the firm's vastly improved profit position. Basically, the warranty guaranteed AMC cars against all defects, with the exception of tires, for one year or 12,000 mi. If a customer had to leave his car for repair overnight or longer, AMC dealers were required to lend him another car at no cost. Each AMC car included in its price "dealer preparation costs" and every car was road-tested by dealers before customer delivery. AMC also had an "800" free telephone hotline directly to its home office in Detroit for special problems. In 1973 the warranty was to include payment of up to $150 to an owner who incurred motel charges because his car broke down 100 mi. or more from home.

A big step forward in consumer protection on major household appliances in France was taken with the introduction of a standard maintenance contract called "X50." The contract had been devised jointly by the Association for Standardization, the National Institute on Consumption, and the National Union of Household Appliance Retailers. It stated the business making the sale, gave guarantees on after-sales service, and set out the rights and obligations of the parties.

A number of developments took place in the trading-stamp and coupon-redemption fields in the U.K. Crusader Bonds announced a plan similar to the successful blue stamp scheme of the cooperative movement. The stamps were redeemable against the goods of the retailer issuing them and were said to cost 2% less than Greenshield stamps. The Sainsbury and Waitrose food-store chains, renowned for their opposition to trading stamps, took up the cudgels against manufacturers' money-off coupons. They announced that these coupons would be redeemed against any goods they sold and not just against the product named on the coupon.

Given the desire to establish common forms of taxation and social benefits throughout the EEC, the rather curious suggestion of the French that a levy should be imposed on large stores to help finance pensions and benefits for small retailers created a stir. The Self-Service Institute of France brought together major stores, voluntary chains, supermarkets, and associations of department and variety stores to oppose the suggestion by means of a joint public relations and advertising campaign.

Italy once more postponed, to Jan. 1, 1973, the introduction of the value-added tax (VAT), to the annoyance of its EEC partners. Britain announced the introduction of a flat-rate tax, probably of 10%, to go into effect in April 1973. For the retailer this change was far more radical than the changeover to decimal currency in 1971, and fears were expressed that too little was being done to prepare for it.

In August 1972 the prefect of Rome signed a decree aimed at regulating food prices in the city. Prices of basic articles in shops could not be higher than those in the 305 city-run street stalls. There was skepticism about the success of the measure, which had no controls or penalties built into it. The basic trouble was an antiquated food-distribution system, said to be dominated by the Mafia.

In Sweden the Buketten group had been raising and selling flowers for about ten years and had some 70 outlets. In 1972 it started to operate in Britain. The franchise was held by Frampton Nurseries, with two shops in Wembley and Croydon and a group of ten outlets planned. The organization aimed at vertical integration—growing, distributing, and selling flowers and plants at retail. It claimed to be able to provide lower prices and fresher stock, the latter by having the plants prepacked at the nursery and delivered to the store in temperature-controlled transport. The group's aim—a difficult one—was to shift flowers from the luxury class to the weekly shopping list.

While the conference of the International Garden Centre Institute, held near Munich, W.Ger., was able to report increasing sales and possibilities for further expansion, experience varied considerably. Syon Park Garden Centre near London had only 300,000 visitors instead of the expected million in 1971 and sustained substantial losses. The conference produced figures showing that Switzerland and the Netherlands had one garden centre for every 135,000 inhabitants; Norway one for 173,000; West Germany one for 263,000; and Britain and Austria one for every 400,000.

Marks & Spencer and Woolworth were both in the news in Britain. Marks & Spencer was trying out a line of toiletries in nine of its branches and, if successful, the range would be sold at all of its outlets. Woolworth, which had recently begun stocking furniture and consumer durable goods in its larger U.K. branches, was extending these lines to its smaller branches by mail order.

Karl Schweri, the sole owner of the Swiss Denner chain, who could claim much of the credit for the abandonment of retail price maintenance in Switzerland in 1967, moved in 1972 against the monopoly of the chemists (pharmacists) and also led a national campaign for cheaper housing. His philosophy of only 1.5% profit on sales, which had made him a multimillionaire, and his habit of giving away profits in excess of this figure to his customers, had not made him popular with his competitors. Between 1967 and 1970 his gross sales more than doubled, to some SFr. 261 million, and sales in 1971 were thought to be up by about one-third.

Schweri's giveaway in 1972 was SFr. 1 million worth of vitamin-C tablets in January and February. One tube of ten capsules was given free with each purchase of SFr. 19.50. Schweri planned to sell the capsules later at about one-third the price charged by pharmacists. This exploited a loophole in the law which permitted the unrestricted sale of tablets of 225 mg. or less, and was expected to be the start of a campaign to sell a wide range of medicinal products.

The campaign for cheaper housing started with the collection by Schweri's stores of the 50,000 signatures necessary for the holding of a national referendum. He wanted the government to create a special fund of SFr. 15 billion to be used to finance the construction of economy-priced accommodations. He had some controversial proposals for raising the money, including a special tax on all companies with reserves above $2.5 million, an 8% levy on all export shipments, and an annual tax on employers of $125 for every foreign worker on the payroll. Possibly in response to all this, the government began to prepare its own low-cost housing program.

In 1973 Pepsi-Cola was to become the first U.S. consumer product manufactured and sold in the Soviet Union. Donald M. Kendall, chairman of Pepsico, Inc., producers of the soft drink, announced in November 1972 that an agreement to place the soft drink on the Soviet market had been concluded with the Soviet Ministry of Trade.

(G. C. HOCKLEY; M. BERNARD SMITH)

See also Advertising; Consumer Affairs; Cooperatives; Industrial Review; Prices.

Merchant Marine:
see Transportation

Mercury:
see Mining

Metals:
see Industrial Review; Metallurgy; Mining

Metallurgy

Environmental protection and cost control continued to be the chief concerns in metallurgy during 1972. There were few new developments in methods of extracting valuable minerals from ore, possibly because the worldwide exploration effort had provided ample ore of most metals of a grade that could be treated by existing methods. Possible exceptions were hydrometallurgy and solution mining (dissolving underground materials and pumping them to the surface), since they held promise of solving such pollution problems as sulfur dioxide emission from the metallurgical treatment by heat of sulfide ores, reducing mining costs where leaching at the site could be used, and possibly treating submarginal ores economically. Research was becoming more sophisticated and better financed, but few practical applications had appeared. Australian work showed that very inexpensive brown coal would absorb from ammoniacal leach solutions many metals, including copper, nickel, and zinc; zinc absorbed on such coal was much more efficient than powdered zinc for precipitating gold from solution. The metals were recovered by burning the coal.

Combining purification with recovery was solvent extraction, in which a liquid that will selectively absorb the desired kind of metal is brought into contact with the leach solution and then separated with the consequent recovery of the metal. The method was finding greater use as an increasing number of satisfactory extraction liquids were discovered. As sulfuric acid production increased due to sulfur dioxide recovery to meet emission standards, interest increased in its possible use as a leaching reagent. A recent development of the flotation of low-grade, fine-grained hematite ore made possible a four-million-ton-per-year pellet plant using ore from a previously uneconomic iron deposit in Michigan.

The diminishing supplies of coal for metallurgical coke encouraged efforts to reduce coke consumption in iron making. Another U.S. blast furnace was being modified to inject powdered boiler-grade coal to replace 30% of the coke. Fuel-oil injection into the blast furnace was also being used, and the possibility of using externally generated reducing gas was being investigated. A prototype natural gas-fired foundry furnace which used no coke was producing eight tons of liquid iron per hour. A channel induction furnace superheated the metal for casting. When melting clean scrap no visible emission was produced.

Use of prereduced ore pellets, which could substitute for scrap and increase steel production without requiring additional coke, was not growing as rapidly as many had expected. A prereduced pellet plant in South America did start production to supply a U.S. steelmaker. An experimental continuous steelmaking process in France was producing 500 tons per day with close control of the carbon content, satisfactory reduction in phosphorus, and no increase in sulfur. The yield was higher than for steelmaking with oxygen, and both capital and operating costs were lower than for conventional processes. Up to 32% scrap could be utilized, which was comparable to the basic oxygen process.

There was an upswing in the use of steels that can be easily machined (turned, bored, planed, milled, etc.). A Japanese producer employed a calcium treatment to improve machinability without affecting other properties, and a U.S. firm by variation of its refining and processing was producing a steel that gave up to 30% higher machining production with no change in chemistry. Improved tooling was also stressed. A new high-speed tool steel produced by powder metallurgy (fabrication from a metal powder or mixture of powders) had the highest hardness at red heat of any available steel and had up to twice the life of any competing steel. The very fine and uniform dispersion of the carbides in the steel was the main reason for its superior performance.

There was widening use of the superplastic alloys, which in warm forming could be stretched to several times their original length with very little force yet had good strength at normal temperature. In addition to the original aluminum-zinc alloy, superplastic bronze, stainless steel, nickel, and titanium alloys were available. Full utilization of the steel and titanium alloys awaited development of tooling that could tolerate the higher working temperatures.

Development of cladding, coating, and treating to reduce material costs or obtain special combinations of properties continued vigorously. Large tantalum sheets that could be explosive-bonded to steel became available, making possible large moderate-cost vessels with the outstanding corrosion resistance of tantalum. A ferritic stainless steel surface was being produced on carbon steel by depositing ferrochrome powder on the adhesive-coated steel in a fluidized bed and then rolling the powder into the surface and heating so that diffusion could bond the particles to the surface and bring the chromium content of the surface to the desired level.

Coating with polymers was replacing painting to an appreciable extent. A short immersion of the metal at the melting temperature of the polymer in a fluidized bed of polymer particles produced a uniform coating and avoided the pollution problem encountered with spray painting. (DONALD F. CLIFTON)

See also Industrial Review; Mining; Physics.

ENCYCLOPÆDIA BRITANNICA FILMS. *The Miner* (1967); *Problems of Conservation—Minerals* (1969).

Meteorology

The atmospheric sciences saw many new technological advances in 1972, but the main goals—more accurate and longer-range forecasting, positive means for modifying storms, and reduction of the disastrous losses in life and property caused each year by weather anomalies—remained beyond reach. Among the facets of meteorology being emphasized by research geophysicists during the year were dynamic climatology and mathematical modeling of a variety of weather phenomena from macroscale forms to local thunderstorms.

Dynamic Climatology. Scientists have long studied the known epochs in the history of the earth's climate, ranging from the Ice Ages at one extreme to the hot, humid eras at the other. Notwithstanding this knowledge, the general public and most climatologists have tended to regard climate as comparatively stable, with epochal shifts remote in time and with any "permanent" change occurring only gradually. Attempts by a few research geophysicists early in the century to develop a dynamic climatology and examine the forces that might produce cataclysmic changes soon petered out for lack of both data and adequate theory. Soon after 1950, however, increasing concern about the possible effects of air pollution, growing interest in weather modification, and the development of space satellites capable of measuring fluctuations in solar radiation and other cosmic sources of radiant energy

Table I. Selected Weather Headlines, 1972

Date	Place	Kind of storm	Casualties, damage, or nature
Feb. 13	Oklahoma and Texas	Tornadoes and severe thunderstorm	Earliest tornadoes of the season; timely warnings; no loss of life
June 9–10	Rapid City, S.D., and vicinity	"Cloudburst"; unusual stationary coincidence	235 persons drowned; thousands of homes swept away in flooded river; damage over $100 million
June 21–23	Pennsylvania and adjacent states	Remains of Hurricane Agnes plus fresh cyclone circulation	At least 134 known drowned; more than $700 million in property losses. Wyoming Valley (Pa.) and others devastated
July–Aug.	Luzon, P.I.	Heavy monsoon rains plus typhoon	At least 427 drowned; 800,000 made homeless; worst flooding in 100 years
Aug.–Sept.	South Korea	Prolonged rains from typhoons	Over 700 drownings; 600,000 homeless; 18 in. of rain in 5 hours
Oct. 21–24	Fiji Islands	Typhoon winds 180 knots	"All buildings blown down" (press report); 13 persons drowned
Nov. 13	Netherlands and northwest Europe	Intense "low"	Death toll at 25; heavy property damage in a few localities

Note: The year was exceptional in the Caribbean and West Indian areas in that there were no noteworthy destructive hurricanes.

Table II. Meteorological Space Satellites

Item	ESSA-8	ESSA-9	NOAA-2	ATS-1	ATS-3
Date of launching	12/15/68	2/26/69	10/15/72	12/6/66	11/5/67
Days in operation as of 11/1/72	1,416	1,371	16	2,156	1,821
Average altitude (statute miles)	892	910	902	22,237	22,237
Nephanalysis (cloud analysis)	Not equipped	11,191	...	...	...
Storm advisories based on nephanalysis	...	4,519	...	...	...
Usable pictures up to Oct. 1972	...	147,526	...	More than 10,000	14,365

led to more serious research into the dynamics of the earth's atmosphere.

A study conducted in Israel and reported in the *Journal of Applied Meteorology* (June 1972) examined the climatic effects of aerosol layers in relation to solar radiation. Using a mathematical model, the researchers studied the effects of the dust and other pollutants that entered the atmosphere following the eruption of the Agung volcano in the Philippines in 1963. They concluded that, if this had continued, 6% of the sun's energy reaching the lower atmosphere would have been absorbed or backscattered. The study enabled rough estimates to be made of the probable consequences of industrial effluents, discharge of water vapour into the stratosphere by jet aircraft, and other large sources of air pollution that may eventually produce major changes in the composition and structure of the atmosphere as a whole.

Even more pessimistic was the research of M. I. Budyko of the U.S.S.R. (*EOS,* October 1972) concluding that change in global climate may come in the relatively near future. Pointing out that the present regime of climate on earth is highly sensitive to small changes in incoming radiation, Budyko noted that a 2% decrease in radiation would lead to an ice sheet covering the entire earth, while a 1% increase would cause all the Arctic and Antarctic ice to melt and raise the sea level more than 200 ft. The study speculated that increased combustion of fuels and the resulting higher level of carbon dioxide in the atmosphere might bring such critical changes in the earth's heat balance within 30 years.

Among many scientific reports on studies of radiation fluxes in the atmosphere and oceans was a brief nontechnical article in *Weather* (June 1972) calling attention to the many factors that modify the effective radiation received and retained as heat on the surface of the earth. There had been many reports of a reduction in solar radiation received on the ground in industrial areas with marked air pollution.

Mathematical Models. In 1915 L. F. Richardson of England had deduced formulas for predicting changes in temperature for a period of six hours, but the computations were so lengthy and laborious that his staff, working with the speediest manual methods available at the time, took weeks to do the computing. High-speed computers revolutionized numerical weather prediction and made it possible to construct mathematical models of cyclones, thunderstorms, and climatic and hydrologic regimes. Reports of such models of weather phenomena dominated the technical literature in 1972.

The January 1972 issue of the U.S. National Oceanic and Atmospheric Administration quarterly, *NOAA,* described the aims and scope of the Geophysical Fluid Dynamics Laboratory, Princeton, N.J. In its comprehensive research on what man is doing to his planet, the laboratory hoped to separate fact from fancy and to determine how serious the environmental crisis is likely to become within the 20th century. Another NOAA laboratory found a relatively inexpensive design for a model that improved local, short-range weather forecasts.

The mathematical model method of research was also put to use in studying the mysteries of clear air turbulence (CAT). This baffling discontinuity, found most frequently at stratospheric altitudes, had become a threat to air safety when high-altitude supersonic jet planes came into use, but its sporadic and transitory occurrence made it hard to observe, measure, and analyze. By 1972 research had established that the most common cause of CAT was the instability associated with the billowing of waves in the free air on the interface between two wind streams, one above the other. Horizontal waves in the stratosphere vary greatly in wavelength and amplitude, and when they crest and break the resulting instability creates turbulence in the air. If the wave is of dimensions critical for structures the size of aircraft, wing damage or fracture may result. Among many studies of CAT, *Nature* magazine (Sept. 29, 1972) reported that British investigators, using high-power radar, were able to identify and fix the location of CAT and to measure the length and amplitude of waves with which the turbulence was associated.

Other Atmospheric Research. Progress in investigating the solar wind was reported by the National Center for Atmospheric Research, Boulder, Colo. (*NCAR Quarterly,* February 1972). Although the effects of this stream of solar plasma on the high atmosphere and, indirectly, on circulation and storms in the troposphere were still unknown, studies of the solar wind by astrophysicists and geophysicists in recent years had contributed much to knowledge of the constituents of solar energy intercepted by the earth. A surprising finding by NCAR researchers in a different sector of meteorology was that mountain-induced waves in the atmosphere may influence weather and climate significantly.

Radar techniques for storm identification and partial analysis were among the comparatively few great advances in meteorology. Radar pictures reveal otherwise invisible internal features of storms, and their importance in modern storm-warning systems gave rise to annual international conferences designed to gather the newest ideas and technical improvements and to agree on further research and coordination of knowledge and systems. The 15th such conference on radar meteorology took place in Champaign, Ill., Oct. 10–12, 1972. Among the 77 research papers presented were several that reported progress in radar detection of hail forming within cumulonimbus clouds, information needed not only for warnings and protective measures but also for hail-suppression operations.

Also reported were new techniques for measuring precipitation over a wide area, for determining dropsize distribution of rainfall for theoretical studies, for examining atmospheric structure and turbulence, and for echo penetration of tornadoes.

John Magill of Dearborn, Mich., attempts to rescue a bobbing TV set from his flooded basement. During June 1972 torrential rains followed by severe flooding caused extensive property damage and left hundreds dead in many parts of the U.S.

UPI COMPIX

Weather Modification. After 1955 a staggering amount of research effort and many millions of dollars were put into comprehensive and exhaustive programs of weather modification. In a limited way, these programs had been turned to practical use in many parts of the world, but weather control in 1972 was still in a relatively early experimental stage. Hail suppression was practiced locally in many countries, and numerous successes had been reported, but gaps in analysis and verification remained, and there were scientists who questioned the validity of optimistic reports. The U.S.S.R. was a leader in the use of cloud seeding with dry ice or silver iodide to reduce the size of hailstones or suppress hail altogether.

One of the best organized and best equipped programs was Project Stormfury, organized in 1962 by the U.S. Weather Bureau and the U.S. Navy to test the effects of cloud seeding on hurricanes. The project had contributed much to the advancement of seeding techniques and to the knowledge of atmospheric phenomena, but its potential for combating hurricanes remained in doubt. Many meteorologists were convinced that the project had beneficially modified one or two hurricanes, but most scientists found the evidence inconclusive.

A few kinds of weather modification had proved to be successful and were widely used; for example, the use of cloud-seeding techniques to clear the fog from airport runways when the air temperature of the fog layer was below freezing. It had also been demonstrated that under certain favourable conditions rainfall could be increased or decreased. Nevertheless, the circumstances required for success and the extent to which amounts of precipitation could be artificially changed were still matters of debate. These uncertainties were apparent in the controversy surrounding the accusations of Vietnam war critics that the U.S. Air Force had intensified the monsoon rains by seeding the clouds over Southeast Asia. Added to the doubts inherent in any test made in the absence of suitable scientific monitoring were the secrecy and strategic objectives of the military authorities who desired to stress their ability to control the weather for propaganda purposes.

Data Collection. A new environmental spacecraft, NOAA-2, was launched October 15 into a circular orbit 785 nautical miles above the earth. Its sensors included scanning and vertical temperature-profile radiometers, solar-proton monitors, high-resolution radiometers, and other elements. By 1972 satellite data had become a vital component of weather information exchanged among weather forecasting services throughout the world and carried on the direct "hot line" weather communications channel linking Moscow and Washington. The contributions that satellite meteorology was making to science were especially prominent in the geophysical literature. (*See* Table II.)

Based on the long-recognized linkages of land-sea-air changes and the worldwide interrelationships of the global atmosphere, climate, and weather, the World Weather Watch, under the aegis of the World Meteorological Organization, and the Global Atmospheric Research Program (GARP) continued their buildup of reporting facilities with the aim of providing a "complete weather analysis" facility during the 1970s.

(FRANCIS W. REICHELDERFER)

See also Astronautics; Disasters; Oceanography.

ENCYCLOPÆDIA BRITANNICA FILMS. *Whatever the Weather* (1967); *Reflections on Time* (1969).

Mexico

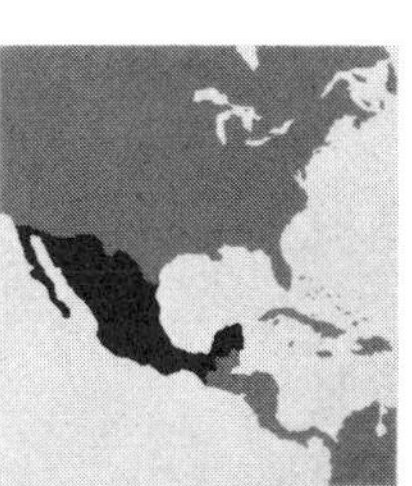

A federal republic of Middle America, Mexico is bounded by the U.S., British Honduras, and Guatemala. Area: 761,600 sq.mi. (1,972,547 sq.km.). Pop. (1972 est.): 52,641,334, including about 55% mestizo and 29% Indian. Cap. and largest city: Mexico City (pop., 1970, 2,902,969). Language: Spanish. Religion: predominantly Roman Catholic. President in 1972, Luis Echeverría Álvarez.

Foreign Relations. Declared "Benito Juárez Year" to mark the centenary of the death of the revered Zapotec Indian who rose to Mexico's highest office, 1972 was a year of political and economic consolidation for President Echeverría's administration. It was also a period of breaking away from the relative isolation of the past and intensifying direct contacts with other countries. Such action was predicated on a desire to promote trade with other states; the president himself visited Chile, Japan, and the U.S.

Close ties were strengthened with other Latin-American countries and, in October, Mexico became a "working partner" of the Andean Group. This organization had been formed in 1969 when a subregional integration agreement was signed in Bogotá by Bolivia, Chile, Colombia, Ecuador, and Peru. A monetary stabilization agreement between the central bank of Mexico and those of the five other republics had already been signed earlier in 1972.

During his visit to Washington in June, President Echeverría was refreshingly blunt in describing the damage caused to agriculture throughout the Valley of Mexico from U.S. industrial effluent pouring into the Colorado River. President Nixon promised to alleviate the plight of the Mexican farmers affected and a commission began to investigate a more permanent solution to the problem.

Domestic Affairs. In the political sphere, the government continued to pursue the twin objectives of modernizing the image of the official Partido Revolucionario Institucional (PRI) and keeping open the dialogue with the nation. Jesús Reyes Heroles, a man with a reputation for integrity and well known for his progressive views, was appointed chairman of the party, and efforts were made to attract and secure the participation of younger age groups in the country's political life. To this end a bill was put before Congress lowering (by four years) to 21 the minimum age for candidates for deputy and (by five years) to 30 the minimum age for senators. To give greater weight to the opposition, changes were also made in the electoral system entitling five deputies to each party that received 1.5% of the total votes cast instead of the previous 2.5%. Moreover, 1 additional deputy up to a maximum of 25 (formerly 20) would be allowed for every additional 0.5% of votes cast. Firm action continued to be taken against abuses of power by individuals in privileged positions, regardless of their "revolutionary" past. Although reaction and opposition remained strong, the changes—prompted partly by a genuine desire to democratize the regime and partly to forestall violent reactions in the future—seemed to be taking place with considerably less obstruction than had at first been feared.

Much of the legislative action in 1972 was designed to remedy some of the country's social and economic deficiencies. Of major significance was the adoption early in the year of a nationwide project to provide

Methodists: *see* Religion

low-cost housing for the working class. The project, under which the state would relieve employers of this responsibility, was foreshadowed in the Federal Labour Law of May 1, 1970. Mexicans with income not exceeding ten times the statutory minimum wage could obtain loans at favourable rates of interest, repayable over a period of 15 years, to buy, build, or improve their homes. About 100,000 dwellings were expected to be financed in this way in 1972, increasing to 500,000 by 1975. Funds would be provided by an initial government contribution of 2 billion pesos supplemented by a special payroll tax on most companies that was expected to raise an additional 3 billion pesos yearly. Quite apart from the social implications of the plan, the scheme was also welcomed for the stimulus that it would give to construction and other industries.

Another important piece of legislation was a decree in July establishing a program for decentralization and regional development and laying down conditions and incentives offered to new industries in the development areas. When the scheme was introduced, the Federal District housed 14.6% of the total population and contributed 46% of the gross domestic product; moreover, 56% of Mexico's industrial output was produced there. Implicit in those percentages was a great disparity in the distribution of industrial plant, an imbalance that the new legislation was designed to correct. For this purpose, the country was divided into three zones offering graded incentives in an effort to attract new industrial plant away from the capital, where overconcentration was creating problems of pollution and overcrowding.

The Economy. During 1972 the economy began to recover from the recession that had set in during mid-1970. In part, the recession had been a consequence of the temporary slowdown normally accompanying a change of administration, and in part it had been induced by the need to restrain rising prices and to prevent a repetition of the large balance of payments deficit on current account recorded in 1970. The figures for 1971 were satisfactory on both counts, but the 3.7% growth rate in gross national product was the lowest for many years. Because recovery was proceeding slowly in 1972, anti-inflation policies were relaxed somewhat to bring the growth rate up to a more normal level. Public investment was raised by 16.4%, and with higher receipts from tourism, increased export earnings, and good harvests, as well as the new housing program and the greater purchasing power resulting from wage and salary increases, business conditions gradually rose to a satisfactory buoyancy by the end of the year. On June 30 the gross domestic product had risen by 6.4%, double the rate achieved in the first half of 1970.

Despite the increased demand, prices seemed not to have risen unduly: the wholesale index for Mexico City showed an increase of 2.1% in the first eight months of 1972, comparing favourably with the 4.2% recorded for the same period of 1971. Foreign trade, on the other hand, began to reflect the increasing buoyancy of the business sector: in January–September, exports rose by 26.9% to $1,338,700,000 (compared with an increase of only 2% in the first eight months of 1971), although imports also rose by 19.2% to $2,129,900,000 as against 1.4% for the same period of 1971. These results underlined the relationship between economic growth and import levels characteristic of developing countries, one of the problems that at the close of 1972 faced the Mexican government in its commitment to reduce unemployment and to achieve a more equitable distribution of wealth in the future.

As President Echeverría reminded the nation in his annual address on September 1, the government's efforts over the preceding 18 months had been directed toward checking inflation and improving the balance of payments position. Both of these short-term objectives had been achieved in less time than had been expected. Mexico was emerging from the stage when growth was almost exclusively directed toward a protected internal market, and in the future industry would have to prove itself internationally competitive.

(MANUEL PULGAR)

Middle East

No major military encounters between Arabs and Israelis occurred in 1972 although Israel launched some heavy raids against Lebanon and Syria in retaliation for Palestinian guerrilla actions in Israel and elsewhere. The political situation remained deadlocked, and there were even fewer signs of a break than in 1971. The only new initiative from any source was King Husain of Jordan's proposal for a United Arab Kingdom on both banks of the Jordan, and this met an almost universally hostile reception. Egypt's expulsion of its Soviet military advisers in July, although an event of some importance, did not lead to

MEXICO

Education. (1969–70) Primary, pupils 8,539,462, teachers 182,851; secondary, pupils 1,063,365; teachers 75,977; vocational, pupils 361,167, teachers 26,103; teacher training, students 59,324, teachers 5,449; higher (including 38 universities), students 188,011, teaching staff (1968–69) 21,087.

Finance. Monetary unit: peso, with (Sept. 18, 1972) a par value of 12.50 pesos to U.S $1 (free rate of 30.53 pesos = £1 sterling). Gold, SDRs, and foreign exchange, central bank: (April 1972) U.S. $1,054,000,000; (April 1971) U.S. $738 million. Budget (1971 est.) balanced at 79,656,000,000 pesos. Gross domestic product: (1970) 423.1 billion pesos; (1969) 374.9 billion pesos. Money supply: (Sept. 1971) 47,970,000,000 pesos; (Sept. 1970) 44,610,000,000 pesos. Cost of living (Mexico City; 1963 = 100): (May 1972) 135; (May 1971) 130.

Foreign Trade. (1971) Imports 30,090,000,000 pesos; exports 18,761,000,000 pesos. Import sources: U.S. 61%; West Germany 9%. Export destinations: U.S. 73%; Japan 5%. Main exports: metal ores 9%; cotton 8%; chemicals 7%; sugar 7%; coffee 6%; shrimps 5%. Tourism (1970): visitors 2,245,500; gross receipts U.S. $1,454,000,000.

Transport and Communications. Roads (1971) 71,568 km. (including 930 km. expressways). Motor vehicles in use (1971): passenger 1,326,200; commercial 557,900. Railways: (1969) 19,780 km.; traffic (1970) 4,534,000,000 passenger-km., freight 22,863,000,000 net ton-km. Air traffic (1970): 2,939,000,000 passenger-km.; freight 41,678,000 net ton-km. Shipping (1971): merchant vessels 100 gross tons and over 185; gross tonnage 400,665. Telephones (Dec. 1970) 1,506,000. Radio receivers (Dec. 1970) 14,005,000. Television receivers (Dec. 1970) 2,978,000.

Agriculture. Production (in 000; metric tons; 1971; 1970 in parentheses): corn *c.* 9,500 (9,000); wheat 1,919 (2,436); sorghum 2,682 (2,565); rice 441 (383); potatoes 395 (385); dry beans 679 (1,000); bananas 1,219 (1,136); oranges 1,610 (1,020); lemons 179 (199); coffee *c.* 192 (184); sugar, raw value (1971–72) *c.* 2,510, (1970–71) *c.* 2,556; tobacco *c.* 83 (78); sisal (1970) 150, (1969) 128; cotton, lint 369 (312); fish catch (1969) 353, (1968) 364. Livestock (in 000; Dec. 1970): cattle 25,124; sheep 5,321; pigs 11,721; horses 5,026; mules 3,603; asses 3,199; chickens *c.* 142,900.

Industry. Production (in 000; metric tons; 1971): cement 7,722; crude oil (1970) 21,973; coal (1969) *c.* 1,500; natural gas (cu.m.) 18,221; electricity (kw-hr.) 30,884,000; iron ore (metal content) 2,851; pig iron 1,771; steel 3,758; sulfur (1970) 1,441; sulfuric acid 1,426; nitrogenous fertilizers (1970–71) 397; lead 137; zinc 78; copper, smelter 74; aluminum 40; manganese ore (metal content; 1970) 99; antimony ore (metal content; 1970) 4.5; gold (troy oz.; 1970) 200; silver (troy oz.) 38,000; cotton yarn (1970) 127; woven cotton fabrics (1970) 115.

any major realignment in the Middle East; it did little to improve relations between the U.S. and the Arabs and, in any case, Syrian mediation helped to achieve a partial reconciliation between Egypt and the U.S.S.R. before the end of the year. An Arab diplomatic campaign to win support for their cause in Western Europe received a severe setback when 11 Israeli athletes were killed by Palestinian terrorists at the Olympic Games in Munich, W.Ger., in September. Meanwhile, Israel continued to consolidate its hold on the occupied territories.

Arab-Israeli Conflict. In January the U.S. revived its plan for a partial Middle East settlement on the basis of the reopening of the Suez Canal. The Israeli Cabinet agreed to indirect "close proximity" talks with the Egyptians on the subject, but Pres. Anwar as-Sadat ruled out such discussions with the U.S. as mediator. The Egyptian president said he pinned his faith on the mission of the UN mediator Gunnar Jarring. In a review of Middle East policy to Congress on February 9, Pres. Richard Nixon placed most of the blame for the lack of a settlement on the U.S.S.R.

After talks with Jarring, Pres. Léopold Senghor of Senegal, who had led the Organization of African Unity (OAU) mission to the Middle East in November 1971, said in February that Egypt had already made its maximum concessions and that Israel should ease the problem by publicly renouncing its intentions to annex Arab territories. The U.S. agreed to increase the number of Phantom and Skyhawk aircraft it would sell to Israel, and delivery over a three-year period began in March. Egypt, on the other hand, began to show increasing dissatisfaction with the Soviet Union's continued failure to supply it with offensive weapons, although Israel protested that Egypt was in fact receiving deliveries of French Mirages through Libya.

Jarring visited Egypt, Jordan, and Israel in February. He said his talks had been fruitful, but it was clear that there had been no break in the deadlock. UN Secretary-General Kurt Waldheim said there was still a basis for continuation of the Jarring mission, which was temporarily suspended until May 1. On February 28 the UN Security Council unanimously condemned Israel for conducting raids against Lebanon.

King Husain's March 15 announcement of his proposal for a United Arab Kingdom with regional governments on the East and West banks of the Jordan River was rejected by Israel and condemned by the Palestinian organizations and most Arab governments. The Palestinian guerrilla organizations, seriously weakened by their suppression in Jordan in 1970 and 1971, attempted to resolve their internal differences. On April 4 the Palestine Liberation Organization (PLO) executive committee announced agreement on a plan whereby all guerrilla units would be unified in a single Revolutionary People's Army and all those political groups that wished to do so would join a United National Front. A Palestine Popular Congress with 500 delegates was held in Cairo April 6–10 to consider the Palestinian situation in the wake of King Husain's proposals.

U.S. Secretary of State William Rogers told a Senate committee on May 15 that the U.S. would only supply Israel with the arms necessary for its security, in order not to give the appearance of a military challenge to Egypt. He continued to express hopes that Egypt would respond to U.S. invitations to join "proximity" talks with Israel. The communiqué issued after the Soviet-U.S. summit meeting in Moscow on May 30 reaffirmed support for a peaceful settlement of the Middle East conflict "in accordance with UN Security Council Resolution 242." The Egyptian government showed disappointment that nothing more concrete had come out of the meeting, although it noted that Israel's demand for direct Israeli-Arab negotiations had been ignored by the two superpowers.

On May 30 Middle East tension was sharply increased by an attack at Lod Airport, near Tel Aviv, in which 28 people, including 16 Puerto Rican pilgrims, were killed and 78 injured by three members of the Japanese extremist Red Army on behalf of the Popular Front for the Liberation of Palestine. The PFLP announced that it did not regard tourists visiting Israel as civilians and that the operation was in revenge for the Israeli killing of innocent people in Egypt, Jordan, and Lebanon. Despite strong Lebanese denials of responsibility, the Israeli government blamed Lebanon for allowing the PFLP to maintain its headquarters on Lebanese territory. King Husain condemned the attack as a sick crime, but the Egyptian prime minister, Aziz Sidky, saw it as a sign that Israel was not invincible.

Israeli attacks on Lebanon on June 21 and 23, in which some 70 guerrillas and civilians were killed, were generally seen as reprisals for the Lod massacre. The action produced a crisis between Lebanon and the Palestinian guerrillas, who agreed to freeze their activities in Lebanon and discipline their various groups. The UN Security Council passed a resolution on June 27 condemning Israel's action and calling for the return of Syrian and Lebanese officers captured during the engagement. The U.S. abstained on the ground that the resolution was not fair and balanced, and Israel rejected it. Lebanon and Syria again raised the question of the prisoners on July 5, but Israel refused to return them except as part of a general exchange of prisoners. On July 8 a leading member of the PFLP, Ghassan Kanafani, was killed when a bomb exploded in his car in Beirut. The PFLP blamed Israel.

On June 5 the Israeli defense minister, Moshe Dayan, said in an interview that if the U.S. were to exert all its pressure on Israel then Israel would have to respond, but that this was a "hypothetical situation." In an interview with a Swedish newspaper three days later, the Israeli foreign minister, Abba Eban, said that Gunnar Jarring had adopted a position Israel could not accept in his February 1971 memorandum asking Israel to agree in advance to withdraw all its forces to the pre-1967 armistice lines. On June 13 the UN secretary-general said the Jarring mission had reached an impasse.

A resolution passed by the ninth summit meeting of the OAU, held in Rabat, Morocco, on June 14, deplored Israel's "negative and obstructive attitude" and called for an immediate withdrawal from occupied Arab territories. The Israeli foreign minister commented that after every such resolution the African leaders "implore us to take no notice of it." His statement was condemned by Pres. Mobutu Sese Seko of Zaire as a direct insult to the African countries.

On June 16 the Democratic candidate in the U.S. presidential election, Sen. George S. McGovern, whose attitude toward Israel had been questioned by Jewish voters, declared his full support for Israel in a letter to the *New York Times*. President Nixon also reaffirmed the commitment of the U.S. to Israel in a message to the Zionist Organization of America on July 15. On July 10 it was announced that Jarring would again resume his mission in August. The British

Microbiology: *see* Life Sciences

MICHA BAR-AM—MAGNUM

Israeli infantry destroy suspected commando bases in Al Habbariyah, an Arab guerrilla stronghold in southern Lebanon, Feb. 26, 1972. An official Israeli announcement stated that Israel had retaliated after a guerrilla ambush had killed three soldiers and two civilians.

government strongly supported the move, but the U.S. expressed skepticism about its value.

President Sadat's announcement on July 18 that he had asked for withdrawal of his Soviet military advisers seemed to offer hope of a break in the Arab-Israeli deadlock. The initial Israeli reaction was cautiously favourable. Israeli Prime Minister Golda Meir said the act was significant, although it did not indicate the end of the Soviet role in Egypt. She appealed to President Sadat to meet her as an equal in a supreme effort to reach an agreed solution. Sadat continued to reject direct negotiations of this kind. Nevertheless, several leading Israelis expressed the view that a new situation had arisen, although no new initiative could be expected until after the U.S. presidential election. Meanwhile Secretary Rogers continued to urge negotiations between Israel and Egypt. The UN secretary-general's annual report to the General Assembly on August 13 barely mentioned the Middle East, except to say that less progress had been made there than on the Cyprus problem.

On August 17 Dayan suggested that Israel would be willing to make a partial withdrawal from Sinai as part of either a temporary or a permanent settlement. He also told an Israeli Labour Party meeting in late August that the time had come for Israel to make a separate peace with Jordan. Persistent reports of Saudi Arabian attempts to mediate between King Husain and the PLO were denied on August 27 by the PLO leader, Yasir Arafat, who said that if the king was sincere he would first allow the reactivation of the eastern front by enabling the guerrillas to return to their positions in Jordan.

Following the expulsion of the Soviet advisers, Egypt planned a wide-ranging diplomatic offensive, aimed especially at Western Europe. This was to precede the EEC foreign ministers' meeting in Rome on September 11 and the new session of the UN General Assembly later in the month. The Egyptians also hoped to find alternative sources of arms in Europe. However, the campaign was severely compromised as a result of the Palestinian guerrilla attack on the Israeli Olympic team in Munich, for which the Black September organization claimed responsibility. (*See* SPORTING RECORD: *Special Report.*) In particular, this led to a sharp deterioration in relations between the Arabs and West Germany, which had been improving. The Egyptian government blamed the Bonn regime for its handling of the affair, and the West German government took strong action against Palestinians and other Arabs resident in West Germany. Arab-West German relations recovered to some extent in late October when the West German authorities allowed the three surviving Black September guerrillas involved in the Munich affair to escape to Tripoli, Libya, during negotiations over the ransom of a hijacked plane. Israel's bitter reaction to this caused some resentment in West Germany.

Israeli spokesmen said Israel would fight terrorists wherever they were, and the PLO declared they would increase their activities. An Israeli attack of unprecedented severity on villages and guerrilla bases in southern Lebanon was regarded as a reprisal for Munich. The Arab states unanimously expressed support for Lebanon, but were unable to give assistance. Later there was heavy fighting along the Israel-Syrian border. In December a leftist-backed Arab Front for Participation in the Palestine Resistance was set up, with Kamal Jumblatt of Lebanon as secretary-general.

On October 3 Defense Minister Dayan called for an "open bridges" policy with Lebanon, similar to that with Jordan which had allowed more than 150,000 Arab visitors to cross the Jordan River in the summer. He also repeated his view that if the choice for Israel was between a return to the old frontiers and no peace he would prefer no peace. On October 14 Prime Minister Meir said she saw no hope of peace in the near future and that nothing would move for at least the next six months. This view was widely endorsed by all the parties to the Middle East conflict.

Inter-Arab Relations. There were few signs of harmony between the Arab states of the Middle East in 1972. The new Arab League secretary-general, the former Egyptian foreign minister Mahmoud Riad, who took over the post when Muhammed Abd-al-Khalek Hassuna retired for health reasons on June 1, endeavoured to breathe new life into the organization. However, his appointment was criticized in several countries, notably Jordan and Libya.

The still somewhat shadowy federation of Libya, Egypt, and Syria survived the strain of Egypt's dismissal of the Soviet military advisers, an action that was endorsed by Libya, Tunisia, and Jordan but not by Syria or Iraq. There was speculation that the Soviet Union would switch its main interest in the Arab world from Egypt to Syria and Iraq. A treaty with Iraq was concluded in April. The federal Cabinet under its Syrian prime minister, Ahmed al-Khatib, was sworn in on January 4 by President Sadat. A meeting of the Presidential Council, scheduled for February 7 in Tripoli, was canceled because of Libyan-Syrian differences over Libyan Pres. Muammar al-Qaddafi's attacks on the U.S.S.R. The meeting finally took place in Cairo in March, and at the same time the 60 members of the federation's National Assembly held their first session. On March 18 the federation's Presidential Council declared its categorical rejection of King Husain's plan for a United Arab Kingdom on the grounds that it was put forward without consultation with the Palestinians and aimed to create a Palestinian entity under Israeli influence.

Pres. Gaafar Nimeiry of Sudan, who had been closely associated with plans for the Arab federation in 1970, called for an Arab summit to discuss King Husain's proposal. Relations between Egypt and Libya and Sudan deteriorated sharply during 1972. Egypt and Libya criticized Sudan for refusing to join the federation and for taking diplomatic initiatives, such as resuming diplomatic relations with the U.S., without consultation. In October Sudan withdrew its troops that had been stationed on the Suez Canal since 1967.

Talks in Cairo in July between the Arab Socialist Union (ASU) and the Libyan Socialist Union prepared the way toward a complete merger of Egypt and Libya. President Qaddafi announced a deadline of July 31 for a final decision on the merger, and President Sadat arrived in Tobruk on that day for talks with the Libyan president. The talks were continued in Benghazi, where it was announced on August 2 that the two leaders had agreed on the full unity of their countries at the earliest possible time and on the strongest possible basis. The unified political command would be established at once, and draft measures for the full union would be put to a public referendum in each country before Sept. 1, 1973.

After an extensive tour of the Arab states in August, Secretary-General Riad proposed the holding of an Arab summit. This was endorsed by Kuwait but received little support from other countries. Arab League foreign ministers met in Cairo September 9–13 and issued a statement strongly condemning U.S. support for Israel. Commenting on the meeting, President Qaddafi declared that all attempts to draw up a joint Arab plan were a waste of time.

At the meeting, the foreign ministers decided to send a delegation, headed by the League's assistant secretary-general, Salim al-Yafi, to mediate the dispute between Yemen (San'a') and Yemen (Aden), which had erupted into border fighting. The delegation succeeded in obtaining a cease-fire on October 13, and talks in Cairo between the two disputants resulted in agreement to unite the two Yemens.

Directors of Arab League offices in Western Europe held a meeting in London in late September to discuss what they described as the current anti-Arab campaign in Europe. The three presidents of the Arab Confederation met again in Cairo October 5–6 to discuss the Yemen situation and West German treatment of Arab citizens. They signed several decrees guaranteeing the right of all federation citizens to work and to own land and property in all parts of the federation. The federal budget of about $55 million for 1973 was also approved.

Economic Development. In the continuing "no peace, no war" situation, nearly all countries in the area continued to spend a high and rising proportion of their budgets on arms. The effects of this were offset to some extent by an increase in oil revenues, the result of greater output and higher prices. Among major oil producers, only Iraq suffered a severe cut in income following its nationalization of the Iraq Petroleum Company in June. The oil-producing states were more concerned with securing participation in the oil companies' concessions than with increasing their revenues. On October 5 it was announced that five Persian Gulf oil-producing states—Abu Dhabi, Qatar, Kuwait, Iraq, and Saudi Arabia—had reached a provisional agreement with nine Western oil companies in New York on an eventual 51% share in ownership of oil companies in their countries.

Despite the high arms expenditure, the development of the economic infrastructure of the Middle East made substantial progress in several areas—notably in the Persian Gulf. The 1972 cereals and cotton harvests were generally good in the area, but the citrus season was poor. (PETER MANSFIELD)

See also Defense; articles on the various political units.

Migration, International

In recent years intracontinental migration, often temporary, had assumed more importance than intercontinental migration; this trend continued in 1972, but with some deceleration because of economic uncertainty and sociopolitical resistance. There was a definite tendency to raise stronger barriers against free movement in Western Europe. This was reflected in October at a private conference in Bonn, W.Ger., attended by labour and employment officials from the nine nations of the enlarged EEC plus Sweden and Switzerland. The conferees noted that, despite foreign workers' contributions to economic growth over the decade 1962–72, the law of diminishing returns was now operating; most "guest workers" wanted to stay and bring their families, thereby necessitating extra expenditures for housing, education, and welfare.

By early 1972 an estimated 11 million migrants were living in Western Europe, 90% of them in France, West Germany, Switzerland, and Britain. About 66% came from southern Europe, but there were substantial numbers from the third world, particularly in France and Britain. Xenophobic and restrictionist trends were increasing. There were riots against Turkish workers and landlords in Rotterdam, Neth., and in the fall official steps were taken to regulate the recruitment and sojourn of foreign workers. In Sweden resentment was particularly focused on Croats because of terrorist activities by a small minority of extremists. Switzerland made certain concessions to Italian workers in connection with a free-trade agreement with the EEC, but xenophobic feeling remained high. In West Germany, where one in every ten workers was a foreigner, the authorities were stopping foreigners from entering via a visa loophole through France. The massacre of Israeli team members at the Olympic Games in Munich in September demonstrated a laxity of control over the entrance and movement of "guest workers" and other foreigners, and prompted calls for greater restrictions and more searching checks on individuals, particularly Muslims and bearers of passports from Arab states.

Britain opened its doors wide enough to let in more than 25,000 Asians expelled from Uganda, but on Jan. 1, 1973 (the date of its entry into the EEC), the Immigration Act, 1971, would place Commonwealth citizens (except "patrials") on a similar footing with aliens other than EEC nationals. The latter would have the same right of free labour movement into the U.K. as British subjects would have in the Community. This was not expected to lead to any major inflow to Britain, because of high unemployment and comparatively unattractive wages and working conditions, but the West German federal employment office expected a big rise in the movement of British workers into Germany (18,700 in late 1972).

Of the labour-exporting countries, Turkey reported that nearly 590,000 workers had emigrated to Europe during 1971–72. Of these nearly 500,000 went to West Germany. Although it exported its own citizens, Spain was also reported to have over 100,000 foreign workers on its soil, including Portuguese in the Asturias and some 40,000 Moroccans and Algerians, mostly illegal entrants, in the Barcelona region.

A major report was published giving the findings of surveys conducted by the Working Party on Migra-

Immigration and Naturalization in the United States

Year Ended June 30, 1971

Country or region	Total immigrants admitted	Quota immigrants	Nonquota immigrants: Total	Nonquota immigrants: Families of U.S. citizens	Aliens naturalized
Africa	6,772	5,672	1,100	1,012	795
Egypt	3,643	3,429	214	182	355
Asia*	103,461	74,650	28,811	26,718	17,839
China†	14,417	11,850	2,567	2,282	2,880
Hong Kong	3,205	2,748	457	415	...
India	14,310	13,727	583	489	443
Iran	2,411	1,784	627	620	501
Japan	4,457	1,595	2,862	2,554	1,716
Korea	14,297	9,073	5,224	4,906	2,083
Pakistan	2,125	1,960	165	154	80
Philippines	28,471	19,197	9,274	8,710	5,488
Thailand	2,915	933	1,982	1,860	135
Vietnam	2,038	219	1,819	1,672	366
Europe‡	96,506	72,627	23,879	21,840	45,065
France	2,001	1,285	716	665	1,328
Germany	7,519	2,435	5,084	4,749	8,455
Greece	15,939	13,666	2,273	2,160	2,614
Italy	22,137	17,827	4,310	4,086	7,637
Poland	2,883	2,204	679	603	3,318
Portugal	11,692	10,642	1,050	1,003	1,306
Spain	4,125	3,048	1,077	906	776
United Kingdom	10,787	6,545	4,242	3,803	6,983
Yugoslavia	6,063	5,496	567	526	1,694
North and Central America	140,114	108,594	31,520	27,299	36,941
Canada	13,128	8,152	4,976	4,200	5,915
Cuba	21,611	20,891	720	402	19,754
Dominican Republic	12,624	10,445	2,179	2,018	752
Guatemala	2,194	1,833	361	317	255
Haiti	7,444	7,212	232	170	554
Jamaica	14,571	13,440	1,131	1,043	500
Mexico	50,103	31,710	18,393	16,221	6,361
Trinidad and Tobago	7,130	6,549	581	559	241
Oceania	2,923	1,804	1,119	979	466
South America	20,700	17,278	3,422	2,997	5,713
Colombia	6,440	5,700	740	600	1,182
Ecuador	4,981	4,538	443	403	737
Guyana	2,115	1,863	252	236	195
Total	370,478	280,626	89,852	80,845	108,407

Immigrants listed by country of birth; aliens naturalized by country of former allegiance.
*Includes Turkey. †Includes Taiwan. ‡Includes U.S.S.R.
Source: U.S. Department of Justice, Immigration and Naturalization Service, 1971 Annual Report.

tion of the Organization for Economic Cooperation and Development's Manpower and Social Affairs Committee. In the emigration areas (a number of localities in Spain, Greece, Italy, Portugal, and Turkey), the traditional balance of "underemployment" in the rural sectors had been deeply disturbed; the agricultural labour market had become tighter, and the migration flow into regional towns had been deflected. It was difficult to trace the effect of the returning migrants, since they tended to be assimilated back into the traditional economy. In general, emigration adversely affected the quality of the regional labour force. In two immigration areas (Lyons in France and Cologne in West Germany), it was found that many foreign workers came for a couple of years to earn enough money to achieve higher living standards in their own societies. The problem was therefore one of temporary adjustment to the receiving society, not of permanent settlement and integration. Most were restricted to unskilled, badly paid, and inferior jobs, in which they did not compete with native workers.

In France illegal entry posed additional problems for recent Portuguese and North African immigrants, and increased their isolation. French statistics, nevertheless, showed that an increasing number of Portuguese immigrants were bringing in their families; figures for Algerian and other North African families were predictably much lower. In West Germany a special International Labour Office inquiry into the family situation of migrant workers showed that, for the six main migrant groups (Turks, Yugoslavs, Italians, Spaniards, Greeks, and Portuguese), 70% of male workers were married and, of these, half had their spouses with them in Germany (one-quarter of these spouses were German girls).

Military Affairs:
see Defense

Australia's immigration target for 1972 was between 135,000 and the originally planned target of 140,000. This was 30,000 lower than the 1971 figure of 170,000, and was attributed to unemployment, which in January 1972 had reached 120,000. Canada received 121,900 immigrants in 1971, nearly 18% below the 1970 total, also reflecting reduced employment opportunities. For the first time the U.S. was the major source country, contributing 20% of the intake. The flow from Britain fell by 41% from 1970. In recent years the intake from Europe had decreased while the Asian and North and Central American contingents had risen. Despite high unemployment, Canada responded more positively and generously than any other country to appeals from Britain and the UN High Commissioner for Refugees by taking in several thousand Ugandan Asians.

In 1971, 370,478 immigrants entered the U.S., some 4,000 fewer than in the previous year. The publication of the interim report of the Commission on Population Growth and the American Future in March 1972 stimulated renewed demographic interest in the topic of U.S. immigration. One surprising finding was that about 20% of U.S. population growth in recent years had been due to net civilian immigration. Several immigration bills were considered by Congress. An administration bill proposed continuing special treatment for Canada and Mexico (an annual quota of 35,000 each but a preferential system to facilitate family reunion) while reducing the ceiling for the remainder of the Western Hemisphere from 120,000 to 80,000 per year; the Eastern Hemisphere ceiling would be 170,000. Another proposal would establish a worldwide annual ceiling of 300,000, with a uniform preference system, from July 1, 1974.

Migration into Brazil had declined over the decade 1962–72, and some 2,000 Brazilians (mostly sons of German settlers) even migrated to West Germany as workers in 1971. Over a 150-year period more than 5.5 million people had immigrated to Brazil, the most numerous groups being Portuguese (32%) and Italians (29%). (SHEILA PATTERSON)

See also Israel: *Special Report;* Refugees.

Mining

A strengthening but irregular and uncertain world economy supported the mineral production industries in 1972 at about the same overall level of activity as in 1971. Although mineral output continued to be impeded by environmental problems and by political uncertainties, there were no significant shortages. Public concern in the U.S. focused on the energy mineral situation, which included the conflicts between rising energy demand and the environmental impacts of strip coal mining, offshore oil and gas production, nuclear energy generation, and air pollution from burning of fossil fuels in their many applications.

Despite the relative stability in 1972 there was growing recognition that a potentially serious U.S. mineral supply deficiency could develop unless governmental and industrial policies and research anticipated the problems in time for their orderly resolution. An analysis of this situation was presented to the U.S. Congress early in 1972 in a report of the U.S. secretary of the interior. The report concluded: "It is mandatory, therefore, as a matter of urgency, that policies be established and programs formulated and undertaken, to create the social and economic environment necessary to foster optimum development of our mineral resources . . . within prudent environmental constraints . . . to meet projected future mineral and energy requirements."

For most minerals both global supply capacity and demand were disrupted by a number of political and general economic events. Although there was a turnaround in the downward slide in world industrial activity, the slowness of the reversal and the availability of reserve stocks delayed any significant rise in demand. Furthermore, the fluidity in foreign exchange rates following the U.S. upward revaluation of gold from $35 to $38 per ounce disrupted world trade, raised investment uncertainties, and resulted in fragmented international mineral commodity markets. On the supply side, the main deterrents were environmental restraints, mainly in mineral processing, but the supply of copper was impeded by nationalistic policies of major producers, and newly mined gold was withheld from the free market by South Africa and the U.S.S.R.

The price of gold was too erratic and uncertain during the year to stimulate serious interest in major new production capacity. The principal effect on mining may have been to reduce South African output, as companies mined more profitable lower-grade ore.

Silver shared the same volatility as gold in the marketplace. Having dipped to $1.29 per ounce in November 1971, it advanced steadily to about $1.80 an ounce by July 1972 and then rose irregularly to a four-year high of $2.03 late in December. There was a fragmented market, however, as the price ceiling on U.S. mined silver was held at $1.61 until August 10 when silver became exempt from price controls. The stronger outlook sparked renewed speculation. Copper, lead, and aluminum markets all displayed weakness in the second half of 1972. The confused mercury market dropped to a low of about $165 a flask in April but had rebounded to $275 by late in the year. Platinum prices fluctuated in response to reports from automobile manufacturers on the metal's use in catalytic devices to curb air pollution from automobile exhausts. The elevated prices of $142 an ounce for platinum and $60 an ounce for palladium were reached in October.

Industry Developments. The large international mining firms that emerged during the 1960s continued their worldwide search for and appraisal of new sources of mineral supply. The increased amount of time needed to explore, develop, and construct huge low-grade mineral projects forced industry to make long-range policy-planning decisions. A great deal of corporate technical and management effort was diverted to tackling the difficult and costly aspects of environmental control.

Profitability of mining declined, and industry moved toward massive low-profit operations. At the same time, the cyclic nature of mineral markets continued, and mining risks remained great.

In Arizona the discovery of about 250,000 tons of copper ore at the Bagdad mine led to plans for expansion. The project was curtailed, however, due to the lack of smelting capacity. In the Miami, Ariz., area City Service Ltd. began stripping at its Pinto Valley mine at midyear. Sixty million tons of preproduction stripping were to be done, and the 40,000-ton-per-day mine operation was scheduled to start in 1975. At the Pima mine, facilities were completed in February to raise capacity from 40,000 to 54,000 tons per day. At the nearby Twin Buttes mine American Metal Climax,

UPI COMPIX

Tom Wilkinson and Ron Flory emerge from the Sunshine Silver Mine near Kellogg, Ida., where they were trapped for a week. They were the sole survivors of the tragedy, which killed 91 miners in May 1972.

Inc., the Banner Mining Co., and the Anaconda Co. were negotiating a joint venture to expand the operation partly through development of new reserves.

Iron ore mining in Michigan's Upper Peninsula was expected to expand greatly under a $275 million program by Cleveland-Cliffs Iron Co. Heart of the expansion was the Tilden project to mine and process ten million tons of low-quality siliceous ore annually and produce four million tons of high-grade pellets by 1974. The project became economically feasible as a result of research in removing silica from the ore. Another element of the expansion was a 50% enlargement of the Empire mine output of pellets to reach 5.3 million tons per year.

Higher gold prices led to a revival of interest in the famous Cripple Creek district in Colorado, closed since 1961. Engineers anticipated that two or three years would be needed for mine reopening, exploration, and plant design and construction. Work began in 1972 to open the Carlton drainage tunnel. Mine and mill dumps also were being investigated for potential profits if gold should continue its price rise.

On May 2 a tragic fire at the Sunshine Silver Mine in Idaho resulted in the deaths of 91 men. The men were trapped underground by the fire and could not escape the poisonous carbon monoxide that spread through the workings. Only two men escaped, almost a week after the fire started, through a remote opening. The fire began in old workings near the 3,400-ft. level and a thorough investigation failed to establish its cause. The Sunshine was the leading U.S. silver producer, and its shutdown until late in the year was estimated to have resulted in a loss in production of about 5.4 million ounces of silver.

The lull in Canadian mining developments in 1971 was reversed. Exploration activity increased, particularly in western Canada, and there were major new mines or expansion projects. The huge, rich Texas Gulf, Inc. (TG), mine at Timmins, Ont., said to be the world's largest silver and zinc producer, was being changed progressively from open-pit to underground mining. TG began shipping zinc ingots from its new 120,000-ton-per-year zinc refinery at Timmins in May. In the Highland Valley area of British Columbia the copper-molybdenum potential continued to expand. The Lornex mine, fourth producer in the area, began concentrate shipments to Japan early in 1972.

African mine development progressed despite the

political uncertainties affecting all business. The sharp rise in gold prices gave a boost to South Africa and was expected to extend the life of the world-famous Witwatersrand goldfields. The quantity of gold recovered dropped somewhat because lower grade ore was being mined, but the total value rose sharply. In Botswana two major events took place. The Orapa diamond mine was officially dedicated in May, 12 years having been required to bring the mine into production. The Orapa deposit was the second largest known kimberlite pipe (vertical mass of volcanic agglomerate) in the world, the largest being in Tanzania. Commitments were made to bring the Selebi-Pikwe copper-nickel mine into production in 1974.

Although the vigorous phase of its mining boom abated, Australia remained one of the prime world areas of ore search. However, lower mineral demand, chiefly from Japan, and governmental concern over the magnitude of foreign investment added new deterrents. Thus, while exploration continued, some expansion plans were curtailed. One of the major projects to receive a green light was the $265 million lateritic nickel-cobalt Greenvale mine in Queensland. The 44 million-ton nickel deposit was expected to start producing 46 million lb. of nickel per year in 1975.

The giant Bougainville copper mine in Papua New Guinea began production early in 1972 and reached an output rate of 120,000 tons of copper a year. In Indonesia the development of the Ertsberg copper mine continued ahead of schedule.

Other major southern Asia and Pacific mineral developments centred on nickel. Lateritic-type deposits were being investigated or developed in Indonesia, the Philippines, and on a large scale in New Caledonia. New laterite-ore nickel producers were gradually eroding the preeminent world position Canada had long held in nickel output.

Operations and plans in the Chilean-Peruvian copper region continued to be disrupted by problems stemming from nationalization of the mines. The compensation offered by Chile when properties were nationalized was challenged, and Kennecott Copper Corp. attempted to block sales in France of copper from its former mines. Brazil, on the other hand, continued to encourage foreign participation in developing its minerals. Development was focused on iron ore and manganese, but a promising copper area was being developed in the state of Bahia, and tin, chromium, tungsten, and columbium deposits attracted attention.

Relatives, rescue workers, and officials of the Wankie Colliery in northwestern Rhodesia wait anxiously with stretchers and first-aid supplies following an explosion in the main shaft on June 6, 1972. A total of 427 men died, making this the fifth worst mining disaster in history.

JOHN MCGEORGE—GAMMA

Technology. The emphasis in mining and mineral processing research shifted further toward environmental and health and safety problems, but the stable and relatively low level of mineral raw materials also forced continual improvements in production engineering to hold costs down. The trend continued toward more surface mining of metals, minerals, and coal, but at the same time it was recognized that underground mining would increase in absolute quantities.

The effectiveness of resin-anchored rock bolts in soft ground was demonstrated at a clay mine in West Virginia, the first U.S. mine using this method as its main roof support. The bolts not only stopped roof falls but the resin sealed the bolt holes, stopping an ingress of water which had made mining and haulage more difficult.

Rotary tunneling and raising machines found wide application in mining and in subway and aqueduct construction. In one instance a 6-mi.-long, 16-ft.-diameter aqueduct drilled under Lake Huron was completed in 15 months, about half the time it would have taken by conventional methods. The record monthly advance was 3,500 ft., and a rate of 19 ft. per hour was achieved on one occasion.

The potential of deep-sea ocean mining attracted wide attention. The technology to accomplish it was under study, but economic feasibility was highly controversial. The extension of tin dredging into deep water took place when a $15 million suction dredge, the world's largest, began operating in January off Thailand.

Giant open-pit mining equipment grew even larger. Six manufacturers reportedly would soon be offering 200-ton capacity, $500,000 ore-haulage units. Meanwhile, designers were at work on 400-to-600-ton units.

Several large new ore carriers entered service. At Tubarão, Braz., 166,000 long tons of iron ore fines were loaded on the "Berge Istra," an ore/oil carrier. In Australia a 147,000-ton iron ore shipment was loaded at Dampier. (P. F. YOPES)

Production. The effects of the worldwide economic recession that began in 1970 were still being felt in the mineral industries in 1972, both because the recession itself varied, with some countries only reaching their lowest point after others were well on the way to recovery, and because there is an inevitable lead time before economic trends make an impact on the mineral industries. Thus, in 1971, the latest year for which reasonably complete figures were available, overall world mineral production continued to rise although at a slower rate than in previous years. Of the 73 mineral commodities for which relatively complete international statistics were available for 1971, the output of 42 increased by an average of 6.8% and the production of 31 declined by an average of 8.59%.

Despite temporarily discouraging economic conditions, there remained a long-term upward trend in world demand for minerals, and the exploration programs necessary to provide the new mineral deposits from which production would have to come continued during 1972. Australia and Indonesia continued to be important centres of exploration, and there was considerable activity in Brazil and Mexico. There was activity in western Africa and South Africa. Exploration tended to be curtailed in the U.S. for a combination of reasons, including federal and state fiscal, environmental, and land use policies.

In 1971 the United States led the world in the production of 26 minerals, including petroleum and natural gas; the Soviet Union in 17, including all forms of coal; Canada in 6; South Africa in 4; Australia and Zaire in 3 each; Brazil, Japan, and Malaysia in 2 each; and 7 other countries in 1. Australia and India tied in the production of monazite.

Aluminum. World primary aluminum production in 1971 was 10.3 million metric tons, an increase of only 605,000 metric tons (6.1%) over 1970. Existing surplus productive capacity resulting from overdevelopment in 1969 and 1970 was exacerbated by the widespread economic slowdown, which depressed world demand for aluminum throughout 1971 and early 1972. Producer inventories increased, output was curtailed, and several large new projects were postponed for a year or two. Prices reflected conditions. Despite extensive discounting the U.S. producer primary ingot list price remained at 29 cents per pound through 1971 and into 1972. By May 1972 it had fallen to 25 cents, closer to the actual sales price of about 22 cents. In 1971 there was no change in the relative rank of the leading aluminum-producing countries, seven of which accounted for 78% of total output. Leaders were the U.S., 3.6 million metric tons (34.7%); U.S.S.R., 1.2 million (11.5%); Canada, 1 million (9.8%); and Japan, 900,000 (8.7%).

Antimony. Revised figures showed that, compared with 1970, world antimony production in 1971 declined 7.4%, to 63,747 metric tons. The five leading producers maintained their relative positions: South Africa, 14,246 metric tons (22.3%); China, estimated 12,000 (18.8%); Bolivia, 11,667 (18.3%); U.S.S.R., 6,900 (10.8%); and Mexico, estimated 3,200 (5%). World demand for antimony remained depressed through 1971 and most of 1972 not only in response to economic conditions but as a consequence of abnormally high prices in 1969 and 1970. From the January 1971 level of 96 cents per pound, the U.S. domestic price had fallen to 57 cents by July 1971, where it remained through 1972. By the end of 1972 supply and demand were in better balance, and some new production was being planned in several parts of the world.

Asbestos. World asbestos output rose 2.8% to 3,580,000 metric tons in 1971, a clear indication of the prevailing economic and business climate. There was no change in relative position among the leading producers: Canada, 1,480,000 metric tons (41.4% of total); U.S.S.R., 1.2 million (32.1%); and South Africa, 300,000 (8.9%). Consumption appeared to have increased somewhat during 1972 as economic conditions improved, and new mines came into production or were being planned. Prices, however, held steady or showed only slight gains through the year.

Cement. At 590,220,000 metric tons, 1971 world cement production was 18.3 million metric tons (3.2%) above 1970 levels. Leading producers maintained their relative positions: U.S.S.R., 100.3 million metric tons (17%); U.S., 72.9 million (12.3%); Japan, 53.8 million (9.1%); and West Germany, 32.7 million (5.5%). The comparatively small increase in output of so basic an industrial mineral was indicative of general economic conditions. No significant change was observed in 1972, although demand in the U.S. appeared to be strengthening toward the end of the year and prices were firming.

Chromium. Estimated world chromite production in 1971 was 6,360,000 metric tons, an increase of about 5% over 1970. As regards individual producers, the Soviet Union (1.8 million metric tons, 28.3% of the total) and South Africa (1.6 million, 25.9%) retained their relative positions, but the Philippines, once third, was pushed to fifth place by Turkey (600,000, 9.5%) and Albania (600,000, 9.5%). Relaxation in the U.S. of restrictions against imports of Rhodesian chromite under sanctions imposed by the UN in 1967 brought 1972 prices down to about $55 per ton, compared with 1971 highs of $72.

Cobalt. World production of cobalt metal was 22,738 metric tons in 1971, an increase of 903 metric tons (4.1%) over the preceding year. There was no change in the relative order of producers: Zaire, 14,518 metric tons (63.8%); Zambia, 1,886 (8.3%); U.S.S.R., 1,588 (7%); and Canada (actually second in mine production to Zaire), with 1,395 (6.1%). List prices in 1972 held firm at $2.45 per pound, although sales were made at lower rates ($2.36 per pound) as a result of weak demand and somewhat increased output.

Copper. World mine and smelter output of copper rose 31,000 metric tons (0.5%) and 9,500 metric tons (0.2%), respectively, in 1971 to 6 million and 6,110,000 metric tons. Apart from some curtailment of production due to world economic conditions, a significant portion of 1971 U.S. production was lost because of a protracted strike. Among the leading producers of mine copper in 1971, Canada edged Zambia for third place. Mine production in the U.S. was 1.4 million metric tons (22.8%); Chile, 720,000 (11.9%); Canada, 650,000 (10.8%); Zambia, 650,000 (10.8%); and U.S.S.R., 620,000 (10.2%). Japan, 11th among mine producers, was second only to the United States in output of smelter copper: 660,000 metric tons (10.8%) to 1,360,000 (22.3%). The general condition of surplus productive capacity relative to demand that characterized the industry late in 1970 and 1971 persisted throughout 1972, and prices remained weak, hovering about the 50 cents-per-pound mark in the U.S. Nevertheless, by the year's end demand appeared to be strengthening as world economic activity increased, and several large new mines were in various stages of development including Cuajone in Peru, Tenke-Fungurume in Zaire, and Sar Chesma in Iran.

Diamonds. Total world diamond production in 1971 was 42.2 million carats, nearly 1% (397,000 carats) less than in 1970. Production of gem diamonds declined about 500,000 carats (4.1%), especially in South Africa, though it remained the leading producer with 3.1 million carats, 17.5% less than in 1970. Output of industrial diamonds, however, increased slightly (149,000 carats, up 0.5%) to 29.4 million carats. In total production, Zaire continued to lead (13.7 million carats, 32.5%), while the U.S.S.R. (8.8 million carats, 20.9%) edged South Africa (7 million carats, 16.7%) out of second place. South Africa led in gem production followed by a second-place tie between South West Africa and the U.S.S.R., each with 1.8 million carats, or 14.1% of world output. Zaire maintained a strong lead in industrial diamond output (12 million carats, 30.8% of total) over U.S.S.R. (7 million carats, 23.8%) and South Africa (3.9 million carats, 13.3%).

Gold. World gold production declined 1,020,000 troy ounces (2.1%) to 46,510,000 troy ounces in 1971. There was no change in the relative positions of major producers: South Africa, 31,390,000 troy ounces (67.5%); U.S.S.R., 6.7 million (14.4%); Canada, 2,240,000 (4.8%); and the U.S., 1.5 million (3.2%). Except in South Africa and probably in the Soviet Union, the majority of the world's gold output in the major producing countries occurred as a by-product of other types of mining. In the United States, for example, the 1971 decline of nearly 14% (240,000 troy ounces) was attributable almost entirely to a strike in the copper mines, which produced nearly 30% of U.S. gold as a by-product. In South Africa, the lower output resulted in part from flooding of the West Driefontein mine and in part from declining grades of ore. The free market price of gold rose into the middle and high $40 range during 1971, exceeded $50 in May 1972, and reached a high of $72.25 on August 2 on the London Exchange. For the balance of the year, prices varied about the $60 level.

Iron and Steel. World output of iron ore in 1971 (785.8 million metric tons) declined 2.5%; pig iron (430,120,000 metric tons) fell 3.9%; and raw steel (582,120,000 metric tons) was down 2.1%, all as a direct result of lessened world economic activity. For the second consecutive year the Soviet Union led the U.S. in production of iron ore, 203 million metric tons (25.8%) to 82.1 million (10.4%), and of pig iron, 88.3 million metric tons (20.5%) to 73,830,000 (17.2%). Australia (62.1 million, 7.9%) edged France out of third place in iron ore production. For the first time the U.S.S.R. surpassed the U.S. in the production of steel, 121 million to 109,260,000 metric tons (20.8 to 18.8%), followed by Japan with 88,560,000 and West Germany with 40,310,000. Some improvement in production took place in 1972, with world steel output expected to rise about 8% over 1971.

Lead. World smelter production of lead declined 3.6% to 3,170,000 metric tons, but world mine production rose nearly 1% to 3.4 million metric tons. Environmental considerations tended to reinforce adverse economic factors in lowering smelter output. There were no relative changes among the largest producers apart from Australia falling behind the U.S.S.R. in mine output. The U.S. led in ore production, 524,900 metric tons (15.4%); U.S.S.R. 450,000 (13.2%); Australia 398,700 (11.7%); and Canada, 387,200 (11.4%). The same order was maintained in smelter output. Prices, which began the year at 14–14.5 cents (New York), strengthened gradually to a 15–16 cent level in late August, but by the year's end were down again to the 14.5–15 cent range.

Manganese. In contrast to steel production to which it is intimately related, world output of manganese rose nearly 14% in 1971 to 20,690,000 metric tons. The three largest producers maintained their relative positions: U.S.S.R., 6,990,000 metric tons (33.8%); South Africa, 3,240,000 (15.6%); and Brazil, 2.6 million (12.6%). Prices held steady throughout 1972 at a nominal 63–68 cents per long ton. The world's first manganese ore pelletizing plant was under construction and nearly ready for commissioning in Brazil.

Mercury. World mercury production increased 7.7% during 1971, reaching 305,720 flasks. No change took place in relative positions among major producers. Spain produced 67,500 flasks (22%); U.S.S.R. 50,000 (16.4%); Italy 42,670 (14%), a decline from 1970; and Mexico, 35,390 (11.6%). Prices in 1972 continued their two-year decline, dropping from about $260–$270 per flask at the end of 1971 to a low of about $150 in mid-1972. Some recovery began in midyear, and prices climbed slowly to a $250–$260 range toward the end of 1972. The rise, however, was essentially artificial and indicated no fundamental strength in the mercury market. It resulted primarily from a combination of producer cutbacks (Canada's Pinchi Lake Mine) and failures (the largest Mexican producer) and the withholding of stocks by producers, particularly the Italians and Spanish, in an effort to improve prices.

Molybdenum. World molybdenum production declined 2.7% to 78,500 metric tons in 1971. Major producers, in their usual order, were U.S., 49,700 metric tons (63.3%); Canada, 12,800 (16.3%); and U.S.S.R., 8,000 (10.2%). Output was believed to have fallen even more in 1972 as several marginal producers ceased operations. List prices remained constant through 1972, but discounting was prevalent. Never-

COURTESY, AUSTRALIAN NEWS AND INFORMATION BUREAU

Ore vessels load bauxite at Weipa on Cape York Peninsula, Australia, where an estimated 2,500,000,000 tons of ore —20% of the world's known bauxite reserves— lie close to the surface. An international consortium of companies was considering constructing the world's largest alumina refinery at the site.

theless, plant shutdowns, reduction of inventories, and improved economic activity appeared to have strengthened both demand and prices in 1972, although a list price increase was not expected for some time.

Nickel. World output of nickel, 640,500 metric tons, rose nearly 2% over 1970. In descending order, the leading producers were, as usual, Canada, 266,700 metric tons (41.6%); U.S.S.R., 117,900 (18.4%); and New Caledonia, 102,300 (16%). As reflected by the producer's price of $1.33 per pound, continued from 1971, demand remained weak through the early part of 1972. A percentage of productive capacity that had been idled in 1971 remained so despite the commissioning of new productive facilities. Toward the end of the year demand began to improve, and on September 1 producers raised their price to $1.53 per pound.

Phosphate. World production of phosphate rock rose 2.1% to 87.5 million metric tons in 1971. As usual, the leading producers were U.S., 35.3 million metric tons (40.3%); U.S.S.R., 21.7 million (24.7%); and Morocco, 12 million (13.7%). During the past several years, the world phosphate industry underwent severe cutbacks brought about by weak demand and greatly excessive productive capacity. During 1972, a much leaner industry saw demand increasing and most surplus capacity and inventories worked down. Although there was no significant increase in price, the market by the end of 1972 was such as to have encouraged the commissioning of several large new phosphate projects.

Platinum Group Metals. World platinum output decreased by 160,000 troy ounces (3.8%) to 4,080,000 troy ounces in 1971. The three largest producers maintained their traditional sequence: U.S.S.R., 2.3 million troy ounces (56.4%); South Africa, 1,250,000 (30.6%); and Canada, 470,000 (11.5%). The reduced output that began in 1971 in response to weakened demand lasted until about mid-1972. Producer prices continued their 1971 slide to $115 per troy ounce in January 1972 and $110 by midyear. In late June 1972, an announcement concerning antipollution requirements for automobile exhaust systems resulted in a long-term contract in which a major U.S. automobile manufacturer agreed to purchase platinum for catalytic pollution control devices from a South African producer. Platinum prices promptly rose and by the end of the year were about $140 per troy ounce.

Potash. World production of potash reached 20.1 million metric tons in 1971, an 8.3% increase. With no change in relative positions from 1970, the leading producers were U.S.S.R., 5.4 million metric tons (26.7%); Canada, 3.5 million metric tons (17.5%); and West Germany, 2.9 million metric tons (14.5%). Excessive overcapacity, which was about 50% in Canada, continued. In 1972 world productive capacity was estimated to be 27.6 million tons, and the excess was expected to linger through the decade.

Silver. World silver production in 1971 fell 3% to 294.7 million troy ounces. For the first time, Canada (45,950,000 troy ounces, 15.6%) led the U.S. (41,560,000, 14.1%), largely because much U.S. silver originates as a by-product of copper mining, which was curtailed by a strike. The Soviet Union (39 million, 13.2%) rose from fifth to third followed by Peru (38.4 million, 13%) and Mexico (36,660,000, 12.4%). Demand continued to be fairly strong through 1972, and, as usual, appeared to outstrip primary production by a significant amount. Prices in 1972 seemed more influenced by industrial than speculative considerations and from a January low of $1.47 per troy ounce (New York) rose more or less steadily to $1.85 in August before falling back slightly to about $1.80.

Sulfur. World sulfur output from all sources rose 3.5% in 1971 to 22,880,000 metric tons. The major producers retained their relative positions: U.S., 8,750,000 metric tons (38.2%); Canada, 4,890,000 (21.4%); and Poland, 2,820,000 (12.3%). Surplus capacity and lower demand depressed the industry. The two major producers of sulfur by the Frasch process, Mexico and the U.S., were severely affected by the rising flood of recovered sulfur extracted from sour gas, especially in Canada, and the anticipated supplies that would result from various stack gas and other antipollution measures. In 1972 the U.S. and Mexican Frasch industries continued to decline, and several producing mines closed.

Tin. World mine tin production held virtually steady at 229,500 long tons, an increase of about 100 tons over 1970. Malaysia continued in first place (74,200 long tons, 32.3%), but the U.S.S.R. (28,000, 12.2%) pushed Bolivia (27,400, 11.9%) from second into third, with Thailand (21,300, 9.3%) continuing as fourth. Demand during 1972 appeared to be fairly strong and the New York price, which had averaged about $1.67 per pound, began slowly to increase, reaching $1.82 in September and holding near that level for the balance of the year. A number of offshore alluvial deposits were being evaluated in Indonesia during the year.

Titanium. Aggregate world production of the titanium minerals, ilmenite and rutile, declined 6% to about 3,750,000 metric tons. Australia continued to be the major producer with 814,800 metric tons of ilmenite (24.1%), down slightly from 1970, and 366,700 metric tons of rutile (90%). Canada and Norway, respectively, produced 775,300 metric tons (23%) and 641,600 metric tons (19%) of ilmenite. The only other rutile producer, Sierra Leone, was down to 12% of its 1970 output due to technical problems at the one producing property. The market for titanium remained weak and uncertain, especially as it depended largely on the aircraft industry. However, the use of ilmenite in pigments was increasing, to some extent at the expense of rutile, and several new mining projects were under consideration in different parts of the world.

Tungsten. World tungsten production increased 9% in 1971 to 36,618 metric tons. China, the U.S.S.R., and the U.S. maintained their respective positions with 7,983 (21.8%), 6,985 (19.1%), and 3,130 (8.5%). Thailand, however, jumped from 12th to 4th place, producing 2,508 metric tons in 1971 compared with 711 in 1970. The increase was due to discovery and development of two new deposits of wolframite. U.S. tungsten demand fell about 30% in 1971 but recovered and increased 15–20% in 1972.

Uranium. Reported non-Communist world output of uranium oxide (U_3O_8) increased 3% in 1971 to 22,300 metric tons. The major producers maintained their relative standings: U.S., 11,709 metric tons (52.5%); South Africa, 3,800 (17%); and Canada, 3,638 (16.3%). Niger joined the ranks of important producers (506 metric tons). Although world demand for nuclear power developed more slowly than originally forecast, since the late 1960s exploration for new uranium deposits in order to meet forthcoming nuclear fuel requirements has been increasing. Low-grade reserves in Canada and the U.S. were enlarged, and a potential high-grade region was found in central Africa, where the Arlit deposit was developed in Niger. The most important area, however, was the Northern Territory in Australia, where several large, high-grade deposits were found and were under development. The price of uranium was also rising. Future contracts in 1972 were being made at $8 per pound contained uranium and up, compared with the recent U.S. average of about $6.80.

Zinc. World output of smelter zinc declined 5.5% to 4,610,000 metric tons, while mine zinc output rose 2% to 5,560,000 metric tons. Major smelter producers were the U.S., 695,300 metric tons (15%); U.S.S.R., 650,500 metric tons (14%); and Japan, 601,100 metric tons (13%), with the U.S.S.R. rising to second from third place. Mine producers include Canada, 1,270,000 metric tons (22.8%); U.S.S.R., 650,450 tons (11.7%); Australia, 448,200 tons (8.1%); and U.S., 445,800 tons (8%). Unlike virtually all other minerals recently, the decline in smelter zinc production was almost wholly due to environmental considerations rather than business conditions. (FRANK H. SKELDING)

See also Fuel and Power; Geology; Industrial Review; Metallurgy.

Monaco

A constitutional monarchy on the northern Mediterranean coast, Monaco is bounded on all land sides by the French *département* of Alpes-Maritimes. Area: 0.65 sq.mi. (1.68 sq.km.). Pop. (1972 est.): 24,500. Language: French. Religion: Roman Catholic. Prince, Rainier III; ministers of state in 1972, François-Didier Gregh and, from May 24, André Saint-Mleux.

Monaco continued its lively program of the arts and its sponsorship of cultural and sporting events during 1972. These included the 30th running of the Monte Carlo Grand Prix, won by Jean-Pierre Beltoise of France. As a result, tourism continued to produce a substantial portion of the national income. Development of modern facilities progressed and the economic future looked brighter. Prospects for offshore petroleum exploitation appeared excellent for the entire coastal area from Marseilles to the Italian border. However, many people feared that the sight of off-

MONACO

Education. (1969–70) Primary, pupils 1,446, teachers 49; secondary, pupils 1,847, teachers 116; vocational, pupils 331, teachers 29.

Finance. Monetary unit: French franc, with (Sept. 18, 1972) a par value of Fr. 5.12 to U.S. $1 (free rate of Fr. 12.24 = £1 sterling), a "commercial" rate, and a free "financial" rate of Fr. 5 to U.S. $1 (Fr. 11.92 = £1 sterling). Budget (1970 est.): revenue Fr. 188,243,000; expenditure Fr. 176,083,000.

Foreign Trade. Included with France. Tourism: visitors (1970) 88,700; gross receipts (1966) U.S. $6.1 million.

Missiles:
see Defense

Molecular Biology:
see Life Sciences

Molybdenum:
see Mining

shore rigs and the threat of oil spills might have unhappy effects on tourism.

The tenth conference of the International Hydrographic Organization was held in Monaco from April 10 to 22. Representatives of 36 member nations, observers from 5 additional states, and representatives of 26 scientific and technical organizations attended.

On May 24, André Saint-Mleux, a French career diplomat, succeeded François-Didier Gregh as the minister of state. The minister is the chief representative of France as well as principal adviser to the crown. (ROBERT D. HODGSON)

Money and Banking

The international monetary system entered a new phase in 1972, following the realignment of exchange rates agreed upon among the Group of Ten countries and Switzerland at the Smithsonian Institution in Washington, D.C., in December 1971. This agreement provided for the devaluation of the U.S. dollar and a reshuffling of the other currencies involved, for lifting of the U.S. import surcharge, and for a widening of the margins within which exchange rates could be permitted to fluctuate. It brought to an end the uncertainties of the preceding year and set the stage for economic recovery in most of the major industrial countries.

The expected post-devaluation reflux of funds to the U.S. failed to materialize. With unemployment in the U.S. high and with monetary policy designed primarily to promote domestic recovery, short-term interest rates there fell to low levels in the early months of 1972. In addition, lingering doubts concerning the durability of the new exchange-rate relationships intensified in June when the pound sterling was set free to float and depreciated sharply in the exchange markets. Another factor was that the U.S. had not entered into any commitment to restore the convertibility of the dollar into gold or other reserve assets. Since the U.S. external trade deficit continued to be very large, it seemed that foreign central banks might have to acquire additional large amounts of dollars.

In February and March funds began to flow from the U.S. to Western Europe and Japan, partly through the Eurocurrency markets. After a short lull they surged up again in June and July, provoking recipient countries to strengthen controls over capital imports. In addition, there were substantial flows of funds to the EEC countries from the U.K. when a short-lived attempt was made to support sterling within the narrow margin of exchange-rate fluctuations agreed on in April by the EEC countries and prospective members.

However, monetary authorities in continental Europe and Japan showed their determination to defend existing parities by exchange controls and, if necessary, by substantial purchases of dollars. In July, after the U.S. authorities had announced the reactivation of the central-bank swap network, suspended since August 1971, and had helped to support the dollar by intervention in the exchange market, a substantial reflux of funds across the Atlantic finally began.

A striking feature of 1972 was the rapid, almost explosive growth of money and credit in most industrial countries. Faced with high or rising unemployment, the authorities in most cases had turned to easier monetary policies and adopted expansionary government budgets. There was a marked strengthening of economic expansion in the U.S. and Canada, while in Europe and Japan a slowing down or pause gave way to unexpectedly rapid recovery. In North America the demand for business loans strengthened considerably. Elsewhere a large part of the increase in bank lending went for housing construction and personal consumption. The main exception was Italy, where economic activity remained depressed.

The year also saw a very rapid growth of money and, especially, of time and savings deposits. Even in the U.S., where containing the growth of the money supply was given priority throughout the year, money plus time deposits expanded at annual rates averaging about 10%. The rise was much faster in Western European countries, Canada, and Japan. (*See* Table I.) Hence there was a gradual return to credit restraint in most countries.

In the U.S. the Federal Reserve began to lower its target for the growth of bank reserves in the spring, and from March onward short-term interest rates rose considerably. In the U.K. the authorities permitted short-term interest rates to go up after outflows of funds had developed in June. In most continental European countries, monetary policies were made more restrictive during the spring and summer. In particular, measures were taken to check the increase in bank liquidity caused by substantial inflows of funds.

Until late summer, short-term interest rates in continental Europe and Japan fell or remained low. Later, as U.S. interest rates continued to rise and the dollar strengthened, monetary authorities in Europe were able to get bank liquidity under control and short-term interest rates there began to rise, sometimes quite sharply. In late October the Bank of England's minimum lending rate, determined according to a new procedure, was raised from 6 to $7\frac{1}{4}$%, and in October and November there were increases in central-bank discount rates in Belgium, France, West Germany, and the Netherlands.

In the latter months of 1972 there were signs of a slowdown in the growth of the money supply in the U.S. and Canada. Rates of increase were still very high in Europe, however. In late October the EEC countries agreed that, as part of a joint anti-inflationary program, each member country would lower the rate of growth of the money supply during 1973 and 1974 to a figure equal to the growth of its real gross national product (GNP) plus 4%, the norm to which they would each seek to reduce the increase in consumer prices during 1973.

Eurocurrency and Eurobond Markets. In marked contrast to the wide fluctuations in 1971, Eurodollar rates were relatively stable in 1972 except for brief periods when speculative influences and uncertainties on the exchange market exerted upward pressures. The London three-month deposit rate moved downward from the beginning of the year and, after a strong but

Table I. Rates of Growth of Money plus Quasi-Money

	1970		1971		1972		
Country	June	Dec.	June	Dec.	March	June	Sept.
United States	2.8	8.0	13.2	11.0	9.9	8.9	10.1
Canada	5.6	10.3	16.2	16.4	16.6	16.9	16.6
Japan	18.1	16.9	20.6	24.3	24.0	26.2	22.0
United Kingdom	7.3	9.5	10.4	13.0	15.4	23.4	26.4
Belgium	7.4	8.2	10.4	12.9	14.7	14.8	14.0
France	6.9	15.0	18.1	17.7	17.5	15.3	19.8
Germany, West	9.3	10.5	12.9	14.5	13.4	14.0	15.7
Italy	11.3	15.0	18.9	16.6	18.4	18.0	17.1
Netherlands	11.1	10.5	8.1	9.4	9.8	11.5	11.0

brief recovery in March, reached a trough of around 4½% in early June. Over this period the differential between Eurodollar rates and domestic U.S. rates was gradually reduced. The three-month Eurodollar rate rose to 5¾% again during the sterling crisis. Rates eased afterward and remained stable until late September, when they moved to a somewhat higher level in a late and still partial adjustment to the higher rates prevailing on domestic money markets.

Demand for Eurodollars was influenced during the year by new regulations in European countries limiting the access of domestic borrowers to the market and by restrictions on the conversion of dollars into domestic currencies by banks. However, much of the effect of this was offset by increased lending to non-European and Eastern European borrowers. On the supply side the central banks of the Group of Ten countries were bound by their agreements in 1971 not to place additional dollar balances in the market, but the monetary authorities of a number of other countries offered funds as their foreign exchange reserves rose.

The Eurobond market was generally characterized by strong and accelerating issuing activity and stable or declining interest rates. Not only were monetary conditions easier, but measures taken in West Germany, Switzerland, Japan, and, earlier, in the Netherlands diverted foreign demand away from domestic securities. In the January–October period, issues totaled $4.9 billion, compared with $2.9 billion in the corresponding period of 1971. Issues in U.S. dollars maintained their share of the total at 56%.

United States. Monetary policy had been eased in 1971 following announcement of U.S. Pres. Richard Nixon's stabilization program in August. With cost inflation being met by direct controls and with external constraints reduced, monetary policy could be directed primarily toward promoting domestic recovery. Banks were liberally provided with reserves, and short-term interest rates fell gradually. At the same time monetary expansion slowed down. Federal Reserve discount rates were lowered to 4½% in November and December. By mid-February 1972 the Treasury bill yield was down to almost 3% and the prime lending rate of several major banks stood at 4½%.

The growth of the money supply quickened again at the beginning of 1972. Business recovery was at last gaining momentum, and unemployment was declining slowly. The rise in wages and consumer prices remained modest, but wholesale prices began to go up more rapidly. Fiscal policy continued to give a strong stimulus to the economy; the federal budget deficit, which came to $23 billion in 1971–72, was expected to be even larger in 1972–73.

Against this background and with the dollar still weak, the authorities began to reduce the stimulus from monetary policy during the spring and summer. The Federal Reserve Open Market Committee set progressively lower objectives for the growth in bank reserves. Since demand for credit remained strong, short-term interest rates moved upward from March onward. By mid-October the Treasury bill yield had risen to about 4.8%, and banks had increased their prime lending rates to 5¾–5⅞%. Policy was then geared to avoid too sharp a credit squeeze, so that money-market conditions eased somewhat and short-term rates leveled off.

The tightening of monetary policy was reflected in a slackening in the growth of the monetary aggregates. Thus, in the third quarter, currency and demand deposits went up to an annual rate of 8.6%, compared with 9.2% in the first quarter, while the growth of money and time deposits rose at a rate of 9.2%, compared with 13.3%. However, the effect of this slowdown on the growth of banks' total resources was largely offset by a rapid expansion in their sales of large certificates of deposit.

The nonbank financial institutions also benefited from a substantial increase in savings deposits, which rose at an annual rate of $48 billion in January–September, following gains of $41 billion in 1971 and $17 billion in 1970. They channeled a record volume of funds to the mortgage market and this, combined with the large contribution from the banks, caused total mortgage credit to rise at an annual rate of $65 billion in January–September.

United Kingdom. Despite strong fiscal and monetary stimulants, growth of output in 1971 had remained well below the economy's potential. Although wage settlements escalated following the miners' strike in January and February 1972, the government decided that the need to promote faster growth was imperative. The March budget provided for sweeping tax cuts totaling £1,200 million in 1972–73. Together with higher government expenditure announced in late 1971, these concessions were expected to bring the central government's borrowing requirement to £3,100 million in 1972–73, compared with £700 million in 1971–72.

In September 1971 new arrangements for the control of bank credit had been introduced; quantitative credit controls were replaced by a new system of reserve asset ratios for banks and finance houses. This put the banks in a better position to compete for funds. Moreover, the banks entered the new regime with comfortable reserve ratios. Some acceleration in the growth of money and bank credit was to be expected, therefore, and, indeed, was felt to be essential in order to accommodate faster growth of output. The ensuing expansion was particularly rapid, however; money and sterling fixed deposits went up by 26% in the year ended in September, and clearing

Table II. Selected Interest Rates

Country		1970 June	1971 June	1971 Sept.	1971 Dec.	1972 March	1972 June	1972 Sept.
Belgium	A	7.50	6.00	5.50	5.50	4.00	4.00	4.00
	B^1	6.34	2.34	3.88	4.10	1.69	2.00	1.73
	C	7.77	7.35	7.15	7.17	7.01	7.07	6.93
France	A	8.00	6.75	6.75	6.50	6.00	5.75	5.75
	B^1	9.35	6.45	5.98	5.27	4.77	3.85	3.88
	C	8.47	8.12	8.13	8.01	7.83	7.56	7.61
Germany, West	A	7.50	5.00	5.00	4.00	3.00	3.00	3.00
	B^2	7.00	4.25	4.25	3.25	2.75	2.75	2.75
	C	8.70	8.20	8.10	7.90	7.40	7.90	7.90
Italy	A	5.50	5.00	5.00	4.50	4.50	4.00	4.00
	B^2	6.95	5.54	6.04	6.04	6.04	5.54	4.40
	C	7.95	7.11	7.14	6.76	6.67	6.42	6.52
Netherlands	A	6.00	5.50	5.00	5.00	4.00	4.00	3.00
	B^2	6.18	4.51	4.49	3.99	2.30	1.94	1.13
	C	8.52	7.22	7.58	7.48	6.62	7.25	6.39
Switzerland	A	3.75	3.75	3.75	3.75	3.75	3.75	3.75
	B^1	2.38	1.88	0.38	1.19	0.12	1.38	1.56
	C	5.87	5.38	5.10	4.99	4.77	5.06	4.98
United Kingdom	A	7.00	6.00	5.00	5.00	5.00	6.00	6.00
	B^2	6.87	5.60	4.83	4.36	4.34	5.21	6.44
	C	9.40	9.30	8.49	8.45	8.79	9.47	9.57
United States	A	6.00	4.75	5.00	4.50	4.50	4.50	4.50
	B^2	6.47	4.70	4.67	4.02	3.72	3.87	4.59
	C	6.99	5.94	5.56	5.62	5.66	5.59	5.70
Canada	A	7.00	5.25	5.25	4.75	4.75	4.75	4.75
	B^2	5.90	3.15	3.93	3.25	3.50	3.58	3.57
	C	8.03	7.30	6.97	6.56	7.24	7.46	7.46
Japan	A	6.25	5.50	5.25	4.75	4.75	4.25	4.25
	B^1	8.00	6.25	5.75	5.21	5.00	4.39	4.25
	C	9.38	7.95	7.44	7.38	6.66	6.45	6.64

A = Central bank's discount rate.
B = Money-market rate.
B^1 = Day-to-day money.
B^2 = 90-day Treasury bills; one-year bills in the case of Italy.
C = Long-term government bond yield.

banks' advances rose by no less than 64%. There was little increase in bank lending to manufacturing industry, but a very sharp rise in personal lending accompanied the consumption boom.

Besides a worsening of inflation, the first half of 1972 witnessed a sharp reduction in the external current-account surplus. Growing industrial unrest led to a massive flight from sterling in mid-June. After the authorities had borrowed £1,000 million from EEC central banks for support operations, the pound was set free to float on June 23 and promptly depreciated by almost 7%.

Money-market interest rates began to move up in May, and the bank rate was raised from 5 to 6% during the June crisis. The three-month interbank rate rose from a trough of $4\frac{1}{2}$% in April to $8\frac{1}{2}$% at the end of July, and during the same period the clearing banks progressively raised their base lending rates from $4\frac{1}{2}$ to 7%. In October the bank rate in its traditional form was replaced by a variable minimum rate for Bank of England lending to the discount market. The new rate, normally to be set weekly at a fixed margin above the Treasury bill tender rate, initially came to $7\frac{1}{4}$%. In early November, shortly after the government had announced a 90-day wage and price freeze, the Bank of England called on the banks to lodge with it special deposits equivalent to 1% of their deposit liabilities.

EEC Countries. In West Germany monetary policy was eased somewhat in late 1971, and this, together with a slowdown in wages and the realignment of exchange rates, helped to dispel business pessimism. A rebound in output in early 1972 brought recovery much sooner than had been expected. The reappearance of large capital inflows in early 1972, superimposed on an already rapid monetary expansion, was most unwelcome. In February the authorities lowered the discount rate to 3%, cut the banks' rediscount quotas by 10%, and increased from 30 to 40% the reserve requirements against the growth of banks' foreign liabilities. In March a new scheme was introduced under which West German companies had to hold cash deposits at the central bank in amounts equivalent to 40% of their new borrowing abroad.

Inflows again reached massive proportions in conjunction with the sterling crisis and the subsequent pressures on the dollar. Rejecting a return to floating, the authorities increased the cash deposit coefficient from 40 to 50% and closed certain loopholes. With West German interest rates high and speculative considerations prominent, the long-standing 25% interest-withholding tax on Deutsche Mark bonds issued by residents no longer served as an effective deterrent to purchasing by foreigners. The government therefore decided to ban the sale of domestic bonds to nonresidents outright. Reserve requirements against banks' liabilities to residents and nonresidents were increased, and the banks' rediscount quotas were cut in two stages, each time by 10%.

These measures absorbed the increase in bank liquidity that had resulted from the inflow of funds and the repayment of the countercyclical tax surcharge, and monetary expansion slowed down. Nevertheless, in September currency and demand deposits stood 14% higher than a year earlier, while money and time deposits had increased by 16% and bank credit was expanding strongly. Moreover, consumer prices had risen faster during the summer, and it also seemed likely that strains on productive resources might reappear. The authorities raised the discount

THOMAS A. JOHNSON—THE NEW YORK TIMES

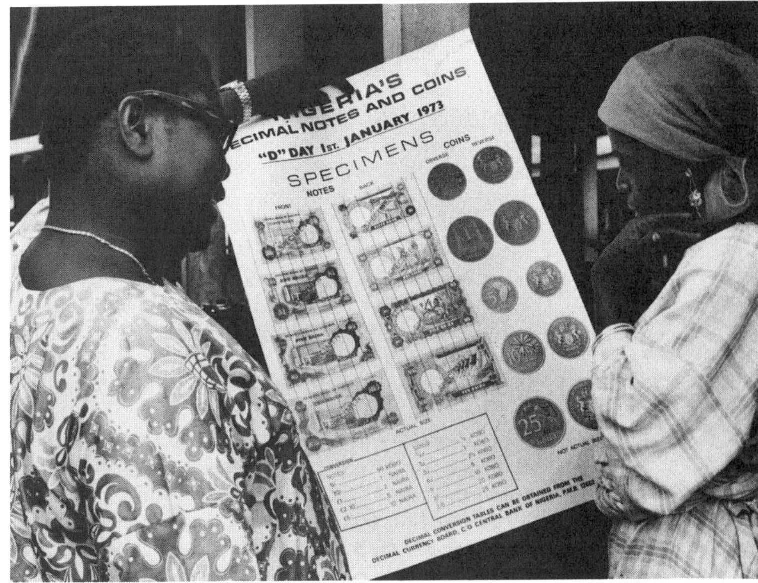

Emanuel Adeleye explains a poster illustrating the Nigerian decimal currency system, which was to be instituted on Jan. 1, 1973. Because 85% of the population is illiterate, Adeleye used movies, music, sound trucks, and drummers to prepare the nation for the transition.

rate from 3 to $4\frac{1}{2}$% in three stages between October and early December, and raised the official selling rates for money-market paper. A general rise in interest rates ensued.

In France the slowdown in economic growth in 1971 had been less marked than in most other countries, and the stimulatory measures adopted were deliberately limited. Monetary policy was eased slightly around the turn of the year; the banks' reserve requirements were lowered in December; and steps were taken to increase the availability of credit for industrial investment and housing. In addition, the authorities reduced money-market rates and sought to bring other domestic interest rates down. On the fiscal side, the government offered some investment incentives and announced a bringing forward of certain public expenditure, but did not depart from its objective of overall budgetary balance. In March reserve requirements against banks' domestic liabilities were lowered further, to 8% in the case of sight deposits.

Conditions soon began to change, however. In the first nine months of the year the money supply and bank credit to the private sector expanded at annual rates of about 25%. In addition, consumer prices began to rise more rapidly in the summer. The dual-exchange market system introduced in 1971 provided a good measure of protection against inflows of funds, but official purchases of foreign exchange, necessary to lend support to sterling in June, resulted in a considerable increase in bank liquidity.

In these circumstances reserve requirements against banks' liabilities to residents and nonresidents were increased. The reserve requirement relating to the increase in the granting of credit by financial institutions was raised from 2 to 4% in June, to 15% in September, and finally to 33% in November. Shortly afterward restrictions were placed on the terms for granting personal and housing credit. In view of the risk of inflows, steps were taken to keep money-market rates down in the spring and summer. Later in the year, with Eurodollar rates higher and domestic credit expanding strongly, the authorities sought to bring about a general rise in interest rates. The discount rate was raised from $5\frac{3}{4}$ to $7\frac{1}{2}$% in two stages in November.

In Italy industrial output had stopped falling by the

beginning of 1972, but recovery continued to be hindered by rising wage costs, industrial unrest, and political uncertainties. The government's budget was highly expansionary; support for the economy also came from investment financed by public funds and capital spending by the semipublic enterprises. Credit policy was kept very easy with the aim of encouraging a revival of private investment. In April, when the official discount rate was lowered from 4½ to 4%, the Bank of Italy curtailed the interest-bearing deposit facilities it had previously offered to the banks. When the banks responded by increasing their security investments, the authorities used moral suasion to encourage lending to the private sector. In August it liberalized the restrictions on credits of over 18 months.

In the wake of the sterling crisis, the EEC countries agreed, as an interim measure, to permit the Italian authorities to sell dollars instead of EEC currencies as a means of keeping the exchange rate within the narrow EEC margins. At the same time, steps were taken to stop capital outflows via the illegal export of banknotes, which had again assumed massive proportions, and the banks were authorized to incur net foreign deficits with the aim of increasing both official foreign exchange reserves and domestic bank liquidity.

In Belgium monetary restrictions were relaxed in late 1971 and early 1972 when a recession seemed imminent. Somewhat unexpectedly, economic activity accelerated in the spring, and credit demands strengthened. In the year ended June 1972, bank lending to the private sector increased by 16% and the money supply went up by 13%. To offset inflows of funds in June and July, the banks' rediscount quotas were cut, and the authorities arranged for the banks to make blocked deposits with the National Bank. The government continued to borrow in the domestic market in excess of its current financing requirement, and used the proceeds to retire its indebtedness abroad. To help slow down the expansion of money and credit, a further substantial part of the financial institutions' liquid funds was blocked at the central bank in November. Following a rise in market interest rates, the official discount rate was raised to 4½%.

Industrial output in the Netherlands rebounded at the beginning of 1972, but the economy continued to be plagued by growing unemployment, wage inflation, and inflows of funds. The government sought to meet its financial needs in the capital market, so that monetary policy could serve to keep domestic liquidity in check. The ceilings on bank credit were suspended in March, and the official discount rate was lowered from 5 to 4% in two stages during the first quarter. When speculative inflows emerged nonetheless, exchange restrictions were tightened. In July the countercyclical tax surcharge, which had been increased from 3 to 5% in January, was put back to 3%. Inflation was tackled directly by the use of price controls and by influencing central wage agreements.

Short-term interest rates having fallen under the influence of inflows of funds, the official discount rate was lowered to 3% in September. At the same time, minimum cash reserve requirements for banks, not used since 1963, were reintroduced, and open-market operations were employed to absorb the maximum of liquidity consistent with avoiding further inflows. After this, external constraints became less severe and the discount rate was raised to 4% in November.

Canada. Although recovery had been under way since late 1970, high unemployment dictated a continuation of fairly liberal monetary and fiscal policies in 1972. Since the Canadian dollar was continuing to float and was now above parity with the U.S. dollar, consideration also had to be given to preventing too sharp a rise in the exchange rate. The government's 1972–73 budget, presented in May, included measures to stimulate investment. For its part, the Bank of Canada, while generally acting to contain bank liquidity, eased the bank's positions when short-term interest rates rose in March and again in May. Partly to discourage inflows, the authorities in June secured the agreement of the chartered banks to a limit on the interest rates they paid on large short-term time deposits. Money-market interest rates later declined, but they remained higher than at the beginning of the year.

Total funds borrowed by nonfinancial sectors had risen sharply in 1971 and remained at a high level. In the first half of 1972 the government more than met its financing requirement by running down cash balances, and it was able to retire some outstanding debt. Nonfinancial businesses and other private borrowers raised funds on roughly the same scale as in 1971, while provincial and municipal governments further increased their borrowing.

Total currency and Canadian dollar deposits held by the public went up at an annual rate of about 18% in January–September. However, this partly reflected a sharp rise in time deposits in the first half of the year and was largely balanced by a decline in activity in the commercial paper market. A marked slowdown in monetary expansion occurred in the third quarter. Over the January–September period chartered banks' lending to the private sector expanded by over 23%, while their domestic liquid assets and foreign positions declined.

Japan. Influenced by expansionary monetary and fiscal policies and a return of confidence following the Smithsonian agreement, the two-year-old recession gave way to renewed general expansion early in 1972. Nevertheless, the authorities sought to stimulate growth still further in order to reduce the huge external trade surplus. A series of supplementary budgets during the year provided for large new investment programs and raised to 26% the planned increase in government general account spending in the 1972–73 fiscal year (April–March). In addition, monetary policy was kept easy; the discount rate was lowered from 5¼ to 4¾% in December 1971 and then to 4¼% in June 1972.

Total bank loans and discounts went up by almost 25% in the year ended September 1972, compared with something over 22% in the preceding 12 months. The growth of time and savings deposits accelerated but efforts to contain the rise in official reserves slowed growth of currency and demand deposits to an annual rate of 20% by September 1972. These efforts included proposals for direct export controls, lower tariffs, and a liberalization of restraints on both imports and capital outflows. On the financial side, privileged credit facilities for exporting were abolished, and greater scope was given to foreign bond issues in Japan. With more immediate effect, exchange controls over inflows were tightened, new foreign deposits with Japanese banks were made subject to a 50% reserve requirement, and the authorities provided the banks with funds to improve their net foreign positions.

(JOHN KNEESHAW)

See also Cooperatives; Economics; Economy, World; Government Finance; Housing; Investment, International; Merchandising; Payments and Reserves, International; Stock Exchanges.

Mongolia

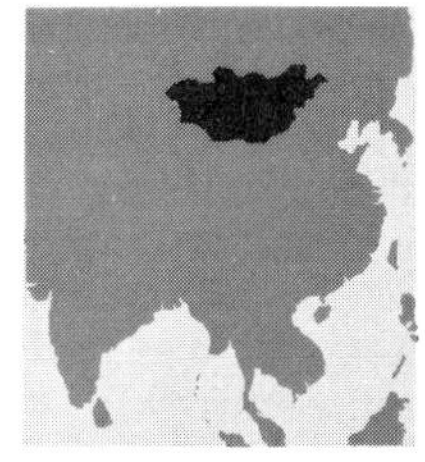

A people's republic of Asia lying between the U.S.S.R. and China, Mongolia occupies the geographic area known as Outer Mongolia. Area: 604,000 sq.mi. (1,565,000 sq.km.). Pop. (1972 est.): 1,301,000. Cap. and largest city: Ulan Bator (pop., 1969 est., 262,600). Language: Mongolian. Religion: Lamaistic Buddhism. First secretary of the Mongolian People's Revolutionary (Communist) Party and chairman of the Council of Ministers (premier) in 1972, Yumzhagiyen Tsedenbal; chairman of the Presidium of the Great People's Hural until May 20, Zhamsarangibin Sambuu.

The 76-year-old chairman of the Presidium of the Great People's Hural, Zhamsarangibin Sambuu, died on May 20, 1972. No successor had been elected by the year's end, but Sonomyn Luvsan, a party Politburo member and first deputy chairman of the Council of Ministers, was appointed deputy chairman of the Presidium. Tumenbayaryn Ragcha, one of the six deputy chairmen of the government, was promoted to first deputy chairman; he ceased to preside over the State Planning Committee, being replaced in this capacity by Byambyn Rinchinpelzhe. Damdinakhavin Maidar, a member of the Politburo and one of the deputy chairmen of the Council of Ministers, was also appointed a first deputy chairman, while Sonomyn Luvsangombo was appointed a deputy chairman of the Council of Ministers.

All these changes were probably connected with the unsatisfactory performance of the national economy, in particular the traditionally inefficient livestock sector on which the U.S.S.R. depended for much of the meat needed for the growing population in eastern Siberia and the Soviet Far East territories. By mid-1972 the total number of livestock amounted to 22,595,000, including 13,312,000 sheep, 4.2 million goats, 2,330,000 horses, 2,120,000 cattle and 633,000 camels.

(K. M. SMOGORZEWSKI)

MONGOLIA

Education. (1969–70) Primary, pupils 137,420, teachers 4,362; secondary, pupils 74,344, teachers 3,566; vocational, pupils 8,254; teacher training, pupils 2,239; higher (including University of Ulan Bator), students 7,226, teaching staff (1968–69) 700.

Finance. Monetary unit: tugrik, with (Sept. 18, 1972) an official exchange rate of 3.68 tugriks to U.S. $1 (9.60 tugriks = £1 sterling) and a tourist rate of 14.40 tugriks to £1 sterling. Budget (1972 est.): revenue 2,136,000,000 tugriks; expenditure 2,124,000,000 tugriks.

Foreign Trade. (1962) Imports 410 million tugriks; exports 274 million tugriks. Import sources (1960): U.S.S.R. 62%; China 23%; Czechoslovakia 5%. Export destinations (1960): U.S.S.R. 75%; Czechoslovakia 8%; China 5%. Main exports (1970): agricultural raw materials 58% (wool 44%, hides 6% in 1960); foodstuffs raw materials 20% (cattle 34% in 1960); foodstuffs 10% (butter and meat 8% in 1960).

Transport and Communications. Roads (1970) c. 75,000 km. (including c. 8,600 km. main roads). Railways (1971) 1,423 km. Telephones (Jan. 1971) 19,000. Radio receivers (Dec. 1970) 166,000. Television receivers (Dec. 1970) 20,000.

Agriculture. Production (in 000; metric tons; 1971: 1970 in parentheses): wheat c. 260 (c. 250); barley c. 9 (c. 9); potatoes c. 23 (c. 22). Livestock (in 000; Dec. 1970): cattle 2,108; sheep c. 13,312; goats c. 4,204; horses c. 2,320; camels c. 670.

Industry. Production (in 000; metric tons; 1970): coal 84; crude oil (1969) 4; electricity (kw-hr.) 516,000.

Morocco

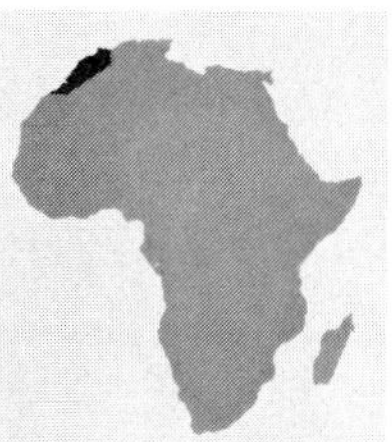

A constitutional monarchy of northwestern Africa, on the Atlantic Ocean and the Mediterranean Sea, Morocco is bordered by Algeria and Spanish Sahara. Area: 177,116 sq.mi. (458,730 sq.km.). Pop. (1971): 15,379,259. Cap.: Rabat (pop., 1971, 374,809). Largest city: Casablanca (pop., 1971, 1,506,373). Language: Arabic; Berber. Religion: Muslim. King, Hassan II; prime ministers in 1972, Muhammad Karim Lamrani and, from November 2, Ahmed Osman.

For the second consecutive year King Hassan survived an attempted coup. On August 16, 1972, as he returned from a private visit to France, his civil aircraft was attacked by Royal Moroccan Air Force fighters. The royal plane landed safely at Rabat, where Hassan escaped further strafing unscathed, attributing his survival to "divine providence." As in 1971, the coup plot was said to have been masterminded by one of the king's closest aides. This time it was Gen. Muhammad Oufkir, minister of defense, former minister of the interior, and a personal adviser of Hassan throughout his reign; Oufkir died at the royal palace the same night, supposedly by his own hand. Two

MOROCCO

Education. (1969–70) Primary, pupils 1,142,810, teachers 33,238; secondary, pupils 283,791, teachers 12,792; vocational, pupils 8,021, teachers 679; teacher training, students 3,622, teachers 121; higher, students 12,770, teaching staff (full-time) 571.

Finance. Monetary unit: dirham, with (Sept. 18, 1972) a par value of 4.66 dirhams to U.S. $1 (free rate of 11.40 dirhams = £1 sterling). Gold, SDRs, and foreign exchange, central bank: (June 1972) U.S. $251 million; (June 1971) U.S. $180 million. Budget (1972 est.): revenue 5,799,000,000 dirhams; expenditure 6,197,000,000 dirhams. Gross domestic product: (1970) 16,890,000,000 dirhams; (1969) 15,920,000,000 dirhams. Money supply: (June 1972) 6,715,000,000 dirhams; (June 1971) 5,804,000,000 dirhams. Cost of living (Casablanca; 1963 = 100): (June 1972) 117; (June 1971) 114.

Foreign Trade. (1971) Imports 3,532,000,000 dirhams; exports 2,520,000,000 dirhams. Main import sources: France 31%; U.S. 14%; West Germany 8%; Italy 6%. Main export destinations: France 36%; West Germany 8%; U.K. 5%; Italy 5%. Main exports: phosphates 23%; citrus fruit 15%; tomatoes 6%; fish 6%. Tourism (1970): visitors 701,000; gross receipts U.S. $134 million.

Transport and Communications. Roads (1971) 25,087 (including 14 km. expressways). Motor vehicles in use (1971): passenger 242,100; commercial (including buses) 90,500. Railways: (1969) 1,756 km.; traffic (1971) 541 million passenger-km., freight 2,775,000,000 net ton-km. Air traffic (1971): 486.8 million passenger-km.; freight 6,590,000 net ton-km. Shipping (1971): merchant vessels 100 gross tons and over 39; gross tonnage 55,585. Telephones (Dec. 1970) 168,000. Radio licenses (Dec. 1970) 935,000. Television receivers (Dec. 1970) 174,000.

Agriculture. Production (in 000; metric tons; 1971; 1970 in parentheses): wheat 2,188 (1,901); barley c. 2,570 (1,955); corn 390 (320); potatoes c. 300 (c. 300); oranges (1970) 876, (1969) 729; dry peas c. 42 (33); dry broad beans c. 190 (190); chick-peas c. 100 (137); wine c. 110 (125); olive oil c. 50 (c. 26); figs c. 65 (c. 65); dates c. 90 (c. 90); tomatoes c. 250 (c. 250); fish catch (1970) 256, (1969) 227. Livestock (in 000; 1970–71): cattle c. 3,630; sheep c. 17,500; goats c. 8,850; horses c. 400; mules c. 410; asses c. 940; camels c. 230; poultry c. 15,800.

Industry. Production (in 000; metric tons; 1971): coal 474; crude oil 23; cement 1,475; iron ore (55–60% metal content) 623; phosphate rock (1970) 11,424; manganese ore (metal content; 1970) 60; lead concentrates (metal content) 77; zinc concentrates (metal content) 13; electricity (excluding most industrial production; kw-hr.) 2,084,000.

Mormons:
see Religion

Tail section of Boeing 727 jet was damaged when the plane was attacked by Moroccan F-5 jet fighters in an assassination attempt on King Hassan II. The attack occurred when the plane carrying the king was returning to Rabat from France.

junior Air Force officers involved in the shooting flew to Gibraltar after the coup had failed but were returned to Morocco. Almost the entire staff of the Kenitra air base was suspended from duty, but it was not until October that 220 officers and men from the base were brought to trial. Eleven were sentenced to death on November 7, and 32 others received prison terms ranging from 3 to 20 years.

The Moroccan people had not been allowed during 1972 to forget the attempted coup of the previous year. More than 1,000 officers and men were tried for complicity in the 1971 attempt; one officer was given the death sentence and 88 others received prison terms. In other government action King Hassan promised to end corruption in the administration, and minor officials were sent to prison for embezzlement at trials in February and April. In December several former ministers were convicted of misuse of public funds and received sentences of up to 12 years' imprisonment and heavy fines.

King Hassan had also promised political reform, and in March he presented a new constitution which was duly approved by popular referendum. The constitution provided for the Cabinet to have increased executive powers and for two-thirds of the members of a new National Assembly to be elected. However, in April the king announced postponement of the proposed elections—on grounds that some two million voters were not registered. In November Prime Minister Karim Lamrani was replaced by Ahmed Osman, the king's brother-in-law, who formed a government of "national unity."

It was also an uncertain year in the schools. In January high-school students went on strike and, after months of demonstrations, arrests, and concessions, classes were only resumed at the end of April. Out of a total of 290,000 students, 40,000 remained absent, and the academic year had to be extended.

No serious effort was made to carry through a promised agrarian reform program until September, when King Hassan initiated the transfer of 90,000 ha. of formerly foreign-owned farming land to Moroccan peasants.

The holding of the summit conference of the Organization of African Unity (of which Hassan was chairman in 1972) in Rabat in June provided Morocco with the opportunity to continue its policy of mending fences with its neighbours. The border dispute with Algeria was finally settled (*see* ALGERIA); the presence at the conference of Pres. Habib Bourguiba of Tunisia brought the promise of closer cooperation between the Maghreb states; but, despite King Hassan's pressing invitation to Pres. Muammar al-Qaddafi of Libya to attend in "a spirit of reconciliation," Qaddafi stayed away and continued to be a fierce critic of the Moroccan monarchy. (PETER KILNER)

Motion Pictures

The major film festivals, usually indicative of current trends, exhibited only a few dominating works in 1972, such as Federico Fellini's *Roma,* or box-office marvels like *The Godfather,* that set aside the rest in a category of mediocrity. Both art and industry seemed to remain in a watershed between old and no-longer-viable creative and economic formulas and the confirmation of new modes of expression and new means of production that might solve the dilemma the previous two decades had produced: continuing inflation of costs paralleled by continual diminution of audiences in most sectors of the cinema world.

Co-production remained a prominent feature of world film production, an outstanding example being the coverage of the Olympic Games, held in Munich, W.Ger., by a team of directors from nine countries: Milos Forman (Czechoslovakian expatriate), Kon Ichikawa (Japan), Claude Lelouch (France), Yuri Ozerov (U.S.S.R.), Arthur Penn (U.S.), Michael Pfleghar (West Germany), John Schlesinger (U.K.), Ousmane Sembene (Senegal), and Mai Zetterling (Sweden).

An odd sidelight of the year was the poll held every decade by the British film magazine *Sight and Sound,* in which film critics of the whole world voted on the ten best films in the history of cinema. The top three in the 1972 poll were: Orson Welles's *Citizen Kane* (1941), Jean Renoir's *La Règle du Jeu* (1939), and Sergei M. Eisenstein's *The Battleship Potemkin* (1925). *Citizen Kane* had also been voted best film in 1962, with Michelangelo Antonioni's *L'Avventura* (1960) and *La Règle du Jeu* in second and third place. In 1972 *L'Avventura* fell to fifth place.

The year saw the deaths of John Grierson, 73, the architect of the British documentary cinema; Maurice Chevalier, 83, the veteran French entertainer; Lord Rank, 83, who as producer J. Arthur Rank was a major force in British film production in the 1940s and 1950s; and, among others, actors and actresses Betty Blythe, 72; Bill Boyd, 74; Brian Donlevy, 69; Miriam Hopkins, 70; Margaret Rutherford, 80; George Sanders, 66; and Brandon de Wilde, 30. (*See* OBITUARIES.) The animated film lost Max Fleischer, 83, whose creations included Koko the Clown, Betty Boop, and Popeye.

The English-Speaking Cinema. *United States.* In 1971 the phenomenal box-office success of *Love Story* gave an unexpected injection of optimism to the old, commercial Hollywood. In 1972, against all odds and expectations, a single film surpassed the success of *Love Story*—*The Godfather* was confidently expected to gross more than $150 million to become the biggest money earner in cinema history. The two successes made Paramount (whose founder, Adolph Zukor, was still living in 1972—his 100th year) one of the most prosperous of the surviving old Hollywood companies. Based on Mario Puzo's novel about a Mafia family,

The Godfather was on the surface no more than an accomplished commercial entertainment—well scripted, tautly directed by Francis Ford Coppola, and finely played, principally by Al Pacino and Marlon Brando (*see* BIOGRAPHY). Its phenomenal success was hard to explain. Perhaps audiences were eager to identify with those who create for themselves life-and-death power over others, or perhaps the essentially romantic view of the Mafia provided a false solace for the social conscience.

A striking feature of U.S. production in 1972 was the number of new directors from other fields of activity within or without the industry. Among the most interesting were the actors Alan Arkin, who filmed Jules Feiffer's play *Little Murders;* Clint Eastwood, whose *Play Misty for Me* told of a philandering disc jockey terrorized by one of his "victims," a psychopathic woman; Jack Lemmon, who directed his ofttimes partner Walter Matthau in *Kotch,* a comicpathetic study of an unwanted old man who asserts a new role in life for himself; Peter Fonda, whose *The Hired Hand* was a stylish if overly symbolic Western; and Charlton Heston, who made a rather overly reverent *Antony and Cleopatra.* Elaine May, who as an entertainer had partnered Mike Nichols, played (as partner to Walter Matthau) in her own film *A New Leaf,* an extremely funny pastiche of the 1930s situation comedy.

Producers Floyd Mutrux and Larry Turman turned directors and filmed, respectively, *Dusty and Sweets McGee,* a horrifying exposé of narcotics abuse, which used actors alongside actual drug addicts, and *The Marriage of a Young Stockbroker,* from a novel by Charles Webb, about a man whose marriage is threatened by his voyeuristic tendencies. Douglas Trumbull, a special effects director who had worked on Stanley Kubrick's *2001: A Space Odyssey,* directed his first feature film, *Silent Running,* which treated the currently fashionable theme of ecology through a science-fiction projection of a future in which the earth is deprived of all vegetation.

British directors continued to work in the U.S. with varying success: Peter Yates's *The Hot Rock* was a very fast and witty variation on the theme of a minutely planned theft that goes disastrously wrong. Anthony Harvey's *They Might Be Giants,* an attractive fantasy about a lawyer who fancies himself Sherlock Holmes but finally proves a good deal saner than anyone else in his immediate neighbourhood, suffered from severe cutting by its distributors. John Boorman's *Deliverance* was an able adaptation of James Dickey's novel about four men whose sporty weekend on the river becomes a fight for survival against primitive human forces; like Boorman's previous films, it tended to suggest more philosophical depth than it could ultimately claim. Peter Watkins continued to explore his burning concern with the perils of the contemporary world in *Punishment Park,* a fantasy set in a not-too-far-distant future America where nonconformists are herded into a disciplinary area and hounded to death or into conformity.

A group of attractive films by already established American directors might be loosely linked by their concern to examine man's individual personality in relation to his historical and social heritage. For his first film since *Butch Cassidy and the Sundance Kid,* George Roy Hill directed *Slaughterhouse-Five.* An adaptation of the best-selling novel by Kurt Vonnegut, Jr., about the life and death of a nonentity, centring on the traumatic moment of his presence at the bombing of Dresden, the film failed to capture the anarchy and unsparing absurdity of the original. Sam Peckinpah, having provoked heated controversy, particularly in Britain, with the extreme violence of *Straw Dogs,* turned to an unusually quiet, reflective, and beautifully controlled subject in *Junior Bonner,* about a father and son whose stubborn loyalty to older values of individual physical and personal accomplishment sets them apart from contemporary society and from their own family. Paul Newman's second feature film as a director, *Sometimes a Great Notion* (in Britain: *Never Give an Inch*), was also about individualism: a highly intelligent, taut drama about the relationship within a family that antagonizes a whole community by defying the union in the lumber camp that is their livelihood. (Not the least attraction of the film was its documentary detail of the lumberjack's work.) Veteran John Huston created one of the most appealing American pictures of the year with *Fat City.* Returning to the scenes and style of his earliest films, it told the story of two fighters in the seedier lower reaches of boxing—one on his way up, the other on his way down, but not so very far apart in ultimate prospects.

Turning to specific genres, there seemed to be a revival of interest in police thrillers following the runaway success late in 1971 of *The French Connection,* a fast, deglamorized drama of a real life investigation of narcotics smuggling. Don Siegel's *Dirty Harry* had Clint Eastwood as a tough cop with unconventional personal methods; *Shaft* and *Shaft's Big Score,* directed by Gordon Parks (*see* BIOGRAPHY), offered a black detective (Richard Roundtree). There were also comic variations on the theme, such as Richard A. Colla's *Fuzz,* which peopled a realistic police station with convincingly incompetent cops.

A major phenomenon during the year was the box-office success of movies featuring black actors and playing primarily to black audiences. Pioneered by *Cotton Comes to Harlem* in 1970, the films constituted a major part of the U.S. market in 1972. Many were criticized by both blacks and whites for their violence, their stereotyped "supercool" heroes, and their tendencies to exacerbate black-white relations and to glorify undesirable activities. Chief among the

COURTESY, UNIVERSAL STUDIO

In a poignant moment from the movie "Sometimes a Great Notion," Paul Newman realizes that his cousin, played by Richard Jaeckel, is doomed by a rising river and a log that has him pinned. Adapted from the Ken Kesey novel and directed by Newman, the film explores the rugged individualism of a logging family.

latter was Gordon Parks, Jr.'s *Super Fly,* about a cocaine pusher in Harlem; it raised a storm of protest but set box-office records. Other successes in these categories included the above-mentioned *Shaft* and *Shaft's Big Score, Melinda* with Calvin Lockhart as a Los Angeles disc jockey killing white gangsters who had murdered his girl friend, and *Slaughter* with Jim Brown also fighting the mob. Black Westerns included *Buck and the Preacher* with Sidney Poitier and Harry Belafonte and *The Legend of Nigger Charley* starring Fred Williamson.

Proponents of these movies claimed that blacks were starved for screen heroes and denied that the film violence against whites would be translated to the real world. At the year's end *Sounder,* directed by Martin Ritt and written by Lonne Elder III, provided a contrast to its violence-filled predecessors. It told a quiet and moving story about a boy's search for his father in rural Louisiana in the 1930s.

The biggest musical, Bob Fosse's *Cabaret,* was a disappointing version of the stage musical in turn adapted from the John Van Druten stage play based on Christopher Isherwood's *Goodbye to Berlin* stories. In its determination to provide a vehicle for the unquestionable talents of Liza Minnelli (*see* BIOGRAPHY), it compromised the original, crudely overstating the background of the rise of Nazism, which Isherwood had presented only as a subtle, if increasingly asphyxiating, atmosphere. The year's other major musical was Arthur Hiller's *Man of La Mancha,* again adapted from the stage. Outstanding among comedies was Peter Bogdanovich's *What's Up, Doc?,* starring Barbra Streisand and Ryan O'Neal and patterned after the "screwball comedies" of the 1930s.

Fritz the Cat, doyen of underground comic strip characters, made his film debut in a feature-length animated cartoon directed by Ralph Bakshi. Robert Crumb's original creature, a would-be hippie feline, retained a fair amount of his social bite and sexual outspokenness. Although inevitably a little less outrageous than in the original magazine drawings, Fritz still presented a striking contrast to the days when udders were censored off Walt Disney cows.

In the realm of *cinéma vérité,* Robert Kaylor's *Roller Derby* exposed the bleak glory of the stars of a brutal popular sport; Elliott Erwitt's *Beauty Knows No Pain* detailed the rigorous training and fanatical credo of a Texan breed of drum majorettes; *Marjoe,* directed by Howard Smith and Sarah Kernochan, was the confessions of a one-time infant-prodigy Pentecostal preacher and healer; and *Gimme Shelter,* directed by David and Albert Maysles and Charlotte Zwerin, described the Rolling Stones' U.S. tour and the 1969 Altamont concert that ended in a fatal stabbing. The richly gifted Fred Wiseman continued his reflective examinations of U.S. institutions with *High School, Law and Order* (on the police force), and *Essene,* which described the tensions underneath the apparently quiet surface of contemporary monastic life.

The U.S. Academy of Motion Picture Arts and Sciences presented its annual Academy Awards in April. *The French Connection* took the Oscars for best movie, best screenplay from nonoriginal material, best direction (William Friedkin), and best actor (Gene Hackman). Awards for best original screenplay went to Paddy Chayefsky for *The Hospital;* for cinematography to Oswald Morris for *Fiddler on the Roof;* for best actress to Jane Fonda for her performance in *Klute;* and for best supporting actor and actress to Ben Johnson and Cloris Leachman for their roles in Peter Bogdanovich's *The Last Picture Show.* Vittorio de Sica's *The Garden of the Finzi-Contini*s was voted best foreign-language film, and Walon Green's *The Hellstrom Chronicle,* the best documentary of the year. Charlie Chaplin, returning to the U.S. for the first time in 20 years, received a special award (*see* BIOGRAPHY).

Britain. The biggest British production of the year was Carl Foreman's *Young Winston,* directed by Richard Attenborough. The film's box-office success might promise further episodes of the long saga of Winston Churchill's extraordinary career. As portrayed by Simon Ward, the young Churchill lacked something of the aggressive ruthlessness that in real life won him a good deal of contemporary unpopularity. Evidently recognizing that a more warty picture of the hero would be bad for business, the film makers concentrated rather on his sad relationship with his father, the ill-fated Lord Randolph Churchill, and his American mother.

Historical and costume pictures were very much in vogue. U.S. director Franklin Schaffner's *Nicholas and Alexandra* proved a pedestrian pictorialization of the last days of the Romanovs, sacrificing invention to a hollow quest for distinction. Waris Hussein's *Henry VIII and His Six Wives* distinctly betrayed its origins as a television series, while Charles Jarrott made a very overly upholstered *Mary, Queen of Scots.* On the literary side Roman Polanski's *Macbeth* was a bewildering mixture of visual magnificence and plodding interpretation.

Writer Robert Bolt chose a historical theme for his debut as a director in *Lamb,* a fictionalized biography of Lady Caroline Lamb, starring the director's wife, Sarah Miles. A rather more modest first film was actor

Annual Cinema Attendance

Country	Total in 000	Per capita
Afghanistan	6,100	0.4
Albania	7,800	4
Algeria	28,700	2.3
Angola	2,800	0.5
Argentina	98,000	4
Australia	32,000	3
Austria	50,600	7
Bahrain	1,400	7
Barbados	1,200	5
Belgium	31,500	3
Bhutan	500	0.6
Brazil	234,700	3
British Honduras	2,000	18
Bulgaria	110,200	13
Burma	218,000	8
Burundi	500	0.2
Cambodia	20,000	3
Canada	97,600	5
Central African Republic	500	0.4
Chad	1,300	0.4
Chile	66,500	7
Colombia	92,800	5
Congo	1,700	2
Cyprus	6,000	10
Czechoslovakia	120,600	8
Dahomey	1,200	0.4
Denmark	26,000	5
Ecuador	15,100	3
Egypt	59,300	1.9
Equatorial Guinea	500	1.7
Faeroe Islands	200	7
Falkland Islands	20	10
Finland	10,000	2
France	215,700	4
French Guiana	700	14
Germany, East	100,600	6
Germany, West	181,000	3
Ghana	18,700	2
Greenland	400	11
Guam	500	5
Guatemala	9,000	2
Hong Kong	84,900	21
Hungary	82,200	8
Iceland	2,300	1.2
India	2,190,000	4
Iran	16,400	0.6
Iraq	8,300	1.3
Israel	49,100	17
Italy	557,000	10
Jamaica	3,600	2
Japan	287,000	3
Jordan	6,100	3
Korea, South	168,400	5
Kuwait	3,800	6.7
Laos	1,000	0.3
Liberia	900	0.8
Luxembourg	1,900	6
Malagasy Republic	4,500	0.7
Malaysia	99,100	9.4
Mali	2,500	0.5
Malta	3,500	11
Mauritius	8,300	10
Mexico	358,700	7
Monaco	100	6
Morocco	18,200	1.3
Mozambique	4,100	0.6
Netherlands	34,300	3
New Caledonia	1,000	11
New Zealand	19,600	7
Niger	800	0.2
Norway	15,000	4
Pakistan	276,600	3
Panama	5,000	4
Poland	141,300	4
Portugal	26,700	3
Qatar	500	5
Réunion	1,200	3
Romania	200,400	10
St. Kitts-Nevis-Anguilla	70	1.1
Senegal	5,200	1.5
Sierra Leone	100	.05
Singapore	28,900	14
Somalia	3,200	1.3
Spain	383,800	12
Sri Lanka (Ceylon)	97,700	8
Surinam	1,700	5
Swaziland	100	0.2
Sweden	28,200	4
Switzerland	33,000	5
Taiwan	868,100	66
Trinidad and Tobago	8,400	8
Tunisia	8,000	1.6
Uganda	2,000	0.3
U.S.S.R.	4,655,900	19
United Kingdom	215,000	4
United States	1,300,000	7
Upper Volta	1,000	0.2
Venezuela	37,700	4
Vietnam, South	25,500	1.4
Western Samoa	500	3
Yemen (San'a')	1,800	0.4
Yugoslavia	90,300	4

KEYSTONE

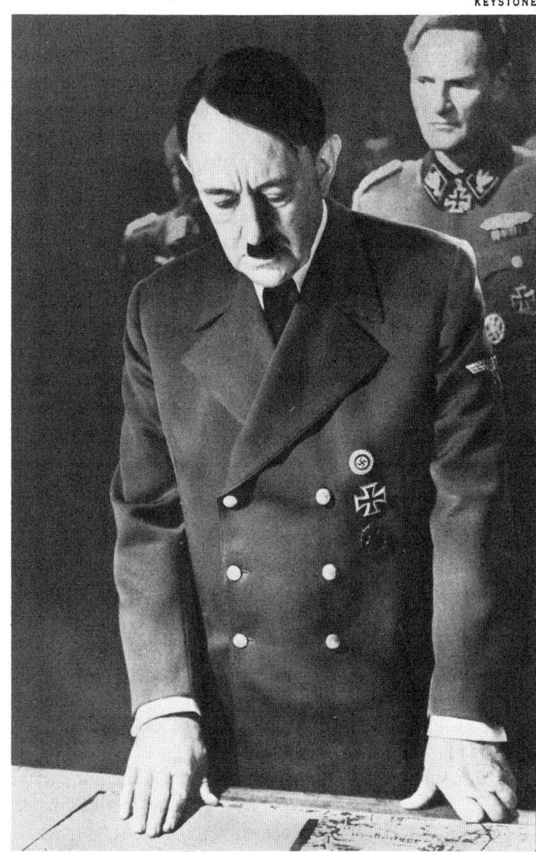

Sir Alec Guinness bears a chilling resemblance to the führer in the title role of "Hitler: The Last Ten Days," filmed in 1972.

David Hemmings' *Running Scared,* a stylish if mannered morality play about a young man's self-discovery through his first encounter with death.

Two distinguished veterans made new films in their native Britain. Working there for the first time in 20 years, Alfred Hitchcock directed *Frenzy,* an old-style piece of Grand Guignol, with archaic charm, rich humour, and incomparable virtuosity. Peter Shaffer's play *The Public Eye* provided a rather stage-bound and inadequate screenplay for Sir Carol Reed's *Follow Me.*

Ken Russell continued to display a bemusing and erratic variety. *The Boy Friend* presented Sandy Wilson's stage musical within the film as if by an indifferent seaside theatrical company to launch a pastiche of 1930s Busby Berkeley musicals. *Savage Messiah* was a fictional re-creation of the life and career of the French-born Vorticist sculptor Henri Gaudier-Brzeska and his loyal Polish companion, Sophie Brzeska.

However, the year's most interesting work was to be found in offbeat and shoestring productions. Philip Trevelyan's *The Moon and the Sledgehammer* was a closeup view of a family of eccentrics, living reclusive lives in a forest, deeply involved in love affairs with ancient machinery of one sort or another. Bill Douglas' *My Childhood,* a deeply felt autobiographical reminiscence of a boyhood in a poor Scottish home, won the Silver Lion of the Venice Film Festival. Christopher Mason's *All the Advantages* was much praised in the Quinzaine des Réalisateurs at the Cannes festival in May. In this film the child of a broken home was rich, but ultimately more solitary and tragic than the child from the Scottish slums. Mike Leigh's *Bleak Moments* provided an unsparingly accurate, funny, and pathetic observation of a sad suburban life—a friendless girl, stuck with her loyalty to a mentally defective sister, failing miserably to establish relationships with men.

Western Europe. *France.* The directors who had emerged as the "new wave" of the early 1960s remained at the centre of progressive cinema activity. After several years of silence, Jean-Luc Godard reappeared, collaborating with Jean-Pierre Gorin as co-director of *Tout Va Bien.* Starring Yves Montand and Jane Fonda, this allegory of a film maker and a journalist and their researches into the state of French labour relations made more concessions to the audience than other recent works, which had tended to take the form of uncompromising political tracts. François Truffaut turned to the English scene for *Anne and Muriel* (in the U.S.: *Two English Girls*), a tender tale of two sisters in love with the same man. Following a brilliant series of thrillers, Claude Chabrol's *Ten Days' Wonder* was something of a disappointment: the director's quirky invention and observation seemed somehow inhibited by the indifferent Ellery Queen original. Luis Buñuel added a further masterly work to his record with *Le Charme discret de la Bourgeoisie,* a surrealist nightmare about a group of middle-class people whose constantly frustrated efforts to arrange a dinner together serve to expose all their pretenses and pretensions.

Italy. The year's most outstanding film was undoubtedly Fellini's *Roma,* an impressionistic picture of the Eternal City itself, nostalgically interwoven with a self-portrait of Fellini at the time of his first encounter with Rome at the end of the 1930s. A mounting crescendo of spectacle and fantasy, the film culminates in an ecclesiastical fashion show and an eerie ballet of motorcycles in the empty night city.

Rather oddly, Pier Paolo Pasolini's *Canterbury Tales,* largely shot in England, won the main prize at the Berlin Film Festival before it was actually finished. The version seen in Berlin, virtually a rough-cut, was a formless and scatological affair. By the end of 1972 the definitive version still had not appeared. While Pasolini was shooting in Britain, Joseph Losey was shooting *The Assassination of Trotsky* in Italy. The historical facts proved to give Losey and his writer, Nicholas Mosley, all too little to work on. However, while the historical limits of the character reduced Richard Burton's Trotski to something of a mannequin, the mysterious, never properly identified assassin (played by Alain Delon) turned out a familiar Losey hero—weak, uncertain of his own motives, driven to betrayal and destruction.

West Germany. Rainer Werner Fassbinder consolidated his reputation with *The Bitter Tears of Petra von Kant,* a claustrophobic chamber piece adapted from a play of the director's own experimental theatre. *The Merchant of Four Seasons,* an equally claustrophobic drama and almost a parody of the German "street films" of the mid-1920s, was a brilliant and merciless denunciation of middle-class conventions, ambitions, and relationships. New talents appeared in Klaus Emmerich, whose *Rosa and Lin,* originally made for television, was an anarchic exposé of current cultural attitudes through the affairs of a glossy-magazine couple in a glossy-magazine home, and in Wim Wenders' strange existentialist anecdote, *The Goalkeeper's Fear of the Penalty.*

Sweden. While Ingmar Bergman was finishing *Cries and Whispers,* released at the end of 1972, Sweden enjoyed one of its biggest box-office successes with *The Emigrants,* Jan Troell's film version of Vilhelm Moberg's saga of the 19th-century Swedish emigration to North America. The film's income reputedly saved Svensk Filmindustri, the world's oldest film company still in active production, from financial ruin. To non-Swedish audiences it seemed a somewhat pedestrian though dazzlingly spectacular costume piece.

Denmark. Jørgen Leth's *Life in Denmark* adopted a Godardian style to produce an alarmingly sardonic image of contemporary life in Denmark through a

On assuming his father's title as the godfather, Michael Corleone, played by Al Pacino, receives the pledge of loyalty—a kiss on the hands—from Clemenza, played by Richard Castellano, in the 1972 box-office hit "The Godfather," based on Mario Puzo's best-selling novel.

UPI COMPIX

COURTESY, WARNER BROS.

Scene from "Deliverance," adapted from James Dickey's best seller, shows a dead man being carried to his grave as Burt Reynolds disposes of the arrow that killed him.

series of *cinéma vérité* interviews introduced by brief, bald titles.

Norway. Finnish-born director Caspar Wrede made a brave attempt at an adaptation of Aleksandr Solzhenitsyn's *One Day in the Life of Ivan Denisovitch,* played in English with Tom Courtenay in the leading role, but ultimately failed to capture the authentic feel of the Siberian labour camp.

Finland. Having suffered a serious decline in the middle 1960s, Finnish cinema showed clear signs of recovery, thanks to the efforts of the Finnish Film Foundation, formed on somewhat similar lines to the Swedish Film Institute. At the same time, Jorn Donner, Finland's most active and internationally successful director, launched his own production company. The year saw a number of films of quality, including Risto Jarva's *When the Skies Fall,* Eija-Elina Bergholm's *Little Marja,* and Mikko Niskanen's *Eight Deadly Shots,* which made masterful use of a recent real-life murder to illuminate the spiritual poverty of rural Finland.

Eastern Europe. *U.S.S.R.* In August the longtime head of Soviet cinema, Aleksei Romanov, was replaced. Never a notable progressive, Romanov was charged with being too liberal and lax in applying the rigid rules of socialist realism. The appointment of a successor with more party than cinema experience suggested unpromising prospects for the immediate future of Soviet movies.

However, Larissa Shepitko's *You and Me* provided a sympathetic and refreshing study of a medical scientist's failure to come to terms with contemporary society or with his own emotional needs. Andrei Tarkovski's science fiction *Solaris,* based on the novel by Polish writer Stanislaw Lem, was a fascinating exploration of time and space on a planet in whose hallucinatory atmosphere phantoms are conjured and human time is turned upside down.

Hungary. Miklos Jancso won the director's prize at Cannes for *Red Psalm,* in which Hungary's political dilemma at the turn of the century was transformed into a strange ballet played out on the endless plains by groups of peasants, landowners, soldiers, and priests, gyrating around one another and around the camera, humiliating, killing, singing. A masterpiece of mise-en-scène, the film nevertheless left doubts as to whether Jancso had not reached an impasse, repeating effects rather than creating new styles. Zoltan Huszarik's first feature, *Sindbad,* was a stylish, virtuoso re-creation of the Budapest of Gyula Krudy, the early 20th-century impressionist writer.

Yugoslavia. The Yugoslav capacity for self-criticism of socialist society continued, even though Dusan Makavejev had not completed a film since his *WR—Mysteries of the Organism.* An evident follower of Makavejev, Bata Cengic made *Scenes from the Life of Shock Workers,* which subjected the creation of the Revolution to some biting, though humorous, criticism.

Romania. A film by a Romanian director emerged, exceptionally, on the international scene in 1972. Julian Mihu's *Felix and Otilia,* though handicapped by being adapted from a sprawling Romanian classic, revealed a distinctive decorative style and a feeling for the bizarre.

Asia. *Japan.* The avant-garde poet, playwright, and theatre director Shuji Terayama turned to the screen with two startling films. *Emperor Tomato Ketchup,* cut for propriety's sake from feature length to a mere 28 minutes, posited the notion of bloody revolution by children against the repression by adults. A full feature film, *Throw Away Your Books, Run into the Streets,* based on a stage play, was an equally startling visualization of some of the obsessions of the contemporary young.

Nagisa Oshima, the most prominent progressive in the cinema, made *Dear Summer Sister.* As in *The Ceremony,* Oshima used personal affairs as metaphors for historical situations: the relationship between Japan and Okinawa is paralleled in the story of a girl in search of a long-lost half brother.

India. In *Company Limited* Satyajit Ray examined a new sector of Bengali society, the world of advertising and executive infighting in a mock-Western industrial empire. An ambitious young executive provokes a strike to cover up executive failure, and in the process discovers the limitations of his own conscience.

Iran. Teheran's first international film festival gave foreign critics an opportunity to see the work of the emergent young cinema of Iran. Daryush Mehrjui followed *The Cow,* which had attracted attention in 1971, with *The Postman,* a visually rich comedy-drama about working-class life in contemporary Iran. Bahram Baizai's *Hard Rain* was a quirky, personal, and firmly constructed story of a young schoolmaster's successful effort to win over the pupils in a forbidding slum school.

Other Areas. While little significant new work came out of Latin America in 1972, the year brought good films from several countries with no previous established film tradition. From Kuwait came Khalid Siddik's *The Cruel Sea,* a harsh critique of the life and rituals of rural society. From Jamaica, Perry Henzell's *The Harder They Come* was an assured, tragic, and funny tale about a slum boy whose ambitions are inevitably thwarted by a corrupt establishment. Of the emergent African cinemas, Senegal clearly took the lead. Ousmane Sembene's *Emitai* dramatized the abortive resistance of a Senegalese village to French Army attempts to requisition its rice in 1944. A highly sophisticated film, its political purpose was the more effective for its scrupulous fairness and rich humour.

(DAVID ROBINSON)

Nontheatrical. Perhaps the most colourful film event of the year was the World Film Festival of Animated Films held at Zagreb, Yugos., June 19–24. It was most appropriate that this festival should be held in Yugoslavia, as in recent years the Yugoslav film makers and their neighbours in Czechoslovakia and Poland had been distinguishing themselves in creating films in animation. However, 25 countries were represented, including the U.S., which led in the number of films selected for showing.

Although the principal focus of the meeting was on films for entertainment and the exercise of sheer artistic imagination, a number of nontheatrical films designed for use in education or industry were also shown. Several films in this category received top awards. Among these were *Hot Stuff,* produced by the National Film Board of Canada, which received first prize in educational animated film. *Bathtub,* a Sesame Street production, won second prize.

Trends in U.S. nontheatrical films indicated that the industry was pulling out of the slump of the past two years. Spending in all markets for nontheatrical pictures, which had shown a slight decline in 1970, had an increase in 1971 of 8% according to reliable reports. Spending for materials and equipment in all audiovisual media, including 8-mm. film, filmstrips, and cassettes as well as 16-mm. film, also gained 8%, amounting to an estimated $1.4 billion in 1971.

The number of films produced for these major markets increased only moderately, with sharp declines in some fields. Production for schools gained 6% with 1,390 films released, while output for universities and colleges had a similar increase with 880 films. There were 9,630 films produced for business and industry, an increase of 7%. However, films for the medical field declined 19%, while those for community agencies fell by 48%. The production of avant-garde, experimental, and student films, which had been having notable growth in recent years, also appeared to have declined by about one-third. The production and distribution of 8-mm. films continued strong with some 2,630 released.

Perhaps the most significant trend indicated by these reports is that in recent years there has been no dramatic growth in the use of 16-mm. films in schools and educational agencies. At the same time, there has been a sharp growth in related media, such as filmstrips, which had a 17% increase in sales in 1971.

(JOHN T. BOBBITT)

See also Photography; Television and Radio.

ENCYCLOPÆDIA BRITANNICA FILMS. *Let Them Learn* (1967); *Growing* (1969)—a computer-animated film; *Practical Filmmaking* (1972).

Motor Sports

Automobiles. International Formula One grand prix racing in 1972 again operated under rules that limited engine capacity to a maximum of three litres. Much attention was paid to safety, with the banning of full-scale airfoils (which increase road adhesion of the wheels and thus promote improved controlability), as they were apt to break away and cause danger, and with precautions taken against fire. Safety considerations instituted by the Grand Prix Drivers' Association (GPDA) and originated for the protection of spectators were now concentrated on the safety of the participants, and modifications costing much money proved an embarrassment to many race organizers and circuit owners. The GPDA refused to allow racing to take place over the Spa circuit in Belgium because it was regarded as potentially dangerous, but did return to the Nürburgring for the German Grand Prix and moved the Belgian race to Nivelles-Baulers. Race sponsorship moved into an advanced sphere when Colin Chapman permitted his Team Lotus cars to race as John Player specials because of the financial support Lotus received from the Player tobacco company, and the British Grand Prix race held at Brands Hatch, Kent, took the title of the John Player Grand Prix.

The 1972 season was scheduled to comprise 15 major grand prix counting toward the world drivers' championship. The Mexican Grand Prix did not materialize, however, because officials could not ensure spectator safety. Before all the point-earning contests had been held Emerson Fittipaldi from Brazil, driving one of the John Player Lotus 72 cars powered with the still-effective Cosworth-Ford V-8 engine, had won the title of world champion with a convincing series of victories. The 1971 world champion, Jackie Stewart of Scotland, did not get the Tyrrell cars he wanted until late in the season and was also ill for part of the year. He also became a centre of controversy over his pronounced concern for driver protection in terms of safer circuits and racing conditions.

The Formula One championship racing opened with the Argentine Grand Prix at Buenos Aires. Driving a Tyrrell 003, Stewart won with a time of 160.56 kph. Second place was filled by the New Zealand driver Denis Hulme, who was in a McLaren M19A/2, the McLaren team continuing to race in spite of the death of Bruce McLaren in a test-drive accident the previous year and being sponsored by the cosmetics firm of Yardley. Third place was taken by Jackie Ickx of Belgium, who was driving for Ferrari in a 312B2 car with Ferrari's own horizontally opposed 12-cylinder engine. In the South African Grand Prix over the Kyalami circuit the McLaren M19A was victorious in the hands of Hulme, who averaged 183.83 kph. Fittipaldi began his successful season there with second place, third position going to Peter Revson of the U.S., driving another McLaren M19.

The Spanish Grand Prix at Jarama, near Madrid, indicated the shape of future events when Fittipaldi won, at 148.627 kph, in a torsion bar-sprung Lotus 72D with inboard brakes, revised rear springing, and a rear airfoil mounted above the transmission. Although fastest lap was set by Ickx' Ferrari at the record speed of 151.284 kph, the Lotus and Fittipaldi's driving put the Italian cars second and third at the finish. The Monaco Grand Prix which followed was not significant, as it was run under conditions of heavy rain and mist. The Frenchman Jean-Pierre Beltoise contrived to keep his BRM P160 in front, chased unenthusiastically by Ickx and Fittipaldi.

The Belgian Grand Prix, which lost most of its character by being transferred to the Nivelles-Baulers course, consolidated Fittipaldi's position as he won at 182.483 kph from François Cevert's Tyrrell and Hulme's McLaren. Chris Amon entered the picture by putting up the best race lap in a Matra-Simca MS120. The next fixture should have been the traditional Dutch Grand Prix at the Zandvoort circuit, but the GPDA was frightened of having to race there and moved on to the French Grand Prix, held at Clermont-Ferrand, but not to the full satisfaction of the barrier-conscious modern racing driver. The Charade circuit was a real test of driving skill, and it is to his credit that there Stewart showed a return to form, the Tyrrell he was driving winning at an average speed of 163.453 kph from Fittipaldi's John Player Lotus.

The competition next moved to Brands Hatch circuit for the John Player race, which was in reality the

Motorboating:
see Motor Sports

Motor Industry:
see Industrial Review

British Grand Prix. It proved an uninspiring event that Fittipaldi had no difficulty in winning from Stewart, the winner's speed being 180.34 kph, although it had been Stewart who had made the fastest lap, at 182.78 kph in a race in which 26 cars started but only 13 survived. Another testing race was the German Grand Prix—back on the twisting, undulating Nürburgring—which proved a resounding triumph for Ferrari. The red Italian cars, both 312Bs, finished in first and second and were driven, respectively, by Ickx and the Swiss Gianclaudio (Clay) Regazzoni. That it was no idle victory was demonstrated by Ickx setting a new lap record for the famous circuit, at 189.6 kph. The Austrian Grand Prix over the Österreichring was a fast race, won by Fittipaldi from Hulme and Revson. Safety was again the prevailing note at Monza, where the 43rd Italian Grand Prix was held, obstacles having been introduced to reduce the speed of the cars as they went into what were formerly fast bends. Again Fittipaldi demonstrated his mastery, and by winning this race, at the high speed of 211.812 kph, from Mike Hailwood and Hulme, he clinched the 1972 drivers' world championship though there were still two more races to go.

With the championship settled and the Mexican Grand Prix canceled, only the United States and Canadian grand prix remained. The former, held at Watkins Glen, N.Y., saw the Tyrrell team overcome its earlier troubles with Stewart the winner at 185.22 kph. His teammate Cevert was second, and Hulme finished third. Stewart established a fresh Formula One record for the course. The same pattern was seen at Mosport Park, Ont., where Stewart not only won the Canadian Grand Prix, at a speed of 183.92 kph for the 80 laps in dry but misty weather, but also set a new Formula One lap record of 189.207 kph. This proved that the Cosworth-Ford V-8 engine could continue to win important races.

The great sports car-racing long-distance races rivaled the grand prix competition, being run over the traditional circuits for longer durations or greater distances and at notably high speeds. Before the longest of them all, the 24-hour race at Le Mans, France, was held, Ferrari had already won the sports car championship and so did not compete in the French classic. Ferrari's withdrawal robbed the race of some of its fire, but out of 55 starters a French Matra-Simca MS670 shared by Graham Hill of Great Britain and Henri Pescarolo of France gained the first victory in this race for France since 1950. Another of these three-litre V-12 cars was second, ahead of a three-litre flat-8 Porsche. Mario Andretti and Ickx teamed to win the Daytona Continental, the final Sebring (Fla.) 12-hour race, and the BOAC 1,000 at Brands Hatch. International rallying flourished during 1972, with the much-publicized Monte Carlo Rally being won by Sandro Munari and Mario Manucci of Italy in a Lancia Fulvia and the East African Safari by Hannu Mikkola of Finland and Gunnar Palm of Sweden in a Ford. (WILLIAM C. BODDY)

Large purses and few surprises in the winner's circle marked U.S. automobile racing in 1972. The champions were well-known names, Joe Leonard repeating as United States Auto Club (USAC) titleholder, Richard Petty winning an unprecedented fourth National Association for Stock Car Auto Racing (NASCAR) Winston Cup crown, and—a mild surprise—George Follmer winning the Canadian-American Challenge Cup, premier series of the Sports Car Club of America (SCCA). Mark Donohue won the Indianapolis 500, and at Daytona Beach, Fla., veteran A. J. Foyt won the Daytona 500 classic, setting a record stock-car speed for the race of 161.5 mph.

Even in racing machinery, well-known names dominated and the surprises were small ones. In USAC championship car competition, the Dan Gurney Eagles, powered by what were still called Offenhauser engines, set an enviable record for top qualifying speed thanks to Bobby Unser and Jerry Grant, but the McLaren-Offenhausers and the Maurice Phillippe-designed Parnelli Offenhausers won more victories. In NASCAR racing, the battle was among the Wood Bros. Mercury, the Junior Johnson-prepared Chevrolet intermediates, and the Petty Engineering Chrysler products, which were as much Dodge as Plymouth in 1972.

Once again the most important race, the Indianapolis 500, was mired in controversy. That Donohue in his Sunoco Penske McLaren-Offenhauser won $218,767 for setting a new race record of 163.46 mph was overshadowed by USAC officials taking second place away from Gurney driver Jerry Grant for having his tank filled from the fuel supply of teammate Bobby Unser. Grant had made a pit stop 12 laps from the end to change a tire as a precaution, and only a check of TV film footage revealed the pit crew's error. For that he was penalized 12 laps, losing $70,000 in prize money and ten places. The furious protest at the severity of the penalty for such a minor infraction was futile.

The second major race of the USAC 500-mi. Triple Crown had its own kind of controversy because of Hurricane Agnes, which flooded Pocono Raceway in northeastern Pennsylvania. The race was postponed at the behest of the state's governor after drivers had taken time trials. A month later, Joe Leonard was made the winner of $84,080 after teammate Al Unser, who crossed first, was penalized a lap for passing on a caution light. This was a key victory in helping Leonard to his second national championship. He also

Driving number 66, Mark Donohue roars past Joe Leonard in the Indianapolis 500. Donohue won with an average speed of 163.46 mph, a record.

AUTHENTICATED NEWS INTERNATIONAL

won the Milwaukee 150 and the Michigan 200 and finished consistently in the top ten most of the year.

Veteran Roger McCluskey scored his first 500-mi. victory in the third race of the Triple Crown at Ontario, Calif. The event was delayed by rain and slowed as pit personnel chased jackrabbits off the course, but McCluskey took home $127,600 for his 151.54 mph race speed. Rookie Mike Hiss finished second.

Richard Petty set the racing tone for NASCAR competition by winning the opening event, the Winston Western 500 at Riverside, Calif., over Bobby Allison in Junior Johnson's Coca-Cola Chevrolet. In moving to his fourth NASCAR crown and the Winston Cup money, Petty, driving Plymouths and Dodges, won eight races, mostly on shorter tracks, and campaigned the entire circuit. Even so, he did not clinch the crown until the Texas 500, final race of the season (won by his former teammate, Buddy Baker, in the K&K Dodge that had been evacuated by Bobby Isaac). Bobby Allison won ten races and the most prize money, $271,395, but by finishing fourth to Petty's third in the Texas race he missed the crown. He was, however, named Driver of the Year in a poll of automotive sports writers.

When the season began, it seemed that it was Petty *v.* the Wood Bros. Driving the Mercury of the latter, Foyt won the Daytona 500 and the rich Miller High Life 500 at Ontario, Calif., and then turned the car over to David Pearson who proceeded to win the Rebel 400 at Darlington, S.C., Daytona's Firecracker 400, the first Talladega, Ala., race, two at Michigan International Speedway, and at Dover, Del.

But by that time Allison had begun his depredations, beating Foyt by 0.16 sec. at Atlanta, Ga., winning twice at Bristol, Tenn., and triumphing at Trenton, N.J., Atlanta, Dover, Del., and in the Southern 500 and National 500 at Charlotte, N.C.

The SCCA's Canadian-American Challenge Cup series was interesting because the domination of Denis Hulme and the McLaren Chevrolets was shattered and because there was a clear changing of the guard, from the nonturbocharged Chevrolet to the 900-hp turbocharged Porsche. Mark Donohue of the Penske Porsche-Audi team did all the development driving on the turbo-Porsche and came into the series as the favourite. But he finished second in the opening race to Hulme because of turbocharger woes. The demise of the St. Jovite, Que., track forced a wait of a month until the next event at Road Atlanta, and when that came about, George Follmer was the Porsche hope with Donohue sidelined because of a practice injury. Follmer won easily, starting his march to the title, which included victories at Mid-Ohio, Elkhart Lake, Wis., Monterey, Calif., and Riverside. Before the Can-Am series Follmer also won the SCCA Trans-Am series for Javelin, the American Motors car that was the series' only factory entry. In the 2.5 Challenge for smaller cars, the BRE Datsuns swept to a convincing victory. (ROBERT J. FENDELL)

Motorcycles. In the early grand prix counting toward the 1972 road-race championships, MV Agusta's star rider, Giacomo Agostini, champion for several successive years in the 350- and 500-cc classes, appeared to be in danger of losing his crown to Yamaha-mounted Jarno Saarinen of Finland. But the Italian rallied and by the middle of the season was occupying his customary place at the top. Results were: 500 cc and 350 cc, G. Agostini (MV Agusta); 250 cc, J. Saarinen (Yamaha); 125 cc and 50 cc, A. Nieto (Derbi); and sidecar, K. Enders (BMW).

UPI COMPIX

Moto-cross champion Åke Jonsson of Sweden displays his winning form in the Trans-American Motorcycle Association Championship on Oct. 29, 1972, in Houston, Tex. Jonsson won the three 30-minute events to take first place.

In the Isle of Man Tourist Trophy (the British round of the championship), Agostini won the 500 cc, six-lap, 226-mi. Senior race, at 104.02 mph, with another Italian MV rider, A. Pagani, placing second at 98.13 mph. A few days earlier Agostini had scored his ninth Tourist Trophy victory in winning the 350-cc Junior event at 102.03 mph, a record speed for the five-lap race. He was followed by eight Yamaha-mounted riders. Other Isle of Man winners were: 125 cc, C. Mortimer (Yamaha), 87.49 mph; 250 cc, P. W. Read (Yamaha), 99.68 mph; sidecar (500 cc), S. Schauzu (BMW), 91.85 mph; 750 cc, Schauzu (560 BMW), 90.97 mph; and Formula 750, R. Pickrell (Triumph), 104.23 mph. The production-machine classes were won as follows: 750 cc, R. Pickrell (Triumph), 100 mph; 500 cc, S. Woods (Suzuki), 92.20 mph; and 250 cc, J. Williams (Honda), 85.32 mph.

In British national racing the class winners were: 125 cc and 250 cc, S. Machin; 350 cc, M. Grant; 500 cc, J. Harvey; and 750 cc, D. Potter. The prestigious "Superbike" contest promoted by the weekly newspaper *Motor Cycle News* was won by J. Cooper. The chief amateur racing event of the year, the Manx Grand Prix, held on the Isle of Man in September, was won by D. Hughes (Matchless), 500 cc; K. J. Huggett (Aermacchi), 350 cc; and W. P. Carpenter (Yamaha), 250 cc.

The 750-cc class gained rapidly in importance during the year, with Norton Villiers fielding a factory team of three sponsored by the tobacco company John Player and Sons, Ltd., and BSA-Triumph having partially factory-supported riders. At the end of the season, however, BSA-Triumph, hard hit by financial troubles since late 1971, announced its withdrawal from race participation.

In the world moto-cross championship both the 500-cc and 250-cc classes were dominated by the Japanese Suzuki concern, with machines ridden by Joel Robert (250 cc) and Roger de Coster (500 cc) of Belgium.

1972 U.S. National Motorboat Racing Champions

Inboard

Class/Owner (Champion)
7 Litre (division I) Leonard R. Ryden Elk Grove Village, Ill.
7 Litre (division II) Antonio G. Rodrigues Valley Stream, N.Y.
5 Litre George E. Fox Van Nuys, Calif., Wayne Thompson Northridge, Calif., and John R. Wolf Sherman Oaks, Calif.
280 Hydro Anthony Scartine New Castle, Del.
225 Hydro John R. Woods St. Louis, Mo.
150 Hydro Richard L. Snider Columbus, Ind.
145 Hydro Willard S. Wilson, Jr. Wilmington, Del.
850 Hydro F. C. Moor Hialeah, Fla.
98 Hydro Richard L. Cooper Miami Shores, Fla.
44 Runabout William R. Overby Metairie, La.
Cracker Box Danny Edward Mang Glendale, Calif.
Jersey Speed Skiff Arthur Cummins, Jr. Highlands, N.J.
Super Stock James L. Gaskins, Jr. Denton, N.C.
Ski Racing Runabout John F. Kiely, Jr. Long Branch, N.J.
B Racing Runabout Ernest Rose Patterson, Calif.
E Racing Runabout Wes Knudsen Provo, Utah
K Racing Runabout Charles E. Boyd Commerce, Calif.
E Service Runabout Otis Benjamin Geiger Coral Springs, Fla.
F Service Runabout Curt Brayer Miami, Fla.

Outboard

Class/Driver
A Racing Runabout Alan Ishii Pasadena, Calif.
B Racing Runabout Bill Seebold, Jr. St. Louis, Mo.
C Racing Runabout Rich Fuchslin Dixon, Calif.
D Racing Runabout Bill Seebold, Jr. St. Louis, Mo.
F Racing Runabout Douglas W. Bindrim Lindenhurst, N.Y.
A Hydro Tim Butts Mount Clemens, Mich.
B Hydro Douglas Thompson Bloomfield, Ont.
C Hydro Fred Hauenstein, Jr. San Jose, Calif.
D Hydro Dan Kirts Elkhart, Ind.
F Hydro Wayne Walgrave Beaver Creek, Minn.

Motor Vehicles:
see Disasters;
Industrial Review;
Motor Sports;
Transportation

The International Six Days' Trial, highlight of the trials calendar, was held in Czechoslovakia, with both the top award, the World Trophy, and the secondary Silver Vase contest going to the home team, mounted on Jawa-CZ machines. (CYRIL J. AYTON)

Motorboats. Unlimited hydroplane racing was dominated in 1972 by a 44-year-old marketing executive from Seattle, Wash. Bill Muncey, a veteran of 15 years on the thunderboat circuit, piloted "Atlas Van Lines" to victory in every event but one. His string included the prestigious Gold Cup, established in 1904. With this triumph Muncey had won the trophy five times—a record equaled only by Gar Wood, who won five straight in the 1920s.

Muncey opened the season on May 21 by winning the Championship Spark Plug Regatta in Miami's Marine Stadium. He then went on to take the Kentucky Governor's Cup two weeks later at Owensboro, Ky.; the Gold Cup at Detroit June 25; and the American Power Boat Association World Championship in Madison, Ind., July 4.

Meanwhile, the runner-up boat in the early season standings lost its driver when Billy Schumacher withdrew from the cockpit of "Pride of Pay 'N Pak." Bill Sterett, Sr., took the helm at Madison, but could do no better than sixth. His son, Bill, Jr., moved into the driver's seat for the President's Cup race at Washington, D.C., the following week. Young Sterett's chances were so lightly regarded that the boat's owner, Dave Heerensberger, scheduled an early departure to catch a plane. It left without him, however, as Sterett out-dueled Muncey in the final race of the event, trading the lead several times over the 15-mi. distance before winning in a final charge to the finish.

It was Muncey's only loss, depriving him of a clean sweep for the season, as he later went on to win the Tri-Cities Atomic Cup at Pasco, Wash., and the Seafair Trophy at Seattle. He won $46,200 on the tour and earned his fourth national driver's championship. "Atlas Van Lines" was the top boat, with "Pride of Pay 'N Pak" second. But due to the change of drivers in mid-season, Terry Sterett aboard "Miss Budweiser" became runner-up on the roster of drivers.

Outboard marathon racing, growing steadily in recent years, gradually acquired strong overtones of stock-car racing as outboard manufacturers fielded professional teams. Jimbo McConnell, with Evinrude power, won the Parker Nine Hour for Outboard Marine Corp. Mercury bounced back after de-bugging a six-carburetor racing engine delivering 200 hp. Bob Hering, a Mercury factory driver, won the Milan Three Hour in April; the Miami "225" in July; returned to Europe to win the Amsterdam Three Hour in September; and teamed with Italian driver Renato Molinari to win the Six Hours of Paris in October.

Tommy Posey put Johnson Outboards in the win column with victories in August at Provo, Utah, and St. Louis, Mo., but Mercury took the rest of the major races. Bill Seebold, Jr., won at Morgan City, La., and St. Marys, O.; Bill Sirois triumphed at Dayton, O.; and Don Pruett won a pair in California. Johnnie Sanders won the outboard world championship at Lake Havasu, Ariz., in November; his record 87 mph was nearly 5 mph faster than Sirois' winning time in 1971.

Offshore powerboat racing closed its year with a storybook finish. Bobby Rautbord, of Miami Beach, Fla., began his expensive chase after the world driving title with winter victories in Argentina and Uruguay. He missed winning the Sam Griffith Memorial in Florida by scant seconds but then won abroad in Spain, Norway, and Sweden. Italy's Carlo Bonomi won at Naples, in France, and two British events: the Poole Offshore race and the prestigious Cowes run. Winning the mid-October Miami–Nassau race would have allowed Bonomi one final chance for the title in the Hennessy Key West race, final event of the year in November.

Meantime, a ruckus over engines, simmering for months, erupted just before the Nassau run. Many drivers were using exotic—and costly—racing crankshafts with the required stock blocks and heads. Ten protests were filed prior to the race, and a mass dismantling of engines was in prospect when the race was over.

Bob Magoon of Miami Beach mediated the dispute, and it was agreed that the protests would be withdrawn and only the winning boat checked. Magoon, who wrapped up the U.S. offshore inboard title earlier in the year, went on to win the race. His boat, a Cigarette with Kiekhaefer Aeromarine engines, was generally accepted as completely legal. Magoon finished 29 minutes ahead of runner-up Bonomi, and by edging the Italian driver he clinched the world title for Rautbord. (J. E. MARTENHOFF)

Mountaineering

Of note during the 1972 season was the failure of two expeditions to Mt. Everest, both attempted on the yet unclimbed southwest face of the mountain. The first of these was the international West German-Austrian-British attempt. The failure was blamed in part on a high incidence of illness in the party and also, as with the 1971 international expedition with the same objective, on differences of opinion between the leaders and the members of various nationalities as to the conduct of the expedition. These differences, which were aired in the world press, tended to confirm the impression given by the 1971 and previous international expeditions to the Himalayas that the scales are weighted against success for parties of mixed nationalities attempting major objectives. The leader of the expedition, Karl Herrligkoffer, was forced to retire on May 5 because of ill health. Under climbing leaders Michel Anderl (W.Ger.), Felix Kuen (Aus.), and Don Whillans (U.K.) the expedition pressed on to reach camp six at 26,896 ft. when the attempt on the summit had to be abandoned, on May 23.

The 11-man British expedition led by Chris Bonington had to give up its autumn attempt on Everest on November 14, after pitching its sixth and last camp at 27,000 ft.—the highest point ever reached by the southwest route. Heavy snows and continuing bad weather, which had already put the expedition three weeks behind schedule, caused the failure. A large number of Japanese expeditions again attempted the Himalayas, with a heavy toll of fatal accidents.

Meanwhile, in the Alps, the urge for first solo ascents and first winter ascents went on. Descents of major faces on skis became a new fashion.

Ascents were made in the summer of 1971 by new routes on Punta Gugliermina, Mont Blanc (Brenva face by a new route near Route Major), Dent d'Hérens (north face), Scheidegg Wetterhorn (north face), and Dent Blanche (north face, two new routes). New routes were made on the following in the Dolomites: Cima della Terra Nova, Sorelle de Sorapis, Pala di San Martino, Cima di Lastei, Cima Sant' Anna,

Torre Margherita, and Cima di Pravecchio. Notable climbs were made in the Alps on the Grosshorn (north face), Gross Schlossberg (west ridge, Engelhörner), Col Maudit (east face), Monte Rosa, Piz Roseg, and other peaks. In winter 1971–72 first winter ascents were made in the Alps on Mont Blanc de Tacul (northeast face, three new routes), Aiguille du Midi and other pinnacles of the western Alps, the Matterhorn (south face), Mont Dolent (north face), Scheidegg Wetterhorn (northwest face), and Torstein (south face). In the summer of 1972 a new line was climbed on the Aiguille d'Argentière (northeast face).

In the U.S.S.R. and Asia climbs along new routes were made in the summer of 1971 in the Caucasus (Dombai Ulgen, Ushba west face, Ushba east face, and Koshtan Tau south spur), Iran (Alam Kuh), Pamirs (Pik Communism), and Hindu Kush (Mir Samir). In the Himalayas, in the post-monsoon season of 1971, nine expeditions failed: on Everest (Arg.), Makalu II (Jap.), Dhaulagiri V (Jap., one killed), Rakaposhi (W.Ger.), Annapurna South (Jap.), Patrosi Himal (U.K.), Kanjiroba (Jap.), Hiunchuli (U.S.), and Fluted Peak (U.S.). The Japanese, however, succeeded in climbing Gangapurna at a cost of eight lives. In 1972, in addition to the two Everest expeditions mentioned above, the following Himalayan attempts were made and failed: Lhotse Shar (W.Ger.), Makalu II (Jap.), Manaslu (S.Kor., with 15 killed), and Dhaulagiri IV (Jap., one killed). Successful climbs were made on Manaslu west face (Aus., two killed) and Nampa (Jap., one killed).

In Alaska during the 1972 summer, new routes were climbed on Mt. McKinley south face, Huntingdon east ridge, and St. Elias east ridge; failures occurred on Moose's Tooth east face. In Canada during the summer of 1971, new routes were ascended in the Purcells, Selkirks, and Coast Range (Peak 8,000 and Raleigh eastern ice face and southeast ridge); and the Misty Icefields and Whitemantle Icecap were explored, with many peaks climbed. In the United States during the summer of 1971, climbers ascended the northeast face of Mt. Redoubt in the Cascades and many new routes in the Sierra Nevada. In the Andes Tumarinaraju and Milpocraju in Bolivia were climbed in 1972. Sword and Cueno Norte were ascended in Patagonia in 1971–72, while failures took place on Cerro Torre, Fitzroy, Cerro Huemul, and Paine Central Tower east face. (JOHN NEILL)

Museums and Galleries

Works of art came under increasing risk of theft, pillage, vandalism, and illicit export in 1972. Michelangelo's marble "Pietà" in St. Peter's, Rome, was seriously damaged by a vandal wielding a hammer. (*See* VATICAN CITY STATE.)

The "reported stolen" columns in professional art reviews made increasingly pessimistic reading. In Italy an average of 16 works were stolen every day from museums, churches, and galleries—a total of 7,560 in 1971. In France 440 pictures were reported stolen in 1969, 1,500 in 1970, and 3,000 in 1971. The term "art drain" was coined in Italy to describe the migration of works of art from artistically rich to monetarily rich countries.

To study the risks incurred by works of art, UNESCO and the Belgian National Commission for UNESCO held a three-day meeting near Brussels that recognized the need for international cooperation in reinforcing anticrime efforts. In cooperation with insurance experts and the police, the International Council of Museums (ICOM) began making an inventory of available security equipment to facilitate use of the most efficient systems. A 1959 Interpol international study on the subject was to be brought up to date. In the U.S. the National Endowment for the Arts provided funds for a study of security programs. (*See* CRIME.)

Less dramatic but perhaps even more vexing were the many smaller acts of vandalism and theft reported by U.S. museums. Full-scale electronic devices, formerly considered a luxury, were added by the Kimbell Art Museum in Fort Worth, Tex., and the Lowe Art Museum in Miami, Fla. Problems of security were especially disturbing as museums, in the face of financial difficulties, were attempting to enhance their image as public service institutions. Despite the difficulties it posed for security, the Metropolitan Museum of Art, New York City, decided to rescind the ban against "Sunday painters" copying works of art directly in the museum's public galleries.

The pressures of current museum life were clearly responsible for the vacancies in the directors' ranks of important museums in the U.S. The resignations of the directors of the Boston Museum of Fine Art, the Museum of Modern Art, New York City, and the Art Institute of Chicago, although each related to factors peculiar to the institution involved, pointed up a problematical situation. The director of a large museum was called upon to work in the complex areas of business and politics, as well as art. On the—perhaps unrealistic—theory that business matters are best handled by an administrator while artistic affairs are left to specialists, the Art Institute of Chicago changed the title of director to president and appointed E. Laurence Chalmers, Jr., a former chancellor of the University of Kansas with little previous experience in the art world.

A major controversy during the year began when the art editor of the *New York Times* questioned the right of the Metropolitan Museum of Art to auction off several dozen works of art in order to raise funds for future acquisitions. The process, euphemistically referred to as "deaccessioning," was, in fact, common. Museums frequently sold works that were thought to be declining in value in terms of the totality of the collection or when they needed funds. During 1972, for instance, the Brooklyn Museum raised $50,000 with an auction of 56 master prints, and the recently formed Museum of American Folk Art, New York City, supported its new building fund with an auction of 100 major items. In line with the current opinion that a museum is accountable to the public, critics of the sales policy hoped, at least, for a less secret approach. In an effort to mollify the critics, the Metropolitan planned an exhibition of recent acquisitions with a catalog describing the details of the transactions.

Many felt that museums in the U.S. could no longer depend on private and local donations for support but would have to look to extensive aid from the federal government. This view was expressed in congressional hearings on the Museum Services Act. Cosponsored by John Brademas (Dem., Ind.) and Dan Rostenkowski (Dem., Ill.), the bill would provide $40 million annually to assist museums in meeting general operating expenses. As of 1972 the federal government provided less than 1% of museum operating costs. The Museum Services Act would make it possible for the fed-

LEE ROMERO—THE NEW YORK TIMES

An employee of the Metropolitan Museum of Art in New York City protests proposed staff layoffs and program cuts announced by director Thomas Hoving on May 8, 1972.

Mozambique: *see* Dependent States

Muhammadanism: *see* Religion

Municipal Government: *see* Cities and Urban Affairs

THE NEW YORK TIMES

Blind children excitedly explore tactile and auditory stimuli at the Tactile Gallery of the Wadsworth Atheneum in Hartford, Conn.

eral government to assume up to 50% of the cost of renovating museum facilities, constructing exhibitions, and general administrative costs. In Canada a new museum policy was proposed by the government; it included a $1 million emergency purchase fund to retain national treasures in Canada and $1.5 million for a conservation network.

In London the trustees of both the National Gallery and the Tate Gallery announced publicly that if the British government persisted in plans to impose charges for visiting museums and galleries, they would openly defy governmental ruling by instituting free days.

New Museums. The U.S. Congress unanimously agreed to the establishment of a museum devoted to the Polish-American hero Tadeusz Kosciuszko. The new Costume Institute of the Metropolitan Museum of Art opened its doors in October 1971. In Texas five new museum buildings were either completed or under construction: the Contemporary Arts Museum, Houston; the Tyler Museum of Art, Tyler; the Kimbell Art Museum, Fort Worth; the Art Museum of South Texas, Corpus Christi; and the Amarillo Art Center. At the Museum of Art, Rhode Island School of Design, Providence, a redesigned gallery to house selections from the museum's collection of African, pre-Columbian, North American, Indian, Eskimo, and Oceanic art opened in September.

A new museum in São Paulo, Braz., the Museu da Casa Brasileira (Museum of the Brazilian Home), was to be installed in the Fabio Prado Palace at the request of Fabio Prado. The museum planned to regroup, classify, and number all objects of value connected with the customs and habits of Brazil, with emphasis on the São Paulo area. In February 1972 the French National Museum of Folk Arts and Traditions opened in Paris. When complete, its cultural gallery would present an overall view of French ethnology.

A new wing of the Boymans-van Beuningen Museum in Rotterdam, Neth., housed the museum's modern art collection comprising paintings by Picasso, Kandinsky, Dali, Magritte, Vasarely, and others.

The new Neptune Hall at the British National Maritime Museum, Greenwich, London, opened on July 21, and the adjoining Barge House, with its Hage Barge, built by 18th-century architect William Kent for Frederick Louis, prince of Wales, reopened at the same time. A new Hall of Primitive Art costing £220,000 opened in the Royal Scottish Museum, Edinburgh. The Carnegie Trust offered the Singleton Open Air Museum, Chichester, Sussex, a grant of £3,300 toward rebuilding and equipping an 18th-century barn as an educational centre. In West Germany the new and up-to-date rooms of the Museum of Bavaria reopened in Munich. The new Ethnology Museum in West Berlin's Dahlen complex of galleries had an inventory of 330,000 objects and could show 5,000 displays. Plans were well under way for a National Antarctic Exhibition, Research, and Reference Centre to be incorporated into the Canterbury Museum, Christchurch, N.Z. In India the Nehru Children's Museum in Calcutta opened in November.

At the Carnegie Institute in Pittsburgh Edward Larrabee Barnes, architect of the Walker Art Center in Minneapolis, Minn., was chosen to design a $12 million addition to the present structure. The relatively little-known Museum of the City of New York announced a $6 million expansion program. The Smithsonian Institution, Washington, D.C., opened the Renwick Gallery after an extensive restoration; it would serve both as a museum and as a locale for official government entertainment. In New York City the Carnegie Corporation presented the Fifth Avenue mansion of Andrew Carnegie as a future home for the Cooper-Hewitt Museum of Decorative Arts and Design. Also in New York City the American Museum of Immigration opened at the base of the Statue of Liberty in New York Harbor.

Acquisitions. The British Museum was given two exceptionally important William Blake watercolours: "Angels Hovering over the Body of Jesus" and "The Angels Rolling Away the Stone." With the help of the National Art Collections Fund, the Ashmolean Museum, Oxford, acquired an important drawing in silverpoint by Hans Holbein the Elder.

The "Overlord Embroidery," the most monumental piece of needlework since the Bayeux Tapestry, was shown for the first time at the Imperial War Museum in London. The embroidery, commemorating Britain's D-Day landings in Normandy in 1944, had been commissioned by Lord Dulverton for presentation to the museum.

The Metropolitan Museum of Art acquired "A Dance Lesson" by Degas (about 1879) in pastel, Fragonard's "Fanfan Playing with Polichinelle and Friends," and, from Mme Umberto de Martini, a portrait of a child by Goya. Joseph Hirshhorn and the Hirshhorn Foundation donated 166 sculptures and 160 paintings worth about $7 million to the Hirshhorn Museum and Sculpture Garden, under construction in Washington, D.C. A 1929 Model A Ford mail truck, valued by the Antique Automobile Club of America at $11,000, was acquired by the Museum of Science and Industry, Chicago. W. Averell Harriman gave his collection of 23 French Impressionist paintings to the National Gallery in Washington, including works by Cézanne, Gauguin, Picasso, Rousseau, Seurat, Courbet, Degas, and Matisse. The Los Angeles County Museum of Art received the $1 million Hammer Collection of works by Rembrandt, Renoir, Modigliani, and van Gogh. The Norton Simon Foundation purchased a still life by Zurbaran (1633) for $3 million, the highest price ever paid for a still life painting. The Museum of Modern Art announced that Picasso had donated to the museum a model of a sculpture, "Construction in Wire" (1928–29), which was to be constructed as a 15-ft.-high Cor-ten steel sculpture for the museum's garden.

International Cooperation. Under its Participation Program, UNESCO sent experts in the development of museums to a number of less developed countries. An international round table was held at Santiago, Chile, on the adaptation of museums to the contemporary world. More than 50 holders of UNESCO fellowships carried out training programs at one of UNESCO's regional training centres in the conservation of cultural property and museography.

The first Conference of African Museums, at Livingstone, Zambia, in July, discussed the lack of cooperation between African museums. A small secretariat was established to coordinate efforts toward the formation of an Association of African Museums with the Provisional Board of the African Museums Association (established in 1969). The Indian National Committee of the International Council of Museums adopted resolutions requesting all Indian museums, archives, and surveys to express solidarity with their counterparts in Bangladesh and to provide assistance for reconstruction, restoration, and conservation. The committee also requested all museums and similar institutions in India not to purchase artistic or archaeological treasures or rare documents that might have been stolen from Bangladesh, and invited the Bangladesh authorities to cooperate closely with the museums.

In Los Angeles, in March, the Executive Committee of the American Association of Museums (AAM) discussed the growing fear that the war in Southeast Asia would jeopardize archaeological and cultural treasures. Member institutions and collectors of Asian art were urged to be especially careful about proper documentation when acquiring objects of Cambodian art. The AAM's annual meeting, held in Mexico City in June, was devoted to the international exchange of cultural objects and the need to provide orderly legal means for their export and import.

(JOSHUA B. KIND; ANDREW SZPAKOWSKI)

See also Art Exhibitions; Art Sales.

Music

The musical world celebrated several centenaries and significant birthdays in 1972. The two most important were those of Aleksandr Scriabin, the Russian composer whose stature had come to be more fully recognized during the course of the previous decade or two, and Ralph Vaughan Williams, the English composer who, though his music had never penetrated very deeply beyond his native land, was nonetheless recognized by many eminent musicians as a figure of considerable importance in 20th-century music. Predictably, Scriabin's centenary was celebrated a good deal more widely, while that of his English contemporary was more or less confined to Great Britain. The most frequently heard works by the Russian composer were perhaps those for the piano, which were widely performed during the year, particularly by his compatriot Vladimir Ashkenazy, who played several of the sonatas at recitals in various major cities, and also by John Ogdon. All of Vaughan Williams' operas were broadcast in Britain by the BBC, his nine symphonies were recorded by André Previn (*see* BIOGRAPHY) and the London Symphony Orchestra, and many of his choral works were revived in performances up and down the English countryside, in which his music was so firmly rooted.

The 70th birthday of Sir William Walton on March 29 was also the occasion of musical celebrations in Great Britain. Both familiar and less well known works were performed in a number of concerts arranged to mark the event. Several articles in the March issue of *Musical Times* were devoted to a reassessment of Walton's work and his contribution to 20th-century music. On March 28, a special birthday concert given by the London Symphony Orchestra included his *Improvisations* on a Britten theme, his concerto for viola, and the dramatic work for baritone, chorus, and orchestra, *Belshazzar's Feast.* On BBC television "Herodiade's Flea," a previously discarded number from *Façade,* received its first performance in a special birthday tribute; the program also included a garland of pieces by Malcolm Arnold, Hans Werner Henze, Previn, and Malcolm Williamson.

On Nov. 26, 1971, at London's Royal Festival Hall, British Prime Minister Edward Heath made musical history by conducting the London Symphony Orchestra in Elgar's *Cockaigne* overture, and indeed making quite a good job of it. On Dec. 7, 1971, the same orchestra gave the London premiere of Hans Werner Henze's Sixth Symphony, with the composer himself conducting. The work was first performed in Havana, Cuba, and was deliberately intended as an expression of Henze's left-wing political thought. It required a large orchestra divided into two groups, one including an electric guitar and the other an amplified violin, the two instruments both playing important parts in the symphony. A quotation from the song of the Vietnamese National Liberation Front was also worked into the texture of the piece.

Also at the end of 1971, the Fellowship of Australian Composers gathered in Sydney to ratify a manifesto of objectives first aired earlier in the same year at Perth in a seminar entitled "The Contemporary Australian Composer and Society." The International Music Council's 14th Assembly took place in Moscow in October 1971. The assembly approved the activities of the council during the previous two years and considerable attention was devoted to the expansion of creative contacts between musicians from East and West.

The trend toward fairly informal presentation of modern scores in the concert hall, instigated by Pierre Boulez, continued both in London and in New York. In January 1972 Boulez opened a season with the BBC Symphony Orchestra at the Roundhouse experimental theatre in north London. This included the London premiere of Karlheinz Stockhausen's (*see* BIOGRAPHY) *Mixtur* for tape and instruments and the world premiere of Justin Connolly's *Tetramorph* for a similar combination. A similar series that took place in New York was entitled "Prospective Encounters."

Two other London groups concerned with the propagation of new music were the London Sinfonietta and the Fires of London, who presented Bruce Cole's music-theatre piece *Pantomimes* for the first time on February 12. In Steve Reich's *Drumming,* a two-hour piece heard on February 4 at the Hayward Gallery in London, 12 players moved around, constantly separating and reforming as they beat out relentless ostinatos and a flood of exotic rhythmic figures. The overall effect of the piece was said to be a conflicting mixture of hypnotism, boredom, and personal inadequacy.

On April 15, Hans Werner Henze's dramatic oratorio *Das Floss der Medusa* received its first stage performance at the Nürnberg Opera, W.Ger. The work related a shameful, real-life episode about a 19th-century sea captain who deserted his ship together with his officers; the few members of the crew who survived on a raft were eventually rescued. The main roles of the piece were those of the mulatto leader of the crew and the figure of Death; between them they carried the main burden of the argument. The hysterical words of the living were accompanied by short, fragmentary wind writing and the narration by fierce percussion; the work as a whole created a compelling dramatic experience.

Shostakovich's Fifteenth Symphony received its first performance by the U.S.S.R. Radio Symphony Orchestra under the composer's son Maxim Shostakovich on January 8. A tape recording of the premiere was broadcast by the BBC in Britain on April 16. Far from being an optimistic work of socialist realism, the symphony, particularly in its final movement, was specifically concerned with the idea of death as it grew out of the motif heard in Wagner's *Ring* preceding Siegfried's funeral march. Twelve-tone methods were used within a primarily tonal context and the ideas were developed on a broad scale, mainly at a fairly leisurely pace. There were also the usual moments of biting wit to contrast with the bleak urgency of the rest.

In London the Royal Choral Society celebrated its centenary with a program consisting of works by Elgar, Britten, and Walton and a revival of Coleridge-Taylor's *Hiawatha's Wedding Feast,* a selection that scarcely suggested that this ancient institution was really facing up to the challenges of the last quarter of the 20th century.

Sir Michael Tippett's Third Symphony received its first performance in a concert given by the London Symphony Orchestra at the Festival Hall on June 22. The second of its two parts introduced a soprano and confirmed the composer's statements about the nature of universal human relationships. On June 7 the New York Philharmonic Promenade presented the premiere of Aaron Copland's *Three Latin American Sketches,* and on August 18 Eugene Ormandy directed the Philadelphia Orchestra in a concert of specifically American music that included works by Gian Carlo Menotti, Roy Harris, Leonard Bernstein, and Samuel Barber. On August 27 Carlos Chavez conducted the premiere of his new work, *Prometheus,* a cantata for chorus, solo voices, and orchestra, at the Cabrillo Festival in California.

The Gulbenkian Festival in Lisbon, Port., was sadly in abeyance in 1972. Nevertheless, the Gulbenkian Foundation continued to encourage performances of new music. Performances in 1972 included the premieres of works by Luciano Berio in June and Penderecki in October. Berio's *Recital I* was also given at the Holland Festival in July. This collage of vocal pieces by many composers was specially written for Cathy Berberian and superbly performed by her.

Malcolm Williamson's setting of a dramatic poem by Ursula Vaughan Williams entitled *The Icy Mirror,* a substantial work in three movements, received its first performance at the Cheltenham Festival on July 9. Gordon Crosse's *Ariadne,* a concertante for solo oboe and 12 players, received its premiere at the same festival. Crosse also wrote a short piece for the last night of the Proms, which continued to extend its horizons.

The Israel Festival, which took place in July and August, included first performances of Sergiu Natra's *Dedication* for mezzo-soprano and orchestra and Zvi Adni's *Meditations on a Drama* for orchestra. The Osaka International Festival in April featured the premiere of Ikuma Dan's orchestral work *Lightning in Moss.* The English Bach Festival, which took place in London and Oxford during April and May, included performances of new works by Karlheinz Stockhausen and Iannis Xenakis. The Warsaw Festival of Contemporary Music in September once again included many new works for both electronic and conventional instruments, as did the Graz, Aus., Festival in October. The Leeds International Pianoforte Competition in September was won by the American pianist Murray Perahia.

Opera. *United States.* Goeran Gentele, who had been appointed director of the Metropolitan Opera in New York in December 1970, was killed in a car accident in July, just after taking up his new post (*see* OBITUARIES). Nevertheless, the company's new season opened in September with a production of *Carmen* carefully based upon Gentele's ideas. The performance was conducted by Leonard Bernstein, with Marilyn Horne in the title role. The original version with dialogue rather than recitatives was used. The end of Gentele's predecessor Sir Rudolf Bing's regime had been celebrated by a gala that went on well into the small hours, with contributions by most of the major singers whom Bing had brought to the Metropolitan.

A production of *Pelléas et Mélisande* in February was conducted by Colin Davis and featured Judith Blegen as a delightful Mélisande. In March a production of *Otello* was staged with Karl Böhm conducting. In June a Verdi festival featuring many of the company's best productions was held at the Metropolitan to replace the planned Verdi conference, which was transferred to Italy.

The New York City Opera presented Donizetti's *Maria Stuarda* with Beverly Sills and Pauline Tinsley in the main roles on March 7, and on March 19 the company presented Lee Hoiby's *Summer and Smoke,* a not altogether successful setting of a minor Tennessee Williams play. The fall season began with a poor production of *Don Giovanni.*

At the Juilliard American Opera Center in New York, Virgil Thomson's new opera *Lord Byron* was given its first performance on April 20. The opera began and ended in Westminster Abbey after the poet's death and concerned the placing of his statue there. The large-scale use of flashback techniques brought in details of Byron's various love affairs from the memoirs. Concerning as it did the public and private life of a creative artist, the composer's own feelings were also clearly involved in the work. His intentions were

The silhouette of Leonard Bernstein in rehearsal of "Carmen," which opened the Metropolitan Opera's 88th season.

NEAL BOENZI—THE NEW YORK TIMES

STUART ROBINSON

The Wheel of Fortune from Act II of Peter Maxwell Davies' opera "Taverner."
The provocative tragedy premiered July 12, 1972, at Covent Garden, London.

carried out by careful matching of words and music in a musical idiom that remained conservative and melodic, and the work thus represented an addition to the small stock of worthwhile American operas.

At the Chicago Lyric Opera, the 1972 season opened on September 25 with a rare production of Verdi's early opera *I due Foscari,* introducing to the U.S. the very promising young Italian soprano Katia Ricciarelli. The San Francisco season, from September to December, offered an interesting new production of *Le nozze di Figaro,* Joan Sutherland in *Norma,* and, on October 26, the first American production of Gottfried von Einem's *Der Besuch der alten Dame.* A complete performance of Berlioz' epic *Les Troyens* was given in Carnegie Hall on March 17 and proved a night of success for the young conductor John Nelson. Frederick Delius' opera *A Village Romeo and Juliet* received its first American performance at the Kennedy Center for the Performing Arts, Washington, D.C., on April 26.

United Kingdom. A lively and very pointed new production of *Le nozze di Figaro* staged by John Copley was presented at the Royal Opera House, Covent Garden, on Dec. 1, 1971, and on March 23 the house's new musical director, Colin Davis, conducted a much-criticized production of Verdi's *Nabucco.* The final production of the 1971–72 season at Covent Garden was of Peter Maxwell Davies' new opera *Taverner,* loosely based on his 16th-century predecessor the composer John Taverner. The critics were divided in their reactions to the work, some finding in it a highly original and relevant piece about the creative artist's relationship with society, others an imbalance between the tenour of the words and the music—a failure to provide sufficiently worthy music to match the complicated subject matter. All, however, praised Michael Geliot's complex but easily comprehended production and Edward Downes's intelligent conducting.

Another new opera that caused controversy was Elisabeth Lutyens' *Time Off? Not a Ghost of a Chance!,* an offbeat comedy with serious implications that was given its first performance by the New Opera Company at Sadler's Wells Theatre in London on March 1. The work was presented in a double bill with Anthony Gilbert's underrated *The Scene-Machine,* another opera very much of its time.

The Sadler's Wells Opera company's administrator at the Coliseum, Stephen Arlen, died in January (*see* OBITUARIES) and was succeeded by Lord Harewood. The company's achievements continued to be considerable. A production of *Das Rhinegold* conducted by Charles Mackerras was the third of the operas of *The Ring* cycle to be produced at the Coliseum and proved as successful as its predecessors. The first new production of the 1972–73 season was *Il trovatore* in August. The first British performance on stage of Prokofiev's epic *War and Peace* followed in October. This was something of a tour de force, excitingly produced by Colin Graham and conducted by David Lloyd-Jones. No truly authentic version of the opera existed, as the composer had been continually revising the work right up to the time of his death; moreover, in the composition of certain scenes he was influenced to some extent by the necessity of conforming with patriotic needs. The version performed by the Sadler's Wells company was a very full one that was on the whole justified by its theatrical effectiveness.

In May Glyndebourne Festival Opera distinguished itself with a marvellous production of Monteverdi's *Il ritorno d'Ulisse in patria* staged by Peter Hall. Janet Baker, who also sang an arresting Dido in *The Trojans* with the Scottish Opera at the Edinburgh Festival in August and at Covent Garden in September, gave the important role of Penelope great feeling and presence. The performances crowned the series of Baroque revivals that had been presented at Glyndebourne.

At the Wexford Festival in October, Carl Maria von Weber's *Oberon* was revived, conducted by Kenneth Montgomery. On May 17 at the Camden Festival in London a production of Delius' *Koanga* was presented, conducted by that eminent Delian Charles Groves. The same festival also included Smetana's rarely heard *The Secret* and a double bill comprising Rachmaninoff's *Aleko* and Massenet's *La Navarraise.* Scottish Opera's new productions for the year were

PETER L. GOULD

Reflecting the phenomenon of 1950s nostalgia, rock 'n' roll groups such as Sha-Na-Na were successful on the concert circuit in 1972.

Britten's *A Midsummer Night's Dream* and Donizetti's *Don Pasquale*. A complete cycle of *The Ring* was given by the company in December 1971. The Welsh National Opera Company presented a new production of Britten's *Billy Budd* in October, excellently staged by Michael Geliot.

Austria. The Salzburg Festival in July and August returned to its own love, Mozart, with new productions of *Così fan tutte* and *Le nozze di Figaro*. The former was notable for Karl Böhm's firm conducting and a fine ensemble of singers, while in the latter Jean-Pierre Ponnelle's fine staging provided a new illumination of a well-known opera. The outstanding revival of the festival remained the production of Alban Berg's *Wozzeck*, produced by Gustav Rudolf Sellner and conducted by Karl Böhm. At the Easter Festival Herbert von Karajan produced and conducted *Tristan und Isolde*. At the Vienna Festival in May, Böhm conducted a successful revival of Weber's *Der Freischütz* with Gundula Janowitz as a lovely Agathe. During the normal season Leonie Rysanek created a dramatically convincing Medea in the title role of a new production of Cherubini's opera while Ileana Cotrubas was an affecting Violetta in *La traviata*.

West Germany. The Bayreuth Festival made headlines with a Marxist version of *Tannhäuser* produced by Götz Friedrich from East Berlin that might or might not have shocked Wagner. At the Munich Festival, Korean composer Isang Yun's *Sim Tjong* was given its first performance. The festival also included a fine new production of *Der Rosenkavalier*, first seen in April, by Otto Schenk with sets by Jürgen Rose. These performances were both at the National Theatre. At the smaller Theater am Gärtnerplatz, Prokofiev's rarely seen *Betrothal in a Monastery* was produced. The West Berlin Festival in September included the first performance of Wolfgang Fortner's *Elisabeth Tudor* with Helga Dernesch in the title role.

Italy. The most important event of the Italian season was the revival, in its complete form, of Rossini's *William Tell* at the Florence Festival in May. Nicolai Gedda sang the title role, which he later recorded in London. At Venice Menotti produced *La traviata* with Beverly Sills as Violetta. In April, also at Venice, Ricciarelli took over the title role in Verdi's *Giovanna d'Arco*. The most exciting production of the season at La Scala was *Aida* conducted by Claudio Abbado. Renzo Rossellini's *L'Annonce faite à Marie* received its first performance at the San Carlo in Naples on April 6. A revival of Donizetti's *Caterina Cornaro* was staged at the same house the following month. The Verona Arena season opened on July 15 with the first performance there of Verdi's *Ernani*.

France. At the Aix Festival, Darius Milhaud's 80th birthday was celebrated with a revival of *Les Malheurs d'Orphée*. An arresting performance of *Pelléas et Mélisande* was also given at the festival. At the Paris Opéra, a new production of Berlioz' *Benvenuto Cellini* was presented on May 18, and on June 29 Hans Hotter bade farewell to the role of Wotan in *Die Walküre*. In October Montserrat Caballé appeared in *Norma* and Karl Böhm conducted the first French performance of *Die Frau ohne Schatten*. Also in October, Georg Solti conducted a concert performance of Schoenberg's *Erwartung* with Anja Silja in the only sung role. Two new operas were given at the Lyons Opéra: Maurice Ohana's *Autodafe* was presented on May 18 and Husson's *Lysistrata* on June 12. At the Bordeaux Festival, Jean-Michel Damase's opera *Eurydice* received its first performance on May 26. The Orange Festival took on an international hue with a production in the Arena on July 23 of *Il trovatore* in which the cast included Montserrat Caballé, the Russian mezzo Irina Arkhipova, and Ludovico Spiess. The festival also included a performance of *La Damnation de Faust*, which took place on July 28.

Australia. The appointment of Edward Downes as musical director gave a new lease on life to the Australian Opera, and the first local production of *Der Rosenkavalier* in the spring showed how much he had already achieved in a relatively short period of time. Another highly successful production was John Copley's staging of *Rigoletto*. Meanwhile, argument continued over the opening of the new Sydney Opera House, due to take place in 1973. (ALAN BLYTH)

Jazz. The dramatically fissiparous nature of jazz continued to be marked throughout 1972 in a number of highly significant ways. While experimentalism continued to tilt even further toward anarchy, the masters of more traditional methods struggled to find audiences large enough to sustain that chimera, a jazz career. It was perhaps hardly surprising that the avant garde should be reduced to such desperate expediencies in its search for a public support comparable to that which had once supported earlier, more naïve methods of jazz-making. But what was far more shocking was the way in which irrefutable evidence continued to present itself to the effect that people were now staying away even from old favourites whose box-office appeal had once seemed secure.

Through the 1960s it had seemed as though Europe might be the salvation for the aging jazz master, but by 1972 there was no longer any doubt that this Jamesian dream had faded. Tours by American concert groups became rare, and sellouts for their performances no longer to be taken for granted. This economic crisis was reflected most vividly in the attempts of one or two leading jazz figures to rid themselves of the jazz label, and to change their identity if not their style of music. The vibraharpist Gary Burton continued to compromise between jazz and pop with such skill as to baffle anyone who might feel inclined to criticize his tactics, but in the case of an older-established musician like Miles Davis, attempts to fuse jazz training and achievement with the more fashionable and transient devices of pop music proved quite disastrous.

Once again the great irony of the situation became obvious whenever one of the remaining jazz virtuosi chose to show his paces. It appeared that in the midst of a declining and perhaps even expiring art, there were a few instances where instrumental virtuosity either reached or sustained unprecedented peaks. Whenever Oscar Peterson began to play the piano, or Stan Getz the tenor saxophone, or Buddy Rich to thunder at the drums, the listener was privileged to witness jazz masterworks. For the Canadian-born Peterson 1972 was an especially important year; by finally jettisoning the string bass and drums that had supported him over so many thousands of concerts and recordings over the years, he accepted the ultimate challenge of jazz piano playing, which is that the soloist become his own rhythm section. It was a challenge that perhaps Art Tatum, James P. Johnson, and Earl Hines had measured up to in the past, but Peterson, with his Tatum-inspired aesthetic, rose most magnificently to the occasion.

Most of the older players fought as best they could against advancing musical senility, but at least one exception to this rule was the Parisian veteran Stephane Grappelly, whose violin playing, for so many years in the long shadow of his guitarist-partner Django Reinhardt, persisted in maturing in a most surprising way, so that to most other musicians, Grappelly in his 60s appeared to be in his prime. The hint of effeteness that had once tended to blur his style had vanished, and Grappelly could now be counted among the most buoyant of practicing soloists. Less happy was the fate during the year of the singer Ella Fitzgerald, whose acute crisis over eyesight resulted in the temporary disappearance of her thistledown voice from the concert stage. A series of operations apparently restored her sight at least partially, but although she became happily active once more, it seemed highly unlikely that she would ever work as extensively as before.

From the instrumental viewpoint the saddest death of the year was that of the tenor saxophone virtuoso Don Byas, who, after a brilliant early career with the Count Basie orchestra and among the pioneers of the new modernism of the early 1940s, chose to exile himself to Europe for the rest of his life. Although risking in this way the stylistic damage that can follow the loss of stimulus that comes with interchange of ideas in a native environment, Byas appeared to suffer no diminution of his great powers; indeed, by his self-imposed exile he may have prolonged his artistic life considerably, for by inadvertently detaching himself from the bitter doctrinal squabbles of recent years, he escaped the tendency to neo-primitivism that had so disfigured the face of jazz over the last decade. A rhapsodist in the school of Coleman Hawkins, Byas nonetheless developed along highly original lines, and by the time of his death was one of the most complex and sophisticated soloists in all jazz.

In some ways the year's most significant death was that of the clarinet pioneer Mezz Mezzrow (Milton Mesirow), an indifferent soloist who would perhaps never have been taken quite so seriously as a musician had it not been for the heightened romanticism of the Chicago bootleg background of his emergent years. But in middle age Mezzrow most unpredictably transcended himself by writing one of the most widely read of all jazz books, and perhaps the most remarkable of all its autobiographies, *Really the Blues*. In this book, Mezzrow's life became transmuted into a lurid if slightly uneasy compromise between fact and fiction, between truth and falsehood, between documentation and pure moonshine. Without doubt *Really the Blues* would continue to stand as a monument to that raffish bohemianism that so characterized the early jazz years. (BENNY GREEN)

Popular. After a period of introversion, entertainment returned to popular music in 1972. Artists regained contact with their public, and genuine stars glittered in all their charismatic glory. There was much emphasis on presentation, some musicians adopting costumes and makeup. Foremost of these "theatricals" was Alice Cooper, an American male singer originally under the auspices of Frank Zappa. Hitherto his audience had been confined to the underground, but in 1972 he burst upon the business with a violent stage act involving simulated killings and rough rock music.

Britain's theatrical king was David Bowie, whose colourful presentation implied a sexual ambiguity not unmixed with satire. Bowie had been in show business since leaving school, working through rock, folk, and mime, and had achieved a hit in 1969 with "Space Oddity." In 1972 two fine LPs and a series of sensational live shows established him as a star. The younger teen-agers favoured Marc Bolan, leader of the group T. Rex, whose performances triggered near-Beatlemanic hysteria. With his curly hair, satin suits, and glitter eyeshadow, Bolan exuded a fairytale fragility that his British fans adored, but U.S. audiences were less enthusiastic.

Amid all the glamour there were many bands who put music before maquillage. One of the best was Lindisfarne, a five-man group from Newcastle upon Tyne, whose versatility, good humour, and straightforward style made them very popular. They so impressed U.S. producer Bob Johnston that he visited England especially to work with them; their first collaboration, "Fog on the Tyne," became one of 1971's best-selling LPs. The Faces, perhaps the most successful group of all, combined showmanship with good rock music. They had in Rod Stewart one of the world's outstanding singers—a soloist in his own right, with two chart-topping albums to his credit during the year—whose extrovert stage manner belied his emotional vocal style. Another British group successfully combining "rock and flash" was Slade, who packed concert halls and had a string of hit singles.

The old-style idol returned in the shape of 21-year-old David Cassidy, whose appearances in "The Partridge Family" television series prompted the launching of his singing career. He soon became the teen-agers' favourite, mobbed wherever he went. Donny Osmond, youngest of the five Osmond Brothers, at 14 became the darling of the subteens with records such as "Puppy Love."

While theatricalism was invading pop, pop was invading the theatre with two musicals on religious themes. *Jesus Christ Superstar,* by Andrew Lloyd Webber and Tim Rice, had first appeared as a record in 1970; 1972 saw stage productions in the U.S. and London, although its secularized portrayal of the Passion of Christ caused some controversy. On a smaller scale was the charming *Godspell,* based on St. Matthew's Gospel. It was a good year for live music. The shortage of suitable concert venues was lessened by the conversion of old theatres, such as the DeMille in New York and London's Rainbow. Many top stars toured—notably the Rolling Stones, who emerged from "exile" to tour North America. One of the highlights of the year was Elvis Presley's concert at Madison Square Garden, New York.

Several stars of the early 1960s made comebacks,

PETER L. GOULD

Folk singer Don McLean created the popular 1972 recording "American Pie," an exciting, symbolic work that elicited myriads of interpretations.

notably Neil Sedaka, Rick (formerly Ricky) Nelson, and ex-Zombies Colin Blunstone and Rod Argent. The Beatles, though separated, were still active; John Lennon made two LPs, Paul McCartney returned to live performance with his new group, Wings, George Harrison supervised the release of the record and film of his concert for Bangladesh, and Ringo Starr made a film of T. Rex. Also on his own was Paul Simon, whose partnership with Art Garfunkel had ended when Garfunkel went into acting; Simon's first solo album was released in March.

Musical activity was not confined to Britain and America. Canada's Anne Murray, the Dutch quartet Focus, and the West German group Can all met with success at home and abroad. Of the singer-songwriters —especially women—who had dominated pop in 1971, less was heard; only Joni Mitchell and Melanie ventured beyond home to tour. Apart from Motown's Valerie Simpson, the most notable newcomers were men: Jackson Browne, who toured with Joni Mitchell; Labi Siffre; Hurricane Smith, record producer turned performer; and Don McLean, whose song "American Pie" summed up a generation's feelings on the "death" of 1960s pop music. There was still a big nostalgia market. In northern England imported copies of old soul numbers such as the Tams' "Hey Girl Don't Bother Me" were played in discothèques and their reissue prompted. Much interest was taken in pop history; over the year a series of records entitled "Cruisin'" was released, tracing the development of American pop radio from 1955 to 1963.

Nostalgia notwithstanding, a wind of change was blowing through the business—even in such establishments as Tamla Motown, which moved its headquarters from Detroit to Los Angeles. Tamla singer Stevie Wonder was among several musicians to experiment with synthesizers; the new British group Roxy Music used one as an integral part of their sound. The year was not without novelties; in February Coca-Cola's commercial "I'd Like to Teach the World to Sing" became a single hit, and in June the charts resounded to the Royal Scots Dragoon Guards's "Amazing Grace" played on bagpipes. An interesting innovation in recording was quadraphonic (4-channel) stereo.

All in all, popular music was healthier during 1972 than it had been for some time; it was truly popular, and musicians were judged more by their performances than by record sales. No "revolution" had occurred, but pop was shaking off the past and allowing new music to emerge. (HAZEL MORGAN)

Namibia:
see Dependent States; South Africa

Narcotics:
see Drugs and Narcotics

NATO:
see Defense

Folk Music. Folk festivals continued to gain popularity in 1972, yet retained local, regional, even national distinctions, both functional and stylistic. Thus in Ghana planting and harvesting celebrated with music in local village festivals, everyone participating, contrasted with the 11th annual National Festival of Arts held in Kumasi, with traditional and contemporary, local and foreign musicians and dancers, and workshops and scholarly papers. Across the globe in Suva, the government of Fiji played host in May to the South Pacific Festival of Arts, the most significant in Oceania.

North America's urban culture produced countless festivals, the largest national ones being the 34th National Folk Festival in Vienna, Va., and the Smithsonian Institution's sixth Festival of American Folklife, in Washington, D.C. The former sought to know Americans and their folk heritage, diversity in unity. The latter associated folk singers, instrumentalists, dancers, and craftsmen, emphasizing informality and audience interaction.

The rapidly urbanizing Eastern European scene seemed to prefer professional folk troupes like the Russian Moiseyev or Piatnitsky, or the Bulgarian Koutev ensemble. The state-supported folk music research institutes and university departments of Eastern Europe studied archaic and acculturated rural and urban folk traditions.

In Ottawa the National Museum of Man's Canadian Centre for Folk Culture Study expanded its activities, reflecting 1971 governmental recognition of Canada's multiculturalism. Ethnic group investigations included folk songs, and Lithuanian and New Brunswick song collections were published. The Archive of American Folk Song in Washington continued to issue bibliographies and authentic records. In Caracas, Venezuela, the Inter-American Institute of Ethnomusicology and Folklore carried out research on Venezuelan and Latin-American traditional music and dance, especially that of South American Indians.

Interest in traditional folk music was spreading and deepening in the industrialized countries among the public, especially youth. In Sweden this became so marked that radio and television programs were increased, and over 20 television documentaries on folk music were produced in 1972.

In the U.S. a special issue of the *Music Educators' Journal* was devoted to ethnomusicology, to stimulate more use by teachers of the musics of the world, and to prod academic specialists into selecting good materials suitable for schools.

An international symposium on African and Afro-American music took place in May at the University of Ghana. The Society for Ethnomusicology, U.S.-based, met in Toronto, emphasizing Canadian traditional music and research there and in the special September issue of its journal *Ethnomusicology*. The society's membership of 1,500 reflected the professional growth of the field, above all in U.S. universities. The International Folk Music Council, the senior world organization devoted to the study, dissemination, and practice of folk music, was 25 years old in 1972. (BARBARA KRADER)

See also Dance; Motion Pictures; Television and Radio; Theatre.

Nauru

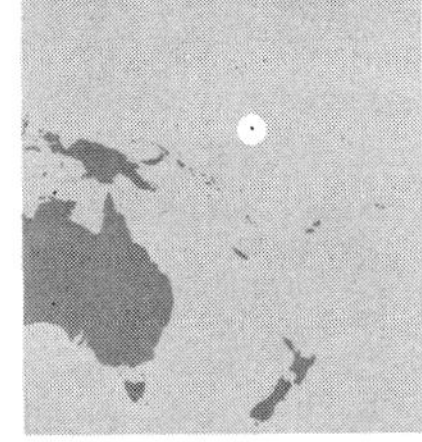

An island republic in the Pacific Ocean, Nauru lies about 1,200 mi. E of New Guinea. Area: 8.2 sq.mi. (21 sq.km.). Pop. (1972 est.): 6,768. Seat of government: Uaboe District. Language: English and Nauruan. Religion: Christian. President in 1972, Hammer de Roburt.

At the March 1972 elections all nine members of the Nauru Local Government Council, which oversaw Nauru's various commercial enterprises, were returned to office. Economic development continued to be President de Roburt's major preoccupation. He attended a meeting of the South Pacific Forum in Canberra, Austr., where the five Forum members, Nauru, Fiji, Western Samoa, Tonga, and the Cook Islands, decided to investigate the possibility of developing free trade among themselves. The U.S. Trust Territory of the Pacific Islands caused problems for the Nauruan Pacific shipping line by placing a 15% tariff upon Nauru's trade with Micronesia in order to protect its own shipping line. (A. R. G. GRIFFITHS)

NAURU

Education. (1970) Primary, pupils 1,465, teachers 94; secondary, pupils 371,368, teachers 28.

Finance and Trade. Monetary unit: Australian dollar, with (Sept. 18, 1972) a free rate of A$0.84 to U.S. $1 (A$2.06 = £1 sterling). Budget (1970–71): revenue A$10,842,000; expenditure A$9,789,000. Foreign trade (1968–69): imports A$5,225,000 (72% from Australia, 7% from New Zealand); exports (phosphates) A$24,046,000 (65% to Australia, 24% to New Zealand, 7% to Japan by tonnage).

Industry. Production: phosphate rock (1969–70) 2.2 million metric tons; electricity (1968) 19.3 million kw-hr.

Nepal

A constitutional monarchy of Asia, Nepal is in the Himalayas between India and Tibet. Area: 54,362 sq.mi. (140,797 sq.km.). Pop. (1971): 11,289,968. Cap. and largest city: Kathmandu (pop., 1971, 153,405). Language: Nepali (official); also Newari and Bhutia. Religion (1970): Hindu 90%; Buddhist 9%. Kings, Mahendra Bir Bikram Shah Deva and, from Jan. 31, 1972, Birendra Bir Bikram Shah Deva; prime minister, Kirti Nidhi Bista.

The accession to the throne of Prince Birendra (*see* BIOGRAPHY) following the death of his father, King Mahendra (*see* OBITUARIES), in January 1972 raised hopes for political and economic reforms after more than a decade of near-feudal rule. Food shortages, spiraling prices, student unrest, and political agitation followed in quick succession, however, creating a difficult situation for the 26-year-old king. By August the partyless panchayat (legislative) system was under serious pressure. The king, who had earlier promised changes in keeping with modern times, sensed a threat to the monarchy itself. Consequently, students and political leaders were detained, and

NEPAL

Education. (1969–70) Primary, pupils 449,141, teachers 18,250; secondary, pupils 96,704, teachers 5,257; vocational, pupils 6,000, teachers 151; teacher training, students 365, teachers (1966–67) 19; higher, students 17,025, teaching staff 1,058.

Finance. Monetary unit: Nepalese rupee, with (Sept. 18, 1972) a par value of NRs. 10.12 to U.S. $1 (free rate of NRs. 24.78 = £1 sterling). Gold, SDRs, and foreign exchange, central bank: (June 1972) U.S. $108.5 million; (June 1971) U.S. $99.6 million. Budget (1971–72): revenue NRs. 561 million; expenditure NRs. 368 million (excluding development expenditure of NRs. 769 million partly financed by foreign aid of NRs. 352 million).

Foreign Trade. (1968–69) Imports NRs. 744.3 million (98% from India in 1964–65); exports NRs. 568 million (99% to India in 1964–65). Main exports: food and livestock 45%; crude materials (including timber and jute) 29%; manufactures 24%.

Agriculture. Production (in 000; metric tons; 1971; 1970 in parentheses): rice *c.* 2,300 (*c.* 2,500); millet and sorghum *c.* 115 (*c.* 115); jute *c.* 35 (*c.* 35). Livestock (in 000; 1970–71): cattle *c.* 6,330; pigs *c.* 300; sheep *c.* 2,200; goats *c.* 2,280.

erring newspapers were punished. Among the political detainees were former prime minister Surya Bahadur Thapa and Panchayat member and Supreme Court lawyer Ram Raj Prasad. In an unprecedented move, the king also expelled 12 elected members of the Panchayat. Former prime minister K. I. Singh and 20 of his followers began a boycott of the Panchayat sessions as their attempt to censure the prime minister and finance minister, Kirti Nidhi Bista, proved abortive. Severe food shortages, caused by the failure of two successive monsoons, hit the entire northern belt, and India rushed 70,000 tons of food grains for distribution among the one million people affected.

Friendly relations with China and India continued, and Peking granted credits totaling NRs. 15.4 million for the import of consumer goods. Nepal was one of the first countries to recognize Bangladesh. (GOVINDAN UNNY)

Netherlands

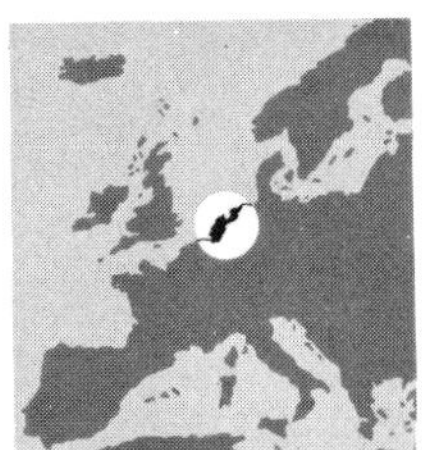

A kingdom of northwest Europe on the North Sea, the Netherlands, a Benelux country, is bounded by Belgium on the south and West Germany on the east. Area: 15,892 sq.mi. (41,160 sq.km.). Pop. (1972 est.): 13,269,563. Cap. and largest city: Amsterdam (pop., 1972 est., 807,742). Seat of government: The Hague (pop., 1972 est., 525,368). Language: Dutch. Religion (1960): Roman Catholic 40.4%; Dutch Reformed 28.3%; Reformed Churches 9.3%. Queen, Juliana; prime minister in 1972, Barend W. Biesheuvel.

After one year and 14 days in office, the government of Barend W. Biesheuvel resigned on July 20, 1972, following the resignation from the Cabinet of Willem Drees, Jr., and Jonkheer Maurits L. de Brauw, both members of the Democratic Socialists-70 (DS-70) Party. They had resigned over cuts in expenditure to their departments and the Cabinet's refusal to impose wage and price controls in the face of rising inflation. Efforts to repair the coalition failed, and the Cabinet decided to remain in office and to call elections for the lower house on November 29.

The electoral roll included about 750,000 new voters between 18 and 21. Nearly 83% of the electorate voted. The results were indecisive. Biesheuvel's original five-party coalition lost six seats (from 82 to

Navies: *see* Defense

Shipyard workers near Rotterdam went on strike for higher wages and the right to strike in February 1972, in defiance of a court decision.

76) while the left-wing coalition led by Joop den Uyl gained four (from 52 to 56), but neither obtained a clear majority. On December 1 Queen Juliana began consultations looking toward the formation of a new government. Meanwhile, Biesheuvel's Cabinet remained in office in a caretaker capacity. The composition of the new lower house (with 1971 results in parentheses) was: Labour Party 43 (39); Catholic People's Party 27 (35); People's Party for Freedom and Democracy 22 (16); Antirevolutionary Party 14 (13); Christian Historical Union 7 (10); Communists 7 (6); Radical Political Party 7 (2); DS-70 6 (8); Democrats '66 6 (11); Farmers' Party 3 (1); others 8.

Queen Juliana opened the new session of Parliament on September 19. The budget for 1973, presented by Finance Minister Roelf J. Nelissen, forecast revenue of 41,115,000,000 guilders and expenditure of 43,081,000,000 guilders, the deficit to be met by tax increases.

In April the president of the Netherlands Bank, Jelle Zijlstra, admitted that government attempts to control inflation were not proving effective. The government's aim had been to obtain a voluntary "social contract" between itself, employers, and trade unionists, without resorting to statutory measures. After hard bargaining and mutual concessions, the three parties reached an agreement on October 30, but a split within the powerful National Federation of Labour threatened to undermine the bargain.

The minister of justice, Andreas A. M. van Agt, caused a public outcry when he announced, in February, the government's intention to pardon the last three Nazi war criminals remaining in Dutch prisons, Ferdinand Hugo Aus der Fünten (former head of the German Central Office for Jewish Emigration), Franz Fischer (*Kriminal-Oberassistent* at the Judenreferat in The Hague), and Joseph Johann Kotälla (assistant commandant of Amersfoort concentration camp). Van Agt and other supporters of the move had to be placed under police protection. After an emotional session, the majority of the lower house voted against the proposal and the government decided to revoke its decision.

At the beginning of the year the government announced that fees to university lecturers would be increased from 200 to 1,000 guilders and registration fees from 10 to 100 guilders. Both chambers eventually voted for the measures after the Cabinet made known that it would not accept a refusal. The majority of university students boycotted official registration, and the faculties of the universities distributed registration cards without accepting fees.

On May 17 the governments of the Netherlands and China announced their mutual decision to exchange ambassadors. A treaty of economic, industrial, and technical cooperation with the U.S.S.R. was signed during the visit (July 5–7) of Soviet Foreign Minister Andrei Gromyko. In January Biesheuvel visited the Netherlands Antilles and Surinam. Before returning, he paid a visit to the U.S.

On February 13, in an attempt to strengthen his influence over the Dutch Catholic Church, Pope Paul VI personally consecrated the conservative Johannes M. Gijsen as bishop of Roermond over the objections of the chapter of the Dutch cathedral.

From August 9 to August 16 the inhabitants of a workers' quarter in Rotterdam rioted against Turkish workers in their district. Household goods and win-

NETHERLANDS

Education. (1969–70) Primary, pupils 1,450,647, teachers 47,841; secondary, pupils 569,738, teachers 36,912; vocational, pupils 536,460; teacher training, students 10,822, teachers (1967–68) 1,149; higher (including 9 universities), students 211,513.

Finance. Monetary unit: guilder or florin, with (Sept. 18, 1972) a par value of 3.24 guilders to U.S. $1 (free rate of 7.90 guilders = £1 sterling). Gold, SDRs, and foreign exchange, central bank: (June 1972) U.S. $3,792,000,000; (June 1971) U.S. $2,975,000,000. Budget (1972 est.): revenue 36,659,000,000 guilders; expenditure 38,931,000,000 guilders. Gross national product: (1970) 113.4 billion guilders; (1969) 102,340,000,000 guilders. Money supply: (May 1972) 34,970,000,000 guilders; (May 1971) 30.4 billion guilders. Cost of living (1963 = 100): (June 1972) 163; (June 1971) 151.

Foreign Trade. (1971) Imports 53,910,000,000 guilders; exports 48,518,000,000 guilders. Import sources: EEC 54% (West Germany 27%, Belgium-Luxembourg 15%, France 8%); U.S. 10%; U.K. 6%. Export destinations: EEC 63% (West Germany 34%, Belgium-Luxembourg 13%, France 10%, Italy 5%); U.K. 7%. Main exports: chemicals 13%; petroleum products 10%; electrical machinery and equipment 8%; machinery (nonelectrical) 7%; meat products 6%; textile yarns and fabrics 6%; dairy products 5%. Tourism (1970): visitors 2,398,000; gross receipts U.S. $421 million.

Transport and Communications. Roads (1971) 79,903 km. (including 524 km. expressways). Motor vehicles in use (1971): passenger 2,902,600; commercial 332,960. Railways: (1970) 3,147 km. (including 1,645 km. electrified); traffic (1971) 8,154,000,000 passenger-km., freight 3,232,000,000 net ton-km. Air traffic (1971): 6,360,000,000 passenger-km.; freight 427,580,000 net ton-km. Navigable inland waterways (1970): 5,598 km. (including 2,421 km. for ships of 1,000 tons and over); freight traffic 30,743,000,000 ton-km. Shipping (1971): merchant vessels 100 gross tons and over 1,539; gross tonnage 5,269,145. Ships entered (1970) vessels totaling 123,875,000 net registered tons; goods loaded (1971) 67,693,000 metric tons, unloaded 208,910,000 metric tons. Telephones (Dec. 1970) 3,410,000. Radio licenses (Dec. 1969) 4,036,000. Television licenses (Dec. 1969) 2,869,000.

Agriculture. Production (in 000; metric tons; 1971; 1970 in parentheses): wheat 706 (640); rye 203 (172); barley 373 (329); oats 199 (201); potatoes 5,749 (5,604); tomatoes (1970) 392, (1969) 358; apples 480 (450); pears 100 (160); sugar, raw value (1971–72) 839, (1970–71) 713; dry peas 39 (39); rapeseed 32 (22); linseed *c.* 5 (*c.* 3); flax fibre 14 (8); milk 8,335 (8,239); butter 121 (121); cheese 292 (279); eggs 276 (279); beef and veal *c.* 320 (318); pork *c.* 720 (705); fish catch (1970) 301, (1969) 323. Livestock (in 000; May 1971): cattle *c.* 4,450; pigs 6,158; sheep 572; horses used in agriculture *c.* 96; chickens 60,125.

Industry. Index of production (1963 = 100): (1971) 188; (1970) 176. Production (in 000; metric tons; 1971): coal 3,610; crude oil 1,715; natural gas (cu.m.) 43,799,000; manufactured gas (cu.m.) 755,000; electricity (kw-hr.) 44,802,000; pig iron 3,760; crude steel 5,084; zinc (1970) 46; cement 4,045; cotton yarn 47; wool yarn 17; rayon, etc., filament yarn 38; nylon, etc., filament yarn and staple fibres (1970) 901. Merchant vessels launched (100 gross tons and over; 1971) 821,000 gross tons. New dwelling units completed (1971) 138,000.

dows were smashed and some Turks had to flee. Inadequate housing and a general feeling of impotence and discontent were blamed for the outbreak.

After the failure of negotiations between the huge AKZO chemical and fibre concern and the trade unions regarding the proposed closing of the ENKA-Glanzstoff factory at Breda, an AKZO subsidiary employing 1,700 workers, strategic sections of the factory were occupied by employees and production was halted on September 18. The occupation ended on September 23 after the closure plan had been abandoned.

Queen Juliana and Prince Bernhard paid a state visit to Great Britain in April and an official visit to France in June. On March 22 a third son, Pieter Christian Michiel, was born to Princess Margriet and Pieter van Vollenhoven. On October 13 twins were born to Princess Irene and Prince Hugo of Bourbon Parma; the girl was named Margarita Maria Beatriz, the boy, Jaime Bernardo. (DICK BOONSTRA)

See also Dependent States.

New Zealand

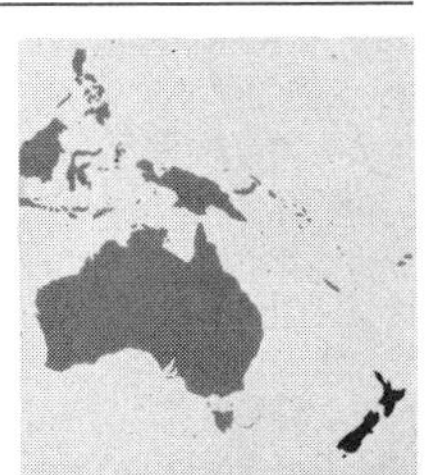

New Zealand, a parliamentary state and member of the Commonwealth of Nations, is in the South Pacific Ocean, separated from southeastern Australia by the Tasman Sea. The country consists of North and South islands and Stewart, Chatham, and other minor islands. Area: 103,736 sq.mi. (268,675 sq.km.). Pop. (1972 est.): 2,909,916. Cap.: Wellington (pop., 1972 est., 136,400). Largest city: Christchurch (pop., 1972 est., 166,800). Largest urban area: Auckland (pop., 1972 est., 670,300). Language: English, Maori. Religion (1966): Church of England 33.7%; Presbyterian 21.8%; Roman Catholic 15.9%. Queen, Elizabeth II; governors-general in 1972, Sir Arthur Porritt and, from September, Sir Denis Blundell; prime ministers, Sir Keith Holyoake until February 2, John Ross Marshall from February 7, and, from December 8, Norman E. Kirk.

The year was one of political change for New Zealand. For some years, change had been expected within the ruling right-wing National Party. It came in February, when the prime minister, Sir Keith Holyoake, who had been party leader for 15 years (12 of them as prime minister), offered his resignation to give the party the opportunity, if it wished, to appoint a new man to contest the general election of November 25. The National Party members of Parliament accepted and elected his deputy, John Ross Marshall, in preference to the other contender, Finance Minister Robert David Muldoon, whom Marshall named as his deputy. Marshall dropped Cabinet members who had already announced intentions of retiring or who now began to announce them. In a major ministerial shake-up Sir Keith Holyoake received the foreign affairs portfolio.

The November election resulted in an upset victory for the Labour Party under Norman Kirk (*see* BIOGRAPHY). Out of power for 12 years, Labour obtained 56 seats in the 87-seat House of Representatives, while the National Party succeeded in winning only 31. On December 8 Kirk formed a 22-member Cabinet, including two Maoris. The new government was expected to emphasize expansion of social services, tax relief, and regional development. In foreign affairs, Kirk indicated that New Zealand would end its participation in the Southeast Asia Treaty Organization and would seek to establish diplomatic relations with China. Acting in concert with the new Labor government in Australia, New Zealand on December 11 announced withdrawal of its military training teams from Vietnam.

In an economy still dependent on overseas markets for pastoral products, wool became the great provider again when international shortages caused it to recover dramatically at auction. At an early October sale, fleeces sold at 66 cents a kilo the previous year went for 231 cents a kilo—the highest price in 22 years. Ironically, the nation had just emerged from months of argument over a Wool Board proposal (adopted as a legislative bill by the government) to set up a corporation that would acquire all the clip from the farmers and sell it more systematically. So vehement was the opposition of a group of big sheep farmers, working through an action committee, that the government shelved the acquisition proposal. As the controversy reached its climax Sir John Acland, chairman of the Wool Board for the previous 12 years, resigned and was succeeded by John Clarke.

The sensation of the year was the collapse in May of the Jeffs Brothers Ltd. group of companies, which had diverse operations including fisheries, exploration, building, and cosmetics. The firm failed because of what the government receiver described as "gross mismanagement."

NEW ZEALAND

Education. (1969) Primary, pupils 514,774, teachers 18,769; secondary and vocational, pupils 184,301, teachers 9,541; higher (including 6 universities), students 56,353, teaching staff 3,132.

Finance. Monetary unit: New Zealand dollar, with (Sept. 18, 1972) a free rate of NZ$0.84 to U.S. $1 (NZ$2.05 = £1 sterling). Gold, SDRs, and foreign exchange, central bank: (June 1972) U.S. $504 million; (June 1971) U.S. $210 million. Budget (1970–71 est.): revenue NZ$1,547,000,000; expenditure NZ$1,561,000,000. Gross national product: (1970–71) NZ$5,432,000,000; (1969–70) NZ$4,741,000,000. Cost of living (1963 = 100): (2nd quarter 1972) 160; (2nd quarter 1971) 149.

Foreign Trade. (1971) Imports NZ$1,186,200,000; exports NZ$1,199,800,000. Import sources: U.K. 29%; Australia 22%; Japan 11%; U.S. 10%. Export destinations: U.K. 32%; U.S. 17%; Australia 9%; Japan 9%. Main exports: wool 16%; lamb and mutton 15%; butter 11%. Tourism (1969): visitors 148,100; gross receipts (1970) U.S. $34 million.

Transport and Communications. Roads (1971) 89,345 km. Motor vehicles in use (1971): passenger 941,600; commercial 185,300. Railways: (1971) 4,847 km.; traffic (1970–71) 507 million passenger-km., freight 3,212,000,000 net ton-km. Air traffic (1971): 1,878,700,000 passenger-km.; freight 43,424,000 net ton-km. Shipping (1971): merchant vessels 100 gross tons and over 118; gross tonnage 181,046. Telephones (Dec. 1970) 1,262,000. Radio licenses (Dec. 1970) 678,000. Television licenses (Dec. 1970) 661,000.

Agriculture. Production (in 000; metric tons; 1971; 1970 in parentheses): wheat 324 (287); barley 227 (174); oats 49 (58); potatoes *c.* 325 (250); dry peas 50 (50); apples 128 (148); milk 5,986 (6,400); butter 233 (240); cheese 108 (100); mutton and lamb 558 (563); beef and veal 397 (393); wool *c.* 236 (238); timber (cu.m.; 1970) 8,700, (1969) 8,400; fish catch (1969) 49, (1968) 59. Livestock (in 000; Jan. 1971): cattle 8,819; sheep (June) 58,913; horses *c.* 81; pigs 617; chickens (April) *c.* 5,500.

Industry. Fuel and power (in 000; metric tons; 1971): coal and lignite 2,124; crude oil (1970) 68; natural gas (cu.m.; 1970) 107,000; manufactured gas (cu.m.) 218,000; electricity (excluding most industrial production; kw-hr.) 14,664,000. Production (in 000; metric tons; 1971): cement 823; phosphate fertilizers (1970–71) 321; wood pulp 569; newsprint (1970–71) 214; other paper (1970–71) 248.

Netherlands Overseas Territories:
see Dependent States

New Guinea:
see Dependent States; Indonesia

Newspapers:
see Publishing

Finance Minister Muldoon in his June budget included large increases in welfare benefits in a 16.2% increase in government spending. He introduced a measure of relief for companies struggling under a payroll tax: this special tax was to be deductible for annual income tax purposes.

Controversial issues were more numerous, and they were argued with greater vigour than usual. French nuclear testing southwest of Tahiti provoked the most emotional protest, with the Federation of Labour blacklisting the handling of French civil airliners and shipping during the testing period. The government had already made its protests against the testing but had not succeeded in arranging a conference of Pacific countries as demanded by some of the protesters. A continuing controversy on whether South Africa's traditional Springbok (all white) Rugby team should be permitted to tour in 1973 drew a detailed statement of policy from Prime Minister Marshall, who expressed abhorrence of that nation's racial policies but said nothing would be gained by isolating South Africa.

The sacking by the New Zealand Broadcasting Corp. of Alexander MacLeod, editor of its journal, the *New Zealand Listener,* at the same time that the corporation was considering political aspects of his editorials, led to a lengthy public inquiry into possible political influence on the board of the corporation.

A New Zealand barrister and solicitor serving in London as high commissioner, Sir Denis Blundell, arrived home in Wellington in September to succeed another New Zealander (but an expatriate), Sir Arthur Porritt, as governor-general.

(JOHN A. KELLEHER)

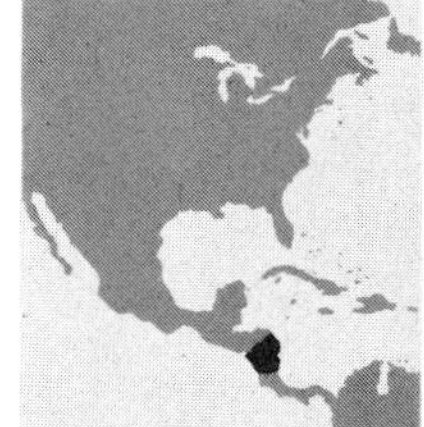

Nicaragua

The largest country of Central America, Nicaragua is a republic bounded by Honduras, Costa Rica, the Caribbean Sea, and the Pacific Ocean. Area: 49,759 sq.mi. (128,875 sq.km.). Pop. (1971): 1,911,540. Cap. and largest city: Managua (pop., 1971, 398,514). Language: Spanish. Religion: Roman Catholic. President in 1972 until May 1, Brig. Gen. Anastasio Somoza Debayle; from May 1, a ruling triumvirate: Roberto Martínez Lacayo, Alfonso Lovo Cordero, and Fernando Agüero Rocha.

According to plan, President Somoza (*see* BIOGRAPHY) stepped down peacefully from his position of direct rule on May 1, marking the first time in 35 years that a Somoza would not govern Nicaragua. He was replaced by a triumvirate consisting of two leaders of the powerful Liberal Party (PLN), Roberto Martínez Lacayo and Alfonso Lovo Cordero, and the acknowledged leader of the Conservative Party, Fernando Agüero Rocha. They were to govern the country until the presidential elections scheduled for September 1974.

Prior to the change in government the nation had elected a constituent assembly in February. The Liberal Party won with 534,171 votes, while the Conservatives totaled 174,897. The parties had combined in a "National Front" and had agreed that, regardless of the vote, the winning party would gain 60 seats in the assembly and the loser would take the remaining 40. Before the elections three small opposition groups and part of the Roman Catholic Church urged voters to remain away from the polls, calling the election a "falsification of the electoral process." Apparently this urging had some effect, for one-third of the electorate abstained from voting. The charge was made that the PLN members of the triumvirate would still answer to Somoza, who retained leadership over the Guardia Nacional (Nicaragua's only armed force).

On December 23 the capital city of Managua was devastated by a series of earth tremors, the strongest of which measured 6.25 on the Richter scale. Early estimates placed the death toll between 10,000 and 12,000, while some 200,000 or more persons were reported to be homeless. The city was without electricity or water, and fires ignited by the quake added to the destruction. General Somoza ordered the city evacuated; a large portion of it was declared to be "contaminated," and orders were issued to level it and cover it with lime. A major international relief effort was mounted, including $3 million in aid from the U.S. However, the disruption of communications and transportation made distribution of relief supplies difficult, and there was criticism of official mismanagement. Managua had also suffered disastrous earthquakes in 1885 and 1931.

During the year, U.S. billionaire Howard Hughes took up temporary residence in the Intercontinental Hotel in Managua, ostensibly to discuss a merger of two airlines, Hughes's Air West and LANICA, owned by the Somoza family. Hughes acquired 25% of the Nicaraguan airline in a deal that was part of a joint hotel-tourist resort venture by Hughes and Somoza. Hughes left Nicaragua for London following the earthquake.

(GEORGE P. PATTEN)

NICARAGUA

Education. (1969–70) Primary, pupils 266,346, teachers (including preprimary) 7,535; secondary, pupils 38,149, teachers 1,671; vocational, pupils 4,221; teachers 297; teacher training, students 3,254, teachers 259; higher (including 2 universities), students 7,682, teaching staff 487.

Finance. Monetary unit: córdoba, with (Sept. 18, 1972) a par value of 7 córdobas to U.S. $1 (free rate of 17.21 córdobas = £1 sterling). Gold, SDRs, and convertible currency, central bank: (June 1972) U.S. $74,260,000; (June 1971) U.S. $60,280,000. Budget (1970 est.): revenue 686.2 million córdobas; expenditure 680.3 million córdobas. Gross national product: (1970) 5,786,000,000 córdobas; (1969) 5,367,000,000 córdobas. Money supply: (June 1972) 704.1 million córdobas; (June 1971) 618.6 million córdobas. Cost of living (Managua; 1963 = 100): (1971) 131; (1969) 117.

Foreign Trade. (1971) Imports 1,473,100,000 córdobas; exports 1,283,900,000 córdobas. Import sources: U.S. 33%; Guatemala 9%; Japan 8%; Costa Rica 8%; El Salvador 8%; West Germany 7%; Venezuela 5%. Export destinations: U.S. 35%; Japan 18%; Costa Rica 13%; West Germany 8%; Guatemala 5%; El Salvador 5%. Main exports: cotton 23%; coffee 16%; meat 16%; sugar 6%.

Transport and Communications. Roads (1970) 6,124 km. (including 368 km. of Pan-American Highway). Motor vehicles in use (1970): passenger 34,400; commercial (including buses) 8,900. Railways: (1969) 348 km.; traffic (1968) 35 million passenger-km., freight 13 million net ton-km. Air traffic (1970): 76,990,000 passenger-km.; freight 1.1 million net ton-km. Telephones (Jan. 1971) 26,000. Radio receivers (Dec. 1970) 109,000. Television receivers (Dec. 1970) 55,000.

Agriculture. Production (in 000; metric tons; 1971; 1970 in parentheses): corn *c.* 210 (*c.* 225); rice 74 (109); sorghum *c.* 60 (*c.* 60); dry beans *c.* 57 (53); coffee *c.* 36 (*c.* 33); sugar, raw value (1971–72) *c.* 196, (1970–71) *c.* 170; cotton, lint *c.* 87 (73). Livestock (in 000; 1970–71): cattle *c.* 2,550; pigs *c.* 630; chickens *c.* 3,000.

Industry. Production (in 000; 1970): cement (metric tons) 136; gold (troy oz.) *c.* 110; electricity (kw-hr.; 1969) 551,000.

Niger

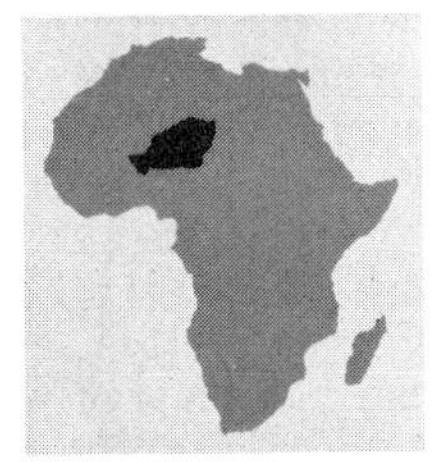

A republic of north central Africa, Niger is bounded by Algeria, Libya, Chad, Nigeria, Dahomey, Upper Volta, and Mali. Area: 458,072 sq.mi. (1,186,408 sq.km.). Pop. (1972 est.): 4,242,682, including (1970 est.) Hausa 53.7%; Zerma and Songhai 23.6%; Fulani 10.6%; Beriberi-Manga 9.1%. Cap. and largest city: Niamey (pop., 1972 est., 102,000). Language: French, and Sudanic dialects. Religion: Muslim, animist, Christian. President in 1972, Hamani Diori.

On January 24–26, French Pres. Georges Pompidou paid an official visit to Niamey in the course of his second African tour since his accession to the French presidency. During the visit, President Diori informed his French counterpart of Niger's desire for a revision of the cooperation agreements between the two countries, particularly those relating to the exploitation of Niger's substantial uranium deposits. Similar demands for the revision of cooperation agreements were made during the year by other former French colonies in Africa, notably Mauritania and Congo. Monetary relations within the franc zone—and, in particular, Mauritania's intention to create its own currency, were discussed when the seven-member council of the West African Monetary Union met in Niamey in December.

In August President Diori visited France to undergo a course of medical treatment at Contrexéville. During his stay in France he took the opportunity to visit Paris for further talks with President Pompidou. Once again, the discussions centred mainly on the question of the cooperation agreements, though without any conclusive decisions being reached. The matter was to be further examined by a joint commission later in the year.

In April, Niamey was the scene of a reconciliation between Libya and Chad. Diplomatic relations were resumed for the first time since August 1971, when Libya was accused of participating in an attempted coup in Chad. The reconciliation was largely due to persistent attempts at mediation on the part of President Diori. (PHILIPPE DECRAENE)

NIGER

Education. (1969–70) Primary, pupils 84,248, teachers (1968–69) 2,176; secondary, pupils 5,587, teachers 277; vocational, pupils 137, teachers 21; teacher training, students 548, teachers 37.

Finance. Monetary unit: CFA franc, with (Sept. 18, 1972) a parity of CFA Fr. 50 to the French franc (CFA Fr. 255.79 = U.S. $1; free rate of CFA Fr. 612.37 = £1 sterling). Budget (1970–71 est.) balanced at CFA Fr. 10,903,000,000.

Foreign Trade. (1970) Imports CFA Fr. 16,213,000,000; exports CFA Fr. 8,795,000,000. Import sources: France 46%; West Germany 8%; U.S. 5%; Netherlands 5%. Export destinations: France 47%; Nigeria 20%; Italy 15%. Main exports: peanuts 56%; livestock 16%; peanut oil 6%.

Transport and Communications. Roads (1971) 6,998 km. Motor vehicles in use (1971): passenger 6,120; commercial 2,070. Telephones (Dec. 1970) 4,000. Radio receivers (Dec. 1970) 100,000.

Agriculture. Production (in 000; metric tons; 1971; 1970 in parentheses): millet 800 (901); sorghum 300 (337); cassava (1970) *c.* 200, (1969) 199; rice 40 (37); peanuts *c.* 240 (*c.* 235); dates *c.* 5 (*c.* 5). Livestock (in 000; 1970–71): cattle *c.* 4,400; sheep *c.* 2,800; goats *c.* 6,200.

Nigeria

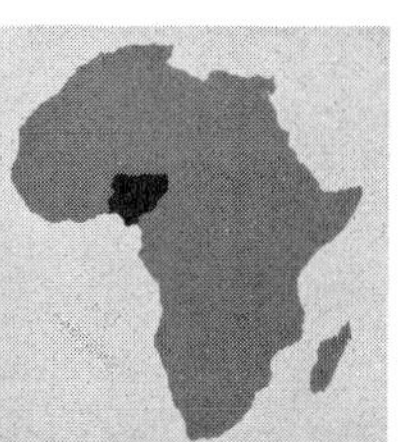

A republic and a member of the Commonwealth of Nations, Nigeria is located in Africa on the north coast of the Gulf of Guinea, bounded by Dahomey, Niger, Chad, and Cameroon. Area: 356,669 sq.mi. (923,768 sq.km.). Pop. (1972 est.): 69,252,709, including: Hausa 21%; Ibo 18%; Yoruba 18%; Fulani 10%. Cap. and largest city: Lagos (pop., 1972 est., 682,223). Language: English (official). Religion (1963): Muslim 47%; Christian 34%. Head of provisional military government in 1972, Maj. Gen. Yakubu Gowon.

In 1972 Nigeria continued to win the peace through successful reabsorption of the Ibo people from the defeated breakaway state of Biafra into national life, including many rebel officers accepted into the Army. Reconciliation problems remained, especially in the Rivers State where East Central Ibo claims to property in the Port Harcourt area were not completely resolved. The military government showed no signs of moving toward civilian rule and appeared to be accepted by the country as cheaper, more efficient, and less corrupt than a civilian equivalent. The government also benefited from an economic boom based on oil. Outstanding problems remained, however, including the lack of skilled administrators and technologists and some tension between statism and federal patriotism.

Nigeria's position in relation to Europe, especially the EEC, was uncertain as was its claim to African leadership. A tentative attempt to take the lead in West African regionalism was forestalled by the formation on June 3 of the Economic Community of West Africa by seven former French African states. This and the proposed highway linking Lagos with Mombasa began to turn Nigerian eyes toward eastern and central Africa. Nigeria continued to maintain a leading place in the Organization of African Unity because of its large Army, reputation for moderation, and economic strength.

The Nigerian economy continued to expand more rapidly than anticipated in both growth rate and capital investment. The 1972–73 federal budget, showing a 12% growth over the previous period (nearly half attributable to oil), envisaged recurrent expenditure of N£499.1 million. Recurrent revenue estimates stood at N£639.9 million (of which N£343 million came from oil), a total budget increase of over 40%. The first progress report of the second national development plan, for which N£1,596,000,000 was earmarked, also exceeded expectations both in financial resources available and in the dynamism of the private sector. The rate of investment in Nigeria (N£465.4 million in 1971–72) was N£66.4 million above the plan figure, with an increasing amount going to the industrial sector. The volume of savings also exceeded estimates. Trade and cooperation agreements with China were signed in August.

Among Nigeria's major economic problems were unemployment and the creation of labour-intensive industry, with more than 2 million (7.8% of the labour force) jobless. There was also a disappointingly slow rate of growth in the agricultural sector, which still employed over 70% of the population and contributed more than half the gross national product, remaining the second largest earner of foreign exchange after oil. Palm products, most affected by the

Nickel: *see* Mining

NIGERIA

Education. (1966–67) Primary, pupils 3,025,981, teachers 91,049; secondary, pupils 202,638, teachers 11,055; vocational, pupils 26,092, teachers 1,378; teacher training, students 28,673, teachers 1,738; higher (universities only; 1968–69), students 9,705, teaching staff 1,328.

Finance. Monetary unit: Nigerian pound, with (Sept. 18, 1972) a free rate of N£0.33 to U.S. $1 (N£0.80 = £1 sterling). Gold, SDRs, and foreign exchange, official: (June 1972) U.S. $311 million; (June 1971) U.S. $333 million. Federal budget (1971–72): revenue N£475 million; expenditure N£465 million. Money supply: (May 1972) N£325.6 million; (May 1971) N£320.3 million. Cost of living (Lagos; 1963 = 100): (June 1972) 170; (June 1971) 166.

Foreign Trade. (1971) Imports N£537.8 million; exports N£585.9 million. Import sources: U.K. 32%; U.S. 14%; West Germany 12%; Japan 8%. Export destinations: U.K. 22%; U.S. 18%; France 15%; Netherlands 14%; West Germany 5%. Main exports: crude oil 71%; cocoa 12%.

Transport and Communications. Roads (1971) 89,000 km. Motor vehicles in use (1969): passenger 41,086; commercial (including buses) 23,600. Railways: (1969) 3,505 km.; traffic (1971) 908.5 million passenger-km., freight 1,264,000,000 net ton-km. Air traffic (1970): 213,623,000 passenger-km.; freight 6,933,000 net ton-km. Shipping (1971): merchant vessels 100 gross tons and over 51; gross tonnage 95,938. Telephones (Dec. 1970) 80,000. Radio licenses (Dec. 1970) 1,275,000. Television licenses (Dec. 1970) 75,000.

Agriculture. Production (in 000; metric tons; 1971; 1970 in parentheses): millet *c.* 2,800 (*c.* 2,800); sorghum *c.* 3,500 (*c.* 3,500); corn *c.* 1,220 (*c.* 1,220); rice 580 (490); sweet potatoes (1970) *c.* 13,500, (1969) *c.* 12,500; cassava (1970) *c.* 6,800, (1969) *c.* 6,800; peanuts *c.* 1,100 (*c.* 780); palm oil *c.* 500 (*c.* 488); cocoa (1971–72) 284, (1970–71) 300; cotton, lint *c.* 40 (*c.* 91); rubber (exports) *c.* 60 (59). Livestock (in 000; 1970–71): cattle *c.* 11,600; sheep *c.* 8,100; goats *c.* 23,500; pigs *c.* 840; poultry *c.* 83,000.

Industry. Production (in 000; metric tons; 1971): crude oil 74,639; cement 665; tin 7.4; electricity (kw-hr.) 1,811,000.

war, were expected to reach prewar figures by 1974; peanuts were affected by late planting and poor weather, while cocoa producers reduced planting following 1971 record crops and low prices. Two major projects, the Niger-Benue River Basin Development Scheme, providing 3 million ac. for rice and sugar, and the Chad Basin Development Plan, were expected to revolutionize agricultural development.

The policy of indigenization was reinforced by the Nigerian Enterprises Promotion Decree of February 29. This reserved for Nigerians exclusively 22 types of enterprise, including retail trade and small-scale services. Aliens were also barred as of March 31, 1974, from another 33 types of enterprise with capital of less than £200,000. Where the paid-up capital exceeded this, equity participation by Nigerian citizens had to be at least 40%. The policy of nigerianization rather than nationalization was also followed in the all-important oil industry, which at nearly 2 million barrels a day made Nigeria one of the world's largest producers and accounted for 74% of its 1971 foreign exchange earnings and 70% of federal government revenue. Aiming at more than 50% control of the Nigerian National Oil Corporation, Nigeria increased its share in the Port Harcourt petroleum refinery to 60%, and via OPEC (Organization of Petroleum Exporting Countries) obtained price increases of more than N£1 per barrel in 1971–72. A Soviet-run petroleum training institute for Nigerians, and the February 1972 Industrial Training Decree, by which the petroleum and other companies were obliged to allocate 2.5% of their annual turnover toward training Nigerians, were temporary sops to political demands for immediate nationalization, recognized by responsible leaders as technically unfeasible.

(MOLLY MORTIMER)

Nobel Prizes

The Nobel Prize selections might almost have been dubbed the Oxford-American sweepstakes in 1972. Of 11 laureates in five disciplines, 2 were professors at the ancient English university and 8 were U.S. citizens. Only German novelist Heinrich Böll's citation for literature precluded an English-speaking monopoly dominated by Rockefeller University in New York City and the University of Illinois.

It was at the latter institution 15 years before that three physicists performed the work that earned them the physics prize: uncovering and describing the miniscule mechanics of superconductors, metals with perplexing electrical properties. *Science* magazine, journal of the American Association for the Advancement of Science, termed this BCS theory, named for its formulators, John Bardeen, Leon N. Cooper, and John Robert Schrieffer, "one of the major achievements in physics of this century." The decision to award a Nobel Prize to three associates who cooperated on a single project was rare enough, but the situation was unique in one respect: Bardeen, having shared the physics prize in 1956, became the first person to win two Nobels in the same discipline (Marie Curie had shared the 1903 physics prize and won the chemistry award eight years later; Linus Pauling had won the chemistry prize in 1954 and the peace prize eight years later; and the International Red Cross had received the peace prize twice).

Two of the year's Rockefeller University laureates were professors Stanford Moore and William Howard Stein, who shared the chemistry prize with Christian Boehmer Anfinsen, a biochemist at the National Institutes of Health, Bethesda, Md. They were cited for "pioneering studies" into the structure of enzymes, the basic elements of biochemical reaction. The third Rockefeller winner, molecular biologist Gerald M. Edelman, shared the prize for medicine or physiology with Oxonian biochemist Rodney R. Porter, for their independent antibody studies. Oxford economist John R. Hicks shared the economics prize with Kenneth J. Arrow of Harvard.

The honorarium for each discipline was approximately $100,000, a significant increase over recent years and, reportedly, the result of newly adroit management of Alfred Nobel's estate, now estimated at $16 million. Nonetheless, with inflation rates taken into account, the prizes would have to be $170,000 if they were to match their original value. The Swedish inventor's will had established the annual prizes that since their inception in 1901 had become the ne plus ultra of international distinctions, particularly in the sciences. Surprising choices of literature laureates during the past decade had somewhat undermined the stature of that prize but its credibility was again on the rise. The economics prize was well regarded but young, having been established only in 1968 and endowed by the Bank of Sweden to mark its third centennial. The peace prize, capstone of both the awards and the legacy of dynamite's inventor, was not given in 1972.

PRIZE FOR PHYSICS

John Bardeen shared his first Nobel Prize for Physics with two other scientists for developing the transistor, the "chip" that revolutionized applied electronics by replacing hot, fragile, short-lived vacuum tubes with components that were cool, durable, tiny, efficient, and cheap. Bardeen's second Nobel was earned for probing the mysterious micromechanics of superconductors—a distant pew of the same electromagnetic church.

Superconductors, certain metals and alloys that, when supercooled to temperatures near absolute zero, lose almost all resistance to electric currents, were first described by Dutch physicist Kamerlingh Onnes early in the 20th century. But their anomalous behaviour was not understood until Bardeen, Leon N. Cooper, and John Robert Schrieffer probed it.

To do so the University of Illinois team had to scrap conventional wisdom regarding the atom's tiny components and make what has been described as "a brilliant intuitive leap." Together they demonstrated that negatively charged electrons in a superconductor, instead of dispersing their energy and momentum through random collisions, arrange themselves in "Cooper pairs" and act in a complementary manner, moving coherently in the same direction at the same speed. This occurs because of a thermodynamically triggered harmony between the natural vibrations of the metal's atoms and the kinetic electrons.

If their thought was unconventional, the association of the three was atavistic in its hierarchical arrangement. The team was headed by Bardeen, already a Nobel laureate before its completion; Cooper, then 27, had come to Urbana, Ill., to perform postdoctoral work at the feet of the preeminent professor; and Schrieffer, a brilliant student, was still working toward his Ph.D. While Bardeen did not expect superconductors to have the catholic application of transistors, he appreciated the importance of his team's discovery. "The theory and its applications can help us understand other physical phenomena," said "Whispering John" with characteristically modest understatement.

Bardeen was born in Madison, Wis., on May 23, 1908, the son of the medical school dean at the University of Wisconsin, where he took his bachelor's and master's degrees in electrical engineering. After working for Gulf Research and Development Company in Pittsburgh, Pa., he earned a doctorate in mathematical physics at Princeton. During World War II he worked on Navy electronics projects, and then joined Bell Telephone Laboratories to invent and develop the transistor with Walter Brattain and William Shockley. He joined the faculty of the University of Illinois in 1951 where protégés Schrieffer and Cooper joined him for a brief, productive period that ended in 1957. On the day his second Nobel was announced Bardeen could not reach the campus because his automatic garage door, controlled by transistors, was stuck.

Cooper, since 1966 Ledyard Goddard university professor at Brown University, Providence, R.I., was that university's first Nobel laureate. He was born in New York on Feb. 28, 1930, and educated at Columbia. After a National Science Foundation fellowship at Princeton's Institute for Advanced Study, he joined Bardeen as a research associate in 1955. Two years later he became an assistant professor at Ohio State University, and went on to Brown in 1958. A "swinging scientist," who dressed modishly and appreciated the arts and literature, Cooper taught an undergraduate physics course for humanities majors, one proof of his interest in relating the disciplines. He also worked frequently in Europe, notably at Varenna, Italy, and the École Normale Supérieure in Paris.

Schrieffer was born in Oak Park, Ill., on May 31, 1931, and earned his bachelor's degree at MIT in 1953. He went directly to Urbana where he won a master's and, in 1957, a doctorate. Like Cooper he was a National Science Foundation fellow, at the University of Birmingham (Eng.) and the Niels Bohr Institute, Copenhagen. He taught at the University of Chicago and the University of Illinois before joining the faculty of the University of Pennsylvania, where he was Mary Amanda Wood professor of physics since 1964. Winner of a Guggenheim fellowship and the National Academy of Sciences' Comstock Award, he shared with Cooper a dedication to nonscientific concerns and helped establish Penn's Afro-American Studies Program.

PRIZE FOR CHEMISTRY

The three scientists who won the Nobel Prize for Chemistry were cited for their studies into the composition and functioning of the enzyme ribonuclease. Like the work that prompted the physics prize and many others in recent years, their investigations were not recent. Christian B. Anfinsen, chief of the chemical biology laboratory at the National Institute of Arthritis, Metabolism, and Digestive Diseases, had first discovered the composition of ribonuclease 20 years before. And between 1949 and 1963 Rockefeller University professors Stanford Moore and William H. Stein had deciphered how it catalyzes digestion of food. It was for this that they won the Nobel, though a week before the prize was announced they unraveled deoxyribonuclease, which is twice as complex a molecule.

While acknowledging that enzyme studies may eventually lead to genetic repair or disease control, Anfinsen finessed their immediate practical significance. "This is groundwork in a sense," he said, "but all scientific work requires basic groundwork first. It's pretty mundane stuff when it comes to practical applications. But without the tools you can't have any applications." Still, deciphering the biochemical anatomy of an enzyme paves the way for its eventual synthetic manufacture. "If you want a certain catalytic job done or perhaps a certain replacement of a missing protein in an animal, you might be able to design in advance the three-dimensional structure."

Born in Monessen, Pa., on March 26, 1916, Anfinsen studied at Swarthmore, the University of Pennsylvania, and Harvard where he took a Ph.D. in biochemistry in 1943. Recipient of several honorary degrees and fellowships, he worked and taught at the Carlsberg Laboratories in Copenhagen, the Nobel Institute in Stockholm, and the Weizmann Institute in Israel. He took his present job in 1963. In a free-wheeling press conference Anfinsen took the federal government to task for its research priorities and articulated the frustrations of many whose work was supported by "chicken feed" he said, in comparison to the billions spent on applied scientific research and development for defense projects.

Moore, born in Chicago on Sept. 4, 1913, studied at Vanderbilt and took a doctorate in organic chemistry in 1938. The following year he joined the staff of the Rockefeller Institute of Medical Research, the University's antecedent. Holder of honorary degrees from the university of Brussels (where he had been a visiting professor) and the University of Paris, he also taught at Vanderbilt and was a visiting researcher at Cambridge (Eng.). He served as president of the Society of Biological Chemists, and chaired a National Research Council panel. A white-haired bachelor, he, too, emphasized the need for accelerating basic research. "It is fundamental to medicine to know the structure of 2,000 enzymes by the year 2000," he told the press. "Man's understanding of man is an even higher priority of research than man's understanding of the universe."

Stein was born in New York on June 25, 1911, educated at Phillips Exeter, Harvard, and Columbia, where he earned his doctorate in 1938, the year he joined Rockefeller Institute. He also taught at the University of Chi-

UPI COMPIX

AUTHENTICATED NEWS INTERNATIONAL

(LEFT, RIGHT) KEYSTONE

Nobel Prize winners in 1972 included John Bardeen (top, left), Leon Cooper (top, right), and John Robert Schrieffer (above, left), winners of the prize for physics, and Rodney Porter (above, right), who shared the prize for physiology or medicine.

cago and Harvard and was a member of the medical advisory board of the Hebrew University-Hadassah Medical School and a trustee of Montefiore Hospital in New York.

PRIZE FOR PHYSIOLOGY OR MEDICINE

The American Gerald M. Edelman and the Briton Rodney R. Porter won the Nobel medical prize for, essentially, rewriting the book on antibodies. "Up to the year 1959," said their citation, "our knowledge of the nature and function of antibodies was very vague and incomplete." Their continued researches "represent clearly a breakthrough that immediately incited a fervent research activity the world over in all fields of immunological science, yielding results and practical value for clinical diagnostics and therapy."

Following procedures he preferred, Porter used an enzyme to fragment the blood's gamma globulin molecule into its composite parts. Following a different approach, Edelman spent 12 years using chemical compounds to do the job. As a result, each identified different pieces of the same biochemical puzzle. Early results demonstrated that instead of being a single chain of amino acids, the gamma globulin molecule comprises several strands of components. The two men, and other immunologists, met as often as twice a year in informal "antibody workshops" to compare notes. As published papers described their progressive success, other teams joined the effort. Then Porter began studying the heavy chains of the molecule while Edelman's team, "mad as we were, started on the whole molecule, a ghastly big job." By 1969 Edelman could make a complete model of the biochemical entity that comprises 19,960 atoms and has an atomic weight of 150,000. "Neither of us could claim that we were solely responsible," Edelman said, "even as a pair of people."

Their different approaches and methods reflected the respective training and scientific backgrounds of the two men. Porter was a biochemist. Born Oct. 8, 1917, he was trained at Liverpool University and Cambridge. "I don't know why I became interested in this work," said Porter, son of a British Railways clerk, "It didn't run in my family." In 1967 he became Whitley professor of biochemistry at Trinity College, Oxford.

Edelman was a physician with an interest in physical chemistry. Born in New York on July 1, 1929, he reportedly had trouble getting into college during the postwar rush. He received a bachelor's degree in chemistry from Ursinus College, Collegeville, Pa., and after taking an M.D. at the University of Pennsylvania, trained at Massachusetts General Hospital, and then spent two years in Paris with the Army Medical Corps. He received his doctorate from Rockefeller University in 1960, when he joined the faculty.

PRIZE FOR ECONOMICS

Sir John R. Hicks, professor emeritus at All Souls College, Oxford, and Kenneth J. Arrow of Harvard University shared the Nobel economics prize for erudite and fundamental theories about complex economic events and ways to predict them. They were cited for the "pioneering contributions to general economic equilibrium theory" they had made through diverse and abstruse writings. A Swedish Academy of Science spokesman said it was Sir John's now classic *Value and Capital* (1939) that resolved basic conflicts between business cycle theory and the equilibrium theory, which holds that economic forces tend to balance each other, rather than simply reflecting cyclical trends. Both men had demonstrated that active forces, not passive ones, strike economic balances when the forces cancel each other out. The foundations they had laid in arcane theory were used widely by public and private interests to determine foreign trade, investment policies, and prices. Other aspects of their copious works have had implications for public welfare policies.

Hicks, who was born on April 8, 1904, studied at Balliol College, Oxford, taking honours in politics, philosophy, and economics. Before returning to Oxford, he taught at the University of Manchester and the London School of Economics, to which he planned to donate his prize money. Married to an economist with whom he collaborated on several books, he was in Japan preparing for a television appearance when the prize was announced. Knighted in 1964, the year before his retirement from teaching, he was regarded as "rather a lone wolf in his thinking." He retired as a fellow of All Souls College in 1972, 40 years after publication of his first book, *The Theory of Wages*.

Arrow, who was born in New York on Aug. 23, 1921, established his reputation at Columbia in 1951 with his doctoral dissertation, "Social Choice and Individual Values." Paul A. Samuelson, winner of the prize in 1970 and pleased that the new laureates were "economists' economists," explained: "It used to be said that only 10 men understood Einstein's theory of relativity. . . . But it is no exaggeration to say that only a score of scholars were able to follow Arrow's early research in these esoteric fields." Perhaps his most startling thesis was the "impossibility theory," which proved that perfectly responsive representative government is impossible. As a colleague explained, "Arrow raised the question of whether there was any democratic way—by voting or otherwise—to achieve a consensus. . . . He was able to show, by using fairly elementary mathematics of a sort that had never been applied before to such a question, that the answer is no."

Arrow began teaching at the University of Chicago, and then went to Stanford from 1949 until his Harvard appointment in 1968, where he inspired the development of a first-rate school of economic theorists. He said he was especially pleased that the award was conferred for theoretical work in view of constantly popular pressure "for relevance. . . . I'm thoroughly in favour of action but I think everything needs to be seen in broader relations that perhaps are not obvious to the eye."

PRIZE FOR LITERATURE

Heinrich Böll was widely regarded as "the conscience of modern Germany," the literary heir of Thomas Mann, and the outstanding humanist interpreter of World War II vis-à-vis his nation's experience. In announcing him as recipient of the literature prize, the Swedish Academy said, "It is not the smallest German miracle that after such years of destitution a new generation of writers, thinkers, and researchers was ready so soon to shoulder their country's and their own essential task in the spiritual life of our time."

Born in Cologne on Dec. 21, 1917, the child of one war and foot soldier of another, Böll was captured by U.S. forces in April 1945 and imprisoned in France. The experience was central to the life and art of a writer who remembered the "frightful fate of being a soldier and having to wish that the war might be lost." Following repatriation, he enrolled in the University of Cologne in order, some said, to qualify for a ration card. His first stories were published in 1947; his first novel, *The Train Was on Time,* two years later. *Acquainted with the Night* brought his first simultaneous critical and popular success in 1953. By 1972 his 40 books had sold four million copies in West Germany and 300,000 in East Germany and his most celebrated novels, *The Clown* and *Billiards at Half-Past Nine,* had been translated into 30 languages.

Böll's frequent theme was the individual's acceptance or refusal of personal responsibility. He used spare prose and frequently sharp satire to present his antiwar, nonconformist point of view. Personally he was an outspoken proponent of causes who campaigned widely for the re-election of Chancellor Willy Brandt in 1972, refused to pay church taxes and publicly criticized the narrow conservatism of the German Roman Catholic Church, and announced he would contribute much of the $100,000 prize to a fund to free writers imprisoned the world over for political reasons. (PHILIP KOPPER)

Norway

A constitutional monarchy of northern Europe, Norway is bordered by Sweden, Finland, and the U.S.S.R.; its coastlines are on the North Sea, the Norwegian Sea, and the Arctic Ocean. Area: 125,052 sq.mi. (323,886 sq.km.), excluding the Svalbard Archipelago, 23,957 sq.mi., and Jan Mayen Island, 144 sq.mi. Pop. (1972 est.): 3,917,773. Cap. and largest city: Oslo (pop., 1972 est., 475,563). Language: Norwegian. Religion: Lutheran (96.2%). King, Olav V; prime ministers in 1972, Trygve Bratteli until October 7 and, from October 18, Lars Korvald.

The Norwegian people on Sept. 25, 1972, voted

Northern Ireland:
see United Kingdom

Norwegian Literature:
see Literature

Nuclear Energy:
see Defense; Fuel and Power; Industrial Review

Numismatics:
see Philately and Numismatics

Nutrition:
see Food

Nuts:
see Agriculture

against their country's membership in the EEC in a national referendum. Of the 77.7% of the electorate who voted, 53.5% (1,099,398) voted against entry and 46.5% (956,043) in favour. The referendum was advisory only, but the Storting (parliament) had agreed it would respect the wishes of the people. Prime Minister Bratteli, who had signed the treaty of accession in Brussels in January, had said that in the event of a negative decision his government would resign.

Even without the referendum, it seemed unlikely that a parliamentary vote on joining the EEC would have achieved the necessary three-quarters majority. While the Labour government was strongly pro-EEC, a considerable minority of Labour members of the Storting opposed it, as did a large minority of the Liberals and most of the Centre and Christian People's Party members. Only the Conservatives were united in support of accession.

The People's Movement Against Norwegian Membership of the EEC was a conglomerate of disparate elements, from intellectuals to fishermen, motivated by a variety of factors from political opposition to NATO to simple concern about job security and from ultraconservative nationalism to religious mysticism. United on a negative level, the movement was ably organized, and the subsequent referendum result was hailed by its leaders as an outstanding example of popular resistance to the political and economic establishment.

The highest proportion of no votes (72.7%) came from the northern fishing province of Nordland, while the highest proportion of yes votes (66.9%) came from the commercially oriented capital. However, heavily industrial districts such as Porsgrunn in the south also registered a strong no vote, suggesting that official trade-union support for EEC membership was by no means wholly shared by the more militant rank and file. With the Centre (formerly Agrarian) Party strongly opposed to membership, the rural communities generally voted against it.

While the Movement Against Membership had succeeded in uniting divergent groups in its prereferendum campaign, it could not easily provide the basis for a new anti-EEC administration. The three non-Labour and non-Conservative parties in the Storting finally agreed on a government under the premiership of Lars Korvald of the Christian People's Party. The new administration, which took office on October 18, included seven members of the Centre Party, five from the minority (anti-EEC) wing of the Liberals, and four from the Christian People's Party. While the new government could claim the support of only 47 of the Storting's 150 members, Korvald expressed confidence that it would be able to count on the votes of various segments of the House on particular issues. The split in the Liberal Party became final on December 9 with the formation of the People's New Liberal Party.

The new government's most urgent task was to open negotiations to secure a free-trade agreement with the EEC, preferably effective from April 1973 when similar agreements with Sweden and other EFTA countries would come into force. Industrialists recognized that such an agreement would be much less favourable than full membership, and concern was expressed about the future development of exports, particularly "sensitive" products such as ferroalloys, aluminum, and paper.

Meanwhile, the economy showed considerable resilience despite relatively slack demand abroad. Commodity exports grew faster than imports, and the first half of 1972 showed a balance of payments surplus of 375 million kroner on current account, compared with a deficit of 1,350,000,000 kroner for the first half of 1971. Foreign currency holdings rose to record levels, and the krone remained strong.

Despite the depressed demand abroad for aluminum, ferroalloys, and certain other products, full employment was maintained almost unimpaired, and industries from engineering to fishing reported good outputs and sales. There was growing concern about rising labour costs and prices; wage increases were limited to 5.6%, but built-in safeguards provided for further increases if the cost of living continued to rise. In the 12 months up to mid-August prices had risen by 8%, and to counter this a price freeze was imposed from September 7.

The Bratteli government's 1973 budget proposals, presented before its resignation, involved heavy increases in state expenditure, particularly in the social insurance sector. For the first time there was a separate "social" budget, proposing a 20% increase in expenditure to 14.7 billion kroner (one-third of total state expenditure), chiefly to meet the cost of lowering the retirement age from 70 to 67 as of Jan. 1, 1973.

Considerable discussion in the Storting followed an incident in November when an unknown submarine was detected in Sogne Fjord. The craft disappeared after 14 days. Highly placed sources said privately that it was a Soviet ship and had been allowed to escape to avoid an international incident.

For the first time the government was able to budget royalty receipts from North Sea oil at the Ekofisk site. (OLE F. KNUDSEN)

NORWAY

Education. (1969–70) Primary, pupils 390,046, teachers 19,448; secondary, pupils 234,449, teachers 17,493; vocational, pupils 65,875, teachers 9,805; higher (including 4 universities), students 46,715, teaching staff 4,922.

Finance. Monetary unit: Norwegian krone, with (Sept. 18, 1972) a par value of 6.65 kroner to U.S. $1 (free rate of 16.09 kroner = £1 sterling). Gold, SDRs, and foreign exchange, central bank: (June 1972) U.S. $1,222,100,000; (June 1971) U.S. $869.7 million. Budget (1972 est.): revenue 24,010,000,000 kroner; expenditure 27,343,000,000 kroner. Gross national product: (1970) 81,370,000,000 kroner; (1969) 70,280,000,000 kroner. Money supply: (June 1972) 20,250,000,000 kroner; (June 1971) 18,510,000,000 kroner. Cost of living (1963 = 100): (June 1972) 159; (June 1971) 148.

Foreign Trade. (1971) Imports 28,722,000,000 kroner; exports 17,988,000,000 kroner. Import sources: Sweden 19%; West Germany 14%; U.K. 12%; Denmark 6%; U.S. 6%; Japan 5%; Canada 5%. Export destinations: U.K. 19%; Sweden 17%; West Germany 15%; Denmark 7%; U.S. 7%. Main exports: ships 10%; machinery 10%; aluminum 10%; fish 9%; iron and steel 8%; chemicals 8%; paper 7%; nickel 5%.

Transport and Communications. Roads (1971) 73,112 km. (including 106 km. expressways). Motor vehicles in use (1971): passenger 806,600; commercial 153,400. Railways: (state only; 1970) 4,242 km. (including 2,440 km. electrified); traffic (state only; 1971) 1,600,000,000 passenger-km., freight 2,600,000,000 net ton-km. Air traffic (including Norwegian apportionment of international operations of Scandinavian Airlines System; 1971): 2,134,600,000 passenger-km.; freight 75,537,000 net ton-km. Shipping (1971): merchant vessels 100 gross tons and over 2,814; gross tonnage 21,720,202. Ships entered (1970) vessels totaling 15,722,000 net registered tons; goods loaded (1971) 34,546,000 metric tons, unloaded 17,923,000 metric tons. Telephones (Dec. 1970) 1,145,000. Radio licenses (Dec. 1970) 1,191,000. Television licenses (Dec. 1970) 854,000.

Agriculture. Production (in 000; metric tons; 1971; 1970 in parentheses): barley 569 (581); oats *c.* 275 (228); potatoes 708 (857); apples *c.* 50 (48); milk *c.* 1,724 (1,730); butter *c.* 19 (19); cheese 54 (52); beef and veal *c.* 59 (56); pork *c.* 68 (65); timber (cu.m.; 1970) 8,600, (1969) 8,100; fish catch (1970) 2,980, (1969) 2,481. Livestock (in 000; June 1971): cattle 917; sheep 1,673; pigs 677; goats *c.* 83; chickens *c.* 5,900.

Industry. Fuel and power (in 000; metric tons; 1971): crude oil 311; coal (Svalbard mines; Norwegian operated only) 466, (U.S.S.R. operated; exports; 1970) 443; manufactured gas (cu.m.) 29,800; electricity (kw-hr.) 62,681,000. Production (in 000; metric tons; 1971): iron ore (65% metal content) 3,910; pig iron 1,274; crude steel 863; aluminum 529; zinc 62; copper 28; cement 2,721; sulfur (1970) 340; nitrogenous fertilizers (N content; 1970–71) 370; mechanical wood pulp (1970) 1,268; chemical wood pulp (1970) 942; newsprint 530; other paper (1970) 868. Merchant vessels launched (100 gross tons and over; 1971) 831,000 gross tons. New dwelling units completed (1971) 38,000.

Obituaries 1972

The following is a selected list of prominent men and women who died during 1972.

ALINSKY, SAUL, U.S. social organizer (b. Chicago, Ill., 1909—d. Carmel, Calif., June 12, 1972), a controversial poverty fighter who attained prominence during World War II with his Chicago "Back-of-the-Yards" movement. He organized the predominantly lower-class white neighbourhood to make concerted demands for better jobs, housing, and schools, and later used the same techniques to form The Woodlawn Organization in a Chicago black ghetto area. His successful methods were later employed in other parts of the country. For a short time during 1965–66 he was involved in the U.S. government's "war on poverty" as a leader in the training centre at Syracuse (N.Y.) University.

ANDERSEN, LALE (LISELOTTE HELEN BEUL), German singer (b. Bremerhaven, Ger., 1913—d. Vienna, Aus., Aug. 29, 1972), gained world fame by her recording of "Lili Marlene," used as the theme song of the German Army radio station in occupied Belgrade during World War II.

ARLEN, STEPHEN, British theatre administrator (b. Birmingham, Eng., Oct. 31, 1913—d. London, Eng., Jan. 19, 1972), managing director of Sadler's Wells Opera from 1966, became general manager of the Old Vic in 1945 and of Sadler's Wells Theatre in 1951. In 1962 he became administrative director of the new National Theatre during its formative period, afterward returning to Sadler's Wells. He was chairman of the British Centre of the International Theatre Institute, and in 1959 advised on the formation of the Belgian national opera.

ARNSTEIN, MARGARET G., U.S. nurse and educator (b. New York, N.Y., Oct. 27, 1904—d. New Haven, Conn., Oct. 8, 1972), dean of the Yale University School of Nursing, was chief of nursing for the U.S. Public Health Service (1960–64) and nursing adviser for international health, Office of the Surgeon General (1965).

ASGEIRSSON, ASGEIR, Icelandic statesman (b. Iceland, 1894—d. Reykjavik, Iceland, Sept. 15, 1972), was president of Iceland from 1952 until 1968. A member of the Althing (parliament) from 1923, he was its speaker at the 1930 millennial celebration. He was minister of finance (1931–34) and prime minister (1932–34). In 1944 he attended the Bretton Woods economic and monetary conference as Icelandic delegate, and was a governor of the International Monetary Fund (1946–52).

ASHBY, W(ILLIAM) ROSS, British cyberneticist (b. London, Eng., Sept. 6, 1903—d. Nov. 15, 1972), an outstanding pioneer in the study of the organization and control of complex systems, was director (1947–59) of research at Barnwood House Hospital, Gloucester. He wrote *Design for a Brain* (1952) and *An Introduction to Cybernetics* (1956), both classics in their field. Director of the Burden Neurological Institute in Bristol (1960–61), and professor of cybernetics in the Department of Electrical Engineering at the University of Illinois, Urbana (1961–70), he was elected a fellow of the Royal College of Psychiatry in 1971.

ASHFORD, DAISY, British author (b. Petersham, Eng., 1881—d. Norwich, Eng., Jan. 15, 1972), was nine when she wrote *The Young Visiters*, an erratically spelled romance of Victorian English "high life" as seen from the nursery. Rediscovered by the author some 30 years later, it was published in 1919 with a preface by Sir James Barrie (who was at first suspected of having written it himself) and subsequently sold half a million copies. *The Young Visiters* was dramatized in 1920 and a musical adaptation was staged in London in 1968. Daisy Ashford wrote several other stories while still a child, some of which appeared in *Daisy Ashford: Her Book* (1920) and in *Love and Marriage* (1965).

ATHENAGORAS I, ecumenical patriarch of the Eastern Orthodox Church (b. Terraplana [Vasilikón], Turk. [now Greece], March 25, 1886—d. Balikli, Turk., July 6, 1972), leader of 126 million Byzantine Christians, was archbishop of Constantinople and New Rome from 1948. Until 1922 he was chief secretary to the Holy Synod at Athens, then was metropolitan of Corfu (1923–30). During his tenure as archbishop of North and South America (1930–48) he became a U.S. citizen (1938), although some years later he was obliged to resume Turkish citizenship. He was deeply influenced by his long stay in the U.S., where he founded the theological college of Sainte-Croix, Conn., and the Saint-Basile Academy in Boston. Athenagoras was often criticized by Athens for his efforts to reach an understanding with the Roman Catholic Church. He met Pope Paul VI in Jerusalem in 1964, in Istanbul in 1967, and again that year when he visited the Vatican.

ATLAS, CHARLES (ANGELO SICILIANO), U.S. body builder (b. Calabria, Italy, Oct. 30, 1893—d. Long Beach, N.Y., Dec. 24, 1972), was in 1922 named by Bernarr Macfadden, publisher of health magazines, the "World's Most Perfectly Developed Man." In 1921 he devised a system of muscle building, called Dynamic Tension, an early form of isometrics, which became the basis for a mail-order course that, by 1972, was available in seven languages and sold at the rate of 70,000 courses a year.

AUSTIN, GENE (EUGENE LUCAS), U.S. singer (b. Gainesville, Tex., June 24, 1900—d. Palm Springs, Calif., Jan. 24, 1972), popular crooner of the 1920s, whose recording of "My Blue Heaven" sold more than 12 million records.

BALDICK, ROBERT, British scholar (b. Huddersfield, Eng., Nov. 9, 1927—d. April 24, 1972), a foremost British expert in French literature and culture, produced in 1955 a widely acclaimed biography of Joris-Karl Huysmans based on his 1952 doctorate. Baldick became a fellow of Pembroke College, Oxford, in 1958. Other works included *The Goncourts* (1960), *The First Bohemian: The Life of Henry Murger* (1961), *The Life and Times of Frédéric Lemaître* (1959), *The Siege of Paris* (1964), and *Dinner at Magny's* (1971). He was joint editor of Penguin Classics from 1964 and was a contributor to *Encyclopædia Britannica*.

BALENCIAGA, CRISTÓBAL, Spanish couturier (b. Guetaria, Spain, Jan. 21, 1895—d. Valencia, Spain, March 23, 1972), greatly influenced fashion trends in the post-World War II era, and was called "the designer's designer." After running his own dressmaking establishment at San Sebastian from the age of 20, he set up in Paris in 1937.

BANCROFT, DAVID J. ("DAVE"), U.S. baseball player (b. Sioux City, Ia., April 20, 1892—d. Superior, Wis., Oct. 9, 1972), a major league shortstop for 16 years, played with the Philadelphia Phillies (1915–18) and with the New York Giants (1920–23). He later played for Boston and Brooklyn, and again for the Giants in his last season (1930). Bancroft's lifetime batting average was .279; he was elected to the Baseball Hall of Fame in 1971.

BARLOW, HOWARD, U.S. conductor (b. Plain City, O., May 1, 1892—d. Bethel, Conn., Jan. 31, 1972), led the Firestone Orchestra on the radio and television feature "Voice of Firestone" from 1943 through 1961. He began his musical career with the Columbia Broadcasting System in 1927 as the network's top musical director; in 1943 he went to the National Broadcasting Company as conductor of the Firestone show. Later the program was taken over by the American Broadcasting Company and aired simultaneously on radio and TV.

BATES, TED (THEODORE L.), U.S. advertising executive (b. New Haven, Conn., Sept. 11, 1901—d. New York, N.Y., May 30, 1972), founder (1940) and head of Ted Bates & Co., based his success on the hard-sell techniques he devised for early television commercials. Bates was president of his company until the late 1950s when he assumed honorary chairmanship.

BERRYMAN, JOHN, U.S. poet (b. McAlester, Okla., Oct. 25, 1914—d. Minneapolis, Minn., Jan. 7, 1972), was regents professor at the University of Minnesota, where he had been a faculty member from 1955. He won the 1965 Pulitzer Prize in poetry for his *77 Dream Songs* (1964); the National Book Award in 1969 for *His Toy, His Dream, His Rest* (1968), and in 1969 shared the Bollingen Prize in Poetry with Karl Shapiro. Berryman's last volume of poetry, *Delusions, etc.,* was published in 1972.

BLOCKER, DAN, U.S. television actor (b. Bowie County, Tex., 1929—d. Inglewood, Calif., May 13, 1972), starred as Hoss Cartwright in the "Bonanza" series from the time of its inception in 1959.

BLYTHE, BETTY, U.S. screen star (b. Los Angeles, Calif, 1900—d. Woodland Hills, Calif., April 7, 1972), appeared in about 60 silent films and more than 50 talkies, including *The Helen Morgan Story* and *My Fair Lady,* her last, in 1964.

BONNIER, JOAKIM, Swedish racing driver (b. Stockholm, Swed., Jan. 31, 1930—d. Le Mans, France, June 11, 1972), was a founder and president of the Grand Prix Drivers' Association and a leading campaigner for greater safety in motor

Betty Blythe

WIDE WORLD

William Boyd

UPI COMPIX

Bruce Cabot

UPI COMPIX

racing. He was killed during the Le Mans 24-hour race when his Lola T280 touched a GT Ferrari while both were traveling at 180 mph on a right-hand curve.

BOYD, WILLIAM, U.S. film actor (b. Hendrysburg, O., June 5, 1898—d. South Laguna Beach, Calif., Sept. 12, 1972), who portrayed the good-guy cowboy Hopalong Cassidy, began his career with romantic parts in some of the most popular films of the 1920s, including *The Volga Boatman* and *King of Kings.*

BRAUNTHAL, JULIUS, Austrian socialist (b. Vienna, Aus., 1891—d. Teddington, Surrey, Eng., April 28, 1972), was secretary of the Socialist International (1949–56).

BRIAN, (WILLIAM) HAVERGAL, British composer (b. Dresden, Staffordshire, Eng., Jan. 29, 1876—d. Shoreham, Sussex, Eng., Nov. 28, 1972), who enjoyed a high reputation in the early years of the century, was thereafter largely neglected until the 1960s brought a revival of interest in his music. By the age of 93 he had written 32 symphonies and many other works, but much of his vast output remained unplayed and unpublished. Notable among his performed works were the *Gothic Symphony* of 1919 (No. 2), performed in London's Albert Hall in 1966, *A First English Suite,* the overture *For Valour,* the symphonic poem *Hero and Leander, Variations on an Old Rhyme, Festal Dance, Doctor Merryheart, By the Waters of Babylon,* the cantata *A Vision of Cleopatra,* the satiric opera *The Tigers,* composed during World War I, and the 12th and 26th symphonies.

BRODA, WALTER ("Turk"), Canadian hockey player (b. Brandon, Man., 1914—d. Toronto, Ont., Oct. 17, 1972), was goaltender for the Toronto Maple Leafs hockey team from 1935 until 1952, with two seasons out for military service in World War II. Broda was signed by the Maple Leafs shortly after he turned professional in 1935. He played in 101 Stanley Cup play-offs, allowing only 211 goals (averaging 2.08 per game), and twice won (1941, 1948) the Vezina Trophy for allowing the fewest goals of any National Hockey League goalie.

BYRNES, JAMES FRANCIS, U.S. statesman (b. Charleston, S.C., May 2, 1879—d. Columbia, S.C., April 9, 1972), began his 50-year political career in 1908 as a small-town prosecutor. In 1910 he was elected to Congress and served in the House for 14 years. After losing a race for the Senate in 1924, he waged a successful campaign in 1930 and two years later was a trusted legislative supporter of Pres. Franklin D. Roosevelt's New Deal program. After World War II erupted in Europe, Byrnes was instrumental in obtaining revision of the Neutrality Act and passage of the Lend-Lease bill for aid to the Allies. In 1941 Roosevelt appointed Byrnes to the U.S. Supreme Court, but after serving 16 months he stepped down to head the wartime Office of Economic Stabilization and from May 1943 until April 1945 the Office of War Mobilization. After Roosevelt's death, Pres. Harry S. Truman appointed Byrnes as secretary of state, and as such he accompanied Truman to the Potsdam Conference in July 1945. As a delegate he also attended the early meetings of the United Nations in London and New York, and conferences in Paris during 1945–46. He left the Cabinet in 1947 and returned to private life in South Carolina, but in 1950 was elected governor of his state and served in that office until 1955.

CABOT, BRUCE (Jacques de Bujac), U.S. screen actor (b. Carlsbad, N.M., 1903—d. Woodland Hills, Calif., May 3, 1972), who co-starred in the original *King Kong* movie of 1933, later played character roles in numerous successful films including *The Green Berets* (1968), *Big Jake* (1971), and *Diamonds Are Forever* (1971).

CARROLL, LEO G., U.S. actor (b. Weedon, Eng., 1892—d. Hollywood, Calif., Oct. 16, 1972), played the role of Cosmo Topper in television's "Topper" series of the 1960s, and also appeared in numerous other TV shows.

CASADESUS, ROBERT MARCEL, French pianist and composer (b. Paris, France, April 7, 1899—d. Paris, Sept. 19, 1972), began his career as a virtuoso concert pianist in 1920, and toured Europe, South and North America, Asia, and Africa. In 1958 he won the Brahms Medal. One of the latest of his symphonies, Symphony No. 7, "Israel" (Op. 68), was first performed Nov. 8, 1972, at Tully Hall.

CHANDOS, OLIVER LYTTELTON, 1st Viscount, British politician and industrialist (b. March 15, 1893—d. London, Eng., Jan. 21, 1972), during World War II was a member of the British War Cabinet as minister of state in the Middle East (1941–42) and minister of production (1942–45).

CHEN YI, Chinese government official (b. Szechwan Province, China, 1901—d. Peking, China, Jan. 6, 1972), a deputy premier and foreign minister (1958–68) of China, in 1941 became commander in chief of the Communist New 4th Army that waged the war with Japan.

CHEVALIER, MAURICE, French entertainer (b. Paris, France, Sept. 12, 1888—d. Paris, Jan. 1, 1972), who popularized the songs "Louise," "Valentine," and "Mimi," was primarily a revue artist but appeared in some 40 French and U.S. films during his career of more than 60 years. Chevalier's first success came in 1909 with the Folies-Bergère. In 1929 he appeared in his first American film, *Innocents of Paris,* and in the same year played the irresistible lover in *The Love Parade.* Another popular role was that of the dashing Captain Danilo in *The Merry Widow* (1934), opposite Jeanette MacDonald. He again appeared in the U.S. in 1947 with his one-man show. During the 1950s he made a film comeback in the U.S. productions *Love in the Afternoon* (1957) and *Gigi* (1958). Chevalier staged successful farewell tours in Europe and America in the 1960s and in 1970 published *Les Pensées de Momo,* a last volume of thoughts and memoirs.

CHICHESTER, SIR FRANCIS, British circumnavigator (b. Barnstable, Devon, Eng., Sept. 17, 1901—d. Plymouth, Eng., Aug. 26, 1972), internationally famous flyer and sailor. At 18 he emigrated to New Zealand, where his interest in flying led to his becoming in 1929 the first second man to make a solo flight from England to Australia, covering 12,600 mi. in 180.5 hours. This was followed in 1930 by the first east-to-west 1,450-mi. solo flight across the Tasman Sea. In 1960 he won the first single-handed transatlantic yacht race, in 40½ days in "Gipsy Moth III." Two years later he cut his record by almost a week. In the 1964 race he came in second, but succeeded in cutting his time to under 30 days. On Aug. 23, 1966, Chichester set forth on a round-the-world voyage in "Gipsy Moth IV," reaching Sydney and a tumultuous welcome on December 12, in 7 days more than his intended 100. He rounded Cape Horn on his return journey on March 20, 1967, and completed the 28,500-mi. journey on May 28, 119 days out from Sydney. On July 7 Queen Elizabeth II dubbed him knight in a special ceremony in the Grand Square of the Royal Naval College, Greenwich, and he was fêted by the City of London. In 1971 Chichester sailed 4,000 mi. from Portuguese Guinea to Nicaragua in just over 22 days. In July 1972, on his last singlehanded transatlantic race, he became ill and was forced to drop out. Chichester's autobiography, *The Lonely Sea and Sky,* was published in 1964.

CHURCH, RICHARD THOMAS, British poet, critic, and novelist (b. London, Eng., March 26, 1893—d. Cranbrook, Kent, Eng., March 4, 1972), first gained attention in 1926 with his dramatic monologue *Portrait of the Abbot.* His outstanding prose included the autobiographical sequence *Over the Bridge* (1955), *The Golden Sovereign* (1957), and *The Voyage Home* (1964). Of his novels, *The Porch* (1937) was the most impressive and won the Femina-Vie Heureuse prize.

CHURCHILL, PETER MORLAND, British intelligence agent (b. Jan. 14, 1909—d. Cannes, France, May 1, 1972), was a captain in the Special Operations Executive (SOE) of the British Army during World War II and played a prominent part in the organization of resistance within France to the German occupation.

CLEMENTE, ROBERTO, U.S.-Puerto Rican baseball player (b. Carolina, P.R., Aug. 18, 1934—d. off San Juan, P.R., Dec. 31, 1972), was killed when a cargo plane loaded with relief supplies for survivors of earthquake-devastated Managua, Nicaragua, went down at sea. Clemente was drafted by the Pittsburgh Pirates from the Brooklyn Dodgers farm team at Montreal following the 1954 season and had just completed his 18th season with the Pirates. During that season the popular outfielder became the 11th major league player to get 3,000 hits for a career total. He won four batting championships in the 1960s, and his lifetime average was .318, the highest among active players. Clemente was chosen for 12 All-Star teams, he was named the NL's most valuable player in 1966, and in 1971, when the Pirates defeated the Baltimore Orioles in seven games, he was chosen the World Series' most valuable player.

Leo G. Carroll

WIDE WORLD

Maurice Chevalier

WIDE WORLD

Roberto Clemente

UPI COMPIX

COLUM, PADRAIC, Irish-American poet (b. Longford, Ire., Dec. 8, 1881—d. Enfield, Conn., Jan. 11, 1972), as a young man took part in the Irish literary renaissance and was associated with W. B. Yeats and Lady Gregory in the early days of the Abbey Theatre in Dublin. He wrote several plays, including *Broken Soil* (1903) and *The Land* (1905), but made his name as a poet and as a writer of children's stories. Poetry collections included *Wild Earth* (1907), *Dramatic Legends* (1922), *Flower Pieces* (1939), *Collected Poems* (1953), and *Images of Departure* (1968). Among numerous volumes of Irish and other folktales retold for children were *The King of Ireland's Son* (1916), *The Adventures of Odysseus and The Tale of Troy* (1918), *Orpheus, or Stories from the Mythologies of the World* (1929), and *Where the Winds Never Blew and the Cocks Never Crew* (1940). A visit to Hawaii in 1923 to study and record native myth and folklore resulted in *At the Gateways of the Day* (1924) and *The Bright Islands* (1925). With his wife, Mary Colum, he published *Our Friend James Joyce* (1958).

CORRELL, CHARLES J., U.S. radio entertainer (b. Peoria, Ill., Feb. 3, 1890—d. Chicago, Ill., Sept. 26, 1972), who, with Freeman Gosden, created the popular, long-running radio series "Amos 'n' Andy." Correll played the role of Andy.

CROOKS, RICHARD, U.S. operatic tenor (b. Trenton, N.J., 1900—d. Portola Valley, Calif., Oct. 1, 1972), a star of the New York Metropolitan Opera Company from 1933 until the early 1950s, was also a featured singer on the "Voice of Firestone" radio series during the 1930s and '40s.

CROWTHER, GEOFFREY CROWTHER, Baron, British economist and educator (b. Leeds, Eng., May 13, 1907—d. London, Eng., Feb. 5, 1972), editor of *The Economist* (1938–56), chairman of The Economist Newspaper Ltd. and of Trust Houses Forte Ltd. (1970–72), was vice-chairman of *Encyclopædia Britannica*'s board of editors. Crowther joined *The Economist* in 1932 and became assistant editor in 1935. As editor, he widened the journal's readership and transformed it into one of the world's most influential weeklies. During World War II he served in the ministries of Supply, Information, and Production. He was chairman (1956–60) of the Central Advisory Council for Education (England), giving his name to its important report; chairman of the Committee on Consumer Credit (1968–71); and (from 1969) chairman of the Commission on the Constitution. In 1969 he also became first chancellor of the Open University. The most important of his business ventures was the Trust Houses hotel chain, which in 1970 merged with the catering and entertainment empire of Sir Charles Forte.

DAVIES, STEPHEN OWEN, Welsh politician (b. Wales, November 1886—d. Merthyr Tydfil, Wales, Feb. 25, 1972), MP for Merthyr Tydfil from 1934, was a strong advocate of Welsh home rule and a left-wing "rebel" of the British Labour Party.

DAY-LEWIS, CECIL, British poet (b. Ballintogher, Ire., April 27, 1904—d. Hadley Wood, Hertfordshire, Eng., May 22, 1972), who in 1968 succeeded John Masefield as Britain's poet laureate, was in the 1930s one of the group of socially aware, left-wing poets centred around W. H. Auden. Dedicated to poetry from his youth, Day-Lewis first attracted attention with *Transitional Poems* (1929), followed by *From Feathers to Iron* (1931), *The Magnetic Mountain* (1933), *A Time to Dance* (1935), *Overtures to Death* (1938), *An Italian Visit* (1953), *Collected Poems* (1954), and other collections. In 1946 he was Clark lecturer at Cambridge (*The Poetic Image*, 1947) and afterward professor of poetry at Oxford (1951–56) and Charles Eliot Norton professor at Harvard (1964–65). He made numerous verse translations from the Latin of Virgil, and as "Nicholas Blake" also wrote detective novels. He was a director of the publishing company Chatto and Windus Ltd.

DE BEER, SIR GAVIN (RYLANDS), British zoologist (b. Nov. 1, 1899—d. June 21, 1972), was professor of embryology, University College, London, from 1945 to 1950, and director of the British Museum (Natural History) from 1950 to 1960. He was president of the Linnean Society (1946–49) and was awarded both the Linnean Gold Medal and the Darwin Medal of the Royal Society in 1958. He was a prolific writer of wide scholarship—a contributor to *Encyclopædia Britannica* and to many scientific, military, literary, and alpine journals. A fellow of the Royal Society from 1940, he was knighted in 1954.

DELACOURT-SMITH, CHARLES GEORGE PERCY SMITH, Baron, British trade union leader (b. Windsor, Eng., April 25, 1917—d. Windsor, Aug. 2, 1972), was general secretary of the Post Office Engineering Union from 1953, after having served as Labour MP for Colchester (1945–50). He became a life peer in 1967 and in 1969 was appointed minister of state in the Ministry of Technology. He returned to the union when Labour went out of office in 1970.

DELL'ACQUA, ANGELO CARDINAL, Italian prelate of the Roman Catholic Church (b. Milan, Italy, Dec. 9, 1903—d. Lourdes, France, Aug. 27, 1972), was vicar-general of Rome, and one of Pope Paul's closest collaborators and firmest supporters. He was ordained on May 9, 1926, served abroad in the Vatican diplomatic corps, and was substitute secretary of state under Pope Pius XII. He was elevated to cardinal by Pope Paul VI in 1967, acted as the Vatican's minister of finance, and was an administrator during both sessions of the second Vatican Council.

DEVAL, JACQUES (Jacques Boularan), French playwright (b. Paris, France, June 27, 1890—d. Paris, Dec. 19, 1972), was the author of many long running successes of which the best known outside France was probably *Tovarich*, in Robert Sherwood's translation. A film version starred Charles Boyer and Claudette Colbert in the roles of two Russian aristocrats employed as servants in a Parisian bourgeois family.

de WILDE, BRANDON, U.S. actor (b. Brooklyn, N.Y., April 9, 1942—d. Lakewood, Colo., July 6, 1972), who began his career as a child star, was killed in a traffic accident. De Wilde appeared in 492 performances of the Broadway play *Member of the Wedding*, which opened in 1950. He starred in the TV series "Jaimie" in 1953–54, following his fine performance as the son in the film *Shane* (1953).

DIES, MARTIN, U.S. congressman (1931–58) from Texas (b. Colorado City, Tex., Nov. 5, 1901—d. Lufkin, Tex., Nov. 14, 1972), was founder and first chairman (1938–45) of the U.S. House Committee on Un-American Activities.

DONLEVY, BRIAN, U.S. actor (b. Portadown, N.Ire., Feb. 9, 1903—d. Hollywood, Calif., April 5, 1972), who began his career in the early 1920s on the Broadway stage in *What Price Glory*, went to Hollywood in the mid-1930s to begin his film career. He played in dozens of movies and was the lead in the television series "Dangerous Assignment."

ELLENDER, ALLEN JOSEPH, U.S. senator (from 1937) from Louisiana (b. Montegut, La., Sept. 24, 1890—d. Bethesda, Md., July 27, 1972), chairman of the Senate Appropriations Committee, held the title of president pro tempore of the Senate by right of his position as that body's senior Democrat. The dean of the Senate—in age as well as in length of service—he had served in the Louisiana state legislature 1924–36.

ERIKSEN, ERIK, Danish politician (b. Denmark, 1903—d. Esbjerg, Den., Oct. 7, 1972), was prime minister from 1950 until 1953 in a coalition of Liberals and Conservatives. Elected to the Folketing first in 1935, he served twice as minister for agriculture. His greatest achievement was the reform of the Danish constitution in 1953, in which the upper chamber (Landsting) was abolished, the voting age reduced to 21, and female succession to the throne introduced.

FELTRINELLI, GIANGIACOMO, Italian publisher (b. Milan, Italy, June 19, 1926—d. near Milan, March 15, 1972), was responsible for publication in the West of Boris Pasternak's *Doctor Zhivago*.

FISHER OF LAMBETH, THE MOST REV. AND RT. HON. GEOFFREY FRANCIS FISHER, Baron, prelate of the Church of England (b. Nuneaton, Eng., May 5, 1887—d. Sherborne, Dorset, Eng., Sept. 15, 1972), was archbishop of Canterbury from 1945 until 1961 and president of the World Council of Churches (1946–54). During his primacy he raised the stipends of the clergy, inaugurated an elaborate revision of the canon law, and worked for the unity, though not the union, of the various Christian churches; he also carried out the coronation ceremonies of Queen Elizabeth II. After ordination, in 1914 he was appointed headmaster of Repton School, where he remained until 1932, when he received the bishopric of Chester. He was bishop of London (1939–45) and dean of the Chapels Royal.

Cecil Day-Lewis

KEYSTONE

Brian Donlevy

WIDE WORLD

Frederik IX

KEYSTONE

His visit to Pope John XXIII in December 1960 revolutionized the atmosphere of relations between the Church of England and Rome. On his retirement in 1961 he was created a life peer.

FLEISCHER, NAT ("MR. BOXING"), U.S. publisher (b. New York, N.Y., 1888?—d. New York, June 25, 1972), founder (1922) and publisher of *The Ring* magazine, also wrote *Training for Boxers* (1929) and published the *Ring Record Book and Boxing Encyclopedia.*

FREDERIK IX, king of Denmark (b. Sorgenfri Castle, Den., March 11, 1899—d. Copenhagen, Den., Jan. 14, 1972), succeeded his father, King Christian X, in 1947. As a youth he joined the Royal Danish Navy, rising from cadet to rear admiral's rank. In 1935 he married Princess Ingrid, daughter of Crown Prince Gustaf Adolf of Sweden. King Frederik, a popular monarch, took every opportunity to mix with his subjects as informally as possible. His two main interests were the sea and music: he made frequent cruises in the royal yacht "Dannebrog," and he liked to conduct at private orchestral concerts. King Frederik and Queen Ingrid had three daughters. The oldest, Princess Margrethe (b. 1940), became heir to the throne following a 1953 constitutional amendment permitting female succession.

FRIML, RUDOLF, U.S. composer (b. Prague, Czech., Dec. 7, 1879—d. Hollywood, Calif., Nov. 12, 1972), whose 33 romantic operettas were based on themes of the swashbuckling past, began his musical education at the Prague conservatory where he studied under Antonin Dvorak. After a second visit to the U.S. (in 1906) Friml became a permanent resident and became a citizen in 1925. His first successful operetta, *The Firefly,* which opened on Broadway in 1912, was followed by *Rose Marie* (1923), with its well-remembered song "Indian Love Call," *The Vagabond King* (1925), and *The Three Musketeers* (1928).

GANZ, RUDOLPH, U.S. pianist and composer (b. Zürich, Switz., Feb. 24, 1877—d. Chicago, Ill., Aug. 2, 1972), was president (1933–54) of the Chicago Musical College, becoming emeritus in 1954 after the college joined Roosevelt University. He conducted the St. Louis Symphony Orchestra (1921–27), directed the young people's programs for the New York Philharmonic and the San Francisco Symphony (1939–49).

GENTELE, GÖRAN, Swedish conductor (b. Stockholm, Swed., Sept. 20, 1917—d. Olbia, Sardinia, July 18, 1972), killed in an auto accident during a vacation trip, was appointed director of the Metropolitan Opera Company in December 1970 to succeed Rudolf Bing as of the 1972–73 season. Gentele served as director of Stockholm's Royal Opera House from 1963 through 1971, during which time he presented several modern works including Alben Berg's *Wozzek* and Karl-Birger Blomdahl's *Aniara.*

GILBRETH, LILLIAN MOLLER, U.S. industrial engineer (b. Oakland, Calif., May 24, 1878—d. Phoenix, Ariz., Jan. 2, 1972), who pioneered in time-motion studies, was the inspiration for the popular book *Cheaper by the Dozen* (1948). The book, written by her two oldest children, Frank Gilbreth, Jr., and Ernestine Gilbreth Carey, recounted their parents' methods of applying their knowledge of industrial management to running a family of 12 children.

John Grierson

WIDE WORLD

GIOBBE, PAULO CARDINAL, Italian prelate of the Roman Catholic Church (b. Rome, Italy, Jan. 10, 1880—d. Vatican City, Aug. 14, 1972), was a leading member of the Vatican diplomatic corps, and oldest member of the Sacred College of Cardinals. He was ordained on Dec. 4, 1904, and soon entered the Sacred Congregation for the Propagation of the Faith. He served as papal nuncio to Colombia from 1925 to 1936, then to the Netherlands until Dec. 15, 1958, when Pope John XXIII made him a cardinal.

GLUECK, ELEANOR TOUROFF, U.S. criminologist (b. New York, N.Y., April 12, 1898—d. Cambridge, Mass., Sept. 25, 1972), who with her husband, Sheldon Glueck, whom she married in 1922, pioneered in studies on crime and delinquency conducted at the Harvard Law School. Eleanor Glueck joined the Law School staff in 1928 and retired in 1964. The Glueck team worked on a number of major crime studies over a 40-year period. One important study, *Unraveling Juvenile Delinquency,* a comparison of 500 delinquent and 500 nondelinquent boys (published in 1950), included the controversial Social Prediction Tables by which the Gluecks endeavoured to show that potential delinquents could be identified by the time they were six years of age.

GOODMAN, PAUL, U.S. social critic, author, and lecturer (b. New York, N.Y., Sept. 9, 1911—d. North Stratford, N.H., Aug. 2, 1972), known as the "father figure of the New Left," displayed keen interest in numerous fields of human endeavour. His versatility led him to probe into psychotherapy, linguistics, environmental and educational problems. Goodman's writings covered all these fields and many more, with his scores of books falling into 21 categories. Among his better known works was the popular study of the young, *Growing Up Absurd,* published in 1960. Others were: *The Empire City,* a novel (1959); *Drawing the Line,* essays on civil disobedience (1962); *Compulsory Mis-Education* (1964); his journal *Five Years: Thoughts in a Useless Time* (1966); and *Hawkweed* (1967), a collection of his poetry.

GORBACH, ALFONS, Austrian statesman (b. Imst, Aus., Sept. 2, 1898—d. Graz, Aus. July 31, 1972), was chancellor of Austria from 1961 to 1964. For five years during World War II he was imprisoned by the Nazis in the Dachau concentration camp. In 1945 he settled in Graz and joined the newly formed People's Party. The next year he was elected to the National Council, and shortly took the post of chairman of the People's Party. On April 11, 1961, he became chancellor. He ran unsuccessfully for the presidency of Austria in 1965.

GOVE, PHILIP BABCOCK, U.S. editor (b. Concord, N.H., June 27, 1902—d. Warren, Mass., Nov. 15, 1972), editor of *Webster's Third New International Dictionary* (1961), became consultant to G. & C. Merriam Co. following his retirement in 1967. Gove was a member of the editorial board of *Encyclopædia Britannica.*

GRIERSON, JOHN, British film producer (b. Kilmadock, Scot., April 26, 1898—d. Bath, Eng., Feb. 19, 1972), associated with the documentary film movement and influenced the worldwide development of mass media in public services. For Britain's Empire Marketing Board and Post Office film units, he produced the outstanding documentaries *Drifters* (1929) and *Night Mail* (1936). From 1957 until 1968 he produced a television series, "This Wonderful World."

GRIFFITH, JOHN STANLEY, British chemist and biophysicist (b. Cambridge, Eng., July 13, 1928—d. Cambridge, April 23, 1972), whose book *The Theory of Transition-Metal Ions* (1961) had a lasting effect on the development of inorganic chemistry, was a fellow of King's College, Cambridge, and had held chairs in the universities of London, Manchester, Pennsylvania, and Indiana. In January 1972 he joined the Basel (Switz.) Institute for Immunology, but illness forced him to return to England. He received the Marlow Medal of the Faraday Society in 1961. Among his later books were *A View of the Brain* (1967) and *Mathematical Neurobiology* (1971).

GRISEWOOD, FREDERICK HENRY ("FREDDIE"), British broadcaster (b. Daylesford, Eng., April 11, 1888—d. Hampshire, Eng., Nov. 15, 1972), pioneer radio announcer of the BBC (1929–48), was known to millions of listeners, especially in his role of compere of the long-running "Any Questions?" program. He wrote an autobiography, *The World Goes By* (1952), and *My Story of the BBC* (1959).

GROFÉ, FERDE (FERDINAND RUDOLPH VON GROFÉ), U.S. composer (b. New York, N.Y., March 27, 1892—d. Santa Monica, Calif., April 3, 1972), whose five-part *Grand Canyon Suite,* written in 1931, became a classic of musical Americana. Other popular works were *Death Valley Suite, Broadway at Night, Mississippi Suite, Symphony in Steel,* and *Hollywood Suite.* His arrangement and orchestration of George Gershwin's *Rhapsody in Blue* was first heard when Paul Whiteman's jazz orchestra made its debut in New York's Aeolian Hall in 1924.

GROSSINGER, JENNIE, U.S. resort executive (b. Galicia, June 16, 1892—d. Grossinger, N.Y., Nov. 20, 1972), was for half a century a familiar figure at Grossinger's 1,300-ac. resort in the Catskill Mountains.

HARTLEY, SIR HAROLD, British scientist (b. London, Eng., Sept. 3, 1878—d. London, Sept. 9, 1972), who contributed to the study of crystallography and electrolytes, was in succession tutorial fellow, senior research fellow, and honorary fellow of Balliol College, Oxford. In 1966 he received the Kelvin Medal in recognition of his great services in furthering the union of science and technology, and in 1967 he was made a Companion of Honour.

HARTLEY, L(ESLIE) P(OLES), British novelist and critic (b. Whittlesea, Eng., Dec. 30, 1895—d. London, Eng., Dec. 13, 1972), was a writer whose affectionate depiction of life's quotidian pleasures and miseries veiled a powerful tragic vision, best expressed in the trilogy *Eustace and Hilda* (1947), and *The Go-Between* (1953), which in 1971 was made into a film. His first novel, *The Shrimp and the Anemone* (1944), part of the *Eustace and Hilda* trilogy, was followed by *The Sixth Heaven* (1946). Hartley's further output included *The Travelling Grave* (1951), *My Fellow Devils* (1951), *A Perfect Woman* (1955), *The Hireling* (1957), and *The Betrayal* (1966).

HARTNETT, CHARLES LEO ("GABBY"), U.S. baseball player (b. Woonsocket, R.I., Dec. 20, 1900—d. Park Ridge, Ill., Dec. 20, 1972), National League catcher, played with the Chicago Cubs for 19 (1922–40) of his 20-year career. At the time of his retirement, at the end of the 1941 season, Hartnett had hit more home runs (236) than any other catcher in the majors, he held the games-caught record with 100 or more games for 12 seasons (8 consecutively), and was named the NL's most valuable player in 1935. His major league lifetime batting average was .298, with a season high of .354 (1937). In 1955 Hartnett was inducted into the Baseball Hall of Fame.

HAYDEN, CARL TRUMBULL, U.S. senator (1927–69) from Arizona (b. Hayden's Ferry [now Tempe], Ariz., Oct. 2, 1877—d. Mesa, Ariz., Jan. 25, 1972), president pro tempore of the Senate from 1957 until 1969 and chairman of the Senate Appropriations Committee, spent a total of 56 years in the U.S. Congress. After beginning his political career as sheriff of Maricopa County, Ariz., Hayden first won a seat in the House of Representatives as a Democrat in 1912 in Arizona's first election upon attaining statehood. He served six more terms in the House; then, in 1926, he was elected to the Senate, where he remained for 42 years before retiring. Among many pieces of legislation that Hayden sponsored were the Nineteenth Amendment to the Constitution (1920), which gave women the right to vote, and the House bill that established Grand Canyon National Park.

HEATTER, GABRIEL, U.S. newscaster (b. New York, N.Y., 1890—d. Miami Beach, Fla., March 30, 1972), whose nightly broadcasts, opening with the phrase "Ah, there's good news tonight!," were heard by millions of listeners during the 1930s, '40s, and '50s.

HODGES, GILBERT RAYMOND ("Gil"), U.S. baseball manager (b. Princeton, Ind., April 4, 1924—d. West Palm Beach, Fla., April 2, 1972), who guided the New York Mets to their first pennant and the World Series championship in 1969. Hodges began his baseball career in 1947 with the Brooklyn Dodgers and earned a regular place at first base a year later. He played in 2,006 games with the Dodgers and in 65 with the newly formed Mets, which he joined in 1962. He appeared in seven World Series and six All-Star games. His all-time batting average was .273, with 1,274 RBIs and 370 homers.

Hodges' career as a manager began in May 1963 with the Washington Senators. After four full seasons with the Senators he returned to the Mets in 1968 and set that proverbially last-place team on its way to the 1969 championship.

HOOVER, J(OHN) EDGAR, U.S. crime fighter (b. Washington, D.C., Jan. 1, 1895—d. Washington, May 2, 1972), director of the U.S. Federal Bureau of Investigation from 1924 until the time of his death, had been associated with the bureau for over five decades, under eight U.S. presidents. Hoover graduated from George Washington University, Washington, D.C., in 1916 with a degree in law, and a year later joined the U.S. Department of Justice. In 1921 he was appointed an assistant director of the Bureau of Investigation. On May 10, 1924, under Pres. Calvin Coolidge, Hoover was made acting director of the bureau, and immediately the organization underwent the modernization that was to make the FBI a powerful and "untouchable" force in the fight against crime.

In a matter of two years in the 1930s, Hoover's agents rounded up, or killed, dozens of notorious criminals including such figures as John Dillinger, "Pretty Boy" Floyd, the Barker gang, and Alvin Karpis. During World War II Hoover turned his attention to German spies and fifth columnists and his men caught scores of them; later Soviet spies and Communists were hunted down with the same relentlessness. In the 1960s Hoover came under public pressure to resign as a result of his quarrels with certain political figures he deemed to be leftists. Later controversies concerned civil rights cases, government wiretapping, and charges against antiwar activists. Hoover was the author of several books, including *Persons in Hiding* (1938) and *Masters of Deceit* (1958).

HOPKINS, (ELLEN) MIRIAM, U.S. stage and screen star (b. Bainbridge, Ga., Oct. 18, 1902—d. New York, N.Y., Oct. 9, 1972), who played in more than 35 motion pictures, was probably best remembered for her role in *Becky Sharp* (1935).

HOWES, BOBBY, British comedian (b. London, Eng., Aug. 4, 1895—d. London, April 27, 1972), the "humble but hopeful" centrepiece of British musical comedies of the 1930s, was given his first variety break by Jack Hylton. Jack Hulbert then introduced him to the West End in intimate revues, and in 1927 he appeared in *The Blue Train,* a sentimental musical comedy.

HSIEH, FU-CHIH, Chinese politician (b. Hupeh Province, China, 1898—d. [announced] Peking, China, March 29, 1972), was first secretary of the Peking Committee of the Communist Party (from March 1971).

HUGHES-HALLETT, JOHN, vice admiral (ret.), Royal Navy (b. Dec. 1, 1901—d. Slindon, Sussex, Eng., April 5, 1972), was naval commander of the Dieppe raid in 1942 and later served as commodore commanding the Channel Assault Force and as navy chief of staff. He was the first to suggest the use of an artificial harbour for the Normandy landings of 1944. In December 1943 he took command of the cruiser "Jamaica" and was present at the sinking of the German battleship "Scharnhorst." He commanded the aircraft carrier "Illustrious" (1948–49) and was promoted to rear admiral in 1950.

HUTCHINSON, JOHN, British botanist (b. Blindburn, Northumberland, Eng., April 7, 1884—d. Kew, Surrey, Eng., Sept. 2, 1972), who began work as a gardener at the Royal Botanic Gardens, Kew, in 1904, became keeper of the museums at Kew (1936–48) and a fellow of the Royal Society (1947). His outstanding contributions to the study of the classification and evolution of flowering plant families included *Flora of West Tropical Africa, Families of Flowering Plants, Common Wild Flowers, More Common Wild Flowers, Uncommon Wild Flowers, The Genera of Flowering Plants,* and *Evolution and Phylogeny of Flowering Plants.* He was also a noted artist who illustrated his own books. He received many honours including the Victoria Medal of Honour of the Royal Horticultural Society and the Linnaean Gold Medal.

JACKSON, MAHALIA, U.S. gospel singer (b. New Orleans, La., Oct. 26, 1911—d. Evergreen Park, Ill., Jan. 27, 1972), became a symbol of black protest through her association with the civil rights movement of the 1960s. Her extraordinary voice first came to public attention in the 1930s when she participated in a cross-country gospel tour singing such songs as "He's Got the Whole World in His Hands," "I Can Put My Trust in Jesus," and her first recording (1934), "God Gonna Separate the Wheat from the Tares." Later Jackson records sold in the millions and with them came the recognition of the white community. This brought about her first appearance at Carnegie Hall on Oct. 4, 1950. Radio and TV appearances were followed by tours abroad and in the U.S., including the 1958 Newport Jazz Festival where she joined with Duke Ellington in his gospel interlude *Black, Brown, and Beige.*

JIGME DORJI WANGCHUK, "Dragon King" of Bhutan (b. Bhutan, 1928—d. Nairobi, Kenya, July 21, 1972), ascended the throne in 1952 on the death of his father, and was responsible for opening his tiny Himalayan kingdom to outside influences. He began by freeing the remaining serfs who had worked the estates of the monasteries and royal family. The reassertion of Chinese authority over Tibet prompted the king to close his northern border and strengthen his country's links with India, which in 1959 agreed to increase aid to Bhutan and to begin a road building program. The effect of this was to stimulate the previously static economy; cash began to replace barter and the wheel was introduced. Although in 1964 the king's right-hand man, Prime Minister Jigme Dorji, was assassinated, the Army remained loyal. The National Assembly was gradually given increasing powers and the king's popularity grew. King Jigme Dorji Wangchuk was succeeded by his son Jigme Singye Wangchuk.

JOHNSON, HOWARD DEARING, U.S. executive (b. 1897—d. New York, N.Y., June 20, 1972), founder and former board chairman of the Howard Johnson Co. restaurant chain.

KALLET, ARTHUR, U.S. author and publisher (b. Syracuse, N.Y., Dec. 15, 1902—d. New Rochelle, N.Y., Feb. 24, 1972), was founder (1936) of Consumers Union, a leading consumer testing organization, and publisher of its monthly *Consumer Reports.*

KARUME, SHEIKH ABEID AMANI RASHID, ruler of Zanzibar (b. Belgian Congo, *c.* 1905—d. Zanzibar, April 7, 1972), was chairman of the Zanzibar Revolutionary Council and first vice-president of Tanzania. He came to power in 1964 following an anti-Arab revolution and after three months he negotiated an Act of Union with Tanganyika, thereafter called the United Republic of Tanzania.

KATZIR, AHARON (Aharon Katchalsky), Israeli molecular biologist (b. Poland, 1914—d. Tel Aviv-Yafo, Israel, May 30, 1972), was among those killed by Japanese terrorists, working for the Popular Front for the Liberation of Palestine, when he arrived back at Lod Airport from an overseas scientific conference. Head of the polymer research department of the Weizmann Institute of Science and internationally famous for his work on polymers and membranes, he was also involved in Israel's military research program.

KAWABATA, YASUNARI, Japanese novelist (b. Osaka, Jap., June 11, 1899—d. Tokyo, Jap., April 16, 1972), winner of a Nobel Prize for Literature, took his own life possibly because of a lingering depression over the suicide (Nov. 25, 1970) of his friend and protégé Yukio Mishima. Kawabata graduated in 1924 from the Tokyo Imperial University, and for a time was a member of the avant-garde movement before reverting to traditional Oriental forms of writing. He established his literary reputation with a short novel, *The Izu Dancer,* then started work in 1934 on *Snow Country,* which he did not finish until 1948. This book and *A Thousand Cranes,* written somewhat later, were best known to the Western world and were cited in awarding Kawabata the Nobel Prize for Literature in 1968.

KEDROV, MIKHAIL NIKOLAEVICH, Soviet actor and director (b. Russia, 1893—d. Moscow, U.S.S.R., March 22, 1972), was principal director at the Moscow Art Theatre (1960–71). He was awarded the title of People's Artist in 1948 and was the winner of four Stalin Prizes.

KELLY, SIR GERALD FESTUS, British portrait painter (b. London, Eng., April 9, 1879—d. London, Jan. 5, 1972), was president of the Royal Academy (1949–54). His state portraits of King George VI and Queen Elizabeth were shown in 1945 and he was knighted that year.

KENDALL, EDWARD CALVIN, U.S. chemist (b. South Norwalk, Conn., March 8, 1886—d. Princeton, N.J., May 4, 1972), winner of a Nobel Prize, was visiting professor of chemistry at Princeton University from 1951. Before that he headed the biochemistry section for 37 years at the Mayo Clinic in Rochester, Minn., and also served as a professor in the University of Minnesota's graduate school from 1921 to 1951.

While at the Mayo Clinic, Kendall isolated the hormone of the thyroid gland (thyroxin), which can correct glandular deficiencies and permit normal growth in human beings. In 1930 he began extensive studies on adrenal cortex hormones. Within ten years he had isolated six of these hormones and named them compounds A, B, C, D, E, and F; compound E later became known as cortisone, widely used in the treatment of rheumatoid arthritis and other related or associated ailments. For his work on adrenal cortex compounds, Kendall (with P. S. Hench and T. Reichstein) received the 1950 Nobel Prize for Physiology or Medicine.

Gil Hodges

WIDE WORLD

J. Edgar Hoover

UPI COMPIX

KING, HETTY, British music hall artist (b. New Brighton, Eng., 1883—d. London, Eng., Sept. 28, 1972), whose career spanned the golden Edwardian age of the British music hall, rose to fame as a male impersonator, appearing most frequently at the Tivoli Theatre in the Strand, London. One of her best-known songs was "All the Nice Girls Love a Sailor."

KLEIN, ABRAHAM MOSES, Canadian poet (b. Montreal, Que., Feb. 14, 1909—d. Montreal, Aug. 21, 1972), received the Governor-General's Medal for Poetry for *The Rocking Chair* (1948). Other works included *Hath Not a Jew* (1940), *Poems* (1944), and *The Second Scroll,* a novel (1951).

KRYLOV, NIKOLAI IVANOVICH, marshal of the Soviet Union (b. 1903—d. Moscow, U.S.S.R., Feb. 9, 1972), was chief of the Soviet Strategic Missile Forces from 1963 and a member of the Central Committee of the Communist Party from 1961.

LARSEN, AKSEL, Danish politician (b. Brændekilde, Den., Aug. 5, 1897—d. Copenhagen, Den., Jan. 10, 1972), was leader of the Danish Communist Party from 1932 until 1958, when he was expelled for "Titoist revisionism." In 1959, with other dissidents, he formed the Socialist People's Party, which in the 1960 election won 11 seats while the Communists lost all 6 of theirs. The new party became a powerful force in the Folketing (parliament) and held 17 seats following the 1971 election.

LAZAREFF, PIERRE, French journalist (b. Paris, France, April 16, 1907—d. Paris, April 21, 1972), was managing director from 1945 of the evening newspaper *France-Soir.*

LEAKEY, LOUIS SEYMOUR BAZETT, British anthropologist (b. Kabate, Kenya, Aug. 7, 1903—d. London, Eng., Oct. 1, 1972), one of the foremost authorities on prehistoric archaeology and paleontology, was also an expert on handwriting, the Kikuyu tribe (of which he was accepted as a member), and animal life. The elder son of a missionary couple working among the Kikuyu, he graduated from St. John's College, Cambridge, Eng., with firsts in modern languages and archaeology and anthropology. During four expeditions to East Africa between 1926 and 1935 he worked out the main sequence of prehistoric cultures in Kenya. In 1937 he began a two-and-a-half-year study of the Kikuyu, and during the Mau Mau troubles of the 1950s acted as official interpreter to Jomo Kenyatta at his trial. In 1945 Leakey became curator of the Coryndon Museum, Nairobi, Kenya; he later founded the National Museums Centre for Palaeontology and Prehistory adjoining the museum. His discoveries included the Kanam jaw and Kanjera skulls, remains of Miocene apes on Rusinga Island, and an almost complete skull of *Proconsul africanus,* the earliest ape skull yet known. In 1959, at Olduvai Gorge, Tanganyika (Tanzania), his wife Mary Leakey discovered the skull of *Australopithecus (Zinjanthropus) boisei,* and the following year their son Jonathan found the first remains of another hominid closer to the human line, named *Homo habilis.* In 1961 Leakey discovered the upper jaw of *Kenyapithecus wickeri,* 14 million years old and thought to be one of the earliest hominids. For his researches Leakey won numerous scientific awards. His writings included: *The Stone Age Cultures of Kenya Colony* (1931); *The Stone Age Races of Kenya* (1935); *Adam's Ancestors* (1935); *Stone Age Africa* (1936); *Olduvai Gorge* (1951); and *Olduvai Gorge 1951–61* (1965).

LEDUC, VIOLETTE, French novelist (b. France, 1907—d. Faucon, France, May 28, 1972), whose illegitimacy, physical ugliness, and sexual nonconformity were the burden of her writings, was probably best known for her autobiographical *La Bâtarde.* She became a secretary in a Paris publishing house and during the Nazi occupation met the writer Maurice Sachs, whose work reinforced her own pessimism. For many years she lived in poverty until Simone de Beauvoir befriended her and persuaded Albert Camus to publish her novel *L'Asphyxie.* Her other books included another autobiographical volume, *La Folie en tête,* and *L'Affamé, Thérèse et Isabelle, La Femme au Petit Renard,* and *Le Taxi.*

LESKINEN, VÄINÖ OLAVI, Finnish politician (b. Helsinki, Fin., March 8, 1917—d. Helsinki, March 8, 1972), foreign minister during 1970–71 and previously minister for social affairs (1952–53, 1958–59) and of the interior (1954–56), was secretary-general of the Finnish Social Democratic Party from 1946 until 1957.

LEVANT, OSCAR, U.S. pianist, humorist, film actor, and author (b. Pittsburgh, Pa., Dec. 27, 1906—d. Beverly Hills, Calif., Aug. 14, 1972), who won an Academy Award for his song "Until Today," was a close friend of George Gershwin and recorded many of Gershwin's works. Levant made his film debut in *The Dance of Life* (1929), then appeared in a number of other movies including *Rhapsody in Blue* (1945).

LIMÓN, JOSÉ ARCADIA, U.S. dancer (b. Culiacan, Mex., Jan. 12, 1908—d. Flemington, N.J., Dec. 2, 1972), a major force in the development of modern dance in the mid-20th century, was noted for his virility, his dignity of bearing, and for his substantial contributions to the increased interest of the American male in modern dance. After studying with Doris Humphrey and Charles Weidman, who were pioneers in modern dance, Limón began his professional career in New York City in 1929 when he appeared in Norman Bel Geddes' production of *Lysistrata.* After dancing in several other Broadway shows, Limón choreographed some of the dances for *Roberta* (1935). In 1937 he composed his first group work, "Danza de la Muerta," and in 1939 presented "Danzas Mexicanas." Limón's first major work, *The Moor's Pavane,* was performed in 1949; other works included *La Malinche* (1949), *The Exiles* (1950), *The Traitor* (1954), and *Emperor Jones* (1956). In 1964 Limón won the Capezio Award, presented by the U.S. State Department for his dance tours abroad.

LIN PIAO (LIN LU-YUNG), Chinese politician and soldier (b. Hupeh Province, China, 1908—d. reported July 28, 1972), whose death in an airplane crash in Mongolia on Sept. 12, 1971, was confirmed by official Chinese sources more than ten months after the crash. Lin had emerged in 1969 as heir apparent to Mao Tse-tung. He was a graduate of the Whampoa Military Academy, and in the 1930s as a guerrilla general he led the vanguard of Mao's forces on the legendary "Long March" from Kiangsi to Yenan in 1934–35. He was wounded in action in 1937 during the Japanese invasions of China and spent the next four years in the Soviet Union, but was again with the Red Army in Manchuria, after the civil war was resumed in 1946. After subduing the opposing Kuomintang troops, Lin became a deputy premier (1954), a member of the Politburo and a marshal (1955), and in 1958 he was elected to the Standing Committee of the Politburo. In 1959 he succeeded P'eng Teh-huai as minister of national defense and began a program of political indoctrination to ensure the Army's loyalty to Mao. In 1965 Lin published his 30,000-character essay *Long Live the Victory of the People's War* prophesying the successful global application of Mao's policy of "encirclement." By 1966, at the time of the Cultural Revolution, Lin had established himself as Mao's "closest comrade in arms" and second in the party hierarchy, and in April 1969 at the ninth party congress he was officially designated Mao's successor. In 1970 Marshal Lin opposed a change of policy which would build up the mechanization of agriculture at the expense of the army forces and, therefore, possibly downgrade his own role in the party. In early September 1971 Lin allegedly plotted the "removal" of Chairman Mao and his own seizure of power. With the discovery of the plan Lin attempted to flee to the Soviet Union, with the resultant crash and his own death.

LONGMAN, MARK FREDERIC KERR, British publisher (b. Nov. 12, 1916—d. Bishopstone House, near Salisbury, Eng., Sept. 6, 1972), was president and former chairman of the Longman Group of Publishing Companies, a director of Pearson Longman Ltd., and vice-chairman of the Penguin Publishing Company. He was president of the Publishers' Association (1969–71), chairman of the National Book League, and of the Fine Arts Society.

LÜBKE, HEINRICH, West German politician (b. Enkhausen, Westphalia, Ger., Oct. 14, 1894—d. Bonn, W.Ger., April 6, 1972), was president of the Federal Republic of Germany (1959–69) in succession to the first president, Theodor Heuss.

LYNCH, WILLIAM ALOYSIUS, U.S. physicist (b. Brooklyn, N.Y., June 21, 1892—d. Darby, Pa., Feb. 14, 1972), an expert on earthquakes, was emeritus professor of physics at Fordham University, the Bronx, N.Y., from 1961.

McKENNEY, RUTH, U.S. author (b. Mishawaka, Ind., Nov. 18, 1911—d. New York, N.Y., July 25, 1972), who was best known for her collection of short stories titled *My Sister Eileen,* began writing the stories for *The New Yorker* magazine

Mahalia Jackson

UPI COMPIX

Oscar Levant

UPI COMPIX

Heinrich Lübke

KARSH OF OTTAWA—CAMERA PRESS/PICTORIAL PARADE

in the 1930s, then published the collection in 1938. The best seller was made into a play (1941) and a movie (1942), then became a Broadway musical hit as *Wonderful Town* in 1953.

MACKENZIE, SIR (EDWARD MONTAGUE) COMPTON, Scottish novelist (b. West Hartlepool, County Durham, Eng., Jan. 17, 1883—d. Edinburgh, Scot., Nov. 30, 1972), who suffered critical acclaim and neglect with equal indifference, left a prodigious output of more than 100 novels, plays, and biographies, including many best sellers. He showed a mastery of cockney humour in *Carnival* (1912) and *Sinister Street* (1913–14); a satiric sting in *Water on the Brain* (1933), attacking the British secret service which had prosecuted him under the Official Secrets Act for his autobiographical *Greek Memories* (1932); and a love of pure fun in *The Monarch of the Glen* (1941) and *Whisky Galore* (1947). Other novels included *Poor Relations* (1919), *Rich Relatives* (1921), *Extraordinary Women* (1928), and plays *The Gentleman in Grey* (1906), *Columbine* (1920), and *The Lost Cause* (1931). The first volume of his memoirs, *My Life and Times: Octave One,* appeared in 1963, and *Octave Ten* in 1971. An ardent Scottish nationalist, he was knighted in 1952.

MAHALANOBIS, PRASANTA CHANDRA, Indian statistician (b. Calcutta, India, June 29, 1893—d. June 28, 1972), was statistical adviser to the Indian government from 1949, and a leading light in the scientific and cultural life of his country. His early manifested abilities in mathematics and physics brought him to the directorship of the physics department of Presidency College, Calcutta, in 1922, a post he held until 1945, when he became principal, and in 1948 professor emeritus. He was a founder of the UN Subcommission on Statistical Sampling, established the Indian National Sample Survey, and was active in the Indian Academy of Sciences and Indian Science Congress. He was elected a fellow of the British Royal Society in 1945, in 1957 honorary president of the International Statistical Institute, and in 1958 a foreign member of the U.S.S.R. Academy of Sciences.

MAHENDRA, KING (MAHENDRA BIR BIKRAM SHAH DEVA), ruler of Nepal (b. 1920—d. Bharatpur, Nepal, Jan. 31, 1972), was responsible for restoring the Nepali monarchy to full power after his accession in 1955. After more than a century of rule by the Ranas, a line of hereditary prime ministers, Mahendra staged a royal coup in 1960, dissolving the National Assembly, abrogating the constitution, and imprisoning political leaders. He was succeeded by his eldest son, Crown Prince Birendra (*see* BIOGRAPHY).

MARLBOROUGH, JOHN ALBERT EDWARD WILLIAM SPENCER-CHURCHILL, 10TH DUKE OF (b. London, Eng., Sept. 18, 1897—d. London, March 11, 1972), was responsible, with government aid, for the restoration of Blenheim Palace in Oxfordshire, presented by Queen Anne to his forebear John Churchill, the 1st duke, in recognition of the latter's victory at the Battle of Blenheim (1704). The 10th duke served as an officer in the Life Guards (1916–27) and as a liaison officer with U.S. forces (1942–45). In 1950 he opened Blenheim Palace, birthplace of Sir Winston Churchill, and its grounds to the public.

MAXWELL, MARILYN, U.S. actress (b. Clarinda, Ia., Aug. 3, 1922—d. Beverly Hills, Calif., March 20, 1972), began her career as a vocalist with the Buddy Rogers and Ted Weems bands in the 1930s. In films she starred in *Stand by for Action* (1942), *Summer Holiday* (1947), and *The Lemon Drop Kid* (1951).

MAYER, MARIA GOEPPERT, U.S. theoretical physicist (b. Kattowitz, Ger. [now Katowice, Pol.], June 28, 1906—d. San Diego, Calif., Feb. 20, 1972), Nobel Prize winner, was a professor of physics at the University of California at San Diego from 1960. Previously at Johns Hopkins University (1930–39) and Columbia University (1939–45), she was, during 1945–60, a professor at the University of Chicago and at the Institute of Nuclear Studies (under Enrico Fermi), at the same time serving as a senior physicist of the Argonne National Laboratory near Chicago.

Early investigations into theories of nuclear structure came into sharp focus for Mayer in 1948 and led to the explanation that a measured spin of a nuclear particle could correspond to one of two different orbits. This made possible a description of the nucleus in terms of orbits of single particles. Mayer worked out a "shell model" of how nuclei absorb neutrons in high-energy physics. This work paralleled that of J. Hans D. Jensen at the University of Heidelberg, and the two scientists met in 1950 to collaborate on a book advancing their theories. Their investigations brought Mayer and Jensen the 1963 Nobel Prize for Physics (which they also shared with E. P. Wigner).

MAYER, RENÉ, French politician (b. Paris, France, May 4, 1895—d. Paris, Dec. 13, 1972), twice finance minister under the Fourth Republic and France's 18th postwar premier (January–May 1953), was among those responsible for modernizing the French economy. In 1955 he succeeded Jean Monnet as president of the High Authority of the European Coal and Steel Community.

MONTHERLANT, HENRY-MARIE-JOSEPH-MILLON DE, French playwright and novelist (b. Neuilly-sur-Seine, France, April 21, 1896—d. Paris, France, Sept. 21, 1972), was one of the greatest contemporary French dramatists, whose diversity of gifts, both physical and intellectual, earned him the title of "a man of the Renaissance." His first novel, *Le Songe* (1922), drew on his World War I experiences. Two years later came a series of essays and poems on sport, *Les Olympiques,* followed in 1926 by a second novel, *Les Bestiaires.* The next ten years were spent mostly in North Africa and Montherlant's conscious self-subjection to the most conflicting elements of experience resulted in an alternating sensualism and asceticism in works written at the time. His dramatic output included *La Reine morte* (1942), *Malatesta* (1946), *Le Maître de Santiago* (1947), *La Ville dont le prince est un enfant* (1951; first performed 1968), *Port-Royal* (1954), and *La Guerre civile* (1965). Notable among his prose works were *Le chaos de la nuit* (1963) and *Les Garçons* (1969). He was elected to the Académie Française in 1960. Having lost the sight of one eye, and fearing complete blindness, Montherlant shot himself.

MOORE, MARIANNE CRAIG, U.S. poet (b. Kirkwood, Mo., Nov. 15, 1887—d. New York, N.Y., Feb. 5, 1972), Pulitzer Prize winner, wrote only 120 poems; *The Complete Poems of Marianne Moore* (published in 1967) occupied but 242 pages. The work of 50 years, however, was widely acclaimed for its rhythms, patterns, and subtle imagery. Her first verses appeared in *The Egoist,* a London magazine, and in Harriet Monroe's *Poetry* magazine. A small collection, *Poems,* published by friends in London in 1921, preceded her first U.S. volume, *Observations* (1924), which received the Dial Award. *Selected Poems* (1935), winner of the Ernest Hartsock Memorial Prize, was followed by *What Are Years* (1941) and other slim books that won for their author most of the major poetry awards: the Harriet Monroe Poetry Award (1944); the Bollingen Prize, the National Book Award for Poetry, and the Pulitzer (all in 1952); the M. Carey Thomas Memorial Award and the Gold Medal of the National Institute of Arts and Letters (1953); and the MacDowell Medal (1967). France bestowed the Croix de Chevalier des Arts et Lettres for her translations in verse of *The Fables of La Fontaine* (1954).

NIELSEN, ASTA, Danish film star (b. Copenhagen, Den., 1882—d. Copenhagen, May 25, 1972), won fame through her lead roles in many German silent films of the 1920s, after making her screen debut in Denmark in 1910. Most notable of her 73 films were *Miss Julie* (1921), *Hedda Gabler* (1924), *Hamlet* (1920), and *Pandora's Box* (1928).

NIJINSKA, BRONISLAVA, U.S.-Polish choreographer (b. Warsaw?, Pol., Jan. 8, 1891—d. Pacific Palisades, Calif., Feb. 21, 1972), younger sister of Vaslav Nijinsky (d. 1950), was a dancer and later chief choreographer for Sergei Diaghilev's Ballets Russes in the 1920s.

NKRUMAH, KWAME (FRANCIS NWIA KOFI), Ghanaian nationalist leader (b. Nkroful, Gold Coast, Sept. 21, 1909—d. Conakry, Guinea, April 27, 1972), who served as president of his country from 1960 to 1966, spearheaded the Gold Coast's emergence from British colonial rule as the independent state of Ghana. In 1947, while in Britain, Nkrumah became general secretary of the United Gold Coast Convention. In 1949 he founded the Convention People's Party (CPP) and the following year declared a policy of "positive action." Following a 12-month prison term for incitement to strike, he became leader of government business, and in 1952 was appointed first prime minister of the Gold Coast. On March 6, 1957, political independence was finally achieved. In 1960 Ghana became a republic with Nkrumah its first president. A series of attempts to assassinate Nkrumah failed, but in 1966, while he was visit-

Marilyn Maxwell

WIDE WORLD

Norman Norell

WIDE WORLD

Louella Parsons

WIDE WORLD

ing Peking, a coup removed him from office and he went into exile in Guinea, where he was given the title of "co-president."

NOLDE, THE REV. O(TTO) FREDERICK, U.S. religious leader (b. Philadelphia, Pa., June 30, 1899—d. Philadelphia, June 17, 1972), was dean of the Graduate School of the Lutheran Theological Seminary in Philadelphia from 1943 until 1962, when he assumed active duty as director of the Commission on International Affairs of the World Council of Churches.

NORELL, NORMAN (Norman Levinson), U.S. fashion designer (b. Noblesville, Ind., April 20, 1900—d. New York, N.Y., Oct. 25, 1972), died a few days after the opening (October 16) of a 50-year retrospective showing of his designs at the Metropolitan Museum of Art. Called America's foremost designer, Norell depended on simplicity and timelessness in his styles, many of which could be worn for as long as 20 years. Norell won his first Coty Award in 1943 and another in 1951; in 1958 he was elected to the Coty Award Hall of Fame.

OUFKIR, MUHAMMAD, Moroccan Army general (b. Bou Denib, Mor., 1920—d. Skhirat Palace, Rabat, Mor., Aug. 17, 1972), minister of defense from 1971, was long regarded as the strong man of Moroccan politics. In 1960 he was appointed director general of national security and in 1965 became minister of the interior. He was later sentenced in absentia to life imprisonment by a French court for his alleged part in the presumed murder in France of the left-wing Moroccan politician Ben Barka. In 1970 he was chiefly responsible for the success of a referendum on a new constitution and the following year apparently foiled an attempted coup by a group of officers and cadets. After the failure of a second coup attempt in 1972, when Moroccan Air Force pilots tried to shoot the king down in his royal aircraft, General Oufkir was reported to have shot himself.

OWEN, REGINALD, British-U.S. actor (b. Hertfordshire, Eng., Aug. 5, 1887—d. Boise, Ida., Nov. 5, 1972), made his London debut in *The Tempest* in 1905. He went to the United States in 1924. Major films included *Mrs. Miniver* and *Random Harvest* in 1942, *The Valley of Decision* and *National Velvet* in 1945, and *Of Human Bondage* in 1946. He last appeared on the stage in the spring of 1972 in the Broadway revival of *A Funny Thing Happened on the Way to the Forum.*

PARKER OF WADDINGTON, HUBERT LISTER PARKER, Baron, British jurist (b. May 28, 1900—d. Donhead, Dorset, Eng., Sept. 15, 1972), lord chief justice from 1958 to 1971, was called to the bar in 1924. He became junior counsel in common law first to the Admiralty (1934) and then to the Treasury (1945–50), a judge of the King's Bench Division of the High Court (1950–54), and a lord justice of appeal (1954–58).

PARRY, SIR (WILLIAM) EDWARD, admiral (ret.), British Navy (b. April 8, 1893—d. Wittersham, Kent, Eng., Aug. 21, 1972), captained the New Zealand Navy's light cruiser "Achilles," which with the "Exeter" and "Ajax" on Dec. 13, 1939, took part in the Battle of the River Plate, which resulted in the scuttling of the German pocket battleship "Admiral Graf Spee." Promoted admiral in 1951, he retired in 1952.

PARSONS, LOUELLA, U.S. movie columnist (b. Freeport, Ill., Aug. 6, 1881?—d. Hollywood, Calif., Dec. 9, 1972), was queen of the top Hollywood gossip columnists during the heyday of that motion-picture colony. At the height of her career she was syndicated in 407 daily and Sunday newspapers with a salary of $52,000 a year in her position as movie editor of International News Service. She joined the Hearst organization in 1922 and a few years later started writing her Hollywood column. She retired in 1965. Parsons was the author of *The Gay Illiterate* (1944) and *Tell It to Louella* (1961).

PATTERSON, JAMES, U.S. stage star (b. Derry, Pa., 1932—d. New York, N.Y., Aug. 19, 1972), won the 1967 Tony, or Antoinette Perry, Award for the role of Stanley in Harold Pinter's *Birthday Party,* having received a previous Obie, or Off Broadway, Award for his performance as Bill in Pinter's *The Collection* (1965).

PAYE, LUCIEN, French educator, politician, and diplomat (b. Vernoil-le-Fourrier, France, June 28, 1907—d. Paris, France, April 25, 1972), was minister of education (1961–62) and France's ambassador to Peking (1964–69).

PEARSON, LESTER BOWLES, Canadian statesman (b. Newtonbrook, Ont., April 23, 1897—d. Ottawa, Ont., Dec. 27, 1972), winner of the 1957 Nobel Peace Prize, was 14th prime minister of Canada (1963–68), head of the Liberal Party (1958–68), and president of the United Nations General Assembly (1952). Pearson, educated at the University of Toronto and at Oxford, began his career in the Department of External Affairs in 1928, and later served as ambassador to London and to Washington (1945–46). He was senior adviser to the Canadian delegation when the United Nations came into being, at San Francisco in 1945, and aided in the partition of Palestine in 1947. Pearson was elected to Parliament in 1948 and on September 10 was sworn in as secretary of state for external affairs. Always a powerful force in the UN, he was elected president of the General Assembly in 1952, the same year he was chairman of the North Atlantic Council. In 1953 he was instrumental in bringing about the Korean truce. When Israel attacked Egypt and the Suez Canal in 1956 Pearson went before the UN with a plan for keeping peace in the troubled area. For this act of diplomacy he was awarded the Nobel Peace Prize.

The Liberals were defeated in 1957 and Pearson relinquished the post of secretary for external affairs. He was chosen as leader of the Liberal Party in 1958; that same year the party suffered another bitter defeat and Pearson had to start rebuilding for a return to power in 1963. With victory Pearson became prime minister. During his administration the national pension plan and a family assistance program were introduced, the old-age security benefits broadened, and groundwork laid for the National Free Medical Service; a royal commission was established for the study of French-English bilingualism and biculturalism; and the Columbia River Treaty with the United States was completed. Pearson, himself, considered one of his greatest achievements to have been the introduction of Canada's first distinctive national flag, along with the adoption of an official national anthem and the creation of the Order of Canada.

Following his retirement from government in 1968 Pearson joined the faculty of Carleton University in Ottawa, where he lectured on international affairs. A short time later he accepted an appointment as chancellor of Carleton. He spent considerable time on his memoirs, with the first volume, *Mike,* being published in 1972.

POPOVIC, VLADIMIR, Yugoslav diplomat (b. Centinje, Montenegro, Jan. 27, 1914—d. London, Eng., April 1, 1972), was a member of the Council of the Federation of Yugoslavia.

POUND, EZRA WESTON LOOMIS, U.S. expatriate poet (b. Hailey, Ida., Oct. 30, 1885—d. Venice, Italy, Nov. 1, 1972), a giant force in 20th-century literature, was also a controversial figure whose activities during World War II brought charges of treason. After a brief teaching career Pound left the U.S. for Europe in 1908, and the following year published his first major book of poetry, *Personae.* The masterful work he produced between 1910 and 1920 included the two cycles *Homage to Sextus Propertius* (1919) and *Hugh Selwyn Mauberley* (1920). Pound encouraged some of the greatest literary figures of his period, discovering T. S. Eliot and assuring publication of James Joyce's novel *Ulysses.* After living in London and Paris for a time, in the mid-1920s Pound took up permanent residence in Italy and subsequently espoused the economic policies of Mussolini. During the war in Europe he conducted a series of radio broadcasts on behalf of the Fascists, airing his adverse views of the U.S. At war's end he was taken into custody and, although he did not stand trial, was committed to St. Elizabeth's Hospital in Washington, D.C., as mentally unfit to answer indictments for treason. After Pound had been confined for 13 years (1945–58), the indictments against him were dropped, and he returned to Italy. In 1967 the *Selected Cantos of Ezra Pound* was published. In 1972 Pound was proposed for the Emerson-Thoreau Medal of the American Academy of Arts and Sciences but, still the centre of literary controversy, was denied the award.

POWELL, THE REV. ADAM CLAYTON, JR., U.S. Baptist minister and congressman (1945–70) from New York (b. New Haven, Conn., Nov. 29, 1908—d. Miami, Fla., April 4, 1972), a controversial public figure who was a prominent spokesman for the civil rights movement in its early days. Powell received his B.A. from Colgate University, Hamilton, N.Y., in 1930 and his M.A. from Columbia in 1932. He was early affiliated with his father's church, the Abyssinian Baptist Church, and alternated with the elder Powell in preaching to its congregation, the largest in the U.S. Powell was elected to the New York City Council in 1941. In 1945 he became

Lester Pearson

UPI COMPIX

Ezra Pound

WIDE WORLD

Adam Clayton Powell

WIDE WORLD

a member of the U.S. House as the Democratic representative from Harlem and began his long fight against segregation. During his 11 successive terms in the House he distinguished himself as chairman of the Committee on Education and Labor (1960–67) and played a leading role in the passage of the 1961 Minimum Wage Act, the Manpower Development and Training Act, and the antipoverty bill, as well as almost 50 other pieces of major social legislation. During the early 1960s, Powell became involved in a lawsuit with a woman who claimed he had wrongly accused her of collecting police graft. Found guilty of civil contempt of court and, later (1966), of criminal contempt, he left the country to avoid arrest. On March 1, 1967, the House voted to exclude Powell from the 90th Congress. In 1969, having satisfied the debt imposed by the court, Powell was seated in the 91st Congress but the following year was defeated for reelection in the Democratic primaries. Powell was the author of a book of sermons, *Keep the Faith, Baby!*, published in 1967.

PRITT, DENIS NOWELL, British lawyer (b. Billericay, Essex, Eng., Sept. 22, 1887—d. May 23, 1972), a confirmed Marxist, played a part in almost every left-wing cause. He was called to the bar in 1909 and took silk in 1927. A leading figure in the Howard League for Penal Reform, the Bentham Committee for Poor Litigants, the National Council for Civil Liberties, and the Haldane Society, he was a sponsor of the World Peace Movement and president of the International Association of Democratic Lawyers. He joined the Labour Party immediately after World War I, became Labour MP for Hammersmith North in 1935, in 1940 was expelled from the party for a book defending entry of Soviet troops into Finland, and in 1945 held his constituency seat as a Labour Independent. He was presidential professor of law in the University of Ghana from 1965 until Kwame Nkrumah's deposition in 1966, and produced many books and pamphlets on political causes. He was awarded a Stalin Peace Prize in 1954.

RAJAGOPALACHARI, CHAKRAVARTI, Indian politician (b. Madras, India, 1878—d. Madras, Dec. 25, 1972), was governor-general of India from 1948 to 1950, when the country became a republic. A graduate of the University of Madras, he practiced as a lawyer before becoming involved in politics as a devoted follower of Mohandas Gandhi. In 1921 he became general secretary of the Indian National Congress and later a member of its working committee. After Congress' success in the 1937 elections he became chief minister (then called prime minister) of Madras. In 1939 the Congress ministries resigned and he was chosen by Gandhi to be one of the first to offer individual civil disobedience to the British authorities, for which he was jailed in 1940—one of five occasions on which he was imprisoned during the struggle for independence. After World War II, in which he opposed Gandhi by pressing for conditional support of the Allies' cause, he became a member of the interim government in Delhi before succeeding Lord Mountbatten as governor-general. During 1952–54 he was again chief minister of Madras and in 1959 he became leader of the newly formed, right-wing Swatantra (Freedom) Party.

RAMSEY, THE RIGHT REV. IAN THOMAS, British clergyman (b. Bolton, Eng., Jan. 31, 1915—d. Oct. 6, 1972), Anglican bishop of Durham from 1966, became chairman of the Archbishops' Commission on Doctrine at its foundation in 1967.

RANK, J(OSEPH) ARTHUR RANK, 1st Baron, British industrialist and film magnate (b. Hull, Eng., Dec. 23, 1888—d. Winchester, Eng., March 29, 1972), founder (1937) and chairman (until 1962) of the Rank Organisation Ltd., played an influential part in the development of the British film industry from the mid-1930s onward. On leaving school he entered the family flour milling business; this grew into the giant Rank Hovis McDougall Ltd., whose life president he became in 1969. Rank entered the film industry through his interest in the Religious Film Society, which he founded in 1933. By the 1950s he was in control of virtually all film production and distribution in Britain. The Rank Organisation ran a chain of theatres and extended into other branches of entertainment, including dance halls, bingo parlors, and bowling alleys.

RICE, DAVID TALBOT, British art historian (b. July 11, 1903—d. March 12, 1972), Watson-Gordon professor of the history of fine art at the University of Edinburgh from 1934 and the university's vice-principal (1967–71), was a leading authority on Byzantine art. He took part in the British Academy expedition to Istanbul (1927–32) and later traveled in the Near East studying Byzantine and Islamic art and archaeology. During 1932–38 he lectured at the Courtauld Institute in London. Among his many publications were *The Birth of Western Painting* (with Robert Byron; 1930), *The Icons of Cyprus* (1937), *Byzantine Painting* (1948), *The Art of Byzantium* (1959), *Art of the Byzantine Era* (1963), and *Islamic Art* (1965). He was a contributor to *Encyclopædia Britannica.*

RIEU, EMILE VICTOR, British publisher and translator (b. London, Eng., Feb. 10, 1887—d. London, May 11, 1972), was editor of the Penguin Classics series (1944–64). In 1912 he was appointed manager of the Oxford University Press in India. In 1923 he became educational manager of Methuen & Co. Ltd., and held that post for ten years, becoming managing director in 1933. He resigned the directorship in 1936 to make a professional career of a long-standing hobby of translating the classics. By the end of 1945 he had completed the *Odyssey*, which, on publication by Sir Allen Lane's Penguin Books, became an immediate best seller in the U.K. and the U.S. The *Iliad* followed in 1950 and thereafter Rieu continued to edit Penguin translations for 20 years. In 1952 he produced a new translation of *The Four Gospels.*

ROBINSON, JACKIE ROOSEVELT, U.S. baseball player (b. Cairo, Ga., Jan. 31, 1919—d. Stamford, Conn., Oct. 24, 1972), who broke baseball's colour line, was handpicked by Branch Rickey, manager of the Brooklyn Dodgers, as the man most likely to succeed in surmounting the race barrier. Robinson was signed in the fall of 1945 for a $3,500 bonus and a $600-per-month contract to play for the Montreal farm club. He came up to the major league Brooklyn club in 1947 and for his entire ten-year career stayed with the Dodgers, during which time the team won six National League pennants (1947, 1949, 1952, 1953, 1955, 1956). At the end of his first season, with an average of .297, Robinson was voted the rookie of the year, and in 1949 he won the NL's most valuable player award with a .342 average. He played all three bases as well as the outfield and excelled as a base runner, chalking up a total of 197 stolen bases. Robinson was a member of six NL All-Star teams, 1949 through 1954, and when he retired in 1956 his lifetime average was .311, with 734 RBIs and 137 home runs. In 1962 he was elected to the Baseball Hall of Fame. His autobiography, *I Never Had It Made*, was published in November 1972.

ROMAINS, JULES (Louis Farigoule), French novelist and playwright (b. Saint-Julien Chapteuil, France, Aug. 26, 1885—d. Paris, France, Aug. 14, 1972), was author of the 27-volume novel series *Les Hommes de bonne volonté*, and from 1946 a member of the Académie Française. In 1911 he published *Mort de quelqu'un*, a psychological drama. This was followed in 1914 by the picaresque *Les Copains.* In 1923 he produced the brilliant farce *Knock ou le triomphe de la médecine.* Later plays included *Le Mariage de M. le Trouhadec* (1925); *La Scintillante* (1925), *Demetrios* (1926). and *Le Dictateur* (1926). His long novel *Le Dieu des corps* (1928) was well received and in 1932 was followed by the first volume of *Les Hommes de bonne volonté*, entitled *Le 6 Octobre*; this vast work covered the period 1908 to 1933.

ROSENHEIM, MAX LEONARD ROSENHEIM, Baron, British physician (b. London, Eng., March 15, 1908—d. London, Dec. 2, 1972), was emeritus professor of medicine at London University, and president of the Royal College of Physicians (1966–72).

RUTHERFORD, DAME MARGARET (Mrs. Stringer Davis), British stage and screen actress (b. Balham, London, Eng., May 11, 1892—d. Gerrards Cross, Eng., May 22, 1972), specialized in playing robust female eccentrics of a certain age. At the late age of 33 she became a student player with the Old Vic Company, later understudying at the Lyric, Hammersmith. From there she worked in weekly repertory and made the acquaintance of Tyrone Guthrie, under whose direction she first caught the critics' eyes in a comedy by Robert Morley. Her role of Miss Bijou in *Spring Meeting* (1938) and that of Miss Prism in *The Importance of Being Earnest* (1939) established her as a star performer. Later roles included Lady Bracknell, Madame Arcati, the medium, in Noel Coward's *Blithe Spirit*, the White Queen in *Alice in Wonderland*, and Mrs. Candour in *The School for Scandal.* Among her many film parts was Miss Marple in *Murder She Said* (1962). In 1963 she won an Oscar as best supporting actress for her part in *The VIPs.* She was created DBE in 1967.

SA'ID IBN TAIMUR, former sultan of Muscat and Oman (b. Oman, 1910—d. London, Eng., Oct. 19, 1972), in 1932 succeeded to the throne of the independent sultanate. Until deposed by his son Qabus ibn Sa'id in 1970, the sultan spent most of his time shut up in his remote palace at Salaleh. Although supplied with ample funds from an oil concession to an international consortium, Sa'id ibn Taimur was opposed to their use for the benefit of his subjects, whom he ruled autocratically. In 1957 British troops crushed a Saudi- and Egyptian-backed attempt to seize part of Oman. In 1965 a revolt broke out in the province of Dhofar and in 1966 the sultan narrowly escaped assassination. Following the palace coup of July 1970 he was exiled to London.

SALISBURY, ROBERT ARTHUR JAMES GASCOYNE-CECIL, 5th Marquess, British statesman (b. Aug. 27, 1893—d. Feb. 23, 1972), regarded as the Conservative Party's leading "kingmaker," became undersecretary to Anthony Eden (Lord Avon) during the latter's first term as foreign secretary (1935–38) and resigned with him over the Abyssinian issue. During World War II he held various Cabinet posts, including that of secretary of state for the dominions (1940–42; 1943–45). Following his assumption of the barony of Cecil of Essendon, he served as leader of the House of Lords from 1942 until 1945. When the Conservatives returned to power in 1951, he again became leader of the House of Lords and supported Eden's Suez policy during the latter's premiership. When Eden resigned in 1957, Salisbury's own resignation soon followed in protest against the new government's plans for accelerating decolonization. He was chancellor of the Order of the Garter from 1960, chancellor of the University of Liverpool (1951–71), and a fellow of the Royal Society.

SAMBUU, ZHAMSARANGIBIN, Mongolian head of state (b. Mongolia, 1895—d. Mongolia, May 20, 1972), was chairman of the Presidium of the Great People's Hural (the Mongolian national assembly) and a member of the Politburo of the Mongolian People's Revolutionary Party.

SANDERS, GEORGE, British film actor (b. St. Petersburg, Russia, July 3, 1906—d. near Barcelona, Spain, April 25, 1972), who depicted a long succession of suave and supercilious cads, crooks, and romantic heroes, took his own life "because I am bored." His portrait of the dramatic critic Addison de Witt in *All About Eve* (1950) won him an Academy Award for best supporting actor. Sanders' American film debut came in 1936 with *Lloyds of London.* Among his later films were *A Shot in the Dark* (1964), *The Quiller Memorandum* (1966), and *The Kremlin Letter* (1970). In 1960 he published *Memoirs of a Professional Cad.*

SCHAROUN, HANS BERNHARD, West German architect (b. Bremen, Ger., Sept. 20, 1893—d. West Berlin, Ger., Nov. 25, 1972), designed the Philharmonic concert hall in West Berlin (inaugurated 1963).

SCHLUMBERGER, DANIEL THEODORE, French archaeologist (b. Mulhouse, France, Dec. 19, 1904—d. Princeton, N.J., Oct. 20, 1972), was assistant inspector and then inspector of antiquities for the French High Commission in the Levant (1929–41), director of the French archaeological delegation to Afghanistan (1945–64), professor in the Faculty of Letters at the University of Strasbourg (from 1955), and later director of the French Institute of Archaeology in Beirut, Lebanon. His excavations included the Umayyad palace of Qasr al-Hayr al-Gharbi in the Syrian desert, the fabled site of Balkh, capital of the Hellenistic successors of Alexander the Great in Afghanistan, and the Mazdean fire temple at Sorkh Kowtal, Afghanistan.

SCHMITT, GLADYS, U.S. novelist and educator (b. Pittsburgh, Pa., 1909—d. Pittsburgh, Oct. 3, 1972), Thomas S. Baker professor of literature at Carnegie-Mellon University in Pittsburgh from 1970, was the author of *David the King* (1946) which sold more than 900,000 copies.

SCOTT, ELISABETH WHITWORTH, British architect (b. Bournemouth, Eng., 1898—d. Dorset, Eng., June 19, 1972), was designer of the Shakespeare Memorial Theatre, Stratford-upon-Avon. She won the international competition of 1928 for the design of a new theatre on the site of the old Gothic Shakespeare Memorial Theatre, which had been destroyed by fire.

SEGNI, ANTONIO, Italian statesman (b. Sassari, Sardinia, Feb. 2, 1891—d. Rome, Italy, Dec. 1, 1972), was the 14th president of the Italian Republic (1962–64) and a principal representative of the right wing of the Christian Democratic Party. A militant Roman Catholic, he became known as a "white Bolshevik" for his post-World War II introduction of agrarian reform while minister of agriculture (1946–51). He was president of the Council of Ministers (premier; 1955–57, 1959–60), minister of defense (1958), and foreign minister (1960–62). He was awarded the Charlemagne Prize in 1964 and retired the following year.

SHAPLEY, HARLOW, U.S. astronomer (b. Nashville, Mo., Nov. 2, 1885—d. Boulder, Colo., Oct. 20, 1972), called the dean of American astronomers, was associated with Harvard University as director of the observatory (1921–52) and as Paine professor of astronomy (1952–56; emeritus from 1956). He received his B.A. (1910) and M.A. (1911) degrees from the University of Missouri; in 1912 he was granted a fellowship at the Princeton Observatory, and in 1913 earned his Ph.D. there. For the next seven years Shapley was on the staff at the Mount Wilson Observatory in California, where he studied the Cepheid variables. After World War II Shapley became interested in public affairs and certain of his political beliefs drew fire from the U.S. House Committee on Un-American Activities. The astronomer, however, faced the committee undaunted and continued his efforts to bring about world unity. Shapley's works included *The Inner Metagalaxy* (1957), *Of Stars and Men* (1958), and *The View from a Distant Star* (1964).

SHAWN, TED (EDWIN MEYERS SHAWN), U.S. dancer (b. Kansas City, Mo., Oct. 21, 1891—d. Orlando, Fla., Jan. 9, 1972), called the "father of modern dance," founded (1915) the Denishawn School of Dance with his wife, Ruth St. Denis (d. 1968), the famed dancer whom he married in 1914. During the 1920s the couple made many tours of the U.S. with their troupe of dancers; they also spent an 18-month period in the Orient dancing and gathering new material. In 1932 Shawn founded the Jacob's Pillow Dance Festival at Lee, Mass., which by the 1970s was attended by 50,000 persons during the season. Shawn was the author of a number of books including *Ruth St. Denis: Pioneer and Prophet.*

SIBYLLA, PRINCESS, of Sweden (b. Coburg, Ger., 1908—d. Stockholm, Swed., Nov. 28, 1972), daughter of Charles Edward, duke of Saxe-Coburg and Gotha (a grandson of Queen Victoria), married Prince Gustaf Adolf of Sweden, son of King Gustaf VI Adolf, in 1932. They had four daughters, known in Sweden as "the Haga princesses," from the castle where the family lived, and a son, Carl Gustaf (b. 1946), who, following his father's death in an air crash in 1947, became heir to the Swedish throne.

SIEFF, ISRAEL MOSES SIEFF, BARON, British business executive and Zionist (b. Manchester, Eng., May 4, 1889—d. London, Eng., Feb. 14, 1972), was president (from 1967) of Marks and Spencer Ltd., multimillion dollar department store chain. Sieff joined the company in 1915, becoming vice-chairman and joint managing director in 1926 and chairman after the death of Simon Marks in 1964. After being influenced by Chaim Weizmann at the University of Manchester, Sieff and Marks worked in the Zionist cause.

SIKORSKY, IGOR IVANOVICH, U.S. aviation pioneer (b. Kiev, the Ukraine, May 25, 1889—d. Easton, Conn., Oct. 26, 1972), whose achievements included the building of a multiple-engine plane and the creation of a flying boat, was the prime developer of the helicopter. His first attempt at flying a helicopter, which he built in Russia in 1909, resulted in failure, but a later American-made model, the VS-300, got off the ground in 1939. Sikorsky designed the two-engine and four-engine planes, used as bombers in World War I, before he went to the U.S. in 1919. By 1923 he had founded the Sikorsky Aero Engineering Corp., which produced in 1924 his first successful twin-engine, 14-passenger plane. This was followed in 1928 by the S-38, a ten-seater amphibian used by the U.S. Navy and by Pan American. In 1929 the Sikorsky company joined United Aircraft Corp. and in 1931 brought out the S-40, a four-engine, single-wing flying boat. The S-40, largest plane at that time, was flown by Pan Am on its Latin-American runs. The VS-300 helicopter, first displayed to the public in 1940 and later much modified, was to become the all-purpose workhorse of military flying.

SILKIN, LEWIS SILKIN, 1ST BARON, British politician (b. London, Eng., Nov. 14, 1889—d. London, May 11, 1972), was Labour MP for Peckham (1936–50), minister of town and country planning (1945–50), deputy leader of the official opposition in the House of Lords (1955–64), and chairman (1940–45) of the Town Planning Committee of the former London County Council (LCC). He was raised to the peerage in 1950.

SIMON, PIERRE-HENRI, French literary critic and scholar (b. Saint-Fort-sur-Gironde, France, Jan. 16, 1903—d. Paris, France, Sept. 20, 1972), was professor of French literature at the University of Fribourg, Switz. (1949–63).

SINGH, SANT FATEH, Sikh leader (b. 1908—d. Amritsar, India, Oct. 30, 1972), was a central figure in the campaign for a Sikh-dominated Punjabi-speaking state in the early 1960s and took over from his leader, Master Tara Singh, the threat to fast unto death as a political weapon. He began a fast in 1965, threatening to burn himself to death if his demands were not met, but called off the threat because of the war with Pakistan. Subsequently the Punjab was split into two states—one mainly Sikh and Punjabi-speaking. In 1966 he again threatened to burn himself if the city of Chandigarh was not made capital of the Punjab. After a further threat in 1970 Chandigarh was made joint capital of both the new states. Singh resigned from politics after the defeat of his Akali Dal party in the state elections of March 1972.

SMITH, BETTY (ELIZABETH KEOGH), U.S. author (b. Brooklyn, N.Y., Dec. 15, 1896—d. Shelton, Conn., Jan. 17, 1972), whose best-selling book *A Tree Grows in Brooklyn* (1943) was based on her own life as a child in Brooklyn. The novel, which sold six million copies, was adapted for the screen (directed by Elia Kazan and released in 1945) and later (1951) made into a Broadway play.

SMITH, JOSEPH FIELDING, U.S. religious leader (b. Salt Lake City, Utah, July 19, 1876—d. Salt Lake City, July 2, 1972), the tenth president of the Church of Jesus Christ of Latter-day Saints, was a descendant of the prophet Joseph Smith who founded the church in the 1830s. After serving as a Mormon missionary to Britain (1904–06), Smith became a church historian. In 1910 he was named to the church's Council of the Twelve Apostles and in 1951 was appointed president of the council. In 1970 Smith, then 93 years of age, was elected president of the Mormons, upon the death of David C. McKay, the ninth president.

SNOW, EDGAR PARKS, U.S. author and expert on China (b. Kansas City, Mo., July 19, 1905—d. Eysins, Switz., Feb. 15, 1972), was the first U.S. journalist to interview Mao Tse-tung after the Chinese Red Army leader, with Chou En-lai, had set up his headquarters in the Yenan caves in Shensi Province in 1935. Snow first went to China in 1928 and remained for 12 years, working a short time for the *China Weekly Review,* then as foreign correspondent for a number of big U.S. dailies and the *London Daily Herald,* as well as for the *Saturday Evening Post, Fortune,* and *Look* magazines. Snow's last trip to China, in 1970, was thought to have paved the way in some part for Pres. Richard Nixon's visit in 1972. Snow's authoritative book *Red Star over China* (1937), recounting his first visit with Mao, was revised to include his later observations and reissued in 1968. Another book, *The Other Side of the River,* concerning Snow's impressions of Communist China 11 years after the revolution, was published in 1962; his last work, *The Long Revolution,* was published in 1972.

SPAAK, PAUL-HENRI, Belgian statesman (b. Schaerbeek, Belg., Jan. 25, 1899—d. Brussels, Belg., July 31, 1972), was a "founding father" of the European Economic Community and played a leading part in post-World War II European politics. Throughout a long and distinguished

Jackie Robinson

WIDE WORLD

Dame Margaret Rutherford

WIDE WORLD

George Sanders

UPI COMPIX

career covering three periods as prime minister and six as foreign minister, he was intimately involved in the major crises of his own country—the German invasion of 1940, the abdication of Leopold III, and the break with the Congo—as well as being in the forefront of the campaign for European integration. A lawyer by training, in 1932 he was elected as a Socialist deputy for Brussels; three years later he became minister of transport, then foreign minister, and in May 1938 Belgium's first Socialist prime minister. As prime minister and again as foreign minister, he strove to keep Belgium neutral. When the Germans invaded, Spaak escaped to England with Prime Minister Hubert Pierlot, and during the government's exile in London he laid the foundations of Benelux. After the war came the long conflict with the king over his having decided to remain in occupied Belgium, and in 1950 Spaak forced Leopold's abdication in favour of his son Baudouin.

The war had convinced Spaak of the necessity for a united Europe. In 1946 he became president of the first UN General Assembly; in 1948, while still prime minister and foreign minister of Belgium, he was elected chairman of the newly founded Organization for European Economic Cooperation; in 1949 he became president of the Consultative Assembly of the Council of Europe, and one year later he commended the Schuman plan for a supranational coal and steel pool to the assembly. In 1954 he threw all his efforts into the creation of a European common market, helping to draft the Rome treaties that established the EEC and Euratom. In 1957 Spaak became secretary-general of NATO, from which he resigned in 1961 to become Belgium's deputy prime minister and foreign minister in a Christian Social-Socialist coalition. He did much to achieve a merger between breakaway Katanga Province and the Congo's central government, and in 1965 signed a treaty with the Congo's prime minister, Moise Tshombe. He retired from active politics in 1966. In 1957 he was awarded the Charlemagne Prize for his work toward realizing the ideal of European unity.

SPECTORSKY, A(UGUSTE) C(OMTE), U.S. publisher (b. Paris, France, Aug. 13, 1910—d. St. Croix, Virgin Islands, Jan. 17, 1972), was associate publisher and editorial director of *Playboy* magazine. After joining the *Playboy* staff in 1956, he was responsible for persuading important writers to let their work appear in the magazine. He made *Playboy* an enormous success by striking a balance between good centerfolds and good writing. Spectorsky was the author of *The Exurbanites,* a best seller of 1955.

SPOFFORD, THE REV. WILLIAM B., U.S. clergyman (b. Claremont, N.H., April 5, 1892—d. Tunkhannock, Pa., Oct. 9, 1972), editor from 1919 of *Witness,* national weekly of the Protestant Episcopal Church, was executive secretary of the Church League for Industrial Democracy, and director and trustee of the American Civil Liberties Union during the 1930s.

STARK, HAROLD RAYNSFORD, admiral (ret.), U.S. Navy (b. Wilkes-Barre, Pa., Nov. 12, 1880—d. Washington, D.C., Aug. 21, 1972), was chief of naval operations at the time of the Japanese attack on Pearl Harbor. He received the rank of admiral in 1939 with the assignment to build a two-ocean navy to counterbalance the threat of Germany and Japan. He was superseded in the top command shortly after Pearl Harbor but was given command of the U.S. naval forces in Europe until the surrender of Germany in 1945. Although officially absolved of any blame for the success of the Japanese attacks on Pearl Harbor, Admiral Stark, like many of his contemporaries, suffered the consequences of the military establishment's ineptitude in the entire disaster. He retired in 1946.

SUSINI, PIERRE, French diplomat (b. Algiers, Dec. 12, 1919—d. Paris, France, Oct. 19, 1972), was French delegate general in Hanoi, North Vietnam, from 1970. He entered the French foreign service in 1944 and served in various capacities in San Sebastian (Spain), Ankara, Reykjavik, Belgrade, Beirut, Damascus, and Cairo before being sent to Hanoi. He received fatal injuries when the French mission buildings in Hanoi were hit during a U.S. bombing raid in October 1972.

SWINTON, PHILIP CUNLIFFE-LISTER, 1st Earl, British politician (b. Bridlington, Yorkshire, Eng., May 1, 1884—d. Masham, Yorkshire, Eng., July 27, 1972), was elected Conservative MP for Hendon, and retained the seat until he received his peerage in 1935. He was minister resident in West Africa (1942–44), minister for civil aviation (1944–45), chancellor of the duchy of Lancaster and minister of materials (1951–52), and secretary of state for Commonwealth relations (1952–55). He was also deputy leader of the House of Lords (1951–55).

SZAMUELY, TIBOR, Hungarian-British scholar (b. Moscow, U.S.S.R., 1925—d. London, Eng., December 1972), was vice-chancellor of Budapest University (1958) and later lecturer in politics at Reading (Eng.) University. He attended school in England, then returned to the U.S.S.R. and was graduated from Moscow University. In 1951 he was arrested and sent to a labour camp; on his release he went to Hungary, then to Ghana, and in 1964 to England, where he made a name for himself in political journalism and as a broadcaster. He became a British citizen in 1969. Before his death he completed a major work, *The Russian Tradition,* to be published in 1973.

TALAL, IBN ABDULLAH, former king of Jordan (b. Mecca, Hejaz, 1909—d. Istanbul, Turk., July 8, 1972), was proclaimed king on Sept. 5, 1951, but abdicated the following year in favour of his son Husain. Talal, privately educated in Amman, joined the Arab Legion in 1927 as a lieutenant, and rose to general of the Legion in 1948. He became ruler after his father, King Abdullah, was assassinated on July 20, 1951. Already suffering mental distress, Talal became increasingly ill, and on Aug. 11, 1952, the Jordanian Parliament declared him mentally unfit and removed him from office. His son Crown Prince Husain was proclaimed successor. Talal spent the remainder of his life in a mental institution.

TAMIROFF, AKIM, U.S. actor (b. Baku, Russia, 1900—d. Palm Springs, Calif., Sept. 17, 1972), was twice nominated for an Academy Award: in 1936 for his portrayal of a Chinese general in *The General Died at Dawn* and in 1943 for his role as a guerrilla leader in *For Whom the Bell Tolls.* In 1959 he was chosen to play the lead in the long-running Broadway play *Rashomon.*

TAZEWELL, CHARLES, U.S. writer (b. Des Moines, Ia., 1900—d. Chesterfield, N.H., June 26, 1972), was the author of the beloved Christmas story *The Littlest Angel,* written in three days in 1939 for *Coronet* magazine, published in book form in 1946, and by 1972 in its 38th printing. Tazewell's other children's books included *The Littlest Snowman,* winner of the Thomas A. Edison prize for the best children's book of 1956.

THEILER, MAX, South African-U.S. immunologist (b. Pretoria, S.Af., Jan. 30, 1899—d. New Haven, Conn., Aug. 11, 1972), winner of a Nobel Prize, was associated with the Rockefeller Foundation from 1931 until 1964, when he became professor of epidemiology and microbiology at Yale University. Theiler studied at the London School of Tropical Medicine, taught at Harvard University (1922–30), then transferred to the virus laboratory of the Rockefeller Institute for Medical Research (which later became Rockefeller University); he was named director of the lab in 1951. At the Rockefeller Institute he pursued his research into the cause of yellow fever and aided in proving that a filterable virus was the causative agent. By 1936 Theiler and his co-workers had succeeded in producing a vaccine, known as 17-D virus, which they tested on themselves to prove its effectiveness. Further successful testing led to mass production of the vaccine in the mid-1940s. For his work in developing the yellow fever vaccine, Theiler was awarded the 1951 Nobel Prize for Physiology or Medicine.

THOMPSON, LLEWELLYN E., JR., U.S. diplomat (b. Las Animas, Colo., Aug. 24, 1904—d. Bethesda, Md., Feb. 6, 1972), was twice ambassador to Moscow, 1957–62 and 1967–69. He served on the U.S. delegation to the strategic arms limitation talks (SALT) at both the Helsinki and Vienna sessions, 1969–71.

THORNDIKE, (ARTHUR) RUSSELL, British actor and author (b. Rochester, Eng., Feb. 6, 1885—d. London, Eng., Nov. 7, 1972), who wrote the *Dr. Syn* novels, was a well-known figure on the London stage for nearly 40 years. His writings include the *Dr. Syn* books about a smuggling parson of the Romney marshes, the first of which was published in 1915 and brought fame to its author (a film based on the stories was later made); other works were *The House of Jeffreys* (1943), and *Sybil Thorndike* (1929), a biography of his sister.

TISSERANT, EUGÈNE GABRIEL GERVAIS LAURENT CARDINAL, French Roman Catholic prelate (b. Nancy, France, March 24, 1884—d. Albano, Italy, Feb. 21, 1972), dean of the Sacred College of Cardinals from 1951, was one of the greatest experts on the history of the Near East and held the title of "librarian and archivist of the Holy Roman Church." Ordained in 1907, he became curator of Oriental manuscripts in the

Akim Tamiroff

WIDE WORLD

Eugène Cardinal Tisserant

KARSH OF OTTAWA—CAMERA PRESS/PICTORIAL PARADE

Helen Traubel

WIDE WORLD

Vatican Library the following year and also professor of Assyrian at the Apollinarian University, Rome (1908–13). Tisserant, who served under six popes, was created cardinal by Pius XI in 1936 and held the dioceses of Ostia and Porto and Sta. Rufina. In 1961 he was elected to the Académie Française.

TRAUBEL, HELEN, U.S. opera and concert star (b. St. Louis, Mo., 1903—d. Santa Monica, Calif., July 28, 1972), famed Wagnerian soprano of the New York Metropolitan Opera Company from 1939 until 1953, made her professional singing debut in the early 1920s with the St. Louis Symphony Orchestra under the baton of Rudolph Ganz (*q.v.*). She first sang Sieglinde in *Die Walküre* in Chicago in 1939, repeating her performance at the Met later that same year when she became a member of the company. Her appearances in nightclubs, films, and on radio and TV led to clashes with Rudolph Bing, the Met's general manager, over their propriety, and in 1953 Traubel left the company. For the next decade or so she worked with the popular entertainers of the day.

TRAYNOR, HAROLD JOSEPH ("Pie"), U.S. baseball player (b. 1900—d. Pittsburgh, Pa., March 16, 1972), who was elected to the Baseball Hall of Fame in 1948, spent his 17-year major league career with the Pittsburgh Pirates. Traynor broke in as a regular with the Pirates in 1922, playing both shortstop and third base. In 1934 he was named player-manager of the Pirates; he retired as a player in 1937 but continued to manage the club until after the 1939 season. Traynor had a lifetime batting average of .320 and a fielding average of .921. In 1969 the baseball writers named him the greatest third baseman of all time and chose him as a member of the all-time major league All-Star team.

TROUT, PAUL HOWARD ("Dizzy"), U.S. baseball player (b. 1916—d. Chicago, Ill., Feb. 28, 1972), star pitcher with the Detroit Tigers from 1939 until 1952, posted a 20–12 record in 1943 and had a 2.22 earned-run average in 1944, his peak season. In 1945 he led the Tigers to the American League pennant and, during the World Series against the Chicago Cubs, won four games out of six that he pitched in nine days. His overall record was 170 won to 161 lost.

TRUMAN, HARRY S.: *see* page 520.

TUPOLEV, ANDREI NIKOLAEVICH, Soviet aircraft designer (b. Pustomazovo, Russia, Nov. 11, 1888—d. Moscow, U.S.S.R., Dec. 23, 1972), was responsible for the design of a wide variety of civil and military aircraft, culminating in the Tu-144 supersonic transport (SST), which first flew on Dec. 31, 1968, two months ahead of the Anglo-French Concorde SST. Educated at the Moscow Higher Technical School, Tupolev in 1918 became assistant director of the Central Aerohydrodynamics Institute. He designed his first aircraft in 1922, and a later model made a historic Moscow–New York flight via Siberia in 1926. His most significant designs came after the advent of jet propulsion and included the twin-jet Tu-104, and the Tu-114, powered by four turboprops, which when introduced in 1961 was the largest and heaviest commercial aircraft in use. Tupolev was a member of the Soviet Academy of Sciences and an honorary fellow of the Royal Aeronautical Society. He received numerous state prizes and in 1959 was awarded the Gold Medal of the Fédération Aéronautique Internationale.

VAN DOREN, MARK, U.S. poet and teacher (b. Hope, Ill., June 13, 1894—d. Torrington, Conn., Dec. 10, 1972), winner of the Pulitzer Prize in 1940 for his *Collected Poems,* was the prolific writer of more than 50 books, including verse, novels, and critical essays. He graduated from the University of Illinois in 1914 and was granted his master's degree the following year. After receiving his doctorate from Columbia University in 1920 Van Doren began his 39-year teaching career at that institution, where he was professor of English until retiring in 1959. Van Doren's fiction was not as impressive as his other writings, but *The Transients* (1935), *Windless Cabins* (1940), and *Tilda* (1943) were well known. His critical works included studies on Thoreau and Dryden, as well as *Shakespeare* (1939), *Nathaniel Hawthorne* (1949), and *Introduction to Poetry,* a critical anthology (1951). As a poet Van Doren received universal acclaim for his fine craftsmanship and for the lyricism and cool intellectuality of his verse. His first volume, *Spring Thunder and Other Poems,* was published in 1924; among his later works were *Collected and New Poems* (1963) and *That Shining Place* (1969). Van Doren also wrote *The Autobiography of Mark Van Doren* (1958) and a play, *The Last Days of Lincoln* (1959). Among his many awards, in addition to the Pulitzer Prize, was the Emerson-Thoreau Medal of the American Academy of Arts and Sciences (1963).

von BEKESY, GEORG, U.S. physicist (b. Budapest, Hung., June 3, 1899—d. Honolulu, Hawaii, June 13, 1972), professor of sensory sciences at the University of Hawaii from 1966, was the recipient of a Nobel Prize in 1961 while a faculty member at Harvard University. Von Bekesy received a Ph.D. in physics from the University of Budapest in 1923 and became an engineer with the Hungarian telephone system, where he began his research work into the mechanics of hearing. In 1947, after spending several years at the Royal Caroline Institute in Stockholm, Von Bekesy went to the United States and joined the faculty at Harvard. He continued his experiments with the human ear and discovered how the ear distinguishes the pitch of sounds in the cochlea, that part of the inner ear shaped like a snail's shell. He demonstrated the role of the cochlea as a sort of microphone that converts the mechanical energy of sound into electrical impulses received by the brain. For this, and for pointing the way toward advances in the diagnosis and correction of damaged hearing, Von Bekesy was awarded the 1961 Nobel Prize for Physiology or Medicine.

WADDAMS, THE REV. CANON HERBERT MONTAGUE, British Anglican clergyman (b. Nov. 15, 1911—d. May 13, 1972), was general secretary of the Church of England Council on Foreign Relations (1945–59). Ordained in 1935, he was assistant missioner at Corpus Christi College, Cambridge, until 1937, when he became assistant priest at the Grosvenor Chapel and chaplain of Liddon House. In the early 1940s he worked in the Religious Division of the Ministry of Information. In 1959 he went to Canada as rector of Manotick, Ont. In 1962 he was appointed canon residentiary of Canterbury Cathedral. He was chairman of the Hansard Society for Parliamentary Government from 1970. A prolific writer, he was a contributor to *Encyclopædia Britannica.*

WATSON-JONES, SIR REGINALD, British orthopedic surgeon (b. 1902—d. London, Eng., Aug. 9, 1972), was orthopedic surgeon to King George VI (1946–52) and to Queen Elizabeth II from 1952. Outstanding contributions to orthopedic surgery were his world-famous textbook on *Fractures and Joint Injuries* (1940) and his founding of the *British Journal of Bone and Joint Surgery.* He was knighted in 1945 and was a member of the council of the Royal College of Surgeons.

WEBSTER, MARGARET, British actress and stage director (b. New York, N.Y., March 15, 1905—d. London, Eng., Nov. 13, 1972), who in the 1950s became the first woman to direct productions (*Don Carlos* and then *Aïda*) at the Metropolitan Opera House, New York, began her career understudying Dame Sybil Thorndike in *Saint Joan,* reaching the Old Vic in 1929. She began directing plays on the London stage in 1935. She was invited to New York to direct *Richard II* (1937), *Hamlet* (1938), and *Henry IV, Part I* (1939). In 1943 she directed *Othello,* playing Emilia herself to Paul Robeson's lead. In 1946 she was elected one of the ten outstanding women of the year by the Women's National Press Club of America. She was the author of *Shakespeare Today* (1957) and *The Same Only Different* (1969), her autobiography.

WEISS, GEORGE MARTIN, U.S. baseball executive (b. New Haven, Conn., June 23, 1894—d. Greenwich, Conn., Aug. 13, 1972), general manager of the New York Yankees during the team's peak years, from 1947 through 1960, when it chalked up ten pennants and seven World Series. Weiss became the first president of the New York Mets in 1961 and remained in that post until 1966 when he retired. He was inducted into the Baseball Hall of Fame in a special executive category.

WELLINGTON, GERALD WELLESLEY, 7th Duke of, British architect and iconographer (b. Aug. 21, 1885—d. Stratfield Saye, Berkshire, Eng., Jan. 4, 1972), an authority on his ancestor, the "Iron Duke," practiced for a number of years as an architect. An expert in the arts and literature of the Regency period, he was a trustee of the National Gallery (1950–57).

"Pie" Traynor

UPI COMPIX

Mark Van Doren

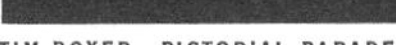

TIM BOXER—PICTORIAL PARADE

George Weiss

WIDE WORLD

UPI COMPIX

TRUMAN, HARRY S., 33rd president of the U.S. (b. Lamar, Mo., May 8, 1884—d. Kansas City, Mo., Dec. 26, 1972), led the U.S. to a new role of international leadership and kept Franklin D. Roosevelt's New Deal tradition at home. Son of John Anderson Truman, a horse-and-mule trader and farmer, Truman received a high school education at Independence, Mo., but did not attend college. Poor eyesight kept him from West Point, but during World War I he served in France with the Missouri National Guard, becoming commander of Battery D, 129th Field Artillery, 35th Division. In 1919 he returned to Kansas City where he married his high school sweetheart, Bess Wallace, and, with his ex-sergeant, opened a haberdashery. The business failed during the depression of 1921, and Truman, refusing to file bankruptcy proceedings, continued to pay off his debts for more than a decade.

In his first attempt at elective office, Truman ran successfully in 1922 for judge of the County Court, with the support of the Kansas City Democratic machine of Thomas J. Pendergast. Subsequent elections, as presiding judge of the County Court in 1926 and, in 1934, to the U.S. Senate, were also won under Pendergast's tutelage.

A more prominent political role began in 1941 when Truman proposed formation of a special Senate investigating committee. As its chairman, he helped expose graft and waste, urged more comprehensive planning of the war effort and postwar reconstruction, and won for himself an important place in the Democratic Party. In 1944 he was picked to replace the controversial Henry A. Wallace as vice-presidential running mate for Roosevelt, who was seeking his fourth term as president.

On April 12, 1945, Roosevelt died, and Truman became leader of a nation faced with staggering problems: World War II had yet to be successfully concluded and conflicts within the wartime alliance resolved; a wartime economy threatened inflation or depression. Truman's record stands as the achievement of a man who did his best "according to his lights" and who himself accepted the responsibility for leadership he had not sought. Within the nearly eight years that he held office, Truman made the decisions to: Use atomic bombs on Hiroshima (Aug. 6, 1945) and Nagasaki (Aug. 9, 1945) in an effort to conclude World War II immediately; authorize development of the hydrogen bomb; provide $400 million aid to Greece and Turkey, beginning in 1947, and establish the Truman Doctrine of support for nations "threatened by Communism"; establish in 1947 the postwar Marshall Plan; operate a $250 million airlift to West Berlin, breaking a 324-day Soviet blockade begun in June 1948 to force Western powers out of the city; begin the Point Four program of technical aid to less developed non-European nations; continue U.S. leadership in creation of the UN; join NATO in 1949, the first military alliance between European nations and the U.S.; and send U.S. troops to Korea in 1950 to defend South Korea against invasion by Communist North Korea. These foreign policy decisions overshadowed the decades that followed, initiating as they did the "cold war" and a long period of U.S. activity abroad.

At home, Truman suffered from congressional opposition and the sometime support of labour. During his administrations, concern for security led to implementation of a stringent "loyalty program" within government; the trial of Alger Hiss; passage in 1950 of the McCarran Internal Security Act, and eventual confrontation with Wisconsin Sen. Joseph McCarthy.

His upset victory in 1948 over New York Gov. Thomas E. Dewey was perhaps a sign of his fluctuating popularity with the public. Forecast as an easy win for Dewey, the election instead returned Truman to office with 49.5% of the popular vote and 303 electoral votes to Dewey's 45.1% and 189 electoral votes.

In 1952 President Truman announced that he would not seek reelection and, having supported Illinois Gov. Adlai E. Stevenson in an unsuccessful bid for the presidency, retired to Independence, where he took a great interest in the Harry S. Truman Library, the depository for his presidential papers.

After voting in the 1968 presidential election, former president Harry S. Truman, then 84, walks briskly back to his home in Independence, Mo. During his presidency, Truman kept newsmen huffing from following the chief executive on daily morning constitutionals.

WIDE WORLD

UPI COMPIX

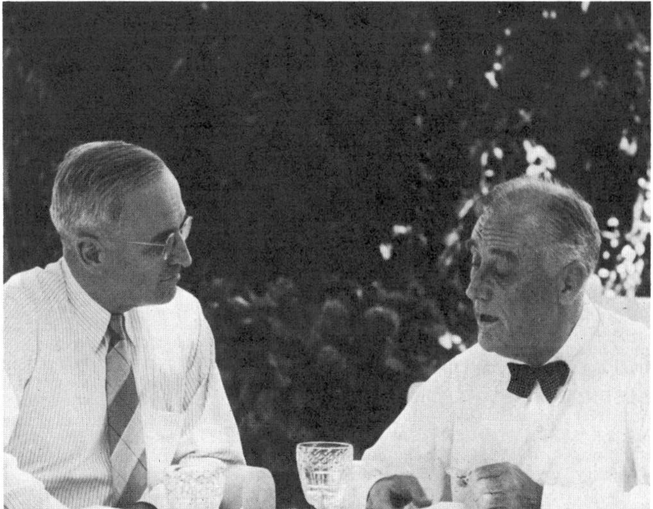

EB INC.

Just two months before he was to become president on the death of Franklin D. Roosevelt, Vice-President Truman (above) made this appearance at the National Press Club in Washington with actress Lauren Bacall. Shortly after the Democratic national convention in 1944, candidates Truman and Roosevelt (right) confer at the White House, the first such conference the two leaders had since Truman had become the surprise vice-presidential nominee over incumbent Henry A. Wallace. Truman, Churchill, and Stalin (below) at the Potsdam meeting in 1945. The famous picture (above right) of Truman in 1948 after his stunning upset election over Thomas E. Dewey.

EB INC.

WHEAT, ZACHARY DAVIS ("ZACK"), U.S. baseball player (b. Hamilton, Mo., May 23, 1888—d. Sedalia, Mo., March 11, 1972), outfielder for the Brooklyn Dodgers from 1909 until 1926, held a lifetime batting average of .317. He was elected to the Baseball Hall of Fame in 1959.

WILLIAM OF GLOUCESTER, PRINCE WILLIAM HENRY ANDREW FREDERICK, ninth in succession to the throne of the United Kingdom (b. Barnet, Eng., Dec. 18, 1941—d. Halfpenny Green, Staffordshire, Eng., Aug. 28, 1972), elder son of the duke of Gloucester (uncle of Queen Elizabeth II), was appointed a counselor of state in 1963, third secretary at the British High Commission at Lagos, Nig., in 1965, and second secretary (commercial) at the British embassy in Tokyo in 1968. He had been a page at the wedding of Princess (later Queen) Elizabeth to Lieut. Philip Mountbatten in 1947. In 1970 the prince resigned from the diplomatic service having become president of the British Light Aviation Centre in 1969. Prince William, a participant in several 1972 international air races, was killed, along with his co-pilot Vyrell Mitchell, in the seventh annual Goodyear International Air Trophy Race.

WILLIAMS, BILLY, U.S. singer (b. Texas, 1911—d. Chicago, Ill., Oct. 12, 1972), entered show business in 1938 with the Broadway hit *Hellzapoppin'*. In 1950 he formed the Billy Williams Quartet, which became a regular feature on the Sid Caesar Saturday night TV "Show of Shows." Williams' hit songs included "Too Young," "Shanghai," and "I'm Gonna Sit Right Down and Write Myself a Letter."

WILLIAMS, SIR (ARTHUR) LEONARD, British politician (b. Birkenhead, Eng., Jan. 22, 1904—d. Mauritius, Dec. 27, 1972), was general secretary of the British Labour Party (1962–68) and from 1968 governor-general of Mauritius. In 1936 he became secretary of the Leeds Labour Party branch and later regional organizer for Yorkshire. In 1946 he transferred to Labour Party headquarters in London as assistant national agent, becoming national agent in 1951.

WILSON, EDMUND, U.S. literary figure (b. Red Bank, N.J., May 8, 1895—d. Talcottville, N.Y., June 12, 1972), often called America's foremost critic, was also the author of dozens of books on history, literature, and economics, as well as a novel, plays, and poetry. He was a graduate of Princeton University (1916) and for a time was an editor for *Vanity Fair* and an associate editor for *The New Republic* (1926–31). In 1931 Wilson published his widely acclaimed *Axel's Castle: A Study in the Imaginative Literature of 1870–1930*. Something of a leftist, Wilson studied in the Soviet Union under a Guggenheim fellowship (1935) and produced *Travels in Two Democracies* (1936), based on his experiences of that period, and *To the Finland Station* (1940). *Boys in the Back Room* and *The Wound and the Bow* came out in 1941; *Notebooks of Night* in 1942; and *The Shock of Recognition* in 1943. Heightened acclaim came with the publication in 1946 of *Memoirs of Hecate County,* which for a time was banned in New York state. From 1944 to 1948 Wilson was a book reviewer for *The New Yorker*. In 1962 he published *Patriotic Gore,* a study of Civil War literature on which he had spent 15 years. Among his last books were *Upstate: Records and Recollections of Northern New York* (1971) and *A Window on Russia,* on Russian literature (August 1972). Wilson was presented the Presidential Medal of Freedom, highest U.S. civilian award, in 1963; he received the National Medal for Literature in 1966 and the $30,000 Aspen Award in 1968.

WILSON, MARIE, U.S. actress (b. Anaheim, Calif., 1917—d. Hollywood, Calif., Nov. 23, 1972), who was noted for her "dumb blond" roles, played the character of Irma in "My Friend Irma," a popular radio and TV series of the 1940s and 50s.

WINCHELL, WALTER, U.S. newspaper columnist and newscaster (b. New York, N.Y., April 7, 1897—d. Los Angeles, Calif., Feb. 20, 1972), whose familiar greeting, "Good evening, Mr. and Mrs. America and all the ships at sea, let's go to press!" opened each broadcast, began his working career in vaudeville at age 12. In the early 1920s he began his gossipy show-business column for the *New York Evening Graphic* newspaper. After 1929, he moved to Hearst's *New York Mirror* and introduced more political items into his "On Broadway" column, which was syndicated in about 800 newspapers by the early 1930s. The *Mirror* ceased publication in 1963, and Winchell's column expired with it, although he later wrote a weekly column for the *New York World Journal Tribune.* Winchell's weekly newscast started on network radio in 1932 and ended on TV in the early 1960s. He was the narrator for the highly successful TV series "The Untouchables."

WINDSOR, DUKE OF, PRINCE EDWARD ALBERT CHRISTIAN GEORGE ANDREW PATRICK DAVID, king of Great Britain and Northern Ireland from Jan. 20, 1936, until his abdication on Dec. 11, 1936 (b. White Lodge, Richmond Park, Eng., June 23, 1894—d. Paris, France, May 28, 1972), was, as Edward VIII, a popular and progressive monarch whose convictions, particularly on marriage, caused him to become the only British sovereign ever voluntarily to resign the crown.

In 1907 he attended the Royal Naval College, Osborne, as a cadet and in 1909 passed on to Dartmouth College. The following year King Edward VII died and the prince became duke of Cornwall and heir to the throne. He was admitted to the Order of the Garter on June 10, 1911, and wore the robes at the coronation of his father, George V, on June 22. On his 16th birthday he was created prince of Wales, and was formally invested at Caernarvon Castle in July 1911. In October 1912 he went up to Magdalen College, Oxford, but it was soon decided that he should join the Army.

At the outbreak of World War I he was commissioned in the Grenadier Guards (Aug. 6, 1914) and gained a staff posting that took him to France and Italy. In the 1920s he undertook extensive goodwill tours of the empire and, after an illness his father suffered in 1928, the prince took an increasing interest in national affairs. In 1932, after unemployment had reached unprecedented levels, he toured workingmen's clubs throughout Britain and enlisted over 200,000 men and women in occupational schemes.

In 1930 the prince's friendship with Mrs. Wallis Warfield Simpson began. Mrs. Simpson, divorced from a U.S. Navy lieutenant in 1927, married Ernest Simpson in 1928. Members of a private circle of friends, the Simpsons were frequently in the company of the prince and by 1934 he was deeply in love with Mrs. Simpson. It was at this point, before he could discuss the matter with his father, that George V died (Jan. 20, 1936) and Edward was proclaimed king.

As king, Edward VIII set in motion drastic economies in the royal estates. In November he opened Parliament and then toured distressed areas in South Wales. Meanwhile his attempts to gain the royal family's acceptance of Mrs. Simpson, who had obtained a divorce Oct. 27, 1936, met with firm opposition, backed by the Church of England (of which he was the head), the politicians, and later the press. Prime Minister Stanley Baldwin attempted to impress upon the king the peril to the integrity of the monarchy caused by the private friendship. Discussions of a morganatic marriage were pursued but on December 2 Baldwin assured him that this was impracticable. The king therefore made his final decision and abdicated on Dec. 10, 1936; the instrument of abdication was endorsed by Parliament on December 11 and thus the reign of Edward VIII ended. The new king, George VI, created his brother Edward duke of Windsor, and accorded him the right to the title of royal highness.

On June 3, 1937, Wallis Simpson and the duke were married under French law at the Château de Candé near Tours. No member of the royal family was present. The duke and duchess lived mainly in France and despite the couple's desire to resettle in England they spent the rest of their married life in exile. The duke accepted Winston Churchill's offer of the governorship of the Bahamas during World War II, then returned to France. Short visits to England followed in succeeding years—to attend the funerals of his brother King George VI (1952) and their mother Queen Mary (1953)—but it was not until 1967 that, for the first time, the duke and duchess were invited to attend an official public ceremony with other members of the royal family—the unveiling of a plaque to Queen Mary at Marlborough House.

The duke of Windsor published his memoirs, *A King's Story,* in 1951; those of the duchess, *The Heart Has Its Reasons,* were published in 1956.

YALMAN, AHMED EMIN, Turkish journalist (b. Salonika, Turk. [now Greece], May 14, 1888—d. Istanbul, Turk., Dec. 19, 1972), one of the most courageous political commentators in his country, entered journalism shortly before the Young Turks' revolution of 1908; he supported the movement of national revival under Mustafa Kemal, and was arrested by the British in 1920 and interned in Malta. In 1922 he became part proprietor and editor of *Vatan* ("The Fatherland"), but after four years the paper was suspended for criticism of Mustafa Kemal. In 1950 he supported the advent of parliamentary government but later became a strong critic of the dictatorial and reactionary tendencies of Pres. Celal Bayar and Premier Adnan Menderes. In May 1960 Yalman was sentenced to 15 months' imprisonment, but was released following the military coup of May 27. In 1961 Yalman founded *Hur Vatan* ("The Free Fatherland"). He wrote two important books: *The Development of Turkey as Measured by Its Press* (1914) and *Turkey in the World War* (1928).

YOULOU, FULBERT, Congolese politician (b. 1917—d. Madrid, Spain, May 5, 1972), was president of the People's Republic of the Congo (former French Congo), 1960–63. Ordained a Roman Catholic priest in 1946, he served as mayor of Brazzaville (1956–63), minister of agriculture (1957–58), and president of the Council of Ministers (1958–60) before being elected president in 1960, just after the country had gained its independence from France as the Republic of Congo. When France cut off its annual aid in 1963 Youlou raised taxes, food prices doubled, and unemployment soared. Youlou intended to proclaim a single-party government but trade union opposition forced his resignation. He was imprisoned by revolutionaries but escaped into the Democratic Republic of the Congo (later Zaire) on April 1, 1965. The Spanish government granted him asylum in 1966.

Walter Winchell

WIDE WORLD

The duke of Windsor

KARSH OF OTTAWA—CAMERA PRESS/PICTORIAL PARADE

Oceanography

A striking aspect of oceanography in 1972 was the increasing commitment of research effort to very large cooperative projects, designed to investigate vital scientific questions too extensive to be addressed by any single institution or laboratory. Many of these projects were the direct result of the International Decade of Ocean Exploration (IDOE), a planned decade (the 1970s) of international oceanographic research first proposed by Pres. Lyndon Johnson in 1968 and endorsed by the UN in the same year.

IDOE projects were divided into the three categories of environmental quality, environmental forecasting, and seabed assessment. Research in the first category was broadly concerned with the establishment of existing concentrations of both naturally occurring substances and pollutants in the world's oceans. This knowledge would constitute a baseline against which future effects of human intervention in the sea could be measured. Possibly harmful substances under study included heavy metals (such as mercury, cadmium, and lead), chlorinated hydrocarbons such as DDT, and crude oil. A global study of dissolved substances in the sea was being carried out by the international Geochemical Ocean Sections (Geosecs) project.

The first of a series of cruises planned as the central part of Geosecs began on July 18, 1972, when the research vessel "Knorr," operated by the Woods Hole (Mass.) Oceanographic Institution, started a nine-month voyage that would take it from above the Arctic Circle to Antarctica. The cruise was planned to follow a major flow of bottom ocean water believed to originate in the Norwegian Sea and to traverse the entire Atlantic Ocean to the Antarctic Circumpolar Current. The scientific novelty of Geosecs sprang from the very complete chemical analysis for dissolved constituents (such as oxygen, nitrogen, nutrients, trace elements, organic and inorganic carbon), radionuclides, and chemical properties (such as alkalinity) that would be made on all water samples. Many of the analytical operations were entirely automated and were under computer control.

Environmental forecasting in the marine environment requires the development of sound theoretical understanding of the most important physical processes in the sea before successful predictive models can be formulated. Among the large-scale IDOE projects aimed at improving such understanding were the Mid-Ocean Dynamics Experiment (MODE), the Coastal Upwelling Experiment (CUE), the Paleoceanography Study, and a program of computer modeling of ocean flow.

While Geosecs would yield much information about ocean currents by showing how they transport and mix dissolved constituents, MODE would examine the detailed structure of the flow in one particular region for a period of more than three months in 1973. The irregularly shaped experimental region, roughly 350 km. (217 mi.) across and located slightly south and west of Bermuda, was chosen to provide information about flow properties typical of mid-ocean regions. The central purpose of MODE was to evaluate the importance, for the overall circulation and mixing of the oceans, of small (perhaps 100- to 200-km. [62 to 124 mi.] wide) but intense quasi-geostrophic eddies that make the greatest contribution to most deepwater current records after tidal and similar currents have been subtracted. ("Geostrophic" refers to the effect of the earth's rotation.)

A program of preliminary shipboard and buoy observation at the MODE site was pursued vigorously during 1972. Simultaneously, theoretical studies of the effects of bottom relief, of density stratification, and of large-scale currents on the eddy field were pursued. The preliminary observations suggested that the eddy flows have, on the average, a much simpler

Current production of major ocean resources with areas of petroleum and gas exploration.

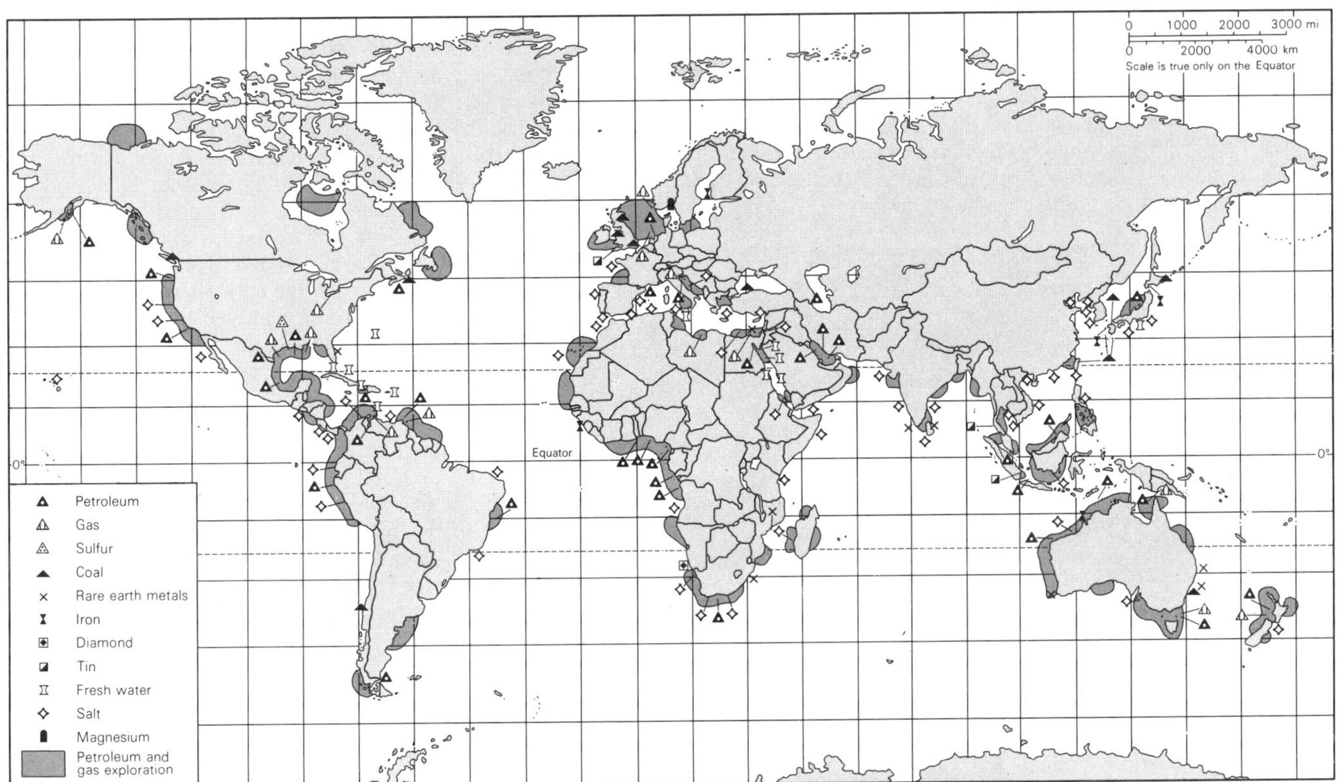

vertical profile than had been expected. Preliminary theoretical work emphasized the effects of bottom relief on the flow and suggested that, under some circumstances, bottom relief may enhance the eddy field.

Upwelling, a process common along the west coast of the Western Hemisphere continents as well as along other long coastlines, was the subject of the CUE project. Upwelling typically occurs during local summer, when prevailing winds force warm surface waters away from the coast. Cold, deep water then rises or "upwells" to replace the wind-displaced surface water, bringing with it rich supplies of nutrients and causing an increase in the production of living organisms. Coastal upwelling areas support over 50% of the oceans' fish, so that a study of the subject had great practical as well as scientific interest.

CUE was initially concentrating on upwelling off the Oregon coast, both for logistic reasons and because enough was known about upwelling there to permit optimal design of the fieldwork. The major field program ended on Aug. 1, 1972. Shipboard measurements of temperature and salinity from three ships, plus measurements of water currents at various levels and of meteorological variables at the sea surface from more than ten moored buoys, made up the central part of the program of measurements, although a number of other techniques were employed. Atmospheric conditions, sea-surface temperature, and sea-surface chlorophyll were monitored from an aircraft. The extent to which the presence of cold, upwelled water was reflected in satellite photographs of cloud patterns was studied, using satellite data supplied by the U.S. National Oceanic and Atmospheric Administration.

Analysis of the data was not yet completed. Preliminary results included confirmation of the existence of a deep poleward current below the Equatorward surface flow that generally prevails in upwelling areas. Upwelling appeared to be set up rather rapidly at the beginning of the season, after which it persisted, even though the wind might reverse itself for periods of several days.

The Paleoceanography Study was concerned with fluctuations in ocean conditions over hundreds or thousands of years, with the aim of learning more about climatic changes. Ocean bottom sediments would be examined to learn how current patterns and water properties in the Atlantic and Pacific changed during a major glaciation.

John Ryther, of the Woods Hole Oceanographic Institution, examines a bay scallop culture in an experimental aquaculture-sewage treatment tank. It was hoped the system ultimately would utilize the sewage from a town of 50,000 to produce 900 tons of oyster meat annually.

WIDE WORLD

Prediction of the behaviour of the ocean would ultimately be done by means of large computer models. Such ocean models were being developed, and preliminary simulation of the flow in the world's oceans had been obtained. Computer models were especially useful in that the importance of such factors as winds, surface heating or cooling, bottom relief, density stratification, and flow intensity could be studied easily either singly or in combination.

The third category of IDOE studies, seabed assessment, combined economic interests with basic research in a three-part exploration of continental margins, mid-ocean rifts and trenches, and the deep sea floor. All current exploitation of marine mineral and petroleum resources was being carried out over continental shelves, yet few continental margins were well mapped geologically. Fieldwork for a study of the eastern Atlantic continental margins began in 1972 with a cruise of the Woods Hole Oceanographic Institution's research vessel "Atlantis II" to the African part of the east Atlantic continental margin. The resulting data would resolve many questions about the ancient opening of the southern Atlantic Ocean and would also show whether the sedimentary pattern indicated the presence of petroleum deposits.

The processes that occur at the edges of a lithospheric plate were being studied in surveys of the Nasca Plate between South America and the East Pacific Rise. The convergence zone, where the plate is forced below the South American continent, was of particular interest, not only for possible mineral deposits but because it was one of the most seismically active regions on the earth. The distribution of manganese on the deep sea floor was being studied in an effort to understand the conditions under which manganese nodules are formed.

Large cooperative projects being conducted independently of IDOE included the North Pacific Experiment (Norpax) and the Deep Sea Drilling Project (DSDP). The purpose of Norpax was to develop an understanding of the processes that control large-scale fluctuations in the atmosphere and the ocean in the mid-latitudes of the North Pacific, which may have a profound effect on the weather of North America. Attention was being focused on the possibility that the ocean and atmosphere react on one another in such a way as to enhance certain abnormal meteorological situations. Measurements of such variables as air temperature, wind speed, and temperatures in the near surface layers of the ocean were being taken, using a network of moored buoys that would ultimately span the entire North Pacific.

The DSDP program, managed by the Scripps Institution of Oceanography, La Jolla, Calif., with scientific guidance from a panel of universities and oceanographic institutions, continued its exploration of the sediments of the ocean floors. The specially outfitted drilling ship "Glomar Challenger" took deep-sea cores in the Coral and Tasman seas and then worked in the Indian Ocean and the Red Sea. The overall result of this project had been to confirm the idea of sea-floor spreading, according to which the ocean's crust spreads from mid-ocean rises at speeds of several centimetres per year and moves toward trenches and zones of convergence where it plunges beneath the surface. (MYRL C. HENDERSHOTT)

See also **Antarctica; Geology; Law; Life Sciences; Meteorology; Seismology.**

ENCYCLOPÆDIA BRITANNICA FILMS. *How Level Is Sea Level?* (1970).

Oman

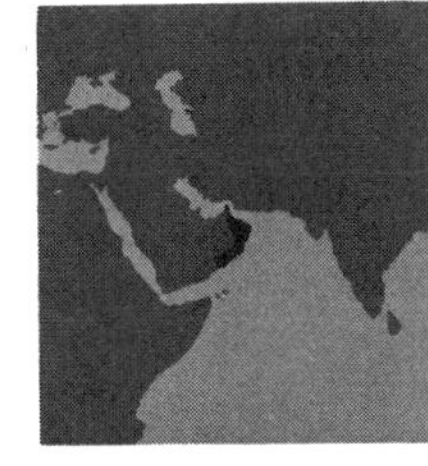

An independent sultanate, Oman occupies the southeastern part of the Arabian Peninsula and is bounded by the United Arab Emirates, Saudi Arabia, the Gulf of Oman, and the Arabian Sea. A small part of the country lies to the north of the rest of Oman and is separated from it by the United Arab Emirates. Area: 82,000 sq.mi. (212,380 sq.km.). Pop. (1970 est.): 750,000. Cap.: Muscat (pop., 1969, 9,973). Largest city: Matrah (pop., 1960, 14,119). Language: Arabic. Religion: Muslim. Sultan in 1972, Qabus ibn Sa'id.

Oman underwent rapid social and economic change in 1972, although development was handicapped by military spending. In January it was announced that the sultan's uncle, Tariq ibn Taimur, who was abroad, had resigned as prime minister owing to ill health and that his functions would be taken over by the sultan's office. Tariq returned to Oman in February and was appointed foreign affairs adviser. Fighting continued against the Marxist-led Dhofari rebels in the southwest, who were receiving aid from China, the Soviet Union, and Yemen (Aden). On May 5 the Omani Air Force attacked Southern Yemeni gun sites after the Omani fort of Habrut had been fired on from across the border. The sultan's British-officered forces scored some successes against the rebels, but the rebellion continued and about half the country's $125 million oil revenues were absorbed by the military. During the year Oman's first airport capable of handling jet aircraft was opened near Muscat.

Sa'id ibn Taimur, sultan of Muscat and Oman from 1932 until his deposition by his son in 1970, died in London on October 19. (*See* OBITUARIES.)

(PETER MANSFIELD)

OMAN

Finance and Trade. Monetary unit: Saudi riyal, with (Sept. 18, 1972) a free rate of U.S. $2.60 to 1 riyal (0.94 riyal = £1 sterling). Budget (1971 est.) revenue *c.* 50 million riyals. Foreign trade (1969 est.): imports 260 million riyals; exports 1,450,000,000 riyals. Import sources: France 51%; West Germany 13%; U.K. 13%; Netherlands 8%; Italy 5%. Export destinations: France 16%; West Germany 15%; Japan 10%; Netherlands 5%; Sweden 5%. Main export crude oil.

Industry. Crude oil production (1971) 14,312,000 metric tons.

Pakistan

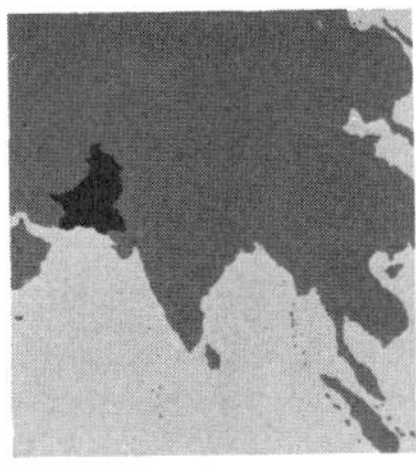

A federal republic, Pakistan is bordered on the south by the Arabian Sea, on the west by Afghanistan and Iran, on the north by China, and on the east by India. Area: 310,915 sq.mi. (805,266 sq.km.), excluding the Pakistani-controlled section of Jammu and Kashmir. Pop. (1972 est.): 60 million. Cap.: Islamabad (pop., 1972 est., 250,000). Largest city: Karachi (pop., 1972 est., 2,500,000). Language: Urdu and English. Religion: Muslim 90%; Hindu and Christian minorities. President in 1972, Zulfikar Ali Bhutto.

The gloom in which 1971 had ended for Pakistanis was gradually dispelled in the early months of 1972. President Bhutto (*see* BIOGRAPHY) showed himself an extremely able administrator, closely in touch with the needs and aspirations of all classes. His two main tasks were to restore confidence at home, bruised by defeat in a war with India and by the unconditional surrender of East Pakistan (Bangladesh), and to convince the world outside that his country possessed in full measure the determination and resources to maintain its position in the comity of nations.

During his first few months of power, Bhutto reminded his people constantly that, in spite of the secession of the eastern wing, the future of the nation was bright. He announced a series of measures that were designed to secure a more just and equitable distribution of national resources among those who were creating them, while at the same time carefully preserving the international confidence necessary to ensure the flow of foreign investment and external aid. In January large-scale industrial reforms were announced; ten categories of industries were nationalized, including iron and steel, heavy engineering, cement, petrochemicals, electricity, gas, and oil refineries, without affecting foreign investment and foreign credit. A Board of Industrial Management was

PAKISTAN

Education. (1969–70) Primary, pupils *c.* 5.1 million; secondary, pupils *c.* 530,000; vocational, pupils *c.* 28,000; primary, secondary, and vocational, teachers (1966–67) 131,925; teacher training, students *c.* 3,000; higher (including 7 universities with 14,425 students in 1966–67), students *c.* 97,090.

Finance. Monetary unit: Pakistan rupee, with (Sept. 18, 1972) a par value (following devaluation of May 11, 1972) of PakRs. 11 to U.S. $1 (free rate of PakRs. 26.61 = £1 sterling). Gold, SDRs, and foreign exchange, state bank: (June 1972) U.S. $289 million; (June 1971) U.S. $215 million. Budgets (1970–71 est.): central (including Bangladesh), revenue PakRs. 7,161,200,000, expenditure PakRs. 5,572,300,000; Pakistan government (former West Pakistan only), revenue PakRs. 1,872,100,000, expenditure PakRs. 2,172,700,000. National income: (1969–70) *c.* PakRs. 45 billion; (1968–69) *c.* PakRs. 41.6 billion. Cost of living (Karachi; 1963 = 100): (May 1972) 160; (May 1971) 142.

Foreign Trade. (Excluding trade with Bangladesh; 1970–71) Imports PakRs. 3,602,000,000; exports PakRs. 2,111,000,000. Import sources: U.S. 29%; West Germany 11%; U.K. 11%; Japan 10%; Italy 5%. Export destinations: Hong Kong 12%; Japan 10%; U.K. 9%; U.S.S.R. 8%; U.S. 6%. Main exports: cotton yarn 18%; cotton fabrics 16%; cotton 14%; rice 9%; leather 5%.

Transport and Communications. Roads (1970) *c.* 150,000 km. (mainly fair-weather tracks; 20,400 km. with improved surface). Motor vehicles in use (1969): passenger 107,200; commercial 34,900. Railways (1969–70): 8,600 km.; traffic 8,732,000,000 passenger-km., freight 6,892,000,000 net ton-km. Air traffic (including Bangladesh; 1971): 2,393,000,000 passenger-km.; freight 71,031,000 net ton-km. Shipping (including Bangladesh; 1971): merchant vessels 100 gross tons and over 177; gross tonnage 581,800. Telephones (including Bangladesh; Jan. 1971) 207,000. Radio licenses (June 1969) 1,339,000. Television receivers (including Bangladesh; Dec. 1970) *c.* 80,000.

Agriculture. Production (in 000; metric tons; 1971; 1970 in parentheses): wheat 6,503 (7,295); barley *c.* 95 (*c.* 110); corn 717 (668); rice 2,077 (2,346); sugar, raw value (1971–72) *c.* 380, (1970–71) *c.* 550; tobacco 125 (123); cotton, lint *c.* 600 (*c.* 500). Livestock (including Bangladesh; in 000; 1970–71): cattle *c.* 44,000; sheep *c.* 15,000; goats *c.* 19,000; buffalo *c.* 12,000; horses *c.* 500; asses *c.* 950; camels *c.* 900.

Industry. Production (in 000; metric tons; 1969–70): cement 2,606; crude oil 480; coal and lignite 1,249; natural gas (cu.m.) *c.* 3,500,000; electricity (excluding most industrial production; kw-hr.; 1965–66) 2,910,000; steel 175; sulfuric acid 31; soda ash 68; cotton yarn 273; woven cotton fabrics (m.) 718,000.

Oil:
see Fuel and Power; Industrial Review

Opera:
see Music

Organization for Economic Cooperation and Development:
see Development, Economic

Organization of African Unity:
see Africa

Organization of American States:
see Inter-American Affairs

Ornithology:
see Life Sciences

Orthodox Churches:
see Religion

Painting:
see Art Exhibitions; Art Sales; Museums and Galleries

Paints and Varnishes:
see Industrial Review

set up to replace the ancient managing agency system, much of which had been in the hands of a few wealthy families.

This step was quickly followed by far-reaching labour reforms that increased labour's participation at management level to 20%, freed workers from salary deductions for welfare programs, and gave them the right to appoint workers' auditors and shop stewards and to appeal to an "ombudsman" for redress of grievances. Increased security of employment and better social services, including housing, completed a package deal to enlist the solid support of labour.

In March a new land reform program was announced, drastically reducing the ceiling on individual and family holdings and closing all the loopholes that had reduced the effectiveness of earlier efforts at agrarian reform. Some 3.5 million ac. were taken over by the state for distribution to more than two million landless peasants. This was followed by a program of extended educational facilities based on the nationalization of private schools and colleges and on a drive to promote equality of opportunity among all classes, the extension of university education, and the ending of unemployment among educated youth. There followed the establishment of an extended health service, and a number of administrative reforms covering the police, the banking system, and the legal structure.

The effect of these measures was to strengthen the hand of the president in his efforts to reconcile in a new democratic constitution the wishes of the four constituent provinces for a large measure of local autonomy with the need for an effective federal government. His Pakistan People's Party (PPP) had a majority in the now truncated National Assembly and in the Punjab and Sind provinces, but was poorly represented in the North West Frontier Province and Baluchistan, where the National Awami Party and the Jamiat-ul-Ulema-i-Islam were strong. There was a feeling in the latter two units that they lagged behind the Punjab and Sind, and had not received their fair share of attention from the development agencies. Their anxiety was temporarily allayed by assurances that both provinces would be helped to make up any past inequities and by a political agreement reached between the PPP and the other political groupings in March that was meant to quiet threats of secession. In September there was further unrest, however, and allegation of a "London plot" by opposition leaders to dismember the country.

Pending the drafting of a new democratic constitution by the National Assembly, government, both central and provincial, was to be formed on the basis of the parliamentary majority, and the relations between the central government and the provinces would be determined on the basis of a modified 1935 act. In April the National Assembly passed an overwhelming vote of confidence in the president, who found himself able to abolish in the same month the martial law regime that had lasted since 1958. Shortly afterward, parliamentary provincial governments took office in all four provinces for the first time since 1955.

Great public anxiety was manifested over the continued detention by India of the Pakistani prisoners of war and by the occupation of Pakistani territory by Indian forces. After careful preliminary exchanges, a summit conference took place between President Bhutto and Indian Prime Minister Indira Gandhi at Simla, India, which laid down a step-by-step procedure for settling bilaterally the differences between their two countries, including a working agreement over Kashmir without prejudice to the stands on principle taken up by each side. Pakistan was disappointed that India insisted on making Bangladesh a party to the settlement of the prisoners of war affair, holding that it was to the Indian Army alone that they had surrendered. In November more than 600 Indian POWs being held in Pakistan were released as a goodwill gesture. Demarcation of the truce line in Kashmir was completed in December, and withdrawal of Indian and Pakistani forces in accordance with the new line began immediately.

A marked feature of 1972 was an upsurge in the national economy, caused by the diversion to external countries of exports formerly taken by East Pakistan. These rose spectacularly and were helped by a realistic (56.7%) devaluation of the rupee in May. As conditions became stable once more, external aid began to flow strongly. Early in the year, China had written off a $100 million loan, deferred for 20 years repayment of PakRs. 10 billion for material supplied, and made a further large investment in the great industrial complex at Taxila. The U.S. and the World Bank Aid to Pakistan Consortium, along with the International Monetary Fund, supplied extensive aid from June onward. The new budget presented in June included a record sum for defense expenditure (PakRs. 4,463,000,000), relieved poorer taxpayers, and increased taxation on capital and wealth. Revenue was estimated at PakRs. 8,510,000,000 with a surplus of PakRs. 250 million on revenue account.

Retaining the portfolio of foreign affairs in his own hands, President Bhutto displayed the same energy in the international field as in the domestic sphere. He toured the Islamic countries, strengthened friendship with China, reached an understanding with Moscow, cemented good relations with Afghanistan, and cooperated with Turkey and Iran in further Regional Cooperation for Development activities. He withdrew Pakistan from the Commonwealth of Nations in January without adversely affecting everyday relations with member countries and on November 8 formally announced Pakistan's withdrawal from SEATO. (L. F. RUSHBROOK WILLIAMS)

Panama

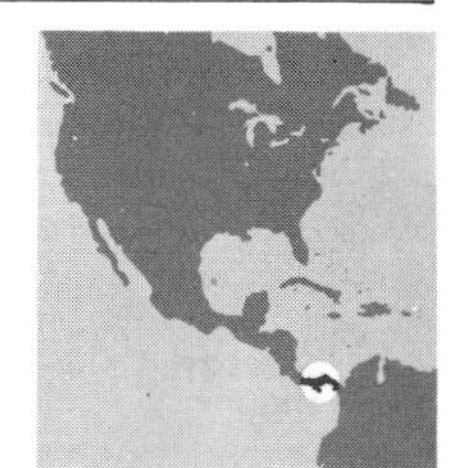

A republic of Central America, bisected by the Canal Zone, Panama is bounded by the Caribbean Sea, Colombia, the Pacific Ocean, and Costa Rica. Area: 29,208 sq.mi. (75,650 sq.km.). Pop. (1972 est.): 1,523,500. Cap. and largest city: Panama City (pop., 1972 est., 364,130). Language: Spanish. Religion (1967 est.): Roman Catholic 87%. President in 1972, Demetrio Lakas Bahas.

Throughout 1972 Panama had a facade of domestic peace. Beneath the exterior was a population living without freedom of speech and press, without independent radio and television news, without political agitation, without election choices, and even without political parties. Omar Torrijos, the youthful general who headed the National Guard, was in complete command of his nation. The loyalty and efficiency of the guardsmen were achieved by lavish rewards, which had been multiplied several times in the course of his rule since 1968. Citizens lived in fear of publicly voicing objections to the political climate or of com-

Palestine:
see Israel; Jordan

plaining about increased gasoline and cigarette taxes.

That there was an undertone of discontent did not go unrecognized in the ruling circles. To counter its spread Torrijos had staged a massive celebration in Panama City in October 1971 of the third anniversary of his advent to power. There, before a crowd variously estimated at 60,000–200,000, he declared that the time had arrived for Panamanians to die to regain sovereignty over the Canal Zone. He also promised an election for August 1972, for an assembly of 500 to decide the political course of his country.

The delegates or "corregidores" to this assembly, chosen in a massive voter turnout, began their deliberations on September 11. They reelected the incumbent president, Demetrio Lakas, to a new six-year term, and in other constitutional changes resolved that national territory could not be transferred or sold and that treaties concerning the canal must be submitted to a national plebiscite. Most spectacular of its pronouncements was a denial that the Canal Zone had ever been purchased or ceded or that its sovereignty had ever been transferred to the United States. It voted to refuse to accept the canal annuity from the U.S. On a temporary basis it vested the control of foreign affairs and the National Guard, and the appointment of heads of government and the Supreme Court, in the "chief of government," namely Torrijos.

In June Panama seized the Panamanian Light and Power Co., largely owned by the Boise Cascade Corp. of the U.S. Compensation for the plant, which was valued at approximately $74 million, was set at $22.5 million. The nationalization of the light and power works fitted into the pattern of Torrijos' state capitalism. This included the allocation of $60 million for a new airport, $40 million for the hydroelectric dam at Bayano, and $150 million for the last segment of road, the Darien Gap, in the Inter-American Highway. Government efforts were also directed to increasing the exports of bananas, sugar, and petroleum derivatives. Money continued to be available in reduced amounts for land expropriation, irrigation systems, and health and education programs. The Inter-American Development Bank authorized a loan of nearly $7 million for the benefit of the University of Panama, which was engaged in expanding its facilities and improving its teaching and administration.

(ALMON R. WRIGHT)

PANAMA

Education. (1969–70) Primary, pupils 238,593, teachers 8,658; secondary, pupils 46,196, teachers 2,327; vocational, pupils 25,449, teachers 1,095; teacher training, students 1,726, teachers 81; higher (including 2 universities), students 7,252, teaching staff 413.

Finance. Monetary unit: balboa, at par with the U.S. dollar, with a free rate (Sept. 18, 1972) of 2.45 balboas to £1 sterling. Gold, SDRs, and foreign exchange: (1971) U.S. $475.6 million; (Dec. 1970) U.S. $302.8 million. Budget (1971 est.) balanced at 186 million balboas. Gross domestic product: (1970) 1,048,600,000 balboas; (1969) 945.4 million balboas. Money supply (deposits only): (Dec. 1971) 103.9 million balboas; (Dec. 1970) 112.6 million balboas. Cost of living (Panama City; 1963 = 100): (2nd quarter 1972) 120; (2nd quarter 1971) 113.

Foreign Trade. (1971) Imports 390,820,000 balboas; exports 120,560,000 balboas. Net service receipts from Canal Zone (1970) 121 million balboas. Main import sources (1970): U.S. 39%; Venezuela 19%; Panama Free Zone 13%; Japan 6%. Main export destinations (1970): U.S. 62%; West Germany 16%. Main exports: bananas 56%; refined petroleum 21%; shrimps 10%.

Transport and Communications. Roads (1969) 6,717 km. Motor vehicles in use (1970): passenger 48,300; commercial (including buses) 14,500. Railways (1970) 671 km. Shipping (1971): merchant vessels 100 gross tons and over 1,031 (mostly owned by U.S. and other foreign interests); gross tonnage 6,262,264. Telephones (Dec. 1970) 85,000. Radio receivers (Dec. 1970) 230,000. Television receivers (Dec. 1969) 125,000.

Agriculture. Production (in 000; metric tons; 1971; 1970 in parentheses): rice *c.* 135 (124); sugar, raw value (1971–72) *c.* 91, (1970–71) 90; bananas (1970) *c.* 900, (1969) 1,019; oranges (1970) *c.* 42, (1969) 42; coffee *c.* 5.5 (5.2); cocoa (1971–72) 0.4, (1970–71) 0.5. Livestock (in 000; 1970–71): cattle 1,240; pigs 147; horses *c.* 157.

Industry. Production (in 000; 1969): cement (metric tons) 174; manufactured gas (cu.m.; 1970) 19,000; electricity (kw-hr.) 859,000.

Paraguay

A landlocked republic of South America, Paraguay is bounded by Brazil, Argentina, and Bolivia. Area: 157,047 sq.mi. (406,752 sq.km.). Pop. (1972): 2,328,790. Cap. and largest city: Asunción (pop., 1972, 387,676). Language: Spanish (official), though Guaraní is the language of the majority of the people. Religion: Roman Catholic. President in 1972, Gen. Alfredo Stroessner.

In 1972 Paraguay remained under the firm control of President Stroessner, supported by the ruling Colorado Party, the Army, and a small oligarchy of business leaders. Criticism was heard, however, from the Roman Catholic Church, which objected to the expulsion of two Jesuits, allegedly for "subversion." This followed government criticism of the church for supporting various agrarian leagues; in retaliation the archbishop of Asunción canceled the traditional Te

PARAGUAY

Education. (1969) Primary, pupils 408,524, teachers (including preprimary) 12,951; secondary, pupils 44,514, teachers (1968) 3,596; vocational (1968), pupils 2,507, teachers 621; teacher training, students 4,115, teachers (1968) 1,021; higher (at 2 universities; 1971), students *c.* 8,100, teaching staff *c.* 880.

Finance. Monetary unit: guaraní, with a free rate (Sept. 18, 1972) of 126 guaranies to U.S. $1 (306 guaranies = £1 sterling). Gold, SDRs, and foreign exchange, central bank: (June 1972) U.S. $19,820,000; (June 1971) U.S. $14,750,000. Budget (1971 est.) balanced at 8,001,000,000 guaranies. Gross national product: (1970) 73.1 billion guaranies; (1969) 68,550,000,000 guaranies. Money supply: (May 1972) 8,039,000,000 guaranies; (May 1971) 6,966,000,000 guaranies. Cost of living (Asunción; 1964 = 100): (June 1972) 124; (June 1971) 116.

Foreign Trade. (1971) Imports 8,836,600,000 guaranies; exports 8,057,300,000 guaranies. Import sources: U.S. 25%; Argentina 14%; West Germany 12%; U.K. 10%. Export destinations: Argentina 27%; U.S. 16%; Netherlands 8%; U.K. 7%; West Germany 6%; France 5%; Belgium-Luxembourg 5%. Main exports: meat 32%; timber 16%; oilseeds 13%; tobacco 7%.

Transport and Communications. Roads (1970) 11,225 km. Motor vehicles in use (1970): passenger 7,400; commercial (including buses) 10,100. Railways: (1970) 498 km.; traffic (1968) 28 million passenger-km., freight 22 million net ton-km. Navigable inland waterways (including Paraguay-Paraná river system; 1966) *c.* 3,000 km. Telephones (Dec. 1970) 24,000. Radio receivers (Dec. 1970) 169,000. Television receivers (Dec. 1970) 18,000.

Agriculture. Production (in 000; metric tons; 1971; 1970 in parentheses): corn 255 (159); cassava 1,690 (1,782); sweet potatoes (1970) 99, (1969) 94; peanuts 20 (17); dry beans 37 (35); sugar, raw value (1971–72) *c.* 61, (1970–71) 53; oranges 228 (*c.* 225); bananas (1970) 249, (1969) *c.* 250; tobacco 18 (18); cotton, lint 9 (13); beef and veal *c.* 116 (*c.* 116). Livestock (in 000; 1970–71): cattle *c.* 5,800; sheep *c.* 320; pigs *c.* 560; horses *c.* 740; chickens *c.* 6,350.

Industry. Production (in 000; metric tons; 1970): cement 63; cotton yarn (1969) 13; electricity (kw-hr.) 220,000.

Panama Canal Zone: *see* Dependent States; Panama

Paper Industry: *see* Industrial Review; Timber

Papua New Guinea: *see* Dependent States

Deum to celebrate Paraguayan independence (achieved in 1811).

There was also trouble from the United States in connection with a U.S. attempt to curtail drug trafficking in various parts of the world. In this context the Paraguayan authorities arrested Auguste-Joseph Ricord, a Frenchman alleged to be a leading figure in the international illegal narcotics trade, but at first refused to extradite him to the U.S. as requested. Following threats to cut back on aid, including suspension of a sugar quota, Ricord was eventually extradited, and normal relations were restored. Meanwhile, Paraguay's awareness of its dependence on the U.S. perhaps led to a visit by President Stroessner to Japan in April that succeeded in establishing useful contacts for alternative sources of aid. The foreign trade position for 1972 appeared to show an improvement over the previous year's deficit of $5 million. The returns for the first six months of 1972 showed a surplus of $8.2 million, with exports ($40.4 million) already two-thirds of the annual figure for 1971; imports were running at approximately the same level as the previous year.

With the country's economic situation thus beginning to show signs of improvement, the government introduced banking legislation designed to facilitate development credit. Banks were to direct their lending in given proportions toward specified sections of the economy: 10% of the loan portfolio to agriculture, 20% to exporters, and 25% to industry. A long-term boost to the economy was also expected to result from the completion of several hydroelectric projects, which were mainly designed to export electricity to Brazil and Argentina.

Unfortunately, as the economy began to move the rate of inflation began to move with it. In 1971 an increase of 6% in the cost of living was recorded, and a comparable figure seemed likely for 1972.

(M. J. SPENCE)

Payments and Reserves, International

When 1972 began, the currency realignments agreed upon at the Smithsonian Institution in Washington, D.C., in December 1971 had several immediate results. First, they ended the chaotic conditions that arose from the rather general regime of floating exchange rates from August through mid-December 1971—conditions that, it was feared, might hurt the economic well-being and the cohesion of the world outside the Soviet Union, China, and the countries in their spheres of influence. Second, the reshuffling of the world's exchange rate structure—the most widespread realignment since 1949, coupled with the only change in the gold content of the U.S. dollar since 1934—established a new basis for conducting international business. And, third, the simultaneous and multilateral readjustment, the first ever accomplished, was regarded as reassurance that the key governments would handle international monetary and economic matters in a spirit of cooperation and compromise.

How Currencies Fared. In the nature of things, the Smithsonian package—*i.e.,* the effective 11% devaluation of the U.S. dollar relative to other major currencies (weighted by trade) and the upvaluation to varying degrees of most other major currencies, together with the removal of the U.S. import surcharge imposed in August 1971—was the product of bargaining between the U.S. administration and other governments. In a world in which relative costs and prices among the key countries were rising unevenly, markets were quick to sense that the rates for some currencies might prove incompatible with the Smithsonian structure. It was not surprising that, at times, they were tense and disturbed. Markets also sensed that since the waves of currency crises stemmed principally from shifts of funds out of some currencies into others in search of protection against devaluation or as outright speculation, the relief for 1972 depended vitally on confidence in monetary, fiscal, and wage conditions, and government postures and policies, in each of the major countries.

In the immediate aftermath of the Smithsonian agreement, it was hoped that funds would begin to return in massive amounts from foreign currencies into dollars; but these hopes failed to come true. On the contrary, during most of January and into February 1972, new funds flowed out of dollars as an accelerated growth of money supply in the U.S., a big drop in U.S. interest rates, and a huge federal budgetary deficit made it appear as if the U.S. were treating with benign neglect the consequences of its domestic monetary and fiscal conditions and policies on confidence in the dollar internationally. As the dollar appeared to be heading for another crisis, West Germany, Japan, and other countries strengthened the controls they had established in 1971 to ward off unwanted dollars. From early March to early June, the exchange markets stabilized. In mid-June, however, as a sterling crisis broke out and the pound was allowed to float, funds in excess of $5 billion sought refuge out of dollars into continental and Japanese currencies. To repel the avalanche, the continental countries and Japan strengthened controls still further, while making substantial purchases of dollars to hold down the appreciation of their currencies.

The pressure on the dollar eased only after mid-July when the markets came to realize that the existing exchange rate relationships between the dollar and the continental currencies would not be changed in the foreseeable future and would, if necessary, be defended through market intervention by European central banks. The Federal Reserve itself exemplified the willingness of the U.S. to play its part by announcing, on July 19, that it would support the dollar—for the first time since the dollar convertibility was suspended in August 1971; it reactivated its mutual credit arrangements with other central banks.

Thereafter, as short-term funds began to return, the dollar firmed steadily and appreciably against the currencies of the industrial countries other than Japan (*see* Graph 1). The October sterling crisis had no effect on the dollar. The backflow of short-term funds into dollars from European currencies was not big enough to offset the outflow of dollars into yen, which, together with the Japanese trade surplus, accounted for further additions to Japan's dollar holdings. Indeed, the backflow, however beneficial for confidence in the dollar, merely, in effect, financed the U.S. basic deficit, which was diminishing much more slowly than had been hoped (*see* Table). The strengthening of the dollar also owed something to the realization that the performance of the U.S. economy—as appraised by growth and stability—was better than that of other industrial countries.

The counterpart of the continuing U.S. payments deficit was found in surpluses of other countries. West

Germany had a small current-account deficit; but since it experienced net inflows of long-term capital, the basic balance showed an even larger surplus than in 1971. During the first half of the year, it also accumulated dollars that originated from the capital flight into marks motivated by the belief that West Germany would once more be obliged to upvalue, as in 1961, 1969, and 1971. From midyear on, as there appeared unmistakable evidence throughout continental Europe of renewed inflationary increases in prices and costs, short-term fund flows were reversed and several countries, especially West Germany and Switzerland, experienced a sizable decline in dollar reserves.

With a rapid expansion in its economy, Canada found itself with a current account deficit—a condition contrasting with surpluses during the previous two years; the change came largely from a decline in the merchandise trade surplus. But capital inflows remained the critical factor behind the exchange rate. By the year's end, the Canadian dollar, which had been floating for over two and a half years, was regarded as very unlikely to be repegged before both the international situation and Canadian-U.S. relationships achieved a higher degree of stability.

The only currency that remained under heavy upward pressure during the entire year was the Japanese yen. Japan recorded in 1972 an even more massive trade surplus than previously—a trade surplus that more than offset the nation's sizable long-term capital investments abroad with the result that the basic balance on current account and long-term capital was also heavily in surplus. On top of this basic surplus, capital inflows—above all, leads and lags in payments and speculative dollar sales from all over the world, including Japan itself—were extraordinarily large. Not too surprisingly, this state of affairs triggered expectations of a second upvaluation of the yen.

Loath to permit any further erosion of the profitability of Japanese industry, which had a substantial surplus capacity, Japanese authorities wanted to buy time at least until the effects of the 1971 yen upvaluation were clear. To hold the yen down, therefore, they bought dollars, and to minimize increases in official dollar reserves, they used the carrot and the stick in a piecemeal sequence. Thus, they agreed to import over several years additional amounts of goods from the U.S.; they encouraged outflows of long-term Japanese capital; and they transferred dollars out of official reserves by "recycling" them into private Japanese banks for loans to foreign borrowers and into the financing of Japanese imports. At the same time, they made a number of moves to restrict exports.

The concern over the future of the Smithsonian exchange rate pattern centred not only around the possible appreciation of the Japanese yen but also around the actual depreciation of the British pound. The U.K. had become afflicted by severe wage-price inflation in the midst of intensive monetary and fiscal stimulation of the economy—stimulation that meant higher imports and a diversion of output from export markets to a more buoyant domestic economy. The deficit in Britain's foreign trade reappeared in February and, by May, it was taken as a sign that the huge current account surplus of the previous three years would soon be eroded, as actually happened in the third quarter. Another unsettling factor in the exchange market was the large rise in export prices. Inflows of short-term funds, which in 1971 contributed decisively to the rise in Britain's official monetary reserves, were reversed dramatically. Enormous amounts of sterling were dumped on the exchanges and, from June 15 to 22, official support for the pound cost the authorities the equivalent of $2.5 billion. With no end to the reserve loss in sight, the government on June 23 allowed the pound to float "as a temporary measure."

While this first phase of sterling depreciation was brought about by market expectations of the float, the second phase, which took place in October, reflected a novel kind of crisis—one stemming from the fear that sterling was about to be repegged at a still lower level than was indicated by the market rates. This fear arose out of a morass of fruitless efforts to intro-

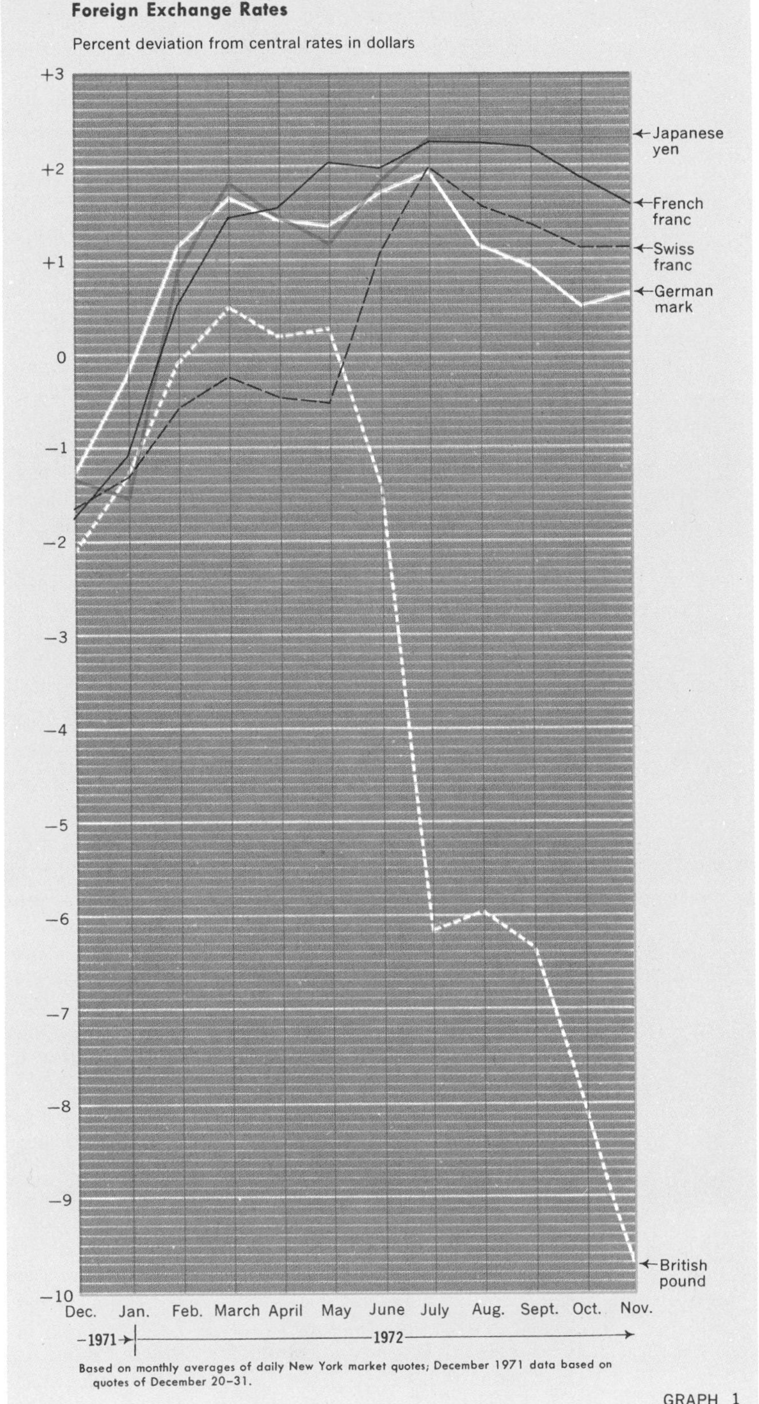

Based on monthly averages of daily New York market quotes; December 1971 data based on quotes of December 20–31.

GRAPH 1

duce voluntary price and wage controls—efforts abandoned early in November when the government called a halt by imposing statutory controls. At year's end, the pound's depreciation was about 9.6% on its former $2.60 parity, compared with the 14% devaluation of November 1967.

The governments of several nondollar countries that purchased dollars to prevent the appreciation of their currencies expanded their international monetary reserves substantially. Altogether, official international liquidity—the holdings by governments and central banks of gold, foreign exchange, Special Drawing Rights (SDRs), and reserve positions in the International Monetary Fund (IMF)—increased during January–September by $19 billion to somewhat over $150 billion (expressed in the devalued 1972 dollars, *i.e.,* dollars at $38 per ounce of gold). This 1972 rise took place on top of a record increase of almost $40 billion during 1971 (including SDRs), which itself followed a year of sharp acceleration in the creation of official international liquidity. SDRs, which were in 1972 in the third year of their existence, were allotted in the amount of $3 billion, which brought their total to $9.5 billion. The entire period would go down in history as one of an explosion of international monetary reserves—by 63% from January 1970 through September 1972. Private international liquidity also continued to increase in 1972.

As in the preceding two years, the expansion of international monetary reserves during 1972 had its counterpart largely in a sharp increase in U.S. monetary liabilities to governments and central banks of other countries; during the first nine months of 1972, these rose by $9 billion to $60 billion (*see* Graph 2). The extent of the weakening in the U.S. liquidity position stood out when the $60 billion of U.S. liabilities to foreign governments was compared with the $13 billion of U.S. international reserve assets.

Gold holdings by governments, central banks, and international financial institutions remained at the $45 billion level (as computed in devalued dollars), around which they had recorded only minor fluctuations since 1968. They were, in effect, immobilized as "a last-ditch reserve" with which governments were most unwilling to part. For gold had become too precious to be sold at the $38 price as the London private market price was much higher—$64.90 per fine ounce at the year's end; it had reached $70 in August. The immobilization of monetary gold was fostered in 1971 by the U.S. decision to suspend what remained of the formal convertibility of the dollar into gold and thus protect the remainder of gold as a national emergency reserve. In 1972, Italy, the U.K., and other countries also refused to pay out gold to settle official debts.

The explosion of international liquidity from 1970 contrasted sharply with fears of scarcity of international monetary reserves that were prevalent as recently as 1969, when the governments decided to embark upon regular allocations of SDRs—allocations that were carried out in 1971 and 1972 as if nothing had happened, but were suspended for 1973. The inordinate expansion of international liquidity was a critical factor in the world's inflation—critical, but by no means the sole force, for domestic factors, above all the expansion of credit to the private economy and government deficit financing, were decisive in Europe and elsewhere.

How International Monetary Reforms Were Approached. In the first year after the breakdown of international monetary arrangements, there was an understandable desire for reforms. The optimists hoped that the international monetary system could be overhauled in a year or two; the skeptics doubted that a reformed system could spring forth full blown like Athena from the head of Zeus. The complexity and the political sensitivity of these issues were exemplified in two reports: one, "Reform of the International Monetary System," by the executive directors of the IMF to its board of governors, published in September, and the other, "Possible Perspectives for International Trade and Economic Relations," presented in August by a group of experts to the secretary-general of the Organization for Economic Cooperation and Development (OECD). Neither report made any attempt to gloss over the differences in attitude and viewpoint among governments or to minimize the diversity of national positions and interests.

To prepare monetary reforms, a special committee of IMF's board of governors was established under the chairmanship of Jeremy Morse of the Bank of England. The group was composed of 20 members—hence the name Group of Twenty—of which 11 were from industrial countries; it replaced the more exclusive Group of Ten formed by the industrial countries, which had concluded the Smithsonian agreement. But, at their first meeting before the end of the year, it had already become evident that the Twenty would find it more than twice as difficult to reach agreement than the Ten.

Return to Fixed Exchange Rates. The governments of the industrialized countries returned in December 1971 to the so-called par value system—fixed parities or central rates, but adjustable in cases of "fundamental disequilibrium," subject to stipulated safeguards as protection against competitive devaluations or competitive non-upvaluations. The emphasis was not on greater flexibility of exchange rates but on less rigidity in holding onto parities that involve fundamental disequilibrium. The margins for fluctuation of market exchange rates were widened from 1 to $2\frac{1}{4}$% on either side of par; but acceptance of these wider margins was not obligatory, although in practice they were at once adopted for all major currencies.

The U.S., as Treasury Secretary George Shultz stated at the IMF meeting, was ready to accept, for the future, the basic fixity of exchange rates; but, in order to facilitate the adjustment of payments imbalances and to help moderate short-term capital flows, the permissible margins for fluctuation should be widened still further. This proposal encountered opposition, however, on the ground that wider bands might become devices for seeking a lower effective exchange rate for a currency. While opposing still wider bands generally, the governments of the nine member countries of the EEC moved toward eliminating the fluc-

The U.S. Balance of Payments
In U.S. $000,000,000

Item	1970	1971	1972
Goods and services	3.6	0.7	−4.6
U.S. government grants and credits	−5.2	−6.0	−5.4
Private long-term capital	−1.4	−4.1	0.0
Basic balance	−3.0	−9.4	−10.0
Repayments to foreign branches of U.S. banks	−6.3	−4.9	−0.4
All other short-term capital outflows*	−1.4	−16.2	0.0
Allocations of SDRs	0.9	0.7	0.7
Balance on official settlements basis	−9.8	−29.8	−9.7

*Including errors and omissions.
Source: Adapted from U.S. Department of Commerce, *Survey of Current Business.*

tuations in the exchange rates of their own currencies.

Special Drawing Rights. A system of basically fixed exchange rates must be supported by convertibility of national currencies into internationally agreed reserve assets. It requires, therefore, a reasonably regular growth in total world reserves because the swings in the balances of payments are apt to be wider with the expansion of international trade, services, and investment. To meet these aggregate needs for reserves, SDRs should increase in importance and should be periodically created in the necessary amounts. In the U.S. view, SDRs should also become the common denominator or the *numéraire* for national currencies.

The future of SDRs gave rise to much soul-searching. First, to make SDRs the principal means of reserve growth called for a more finely tuned adjustment process than in the past. Obviously, a continuous financing of persistent deficits by SDRs would tend to undermine the whole SDR arrangement. Second, the U.S. proposed that SDRs should cease to be partly repayable, that the limits beyond which the participants are not obliged to accept SDRs in settlement of other countries' deficits should be lifted, and that the gold guarantees presently attached to SDRs should be eliminated (for a description of present SDRs, *see* the 1970 *Book of The Year*). Against this view, it was pointed out that the removal of safeguards like these would make the donations of liquidity through SDRs even more inflationary. And, third, many of the less developed countries wanted to "link" the creation of SDRs to distribution of economic aid by the industrial nations. Presently, SDRs were, for the most part, given to the U.S. and other industrial countries responsible for the maintenance of expanding world trade and the functioning of the international monetary system. The primary need of the less developed countries was long-term capital—domestic as well as funds obtained through capital imports.

Gold. The prevalent view in official circles was that gold would be retained as an international monetary instrument but its importance would gradually diminish. The U.S. Treasury, which saw its holdings decline from its record high of $26.9 billion in August 1949 to $10.5 billion in December 1972 (at the $38 price), sought to deemphasize the role of gold more rapidly than the European countries and Japan, which almost quadrupled their gold stocks over the same period to $23 billion, or one half of the world's total monetary gold reserves.

In May 1972, the monetary price of gold in terms of the U.S. dollar was raised to $38 per fine ounce. This was 8.6% higher than the $35 price fixed in 1934; meanwhile, however, the dollar had lost 68% of its buying power (as measured by consumer prices). In terms of what it buys, the dollar had, therefore, depreciated much more than had thus far been recognized in raising the official monetary price of gold.

The Bretton Woods system of 1945 had been patched up in December 1971; but since it was based on gold, it could not work without a rise in the official value of gold. Conceivably, the Bretton Woods system could be replaced by arrangements that would be equally systematic, such as a full-fledged SDR standard; but this would be a veritable monetary revolution.

The Dollar. The huge increase in dollar reserves during 1970–72 was a serious and disturbing development in international monetary relationships. Governments outside the U.S. generally agreed that the future reserve growth should not depend on U.S. payments deficits, as it had in the past quarter century. The U.S. itself expressed the view that the new system should neither ban nor encourage dollar holdings in international monetary reserves; but it conceded that the dollar should not be required to play so prominent a role in the operation of the new system.

During 1972, nondollar currencies became, in effect, pegged to an inconvertible dollar. Clearly, dollars were convertible into other currencies and could be used to settle debts, at exchange rates maintained by other countries within specified limits of parity. But, unlike other countries, the U.S. financed its deficits not by using its reserves, but by issuing "IOUs." In

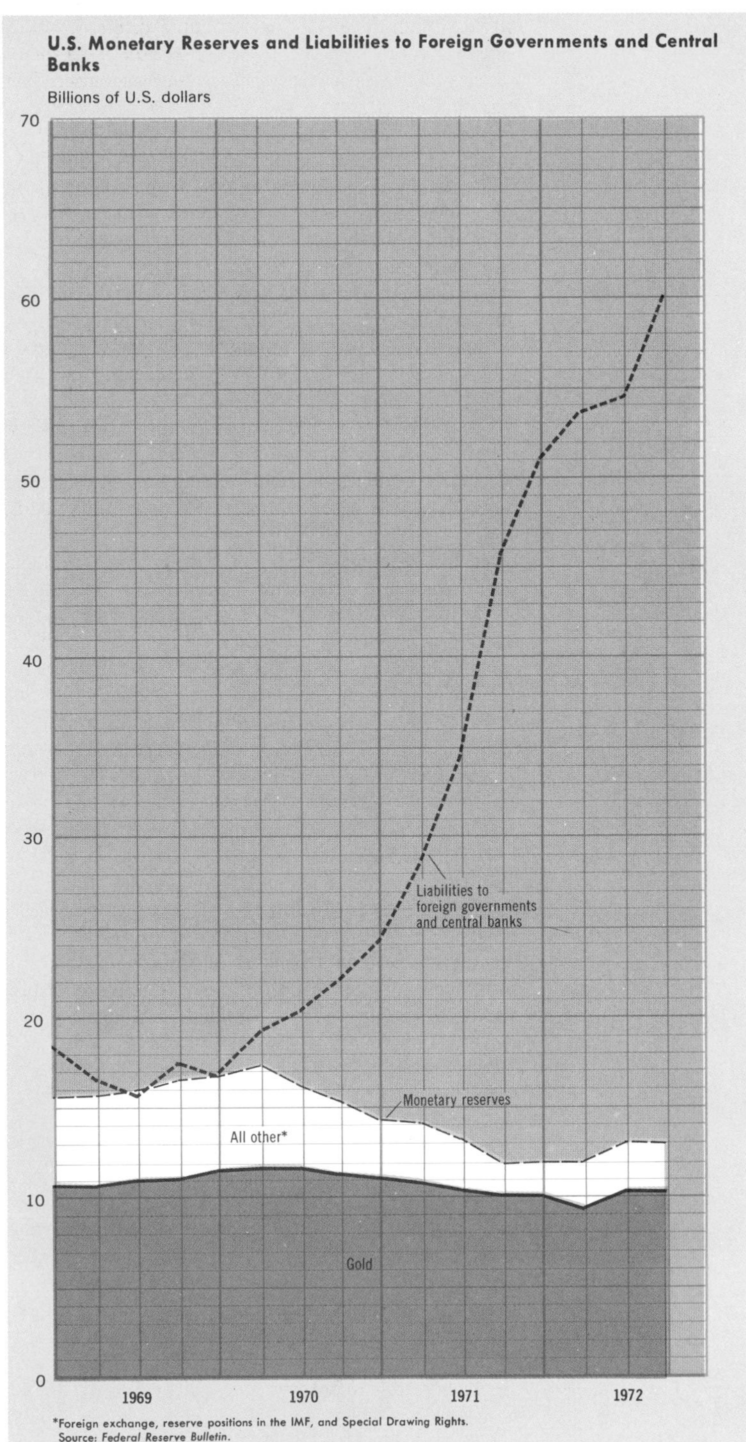

*Foreign exchange, reserve positions in the IMF, and Special Drawing Rights.
Source: *Federal Reserve Bulletin.*

GRAPH 2

the first nine months of 1972, the U.S. actually added little to its reserves (including the SDR allocation) although the overall settlements deficit amounted to $8.7 billion; in 1971 as a whole it used $2.3 billion of its reserves but had a $29.8 billion deficit. Not astonishingly, therefore, other major countries regarded the restoration of dollar convertibility into internationally agreed assets—gold, SDRs, and reserve positions in the IMF—as an indispensable step toward a reformed international standard. While the U.S. embraced dollar convertibility as an objective, there was no early prospect for its restoration.

Improving the Processes of Balance of Payments Adjustment. A deep-seated difficulty in the past was the unwillingness of governments to face up even to obvious situations of "fundamental disequilibrium." They delayed far too long the correction of payments deficits and—perhaps even more—of surpluses. This was not the fault of the international institutional arrangements, for the IMF Charter stipulated parity changes in cases of fundamental disequilibrium. But there was no agreement about responsibilities for initiating the balance of payments adjustment—the ways and means by which countries achieve and maintain an equilibrium in their economic relationships with other countries through timely devaluations or upvaluations of exchange rates and through other steps with similar balance of payments effects. The end result was monetary instability, speculation, and even political friction.

From the start of the discussions about reforms, the governments envisaged—as already noted—convertibility of currencies, including the dollar, into internationally agreed reserve assets. Convertibility itself, however, was not enough. Surely, losses of reserves force a persistent deficit country to take remedial action sooner or later. But a deficit country can delay adjustment through extensive borrowing and by restricting imports and capital outflows. The discipline is even less effective in the case of a country with a balance of payments surplus, for it can accumulate reserves more or less indefinitely. In actual experience, the pressure on countries gaining reserves excessively to upvalue their currencies (or to take other action with a similar balance of payments effect) was in the past much smaller than the pressure to devalue on countries losing reserves heavily. In the U.S. view, there was a crucial asymmetry between deficit and surplus countries—a gap that had to be corrected.

Reliance could not be placed entirely on the discretion of governments to initiate timely or equitable adjustment policies. Similarly, no reliance could be placed on the international bodies to induce national governments to adjust domestic policies. What was needed was to devise "objective criteria" to identify serious imbalances. In the U.S. view, "the most equitable and effective single indicator" consisted of "disproportionate gains or losses in monetary reserves." At some point, for instance, a country piling up reserves should lose its right to demand conversion; and should it fail to take effective adjustment measures, other countries should be permitted to protect their interests by such steps as special surcharges on imports from the chronically surplus country. On the other hand, a deficit country consistently refusing to initiate adjustment measures might be penalized by the withdrawal of borrowing privileges or SDR allocations.

The U.S. position encountered determined resistance. The surplus countries warned against a possible misunderstanding, for even though the deficits and surpluses are arithmetically equal, this gives no insight into causal relationships. A country that, by its action or inaction, creates its own deficit or surplus should subject itself to adjustment, but not a country that merely finds itself in imbalance because of conditions and policies, or lack of policies, in some other country.

For deficit countries, the adjustment process meant until quite recently that they should make a stronger domestic effort to regain stability, including domestic monetary, fiscal, and wage self-discipline, however unpopular. The shift of emphasis on the easy way out through devaluation of the external value of the currency was discomforting and disquieting. Similarly, surplus countries could not be expected to accept upvaluation of their currencies as the simplest and most expedient way to help restore international balance. If this were to become the international rule, hard-working nations, practicing at least a measure of monetary and fiscal discipline, would be penalized for the inflationary behaviour of countries that were less disciplined. If certain nations could inflate with impunity, the world as a whole would be increasingly prone to inflation.

Encouraging Freer Trade and Capital Flows. The process of orderly balance of payments adjustment through exchange rate changes would be made more difficult if countries or groups of countries were insulated from foreign price competition. The U.S. sought, therefore, to approach monetary reforms along with reforms of the world's trading arrangements and practices. It wanted a "one world" solution that was nondiscriminatory and multilateral in money and trade alike.

In fact, the trading relations between the U.S., on the one side, and Europe and Japan, on the other, were severely strained in 1972. There were also disagreements between the U.S. and some of the industrialized countries about the role and desirability of long-term capital flows and their financing. The U.S. appeared to be inclined to let other countries take the dollars or take the consequences in the guise of the appreciation of their currencies; on the other hand, Canada, Europe, Japan, and Australia seemed unwilling to accept U.S. investments without limit and thus, in effect, sell factories for more U.S. merchandise exports, let alone in return for dollars accumulated on the central bank books.

Another clash centred around the rapid movements of large amounts of short-term funds through the exchanges. The U.S. put forward the view that movements of capital should be allowed to exert their full influence within the wider margins around the established central rates. The European countries and Japan, which had gradually built up controls on unwanted dollar inflows, appeared resigned to even more restrictions, including those on the Eurodollar market, as one way of dealing with the problem. No convertible fixed-rate system could be counted on to hold together if subjected to vast movements of funds from one currency to another.

Conclusion. On the eve of 1973, the scope and the nature of international monetary reforms were nebulous. "The brave new world of SDRs" was not around the corner. While there was scope for formal reform of the system, governments of all large countries realized that their freedom of action in all matters affecting international payments and reserves was limited. It appeared, therefore, that there would be no rash and irrevocable changes in the presently accepted or acceptable monetary rules. More than ever, the needed changes were in the behaviour of currencies under these rules.

The most encouraging development on the international monetary horizon was the strengthening of the dollar—at home, since the loss of its buying power slowed down perceptibly, as well as in its relationships with other currencies. A reliably stable dollar would help other major countries avoid inflation, for they wanted to maintain fixed dollar parities for their currencies. At the same time, a dollar that was above suspicion would restore to the international monetary structure its main pillar.

(MIROSLAV A. KRIZ)

See also Commercial Policies; Commodities, Primary; Economy, World; Investment, International; Money and Banking; Prices; Trade, International.

Peace Movements

The context of peace movement activities in 1972 was marked by a series of paradoxes. While peace spokesmen applauded Pres. Richard Nixon's efforts to reduce tensions with China and the Soviet Union, they also stressed the need to terminate U.S. military involvement in Indochina. While direct troop involvement in Indochina decreased, U.S. air and naval power continued to play a dominating role. While a significant arms limitation treaty was signed with the Soviet Union, this act was accompanied by an administration request for increased defense spending. While mass protest as a tactic suffered a severe decline, the gathering of oppositional currents into the Democratic Party boosted the preconvention campaign of Sen. George McGovern. While McGovern's candidacy marked the highwater point of the electoral peace effort, the larger U.S. electorate was reluctant to support many of the movement's key assumptions.

Despite the breakup of several of the more radical components of the antiwar movements of the '60s, peace advocates were often successful in linking up with significant environmental, consumer, civil liberties, and legislative efforts. Beyond this, peace leaders continued to focus on control and reversal of the arms race, the reduction of tension in crisis areas, humanitarian and emergency relief, and the development of structures to promote a stable peace.

McGovern's difficulties in translating his convention successes into a national victory could not efface the fact that, for the first time in post-World War II politics, the U.S. peace movement could readily identify a major party contender who articulated many of their deepest concerns. In Congress, however, the two branches persisted in their disagreement over ending U.S. involvement in Southeast Asia. While the Brooke Amendment, cutting off funds for carrying on the war, narrowly passed the Senate, 49–47, the House turned down, 178–228, an end-the-war proposal recommended by its own Foreign Affairs Committee. Further legislative attempts to end the war became entangled in election-year politics. Nevertheless, organizations such as Common Cause, Americans for Democratic Action, SANE, and the Council for a Livable World lobbied intensively for a reassertion of congressional initiative.

In their efforts to mobilize public opinion on the war issue, peace groups targeted key U.S. corporations involved in war industry. In particular, Clergy and Laymen Concerned submitted resolutions for debate at the spring stockholders' meetings of General Electric, Honeywell, Standard Oil of New Jersey, and the International Telephone and Telegraph Co., each of which was engaged in producing air-war and antipersonnel materials. CALC urged such proposals as cessation of the production of antipersonnel weapons and the creation, in each corporation, of committees on conversion to peacetime work. Other bodies, such as the Church of the Brethren, chose to divest themselves completely of all investments in corporations producing weapons and defense-related products.

In a related development, a coalition of agencies from five major Protestant denominations challenged General Motors, Goodyear Tire and Rubber, and Mobil Oil to provide complete disclosure of their policies and operations in South Africa. Gulf Oil was challenged concerning its operations in Angola, while a fifth corporation, IBM, volunteered to provide a full report to its stockholders. The project marked an unusual collaboration among churches; the challengers included the Episcopal Church, the United Church of Christ, the American Baptist Convention, the United Presbyterian Church, and the United Methodist Church.

Although significant portions of organized labour were severely critical of peace movement strategies, over 20 unions representing over four million workers supported Labor for Peace, a voluntary organization of trade unionists aimed at mobilizing labour opposition to the Indochina war. Besides the Teamsters and the United Auto Workers (the two largest independent unions in the U.S.), Labor for Peace included representatives from 15 AFL-CIO affiliates and four additional independent unions. The founding conference of 985 representatives in St. Louis, Mo., demanded immediate military withdrawal from Indochina and urged attention to the task of reconverting the economy to a full-employment, peacetime basis.

Reflecting the mounting effort to organize and focus economic pressures to achieve social justice, a Boycott Center was established in Atlanta, Ga. A development of the Martin Luther King Institute for Nonviolent Change, the centre planned to develop a national network alert to respond swiftly in support of just requests for aid. The centre was already assisting the United Farm Workers Organizing Committee in their boycott of nonunion iceberg lettuce.

Other peace organizations advanced varied tactics and strategies to build the antiwar movement. The Quaker-related American Friends Service Committee issued a new White Paper entitled "Indochina 1972: Perpetual War," which condemned the U.S. role, outlined the growing pattern of "automated warfare" on an "electronic battlefield," and termed U.S. withdrawal a "logical, ethical necessity." The AFSC also designated an "Indochina Summer" of intensified peace education and protest. The Vietnam Veterans Against the War were highly visible in protests that followed the intensified bombardment of North Vietnam. The Committee of Liaison, which administered the flow of mail to U.S. prisoners of war in North Vietnam, facilitated the release of three U.S. prisoners by Hanoi in September. The men were accompanied on their return trip to the U.S. by three committee members, William Sloane Coffin, Jr., David Dellinger, and Cora Weiss.

SANE focused on lobbying, electoral politics, and educational efforts during the year, while United World Federalists stressed the need for full funding of the U.S. share of UN expenses, world environmental

BETTYE LANE—
NANCY PALMER PHOTO AGENCY

JESSICA SAMUELS—NANCY PALMER PHOTO AGENCY

Above, Jane Fonda speaks at press conference after returning from North Vietnam, where she had delivered a radio appeal to U.S. pilots regarding their bombing of North Vietnamese hospitals, schools, and dikes. Right, the Rev. Daniel J. Berrigan holds a prayer service on the steps of St. Patrick's Cathedral in New York City. He charged that he had been excluded from preaching at a peace mass inside the church on June 4, 1972.

laws, and forceful international action to curb air piracy. The UWF also supported former UN secretary-general U Thant's call for a "second allegiance to the human community" by means of individual declarations and enrollments as "planetary citizens." Several groups assisted the "Unsell the War" effort of advertising and media specialists to utilize mass persuasion techniques to challenge the war. In the House of Representatives, a group of members introduced the "World Peace Tax Fund Act," which would permit citizens opposed to war on moral and religious grounds to reroute their federal income, gift, and inheritance taxes from military to peace-related activities.

Despite the failure of the U.S. government to convict Father Philip Berrigan and the other Harrisburg Seven antiwar activists on major conspiracy charges, antiwar leaders decried the pattern of surveillance of civilian political dissenters, harrassment, and politically motivated trials that they saw as a growing strategy within the federal government. They especially cited the forthcoming trial of Daniel Ellsberg and his associate, Anthony Russo, on charges of stealing classified documents, defrauding the government of their custody, and violating the Espionage Act. Many anticipated that the "Pentagon papers trial" would intensify debate over the people's right to know and challenge the prevalent system of classifying sensitive documents to place them beyond the reach of public exposure and debate.

A number of peace organizations operating under the aegis of the People's Coalition for Peace and Justice sponsored small nongovernmental "delegations" of Americans who met unofficially with representatives of North Vietnam, the provisional government of South Vietnam, and other nongovernmental groups. Similarly, three U.S. labour leaders, Clifton Caldwell of the Amalgamated Meat Cutters, Harold Gibbons of the Teamsters, and David Livingston of the Distributive Workers Union, visited North Vietnam at the invitation of their counterparts in the North Vietnamese labour movement.

Internationally, 1972 witnessed a striking convergence of the ecological and peace issues, most notably at the UN Conference on the Human Environment, held in Stockholm in June. (*See* ENVIRONMENT.) The deliberations of the conference were far from unanimous, but peace activists were encouraged by the numerous nongovernmental conferences occurring parallel to the Stockholm venture. The most significant was the transnational Dai Dong effort, sponsored by the International Fellowship of Reconciliation (IFOR). Dai Dong participants stressed the interrelatedness of all problems threatening human survival, especially war, and drafted an "Independent Declaration on the Environment" that was presented to the larger UN conference.

The IFOR continued to sponsor the Costa Rica Conference on Revolutionary Nonviolence, which gathered leaders from labour and the church from throughout Latin America and anticipated a continent-wide organization oriented toward nonviolence. IFOR also subsidized experiments in organizing nonviolent peace-keeping forces in Northern Ireland and studied possible techniques of nonviolent intervention in neocolonialist situations in Africa. The World Council of Churches and the All-Africa Conference of Churches played a crucial role in securing negotiations that resulted in a cease-fire in the Sudan, where civil conflict had festered since 1955.

In mid-February, 800 delegates from 80 nations participated in the World Assembly for Peace held in Versailles, France. While the call for the assembly was patterned after several previous Communist-initiated world gatherings, a broader range of groups was represented. A lengthy series of resolutions was adopted, including support for an intensive six-week campaign in the U.S. against the air war in Indochina. In a separate action, the International Commission of Inquiry into War Crimes focused on evidence that the U.S. had bombed dikes in the Red River Delta.

Peace spokesmen in Great Britain struggled to formulate nonviolent alternatives to the violence in Northern Ireland, debated the desirability of continued British association with NATO, and pressured the government to disengage itself more fully from U.S. policy in Vietnam. In Japan debate mounted over anticipated increases in the budget for the so-called self-defense forces and continued U.S. use of military bases on Japanese soil. In India peace advocates were torn between their empathy for newly emergent Bangladesh and their aversion to the violence that accompanied its birth. Their basic energies were devoted to assisting the organization of a massive emergency relief program for the new nation. The murder of members of the Israeli Olympic team at Munich by Palestinian terrorists led some peace leaders to question the nationalist emphasis of the Olympic Games themselves. (RICHARD O. HATHAWAY)

Peru

A republic on the west coast of South America, Peru is bounded by Ecuador, Colombia, Brazil, Bolivia, Chile, and the Pacific Ocean. Area: 496,-222 sq.mi. (1,285,215 sq.km.). Pop. (1972 est.): 13.6 million, including approximately 52% whites and mestizos and 46% Indians. Cap. and largest city: Lima (pop., 1972 est., 3.3 million). Language: Spanish; Indians speak Quechuan or Aymara. Religion: Roman Catholic. President of the military government in 1972, Juan Velasco Alvarado.

Politically 1972 was uneventful, and the government's policy of pragmatism and consolidation continued. On January 3 Gen. Edgardo Mercado Jarrín resigned as minister of foreign affairs and was appointed army chief of staff. This was seen as a move to put him in line to succeed President Velasco on his retirement.

Sinamos, the government agency set up in 1971 to mobilize the people behind the government, was increasingly active during the year, reflecting the government's concern over the prevailing sense of apathy. It was hoped that under the leadership of one of the more radical generals, Leonidas Rodríguez, Sinamos might do something to fill the political vacuum created by the regime. Sinamos and the government talked in terms of creating a participatory and pluralistic society, based on three sectors: state; private—reformed by the workers' communities; and social—presumably something akin to cooperatives.

Economically, 1971 had not been a very satisfactory year. The trade surplus fell to U.S. $141 million, and the gross national product rose by only 5.9%, compared with 7.7% in 1970. The trade balance for January–June 1972 was U.S. $112.7 million, compared with U.S. $48 million in the first half of 1971, a recovery based on heavy shipments of fish meal and a revival in the flow of mineral exports. However, prospects for the economy diminished with the arrival and continued presence of the warm El Niño Current, which killed or drove away the anchoveta that provided so much of Peru's foreign exchange. Anchoveta supplies fell to minimal levels. Most fishing was suspended, and in late September the government decreed a ban on all further shipments of fish meal and fish oil until further notice. Three major buyers of fish meal, the U.S., China, and Cuba, did not ask for penalties, but Peru's largest customer, West Germany, demanded compensation if its orders were not filled. In December fishing was resumed on a limited basis, but the results were reported to be poor, and the UN Food and Agriculture Organization predicted that these conditions would continue at least until March 1973. Worries over the probable detrimental effect on Peru's international payments position led to speculation about a possible devaluation of the sol, although the minister of economy denied this. The government succeeded in stabilizing internal prices after a large increase of 5.8% in the cost of living in the first three months of 1972. The 1972 cost of living rise was expected to be in the neighbourhood of 10–12%, and it seemed unlikely that the national growth rate would reach the 7.5% target.

Other events in 1972 did help to ease Peru's longer-term problems. Following the refusal of Peru's creditors in 1971 to agree to a rescheduling of the country's foreign debt, a financial mission visited Paris in February to seek financial backing for 94 projects listed in the 1971–75 development plan. These included irrigation works, petrochemicals, copper mining, and telecommunications. The mission met with representatives of leading industrial countries, and in July these nations agreed in principle to provide loans totaling U.S. $1,077,000,000.

The trend toward foreign participation in the petroleum sector continued, and several foreign companies, including the British Petroleum Co., signed contracts similar to the one signed by Occidental Petroleum in June 1971. These companies were to develop and explore areas in the northeastern jungle region in return for a straight percentage of wellhead output. In May the government announced the proving of Pavayacu X-3, the third productive exploratory well in the remote Amazon fields, which had been discovered by the state company, Petroperú. Plans for a 400-mi., U.S. $250 million pipeline across the western Amazon jungle and over the Andes to the Pacific coast would now definitely proceed.

The state mining company, Mineroperú, signed a contract with a Japanese consortium in October for the construction of a copper refinery at the port of Ilo on the far south coast. On November 30 local assets of the Peruvian Corp. were auctioned in a paper operation by which the government formally took over the country's main railways. (JEREMY WILLOUGHBY)

PERU

Education. (1968) Primary, pupils 2,334,982, teachers (including preprimary) 68,089; secondary, pupils 470,664, teachers 26,915; vocational, pupils 93,034, teachers 8,439; higher, students 101,099, teaching staff 11,649.

Finance. Monetary unit: sol, with a principal official exchange rate (Sept. 18, 1972) of 38.70 soles to U.S. $1 (nominal rate of 95 soles = £1 sterling). Gold, SDRs, and foreign exchange, central bank: (April 1972) U.S. $246.3 million; (April 1971) U.S. $292.3 million. Budget (1970 rev. est.): revenue 45 billion soles; expenditure 45,531,000,000 soles. Gross national product: (1969) 198,320,000,000 soles; (1968) 181,240,000,000 soles. Money supply: (June 1971) 31,540,000,000 soles; (June 1970) 27,250,000,000 soles. Cost of living (Lima and Callao; 1963 = 100): (May 1972) 233; (May 1971) 217.

Foreign Trade. (1971) Imports 23,323,000,000 soles; exports 34,492,000,000 soles. Import sources: U.S. 29%; West Germany 12%; Japan 10%; U.K. 5%; Canada 5%. Export destinations: U.S. 29%; West Germany 15%; Japan 12%; Netherlands 7%. Main exports: fish meal 31%; copper 19%; sugar 8%; iron ore 7%; silver 5%; zinc 5%; cotton 5%.

Transport and Communications. Roads (1969) 50,056 km. Motor vehicles in use (1970): passenger 230,400; commercial (including buses) 117,500. Railways (1969): 1,752 km.; traffic 254 million passenger-km., freight 591 million net ton-km. Air traffic (1970): 788,783,000 passenger-km.; freight 25,722,000 net ton-km. Shipping (1971): merchant vessels 100 gross tons and over 601; gross tonnage 420,656. Telephones (Dec. 1970) 208,000. Radio receivers (Dec. 1970) 1,819,000. Television receivers (Dec. 1970) 395,000.

Agriculture. Production (in 000; metric tons; 1971; 1970 in parentheses): rice 587 (587); corn 578 (615); wheat 114 (125); barley 150 (170); potatoes 1,900 (1,929); cassava (1970) 498, (1969) 450, dry beans *c.* 65 (63); sugar, raw value (1971–72) *c.* 900, (1970–71) *c.* 877; grapes *c.* 58 (57); coffee *c.* 74 (65); cotton, lint *c.* 92 (92); fish catch (1970) 12,613, (1969) 9,244. Livestock (in 000; 1970–71): cattle *c.* 4,150; sheep 17,063; pigs 1,930; goats 1,860; horses *c.* 600; poultry *c.* 22,000.

Industry. Production (in 000; metric tons; 1970): cement 1,144; crude oil (1971) 3,048; coal (1969) *c.* 162; iron ore (metal content) 6,119; pig iron 180; steel (1969) 194; lead (1969) 78; zinc 64; copper 33; tungsten concentrates (exports; oxide content; 1969) 0.6; gold (troy oz.) 95; silver (troy oz.) 38,000; fish meal 2,253; electricity (kw-hr.) 5,324,000.

Philately and Numismatics

Philately. Many national post offices improved their press information services and set out to capture new philatelic markets in 1972. One bad example of this effort was the lavish volume titled *The Sea,* issued by the U.S. Postal Service. Priced at $300, the work contained nine common U.S. stamps and some fine

Penology: *see* Prisons and Penology

Pentecostal Churches: *see* Religion

Petroleum Industry: *see* Fuel and Power; Industrial Review

A.F.P. / PICTORIAL PARADE

French medal (above) was issued to coincide with the dedication of Charles de Gaulle's memorial at Colombey-les-Deux-Églises on June 18, 1972. The medal was designed by Albert de Jaeger and stamped by la Monnaie de Paris.

WIDE WORLD

Right, Leonard Nathanson of Southfield, Mich., examines a flawed sheet of eight-cent Eisenhower stamps purchased from his local post office. A rare preprinting paper fold running along the eighth row made the sheet a valuable collector's item.

AUTHENTICATED NEWS INTERNATIONAL

UPI COMPIX

UPI COMPIX

Far left, U.S. stamp issued in 1972 depicts a favourite scene from Mark Twain's "Tom Sawyer." Left, stamp issued in support of family planning aroused criticism from Roman Catholic spokesmen. Above, stamp issued to commemorate the 75th anniversary of the Parent-Teacher Association.

seascape photography, but did not justify its official description as "the first major philatelic publication of the U.S. Postal Service."

In Great Britain the long negotiations for the amalgamation of the British Philatelic Association Ltd., the National Philatelic Society, and the Philatelic Traders Society Ltd. were finally abandoned; the three organizations pledged that they would continue to cooperate in the overall interests of philately. After more than a century, the parent company of Stanley Gibbons Ltd. changed its name to Stanley Gibbons International Ltd. and became a holding company. The old name was retained for the stamp selling division. Gibbons also abandoned its incomplete sectional catalog and began to issue a three-part European catalog and a three-part catalog covering the rest of the world. The Great Britain and Commonwealth catalog remained as a separate volume.

The major international exhibition, held in Brussels under the patronage of King Baudouin, opened at the end of June. Baudouin donated the Grand Prix d'Honneur (a large gold medal) to E. Antonini of Switzerland for his collection of French stamps. The Grand Prix International in the open competition classes went to Count A. Gerli of Italy for a fine collection of Tuscany stamps, and the Grand Prix National for the best entry of Belgian stamps was awarded to M. Zhigne of Belgium. At the exhibition, Stanley Gibbons sold a Mauritius *2d.* blue "Post Office" for £20,000, a new record price for this stamp.

The establishment, on August 1, of a new postal service for the United Arab Emirates brought promise of an end to the unnecessary speculative issues put out by the separate sheikhdoms of the former Trucial States. There was a delay in producing a unified issue, however, giving private operators the chance for a final fling that put a flood of worthless stamps on an already sated philatelic market. The Olympic Games at Munich, W.Ger., resulted in the biggest-ever worldwide "omnibus" issue, with stamps from countries having the smallest participating teams (or no teams at all) being the most numerous.

An international sensation was caused by the disclosure that about 400 unauthorized envelopes had been carried to the moon and back by the crew of Apollo 15 and that 100 had been sold by Hermann Sieger in West Germany at about $1,500 each. The National Aeronautics and Space Administration confiscated the remaining 300. (*See* ASTRONAUTICS.)

At the Central Criminal Court, London, on September 5, James Alexander Mackay, assistant keeper in the Department of Printed Books and curator of the British Museum's philatelic collections, pleaded guilty to five charges of stealing stamp proofs loaned to the museum by the Crown Agents and was fined £1,000. Just before the trial, Thomas De La Rue and Co. Ltd. announced that their 85-volume record collection of stamps would be withdrawn from loan to the British Museum (which did not have facilities for making the collection available to students) and transferred to the National Postal Museum in the Chief Post Office in London.

The 1972 signatories to the Roll of Distinguished Philatelists were Lucien Berthelot (France), Sir

Athelstan Caroe (U.K.), J. E. H. P. J. Crustin (Belgium), and John B. Marriott (U.K.), the keeper of the Royal Philatelic Collections at Buckingham Palace. The Philatelic Congress Medal was awarded to F. P. H. Parsons of London.

(KENNETH F. CHAPMAN)

Numismatics. Although the U.S. Mint did not issue any new types or designs of coins in 1972, it did produce the first in a series of dollar-size bronze medals observing the bicentennial of the American Revolution. The series of medals were being planned and issued by the American Revolution Bicentennial Commission, established by Congress.

At the annual convention of the American Numismatic Association (ANA), held in New Orleans, La., in August, Mint Director Mary T. Brooks announced that the cupronickel Eisenhower dollar would be included in the 1973 proof sets. Limited numbers of these specially struck sets would be available from the U.S. Assay Office, Numismatic Service, in San Francisco until the limit of production capacity was reached. The 40% silver proof and the uncirculated dollars would be struck again in 1973.

Many countries struck coins in new designs or values during the year. This was particularly true of small, new countries, some of which issued coins primarily for collectors and at premium prices. Somewhat surprisingly, there was an increase in the number of silver coins being issued, especially those intended to appeal to collectors. Iran, for example, put out a set of five coins containing nearly five ounces (avoirdupois) of commercially pure silver.

Numismatists interested in history and art were offered a wide variety of medals, mostly from private firms. Among the hundreds of issues in 1972 were medals commemorating Moses and the Ten Commandments, Sir Walter Raleigh, Walt Whitman, James Fenimore Cooper, the Baha'i House of Worship, the Apollo 16 moon mission, the 75th anniversary of Lincoln Memorial University, and a series of four relating to physicians. The ANA selected Elizabeth Jones of Rome as the recipient of its annual Numismatic Art Award for Excellence in Medallic Sculpture and presented the gold award medal to her at its New Orleans convention.

Interest in the hobby continued to grow, with the ANA showing a net increase in membership of more than 1,000 for the third consecutive year. Most dealers reported good business and advancing prices. A 1794 U.S. penny reportedly brought $15,000 at an auction sale, a new record price for a copper coin. New records were set also by the reported sales of an 1894-S dime at $50,000, an 1804 silver dollar at $80,000, and a 1913 Liberty Head nickel at $100,000. Some 1972 U.S. pennies struck from dies that had a double outline of the lettering and date were selling at around $100 each. Activity in all forms of paper money was also strong, and the collecting of old checks as an adjunct to paper money was gaining impetus.

In spite of efforts by the ANA and other organizations, particularly the numismatic publishers, counterfeit, altered, and other specious coins were still being offered to collectors. Modern manufacturing techniques permitted the production of fakes that were very difficult to detect. The ANA established a certification service where collectors could have their coins checked (at a modest fee) for authenticity, and this was expected to slow the sale of false coins somewhat.

The ANA took two other major steps in 1972. It issued a catalog, based on a library classification system devised especially for numismatic literature, listing the material in its extensive library. After several years in the embryo stage, its numismatic museum in Colorado Springs, Colo., had been developed into a tourist attraction and an aid to students.

(GLENN B. SMEDLEY)

See also Postal Services.

Philippines

Situated in the western Pacific Ocean off the southeast coast of Asia, the Republic of the Philippines consists of an archipelago of about 7,100 islands. Area: 115,800 sq.mi. (300,000 sq.km.). Pop. (1972 est.): 39,102,000. Capital: Quezon City (pop., 1970, 754,452). Largest city: Manila (pop., 1970, 1,330,788). Language: Pilipino (based on Tagalog), English, Spanish, and many dialects. Religion (1960): Roman Catholic 84%; Aglipayan 5%; Muslim 5%; Protestant 3%. President in 1972, Ferdinand E. Marcos.

On Jan. 12, 1972, President Marcos lifted a state of emergency imposed in August 1971 following a bomb attack on a political rally held in Manila. The proclamation also restored the suspended rights of habeas corpus except for persons currently under detention "for the crimes of insurrection or rebellion." After the bombing President Marcos had vowed to "impose martial law if necessary" to "liquidate the Communist apparatus," which he blamed for the attack.

Marcos had repeatedly expressed alarm at what he titled the "Communist menace." Indeed active Maoist dissidents within the country had undertaken to point out what they considered the inability of the government to focus adequately on the problems of the nation. Unemployment, in a country with a population growth rate of 3.3%; widespread corruption among government officials, some of whom employed private armies to further their political ambitions and business goals; and the large number of tenant farmers in

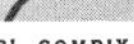
UPI COMPIX

After ordering emergency security measures in the Philippines on Aug. 24, 1972, Pres. Ferdinand Marcos displays a rifle he claimed was furnished to Communist Huks by a political opponent. Marcos imposed martial law on September 23 following an assassination attempt on Defense Secretary Juan Ponce Enrile.

JOHN CHUA, JR.—
NANCY PALMER PHOTO AGENCY

This was the scene in a Manila street after weeks of torrential rains devastated over 4,000 sq.mi. of Luzon. Reported to be the worst natural calamity in Philippine history, the rains caused the deaths of at least 427 persons.

this predominantly agricultural country were some of the nation's ills under criticism.

Throughout most of the year these social and economic problems remained unabated. Joblessness for 20% of the labour force (one out of every four men between the ages of 15 and 24 was unemployed); a gross national product of under $8 billion, ranking 42nd in the world; a steadily widening gap between rich and poor, with the income of the richest 20% amounting to 15 times that of the poorest 20%—all made intolerable the effects of the floods that came in July and August to destroy the country's rice crop. In the worst natural disaster in Philippine history, floodwaters swept through Manila and 14 provinces of Luzon Island. The 25-day storm left an estimated 2.6 million people without food or means of earning it. More than 400 lives were lost, and the nation's economy was said to have been set back five years.

On September 23, in a move that took most of the country by surprise, President Marcos declared martial law in the Philippines. In an effort to "save the Republic and to reform the society" Marcos hoped to "completely dismantle the entire apparatus of the Communist Party" in the country. Metropolitan police in Manila closed most of the newspapers and radio and television stations. A series of "general orders" from the Presidential Palace, aimed at creating a "new society," included: censorship of all domestic and international news media; a temporary ban on unofficial travel abroad by Filipinos; national control of airlines and sky marshals aboard all planes to prevent the possibility of hijacking; closing of all schools for a week; the imposition of the death penalty for the illegal possession of firearms; a ban on all public demonstrations, rallies, and labour strikes; imposition of a midnight to 4 A.M. curfew; and the arrest of "those directly involved in the conspiracy to overthrow the government."

Two months after martial law was declared, the list of people in detention camps had exceeded 6,000. Included were politicians, journalists, student activists, educators, businessmen, and a number of suspected gangsters. Most of these were alleged to have engaged in subversive activities. The secretary-general of the opposition Liberal Party, Sen. Benigno Aquino, Jr., was most prominent among the arrested political leaders. The publisher of the largest daily newspaper and editors of several others had likewise been detained.

On November 29, the constitutional convention delegates approved a draft constitution, which offered the Filipinos a parliamentary form of government. The 317 convention members, chosen in nationwide elections in 1970, voted 271 to 14 for the draft. There was one abstention and the rest were absent, some in detention camps. A national referendum to approve the new charter was set for early 1973. The new constitution was designed to provide for an interim national assembly consisting of convention members who approved of the draft and incumbent senators and congressmen who wished to serve.

In December Marcos relaxed some of the martial law restrictions, lifting newspaper censorship and releasing some of those in detention camps. Also during the month insurgent Muslims clashed with government troops in Mindanao.

On December 7, Imelda Marcos, wife of the president, was attacked by a man armed with a foot-long bolo knife at a public gathering. She survived, with injuries on her arms and hands reportedly requiring 75 stitches. At least two other persons were wounded by the assailant before he was shot dead by guards. The attacker was identified later as an engineer from the southern Philippines. (RAFAEL PARGAS)

PHILIPPINES

Education. (1967–68) Primary, pupils 6,406,826, teachers 207,557; secondary, pupils 1,273,120; vocational, pupils 90,009; secondary and vocational, teachers 46,171; higher (including 33 universities), students 600,787, teaching staff 25,325.

Finance. Monetary unit: peso, with (Sept. 18, 1972) an official rate of 3.90 pesos to U.S. $1 and a free rate of 6.80 pesos to U.S. $1 (16.65 pesos = £1 sterling). Gold, SDRs, and foreign exchange, central bank: (June 1972) U.S. $463 million; (June 1971) U.S. $299 million. Budget (1971 actual): revenue 5,980,000,000 pesos; expenditure 6,166,000,000 pesos. Gross national product: (1970) 38.7 billion pesos; (1969) 31,480,000,000 pesos. Money supply: (June 1972) 5,364,000,000 pesos; (June 1971) 4,820,000,000 pesos. Cost of living (Manila; 1963 = 100): (June 1972) 211; (June 1971) 174.

Foreign Trade. (1971) Imports 8,525,000,000 pesos; exports 7,043,000,000 pesos. Import sources: Japan 29%; U.S. 25%; West Germany 7%; U.K. 5%. Export destinations: U.S. 40%; Japan 35%; Netherlands 7%. Main exports: coconut products 23%; sugar 20%; timber 19%; copper 17%.

Transport and Communications. Roads (1970) 77,950 km. Motor vehicles in use (1970): passenger 279,200; commercial (including buses) 179,400. Railways (1969): 1,144 km.; traffic 584 million passenger-km., freight 115 million net ton-km. Air traffic (1970): 1,456,200,000 passenger-km.; freight 26,242,000 net ton-km. Shipping (1971): merchant vessels 100 gross tons and over 318; gross tonnage 945,508. Telephones (Jan. 1971) 310,000. Radio receivers (Dec. 1968) 1,633,000. Television receivers (Dec. 1970) 400,000.

Agriculture. Production (in 000; metric tons; 1971; 1970 in parentheses): rice 5,168 (5,343); corn 2,039 (2,005); sweet potatoes (1970) 731, (1969) 718; cassava (1970) 442, (1969) 506; copra *c.* 1,626 (1,325); sugar, raw value (1971–72) *c.* 1,880, (1970–71) 2,058; coffee 51 (49); bananas (1970) *c.* 900, (1969) *c.* 896; tobacco 56 (61); rubber *c.* 20 (19); abaca *c.* 60 (*c.* 70); pork *c.* 200 (*c.* 200); timber (cu.m.; 1970) 33,700, (1969) 35,500; fish catch (1970) 990, (1969) 978. Livestock (in 000; March 1971): cattle *c.* 1,700; buffalo *c.* 4,500; pigs *c.* 6,500; goats 775; horses *c.* 295; chickens *c.* 60,000.

Industry. Production (in 000; metric tons; 1971): coal 40; iron ore (55–60% metal content) 2,249; chrome ore (oxide content; 1970) 199; manganese ore (metal content) 2.5; copper concentrates (metal content) 197; gold (troy oz.; 1970) 603; silver (troy oz.; 1970) 1,701; cement 3,115; electricity (kw-hr.; 1969) 8,213,000.

Phosphate:
see Mining

Philosophy

The logic of moral judgments, methodology in moral and social philosophy, and theories of the nature of the good and the right were common themes in 1972. Moreover, the concern of philosophy with practical moral and social issues was exhibited widely. A historical background of that concern in the U.S. was presented by Morton White in *Science and Sentiment in America. On the Dialectics of Moral Consciousness,* by Maria Makai, raised the question of the beginning and essence of moral evaluation. The relevance of philosophy for public affairs was argued by several essayists in *Philosophy and Political Action,* edited by Virginia Held, Kai Nielsen, and Charles Parsons.

Civil Disobedience, by Carl Cohen, analyzed the moral and legal justifications of civil disobedience and described its appropriate political uses. John Rawls, in *A Theory of Justice,* argued that the meaning of justice should be found in the natural rights theory of the contract tradition rather than in utilitarianism. *Normative Systems,* by Carlos E. Alchourron and Eugenio Bulygin of Brazil, was an adaptation of general concepts of the meta-theory of science to normative and legal discourse. The relevance of philosophy to practical issues was the substance of four volumes of *New Studies in Practical Philosophy,* by R. M. Hare of Oxford.

The theory of the nature of the mind, especially in its relation to the body, occupied a large place in philosophic thought. In *Biology and Knowledge,* Jean Piaget of Geneva held that the loss of instinct in man produced an intellectual revolution. Zeno Vendler, of the University of Calgary, Alta., in *Res Cogitans,* rejected the behaviourist and empiricist view of the mind in favour of a rationalistic view fashioned on a revision of the position of Descartes. The Eddington Memorial Lecture of John Hick, *Biology and the Soul,* and Keith Campbell's *Body and Mind* were further expressions of the increasing interest in this problem. A romantic theory of the mind as a creative source of human behaviour was developed by Guy Sircello in *Mind and Art.*

In *Probability and Evidence,* A. J. Ayer of Oxford presented a new interpretation of nontruth-functional conditionals. A criticism of philosophy for its general failure to come to grips with the factual data of empirical science was set forth by Jean Piaget in *Insights and Illusions of Philosophy,* translated into English by Wolfe Mays. In the first volume of *Human Understanding,* Stephen Toulmin held that "adaptation" and "demand" rather than "form" and "validity" are the keys to the development of modern patterns of analysis. *A General Interpreted Modal Calculus,* by Aldo Bressan of Padua, Italy, suggested original approaches to the problems of prediction, description, and substance.

In *Reason Revisited,* Sebastian Samay of Dublin undertook a systematic and critical presentation of the philosophy of Karl Jaspers. *Contemporary Philosophy in Scandinavia,* edited by Raymond E. Olson and Anthony M. Paul, was the first full-scale effort to present current Scandinavian thought in English. J. Preston Cole's *The Problematic Self in Kierkegaard and Freud* undertook to place psychoanalysis within an existential framework. A. J. Ayer's volume *Russell and Moore: The Analytical Heritage* was an exposition and critique of the chief creators of the analytical movement that returned British thought from Hegelianism to empiricism. *The Metaphysical and Geometrical Doctrine of Bruno,* by the Yugoslav philosopher Ksenija Atanasijevic, was published in an English translation by George Vid Tomashevich.

The Academy of Athens published the first volume of *Philosophia,* a yearbook of ancient and modern philosophy. The first issue of *Neue Hefte für Philosophie* was edited by R. Bubner, K. Cramer, and R. Wiehl at Heidelberg. *Second Order,* dedicated to the cultivation of philosophy in relation to African life and institutions, was initiated at the University of Ife, Nigeria. *Philosophy and Public Affairs* was established by Marshall Cohen at Princeton and *Idealistic Studies,* edited by Robert N. Beck, was established at Clark University, Worcester, Mass.

The Society for Women in Philosophy held its first conference in Chicago. Among philosophical conferences held in 1972 were a centenary observance of the birth of Bertrand Russell at McMaster University in Ontario and the second conference of the International Husserl and Phenomenological Research Society. (STERLING M. MCMURRIN)

ENCYCLOPÆDIA BRITANNICA FILMS. *The Medieval Mind* (1969); *Spirit of the Renaissance* (1971).

Photography

The world photographic market, amateur and professional, amounted to DM. 12.3 billion (about U.S. $4 billion) in 1972, according to statistics compiled by AgfaGevaert. North America accounted for 57% of the total, and Europe for 28%. Photochemical products comprised 60% of the market and, of this, 58% went for still photography films. Of the approximately 40% devoted to equipment, still cameras accounted for 49% and motion-picture cameras for 20%.

The West German photographic industry, which normally exports about 56% of its production, was considerably influenced by changes in international currency regulations adopted in 1971. Although total West German exports, at DM. 1,240,000,000, were approximately the same as in 1970, exports to the U.S. fell by some 20%, and the industry was concentrating on nations belonging to the EEC.

During 1972 it became increasingly clear that rising labour costs were making it uneconomic for some West German firms to continue manufacturing cameras and allied mechanical products domestically. Rollei had begun production in Singapore in 1971, and this was expanded substantially in 1972. Zeiss Ikon implemented its earlier decision to stop the manufacture of inexpensive and medium-priced photographic products and, in a surprise move, Ernst Leitz Ltd. of Wetzlar, W.Ger., entered into a manufacturing agreement with the Minolta Camera Co. Ltd. of Osaka, Jap. U.S. firms were also using Japanese manufacturing facilities. A good example was the Vivitar Corp. which utilized U.S. marketing and finance and Japanese fabrication, with lens design as a joint enterprise.

Japanese photographic production was valued at U.S. $445 million in 1971, an increase of 6.9% over the previous year. The value of still cameras remained

"Identical twins, Roselle, N.J., 1967" from the Diane Arbus retrospective photographic exhibition at the Museum of Modern Art in New York City.

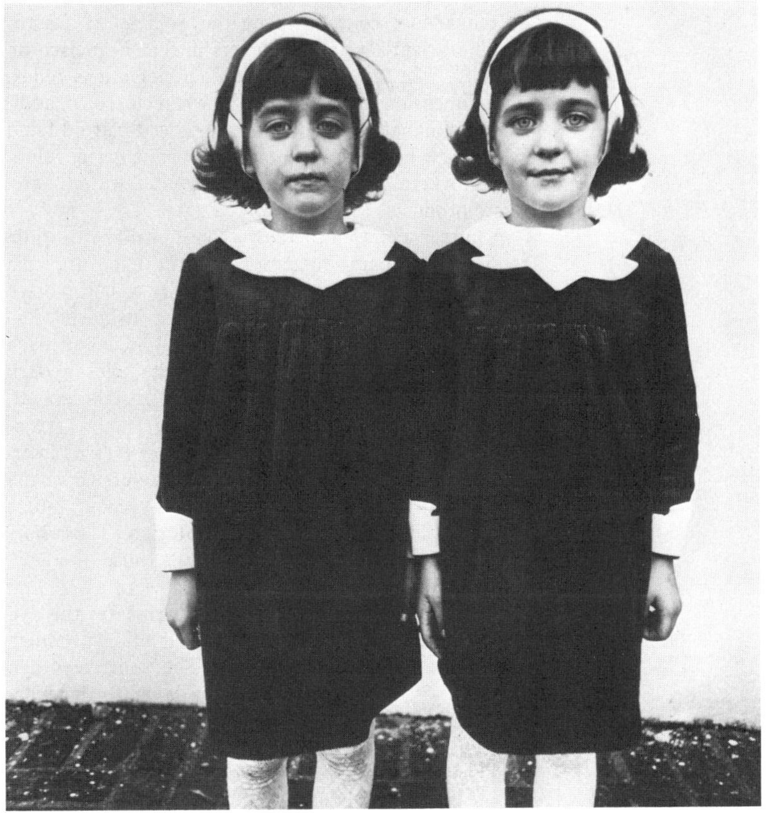

DIANE ARBUS, LENT BY DOON ARBUS

JERRY N. UELSMANN PORTFOLIO—PUBLISHED BY WITKIN-BERLEY, LTD.

"All American Sunset, 1971" by Jerry Uelsmann was included in his show at the Witkin Gallery, New York, in April 1972. Typical of the incongruous juxtaposition present in much of his work, this image displays a rather heavy-handed surrealistic influence.

about the same, at $269 million, although unit production fell 8.9%. Exports to the U.S. rose 15% to $267 million. The U.S. continued to be the main market for Japanese products, taking 38% of the total.

Processes and Equipment. A new compact Polaroid camera was introduced in 1972. The announcement was made on April 25 by Edwin Land to a meeting of Polaroid stockholders, sorely in need of reassurance since key Polaroid patents would shortly expire and Kodak, which previously had manufactured Polaroid film under contract, had announced its intention to enter the instant-photography field itself.

Technical details of the new camera were revealed at the annual conference of the Society of Photographic Scientists and Engineers in San Francisco on May 10. The camera was a folding single-lens reflex, with dimensions of 1 × 4 × 7 in. when closed. In addition to eliminating the bulk of the older Polaroid Land cameras, it had the advantage of permitting development to take place without timing and without any waste products.

A mirror was used to allow a long focal length while retaining compact dimensions. After exposure, the print was expelled from the camera by a motor drive and the image began to appear almost instantly. The print was about 8 × 8 cm. ($3\frac{1}{4} \times 3\frac{1}{4}$ in.) and each film pack contained ten of these units, plus a dark slide and the battery needed to energize the camera. The sensitive material consisted of an integral structure of about 17 layers, including a mordant or fixer. A wide margin on the print contained a version of the Polaroid processing pod which held, among other reagents, the viscous processing solution. The whole inner structure was less than two mils thick.

The major ingredients of the pod were alkali and titanium dioxide. The alkali, which permeates the dye layers, becomes oxidized, and the oxidation products immobilize the dye on the image. The unoxidized dye pigment passes through the titania layer to the mordant, where it is held and appears as a positive image against the white background. New kinds of indicator dyes were synthesized which absorb light at low pH values but become colourless in conjunction with alkali. These dyes were incorporated into the viscous reagent so that, in effect, development takes place under a dark curtain that is bleached away during the process. It was emphasized that this method could be used with existing Polaroid Land equipment if competitive pressure made it necessary.

Kodak's Pocket Instamatic cameras were introduced during the year and received wide commercial acceptance. The cameras take 16-mm. film in cartridges, utilizing an "easy-load" principle similar to that of the original Instamatic produced in 1963. There was nothing new about either subminiature formats or 16-mm. cartridges, but Kodak introduced not only a complete range of cameras but also accessories, projectors, and sophisticated processing equipment for the photofinishing houses. Since the negative size was 13 × 17 mm., an improved emulsion was necessary to produce colour prints of good quality in the 9 × 11.5 cm. ($3\frac{1}{2} \times 4\frac{1}{2}$ in.) size. The Kodak monochrome film, Verichrome pan, was altered to give finer grain and a sharper image and—even more important considering the rising popularity of colour—Kodacolor II was introduced, with corresponding improvements over the original Kodacolor. As manufacturing capacity increased, it was planned to introduce Kodacolor II in larger sizes.

Among cameras generally, electronic shutters were being used more widely than ever before. Of particular interest was the electronically timed shutter in which the aperture is set first and the exposure controlled by continuously variable shutter speeds. The key component was the electrical memory circuit which retains, as an exposure factor, the light intensity reading of the subject. The Pentax ES, Yashica Electro AX, and the Minolta SLR all incorporated this principle.

The Fujica ST 701 and 801 incorporated a new method of light measurement employing silicon cells, heavily filtered to give correct colour response and using a field effect transistor circuit to restore sensitivity. An advantage of this system was that the silicon cell does not display the "memory" of the conventional cell. In addition, meter response in dim light is appreciably faster. A novelty shown at Photokina '72 in Cologne, W.Ger., was the Domnick double cassette camera for 6 × 6 cm. and 4 × 4 cm. formats. These cameras had a cassette on each side of the camera and electric motors that drove the selected film into the exposing position, retracting it after use. The photographer thus had a choice of two emulsions, although the system had some disadvantages of weight and cost.

Two special-purpose transparency colour films were introduced by Eastman Kodak. SO-456 was a slow, high-contrast material with the green-sensitive layer at the top of the monopack in order to achieve high sharpness. Ektachrome Duplicating Film 6120 replaced the firmer 6119 and was from one to two stops faster than the earlier material. No masking or other means of contrast adjustment was needed for making duplicate transparencies.

Electronic flash units with automatic exposure control became increasingly popular. A fundamental advance in design was introduced in the Rollei E36RE and subsequently incorporated in other models. The previous system depended on a light sensor which, when activated by reflected flash light from the subject, actuated a shorting device in parallel with the capacitor storing the electrical energy. This meant that when a flash was interrupted before the capacitor was completely discharged, the energy not converted into light was dissipated as heat. The new system had a switch-off device in series with the capacitor, so that unexpended charge remained in the capacitor. Under extreme conditions—as when making close-up flash pictures in rapid succession—this new principle could result in recycling times as low as 0.3 seconds, and as many as 500% more flashes could be obtained from one set of batteries or one charge.

Another idea, shown in Honeywell and Rollei units, involved placing the sensor on a lead instead of having it built into the casing. It is common practice to bounce flash light from a ceiling or wall in order to obtain diffused lighting. However, if the light cell is mounted in the casing, exposure is based on the light reflected back from that ceiling or wall rather than from the subject, and the automatic exposure measurement is incorrect. With the sensor separated, it can be pointed toward the subject, irrespective of where the flash head is directed. Several flash units were shown that allowed a choice of apertures for automatic flash operation.

During 1972 more firms adopted multicoating of lens elements to achieve reduction in flare and avoid internal reflections. Carl Zeiss of Oberkochen introduced 23 new lenses at the '72 Photokina. The Sonnar Superachromat 250-mm. *f*/5.6 lens virtually eliminated the secondary spectrum, a feature that was of particular value with high-sensitivity panchromatic film, infrared film, or false-colour film. No refocusing was needed when the sensitivity of the film extended beyond the visible spectrum. The 15-mm. *f*/8 three element Hologen, covering the amazingly wide angle of 110° with minimum distortion, was introduced in a new focusing version for the Leica Model M. In 1966 such a modification had been said to be impossible.

Another lens of extreme wide angle was the Zeiss 15-mm. *f*/3/5 Distagon, with 14 elements. A filter turret built into the lens permitted the use of four filters, and the lens could be used in single-lens reflex cameras. The 16-mm. *f*/2.8 F Distagon was a fisheye lens for the 35-mm. format covering an angle of 180° from corner to corner. The Zeiss 35-mm. *f*/1.4 Distagon was remarkable for its high speed as well as excellent close-up performance. A general trend was the inclusion of floating elements that do not move with the rest of the lens during focusing, thus retaining lens corrections through an extended focusing range.

Many Japanese firms introduced new lenses, although most of them were slightly improved versions of previous types. However, the Asahi Optical Co. Ltd. of Tokyo exhibited a 135–600-mm. *f*/6.7 zoom with 15 elements and a 1,000-mm. mirror lens for the 6 × 7 cm. format. Canon made extensive use of floating element construction in many of their new lenses and employed fluorite elements in a 300-mm. *f*/2.8. Nikon showed an 80-mm. *f*/4.5 lens that automatically focuses on a subject in the centre of the viewfinder. Sun Optical Co. introduced an 80–240-mm. *f*/4 zoom lens with a macro focusing movement allowing focus on a plane 250 cm. away from the front surface.

"Behind the Great Wall," an exhibit at New York's Metropolitan Museum of Art documenting a century of Chinese history, included (left) John Thomson's 1870 portrait of Prince Kung and (right) Henri Cartier-Bresson's image of a bewildered father searching for his son among the ranks of the Kuomintang recruits in 1949.

COURTESY, METROPOLITAN MUSEUM OF ART

HENRI CARTIER-BRESSON—MAGNUM

Kodak Ektacolor 30 and 37 colour printing papers received wide acceptance. They were designed for three-bath processing, necessitating changes in finishing machines intended for the Ektacolor 20 and 47 papers which needed five solutions. Ektacolor 30 and 37 had resin-coated bases, shortening the processing time since the paper did not absorb chemicals that subsequently needed to be washed away. Since the Ektaprint 3 processing system works at 88° F (31° C), with a highly active colour developer, print-processing times could be reduced by up to 60%, compared with Ektacolor 20 and 47. Another difference was the reduced effluent from the bleach bath. A bleach-fix regeneration unit could be used, so that the solution was recycled continuously. The regenerator unit consisted of two silver recovery units, and since ferrocyanide and zinc sulfate were excluded from the bleach-fix and stabilizer formulations, there was a reduction in the contamination of waste water.

GAF announced a new colour print paper, Type 7201, designed for three-bath processing and, like Ektaprint 3, having bleach-fix regeneration. Agfa-Gevaert introduced a new paper, MCN 310, with a resin-coated base, also designed for three-bath processing at high temperatures and bleach-fix regeneration.

Processing houses faced considerable turmoil as a result of the introduction of the 110-size film, together with the changeover from 022 to Flexicolor processing. In addition, since Kodacolor II had higher overall green and blue densities than the older Kodacolor, changes in printing machines were required. Complete new equipment lines were needed for processing 110, including machines to open cassettes, splice films, cut film strips, and mount transparencies, as well as to process and print films.

The Colorapid processor, a compact batch machine, utilized the principle of cascading liquids over the material, rather than moving the film through the solutions. Timing and sequence of solutions and washes were controlled automatically by punch card. A useful result of the three-batch process was that chemicals for colour negative film and colour paper could both be stored in the machine at the same time.

Exhibitions. Contemporary work over the past few years had shown a tendency to high contrast and a fondness for thin black borders. Of more significance was the trend toward inclusiveness—showing the surroundings of the subject rather than excluding as much as possible. To some extent, this might stem from a habitual use of lenses with wider angles, but it remained an open question whether equipment influences pictorial form or whether preconceived ideas of form dictate the choice of equipment.

The major pictorial exhibitions, the Royal Photographic Society's exhibition and the London Salon, showed little that was new. Trends in Europe and, to some extent, in the U.S. were shown at Photokina. The outstanding colour exhibition was "The Creation" by Ernst Haas of New York, which included 48 dye-transfer prints corresponding to or congenial with the text of Genesis. "Sequences," selected by Alan Porter, attempted to show how a selection of pictures around a theme could convey more to the viewer than a single photograph. "Universalists" displayed the work of chief photographers from leading European magazines. "Women Photographed by Women" was held in cooperation with the magazine *Photo* of Paris.

The exhibition "Society 12" was designed to show work by young people placing on record their attitudes toward modern society. "Creative Photographers" was organized by the Union of Polish Art Photographers with the stated aim of showing experimental prints designed, not as finished two-dimensional works, but as part of a more complete display containing its own logic.

The International Amateur Photographers Championship was compiled from prizewinners of the preceding ten years. "By the Light of Earth," organized by the European Space Research Organization, was intended to symbolize rather than to describe. "Anti-Photokina" was an experiment intended to provide those who deride the pictures generally shown in exhibitions with an opportunity to display their own work. Blank walls were left and anyone who cared to was invited to put up his own display. Unfortunately, virtually nothing appeared. Keystone Press of Munich cooperated with Volkswagenwerk AG and the Federation of German Amateur Photographers in setting up "The Love Bug." More than 1,000 photographers submitted prints and the results showed remarkable ingenuity. (N. F. MAUDE)

See also Motion Pictures.

Pipelines:
see Fuel and Power; Transportation
Plastics Industry:
see Industrial Review
Platinum:
see Mining
Poetry:
see Literature

Physics

Fusion for Power Production. The search continued for cheaper, cleaner, nonexpendable sources of energy. During 1972 the laser-produced fusion technique seemed the most promising. The basic energy-producing reaction in this method is the fusion of two deuterium nuclei to produce helium nuclei and high-energy neutrons. However, for the reaction to occur the material containing the deuterium must be at a temperature of 2×10^8 K and hence must be in the form of a plasma. (In a plasma the constituent particles of atoms—electrons and nuclei—break free of each other.) The fusion reaction is "helped" if the plasma is maintained at a sufficiently high density to overcome the force of repulsion between the nuclei. Adding tritium to the deuterium can lower the required plasma temperature to 5×10^7 K.

This approach would satisfy at least two of the criteria for power production since deuterium is in abundant supply in ordinary water and the fusion process develops less radioactive waste than the conventional fission nuclear reactor. The practical problem, of course, is to produce the high-temperature, high-pressure plasma that is necessary for the energy output from the fusion process to exceed the energy input to the system.

Until 1972 the majority of the research effort went into two different plasma heating processes. In the first, a low-temperature plasma is contained in a magnetic field and then heated and compressed by passing electric currents through it. In the second, a solid particle or droplet, containing deuterium, is heated by a high-energy, very short laser pulse and the plasma so formed is then contained by a magnetic field. The major problems with these techniques are that the containment of the plasma by a magnetic field is never perfect—the Soviet Tokamak system maintained fusion for 0.1 sec., the best so far achieved—and the lasers available in 1972 did not have sufficient power to produce a high enough plasma temperature.

A further problem with the laser heating method is that the solid deuterium pellets are perfect reflectors of the incident light, thus preventing any absorption of that light. Without any absorption there would be no heating, all the energy being reflected away from the pellet. However, a laser pulse with a very carefully shaped leading edge or with a smaller introductory pulse was found to produce absorption (*Phys. Rev. Lett.,* 28:85, 1972). The initial laser pulse produces local heating and expansion of the surface of the pellet, and the major pulse is then reflected from the high-density core of the deuterium pellet and absorbed by the outer layers.

This laser heating process was taken a step further in 1972 by workers in the U.S. and the Soviet Union (*Nature,* 239:139, 1972; *Physics Today,* August 1972). The proposals, which by the year's end had no experimental justification, indicated that with a sufficiently powerful laser the deuterium/tritium pellet can be caused to implode. This increase in density of the pellet reduces by many orders of magnitude the laser power required to produce the necessary heating.

Power Transmission. A novel approach that would revolutionize the transmission of power from a nuclear source was suggested during the year (*Science,* 176: 1323, 1972). First, the "power station" should be located at sea to enable the excess heat generated by the nuclear process to be readily dissipated, and, second, the power should be transmitted in the form of hydrogen rather than electric current. The hydrogen is formed by electrolysis at the source and could be piped to the consumer, who, using fuel cells to reverse the process, would then produce direct current with a side product of pure water.

Gravity Waves. Joseph Weber's detection of gravity waves in 1969 provided a great stimulant to work on the subject. Scientists in Israel (*Physics Today,* June 1972) used the earth as a detector and monitored gravity waves from a pulsar, using a seismometer to detect the surface accelerations of the earth which, when analyzed by applying a Fourier series to the data, correspond to the characteristic frequency of the pulsar.

Theoreticians hotly debated Weber's results (*Phys. Rev. Lett.,* 28:991, 1972; 28:994, 1972; 28:998, 1972), which indicate that the source of the waves, in the centre of our galaxy, must be radiating preferentially in the plane of the galaxy. Meanwhile, gravity-wave observation posts were completed or were under construction in several countries.

Lasers. Significant progress was made in 1972 toward the goal of an X-ray laser. A multistage, Q-switched, neodymium-glass laser was used to produce hard (short-wavelength) X rays from a solid target (*Physics Today,* January 1972). As in the nuclear fusion experiments, the main laser pulse was preceded by a pulse of low power, which formed a plasma at the metal surface. This plasma was then heated by the main laser pulse, causing it to emit X rays. With no precursor pulse, the resultant X rays are only of long wavelength, but if there is a long precursor pulse some hard X rays are emitted. The work is directed toward hard X rays since they are more energetic and penetrate deeper into solid materials than longer wavelength radiation.

U.S. physicists also claimed to have produced coherent X rays from an aqueous copper sulfate gel pumped with a three-stage neodymium-glass laser (*Proc. Nat. Acad. Sci., U.S.A.* 69:1744, 1972). The gel was contained between two microscope cover glasses, and the coherence of the resulting X rays was inferred from the fact that the X-ray beam was automatically collimated at a diameter of 0.02 cm. over a distance of 110 cm. The wavelength of these X rays was not measured, but they were shown to be hard by their penetration through several layers of aluminum foil. More recent work, however, in several laboratories around the world cast some doubt on these measurements. Very careful studies have failed to reveal any coherent X-ray production from the copper sulfate gel and the U.S. experiments are thought to be troubled by photographic problems. The X-ray laser was expected to be especially useful in such fields as crystallography and medical holography.

(S. B. PALMER)

See also Astronautics; Astronomy; Chemistry.

Poland

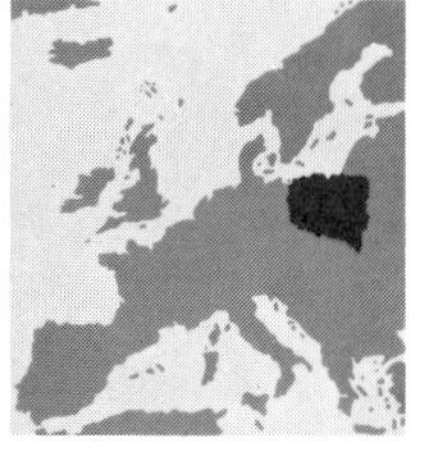

A people's republic of Eastern Europe, Poland is bordered by the Baltic Sea, the U.S.S.R., Czechoslovakia, and East Germany. Area: 120,725 sq.mi. (312,677 sq.km.). Pop. (1971 est.): 32,852,400. Cap. and largest city: Warsaw (pop., 1971 est., 1,326,000). Language: Polish. Religion: predominantly Roman Catholic. First secretary of the Polish United Workers' (Communist) Party in 1972, Edward Gierek; chairmen of the Council of State, Jozef Cyrankiewicz and, from March 28, Henryk Jablonski; chairman of the Council of Ministers (premier), Piotr Jaroszewicz.

To complete the reshuffle in party and state administration that he had inaugurated soon after he came to power in 1970, Edward Gierek dissolved the Sejm 15 months before its four-year term was to expire and held new elections on March 19, 1972: in 80 constituencies there were 625 candidates for 460 seats; 280 deputies were elected to the Sejm for the first time. The Polish electoral system was unique in the socialist bloc in that electors were able to indicate the relative popularity of the candidates. For instance, in the Sosnowiec constituency Gierek received 99.8% of the votes, but Jozef Kepa, first secretary of the Warsaw party organization, obtained only 93.3%. However, the political composition of the sixth Sejm was the same as that of its predecessor: the Polish United

Shoppers browse in privately owned shops in Warsaw. In contrast to some Eastern European countries, private enterprise was being encouraged in Poland.

UPI COMPIX

Workers' Party (PUWP) got 255 seats, the United Peasants' Party (UPP) 117, the Democratic Party 39, and nonparty members 49.

The new Sejm assembled for a short session on March 28, and elected as "marshal" (speaker) Stanislaw Gucwa, chairman of the Supreme Executive of the UPP, to replace Dyzma Galaj, a prominent member of the same party, elected to that post in February 1971. The latter was probably replaced because he insisted too loudly that the constitutional prerogatives of the Sejm should not be curtailed. The Sejm also elected Henryk Jablonski (*see* BIOGRAPHY) as chairman of the Council of State to succeed Jozef Cyrankiewicz. In all, 10 out of 17 members of the Council of State were new. There were more changes, too, in the composition of the Council of Ministers. Since the dramatic food riots of December 1970, 21 of the 33 portfolios had changed hands. Among the most recent changes Tadeusz Olechowski succeeded Kazimierz Olszewski as minister of foreign trade and Jerzy Kuberski succeeded Jablonski as minister of public instruction and higher education. On May 6 Stanislaw Wronski, minister of culture and art, succeeded Mieczyslaw Moczar as chairman of the Central Board of the Union of Fighters for Freedom and Democracy (ZBOWID). Moczar's removal as head of the organization he had created was followed on June 2 by the appointment of Gen. Wladyslaw Grudzien as minister of combatants' affairs.

Premier Jaroszewicz presented to the Sejm the revised draft five-year plan for 1971–75. The plan, approved on June 8, aimed to satisfy the needs and aspirations of workingmen and to establish solid foundations for the further rapid development of the socialist economy. The plan envisaged a 40% growth of the national income as compared with a 33% growth in 1966–70. On May 10 and 11 the Central Committee of the PUWP discussed the long-term housing program that was to absorb 18% of the total investment in the current five-year period, growing to 23% in the following period; 1,080,000 apartments were to be built in the current five-year plan, and a total of 7.3 million by 1990.

On October 31 the ruling party and the government decided to extend for at least a year the freeze on food prices introduced on Jan. 8, 1971. Premier Jaroszewicz explained that this decision was made possible by a 20% increase in industrial production and an 11% rise in agricultural output in 1971 and 1972. During these two years the total number of employed had risen by more than 700,000; real wages grew by 5.5% in 1971 and by 6% in 1972.

In foreign policy the most important event was the ratification on May 17 by the West German Bundestag of the Warsaw treaty of Dec. 7, 1970, by which West Germany recognized the "inviolability now and in the future" of the western frontier of Poland along the Oder and Neisse rivers. Diplomatic relations with West Germany were established in November. The Holy See, drawing its own conclusions from this act, decided on June 28 to adjust the external borders of the new western Polish bishoprics with the internationally recognized frontier, to reappoint the apostolic administrators in Wroclaw, Opole, Olsztyn, and Gorzow as residential bishops, and to divide the huge diocese of Gorzow into three, thus creating two new bishoprics in Pomorze.

The most important foreign visitor to Warsaw during the year was U.S. Pres. Richard M. Nixon. The talks between the Polish and U.S. statesmen on May 31 and June 1 were "frank, businesslike, and constructive." Both sides welcomed the treaty between Poland and West Germany. In order to increase commercial and other economic links between the two countries, both sides decided to create a Polish-U.S. Trade Commission. On November 9 in Washington, Peter Peterson, U.S. secretary of commerce, and Tadeusz Olechowski signed a long-term agreement aimed at trebling Polish-U.S. trade. Just prior to this it was announced that U.S. Export-Import Bank credits would be made available to Poland.

Between October 2–6 Gierek paid an official visit to France. He and Pres. Georges Pompidou signed a declaration of friendship and collaboration between the two countries, while a ten-year agreement on economic cooperation provided for the doubling of Franco-Polish trade. France granted Poland a three-year credit of Fr. 1.5 billion.

John Davies, British secretary of state for trade and industry, visited Poland October 16–19. He had talks with Premier Jaroszewicz, and discussed Polish-British trade relations with Olechowski. Both sides stressed their interest in a substantial increase in trade between the two countries. A five-year trade agreement was signed with Sweden in October.

(K. M. SMOGORZEWSKI)

POLAND

Education. (1969–70) Primary, pupils 5,443,132, teachers 229,225; secondary, pupils 309,706, teachers 19,412; vocational, pupils 905,781, teachers 128,775; teacher training, pupils 39,270, teachers 5,243; higher (including 9 universities), students 322,464, teaching staff 31,377.

Finance. Monetary unit: zloty, with (Sept. 18, 1972) an official exchange rate of 3.68 zlotys to U.S. $1 and a tourist rate of 38 zlotys to U.S. $1 (87.90 zlotys = £1 sterling). Budget (1971 est.): revenue 379.4 billion zlotys; expenditure 376.6 billion zlotys. National income (net material product): (1970) 738.4 billion zlotys; (1969) 696.1 billion zlotys.

Foreign Trade. (1971) Imports 16,151,000,000 zlotys; exports 15,489,000,000 zlotys. Import sources: U.S.S.R. 35%; East Germany 11%; Czechoslovakia 9%; West Germany 5%; Hungary 5%. Export destinations: U.S.S.R. 36%; East Germany 8%; Czechoslovakia 7%; West Germany 5%. Main exports (1970): machinery 31%; coal and coke 11%; transport equipment 8%; iron and steel 7%; textiles and clothing 6%; meat and products 5%.

Transport and Communications. Roads (1971) 303,750 km. (including 139 km. expressways). Motor vehicles in use (1971): passenger 555,600; commercial 277,300. Railways: (1970) 23,311 km. (including 3,872 km. electrified); traffic (1971) 37,228,000,000 passenger-km., freight 104,334,000,000 net ton-km. Air traffic (1971): 655.3 million passenger-km.; freight 8,142,000 net ton-km. Shipping (1971): merchant vessels 100 gross tons and over 606; gross tonnage 1,760,397. Telephones (Dec. 1970) 1,867,000. Radio licenses (Dec. 1970) 5,658,000. Television licenses (Dec. 1970) 4,215,000.

Agriculture. Production (in 000; metric tons; 1971; 1970 in parentheses): wheat 5,453 (4,608); rye 7,840 (5,433); barley 2,449 (2,149); oats 3,200 (3,209); potatoes 39,928 (50,301); sugar, raw value (1971–72) 1,713, (1970–71) 1,505; rapeseed 633 (566); linseed *c.* 55 (65); dry peas *c.* 63 (61); onions (1970) 365, (1969) 315; apples *c.* 730 (691); tobacco *c.* 78 (85); flax fibre *c.* 55 (52); hemp fibre *c.* 16 (14); butter *c.* 205 (201); cheese *c.* 250 (245); beef and veal *c.* 555 (544); pork *c.* 1,300 (1,292); timber (cu.m.; 1970) 18,300, (1969) 18,100; fish catch (1970) 469, (1969) 408. Livestock (in 000; June 1971): cattle 10,213; horses *c.* 2,570; pigs *c.* 13,870; sheep *c.* 3,400; chickens *c.* 151,000.

Industry. Index of industrial production (1963 = 100): (1971) 192; (1970) 177. Fuel and power (in 000; metric tons; 1971): coal 145,490; brown coal 34,517; coke (1970) 15,212; crude oil (1970) 424; natural gas (cu.m.) 5,383,000; manufactured gas (cu.m.; 1970) 7,085,000; electricity (kw-hr.) 68,867,000. Production (in 000; metric tons; 1971): cement 13,084; iron ore (30% metal content) 2,080; pig iron 7,497; crude steel 12,738; aluminum (1970) 99; zinc (1970) 209; copper (1970) 72; lead (1970) 54; sulfuric acid 2,254; nitrogenous fertilizers (1970) 1,030; processed phosphate fertilizers (1970) 599; cotton fabrics (m.) 906,000; woolen fabrics (m.) 99,000; rayon and synthetic fabrics (m.; 1970) 116,000; passenger cars (units) 85; commercial vehicles (units) 56. Merchant vessels launched (100 gross tons and over; 1971) 489,000 gross tons.

Police

The 41st General Assembly of the International Criminal Police Organization (Interpol), to which 114 countries were affiliated in 1972, was held in Frankfurt am Main, W.Ger., September 19–26, under the shadow of increasing political terrorism. Although Interpol's constitution forbade the organization's intervention in cases of racial or political character, many members were prepared to argue that terrorism was a criminal offense that could not be condoned for its political motives. The Israeli delegates failed in an attempt to have the question raised before the assembly. Had they succeeded it was expected that the Arab delegations would have left both the conference and the organization, and the French, who had close links with Algeria, pursued a policy of friendship to the Arabs, and had contributed greatly to Interpol, would have been extremely embarrassed. Many members considered that the constitution needed revision; a majority were reportedly in favour of establishing a special international service to fight terrorist activities, with proposed headquarters at Scotland Yard, London, under the charge of Robert Mark, the new London metropolitan commissioner of police. Reports were submitted to the 270 delegates on international illicit drug traffic, international currency counterfeiting, illicit traffic in diamonds, cooperation with regard to currency offenses, and a rash of counterfeiting of watches and clocks by putting the faces or names of fine watches on cheap workings.

A symposium on organized crime, held at Interpol headquarters in Saint-Cloud, France, in November 1971, was attended by 89 participants from 40 countries. A second symposium in December 1971, on the use of electronic data processing in criminal police work, was attended by 82 experts from 30 countries. In November 1971 Interpol was represented at a conference on drug abuse and traffic for Southeast Asian countries held in Canberra, Austr.

Various studies were made during the year; topics included firearms regulations, powers and duties of the police, search of persons and premises and the seizure of property, evolution of the problem of combating slavery, and juvenile delinquency. There was an increase in the work of most of the National Central bureaus during 1971; 2,214 arrests were made as a result of collaboration between NCBs, which exchanged 154,904 items of information. Between June 1971 and June 1972, the General Secretariat studied 15,971 cases, resulting in 846 arrests. NCBs were supplied with 9,180 items of information and 371 persons were subjects of international notices. In 1971 the Interpol radio network carried 160,719 messages, an increase of 6% over 1970.

In accordance with long-standing tradition, Interpol followed the work of the UN Commission on Narcotic Drugs in Geneva. The General Secretariat was also represented at a seminar organized by the U.S. Bureau of Narcotics and Dangerous Drugs in Washington, D.C., in September 1971. Within the framework of its relations with the International Civil Aviation Organization, Interpol took part in the work of a committee that met in Montreal; it also attended an International Air Transport Association seminar.

West Germany. Public pressure on police forces was probably most intense in West Germany in 1972. Under the impact of a spate of bank robberies and anarchist bombings throughout 1972, especially by the so-called "Baader-Meinhof group" (*see* BIOGRAPHY: *Meinhof, Ulrike*), the federal and state ministers of the interior decided to implement a security program. The police were to be reinforced by 10,000 men, cooperation between the regular police force (Schutzpolizei) and the criminal police improved, unnecessary activities reduced, and legislative measures introduced to enable Länder (state) police forces to call in support from the Bundesgrenzschutz (federal border guard) where necessary. The powers of the Bundeskriminalamt (Federal Office of Criminal Investigation) were to be extended. Certain parts of the security program had been carried out by August 1972, particularly enactment of the Bundesgrenzschutz law. New regulations were also introduced for the training of senior police officers, a new, stricter firearms law was to become effective Jan. 1, 1973, and a new explosives law was in preparation.

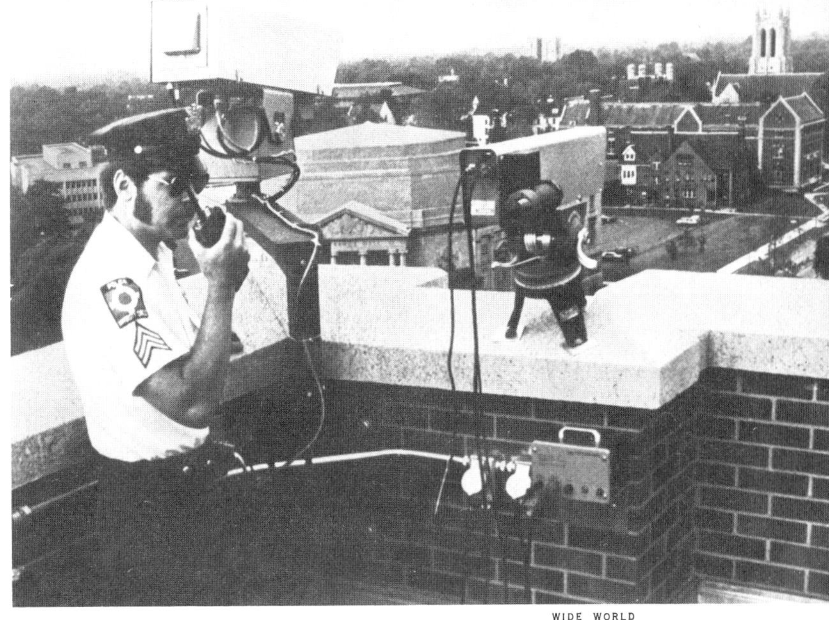

WIDE WORLD

Approaching Dick Tracy technology, a Cleveland, O., policeman uses a walkie-talkie, while a television camera (left) scans the street below. The TV signals are transmitted to headquarters via the laser equipment at right.

Eleven West German policemen were killed while on duty during the first six months of 1972. North Rhine-Westphalia decided to train 700 sharpshooters and to spend DM. 700,000 on new weapons and ammunition, and Lower Saxony passed a law enabling police to shoot when the situation justified it even if hostages' lives were endangered. A girl hostage had already been killed by police in Munich during a bank robbery in 1971, and in 1972 a British salesman was killed when plainclothes police with submachine guns stormed his quarters by mistake.

Then, on September 5, at 4:30 A.M. in the Olympic Village, Munich, eight members of the Black September guerrilla organization stormed the Israeli quarters, killing two members of the Israeli team and holding nine others hostage for the release of 200 Palestinian guerrillas held in Israel. After the Israeli government had refused to bargain and negotiations with West German officials had failed, the guerrillas, led to believe they would be flown to an Arab country, were taken to Fürstenfeldbruck military airfield where police sharpshooters opened fire on the guerrillas in a rescue attempt; all the hostages, five guerrillas, and one policeman were killed. (*See* SPORTING RECORD: *Special Report.*) An inquiry into the incident by the federal and Bavarian officials involved exonerated the police and themselves. Under the West German constitution, formulated after World War II, the Army was forbidden to aid the civil power. Nonetheless, the Bundesgrenzschutz, which had military equipment and training, could have been called in but was not. The government subsequently decided to train a special unit of the Bundesgrenzschutz as an antiterrorist force; a number of Arabs were expelled and restriction and surveillance of all others in West Germany intensified. Three Arabs captured at the airfield were released in response to hijackers' demands on October 30.

United Kingdom. Immediately following his appointment as commissioner of the Metropolitan Police on April 17, 1972, Robert Mark set in motion radical changes in the structure of his forces. These included the rotation of five top Criminal Investigation Department officers, which presaged further switching at senior levels to increase experience and keep men fresh. There were also plans to assign one-third of the Flying Squad officers to divisional CID offices annually, with a complete change of staff every three years. A new 24-hour service, "A 10," was set up to receive public complaints concerning police behaviour. Henceforth local CID officers were to be directly answerable to the uniformed officer in charge of their division instead of to Scotland Yard and all branches were to become interchangeable in their duties; promotion prospects would be greatly improved by this increased flexibility.

The number of indictable offenses known to the police in England and Wales during 1971 was 1,646,081. At the end of 1971 the strength of the police was 96,844. A recruitment campaign continued throughout 1972, bringing strength up to about 100,000. The first part of a report on the rank structure of the police was published and in September a number of changes recommended in it were introduced. Police force boundaries were to be altered to conform with the new local authority areas proposed in a government reorganization bill.

In a report published in September 1972 the House of Commons Select Committee on Race Relations and Immigration urged the establishment of independent tribunals to look into immigrants' complaints against the police. A national crime prevention campaign during the year placed special emphasis on the protection of dwellings and cars; a second national conference of crime prevention panels was held in London in July. In September the Association of Chief Police Officers expressed apprehension that with Britain's entry into the EEC British hijackers and experts in fraud would be tempted to the less sophisticated continent for fresh pickings.

France. The penalties imposed in the fall of 1971 by the minister of the interior, Raymond Marcellin (by which one police union leader was discharged and four others were retired), did nothing to decrease the potential militancy of the police in 1972. Nonetheless there was a relative slackening of tension, which allowed Marcellin to withdraw all but one of the penalties. Some satisfaction was given to police demands: numbers were increased, certain bonuses were raised, and two new cadres were set up to facilitate promotion from within the force. At the second congress of the Federation of Police Unions, held in June 1972 in Paris, participants attacked the manner in which police forces were used to suppress demonstrations, condemned the militia or auxiliary police set up by some major enterprises such as Renault, and protested low police wages. Days of protest to demand higher wages and salaries were to be organized in cooperation with other public service unions. The "moral defense" of the police service remained a priority, but scandals in the fall of 1972 in the region of Lyons, which revealed the involvement of certain police officers in cases of prostitution, were not of a type to improve the police's public image. In a communiqué dated Sept. 1, 1972, the minister of the interior admitted that there had been "some deplorable weaknesses" and announced a reorganization of the central body concerned with the suppression of the white-slave trade. A proposal for reforming the judicial police (Garde des Sceaux) was under review. This corps was once more to be named "criminal police"; its 17 regional bodies were to be replaced by nine directorates and 42 mobile brigades.

Police beat a University of Minnesota student during a campus protest in May 1972 over a step-up of the war in Vietnam. Tear gas was used by police, rocks and bottles by the students.

UPI COMPIX

Italy. Interior Minister Mariano Rumor announced in March that he was determined "to break the chain of robberies and crime" flourishing in Italy. The two major, often rival law enforcement agencies, the Public Security Police and the paramilitary Carabinieri, were under orders to coordinate efforts. Police were advised not to ask for days off during the electoral campaign.

Scandinavia. Total strength of the Danish police on Jan. 1, 1972, was 8,196. Reported offenses increased from 263,000 in 1970 to 299,000 in 1971 and included 2,700 sexual offenses, up from 2,460 in 1970 after five years of modest but regular decreases. After nearly five years of deliberation and debate, a bill reducing the number of police districts from 72 to 54 was passed in June. The power of chief constables was extended when they were ruled competent to prosecute cases of drunken or careless driving, in addition to other more minor offenses. This reform, it was hoped would reduce the work of the seven local public prosecutors by some 50%.

In Norway serious thefts reported to the police had almost doubled in number between 1962 and 1972 and violence among the young was increasing even in small townships. After much controversy over the arming of the police, in the spring the Department of Justice decided that special police patrols should carry guns on duty. To combat the rising toll of road accidents the police inaugurated experimental traffic patrols consisting of a civilian police car and a uniformed constable on a motorcycle in continuous radio contact. Serious traffic offenses could be reported by the car driver to the motorcyclist, who would then overtake and apprehend the offender. Protesting inadequate resources for development, the director of Norway's only police academy resigned in 1972.

U.S.S.R. The number of crimes reported in 1972 declined sharply. Experimental teams were established to concentrate on preventive and corrective work among individuals who violated public order but did not commit crimes, and among those whose punishment did not involve imprisonment. The Ministry of Internal Affairs increased its street patrols, especially at night, and continued to furnish shops, storehouses, and homes with burglar alarm systems. Research continued to optimize traffic control and minimize road accidents. Booklets and articles describing the role and history of the militia were being prepared for issue on the 50th anniversary of the U.S.S.R.

Australia. While the crime rate continued to increase in 1972, police had fewer public demonstrations and protests to deal with than in recent years. Problems of recruiting, promotion, and conditions of employment received renewed attention. Although the Victoria police reported that applications to join the force had doubled since the 1971 St. Johnston report was published, the forces in South Australia, the Northern Territory, and New South Wales recorded recruiting difficulties. Changes in police leadership occurred in New South Wales and South Australia with the retirement of two veteran commissioners. A former English chief constable was appointed to head the South Australia force. Shortly after assuming office he was confronted with a major scandal involving allegations of police brutality.

A disturbing increase was noted in the number of Australian police killed in the execution of their duties. Responding to police concern about the deaths of three officers in 1971, the New South Wales government announced it would provide increased compensation to police widows; modern firearms were also issued to police. Following reports that figures from the U.S. organized crime world were becoming involved in Australian gambling and club activities, the improvement of crime intelligence operations formed one of the main subjects of discussion among police chiefs in 1972. Despite three years of discussion and the enactment of enabling legislation, the establishment of a Commonwealth Institute of Criminology remained stalled in 1972 because of political difficulties between the various state governments and the Commonwealth. (x.)

United States. FBI Uniform Crime Reports revealed that in 1971 U.S. cities had an average of 2.4 police employees per 1,000 inhabitants, an increase of 4% over 1970; civilian employees comprised 13.7% of all city police personnel. Males represented 99% of all sworn personnel in cities, 97% in suburban areas, and 94% in rural areas. However, the use of women to patrol the streets appeared to be a new development in urban law enforcement. A report on "Women in Policing" published in June 1972 by the Police Foundation indicated a reduction of "the incidence of violence between police officers and citizens when women are assigned to patrol." Despite the apparent benefits of using policewomen for a wider range of duties, there was deep resentment against the concept in many departments.

U.S. law enforcement agencies made an estimated 8.6 million arrests nationally in 1971 for all criminal acts except traffic offenses, an increase of 3% over 1970. This also represented an increase of 26% over the past five years, with the arrests of persons under 18 up 40%. Law enforcement agencies solved 84% of the murder offenses, 55% of forcible rapes, 66% of aggravated assaults, and 27% of robbery offenses. In the property crime categories, however, they cleared only 19% of the burglaries, 19% of the larcenies, and 16% of the auto thefts. In an effort to counter the low solution rate for burglaries New York City became one of 400 cities initiating a burglary prevention program. In eight precincts electric engraving pencils were loaned to residents who could mark personal property with their Social Security numbers, inventory the property, and deposit the records with the police. In Dallas, Tex., which started the program in November 1971, only 900 persons had taken advantage of it. Cities and counties across the U.S. were also following the lead of Oakland, Calif., by adding minimum security requirements to their building codes. In Baltimore, Md., a bicycle patrol was initiated following an epidemic of burglaries in residential areas where patrol cars had difficulty operating in alleys.

State police and highway patrol organizations employed 57,131 persons in 1971, an increase of 4% over 1970. In April 1972, the *New York Times* revealed that only five states—California, Illinois, Maryland, New Jersey, and Pennsylvania—had more than ten blacks in their uniformed state police forces. Illinois, with 28, had the highest percentage but these men represented only 1.64% of the 1,700 men on the force. In February a federal district court ordered the Alabama Department of Public Safety to begin an immediate campaign of black recruitment that was to continue until the presently all-white state police force was 25% black. Security personnel for private companies totaled 289,000 and cost $2.5 billion a year. A study for the Justice Department released in April concluded that private personnel were frequently ill-trained, sometimes corrupt, and in many states virtually unregulated.

There were 126 law enforcement officers killed due to felonious criminal action in 1971, compared with 100 in 1970 and 86 in 1969. Of these murders 121 were perpetrated by firearms—94 by handguns. On March 9, 1972, three Detroit policemen burst into an apartment where five sheriff's deputies were playing cards, killing one deputy and wounding three others. At their trial the three officers said they had seen a man with a gun enter the apartment building and had followed him; they were acquitted on August 11. Both the Detroit Police Department and the Wayne County sheriff's office called the shooting a "tragic mix-up." The policemen were members of a special unit called STRESS, for "Stop the robberies—enjoy safe streets," to reduce street crime. Since the unit's inception in January 1970, 14 persons, 13 of whom were black, had been shot to death by STRESS officers. Many black leaders denounced the program and demanded its abolishment.

In January 1972 it was reported that police corruption, including charges of selling heroin and accepting payoffs from gamblers and prostitutes, had been uncovered in police departments and sheriffs' offices in at least 23 states; grand juries in the District of Columbia investigated allegations of kickbacks, shakedowns, and perjury involving at least 16 policemen. In Chicago, several policemen were indicted by federal grand juries in connection with alleged shakedowns of taverns and in June a federal source reported that five Chicago policemen were considered suspects as members of an "assassin squad" that was part of a nationwide war to gain control of narcotics traffic in big city ghettos.

In August the New York City Police Department was accused of failing to investigate reports given to it by a federal agency between 1968 and 1970 that 72 policemen—from patrolman to captain—were "improperly engaged in the narcotics traffic."

The Knapp Commission, a blue ribbon panel of

private citizens headed by Whitman Knapp and appointed in May 1970 to investigate the New York City Police Department, reported on Aug. 6, 1972, that it found a pattern of widespread corruption in the department ranging from free meals to "staggering" payoffs in narcotics. Mayor John Lindsay's office was also criticized for having failed to take adequate steps when charges of extensive corruption had been made four years earlier. On September 19 New York Gov. Nelson Rockefeller announced that he was appointing a "superprosecutor" to investigate corruption among policemen, prosecutors, and judges.

A report filed with Congress on May 1, 1972, disclosed that court-approved wiretapping rose by 37% in 1971. Of the 816 wiretaps authorized, 570 involved gamblers and 126 persons in narcotics; they were used mostly in New York and in New Jersey, with the remainder concentrated in cities where federal strike forces against organized crime had been active.

(VIRGIL W. PETERSON)

See also Crime; Law; Prisons and Penology; Race Relations.

ENCYCLOPÆDIA BRITANNICA FILMS. *Our Community Services* (1969).

Political Parties

The following table is a general world guide to political parties. All countries that were independent on Dec. 1, 1972, are included; there are a number for which no analysis of political activities is given.

Parties are included in most instances only if represented in parliaments (in the lower house in bicameral legislatures), but the figures in the last column of the table do not necessarily add up to the total number of seats in parliament because independents and certain small political groupings are sometimes omitted. The date of the most recent general election follows the name of the country.

The code letters in the affiliation column show the relative political position of the parties within each country; there is, therefore, no entry in this column for single-party states. There are obvious difficulties involved in labeling parties within the political spectrum of a given country. The key chosen is as follows: F—fascist; ER—extreme right; R—right; CR—centre right; C—centre; L—non-Marxist left; SD—social-democratic; S—socialist; EL—extreme left; and K—Communist.

The percentages in the column "Voting strength" indicate proportions of the valid votes cast for the respective parties, or the number of registered voters who went to the polls in single-party states.

COUNTRY AND NAME OF PARTY	Affiliation	Voting strength	Parliamentary representation
Afghanistan (1969)			
Royal government with an elected House of the People (Wolesi Jirga)	—	—	216
Albania (1970)			
Albanian Labour (Communist)	—	100%	214
Algeria			
Military government since June 19, 1965	—	—	—
Andorra (1969)			
No parties	—	—	24
Argentina			
Military government since June 28, 1966	—	—	—
Australia (1972)			
Country (Conservative)	R	...	20
Liberal	CR	...	38
Democratic Labor (DLP)	C	...	—
Australian Labor (ALP)	L	...	67
Austria (1971)			
Freiheitliche Partei Österreichs	R	5.4%	10
Österreichische Volkspartei	C	43.0%	80
Sozialistische Partei Österreichs	SD	50.0%	93
Kommunistische Partei Österreichs	K	1.4%	0
Bahrain			
Emirate	—	—	—
Bangladesh			
Provisional government formed in December 1971	—	—	—
Barbados (1971)			
Democratic Labour Party	C	...	18
Barbados Labour Party	L	...	6
Belgium (1971)			
Volksunie (Flemish)	R	11.0%	21
Front Démocratique des Bruxellois Francophones / Rassemblement Wallon	R	11.4%	24
Parti pour la Liberté et le Progrès	CR	16.7%	34
Parti Social-Chrétien / Christelijk Volks-Partij	C	30.0%	67
Parti Socialiste Belge	SD	27.2%	61
Parti Communiste Belge	K	3.2%	5
Bhutan			
No parties	—	—	130
Bolivia			
Military government since Sept. 26, 1969	—	—	—
Botswana (1969)			
Botswana Democratic Party	C	...	24
Botswana People's Party	L	...	3
Botswana National Front	EL	...	3
Botswana Independent Party	L	...	1
Brazil (1970)			
Aliança Renovadora Nacional	CR	...	223
Movimento Democratico Brasileiro	L	...	87
Bulgaria (1971)			
Bulgarian Communist 266, Agrarian Union 100, Nonparty 34 (Fatherland Front)	—	99.9%	400
Burma			
Military government since March 2, 1962	—	—	—
Burundi			
Military government since Nov. 28, 1966	—	—	—
Cambodia (1972)			
Socio-Republican Party	—	...	26
Cameroon (1969)			
Union Nationale Camérounaise	—	...	50
Canada (1972)			
Social Credit	R	7%	15
Progressive Conservative	CR	35%	107
Liberal	C	38.3%	109
New Democratic	L	17.8%	31
Central African Republic			
Military government since Jan. 1, 1966	—	—	—
Ceylon (Sri Lanka; 1970)			
United National	R	34.2%	17
Sri Lanka Freedom	CR	33.0%	91
Federal (Tamil)	C	4.4%	13
Lanka Sama Samaja (Trotskyist)	S	7.9%	19
Communist	K	3.0%	6
Others	—	...	5
Chad (1969)			
Union pour le Progrès du Tchad	—	...	75
Chile (1969)			
Partido Nacional	R	20.9%	34
Partido Radical	C	13.4%	24
Partido Demócrata-Cristiano	C	31.1%	55
Partido Socialista Chileno	S	12.8%	15
Partido Comunista de Chile	K	16.6%	22
China, People's Republic of			
Communist (Kungchan-tang)	—	—	—
Colombia (1970)			
Alianza Nacional Popular	R	...	72
Partido Conservador	R	...	90 (Conservador and Liberal together)
Partido Liberal	C		
Congo			
Military government since September 1968	—	—	—
Costa Rica (1970)			
Partido de Liberación Nacional	R	...	32
Partido de Unificación Nacional	C	...	22
Acción Socialista	L	...	2
Cuba			
Partido Comunista de Cuba	—	—	—
Cyprus (1970)			
Greek-Cypriot			
Progressive Front	R	...	7
Unified Party	C	...	15
Democratic Centre Union	L	...	2
Independents	—	...	2
Progressive Party of Working People	K	...	9
Turkish-Cypriot			
National Solidarity	—	...	15
Czechoslovakia (1971)			
National Front	—	99.8%	350
Dahomey			
Military government since Oct. 26, 1972	—	—	—

COUNTRY AND NAME OF PARTY	Affiliation	Voting strength	Parliamentary representation
Denmark (1971)			
Conservative	R	16.7%	31
Liberal Democratic (Venstre)	C	15.6%	30
Radical-Liberal	C	14.3%	27
Social Democratic	SD	37.3%	70
Socialist People's	S	9.1%	19
Communist	K	1.4%	0
Faeroe Islands and Greenland	—	...	2
Dominican Republic (1966)			
Partido Reformista	R	...	48
Partido Revolucionario Dominicano	C	...	26
Ecuador (1968)			
Alianza Popular	R	...	...
Izquierda Democrática	L	...	...
Egypt (1971)			
Arab Socialist Union	—	...	338
El Salvador (1972)			
Partido de Conciliación Nacional	R	...	38
Union Nacional de Oposicion	C	...	7
Partido Popular Salvadoreño	L	...	6
Equatorial Guinea (1968)			
Movimiento por Unión Nacional de Guiné Ecuadorial (MUNGE) } Idea Popular de Guiné Ecuadorial (IPGE) } Movimiento Nacional por Liberación de Guiné Ecuadorial (MONALIGE)	—	...	35
Ethiopia (1965)			
Imperial government with an elected Yeheg Memria (lower chamber)	—	—	250
Fiji (1972)			
Alliance Party (mainly Fijian)	—	...	33
National Federation Party (mainly Indian)	—	...	19
Finland (1972)			
Kansallinen Kokoomus Poulue (Cons.)	R	17.5%	34
Svenskapartiet (Swedish Party)	R	5.3%	10
Keskusliitto (Centre, ex-Agrarian)	C	16.4%	35
Christian League	C	2.5%	4
Kansan Poulue (Liberal)	C	5.1%	7
Rural Party	L	9.2%	18
Sosialidemokraatinen Poulue	SD	25.8%	55
People's Democratic League	K	17.1%	37
France (1968)			
Extreme right	ER	0.2%	—
Union des Démocrates pour la République (Gaullists)	CR	38.1%	292
Independent Republicans	CR	5.1%	61
Centre Démocrate	C	10.8%	33
Fédération de la Gauche Démocrate et Socialiste	L	18.0%	57
Parti Socialiste Unifié	EL	4.1%	10
Parti Communiste Français	K	22.1%	34
Gabon (1969)			
Parti Démocratique Gabonais	—	—	—
Gambia, The (1972)			
People's Progressive Party	C	...	28
United Party	L	...	3
German Democratic Republic (1971)			
National Front	—	99.9%	434
Germany, Federal Republic of (1972)			
Nationaldemokratische Partei Deutschlands	F	0.6%	—
Christlich-Soziale Union	R }	44.8%	{ 48
Christlich-Demokratische Union	R }		{ 177
Freie Demokratische Partei	C	8.4%	41
Sozialdemokratische Partei Deutschlands	SD	45.9%	230
Deutsche Kommunistische Partei	K	0.3%	—
Ghana			
Military government since Jan. 13, 1972	—	—	—
Greece			
Military government since April 21, 1967	—	—	—
Guatemala (1970)			
Movimiento de Liberación Nacional	R	...	31
Partido Institucional Democrático	CR	42.9%	19
Democracia Cristiana Guatemalteca	C	21.5%	5
Partido Revolucionario	L	35.6%	...
Guinea (1968)			
Parti Démocratique de Guinée	—	—	75
Guyana (1968)			
People's National Congress	C	...	30
United Force	L	...	4
People's Progressive Party	EL	...	19
Haiti			
Presidential dictatorship since 1957	—	—	—
Honduras (1971)			
Partido Nacional	R	...	33
Partido Liberal	C	...	32
Hungary (1971)			
Patriotic People's Front	—	98.9%	352
Iceland (1971)			
Independence (Conservative)	R	36.2%	22
Progressive	C	25.2%	17
Liberal Left	L	8.9%	5
Social Democratic	SD	10.4%	6
People's Union	EL	17.1%	10
India (1971)			
Jan Sangh (Hindu Nationalist)	ER	...	22
Swatantra (Freedom)	R	...	7
Dravida Munnetra Kazhagam	R	...	23
Ruling Congress	C	...	349
Opposition Congress	C	...	16
Praja Socialist	SD	...	2
Samyukta Socialist	S	...	3
Communist (pro-Soviet)	K	...	24
Communist (pro-Chinese)	K	...	25
Independents and others	—	...	43
Indonesia (1971)			
Sekber Golkar (Functional Groups)	—	...	261
Partai Nasional Indonesia	R	...	20
Nahdatul Ulama (Muslim Teachers)	R	...	58
Partai Sarikat Islam Indonesia (United Muslims)	C	...	10
Perti (Islamic Party)	C	...	2
Parmusi (Liberal Muslims)	C	...	24
Partai Keristen Indonesia (Protestants)	C	...	7
Partai Katholik	C	...	3
Partai Murba (Party of the Masses)	EL	...	0
West Irian	—	...	9
Iran (1971)			
Iran Novin (New Iran)	R	...	226
Mardom (People's) Party	C	...	36
Pan-Iranian Party	C	...	1
Religious groups	—	...	5
Iraq			
Military governments since 1958	—	—	—
Ireland (1969)			
Fianna Fail (Sons of Destiny)	C	...	75
Fine Gael (United Ireland)	C	...	50
Labour	L	...	18
Israel (1969)			
Free Centre	ER	1.2%	2
Gahal (Herut-Liberal Alignment)	R	21.7%	26
National Religious	C	9.7%	12
Agudat Israel	C	3.2%	4
Poalei Agudat Israel	C	1.8%	2
Independent Liberal	C	3.2%	4
State List (Ben-Gurion)	L	3.1%	4
Maarakh (Labour Alignment)	L	46.2%	56
Two Arab lists	L	...	4
Haolam Hazé (Avnery)	L	1.2%	2
Communist (Maki or pro-Israel)	K	1.2%	1
Communist (Rakah or pro-Arab)	K	2.8%	3
Italy (1972)			
Movimento Sociale Italiano	F }	8.7%	56
Partito di Unita Monarchica	R }		
Partito Liberale Italiano	CR	3.9%	20
Democrazia Cristiana	C	38.8%	267
Partito Repubblicano Italiano	C	2.9%	15
Partito Social-Democratico Italiano	L	5.1%	29
Partito Socialista Italiano	SD	9.6%	61
Partito Comunista Italiano	K	27.2%	179
Südtiroler Volkspartei	—	0.5%	3
Ivory Coast (1970)			
Parti Démocratique de la Côte d'Ivoire	—	...	100
Jamaica (1972)			
People's National Party	L	...	37
Jamaica Labour Party	L	...	15
Japan (1972)			
Komeito	CR	8.5%	29
Liberal-Democratic	CR	46.9%	271
Democratic Socialist	SD	7.0%	19
Socialist	S	21.9%	118
Communist	K	10.5%	38
Independents	—	—	16
Jordan			
Royal government, no parties	—	—	60
Kenya (1969)			
Kenya African National Union	—	—	171
Korea, North (1967)			
Korean Workers' (Communist) Party	...	100%	300
Korea, South			
Presidential dictatorship since Oct. 17, 1972	—	—	—
Kuwait			
Princely government	—	—	30
Laos			
Royal government; pro-Communist Neo Lao Hak Sat party controls area bordering North Vietnam	—	—	—
Lebanon (1972)			
Maronites (Roman Catholics)	—	...	30
Greek Catholics (Melchites)	—	...	6
Armenian Catholics	—	...	1
Armenian Orthodox	—	...	4
Greek Orthodox	—	...	11
Other Christians	—	...	2
Sunni Muslims	—	...	20
Shia Muslims	—	...	19
Druzes (Muslim heretics)	—	...	6

COUNTRY AND NAME OF PARTY	Affiliation	Voting strength	Parliamentary representation
Lesotho (1970)			
Constitution suspended Jan. 30, 1970, following the apparent defeat of the ruling National Party in the Jan. 27 general election	—	—	—
Liberia (1968)			
True Whig Party	—	...	41
Libya			
Military government since Sept. 1, 1969	—	—	—
Liechtenstein (1970)			
Vaterlandische Union	CR	...	8
Fortschrittliche Burgerpartei	C	...	7
Christlich-Soziale Partei	C	...	—
Luxembourg (1968)			
Parti Chrétien-Social	CR	35.3%	21
Parti Libéral	C	16.6%	11
Parti Ouvrier Socialiste	SD	32 3%	18
Parti Communiste	K	15.5%	6
Malagasy Republic			
Military government since Oct. 13, 1972	—	—	—
Malawi (1971)			
Malawi Congress Party	CR	...	58
Malaysia			
Malaya (1969)			
Federal Alliance Party	R	...	66
Panmalayan Islamic Party	R	...	12
Gerakan Rakyat Malaysia	C	...	8
Democratic Action (Chinese)	L	...	13
People's Progressive Party	K	...	4
Sarawak (1970)			
Federal Alliance Party	R	...	10
Opposition groups	L	...	14
Sabah (1970)			
Federal Alliance Party	R	...	6
Opposition groups	L	...	10
Maldives (1965)			
Government by the Didi family	—	...	54
Mali			
Military government since Nov. 19, 1968	—	—	—
Malta (1971)			
Nationalist Party	R	48.1%	27
Malta Labour Party	SD	50.8%	28
Mauritania (1965)			
Parti du Peuple Mauritanien	—	92%	40
Mauritius (1967)			
Independence Party (Indian-dominated)	C	...	39
Parti Mauricien Social-Démocrate	L	...	23
Mexico (1970)			
Partido Acción Nacional	CR	13.8%	20
Partido Revolucionario Institucional	C	84.4%	178
Partido Auténtico de la Revolución Mexicana	L	0.9%	5
Partido Popular Socialista	S	0.5%	10
Monaco (1968)			
Union Nationale et Démocratique	—	...	18
Mongolia (1967)			
Mongolian People's Revolutionary Party	—	99%	295
Morocco (1970)			
Independents (pro-government)	CR	...	159
Popular Movement	C	...	60
Istiqlal	C	...	8
National Union of Popular Forces	L	...	1
Others	—	...	12
Nauru (1971)			
No political parties	—	...	18
Nepal			
Royal government since December 1960	—	—	—
Netherlands (1972)			
Statkundig Gereformeerde Partij	R	2.2%	3
Boerenpartij (Farmers' Party)	R	1.9%	3
Anti-Revolutionaire Partij (Calvinist)	CR	8.8%	14
Christelijk Historische Unie (Protestant)	CR	4.8%	7
Katholieke Volkspartij	C	17.7%	27
Volkspartij voor Vrijheid en Democratie	C	14.4%	22
Democraten '66 (Nonconformist reformers)	C	4.2%	6
Democraten Socialisten-70	L	4.1%	6
Partij van de Arbeid	SD	27.4%	43
Pacifistisch Socialistische Partij	S	1.5%	2
Communistische Partij	K	4.5%	7
Five other parties	—	8.5%	10
New Zealand (1972)			
National (Conservative)	CR	41.0%	31
Labour Party	L	48.4%	56
Nicaragua (1967)			
Partido Liberal Nacionalista (Somoza)	R	...	36
Partido Conservador Tradicionalista	R	...	15
Partido Demócrata Cristiano	C	...	2
Partido Liberal Independenta	C	...	1
Niger (1970)			
Parti Progressiste Nigérien	—	...	50
Nigeria			
Military governments since Jan. 15, 1966	—	—	—
Norway (1969)			
Høyre (Conservative)	R	19.4%	29
Kristelig Folkeparti	CR	9.4%	14
Senterpartiet (ex-Agrarian)	C	10.6%	20
Venstre (Liberal)	C	9.3%	13
Arbeiderpartiet (Labour)	SD	46.7%	74
Sosialistisk Folkeparti	S	3.5%	—
Norges Kommunistiske Parti	K	1.0%	—
Oman			
Sultanate	—	—	—

COUNTRY AND NAME OF PARTY	Affiliation	Voting strength	Parliamentary representation
Pakistan			
Provisional government since December 1971	—	—	—
Panama (1972)			
No political parties	—	—	505
Paraguay (1967)			
Partido Colorado (Stroessner)	R	69.4%	80
Partido Liberal Radical	C	21.5%	29
Partido Liberal	C	6.2%	8
Partido Revolucionario (Febrerista)	SD	2.8%	3
Peru			
Military government since Oct. 3, 1968	—	—	—
Philippines			
Martial law since Sept. 21, 1972	—	—	—
Poland (1972)			
Front of National Unity:	—	99.5%	
Polska Zjednoczona Partia Robotnicza			255
Zjednoczone Stronnictwo Ludowe			117
Stronnictwo Demokratyczne			39
Nonparty			49
Portugal (1969)			
Acção Nacional Popular	—	...	130
Qatar			
Emirate	—	—	—
Rhodesia (1970)			
Rhodesian Front (European)	R	70%	50
Centre Party (mainly African)	C	10%	7
National People's Union (African)	L	...	1
Others (elected by councils of chiefs)	—	...	8
Romania (1969)			
People's Front: Partidul Comunist Romîn; Nonparty	—	99.75%	465
Rwanda (1965)			
Parmehutu Party	—	...	47
San Marino (1969)			
Partito Democratico-Cristiano	CR	...	27
Partito Social-Democratico	SD	...	11
Partito Socialista	S	...	7
Partito Communista (pro-Soviet)	K	...	14
Partito Communista (pro-Chinese)	K	...	1
Saudi Arabia			
Royal government	—	—	—
Senegal (1968)			
Union Progressiste Sénégalaise	—	...	80
Sierra Leone (1967)			
All People's Congress	—	...	48
Sierra Leone People's Party	—	...	12
Singapore (1972)			
People's Action Party	C	...	65
Four opposition parties	—	—	—
Somalia			
Military government since Oct. 21, 1969	—	—	—
South Africa (1970)			
Nationalist Party	R	...	117
United Party	C	...	47
Progressive Party	L	...	1
Spain (1971)			
Movimiento Nacional	—	...	558
Sudan			
Military government since May 25, 1969	—	—	—
Swaziland (1972)			
Imbokodvo Party	...	...	21
Congress Party	...	...	3
Sweden (1970)			
Moderata Samlingspartiet (ex-Höger)	R	11.5%	41
Centerpartiet (ex-Agrarian)	CR	19.9%	71
Folkpartiet (Liberal)	C	16.2%	58
Socialdemokratiska Arbetarepartiet	SD	45.3%	163
Vänsterpartiet Kommunisterna	K	4.8%	17
Switzerland (1971)			
National Action	R	...	4
Republican Movement	R	...	7
Conservative Christian Social People's	R	20.4%	44
Evangelical People's	R	1.9%	3
Swiss People's (formerly Farmers and Artisans)	CR	11.4%	23
Radical Democratic (Freisinnig)	C	21.3%	49
League of Independents	C	7.6%	13
Liberal Democratic	L	2.3%	6
Social Democratic	SD	23.1%	46
Communist (Partei der Arbeit)	K	2.7%	5
Syria			
Baath and military government	—	—	—
Taiwan (Republic of China)			
Nationalist (Kuomintang)	—	—	773
Tanzania (1970)			
Tanganyika African National Union (elected)	C	...	120
Zanzibar Afro-Shirazi Party (nominated)	L	—	52
Thailand			
Royal and military government	—	—	—
Togo			
Military government since Jan. 13, 1967	—	—	—
Tonga (1972)			
Legislative Assembly of seven nobles, seven ministers, and seven elected delegates	—	—	21

COUNTRY AND NAME OF PARTY	Affiliation	Voting strength	Parliamentary representation
Trinidad and Tobago (1971)			
People's National Movement	C	...	36
Action Committee for Dedicated Citizens	L	—	—
Tunisia (1969)			
Destourian Socialist Party	—	—	101
Turkey (1969)			
Turkish Justice	R	56.9%	257
Republican Nation's	R	1.3%	6
Republican People's	C	31.8%	144
Reliance (breakaway from RPP)	C	3.3%	15
Union	C	1.8%	8
New Turkey	C	1.3%	6
Nationalist Action (Peasants)	L	0.2%	1
Turkish Workers'	EL	0.4%	2
Uganda			
Uganda People's Congress	—	...	...
Union of Soviet Socialist Republics (1970)			
Communist Party of the Soviet Union	—	99.74%	767
United Arab Emirates			
Emirate	—	—	—
United Kingdom (1970)			
Conservative and Unionist	R	46.4%	330
Liberal	C	7.4%	6
Labour	L	43.0%	287
Others	—	...	7
United States (1972)			
Republican	CR	...	191
Democratic	C	...	244
Upper Volta (1970)			
Union Démocratique Voltaique	CR	...	37
Parti du Regroupement Africain	C	...	12
Mouvement de Libération Nationale	L	...	6
Uruguay (1971)			
Partido Nacional (Blanco)	R	40.3%	...
Partido Colorado (Liberal)	C	41.0%	...
Frente Amplio	EL	18.7%	...
Venezuela (1968)			
Cruzada Cívica Nacional	ER	11.4%	21
Unión Republicana Democrática	R	9.6%	17
Frente Nacional Democrático	R	2.6%	5
Fuerza Democrática Popular	C	5.5%	10
Comitado Organización Política Electoral Independiente (COPEI; Social Christians)	C	25.4%	57
Acción Democrática	C	28.0%	68
Movimiento Electoral del Pueblo	L	14.5%	27
Unión para Avanzar (Communist)	K	2.8%	5
Vietnam, North (1971)			
Lao Dong (Communist Party)	—	...	420
Vietnam, South (1971)			
National coalition	—	...	152
Western Samoa (1970)			
No political parties	—	...	45
Yemen (Aden)			
National Liberation Front	—	—	—
Yemen (San'a')			
Republican regime since November 1967	—	—	—
Yugoslavia (1969)			
League of Communists of Yugoslavia / Socialist Alliance of the Working People	—	...	670
Zaire (1970)			
Mouvement Populaire de la Révolution	—	98.3%	420
Zambia (1968)			
United National Independence Party	—	—	—

(K. M. SMOGORZEWSKI)

Political Science

The research, teaching, and writings of political scientists in 1972 continued to be affected by the rapid evolution of the international scene and of national political patterns in many countries. U.S. Pres. Richard Nixon's visit to Peking and the implementation of West German Chancellor Willy Brandt's *Ostpolitik* opened the way to a major rearrangement of power relations throughout Asia and Western Europe. Analyzing and explaining these changes and their effects on domestic politics proved to be a major challenge for political science, only too prone in recent years to present as timeless the carefully drawn conclusions of highly refined research carried out with little concern for the historical context.

The relative calm prevailing in most universities, in contrast with previous years, was in itself a surprise. Agitation and militancy had often been explained in terms that seemed to imply they had become relatively permanent phenomena. The lowering of international tensions, at least among the big powers, and the slow progress toward peace in Vietnam clearly had something to do with the unexpected quiet. Political scientists who were not actively engaged in explaining such immediate events were encouraged to get down again to serious specialist work, but most of them could not be oblivious to the effect of international relations on domestic political behaviour.

In the U.S. many political scientists took an active part in the primary elections, the conventions of the major parties, and the campaign efforts of President Nixon and Sen. George McGovern—in much larger numbers, as usual, on the Democratic side. As in previous years, however, the liberalism of the discipline excluded "radical" control of the American Political Science Association. In the mail ballot closed on Nov. 17, 1971, Robert E. Ward, the candidate of the APSA nominating committee for the presidency of APSA for 1972–73, was elected by 4,200 votes, as against 3,035 for Richard A. Falk, an outspoken opponent of the Vietnam war who later became vice-chairman of the National Committee for Impeachment (of President Nixon).

Among new fields of professional attention was that of scientific information. Under APSA auspices, a group headed by Carl Beck of the University of Pittsburgh compiled a thesaurus of political science descriptors and made plans for the establishment of a U.S. centre for political science abstracts, to work in close cooperation with the *International Political Science Abstracts*.

The newly established European Consortium for Political Research held several meetings, workshops, and summer schools. Participation in its activities and the increase in its institutional membership (to 40 institutions by the end of the year) proved that it had filled a real need. Its executive committee met in Paris on September 29 and decided to hold eight simultaneous workshops, on a variety of topics, at Mannheim, W.Ger., in April 1973.

The Executive Committee of the International Political Science Association, meeting on September 14 at Bucharest, Rom., made final preparations for the ninth World Congress of Political Science, to be held in Montreal, Aug. 18–25, 1973. More than a thousand political scientists were expected to attend the congress, which would be organized around two major themes: "politics between economy and culture" and "key issues in international conflict and peace research." The committee unanimously nominated Jean Laponce of the University of British Columbia as candidate for the presidency of IPSA.

The striking increase in political science journals noted in 1971 continued. Among recent additions were: *American Political Quarterly* (Riverside, Calif.); *Année politique en Belgique* (Brussels); *Boletín de Ciencias políticas y sociales* (Mendoza, Arg.); *Boletín informativo de Ciencia política* (Madrid); *Comparative Politics* (Chicago); *Estudios internacionales* (Santiago, Chile); *Indian Journal of Politics* (Aligarh, India); *Indian Political Science Review* (Delhi, India); *International Relations* (London); *Journal of Political Studies* (Jullundur, India); *Policy Sciences* (New York City); *Preuves* (Paris); *P.S. Political Science Newsletter* (Washington, D.C.); *Revista de Ciencia política* (Rio de Janeiro, Braz.); *Verfassung und Verfassungswirklichkeit* (Opladen, W.Ger.); and *Zeitschrift für Parlamentsfragen* (Opladen). (SERGE HURTIG)

ENCYCLOPÆDIA BRITANNICA FILMS. *The Presidency—Search for a Candidate* (1970); *The Progressive Era* (1971); *The Modern Presidency and the Limits of Power* (1971); *Where's Your Loyalty?* (1972); *Who Needs Rules?* (1972).

Populations and Areas

World population continued to grow at a rapid 2% annual rate, despite increasing action by individuals and many national programs to curb high fertility through birth control programs. Estimated world population for mid-1972 was 3,782,000,000. That was an increase over the midyear estimate for 1971 of 76 million people, which was the current population of East and West Germany combined. If the present rate of growth continued, the world population would double in 35 years. This would be in sharp contrast to the 1,800 years it took for the population to grow from approximately 210 million to the current level. Not surprising, then, was the current view that more population would mean more problems of pollution, economic stagnation, and misery, since most of the growth was occurring in less developed countries, where the growth of human numbers was outstripping ability to feed, clothe, house, or employ.

Latin America, with 300 million people, was growing faster than any other area in the world. At its current annual growth rate of 2.8% a year, the population of the area would double in 25 years. On the other hand, Asia, with 2,000,000,000 people, was responsible for two-thirds of the world population increase during the year. Although its 2.3% growth rate was lower than that of Latin America, its population could double in only 30 years.

LEIF SKOOGFORS—CAMERA PRESS/PICTORIAL PARADE

Feminist groups sell these pro-abortion buttons to raise money for their fight to legalize abortion in the U.S.

Two Asian countries, China and India, were the most populous countries of the world. China was growing at a rate that could double its 787 million population in 41 years. And India, growing faster, could double its 548 million people in only 28 years. The new nation of Bangladesh, formerly East Pakistan, was estimated to have about 75 million people. Pakistan, from which Bangladesh separated, had 67 million. The best estimate suggested a doubling of the population in 21 years.

The total population of Africa was estimated to be 375 million. With a growth rate of 2.6% per year the continent could add another 364 million in 27 years. While this growth was high, Africa's growth could be substantially higher, since the world's highest death rates (21 per 1,000) inhibited the effects of the world's highest birthrates (47 per 1,000). Improved medical programs in Africa could lower death rates.

The countries in the industrial world stood in contrast to Latin America, Asia, and Africa, for in them in general fertility had been dropping over the past decade. In fact, the populations of some European countries were at, or close to, stabilization. These included East and West Germany, Austria, Belgium, Luxembourg, and Hungary. An interesting but special case was West Berlin, which was estimated to be losing population at a rate of 1% per year. The decrease was largely a result of a high death rate and a low birthrate, which stemmed from the unusually large proportion of older people in the population. More than one-fifth of West Berliners were 65 years or older.

Population growth in the Soviet Union and elsewhere among the member countries of the Warsaw Pact was reported to have slowed, primarily as a result of marked drops in birthrates in these countries beginning in the mid-1950s when abortion laws were liberalized. Romania was thought to be typical of the entire bloc. The birthrate had dropped to 12 per 1,000 in December 1966; a tightening of the abortion laws at that time led to an increase by September 1967 to 40 births per 1,000. Since then, however, presumably because of increased use of contraceptives and recourse to illegal abortions, the rate had dropped to 20 per 1,000 in the first quarter of 1971.

The other members of the Warsaw Pact were the U.S.S.R., Poland, East Germany, Bulgaria, Czechoslovakia, and Hungary. Together their total population in 1970 was 348.8 million. An estimated 60% of all pregnancies in Hungary were being aborted, 44% in Bulgaria, 36% in Czechoslovakia, and 23% in Poland. In the Soviet Union itself, with 70% of the total population, the abortion rate was believed to be 60%. One of the most notable effects of the declining birthrate would be its impact on the labour force in upcoming years. With the number of young people entering the work force declining, and with the reserve of peasants and women that was once recruited heavily to help expand industrial output virtually exhausted, future industrial growth in these countries would have to depend on higher output per man-hour.

In the U.S. fertility had also dropped for more than a decade, and the January 1972 birthrate of 17.2 per 1,000 was the lowest on record. The birthrate continued to drop during the first nine months of the year to 16.6 per 1,000, 11% below the rate of a year before. This decrease brought the fertility rate down from 2.39 children per family for the first nine months of 1971 to 2.08 children, a figure below the 2.1 rate necessary for zero population growth, that is, for a population to do no more than replace itself. Factors cited as contributing to the continuing decline included the growing proportion of young women staying single, the number of married women having children later and working longer, and a general desire of women to have smaller families. Other factors might also be the depressed state of the economy in 1972, the increasing use and effectiveness of contraceptives, and the liberalization of abortion laws in several states.

Still, the large number of children that were born during the baby boom years of the 1950s were now entering reproductive ages, and the possibility of an upsurge in the birthrate was strong. In 1972 there were 500,000 more women aged 18 than there had been in 1962 and 900,000 more than in 1952. Any slight upward shift in the fertility rate among these women would cause a significant increase in the population growth rate.

Using the new figures, the U.S. Census Bureau revised its projection of future population growth. With

continued on page 556

Table I. The Ten Largest Nations by Area and Population*

Rank	Area in sq.mi.	Rank	Population
1 U.S.S.R.	8,600,340	1 China	787,176,000†
2 Canada	3,851,809	2 India	547,949,809†
3 China	3,691,500	3 U.S.S.R.	245,066,000†
4 United States	3,615,122‡	4 United States	208,232,000
5 Brazil	3,286,470	5 Indonesia	119,232,499†
6 Australia	2,967,909	6 Japan	106,251,000
7 India	1,261,810	7 Brazil	98,854,300
8 Argentina	1,072,157	8 Bangladesh	75,000,000
9 Sudan	967,494	9 Nigeria	69,252,709
10 Zaire	905,360	10 Germany, West	61,280,600†

*Areas are latest official data available; populations are for 1972.
†1971.
‡Excludes Great Lakes waters and territorial sea.

Table II. Populations and Areas of the Countries of the World

Continent and state	Area in sq.mi.	Population in 000	Persons per sq.mi.
World total	57,901,554	3,707,232	70.7*
AFRICA	11,637,607	375,713	32.3
Algeria	896,588	14,644	16.3
Botswana	220,000	667	3.0
Bouvet Island (Norwegian)	23	—	—
British dependencies	311	61	—
Burundi	10,759	3,615	336.0
Cameroon	179,557	5,836	32.5
Central African Republic	240,377	1,637	6.8
Chad	495,752	3,791	7.6
Congo	132,000	1,089	8.3
Dahomey	43,483	2,792	64.2
Egypt	386,900	34,076	88.1
Equatorial Guinea	10,830	289	26.7
Ethiopia	471,800	25,564	54.2
French dependencies	10,733	830	—
Gabon	103,346	950	9.2
Gambia, The	4,467	375	83.9
Ghana	92,100	8,559	92.9
Guinea	94,925	4,010	42.2
Ivory Coast	123,483	4,420	35.8
Kenya	224,960	12,068	53.6
Lesotho	11,720	1,081	92.2
Liberia	43,000	1,571	36.5
Libya	675,000	2,010	3.0
Malagasy Republic	226,442	7,424	32.8
Malawi	45,747	4,552	99.5
Mali	478,822	5,143	10.7
Mauritania	398,000	1,200	3.0
Mauritius	720	856	1,188.9
Morocco	177,116	15,379	86.8
Niger	458,072	4,243	9.3
Nigeria	356,669	69,253	194.2
Portuguese dependencies	800,300	14,816	—
Rhodesia	150,803	5,590	37.1
Rwanda	10,169	3,842	377.8
Senegal	78,684	4,022	51.1
Sierra Leone	27,699	2,627	94.8
Somalia	246,154	2,864	11.6
South Africa	471,445	22,092	46.9
South West Africa (Namibia)	318,261	746	2.3
Spanish Sahara	102,703	76	0.7
Sudan	967,494	16,489	17.0
Swaziland	6,704	446	66.5
Tanzania	364,943	14,028	38.4
Togo	21,900	1,960	89.5
Tunisia	63,378	5,137	81.1
Uganda	91,452	10,127	110.7
Upper Volta	105,870	5,491	51.9
Zaire	905,360	22,860	25.2
Zambia	290,586	4,515	15.5
ANTARCTICA	5,500,000†	‡	—
Australian Antarctic Territory	2,472,000	—	—
British Antarctic Territory§	650,000	—	—
French Southern and Antarctic Lands	202,916	—	—
Norwegian dependencies	96‖	—	—
Ross Dependency (New Zealand)	160,000	—	—
ASIA (exclusive of U.S.S.R.)	10,720,817	2,082,441	194.2
Afghanistan	250,775	17,480	69.7
Australian dependencies	58	3	—
Bahrain	256	220	859.4
Bangladesh	55,126	75,000	1,360.5
Bhutan	18,000	854	47.4
Brunei (British protected state)	2,226	136	61.1
Burma	261,789	27,600	105.4
Cambodia (Khmer Republic)	69,898	6,968	99.7
China	3,691,500	787,176	213.2
Cyprus	3,572	639	178.9
Hong Kong (British)	400	3,948	9,870.0
India (incl. Jammu and Kashmir)	1,261,810	547,950	434.3
Indonesia	782,658	119,232	152.3
Iran	635,932	30,151	47.4
Iraq¶	168,927	10,074	59.6
Israel	7,992	3,066	383.6
Japan	143,818	106,251	738.8
Jordan	37,737	2,383	63.1
Korea, North	46,800	14,281	305.1
Korea, South	38,022	33,167	872.3
Kuwait	6,880	815	118.5
Laos	91,400	3,033	33.2
Lebanon	3,950	2,126	538.2
Malaysia	127,316	12,324	96.8
Maldives	115	114	991.3
Mongolia	604,000	1,301	2.2
Nepal	54,362	11,290	207.7
Neutral Zone	7,000	...	—
Oman	82,000	750	9.1
Pakistan	310,915	60,000	193.0
Philippines	115,800	39,102	337.7
Portuguese dependencies	5,769	935	—
Qatar	4,400	160	36.4
Saudi Arabia¶	865,000	7,965	9.2
Sikkim (Indian protected state)	2,744	202	73.6
Singapore	226	2,129	9,420.4
Sri Lanka (Ceylon)	25,332	12,711	501.8
Syria	71,498	6,303	88.2
Taiwan	13,892	15,090	1,086.2
Thailand	198,500	35,335	178.0
Turkey	301,380	36,110	119.8
United Arab Emirates	32,300	197	6.1
Vietnam, North	63,360	21,595	340.8
Vietnam, South	67,108	18,900	281.6
Yemen (Aden)	111,074	1,475	13.3
Yemen (San'a')	77,200	5,900	76.4
EUROPE (exclusive of U.S.S.R.)	1,904,687	462,802	243.0
Albania	11,100	2,226	200.5
Andorra	179	21	117.3
Austria	32,375	7,456	230.3
Belgium	11,781	9,695	822.9
British dependencies	298	211	—
Bulgaria	42,823	8,565	200.0
Czechoslovakia	49,373	14,436	292.4
Denmark (incl. Faeroe Islands)	17,169	5,033	—
Finland	130,128	4,634	35.6
France	210,038	51,487	245.1
Germany, East	41,768	17,041	408.0
Germany, West (incl. W. Berlin)	95,979	61,281	638.5
Greece	50,944	8,769	172.1
Hungary	35,919	10,374	288.8
Iceland	39,768	207	5.2
Ireland	27,136	2,978	109.7
Italy	116,313	54,025	464.5
Liechtenstein	62	23	371.0
Luxembourg	999	342	342.3
Malta	122	322	2,639.3
Monaco	0.6	24	40,000.0
Netherlands	15,892	13,270	835.0
Norway (incl. Svalbard and Jan Mayen)	149,153	3,921	—
Poland	120,725	32,852	272.1
Portugal	35,383	8,870	250.7
Romania	91,700	20,470	223.2
San Marino	24	20	833.3
Spain	194,881	34,003	174.5
Sweden	173,731	8,115	46.7
Switzerland	15,941	6,270	393.3
United Kingdom	94,216	55,355	587.5
Vatican City	0.2	0.6	3,000.0
Yugoslavia	98,766	20,505	207.6
NORTH AND CENTRAL AMERICA	9,360,419	325,145	34.7
Barbados	166	244	1,469.9
British dependencies	15,749	889	—
Canada	3,851,809	21,830	5.7
Costa Rica	19,652	1,832	93.2
Cuba	42,827	8,657	202.1
Dominican Republic	18,658	4,305	230.7
El Salvador	8,098	3,649	450.6
French dependencies	1,211	679	—
Greenland (Danish)	840,000	47	0.05
Guatemala	42,042	5,604	133.3
Haiti	10,714	4,244	396.1
Honduras	43,277	2,756	63.7
Jamaica	4,244	1,911	450.3
Mexico	761,600	52,641	69.1
Netherlands Antilles (Dutch)	385	229	594.8
Nicaragua	49,759	1,912	38.4
Panama (excl. Canal Zone)	29,208	1,523	52.1
Trinidad and Tobago	1,980	1,030	520.2
United States	3,615,122	208,232	57.6
United States dependencies	3,918	2,931	—
OCEANIA	3,285,509	19,916	6.1
Australia	2,967,909	12,944	4.4
Australian dependencies	178,467	2,466	—
British dependencies	11,311	232	—
Canton and Enderbury Islands (U.K.-U.S.)	27	—	—
Fiji	7,055	535	75.8
French dependencies	8,725	249	—
Nauru	8	7	875.0
New Hebrides (Fr.-U.K.)	5,700	86	15.1
New Zealand	103,736	2,910	28.1
New Zealand dependencies	197	28	—
Tonga	225	90	400.0
United States dependencies	1,016	221	—
Western Samoa	1,133	148	130.6
SOUTH AMERICA	6,892,175	196,149	28.5
Argentina	1,072,157	23,552	22.0
Bolivia	424,165	5,062	11.9
Brazil	3,286,470	98,854	30.1
Chile	292,257	8,835	30.2
Colombia	439,735	22,490	51.1
Ecuador	109,483	6,598	60.3
Falkland Islands (British)	6,150	2	0.3
French Guiana	34,750	50	1.4
Guyana	83,000	714	8.6
Paraguay	157,047	2,329	14.8
Peru	496,222	13,600	27.4
Surinam (Dutch)	70,060	385	5.5
Uruguay	68,536	2,956	43.1
Venezuela	352,143	10,722	30.4
U.S.S.R.	8,600,340	245,066	28.5

Note: Populations given are latest available UN estimates. A dash (—) in the population column indicates none or negligible; a dash in the density column indicates figure not relevant; three dots (...) indicate not available.

*In computing the world density the area of Antarctica is omitted.

†Estimated area, including some unclaimed territory.

‡Less than 1,000 persons.

§Includes some territory claimed by Argentina and Chile.

‖Insular dependencies only. Norwegian claims to continental Antarctica are undefined.

¶Excluding Iraq-Saudi Arabia neutral zone of 7,000 sq.mi.

Table III. World Census Data

POLITICAL UNIT	Year of census	ENUMERATED POPULATION Total	Male	Percent urban*	AGE DISTRIBUTION 0 to 14	15 to 44	45 and over	ECONOMICALLY ACTIVE Total	Agriculture	Mining and manufacturing
Afars & Issas	1964	82,100	...	57.4	...	...	...	...	...	...
Albania	1960	1,626,315	834,384	30.9	...	...	...	730,800	...	...
Algeria	1966	11,833,126	6,079,900	...	5,947,800†	4,387,700†	1,744,800†	2,335,200	1,300,000	183,500
American Samoa	1970	27,159	13,682	28.3	12,879	10,872	3,408	5,094	110	1,166
Angola	1960	4,830,449‡	2,459,015	10.6	2,011,378	2,177,631	641,440	1,421,966	944,716	26,508
Antigua	1960	54,060‡	25,230	60.1	23,154†	20,964†	9,942†	16,873	12,564	4,084
Argentina	1960	20,008,945	10,034,544	...	5,772,043§	10,486,674§	3,663,094§	7,599,071	1,460,541	1,959,041
Australia	1966	11,550,462	5,816,359	83.2	3,392,488†	4,873,899†	3,284,073†	4,856,455	...	1,368,468
Austria	1961	7,073,807	3,296,400	50.1	1,660,615†	2,729,599†	2,683,593†	3,369,815	767,604	1,093,046
Bahamas	1970	168,812‡	83,661	...	73,601	69,316	25,895	69,791	4,791	3,902
Bahrain	1971	216,078	116,314	...	95,640	90,994	29,444	60,301	3,990	8,464
Barbados	1960	232,327	105,519	40.3	88,882	88,636	54,809	85,040	22,440	13,468
Belgium	1961	9,189,741	4,496,860	66.4	2,333,846†	3,543,729†	3,312,166†	3,512,463	253,922	1,326,732
Bermuda	1970	52,330‡	26,293	7.0	15,520	24,206	12,604	33,948	983	5,837‖
Botswana	1964	543,105	264,535	...	242,424†	204,797†	80,198†	250,678	227,009	1,800¶
Brazil	1970	93,204,379‡	46,330,629	55.9	38,865,773♀	44,048,881♀	10,289,725♀	29,545,293	13,071,385	5,263,805‖
British Honduras	1970	119,934	60,091	54.5	59,138	42,591	18,176	31,306	11,207	4,633
British Solomon Islands	1970	160,998	85,179	...	71,761	66,326	22,911	13,690¶	3,182¶	960¶
British Virgin Islands	1970	10,298	5,481	21.9	3,788	4,237	1,647	3,842	298	195
Brunei	1971	136,256	72,772	63.6	59,136	59,555	17,256	40,012	4,776	4,666
Bulgaria	1965	8,227,866	4,114,167	46.4	2,112,364†	3,789,130†	2,326,372†	4,267,793	1,891,398	1,124,885
Cambodia (Khmer Rep.)	1962	5,740,115	2,880,780	16.0	2,513,300	2,381,215	845,600‡	...	...	...
Canada	1971	21,568,315‡	10,795,370	...	6,380,900	9,419,695	5,767,725	6,458,156δ	648,910δ	1,101,553δ
Canal Zone	1970	44,198	24,254	5.8	14,061	22,588	7,549	9,776	123	281
Cape Verde Islands	1960	199,661	94,027	23.2	99,023□	69,816□	29,358□	105,570	42,387	1,294
Cayman Islands	1960	8,511‡	3,974	41.4	3,020†	3,515†	1,976†	3,132	...	...
Channel Islands										
Guernsey	1971	53,734	25,878	...	12,401	20,456	20,877	23,813	5,494	2,486
Jersey	1961	63,550	30,715	...	12,534†	25,643†	25,373†	30,696	3,259	2,028
Chile	1970	8,853,140	4,321,500	76.0	3,456,700	3,729,320	1,547,300	2,607,360	552,340	490,740
Christmas Island	1971	2,691	1,732	...	829	1,523	339	...	...	...
Colombia	1964	17,484,508	8,614,652	52.8	8,155,529◇	7,022,627◇	2,306,508◇	5,134,059	2,427,059	81,279
Comoro Islands	1966	244,905‡	120,385	13.9	109,364	95,358	42,183	82,090	52,415	11,035
Cook Islands	1971	21,317	10,910	...	10,996	7,463	2,858	5,581	1,224	509
Costa Rica	1963	1,336,274‡	668,957	34.5	636,665	516,395	183,214	395,273	194,309	46,459
Cuba	1970	8,553,395‡	4,374,624	60.5	3,140,712▲	4,919,673▲	493,010▲	...	...	...
Cyprus	1960	573,566‡	281,983	35.9	221,656	226,612	125,298	241,823	93,287	37,718
Czechoslovakia	1970	14,361,557‡	6,990,000	55.6	3,289,533	6,192,976	4,879,048	6,989,000	1,141	3,359+
Denmark	1970	4,937,784	...	79.9	1,146,400¶	2,049,700¶	1,757,400¶	2,409,100¶	257,000¶	677,400¶
Dominica	1970	69,549	32,968	46.2	34,118	22,543	12,888	19,617	7,720	1,551
Dominican Republic	1970	4,006,405	1,998,990	39.8	1,904,425	1,610,915	491,065	...	...	...
Ecuador	1962	4,476,007	2,236,476	36.0	2,014,505†	1,838,160†	623,342†	1,442,591	800,390	215,617
Egypt	1966	30,053,861	15,168,000	40.5	...	...	...	...	...	...
El Salvador	1961	2,510,984	1,236,728	38.5	1,176,744†	1,011,819†	322,421†	807,092	486,213	104,227
Equatorial Guinea	1960	245,989	132,293	...	...	...	...	...	...	...
Faeroe Islands	1970	38,612‡	...	...	...	...	...	...	...	...
Falkland Islands	1962	2,172	1,195	49.4	568⊕	1,134⊕	470⊕	930	359	...
Fiji	1966	476,727	242,747	33.4	232,826†	190,543†	53,112†	125,809	656,921	10,451
Finland	1970	4,622,299‡	2,233,658	50.9	1,120,287	2,068,345	1,433,527	2,128,537	428,991	722,796
France	1968	49,654,556‡	24,196,528	70.0	11,790,960	20,655,544	17,208,052	19,961,852	3,131,320	7,903,324
French Guiana	1961	33,295‡	16,288	75.1	12,127♀	14,296♀	6,872♀	11,981	3,273	...
French Polynesia	1962	84,550	43,106	...	45,232†	34,591†	3,643†	25,593	9,484	5,715
Gabon	1970	950,009	455,339	26.9	336,493	393,875	219,641	...	...	...
Gambia, The	1963	315,486	160,849	8.8	118,586	155,834	41,066	160,000¶	135,000¶	2,500¶
Germany, East	1964	17,011,931‡	7,751,862	72.9	4,262,941†	6,338,075†	6,410,915†	7,657,786	1,267,257	3,140,721
Germany, West	1970	60,650,599	28,866,724	...	14,058,277	24,821,962	21,770,360	26,493,512	1,990,514	12,956,672
Ghana	1970	8,559,313‡	4,247,809	28.9	4,015,965	3,439,456	1,103,892	3,133,047	1,790,806	...
Gibraltar	1970	26,833	12,914	...	2,865	6,333	3,716	11,748	...	258
Gilbert and Ellice Islands	1968	53,517	26,404	14.9	20,323	17,130	7,187	13,121	8,601	496
Greece	1971	8,768,640	4,280,060	53.2	2,180,220	3,710,960	2,877,460	3,283,880	1,330,320	560,860
Greenland	1965	39,600	20,354	...	19,091†	15,752†	4,757†	13,248	3,651	300
Grenada	1960	88,677	40,660	8.2	42,268	30,472	15,937	15,219	10,895	2,657
Guadeloupe	1967	312,724‡	159,760	45.8	139,346	126,281	59,412	...	...	...
Guam	1970	84,996	47,362	25.5	33,701	41,162	10,133	22,112	157	1,386
Guatemala	1964	4,287,997	2,172,456	33.6	1,949,395	1,786,505	551,519	1,362,669	...	...
Guyana	1960	560,330	279,128	15.5	259,228	215,228	85,874	174,730	59,790	32,371
Honduras	1961	1,884,765	939,029	23.2	940,827†	730,153†	213,785†	567,988	379,125	45,779
Hong Kong	1971	3,948,179	2,000,602	...	720,120	880,204	399,278	1,654,907	34,013	737,117
Hungary	1970	10,315,600	4,998,300	45.1	2,167,000	4,564,000	3,584,600	5,001,200	1,287,800	1,828,800
Iceland	1970	204,930‡	...	...	...	...	...	...	...	...
India	1971	547,949,809	283,936,614	19.9	...	...	...	183,605,325	126,011,684	...
Indonesia	1971	119,232,499‡	58,279,166	17.4	52,261,306	50,399,092	15,791,588	40,100,070	24,772,230	3,021,868
Iran	1966	25,078,923	12,981,665	38.1	11,639,200†	9,861,700†	3,642,800†	7,584,085	3,168,515	1,293,912
Iraq	1965	8,261,527	4,205,201	44.1	...	...	...	...	...	...
Ireland	1966	2,884,002	1,449,032	49.2	...	...	...	1,106,000	330,000	277,000
Isle of Man	1971	56,289	26,461	55.7	...	...	...	...	...	...
Israel	1961	2,179,491‡	1,106,069	77.9	786,196	869,045	524,250	751,230	96,420	168,895
Italy	1961	50,623,569‡	24,791,683	47.7	11,549,626◇	22,903,305◇	16,170,638◇	20,096,693	5,657,446	7,886,181‖
Jamaica	1960	1,609,814‡	773,439	32.0	662,508	646,281	301,025	677,003	229,718	94,172
Japan	1970	104,665,171‡	51,238,700	72.1	25,081,700	52,929,100	26,305,900	52,409,200	10,149,000	13,695,700
Jordan	1961	1,706,226	867,597	47.4	815,910**	638,732**	251,584**	389,978	137,757	41,932
Kenya	1969	10,943,000	5,482,000	10.1	5,293,000	4,237,000	1,413,000	...	...	...
Korea, South	1966	29,207,856	14,700,966	33.5	12,851,456	11,975,220	4,381,178	9,325,000	4,826,000	940,000
Kuwait	1970	738,663	419,886	...	319,299	353,210	66,154	233,534	4,060	39,263
Lesotho	1966	969,634	465,784	...	370,390	306,208	172,756	...	...	...
Liberia	1962	1,016,443	503,588	19.7	394,509†	471,553†	150,381†	411,794	298,404	22,913
Libya	1964	1,564,369‡	813,386	...	683,431	630,379	249,160	405,258	146,709	43,636
Liechtenstein	1970	21,350	10,616	...	5,961▲	13,708▲	1,681▲	10,251	634	...
Luxembourg	1966	334,790	164,575	...	75,450	138,781	120,559	164,575	14,554	45,864
Macau	1960	169,299‡	83,897	95.2	68,556†	60,472†	40,271†	37,905	1,717	22,000‡
Malawi	1966	4,039,583	1,913,262	5.0	1,774,766	1,645,740	619,077	...	...	...
Malaysia										
West Malaysia	1957	6,278,758	3,237,579	26.5	2,752,208	2,576,252	950,298	2,164,861	468,317	58,499
East Malaysia	1960	1,198,950	612,462	15.0¶	197,826	199,091	57,504	470,911	381,941	7,451
Maldives	1967	103,801‡	55,346	...	46,086	45,422	12,293	...	...	...

Table III. World Census Data *(Continued)*

POLITICAL UNIT	Year of census	ENUMERATED POPULATION Total	Male	Percent urban*	AGE DISTRIBUTION 0 to 14	15 to 44	45 and over	ECONOMICALLY ACTIVE Total	Agriculture	Mining and manufacturing
Malta	1967	314,216‡	150,598	...	93,759	136,884	83,573	94,367	7,109	22,893
Martinique	1967	320,030	155,212	45.8	139,262	120,406	60,211	89,464	22,746	8,091
Mauritius	1962	681,619	342,306	34.2	323,007†	258,285†	100,327†	187,401	70,866	27,560
Mexico	1970	48,377,363‡	24,140,309	58.6	22,359,416	19,446,516	6,571,029	12,994,395	5,131,666	2,353,814
Monaco	1968	23,035‡	10,424	100.0	2,979	8,273	11,783	10,093	11	2,170
Mongolia	1963	1,018,800‡	508,800	39.5	411,300†	378,100†	227,700†	483,400	279,200	41,900
Montserrat	1970	11,458‡	5,374	11.1	2,285	...	1,281	3,769	759	218
Morocco	1960	11,626,232‡	5,809,172	29.3	5,307,824†	4,738,350†	1,580,058†	3,290,950	1,721,000¶	...
Mozambique	1960	6,578,604‡	3,149,270	...	...	...	...	...	...	...
Nauru	1966	6,048	3,696	...	...	...	...	...	...	...
Nepal	1961	9,387,661	4,619,973	2.8	3,684,000¶	4,258,000¶	1,445,000¶	...	...	...
Netherlands	1960	11,461,964‡	5,706,874	55.4	3,516,623▲	6,952,166▲	993,175▲	4,168,626	446,695	1,306,480
Netherlands Antilles	1960	192,538‡	94,811	...	79,683	77,069	35,786	59,806	1,029	16,059
New Caledonia	1969	100,579‡	52,591	41.6	34,964	46,028	19,587	39,185	13,357	7,152
New Guinea, Territory of	1966	1,578,650	821,899	47.3	694,633†	700,669†	183,348†	889,287	818,739	9,023
New Zealand	1971	2,862,631	1,430,856	81.4	905,775	1,160,350	786,012	1,102,000¶	139,100¶	353,600¶
Nicaragua	1963	1,535,588	757,922	40.9	740,729†	603,072†	191,787†	474,960	283,106	59,644
Nigeria	1963	55,670,046	28,112,118	16.1	25,514,354†	25,980,055†	4,175,637†	18,267,669	10,209,122	2,205,476
Norway	1960	3,591,234‡	1,789,406	32.1	989,927†	1,396,484†	1,204,823†	1,406,358	188,431	367,296
Pakistan	1961	93,831,982‡	49,308,645	13.1	40,178,518†	36,322,838†	13,781,318†	30,205,981	22,441,788	...
Panama	1970	1,428,082	723,749	47.6	620,454	589,133	218,495	488,668	...	...
Papua	1966	606,336	318,460	87.7	274,873†	270,698†	60,765†	312,748	269,076	4,375
Paraguay	1962	1,816,890	895,551	36.1	866,052†	684,563†	266,275†	596,555	312,647	91,077
Peru	1961	10,420,351††	4,925,518	47.4	4,290,084♀	4,143,473♀	1,468,200♀	3,124,579	1,555,560	477,393
Philippines	1970	36,684,486‡	18,250,351	...	17,858	15,422	4,679	...	...	...
Poland	1970	32,589,000	15,834,000	52.2	8,605,000	14,965,000	9,019,000	16,442,100	5,999,600	...
Portugal	1960	8,889,392‡	4,254,373	22.6	2,757,895†	3,792,171†	2,339,326†	3,316,472	1,393,624	717,117
Portuguese Guinea	1960	521,336	260,650	...	...	...	...	...	...	...
Portuguese Timor	1960	517,079	267,783	...	...	...	...	...	...	...
Puerto Rico	1970	2,712,033‡	1,329,949	58.1	990,920	1,138,462	582,551	...	...	...
Réunion	1967	416,525	203,497	42.8	189,997	163,253	62,166	94,334	27,845	6,910
Rhodesia	1969	5,099,340	2,567,081	16.8	2,385,907	2,082,996	591,194	110,363††	8,351††	30,235‡‡‖
Romania	1966	19,103,163‡	9,351,075	38.2	4,968,524	8,864,512	5,253,555	10,362,300	5,889,591	2,013,525
Rwanda	1965	3,744,723‡	1,493,963	...	1,397,928°	1,235,648°	487,147°	1,136,378	...	...
St. Helena	1966	4,649	2,233	...	1,944♀	1,501♀	1,204♀	1,562	...	...
St. Kitts-Nevis and Anguilla	1960	56,693‡	26,149	32.9	25,920†	19,378†	11,395†	32,023	8,565	2,078
St. Lucia	1960	86,108	40,693	24.9	38,109†	33,122†	14,877†	28,544	15,144	3,485
St. Pierre and Miquelon	1967	5,186	2,593	...	1,676	2,216	1,294	1,876	...	374
St. Vincent	1960	79,948	37,561	...	39,305	28,267	12,376	23,310	9,954	2,868
São Tomé and Príncipe	1960	63,485‡	35,259	...	...	...	...	...	...	...
Seychelles	1971	52,650	26,244	26.1	22,856	18,966	10,656	17,868	5,077	1,168§§
Sierra Leone	1963	2,180,355	1,081,123	...	800,404	1,016,240	363,711	...	682,588	88,846
Sikkim	1961	162,189	85,285	4.2	68,019†	73,748†	20,422†	2,728	249	64
Singapore	1970	2,074,500	1,062,100	...	804,800	933,100	336,600	...	...	...
South Africa	1960	16,002,797	8,043,493	46.7	6,418,492	6,945,380	2,638,925	5,696,060	1,700,958	1,285,113
South West Africa (Namibia)	1960	526,004	265,312	21.9	217,541†	227,238†	81,225†	203,271	118,996	18,647
Spain	1960	30,430,698	14,763,388	42.5	8,365,000†	13,506,800†	8,652,900†	11,634,214	4,803,316	2,749,419
Spanish Sahara	1970	76,425	43,981	45.3	32,804	33,265	10,356	...	...	...
Sri Lanka (Ceylon)	1963	10,624,507	5,503,000	18.8	4,616,920†	4,408,550†	1,564,590	2,542,920	1,272,800	258,170
Surinam	1964	324,211	161,855	40.1	147,927	122,897	46,668	80,199††	19,922††	12,713††
Swaziland	1966	374,571	178,795	12.5	174,455†	145,618†	54,498†	121,063	85,103	23,480
Sweden	1970	8,076,903‡	4,033,937	81.4	1,665,989	3,249,047	3,161,867	3,908,000¶	327,000¶	1,451,800‖¶
Switzerland	1970	6,269,783	3,089,326	52.0	1,466,533	2,750,816	2,052,434	3,005,139	229,293‖‖	1,451,975‖‖
Syria	1970	6,303,000	3,233,000	43.5	2,899,000	2,552,000	852,000	1,796,000¶	1,323,000¶	150,000¶
Taiwan	1966	13,348,096‡	7,031,644	59.2	5,775,194	5,622,590	1,950,312	8,619,952	1,437,944	592,082
Tanzania	1967	12,313,469	6,005,894	...	5,398,445	4,932,236	1,960,130	5,577,567	5,078,038	96,502
Thailand	1960	26,257,916	13,154,149	12.5	11,823,535†	10,949,932†	3,484,393†	13,836,984	11,334,382	500,595
Togo	1958–60	1,439,772	689,556	9.6	695,411†	558,839†	185,550†	566,868	452,889	...
Tonga	1966	77,429	39,157	...	...	...	...	...	...	...
Trinidad and Tobago	1960	827,957	411,580	17.0	351,050	336,730	140,177	262,570	52,528	53,617
Trust Territory of the Pacific Islands	1960	75,836‡	38,721	...	33,332†	27,139†	15,092†	...	...	...
Tunisia	1966	4,533,351	2,314,419	40.1	2,191,088†	1,678,465†	663,798†	1,093,735	448,296	103,582
Turkey	1970	35,666,549	18,063,001	...	14,888,793	15,023,899	6,753,857	14,533,725	9,730,469	1,742,282
Turks and Caicos Islands	1960	5,668‡	2,667	...	2,557†	1,975†	1,136†	2,034	393	...
Uganda	1969	9,548,847	4,818,449	7.7	4,404,291	3,781,156	1,350,865	...	...	...
Union of Soviet Socialist Republics	1970	241,720,000	111,399,000	56.0	74,710,000**	104,880,000**	61,861,000**	...	...	...
United Kingdom	1961	52,708,934	25,480,791	79.0	12,335,703	20,784,033	19,589,198	23,616,620	865,129	6,975,166
United States	1970	203,211,926	98,912,192	73.5	57,900,052	83,436,603	61,875,271	85,903,000¶	3,674,000¶	22,467,000¶
Uruguay	1963	2,592,563	1,289,454	...	721,500	1,143,600	727,500	1,015,500	181,800	213,600
Venezuela	1971	10,721,522	5,364,365	75.5	4,845,431†	4,464,357†	1,411,734†	3,068,784	645,027	619,285
Vietnam, North	1960	15,916,955	7,687,814	9.5	7,055,544¶¶	7,556,129¶¶	1,305,282¶¶	8,119,286	6,377,024	537,761
Virgin Islands of the United States	1970	62,468‡	31,157	24.4	22,311	29,766	10,391	24,501	172	2,263
Western Samoa	1966	131,379	67,809	19.2	...	...	...	...	...	...
Yugoslavia	1961	18,549,291‡	9,043,424	28.8	5,770,817	8,168,259	4,610,215	8,340,400	4,674,856	1,137,848
Zambia	1969	4,056,995	1,987,011	29.6	1,878,861	1,646,486	527,648	1,159,698	...	...
DEMOGRAPHIC AND/OR SAMPLE SURVEYS										
Burundi	1962	2,319,540	1,104,266	...	...	...	...	...	...	...
Central African Republic	1959–60	1,177,000	577,000	6.8	429,000	661,000	81,000	610,000	461,000	52,000
Chad	1964	3,254,000	1,567,000	7.8	...	...	...	950,000	600,000	60,000
Congo	1960–61	794,400‡	...	...	...	...	...	...	...	...
Cuba	1965	7,630,700	2,895,155	53.0	2,808,190♀♀	4,009,110♀♀	813,400♀♀	2,546,000	838,000	390,000
Dahomey	1961	2,106,000	...	...	...	...	...	...	...	...
Malagasy Republic	1966	6,200,000	3,049,000	...	2,882,000	2,326,000	992,000	2,733,000	2,396,000	337,000
Mali	1960–61	4,100,000	...	...	1,763,000†	2,127,900†	209,100†	...	...	...
Niger	1959–60	2,556,211	...	...	...	...	...	1,506,490	703,610	4,510
Senegal	1960–61	3,109,840‡	1,531,760	23.7	1,320,680†	1,641,420†	147,720†	1,317,580	1,087,020	73,800
Upper Volta	1960–61	4,400,000	2,208,800	4.6	1,830,400†	1,892,000†	677,600†	2,627,000	1,300,000	...

Note: Data reflect results of enumerations conducted 1957 to 1971, as available. Age groups may not add to country total due to ages not specified in census.
*That population defined as urban by the political unit.

†0–15, 16–45, 46 and over.
‡De jure population.
§0–13, 14–49, 50 and over.
‖Includes public utilities and construction.
¶Estimate.
♀0–14, 15–49, 50 and over.

δ1966 census.
□0–19, 20–49, 50 and over.
°0–14, 15–45, 46 and over.
▲0–14, 15–64, 65 and over.
+Includes construction.
⊕0–15, 16–49, 50 and over.
**0–15, 16–44, 45 and over.

††Excludes Amerindian.
‡‡Excludes African population.
§§Includes utilities.
‖‖Mining included in agriculture.
¶¶0–15, 16–55, 56 and over.
♀♀0–14, 15–54, 55 and over.

continued from page 552

the current population set at 209.3 million, it had been estimated that in the year 2000 the population would be 322.3 million, if the average family had 3.1 children, or 271.1 million if it had 2.1 children. These projections were abandoned in 1972 for estimates that set the population in 2000 at 300.4 million, if the fertility rate was 2.8 children per family, or at 250.7 million, if it was 1.8 children. The Census Bureau admitted that the low 1.8 rate was "entirely arbitrary" but felt that it reflected a clearly discernible trend "into a period of notably slower population growth."

A major change that would be brought about by the declining fertility rate would be a substantially older population. If the current birthrate were maintained the part of the population under 30, for example, would drop from 53% in 1972 to 44% in 2000. The median age, or midpoint of the age span, would also be adjusted from the current 28.1 years to 34 years. Such changes would carry others with them. Average family income would climb, with significant changes in the quality of life. With nonworking children constituting a smaller proportion of the population, an increasing part of it would be working.

Canada's population, according to the Canadian five-year census taken on June 1, 1971, and reported on April 22, 1972, increased by 7.8%, during the five years covered, to 21,568,315. This figure indicated that the decline in the rate of growth noted over the last 20 years had continued. Canada's population had grown 14.8% between 1951–56, 13.4% between 1956–61, and 9.7% between 1961–66. The only province to show a decline was the predominantly rural prairie land of Saskatchewan. The fastest growing populations were recorded in the Yukon, up 27.9%, and the Northwest Territories, up 21.1%. Most of the growth, however, was in Ontario (47.8%) and Quebec (16%).

In the U.S. per capita gross national product was $4,240 in 1969. In most of the more developed world, where rates of population growth tended to be under 1% annually, the per capita GNP was over $1,000, as a rule. In the less developed nations the reverse was true. Rates of growth were frequently over 3% annually, with per capita GNPs of under $200.

What was more, countries with high rates of population growth were characterized by high proportions of young people and low proportions of the aged. For example, 44% of Africa's population was estimated to be under 15 years of age and only 3% to be 65 years and older. In Europe, on the other hand, only 25% of the population was under 15 and 12% was 65 or older. In the United States the proportions were 29% under 15 years and 10% 65 years and older.

While the rates of growth varied sharply between more developed and less developed countries, urbanization was a phenomenon common to both worlds. Despite this trek to the cities, the less developed world remained predominantly rural or small-town oriented.

In fact, only 16% of Asia's vast population of 2,000,000,000 lived in urban areas greater than 100,000 population. In Africa, where urbanization was less pronounced, only 11% of the continent's 375 million people lived in large urban areas. At the other end of the scale was the United States, with 58% of its people living in communities of over 100,000. The same proportion lived in large urban areas in northern Europe. Moreover, the highest large-city concentration (71%) was found in the United Kingdom.

Although the politics of population growth had long been dominated by religious attitudes and national notions that sizable numbers of people spell power, wealth, and a "place in the sun," the voice for slower world growth had become stronger. Proclaiming the convening of a world population conference in 1974, United Nations Secretary-General Kurt Waldheim called, on July 20, 1972, for a formulation of national plans to broadcast information about family planning and its practice and for "action appropriate to the emphasis on population as a major factor in economic development, social progress, and improvement of the quality of life both in developed and developing countries." (WARREN W. EISENBERG)

Portugal

A unitary corporative republic of southwestern Europe, Portugal shares the Iberian Peninsula with Spain. Area: 35,383 sq.mi. (91,641 sq.km.), including the Azores (905 sq. mi.) and Madeira (308 sq.mi.). Pop. (1971 est.): 8,869,800. Cap. and largest city: Lisbon (pop., 1971 est., 786,500). Language: Portuguese. Religion: Roman Catholic. President in 1972, Rear Adm. Américo de Deus Rodrigues Tomás; premier, Marcello José das Neves Alves Caetano.

Portugal remained politically stable in 1972, but economic progress was again limited. The main political event of the year was the election on July 25 of 77-year-old Rear Adm. Américo Tomás for a third seven-year term as president of the republic. This was followed early in August by a reorganization of the Cabinet: Manuel Artur Cotta Dias was appointed minister of economy and finance in place of João Augusto Dias Rosas, and Rogério Martins and Xavier Pintado were replaced as secretaries of state for industry and commerce, respectively, by Azevedo de Pinto and Hermes Augusto dos Santos.

Many commentators agreed that the reelection of Tomás signaled a formal end to Premier Caetano's attempt to introduce a measure of political liberalization. Martins and Pintado were widely regarded as the two principal reformers in the Cabinet, and several other liberals in the second rank of the administration were removed from their posts during the year. It was believed that Caetano had sought the presidency for himself, but that this had been vetoed by the armed forces high command. According to this view, he then compromised and supported Tomás in preference to a more active senior officer.

There were other signs during the year that no meaningful civilian political activity would henceforth be permitted. A new press law came into effect on June 1, under which official censorship before publication was abolished and owners and editors of newspapers became responsible for voluntary censorship. However, the government reserved the right to the "official preexamination of news" while Portugal and its overseas territories were still in "a state of subversion." Outside official circles, it was generally agreed that the new system was less rigid than the old but that much depended on how the government viewed the needs of "national security." A decree published in midyear reorganized the General Department of Security, granting to it powers similar to those of the old secret police, the PIDE. Early in May the National Assembly approved a new organic law giving greater autonomy to the African territories; it was clear, however, that control still firmly resided in Lisbon.

The performance of the Portuguese economy was uneven during 1972. The growth rate for the year was estimated at 7%, against 5.3% in 1971. The uptrend in economic activity of 1971 gathered momentum, demonstrated by increased consumption and public and private investment and a substantial rise in imports of machinery, equipment, and raw materials. Large projects were initiated for ports, roads, shipyards, steel, oil refining, and petrochemicals. Measures were introduced to strengthen the capital market, including the establishment of an advisory service for investors and controls over share issues by large private companies. On the other hand, growing inflationary pressures, which had mounted steadily since 1966, gave increased grounds for concern. Basically these were caused by the stimulation of domestic demand without a compensating increase in the general level of productivity. In midyear the secretary of state for commerce was granted powers to control the prices of goods and services and to suspend regulations that prevented the sale and distribution of foodstuffs and other essential goods. The external position remained strong. The traditionally large trade deficit was offset mainly by emigrants' transfers and proceeds from tourism.

It was officially recognized that prosperity could be sustained in the long run only if the metropolitan economy became fully competitive with the advanced industrial countries of Western Europe and North America. Two important steps were taken with this in view. Early in June an industrial reform law was published containing a wide range of incentives for new projects and the expansion of existing ones. Late in July an agreement was signed with the EEC providing for mutual tariff reductions on most industrial goods over a specified period.

The government continued its efforts to develop the overseas provinces, while successfully maintaining their security against guerrilla attacks. The economy of Angola maintained its rapid expansion, but there were some doubts as to future prospects for growth in Mozambique. (ROBIN CHAPMAN)

See also Dependent States.

PORTUGAL

Education. (1968–69) Primary, pupils 961,546, teachers 29,266; secondary, pupils 224,058, teachers 14,771; vocational, pupils 151,572, teachers 9,103; teacher training, students 2,647, teachers 289; higher (including 4 universities), students 42,560, teaching staff 1,864.

Finance. Monetary unit: escudo, with (Sept. 18, 1972) a par value of 27.25 escudos to U.S. $1 and a free rate of 26.80 escudos to U.S. $1 (65.57 escudos = £1 sterling). Gold, SDRs, and foreign exchange, official: (June 1972) U.S. $1,971,000,000; (June 1971) U.S. $1,529,000,000. Budget (1971 est.): revenue 32,053,000,000 escudos; expenditure 32,050,000,000 escudos. Gross domestic product: (1970) 180.7 billion escudos; (1969) 162.1 billion escudos. Money supply: (March 1972) 97,570,000,000 escudos; (March 1971) 87,010,000,000 escudos. Cost of living (Lisbon; 1963 = 100): (June 1972) 179; (June 1971) 161.

Foreign Trade. (1971) Imports 52,416,000,000 escudos; exports 30,248,000,000 escudos. Import sources: West Germany 16%; U.K. 14%; Angola 10%; U.S. 7%; France 7%; Italy 5%; Spain 5%. Export destinations: U.K. 23%; Angola 14%; U.S. 10%; Mozambique 7%; West Germany 6%; Sweden 6%; France 5%. Main exports: textile yarns and fabrics 28%; chemicals 8%; machinery 8%; wine 7%; cork 6%. Tourism (1970): visitors 3,342,900; gross receipts U.S. $237 million.

Transport and Communications. Roads (continent; 1970) 30,165 km. (including 77 km. expressways). Motor vehicles in use (1970): passenger 513,500; commercial 27,600. Railways: (continent; 1970) 3,563 km.; traffic (1971) 3,568,000,000 passenger-km., freight 812 million net ton-km. Air traffic (1971): 2,995,000,000 passenger-km.; freight 58,940,000 net ton-km. Shipping (1971): merchant vessels 100 gross tons and over 384; gross tonnage 925,793. Telephones (Dec. 1970) 750,000. Radio licenses (Dec. 1969) 1,406,000. Television licenses (Dec. 1970) 368,000.

Agriculture. Production (in 000; metric tons; 1971; 1970 in parentheses): wheat 794 (540); barley 84 (54); oats 132 (72); rye 163 (157); corn 529 (581); rice 164 (195); potatoes 1,165 (1,220); dry broad beans 32 (27); other dry beans 52 (55); chickpeas 15 (20); figs (1970) *c.* 220, (1969) 221; oranges (1970) 90, (1969) 124; apples *c.* 55 (58); pears *c.* 45 (56); wine 854 (1,162); olive oil 47 (67); meat 216 (210); timber (cu.m.; 1970) 6,400, (1969) 5,900; fish catch (1969) 457, (1968) 506. Livestock (in 000; 1970–71): sheep 5,690; cattle *c.* 1,300; pigs *c.* 1,400; goats *c.* 525; asses *c.* 153; chickens *c.* 13,000.

Industry. Fuel and power (in 000; 1971): coal (metric tons) 253; manufactured gas (Lisbon only; cu.m.) 125,000; electricity (kw-hr.) 7,877,000. Production (in 000; metric tons; 1971): iron ore (50% metal content) 102; sulfur (1970) 221; cement 2,270; tin 0.5; manganese ore (metal content; 1970) 2.2; tungsten concentrates (oxide content; 1970) 1.9; gold (troy oz.; 1970) 13; cotton yarn 83; woven cotton fabrics 47; preserved sardines (1970) 25; cork products (1970) 300.

Postal Services

The number of member states of the Universal Postal Union (UPU) rose to 146 with the admission of Tonga on Jan. 26, 1972. Among topics discussed at the May session of the Executive Council were further technical assistance to less developed countries (also a topic of the Consultative Council for Postal Studies at its meeting in Bern, Switz., in November), simplification of customs and tariffs, procedure in cases of diplomatic hostility or outright war, and maximum use and security of airmail services. The 17th UPU Congress was scheduled to be held in Lausanne, Switz., in 1974.

In November 1971 Britain's Post Office Corporation had published proposals for restructuring the inland postal services by withdrawing or modifying those services that had proved persistently unprofitable. The proposals (designed to save £13 million per year at March 1971 prices) were referred to the Post Office Users' National Council in accordance with the Post Office Act of 1969. The Post Office accepted the council's recommendations for withdrawal of Saturday afternoon collections; abolition of third letter delivery and second weekday parcel delivery in London; closure of post office counters on Saturday afternoons or early closing days where conditions were suitable; and replacement of the registered parcel service and introduction of new compensation arrangements. The estimated saving on these changes was £1.5 million per year. The third letter and second parcel deliveries in London and Saturday afternoon collections nationally were abolished during August 1972; the registered parcel service was replaced by the new compensation arrangements on September 4.

Postal headquarters was reorganized during the year. Separate managerial units were introduced for the letter and parcel services. Marketing and management services departments were set up to improve profitability by bringing in new business and improving efficiency. Management consultants were engaged with a view to introducing additional efficiency audits of mail work in sorting offices and a reappraisal of the handling arrangements for overseas mail.

A new air letter form conforming to the interna-

Portuguese Overseas Provinces:
see Dependent States

UPI COMPIX

The president of the National Association of Professional Bureaucrats (Nataprobu) arrives in Washington, D.C., with mail from Philadelphia. James H. Boren and five other riders made the trip in relays, delivering the mail faster than the U.S. Postal Service.

tional A4 size was introduced in April as an alternative to the smaller form issued in 1968. It was of thicker, heavier paper than the 1968 design and could be completely sealed. Fully mechanized parcel offices were opened at Birmingham and Leicester; the former, with 13 parcel-sorting machines, was the largest in the country. On the letters side, 13 offices were equipped with code-sorting machinery, although not all were fully operational. Almost every address in the U.K. was expected to be postcoded by early 1973.

In France the CIDEX system for special delivery of individual mail was adopted by the postal service for the distribution of letters in rural districts. Every customer who agreed to take part in the project would be given, free of charge, a large letter box with a lock. The individual boxes could be grouped in sets and placed in easily accessible places near the customers' homes. A signal on the box allowed the customer to show the postman that he wanted him to come to his home. A box reserved for outgoing correspondence could be attached. Under the new system, applied experimentally at Plouarzel in the *département* of Finistère, the traditional method of delivery was reorganized to ensure two successive rounds. In the first, the postmen put normal mail into the boxes. A second round, beginning immediately after the first round had ended, was reserved for delivery of special mail, for supplying customers who wished to continue to receive their mail at home, and for visiting those who had asked to see the postman.

The first experiments with CIDEX were encouraging and gained wide support from the customers involved. In addition, the new system markedly decreased the postman's work. Enough time was saved to permit a rural postman on a CIDEX round to handle most of the postal services usually transacted across the counter and to take an active part in collecting savings. Finally, CIDEX was expected to solve the problems of postal deliveries in rural and semiurban districts and to help surmount the increase in the volume of mail, which was roughly doubling every 15 years.

In furtherance of the West German government's plans to transform the Deutsche Bundespost (federal postal services) into a public service enterprise, the Federal Ministry of Transport, Post, and Telecommunications was reorganized so that the "posts" and "telecommunications" sectors became individually responsible for their economic operation. Special organizational units were established to deal with certain tasks common to both sectors, and staffs were set up to advise and support the management.

West German posts and telecommunications traffic rose 7.9% during the year. In spite of this increase, the quality of service was maintained, and services and facilities were improved and expanded. At the beginning of 1972 it was possible to handle 92.8% of the entire international telephone traffic via the subscriber trunk dialing service. Preparations continued for the introduction of an electronically controlled dialing system for the local networks and of an electronic data-transmission system. A second shortwave transmitter was constructed in Wertachtal.

Efforts to run the posts and telecommunications services economically led to the elimination of 4,500 jobs. Total personnel increased to 468,921, however, and the number of vacant posts rose to more than 28,000, primarily because of the growth of traffic volume and the introduction of the 42-hour week. In view of the strained situation on the labour market, personnel planning methods were refined and the first phase of a computerized personnel data system was introduced.

In Sweden the Post Office Bank and other banks continued to cooperate in an integrated on-line payments system and in the installation of mechanical cash dispensers, through which a customer could cash banknotes, with the aid of a special card, at any time of the day. A number of such machines were installed in 1972 and were to be made available to account holders in all banks participating in the scheme.

The Spanish postal service handled 4,200,000,000 items during 1971, an increase of 3% over 1970. Postal revenues totaled 7,198,000,000 pesetas and expenses, 7,150,000,000 pesetas. During the first six months of 1972 a fourth postal mail train began operating, between Madrid and Levant. There was a spectacular increase in the telex service and the number of subscribers rose from 5,700 to 7,100. Of the 54,000 Spanish postal and communications employees, 25,000 were rural and urban postmen and 11,000 worked in communications. There were 230 buildings under construction in the postal and communications services. Some 2,660,000 persons held postal savings books with 45,784,000,000 pesetas invested.

More than 44,000,000,000 postal items were handled by the Soviet postal service in 1971, and 100 million persons were served daily. Over 80,000 permanent and mobile post offices were in use. The principal operations of mail processing were mechanized at 22 large post offices and at more than 400 production shops and divisions. The techniques of mail processing were undergoing simplification and automation, and a whole range of automatic equipment was introduced. To facilitate the task of postal workers, mail in low-temperature zones in winter was delivered via so-called exchange hatches, which were provided with special shields to keep out the cold. Preparations were being made for the introduction of postal coding. Automated letter-sorting machines using a six-digit indexing system were being developed. Each postal establishment was assigned its six-digit index, and explanatory work among the population was being carried out through films and manuals.

To enable the New Zealand Post Office to pay its way in the face of rising costs (principally from increased salaries and wages), charges for most of its services were increased from Oct. 1, 1971. Telephone and toll charges rose by approximately 20%, but charges for domestic mail services remained unchanged. For the year ending March 31, 1972, income exceeded expenditure by NZ$300,000. During 1972 the government approved the progressive introduction of subscriber toll dialing. A new direct radiotelephone service with Niue and a telex service with Rarotonga were introduced, enabling Niue and Rarotonga to make calls to other countries through the New Zealand international exchange at Auckland.

In South Africa more than 1,700,000,000 items of mail were handled in 1972, and were conveyed over an integrated network of road, rail, air, and sea services. Mail conveyance costs totaled R 10.7 million during the financial year ended March 31, 1972. At the larger centres, automated equipment expedited the facing and date-stamping of mail posted locally. South African postage stamps (except the very highest denominations) were treated with a luminous substance that glowed under ultraviolet light, enabling the facing and canceling machines to locate the stamps and to perform the required functions. (X.)

A major cost-cutting effort and a campaign to improve mail delivery occupied the U.S. Postal Service in its first full year as a corporate-style, semi-independent government agency. The economy drive began soon after Elmer T. Klassen, former president of American Can Co., became the nation's 63rd postmaster general in January 1972, succeeding Winton M. Blount. Klassen, who had been deputy postmaster general in 1969–71, outlined his plans on March 29 in a filmed speech to the Postal Service's 720,000 employees. He announced a temporary hiring freeze and other economy moves and explained that his aim was to avert a $450 million increase in mail rates, included in the service's fiscal 1973 budget.

Complaints about deteriorating delivery service mounted as the employment freeze extended through August. However, on August 28 Klassen announced that economies realized from the freeze and from other measures had eliminated the need to raise first-class letter rates from eight to nine cents per ounce in January 1973. The ban on hiring—which had trimmed the postal work force by 33,000 to 687,000—was lifted in certain areas.

In its campaign to provide faster mail service, the Postal Service had succeeded in raising employee productivity and improving delivery of airmail and certain first-class letters, but other cutbacks in service and sporadic delivery performance aided its growing number of competitors. For the first time since the 1930s, the rate of growth of mail volume fell, to 0.1%. Volume of first-class letters actually declined from the previous year's 50 billion pieces.

For the first time, United Parcel Service surpassed the Postal Service in the number of packages delivered. The Independent Postal System of America and other private firms, primarily involved in delivering advertising circulars door-to-door, began a court battle to try to break the service's monopoly on first-class letters. Magazine publishers began testing alternative delivery methods, and several utility companies started delivering bills on their own.

The move to other mail systems gained impetus when the Postal Rate Commission, which reviews the service's rate requests, approved $1,370,000,000 in higher annual postal fees on June 5, 1972. Most of the increases had been put into effect on a temporary basis in May 1971, pending a final decision by the commission. Rates for third-class mail items, chiefly advertising circulars, were raised an average 24% on March 12, 1972, after a successful appeal by the Postal Service ended a court ban on the higher rates.

Major users of the mails urged congressional post office committees to investigate mail rates, and more than 20 individuals and groups, primarily representing magazine, newspaper, and book publishers, testified before a House subcommittee. Attempts to legislate relief failed, but some congressmen vowed to try again in the next session.

As part of its mail improvement program, the Postal Service expanded evening mailbox collection services, which had been drastically reduced in recent years. A jet air taxi service was begun between major eastern cities, and faster mail trains were added to transport packages and other bulk-mail items between the Middle West and the West Coast.

Another new service introduced in late 1972 enabled individual customers to make small purchases of stamps through the mail and pay for them by check. In ten post offices around the country, the Postal Service opened retail outlets, called "Postiques," which offered, in addition to inexpensive postal-related items, such products as reproductions of paintings in the National Gallery of Art and books and pamphlets published by the Government Printing Office.

Work continued on a $1 billion network of 33 major facilities to process bulk mail. In January 1972 the service successfully sold its first public offering, $250 million in 25-year bonds, with proceeds earmarked for the mechanization program. The service's first major mail reclassification proposal was to be presented to the Postal Rate Commission in mid-January 1973. In preparing the proposal the Postal Service polled 10,000 households and 40,000 businessmen.

The Postal Service deficit in fiscal 1972 was slightly above $150 million, compared with $2.6 billion the previous year. (TIMOTHY D. SCHELLHARDT)

See also Philately and Numismatics; Telecommunications.

Prices

There was little sign in 1971–72 of any general deceleration in the rate of inflation in either developed or less developed countries. The best that could be said about the performance of industrial nations was that, on average, they had managed to stop the acceleration of their price increases. Less developed countries were less fortunate in this respect; the situation worsened in many of them at both the wholesale and the retail levels, often seriously.

Consumer Prices. Taking developed market economies as a whole, the average increase in the cost of living between 1971 and 1972 was just over 6%, exactly the same as a year earlier. The rates of inflation varied from country to country, but there were only one or two cases of deterioration similar to those that marked 1969–70 and 1970–71.

As Table I shows, the biggest increases occurred in New Zealand (8.2%), the Netherlands (8.1%), the U.K. (7.6%), Finland (7.3%), and Australia (7%). In New Zealand the combined effect of recession and stringent controls of prices and wages (the freeze of 1971 was followed early in 1972 by severe controls) appeared to have helped to check the rise in prices somewhat. In the Netherlands the index-linking system seemed to have caused considerable problems over the last two years. Almost all wages, social security premiums, pensions, sickness benefits, and national

Potash: *see* Mining
Poultry: *see* Agriculture
Power: *see* Engineering Projects; Fuel and Power; Industrial Review
Presbyterians: *see* Religion

assistance payments were included in the system. Toward the end of 1972 the authorities had little choice but to resort again to price controls. There was a noticeable and continuous improvement in the rate of inflation in the U.K. early in 1972, but the situation deteriorated in the second half of the year. In November a freeze was introduced for 90 days on all incomes and prices. Only certain foodstuffs and imported raw materials that are normally subject to strong seasonal fluctuations were exempted. The freeze was regarded as the first stage in the government's program for controlling inflation. In Finland new legislation was passed enabling the government to control prices and rents. Despite a mild recession, inflation worsened in Australia.

An interesting fact that emerges from Table I is the extent to which price increases were becoming similar in many developed market economies. In no fewer than half of the countries included in the table, the increase was fairly close to the average. The biggest rise in this group was recorded by Norway (6.8%), where the price freeze was followed by a law to control prices indefinitely. In Denmark (6.4%) domestic costs and prices continued to rise rapidly despite sluggish growth. A similar problem was experienced by Sweden (6.3%), though in this case higher import prices and indirect taxes added to the inflationary tendencies. In December the Swedish government froze the prices of dairy and meat products, effective Jan. 1, 1973. Austria (6.1%) and Switzerland (6%) were rather exceptional in this group of countries, since both of them had experienced a very high level of economic activity and considerable pressure on productive resources. The Swiss Parliament adopted a series of anti-inflationary measures in December; although the government had asked only for the power to control prices, it was given authority to control wages and profits as well.

In France, where food prices played an extremely important role in the inflationary process, there were substantial increases in prices of a number of important foodstuffs. Consequently, the fact that the cost of living did not go up much faster in 1972 than during the two previous years could probably be attributed, at least partly, to the policies employed to stabilize other prices, notably those of industrial products. Early in 1972, as soon as the anti-inflationary contracts signed in 1971 expired, the government introduced a "price programming" policy that set target

Basic Consumer Expenditures of Selected Countries, 1970

As percent of total consumer expenditures

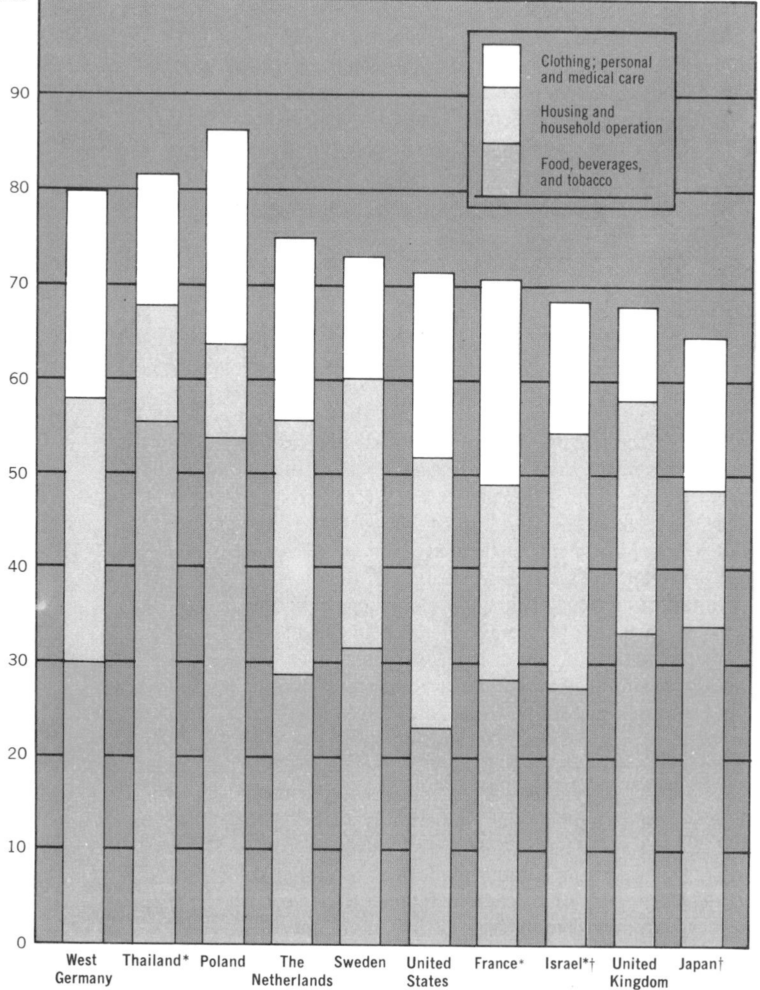

*1969.
†Average consumption expenditures of urban households.
Source: Country statistics.

Table I. Cost of Living—Selected Countries

Country	Index (1963 = 100) 1970	1971	1972*	Annual % change 1963–69 (Average)	Annual % changes over preceding year 1970	1971	1972†
Developed market economies							
Denmark‡	150	159	166	5.9	6.4	6.0	6.4
Finland	145	154	162	5.9	2.8	6.2	7.3
Netherlands	141	152	161	5.1	4.4	7.8	8.1
New Zealand	136	150	159	4.2	6.2	10.3	8.2
Japan	144	153	158	5.0	7.5	6.3	4.6
Norway	140	149	157	4.1	10.2	6.4	6.8
U.K.	135	148	156	4.1	6.3	9.6	7.6
Sweden	135	145	152	3.9	7.1	7.4	6.3
France	131	138	144	3.7	5.6	5.3	5.9
Switzerland	126	135	141	3.4	3.3	7.1	6.0
Austria	128	134	140	3.5	4.1	4.7	6.1
Belgium‡	129	134	139	3.7	4.0	3.9	5.3
Italy	128	134	139	3.4	4.9	4.7	4.5
Australia	124	132	138	3.1	3.3	6.4	7.0
U.S.	127	132	135	3.1	5.8	3.9	3.1
Canada	126	130	134	3.4	3.3	3.2	4.7
Germany, West	120	127	132	2.5	3.4	5.8	5.6
Less developed countries							
Brazil	1,047	1,268	1,440	43.7	19.1	21.1	18.8
Chile	598	718	924	28.6	32.3	20.1	34.9
Vietnam, South	590	698	820	27.6	36.6	18.3	20.6
Argentina	380	512	724	22.3	13.4	34.7	53.4
Yugoslavia	248	286	325	14.4	10.7	15.3	15.2
Korea, South	249	280	308	14.1	12.7	12.4	12.0
Cambodia	132	227	244	2.8	11.9	72.0	32.6
Peru	206	220	235	11.9	5.1	6.8	8.8
Colombia	197	214	234	10.7	7.1	8.6	12.5
Philippines	149	177	204	4.1	17.3	18.8	22.9
India	169	175	179	8.3	5.6	3.6	5.9
Spain	155	168	178	6.6	5.4	8.4	7.9
Portugal	146	163	178	5.4	6.6	11.6	13.4
Nigeria	140	159	170	3.7	12.9	13.6	9.0
Israel	138	154	170	4.5	6.2	11.6	13.3
Ireland	145	158	168	5.0	8.2	9.0	9.1
Zambia	150	159	166	6.5	2.7	6.0	5.1
Ecuador	135	146	153	4.2	5.5	8.1	7.0
Pakistan	137	144	151	4 5	5.4	5.1	7.1
Jamaica	136	145	149	3.7	9.7	6.6	4.9
Tanzania‡	125	130	141	3.4	2.4	4.0	11.0
South Africa§	125	133	139	2.9	5.0	6.4	6.1
Tunisia	128	135	138	4.1	0.8	5.5	1.5
Sri Lanka (Ceylon)	127	130	137	3.1	5.8	2.4	7.0
Mexico‡	126	130	135	3.1	5.0	3.2	4.7
Ethiopia‡	143	143	135	4.5	10.0	0.0	−7.5
Puerto Rico	123	128	132	2.9	3.4	4.1	3.9
Iran	114	119	128	1.9	1.8	4.4	7.6
Iraq	117	121	127	1.9	4.5	3.4	4.1
Greece	118	121	125	2.2	3.5	2.5	3.3
Costa Rica	116	120	123	1.8	4.5	3.4	3.4
Kenya‡	113	117	123	1.6	2.7	3.5	8.8
Thailand	117	119	122	2.5	0.9	1.7	3.4
Morocco	111	115	120	1.4	1.8	3.6	4.3
Cyprus	110	114	119	1.1	2.8	3.6	5.3
Venezuela	112	115	118	1.6	1.8	2.7	3.5
Malta	114	116	117	1.6	3.6	1.8	0.0
Malaysia (West)	109	111	113	1.1	1.9	1.8	1.8
Singapore	108	110	111	1.3	0.0	1.9	0.9
Guatemala	107	106	106	0.7	2.9	−0.9	0.0

*January–June (average).
†First half 1972 over first half 1971.
‡Excluding rent.
§White population only.
Sources: International Monetary Fund, *International Financial Statistics;* United Nations, *Monthly Bulletin of Statistics;* International Labour Office, *Bulletin of Labour Statistics.*

price increases for the next 12 months. Moreover, a number of companies had been required to reduce their prices by government decree. In West Germany (5.6%) a relatively brief recession and moderation in cost increases were apparently not sufficient to reduce the rate of inflation from its unusually high level. Food prices made an important contribution to the increase in the cost of living. Nevertheless, West Germany remained one of the very few industrial countries in which the authorities refused to resort to stringent controls over incomes and prices, preferring, instead, to rely mainly on monetary measures.

The rate of inflation slowed down noticeably in Japan (4.6%) and to a lesser extent in Italy (4.5%), but probably the most noteworthy improvement took place in the U.S. (3.1%), where increases in the cost of living were almost halved between 1970 and 1972. It was difficult to say how much of the improvement was attributable to the anti-inflationary measures introduced in 1971, but Phase Two of the prices and incomes policy was in force during most of the period under analysis. Wage increases were limited to 5.5% and price controls were applied selectively, with the aim of holding the overall increase to about 2–3%. Prices of most raw agricultural products were excluded from the controls.

Among less developed countries, the worst rates of inflation were again experienced by Latin-American countries, notably Argentina (53.4%) and Chile (34.9%), and the two countries ravaged by war, South Vietnam (20.6%) and Cambodia (32.6%). However, Yugoslavia (15.2%), Portugal (13.4%), and Israel (13.3%) were rapidly approaching rates that are normally rare outside South America. Of the three, Yugoslavia had suffered for some years from the most serious inflation in Europe. Between 1970 and 1972 the authorities imposed several price freezes, but none of the measures appeared to be very effective. In Portugal increases in wages and prices were aggravated by labour shortages and production bottlenecks, and prices continued to rise sharply despite the introduction of price controls at the retail level. There was also a good deal of overheating in the Israeli economy, mainly as a result of rapid growth of investment. A number of monetary measures were introduced to curb increases in prices, and attempts were made to restrain growth of public expenditure. At the same time, some of the most stable price indices in the world were achieved by a number of less developed countries—the result of tight controls and the much narrower coverage of their indices as compared with those of the industrial nations.

What made inflationary trends so serious in many countries was that food prices were making such an important contribution to the overall increase in the cost of living. This can be seen from Table II. (An index number of 100 for any particular year shows that food prices and the cost of living—including food—had increased at the same rate between 1963 and that year. Numbers greater or smaller than 100

Table II. Indices of Food Prices in Relation to Cost-of-Living Index

1963 = 100

Country	1969	1970	1971	1972*
Developed market economies				
Denmark	102	104	104	110†
Sweden	101	102	104	106†
Japan	103	105	105	104
Finland	105	104	101	103†
Norway	101	103	103	102†
U.K.	98	99	100	101†
France	98	98	99	100
Belgium	102	101	99	99†
U.S.	100	99	98	99
New Zealand	101	101	99	98
Austria	100	100	99	98†
Canada	99	98	97	98†
Australia	101	101	99	97
Italy	97	96	96	95
Germany, West	96	95	94	94†
Netherlands	98	98	94	93†
Less developed countries				
Vietnam, South	135	134	129	131†
Nigeria	103	113	126	128‡
Philippines	113	118	116	118
Cambodia	94	101	115	112
Thailand	111	111	109	110
Chile	99	101	105	110
Costa Rica	105	108	108	108
Pakistan	104	106	106	108‡
Tunisia	103	103	108	108
Iran	101	100	102	108‡
Puerto Rico	105	106	107	107†
India	109	109	107	106†
Kenya	103	103	104	106†
Argentina	96	99	104	106
Greece	102	102	104	105‡
Yugoslavia	99	100	101	104‡
Sri Lanka (Ceylon)	104	104	104	103†
Cyprus	103	102	103	103
Morocco	100	99	101	103
Ethiopia	104	109	109	102†
Iraq	99	99	99	102
South Africa§	103	102	101	101
Mexico	101	102	101	101‡
Malta	103	103	101	100
Zambia	99	100	100	100
Paraguay	97	96	99	100†
Guatemala	100	101	100	99‡
Singapore	99	98	99	99†
Colombia	99	97	96	97‡
Venezuela	97	96	96	97
Ireland	97	96	95	97
Portugal	99	98	95	95†
Spain	96	94	94	94‡
Israel	96	93	95	93
Brazil	92	91	93	93†

*January–June (average) except where stated otherwise.
†January–July (average).
‡January–May (average).
§White population only.
Sources: United Nations, *Monthly Bulletin of Statistics;* International Labour Office, *Bulletin of Labour Statistics.*

Table III. Wholesale Prices for Selected Countries

Country	Index (1963 = 100) 1970	1971	1972*	Annual % change 1963–69 (Average)	Annual % changes over preceding year 1970	1971	1972†
Developed market economies							
Finland	142	149	157	5.3	4.4	4.9	6.8
New Zealand	127	138	148	3.2	5.0	8.7	10.4
U.K.‡	128	138	142	3.1	6.7	7.8	4.4
Denmark	127	132	136	2.7	8.5	3.9	4.6
Sweden	126	130	136	2.8	6.8	3.2	6.2
Austria	122	128	131	2.5	5.1	4.9	2.3
Norway	123	129	131	2.5	6.0	4.9	3.1
France§	124	127	130	2.5	6.9	2.4	3.2
Netherlands	124	125	127	2.7	6.0	0.8	1.6
Italy	119	123	126	1.8	7.2	3.4	3.3
U.S.	117	120	124	2.1	3.5	2.6	3.3
Canada	117	118	124	2.5	0.9	0.9	6.0
Belgium	118	117	120	2.1	4.4	−0.8	2.6
Switzerland	112	114	117	1.1	4.7	1.8	2.6
Germany, West	107	112	114	0.2	5.9	4.7	2.7
Japan	112	112	111	1.3	3.7	0.0	−0.9
Less developed countries							
Brazil	902	1,087	1,235	39.6	22.1	20.5	19.2
Chile	666	785	1,019	30.3	36.1	17.9	35.3
Argentina	313	436	673	18.3	14.2	39.3	72.1
Vietnam, South	312	372	466	16.6	24.3	19.2	33.5
Korea, South	216	235	264	12.1	9.1	8.8	16.3
Colombia	195	214	231	10.4	7.7	9.7	11.1
Yugoslavia§	156	178	193	6.0	9.8	14.1	12.2
India	166	172	179	7.7	6.4	3.6	5.9
Ireland	139	147	157	4.7	5.3	5.8	7.5
Israel	124	136	155	2.5	6.8	9.7	16.5
Tunisia	138	146	154	4.9	3.8	5.8	6.9
Spain	125	132	141	3.5	1.6	5.6	6.8
South Africa	120	125	132	2.5	3.4	4.2	6.5
Morocco	116	121	132	1.3	7.4	4.3	7.3
Iran	113	120	128	1.4	3.7	6.2	6.7
Greece	117	120	124	2.2	2.6	2.6	4.2
Venezuela	116	120	123	2.2	1.7	3.4	4.2
Costa Rica	118	121	122	1.4	8.2	2.5	0.0
Thailand	117	117	122	2.7	0.0	0.0	5.2
Iraq	113	121	117	0.5	9.7	7.1	−4.9
El Salvador	114	108	110	0.8	8.5	−5.3	1.9

*January–June (average).
†First half 1972 over first half 1971.
‡Prices of finished goods only.
§Prices of industrial products.
Sources: International Monetary Fund, *International Financial Statistics;* United Nations, *Monthly Bulletin of Statistics.*

indicate the extent to which food prices had increased at a relatively higher or lower rate.) Among developed market economies, increases in food prices were becoming rather serious in the Scandinavian countries, Japan, the U.K., and, to a relatively lesser extent, France. Again, the problem was much more acute in many less developed countries, where by far the biggest proportion of consumer expenditure went to foodstuffs. As one would expect from the indices in Table I, the most serious situations were in South America, South Vietnam, Cambodia, and two countries that had experienced considerable deterioration recently in their price levels, Nigeria and the Philippines.

Wholesale Prices. Probably the most encouraging sign in many industrial countries in 1971–72 was the noticeable slackening in the rates at which their wholesale prices were increasing. It was difficult to say how much of this improvement was due to reductions in the prices of many primary commodities and how much to various price controls that, by concentrating on industrial products, tended to be much more effective at the wholesale than at the retail level. Whatever the causes, the fact remained that wholesale prices were considerably more stable in 1971 and 1972 than the cost of living index. (*See* Table III.) In 1972 this was true even of a number of industrial countries that were experiencing very high rates of inflation; *e.g.*, the Netherlands, Norway, and the U.K.

The improvement was not shared by many less developed countries. In fact, 1971 and 1972 almost certainly provided a classic example of inflation being exported from high- to the low-income nations. The increasing difficulties of many less developed countries can be seen clearly in Table III. In 1970 there were only four instances in which wholesale prices were rising by more than 10%. In 1972 this happened in almost half of the countries included in the table, with increases ranging from 72.1% in Argentina to 11.1% in Colombia. (MILIVOJE PANIC)

See also Commodities, Primary; Economy, World; Employment, Wages, and Hours; Income, National; Industrial Review; Investment, International; Merchandising; Money and Banking; Payments and Reserves, International; Stock Exchanges; Trade, International.

Prisons and Penology

Prison riots and demonstrations continued in 1972—though none as bad as those in Attica, N.Y., in 1971. The worst, in Trieste, Italy, in August, resulted in three deaths. Two of the dead were minors who suffocated when a group of young prisoners set fire to bedding and furniture. The third was a middle-aged Roman arrested in Rimini for stealing a wallet. He, too, suffocated.

Riots had beset other Italian jails, including the modern Rebibbia prison in Rome despite its football fields, libraries, carpentry workshops, and 175 television sets. Proceedings were later opened against the governor, deputy governor, and several wardens for alleged mass beatings. In the United States there were uprisings in the maximum security wing of the Passaic County (N.J.) jail, and at both the State Penitentiary and the House of Correction in Maryland. Inmates at the District of Columbia jail protested the length of time they were held awaiting trial or transfer by seizing the director of the Washington Department of Corrections and nine other hostages. After two groups of inmates were processed through the U.S. District Court, the hostages were released.

The New York State Special Commission, whose inquiry into the disastrous Attica riots was published in September, found that the riot did not arise from a revolutionary conspiracy but was rather a "spontaneous burst of violent anger" by a new type of prisoner—mainly young blacks no longer prepared to accept the "petty humiliations and racism that characterize prison life." The report criticized Gov. Nelson Rockefeller of New York for not personally appearing on the scene and satisfying himself that there was no alternative to armed intervention and that all precautions against excessive force had been taken; it condemned both the taking of hostages by the prisoners and the arming of the guards, state troopers, and sheriff's deputies with lethal weapons only.

In Argentina, 16 detained guerrillas were killed in August by police fire while attempting to escape from a military base in Patagonia. One of the dead was the wife of Mario Roberto Santucho, a guerrilla leader who, with five others, had hijacked a jet to Chile the previous week.

Two prisoners in Brazil were shot dead, also in August, during a riot by 54 prisoners detained at a police station in the centre of Rio de Janeiro. Five hours of submachine gun fire by troops and police persuaded the remaining prisoners to surrender.

In France, the serious riot at Toul prison in 1971 resulted in a whole range of penal reform measures announced early in 1972. These included more suitable work and higher pay for prisoners, social security for prisoners' families, and a much more precise definition of inmates' rights so as to allow less arbitrary powers to the authorities.

The most noteworthy feature of the widespread but mainly passive demonstrations in many English prisons was the fact that they were triggered by the outside organization PROP (Preservation of the Rights of Prisoners), modeled on KRUM, an organization of ex-prisoners and academics in Sweden and Norway. PROP had extremely effective publicity methods. It began by calling itself a trade union for prisoners and sought to force negotiations with the Home Office over grievances and rights by calling for strikes and demonstrations. The Home Office refused to negotiate, but otherwise responded calmly and avoided any serious confrontation. At one time, it was also faced by strike and go-slow threats by the Prison Officers Association, the trade union for guards, unless firm action was taken against demonstrations.

Causes of Unrest. The overt causes of these phenomena included sometimes out-of-date prison rules and, often, overcrowding, old and unsuitable buildings, lack of suitable work, and shortage of staff. In Britain, with a higher daily average prison population than in other Western European countries, guards sometimes had to work as many as 70 hours a week.

There were probably also deeper and less overt reasons. Any prison contains, on the one hand, unwilling captives, often socially and psychologically deprived, and, on the other, staff whose task it is to keep prisoners contained. The fundamentally different basic aims of the two groups are reinforced by two very different value systems. The inmate culture is both criminal and antiauthoritarian. Its values are so hostile to authority that punishments by those in charge may bestow status on defiant prisoners, and rewards may produce suspicion or worse among fellow inmates.

By contrast, the staff culture is authoritarian and, sometimes without recognizing it, concerned with emphasizing the status superiority of staff over all

Printing:
see Industrial Review

LEFT, JERRY CABLUCK—THE NEW YORK TIMES; RIGHT, EDWARD HAUSNER—THE NEW YORK TIMES

The disparity in prison life in the U.S. is dramatically illustrated by these two prison scenes. At left, a prisoner at the Federal Correctional Institution at Fort Worth, Tex., picnics with visitors. The photograph at right was taken in the Brooklyn House of Detention for Men while a group seeking support for reforms in New York prisons and courts toured the facility. The man lying on the floor is manacled to a cell bar.

inmates. The reluctance to embrace fundamental reforms, which is common among basic grade staff, appears to stem from the fact that while both guards and prisoners often come from a working-class background, one group blatantly disregarded the law and the other did not. And, such is human nature that the faithfully law-abiding may sometimes secretly envy the daring lawbreaker—all the more reason for the former to require dramatic demonstrations that crime does not pay. Improving the lot of the prisoner may seem a psychological threat to the guards, who of necessity find themselves in close physical proximity to criminals whom they therefore need to repudiate all the more strongly. The presence among prisoners of violent and unstable men may also prove a real physical threat. It is no wonder the two groups tend frequently to be in a state of undeclared warfare.

Reforms, therefore, have to take into account the problems of the staff—their need for support, status, and a more constructive role before they can willingly tolerate attempts to tackle the problems of inmates. The opening of communications among all levels of staff and between staff and inmates is essential so that grievances can be voiced and difficulties recognized before they blow up. But the inhibitions to open communications are not only psychological.

Prison Alternatives. Throughout 1972 there was, however, a growing body of opinion that the main task for penology was not to build more prisons but to devise treatment-intensive alternatives to imprisonment in the community in which many relatively harmless offenders could be dealt with. This led to the emergence, in the U.K., of such bodies as RAP (Radical Alternatives to Prison), which wanted virtually all prisons abolished, and to more modest new legislation such as the Criminal Justice Act 1972, which did, in fact, provide alternatives such as community service and day centres for offenders and bail hostels for those without fixed address who would otherwise be remanded in custody.

A statistical glimpse of imprisonment was given by René Pleven, the French minister of justice, in a speech made in June. According to Pleven, the Netherlands led the league table in Western Europe with only 25.4 prisoners per 100,000 population; Belgium had 64.2, France 66, Denmark 71.7, and the U.K. 72.5. To make any real impact on reducing the prison population, major new resources would have to be developed within the community itself. Much of this would have to be social work in one form or another. The techniques and, to some extent, the nature of social work continued to change in 1972, which also saw the emergence of social work management as a profession equal in status and skill to medical administration, at least in the U.K. The Butterworth report, published in August, extended this development to probation and aftercare. Salaries were massively increased to a level that gave probation work recognition as a genuine profession, and the drain away from it and toward the new unified and large local authority social work departments consequently was expected to dry up.

On Feb. 16, 1972, in Strasbourg, France, heads of the prison services of all 17 member states of the Council of Europe accepted the principle that "deprivation of liberty shall be effected in material and moral conditions which ensure respect for human dignity"; they agreed on a set of minimum prison standards ranging from concerns about food and bedding, cell space, medical care, and visits to legal protection of prisoners and their preparation for reintegration in the outside world.

But how should authorities plan over the long run for resources for the prevention of crime and the treatment of offenders? As part of its work in this field, the Council of Europe set up an expert committee to study forecasting and prediction methods. The Harvard University criminologists Eleanor Glueck (*see* Obituaries) and Sheldon Glueck, years previously, had pioneered prediction methods to forecast the occurrence of juvenile delinquency with considerable success. Other work had concentrated on the incidence of future crime on the basis of presently known criminality. During the Council of Europe meetings, French experts demonstrated accurate forecasting methods based on past correlations between major socioeconomic factors and the incidence of crime. Whether such methods could also lend themselves to forecasting the future needs for human and material resources to prevent crime or to treat offenders remained to be seen. For they could not take accurate account of the development of future preventive or treatment techniques and the possible success these might achieve.

It was encouraging to note that the California Probation Subsidy program seemed to continue its success in 1972. Begun in the mid-1960s, this program subsidized offenders on probation with money that otherwise would have been spent on penal institutions. The need to build many new institutions was thus avoided. Another California project that saw itself transplanted to Europe was the New Careers idea, in which selected offenders were supported in their attempt to achieve a high degree of legitimate success. Allied to this notion of self-help was the spreading practice of encouraging some offenders to help others like themselves. For in so doing, they often helped themselves. In the U.K., for example, some ex-offenders continued to be trained as wardens for hostels for homeless offenders.

In an effort to tackle the problem from yet a different angle, the Council of Europe set up another expert committee to study the question of decriminalization and depenalization. In some countries, matters such as homosexual behaviour or abortion had ceased, usually within certain limits, to be offenses (with a consequent reduction in the offenders who had somehow to be dealt with). Then there was behaviour that, though formally still an offense, would not be prosecuted unless there were special circumstances.

In June the Supreme Court of the United States struck down the death penalty in virtually all cases on the grounds that, as currently administered, it violated the constitutional ban on "cruel and unusual punishment." For practical purposes this meant that the U.S. joined Britain as yet another abolitionist country. Almost all Western European countries had abandoned the death penalty, or kept it on the statute book without using it. But it continued to be applied in other parts of the world, including the U.S.S.R. and the continent of Africa. (HUGH J. KLARE)

See also Crime.

Profits

At the beginning of 1972, the cyclical divergences of the two preceding years gave way to renewed expansion in nearly all the Western industrialized economies. The recession in the U.S. was more than a year past its trough. Canada, which had suffered a slowdown, already had a full year of renewed, rapid growth behind it. West Germany's minor recession reached its low point in the final quarter of 1971. France, after a temporary deceleration early in 1970, continued to expand into 1972. The Japanese economy bottomed out early in 1972, after suffering its longest recession of the postwar period (albeit only a growth recession). Britain, where efforts at reflation had boosted prices more than growth, appeared to be coming out of the doldrums. Even Italy gave some tentative indications of breaking out of its two-year stagnation.

This convergence of cyclical patterns was highly favourable to profit expansion. A mitigating factor for some countries was the currency realignment of 1971, which in the main benefited the U.S. at the expense of Japan and West Germany, but the available evidence suggested that any adverse effects on this score were offset by the coincident elimination of the U.S. import surcharge and the beneficial effects of the underlying cyclical recovery. All five of the countries with current profits data—the U.S., U.K., Canada, West Germany, and Japan—reported rising earnings in 1972. Moreover, it appeared reasonable to infer that a general increase in profits was also in process elsewhere. This was suggested not only by the fact of widespread economic resurgence but also by the rise of equity prices on the world's stock markets. Most notable, perhaps, was the surge of the U.S. Dow Jones industrial average beyond the 1,000 mark in November. Italy, where the market hovered around the lowest levels in 13 years, was the only major exception.

In the U.S. the recovery of profits gained momentum in 1972. By the second quarter, the rate of profits, both before and after taxes, exceeded the earlier records established in the second half of 1968. (*See* Table II.) By the third quarter, profits before taxes reached $90 billion (all profits figures are seasonally adjusted annual rates) and after-tax profits were $48 billion. These figures were 14 and 15%, respectively, higher than the results of the corresponding quarter of 1971 and 39 and 47%, respectively, above the lowest level of recent years, reached in the final quarter of 1970. In real terms—after adjustment for inflation—the behaviour of profits appeared more subdued. Unlike real gross national product (GNP), which exceeded its prerecession peak (third quarter 1969) by 9% in the third quarter of 1972, corporate profits after taxes in constant dollars were still some 13% below their peak (1966).

The improvement of profits in 1972 rested on a strong foundation of rising volume, productivity gains, and higher prices. In the third quarter of 1972, the physical output of nonfinancial corporations, which account for 80% of all corporate profits, exceeded that of the corresponding quarter of 1971 by 9.2%. A 5% increase in productivity permitted this expansion of output to take place with no more than a 4% gain in the number of man-hours worked. As a result, a 5.8% increase in compensation per man-hour raised unit labour costs by only 0.8%. At the same time, unit nonlabour costs rose no more than 0.3%, while unit

Table I. Canada: Profits and Related Measures
Seasonally adjusted

Period	Corporation profits before taxes at annual rates (Can$000,000)	Profit margin, all industries (%) Before taxes	After taxes	Unit labour costs 1962=100
1970: First quarter	8,216	6.2	4.0	136.0
Second quarter	7,748	5.8	3.6	137.1
Third quarter	7,912	5.8	3.7	138.8
Fourth quarter	7,360	5.4	3.5	140.8
1971: First quarter	7,860	5.8	3.6	142.2
Second quarter	8,660	6.2	3.9	145.7
Third quarter	9,752	6.2	4.0	145.9
Fourth quarter	9,928	6.2	4.2	147.6
1972: First quarter	10,196	6.7	4.4	151.0
Second quarter	10,260	—	—	152.1

Sources: Statistics Canada, *Canadian Statistical Review* (October 1972), *Industrial Corporations, Financial Statistics, First Quarter 1972* (October 1972); Bank of Canada, *Monthly Review* (October 1972).

prices gained 1.3%. The result was a 7% increase in unit profits.

The upsurge of profits in Canada that began at the end of 1970, after two years of decline, continued into 1972, notwithstanding some further appreciation of the exchange rate. The pace of the increase was somewhat slower, however. Corporation profits before taxes reached a record level of Can$10.3 billion (seasonally adjusted annual rate) in the second quarter of 1972, 18% above the year-earlier level and 39% higher than at the cyclical turning point of 1970. (*See* Table I.) Inventory profits were roughly the same in the two periods, indicating that the recorded change in profit levels reflected essentially an improvement in returns from operations. Seasonally adjusted data further reveal a steadily rising trend in profit margins.

Despite a temporary interruption of economic growth in the United Kingdom because of inventory liquidation at the beginning of the year, profits extended their gains into 1972. Worldwide income of resident companies reached a record seasonally adjusted quarterly rate of £2,900 million in the second quarter, 9% higher than in the corresponding quarter of 1971. (*See* Table III.) Gross trading profits (operating income before inventory valuation adjustment, depreciation, interest expense, and income taxes) arising in the U.K. also rose 9% in the second quarter to surpass earlier records. The fastest growth, however, occurred in rent and nontrading income arising in the U.K., which increased 16%.

Profits might have increased even more in the absence of the July 1971 commitment by Britain's leading companies to hold price increases to 5% over the subsequent 12 months. Indeed, Britain's severe inflation, which frustrated government measures to spur real growth, contributed to the exchange crisis and the sterling float of June, and finally brought about a wage and price freeze in November, came mainly at the retail end.

Mirroring the renewed economic expansion that began in West Germany at the end of 1971, profits in West Germany appeared to be on a rising trend in 1972, notwithstanding the 14% upvaluation of the mark in December 1971. Tracking profits in Germany is difficult, because the published data aggregate corporate profits with income from professional activities, farming, rental, and interest (called income from entrepreneurial activity and property; IEP). However, the Bundesbank in its October 1972 *Monthly Report* noted that the earnings of enterprises reached their low point in the second half of 1971 and recovered thereafter on the strength of higher production, productivity, and prices. IEP reportedly grew 6.5% in the first half of 1972, seasonally adjusted. The published figures, which are not seasonally adjusted, indicate that IEP before taxes reached DM. 91.3 billion in the first half of 1972, up 7% over the corresponding period of 1971. (*See* Table IV.) At the same time, after-tax IEP rose 9.6% to DM. 73.7 billion. The dynamics of West Germany's profits recovery can be seen in an 8.8% increase in industrial output per man-hour (seasonally adjusted annual rate) during the first half of 1972, while wages and salaries per man-hour rose 8.5%.

Table II. United States Corporate Profits and Related Indicators

Seasonally adjusted annual rates

Period	Profits (in $000,000,000) Before taxes	Less inventory profits	After taxes	Profits per dollar of sales (cents)*	Ratio of profits to income originating in corporations (%)†	Ratio of price to unit labour cost index‡
1970: First quarter	70.7	64.3	36.4	4.1	8.4	97.1
Second quarter	70.8	67.1	36.2	4.2	8.3	97.0
Third quarter	71.9	67.3	36.5	4.0	8.3	96.6
Fourth quarter	64.9	62.2	32.7	3.6	7.5	96.4
1971: First quarter	76.5	71.8	38.4	4.0	8.5	96.7
Second quarter	78.1	73.8	39.5	4.3	8.5	97.4
Third quarter	79.1	73.3	41.6	4.2	8.9	97.9
Fourth quarter	76.1	72.2	40.8	4.0	8.7	98.1
1972: First quarter	82.9	76.5	44.2	4.1	9.0	97.8
Second quarter	85.9	80.3	45.8	4.3	9.1	98.2
Third quarter	90.0	83.9	48.0	—	9.3	99.2

*After taxes, all manufacturing.
†All industries.
‡Manufacturing; 1967 = 100.
Sources: *Survey of Current Business* (July and November 1972); *Business Conditions Digest* (November 1972).

Table III. United Kingdom: Company Income and Related Indicators

Period	Seasonally adjusted quarterly rates company income (£000,000): Total	Income arising in the United Kingdom: Gross trading profits of companies	Rent and nontrading income	Income from abroad	1963=100 Seasonally adjusted: Output per person employed at 1963 prices All production industries	Wages and salaries per unit of output, whole economy
1970: First quarter	2,331	1,277	524	530	126.6	130.6
Second quarter	2,371	1,273	541	557	127.0	132.9
Third quarter	2,365	1,272	554	539	128.9	136.2
Fourth quarter	2,489	1,339	575	575	130.2	140.2
1971: First quarter	2,570	1,360	589	621	130.5	145.9
Second quarter	2,674	1,427	604	643	133.2	148.2
Third quarter	2,776	1,520	635	621	135.2	151.2
Fourth quarter	2,721	1,462	629	630	136.2	152.6
1972: First quarter	2,800	1,480	651	669	135.0	158.5
Second quarter	2,902	1,553	698	651	143.7	159.3

Source: Central Statistical Office, *Economic Trends* (October 1972).

Table IV. West Germany: Profit and Income Developments

	Income from entrepreneurial activity and property In DM. 000,000; without adjustment for seasonal variation: Before income taxes	After income taxes	Share of national income (%)	1962=100; Seasonally adjusted: Output per man-hour in industry	Unit labour costs	Industrial wholesale prices
1970: First half	82,150	65,460	33.1	158	124	106.6
Second half	93,850	75,580	33.4	158	132	108.5
1971: First half	85,310	67,210	30.9	164	136	112.0
Second half	97,200	78,150	31.7	166	142	113.1
1972: First half	91,280	73,660	30.4	173	142	115.0

Sources: *Wirtschaft & Statistik* No. 9 (1972); *Statistische Beihefte zu den Monatsberichten der Deutschen Bundesbank, Reihe 4* (October 1972).

In Japan corporate profits bottomed out around the beginning of 1972 and were rising strongly by the second half of the year. A survey based on 546 corporations listed on the first and second sections of the Tokyo Stock Exchange indicated that, in the half-year period ended in March 1972, after-tax profits were down 2.5% relative to the immediately preceding six months. This was the third consecutive period of falling after-tax profits. The turnabout, however, was evident in pretax ordinary profits, which rose 1.4% in the October 1971–March 1972 period, and the rebound gathered more momentum in April–September 1972 than had been expected. A survey of 548 companies listed on the two stock exchange sections showed pretax and post-tax profits up 10.7 and 8.6%, respectively. The recovery of profits among manufacturing companies was particularly notable.

(GERALD A. POLLACK)

See also Stock Exchanges.

Propaganda

The year 1972 was one of important change in international propaganda, marked by more moderate, more subtle patterns in the attitudes of the great powers toward each other. The most obvious occurred in the propaganda relationship between the U.S., the Soviet Union, and China. In general, it reflected their improved relations, most strikingly illustrated by U.S. Pres. Richard Nixon's visits to Moscow and Peking.

Both China and the Soviet Union softened their propaganda images of the U.S. without sacrificing their fundamental political positions. The change was most dramatic in the case of China, chiefly because Peking's language had been more strident. The new language first became evident in 1971, when such familiar phrases as "running dogs of imperialism" were dropped from references to U.S. leaders. In 1972 "imperialism" still described U.S. policy, especially with regard to Southeast Asia, but the tone was noticeably more subdued.

While the changing realities dictated an abrupt turn by China, Moscow's propaganda line on the U.S. had been undergoing slow modification since the depths of the cold war. The process became even more pronounced as Nixon's visit neared. The U.S.S.R. was not prepared to cast the U.S. leadership in a generally favourable light, but it had reached the point of crediting the U.S. with wisdom on specific issues, such as arms control and trade.

Moscow and Peking found it easier to treat Washington with moderation than each other. As propaganda lines toward the U.S. became more judicious, the bitterness of their feud stood out more clearly. Each accused the other of betraying the world Communist revolution and of plotting aggression against neighbouring countries. Peking specifically named the Soviet Union as its number one enemy, a distinction once accorded the U.S. One subject on which the two seemed to agree was the war in Vietnam. In remarkably parallel fashion, they softened their tones on this theme. Neither protested when U.S. leaders in 1972 began to state publicly their judgment that both Peking and Moscow wanted the war to end with a just, negotiated solution.

A more interesting propaganda exercise on the war was conducted by North Vietnam itself. By 1972 Hanoi had learned the usefulness of wider reporting by U.S. correspondents, who tended to emphasize the human side of the conflict. From Hanoi's standpoint such reporting could be regarded only as a decided propaganda plus. North Vietnam also scored a short-term propaganda success with its charges that the U.S. was bombing dikes deliberately, threatening to flood much of the country's rice-growing land and most heavily populated areas. U.S. officials flatly denied the accusations, which decreased as the flood season passed. U.S. specialists judged that Hanoi had bungled one propaganda opportunity by its overly blatant attempts to exploit three captured U.S. flyers, who were released into the custody of U.S. antiwar activists in September. However, the subsequent highly publicized tug-of-war between the activists and the U.S. Defense Department, which claimed jurisdiction over the airmen, largely nullified any U.S. effort to capitalize on Hanoi's blunder.

In the volatile Middle East, Egyptian Pres. Anwar as-Sadat's expulsion of Soviet advisers and military forces greatly reduced the credibility of any Egyptian threat against Israel. It also automatically created pressures on Israel for a corresponding gesture, and Israeli leaders, almost immediately, began to spell out their terms for a settlement more clearly than before. While they offered little that was specific in the way of compromise, they did establish the point that they remained flexible.

U.S. propaganda required less adjustment in 1972 than that of Washington's propaganda opponents, probably because it relied more on selective application of fact and interpretation and normally avoided intemperate language. One of the most delicate U.S. propaganda undertakings of the year was the public presentation of the Nixon administration's approach to peace in Vietnam. In essence, the administration represented its gradual withdrawal of U.S. forces while attempting to negotiate a political settlement as the most that could be expected of a nation that honoured its commitments.

Content aside, there were few substantial changes in the scope of international government information programs. The U.S. Information Agency spent $196.8 million, about the level of the previous year, for activities ranging from broadcasting, film production, and publishing through escort service for visiting journalists. In addition, the Department of State spent an estimated $40.5 million for propaganda. There was no official U.S. estimate of the comparable Soviet outlay, though privately U.S. officials believed it was somewhat less than their own. Among other Western nations France was estimated to spend $313 million annually for external propaganda, a figure swollen by the cost of thousands of teachers and technical advisers in former colonies.

In one of the key measurements of propaganda effort, the Voice of America broadcast more than 800 hours per week in 36 languages through its global network. The campaign directed at North Vietnam was stepped up after Hanoi opened its April offensive. Uzbek was added to the Russian, Ukrainian, and Georgian languages in programs beamed to the Soviet Union. In addition, Radio Liberty and Radio Free Europe, propaganda organizations privately operated but with U.S. government support, broadcast almost 1,100 hours per week to Eastern Europe. Other nations with major propaganda broadcast programs were the Soviet Union with 1,900 hours per week, China with 1,250 hours, West Germany with 625 hours, and Egypt with 950 hours. Egypt, in fact, provided a dramatic illustration of propaganda's importance to some countries. U.S. intelligence sources estimated that Egypt spent 2.3% of its budget—by far the world record in comparative effort—or about $112 million for external propaganda in 1972.

(HENRY L. TREWHITT)

Psychology

The concept of human behaviour control had come a long way in the more than 30 years since B. F. Skinner and a few associates had formed its basic principles by observing pigeons and rats in Skinner Boxes. In 1972, it was being used in schools, mental hospitals, rehabilitation wards, industry, national parks, and by that nice couple down the street in raising their children. The behavioural techniques used and refined in the work by the University of Kansas Bureau of Child Research at Juniper Gardens, a black housing project in the poorest section of Kansas City, had been spread to many parts of the U.S. through workshops, books, and teaching programs.

The long-simmering controversy over the meaningfulness of intelligence tests grew hotter as researchers disputed the claims of racial and sex-related differences in intelligence made by Arthur Jensen of the University of California, Richard Herrnstein of Harvard, and William Shockley of Stanford. Most of the new work contended that IQ tests were culture-loaded

Public Utilities:
see Cooperatives;
Fuel and Power;
Industrial Review;
Transportation

in favour of middle class whites, leading to the unfair classification of thousands of black and Chicano children as retarded. Psychologist George Mayeske of the U.S. Office of Education reported that 20–30% of the answers on achievement and IQ tests reflected cultural background rather than native intelligence, and that this was enough to account for the significant differences in test scores of different culture groups.

The 1972 International Congress of Primatology brought the world's leading researchers together in the U.S. for the first time. A significant finding was reported by J. S. Gartlan of the University of Bristol, Eng., and the Federal University of Cameroon. Social structures maintained by five species of monkeys and baboons living in mountains, savannas, lake basins, and rain forests were found, contrary to previously held assumptions, to vary depending on the surroundings and, within the same surroundings, over a period of time. Changes within a structure seemed to be most affected by rapid ecological changes, especially deforestation, and by marked changes in the mode and efficiency of hunting.

The value and effectiveness of encounter groups and other forms of sensitivity training came under close scrutiny. One study, by psychologists M. A. Lieberman and M. B. Miles and psychiatrist Irvin Yalom, found that 9.6% of the participants in the groups studied experienced psychiatric breakdowns following encounter therapy. Most casualties appeared within groups with "charismatic and authoritarian" leaders; low-risk groups were those with "loving leaders."

Psychological research on social unrest covered violence, women's liberation, minorities, drugs, alcoholism, and the poor. Violence was scrutinized by a team at the University of Michigan headed by Monica Blumenthal, which found that institutional violence, such as war or police activity, was not considered violence by nearly all the 1,400 men surveyed. The report of the U.S. surgeon general's Scientific Advisory Committee on Television and Social Behavior noted a limited link between violence seen on television and the actions of the already aggressive child. Researchers on the committee asked that some type of violence scale be established for use in regulating television programming. Many women scientists asked that research on women be done by women, advancing the same argument used by other minority groups: that research by nonmembers is done from a different viewpoint and, therefore, measures the group unfairly. The importance being assigned to drug and alcoholism studies in the U.S. had been underscored in 1971 by the establishment of a Special Action Office for Drug Abuse Prevention to coordinate the activities of 14 federal departments. Reports done for various governments on the use and abuse of marijuana, which generally neither condemned nor condoned the drug, brought a rash of pro-legalization movements throughout the world.

Renewed attention was paid to the works of Carl Jung, Wilhelm Reich, and others as part of a general growth of interest in mysticism and mystical phenomena. Research on transcendental meditation, alternate life-styles, and religious movements such as the "Jesus people" reflected the continuing popular interest in this area.

Do the Poor Want to Work, by social psychologist Leonard Goodwin of the Brookings Institution, said yes they do, quite emphatically. Goodwin surveyed 4,000 welfare recipients and found they had the same strong life expectations, work ethic, and identification with work as a means of self-respect and personal development as the middle class worker. Goodwin charged that the middle class misconception that the poor do not want to work distorted public policies and distracted attention from the real problems of unemployment. (PATRICE DAILY HORN)

See also Medicine.

Publishing

Harassment and censorship were all too common experiences in publishing in many parts of the world in 1972. In the International Press Institute's annual review, published in December and entitled *Another Year of Lost Battles,* director Ernest Meyer stated that scarcely one-fifth of UN member countries enjoyed what could genuinely be called freedom of information. Referring to continuing governmental intimidation of journalists and manipulation of the mass media, Meyer stressed the danger in the acceptance, by growing numbers of governments and individuals, of attacks on freedom of expression as justifiable. The report cited as most serious the silencing of the Philippines press on the pretext that it "consciously or unconsciously" favoured Communism. (*See* PHILIPPINES.)

In the U.S. the issue centred around a 5–4 ruling made on June 29 by the Supreme Court that grew out of three incidents in which reporters, most notably Earl Caldwell of the *New York Times,* had refused to testify when subpoenaed by grand juries, saying that any appearance before a secret panel would destroy their credibility among confidential news sources. Writing for the majority, Justice Byron R. White denied the reporters' claim to constitutional protection: "The First Amendment interest asserted by the newsmen was outweighed by the general obligation of a citizen to appear before a grand jury or at a trial, pursuant to a subpoena, and give what information he possesses." In dissenting Justice Potter Stewart maintained that "the court's crabbed view of the First Amendment reflects a disturbing insensitivity to the critical role of an independent press in our society [and] invites state and federal authorities to undermine the historic independence of the press by attempting to annex the journalistic profession as an investigative arm of government."

The first test of the decision came in October, when reporter Peter Bridge (*see* BIOGRAPHY) was jailed for 21 days after being held in contempt of court for refusing to amplify in secret session what he had reported about a New Jersey political scandal. Ironically, Bridge no longer represented a paper; the *Newark Evening News,* once New Jersey's largest, had been crippled by inept management and union troubles and ceased publication on August 31. In November the court's ruling was invoked again when Los Angeles newsman William T. Farr received an open-ended jail sentence for refusing to disclose his sources for an article on the Charles Manson murder trial. It was also used later to jail briefly the general manager of New York radio station WBAI-FM, Edwin A. Goodman, who refused to turn over tapes made during a 1970 prison riot, and John F. Lawrence, Washington, D.C., bureau chief of the *Los Angeles Times.* The *Times* refused to release tapes of an interview concerning the Watergate affair until released from its promise of secrecy by the person interviewed.

With an irony that plagued U.S. journalism throughout 1972, the "Newark (N.J.) Evening News" announced on Aug. 29, 1972, that it would cease publication on August 31, six weeks before its reporter Peter Bridge was jailed for refusing to reveal to a grand jury his source in a local bribery story. A June 1972 Supreme Court decision declared that journalists could not be guaranteed professional immunity from compelled testimony under the First Amendment, a ruling that many felt would seriously hamper investigative reporting.

(TOP) WIDE WORLD; (BOTTOM) TYRONE DUKES—THE NEW YORK TIMES

World Daily Newspapers and Circulations, 1971–72*

Country	Daily newspapers	Circulation per 1,000 of population
AFRICA		
Algeria	4	14
Angola	5	10
Cameroon	2	3
Central African Republic	2	0.6
Ceuta	1	58
Chad	1	0.2
Congo (Brazzaville)	3	0.7
Dahomey	2	1
Egypt	15	23
Ethiopia	6	1
Ghana	3	46
Guinea	1	1
Ivory Coast	1	10
Kenya	3	14
Liberia	2	6
Libya	7	20
Malagasy Republic	13	8
Mali	3	0.6
Mauritius	13	78
Melilla	1	60
Morocco	7	14
Mozambique	6	7
Namibia	2	12
Niger	1	0.5
Nigeria	11	7
Portuguese Guinea	1	4
Réunion	1	64
Rhodesia	2	16
Senegal	1	5
Seychelles	2	31
Sierra Leone	2	16
Somali Republic	2	2
South Africa	23	40
Sudan	13	8
Tanzania	7	5
Togo	3	7
Tunisia	4	16
Uganda	4	8
Zaire	7	1
Zambia	2	13
Total	188	
NORTH AMERICA		
Bahama Islands	3	163
Barbados	1	90
Bermuda	1	233
British Honduras	2	32
Canada	118	206
Costa Rica	5	101
Cuba	8	...
Dominican Republic	7	32
El Salvador	7	103
Guadeloupe	1	139
Guatemala	9	27
Haiti	6	5
Honduras	7	17
Jamaica	2	66
Leeward Islands	3	33
Martinique	2	138
Mexico	200	...
Netherlands Antilles	5	149
Nicaragua	7	51
Panama (incl. Canal Zone)	13	103
Puerto Rico	4	182
Trinidad and Tobago	3	119
United States	1,748	302
Virgin Islands (U.S.)	3	221
Total	2,165	
SOUTH AMERICA		
Argentina	84	182
Bolivia	14	42
Brazil	257	36
Chile	122	86
Colombia	34	53
Ecuador	16	41
French Guiana	1	29
Guyana	3	58
Paraguay	11	41
Peru	85	122
Surinam	5	52
Uruguay	31	140
Venezuela	38	71
Total	701	
ASIA		
Afghanistan	8	6
Burma	28	9
Cambodia	26	22
China	392	19
Cyprus	10	108
Hong Kong	14	485
India	593	14
Indonesia	85	7
Iran	33	8
Iraq	5	...
Israel	24	208
Japan	168	511
Jordan	5	24
Korea, North	7	...
Korea, South	43	66
Kuwait	5	35
Laos	7	3
Lebanon	52	...
Macao	6	114
Malaysia	32	74
Mongolia	2	103
Nepal	16	3
Pakistan	139	6
Philippines	23	27
Ryukyu Islands	10	284
Saudi Arabia	5	10
Singapore	8	201
Sri Lanka (Ceylon)	19	49
Syria	5	...
Taiwan	32	64
Thailand	24	21
Turkey	400	41
Vietnam, North	7	...
Vietnam, South	56	67
Yemen	5	18
Total	2,294	
EUROPE		
Albania	2	52
Austria	25	268
Belgium	44	260
Bulgaria	12	193
Czechoslovakia	25	252
Denmark	90	364
Finland	67	358
France	106	238
Germany, East	40	445
Germany, West	393	319
Gibraltar	2	231
Greece	110	79
Hungary	27	214
Iceland	5	448
Ireland	7	233
Italy	70	127
Luxembourg	7	412
Malta	7	...
Netherlands	94	307
Norway	81	383
Poland	43	209
Portugal	20	71
Romania	55	169
Spain	116	104
Sweden	114	534
Switzerland	117	375
U.S.S.R.	639	336
United Kingdom	106	488
Vatican City (Holy See)	1	†
Yugoslavia	24	85
Total	2,449	
OCEANIA		
American Samoa	1	90
Australia	58	321
Cook Islands	1	38
Fiji	1	30
French Polynesia	4	93
Guam	2	168
New Caledonia	1	71
New Zealand	38	376
Niue	1	60
Tonga	2	16
Total	109	
Grand total	7,906	

*Only newspapers issued four or more times weekly are included. Areas not listed had no known daily newspapers.
†Circulation largely outside territory.
Sources: *UN Statistical Yearbook 1971 (1972); Newspaper Press Directory 1972; Editor & Publisher International Yearbook 1971*; other secondary sources.

(WILLIAM A. HACHTEN)

In the U.K. in September the Franks Committee on the Official Secrets Act recommended repeal of the catchall clause making it an offense to give or receive government information without official authority and formulation of a new Official Information Act defining official secrets more precisely. In July the Younger Committee reported that it found it impossible to devise a yardstick by which to judge when considerations of public importance should override respect for privacy and advised that the Press Council should judge each case on its merits. In contrast, trade union pressures caused concern. In October Anthony Wedgwood Benn (then Labour Party chairman) made public comments widely taken to mean that unions should take industrial action to restrict reporting unfavourable to the Labour Party. Party leader Harold Wilson repudiated any such idea in a formal statement. In December, following leakages of government documents on possible future closures of up to 40% of Britain's railway system, the offices of the *Railway Gazette* were searched by police, who were alleged to have tapped the paper's telephones.

Harassment of journalists took several forms. In Uganda in September, 16 U.K. journalists were imprisoned by order of Pres. Idi Amin and held for some days before being deported. Earlier David Bonavia, correspondent in Moscow since 1969 for *The Times* of London, was expelled from the Soviet Union for "systematic activities incompatible with the status of a foreign correspondent." In Czechoslovakia an Italian journalist was held in Prague for 43 days without trial.

Other infringements reported in 1971–72 included the sentencing in Greece, in November 1971, of the publisher of the English-language *Athens News* to seven months' imprisonment for publishing an inaccurate headline about U.S. Vice-Pres. Spiro Agnew's visit. In May 1972 the editor won an appeal of further charges. In Lebanon one newspaper manager was imprisoned and two fined heavily for publishing articles criticizing heads of other Arab states. In Pakistan editors, publishers, and printers were fined and imprisoned for "objectionable writings," and the *Sun*, a leading Karachi daily, was closed for violating censorship regulations. In Portugal revised press laws imposed tighter censorship and stiffer penalties. In Spain the influential liberal evening paper *Madrid* finally closed after suspension for political reasons in November 1971, and its publisher fled to France.

In Tanzania Pres. Julius Nyerere dismissed the editor of the government-owned *The Standard* and that paper and the *Nationalist*, both English-language dailies, were to be merged "in the interests of rationalization and consolidation of the Socialist revolution." In Turkey *Aksam*, one of the oldest daily papers, was closed by the military authorities for derision of martial law. In Zambia the editor of *The Times of Zambia* and *Sunday Times of Zambia* was replaced, under political pressure, by a diplomat with no journalistic experience.

Newspapers. Economic pressures shaping the fortunes of newspapers in the West were accentuated in 1972 by "stagflation"—inflation combined with a low level of business activity. Production costs continued to rise, notably as a result of demands for higher wages and salaries; sales remained stagnant, and advertising revenues were depressed. Several governments took measures to support newspapers.

In the U.K., however, inflation operated, temporarily, at least, to relieve economic pressures. Decimalization of the coinage in February 1971, which coincided with the inflationary effects of wage increases, enabled some newspaper owners to retrieve losses by doubling their prices from six pence in 1969 to five new pence (one shilling in predecimal coinage) without losing sales. A further boost came from an advertising boom associated late in 1972 with the inflationary tendencies of consumer spending. The most successful national paper was the *Sun,* relaunched in 1969 as a popular, picture-filled tabloid, which approached the three million circulation mark by the end of 1972. Two quality papers, *The Times* and the *Guardian,* reported greatly improved financial situations. Regional dailies and local weeklies were doing well, many with record sales and advertising revenues. The only national stoppage was one of four days in July, when printing unions joined a protest against imprisonment of five dockers for infringement of the 1971 Industrial Relations Act. (*See* LABOUR UNIONS; UNITED KINGDOM.) The U.K.'s entry into the EEC prompted closer relations between British and continental papers. In February *The Times* began joint and simultaneous publication with the French *Le Monde,* Italian *La Stampa,* and West German *Die Welt* of a series of special European reports; and the *Guardian* made permanent its publication of dispatches from *Le Monde* in the *Guardian Weekly.*

In continental Europe many newspapers were in difficulties, some because of high costs and low revenues, others because of industrial unrest; during 1972 several were forced to close. The perilous state of French newspapers was highlighted early in the year when the popular *Paris-Jour* (founded in 1959) was forced to close. Of France's national dailies only *Le Monde* was reported making a profit, and even it had lost ground in 1971. Most papers raised prices by at least 40%, an action requiring governmental approval. The government aided the press by preferential postal rates, tax exemptions, and subsidies. In the provinces papers, mainly in monopoly positions, were in less severe difficulties. *Sud-Ouest,* southwest France's leading daily, ran into trouble in February, when printers struck against the installation of new machinery.

France-Dimanche, the French weekly scandal sheet whose obituary notice on actor Maurice Chevalier, printed at the end of 1971, had preceded the entertainer's death by several days, scored another "scoop" in December 1972 when it reported the "secret remarriage of the duchess of Windsor." The duchess obtained a court order for the withdrawal of the issue carrying the story.

In the Netherlands public opinion opposed mergers as a threat to diversity and most papers, running at a loss, were sharing printing presses and cutting staffs to reduce costs. In July the government, already compensating the press for loss of advertising to commercial broadcasting, announced a subsidy of some 50 million guilders. In Denmark the trade unions made grants to help Social Democratic papers; in Norway the government introduced a loan fund to provide credit for papers threatened by rising costs; in Sweden the government introduced a subsidy, financed by a 10% advertising levy, to help weaker papers. Rising costs caused West German newspaper proprietors to demand tax and postage concessions. Even the giant Axel Springer group had suffered in 1971, when sales rose by only 2% and profits were more than halved; by mid-1972, however, it reported improvement, with the help of a big investment program. None of Italy's 81 dailies recorded a profit in 1971, and the govern-

WIDE WORLD

UPI COMPIX

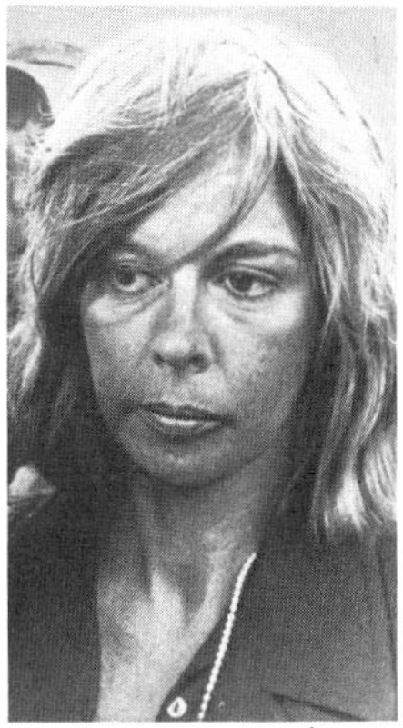

LONDON DAILY EXPRESS/ PICTORIAL PARADE

The Feb. 4, 1972, "Life" magazine cover story related the history of Clifford Irving's biography of Howard Hughes. On February 11, "Life" denounced the biography as a hoax and announced cancellation of its $250,000 agreement with McGraw-Hill to publish excerpts. Irving and his wife, Edith, pleaded guilty to federal conspiracy and state grand larceny and conspiracy charges.

ment, already providing indirect support and some subsidies for the press, voted some $15 million in tax concessions, subsidies, and grants, some to continue to 1986. Strikes caused national stoppages in June–July, when publishers gave up Monday morning editions to save overtime pay for Sunday work.

Economic problems of a different kind troubled newspaper publishers in India, where almost all newsprint was imported from the U.S., which suspended aid during the 1971 Indo-Pakistani war. The government ordered restriction of newspaper size to ten pages, but publishers, fearing that newsprint shortage was an excuse to destroy their independence and viability, opposed the order; in April the Supreme Court rescinded it.

In Australia Rupert Murdoch significantly expanded his press interests. In June he bought from Sir Frank Packer, chairman of Australian Consolidated Press, Ltd., the *Sydney Daily Telegraph* and *Sunday Telegraph,* thus reducing Australia's news media ownership from four empires to three. Murdoch immediately merged his quality *Sunday Australian,* founded in 1971, with the tabloid *Sunday Telegraph.* He had already closed the *Finance Week,* a promising beginner, after only three months. (HARFORD THOMAS)

Despite the Supreme Court decision, secret sources remained the mainstay of investigative reporting in the U.S. The story of the Watergate affair, begun with the arrest of men planting electronic "bugs" in the Democratic National Committee headquarters, involved a host of unnamed informants. Digging by *Washington Post* reporters Bob Woodward and Carl Bernstein prompted investigations by courts, Congress, and the FBI; in turn, anonymous sources close to the investigations provided material for new stories, including relationships between the original "buggers" and Republican campaign officials and a sabotage operation against Democratic candidates. One trick laid at the White House door by the *Post* involved the notoriously biased *Manchester* (N.H.) *Union Leader,* whose publisher, William Loeb, trumpeted a letter, purportedly written by a Florida pensioner, accusing presidential contender Sen. Edmund S. Muskie (Dem., Me.) of a racial slur against New Englanders of French-Canadian descent.

In May syndicated columnist Jack Anderson (*see* BIOGRAPHY) won a Pulitzer Prize for reporting secret proceedings of inner government councils on the Indo-Pakistani war. The columnist became a celebrated authority whom many found more credible than government officials. Among his stunning disclosures was the connection between the quashing of Justice Department action against the International Telephone and Telegraph Corp. (ITT) and the giant company's offer to defray Republican convention costs. Later, however, Anderson was guilty of a sloppy bit of mud-slinging when, acting on uncorroborated evidence, he accused the Democratic vice-presidential candidate, Missouri Sen. Thomas Eagleton (*see* BIOGRAPHY), of having a police record for drunk and reckless driving. Eagleton's history of mental depressions had been unearthed and handled responsibly by Bob Boyd and Clark Hoyt of the Knight Newspapers.

It had, of course, been a "secret" source that provided *New York Times* reporter Neil Sheehan with the Pentagon papers a year earlier (though the source's identity later became known). The *Times* won its 38th Pulitzer Prize, for meritorious public service, for its series on the documents; Sheehan, however, came away empty-handed, to the dismay of many journalists.

UPI COMPIX

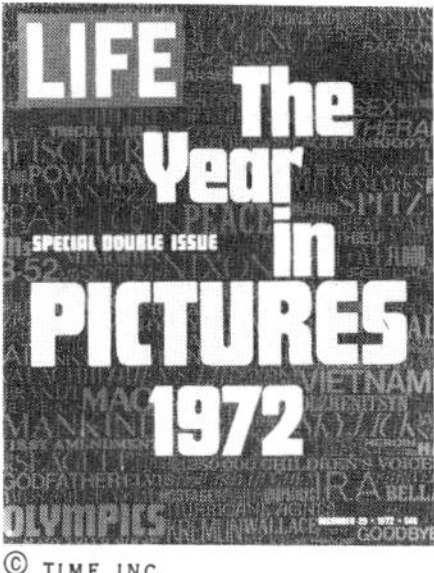

"Life" magazine: born Nov. 23, 1936; died Dec. 29, 1972. A spectacular era in American journalism closed with the announcement that "Life" would cease publication with its year-end issue. Soaring costs and increasing competition from television finally doomed the magazine, which, for 36 years, gave its readers intimate close-ups of world leaders and beautiful women, explored the meanings of art and religion, and revealed the wonders of science.

Among the signs indicating a healthy North American newspaper industry was the modest increase in U.S. daily newspaper circulation of 123,731, to a new high of 62,231,258, reported as of Sept. 30, 1971, by *Editor & Publisher Year Book.* Morning dailies increased in number from 334 to 339 and absorbed most of the circulation gains; evening papers lost 58,617 copies per day and declined in number from 1,429 to 1,425. Among the papers folding in 1972 were the *Boston Herald & Traveler* and the *Washington* (D.C.) *Daily News.* The *Herald & Traveler,* a leading New England conservative journal, collapsed after a 25-year-old civil suit divested it of the profitable television station that was keeping it afloat. The *Daily News* had shared the evening market with the *Evening Star,* with both losing money; the bigger *Star* purchased the tabloid from Scripps-Howard with the hope that the consolidated *Star-News* would compete vigorously against the *Post*'s morning monopoly. The number of newspapers with Sunday editions increased by four during 1971, to 590. The addition of at least one more in 1972, that launched on April 9 by Long Island's *Newsday,* the country's biggest suburban newspaper (440,765 circulation), would be balanced against the discontinuance in 1973 of *Chicago Today*'s weekend editions. Canada's 115 dailies, three less than in 1970, reported slight circulation declines to 4,604,-679 in 1971. With an increase in the number of Sunday papers from 9 to 12, however, Sunday circulation rose 23.2% to 1,046,783, topping the one million mark for the first time. (PHILIP KOPPER)

In the comparatively brief time since March 1970, when an experimental optical character recognition scanner (OCR) was installed at the *Worcester* (Mass.) *Telegram & Gazette* plant, technological revolution had swept through the newsrooms of U.S. newspapers. In 1972 many reporters were typing their stories on special electric typewriters with a font that could be "read" by the OCR and translated into magnetic or paper tape at a column a minute. This tape would then be fed into typesetting equipment. In other newsrooms, video display terminals (VDTs) were being used. With these a reporter could type his story directly onto the screen of the terminal, use a cursor (a small beam of light on the screen) to make corrections or changes, and then send his story to the computer. Editors could recall this story on their VDTs, make changes, and then, through a computer that operated in billionths of a second, release the story for typesetting. At newspapers where electronic installations had not yet been made, contracts had been let for such systems or intraoffice committees were debating the comparative merits and costs of OCRs and VDTs. (M. BERNARD SMITH)

Magazines. *Life* magazine died late in 1972. Time Inc. announced on December 8 that the last issue of the magazine would bear the date December 29. The announcement sent shock waves beyond the worlds of journalists and publishers. Millions in the U.S. had come to look upon the magazine's name as a household word. In every major city in Europe and the Far East, editions of *Life* could be found on newsstands. Founded in 1936 out of the fertile mind of Henry Luce, the magazine was an instant success, so much so that weekly demand grew far faster than anticipated and fulfillment costs nearly pulled the fledgling enterprise under. *Life* brought the emerging art of photojournalism into its own; it was a classic example of an idea whose time had come. Throughout the Spanish Civil War, World War II, the Korean War, and Vietnam, *Life* brought a new awareness of war to its millions of readers. From Robert Capa's shattering photograph of a Spanish soldier being shot in action to Larry Burrows' photographs of the tragic struggle in Southeast Asia, the magazine was brilliant and unyielding in journalistic responsibility and imaginative enterprise.

Life could be and was tender and full of the matter of living. In a day when sex stayed behind closed doors, it published photographs of the birth of a baby. The *Life* photographic essay often went deep into the minds and hearts of all people, how they lived, how they succeeded, how they grew old, what they thought, what they cared about. The world's greatest names in photography appeared on its pages and often on its masthead: Alfred Eisenstaedt, Margaret Bourke-White, Leonard McCombe, Mark Kauffman, Henri Cartier-Bresson, David Douglas Duncan, Capa, Gjon Mili, and Gordon Parks. And, too, *Life* spawned great editors, writers, and reporters. Edward K. Thompson was managing editor for 12 years of the magazine's greatest growth and strength. He was succeeded in the early 1960s, when television began to eat into *Life*'s dominance, by George P. Hunt. All over the world there were men and women who had once worked for *Life* in one capacity or another. It was a huge fraternity with only one initiation—be excellent. Now, with the death of *Life,* that fraternity, through the inevitability of natural attrition, would become more and more exclusive.

Other magazines both in the U.S. and elsewhere fared better. In continental Europe mass-circulation picture weeklies flourished; France's *Paris-Match,* West Germany's *Der Spiegel,* and Italy's *Oggi* had circulations of at least one million; *l'Express,* France's weekly news magazine, sold more than 500,000 copies. In the U.S. the Postal Service imposed substantial postage increases that threatened the existence of many financially marginal smaller magazines and ate into profits in general. One reason for *Life*'s demise, most certainly, was the postage increase. Second-class magazine rates would go up 127% over five years, equivalent to about 25% annually.

Women's magazines based on sensible feminist editorial content began to appear, most notably *Ms.*, the first with a big circulation (350,000). Less forceful, *W* made its appearance in April, a consumer's model of *Women's Wear Daily*. In the U.K. women's magazines continued their domination of the market and sales rose for the first time since 1959. Though smaller specialty hobby and sports magazines were more profitable, decimalization and higher advertising revenues provided money for revamping and for sales promotion, especially at International Publishing Corp. (IPC), leading publisher of mass-circulation women's weeklies and monthlies. The sale of *Vanity Fair,* a money-losing monthly, to IPC, where it was merged with the popular *Honey,* apparently provided the National Magazine Co. with the funds to launch *Cosmopolitan,* an anglicized version of the U.S. monthly.

Magazines for blacks grew fastest in the special audience field in the U.S. There were 50 different titles directed to black audiences, ranging from small literary magazines to *Black Sports, Essence* (for women), and *Foxtrapper,* a publication patterned after *Playboy*. Consumers Union, publishers of *Consumer Reports,* began a new magazine titled *Media & Consumer* that would discuss press coverage of consumer issues. Time Inc. introduced *Money,* a magazine that would tell its readers how best to spend, save, and invest dollars. Other publications with specialized audiences were noted. The U.S. Information Agency admitted using comic books as a propaganda medium. The widely successful *Whole Earth Catalog* called it quits as promised but there were plenty of substitutes, including *Place,* a publication for "alternative living." Specialization did not mean automatic success. *Book World,* a weekly literary review distributed in the *Washington Post* and the *Chicago Tribune,* ceased publication; *New Woman* suspended publication temporarily, with a promise to return in 1973; and *Electronics Illustrated,* begun in 1958, was to be axed at the end of 1972.

The changing shape of magazines took many forms. *Good Housekeeping* studied the possibility of a television series. Two new poetry magazines were to be issued exclusively on record or cassette. *Doctors' Finances,* which printed condensed articles, offered readers cassette supplements. *Current Audio Magazine* was available only on record, eight-track tape, and cassette. Kodak Microfilm Systems urged original publication on microfiche. And the publishers of *Library Journal* began publication of *News and Reviews of Non-Print Media. Fortune* switched its format to a smaller size to cut paper and production costs. The new forms and formats added to the headaches of copyright revision, already bogged down over the frustrations brought on by photocopying. (See *Books,* below.)

One of France's few remaining literary weeklies closed during the year: *Les Lettres françaises,* founded secretly in 1941 by two heroes of the Resistance and edited since 1955 by the poet Louis Aragon. It was feared that *Les Nouvelles littéraires,* celebrating its 50th anniversary, might also have to close. Underground and "fringe" magazines were in difficulties and several closed, among them *l'Idiot internationale,* founded in 1969 and forced under by the number of legal actions against it, and, in the U.K., *7 Days,* a revolutionary weekly begun in October 1971. On the other hand, *Time Out* had established itself in London as the voice of the "alternative society." Among magazines impounded during numerous police raids in Britain in September were *Men Only* and *Club International,* both cited as being obscene by the Longford report on pornography. Police denied any connection between the report and the raids, saying they resulted from an inquiry begun in 1971 (see *Books,* below). In the U.S. Ralph Ginzburg served eight months of a three-year prison term nine years after he was convicted of using the mails for obscene promotional materials in connection with his magazine *Eros*.

Playboy's preeminence remained intact in spite of impressive circulation and advertising gains made by Britain's *Penthouse* in the U.S. in 1972. Playboy Enterprises Inc., *Playboy*'s parent company, launched *Oui* to compete with the earthy approach of *Penthouse* and reach a younger generation without diluting *Playboy*'s image as a thinking man's magazine. In Italy, Hugh Hefner launched an Italian edition of *Playboy* and the entrenched Italian girlie magazine *Playmen* struck back with a nine-page layout of nude photographs of Jacqueline Onassis. In Chicago attorney F. Lee Bailey entered the *Playboy* arena with *Gallery,* whose first three covers looked so much like *Playboy* magazine that there was dark talk of lawsuits.

One of the U.K.'s best-known weeklies, the left-wing *New Statesman,* changed editors in March, when Richard Crossman resigned over a dispute with the board on editorial policy. Crossman's successor was Anthony Howard. Norman Cousins seemed off to a good start again in the U.S. with *World,* a "review of ideas, the arts, and the human condition." The *Saturday Review* that Cousins edited for 31 years, meanwhile, was undergoing substantial change in the hands of Nicolas Charney and John Veronis. The two, who had founded *Psychology Today,* sold it to Boise-Cascade Corp. for $21.5 million, and then left the enterprise when Boise refused their request to purchase *Saturday Review,* were attempting to turn *Saturday Review* into four separate magazines with subtitles of *The Arts, Science, The Society,* and *Education. Psychology Today,* meanwhile, boosted its circulation rate-base from 750,000 to 800,000. Its parent company, Communications Research Machines Inc. (a wholly owned subsidiary of Boise), sold off the fledgling *Intellectual Digest* to its publisher, James Horton, and a group of investors. Helen Gurley Brown finally kept her promise and published a nude male centrefold in *Cosmopolitan*. The model was actor Burt Reynolds.

The year's most sensational encounters between magazines and government took place in West Germany. In August police searched the offices of the popular picture weekly *Quick* on grounds of suspected bribery and tax offenses. Observers believed, however, that the action was in retribution for *Quick*'s opposition to the government of Willy Brandt, and particularly because the magazine published the letter of resignation of Karl Schiller, minister of economics and finance. Later, *Quick*'s editor and 35 other journalists refused to give evidence about their publication of a secret telegram from the West German embassy in Washington, D.C., to the Foreign Office in Bonn.

(WILLIAM A. KATZ; MICHEL SILVA; HARFORD THOMAS)

Books. Although world production continued to rise in 1971–72, in some big book-producing countries output of titles and export values fell, and when the general rise in book prices was taken into account, even in those countries where values were rising, the number of books exported might be falling. The declines did not indicate glutted markets, however. In the less developed countries demand for books was growing as mass-education programs took effect; and even in the so-called fully literate countries consumer research revealed high market potentials.

Decline in output reflected the need for publishers to cut losses, reorganize production, and concentrate resources. Reasons for declining exports were more complex. Some direct exports were eliminated by the growth of multinational publishing and distribution networks, such as France's Hachette, Italy's Fabbri, West Germany's Bertelsmann, the U.K.'s Oxford University Press and Hamlyn, Granada, and Longman groups, and the U.S.'s Doubleday, Time-Life, McGraw-Hill, and Crowell-Collier & Macmillan. U.K. entry into the EEC encouraged further linkups: Longman, for instance, formed joint subsidiaries with Armand Colin of Paris and Langenscheidt of Munich. Growth of national publishing industries also helped to explain declining exports. Book exports to India from the U.K., for example, fell in 1971, when the Indian government recognized publishing as an industry, with a right to tax incentives.

Another change in the pattern of book publishing was the new status of the paperback. In West Germany, where total output fell in 1971 by 5,141 titles to 42,959, paperbacks continued to account for 8.3% of the output. In Denmark, where titles rose again, by 277 to 5,339, paperbacks rose by nearly 100 titles to a record 733. In the U.K., where the number of titles fell in 1971 for the first time since 1959, by 1,891 to 31,598, the "big four" paperback publishers—Penguin, Fontana, Pan, and Corgi—claimed world sales of 88.5 million copies at a value of more than £15 million.

The Longford report on pornography, published as a 60-pence Coronet paperback, proved a best seller, with 125,000 copies sold within a few days of publication. It had been awaited with anxiety, but its proposals for amendment of the Obscene Publications Acts of 1959 and 1964 were fairly well received. Its definitions of "obscene" publications, etc., as those likely to "outrage contemporary standards of decency or humanity accepted by the public at large," and of pornography as that which "exploits and dehumanizes sex so that . . . women in particular are treated as sex objects" seemed, however, likely to prove difficult in practice; and its proposal that the teaching of sex education in schools be made subject to the obscenity laws was widely criticized. The report's publication was followed by an "entirely coincidental" wave of police raids on publishers and distributors of "porn" that roused public feeling against "Gestapo" methods.

A U.K. working party reported in May on the possibility of amending the 1956 Copyright Act to restrict lending to the public as an offense against copyright and to introduce Public Lending Right (PLR) under cover of a new act. In Denmark, where a PLR system had been in force since 1945, authors were demanding higher rates of subsidy, and publishers, who received no benefit under the existing law, were demanding to be included.

Although U.K. output of titles had continued to fall in January–June 1972, by the end of September the total had risen to 24,680. The rate of increase in new book prices was also slowing down, to about 3.5% in 1971–72. Total turnover for 1971 was expected to be up, from £153.7 million to some £160 million, with some £72 million in foreign exchange. The most striking change was in number of publishers, up from 1,581 in 1971 to 1,673 in 1972. More small, independent firms were being launched, and were succeeding.

Take-overs and mergers continued to erode the pattern of Australian publishing, and by the end of 1972, of the country's 76 publishing firms, 35, all major companies, were under U.S. or U.K. control. The rejection in April by the Trade Practices Tribunal of the publishers' association's appeal to exempt books from the 1971 act abolishing retail price maintenance destroyed the traditional fabric of book publishing in Australia.

In Western Europe, Swiss publishing remained the most consistently successful. Although output was marginally down in 1971 to 6,087 titles (mainly because of a 12% drop in publication for the home market of books in French), exports were up by 22.5% to a value of SFr. 187.5 million. In West Germany both exports and imports were up, but their reported values took no account of steeply rising book prices. In Denmark, where book prices were 7–8% higher in 1970 than in 1969, real turnover was decreasing. Imports of books into Spain increased dramatically in 1971 to a value of U.S. $22.7 million, 36.5% above the 1970 figure. Book exports totaled $80.7 million in 1971, mainly (76%) to Spanish-speaking countries. In connection with UNESCO's International Book Year 1972, Spanish publishers undertook considerable promotional activities in Latin America.

In the first year of a five-year plan that set higher targets for book production and quality, the Soviet Union published a record 85,000 titles, 6,692 more than in 1970.

Celebrations of International Book Year were worldwide and various. The most original, perhaps, was the gift, announced in March by the French minister of education, of six French classics to each couple married during the year. Jamaica's celebrations included the holding of its first book fair; Poland took as the theme of its 17th Warsaw International Book Fair UNESCO's slogan for the year, "A Book for Everyone"; Switzerland gave away 50,000 copies of a specially produced paperback; New Zealand founded a National Book Council; the Soviet Union held an international symposium in Moscow in September; and Kenya's publishers' association inaugurated two annual Kenyatta Awards for Literature. In the U.K. there was general concern at lack of governmental support; the main national event was the holding of the first National Book Week (November 4–11), organized by the National Book League. In the U.S. the program was observed with exhibits, conferences on books as tools in economic development abroad, and projects to end functional illiteracy in the U.S.

As part of West Germany's celebrations the Frankfurt International Book Fair invited members of the book trades of 15 African, Asian, and Latin-American countries to the fair as guests. Frankfurt also organized a special exhibition, "Books About Books," that went on to Paris for UNESCO's General Assembly. Frankfurt's fair, as usual, broke all records with 3,683 publishers present, 121 more than in 1971, and 148 more from abroad. (DOROTHY M. PARTINGTON)

U.S. book publishers referred to 1972 as "the year of the gull and the gulled." The gull was celebrated in aviation writer Richard Bach's *Jonathan Livingston Seagull,* an illustrated allegory that sold more than a million copies. The "gulled" were the McGraw-Hill Book Co. and *Life* magazine (among others), victims of a flamboyant and expensive ($750,000) literary hoax, Clifford Irving's (*see* BIOGRAPHY) spurious *The Autobiography of Howard Hughes.*

The "taped reminiscenses" of the millionaire recluse were originally due to be published on March 27, 1972, with *Life* to publish parts of them in three installments beginning on March 10. Charges and countercharges that flew about from late December 1971 to mid-February 1972 included a description of the book as a "fantastic fiction" by a voice claiming to be Hughes; claims by a Nevada firm that it had purchased exclusive rights to Hughes's autobiographical materials in 1965 for $10; the filing of lawsuits by the firm seeking to prevent publication of the Irving manuscript and another edited by Robert P. Eaton to be exerpted in *Ladies' Home Journal;* advancement by McGraw-Hill and *Life* of the release dates to coincide with the release of the Eaton book and of yet another by a long-time Hughes aide, Noah Dietrich; hints of a link between Hughes and Pres. Richard Nixon (which proved to be nothing that was not already known); the questioning by Swiss authorities of the identity of the "H. R. Hughes" who had cashed the advance payments; the acknowledgment by Irving that his wife, Edith, had, as "Helga R. Hughes," deposited and withdrawn the funds using a forged passport; reports by two women that Irving had been with them at the times he claimed to have been interviewing Hughes; and finally announcements that the manuscript was indeed a hoax, that neither McGraw-Hill nor *Life* would publish it, and that it appeared to have been taken mainly from the Dietrich manuscript.

The case was wrapped up on March 14 when the Irvings pleaded guilty to charges of conspiracy in the swindle. They and Irving's researcher, Richard Suskind, received light sentences with Mrs. Irving facing Swiss forgery charges. At about that same time, however, McGraw-Hill agreed to pay damages to the estate of James H. McGregor, parts of whose 1940 book describing the Wounded Knee massacre had been reproduced almost verbatim in *The Memoirs of Chief Red Fox,* a best seller by a self-styled Sioux Indian chief. In April Praeger Publishers, Inc., took the unusual move of withdrawing from circulation a book on the tobacco industry because another publisher charged it contained "substantial plagiarism."

There was a decrease in the total number of new books and new editions published in the U.S. in 1972. During the first nine months 24,703 titles were published, compared with 28,494 at that point in 1971. This modest decline reflected diminishing markets for fiction and literature, textbooks, histories, and scholarly reprints and a deliberate effort to reduce the highly speculative publication of novels and other trade books. Best sellers in 1972 included:

Nonfiction: *I'm O.K.-You're O.K.* by Thomas Harris; *Eleanor and Franklin* by Joseph P. Lash; *O Jerusalem!* by Larry Collins and Dominique LaPierre; *Open Marriage* by Nena and George O'Neill; and *The Boys of Summer* by Roger Kahn.

Fiction: *Jonathan Livingston Seagull* by Richard Bach; *The Winds of War* by Herman Wouk; *The Word* by Irving Wallace; *August 1914* by Aleksandr Solzhenitsyn; and *Captains and the Kings* by Taylor Caldwell.

As elsewhere, the publishing of mass-market paperbacks in the U.S. leaped forward—from 2,393 titles in 1970 to 2,985 in 1971, with the estimated total for 1972 somewhat in excess of 3,500. More spectacular than the bulge in quantity were the new peaks reached in the purchase prices of paperback reprint rights, including bids of over $1 million for *I'm O.K.-You're O.K.* and *Jonathan Livingston Seagull.* Textbook publishing, however, suffered from the effects of the decline in the U.S. birthrate in the late 1960s. The dollar volume of educational publishers of under $900 million represented an increase in sales over 1971 but also a substantial decrease in profits due to increased costs and unusually heavy (18%) "returns" from college bookstores. The 80-odd university presses, responsible for at least 10% of the titles published annually, again experienced the downward trend that began in 1967. In February the director of Harvard University Press was dismissed, presumably because of the serious deficit. Late in September the Andrew W. Mellon Foundation announced grants totaling $2,125,000 to aid the university presses.

COURTESY, THE MACMILLAN CO.

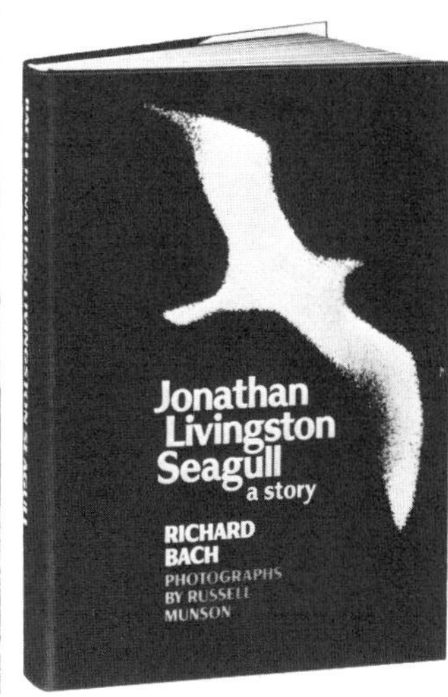

Richard Bach and his "Jonathan Livingston Seagull," which rose from initial rejection to the top of the 1972 best-seller list, breaking all hardback sales records since "Gone with the Wind."

Serious controversy again marked the selection of a winner of the National Book Awards. Stewart Brand's *The Last Whole Earth Catalog: Access to Tools,* published by the Portola Institute, was described as a nonbook by some, including NBA juror Garry Wills, who resigned when the oversized paperback was nominated. The prevailing view, however, was that of juror Harrison E. Salisbury, who said, "this creation is unique. It is what our society is about."

Censorship was in the news again in book publishing in 1972 and twice involved the U.S. Central Intelligence Agency. Victor L. Marchetti, a former CIA agent, had contracted with Alfred A. Knopf for a nonfiction work about the agency. A federal judge, acting at the request of the Justice Department, issued a temporary restraining order to prevent publication of the work. In the second incident the CIA requested the right to see proofs of *The Politics of Heroin in Southeast Asia,* written by Alfred W. McCoy with Cathleen B. Reed. The publishers, Harper & Row, found nothing in the ten pages of criticism filed by the CIA to warrant changing the text, and the book was published on August 28. The Unitarian Universalist Association's affairs became the subject of three federal investigations because its publishing arm, Beacon Press, had printed the edition of the Pentagon papers that was read into a congressional subcommittee's records. (*See* RELIGION.)

Failing again to revise copyright legislation to modernize it and to bring it into line with the Bern Convention (which, among other things, granted copyright protection for the life of the author plus 50 years), the U.S. Congress extended existing copyright protection for the seventh time, this time through the end of 1974. By that date, Congress assumed, a revision bill would be passed. If so, it would have to solve such questions as the use of network television programs by cable television and the knottier matter of photocopying. Most publishers insisted that the common practice of photocopying pages or chapters of books, magazine or newspaper articles, or even entire works infringed on copyright and/or deprived publisher and author of income and property. In a landmark case, in March, a commissioner of the U.S. Court of Claims upheld assertions by William & Wilkins, the medical and scientific publisher, that the National Institutes of Health and the National Library of Medicine had indulged in "wholesale" photocopying of the firm's journals. (LEONARD R. HARRIS)

See also Literature.

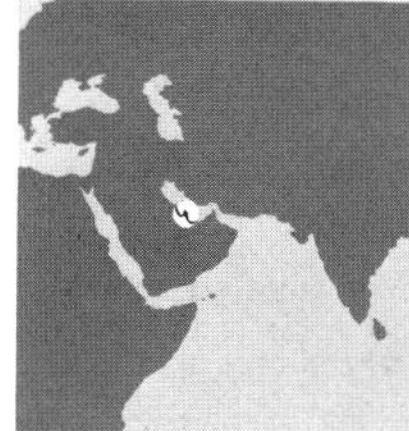

Qatar

An independent emirate on the west coast of the Persian Gulf, Qatar occupies a desert peninsula east of Bahrain, with Saudi Arabia and the United Arab Emirates bordering on the south. Area: 4,400 sq.mi. (11,400 sq.km.). Pop. (1971 est.): 160,000. Capital: Doha (pop., 1971 est., 95,000). Language: Arabic. Religion: Muslim. Emirs in 1972, Ahmad ibn Ali ibn Abdullah ath-Thani and, from February 22, Sheikh Khalifah ibn Hamad ath-Thani; prime minister, Sheikh Khalifah ibn Hamad ath-Thani.

Qatar's first year as a fully independent state saw the overthrow of Emir Ahmad by his cousin, the deputy ruler and prime minister, Sheikh Khalifah, in a bloodless coup on Feb. 22, 1972, while Ahmad was away on a hunting trip. The new ruler at once announced a 20% increase in salaries for the civil service, Army, and police force and cuts in the expenditures of the ruling family, whose several hundred members absorbed a major part of Qatar's oil revenues. In April Sheikh Khalifah appointed a 20-member advisory council, which he described as Qatar's "first experiment in democracy."

Oil revenues were expected to exceed $175 million in 1972 although the national budget remained at about $50 million. In March it was announced that Qatar Petroleum and Shell Qatar had agreed to the government's acquiring a 20% share in their concessions. The Qatar Petroleum National Co. was established in April to manage the government's 20% share in the foreign companies as well as to refine and market oil on its own. (PETER MANSFIELD)

QATAR

Education. (1969–70) Primary, pupils 13,668, teachers 677; secondary, pupils 3,109, teachers 198; vocational, pupils 244, teachers 44; teacher training, students 205; teachers 27.

Finance and Trade. Monetary unit: Qatar-Dubai riyal, with (Sept. 18, 1972) a free rate of 4.37 riyals to U.S. $1 (10.70 riyals = £1 sterling). Oil revenues (1971 est.) 900 million riyals; development expenditure (1972 est.) 730 million riyals. Foreign trade: imports (1971) 515,869,000 riyals; exports (1969 est.) 1.2 billion riyals. Import sources: U.K. 37%; Japan 10%; U.S. 10%; Lebanon 8%; West Germany 5%. Export destinations: U.K. 21%; Italy 18%; France 12%; Australia 11%. Main export crude oil.

Industry. Crude oil production (1971) 20,201,000 metric tons.

Puerto Rico:
see Dependent States

Quakers:
see Religion

Race Relations

Intended as an international festival of peace and goodwill, at which the world's best athletes would compete as individuals, the revived Olympic Games had increasingly become an additional arena for nationalistic display, political wrangling, ideological demonstrations, and violence. The 1964 Games in Japan saw the exclusion of South Africa and the withdrawal of North Korea and Indonesia. In Mexico in 1968 student riots were put down ruthlessly by police, and victorious black U.S. athletes introduced "black power" gestures. At the Munich Games of 1972, the West German hosts hoped to create a new image to replace the memory of the militaristic performance of German athletes at the Berlin Games in 1936. In 1972, however, a group of African states forced a last-minute decision to evict a multiracial Rhodesian team from the Games altogether, and ten days later the Palestinian Black September organization's kidnapping and murder of 11 Israeli athletes struck what seemed to many a lethal blow at the Olympic ideal. It also demonstrated to the world the rise of a dangerous by-product of rabid nationalism and militant ethnicity: the urban guerrilla or terrorist group.

The events at Munich reflected not only black-white and Arab-Israeli conflicts but also the double standards prevailing in international relations. Of all the Arab states, Jordan alone condemned the Munich killings, and of the African states that had successfully expelled the Rhodesian team only Tanzania's Pres. Julius Nyerere held to a single standard in rebuking Pres. Idi Amin for racism over his expulsion of Uganda's Asian minority. (*See* SPORTING RECORD, *Special Report*.)

The noncitizen Uganda Asian refugees, particularly the thousands who found themselves stateless, were the publicized tip of a very large iceberg of old and new refugees in Africa, the Near East, Asia, and elsewhere, mostly the victims of ethnic, religious, or political persecution. Uganda itself was sheltering many thousands of African refugees from tribal enemies in Rwanda and the Sudan. The ending of the war in East Pakistan and the subsequent establishment of an independent Bangladesh meant that millions of displaced Bengalis were returned to their homeland; on the other hand, 1.5 million Urdu-speaking Muslim Biharis, who had migrated to East Pakistan when it became independent in 1946–47, became a potential target for collective vengeance on account of the preferential treatment enjoyed by them under the Pakistanis and the collaboration by some in the earlier terror inflicted on the Bengalis by the Pakistani Army.

In the Soviet Union harassment of human rights campaigners and members of some ethnic minorities, particularly Jews, continued. An increased exodus of Jews to Israel was, however, permitted, although attempts were made to impose fees for such permits. Just over its borders, the Soviet Union was exploiting Kurdish minority grievances in Turkey's Asian provinces, while stepping up its support of the terrorist Turkish People's Liberation Army and distributing propaganda via East Berlin among the half-million Turkish citizens working in Western Europe.

A number of other long-standing minority situations were tense, notably in Northern Ireland; in Croatia (and among Croat settlements abroad in such countries as Sweden and Australia); in Brittany and Wales (over the language issue); and in Quebec, where the extremist nationalist minority could look forward to gaining maximum publicity for their cause at the 1976 Olympic Games in Montreal.

South Africa. In 1971–72 the Afrikaner Nationalist government once again lurched heavily to the right. After losing political ground for some years among Nationalist supporters because of its more "outward-looking" and "enlightened" policies, including concessions to racial mixing in sports, it won a massive by-election victory in rural Oudtshoorn in April by using all the old tribal cries of fear and hatred against the mainly English-speaking opposition. In June, white students at the English-language universities demonstrated in sympathy with nonwhites who had been protesting at their "ethnic" universities the country's system of segregated and unequal education. Instead of moving in strength into the "ethnic" campuses, the government chose to exert indirect pressure on them by deploying police with brutal force against white students and onlookers in Cape Town. Disquiet and apprehension were expressed among the white opposition, but Prime Minister B. J. Vorster probably spoke for most Afrikaner Nationalists when he expressed full approval of the police action.

The swing to the right and to "police state" methods resulted from a tardy realization of the basic instability of the apartheid system; it became clear that any relaxation of pressure would lead to the disintegration of the system. For some years, under adroit leaders such as Chief Kaiser Matanzima and Chief Gatsha Buthelezi, the Bantustans (African homelands) had been slipping out of control, using the logic of separate development to demand equal rights and more land for the establishment of "separate nationhoods." A common front was slowly forming among Bantustan leaders, and there was increasing talk of the logic of unity among the "black ethnic groups."

A broader black-white polarization was reflected in the announcement in August by the South African Institute of Race Relations and the *Rand Daily Mail* that they would no longer use the term "nonwhite" to describe the country's African, Coloured (mixed), and Indian groups; instead, they would use the term "black." Until recently this would have been unacceptable to most of the Cape Coloured and Indian population, who regarded themselves as culturally superior to and politically different from black Africans. Recently, however, many were preferring to call themselves "black" out of bitterness at rejection and as an emotive political slogan to bring about nonwhite solidarity. In the political sphere there was growing rapprochement among the legalized separate institutions of the Bantustans, the Indian Council, and the Coloured Persons Representative Council. Another instance of growing polarization was the disbanding of the multiracial University Christian Movement after a turbulent five years of existence, under pressure both from the government and from all-black organizations no longer willing to work within a multiracial organization.

A major factor behind the unworkability of apartheid had always been that its success depended upon rapid and consistent economic expansion, which in turn could only be achieved through fuller economic integration and the creation of a better-paid and better-qualified African urban working class to provide a stable home market. That in turn would mean the end of apartheid. In 1971–72, for the first time since South African railways became a "white labour" preserve to provide jobs for poor whites, 2,300 African workers were working in "white" jobs that could not be filled in the marshaling yards. They were paid half the shunters' wage and were called "marshalers" rather than "shunters." In less ideologically pure industries, the process had gone even further; despite the rigid opposition of most white unions, an estimated overall shortage of 100,000 skilled workers was forcing employers to reinterpret, evade, or simply pay regular fines for contravening job reservation rules. The government's policy of encouraging the establishment of industries in the homelands or on their borders was ineffective. Yet, despite the small concessions and evasions, the gap between white and African wages had widened over the past five years from 5.1:1 to 5.7:1 in manufacturing, and from 17.5:1 to over 20:1 in mining.

South Africa's "outward looking" policy of promoting dialogue with black African countries was checked not only by increasing internal opposition from conservative sections of the ruling Afrikaner Nationalist Party but also externally through a change of leadership in Malagasy and an intensification of the black African states' antiapartheid stance. Still striving for realistic contacts were the Ivory Coast and the new UN secretary-general, Kurt Waldheim, in his attempt to end the dispute over the control of South West Africa. Nearer home, Lesotho's prime minister, Chief Leabua Jonathan, said that dialogue had foundered because of racial discrimination.

United Kingdom. For a year or so immigration and race relations had receded as major political issues in Britain, despite an increasing polarization between liberals and reformers and a neo-Marxist or black power minority. How superficial the calm and how deep the fears and anxieties felt by many Britons was dramatically demonstrated in August by the swelling tide of public hostility after Pres. Idi Amin of Uganda announced his intention to expel within three months all Asians who did not possess Uganda citizenship, on the ground that they were "sabotaging the economy." The bulk of these Asians, then estimated at approximately 50,000–60,000, held U.K. passports, and President Amin called upon Britain to take responsibility for them. The hostile public response in Britain was

Militant Indians demonstrate in the Bureau of Indian Affairs building in Washington, D.C., which they occupied on Nov. 2–8, 1972. A violent confrontation was avoided when the government promised to consider their protest.

WIDE WORLD

CAMERA PRESS/PICTORIAL PARADE

Two children sit peacefully together at a London rally organized by the Rhodesia Emergency Campaign Committee to protest the Smith–Douglas-Home settlement for Rhodesia. A study commission headed by Lord Pearce reported against the agreement in May 1972.

partly due to the fact that no immediate firm response to the situation was made, many ministers and officials being dispersed for the summer vacation. On August 15, however, the British government accepted its "legal and moral responsibility" to those holding British passports, and subsequently set up a Uganda Resettlement Board under the chairmanship of Sir Charles Cunningham, a retired civil servant who had worked with the Anglo-Egyptian Resettlement Board to assist nearly 7,000 British citizens expelled from Egypt.

An airlift was organized and the resettlement machinery got under way, with civil service teams working with uniformed professional organizations (the Women's Royal Voluntary Service, the Red Cross, and the St. John Ambulance Association) and aided, not without administrative friction, by a coordinating committee linking approximately 60 voluntary agencies, a few of whom had regarded coloured immigrants as their special preserve. By October it had become clear that many thousands of Asians had left Uganda quietly since the 1969 census, and that at most some 25,000–28,000 might come to Britain.

Most refugees arrived with little or no money, but many had skills or qualifications and the resettlement program included finding houses, jobs, opportunities to complete educational courses, and possibly loans to start up businesses. By September considerable public sympathy had been aroused, despite the long silence of the Labour Party opposition and an emotional debate at the Conservative Party conference led by Enoch Powell, whose views were "utterly repudiated" by Home Secretary Robert Carr.

The arrival of the Uganda Asians seemed likely to introduce some diversity and a possible change of direction into the race relations scene in Britain. Victims of black racialism, they were political refugees rather than economic migrants, urbanized, highly adaptable, and middle-class and settler-minded in orientation. It remained to be seen how well British society would accept them as a pacemaking group for the rest of the coloured immigrant minorities. In the background there remained the awareness that there were still about a quarter of a million people with British and no other citizenship living in various parts of the Commonwealth (including about 120,000 in other East African countries and 140,000 in Malaysia and Singapore).

In its annual report in June the Race Relations Board called for an extension of its powers, granted under the 1968 Race Relations Act, to allow the board to investigate without requiring it to suspect that any individual unlawful act had been committed. While discrimination in places offering services and accommodations to the public had greatly diminished, and discriminatory advertisements had virtually vanished, there was a lack of firm knowledge in the crucial fields of employment and housing.

Relationships between minority groups, particularly young West Indians, and the police continued to be delicate, despite increasing initiatives by police authorities to improve training and to appoint more community liaison officers. Recruitment of coloured officers remained low, with only 41 in England and Wales out of a total of 92,925. The House of Commons Select Committee on Race Relations and Immigration reported on police-immigrant relations in September 1972. Detailed recommendations were made under a number of headings, including community liaison, work in schools, training, recruitment of coloured police and wardens, promoting proficiency and communication in Asian languages, information on citizens' rights, and a complaints procedure.

(SHEILA PATTERSON)

United States. The year 1972 was not marked by a general improvement in U.S. race relations. The momentum of the civil rights movement of the 1960s had spent itself; and public officials failed to provide positive leadership for the nation. Indeed, a historian looking back a generation later might well conclude that 1972 was a year of retrogression.

Employment remained a troubled area. The National Association for the Advancement of Colored People (NAACP) at its annual convention in July described the employment situation of urban black Americans as worse "than at any time since the Great Depression." The NAACP estimated that one-third of the urban black youths under 21 and out of school were without jobs. For the entire labour market, the U.S. Department of Labor released data showing that recorded black unemployment rates had fluctuated between 9.3 and 10.3% throughout 1971 and 1972. While the white rate had declined from a 1971 average of 5.4% to 4.6% by November 1972, the black rate held firm at 9.8%.

Part of the problem lay in the failure of federal efforts. A ten-month probe of the Rural Manpower Service released in April by the Department of Labor disclosed widespread evidence of discrimination by the Service against blacks, women, and Chicanos. In October, 17 farm worker and civil rights groups followed up this probe by suing in the U.S. District Court for the District of Columbia to enjoin the secretary of labour from financing state rural manpower programs. In June, George Holland resigned as director of the Labor Department's Office of Federal Contract Compliance; he branded federal efforts to ensure nondiscrimination in hiring by general contractors as "ineffective."

The U.S. Civil Service Commission reported in July that the percentage of minority employees in federal civilian jobs had declined slightly, from 19.6 to 19.5%, largely because of deep job cuts in the Postal Service. The Federal Power Commission ruled in July that it did not have the power to enforce fair employment practices by utilities. This action came after 12 civil rights organizations had charged "rampant discrimination" in employment by utilities against blacks, women, and Spanish-surname Americans. In August U.S. Pres. Richard Nixon publicly opposed job quotas, a chief mechanism used by his own administration to fight discrimination. The much-heralded "Philadelphia Plan," a federal effort to combat discrimination in the building trades by using required minimum minority job quotas, began to be quietly discarded after the president's statement. Nevertheless, the Labor Department announced in October an agreement signed by 15 building trades unions in Chicago with 41,000 members to employ 9,820 more minority workers by 1976. Quotas were not mentioned, but each trade would have specific annual hiring "goals."

The U.S. Congress in March passed the 1972 Employment Act, thereby strengthening the U.S. Equal Employment Opportunity Commission (EEOC). First, the new act expanded the commission's jurisdiction to cover the employees of private educational institutions, state and local governments, and all companies and unions with at least 15 (rather than 25) workers. Second, the act empowered the EEOC to

continued on page 580

SPECIAL REPORT

AMERICAN INDIANS: THE END OF THE FIFTH CENTURY OF CONTACT

By Vine Deloria, Jr.

The very stability of Indian affairs in 1972 belied important developments for American Indian people. As the fifth century of contact with European peoples drew to a close, Indian people in the continental United States could look back upon a fairly successful resistance to the powerful forces of change initiated by the multitude of non-Indians who had come to dwell on the continent with them.

Nations Within a Nation. The background to the American Indian historical outlook is in itself fascinating. From 1492 until the end of the French and Indian War in 1763, the tribes of the eastern Atlantic seaboard, with rare exceptions, had compelled the intruding Europeans to treat them as sovereign nations. The Iroquois, particularly, maintained their political independence as long as there were two nations competing for control of the continent.

Until 1871 the tribes of the interior forced the United States to deal with them as quasi-sovereign entities. Ignoring the U.S. purchase of the Louisiana Territory from France, the tribes of the Great Plains and Rocky Mountains insisted on extinguishment of their aboriginal title by treaty, thus placing on the U.S. legal burdens and responsibilities for the future.

By the end of the 19th century, however, the tribes had been forced onto reservations amounting to a fraction of their original landholdings. The large areas reserved by treaty were further eroded by the General Allotment Act of 1887, which aimed at reducing tribal solidarity by individualizing the sources of wealth and income. The tribal estates were divided, with individual tribal members receiving allotments generally comparable to the farms given to non-Indians under the Homestead Act. Off-reservation boarding schools were created, designed to reduce Indian children's knowledge of their own culture and prepare them for assimilation into the larger society.

As the 19th century ended, government officials congratulated themselves on the solution of the "Indian problem." One Indian commissioner wrote in 1910 that the conclusion of Indian Affairs was now simply a matter of administration of the few property rights remaining to the tribal members. For several decades it appeared that the commissioner's prophecy was being fulfilled.

American Indians served with distinction in World War I, earning the gratitude of the nation and the U.S. citizenship act of 1924. If the war earned them citizenship, it also served to expand their horizons to include the world and a fair knowledge of the U.S. political structure. Indians participated in government to an increasing degree. Charles Curtis, a Kaw Indian, became vice-president of the United States under Herbert Hoover in 1928.

Vine Deloria, Jr., is a Standing Rock Sioux from Martin, S.D. He is a former executive director of the National Congress of American Indians and is author of the best-selling book Custer Died for Your Sins.

CHIE NISHIO—NANCY PALMER

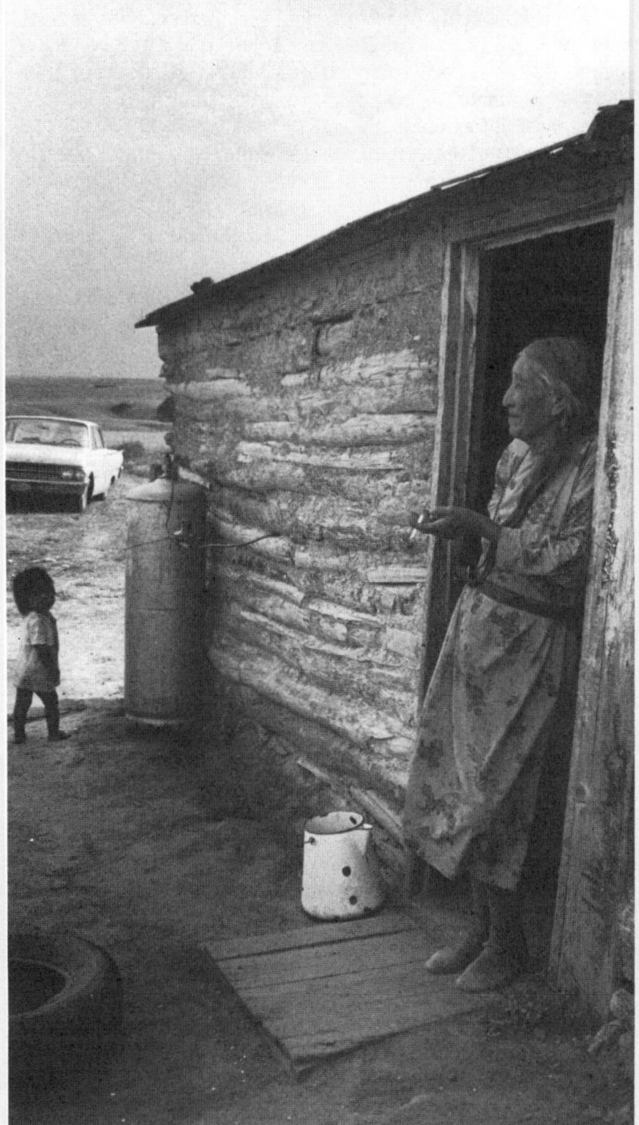

But things were not going well on the reservations. Schools were deteriorating. The increasing technology of American society drove the cost of living beyond the reach of the reservation people, and they were the first group to suffer from the impending depression of the 1930s. Allotment continued to reduce the Indian land base, and ownership of the lands became so fractionated that the people were forced to lease them instead of ranching or farming them, thus further reducing their income.

In 1934, under the administration of Franklin D. Roosevelt, the reservation people were given an opportunity to form quasi-independent governments for the purposes of improving their conditions and reversing the drastic erosion of the tribal land base. A revolving fund for land acquisition programs and economic development was established, and tribes were allowed to draw up constitutions and bylaws for self-government.

The Indian Reorganization Act was nearly stillborn, however. Its implementation required congressional appropriations, and the sudden shift from depression to World War II practically eliminated funds for reservation development. Following the war, New Deal programs came under heavy attack. The Bureau of Indian Affairs was subjected to particularly severe scrutiny, and critics of the bureau developed an ideology looking toward dissolution of the traditional responsibilities borne by the federal government on behalf of the Indian tribes.

In the 1950s this ideology surfaced in a policy of termination of federal services to selected tribes. An effort was made to repeal the self-government provisions of the Indian Reorganization Act, and Indian opponents of termination were harassed and investigated by senators and congressmen advocating the new policy. Several tribes lost their treaty rights by unilateral action of Congress, and a number of laws were passed attempting to push federal responsibilities upon the states.

The Growth of Activism. By the beginning of the 1960s, the Indian tribes had formed a determined voting bloc advocating self-determination instead of termination and demanding a review of federal policies. The Indian people pointed out that the federal government had never invested any substantial sums in development of ordinary municipal services on the reservations and, by law and rigid administrative practice, had prevented any development of reservation resources by either tribal governments or individual Indians.

As the socially progressive programs of Presidents John Kennedy and Lyndon Johnson passed into law, Indian tribes were demanding that provisions be included allowing tribes a legal status comparable to that of states and municipalities. The result was to enhance the status of reservation governments and make them eligible to become sponsoring agencies for a number of programs. By the mid-1960s Indian tribes were developing programs of amazing breadth.

Although not directly affected by the civil rights movement of the 1960s, the Indian tribes were greatly influenced by the movement's sentiment. The Poor People's Campaign of 1968, especially, forced a reconsideration of tactics. The vast majority of reservation people rejected involvement in the campaign, but Indians living in the cities took notice of it and began to organize for action.

In 1969 the first of the notable Indian activist efforts began as 89 Indians captured Alcatraz Island in San Francisco Bay in a stunning midnight invasion. Within the next two years nearly every large city had one or more Indian groups attempting to gain a foothold on surplus federal property near or within the city limits. Whether the Indian activists recognized it or not, their attempted captures of radar stations and military bases raised the more fundamental question of the restoration of lands illegally taken by government agencies earlier in the century.

Among the most controversial problems was the restoration of religious shrines to the people of the Taos Pueblo and Yakima tribes. In the former instance the U.S. Forest Service had placed the Blue Lake area in a national forest and allowed the Taos religious leaders only temporary use of the area. In the latter case the Forest Service denied the rights of the Yakima people to access altogether. By 1972 the Nixon administration had returned both areas to the tribes concerned and, in addition, had settled the long-standing claim of the Alaska natives to their lands in that state. As to land restoration, the administration was regarded as the most progressive in history.

A Question of Identity. The activist movement began to sputter in 1971 and underwent rather extensive transformations in 1972, perhaps indicating that the changes of the 1960s, while in general progressive, had revealed fundamental flaws in the drive for Indian unity. Many young people who had begun as daring protesters became more interested in the resurgence of Indian tribal religions, and some of the best leadership left the political arena.

The federal government, especially the Bureau of Indian Affairs, continued to place its major emphasis on grants to tribal governments for economic development. This course of action had been urged repeatedly during the 1960s but had not been implemented until the Nixon administration took office. Yet the grants came too late in most instances. The action had passed from the area of economic development, and internal struggles for definition of tribal identities began to jeopardize the programs.

Chief irritant among reservation people was the application of the Bill of Rights with respect to the functioning of tribal courts, an innovation required by the 1968 Indian civil rights

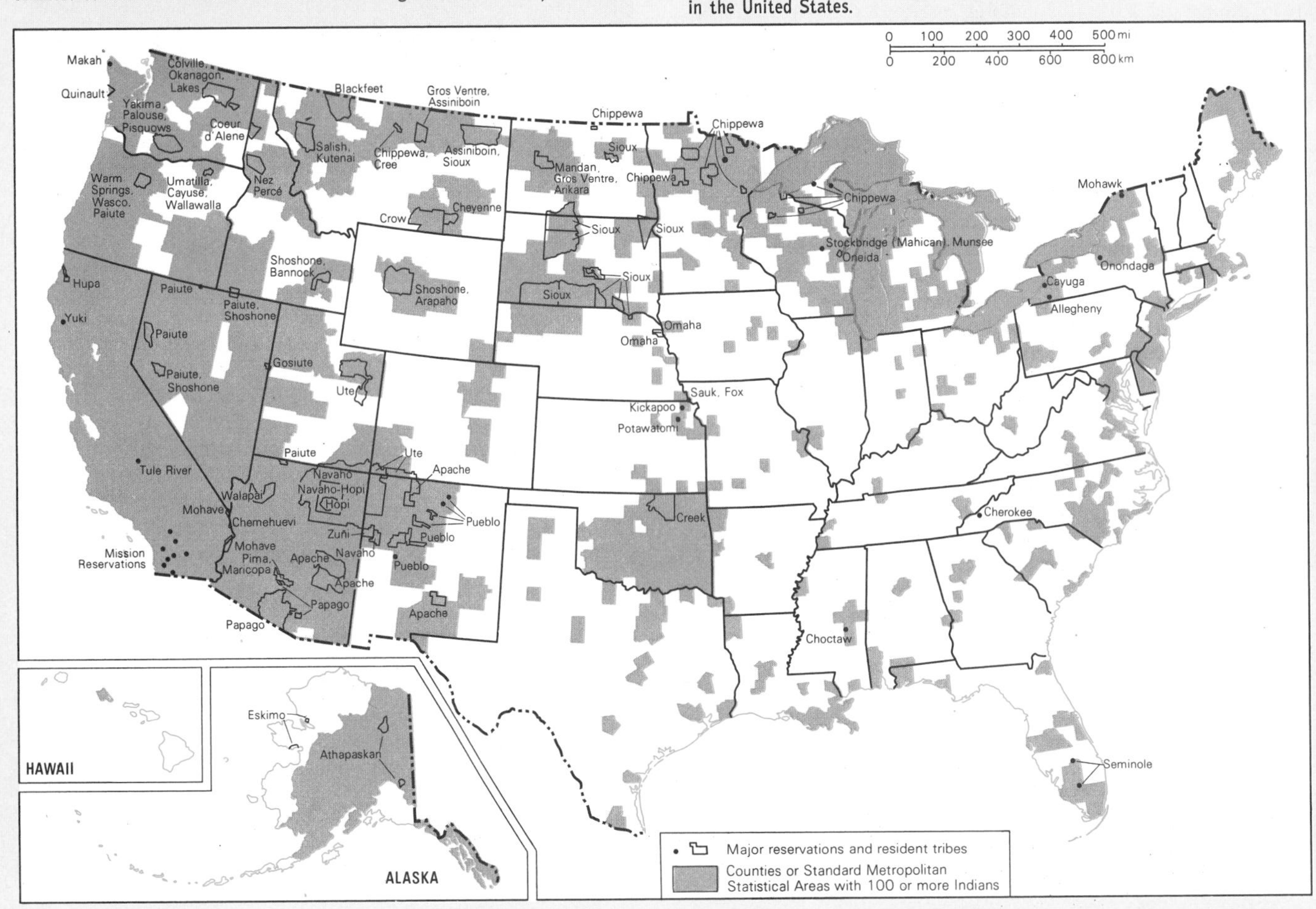

Distribution and concentrations of American Indians in the United States.

legislation. Tribal courts were required to conform to constitutional procedures guaranteed in the federal courts. Development of new law interpreting this requirement placed the tribal courts on a collision course with state and federal courts as to matters of jurisdiction.

Tribal enrollment procedures gave rise to fundamental questions about the existence and identity of the tribe itself. In precontact times, when a band grew too large to support itself it split into two fairly equal independent groups. The treaties, however, had required the establishment of tribal rolls for the purpose of distributing annuities according to the treaty articles. As time passed the tribe was regarded as being legally composed of individuals whose names were on these rolls or their direct descendants. By 1972 the problem had become acute for many tribes. Changes in constitutions required a positive vote of 30% of the tribal members. Some tribes had only 300 people living on the reservation but had close to 7,000 people on their rolls. Constitutional amendment was impossible, of course, under such conditions.

Many reservations had populations in excess of 10,000, with large numbers of people coming and going in search of employment, better educational opportunities for their children, or because of dissatisfaction with existing tribal programs. Developing and maintaining a consistent tribal program for reservation residents became an extremely difficult task. Programs might be approved by one constituency and overturned a couple of years later by another group of constituents. The avowed policy of the federal government to create Indian-controlled school boards produced additional conflicts. To many Indian people, Indian control meant that parents in the local communities could serve on school boards. To tribal officials, local control meant at least appointment by tribal councils and conceivably political patronage.

The churches had come to the reservations at an early period. Many had received lands in exchange for providing schools and hospitals. By the mid-1960s the national church bodies had created Indian advisory councils, and most had been successful, but by 1972 a general backlash had developed that boded ill for any future mission activity. Churches had to pull back expenditures in all areas, and this retrenchment was considered as a betrayal by many Indian people who were now weighing the relative merits of Christianity against a total return to Indian values and beliefs.

Education at the college and postgraduate levels appeared to be the most solidly established program in Indian Affairs. Some 100 students were in law school under a program jointly funded by the Bureau of Indian Affairs and the Office of Economic Opportunity. Over 7,000 Indian young people were attending college, and a number of graduate programs had opened up for Indian people. New ethnic studies and Indian programs at the college and university level absorbed every graduate, and more were needed. Yet even here the calm was about to end. The development of Indian studies programs raised severe identity questions. Older people and traditional Indians felt that no one could learn about tribal customs and traditions in a classroom. Nearly educated Indians, more optimistic than realistic, continued to work hard to transform tribal culture into a respectable academic discipline.

The political unity that had been developed in the previous two decades showed severe strains. The Nixon administration had been generally progressive and very keenly aware of Indian desires to regain cherished tribal lands. Yet the general tone of the administration, particularly in its federal court appointments, created a distinct sense of uneasiness among Indians. In an election year, they indicated a reluctance to support either candidate.

At the same time, Indians were becoming increasingly aware of world movements. A substantial number went to Sweden to protest the treatment of aboriginal peoples. The condition of Indians in Brazil worried many North American Indians, and they no longer regarded the borders between nations as having any lasting significance. A countermovement of aboriginal peoples encompassing the Western Hemisphere, Australia, the Pacific, and the Lapps of northern Scandinavia appeared to be in the making.

The fundamental religious problem of non-Western peoples, which had affected nearly all of the relationships between Indians and non-Indians, manifested itself in concern for ecology by traditional Indians. In most instances this concern was diametrically opposed to tribal council plans for reservation development. Thus the question of 20th-century Indian identity was being raised at the most elemental level.

The Indian understanding of history undergirded every problem, and few were able to articulate any direction for the future. On the brink of success that had seemed impossible two decades before, many Indian people discovered that they had been measuring progress according to non-Indian standards. The only apparent consolation to many Indians was the continual crumbling of the institutions of non-Indian society.

The immediate future would probably determine how much tribal culture has been lost and how much had transformed itself into as yet unrecognized techniques of community survival. One could only say that 1972 was a year of intense bewilderment and reflection, in which Indians suddenly paused and poised. Where they would go was another question. In view of their amazing revival and determination to survive as Indians gradually reclaiming their homelands, they had at last become a group that could not be administered. Perhaps this is all that many people had wanted.

E'LOIS KINNON

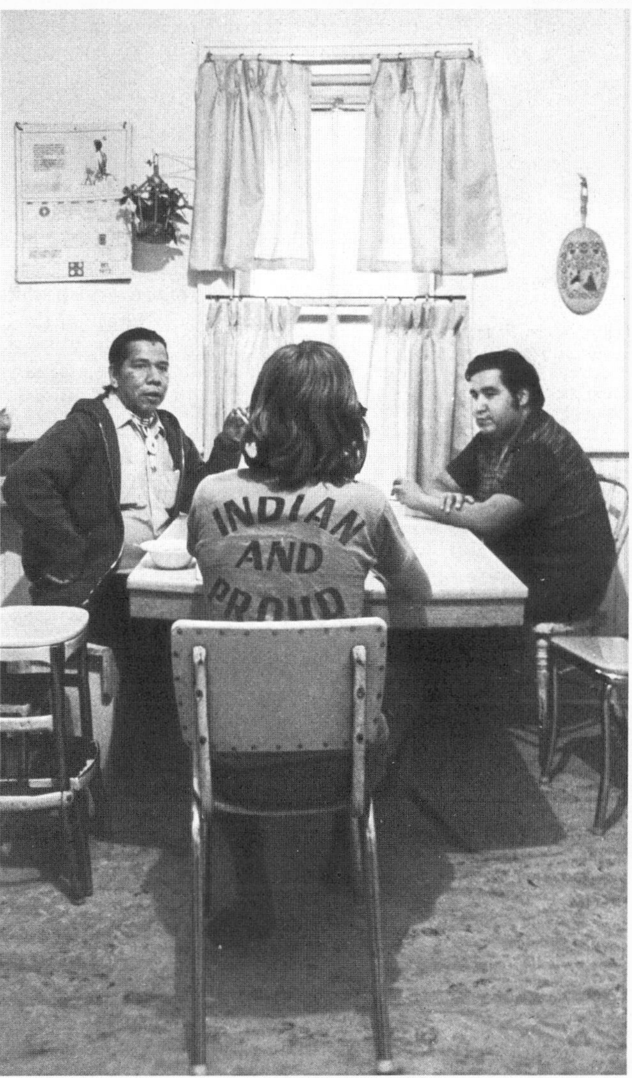

Mike Chosa (left), militant Indian organizer, confers with associates in Milwaukee, Wis.

continued from page 576

seek federal court action against employment discrimination, though a filibuster prevented passage of an additional provision to allow the commission to issue binding cease-and-desist orders against discriminators. The Department of Health, Education, and Welfare followed in October with 17 pages of guidelines for minority employment directed at 2,500 colleges and universities with federal contracts. No quotas were set, though numerical "goals and timetables" would be required. The EEOC used its new court powers in May by filing suit in Jacksonville, Fla., against the Container Corp. of America and related unions, for alleged job discrimination against both blacks and women. In August the cities of Montgomery, Ala., and Los Angeles were sued for racial discrimination in hiring for public jobs.

But a January decision in New York City demonstrated that progress via the courts could be slow. A federal judge ordered steamfitters' union Local 638 to upgrade 169 black and Puerto Rican apprentices to journeyman status. This small number represented the most reclassifications ever ordered in a suit brought by the federal government. By contrast, a U.S. District Court judge in San Diego, Calif., in September demonstrated how the courts can obtain faster results. The Imperial Irrigation District was ordered to hire Chicanos and blacks to fill two-thirds of all new job vacancies until the minority proportion of the district's work force rose to Imperial County's minority population proportion (49.5%). Of interest, too, was a job discrimination case brought to the U.S. District Court in Montgomery, Ala., by two Air Force blacks. Judge Frank Johnson ruled that the federal government, in invoking the doctrine of sovereign immunity, could not be sued but that Cabinet officers could.

Not surprisingly, black income did not close the wide gap with white income. After significant relative gains during the 1960s, the median black family income reached 61% that of the median white family by 1970, according to the U.S. Bureau of the Census. But by 1971 this percentage actually declined slightly to 60%; black family earnings rose to $6,440 while white family earnings rose more rapidly to $10,672. These totals, however, hid the polarization of wealth within the black community. About a quarter of black families made more than $10,000 during 1971 (compared with about a half of white families); yet a fifth of black families received less than $3,000.

Police in Baton Rouge, La., hold two black demonstrators following a bloody melee on Jan. 10, 1972, in which two black men and two sheriff's deputies were killed. A rally organized by members of a Black Muslim organization precipitated the confrontation.

UPI COMPIX

Federal aid to minority businesses rose from $200 million in 1969 to $360 million in 1971. Yet minority-owned firms, especially among blacks, remained a minuscule phenomenon in the nation's vast economic system. Black-owned firms constituted only 2% of all companies and less than 0.5% of gross receipts.

With black income gains minimal in a time of continuing high inflation, trends in housing and health were understandably not encouraging. Federally aided low- and medium-income housing starts did increase, with the U.S. Department of Housing and Urban Development (HUD) announcing in February a hoped-for goal of 566,000 such starts by 1973, compared with only 156,000 in 1969. HUD also guaranteed in July $14 million in land development bonds for Floyd McKissick's "Soul City," a proposed new town development in Warren County, N.C. It marked the first such guarantee for a black-owned venture and the first outside of a metropolitan area. But few changes in the actual living conditions of blacks occurred during the early 1970s. As in 1970, black families were still about three times more likely than white families to be living in an overcrowded unit and only two-thirds as likely to own their unit.

Americans were outraged and embarrassed to learn that in 1932, 600 poor black men participated in a Public Health Service project at Tuskegee, Ala., that was designed to learn how untreated syphilis ravaged the body. The method was through autopsies. Of the 600 men, 400 were syphilitics who went untreated and 200 were an uninfected control group. In 1942 a cure for syphilis—penicillin—was discovered, yet the infected men were not treated. At least seven of the men died of the disease and 154 more of heart failure "not specifically related" to the disease.

Politics in the presidential election year of 1972 involved race relations in numerous ways. U.S. Rep. Shirley Chisholm of Brooklyn (*see* BIOGRAPHY) formally announced in January her candidacy for the Democratic presidential nomination, the first black woman to do so. Other blacks served in key roles. Yvonne Braithwaite Burke of California was co-chairperson of the Democratic Party convention and became nationally known through television. Former New York state senator Basil Paterson was elected vice-chairman of the Democratic National Committee, the first black in a national leadership role in a major party. Patricia Harris, former dean of the Howard University Law School, was elected permanent chairperson of the Democratic Party's powerful Credentials Committee. Approximately 4% of the delegates at the Republican convention and 14% at the Democratic convention were black. Though President Nixon won reelection easily, black voters continued to follow their strong Democratic leanings at a roughly 7–1 margin.

Blacks scored political successes in 1972. The Black Caucus of the House of Representatives swelled from 13 to 16. Mrs. Burke, a former state assemblywoman, won a seat from Los Angeles; Barbara C. Jordan, a former state senator, won a seat from Houston; and the Rev. Andrew Young (*see* BIOGRAPHY), a former aid to Martin Luther King, Jr., won a seat from Atlanta. Jordan and Young were the first black representatives from the South since the post-Reconstruction era. Two young black mayors were elected in Alabama: John Ford in Tuskegee, a town of 11,000 of whom 80% were black; and A. J. Cooper in Prichard, a blue-collar suburb of Mobile of 41,000 of whom 52% were black. In Selma, Ala., the scene of civil rights confrontations in the 1960s, five blacks were elected to a ten-member city council because a new state law allowed voters to choose their councilmen by wards rather than in community-wide contests.

Such changes in political structures were often critical for black political gains. In January a three-judge federal court in Montgomery, Ala., ordered the adoption of a new reapportionment plan that would divide the Alabama legislature into single-member districts. This shift was believed to favour both blacks and Republicans, who had only two legislators each at the time. In similar federal court actions, a new redistricting plan in Virginia was approved and plans in New Jersey and Connecticut were overturned—all with the potential effect of increasing the political voice of minorities.

The political campaigning made the controversial issue of busing to achieve the racial desegregation of public schools the prime symbol of the year's resistance to racial change. Opponents argued that the federal courts had "gone too far" in ordering "massive" busing at great public expense to achieve racial balance. A March Gallup survey found that about 70% of the nation's whites opposed busing for desegregation, though approximately 66% supported desegregation; it also found that only 3% of the parents of school-aged children were actually affected. Agreeing with the antibusing majority, President Nixon advantageously labeled it "one of the burning social issues of the past decade."

Proponents pointed out that 43.5% of America's schoolchildren were bused regularly. Annually, about 256,000 school buses carried 19 million pupils 2,200,000,000 mi. at a cost of $1.7 billion. Clearly, argued integrationists, Americans did not object to school busing per se, and only did so when the busing was for racial desegregation. School busing, concluded the chairman of the U.S. Commission on Civil Rights, Father Theodore Hesburgh (*see* BIOGRAPHY), "is the most phony issue in the country."

"Burning" or "phony," the issue dominated the racial headlines throughout the year. President Nixon on February 10 ordered a study to determine the best means to prevent the courts from employing busing for desegregation. At issue were antibusing legislative proposals that many observers considered unconstitutional versus an initiative for a constitutional amendment that would read: "No public school student shall, because of his race, creed, or color, be assigned to or required to attend a particular school." Father Hesburgh called the proposed amendment "fundamentally anti-black." Meanwhile, the antibusing forces staged a 3,300-car protest motorcade from Richmond, Va., to Washington, D.C., and a six-week, six-person march from Pontiac, Mich., to Washington.

After stormy sessions throughout late February, the Senate passed a combined higher education and desegregation aid bill with a relatively mild antibusing provision. But Nixon demanded more in a nationwide evening address over television and radio on March 16. Condemning the practice in strong terms, he proposed legislation: (1) to deny courts the power to order busing to achieve elementary school desegregation; (2) to impose a moratorium on all new court-ordered busing; and (3) to begin a program to concentrate federal educational aid in poor districts so as to substitute "equal educational opportunity" for racial integration. New York's Mayor John Lindsay called it a "cave-in" to the segregationist views of Alabama Gov. George Wallace, and opposition even

WIDE WORLD

Wounded plainclothesman is dragged to safety by a colleague during a street battle in New York City's Harlem on April 14, 1972, in which five policemen and three civilians were injured. Tempers of neighbourhood residents flared when two white officers entered a Black Muslim mosque.

came from inside Nixon's administration. A signed public letter from 95 of the 148 lawyers in the Justice Department's Civil Rights Division opposed the proposals as being of dubious constitutionality and "inconsistent with our national commitment to racial equality." Nevertheless, the department began to intervene in numerous school desegregation suits to argue for segregation.

Before turning to these new proposals, however, the Senate (63–15) and the House (218–180) passed in May and June the original Higher Education Bill with three antibusing riders. These riders delayed all new court busing orders until all appeals were exhausted or until Jan. 1, 1974; banned the use of federal funds for desegregation busing unless requested by local authorities; and banned the encouragement of busing by federal officials "unless constitutionally required."

The political pressure for these elaborate maneuvers derived largely from a set of significant desegregation rulings by the federal courts. In January the Supreme Court agreed to hear an appeal by black and Chicano parents for desegregation of Denver's public schools. It marked the first Supreme Court action concerning a large city outside of the South, and a decision was due at the year's close. The Supreme Court upheld a Nashville-Davidson County desegregation plan requiring the busing of 49,000 children and refused 8–0 to review an order requiring Norfolk, Va., to provide free transportation to school for 24,000 children under a desegregation plan.

In Richmond, Va., U.S. District Court Judge Robert Merhige, Jr., ordered in January that the city's schools (70% black) be consolidated with those of two adjoining counties (9% black) to form one desegregated system (34% black). Merhige's order probably would not entail additional busing. The 4th Circuit Court of Appeals overturned (5–1) this ruling in June. In Detroit U.S. District Court Judge Stephen Roth in June ordered the consolidation of the public schools of Detroit (65% black) and its 52 surrounding suburbs (29 of them all white), with each school attaining at least 25% black enrollment. Roth's order would cause 310,000 children to be bused across Detroit's city lines. In December the 6th Circuit Court of Appeals upheld Roth's decision. Both the Richmond and Detroit cases were appealed to the Supreme Court.

The effects of this extensive court action were reflected in federal data. Black children in completely segregated schools declined from 40% in 1968 to 12% in 1971–72, and those in predominantly white schools rose from 18% in 1968 to 44% in 1971–72. But resegregation was taking place in many Southern and Northern cities, making further progress increasingly dependent on a metropolitan approach. The National Education Association announced in May that 30,000 teaching jobs for blacks had been eliminated in 17 Southern and border states since 1954. The first black teacher to be honoured, however, as "National Teacher of the Year," James Rogers, Jr., was a high-school instructor in Durham, N.C. And the Census Bureau reported that the high school dropout rate for blacks 14 to 19 years old declined in 1971 to 11.1% from 14.6% in 1970.

In higher education, James C. Bond was named president of California State University at Sacramento and thus became the first black president of a major Western college. At two overwhelmingly white universities, Louisiana State and Arkansas, the first black student presidents were elected. Black protests in general subsided on the campuses during 1972, but tensions at Southern University in Baton Rouge, La., led to tragedy in November. Two 20-year-old black students were shot and killed after East Baton Rouge Parish police ordered protesting students to leave an administration building and began firing tear-gas canisters. An official state inquiry commission concluded that the students had been killed by one shotgun blast fired from an area occupied by sheriff's deputies. In January Baton Rouge had been the scene of a wild gunfight that left two white deputy sheriffs and two young black men dead and 31 injured when police attempted to stop a street rally in a black neighbourhood. Racial disturbances continued to flare in the military, with tensions in the Navy gaining publicity. (*See* DEFENSE.)

American Indians also attracted attention with a November protest at the Washington, D.C., headquarters of the U.S. Bureau of Indian Affairs. Led by activists of the American Indian Movement, 500 young Indians barricaded themselves in the BIA building for six days. The negotiated agreement broke down after it was discovered that considerable damage and apparent thefts had been committed in the building. Subsequently, the commissioner and deputy commissioner of the BIA were removed from their positions. For an extended discussion of Indian affairs, *see* SPECIAL REPORT.

Militants also figured prominently in numerous court cases. The most publicized involved Angela Davis (*see* BIOGRAPHY), a young black Communist accused of murder, kidnapping, and conspiracy. Her long-delayed trial finally began in March in San Jose, Calif.; it ended in June with her acquittal by an all-white jury after 13 hours of deliberation. Likewise, in a related trial in March, an all-white jury in San Francisco found two of the black "Soledad Brothers" innocent of the 1970 slaying of a Soledad prison guard. H. Rap Brown, a well-known black militant from Baton Rouge, was sentenced in New Orleans in June to five years in prison and fined $2,000 for a 1968 conviction of carrying a rifle while under indictment. He faced other criminal charges in New York. In Chicago, State's Attorney Edward V. Hanrahan and 13 codefendants were acquitted in October of conspiring to obstruct justice in the slaying of Black Panther leaders Fred Hampton and Mark Clark in 1969. But when he ran for reelection the next month, Hanrahan was defeated by an aroused black electorate.

In related developments, two lower federal courts tackled the issue of discrimination in hiring by the police. Philadelphia's police were ordered to hire at least one black for every two whites, and Alabama was ordered to hire an equal number of whites and blacks until a quarter of its state police were black. None of the 644 Alabama state police was then black; indeed, a check of eight Southern states found only 27 blacks out of 5,000 state policemen.

Not all federal court rulings favoured black contentions. The Supreme Court, for example, ruled 6–3 in June that Pennsylvania could grant a liquor license to a private club with racially restrictive guest practices; soon afterward, the Elks voted to continue to exclude blacks from their membership. The court also unanimously rejected appeals by black voters to invalidate Mississippi's 1971 legislative elections because of malapportionment and racial discrimination. But a three-judge federal court in the District of Columbia struck down some of the tax benefits of segregated fraternal organizations.

The racial frustrations of the year were dramatized by the actions of the first national black political convention, held in Gary, Ind., in March with over 3,300 voting delegates and some 5,000 observers. During attempts to set the future direction for black political actions, a split emerged between those who would reject the political system and those who would work within it. A wide variety of sometimes conflicting resolutions were passed, including support for more black community control, an Urban Homestead Act to distribute land and housing, a $5 billion black development agency, and a constitutional amendment to guarantee proportional black congressional representation.

A final note that appeared ominous to many was struck in November when the Nixon administration forced Father Hesburgh to resign as chairman of the Commission on Civil Rights. Hesburgh, the president of Notre Dame University, had called earlier for moral leadership in civil rights both inside and out of government. (THOMAS F. PETTIGREW)

See also Cities and Urban Affairs; Police; United States.

Six hundred white parents and students in Memphis, Tenn., pelt a school bus with dirt in March 1972 during a symbolic burial ceremony protesting court-ordered busing.

UPI COMPIX

Refugees

A refugee was once described as a man who votes with his feet. In 1972 this voiceless plebiscite continued in many parts of the world as hundreds of thousands fled their homelands in fear of persecution to seek asylum elsewhere. By far the largest refugee problem facing the international community at the end of 1971 was solved with the repatriation between January 1 and March 25, 1972, of the East Bengali refugees (reported by the government of India to number some ten million) who had crossed from East Pakistan into India beginning in March 1971. In this emergency, the Office of the United Nations High Commissioner for Refugees (UNHCR) acted as a focal point for assistance from and through the UN system, helping to mobilize funds from governments and private sources both for the relief action in India and for the repatriation movements. In all, approximately $185 million was channeled through UNHCR.

The way was opened to the solution of another refugee problem when the Sudan government and the South Sudan Liberation Movement signed an agreement in February in Addis Ababa, Eth., ending 16 years of civil conflict. At that time, approximately 200,000 Sudanese refugees had been living in the Central African Republic, Ethiopia, Uganda, and Zaire for as long as nine years. To create the necessary economic and social conditions for their return—as well as that of about 500,000 persons displaced within the country who were living in the bush—the Sudan government asked the UN for help. The secretary-general designated the UNHCR to coordinate immediate relief measures in the southern Sudan, much as it had done in India, and implementation of a one-year plan began in July. By mid-November about $14 million had been raised toward the $17.7 million target for the operation, which involved mounting an airlift to bring food and supplies from northern Sudan as well as providing earth-moving equipment to repair the roads and funds to rebuild schools and medical facilities destroyed during the fighting. Shortly before the end of the year approximately 220,000 displaced persons and 30,700 refugees had returned.

These coordinating tasks, both in India and the Sudan, were special assignments entrusted to the UNHCR over and above the office's normal responsibilities. The total number of refugees within the High Commissioner's competence (meaning persons who were outside their country of origin owing to well-founded fear of persecution) stood in 1972 at approximately 2.5 million spread over five continents: Africa, 1 million; the Americas, 630,000; Asia, 200,000; Europe, 616,000; and Oceania, 38,000. These figures included both persons who had become self-supporting but had not yet acquired a new nationality and those still in need of assistance. They did not include people who had fled their homes but remained within their native country, as was the case with thousands in Vietnam and Cambodia.

As in the past several years, well over half of UNHCR's regular budget, which in 1972 was $8 million, was allocated for assistance to African refugees, in many cases for persons from areas still under colonial administration. Thus, the great majority of the more than 250,000 persons who benefited from UNHCR's aid were Africans.

The largest new emergency in Africa to require international assistance concerned approximately 48,000 refugees from Burundi, who because of intertribal hostilities crossed into Tanzania, Rwanda, and Zaire in May. In response to appeals from the countries of asylum, UNHCR made available $1.2 million during 1972 for this group of refugees, and an additional $1,350,000 was provided in the 1973 budget.

UPI COMPIX

Frightened faces of a mother and her child in Hue, South Vietnam, reflect the misery of refugees escaping from battles to the north. Shortly after their arrival in May 1972, Communist troops attacked in the area of the old imperial capital, and the refugees were forced to seek a new sanctuary.

In October approximately 10,000 Jehovah's Witnesses fled a purge by the government in Malawi and arrived in the eastern part of Zambia. By mid-December the number had grown to 18,000, and UNHCR made an emergency allocation of $39,200 for them.

Another situation requiring international action developed when Pres. Idi Amin of Uganda ordered the expulsion by November 7 of all Asians not holding Ugandan nationality. While the great majority of those affected held British passports and approximately 25,000 went directly to the U.K., there remained about 6,000–7,000 stateless persons for whom the UN had to take responsibility. This was done by arranging for them to receive Red Cross travel documents in Uganda and then by trying to find permanent resettlement opportunities. By November 9, all of the stateless persons had been moved from Uganda. Approximately 2,500 were accepted on a permanent basis by Canada, Switzerland, and the U.S., and 3,600 were admitted to temporary transit centres in Europe. By mid-November the UNHCR had received offers of permanent resettlement for about 1,400 of this latter group and was continuing its efforts both to find places for the remaining 2,200 and to raise the funds needed to cover their care and maintenance in transit.

In Europe, the flow of persons of European origin seeking asylum elsewhere diminished. However, a general slowdown in openings for migrants, caused by unemployment in overseas countries, obliged refugees to wait longer in reception centres before moving on.

Efforts in the field of international protection continued during 1972. The number of countries acceding to the 1951 Convention Relating to the Status of Refugees, which defined the rights of refugees and

Radio:
see Television and Radio

Railroads:
see Transportation

Recordings:
see Music

Reformed Churches:
see Religion

established a standard of treatment for them, increased to 63. Moreover, a group of independent legal experts, brought together at the initiative of the Carnegie Endowment for International Peace, drew up the draft text of a binding Convention on Asylum. It would formally prevent states from turning back persons seeking asylum at the frontier except on extremely serious grounds. (UNHCR)

See also Migration, International.

Religion

Organized religion in 1972 reflected the uneasiness in the world at large. Churches continued to agonize over the conflicts in Southeast Asia, the Middle East, Bangladesh, Northern Ireland, and Uganda. Massive relief drives for clothing, food, and money were undertaken, especially for the victims of the war in Bangladesh. The civil war in Northern Ireland continued to occupy the attention of concerned Protestant and Roman Catholic churchmen. Despite conferences and united prayer services, the Irish antagonists apparently paid little attention to the efforts of church people to effect a reconciliation.

Among the various movements to achieve unity among the churches, 1972 was a year of advance, retreat, and, quite often, stalemate. A drop in contributions from member churches forced such ecumenical organizations as the World Council of Churches and, in the U.S., the National Council of Churches to cut back on staff, drop or curtail some programs, and generally reconsider their role in the life of the church. In what amounted to a gesture of recognition toward the third world, the WCC chose, as its general secretary, the Rev. Philip Potter (*see* BIOGRAPHY), a Methodist from Dominica in the West Indies. The National Council of Churches also elected its first black president, the Rev. W. Sterling Cary of the United Church of Christ.

One favourable ecumenical development was the Anglican-Roman Catholic agreement on the meaning of Holy Communion. (See *Anglican Communion,* below.) The document, released at the end of 1971 and approved by Pope Paul VI and Michael Ramsey, archbishop of Canterbury, explicitly stated that "we have reached substantial agreement." The *Church Times,* an Anglican newspaper published in London, expressed the hope that this might lead to eventual Vatican recognition of Anglican orders. Roman Catholic refusal to recognize priests ordained in the Anglican Communion after the Reformation as part of the Apostolic Succession had been a major source of disagreement between the two churches.

Another significant breakthrough occurred when an official dialogue group of Lutheran and Roman Catholic theologians reported the possibilities of "concord" on the issue of papal primacy. (See *Lutherans,* below.) Still to be discussed, however, was the dogma of papal infallibility, regarding which there was sharp disagreement. Earlier the two groups found themselves in fundamental accord on the Nicene Creed and on the significance of Holy Communion.

Less progress was reported in the area of organic union. In Britain the Congregational Church in England and Wales and the Presbyterian Church of England merged into the United Reformed Church with nearly 250,000 members, but the scheme for union between British Anglicans and Methodists was voted down decisively by the Anglicans in May. In Canada a proposed union of the United Church of Canada, the Anglicans, and the Christian Church (Disciples of Christ) appeared to be virtually dead. (See *United Church of Canada,* below.) Perhaps the biggest setback to U.S. church unity occurred when the United Presbyterian Church in the U.S.A. voted to withdraw from the Consultation on Church Union (COCU), an attempt to unite nine Protestant denominations into a church body of some 25 million members. (See *Presbyterian, Reformed, and Congregational,* below.) The eight remaining members of COCU were the United Methodist Church, the Presbyterian Church in the U.S., the Episcopal Church, the Christian Church (Disciples of Christ), the African Methodist Episcopal, African Methodist Episcopal Zion, and Christian Methodist Episcopal churches, and the United Church of Christ. The United Church of Christ had voiced some reservations about the plan of union and proposed several revisions.

Churchmen could not agree on definitive reasons for the cooling of enthusiasm for merger movements within Christianity. Some felt there was a decline in ecumenical zeal. Others said that conservative churchmen as a whole disliked sacrificing or compromising traditional confessions for the sake of a larger church body. There also seemed to be a general consensus that a merger of church bodies did not necessarily guarantee a more effective working church. Finally, there was the fear that the creation of a superchurch would necessitate more elaborate bureaucracies. These setbacks did not necessarily mean that the ecumenical movement was doomed, however. Large segments of Protestantism, Roman Catholicism, and Eastern Orthodoxy had ecumenical relationships although they had never pursued organic unity. In late September a plan to unite five of New Zealand's Protestant denominations was approved by the membership of the churches involved, though a final vote would have to be taken in 1974.

Christianity, especially in the U.S., continued to witness the paradox of declining membership in the mainline churches, even as they struggled to make themselves more "relevant" to current social problems, and growth among the fundamentalist and evangelical denominations. Nowhere was this more evident than among young people, many of whom seemed drawn to the certainties of the "old-time religion." That the so-called Jesus Freaks were only the most visible and widely publicized fringe of the movement was apparent at Explo 72, a massive revival meeting that attracted some 75,000 people, most of them young, to the Cotton Bowl in Dallas, Tex., in June. Evangelist Billy Graham called the meeting a "religious Woodstock," in reference to the 1969 rock concert in upstate New York that was one of the landmarks of the youth culture, but the young people at Dallas appeared predominantly neatly dressed and middle class. The fringe still flourished, however. Several parents instituted legal proceedings against the Children of God sect, which demanded that its young adherents leave their families and take up a rigidly structured communal way of life. The aggressiveness of some groups toward the conversion of Jews and the appearance of "Jewish Christian" sects aroused some apprehension among Jewish leaders. (See *Judaism,* below.)

The year also saw continued interest in the so-called charismatic revival, involving the traditional Pentecostal practices of speaking in tongues, faith healing, and "baptism in the Spirit." Long confined to the

Pentecostal churches (which were themselves growing rapidly), these phenomena had appeared in the mainline churches, where they constituted a burgeoning movement. (*See* Special Report.) Both the growth of fundamentalism and the charismatic revival probably shared some basic social causes, and they overlapped at some points. That they were not synonymous had been demonstrated in 1971, when the singer Pat Boone was expelled from the fundamentalist Churches of Christ for participating in charismatic experiences.

Conservative-liberal splits within some of the major denominations appeared to be widening. Such issues lay behind the struggle between the conservative president of the Lutheran Church-Missouri Synod and the president and faculty of the denomination's largest theological seminary. (See *Lutherans,* below.) Several conservative congregations in the Presbyterian Church in the U.S. announced formation of an independent presbytery. (See *Presbyterian, Reformed, and Congregational,* below.) The Rt. Rev. John Hines, who as presiding bishop of the Episcopal church had instituted controversial social programs (and had seen membership, attendance, and giving decline), announced that he would leave his post before retirement age "to make way for a younger man."

Taking all these indications together, some observers foresaw not ecumenism on the grand scale proposed by COCU, but rather a blurring of traditional denominational distinctions and a realignment, possibly along liberal-socially oriented–fundamentalist-conservative lines. In a book that attracted considerable attention during the year, *Why Conservative Churches Are Growing,* Dean M. Kelley, a staff executive of the National Council of Churches, put forward the thesis that strict churches making heavy demands on their members were growing while tolerant, undemanding churches were either static or declining. Among his examples was the contrast between the pre- and post-Vatican II Roman Catholic Church.

The 1972 *Yearbook of American Churches* reported that membership in U.S. churches and synagogues stood at 131,045,953, a slight rise from the 62.4% of the total U.S. population reported in the 1970 *Yearbook.* This statistic could not be considered conclusive, however, because of the addition of some denominations to the 1972 *Yearbook* tabulations. The Roman Catholic Church recorded an increase of only 0.7%. Losses were reported by many mainline Protestant denominations, but the Southern Baptist Convention rose by 1.2% to become the nation's largest Protestant body (11,628,032 members). The 13-year downtrend in churchgoing continued, according to a Gallup Poll released in January 1972. The falloff was greatest among Roman Catholics; attendance among Protestants and Jews had remained fairly steady since 1964.

Figures released in 1972 revealed that Americans gave more money to religion in 1971 than ever before, but they were giving a smaller share of their charitable dollars than in previous years. While giving to religion increased $300 million to $8.6 billion in 1971, religion received only 40.7% of the charitable dollar, a sharp drop from the 42.6% given in 1970. Harlan F. Lang, editor of *Giving USA,* attributed the trend to inflation, the competition for the dollar, and declining church attendance.

The U.S. Supreme Court's ruling that Old Order Amish parents do not have to send their children to public schools was hailed by churchmen of all faiths as a victory for religious freedom. The ruling reversed lower court decisions in Wisconsin that had refused to make special allowances for Amish children. The Supreme Court clearly stated that religious freedom takes precedence over educational statutes on attendance. The case began when three Old Amish fathers in New Glarus, Wis., were charged with violating a state law by removing their children from school before the age of 16. The Amish believe that to send children to high school would expose the parents to "censure of the Church community" and also "endanger their own salvation and that of their children."

LEE ROMERO—THE NEW YORK TIMES

The Right Rev. Paul Moore, Jr., addresses a congregation of 4,000 at the Cathedral Church of St. John the Divine during an eight-hour ceremony on Sept. 23, 1972, celebrating his enthronement as the 13th Episcopal bishop of New York.

There was continued discussion on the ordination of women to the ministry. Most Protestant denominations already permitted the ordination of women (among major holdouts were the Episcopalians and the Lutheran Church-Missouri Synod), but ordination did not always guarantee a position in a church. Pope Paul VI issued a motu proprio—a decree by his own hand—barring women from formal participation in the Mass, although women might perform certain functions upon occasion when authorized to do so.

(ALFRED P. KLAUSLER)

PROTESTANTS

Anglican Communion. The elaborate scheme for Anglican-Methodist reunion in Britain finally collapsed in 1972. Concocted by distinguished leaders of the two churches after years of negotiations, the plan, accepted by the Methodists but rejected by the Anglicans in 1969, was brought back to the Church of England's supreme governing body, the General Synod, in May at the instigation of Archbishop Ramsey. It had been decided in advance that a favourable vote of at least 75% would be required, and the vote in favour proved to be only 65%. The archbishop, who had thrown the whole weight of his office behind the scheme, dismissed any suggestion that he should resign because of this failure of his personal policy. However, one diocesan bishop (Cyril Easthaugh of Peterborough) soon afterward declared that the defeat of the scheme had been "a serious setback to bishops' leadership" insofar as the majority of his fellow bishops (unlike himself) had espoused a cause that had proved unacceptable to a large proportion of the clergy and laity of the church.

UPI COMPIX

William Johnson, an admitted homosexual and a ministerial candidate in the United Church of Christ, awaits a decision on his ordination by lay and clergy delegates of San Francisco area churches. On April 30, 1972, his application was approved by nearly a two-to-one margin.

Elsewhere in the field of ecumenical relations, the Church of England took a historic decision in legislating for the admission of all baptized Christians in good standing to Holy Communion in its own churches. The Anglican Church in Wales favoured discussion of "a covenant for union by 1974" with Methodists, Congregationalists, and Presbyterians. Official schemes for uniting Anglicans with other churches in Canada, New Zealand, Australia, and Sri Lanka (Ceylon) remained uncertain. (See *United Church of Canada,* below.)

The text of the agreement reached between Anglican and Roman Catholic theologians, announced in the preceding September but only published on the last day of 1971, revealed a "startling" consensus on vital issues that had divided the two churches for more than four centuries, including the Real Presence of Christ in the sacrament of the Lord's Supper or Eucharist. There were hopes that this agreement might pave the way to possible intercommunion, but the Vatican appeared to remain lukewarm.

In the sensitive area of race relations, Anglicans were deeply divided over the wisdom of the World Council of Churches in making financial grants to guerrilla organizations in southern Africa, even though the grants were specifically not to be used for military purposes. But Anglican detestation of the theory and practice of white supremacy there was amply demonstrated by the expulsion of the bishop of Damaraland (Colin Winter) from his diocese by the South African government; the long ordeal of the dean of the Johannesburg cathedral (Gonville A. ffrench-Beytagh), who was finally acquitted on appeal after having been sentenced to imprisonment; and by the subsequent unsuccessful prosecution of the dean of the Cape Town cathedral (Edward King) for joining in demonstrations against racial segregation.

The issue of the ordination of women to the Anglican priesthood continued to simmer after the bishop of Hong Kong's ordination of two women in November 1971. In New Zealand the General Synod of the Anglican Church rejected a proposal to ordain women, but only by a very narrow majority. In England one diocese (Southwark) voted in favour of this innovation, but the Church of England as a whole remained undecided. In the U.S., where the 1970 General Convention of the Episcopal Church had approved the ordination of women as deacons (normally a first step toward becoming a priest), the House of Bishops voted to admit women to the priesthood. Before taking effect, the move would have to be approved by the next General Convention in 1973.

In the internal affairs of the Church of England, a notable development was the initially favourable reaction of the General Synod to new proposals affecting the parochial clergy. The suggestions included compulsory retirement at the age of 70; a leveling of stipends; the abolition of the right of private patrons to appoint clergymen to benefices; and the erosion of the traditional "parson's freehold" by measures to allow the expulsion of a parson from his parish if "a deterioration in pastoral relationships" between him and his people could be proved. These and other measures during the year confirmed the impression among many observers that Anglicanism, under pressure of the modern demand that the church be run as a professional organization on lines of business-like efficiency, was moving away from the traditional view of the church as a supernatural body and of its priesthood as a unique vocation. (R. L. ROBERTS)

Baptists. According to the Baptist World Alliance, Baptist churches in 115 countries had a total membership of 31,432,130 in 1972. This was a gain of 390,493 over a year earlier and reflected increases in every continent except Asia and Europe.

Though Baptists were declining in Europe as far as numbers were concerned, there was considerable vitality in such nations as Romania, where the first national conference in seven years was held in Bucharest. The conference reported over 4,000 baptisms in the preceding year, and it was estimated that twice that number had gone unreported. The Rev. Andrew MacRae, secretary of the Scottish Baptist Union, completed his two-year term as president of the European Baptist Federation when the federation met in council in August in Yugoslavia, the first such meeting ever held in a Communist country. Claus Meister of Switzerland was elected to succeed him. Plans were being completed for the European Baptist Federation Congress to be held in July 1973 in Zürich, Switz.

In Italy a rift—often found in U.S. Baptist circles—between social activists and those who would confine church activities to traditional religious practices, was evident. The U.S. missionaries in Italy, most of whom were affiliated with the conservative Southern Baptist Convention, took sides against the activists. The Rev. José Cardon, Baptist minister and secretary of the Evangelical Defense Committee in Spain, reported that the five-year-old law on religious freedom was working more satisfactorily than had been anticipated. In 1971 evangelicals in Spain published, with official approval, nearly 1,250,000 copies of some 500 different religious books and pamphlets. The Moscow Baptist Church was visited by U.S. Pres. and Mrs. Richard Nixon during the president's trip to the U.S.S.R. No head of state had ever visited the Moscow church before.

In Liberia, where William Tolbert (*see* BIOGRAPHY), a former president of the Baptist World Alliance, was president, Baptists were seeking to erect dormitories and to increase faculty personnel to meet a rapid increase in the student population. Missionaries in East Africa appealed to the Baptist World Alliance for financial and other aid for nearly 3,000 Baptists in Burundi, where at least 50,000 persons had been killed in an intertribal war. Burundi Baptists, most of whom were members of the Hutu tribe, appeared to have been killed because of their leadership roles rather than because of religious persecution.

The two largest white Baptist groups in the U.S., the Southern Baptists and the American Baptists, held their annual meetings in Philadelphia and Denver, Colo., respectively. The Southern Convention defeated an effort by ultraconservatives to recall the 12-volume Broadman Bible Commentary, published by the Convention's Sunday school board, on grounds that it was overly liberal.

The American Baptists' meeting was the last to be held annually; biennial meetings would be held beginning in 1973. The decision to meet every other year was part of a reorganization that included greater centralization of authority, although representative government was ensured by a carefully balanced system of electing delegates to the biennial meetings and the General Board. Robert C. Campbell, former dean of the American Baptist Seminary of the West, Covina (Calif.) Campus, was elected to the post of general secretary, and the name of the denomination was changed from the American Baptist Convention to the American Baptist Churches in the U.S.A.

David Shannon of the American Baptists became dean of Pittsburgh Theological Seminary, the first black to be so named by a predominantly white seminary. Another precedent was set when the American Baptists joined with the black Progressive National Baptist Convention in a $7.5 million Fund for Renewal to provide vocational opportunities for minority youth.

The American Baptists temporarily withdrew their endorsement of all Navy chaplains when chaplain Andrew Jensen was accused of adultery and court-martialed for "moral turpitude." General endorsement procedures were restored after Jensen was acquitted, but not before the question of who is the final administrator of the military chaplain had been thoroughly examined.

Many North American Baptist groups entered into Key '73, a continent-wide program in evangelism made up of predominantly conservative groups with a strong emphasis on traditional evangelism. Some groups, the American Baptists among them, insisted that their participation would provide an opportunity for people of all theological persuasions to express themselves in outreach and mission.

(NORMAN DE PUY; R. W. THOMSON)

Christian Church (Disciples of Christ). In an effort to achieve a better understanding of growing Asian resistance to Western paternalism and what it means to the overseas work of churches, Moderator Walter D. Bingham of Louisville, Ky., led a church delegation to the Orient in October 1972 for dialogue with political and social leaders as well as church officials.

The church's 222-member General Board urged some form of amnesty for draft law violators at the end of the Vietnam war, reiterated support of COCU, and called for an end to the U.S. embargo on trade with Cuba. Controversy surrounded its reversal of an earlier decision to hold the church's 1975 General Assembly in Salt Lake City, Utah. The reversal came after blacks on the board objected to the racial policies of the Church of Jesus Christ of Latter-day Saints, a dominant force in Utah, which excludes blacks of African descent from the priesthood.

Three teen-agers were elected to the General Board and one of them, Miss Pat Villars of Minden, Neb., became the youngest person ever to be named to the 45-member administrative committee.

In August, Canadian Disciples, an integral part of the church's organization in North America, celebrated the 50th anniversary of their All-Canada Committee.

For the second year in a row the church showed a 2% increase in receipts for world work, though the membership had fallen by about the same percentage, to 1,391,210, in 1971. Feasibility studies were begun on a multimillion-dollar campaign for both capital and ongoing projects in 1975–79. The church closed out its Reconciliation race and poverty crisis program after four years, during which $2 million had been raised, but an annual special offering for race and poverty work was established with a first-year goal of $750,000. (ROBERT L. FRIEDLY)

Christian Science. In May 1972 the board of directors of the First Church of Christ, Scientist, in Boston requested that church members throughout the world give earnest consideration to prayer for the peaceful and prompt solution of troubling world conditions. Announcements of this were read in some 3,200 branch churches in 58 countries, and an editorial supporting the call to prayer appeared in the *Christian Science Monitor*. The immense power for good inherent in unselfed prayer was also emphasized at regional youth meetings held in 17 cities throughout the world.

At the denomination's annual meeting in June, church members were urged to dedicate themselves anew to the practice of Christian healing, or healing through prayer. This theme was stressed throughout the year in conferences, public lectures, films, periodicals, and radio programs.

For the first time in the denomination's history, a director from an overseas area was named to the board of directors in April. Otto Bertschi of Zürich, Switz., succeeded Clayton Bion Craig of Boston, who retired after 23 years' service. The chairman of the board of directors for 1972 was Arthur P. Wuth, who had served on the board since 1964. In October David E. Sleeper became the first member of the denomination's top administrative body to make an official tour of Latin America. At the annual meeting George Nay of Boston was named the new president of the Mother Church. Construction neared completion on the new 15-ac. Christian Science Center in Boston.

(J. BUROUGHS STOKES)

Churches of Christ. World evangelism, youth involvement, and media utilization were the primary concerns of the Churches of Christ in 1972. A mission centre was opened in the new World Trade Center in New York City to contact foreigners visiting the U.S. A new modern-language translation of the New Testament into Italian was completed. Translation of the New Testament into Farsi (modern Persian) was begun, and work was under way on translating teaching materials into Swahili and Japanese. As part of the continuing effort to train indigenous leadership overseas, a program of training in personal evangelism for preachers was carried out in Japan and a series of leadership training courses was held in Africa.

Youth groups, both at home and abroad, were being utilized in evangelistic efforts. Graduates of a preacher training school in Mexico City were engaged in founding churches and then revisiting and encouraging the new Christians. Young people from schools in Korea and the Philippines conducted regular evangelistic campaigns.

A new 490-ac. campus of Pepperdine University, a university related to the Churches of Christ, opened at Malibu, Calif., and its original Los Angeles campus was dedicated to the needs of the urban community.

The syndicated column begun by the Druid Hills Church in Atlanta, Ga., was appearing in over 325 U.S. newspapers, and the church was planning a prime-time nationwide television program. The televised Amazing Grace Bible Class of the Madison, Tenn., church was accepted for showing on the 90-station Armed Forces Television Service. World Radio began beaming Russian-language broadcasts into the U.S.S.R. (M. NORVEL YOUNG)

Church of Jesus Christ of Latter-day Saints. Several important changes in the leadership of the church occurred in 1972. Pres. Joseph Fielding Smith (*see* OBITUARIES) died on July 3, and on July 7, Harold B. Lee (*see* BIOGRAPHY) became first president, with N. Eldon Tanner and Marion G. Romney as counselors. In April, Victor L. Brown was appointed presiding bishop of the church, with H. Burke Peterson and Vaughn J. Featherstone as counselors. Bruce R. McConkie became a member of the Council of Twelve Apostles in October.

The year also witnessed important developments in the departments of the church. In January, Leonard J. Arrington, an economic historian of the American West, was named church historian. Following the death of Richard L. Evans in November 1971, J. Spencer Kinard was appointed as narrator for the Sunday morning broadcasts of the Mormon Tabernacle Choir. All missionary services were put under the direction of the First Council of the Seventy.

World membership totaled approximately 3,150,000 in 1972, comprising over 7,000 congregations throughout the world. As an indication of the church's growing international base, the second area general conference was held Aug. 25–27, 1972, at Mexico City. The first such conference had been held in 1971 at Manchester, Eng. Two new temples were dedicated for sacred ordinance work at Provo and Ogden, Utah.

(LEONARD JAMES ARRINGTON)

Jehovah's Witnesses. The society of Christian ministers known as Jehovah's Witnesses was active in 208 countries and territories in 1972. This work was organized by 28,407 congregations, supervised by the Governing Body of Jehovah's Witnesses through 95 branch offices of the Watch Tower Bible and Tract Society.

Some 163,123 new ministers (members) were baptized during 1972, bringing the worldwide total to 1,658,990. During the summer 163 "Divine Rulership" district assemblies were held in the U.S., Canada, the British Isles, and 13 countries of Western Europe; over 1,280,000 persons attended the public talk entitled "Divine Rulership—the Only Hope of Mankind." Attendance at the annual celebration of the Lord's Evening Meal totaled 3,662,407, an increase of some 210,000 over 1971.

Reports late in the year indicated that approximately 18,000 Jehovah's Witnesses in Malawi had been forced to flee into Zambia as a result of government persecution.

Printing presses were installed in Watch Tower Society offices in Japan, the Philippines, Australia, and Ghana during the year. The Brooklyn printing plant produced 30,449,715 Bibles and bound books and over 237 million magazines. Circulation of *The Watchtower,* the official journal of Jehovah's Witnesses, rose to 7,850,000 in 74 languages, and its companion magazine, *Awake!,* attained a new record circulation of 7.5 million in 29 languages. New books released included *Paradise Restored to Mankind—By Theocracy!,* containing a verse-by-verse discussion of the Old Testament books of Haggai and Zechariah, and a new easy-to-read Bible translation, *The Bible in Living English* by Steven T. Byington. (N. H. KNORR)

Lutherans. Significant results of several ecumenical dialogues were reported during the year. Internationally, a Lutheran-Roman Catholic commission completed a four-year study on "The Gospel and the Church" by noting a "remarkable degree of agreement on the understanding of the ministerial office in the church" and "general agreement that the long-standing . . . issue of justification need no longer divide our churches." Also, it was said, Lutherans and Catholics can accept the office of the papacy "as a visible sign of the unity of the churches . . . insofar as it is subordinated to the primacy of the Gospel by theological reinterpretation and practical restructuring." In the U.S., Lutheran and Catholic theologians prepared to issue a report in 1973 on papal primacy and the universal ministry.

On a world level, Lutheran and Anglican theologians called upon their churches to welcome communicants from the other church and to encourage their own members to receive the Lord's Supper in congregations of the other tradition. A similar report was issued by participants in the Lutheran-Episcopal dialogue in the U.S. A second round of talks began in the U.S. between Lutheran and Reformed theologians to explore the possibilities of a "consensus statement which aims at affecting fuller expressions of Church fellowship, witness and service." In Europe, Lutheran and Reformed churchmen concluded that enough agreement existed between the two major branches of the Reformation to declare altar and pulpit fellowship and mutual recognition of ministries. Lutherans and Roman Catholics in the Philippines reached formal agreement expressing mutual recognition of the baptismal ceremony administered by either church.

The Evangelical Church of the Union (EKU), representing some 19 million Christians, the large majority Lutheran, was being divided administratively into East and West German regions. The seven regional churches in the union dated back to the Middle Ages.

The Lutheran World Federation, in its 25th anniversary year, accepted as members the 7,500-member Batak Christian Church of Indonesia and the 950-member Korea Lutheran Church. The LWF now had 86 member bodies, representing some 54 million of the world's 73.5 million Lutherans.

Lutheran Bishop Leonard Auala of South West Africa, an outspoken foe of South Africa's apartheid policies, visited the U.S. In contrast to the stand of leading U.S. denominations and church agencies, Bishop Auala warned that withdrawal of U.S. industry's $1 billion investment in South Africa would create serious suffering, with thousands of black Africans losing their jobs. The Lutheran World Federation said it would withdraw its deposits from banks that pursue "policies and practices that contribute to the worsening of the non-whites' position in South Africa."

The Lutheran Church in America's biennial convention approved a massive restructuring plan to streamline its operations and enable the 3.1 million-member denomination to fulfill its role more effectively in meeting the emerging needs of church and society. A similar revision of its national structure took place in the 2.5 million-member American Lutheran Church, and some saw these moves as a prelude to merger of the two bodies. The ALC, which with the LCA voted to ordain women in 1970, declined a request from the Lutheran Church-Missouri Synod to reconsider its action as divisive of the fellowship between the two bodies. At year's end, the LCA had ordained four women, the ALC only one.

A long-simmering controversy over doctrinal orthodoxy erupted in the Lutheran Church-Missouri Synod, centred on Concordia Seminary in St. Louis, Mo., the largest Lutheran and third largest Protestant theological school in the world. Shortly after his upset election to the Synod's presidency in 1969, as a candidate of conservatives, the Rev. Jacob A. O. Preus named a fact-finding committee to investigate charges of heretical teaching at the seminary. The American Association of Theological Schools entered the dispute by placing Concordia's accreditation on probation for two years because, it said, the Synod does not ensure "adequate authority" of the seminary's board of control. Then Preus issued a "Statement of Scriptural and Confessional Principles" in which he said, among other things, that all Synod members must believe that every word of the Bible is literally true.

When the fact-finding committee's long-delayed report was released, Preus said it made it "abundantly clear that some professors at the seminary hold views contrary to the established doctrinal positions of the Synod." He demanded that Concordia's board of control "deal with those professors" and "deal personally and first of all" with John Tietjen, the seminary president. In a sharp rebuttal, sent to all pastors of the Synod, Tietjen denounced the investigation as "unfair, untrue, less than Scriptural, and un-Lutheran." The issue was likely to come to a head at the 2.8 million-member denomination's next biennial convention at New Orleans in July 1973.

For the third successive year, membership of Lutheran church bodies in North America decreased, to a total of 9,120,352, with 8,815,852 baptized children and adults in the U.S. and 304,500 in Canada.

(ERIC W. MODEAN)

Methodists. The year's focal point for the United Methodist Church was the Quadrennial General Conference in Atlanta, Ga., where 1,000 delegates voted overwhelmingly to revamp the organization, as well as to revise the denomination's doctrinal statements and to rewrite its statement of social principles.

The greatest structural change involved combining nine national program agencies into four boards—Discipleship, Global Ministries, Church and Society, and Higher Education and Ministry. As nearly as possible, the boards were to consist of one-third laymen, one-third laywomen, and one-third clergy, rather than the traditional half lay and half clergy. Each agency was also to include representation from major ethnic groups, youth (under 18), and young adults (19–30). The thrust toward ending all structures determined by race was accelerated by the General Conference, which decreed that no more such conferences could exist after mid-1973. Black conferences in several Southern states merged with their white counterparts during the year. In November the last white conference in the nation to approve a merger plan, the North Mississippi Conference, voted to merge with the black Upper Mississippi Conference.

The number of women delegates at the General Conference increased to a new high of 13%. The church established a Commission on the Status and Role of Women, and the Women's Society of Christian Service and the Wesleyan Service Guild were merged into the new United Methodist Women. For the second time the General Conference seated ten nonvoting youth, along with several seminary students. A constitutional amendment removing any age requirement for delegates was passed, subject to annual (regional) conferences' approval, and action was completed on an amendment removing the age minimum for full participation in the annual conferences.

The General Conference overwhelmingly adopted a new statement of doctrine. Instead of replacing or revising traditional creeds, it sets up guidelines to help church members understand their beliefs and apply them to life. The legislative session also adopted a Statement of Social Principles, the latest revision of a social-action document first approved in 1908. A long-time emphasis on peace action was strengthened by General Conference condemnation of U.S. involvement in the Vietnam war; establishment of a special effort known as "Call for Peace and the Self-Development of Peoples"; and authority for church agencies to use their investments to try to dissuade industry from producing weaponry for the Indochina war.

JACK MANNING—THE NEW YORK TIMES

Students and faculty of the General Theological Seminary (Episcopal) participate in an "allegorical procession" preceding a Solemn Requiem Mass celebrated at the Cloisters in New York City on Feb. 14, 1972, in honour of the Vietnamese war dead.

Ecumenically, the year saw reaffirmation of United Methodist participation in COCU and in the World and National Councils of Churches; approval for the initiation of dialogue with Jewish communities; support for the evangelistic effort known as Key '73; final approval by the denomination for its churches in Northern India to join a new united church; and authorization for units in Sierra Leone, Costa Rica, Panama, Taiwan, and North Africa to become autonomous.

U.S. membership dropped about 1.5% to 10,509,198, and giving for church-wide administration and benevolence fell 1% to $45,368,431.

Hopes of a decisive step toward union between the Anglican and Methodist churches in Britain received a sharp setback in 1972. (See *Anglican Communion,* above.) Nevertheless, ecumenical initiatives continued. A number of churches were being shared with other denominations, and plans were made for a new ecumenical centre at Skelmersdale, in the Liverpool district. In Paris the Methodist Church and St. George's Anglican Church unanimously agreed to share one building, and in Belize, British Honduras, the Roman Catholics were included in a joint ecumenical centre. The scheme for church union in Sri Lanka was confirmed by both ministerial and representative sessions of the Ceylon Methodist Conference. Six churches were involved.

Officers of the World Methodist Council met for a consultation in Tonga at the beginning of the year. A watchnight service was attended by the king of Tonga and his entourage. The first meeting of the newly constituted Executive Committee of the World Methodist Council, presided over by Bishop Prince Taylor, was held at Wesley College, Bristol, Eng., at the end of August. Hugh Sherlock, first president of the Methodist Church in the Caribbean and the Americas, took up his appointment as one of the secretaries of the World Methodist Council in July.

(WINSTON H. TAYLOR; MAX W. WOODWARD)

Pentecostal Churches. The Pentecostal movement around the world continued to exhibit impressive growth and development in 1972. Events during the year indicated a growing theological maturity within the movement and greater acceptance by other churches.

In contrast to membership declines in most of the traditional Protestant bodies, the Pentecostal churches in the U.S. grew from 2,264,771 adult members in 29,475 churches in 1971 to 2,357,514 members in 30,035 churches in 1972. The largest Pentecostal denomination, the Assemblies of God, grew by 5%, from 645,000 to 679,000, and this rate was generally matched by the other major bodies: the Church of God (Cleveland, Tenn.), the Pentecostal Holiness Church, the International Church of the Foursquare Gospel, the Church of God in Christ, the Open Bible Standard Churches, the Pentecostal Church of God of America, and the United Pentecostal Church, Inc.

Growing maturity was indicated by the meeting in November of the Society for Pentecostal Studies in Oklahoma City, where Catholic, Protestant, and Pentecostal scholars explored the expanding perspectives of the burgeoning charismatic movement in the traditional denominations. (*See* Special Report.) Another highlight was the meeting in June of the first Catholic-Pentecostal dialogue in Zürich, Switz.

The image of Pentecostalism was enhanced by the phenomenal growth of such charismatic-oriented publishing houses as Logos and Creation House. However, the film *Marjoe,* concerning a preacher and healer who admitted he was motived by a desire for money rather than by faith, proved an embarrassment to the movement.

Of great interest to Pentecostals were the June meeting of Pentecostal-Catholics at the University of Notre Dame, where 11,000 gathered, and the meeting of 8,000 Pentecostal-Lutherans in Minneapolis in August. The Council on Spiritual Life conducted by the Assemblies of God, also in Minneapolis, gave tentative approval to the charismatic movement in other churches.

Ray Hughes became general overseer of the Church of God (Cleveland, Tenn.), succeeding Leonard Carroll, who died in January. The Church of God in Christ, the largest black Pentecostal group, was suffering a major schism; a faction of the church had set up offices in Evanston, Ill., and efforts at reconciliation had failed to restore unity at year's end.

The year 1972 proved an outstanding one for the autonomous local Assemblies of God in Great Britain and Ireland. The fellowship had grown rapidly after its inception in 1924, but progress had slowed after World War II. However, at the 1972 annual general conference, held at Minehead, Somerset, and attended by some 6,000 people, it was reported that the number of churches had increased by 14 to 549, the greatest annual addition in 15 years. There were 427 accredited ministers, 64 probationers, 49 retired ministers, and 51 church representatives.

Overseas missionary activities extended to Ireland, India, Kenya, Malaysia, Nigeria, Sierra Leone, South Africa, Spain, Tanzania, Uganda, Pakistan, and Zaire. Home missions also pursued a vigorous policy; seven major crusades were held in towns and cities in 1971, and eight were planned through 1972. Regular broadcasts were made over Radio WIVV (Puerto Rico), Radio ELWA (Liberia), IBRA Radio (Portugal), and the Far East Broadcasting Corporation (Manila). The official organ, *Redemption Tidings,* had a weekly circulation of 8,800.

(AARON LINFORD; VINSON SYNAN)

Presbyterian, Reformed, and Congregational. The 1972 meeting of the Executive Committee of the World Alliance of Reformed Churches (Presbyterian and Congregational), held in Jakarta, Indon., July 20–25, provided the first opportunity to implement decisions taken at the 1971 meeting. In order to intensify relationships within the Alliance family, members had agreed, among other things, "that the agenda and timetable of future Executive Committee meetings be arranged in such a way as to make possible consultations with representatives and experts from member churches in the region."

Immediately following the Jakarta meeting, a consultation was held at the ecumenical centre in Sukabumi, attended by WARC executives, delegates from all 20 Indonesian member churches of the Alliance, and representatives of the Council of Churches in Indonesia. Alliance staff and committee members visited nearly all the member churches in Indonesia and also participated in a coordinated visitation program to WARC churches in 15 countries en route to and from Indonesia.

Through a technical adjustment of membership criteria, the number of Indonesian churches in the Alliance increased from 13 to 20. One European church was admitted into membership: the Conference of Reformed Ministers and Congregations in the German Democratic Republic, with an estimated membership of 10,000. On Oct. 5, 1972, the Congregational Church in England and Wales and the Presbyterian Church of England merged to form the United Reformed Church. The merger was the first union across confessional boundaries in England since the Reformation.

On the interconfessional level, talks between the Lutheran World Federation and WARC continued through the Joint Committee. (See *Lutherans,* above.) Dialogues continued with the Roman Catholic Church on the general theme of "the Presence of Christ in Church and World," and on the specific issue of the theology of marriage, the latter conducted jointly by WARC and the LWF. The possibilities of a theological dialogue with the Baptist World Alliance were to be investigated.

In what was interpreted as a severe setback to the ecumenical movement, the 184th General Assembly of the United Presbyterian Church in the U.S.A. voted (411–310) to pull out of COCU. The move carried a special irony, since COCU had first been proposed by Eugene Carson Blake, then stated clerk of the denomination and later general secretary of the World Council of Churches, together with the late Episcopal Bishop James Pike. The assembly approved continued efforts toward union with the Presbyterian Church in the U.S. In other moves it supported busing as a means to achieve integration, reaffirmed a liberal stand on abortion, and adopted a revision of the rules permitting laymen to assist at Communion. After a heated debate, the assembly voted to centralize its national offices in a single location in New York City.

The Presbyterian Church in the U.S. (Southern Presbyterians) voted to remain in COCU, but its principal attention was centred on the possibility of schism within its ranks. For some years the more conservative members had claimed that the church leadership was deviating from "historic Presbyterian doctrine" and had objected to its involvement with social issues and to the moves toward union with the United Presbyterian Church in the U.S.A. In the fall of 1972 several conservative congregations joined with some five independent Presbyterian churches to form a group known as the Vanguard Presbytery, a Provisional Presbytery for Southern Presbyterians and Reformed Churches Uniting.

The Orthodox Presbyterian Church and the Reformed Presbyterian Church, Evangelical Synod, moved closer toward the development of a plan of union. Approval was given to initial plans to realign mission agencies, to unite presbyteries, and to centralize control of educational institutions and publications. Women continued to play an increasingly important role in the church. Thirty of the 44 classes (which met the two-thirds requirements for an amendment to the constitution) in the Reformed Church in America voted to approve the ordination of women as elders and deacons. During the year the United Presbyterian Church in the U.S.A. announced that 72 women were preparing for the ministry and 103 women were already ordained.

Membership in the United Presbyterian Church in the U.S.A. declined by 66,422 to approximately 3.1 million, although total contributions increased more than $11 million to $368,464,703 and per-member giving set a new high of $121.95. Benevolences at the General Assembly level for the Presbyterian Church in the U.S. (about one million members) totaled $7,510,502, 88.36% of the amount requested but less than the year before. The 186,500 members of the Presbyterian Church in Canada gave a record $2,634,000 to national and overseas benevolences.

(FREDERIK H. KAAN; WILLIAM B. MILLER)

Religious Society of Friends. British Friends cooperated energetically with other bodies in the emergency reception of Asians expelled from Uganda by Pres. Idi Amin. Full support was given to work for reconciliation in Northern Ireland, including social service projects of Ulster Friends in Belfast. Some £75,000 was raised during 1972 toward the establishment of a chair of peace studies at the University of Bradford, Yorkshire; the university agreed to contribute a like sum.

With the support of Friends in other countries, British Friends and the American Friends Service Committee undertook an emergency feeding program in Bangladesh. The AFSC issued another White Paper on the war in Vietnam, "Indochina 1972: Perpetual War," and participated in a study of the black student in Southern U.S. schools, published under the title *It's Not Over in the South.* Altogether, the AFSC spent $8,380,000 for programs in the U.S. and 16 other countries. In May, 11 representatives of the AFSC visited China.

More than 1,400 persons gathered for the Friends General Conference sessions at Ithaca, N.Y., June 24–July 1, to explore the theme "Where Should Friends Be Pioneering Now?" The Friends United Meeting met at Green Lake, Wis., July 8–15, for business sessions combined with a conference-type experience.

The One Per Cent Fund set up by London Yearly Meeting—financed by members who undertook to contribute 1% of their income annually—made further grants to projects in less developed countries. More than £100,000 had been distributed in this way by 1972. (EDWIN BRONNER; CLIFFORD HAIGH)

Salvation Army. The Salvation Army's spirit of service was typified by the death in 1972 of Maj. G. William Medley, commanding officer in Rapid City, S.D., who perished while helping to evacuate people trapped during the flood that devastated the city in June. At the height of the disaster, the Army was feeding 5,000 people a day. An agreement for full cooperation during a major disaster, signed by the Salvation Army and the U.S. Office of Emergency Preparedness, helped to speed relief efforts in the Eastern states in June when major flooding followed in the wake of Hurricane Agnes.

During the year Gen. Erik Wickberg toured Salvation Army centres in South America, Japan, New Zealand, and Australia, visited West Berlin, and Neuchatel, Switz., and inaugurated the new national headquarters in Amsterdam. In the course of Commissioner Arnold Brown's tour of European countries, a social-medical team of six Salvationists led by Major Eva den Hartog was dedicated for service in Bangladesh.

The British Congress of Salvationists initiated its "Save Britain" campaign in July. A new wing was opened at Booth House, London, for the purpose of enabling bail to be given to young men remanded from Bow Street and Marlborough Street magistrates courts.

"Every Child Matters" was the theme of the year in the U.S. A new national commander, Commissioner Paul J. Carlson, was named to succeed Commissioner Edward Carey, who retired. One of the featured speakers at the 1972 conference of the American Correctional Association was Commissioner Charles Pean, formerly Salvation Army territorial commander in France, who was best known for his work, done as a young man, to acquaint the world with the horrors of Devil's Island. (C. EMIL NELSON; HARRY READ)

Seventh-day Adventists. Mission '72, the largest coordinated program of evangelism ever attempted by the church, began on March 4 and continued throughout the year. Attendance on the first night of the 2,000 three-week meetings held in North America was about 250,000. Mission '72 meetings also were held in Australia, Africa, and Latin America. In Jamaica 7,000 persons were baptized on a single day in October.

During the year nearly 190,000 members were added to the church worldwide, bringing total membership to about 2.2 million. At the autumn meeting of church administrative leaders, held in Mexico City, October 14–21, a record $59 million was appropriated for educational, evangelistic, medical-welfare, and building projects around the world.

Steps were taken to consolidate the church's television and radio production facilities. The "Faith for Today" and "It Is Written" television programs moved from New York City and Washington, D.C., respectively, to a new multimillion-dollar radio, TV, and film centre at Thousand Oaks, Calif. The "Voice of Prophecy," currently in Glendale, Calif., would move into the complex when it was completed.

A major reorganization was effected in the overseas operation of the church when the Southern and Central European divisions were merged into the Euro-Africa Division, with headquarters in Bern, Switz. The first international congress of the International Commission for the Prevention of Alcoholism was held in Afghanistan, August 27–31. The meeting attracted delegates from 30 countries. A ten-story administrative building to house the church's headquarters in Washington, D.C., was completed in June.

(KENNETH H. WOOD)

Unitarians and Universalists. For the Unitarian Universalist Association, the two most dramatic in-

continued on page 593

THE PENTECOSTAL PHENOMENON

By Martin E. Marty

Pentecostalism is a form of expressing the Christian faith; it accents "baptism in the Holy Spirit" and the receipt of spiritual power. Pentecostalists have in some cases formed new denominations, church bodies that are among the fastest-growing in the world. More recently, many have remained inside the major denominations where they make up a "charismatic" movement, named after the "charisms" or gifts of the Holy Spirit. These gifts are described in the New Testament as being received by early followers of Jesus Christ. They included the ability to heal, to "discern the spirits," to prophesy, and to "speak in tongues." Speaking in tongues—uttering ecstatic and unintelligible speech—has done the most to draw attention to Pentecostalism, though not all adherents of the movement make it the centre of their activity.

Pentecostalism as it is known today has three histories: one begins in 1960, the second in 1900, and the third at the start of the Christian era, around A.D. 30. They have much in common, but their contexts differ somewhat. The 1960s movement drew attention to Pentecostalism because of its spread into churches that historically gave little attention to this version of "baptism in the Holy Spirit." These include the Episcopal, the Lutheran, and the Roman Catholic.

An Unexpected Outpouring. The brief prehistory of "neo-Pentecostalism" in the mainline American churches began in the later 1950s. A number of Episcopal and other conventional Protestant bodies were being stirred by news that some of their clerical leaders had come under the influence of prayer groups in the older Pentecostal denominations. When, in 1960, Father Dennis Bennett announced to his congregation, St. Mark's Episcopal at Van Nuys, Calif., that he had experienced a new outpouring of God's spirit, the recent movement can be said to have begun.

Father Bennett's announcement was dramatic. His colleagues at St. Mark's dissociated themselves from his activities and his ministry. The major media picked up the story. The Episcopal Church authorized inquiries, particularly as the movement began to spread along the West Coast. Before long, "charismatic renewal" became an issue across the land.

If Father Bennett was best known for advocating speaking in tongues, another element of the renewal had already become familiar to his fellow Episcopalians through the activities of the Order of St. Luke, founded in 1947. This order, which also attracted non-Episcopalians, believed that the New Testament practices of "healing in the Spirit" and the biblical promises concerning such healing should remain in effect. In the order, and in a minor way elsewhere, these modern Christians engaged in their own version of what the public called faith healing. They often held services involving prayer and "the laying on of hands" or the application of healing oils.

While Pentecostalism aims to give expression to the Holy Spirit's uniting power, it has, almost everywhere, engendered mistrust and division in the churches. Sometimes the Pentecostalists are simply misunderstood by their more traditional fellow believers, who have not focused their own Christian experience around baptism in the Holy Spirit. At other times adherents of the movement, impatient with those who seem to them to be half-believers, invite opposition by speaking out critically. In any case, reaction by outsiders soon inspired the tongue-speakers, the healers, and those who experienced other forms of the charisms or gifts to seek out each other. One form of association was the Blessed Trinity Society, which from 1961 to 1966 published a magazine, *Trinity*. A more popular form of gathering has been the Full Gospel Business Men's Fellowship International (FGBMFI), an organization that since 1953 has attracted thousands of small businessmen who advocate Pentecostal gifts and practices.

A Growing Phenomenon. Before long a number of denominations were reporting outbreaks of tongue-speaking or other phenomena connected with Pentecostalism. Both on the West Coast and around Minneapolis, Minn., the Lutherans were stirred or disturbed over reports of such events in their midst. The American Lutheran Church authorized a study in 1962, and the Lutheran Church-Missouri Synod found it had to deal with the subject after one of its Minnesota congregations divided over the issue of its pastor's involvement.

Both synods took circumspect and rather critical views of Pentecostalism. They recognized the presence of special gifts of the Spirit in the New Testament and did not deny the possibility of their continuance. But they were aware that devotion to these gifts in the modern world could lead to divisiveness within congregations, and they found in Lutheran theology some reasons for caution. The two major Presbyterian church bodies in the United States reacted similarly, even though Pentecostalism did not spread widely there or in the American Baptist Convention, the other church touched by the movement.

The Roman Catholic Church, through its long history, had known outbreaks of activities similar to modern Pentecostalism, but Pentecostalism had been a Protestant movement and until the Second Vatican Council (1962–65) it would have been almost inconceivable for Catholics to identify with an expression of Christianity that derived from Protestant influences. The new ecumenical spirit, however, permitted Catholics to acknowledge such debts, to associate with non-Catholics, and to develop a version of charismatic renewal appropriate to Catholicism.

While earlier Pentecostalism had long been associated with Christians of lower economic classes, people who—it was thought—were often barely literate, it is interesting to note that Catholic renewal was born largely on college campuses. There had been numerous earlier attempts to start prayer cells, to engage in *cursillos* (brief, intense, spiritual retreats), and to encourage a more lively response to the Spirit. In the mid-1960s the movement surfaced at Duquesne University in Pittsburgh, Pa., and then—most notably—at the University of Notre Dame in Indiana. As it spread to the University of Michigan and elsewhere, the need for organization was recognized. A National Conference on Charismatic Renewal in the Catholic Church was soon formed, and early in the 1970s annual conferences held at Notre Dame could attract well over 10,000 people, Catholic and non-Catholic alike.

The various denominations gave differing flavours to their expressions. While the older Pentecostalism had ordinarily downgraded infant baptism and had given little devotion to the sacrament of the Lord's Supper or the Eucharist, the "high church" Protestants and the Roman Catholics did nothing radical to reject infant baptism. But they did believe that when Christians gathered in prayer and experienced the Pentecostal event, this was a "second baptism" in the Spirit. They also made much of the rite of confirmation.

The older Pentecostalism, which concerns us less here, was born with the 20th century when followers of Charles Parham, an evangelist in the Holiness movement at Topeka, Kan., found one of their number, Agnes Ozman, speaking in tongues at a gathering on New Year's Eve, 1900. The Holiness movement,

Martin E. Marty is professor of church history at the University of Chicago, associate editor of The Christian Century, *and author of* Protestantism.

which derived from Wesleyan Methodism, stressed Christian perfection and renewal. The Pentecostal version soon spread from Topeka throughout Kansas and the Southwest and made its way to California. It began as an integrated movement, but in the course of time, its black and white followers tended to form separate denominations.

Throughout the 1950s Henry Pitney van Dusen, then president of Union Theological Seminary in New York, tried to bring this "Third Force Christendom," which was neither conventionally Protestant nor Catholic, to the attention of the mainline churches. It was growing in the Caribbean, in Central and South America, in North America's urban ghettos and remote backlands. Some of its spokesmen, most notably one David du Plessis, were even talking to leaders of the World Council of Churches.

Seekers After the Spirit. Both of the modern movements claim that they keep alive practices depicted in the Book of Acts, discussed in the writings of St. Paul, and recurrent in later Christian history. Intense partisans resist any efforts by either sympathetic or hostile observers to locate them sociologically or to account for them psychologically. They simply experience supernatural gifts that natural man cannot explain, and these gifts can come anywhere at any time. They point out that Pentecostalism has been effective among the poor in the third world nations and that it has been recognized on Ivy League and Catholic campuses. Modern-day peasants have been drawn to it, while the FGBMFI testifies to the participation of businessmen.

Social analysts, however, cannot rest content with these claims, and they have tried to account for the outbreak in various sets of terms. Some attribute Pentecostalism to the attempt of moderns to break out of the boredom and emptiness of life, thus accounting for the movement's latter-day popularity among the rootless in prosperous suburbs. Some point out that witness to the Spirit has occurred again and again in times of societal upheaval; the 1960s and 1970s certainly have been unsettling, providing fertile soil for ecstatic and enthusiastic movements. Still others see Pentecostalism as one among many attempts to achieve spiritual experiences in an age often described as secular. A similar release has been sought in African religion, in Asian religion, Zen Buddhism or Yoga, and in the "Jesus Movement"—which bears some resemblances to Pentecostalism.

Nothing fascinates the non-Pentecostal or inspires the Pentecostal more than does the practice of "speaking in tongues." This phenomenon, not easily explained, permits Christians—usually when gathered in conducive circumstances—to utter unintelligible sounds just as the early Christians were pictured as doing in the time of St. Paul. Paul was familiar with the practice and was inclined toward it himself. He was cautious about the problems it could create for communication and fellowship, however; he located it among the lesser gifts of the Spirit and asked for devotion to clear speech. But Pentecostals today enjoy this overlooked gift and stress that it is a special evidence of God's visitation.

This "ecstatic speech that is usually unintelligible to the hearer" has been viewed in various ways by anthropologists and psychologists. The former have tape-recorded and analyzed tongue-speaking (glossolalia) in both the Christian and non-Christian worlds. Almost all find that there is nothing distinctive in the Christian version. Psychologists have observed that, in some cases, tongue-speaking bears parallels to hallucinations, trances, or conjured experiences. Some relate it to the idea of release from repression, while others see it as a regression to the preintellectualized speech of the child, expressive of a kind of innocence in the midst of modern complexity. It is not likely that debate on the subject will be resolved soon or easily.

In the meantime many people are drawn to Pentecostalism as a means of renewing and spreading the Christian faith. Let others, they will say, locate them among the many movements that seek immediacy and ecstasy; their expression differs from all others in that it is a unique supernatural visitation from God and a fresh bestowal of his Spirit.

continued from page 591
cidents of 1972 concerned the U.S. government's reaction to publication of the Pentagon papers by the denomination's Beacon Press and the introduction of an explicit new sex education course in the Sunday schools of many of the 958 U.S. and Canadian Unitarian Universalist churches and fellowships.

Justice Department attempts to subpoena the UUA's bank account records were being challenged as a violation of religious freedom, association, and expression. The government action appeared to be in retaliation for printing 7,000 pages of classified background information on U.S. involvement in Vietnam, which had already been read into a congressional subcommittee's records by Sen. Mike Gravel, an Alaska Unitarian. Prior to this, a somewhat shorter version of the papers had been issued by the *New York Times*.

After a year of testing, an audiovisual education kit titled *About Your Sexuality* was released for widespread use. It was reviewed by a New York law firm, and 3,000 persons were trained in the use of the materials. Citizen petitions to district attorneys in Waukesha County, Wis., and Nassau County, N.Y., claimed that the kit violated obscenity laws. The denomination believed that this represented a threat to voluntary courses offered by religious movements within their own institutions.

The annual General Assembly of the UUA met in Dallas, Tex., from May 30 to June 4, 1972, and attracted 678 delegates, the smallest number in years. Lack of enthusiasm for the meetings was attributed to weariness over annual confrontations, fewer resources in local churches for sending representatives, and the absence of any key, burning issue. After years of trying, the assembly came within three votes of the two-thirds majority required to change the bylaws and introduce biennial assemblies. The bylaws were to be revised to remove such discriminatory language as "brotherhood of man" and "mankind."

The delegates voted to urge the association and all its members and churches to refuse payment of the 10% telephone excise tax levied by the U.S. Congress in 1966 specifically to finance the war in Vietnam. The Board of Trustees was asked to cooperate with other bodies to foster social responsibility in the investment of endowment funds. The annual Holmes Weatherly Award for outstanding efforts in social action was presented to the United Farm Workers, AFL-CIO. The General Assembly backed up this award with a resolution to boycott iceberg lettuce until a meaningful contract was established between the UFW and the growers.

The abrasive confrontations over black empowerment that had split the movement for several years were resolved. A $250,000 grant from the Veatch Committee and the North Shore Unitarian Society of Plandome, N.Y., was divided between the Black Affairs Council and Black and White Action, with smaller amounts for other, similar programs.

The British General Assembly met in London, April 7–10, 1972; among the subjects discussed were alcoholism and "The Limits of Sexual Freedom." A resolution was carried expressing sympathy to a sister organization, the Non-Subscribing Presbyterian Church of Ireland, during the difficulties in Ulster. Later in the year Protestant and Roman Catholic children were entertained at a week's holiday at the Unitarian Holiday Home in Derbyshire. A historically significant conference was held with high-ranking representatives of the Roman Catholic Church on "The Authority of the Religious Conscience." It was to be followed by a further meeting on the theme "Natural Theology and the Liberal Religious Doctrine of Man."

(JOHN NICHOLLS BOOTH; BRIAN L. GOLLAND)

United Church of Canada. The movement toward union with the Anglican Church of Canada came to a standstill in 1972, and some United Church ministers expressed the belief that the Anglicans were backpedaling. The second largest diocese in the Anglican Church of Canada rejected intercommunion with the United Church and recognition of its ministerial order. In the United Church there was disappointment, but in August its General Council overwhelmingly rejected a motion that it should suspend negotiations and recommended that the revision of the draft *Plan of Union* be continued.

The sharpest criticism of the *Plan of Union* was that it proposed nothing more than the "merger of two existing bodies," whereas the original goal had been "a new manifestation of the Church." It was suggested that, instead of the direct organizational approach to union, the churches might better have encouraged united action "in relation to realizable goals addressed to human needs."

In spite of the ho-hum attitude of many churchmen to union, a sense of unity was developing where opportunities arose for cooperation. Some church buildings housed Anglican and United Church congregations, and sometimes Roman Catholic and Presbyterian congregations were involved. In many cases the work of Christian education was shared, though the congregations worshiped separately at agreed times. In one area a Lutheran pastor was serving the Anglicans, Lutherans, Mennonites, Presbyterians, and United Church people with the blessing of the churches.

The 1972 General Council of the United Church had as its moderator the Rt. Rev. Norman Bruce McLeod; at 43 he was the youngest moderator in the church's history and the first to have been born after the church's formation in 1925 by a union of Congregationalists, Methodists, and Presbyterians. Four-fifths of the council's 450 members were attending for the first time and one-third were women. Dissatisfaction with the 1971 council's liberal view of abortion required a new debate but, with the exception of some qualifying statements, the result was the same. Essentially, the council had held that abortion was a private matter between a woman and her doctor but that it should only be used as a last resort. The council opposed the death penalty for murder but asked the government to find alternatives to capital punishment as a deterrent to murder. In the most emotional issue of all, it decided that the church should be prepared to respond creatively either to the continuance of Canada's present makeup or to the secession of Quebec. (ARTHUR G. REYNOLDS)

United Church of Christ. The membership of the United Church of Christ in 1972 stood at 6,688 congregations and 1,928,674 members. When the denomination came into being in 1957, it brought together four U.S. churches, the Congregational and Christian churches, which had united in 1931, and the Evangelical Synod of North America and the Reformed Church in the United States, which had merged in 1934.

During 1972 the denomination moved toward implementation of the four priorities adopted by the General Synod of 1971: meeting the faith crisis; racial justice; peace; and strengthening the local church. To help meet the faith crisis, a program entitled "Faith Exploration" was developed for use at the local and regional levels; it was hoped that at least 30,000 members would be involved in the program during 1972–73.

The denomination embarked on a $17 million campaign on behalf of the six black colleges related to the church, as well as a number of overseas projects in areas of racial conflict. In reviewing its investments, it worked particularly with the Mobil Oil Corp., which agreed to make a full disclosure of its operations in South Africa. The work of the church relating to American Indians was turned over to the newly formed Council on American Indian Ministry, with the aim of providing greater self-determination within the Indian churches.

An interstaff peace team planned and carried out an interchange of pastors between the United Church of Christ and the Evangelical Church in East Germany, participated in the National Council of Churches' Inquiry on War Crimes, and helped to fund the National Council's Emergency Ministry Concerning the (Vietnam) War. Two task forces were engaged in developing proposals on strengthening the local church. The Task Force on Leadership Development proposed that programs for professional and lay leadership in the church be brought together administratively and that the new national office charged with this responsibility be regionalized. The Task Force on the Status of Women in Church and Society requested moves to ensure that at least 50% of the delegates to national meetings and of the members of national boards and councils be women.

In March 1972 the Council for Christian Social Action, the national agency with responsibility in this area, dismissed its entire staff, partly for financial reasons and partly in order to redirect its program. The Executive Council of the church placed the Council for Christian Social Action on an interim operating basis until a reassessment could be made of the appropriate style for Christian social action in the church today. A decision would be made at the 1973 General Synod.

During 1972 the Executive Council raised some questions about the future of COCU and suggested that a way should be found for the Consultation to determine its course in the light of ecumenical developments at the local level rather than on the basis of a nationally drafted plan of union. (See *Presbyterian, Reformed, and Congregational,* above.)

(ROBERT V. MOSS)

ROMAN CATHOLIC CHURCH

Toward the end of 1971, the third international Synod of the Roman Catholic Church, meeting in Rome, had made the church aware of the increasing differences between local churches. In many places, especially in less developed countries, the important question was whether the church was a spur or a hindrance to national identity. Elsewhere, the issues causing tension were mainly substantial questions concerning the church's message and the way to communicate it. The year that followed was one of fundamental questioning.

In Africa, Zaire was the setting for an inconclusive skirmish, in January, between Pres. Mobutu Sese Seko and Joseph-Albert Cardinal Malula, archbishop of Kinshasa. The ostensible issue was "africanization" and the particular flashpoint, the president's abolition of "Christian names." An article in *Afrique Chré-*

tienne, supported by the cardinal, opposed the return to "an original African philosophy which had value only for that past." The weekly publication was suppressed for six months, the cardinal ordered to abandon his residence, and the John XXIII seminary was closed down. The cardinal slipped out of Zaire secretly, but later returned with assurances of safe-conduct.

By 1972 over 30 million Catholics in Asia obtained an official forum to deal with local problems. In February it was announced that the Federation of Asian Bishops' Conferences (FABC) was almost ready to start functioning. The Asian bishops went ahead with the project, jumping many of the red-tape barriers set by Rome because, they said, "any sign of indecision or further delay among the leaders of the Church . . . would undermine the credibility of the Church and inflict wounds on many."

The church in India was especially concerned with liturgy and minority rights. The Vatican approved a plan for adapting the liturgy to India, with the use of Hindu symbols in the Mass. The Indian Bishops' Conference was concerned that relations between Christians and other Indians were being damaged because Christianity was still presented in "Western garb." India's first convention for the rights of minority groups was organized by the Catholic bishops. Art. 30 of the constitution, ensuring the right of religious minorities to educational establishments supported by government grants, had been attacked as conflicting with the socialist society emerging in India.

Lithuanian Catholics sent a protest with 17,000 signatures to Soviet Communist Party leader Leonid I. Brezhnev, complaining that "in violation of Lithuania's criminal code, believers suffer discrimination because of their faith." A copy was sent to UN Secretary-General Kurt Waldheim, and the text was made public on March 27. This protest followed a number of other appeals by Catholics, who were often linked in the U.S.S.R. with nationalist and separatist movements. Later in the year, following reports of riots in Kaunas, the Catholic bishops warned their people not to "protest too strongly."

In Chile, Christianity and Marxism were able to coexist more peacefully and even to cooperate. Concurrently with the third UN Conference on Trade and Development in April and May, the first Latin-American meeting of "Christians for Socialism" was held in Santiago. The organizer, Father Correa Arroyo, a Jesuit priest and professor of agriculture in the Catholic University of Chile, wanted, he said in his opening address, "to show the revolutionary attitude of Christians in face of the injustices of world imperialism." Clergy and laity from all the Latin-American countries attended, as well as observers from the U.S., Canada, and Europe. The final document supported the socialist experiments of Cuba and Chile, had reservations about Mexico and Brazil, and denied that Christians could have their own characteristic way of liberating the Latin-American peoples from the oppression of imperialism; it invited them to unite their forces with Marxists, who were urged to take up a new attitude to Christianity.

In the U.S. the striking growth of Pentecostalism was reflected in the sixth International Conference on Charismatic Renewal held on the campus of the University of Notre Dame at the end of June. Numbers were greater than ever before. The Catholic charismatic renewal movement was still perhaps viewed rather uneasily by the hierarchy, but the conference

UPI COMPIX

Pope Paul VI waves to a welcoming crowd along the Grand Canal in Venice on Sept. 16, 1972. His visit was the first by a reigning pope in 172 years.

was attended by Bishop Joseph McKinney, auxiliary bishop of Grand Rapids, Mich. The official voice of the church in the U.S. was heard in April, when the bishops at their Atlanta, Ga., spring meeting issued a statement criticizing Pres. Richard Nixon's Commission on Population Growth and the American Future, especially as regards its position on abortion; throughout the year the church was active in opposing the liberalization of abortion laws, though an effort was made to shift emphasis to a more positive "right to life." In May six bishops strongly criticized the U.S. mining of North Vietnamese ports and the intensification of the war.

In Europe the recognition by the Vatican on June 28 of the Polish dioceses in the "recovered territories" (former German territories annexed by Poland in 1945) put an end to a long-standing Polish complaint and helped the Polish authorities in their policy of "normalization" toward the church. The outlook was less encouraging in other Communist countries of Eastern Europe, especially in Yugoslavia and Czechoslovakia. In June the journal of the Czechoslovak Ministry of Defense launched an attack on the Vatican, which was seen as possibly heralding a new wave of persecution.

Western Europe's problems seemed slighter by comparison. Tensions, misunderstandings, and conflict within the church took different forms in Spain, Great Britain, the Netherlands, and Italy. The Spanish episcopacy decided to continue the policy of the September 1971 assembly of bishops and priests, which had claimed greater independence of the church from the state. On the eve of the bishops' meeting in March, a document from the Sacred Congregation for the Clergy was published, attacking the new approach. The Spanish bishops treated it with reserve, and went ahead with their program. The document later turned out to be somebody's mistake.

In Great Britain the resignations of the entire teaching staff of Corpus Christi catechetical college were accepted, much to their surprise, by John Cardinal Heenan. He later stated that he had no worries about the orthodoxy of teaching there, but he had to accept

TIKHOMIROFF—RAPHO GUILLUMETTE

Russian Orthodox pilgrims worship at the monastery of Troitsa in Zagorsk, near Moscow. "A church dictatorially directed by atheists is a spectacle that has not been seen for 2,000 years," mourned Aleksandr Solzhenitsyn, winner of the 1970 Nobel Prize for Literature. Soviet authorities refused to allow Solzhenitsyn to receive the $79,000 award, thus thwarting his dream of building a church in the U.S.S.R.

that "their understanding of religious education was incompatible with my own." Religious teaching also proved a sensitive area in the Netherlands. After a controversy over the appointment of conservative Bishop J. M. Gijsen in Roermond early in the year over the strong opposition of the liberal Dutch hierarchy, the Netherlands seemed to become very quiet until, in June, there was news of a new "Dutch Catechism" intended for secondary pupils. Father Jean Galot, in *Civiltà Cattolica,* condemned the doctrinal content as not representing the "authentic teaching of the Church."

In Italy in August there was shock over the Vatican decision to dismiss the whole governing body of the Benedictine monks of Cassino, apparently because they had refused to remove from office the progressive abbot of St. Paul's-Without-the-Walls, Dom Giovanni Franzoni. He commented, "In Rome the ecclesiastical system in the pure state does not exist. It is tied to the political and economic power. It is clear that we have touched the nerves of this power."

The year witnessed steady progress in ecumenism, hard to document but exemplified by the Anglican-Roman Catholic agreed statement on the Eucharist, released Dec. 31, 1971. (See *Anglican Communion,* above.) A book prepared by the Vatican Council for the Application of the Liturgy and published in February outlined a procedure whereby converts could enter the church step by step over a period of years. From the Vatican came new norms, promulgated in July, for the annulment of lawful but nonconsummated marriages, the effect of which was to speed up the procedure. On July 13 a statement was issued clarifying the circumstances in which Catholics could obtain forgiveness of their sins when private confession was impossible or seriously difficult. The statement was apparently designed to discourage the growing practice of granting absolution for grave sins in communal penitential rites. Other Roman documents strengthened the hand of the Holy See in the appointment of bishops, warned nuns that they should wear their religious habits, set discouraging limits on intercommunion, and barred women from any formal role in the ministry. Some began to speak of a backlash.

On September 22 the pope took the opportunity of a state visit by Italy's new president, Giovanni Leone, to demand the abolition of divorce. (*See* VATICAN CITY STATE.) (PETER HEBBLETHWAITE)

EASTERN CHURCHES

The Orthodox Church. On July 6, 1972, the Ecumenical Patriarchate of Constantinople, which enjoys a traditional honorary primacy in the Orthodox world, lost its incumbent, Patriarch Athenagoras I (*see* OBITUARIES). A prestigious personality, Athenagoras had been projected into the limelight on the occasion of his three successive meetings with Pope Paul VI in Jerusalem, Istanbul, and Rome. The funeral, on July 11, was attended by Christian leaders from both Eastern and Western Europe. Immediately after the patriarch's death, the Turkish government issued several public statements requiring that a successor be elected without delay and barring several leading candidates from running.

On July 16 the Holy Synod of the Patriarchate, composed mostly of titular bishops, elected Dimitrios (*see* BIOGRAPHY), metropolitan of Imbros and Tenedos, by a 12 to 3 vote. The new patriarch was immediately enthroned. Aged 58, the new patriarch was born and raised in Istanbul. His name had never been mentioned among possible successors to Athenagoras. Observers explained the circumstances of the election by the Turkish desire to lower the prestige of the Patriarchate as an international centre and as the only remaining symbol of Greek presence in Asia Minor. International commentators expressed the view that if the Orthodox Church was to establish a functioning centre of common action, it would have to be located outside Turkey. Others feared that such a move would unduly enhance the prestige of the Russian Church, although the latter had never formally tried to supplant Constantinople. Undoubtedly, this issue would dominate Orthodox ecclesiastical politics in the years to come.

Ephrem II, the Orthodox patriarch of Georgia—an ancient autocephalous church located in the U.S.S.R. —died on April 7. He was succeeded by Metropolitan David.

The problem of the survival of religion in the U.S.S.R. was agitated both in the Soviet press and abroad. Soviet antireligious commentators complained about the lasting influence of the Orthodox Church, illustrated by the fact that, during the 1960s, 25 bishops below the age of 40 were consecrated. However, Aleksandr Solzhenitsyn, the Nobel Prize-winning novelist, addressed a "Lenten Letter" to Patriarch Pimen of Moscow, accusing the hierarchy of unnecessary servility to the demands of the state.

The session of the Pan-Orthodox Commission for the preparation of a "great council" of the Orthodox Church was postponed. However, the Pan-Orthodox Commission for a Dialogue with Anglicanism met with its Anglican counterpart in Geneva on September 11–14. The results were described as "promising" in the official communiqué, and another meeting was scheduled for July 1973. Much inter-Orthodox activity took place throughout 1972 on the level of theological education. International conferences of Orthodox theologians were held in Athens (May), Thessaloniki (September), and New York City (September).

Metropolitan Vladimir Nagosky, American-born primate of the autonomous Japanese Church, resigned and retired to the U.S. He was replaced on March 19 by Theodosius Nagashima, the first native Orthodox primate. However, another American, Serafim Sigrist, was appointed bishop of Sendai. In the U.S. the 39-year-old, American-born Theodosius Lazor was elected bishop of Pittsburgh, Pa.

On April 22 the Orthodox Church in America accepted into its fold as an exarchate the Iglesia Ortodoxa Catolica of Mexico (also known as the Mexican National Church). This 20,000-member body, headed by the Mexican Bishop José Cortes y Olmos, was the first sizable group of Spanish-speaking Orthodox Christians. In France the Orthodox Patriarchate of Romania accepted into its jurisdiction the group previously known as Église Orthodoxe de France, which uses a Western liturgical rite.

Eastern Non-Chalcedonian Churches. In the fall of 1971 the most important of the ancient Non-Chalcedonian Churches, the Coptic Church of Egypt, chose a new head, Patriarch Amba Shenouda III. The new patriarch was one of the leading intellectuals of the Coptic Church, and during his earlier career had exercised marked influence among the younger generation. Upon his enthronement, he declared his readiness to develop ecumenical ties with other Christians and to improve relations with the Muslim majority. On Dec. 15, 1971, Shenouda III received a delegation of the United Evangelical Church (U.S.). He also exchanged visits with the Greek Orthodox patriarch of Alexandria, Nicholas VI, who promised to allow the Copts the use of 30 Greek Orthodox churches on the lower Nile where an Orthodox population no longer existed.

The Ethiopian Church, a daughter church of the Egyptian Copts, showed equal interest in international relations and an even more marked concern for developing relations with the Chalcedonian Orthodox Church. Patriarch Theophilus of Ethiopia paid visits to Patriarch Athenagoras (November 1971) and to the Church of Greece. (JOHN MEYENDORFF)

JUDAISM

No significant new data on the size and distribution of the world Jewish population became available in 1972. The increased flow of immigration to Israel from the U.S.S.R. (an estimated 31,000 in 1971–72, as against an estimated 1,000 in 1970) was of significance as a pointer to possible developments in the future, but did not change the existing distributional pattern. (*See* ISRAEL: *Special Report.*)

Soviet Jewry remained the focus of Jewish collective concern. The promise given by Soviet Premier Aleksei N. Kosygin during his visit to Canada at the beginning of 1972 was kept, and Jews were allowed to leave, although many applicants for visas and Jews manifesting sympathy with Israel were harassed inside the Soviet Union. Then, on August 3, the Presidium of the Supreme Soviet issued a decree requiring "reimbursement by U.S.S.R. citizens leaving for permanent residence abroad of state expenditure on education." This meant that anyone with academic training would have to make a payment for an exit visa varying from 12,250 rubles ($15,000) for a graduate of Moscow State University to 1,700 rubles ($2,150) for a holder of the "candidate of science" degree, amounts that few could ever hope to raise.

Jews in the U.S.S.R., like Jews in the rest of the world, had a disproportionately high percentage of academically educated persons, and the new regulation affected a large number of families wishing to emigrate. There were worldwide protests by representatives of Jewish and non-Jewish organizations, institutions, and personalities against the tax, but it was far from certain whether these representations would have any influence on the Soviet authorities, and it was not yet known to what extent the tax would alter the flow of Jewish emigration.

Moscow's yeshiva (rabbinical college), the only place in the U.S.S.R. where Jewish religious functionaries could be trained, was reopened. It had six students aged from 23 to 52, none of whom was studying to be a rabbi; they attended courses in *shehita* (slaughtering) and *hazanut* (cantorial music). Shulem Royzen, the chairman of the Moscow Jewish congregation, stated that it was hoped to bring the number of students to 25, but emphasized the acute shortage of teachers.

There was no appreciable change in the situation of Jewish communities in other Eastern European countries. In Czechoslovakia, Vilem Benda was dismissed from his post as director of the Jewish Museum in Prague for resisting pressure to rearrange the museum's contents in order to impart political propaganda. The museum housed one of the richest collections of Jewish art and historical relics in the world.

The position of the residual Jewish communities in the Arab world remained precarious. Reports were received from Syria that Jews were "considered to be hostages," that they "lived in constant fear of governmental measures against them," and that Jews were imprisoned and allegedly tortured. It was also reported that Albert Elia, the leader of the Lebanese Jewish community, had been kidnapped and held in Syria. The plight of the Syrian Jews evoked protest demonstrations in many parts of the world. The second attempt to assassinate King Hassan II of Morocco, and the death of Morocco's strong man, Muhammad Oufkir, greatly disturbed the Moroccan Jewish community, since King Hassan and Oufkir had been their main defenders against the hostility of pan-Arab nationalists. However, King Hassan promised that Jews would continue to enjoy equal rights with the rest of the Moroccan population. The massacre of passengers at Lod Airport by Japanese gunmen in May and the Olympics tragedy in Munich, W.Ger., in September, in which 11 Israeli sportsmen were killed, made a deep impact on the diaspora Jewish communities as well as in Israel. (*See* ISRAEL; SPORTING RECORD: *Special Report.*)

The perennially smoldering issue "Who is a Jew?" brought religious circles of all trends to a deeper involvement in the problem and to a clearer realization that it was impossible to draw a clear distinction between Jews inside and outside Israel. The issue, involving the problems of conversions and mixed marriages, tended to polarize attitudes of Orthodox, Reform, and Liberal Jews, especially in Great Britain. Immanuel Jacobovits, the chief rabbi of the United Hebrew Congregations of the British Commonwealth, admitted that "we have no special interest in swelling our numbers by conversions" and that London's Beth-Din standards were stricter than in many other countries.

Diverse local conditions could have an important bearing on the decision to admit proselytes; in Israel, where there was hardly any opportunity of becoming integrated into non-Jewish society, it was obviously far easier to accept converts (and harder to reject them) than in the diaspora. Nevertheless, the problem of conversion continued to be a political issue. The Orthodox parties were under pressure from their own extremists to insist that only "conversion accord-

COURTESY, SOKA GAKKAI

Sho-Hondo, a shrine built on the lower slopes of Mt. Fuji by devotees of the Japanese Soka Gakkai sect of Buddhism, was opened in October 1972. Membership in the sect grew phenomenally from 3,000 in 1945 to eight million in 1972.

ing to Halachah" (*i.e.,* Orthodox law and practice) be recognized by the Israeli government as a determination of Jewish status, while the leftist parties in the Knesset were pressing for restriction of the role of the rabbinate in public life and the recognition of civil marriage.

In the U.S. the American Jewish Committee established a task force to study the problem of Jewish identity. The Conference of Jewish Federations and Welfare Funds had launched a similar project in 1971. The emergence of this issue in American Jewish life was due to two antithetical factors. On the one hand, the importance of the "ethnic," or "heritage" factor in public life had greatly intensified in the past decade. Children and grandchildren of immigrants had become eager to cultivate their historic heritage, in order to enrich their lives by the feelings of rootedness in an ancient culture and to counteract the aimless turbulence of drifting youth in recent years.

On the other hand, the youth rebellion of the late 1960s had placed all the customs and values of the past into question. Apart from the extremist groups, great numbers of young people had come to feel that the adult establishment had somehow gone astray. While deeply interested in religious experience as a source of ethical values, they were skeptical of the value of established institutions in religion, education, and philanthropy. The younger generation was uncertain about its own Jewish identity and was often described (and described itself) as "post-Jewish." A new religious phenomenon made some impact on marginal Jewish youth. Growing up in the ecumenical atmosphere in which the Jewishness of Jesus was often stressed, a number of young Jews joined a Jewish-Christian movement that turned to some Jewish customs but regarded Jesus as a saviour. Most older Jews regarded this as a passing fad, but it gained an unexpectedly large number of adherents, however temporary and tenuous.

The *Encyclopedia Judaica* was published during the year. Begun in pre-Hitler Germany, continued in the U.S., and completed in Israel, it reflected the worldwide distribution of Jewish scholars. Sally Priesand, who graduated from the Hebrew Union College-Jewish Institute of Religion in Cincinnati, O., was ordained as the first female rabbi in the U.S.

(JACOB B. AGUS; PAUL GLIKSON)

BUDDHISM

In the early 1950s many Buddhists in Asia were jubilant over the renewed vitality of their faith. The "resurgence of Buddhism," as it was called then, had two separate but related thrusts. The first concerned the future of Buddhism in the so-called Buddhist nations, from Ceylon to Vietnam, that had attained independence after the end of World War II. The second involved an exaggerated view on the part of Asian Buddhists concerning the spiritual bankruptcy of the West and the potential of Buddhism to fill the spiritual vacuum. In both respects, this optimism had been dampened by recent events. A Buddhist layman in Sri Lanka, N. Gunaratne, openly stated that "Buddhism as a religion has proved to be a failure in Western countries," while the Buddhist communities in Asia were facing a number of external and internal crises.

In Ladakh, India, the construction of the Srinagar-Leh highway had effectively broken down the isolation of the Tibetan refugee community, among whom were 2,000 monks (lamas) and 7,000 nuns (chomos). Internally, the Tibetan community was split by the revolt of the 25,000-strong Khanpas against the Dalai Lama's brother, Gyalpo Thondup, on the ground that he was secretly collaborating with Peking. Elsewhere in India, Buddhism continued to attract the "scheduled caste" people (untouchables), as was evidenced by several cases of mass conversion that took place in 1971 in the Lucknow area.

Of the ten million refugees who fled their homes in East Pakistan in 1971, 500,000 were Buddhists. Many fled to India, but 20,000 sought refuge in the Chin Hills Special Division in Burma and 15,000 in the Mizo Hills in Assam. D. P. Barooah, general secretary of the Pakistan Centre of the World Fellowship of Buddhists, and his family were killed by Pakistani soldiers; the Venerable Abhayatissa Maha Thera, the senior Buddhist leader in Pakistan, was mercilessly beaten, and many temples were ransacked. Two gold Buddha statues in monasteries in Chittagong were cut into pieces and taken to West Pakistan.

The Theravada Buddhist nations were also confronted by many difficulties. Ceylon, officially known as the Republic of Sri Lanka after May 1972, had not yet recovered from the aftermath of the 1971 revolt by the Peoples Liberation Front. According to a leading prelate, "Ninety-five percent of those who engaged in violent activities were Buddhists," and the position of the bhikkhus (monks) and the temple had deteriorated after the revolt was suppressed. The Ceylonese government took advantage of the emergency regulations to abandon the Buddhist Poya holidays and introduce the Saturday-Sunday weekend.

In Burma Ne Win's Revolutionary Council was urging the updating of the *dhammathats* (traditional law). In Thailand, where government troops were fighting guerrillas in the northern border area, the first Buddhist mission to the Karen minority was established in Chieng Mai Province in 1971. A new Buddhist university was to be built in Aitthaya Province, about 70 mi. from Bangkok. In December 1971 the first International Buddhist Youth Conference was held in Bangkok as a prelude to the tenth General Conference of the World Fellowship of Buddhists.

In Japan the new religions of Buddhist origin, especially the Nichiren Shoshu (Soka Gakkai) and the Rissho Koseikai, seemed to be more active than traditional Buddhist denominations. Plans were being made to develop Lumbini, the legendary birthplace of the Buddha in Nepal; the architect Kenzo Tange, who had designed Expo 70 in Osaka, Jap., was assigned to the Lumbini project.

In the West a Centre of Zen Buddhist Studies was established in Venice, Italy. Publication of an Italian version of the *Dhammapada,* an important part of the Theravada Buddhist canon, was begun by the Associazione Buddhista Italiana. A new film entitled *Buddham Saranam Gocchami* ("I take my refuge in the Buddha") was completed in England; it featured Ceylonese paintings and sculptures up to the 12th century. (JOSEPH M. KITAGAWA)

ISLAM

As had been the case so often in recent years, political events affecting Muslims seemed to overshadow more specifically religious developments. Much of the Muslim world's interest centred around the aftermath of the 1971 Indo-Pakistani war and the formation of independent Bangladesh. (*See* BANGLADESH; PAKISTAN; *Religions of Asia,* below.) In December 1971 the Muslim World League, meeting in Mecca, called for a jihad (holy war) against India, but the call had little effect.

Attention of Muslims in the Middle East continued to focus on the Arab-Israeli situation and the political maneuvers among the various Arab governments. (*See* MIDDLE EAST.) A related incident was the Saudi Arabian government's continuation of a ban against Israeli Arab Muslims attending the pilgrimage to Mecca, despite an announcement the previous November by the mayor of Hebron in Israel that an agreement had been reached allowing participation.

Early in January the first Islamic conference on family planning was held in Rabat, Morocco, under the auspices of the Planned Parenthood Federation. It was announced that modern family-planning techniques are not contrary to Muslim law, though abortion and sterilization are. In March a conference of 31 foreign ministers of Islamic countries meeting in Jiddah, Saudi Arabia, decided on the founding of an Islamic bank, though questions relating to some transactions, such as interest on loans, were not yet clarified. The conference also called for sending delegations to Pakistan and the Philippines to mediate disputes involving Muslims. In New York City prisons were ordered to respect Muslim dietary laws.

(R. W. SMITH)

RELIGIONS OF ASIA

In the autumn of 1970 delegates at the World Conference on Religion and Peace, held in Kyoto, Jap., had resolved that all religions must come to grips with both the spiritual and the temporal needs of humanity —*e.g.,* peace, human rights, economic development, and racial brotherhood. But the events of 1972 indicated that the religions of Asia were finding it extremely difficult to implement these resolutions. Moreover, religious enthusiasm often seemed to intensify conflicts between political, economic, national, and racial groups.

On the Indian subcontinent Muslim-Hindu feuds were nothing new. Since the partition of the subcontinent into India and Pakistan in 1947 resulted in the flight of more than 16 million refugees who crisscrossed the border, tensions had continued to exist between the two countries on a political level and between Hindus and Muslims on a religious level. To complicate the matter further, the December 1971 war found predominantly Hindu India coming to the aid of Muslim East Pakistan in its ultimately successful struggle for independence against West Pakistan. The new nation of Bangladesh faced a number of serious problems, not the least of which was the animosity existing between the Biharis, a Muslim minority of north Indian origin, and the Bengali majority, which also professed the Islamic faith.

India was beset by the widespread violent activities of bandit gangs, although the Sarvadaya Brotherhood, led by Jayaprakash Narayan, claimed a measure of success in pacifying some of them. Followers of the extremely nationalistic Hindu party Jan Sangh were unhappy about the Simla accord between India and Pakistan. (*See* INDIA; PAKISTAN.) In June, following nationalization of the Muslim university in Aligarh, a series of riots took place in the cities of Varanasi, Allahabad, and Aligarh, all in the northern Indian state of Uttar Pradesh.

Admittedly, this was a difficult time for the peoples in Asia, whether they were religiously oriented or not, because rapid change was affecting all dimensions of life. The swift turnabout of the U.S. attitude toward Peking confused many Communists as well as religious leaders. Some political leaders prepared to meet the changing situation. In April the Association of Southeast Asian Nations stressed the need for strengthening national economies in order to increase economic and political stability in the entire region, and in June the Asian and Pacific Council indicated its willingness to invite nations with different ideologies and political systems. (*See* SOUTHEAST ASIA.) At the ASPAC meeting Pres. Park Chung Hee of South Korea openly stated that "We cannot afford to cling fondly to fixed ideas and notions which contravene the emerging currents of a new era," and Park's South Korea subsequently began serious discussions with Communist North Korea.

Nevertheless, religious prejudices died hard. In Mindanao, the second largest island of the Philippines, the Muslim minority was being persecuted by a Catholic organization that the Muslims claimed was operating with the tacit support of the local Roman Catholic Church. Some of the Arab Muslim nations, notably Libya and Egypt, expressed a desire to help the Muslims in the Philippines, and three Soviet Muslim officials who visited Mindanao promised aid and relief. Tension also remained high in Sri Lanka, where the Hindu Tamil minority and the Sinhalese Buddhist majority had not worked out a satisfactory formula for coexistence. (See *Buddhism,* above.)

By far the most troublesome problem for Asia was the tortured situation in Indochina. In South Vietnam Pres. Nguyen Van Thieu represented the small but powerful Roman Catholic minority in a predominantly Buddhist country. Regardless of the eventual outcome, relations between the Buddhists and Roman Catholics in Vietnam, as well as between the Buddhist majority and the various non-Buddhist ethnic minorities throughout the Indochinese Peninsula, had been irreparably damaged.

The unknown quantity in Asia was Communism, which had always portrayed itself as a semireligious revolutionary movement. To be sure, the once powerful Indonesian Communist Party had been smashed; Communists were suppressed in South Korea and Taiwan and divided in India. In Japan and elsewhere,

Estimated Membership of the Principal Religions of the World*

Religions	North America†	South America	Europe‡	Asia	Africa	Oceania§	World
Total Christian	224,139,000	176,731,500	415,097,000	85,654,000	107,530,000	14,955,000	1,024,106,500
Roman Catholic	126,205,000	171,125,000	192,142,000	46,121,000	37,890,500	4,150,000	577,633,500
Eastern Orthodox	4,100,000	50,000	92,445,000	1,510,000	25,000,000‖	80,000	123,185,000
Protestant¶	93,834,000	5,556,500	130,510,000	38,023,000	44,639,500♀	10,725,000	323,288,000
Jewish	6,281,900	769,800	3,996,280	2,664,170	200,500	77,000	13,989,650
Muslimδ	200,000	85,000	25,065,000	376,269,500	126,735,000	525,000	528,879,500
Zoroastrian□	—	—	—	180,000	—	—	180,000
Shinto◇	25,000	60,000	—	60,000,000	—	—	60,085,000
Taoist△	15,000	18,000	—	51,850,000	—	—	51,883,000
Confucian△	90,000	100,000	50,000	305,175,000	—	40,000	305,455,000
Buddhist+	300,000	160,000	20,000	267,185,000	—	—	267,665,000
Hindu⊕	60,000	710,000	200,000	475,541,500	772,000	375,000	477,658,500
Totals	231,110,900	178,634,300	444,428,280	1,624,519,170	235,237,500	15,972,000	2,729,902,150
Population**	327,000,000	195,000,000	711,000,000	2,104,000,000	354,000,000	19,700,000	3,706,000,000

*Religious statistics are directly affected by war and persecution; for example, the expulsion of Asians from Uganda changes the estimate of the number of Hindus in Africa. World refugees approximate 25 million.

†Includes Central America and the West Indies.

‡Includes the U.S.S.R., in which the effect of a half century of official Marxist ideology upon religious adherence is much disputed among specialists. The same difficulty in estimating continuing religious adherence obtains in other nations with officially Marxist governments.

§Includes New Zealand and Australia as well as islands of the South Pacific.

‖Including Coptic Christians.

¶Protestant statistics outside Europe usually include "full members" only, rather than all baptized persons, and are not comparable to those of ethnic religions or churches counting all adherents.

♀Including many sects and cults of recent appearance and rapid growth.

δThe chief base of Islam is still ethnic, although some missionary work is now carried on in Europe and America (viz., Black Muslims). In countries where Islam is the state religion, minority religions are frequently persecuted and statistics are difficult to obtain.

□Zoroastrians are found in Iran, India, and Pakistan.

◇A Japanese ethnic religion, Shinto has declined markedly since the Japanese emperor gave up claim to divinity (1947). In contrast to Japanese branches of Buddhism, Shinto does not survive well among emigrants outside the homeland. Japanese religious statistics are problematical because adherents frequently are related to several different religions simultaneously.

△Figures on China are highly speculative, since the abiding effects of the Maoist-Marxist revolution upon Taoism, Confucianism, Christianity, and Islam are yet to be measured.

+Buddhism has produced several modern renewal movements that have gained adherents in Europe and America, areas not formerly ethnic-Buddhist.

⊕Hinduism's strength in India has been enhanced by nationalism; modern Hinduism has also developed renewal movements that have reached into Europe and America for converts.

**Source: United Nations, *Population and Vital Statistics Report* (July 1, 1972); world total adjusted for discrepancies in migration data; unadjusted total is 3,710,700,000.

(FRANKLIN H. LITTELL)

however, the Communists were given credit for fighting high prices, pollution, housing shortages, and other social ills, all of which should greatly concern religious leaders. The phenomenon of New Religions in Japan, which was by no means confined to that country, might be partly explained by the vacuum created by the inactivity of the traditional religions in Asia.

(JOSEPH M. KITAGAWA)

WORLD CHURCH MEMBERSHIP

With the expansion of the ecumenical movement, scholarly representatives of world religions, confronting each other, in many cases for the first time, have often discovered that they lacked a common language. Nowhere is this more evident than in the matter of statistics.

Even in the West there is a wide variety in styles of reckoning. In the U.S. and in other areas where religious liberty and voluntary adherence obtain, the relationship of the individual to his faith community is termed "membership," comparable to membership in a union or professional association. In European Christendom, where state churches long dominated the scene, those in traditional relationship are termed "communicants" or "constituents."

In the Eastern religions, even these terms are too precise. Hinduism and Buddhism have "adherents." In Confucianism, Taoism, and Shinto, philosophy and life-style are so intertwined that no terms implying a separation of the religious relationship from other functional roles can be used accurately. In modern Japan, for example, the total of religious adherents runs to nearly four times the total population; a considerable number of Japanese "belong" to one or more Buddhist sects, observe festivals at Shinto shrines, and are perhaps also counted as "members" of one of the unique universal cults that have sprung up in the Orient since World War II.

Clearly the compilation of reliable religious statistics is severely compromised by the different ways of counting. The membership of the Zen Buddhist Society in Boston can be determined exactly; the number of Buddhist adherents in Burma is often based on rough estimates of population and population growth. The membership of Lutheran congregations in Chicago can be totaled precisely; in Sweden and Denmark the state churches reckon over 98% of each population as Lutheran, though official studies show that less than 5% are in effective connection. Similar problems exist in all countries where some form of religious establishment still prevails.

The problem of totaling Christian statistics reaches its ultimate level of speculation when attention is turned to areas where Marxism is the official ideology. For example, some Eastern Orthodox tables still count 100 million Russians. Accordingly, although the accompanying table is revised regularly to reflect the latest surveys and estimates, readers are advised to use it with consciousness that mixed styles of reckoning are necessarily incorporated.

(FRANKLIN H. LITTELL)

Rhodesia

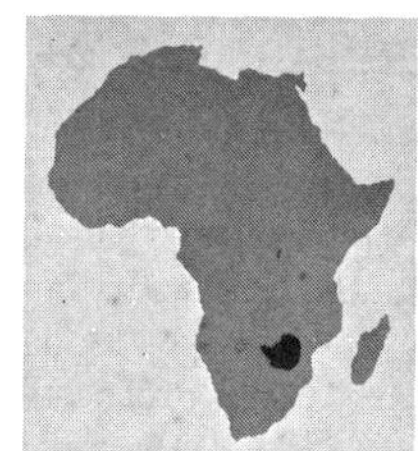

Though Rhodesia declared itself a republic on March 2, 1970, it remained a British colony in the eyes of many other nations. It is bounded by Zambia, Mozambique, South Africa, and Botswana. Area: 150,803 sq.mi. (390,580 sq.km.). Pop. (1971 est.): 5,590,000, of whom 94% are African and 5% white. Cap. and largest city: Salisbury (pop., 1969, 354,000). Language: English (official) and Bantu. Religion: predominantly traditional tribal beliefs; Christian minority. President in 1972, Clifford Dupont; prime minister, Ian D. Smith.

In January 1972 a commission led by Lord Pearce, a former lord of appeal, arrived in Salisbury from

Resources, Natural: *see* Environment

Retail Sales: *see* Merchandising

Britain to put to the test of public opinion the proposals agreed upon in November 1971 by the British foreign secretary, Sir Alec Douglas-Home, and Ian Smith (*see* BIOGRAPHY) for a settlement of Rhodesia's future. The agreement provided for the African population to achieve, slowly and gradually, political parity with the whites. Almost immediately there were outbreaks of violence by Africans in Shabani, Gwelo, Fort Victoria, Salisbury, and Umtali. For a time the commission's work appeared to be in jeopardy, but the chairman stubbornly refused to be deterred from his task. Smith's government reacted harshly to the rioting; a number of Africans were killed by police and a former prime minister of Southern Rhodesia, Garfield Todd, and his daughter Judith were arrested on Smith's order, as was Josiah Chinamano, treasurer-general of the African National Council formed in December 1971 to oppose the settlement proposals. In March the government banned the sale of ANC membership cards, and 60,000 of them were seized by security police. Both the government and the ANC made allegations of intimidation against their opponents, and the government submitted to the commission evidence of intimidation which it thought would carry considerable weight in determining the commission's attitude toward the evidence it had heard. ANC sympathizers, meanwhile, compiled a body of evidence indicating persistent harassment by the government at a time when freedom of political expression was supposed to be guaranteed.

In the interval before the publication of the commission's report there was a swing to the right in the political sympathies of some of the white population of Rhodesia who were critical of Smith for having taken part in any discussions which might have

WIDE WORLD

A Rhodesian tribesman on the banks of Lake Kariba listens as officials explain terms of a proposed settlement between Britain and the white Rhodesian government. His face reflects the predominant black dissatisfaction with terms of the accord.

compromised the position of Europeans in the country. This led to a strengthening of the recently formed United Front Against Surrender Party, which had pledged itself to ensure that the interests of the white population would remain paramount. Early in May another right-wing party, the Democratic Party, was formed with the goal of preserving the white man and his "civilization" in Rhodesia. Smith's Rhodesian Front Party reacted swiftly to these challenges by sending ministers to tour the country to present the government's case to the people, but there was in fact no serious threat to the Front's domination. The right wing's criticisms of Smith and the more widely felt concern among whites that the terms of settlement might involve politically dangerous concessions were tempered by a general anxiety regarding the country's economic future and the threat to Rhodesian security arising from FRELIMO (Mozambique Liberation Front) activities along the eastern border should sanctions continue.

The commission's report, published on May 23, concluded that while the proposals appeared acceptable to the majority of whites they were rejected by the majority of Africans and that thus the people of Rhodesia as a whole could not be said to have accepted the proposals as a basis for independence. Smith claimed that the report contained many misrepresentations of the true position and expressed the view that the conclusion was a mistaken one. He informed the British government that he was still prepared to implement the settlement but would not do so unilaterally nor would he reopen negotiations with a view to amending the terms of the settlement. The British foreign secretary, meanwhile, said that the Rhodesian people should be given time to reflect on the problem in the hope that they would come to accept some compromise that would lead to orderly political change. In the meantime, the status quo would be preserved, including sanctions.

While the white population tended to rally to Smith's government in reaction to the commission's

RHODESIA

Education. (1970) African: primary, pupils 677,415, teachers 16,958; secondary, pupils 24,201, teachers 1,027; vocational and teacher training, students 2,113, teachers 121. Non-African: primary, pupils 39,504, teachers 1,588; secondary, pupils 26,462, teachers 1,539; vocational and teacher training, pupils 2,818, teachers 189. African and non-African: higher (University of Rhodesia), students 867, teaching staff 162.

Finance. Monetary unit: Rhodesian dollar, with (Sept. 18, 1972) a free rate of R$0.70 to U.S. $1 (R$1.60 = £1 sterling). Budget (1970–71 rev. est.): revenue R$206,675,000; expenditure R$215,715,000. Gross national product: (1969) R$930 million; (1968) R$816 million.

Foreign Trade. (1969) Imports R$199.4 million; exports R$226.9 million. Import sources (1965): U.K. 30%; South Africa 23%; U.S. 7%; Japan 6%. Export destinations (1965): Zambia 29%; U.K. 20%; South Africa 11%; West Germany 8%; Malawi 6%; Japan 5%. Main exports (1965): tobacco 51%; asbestos 12%; machinery 9%; clothing 6%; chemicals 5%.

Transport and Communications. Roads (1969) 78,064 km. Motor vehicles in use (1969): passenger 126,600; commercial (including buses) 52,000. Railways (1971): 3,250 km.; freight traffic (including Botswana; 1969–70) 6,501,000,000 net ton-km. Telephones (Jan. 1971) 132,000. Radio receivers (Dec. 1970) 145,000. Television receivers (Dec. 1970) 50,000.

Agriculture. Production (in 000; metric tons; 1971; 1970 in parentheses): corn *c.* 900 (*c.* 700); millet *c.* 220 (*c.* 220); peanuts *c.* 122 (*c.* 104); tobacco *c.* 62 (*c.* 62); tea *c.* 2.3 (*c.* 2.3); sugar, raw value (1971–72) *c.* 196, (1970–71) *c.* 142; beef and veal (1970–71) *c.* 72, (1969–70) *c.* 70. Livestock (in 000; 1970–71): cattle *c.* 4,000; sheep *c.* 460; goats *c.* 700; pigs *c.* 145.

Industry. Production (in 000; metric tons; 1970): asbestos 80; coal (1969) 3,332; chrome ore (oxide content; 1965) 281; iron ore (metal content; 1966) *c.* 830; gold (troy oz.) *c.* 500; electricity (kw-hr.) 6,410,000.

report, they remained anxious about the future. It was thought that the African politicians who had led the campaign against the settlement might become more aggressive. In November the government announced removal of segregationist clauses from the 1970 Land Tenure Act. The clauses, which it had been feared would end interracial religious services and education, had been strongly opposed by church groups.

(KENNETH INGHAM)

Romania

A socialist republic on the Balkan Peninsula in southeastern Europe, Romania is bordered by the U.S.S.R., the Black Sea, Bulgaria, Yugoslavia, and Hungary. Area: 91,700 sq.mi. (237,500 sq.km.). Pop. (1971 est.): 20,470,000, including (1968) Romanian 87.8%; Hungarian 8.4%. Cap. and largest city: Bucharest (pop., 1970 est., 1,475,050). Religion: Romanian Orthodox 70%; Greek Orthodox 10%. General secretary of the Romanian Communist Party and president of the State Council in 1972, Nicolae Ceausescu; chairman of the Council of Ministers (premier), Ion Gheorghe Maurer.

During 1972 President Ceausescu continued to proclaim at home and abroad that the existence of national states was consistent with Marxist internationalism, and that international peace and security had to be based on the observance of every state's right to freedom, independence, and sovereignty. Between March 11 and April 6 Ceausescu visited eight African countries beginning with Algeria (to which Romania granted a U.S. $100 million credit for industrial equipment), followed by the Central African Republic, Congo, Zaire, Zambia, and Tanzania, and ending with Sudan and Egypt.

Jeno Fock, the Hungarian premier, paid an official visit to Bucharest February 24–26, during which he and Maurer, his Romanian opposite number, signed a 20-year treaty of friendship. On May 12 a similar and long-postponed treaty was signed with East Germany. On May 16 Presidents Ceausescu and Tito of Yugoslavia opened the giant hydroelectric dam that the two countries had constructed on the Iron Gate stretch of the Danube. The project, which had cost some $450 million, was started in 1964. On September 27–28 Ceausescu and Maurer visited Bulgaria, and a protocol was signed concerning the joint building of the Cioara-Belene hydroelectric dam across the lower Danube.

To underline Romania's independence, Ceausescu sent a military delegation, headed by Gen. Emil Bodnaras, to China. Between May 4 and 7 the Romanian president was host to Prime Minister Golda Meir of Israel. In spite of this maneuvering—and despite the report that Gen. Ion Serb, chief of the Bucharest military garrison, had been shot earlier in the year for passing information on Romanian defense deployments to Moscow—Ceausescu was invited by Soviet party leader Leonid I. Brezhnev to the meeting of Communist leaders in the Crimea July 31.

Ceausescu's state visit to Belgium in October was his second to a Western European country (the first was to France in June 1970). Earlier it had been revealed that, in February, Romania had become the first Comecon member to ask to join the EEC's generalized trade preference system for less developed countries—a request that France opposed on the ground that Romania was not a less developed country in the usual sense of the term. On September 20 Romania became the first member of Comecon to apply for membership in both the International Monetary Fund and the World Bank. The formal Romanian requests were delivered by Corneliu Bogdan, the Romanian ambassador to the U.S., to Pierre-Paul Schweitzer, managing director of the IMF, and World Bank Pres. Robert McNamara. Romania signed the "instrument of acceptance" to the IMF in a ceremony in Washington on December 16.

In April Paul Niculescu-Mizil, a member of the party Presidium, was dropped from the party's seven-man secretariat and shifted to the less important post of deputy premier; in October he was appointed minister of education. There were reasons for believing that he had become an impediment to the improvement of Romanian relations with the U.S.S.R. and Hungary. On October 18 Corneliu Manescu, foreign minister since March 1961, was replaced by his deputy, George Macovescu. It was believed that Manescu had been dismissed as a result of pressure from Moscow.

(K. M. SMOGORZEWSKI)

Rice:
see Agriculture

Roads:
see Engineering Projects; Transportation

Rockets:
see Astronautics; Defense

Rodeos:
see Fairs and Shows

Roman Catholic Church:
see Religion

ROMANIA

Education. (1969–70) Primary, pupils 2,886,855, teachers 133,842; secondary, pupils 261,749, teachers 13,679; vocational, pupils 366,239, teachers 20,994; teacher training, students 22,494, teachers 171; higher (including 11 universities), students 151,705, teaching staff 13,166.

Finance. Monetary unit: leu, with (Sept. 18, 1972) an official exchange rate of 5.53 lei to U.S. $1 (13.39 lei = £1 sterling) and a tourist rate of 16 lei to U.S. $1 (38.74 lei = £1 sterling). Budget (1970 est.): revenue 133,342,000,000 lei; expenditure 130.9 billion lei.

Foreign Trade. (1970) Imports 11,761,000,000 lei; exports 11,105,000,000 lei. Import sources: U.S.S.R. 26%; West Germany 8%; Czechoslovakia 8%; East Germany 6%; France 6%; U.K. 5%; Italy 5%. Export destinations: U.S.S.R. 29%; West Germany 9%; Czechoslovakia 7%; Italy 6%; East Germany 6%. Main exports: machinery 23%; foodstuffs 12%; raw materials (minerals, metals, etc.) 13%; petroleum products 7%; chemicals 7%.

Transport and Communications. Roads (1970) 75,879 km. Motor vehicles in use: passenger (1969) *c.* 35,000; commercial (1970) 45,100. Railways: (1970) 11,012 km.; traffic (1971) 18,800,000,000 passenger-km., freight 50,830,000,000 net ton-km. Air traffic (1971): 357.5 million passenger-km.; freight 6,266,-000 net ton-km. Inland waterways in regular use (1970) 1,673 km. Shipping (1971): merchant vessels 100 gross tons and over 71; gross tonnage 363,996. Telephones (Dec. 1970) 639,000. Radio licenses (Dec. 1970) 3,075,000. Television licenses (Dec. 1970) 1,484,000.

Agriculture. Production (in 000; metric tons; 1971; 1970 in parentheses): wheat 5,585 (3,351); barley 665 (513); oats *c.* 150 (117); corn *c.* 7,762 (6,536); potatoes *c.* 3,000 (2,036); onions (1970) 223, (1969) 208; tomatoes (1970) 720, (1969) 676; sugar, raw value (1971–72) *c.* 499, (1970–71) 374; sunflower seed *c.* 900 (770); dry beans *c.* 115 (73); soybeans *c.* 180 (91); dry peas *c.* 142 (155); plums (1970) 697, (1969) 962; apples *c.* 260 (176); wine *c.* 700 (*c.* 476); tobacco *c.* 30 (22); linseed *c.* 35 (42); hemp fibre *c.* 20 (*c.* 14). Livestock (in 000; Jan. 1971): cattle 5,215; sheep 13,818; pigs 6,359; horses *c.* 665; poultry 54,333.

Industry. Index of production (1963 = 100): (1970) 229; (1969) 201. Fuel and power (in 000; metric tons; 1971): coal 6,793; lignite 13,808; coke (1970) 1,070; crude oil 13,794; natural gas (cu.m.) 26,487; manufactured gas (cu.m.) 536,000; electricity (kw-hr.) 38,321,000. Production (in 000; metric tons; 1971): cement 8,523; iron ore (30–35% metal content) 3,467; pig iron 4,382; crude steel 6,802; sulfuric acid 1,048; nitrogenous fertilizers (nitrogen content; 1970) 647; cotton yarn 121; cotton fabrics (sq.m.) 481,000; wool yarn 38; woolen fabrics (sq.m.) 70,000; newsprint 53; other paper (1970) 462; passenger cars (units) 9.1; commercial vehicles (units) 38. New dwelling units completed (1970) 159,000.

Rowing

East Germany claimed the principal honours in the 1972 Olympic Games rowing competition with medals in every race—finishing with three golds, a silver, and three bronzes. The U.S.S.R. qualified for six finals and won two of them. Other Eastern European medalists were Czechoslovakia with a silver and a bronze from four finals and Romania with a bronze after three finals. West Germany appeared in five finals and collected a gold and a bronze. New Zealand reached three finals and distinguished itself with a gold and a silver. A third triple finalist was the United States, which earned a silver in the eights.

The finest performance by East Germany was the triumph of Etuf Essen, the 1968 Olympic gold medalists in coxless fours, in retaining their title. They succeeded in rowing New Zealand down in the last 50 m. to win by 1.37 sec., after trailing by more than a length 500 m. from the finish. The famed "Bulls of Konstanz" won the coxed fours for West Germany after leading comfortably from the halfway mark. In single sculls victory went to the 25-year-old Soviet student Yuri Malishev. The favourite, Alberto Demiddi (Arg.), tried in vain to unsettle him by starting with 47 strokes in the first minute, but Malishev, with a more economical and effective rate of 34, had the measure of Demiddi from start to finish and lowered the 1928 record by 0.48 sec. The U.S.S.R. also won the double sculls from Norway.

Both classes of pairs were won easily by East Germany to complete their gold-medal hat trick. In the coxless event the 19-year-old winners, Siegfried Brietzke and Wolfgang Mager, produced the first Olympic fruits from a nationwide recruiting campaign for rowers launched in 1968. New Zealand led the field in the eights final by a length after 750 m.

Soviet oarswomen won three events and also collected a silver medal in the Women's European championships held in Brandenburg, E.Ger. The Netherlands, with a gold, silver, and bronze medal, finally broke the Eastern European domination of the meet with Romania also earning distinction by collecting a gold and a silver. The performance of the Dutch girls was the best by a Western European country since the championships were founded in 1954. France also did well with a silver and a bronze. The Soviet women took the eights, double sculls, and coxed fours; Romania triumphed in quadruple sculls; and the Netherlands, in single sculls, won a European title for the first time.

Although East Germany was not in the forefront at Brandenburg, its athletes won three gold and two silver medals in the world youth rowing championships in Milan, Italy. Czechoslovakia, the Netherlands, West Germany, and the U.S.S.R. were the other gold medalists. West Germany won four silver medals and one bronze, while the Soviet Union took a silver and three bronze.

In the U.K., eight events at Henley Royal Regatta were won by overseas entries. A. Timoschinin became the first Soviet sculler to win the Diamond and his countrymen from W.M.F. Moscow and Spartak Moscow triumphed in the Grand and Stewards' challenge cups. Poland took the Silver Goblets; St. Catherine's Rowing Club became the first Canadian winners of the Prince Philip Cup; Kent School, U.S., celebrated its 50th season with its first success in the Princess Elizabeth Cup; and Harvard University, in retaining the Thames Cup, became the 154th overseas winner at Henley. In the 118th boat race, Cambridge recorded its 66th victory over Oxford, by 9½ lengths.

(KEITH OSBORNE)

SPORT & GENERAL/PICTORIAL PARADE

The Cambridge boat crew pulls away from Oxford at Hammersmith Bridge to win the University Boat Race for the fifth straight year.

Rubber

World production of natural rubber in 1971 was estimated at 3,002,000 metric tons, an increase of 105,000 metric tons over 1970. Production for the first six months of 1972 was estimated at 1,432,500 metric tons, up 31,500 metric tons from the corresponding period in 1971. The management committee of the International Rubber Study Group (IRSG), meeting in London in June 1972, estimated world production of new rubber as follows: natural rubber supplies, including delivery from governmental surplus stocks, 3,180,000 metric tons; synthetic rubber, 5,420,000 metric tons. It was estimated that some 3,180,000 metric tons of natural rubber and 5,270,000 metric tons of synthetic rubber would be consumed (*i.e.,* turned into manufactured products) in 1972. (Estimates for synthetic rubber production do not include the U.S.S.R., non-IRSG countries in Eastern Europe, or China.)

The New York spot price for no. 1 smoked sheet rubber was 18⅞ cents per pound on Oct. 1, 1972, compared with 18 cents a year earlier. The price structure of natural rubber remained about the same as in 1971, with little spread between no. 1 ribbed smoked sheets and the lower grades. The increased world capacity for production of synthetic polyisoprene seemed to have had little effect on the price of the natural product, although this may have been behind the decline to 16½ cents per pound earlier in the year.

The area under cultivation of plantation (natural) rubber was estimated at 5,950,000 ha. (14,700,000 ac.). West Malaysian production of natural rubber in 1971 totaled 1,276,331 metric tons, and world output in the same year was estimated at 3,002,000 metric tons—both records. The U.S. remained the largest single buyer. World consumption of natural rubber latex (dry basis) in 1971 was estimated at 265,250 metric tons. Figures for the consumption of synthetic latices were incomplete, but the U.S. alone consumed 121,217 metric tons (dry basis) of the SBR (styrene-butadiene rubber) type. World production of all types of synthetic rubbers in 1971 (excluding countries not reporting) was estimated at 5,136,000 metric tons, of which the U.S. produced 2,277,024.

Production of all types of reclaimed rubber in 1971 amounted to 291,255 metric tons. Reclaimed rubber production had been decreasing since the early 1960s due to pollution problems inherent in the manufacturing method and changing trends in rubber compounding.

Research expenditure by the U.S. rubber industry was estimated at $295 million for 1972, an increase of 5% over 1971. Tire uniformity and quality were being emphasized by both tire manufacturers and automobile makers. All original equipment tires were being tested by the rubber companies, prior to shipment, for radial and lateral force variation as well as balance. X ray, an old tool, was still widely used for locating defects that could cause failure, but the development of infrared heat-detecting devices had progressed to a point where hot spots in a loaded running tire could be detected easily. The tire then was usually stopped short of failure and dissected to determine the cause of the hot spot.

Radial tires, which accounted for the majority of tires sold in Europe, were being offered as original equipment on a number of U.S. passenger cars. Formerly, they had been produced and sold on the U.S. replacement market. Both all-textile cord-reinforced tires and tires with textile radial plies and one or more steel cord belts were being manufactured. Development of an all-glass radial tire was reported. Meanwhile, rubber was being used in the bumpers under development to meet the U.S. requirement that they withstand a five-mile-per-hour impact with no damage.

(J. R. BEATTY)

Table I. Natural Rubber Production

In 000 metric tons

Country	1967	1968	1969	1970	1971
Malaysia	998	1,100	1,268	1,269	1,324
Indonesia	762*	752*	790	780*	834*
Thailand	214	259	282	287	316
Africa*	164	170	181	213	195
Sri Lanka (Ceylon)	143	149	151	159	141
India	63	69	80	90	99
Vietnam	41	29	26	29	35
Brazil	21	23	24	25	24
Cambodia	53	51	52	13	1
Others*	28	31	31	32	33
Total*	2,487	2,633	2,885	2,897	3,002

*Estimate.

Table II. Synthetic Rubber Production

In 000 metric tons

Country	1967	1968	1969	1970	1971
United States	1,943	2,165	2,286	2,232	2,277
Japan	281	381	526	697	759
France	189	223	275	316	323
Germany, West	190	238	292	302	306
United Kingdom	204	237	273	306	277
Netherlands	125	163	214	206	211
Canada	200	197	199	205	197
Italy*	118	125	135	155	160
Germany, East	109	102	114	118	129
Brazil	52	59	62	75	78
Poland	40	41	48	62	66
Romania	51	54	55	61	...
Belgium	20	25	35	50	60
Czechoslovakia*	33	35	40	50	52
Mexico*	20	34	36	40	45
Spain	11	26	34	40*	45*
Argentina	17	23	38*	39*	45*
Australia	26	30	33	33*	43*
India	22	25	25	30	33
South Africa	24	25	24	29	30
Total*	3,675	4,208	4,744	5,046	5,136

*Estimate.
Source: International Rubber Study Group.

Rugby Football:
see Football

Russia:
see Union of Soviet Socialist Republics

Russian Literature:
see Literature

Sabah:
see Malaysia

Rwanda

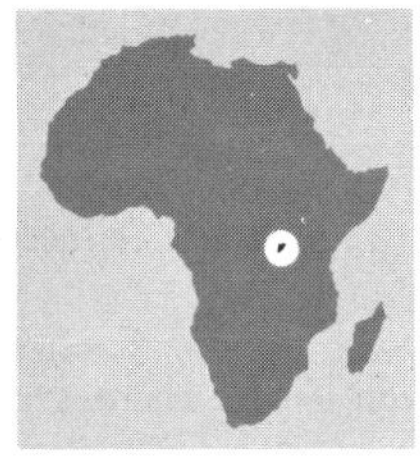

A republic in eastern Africa, Rwanda is bordered by Zaire, Uganda, Tanzania, and Burundi. Area: 10,169 sq.mi. (26,338 sq.km.). Pop. (1971 est.): 3,841,676, including (1970) Hutu 90%; Tutsi 9%; and Twa 1%. Cap. and largest city: Kigali (pop., 1971 est., 60,000). Language (official): French and Kinyarwanda. Religion (1970): animist 43%; Roman Catholic 46%; Protestant 7%; Muslim 1%. President in 1972, Grégoire Kayibanda.

Rwanda stood on the fringe of neighbouring Burundi's tribal war in early 1972. With the same tribal makeup as Burundi but with power in Hutu rather than Tutsi hands, it became the destination of many Hutu refugees fleeing from Tutsi terrorism. Notwithstanding Rwanda's long feud with Burundi, President Kayibanda counseled moderation. (*See* BURUNDI.) Uganda's closure of the common border forced Rwanda to extend trade links via Tanzania, and in August Ugandan Pres. Idi Amin threatened to destroy Kigali if Rwanda supported alleged anti-Ugandan subversion by Israel. Despite these alarms and some Cabinet reshuffles, Rwanda itself remained comparatively peaceful. Its principal initiatives were the establishment in November 1971 of diplomatic links with China, the exploration of further technical contacts with that country, and the issuance of conventional statements against colonialism.

Rwanda continued to rely heavily on foreign aid. During 1972 both the UN Development Program and the International Development Association provided substantial assistance, including $3 million for highway maintenance.

(MOLLY MORTIMER)

RWANDA

Education. (1967–68) Primary, pupils 372,184, teachers 5,921; secondary, pupils 6,466; vocational, pupils 912; teacher training, students 1,464; secondary, vocational, and teacher training, teachers 580; higher (1969–70), students 287, teaching staff 58.

Finance. Monetary unit: Rwanda franc, with (Sept. 18, 1972) a par value of RwFr. 92.11 to U.S. $1 (official rate of RwFr. 242.7 = £1 sterling). Gold, SDRs, and foreign exchange, central bank: (June 1972) U.S. $4,620,000; (June 1971) U.S. $3,040,000. Budget (1969 est.): revenue RwFr. 1,636,618,000; expenditure RwFr. 1,664,000,000.

Foreign Trade. (1971) Imports RwFr. 3,298,300,000; exports RwFr. 2,220,800,000. Import sources (1969): Belgium-Luxembourg 15%; Japan 14%; Uganda 12%; West Germany 11%; Kenya 7%; U.S. 7%; France 5%. Export destinations (1969): Belgium-Luxembourg 29%; Uganda 8%; Kenya 6%. Main exports: coffee 50%; tin 20%.

Agriculture. Production (in 000; metric tons; 1971; 1970 in parentheses): sorghum *c.* 140 (156); dry beans *c.* 140 (144); dry peas *c.* 63 (65); potatoes *c.* 126 (126); sweet potatoes (1970) 417, (1969) 324; cassava (1970) 345, (1969) 283; coffee *c.* 12 (*c.* 14); tea *c.* 2 (1.2). Livestock (in 000; July 1971): cattle *c.* 740; sheep *c.* 230; pigs *c.* 60.

Sailing

The year 1972 was a good one for multihulled boats. Alain Colas of France won the single-handed transatlantic race in his trimaran "Pen Duick IV"; the knifelike 60-ft. proa "Crossbow" won the speed record sailing time trials at Weymouth, Dorset, averaging 26.3 knots; and the Tornado catamaran was selected by Great Britain as a new class for the 1976 Olympic Games.

As usual, the year began with the Southern Cross Cup Series, culminating in the Sydney–Hobart race. New Zealand, represented by its highly tuned one-tonners "Pathfinder," "Runaway," and "Wai-Aniwa," easily won the team series. In addition, "Pathfinder" collected the Sydney–Hobart trophy, and "Wai-Aniwa" was the top point scorer of the series. Britain's strong team of "Cervantes IV," "Morning Cloud," and "Prospect of Whitby" finished second, with New South Wales' "Pilgrim," "Polaris," and "Ragamuffin" comfortably in third place.

Also in Australia, "Quest III," sporting the most sophisticated rig the sailing world had yet seen, trampled all over its U.S. challenger, "Weathercock," to defend the International C Class catamaran challenge trophy (Little America's Cup) successfully for Australia. Bruce Proctor and Graeme Ainslie sailed a superb series; however, top honours should perhaps have gone to Lindsay Cunningham, who invented and engineered the complicated but effective rig, which took an hour and a half to set up each day.

During February and March eyes were turned toward the Southern Ocean Racing Conference (SORC) series, based in Florida and the Caribbean, for any new 1972 winning designs. However, it was the much used and very secondhand-looking "Condor," a four-year-old Redline 41 Class D boat sailed by Hill Blackett of Chicago, that firmly put the blue-water experts in their places in a series marked by light winds. Second was the new aluminum S & S 49 "Aura," the Class B winner, and third the PJ-37 "Elixir," the Class E winner. During the series the overall race winners were: in the Lipton Cup, "Neat Package," Ronald Hume; the Miami–Nassau race, "Charisma," Jesse Phillips; the Nassau Cup race, "Arieto," Buzz Schofield; the Miami–Lucaya race, "Sorcery," James Baldwin; and the St. Petersburg–Fort Lauderdale race, "Celerity II," William Hough.

The classic Newport–Bermuda race was a triumph for Britain's "Noryema," breaking the U.S. domination of this race for the first time. But it must have been a bitter disappointment for owner Ron Amey—because of imminent take-over bids for his company in England, he was not aboard to celebrate the victory. First to finish was the new Class A C & C 61 "Robon," owned by Robert Grant, sailing in ahead of the giant Class A boats "Windward Passage," "Blackfin," "Baccara," "Ondine," and "Buccaneer." "Noryema," a Class C boat, won the race on corrected time. The Newport–Bermuda race concluded the Onion Patch series, which was won by the U.S. with Britain the runner-up.

After the Bermuda event a record number of 48 yachts took part in the Discovery race to Bayona, Spain. Winner of a slow race was Richard Nye in his latest "Carina" in Class B, runner-up being the Class D yacht "Prim" owned by M. Gibbons-Neff. "Noryema" won Class C and fifth place overall.

The half-ton cup series, dominated for the past three years by Peter Norlin in his Scampi for Sweden, was won by Paul Elvstrøm of Denmark in a new creation put together only hours before the first race. This new Elvstrøm half-tonner was clearly a flier in light winds, and though Bruce Banks of Britain put up a fine show in his Scampi he could not match Elvstrøm, who won four of the five races. Some modification of Elvstrøm's lifelines was required before he was allowed to compete.

The quarter-ton series was once more a triumph for the French in their stripped-down racing machines, the winner being Laurent Cordelle's much-modified Écume de Mer, "Petite Fleur"; however, the Swedish Little Scampi "Genant GT," sailed by Leif Erikson, finished second ahead of the 1971 series winner, "Juliénas 71," to break the French stranglehold.

In the single-handed transatlantic race, Alain Colas triumphed in his trimaran "Pen Duick IV" over the huge 128-ft. Carter-designed prerace favourite monohull "Vendredi 13," sailed by J. Y. Terlain; third was another trimaran, "Cap 33," sailed by J. M. Vidal. The French thus finished first, second, and third. Winner on handicap was Britain's Royal Marine officer Mike McMullen in his 32-ft. Contessa, "Binkie II." Sir Francis Chichester also competed but was forced to give up because of ill health and died several weeks later (*see* OBITUARIES).

For many international yachtsmen the year was a buildup for the Olympic Games in Kiel, W.Ger., in which six classes were involved: Finn, Flying Dutchman, Tempest, Star, Soling, and Dragon. Only one boat could represent each country in a class, and in some countries competition for selection was almost harder than the Olympics themselves. In the smallest class, the single-handed Finn, there was a draw for boats, which were supplied by the host nation. The winner, Serge Maury of France, had been sailing a boat similar to the supplied boat for some months and had finished third in competition at Kiel in June. However, Ilias Hatzipaulis of Greece and Victor Potapov of the U.S.S.R. pulled off somewhat of a surprise in the light winds to take the silver and bronze medals. In the Flying Dutchman class Rodney Pattisson once more finished first; since winning a gold medal in the 1968 Olympics this British yachtsman had won every Flying Dutchman world and European title series raced, and he started out a clear favourite. The battle was really for second and third places, the Pajot brothers from France finally defeating the 1968 silver medalist, Ulli Libor of West Germany. For much of

Dramatic early lead of "Red Rock II" was not enough to win the Newport–Bermuda race, in which Britain's "Noryema" triumphed.

UPI COMPIX

the Tempest series Britain appeared likely to add a second gold medal to its tally through Allan Warren and David Hunt, but the 1968 Finn-class gold medalist, Valentin Mankin of the U.S.S.R., thought otherwise and came back strongly to snatch the gold from the British pair by finishing third in the final race. Glen Foster, the pre-series favourite, took the bronze for the U.S.

Star-class winner David Forbes of Australia sailed a remarkable series; after a poor season he borrowed a new European-built boat from Sweden's Pelle Petterson only two weeks before the Olympics and proceeded to finish ahead of Petterson, leaving reigning world champion Willi Kuhweide of West Germany to take the bronze medal. The big surprise in this class was the poor showing of the U.S. entry. The Soling class was completely dominated by Bud Melges of the U.S., with Stig Wennerström of Sweden an easy silver medalist; David Miller of Canada finally won the scramble for the bronze. Most of the Dragon-class competitors never seemed to recover from the shock of seeing John Cuneo of Australia walk away with the first three races and so virtually sew the series up before the others had realized it had started. Pre-series favourite and European champion Paul Borowski of East Germany managed with a late run to take the silver medal ahead of Don Cohan of the U.S.

(ADRIAN JARDINE)

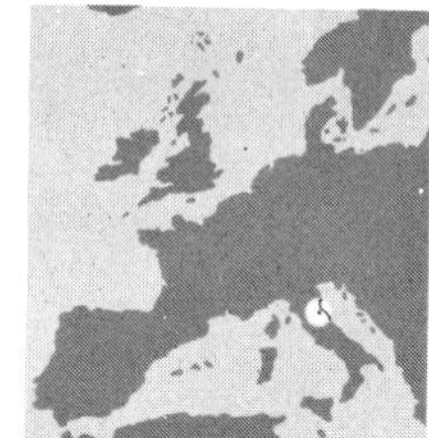

San Marino

A small republic, San Marino is an enclave in northeastern Italy, 14 mi. SW of Rimini. Area: 25 sq.mi. (61 sq.km.). Pop. (1972 est.): 20,000. Cap.: San Marino (metro. pop., 1971 est., 4,400). Language: Italian. Religion: Roman Catholic. San Marino is united with Italy by a customs union. The country is governed by two *capitani reggenti,* or coregents, appointed every six months by a Grand and General Council. Executive power rests with two secretaries of state: foreign and political affairs and internal affairs. In 1972 the positions were filled, respectively, by Giancarlo Ghironzi and Gian Luigi Berti.

Late in 1971 Federico Bigi announced his intention to resign as secretary of state for foreign and political affairs, a post he had held for nearly 15 years. He was recognized as the major figure in San Marino's government and in the dominant Christian Democratic Party. Giancarlo Ghironzi, a physician and secretary of state for the treasury, was nominated on Jan. 10, 1972, to succeed Bigi but failed by one vote to obtain the necessary majority on the first ballot. He was elected, however, on January 17.

No change in foreign policy was anticipated. In internal affairs San Marino was struggling with increased expenditures and stable revenues. Ghironzi, a liberal, might introduce more progressive measures, but his difficulty in being elected might indicate a period of instability within the government.

(ROBERT D. HODGSON)

SAN MARINO

Education. (1969–70) Primary, pupils 1,580, teachers 89; secondary, pupils 843, teachers 62.

Finance. Monetary unit: Italian lira, with (Sept. 18, 1972) a par value of 581.50 lire to U.S. $1 (free rate of 1,423 lire = £1 sterling). Budget (1970–71 est.) balanced at 6,475,000,000 lire. Tourism (1970) *c.* 3 million visitors.

St. Lucia: *see* Dependent States

Salvador, El: *see* El Salvador

Salvation Army: *see* Religion

Samoa: *see* Dependent States; Western Samoa

Sarawak: *see* Malaysia

Satellites, Space: *see* Astronautics

Saudi Arabia

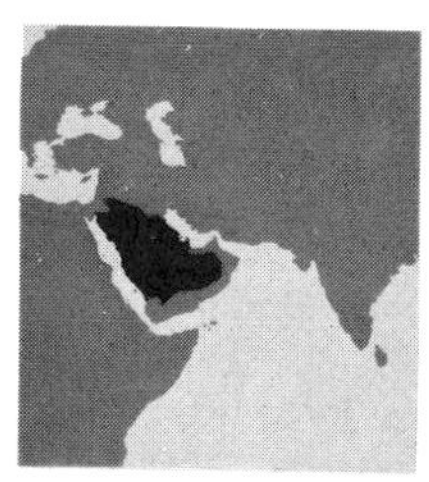

A monarchy occupying four-fifths of the Arabian Peninsula, Saudi Arabia has an area of 865,000 sq.mi. (2,240,000 sq.km.). Pop. (1971 est.): 7,965,000. Cap. and largest city: Riyadh (pop., 1965 est., 225,000). Language: Arabic. Religion: Muslim. King and prime minister, Faisal ibn 'Abd al-'Aziz ibn 'Abd ar-Rahman Al Sa'ud.

In 1972 King Faisal, as leader of the conservative forces in the Arab world, pursued a fairly unobtrusive diplomacy except in South Arabia, where he actively supported the Northern Yemenis (Yemen [San'a']) and Southern Yemeni exiles against the Marxist regime in Yemen (Aden). In his public statements the king attacked both Zionism and Communism with great vehemence; at one press conference he blamed the Jews for most of the ills in the world. On February 29 the third conference of Islamic foreign ministers opened in Jedda with 31 Muslim countries represented. The king provided funds for the establishment of an international Islamic news agency based in Jedda. On March 8 Pres. Anwar as-Sadat of Egypt visited Faisal in Jedda for talks on strengthening the Arab front and gave details of his recent discussions in Moscow. Saudi Arabia declared itself ready to continue its joint efforts with Egypt to mediate between the Jordanian government and the Palestinian guerrillas. In contrast to Libya and Kuwait, Saudi Arabia continued to provide financial aid to Jordan and was the only major Arab state to maintain good relations with that country, although it did not publicize this.

Like other Middle East oil-producing states, Saudi

SAUDI ARABIA

Education. (1969–70) Primary, pupils 397,153, teachers (including preprimary) 17,245; secondary, pupils 67,817, teachers (public only) 3,820; vocational, pupils 1,777, teachers 341; teacher training, students 9,875, teachers 570; higher, students 6,942, teaching staff 573.

Finance. Monetary unit: riyal, with (Sept. 18, 1972) a par value of 4.14 riyals to U.S. $1 (free rate of 10.06 riyals = £1 sterling). Gold, SDRs, and foreign exchange, official: (June 1972) U.S. $1,915,000,000; (June 1971) U.S. $912 million. Budget (1972–73 est.) balanced at 13.2 billion riyals. Money supply: (Jan. 1972) 2,846,000,000 riyals; (Jan. 1971) 2,307,000,000 riyals.

Foreign Trade. (1970) Imports 3,974,000,000 riyals; exports 10,906,000,000 riyals. Import sources: U.S. 14%; Lebanon 9%; Japan 8%; West Germany 8%; U.K. 6%. Export destinations: Japan 21%; Italy 11%; Netherlands 9%; U.K. 8%; France 6%; Bahrain 5%. Main exports: crude oil 78%; petroleum products 16%.

Transport and Communications. Roads (1971) *c.* 22,000 km. (including 13,120 km. with improved surface). Motor vehicles in use (1971): passenger 47,800; commercial 34,700. Railways (1970) 606 km. Shipping (1971): merchant vessels 100 gross tons and over 33; gross tonnage 45,492. Telephones (Jan. 1969) 44,000. Radio receivers (Dec. 1970) 85,000. Television receivers (Dec. 1969) *c.* 50,000.

Agriculture. Production (in 000; metric tons; 1971; 1970 in parentheses): wheat *c.* 150 (*c.* 150); barley *c.* 35 (*c.* 34); millet *c.* 16 (*c.* 16); sorghum *c.* 52 (*c.* 52); dates *c.* 220 (*c.* 220). Livestock (in 000; 1970–71): cattle *c.* 320; sheep *c.* 3,300; goats *c.* 2,050; camels *c.* 560; asses *c.* 135.

Industry. Production (in 000; metric tons; 1970): cement 675; crude oil (1971) 223,412; electricity (excluding most industrial production; kw-hr.) 770,000.

Arabia was seeking 20% participation in the operation and management of foreign oil companies. On February 1 talks opened on the issue between Aramco Pres. Frank Jungers and the Saudi oil minister, Ahmed Zaki al-Yamani, with the latter acting as representative of all the oil-producing nations in the Persian Gulf area. On March 11 Saudi Arabia announced that Aramco had agreed to the principle of participation, the first foreign oil company to do so.

Saudi Arabia's wealth continued to increase at a spectacular rate in 1972. The nation in 1971 had had a 29.6% share in total Middle East oil output, and production in 1972 was running at about 30% above that of 1971. In September Yamani announced that Saudi Arabia, which owned an estimated 25% of the world's proved oil reserves, planned to increase output from 6 million to 20 million bbl. per day by 1980. This would increase Saudi oil revenues to an estimated $15 billion in 1980, compared with $2,160,000,000 in 1971. At the same time, Yamani proposed that Saudi Arabia should be given a special place in the U.S. market, free from duties and quota restrictions, and that this would encourage large-scale Saudi investment in oil marketing facilities in the U.S.

In the record Saudi budget of $3.2 billion for 1972–73, 28% of the expenditure was allocated to defense, 14% to transport and communications, and 18% to social services. Plans were announced during 1972 to build up a navy to protect Saudi Arabia and other Arab states in the area. (PETER MANSFIELD)

Savings and Investment

Investment and savings in 1972 rose sharply in spending at home on fixed assets, such as plant, machinery, buildings, and houses, and on inventories in the U.S., Canada, and the U.K. Relative stability or modest declines in West Germany, France, Italy, and Japan occurred in the same areas. Marked differences in foreign balance—investment or disinvestment abroad—were noted both in relation to 1971 and between various countries.

Changes in domestic and foreign investment and savings tend to reflect cyclical influences and policies pursued by the authorities in different countries. The latter, in addition to aiming at accelerating or slowing down the pace of expansion in total output of goods and services, also try to improve their external accounts and, especially in recent years, contain inflationary pressures.

In broad terms 1972 was a year in which economic recovery in the U.S. and Canada continued on its upward course; the U.K. began to emerge from a period of stagnation; and authorities of the principal industrial countries of Europe and Japan reversed their policies of retrenchment and tried to generate and help the cyclical upswing.

In the U.S. and Canada the rather marked increase in domestic investment in 1972 represented a continuation of the cyclical recovery that had begun in 1971, partly as a result of a substantial advance in federal expenditures. But whereas in 1971 the bulk of additional investment spending was concentrated on housing, the expansion in investment outlays in 1972 comprised dwellings, purchases of new productive assets by the manufacturing and nonmanufacturing sectors, and an acceleration in inventory buildup. However, despite the hopes expressed in December 1971, when the U.S. dollar was devalued in terms of other currencies, the U.S. experienced no improvement in its net foreign balance (balance on current account). Instead, there was a further increase in deficit on current account, indicating that U.S. spending on fixed assets at home continued to rely on real resources provided, even to a greater extent than in 1971, by other countries.

In the U.K., following a period of stagnation of total output and investment in 1971, there was a substantial rise in 1972 in outlays on additional productive equipment, residential buildings, and stock inventories. The momentum of additional spending was especially pronounced in housing and the public sector, and was more modest as regards spending on fixed assets by industry and commerce. As in the case of the U.S., an increase in domestic investment was accompanied by a further worsening of the nation's external account, reflecting another contraction in the volume of real resources made available on balance to overseas by way of transfer of savings.

Among the three continental European countries, Italy's experience with investment and savings was in some ways similar to that of the U.K. Following the recession of 1971, when total spending on productive assets and dwellings as well as additions to inventory slumped, there was some revival, although of modest dimensions. This was due almost entirely to a large expansion in expenditure on new equipment in the public sector, including nationalized industries and public corporations. There was no significant improvement in housing, but private industry started to add to the volume of its inventories. This development, as in the U.K. and the U.S., was accompanied by some decline in net foreign balance, thus reducing the volume of savings and consequently the command over real resources that the Italian economy put at the disposal of other countries.

In France year-to-year fluctuations in the rate of growth in total investment and savings and total output tend to be much smaller than in other industrial countries. This remained true in 1972, which showed little change in the pace of spending on fixed assets

Table I. Changes in Gross National Product, Fixed Domestic Investment, Stock Building, and Foreign Balance in Selected Countries

In percent

Country	Year	Increase in GNP	Change in total fixed domestic investment	Change in stock building*	Change in foreign balance*
U.S.	1970	−0.6†	−3.2‡	−0.6	0.3
	1971	2.7†	6.4‡	0	−0.3
	1972§	5.75†	10.75‡	0.25	−0.25
Canada	1970	3.3†	2.9	−1.4	2.6
	1971	5.4†	5.9	0.2	−1.2
	1972§	5.75†	6.0	1.0	−1.25
U.K.	1970	2.2‖	1.3	0	0
	1971	1.7‖	1.0	−0.4	−0.1
	1972§	3.25‖	4.5	0.5	−1.5
West Germany	1970	5.5†	11.5	−0.3	−1.5
	1971	2.8†	4.0	−1.4	−0.7
	1972‡	2.0†	−1.0	0	−0.25
France	1970	5.8‖	7.5	−0.7	1.5
	1971	5.1‖	5.1	−0.3	0.1
	1972‡	5.0‖	5.0	0.5	0
Italy	1970	5.0‖	2.5	1.0	−1.6
	1971	1.2‖	−5.3	−1.2	1.3
	1972‡	3.75‖	1.25	0.5	0.5
Japan	1970	10.2†	13.5	1.3	−0.2
	1971	6.1†	7.6	−2.7	1.8
	1972‡	6.5†	6.5	0	−0.25

*As percentage of GNP in the previous year.
†Gross national product at market prices.
‡Private fixed investment.
§All 1972 figures are estimates.
‖Gross domestic product at market prices.
Source: Organization for Economic Cooperation and Development, *Economic Outlook* (July 1972).

but a fair increase in the buildup of inventories. Foreign balance remained almost unchanged as compared with 1971.

In contrast, West Germany experienced an appreciable decline in spending on fixed assets, which was particularly marked in industry. This decline, following that of 1971, was the principal factor responsible for another slowing down in the rate of advance in total output. It was accompanied by a rise in spending on fixed assets by the public sector, which expanded after a sharp decline in the preceding year, the change reflecting the authorities' policy of trying to generate economic recovery. Partly because of the rise in the external value of the mark, agreed upon in the U.S. in December 1971, there was another reduction in net foreign balance, which, although still positive, showed that a larger part of domestically generated savings was used up at home.

In many ways the behaviour of investment and savings in Japan, another country with a large surplus on current account, resembled that of West Germany. In the wake of the restrictive policies adopted by the authorities in 1970 and 1971, total spending on fixed assets in 1972 showed another deceleration. The main factor responsible for this was a decline in outlays on productive assets by private industry sufficiently sharp to offset expansion in spending on housing and an almost unchanged rate of growth in purchases of fixed assets by the public sector. However, a shift in emphasis in official policies, associated with the upvaluation of the yen in December 1971, led to a reversal in spending on inventories and to a reduction in foreign balance.

In the U.S. in 1971, when domestic investment and economic recovery were getting under way, additional savings came from financial institutions at home and, above all, from overseas. While households made a net contribution to the requirements of nonfinancial enterprises and of the public sector, which increased because of additional investment outlays, it was in absolute and relative terms smaller than in 1970. This was mainly because of rising spending on housing, itself an important element of additional investment. The financial institutions, whose net savings rose by about 150%, contributed in relative terms a small proportion of the new requirements, with the bulk of savings needed coming from overseas in the form of a much greater deficit on current account.

In the U.K., which in 1971 experienced a marked slowing down in domestic investment and in economic growth, the requirements for total savings on the part of nonfinancial enterprises declined as did also those of financial institutions. Although the public sector became a net borrower, the volume of additional savings generated domestically was adequate to provide for all domestic requirements and to raise the amount transferred abroad.

The behaviour of savings in 1971 in West Germany, France, and Italy, all of which were then going through a period of slowing down in total output and domestic investment, resembled in some ways that of the U.K. In two of these countries, West Germany and Italy, the net financial savings of the household sector rose quite substantially and the increase in their holdings of financial assets in this sector exceeded by a comfortable margin the additions to financial liabilities.

(T. M. RYBCZYNSKI)

See also Money and Banking; Profits; Stock Exchanges.

Table II. Savings and Investment in Selected Industrial Countries in 1971

Country	House-holds	Enter-prises	Public sector	Financial institutions	Foreign sector	Total
U.S. (in $000,000,000)						
Gross saving	+186.1	+89.8	−26.7	−7.8	+2.8	+259.9*
Gross physical investment	−134.9	−118.0	—	−2.5	—	−259.9*
Capital transfers and adjustments	−4.7	−19.8	−4.1	+0.3	+10.8	—
Net financial savings	+46.5	−48.0	−30.8	+5.6	+13.6	—
Financial assets	−91.3	−23.4	−19.3	−149.6	−22.2	−318.9
Indebtedness	+44.8	+71.4	+50.1	+144.0	+8.6	+318.9
U.K. (in £000,000)						
Gross saving	+2,787	+2,767	+4,333	+372	−952	—
Gross physical investment	−1,393	−3,227	−4,596	−565		
Capital transfers and adjustments	+832	+150	−292	+213	−429	—
Net financial savings	+2,226	−310	−555	+20	−1,381	—
Financial assets	−4,797	−1,834	−4,060	−10,448	−3,026	−24,165
Indebtedness	+2,571	+2,144	+4,615	−10,428	+4,407	+24,165
West Germany (in DM. 000,000,000)						
Gross saving	+59.76	+93.68	+46.24	+8.68	+0.58	+208.94
Gross physical investment	—	−173.79	−31.30	−3.85	—	−208.94
Capital transfers and adjustments	−6.48	+19.79	−13.87	−6.84	+7.40	—
Net financial savings	+53.28	−60.32	+1.07	−2.01	+7.98	—
Financial assets	−59.56	−29.46	−15.90	−113.30	−19.93	−238.14
Indebtedness	+6.28	+89.78	+14.83	+115.32	+11.95	+238.14
Italy (in 000,000,000 lire)						
Gross saving	+9,152	+5,554	−1,461	+708	−1,203	+12,753†
Gross physical investment	—	−10,702	−1,795	−253	—	−12,750†
Capital transfers and adjustments	—	+955	−973	—	+18	—
Net financial savings	+9,152	−4,193	−4,229	+455	−1,185	—
Financial assets	−9,290	−3,684	−2,571	−17,285	−2,419	−35,033
Indebtedness	+138	+7,841	+6,800	+16,830	+3,604	+35,033
France (in Fr. 000,000,000)						
Gross saving	+104.48	+94.47	+18.84	+28.90	+1.76	+273.51
Gross physical investment	−69.07	−147.39	−21.47	−10.52		
Capital transfers and adjustments	+1.26	+8.55	−0.19	+2.63	−12.24	−273.51
Net financial savings	+36.66	−44.37	−2.83	+21.01	−10.47	—
Financial assets	−64.60	−31.81	−5.90	−133.81	−3.77	−239.89
Indebtedness	+27.94	+76.17	+8.72	+112.80	+14.24	+239.89

Note: For gross saving, gross physical investment, and capital transfers and adjustments, + means receipts and — means expenditure; for financial assets, — means spending on assets; for indebtedness, + means increase in indebtedness.

For the U.S., public sector includes federal, state, and local governments and financial institutions includes monetary authorities, commercial banks, other private financing institutions, and government-sponsored lending agencies; for the U.K., public sector includes central government, local authorities, and public corporations; for West Germany, enterprises includes housing and public sector includes social security funds; for Italy, public sector includes local authorities, social security funds, and autonomous government agencies.

*The total includes discrepancy of 1.5 in physical investment and −1.7 in adjustments.

†The total includes discrepancies pertaining to public sector and financial institutions of +137 for financial assets and −180 for financial liabilities.

Source: Organization for Economic Cooperation and Development, *Financial Statistics*, no. 5/1, 5/A and 5/B, 1972.

Schools: *see* Education

Scotland: *see* United Kingdom

Sculpture: *see* Art Exhibitions; Art Sales; Museums and Galleries

Securities: *see* Savings and Investment; Stock Exchanges

Seismology

Large nuclear test explosions have provided seismologists with unique opportunities to study the interior of the earth and the causative mechanisms of earthquakes. With uncertainties as to time and location removed, the behaviour of the earth, the seismic wave characteristics and path, and many other aspects of seismic activity can be measured with great accuracy. Explosions in the Aleutian Islands such as Longshot (1965), Milrow (1969), and Cannikin (1971) have been especially productive since they occurred in a highly seismic region that is also a classic island arc structure, typical of many seismic areas in the circum-Pacific belt.

Even though seven years had passed since Longshot, analysis of data resulting from it continued. Katsuyaki Abe of Japan revealed that Longshot produced evidence of lithospheric tearing beneath the Aleutian arc. His analysis of anomalies in seismic velocity suggests that when the arc was being formed an underthrusting lithospheric plate beneath it was torn by overthrusting lithospheric material, forming the atypical structure of Bowers Ridge which stretches northward, perpendicular to the arc. Similarly, a recent report on Milrow, comparing underwater sound signals from this one-megaton explosion on Amchitka Island and a 340-ton test explosion offshore, indicated that the smaller test shot produced higher values of peak pressure, higher frequency content, and longer duration of disturbance. This experiment provided important clues for distinguishing between earthquakes, underground explosions, and underwater explosions.

Cannikin provided far more exact and pertinent information than its predecessors, both because of its greater size and because of the extensive instrumentation used to measure it. While analysis of it would continue for several years, much significant information had already been obtained. The contention that explosions can be distinguished from earthquakes by the difference in the energy ratio between body waves (transmitted through the earth's interior) and surface waves was given dramatic support. For earthquakes, magnitudes derived independently from body-wave amplitudes and surface-wave amplitudes are very nearly equal, but for Cannikin the body-wave magnitude was 6.8 and the surface-wave magnitude was 5.7, or more than 100 times smaller. This indicates that a much larger proportion of the explosion energy is converted to body waves than is the case for natural earthquakes.

A study by E. P. Hasbrouck and J. H. Allen of the National Oceanic and Atmospheric Administration indicated magnetic detection of stress release in the tectonic block containing the shock, a stress increase across the White Alice fault, which passes within one kilometre of the shot point, and a stress pattern consistent with a displacement along the fault. The conclusion was based on records from 200 locations along the fault, which showed changes in the magnetic field to be oriented along the trace rather than radially from the shot point. E. R. Engdahl of the Cooperative Institute for Research in Environmental Sciences in Boulder, Colo., found that Cannikin did not interfere with the natural earthquake-causing processes. There was continuous aftershock activity until the collapse of the explosion-generated cavity 38 hours later, but it then diminished abruptly. This is typical of previous explosion sequences. Aftershock activity is confined to the shot point area and does not represent a change in natural seismicity.

HUGUES VASSAL—GAMMA

A bewildered child sits in the rubble of her home after an earthquake that killed more than 4,000 persons in southern Fars Province in Iran. The quake struck in April 1972.

The San Fernando, Calif., earthquake of Feb. 9, 1971, was recorded on over 200 accelerographs of the southern California strong motion network, making it the most completely recorded earthquake in U.S. history. All aspects of this spectacular shock were still under intensive study. Although the shock was of moderate size (magnitude 6.6 on the Richter scale), its effects on structures were so startling that major revisions in planning and engineering practices were being considered. The accelerogram recorded at Pacoima Dam was especially significant, since it showed peak accelerations and velocities more than twice those produced by the previous "standard" earthquake of 1940. Since relatively little damage occurred at the site of the instrument, a reevaluation of the significance of peak accelerations was necessary. It was clear that duration of shaking is an important factor in causing damage and must be considered, along with peak acceleration (the previously used standard criterion), in determining shock severity.

For some time it had been possible to obtain amplifications of 500,000 or more in recording body waves, but until recently the best surface-wave amplification rarely exceeded 7,000. In 1972, 11 of the stations in the U.S. government's worldwide network of standard seismograph stations (WWNSS) were being equipped with ultra-long-period, high-gain seismographs, developed by the Lamont-Doherty Geological Observatory of Columbia University, that would permit seismic surface waves with periods of 20–100 seconds to be amplified several hundred thousand times. This would have a profound effect on the study of several aspects of seismology, including detection of seisms in the lower magnitude ranges, determination of earthquake magnitude and of earthquake source mechanisms and the extent and behaviour of fault systems.

Most of the seismograph stations installed in Antarctica as part of the International Geophysical year (1957–59) were subsequently abandoned or were functioning with very limited resources. There was new hope for future operations, however, following development of the unmanned geophysical observatory (UGO), an automatic station that collects data from a variety of passive sensors and relays them to the U.S. via commercial satellite. The first UGO was installed at McMurdo and operated continuously from Jan. 4, 1972. This station did not have seismographs, but they were included in plans for future installations. (RUTLAGE J. BRAZEE)

See also Disasters.

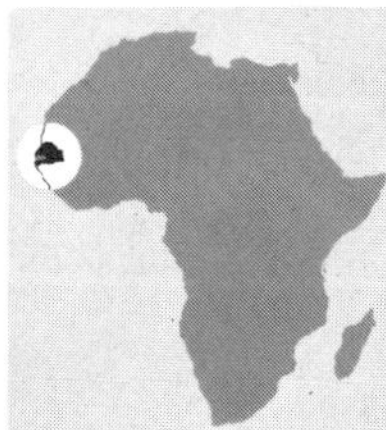

Senegal

A republic of northwestern Africa, Senegal is bounded by Mauritania, Mali, Guinea, and Portuguese Guinea, and by the Atlantic Ocean. The independent nation of The Gambia forms an enclave within the country. Area: 78,684 sq.mi. (203,793 sq.km.). Pop. (1971 est.): 4,022,000. Cap. and largest city: Dakar (pop., 1970 est., 580,000). Language: French (official); Wolof; Serer; other tribal dialects. Religion: Muslim 90%; Christian 6%. President in 1972, Léopold Sédar Senghor; premier, Abdou Diouf.

In April 1972 President Senghor commuted the life sentence imposed upon former premier Mamadou Dia for plotting against the security of the state to 20 years in prison. Two government reshuffles took place during the year, the first in June and the second in July. There was also some reorganization of top posts in the armed forces, largely occasioned by the impending retirement of Gen. Jean-Alfred Diallo, who had been in overall command of the armed forces.

Senghor continued to pursue the intense diplomatic activity that had characterized his foreign policy for several years. In January both Pres. Mokhtar Ould Daddah of Mauritania and Gunnar Jarring, UN mediator in the Middle East, were received in Dakar, followed in February by Walter Eytan of the Israeli Foreign Office and Pres. Albert Bernard Bongo of Gabon.

In May President Senghor visited Liberia, where a spectacular reconciliation took place between himself and Pres. Sékou Touré of Guinea. This brought a respite from the mounting tension that had characterized relations between the two countries since November 1970. Meanwhile, Senghor's appointment as chairman of the Common Organization of Africa, Malagasy, and Mauritius (OCAM) in April provided increased opportunities for him to exercise his talents as a mediator.

During the year border incidents increased the tension between Senegal and neighbouring Portuguese Guinea. In May six Senegalese lost their lives in an incident in Casamance, and in October the Senegalese authorities denounced an incursion into their territory by Portuguese armoured vehicles.

(PHILIPPE DECRAENE)

SENEGAL

Education. (1968–69) Primary, pupils 255,493, teachers 5,608; secondary, pupils 42,228, teachers 1,568; vocational (1967–68), pupils 10,608, teachers 354; teacher training, students (1966–67) 821, teachers (1965–66) 80; higher (University of Dakar; 1969–70), students 3,559.

Finance and Trade. Monetary unit: CFA franc, with (Sept. 18, 1972) a parity of CFA Fr. 50 to the French franc (CFA Fr. 255.79 = U.S. $1; free rate of CFA Fr. 612.37 = £1 sterling). Budget (1971–72 est.) balanced at CFA Fr. 57,040,000,000. Foreign trade (1971): imports CFA Fr. 60,560,000,000; exports CFA Fr. 34,710,000,000. Import sources: France 47%; U.S. 6%; West Germany 6%; Thailand 5%; Ivory Coast 5%. Export destinations: France 52%; Ivory Coast 7%; Mauritania 6%. Main exports: peanut oil 21%; phosphates 12%; peanut oil cake 9%; fish and products 8%; peanuts 5%.

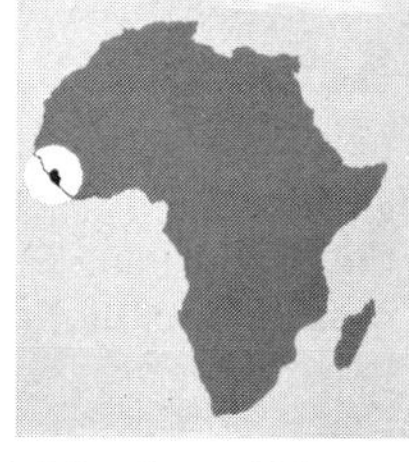

Sierra Leone

A republic within the Commonwealth of Nations, Sierra Leone is a West African nation located between Guinea and Liberia. Area: 27,699 sq.mi. (71,740 sq.km.). Pop. (1972 est.): 2,626,800, including (1963) Mende and Temne tribes 60.7%; other tribes 38.9%; non-African 0.4%. Cap. and largest city: Freetown (pop., 1972 est., 195,800). Language: English (official); tribal dialects. Religion: animist 66%; Muslim 28%; Christian 6%. President in 1972, Siaka Stevens; prime minister, Sorie Ibrahim Koroma.

Although the 1970 state of emergency remained in effect, some degree of peace and stability returned in 1972. District councils, suspended in April because of alleged misappropriation of funds, were replaced as administrative agencies by the central government and the chiefs. Although elections were due in 1973, opposition remained virtually impossible. The officially recognized Sierra Leone People's Party was small and cautious, while the United Democratic Party was banned and its leaders were jailed. The many petitions favouring a one-party state submitted by the ruling All People's Congress Party and 130 paramount chiefs lent some credence to the suspicion of stage management.

Close relations with Guinea remained central to foreign policy, and friendly gestures were made in the direction of the U.S.S.R. and China. Sierra Leone had recognized China in 1971. Arms were provided by China, and motor patrol boats were promised for Sierra Leone's territorial waters, newly extended to 200 mi.

Economic life continued to be dominated by wasting diamond assets (with wastage hastened by increased illicit mining). In February the third largest diamond in the world was found. The stone, weighing 968.8 carats and valued at more than $10 million, was acquired by a New York diamond merchant. The 1971 trade balance showed a 10 million leone deficit as the value of agricultural exports declined. Negotiations for a share in Swiss-controlled bauxite developments were begun, but U.S. interests in rutile

SIERRA LEONE

Education. (1969–70) Primary, pupils 154,848, teachers 5,011; secondary, pupils 29,058, teachers 1,364; vocational (1968–69), pupils 1,732, teachers 97; teacher training, students 879, teachers 129; higher, students 1,119; teaching staff 202.

Finance and Trade. Monetary unit: leone, with (Sept. 18, 1972) a free rate of 0.82 leone to U.S. $1 (par value of 2 leones = £1 sterling). Budget (1970–71 est.): revenue 51 million leones; expenditure 46.3 million leones. Foreign trade (1971): imports 94,020,000 leones; exports 83,130,000 leones. Import sources: U.K. 29%; Japan 10%; U.S. 7%; West Germany 6%; Nigeria 6%; France 5%; Netherlands 5%. Export destinations: U.K. 62%; Netherlands 8%; Japan 6%; U.S. 6%; West Germany 5%. Main exports: diamonds 59%; iron ore 13%; palm kernels 7%.

Agriculture. Production (in 000; metric tons; 1971; 1970 in parentheses): rice *c.* 450 (*c.* 425); cassava (1970) *c.* 65, (1969) *c.* 65; palm kernels *c.* 55 (*c.* 59); palm oil *c.* 60 (*c.* 53); coffee *c.* 6 (*c.* 7.5). Livestock (in 000; 1970–71): cattle *c.* 250; sheep *c.* 58; goats *c.* 158; chickens *c.* 3,000.

Industry. Production (in 000; metric tons; 1970): iron ore (metal content) 1,355; bauxite 449; diamonds (exports; metric carats) 1,955; electricity (kw-hr.) 197,000.

remained untouched. Tourism showed signs of expansion, with the Commonwealth Development Corporation providing a first-class hotel and water supplies. In June the Bank of Sierra Leone Working Party Report severely condemned Sierra Leone business operatives for alleged inefficiency and corruption.

(MOLLY MORTIMER)

Singapore

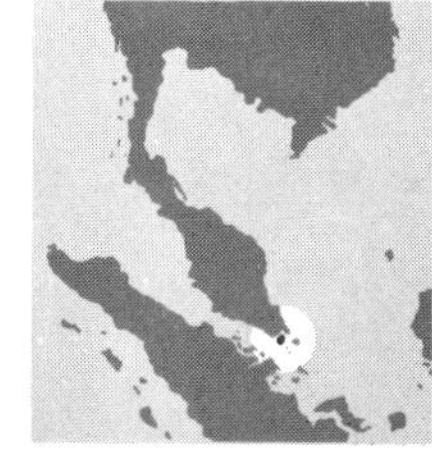

Singapore, a republic within the Commonwealth of Nations, occupies a group of islands, the largest of which is Singapore, at the southern extremity of the Malay Peninsula. Area: 226 sq.mi. (584 sq.km.). Pop. (1971 est.): 2,129,300, including 76% Chinese, 15% Malays, and 7% Indians. Language: official languages are English, Malay, Mandarin Chinese, and Tamil. Religion: Malays are Muslim; Chinese, mainly Buddhist; Indians, mainly Hindu. President in 1972, Benjamin Henry Sheares; prime minister, Lee Kuan Yew.

The People's Action Party (PAP) of Prime Minister Lee Kuan Yew, which had been in power since 1959 and unopposed since 1965, dissolved Parliament in August 1972 and sought a new five-year mandate eight months before the expiration of its term. In the subsequent general elections held in September it won all 65 seats, its share of the vote having risen from 46.9% in 1963 to almost 70% in 1972. After the elections, the government announced constitutional amendments to prevent any surrender of Singapore's sovereignty through incorporation into or federation with another country unless approved by two-thirds of the population in a referendum. The contemplated legislation would not, however, prevent the nation from entering into arrangements for mutual security and economic cooperation with other countries in the region or outside it.

The government also announced measures to penalize couples for having more than two children by increasing hospital charges for deliveries after the second child, reducing income tax relief from the existing five to the first three children, and reducing paid maternity leave from three to two confinements. These measures were to come into force in August 1973.

SINGAPORE

Education. (1969–70) Primary, pupils 366,881, teachers 12,213; secondary, pupils 131,475, teachers 5,974; vocational, pupils 20,635, teachers 1,221; higher (including 2 universities), students 12,659, teaching staff 1,074.

Finance and Trade. Monetary unit: Singapore dollar, with (Sept. 18, 1972) a par value of Sing$2.82 to U.S. $1 (free rate of Sing$6.78 = £1 sterling). Budget (1971–72 est.): revenue Sing$1,307,000,000; expenditure Sing$1,306,800,000. Foreign trade (1971): imports Sing$3,656,500,000; exports Sing$5,371,200,000. Import sources: Japan 20%; Malaysia 17%; U.S. 13%; U.K. 7%; China 5%; Kuwait 5%. Export destinations: Malaysia 23%; U.S. 12%; South Vietnam 7%; Japan 7%. Main exports: petroleum and products 21%; rubber 18%; machinery 10%.

Transport and Communications. Roads (1971) 1,938 km. Motor vehicles in use (1970): passenger 148,300; commercial 34,100. Railways (1970) 45 km. Railway and air traffic: *see* MALAYSIA. Shipping (1971): merchant vessels 100 gross tons and over 185; gross tonnage 581,777. Shipping traffic (1971): goods loaded 19,578,000 metric tons; unloaded 29,330,000 metric tons. Telephones (Dec. 1970) 161,000. Radio licenses (Dec. 1970) 101,000. Television licenses (Dec. 1970) 157,000.

JAMES P. STERBA—THE NEW YORK TIMES

Skyscrapers abuilding loom over Singapore's famous waterfront. Construction was booming in Singapore more than anywhere else in Southeast Asia.

Singapore had a birth rate of 22.8 per thousand in 1971 and the aim was to reduce this to 18.4 by 1975 and 14.8 by 1980.

Although Singapore had yet to absorb the full impact of the British military withdrawal, 1972 proved another happy milestone in its history. Instead of massive unemployment, economic hardship, and gloom following the withdrawal, there was full employment, economic buoyancy, and the prospect of rapid industrial expansion. The republic's concern, according to the prime minister, was no longer to create more jobs but to upgrade the skills of its workers, to increase productivity, and to generate more revenue. Every sector of the economy recorded notable progress in 1971. Singapore's gross domestic product grew by 14.1%—just 1% short of the target. The country's overseas assets backing its currency had multiplied almost 13 times in the 13 years of PAP government —from Sing$336.2 million in 1959 to Sing$4,230,000,000 in June 1972. The per capita gross national product grew from Sing$2,960 in 1970 to Sing$3,317 in 1971, the second highest in Asia after Japan. Barring economic upsets, Singapore hoped to achieve an annual 10% growth rate, which would in turn allow for a 5% annual wage increase.

(MAHINDER SINGH RANDHAVA)

Skiing

Holiday recreational skiing remained popular during 1972, with expanded facilities at many winter resorts, particularly in North America and the European Alps. Spain, although not so readily linked in people's minds with snow, developed a potential in the Pyrenees and in the mountains around Madrid and Granada. Notable advances were made in Alaska at Mt. Alyeska, in Australia at Thredbo, New South Wales, in Czechoslovakia at Tatranská Lomnica, in Japan at Sapporo, and in Yugoslavia at Kranjska Gora, Slovenia. Skiing in Scotland was enhanced by international recognition of a slalom course near Aviemore.

Gaining increased popularity for beginners was instruction on a graduated series of short skis. The still-expanding networks of mechanical ascent brought more resorts within reach of higher snow, thus appreciably lengthening the season. Ski bobbing (skiing while seated on a low, bikelike sled) was promoted

Sikkim: *see* Dependent States

Silk: *see* Industrial Review

Silver *see* Mining

Skating: *see* Hockey; Ice Skating; Sporting Record

LONDON DAILY EXPRESS/ PICTORIAL PARADE

Some of the 8,500 competitors are an incredible sight at the start of the 49th Vasa race in Sweden. The race, which follows the route taken by King Gustavus Vasa of Sweden in his flight from the Danes in 1519, was won by Swedish skier Lars-Arne Bolling.

at more winter sports centres, realizing a greater following both as a recreation and as a racing sport. General public interest in skiing was intensified by the wider publicity given to World Cup and Olympic events.

The International Ski Federation (FIS) and the International Olympic Committee (IOC) never completely resolved their differences concerning eligibility and amateur status. The last-minute Olympic exclusion of the Austrian Alpine racer Karl Schranz by a 28–14 vote of IOC members proved an act of brinkmanship threatening to disrupt all championship competition. A request from the FIS to study the IOC evidence was rejected, and, although the FIS made it clear that Schranz was still eligible for subsequent events under its jurisdiction, the Austrian champion decided to retire.

The world championship titles in both Alpine and Nordic disciplines were decided concurrently with those of the Winter Olympic Games. (*See* SPORTING RECORD: *Special Report.*)

Alpine Racing. The prestige of the annual World Alpine Ski Cup competition, in its sixth season, became more significant than the 22nd Alpine World Ski Championships, the reason being that the latter depended on the outcome of one meeting, and the final World Cup results reflected much longer consistency of form. In any case, no one could dispute who were the outstanding Alpine racers of the year: Gustavo Thoeni of Italy and Annemarie Proell of Austria won the men's and women's overall world championship titles, and both also retained their World Cup honours won in 1971.

In the world championship Alpine combination results, Thoeni's runner-up was Walter Tresch of Switzerland, with the Canadian Jim Hunter third. Miss Proell owed her success to the fact that Marie-Thérèse Nadig, the Swiss schoolgirl who won both the downhill and giant slalom, did not finish in the slalom and thus failed to qualify. Florence Steurer of France placed second, followed by the Norwegian Thorild Foerland.

The World Cup races, maintaining continuity of interest throughout a four-month series, were based on each racer's highest score in 15 of 42 selected top international events, 21 each for men and women, at nine European and three North American sites, ending at Pra-Loup, France, on March 19. Thoeni led in the slalom and giant slalom to offset his relative weakness in the downhill. Henri Duvillard (France) and Edmund Bruggmann (Switz.) finished overall second and third, respectively. The men's issue was not settled until the final race, but Miss Proell's success was ensured a month earlier at Banff, Alta., when she gained an unassailable lead with seven races still to go. The runner-up, Françoise Macchi of France, had been a serious rival until she badly injured a knee during Olympic training at Sapporo. Another French girl, Britt Lafforgue, finished third and was top scorer in the slalom, Miss Proell having led comfortably in the giant slalom and downhill. With an equal number of races counting in all three events, the contests provided a fair test of all-around ability. France won the Nations' Cup, awarded for the highest aggregate points from the 42 races on the World Cup calendar. Two-thirds of the French total was scored by women racers. Austria finished second and Switzerland third.

The second annual Canadian-American Ski Trophy Alpine competition, spread over 12 sites with rules similar to those of the World Cup, resulted in victories for Don Rowles and Cheryl Bechdolt, both of the U.S.

Lasse Hamre of Norway won the Lange Cup, the season's major professional Alpine event, at Vail, Colo., held March 31–April 2, but the U.S. racer Spider Sabich was again the season's most successful professional, netting a record $50,650 in prize money in nine meetings. All professional competition took place in North America, since efforts to promote events elsewhere had not succeeded.

Nordic Events. Cross-country skiing, traditionally a Scandinavian recreation, attracted increased participation during the year. More cross-country courses were provided for holiday skiers in Switzerland and the U.S., with special cross-country ski packs more readily available. Expansion of the more specialized sport of ski jumping was stressed by FIS recognition of 138 jumping hills in 18 countries as suitably sanctioned for competitions.

The 29th world championships in Nordic events (cross-country and jumping) were determined concurrently with the Olympic results at Sapporo, and the widening appeal of ski jumping throughout the world was further underlined by the first Japanese and Polish victories. Switzerland was the only country whose skiers at Sapporo won world championship medals in jumping and cross-country events as well as in both men's and women's Alpine races, a unique demonstration of national versatility. The next world championships, in 1974, were allocated to Falun, Swed., for the Nordic events and St. Moritz, Switz., for the Alpine races.

The first world championship in ski flying, a technique differing from conventional ski jumping by emphasis on distance rather than style, was held on a giant 120-m. hill at Planica, Yugos., on March 24–26. Walter Steiner of Switzerland made jumps of 508 ft. and 518 ft. for a comfortable victory over the East German Heinz Wossipivo, with Jiri Raska of Czechoslovakia finishing third. (HOWARD BASS)

Soccer: *see* Football

Social Services

With at least some form of social security scheme operating in all but the least developed countries, the tendency in 1972 was to make existing plans more advantageous to the recipients. Continual increases in the cost of living posed a special problem, and there was a growing trend, except in the U.K., to meet it by an escalating process rather than by the enactment of new legislation from year to year. The International Labour Conference called on the International Labour Office to intensify its efforts to extend social security protection, especially to vulnerable groups such as rural and migrant workers. Total costs necessarily increased. In Canada, for example, expenditure by all levels of government on health and social welfare rose from $3,898,500 in the year ended March 31, 1963, to an estimated $8,547,500 in the year ended March 31, 1970.

The 16th International Conference on Social Welfare, entitled "Developing Social Policy in Conditions of Rapid Change," was held at The Hague, Neth. Nearly 3,000 representatives from all parts of the world attended. Regional reports prepared for the conference showed that interest in social planning was increasing throughout Europe, but that there was no adequate data base for most decision-making in social policy areas.

United Kingdom. British national insurance pensions were payable anywhere in the world, but increases in pensions awarded after a pensioner had left the U.K. or after a person living abroad had qualified were paid only where there was a reciprocal agreement with the other country or territory involved. Reciprocal agreements covering payment of pension increases had been negotiated with Austria, Belgium, Bermuda, Cyprus, France, West Germany, Guernsey, the Isle of Man, Ireland, Israel, Italy, Jersey, Luxembourg, Malta, the Netherlands, Northern Ireland, Switzerland, Turkey, the U.S., and Yugoslavia. Negotiations with Japan were in progress.

The National Insurance Act, 1972, established the first annual upgrading of retirement pensions and other benefits, a matter previously dealt with at irregular intervals, usually of about two years. The act also provided for increases in flat-rate benefits, and supplementary benefits (for which the only qualification was need) were raised by regulations of the Supplementary Benefits Commission. The standard rate for a single person was increased by 12½%, from £6 to £6.75. The benefit paid to a wife or adult dependent and to a married woman on her husband's insurance was increased from £3.70 to £4.15, so that the benefit for a married couple rose from £9.70 to £10.90. Pensioners over 80 continued to receive the 25 pence age addition. The rates of benefit for dependent children, supplementary benefits, and attendance allowances were increased proportionately. The old persons' pension, payable to those who were too old to enter the national insurance scheme in 1948 or to people who had reached the age of 80 and for some reason did not qualify for retirement pensions, was also raised by 12½%, from £3.60 to £4.05 a week. In the six months since the last increase, in September 1971, the general retail price index had risen by 2.8% and the special index for pensioners by 3.8%. The government believed that the 12½% increase in pension rates and benefits, which became payable in October, would be sufficient to meet further price rises. Contribution rates were raised to cover the cost of the increased benefits, but the 7.5 million people earning less than £18 a week were not affected.

There was criticism in the House of Commons over the policy of granting supplementary allowances to the families of men on strike. In Great Britain benefit was payable to families but not to the strikers themselves. In West Germany and Sweden strike pay was usually sufficient to support the striker and his family. Public relief could be provided by the local authorities as a last resort and might be repayable. In the Netherlands and Belgium there was no legal provision removing strikers from eligibility for locally administered relief, but in practice the granting of assistance to strikers was not encouraged. In France and Italy the brevity of most strikes meant that there was usually no question of strikers being subsidized from public funds. Where this was necessary, France generally restricted relief to a continuation of family and lodging allowances.

The Supplementary Benefits Commission took special action to eliminate possible abuses caused by persons who were working while drawing supplementary benefit, undisclosed cohabitation, fictitious desertion, or false statements by a wife that her husband had left her. Some 9,000 such cases were investigated during the six months ended March 31, 1972. Of these, about 25% in Scotland and about 45% in England and Wales involved fraud. The resultant gross saving totaled more than £2 million in 1971, of which about £887,000 related to cohabitation abuses.

On average, the number of benefits and allowances (including supplementary benefits) being paid in any one week was about 17 million. At the end of 1971 retirement pensions (including old-age pensions) numbered 7,647,000 (1970, 7,525,000) and supplementary benefits nearly 3 million, slightly more than in 1970. There were about 25 million persons within the scope of the contribution provisions of the national insurance scheme, of whom nearly 15 million were employed men and over 8 million were employed women. Of these, about 4.75 million men and more than one million women who were either self-employed or nonemployed paid graduated contributions at reduced rates. Of those receiving supplementary pensions and allowances, 66% were old people. Of supplementary pensioners without retirement pensions, 67.8% had received benefits for more than five years. So had 50.6% of sick persons below pension age who were not eligible for national insurance benefit; such persons were not required to register for employment. Of supplementary benefits being paid, 14.6% included an exceptional circumstances addition ranging from a few pence to £3 or more.

Part of the reason elderly Italian Americans like 86-year-old Mrs. Maria Ferrara get little public help is their reluctance, out of their own sense of pride, to accept "charity." Picture was taken in her small apartment during visit from the Rev. Silvano Tomasi of the Center for Migration Studies on Staten Island in New York. Jewish and Italian poor have been ignored by New York's antipoverty program, it was charged.

NEAL BOENZI—THE NEW YORK TIMES

With the agreement of the Department of Employment, arrangements were made for certain unemployed claimants over 55 (50 for women), who were required to register for work, to report to the employment exchange quarterly instead of weekly, and to receive their supplementary benefit by order book instead of by weekly payments from the exchange.

(JOHN MOSS)

United States. On Sept. 1, 1972, Social Security benefits (Federal Old Age, Survivors, and Disability Insurance) rose 20% across the board, as a result of legislation passed in June. This meant an increase of $336 a year for the average retired worker and $564 for the average retired couple. The same bill provided for automatic increases in Social Security benefits whenever the cost of living rose more than 3% in a calendar year, beginning with 1975.

Just before it adjourned in October, Congress passed a $5.4 billion Social Security and welfare bill that contained 144 additional changes in Social Security, welfare, and health benefits. Conspicuously missing from the measure, however, was the major overhaul of the welfare system that Pres. Richard Nixon had called "White House Priority Number One" in 1971.

The main provisions of the law included the following: benefits for 3.8 million widows and dependent widowers would rise from 82.5% of the amount received by the deceased spouse to 100%, starting Jan. 1, 1973. As of the same date, a Social Security retiree under 72 would be allowed to earn $2,100 a year instead of $1,680 and still receive full pension benefits; benefits would be reduced $1 for each $2 earned over $2,100. Every person who had worked in a job covered by Social Security for at least 30 years would receive minimum benefits of $170 a month (or $255 for a couple), an increase from $84.50 effective Jan. 1, 1973. Starting Jan. 1, 1974, Social Security benefits would be increased 1% for each year a person delayed his retirement after age 65. Starting July 1, 1973, Medicare would be offered to about 1.7 million disabled Social Security beneficiaries, regardless of age, after they had been on disability for 24 months, and to 10,000 persons suffering from chronic kidney disease. Medicare beneficiaries would be allowed to enroll in a health maintenance organization providing

Social Security Programs, by Country, 1972*

Type of program available

Country	Old age, invalidity, survivors	Health, sickness, maternity	Work injury	Unemployment	Family allowances
Afghanistan			X		
Albania	X	X	X		X
Algeria	X	X	X		X
Argentina	X	X	X		X
Australia	X	X	X	X	X
Austria	X	X	X	X	X
Barbados	X	X	X		
Belgium	X	X	X	X	X
Bolivia	X	X	X		X
Botswana			X		
Brazil	X	X	X	X	X
Bulgaria	X	X	X	X	X
Burma		X	X		
Burundi	X		X		
Cambodia			X		X
Cameroon	X	X	X		X
Canada	X	X	X	X	X
Central African Rep.	X	X	X		X
Chad		X	X		X
Chile	X	X	X	X	X
China	X	X	X		
Colombia	X	X	X		X
Congo	X	X	X		X
Costa Rica	X	X	X		
Cuba	X	X	X		
Cyprus	X	X	X	X	
Czechoslovakia	X	X	X		X
Dahomey	X	X	X		X
Denmark	X	X	X	X	X
Dominican Rep.	X	X	X		
Ecuador	X	X	X	X	
Egypt	X	X	X	X	
El Salvador	X	X	X		
Ethiopia			X		
Finland	X	X	X	X	X
France	X	X	X	X	X
Gabon	X		X		X
Gambia, The			X		
Germany, East	X	X	X	X	X
Germany, West	X	X	X	X	X
Ghana	X	X	X	X	
Greece	X	X	X	X	X
Guatemala	X	X	X		
Guinea	X	X	X		X
Guyana	X	X	X		
Haiti	X	X	X		
Honduras	X	X	X		
Hungary	X	X	X	X	X
Iceland	X	X	X	X	X
India	X	X	X		
Indonesia		X	X		
Iran	X	X	X		X
Iraq	X	X	X		
Ireland	X	X	X	X	X
Israel	X	X	X	X	X
Italy	X	X	X	X	X
Ivory Coast	X	X	X		X
Jamaica	X		X		
Japan	X	X	X	X	
Jordan		X	X		
Kenya	X	X	X		
Korea, South			X		
Laos			X		
Lebanon	X	X	X		X
Liberia			X		
Libya	X	X	X		
Luxembourg	X	X	X	X	X
Malagasy Rep.	X	X	X		X
Malawi			X		
Malaysia	X	X	X		
Mali	X	X	X		X
Malta	X	X	X	X	
Mauritania	X	X	X		X
Mauritius	X		X		X
Mexico	X	X	X		
Morocco	X	X	X		X
Nauru	X	X	X		X
Netherlands	X	X	X	X	X
New Zealand	X	X	X	X	X
Nicaragua	X	X	X		
Niger	X	X	X		X
Nigeria	X	X	X		
Norway	X	X	X	X	X
Pakistan		X	X		
Panama	X	X	X		
Paraguay	X	X	X		
Peru	X	X	X		
Philippines	X	X	X		
Poland	X	X	X		X
Portugal	X	X	X		X
Romania	X	X	X		X
Rwanda	X		X		
Saudi Arabia	X		X		
Senegal		X	X		X
Sierra Leone			X		
Singapore	X	X	X		
Somalia			X		
South Africa	X		X	X	X
Spain	X	X	X	X	X
Sri Lanka (Ceylon)	X	X	X		
Sudan			X		
Swaziland			X		
Sweden	X	X	X	X	X
Switzerland	X	X	X	X	X
Syria	X		X		
Taiwan	X	X	X		
Tanzania	X	X	X		
Thailand			X		
Togo	X	X	X		X
Trinidad and Tobago	X		X		
Tunisia	X	X	X		X
Turkey	X	X	X		
Uganda	X		X		
U.S.S.R.	X	X	X		X
United Kingdom	X	X	X	X	X
United States	X	X	X	X	
Upper Volta	X	X	X		X
Uruguay	X	X	X	X	X
Venezuela	X	X	X		
Vietnam, North	X	X	X		X
Vietnam, South		X	X		X
Western Samoa			X		
Yugoslavia	X	X	X	X	X
Zaire	X		X		X
Zambia	X		X		

*Data as of mid-1972.

Source: U.S. Department of Health, Education, and Welfare, Social Security Administration, Office of Research and Statistics, *Social Security Programs Throughout the World.*

comprehensive prepaid health care, and the government would pay the premium if the plans provided federally approved services. Chiropractor care would be included under Medicare. The federal-state program of aid to the aged, blind, and disabled would be replaced on Jan. 1, 1974, with a new program financed and administered entirely by the federal government. It would guarantee a minimum of $130 a month for aged, blind, and disabled individuals who had no outside income ($195 a month for couples).

The annual expenditure for Social Security was expected to increase from $43.2 billion in 1972 to $59 billion in 1975. To meet the cost, Congress also raised payroll taxes. The maximum tax in 1973 would be $631.80 each for employees and employers, based on a rate of 5.85% on the first $10,800 of salary. In 1974 it would go up to $702, based on 5.85% on the first $12,000. In 1972 the rate was 5.2% on the first $9,000, or a maximum of $468 each for employees and employers.

While making these important changes, Congress could not reach agreement on reforming the basic family welfare program, Aid to Families with Dependent Children (AFDC). In 1971 the House had passed a reform measure that included President Nixon's Family Assistance Plan, guaranteeing an annual payment of $2,400 for a family of four with no outside income. In the Senate one faction backed the administration plan, a second, led by Sen. Abraham A. Ribicoff (Dem., Conn.), favoured a more liberal program, while a third supported a more conservative bill containing a "workfare" provision. None of the approaches could muster a majority.

Meanwhile, welfare rolls continued to grow. The Department of Health, Education, and Welfare (HEW) reported that 15,057,000 persons were receiving public assistance payments on June 30, 1972, representing an increase of 719,000 or 5% over the previous year. Expenditures for money payments and medical assistance under federally aided programs were up 17.4% to $18,242,169,053. However, both percentage rises were lower than those recorded a year earlier. In June 1972, 10,919,000 persons, including 7,889,000 children, received money payments under AFDC. The number of recipients in the other welfare categories were: old-age assistance 2,025,000; aid to the permanently and totally disabled 1,136,000; blind 81,000; and general assistance (no federal funds) 896,000. According to a government-sponsored study cited by Senator Ribicoff, less than 1% of persons on welfare were able-bodied, unemployed adult males.

The administration announced in December that, effective Jan. 1, 1973, states whose welfare management systems were judged inadequate would be penalized by losing some of their federal funds. The loss to the states in fiscal 1974 was expected to be $465 million, or 8.3% of the federal share of AFDC.

A two-year extension of the Office of Economic Opportunity (OEO) antipoverty programs was authorized, with funding at $2,360,000,000 in fiscal 1973 and $2,390,000,000 in fiscal 1974. The extension provided that handicapped children were to receive at least 10% of the enrollment opportunities in the Head Start program for preschoolers and that children from families with annual incomes under $4,320 could take part in Head Start at no charge. Despite some opposition, the legal services program would be kept within OEO. Another provision established consumer action and education programs for low-income persons.

Congress overrode a presidential veto to raise pensions for more than 900,000 retired railroad workers to match the boost in Social Security benefits. Child nutrition programs were expanded and strengthened. The basic federal reimbursement rate was increased from 6 to 8 cents for every school lunch served, and more liberal eligibility guidelines were set, under which all children below the federal poverty level would receive free lunches. The nonschool food program and school breakfast program were extended for three years. Congress imposed a $2.5 billion annual ceiling on matching grants to states for social services under a public-assistance program. The action was taken after several states discovered an obscure provision of the 1967 amendments to the Social Security law authorizing $3 of federal money for each $1 that states and local governments spent on such services as child care and family planning and counseling. State requests for funds had leaped from $370 million in fiscal 1969 to nearly $5 billion in fiscal 1972.

The Older Americans Act of 1965 was amended to provide grants to the states to establish nutrition programs for low-income elderly. However, President Nixon vetoed another set of amendments to the 1965 Act authorizing $2.2 billion over three years for a variety of social service programs and a measure that would have established a National Institute on Aging.

The Supreme Court upheld a Texas law that paid families with dependent children 75% of their estimated need while giving aged and disabled welfare recipients 95 to 100%. In another decision, the court declared that an illegitimate child has as much right to Social Security benefits earned by his father as does a legitimate child. California began a test of its controversial "work-or-else" welfare program, under which able-bodied welfare recipients who could not be placed in permanent jobs or job training had to work for a government or nonprofit agency for up to 80 hours a month to be eligible for aid. A similar program in New York was halted by a court restraining order.

The National Commission on State Workmen's Compensation Laws, set up by Congress, issued a report calling for massive reforms. It said that, in most states, most payments by employers and insurance plans for work-related injuries, disabilities, and deaths were insufficient and unfairly distributed. The report did not suggest a federal take-over of the program, but urged states to move quickly to broaden coverage, liberalize benefits, and improve medical and rehabilitation service. (DAVID M. MAZIE)

Canada. Under the Canada Pension Plan, the maximum pensionable earnings used to calculate retirement benefit were originally $5,000 a year. By 1971 this figure had risen to $5,400, and during 1972–75 it would be adjusted in line with changes in the pension index, which was based on the consumer price index. Beginning in 1976 it would also be adjusted to reflect changes in average wage and salary levels. From 1970, retirement pensions became payable to contributors who were 65 years of age or over provided that, if under 70, they had retired from regular employment. They would become payable at the full rate from January 1976. This would be 25% of contributors' pensionable earnings, averaged since January 1966 or from age 18, whichever was later.

The Federal Medical Care Insurance Programme (Medicare), under which costs were shared by the federal government and the provinces, was extended to include all the provinces. Originally the Medical Care Insurance Commission had paid for approved services on the basis of 85% of the fees listed in the

KEYSTONE

Mrs. Florence Bushby, 96 years old and an original member of the Orpington Nurses and Citizens Association, cheerfully pickets in favour of a new hospital for Orpington, which is in Kent, Eng.

physicians' fee schedule. This was changed to 100% for most office and home visits.

The old-age security pension and the Guaranteed Income Supplement programs were amended to provide that the flat-rate pension of $80 per month, established in 1971, should be increased as of January 1972 to reflect the full increase in the consumer price index. The monthly old-age pension thus became $82.88, and beginning in 1973 it would be increased from April 1 of each year. The provision for full escalation equivalent to the increase in the consumer price index also applied to the guaranteed income supplement. In 1972 the maximum monthly amount guaranteed became $66.12 to a single pensioner and $59.62 to each spouse for married couples who were both pensioners.

Oceania. The August 1972 Australian budget provided for increases in pensions. If the necessary legislation was passed, pensions for single people and widows would increase by about 10%. A promise was given that, within three years, pensioners earning an income above their pensions would be eligible for full pension without any means test.

In New Zealand total expenditure on social security cash benefits, including supplementary assistance, increased from NZ$288,030,742 for the year ended March 31, 1971, to NZ$327,053,217 in the year ended March 31, 1972; 58% of cash benefits were paid without a means test. The Social Security Department and the Child Welfare Division of the Department of Education were amalgamated to form a new Department of Social Welfare. The Royal Commission on Social Security, appointed in September 1969, made 110 recommendations in its report, 81 of which affected payment of benefits and pensions. Although the recommendations did not represent a major reconstruction of the social security system, they did include proposed changes to ensure that the scheme adequately met the needs of present-day society.

Other Countries. In Austria the contribution basis for pensions generally was raised. Widows' pensions were increased by 10% to 60% of the deceased husband's entitlement, but if the widow had other substantial income it was reduced by one-sixth. In Czechoslovakia the rates of allowances and pensions were raised. A national social security plan for old people was introduced in Spain. It included the establishment of pensioners' clubs, residential accommodation and geriatric centres, and provision of vacations and home help in cooperation with private groups. In Turkey a new scheme was introduced covering old-age, disability, and survivors' insurance and providing benefits for self-employed persons other than farmers.

Contribution and benefit levels were raised in Mexico, and coverage was extended to a larger number of independent farmers. In Japan a flat-rate social security scheme for dependent children was established. Unlike other social security schemes in Japan, this one covered all persons irrespective of their employment, but only where there were three or more dependent children under 18. A new pension plan was introduced for farmers. In Algeria a new social security scheme for agricultural workers and their families covered sickness, maternity, family allowances, invalidity, old age, and death. Pension increases were approved for collective farm and state enterprise workers in the Soviet Union. (JOHN MOSS)

See also Education; Housing; Insurance; Medicine; Race Relations; Refugees; Taxation.

Sociology

In 1972 sociology entered a state of heightened self-consciousness. From the onset of the discipline, sociologists had taught that man is a product of his culture. This fundamental proposition was what distinguished a sociological from a psychological interpretation of human behaviour. Yet an examination of the epistemologies of sociology left the distinct impression that sociologists saw their discipline as one in which "objective detachment" freed the social scientist from the encapsulating influence of his own culture. It now appeared that the 1970s would be the decade in which sociologists discovered that they, too, were products of the culture in which they laboured. From the outside this might seem trivial and esoteric, but the internal navel-gazing of sociologists appeared to be the biggest development in the discipline since the initiation of government research grants.

The critical reassessment of the sociological enterprise was stimulated by the publication in paperback of two notable works, both of which were substantially intelligible to the layman. Alvin W. Gouldner's *The Coming Crisis of Western Sociology* was imbued with polemics against the sociological establishment. Robert W. Friedrichs' *A Sociology of Sociology,* which won the American Sociological Association's Sorokin Award in 1971, read as a more sober and detached analysis. Yet the two authors were in substantial agreement on a number of points: the functionalism of Talcott Parsons, which had dominated the discipline, was under heavy attack, and several new theoretical models were struggling for acceptance; the value-free posture of neutrality in sociology must be critically reexamined.

The source of the trauma lay in the upheavals of the 1960s. Never before had sociologists been called upon with greater frequency to interpret and propose remedies for so many social ills. But like politicians, government bureaucrats, and university administrators, sociologists had been taken by surprise by most of the significant developments of the decade. If some sociologists were embittered because their prescriptions had not been followed, others viewed this as a species of benign neglect, for they were less certain than they had been a decade earlier that they possessed any magic potions.

The "new breed" of sociologists that had emerged amid the turmoil were bound together by the belief that sociology was neither liberal nor reform minded. Sociologists had sold their wares to the highest bidder, and their knowledge, far from being used for human betterment, had been used to manipulate those who challenged the status quo. Further, sociologists could not even envisage social change because their very consciousness had been molded by reactionary theories.

Some argued for the abandonment of "objectivity," contending that, since sociological knowledge is ultimately political rhetoric, the goal was to develop a political rhetoric for the oppressed. Others, less radical, argued that sociologists must become more self-conscious about their underlying presuppositions and more politically astute about the potential uses and misuses of their knowledge. Many other disciplines were experiencing the same restlessness, paralleling the convulsions within society. The significance of the turmoil within sociology, however, seemed to be the increasing application of sociological knowledge to the discipline itself—in a sense, the sociology of sociology. To a growing number of sociologists, there was hope that this would lead to the attainment of deeper insights about society.

In at least one area, the discipline was taking some long-overdue practical steps. At the 1972 annual meeting of the ASA, held in New Orleans, La., in late August, William J. Goode of Columbia University relinquished the presidency to Mirra Komarovsky, also of Columbia, and women were represented on the new governing council in greater proportion than ever before. Even so, representatives of the ASA's Committee on the Status of Women in the Profession and of Sociologists for Women in Society pointed out that women still constituted a minority on the council, and that even this advancement had not been matched in the sociology faculties of most major universities.

(JEFFREY K. HADDEN)

See also Psychology; Social Services.

ENCYCLOPÆDIA BRITANNICA FILMS. *Operation Bootstrap* (1968); *Heritage in Black* (1969); *The House of Man, Part II—Our Crowded Environment* (1969); *Manuel from Puerto Rico* (1969); *Chicano from the Southwest* (1970); *Linda and Billy Ray from Appalachia* (1970); *Jesse from Mississippi* (1971); *Johnny from Fort Apache* (1971); *Irish Boy: The Story of Sean* (1972).

Somalia

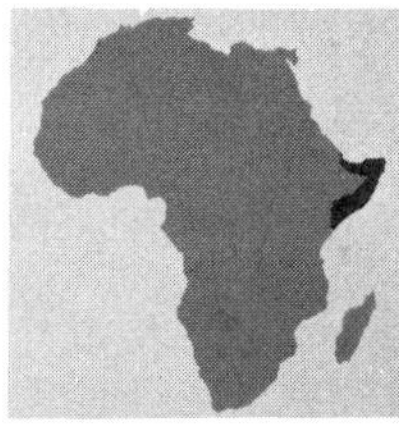

A republic of northeast Africa, the Somali Democratic Republic, or Somalia, is bounded by the Gulf of Aden, the Indian Ocean, Kenya, Ethiopia, and Afars and Issas. Area: 246,154 sq.mi. (637,541 sq.km.). Pop. (1971 est.): 2,864,000, predominantly Hamitic, with Arabic and other admixtures. Cap. and largest city: Mogadiscio (pop., 1969 est., 200,000). Language (official): Arabic, English, Italian; also Somali. Religion: predominantly Muslim. President of the Supreme Revolutionary Council in 1972, Maj. Gen. Muhammad Siyad Barrah.

Somalia in 1972 continued its three-year development plan, which had been published in 1971. Projects of the plan included road building, irrigation works, and the construction of a new airport. In January 1972 a fresh campaign was launched to implement the principles of "scientific socialism" in the country. A law was promulgated forbidding government employees to deal in property or own more than one house. Another law stopped physicians from practicing privately; instead, they were to be employed by the state. President Siyad openly denied that there was any conflict between socialism and the Islamic faith.

Siyad paid state visits to the U.S.S.R. and to several Arab and African countries. In June he was elected one of the vice-chairmen at the Organization of African Unity assembly of heads of state in Rabat, Morocco. A meeting was held in July at Baidoa in southern Somalia between President Siyad and Presidents Gaafar Nimeiry of the Sudan and Idi Amin of Uganda. During October, negotiations between Uganda and Tanzania were held at Mogadiscio after border clashes, with Somalia acting as mediator.

The former vice-president of the Supreme Revolutionary Council, Muhammad Ainanshe Guleid, and two associates, arrested in 1971 and charged with conspiracy, were condemned to death in May. On July 3 the three men were publicly executed by firing squad.

(VIRGINIA R. LULING)

SOMALIA

Education. (1969–70) Primary, pupils 31,589, teachers (including preprimary) 915; secondary, pupils 22,360, teachers 872; vocational, pupils 906, teachers 79; teacher training, students 168, teachers 10; higher, students 548, teaching staff 48.

Finance. Monetary unit: Somali shilling, with (Sept. 18, 1972) a par value of 6.93 Somali shillings to U.S. $1 (free rate of 18.05 Somali shillings = £1 sterling). Gold, SDRs, and foreign exchange, central bank: (March 1971) U.S. $21.7 million; (March 1970) U.S. $15 million. Budget (1971 est.): revenue 316.3 million Somali shillings; expenditure 306.3 million Somali shillings. Cost of living (Mogadiscio; 1963 = 100): (May 1972) 132; (May 1971) 141.

Foreign Trade. (1971) Imports 446.9 million Somali shillings; exports 246.2 million Somali shillings. Import sources (1970): Italy 29%; West Germany 9%; U.S. 8%; Japan 7%; U.S.S.R. 7%; U.K. 6%; Kenya 5%; Singapore 5%. Export destinations (1970): Saudi Arabia 52%; Italy 26%; Yemen (Aden) 10%. Main exports: livestock 50%; bananas 26%; hides and skins 7%.

Transport and Communications. Roads (1969) 13,396 km. Motor vehicles in use (1969): passenger 5,900; commercial 8,000. There are no railways. Shipping (1971): merchant vessels 100 gross tons and over 109; gross tonnage 592,664. Telephones (Jan. 1971) *c.* 5,000. Radio receivers (Dec. 1970) 50,000.

Agriculture. Production (in 000; metric tons; 1970; 1969 in parentheses): millet and sorghum *c.* 50 (*c.* 63); cassava *c.* 25 (*c.* 23); sugar, raw value (1971–72) *c.* 49, (1970–71) *c.* 49; bananas *c.* 150 (*c.* 150). Livestock (in 000; 1970–71): cattle *c.* 2,350; sheep *c.* 3,950; goats *c.* 5,000; camels *c.* 3,000.

South Africa

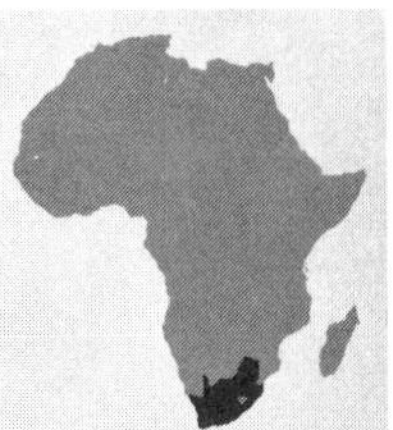

A republic occupying the southern tip of Africa, South Africa is bounded by South West Africa, Botswana, Rhodesia, Mozambique, and Swaziland. Lesotho forms an enclave within South African territory. Area: 471,445 sq.mi. (1,221,037 sq.km.), excluding Walvis Bay, 372 sq.mi. Pop. (1971 est.): 22,092,000, including (1970) Bantu 70.2%; white 17.5%; Coloured 9.4%; Asian 2.9%. Executive cap.: Pretoria (metro. pop., 1970, 561,703); judicial cap.: Bloemfontein (pop., 1970, 180,179); legislative cap.: Cape Town (metro. pop., 1970, 1,096,597). Largest city: Johannesburg (metro. pop., 1970, 1,432,643). Language: Afrikaans and English. Religion: mainly Christian. State president in 1972, Jacobus J. Fouché; prime minister, B. J. Vorster.

Domestic Affairs. A Cabinet reorganization affecting one-third of government ministers occurred in August 1972 following the resignation in June of T. J. A. Gerdener, minister of the interior. Gerdener announced plans for the formation of a multiracial organization for furthering aid to and cooperation with neighbouring black states in southern Africa and the various racial groups in South Africa. Four other ministers retired. Constitutional proposals for establishing a South African federal state to replace the existing unitary system were outlined by the opposition United and Progressive parties.

A parliamentary select committee, later converted into a commission, was set up to inquire into the activities of various student organizations. Legislation was passed putting into effect recommendations of the one-man (Potgieter) judicial commission on state security and the establishment of a security council directly responsible to the prime minister. Telephone tapping and the interception of mail in the interests of na-

Soil Conservation: *see* Environment

Sorghum Grains: *see* Agriculture

tional security were authorized by law. A Civil Aviation Act prescribed heavy penalties for the hijacking and sabotage of aircraft.

Authorized defense expenditure for 1972–73 rose by R 25.9 million to R 335.3 million. In pursuance of the policy of self-sufficiency in armaments, H. J. Samuels, head of the Armaments Board, reported that Mirage jet aircraft were being built by the Atlas Aircraft Corporation near Pretoria, and the feasibility of building naval shipping was being investigated. A submarine base was opened at Simonstown and a third submarine, constructed in France, was commissioned. It was decided to build a R 20 million dry dock at Saldanha to advance a project for shipping semiprocessed steel and manganese produced at Sishen in the northwestern Cape. Plans for constructing the country's first nuclear power station at Koeberg near Cape Town, to become operational by 1981, were proceeding. Television service, on a noncommercial basis and with a single bilingual channel, was scheduled for 1976.

Continuing the policy of partial self-government in the Bantu homelands (so-called Bantustans), with a view to ultimate independence, the government established a legislative assembly for the Tswana ethnic unit. This step followed a general election in which Tswanas in and outside the homeland gave the party of Chief Lucas Mangope a substantial majority. Tswanaland was renamed Bophutatswana, with Mafeking as the capital and Mangope as chief minister. Provision was made for the establishment of legislative assemblies in the Ciskei and Zululand (renamed KwaZulu). In the Ciskei (capital Zwelitsha) the Cabinet was headed by Chief Justice Mbandla. KwaZulu (capital Nongoma) was designated a constitutional monarchy, with Paramount Chief Zwelithini Goodwill as king and Chief Gatsha Buthelezi as chief executive councillor. Other homelands were also on the way toward territorial self-government.

Detailed plans and maps were published by the government for the consolidation of the scattered areas of the homelands. The affected populations, both white and black, were given the opportunity to make representations to the Bantu Affairs Commission. The strongest objections came from white farmers in Zululand and from the Zulus themselves. Buthelezi demanded more land and more consultation by the government in the demarcation of the boundaries of KwaZulu. Paramount Chief Kaiser Matanzima of the Transkei also asked for the inclusion of a number of districts reserved for white occupation, as well as for Port St. Johns, and proposed a union with the Ciskei to form a single Xhosaland that would include the port of East London and King William's Town. The Transkei and KwaZulu requests were rejected; Prime Minister B. J. Vorster said there would be no land allocations to the homelands other than those set aside in 1936, which amounted to 13% of South Africa.

In the urban areas the policy of "endorsement out" and repatriation to the homelands was continued, though with some relaxation in the influx control regulations. To meet public criticism of the hundreds of thousands of Bantu who served short terms of imprisonment every year for mainly technical offenses under the pass laws, a network of aid centres was brought into operation with the aim of keeping such persons out of jail.

In the Coloured Persons' Representative Council opposition by the antiapartheid Labour Party to the ruling Federal Party led to legislation empowering the central government to intervene if the council was prevented from discharging its budgetary and financial functions because the Federal Party had lost its majority. The government rejected as impracticable proposals for creating a separate Coloured homeland. Plans were announced for the development of growth points for the Coloured People in the western Cape. A Coloured corps special service battalion was established providing for a 12-month period of training youths similar to that of white national servicemen.

Student disturbances that began at nonwhite university institutions spread to white universities in Cape Town, Johannesburg, Grahamstown, and Natal. About 600 students and others involved in protests against aspects of the government's race policy were arrested in clashes with the police. A number charged under the Riotous Assemblies Act were acquitted, several as a result of successful Supreme Court appeals upholding the right of lawful protest. Four Indians—three men and a woman—were tried under the Terrorism Act and sentenced in Pretoria to the minimum penalty of five years' imprisonment. Evidence showed that they were associated with the Indian teacher Ahmed Timol who had died in October 1971 while being detained with them, seemingly by jumping from a window of the Johannesburg police headquarters. On April 14 the five-year prison sentence imposed on the Anglican dean of the Johannesburg cathedral, G. A. ffrench-Beytagh, was set aside by the Appeal Court,

SOUTH AFRICA

Education. (1967) European: primary, secondary, and vocational, pupils 793,189, teachers 33,235; teacher training, students 9,985, teachers 772; higher (1966), students 44,184, teaching staff 8,013. African and other non-European: primary, secondary, and vocational, pupils 2,853,837, teachers 59,000; teacher training, students 8,173, teachers *c.* 4,600; higher (1966), students 4,218, teaching staff 398.

Finance. Monetary unit: rand, with (Sept. 18, 1972) a free rate of R 0.80 to U.S. $1 (par value of R 1.95 = £1 sterling). Gold, SDRs, and foreign exchange, official: (June 1972) U.S. $982 million; (June 1971) U.S. $804 million. Budget (1971–72 est.): revenue R 2,495,000,000; expenditure R 2,503,000,000. Gross domestic product: (1970) R 12,404,000,000; (1969) R 11,339,000,000. Money supply: (May 1972) R 2,406,000,000; (May 1971) R 2,195,000,000. Cost of living (1963 = 100): (June 1972) 140; (June 1971) 133.

Foreign Trade. (1971) Imports R 2,880,500,000; exports (excluding gold) R 1,573,500,000 (outflow of gold U.S. $1,541,000,000). Import sources: U.K. 23%; U.S. 16%; West Germany 14%; Japan 10%. Export destinations: U.K. 27%; Japan 12%; U.S. 8%; West Germany 7%; ship's and aircraft stores 5%. Main exports (excluding gold): diamonds 11%; fruit and vegetables 11%; metal ores 6%; copper 6%; iron and steel 6%; textile yarns and fabrics 5%.

Transport and Communications. Roads (1971) *c.* 320,000 km. (including *c.* 185,000 km. main roads and *c.* 32,000 km. with improved surface). Motor vehicles in use (1970): passenger 1,653,000; commercial 394,000. Railways: (1969) 19,796 km. (excluding Namibia 2,354 km.); freight traffic (including Namibia; 1970–71) 57,178,000,000 net ton-km. Air traffic (1971): 3,071,000,000 passenger-km.; freight 73,630,000 net ton-km. Shipping (1971): merchant vessels 100 gross tons and over 249; gross tonnage 538,493. Telephones (Jan. 1971) 1,554,000. Radio receivers (Dec. 1967) 2.7 million.

Agriculture. Production (in 000; metric tons; 1971; 1970 in parentheses): corn 8,600 (6,133); wheat 1,620 (1,396); sorghum 650 (445); oats 89 (122); peanuts 399 (318); sunflower seed 127 (96); potatoes *c.* 650 (586); sugar, raw value (1971–72) 1,875, (1970–71) 1,399; oranges *c.* 530 (*c.* 506); apples *c.* 250 (*c.* 230); wine 577 (419); tobacco *c.* 34 (34); wool 53 (*c.* 57); meat *c.* 617 (*c.* 610); milk *c.* 2,840 (2,820); fish catch (1970) 862, (1969) 1,091. Livestock (in 000; June 1971): cattle *c.* 12,320; sheep 30,671; pigs *c.* 1,350; goats *c.* 5,600; horses *c.* 430; chickens (on farms and estates) *c.* 12,400.

Industry. Index of manufacturing production (1963 = 100): (1971) 163; (1970) 159. Fuel and power (in 000; 1971): coal (metric tons) 58,781; manufactured gas (cu.m.; 1970) 1,618,000; electricity (kw-hr.) 52,716,000. Production (in 000; metric tons; 1971): cement 5,859; iron ore (60–65% metal content) 10,476; pig iron 4,456; crude steel 4,960; copper ore (metal content) 158; asbestos (1970) 287; chrome (oxide content; 1970) 642; antimony concentrate (metal content; 1970) 17; manganese ore (1970) 1,178; gold (troy oz.) 31,370; diamonds (metric carats; 1970) 8,112; fish meal (including Namibia; 1970) 309.

which found him not guilty of offenses under the Terrorism Act; he left for Britain on the same day.

In the 12 months prior to June, 12 persons were banned under the Suppression of Communism Act, including a Catholic priest, Cosmas Desmond, author of *Discarded People,* which described conditions in resettlement areas at Dimbaza and Sada in the eastern Cape. Helen Joseph, the first person to have been placed under house arrest, was freed from restrictions after 15 years. She continued to be "listed" and could not be quoted. A new political organization, the Black People's Convention, was formed in Pietermaritzburg, with the object of uniting African, Coloured, and Indian people and implementing "black consciousness." The African Students' Organization proclaimed an ideology of black self-reliance, resembling that of the "black power" movement in the U.S.

Foreign Affairs. After a month-long tour of South West Africa (Namibia) by Alfred Escher, UN Secretary-General Kurt Waldheim's special representative, a compromise agreement on the fate of the territory was announced in mid-November (*see* DEPENDENT STATES). Resolutions condemning South Africa's race policies and calling for total sanctions against the country were adopted by the UN General Assembly in November. South Africa, with Portugal, withdrew from the proceedings of the Trusteeship Committee in protest against a decision by it to allow representatives of "liberation movements" in southern Africa, characterized by the two countries as "terrorists," to attend committee sessions as observers. South Africa dissociated itself from a General Assembly resolution urging international aid for "freedom fighters" in colonial territories. A decision by the World Council of Churches to give financial aid to such movements in Africa was condemned by the government and a number of churches in South Africa. These for the most part, however, refused to resign from the World Council of Churches. The WCC resolved in August to withdraw its funds from countries trading with South Africa, Rhodesia, and the Portuguese territories in Africa. U.S. business firms operating in South Africa resisted pressure to withdraw their investments.

South Africa's relations with neighbouring African states under the policy of "dialogue" suffered a setback when Malagasy broke off contacts after a change of regime on the island. In July the U.S. appointed a black diplomat, James Baker, as economic and commercial counselor in its embassy in Pretoria.

South Africa's participation in international sporting events continued to be affected by opposition to its race policies. Efforts to seek readmission to the Olympic Games were unsuccessful.

The Economy. In his budget for 1972–73 introduced in March, the minister of finance, N. J. Diederichs, announced a number of measures aimed at revitalizing the economy by easing credit and stimulating the growth rate while continuing to curb inflationary pressures and the rate of increase in state spending. Concessions were made to industry in the use of African labour, to meet the shortage of other labour and the anticipated improvement in industrial production and exports. It was announced in November that the retail and distributive trade was to offer its black workers wage increases of up to 46%. Restrictions on the borrowing of money from abroad for industrial expansion were modified. Interest rates were lowered and all lending restrictions were removed in October, mainly to encourage industrial production. The government also guaranteed all necessary tariff protection to industry, on a selective basis, in spite of provisions of the General Agreement on Tariffs and Trade. Import controls and installment buying restrictions were lifted on a number of commodities.

WIDE WORLD

A student hurls a tear gas canister back at police during rioting in Cape Town on June 5, 1972. About 10,000 people were involved in the antiapartheid protest.

The effect of the devaluation of the rand by 12.28% in December 1971 was apparent in the improvement of the balance of payments and the gold and foreign exchange reserves. In June the trade deficit (excluding gold) had fallen to R 450 million, from R 1,017,000,000 in October 1971. The floating of the British pound in June had a further impact on the Reserve Bank's gold and foreign assets, which rose from less than R 500 million in November 1971 to R 938 million a year later. When the continued drop in the value of the pound resulted in an 8% de facto devaluation of the rand in October, Diederichs announced that the rand would no longer be linked with sterling but would be at a fixed parity rate with the U.S. dollar.

(LOUIS HOTZ)

Southeast Asia

Visiting Jakarta, Indon., in July 1972, British Foreign Secretary Sir Alec Douglas-Home said that it was likely that the rivalry among the major nations for world power and influence would now be decided in Asia. Southeast Asian governments did not seem to have any precise notions as to how they were going to be involved in the rivalries, but a tendency to agree with Sir Alec informed their policies during 1973.

The year began with U.S. Pres. Richard Nixon's visit to China in February. When Nixon's new policy of normalizing relations with China was announced in 1971, it had unsettled many Southeast Asian governments which in the past had hitched their wagons to the star of Washington and adopted a hostile attitude toward Peking. When Nixon followed up his China initiative with a visit to Moscow, and when neither China nor the Soviet Union did anything to stop the U.S. from bombing Hanoi or blockading North Vietnam's ports, the impression grew in Southeast Asia that small nations would be increasingly on their own.

At various panel discussions, seminars, and conferences, Southeast Asian leaders began advising one another and the peoples of the region in general on how to meet the developing challenge. The Malaysian prime minister, Tun Abdul Razak, said that Southeast Asia must develop the strength to stand on its own

CAMERA PRESS/
PICTORIAL PARADE

A crucifix remains on the wall of a Roman Catholic Church in Quang Tri, South Vietnam, which was virtually destroyed after weeks of fighting between South Vietnamese and North Vietnamese, who finally were driven away.

feet and to defend its sovereignty and integrity if it wanted the respect of the big powers. Indonesian Foreign Minister Adam Malik asked Southeast Asian nations to avoid developing a ghetto mentality but to guard against manipulations by the richer nations to use them as tools to wage other people's wars. Singapore Foreign Minister Sinathamby Rajaratnam wanted Southeast Asian nations to create a situation in which big powers would find it essential to secure their assistance in ensuring world peace and stability.

The groping for effective policies assumed another dimension of urgency with the visit to China in September by Japan's new prime minister, Kakuei Tanaka (*see* BIOGRAPHY). The resultant establishment of diplomatic relations between the two countries struck Southeast Asia as an event of even greater significance than the détente between China and the U.S. The main reason for this feeling was that the U.S. was thought to be in a mood to disengage itself from Asia, while Japan was seen as further entrenching itself in the region.

The question being asked in Southeast Asian capitals in the wake of the Tanaka visit to Peking was how the reconciliation of the traditional enemies would affect the region. The joint statement issued at the end of Tanaka's visit specifically mentioned that neither Japan nor China would aim at gaining hegemony in the region. Nevertheless, it was recognized by Southeast Asian governments that both countries were already too involved in the region to leave it alone. Maoist underground movements existed in most of the countries of the region, and, although Peking did not overtly assist them, they were widely believed to have links with China. Japan's tendency to see the region as indispensable to its economy was emphasized when it took a firm stand against an Indonesian-Malaysian move early in the year to declare the Strait of Malacca a territorial waterway. Japan was the first "outside" power to show interest in getting diplomatically involved in the Indochina cease-fire moves in October.

A short-term fear which seemed to grow in Southeast Asia was strictly economic in origin. Many Southeast Asian countries had been supplying vast quantities of raw materials to Japan and receiving substantial capital investment from Japanese sources. These countries began worrying whether Japan would turn now to China both for some of the raw materials and as a destination for investment capital. This could leave Southeast Asia merely as a market for Japanese goods, further tilting the balance of payments position against the countries of the region.

At the political and military levels also, an air of uncertainty held sway. Most countries made friendly overtures to China and tried to maintain friendly relations with all big powers. However, there were significant differences of opinion among the governments on basic policies.

Malaysia steadfastly campaigned for a neutral Southeast Asia, arguing that it would not only safeguard the interests of Southeast Asian countries but also help the big powers disengage from the Indochina conflict without loss of prestige. However, Tun Abdul Razak, during an official visit to Moscow in October, found little encouragement from the Soviet Union, one of the countries asked to guarantee neutralization.

On the other hand, the neutralization plan appeared to have a direct impact on the five-power defense arrangement between Malaysia and Singapore on the one side and Britain, Australia, and New Zealand on the other. Singapore was vehemently in favour of continuing the arrangement because it guaranteed the security essential to maintain international business confidence in the stability of the region. But Malaysia made it clear that it opposed all defense pacts and that the five-power arrangement ran counter to the spirit of neutralization. In an interview in Leningrad in October, Prime Minister Razak said that all foreign bases in the region would have to be phased out before big-power guarantees were sought for neutralization; he indicated there was an agreement to this effect among the five member countries of the Association of Southeast Asian Nations (ASEAN). He added that Malaysia would quit the five-power arrangement before asking the big powers to guarantee neutralization.

The coolness toward the arrangement evinced by the new Labour governments in Australia and New Zealand cast a shadow that could not be ignored. Late in the year, however, the new Australian prime minister, Gough Whitlam, told a news conference there was no urgent need for a review and that the Australian battalion stationed in Singapore would remain there until its term ended in 1974.

Meanwhile, the nonalignment lobby in Southeast Asia received a jolt at the conference of foreign ministers of nonaligned nations at Georgetown, Guyana, in August. The conference voted to grant full membership to the Viet Cong delegation from South Vietnam, which had previously held only observer status. Charging that the vote violated the principle of consensus, Indonesia, Malaysia, and Laos walked out of the conference but explained they were not abandoning the nonaligned movement altogether.

Another bitter argument in Georgetown involving Asian members was over the site of the fourth nonaligned summit, to be held in 1973. The first three having been held in Belgrade, Cairo, and Lusaka, Asian countries wanted the 1973 meeting to be held in a city on their continent. But the Georgetown conference decided on another African capital, Algiers. Indonesia and Malaysia hinted that they might not participate, and Indonesian Foreign Minister Malik said that the future of the nonaligned group was in great jeopardy because the African nations were trying to force majority decisions on the Asian minority.

ASEAN. The air of uncertainty that surrounded the five-power defense arrangement extended to other regional organizations as well. For the most significant of these, the Association of Southeast Asian Nations, it was another year of much talk with little action. The ASEAN summit idea, vigorously pushed by the Philippines in 1971, was indefinitely put off when senior ministers of the five member countries (Thailand, Malaysia, Singapore, Indonesia, and the Philippines) met in Manila in July and failed to reach an agreement.

In April the foreign ministers of the five countries had met in Singapore for ASEAN's fifth ministerial meeting. At the end of the two-day conference they proposed that new guidelines and criteria of priorities be formulated to make the association a more effective instrument for cooperation.

One idea that gained ground during the year was that ASEAN should coordinate discussions between member countries and the EEC. A special coordination committee was set up for the purpose. The basic issues were European tariff discrimination against products from ASEAN countries and associate membership status for ASEAN countries in the EEC.

With a view to strengthening the collective bargaining position of ASEAN countries, chambers of commerce executives from member countries met in Jakarta in April to set up an ASEAN Chamber of Commerce and Industry. Elimination of unhealthy competition among member countries was stated to be one of the objectives of the conference.

Although avowedly an economic association, ASEAN continued to chase political shadows. Thailand's Thanat Khoman said that the member countries were slowly developing a common foreign policy, but evidence pointed to the contrary; Thanat Khoman himself vacated his long-held position as Thailand's foreign minister and went into political oblivion. The most serious potential source of friction arose over the Strait of Malacca early in the year when the Indonesian and Malaysian governments jointly claimed it as their property. The U.S., Britain, Japan, and the Soviet Union asserted that the strait was an international passageway. The one country that kept conspicuously silent was Singapore, the principal port commanding the Malacca strait. Reports circulated that Indonesia and Malaysia had in fact joined hands to reduce the importance of Singapore. These reports were strengthened when Thailand later came out with "concrete" plans to cut a canal across the Kra Isthmus, which, if it materialized, would seriously reduce Singapore's trade. In September an Indonesian Defense Ministry official added another note to the internecine rivalry by saying that the existence of a big-power naval base in Singapore would obstruct the creation of a neutral Southeast Asia. This comment stemmed from reports that Singapore had threatened to permit the Soviet Union to replace Australia if Australia withdrew its forces stationed in Singapore.

SEATO. In the wake of improved U.S. and Japanese relations with China, questions were raised about the relevancy of the Southeast Asia Treaty Organization, formed primarily for the containment of China-based Communism. On November 8, Pakistan gave notice of its intention to withdraw from the organization. The review of foreign policy commitments promised by the Labour governments of Australian Prime Minister Whitlam and New Zealand Prime Minister Norman Kirk included scrutiny of SEATO, and it seemed highly probable that the two countries would reduce their participation in the organization to observer status. Prior to his election, Whitlam, then leader of the opposition, had referred to SEATO as moribund. Gen. Jesús Vargas, retiring secretary-general of SEATO, was replaced by Sunthorn Hunthorn Hongladarom, Thailand's ambassador to the U.S.

A two-day military advisers' conference in Canberra, Austr., in July resolved that the military effectiveness of SEATO should be strengthened in the face of continuing Communist subversion in the treaty area. However, there was no evidence during the year of SEATO making its presence felt in any way in any area. A two-day military exercise in Thailand in June left the insurgency problem in northern and northeastern Thailand as vexatious for Thailand as ever.

ECAFE. Having achieved little more than accumulating a vast collection of paper plans over the years, the UN Economic Commission for Asia and the Far East received a slight boost during 1972 with the prospects of China becoming an active member. By year's end China had not participated in any ECAFE meeting, but Executive Secretary U Nyun was invited to visit Peking in November.

On the occasion of its 25th anniversary in September, ECAFE had only an increase in membership from the original 10 to 29 to report. However, with the prospects of peace in Indochina improving, there were fresh hopes that one of ECAFE's many projects, the Mekong River development scheme, might receive a shot in the arm. An expert group met in Bangkok in September and suggested the formation of a new permanent forum to promote economic cooperation in the Mekong area. (T. J. S. GEORGE)

UPI COMPIX

A dazed civilian walks away from his burning home during a Communist rocket and artillery attack on Phnom Penh, Cambodia, on March 21, 1972.

Soviet Bloc Economies

During 1972 the 26th plenary session of the Council for Mutual Economic Assistance (CMEA, or Comecon) was held in Moscow from July 10 to 12; the executive committee, in which the member countries were represented by deputy heads of governments, met five times at its Moscow headquarters.

The plenary session welcomed Cuba as the second non-European member, the first being Mongolia. Thereafter, economic aid to Cuba became the collective responsibility of all seven European members of the CMEA, as had been the case for Mongolia since 1962. The main task of the plenary session was to examine the progress of the comprehensive program for economic integration of the member countries, which had been adopted in July 1971 by the 25th plenary session in Bucharest. The session approved a program of cooperation in forecasting and coordinating the members' five-year plans for 1976–80, and of joint planning of special types of industrial production.

At its successive meetings, the executive committee endorsed a few proposals of specialized standing subcommittees aimed at stepping up the production of new machinery and electronic equipment; it also instructed its subcommittees to draft the necessary measures for increasing cooperative economic efficiency, improving the socialist division of labour, and accelerating scientific and technological progress. Some congratulations were deemed necessary, too, and the executive committee was glad to recognize that the turnover of machinery and equipment among the

Southern Rhodesia: *see* Rhodesia

Southern Yemen: *see* Yemen, People's Democratic Republic of

South West Africa: *see* Dependent States; South Africa

member countries had almost tripled from 1960 to 1970, and that CMEA chemical industries' output had risen 3.2 times during that period.

Nikolai Patolichev, Soviet foreign trade minister, said in May in an interview with the Novosti Press Agency that the comprehensive program of economic integration was developing successfully. The CMEA countries ranked first in Soviet foreign trade, accounting for more than half of Soviet exports and imports. Deliveries from the U.S.S.R. over the previous five years had almost fully met their import requirements for crude petroleum, natural gas, and cast iron. The U.S.S.R. supplied 85% of their needs in iron ore, and a substantial share of their requirements for petroleum products, fertilizers, rolled steel, nonferrous and rare metals, timber, and cotton. In return during the same period the U.S.S.R. had received from its CMEA partners 1,154 oceangoing ships; about 34,000 railway freight cars, 5,000 railway passenger cars, over 1,600 electric and diesel locomotives, complete sets of equipment for 54 chemical plants, as well as vast quantities of farm machinery and consumer goods.

Aleksandr Alekseyev, a member of the CMEA joint economic research department, said in October in an interview with *Krasnaya Zvezda* that the CMEA industrial complex was far bigger than the combined industrial capacity of the EEC. Industrial output of the EEC countries rose in 1971 by only 2.6% as compared with 1970, while the rate of industrial growth of the CMEA countries was 7.8%.

According to V. Kudrov, writing in *Sotsialisticheskaya Industria* (October 12), from 1950 to 1970 the share of the CMEA countries in the world's industrial output expanded from 18 to 32%. Of particular interest, Kudrov added, were comparisons of the gross production of the U.S.S.R. and the U.S. The total national income of the U.S.S.R. rose in the period 1960–71 from 58 to 65% of the U.S. total, while the ratio of Soviet industrial output compared with that of the U.S. rose from 55 to 75%. Nevertheless, a considerable discrepancy persisted between the existing level of industrial production of the CMEA countries and the rather modest volume of their trade with the capitalist world. In 1971 the world's imports reached a total of $357 billion, including only $32.2 billion (9%) for the seven European CMEA countries; their part in the $343.1 billion world's exports was $33.9 billion (9.9%). About 67% of the total goods turnover of the CMEA countries was trade with each other.

Spokesmen for the CMEA governments complained that the discrepancy in trade between the socialist and developed capitalist countries was the result of discriminatory obstacles by the latter. They mentioned the refusal to grant most-favoured-nation status to most of the Eastern European countries; the quotas on imports of their finished goods, particularly of machinery and equipment; and the embargo system on "strategic" goods operated by NATO powers since the early 1950s—though this system had been gradually reduced in scope. Replying to this criticism, spokesmen of the Western industrial countries retorted that there were three main obstacles facing any expansion of East–West trade: first, the CMEA countries had no convertible currency; second, they stuck to their arbitrary and complicated system of costing and pricing; third, Western exporters or importers never came in contact with their Communist suppliers or customers but had to negotiate with state combines hesitant in taking responsibility.

In spite of all the difficulties inspired by national ambitions and jealousies, integration of the CMEA area was progressing. The International Bank for Economic Cooperation, founded in 1963, announced in 1972 that of the initial capital of 300 million "convertible" rubles approximately 120 million rubles had been paid in by member countries, including 20 million in gold and hard currencies; the amount of short-term credits granted to member countries amounted in 1971 to 3 billion rubles.

The International Investment Bank, created in 1970 with an initial capital of 1 billion rubles, of which 184 million had been paid up in 1971, granted in that year medium- and long-term credits to finance the building of 16 industrial plants, of which 6 were to be in Romania, 5 in Poland, 3 in Hungary, 1 in Czechoslovakia, and 1 in East Germany. "Intermetal," created in 1964, was a coordinating body covering rolled goods, steel pipes, and secondary metallurgical products. Its headquarters was in Budapest, and all European CMEA members except Romania joined this organization whose turnover in steel products rose in eight years from 950,000 to 2,110,000 tons. "Interchim," created in 1969, with headquarters in Halle, E.Ger., united all the European CMEA members, and aimed at coordinating the production and distribution of small-tonnage but valuable chemicals. Beginning in 1962 a central dispatch service for electric power covering all European CMEA members functioned in

Table I. Growth of National Income in Eastern Europe

Country	1965 actual (1960=100)	1971 actual (1970=100)	1975 plan (1970=100)
U.S.S.R.	137	106.0	140
Germany, East	118	104.5	128
Czechoslovakia	110	105.8	128
Poland	135	107.5	139
Hungary	122	107.0	132
Romania	154	112.5	182
Bulgaria	138	109.0	150

Table II. Rates of Industrial Growth in Eastern Europe*

Country	1961–65 actual	1966–70 actual	1971 actual	1971–75 plan
U.S.S.R.	8.6	8.5	7.8	7.9
Germany, East	5.9	6.4	5.5	6.3
Czechoslovakia	5.2	6.3	6.9	6.3
Poland	8.6	8.3	8.0	8.5
Hungary	8.1	6.1	5.0	7.3
Romania	13.0	11.8	11.5	11.0
Bulgaria	11.7	11.2	9.5	9.9

*Yearly average percentages.

Table III. Growth of Agricultural Production in Eastern Europe

Country	1961–65 actual (1960=100)	1966–70 actual (1961–65=100)	1971 actual (1970=100)	1971–75 plan (1966–70=100)
U.S.S.R.	112	121	100	122
Germany, East	104	120	102.4	...
Czechoslovakia	97	119	102.8	114
Poland	115	116	103.7	121
Hungary	106	116	109	116
Romania	113	123	118	149
Bulgaria	117	126	103	120

Table IV. Basic Industrial Products in Eastern Europe*

Product	1951	1966	1971
Electric power (000,000 kw-hr.)	143.8	729.9	1,062.0
Coal† (000,000 metric tons)	444.8	1,152.2	1,272.9
Crude petroleum (000,000 tons)	49.6	280.6	393.4
Natural gas (000,000,000 cu.m.)	...	162.8	247.4
Crude steel (000,000 tons)	41.4	127.0	162.4
Sulfuric acid (000 tons)	3,524	13,684	19,290
Cement (000,000 tons)	21.3	114.0	145.0

*U.S.S.R., East Germany, Czechoslovakia, Poland, Hungary, Romania, and Bulgaria.
†Hard coal, brown coal, and lignite.
Source: National statistics.

Soviet Literature: *see* Literature

Soviet Union: *see* Union of Soviet Socialist Republics

Soybeans: *see* Agriculture

Spacecraft: *see* Astronautics

Space Exploration: *see* Astronautics

Prague, which was also from 1962 the CMEA central depot for rolling stock.

The building of the second 4,350-km. Druzhba ("Friendship") pipeline between Almetyevsk (U.S.S.R.) and Plock (Poland), Schwedt (East Germany), Hrdlo (Czechoslovakia), and Szaszhalombatta (Hungary) was progressing and would be completed in 1974. The building of the "Transgas" pipeline to carry natural gas from Uzbekistan, Turkmenia, and Kazakhstan through Czechoslovakia to central Europe began in 1971, and gas was expected to start flowing through it during 1973. Among the most recent CMEA coordinating bodies was the "Interatominstrument," founded on March 1, 1972, with headquarters in Warsaw; it grouped six European CMEA countries, Romania excepted, and its aim was to develop and standardize the apparatus necessary for peaceful uses of atomic energy.

In July six European CMEA countries, Czechoslovakia excepted, signed an agreement in Moscow to finance jointly the building of a mill at Ust-Ilim, in eastern Siberia, expected to produce 500,000 tons of cellulose annually. A much more important joint enterprise was the proposed financing of a CMEA metallurgical combine based on the great iron ore deposits near Kursk. (K. M. SMOGORZEWSKI)

See also Communist Movement.

Spain

A nominal monarchy of southwest Europe, Spain is bounded by Portugal, with which it shares the Iberian Peninsula, and by France. Area: 194,881 sq.mi. (504,741 sq.km.), including the Balearic and Canary islands. Pop. (1971 est.): 34,003,178, including the Balearics and Canaries. Cap. and largest city: Madrid (pop., 1971 est., 3,197,336). Language: Spanish. Religion: Roman Catholic. Prince of Spain and king-designate, Don Juan Carlos de Borbón y Borbón; chief of state and premier in 1972, Gen. Francisco Franco Bahamonde.

Franco's hold on the reins of government showed no signs of weakening in 1972. Although he reached his 80th birthday during the year, he did not delegate any major decision-making functions to his Cabinet. In July, however, a decree was published virtually naming Adm. Luis Carrero Blanco (*see* BIOGRAPHY) as the general's successor as premier, at least for the interim period after Franco's death or withdrawal from political life. Some sort of framework was evidently being constructed for the perpetuation of the regime, with a division of the functions currently held by Franco alone.

The events of the year again demonstrated the regime's ability to survive despite considerable opposition, as evidenced by the number of strikes (still illegal in Spain) and worker demonstrations. The killing of two shipyard workers at El Ferrol in March by the Civil Guard, while controlling a demonstration in connection with a strike, was the most extreme example of the government's firm treatment of such problems. The largely Communist-run illegal "worker's commissions"—the nearest thing in Spain to genuinely free labour unions—continued to find support in the heavily industrialized areas.

The violence was by no means one-sided, however. Bombs were continually being planted by members of the ETA, the Basque nationalist movement, and in November students attacked the French consulate in Saragossa and killed the consul, evidently as a protest against the French government's outlawing of Basque rebel leaders hiding in France. Discontent was rife in the universities, where problems of discipline among students, caused by crowding and a severe shortage of teachers, were spreading to the academic staff. The government issued regulations requiring prospective teachers to produce certificates, issued by the police, certifying to their good character. The regulations also allowed the government to appoint rectors, who had formerly been elected from within the universities themselves. The armed police were withdrawn from the campus of Madrid University, where their presence since 1969 had been a continual provocation. It was presumably hoped that the new measures would act more subtly and that the 1973 budget, in which education was the largest item, would enable academic conditions to be improved, thus removing at least the more obvious causes of complaint.

In recent years Spain had made increasing efforts to improve its relationships with foreign countries, seeking cooperation in cultural matters, economic ad-

SPAIN

Education. (1968–69) Primary, pupils 3,664,823, teachers 108,195; secondary, pupils 1,210,017, teachers (1967–68) 34,119; vocational, pupils 338,266, teachers (1967–68) 22,688; teacher training, students 54,249, teachers 2,666; higher (including 27 universities), students 178,255, teaching staff (1967–68) 10,894.

Finance. Monetary unit: peseta, with (Sept. 18, 1972) a par value of 64.47 pesetas to U.S. $1 (free rate of 155.32 pesetas = £1 sterling). Gold, SDRs, and convertible currencies, central bank: (June 1972) U.S. $3,991,000,000; (June 1971) U.S. $2,254,000,000. Budget (1970) balanced at 309,758,000,000 pesetas. Gross national product: (1970) 2,258,000,000,000 pesetas; (1969) 2,011,000,000,000 pesetas. Money supply: (March 1972) 886.9 billion pesetas; (March 1971) 706.8 billion pesetas. Cost of living (1963 = 100): (June 1972) 182; (June 1971) 167.

Foreign Trade. (1971) Imports 345.8 billion pesetas; exports 205.7 billion pesetas. Import sources: EEC 33% (West Germany 12%, France 10%, Italy 5%); U.S. 16%; U.K. 8%; Saudi Arabia 5%. Export destinations: EEC 37% (West Germany 12%, France 11%, Italy 7%, Netherlands 5%); U.S. 15%; U.K. 8%. Main exports: machinery 11%; fruit 8%; vegetable oils 6%; footwear 6%; ships and boats 5%; chemicals 5%. Tourism (1970): visitors 22,657,100; receipts U.S. $1,681,000,000.

Transport and Communications. Roads (1971) 139,400 km. (including 417 km. expressways). Motor vehicles in use (1971): passenger 2,784,700; commercial 760,400. Railways: (1970) 16,592 km. (including 3,769 km. electrified); traffic (1971) 13,534,000,000 passenger-km., freight 9,108,000,000 net ton-km. Air traffic (1971): 7,066,000,000 passenger-km.; freight 152,693,000 net ton-km. Shipping (1971): merchant vessels 100 gross tons and over 2,279; gross tonnage 3,934,129. Telephones (Dec. 1970) 4,569,000. Radio receivers (Dec. 1969) 7,042,000. Television receivers (Dec. 1970) 5.8 million.

Agriculture. Production (in 000; metric tons; 1971; 1970 in parentheses): wheat 5,387 (4,064); barley 4,783 (3,069); oats 577 (395); rye 271 (259); corn 2,058 (1,883); potatoes 4,629 (4,937); rice 361 (382); sorghum 148 (192); chick-peas 75 (97); dry broad beans 128 (132); other dry beans *c.* 120 (110); tomatoes (1970) 1,560, (1969) 1,398; onions (1970) *c.* 970, (1969) 960; apples *c.* 430 (*c.* 416); pears *c.* 200 (194); oranges (1970) 2,260, (1969) 2,463; lemons (1970) 130, (1969) 130; sugar, raw value (1971–72) *c.* 1,067, (1970–71) 781; sunflower seed 254 (153); bananas (1970) 330, (1969) 432; dates *c.* 17 (*c.* 17); figs (1970) 148, (1969) 158; olive oil 360 (434); wine 2,333 (2,501); tobacco 28 (25); cotton, lint 49 (59); meat *c.* 1,000 (940); fish catch (1970) 1,497, (1969) 1,496. Livestock (in 000; 1970–71): cattle 4,235; pigs 6,917; sheep 18,443; goats 2,636; horses *c.* 270; mules *c.* 550; asses *c.* 360; chickens *c.* 47,000.

Industry. Index of industrial production (1963 = 100): (1971) 216; (1970) 205. Fuel and power (in 000; metric tons; 1971): coal 10,549; lignite 2,952; crude oil 120; manufactured gas (cu.m.) 2,410,000; electricity (kw-hr.) 59,920,000. Production (in 000; metric tons; 1971): cement 16,990; iron ore (50% metal content) 7,329; pig iron 4,950; crude steel 7,759; aluminum 127; copper 73; zinc 89; lead 72; sulfur (1970) 1,242; nitrogenous fertilizers (1970–71) 580; phosphate fertilizers (1970–71) 499; potash fertilizers (1970–71) 525; cotton yarn 83; cotton fabrics 82; wool yarn 37; rayon, etc., yarn and fibres 59; nylon, etc., yarn and fibres 77. Merchant vessels launched (100 gross tons and over; 1971) 916,000 gross tons.

KEYSTONE

Gen. Francisco Franco (left) witnesses the marriage of his granddaughter, Maria del Carmen Martinez-Bordiu Franco, to Prince Alfonso de Borbón y Dampierre, grandson of Spain's last king, Alfonso XIII, at the Pardo Palace on March 8, 1972.

vantages, and increased international influence. The most notable move in this direction in 1972 was the signing on September 15 of a trade agreement with the Soviet Union, the first open contact between the two countries since the Spanish Civil War. The pact was a source of great disappointment to the illegal Spanish Communist Party, which felt the Soviets had let them down badly by thus recognizing the Franco regime. Visits to Madrid in February and November by the British foreign secretary, Sir Alec Douglas-Home, suggested the possibility of a negotiated settlement of the Gibraltar dispute.

The issue that dominated Spain's foreign affairs in 1972, however, was the question of the country's relationship with the EEC. It had been stated unequivocally by European politicians (notably by Sicco Mansholt, president of the EEC Commission) that since the EEC was a union of democratic countries, Spain could not qualify for membership with its existing form of government. A prominent Spanish politician denounced this view as undemocratic. Nevertheless, advantageous though membership would be for Spain, there appeared to be no chance of a cordial political relationship developing for the time being. Closer trade ties were being sought, nonetheless. The nine members of the enlarged Common Market accounted for more than half of all Spanish foreign trade, and Spain stood to suffer badly if a new and more advantageous agreement could not be reached. The existing agreement, signed in 1970, presupposed a six-member EEC, not a Community that included the United Kingdom, Denmark, and Ireland.

The economy progressed satisfactorily during the year. After the setback of 1970–71, production rose strongly in 1972—at a rate approaching 8%, compared with 5.1% in 1971. The resumption of faster growth rates did nothing to decrease the pace of inflation, which had already caused concern in 1971. Toward the end of the year the government took steps to keep prices down, including direct controls, margin limitations, and increased imports. This last was made possible only by the fact that Spanish gold and foreign currency reserves had reached a very high level (U.S. $4,782,000,000 at the end of October), largely because of the continued success of the tourist industry. By the end of September tourism had already brought in nearly as much foreign currency income as in the whole of 1971. With increased remittances from Spanish emigrant workers, the overall balance of payments ended the year on a strong note. (RALPH DEANE)

Spanish Literature: *see* Literature

Spanish Sahara: *see* Dependent States

Spices: *see* Agriculture

Spirits: *see* Alcoholic Beverages

Speleology

The link between the Flint Ridge cave system and Mammoth Cave in Kentucky, long believed to exist, was discovered in September 1972 by a party of U.S. explorers that included five men and a woman. Entering the Flint Cave system, the group spent five hours traversing the narrow passageways, sometimes in water up to their chins, before they emerged at a Mammoth Cave tourist trail. Prior to the discovery, the length of the Flint Ridge system was set at approximately 93 mi. while the length of Mammoth Cave was believed to be more than 55 mi. New discoveries in Jewel Cave, South Dakota, brought its length to 43.1 mi., and in Pulaski County, Ky., the Sloans Valley cave system increased to 23 mi.

In September 1971 a British expedition led by John Middleton reached a depth of 2,400 ft. in Ghar Parau in the Zagros Mountains of Iran. A 1972 expedition found that the cave ended in a sump a short distance farther on. Early in 1972 the Gorgoroth Cave in the Mt. Arthur region of New Zealand was explored to a surveyed depth of 1,140 ft., making it the second deepest in the Southern Hemisphere. The Khazad-Dum cave in Tasmania was extended in December 1971, and the terminal sump was reached at a depth of 1,020 ft.; it was now the deepest cave in Australia. Poloska Jama in Yugoslavia was explored by a club from Ljubljana; its overall depth was 2,218 ft. and its length, 6.25 mi. In January the newly discovered Abisso Carlo Pelagalli in Italy was descended to 1,158 ft.

In December 1971 J. Parker and J. Phillips of the Cave Diving Group of Great Britain dived through six sumps in Ogof Agen Allwedd, South Wales, and explored some three-quarters of a mile of new passage; further extensive discoveries were made there in the summer of 1972. Also late in 1971 another half-mile of passage was entered in Gaping Gill, Yorkshire, making the cave about seven miles long. Michel Siffre of France once again spent a long period isolated in a cave to investigate the natural cycle of human sleeping and waking; this time he was in Midnight Cave in Texas and stayed down for nearly seven months, from February 14 to September 5.

A new biospeleological cave laboratory was opened in the Atabex Cave in Cuba. The former Speleological Society there was incorporated into the Department of Speleology of the Cuban Academy of Sciences. A historical study of the development of all aspects of cave science was under way at the University of Leicester, Eng. Two major new textbooks on speleology appeared: *Karst Geology* by M. M. Sweeting and *Karst: Important Karst Regions of the Northern Hemisphere*, edited by M. Herak and V. T. Stringfield. (T. R. SHAW)

WILL THE OLYMPIC FLAME BE LIGHTED AGAIN?

By Howard Bass and
Norris and Ross McWhirter

Many of the 80,000 spectators who attended the closing ceremonies of the games of the XX Olympiad in Munich, West Germany, on Sept. 11, 1972, believed they would never again see the Olympic flame cast its symbolic light over young men and women gathered together from the world over to display their best athletic abilities. The murder of 11 Israeli Olympic competitors was a tragedy too great, too incredible, too filled with terror for the already shaky structure of the Olympic Games to cope with.

The infamous day of terror began at 4:30 A.M. on Sept. 5, 1972, when a Palestinian commando squad apparently affiliated with the Black September movement scaled a wall in the Olympic Village in Munich and forced their way into the quarters of the Israeli Olympic team. Moshe Weinberg, wrestling coach, and Joseph Romano, a weight lifter, resisted and were killed immediately. Nine other Israelis were held hostage while West German authorities surrounded the building housing the Israeli quarters. The terrorists demanded the release of 200 Arabs held in Israeli prisons, and an airplane to fly them to safety. About 10 o'clock P.M. on Sept. 5, believing they had reached an agreement, the Arab terrorists led their bound and blindfolded hostages from their quarters into buses that transported them to waiting helicopters. The helicopters lifted them to Fürstenfeldbruck air base, 20 miles from Munich, where West German police were lying in ambush. Two terrorists descended from a helicopter and walked to inspect a Boeing 727 jetliner they expected to use for their flight to the Middle East. West German sharpshooters fired upon them. One Arab tossed a hand grenade at one of the helicopters, killing all the Israeli hostages aboard. By the time the shooting was over, all nine hostages were dead. The 20-hour reign of terror resulted in the death of the 11 Israelis, one Munich policeman, and 5 Arab guerrillas. Three of the terrorists were captured. For the first time in history, the Olympic Games were suspended for 24 hours (Sept. 5–6) so that memorial services could be held for the murdered athletes.

The modern Olympics were revived in 1896, centuries after their abolition by Roman Emperor Theodosius I in A.D. 393. Management of the Games in the modern era had not built a strong, unified structure and organization under which athletes could compete with one another in the spirit that was born 28 centuries ago in Greece. The 1972 Games marked the first return of the Olympics to a German city since the 1936 Games, hosted by Adolf Hitler and roundly criticized for their blatant chauvinism. The West German invitation had been extended, in part at least, to offer the world a contrast. Yet chauvinism, this time with new actors, once again intruded.

The figure of Avery Brundage (*see* BIOGRAPHY) has to millions of followers of the Games often been one of controversy. Brundage has failed to come to grips with the strong commitment so many athletes have made toward the idea of freedom and equality. Although the International Olympic Committee barred Rhodesia from competition because of its racist policies after black African athletes threatened to leave the 1972 Summer Games, Brundage seemed to take it as a personal attack. Many in the stadium and throughout the world were shocked when, speaking at the memorial services, he equated this "attack" with the killing of the 11 Israelis, a statement for which he later apologized. But Brundage is out now and it is up to Lord Killanin of Ireland, the new head of the International Olympic Committee, to put the Games back in order. He and his fellow Olympic officials should once and for all straighten out the long-standing hypocrisy over what "professionalism" really means. They will have to deal squarely with the issues of racism and nationalism. They will have to see that the rules fit the times and that they are applied equally and generally, not selectively.

Howard Bass is the editor of the Winter Sports Annual *and winter sports correspondent for* The Daily Telegraph *of London.*

Norris and Ross McWhirter are compilers and editors of the Guinness Book of World Records *and* Dunlop Book of Facts.

WIDE WORLD

RAYMOND DEPARDON—GAMMA

KEYSTONE

The charred remains of a Huey helicopter (left) seem out of place in Munich, W.Ger., where peace had prevailed for 27 years. But on Sept. 5, 1972, an insidious kind of war occurred. At the height of the conflict, a Palestinian guerrilla tossed a grenade into the craft, killing the Israeli athletes held captive there.
The hooded figure (above, left) was out of place, too but it stayed outside the Israeli team's Olympic Village apartment for what seemed like an eternity to the world watching on live TV. The wreath at the dead athletes' door (above, right) was from the burgomaster of Munich.

Winter Olympics. For the first time in history, the Winter Olympic Games were held in Asia. On Feb. 3, 1972, Emperor Hirohito declared the XI Winter Olympic Games open at Sapporo, Japan. Biting winds that had shaped the weather days before the opening of the Games gave way to bright, benevolent sunshine on opening day. Thirty-five nations were represented by 1,130 competitors (912 men and 218 women; these figures had previously been exceeded in 1964 at Innsbruck, Austria, and in 1968 at Grenoble, France). The festive mood of a colourful opening ceremony before 50,000 spectators at the outdoor Makomanai speed skating arena was a contrast to the anger of the week before, when the Austrian alpine skier Karl Schranz was banned for alleged professionalism. The decision penalized one man for breaking a rule widely believed to be outdated and impractical to enforce properly.

Ard Schenk (*see* BIOGRAPHY), a Dutch speed skater, stole the individual thunder of these Games just as the French alpine skier Jean-Claude Killy had done in 1968. Schenk's long strides down the straight stretches, fast cornering, and stylishly smooth economy of energy won him gold medals in the 1,500, 5,000, and 10,000 m., shattering two Olympic records in the process. Kees Verkerk helped Schenk to emphasize Dutch supremacy, but Roar Grønvold and Sten Stensen placed well to retain respect for Norway. In the more specialized 500-m. sprint, Erhard Keller, after two false starts, broke another Olympic best time in successfully defending his title for West Germany.

Olympic speed skating records were also smashed in all four women's events, underlining the improvement of technique in four years. In the 1,500 m. three Dutch stars, Stien Baas-Kaiser, Atje Keulen-Deelstra, and Elly van de Brom, were unexpectedly outpaced by Dianne Holum of the U.S., hitherto more renowned as a sprinter. The U.S. victory stunned the chartered plane-loads of avid Dutch supporters.

OLYMPIC CHAMPIONS, 1972 WINTER GAMES, SAPPORO

	Nordic Skiing	
	Men	
15-km. cross-country	S. Lundback (Swed.)	45 min. 28.24 sec.
30-km. cross-country	V. Vedenin (U.S.S.R.)	1 hr. 36 min. 31.15 sec.
50-km. cross-country	P. Tyldum (Nor.)	2 hr. 43 min. 14.75 sec.
40-km. ski relay	U.S.S.R.	2 hr. 4 min. 47.94 sec.
70-m. ski jump	Y. Kasaya (Jap.)	244.2 pt.
90-m. ski jump	W. Fortuna (Pol.)	219.9 pt.
Nordic combined	U. Wehling (E.Ger.)	413.340 pt.
	Women	
5-km. cross-country	G. Kulakova (U.S.S.R.)	17 min. 0.5 sec.
10-km. cross-country	G. Kulakova (U.S.S.R.)	34 min. 17.82 sec.
15-km. ski relay	U.S.S.R.	48 min. 46.15 sec.
	Alpine Skiing	
	Men	
Downhill	B. Russi (Switz.)	1 min. 51.43 sec.
Slalom	F. Fernandez Ochoa (Spain)	1 min. 49.27 sec.
Giant slalom	G. Thoeni (Italy)	3 min. 09.62 sec.
	Women	
Downhill	M. Nadig (Switz.)	1 min. 36.68 sec.
Slalom	B. Cochran (U.S.)	1 min. 31.24 sec.
Giant slalom	M. Nadig (Switz.)	1 min. 29.90 sec.
	Biathlon	
Individual	M. Solberg (Nor.)	1 hr. 15 min. 55.50 sec.
Relay	U.S.S.R.	1 hr. 51 min. 44.92 sec.
	Figure Skating	
Men	O. Nepela (Czech.)	2,739.1 pt.
Women	T. Schuba (Aus.)	2,751.5 pt.
Pairs	I. Rodnina and A. Ulanov (U.S.S.R.)	420.4 pt.
	Speed Skating	
	Men	
500-m.	E. Keller (W.Ger.)	39.44 sec.*
1,500-m.	A. Schenk (Neth.)	2 min. 02.96 sec.*
5,000-m.	A. Schenk (Neth.)	7 min. 23.61 sec.
10,000-m.	A. Schenk (Neth.)	15 min. 01.35 sec.*
	Women	
500-m.	A. Henning (U.S.)	43.33 sec.*
1,000-m.	M. Pflug (W.Ger.)	1 min. 31.40 sec.*
1,500-m.	D. Holum (U.S.)	2 min. 20.85 sec.*
3,000-m.	S. Baas-Kaiser (Neth.)	4 min. 52.14 sec.*
	Ice Hockey	
	Winning team U.S.S.R. (beat Czechoslovakia 5–2 in final)	
	Bobsledding	
Two-man	West Germany	4 min. 57.07 sec.
Four-man	Switzerland	4 min. 43.07 sec.
	Tobogganing (Luge)	
Single (men)	W. Scheidel (E.Ger.)	3 min. 27.58 sec.
Two-man	Italy and East Germany (tie)	1 min. 28.35 sec.
Single (women)	A. Muller (E.Ger.)	2 min. 59.18 sec.

*Olympic record.

Anne Henning captured a second gold medal for the United States in an incident-packed 500-m. sprint. She completed the distance in record time even after being balked, which allowed a second run in which she clocked a still faster time. Miss Henning thus became the only athlete to set a new Winter Olympic record time twice in the same event. At 16, she was also the youngest victor at Sapporo.

Miss Baas-Kaiser finished nearly 7 sec. ahead of Miss Holum in the 3,000 m., while Monika Pflug took the 1,000 m. for West Germany. In the latter race a mere 0.01 sec., the smallest recordable margin, separated the second and third finishers, Miss Keulen-Deelstra and Miss Henning. The previous best Olympic figures were lowered no fewer than 29 times in the eight men's and women's events.

Trixi Schuba of Austria won the women's figure skating with some of the best compulsory figures ever traced, giving her an unprecedented lead at the halfway mark. Her relatively moderate freestyle was anticlimactic but adequate for overall victory. Karen Magnussen of Canada took the silver medal as best all-rounder, while the third-placed U.S. skater Janet Lynn was top freestyle scorer, her marks from one judge including a controversial six, which implied perfection.

Ondrej Nepela became the first Czechoslovak to win an Olympic figure skating title. He included a masterly triple Salchow jump but fell when attempting a triple toe-loop jump. Sergei Chetverukhin's second place was the highest achieved by a Soviet man in international solo figure skating. In the pairs event, Aleksei Ulanov and Irina Rodnina narrowly defeated their Soviet compatriots Andrei Suraikin and Ludmila Smirnova.

In contrast to the figure skating, the alpine ski racing provided several major upsets. Swiss skiers showed a resurgence of strength, while the Austrians and injury-handicapped French had less success than expected.

Bernhard Russi and Roland Collombin finished first and second for Switzerland in the men's downhill on Mt. Eniwa. Gustavo Thoeni of Italy predictably won the first Olympic men's giant slalom to be decided by two descents, but a big surprise was the slalom victory of Francisco Fernandez Ochoa, the first Spaniard to win a medal in any Winter Olympics.

Marie-Thérèse Nadig, 17, a chubby Swiss schoolgirl without a previous race victory in the season, narrowly defeated Annemarie Proell, the firm Austrian favourite, in the women's downhill. As if to prove this was no fluke, Miss Nadig also won the giant slalom, again with Miss Proell second, on a course slowed by heavy snow. On the steep Mt. Teine slalom course less than half the field of 42 finished, and the winner, Barbara Cochran, gained the first alpine skiing gold medal for the U.S. in 20 years.

In Nordic skiing, the customary domination of north Europeans persisted on the cross-country course but not in the jumping. Pål Tyldum, a Norwegian farmer, made a late spurt in warm sunshine to take the grueling 50-km. marathon with a notably fast time, followed by his teammate, Magne Myrmo. Vyacheslav Vedenin, a Soviet soldier, took the 30 km., while Sven-Åke Lundback, a Swedish electrician, led from start to finish in the 15 km. The 40-km. men's relay went to the Soviet quartet, less than 10 sec. better than the Norwegians.

A tremendous first leap of 111 m. from the big tower at Ohkurayama clinched the 90-m. ski jump for Wojciech Fortuna of Poland. Home ground advantage proved decisive for the Japanese in the Miyanomori 70-m. jump, with Yukio Kasaya leading his teammates to a clean sweep. Neither Poland nor Japan had previously won medals for Olympic jumping.

After a 24-hour postponement because of poor visibility, Magnar Solberg of Norway successfully defended the individual

KEYSTONE
Vasily Alekseyev

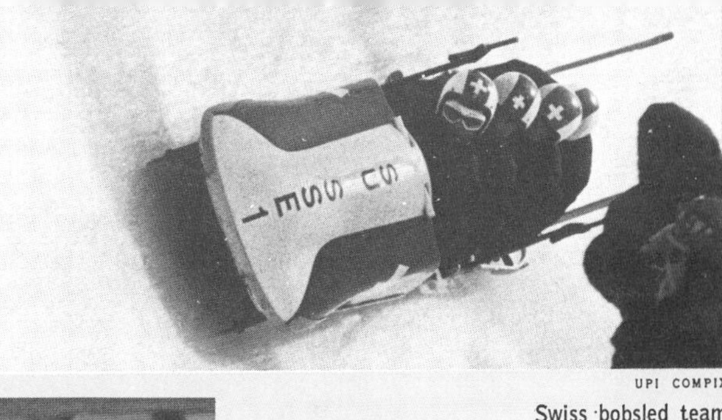

UPI COMPIX
Swiss bobsled team

WIDE WORLD
Mark Spitz

KEYSTONE
Frank Shorter

UPI COMPIX
Barbara Cochran

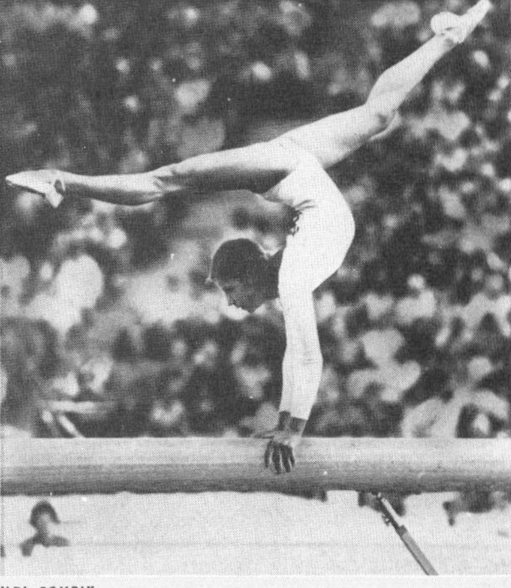

UPI COMPIX
Olga Korbut

KEYSTONE
Mary Peters

biathlon title. The Soviets retained the biathlon team relay. Galina Kulakova, a stocky Soviet physical education teacher, was the most successful woman competitor in the games, winning both the 5-km. and 10-km. cross-country ski events and sharing a third gold medal as a member of the winning relay team.

Italy failed to retain either of the bobsled titles. West German crews gained the first two places in the two-man event. Wolfgang Zimmerer, with Peter Utzschneider his brakeman, made the best time in each of the first three heats, exercising prudent caution in the fourth to ensure a winning score. Horst Floth, braked by Pepi Bader, earned the silver medal after breaking a course record that would last forever because the difficult but not very dangerous Mt. Teine track, specially built for the meeting, was afterward broken up. In the four-man event, Jean Wicki steered his Swiss team to a narrow victory over Nevio De Zordo's Italian sled.

East Germans scored victories in both the men's and women's luge tobogganing singles, Wolfgang Scheidel and Anna Muller gaining the titles by negotiating the 14 hazardous curves with consistently superior steering and weight transference. An East German monopoly was prevented when, in the men's two-seater luge, Horst Hornlein and Reinhard Bredow were held to a dramatic first place tie with Paul Hildgartner and Walter Plaikner of Italy. The teams had identical aggregates for the two runs, and so two gold medals were awarded.

As in every Winter Olympics, ice hockey proved the biggest crowd-puller. Winner for the third consecutive time was the Soviet Union. With a more vulnerable defense than in the two previous Olympics, the Soviet team could no longer outclass its opponents. Nevertheless, the U.S.S.R. dropped only one point in a 3–3 draw with Sweden. A startling 5–1 victory by the United States over Czechoslovakia earned an unexpected silver medal for the youngest-ever U.S. team. The competition's leading scorer was the Soviet winger, Valery Kharlamov, with 9 goals and 6 assists, but the outstanding individual was Michael Curran, the U.S. goalkeeper, credited with 194 saves in 5 matches.

Summer Olympics. The XX Olympic Games were the largest and most expensive ever staged. Over 10,000 athletes from 124 countries participated in 21 sports during 16 days that rewrote the record books. The most successful overall team, by the yardstick of medals won, was that of the U.S.S.R., which took 50 of the 195 gold medals at stake. When weighted for size of population, however, by far the most powerful team was that of East Germany, where sports had been intensively encouraged for years. Competitors from only 25 countries won titles of any kind, while another 23 had to be content with silver and/or bronze medals. This left more than half the national teams (76) to return home empty-handed.

As in all the preceding 16 Olympic Games (3 were canceled due to World Wars), "superstars" emerged. The three men of the 1972 Games were Lasse Viren of Finland (*see* BIOGRAPHY), winner of the 5,000- and 10,000-m. runs; Valery Borzov (U.S.S.R.), winner of the 100- and 200-m. dashes; and Mark Spitz of the U.S. (*see* BIOGRAPHY), the fastest swimmer in history and the first man able to win seven gold medals in one Games. On the feminine side were Olga Korbut, the tiny gravity-defying Soviet gymnast (*see* BIOGRAPHY), and West Germany's Ulrike Meyfarth, who at 16 became the youngest track competitor ever to win a gold medal with her world record equaling 6 ft. $3\frac{1}{2}$ in. (1.92 m.) high jump.

World records were bettered or equaled in 12 of the 38 track and field events. Of these perhaps the most impressive was that of the 400-m. hurdler John Akii-Bua (Uganda), who lowered by 0.3 sec. the record set against 20% less atmospheric resistance by David Hemery (U.K.) at the Mexico City Games of 1968. Akii-Bua, one of a family of 43 and with 8 brothers or half-brothers who represented Uganda at the Games, served notice that African athletes would soon be more fully represented in the roll of world record holders.

The sprints were dominated by Borzov, who won the 100 m. by a full metre from Robert Taylor (U.S.) and the 200 m. by 2 m. from Larry Black (U.S.). Consternation had occurred at the afternoon session on August 31 when only one (Taylor) of the

OLYMPIC CHAMPIONS, 1972 SUMMER GAMES, MUNICH

Archery

Men's round	J. Williams (U.S.)	Women's round	D. Wilber (U.S.)

Basketball

Winning team U.S.S.R. (beat U.S. 51–50 in final)

Boxing

Light flyweight	G. Gedo (Hung.)	Welterweight	E. Correa (Cuba)
Flyweight	G. Kostadinov (Bulg.)	Light middleweight	D. Kottysch (W.Ger.)
Bantamweight	O. Martinez (Cuba)	Middleweight	V. Lemechev (U.S.S.R.)
Featherweight	B. Kousnetsov (U.S.S.R.)	Light heavyweight	M. Parlov (Yugos.)
Lightweight	J. Szczepanski (Pol.)	Heavyweight	T. Stevenson (Cuba)
Light welterweight	R. Seales (U.S.)		

Canoeing

	Men	
1,000-m. Canadian singles	I. Patzaichin (Rom.)	4 min. 08.94 sec.
1,000-m. Canadian pairs	U.S.S.R.	3 min. 52.60 sec.
1,000-m. kayak singles	A. Shaparenko (U.S.S.R.)	3 min. 48.06 sec.
1,000-m. kayak pairs	U.S.S.R.	3 min. 31.23 sec.
1,000-m. kayak fours	U.S.S.R.	3 min. 14.02 sec.
Slalom Canadian singles	R. Eiben (E.Ger.)	315.84 pt.
Slalom Canadian pairs	East Germany	310.68 pt.
Slalom kayak singles	S. Horn (E.Ger.)	268.56 pt.
	Women	
500-m. kayak singles	Y. Ryabchinskaya (U.S.S.R.)	2 min. 03.17 sec.
500-m. kayak pairs	U.S.S.R.	1 min. 53.50 sec.
Slalom kayak singles	A. Bahmann (E.Ger.)	364.50 pt.

Cycling

1,000-m. sprint	D. Morelon (France)	11.25 sec. (Best 200 m.)
1,000-m. time trial	N. Fredborg (Den.)	1 min. 06.44 sec.
2,000-m. tandem	U.S.S.R.	10.52 sec. (Best 200 m.)
4,000-m. individual pursuit	K. Knudsen (Nor.)	4 min. 45.74 sec.
4,000-m. team pursuit	West Germany	4 min. 22.14 sec.
100-km. team time trial	U.S.S.R.	2 hr. 11 min. 17.8 sec.
Road race (200-km.)	H. Kuiper (Neth.)	4 hr. 14 min. 37.0 sec.

Equestrian Sports

	Individual	*Team*
Dressage	L. Linsenhoff (W.Ger.) on Piaff	U.S.S.R.
3-day event	R. Meade (U.K.) on Laurieston	United Kingdom
Show jumping	G. Mancinelli (Italy) on Ambassador	West Germany

Fencing

	Individual	*Team*
Foil	W. Woyda (Pol.)	Poland
Épée	C. Fenyvesi (Hung.)	Hungary
Sabre	V. Sidiak (U.S.S.R.)	Italy
Women's foil	A. Ragno (Italy)	U.S.S.R.

Football (Soccer)

Winning team Poland (beat Hungary 2–1 in final)

Gymnastics

	Men	*Women*
Combined exercises		
individual	S. Kato (Jap.)	L. Tourischeva (U.S.S.R.)
team	Japan	U.S.S.R.
Parallel bars	S. Kato (Jap.)	—
Uneven parallel bars	—	K. Janz (E.Ger.)
Horizontal bar	M. Tsukahara (Jap.)	—
Long horse	K. Koeste (E.Ger.)	K. Janz (E.Ger.)
Pommeled horse	V. Klimenko (U.S.S.R.)	—
Rings	A. Nakayama (Jap.)	—
Balance beam	—	O. Korbut (U.S.S.R.)
Floor exercises	N. Andrianov (U.S.S.R.)	O. Korbut (U.S.S.R.)

Handball

Winning team Yugoslavia (beat Czechoslovakia 21–16 in final)

Hockey (Field)

Winning team West Germany (beat Pakistan 1–0 in final)

Judo

Lightweight	T. Kawaguchi (Jap.)	Light heavyweight	S. Chochoshvili (U.S.S.R.)
Welterweight	T. Nomura (Jap.)	Heavyweight	W. Ruska (Neth.)
Middleweight	S. Sekine (Jap.)	Open class	W. Ruska (Neth.)

Modern Pentathlon

Individual	A. Balczo (Hung.)	5,412 pt.
Team	U.S.S.R.	15,968 pt.

Rowing

Single sculls	Y. Malishev (U.S.S.R.)	7 min. 10.12 sec.
Double sculls	U.S.S.R.	7 min. 01.77 sec.
Coxed pairs	East Germany	7 min. 17.25 sec.
Coxless pairs	East Germany	6 min. 53.16 sec.
Coxed fours	West Germany	6 min. 31.85 sec.
Coxless fours	East Germany	6 min. 24.27 sec.
Eights	New Zealand	6 min. 08.94 sec.

Shooting

Free pistol	R. Skanaker (Swed.)	567 pt.*
Free rifle	L. Wigger (U.S.)	1,155 pt.
Small-bore rifle (prone)	Ho Jun Li (N.Kor.)	599 pt.†
Small-bore rifle (3-position)	J. Writer (U.S.)	1,166 pt.†
Rapid-fire pistol	J. Zapedzki (Pol.)	595 pt.*
Trapshooting	A. Scalzone (Italy)	199 pt.†
Skeet shooting	K. Wirnhier (W.Ger.)	195 pt.
Moving target	L. Zhelezniak (U.S.S.R.)	569 pt.†

Swimming and Diving

	Men	
100-m. freestyle	M. Spitz (U.S.)	51.22 sec.†
200-m. freestyle	M. Spitz (U.S.)	1 min. 52.78 sec.†
400-m. freestyle	B. Cooper (Austr.)	4 min. 00.27 sec.*
1,500-m. freestyle	M. Burton (U.S.)	15 min. 52.58 sec.†
100-m. breaststroke	N. Taguchi (Jap.)	1 min. 04.94 sec.†
200-m. breaststroke	J. Hencken (U.S.)	2 min. 21.55 sec.†
100-m. butterfly	M. Spitz (U.S.)	54.27 sec.†
200-m. butterfly	M. Spitz (U.S.)	2 min. 00.70 sec.†
100-m. backstroke	R. Matthes (E.Ger.)	56.58 sec.*
200-m. backstroke	R. Matthes (E.Ger.)	2 min. 02.82 sec.§

Swimming and Diving (continued)

	Men	
200-m. individual medley	G. Larsson (Swed.)	2 min. 07.17 sec.†
400-m. individual medley	G. Larsson (Swed.)	4 min. 31.98 sec.*
400-m. freestyle relay	United States	3 min. 26.42 sec.†
800-m. freestyle relay	United States	7 min. 35.78 sec.†
400-m. medley relay	United States	3 min. 48.16 sec.†
Platform diving	K. Dibiasi (Italy)	504.12 pt.
Springboard diving	V. Vasin (U.S.S.R.)	594.09 pt.
	Women	
100-m. freestyle	S. Neilson (U.S.)	58.59 sec.*
200-m. freestyle	S. Gould (Austr.)	2 min. 03.56 sec.†
400-m. freestyle	S. Gould (Austr.)	4 min. 19.04 sec.†
800-m. freestyle	K. Rothhammer (U.S.)	8 min. 53.68 sec.†
100-m. breaststroke	C. Carr (U.S.)	1 min. 13.58 sec.†
200-m. breaststroke	B. Whitfield (Austr.)	2 min. 41.71 sec.*
100-m. butterfly	M. Aoki (Jap.)	1 min. 03.34 sec.†
200-m. butterfly	K. Moe (U.S.)	2 min. 15.57 sec.†
100-m. backstroke	M. Belote (U.S.)	1 min. 05.78 sec.*
200-m. backstroke	M. Belote (U.S.)	2 min. 19.19 sec.†
200-m. individual medley	S. Gould (Austr.)	2 min. 23.07 sec.†
400-m. individual medley	G. Neall (Austr.)	5 min. 02.97 sec.†
400-m. freestyle relay	United States	3 min. 55.19 sec.†
400-m. medley relay	United States	4 min. 20.75 sec.†
Platform diving	U. Knape (Swed.)	390.00 pt.
Springboard diving	M. King (U.S.)	450.03 pt.

Track and Field

	Men	
100-m. dash	V. Borzov (U.S.S.R.)	10.14 sec.
200-m. dash	V. Borzov (U.S.S.R.)	20.00 sec.
400-m. dash	V. Matthews (U.S.)	44.66 sec.
800-m. run	D. Wottle (U.S.)	1 min. 45.9 sec.
1,500-m. run	P. Vasala (Fin.)	3 min. 36.3 sec.
5,000-m. run	L. Viren (Fin.)	13 min. 26.4 sec.*
10,000-m. run	L. Viren (Fin.)	27 min. 38.4 sec.†
Marathon	F. Shorter (U.S.)	2 hr. 12 min. 19.8 sec.
110-m. hurdles	R. Milburn (U.S.)	13.24 sec.§
400-m. hurdles	J. Akii-Bua (Uganda)	47.82 sec.†
3,000-m. steeplechase	K. Keino (Kenya)	8 min. 23.6 sec.*
400-m. relay	United States	38.19 sec.§
1,600-m. relay	Kenya	2 min. 59.8 sec.
20-km. walk	P. Frenkel (E.Ger.)	1 hr. 26 min. 42.4 sec.*
50-km. walk	B. Kannenberg (W.Ger.)	3 hr. 56 min. 11.6 sec.*
High jump	Y. Tarmak (U.S.S.R.)	2.23 m.
Long jump	R. Williams (U.S.)	8.24 m.
Pole vault	W. Nordwig (E.Ger.)	5.50 m.*
Triple jump	V. Saneyev (U.S.S.R.)	17.35 m.
Shot put	W. Komar (Pol.)	21.18 m.*
Discus	L. Danek (Czech.)	64.40 m.
Hammer throw	A. Bondarchuk (U.S.S.R.)	75.50 m.*
Javelin	K. Wolfermann (W.Ger.)	90.48 m.*
Decathlon	N. Avilov (U.S.S.R.)	8,454 pt.†
	Women	
100-m. dash	R. Stecher (E.Ger.)	11.07 sec.§
200-m. dash	R. Stecher (E.Ger.)	22.40 sec.§
400-m. dash	M. Zehrt (E.Ger.)	51.08 sec.*
800-m. run	H. Falck (W.Ger.)	1 min. 58.6 sec.*
1,500-m. run	L. Bragina (U.S.S.R.)	4 min. 01.4 sec.†
100-m. hurdles	A. Ehrhardt (E.Ger.)	12.59 sec.*
400-m. relay	West Germany	42.81 sec.§
1,600-m. relay	East Germany	3 min. 23.0 sec.†
High jump	U. Meyfarth (W.Ger.)	1.92 m.§
Long jump	H. Rosendahl (W.Ger.)	6.78 m.
Shot put	N. Chizhova (U.S.S.R.)	21.03 m.†
Discus	F. Melnik (U.S.S.R.)	66.62 m.*
Javelin	R. Fuchs (E.Ger.)	63.88 m.*
Pentathlon	M. Peters (U.K.)	4,801 pt.†

Volleyball

Winning men's team Japan (beat East Germany 3–1 in final)	Winning women's team U.S.S.R. (beat Japan 3–2 in final)

Water Polo

Winning team U.S.S.R.
(tied Hungary 3–3 in final; U.S.S.R. declared winner because it outscored its opponents 22–16 over last five matches; Hungary's goal record was 23–18)

Weight Lifting

Flyweight	Z. Smalcerz (Pol.)	337.5 kg.*
Bantamweight	I. Foeldi (Hung.)	377.5 kg.†
Featherweight	N. Nourikian (Bulg.)	402.5 kg.§
Lightweight	M. Kirzhinov (U.S.S.R.)	460.0 kg.†
Middleweight	Y. Bikov (Bulg.)	485.0 kg.†
Light heavyweight	L. Jenssen (Nor.)	507.5 kg.*
Middle heavyweight	A. Nikolov (Bulg.)	525.0 kg.*
Heavyweight	Y. Talts (U.S.S.R.)	580.0 kg.*
Super heavyweight	V. Alekseyev (U.S.S.R.)	640.0 kg.*

Wrestling

	Freestyle	*Greco-Roman*
Paperweight	R. Dmitriev (U.S.S.R.)	G. Berceanu (Rom.)
Flyweight	K. Kato (Jap.)	P. Kirov (Bulg.)
Bantamweight	H. Yanagida (Jap.)	R. Kazakov (U.S.S.R.)
Featherweight	Z. Abdulbekov (U.S.S.R.)	G. Markov (Bulg.)
Lightweight	D. Gable (U.S.)	S. Khisamutdinov (U.S.S.R.)
Welterweight	W. Wells (U.S.)	V. Macha (Czech.)
Middleweight	L. Tediashvili (U.S.S.R.)	C. Hegedus (Hung.)
Light heavyweight	B. Peterson (U.S.)	V. Rezantsev (U.S.S.R.)
Heavyweight	I. Yarygin (U.S.S.R.)	N. Martinescu (Rom.)
Super heavyweight	A. Medved (U.S.S.R.)	A. Roshin (U.S.S.R.)

Yachting

Finn class	S. Maury (France)
Flying Dutchman class	R. Pattisson (U.K.) in "Superdoso"
Tempest class	V. Mankin (U.S.S.R.) in "Eskimo"
Soling class	H. Melges (U.S.) in "Teal"
Star class	D. Forbes (Austr.) in "Simba V"
Dragon class	J. Cuneo (Austr.) in "Wyuana"

*Olympic record.
†World record.
‡Equals Olympic record.
§Equals world record.

three U.S. sprinters appeared for the second qualifying round of the 100 m. Both Rey Robinson and his fellow co-holder of the world's record in the 100 m., Eddie Hart, failed to appear on time. It transpired that both were watching television in the Olympic Village thinking they were viewing a replay of the first-round heats. Unfortunately, a team official had been using an out-of-date schedule of events.

The U.S. track and field team suffered a succession of other disasters quite beyond the laws of chance. The uncanny number of athletes who fell, including Jim Ryun in the 1,500-m. run, was believed to be related to the bounciness of the Rekordtan surfaced track and to the fact that it was so silent that athletes, who normally can gauge an opponent's whereabouts by sound, were continuously looking over their shoulders.

The U.S. team won only five of the men's track events. Vince Matthews took the 400 m. in 44.66 sec., but was later banned from the 1,600-m. relay for unseemly behaviour on the victory stand. David Wottle, whose golf cap caused as much interest as the monocle of a British sprinter in 1928, came from behind to win the 800 m. by a whisker. A third U.S. victor was the incomparable Rod Milburn, who flashed over the high hurdles in 13.24 sec. to equal the world record and win by a clear metre from the taller Frenchman Guy Drut. The fourth U.S. gold medal came in the 400-m. relay, run in a world record equaling time of 38.19 sec. by Black, Taylor, Gerald Tinker, and Hart. There was some solace for the Americans, who had so overpowered the rest of the world in all previous Olympics, when Frank Shorter won the 26 mi. 385 yd. marathon by more than 2 min. His time was less than 9 sec. over the fastest Olympic marathon, set by Abebe Bikila of Ethiopia in 1964.

In the field events there was controversy over the vacillation of the International Amateur Athletic Federation (IAAF) on the use of high-density vaulting poles. After a ban followed by a relaxation, there was a further ban, from which the world record holder, Bob Seagren (U.S.), was the most conspicuous sufferer. The winner was the East German Wolfgang Nordwig who set an Olympic record of 5.5 m. This ended the monopoly of this Olympic event by U.S. vaulters.

The expanded women's program of 14 events produced 7 new or equaled world records, 4 on the track, 2 in the field, and 1 in the pentathlon. Most outstanding of those on the track were the 1,500-m. victory of Ludmila Bragina (U.S.S.R.), whose time of 4 min. 1.4 sec., would have won the men's event as recently as 1920, and the 1,600-m. relay win by 15 yd. by the East Germans despite Kathy Hammond's astounding anchor stage of 49.2 sec. for the U.S. Perhaps the most emotional scenes in the stadium came in the women's high jump in which the 16-year-old West German girl Ulrike Meyfarth held the crowd spellbound while she successively raised her personal best to the point that she equaled the world record height of 1.92 m. The women's pentathlon was won by Mary Peters (U.K.; *see* BIOGRAPHY).

The staging of the 34 swimming, diving, and water polo events broke new ground technologically because of the astounding success of the swimming stadium's design in diminishing the wake of the swimmers. In the men's 15 individual and relay races, world records were set or equaled in all but the 400-m. freestyle, 100-m. backstroke, and 400-m. individual medley; in the 14 women's events there were new records in all but the 100-m. freestyle and backstroke and in the 200-m. breaststroke.

The domination of Mark Spitz was total. He either won or shared seven gold medals and seven new world records, and he emerged in the 100-m. freestyle as the fastest swimmer in history. He first took the 200-m. butterfly (2 min. 0.7 sec.) and followed with a time of 50.90 sec. as the anchor man on the winning U.S. 400-m. freestyle relay team. The next day he took the 200-m. freestyle in 1 min. 52.78 sec. His fourth gold medal came in the 100-m. butterfly with a time of 54.27 sec., and his fifth was won by swimming the anchor stage of the 800-m. freestyle relay. Spitz's sixth triumph was the 100-m. freestyle in which he set a world record 51.22 sec., and he gained his seventh and final gold medal in the third (butterfly) stage in the 400-m. medley relay.

The campaign of Australia's Shane Gould to sweep six women's titles got off to a fine start when she won the 200-m. individual medley with a world record of 2 min. 23.07 sec. But she received a setback in the 100-m. freestyle, finishing third behind Sandra Neilson and Shirley Babashoff of the U.S. Miss Neilson's winning time was 58.59 sec. The next day, however, the Australian came back to win the 400-m. freestyle in the world record time of 4 min. 19.04 sec. On September 1 she took her third gold medal, in the 200-m. freestyle, again in world record time (2 min. 3.56 sec.). Her bid for the 800-m. title was thwarted by Keena Rothhammer (U.S.), who won in a world record 8 min. 53.68 sec. with Miss Gould finishing second.

Controversy entered the swimming arena when Rick DeMont of the U.S. was stripped of his 400-m. freestyle gold medal for taking an improper asthma medication before the race. DeMont was also prevented from entering the 1,500-m. freestyle, as U.S. Olympic officials again drew criticism. Controversy also surrounded the judging of some of the diving events.

The return of archery after an absence of 52 years from the Olympic program produced an entry of 95 archers from 27 countries, and the top 3 men and 5 women equaled or beat the existing world records. The winners were the U.S. competitors John Williams (2,528 pt.) and Doreen Wilber (2,424 pt.). Canoeing was expanded to 11 events by the inclusion of 4 "white water" slalom events. These predictably attracted far greater interest than the "flat" kayak and Canadian events. The Soviets took six out of seven of the gold medals in the "flat" events, and East Germany won all the new slalom races.

Gymnastics made a tremendous impact on television audiences the world over and no single competitor more than a diminutive Soviet girl, Olga Korbut. She won gold medals for the floor exercises and the balance beam and was in the winning combined team exercises. She also performed dazzlingly on the uneven parallel bars to tie for second. In the men's events Sawao Kato of Japan and Viktor Klimenko (U.S.S.R.) were outstanding. Kato won the parallel bars and the individual combined exercises, helped Japan win the combined team exercises, and took home silver medals in the horizontal bar and pommeled horse. Klimenko won the pommeled horse.

Perhaps the ugliest scenes of the whole Games took place in the field hockey finals when the once-invincible players from India and Pakistan found themselves shunted to an unaccustomed bronze and silver medal, respectively, by West Germany. The Pakistanis behaved with ill grace in what was their only medal of the Games and the 11 members of the team were barred from future Olympic competition.

The United States' record of never having lost a basketball match since the Olympic inception of this sport in 1936 ended with a loss during confusion over the elapse of playing time. The Soviet team won the final 51–50 literally in the last second in a match that was restarted after it was pointed out by the Brazilian and Bulgarian referees that there were still three seconds left although the U.S. team was already celebrating a triumph.

Cuba, with 3 (bantamweight, welterweight, and heavyweight) out of the 11 gold medals, was the most successful country in boxing. The only other country with more than a single success was the U.S.S.R., whose men took the featherweight and middleweight divisions and, ironically, supplied the coaches for the Cuban squad. The greatest of the Cubans was the heavyweight winner Teofilo Stevenson.

The wrestling program, extended to ten body weights in each of the styles (free and Greco-Roman), saw a great shifting of national fortunes. The U.S.S.R. grabbed nearly half the gold medals (nine) compared with three at Mexico City, while the Japanese were reduced from four in 1968 to two at Munich and the traditionally strong Turks and East Germans went home empty-handed. The U.S. had its best performance ever with three gold medals.

Sporting Record

AEROBATICS

Event	Winner	Country
WORLD CHAMPIONS		
Men	R. Hilliard	U.S.
Women	M. Gaffaney	U.S.
Team	U.S.	

ARCHERY

Event	Winner	Country
EUROPEAN CHAMPIONS		
Men's individual	G. Jarvil	Sweden
Men's team	Sweden	
Women's individual	K. Lossaberidze	U.S.S.R.
Women's team	U.S.S.R.	
MUNICH PRE-OLYMPIC TOURNAMENT WINNERS		
Men's individual	A. Jacobsen	Denmark
Women's individual	E. Gapchenko	U.S.S.R.

BADMINTON

Event	Winner	Country
EUROPEAN CHAMPIONS		
Men's singles	W. Bochow	West Germany
Men's doubles	W. Braun, R. Maywald	West Germany
Women's singles	M. Beck	U.K.
Women's doubles	G. Gilks, J. Hashman	U.K.
Mixed doubles	D. Talbot, G. Gilks	U.K.
Team	U.K.	
OLYMPIC GAMES DEMONSTRATION TOURNAMENT WINNERS		
Men's singles	R. Hartono	Indonesia
Men's doubles	A. Chandra, C. Handrinata	Indonesia
Women's singles	N. Nakayama	Japan
Mixed doubles	D. Talbot, G. Gilks	U.K.
UBER CUP (World team championship, women)		
World champions	Japan	
European champions	Denmark	
North American champions	Canada	

BOBSLEDDING

Event	Winner	Country
EUROPEAN CHAMPIONS		
Four-man	H. Müller, H. Ott, R. Born, H. Hiltebrand	Switzerland
Two-man	W. Zimmerer, P. Utzschneider	West Germany

CROSS-COUNTRY

Event	Winner	Country
INTERNATIONAL CHAMPIONS		
Senior, individual	G. Roelants	Belgium
Senior, team	England	
Junior, individual	A. Tomasoni	Italy
Junior, team	Italy	
Women, individual	J. Smith	England
Women, team	England	
EUROPEAN CLUB CHAMPIONS		
Individual	K. Lismont	Belgium
Team	FC Liegois	Belgium
NATIONAL CHAMPIONS—MEN		
Belgium	G. Roelants	
Canada	R. Munro	
Czechoslovakia	P. Penkava	
East Germany	M. Kuschmann	
England: Senior	M. Thomas	
Junior	D. Black	
Ireland: Senior	J. Buckley	
Junior	D. O'Connor	
Morocco	H. Jaddour	
Netherlands	J. Hermens	
Northern Ireland	M. Teer	
Norway	A. Risa	
Scotland: Senior	I. McCafferty	
Junior	J. Brown	
Wales	M. Thomas	
West Germany	L. Philipp	
NATIONAL CHAMPIONS—WOMEN		
Canada	G. Reiser	
Czechoslovakia	E. Privrelova	
East Germany	G. Hoffmeister	
England	R. Ridley	
Ireland	M. Lynch	
Netherlands	B. Boxem	
Scotland	M. Coomber	
U.S.	D. Brown	
Wales	B. Cardy	
West Germany	E. Tittel	

WIDE WORLD

CURLING

Event	Winner
WORLD CHAMPIONS	Canada

CYCLING

Event	Winner	Country
WORLD CHAMPIONS—PROFESSIONAL		
Sprint	R. van Lancker	Belgium
Individual pursuit	H. Porter	U.K.
Motor-paced	T. Verschueren	Belgium
Road	M. Basso	Italy
WORLD CHAMPIONS—AMATEUR		
Sprint	Not held	
Individual pursuit	Not held	
Team pursuit	Not held	
Motor-paced	H. Gnas	West Germany
Road	Not held	
WORLD CHAMPIONS—WOMEN		
Sprint	G. Ermolayeva	U.S.S.R.
Individual pursuit	T. Garkushina	U.S.S.R.
Road	G. Gambillon	France
MAJOR PROFESSIONAL ROAD-RACE WINNERS		
Critérium des As	R. Poulidor	France
Flèche Wallonne	E. Merckx	Belgium
Four Days of Dunkirk	Y. Hezard	France
Liège–Bastogne–Liège	E. Merckx	Belgium
Midi-Libre	C. Guimard	France
Milan–San Remo	E. Merckx	Belgium
Paris–Roubaix	R. de Vlaeminck	Belgium
Paris–Tours	N. van Tyghem	Belgium
Paris–Nice	R. Poulidor	France
Tour of Belgium	R. Swerts	Belgium
Tour of the Dauphiné	L. Ocana	Spain
Tour of Flanders	E. Leman	Belgium
Tour of France	E. Merckx	Belgium
Tour of Emilia	E. Merckx	Belgium
Tour of Italy	E. Merckx	Belgium
Tour of Lombardy	E. Merckx	Belgium
Tour of Luxembourg	R. Rosiers	Belgium
Tour of Portugal	J. Agostinho	Portugal
Tour of Normandy	B. Thevenet	France
Tour of Spain	J.-M. Fuente	Spain
Tour of Switzerland	L. Pfenninger	Switzerland
Grand Prix des Nations	R. Swerts	Belgium
MAJOR AMATEUR ROAD-RACE WINNERS		
Paris–Roubaix	Y. Benaets	Belgium
Tour de l'Avenir	F. den Hartog	Netherlands
Tour of Britain	H. Kuiper	Netherlands
Tour of the U.S.S.R.	R. Kalieniecs	U.S.S.R.
Warsaw–Berlin–Prague	V. Moravec	Czechoslovakia
William Tell Grand Prix	D. Lloyd	U.K.
Grand Prix des Nations	G. Bischoff	Switzerland
NATIONAL ROAD-RACE CHAMPIONS		
Belgium	W. Godefroot	
France	R. Berland	
Italy	F. Gimondi	
Luxembourg	R. Gilson	
Netherlands	T. Tabak	
Portugal	J. Agostinho	
Spain	L. Ocana	
Switzerland	J. Fuchs	
U.K.	G. Crewe	
West Germany	W. Peffgen	

FENCING

Event	Winner	Country
EUROPEAN CUP WINNERS		
Men's foil, team	A. S. Melun	France
Women's foil, team	Steaua Bucharest	Romania

FOOTBALL, ASSOCIATION

Event	Winner	Country
MAJOR INTERNATIONAL TOURNAMENTS (National teams)		
Asian Nations' Cup	Iran	
African Nations' Cup	Congo	
Brazilian Independence Trophy	Brazil	
Central American Championship	Mexico	
European Under 23 Championship	Czechoslovakia	
European Youth Championship	England	
British Isles international championship	England	
MAJOR INTERNATIONAL TOURNAMENTS (Clubs)		
World Champions' Cup	Ajax Amsterdam	Netherlands
European Champions' Cup	Ajax Amsterdam	Netherlands
European Cup-Winners' Cup	Glasgow Rangers	Scotland
South American Champions' Cup	Independiente	Argentina
UEFA Cup	Tottenham Hotspur	England

NATIONAL CHAMPIONS (National Cup and League Winners)		
Albania	League	Vlaznia
Algeria	Cup	Hamra Annaba
Argentina	League	Rosario Central
Austria	Cup	Vienna FC
	League	Wacker Innsbruck
Belgium	Cup	SC Anderlecht
	League	SC Anderlecht
Brazil	League	Atletico Mineiro
Bulgaria	Cup	CSKA Sofia
	League	CSKA Sofia
Chile	League	Union San Felipe
Colombia	League	Millionarios
Czechoslovakia	Cup	Sparta Prague
	League	Spartak Trnava
East Germany	Cup	Carl Zeiss Jena
	League	FC Magdeburg
Ecuador	League	Barcelona FC
England	FA Cup	Leeds United
	League Cup	Stoke City
	League	Derby County
Finland	Cup	Reipos Lahti
	League	TPS Turku
France	Cup	Olympique Marseilles
	League	Olympique Marseilles
Greece	Cup	Salonika
	League	Panathinaikos
Hungary	Cup	Ferencvaros
Ireland	Cup	Cork Hibernians
	League	Waterford
Israel	League	Maccabi Tel-Aviv
Italy	Cup	FC Milan
	League	Juventus
Luxembourg	Cup	Red Boys Differdingen
Netherlands	League	Ajax Amsterdam
Northern Ireland	Cup	Coleraine
Norway	Cup	Brann Bergen
	League	Viking
Paraguay	League	Olimpia
Peru	League	Universitario
Poland	Cup	Gornik Zabrze
	League	Gornik Zabrze
Portugal	Cup	Benfica
	League	Benfica
Romania	Cup	Rapid Bucharest
	League	Pitesti
Scotland	Cup	Glasgow Celtic
	League	Glasgow Celtic
Spain	Cup	Atletico Madrid
Sweden	Cup	Landskrona
Switzerland	Cup	FC Zürich
	League	FC Basel
Turkey	League	Galatasaray
Uruguay	League	Nacional
Wales	Cup	Wrexham
West Germany	Cup	Schalke 04
	League	Bayern Munich
Yugoslavia	Cup	Hajduk Split
	League	Zeljeznicar

GLIDING

Event	Winner	Country
WORLD CHAMPIONS		
Standard class	J. Wroblewski	Poland
Open class	G. Ax	Sweden

HANDBALL

Event	Winner
WORLD CHAMPIONS	
Men's team	Romania
Women's team	East Germany

JUDO

Event	Winner	Country
WORLD UNIVERSITIES' CHAMPIONS		
Lightweight	Y. Ishime	Japan
Light-middleweight	F. Mitsumoto	Japan
Middleweight	H. Yoshinaga	Japan
Light-heavyweight	K. Eya	Japan
Heavyweight	H. Uemara	Japan
Unlimited weight	T. Nakamura	Japan
Team	Japan	
EUROPEAN CHAMPIONS		
Lightweight	J.-J. Mounier	France
Light-middleweight	H. Hotgen	East Germany
Middleweight	J.-P. Coche	France
Light-heavyweight	A. Parisi	U.K.
Heavyweight	W. Ruska	Netherlands
Unlimited weight	W. Ruska	Netherlands
Team	U.S.S.R.	

KARATE

Event	Winner	Country
WORLD CHAMPIONS		
Individual	L. T. Watarabe	Brazil
Team	France	

KARTING

Event	Winner	Country
WORLD CHAMPION	F. Goldstein	Belgium

MODERN PENTATHLON

Event	Winner	Country
WORLD JUNIOR CHAMPIONS		
Individual	G. Plank	Hungary
Team	Hungary	
U.S. CHAMPION	C. Richards	
U.K. CHAMPION	J. Fox	

MOTORCYCLING

Event	Winner	Country
WORLD CHAMPIONS		
50 cc.	A. Nieto	Spain
125 cc.	A. Nieto	Spain
250 cc.	J. Saarinen	Finland
350 cc.	G. Agostini	Italy
500 cc.	G. Agostini	Italy
Sidecar	K. Enders	West Germany

ORIENTEERING

Event	Winner	Country
WORLD CHAMPIONS		
Men's individual	A. Hadler	Norway
Men's team	Sweden	
Women's individual	S. Monspart	Hungary
Women's team	Finland	

PARACHUTING

Event	Winner	Country
WORLD CHAMPIONS—MEN		
Jumping	J. Armaing	France
Precision	I. Majer	Czechoslovakia
Combined	R. Schoelpple	U.S.
Precision, team	Switzerland	
Combined, team	U.S.S.R.	
WORLD CHAMPIONS—WOMEN		
Jumping	M.-F. Baulez	France
Precision	L. Dyuyova	U.S.S.R.
Combined	D. Karkoschka	East Germany
Precision, team	Bulgaria	

RACKETS

Event	Winner	Country
World Open championship	W. Surtees	U.K.
U.K. amateur championship	H. Angus	U.K.
U.K. amateur championship doubles	H. Angus, C. Hue-Williams	U.K.
U.K. open championship doubles	F. Willis, C. Emms	U.K.

ROLLER HOCKEY

Event	Winner
WORLD CHAMPIONS	Spain

ROLLER SKATING

Event	Winner	Country
WORLD CHAMPIONS		
Men	M. Obrecht	West Germany
Women	P. Hausler	West Germany
Pairs	G. Robowitsky, D. Robowitsky	U.S.
Dance	D. Lambert, F. Straker	U.S.

SAILING

Class	Helmsman	Country
WORLD CHAMPIONS		
Cadet	G. Owens	U.K.
Contender	P. Hollis	Australia
Dragon	A. Birch	Denmark
Enterprise	R. Hance	U.K.
Finn	J. Bruder	Brazil
Fireball	J. Diesch	West Germany
5.5 m.	C. Bigar	Switzerland
5-0-5	N. Loday	France
4-2-0	D. Johnsen	West Germany
4-7-0	J. Vollebregt	Netherlands
Hornet	M. Goodwin	U.K.
Moth	J. Faroux	France
O.K.	K. Axroth	Sweden
Star	W. Kuhweide	West Germany
Tornado	R. Jessenig	Austria
Vauriens	J. Quemeneur	France
EUROPEAN CHAMPIONS		
Finn	C. Schröder	East Germany
Fireball	J. Vuithier	Switzerland
Finn Junior	R. Blaszka	Poland
Flying Dutchman	R. Pattisson	U.K.
5-0-5	S. Sjöstrom	Sweden
4-7-0	J. van Werkoven	Netherlands
Moth	C. Hervet	France
Soling	C. Schwartz	East Germany
Star	P. Pettersson	Sweden
Tornado	I. Fraser	U.K.
Tempest	B. Staartjes	Netherlands

WIDE WORLD

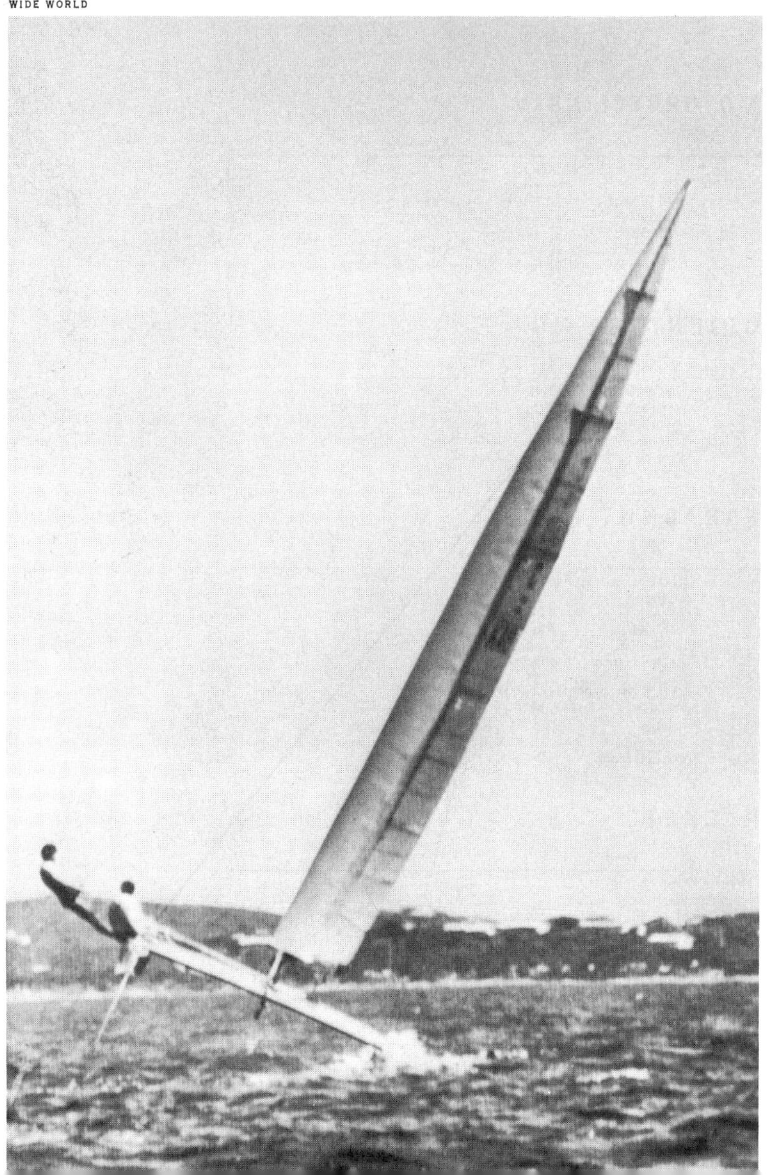

PRE-OLYMPIC REGATTA WINNERS		
Finn	T. Lundquist	Sweden
Flying Dutchman	R. Pattisson	U.K.
Soling	Crown Prince Harald	Norway
Tempest	H. Laprell	West Germany
Dragon	P. Jensen	Denmark
Star	J. Bruder	Brazil

SPEEDWAY

Event	Winner	Country
WORLD CHAMPIONS		
Individual	I. Mauger	New Zealand/U.K.
Pairs	T. Betts, R. Wilson	England
Team	T. Betts, J. Louis, I. Mauger, R. Wilson	Great Britain

SQUASH RACKETS

Event	Winner	Country
British open, men	J. Barrington	U.K.
British open, women	H. McKay	Australia
British amateur, men	G. Alauddin	Pakistan

TABLE TENNIS

Event	Winner	Country
EUROPEAN CHAMPIONS		
Men's singles	S. Bengtsson	Sweden
Men's doubles	I. Jonver, P. Rozsas	Hungary
Women's singles	Z. Rudnova	U.S.S.R.
Women's doubles	J. Magos, H. Lotaller	Hungary
Mixed doubles	S. Gomozkov, Z. Rudnova	U.S.S.R.
Men's team	Sweden	
Women's team	Hungary	
BRITISH OPEN CHAMPIONS		
Men's singles	S. Bengtsson	Sweden
Men's doubles	A. Stipancic, D. Surbek	Yugoslavia
Women's singles	M. Alexandru	Romania
Women's doubles	M. Alexandru, E. Vlaicov	Romania
Mixed doubles	A. Stipancic, M. Alexandru	Yugoslavia, Romania
Men's team	Sweden	
Women's team	Czechoslovakia	
WEST GERMAN OPEN CHAMPIONS		
Men's singles	K. Johansson	Sweden
Men's doubles	S. Bengtsson, K. Johansson	Sweden
Women's singles	Z. Rudnova	U.S.S.R.
Women's doubles	M. Alexandru, C. Crisan	Romania
Mixed doubles	J. Secretin, C. Bergeret	France
Men's team	Sweden	
Women's team	Hungary	
ASIAN CHAMPIONS		
Men's singles	N. Hasegawa	Japan
Women's singles	Li Li	China
Mixed doubles	M. Kono, T. Inoue	Japan

TOBOGGANING

Event	Winner	Country
EUROPEAN CHAMPIONS		
Men's singles	W. Fiedler	East Germany
Women's singles	U. Rührold	East Germany
Men's pairs	H. Hörnlein, R. Bredow	East Germany

TRACK AND FIELD

Event	Winner, affiliation	Performance
U.S. NATIONAL AAU CHAMPIONS—MEN (OUTDOORS)		
100 m.	R. Taylor, Texas Southern	10.2 sec.
200 m.	C. Smith, Southern California Striders	20.7 sec.
400 m.	L. Evans, Bay Area Striders	45 sec.
800 m.	D. Wottle, Bowling Green State	1 min. 47.3 sec.
1,500 m.	J. Howe, Kansas State	3 min. 38.2 sec.
5,000 m.	M. Keogh, Manhattan	13 min. 51.8 sec.
10,000 m.	G. Fredericks, Penn State	28 min. 8 sec.
3,000-m. steeplechase	J. Dare, U.S. Navy	8 min. 33.8 sec.
110-m. hurdles	R. Milburn, Southern University	13.4 sec.
400-m. hurdles	D. Bruggeman, Ohio Track Club	50 sec.
High jump	B. Schur, Kansas	7 ft. 2 in.
Pole vault	D. Roberts, Rice	18 ft. ¼ in.
Long jump	A. Robinson, Fort McArthur	26 ft. 5¾ in.
Triple jump	J. Craft, U. of Chicago Track Club	54 ft. 10 in.
Shot put	R. Matson, Texas Striders	69 ft. 6½ in.
Discus	J. Silvester, Intermountain Track Club	213 ft.
Hammer throw	A. Schoterman, Kent State	228 ft. 1 in.
Javelin	F. Luke, Husky Spike Club	277 ft. 5 in.
U.S. NATIONAL AAU CHAMPIONS—WOMEN (OUTDOORS)		
100 m.	A. Annum, Ghana	11.5 sec.
200 m.	A. Annum, Ghana	23.4 sec.
400 m.	K. Hammond, Sacramento Road Runners	52.3 sec.
800 m.	C. Hudson, Albuquerque Olympic Club	2 min. 6.7 sec.

UPI COMPIX

Event	Winner, affiliation	Performance
1,500 m.	F. Larrieu, San Jose Cindergals	4 min. 18.4 sec.
3,000 m.	T. Anex, Will's Spikettes	9 min. 42.6 sec.
1,500-m. walk	J. Bocci, Wolverine Track Club	6 min. 59.1 sec.
100-m. hurdles	M. Rallins, Tennessee State U.	13.5 sec.
200-m. hurdles	P. Hawkins, Atoms Track Club	26.3 sec.
800-yd. medley relay	Sports International Track Club	1 min. 40.6 sec.
440-yd. relay	Sports International Track Club	45.4 sec.
1-mi. relay	Canton (O.) Track Club	3 min. 45.3 sec.
2-mi. relay	San Jose Cindergals	9 min. 7.3 sec.
High jump	A. Reid, Texas Women's U.	6 ft. ½ in.
Long jump	W. White, Mayor Daley Youth Foundation	20 ft. 6¼ in.
Shot put	M. Seidler, Mayor Daley Youth Foundation	52 ft. 9 in.
Discus	J. De la Vina, Mayor Daley Youth Foundation	172 ft. 9 in.
Javelin	S. Calvert, Los Angeles Track Club	184 ft.
Team	Los Angeles Track Club	64 pt.
U.S. NATIONAL AAU CHAMPIONS—MEN (INDOORS)		
60 yd.	D. Meriwether, unattached	6.2 sec.
600 yd.	L. Evans, Bay Area Striders	1 min. 11.3 sec.
1,000 yd.	J. Plachy, Czechoslovakia	2 min. 9.8 sec.
1 mi.	B. Dyce, United Athletic Association	4 min. 1.8 sec.
3 mi.	E. Puttemans, Belgium	13 min. 18.4 sec.
60-yd. hurdles	R. Milburn, Southern University	7.1 sec.
1-mi. relay	Brooklyn Over the Hill Athletic Association	3 min. 14.7 sec.
2-mi. relay	Manhattan College	7 min. 32.4 sec.
Sprint medley relay	Adelphi	2 min. 5.5 sec.
High jump	G. White, Penn State	7 ft. 2 in.
Pole vault	K. Isaksson, Sweden	17 ft. 10½ in.
Long jump	H. Hines, Southern California Striders	25 ft. 11¼ in.
Triple jump	J. Craft, U. of Chicago Track Club	54 ft. 4½ in.
Shot put	F. DeBernardi, U. of Texas, El Paso	66 ft. 1½ in.
35-lb. weight throw	G. Frenn, Pacific Coast Club	72 ft. 4 in.
U.S. NATIONAL AAU CHAMPIONS—WOMEN (INDOORS)		
60 yd.	I. Davis, Tennessee State U.	6.9 sec.
220 yd.	E. Stroy, Sports International Track Club	24.6 sec.
440 yd.	K. Hammond, Sacramento Road Runners	54.9 sec.
880 yd.	C. Toussaint, Atoms Track Club	2 min. 8.2 sec.
1 mi.	D. Brown, Falcons Track Club	4 min. 44 sec.
60-yd. hurdles	P. Johnson, Angels Track Club	7.5 sec.
640-yd. relay	Atoms Track Club	1 min. 10.4 sec.
880-yd. relay	Los Angeles Mercurettes	1 min. 46.2 sec.
1-mi. relay	New York Police Athletic League	3 min. 51.6 sec.
High jump	D. Van Kiekebelt, Canada	5 ft. 8 in.
Long jump	M. Watson, Los Angeles Track Club	20 ft. 11¾ in.
Shot put	M. Seidler, Mayor Daley Youth Foundation	50 ft. 11½ in.
Team	Atoms Track Club	16 pt.

TRAMPOLINE

Event	Winner	Country
WORLD CHAMPIONS		
Men's singles	P. Luxon	U.K.
Men's pairs	P. Luxon, R. Hughes	U.K.
Women's singles	A. Nicholson	U.S.
Women's pairs	M. Steig, R. Grant	U.S.

WATER SKIING

Event	Winner	Country
EUROPEAN CHAMPIONS—MEN		
Jumping	P. Seaton	U.K.
Figures	M. Stelno	Czechoslovakia
Slalom	R. Zucchi	Italy
Overall	P. Seaton	U.K.
EUROPEAN CHAMPIONS—WOMEN		
Jumping	W. Staehle	Netherlands
Figures	W. Staehle	Netherlands
Slalom	W. Staehle	Netherlands
Overall	W. Staehle	Netherlands
EUROPEAN CHAMPIONS—TEAM		
Men's and women's combined		France

WEIGHT LIFTING

Event	Winner, country	Performance
EUROPEAN CHAMPIONS		
Flyweight	Z. Smalcerz, Poland	749¼ lb.
Bantamweight	R. Belenkov, U.S.S.R.	793¼ lb.
Featherweight	D. Shanidze, U.S.S.R.	870½ lb.
Lightweight	M. Kuchev, Bulgaria	986¼ lb.
Middleweight	Y. Bikov, Bulgaria	1,057¾ lb.
Light-heavyweight	B. Pavlov, U.S.S.R.	1,129½ lb.
Middle-heavyweight	D. Rigert, U.S.S.R.	1,228¾ lb.
Heavyweight	Y. Talts, U.S.S.R.	1,295 lb.
Super-heavyweight	V. Alekseyev, U.S.S.R.	1,394¼ lb.
Team	U.S.S.R.	
INAUGURAL WORLD RECORD TOTALS (Excluding press, which is to be banned from international competition)		
Flyweight	V. Smetanin, U.S.S.R.	511.5 lb.
Bantamweight	G. Chetin, U.S.S.R.	
	M. Nassiri, Iran	561 lb.
Featherweight	Y. Miyake, Japan	
	Hsiao Ming-siang, China	
	D. Shanidze, U.S.S.R.	610.5 lb.
Lightweight	W. Baszanowski, Poland	
	M. Kirzhinov, U.S.S.R.	671 lb.
Middleweight	V. Kurentsov, U.S.S.R.	
	M. Ohuchi, Japan	715 lb.
Light-heavyweight	V. Shary, U.S.S.R.	770 lb.
Middle-heavyweight	D. Rigert, U.S.S.R.	819.5 lb.
Heavyweight	P. Pervushin, U.S.S.R.	863.5 lb.
Super-heavyweight	V. Alekseyev, U.S.S.R.	913 lb.

WRESTLING

Event	Winner	Country
EUROPEAN FREESTYLE CHAMPIONS		
Light-flyweight	S. Baigin	Turkey
Flyweight	A. Alakhverdiev	U.S.S.R.
Bantamweight	I. Kuleshov	U.S.S.R.
Featherweight	R. Pliev	U.S.S.R.
Lightweight	I. Yusseinov	Bulgaria
Welterweight	A. Seger	West Germany
Middleweight	V. Suilzhin	U.S.S.R.
Light-heavyweight	G. Strakhov	U.S.S.R.
Heavyweight	I. Yarygin	U.S.S.R.
Super-heavyweight	A. Medved	U.S.S.R.
EUROPEAN GRECO-ROMAN CHAMPIONS		
Light-flyweight	G. Berceanu	Romania
Flyweight	J. Mihalek	Poland
Bantamweight	K. Traikov	Bulgaria
Featherweight	G. Markov	Bulgaria
Lightweight	J. Henkel	East Germany
Welterweight	P. Galaktopoulos	Greece
Middleweight	A. Nasarenko	U.S.S.R.
Light-heavyweight	S. Nikolov	Bulgaria
Heavyweight	N. Yakovenko	U.S.S.R.
Super-heavyweight	A. Tomov	Bulgaria

(D. K. R. PHILLIPS)

See also Baseball; Basketball; Bowling and Lawn Bowls; Boxing; Chess; Contract Bridge; Cricket; Cycling; Football; Golf; Hockey; Horse Racing; Ice Skating; Motor Sports; Rowing; Sailing; Skiing; Swimming; Tennis; Track and Field Sports.

Sri Lanka: *see* Ceylon

Stamp Collecting: *see* Philately and Numismatics

Steel Industry: *see* Industrial Review

Stock Exchanges

Stock exchanges throughout the world staged broad-based advances in 1972. All of the major stock price indexes registered gains (*see* Table I). Even among those nations with relatively minor stock exchange operations, bull markets prevailed as a rule.

Stock price movements are generally determined by a mixture of economic developments and psychological factors. In 1972 the favourable conditions outweighed the negative factors. Industrial production in most countries was on the upswing. Corporate profits were rising, and consumer confidence about the outlook for world peace was generally high. In addition, yields on fixed-income securities were not so high as in the previous year, thereby enhancing the relative attractiveness of stocks. But the most fundamental reason for the widespread bullish performance of stock prices was the interim international monetary settlement worked out in December 1971 between the U.S. and its principal trade partners. Altogether, these considerations overshadowed concern about the inability of governments to cope with inflationary pressures and social unrest.

The Dec. 18, 1971, Smithsonian agreement, which realigned exchange rates among the world's major currencies, raised investor hopes that peace had been achieved on the international monetary front. Not only did this agreement avert the immediate threat of a world financial crisis but it was followed in February by trade agreements between the major nations that offered prospects for a renewed surge in the growth of international trade and commerce. Stock markets throughout the world responded to these events in a bullish manner. Nearly all of the known stock price indexes experienced significant gains in the first half of 1972.

New York Stock Exchange prices and average daily volume, 1972.

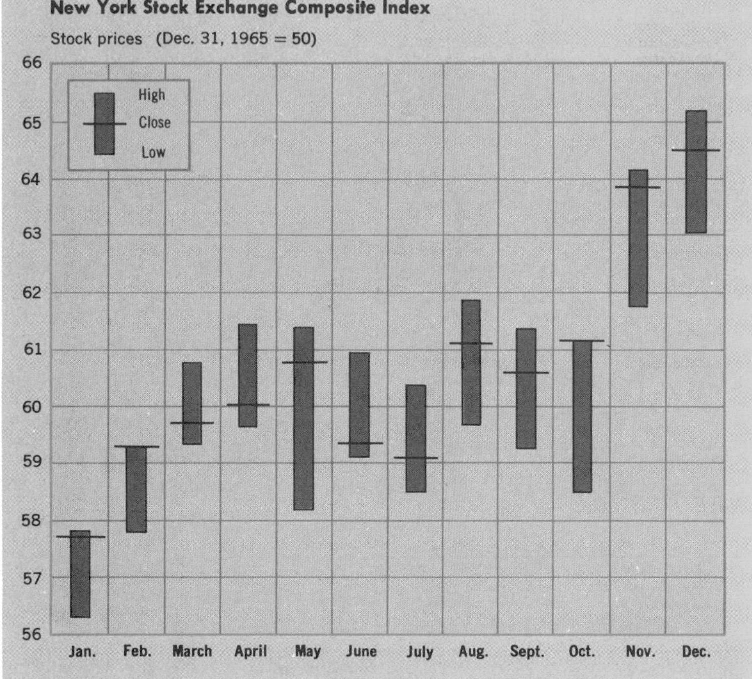

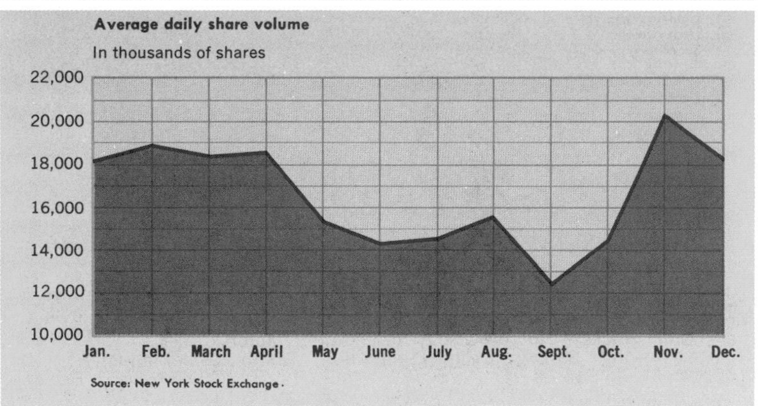

The general rise in equity values was halted temporarily when the British government announced on June 23 that it would let the pound float in value on the world market. This reminded investors that international monetary problems were not quite solved, despite the 1971 devaluation of the U.S. dollar and realignment of world currencies.

However, the underlying upward trend in stock prices had been established. Moreover, gathering signs of business improvement and growing investor confidence in the long-run economic outlook enabled stock markets to forge ahead. As 1972 came to a close, many governments were attempting to overcome the inflationary pressures in their economies. The resulting uncertainties generally left equity values below the peaks reached in October.

In Europe stock markets were uniformly strong during 1972. Among the countries for which full year's data were available, bull markets were prevalent in the Netherlands, Belgium, Austria, Switzerland, France, Sweden, Italy, West Germany, and Great Britain. Where only partial information on stock prices was available, rising markets were in progress in Ireland, Finland, Spain, Norway, Portugal, and Denmark.

Outside of Europe, Japan, Australia, South Africa, and Hong Kong revealed strong performances. Limited price information on non-European countries showed higher markets prevailing in Israel, New Zealand, Venezuela, and India, while the Philippines experienced a mixed market, and Ceylon had lower stock prices.

United States. The stock markets of the U.S. were remarkably bullish and nonspeculative during most of 1972 as new highs were achieved on most of the important indexes. The Dow Jones industrial average, the most popular barometer of securities prices, for the first time in history broke through the 1,000 level on November 14, rising to 1,036.27 on December 11 before falling back moderately to close the year at 1,020.02. The final session of the year was the third busiest in history at the New York Stock Exchange (NYSE), with a total of 27,550,000 shares changing hands. The only two days with heavier trading occurred in 1971.

There were two prolonged rallies in securities prices in 1972. The first began in November 1971 and extended into April 1972, while a second started in mid-October and lasted for two months before faltering, largely as a result of disappointment over the failure of the peace talks between the U.S. and North Vietnam. Early in the year the market followed an upward path in response to favourable international currency developments and a steady stream of positive business reports. For several months at midyear, prices moved erratically with little change in response to uncertainties about the possible course of prices, the scope of the economic recovery, the failure to end the war in Southeast Asia, and the economic controls program. It was a blue-chip stock market in that only between 20 and 25% as much trading was done on the American Stock Exchange (ASE), which generally features smaller companies, as on the NYSE. A ratio of 40 to 50% is considered speculative by many analysts.

The bond market did not participate in the boom as actively as did equity securities. Public offerings of corporate bonds, including convertibles, declined about 27% during 1972 to approximately $18.1 billion from $24.8 billion in 1971, while municipal issues dropped about 7% to $22.8 billion from the record $24.4 billion of 1971. Bond trading was off sharply on both the NYSE and the ASE. With the demand for funds reduced and inflation curbed, interest rates held steady in 1972 following several years of wide variation. Rates on high-quality bonds ranged from about $7\frac{1}{4}$ to $7\frac{3}{4}$% and yields on tax exempts from 5 to $5\frac{1}{2}$%. Short-term Treasury bill rates rose sharply from 3% in February to 5% in December. The prime bank lending rate ranged between $4\frac{3}{4}$% in February to 6% in December.

Average prices on the NYSE were higher for industrials in 1972 than in any previous year, while prices of public utilities and railroad stocks lagged (*see* Table II). The 500 stocks in the composite index moved from a November 1971 low of 92.78 to close that year at 99.17. The index advanced to 103.30 in January 1972 and to 108.81 in April before stalling for several months preliminary to its end-of-the-year spurt. The composite index achieved an all-time high of 119.12 in 1972 and recorded a gain during 1972 of 15.63%, compared with the 1971 gain of 10.79%.

The 425 stocks in the industrial group advanced unsteadily through the year, rising from a January level of 114.12 to 121.34 in April after which there was some uncertainty, a short boom in August, and a year-end rally. The high for the year was 132.95 and the year-end close was 131.87, a gain of 16.99% over the corresponding figure for 1971.

Public utility stocks were disappointing in 1972 as they declined to levels below those of the previous year. From a January 1972 high of 60.19, the average of 55 public utilities dipped to a low of 53.47 in July, contrasted with 60.08 on Standard and Poor's index for July 1971. The high for the year was 62.99 and the low 52.95, both figures below their 1971 counterparts of 64.81 and 54.48. However, the December closing figure was 61.05, a net gain of 2.04% above the 1971 closing average.

The index of railroad stock prices began the year at 45.16, compared with 36.64 in 1971. After a slight gain to 47.38 in April, the average drifted lower and by the summer was below the corresponding 1971 figure. At the close of 1972 the railroad index had declined to a level about 0.78% below that of the previous year. In large measure, the performance of the railroad stocks was attributed to the continuing losses sustained on passenger traffic along with inactive trackage, labour problems, and the continuing effect of the Penn Central bankruptcy.

Common stock yields declined throughout most of 1972 from a level of 3.16% in January to a low of 2.98% in November. The spread in yields between high-grade stocks and bonds was the highest in the annals of the stock market, with bonds yielding more than double the returns of blue-chip stocks.

Government bond prices were relatively unchanged in 1972 as compared with 1971 (*see* Table III). In January long-term government issues averaged $68.79 per $100 bond; this figure then declined slightly to $67.66 in April, after which it fluctuated within narrow limits in the range of $68 and $69. Yields on government bonds were lower during the first half of 1972 than they had been a year earlier, but they advanced in the second half of the year. In October the average long-term yields were 5.69%, contrasted with 5.46% the previous year. Short-term yields moved upward more rapidly, and by December 90-day Treasury bill yields were achieving sharp gains.

Corporate bond prices remained relatively unchanged in 1972. Starting from a high of $67.10 in January, prices slid slowly to an April low of $65.10 and then fluctuated about the $65.50 level through most of the remainder of the year (*see* Table IV).

continued on page 638

Table I. Selected Major World Stock Price Indexes*

Country	1972 range High	1972 range Low	Year-end indexes 1971	Year-end indexes 1972	Percent increase
Australia	639	490	504	605	20
Austria	2,406	1,993	1,991	2,386†	20
Belgium	121	97	97	121	25
France	89	68	67	78	16
West Germany	121	97	98	110	12
Italy	57	44	47	53	13
Japan	5,208	2,712	2,714	5,208	92
Netherlands	156	105	106	156	47
South Africa	270	183	192	270	41
Sweden	369	309	306	356	16
Switzerland	425	347	343	406	18
United Kingdom	544	462	477	505	6

*Index numbers are rounded, and limited to countries for which full year's data were available.
†As of Dec. 22, 1972.
Sources: *Barron's, The Economist, Financial Times, New York Times.*

Table II. U.S. Stock Market Prices and Yields

Month	Railroads (20 stocks) 1972	Railroads (20 stocks) 1971	Industrials (425 stocks) 1972	Industrials (425 stocks) 1971	Public utilities (55 stocks) 1972	Public utilities (55 stocks) 1971	Composite (500 stocks) 1972	Composite (500 stocks) 1971	Yield (200 stocks; %) 1972	Yield (200 stocks; %) 1971
January	45.16	36.64	114.12	102.22	60.19	63.43	103.30	93.49	3.16	3.47
February	45.66	38.78	116.86	106.62	57.41	62.49	105.24	97.11	3.12	3.41
March	46.48	39.70	119.73	109.59	57.73	62.42	107.69	99.60	3.08	3.29
April	47.38	42.29	121.34	113.68	55.70	62.06	108.81	103.04	3.07	3.19
May	45.06	42.05	120.16	112.41	54.94	59.20	107.65	101.64	3.06	3.35
June	43.66	42.12	120.84	110.26	53.73	57.90	108.01	99.72	3.13	3.38
July	42.00	42.05	119.98	109.09	53.47	60.08	107.21	99.00	3.11	3.51
August	43.28	43.55	124.35	107.26	54.66	57.51	111.01	97.24	3.03	3.34
September	42.37	47.18	122.33	109.85	55.36	56.48	109.39	99.40	3.05	3.35
October	41.20	44.58	122.39	107.28	56.66	57.41	109.56	97.29	3.04	3.48
November	42.41	41.19	128.29	102.21	61.16	55.86	115.05	92.78	2.98	3.47
December		43.17		109.67		57.07		99.17		3.21

Source: U.S. Department of Commerce, *Survey of Current Business*. Prices are Standard and Poor's monthly averages of daily closing prices with 1941–43=10. Yield figures are Moody's index of 200 stocks.

Table III. U.S. Government Long-Term Bond Prices and Yields
Average price in dollars per $100 bond

Month	Average 1972	Average 1971	Yield (%) 1972	Yield (%) 1971	Month	Average 1972	Average 1971	Yield (%) 1972	Yield (%) 1971
January	68.79	66.10	5.62	5.91	July	69.23	66.16	5.57	5.91
February	68.32	66.78	5.67	5.84	August	69.55	67.33	5.54	5.78
March	68.43	67.94	5.66	6.71	September	68.06	69.35	5.70	5.56
April	67.66	67.57	5.74	5.75	October	68.09	70.33	5.69	5.46
May	68.59	65.72	5.64	5.96	November	69.87	70.47	5.50	5.44
June	69.05	65.84	5.59	5.94	December		68.80		5.62

Source: U.S. Department of Commerce, *Survey of Current Business*. Average prices are derived from average yields on the basis of an assumed 3% 20-year taxable U.S. Treasury bond. Yields are for U.S. Treasury bonds that are taxable and due or callable in ten years or more.

Table IV. U.S. Corporate Bond Prices and Yields
Average price in dollars per $100 bond

Month	Average 1972	Average 1971	Yield (%) 1972	Yield (%) 1971	Month	Average 1972	Average 1971	Yield (%) 1972	Yield (%) 1971
January	67.1	66.5	7.19	7.36	July	65.6	63.2	7.21	7.64
February	66.7	66.8	7.27	7.08	August	65.8	63.4	7.19	7.59
March	66.2	65.8	7.24	7.21	September	65.6	64.2	7.22	7.44
April	65.1	65.0	7.30	7.25	October	65.5	65.2	7.21	7.39
May	65.2	63.7	7.30	7.53	November	65.9	66.4	7.12	7.26
June	65.6	63.5	7.23	7.64	December		66.5		7.25

Source: U.S. Department of Commerce, *Survey of Current Business*. Average prices are based on Standard and Poor's composite index of A1+ issues. Yields are based on Moody's Aaa domestic corporate bond index.

SPECIAL REPORT

PORK BELLIES, PLYWOOD, AND SILVER COINS

By Barry J. Lind

When the Chicago Mercantile Exchange organized the International Monetary Market and began offering futures trading in foreign currencies on May 16, 1972, the commodities markets experienced another of the revolutionary developments that have marked them in recent years. Once confined mainly to grains, butter, eggs, the major metals, sugar, and cocoa, the markets now deal in such goods as plywood, live cattle and hogs, frozen pork bellies, frozen orange juice, and silver coins. Such other "way out goods" as real-estate mortgages and stock options are also under consideration for trading. Major brokerage firms have established separate commodities departments to keep them competitive with firms dealing exclusively in commodity futures. Computers have played an important role in meeting the demands for instant quotations and eliminating back office backlogs.

One measure of public interest in commodities trading is 1971's record $98 billion trading volume in the U.S. alone. This followed a record year in 1970, and it appears that 1972 has set still another record. Among the reasons for this increased interest are the large and quick profit potential, the relatively small margin requirements, and the far wider selection of commodities now available for trading.

Hedgers and Speculators. Commodity trading has been a practice for more than 300 years. It is done at exchanges throughout the U.S. and in important cities in other countries. Commodity traders fall into two basic categories, the hedgers and the speculators. Originally, food processors or merchants would bid for a farmer's crop even before it was planted. They were hedging—protecting themselves against drastic price rises in the future. Conversely, by accepting such a bid, the farmer was able to hedge and protect himself against adverse price movements.

Today the businessman who produces, processes, or markets various commodities may trade futures contracts to avoid risking his business capital. In anticipation of a possible change in his physical inventory, he tries to cover himself with an offsetting position in the futures market. For example, a processor may contract to sell a certain quantity of a manufactured product at a specified price for future delivery. When the time of manufacture arrives, he must buy specified amounts of raw materials. To protect himself against a rise in the price of the raw materials in the interim, as compared with the price when he made the original contract, he buys futures contracts equal in quantity to his forward contract. If the price of the materials does rise, he can sell the futures contract at a profit and thus offset the loss on his contract to sell the manufactured product.

The other category of commodity trader is the speculator ready to risk his capital to make a profit. He simply buys when he thinks the price is too low and sells when he thinks it is too high.

Barry J. Lind is owner and president of B. J. Lind & Company, Chicago, Ill., the largest commodity futures brokerage firm in the U.S. He is a member of the Chicago Mercantile Exchange Board of Governors.

The entry of the speculator into commodity futures trading brought with it enormous amounts of capital, activity, and market liquidity (ready convertibility into cash). The speculator is the risk bearer—the one who assumes the risks the hedger seeks to avoid. Because of his continuous trading activity, he keeps the market broad and active—a vital necessity for effective hedging.

Exchanges. Commodity exchanges consist of members who buy their memberships (also called seats) and who are either engaged in marketing, processing, or producing commodities, or are brokers executing orders for others or trading for themselves. The exchanges are supported by dues and assessments on members and by fees charged for handling each transaction. They have their own governing bodies which police the business to make sure that it is being carried on under a set of rules equally fair for large and small business interests and for speculators. Exchanges do not buy or sell, nor do they set prices. All prices are determined through open trading in "pits" provided by the exchanges.

These pits are usually octagonal in shape and consist of a series of steps on which brokers and traders stand and face each other on the trading floor. Although there are different pits for different commodities, the method of trading is consistent. Every offer to sell or bid to buy must be called or cried out publicly. Consequently, to the uninitiated, pandemonium reigns on every trading floor as hundreds of brokers are shouting out bids and offers. To make certain they are understood, the brokers supplement their shouts with hand signals. A palm turned away from the person trading indicates an offer to sell. A palm turned in means a bid to buy. As each transaction is made, it is relayed by telephone to blackboards, where, in full view of all, the price is chalked up. If there is a price change from preceding transactions, it is reported on quotation boards throughout the country and by cable throughout the world.

Futures. All commodities are traded on the basis of a futures contract, which requires delivery of a commodity in a specific month in the future. At any time before that contract matures, the buyer may close out his obligation through an equal but opposite trade. He may buy a contract to offset a short sale (selling a contract at today's price in the hope of purchasing an equal quantity at a lower price before liquidation date) or sell a contract to offset a long buy (a purchase in anticipation of a higher market price in the future). The difference between the purchase and selling price, minus commission, is the trader's profit or loss. Reduced to its most understandable form, a commodity futures contract is an agreement to buy or sell a specified amount of a product during a certain month at a price determined at the time the agreement is made.

The old story of a contract of soybeans being delivered to the home of a trader who failed to sell off his contract is sheer nonsense. Less than 2% of all futures contracts traded are ever held to delivery. If for any reason a contract must be delivered, it remains in storage, where daily storage rates plus insurance are paid until the commodity can be redelivered on the exchange or sold on the cash market.

There is uniformity in commodity futures contracts in that they all are of a specific unit for each commodity. For example, a live hog contract is 30,000 lb., a frozen pork belly contract is 36,000 lb., and a wheat contract is 5,000 bu. All commodity futures are traded in multiples of one contract.

Margins on commodity trades are not like margins on securities accounts, which represent an ownership interest for the buyer of the security. Margins on commodity trades are predetermined money deposits required per exchange rules by the brokerage firm for each individual contract to ensure performance of contract commitments. In trading commodities, the margin deposit generally runs about 10% of the total value of the contract, thereby providing the kind of leverage that continually attracts new speculators into the market. This contrasts with a 65% margin required for buying stocks.

FRED KLIGMAN

". . . to the uninitiated, pandemonium reigns on every trading floor as hundreds of brokers are shouting out bids and offers." The author is in centre of picture with both arms in air.

Most commodities are quoted at one one-hundredth of a cent. Grains are quoted in fluctuations of eighths of a cent per bushel. In the value of the contract, each point (based on one one-hundredth of a cent) varies according to the commodity. For instance, in trading cocoa one point represents $3. In cotton each point equals $5, while in domestic raw sugar each point equals $11.20.

Trading. Professional commodity traders do not operate in a haphazard way. Most of them follow a plan or a pattern that they have determined is the most successful for their particular type of operation. Specific guidelines must be established and adhered to if a trader is to meet with success. In many instances, these guidelines go completely against human nature, but a trader knows that he stands the best chance for success if he adheres to his particular method. A professional trader never measures the number of profitable trades he makes against the number of losing trades. He measures the total dollars that are taken as profit against the total dollars taken as losses over a period of time.

For the speculator trading in commodity futures, it is possible to be wrong 75% of the time and still realize an excellent profit in his overall operation. The reason is that in commodity trading, as in practically no other field, it is essential to cut losses as quickly as possible and let profits ride. It is not advisable to hold onto a loser in the hope that it will come back, nor is it wise to cash in a winner immediately until seeing what kind of pattern is emerging.

Because the commodity market constantly strives for stability in operation, daily predetermined price limits are set on futures contracts. Trading may not take place outside these limits on a given day. This prevents sudden demoralization of the market and unnecessary fluctuations caused by hysteria or exaggerated hopes or fears. For example, the limitation in frozen pork bellies is 1½ cents per pound, or 150 points up or down—representing $540 per contract from the previous day's close; in cocoa it is 1 cent per pound, or 100 points up or down, equal to $300; and grains are eight to ten cents, representing $400 to $500 per contract. This system contrasts with the stock market, where security prices may take unlimited swings up or down on any particular day.

Another vital difference between trading stocks and trading commodity futures is in the area of broker commissions. In trading stocks, a commission is paid upon purchase and upon sale. In trading commodities, only one commission is paid and that is a round-turn commission—paid only when a transaction has been completed, either a purchase and a sale, or a sale and a covering purchase. Each commission is specified per contract.

Commodity prices reflect the opinion of the market with respect to the forces of supply and demand. Trades are made in open auction with buyers and sellers bidding for the best competitive prices. Influencing factors can range from weather conditions and crop reports to labour relations, export opportunities, government controls, transportation, and national and international political conditions, but in the end it all comes down to supply and demand.

Commodity trading can be accomplished through most major stock brokerage firms and through firms specializing only in commodity futures trading. Transactions for commodity futures in the United States are under the constant scrutiny and supervision of the Commodity Exchange Authority, an agency of the U.S. Department of Agriculture, which administers and enforces the Commodity Exchange Act to protect not only member brokers but the general public as well.

Because trading commodities is the truest form of speculation, just as it presents opportunity for high profits it also provides equal opportunity for high losses. For the ill-financed, the uninformed, and the highly emotional trader, commodity futures trading can be extremely risky. But for the investor who has risk capital available, understands the principles of commodity trading, and can accept profits and losses intelligently and calmly, trading commodities offers excellent profit opportunities with minimal capital investment.

continued from page 635

Yields were above the corresponding 1971 values in only three months of 1972. Trading volume in bonds was surprisingly off in 1972 on both leading exchanges. The NYSE reported sales of $5,444,117,100 in 1972, compared with $6,563,822,400 in 1971, a decline of 22% in volume. On the ASE the drop was from $867,-046,000 in 1971 to $728,524,000 in 1972. The U.S. Treasury reported that 1972 represented the greatest annual growth in bond holdings since World War II. The government sold $6.2 billion in savings bonds, the best one-year sales since 1948. At the year's end, investors held $58.1 billion in Series E and H bonds and in Freedom Shares, $3.3 billion more than in the previous year.

Aggregate volume on the NYSE for the 12 months of 1972 totaled 4,138,187,706 shares, compared with 3,891,317,731 in 1971. A record 2,022 different issues were traded. On the ASE 1,616 issues were traded, compared with 1,512 in 1971, and the volume was 1,117,989,153 in 1972, compared with 1,070,871,185 the previous year. A similar gain in volume of trading activity was reported by the Pacific Coast Stock Exchange, where there were 260,526,993 transactions in 1972 and 223,208,082 in 1971. The National Association of Securities Dealers indicated that the 1972 volume for stocks quoted on its automated system for over-the-counter securities was 2.2 billion shares, nearly twice the annual ASE volume and half that of the NYSE.

The profitability of Wall Street brokerage firms was severely affected by a combination of adverse factors in 1972. Under pressure from the Securities and Exchange Commission (SEC), the New York Stock Exchange had ordered brokers to negotiate commissions on trades above $500,000 from April 1971. A year later this figure was reduced to $300,000. Negotiated commissions resulted in price cutting and consequent losses to brokerage firms. A large number of low-volume trading days also contributed to poor profitability for the brokers.

Index of industrial ordinary share prices on the London Stock Exchange, 1950-72.

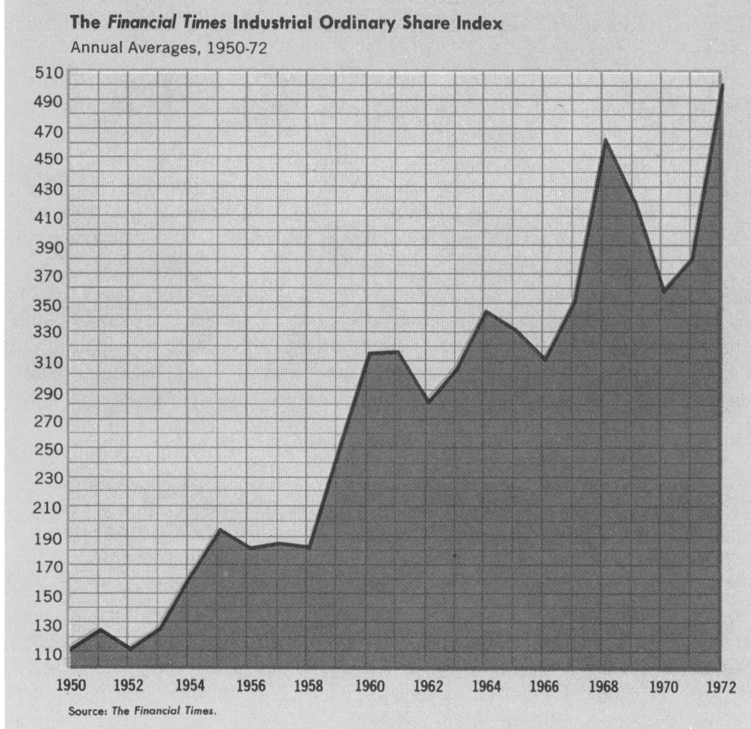

The mutual fund industry fared badly in 1972 as customers continued to sell more shares than they bought. Net redemptions prevailed during most of the year, and in November they set a record of $258 million.

The SEC played an active role in policy issues during 1972. It recommended membership on the exchanges for broker-dealers affiliated with financial institutions provided that at least 80% of the business of such dealers was with unaffiliated public investors; fuller disclosures on new stock issues in "meaningful" language that nonlawyers could understand; increased fiduciary isolation of cash and securities of customers from the risks of the brokerage firms; a centralized ticker-tape service; and greater involvement by the public in the activities of the securities exchanges.

In a major shift of emphasis, both the NYSE and the ASE were reorganized in 1972 with full-time salaried chairmen and reorganized boards of directors whose membership gave the public an equal voice. Each board was reformed with ten representatives of the public and ten from the securities industry plus a chairman.

Canada. The Canadian securities markets paralleled those of the U.S. as economic recovery carried the gross national product beyond the $100 billion mark for the first time, a gain of 10% for the year. Price increases accounted for a little over 4% of this gain, and real income rose about 6%. Unemployment continued above the 7% figure, which was regarded as much too high. Despite considerable political uncertainty and nationalist feeling about foreign ownership of Canadian enterprises, the market moved ahead vigorously, Canadian stock prices rising by 26% in 1972.

The 150 industrials on the Toronto Stock Exchange rose sharply in January and February, leveled off until July with about a 10% gain, moved up an additional 8% in September, and then fell back slightly in November. By the end of 1972 the index had gained 20% over the year-end 1971 level. Western oil and gas stocks attracted more investor interest than mining shares, and brokers in Toronto, Montreal, and Vancouver reported bullish sentiments in the last part of the year.

The Canadian bond market made strong progress as heavy buying interest from both foreign and domestic sources along with optimism about a Vietnam peace settlement worked to boost prices sharply higher. Short-term interest rates remained stable throughout most of 1972. (IRVING PFEFFER)

Western Europe. The Netherlands stock market was a star performer in 1972. Reversing a two-year decline, the price index of shares traded on the Amsterdam Stock Exchange increased 47% from the end of 1971 to the end of 1972. This was the strongest performance of the EEC countries and the second largest gain among the selected major stock price indexes.

Among the major Western European nations Belgium was the only one that had avoided a general stock market decline since 1968, although its stock prices were unchanged in 1970. The 1972 rise on the Brussels Stock Exchange amounted to 25%. Government moves to end the "stagflation" (lower competitiveness of industry because of fast-rising wages, reduced export growth, and less demand for capital goods) were largely responsible for the bullish performance.

After falling 3% in 1971, the Austrian stock market reversed its bearish trend in 1972. For the year as a whole, prices on the Vienna Stock Exchange rose 20%. During the first four months of 1972, the index of stock prices fluctuated around the December 1971 levels without any apparent trend. In mid-April prices were virtually unchanged from the beginning of the year. The subsequent rise from April 14 to June 16 was relatively moderate (4%). But the uptrend gathered momentum once the British sterling crisis had passed.

The stock market in Switzerland traced out a pattern similar to its European neighbours. From the end of 1971 to the end of 1972, prices on the Zürich Stock Exchange increased 18%.

The broad trend of prices on the Paris Bourse in 1972 was sharply upward (+16%). The year began with stock prices continuing the gains recorded following the Smithsonian agreement in December 1971. In midyear, prices experienced a mild decline in response to the floating pound. A rally took place after that crisis had passed, but it failed to carry through to the end of the year. As 1972 came to a close, stock prices were 12% below the 1972 high reached on October 6.

The Swedish stock market also experienced a bull market in 1972 (+16%). The stock price index of the Stockholm Exchange jumped 6% during the first three weeks of January, but the gain was cut in half by the end of March. The rebound lasted into early May and put stock prices 16% ahead of the final figures in 1971. The market was temporarily upset in June by the sterling crisis, but the subsequent upturn was broad-based enough to carry the index in early December to less than 2% below its all-time high set in 1968. During the final weeks of 1972, stock prices were cut by the reinstatement of price freezes on meat and dairy goods.

After experiencing a bearish trend since November 1969, the Italian stock market turned to the plus side in 1972. The recovery in equity values began in March, but prices on the Milan Stock Exchange did not move above the 1971 close until near the end of April. Government predictions of strong business activity, including improved export performance, sparked the advance. Prices finished the year 13% above the 1971 close but 7% below the November highs.

West German stock markets were generally strong in 1972. The bullish tone established by the Smithsonian monetary accord created an upsurge in investor confidence. Moreover, the Bundesbank moved to bolster a sagging economy by lowering the bank rate, first to 4 from 4½%, then to 3%, its lowest level since the 1967 recession. Stock prices finished the year 12% higher than the year before, but 9% below the August high.

Wide fluctuations characterized the London Stock Exchange in 1972. The *Financial Times* index of 30 industrial stocks at the end of March was up 7% from the 1971 close. This strong performance occurred despite relatively high unemployment, severe wage and price inflation, and a nationwide coal miners' strike. However, bullish expectations were generated by the prospects for British business raised by entry into the EEC in January 1973 and by the Smithsonian agreement, which eliminated uncertainties surrounding monetary and trade questions.

In mid-March the British government announced the biggest tax reduction in the country's history. This, combined with the encouraging first quarter earnings reports of leading British companies, caused stock prices to move sharply upward, reaching an all-time high on May 19. Following several weeks of profit-taking, stock prices entered into a significant downtrend. Lagging economic growth, repeated warnings that inflation threatened the government's economic goals, and a dock workers' strike were important influences. But the major part of the decline was precipitated by the British Treasury's announcement on June 23 that it would let the pound float in value on the world market for an indefinite period. This threatened to destroy the effectiveness of the Smithsonian agreement. The entire gain in the stock price index from the beginning of the year was virtually wiped out. At the end of June stock prices were less than 1% above the 1971 close.

In mid-July a monetary conference of the EEC agreed that, except for the pound, existing currency relationships among the Common Market countries would be maintained. This restored confidence to the

UPI COMPIX

A man on the floor of the New York Stock Exchange tosses paper and ticker tape into the air in celebration of the Dow Jones industrial average's closing above 1,000 for the first time in history. The final closing figure on November 14 was 1,003.16.

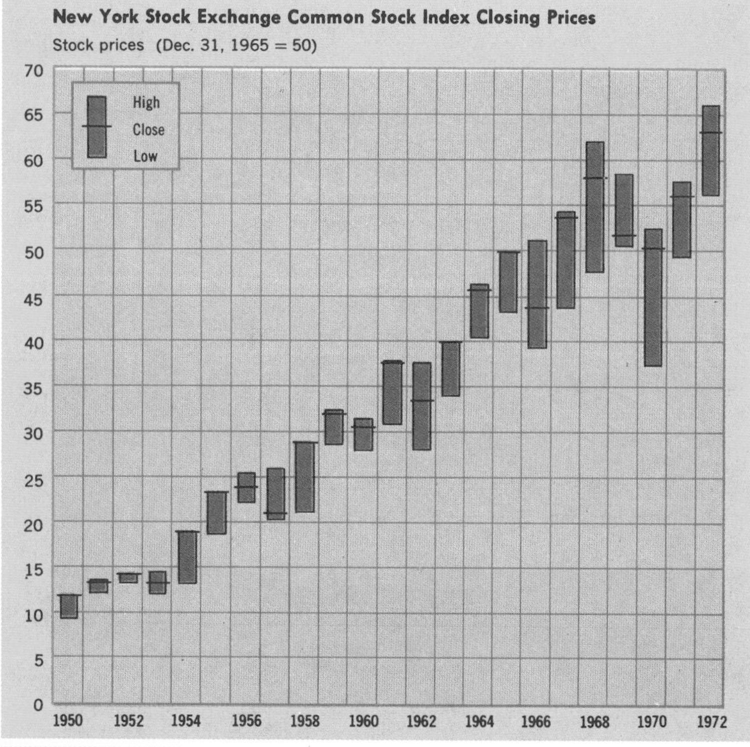

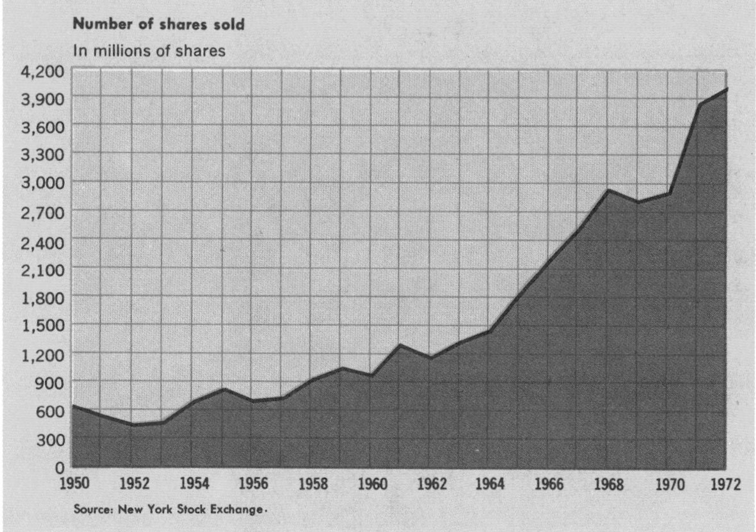

Stock trading on the New York Stock Exchange: yearly range of prices and number of shares sold, 1950-72.

crisis-plagued financial centres of Europe and renewed the upward trend of stock prices on the London Exchange. The rally, which lasted through August, pushed the index 11% above the June close. Stock prices moved lower during the remainder of the year, and at its December close the *Financial Times* industrial share index was off 7% from its all-time high.

Bullish trends were also evident in European countries where full year's data were not as yet available. Average stock prices in Finland in July were 48% higher than in December 1971. In Ireland share prices through June were up 35%. The stock price indexes in Spain and Portugal on average rose 26 and 8%, respectively, through July. The Oslo Stock Exchange in Norway through September was 19% higher than in the final month of 1971, despite the government's failure to obtain voter approval for entry into the EEC. And in Denmark, where Common Market entry was accepted, average stock prices increased 39% through August.

Other Countries. The Tokyo Stock Exchange outperformed all the major markets of the world in 1972 (+92%). Its index of 225 common stocks ended 1972 at an all-time peak, more than four times higher than when the bull market started at the beginning of 1968. Prices rose virtually without pause throughout the year; not even the pound crisis could stop the rampaging bull market.

The 1971 Smithsonian agreement resulted in a 17% upward revaluation of the Japanese yen. At the same time, however, the U.S. removed its import surcharge, which had been particularly damaging to Japanese exporters. Nevertheless, to counteract fears of recession the government authorized stepped-up spending for military goods, public works, and social services. Its announced objective was to spur the economy to a better than 7% growth rate for the year ending March 1973.

During the first five months of 1972, stock prices rose 34%. By mid-April it was evident that the Japanese economy was operating at much higher levels than the government's projections. The floating British pound had no lasting effect on the stock market as brief periods of falling prices seemed more tied to profit-taking than to external developments.

The improvement of business conditions throughout the summer and early fall added fuel to an already overheated stock market. Investors from throughout the world poured money into Japanese stock markets. In November it appeared that Japan's gross national product would be up more than 9% for fiscal 1973. Volume on the Tokyo Stock Exchange surged to record levels. In fact, activity was so great that a number of controls had to be imposed to cool the speculative enthusiasm of investors, including reduced trading hours to allow brokers to catch up with their paper work and increased margin requirements for purchasing stock.

Australia also experienced a bull market, its first since 1969. Prices on the Sydney Stock Exchange rose 20% from the end of 1971 to the end of 1972. Much of the gain was achieved in the first six months. From the year's low on January 17, the index of stock prices surged 30% almost without interruption to reach a high on June 23. Following the Smithsonian agreement, Australia revalued its currency 6% against the dollar. However, on a trade-weighted average basis, this amounted to a devaluation of 2% vis-à-vis the major trading countries. The resulting foreign trade surplus pushed the country's balance of payments into a favourable position for the second quarter of 1972, the first such surplus since early 1964.

The trend of stock prices in South Africa followed a pattern generally similar to the Netherlands and Belgium. From year-end 1971 to year-end 1972 industrial share prices on the Johannesburg Stock Exchange rose 41%, the third best performance among the major stock price indexes.

Where only limited information on stock markets was available, rising prices were generally the rule. The performance of the Israeli stock exchange in Tel Aviv was particularly strong. Stock prices were up 35% through July, with the biggest monthly gain recorded in January (14%). In New Zealand prices had risen 7% through August, while the rise in Venezuela amounted to 6%. Average share prices in India showed a 3% gain through August.

(ROBERT H. TRIGG)

See also Economy, World; Investment, International; Money and Banking; Savings and Investment.

Strikes:
see Labour Unions

Sugar:
see Agriculture

Sulfur:
see Mining

Surgery:
see Medicine

Surinam:
see Dependent States

UPI COMPIX

Students concentrate on a reading lesson at a bush school in Matu, one of the few such schools that remained in session during civil warfare in 1972.

Sudan

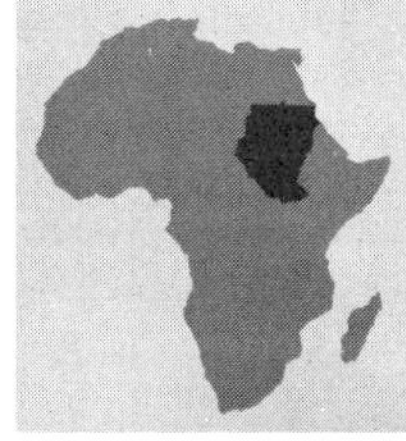

A republic of northeast Africa, the Sudan is bounded by Egypt, the Red Sea, Ethiopia, Kenya, Uganda, Zaire, the Central African Republic, Chad, and Libya. Area: 967,494 sq.mi. (2,505,813 sq.km.). Pop. (1972 est.): 16,489,000, including Arabs in the north and Negroes in the south. Cap. and largest city: Khartoum (pop., 1972 est., 300,000). Language: Arabic; various tribal languages in the south. Religion: Muslim in the north; predominantly animist in the south. President and prime minister in 1972, Maj. Gen. Gaafar Nimeiry.

Peace was restored to the southern Sudan in 1972, after more than 16 years of insurgency. Under an agreement signed at Addis Ababa, Eth., in February between the government and representatives of the South Sudan Liberation Movement (SSLM), an immediate cease-fire was ordered and the three southern provinces were granted autonomy as a region that would have its own president, council of ministers, and, after an interim 18 months, regional assembly. During the following six months 6,000 members of the Anya-Nya, the military wing of the SSLM, were integrated with an equal number of regular soldiers from the north to form a balanced force for the south.

It was fortunate that the 200,000 southern refugees in neighbouring countries did not rush home once the peace agreement was ratified. The new regional government already had the immense task of resettling an estimated half million people who had fled from their villages into the countryside during the years of fighting. In this task the world community was at first slow to provide assistance, but by the end of the year the Office of the United Nations High Commissioner for Refugees (UNHCR) was coordinating a relief program. (*See* REFUGEES.)

Estranged from the Soviet Union and Eastern Europe since the abortive pro-Communist coup of 1971, Sudan obtained little development aid from those countries, and promises of help from Libya were not fulfilled. Diplomatic relations were reestablished with the United States and West Germany, and these two countries, together with Britain, responded quickly with loans and credits, as did also Kuwait, Saudi Arabia, and Abu Dhabi among the Arab states.

Sudan's concentration on its two chronic internal problems—the south and development needs—caused the regime to fall foul of its erstwhile close friends in the Arab world. Sudan had no wish to join the Confederation of Arab Republics, linking Egypt, Libya, and Syria, and the Sudanese action in September in turning back a Libyan contingent sent by air to assist Pres. Idi Amin of Uganda brought heated recriminations from both Libya and Egypt.

The Sudanese Socialist Union, the country's sole permitted political organization, held its first congress in January and drew up a national charter. In October a People's Assembly met for the first time and was given the task of drawing up, within six months, a permanent constitution. (PETER KILNER)

SUDAN

Education. (1969–70) Primary, pupils 610,798, teachers 12,370; secondary, pupils 172,486, teachers 9,030; vocational, pupils 1,181, teachers 151; teacher training, students 2,291, teachers 156; higher (including University of Khartoum), students 11,691, teaching staff 1,107.

Finance. Monetary unit: Sudanese pound, with (Sept. 18, 1972) a par value of Sud£0.348 to U.S. $1 (nominal free rate of Sud£0.852 = £1 sterling). Gold, SDRs, and foreign exchange, official: (June 1972) U.S. $34.4 million; (June 1971) U.S. $27.6 million. Budget (1971–72 est.): revenue Sud£189 million; expenditure Sud£178 million. Money supply: (May 1972) Sud£118,880,000; (May 1971) Sud£115,570,000. Cost of living (1963 = 100): (April 1972) 120; (April 1971) 119.

Foreign Trade. (1971) Imports Sud£123,660,000; exports Sud£115.2 million. Import sources: India 17%; U.K. 12%; U.S.S.R. 7%; China 7%; West Germany 5%; Egypt 5%. Export destinations: U.S.S.R. 15%; India 11%; China 10%; Italy 8%; West Germany 7%; Japan 7%; Egypt 6%; U.K. 5%. Main exports: cotton 61%; peanuts 8%; gum arabic 7%.

Transport and Communications. Roads (1970) *c.* 50,000 km. (mainly tracks, including 335 km. asphalted). Motor vehicles in use (1970): passenger 27,400; commercial (including buses) 16,500. Railways: (1969) 4,725 km.; freight traffic (1970) 2,684,000,000 net ton-km. Air traffic (1970): 155,529,000 passenger-km.; freight 3,082,000 net ton-km. Navigable waterways (1970) 4,068 km. Telephones (Dec. 1970) 45,000. Radio licenses (Dec. 1968) *c.* 180,000. Television receivers (Dec. 1970) 35,000.

Agriculture. Production (in 000; metric tons; 1971; 1970 in parentheses): millet 325 (460); sorghum 2,152 (1,529); dry broad beans *c.* 13 (*c.* 12); peanuts *c.* 353 (*c.* 353); durra (1969) 619, (1968) 1,980; sesame *c.* 350 (*c.* 329); sugar, raw value (1971–72) *c.* 78, (1970–71) *c.* 79; dates *c.* 72 (*c.* 72); bananas *c.* 10 (*c.* 10); cotton, lint *c.* 238 (225); beef and veal *c.* 141 (*c.* 139); mutton and lamb *c.* 84 (*c.* 83). Livestock (in 000; 1970–71): cattle *c.* 13,650; sheep *c.* 13,200; goats *c.* 10,100; camels *c.* 3,100; asses *c.* 640.

Industry. Production (in 000; metric tons; 1970): cement 156; salt 63; electricity (kw-hr.) 392,000.

Swaziland

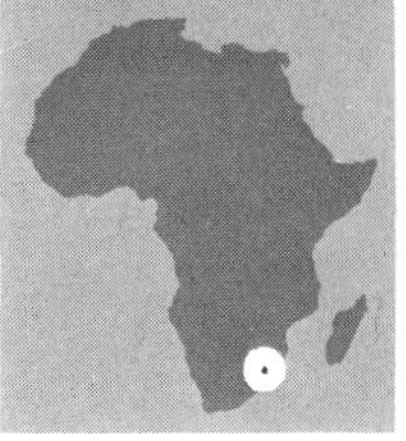

A landlocked constitutional monarchy of southern Africa, Swaziland is bounded by South Africa and Mozambique. Area: 6,704 sq.mi. (17,364 sq.km.). Pop. (1972 est.): 446,000. Cap. and largest city: Mbabane (pop., 1972 est., 17,850). Language: English and siSwati (official). Religion: Christian 60%; animist 40%. King, Sobhuza II; prime minister in 1972, Prince Makhosini Dlamini.

SWAZILAND

Education. (1969) Primary, pupils 64,955, teachers 1,712; secondary, pupils 6,911, teachers 365; vocational, pupils 144, teachers 10; teacher training, students 296, teachers 31; higher (1968), students 69, teaching staff 15.

Finance and Trade. Monetary unit: South African rand, with (Sept. 18, 1972) a free rate of R 0.80 to U.S. $1 (par value of R 1.95 = £1 sterling). Budget (1971–72 est.): revenue R 17,241,000; expenditure R 16,505,000. Foreign trade (1970): imports R 42,-750,000; exports R 50.2 million. Main exports: sugar 24%; iron ore 22%; wood pulp 19%; asbestos 10%; citrus fruit 7%.

Agriculture. Production (in 000; metric tons; 1970; 1969 in parentheses): corn 63 (58); rice 7 (8); sugar, raw value (1971–72) *c.* 150, (1970–71) *c.* 170; cotton, lint 2 (2). Livestock (in 000; 1970–71): cattle *c.* 560; sheep *c.* 41; pigs *c.* 13; goats *c.* 270; chickens *c.* 360.

Industry. Production (in 000; metric tons; 1970): coal 130; iron ore (metal content) 1,470; asbestos 33; electricity (kw-hr.) 90,000.

The Swazi elections of May 1972, the first since independence, were won by Prince Makhosini Dlamini's royalist Imbokodvo National Movement, based on the traditional Swazi National Council. Five parties contested the 24 seats in the House of Assembly. The main opposition branch of the Ngwane National Liberatory Congress won three seats, but even it was torn by internal rivalry and presented only its 1964 manifesto. Following the elections King Sobhuza, who with a reign of 51 years was the world's longest-ruling living monarch, commented that the advent of an official opposition was "a new thing in Swaziland."

Swaziland's economy was becoming less dependent on remittances from workers in South Africa, although it remained closely tied to the republic through a customs union and integrated power supplies, and South Africa was stepping up investment in Swazi industry. The proposed rail link between the two countries did not materialize, however. Some 90% of Swaziland's imports (about R 46.1 million in 1971) came from South Africa, but exports (R 54.5 million in 1971) were routed via Lourenço Marques in Mozambique. On May 31 V. T. Ngwanya, an elected representative of the House of Assembly, was handed over to the South African police after having been declared a prohibited immigrant. (MOLLY MORTIMER)

Sweden

A constitutional monarchy of northern Europe lying on the eastern side of the Scandinavian Peninsula, Sweden has common borders with Finland and Norway. Area: 173,731 sq.mi. (449,964 sq.km.). Pop. (1971 est.): 8,115,426. Cap. and largest city: Stockholm (pop., 1972 est., 724,000). Language: Swedish, with some Finnish and Lapp in the north. Religion: predominantly Lutheran. King, Gustaf VI Adolf; prime minister in 1972, Olof Palme.

The economic recession of 1971—the most serious since World War II—continued into 1972, marked by inflation, high taxes, a worrisome level of unemployment (2.8% in October), and frequent factory closings. In contrast to earlier recessions, mainly caused by international developments, these difficulties were to a large extent the result of tight fiscal policies taken to alleviate the inflationary tendencies of 1969–70. During the winter of 1972 it seemed that the bottom had been reached, and the Social Democratic minority government predicted an improvement by spring.

The budget for 1972–73, presented to the Riksdag in January 1972, was notable for a tighter fiscal policy, restrictions on expenditure, and the absence of tax increases. Revenue was estimated at 55,831,000,-000 kronor, an increase of 7% over 1971–72, and expenditure at 59,110,000,000 kronor, an increase of 4.5%. The deficit was about 100 million kronor less than that for the previous year. For most of the year, the government remained unusually cautious despite sluggish growth in investment and production (in 1971 production actually dropped slightly for the first time since World War II, though to some degree this was due to a reduction of the work week to 40 hours), weak demand, and unemployment aggravated by rising prices (food prices had risen 16% between December 1970 and April 1972). Opposition spokesmen, especially from the non-Socialist parties, repeatedly called for strong general measures, such as a reduction of the employer's tax, to improve profitability and investment. The government, however, continued to institute selective measures with limited effects, such as extra appropriations to the Labour Market Board, although there was a notable lack of evidence of their success. Late in the year stronger proposals were introduced, including postponement of an earlier decision to increase employers' pension payments and a freeze on meat and dairy products effective Jan. 1, 1973.

Behind the recession lay a serious long-term problem. Unemployment had been rising continually since 1965, regardless of the state of the economy. Low-wage industries were being phased out gradually, and their labour force, after retraining, transferred to high-wage industries. Unfortunately, the expansion of high-wage industries had not kept pace with the closing of low-wage industries. High labour costs had forced companies to increase the speed of production, which caused increased unemployment among older workers, the handicapped, and other groups considered to be in the low-production category. This had been accompanied by a slow rate of investment and sinking profitability. All this posed a tough problem for the Social Democratic government, committed as it was to the creation of a more equitable society. High profits would have a negative effect on efforts to achieve equality, but without them there would be no industrial expansion. There were no easy solutions to this dilemma.

The government had a relatively easy year in the Riksdag. Although it held fewer seats than the non-Socialist opposition parties, it could usually rely on the support of the Communists. There was one serious exception; in March it proposed a number of important measures, scheduled to take effect on Jan. 1, 1973—an increase in the value-added tax (VAT) from 17.65 to 20%; higher duties on tobacco, gasoline, wine, and spirits; a reduction in the income tax; and a two-year freeze on local government taxes. The change in VAT was highly controversial. The opposition parties, especially the Communists, were strongly against any increase, since it would automatically lead to higher food prices, and in fact had been campaigning for a reduction. The government assumed that the lowering of the income tax would be enough to guarantee support for the increase in VAT, but it seriously misjudged the mood of the opposition.

Confronted with this unexpected development, the government put forward an alternative proposal: instead of increasing VAT, it would raise the employer's

Swedish Literature:
see Literature

tax from 2 to 4%. This was hardly calculated to please the non-Socialist parties, but it was exactly what the Communists wanted and therefore ensured a majority for the government. The increase in the employer's tax, together with the imposition of a tax ceiling on local authorities, struck many observers as dangerous, since both measures would have a further dampening effect on an already listless economy.

Sweden had made it clear that full membership in the EEC was incompatible with its policy of neutrality, a viewpoint shared by all political parties, and for some time it had been negotiating for a favourable free-trade agreement. This was eventually signed in July, and was the most comprehensive agreement in the field of trade policy in Sweden's history. It meant that all Swedish industrial goods would become duty-free within the EEC, in five stages, by 1977, with two serious exceptions: special steels would not be duty-free until 1979, and paper would have to wait until 1983; agricultural products were not included.

In March it was proposed that the official Church of Sweden be disestablished as of 1983. The church would retain its property but would lose its taxing power. In November the government announced an important regional program which, if implemented, would have a major effect on Sweden's development. Its aim was to ensure that every province would retain at least its 1972 population and that all would have equal opportunities with regard to employment, environment, and social, commercial, and cultural services.

The UN Conference on the Human Environment, held in Stockholm in June, attracted some 1,200 delegates, 1,000 journalists, and thousands of other visitors. (*See* ENVIRONMENT.) In December 1971 the government published a draft of an ambitious plan to control the exploitation and preservation of Sweden's land, coastline, lakes, and waterways. Two months later the maximum permissible content of lead in gasoline was reduced from 0.7 gram per litre to 0.4 gram, effective Jan. 1, 1973. Expenditure on the environment increased steadily, reaching 1.2 billion kronor in the first half of 1972.

In September Sweden experienced its first hijacking, when an SAS DC-9 carrying 90 persons on a scheduled flight between Stockholm and Göteborg was hijacked by three Croatian extremists. The hijackers demanded the release of seven Croatian convicts held in Swedish prisons (including the two men responsible for the murder of the Yugoslavian ambassador in Stockholm in 1971) and 500,000 kronor. It was decided to accede to their demands in return for the release of the passengers. The hijackers and released convicts then forced the crew of the DC-9 to fly to Madrid, where they eventually surrendered to the Spanish police.

SVENSKT PRESSFOTO / KEYSTONE

From the throne at the royal castle in Stockholm, the beloved King Gustaf Adolf delivers a speech at the opening of the Riksdag on Jan. 11, 1972. The king turned 90 in 1972.

Early in November it was announced that the Facit office machine group, one of Sweden's best-known companies, which was in serious economic difficulties, was to be taken over by Electrolux, a rapidly expanding producer of domestic appliances and ecological equipment. King Gustaf VI Adolf celebrated his 90th birthday on November 11.

The renewed bombing of Hanoi by the United States in December met with exceptionally strong public and official protest in Sweden and normal diplomatic relations between the two countries were virtually suspended. (ALAN WILSON)

SWEDEN

Education. (1969–70) Primary, pupils 606,220, teachers 30,620; secondary, pupils 415,939, teachers (1968–69) 36,701; vocational, pupils 227,876, teachers (1967–68) 16,019; teacher training, students 11,514; higher (including 9 universities), students 114,875, teaching staff (1964–65) 2,296.

Finance. Monetary unit: krona, with (Sept. 18, 1972) a par value of 4.81 kronor to U.S. $1 (free rate of 11.56 kronor = £1 sterling). Gold, SDRs, and foreign exchange, central bank: (June 1972) U.S. $304 million; (June 1971) U.S. $873 million. Budget (1972–73 est.): revenue 55,831,000,000 kronor; expenditure 59,110,000,000 kronor. Gross domestic product: (1970) 168,660,000,000 kronor; (1969) 151,840,000,000 kronor. Money supply: (June 1972) 18,870,000,000 kronor; (June 1971) 16,910,000,000 kronor. Cost of living (1963 = 100): (June 1972) 153; (June 1971) 143.

Foreign Trade. (1971) Imports 36,193,000,000 kronor; exports 38,152,000,000 kronor. Import sources: West Germany 19%; U.K. 14%; U.S. 8%; Denmark 8%; Norway 6%; Finland 5%. Export destinations: U.K. 14%; West Germany 11%; Norway 10%; Denmark 10%; U.S. 7%; Finland 6%; France 5%. Main exports: machinery 26%; motor vehicles 10%; paper 8%; iron and steel 8%; wood pulp 7%; timber 6%; ships and boats 5%.

Transport and Communications. Roads (1971) *c.* 174,000 km. (including 441 km. expressways and 62,000 km. of subsidized private roads open to the public). Motor vehicles in use (1971): passenger 2,356,600; commercial 142,300. Railways (1970): 12,208 km. (including 7,520 km. electrified); traffic 4,775,000,000 passenger-km., freight 17,311,000,000 net ton-km. Air traffic (including Swedish apportionment of international operations of Scandinavian Airlines System; 1971): 2,630,000,000 passenger-km.; freight 114,336,000 net ton-km. Shipping (1971): merchant vessels 100 gross tons and over 937; gross tonnage 4,978,278. Telephones (Dec. 1970) 4,307,000. Radio receivers (Dec. 1970) 2,846,000. Television licenses (Dec. 1970) 2,513,000.

Agriculture. Production (in 000; metric tons; 1971; 1970 in parentheses): wheat 995 (962); barley 2,029 (1,904); oats 1,867 (1,686); rye 301 (228); potatoes 1,242 (1,490); sugar, raw value (1971–72) 267, (1970–71) 218; rapeseed 228 (191); butter 43 (42); cheese *c.* 69 (63); beef and veal *c.* 164 (164); pork *c.* 235 (229); timber (cu.m.; 1970) 60,400, (1969) 52,500; fish catch (1970) 294, (1969) 278. Livestock (in 000; June 1971): cattle 1,840; sheep *c.* 330; pigs 2,155; horses 54; chickens 7,017.

Industry. Index of industrial production (1963 = 100): (1971) 161; (1970) 156. Production (in 000; metric tons; 1971): cement 3,826; coal (1969) 22; electricity (68% hydroelectric in 1970; kw-hr.) 66,502,000; iron ore (60–65% metal content) 33,277; pig iron 2,580; crude steel 5,260; aluminum 76; copper 50; lead (1970) 43; gold (troy oz.; 1970) 44; silver (troy oz.; 1970) 3,948; cotton yarn 9.5; rayon, etc., yarn and fibres 36; mechanical wood pulp (1970) 1,540; chemical wood pulp (1970) 6,603; newsprint 970; other paper (1970) 3,329. Merchant vessels launched (100 gross tons and over; 1971) 1,837,000 gross tons. New dwelling units completed (1971) 107,000.

Swimming

An Olympic year always produces many new world swimming records, and 1972 was no exception. Including those at the Olympic Games, 23 were set by the men (17 by U.S. swimmers) beginning with 8 min. 23.8 sec. for the 800-m. freestyle by 17-year-old Brad Cooper of Australia at the New South Wales Australian Championships on January 12. The women were only slightly less prolific as they set 19 world marks (12 by U.S. swimmers) inaugurated by Australia's Shane Gould, 15, who lowered the 100-m. freestyle to 58.5 sec. at the New South Wales Championships on January 8.

In Europe, East Germany served notice that its swimmers too would be a threat for medal honours at the Olympics. In a dual meet with the Soviet Union at Moscow on April 7–9, the East Germans defeated the Soviets for the third successive year, 184–160. On the final day of the meet East German star Roland Matthes, 21, lowered his own 100-m. backstroke world record to 56.3 sec. Three months later, at Leipzig, E.Ger., in the German Championships, Matthes was timed in 2 min. 2.8 sec. to lower his 200-m. backstroke record almost beyond reach of any other competitor, about four seconds faster than his closest rival. Matthes was the star of the Leipzig tournament as he won the 100-m. freestyle in 53.6 sec., 100-m. butterfly in 56.5 sec., and the 100-m. backstroke in 56.8 sec. Rosemarie Kother, 16, was also impressive as she set a new European record for the 200-m. butterfly at 2 min. 19.5 sec.

Italy unveiled an Olympic threat in its national championships at Turin on July 23–24. Novella Calligaris, 15, set European records in the 400-m. freestyle, 4 min. 26.7 sec., and 800-m. freestyle, 9 min. 6 sec. She also won the 200-m. freestyle, the 400-m. individual medley, and 200-m. butterfly. In Japan, Mayumi Aoki, 19, at Tokyo on July 21 lowered the 100-m. butterfly world record to 1 min. 3.9 sec. as girls from both sides of the ocean were beginning to close the gap on the previously dominant U.S. swimmers.

At the Canadian Olympic Trials at Winnipeg, Man., on August 7–10, 17 new Canadian records were set as well as four Commonwealth marks. Outstanding were Leslie Cliff and Donna Marie Gurr, both 17. Miss Cliff won five events, setting Canadian records in the 200-m. butterfly at 2 min. 26 sec. and in the 200-m. individual medley at 2 min. 25.7 sec. Miss Gurr swam the fastest 100-m. backstroke going into the Olympics, clocking 1 min. 6.4 sec. Her 2 min. 22.5 sec. for the 200-m. backstroke also set a Canadian mark. Bruce Robertson, 19, a student at the University of British Columbia, was timed at 56.6 sec. for the 100-m. butterfly to set a Canadian record.

Swimmers in the United States were not idle. The first major competition was the 49th annual National Collegiate Athletic Association (NCAA) swimming and diving championships at West Point, N.Y., March 23–25. For the fifth straight year Indiana University won, scoring 390 points to 371 for runner-up University of Southern California. The championship produced 12 short-course (25-yd. pool) U.S. records and 13 NCAA marks. Indiana captain Mark Spitz (*see* BIOGRAPHY) won two events, both in record time, to lead his Hoosiers to their title.

The U.S. Olympic swimming trials were held at Portage Park pool in Chicago, August 2–6, and this qualifying meet replaced the annual Amateur Athletic Union (AAU) long-course (outdoor) national championships. Seven world and ten U.S. records were set by the men, and four world and seven U.S. marks by the women. All of them except the 400-m. freestyle record of 4 min. 0.1 sec. by Kurt Krumpholz, 18, of Corona del Mar, Calif., were later to be lowered at the Olympic Games. Krumpholz achieved his time in a preliminary heat, but in the finals failed to qualify for the Olympic team.

Diving. U.S. divers learned early in the year that they would have a hard battle to retain the dominance that they had enjoyed in previous Olympics. At the National AAU Indoor Diving Championships, March 26–April 1, at Dallas, Tex., Capt. Micki King of the U.S. Air Force and Cynthia Potter won the 1-m. and 3-m. springboard titles, respectively, while Sweden's 17-year-old Ulrika Knape began her climb toward world supremacy by winning the 10-m. platform event. Don Dunfield and Lieut. Phil Boggs divided the springboard championships, with Dunfield taking the 1-m. and Boggs the 3-m. Dick Rydze won the platform event.

The next test took place at Winnipeg, Man., April 8–9, with divers from the Soviet Union, Sweden, Czechoslovakia, Australia, Colombia, Brazil, Mexico, Canada, and the U.S. participating. The Canadians Beverly Boys and Liz Carruthers finished first and second in the 3-m. springboard, followed by Ulrika

World Records Set in 1972

Event	Name	Country	Time
MEN			
100-m. freestyle	Mark Spitz	U.S.	51.5 sec.
100-m. freestyle	Mark Spitz	U.S.	51.2 sec.
200-m. freestyle	Mark Spitz	U.S.	1 min. 52.8 sec.
400-m. freestyle	Brad Cooper	Australia	4 min. 1.7 sec.
400-m. freestyle	Kurt Krumpholz	U.S.	4 min. 0.1 sec.
800-m. freestyle	Brad Cooper	Australia	8 min. 23.8 sec.
1,500-m. freestyle	Rick DeMont	U.S.	15 min. 52.9 sec.
1,500-m. freestyle	Michael Burton	U.S.	15 min. 52.6 sec.
100-m. backstroke	Roland Matthes	East Germany	56.3 sec.
200-m. backstroke	Roland Matthes	East Germany	2 min. 2.8 sec.
100-m. breaststroke	Nobutaka Taguchi	Japan	1 min. 4.9 sec.
200-m. breaststroke	John Hencken	U.S.	2 min. 22.8 sec.
200-m. breaststroke	John Hencken	U.S.	2 min. 21.6 sec.
100-m. butterfly	Mark Spitz	U.S.	54.6 sec.
100-m. butterfly	Mark Spitz	U.S.	54.3 sec.
200-m. butterfly	Mark Spitz	U.S.	2 min. 1.5 sec.
200-m. butterfly	Mark Spitz	U.S.	2 min. 0.7 sec.
200-m. individual medley	Gary Hall	U.S.	2 min. 9.3 sec.
200-m. individual medley	Gunnar Larsson	Sweden	2 min. 7.2 sec.
400-m. individual medley	Gary Hall	U.S.	4 min. 30.8 sec.
400-m. medley relay	U.S. Olympic team (Mike Stamm, Tom Bruce, Mark Spitz, Jerry Heidenreich)		3 min. 48.2 sec.
400-m. freestyle relay	U.S. Olympic team (Dave Edgar, John Murphy, Jerry Heidenreich, Mark Spitz)		3 min. 26.4 sec.
800-m. freestyle relay	U.S. Olympic team (John Kinsella, Fred Tyler, Steve Genter, Mark Spitz)		7 min. 35.8 sec.
WOMEN			
100-m. freestyle	Shane Gould	Australia	58.5 sec.
200-m. freestyle	Shirley Babashoff	U.S.	2 min. 5.2 sec.
200-m. freestyle	Shane Gould	Australia	2 min. 3.6 sec.
400-m. freestyle	Shane Gould	Australia	4 min. 19.0 sec.
800-m. freestyle	Jo Harshbarger	U.S.	8 min. 53.8 sec.
800-m. freestyle	Keena Rothhammer	U.S.	8 min. 53.7 sec.
200-m. backstroke	Melissa Belote	U.S.	2 min. 20.6 sec.
200-m. backstroke	Melissa Belote	U.S.	2 min. 19.2 sec.
100-m. breaststroke	Cathy Carr	U.S.	1 min. 13.6 sec.
100-m. butterfly	Mayumi Aoki	Japan	1 min. 3.9 sec.
100-m. butterfly	Mayumi Aoki	Japan	1 min. 3.3 sec.
200-m. butterfly	Karen Moe	U.S.	2 min. 16.6 sec.
200-m. butterfly	Karen Moe	U.S.	2 min. 15.6 sec.
200-m. individual medley	Shane Gould	Australia	2 min. 23.1 sec.
400-m. individual medley	Gail Neall	Australia	5 min. 3.0 sec.
400-m. medley relay	U.S. Olympic team (Melissa Belote, Cathy Carr, Deena Deardurff, Sandy Neilson)		4 min. 25.3 sec.
400-m. medley relay	U.S. Olympic team (same team as above)		4 min. 20.8 sec.
400-m. freestyle relay	U.S. Olympic team (Kim Peyton, Sandy Neilson, Jane Barkman, Shirley Babashoff)		3 min. 58.1 sec.
400-m. freestyle relay	U.S. Olympic team (Sandy Neilson, Jennifer Kemp, Jane Barkman, Shirley Babashoff)		3 min. 55.2 sec.

UPI COMPIX

Mark Spitz swims his way to a world record of 2 min. 1.53 sec. in the 200-m. butterfly during Olympic trials in Chicago on Aug. 2, 1972. He lowered this mark to 2 min. 0.7 sec. in the Olympic Games.

Knape. Miss Knape turned the tables in the platform event with Miss Boys and Milena Duchkova, the 1968 Olympic champion from Czechoslovakia, as runners-up. In the men's competition, Mike Finneran of the U.S. won both the springboard and platform events. In the springboard he was followed by Vladimir Vasin of the Soviet Union and Craig Lincoln of the U.S. In the platform, Volodu Kapirulin of the Soviet Union was runner-up followed by Mike Brown of the U.S.

The U.S. National AAU Outdoor Championships were held at Lincoln, Neb., July 11–15. Cynthia Potter successfully defended her 1-m. and 3-m. springboard titles, while Janet Ely won the 10-m. platform. Don Dunfield won the men's 1-m. and Mike Finneran the 3-m. springboard titles with Rick Early taking the platform.

The U.S. Olympic diving trials held at Oak Park, Ill., July 18–20, produced a team of eight divers to represent the U.S. at Munich, W.Ger. Three girls, Micki King, Cynthia Potter, and Janet Ely qualified to compete in the Olympics in both the springboard and platform. Craig Lincoln, Mike Finneran, and David Bush were the springboard competitors for the games, and Dick Rydze, Rick Early, and Finneran qualified for the platform.

The Olympics. For the first time, a swimmer was named the outstanding athlete of the Olympic Games. This honour was bestowed upon 22-year-old Mark Spitz from Carmichael, Calif., who in eight days of competition in a feat unmatched in Olympic history won seven gold medals, set four individual world records, and participated in three world-record-setting relays. Almost as brilliant as Spitz was Australia's 15-year-old Shane Gould. The blonde teen-ager competed in five individual races and won three, was runner-up in one, and third in the other. Her three gold medals were world record performances, as the women set 11 new world marks out of 14 events.

For the results of swimming and diving competition in the Olympics, *see* SPORTING RECORD: *Special Report*.

(ALBERT SCHOENFIELD)

Switzerland

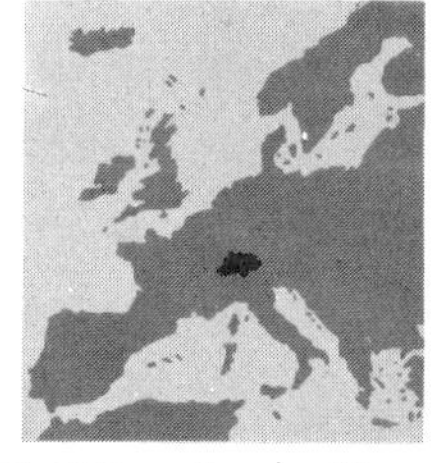

A federal republic in west central Europe consisting of a confederation of 25 cantons, Switzerland is bounded by West Germany, Austria, Liechtenstein, Italy, and France. Area: 15,941 sq.mi. (41,288 sq.km.). Pop. (1970): 6,269,783. Cap.: Bern (pop., 1970, 162,405). Largest city: Zürich (pop., 1970, 422,640). Language: French, German, Italian, Romansh. Religion (1967): Roman Catholic 49.4%; Protestant 47.7%. President in 1972, Nello Celio.

In June 1972 the ten-member group appointed in 1967 under the chairmanship of former federal councillor F. T. Wahlen announced that it was putting the finishing touches to its final report on the forthcoming total revision of the federal constitution. On the basis of this report the Federal Council would draw up its formal project for submission to the people in 1974.

Meanwhile, the two houses of the federal Parliament discussed and approved one of the major changes to be made in the existing constitution: the abrogation of articles 51 and 52, which imposed restrictions on the Jesuits and on the founding of new (Roman Catholic) convents. This amendment was to be submitted to a popular referendum in 1973; its adoption was a precondition to ratification of Switzerland's signature, on Dec. 21, 1972, of the European Convention on Human Rights.

In February a working group under the auspices of the Forum Helveticum, representing a wide range of public opinion, completed a study in which a majority expressed itself in favour of introducing some form of civil service for conscientious objectors. Early in November the Federal Council announced its approval of the so-called Muenchenstein initiative calling for the substitution of civil for military service by conscientious objectors, and agreed to submit a pertinent report to the federal Parliament in January 1973, with a view to the latter's working out the necessary constitutional amendment.

In anticipation of the coming into force of the 1971 constitutional amendment for the protection of the environment, Parliament in the spring approved a set of federal emergency measures to prohibit or restrict building in certain areas. In October the Federal Council proposed an additional amendment to strengthen the government's powers over water resources.

On November 23 the Bernese cantonal government published a long-awaited draft statute for its Jura region. It was hoped that the statute, by granting a large measure of autonomy to the French-speaking Catholic districts, would provide a workable compromise between the separatist and antiseparatist camps.

In the spring the people voted by a massive majority in favour of a constitutional amendment calling for the promotion of housing and the protection of tenants. In September a popular initiative to impose stricter controls on the manufacture of armaments and to prohibit their exportation was defeated by a narrow margin (593,199 to 584,726, 32.7% of the electorate voting). The Federal Council, emphasizing the necessity of maintaining a credible military defense, was now free to pursue its own, less stringent, project of controlling the manufacture and exportation of arms.

The federal Parliament during the summer approved an official report on Switzerland's relations with the UN and its specialized agencies during the period 1969–71. The debate revealed a slight increase of support for Switzerland's eventual full membership in the UN. A public opinion poll suggested that about 45% of the population were for and 35% against full membership; the rest were undecided.

Toward the end of the year, the most important public issue was the conclusion, after two years of negotiations, of a free-trade agreement between Switzerland and the EEC in Brussels. As the Federal Council explained, the agreement respected Switzerland's neutrality; it entailed no modification of the country's internal political structure; it in no way impaired the country's freedom to conclude treaties with third countries; the policy of limiting the volume of foreign labour was not affected; and it provided for the possibility of other than free-trade arrangements, as in transportation. It was submitted to referendum on December 3 and was approved by a vote of 1,345,057 to 509,350.

The country's economy continued to be characterized by boom conditions and a strong inflationary trend, which in 1972 attained 7.3%, while all the indexes pointed to a further increase. A revision of the constitutional article 315, the basis of the government's powers in the field of economic policy, was under discussion. Meanwhile, the government prohibited the investment of foreign funds in Swiss securities and in mortgages on real estate as well as the acquisition of Swiss real estate by foreigners residing abroad.

(MELANIE F. STAERK)

SWITZERLAND

Education. (1969–70) Primary, pupils 487,583, teachers (excluding craft teachers; 1961–62) 23,761; secondary, pupils 306,786, teachers (full-time; 1961–62) 6,583; vocational, pupils 145,937; teacher training, students 11,300; higher (including 8 universities), students 40,083, teaching staff 3,500.

Finance. Monetary unit: Swiss franc, with (Sept. 18, 1972) an official rate of SFr. 3.84 to U.S. $1 (free rate of SFr. 9.27 = £1 sterling). Gold, SDRs, and foreign exchange, central bank: (June 1972) U.S. $7,018,000,000; (June 1971) U.S. $5,083,000,000. Budget (1971 est.): revenue SFr. 8,517,000,000; expenditure SFr. 8,609,000,000. Gross national product: (1971) SFr. 100.6 billion; (1970) SFr. 88.1 billion. Money supply: (May 1972) SFr. 54,270,000,000; (May 1971) SFr. 47,140,000,000. Cost of living (1963 = 100): (June 1972) 143; (June 1971) 134.

Foreign Trade. (1971) Imports SFr. 29,636,000,000; exports SFr. 23,543,000,000. Import sources: EEC 59% (West Germany 30%, France 13%, Italy 10%); U.K. 8%; U.S. 7%; Austria 5%. Export destinations: EEC 38% (West Germany 15%, Italy 9%, France 9%); U.S. 9%; U.K. 7%; Austria 6%. Main exports: machinery 30%; chemicals 22%; watches and clocks 11%; textile yarns and fabrics 9%. Tourism (1970): visitors 6,839,900; gross receipts U.S. $905 million.

Transport and Communications. Roads (1971) 59,808 km. Motor vehicles in use (1971): passenger 1,482,000; commercial 137,500. Railways: (state; 1970) 2,926 km. (including 2,911 km. electrified), (private; 1969) 2,082 (including 2,070 km. electrified); traffic (state railways; 1971) 7,921,000,000 passenger-km., freight 6,622,000,000 net ton-km., (private railways; 1970) 1,171,000,000 passenger-km., freight 417 million net ton-km. Air traffic (1971): 5,199,000,000 passenger-km.; freight 201,033,000 net ton-km. Shipping (1971): merchant vessels 100 gross tons and over 32; gross tonnage 199,591. Telephones (Dec. 1970) 3,026,000. Radio licenses (Dec. 1970) 1,852,000. Television licenses (Dec. 1970) 1,274,000.

Agriculture. Production (in 000; metric tons; 1971; 1970 in parentheses): wheat 441 (348); barley 170 (136); oats 29 (30); rye *c.* 40 (46); potatoes 950 (1,090); apples *c.* 430 (*c.* 360); pears *c.* 190 (*c.* 185); sugar, raw value (1971–72) *c.* 74, (1970–71) 58; wine 82 (118); milk *c.* 3,270 (3,230); butter *c.* 35 (32); cheese *c.* 88 (87); beef and veal 131 (135); pork 206 (196). Livestock (in 000; April 1971): cattle 1,890; sheep 292; pigs 1,872; horses *c.* 50; chickens 6,265.

Industry. Index of industrial production (1963 = 100): (1971) 146; (1970) 143. Production (in 000; metric tons; 1971): cement 5,217; aluminum 94; rayon, etc., yarn and fibre (1970) 12; nylon, etc., yarn and fibre (1970) 48; cigarettes (units; 1970) 29,229,000; watches (units; 1970) 52,607; manufactured gas (gasworks only; cu.m.; 1970) 396,000; electricity (kw-hr.) 31,594,000.

Syria

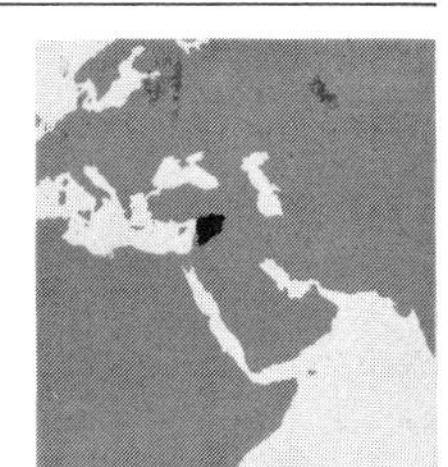

A republic in southwestern Asia on the Mediterranean Sea, Syria is bordered by Turkey, Iraq, Jordan, Israel, and Lebanon. Area: 71,498 sq.mi. (185,180 sq.km.). Pop. (1970): 6,303,000. Cap. and largest city: Damascus (pop., 1970, 836,000). Language: Arabic (official); also Kurdish, Armenian, Turkish, and Circassian. Religion: predominantly Muslim. President in 1972, Gen. Hafez al-Assad; premier, Abdul Rahman Khleyfawi.

In 1972 the modest liberalization of the Syrian regime of the previous year was continued and relations with most Arab states improved, although those with Egypt and Libya, Syria's partners in the tripartite Arab federation, underwent some strain. There was a partial rapprochement with the rival Baathist

SYRIA

Education. (1969–70) Primary, pupils 845,130, teachers 23,431; secondary, pupils 281,254, teachers 10,651; vocational, pupils 10,445, teachers 892; teacher training, students 4,018, teachers 398; higher (including 2 universities), students 37,540, teaching staff 1,056.

Finance. Monetary unit: Syrian pound, with (Sept. 18, 1972) an official exchange rate of S£3.82 to U.S. $1 and a free rate of S£4.32 to U.S. $1 (S£10.44 = £1 sterling). Gold, SDRs, and foreign exchange: (May 1972) U.S. $119 million; (May 1971) U.S. $61 million. Budget (total; 1972 est.) balanced at S£3,188 million. Money supply: (May 1972) S£2,528 million; (May 1971) S£2,387 million. Cost of living (Damascus; 1963 = 100): (Feb. 1972) 125; (Feb. 1971) 132.

Foreign Trade. (1971) Imports S£1,677 million; exports S£743.3 million. Import sources: Lebanon 9%; Italy 7%; U.S. 7%; West Germany 6%; U.S.S.R. 6%; Iraq 6%. Export destinations: Italy 28%; U.S.S.R. 15%; Lebanon 8%. Main exports: cotton 42%; crude oil 24%; fruit and vegetables 5%.

Transport and Communications. Roads (1971) 16,710 km. (including 63 km. expressways). Motor vehicles in use (1971): passenger 31,700; commercial 17,500. Railways: (1970) 1,100 km.; traffic (1971) 83,750,000 passenger-km., freight 120,890,000 net ton-km. Air traffic (1970): 219,932,000 passenger-km.; freight 1,238,000 net ton-km. Ships entered (1970) vessels totaling 16,544,000 net registered tons; goods loaded (1971) 31,431,000 metric tons, unloaded 2,447,000 metric tons. Telephones (Dec. 1970) 111,000. Radio receivers (Dec. 1970) 1,367,000. Television receivers (Dec. 1970) 116,000.

Agriculture. Production (in 000; metric tons; 1971; 1970 in parentheses): wheat 846 (625); barley 262 (235); millet and sorghum *c.* 20 (14); chick-peas 24 (15); lentils 87 (58); grapes *c.* 215 (206); raisins *c.* 9 (9); figs (1970) 44, (1969) 50; sugar, raw value (1971–72) *c.* 37, (1970–71) *c.* 26; olive oil *c.* 18 (16); tobacco *c.* 8.9 (6.7); cotton, lint *c.* 156 (148); wool *c.* 7.5 (7). Livestock (in 000; 1970–71): cattle *c.* 550; sheep *c.* 6,200; goats *c.* 770; horses *c.* 70; asses *c.* 230; chickens (Dec. 1970) 3,669.

Industry. Production (in 000; metric tons; 1970): petroleum products 1,826; cement (1971) 910; cotton yarn 20; electricity (kw-hr.) 947,000.

regime in Iraq, but several major Syrian-Iraqi differences remained.

In March President Assad gave evidence of Syria's new flexibility when he said for the first time that Syria accepted UN Security Council Resolution 242 as a basis for a political settlement in the Middle East provided it meant a complete Israeli withdrawal from territories occupied in 1967 and full restitution of Palestinian rights. During the year Syria took steps to improve relations with the more conservative Arab states. It established diplomatic ties with the newly independent Qatar, Bahrain, and United Arab Emirates; a Syrian trade mission to Saudi Arabia settled various outstanding difficulties between the two countries; and after Assad's visit to Kuwait in April the Kuwaiti government agreed to provide approximately $30 million to augment Syria's general reserves in its struggle with Israel. Relations with Jordan showed no sign of improvement, although the partial closing of the frontier was ended December 1.

The ideological war between Syrian and Iraqi Baathists continued during the first part of the year, but following Syria's nationalization of Iraq Petroleum Co. installations in the wake of Iraq's nationalization of the Western-owned company on June 1, there was a marked improvement in relations between the two countries. The Iraqi foreign minister visited Damascus, and agreement was reached to increase trade and to settle several outstanding problems. However, the new rapport was severely shaken on October 13 when a dispute arose over the level of Syria's transit revenues for Iraqi oil, which before nationalization had accounted for 10% of Syria's foreign exchange earnings.

Relations with the Soviet Union and Eastern Europe remained close, and a Syrian delegation visited China in May. In August Assad declared it was not Syria's intention to follow the example of Pres. Anwar as-Sadat of Egypt by expelling the Soviet military advisers from Syria. Indeed, it was announced in September that the Soviet Union and Syria had agreed on a military buildup in Syria, and it was widely forecast that the U.S.S.R. would henceforth concentrate its military aid to the Arab world on Syria. Assad was, however, anxious to avoid a complete breach between Egypt and the Soviet Union. He made a secret visit to Moscow at the end of September which prepared the ground for the partial Egyptian-Soviet rapprochement that followed. After the massacre of Israeli Olympic athletes at Munich, W.Ger., in September, the plane hijacking in October that secured the release of Palestinian terrorists responsible for the massacre, and again in November and December, Syria suffered severe Israeli bombing raids. In December it was reported that the Syrian government was attempting to curb guerrilla activities.

On March 7 the long-awaited undertaking to form a left-wing coalition to replace the former exclusively Baathist political control was carried out when a National Progressive Front was created. It comprised an 18-member central leadership, including President Assad, nine other Baathists, and two members from each of four non-Baathist parties. The Baathists had suffered setbacks in provincial elections in March.

The powers of the Syrian president, which had been greatly increased in February 1971 to make them similar to those of the Egyptian president, were further extended by the Syrian Baathist Regional Command in May. At that time, amendments to the 1969 provisional constitution authorized the president to assume legislative powers when the National Assembly was not in session, or in times of emergency.

Mild but significant measures of economic liberalization were pursued. Import restrictions were relaxed, private enterprise and foreign tourism encouraged, and further steps taken to attract expatriate Syrian and Arab capital. The sharp reduction of oil transit revenues following the nationalization of the Iraq Petroleum Co. were at least partly offset by the above-average 1972 grain harvest. Work on the Euphrates Dam was reported on schedule with blocking of the main stream due for July 1973. (PETER MANSFIELD)

Taiwan

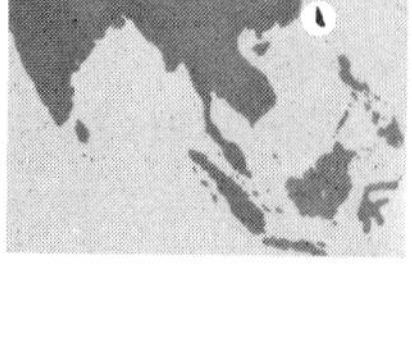

Taiwan, which consists of the islands of Formosa and Quemoy and other surrounding islands, is the seat of the Republic of China (Nationalist China). It is situated north of the Philippines, southwest of Japan and Okinawa, and east of Hong Kong. The island of Formosa has an area of 13,087 sq.mi.; including its 77 outlying islands (14 in the Taiwan group and 63 in the Pescadores group), the area of Taiwan totals 13,892 sq.mi. (35,980 sq.km.). Pop. (1972 est.): 15,089,756. Cap. and largest city: Taipei (pop., 1972 est., 1,864,697). President in 1972, Chiang Kai-shek; premier (president of the Executive Yuan), C. K. Yen until March 21 and, from June 1, Chiang Ching-kuo.

In 1972 the international position of Nationalist China suffered a devastating blow from U.S. Pres. Richard Nixon's visit to mainland China in February. This came on the heels of Taiwan's ouster from the UN in late October 1971. After that, more than 20 countries shifted diplomatic ties from Taipei to Peking, reducing the Chinese Nationalist government's recognition roster from nearly 70 to less than 50 by late 1972.

President Nixon's journey to Peking marked a low point in the diplomatic status of Taiwan. On February 9, about a week before his departure for Peking, Nixon stated: "The ultimate relationship between Taiwan and the mainland is not a matter for the United States to decide." He urged the parties concerned to seek a peaceful solution to the problem in order to reduce tensions in the Far East. Although Nixon did not suggest any particular course for either party to follow, he declared that "with the Republic of China we shall maintain our friendship, our diplomatic ties, and our defense commitment."

KEYSTONE

The Tsengwen reservoir under construction in Taiwan was to be completed in March 1973. The dam's volume would be 12,560,000 cu.yd., and its annual power output 212,600,000 kw-hr. It would provide 228,000 tons of running water per day, enough to supply cities and towns with an aggregate population of 1.5 million.

Despite Nixon's assurance on the maintenance of existing diplomatic relations and his statement that talks with Chou En-lai would concern only issues between the U.S. and China, Nationalist officials were naturally apprehensive about the summit talks in Peking. They made no secret of their strong opposition to Nixon's visit, but their formal complaints were cautious and restrained. On February 17, the Ministry of Foreign Affairs issued a statement declaring that "it will consider null and void any agreement involving the rights and interests of the government and people of the Republic of China which may be reached between the government of the United States and the Chinese Communist regime as a result of that visit." Furthermore, the statement said that "the Chinese government trusts that the American President will live up to the solemn assurances that he has repeatedly made."

The joint communiqué of February 27, issued by President Nixon and Chinese Premier Chou En-lai, dealt with the question of Taiwan mainly in principle, not in terms of immediate actions. The U.S. committed itself to the proposition that there is only one China, that, by implication, the mainland regime is the de jure as well as de facto government of all China, and that Taiwan is a part of that one China. Furthermore, the U.S. agreed not to interfere in relations between China and Taiwan, and to withdraw its military forces and installations from Taiwan as soon as tensions ceased in the area. The communiqué made no mention of the mutual defense treaty of 1954 between the U.S. and Taiwan since such a reference would have been objectionable to Peking.

The Nationalist government lost no time in registering its disapproval of the communiqué. In comparison with the disapproval and protest in the press the government statement was rather mild, as the officials fully realized the importance of the goodwill of the U.S. government to the Nationalist cause. A U.S. Department of State spokesman, Charles W. Bray, reaffirmed the defense commitment of the U.S. to Nationalist China.

The so-called "Nixon shocks" on China and economic policy pushed Japan to take early and independent action to normalize its relations with mainland China. Since the Sino-Japanese peace treaty of 1952 had formed the basis for all relations between the two countries and recognized the Nationalist regime as the government of China, the Nationalists regarded the normalization of Peking-Tokyo ties as contrary to the pledges of Japan to respect its treaty obligations. On September 29, Japanese Prime Minister Kakuei Tanaka (*see* BIOGRAPHY) agreed to immediately establish diplomatic relations with Peking, and as a result Japan severed its diplomatic ties with Taiwan.

Prior to Nixon's visit to Peking, Chiang Kai-shek, after 24 years as president, had made known his decision not to seek another term. Chiang reached the age of 85 on October 31. In view of the diplomatic setbacks, however, government and party officials considered Chiang's prestige essential to guide the destiny of the country. Immediately after he announced his intention to step down in an address to the National Assembly on February 26, a nationwide movement was initiated to draft him. On March 21 he was reelected for a fifth six-year term with 1,308 votes, only 8 votes short of unanimity.

Yen resigned as premier immediately after taking the oath of office for a second term as vice-president; he was replaced by Chiang Ching-kuo (*see* BIOGRAPHY). On December 23, 36 new members of the Legislative Yuan and 53 new members of the National Assembly were elected; most of the successful candidates were members of the Kuomintang, although several independents were also chosen. The election of the additional members of the two bodies was made possible by a revision of the constitution earlier in the year. Their terms of office would be three years for the Legislative Yuan and six years for the National Assembly; the incumbent members, most of whom had been elected before the Nationalist government left the mainland, would continue to serve indefinite terms.

(HUNG-TI CHU)

See also China.

TAIWAN

Education. (1969–70) Primary, pupils 2,428,041, teachers 57,935; secondary, pupils 872,277, teachers 32,244; vocational, pupils 155,947, teachers 7,308; teacher training, students 528, teachers 14; higher (including 9 universities), students 184,215, teaching staff 20,515.

Finance. Monetary unit: New Taiwan dollar, with (Sept. 18, 1972) a par value of NT$40 to U.S. $1 (free rate of NT$98 = £1 sterling). Gold, SDRs, and foreign exchange, official: (June 1972) U.S. $606 million; (June 1971) U.S. $504 million. Budget (1970–71 est.): revenue NT$51,757,000,000; expenditure NT$50,068,000,000. Gross national product: (1970) NT$217,640,000,000; (1969) NT$190,810,000,000. Money supply: (June 1972) NT$50,980,000,000; (June 1971) NT$40,530,000,000. Cost of living (1963 = 100): (June 1972) 131; (June 1971) 126.

Foreign Trade. (1971) Imports U.S. $1,844,000,000; exports U.S. $1,997,700,000. Import sources (1970): Japan 43%; U.S. 24%. Export destinations (1970): U.S. 40%; Japan 15%; Hong Kong 10%; West Germany 5%. Main exports (1970): clothing 15%; textile yarns and fabrics 14%; fruits and vegetables 12%; telecommunications equipment 9%; plywood 5%; small plastics manufactures 5%.

Transport and Communications. Roads (1970) 15,382 km. Motor vehicles in use (1970): passenger 49,500; commercial 41,000. Railways (1970): *c.* 4,400 km.; traffic 6,212,000,000 passenger-km., freight 2,631,000,000 net ton-km. Air traffic (1970): 954 million passenger-km.; freight 25,175,000 net ton-km. Shipping (1971): merchant vessels 100 gross tons and over 316; gross tonnage 1,321,758. Telephones (Jan. 1971) 403,000. Radio licenses (Dec. 1969) 1,428,000. Television licenses (Dec. 1968) 193,000.

Agriculture. Production (in 000; metric tons; 1971; 1970 in parentheses): rice *c.* 2,987 (3,226); sweet potatoes (1970) 3,441, (1969) 3,702; cassava (1970) 308, (1969) 316; peanuts 140 (122); oranges (1970) *c.* 156, (1969) 123; tea *c.* 28 (28); sugar, raw value (1971–72) *c.* 750, (1970–71) 843; bananas (1970) 462, (1969) 586; tobacco 12 (21); sisal *c.* 11 (11); jute 14 (14); pork *c.* 360 (354). Livestock (in 000; Dec. 1970): cattle 75; pigs *c.* 3,080; goats 167; chickens 14,269.

Industry. Production (in 000; metric tons; 1970): coal 4,473; crude oil 90; natural gas (cu.m.) 918,000; electricity (kw-hr.) 13,554,000; cement 4,305; pig iron 61; crude steel 294; salt 535; caustic soda 126; petroleum products 5,030; cotton yarn 86; paper 461.

Tanzania

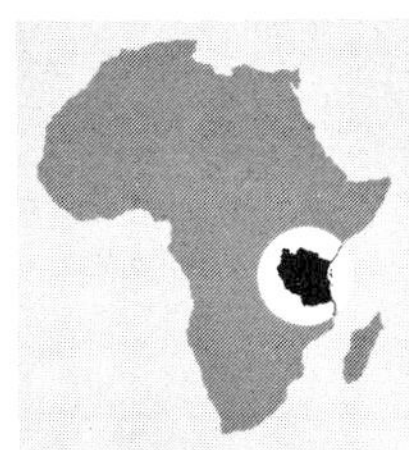

This republic, an East African member of the Commonwealth of Nations, consists of two parts: Tanganyika, on the Indian Ocean, bordered by Kenya, Uganda, Rwanda, Burundi, Zaire, Zambia, Malawi, and Mozambique; and Zanzibar, just off the coast, including Zanzibar Island, Pemba Island, and small islets. Total area of the united republic: 364,943 sq.mi. (945,203 sq.km.). Total pop. (1972 est.): 14,027,879, including (1966 est.) 98.9% Africans and 0.7% Indo-Pakistani. Cap.

and largest city: Dar es Salaam (pop., 1972 est., 396,700) in Tanganyika. Language: English and Swahili. Religion (1967): traditional beliefs 34.6%; Christian 30.6%; Muslim 30.5%. President in 1972, Julius Nyerere.

On Dec. 9, 1971, Tanzania celebrated ten years of independence. At a press conference later in December President Nyerere declared that during the next decade the government intended to encourage wide-ranging decentralization, although money would still be voted by Parliament and the regions would not become autonomous. The president's optimism received a setback on Christmas Day when Regional Commissioner Wilbert Klerruu was shot dead by a Hehe farmer, who, with a number of other prosperous farmers in the Iringa region, opposed the government's rural reconstruction program.

In January the first vice-president and leader of the Revolutionary Council of Zanzibar, Sheikh Abeid Karume, released about 600 petty criminals from prison to mark the eighth anniversary of the revolution which had brought him to power. In April, Karume was assassinated (*see* OBITUARIES). Four of his assailants, all members of the Army, were killed. Of those killed two were said to have been supporters of the former Umma Party, which had merged with Karume's Afro-Shirazi Party after the revolution that overthrew the sultan in 1964. Abdul Rahman Muhammad Babu, who had been leader of the Umma Party, was arrested by Tanzanian security police on April 14, suspected of complicity in the plot. Karume's death was not followed by any marked change in the character of the regime, for Nyerere felt constrained to appoint as Karume's successor Aboud Jumbe, who had been a leading member of Karume's government.

CAMERAPIX/KEYSTONE

The coffin of the first vice-president, Sheikh Abeid Karume, is escorted by heavily armed soldiers during Karume's funeral in Zanzibar. He was assassinated on April 7, 1972.

Relations between Britain and Tanzania showed signs of improvement after the publication of the Pearce commission report on Rhodesia in May. This improvement received further indirect encouragement as a result of the cooling of Britain's relations with Uganda, where Pres. Idi Amin was making accusations of plots against his regime by Nyerere on behalf of Milton Obote, former president of Uganda, and by Britain in pursuit of its own interests. When Amin in August ordered all British Asians to leave Uganda within three months, Nyerere denounced his action as lacking humanity and Amin's criticism of the Tanzanian leader increased. On September 17 an armed force consisting of supporters of Obote crossed into Uganda from northwestern Tanzania. Amin at once accused Tanzania of sending its own soldiers against his country and launched aerial attacks on the Tanzanian lake ports of Bukoba, Mwanza, and Musoma. Nyerere denied that Tanzanian troops had been in any way involved. The invasion soon proved unsuccessful and, following the intervention of the president of Somalia, Muhammad Siyad Barrah, peace terms were agreed on October 5 between the two countries although relations remained strained.

(KENNETH INGHAM)

TANZANIA

Education. (1968) Primary, pupils 833,898, teachers 17,893; secondary, pupils 34,551, teachers 1,668; vocational, pupils 1,064, teachers 83; teacher training, students 2,673, teachers 231; higher (University of Dar es Salaam; 1970), students 1,194, teaching staff 123.

Finance. Monetary unit: Tanzanian shilling, with (Sept. 18, 1972) a par value of TShs. 7.14 to U.S. $1 (free rate of TShs. 17.50 = £1 sterling). Gold, SDRs, and foreign exchange: (June 1972) U.S. $81.1 million; (June 1971) U.S. $66.1 million. Budget (1970–71 est.): revenue TShs. 1,654,000,000; expenditure TShs. 1,652,000,000. Money supply: (May 1972) TShs. 1,935,000,000; (May 1971) TShs. 1,833,000,000. Cost of living (Dar es Salaam; 1963 = 100): (June 1972) 142; (June 1971) 126.

Foreign Trade. (Excluding trade with Kenya and Uganda; 1971) Imports TShs. 2,414,000,000; exports TShs. 1,792,000,000. Import sources: China 25%; U.K. 20%; West Germany 7%; Japan 6%; Iran 6%; Italy 5%. Export destinations: U.K. 24%; Zambia 10%; India 8%; U.S. 8%; Hong Kong 7%; China 5%. Main exports: coffee 17%; cotton 14%; diamonds 12%; sisal 7%.

Transport and Communications. Roads (1969) 16,743 km. Motor vehicles in use (1970): passenger *c.* 33,300; commercial (including buses) *c.* 33,700. Railways (1970) *c.* 2,580 km. (for traffic *see* KENYA). Construction of a *c.* 1,800-km. railway linking Dar es Salaam and Kapiri Mposhi in Zambia began in 1970; completion was planned for 1976 (a first 500-km. section of track had been laid at the beginning of 1972). Air traffic: *see* KENYA. Shipping traffic (mainland only; 1970): goods loaded 1,399,000 metric tons; unloaded 2,290,000 metric tons. Telephones (Dec. 1970) 36,000. Radio receivers (Dec. 1970) 150,000. Television licenses (Dec. 1969) 4,000.

Agriculture. Production (in 000; metric tons; 1971; 1970 in parentheses): corn *c.* 541 (650); sweet potatoes (1970) 310, (1969) 213; millet *c.* 138 (138); sorghum *c.* 107 (107); sugar, raw value (1971–72) *c.* 108, (1970–71) *c.* 99; rice *c.* 185 (182); cassava (1970) *c.* 1,500, (1969) *c.* 1,300; coffee *c.* 64 (64); cotton, lint *c.* 75 (71); sisal *c.* 181 (*c.* 202); timber (cu.m.; 1970) 31,500, (1969) 30,500. Livestock (in 000; 1970–71): cattle *c.* 13,300; sheep *c.* 2,800; pigs *c.* 22; goats *c.* 4,450; asses *c.* 160; poultry *c.* 20,600.

Industry. Production (in 000; metric tons; 1970): cement 177; salt 42; magnesite (exports) 0.8; gold (troy oz.) 7.9; diamonds (metric carats) 708; electricity (excluding most industrial production; kw-hr.) 396,000.

Taxation

"Tax reform" was frequently mentioned in the 1972 U.S. presidential campaign, but because all candidates favoured it, at least in abstract terms, it never became an issue. Taxpayer discontent was apparent, nonetheless, and serious consideration of a number of aspects in the tax structure was expected in the near future. In Europe most changes were related to efforts to harmonize taxation within the EEC. A drastic revision of Britain's tax structure was put forward in the 1972 budget.

United States. The year 1972 was one of much discussion and little action in tax legislation in the U.S. The Democratic presidential candidate, Sen.

Tariffs:
see Commercial Policies; Trade, International

George McGovern, made specific suggestions, some of which were promptly disavowed by congressional leaders of his own party. Pres. Richard Nixon withheld any definite recommendations until after the election.

Earlier in the year, the chairman of the House Ways and Means Committee, Wilbur D. Mills (Dem., Ark.), sponsored legislation to repeal, effective over the three years 1974–76, more than 50 provisions of the income and estate taxes that had become the subject of criticism and controversy. This was a temporizing action that relieved the political pressure on members of Congress to act hastily in an election year. It was generally presumed that after committee hearings many if not most of the provisions would be reenacted in the same or a modified form.

Continued reliance on property taxation as a principal source of revenue for school finance was challenged by decisions in several state and federal courts, based on the finding that differences in fiscal capacity between districts denied equal opportunity to children. A decision on the issue by the U.S. Supreme Court was expected in 1973. Early in 1972 President Nixon requested the Advisory Commission on Intergovernmental Relations to analyze the possibility of establishing a program of federal grants for school expenses to states and localities that renounced the use of property taxes on residences for this purpose, with the federal funds to come from a new federal value-added tax. Such a program would have brought together in one package three significant changes: a new federal tax, a form of revenue sharing for a particular purpose (education); and property tax relief on residences.

Various studies in 1972 indicated the prospect for continued large federal deficits under current programs. The administration publicly accepted the 1972–73 deficits as appropriate stimulation under existing economic conditions, thereby giving bipartisan political respectability to deficit spending in conditions short of full employment. Congressional appropriations were so large, however, that it became apparent the deficit would be excessive by any standard. To forestall a manifest need for a tax increase, the House Ways and Means Committee, in conjunction with the White House, proposed legislation giving the president authority to reduce expenditures as needed to keep the total at $250 billion. This, in effect, would have established an item veto under which the president could cut back programs at his discretion. The legislation was adopted by the House but rejected by the Senate in the closing hours of the Congress.

An administration commitment not to propose tax increases in 1973 was conditioned on a limitation of expenditures that was widely regarded as unattainable. Two publications in 1972 were especially significant in setting the background for tax policy. In the Brookings Institution study *Setting National Priorities: The 1973 Budget*, it was recognized that larger government expenditures—that is, more expensive programs—are not necessarily more effective in dealing with social problems; new social concerns can be satisfied only by changing the behaviour of individuals and institutions. Significantly, the Brookings study was written by some of those who had had important government positions during the 1960s and had been sympathetic to programs that, in 1972, they recognized as unsuitable. Their forthright recognition that a larger public expenditure will not necessarily be more effective than a smaller one could lay a base for more critical analysis and greater economy in government spending.

The second significant publication, by Roger A. Herriott and Herman P. Miller, "Tax Changes Among Income Groups—1962–68" (*Business Horizons*, February 1972), showed that people with lower incomes received substantially larger proportionate benefits from government expenditures than those with middle and larger incomes. Earlier studies had reached similar conclusions but the subject had received little attention. For many years estimates had been made of the distribution of the tax burden by income classes and, though the conclusions differed somewhat, in general it appeared that the tax burden as a proportion of income is heavy on those with quite small incomes, becomes smaller for those in the middle income brackets, and then rises substantially for those with large incomes. It was widely, but not universally, believed that government policies should redistribute income in favour of those with smaller incomes, a goal that had been thought to require progressive taxation—that is, taxation that takes a larger fraction of larger incomes. However, an analysis of the combined effects of taxation and government expenditures showed that there would be a redistribution of income if the burden of taxation was proportional to income or even slightly regressive. Additional analysis of the combined effects of taxation and expenditures on the distribution of income would clearly be needed for rational policy decisions.

Value-Added Taxation. The value-added tax (VAT), first introduced in France in the 1950s, was the subject of much discussion in the U.S. in 1972, as the EEC countries moved toward universal adoption of it by 1973 as a principal source of revenue. Though the name "value-added" suggested a complicated process of addition to determine the base of the tax, in practice the calculations were very simple. The tax is applied to a company's net sales with an offsetting credit for the tax paid on all its purchases. With a 3% tax, for example, a company with sales of $100,000 and purchases of $70,000 would owe a tax of $900 ($3,000 on sales less a credit of $2,100 for the tax on purchases).

Unlike most other taxes, VAT is neutral in many respects. It is applied at all levels of business, including sales to final consumers. It can be applied to all types of business, including the service industries and professional activities. It falls equally on incorporated and unincorporated business. It avoids the artificial inducement to financing with borrowed funds that is an unfortunate result of the corporate income tax. It falls equally on capital-intensive and labour-intensive methods of production. It is neutral with respect to foreign trade, in contrast to income and payroll taxes, which place domestic producers at a disadvantage in comparison with foreign producers both in the home market and abroad.

VAT had been discussed as an alternative to part of the corporation income tax for several years, but changed circumstances in 1972 placed it in a new context as a possible source of additional revenue, a source of funds for partial relief of state and local property taxes, or both. Interestingly, the positions of various people regarding the tax also changed. Prior to 1972, those who opposed the corporation income tax because of the distortion it introduced into business decisions favoured VAT as a partial substitute. Like the corporation income tax, VAT would be reflected in higher prices, but it would have the advantage of substituting a neutral, nondistorting tax for one that had numerous adverse effects on the domestic economy and the country's international position. Opponents argued that VAT would be regressive and that a reduction in the corporation income tax would give windfall gains to stockholders.

In 1972 many of those who had favoured VAT also objected to large increases in government expenditures. Since VAT would produce something like $5 billion for each percentage point of tax, its availability would reduce the pressure to limit spending. Thus some previous advocates of VAT dropped their support for it because they feared it would be used to support enlarged spending programs. By contrast, some of those who had supported various changes in the income and estate taxes, along the lines adopted by Senator McGovern, came to believe that enactment of VAT, which would be criticized as regressive, would provide an opportunity, politically, to secure acceptance of the progressive tax changes they favoured. Accordingly, they began to recognize the possibilities of a tax package that would give them the changes they had not been able to secure in separate legislation.

Proposed Changes in Income Taxation. High on the list of proposed changes in income taxation was full inclusion of capital gains in taxable income. For over 50 years, capital gains—that is, the profits on the sale of capital assets such as stocks and bonds and real estate—had been taxed at lower rates than ordinary income. This reflected a belief that, though capital gains represented a tax-paying capacity, they did not constitute income.

In distinguishing between capital and income, the tax law conformed to general corporate law, trust law, and the familiar attitudes of families in handling their personal affairs. A quite different concept had developed in tax theory whereby income was regarded as the net accretion to a person's wealth, plus his consumption during a year. For purposes of taxation, appreciation in the value of an asset was deemed to be similar to salaries, interest, and rent. Ideally, those holding this concept favoured annual taxation of unrealized gains, offset by unrealized losses. Most of them recognized, however, that problems of annual valuations and the absence of cash with which to pay the tax on assets that had merely risen in value without being sold would make this impractical. Full taxation on sale or at death was a second-best procedure.

Senator McGovern, in advocating full taxation of gains, stated that "money made by money should be taxed at the same rate as money made by men." Herbert Stein, chairman of the Council of Economic Advisers, noted that money made by money is already taxed more heavily because it is also subject to the corporation income tax, inheritance taxes, and property taxes. More fundamentally, critics of full taxation of capital gains regarded a tax on a mere shift from an appreciated investment to a new investment as a capital levy rather than an income tax. Ideally, they would distinguish gains that were reinvested to maintain a capital sum intact from profits used to finance current consumption, but this was not practical without annual personal balance sheets. Taxation of capital gains also raised issues of economic policy on which tax experts differed. To what extent does the existence of a capital gains tax reduce the mobility of capital from one investment to another? To what extent does it reduce the total amount of capital and the direction of investment?

A second major issue in tax policy concerned the appropriate allowances for depreciation—that is, recovery of the cost of investments in machinery and buildings. In measuring income for business purposes, the cost of machinery is spread over the estimated useful life of the property. Since replacement of depreciable property depends on economic conditions and technological changes that cannot be predicted with assurance, estimates of useful lives are inevitably inaccurate.

A fast write-off for tax purposes is desired by taxpayers. Though the total deductions are the same regardless of the time over which they are spread, an earlier deduction permits taxpayers to recover their investment sooner and reinvest the funds to earn additional income. The prospect of a faster recovery of an investment also reduces the element of risk. U.S. tax law and administration had tended to restrict tax deductions for depreciation to rates based on a presumption of relatively long useful lives.

In a succession of legislative and administrative actions starting in 1954 and culminating in 1971, U.S. depreciation allowances were made more liberal, though in 1972 they were still more stringent than those in most other industrial countries. In 1972, however, Senator McGovern proposed a reversal of this trend, and it was expected that the issue would be reopened for discussion in 1973.

Critics of rapid depreciation believed, at least implicitly, that the final burden of the corporation income tax is on the corporation and its stockholders. On this assumption, any relief from the tax, through lower rates, more rapid depreciation, or other deductions, benefits business and stockholders rather than the general body of citizens. Others believed that the corporation income tax is a cost of doing business and is ultimately reflected in the prices paid by final consumers. To the extent that the tax is shifted, lower tax rates or more generous deductions of any sort will benefit the general public. Numerous theoretical and statistical analyses had not produced conclusive answers, though the preponderance of opinion appeared to be that business income taxes are, in large part, shifted forward.

A closely related issue involved depletion and other deductions for the oil, gas, and mining industries. Since 1926 companies in the extractive industries had been permitted to take depletion for tax purposes based on percentages of gross and net income as an alternative to depletion intended to recover the cost of a property as its deposits became exhausted. The percentage depletion allowance was often many times the cost of a property. Percentage depletion was defended on the grounds of high risk in the industries, their importance to national defense, and the fact that their assets are irreplaceable. It was criticized as permitting some corporations and individuals to escape their fair share of taxes and as giving an indirect government subsidy to an industry that may not need it.

In 1972 the developing shortages of energy and of certain other natural resources were being widely discussed, but virtually no attention had been given to their tax implications. Future discussions of the tax treatment of extractive industries would need to include systematic consideration of current and future needs and availabilities, the importance of discoveries of new sources and forms of energy, the effect of energy imports on the balance of payments, and the relative importance and control of domestic and foreign sources.

THE TIMES, LONDON/PICTORIAL PARADE

British purchase tax cuts effective March 22, 1972, were passed on to consumers, as is evident in this scene at an F. W. Woolworth chain store in Cheapside, London.

A third major area of controversy in 1972 concerned the tax treatment of business income from subsidiary corporations located outside the U.S. The income of foreign subsidiaries was taxed abroad where and when it was earned; it was also taxed in the U.S. when it was received by the parent corporation as dividends or in some other form. Foreign governments ordinarily imposed an additional income tax on dividends as they left the country. The income taxes paid abroad were allowed as a credit against the U.S. tax; thus if the combined foreign taxes were equal to or exceeded the U.S. tax, no net U.S. tax was due.

It was proposed by, among others, the AFL-CIO that the U.S. corporation income tax be applied against the income of all foreign subsidiaries, whether it was retained abroad for business expansion or remitted to the parent corporation. Those favouring the change argued that the present law provided a tax inducement for investment abroad that was likely to be at the expense of investment and employment at home. Opponents argued that U.S.-owned subsidiaries abroad must be able to compete with local business firms and that, if foreign subsidiaries were no longer competitive, the U.S. would fail to receive the profits from them. They contended, further, that investment abroad was not made to escape U.S. taxes, nor did plants abroad fill demands that would otherwise be met by exports from the U.S.

Other Areas of Possible Tax Revision. The estate tax might also be reviewed in 1973–74. Among the many proposals for fundamental revision were: a combination of gift and estate taxes into a single transfer tax, with the rates applicable to transfers at death being dependent on lifetime gifts; a shift from an estate tax based on the total amount left by a decedent to an inheritance tax based on the amount received by individual heirs; a capital gains tax at death on the assumption that all gains were realized at that time; abolition of the tax on bequests to a surviving spouse; and higher rates of tax on bequests to grandchildren or collateral relatives than to a spouse or children.

Somewhat surprisingly, there had been little discussion about the so-called double taxation of corporations and stockholders. Most of the major European countries, Canada, and Japan provided in one way or another for partial relief. France, for example, gave stockholders a credit against their individual taxes for part of the corporate tax. The U.S. allowed only a $100 exemption for dividends.

State and local property taxes were subject to increasing criticism. They had risen rapidly and had become especially burdensome for elderly homeowners living on fixed incomes. Some relief from property taxes on residences was in prospect, possibly through federal grants for education or other purposes, conditioned on reduction of property taxes on some or all classes of residences, or through assumption by the states of some expenditures currently met by localities. Proposals had also been made for substantial changes in the structure of property taxes, quite unrelated to relief for homeowners. The large increases in values of land, arising from the growth of population and urbanization, led to revived interest in attempts to tax land more heavily than improvements on land. With taxes so high, improved methods of assessment had become urgent. Systematic planning and regional control of land use, widely recognized as necessary, could also have a bearing on property taxation.

(DAN THROOP SMITH)

United Kingdom. The March 1972 budget, though it gave back considerable sums to taxpayers, chiefly by way of increased tax allowances and purchase tax reductions, made few structural changes. However, future changes of major importance were spelled out. The firm intention to introduce VAT in April 1973 at a flat rate of 10% ended speculation on the form this tax would take. The purchase tax would then be abolished. There would be a general exemption for all businesses whose taxable turnover did not exceed £5,000 a year. In addition to VAT, new and imported cars would carry a tax of 10% of the wholesale value to offset the loss of the purchase tax. There would be exemptions for insurance, postal services, education, health services, newspapers, periodicals, and books, and all food other than that currently subject to the purchase tax. New housing would be wholly relieved from the tax, and rents would be exempt.

April 1973 would also see abolition of the dual system of income tax and surtax. Relatively few people paid tax at the full rate of 38.75% on earned income because of an allowance of two-ninths on income up to £4,005 and 15% of the excess over £4,005. The proposed change would abolish earned income relief and, instead, would impose a surcharge on investment income over and above the standard rate. The combined tax on income would be at the rate of 30% on the first £5,000 of taxable income (about the same as the current rate with earned income relief). For incomes between £5,000 and £6,000, the rate would be 40%. Above that amount, rates would rise in steps of 5% until a maximum of 75% was reached at the level of £20,000. Higher income groups would benefit most under the proposed rates, as well as from the proposal to exempt the first £2,000 of investment income from the 15% unearned income charge. The budget also made stock option schemes, approved by the Inland Revenue, exempt from tax. These concessions to the wealthy and the fact that VAT was expected to hit the poor the hardest led to considerable criticism in a year when the government was trying to limit pay increases.

The budget crystallized changes in the corporation tax that had been proposed in a Green Paper (a Green Paper is a government paper meant to project the broad outlines of change and stimulate public discussion) the previous year and considered by a select committee. The decision was made to adopt the imputation system of tax, putting Britain in line with France and West Germany. The existing system of company tax, introduced in 1965, made a complete separation between the company and its stockholders; company profits were taxed at 40% and dividends were taxed at the standard rate. Under the new system, which would take effect in April 1973, a single rate of corporation tax was proposed (probably 50%), payable on all taxable profit, whether distributed or not. Income tax would no longer be deducted from dividends. A company paying out dividends would be required to make an advance payment of corporation tax at a rate of three-sevenths of the dividend, but this payment would be set off against its corporation tax due for that accounting period. If a company declared a dividend of £100, a U.K. stockholder would receive a dividend of £70 and a tax credit of three-sevenths of £70, or £30. The stockholder would have no tax adjustment to make unless he could claim a refund because he was not liable to tax or unless his tax was above the basic rate of 30%, in which case he would be liable for the difference. A substantial concession was proposed for small companies (defined as those whose taxable profits in the year were below £15,000). Capital gains of companies would be taxed at what would be, in effect, a rate of 30%, and special provisions were to be made for building societies and cooperative societies.

Two important Green Papers were published in 1972. The first, in March, proposed to sweep away the current system of estate duty. The existing estate duties specified rates of up to 75% on estates over £500,000, but there were numerous loopholes and a growing number of accountants, lawyers, and tax experts spent their time searching for them. The paper suggested that the beneficiary be taxed on the sum he received, rather than the current system, under which a tax was levied on the value of the property left by the deceased. The paper put forward a number of alternatives for discussion including the question of whether gifts as well as bequests should be included in the tax base.

The second Green Paper, published in October, put forward the idea of tax credits. If carried out, it would represent the most important tax change since pay-as-you-earn was introduced in 1943. The principle of tax credits had long been advocated in the public finance field as a way of eliminating some of the glaring anomalies of the tax allowance system. Those whose incomes were too low to pay tax gained little or no benefit from tax allowances, while those with the highest incomes gained the most because allowances had the effect of reducing their high rates. Under a tax credit scheme, tax would be payable on all income and all persons in similar circumstances would have the same tax credit. Those who did not earn enough to exhaust the credit would receive the difference in cash. In addition to social benefits, such a system would result in simplification and considerable administrative savings.

One danger inherent in these proposals was that they could not be fully implemented before the 1978 budget. Existing problems of poverty needed immediate attention and, in any case, the tax credit scheme as proposed was not intended as a wholesale attack on poverty.

European Economic Community. One of the stated aims of the EEC was to harmonize taxation in order to avoid distortions between member countries

Table I. Taxes (Including Social Security Contributions) as a Percentage of GNP at Factor Cost, 1970

Country	Percent
West Germany	40.5
France	41.4
Italy	32.8
Netherlands	45.0
Belgium	38.2
United Kingdom	42.7

caused by differing tax structures—the most likely distortions being those concerned with movements of labour and capital and with trade patterns. This did not necessarily require (and was not likely to achieve) similar tax structures in all member countries. For example, as long as taxes on corporations, which could be rebated on exports, were roughly proportional in each country, the actual type of tax imposed did not matter from the point of view of trade. Where harmonization was required, one of the main difficulties was whether to harmonize a tax toward the level of the highest country or toward the lowest, or to exclude some items from the tax altogether.

The Commission for Tax Harmonisation had presented its first-stage proposals to the EEC ministers of finance in 1971. In the case of VAT, the first priority was harmonization of the taxable bases, not only to reduce fiscal trade barriers between members but to ease the passage to the time when the Community itself would administer some of the tax revenue of its members. By the end of 1973, the commission was expected to present its recommendations on harmonization of taxes on tobacco, alcohol, and petroleum products, as well as proposals for the principal excise taxes and on the complex problems involved in securing harmonization of company taxation.

Comparisons of the tax structures of five of the six original EEC countries and the U.K. are shown in Tables I and II. Social security contributions have been included on the ground that this provides a more meaningful comparison; both are compulsory exactions by the government and, as a general rule, social security payments are not tied precisely to benefits but are used to raise revenue when this seems convenient. In Table I, Italy stands out as the country with the lowest level of taxation, while the U.K. falls in the middle range. Interestingly enough, the percentage figure for Italy (32.8), a relatively poor country, was comparable to that of the U.S. (33).

Table II shows that there were considerable differences in the tax structures of the various EEC countries. France, in particular, had a relatively low tax on incomes but a high tax on employers for social security purposes. The Netherlands showed the lowest percentage of tax on expenditures, but again this was counterbalanced by a high yield from social security contributions by employers. In the U.K. it was noticeable that, taking taxes on corporations and employers'

Table II. Structure of Taxes and Social Security Contributions as a Percentage of Total Taxes, 1970

Item	West Germany	France	Italy	Netherlands	Belgium	United Kingdom
Taxes on income						
Households	25.5	12.8	16.3	27.6	25.6	32.1
Corporations	5.0	6.6	5.0	6.7	7.0	8.0
Taxes on expenditure	37.4	40.5	41.2	28.9	37.5	45.6
Social Security						
Persons	14.8	11.5	37.5	10.0	10.0	7.1
Employers	17.4	28.7		26.8	20.0	7.3

social security payments together, companies were relatively lightly taxed, while taxes on expenditures were high. Italy was in the process of overhauling its tax system to bring it more into line with its EEC partners (*see* below). Taxes on capital, mainly death and gift taxes, are not included in the table since they were relatively minor sources of revenue for all the countries listed.

The wider community of Organization for Economic Cooperation and Development (OECD) countries extended its operations in the field of fiscal harmonization in 1971 by setting up a new Committee on Fiscal Affairs. The increased importance of international companies and the increased flows of investment funds across borders lent some urgency to this matter. The OECD had been concerned mainly with the avoidance of double taxation, demand-management aspects of fiscal policy, broader tax adjustments, and VAT. The new committee had as its first priority a consideration of taxation and international capital flows, international aspects of company taxation, and the standard classification of tax revenues.

West Germany was planning a general tax reform, probably for 1974. It was expected that the much criticized "two-rate system," whereby a corporation and its stockholders are separate legal persons subject to separate taxation, would be changed. The Scientific Advisory Committee of the Office of the Minister of Finance, which considered several proposals on this subject, favoured a plan whereby the total taxable profit of a company would be taxed at the highest rate of the individual income tax. The stockholder would receive any dividend paid out by the company, plus a credit for the proportion of the corporation tax paid by the company. Both would be taxable income in the hands of the stockholder, but he could use the tax credit to offset against his own tax.

The Netherlands government's 1972 budget represented an effort to reduce the level of inflation being experienced by so many European countries. The excise tax on gasoline was increased, and a new excise tax on soft drinks was introduced that would harmonize with other Benelux countries. A number of changes were made in VAT, one of which was to subject electricity to taxation at the standard rate of 14% instead of 4%. A 60% surcharge was imposed on motor vehicles, which were taxed according to weight. An automatic inflation correction devised for the income tax would be applied for the first time in 1972.

After ten years of debate, Italy's tax reform bill was enacted on Oct. 7, 1971. Its main aims were to simplify the tax structure and to introduce VAT in accordance with the country's EEC obligations. About 18 old taxes would be replaced by three different income taxes—for the individual, for the corporation, and a local income tax—and a capital gains tax on immovable property. The VAT would replace about 23 other indirect taxes, including the turnover tax, and death duties were radically changed. VAT and certain other provisions of the bill were to become effective on Jan. 1, 1973, while the individual and corporate income taxes would become effective on Jan. 1, 1974. Transitional measures with respect to VAT were designed to avoid postponement of new purchases by entrepreneurs. Modifications in income tax to help those in low income groups were to be made to offset the slight increases in prices expected from the change to VAT. Taxable income of up to 2 million lire (approximately U.S. $3,500) would be subject to a 10% tax, rising to 72% on incomes over 500 million lire. The standard rate proposed for the tax on added value was 12%. (G. C. HOCKLEY)

See also Economics; Economy, World; Employment, Wages, and Hours; Government Finance; Social Services.

Tea:
see Agriculture

Telecommunications

The telecommunications industry found 1972 a bewildering year. Long-range studies were forecasting almost costless telecommunications, British telephone traffic was reaching an all-time high growth rate, and the U.S. Federal Communications Commission (FCC) finally made a policy for a U.S. domestic satellite system. On the other hand, telephone costs increased, the British public was finding trouble-free calls more difficult, and commercial interest in domestic satellites diminished.

Specialized Common Carriers. The 1971 FCC decision allowing virtually any company, or common carrier, to enter the microwave transmission field as long as certain financial and technical specifications were met was taken advantage of for the first time in 1972. The first specialized common carrier to take the field with actual commercial service was Microwave Communications, Inc. (MCI), between Chicago and St. Louis, in January. The firm reported doing a modest volume of private line business, in which a customer leases one or more links of varying bandwidth between his own premises.

As the year progressed, MCI's lawyers and economists were even busier than its technicians. Repeatedly voicing its fear that the established common carriers (such as the Bell System) would interpret the "full and fair competition" ruling of the FCC to engulf it, MCI became involved in a series of rate and tariff regulatory proceedings. A direct confrontation came first, not from the Bell System as originally expected, but from the other, and much smaller, established nationwide carrier, the Western Union Telegraph Co. Western Union, which by 1972 obtained appreciably less than half its revenue from the familiar message telegram, filed reduced private line rates with the FCC just for the Chicago–St. Louis route to "match" the lower charges of MCI.

Since MCI first proposed specialized service a decade earlier, the established telecommunications carriers had contended that it and others would "cream skim" business on high-volume and low-cost routes, leaving the Bell System and Western Union to serve thinly populated and, therefore, high-cost areas. Until 1972 established policy for the common carriers called for nationwide averaging of interstate service costs and rates. Thus, service between two small towns in the Rocky Mountains cost the customer no more than for the same mileage between two large cities in the East, although it cost much more to provide the former.

Western Union's Chicago–St. Louis private line rates marked the first departure from that policy, and the FCC immediately ordered an investigation. Authorities generally agreed that the outcome of the case would fix the rules for future price competition between the nationwide general carriers and the specialized systems. The inquiry began at the end of 1972, and was not expected to reach a decision at least until well into 1973.

During 1972 a number of specialized common carrier systems were authorized, including much of the projected nationwide system of the Data Transmission

continued on page 657

CABLE COMMUNICATIONS—A SPRINGBOARD TO TOMORROW

By Mary Alice Mayer Phillips

Just as the automobile crank and the Victrola have been relegated to museums, and washing machines, iceboxes, and stoves have evolved, "cable communications" has and will continue to develop form, function, impact, sophistication, and glamour conceivable only by today's most imaginative dreamers. Through his cable equipment a future subscriber may have available on his home screen such services as books on microfilm, news and weather data, market information, movies and sports events, shopping services, remote public utility meter readouts, currency and checking system services, mail service, central security protection against fire and burglary, automated typing, and optical character recognition for such information parcels.

Cable communications can only be considered as an integrated part of a comprehensive communications system and should be recognized as deriving from the CATV (community antenna television) service concept. "CATV" is the term applied by the U.S. Federal Communications Commission (FCC) to facilities that receive signals over the air from television stations, modify them, and distribute them over cable or wire to subscribing members of the public who pay for such service. The CATV industry is also popularly known as "cable TV," "cablecasting," or even "broadband communications." The designation "community antenna television" can be misleading, implying as it does that CATV is no more than an antenna owned by the community. The fact is that drastic changes in form and function, technology, and services have made this assumption obsolete.

Growth of a New Industry. The community antenna television industry has become a phenomenon on the American scene. The service grew out of a need by disenfranchised members of the public rather than from any design or marketing plan of a large manufacturer. Historically, certain geographic locations, due to terrain or remote position, were particularly difficult to serve by air transmission. Mountains could not be pierced by airwave communications signals. Sparsely populated areas were for economic reasons impractical for television station construction, establishment, and maintenance.

The interest of the large manufacturer of electronic equipment was not sufficiently attracted to the needs of the people in the television reception fringe areas, for generally they did not appear to constitute a market sufficiently large. Rather, individuals were responsible for the practical implementation of the dream of community antenna television. The personalities responsible for early-day CATV were in some cases colourful, in others conservative—the combination offering a healthy blend for a young industry.

Mary Alice Mayer Phillips is a lecturer and consultant on mass communications and author of CATV: A History of Community Antenna Television *and* British Commercial Television: Advertising, Revenues, Taxes.

By 1948 television was on its way to national popularity. Production and factory-value figures indicate that from 1946 to 1948 factory production of television sets increased from 6,000 to 1,160,000; sales to consumers climbed from 6,000 to 977,000; and the statistics on sets in use went from 5,000 to 975,000. Television master distribution systems had been developed and were installed in multiple dwellings and hotels, such as the Waldorf-Astoria in New York City. Although the Roller Derbys, the Hopalong Cassidys, and the Milton Berles gained national acclaim over television, it is contended that the real captivating power of television lay in the medium itself rather than in the programming it transmitted.

Television at this point was offering only limited service in the large cities and virtually no service in rural areas or towns more than 50 mi. from the metropolitan centres with broadcasting stations. Geographic factors, such as terrain or distance from a television transmitter, and the 1948 FCC freeze on the licensing of new TV stations, threatened to restrict television to a few privileged urban areas. Although equipment manufacturers were distributing television receivers in rural and fringe areas, they had not tried to resolve the peculiar reception problems in these areas. Consequently, local distributors had an oversupply of television sets which they could not sell until special receiving and distribution system equipment was designed, developed, and installed. Thus, both the populace and the appliance dealers wanted television to come to town. Community antenna television was a product of this demand.

Special note should be made regarding the 1948 FCC freeze. In 1948, after public hearings, the FCC established a television allocations program that proposed a distribution of 12 very-high-frequency (VHF) channels to 340 cities. The allocations were based on engineering predictions that television signals would be limited to 35 mi. It was soon found, however, that television signals carried farther than had been anticipated and that stations had been spaced too closely together. Accordingly, later in 1948, the commission declared a temporary freeze on all new television applications and commenced further rule-making proceedings. The hearings continued until the fall of 1951, and in April 1952, the commission issued its order setting a new table of television allocations. During this freeze period the demand for television increased, and thus the CATV industry, with its ability to supply television service to many areas without local stations, was given impetus.

No one man was solely responsible for the development of CATV. Although there is some question about who did what precisely where and when, there is no question that CATV pioneers were involved with similar concerns at about the same time. Each of these small businessmen took steps initially to solve the problems. L. E. Parsons is the recognized father of cable television for having devised in Astoria, Ore., the first experimental community antenna system. He possessed technical handyman qualities, but did not have the business acumen necessary for sustaining his enterprise.

Unlike many others who were active in the early days of the industry, Milton Jerrold Shapp (later governor of Pennsylvania) possessed some degree of technical training. Furthermore, he was able to devise a situation in which he could develop a reliable CATV system. Although Shapp and his associates initially lacked funds, with $500 and a reciprocal association with Robert Tarlton of Lansford, Pa., they constructed and built the Panther Valley Television Co. (PVTV). For Shapp, PVTV was a field testing site which brought national attention and consequent encouragement to Jerrold Electronics Corp. as a viable enterprise engaged in the construction and installation of community antenna system equipment. Shapp subsequently built Jerrold Electronics into one of the leading CATV equipment manufacturing operations in the country. Martin F. Malarkey, Jr., of Pottsville, Pa., formerly in the music store business and without any appreciable electronic background, developed a CATV business management consultant enterprise in Washington, D.C.

In the late 1940s and early 1950s, although relatively unknown throughout the country, CATV was being watched carefully by many concerned parties. The industry grew rapidly in miles of cable, in numbers of subscribers, in its effect on the habits of individual subscribers, and, perhaps most importantly and impressively, in the degree of entrenchment in the life of each local community it was serving.

Government Regulation. A number of important pronouncements at the federal level by the FCC and the courts warrant consideration in the development of CATV. In the significant case of *Frontier Broadcasting Company* v. *Collier,* the FCC in 1958 held that CATV systems were not common carriers. Later, in the *Carter Mountain Transmission Corp.* opinion, the FCC refused to grant to a common carrier by radio the right to construct facilities for carriage of signals on behalf of CATV systems because of the impact thereof on an existing local television station, provided, however, that the commission would reconsider the matter if and when it could be shown that the CATV systems would carry the signal of the local TV station and would not duplicate its programming. The FCC's First Report and Order (1965) provided that, in order to protect the programming of the local station, CATV systems using microwave facilities must carry the local signals and may not within 15 days duplicate local programming. The Second Report and Order (1966) limited the time to the same day and extended these requirements to all CATV systems, regardless of whether microwave was used.

In June 1968, two cases decided by the U.S. Supreme Court and two by the FCC were extremely important to the CATV industry: (1) in *United States* v. *Southwestern Cable Co.,* the Supreme Court held that CATV systems are engaged in interstate commerce, and that under the Communications Act the commission has the authority to regulate the CATV industry; (2) in *Fortnightly Corporation* v. *United Artists Television, Inc.,* the court stated that a CATV system's retransmission of a broadcast does not amount to a performance under the Copyright Act, and, consequently, CATV operators are not liable for copyright fees to television broadcasters; (3) in *General Telephone Company of California,* the FCC decided that a certificate of public necessity and convenience pursuant to the Communications Act must be obtained by a telephone company before commencing construction of distribution facilities to provide channel service to a CATV system; and (4) in *Midwest Television, Inc.,* the commission barred San Diego CATV systems from carrying Los Angeles signals (except for certain existing situations); San Diego systems were allowed to furnish local programming but without advertising.

Finally, in the area of federal regulation, the commission's Notice of Proposed Rule Making and Notice of Inquiry, released Dec. 13, 1968, expressed the intention to explore on a broad scale the question of how to procure most effectively, consistent with the public interest, the full benefits of CATV potential services and what regulations might be adopted to further this goal.

On June 16, 1972, the FCC adopted amendments to its CATV rules of Feb. 2, 1972. Essentially, these rules require that systems in the top 100 markets must have at least 20 broadcast channels including an origination (production) or subscription (leased) channel for each off-air channel and nonvoice return communication capacity. At least one access channel each must be dedicated to public use, to education, and to government. After fulfillment of these obligations, channels may be leased. Systems with 3,500 or more subscribers must have at least one origination channel, have nonautomated facilities for local production, and be a local outlet "to a significant extent."

Channel use charges for political advertising must be uniform and comparable to charges for other uses and also be nondiscriminatory and nonpreferential. No charges are to be made for at least five years for either the education or the government access channels. On the public-access channels, one channel may charge only for use exceeding five minutes of line production. No provisions were made for the leased channels.

The FCC laid out some special use requirements for nonsubscription and subscription channels. Origination channels are usable for such purposes only. Commercial advertising is permitted at the beginning and end of a program and in natural breaks that are not controlled by the system operator. Outside the top 100 markets, systems cannot restrict the use of substantial portions of time for controversial local issues. Public and leased access channels must be made available on a nondiscriminatory, first-come first-served basis. On the government access channels there is to be no censorship, and no restrictions can be laid down except as state or federal laws may otherwise provide. No provisions were made for the educational access channels.

Subscription TV is permitted and divided into five categories of consideration. Series—programs with an interconnected plot or the same cast of principal characters—are not permitted. Feature films are not permitted until two years after their first U.S. general theatrical release. Subscription cablecasting of sports is not permitted within two years of the sports event telecast live on a regular basis on a Grade A (service at least 90% of the time for at least 70% of the receiving locations) signal in the system community, or within two years of the specific sports event telecast in the community when it occurred. No advertising on feature or sports programs on subscription channels is permitted except before and after the program, and it can only advertise other subscription programs.

General broadcasting regulations related to such concerns as the fairness doctrine and sponsorship identification were extended to cablecasting. Also, a restriction was made as follows: systems in the top 100 markets operating on March 31, 1972, are "grandfathered"—not required to conform to new regulations—until March 31, 1977. If prior to March 31, 1977, access channel operations commence or if television signals are added to fill quotas in the top 100 markets, operations shall conform to applicable requirements. Each system must add one access channel for each such added signal in the following order of priority: public, educational, government, leased.

At the state level, the overwhelming majority of state tribunals and authorities have taken the position that essential jurisdiction is vested in the FCC, that the states are preempted in this general area, that CATVs are not public utilities, and that CATV systems are interstate in character. However, this is not to say that state or local authorities may not levy reasonable use or permit taxes on CATV facilities or require them to pay rent for the use of streets, alleys, or other public facilities. In regard to municipalities, their taxes or charges are sustained where they are reasonable and are levied, not for the privilege of doing business or as a revenue device, but for the enforcement of appropriate local government supervision, as a rental for permitting use of the public ways, or for the expense of inspection.

The Future—A Cable-Air Blend? As the residents of rural areas had felt faulted in the late 1940s by the lack of available television channels, in the late 1960s and into the 1970s the urban dweller has been disturbed by the inadequacy and/or unreliability of the communications services he is receiving. Television reception is often disintegrating to little more than snow and ghosts with pictures sometimes obliterated and indiscernible. Telephone service likewise is breaking down where and when it is needed the most.

The present allocations table issued in the FCC's 1952 Sixth Report and Order has come to be recognized as inadequate to meet communications demands. Possible and needed services for the public using the portion of the electromagnetic spectrum presently allocated to television far outstrip the capability of the current assignments chart to carry such traffic. Consequently, analysis or projection of any aspect of communications as it might use the airwaves must relate directly to the carriage potential of the electromagnetic spectrum.

continued from page 654
Co. (Datran). Datran, while planning to open its first commercial service by 1974, modified its original plans so as to reduce the previously estimated $300 million investment to below $200 million. It planned to do this by leasing initial local distribution facilities from telephone companies, instead of building them.

Others getting government approval to build systems included an affiliate of MCI, Interdata Communications, Inc., between New York and Washington; the Nebraska Consolidated Communications Corp., which started with a microwave radio system for the Nebraska state government and planned to cover much of the country; and Western Tele-Communications, Inc., mainly a transmitter of television broadcast program material in the West. As the year drew to a close, MCI's Chicago–St. Louis system remained the only specialized carrier in actual commercial operation.

Although all concerned were proceeding on the basis of the FCC's "open entry" policy, a federal court test of that policy remained pending. Not yet decided by the Court of Appeals in San Francisco were the protests of the National Association of Regulatory Utility Commissioners, representing state public service commissions, and the Washington state commission. They argued that the new specialized carriers would siphon off the business service revenues of the established telephone companies to the detriment of the companies' "less affluent" residential and small business users.

"Interconnects." Taking almost equally as long to establish itself as a going business was the "interconnect" market. This slowly burgeoning field, the product of a 1968 FCC decision in the landmark "Carterfone" case, comprised the provision by private entrepreneurs of private branch exchange switchboards, key systems, and other telephone facilities on the premises of customers, usually businesses. Although the private systems had intercommunicating,

Today the most promising answer to the channel allocations problem and the desire and requirements of the public for increasing communications service is a hybrid cable-air communications blend. The requirements of colour reception, the growth of ultrahigh-frequency (UHF) transmission, and the inability of apartment house master antenna systems to meet current demands put cable-air experimentation on exceptionally favourable footing. Furthermore, a microwave link-cable communications merger concept holds significant promise of bringing required and luxury communications services to both mass and specialized audiences.

This hybrid technological design must meet the following functional specifications: (1) it must carry multiple channels to multiple receivers in a designated area in such a way as to avoid the expensive project of tearing up the streets to lay cable; (2) it must function as a system for point-to-point operation to satellite cities; and (3) it must be able to transcend such barriers as rivers. To this point, highly successful operational experiments have been conducted at the 18- and 40-gigaHertz (1 gigaHertz = 1 billion Hz) and 2,150- and 2,160-MHz regions of the electromagnetic spectrum. As a short-haul, high-volume, low-noise, high-power microwave link, such systems seem to hold promise of assuming a significant role in communications.

Technological advance is exceptionally expensive and will become increasingly so in terms of financial and skill resources and technical and programming capabilities. Consequently, equipment and systems characteristics will describe patterns substantially modified from those of the less expensive founding days of community antenna television. At this time the capital outlay for research and development is usually so significant that only the corporate giants can afford it. Mergers in a formal and fiscal sense, together with outside financing, are the current trend and will probably continue to occur.

Reasonable speculation indicates that the CATV industry will describe a growth pattern similar to that of the automobile industry. In the 1920s and 1930s there were many car manufacturers who eventually disappeared or were absorbed by a few major companies. Similarly, by the year 2000 the CATV industry will probably bear less than a score of names, with about ten leading the pack in general public reputation, awareness, sales, and service.

Although studies have been prepared proposing or assuming the end of over-the-air broadcasting in favour of cable, such efforts seem hardly more than academic exercises. Contemporary political, legal, and economic realities suggest neither the disappearance nor the obsolescence of other media but rather a dilution of some of the media in the consumption patterns of individuals. Just as people did not stop buying newspapers when radio was introduced or dispose of their radios with the advent of television, so it will predictably be with the broadcast service of cable communications. The media mix of the future will involve the blend of an increasing number of media and will vary to satisfy the requirements and desires of each person. The difference will lie in the fact, however, that most of these services will be efficiently channeled through broadband facilities.

The cable communications industry projected into and beyond the 1970s will continue its dynamic growth and development. The predominant domestic and multinational need is for a widely available two-way communications system that can rapidly handle large amounts of information in both directions. It need not compete destructively with existing media but must complement and utilize the presently available communications services.

Consistent with the history of CATV, experimental innovations initiated in the industry illustrate what is technically feasible and reflect its consistently progressive character. Innovations in technology and service will probably be witnessed primarily in systems constructed in major markets, especially as they evolve into both home and urban communications systems.

The potential for intervention by statute or regulation of so many diverse governmental and regulatory bodies and commissions, together with the resultant impact for good or ill, warrants intelligent and imaginative planning on the part of interested and influential persons in government, politics, and communications. As the industry has become an obvious potentially effective public servant, in addition to the federal, state, and local regulatory layers discussed above, a fourth regulatory layer with a function of information and counsel has become apparent. It includes the Office of Telecommunications Policy, the Cable Television Information Center, and presidentially appointed study committees. These agencies of the fourth regulatory layer pose a significant danger to the activities of the industry in that their many reports emphasize the glamorous and idealistic phases of the business rather than the basic technical, regulatory, and political problems. If adequately staffed with intellectual and ethical persons who are politically effective, their function will result in a positive contribution. On the other hand, if staffed with people who might have been disheartened or disenfranchised in other areas of the communications industry, or who are either intellectually or ethically less than eminent, their efforts could at best be wasted or their impact might be seriously detrimental to the public interest.

Finally, it is necessary at this time for the communications industry to talk and think and plan in nothing less than global terms. If hardware and technical designs are exploited to serve ethically and philosophically idealistic objectives, communications media may serve as a circuitry of peace.

conference, and other internal features, they became most useful when they were interconnected with the general switched telephone network. In this manner, business A, with its own private system, could talk with business B, whose system was provided by the telephone company, just as though both were entirely served by the telephone company.

Following the Carterfone decision, the Bell System filed tariffs (the rules and rate sheets under which they did business) requiring that customer-provided devices be connected with the telephone network through "interface" devices furnished by the phone companies. These devices were intended to protect the telephone system, its employees, and other customers from a variety of harms, ranging from surging electrical voltages to tying up telephone central switching offices so that other customers had no service.

Frequent protests by nontelephone company suppliers led to an extended study of the situation. The independent "interconnect" suppliers contended that the telephone companies' requirements were too costly and cumbersome, and gave the utilities an unfair competitive advantage over independent firms.

Telephones. The growth curve for telephone traffic is fairly standard, and the U.K. in 1972 hit the steepest part of it, the same rate of growth experienced by the U.S. in the early 1960s. Investment in telecommunications by the British Post Office in 1972 ran at £500 million a year, and one in three householders owned a telephone. Unfortunately, at this very time of greatest demand the British public started to reap the rewards of a technical decision made by the Post Office in the 1950s that by 1972 everyone admitted was wrong. Equipped at that time with aging Strowger exchanges, the Post Office courageously but rashly decided to bypass the U.S. adoption of crossbar techniques and go directly into electronic exchanges. After some years of experiment, this decision turned out to be a complete failure and, having missed the boat with crossbar, the Post Office found itself having to replace worn-out old-fashioned Strowger equipment with new old-fashioned Strowger equipment. As a result, the system snarled up because the slow Strowger could not cope with the increased traffic demand of 1972.

Countries Having More Than 100,000 Telephones

Telephones in service, 1971

Country	Number of telephones	Percentage increase over 1961	Telephones per 100 population	Country	Number of telephones	Percentage increase over 1961	Telephones per 100 population
Algeria	184,063	...	1.28	Lebanon	192,000	189.2	6.78
Argentina	1,746,015	34.7	7.17	Luxembourg	111,437	117.0	32.68
Australia*	3,913,167	72.7	31.18	Malaysia*	168,826	121.7	1.58
Austria	1,427,333	103.5	19.29	Mexico	1,507,363	188.3	2.97
Belgium	2,018,827	76.7	20.83	Morocco	169,614	30.8	1.08
Brazil	2,000,726	86.9	2.17	Netherlands	3,409,842	111.4	26.00
Bulgaria	473,047	...	5.54	New Zealand	1,262,427	69.5	44.14
Canada	9,752,537	70.3	45.23	Norway	1,144,795	54.6	29.41
Chile	369,198	91.1	3.78	Pakistan	207,281	160.4	0.18
Colombia	974,415	228.5	4.54	Peru	222,776	105.0	1.61
Cuba	291,264	45.7	3.44	Philippines	309,922	173.2	0.81
Czechoslovakia	2,003,421	97.2	13.82	Poland	1,867,086	111.8	5.67
Denmark	1,696,765	58.2	34.42	Portugal	749,963	89.9	7.76
Egypt†	365,000	49.3	1.14	Puerto Rico	333,738	252.8	12.18
Finland	1,180,785	94.7	25.21	Rhodesia	131,572	63.7	2.44
France	8,774,261	101.3	17.19	Romania†	596,000	...	2.99
Germany, East	2,089,216	61.2	12.11	Singapore	161,310	170.1	7.78
Germany, West	13,834,827	130.8	22.43	South Africa	1,553,825	65.7	7.06
Greece	1,044,777	369.9	11.96	Soviet Union	11,000,000	155.8	4.51
Hong Kong	583,222	435.8	14.76	Spain	4,604,368	156.9	13.56
Hungary	823,600	84.1	7.96	Sweden	4,505,802	63.2	55.67
India	1,245,352	164.7	0.23	Switzerland	3,025,779	82.4	48.26
Indonesia	200,514	64.4	0.17	Syria	114,590	108.6	1.84
Iran	307,500	190.4	1.06	Taiwan	403,348	311.5	2.75
Iraq	119,650	120.6	1.24	Thailand*	152,959	258.7	0.42
Ireland	307,497	103.4	10.44	Turkey	576,943	137.4	1.62
Israel	510,550	334.1	17.47	United Kingdom	14,966,748	81.0	26.68
Italy	9,368,732	142.7	17.38	United States	120,218,000	61.7	58.35
Japan	26,233,360	280.1	25.14	Uruguay	215,299	52.2	7.42
Korea, South	633,818	480.2	2.01	Venezuela	405,613	100.8	3.90
				Yugoslavia	736,045	183.6	3.57

*1970. †1969.
Source: American Telephone and Telegraph Co., *The World's Telephones*, 1961 and 1971.

Meanwhile, the British firms developed their own crossbar systems and managed to press a few on the Post Office. At the same time, one firm, Standard Telephone & Cables, Ltd., went ahead with a partially electronic telephone exchange, the TXE-4. Then in November 1971, the Post Office announced that it had placed a £15 million contract with STC for 18 TXE-4s. This precipitated a major row which reverberated through Parliament. Two companies making crossbars, British General Electric Co., Ltd., and the Plessey Co., Ltd., claimed that the TXE-4 decision was the wrong one for Britain, pointing out that a decision for crossbar would help the export situation. The Post Office countered by claiming that its decision was the result of a massive computer study. Tempers were not calmed when in April the Post Office placed a £14 million order for crossbars—with the Swedish L. M. Ericsson Co.

Private automatic branch exchanges (PABX) had remained stubbornly electromechanical in the face of developments in electronics and despite their being the most used telecommunications device. British firms and International Telephone and Telegraph (ITT) had failed to produce usable systems. Consequently, it came as a rude shock in March when IBM took the wraps off a PABX which far outperformed the most advanced electromechanical equipment. The extension facilities of the normal PABX are usually limited to dialing another extension, dialing the public network, transferring calls, and holding them while making an inquiry on another extension. By comparison, the IBM 3750 PABX used stored program control and silicon-controlled rectifiers for high-speed switching to provide the user with an enviable and flexible range of facilities. For example, by pressing an abbreviated dialing prefix digit plus only two other digits on the pushbutton dial, a user can call any one of a hundred outside telephone numbers. The annoying business of dialing long numbers repeatedly because the number is busy is eliminated; when the 3750 "hears" the busy tone, it remembers the number and all the user has to do to try the call again is press the "external number repetition" digit.

Satellites. The assumption that Communications Satellite Corp. (Comsat) would run the U.S. domestic satellite system was shown to be ill-founded when the FCC in June insisted on an "open skies" policy and asked for proposals from any organization with the necessary technical and financial resources. The result was a flood of new ideas embodied in eight formal proposals.

The American Telephone and Telegraph Co. (AT & T) had planned to use the satellite to tie together its so-called "data islands" on the East Coast, West Coast, and around Chicago, but the FCC ruled that the company could only use the satellite for telephone traffic. Financially, the most desirable users would have been the three national television networks which had to spend $75 million a year sending their programs across the country using microwave links. However, calculations showing that they could save half this amount by going over to domestic satellite appeared to be overly optimistic. Technically, the most interesting proposals came from Fairchild Industries, which submitted plans for a giant satellite powerful enough to beam signals into small aerials that could, for example, be used by schools.

Fairchild was already developing Applications Technology satellites F and G for the U.S. National Aeronautics and Space Administration (NASA). They were more powerful than anything previously in service, and instead of the 80-ft. ground dish aerials required by Intelsat satellites, they needed only 12-ft. dishes to collect television signals and relay them to local receivers.

Impatient at the delay in completing a U.S. satellite system, a U.S. firm, RCA Global Communications, signed an agreement with Canada's domestic satellite company early in December. Subject to approval by Canadian and U.S. regulatory agencies, Telesat Canada would allow RCA to use one full-time channel of the Anik 2 satellite. This service would permit voice and television transmission between the U.S. East and West coasts and between both coasts and Alaska. It was scheduled to begin in June 1973.

Two more satellites of the Intelsat 4 class went into service, and development began on the new, higher capacity Intelsat 5. The increasingly mature international satellite service not only continued to provide more telecommunications service to business and government users, but its progress also became steadily more apparent to television viewers in the home. Television service from two of the year's major news events, U.S. Pres. Richard Nixon's visit to China and the violence-marred Olympic Games, was brought to homes throughout the world, almost routinely.

Cable Communications. Mostly evolution, and not revolution, continued to be the word during the year for cable television (CATV) systems. Growth of new systems, held up for more than two years while basic rules for CATV operation were considered by the U.S. government, began to move again after the FCC issued a whole new set of rules for cable TV.

Basically, the FCC said, it is striving toward attaining cable TV systems in local communities that will be "something more than an antenna service." (*See* Special Report.) (DON BYRNE; LAURIE JOHN)

International Telecommunication Union. During 1972 membership in the International Telecommunication Union (ITU) increased to 143 with the accession to the International Telecommunication Convention of Tonga, Oman, and the United Arab Emirates. The 27th session of the Administrative Council was held at ITU headquarters in Geneva, May 27–June 16. The council passed a resolution recognizing the representatives of the People's Republic of China as the only legitimate representatives of China at the ITU. The council also agreed upon the calendar of future ITU conferences, the principal ones being: World Administrative Telegraph and Telephone Conference, Geneva (April 2–11, 1973); Plenipotentiary Conference, Torremolinos, Spain (Sept. 14 to Oct. 26, 1973); and World Administrative Radio Conference for Maritime Mobile Telecommunications, Geneva (April 22 to June 7, 1974).

The council examined a report on technical cooperation during 1971. Under the ITU's various technical cooperation programs in less developed countries, 255 experts were on field missions and 448 fellows were undergoing training abroad. The total cost of this assistance amounted to $7,714,261. The three main objectives of ITU's technical cooperation activity continued to be: (1) promoting the development of regional telecommunications networks in Africa, Asia, and Latin America; (2) strengthening the telecommunications technical and administrative services in less developed countries; and (3) developing the human resources required for telecommunications. (ITU)

COURTESY, GTE SYLVANIA

A working model of a sunlight-powered laser is demonstrated by Lloyd Huff, who headed the team of scientists that developed the device. Because it had an operating life of five to seven years, it would have a practical application in communications satellites.

See also Industrial Review; Television and Radio.

ENCYCLOPÆDIA BRITANNICA FILMS. *Getting the News* (1967); *What Is a Computer?* (1971).

Television and Radio

More than 927 million television and radio sets were in use throughout the world in 1972. Some radio service was available in almost every country, and there was some television service in every industrial nation except South Africa, whose government was considering introducing it by 1975. Television sets in the world totaled 261,750,000 and radio sets 665.5 million, according to estimates compiled by *Broadcasting* magazine and *Broadcasting Yearbook*. Approximately 95 million, or 36%, of the television sets were in the United States. The U.S.S.R. had the second largest number, about 30 million, and Japan was third with about 24 million. Other *Broadcasting* estimates showed the United Kingdom with 20 million, West Germany 17 million, France 12 million, Italy 10.8 million, Canada 6.8 million, Spain 4.5 million, Poland 4 million, Argentina 3.5 million, Australia 3.2 million, Czechoslovakia 3.1 million, Sweden 2.7 million, Belgium 2.1 million, Hungary and Yugoslavia 1.8 million each, Austria 1.6 million, Denmark 1.4 million, and Bulgaria 1.2 million. At the other extreme, *Broadcasting* reported Singapore with 185,000, Syria 120,000, Kuwait 110,000, Tunisia 70,000, Malta and the Sudan 65,000 each, Cyprus and Rhodesia 50,000 each, Yemen (Aden) 22,000, Mauritania and Zambia 20,000 each, Bermuda 18,000, Uganda 15,000, Ethiopia 8,000, Liberia 6,500, Gibraltar 6,000, and Sierra Leone 3,500.

About 53% of the world's radio sets, or 353.5 million, were in the U.S. No country of any size lacked some form of radio service, although in a few areas the service consisted only of loudspeakers set up in public places for community listening, and in some cases the broadcasts came from booster or relay stations rather than directly from broadcasting stations.

COURTESY, PBS

Bob (right) and Ray of radio fame satirize TV coverage of rocket launchings in a scene from Kurt Vonnegut's "Between Time and Timbuktu—A Space Fantasy." The program was part of the "Special of the Week" series aired by the Public Broadcasting Service in 1972.

Approximately 6,385 television stations were in operation in the world in 1972, according to *Broadcasting.* Their geographic distribution changed little from 1971. About 2,100 were in the Far East, 2,000 in Western Europe, 1,009 in the U.S., 910 in Eastern Europe, 175 in South America, 81 in Canada, and 35 in Africa. The choice of programs offered viewers ranged from only one in many countries to ten or more in others. In the U.S., according to *Broadcasting,* 97% of all TV households could receive at least three stations, and almost two out of ten (17%) could receive ten or more. Taking radio as well as television into account, *Broadcasting* reported that the program choice in the U.S. ranged from 26 television stations and 104 radio stations for residents of the New York City metropolitan area to 5 television and 8 radio stations for Glendive, Mont., a community of 4,600 homes, and somewhat less than that for some smaller communities.

More than 13,400 radio stations were on the air or under construction throughout the world in 1972. The majority were amplitude modulation (AM) stations, but the number of frequency modulation (FM) stations was growing. In the U.S., which had 7,533, or about 56%, of the world's radio stations, about 42% (3,110) were FM.

Organization. One of the greatest accomplishments in organization in 1972 related to the coordination of international satellite relays for coverage of such events as U.S. Pres. Richard Nixon's visits to China and the U.S.S.R., the U.S. Apollo 16 and 17 moon missions, the Olympic Games, and the U.S. elections. Viewers throughout the world were able to watch these events as relayed through communications satellites "parked" in stationary orbits over the Atlantic and Pacific oceans and, beginning in midyear, one over the Indian Ocean.

Coverage of the summer Olympic Games, August 26 through September 11, led to a record volume of satellite television traffic. The U.S. Communications Satellite Corp. (Comsat), manager of the worldwide International Telecommunications Satellite Consortium (Intelsat), logged 1,005 half-channel hours (hours of one-way transmission, to or from a satellite) of Olympics satellite time, more than twice the 450 half-channel hours used for the Olympic Games in Mexico City four years earlier. Estimates indicated that approximately one billion viewers saw some portions of the Olympics coverage, about 200 million more than were believed to have seen some part of the 1968 Mexican Olympics coverage.

Extensive satellite arrays were also used to display worldwide the coverage of President Nixon's visit to mainland China in February and to Moscow in May. Also seen throughout the world were the Apollo 16 and 17 moon flights in April and December and the U.S. elections in November.

An unprecedented event in broadcasting history was the International Conference of Broadcasting Unions on Communication Satellites which took place in Rome, March 6–11, 1972. Convened by the European Broadcasting Union (EBU), it was the first world meeting of regional broadcasting unions and the major broadcasting organizations of North America. Despite the absence of the Prague-based Organisation Internationale de Radio et Télévision (OIRT), the nearly 100 delegates present represented a virtually worldwide cross section of broadcasting opinion. The conference adopted a number of recommendations in the legal, program, and technical fields, and it was hoped that through these measures collaboration between the various groups would increase in scope. Of particular significance was a technical recommendation which aimed at the adoption of uniform rules for global operations in intercontinental television transmissions by satellites. The rules were to be based on preliminary standardization which had already taken place in Europe–North America transmissions. As a result of the Rome conference's success the Asociacion Interamericana de Radiodifusion invited the participants to meet again in Rio de Janeiro in November 1973.

In August the Soviet Union proposed in the UN an international agreement against transmission by satellite of television broadcasts to countries without their permission. Foreign Minister Andrei A. Gromyko, in his note to Secretary-General Kurt Waldheim, warned against "allowing live television broadcasts to become a source of international conflicts." In October the political committee of the General Assembly voted down the proposal.

On January 14, U.S. Rep. James H. Scheuer (Dem., N.Y.) reported that Alexander B. Chakovsky, editor of *Literaturnaya Gazeta,* journal of the Soviet Writers' Union, had indicated to him that the Soviet Union might be willing to change its attitude toward internal dissent if Western radio propaganda ceased. On June 16, however, the U.S. Senate approved a bill authorizing funds totaling $38,520,000 for fiscal 1973 for Radio Free Europe and Radio Liberty. (*See* PROPAGANDA.)

EBU president Marcel Bezençon retired at the end of the year. This outstanding personality in international broadcasting, who had earlier in the year retired as director general of the Swiss Broadcasting Corp., had originated the idea for the creation of a "program stock exchange" which led to the establishment in 1954 of the worldwide news and program exchange facility by terrestrial and satellite links known as Eurovision. As his successor the EBU elected Charles Curran, director general of the British Broadcasting Corp., an appropriate gesture in the year in which the BBC celebrated its 50th anniversary.

For the first time since the establishment of OIRT the chairmen of individual Radio Program Commission groups met and discussed their common problems in Sofia, Bulg., May 16–18. Two directives were approved, and a number of resolutions and recommendations adopted regarding radio commemoration of the 50th anniversary of the Soviet Union and of the 25th anniversary of the foundation of the Romanian Socialist Republic.

On June 6 the 12th session of the OIRT Television Program Commission met in Warsaw, Pol., with representatives from Bulgaria, Czechoslovakia, Finland, East Germany, Hungary, Poland, Romania, and the U.S.S.R. participating. The session surveyed the work of Intervision during 1972 and determined on methods of further improving cooperation among members. The major events presented over the Intervision network continued to be the congresses of Communist and Workers' parties held in the European socialist countries. Questions of future cooperation with other regional broadcasting unions were also examined.

Plans for the creation of domestic, as opposed to international, satellite systems for relaying programs within rather than between countries were at varying stages of development in several countries in 1972. The Soviet Union's Orbita satellite continued to relay programs from Moscow to distant areas. Canada in November launched a six-channel satellite, designed to serve the entire country. India still hoped to have its much-delayed Satellite Instructional Television Experiment (SITE) in operation in 1974–75: this would use a satellite, to be supplied by the U.S., in a one-year test of the feasibility of carrying a massive educational program into remote villages where special community receivers would be installed.

United States. The number of U.S. households equipped with colour television sets totaled 31.4 million, or 56.1% of all U.S. television households, as of July 1, 1972, according to estimates reported in *Broadcasting.* This was a gain of 4.4 million colour homes since Oct. 1, 1971, when the estimates first indicated that more than half of all TV households had colour television. All three commercial TV networks—the American Broadcasting Co. (ABC), the Columbia Broadcasting System (CBS), and the National Broadcasting Co. (NBC)—transmitted virtually all of their programs in colour, as did most U.S. stations, whether affiliated with networks or not.

On February 3 new rules were announced by the Federal Communications Commission (FCC) regulating the future extension of cable television (CATV), to promote its growth from rural areas into the nation's smaller cities, but to restrict its encroachment into major metropolitan areas. About 9% of the nation's 60 million homes with TV sets carried CATV, which brought programs into the home by coaxial cable instead of by regular broadcast transmissions. (*See* TELECOMMUNICATIONS: *Special Report.*)

The FCC on June 16 voted four to three in favour of ending its ban on domestic satellite communications by private companies. Eight companies had already submitted plans and three—the American Telephone and Telegraph Co. (AT & T), Western Union, and the Hughes Aircraft Co.—declared themselves ready to begin work on telephone, telegraph, and cable TV satellite systems. The FCC barred AT & T from transmitting TV programs by satellite for at least three years in order to prevent it from using revenues from monopolistic telephone services to impede satellite competition. Beginning August 1 the FCC barred the networks from acquiring any financial or proprietary rights in any program they did not exclusively produce. From June 1, 1973, they were also to be barred from distributing any programs to independent stations.

After conservative criticism of nude ballet and antiwar films on public television, on June 30 Pres. Richard Nixon vetoed a bill authorizing funds to the Corporation for Public Broadcasting, on the grounds that the corporation was becoming too powerful and that the bill's funding procedure was faulty. On August 1 the corporation was granted a one-year $45 million authorization.

A November report by the "Alternative Education Foundation" of Bloomington, Ind., on network news treatment of the 1972 Democratic presidential candidates concluded that the desperate urge for the largest possible audience inevitably led to the news being presented in a form considered the most entertaining, a superdramatized political "Peyton Place." (Why did Ed Muskie cry? Would he gain the 50% of votes considered necessary for success by the networks in the New Hampshire primary? Could McGovern come up from nowhere in the California primary? Was there a chance for Hubert Humphrey?) As a result the foundation concluded that there was hardly any considered discussion of policies or real issues; this policy "encourages on the part of the citizens a pervasive cynicism about their political institutions while, at the same time, depriving them of the information that is needed if they were to control these institutions."

Broadcasters, meanwhile, operated under pressures more intense in 1972 than ever before. The number of stations whose license renewals were challenged, either by local minority groups who claimed their interests had not been properly served and wanted the renewals denied, or by groups seeking the licenses to operate the stations themselves, continued to grow. More than 100 such cases were pending before the FCC in mid-1972, according to a count by *Broadcasting.* In many cases the challengers were able to win concessions in programming, employment, and citizens' participation in the operation of the stations they were challenging.

But it was not only stations up for license renewal that were subject to challenge; similar tactics were used more and more against stations being bought and sold, since such transactions also were subject to FCC approval. One would-be new owner agreed to let a challenging group name three members of a seven-member board of directors as the price for withdrawal of challenges to its acquisition of the station involved, KABL-AM-FM in Oakland–San Francisco, Calif. Several prospective buyers planning to change the program formats of their stations—from classical to contemporary music, for example—faced indefinite delays as a result of protests to the FCC by local groups opposing such changes, and in some cases abandoned either the program change or the purchase.

One of the most spectacular settlements was made by McGraw-Hill Inc., the publishing company, which had contracted to buy the five television stations owned by Time Inc., another major publisher, for $69.3 million. Under challenge by eight Mexican-American organizations and one black group, McGraw-Hill not only made extensive commitments in programming, citizen-advisory councils, employment, training programs, and access to the stations' facilities, but also agreed not to buy one of the five stations, WOOD-TV in Grand Rapids, Mich. The challengers contended that acquisition of the Grand Rapids station would violate FCC policy on sales involving major markets, although the FCC had already held that the WOOD-TV transaction should be exempt from the policy and had approved all five sales as originally proposed.

Among other pressures under which broadcasters operated were mounting demands for access to station time to present minority viewpoints. The equal-time law, requiring broadcasters who made time available to one candidate to make similar provision for his rivals, was particularly nettlesome because 1972 was a presidential election year and because Congress had enacted a law requiring broadcasters to sell time for political broadcasts at their lowest rates. The fairness doctrine, construed by earlier court decisions to apply to product commercials as well as controversial issues, raised the threat that broadcasters might be required to provide time for "counteradvertising" in which critics of a particular commercial or advertised product would be free to put their criticisms on the air. Advertisers as well as broadcasters insisted that this would force sponsors to put their advertising money into other media, where no such requirement was proposed.

Clay Whitehead, the principal White House adviser for broadcasting, announced in December that the administration had drafted tough new legislation on television programming, which it intended to present to Congress early in 1973. The proposed legislation would make individual television stations responsible, at the risk of losing their licenses, for the content of all network material they broadcast. Network and station officials sharply criticized the proposal as introducing government censorship. President Nixon also lent his weight to an effort to end local television blackouts of professional football games, but the Supreme Court upheld the practice.

The charge that violence or aggressive behaviour in television programs promotes violence or aggressive behaviour on the part of young viewers continued to be an issue, although it seemed to abate somewhat after a special 12-member Scientific Advisory Committee on Television and Social Behavior, appointed by the U.S. surgeon general in 1969, issued a report on its two-year, $1 million study early in 1972. The report stopped far short of providing the indictment that many critics had made against television; it found some evidence of a causal relationship between aggression on TV and aggressive behaviour, but suggested that such a relationship is strongest among children predisposed to aggression.

Redd Foxx (left) and Demond Wilson show a cynical affection for each other in NBC's series "Sanford and Son," which premiered in January 1972. The successful show, based on the BBC's "Steptoe and Son," followed the pattern of the popular "All in the Family."

COURTESY, NBC

The television networks were the targets of demands by the film craft unions that they be required to increase the number of original episodes in each program series they present and reduce the number of reruns to no more than 25% of nighttime programming. The networks countered that so drastic a reduction in reruns would escalate network production costs to a point 100% higher than profits. The net effect, they said, would not be the increase in Hollywood production that the craft unions were seeking but an increase in production in less expensive locations, to the disadvantage of Hollywood craftsmen.

Pay television remained a source of concern for broadcasters, but more in combination with a larger worry, cable television, than on its own. Zenith Radio Corp., which had developed the Phonevision over-the-air system of subscription television, terminated its plan to establish its own system through acquisition of KWHY-TV in Los Angeles. But Pay Television Corp., whose principals had been associated with Zenith in the past, bought another Los Angeles station, KBSC-TV, subject to FCC approval, and planned to augment the station's broadcasts with Phonevision pay transmissions. Actual pay-TV, however, was offered by a number of cable-television systems.

The news for broadcasters was not all bad in 1972, however. In July the U.S. Court of Appeals for the District of Columbia, which in the past had ruled strongly in favour of local groups in their challenges to existing broadcasters, upheld the FCC's determination that charges made against WMAL-TV in Washington were not specific enough to require a hearing. Broadcasters were heartened, too, by a federal court opinion issued in November urging that the FCC reconsider whether the fairness doctrine may not, in fact, be doing more harm than good.

Europe. Western European broadcasting systems continued to face rising costs because of the need to apply such technical innovations as multichannel, colour, and cable television, and also because of the extension of viewing time and the trend to regional and local services. Pressure on broadcasting authorities from politicians, advertisers, trade unions, libertarians, and puritans continued unabated.

In the United Kingdom the BBC celebrated its 50th anniversary with an exhibition at Langham Place, London, which was opened by Queen Elizabeth II on November 1. The BBC on October 24 revealed an important technical innovation. A new plan had been devised, with the approval of the governors, whereby every TV receiver could be transformed into a potential store of "printed" information, available at the press of a button. From a small digital keyboard the viewer would be able to select any one of about 30 services covering program information, business reports, weather reports, stock (share) prices, news flashes, farming reports, telephone data, foreign language translations, and even subtitles for superimposition on normal programs for deaf viewers. The prototype of the "Ceefax" system, as it was called, was expected to be ready by early 1973, and a public service on these lines could well be in operation by 1976. The provision of adapters was to be left to manufacturers in collaboration with the BBC; a more complex task was to decide just which data services to provide and how to finance them. Since it was technically feasible to record Ceefax signals on videotape, the new technology of the video-cassette could extend the possibilities almost infinitely.

Although the BBC's charter did not expire until 1976, even by the beginning of 1972 the corporation had committed itself heavily to a defense of the status quo. Lord Hill, the chairman, was to retire by year's end, and government concern over program standards was reflected in the search for a "strong man" to replace him (by which was meant one who would toe the government line). According to some government and opposition sources, the corporation had too strong a tendency to take sides and was too far ahead of public taste. Lord Hill dealt with this type of criticism in the foreword to the BBC's *Yearbook:* "I do not believe that the campaign against our independence will succeed. But the danger is there."

In view of the increased number of commercial radio stations allowed in the U.K., the BBC planned to have its reorganized radio service fully operational well before Britain's first commercial local stations went on the air in the spring of 1974. Increased news coverage and provision of medium-wave frequencies to BBC local stations in addition to their existing VHF (very-high-frequency) wavelengths were expected to give the BBC a considerable lead over its commercial rivals. On July 12 the Independent Television Authority (ITA) changed its name to the Independent Broadcasting Authority (IBA) to designate its extended responsibility for the 60 local commercial radio stations which were planned. The stations were to be financed by spot advertising (nine minutes per hour) controlled by the IBA. The first five would operate from London (an entertainment and a specialist news station), Manchester, Glasgow, and Birmingham.

In its most serious clash with the Irish government in its 12-year history, the nine-member governing body of the Irish national broadcasting authority, Radio Telefis Eireann (RTE), was dismissed on November 24. The action came after ministerial protests over a broadcast account of an interview given by IRA Provisional leader Sean MacStiofain (*see* BIOGRAPHY), who was sentenced to six months' imprisonment on November 25. According to the government the nine-man board had ignored a directive restraining it from broadcasting "any matter . . . calculated to promote the aims or activities of any organization which engages in, promotes, encourages, or advocates the attaining of any political objective by violent means." The new chairman of a seven-man replacement board was James A. Scannell, former secretary of the Department of Posts and Telegraphs.

Following sanctions against certain staff members of the state-run Office de Radiodiffusion Télévision Française (ORTF) by its board in March, on June 7 the French government decided to reorganize the top management of ORTF. The chairman of the ORTF board, Pierre de Leusse; the director general, Jean-Jacques de Bresson; and the director of regional stations, Jacques Homery, all resigned. On July 12 Arthur Conte, a Gaullist deputy, a representative of the deeply conservative radicalism of the far south, and a virulent anti-Communist, was named as the new president of ORTF, taking over functions of both chairman and director general for a three-year term. This appointment appeared to have effectively brought to an end the period of relative liberalization of French television that had begun in 1968 under the guidance of Premier Jacques Chaban-Delmas. Henceforth, ORTF was expected to revert to its former habit of ignoring the opposition and slanting the news constantly in the government's favour. These fears were confirmed with the firing on July 17 of Pierre Desgraupes, former director of information of ORTF's first TV channel and a principal proponent of greater freedom of expression.

CAMERA PRESS/PUBLIX

UPI COMPIX

Warren Mitchell (left) portrays Alf Garnett, British prototype of Archie Bunker in Johnny Speight's BBC series "Till Death Us Do Part." Carroll O'Connor (above) stars as Archie Bunker, America's most popular bigot. The CBS series was adapted from its BBC counterpart.

The second international congress on the video-cassette industry in Cannes, France, in March proved something of an anticlimax in comparison with the euphoric tone of the previous year's gathering. Approximately 1,200 delegates attended from 28 countries and 550 societies to hear a courageously self-critical analysis. In the Netherlands products were being marketed in an unfinished state; in the U.S. neither CBS, NBC, nor ABC had really begun to compete in this "gold mine turned air bubble"; and in Japan the most profitable exploitation of the medium was in the field of pornography.

In Italy a dispute over whether to adopt the French SECAM or West German PAL colour television system threatened to topple the government of Premier Giulio Andreotti. Both the French and West German governments appeared to attach great importance to Italy's decision, the SECAM representatives claiming that the future of the entire European electronics industry and of European politico-economic leadership were at stake. According to them French government support for SECAM was based on the desire to thwart the growth of German political and economic power on the continent and to replace it with a Latin partnership. Andreotti's was the 12th Italian government that had been unable to decide which of the two systems to use. Much controversy continued throughout the year, with the National Association of Electrical Industries declaring that the adoption of SECAM would jeopardize 30,000 jobs. In early October the dispute was once more shelved when Andreotti told a parliamentary committee that colour TV would not be introduced in Italy before 1974.

After a prolonged battle by the Nederlandse Omroep Stichting (NOS) to persuade Parliament to increase license fees for TV and radio, on September

28 a bill was introduced proposing increases from 75 to 108 guilders and from 24 to 33 guilders, respectively, beginning Jan. 1, 1973. The fees had remained unchanged since 1969. If these changes were to be implemented, increased revenue for 1973 was estimated at 363.6 million guilders and for 1974 at 369.8 million guilders. Should they not be accepted, the Netherlands broadcasting system would be placed in a financially untenable position.

On September 5 Philips Co. introduced in Eindhoven its latest invention, a video-long-playing (VLP) record system, which made possible the "playing" of a recorded colour program of 30–45 minutes' duration on the screen of a TV set. VLP for the first time brought the laser beam to the consumer market, for Philips had found an inexpensive method of manufacturing a helium-neon laser, whose very fine light spot traced the record track on which all data signals for picture and sound reproduction were stored in microscopic indentations. Reproduction could be retarded, stopped, or even reversed without influencing the quality of the record.

WIDE WORLD

Edwin A. Goodman, general manager of radio station WBAI in New York City, speaks to reporters following his release from jail in March 1972. Goodman, cited for contempt because he refused to release tapes of interviews held with prisoners during the take-over of the Tombs in October 1970, said, "We must resist the government's use of the media for informational purposes."

As of Jan. 1, 1972, the Soviet television receiving network comprised 45 million sets. Besides the TV program studios (of which there were 127), the U.S.S.R. had 145 powerful and 960 low-powered relay stations, and the world's longest cable and relay lines. Both ground and satellite systems were employed for transmissions. The studios of Moscow, Kiev, Tbilisi, Tashkent, Baku, and Leningrad broadcast colour TV for five hours a day to 66 towns in the Soviet Union. Radio broadcasts covered the entire country. Stereophonic broadcasting was assuming greater proportions and by 1972 was being carried out for more than ten hours daily.

Programming. Broadcasting's ability to carry its coverage of news events into homes around the world was shown repeatedly in 1972. One of the most spectacular demonstrations came in TV coverage of President Nixon's February visit to China, which gave millions an unprecedented look at life inside that nation and was witnessed in the U.S. and many other countries in colour that experts rated exceptionally high in quality. The three U.S. television networks transmitted 52 hours of material by satellite from 18 locations, including the Peking and Shanghai airports, the Great Wall of China, the city of Hangchow, reception and banquet halls, and the scenes of public meetings between President Nixon and Premier Chou En-lai and other Chinese leaders.

Less spectacular photographically, but more complicated electronically, was Nixon's visit to the U.S.S.R. in May, to which the U.S. networks devoted more than 20 hours. Much of this coverage was transmitted to countries around the world.

To get the pictures from Moscow to the U.S., the signals first had to be relayed over more than 2,000 mi. by microwave and land lines, from Moscow to Finland, then to Sweden, to Denmark, and finally to the earth station at Raisting, W.Ger., for transmission to the Atlantic satellite. Because of differing transmission standards, the signals had to be transcoded twice. At Helsinki, Fin., the Soviet transmissions, which used the 625-line, 50-frame sequential memory (SECAM) system, were converted to the 625-line, 50-frame phase alternation line (PAL) system widely used in Europe; at Raisting these were converted to the 525-line, 50-frame U.S. standard for transmission to the Atlantic satellite and thence to the earth station at Etam, W.Va.

The Winter Olympics in Sapporo, Jap. (February 3–13), and the Summer Olympics in Munich, W.Ger. (August 26–September 11), provided the major sporting highlights on radio and television during 1972. For the EBU they were the culmination of three years of intensive preparations. The Munich Olympics broadcasts were the most comprehensive ever to be seen and heard. For many people, though, the event likely to remain uppermost in their memories was the dramatic news sequence transmitted over the Eurovision network following the break into the Israeli athletes' quarters by Arab terrorists.

In entertainment programming, mysteries, Westerns, and comedies produced in the U.S. remained among the favourites in most television countries, but foreign sales of U.S. programs in 1972 were again sluggish in comparison with earlier years. Although "Bonanza," "Gunsmoke," "Perry Mason," "Bewitched," "My Three Sons," "The Carol Burnett Show," and other programs were being seen in scores of countries, program sales authorities reported that overseas buyers were becoming more selective, particularly when newer releases were offered. This slackening sales pace, first noticeable in 1971, was attributed primarily to three factors: as they gained experience, local producers in foreign markets were becoming increasingly able to fill their own needs; a sense of "nationalism" continued to be manifest and, with it, emphasis on "localism" in programming continued to grow; and overseas producers were themselves becoming more competitive in the world market. *Broadcasting* reported that U.S. overseas sales slipped from an anticipated $90 million to about $85 million in 1971 and probably would not exceed $85 million in 1972. Two years earlier, the figure had reached $99 million.

United States. The FCC's prime-time access rule, which in effect required TV-network affiliates to program four weekly prime-time hours that formerly were filled by the networks, continued to have a fundamental effect on programming in 1972. It also remained a centre of controversy. In the rule's first year of operation, the 1971–72 season, it was generally agreed that the local programs inserted in these periods—averaging a half-hour each week-night and an hour on Sunday night—tended to attract smaller audiences than the network programs they had replaced. An analysis published in *Broadcasting* concluded that, on the whole, the most successful "access programs"—those bought or produced by the stations for these periods—usually were updated versions of former network hits, such as "The Lawrence Welk Show" and "Hee-Haw."

NBC petitioned the FCC to repeal the rule and was joined by other broadcasters. The FCC did not go that far, but in late October did concede that the rule did not appear to be working as well as it might and, accordingly, called for a broad review of the subject. The repeal question was only one of many that the review was expected to consider. Among others were whether the rule was accomplishing its stated objective of increasing the diversity of program sources, whether it might be improved by one or more of many amendments that had been suggested, and whether even greater limitations on networks—and more stringent requirements on stations—might be desirable. The FCC said it hoped to dispose of the basic issues of the controversy by early 1973.

In the season that started in September 1972, network programs were distinguished by bolder attempts to reflect contemporary problems. The basic program forms were still the Western, mystery/adventure drama, comedy, and variety, but their weekly episodes often undertook to deal with problems and issues that would have been unacceptable on television only a few years earlier. Homosexuality, abortion, embryo transplants, drug abuse, the causes of crime, and prisoner rehabilitation were among the issues introduced into some of the regular series plots. Among the most successful of the new series were "Maude," a spinoff from "All in the Family," and "Bridget Loves Bernie," about a Jewish-Catholic marriage. Other trends moved toward more "mini-series"—series with six or eight episodes on a single subject, such as "Search for the Nile" and "The Six Wives of Henry VIII," rather than the conventional 20 to 24 episodes—and toward longer single shows, 60 minutes or more.

At the 24th annual Emmy Awards ceremony in May the National Academy of Television Arts and Sciences voted "Brian's Song," a story about friendship and death on a professional football team, as the best show of the 1971–72 season. Best dramatic series was "Elizabeth R," while "All in the Family" was named best comedy and "The Carol Burnett Show" the best variety series.

Sports remained a major attraction, as demonstrated both by the rating services' audience estimates and by the prices paid for broadcast rights. ABC-TV's coverage of the Olympics took the first seven places in the A. C. Nielsen Co.'s national ratings for the two weeks ended September 3, pushing CBS-TV's "All in the Family" from its accustomed number one or number two position down to number eight. Similarly, NBC-TV's coverage of two World Series games in prime time took first and second places in the Nielsen report for the week ended October 22. *Broadcasting* reported that radio and TV networks and stations paid $41,185,000 for rights to cover major league baseball during the year, and $68,916,200 for professional and collegiate football rights. The baseball price was about $734,000 more than broadcasters paid in 1971, but the football bill, which had shown some signs of leveling off in 1971, represented an increase of $2.7 million, about $1.5 million of which was in higher charges for ABC-TV's "NFL Monday Night Football." Other sports such as ice hockey, basketball, and golf added thousands of dollars to the sports outlays.

In radio, the diversity of program choice was, if anything, greater in 1972 than it had ever been. Some stations were devoted to all-news and others to all-talk, a format based primarily on calls from listeners on specific subjects, but most radio stations chose a musical format—country-and-western, contemporary, rhythm-and-blues, classical, progressive rock, or whatever.

In noncommercial broadcasting the big hits were "Sesame Street," for preschool children, which was still considered the goal toward which all children's programming might reach, and "The Electric Company," also produced by the Children's Television Workshop, which was aimed at helping second, third, and fourth graders with reading problems. On a broader scale, the Public Broadcasting Service conducted a study of its public-affairs programming for the year and reported in October that three-fourths of its programs had consisted of children's and cultural programs and no more than one-fourth had dealt with public affairs, on which PBS had been accused of exhibiting a left-wing bias.

Europe. A regular biennial event that took place during the year was the EBU workshop for producers and directors of television programs for children and young people. The third of its kind, it was held in Marseilles, France, February 20–25, and the accent this time was on programs for children under seven. Participants from 28 television services examined various themes ranging from the audience and its particular needs to presentation methods.

The EBU's television program screening sessions celebrated their tenth anniversary in October in Milan, Italy, where they had been held regularly since inaugurated in 1963. Over the years, the screening sessions had assumed a steadily increasing importance as a place for buying, selling, or exchanging films produced by EBU active members, and this was shown by the fact that in 1972 more than 225 delegates from approximately 30 EBU active and associate member countries attended, compared with 50 delegates in 1963. With regard to the products offered, two tendencies were noted: the increasing use of colour, which had risen from 50% in 1960 to over 95% in 1972, and the increase in the number of videotape recordings as opposed to films.

The 12th International Festival of Television held in Monte Carlo announced its awards on March 14. First prize (La Nymphe d'or) went to "Leonardo da Vinci," produced by Italy's RAI. The prize for best scenario went to the BBC's "The Snow Goose," based on a story by Paul Gallico; for the best serial to "The Outside," produced by Polish TV; for the best children's program to the Soviet Union's "Chok and Cher"; and for the best social documentary to the BBC's "Gale Is Dead," which also shared the Unda prize of the Catholic Association of Radio and Television with ORTF's "The Drug."

Norway's program output was dominated in 1972 by the government's proposal of membership in the EEC and the September 25 plebiscite, which rejected it. The Sapporo and Munich Olympics attracted wide interest, but the most popular entertainment program of the year was the BBC series "A Family at War," which depicted with sensitive realism the fate of a provincial British family during World War II. The actors and actresses were invited to appear on Norwegian TV. Cooperation with Swedish and Danish TV drama continued.

In West Germany three wildlife documentaries, "Wildlife Safari," "A Place for Animals," and "On the Track of Rare Animals," were among the most popular programs. Live sports programs, especially football matches, continued to win high ratings. The number of stereo transmissions of music and drama increased considerably during the year.

In March 1972 in the U.S.S.R. the All-Union Radio began a new series entitled "Toward the 50th Anniversary of the Formation of the U.S.S.R.," describing the progress of socialism, in honour of the forthcoming jubilee of the Soviet state. The broadcast "Leninist University for Millions" and special series such as "Music of the Peoples of the U.S.S.R.," "Friendship," and "We Are Waiting for You in the Ostankino Concert Studio" were also devoted to this subject.

In Portugal Radiotelevisão Portuguesa (RTP), already reaching 90% of the population, extended transmissions to the 6,000 or so television receivers in the Madeira Islands. Programs continued to be aimed at majority tastes, but included educational, school, and lunchtime broadcasts, as well as information, news and sports, and drama and music.

COURTESY, NET

Glenda Jackson appears as the aged Elizabeth I near the end of her reign in the final episode of the BBC's six-part series "Elizabeth R."

On January 13 viewers in the Netherlands saw a pseudodocumentary, "Rudy Schokker," which dealt with the unhappy fate of a young couple whose child, conceived as a jet plane flew overhead, had inherited the roar of a jet engine instead of a normal child's cry. The family was eventually forced to live in a caravan at the end of a runway at Schiphol airport. So many viewers were affected by what was, in fact, a hoax, that the program studio was flooded with gifts and money from sympathizers.

Other programs that aroused particular interest included an interview with Prince Claus, the first ever given by a member of the Dutch royal family. The European Cup final, Ajax v. Inter-Milan, was played on May 31 in Rotterdam. NOS, with nine cameras on location, retransmitted to 31 other countries, and audience estimates ranged from 200 to 300 million viewers.

Britain's Associated Television (ATV) in March announced the sale of 25 half-hour episodes of a new spy TV film series, "The Adventurers," to the U.S. sponsor, Chevrolet, to be seen on NBC-owned-and-operated stations and on independent stations. ATV also sold a second series of 26 episodes of "The Protectors" to Fabergé. ATV's space fiction show "UFO," which had attempted to entice away viewers of the BBC's "Dr. Who" series, had already earned $1 million in sales outside the U.S. when it brought in another $1.5 million in the two weeks during which it was offered in syndication in that country. In January it was announced that Julie Andrews had been signed by ATV to do two exclusive series, each of 24 one-hour variety shows, and that ABC had already paid $8 million for rights to screen the first one. Export sales in the financial year ended March 1972 were expected to top the previous year's $29 million.

In September the BBC announced an extra 200 hours of children's TV, for 700 hours a year. This was made possible by the removal of restrictions on broadcasting hours. Programs for children were to be provided on Sundays for the first time. Among the new series was "Jackanory Playhouse," which was to feature six plays for children by authors including Henry Livings and Ted Hughes. There was also to be a new twice-weekly news bulletin for children.

A BBC 2 inquiry into "Who Sank the Lusitania?" provoked renewed controversy in October by its suggestion that Winston Churchill as first lord of the Admiralty might have allowed the sinking as a means of persuading the United States to enter World War I. New evidence brought to light in the program pointed strongly to the ship's having been loaded with illicit munitions.

Concern with audience participation remained in the forefront of BBC and ITV planning. ITV introduced "Open Night," giving viewers an opportunity to answer back in the manner of the BBC's "Talkback." However, neither went as far as the Dutch in making available central production facilities to accredited group representatives of minority interests.

Japan. The major event in Japanese broadcasting in 1972 was the XI Winter Olympics held in Sapporo in February. The Japanese network NHK covered all the events and also assumed responsibility for producing films for transmission overseas.

Political events covered included the reversion to Japan of Okinawa and the resignation of Prime Minister Eisaku Sato. There were also series on violent clashes between "Red Army Sect" students and police, and the discovery in Guam of Shoichi Yokoi (*see* BIOGRAPHY), a former Japanese soldier who did not know World War II had ended. The viewing rate of these TV programs was reported to be as high as 90%. From 1971 through mid-1972 a series of children's programs starring masked heroes became very popular and led to large sales of masks.

During the UN Conference on the Human Environment held in Stockholm, NHK took up the problem of environmental pollution and tried to emphasize its seriousness to the general public through various programs, focusing especially on the problem of photochemical smog (a major problem in Japan). In this connection, NHK took a step forward from conventional news coverage toward a scientific investigation linking experts in various scientific and industrial fields in an effort to stimulate more intensive research.

(RUFUS W. CRATER; SOL TAISHOFF; MICHAEL TYPE)

Amateur Radio. In mid-October amateurs put the first of a new series of sophisticated satellites into space. Designed and built by radio amateurs in the U.S. and Australia, the satellite was launched as a "piggyback" package aboard a NASA Delta space rocket from the Western Test Range in California. OSCAR VI (for Orbiting Satellite Carrying Amateur Radio) differed from the five earlier OSCARs in several important respects. Powered by batteries, recharged by solar power, it was designed to remain operational for at least a year in a circular polar orbit at an altitude of 900 mi. Receiving amateur signals on the 2 metre band and retransmitting them on the 10 metre band—both international frequencies—OSCAR VI made possible international communication on frequencies previously limited to short-range operation. Amateurs throughout the world, including those in less developed countries who had not previously had any opportunity for direct experience with space communication via satellite, were able to communicate through OSCAR VI with relatively simple equipment.

Hurricane Agnes, moving up the east coast of the

U.S. early in the summer, brought heavy rains and record flooding to large areas of the middle Atlantic and northeastern states. Hardest hit were southwestern New York and central Pennsylvania. More than 600 amateur radio operators within the disaster area set up their equipment and provided emergency communications until telephone and other communications were restored to normal, in many instances more than a week after the storm struck. Amateur radio operators also provided vital communications links when normal channels were disrupted by the earthquake in Managua, Nicaragua, in December.

Late in the year the FCC issued the most extensive changes in rules and regulations in more than 20 years. Prominent among them were those affecting Novice Class operators. The Novice frequency allocation on the 2 metre band was deleted and a new one assigned on 10 metres. One of the most significant changes was the introduction of rules covering operation of amateur repeaters, devices that retransmit received signals in order to provide improved communications range and coverage. Also of major importance was an expansion of the voice sub-bands on the 75 and 40 metre bands. (MORGAN W. GODWIN)

See also Advertising; Astronautics; Motion Pictures; Music; Telecommunications.

ENCYCLOPÆDIA BRITANNICA FILMS. *Getting the News* (1967).

Tennis

The administrative conflict affecting competition tennis was resolved in 1972. As of January 1 players under contract to World Championship Tennis (WCT), the Dallas-based corporation controlled by Lamar Hunt, were banned from competing in events sanctioned by the International Lawn Tennis Federation (ILTF). This meant that many of the leading male players did not participate in major championships in South Africa, Italy, West Germany, France, Wimbledon, and others run by national associations, although the U.S. championships at Forest Hills, N.Y., were open to all classes of players by arrangement. The arrangement between WCT and the ILTF allowed the former to promote two separate tournament schedules between January and May incorporating 64 players. WCT signed no more contracts with players, and as existing contracts expired the distinction between contract and independent professionals would dissolve and all players would be able to compete freely in major events. Tennis grew as a participants' sport most markedly in the United States, where an annual growth rate of between 10 and 15%, involving approximately 13 million players, was reported.

The shortening of tournament play matches with the "tie breaker" continued, the system varying from one country to another. The British method was the best of 12 points at either six or eight games all, with the final set being played out normally. The U.S. method imposed the best of nine points at six all, with "sudden death" on the ninth point.

More than one attempt was made to organize professional players into a cooperative association. The most substantial appeared to be the Association of Tennis Professionals, with the South African player Cliff Drysdale as its president and Jack Kramer of the U.S. as its executive director. It attracted an initial membership of 56 leading players, each paying a $400 entry fee.

THE TIMES, LONDON/PICTORIAL PARADE

The U.S.'s Stan Smith hammers a shot back at West Germany's Hans Plotz, whom Smith overwhelmed 6–1, 6–1, 6–3 at Wimbledon in June 1972. Smith took the men's singles crown at Wimbledon.

A loosely knit women's professional group had success in organizing a series of sponsored tournaments in the United States with the blessing of the U.S. Lawn Tennis Association, thus boosting the earnings of some women players. Billie Jean King of the U.S. earned $30,300 in prize money in 14 such tournaments early in the year.

Commercial sponsorship became an increasingly integral part of promoting the game, with the notable exception of the Wimbledon championship, which continued to make handsome profits without commercial support.

Men's Competition. *Singles.* At the end of 1971 the Grand Prix series organized by the ILTF was won by the American Stan Smith (*see* BIOGRAPHY) with Ilie Nastase of Romania second. In the subsequent Masters' tournament at Coubertain Stadium in Paris contested by Smith, Nastase, Cliff Richey (U.S.), Pierre Barthes (France), Zeljko Franulovic (Yugos.), Jan Kodes (Czech.), and Clark Graebner (U.S.), Nastase was the unbeaten victor in the all-play-all series, with Smith as runner-up.

Since its starting date was at the end of 1971, the Australian championship, played at Melbourne, had the participation of contract professional players. Ken Rosewall (Austr.) won for the fourth time and second successive year, taking the final from Mal Anderson (Austr.), the winner in 1958. Rosewall's first Australian title was in 1953.

The South African meet in Johannesburg was won by Richey in a final against Manuel Orantes of Spain. Later, Orantes went on to gain his first important success with the Italian championship in Rome, beating Kodes in the final 4–6, 6–1, 7–5, 6–2.

At Dallas in May the last tournament in the WCT series between eight qualifiers, Rosewall, Rod Laver (Austr.), John Newcombe (Austr.), Marty Riessen (U.S.), Drysdale, Arthur Ashe (U.S.), Tom Okker (Neth.), and Bob Lutz (U.S.), was an outstanding event of the year. Rosewall earned $50,000 by beating Laver 4–6, 6–0, 6–3, 6–7, 7–6.

The French championship in Paris had an unexpected winner in the Spaniard Andres Gimeno against an even more unexpected finalist, the Frenchman Patrick Proisy, who had defeated Orantes in the semifinal and Kodes in the quarterfinal. Gimeno had beaten

Alex Metreveli of the Soviet Union in the semifinal and Smith in the quarterfinal.

Orantes took the West German title, again played in the spring in Hamburg. In the final he defeated Adriano Panatta (Italy), a player who continued to show improvement without getting to the top.

The Wimbledon championship, despite the absence of WCT contract players, had an attendance of 298,660, only 220 short of the year before. It was won by Smith, the 1971 runner-up. In the quarterfinal he beat Metreveli 6–2, 8–6, 6–2. He won the semifinal against Kodes 3–6, 6–4, 6–1, 7–5, and, in the final, gained a narrow victory by 4–6, 6–3, 6–3, 4–6, 7–5, after memorable excitement and quality, over Nastase.

The U.S. championship also had a final of outstanding quality. Nastase defeated Ashe 3–6, 6–3, 6–7, 6–4, 6–3 after Ashe appeared to be in command at 4–2 in the fourth set. There were some notable upsets during the tournament. Ashe beat Smith in the quarterfinal 7–6, 6–4, 7–5; Richey defeated Laver in the fourth round, Laver having an injured back; Rosewall lost to Mark Cox of the U.K. in the second round; and Newcombe fell to Fred Stolle of Australia in the third.

Doubles. The most successful pair during 1972 were Bob Hewitt and Frew McMillan of South Africa. They won the South African, French, and Wimbledon titles. Rosewall and Owen Davidson (Austr.) won the Australian championship, while Nastase took the Italian title with his fellow Romanian Ion Tiriac and the West German title with Kodes of Czechoslovakia. Roger Taylor (U.K.) and Cliff Drysdale won the U.S. In WCT events the most consistent partnership was Okker and Riessen.

Davis Cup. Because of a change of rules the U.S., the 1971 Davis Cup winners, played through the entire 1972 tournament instead of competing only in the final. Fifty-two nations took part. The entry of Rhodesia was again refused. South Africa was accepted at first, but expelled later, following the precedent of earlier years. Players under contract to WCT remained ineligible to represent their countries. Australia suffered most from the ban but nonetheless did better than in previous years. Mal Anderson, 37 years old, rejoined the Australian team, having last been a member in 1957 and 1958. Australia defeated South Korea, Japan, and India to win the Eastern Zone.

The Italian team, victors against Austria and the Netherlands before losing to Romania, was again represented by Nicola Pietrangeli, though only in doubles. This brought the total number of rubbers played in the Davis Cup by Pietrangeli, who first played in 1954, to 164, an outstanding individual record. Romania defeated Switzerland, Iran, Italy, and the U.S.S.R. to win the European Zone "A," while Spain beat Bulgaria, France, Monaco, and Czechoslovakia to win Zone "B." The U.S. triumphed over the Caribbean Commonwealth, Mexico, and Chile to win the American Zone.

In the interzone semifinal Romania defeated Australia 4–1 in Bucharest, and the U.S. beat Spain 3–2 in Barcelona. The choice of venue for the final belonged under the rules to the U.S., but the Americans agreed to play in Bucharest because both previous challenge rounds between the two nations had been staged in the U.S. Accordingly, for the first time since competition began in 1900, the decisive match for the Davis Cup took place in a country other than Great Britain, the U.S., France, Australia, or New Zealand. In Bucharest in October the U.S. beat Romania 3–2 to win the trophy for the 24th time. Smith, Tom Gorman, and Erik Van Dillen comprised the U.S. team, while Nastase and Tiriac competed for Romania.

Billie Jean King plays against Evonne Goolagong in the Wimbledon finals. Mrs. King won easily, adding the Wimbledon crown to her impressive list of victories in 1972 and continuing her domination of women's competition.

FOX PHOTOS/PICTORIAL PARADE

Women's Competition. *Singles.* The Grand Prix at the end of 1971 was won by Billie Jean King (U.S.), whose dominance during 1972 was more marked. The Australian title was taken by Virginia Wade (U.K.), who beat Evonne Goolagong (Austr.) in the final. Miss Goolagong avenged the defeat by beating Miss Wade in the final match of the South African championship. Linda Tuero (U.S.) won the Italian title, but she lost the final of the West German meeting to Helga Masthoff (W.Ger.).

Mrs. King won the French championship without losing a set in any round, easily beating Miss Goolagong, the 1971 winner, in the final. Mrs. King also won the Wimbledon championship, losing only one set in the quarterfinal to Miss Wade. She beat Miss Goolagong, the defending champion, in the final, again easily. Mrs. King also won the U.S. title at Forest Hills, losing no sets. In the final she beat Kerry Melville of Australia, who had beaten the young American Chris Evert (*see* BIOGRAPHY) in the round before. Miss Goolagong lost early at Forest Hills to Pam Teeguarden. Margaret Court (Austr.), absent from the game for most of the season after having a baby, became a semifinalist at the U.S. meeting but was beaten 6–4, 6–4 by Mrs. King. Mrs. King also played with great success on the women's professional circuit in the U.S. She was unquestionably the best player of the season.

Doubles. Mrs. King partnered Betty Stove (Neth.) to win both the French and Wimbledon championships. Miss Stove played with Françoise Durr (France) to take the U.S. title. The Australian championship was taken by Helen Gourlay with her fellow Australian Kerry Harris, and the South African championship by Miss Gourlay with Miss Goolagong. The West Germans, Mrs. Masthoff and Heide Orth, dominated their own national title.

Wightman Cup. The U.S. defeated Great Britain 5–2 at Wimbledon. The U.S. team included Miss Evert, Wendy Overton, Patti Hogan, and Valerie Ziegenfuss, while the British consisted of Miss Wade, Joyce Williams, Corinne Molesworth, Nell Truman, and Winnie Shaw.

Federation Cup. In Johannesburg a South African team consisting of Pat Pretorius and Brenda Kirk were first-time winners. They defeated France 2–1 in the quarterfinal, the U.S. 2–1 in the semifinal, and Great Britain 2–1 in the final. (LANCE TINGAY)

Thailand

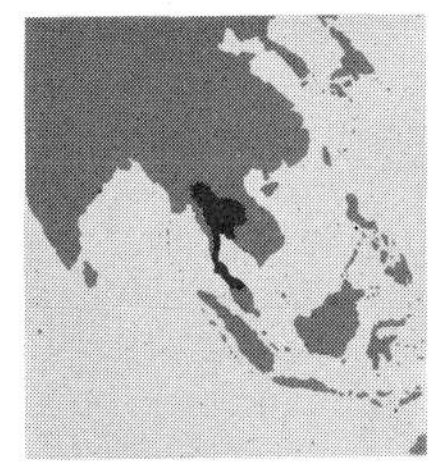

A constitutional monarchy of Southeast Asia, Thailand is bordered by Burma, Laos, Cambodia, and Malaysia. Area: 198,500 sq.mi. (514,000 sq.km.). Pop. (1971 est.): 35,335,000. Cap. and largest city: Bangkok (pop., 1970 est., 2,213,522). Language: Thai. Religion (1964): Buddhist 93.7%; Muslim 3.9%. King, Bhumibol Adulyadej; prime minister in 1972, Field Marshal Thanom Kittikachorn.

Suspicious of China and resentful of Chinese backing of its growing insurgency movement, Thailand nevertheless strengthened relations with Peking in 1972. The military government did not abandon its public posture of extreme reluctance to open any dialogue with the Chinese. Its reaction to U.S. Pres. Richard Nixon's China visit was conspicuously low-key, and live television coverage of the visit was canceled at the last moment.

In the first half of the year, however, Chinese attempts to gain Thai participation in a badminton tournament in Peking found favourable response in Bangkok. Eventually, badminton yielded to the more tested diplomatic sport of table tennis and a Thai team went to Peking in September. Accompanying the team was Prasit Karnchanawat, deputy director of economics, finance, and industry, whose "advisory" role was seen as a cover for political and economic soundings. A month after the table-tennis team had returned home, a Thai trade team journeyed to China to participate in the autumn Canton Trade Fair—a first for Thailand.

Thai suspicions of China, however, continued. In July the director general of secondary education reported a growing number of unauthorized classes at night which were quietly giving Chinese instruction to several hundred students. He said "the authorities are concerned that these classes might indoctrinate the students in some undesirable foreign ideology." Government leaders often commented that China would have to stop supporting the insurgents before friendly relations between the two countries could be established.

The insurgency movement grew in strength and scope during 1972. Government operations against the underground forces escalated from localized clashes to full-scale battles. By March one and a half army divisions were involved in the campaign, supported by fighter-bombers and supply helicopters. In June there were reports that the Thai insurgents had for the first time begun coordinating their activities with Malaysian Chinese guerrillas. At about the same time the authorities made their biggest weapons sweep on record when they captured a shipment of modern arms in the northeastern province of Kalasin. The supreme command had earlier announced plans to increase defense spending by an unspecified amount during the subsequent two years "to counter subversion and insurgency and to ensure Thailand's military capability to meet all threats to our security." The announcement also said that the U.S. had increased its military assistance program to Thailand by $15 million in the current financial year.

The National Executive Council made good use of the martial law proclaimed in November 1971 to make life more conformist in Thailand. One of its earliest decrees banned long hair and permissive dress and curtailed night life, imposing a midnight curfew on places of amusement. This was enforced with no regard even for the important tourist trade.

On the crucial questions of framing a new constitution and appointing a new Cabinet, progress was slow, and the process was not completed until December. At the time of the November 1971 coup it had been announced that an interim constitution would be promulgated immediately, but this was subsequently postponed three times. In July it was announced that Thanom's term as supreme commander of the armed forces would be extended by another year beginning September 30. A new interim constitution was finally promulgated in December. The National Executive Council, which had ruled by decree since the coup, was dissolved; a 299-member assembly, composed mostly of military officers, was appointed to function as a parliament; and on December 18 the king appointed Thanom as prime minister.

Presenting the annual budget on September 29, Thanom announced a partial reorganization of the ministries, under which the Ministry of National Development was scrapped. Budget expenditure for 1973 was envisaged at 31.6 billion baht, a 9% increase over 1972. (T. J. S. GEORGE)

THAILAND

Education. (1968–69) Primary, pupils 5,122,728, teachers (including preprimary) 127,737; secondary, pupils 394,419, teachers (state only) 10,370; vocational, pupils 62,066, teachers 5,768; teacher training, students 22,634, teachers 2,293; higher (including 8 universities), students 41,848, teaching staff 5,470.

Finance. Monetary unit: baht, with (Sept. 18, 1972) a par value of 20.80 baht to U.S. $1 (free rate of 51.24 baht = £1 sterling). Gold, SDRs, and foreign exchange, official: (June 1972) U.S. $1,032,000,000; (June 1971) U.S. $900 million. Budget (1970–71 est.): revenue 21.8 billion baht; expenditure (including capital account) 28,645,000,000 baht. Gross national product: (1969) 115,470,000,000 baht; (1968) 103,220,000,000 baht. Money supply: (March 1972) 22,220,000,000 baht; (March 1971) 20,030,000,000 baht. Cost of living (Bangkok and Thonburi; 1963 = 100): (June 1972) 123; (June 1971) 119.

Foreign Trade. (1971) Imports 26,769,000,000 baht; exports 17,345,000,000 baht. Import sources: Japan 38%; U.S. 14%; West Germany 8%; U.K. 8%. Export destinations: Japan 25%; U.S. 13%; Netherlands 8%; Singapore 7%; Hong Kong 7%. Main exports: rice 17%; corn 13%; rubber 11%; tin 9%; tapioca 7%; kenaf 5%.

Transport and Communications. Roads (main; 1971) 17,105 km. Motor vehicles in use (1971): passenger 246,800; commercial 143,800. Railways: (1969) 3,765 km.; traffic (1970) *c.* 3,860,000,000 passenger-km., freight *c.* 2,250,000,000 net ton-km. Air traffic (1971): 1,032,700,000 passenger-km.; freight 39,641,000 net ton-km. Shipping (1971): merchant vessels 100 gross tons and over 62; gross tonnage 86,222. Telephones (Dec. 1970) 153,000. Radio receivers (Dec. 1970) 2,775,000. Television receivers (Dec. 1969) 241,000.

Agriculture. Production (in 000; metric tons; 1971; 1970 in parentheses): rice 13,570 (13,470); corn *c.* 2,075 (1,950); peanuts *c.* 190 (190); sweet potatoes (1970) *c.* 250, (1969) *c.* 248; sorghum *c.* 100 (120); dry beans *c.* 230 (*c.* 220); soybeans *c.* 90 (*c.* 100); cassava (1970) 1,969, (1969) 1,932; sugar, raw value (1971–72) *c.* 685, (1970–71) *c.* 572; bananas (1970) *c.* 1,200, (1969) *c.* 1,200; tobacco *c.* 95 (93); rubber *c.* 316 (*c.* 287); cotton, lint *c.* 21 (21); jute *c.* 12 (9); kenaf *c.* 330 (*c.* 357); timber (cu.m.; 1970) 19,000, (1969) 18,700; fish catch (1970) 1,595, (1969) 1,270. Livestock (in 000; 1970–71): cattle *c.* 5,300; buffalo *c.* 6,950; pigs *c.* 4,260; chickens *c.* 35,000.

Industry. Production (in 000; metric tons; 1971): cement 2,780; tin concentrates (metal content) 22; tungsten concentrates (oxide content; 1970) 1; lead concentrates (metal content; 1970) 1.2; electricity (kw-hr.; 1969) 3,728,000.

Textiles: *see* Industrial Review

Theatre

Great Britain and Ireland. The National Theatre's difficulties were eased in 1972 by the box-office success of its revival of Eugene O'Neill's *Long Day's Journey into Night* at the Old Vic, and the future of its new home on the South Bank was assured by a government bill increasing the building grant by nearly £2 million to counter the effects of inflation. Michael Blakemore proved a first-rate acquisition to the production team, particularly with his colourful and realistic British premiere of the Ben Hecht-Charles MacArthur *The Front Page*. Another box-office and artistic hit was Tom Stoppard's philosophical romp *Jumpers,* notable for Michael Hordern's absentminded professor and Diana Rigg as his ex-showbiz singer wife and the first actress to bring full frontal nudity to that august stage. Blakemore's way with *Macbeth,* with Diana Rigg as Lady Macbeth, was simple and straightforward, though not quite so denuded of complexities as David William's *Richard II* with its tailor-made title role for Ronald Pickup. Jonathan Miller transported *The School for Scandal* to a filthy Hogarthian world into which Louise Purnell's Lady Teazle fitted snugly. The National's traveling company, a new venture, made its debut with John Ford's *'Tis Pity She's a Whore* directed by Roland Joffé. The play was seen to advantage during the summer at the new Globe Playhouse, a temporary home on the South Bank under Sam Wanamaker's management intended as a future arts centre with ambitious plans for popularizing all the performing arts. At the Young Vic across the road, Frank Dunlop and his colleagues continued to attract young audiences with new and classical plays in modern garb, including *The Alchemist, The Shadow of a Gunman, Julius Caesar,* and John Osborne's first two plays.

The Royal Shakespeare Company set new box-office records with receipts of £1,004,175 from its two theatres and its tour and with attendances at Stratford averaging 95.9% of full capacity. The most sought-after production was the recast revival of Peter Brook's *A Midsummer Night's Dream,* which went on to win laurels abroad as part of a year-long world tour. Two Shakespearean hits taken over from the previous Stratford festival were John Barton's *Othello,* partly updated, with Brewster Mason as the sturdy blackamoor, and *The Merchant of Venice* with Susan Fleetwood as a sly Portia. Edward Albee's *All Over* was finely staged by Peter Hall at the Aldwych. Terry Hands worked wonders breathing new life into T. S. Eliot's *Murder in the Cathedral,* but David Jones's attempts to get English actors to impersonate Russians convincingly in Maksim Gorki's *The Lower Depths* fell short of the previous year's production of *Enemies.* He was far more successful with John Arden and Margaretta D'Arcy's *The Island of the Mighty,* a marathon ballet-drama in which King Arthur and his times were stripped of their legendary romantic trappings, despite acrimonious complaints of betrayal by Arden and his wife, who withdrew their cooperation and picketed the stage door. A less than tactful reply by Jones and manager Trevor Nunn caused one board member to resign.

A similar fate almost befell Frank Norman's exposure of the tourist trade racket, *Costa Packet,* the climax of an enterprising season at Joan Littlewood's Theatre Workshop. However, the author, who charged that the play had been altered beyond recognition, was eventually mollified by its financial success. At the Royal Court Theatre, under the management of Oscar Lewenstein, hopes of expansion were raised when the government indicated its willingness to place the Old Vic at its disposal in 1974, when the National Theatre, under Lord Olivier's designated successor, Peter Hall, would be moving to its new home on the South Bank. Outstanding novelties at the Royal Court were E. A. Whitehead's two-character drama of a broken marriage, *Alpha Beta,* starring Albert Finney (a Lewenstein partner in the management), Charles Wood's parody of commercial film makers, *Veterans,* and the latest plays by Arnold Wesker and John Osborne. Wesker's *The Old Ones* examined the problems of a group of aging Jews, while Osborne's *A Sense of Detachment,* staged by guest director Frank Dunlop, broke countless conventions of stage tradition and common decency in an effort to get the audience's goat. *Romeo and Juliet* at the Shaw rivaled in popular appeal a revival of James M. Barrie's long-neglected *Mary Rose* starring Mia Farrow. The best items in an unusually attractive season at the Mermaid were R. C. Sherriff's *Journey's End,* splendidly revived by Eric Thompson, Harold Pinter's *The Caretaker,* and a collage of Noel Coward works called *Cowardy Custard.*

Despite complaints of rising costs and appeals for various forms of government aid, the commercial theatre thrived as usual. Frank Marcus delivered *Notes on a Love Affair,* a Pirandellian essay on the plight of a middle-aged authoress; John Mortimer a handsomely mounted dramatization of Robert Graves's *I, Claudius;* and Alan Ayckbourn another of his whimsical comedies, *Time and Time Again,* starring Tom Courtenay. Frank Harvey's stage version of Thomas Hardy's *The Day After the Fair* marked Deborah Kerr's return to the West End after a long absence in the U.S., and a newcomer, Charles Laurence, provided a touching study of human foibles entitled *My Fat Friend.* William Douglas Home's misleadingly titled *Lloyd George Knew My Father* also blended pathos and comedy, in a less irritating idiom for once, and provided showy parts for Peggy Ashcroft and Ralph Richardson. Donald Sinden continued to have them "rolling in the aisles" with a commercial revival of Dion Boucicault's *London Assurance,* produced by Ronald Eyre and a former Royal Shakespeare hit. Vanessa Redgrave appeared briefly, leaving the cast prematurely, in Tony Richardson's faithfully Brechtian *The Threepenny Opera,* which acquired an ironic topicality by opening during a bitter industrial dispute and braving the ensuing blackouts.

Offerings from the U.S. included *Company* with Elaine Stritch, *Applause* with Lauren Bacall, *Reunion in Vienna* (transferred from the Chichester Festival), *Jesus Christ Superstar,* the Anglo-American *I and Albert* by Jay Allen about Queen Victoria, and last but by no means least in terms of spectacle and investment of resources the world premiere of *Gone with the Wind.* The outlying playhouses of Greenwich and Hampstead catered to their patrons' needs without any startling innovations, while on the other fringe—cellar, pub, and lunchtime theatres—experimental activity continued unabated, most of it ephemeral though Ed Berman's Almost Free Theatre came up with some promising new material.

In Ireland Eileen Doolan replaced Hugh Hunt as director of the Abbey Theatre, and the Dublin Festival was revived after being closed for a year. The festival included Alan Simpson's production of Brendan

Behan's unfinished third play, *Richard's Cork Leg,* reconstituted by Simpson from posthumous manuscripts. The production later transferred to the Royal Court in London.

France. The main Comédie Française theatre was closed because of industrial disputes concerning systems of work and pay among technical staff. Nothing daunted, the company pitched a tent in the Tuileries gardens where they unveiled their tercentenary tribute to Molière—a new production of *Le Bourgeois gentilhomme* staged by Jean-Louis Barrault, returning to his old theatre after 27 years' absence. Barrault also retained the Récamier Theatre as his own headquarters and as that of the reformed Théâtre des Nations, which ceased to be a festival and became an organization for sponsoring foreign troupes anywhere and at any time with government backing. There, Peter Brook's Experimental Theatre Workshop presented excerpts from Peter Handke's *Kaspar,* and Roland Dubillard's mystifying and poetic *Where the Cows Drink* provided a fine star role for Barrault's wife, Madeleine Renaud. Miss Renaud also appeared in Barrault's production of Paul Claudel's *Beneath the Wind of the Balearic Islands,* the "comic" fourth member of *The Satin Slipper* tetralogy, which had its world premiere in a tent within the precincts of the disused Gare d'Orsay. Other outdoor events under Barrault's aegis included Luca Ronconi's claustrophobic version of the *Oresteia* and the American Robert Wilson's awesomely drawn out *Overture,* which took 24 hours at the Opéra Comique.

The undisputed highlight at the Comédie Française itself was *Richard III,* newly translated by Jean-Louis Curtis and starring Robert Hirsch and Jacques Charon as Gloucester and Buckingham. It was produced by Terry Hands of the Royal Shakespeare, the company's first British guest director, and was the first truly Elizabethan Shakespeare to be seen on this stage. At the Théâtre National Populaire (TNP) the year began haltingly with several offbeat productions, enlivened by Jorge Lavelli's revolutionarily breathtaking production of Fernando Arrabal's antiestablishment musical *Bella Ciao.* However, not only was Georges Wilson's contract not renewed but the TNP was taken out of Paris for good and handed over to Roger Planchon and his colleagues in Lyons. The two empty theatres were taken over by Jack Lang, former director of the Nancy University Theatre Festival; the larger one was closed immediately for 12 months for overhaul and modernization.

The biggest draws at the Théâtre de l'Est Parisien and the Théâtre de la Ville were Guy Rétoré's audience-involving version of Bertolt Brecht's *Saint Joan of the Stockyards* and Jean Mercure's traditional mounting of Albert Camus's *The Possessed.* As a sequel to *1789* Ariane Mnouchkine put on *1793,* dealing with a different facet of the French Revolution, at the Cartoucherie de Vincennes, alternating the two plays in the company's repertory.

There were no great discoveries in the commercial sector. Even Jean Anouilh's latest hit, *The Opera Director,* wearily covered old ground albeit with great skill. André Roussin's *The Slap,* featuring a music critic at odds with a performer who slaps his face, was nothing if not box-office material, while Eugène Ionesco's *Macbett* (so spelled to avoid confusion with Shakespeare's tragedy) was a comic treatment in minor vein of the theme of lust for power. Bernard Kops's semiautobiographical study of a frustrated author, *David It Is Growing Dark,* had its world premiere at Barsacq's Atelier. Among other English playwrights represented, the most outstanding production was Jorge Lavelli's sympathetic treatment of Pinter's *Old Times* with fine acting by Delphine Seyrig.

CENTRAL PRESS/PICTORIAL PARADE

Sir John Gielgud (left) as Sir Geoffrey Kendle and John Mills as Lawrence d'Orsay appear in a scene from Charles Wood's "Veterans," a widely acclaimed 1972 London production.

Switzerland, Germany, Austria, Belgium. In Switzerland Harry Buckwitz increased the stature of the Zürich Schauspielhaus with the world premiere of Rolf Hochhuth's first comedy, *The Midwife,* in which the titular character was not above taking the law into her own hands in a good cause. The play was staged simultaneously in a number of German-speaking theatres with varying degrees of success. Guest director Peter Gill from London's Royal Court had language troubles with *A Midsummer Night's Dream,* but Jerzy Jarocki of the Cracow Stary Theatre scored an artistic bull's-eye with his ingenious staging of Witold Gombrowicz's *The Wedding.* At the nearby small Neumarkt theatre Horst Zankl's new regime began well with a stylized rendering of Handke's *The Ride Across Lake Constance.* The main event in Basel was Dieter Forte's adaptation of *The White Devil,* while Jan Kacer's *Uncle Vanya* showed how close a Czechoslovakian director may come to penetrating the enigmas of the Russian soul.

In West Germany the year was marked by the arrival of new managers and directors and the shifting of well-known ones from one theatre to another. Ivan Nagel's regime at Hamburg produced many highlights: Wilfried Minks's *The Miser;* the inauguration of a new studio stage with several plays by the Englishman Howard Brenton; Hartmut Lange's *Trotsky in Coyoacán,* starring Karl Maria Schley; Gorki's *The Barbarians;* and *The Hypochondriacs,* a first play by Botho Strauss. At Boy Gobert's rival Thalia theatre, Minks's production of *Maria Stuart* was dominated by an outsize figure of Christ. At the Berlin Schiller Theater Heinz Lietzau's new regime opened with an opulent production of Heinrich von Kleist's *The Prince of Homburg,* in which the stage was again dominated, this time by Minks's outsize figure of an avenging angel. Peter Palitzsch's reign at Frankfurt began auspiciously, if horrifyingly, with the West German premiere of Edward Bond's *Lear,* and Hans Peter Doll's at Stuttgart with yet another Minks production, Sean O'Casey's *Cock-a-Doodle-Dandy,* and Alfred Kirchner's *Romeo and Juliet.*

The three-man directorate at Cologne (Geoffrey Reeves from London, Roberto Ciulli from Milan, and resident director Hansgünther Heyme) collapsed almost before it had begun to operate. Reeves turned the George S. Kaufman-Moss Hart *You Can't Take It With You* into a box-office success, but his new methods and those of his closest collaborators foundered on the conservative prejudices of some of the actors. At Darmstadt the Chilean Gaston Salvatore's *The Death of Büchner* disappointed the high hopes placed in him by the new management at the inauguration of the rebuilt City Theatre. Only in Bochum did a newcomer strike gold in his first effort: British director Peter Zadek received a warm welcome from his public (rather warmer than from the critics, however) with sold-out houses for his nostalgic evocation of Berlin in the 1920s in his and Tankred Dorst's musical version of Hans Fallada's *Little Man What Now?* Various productions brought to the fore the name of Franz Xaver Kroetz, a new socio-critical dramatist from Bavaria and a master of the chilling, horror-comic manner. The name of the late Ödön von Horvath also began to figure increasingly in repertories. The most-produced playwright in 1972 was Brecht, taking the lead from Shakespeare for the first time.

In West Berlin von Horvath's *Tales from the Vienna Woods* directed by Klaus Michael Grüber placed the Schaubühne unassailably at the forefront of West Germany's theatrical ensembles, a position that Peter Stein failed to usurp either with his painfully slow-moving, hypnotic version of *The Prince of Homburg* or with his unorthodox staging of the Soviet epic drama *An Optimistic Tragedy*. The final productions of outgoing Schiller Theater manager Boleslaw Barlog's 25th year failed to strike any signal critical or public response, and even the productions at Hansjörg Utzerath's Freie Volksbühne were run-of-the-mill affairs. Only in East Berlin did spirits revive at Benno Besson's Volksbühne and especially at the Deutsches Theater and the Berliner Ensemble. The replacement of Hanns Anselm Perten by Gerhard Wolfram at the Deutsches brought instant relief from an increasingly difficult situation and a succession of poor productions, Manfred Wekwerth's brilliantly conceived *Richard III* notwithstanding. Peter Hacks, too, was rehabilitated, with his election to the Arts Academy and two new productions of his plays, *Amphitryon* at the Deutsches and *Omphale* by the Berliner Ensemble.

Vanessa Redgrave stars as Polly Peachum in a London revival of "The Threepenny Opera."

CENTRAL PRESS/PICTORIAL PARADE

In Vienna major draws were Gerhard Klingenberg's stylish production of Arthur Schnitzler's psychological drama *Liebelei* at the Burgtheater's small stage, Peter Hall's foreign-language debut with Pinter's *Old Times,* and Jean-Paul Roussillon's with *The Lady from Maxim's,* also on the small stage.

In Brussels the season was illuminated by three world premieres: the stage version of Guillaume Apollinaire's *The Rotting Enchanter;* the Cuban Eduardo Manet's *The One-Eyed Man* at the Belgian National Theatre; and Dario Fo and Arturo Corso's *Mistero Buffo,* set to music, a near-profane popularization of the Passion of Christ at the Royal Opera's small stage.

Italy. The big event of 1972 was the return of Giorgio Strehler to the Milan Piccolo, which he had founded and run for nearly a quarter of a century until he walked out in 1969 in protest at the city fathers' broken promise of a new, larger, and better-equipped playhouse. In the light of new guarantees, he launched his new regime with a penetratingly new view of *King Lear* in which Cordelia and the Fool were played by the same actress. At the Valle in Rome the Giovani revived Diego Fabbri's *The Lying Woman* in a revised version that included Rossella Falk in a topless gown, and Luigi Pirandello's *Right You Are If You Think You Are.* Franco Enriquez took the reins of the Argentina or Rome City Theatre, and in Genoa Luigi Squarzina scored a double triumph with *Tonight We Improvise* and *Mother Courage.*

Eastern Europe. Heads continued to roll in a continuing crisis throughout the area. In Prague the Cinoherni Klub's creator Miroslav Vostry lost his post, while the Theatre Behind the Gate closed down following the dismissal of its founder, Otomar Krejca. In Bucharest Liviu Ciulei, brilliant head of the Bulandra City Theatre, was also dismissed, and the production of Nikolai Gogol's *The Government Inspector* by Lucian Pintilie at his theatre had to close. Nevertheless, the troupe won universal acclaim at the East Berlin Arts Festival for Pintilie's rollicking version of Ion Caragiale's *Carnival Tales* a week before the ax fell.

In Moscow Polish director Andrzej Wajda staged David Rabe's Vietnam drama *Sticks and Bones* in Russian at the Contemporary Theatre before going on to stage it in Polish in Cracow. A poetic drama by Evgeni Yevtushenko criticizing the American way of life was staged by Yuri Liubimov at the Taganka Theatre, where a guitar-playing Hamlet also attracted attention. At the Mossoviet Yuri Zavadsky staged a poetic drama about modern Armenia by A. Shagunian, while Evgeni Simonov staged another about Aleksandr Pushkin at the Vakhtangov. Highlights of the year in Poland were a collage of the works of Stanislaw I. Witkiewicz by Jozef Szajna, Ionesco's *Macbett* staged by Erwin Axer, and Janusz Warminski's exciting production of Wesker's *The Kitchen* at the Ateneum.

Scandinavia. All eyes were directed toward Stockholm, where more plays by Swedish authors saw the light of day than ever before. These included Kent Andersson's *Agnes* at the Scala, and at the City Theatre *Harriet and Gunnar,* a musical by Bengt Ernryd and Johan Bergenstråhle, who also directed a fabulous production of *Miss Julie* at Helsinki's Little Theatre at the same time. Ingmar Bergman threw new light on Ibsen's *The Wild Duck* at the Royal Dramatic by having most of the normally unseen off-stage business enacted on an apron in full view of the audience. Ralf Långbacka and Kalle Holmberg, both in Turku after abandoning the Finnish capital, enhanced their reputations with an impressive *King Lear* and Alexis Kivi's *The Seven Brothers.* The National Theatre in Helsinki celebrated the 100th anniversary of the Finnish theatre with a colourful musical version of Teuvo Pakkala's *The Log-Rollers.*

(OSSIA TRILLING)

U.S. and Canada. The man of the year in the American theatre was Joseph Papp (*see* BIOGRAPHY), founder and producer of the New York Shakespeare Festival. *Sticks and Bones,* David Rabe's bitter play about a returned Vietnam veteran, was originally produced at the Festival's downtown Public Theatre; in February it moved to Broadway and subsequently won an Antoinette Perry (Tony) Award as the best play of the season. *That Championship Season* by Jason Miller opened at the Public Theatre in May. An old-fashioned, well-made, wonderfully effective realistic drama, in which the reunion of a high-school basketball team in a small town in Pennsylvania becomes an image of America's moral corruption, it won the New York Drama Critics Circle Award as the best play of the season and moved to Broadway. A musical adaptation of Shakespeare's *Two Gentlemen of Verona,* adapted by John Guare and Mel Shapiro, with music by Galt MacDermot, was originally produced at the Festival's outdoor Delacorte Theatre in Central Park in the summer of 1971; it too transferred to Broadway and won both the Tony Award and the Drama Critics Circle Award as the best musical of the 1971–72 season. None of these three productions was farmed out to Broadway managements; they were reproduced for Broadway by Papp and the Shakespeare Festival.

Meanwhile, at the Public Theatre, Papp concentrated on new plays by American dramatists. During the season he offered, among others, *The Black Terror* by Richard Wesley (set in the future, and concerned with violent black revolution); *Older People* by John Ford Noonan; *The Hunter* by Murray Mednick; and two bills of one-act plays by black playwrights. The 1972 Shakespeare Festival summer season in Central Park featured an admirable *Hamlet,* directed by Gerald Freedman, with Stacy Keach as the Prince, James Earl Jones as Claudius, and Colleen Dewhurst as Gertrude, and a well-received *Much Ado About Nothing,* directed by A. J. Antoon and set in small-town America about the turn of the century. It subsequently followed Papp's other ventures to Broadway.

Joseph Papp's conquest of Broadway made it more clear than ever before that the main sources of theatrical energy and creativity in the U.S. had become the subsidized, noncommercial, professional theatres. The New York Shakespeare Festival was the most active such theatre in New York, but was by no means the only one. The Chelsea Theatre Center, which occupied premises at the Brooklyn Academy of Music, had its most successful season to date in 1971–72. Two Chelsea productions were later given regular off-Broadway runs: *Kaddish,* Allen Ginsberg's multimedia adaptation of his poem on the death of his mad mother, and Gene Lesser's blunt and bawdy staging of *The Beggar's Opera,* John Gay's 18th-century comical-satirical-musical classic.

The Repertory Theatre of Lincoln Center, on the other hand, had an unhappy season in 1971–72, although its revival of Arthur Miller's *The Crucible* was respectfully received. Downstairs in the Forum, its small second auditorium, the Repertory offered the first U.S. performances of *People Are Living There,* by the South African playwright Athol Fugard, and of Peter Handke's *The Ride Across Lake Constance;* the first was realistic and the second Absurdist, but neither was greeted with much warmth. The Forum production of *The Duplex* by Ed Bullins was notable for an angry public dispute between Bullins and the Repertory management. The last Forum production of 1971–72, however, was *Suggs,* an engaging comedy about the pains and terrors of life in New York by a promising young playwright named David Wiltse, with a fine central performance by William Atherton as an innocent in the "big city." The Repertory's 1972–73 season opened with the U.S. premiere of Gorki's *Enemies* on the main stage; and, in the Forum, a Beckett Festival, two bills of one-act plays by Samuel Beckett (including the world premiere of *Not I*) starring Hume Cronyn and Jessica Tandy. Meanwhile, Jules Irving, artistic director of the Repertory Theatre, resigned because his board of directors could not or would not raise enough money to mount further productions in the Forum after the closing of the Beckett Festival.

Three new professional noncommercial theatre companies appeared in New York in 1972. The City Center Acting Company, made up of the first graduating class of the Drama Division of the Juilliard School, with John Houseman as its artistic director, offered a season of six plays in repertory at a church near Lincoln Center. The plays, which varied widely in time and style, were the U.S. premiere of *Women Beware Women* by Thomas Middleton (17th-century, English), *The School for Scandal* by Richard Sheridan (18th-century, English), *The Lower Depths* by Gorki (1902, Russian), and two recent works: *U.S.A.,* adapted from John Dos Passos' novels by Paul Shyre, and *Next Time I'll Sing to You* by James Saunders. The New Phoenix Repertory Company—the third such group to appear in New York under the Phoenix management—presented O'Neill's *The Great God Brown* (directed by Harold Prince) and Molière's

FRIEDMAN-ABELES

In a dream sequence from the nostalgic musical "Grease," a 1972 Broadway production, Marya Small (foreground) envisions rock 'n' roll star Alan Paul (top) leading a roller-crowned choir in a number entitled "Beauty School Dropout."

MARTHA SWOPE

One of Broadway's favourite leading ladies, Gwen Verdon, portrays a babysitter whose charges, Ariane Munker (left), Shawn Campbell, and Johnny Doran, give her the shivers in the 1972 Jack Horrigan thriller "Children! Children!"

Don Juan (directed by Stephen Porter) at the Lyceum, a Broadway theatre. In Queens the Queens Playhouse opened its doors with a production of George Bernard Shaw's *Pygmalion.* And the Circle in the Square, long established off-Broadway, opened its new Broadway headquarters with O'Neill's *Mourning Becomes Electra,* starring Colleen Dewhurst.

A number of black theatres made their presence felt in New York, and two promising playwrights emerged from them. *The Sty of the Blind Pig* by Philip Hayes Dean was presented by the Negro Ensemble Company near the end of 1971, and *Don't Let It Go to Your Head* by J. E. Gaines, a presentation of the New Federal Theatre, opened at the Henry Street Playhouse early in 1972. The former was heavy and sombre, and the latter comic and melodramatic by turns; both were realistic accounts of black American lives. A different sort of racially oriented theatre group, the American Indian Theatre Ensemble, made its debut at the La Mama Experimental Theatre Club.

Noncommercial professional theatres were by no means confined to New York; dozens of them, some long established, continued to function in other cities. The Arena Stage, in Washington, D.C., was represented on Broadway by its production of *Moonchildren* by Michael Weller; the Arena also offered, for local audiences, the U.S premiere of *Uptight,* a quizzical play by the West German writer Günter Grass about the conflict between uneasy liberalism and revolutionary passion, and *The Foursome,* a realistic play about working-class sexuality by the British playwright E. A. Whitehead. The John F. Kennedy Center for the Performing Arts, also in Washington, functioned mainly as a stopping place for touring attractions; nevertheless, it managed to send three productions, all revivals, on to Broadway: *The Country Girl* by Clifford Odets (directed by John Houseman, with Maureen Stapleton, Jason Robards, Jr., and George Grizzard); *Lost in the Stars* (a musical play based on Alan Paton's novel *Cry, the Beloved Country,* with words by Maxwell Anderson and music by Kurt Weill); and *Captain Brassbound's Conversion* by Shaw (a star vehicle for Ingrid Bergman).

In Minneapolis the Tyrone Guthrie Theatre presented Sophocles' *Oedipus the King* in a new adaptation by Anthony Burgess, directed by Michael Langham, with Len Cariou in the title role. The Long Wharf Theatre in New Haven, Conn., offered the U.S. premiere of *The Contractor* by the British playwright David Storey, in November 1971, and the U.S. premiere of Storey's *The Changing Room* in November 1972. The Pittsburgh Playhouse gave the U.S. premiere of *Enter a Free Man* by Tom Stoppard.

Of the professional companies on university campuses, the most vigorous was the Yale Repertory Theatre in New Haven, which presented the U.S. premiere of *Happy End,* a musical play by Bertolt Brecht and Elisabeth Hauptmann, with music by Kurt Weill, and the world premiere of *Are You Now or Have You Ever Been,* Eric Bentley's documentary play dramatized from the records of the U.S. House Committee on Un-American Activities. A new management at Princeton's McCarter Theatre began its administration with two U.S. plays: the world premiere of *Agamemnon,* a rather literary verse play by Harvard University professor William Alfred, and the U.S. premiere of *The Tooth of Crime,* a play about a rock singer by 28-year-old Sam Shepard.

Meanwhile, Broadway continued to exist, but an air of deep malaise hung over it. The Broadway audience —deterred by crime in the streets or high ticket prices or changing habits—seemed to be shrinking. Caught between dwindling audiences and rising costs, producers found it increasingly difficult to turn a profit. Even productions with well-known names attached to them, plus highly favourable reviews, lost money. The most notable of these was *Old Times,* Pinter's elegant study of an ambiguous three-cornered relationship, which came to New York in November 1971, in a production under the auspices of the Royal Shakespeare Company of London. Peter Hall directed, and Rosemary Harris, Robert Shaw, and Mary Ure comprised the entire cast. Other imports from London included *Vivat! Vivat Regina!,* Robert Bolt's history play, with Eileen Atkins as Elizabeth I and Claire Bloom as Mary, queen of Scots, and *Butley* by Simon Gray, in which Alan Bates had a tremendous personal success as a vituperative teacher.

Aside from London imports and transfers from noncommercial theatres, Broadway had little to offer in 1972. At the end of the year there was a new Neil Simon comedy, *The Sunshine Boys.* And there were a few musicals. *Sugar,* based on Billy Wilder's movie *Some Like It Hot,* was mediocre but serviceable, sustained by the exuberant transvestite clowning of Robert Morse. There was a happy revival, imported from Los Angeles, of *A Funny Thing Happened on the Way to the Forum* with the indomitable Phil Silvers. The musical comedy success of the fall season was *Pippin,* an account of the imaginary travails of Charlemagne's son, staged with a great deal of razzmatazz by Bob Fosse.

A headline in *Variety,* the theatrical trade paper, summed up the off-Broadway season as "Punkeroo." There was a new play, transferred from an off-off-Broadway theatre, by the Spanish dramatist Fernando Arrabal, full of anguish and scatology, set in a prison in his native country, and titled *And They Put Handcuffs on the Flowers.* There was a larky double bill by Tom Stoppard, *After Magritte* and *The Real Inspector Hound;* the latter was a parody of a British mystery play, with two critics, seated out front, gradually getting caught up in the action. A new play by Tennessee Williams, titled *Small Craft Warnings* and set in a California bar, proved more successful than most of his recent work.

Off-Broadway presented several musicals, including two by Al Carmines, the amazingly prolific musical minister, transferred from his off-off-Broadway base at the Judson Memorial Church: *Wanted* (book by David Epstein), about some notable American outlaws, and *Joan* (book, lyrics, and music by Carmines), a highly unorthodox account of a modern Joan of Arc. *Grease,* a rock 'n' roll evocation of the 1950s, was so successful that it moved to Broadway, and *Don't Bother Me, I Can't Cope,* an all-black revue written by, and starring, Micki Grant, had a successful run at a "middle theatre," a middle-sized house that was neither Broadway nor off-Broadway. There was also an off-Broadway revue devoted to the songs of Kurt Weill and another devoted to the works of Noel Coward.

In Canada the theatre was swept by a vivifying wave of cultural nationalism. Small theatres, devoted almost exclusively to presenting new Canadian work, were functioning in cities from coast to coast. Among these theatres were Pier I (Halifax), Théâtre d'Aujourd'hui (Montreal), Toronto Free Theatre, Factory Theatre Lab (Toronto), Tarragon Theatre Ltd. (Toronto), Théâtre Passe Muraille (Toronto), Theatre Three (Edmonton), and The Savage God (Vancouver). Two notable plays came out of these theatres: *Creeps* by David Freeman, from the Factory Theatre Lab, about life among cerebral palsy victims, and *Leaving Home* by David French, from the Tarragon Theatre, about a family from Newfoundland living in Toronto.

A new summer festival, Festival Lennoxville at Bishop's University, Lennoxville, Que., came into existence with a policy of doing only Canadian plays—not new ones but Canadian plays that had already been produced and that deserved to be seen again. In its first season, it presented *The Ottawa Man* (Mavor Moore's canadianized adaptation of Gogol's *The Government Inspector*), *Captives of the Faceless Drummer* by George Ryga, and *Lulu Street* by Ann Henry. (JULIUS NOVICK)

See also Dance; Literature; Music.

ENCYCLOPÆDIA BRITANNICA FILMS. *The Cherry Orchard I—Chekhov: Innovator of Modern Drama* (1967); *The Cherry Orchard II—Comedy or Tragedy?* (1967); *A Doll's House I—The Destruction of Illusion* (1967); *A Doll's House II—Ibsen's Themes* (1967); *Shaw vs. Shakespeare Part I: The Character of Caesar, Part II: The Tragedy of Julius Caesar, Part III: Caesar and Cleopatra* (1970).

Timber

The world's forests continued to show a steady increase in yield in 1969, the latest year for which figures were available. Total output was estimated at 2,184,739,000 cu.m. of roundwood, compared with 2,149,775,000 cu.m. in 1968 and 1,908,872,000 cu.m. in 1960 (1 cu.m. = 35.31 cu.ft.). Of the 1969 total, 1,219,428,000 cu.m. were removed for industrial uses, the remainder being used for fuelwood, charcoal, and other domestic and nonindustrial purposes. Removals of coniferous (softwood) roundwood and broad-leaved (hardwood) roundwood were approximately equal in volume, but coniferous roundwood accounted for about 70% of the total removed for industrial use. The estimates were made by the UN Food and Agriculture Organization.

The total value of world production in 1969 was $48.4 billion, compared with $45.5 billion a year earlier. The value of processed wood (sawn wood, railway crossties, and boxboards) was $16.3 billion; pulp products (paper and paperboard) accounted for $20.7 billion; panel products (veneers, plywood, particle board, and fibreboard) for $6 billion; and all other wood products for $5.4 billion. Estimates were in terms of U.S. dollars based on constant 1960 prices.

Sawlogs for lumber and veneer accounted for more than one-third of all roundwood removals and for about three-fourths of removals for industrial purposes. Sawn wood (lumber) production in 1969 totaled 408,528,000 cu.m. (1 cu.m., lumber measure = 424 bd-ft.), about 80% of which was coniferous. Approximately 90% of coniferous sawn wood and nearly two-thirds of broad-leaved sawn wood came from the temperate regions of the Northern Hemisphere.

The U.S.S.R. ranked first among coniferous sawn wood producers in 1969, with a reported total of 95,490,000 cu.m. This slightly exceeded the combined total of 95,441,000 cu.m. for the U.S. and Canada. The U.S. ranked second among individual nations with 69,764,000 cu.m.; Japan was third with 32,450,000 cu.m.; and Canada ranked fourth with 25,677,000 cu.m. Sweden, with 11,405,000 cu.m., was fifth in the world and first among European nations.

The U.S. led in output of broad-leaved sawn wood, with 18,595,000 cu.m. in 1969. The U.S.S.R. was second with 16,850,000 cu.m.; Japan produced 9,107,000 cu.m.; and China's output was estimated at 5.2 million cu.m. Among regions, Asia was the largest producer, followed by North America, Europe, South America, the Pacific area, Africa, and Central America in that order.

Preliminary estimates of U.S. lumber production were available for 1971, based on information compiled by the National Forest Products Association. Total 1971 output was 36,639,000,000 bd-ft., including 30,283,000,000 bd-ft. of softwood lumber and 6,356,000,000 bd-ft. of hardwood lumber. The combined output was some 2,000,000,000 bd-ft. greater than the 1970 figure but still below the postwar high of 38,900,000,000 bd-ft. reached in 1950. In 1971 the U.S. exported 1,096,700,000 bd-ft. of lumber and imported 7,619,300 bd-ft. The wholesale price index of lumber in June 1972 was 159 (1967 = 100), 18.3%

THE NEW YORK TIMES

A seven-foot-thick Douglas fir log (in midair to left of cables) is lifted by a Sikorsky S-64E Skycrane. An innovation in logging, the huge helicopter makes remote timber accessible and eliminates the need for road building and clear-cutting.

Theology: *see* Religion

above a year earlier. U.S. timber production was slowed somewhat in 1972 by a temporary injunction against cutting on certain national forest lands considered to have possible value for designation as wilderness areas. The injunction resulted from a suit filed by the Sierra Club, a conservationist organization. The U.S. Forest Service, meanwhile, adopted a new program for "national forest management in a quality environment," which included restrictions on clear-cutting in certain types of forest.

Canadian lumber production in 1969 was reported at 11,573,900,000 bd-ft., a gain over the 11,343,700,000 bd-ft. (revised figure) of 1968. About 95% of the total was softwood lumber and approximately two-thirds was exported.

World production of wood pulp continued to increase steadily, rising to 98,050,000 metric tons in 1969, compared with the revised estimate of 91.4 million tons in 1968. Chemical (including semichemical) pulp accounted for about 70% of world output, the remainder being mechanical or groundwood pulp used mainly for newsprint. North America accounted for more than half of the 1969 wood-pulp total. Among European producers, Sweden led with 7.6 million tons.

World particle board production in 1969 totaled 16,089,000 cu.m., compared with 13,690,000 cu.m. in 1968. The 1968 figure represented an increase of more than 200% over 1960. Europe continued to account for more than half of the total, with West Germany the leading producer. The U.S. produced 3,017,500 cu.m., a substantial increase over 1968, and the U.S.S.R. ranked third with 1,722,800 cu.m. Production in the U.S. had risen sixfold from 1958 to 1966, while Canada had increased its production by nearly 40% between 1965 and 1968.

(CHARLES EDGAR RANDALL)

See also Environment; Industrial Review.

ENCYCLOPÆDIA BRITANNICA FILMS. *Trees and Their Importance* (1966); *Science Conserves Forests* (1967); *The Coniferous Forest Biome* (1969); *Problems of Conservation—Forest and Range* (1969); *Problems of Conservation—Our Natural Resources* (1970).

Tobacco

World tobacco production in 1971 was estimated at about 10,000,000,000 lb., a drop of 1% from the previous year's figure but still 12% above the 1960–64 average. During the year, production of flue-cured and Oriental tobacco remained approximately at the 1970 levels, but that of the Burley type went up by about 5% as increases in Italy, South Korea, Malawi, and some South American countries more than compensated for a decline in the United States.

Among the major producing countries, output in the U.S. declined 6% to 1,790,000,000 lb., close to the very low level of 1968. The area harvested in the U.S. fell by 5%, and yields were slightly lower than in the previous year. In Canada a record yield of flue-cured leaf in Ontario offset an overall decline in the area harvested, resulting in a relatively unchanged total production. Both the area under cultivation and the size of the crop increased in India in 1971, although production of flue-cured leaf declined as a result of bad weather. In Africa there was another strong increase in production in Malawi, particularly of Burley and flue-cured leaf, while in Zambia there was a partial recovery in the output of the flue-cured variety.

In recent years world tobacco production had exceeded consumption requirements, resulting in a buildup of large stock reserves. This situation caused considerable concern in some areas, forcing governments to introduce policies aimed at adjusting to current demands and international trade. The volume of world trade in tobacco was relatively steady, although significant shifts had occurred in recent years. For example, the continuing sanctions against trade with Rhodesia encouraged many countries to expand their own production, both for domestic use and for export. Also, the effect on world trade patterns of the EEC's common agricultural policy for tobacco, adopted in 1970, was already becoming apparent. The policy provided a 30% subsidy per pound for the purchase of Italian Burley. With no production controls and with the guarantee of a high support price, Italian farmers brought their Burley production up by 17 million lb. in 1971 to 70 million lb. Faced with this competition, Greek exports to the EEC suffered and Greece abandoned plans to expand Burley production. There were similar increases in production in other EEC countries, almost certainly a foretaste of future developments. Of course, other countries also protected their producers, including developed countries like the U.S. where support prices rose in 1971.

World trade in tobacco during 1971 was probably greater than in 1970 in spite of difficulties caused by the U.S. dock strikes. The U.S. was still the principal tobacco exporter, but with competing countries able to undercut on prices its share of total world trade was falling. Its 32% share of the export market in 1969 had declined to 25% in 1971. Among other major tobacco-exporting countries in the non-Communist world, India, Canada, Turkey, and the Philippines all increased their shipments. Total exports of unmanufactured tobacco in the non-Communist world went up by 3% in 1971 to 1,660,000,000 lb. Western Europe, the U.S., and Japan took 85% of the total imports.

World consumption of cigarettes by unofficial estimates increased 3% during 1971, most of the gain coming from the less developed countries. With the growth of world population and of incomes, and the increase in cigarette smoking among young people, it was a trend that seemed likely to continue. In the U.S., despite the health warnings on cigarette packs, cigarette purchases increased by 4%. In Britain, on the other hand, there was a 10% drop in cigarette smoking following the publication of a report on smoking and health by the Royal College of Physicians early in 1971; by the end of the year, however, over half of this loss had been recovered. The report gave a tremendous boost to cigar sales, which rose from 975 million pieces in 1970 to 1,360,000,000 in 1971, and also accounted for a 3% increase in pipe-tobacco sales.

The development of tobacco substitutes continued to preoccupy industry scientists, but it was proving a long, slow job. In Britain the Imperial Tobacco Group, working jointly with Imperial Chemical Industries, estimated that it would possibly be four or five years before their new smoking material, a cellulose-based substance, would be ready to market. Once this stage was reached, however, the product would be offered to all tobacco companies and the process would be available under license. In the U.S. the Celanese Corporation was reported to be well advanced with its synthetic substitute, and in West Germany similar experiments were being conducted by the Bayer group.

Tin: *see* Mining
Titanium: *see* Mining

A joint development of a West German company, Siebe Gorman Holdings, and British American Tobacco was concentrating on the application of charcoal cloth material to cigarette filters. The cloth was originally developed as a filter for military respirators.
(VIVIAN RAVEN)

Togo

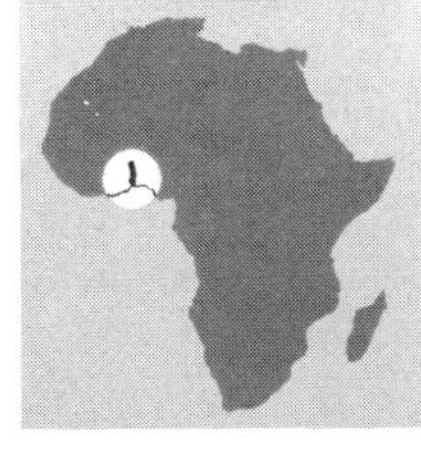

A West African republic, Togo is bordered by Ghana, Upper Volta, and Dahomey. Area: 21,900 sq.mi. (56,600 sq.km.). Pop. (1972 est.): 1,960,000. Cap. and largest city: Lomé (pop., 1970, 148,443). Language: French (official). Religion: animist; Muslim and Christian minorities. President in 1972, Gen. Étienne Eyadema.

In a referendum on Jan. 9, 1972, Gen. Étienne Eyadema was confirmed in his role as president by a total of 867,941 votes out of 868,819 votes cast. A government reshuffle took place a few days later. In December the Central Committee of the ruling Rassemblement du Peuple Togolais decided that the country's labour unions should be reformed into a single union.

During the year the president directed his attention almost exclusively to strengthening cooperation between Togo and France. In February Franco-Togolese military exercises were carried out in the northern part of the country, and in May the French secretary-general for African and Malagasy affairs, Jacques Foccart, paid an official visit to Togo. This was followed in September by a visit from Pierre Billecocq, the French secretary-general for foreign affairs with special responsibility for cooperation.

Finally, in November French Pres. Georges Pompidou visited Togo. During the discussions that took place General Eyadema's demand for a revaluation of the CFA franc received a somewhat dusty answer from the French president. Nevertheless, a cordial atmosphere prevailed and the rapturous welcome given to President Pompidou by the Togolese contrasted favourably with the distinctly cooler reception that he had received in Upper Volta earlier the same week.

In April the conference of heads of state of the Common Organization of Africa, Malagasy, and Mauritius (OCAM) took place in Lomé. The main events of the conference were the appointment of Pres. Léopold S. Senghor of Senegal as president and the withdrawal of Zaire.
(PHILIPPE DECRAENE)

TOGO

Education. (1969–70) Primary, pupils 206,283, teachers 3,689; secondary, pupils 16,688, teachers 556; vocational, pupils 2,072, teachers 157; teacher training, students 119, teachers 13; higher, students 263, teaching staff 21.

Finance. Monetary unit: CFA franc, with (Sept. 18, 1972) a parity of CFA Fr. 50 to the French franc (CFA Fr. 255.79 = U.S. $1; free rate of CFA Fr. 612.37 = £1 sterling). Budget (1971 est.) balanced at CFA Fr. 10 billion.

Foreign Trade. (1971) Imports CFA Fr. 19,455,000,000; exports CFA Fr. 13,626,000,000. Import sources: France 34%; U.K. 12%; West Germany 9%; Netherlands 6%; U.S. 5%; Japan 5%. Export destinations: France 31%; Netherlands 26%; West Germany 13%; U.S.S.R. 10%; Belgium-Luxembourg 6%. Main exports: phosphates 35%; cocoa 31%; coffee 18%.

Tonga

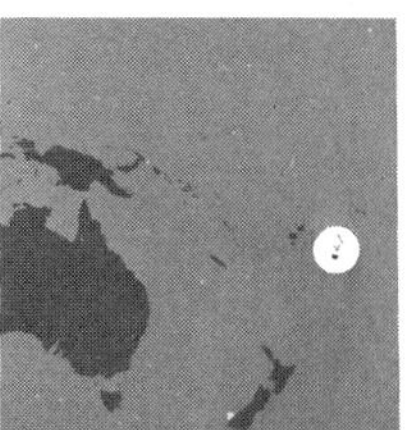

An independent monarchy and member of the Commonwealth of Nations, Tonga is an island group in the Pacific Ocean east of Fiji. Area: 225 sq.mi. (582 sq.km.). Pop. (1972 est.): 90,000. Cap.: Nukualofa (pop., 1972 est., 20,000). Language: English and Tongan. Religion: Christian. King, Taufa'ahau Tupou IV; prime minister in 1972, Prince Tu'ipelehake.

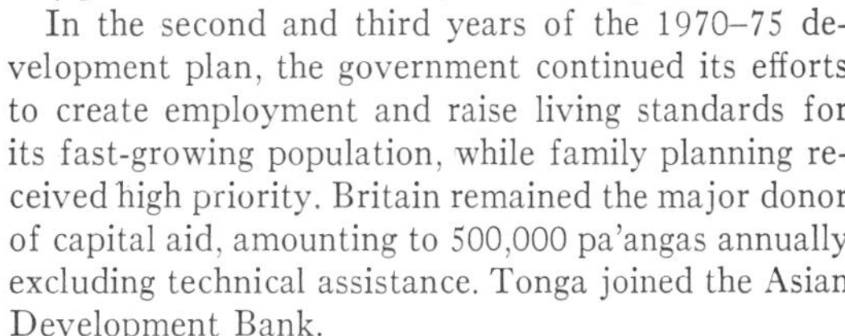

In the second and third years of the 1970–75 development plan, the government continued its efforts to create employment and raise living standards for its fast-growing population, while family planning received high priority. Britain remained the major donor of capital aid, amounting to 500,000 pa'angas annually excluding technical assistance. Tonga joined the Asian Development Bank.

The government's program of controlled tourist development offered the greatest potential for employment and foreign exchange. Fua'amotu airport was improved to medium jet standard, and a new airstrip and international hotel were opened on Vava'u. Trade preferences were to be extended to Tonga by the EEC from Jan. 1, 1973. Tonga's minister of finance, Mahe Tupouniua, became the first director of the South Pacific Bureau for Economic Cooperation.

Seven nobels' and seven peoples' representatives were elected for three-year terms in the Legislative Assembly, one of each for the first time. In June the king raised Tonga's flag on two small, artificial islands built on the Minerva reef to forestall the U.S. Ocean Life Research Foundation's plan for a sea city and tax haven republic.
(MARY BOYD)

TONGA

Education. (1970) Primary, pupils 17,826, teachers 658; secondary (1968), pupils 9,421, teachers (1967) 358; teacher training, students 102, teachers 6.

Finance and Trade. Monetary unit: pa'anga, with a free rate (Sept. 18, 1972) of 0.85 pa'anga to U.S. $1 (2.09 pa'angas = £1 sterling). Budget (1971–72 est.): revenue 3,002,000 pa'angas; expenditure 3,218,000 pa'angas. Foreign trade (1971): imports 6,305,000 pa'angas; exports 2.2 million pa'angas. Import sources: New Zealand 37%; Australia 26%; Fiji 12%; U.K. 12%; Japan 6%. Export destinations: New Zealand 35%; Netherlands 16%; West Germany 11%; U.K. 10%; Sweden 7%; Norway 6%; Australia 6%. Main exports: copra 50%; bananas 17%; desiccated coconut 14%.

Tourism

International travel grew in 1971 even in the face of economic difficulties. This proved to be the case when definitive 1971 statistics of international tourism were published in 1972. International tourist arrivals reached 181 million, up 7% from 1970, while the growth of receipts to more than $20 billion was considerably higher at 14%. A salient feature of 1971 had been the 20% growth of tourism in the Middle East, where effective promotion and new hotel developments combined with a relatively more stable political climate to bring rapid results. Europe recorded an 8% consolidated increase in arrivals, but there were many variations among countries.

In Italy, hotel arrivals reached a total of 10.5 million, an increase of only 1.1%. A shortage of foreign labour in accommodation establishments was

Tornadoes: *see* Disasters; Meteorology

AUTHENTICATED NEWS INTERNATIONAL

Boeing Aircraft is offering a new luxury option to airline companies that own or plan to buy Boeing's giant 747: a spacious 42-ft.-long "downstairs room," which is designed in place of the forward cargo compartment.

credited for Switzerland's sluggish increase of 1.2% for a total of 6.9 million arrivals. However, other European countries rode a tourist boom. Spain recorded 26.8 million arrivals in 1971, an increase of 23%, and receipts topped $2 billion for the first time in that country's dynamic tourist history. France received 14.7 million tourists, 7% more than in the previous year, and earned $1,450,000,000. One of the highest growth rates, more than 30%, was recorded by Greece, with over 2 million tourists, and Israel hosted over 47% more travelers, 617,000.

Africa experienced a strong growth in international tourist arrivals. Tunisia was visited by 608,000 tourists, a 48% increase, while Kenya's tourism grew 20% to reach 410,000. International tourist arrivals in the Americas, however, had an average growth of only 4–5%, while, after the success of Japan's Expo 70, the Pacific region experienced a net zero trend. International tourism in the South Asia region, notably in India and Pakistan, declined in 1971, a fact related to the social and political events that troubled the subcontinent at the close of that year.

Under the influence of the floating U.S. dollar, international tourist receipts (in dollar terms) drifted upward in the third and final quarters of 1971, and were at record levels in many countries. Overall, the experts noted, tourism had performed well in 1971, despite uncertainty in economic conditions generally, again demonstrating its ability to withstand perturbations in the economic climate.

Tourism in 1972. During the first part of 1972 international tourism appeared to grow even faster than in the corresponding period of 1971. Statistics for the early months pointed to another highly successful year. In spite of persisting high unemployment in some countries, the general business outlook was optimistic and consumer spending buoyant. Such conditions favoured the renewed growth of international tourism, and experts predicted that 200 million arrivals would be reached before 1975. Particularly encouraging for the travel trade was the absence of any foreign exchange restrictions which, in another era, might have accompanied the Smithsonian parity agreements reached at the close of 1971.

The year, however, was not without its upsets. As a result of the British government's decision to float the pound sterling, many British tourists abroad found that the pound in their pocket went less far than anticipated, while others, perhaps more fortunate, were politely requested to pay a supplement on the package tour price when they returned home. Significantly, such measures showed little sign of adversely affecting international travel. United States foreign travel, with the dollar buying up to 13% less abroad than during 1971, was reported going strong with departures in the first half of 1972 up 25% over the corresponding period of the previous year.

In the first six months of 1972, arrivals were up 15% in Spain, 11% in the United Kingdom, 42% in Tunisia, 23% in Hong Kong, 28% in Greece, 10% in Italy, 10% in West Germany, 15% in Japan (host to the Winter Olympics in February), and only 5% in Switzerland. Worried hotel proprietors in Switzerland petitioned the federal government for exemption from stringent quota restrictions on foreign labour, and hotels and restaurants adopted the "tip included" basis of pricing. France also appeared to make a good start in the early months of 1972, as did islands from Sri Lanka (Ceylon) to the Seychelles and from Cyprus to the Caribbean. In the U.S. arrivals were up 7.5%, and in Canada arrivals of overseas visitors were double those recorded in the same period of the previous year.

The private automobile remained dominant as the means of transportation for tourists. Considerable expenditure on car ferries, motels, and expressways was planned to accommodate the anticipated future growth of automobile tourism. The volume and share of tourist travel accounted for by airlines sustained a steady increase. Cruise shipping and ferry operations continued to replace regular passenger shipping services in terms of importance for sea journeys, while the general fall in international tourist travel by rail appeared to level off in 1971–72. In the U.S., the establishment of Amtrak marked official determination to preserve and reorganize rail passenger services, and in Europe the enlargement of the EEC scheduled for 1973 would, it appeared, be marked by the beginning of work, at last, on a rail tunnel linking the U.K. and France.

With passenger traffic on International Civil Aviation Organization (ICAO) members' scheduled services only up 4.2% in 1971 over 1970 (excluding the U.S.S.R. and China), airlines faced the lowest level of growth since 1958. Technological improvements, such as "jumbos" and wider-bodied jets, were no longer sufficient to offset continuing low levels of profitability, reduced traffic growth rates, unsatisfactory load factors, and increased unit costs, and the International Air Transport Association (IATA) claimed revenue yields had decreased by an average of 12% over the past ten years. A dialogue developed with the international travel trade on the subject of air fares. Travel research circles were at pains to observe that higher air fares could have adverse consequences for longer-distance travel, as well as delaying the achievement of a truly "mass" air travel market, particularly in Europe, where the great majority

International Tourist Arrivals and Receipts

Region	Arrivals 1970	Arrivals 1971*	Percent change
Africa	2,275,000	2,640,000	+16%
Americas	32,400,000	33,700,000	+ 4%
Europe	126,235,000	136,300,000	+ 8%
Middle East	2,815,000	3,400,000	+21%
Pacific and East Asia	4,435,000	4,430,000	0%
South Asia	850,000	910,000	+ 7%
Total arrivals	169,000,000	181,000,000	+ 7%
Total receipts	$17,900,000,000	$20,400,000,000	+14%

*Estimated.

Source: International Union of Official Travel Organizations, Geneva.

of travelers continued to travel quite close to home. But mass long-distance travel could not be realized unless and until the airline industry was in a state of financial health.

In its *Pilot Study on Long Term Forecasts* (published in 1972) the International Union of Official Travel Organizations (IUOTO) and its specialist forecast team estimated that by 1980 the less developed world would increase its share of world tourist arrivals from the 9% of 1970 to about 13%, an absolute increase of 17 million arrivals and a more than doubling of volume over ten years. For this to be realized it was important that air travel be made available on the most economic basis possible. Practical steps that might increase future profitability included the spreading of seasonal loads through government action to encourage holidays throughout the year, and the "instant" fares pioneered in 1972 by British European Airways (BEA), to attract discretionary traffic at off-peak hours by offering round-trip fares at no more than the one-way price. Some circles criticized the high level of airline advertising aimed at promoting "image," maintaining that it would be more useful to promote "destination" and thus share the cost with tour operators, hotel proprietors, and local tourist offices.

Pricing policy appeared to be the hallmark of the success of the nonscheduled airlines, whose traffic was reported by the ICAO to be increasing at a rate of about 26% annually. The latter part of 1972 saw many airlines settling down to examine the future, encouraged, perhaps, by an upturn of 31% in North Atlantic traffic in the early months. At the same time, IATA's director general put forward a six-point program aimed to promote the orderly and planned development of tourism and air transport, taking account of the "public service" obligations of the airlines, and setting out clearly the responsibility of governments in this field.

The boom in overseas tourism experienced by the United Kingdom over recent years was not without its troubles. Overseas visits reached seven million in 1971, with earnings (mainly from the U.S.) of $1,195,000,000. With this volume of travelers, concentrated in the summer months, some observers wondered whether London might not suffocate under the sudden stampede of overseas tourists. Others observed that the new "mass" tourism was nothing but an illusion created by growth in the general level of the population.

For the president of the London Tourist Board it was "necessary that the tourist butter be spread more evenly." Some even wanted to make foreign tourists pay, via a hotel supplement, for museums and other sights. Pointing out that if prices and taxes were too high tourists would go elsewhere, the British Tourist Authority (BTA) produced comforting statistics to show that although eight out of ten visitors to Britain saw London, the trend was for more and more people to travel outside the capital. Visits to London were declining, but visits to Britain were growing, and there was a real possibility of regions getting a fairer share of tourist earnings, with consequent benefits for employment. The BTA stated that no one should be unwise enough to scare away the foreign tourist by talk of taxes and other retrograde measures. As if to underline the sensitivity of international tourism to adverse publicity, foreign arrivals in the U.K. in the peak summer month, July, were reported down 1% from 1971, with U.S. visitor arrivals down even more strongly, by 9%. The BTA's seasonally adjusted figures also suggested the possibility of some slowing down in the generally upward trend of tourist arrivals experienced by the U.K. in recent years.

Although tourism in Ireland was depressed in 1972 by civil disturbances in the North, the industry was highly satisfied with the achievements of the 1960s. The Irish Tourist Board (Bord Failte Eireann) reported that every $100 of foreign earnings produced, after deduction of imports, a net benefit of about $54 that could be employed to finance the additional imports required for economic development.

Tourism's central role in world invisible trade was underlined by another study carried out in 1972 by IUOTO, showing a very high correlation (exceeding 99%) between the development of exports and tourism receipts during 1960–70. International tourist receipts had grown by an average 10% annually, justifying the claim of travel circles that the industry had become a front-runner of world trade.

Following the UN Conference on the Human Environment held in June 1972 came an antipollution initiative that had tourism very much at heart: the world operation "Message in the Sea," launched in Panama City in December. More than 100,000 floating messages were immersed in the Atlantic and the Pacific on either side of Panama City. The operation, sponsored by the 109 members of IUOTO and by various scientific bodies, aimed to demonstrate the ubiquity of marine pollution, its adverse consequences for tourism, and the interdependence of nations faced with this growing menace to seas and beaches. "Message in the Sea" also hoped to perfect scientists' understanding of ocean currents. The operation was proclaimed as the closing feature of the 1972 "Tourism Year of the Americas," a regional initiative to make the values and cultures of the Western Hemisphere better known throughout the world. In the struggle to foster and preserve environmental values, recalled the operation's director, tourism would be one of the chief beneficiaries.

Organization. During 1972 further progress was made in setting up the new intergovernmental World Tourism Organization (WTO) to succeed IUOTO. By October, 33 nations had formally approved the statutes of the new body, and in other countries the process of ratification was in its final phase. With 51 ratifications required for WTO to come into existence, the inauguration of the organization was anticipated for 1974.

The role of international tourism as a catalyst for economic development was endorsed by the third session of the United Nations Conference on Trade

Geodesic beach houses line the Red Sea beach at Nahama Bay in the Sharm el-Sheikh area of the Sinai Peninsula. The beach house development was intended to meet the demands of Israel's rapidly expanding tourist boom.

KEYSTONE

and Development (UNCTAD) in Santiago, Chile, in April–May 1972. Nevertheless, the bulk of the receipts from international tourism were still earned by the wealthier of the developed countries, the share of all less developed countries having been estimated at 20%.

UNCTAD recognized that widespread access to travel for all segments of the population could contribute to raising standards of living and promoting real awareness of obstacles to economic development. Those states whose national tourism organizations were members of IUOTO were invited to make an early decision on ratifying the WTO statutes so that the new organization "may contribute effectively to the development of tourism in general, and its rapid growth in developing countries in particular."

During the year a number of organizations turned their attention to improving the quality and availability of the statistics of international tourism. Such figures were indispensable for planning and research. A set of Guidelines for Tourism Statistics, prepared in collaboration with IUOTO and the International Monetary Fund, were endorsed by UNCTAD, and in Europe the subject received special attention from a meeting on travel statistics convened in March by the UN Economic Commission for Europe in cooperation with IUOTO's secretariat. A program for standardizing, improving, and extending national statistics was drawn up and subsequently approved by the 20th plenary session of the Conference of European Statisticians, meeting in Geneva in June.

A report of the European Travel Commission, a research body representing 22 Western European countries, stressed that much more could and should be done to improve travel statistics in Europe. More international cooperation was essential, and sampling methods should be more extensively adopted. This needed to be combined with more intelligent and competent interpretation of statistics in planning and forecasting.

The secretary-general of IUOTO had in 1971 appointed an expert on travel statistics to carry out an operational mission to nine African countries. There, he studied methods of collection currently employed and made proposals, in collaboration with the responsible authorities, for improving existing techniques. The expert was able to formulate concrete proposals for increasing cooperation between the different sectors responsible for the collection and publication of tourism statistics.

In anticipation of its future responsibilities as the World Tourism Organization, IUOTO continued to develop its regional representation. Three new regional secretariats (in Lagos, Nig., for Africa; in Cairo for the Middle East; and in Colombo, Sri Lanka [Ceylon], for the South Asian region) opened in October. They complemented the general secretariat in Geneva and the regional office already in operation for the Americas in Lima, Peru. Simultaneously, IUOTO embarked on work for major tourism development studies that would embrace East and West Africa, South Asia, the Mediterranean basin, and the Baltic. The research, to be completed in late 1973, aimed at drawing up an inventory of tourist attractions in each subregion, followed by a market demand forecast. The national tourist offices of the areas concerned were called upon to draw up programs of action to meet the foreseeable developments in tourist travel.

(PETER SHACKLEFORD)

See also Transportation.

Toys and Games

Whatever the reasons—economic inflation, depression, greater public discernment, a lack of production creativity—1972 was marked by caution in toy manufacturing and buying habits on a fairly worldwide scale. Nonetheless, in the two biggest markets, U.S. toy, game, and decoration manufacturers sold $2,351,000,000 of merchandise in 1971 (4.1% over the previous year), and British manufacturers dispatched £94 million worth of goods; sales were expected to be even greater in 1972 and possibly more profitable.

The caution was demonstrated in the switch to staple items, the reliance on old favourites. Among surprise best-selling toys in the U.S. and Britain was the boy's doll GI Joe (called Action Man in Britain)—no more a new toy than was Mattel's Barbie doll, which also did well. Wheeled metal pedal toys and plastic sit-'n'-ride toys, model cars, model kits, bicycles—the substantial toys where value for money was more discernible in the buyer's eye—these were the year's best sellers in 1972. There was a touch of "pandamania" when U.S. Pres. Richard Nixon visited China, a strong move toward chess sets spurred by the Bobby Fischer-Boris Spassky championship, and renewed interest in backgammon, but these also were traditional articles.

Plastic model kits, always good value for money, were extraordinarily successful worldwide. The U.S. kit market alone was valued at $230 million by the Hobby Industry Association of America, and U.S., British, Italian, and Japanese companies had strong home demands accompanied by valuable export markets. Airfix, Britain's leading kit maker, was not only one of the most successful British toy companies, but also one of the most profitable.

The demand for kits also meant a resurgence of war toys, for invariably kit subjects were warships, aircraft, and tanks, and associated with them, especially in Britain, tiny model infantrymen of historic regiments that thousands of enthusiasts painstakingly painted in the original uniform colours and deployed in reconstructed famous battles. So far the call to "ban all war toys" had not been taken up by mothers' consumer groups, perhaps because of a realization that it is the detail of military equipment that children appreciate, not necessarily the violence associated with them.

The trend toward the staple toy was also reflected in the lack of success of television-promoted toys; the public became disenchanted with their value, and retailers equally so by the nontoy shops that buy in the promoted lines at highly favourable quantity prices to sell at "sale" levels over the Christmas selling period only. Activities like this, and the increase in mail-order buying by the public, led to a steady decline in the number of specialist toy shops.

Some supermarket groups found Christmas toy sales so profitable that permanent supermarket toy departments were not now uncommon. Indeed, toy manufacturers almost wholly lost their inhibitions about selling to nontoy outlets.

A measure of this return to old favourites could further be gauged by a resurgence of merchandising Walt Disney characters throughout the world. The only other character line heavily merchandised in 1972 was the Sesame Street Gang from the preschool television series, now popular even in Eastern Europe.

FOX PHOTOS/PICTORIAL PARADE

Penny-farthing bicycles for children were successfully introduced into the 1972 U.S. and U.K. toy markets.

Undoubtedly 1972 was a welcome year of stability for many toy manufacturers, a time to cut back on stocks and replan growth. Growth was anticipated in the enlarged EEC, not necessarily so much for the major European companies which had long maintained high exports within the EEC but for manufacturers in the smaller, expanding "toy" countries. Meanwhile, U.S. firms continued buying European toy companies and opening up subsidiaries.

Nontoy groups also showed a passing interest in the European toy market. The title, often self-bestowed, of Europe's largest toy company was held for a few months of 1972 by a relative newcomer. The situation had its roots in the Lines Bros. collapse of 1971. The Barclay Toy Group, an offshoot of Barclay Securities, one of Britain's most successful finance companies, first built up a moderately strong interest in toys by acquiring the internationally known makers of Mobo and Chad Valley toys and then became Europe's largest firm by purchasing Tri-Ang Pedigree, the major part of Lines Bros. Barely had the announcement gone out that they were ready to expand into Europe than the acquired factories were either sold to other companies or for redevelopment, thousands of employees were laid off, and the Barclay Toy Group operation atrophied.

Toy safety legislation remained an area of activity during the year. The U.S. Food and Drug Administration announced in June that it was recalling more than 200,000 toys banned as hazardous to children. They included toys with parts that could slice, puncture, and be swallowed or inhaled, such as toy lawnmowers, rattles, musical balls, and musical typewriters.

In November the Chicago City Council banned the sale or possession for sale of toys with toxic paint, sharp edges, parts small enough to be swallowed, and with heat or electrical hazards. It also outlawed toys that are too noisy. The Chicago ordinance was believed to be the first such action taken by a municipality and, according to its sponsor, was stricter than existing federal legislation. (DAVID R. JAMES)

Track and Field Sports

The 1972 Olympic Games, held in Munich, W.Ger., produced only two new men's world records on the track, one in the decathlon, and none in the field events, an indication, perhaps, that track and field athletics for men had become highly developed. Women's competition yielded more records.

Finland's middle-distance supremacy of the 1920s and 1930s was reestablished. The U.S.'s dominance in sprinting was upset by the Ukrainian Valery Borzov and its 76-year Olympic monopoly of the pole vault was ended. East Germany demonstrated how a nation of only 17 million could, through the exercise of a state priority, produce an outstanding team within seven years.

International Competition. One of the most significant developments was the demonstration by Lasse Viren of Finland (*see* BIOGRAPHY) that victories in middle distances would not depend on maintaining a fast, level pace but on a prolonged surge many laps from home. Thus, in his Olympic 5,000 m., Viren ran the last mile in 4 min. 01.2 sec., faster than the world mile record up to Roger Bannister's famous run of 1954. In his world record Olympic 10,000 m., Viren's last two laps were negotiated in 1 min. 56.4 sec. despite his fall just before the halfway mark.

Africa, which had produced its first gold-medal winner in the Ethiopian marathon runner Abebe Bikila in 1960, showed that the gap between its best performers and those of Europe and North America had closed, albeit to some extent through the agency of European and American coaches. John Akii-Bua (Uganda) removed three-tenths of a second from the 400-m. hurdle world record set in the highly advantageous altitude of Mexico City in 1968. Other gold-medal winners from Africa included Kipchoge Keino of Kenya in the 3,000-m. steeplechase, and the Kenyan team in the 1,600-m. relay. After three straight victories in the marathon, however, the Africans yielded to Frank Shorter of the U.S.

The year saw 18 ft. bettered by six pole vaulters,

Table I. World 1972 Outdoor Records—Men

Event	Competitor, country, date	Performance
100 m.	Eddie Hart, U.S., July 1	9.9 sec.*
	Rey Robinson, U.S., July 1	9.9 sec.*
800 m.	Dave Wottle, U.S., July 1	1 min. 44.3 sec.*
3,000 m.	Emiel Puttemans, Belgium, September 14	7 min. 37.6 sec.
2 mi.	Lasse Viren, Finland, August 14	8 min. 14.0 sec.
3 mi.	Emiel Puttemans, Belgium, September 20	12 min. 47.6 sec.
5,000 m.	Lasse Viren, Finland, September 14	13 min. 16.4 sec.
	Emiel Puttemans, Belgium, September 20	13 min. 13.0 sec.
10,000 m.	Lasse Viren, Finland, September 3	27 min. 38.4 sec.
10 mi.	Willy Polleunis, Belgium, September 20	46 min. 4.2 sec.
20,000 m.	Gaston Roelants, Belgium, September 20	57 min. 44.4 sec.
One hour	Gaston Roelants, Belgium, September 20	12 mi. 1,610 yd.
110-m. hurdles	Rod Milburn, U.S., September 7	13.2 sec.*
400-m. hurdles	John Akii-Bua, Uganda, September 2	47.8 sec.
3,000-m. steeplechase	Anders Gaerderud, Sweden, September 14	8 min. 20.8 sec.
400-m. relay	United States, September 10	38.2 sec.*
4-mi. relay	New Zealand, February 3	16 min. 2.8 sec.
Pole vault	Bob Seagren, U.S., July 2	18 ft. 5¾ in.
Discus	Rickard Bruch, Sweden, September 10	225 ft.
Javelin	Janis Lusis, U.S.S.R., July 6	307 ft. 8¾ in.
Decathlon	Nikolai Avilov, U.S.S.R., September 7–8	8,454 pt.

*Ties record.

In the triple jump, Viktor Saneyev (U.S.S.R.) recorded 17.44 m. (57 ft. 2¾ in.) in Sukhumi, U.S.S.R., on October 18, but this was not in competition.

Table II. World 1972 Outdoor Records—Women

Event	Competitor, country, date	Performance
100 m.	Renate Stecher, East Germany, June 3	11.0 sec.*
	Ellen Stropahl, East Germany, June 15	11.0 sec.*
	Eva Gleskova, Czechoslovakia, July 1	11.0 sec.*
	Renate Stecher, East Germany, August 20	11.0 sec.*
200 m.	Renate Stecher, East Germany, September 7	22.4 sec.*
400 m.	Monika Zehrt, East Germany, July 4	51.0 sec.*
880 yd.	Madeline Jackson, U.S., May 14	2 min. 2.0 sec.*
1,500 m.	Ludmila Bragina, U.S.S.R., September 9	4 min. 1.4 sec.
100-m. hurdles	Annelie Ehrhardt, East Germany, June 15 and August 13 (twice)	12.5 sec.
	Pamela Ryan, Australia, June 28	12.5 sec.*
400-m. relay	West Germany, September 10	42.8 sec.*
1,600-m. relay	East Germany, September 10	3 min. 23.0 sec.
1-mi. relay	U.S., August 12	3 min. 33.9 sec.
High jump	Ulrike Meyfarth, West Germany, September 4	6 ft. 3½ in.*
	Yordanka Blagoeva, Bulgaria, September 24	6 ft. 4¼ in.
Shot put	Nadyezhda Chizhova, U.S.S.R., September 7	68 ft. 11¼ in.
Discus	Argentina Menis, Romania, September 24	220 ft. 10 in.
Javelin	Ruth Fuchs, East Germany, June 11	213 ft. 5 in.
Pentathlon	Mary Peters, U.K., September 2–3	4,801 pt.

*Ties record.

topped by Bob Seagren (U.S.) with a world record of 18 ft. 5¾ in. New marks in the discus and javelin were set by the erratic Swede Rickard Bruch with 225 ft. in the former, while the consistent Janis Lusis (U.S.S.R.) threw the javelin 307 ft. 8¾ in., more than 10 ft. farther than the next best effort during the season. That next best, ironically, was the 296-ft. 10-in. throw by Klaus Wolfermann (West Germany) that beat Lusis for the Olympic gold medal by less than an inch.

Support for the observation that at the shorter distances the graph of world record track achievements was flattening out was abundant. During the year the world records for the 100 m. (9.9 sec.), the 800 m. (1 min. 44.3 sec.), the 110-m. hurdles (13.2 sec.), and the 400-m. relay (38.2 sec.) were all equaled, but none was beaten.

New records were more abundant in women's competition. World marks were equaled in five short events, with the sprinting of Renate Stecher (East Germany) the outstanding feature. But at 1,500 m. and in all the field events except the long jump new ground was decisively broken. Ludmila Bragina (U.S.S.R.) eventually reduced the 1,500-m. record in her Olympic triumph to 4 min. 1.4 sec. and thus put the first feminine 4-min. 1,500 m. (first broken by men in 1912) within the bounds of near future probability.

The high-jump record, which had long remained the property of Iolanda Balas-Söter (Romania) until Ilona Gusenbauer (Austria) took possession of it in 1971, was first equaled by the 16-year-old West German Ulrike Meyfarth in her Olympic triumph and then beaten two weeks later by Yordanka Blagoeva of Bulgaria who did 6 ft. 4¼ in. Mary Peters of the U.K. (*see* BIOGRAPHY), at the age of 33, edged the pentathlon record over 4,800 points by dint of her high jump, shot put, and hurdling techniques. These overcame her relatively modest talent as a sprinter and long jumper.

The Olympics naturally dominated the 1972 season, but they were sufficiently early for the Belgians in particular to make a later onslaught on the long-distance records. At Brussels on September 20, Emiel Puttemans lowered the 3-mi. record to 12 min. 47.6 sec. and the 5,000-m. to 13 min. 13 sec. The 5,000-m. mark had been lowered only six days previously by Viren to 13 min. 16.4 sec. In a race to attempt the world one-hour distance record, Belgium's old master Gaston Roelants lowered the 20,000-m. record to 57 min. 44.4 sec. and beat his own hour record with 12 mi. 1,610 yd.

The International Amateur Athletic Federation (IAAF) was searching for a new president after the marquess of Exeter announced at its meeting at the Munich Olympics that he would retire because of age after the present term of four years. The IAAF was concerned about its part in what were regarded as inevitable changes of structure and size in the Olympic Games, since track and field athletics maintained its place as the core of the quadrennial celebration. (*See* SPORTING RECORD: *Special Report.*)

As of May 1, 1973, a number of the rules of competition would be changed in international tournaments. The 800 m. would be run in lanes for the first two bends instead of only for the first one. Ties for first place in the high jump and pole vault, when the competitors have had an equal number of jumps, would be broken by an extra trial at the tying height and if the tie still remained, there would be a jump-off with the bar raised or lowered to previously announced heights (one trial each) until the winner emerged. The definition of walking was tightened up to cut out "lifting." But the IAAF declined to insist on electric timing for world sprint records up to 200 yd.

(NORRIS AND ROSS MCWHIRTER)

United States Competition. All competition in the U.S. led toward the Olympic Games, but despite that added incentive the number of new records set by U.S. athletes was relatively small.

Bob Seagren, the veteran pole vaulter of the Southern California Striders, was the only American to set a new record. The 1968 Olympic champion and former world record holder did it twice. Recovering from knee surgery, Seagren started the season late but soon regained his old form. On May 23, in El Paso, Tex., he vaulted 18 ft. 4½ in., 2½ in. over the pending new standard of Kjell Isaksson of Sweden. The latter was in the same competition and also cleared 18 ft. 4½ in. to share the record. Then, at the U.S. Olympic trials in Eugene, Ore., on July 2, Seagren took undisputed possession of the vault record with 18 ft. 5¾ in.

Earlier, Isaksson, who spent most of the winter and spring competing in the U.S., twice upped the record. He vaulted 18 ft. 1 in. at Austin, Tex., April 8 and 18 ft. 2 in. at Los Angeles, April 15.

Table III. U.S. Olympic Trials
Eugene, Ore., June 29–July 9, 1972

Event	Competitor, affiliation	Performance
100 m.	Eddie Hart, Bay Area Striders	9.9 sec.
200 m.	Chuck Smith, Southern Cal. Striders	20.4 sec.
400 m.	Wayne Collett, Southern Cal. Striders	44.1 sec.
800 m.	Dave Wottle, Bowling Green State	1 min. 44.3 sec.
1,500 m.	Jim Ryun, Club West	3 min. 41.5 sec.
5,000 m.	Steve Prefontaine, Oregon	13 min. 22.8 sec.
10,000 m.	Frank Shorter, Florida Track Club	28 min. 35.6 sec.
3,000-m. steeplechase	Mike Manley, Oregon Track Club	8 min. 29.8 sec.
Marathon	Frank Shorter, Florida Track Club, and Ken Moore, Oregon Track Club (tie)	2 hr. 15 min. 57.8 sec.
20,000-m. walk	Larry Young, Columbia College	1 hr. 35 min. 56.4 sec.
50,000-m. walk	Larry Young, Columbia College	4 hr. 13 min. 4.4 sec.
110-m. hurdles	Tom Hill, Arkansas State	13.5 sec.
400-m. hurdles	Ralph Mann, Southern Cal. Striders	48.4 sec.
High jump	Dwight Stones, UCLA	7 ft. 3 in.
Pole vault	Bob Seagren, Southern Cal. Striders	18 ft. 5¾ in.
Long jump	Arnie Robinson, Fort McArthur	26 ft. 4¾ in.
Triple jump	John Craft, U. of Chicago Track Club	56 ft. 2 in.
Shot put	George Woods, Pacific Coast Club	70 ft. 1¼ in.
Discus	Jay Silvester, Intermountain Track Club	211 ft. 2 in.
Hammer throw	Tom Gage, New York Athletic Club	229 ft. 11 in.
Javelin	Bill Schmidt, Fort MacArthur	270 ft. 6 in.
Decathlon	Jeff Bannister, Decathlon Club America	8,120 pt.

Table IV. NCAA Outdoor Championships

Eugene, Ore., June 1–3, 1972

Event	Competitor, affiliation	Performance
100 m.	Warren Edmonson, UCLA	10.1 sec.
200 m.	Larry Burton, Purdue	20.5 sec.
400 m.	John Smith, UCLA	44.5 sec.
800 m.	Willie Thomas, Tennessee	1 min. 47.1 sec.
1,500 m.	Dave Wottle, Bowling Green State	3 min. 39.7 sec.
5,000 m.	Steve Prefontaine, Oregon	13 min. 31.4 sec.
10,000 m.	John Halberstadt, Oklahoma State	28 min. 50.3 sec.
3,000-m. steeplechase	Joe Lucas, Georgetown	8 min. 30.2 sec.
110-m. hurdles	Jerry Wilson, Southern Cal.	13.4 sec.
400-m. hurdles	Bruce Collins, Pennsylvania	49.1 sec.
440-yd. relay	Southern California	39.6 sec.
1-mi. relay	UCLA	3 min. 5.3 sec.
High jump	Tom Woods, Oregon State	7 ft. 3¼ in.
Pole vault	Dave Roberts, Rice	17 ft. 3 in.
Long jump	Randy Williams, Southern Cal.	26 ft. 8¼ in.
Triple jump	James Butts, UCLA	53 ft. 2¼ in.
Shot put	Fred DeBernardi, U. of Texas, El Paso	66 ft. 6½ in.
Discus	Fred DeBernardi, U. of Texas, El Paso	196 ft. 5 in.
Hammer throw	Al Schoterman, Kent State	231 ft. 3 in.
Javelin	Rick Dowswell, Ohio	265 ft. 11 in.
Decathlon	Ron Evans, Connecticut	7,571 pt.
Team	UCLA	82 pt.

Table V. NCAA Indoor Championships

Detroit, Mich., March 10–11, 1972

Event	Competitor, affiliation	Performance
60 yd.	Herb Washington, Michigan State	6.1 sec.
440 yd.	Larance Jones, Northeast Missouri	48.3 sec.
600 yd.	Dale Gibson, Mississippi State	1 min. 11.3 sec.
880 yd.	Dave Wottle, Bowling Green State	1 min. 51.8 sec.
1,000 yd.	Morgan Mosser, West Virginia	2 min. 8.9 sec.
1 mi.	Ken Popejoy, Michigan State	4 min. 2.9 sec.
2 mi.	Sid Sink, Bowling Green State	8 min. 36.5 sec.
60-yd. hurdles	Tom McMannon, Notre Dame	7.2 sec.
1-mi. relay	Adelphi	3 min. 15.8 sec.
2-mi. relay	Illinois	7 min. 29.9 sec.
Distance medley relay	Bowling Green State	9 min. 49.5 sec.
High jump	Chris Dunn, Colgate	7 ft. 2¾ in.
Pole vault	Jan Johnson, Alabama	17 ft. 1¼ in.
Long jump	Henry Hines, Southern Cal.	25 ft. 10 in.
Triple jump	Barry McClure, Middle Tennessee State	52 ft. 10¼ in.
Shot put	Doug Lane, Southern Cal.	64 ft. 3½ in.
35-lb. weight throw	Jacques Accambray, Kent State	71 ft. 3¼ in.
Team	Southern California	19 pt.

The Olympic trials, which were spread over 11 days and which pitted the elite of U.S. track and field talent against each other in the quest of berths on the Olympic team, were very productive. In addition to Seagren's new vault mark, world records were matched in two events by three athletes. And a number of new national bests were achieved.

A close finish in the 100-m. dash saw Eddie Hart of the Bay Area Striders nose out Rey Robinson of Florida A & M. Both clocked 9.9 sec. to tie the world mark first set in 1968. Also on July 1, Dave Wottle of Bowling Green State University was the surprise winner of the 800 m. with a world record-equaling time of 1 min. 44.3 sec. Wottle, who thought he was better at the mile, ran throughout the season wearing a battered white golf cap.

At the Olympics, high hurdler Rod Milburn of Southern University matched the global best at the 110-m. distance, recording 13.2 sec. on September 7. Three days later the U.S. 400-m. relay team tied the world record of 38.2 sec. in winning the Olympic gold medal. Larry Black of North Carolina Central started and was followed by Robert Taylor of Texas Southern, Gerald Tinker of the Kent Track Club, and Hart.

Three other best-ever times were turned in during the season but none could be accepted as an official world record. The University of Southern California twice bettered the 880-yd. relay standard but could not be given the record because one of the team members was not a U.S. citizen and the rules stipulated that all must be from the same country. Leon Brown, Edesel Garrison, Willie Deckard, and Don Quarrie, a native of Jamaica, ran 1 min. 21.1 sec. in Los Angeles on March 4 and 1 min. 20.7 sec. in Fresno, Calif., on May 13.

The distance medley relay record set by Kansas State went unrecognized for another reason—there was no official world record for the event. But the 9 min. 31.8 sec. time put together by Clardy Vinson, Mike Lee, Rick Hitchcock, and Jerome Howe on April 29 at Des Moines, Ia., was the fastest ever. North Carolina Central ran the sprint medley relay in 3 min. 14.8 sec. at Philadelphia on April 29, but did not get official recognition for this fastest time for two reasons. This, too, was an unofficial event internationally, and the team also included runners from two countries. Julius Sang and Robert Ouko of Kenya teamed with Larry Black and Jeff Horsley of the U.S. In still another unrecognized event, George Frenn of the Pacific Coast Club threw the 35-lb. weight 74 ft. 2¾ in. at Richmond, Va., March 17.

U.S. records took more of a battering than world marks, and again a large part of the action took part in the Olympic trials. There, Steve Prefontaine of Oregon ran 5,000 m. in 13 min. 22.8 sec. on July 9, and Ralph Mann of the Southern California Striders was clocked in 48.4 sec. for the 400-m. hurdles on July 2. Larry Young of Columbia College walked 50,000 m. in 4 hr. 13 min. 4.4 sec. on July 4. In the triple jump, John Craft of the University of Chicago Track Club leaped a wind-aided 56 ft. 2 in., followed by Dave Smith of the Bay Area Striders with 56 ft., both surpassing the previous U.S. record.

Prefontaine had lowered the U.S. 5,000-m. record to 13 min. 29.6 sec. at Eugene, Ore., on April 29. And he twice set national bests at 3,000 m., running 7 min. 45.8 sec. at Gresham, Ore., on June 24 and 7 min. 44.2 sec. at Oslo, Nor., on August 3.

The 10,000-m. record was bettered three times. Greg Fredericks of Penn State did it first, running 28 min. 8 sec. at Seattle on June 16, while Frank Shorter of the Florida Track Club did it twice in the Olympic Games. The Olympic marathon winner ran 27 min. 58.2 sec. on August 31 and 27 min. 51.4 sec. on September 3.

North Carolina College bettered the U.S. 1-mi. relay

WIDE WORLD

Finnish runner Olavi Suomalainen crosses the finish line to win the 76th Boston Athletic Association marathon, run on April 17, 1972.

UPI COMPIX

Colgate University high jumper Chris Dunn is a study in body control as he clears 7 ft. 2¾ in. to set a new National Collegiate Athletic Association indoor record at the 1972 national indoor track championships held in Detroit on March 10–11, 1972.

record with 3 min. 3.1 sec. on April 29 in Philadelphia but would not get the record because of the mixed composition of the quartet. The 50,000-m. walk U.S. best was lowered again by Young at Munich, where he did 4 hr. 46 sec. on September 3. Young also had a U.S. record at 20,000 m., walking 1 hr. 30 min. 10 sec. at Columbia, Mo., on May 7.

In team competition, UCLA won the National Collegiate Athletic Association (NCAA) championships with 82 points at Eugene, June 1–3, while North Carolina Central captured the National Association of Intercollegiate Athletics (NAIA) title in Billings, Mont., June 1–2, scoring 68 points.

Indoors, competition was highlighted by the first indoor dual meet ever held between the U.S. and the U.S.S.R. The U.S. outscored the Soviet Union, 76–69, at Richmond, Va., March 17. The NCAA title was claimed by Southern California at Detroit, March 11, with 19 points.

Four major indoor world bests—there are no officially recognized records—were established. Herb Washington of Michigan State ran 60 yd. in 5.8 sec. at East Lansing, Mich., on February 12, and Mark Winzenried of Club West ran 1,000 yd. in 2 min. 5.1 sec. at Louisville, Ky., the same night. Isaksson upped the indoor pole vault record to 17 ft. 10½ in. in New York February 26, and Al Feuerbach of the Pacific Coast Club claimed a new shot put mark with 69 ft. 4¾ in. at Pocatello, Ida., February 5.

In less frequently contested, and therefore nonstandard indoor events, bests-on-record were credited to Marshall Dill of Michigan State, who ran 300 yd. in 29.5 sec., Milburn, who hurdled 120 yd. in 13.4 sec., and Tommie White of the Southern California Striders, who ran the 60-m. hurdles in 7.4 sec. Quarrie and Cliff Branch of Colorado ran 100 yd. in 9.3 sec. to equal the world's indoor best, and Washington and Mel Pender of the U.S. Army did the same by sprinting 50 yd. in 5 sec.

U.S. indoor records went to high jumper Reynaldo Brown of the California Polytechnic Institute, at 7 ft. 4 in., triple jumper John Craft, with 55 ft. 5 in., and Juris Luzins of the U.S. Marine Corps, who ran 600 m. in 1 min. 19.8 sec.

U.S. women were paced by Kathy Hammond and Madeline Manning Jackson. They teamed with Debra Edwards and Mable Fergerson to lower the world 1-mi. relay record to 3 min. 33.9 sec. and performed brilliantly as individuals. Manning equaled the world 880-yd. mark with 2 min. 2 sec., while Hammond lowered national records to 51.6 sec. for 400 m. and 52.2 for 440 yd. Indoors, Hammond claimed world bests of 64.5 sec. for 500 yd. and 1 min. 20.5 sec. for 600 yd.

Other world indoor bests went to Kathy Gibbons, 2 min. 32.2 sec. for 1,000 yd.; Debbie Heald, 4 min. 38.5 sec. for 1 mi.; Patty Johnson, 6.4 sec. for the 50-yd. hurdles and 7.4 sec. for the 60-yd. hurdles (equaling the record). The 60-yd. and 55-m. records of 6.5 sec. were equaled by Mattline Render and Alfreda Daniels.

U.S. outdoor records went to Francie Larrieu, 4 min. 10.4 sec. for 1,500 m.; Patty Johnson, 13 sec. for the 100-m. hurdles; Olga Connolly, 179 ft. 2 in. in the discus; Kathy Schmidt, 200 ft. 6 in. in the javelin; and Gale Fitzgerald, 4,305 points in the pentathlon. Indoors, national records fell to Martha Watson, 21 ft. ¾ in. in the long jump, and Maren Seidler, 52 ft. 7¼ in. in the shot put. (BERT NELSON)

Trade, International

The total value of world trade in 1972 was 12 to 13% higher than in 1971. Growth was somewhat more rapid in the first half of the year, but there were signs that this pace would diminish later on. Expansion of world trade is dependent on cyclical changes in output and imports in the main industrial countries. The large increase in trade during 1969 and 1970 was supported by a rapid increase of demand in Europe and Japan. (*See* Table I.) In 1971 the growth in imports to these areas was reduced, but demand in North America expanded. The economic recovery in Canada and the U.S. provided the main stimulus to world trade during 1972, although European demand was again buoyant.

Although the growth in the value of world trade in 1971 and 1972 was less than in 1969 and 1970, it was still higher than the average rate of 9.5% that prevailed during the 1960s. The important feature of 1971 and 1972 was the extent to which prices of traded goods were rising. Throughout the 1960s world trade prices had risen by less than 10% (*i.e.*, only 1% per year). However, in the three years from mid-1969 to mid-1972 prices rose by no less than 18%, and much of this occurred in 1971 and 1972. In addition to general and persistent inflationary pressures, two special factors contributed to the price rise: agreements between the Organization of Petroleum Exporting Countries and the major international oil companies in early 1971 raised the price of petroleum exports by more than 20%, and the appreciation of several major currencies during 1971 raised the dollar value of world trade by about 2%.

As a result of these large price increases, the growth in volume of world trade was much less than the growth in value. In 1971 and 1972 about half the growth in value was accounted for by price increases and the volume increase was only about 6% per year —much less than the increases in the preceding years and below the average rate of 8.4% prevailing in the 1960s. The low increase in the volume of trade in 1971 was largely due to the slowdown of economic activity in Europe and Japan, which account for about one-half of world trade; in 1971 their volume of imports increased by only 4.5%, compared with 13% in 1970.

Import expansion also fell off sharply in the more developed primary producing countries, but demand growth continued in the less developed areas.

In preceding years the expansion of trade had usually had a more favourable effect on exports from industrial countries than on those of the primary producers. In 1971, and to a lesser extent in 1972, the expansion of trade was shared by industrial countries and primary producers alike, although much of the improved performance of the latter was confined to the oil-exporting nations in the Middle East and North Africa. The less developed primary producers, excluding oil exporters, fared less well than for some time.

Primary Producing Countries. Exports from primary producing countries increased by 11% in value in 1971, only slightly below the 12% growth rate recorded in the two previous years. Their imports rose faster than their exports, so that their overall trade balance deteriorated. (*See* Table II.) Primary producers' exports accelerated in the first half of 1972, however, and there were signs that their trade balance was improving. The volume of trade rose much less than the value of trade in 1971, particularly for the less developed areas. Average prices for primary products (excluding petroleum) fell, and there was a very uneven distribution of changes in export values and trade balances. On the other hand, the 20% increase in petroleum prices was a major influence on the petroleum exporters; although the volume of their exports grew less rapidly in 1972 than previously, the value of their exports increased by 30%.

Dollar prices of primary products increased sharply in 1972 following the realignment of currencies at the end of 1971. In mid-1972 the price index of primary producers' exports was 10% above the level of a year earlier. In 1971 the average price of all agricultural products was the same as in 1970, but food prices were 2% lower while prices of nonfood products were up 3%; both groups of products recorded large increases in 1972. Wool prices made particularly large gains, chiefly as a result of Japanese demand. The prices of most metals and minerals continued to fall from the very high levels of 1969; by mid-1972 the average price was 20% below the 1970 level.

Exports from the more developed primary producers grew less in 1971 than in 1970 in terms of both value and volume. Imports were also growing less rapidly than in the previous year, but this did not prevent a deterioration in the trade balance of this group. (*See* Table II.) Exports accelerated in Australia, New Zealand, and South Africa, and there was a $300 million improvement in the Australian trade balance, due largely to higher wool prices. The export growth of European primary producers as a group slackened in 1971, despite high growth rates in Spain, Turkey, and Ireland. The combined trade deficit of these countries rose by $1 billion.

The less developed primary producing countries (excluding the petroleum exporters) were faced with both falling export prices and a slackening demand for their products in 1971. The rate of growth of their export volume had been falling since the 10% increase in 1968, and in 1971 amounted to no more than 3%. Lower prices, moreover, meant that the value of their exports rose by only 1.5%—the smallest annual increase since 1967. At the same time, the value of their imports continued to grow rapidly. As a result, their trade balances came under considerable pressure, which continued in 1972.

The very favourable trade balance of the oil-producing countries in the Middle East can be seen in Table II. When oil producers in Africa, Asia, and Latin America are included, the combined trade sur-

Table I. World Trade

Percent change from previous year

Country		1968	1969	1970	1971	1972*
Imports						
World	value	11.5	13.9	14.6	11.5	14.3
	volume	12.5	11.4	9.0	5.8	6.1
Industrial countries	value	12.3	15.0	15.2	11.5	18.0
	volume	13.0	12.1	9.2	5.8	7.7
United States	value	22.9	8.5	10.8	14.1	20.2
	volume	21.6	5.3	3.5	8.3	...
Canada	value	13.7	14.5	1.8	15.7	24.0
	volume	9.1	11.7	−3.2	9.6	...
United Kingdom	value	6.5	5.3	8.9	10.5	19.8
	volume	10.6	2.2	5.8	3.5	...
Germany, West	value	16.1	23.7	19.6	15.2	18.7
	volume	18.3	18.0	14.1	10.9	...
Japan	value	11.4	15.7	25.7	4.4	11.2
	volume	13.0	15.9	19.5	1.8	...
Primary producers	value	8.3	10.0	12.5	11.7	15.3
	volume	9.2	7.7	8.8	6.7	11.0
More developed areas	value	4.8	13.8	18.8	9.1	...
	volume	6.6	11.8	13.3	5.4	...
Less developed areas	value	8.8	9.8	11.8	12.0	...
	volume	9.9	6.7	7.7	7.0	...
Oil exporters	value	11.4	9.9	10.2	18.0	...
	volume	12.5	6.8	6.2	12.9	...
Others	value	8.3	9.7	12.3	10.5	...
	volume	9.4	6.6	8.1	5.5	...
Exports						
World	value	11.9	14.6	14.8	11.9	14.5
	volume	12.9	10.9	9.2	5.7	6.2
Irdustrial countries	value	12.5	15.2	15.5	11.8	18.9
	volume	13.1	11.6	9.3	6.0	8.6
U.S.	value	9.5	9.7	13.7	2.1	6.1
	volume	7.9	6.3	7.5	−1.1	...
Canada	value	19.4	9.4	16.6	8.8	13.1
	volume	16.4	6.6	10.8	5.5	...
United Kingdom	value	6.8	14.1	9.9	15.4	19.2
	volume	14.5	10.3	3.6	5.2	...
Germany, West	value	14.3	16.9	17.7	14.2	20.6
	volume	16.0	12.1	8.4	6.7	...
Japan	value	24.2	23.3	20.8	24.3	16.6
	volume	24.1	18.0	14.0	17.0	...
Primary producers	value	9.2	12.2	12.3	11.1	16.4
	volume	9.7	10.0	8.6	5.4	...
More developed areas	value	4.9	15.5	12.3	9.7	...
	volume	9.0	10.7	8.4	6.7	...
Less developed areas	value	9.8	12.1	11.8	11.0	...
	volume	9.8	8.9	8.7	5.0	...
Oil exporters	value	10.7	8.5	11.9	30.0	...
	volume	9.1	13.3	11.4	9.9	...
Others	value	9.1	14.3	11.5	1.5	...
	volume	10.1	7.1	7.6	3.0	...

*First six months compared with first six months of 1971.
Sources: International Monetary Fund, *Annual Report;* United Nations, *Monthly Bulletin of Statistics.*

Table II. Primary Producing Countries' Foreign Trade

In $000,000,000

Area	1971 Exports	1971 Imports*	1971 Balance of trade	1970 Exports	1970 Imports*	1970 Balance of trade
More developed countries†	19.8	29.4	−9.6	18.0	26.9	−8.9
Less developed countries‡	60.1	62.9	−2.8	54.1	55.7	−1.6
Latin America	14.7	15.7	−1.0	13.8	14.1	−0.3
West Indies	2.6	4.2	−1.6	2.4	3.7	−1.3
Middle East	13.5	9.1	4.4	11.2	8.1	3.1
Asia	16.2	21.2	−5.0	14.5	18.9	−4.4
Africa	12.4	11.8	0.6	11.7	10.1	1.6
Total‡	79.9	92.3	−12.4	72.1	82.6	−10.5

*Imports, in most cases, include freight and insurance charges.
†Australia, New Zealand, South Africa, and the less industrialized countries of Western Europe.
‡The total includes Pacific islands not shown separately.
Source: International Monetary Fund, *International Financial Statistics.*

Table III. World Exports of Manufactured Goods

Percent of total value

Year	Total value in $000,000,000*	United States	United Kingdom	West Germany	France	Italy	Japan	Others†
1955	34.0	24.5	19.8	15.5	9.3	3.4	5.1	22.4
1960	52.4	21.6	16.5	19.3	9.6	5.1	6.9	21.0
1965	83.2	20.3	13.9	19.1	8.8	6.7	9.4	21.8
1968	114.8	20.1	11.6	19.4	8.2	7.3	10.6	22.8
1969	134.0	19.3	11.3	19.5	8.2	7.3	11.2	23.2
1970	154.4	18.5	10.8	19.8	8.7	7.2	11.7	23.3
1971	174.0	17.0	11.0	20.1	8.8	7.2	12.8	23.1
1972‡	198.8	16.2	10.6	20.3	9.4	7.4	12.8	23.3

*Excluding special category exports (mostly arms).
†Belgium, Luxembourg, Canada, Netherlands, Sweden, and Switzerland.
‡First half of year (seasonally adjusted); value at annual rate.
Source: National Institute of Economic and Social Research, London.

Table IV. Trade of Industrial Countries

In $000,000,000

Country	1972 Exports	1972 Imports	1972 Balance of trade	1971 Exports	1971 Imports	1971 Balance of trade
United States	47.43	53.92	−6.49	44.14	45.60	−1.46
Canada	19.18	18.08	1.10	17.68	15.46	2.22
EEC	118.65	113.77	4.88	101.00	99.44	1.56
Belgium	14.80	14.38	0.42	12.30	12.67	−0.37
France	24.77	25.87	−1.10	20.52	21.24	−0.72
Germany, West	45.17	38.84	6.33	39.04	34.34	4.70
Italy	17.74	18.19	−0.45	15.12	15.98	−0.86
Netherlands	16.16	16.52	−0.36	14.02	15.19	−1.17
EFTA	54.84	61.70	−6.86	48.41	55.84	−7.43
United Kingdom	24.72	27.74	−3.02	22.34	23.94	−1.60
Japan	26.70	21.74	4.96	24.01	19.70	4.31
Total	266.80	269.21	−2.41	235.24	236.04	−0.80

*First half of year (seasonally adjusted) at annual rate.
Source: Organization for Economic Cooperation and Development, *Main Economic Indicators.*

plus for this group was $5.3 billion in 1970 and, with higher oil prices, $6.7 billion in 1971. The remaining less developed primary producers (most of those outside the Middle East) recorded trade deficits of $6.9 billion in 1970 and $10.4 billion in 1971.

The deterioration in the overall Latin-American balance was accounted for by a sizable increase in the Brazilian deficit, as imports increased by one-third. An increase in the Peruvian deficit of $300 million, caused by falling exports and rising imports, was more than offset by an increased Venezuelan surplus based on higher oil prices. In Africa the overall surplus of $600 million was dominated by the $2.1 billion surplus in Libya; most other countries recorded deficits and in many cases these were larger in 1971 than in 1970. Zambia recorded a $400 million increase in its deficit as exports fell sharply. The trade deficit of primary producers in Asia rose by about $500 million in 1971 for the second consecutive year. Half of this was attributable to a larger Indian deficit.

Industrial Countries. Exports by industrial countries rose 11.9% in value in 1971; the increase in their imports was slightly less and there was a small improvement in their overall trade balance. (*See* Table IV.) In the first half of 1972 exports of the industrial countries were 13% higher than a year earlier while their imports rose by 14%, resulting in a deficit in their trade balance.

These overall figures, however, concealed marked differences between regions and countries—a 24% increase in exports from Japan in 1971 compared with only 4% in those from North America. The slackening in the growth of North American exports was very marked. Exports from the U.S., which had increased by nearly 14% in 1970, rose by only 2% in value in 1971; in volume terms U.S. exports actually fell by 1%. On the other hand, Japanese exports were growing even faster than in 1970, making 1971 the fourth successive year in which Japan recorded an export growth of over 20%. The growth of EEC and the European Free Trade Association (EFTA) exports was somewhat less in 1971 than in 1970.

The most notable decline in import expansion occurred in Japan—from 26% in 1970 to 4% in 1971. Only in North America did imports gather momentum, reflecting not only a cyclical upswing in domestic de-

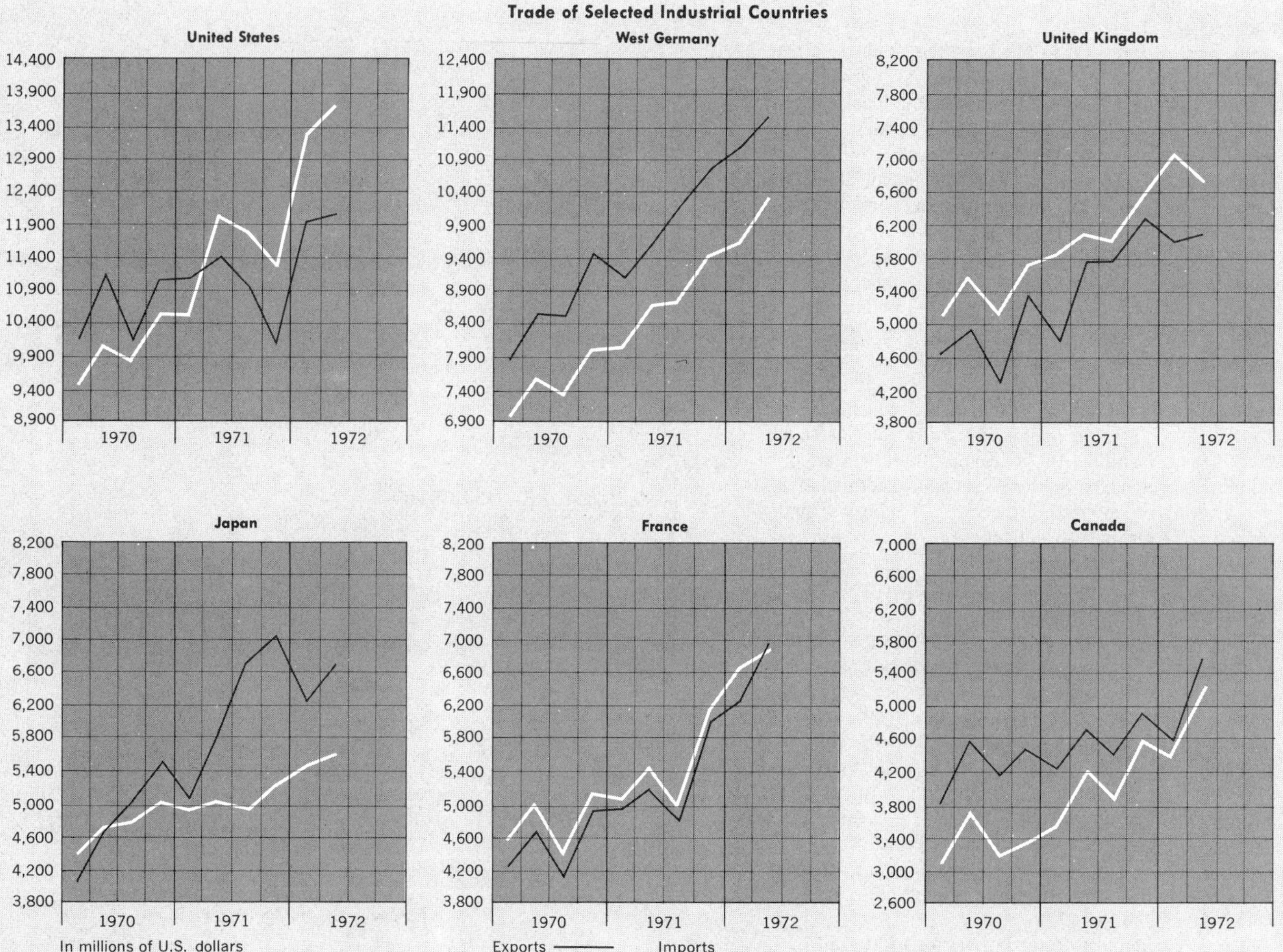

mand but also anticipation of a depreciation of the Canadian and U.S. dollars. This acceleration was particularly notable in Canada, where imports rose by 16% in 1971, compared with less than 2% in 1970. These differences in import and export growth rates continued in the first half of 1972, but they were becoming less marked. The growth of Japanese exports eased off a little; North American exports accelerated, as did exports from Europe.

The divergent movements in imports and exports had a significant effect on the trade balances of the individual countries. The U.S. trade balance moved from a small surplus in 1970 to a sizable deficit in 1972, whereas the EEC countries and Japan recorded sharply increased surpluses. (*See* Table IV.)

The three main trade flows (*i.e.,* industrial countries' exports to, and imports from, primary producers and trade between industrial countries) all grew at much the same rate in 1971. This was in contrast to earlier years, when trade between industrial countries had often grown the fastest. Trade between members of the EEC, which had increased by 26% in 1969 and 19% in 1970, rose by only 15% in 1971. EEC exports to Japan, which had increased by one-third in 1970, fell by 5% in 1971, and the growth of Japanese exports to the EEC was reduced from 41% in 1969 and 35% in 1970 to 26% in 1971. This was still the second fastest growing flow in 1971, next to Japanese exports to North America, which increased by 29%.

The shares of the main industrial nations in the world trade in manufactured goods are given in Table III. West Germany, France, and Italy continued to increase their shares in total exports at the expense of the U.S. and the U.K. The previously uninterrupted increase in the Japanese share was halted in 1972, probably only temporarily, by the revaluation of the yen.

In 1971 the U.S. recorded its first trade deficit since 1935. The coincidence of slow growth in overseas markets and a recovery in domestic production, coupled with what was proving to be an overvalued exchange rate, meant a slow (2%) growth in exports and a fairly rapid (14%) growth in imports. The result was a deficit of $1.5 billion, a deterioration in the trade balance of $4.7 billion compared with 1970. A large increase was recorded in imports of industrial materials and in imports of motor vehicles from Canada, partly as a result of the prolonged General Motors strike. These two product groups between them accounted for two-thirds of the growth in imports. This adverse trend in U.S. trade continued into 1972, when imports were some 20% higher than a year earlier and exports were up only 6%; the trade deficit increased very sharply to an annual rate of $6.5 billion in the first half of the year.

Canada was able to maintain a trade surplus in 1971 and the first half of 1972 despite an accelerating growth in domestic demand. In 1971 exports suffered a little from the decline in world metal prices and grew more slowly than in recent years. In 1972 the rate of growth of imports was very rapid and the trade surplus was reduced considerably.

The combined trade balance of the EEC countries moved from equilibrium in 1970 to a small surplus in 1971 and to a moderately large surplus in 1972. Most of the member countries shared in this improvement, although the largest contribution to both the overall balance and the improvement came from West Germany. Sluggish demand at home and the appreciation of the mark reduced the growth rate of both imports and exports in West Germany in 1971, while the trade surplus improved somewhat. In 1972 exports accelerated once more as West Germany continued to increase its share of world trade in manufactured goods, and there was a consequent substantial increase in its already large surplus. The French deficit was reduced in 1971; exports rose by 15% and imports by 11%. After a slow start, exports of manufactured goods accelerated as sales to other EEC countries increased. In Italy and the Netherlands the trade deficits were steadily reduced in both 1971 and 1972.

UPI COMPIX

Black students from Southern University, Baton Rouge, La., face armed sheriff's deputies at a Mississippi River terminal in Burnside, where Rhodesian chromium ore was being loaded onto barges on March 20, 1972. Two students were arrested during the protest over U.S. trade with countries that maintain policies of racial segregation.

The improvement in the trade balance of the EFTA countries in 1971 largely reflected the reduction in the U.K. deficit. U.K. exports rose only 5% in volume but the value increased by 15% as prices rose about 10%. Imports grew by over 10% despite spare plant capacity and slow growth in home demand. Imports of finished consumer goods rose by 42% and of fuels by 32%, while imports of industrial materials declined slightly. In the first half of 1972 both imports and exports were nearly one-fifth higher than a year earlier although compared with the second half of 1971 imports were up 9% and exports were 1.5% lower. As a result, the U.K. deficit increased.

The marked difference between the growth in Japanese imports (4%) and exports (24%) in 1971 led to an increase in the Japanese trade surplus of $3.9 billion. Exports of machinery and equipment rose by 22% to record a threefold increase in five years. The growth of imports accelerated in the first half of 1972 with the recovery in domestic production and demand, but it remained lower than the growth of exports and the surplus increased further.

(A. G. ARMSTRONG)

See also Commercial Policies; Commodities, Primary; Payments and Reserves, International.

ENCYCLOPÆDIA BRITANNICA FILMS. *Rotterdam—Europort, Gateway to Europe* (1971).

Transportation

The trend toward containerization continued in 1972, together with the concomitant integration of different transport modes. Movement in containers, bulk and unit loads, and by roll-on/roll-off services can involve one continuous transport process by road, rail, sea, and inland waterway—the word transmodality was coined to describe it—and new facilities and handling

Trade Unions: *see* Labour Unions

Traffic Accidents: *see* Disasters

AUTHENTICATED NEWS INTERNATIONAL

Pan American World Airways' new terminal at John F. Kennedy International Airport in New York was completed in 1972 at a cost of $70 million. The terminal has gate positions for six 747s and ten smaller aircraft, and rooftop parking facilities for 500 automobiles.

equipment were being provided on an increasing scale to cope with it. New container berths came into operation at many ports, and more were under construction.

Two concepts that exemplified this development were LASH (lighter aboard ship) and Seabee land-sea bridges. Both involved ships carrying barges that originated and ended their journey by inland waterway. The most extensive intercontinental land-sea bridge for the movement of containers by sea and rail was between Europe and Japan across Siberia. Cargoes in 20-ft. containers were carried by Soviet vessels from European countries to Leningrad, where they were transshipped to trains, carried to the Far Eastern port of Nakhodka, and then taken by Soviet ships to Yokohama.

Despite some interruptions caused by industrial disputes, indications were that overall traffic in 1972 would equal or exceed that of 1971. Passenger traffic on the railways tended to grow as systems were modernized and technological developments gave rise to higher speeds and more convenient services. Rail freight traffic generally declined, however, and few rail networks were operating profitably. The shift to road transport continued and some rail traffic was lost to pipelines. This also affected inland transport, although the St. Lawrence Seaway achieved a new record.

While over-the-road freight traffic more than maintained its growth, the number of passengers carried by road on public transport systems continued to decline. To offset this, several rapid transit systems were under construction and others were projected. The first section of the computer-operated Bay Area Rapid Transit (BART) system in the San Francisco area was brought into operation in September. Reports late in the year indicated that traffic on the line was growing, although there had been some initial difficulties with the computer system. It was hoped that BART's modern, high-speed (70 mph) trains would lure riders from San Francisco's overcrowded freeways, and its performance was being watched closely by other urban transportation authorities.

(ERNEST DAVIES)

AVIATION

The year's events gave some ground for hope that the depression that hit the airlines at the turn of the decade might be ending. Even more important, governments and airlines began to take a fresh look at the structure of the industry and its regulation. Reform of rate systems and redefinition of the traditional roles of scheduled and nonscheduled airlines seemed likely to be the outcome.

The industry's problems stemmed from the depressed state of scheduled traffic, accompanied by a sudden increase in available aircraft capacity resulting from the introduction during 1970 and 1971 of the new high-capacity "wide-body" jets. At the same time, the demand for low-fare travel from the "leisure" market increased enormously. The scheduled airlines were slow to adapt their rates to cater to this market, and the charter carriers were able to attract the bulk of it. However, the ready availability of early-model jets, surplus to the requirements of the scheduled airlines, led to a rapid expansion of charter fleets and depressed charter rates, so that nonscheduled airlines fared little better than their scheduled counterparts.

Scheduled traffic began to pick up in 1972 after meagre growth in 1970 and 1971. On the North Atlantic, generally considered a barometer for the industry, the number of passengers in the first half of the year was 3% higher than in the first half of 1971. The number of flights declined by 2% and the average seating capacity of aircraft rose only 6%, with the result that passenger load factors (the proportion of available seats occupied by passengers) improved significantly. First reports for the second half of the year indicated that the trend was continuing.

Although statistics were sparse, it appeared that charter traffic continued to expand in 1972. Figures released by the International Air Transport Association (IATA), representing the main international scheduled carriers of the West, showed that charter airlines increased their share of the number of passengers on the North Atlantic route from a mere 2% in 1963 to 20% in 1971. Charter services operated by the scheduled airlines accounted for 14% of passengers in 1963 and 10% in 1971. The share of passengers taken by scheduled services fell from 84 to 70% during the period.

World scheduled airline traffic (excluding the U.S.S.R. and China) amounted to 50,130,000,000 ton-kilometres in 1971, a figure only 4.9% higher than in 1970. This compared with an average annual growth of 14% over the decade and was the lowest individual figure during that period. On the basis of first reports for 1972, it was widely believed that the lowest point had been reached in 1971. Short-haul traffic was the one sector of the scheduled industry to maintain reasonable growth throughout the depression. In the case of intra-European traffic, for example, the number of passenger-kilometres in 1971 was nearly 13% higher than in 1970, and for the 12 months ended August 1972 it was 11% higher than in the previous 12-month period.

Nevertheless, a big question mark hung over the scheduled airlines' financial results in 1972. The director general of IATA reported during the year that a continuing deterioration had been apparent during 1971. The operating deficit of the association's members before capital charges was put at 1.1% of revenue, but it was estimated that 1972 would see a swing back to an operating profit of 0.8%. The decline from a figure of 10% in 1965 to the 1971 low point had been fairly steady.

Cost inflation continued to affect the airlines. Also of great concern was the dilution of revenue yield as a result of the growing use of special low fares—period excursions, youth fares, etc. For scheduled airlines the yield (in dollars per ton-kilometre) had decreased slightly over the preceding ten years, even though traffic had increased almost fourfold and revenue more than threefold during the same period. The problem that now faced the scheduled airlines was that of countering the inroads made by charter carriers without sustaining a further decrease in average revenues. On April 1 Qantas of Australia unilaterally slashed fares between Australia and Britain by a third, offering a £196 single fare. Other scheduled airlines were forced to follow suit. Although protected by government restrictions on charter operations into Australia, Qantas had been losing traffic to a flourishing charter operation between Europe and points in the Far East, since passengers could go on to Australia by scheduled flight and still save money on the overall journey.

The most disquieting feature of the world charter scene was the mushroom growth of illicit "affinity-group" charters. The practice of supplying charter facilities to groups of travelers belonging to clubs and associations had been introduced to meet a demand but, at the same time, rules designed to deter passengers who would normally travel at full fare had been imposed. During 1971 and 1972 group "organizers," who had found that the rules could be circumvented profitably and with impunity, moved into the business in a big way. Attempts by governments on both sides of the Atlantic to enforce the rules by demanding cancellation of suspect flights were not successful in stemming the illicit traffic and brought adverse—and often undeserved—publicity for the airline industry. There were numerous cases of passengers being stranded by, and losing their money to, "fly-by-night" travel organizers. In one such incident, some 140 passengers were stranded at Gatwick Airport, London, after a U.S. travel firm had failed to arrange their return flight. Many remained at the airport with little or no money until free return transport to the U.S. was arranged by a London hotel group.

Talks were held several times during the year by government authorities of most Western European countries, the U.S., and Canada, in an effort to agree on a new basis for the regulation of charters. At the end of September the U.S. Civil Aeronautics Board (CAB) announced a scheme that promised to form the basis of charter regulation from 1973 onward. The British Civil Aviation Authority (CAA) announced a similar scheme shortly afterward. They planned to allow airlines to wholesale blocks of 40 or more charter seats to authorized travel organizers, who would retail them to the public. To prevent a massive diversion of passengers from scheduled services, bookings would be closed three months before the flight.

At the same time, the CAA proposed a similar facility for scheduled services. There were signs that the two British long-haul scheduled airlines would introduce this in April 1973, even though not all IATA airlines were in agreement. Meanwhile the CAB's charter rule was challenged in the courts by TWA and others on the ground that it constituted "individually ticketed travel," which under U.S. law was the preserve of the scheduled services.

One result of the instability in the industry was the failure of a number of airlines during 1972 and the merger of others. In the U.S., Delta Air Lines absorbed the financially weak Northeast Airlines in a merger on August 1. In another merger, Allegheny Airlines absorbed Mohawk Airlines in April. On May 3 the U.S. supplemental (charter) carrier Universal Airlines ceased operations because of financial difficulties. Two other charter airlines to cease operating were Lloyd International of Britain and Paninternational of West Germany. The West German charter industry, in particular, displayed symptoms of instability.

In the Far East, Malaysia-Singapore Airlines split, for political reasons, into two—Singapore Airlines and Malaysia Airline System. In Britain further moves by the British Airways Board to bring the two state airlines, British European Airways (BEA) and British Overseas Airways Corp. (BOAC), closer together took effect on September 1 with an integration of top management; a complete merger remained a possibility. On March 29 Austrian Airlines announced the signing of a technical cooperation agreement with Swissair, although this stopped short of the close integration envisaged earlier.

A little-known airline stepped into the international limelight when CAAC, the flag carrier of China, ordered 14 more Trident 2 jets from Hawker Siddeley in Britain, bringing its order to 20; 10 Boeing 707s from the U.S.; and (in a preliminary contract) 3 Anglo-French Concorde supersonic transports. The Chinese airline, which also bought 5 Ilyushin Il-61 long-haul jets, was apparently endeavouring to apportion its reequipment among the major powers. CAAC services to the West were widely anticipated, although no starting date was announced. Traffic-rights negotiations were held between China and a number of countries, including Japan.

BOAC and Air France ordered five and four Concorde SSTs, respectively, during 1972, and a preliminary order for two was received from Iran National Airlines. At the same time, Air Canada and Sabena (Belgium) said they were allowing their options for the aircraft to lapse, Sabena pleading current economic difficulties. Clearly there was still doubt among the airlines as to the economic viability of the aircraft. On September 26 IATA spokesmen forcefully pointed out the inhibiting effect that nighttime antinoise "curfews" at airports would have on supersonic operations. An amendment to a bill passed by the U.S. Senate in October sought to ban SSTs from the U.S., but it did not immediately become law.

A major new aircraft, the Lockheed L-1011 TriStar, entered service with Eastern Airlines in the U.S. on April 26. Its chief rival trijet, the McDonnell Douglas DC-10, had entered service the previous summer, and deliveries of a long-range version, to KLM (Neth.) and Swissair, were expected in December. According to the International Civil Aviation Organization (ICAO), the number of new transport aircraft on order but not yet delivered to airlines stood at 416 at the beginning of 1972, the lowest figure in seven years. However, there were some signs during 1972 that airlines were beginning to buy again. Sales of the Boeing 727 were outstanding, totaling more than 115 during the year; customers included Iberia (Spain), Braniff, and All Nippon (Japan). The European airbus A-300B made its first flight on October 28 at Toulouse, France.

A number of serious accidents occurred during 1972. On October 13 an Aeroflot Il-62 (U.S.S.R.) crashed on final approach to Sheremetyevo Airport, Moscow, with the loss of 176 lives. There was wide criticism in the West of the delay before Soviet authorities released details of the accident, which occurred on an international flight. The disaster was the worst in the history of civil aviation. An Interflug (East Germany) Il-62 crashed at East Berlin on August 14 with the loss of 156 lives. A BEA Trident crashed near London on June 18; all 118 on board were killed. An East African Airways VC10 crashed at Addis Ababa, Eth., on April 18 with the loss of 41 lives. A United Airlines 737 on December 8 missed its approach at Chicago's Midway Airport and crashed into a nearby residential neighbourhood, killing 45. On December 29 an Eastern Airlines L-1011 TriStar went down in the Florida Everglades near Miami, causing 101 deaths. Japan Air Lines and Cathay Pacific Airways were among other international airlines suffering serious accidents. (*See* DISASTERS.) It appeared that the 1972 accident rate, when finally established, might have been worse than that of 1971. Preliminary figures for that year issued by the ICAO indicated a fatality rate per 100 million passenger-miles of 0.35. The 1970 figure, at 0.28, was the lowest since 1950, and the period 1960–70 had shown a steady improvement.

Hijacking and crime continued to give cause for concern in 1972. Typical of a number of incidents was that on July 31, when a Delta Airlines DC-8 was hijacked by a gang over Florida; after payment of a $1 million ransom, the aircraft was flown to Algeria and later released by the authorities there. The hijackers were permitted to remain, but Algeria subsequently returned the ransom money. A study by Sir Frederick Tymms gave the following figures for hijacking incidents worldwide: January–August 1971, 32; 1970, 80; 1969, 80; 1930–68, 90. (*See* CRIME.)

On June 19 a one-day strike of airline pilots, organized by the International Federation of Air Line Pilots Associations and aimed at drawing world attention to the crime situation and governments' inaction, caused considerable disruption of traffic throughout the world. Domestic flights in the U.S., where the airlines obtained a court order forbidding pilots from joining the strike, were largely unaffected. In November the possibility of another such strike was raised after three hijackers captured a Southern Airways DC-9, extorted $2 million from the airline, and took the 31 passengers and crew on a 29-hour marathon flight that included landings at eight airports before a final emergency landing in Havana.

The incident pointed up a number of questions concerning the hijacking problem. Security provisions at most major airports had been strengthened; the three hijackers were said to have fit the "profile" of a possible hijacker and to have been examined with a metal detector, but they still managed to bring what amounted to a small arsenal onto the aircraft. FBI agents shot out the plane's tires as it was taking off from Orlando, Fla., leading to a dispute over whether such potentially dangerous actions should be taken without first consulting the pilot. The ransom payment threatened to endanger the airline's financial stability, though Cuba later indicated that the money would be returned. In addition, Cuba, which for several years had been the major goal of U.S. hijackers, expressed a desire to reach some kind of antihijack agreement with the U.S., and negotiations looking toward such an agreement were begun. An ICAO committee in September considered possible sanctions against countries harbouring hijackers.

(DAVID WOOLEY)

COMMERCIAL MOTOR TRANSPORTATION

With the shift of freight traffic from rail to road continuing, and with the latter claiming an increasing proportion of new traffic, the main developments in road freight were increases in the capacity, weight dimensions, and speed of vehicles, their stricter control, and the easing of the flow of international traffic across frontiers.

Little progress was made toward development of a common transport policy within the European Economic Community. The six member countries and the three acceding countries failed to reach agreement on the size of vehicles; the proposed maximums of 11 tons axle weight and 40 tons gross weight proved unacceptable to some countries concerned. Some agreement was possible on hours of work and other matters, however. The quota system continued in operation, with 15% of European inter-Community traffic carried under Community licenses; the remainder were moved under bilateral systems, which were considerably extended during the year.

The number of trucks in Western Europe had been increasing at a rising rate, approaching 7% per year, and the average carrying capacity was growing by about the same percentage. The total amount of freight carried was increasing at about 3% per year overall, with international traffic rising more rapidly than internal traffic. In the U.K. the latest figures showed that, out of a total of approximately 2,000,000,000 tons of freight moved each year, some 85% went by road, 10% by rail, and 5% by coastal shipping, inland waterway, or pipeline. In terms of ton-miles, trucks were responsible for 75% of the total. Although coal, iron, and steel made up the larger part of rail tonnage, even more of these commodities moved by road. Of 1,500,000,000 tons of general merchandise, only 3% went by rail.

There was a marked increase in roll-on/roll-off traffic. The number of articulated vehicles (semitrailers, etc.) carrying containers rose rapidly, especially in Europe, and an increasing amount of freight passing through the English Channel and North Sea ports was being taken to its ultimate destination by road. The European Conference of Ministers of Transport continued its efforts to harmonize the terms of competition in the road transport field and to mitigate certain distorting factors resulting from differences in the various countries' provisions for taxation of vehicles in transit.

In the U.S. trucks carried some 425,000,000,000 ton-miles of freight in 1971, compared with 411,000,000,000 ton-miles in 1970, and truck mileage accounted for over 19% of total vehicle travel, including that by private car. Traffic rose even further in 1972.

Despite the efforts being made by many countries to improve road passenger transport facilities in large cities and metropolitan areas, patronage in urban areas continued to decline, although at a slower rate. In the U.S. the 1,046 bus systems carried 4.7 million passengers in 1971, compared with 5 million in 1970, and of these only 3,734,800 were revenue passengers, representing a decline of 323,500,000. However, total revenue rose from $1,193,000,000 in 1970 to $1,226,800,000 in 1971, the result of an increase in average fare per revenue passenger to 32.23 cents from 29.41 cents. Total revenue vehicle-miles operated declined from 1,409,000,000 in 1970 to 1,375,000,000 in 1971. Operational fleets fell by 550 buses to 49,150, al-

World Transportation

Country	Railways: Route length in 000 km.	Railways Traffic: Passenger in 000,000 pass.-km.	Railways Traffic: Freight in 000,000 net ton-km.	Motor transport: Road length in 000 km.	Motor transport, Vehicles in use: Passenger in 000	Motor transport, Vehicles in use: Commercial in 000	Merchant shipping, Ships of 100 tons and over: Number of vessels	Merchant shipping: Gross reg. tons in 000	Air traffic: Total km. flown in 000	Air traffic: Passenger in 000 pass.-km.	Air traffic: Freight in 000 net ton-km.
EUROPE											
Austria	5.9*	6,330*	9,600*	94.8	1,197.0	121.0	7	11	13,421	416,200	4,470
Belgium	4.2	8,365	7,350	94.0	2,059.6	226.7	224	1,183	49,336	2,722,000	211,178
Bulgaria	4.2	6,223	14,918	36.1	c.17.0†	c.20.0†	148	704	7,690	305,060	5,560
Czechoslovakia	13.3	17,298	63,465	145.9	766.5	198.6	12	83	20,155	904,800	15,651
Denmark	2.4*	3,637*	1,760*	61.5†	1,076.9	247.4	1,264	3,520	32,168‡	1,616,368‡	71,304‡
Finland	5.9	2,156	5,759	72.7	752.9	118.9	390	1,471	19,938	754,900	26,093
France	36.0	41,033	67,028	789.0	13,130.0	1,795.0	1,399	7,011	211,824	13,587,039	557,780
Germany, East (excluding Berlin)	14.5	18,406	43,650	c.160.0	1,268.0	198.0	430	1,016	...	842,700†	23,319†
Germany, West (excluding Berlin)	33.1	38,810	65,411	417.0	15,476.0§	1,191.0§	2,826	8,679	135,595	8,609,000	573,793
Greece	2.6	1,531	688	35.3	263.0	117.6	2,056	13,066	29,749	2,342,700	36,107
Hungary	8.7	13,637	19,612	109.4	294.0	98.0	18	33	8,071	334,321	6,466
Ireland	2.2	575	521	87.2	393.5	52.8	90	174	24,074	1,812,000	66,270
Italy	20.1	33,943	17,226	287.5	11,350.0	935.0	1,690	8,139	143,977	9,502,000	323,870
Netherlands	3.1	8,154	3,232	79.9	2,902.6	333.0	1,539	5,269	92,775	6,360,000	427,580
Norway	4.2*	1,600*	2,600*	73.1	806.6	153.4	2,814	21,720	40,024‡	2,134,600‡	75,537‡
Poland	23.3	37,228	104,334	303.7	555.6	277.3	606	1,760	15,972	655,300	8,142
Portugal	3.6	3,568	812	30.2	513.5	27.6	384	926	39,328	2,995,000	58,940
Romania	11.0	18,800	50,830	75.9	c.35.0†	45.1	71	364	10,040	357,500	6,266
Spain	16.6	13,534	9,108	139.4	2,784.7	760.4	2,279	3,934	105,140	7,066,000	152,693
Sweden	12.2	4,775	17,311	c.174.0	2,356.6	142.3	937	4,978	51,902‡	2,630,000‡	114,336‡
Switzerland	2.9*	7,921*	6,622*	59.8	1,482.0	137.5	32	200	75,421	5,199,000	201,033
U.S.S.R.	135.2	265,406	2,633,000	1,358.9†	c.1,500.0†	c.4,500.0†	6,575	16,194	...	78,500,000	2,070,000
United Kingdom	19.0‖	35,708‖	21,989‖	357.3	11,887.0	1,667.0	3,785	27,335	327,052	18,646,000	604,762
Yugoslavia	10.3	11,179	19,748	100.4	720.9	107.3	356	1,543	17,195	939,500	7,575
ASIA											
Burma	3.1	2,360	755	c.25.0	29.8	31.0	38	55	5,950	141,159	2,379
Cambodia (Khmer Republic)	0.6	109	83	c.11.0	27.5	11.2	3	4	1,056	30,800	516
China	c.35.0	45,670†	265,260†	c.800.0	c.60.0†	c.400.0†	265	1,022	...	63,882†	1,967†
India	60.0†	113,080*	119,860*	983.0	619.8	333.3	397	2,478	65,690	3,612,000	125,978
Indonesia	7.3†	3,884†	655†	84.4	257.0	112.9	501	619	20,241	1,007,300	18,636
Iran	3.5	1,800	2,758	42.7	285.0	96.3	77	132	11,523	683,810	9,634
Iraq	2.4†	374	1,462	18.6	71.8	33.7	36	46	4,677	249,770	2,164
Israel	0.8	371	419	9.3	174.4	75.3	102	646	30,979	3,026,300	111,978
Japan	28.0†	287,500	62,476	1,022.9	10,572.0	9,280.0	8,851	30,509	224,128	10,430,000	479,660
Korea, South	5.4	8,246	8,473	c.34.0	60.7	64.7	337	940	14,290	445,150	6,900
Malaysia	1.8	647¶	1,208¶	23.7	279.4	72.6	94	85	11,384♀	664,103♀	11,206♀
Pakistan	8.6	8,732	6,892	c.150.0	107.2†	34.9†	177δ	582δ	28,927δ	2,393,000δ	71,031δ
Philippines	1.1†	584†	115†	78.0	279.2	179.4	318	946	40,585	1,456,200	26,242
Syria	1.1	84	121	16.7	31.7	17.5	4	1	4,188	219,932	1,238
Taiwan	c.4.4	6,212	2,631	15.4	49.5	41.0	316	1,322	17,752	954,000	25,175
Thailand	3.8†	c.3,860	c.2,250	17.1	246.8	143.8	62	86	16,668	1,032,700	39,641
Turkey	8.0	5,763	5,747	59.5	168.7	126.8	328	714	13,569	988,100	7,083
Vietnam, South	0.6	85	38	20.9	58.4	29.2	39	32	14,866	485,000	3,928
AFRICA											
Algeria	4.1	1,097	1,327	76.0	137.2	106.0	27	95	10,353	514,873	4,137
Central African Republic	—	—	—	21.3	6.1	2.0	...	...	1,719□	68,914□	6,340□
Chad	—	—	—	30.7	4.8	5.8	...	...	2,373□	78,953□	7,102□
Dahomey	0.6	71	96	6.9	12.5	7.2	...	...	1,329□	64,864□	6,340□
Egypt	4.5†	6,529	3,333	c.50.0	130.7	30.1	127	241	17,263	955,900	18,081
Gabon	0.4	...	...	6.0	7.1	5.8	4	1	2,889□	85,624□	6,520□
Ghana	1.0	543	311	c.31.0	36.5	27.0	73	166	3,462	147,370	3,189
Ivory Coast	0.7	631	424	35.0	55.0	29.1	32	42	1,770□	70,670□	6,416□
Kenya	c.2.3	4,529†◊	3,941◊	44.9	58.0	52.7	24	23	6,340▲	267,630▲	10,587▲
Malawi	0.5	65	202	10.7	10.2	7.6	...	...	1,274	27,662	427
Mali	0.6†	77†	110†	13.2	1.1	0.6	...	...	2,099	45,525	2,592
Morocco	1.8†	541	2,775	25.1	242.1	90.5	39	56	7,974	486,800	6,590
Nigeria	3.5†	908	1,264	89.0	41.1†	23.6†	51	96	5,381	213,623	6,933
Rhodesia	3.2	...	6,501+	78.1†	126.6†	52.0†	...	...	2,834†⊕	72,112†⊕	891†⊕
Senegal	1.0†	245	179	15.4	40.4	18.1	30	14	1,849□	73,594□	6,370□
South Africa	19.8†	...	57,178**	c.320.0	1,653.0	394.0	249	538	41,891	3,071,000	73,630
Tanzania	c.2.6	4,529†◊	3,941◊	16.7†	c.33.3	c.33.7	11	18	6,340▲	267,630▲	10,587▲
Uganda	c.1.0	4,529†◊	3,941◊	24.5†	32.3†	6.0†	1	6	6,340▲	267,630▲	10,587▲
Zaire	5.8	657	1,927	140.0	70.0	27.5	7	39	12,689	595,300	17,977
Zambia	1.4†	...	...	34.7†	48.2†	30.6	1	6	4,725	228,014	5,530
NORTH AND CENTRAL AMERICA											
Canada	72.8	3,657	160,750	810.1	6,602.2	1,736.0	1,228	2,366	242,460	15,397,238	432,009
Costa Rica	0.7	c.55	c.18	18.7	39.3	27.1	6	3	5,978	197,000	12,260
El Salvador	0.6	...	...	8.6	35.1	18.5	16	4	...	...	...
Guatemala	c.0.8	...	106	c.12.0	42.6	24.4	2	4	4,850	104,090	6,820
Honduras	1.0	...	...	5.2†	18.8	16.9	54	70	10,530	163,755	3,870
Mexico	19.8†	4,534	22,863	71.6	1,326.2	557.9	185	401	57,733	2,939,000	41,678
Nicaragua	0.3†	35†	13†	6.1	34.4	8.9	6	11	2,240	76,990	1,100
Panama	0.7	...	...	6.7†	48.3	14.5	1,031	6,262	...	...	...
United States	333.1†	9,830	1,067,712	6,003.0	89,280.0	18,748.0	3,327	16,266	3,887,640	218,544,000	7,479,936
SOUTH AMERICA											
Argentina	39.7†	12,188	12,925	201.1	1,304.3†	714.8†	335	1,312	47,353	2,394,925	55,998
Bolivia	3.6	256†	316†	25.6	c.19.2	c.28.8	...	...	3,580	108,970	1,730
Brazil	32.0†	13,338†	25,207†	1,039.8	2,002.6†	656.1†	420	1,731	95,406	4,983,000	189,666
Chile	10.8	2,338	2,533	70.5	c.220.0	c.70.0	135	388	20,885	1,112,500	47,393
Colombia	3.5	235	1,172	c.45.0†	c.150.5†	c.135.0†	50	209	54,849	1,701,000	64,275
Ecuador	1.0	85	56	17.2	39.6	51.2	18	45	12,301	255,323	10,687
Paraguay	0.5	28†	22†	11.2	7.4	10.1	26	22	...	...	...
Peru	1.8†	254†	591†	50.1†	230.4	117.5	601	421	19,958	788,783	25,722
Uruguay	3.0†	...	...	c.41.6	202.0	84.2	42	163	2,315	63,207	290
Venezuela	0.5	36	13	43.2	708.0	257.0	109	412	30,596	1,424,600	67,947
OCEANIA											
Australia	40.3*	3,504*†,††	25,190*	884.3	3,898.5	971.5	350	1,105	186,427	9,268,445	270,008
New Zealand	4.8	507	3,212	89.3	941.6	185.3	118	181	33,680	1,878,700	43,424

Note: Data are for 1970 or 1971 unless otherwise indicated.
(—)Indicates nil or negligible; (...) indicates not known; (c.) indicates provisional or estimated.
*State system only.
†Data given are the most recent available.
‡Including apportionment of traffic of Scandinavian Airlines System.
§Including West Berlin.
‖Excluding Northern Ireland.
¶Including Singapore.
♀Apportionment of traffic of Malaysia-Singapore Airlines Ltd.
δIncluding Bangladesh.
□Including apportionment of traffic of Air Afrique.
◊Total for Kenya, Tanzania, and Uganda (East African Railways Corp.).
▲Including apportionment of traffic of East African Airways Corp. and Caspair Ltd.
+Including traffic for Botswana.
⊕Including apportionment of traffic of Central African Airways Corp.
**Including South West Africa (Namibia).
††Excluding New South Wales and Queensland.

Sources: UN, *Statistical Yearbook 1971*; *Monthly Bulletin of Statistics*; *Annual Bulletin of Transport Statistics for Europe 1969*; Lloyd's Register of Shipping, *Statistical Tables 1970*; International Road Federation, *World Road Statistics 1972*; *Jahrbuch des Eisenbahnwesens 1971*.

(M. C. MacDONALD)

TERESA ZAMBALA—THE NEW YORK TIMES

UPI COMPIX

Two transit systems made their debut in the U.S. in 1972. The Bay Area Rapid Transit system (BART) trains (above) link San Francisco, Oakland, and suburban counties over a 75-mi. network of subways, tunnels, and elevated and surface lines. A computerized Personal Rapid Transit System (right) links two campuses of West Virginia University at Morgantown, cutting travel time from an hour to less than five minutes for the $1\frac{1}{2}$-mi. trip.

though the average carrying capacity increased slightly. The total number of passenger-kilometres rose in some European countries if long-distance coach travel was included. In Austria it rose by 8%, in Belgium by 6%, and in Spain by 18%.

Measures taken to stimulate patronage included giving buses priority at traffic lights, permitting anti-directional travel on one-way street systems, reserved bus lanes, exemption from turning bans, and the tailoring of services to special needs, including on-demand and commuter express services. In both the U.S. and the U.K. several bus experimental schemes financed with public funds were in operation. In some cases bus licensing was relaxed, and in West Germany 45% of the special fuel tax of 3 pfennigs per litre of gasoline was used to subsidize public passenger transport services.

PIPELINES

Construction of new pipelines and the extension or duplication of existing networks for transporting both crude oil and its products and natural gas accelerated during the year. Steps were taken to add to the capacity of the European network by inaugurating new pumping facilities, by looping, and by the construction of new big-diameter lines parallel to the original systems. The two trunk lines from the North Sea ports of Wilhelmshaven, W.Ger. (the Northwest line), and Rotterdam, Neth., to the lower Rhine-Ruhr area of West Germany were enlarged, and the new Northwest parallel pipeline was scheduled to begin operation in 1973. The crude-oil network from the Mediterranean ports to eastern France, southern Germany, northern Italy, Switzerland, and Austria was being expanded with two parallel lines. The line starting near Marseilles, France, neared completion, and consideration was being given to laying a feeder from the Trans-Alpine pipeline, which begins at Trieste, Italy, to the Yugoslav port of Omisalj, the starting point of a projected pipeline to northern Yugoslavia, Hungary, and Czechoslovakia.

Expansion of the line from Rotterdam to Antwerp, Belg., was begun; when completed, it would increase the carrying capacity from 28 million to 46 million tons per year. In France a second pipeline, 80 km. long, from Berre to the Manosque underground oil storage complex was authorized. The Fos–Strasbourg line to Lyons was completed, as were additions to the Le Havre–Paris products line. A 250-km. products line from Bordeaux south to Agen and Toulouse was under consideration. Also being considered was a massive crude-oil artery extending from Le Havre to the Ruhr.

In the U.S.S.R. progress was made on Druzhba II, which was being laid alongside the original 4,350-km. line transporting crude oil from the European Russia and Ural-Volga areas. It was anticipated that by 1975 50 million tons a year would pass through this network to Poland, East Germany, Czechoslovakia, and Hungary. The line was also to be connected with the recently discovered oil deposits in western Siberia and Kazakhstan. The first 818-km. section of the 4,000-km., 122-cm.-diameter crude-oil pipeline from the Tyumen oil fields to Nakhodka on the Sea of Japan was completed early in 1972; work was started on the next section, which would extend 1,450-km. to Irkutsk and was scheduled for completion in 1973.

In the summer the U.S. Department of the Interior decided to issue a permit for construction of the long-delayed trans-Alaska pipeline, which would bring crude oil from the North Slope fields to the warm-water port of Valdez. Work on the line could not begin, however, pending resolution of court proceedings brought by groups who feared the effects of the pipeline on the delicate Arctic environment. The Interior Department's own environmental impact statement had indicated that the pipeline could have serious adverse effects. In his statement announcing the decision, Secretary of the Interior Rogers Morton pointed to the overriding need of the country for energy and added that the route from Alaska across Canada to the Midwest, favoured by the environmentalists, was "impractical at this time."

With the discovery and exploitation of new natural-gas fields, particularly offshore, the European network of natural-gas pipelines had become even more extensive than that of the oil pipelines and was expanding at a faster rate. The largest unified natural-gas pipeline network outside the U.S.S.R. was that of Ente Nazionale Indocarburi of Italy. This totaled 9,714 km. at the end of 1971, and was being extended by a further 5,000 km. Plans included extensions to border points to receive Soviet gas at Tarvisio and Dutch gas at the Gries Pass. The pipeline from that point through Switzerland to West Germany would be the longest natural-gas line in Europe. Construction of a line across the Messina Strait to Sicily was under study. A 160-km. line from Imatra to Kouvola and Kotka in Finland was scheduled for completion in 1973. In Algeria a third big natural-gas pipeline parallel to the existing 570-km. Hassi R'Mel–Arzew line was begun. New pipeline construction for transport from the Soviet Union's extensive natural-gas fields included a big line from Medvezhye in the northern part of western Siberia to the Urals. The 416-km.-long Czechoslovakian section of the gas line from the U.S.S.R. to Western Europe and the spur to East Germany were completed during the year.

Canada planned to build a 48-in.-diameter pipeline down the Mackenzie Valley with the capacity for delivering 3,500,000,000 cu.ft. of Arctic gas a day. A route for the line through eastern Canada was being surveyed. Expansion of both of Canada's transcontinental systems was authorized. In Bolivia the 530-km. line from the Santa Cruz fields to Yacuiba near the Argentine border was completed in 1972, as were links with the main pipeline from Campo Durán to Argentina. A project for development of the Palm Valley field in central Australia included a large-diameter line that would deliver gas to the coast for shipment to California. Also in the planning stage was a 775-mi. pipeline to deliver Cooper Basin gas to Sydney and other towns in New South Wales.

RAILWAYS

With more traffic carried at generally higher rates, the railway industry in general reported higher gross revenues in 1972. However, in most cases higher costs offset the improvements in revenue, deficits reached even higher levels, and in many countries subsidies were required, especially in order to maintain uneconomic but necessary services. Countering a trend of recent years, passengers carried and passenger-kilometres tended to increase while freight traffic on some systems declined. British Rail, with a deficit of £15 million in 1971, anticipated a £40 million deficit in 1972 and no improvement was foreseen for 1973; government grants and loans to the system totaled £100 million in 1971 and the estimate for 1972 was £160 million. Both the U.S. railroads and the Canadian National railways sustained heavy losses.

Amtrak, the quasi-governmental organization set up in 1971 to take over most intercity passenger services in the U.S., reported a loss of $111 million in its first year of operation, ended April 30, 1972. According to its annual report, the only consistently profitable passenger route in the country was the line between New York City and Washington, D.C., which included the high-speed Metroliner service. In November Amtrak announced that its revenues for the third quarter of 1972 were 13% above those for the comparable period a year earlier; all but three of the 14 railroads participating in Amtrak showed increases.

In August the Interstate Commerce Commission (ICC) authorized merger of the Illinois Central Railroad and the Gulf, Mobile & Ohio. The combined company, to be known as the Illinois Central Gulf Railroad, would operate a 9,400-mi. network extending over 13 states. In other actions, the ICC authorized the Louisville & Nashville Railroad to merge with the Monon, and permitted Central of Georgia to take over four smaller railroad companies. In June the Erie-Lackawanna announced that it was filing for reorganization under the federal Bankruptcy Act, principally because of widespread damage to its lines caused by flooding in the Eastern states in the wake of Tropical Storm Agnes.

A number of technological developments were introduced during the year, including new types of traction and improvements in the riding quality of passenger rolling stock to allow faster speeds on existing tracks. The main handicap to high speeds on curves is carbody tilting, but developments in several countries

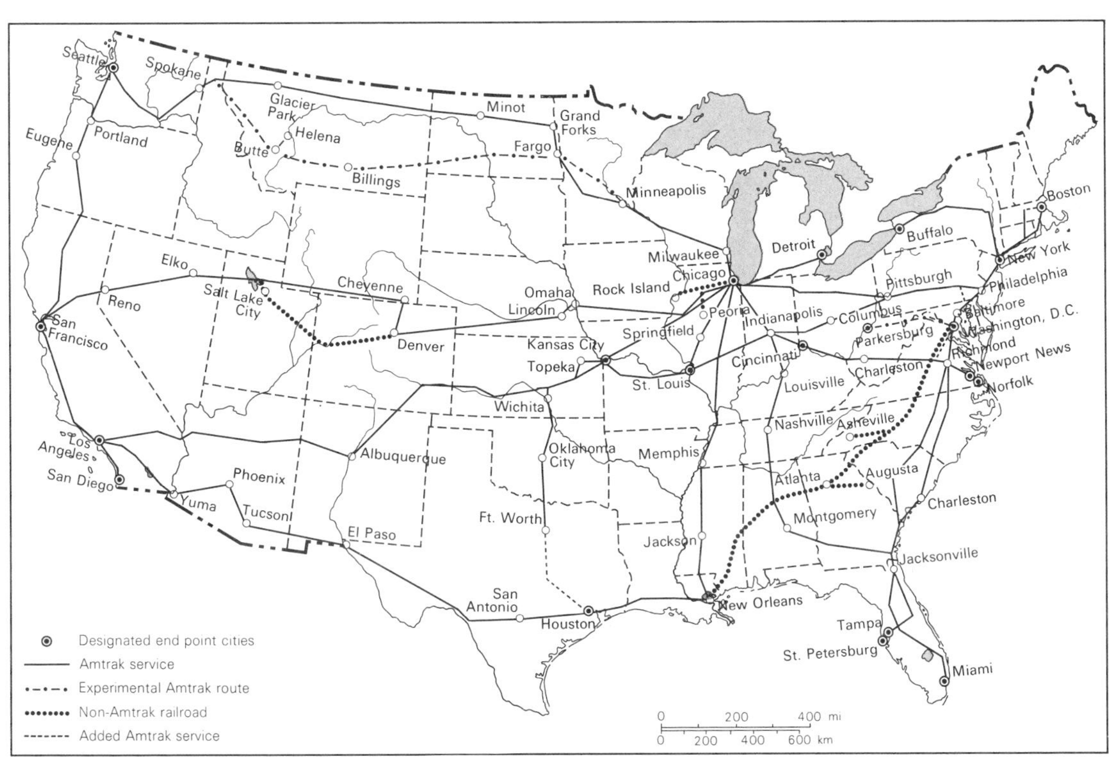

Routes of the National Railroad Passenger Corporation (Amtrak), which operates intercity passenger trains under the terms of the U.S. Rail Passenger Service Act.

gave promise of permitting speeds around bends from 35 to 50% higher than had been possible with older equipment. Most notable was the British gas-turbine-powered advanced passenger train (APT), designed for speeds of up to 250 kilometres per hour (km/h; 155 mph) with a tilt to a maximum angle of 9°; this, added to the superelevation of track, would permit a total tilt of 17° from the vertical. A prototype APT with electric traction was also being developed. Late in 1972 tests were begun on the precursor of British Rail's new intercity trains, which were expected to reach 200 km/h. The first on-track tests of the British Tracked Hovertrain reached 110 km/h.

Canada designed a low-profile, lightweight, push-pull train comprising two 2,700-hp diesel electric locomotives, one at each end, with an electronically controlled hydraulic mechanism incorporated in special swiveling trucks (bogie trucks); this provided automatic tilting of the bodies around curves and allowed a 40% increase in speed. Sweden, West Germany, France, and Japan were also developing tilting mechanisms. Sweden's worked on the principle of exhausting air from springs on the inside of curves and feeding air to those on the outside. Japan's system consisted of a pendulum method of tilting by suspending the cars from the top and supporting them on rollers underneath. In France tests began on an experimental articulated train powered by two gas turbines designed for speeds of 250 to 300 km/h.

Construction of a 26-km. aerotrain line from La Défense, in Paris, to the new town of Cergy was authorized, and introduction of turboprop train service between Nantes, Tours, Vierzon, and Lyons was scheduled for 1973. West Germany was developing a magnetic suspension and linear motor propulsion train with 60 km. of track designed for speeds up to 500 km/h. The U.S.S.R. planned to introduce superheavy trains with a total weight of between 7,000 and 10,000 tons and with booster locomotives positioned in the middle of the train. An experimental train tested over the new San-Yo line in Japan achieved 286 km/h.

The higher speeds made possible by improvements in track construction and maintenance, extension of electrification, more powerful motive power, and better riding qualities were paying off on intercity services. Average speeds of 100–145 km/h were becoming common, while top speeds increased to 200 km/h and were expected to reach 250 km/h in 1973. The Trans-Europ Express services, connecting major European centres of population and industry, consisted of a network of fast, comfortable trains on 27 different routes, served by 35 trains stopping at 125 stations, and carrying 2.5 million passengers annually. Named trains on the French railways averaged 133 to 145 km/h overall and achieved a top speed of 200 km/h. On the 681-km. Tokyo–Okayama (Japan) high-speed line, opened in March 1972, the average speed between the two cities was 164 km/h and the top speed was 209 km/h. In the U.S. the turbo train that began operation in 1972 between Washington, D.C., and Parkersburg, W.Va., covered the 315-m. journey in eight hours, a speed made possible by pendulum suspension and quick acceleration and braking. Canada was planning to resume operation of its turbo trains between Montreal and Toronto early in 1973.

Higher speeds were also being achieved by freight trains. A notable development was the increase in speeds on the Trans-Europ Express-Marchandises network, linking the railway systems of all European countries west of the U.S.S.R. and Finland and comprising some 114 connections. The trains operated at maximum speeds of 85–100 km/h and average speeds of up to 57 km/h.

Some 53,000 route-kilometres were operating with electric traction in Western Europe in 1972. In the U.S.S.R. electrification of the country's rail network of 135,000 km. was proceeding at a rate of 2,000 km. per year. Poland planned to electrify 1,350 km. by 1975 and it was expected that 80% of all the country's traffic would be electrically hauled by 1980. In East Germany, 1,300 km. were to be electrified by 1977.

Most railway systems had greatly reduced their route-mileage during the preceding two decades. By 1972, however, the process had decelerated, and construction of new lines, especially in less developed areas, exceeded closures. Thus the Soviet and Indian systems continued to expand, and new lines were being built in a number of African countries, Australia, and Japan. In the U.S.S.R. 3,179 km. of new lines had been built between 1966 and 1970, and in 1971–72 services were begun on a 115-km. section of the 250-km. line on the Trans-Siberian railway linking Uzbekistan and Tajikistan. Construction was begun on a line from Bam, 2,000 km. W of Vladivostok, to Tyndinskiy in the Amur forest. In Japan the Okayama–Hakata section of the new San-Yo line was scheduled for opening in the spring of 1975. Construction of the Kathua to Jammu and Kashmir line in India neared completion.

The 70-mi. extension of the Vitória and Minas railway in Brazil was completed. In Mexico a feasibility study of a new route across the Isthmus of Tehuantepec was under way. In Canada extensions to the Pacific Great Eastern Railway, totaling 250 mi., were being built from the Dease Lake line to Lower Post, 5 miles south of the Yukon border. Construction of a Trans-Gabon railway was authorized to link iron-ore deposits at Mekambo with the new deepwater port of Owendo. South Africa planned to construct an 843-km. iron-ore line from Sisken to Sabdanha Bay.

Construction of the long-discussed railroad tunnel under the English Channel was scheduled to begin in 1973. (ERNEST DAVIES)

WATER TRANSPORTATION

Shipping. Depressed freight markets, labour troubles, ever rising costs, and the threat of growing interference with shipping on political, economic, and environmental grounds all combined to make 1972 another difficult year for the shipping industry. Stagnant freight markets were partly the result of the continuing flood of new tonnage generated by the gross over-ordering—as it appeared in retrospect—of the boom years of the late 1960s. In the course of 1972 the world fleet expanded by something approaching 20 million tons, taking it well over 250 million tons for the first time. Another significant factor was the low state of Japanese chartering following the floating of the U.S. dollar and the slowdown in the Japanese economy in late 1971. Thus Japan demonstrated that it had become the major force in world shipping, as well as in world shipbuilding, with the largest fleet (after Liberia) and the largest cargo generation.

Japan distinguished itself in another, less satisfactory way with a 90-day seamen's strike that indicated a militance and intransigence new to that country. The strike immobilized the fleet and inflicted substantial damage on the economy, although it failed to have more than a marginal effect on freight markets. On the U.S. West Coast dockers struck for 135 days, while in Britain dockers closed the ports for three weeks in the summer. (*See* LABOUR UNIONS.)

In both Britain and the U.S., the dockers' strikes were basically over containerization which, although firmly established as the prime mode of carrying mixed general cargo on the main trade routes, was still suffering from higher costs, lower or nil profits, and more persistent troubles of various kinds than its protagonists had expected at this late stage. Partly because of this, and partly because the most attractive routes were now containerized, 1972 appeared to mark the beginning of a pause in what had probably been the most costly, far-reaching, and rapidly implemented revolution the shipping industry had ever known. There still remained some routes to be converted to containers—Europe to Africa and South and Central America, for example—but no one seemed in much hurry to get on with it.

In contrast to tramp and tanker owners, liner operators were doing somewhat better in 1972 as a result of more realistic freight charges than they had been able to extract from shippers in many years. With costs rising rapidly in every department of operation, rate increases of 10–30% were essential, but it had taken the cancellation of a proposed £80 million containerization project by Britain–New Zealand lines in 1971—on the ground of inadequate returns—to convince shippers that the lines really meant business. There was continued concern about marine pollution. The Inter-Governmental Maritime Consultative Organization advocated tougher measures that, whatever their effect on cutting down oil spillage into the sea, would probably limit the size of tankers to the current maximum of around 500,000 tons for some time to come. (*See* ENVIRONMENT.)

Meanwhile, the UN Conference on Trade and Development (UNCTAD), meeting in Santiago, Chile, in the spring, brought renewed pressure for control over international shipping, primarily from less developed nations with the possibly conflicting aims of increasing their own merchant fleets and reducing the cost of sea transport on their overseas trade. The traditional maritime states predictably resisted the demand for more state intervention in deep-sea shipping, pressing instead for a commercial code of practice through which shippers and shipowners would keep their own houses in order. However, some further erosion of what was once regarded as the freedom of the seas seemed inevitable.

On the technical front the most striking phenomenon was the emergence of a substantial fleet of huge and enormously expensive gas carriers and barge carriers. (MICHAEL BAILY)

Docks and Harbours. The world's major ports continued to be transformed from assembly points for large numbers of individual cargo items to staging posts in the continuous and integrated movement of goods in containers and bulk loads over various forms of transport. Facilities to meet this changing role were being provided on an ever increasing scale. Apart from the provision of modern container berths, changes in port operations included diminution of the necessity for transit warehouses on the quay and the substitution of open areas and equipment for marshaling the containers for transfer from one transport mode to another—*e.g.*, from road or rail to ship and vice versa.

Equipment for the speedy handling of specialized cargoes in unit loads was needed to match the specialized ships that carried them. Bulk cargo tankers and unit-load and container vessels—steadily increasing in size—were taking the place of cargo liners and tramps. Ports being adapted to handle these large vessels were utilizing completely new methods. The unit-load concept, for example, could involve horizontal loading through large openings in the ship's side, using fork-lift trucks as the main handling equipment. Roll-on/roll-off facilities were required for containers carried throughout the journey by motor vehicles. Both large and small ports were competing for this trade, and there was some danger of excess capacity.

There was no slowdown in capital investment in port development during the year, however. Japan led in the installation of new container facilities, and it was anticipated that some 55 such facilities, each 250–300 m. long, would be operational by 1974–75. Eighty new berths were to be built at the port of Osaka, five of which would be container berths. Among other major ports undergoing improvement, Le Havre, France, began work early in 1972 on an oil terminal that would provide accommodation for tankers of around one million tons; it was expected to be ready in 1974. A new lock, the world's largest in its class, connecting the tidal basin with the channel of the port and capable of taking 250,000-ton vessels, was opened early in the year. Construction of another port, either along the coast or, preferably, offshore, was being considered.

The largest port in the Soviet Union, with a capacity for handling tankers of up to 180,000-tons displacement, was to be built at the Grigoryevzkiy coastal lagoon near Odessa, and a new deepwater port was under construction at Wrangel Bay. A new container port was under construction at Esbjerg, Den.

In the U.K. the £50 million Seaforth dock at Liverpool, with six container berths and a roll-on/roll-off berth, started to receive ships in 1972. A new container terminal serving the Far East came into operation as part of a £14.5 million development at Southampton. Two new roll-on/roll-off terminals at Hull became operational, and others were opened at Sheerness and Plymouth. Ellesmere Port planned further container terminals. Work was in progress on a £15 million dock project at Bristol, and extensions for five new berths at Harwich were authorized. The new container berth at Greenock was able to take the largest container ships operating on the North Atlantic at all states of the tide. At Grangemouth a new lock would accommodate larger oceangoing ships.

In North America investment in new facilities at existing ports continued on a grand scale, and long-term planning of further capacity to cope with the next generation of supersized vessels was undertaken. The U.S. Army Corps of Engineers was directed to study the economic and environmental feasibility of developing a deepwater facility for supertankers and other bulk-cargo carriers to serve the North Atlantic coast between Maine and Virginia. An offshore bulk terminal to serve the East Coast was also under consideration. Meanwhile, the Port Authority of New York and New Jersey brought into operation a new container terminal at Port Jersey, N.J.; located three miles from the sea, it was just inside the harbour at Port Jersey's industrial complex. Work continued on the Elizabeth-Port Authority Marine Terminal and Port Newark complex; upon completion, the complex would have over three miles of berthing space, including three full container-ship berths and nearly 416 ac. of area to handle waterborne cargo. Construction also proceeded on the six-berth passenger ship terminal in

Manhattan, scheduled for completion early in 1974. A $10 million container terminal was opened at Long Beach, Long Island, and two new ship berths were being built at Maryland Port. The second full container berth at New Orleans, La., started receiving ships, and plans for a new lock and channel between the Mississippi River and the Gulf of Mexico to accommodate large modern vessels were under consideration. A new cargo complex was opened at Baltimore, Md. In Canada, Vancouver port was to be expanded to handle container traffic, and Port St. John, N.B., was being modernized at a cost of $17.5 million.

At Madras, India, the outer harbour project was completed, enabling tankers of 70,000–80,000 deadweight tons (dwt) to enter. Other ports where construction was in progress included Mormagoa, Haldi, Kandla, Cochin, Nhava-Sheva, and Bombay. Improvements at Vizagapatam on India's eastern coast, scheduled for completion in 1974, would make it the only port complex between Rotterdam and Tokyo capable of taking ships up to 100,000 dwt.

Inland Waterways. Indications were that the final figures for inland waterway traffic in Europe in 1971 would show little improvement over 1970, when 471.2 million metric tons were carried and international traffic totaled 178.3 million metric tons. Since 1962 international traffic had risen more steeply than internal traffic, and this trend continued into 1972. Rhine traffic crossing the Netherlands frontier with West Germany and through the Basel (Switz.) ports and traffic on the Austrian part of the Danube were all higher in 1972 than 1971. In the U.S.S.R. freight tonnage carried on inland waterways during the first half of 1972 was 7% above the same period in 1971.

In West Germany considerable progress was made on the Rhine-Main-Danube canal, which would link the North and Black seas in the late 1980s. The main construction fell into three parts: canalization of the Main between Aschaffenburg and Bamberg; construction of the Main-Danube canal from Bamberg to Kelheim and canalization of the Danube from Kelheim to Regensburg; and extension of the German Danube from Regensburg to the West German-Austrian frontier. The Main-Danube section was complete to Erlangen. The harbour at Nürnberg was opened in September 1972, and the 133-km. section of the canal between Nürnberg and Regensburg would be ready in 1981. The completed sections on the Main and Main-Danube canal carried 13.7 million tons in 1970, and the German Danube carried 4 million tons; the figures for 1971 were expected to be higher.

In conjunction with the Cabora Bassa hydroelectric scheme in southern Africa, the Zambezi River was to be made navigable for 260 mi. from its mouth up to the city of Tete in Mozambique. Nicaragua was studying a plan to cut a 140-mi. canal parallel to the Atlantic coast to link the major navigable rivers in the region. The canal would take maximum advantage of existing creeks and lagoons and, together with the major rivers, could provide surface communication in the Atlantic region stretching from Bluefields Bay in the south to Puerto Cabezas in the north.

The St. Lawrence Seaway set a new record for traffic in the 1972 shipping season, surpassing the previous record set in 1971. Final figures for 1971 totaled 52.9 million tons in 8,728 transits on the Montreal–Lake Ontario section and 63 million tons in 9,168 transits on the Welland section. Through traffic accounted for 4,265 transits carrying 46.8 million tons. Work on the Welland bypass was well ahead of schedule; portions of the new channel were flooded, the Welland River Syphon and Diversion was put into operation, and the tunnel was completed. The entire bypass was expected to be finished in 1973. (ERNEST DAVIES)

Hovercraft. In February 1972 British Hovercraft Corp. (BHC) announced an order worth £5 million from the Imperial Iranian Navy (already the world's largest user of Hovercraft). The British government announced in March that it was spending £1.5 million in development contracts within the industry and had a further £1 million in reserve. This led to the announcement of several plans to enlarge and modify existing craft such as BHC's SR-N6. BHC launched two stretched SR-N6s with 58 seats instead of the usual 38 in the spring.

In the U.S. trials of two 100-ton surface-effect ship models proceeded, and in April the Advanced Research Projects Agency authorized further studies to develop an effective amphibious Hovercraft for military use in the Arctic. In Canada Bell Aerospace launched a second Voyageur 40-ton amphibious transport and began building four more craft. The company announced in October that it would develop a 15-ton craft known as the Viking in conjunction with the Canadian government. (JOHN BENTLEY)

See also Cities and Urban Affairs; Engineering Projects; Industrial Review.

ENCYCLOPÆDIA BRITANNICA FILMS. *The Mississippi System: Waterway of Commerce* (1970); *The Great Lakes—North America's Inland Seas* (1971); *Rotterdam—Europort, Gateway to Europe* (1971).

Trinidad and Tobago

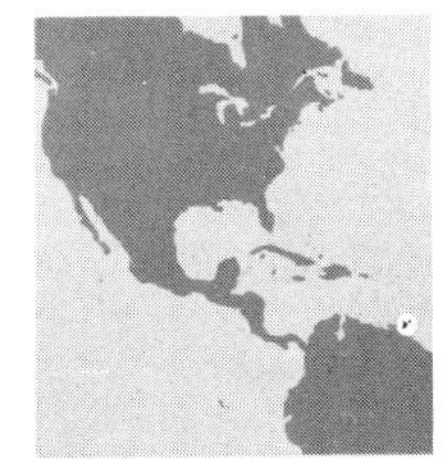

A parliamentary state and a member of the Commonwealth of Nations, Trinidad and Tobago consists of two islands off the coast of Venezuela, north of the Orinoco River delta. Area: 1,980 sq.mi. (5,128 sq.km.). Pop. (1971 est.): 1,030,000, including (1960) Negro 43.3%; East Indian 36.4%; mixed 16.3%. Cap. and largest city: Port-of-Spain (pop., 1970, 67,867). Language: English (official); Hindi, French, Spanish. Religion (1960): Christian 66%; Hindu 23%; Muslim 6%. Queen, Elizabeth II; governor-general in 1972, Sir Solomon Hochoy; prime minister, Eric Williams.

The 1972 budget of TT$497,760,000 announced in January continued the policy of expansion in highway construction, low-cost housing, schools, hospitals, and waterworks, but also provided for further government intervention with risk capital in the productive sectors of the economy. In order not to neglect private enterprise, income from farms of less than 50 ac. was to be tax-free for five years; the Small Business Unit of the Industrial Development Corp. was refinanced; and for the first time in any Commonwealth Caribbean country manpower was subsidized by an employment allowance to medium-sized businesses in the hope of encouraging them to employ more staff and to work second shifts. The first Commonwealth Caribbean Workers' Bank was opened at Port-of-Spain on Dec. 1, 1971. It was exempted for five years from corporation tax and stamp duty, and its stockholders from income tax on their dividends. The government held a 16% interest. The number of unemployed remained at about 50,000, 12% of the labour force.

Under the emergency regulations that resulted from

TRINIDAD AND TOBAGO

Education. (1968–69) Primary, pupils 232,611, teachers (state only; 1969–70) 6,510; secondary, pupils 46,455, teachers 1,824; vocational, pupils 4,679, teachers 273; teacher training, students 714, teachers 81; higher, students 1,267, teaching staff 200.

Finance and Trade. Monetary unit: Trinidad and Tobago dollar, with (Sept. 18, 1972) a free rate of TT$1.96 to U.S. $1 (par value of TT$4.80 = £1 sterling). Budget (1970 est.): revenue TT$295 million; expenditure (excluding TT$99 million capital expenditure) TT$277 million. Foreign trade (1971): imports TT$1,304,800,000; exports TT$1,036,400,000. Import sources: U.S. 17%; Saudi Arabia 15%; Libya 13%; U.K. 13%; Venezuela 10%. Export destinations: U.S. 41%; Sweden 10%; U.K. 9%; ship and aircraft bunkers 8%; Puerto Rico 5%. Main exports: petroleum products 70%; crude oil 7%; sugar 6%.

Transport and Communications. Roads (1970) 6,222 km. (including 2,040 km. main roads). Motor vehicles in use (1970): passenger 74,900; commercial (including buses) 20,200. Air traffic (1970): 510.8 million passenger-km.; freight 10,761,000 net ton-km. Shipping traffic (1969): goods loaded *c.* 21,430,000 metric tons; unloaded *c.* 15,520,000 metric tons. Telephones (Dec. 1970) 56,000. Radio receivers (Dec. 1969) 293,000. Television licenses (Dec. 1970) 54,000.

Agriculture. Production (in 000; metric tons; 1971; 1970 in parentheses): rice *c.* 10 (*c.* 10); sweet potatoes *c.* 18 (*c.* 18); oranges *c.* 12 (*c.* 11); grapefruit *c.* 18 (*c.* 15); sugar, raw value (1971–72) 236, (1970–71) 220; copra *c.* 13 (*c.* 13). Livestock (in 000; 1970–71): cattle *c.* 65; pigs *c.* 53; goats *c.* 37; poultry *c.* 5,340.

Industry. Production (in 000; metric tons; 1971): crude oil *c.* 6,100; petroleum products (1970) 21,286; cement 259; nitrogenous fertilizers (1970–71) *c.* 80; electricity (kw-hr.) 1,226,000.

the dispute between the Oilfield Workers' Trade Union (OWTU), led by Black Power militant George Weekes, and the Seamen and Waterfront Workers' Trade Union (SWWTU), 16 persons were detained, including Weekes. Also, several bills were passed dealing with sedition and control of trade unions.

At a time of high unemployment, rising costs in the important sugar industry, and uncertainty raised by Britain's entry into the EEC, Trinidad's oil discoveries came as a welcome economic boost. By the end of the year offshore wells were providing the government with TT$960,000 a week in royalties, and the country expected to double its 1971 output of 47.5 million bbl. by the end of 1973. (R. J. M. DENNERSTEIN)

Tunisia

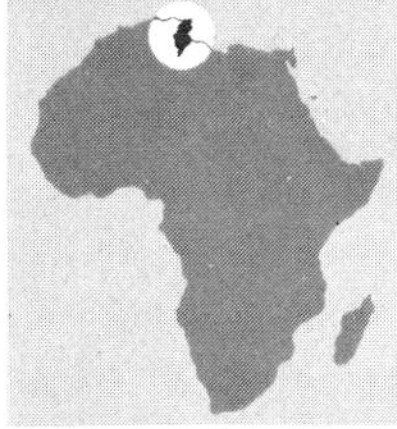

A republic of North Africa, lying on the Mediterranean Sea, Tunisia is bounded by Algeria and Libya. Area: 63,378 sq.mi. (164,150 sq.km.). Pop. (1970 est.): 5,137,000. Cap. and largest city: Tunis (pop., 1966, 468,997). Language: Arabic (official). Religion: Muslim; Jewish and Christian minorities. President in 1972, Habib Bourguiba; prime minister, Hedi Nouira.

Within Tunisia 1972 saw the expulsion of former minister of the interior Ahmed Mestiri from the official Neo-Destour Socialist Party for the second time, and disturbances at the University of Tunis. The main events in foreign affairs were the visit of Egyptian Pres. Anwar as-Sadat in May and President Bourguiba's trip to Paris in June.

Mestiri, leader of the liberal wing of the Neo-Destour party, was expelled for the second time in four years after criticizing the conduct of the 1971 party congress and the policies of Prime Minister Hedi Nouira. He had been reinstated in April 1970 after his first expulsion in 1968 when he resigned from the government as a protest against the collectivization policies of Ahmed Ben Salah.

In February violent clashes between police and students in the streets of Tunis led to the closing of the faculties of law and letters at the University of Tunis and the arrest of about 100 students. By April, however, the situation had improved, and Bourguiba announced that the faculties would reopen several months earlier than originally planned. In September the trial of approximately 40 students by a Tunis disciplinary tribunal was adjourned pending further inquiries.

During President Sadat's visit Bourguiba reaffirmed his country's solidarity with Egypt while expressing doubts about the wisdom of a new Arab-Israeli war. The visit was returned in November by the Tunisian prime minister. Bourguiba's visit to Paris in June set the seal upon the Franco-Tunisian reconciliation, and questions relating to the political development of the Mediterranean area were discussed by Bourguiba and French Pres. Georges Pompidou. The latter, however, had serious reservations about the Tunisian plan for a general conference of Mediterranean states.

A distinct thaw in relations between Tunisia and neighbouring Algeria had been evident for some time, and in the course of the year a complete normalization of relations between the two countries was achieved. In March the Tunisian prime minister visited Algiers and the following month Algerian Pres. Houari Boumédienne was received in the Tunisian capital. This was followed by a visit to Algiers by President

TUNISIA

Education. (1968–69) Primary, pupils 857,514, teachers 16,693; secondary, pupils 90,620; vocational, pupils 50,587; secondary and vocational (1967–68), teachers 5,299; teacher training, students 8,207; higher (at University of Tunis), students (1970–71) 9,811, teaching staff 304.

Finance. Monetary unit: Tunisian dinar, with (Sept. 18, 1972) a par value of 0.48 dinar to U.S. $1 (free rate of 1.13 dinars = £1 sterling). Gold, SDRs, and foreign exchange, central bank: (June 1972) U.S. $165.5 million; (June 1971) U.S. $93.8 million. Budget (1972 est.) balanced at 175 million dinars. Gross domestic product: (1970) 661 million dinars; (1969) 627.2 million dinars. Money supply: (April 1972) 260,270,000 dinars; (April 1971) 210,120,000 dinars. Cost of living (Tunis; 1963 = 100): (June 1972) 138; (June 1971) 133.

Foreign Trade. (1971) Imports 179,960,000 dinars; exports 113.3 million dinars. Import sources: France 36%; U.S. 15%; Italy 9%; West Germany 7%. Export destinations: Italy 19%; France 19%; West Germany 13%; Libya 10%; Spain 6%. Main exports: crude oil 25%; olive oil 21%; phosphates 19%. Tourism (1970): visitors 410,700; gross receipts U.S. $65 million.

Transport and Communications. Roads (1971) 18,267 km. Motor vehicles in use (1971): passenger 72,100; commercial 39,400. Railways: (1969) 1,998 km.; traffic (1971) 469 million passenger-km., freight 1,371,000,000 net ton-km. Air traffic (1971): 316,880,000 passenger-km.; freight 2,107,000 net ton-km. Telephones (Dec. 1970) 76,000. Radio licenses (Dec. 1970) 388,000. Television licenses (Dec. 1970) 51,000.

Agriculture. Production (in 000; metric tons; 1971; 1970 in parentheses): wheat 600 (450); barley 140 (*c.* 150); tomatoes (1970) *c.* 127, (1969) 153; wine *c.* 70 (60); dates *c.* 50 (*c.* 47); figs *c.* 15 (14); olive oil 160 (90); oranges (1970) *c.* 70, (1969) 83; lemons (1970) *c.* 12, (1969) 18. Livestock (in 000; 1970–71): sheep *c.* 3,100; cattle *c.* 670; goats *c.* 450; camels *c.* 280; poultry *c.* 9,000.

Industry. Production (in 000; metric tons; 1971): crude oil 4,097; cement 583; iron ore (55% metal content) 936; phosphate rock (1970) 3,021; lead 19; sulfuric acid 455; electricity (excluding most industrial production; kw-hr.) 768,000.

Trucking Industry: *see* Transportation

Trust Territories: *see* Dependent States

Tungsten: *see* Mining

Bourguiba himself, during which he took the opportunity to reiterate his desire for a general conference of Mediterranean states. In December, Bourguiba publicly rejected a Libyan proposal for union of the two countries. (PHILIPPE DECRAENE)

Turkey

A republic of southeastern Europe and Asia Minor, Turkey is bounded by the Aegean Sea, the Black Sea, the U.S.S.R., Iran, Iraq, Syria, the Mediterranean Sea, Greece, and Bulgaria. Area: 301,380 sq.mi. (780,576 sq.km.), including 9,158 sq.mi. in Europe. Pop. (1972 est.): 36,110,000. Cap.: Ankara (pop., 1970, 1,208,791). Largest city: Istanbul (pop., 1970, 2,247,630). Language: Turkish, Kurdish, Arabic. Religion: predominantly Muslim. President in 1972, Gen. Cevdet Sunay; prime ministers, Nihat Erim until April 17 and, from May 22, Ferit Melen.

Political instability and economic progress characterized Turkey in 1972. Business confidence revived under the second "above party" government formed by Nihat Erim on Dec. 11, 1971. The military authorities pursued their campaign against terrorism and made wide use of their powers under martial law. Terrorist outrages continued, however. On March 26 members of the Turkish People's Liberation Army (TPLA) kidnapped one Canadian and two British radar technicians in an attempt to secure the release of three terrorists condemned to death for the abduction of four U.S. radar technicians in March 1971. The authorities refused to parley, and the hostages and ten of their captors were killed on March 30 in the mountain village of Kizildere in northern Turkey. The TPLA tried again on May 3, hijacking a Turkish airliner on a domestic flight and forcing it to land in Sofia, Bulg. Although concessions were again refused, bloodshed was avoided when the four hijackers surrendered to the Bulgarian authorities. On May 4 another group of TPLA terrorists shot and wounded the Turkish gendarmerie commander, Gen. Kemalettin Eken. The three condemned terrorists were executed in Ankara on May 6. On October 22 a second Turkish airliner was forced to land in Sofia. Turkish authorities refused concessions; the Bulgarian government accused them of being uncooperative, but nevertheless arranged the terrorists' surrender.

In the meantime, the Erim government had resigned on April 17, after the four major political parties had refused to grant it wider powers to rule by decree, as demanded by President Sunay in a memorandum on April 3. On April 29 Sunay entrusted the formation of the new government to veteran independent Sen. Suat Hayri Urguplu, but the president relieved him of his mission on May 13 when military commanders disagreed with his choice of ministers. The political crisis was finally resolved when Ferit Melen (*see* BIOGRAPHY), a member of the small moderate National Reliance Party and minister of defense in the outgoing Erim administration, formed a new government on May 22 and was given a vote of confidence by Parliament on June 5.

The new government included ministers from the National Reliance Party, the majority Justice Party, and the Republican People's Party (RPP). The RPP, however, was split by a feud between 87-year old Ismet Inonu and Bulent Ecevit, leader of the party's left-of-centre policy. On May 8 Inonu resigned from the leadership of the RPP after a special party conference had upheld Ecevit's stand, and Ecevit succeeded him on May 14. The change was followed by a number of resignations from the RPP; the dissidents formed a new Republican Party (RP) on September 4, under the leadership of Kemal Satir. On November 4 the RPP leadership ordered its five members to resign from the Melen government. However, the five preferred to resign from the party, following the lead of Inonu, who left the RPP on November 5. After further resignations, the RPP was left with 103 seats out of the 143 it had had in the Assembly.

Arrests and trials on charges of political subversion and insurrection continued throughout the year. On September 25 it was announced that martial law courts had passed 860 sentences and that another 1,100 people were being tried. The former dean of the Ankara Faculty of Political Science, Mumtaz Soysal, was sentenced to six years and eight months' imprisonment after a retrial, and on December 23 his defense counsel, Ugur Alacakaptan, professor of criminal law at Ankara, received a similar sentence.

Outside Turkey considerable publicity was given to the case of 14-year-old British schoolboy Timothy Davey, who on March 1 was sentenced in Istanbul to six years and three months' imprisonment for conspiracy to traffic in hashish. On October 6 Davey escaped from a reformatory, but was recaptured. The case occasioned widespread protests in Britain, and Prime Minister Erim canceled a planned stopover in London on his way to the U.S. in March.

Erim's visits to France (January 19–22) and the U.S. (March 19–23) reaffirmed Turkey's pro-Western stance. Soviet Pres. Nikolai Podgorny visited Ankara on April 11–17. (ANDREW MANGO)

See also Cyprus.

TURKEY

Education. (1969–70) Primary, pupils 4,905,107, teachers 123,030; secondary, pupils 959,401, teachers 28,864; vocational, pupils 163,263, teachers 11,534; teacher training, students 62,969, teachers 2,351; higher (including 9 universities), students 160,334, teaching staff 9,786.

Finance. Monetary unit: Turkish pound or lira, with (Sept. 18, 1972) a par value of 14 liras to U.S. $1 (free rate of 34.29 liras = £1 sterling). Gold, SDRs, and foreign exchange, central bank: (June 1972) U.S. $829 million; (June 1971) U.S. $443 million. Budget (1970–71 est.): revenue 36,293,000,000 liras; expenditure 37,093,000,000 liras. Gross national product: (1970) 147,940,000,000 liras; (1969) 128,380,000,000 liras. Money supply: (Dec. 1971) 22,660,000,000 liras; (Dec. 1970) 17,620,000,000 liras. Cost of living (Ankara; 1963 = 100): (June 1972) 201; (June 1971) 180.

Foreign Trade. (1971) Imports 16,526,000,000 liras; exports 9,090,000,000 liras. Import sources: West Germany 18%; U.S. 12%; Italy 11%; U.K. 10%; France 7%; U.S.S.R. 6%; Switzerland 5%; Iraq 5%. Export destinations: West Germany 19%; U.S. 10%; Switzerland 10%; France 7%; Lebanon 7%; U.S.S.R. 5%; U.K. 5%. Main exports: cotton 30%; hazelnuts 12%; tobacco 10%.

Transport and Communications. Roads (1971) 59,453 km. Motor vehicles in use (1970): passenger 168,700; commercial 126,800. Railways: (1970) 7,985 km.; traffic (1971) 5,763,000,000 passenger-km., freight 5,747,000,000 net ton-km. Air traffic (1971): 988.1 million passenger-km.; freight 7,083,000 net ton-km. Shipping (1971): merchant vessels 100 gross tons and over 328; gross tonnage 713,767. Telephones (Dec. 1970) 577,000. Radio licenses (Dec. 1970) 3,072,000. Television receivers (Dec. 1969) 25,000.

Agriculture. Production (in 000; metric tons; 1971; 1970 in parentheses): wheat 13,594 (10,081); corn 1,060 (1,040); rye *c.* 900 (630); barley 4,170 (3,250); oats 435 (415); onions (1970) 748, (1969) 691; potatoes 2,000 (1,915); sunflower seed *c.* 396 (375); chick-peas *c.* 120 (109); dry beans *c.* 155 (140); lentils *c.* 105 (92); oranges (1970) 523, (1969) 483; lemons (1970) 126, (1969) 121; apples *c.* 700 (748); pears *c.* 170 (180); grapes *c.* 3,860 (3,850); raisins *c.* 315 (*c.* 310); figs (1970) 214, (1969) 215; sugar, raw value (1971–72) *c.* 913, (1970–71) 645; olive oil 80 (118); tea *c.* 34 (34); tobacco *c.* 168 (138); cotton, lint 497 (400). Livestock (in 000; Dec. 1970): cattle 12,756; sheep 36,471; horses 1,049; asses 1,805; buffalo 1,117; goats 19,483; chickens *c.* 32,600.

Industry. Fuel and power (in 000; metric tons; 1971): crude oil 3,453; coal (1970) 4,573; lignite (1970) 9,246; electricity (kw-hr.) 9,727,000. Production (in 000; metric tons; 1971): cement 7,543; iron ore (55–60% metal content) 2,547; pig iron 882; crude steel 1,122; sulfur (1970) 70; sulfuric acid (1970) 28; nitrogenous fertilizers (1970) 82; phosphate fertilizers (1970) 63; manganese ore (metal content; 1970) 4.7; chrome ore (oxide content; 1970) 295; cotton yarn (factory only; 1970) 47; wool yarn (1968) 28.

Uganda

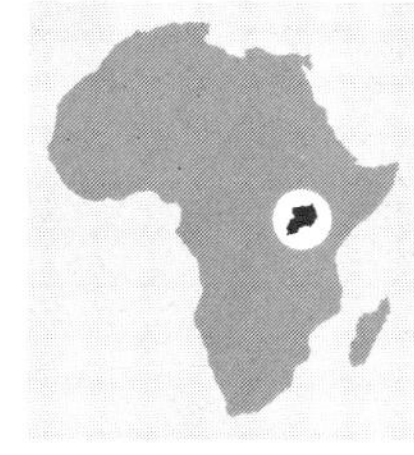

A republic and a member of the Commonwealth of Nations, Uganda is bounded by Sudan, Zaire, Rwanda, Tanzania, and Kenya. Area: 91,452 sq.mi. (236,860 sq.km.), including 15,236 sq.mi. of inland water. Pop. (1971 est.): 10,127,340, about 99% of whom are African. Cap. and largest city: Kampala (pop., 1969, 330,700). Language: English (official), Bantu, Nilotic, Nilo-Hamitic, and Sudanic. Religion: predominantly traditional beliefs, with Hindu, Muslim, and Christian minorities. President in 1972, Gen. Idi Amin.

Events in the final weeks of 1971 had presaged a difficult time for Uganda's Asians in 1972. In November 1971 Pres. Idi Amin criticized the Asian community, numbering about 80,000, for isolating themselves from the African people, and on December 8 he announced that all applications for citizenship outstanding on Jan. 25, 1971, had been canceled. In January 1972 he stated that the Africans should be in control of the economy, but that Asians who were already Uganda citizens had no cause for worry.

On August 9 President Amin delivered his most fundamental attack upon the Asian community when he ordered all Asians of non-Ugandan citizenship to quit the country within three months. He claimed that their presence prevented Uganda's Africans from playing their rightful part in developing the country's economy and that their failure to become Uganda citizens demonstrated their unwillingness to throw in their lot wholeheartedly with a country in which they lived and from which they drew their means of livelihood. Britain protested strongly, but Amin remained adamant, even briefly extending his order to cover Asians who had taken out Uganda citizenship though this was later withdrawn. Later in August, however, the president announced that the take-over of foreign-owned businesses would be extended to European-owned firms. Amin argued that his country was engaged in an economic war, and he accused a number of countries of plotting against his regime and against the well-being of the country as a whole. His policy undoubtedly won the support of many Uganda Africans who hoped to take over the businesses left by the Asians, but others had doubts about the likely effects upon a country that possessed only enough foreign exchange to pay for a month's imports.

Israel, too, came under criticism. Early in the year Libya agreed to assist Uganda in the development of its armed forces if Uganda would reduce its commitment to Israel. Toward the end of March Amin became convinced, as a result of a report in an Israeli newspaper, that Israeli personnel were involved in subversive activities in Uganda. He therefore announced that contracts with Israeli military instructors in Uganda would not be renewed when they expired. Israel countered by immediately recalling its military experts. Amin later publicly endorsed Adolf Hitler's policy of exterminating Jews.

Relations with Britain also received a jolt in mid-June when a BOAC aircraft carrying arms to Zambia was detained for three weeks at Entebbe Airport owing to a dispute over clearance negotiations. More serious, however, for Uganda's external image was the publication early in July of the report of a commission of inquiry into the disappearance of two U.S. citizens in Mbarara in 1971. Justice David Jeffreys Jones of the Uganda High Court, who conducted the inquiry, claimed that he had met with repeated obstruction from army officers in carrying out his task and concluded on the evidence that the two missing men had been killed by army personnel in the military barracks in Mbarara and their bodies and possessions disposed of to cover up the crime. Judge Jones subsequently resigned and left Uganda.

GOKSIN SIPAHIOGLU—JOCELYNE BENZAKIN

Jubilant Ugandans in a village outside Kampala sing anti-Asian songs to celebrate the expulsion of Asians from Uganda.

UGANDA

Education. (1968) Primary, pupils 632,162, teachers (1967) 19,257; secondary, pupils 31,637, teachers 1,304; vocational, pupils 3,527, teachers 272; teacher training, students 4,292, teachers 308; higher (at Makerere University; 1970), students 3,053, teaching staff 350.

Finance. Monetary unit: Uganda shilling, with (Sept. 18, 1972) a par value of UShs. 7.14 to U.S. $1 (free rate of UShs. 17.51 = £1 sterling). Gold, SDRs, and foreign exchange: (June 1971) U.S. $43.4 million; (June 1970) U.S. $64.7 million. Budget (1970–71 est.): revenue UShs. 1,142,000,000; expenditure UShs. 1,121,000,000. Cost of living (Kampala; 1963 = 100): (1st quarter 1972) 169; (1st quarter 1971) 159.

Foreign Trade. (Excluding trade with Kenya and Tanzania; 1971) Imports UShs. 1,362,000,000; exports UShs. 1,680,000,000. Import sources: U.K. 32%; Japan 13%; West Germany 10%; U.S. 7%; Italy 6%; India 5%. Export destinations: U.K. 24%; U.S. 22%; Japan 11%; India 8%; West Germany 7%. Main exports: coffee 58%; cotton 21%; copper 8%; tea 6%.

Transport and Communications. Roads (1969) 24,539 km. Motor vehicles in use (1969): passenger 32,300; commercial (including buses) 6,000. Railways (1970) *c.* 1,000 km. (for traffic *see* KENYA). Air traffic: *see* KENYA. Telephones (Dec. 1970) 30,000. Radio receivers (Dec. 1967) 509,000. Television receivers (Dec. 1969) 12,000.

Agriculture. Production (in 000; metric tons; 1971; 1970 in parentheses): millet *c.* 630 (*c.* 630); sorghum *c.* 332 (*c.* 332); sweet potatoes (1970) *c.* 710, (1969) *c.* 710; cassava (1970) *c.* 2,150, (1969) 2,321; peanuts *c.* 234 (*c.* 234); dry beans *c.* 270 (*c.* 260); coffee *c.* 210 (*c.* 204); tea *c.* 18 (18); sugar, raw value *c.* 154 (166); sesame *c.* 23 (*c.* 23); cotton, lint *c.* 69 (*c.* 75); timber (cu.m.; 1969) 11,300, (1968) 11,000; fish catch (1970) 129, (1969) 125. Livestock (in 000; Dec. 1970): cattle *c.* 4,400; sheep *c.* 880; goats *c.* 1,940; pigs *c.* 77; chickens *c.* 10,200.

Industry. Production (in 000; metric tons; 1970): copper, smelter 17; tin concentra es (metal content) 0.11; tungsten concentrates (oxide content) 0.15; salt (exports) 3; phosphate rock 300; cement (1971) 202; electricity (excluding most industrial production; kw-hr.; 1971) 817,000.

Tunnels: *see* Engineering Projects

Amin's popularity with other African states, which he had been attempting to build up, suffered a setback over his Asian policy. Pres. Julius Nyerere of Tanzania, who had never been very friendly toward Amin, denounced his action as inhumane, and there were further abusive exchanges between the two countries. On September 17 forces loyal to Uganda's former president, Milton Obote, invaded southwestern Uganda from Tanzania and met with some initial success. Amin accused Tanzanian forces of being involved in the campaign, but this was denied by Nyerere. Nevertheless, Amin sent his Israeli-trained Air Force to bomb a number of Tanzanian towns on the shores of Lake Victoria. The invading forces were soon defeated, and although it became clear that Tanzanian troops had not taken part it was difficult for the Tanzanian authorities to deny all knowledge of the preparations for the invasion or to escape the accusation of having assisted them. Through the intervention of Pres. Muhammad Siyad Barrah of Somalia, peace terms were agreed upon between Uganda and Tanzania in October, but relations remained strained.

In spite of the delays occasioned by the fighting, the airlift arranged by Britain and a number of other countries that had agreed to provide homes for expelled Asians began to operate effectively, and it was estimated that by the November 8 deadline imposed by Amin all non-Ugandan Asians apart from about 1,500 stateless persons had left. The president had stated that Asians not out of the country by the required date would be rounded up and put in camps. Those expelled were allowed to take with them a maximum of £50 in currency together with goods not exceeding £500 in value. All other possessions had to be handed over to the government. Late in November Britain retaliated by canceling a credit of £24 million, and subsequently British personnel were ordered to quit the country by December 31. Amin then sought additional aid from China. On December 18, 41 mostly British-owned foreign companies were nationalized and on December 31 a "mass mobilization" of Ugandans was declared. (KENNETH INGHAM)

See also Race Relations; Refugees; United Kingdom.

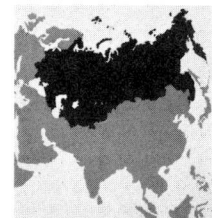

Union of Soviet Socialist Republics

The Union of Soviet Socialist Republics is a federal state covering parts of eastern Europe and northern and central Asia. Area: 8,600,340 sq.mi. (22,274,900 sq.km.). Pop. (1971): 245,066,000, including (1970) Russians 53%; Ukrainians 17%; Belorussians 4%; Uzbeks 4%; Tatars 3%. Cap. and largest city: Moscow (pop., 1970, 6,942,000). Language: officially Russian, but many others are spoken. Religion: about 40 religions are represented in the U.S.S.R., the major ones being Christian denominations. General secretary of the Communist Party of the Soviet Union in 1972, Leonid I. Brezhnev; chairman of the Presidium of the Supreme Soviet (president), Nikolai V. Podgorny; chairman of the Council of Ministers (premier), Aleksei N. Kosygin.

Domestic Affairs. Aside from a growing fascination with the outward manifestations of the consumer society, other trends in social policy that had attracted attention in the West for some time found a positive echo in the Soviet Union. A press conference given in Moscow in October by Mikhail Prokofiev, the minister of education, showed that Soviet educators had become aware of the problem of children's underutilized capacity for learning. The minister forecast the lowering of the school admission age from seven years to six in 1975 (it was reduced from eight to seven in 1957) and the introduction of ten years' compulsory schooling. Earlier in the year, in July, the Central Committee of the Soviet Communist Party met to consider the future of higher education. It deplored the fact that the standards of achievement in some educational establishments had failed to keep up with the demands of scientific and technological progress, particularly in the area of postgraduate education. To improve the coordination of educational standards throughout the country, the Central Committee set up a new Council for Higher Education, and the authorities were given until 1974 to raise the level of scientific and technological training. In the social sciences, more had to be done "to cultivate in the students a class approach to the phenomena and events of public life, and skill in criticizing anti-Marxist views."

In September the U.S.S.R. Supreme Soviet instructed the Soviet government to pay more attention to the protection of the environment and to the proper utilization of the country's natural resources. In the debate, several deputies mentioned measures taken recently to control wind erosion over an area exceeding 44 million ac. in northern Kazakhstan and western Siberia—apparently an attempt to cope with the legacy of Nikita S. Khrushchev's policy of indiscriminate plowing up of "virgin lands." Deputy Premier Vladimir Kirillin advocated closer international cooperation in environmental matters, but did not mention the Soviet Union's refusal to attend the UN Conference on the Human Environment in Stockholm in June. However, an agreement with the U.S. on cooperation in the protection of the environment was concluded as a result of President Nixon's visit to Moscow.

Throughout 1972, as in previous years, Soviet authorities had to face a certain amount of dissent and discontent, expressed at various levels. The rejection of the fundamentally totalitarian nature of the system by relatively small groups of intellectuals manifested itself mainly through the *Chronicle of Current Events* and other clandestinely printed publications. The courage and persistence of the dissidents, who continued to engage in *samizdat*—the clandestine production and circulation of illegal publications—made them the first target of police repression. A particularly widespread wave of arrests followed immediately after U.S. Pres. Richard Nixon's visit in May.

Perhaps the best-known dissenter was the nuclear physicist Andrei D. Sakharov, who published his controversial memorandum calling for greater intellectual freedom in 1968. In an article published in *L'Express* in Paris at the beginning of August 1972, he attacked those "who favour a bigoted bureaucracy and intervention of a totalitarian government in the lives of citizens." Sakharov was also associated with the small self-styled Soviet Action Group for the Defense of Human Rights. This group had made protests several times to the United Nations against the arbitrary arrest and persecution of Soviet citizens, and especially against the practice of confining political dissidents in mental hospitals on trumped-up psychiatric grounds.

The year began with a sentence of 12 years in prison and exile passed in January on Vladimir Bukovsky for crimes against the state, which in the main seemed to consist of informing foreigners about conditions in the so-called psychiatric hospitals. In June the police

Unemployment:
see Employment, Wages, and Hours; Social Services
UNESCO:
see United Nations

took action against some of those associated with the Action Group, but not against Sakharov, who was probably protected by his prominent position within the scientific establishment. One of the leaders of the group, Pyotr Yakir, a well-known historian and son of an army general executed by Stalin, was arrested, together with others accused of tape-recording Western broadcasts and circulating the writings of proscribed authors. (Yakir was later reported to be collaborating with the secret police.) The victims of this purge, which lasted most of the year, included the Leningrad scientist Yuri Melnik, sentenced to three years in June; the sociologist Vatslav Sevruk, confined to a mental hospital; the Moscow astronomer Kronid Lyubarsky; the Kiev cybernetics expert Leonid Plyushch; and the founder of the Action Group, Victor Krasin. Sakharov and the cellist Mstislav Rostropovich were among the distinguished signatories of an appeal delivered to the Supreme Soviet in September calling for abolition of capital punishment and the release of political prisoners. Aleksandr Solzhenitsyn, still living in retirement near Moscow, refused an offer by the Swedish government to award his 1970 Nobel Literature Prize in a private ceremony at the Swedish embassy. (*See* LITERATURE.)

The authorities pursued a fairly rigid policy of control over intellectuals who had some access to the media. In January the Central Committee of the Soviet Communist Party once again denounced the shortcomings of literary and artistic criticism; it complained of lack of vigour "in the struggle against various kinds of non-Marxist views on art and against revisionist aesthetic conceptions" and demanded a strengthening of party control over all aspects of intellectual activity. The head of the Soviet film industry, Aleksei Romanov, was dismissed in August for being "too much influenced by Western trends." The Soviet regime's concern over the influence of the media was reflected even in diplomatic action. In August the Soviet government went as far as to ask the United Nations to place on its agenda a Soviet proposal for an international agreement against transmission by satellite of television broadcasts to countries without their permission. In his note to the UN secretary-general, Soviet Foreign Minister Andrei A. Gromyko warned against "allowing live television broadcasts to become a source of international conflicts."

Throughout 1972 there were reports of the arrest of nationalist elements in the Ukraine, the Baltic republics, and Central Asia. In January several Ukrainian nationalists were imprisoned in Kiev and Lvov. In March the Central Committee of the Soviet Communist Party turned its attention to Stalin's homeland, Georgia, criticizing the municipal leadership in Tbilisi for allowing graft and corruption to affect economic policy. There was a crisis of another kind in Tbilisi in June, when several people were killed and thousands rendered homeless by storms and natural disasters; the first secretary of the Tbilisi municipal party organization, Otar I. Lolashvili, was dismissed soon afterward. In September the first secretary of the Georgian Communist Party and alternate member of the Soviet Politburo, Vasili Mzhavanadze, was retired at the age of 70 and replaced by the energetic 45-year-old Eduard Shevardnadze. The dismissal in May of Petr Shelest from his post as first secretary of the Ukrainian Communist Party and from the Soviet Politburo indicated, among other things, some dissatisfaction with the management of Ukrainian affairs. Shelest was demoted to the relatively unimportant position of deputy premier of the Soviet Union, and his place at the head of the party in the Ukraine was filled by Vladimir V. Shcherbitsky, reputedly a close associate of Brezhnev.

WIDE WORLD

The disastrous 1972 grain harvest caused a shortage of bread in the Soviet Union. Soviet women are shown lined up to buy bread in a Moscow bakery.

Although by Soviet standards the Baltic republics of the U.S.S.R. were allowed a considerable degree of latitude in maintaining their cultural traditions, serious discontent persisted. In March petitions protesting religious persecution were signed by 17,000 Lithuanian Roman Catholics and sent to the UN and to Brezhnev; they referred to the guarantees of freedom of conscience contained in the Soviet constitution. At the same time, the local press in Latvia felt that it had to react to an open letter sent by 17 Latvian Communists, in which they complained of the russification of their country; they were labeled as tools or dupes of the U.S. Central Intelligence Agency. The worst crisis, however, developed in Lithuania. In May a young political protester set himself on fire, and his death led to riots in Kaunas, where thousands of young people shouting for "freedom for Lithuania" battled with troops and police. The Soviet press subsequently described the young suicide as a drug addict and dismissed the riots as hooliganism. Nevertheless, they were important as a major demonstration against official policy in the Soviet Union.

The most prominent minority in the U.S.S.R. consisted of those Jews who obstinately continued to regard Israel as their real fatherland. In 1972 there was a strictly controlled increase in the number of exit permits, although from time to time heavy compensation payments were demanded from scientists and other academically trained Jews. Indeed, even some non-Zionist dissidents were allowed to emigrate in 1972—among them the poet Yesenin-Volpin, the writer Yuri Glazov, and the painter Yuri Titov. (*See* ISRAEL: *Special Report.*)

The Economy. The U.S.S.R. considered itself to be moving into an advanced phase of economic development, when industrial expansion no longer needed to be ruthlessly pursued at the expense of the environment and in complete disregard of human needs. The most prominent feature of the ninth five-year plan (1971–75) was the shift in emphasis toward meeting the wishes of the Soviet consumer. Consumer satisfaction, however, was not proving as easy as might have been expected. Imports of goods from Eastern Europe, especially from East Germany, and also from non-Communist countries gave the customers yardsticks for comparison, and Soviet enterprises were finding it difficult to meet these standards. Service industries had always been inefficient in centrally planned economies, and there were widespread complaints about the slowness and poor quality of service.

The authorities tried to react to these needs. An interdepartmental committee for research into consumer needs was established at the beginning of 1972. The government offered long-term credits for the construction of self-service stores, and by 1975 more than half of the retail outlets were to be converted to self-service. In his major policy speech to the 15th congress of Soviet Trade Unions in March, Brezhnev had to admit that the planned improvement in the provision of consumer goods had not yet materialized. The construction industry had failed to build new factories for the production of consumer goods, and unsold stocks of low-quality goods were disrupting the distribution network. Yet it would be incorrect to paint too gloomy a picture—the Soviet consumer lagged behind his Western counterpart, but his situation had improved greatly in recent years, and the improvement was being maintained.

The major problem posed to the economy in 1972 was the failure of agriculture. The grain harvest was officially 23 million tons below target, and the Soviet Union faced its worst food shortages since the harvest failure of 1963. By October Soviet foreign trade officials were eager to obtain deliveries of more than 11 million tons of U.S. wheat due under their recent trade agreement with the U.S. Apart from the chronic inefficiency of the Soviet Union's collective farming system, the main reason for the crisis was the freak winter weather in 1971–72, when not enough snow fell to insulate the seeds in the ground against frost. The situation was made much worse by the excessively hot weather and drought that prevailed in the summer of 1972 and incidentally caused major forest fires in the Moscow region and elsewhere. The harvest failure meant that the U.S.S.R. had to use hard currencies to finance food imports instead of buying industrial equipment; it was also deprived of the currency earned by grain exports to Western Europe in recent years. But at least people did not starve. The Soviet government was able to import the necessary foodstuffs without undue difficulty. (*See* AGRICULTURE.)

Industry, on the whole, did better than farming. The 1971 plan targets were met, and in October the Central Statistical Board announced that industrial output in the first nine months of 1972 was 6.7% above the total for the same period in 1971; the highest rate of development was in the engineering, chemical, and power industries. Labour productivity was reported to have increased by 5.3%, production costs had been reduced, and the nine-month targets for profits fulfilled. On September 1 the government announced sizable pay increases, averaging over 20% for five million professional salary earners.

One of the most interesting planning innovations in the U.S.S.R. was the Genshema, a general scheme of industrial location for 1971–80. Since 1966 thousands of experts had worked on preparations for the scheme, and computers were busy constructing a large variety of econometric models. It seemed that the policy of locating new industries was to be dictated by the availability of energy resources. The ninth five-year plan provided that by 1975 oil and gas would supply 76% of Soviet fuel and power requirements, but it also called for the completion of seven nuclear power stations, each with a capacity of more than 1,000 Mw. The Genshema paid special attention to the development of the northern regions, which were nearest to the industrial centres of the U.S.

President Nixon's visit to Moscow underlined the significance of the economic rapprochement with the U.S. The agreement for the purchase of $750 million in U.S. grains, concluded during the summer, helped to overcome the effects of the harvest failure. In October the U.S.S.R. concluded a comprehensive trade agreement with the U.S. and, as part of the arrangements, agreed to settle debts to the U.S. totaling $722 million, arising out of the Lend-Lease arrangements of World War II, in annual installments up to the year 2001. Some private U.S. firms were permitted to set up branch offices in Moscow.

The Soviet quest for technological know-how led to agreements with other non-Communist industrial countries. A $300 million contract for the construction of five chemical plants was signed with Japan; purchases from France included a large number of special compressors used in checking sections of new oil pipeline; and the establishment of closer relations with

U.S.S.R.

Education. (1969–70) Primary, pupils 40,483,000; secondary, pupils 4,556,000; primary and secondary, teachers 2,355,000; vocational and teacher training, pupils 4,301,700, teachers (1965–66) 251,000; higher (including 49 main and 57 technical universities), students 4,549,600, teaching staff (1965–66) 201,000.

Finance. Monetary unit: ruble, with (Sept. 18, 1972) an official exchange rate of 0.83 ruble to U.S. $1 (2 rubles = £1 sterling). Budget (1971 est.): revenue 166.3 billion rubles; expenditure 165.1 billion rubles.

Foreign Trade. (1971) Imports 11,231,000,000 rubles; exports 12,426,000,000 rubles. Import sources: Sino-Soviet area 66% (East Germany 15%, Poland 11%, Czechoslovakia 11%, Bulgaria 10%, Hungary 7%, Romania 5%). Export destinations: Sino-Soviet area 65% (East Germany 14%, Poland 10%, Czechoslovakia 10%, Bulgaria 8%, Hungary 7%, Cuba 5%). Main exports: machinery 22%; iron and steel 10%; crude oil 9%; timber 6%; nonferrous metals 5%; petroleum products 5%.

Transport and Communications. Roads (1969) 1,358,900 km. (including 511,600 km. motorable roads in 1970). Motor vehicles in use: passenger (1969) *c.* 1.5 million; commercial (1965) *c.* 4.5 million. Railways (1970): 135,200 km. (including 33,900 km. electrified); traffic 265,406,000,000 passenger-km., freight (1971) 2,633,000,000,000 net ton-km. Air traffic (1970): 78,500,000,000 passenger-km.; freight 2,070,000,000 net ton-km. Navigable inland waterways (1970) 144,500 km.; traffic 174,000,000,000 ton-km. Shipping (1971): merchant vessels 100 gross tons and over 6,575; gross tonnage 16,194,326. Telephones (Dec. 1970) 11 million. Radio licenses (Dec. 1970) 94.6 million. Television licenses (Dec. 1970) 34.8 million.

Agriculture. Production (in 000; metric tons; 1971; 1970 in parentheses): wheat 98,700 (99,734); barley 34,500 (38,172); oats 14,600 (14,200); rye 12,800 (12,972); corn 8,600 (9,428); rice 1,400 (1,280); millet 2,040 (2,100); potatoes 92,296 (96,783); sugar, raw value (1971–72) *c.* 8,220, (1970–71) *c.* 9,293; sunflower seed 5,658 (6,144); linseed *c.* 470 *c.* 525); dry peas *c.* 5,200 (*c.* 4,900); soybeans *c.* 610 (*c.* 603); tea 69 (67); wine 2,820 (2,680); cotton, lint 2,380 (2,343); flax fibre 466 (456); tobacco *c.* 288 (*c.* 270); wool 254 (251); eggs *c.* 2,481 (*c.* 2,222); meat *c.* 8,750 (8,765); milk 83,300 (82,900); butter *c.* 1,140 (1,067); cheese 466 (478); timber (cu.m.; 1970) *c.* 386,000, (1969) *c.* 388,000; fish catch (1970) 7,252, (1969) 6,498. Livestock (in 000; Jan. 1971): cattle 99,142; pigs 67,483; sheep 138,059; goats 5,360; horses 7,400; poultry 652,700.

Industry. Index of production (1963 = 100): (1971) 189; (1970) 175. Fuel and power (in 000; metric tons; 1971): coal and lignite 641,000; crude oil 377,070; natural gas (cu.m.; 1970) 197,945,000; manufactured gas (cu.m.; 1970) 32,899,000; electricity (kw-hr.) 800,000,000. Production (in 000; metric tons; 1971): cement 100,300; iron ore (60% metal content) 203,000; pig iron 89,300; steel 121,000; aluminum (1969) *c.* 1,100; copper (1970) *c.* 1,075; lead (1970) *c.* 440; zinc (1969) *c.* 610; manganese ore (metal content; 1970) 2,446; tungsten concentrates (oxide content; 1970) 8.5; magnesite (1969) *c.* 3,100; gold (troy oz.; 1969) 6,250; silver (troy oz.) *c.* 30,000; sulfuric acid 12,775; caustic soda 2,030; plastics and resins 1,860; nitrogenous fertilizers (plant nutrient content; 1970) 5,423; phosphate fertilizers (plant nutrient content; 1970) 2,500; potash fertilizers (plant nutrient content; 1970) 4,087; newsprint (1970) 1,100; other paper (1970) 5,605; cotton fabrics (sq.m.) 6,400,000; woolen fabrics (sq.m.) 674,000; rayon and synthetic fabrics (finished only; sq.m.) 891,000; passenger cars (units) 529; commercial vehicles (units) 812. New dwelling units completed (1970) 2,283,000.

West Germany, following the ratification of the 1970 treaty between Moscow and Bonn, also opened up new opportunities. The U.S.S.R. State Committee for Science and Technology concluded a number of technological cooperation agreements with capitalist firms, including the BASF and Hoechst chemical concerns and the AEG-Telefunken and Siemens electrical and electronic concerns in West Germany and the Occidental Petroleum Corp. in the U.S. The linkup with Siemens, in particular, was expected to be of some assistance to the relatively backward Soviet computer industry.

In July a long-term trade agreement between the U.S.S.R. and West Germany was agreed in Bonn. This was especially significant, since in 1971 West Germany had moved up to first place among the U.S.S.R.'s Western European trading partners. One of the most interesting aspects of Soviet cooperation with non-Communist countries was the projected exploitation of the Siberian oil and natural gas fields. Esso and Gulf Oil of the U.S. had shown an interest in the area, and negotiations with Japan for credits and technical cooperation in the opening of the Yakut and Tyumen fields and the building of related pipeline systems had been going on for some time.

Foreign Policy. The Soviet Union's policy of underpinning the status quo by negotiating directly with the U.S. culminated in President Nixon's visit to Moscow. There were, of course, many reasons why the Soviet Union needed to achieve a modus vivendi with the U.S.: a joint responsibility for the prevention of nuclear war, a desire to reduce the economic burden of the missile race, fear of China, and the challenges presented to the conduct of foreign policy by the emergence of a multipolar international system. The U.S. decision to come to terms with China changed the climate for negotiations between the superpowers, despite the attempts made by the Soviet propaganda machine to pillory Nixon's journey to China as the result of "the great-power, chauvinist, anti-Marxist policy of the Peking leadership . . . which has brought the Maoists to the role of actual accomplice to imperialist policy" (*Pravda,* March 28, 1972). The president's talks in Moscow, on the other hand, were praised as a sign that "an improvement of relations between the U.S.S.R. and the U.S. in the interests of both nations and the cause of promoting peace and international security is quite possible" (*Pravda,* May 31, 1972).

The most important immediate consequence of Nixon's visit was the signing of the U.S.-Soviet treaty on the limitation of strategic arms. It was agreed to limit the U.S. and the U.S.S.R. to 200 defensive antiballistic missiles each. The U.S., relying on its advantage in multiple independently targeted warheads, allowed the U.S.S.R. to maintain a numerical edge in the total of missile launchers. (*See* DEFENSE.) Other agreements dealt with cooperation in space, trade, and the protection of the environment. The U.S.S.R.'s conciliatory policy toward the Nixon administration extended even to Vietnam. The Soviet government virtually ignored the mining of Haiphong Harbour which preceded the president's visit to Moscow.

Relations with China remained reasonably static, though cool, and polemics were conducted at a fairly low level. For example, on Aug. 7, 1972, the Soviet government newspaper *Izvestia* published an apprehensive and hostile review of a new world atlas recently published in Peking. "Every page reeks with great-power contempt for other countries," claimed

WIDE WORLD

Looming paternally over the "Coat of Arms Square" in Leningrad, this cardboard rendering of Lenin was erected for the anniversary celebration on Nov. 7, 1972, of the Bolshevik Revolution.

the reviewer, who seemed particularly upset that the U.S.S.R. was described as a purely "European" state. Yet in July the Chinese ambassador to the U.S.S.R., Liu Hsin-chuan, undertook an extensive tour of Belorussia, the Baltic area, and Leningrad and was well received everywhere. In October reasonably cordial messages were sent to Peking on the 23rd anniversary of the People's Republic of China, though an authoritative article in *Pravda* on September 3 spoke of the "tactical peculiarities of Peking's present policy" and described China's developing relations with the U.S. as part of "the struggle against the Soviet Union."

It was argued that the unstable situation on the eastern frontier had helped persuade the Soviet Union of the need to maintain stability in Europe. Certainly in May 1972 Moscow welcomed the long-delayed ratification by the Bundestag of the 1970 treaties between West Germany and the Soviet Union. The Soviet leadership had consistently adopted a friendly attitude toward Chancellor Willy Brandt's government, and it encouraged its East German allies in the negotiations for mutual recognition with Bonn. Soviet policy vis-à-vis Germany depended to some extent on the security of the Soviet position in Eastern Europe, and all the potential trouble spots there were quiet in 1972. This was confirmed by the successful Warsaw Pact Shield 72 maneuvers, which took place without difficulty in Czechoslovakia in the fall. A meeting of leaders of the Communist parties of the Warsaw Pact countries, held in the Crimea in August, fully endorsed the Soviet Union's European policy. Elsewhere in Eastern Europe, President Tito's visit to the U.S.S.R. in June seemed to bring to an end the tension between the Soviet Union and Yugoslavia caused by the Warsaw Pact invasion of Czechoslovakia in 1968.

The next step in the Soviet Union's European policy was the proposal for a European security conference, which might institutionalize the existing state of affairs in Europe and which the U.S.S.R. had been urging on an initially reluctant Western alliance for some time. In 1972 the Soviet government continued to press this proposal at all levels. It confirmed Finnish support for the idea during Pres. Urho Kaleva Kekonnen's visit to Moscow in August, and it obtained somewhat lukewarm support from Giulio Andreotti, the Italian premier, during his visit in October. The Soviet foreign minister, Andrei Gromyko, went to Paris in June and obtained Pres. Georges Pompidou's approval. At the 15th Trade Union Congress in March, Brezhnev went beyond the narrow security conference proposal by acknowledging for the first time the existence of the EEC as a viable international reality. The Soviet policy of normalization was even stretched to cover a trade agreement with Francisco Franco's Spain. Finally, on Nov. 22, 1972, preparatory talks for a European security conference began in Helsinki.

While 1972 seemed to bring the Soviet Union closer to the achievement of its short-term policy goals in Europe, events in the Middle East moved in the opposite direction. In the summer, relations with Egypt deteriorated suddenly, as the Egyptians realized that the Soviet Union would not supply all the military equipment they thought they needed to develop the offensive capacity of their armed forces. In July Pres. Anwar as-Sadat told the Central Committee of the Arab Socialist Union that the U.S.S.R. had failed to send weapons that had been promised and had, in consequence, been asked to withdraw its military experts and advisers from Egypt.

The number of Soviet military advisers was estimated to be about 20,000. Some efforts were made to heal the breach, notably by the Egyptian premier, Aziz Sidky, who went to Moscow in October and whose visit was followed by replacement of the anti-Soviet defense minister, Gen. Muhammad Ahmed Sadek. Some weapons systems were delivered early in November, and Soviet-Egyptian relations returned to a semblance of cordiality, but relatively few Soviet military experts returned.

Soviet interests in the Persian Gulf and in the Indian subcontinent continued to await the reopening of the Suez Canal. The Soviet Union maintained reasonably close relations with other Arab and Middle Eastern countries. A friendship treaty with Iraq was concluded in the spring during Premier Kosygin's visit to Baghdad, and the U.S.S.R.'s first stake in Arab oil materialized when, on April 7, the North Rumaylah oil field, developed with Soviet assistance, began production. The Syrian president, Hafez al-Assad, came to Moscow in July. More significantly, in October the shah of Iran paid a state visit to the U.S.S.R.

The independence of Bangladesh had been made possible by Indian military action, and the U.S.S.R., having recognized the new state in January 1972, expected to reap some diplomatic advantage as a result of having backed India throughout the crisis. Sheikh Mujibur Rahman of Bangladesh went to Moscow in March, and he was followed almost immediately by Pres. Zulfikar Ali Bhutto of Pakistan. This was one contest where the Chinese and Americans, who had supported Pakistan, came out on the losing side.

The Soviet reaction to the renewed U.S. bombing of Hanoi in December was comparatively restrained, although Brezhnev, speaking at celebrations marking the Soviet Union's 50th anniversary on December 21, said that the course of U.S.-Soviet relations hinged on the conclusion of the Vietnam war. (OTTO PICK)

See also Communist Movement; Propaganda.

ENCYCLOPÆDIA BRITANNICA FILMS. *The Soviet Union: Epic Land* (1971); *The Soviet Union: A Student's Life* (1972).

Unions: *see* Labour Unions

Unitarians: *see* Religion

United Arab Republic: *see* Egypt

United Church of Canada: *see* Religion

United Church of Christ: *see* Religion

United Arab Emirates

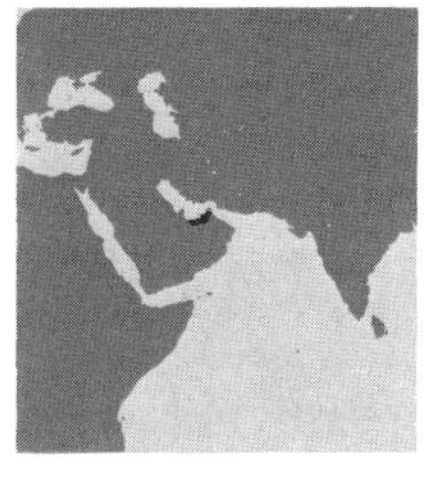

Consisting of seven emirates, the United Arab Emirates (the former Trucial States) is located on the eastern Arabian Peninsula. Area: 32,300 sq.mi. (83,657 sq.km.). Pop. (1971 est.): 197,000. Cap.: Abu Dhabi town (pop., 1968, 22,023). Language: Arabic. Religion: Muslim. President in 1972, Sheikh Zaid ibn Sultan an-Nahayan.

During its first year as an independent state, the United Arab Emirates established diplomatic relations with all the Arab states and most leading Western countries, but a decision on relations with the Soviet Union was delayed, apparently because of Saudi influence. On Jan. 25, 1972, the ruler of Sharjah, Sheikh Khalid, was killed in an attempted coup led by his cousin, Sheikh Saqr, who had been deposed as ruler in 1965. He was replaced by his younger brother, Sheikh Sultan, the UAE educational minister.

On February 10 Ras al-Khaimah, the only one of the seven Trucial States to remain outside the UAE, decided to join. Some 20 people were killed in a tribal land dispute between Fujairah and Sharjah in June. The dispute was settled by a conciliation commission set up by the UAE president, Sheikh Zaid (*see* BIOGRAPHY).

Economic development proceeded rapidly, especially in oil-rich Abu Dhabi and Dubai, and in September plans were announced to build "the biggest dry dock between Europe and the Far East" in Dubai. An offshore oil strike at Abu Musa Island, which according to a recent agreement was shared between Sharjah and Iran, indicated that Sharjah would be the third member of the UAE to become an important oil producer. (PETER MANSFIELD)

UNITED ARAB EMIRATES

Education. Primary and secondary (1968–69), pupils *c.* 12,000 (including 4,387 in Abu Dhabi), teachers (Abu Dhabi only) 223.

Finance. Monetary units: Abu Dhabi, Bahrain dinar with (Sept. 18, 1972) a free rate of 0.44 dinar to U.S. $1 (1.07 dinars = £1 sterling); other states, Qatar Dubai riyal with (Sept. 18, 1972) a free rate of 4.37 riyals to U.S. $1 (10.70 riyals = £1 sterling). Budgets: (Abu Dhabi; 1971 est.) oil revenue *c.* 180 million dinars; (Dubai; 1970 est.) revenue *c.* 4 million dinars; (other states; 1971) revenue *c.* 1 million dinars.

Foreign Trade. Abu Dhabi (1969) imports 59,000 dinars (32% from U.K., 18% from U.S., 7% from Dubai). Main export crude oil. Dubai (1971): imports 1,059,000,000 riyals; exports 135,827,000 riyals (excluding oil and gold; including reexports of 126,942,000 riyals). Import sources: U.K. 18%; Japan 17%; U.S. 12%; Switzerland 9%. Export destinations: Iran 47%; Oman 13%; Qatar 11%. Main export crude oil; other (excluding oil and gold; mainly reexports): foodstuffs 38%; household goods 26%; arms and ammunition 9%; clothing 7%; building materials 6%; drilling materials 6%.

Industry. Crude oil production (in 000; metric tons; 1971): Abu Dhabi 44,614; Dubai 6,340.

United Kingdom

A constitutional monarchy in northwestern Europe and member of the Commonwealth of Nations, the United Kingdom comprises the island of Great Britain (England, Scotland, and Wales) and Northern Ireland, together with many small islands. Area: 94,216 sq.mi. (244,018 sq.km.), excluding 1,188 sq.mi. of inland water and the crown dependencies of the Channel Islands and Isle of Man. Pop. (1971): 55,355,138. Cap. and largest city: London (pop. [Greater London], 1971, 7,392,995). Language: English; some Welsh and Gaelic also are used. Religion: mainly Protestant. Queen, Elizabeth II; prime minister in 1972, Edward Heath.

During 1972 the United Kingdom completed the legislation necessary for its full participation in the European Economic Community on Jan. 1, 1973. Worsening strife between the Protestant and Catholic communities of Northern Ireland led to the imposition of direct rule there, and economic difficulties involving inflation, unemployment, and industrial unrest led to abandonment of a fixed parity for sterling and to a 90-day freeze on wages and prices.

Domestic Affairs. The prime minister, Edward Heath (*see* BIOGRAPHY), who had made few changes in the structure of his government since the Conservatives were elected in June 1970, was forced by events to reshuffle some of his senior Cabinet posts in 1972. The decision to transfer responsibility for the government of Northern Ireland to Westminster, announced on March 24, was accompanied by the appointment of William Whitelaw (*see* BIOGRAPHY) as secretary of state for Northern Ireland—a new office. In changes announced on April 7 Robert Carr (*see* BIOGRAPHY) took over as lord president of the Council and leader of the House of Commons. Carr's post as secretary of state for employment was taken by Maurice Macmillan. Outside the Cabinet a new post of minister of industrial development was taken by Christopher Chataway. A further switch of Cabinet posts came on July 18, when Reginald Maudling resigned as home secretary because of allegations relating to him made in an inquiry into the bankruptcy of John Poulson, former head of an international firm of architects. Carr was made home secretary and continued for the time being as leader of the Commons.

UPI COMPIX

With the help of a gas lantern, a London woman is able to see a greeting-card display during a power blackout in February 1972 caused by a prolonged strike of coal miners.

A more extensive reconstruction followed on November 5 when Heath announced that Peter Walker was to take over the Department of Trade and Industry (DTI) and would be replaced at the Department of the Environment by Geoffrey Rippon, whose responsibilities for Europe were to go to John Davies (moving from the DTI). James Prior became leader of the House of Commons and his post as minister of agriculture was taken by Joseph Godber. A new Cabinet post of minister for trade and consumer affairs was filled by Sir Geoffrey Howe.

Disagreements over entry into the EEC led to changes in the Labour Party hierarchy. Roy Jenkins (*see* BIOGRAPHY), strongly pro-European deputy leader of the party who had been reelected the previous November, resigned from Harold Wilson's shadow cabinet in April, along with George Thomson and Harold Lever, saying he could not join in Labour's decision to vote with anti-Market Conservatives on a proposal to submit entry to the EEC to the test of a referendum. Three other Labour front bench members

UNITED KINGDOM

Education. (1969–70) Primary, pupils 5,835,093, teachers 237,710; secondary and vocational, pupils 3,945,297, teachers 227,981; higher (44 universities only), students 226,733, teaching staff 33,000.

Finance. Monetary unit: pound sterling, with (Sept. 18, 1972) a free rate of £0.41 to U.S. $1 (U.S. $2.45 = £1 sterling). Gold, SDRs, and convertible currencies, official: (June 1972) U.S. $9,164,000,000; (June 1971) U.S. $5,319,000,000. Budget (1972–73 est.): revenue £16,839 million; expenditure £16,624 million. Gross national product: (1971) £855,720 million; (1970) £50,290 million. Money supply (excluding quasi-money): (March 1972) £11,160 million; (March 1971) £8,507 million. Cost of living (1963 = 100): (June 1972) 158; (June 1971) 149.

Foreign Trade. (1971) Imports £9,866 million; exports £9,179 million. Import sources: EEC 21% (West Germany 7%, Netherlands 5%, France 5%); U.S. 11%; Canada 6%; Ireland 5%. Export destinations: EEC 21% (West Germany 6%); U.S. 12%; Ireland 5%. Main exports: machinery 28%; motor vehicles 11%; chemicals 10%; textile yarns and fabrics 5%. Tourism (1970): visitors 6,730,000; gross receipts U.S. $1,039,000,000.

Transport and Communications. Roads (1970) 357,288 km. (including 1,133 km. expressways). Motor vehicles in use (1970): passenger 11,887,000; commercial 1,667,000. Railways (excluding Northern Ireland; 1970): 18,989 km.; traffic 35,708,000,000 passenger-km., freight (1971) 21,989,000,000 net ton-km. Air traffic (1971): 18,646,000,000 passenger-km.; freight 604,762,000 net ton-km. Shipping (1971): merchant vessels 100 gross tons and over 3,785; gross tonnage 27,334,695. Ships entered (1970) vessels totaling 137,888,000 net registered tons; goods loaded 52,818,000 metric tons, unloaded 199,727,000 metric tons. Telephones (Dec. 1970) 14,967,000. Radio receivers (Dec. 1971) *c.* 18.6 million. Television licenses (Dec. 1971) 16,588,000.

Agriculture. Production (in 000; metric tons; 1971; 1970 in parentheses): wheat 4,824 (4,236); barley 8,558 (7,529); oats 1,371 (1,217); potatoes 7,173 (7,482); sugar, raw value (1971–72) 1,179, (1970–71) 984; apples *c.* 595 (612); pears *c.* 80 (80); dry peas *c.* 80 (87); dry broad beans 134 (160); tomatoes (1970) 108, (1969) 94; onions (1970) 144, (1969) 117; eggs 862 (891); milk *c.* 13,310 (12,675); butter 66 (65); cheese 156 (130); beef and veal *c.* 1,005 (997); mutton and lamb *c.* 230 (232); pork *c.* 1,018 (925); wool *c.* 28 (30); fish catch (1970) 1,099, (1969) 1,083. Livestock (in 000; June 1971): cattle 12,806; sheep 25,998; pigs 8,742; chickens 132,929.

Industry. Index of production (1963 = 100): (1971) 126; (1970) 124. Fuel and power (in 000; metric tons; 1971): coal 149,730; crude oil (1970) 83; natural gas (cu.m.) 19,046,000; manufactured gas (cu.m.; 1970) 20,458,000; electricity (kw-hr.) 254,000,000. Production (in 000; metric tons; 1971): cement 17,890; iron ore (25–30% metal content) 10,250; pig iron 15,410; crude steel 24,560; nitrogenous fertilizers (1970–71) 748; passenger cars (units) 1,742; commercial vehicles (units) 456; cotton fabrics (m.) 559,000; woolen fabrics (sq.m.) 186,000; rayon and other synthetic fabrics (m.) 472,000. Merchant vessels launched (100 gross tons and over; 1971) 1,239,000 gross tons. New dwelling units completed (1971) 363,000.

GILLES PERESS—MAGNUM

Two Roman Catholics lie dead in a Londonderry street following the "Bloody Sunday" confrontation with British troops on Jan. 30, 1972, in which 13 civilians were killed.

in the Commons resigned their roles as party spokesmen on this issue, and one, Dick Taverne, subsequently resigned his seat as MP for Lincoln to fight a by-election as an independent. Roy Jenkins' place as deputy leader was taken by Labour's former minister of education, Edward Short, who, although supporting British entry into Europe, had kept clear of the controversy within the party. He defeated Michael Foot, who headed the anti-Market wing of the Labour Party. Barbara Castle, former Labour minister of employment, left the shadow cabinet in November.

British entry into the EEC overshadowed other parliamentary affairs in the opening months of the year. Although the Commons had voted on Oct. 28, 1971, 356 votes to 244, approving British entry on the terms negotiated during 1971, Labour opposition against entry hardened and the party whip was imposed during the debates on the European Communities Bill. This bill was to give the force of law in the United Kingdom to existing and future Community law and to provide for payment of the U.K. share of the Community budget and for implementation of other obligations to the Community. The bill was published with an explanatory memorandum on January 26, shortly after Edward Heath had signed the treaty of accession in Brussels. The government's majority on the second reading debate in February fell to eight votes, and on a number of occasions at the committee stage it fell below ten.

One of the main complaints made by the Labour opposition during the debates was that the power of Parliament was being diminished, particularly in the control of taxation, which Harold Wilson said had dominated every issue of parliamentary freedom for 700 years. Enoch Powell, the principal Conservative opponent of entry, said that the country would be losing its judicial independence. Geoffrey Rippon, however, insisted that ministers would remain responsible to Parliament for what they did in the Community and nothing in the bill prejudiced the ultimate sovereignty of Parliament. The government successfully resisted all attempts to change the bill, which received the royal assent in October.

Soon after the enactment of the bill Heath took part in a summit meeting of the heads of the nine present and future member states in Paris on October 19–20. The meeting agreed on steps to achieve European union by 1980 and on a regional policy of special importance to Britain. The U.K. supplied two members to the enlarged EEC Commission: Sir Christopher Soames and George Thomson (*see* BIOGRAPHY). The Labour Party decided on December 13 that it would not send representatives to the European Parliament in Strasbourg (in which Britain was allotted 36 seats) for at least a year.

By-elections provided small comfort for the government and even less for Labour. Following an earlier win at Rochdale, on December 7 the Liberals swept to a sensational victory at Sutton and Cheam, formerly a Conservative seat, with a swing of over 30% in their favour. The Conservatives held Uxbridge by a greatly reduced majority over Labour on the same day.

Street map of Belfast, the scene of bitter violence throughout the year.

P. MICHAEL O'SULLIVAN

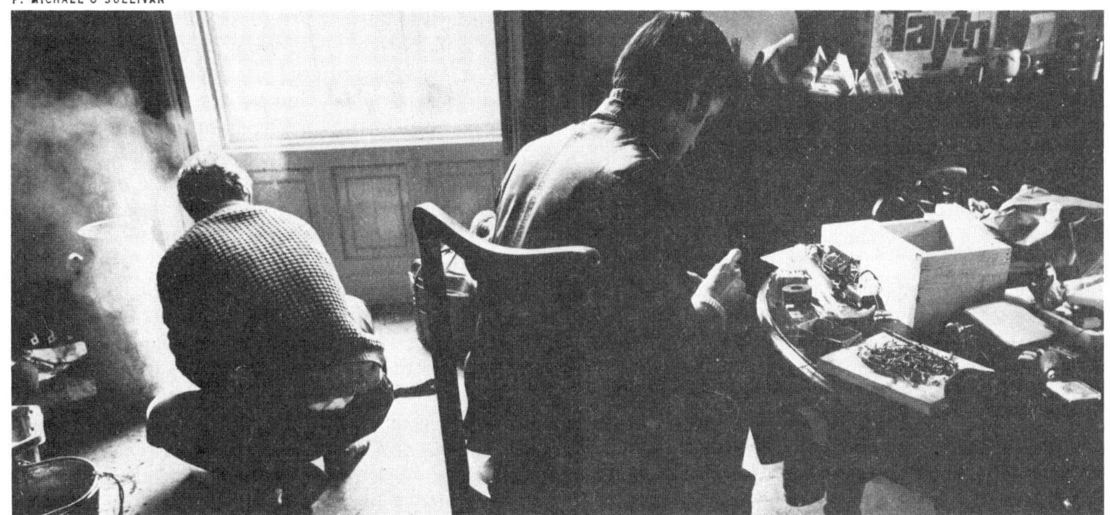

IRA members assemble bombs at an undisclosed location in Northern Ireland.

On November 22 the government was defeated by 275 votes to 240 after a stormy debate on its proposed Commonwealth and EEC immigration rules. Calls for Heath's resignation were ignored and it was expected that new legislation would make concessions to Tory backbench pressure in favour of white immigrants from the "old" Commonwealth countries of Australia, New Zealand, and Canada.

Following a series of bombings, some at the homes of Cabinet ministers, during 1968–71, four members of the self-styled "Angry Brigade," an anarchist movement composed seemingly of left-wing intellectual idealists, were each given sentences of ten years' imprisonment after a 111-day trial ending December 6.

Foreign Policy. Foreign relations were established on a more normal basis with China. The U.K. had voted for China's admission to the UN in October 1971. An exchange of ambassadors followed in March 1972, and in October the foreign secretary, Sir Alec Douglas-Home, paid an official visit to Peking.

A new defense agreement was signed with Malta on March 26 after nine months of negotiations, which at a late stage led to the withdrawal of some British troops. The agreement, made jointly with NATO, was to run seven years, with Britain paying about 40% of the costs. It excluded the Warsaw Pact countries from being given military facilities in Malta.

An attempt to reach a settlement with Rhodesia over its unilateral declaration of independence failed. Terms agreed on in November 1971 had been dependent on their acceptability to the Rhodesian people as a whole. A commission led by Lord Pearce went to Rhodesia from January to March and, in its report published on May 23, said that while the terms were acceptable to Europeans they were rejected by the majority of Africans. Britain decided there was, therefore, no basis for independence and that the status quo should continue, including the UN sanctions.

When Pres. Idi Amin of Uganda ordered the expulsion of all Asians in Uganda, the British government accepted the responsibility to admit those who held British passports (estimated at around 25,000). A Uganda Resettlement Board was set up to supervise their settlement in Britain. (*See* RACE RELATIONS.)

Disagreement over fishing limits caused friction between Britain and Iceland, which unilaterally established a 50-mi. limit September 1. (*See* ICELAND.)

The Economy. The year began with the British economy seemingly in good shape. A substantial balance of payments surplus had been achieved during 1971—£952 million, of which £297 million was on visible trade. This was only the fourth time since World War II that there had been a surplus on visible trade for a whole year. The reserves stood at £2,526 million, more than double what they had been at the beginning of 1971. The parity rate for sterling was confirmed at U.S. $2.60 in the realignment of currencies set out in the Smithsonian agreement in Washington, D.C., in December 1971. Unemployment, however, remained obstinately high, and reached 918,600 in January 1972. There was some slowing down in the pace of inflation early in the year, compared with the 12.6% increase in hourly rates for manual workers and the 9% increase in retail prices during 1971. At the beginning of 1972 the inflation rate had been brought back to 6% per annum. Britain's overseas loans, incurred in coping with the sterling crises of recent years, had been completely repaid by the end of April, yet the reserves reached £2,737 million.

These encouraging trends were offset by a serious worsening of labour relations. A strike of coal miners —the first nationwide coal strike since 1926—lasted from January 9 to February 28. This was accompanied by picketing of coal-fired power stations, which led to extensive power cuts and emergency cuts in industrial use of power affecting the employment of between 1.5 million and 2 million workers. The strike arose out of a pay claim put in by the miners' union for increases of up to 47%. The National Coal Board made a number of offers amounting to overall increases of between 7 and 8%, which were rejected. A state of emergency was declared on February 9 giving the government powers to protect vital services and supplies. Restrictions on the use of electricity followed. The dispute was submitted to a court of inquiry under Lord Wilberforce, which came to the conclusion that public opinion would support the miners' claim for "a general and exceptional increase." The court recommended much larger increases, averaging about 25%, which the miners accepted. On December 11 the government announced subsidies totaling £175 million annually to the coal industry and the writing off of the NCB's deficit of £475 million. This was a dramatic reversal of the industry's long rundown and, with the £1,200 million package of government aid, would allow coal to remain one of Britain's chief energy sources.

When Chancellor of the Exchequer Anthony Barber introduced his budget on March 21 he was still able to show that the rate of price inflation had been cut by half since the summer of 1971. The visible trade surplus, however, had declined sharply, partly because of disruption by the coal strike. While private consumption was rising fast, unemployment remained high and investment was recovering too slowly. Barber, therefore, decided that "a further boost to demand is required." His target was a 5% growth rate. He thought this could be done without damage to the fight against inflation. He argued that there was "a rare opportunity to secure a sustained and a faster rate of economic expansion over a considerable period of years" for five reasons: new opportunities in the Common Market; more unused resources available than at any time since World War II; potential growth of productivity; accelerated growth of public expenditure; the strength of the balance of payments and the reserves.

On this basis Barber made tax cuts amounting to £1,200 million, over 80% of it on income tax. He also announced plans for the introduction of the value-added tax in April 1973 (replacing the purchase tax and the selective employment tax and coming into line with the EEC), restructuring of the corporation tax to discriminate between retained and distributed profits, and a new form of personal income tax. To stimulate investment (which in the U.K. stood at 15% of the national income, compared with 19% in the EEC) Barber made a free depreciation allowance of 100% for the first year for all investment in plant and machinery plus special grants for the backward regional development areas. The 1972–73 tax cuts brought the total of tax reductions made by the Heath government since June 1970 to £3,000 million.

Although Barber's cuts were hailed as a sunshine budget, the sunshine did not last long. On June 23, the government was forced to "float" the pound after a third of the reserves had been lost in three days in a speculative run on sterling. The pound fell from its fixed dollar parity of 2.60 to around 2.45, and steadied there, only to be overtaken by another crisis of nerves in October when for a time it fell below 2.35.

The causes of the new sterling crisis were complex but, in summary, were due to a worsening of industrial unrest, which led to poor trade figures, and to fears that inflation was getting out of control again. Figures for the January–March balance of payments published on June 8 were dismal. Surpluses in the last two quarters of 1971 had been £354 million and £242 million; they were now only £30 million, with a £118 million deficit on visible trade. In addition there had been a net outflow of £195 million in private investment. By December the current account had moved into deficit for the first time since 1968; imports exceeded exports by £280 million during the third quarter, while the surplus on invisibles was no more than £174 million.

This sudden reversal of the 1971 trends could be partly attributed to disruption of industry by the coal strike, followed by sporadic stoppages in the docks, which culminated in a national dock strike in July, when pickets were sent to prison for defying the National Industrial Relations Court. A three weeks' dock stoppage followed over the dockers' claim to work in depots where containers were packed for loading on ship. (*See* LABOUR UNIONS.)

In this climate in July the government began to make new approaches to the Confederation of British Industry (CBI) and the Trades Union Congress (TUC) for a voluntary prices and incomes policy. The CBI was persuaded to extend the price freeze it had agreed to in 1971 for another three months. After a number of preliminary talks, Heath put forward a package proposal on September 26 limiting price increases to 5% and basic wage increases to £2 a week (which after allowing for extras above the basic rate would have been around an 8% increase) on the assumption of a 5% increase in economic growth. The proposals foundered on the insistence of the TUC that while it could not accept control of wages there must be control of prices. After ten sessions the talks broke down on November 2.

Meanwhile the inflationary pressures seemed to be intensifying. The money supply in the third quarter of the year was between 25 and 30% above the previous year, partly because of relaxation of credit restraints. Credit went partly to finance industrial expansion but also to speculators and private individuals. In August bank advances to British residents were reported 46% higher than a year before. The bank rate, which had been fixed by the Bank of England for the previous 270 years and was used as a datum line for other interest rates, was abolished early in October, leaving interest rates to be determined more freely in relation to the market rate for Treasury bills. In an attempt to arrest the inflation, Heath announced on November 6 a 90-day standstill on wages, prices, rents, and dividends. The 90 days would be used to frame a system of statutory price and wage controls. Calls from the Bank of England in December withdrew over £600 million from circulation.

In November unemployment fell by about 85,000 to 744,876 (3.3% of the labour force); this was the largest fall in any similar period for 25 years.

Combating unofficial skepticism at its 5% growth target, the government announced toward year's end a huge increase in planned expenditure during 1972–77, amounting to an extra £2,317 million, over half of which was to go to education and social services. In addition, a £3,000 million, ten-year investment program in the British steel industry was announced.

Legislation. Among the laws enacted by Parliament during 1972 were the Local Government Act, setting up an entirely new structure of counties and districts to replace the Victorian system that had lasted nearly 100 years; the Housing Finance Act, which required "fair" rents to be charged by local authorities and provided for rent allowances for those on low incomes in privately owned as well as local-authority accommodations; the Industry Act, providing selective financial aid for industry and a new scheme of regional development grants; the Sound Broadcasting Act, providing for commercial local radio to be supervised by an Independent Broadcasting Authority; and the Museums and Galleries Admission Charges Act. A Fair Trading Bill introduced on December 1 included major new measures concerning consumer protection, monopolies, and restrictive practices.

Northern Ireland. Terrorism in Northern Ireland intensified toward the end of 1971, to the point where 114 civilians, 48 soldiers, and 11 police had been killed. In Londonderry on January 30 an illegal civil rights march led to a clash with men of the Parachute Regiment in which 13 civilians were killed and 16 wounded. A government inquiry headed by Lord Widgery, the lord chief justice, reported on April 19 that "if the Army had persisted in its 'low key' attitude and had not launched a large-scale operation to arrest hooligans, the day might have passed off without serious incident"; the soldiers were fired on first, but some firing by the soldiers bordered on the reckless, and none of those killed or wounded was proved to have been shot while handling a weapon.

The minister of state for home affairs in the Northern Ireland government, John Taylor, was seriously wounded in an assassination attempt on February 25. On March 4 a bomb exploded in a Belfast restaurant without warning, killing two women and wounding 136 people. It was against this background of escalating violence that, in talks on March 22 and 23, the British government proposed to take over responsibility for law and order, to begin phasing out the internment policy that had proved a provocation to continuing Irish Republican Army (IRA) violence, and to hold periodic plebiscites to determine the wishes of the Northern Ireland population. Brian Faulkner, the Northern Ireland prime minister, refused to accept the transfer of responsibility for law and order. The British government thereupon suspended the Northern Ireland constitution and assumed direct rule, while repeating the assurance that the position of Northern Ireland as part of the United Kingdom would not be changed without the consent of the people. Heath further promised that the Army would stay in Northern Ireland so long as any faction sought to terrorize or intimidate ordinary people.

William Whitelaw, who now became secretary of state for Northern Ireland, was immediately confronted by the militant Protestants of the Vanguard Movement, who called a two-day general strike protesting direct rule by Westminster. Vanguard leader William Craig made common cause with Faulkner. The left-wing and pro-Irish Social Democratic and Labour Party (SDLP) led by Gerard Fitt and the middle-of-the-road Alliance Party welcomed the British move. Whitelaw sought to pacify the militants by releasing internees and lifting the ban on marches. He also pushed ahead with plans for industrial development and reconstruction. An advisory commission was set up with seven Protestant and four Roman Catholic members.

Yet terrorism continued. The Army clashed with Protestants who had formed the paramilitary Ulster Defence Association (UDA). The growing weariness of the bulk of the population led the Official wing of the IRA to declare a truce on May 29; the extremist Provisionals, however, increased their terrorist activities until they too agreed to a truce starting on June 26. But a number of killings occurred during the truce, and the UDA started barricading Protestant "no-go" areas. The truce lasted less than two weeks. It was called off by the Provisionals on July 9, and they resumed an even more violent campaign. On July 21 Belfast suffered its worst day of bombings; 20 bombs were exploded without warning within half an hour, one at a crowded bus station. Eleven people were killed and 96 of 120 wounded were hospitalized.

Having failed in conciliation, the security forces went onto the offensive. Another 4,000 troops were sent to Northern Ireland, bringing the total to 21,000, and on July 31 troops moved into the "no-go" areas of Londonderry, which had been IRA sanctuaries, and cleared them of barricades. Searches uncovered large stocks of arms. Meanwhile Whitelaw had been trying to bring about all-party talks on a political settlement. Discussions were held in September, but the SDLP refused to take part, having made the release of all internees a condition of attendance.

On October 30 the government issued a Green Paper, "The Future of Northern Ireland," as a basis for discussion on the future constitution when direct rule ended. Opinion in Westminster was moving toward some form of regional authority that would provide minority groups with an effective voice in government. A plebiscite on the border question was promised for early 1973. By year's end the total of people killed since the outbreak of the conflict in 1969 had reached 676. (HARFORD THOMAS)

See also Ireland.

United Nations

Secretary-General Kurt Waldheim presented his first report to the General Assembly on the work of the UN in August 1972 and reflected on the eight months since he took office on January 3. He praised the "key role" the UN played "in the co-operative effort to tackle long-term social and economic problems," but noted that "in the political spheres, the Organization's place is more uncertain." In May the secretary-general had called attention to an "alarming" trend among nations away from using UN procedures for solving disputes. Noting that governments seemed to be reverting to traditional secret diplomacy (in relation to Vietnam) or even force (as in the India-Pakistan war of 1971), he stressed the unused UN capacity to assist in keeping the peace. He expressed the hope that the relative lack of interest in the UN among the superpowers was a passing phenomenon and cited a new breed of nonpolitical global issues before the United Nations, including environment, disaster relief, and new international law for the sea and ocean floor.

The first UN Conference on the Human Environment took place in Stockholm June 5–16. It approved 100 recommendations to be embodied in an international Action Plan to protect man's habitat on earth. It also adopted a Declaration on the Human Environment, setting out 26 principles, including, among others, a conviction that mankind had reached the stage where it must shape its actions throughout the world "with a more prudent care for their environmental consequences." (*See* ENVIRONMENT.)

Terrorism. Throughout the year Waldheim attempted to use his good offices to mitigate potential or actual tragedies from terrorism, including airplane hijackings and the massacres in May at the Lod Airport in Israel and in September at the Olympic Games in Munich. A week before the 27th General Assembly opened on September 19, Waldheim declared that the UN could not remain a "mute spectator" in the face of a growing trend toward acts of terror and violence against innocent people. He asked the assembly to include on its agenda an item titled "measures to prevent terrorism and other forms of violence which endanger or take innocent human lives or jeopardize fundamental freedoms."

Assembly debate later demonstrated a division between some states, led by the Arabs, which wished to avoid discussing terrorism except in the most general terms, and others which pressed for immediate action. The Arab nations favoured a draft resolution calling for an assembly committee to study members' suggestions of the best ways to eliminate terrorism and to examine the causes of international terrorism. Another draft, favoured by the U.S., asked the president of the assembly (Stanislaw Trepczynski of Poland) to name a committee to study the underlying causes of terrorism but also asked the International Law Commission to draft a convention against terrorism that a special conference on the subject might adopt in November 1973. On December 18 the first and weaker resolution passed the assembly by a vote of 76–35 with 17 abstentions.

Decolonization. Few continuing issues before the UN aroused such strong feelings as those connected with decolonization, particularly in Africa. International concern for policies being followed by South Africa, Rhodesia, and Portugal was evident in special Security Council meetings, actions by the secretary-general, and in General Assembly resolutions.

To emphasize its concern with colonialism and racial discrimination in southern Africa, the Security Council held a week-long series of meetings in Addis Ababa, Eth., January 28–February 4. It was the first time in 20 years that the council had met away from UN headquarters in New York, and the meetings were the first ever held in Africa.

South Africa. When the General Assembly declared void South Africa's League of Nations mandate to administer South West Africa (Namibia) in 1966, the UN began trying to advance the cause of Namibian independence. On February 4, at its meetings in Ethiopia, the Security Council adopted three resolutions relating to South Africa. One, adopted by a vote of 14–0 (China did not participate), invited the secretary-general to undertake contacts in South Africa designed to further Namibian independence; a second condemned South Africa for refusing to comply with past UN decisions on Namibia and called upon it to withdraw from the territory and turn it over to the UN to administer directly. The council had adopted such resolutions before, but a new provision in this one denounced what the council characterized as repressive measures against African workers and asked for the end of the contract system under which they occurred. The third resolution condemned apartheid, urged South Africa to release all prisoners or others restricted because of it, and requested all states to adhere strictly to the nine-year-old arms embargo against South Africa.

In response to the council's requests, Secretary-General Waldheim went to Cape Town in March, where he talked with South African Prime Minister Vorster and Foreign Minister Hilgard Muller. He also visited Namibia to consult with leaders and groups there. He continued his conversations in New York in May with Muller and others, and on July 20 reported that he had South African consent to send a special representative to South Africa to work for Namibian self-determination and independence. On September 25 Waldheim appointed Alfred Escher of Switzerland as the special representative. On November 15 Escher recommended to the Security Council that the UN maintain continuing contacts with South Africa to help create the necessary conditions for Namibian self-determination and independence. African members of the council later characterized the report as "disappointing" because so little had been accomplished and urged that contacts be broken off.

Rhodesia. At the Security Council meetings in February in Addis Ababa, the African members asked the U.K. to shelve a proposed Anglo-Rhodesian settlement. Their draft resolution received nine affirmative votes, but the U.K. vetoed it because the U.K. would not accept a directive asking it to change a policy still being worked out by a royal commission (the Pearce commission) then canvassing Rhodesian opinion on the subject. In May, the U.K. reported to the council that the commission had found the terms were acceptable to a majority of the 250,000 resident "Europeans" but not to the 5 million Africans, and that the proposed settlement was being abandoned.

On February 28 the Security Council specified that imports of chrome ore from Rhodesia would undermine the UN-imposed boycott of the regime and contravene states' obligations under the UN Charter. U.S. Deputy Ambassador Christopher H. Phillips said that the U.S. Congress had authorized U.S. imports of chrome in 1972 because of growing U.S. dependence on the Soviet Union for the strategic material at the same time that quantities of the cheaper Rhodesian supplies were moving into other countries. He added that the U.S. remained committed to sanctions as a

Table I. Member States of the United Nations

Dec. 31, 1972

Afghanistan	Ecuador*	Liberia*	Sierra Leone
Albania	Egypt*	Libya	Singapore
Algeria	El Salvador*	Luxembourg*	Somalia
Argentina*	Equatorial Guinea	Malagasy Rep.	South Africa*
Australia*	Ethiopia*	Malawi	Spain
Austria	Fiji	Malaysia	Sri Lanka (formerly Ceylon)
Bahrain	Finland	Maldives	Sudan
Barbados	France*	Mali	Swaziland
Belgium*	Gabon	Malta	Sweden
Belorussia*	Gambia, The	Mauritania	Syria*
Bhutan	Ghana	Mauritius	Tanzania
Bolivia*	Greece*	Mexico*	Thailand
Botswana	Guatemala*	Mongolia	Togo
Brazil*	Guinea	Morocco	Trinidad and Tobago
Bulgaria	Guyana	Nepal	Tunisia
Burma	Haiti*	Netherlands*	Turkey*
Burundi	Honduras*	New Zealand*	Uganda
Cambodia (Khmer Rep.)	Hungary	Nicaragua*	Ukraine*
Cameroon	Iceland	Niger	U.S.S.R.*
Canada*	India*	Nigeria	United Arab Emirates
Central African Rep.	Indonesia	Norway*	United Kingdom*
Chad	Iran*	Oman	United States*
Chile*	Iraq*	Pakistan	Upper Volta
China*	Ireland	Panama*	Uruguay*
Colombia*	Israel	Paraguay*	Venezuela*
Congo	Italy	Peru*	Yemen (Aden)
Costa Rica*	Ivory Coast	Philippines*	Yemen (San'a')
Cuba*	Jamaica	Poland*	Yugoslavia*
Cyprus	Japan	Portugal	Zaire
Czechoslovakia*	Jordan	Qatar	Zambia
Dahomey	Kenya	Romania	
Denmark*	Kuwait	Rwanda	
Dominican Rep.*	Laos	Saudi Arabia*	
	Lebanon*	Senegal	
	Lesotho		

*Signatories to original charter.

Table II. Council Membership

Years indicate date membership expires

Country	Security Council	Economic and Social Council	Trusteeship Council
China	Permanent	1974	Permanent
France	Permanent	1975*	Permanent
U.S.S.R.	Permanent	1974	Permanent
United Kingdom	Permanent	1974	Permanent
United States	Permanent	1973	Permanent†
Algeria		1975	
Australia	1974		†
Austria	1974		
Bolivia		1974	
Brazil		1975*	
Burundi		1974	
Chile		1974	
Finland		1974	
Guinea	1973		
Haiti		1973	
Hungary		1973	
India	1973		
Indonesia	1974		
Japan		1974	
Kenya	1974		
Lebanon		1973	
Malagasy Rep.		1973	
Malaysia		1973	
Mali		1975	
Mongolia		1975	
Netherlands		1975	
New Zealand		1973	
Niger		1973	
Panama	1973		
Peru	1974		
Poland		1974	
Spain		1975	
Sudan	1973		
Trinidad and Tobago		1975	
Uganda		1975	
Yugoslavia	1973		
Zaire		1973	

*Reelected.
†Administering authority.

whole and that the council should direct its attention to more serious violators.

These assurances did not entirely placate the Security Council, which on July 28 approved recommendations of its sanctions committee designed to tighten boycott measures against Rhodesia. It then condemned all acts violating the boycott. On December 7 the General Assembly in a resolution adopted 93–8 condemned the importation by the U.S., South Africa, and Portugal of chrome and nickel from Rhodesia. This resolution marked the first time the assembly had ever used the word "condemn" against the United States by name.

Portuguese Territories. At its February meetings in Africa, the Security Council repeated earlier calls for self-determination and independence for the Portuguese territories of Angola, Mozambique, and Portuguese Guinea (Bissau). It urged immediate halt of armed repression and the withdrawal of all armed forces so engaged. States were asked to withhold from Portugal any military supplies that it could possibly use for continued repression in Africa.

Peace-Keeping. The special UN representative for a Middle East peace, Gunnar V. Jarring, met privately several times during the year with Waldheim and with Israeli and Arab representatives to try to bridge the differences between them. In May, however, a representative of the secretary-general characterized the Middle East situation as "stuck."

Most of the peace-keeping problems in the Middle East arose on the Lebanese-Israeli border, and the Security Council had the subject on its agenda several times. The first protest involved a Lebanese complaint of Israeli Army raids and artillery attacks in January and February. On February 28 the council demanded unanimously that Israel stop all its ground and air action against Lebanon and withdraw all its military forces from Lebanese territory. Lebanon on March 29 called for stationing additional UN observers on its border with Israel to assist the seven observers already there. The council agreed on April 19 to station 14 more UN officers in the area, along with 13 additional supporting personnel.

Both Lebanon and Israel urgently requested a meeting of the Security Council in late June because of military activity that flared up between them. Lebanon complained of persistent Israeli "acts of aggression," while Israel protested the "acts of terror and violence" emanating from Lebanon. The council on June 26 condemned Israel's "repeated attacks" against Lebanon. Israel characterized its movements as "self-defense" against Arab terrorist organizations in southeastern Lebanon.

Complaints by Syria and Lebanon about Israeli air raids on their villages brought the Security Council into session again on September 10. The U.S., however, vetoed a draft resolution that would have asked "the parties concerned" to cease all military operations immediately and to exercise "the greatest restraint" in the interest of international security. The U.S. refused to accept the resolution after the council rejected amendments referring to acts of Arab terrorism that had ended in the murder in Munich earlier in the month of 11 athletes on the Israeli Olympic team. The U.S. argued that the council would do no good by adopting a resolution condemning one form of violence while countenancing another.

Budget. Financial problems continued to plague the UN. In the past, the major difficulties arose because France and the U.S.S.R. refused to pay their share of

WIDE WORLD

Huang Hua, China's ambassador to the UN, casts his country's first veto on Aug. 25, 1972. It was the lone vote in the UN Security Council that barred Bangladesh from membership.

peace-keeping costs incurred during UN operations in the Middle East and the Congo. The latest threat to UN solvency arose when the U.S. insisted that its share of the UN budget be reduced from 31.5 to 25%. Faced with the threat of even more drastic losses of U.S. support if it failed to comply with this request, the assembly granted it in a vote of 81–27–22 on December 13, providing that the lowered assessment should come into effect "as soon as practicable."

(RICHARD N. SWIFT)

UNESCO. During the year, UNESCO convened two important conferences. The third International Conference on Adult Education, held in Tokyo during July and August, was attended by nearly 400 delegates from 82 member states plus observers from other countries and some 40 nongovernmental organizations. At the meeting it was unanimously agreed that adult education should be recognized as an indispensable component of lifelong education and that governments should adopt legislative and other measures to support this. The Intergovernmental Conference on Cultural Policies in Europe, held in Helsinki during June, was attended by delegates from 30 countries, including 26 ministers. This conference made it clear that in spite of different political and social structures, culture had become part of man's daily life, making it incumbent on governments to provide greater cultural opportunities.

At the 17th session of UNESCO's General Conference, a delegation from China was seated for the first time; the conference also elected Bangladesh as its 130th member state and East Germany as the 131st. Other countries elected to full membership during the year were Bahrain, Oman, Qatar, and the United Arab Emirates. The withdrawal of Portugal from UNESCO, announced in 1971, took effect at the end of 1972.

(RICHARD D. A. GREENOUGH)

United States

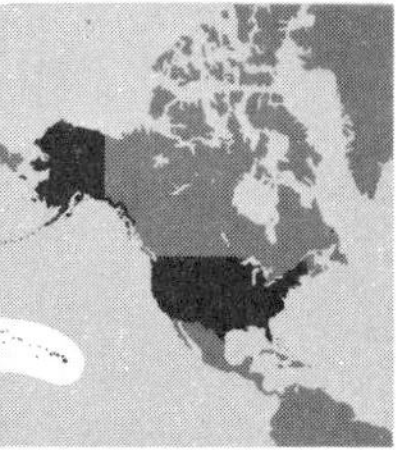

The United States of America is a federal republic composed of 50 states, 49 of which are in North America and one of which consists of the Hawaiian Islands. Area: 3,615,122 sq.mi. (9,363,123 sq.km.), including 78,267 sq.mi. of inland water but excluding the 60,306 sq.mi. of the Great Lakes that lie within U.S. boundaries. Pop. (1972 est.): 208,232,000, including (1970) white 87.3%; Negro 11.1%. Lan-

OLIPHANT, THE DENVER POST 1972 © THE LOS ANGELES TIMES SYNDICATE

This Oliphant cartoon refers to the issues of secrecy in government operations raised in 1972 by columnist Jack Anderson and many other journalists.

guage: English. Religion (1963 est.): Protestant 64,435,000; Roman Catholic 42,877,000; Jewish 5,365,000; Orthodox 2.8 million. Cap.: Washington, D.C. (pop., 1971 est., 741,000). Largest city: New York (pop., 1970, 7,895,563). President in 1972, Richard Milhous Nixon.

For President Nixon (*see* BIOGRAPHY), 1972 was a year of diplomatic and political triumph. His visit to China in February—the first ever to that country by an incumbent president—marked the end of a period of Peking-Washington hostility that had lasted almost a quarter century. Traveling to Moscow in May, Nixon signed a number of agreements with the Soviet Union on strategic arms limitation and other matters. Then, in late October, it was announced that the United States and North Vietnam were near agreement on an Indochina peace plan. These developments no doubt contributed to the president's reelection on November 7 by a near-record margin of popular and electoral votes.

In his landslide reelection, Nixon carried every state except Massachusetts and the District of Columbia, which were won by Democratic nominee George S. McGovern (*see* BIOGRAPHY). Complete, official returns gave the president 47,168,963 popular votes (60.7%) to McGovern's 29,169,615 (37.5%). Nixon won 520 electoral votes, McGovern 17, John Hospers, a Libertarian, 1.

Nixon's overwhelming victory had little impact on congressional and gubernatorial races, however. Amid widespread ticket-splitting, the Democrats had a net gain of two seats in the U.S. Senate and one more governorship; they lost only 13 House seats. The election was, as Republican National Chairman Robert Dole put it, "a personal triumph for Mr. Nixon but not a party triumph." The outcome of the various Senate races widened Democratic control of that chamber to 57–43 from the 55–45 lineup of the 92nd Congress. Republican gains in the House closed the gap to 242–192 (plus one independent) in the Democrats' favour, compared with 255–177 in the old Congress. In the gubernatorial contests, the net Democratic gain of one seat brought the party's margin of power in the statehouses to 31–19.

A number of well-known incumbents lost their seats to challengers. Senate losers included Gordon Allott (Rep., Colo.), J. Caleb Boggs (Rep., Del.), Jack Miller (Rep., Ia.), Margaret Chase Smith (Rep., Maine), and William B. Spong, Jr. (Dem., Va.); they were defeated by Democrats Floyd K. Haskell, Joseph R. Biden, Jr., Dick Clark, William D. Hathaway, and Republican William L. Scott, respectively. The 13 House incumbents defeated on November 7 included John H. Kyl (Rep., Ia.), John S. Monagan (Dem., Conn.), Alvin E. O'Konski (Rep., Wis.), Graham Purcell (Dem., Tex.), and Fred Schwengel (Rep., Ia.), each of whom had served at least six terms. In addition, veterans Wayne N. Aspinall (Dem., Colo.) and Emanuel Celler (Dem., N.Y.) lost out earlier in primary elections. Among the new governors elected in November were Democrats Daniel Walker (Ill.), Philip W. Noel (R.I.), and Dolph Briscoe (Tex.); and Republicans Christopher "Kit" Bond (Mo.), James E. Holshouser (N.C.), and Otis R. Bowen (Ind.).

Faced with a Democratic-controlled Congress, President Nixon enjoyed only limited success with his legislative program in 1972. His greatest victory came when Congress enacted a law providing for general revenue sharing—one of the "six great goals" proposed by Nixon in 1971. The law established a five-year program to share $30.2 billion in federal revenues with state and local governments. It appropriated federal revenues to a trust fund for distribution among the state and local governments at an initial annual level of $5.3 billion. The program was made retroactive to Jan. 1, 1972.

Congress approved three temporary increases in the federal debt ceiling in 1972, the last only after a bitter fight over the president's request for unprecedented authority to cut federal spending without congressional approval to $250 billion in fiscal 1973. Although not controversial in itself, the third temporary debt-ceiling bill became the subject of a partisan dispute when the House Committee on Ways and Means added a rider approving the president's request. An amended version of the president's request was eventually defeated in the Senate, and the debt-ceiling increase was approved without any spending-limit provisions.

In the waning moments of the 92nd Congress, the House and the Senate overrode President Nixon's veto of the Federal Water Pollution Control Act Amendments of 1972, a $24.6 billion measure aimed at cleaning up the nation's waters by 1985. As enacted, the law set a national goal of eliminating all pollutant discharges into the nation's waters by 1985 and making the waters safe for fish, shellfish, wildlife, and recreation by 1983. It included more than $18 billion in federal grants to states for construction of waste treatment plants.

Forty-nine years after the measure was first introduced, Congress completed action in 1972 on a proposed constitutional amendment guaranteeing equal rights for women. The amendment then went to the states where approval of 38 legislatures was required for ratification. The administration did not request the amendment, but it was supported by the president. If ratified, it would become the 27th amendment to the federal Constitution.

A filibuster near the end of the 1972 session successfully prevented the Senate from voting on a tough antibusing bill previously passed by the House and actively supported by the president. The bill would have barred all school busing except to the school closest or next closest to the student's home and would have allowed the reopening of previous desegregation orders to bring them into compliance with the bill's provisions. But the Education Amendments of 1972, a separate, omnibus education measure, contained language that postponed until 1974 the effective date of court orders requiring busing and also limited the use of federal funds for busing intended to overcome racial imbalance or to desegregate schools. (*See* RACE RELATIONS.)

Congress increased Social Security benefits by 20% across the board, provided for further, automatic increases whenever the cost of living rose by more than 3% in a calendar year, and made a number of other increases in Social Security coverage. To pay the costs of these expanded benefits, Social Security contributions made by employees and employers were raised. (*See* SOCIAL SERVICES.)

Congress authorized appropriations of $3.4 billion for the National Aeronautics and Space Administration (NASA) in fiscal 1973, an increase of $59.9 million over the amount for fiscal 1972. The fiscal 1973 figure included $227.9 million for the space shuttle program, which was strongly supported by the administration but opposed by members of Congress desirous of reducing the space budget. The shuttle was to be a reusable vehicle capable of transporting men and equipment to and from earth orbit. Opponents of the program offered amendments in both chambers to delete shuttle funds from the NASA authorization. The opponents were voted down decisively.

A number of significant bills either were killed or died in the 92nd Congress. These included several end-the-war amendments, tax reform, a measure establishing a consumer protection agency, legislation raising the federal minimum wage, a highway-mass transit bill, no-fault insurance, a school prayer amendment, a European troop-withdrawal amendment, and legislation concerning strip mining, land use, power-plant siting, presidential powers to make war, health maintenance organization, the regulation of private pension plans, activities of lobbyists, and nonpublic school tuition tax credits.

Foreign Affairs. While many elements of President Nixon's domestic program were being rebuffed by Congress, his foreign policy initiatives often produced spectacular results. The president's foreign policy was predicated on the assumption that the era of Soviet-U.S. global dominance had come to an end. In a report to Congress on February 9, he stated: "The end of bipolarity requires that the structure of peace must be built with the resources and concepts of many nations." He added that "Our enmities are not immutable, and we must be prepared realistically to recognize and deal with their cause."

Less than two weeks later, Nixon departed for China to meet with leaders of the Peking government. Arriving in the Chinese capital on February 21, President and Mrs. Nixon and their party were greeted by Premier Chou En-lai and other top-level dignitaries. The president conferred for one hour later in the day with Communist Party Chairman Mao Tse-tung, an event that had not been announced beforehand, but that foretold the success of the visit.

The Chinese were hosts at a banquet the evening of February 21 at the Great Hall of the People. Chou offered a toast to the Nixon party in which he said that the president's visit "provides the leaders of the two countries with an opportunity of meeting in person to seek the normalization of relations between the two countries and also to exchange views on questions of concern." Nixon responded by saying that there was "no reason for us to be enemies. Neither of us seeks the territory of the other. Neither of us seeks domination over the other. Neither of us seeks to stretch out our hands and rule the world."

Additional meetings between Nixon and Chou followed. In a joint communiqué released in Shanghai, February 27, the two leaders indicated that their talks had resulted in agreement on the need for increased U.S.-Chinese contacts and for eventual withdrawal of U.S. military forces from Taiwan. The 1,800-word communiqué was divided into five sections, the first three of which dealt with a general account of Nixon's stay in China; a recitation of each party's views on Asian policy issues; and a list of mutually agreed upon rules governing international relations.

The fourth section of the document was given over to statements on Taiwan, whose status was recognized in advance as being the main stumbling block to improved relations between Washington and Peking. For its part, China reaffirmed its traditional claims to the island, emphasizing that the "liberation of Tai-

continued on page 717

UNITED STATES

Education. (1971–72) Primary (including preprimary), pupils 36.7 million, teachers 1,308,000; secondary and vocational, pupils 15,150,000, teachers 1,051,000; higher (including teacher-training colleges), students 8,390,000, teaching staff 617,000.

Finance. Monetary unit: U.S. dollar, with (Sept. 1972) a par value of U.S. $38 to one ounce of gold and a free rate of U.S. $2.42 to £1 sterling. Gold, SDRs, and foreign exchange, official: (Sept. 1972) $12,770,000,000; (Sept. 1971) $11,560,000,000. Federal budget (1971–72 est.): revenue $220.8 billion; expenditure $246.3 billion. Gross national product: (1971) $1,050,400,000,000; (1970) $976.4 billion. Money supply: (June 1972) $232.5 billion; (June 1971) $221.9 billion. Cost of living (1963 = 100): (June 1972) 136; (June 1971) 132.

Foreign Trade. (1971) Imports $45,602,000,000; exports (excluding military aid of $582 million) $43,555,000,000. Import sources: Canada 28%; Japan 16%; West Germany 8%; U.K. 5%. Export destinations: Canada 23%; Japan 9%; West Germany 6%; U.K. 5%. Main exports: machinery 27%; motor vehicles 10%; chemicals 9%; aircraft 8%; cereals 6%.

Transport and Communications. Roads (1971) 6,049,265 km. (including 69,205 km. expressways). Motor vehicles in use (1971): passenger 92,255,000; commercial 18,977,000. Railways: (1970) 331,165 km.; traffic (Class I only; 1971) 9,830,000,000 passenger-km., freight 1,067,712,000,000 net ton-km. Air traffic (1971): 218,544,000,000 passenger-km. (including internal services 179,100,000,000 passenger-km.); freight 7,179,936,000 net ton-km. (including internal services 4,555,000,000 net ton-km.). Inland waterways: freight traffic (1970) 465,000,000,000 ton-km. (including 167,000,000,000 ton-km. on Great Lakes system and 202,000,000,000 ton-km. on Mississippi River system). Shipping (1971): merchant vessels 100 gross tons and over 3,327; gross tonnage 16,265,669. Ships entered (including Great Lakes international traffic; 1970): vessels totaling 254,154,000 net registered tons; freight (1971) loaded 186,340,000 metric tons, unloaded 305,748,000 metric tons. Telephones (Jan. 1971) 120,218,000. Radio receivers (Dec. 1970) 290 million. Television receivers (1971) 92.7 million.

Agriculture. Production (in 000; metric tons; 1971; 1970 in parentheses): corn 140,733 (104,135); wheat 44,620 (37,291); oats 12,712 (13,190); barley 10,070 (8,923); rye 1,294 (986); rice 3,820 (3,758); sorghum 22,739 (17,690); soybeans 31,823 (30,584); dry beans 744 (789); dry peas 237 (179); peanuts 1,357 (1,351); potatoes 14,451 (14,773); sweet potatoes 539 (626); sugar, raw value (1971–72) 5,134, (1970–71) 5,103; apples 2,791 (2,823); pears 665 (487); oranges 7,861 (7,875); grapefruit 2,266 (2,247); lemons 765 (711); wine *c.* 1,400 (*c.* 1,167); raisins *c.* 226 (175); linseed 478 (762); tobacco 810 (865); cotton, lint 2,299 (2,213); wool *c.* 39 (40); eggs *c.* 4,219 (4,184); beef and veal *c.* 10,180 (9,990); pork *c.* 6,500 (6,091); timber (cu.m.; 1970): softwood 249,600, (1969) 242,300; hardwood 87,100, (1969) 88,400; fish landings 2,254 (2,226). Livestock (in 000; Jan. 1971): cattle 114,568; sheep 19,560; pigs 67,540; horses *c.* 7,800; chickens 442,783.

Industry. Index of production (1963 = 100): (1971) 140, (1970) 139; mining (1971) 120, (1970) 123; manufacturing (1971) 139, (1970) 139; electricity, gas, and water (1971) 178, (1970) 171; construction (1971) 114, (1970) 105. Unemployment: (1971) 5.9%, (1970) 4.9%. Fuel and power (in 000; metric tons; 1971): coal and lignite 495,132; crude oil 466,704; natural gas (cu.m.) 636,936,000; manufactured gas (cu.m.) *c.* 24,600,000; electricity (kw-hr.) 1,717,512,000. Production (in 000; metric tons; 1971): iron ore (55–60% metal content) 81,336; pig iron 75,720; crude steel 109,260; cement (shipments) 71,052; newsprint 2,976; sulfuric acid 26,567; caustic soda 8,796; nitrogenous fertilizers (plant nutrient content; 1970–71) 8,103; phosphate fertilizers (plant nutrient content; 1970–71) 5,387; potash fertilizers (plant nutrient content; 1970–71) 2,352; plastics and resins 8,184; synthetic rubber 2,278; passenger cars (units) 8,508; commercial vehicles (units) 2,052. Merchant vessels launched (100 gross tons and over; 1971) 482,000 gross tons. New dwelling units started (1971) 2,084,400.

U.S. ELECTION 1972 NIXON: 520 McGOVERN: 17

By David Maxey

Shortly before the 1972 presidential election, Pres. Richard Nixon told a reporter that "the election was over the day he [Sen. George McGovern] was nominated." South Dakota Senator McGovern (*see* BIOGRAPHY) had announced his candidacy in January 1971 knowing he needed all the time and media attention he could get to overcome what all political observers agreed upon: the certainty that Sen. Edmund Muskie of Maine would be the Democratic Party's nominee.

That month, Frank Mankiewicz, one of McGovern's most trusted aides, sat in McGovern headquarters on Capitol Hill in Washington, D.C. Between flurries of incoming phone calls, he explained the scenario by which McGovern would seize the Democratic nomination. First, a very strong run against the favourite, Senator Muskie, in the nation's first presidential primary in New Hampshire on March 7, 1972. Then, a victory in the Wisconsin primary in early April. That would provide the momentum to go the rest of the way. Mankiewicz ignored the intervening primary in Florida. "Florida," he snorted, "is a mutant, a hybrid." With a high but then unspecified number of Democrats competing, Mankiewicz reasoned, the Florida result would be meaningless.

Early Primaries. Muskie followed a different strategy. As the front-runner, he wanted to snare the nomination early and so was committed to running in all of the first eight presidential primaries. Prominent Democratic politicians lined up eagerly to endorse him. Among them: Gov. John Gilligan of Ohio; Leonard Woodcock, president of the United Auto Workers; Iowa Sen. Harold Hughes; and Pennsylvania Gov. Milton Shapp.

Muskie's front-running strategy stretched his energies and resources thin. Through January and February 1972, he shuttled exhaustingly between New Hampshire, Florida, Wisconsin, and all the other necessary stops. On February 26, in New Hampshire, the pressure began to tell. Mounting the bed of a truck parked outside the offices of the archconservative *Manchester Union Leader*, the state's largest newspaper, Muskie launched an attack on the paper's publisher, William Loeb. As he spoke of Loeb's unflattering remarks about Mrs. Muskie, the senator's voice cracked, and the crowd saw tears form in his eyes. The spectacle badly dented the image Muskie had tried all year to present, that of a calm, trustworthy, serene candidate. When New Hampshire voted on March 7, Muskie won the hollowest of victories, 46.4% of the vote, far below the predicted 65%. George McGovern, reaping the benefit of his early start and vigorous organization, was close behind with 37.1%. The first part of the Mankiewicz scenario had been acted out.

Richard Nixon (*see* BIOGRAPHY), without ever entering the state, received 67.9% of the Republican vote. That resolved the question of whether his opponents on the left and right of the GOP, Rep. Paul McCloskey and Rep. John Ashbrook, had any chance at all of unsettling him. McCloskey withdrew from the race $45,000 in debt. Ashbrook went on, but was never taken seriously as a candidate again.

In Florida the battle over the issue of busing was on. The Richmond, Va., decision handed down in January by U.S. District Court Judge Robert R. Merhige was still fresh in parents' minds. The judge had ordered Richmond's city school system, where 68% of the students were black, merged with two predominantly white, suburban school districts. Students would be bused to and from schools to achieve racial balance in all of them. Gov. George Wallace of Alabama (*see* BIOGRAPHY), with one of the surest instincts for finding the flash points of political pain, saw busing, correctly, as an issue that voters would rage about. His entry into the Florida primary hit the issue squarely.

Florida Gov. Reubin Askew put his enormous political prestige on the line, as he campaigned statewide against an antibusing referendum placed on the presidential primary ballot by the Florida legislature: lacking the votes in the legislature to keep the antibusing question off the ballot, Askew had managed to have another question added: "Do you favor providing an equal opportunity for quality education for all children regardless of

---

David Maxey became editor of Psychology Today *after covering the 1972 U.S. presidential campaign as a staff writer for* Life *magazine. He was managing editor of* Look *magazine when it ceased publication.*

ABBAS-SIPA/JOCELYNE BENZAKIN

J.-P. LAFFONT—GAMMA

Above, Pres. Richard Nixon and Vice-Pres. Spiro Agnew acknowledge cheers after their renomination at the Republican national convention. Many youthful voters, some of whom appeared at the convention (left), helped Nixon win a landslide victory in November 1972. He carried 49 states and won 60.7% of the popular vote.

WIDE WORLD

UPI COMPIX

Above, Democratic presidential candidate Sen. George McGovern (left) meets with his running mate, Sargent Shriver, just prior to Shriver's formal acceptance by the Democratic National Committee. The scene at right was a boisterous moment at the Democratic national convention.

race, creed, color or place of residence, and oppose a return to a dual system of public schools?" Askew's campaign focused the rage of many of his constituents on him, and the Democratic presidential candidates, of which there were 11, found themselves discussing busing much oftener than they wished.

Mayor John Lindsay of New York City, Rep. Shirley Chisholm of New York (*see* BIOGRAPHY), former senator Eugene McCarthy of Minnesota, and Senator McGovern, all liberal candidates, spoke in favour of busing when asked. Sen. Vance Hartke of Indiana, Rep. Wilbur D. Mills of Arkansas, and Mayor Sam Yorty of Los Angeles, although on the ballot, were not campaigning actively. Senator Muskie and Sen. Hubert H. Humphrey of Minnesota bobbed and weaved on the issue. Only Wallace and Sen. Henry M. Jackson of Washington spoke out squarely against busing.

As the race grew hotter, political observers began to doubt that, with 11 names on the Democratic ballot, anyone could win a clear victory. George Wallace proved them wrong by taking 42% of Florida's statewide vote and nearly all of the 81 delegates to the Democratic national convention. Senator Humphrey was second (18%) and got the few delegates Wallace did not. Senator Jackson, the other forthright foe of busing, was third with 13%, just high enough to convince him not to withdraw from the race. Muskie, with 9%, lost his front-runner's status.

Governor Askew watched the returns from his suite in the Sheraton Four Ambassadors Hotel. Earlier, he had mockingly raised a glass of water in a Miami Beach restaurant and intoned: "We, who are about to die, salute you." Unlike Muskie, he had not misread the voters, so there was little shock in seeing the antibusing referendum pass by 75% while the equal-opportunity ballot question also passed with 79% approval. In the excitement over Wallace's stunning victory, few noticed or cared that George McGovern, who had written Florida off early, had finished with 6% of the popular vote, behind Mayor Lindsay and only slightly ahead of Shirley Chisholm.

Muskie Eliminated. The Muskie campaign limped on to Wisconsin. Busing was not an issue there, so George Wallace found another thorny theme: the property tax. His own polling told him that he would not do well in the liberal state of Wisconsin, and so he delayed campaigning there. But he had the issue identified, and so did Senator McGovern. Senators Humphrey and Muskie, both needing victory badly, were slow to see what was bothering the electorate. The voters of 1972, everywhere, were in a sullen, doubting mood; they wanted specifics and plain talk. When he finally arrived in the state, George Wallace gave it to them. But the year-old campaign organization of George McGovern paid off on April 4, as the South Dakotan took 30% of the popular vote, the victory, and the second step of the Mankiewicz plan. To his own considerable surprise, Wallace finished second with 22% of the vote; his tally was boosted by the fact that 35% of the state's Republican voters crossed party lines to vote for him. Humphrey, who had worked 19-hour days in the state where he was supposed to be beloved as "our third senator," finished third with 21%. And Muskie, despite last-minute importations of Polish-surname politicians to help him in Milwaukee's ethnic wards, was a distant fourth with 10%. The Wisconsin vote finished the candidacy of Lindsay.

By now, the primary politics of 1972 had proven kindest to highly organized politicians with a small, devout, active band of followers, and Hubert Humphrey decided to focus his attention and waning resources on Pennsylvania's primary. The large numbers of labour voters there could be relied on not to forget Humphrey's strong support for labour's causes.

Humphrey's decision suited the McGovern forces. Their plan called next for intensive work in Massachusetts, the most liberal state in the country, where they could expect courtesy if not outright public support from Sen. Edward Kennedy. Many Massachusetts Democrats, taking Kennedy's denials of his candidacy at face value, were eager to work for McGovern.

On April 25 the strategies of both Humphrey and McGovern paid off, and the hopes of Senator Muskie were crushed between them. He finished fourth in Pennsylvania, behind winner Humphrey, Wallace, and McGovern, and a distant second to McGovern in Massachusetts. He then withdrew with dignity.

Wallace Shot. In early May, a sick young man named Arthur Bremer altered the politics of 1972. As Governor Wallace campaigned toward certain victory in the Maryland primary, Bremer stepped foward out of a shopping-centre crowd and shot him four times. Wallace survived, but at the cost of being paralyzed from the waist down. Maryland's voters surged out on election day to give Wallace a huge victory, his last of 1972.

From then on, the stricken governor was the focus of many visits from Democratic and Republican politicians. The question was, would he endorse anyone else for the presidency, or would he decide that his particular brand of right-leaning populism could not be found in any of the other candidates? While Wallace recuperated, the millions who would have voted for him as a Democratic or independent candidate began to move in overwhelming proportions behind the candidacy of Richard Nixon.

Final Primaries. In the primaries that followed, McGovern continued to build up a lead in convention delegates. He was even more successful in the nonprimary states, where his devoted followers made certain that delegate-selection caucuses voted his way. But that success overrode the much more basic process that was taking place: the Democratic Party was tearing itself apart. One reason lay in the work of the commission that carried the new front-runner's name. Founded in the wake of the disastrous and violent Democratic national convention in 1968, the McGovern Commission put forth guidelines for the selection of delegates. They were designed to open the party's deliberations to more young people, to blacks, and to women.

The guidelines worked, but they also functioned to diminish the participation of many long-time Democratic Party workers. Prominent national Democrats found themselves, in some cases, unable to find a spot on their own states' delegations.

The rise of McGovern as a potential nominee also scared many Democrats. Mayor Richard J. Daley of Chicago was unhappy, not only because his first choice was Edward Kennedy but also because the slate of delegates that included him was being challenged as lacking representative numbers of women, blacks, and young people. George Meany, president of the AFL-CIO, was publicly choleric about McGovern's antiwar views. John Connally, former governor of Texas, likewise felt that McGovern was departing from traditional Democratic principles.

As George McGovern became more successful, the liberal views that had inspired his young campaign workers became widely known. For many, McGovern was beginning to symbolize a candidacy of radical children, the creators of riots, the smokers of marijuana, the draft dodgers, the freaks.

With the California primary approaching, Hubert Humphrey tried to bring all the objections to McGovern together in a last attempt to save the nomination for himself. He excoriated his old Senate friend for his expensive ideas on welfare and his desire to cut the defense budget. It almost worked. Humphrey closed fast in May and early June, but the McGovern organization held on. McGovern won all of California's giant delegation, and beat Humphrey 44.3% to 39.1% in the popular vote. The margin was not as large as McGovern had hoped for, and the bitterness of the fight, together with the effectiveness of the Humphrey charges, had not been lost on the silent watchers at the Committee to Re-elect the President (CRP).

While the Democrats tore at each other, President Nixon was quietly following the strategy he had decided upon early. His reelection campaign was to rest squarely on the idea that he was the incumbent, too busy with the affairs of state to meddle in partisan matters. The CRP, so named to gain more from the institution of the presidency than from the dubiously popular name of Nixon, found no trouble raising campaign funds. The budget for the Nixon-Agnew ticket was $45 million.

Nixon was beautifully positioned in early June. His sense of timing, of the long view, had allowed New Hampshire voters to mix television reports of their state's primary election campaigns with exciting news film of the president setting foot in China. He was near to a summit meeting with the leaders of the Soviet Union. There was a rising consensus among voters that his handling of the Vietnam war was correct, and that he was winding it down as fast as was prudent.

Watergate Affair. On June 17, five men were apprehended at night at the Watergate Office Building headquarters of the Democratic National Committee and Democratic leaders thought they saw a political break. The intruders were laden with electronic eavesdropping equipment and led by the director of security of the Committee to Re-elect the President, James McCord. CRP's campaign director, former attorney general John Mitchell, quickly fired McCord, but the scandal had only begun to erupt. Eleven days later, Mitchell fired G. Gordon Liddy, a counsel to the finance committee of CRP, because Liddy refused to answer FBI questions about his frequent phone conversations with one of the Watergate bugging team. Mitchell himself resigned a few days later, explaining that his wife, Martha (*see* BIOGRAPHY), demanded that he leave politics, or she would leave him.

The Democratic National Committee, led by Chairman Lawrence F. O'Brien, was vocally indignant, and sued CRP for $1 million. Furore over the Watergate case was stoked by later revelations that money used by Bernard Barker, one of the Watergate five, came from Nixon campaign funds raised in the Midwest. It was cynicism, very likely, that kept the Watergate incident from doing permanent damage to the Nixon cause. *The Hopes and Fears of the American People,* a book published in 1971 by Potomac Associates, a Washington-based research firm, found that a substantial number of citizens felt their own lives were going along well, but that American institutions—the churches, legislative bodies, large corporations—were not especially to be trusted to carry out their roles in an efficient, respectable manner. In short, the study showed, Americans are cynical about the powerful among them.

The Conventions. The McGovern campaign, meanwhile, reached the height of its power and efficiency at the Democratic national convention, held in the heat of July at Miami Beach. McGovern delegates beat back a last-minute try to have the result of the winner-take-all primary in California declared invalid. The Illinois delegation, which was to have been led as usual by Mayor Daley, was replaced with a new delegation that allowed higher proportions of women, young people, and blacks. Daley sensed the coming rebuff and stayed home. Once the delegations were agreed upon and seated, the nomination of McGovern was assured. But from the moment McGovern became the nominee, the mystical luck of his campaign began to fail.

McGovern wanted Sen. Edward Kennedy as his running mate. He alone still had not believed Kennedy's genuine disinterest in 1972 national politics. Kennedy's refusal to join the ticket set off a manhunt. Senator Muskie vacillated for two days, then turned McGovern down. Sen. Abraham Ribicoff of Connecticut said no. Gov. Reubin Askew of Florida had taken himself out of consideration earlier. Finally, McGovern settled on the dynamic junior senator from Missouri, Thomas F. Eagleton (*see* BIOGRAPHY). In the flurry to get the ticket set, McGovern aides had made only a cursory check of Eagleton's background, and the senator himself assured them in a hurried telephone conversation that he had "no skeletons in his closet." Within two weeks the news broke that Eagleton had been hospitalized three times in the past 12 years for nervous exhaustion, had received psychiatric care, and had twice been given electric shock treatments.

McGovern's reaction to Eagleton's news did as much as anything could have to shatter, in the public mind, what he regarded as the core of his candidacy: his openness, candour, and credibility. At first, he said he would have placed Eagleton on the ticket even if he had known about his medical history. In a quote that was to haunt him, he said he was behind Eagleton "1,000 percent." Simultaneously, he began to drop hints to newsmen that Eagleton would be dropped from the ticket. The press, angry at what they viewed as McGovern's attempts to use them, became increasingly critical. They began to headline other inconsistencies they saw between McGovern's utterances and his behaviour. Despite Eagleton's efforts to stay on the ticket, McGovern did persuade him to withdraw.

Sargent Shriver, Senator Kennedy's brother-in-law, became the new vice-presidential nominee, but the shadow of Eagleton remained. The Republicans began to show new interest in the possibility of carrying normally Democratic Missouri, where voters were furious at Eagleton's dismissal. Reporters at the time recorded a curious but deeply felt inconsistency in voter thinking. McGovern, the argument ran, should have known about Eagleton's medical history, but Eagleton had been under no obligation to bring it up himself. The fact that Eagleton had dissembled, and had previously made attempts to mislead Missouri reporters about the nature of his hospital stays, made no negative impression at all.

President Nixon and Vice-Pres. Spiro Agnew (*see* BIOGRAPHY) were nominated by acclamation at the Republican convention in August, and the small but noisy band of antiwar demonstrators outside the Convention Hall in Miami Beach had no effect on the jubilation inside. The Republican convention was a celebration, an advance victory party for what all within the hall felt was to come.

Campaigns and Election. The burden of campaigning for the Republican ticket was carried by a group of 36 "surrogate" candidates, an impressive list of Cabinet officers, senators, and other Republican officials. Vice-President Agnew campaigned sedately, steering away from the rhetoric that four years earlier had made him a national figure. The president had early laid to rest press speculation that Agnew might be dropped from the ticket in favour of John Connally. Connally had found another way to support Nixon, in the founding and operation of "Democrats for Nixon." Connally himself kicked off the effort with a highly effective half-hour explanation on television of why he, a Democrat and long-time friend of former Pres. Lyndon B. Johnson, could not swallow the idea of McGovern in the White House.

The very existence of a thriving Democrats for Nixon organization pointed up the fatal flaw in the McGovern electoral equation. As a candidate from the left wing of the national Democratic Party, his efforts to reform the party's delegate selection procedures had been effective, and the new people had flooded the convention that nominated him. But many more were forced by the same reforms to stay home, not only from the convention but from organization meetings of the newly "McGovernized" state and local parties. In short, the McGovern candidacy shattered the fragile old Democratic coalition founded by Franklin D. Roosevelt. Ethnic voters, blue-collar workers, and Southerners of all income levels did not see guidelines aimed at allowing more of *them* to take part in Democratic deliberations. Urban Jews, loyal Democrats for decades, began to see in McGovern's insistence on numerical balance for minorities in convention delegations something close to the quota system that had been used against them for so long.

Aside from procedural matters, there was also the fact that McGovern's very liberal views were anathema to many Democratic voters. The Democratic Party had presided over two of the most traumatic events of the 20th century: the Vietnam war and the civil rights movement. All the turbulence of those issues, all the anxieties, were easy to lay at the feet of a "permissive" liberal Democrat like McGovern. He wanted to end the war, all right, but would he save the national honour in the process? Would his desire to cut the defense budget leave the country defenseless against aggression from abroad? Were his ideas about welfare just that one step too far in the direction of allowing the poor to lead indolent lives at the expense of the taxpayers?

CRP focused early and often on the more radical-sounding views of McGovern, highlighting his support of amnesty for young people who fled to Canada to avoid the draft, his sometime musings that marijuana might better be legalized, and his purported support of legalized abortion. Whether those views had merit or not, they were not seen as meritorious by the majority of U.S. voters. In a manner not seen before in this century, a Republican president managed to isolate his opponent on the very left of the American spectrum. Only Massachusetts and the District of Columbia kept McGovern from a total eclipse in the Electoral College. He had become, as establishment Democrats feared he would, a "Goldwater of the Left." The popular vote totaled 47,168,963 for Nixon and 29,169,615 for McGovern; the Electoral College figures were 520–17.

The election of 1972 suggested, however, that some semblance of the old Democratic coalition was still there, shaky but viable enough to support a man of the centre. President Nixon's electoral triumph, while impressive, was personal. Voters across the country split tickets with abandon, and the GOP won only 12 new seats in the House of Representatives and lost 2 in the Senate. The Democrats netted one new governorship. That suggests that the Nixon forces did not produce a philosophical shift in the electorate but only a momentary move to keep things in the country more nearly as they were.

continued from page 713

wan is China's internal affair." The U.S. said that it acknowledged that "all Chinese on either side of the Taiwan Strait maintain there is but one China and that Taiwan is a part of China." It added: "The United States government does not challenge that position. It reaffirms its interest in a peaceful settlement of the Taiwan question by the Chinese themselves. With this prospect in mind, it affirms the ultimate withdrawal of all U.S. forces and military installations from Taiwan. In the meantime, it will progressively reduce its forces and military installations on Taiwan as the tension in the area diminishes."

The U.S. statement represented a sharp departure from Washington's long-standing policy of unswerving support for the government of Nationalist Chinese leader Chiang Kai-shek on Taiwan. Thus, the fifth and final part of the Shanghai communiqué came as something of an anticlimax. It stated that both sides had discussed joint contacts "in such fields as science, technology, culture, sports and journalism" and that they planned to "facilitate the further development of such contacts and exchanges." The desirability of increasing "bilateral trade" was stressed.

Nixon's journey to the Soviet Union in May was more productive than the China trip in terms of tangible results. The most important of these were a pair of accords limiting offensive and defensive strategic nuclear weapons. The first—a treaty that required and later received Senate approval—limited the two nations' antiballistic missile systems. The second accord—an executive agreement not requiring Senate approval—froze land- and sea-based missiles at their present levels. (*See* DEFENSE.)

During Nixon's five days of meetings with the chief Soviet negotiator, Communist Party General Secretary Leonid I. Brezhnev, and other Kremlin officials, the leaders approved five other agreements, which for the most part were ready for signing before the summit meeting opened on May 22. The agreements provided for (1) establishment of a joint committee on cooperation in the field of environmental protection; (2) coordinated research on cancer, heart disease, and environmental health; (3) a joint flight with linked Soviet and U.S. spacecraft in 1975; (4) creation of a permanent commission on scientific and technical cooperation that would meet at least once a year to recommend joint projects; and (5) prohibition of mutual harassment on the high seas and establishment of an experimental signal system to avoid naval mishaps.

The Moscow summit led within two months to a major trade deal. Nixon announced on July 8 that the U.S. had concluded a three-year agreement for the sale of at least $750 million of American wheat, corn, and other grains to the Soviet Union. It was the largest grain transaction in history between two countries. One month later, on August 9, the U.S. Department of Agriculture (USDA) said that the sale of U.S. grains to the Soviet Union might top $1 billion. The new estimate was based on the likelihood that the U.S.S.R. would purchase $500 million in wheat alone because of the poor harvest.

Some Democrats later charged that the grain deal had given a windfall profit to exporters and had shortchanged U.S. farmers, consumers, and taxpayers. At an October 5 news conference, President Nixon retorted that the farmers "got $1 billion in more farm income" from the grain deal, the taxpayers "were saved $200 million" that it would have cost to keep the grain in storage, and "thousands of jobs [were] created" on the farm, in the merchant marine, and in processing areas. Reports persisted, however, of windfall profits for grain speculators because the USDA had informed them in advance of a special temporary rise in the export subsidy from 38 to 47 cents per bushel. Observers also charged that farmers lost income from having to sell their wheat and other grains at lower prices than would have prevailed if there had been announcements of the change in the subsidy and of a mid-August Soviet crop report. Estimates of the cost to U.S. taxpayers as a result of the sale ran as high as $120 million.

The nation's most nagging foreign policy problem, the war in Indochina, appeared to move somewhat closer to solution in 1972. President Nixon announced to the nation on May 8 that he had ordered the mining of North Vietnamese ports and bombing of land and sea routes to North Vietnam in an attempt to prevent delivery of war supplies to that country. Five months later, the policy seemed to bear fruit. Presidential adviser Henry A. Kissinger (*see* BIOGRAPHY) stated in Washington on October 26 that "peace is at hand." Reporting on his secret negotiations with the North Vietnamese, Kissinger said a final agreement on a truce and a political settlement could be worked out in one more conference with the North Vietnamese "lasting no more than three or four days." On October 27 U.S. Secretary of Defense Melvin R. Laird confirmed earlier reports that the U.S. had ordered a temporary halt to bombing north of the 20th parallel in North Vietnam.

Hopes for early settlement of the war were frustrated in the following weeks, however, as North Vietnam, South Vietnam, and the U.S. proved unable to reach an agreement satisfactory to all sides. Finally, in mid-December, the White House announced that President Nixon had ordered resumption of full-scale bombing north of the 20th parallel. Despite the order, presidential press secretary Ronald L. Ziegler insisted that "the road to a negotiated peace is wide open. We want a rapid settlement to this conflict." The bombing was the heaviest of the war and surpassed in tonnage virtually all of the famous bombing raids of World War II. Losses of U.S. B-52 bombers, used above the 20th parallel for the first time, were heavy. The U.S. halted its bombing above the 20th parallel on December 30, and the talks between Kissinger and the North Vietnamese were scheduled to resume Jan. 8, 1973.

A treasured gift from the People's Republic of China to the people of the United States, Ling-ling, a female giant panda, draws appreciative crowds at the National Zoo in Washington. Along with Hsing-hsing, a male, Ling-ling was presented to President Nixon during his 1972 Peking visit.

WIDE WORLD

U.S. relations with Cuba, frozen for more than a decade, took a slight turn for the better toward the end of the year. Using the Swiss embassy in Havana as a go-between, the two countries began indirect negotiations in November on an agreement to curb hijacking of airplanes and boats by citizens of the two countries. The decision to begin talks came after four U.S. men diverted an Eastern Airlines jet to Havana on October 29 and three Americans forced a Southern Airways plane to land in the Cuban capital on November 12. Cuban Prime Minister Fidel Castro was reported to have lost all patience with hijackers who sought asylum in his country on the pretext that they were political refugees. At the same time, he was said to be eager to conclude an agreement that would commit the U.S. to extradite Cubans who commandeered boats when fleeing to the U.S.

Domestic Affairs. On the domestic front, the presidential election campaign dominated the news from the start of the primary season in March to the November day of decision. President Nixon's renomination by the Republicans was a foregone conclusion, and his reelection appeared likely all during the campaign. For the Democrats, though, the campaign was full of surprises. The Democrats' troubles began to surface early in the primary season. Sen. Edmund S. Muskie of Maine, the acknowledged front-runner for the Democratic presidential nomination, made a poor showing in the first few primaries and finally withdrew from active campaigning on April 27. Sen. Hubert H. Humphrey of Minnesota, the party's standard-bearer in 1968, announced his candidacy on January 10 and soon won the backing of organized labour and other groups that had supported him in the past. Meanwhile, Sen. George McGovern of South Dakota and Gov. George Wallace of Alabama (*see* BIOGRAPHY) were displaying surprising strength in the early primaries. McGovern and Wallace, it was said in the spring, were spokesmen for a "new populism" that would be an important factor in the election.

On May 15, Wallace, appearing at a campaign rally at a shopping centre in Laurel, Md., was shot and seriously wounded by an assailant later identified as Arthur Bremer, 21, of Milwaukee, Wis. Wallace, paralyzed from the hips down by a bullet that lodged near his spine, won impressive victories in both the Maryland and Michigan Democratic primaries the day after he was struck down. The attack nevertheless had the effect of removing him from the race.

By late June, McGovern had acquired nearly all of the 1,509 delegate votes he needed to be nominated by the Democratic national convention. But the South Dakotan's campaign suffered a potentially serious setback June 29 when the convention's credentials committee, meeting in Washington, voted to ignore California's winner-take-all primary law and award 151 of the 271 McGovern delegates from that state to other candidates in proportion to their primary vote. On June 30 the committee also voted to oust Mayor Richard J. Daley and 58 other Chicago delegates and seat a slate of challengers that included 40–50 McGovern supporters. Both actions were immediately tested in court; on July 7, the U.S. Supreme Court ruled that the convention itself should decide the issue.

Voting on the California and Illinois credentials cases (and others as well) took place during the opening session of the convention in Miami Beach, Fla., on July 10. In every instance, the McGovern forces prevailed, thus removing any lingering doubt as to who would be nominated. McGovern's nomination came on the first ballot July 12. For an extended discussion of the conventions, campaigning, and election, *see* Special Report.

After his election President Nixon made sweeping changes among his top officials as well as the middle echelons of government. Secretary of Health, Education, and Welfare Elliot L. Richardson became secretary of defense, replacing Melvin R. Laird. Caspar W. Weinberger, former head of the Office of Management and Budget, succeeded Richardson. Roy L. Ash, president of Litton Industries, replaced Weinberger. Replacing Peter G. Peterson as secretary of commerce was Frederick B. Dent, a South Carolina textile manufacturer; Peterson went on a foreign trade mission for the president. Peter Brennan, a labour union president in New York City, was chosen to replace Secretary of Labor James D. Hodgson.

George W. Romney resigned as secretary of housing and urban development to form an organization of citizens to attack "life and death" issues before they become crises; he was succeeded by Undersecretary of Commerce James T. Lynn. For secretary of transportation Nixon appointed Claude S. Brinegar, a California oil executive, to replace John A. Volpe, who was appointed ambassador to Italy.

In other top-level changes Nixon named James R. Schlesinger, who was serving as chairman of the Atomic Energy Commission, to be the director of the Central Intelligence Agency. He replaced Richard M. Helms, who was appointed ambassador to Iran. A former White House speech writer, James Keogh, replaced Frank J. Shakespeare, Jr., as head of the United States Information Agency.

In an effort to hold down federal spending White House budget officials late in December announced cutbacks and cancellations of some programs. Eliminated were the 36-year-old Rural Environmental Assistance Program, which offered landowners annual payments to cover in part the cost of antipollution and conservation practices, and the Water Bank Program, which had offered ten-year contracts to protect wetlands for migratory water fowl. The low-cost loans for rural electric and telephone systems were ended, as were emergency loans to farmers for crop and livestock losses due to floods, storms, and other severe weather. Payments to feed-grain producers were expected to be cut about $800 million from 1972.

The U.S. space program reached the end of an era in 1972 with the last two manned flights to the moon under the Apollo program. Two astronauts from Apollo 16 spent a record 71 hours and two minutes on the moon April 20–23 during the first manned mission to the lunar mountains. They walked, worked, and drove an electric vehicle on the lunar surface outside their spaceship for a record total of 20 hours and 14 minutes during three separate sorties.

Apollo 17 was launched from Cape Kennedy on December 7 and returned to earth December 19 with 249 lb. of rock and soil samples. It broke Apollo 16's record by staying more than three days on the moon.

UPI COMPIX

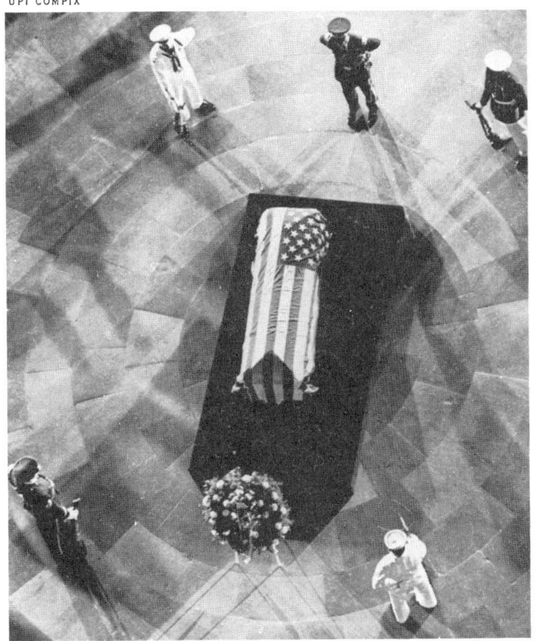

An honour guard composed of one man from each branch of the U.S. military services stands at parade rest around the casket of J. Edgar Hoover in the Capitol rotunda, where it lay in state on May 3, 1972. Hoover, director of the FBI for 48 years, was the first civil service employee to receive such honours.

In a statement issued December 14, President Nixon said: "This may be the last time in this century that men will walk on the moon. But space exploration will continue, the benefits of space exploration will continue, the search for knowledge through the exploration of space will continue, and there will be new dreams to pursue based on what we have learned."

(RICHARD L. WORSNOP)

ENCYCLOPÆDIA BRITANNICA FILMS. *The Industrial Revolution—Beginnings in the United States* (1968); *Midwest—Heartland of the Nation* (1968); *Produce—From Farm to Market* (1968); *Heritage in Black* (1969); *The Pacific West* (1969); *The Rise of Labor* (1969); *The South: Roots of the Urban Crisis* (1969); *Chicano from the Southwest* (1970); *The Industrial Worker* (1970); *Linda and Billy Ray from Appalachia* (1970); *The Mississippi System—Waterway of Commerce* (1970); *The Presidency—Search for a Candidate* (1970); *The Rise of Big Business* (1970); *The Rise of the American City* (1970); *An Essay on War* (1971); *The Great Lakes* (1971); *Jesse from Mississippi* (1971); *Johnny from Fort Apache* (1971); *The Progressive Era* (1971); *Valley Forge* (1971); *President of the USA: Too Much Power?* (1972); *The Shot Heard Round The World* (1972); *Yorktown* (1972); *The Boston Tea Party* (1972).

Upper Volta

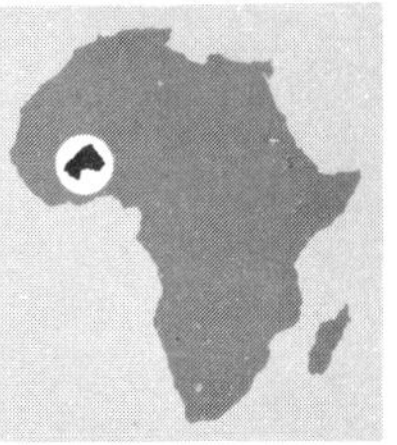

A republic of West Africa, Upper Volta is bordered by Mali, Niger, Dahomey, Togo, Ghana, and Ivory Coast. Area: 105,870 sq.mi. (274,200 sq.km.). Pop. (1971 est.): 5,491,000. Cap. and largest city: Ouagadougou (pop., 1970 est., 110,000). Language: French (official). Religion: animist; Muslim and Christian minorities. President in 1972, Gen. Sangoule Lamizana; premier, Gérard Kango Ouedraogo.

An atmosphere of general lassitude prevailed during 1972, punctuated by disagreements between the civil and military authorities and a constant undercurrent of unrest in the country's secondary schools and colleges. The year was marked by three major events: General Lamizana's official visit to Egypt in February, the Third Festival of African Cinema held in Ouagadougou in March, and finally the official visit of French Pres. Georges Pompidou in November.

During his visit to Egypt President Lamizana pledged his wholehearted diplomatic support to the Cairo government. He gave his solemn recognition of Egypt's right to the Sinai, occupied by Israel since the Arab-Israeli war of 1967.

Universalist Church: *see* Religion
Universities: *see* Education

UPPER VOLTA
Education. (1968–69) Primary, pupils 99,827, teachers (including preprimary) 2,292; secondary, pupils 8,117, teachers 432; vocational, pupils 1,298, teachers (1967–68) 106; teacher training (1967–68), students 1,114, teachers 35; higher, students 122, teaching staff 19.
Finance. Monetary unit: CFA franc, with (Sept. 18, 1972) a parity of CFA Fr. 50 to the French franc (CFA Fr. 255.79 = U.S. $1; free rate of CFA Fr. 612.37 = £1 sterling). Budget (1971 est.): revenue CFA Fr. 10,515,000,000; expenditure CFA Fr. 9,572,000,000.
Foreign Trade. (1971) Imports CFA Fr. 14,050,000,000; exports CFA Fr. 4,410,000,000. Import sources: France 44%; Ivory Coast 11%; West Germany 5%; U.S. 5%. Export destinations: Ivory Coast 38%; France 22%; Ghana 10%; Italy 10%; Japan 5%. Main exports: livestock 36%; oilseeds 22%; cotton 19%; meat 6%; fruits and vegetables 5%.

The Third Festival of African Cinema was attended by film makers from all parts of Africa and contributed substantially to raising Upper Volta's status on the continent. It also contributed substantially to the overheating of tempers in a capital where extremism was becoming more and more prevalent, and the occasion was used by militants, many of whom had been members of the former African Independence Party, to denounce the "cultural alienation" that they believed was afflicting Africa. In its place they preached a form of xenophobic nationalism, especially condemning former colonial rulers in the hope of casting a shadow over President Pompidou's visit scheduled for later in the year.

When Pompidou did arrive, the reception given him was marked by a distinct coolness, especially in comparison with the rapturous welcome given to him in Togo later the same week. Nevertheless, talks between Pompidou and the government of Upper Volta were cordial. Moreover, during his visit Pompidou announced France's decision to write off debts owed by its former African colonies to the extent of Fr. 1 billion. (PHILIPPE DECRAENE)

Uruguay

A republic of South America, Uruguay is on the Atlantic Ocean and is bounded by Brazil and Argentina. Area: 68,536 sq.mi. (177,508 sq.km.). Pop. (1972 est.): 2,956,300, including white 89%; mestizo 10%. Cap. and largest city: Montevideo (pop., 1972 est., 1,459,200). Language: Spanish. Religion: mainly Roman Catholic. Presidents in 1972, Jorge Pacheco Areco and, from March 1, Juan María Bordaberry.

The year 1972 brought a major change in emphasis on the Uruguayan political front. After the spectacular escape of 106 Tupamaro guerrillas from Punta Carretas prison in September 1971, police and Army security forces were reorganized to form a combined antiguerrilla unit. President Bordaberry, who had based his election campaign on a promise to stamp out guerrilla activity, duly took office on March 1, despite a two-month recount and allegations of irregularities in the election in November 1971. The security campaign, which was already beginning to bear fruit, was further strengthened by a declaration of a "state of internal war" on April 15 under which the armed forces were given wide powers of search and arrest and parts of the constitution relating to individual rights were suspended. The campaign led to the discovery of secret arms dumps and "people's prisons," the release of a number of hostages held by the Tupamaros, and the arrest of more than 2,000 guerrillas, including Raúl Sendic, the accredited founder of the movement, who had escaped in the mass breakout from Punta Carretas.

However, as the threat of the Tupamaros gradually receded, the Army began to test its newly acquired influence in other spheres. Acting upon information gleaned from Tupamaros under interrogation, the Army began to investigate the activities of leading businessmen and other prominent persons suspected of "economic crimes," mainly smuggling, corruption, and currency speculation.

At the end of September complaints of torture by four physicians held as suspected guerrillas, together with the Army's refusal to release them, led to a strike by 5,000 doctors and ultimately to the resignation of the minister of defense, Augusto Legnani, and the commander in chief of the Army, Gen. Florencio Graviña. A few days later, Jorge Batlle, editor of a Montevideo newspaper and leader of the "Unidad y Reforma" sector of the ruling Colorado Party, was arrested after a radio broadcast in which he had criticized the role of the Army. After being held incommunicado for two days, he was threatened with charges of "attacking the moral strength of the armed forces," an offense carrying a penalty of 18 months' to 6 years' imprisonment.

In the inevitable reaction, factions of all political parties united in condemning the behaviour of the Army, and the entire Cabinet resigned. Although this was a normal expedient to permit a reshuffle, specula-

URUGUAY
Education. (1968–69) Primary, pupils 369,816, teachers 13,095; secondary, pupils 118,082, teachers 9,715; vocational, pupils 35,648, teachers 3,048; teacher training, students 6,963; higher, students 18,650, teaching staff (1963–64) 2,182.
Finance. Monetary unit: peso, with (Sept. 18, 1972) a principal rate of 625 pesos to U.S. $1 (1,528 pesos = £1 sterling) and a free rate of 880 pesos to U.S. $1 (2,150 pesos = £1 sterling). Gold, SDRs, and foreign exchange, official: (June 1972) U.S. $186 million; (June 1971) U.S. $175 million. Budget (1970 est.): revenue 83,927,000,000 pesos; expenditure 94,973,000,000 pesos. Gross domestic product: (1970) 596.2 billion pesos; (1969) 499.7 billion pesos. Money supply: (Nov. 1971) 123,313,000,000 pesos; (Nov. 1970) 83,335,000,000 pesos. Cost of living (Montevideo; 1963 = 100): (June 1972) 4,822; (June 1971) 2,792.
Foreign Trade. (1971) Imports U.S. $221.9 million; exports U.S. $205.7 million. Import sources: Brazil 16%; Argentina 14%; U.S. 10%; West Germany 10%; U.K. 8%; Kuwait 6%. Export destinations: West Germany 12%; Brazil 12%; Italy 11%; Netherlands 7%; Greece 6%; France 5%; U.S. 5%. Main exports: meat 34%; wool 31%; hides and skins 10%.
Transport and Communications. Roads (1970) *c.* 41,600 km. Motor vehicles in use (1970): passenger 202,000; commercial (including buses) 84,200. Railways (1969) 2,975 km. Air traffic (1970): 63,207,000 passenger-km.; freight 290,000 net ton-km. Shipping (1971): merchant vessels 100 gross tons and over 42; gross tonnage 162,774. Telephones (Jan. 1971) 215,000. Radio receivers (Dec. 1970) 1,081,000. Television receivers (Dec. 1969) 250,000.
Agriculture. Production (in 000; metric tons; 1971; 1970 in parentheses): wheat 316 (388); barley 49 (45); oats 63 (78); sweet potatoes (1970) 74, (1969) 74; corn 160 (139); sorghum 72 (35); linseed 49 (81); sunflower seed 49 (65); rice 122 (142); sugar, raw value (1971–72) 70, (1970–71) 67; oranges (1970) 59, (1969) 64; wine *c.* 85 (*c.* 86); wool 45 (47); beef and veal *c.* 370 (*c.* 360). Livestock (in 000; May 1971): cattle *c.* 8,500; sheep *c.* 19,700; pigs *c.* 390; horses *c.* 420; chickens *c.* 4,900.
Industry. Production (in 000; metric tons; 1969): cement 462; crude steel *c.* 14; petroleum products (1970) 1,600; electricity (excluding most industrial production; kw-hr.; 1970) 2,132,000.

Uranium: *see* Mining

Urban Affairs: *see* Cities and Urban Affairs

tion mounted as to the likelihood of a military coup.

In the economic field, the Bordaberry administration set about tackling the foreign trade situation as soon as it took office. The exchange rate system was overhauled in an attempt to strengthen export earnings and bolster international reserves. The result was a floating rate for financial operations and a carefully manipulated rate for trade transactions, the latter being systematically devalued as the government sought to maintain the balance between internal and external factors. However, the measures had little effect. The economic situation continued to deteriorate, and in July a ban was imposed upon domestic consumption of beef in a further attempt to increase export earnings.

Widespread social unrest in response to raging inflation, which had reached nearly 60% toward the end of the year, caused a spate of general stoppages including a paralyzing transport workers' strike in September. The government sought to counter the unrest by agreeing to a 20% wage raise in the private sector. However, since price increases were also authorized, any increase in purchasing power was likely to be swallowed up almost at once. (M. J. SPENCE)

Vatican City State

This independent sovereignty is surrounded by but not part of Rome. As a state with territorial limits, it is properly distinguished from the Holy See, which constitutes the worldwide administrative and legislative body for the Roman Catholic Church. The area of Vatican City is 108.7 ac. (44 ha.). Pop. (1971 est.): 648. As sovereign pontiff, Paul VI is the chief of state. Vatican City is administered by a pontifical commission of five cardinals, of which the secretary of state, Jean Cardinal Villot, is president.

Diplomatic relations were established with Bangladesh, Tunisia, Algeria, and Sudan in 1972, and the Vatican continued to pursue contacts with Hungary and Poland. Among those granted papal audience were Austrian Pres. Franz Jonas, Irish Foreign Minister P. J. Hillery, and Italy's president, Giovanni Leone, whose meeting enlivened controversy over revision of the 1929 Concordat and the question of a referendum on the recently introduced Italian divorce law.

As part of International Book Year, on July 6 the Vatican displayed 150 rare antique books, including a papal bull of 1520 "against the errors of Martin Luther and his followers."

Michelangelo's "Pietà" in St. Peter's Basilica was damaged by a hammer attack on May 21. The assailant, Hungarian-born Laszlo Toth, claimed that he was Jesus Christ. The left arm of the Madonna was shattered and her nose, left eye, and veil were chipped. Two days later an Italian newsman staged a mock hammer attack on Michelangelo's "Moses" to emphasize the urgent need for protection of Italy's artistic masterpieces. In October it was reported that the "Pietà" had been repaired by Vatican experts to the point where it showed no obvious impairment. In the future it would be housed in a bulletproof glass case.

Deep mourning followed the death on February 21 of Eugène Cardinal Tisserant (*see* OBITUARIES).

(MAX BERGERRE)

See also Religion.

Venezuela

A republic of northern South America, Venezuela is bounded by Colombia, Brazil, Guyana, and the Caribbean Sea. Area: 352,143 sq.mi. (912,050 sq.km.). Pop. (1971): 10,721,522, including mestizo 69%; white 20%; Negro 9%; Indian 2%. Cap. and largest city: Caracas (pop., 1971, 1,035,499). Language: Spanish. Religion: predominantly Roman Catholic. President in 1972, Rafael Caldera.

Although negotiations on Venezuela's accession to the Cartagena Agreement and on the border dispute with Colombia focused much attention on the nation's relations with the Andean countries, a significant decline in petroleum production ensured that the oil industry remained near the centre of political debate during 1972. At the same time, the nomination of candidates for the presidential election in December 1973 heralded the start of what promised to be a long and intense campaign.

The talks on Venezuela's entry into the Andean Group eventually began in March. By August the Venezuelans had become optimistic about the acceptability of their application. The government was reported to be looking on entry into the group by the end of the year as an accomplished fact, and a leading

VENEZUELA

Education. (1969–70) Primary, pupils 1,681,947, teachers 49,730; secondary, pupils 287,952, teachers 12,598; vocational, pupils 146,421, teachers 7,182; teacher training, students 13,841, teachers 1,184; higher (including 8 universities), students 70,185, teaching staff 7,318.

Finance. Monetary unit: bolívar, with (Sept. 18, 1972) an official selling rate of 4.40 bolivares to U.S. $1 (free rate of 10.67 bolivares = £1 sterling). Gold, SDRs, and foreign exchange, central bank: (June 1972) U.S. $1,384,000,000; (June 1971) U.S. $1,089,000,000. Budget (1971 est.) balanced at 10,987,000,000 bolivares. Gross domestic product: (1970) 45,810,000,000 bolivares; (1969) 42,720,000,000 bolivares. Money supply: (April 1972) 8,451,000,000 bolivares; (April 1971) 6,962,000,000 bolivares. Cost of living (Caracas; 1963 = 100): (June 1972) 118; (June 1971) 115.

Foreign Trade. Imports (f.o.b.; 1971) 8,319,000,000 bolivares; exports (1971) 13,759,000,000 bolivares. Import sources (1970 est.): U.S. 47%; West Germany 9%; Japan 8%; Canada 7%; Italy 5%; U.K. 5%. Export destinations (1970 est.): U.S. 35%; Netherlands Antilles 19%; Canada 11%; Trinidad and Tobago 6%. Main exports: crude oil and petroleum products 92%; iron ore 5%.

Transport and Communications. Roads (1971) 43,238 km. (including 569 km. expressways). Motor vehicles in use (1971): passenger 708,000; commercial 257,000. Railways (1970): 475 km.; traffic 36 million passenger-km., freight 13 million net ton-km. Air traffic (1971): 1,424,600,000 passenger-km.; freight 67,947,000 net ton-km. Shipping (1971): merchant vessels 100 gross tons and over 109; gross tonnage 411,696. Telephones (Jan. 1971) 406,000. Radio receivers (Dec. 1970) 1.7 million. Television receivers (Dec. 1970) 720,000.

Agriculture. Production (in 000; metric tons; 1971; 1970 in parentheses): corn *c.* 725 (710); rice *c.* 240 (226); sesame *c.* 126 (126); sweet potatoes (1970) 123, (1969) 118; cassava (1970) 317, (1969) 310; dry beans *c.* 58 (46); coffee *c.* 61 (61); tobacco *c.* 12 (12); cocoa (1971–72) 18, (1970–71) 19; bananas 989 (968); oranges 192 (184); sugar, raw value (1971–72) *c.* 550, (1970–71) *c.* 511; cotton, lint *c.* 15 (13); beef and veal *c.* 199 (*c.* 198). Livestock (in 000; 1970–71): cattle 8,499; pigs 1,671; sheep 104; horses 427; asses *c.* 500; poultry 20,430.

Industry. Production (in 000; metric tons; 1971): crude oil 185,772; natural gas (cu.m.) 9,367,000; petroleum products (1970) 60,670; iron ore (64% metal content) 19,523; cement (1970) 2,520; gold (troy oz.; 1970) 22; diamonds (metric carats; 1970) *c.* 500; electricity (kw-hr.; 1970) 12,631,000.

U.S.S.R.:
see Union of Soviet Socialist Republics

Utilities, Public:
see Cooperatives; Fuel and Power; Industrial Review; Transportation

Venereal Diseases:
see Medicine

Caracas newspaper, *El Nacional,* described negotiations as at an important, almost final stage. The opinion of experts in Lima, however, was somewhat different. They believed that the outcome of the negotiations was still very much in the balance, with the metal products development program one of the principal points to be resolved. This was the only development program on which the members of the group had reached agreement and with Venezuela already producing around half their total output it would, they argued, have to be completely renegotiated.

The first reports of subsequent meetings tended to confirm the reservations expressed in Lima. Although described as positive, the talks did not produce a final agreement. It appeared that in addition to specific questions, such as the metal products development program, there were others of a more general nature, such as foreign investment policy, on which substantial progress had to be made.

Similarly, the talks on border demarcation between Venezuela and Colombia did not result in a substantive agreement. Differences over future procedure also appeared. In mid-August Colombia's chief negotiator indicated that his country would be willing to refer the dispute to the International Court at The Hague if it was not solved by bilateral negotiation. This idea did not find a receptive audience in Venezuela, where the emphasis reportedly lay on a bilateral solution. Moreover, according to some sources, Venezuela wanted to suspend the talks, at least until after the presidential elections in both countries in late 1973 and early 1974, while the Colombians preferred to continue them. Meanwhile the Venezuelan government continued its arms spending with a £6 million order of patrol vessels from the U.K. and an order for 142 AMX-30 tanks from France at a cost of $60 million.

A drop in petroleum production (about 15% in the first half of the year), following one of between 4 and 5% in 1971, provoked considerable comment in both Venezuela and abroad. This, together with the approval by the Chamber of Deputies of the domestic oil marketing bill, kept the petroleum sector well to the forefront of Venezuelan politics. The three main reasons given for the drop were that the demand for oil was lower than expected, owing to a mild winter in Europe and North America; that a decline in freight rates had made it cheaper for European and North American oil companies to transport supplies from the Middle East; and that local taxation increases had made Venezuelan oil more costly to produce.

The effect of a decline in petroleum output on the economy in general, and on government revenue in particular, was difficult to assess because of the introduction by the government in December 1971 of tax penalties for specified quarterly variations in output. Moreover, the position was further obscured by reports that the oil companies had asked the government to waive those penalties because they expected production to increase in the second half of 1972.

The domestic oil marketing bill, passed by the Chamber of Deputies in July, the aim of which was to give the Corporación Venezolana del Petróleo (CVP) complete control of the internal marketing of petroleum products by 1975, was part of a package of measures designed to provide a new framework for the foreign investor in Venezuela. As the year drew to a close, legislation on foreign investment was still being drafted by a presidential commission. This delay was in part due to the desire not to prejudice Venezuela's entry negotiations with the Andean Group, where this topic proved particularly difficult.

By late 1972 the campaign for the 1973 presidential election had been initiated with the nomination of the principal candidates. For the two main parties, the Comitado Organización Politica Electoral Independiente (COPEI) and Acción Democrática (AD), these were Lorenzo Fernández and Carlos Andrés Pérez, respectively. The other contenders were reported to be Paz Galarraga for the Nueva Fuerza, a coalition of the Unión Republicana Democrática (URD), Movimiento Electoral del Pueblo (MEP), and the Communist Party; and José Vicente Rangel for the Movimiento al Socialismo, a splinter group that had broken away from the Communist Party in 1971. In December there were reports that former dictator Gen. Marcos Pérez Jiménez would attempt to return from exile in Madrid (his previous visit in May having caused violent student riots) to direct an extreme nationalist campaign for the Cruzada Cívica Nacionalista (CCN). The platforms on which each candidate hoped to be elected had still to emerge, but the fall in oil production and the low level of reserves suggested that oil policy would be an important issue.

(ROBERT STENT)

Veterinary Medicine

California poultry were struck by a disastrous outbreak of Newcastle disease in 1972. The highly virulent strain of Newcastle disease virus had been brought into the U.S. with ornamental birds imported two years earlier. Following lesser outbreaks in Texas and Arizona, it became established in southern California, reaching such proportions that the U.S. Department of Agriculture declared a national emergency in early 1972. Although many of the poultry flocks had been vaccinated, it was estimated that losses would reach 15 to 20% if the disease was allowed to run its course. The USDA decided on a program of total eradication by slaughter, and from March to October some 7.8 million chickens, turkeys, ducks, and ornamental birds were killed.

Despite widespread vaccination, Venezuelan equine encephalomyelitis (VEE) recurred in Mexico near the U.S. border; 2,366 equine deaths were reported there between January and August 1972. In 1970–71 the disease had spread from Central America to Mexico and into Texas, where about 3,400 horses were affected and 1,500 died. By late November 1971 some 4,000 veterinarians had vaccinated nearly three million horses in 19 states (about 95% of the animals at risk in this area), and 13.5 million ac. of the Gulf Coast had been sprayed by air to kill the mosquito vector. An additional 173,000 horses were vaccinated during 1972, and no cases of VEE were diagnosed in the United States.

The first outbreak of African swine fever in the Western Hemisphere appeared to have been successfully contained. It had begun in Cuba in May 1971 and was confirmed in June, whereupon stringent control measures were introduced. About 12,000 pigs died on 33 farms and 20,000 were destroyed, after which all the swine in Havana Province—more than 500,000—were slaughtered and the meat sterilized for human consumption. No additional cases were recorded after August 1971.

Foot-and-mouth disease occurred in Peruvian llamas, for the first time in any South American

G. BARTL—GAMMA

Eminent Austrian zoologists Richard Holy and Ludwig Wöss perform successful surgery on python to remove a lung carcinoma (cancer).

camelid, and vaccination programs were intensified throughout the continent. Outbreaks were reported in Greece and Turkey, which had been free of the disease for more than five years. Mass vaccination for rinderpest brought this disease under control in the Middle East, where outbreaks in 1969–70 had affected or threatened cattle in most Mid-Eastern countries. In much of Africa, intensive vaccination campaigns had reduced the incidence of rinderpest to its lowest level in many years. By July 1972 the U.S. hog cholera eradication program had progressed to the point where only New Jersey, Texas, and the Carolinas remained infected. Subsequently, sporadic outbreaks occurred in several states, making it unlikely that the goal of total eradication by the end of 1972 would be attained. Following an outbreak of swine vesicular disease, the first of its kind in England, in December, over 3,000 pigs were slaughtered.

During 1971 the incidence of animal rabies in the U.S. increased 34% over that for 1970, to 4,392 cases, and for the first time at least one case was recorded in every state except Hawaii. Most of the increase involved wildlife, with skunks accounting for 46% of the cases. Veterinarians joined with public health officials in warning the public against keeping these animals as pets. In Latin America more than a million horses and cattle died of rabies spread by vampire bats. Earlier control methods involving dynamite and flamethrowers had been unsatisfactory, largely because they also killed beneficial species. A more successful method involved smearing an anticoagulant on captured bats, which were then released. The bats died within 24 hours, but not before they had transferred the compound to 20 or 30 others of their species.

For about 15 years U.S. producers had fed diethylstilbestrol (DES) to cattle to promote growth and increase tenderness of beef, but this practice had come under fire from the Food and Drug Administration. When fed in large amounts, the drug produced cancer in laboratory animals, and concern was expressed that small residues in meat might be carcinogenic. The drug left no residues in meat when it was withdrawn from animal feed before slaughter, but some cattle feeders apparently used it improperly and a few contaminated carcasses were discovered. The FDA banned use of the drug in feed after Jan. 1, 1973. It could still be used in the form of pellets implanted under the skin, though there was some sentiment for banning this practice also. (J. F. SMITHCORS)

Vietnam

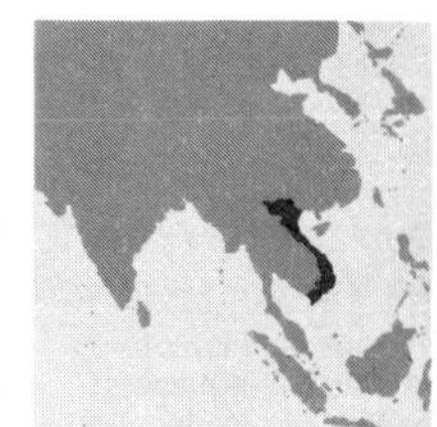

A country comprising the easternmost part of the Indochinese Peninsula, Vietnam was divided de facto into two republics in July 1954.

Republic of Vietnam (South Vietnam). This is bordered by North Vietnam (along the 17th parallel), the South China Sea, Cambodia, and Laos. Area: 67,108 sq.mi. (173,809 sq.km.). Pop. (1972 est.): 18.9 million. Cap. and largest city: Saigon (pop., 1972 est., 2 million). Language: Vietnamese. Religion: Buddhist; pagan; Confucian; Christian. President in 1972, Nguyen Van Thieu; premier, Tran Thien Khiem.

VIETNAM: Republic

Education. (1969–70) Primary, pupils 2,375,982, teachers 45,077; secondary, pupils 636,921, teachers 16,314; vocational, pupils 14,569, teachers 907; teacher training, students 3,923, teachers 92; higher, students 47,296, teaching staff 1,348.

Finance. Monetary unit: piastre, with (Sept. 18, 1972) an official exchange rate of 118 piastres to U.S. $1 and a parallel market rate (for exports and some imports) of 410 piastres to U.S. $1 (free rate of 1,003 piastres = £1 sterling). Gold, SDRs, and foreign exchange, central bank: (June 1972) U.S. $204 million; (June 1971) U.S. $188 million. Budget (1971 est.): revenue 239 billion piastres; expenditure 267 billion piastres. Money supply: (May 1972) 233,920,000,000 piastres; (May 1971) 184,340,000,000 piastres. Cost of living (Saigon; 1963 = 100): (June 1972) 848; (June 1971) 683.

Foreign Trade. (1971) Imports 70,077,000,000 piastres; exports 994 million piastres. Import sources: U.S. 41%; Japan 18%; Taiwan 10%; France 8%; West Germany 6%. Export destinations: France 44%; Japan 14%; West Germany 10%. Main export rubber 76%.

Transport and Communications. Roads (1970) 20,917 km. Motor vehicles in use (1971): passenger 58,400; commercial (including buses) 29,200. Railways: (1970) 625 km. (excluding 653 km. not operated); traffic (1971) 85.5 million passenger-km., freight 38 million net ton-km. Air traffic (1971): 485 million passenger-km.; freight 3,928,000 net ton-km. Telephones (Dec. 1970) 35,000. Radio receivers (Dec. 1969) 1.3 million. Television receivers (Dec. 1970) 450,000.

Agriculture. Production (in 000; metric tons; 1971; 1970 in parentheses): rice 6,324 (5,715); sweet potatoes (1970) 220, (1969) 226; cassava (1970) 216, (1969) 233; peanuts *c.* 32 (32); dry beans *c.* 12 (11); rubber *c.* 34 (33); tea *c.* 5.5 (5.5); coffee *c.* 4 (3.9); fish catch (1970) 577, (1969) 464. Livestock (in 000; 1970–71): cattle 908; buffalo 565; pigs 3,848.

Industry. Production (in 000; metric tons; 1970): cement 286; salt *c.* 118; cotton yarn 12; woven cotton fabrics (m.; 1969) 61,000; electricity (excluding most industrial production; kw-hr.; 1971) 1,343,000.

VIETNAM: Democratic Republic

Education. (1966–67) Primary and secondary, pupils 4,517,600, teachers 86,495; vocational, pupils 101,880, teachers 4,194; higher (including University of Hanoi; 1970), students *c.* 72,000, teaching staff (1966–67) 5,004.

Finance and Trade. Monetary unit: dong, with (Sept. 18, 1972) an official exchange rate of 2.71 dong to U.S. $1 (8.63 dong = £1 sterling) and a "tourist" rate of 13.24 dong to £1 sterling. Budget (1963) balanced at 1,779,288,000 dong. Foreign trade (1965): imports *c.* 530 million dong; exports *c.* 290 million dong. Main import sources: U.S.S.R. *c.* 40%; China *c.* 25%; East Germany *c.* 9%; Czechoslovakia *c.* 8%; Poland *c.* 6%. Main export destinations: China *c.* 40%; U.S.S.R. *c.* 25%; Japan *c.* 9%; Czechoslovakia *c.* 6%; East Germany *c.* 5%.

Transport. Roads (1965) *c.* 9,000 km. Railways (1969) *c.* 780 km.

Agriculture. Production (in 000; metric tons; 1970; 1969 in parentheses): rice *c.* 5,000 (*c.* 4,900); corn *c.* 230 (*c.* 250); sweet potatoes *c.* 900 (*c.* 900); cassava *c.* 730 (*c.* 700); peanuts *c.* 40 (*c.* 46); dry beans *c.* 15 (*c.* 15); tobacco *c.* 4 (*c.* 4); tea *c.* 2.8 (*c.* 2.7). Livestock (in 000; 1970–71): buffalo *c.* 1,700; cattle *c.* 880; pigs *c.* 6,800.

Industry. Production (in 000; metric tons; 1970): coal *c.* 3,300; phosphate rock *c.* 1,050; salt *c.* 150; cement *c.* 500; cotton fabrics (m.; 1964) 105,200; paper (1964) 19; electricity (kw-hr.; 1964) 548,000.

A.F.P./PICTORIAL PARADE

This rare photograph of a North Vietnamese tank unit in training was released by Hanoi. The armoured tank of Soviet design is a 35-ton T-54, first seen in 1947.

A search for peace in the country mercilessly ravaged by war for more than a quarter of a century was spurred during the year by mutual recognition of a military stalemate. The Viet Cong's role in the struggle continued to be overshadowed by the growing participation of North Vietnamese armed forces, whose massive spring offensive failed to administer a decisive blow to the Saigon government whose units, though staggered and crippled at first, survived the assaults in a crucial test. They did not enjoy the benefit of U.S. ground combat support, which was terminated during 1972. However, U.S. air power aided them greatly. North Vietnam's problems were compounded by U.S. military interdiction of its supply lines to the South and the seemingly effective blockade of North Vietnam's ports.

In the four years since their devastating Tet offensive, the North Vietnamese had diligently prepared for another large-scale series of attacks against South Vietnam, which they hoped would be militarily decisive or politically advantageous in any forthcoming settlement. Saigon's hopes were pinned to self-survival, as U.S. troop withdrawals proceeded apace and U.S. strength within the country was reduced to advisory status and logistical support. The 1972 North Vietnamese offensive put the U.S. program of vietnamization to the test of steel.

A large-scale offensive by North Vietnam in early 1972 had been anticipated by U.S. and South Vietnamese officials months before it was actually launched, but no one foresaw its severity or the astounding ability of the North Vietnamese to introduce vast quantities of armour and artillery through the several hundred miles of roads in mountains and jungles. The massive invasion of South Vietnam began on March 30 with assaults across the supposedly demilitarized zone (DMZ). Units of the regular North Vietnamese Army, equivalent in strength to five infantry divisions and supported by five artillery, antiaircraft, missile, and tank regiments, easily swept southward under the cover of the seasonal monsoon, which grounded aircraft. An estimated total of 54,000 North Vietnamese troops moved to establish control over the northernmost provinces of South Vietnam, apparently seeking as their primary objectives the seizure of Quang Tri and of the old imperial capital of Hue. Subsequently, North Vietnam opened other fronts far to the south and in the Central Highlands.

In all, North Vietnam probably employed major portions of 12 of its 15 regular divisions for the massive offensive. Hanoi's troops were supported by Viet Cong units, which operated as terrorist and harassment forces. Captured enemy documents purportedly spelled out the requirement that "two-thirds of the countryside be liberated prior to the end of June 1972." President Thieu proclaimed: "This is the final battle to decide the survival of the people."

Initially, the South Vietnamese were dangerously crushed by the three-pronged offensive. A newly created government division, the Third, was hardest hit and incapable of offering resistance. It abandoned all 12 of its forward bases south of the DMZ in the first two days of fighting. More experienced South Vietnamese units, particularly airborne forces, rangers, and marines, distinguished themselves by offering fierce resistance and holding threatened positions.

The spirited, protracted fight for An Loc, near Saigon, was marked by a ferocity rarely displayed by the regular South Vietnamese Army. In the Central Highlands, Saigon's forces offset initial reversals by an unyielding stand in subsequent battles for territorial control. The performance of government troops after the first setbacks was significant because the North Vietnamese used armour and artillery on an unprecedented scale. While U.S. aircraft, both fixed-wing and helicopters, were instrumental in the destruction of hundreds of tanks, the South Vietnamese ground troops were credited with at least holding their own in the face of awesome enemy firepower.

Quang Tri city was the only provincial capital to fall to the North Vietnamese during the offensive, though others were attacked and constantly threatened. Thus, the outcome was a severe blow to the North Vietnamese because of their inability to win control over urban areas. On the other hand, Saigon's pacification effort of the previous four years was to a great extent undone in the few months of intensified fighting. Official government figures revealed that 40% of the country was directly affected by the offensive, resulting in widespread civilian casualties and creating another million refugees who were forced to flee the ever extended zones of combat.

After five months of fighting, South Vietnam announced that its forces had killed 70,000 North Vietnamese and Viet Cong. Inflated as the figures may have been, it was evident that Hanoi's losses were great. South Vietnam's military losses were acknowledged as 14,000 killed, 5,000 missing, and 50,000 wounded. While Saigon's troops may have won the battle of attrition, their losses were not easy to absorb. Four of their divisions were so decimated as to be judged nonfunctional as combat units.

South Vietnam's efforts were probably intensified by the knowledge that U.S. air and naval units were carrying the war to North Vietnam again. The resumption of full-scale aerial attacks on the North on April 16 and the announcement on May 8 by U.S. Pres. Richard Nixon of the mining of North Vietnam's ports and the blockading of land and sea routes to the South greatly increased Saigon's capacity to resist. The stepped-up U.S. air and naval campaign also achieved some success in limiting the resupply and reinforcement of North Vietnamese forces operating in the South.

In July, the Saigon government announced that it had reestablished control over Quang Tri province. A task force of 20,000 marines, paratroopers, infantrymen, and militiamen fought its way across the northern defense line at the My Chanh River to retake the hard-fought area. This ended the incredible carnage along the 12-mi. road between My Chanh and Quang Tri cities, which had become known as the "Highway of Horror."

Throughout the country, a stalemate was apparent. The North Vietnamese and the Viet Cong controlled slightly larger portions of South Vietnam than they did before the offensive was mounted, but they seemed incapable of pressing additional major attacks. Government forces, meanwhile, were able to exercise authority over most of the country but were unable to oust the Communists from pockets of territory they had dominated for long periods of time, particularly those that adjoined Laos and Cambodia, to which the North Vietnamese could withdraw and regroup without difficulty. A force of 145,000 North Vietnamese remained in South Vietnam in early November when both sides moved to reach a cease-fire and work toward a political solution.

The most recent efforts to achieve peace had begun in earnest in the closing months of 1971. By Jan. 25, 1972, the U.S. and South Vietnamese governments were prepared to offer an eight-point plan for ending hostilities. The joint proposal was aimed at ending the three-year-old impasse in the Paris negotiations. It consisted of the following elements: (1) total withdrawal of all U.S. and other foreign forces within six months of an agreement; (2) the release of all military and civilian prisoners, to begin the day that troop withdrawals were started and to be completed when all foreign troops had been removed; (3) a "free and democratic presidential election" within six months of an agreement, with a caretaker government to assume control after the resignation of the president and vice-president one month before the nationwide balloting; (4) affirmation of the 1954 and 1962 Geneva agreements; (5) the "mutual respect for [the] independence, sovereignty, territorial integrity and non-interference" of the countries of Indochina; (6) a general Indochina cease-fire to begin with the signing of the agreement; (7) international supervision of the cease-fire, troop withdrawals, and prisoner exchanges; and (8) an "international guarantee for the fundamental national rights of the Indochinese peoples."

North Vietnamese and Viet Cong delegates in Paris denounced the eight-point plan the day after it was proposed. While the talks continued for two months, there was no progress in the halting search for an end to the war. On March 23 William J. Porter, U.S. ambassador to the Paris talks, announced an indefinite postponement of the sessions. Though the newest initiative was rebuffed, it still provided a framework for later efforts that were more productive.

Part of the reason for Hanoi's repeated resistance to overtures of peace from the U.S. was its asserted belief that the Nixon administration was unwilling to drop its support of President Thieu. Thieu, on his part, charged that the North Vietnamese were intransigent, feeling that "All the Communists want is for South Vietnam to surrender unconditionally." He reiterated his oft-repeated policy of the "four no's:" no abandonment of territory to the North Vietnamese, no coalition government, no policy of neutrality, and no Communist participation in the political affairs of South Vietnam. Thieu feared that the U.S. would drop him precipitately, a concern heightened during the year's first peace drive when U.S. Secretary of State William P. Rogers on February 3 stated that Washington was "flexible" on the composition of a caretaker government.

The growing distrust between the U.S. and South Vietnam persisted and was further deepened by a resumption of secret talks between White House aide Henry Kissinger (*see* BIOGRAPHY), and North Vietnamese Politburo member Le Duc Tho. In October, South Vietnam learned of the imminence of a U.S.-North Vietnamese breakthrough during Kissinger's visit to Saigon. Hanoi announced the terms of the agreement, which was subsequently confirmed by Kissinger who announced, "We believe peace is at hand." The main points of the plan were: a cease-fire throughout Indochina; an end to U.S. military operations against North Vietnam; the withdrawal of the remaining U.S. forces in South Vietnam (about 32,000 men) within 60 days of the signing; the concurrent release of the U.S. prisoners held by North Vietnam; acknowledgment of authority in areas respectively under government and Communist control; creation of a National Council of National Reconciliation and Concord, to be made up by equal representation of the Saigon government, the Viet Cong, and South Vietnamese neutralists; general elections to determine the nation's future political direction with commissions representing the involved parties, under the general supervision of an International Control Commission, to oversee the balloting and to supervise the cease-fire; and the calling of an international conference to guarantee all provisions within 30 days of the signing of the agreement.

Thieu's opposition to certain points of the plan was made known even before the terms were announced publicly. The president spoke out against a coalition arrangement in the national commission, calling it "unacceptable." His supporters stated that Thieu felt he could never accept "the tripartite proposal." Foreign Minister Tran Van Lam declared that the South Vietnamese government considered the Kis-

A child holds out his empty bowl while waiting for food at a refugee camp near Da Nang that houses many who fled the heavy fighting north of Hue.

UPI COMPIX

BRUNO BARBEY—MAGNUM

The city of An Loc is in ruins after a siege by North Vietnamese that lasted for months. Communist troops isolated the city by cutting off the highway to Saigon, leaving it totally dependent on airlifts for supplies and reinforcements.

singer-Tho agreement a "surrender." Particular objections were voiced by Lam and other government members on the three-sided political arrangement, which Lam called a coalition "in disguise," the lack of a provision ensuring the withdrawal of the 145,000 North Vietnamese troops in the South, and the need for reestablishing the demilitarized zone.

Negotiations between Kissinger and Le Duc Tho took place during November 20–25 and again during December 4–13. Despite the earlier optimistic forecasts, the talks then broke down and no final agreement was reached. Each side blamed new demands and conditions by the other as the cause of the impasse. On December 18 the U.S. resumed full-scale bombing of North Vietnam above the 20th parallel, an area that includes Hanoi and Haiphong. Except for a 24-hour Christmas break, the air attacks, described as the heaviest in the history of warfare, continued until December 30. At that time, the White House announced that the U.S. would halt indefinitely the bombing above the 20th parallel and that the negotiations would resume on January 8. Hanoi and Haiphong suffered severe damage from the bombing, but the U.S. also lost heavily with at least 15 B-52 bombers shot down and more than 80 airmen killed or missing.

Thieu's own hold on the country was strengthened during the year by emergency powers granted him in the wake of the North's offensive. His political opponents feared the consequences of the special powers granted Thieu, and legislative approval came only after what appeared to be subterfuge and chicanery. Thieu in turn attacked his critics, saying, "They are mangy practitioners of treason, Communists in practice if not in name."

Further consolidation of Thieu's rule came in September when he abolished local elections. He reserved for himself the authority to dismiss and to appoint all of the officials who would administer each of the country's hamlets. In December he issued a decree that was expected to eliminate most of the many small opposition parties by setting standards of minimum size and strength. (ROBERT GORALSKI)

Democratic Republic of Vietnam (North Vietnam). This is bordered by China, the Gulf of Tonkin, the South China Sea, South Vietnam, and Laos. Area: 63,360 sq.mi. (164,103 sq.km.). Pop. (1971 est.): 21,595,000. Cap. and largest city: Hanoi (pop., 1965 est., 500,000). Language: Vietnamese. Religion: Buddhist; pagan; Confucian; Christian. Secretary of the Communist Party in 1972, Le Duan; president, Ton Duc Thang; premier, Pham Van Dong.

Having known only war since its birth in 1945, North Vietnam came face to face with the possibility of peace in 1973 only to see that possibility fade by year's end.

Prospects of peace grew in the wake of the heaviest punishment the country had known in 27 years of warfare. There was no indication either of the impending escalation of the war or of the possibility of peace when the year started. U.S. bombers were striking at targets in North Vietnam and Laos, and there were reports of a North Vietnamese military buildup just above the demilitarized zone. These reports led to the belief that the Soviet Union was pressing Hanoi to mount a major offensive against South Vietnam at the time of U.S. Pres. Richard Nixon's China visit.

Toward the end of March a high-level Soviet air defense delegation visited Hanoi. About the same time revised U.S. intelligence estimates claimed that Moscow was the top supplier of arms to North Vietnam. Total military and economic aid to Hanoi by its Communist allies in 1971 was estimated at $775 million. Of this the Soviet Union was said to have contributed military aid worth $100 million and China $75 million. In December the Soviet Union pledged to continue large-scale military and economic aid through 1973.

Nothing happened while Nixon was in China. Soon afterward, during March 20–25, the National Assembly held its second session. The keynote of Premier Pham Van Dong's political report to the Assembly was that "we are in a better position to initiate attacks at the enemy and advance steadily to seize bigger and bigger victories." He reiterated North Vietnam's support for the peace plan announced by the Provisional Revolutionary Government (Viet Cong) of South Vietnam and rejected President Nixon's eight-point counter plan as "the logic of the gangster." He stressed the military solidarity of the Vietnamese, Cambodian, and Laotian peoples and pledged redoubled efforts from the socialist North to help its Indochinese brethren, calling for special efforts on the economic front to help attain immediate revolutionary goals.

Subsequently, the Central Committee of the ruling Vietnam Workers' Party held its 20th plenum and passed various resolutions in support of state policy goals. The plenum emphasized the need to increase party leadership of economic affairs and to improve economic management with a view to turning the economy from a small production base to large-scale socialist production.

As it turned out, Pham Van Dong was preparing the nation for the biggest and most surprising offensive of the long Indochina war—surprising because, abandoning the usual guerrilla techniques, the North Vietnamese command resorted to conventional warfare with tanks and artillery columns. As April dawned, wave after wave of North Vietnamese troops stormed across the demilitarized zone and overran the South Vietnamese provincial capital of Quang Tri. In the Central Highlands and the Mekong Delta the offensive also rapidly gathered momentum. For weeks speculation raged throughout the world over the objectives of the sudden North Vietnamese onslaught. The general view was that the North was not after territorial gain but was out to destroy the U.S. vietnamization plan and facilitate renewed penetration of the countryside by the Viet Cong. It appeared that this objective was largely fulfilled; only intensive U.S. air strikes prevented a South Vietnamese rout, although the Saigon troops later stiffened their resistance.

However, North Vietnam paid an intolerably heavy price for what it gained. On May 8 President Nixon announced he had ordered the mining of all North Vietnamese harbours and gave international shipping three days to leave the area. He also ordered an escalation of U.S. bombing of North Vietnam. Targets in Hanoi city came under attack. Haiphong, the main harbour, was reportedly reduced to flatland. Other population centres were bombed, and Hanoi charged the U.S. with genocide as the elaborate dike system in the Red River Delta which had traditionally kept Hanoi and surrounding areas from being submerged in floodwaters was severely damaged. The bombing continued until the end of September with only a four-day break in mid-June as a U.S. goodwill gesture to the Soviet Union, whose president was visiting Hanoi at the time.

The bombing and blockade did not visibly slow down the North Vietnamese offensive in the South, which apparently had been prepared so carefully that enough supplies had already moved to concentration areas well before the U.S. retaliated. Limited supplies continued to get into North Vietnam, sometimes in Chinese junks hugging the coastline and sometimes through railway and road links, although these were a prime target of U.S. bombers. However, neither China nor the Soviet Union tried to break the U.S. blockade. Much to Hanoi's displeasure, the Nixon visit to Moscow took place on schedule in May while the bombing and the blockade were still going on.

By July there was evidence that the pressure of war was beginning to tell. An editorial in the official newspaper *Nhan Dan,* signed by Deputy Premier Le Thanh Nghi, announced a total mobilization of labour and a crackdown on shirkers; citizens were told to put the national interest above all else, and anyone who failed to obey the regulations on working hours or failed to obtain jobs aiding the national effort might be ordered by the chairman of the local administrative committee to do work useful to society in labour camps

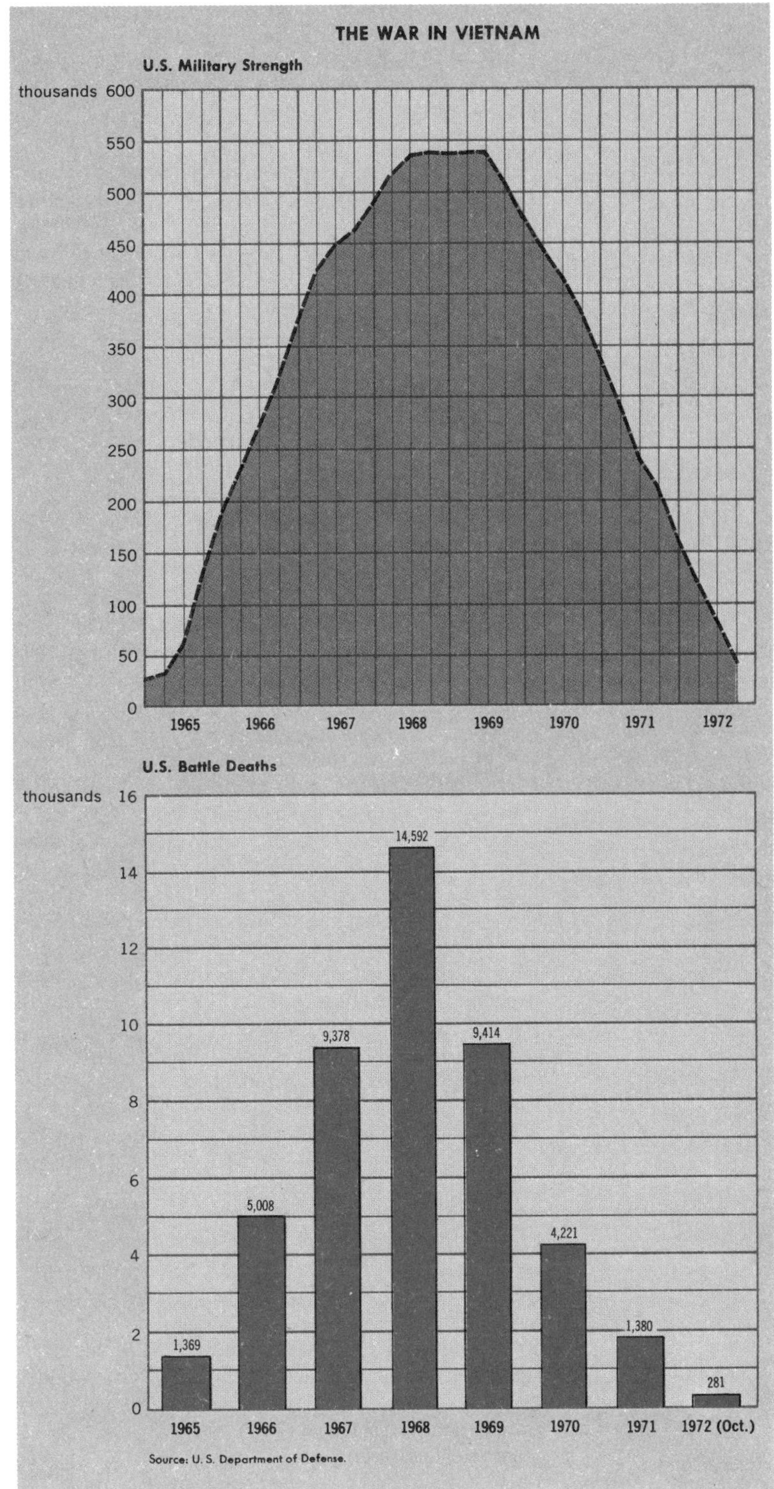

from six months to two years; even elderly or disabled persons retired from the work force might be called back to work if necessary.

Although the North Vietnamese offensive continued with undiminished vigour, it soon became apparent that the U.S. bombing was inflicting crippling damage on North Vietnam. There were reports of a divergence of opinion among the top leaders in Hanoi on the future course of policy. By all accounts, the destruction wrought by the bombing was a contributory factor behind renewal of the peace negotiations that began in Paris in September between Hanoi's Politburo member Le Duc Tho and U.S. presidential adviser Henry Kissinger. The negotiations subsequently broke down in December, and the U.S. began bombing the Hanoi-Haiphong area on an unprecedented scale. Both cities suffered extensive damage before the bombing was again halted on December 30. Negotiations were scheduled to resume January 8.

Official sources claimed that the North Vietnamese economy had progressed despite the ravages of war. The overall rice area was reportedly 10,000 ha. more than in the previous year while the total value of industrial and handicrafts production was said to have increased by 5%. (T. J. S. GEORGE)

See also Defense.

Vital Statistics

For a decade or more the general trend of the birthrate in the U.S., Canada, and most European countries had been downward. After rising moderately from 1968 to 1970, it resumed its decline in 1971 and the early months of 1972. In the few countries of Africa, Asia, and South America that had reliable annual information, the rate had been decreasing slowly. During the same period the death rate in the U.S., Canada, the European countries, and the few other countries with useful statistics had fluctuated within a narrow range. The most significant effect of the birth and death rate movement was a slowing of the rate of population growth in developed countries. The countries for which there was little reliable information were also those in the less developed parts of the world, with much higher birth and death rates and higher rates of population growth. In general, available fragmentary information indicated that the rate, but not the magnitude of population growth, had also fallen moderately in many of these nations. During this same period when the birthrate had been declining, the marriage rate had risen moderately in the U.S., Canada, and most countries of Europe.

Birth Statistics. In the U.S. the provisional crude birthrate declined from 18.2 births per 1,000 population in 1970 to 17.3 in 1971, a decrease of almost 6%. The decline continued in 1972; provisional data for the first eight months showed a nearly 10% fall compared with the same period in 1971. The provisional number of births fell 4.3%, from 3,718,000 in 1970 to 3,559,000 in 1971, while the number in the first eight months of 1972, 2,153,000, was 8.6% below the corresponding 1971 period. Estimated rates by age of mother, based on data available for less than half the states, indicated that the decline had occurred in all age groups except the numerically small group under 15 years. The general fertility rate (births per 1,000 women aged 15–44 years) fell from 87 for the 12 months ended in August 1970 to 85 and 76, respectively, for the corresponding periods of 1971 and 1972.

Virgin Islands:
see Dependent States

Determination of the factors accounting for the fertility decrease awaited final tabulation of the data for 1970, 1971, and 1972, plus information on attitudes and childbearing plans of women that would be provided by the new Family Growth Survey, a nationwide sample survey of married women to be inaugurated by the National Center for Health Statistics of the U.S. Public Health Service in 1973. However, data from the June 1972 Current Population Survey of the Bureau of the Census indicated that whereas in 1967 married women aged 18 to 24 expected, on the average, to have 2.9 births during their childbearing years, in 1972 the corresponding group expected to have an average of only 2.3 births. For wives aged 25 to 29, the expectations were 3 and 2.5 births, respectively. Demographers believed that increased availability and use of contraceptive materials, more liberal abortion laws in some of the states, and a change in prevailing social attitudes were contributing factors.

The rate of natural increase (excess of births over deaths) fell from 8.8 per 1,000 population in 1970 to 8 in 1971, adding 1,638,000 persons to the U.S. population, compared with 1,797,000 in 1970. The rate declined further in the first eight months of 1972—to 6, compared with 7.8 for the same period in 1971.

Among the countries where birth registration was at least 90% complete, UN tabulations indicated that 29 experienced a downward trend of the birthrate from 1965 to 1971. In six countries the rate rose somewhat during this period, and in six it remained stable. Fourteen countries had a lower rate in the early months of 1972 compared with the same period in 1971; only two countries reported higher rates, while four reported no change. As of 1972, birthrates around the world had a wide range from about 13 per 1,000 population to 50 or more. The rate of population growth correlates closely with the magnitude of the birthrate.

Death Statistics. The crude death rate (deaths per 1,000 population) in the U.S. had fluctuated within a very narrow range for over a decade. Year-to-year changes had been small and due chiefly to variations in the incidence of influenza and pneumonia. The provisional number of deaths in 1971 was 1,921,000, the same as in 1970. However, a 3% increase occurred in the first eight months of 1972: 1,322,000 deaths, compared with 1,284,000 in the corresponding months of 1971. The death rate fell from 9.4 in 1970 to 9.3 in 1971, but the rate for the first eight months of 1972, 9.5, was slightly higher than the corresponding 1971 rate of 9.4. Decreases in all of the age-specific rates, except for a slight increase for the 1-to-4-year age group, contributed to the decline in the total death rate between 1970 and 1971. The largest decreases occurred in the 45–54 and 55–64 age groups, 2.9% in both cases.

The ten leading causes of death for the U.S. in 1971 and the estimated death rates are shown below. Each of these causes had the same rank in 1971 as in 1970 except cirrhosis of the liver (9 in 1970) and arteriosclerosis (8 in 1970). Small decreases occurred in the rates for all ten causes.

The total death rate in most European countries had also changed within narrow limits during the preceding decade. In the few countries of Africa, Asia, and South America that had reasonably complete statistics, the trend of the death rate had been steadily downward, reflecting some improvement in health services and/or economic conditions. Among the countries that had at least 90% complete registration, 10 reported slightly higher death rates in 1971 than in 1970, 12 reported slightly lower rates, and in 3 countries the rate did not change. Among the countries for which some 1972 data were available, eight had slightly higher rates in 1972 than in 1971, four reported lower rates, and there was virtually no change in eight countries.

Cause of death	Estimated death rate per 100,000 population
All causes	929.0
Diseases of the heart	358.4
Malignant neoplasms (cancer)	160.9
Cerebrovascular diseases	100.6
Accidents	53.6
Influenza and pneumonia	27.2
Certain causes of mortality in early infancy	19.2
Diabetes mellitus	18.2
Cirrhosis of the liver	15.5
Arteriosclerosis	15.5
Bronchitis, emphysema, and asthma	14.5

The crude death rate is not the best index of differences in the intrinsic mortality experience of different countries. Some type of age-adjusted rate, reflecting a weighted average of the death rates of all the specific age classes in the populations, is needed because the age composition of the populations of countries varies greatly. Countries with higher proportions of older people and lower proportions of younger people may have as high or higher crude death rates than those with populations composed mainly of young people, even when all of the age-specific rates of countries with "older" populations are lower than those of countries with "younger" populations.

Infant and Maternal Mortality. The infant mortality rate (deaths under one year per 1,000 live births) in the U.S. fell in 1971 as it had each year since 1962, and it continued to decline in 1972. The rate was 19.2 in 1971, compared with 19.8 in 1970. The rate for the first eight months of 1972 was 18.5, 3.7% below the 19.2 rate for the same months of 1971. All of the decline in the U.S. occurred among infants under 28 days old, where the rate fell from 14.9 in 1970 to 14.3 in 1971. The rate for the older infant group, 28 days to 11 months of age, was the same in both years, 4.9. In 1971 the infant mortality rate for white infants (16.8) was much lower than for all others (30.2), but the decrease between 1970 and 1971 was larger for the latter group.

Among countries with at least 90% complete registration, the infant mortality rate in 1969, 1970, or 1971 ranged from about 12 to about 92. Some of the differences, however, resulted from differences in the procedures governing inclusion or exclusion of prematurely born infants who die shortly after birth.

The provisional maternal mortality rate for the U.S. fell from 24.7 deaths per 100,000 live births in 1970 to 20.5 in 1971, a decrease of 17%. Comparison between countries of death rates for this cause, as well as other specific causes, is significantly limited by differences in the classifications and assignment rules used.

Table I. Life Expectancy at Birth, in Years, for Selected Countries

Country	Period	Male	Female
Africa			
Burundi	1965	35.0	38.5
Egypt	1960	51.6	53.8
Liberia	1962	36.1	38.6
Nigeria	1965–66	37.2	36.7
Upper Volta	1960–61	32.1	31.1
Asia			
Cambodia	1958–59	44.2	43.3
Hong Kong	1968	66.7	73.3
India	1951–60	41.9	40.6
Israel	1969	69.2	72.8
Japan	1968	69.1	74.3
Jordan	1959–63	52.6	52.0
Korea, South	1955–60	51.1	53.7
Pakistan	1962	53.7	48.8
Taiwan	1965	65.8	70.4
Thailand	1960	53.6	58.7
Europe			
Albania	1965–66	64.9	67.0
Austria	1969	66.5	73.3
Belgium	1959–63	67.7	73.5
Bulgaria	1965–67	68.8	72.7
Czechoslovakia	1966	67.3	73.6
Denmark	1967–68	70.6	75.4
Finland	1961–65	65.4	72.6
France	1968	68.0	75.5
Germany, East	1965–66	68.7	73.7
Germany, West*	1966–68	67.6	73.6
Greece	1960–62	67.5	70.7
Hungary	1964	67.0	71.8
Iceland	1961–65	70.8	76.2
Ireland	1960–62	68.1	71.9
Italy	1960–62	67.2	72.3
Netherlands	1968	71.0	76.4
Norway	1961–65	71.0	76.0
Poland	1965–66	66.9	72.8
Portugal	1959–62	60.7	66.4
Romania	1964–67	66.5	70.5
Spain	1960	67.3	71.9
Sweden	1967	71.9	76.5
Switzerland	1958–63	68.7	74.1
United Kingdom			
England and Wales	1967–69	68.7	74.9
Northern Ireland	1967–69	68.3	73.7
Scotland	1967–69	67.1	73.2
Yugoslavia	1966–67	64.7	69.0
North America			
Barbados	1959–61	62.7	67.4
Canada	1965–67	68.8	75.2
Costa Rica	1962–64	61.9	64.8
Guatemala	1963–65	48.3	49.7
Mexico	1965–70	61.0	63.7
Panama	1960–61	57.6	60.9
Puerto Rico	1959–61	67.1	71.9
United States	1968	66.6	74.0
Oceania			
Australia	1960–62	67.9	74.2
New Zealand	1960–62	68.4	73.8
South America			
Argentina	1959–61	63.1	68.9
Chile	1960–61	54.4	59.9
Peru	1960–65	52.6	55.5
Surinam	1963	62.5	66.7
Uruguay	1963–64	65.5	71.6
U.S.S.R.	1967–68	65.0	74.0

*Not including West Berlin.
Source: United Nations, *Demographic Yearbook* (1970).

Table II. Birthrates and Death Rates per 1,000 Population and Infant Mortality per 1,000 Live Births in Selected Countries, 1971*

Country	Birth-rate	Death rate	Infant mortality	Country	Birth-rate	Death rate	Infant mortality
Africa				Romania†	21.1	9.5	49.4
Egypt	34.9†	15.0†	119.0†	Spain†	19.6	8.5	27.9
Kenya†	17.2	3.9	55.0	Sweden	14.1	10.2	11.7‡
Mauritius†	27.3	7.8	57.6	Switzerland	15.2	9.2	15.1†
Tunisia	36.2†	8.8†	77.7‡	United Kingdom	16.2	11.6	18.0
Asia				England & Wales	16.0	11.6	17.6
Cyprus	21.7	6.4	25.3	Northern Ireland	20.7	10.6	23.0
Hong Kong	19.0	5.0	18.5	Scotland	16.6	11.8	19.9
Israel†	26.8	7.0	22.9	Yugoslavia	18.2	8.7	55.2†
Japan	19.2	6.6	12.4	North and Central America			
Kuwait†	44.7	4.9	39.4	Barbados	21.9	8.6	29.0
Lebanon	26.5	4.5	13.6§	Canada	17.0	7.3†	18.8†
Philippines‡	26.5	6.8	67.3	Costa Rica	33.8†	6.6†	67.1‡
Singapore	22.3	5.4	20.1	Cuba	30.1	6.0	35.5
Thailand‡	32.6	7.0	26.2	El Salvador†	40.0	9.9	66.7
Europe				Guatemala†	39.0	15.0	88.4
Austria	14.5	13.0	25.9	Jamaica	34.8	7.4	26.4
Belgium	14.5	12.2	20.5†	Mexico†	43.4	9.9	68.5
Bulgaria†	16.3	9.1	27.3	Panama	37.1	6.8	36.8
Czechoslovakia†	15.8	11.4	22.1	Puerto Rico†	24.8	6.6	28.6
Denmark	15.2	9.9	14.2†	United States	17.3	9.3	19.2
Finland	13.1	9.8	11.8	Oceania			
France	17.1	10.7	14.4	American Samoa†	34.6	5.4	27.9
Germany, East†	13.9	14.1	18.8	Australia	21.7	8.7	17.9†
Germany, West‖	12.8	11.7	23.2	Fiji	30.3	5.9	18.5†
Greece†	16.5	8.4	29.6	Guam	34.1	4.0	20.5
Hungary	14.5	11.9	34.9	New Caledonia†	35.9	9.6	41.1
Iceland†	19.5	7.1	13.3	New Zealand†	22.1	8.8	16.7
Ireland	22.8	10.6	19.2†	Western Samoa†	34.5	5.4	18.3
Italy	16.8	9.6	28.3	South America			
Luxembourg	13.0	12.9	22.5	Ecuador†	37.8	9.9	76.6
Netherlands	18.8	8.4	11.1	Paraguay†	33.4	5.3	35.6
Norway	16.9	9.9	13.8‡	Uruguay	20.4	9.2†	48.7‡
Poland†	16.8	8.2	33.2	Venezuela†	38.1	6.6	48.7
Portugal	19.0†	10.4†	47.6	U.S.S.R.	17.8	8.2	22.9

*Registered births and deaths only.
†1970.
‡1969.
§1960.
‖Not including West Berlin.
Source: United Nations, *Population and Vital Statistics Report* (July 1, 1972).

Expectation of Life. The estimated average expectation of life for babies born in the U.S. in 1971 was 71.1 years, slightly longer than the 70.8 years for infants born in 1970. This increase was consistent with the general improvement in age-specific death rates noted above. (Expectation of life at birth is the average number of years that an infant could be expected to live if the age-specific death rates observed during the year of its birth were to prevail throughout its lifetime.)

As shown in Table I, life expectancy in Canada, Australia, New Zealand, Israel, Japan, and most European countries was similar to that in the U.S. However, the Scandinavian countries and the Netherlands had the longest life expectancy in the world. In contrast, life expectancy was much lower in most countries of South America, Africa, and Asia.

Marriage and Divorce. The number of marriages in the U.S. rose slightly from 2,179,000 in 1970 to 2,196,000 in 1971, but the crude rate (marriages per 1,000 population) fell marginally from 10.7 to 10.6. However, both the number and the rate increased in the first eight months of 1972; the number of marriages was more than 3% higher and the rate was 10.8, compared with 10.6 for the same months of 1971. Thus the steady increase in marriages that began in 1959 seemed to be continuing. The trend was due primarily to a rise in the number of persons reaching marriageable age, traceable, in turn, to the higher birthrates of the years beginning with 1946.

In 1971 marriages increased in seven of the nine geographic divisions of the U.S. The largest gains, about 5%, occurred in the East South Central and Mountain divisions, while the Middle Atlantic and Pacific divisions showed declines of about 4%. Approximately 21,000 fewer marriages (−8%) were performed in California and Pennsylvania combined, while Florida, Ohio, and Tennessee combined showed a corresponding increase. The rise in Tennessee was apparently influenced by a change in the state law that reduced the legal minimum age for marriage without parental consent from 21 to 18 for both parties.

In most countries with fairly complete reporting, the trend of marriages was upward during the period 1965–71, although most of them showed a slight decrease between 1970 and 1971. However, as in the U.S., a majority of countries reported some increase in the early months of 1972. It was of interest to note that the decade-long decline of the birthrate in most technologically advanced countries had been accompanied by a generally rising crude marriage rate—largely attributable, as in the U.S., to the larger numbers of persons entering the marriageable ages. With more young people, more marriages, and fewer births, age-specific birthrates declined even more than the crude birthrate.

Differences in the marriage rates of different countries are influenced by the age composition of the population, customary age at marriage, and the ratio of legally reportable marriages to common-law or "consensual" marriages, which are not formally reported. The range of reported marriage rates throughout the world is shown below. Most of the available data are for 1970, with a few countries reporting for 1971.

The provisional estimate of the number of divorces in the U.S. in 1971 was 768,000, about 7% more than the 715,000 in 1970. The crude divorce rate (divorces per 1,000 population) was 3.7, approximately 6% above the 1970 rate of 3.5. The trend of divorces had been upward since 1962. During the period 1962–67 the rate increased about 4% per year, and from 1967 to 1970 the yearly increases averaged about 10%. The rate for 1971 was the highest since the all-time peak of 4.4 in 1946, immediately after World War II. Some of the increase was attributed to the size of the young married population. National divorce statistics for the U.S. are estimates based on data from 42 states and the District of Columbia.

Countries	Range of marriage rates per 1,000 population
Argentina*, Costa Rica†, Guatemala, Jamaica, Mauritius, Panama, Sweden	Less than 7
Albania, Austria, Belgium, Bulgaria, Chile*, Finland, France, East and West Germany, Greece, Iceland, Italy, Mexico, Norway, Romania, Spain, Switzerland	7–8.4
Australia, Canada, Czechoslovakia, Denmark, Hungary, Israel, Netherlands, New Zealand, Poland, Portugal, U.S.S.R., United Kingdom, Uruguay‡, Yugoslavia	8.5–9.9
Japan, United States	10 and over

*1968 data.
†1965–70.
‡1969 data.
Source: UN *Monthly Bulletin of Statistics.*

Among the countries reporting divorces, the U.S. had the highest rate, 3.7, in 1971. The U.S.S.R. reported the second highest rate in 1971, 2.6, and Hungary reported a rate of 2.2. Countries with divorce rates between 1 and 1.9 were Australia, Austria, Bulgaria, Czechoslovakia, Denmark, Finland, East Germany, West Germany, Iceland, New Zealand, Poland, Sweden, Switzerland, the United Kingdom, and Yugoslavia. All other countries had rates below 1.

(ROBERT D. GROVE)

See also Populations and Areas.

Western Samoa

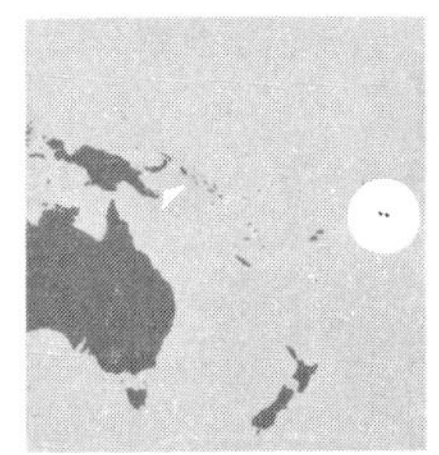

A constitutional monarchy and member of the Commonwealth of Nations, Western Samoa is an island group in the South Pacific Ocean, about 1,600 mi. E of New Zealand and 2,200 mi. S of Hawaii. Area: 1,133 sq.mi. (2,934 sq.km.), with two major islands, Savai'i (662 sq.mi.) and Upolu (435 sq.mi.), and seven smaller islands. Pop. (1972 est.): 148,398. Cap. and largest city: Apia (pop., 1971, 30,266). Language: Samoan and English. Religion: about 80% Protestant, 20% Roman Catholic. Head of state (*O le Ao o le Malo*) in 1972, Malietoa Tanumafili II; prime minister, Tupua Tamasese Lealofi IV.

WESTERN SAMOA

Education. (1969) Primary, pupils 27,596, teachers 902; secondary, pupils 9,522, teachers 369; vocational, pupils 84, teachers 7; teacher training, students 271, teachers 17.

Finance and Trade. Monetary unit: Western Samoan dollar (thaler), with (Sept. 18, 1972) a nominal free rate of WS$0.66 to U.S. $1 (WS$1.60 = £1 sterling). Budget (1971 est.): revenue WS$6,478,000; expenditure WS$6,518,000. Foreign trade (1970): imports WS$9,791,000; exports WS$3,391,000. Import sources: New Zealand 32%; Australia 16%; U.S. 14%; Japan 10%; U.K. 8%. Export destinations: New Zealand 47%; Netherlands 18%; West Germany 13%; U.S. 7%; U.K. 5%; Norway 5%. Main exports: copra 40%; cocoa 31%; bananas 16%.

Wages and Hours: *see* Employment, Wages, and Hours
Wales: *see* United Kingdom
Warsaw Treaty Organization: *see* Defense
Water Resources: *see* Environment
Weather: *see* Meteorology
Welfare: *see* Social Services
West Indies: *see* Barbados; Cuba; Dependent States; Dominican Republic; Haiti; Inter-American Affairs; Jamaica; Trinidad and Tobago

The overall improvement in the economy continued into 1972, despite the drop in world prices for copra. Tourism, the second largest foreign exchange earner, was encouraged by more hotel construction. The greatest amount of aid came from New Zealand, which continued to assist the redevelopment of Apia hospital and the creation of a ferry service linking Upolu and Savai'i. Agreement was reached with the Asian Development Bank on a soft loan of U.S. $2 million for a power project. Western Samoa joined the International Monetary Fund with a quota of U.S. $2 million and took steps toward becoming a member of the World Bank Group.

The government decided to establish formal diplomatic relations with New Zealand and to appoint a resident high commissioner in Wellington. New Zealand's prime minister, John Marshall, attended ceremonies marking the opening of the new Legislative Assembly building and the tenth anniversary of independence. (MARY BOYD)

Words and Meanings, New

With the Apollo program concluding in 1972, plans were made for future collaboration between Kazakhstan and Cape Kennedy whereby the **salyut-skylab** space station might be orbited by Soviet cosmonauts in conjunction with U.S. astronauts. Meantime ESRO, the European Space Research Organization, planned its system of **geostationary** satellites.

Jet lag was the terse phrase adopted to denote that disturbance of one's "biological clock" during long east-west and west-east flights on the assumption that the clock normally operates over a **circadian cycle.** As computer systems became more elaborate and sophisticated, the industry decided on a new tripartite classification of components into **mainframe, peripherals,** and **software.** The computer industry also established a new measurement called the **megabyte,** equal to 2^{20} (1,048,576) bytes, or eight times that number of bits or binary digits.

At the summer UN Conference on the Human Environment in Stockholm, **antitechnology** was acclaimed almost as a cult. **Earthwatch** (echoing a British television program, "Doomwatch") was the name given to the plan of action directed against anything that might lead to **ecocide** or the destruction of a whole countryside (a cacophonous neologism based on genocide). **Immunobiology** was proclaimed as a new counterscience. Pessimists, deliberately ignoring the fact that Thomas More's *Utopia* meant "nowhere," blamed technology for transforming **eutopia** into **dystopia.**

Several of the year's inventions were concerned with the betterment of the human condition. **Bioceramics,** for instance, induced bone regrowth through porcelain implants that provided a natural matrix for renewed ossification. **Arteriografts,** made of platinum and tantalum plastic, replaced defective or worn-out arteries. A saving technique in difficult childbirth was provided by the **cardiotocograph,** recording the heartbeat of the unborn baby by means of a mini-electrode attached to its scalp. The **optacon** enabled a blind person to read print by touch; an electronic minicamera converted printed texts into tactile patterns that could be felt by the blind person's fingertips. It was not unconnected with another electronic invention named the **stereoscan,** a microscope capable of resolving details as small as one-millionth of a centimetre, such as the branching processes of nerve cells. Rapid progress was achieved toward the perfection of **phototropic glass,** valuable in greenhouses because it darkens automatically when the sun shines on it.

Psychosurgery, involving operations on the human brain in the treatment of mental disorders, evoked some hostile criticism on grounds of both professional ethics and public morality. **Zoosemiotics** was adopted as a technical term to cover all systems of communication in the animal world, especially those employed by bees and dolphins. **Anthropozoology** was a grandiose neo-Hellenism created to denote nothing more nor less than Desmond Morris' conception of man as naked ape. More seriously, geophysicists joined with seismologists in approving the term **plate tectonics** to describe the conflicting stresses and strains between rock masses in the cooling-down period that resulted in the earth's present structural formation. Advances were also made in **paleoanthropology,** the study of hominids and other manlike creatures more primitive than *Homo sapiens.*

On at least one occasion a committee meeting was declared **inquorate** because too few members were present to constitute a quorum. The echoic verb **zap,** used to indicate destruction of a target with a single burst of gunfire, rose in status. So, too, did the underworld **fladge,** denoting a violent form of masochism. Some high fidelity radio hobbyists, or **audiophiles,** were the proud possessors of separate loudspeakers for the reproduction of high and low frequencies which they called **tweeters** and **woofers,** respectively, but soon the technicians supplied them with a coaxial two-in-one, or **tweeter-woofer.** For a time the Yiddish verb **gazump** (formerly gazoomph), "to swindle," was on everybody's lips in Britain when estate agents (realtors), taking unfair advantage of cost inflation, raised the prices of houses after offers had been accepted. Indeed, in this narrower sense **gazumping** even found its way into the law courts. Other words that rose in status in Britain, having previously gained currency in the U.S., were **medic,** denoting any member of the medical profession, whether physician, surgeon, specialist, or student; **mugger** for any lawless rough who **mugs** or robs with violence; and **whizkid** for any brilliantly clever executive or consultant. Obstreperous **pre-teens,** children of 12 and under, were described as **stroppy.**

Some colourful portmanteau words also rose in status, notably **snazzy,** "flashy, fancy, stylish," a blend of snappy and jazzy. Certain contestants at the Olympic Games were nicknamed **shamateurs** on the ground that they were sham amateurs, posing as nonprofessionals when it suited them. Television and sound radio were grouped together as **teleradio.** A more sinister portmanteau word was **identikit,** the highly specialized police identification kit, often used metaphorically. The mating of male coyotes with female dogs or bitches produced **coydogs.** A facetious blend of Ivy League (a sports association of eight northeastern universities of the U.S.) with ivory tower (Sainte-Beuve's *tour d'ivoire*) produced **ivy-league tower,** the dwelling place of the academic loner.

Counterproductive, more forcefully negative than unproductive or nonproductive, became a vogue word. Sometimes the prefix **non-,** still hyphenated, implied a subdued negative, as in the already well-known expression **non-event.** A **non-summer** meant a summer that was no summer at all. A **non-answer** was an

continued on page 733

Wheat: *see* Agriculture
Wines: *see* Alcoholic Beverages
Wool: *see* Agriculture; Industrial Review

Words and Meanings, New

The words, phrases, and other forms listed below achieved some currency in the information media during 1972. This list has been prepared by the permanent editorial staff of G. & C. Merriam Company, Springfield, Mass., publishers of *Webster's Third New International Dictionary* and a subsidiary of Encyclopædia Britannica, Inc.

adscape *n* : a scene (as along a highway) in which advertising billboards predominate

air piracy *n* : the hijacking of a flying airplane : SKYJACKING

alternative society *n* : a society of young people whose values and life-styles run counter to those of established society—called also *counterculture*

anticommercial *n* : a commercial against a product advertised in another commercial

bike-in *n* : a gathering of bicyclists for the purpose of demonstrating in favor of the construction of bikeways

blippo *vb* : to subject to failure or disaster : RUIN

brain-fade *n* : a mistake in judgment by a racing driver

carnography *n* : the depiction (as in motion pictures) of gory acts of violence

cephalocide *n* : the systematic liquidation of the intellectual leaders of a group

chicanismo *n, often cap* : strong ethnic pride exhibited by Chicanos

chick-pecked *adj* : subject to persistent nagging or attempts to dominate by a girl friend

conceptual art *n* : art in which the concept conveyed is more important than what is utilized or created

condomaximum *n* : a very large building containing condominiums

crisis center *n* : a facility run by nonprofessionals who counsel those who telephone for help in a personal crisis

cry-print *n* : a spectrographically produced pattern of the cry of an infant that is used for detecting physiological abnormalities—**cry-printing** *n*

dap *n* : a slapping together of the right hands of two people as a greeting or sign of friendship

dingbat *n* : a stupid or unsophisticated person : NITWIT

dope opera *n* : a motion picture whose story deals with the illicit use of drugs

doublespeak *n* : the oral use of two dialects of the same language : BIDIALECTALISM—**doublespeaker** *n*

ecocatastrophe *n* : a major destructive upset in the balance of nature especially when caused by the intervention of man

ecotage *n* : destructive or obstructive action designed to publicize and embarrass environmental polluters

ephebiatrist *n* : a specialist in the medical and emotional treatment of teen-agers

flipping *n* : the charging of interest on interest (as by a loan shark)

futuriasis *n* : a morbid fixation on or fear of the future

Godrock *n* : rock music with lyrics referring to God

God squad *n* : a group of clergymen who volunteer to work part-time with a municipal police department

Green Machine *n* : the administrative structure of the U.S. army : the military establishment

hatchback *n* **1** : a back on a closed passenger automobile (as a coupe) having an upward-opening hatch **2** : an automobile having a hatchback

heightism *n* : discrimination against short people

helicop *n* : a policeman on patrol in a helicopter

hiker-biker *n* : a site (as along a bicycle route) with camping and picnicking facilities

house sitter *n* : one who is paid to live in a house while the occupants are away

hydrolig *n* : a liquid-filled plastic bag that is worn around the knee (as of a football player) to protect the ligaments

interventurism *n* : involvement in power struggles abroad

jay-cycling *n* : riding a bicycle in a careless or illegal manner so as to be endangered by traffic

Jesus boot *n* : one of a pair of hollow box-shaped boots (as of wood and polystyrene) designed to allow the wearer to walk on water—called also *watershoe*

living will *n* : a written declaration in which a person requests that if he becomes disabled beyond reasonable expectation of recovery he be allowed to die in dignity rather than be kept alive by artificial means

MCP *abbr* male chauvinist pig

media ecology *n* : the study of the interaction between people and the mass communications media

mediagenic *adj* : likely to appeal to the audiences of the mass media and especially television

mediography *n* : a list of available audio-visual materials relating to a course of study

micropolis *n* : a very small city

middle college *n* : a 3-year liberal arts program at a university that admits students who have completed the 10th grade and that includes courses normally covered in the last two years of high school and the first two years of college

monster *n, specif* : a drug that stimulates the central nervous system

Moses Freak *n* : a youth who strictly observes traditional Jewish teachings and mores

mud bed *n* : a bed consisting of a wooden frame filled with mud and covered with a vinyl sheet

nastyism *n* : an underhanded or spiteful comment

open classroom *n* : a system of education in which activities involving multidisciplinary skills replace traditional subject courses

open dating *n* : the marking of perishable products (as bakery and dairy items) with the date on which the product was packaged or after which it should not be sold

paintural *n* : a three-dimensional artwork that is a combination of painting and sculpture

performance contracting *n* : a system of education in which a private company contracts to bring the performance of a failing public school student up to an acceptable level in specified subject areas

phone freak *or* **phone phreak** *n* : one who illegally uses an electronic device to make long-distance telephone calls without paying for them

prehumous *adj* : existing or occurring before one's death <a *prehumous* monument>

prequel *n* : a literary work whose narrative sequentially precedes that of an earlier work

psytocracy *n* : a form of government in which the citizens are psychologically manipulated for political purposes

quadraphony *n* : the transmission, recording, or reproduction of sound by techniques that utilize four transmission channels—**quadraphonic** *adj*

saccharinize *vb* : to make agreeable or pleasing

skin-search *vb* : to examine the denuded body of a prisoner for contraband

socspeak n : jargon used by sociologists

tapsichorean *adj* : of or relating to tap dancing <the *tapsichorean* art>

technethics *n* : the responsible use of science, technology, and ethics in a society shaped by technology

telemedicine *n* : the practice of medicine via television

Tio Taco *n* : a Mexican-American who submissively accepts the values of Anglo-American society

upfront *adj* : HONEST, STRAIGHTFORWARD

urbiphobia *n* : a fear of or aversion to cities

visual literacy *n* : the ability to discriminate and interpret the visible actions, objects, and symbols encountered in one's environment

voicespondence *n* : communication between persons by an exchange of tape-recorded messages—**voicespond** *vb*—**voicesponder** *n*

watershoe *n* : JESUS BOOT

windsurfing *n* : riding on a surfboard that is equipped with a sail

yips *n* : a psychological state in a golfer that is characterized by the inability to execute a crucial putt

continued from page 731
answer that failed to give a straight reply. That negatives tend to lose force and so require subsequent reinforcement was shown by the use of **never ever,** "never at any time," an expression that spread with astonishing rapidity throughout the mass media. "There was no doubt whatsoever" became "There was never ever any doubt."

Numerous expressions reflected a popular desire to soften the hardness of reality. **Multinational** suggested a greater degree of integration than international. Allotments (small pieces of land assigned by British town councils for cultivation by individuals) became **leisure gardens.** Delinquent children were no longer sent to penal institutions, or even to approved schools, but to **community homes.**

The use of **answerability** (German *die Verantwortlichkeit*) was greatly extended during the year at the expense of **accountability** (to a particular person or body) and **responsibility** (French *la responsabilité*). The notion spheres of these three important synonyms were seen to be interchanging kaleidoscopically.

As a favourite phrase, **life-style** tended to supersede the slightly earlier **quality of life,** the more definitely economic **standard of living,** and the traditional **way of life,** although all four expressions continued in circulation. More than ever before the **silent majority** were contrasted with the **vocal minority.** Everywhere people were being solemnly admonished to **get their priorities right,** but many seemed only too anxious to **get away from it all.**

(SIMEON POTTER)

Yemen, People's Democratic Republic of

A people's republic in the southern coastal region of the Arabian Peninsula, Yemen (Aden) is bordered by Yemen (San'a'), Saudi Arabia, and Oman. Area: 111,074 sq.mi. (287,680 sq.km.). Pop. (1971 est.): 1,475,000. National cap. and largest city: Aden (pop., 1971 est., 184,000); administrative cap.: Madinat ash-Shab. Language: Arabic. Religion: Muslim. Chairman of the Presidential Council in 1972, Salem Ali Rubayyi; prime minister, Ali Nasir Muhammad Husani.

During 1972 the avowedly Marxist regime of the People's Democratic Republic of Yemen was in conflict with its Omani and North Yemeni neighbours. At home hotels, theatres, and privately owned buildings and shops were all nationalized and, with government approval, poor peasants in the fifth governorate in the eastern part of the country seized lands from the larger landowners.

In May the Omani Air Force bombarded PDRY frontier areas in response to alleged PDRY attacks in support of the Dhofari rebels in Oman. The PDRY government held Britain responsible. The PDRY regime also declared itself threatened from the north, where exiled South Yemenis, including former ruling sheikhs and members of the banned Front for the Liberation of South Yemen (FLOSY) and the South Arabian League, supported by Saudi Arabia, had expressed their determination to overthrow the Aden government. Fighting on the border with the Yemen Arab Republic broke out at the end of September, and on October 8 North Yemeni forces occupied the offshore Kamaran Island belonging to the PDRY. Arab League mediation led to an uneasy cease-fire on October 13, and talks in Cairo to an agreement to unite the two countries, officially signed in Tripoli, Libya, on November 28.

Foreign aid to the PDRY was largely confined to the Communist states, including the U.S.S.R. and China, which were competing for influence. Acute economic difficulties caused by the continued closure of the Suez Canal were reflected in a decision to reduce the salaries of all members of the ruling National Liberation Front.

(PETER MANSFIELD)

YEMEN, PEOPLE'S DEMOCRATIC REPUBLIC OF

Education. (1969–70) Primary, pupils 104,708, teachers 3,453; secondary, pupils 12,305, teachers 681; vocational, pupils 510, teachers 85; teacher training, students 235, teachers 29.

Finance and Trade. Monetary unit: Yemen dinar, with (Sept. 18, 1972) a free rate of 0.37 dinar to U.S. $1 (0.92 dinar = £1 sterling). Budget (1970–71): revenue 13 million dinars; expenditure 18 million dinars. Foreign trade (1971): imports 64.9 million dinars; exports 43.1 million dinars. Import sources (1970): Iran 18%; Kuwait 13%; Japan 11%; United Arab Emirates 5%; U.K. 5%. Export destinations (1970): U.K. 25%; Japan 14%; Thailand 9%; Australia 6%; South Africa 6%; Spain 5%; Yemen (San'a') 5%. Main exports petroleum products 75%.

Transport. Roads (1970) *c.* 4,500 km. (mainly tracks; including 205 km. with improved surface). Motor vehicles in use (1970): passenger 10,200; commercial (including buses) 2,400. There are no railways. Ships entered (1970) vessels totaling 8,299,000 net registered tons; goods loaded (1970) *c.* 6 million metric tons, unloaded *c.* 6.9 million metric tons.

Agriculture. Production (in 000; metric tons; 1971; 1970 in parentheses): millet and sorghum *c.* 75 (58); dates *c.* 8 (*c.* 8); cotton, lint 6 (5). Livestock (in 000; 1970–71): cattle *c.* 92; sheep *c.* 215; goats *c.* 870; camels *c.* 40.

Industry. Production (in 000; metric tons; 1970): salt 88; petroleum products 6,311; electricity (kw-hr.) 194,000.

Yemen Arab Republic

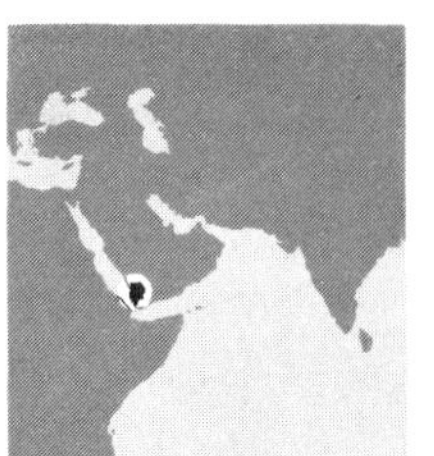

A republic situated in the southwestern coastal region of the Arabian Peninsula, Yemen (San'a') is bounded by Yemen (Aden), Saudi Arabia, and the Red Sea. Area: 77,200 sq.mi. (200,000 sq.km.). Pop. (1971 est.): 5.9 million. Cap. and largest city: San'a' (pop., 1970 est., 130,000). Language: Arabic. Religion: Muslim. President in 1972, Qadi Abdul Rahman al-Iryani; premiers, Mohsin al-Aini and, from December 30, Kadhi Abdullah al-Hagri.

In 1972 the Yemen Arab Republic turned increasingly toward the West and Saudi Arabia, while its conflict with the Marxist regime in Aden led to strained relations with the Soviet Union. However, the premier visited China and North Korea in July and was warmly received. On July 2 Yemen resumed relations with the U.S.—becoming the first of the Arab states that broke relations with the U.S. during the 1967 Middle East crisis to do so—and it was announced that U.S. aid to Yemen would be resumed shortly. Aid from other Western countries helped to alleviate Yemen's severe economic difficulties.

When the situation on Yemen's border with the People's Democratic Republic of Yemen (PDRY) began to deteriorate in March, the premier toured Arab capitals explaining Yemen's view that the PDRY should allow the thousands of political exiles who had sought refuge in north Yemen to return. Fighting

World Bank: *see* Development, Economic

World Council of Churches: *see* Religion

Yachting: *see* Sailing

YEMEN ARAB REPUBLIC

Education. (1969–70) Primary, pupils 72,107, teachers 1,533; secondary (1970–71), pupils 4,934, teachers (1967–68) 115; vocational (1970–71), pupils 640; teacher training, students 497, teaching staff (1965–66) 5.

Finance and Trade. Monetary unit: riyal, with (Sept. 18, 1972) a free exchange rate of 4.69 riyals to U.S. $1 (12.37 riyals = £1 sterling). Budget (1969–70): revenue 109 million riyals; expenditure *c.* 125 million riyals. Foreign trade (1971): imports 184.8 million riyals; exports 31.6 million riyals. Import sources (1970): Yemen (Aden) 23%; Australia 12%; U.S.S.R. 12%; France 12%; U.K. 8%; Japan 6%. Export destinations (1970): Yemen (Aden) 52%; U.S.S.R. 32%; Japan 12%. Main exports (1970): coffee 51%; kat 28%; salt 9%; hides and skins 8%.

Agriculture. Production (in 000; metric tons; 1971; 1970 in parentheses): millet and sorghum *c.* 550 (*c.* 550); wheat *c.* 15 (*c.* 15); dates *c.* 60 (*c.* 60); coffee *c.* 3.6 (*c.* 3.6); cotton, lint *c.* 1 (*c.* 1). Livestock (in 000; March 1971): cattle *c.* 1,380; sheep *c.* 12,400; camels *c.* 59.

broke out at the end of September around the Yemeni town of Qa'tabah. Yemen accused the PDRY of using foreign pilots to bombard Yemeni territory, and on October 8 Yemeni forces occupied the Red Sea island of Kamaran, which lay off its shores but had belonged to the PDRY. Yemen accepted Arab League mediation and on November 28 an agreement to unite the two countries was signed in Tripoli, Libya. On December 28 Premier Mohsin al-Aini resigned, claiming that the Consultative Council (parliament) was obstructing the union agreement. Kadhi Abdullah al-Hagri formed a new government on December 30.

(PETER MANSFIELD)

Yugoslavia

A federal socialist republic, Yugoslavia is bordered by Italy, Austria, Hungary, Romania, Bulgaria, Greece, and Albania. Area: 98,766 sq.mi. (255,804 sq.km.). Pop. (1971): 20,504,516. Cap. and largest city: Belgrade (pop., 1971, 774,744). Language: Serbo-Croatian, Slovenian, and Macedonian. Religion (1953): Orthodox 41.4%; Roman Catholic 31.8%; Muslim 12.3%. President of the republic and president of the League of Communists in 1972, Marshal Tito (Josip Broz); president of the Federal Executive Council (premier), Dzemal Bijedic.

The introduction of political trials and purges and a tightening-up of censorship were the main features of Yugoslavia's internal political scene in 1972. In foreign policy, the rapprochement with the U.S.S.R. continued, but so did efforts to retain political and economic links with the West.

The enforced resignation in December 1971 of top party and government leaders in Croatia who had been accused by President Tito of liberalism and nationalism was followed by a widespread purge of the Croatian party, administration, judiciary, and the university, involving over a thousand people. At the second conference of the League of Communists in January 1972, Tito denied there was a crisis in the party and the country, but the purge continued and widened.

Numerous student leaders, party officials, university intellectuals, and writers accused of Croatian nationalism were arrested and brought to trial during the summer and fall. On October 6 the four main leaders of the Zagreb student strike of November 1971, held in support of the then party leaders' demand that a bigger share of Croatia's foreign currency earnings be returned to Croatia, received sentences of up to four years' imprisonment. On Oct. 26, 1972, the editor of the banned Zagreb paper *Hrvatski Tjednik* ("Croatian Weekly"), Vlado Gotovac, was sentenced to four years. Similar sentences were passed on other intellectuals charged with conducting nationalist propaganda and, in some cases, with having links with Croatian exiles in the West. A group of 19 Croat guerrillas, most of whom were alleged to have come from Australia, entered Yugoslavia illegally in July; the group was destroyed a month later, after it had inflicted 13 casualties on the security forces. This incursion and the hijacking of a Swedish airliner by three young Croats on September 17 led to a vigorous Yugoslav diplomatic campaign aimed at persuading Western governments to ban Yugoslav exile political organizations in their countries.

In October the purge spread to Serbia. The party leader, Marko Nikezic, and the party secretary, Latinka Perovic, resigned after being accused of excessive liberalism in the economic sphere. The foreign minister, Mirko Tepavac, resigned on November 1 and was replaced on December 5 by Milos Minic. Other important resignations included those of Slovenian Premier Stane Kavcic and of Macedonian party secretary Slavko Miloslavlevski.

YUGOSLAVIA

Education. (1969–70) Primary, pupils 2,857,291, teachers 116,930; secondary, pupils 184,068, teachers 10,028; vocational, pupils 500,484, teachers 16,096; teacher training, students 21,194, teachers 1,299; higher (including 8 universities), students 239,701, teaching staff (1967–68) 15,950.

Finance. Monetary unit: dinar, with (Sept. 18, 1972) a par value of 17 dinars to U.S. $1 (free rate of 40.75 dinars = £1 sterling). Gold, SDRs, and foreign exchange, central bank: (June 1972) U.S. $451 million; (June 1971) U.S. $180 million. Budget (1970 est.): revenue 27,672,000,000 dinars; expenditure 25,659,000,000 dinars. Net material product: (1970) 157 billion dinars; (1969) 132 billion dinars. Money supply: (March 1972) 44,960,000,000 dinars; (March 1971) 36.1 billion dinars. Cost of living (1963 = 100): (May 1972) 332; (May 1971) 290.

Foreign Trade. (1971) Imports 48,795,000,000 dinars; exports 26,240,000,000 dinars. Import sources: West Germany 19%; Italy 12%; U.S.S.R. 9%; U.K. 6%; U.S. 6%; Czechoslovakia 5%; Austria 5%. Export destinations: U.S.S.R. 15%; Italy 12%; West Germany 12%; Czechoslovakia 6%; U.K. 6%; U.S. 6%; Poland 5%. Main exports: machinery 13%; nonferrous metals 10%; transport equipment 8%; meat 7%; chemicals 7%; clothing 5%. Tourism: (1970): visitors 4,748,700; gross receipts U.S. $276 million.

Transport and Communications. Roads (1970) 100,359 km. Motor vehicles in use (1970): passenger 720,900; commercial 107,300. Railways: (1970) 10,289 km.; traffic (1971) 11,179,000,000 passenger-km.; freight 19,748,000,000 net ton-km. Air traffic (1971): 939.5 million passenger-km.; freight 7,575,000 net ton-km. Shipping (1971): merchant vessels 100 gross tons and over 356; gross tonnage 1,543,149. Telephones (Dec. 1970) 736,000. Radio licenses (Dec. 1970) 3,372,000. Television licenses (Dec. 1970) 1,796,000.

Agriculture. Production (in 000; metric tons; 1971; 1970 in parentheses): wheat 5,604 (3,792); barley 463 (402); oats 312 (309); rye 134 (127); corn 7,442 (6,928); potatoes 2,916 (2,930); sunflower seed 347 (264); sugar, raw value (1971–72) 429, (1970–71) 357; dry beans *c.* 200 (188); onions (1970) 266, (1969) 212; tomatoes (1970) 313, (1969) 328; plums (1970) 896, (1969) 1,292; apples *c.* 320 (277); pears *c.* 112 (112); figs (1970) 22, (1969) 20; wine 555 (540); tobacco 44 (49); beef and veal *c.* 270 (245); pork *c.* 350 (339); timber (cu.m.; 1970) 17,000, (1969) 16,900; fish catch (1970) 45, (1969) 44. Livestock (in 000; Jan. 1971): cattle 5,138; sheep 8,703; pigs 6,562; horses 1,076; chickens 40,104.

Industry. Fuel and power (in 000; metric tons; 1971): coal 706; lignite 30,194; crude oil 2,961; natural gas (cu.m.) 1,151,000; manufactured gas (cu.m.) 169,000; electricity (kw-hr.) 29,425,000. Production (in 000; metric tons; 1971): cement 4,955; iron ore (35% metal content) 3,725; pig iron 1,630; crude steel 2,443; bauxite 1,973; antimony ore (metal content; 1970) 2; chrome ore (oxide content; 1970) 15; manganese ore (metal content; 1970) 4.6; aluminum 47; copper 93; lead 99; zinc 53; sulfuric acid 808; cotton yarn 100; wool yarn 39; wood pulp (1970) 484; newsprint 80; other paper (1970) 453.

The campaign to eliminate corruption from public life and reduce the growing gap between the lower-paid workers and the middle class led to the publication of lists of Yugoslavia's "new millionaires" in the fall. A number of trials for embezzlement and other financial malpractices were held throughout Yugoslavia. Strikes continued, despite the much-publicized new policy of giving the workers a greater say in running the country. The largest strike occurred in the huge Elektronska Industrija factory in Nis (November 4–7). Management had been unable to pay the workers' wages because the firm was insolvent. For similar reasons about three-quarters of a million workers faced pay cuts of at least 10% at year's end.

Prices of bread, flour, edible oil, and sugar went up by 20% on October 11. Inflation was running at the average annual rate of 15%, but exports had increased by 21% in the first eight months of 1972 and imports fell by 15%. The trade deficit was $570 million, or 50% less than in the corresponding period of 1971. Thanks to hard-currency remittances from Yugoslav workers in the West and good tourist earnings, Yugoslavia had a small balance of payments surplus.

The highlight of the diplomatic year was the state visit October 17–21 by Queen Elizabeth II, the first ever paid by a reigning British monarch to a Communist country. The most significant foreign policy event, however, was President Tito's visit to the U.S.S.R. on June 5–10. On the first day of the visit, which he called a "new turning-point," the 80-year-old Tito was awarded the Order of Lenin, the U.S.S.R.'s highest decoration for foreigners. In mid-July, the Moscow session of Comecon was attended for the first time by the Yugoslav prime minister, Dzemal Bijedic, who announced that Yugoslavia would enter into more intimate collaboration with the organization in various fields, though still formally retaining its observer-member status. On November 3 the U.S.S.R. granted Yugoslavia a $540 million credit at the favourable rate of 2%, the biggest foreign credit ever granted to Yugoslavia by a foreign power. Nevertheless, Yugoslavia's trade with the EEC continued to grow faster than that with Comecon, and Yugoslavia continued to make strenuous efforts to attract further Western capital investment. On November 27 Yugoslavia started negotiations with the EEC for the conclusion of a new trade agreement to replace the one signed in April 1970. At a party meeting in Slovenia in December, Tito denied that Yugoslavia would "return under the Soviet umbrella."

Yugoslavia's relations with Austria deteriorated in October as a result of a campaign in Austria against the bilingual Slovene-German road signs put up in the Austrian province of Carinthia, which had a 25,000-strong Slovene minority. On November 13 President Tito attacked the campaign as "fascist," and the Yugoslav government protested vigorously against apparent police inactivity during riots. (K. F. CVIIC)

Zaire

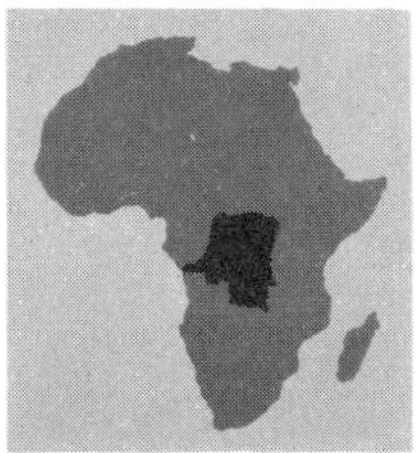

A republic of equatorial Africa, Zaire is bounded by the Central African Republic, Sudan, Uganda, Rwanda, Burundi, Tanzania, Zambia, Angola, Congo, and the Atlantic Ocean. Area: 905,360 sq.mi. (2,344,885 sq.km.). Pop. (1972 est.): 22,860,352. Cap. and largest city: Kinshasa (pop., 1972 est., 1,623,760). Language: French; Bantu dialects. Religion: animist approximately 50%; Christian 43%. President in 1972, Mobutu Sese Seko.

Zaire faced 1972 with serious economic problems. The low prices offered for copper, which accounted for more than half the country's exports, resulted in a considerable reduction in income, while increased spending on salaries and additional capital investment helped to produce a heavy budget deficit. The growth rate in both industrial and agricultural output had slowed in 1971, but there was optimism regarding the prospect of an improvement in the near future.

As part of the continuing campaign to arouse a spirit of nationalism through what was described as a return to African authenticity, Katanga was renamed Shaba on New Year's Day and Stanley Pool became Malebo Pool. President Mobutu himself dropped his Christian names and became Mobutu Sese Seko (*see* BIOGRAPHY). A new nationality bill was approved by the National Assembly which required all Zairean nationals having a Zairean mother and a foreign father to adopt their mother's name in place of that of their father; other Zaireans were required to take local names instead of their Christian names. These changes were followed by a vigorous official attack on the Roman Catholic archbishop of Kinshasa, Joseph-Albert Cardinal Malula, for having allegedly opposed the authenticity campaign, and for four months he was not permitted to return from Rome.

In May the opening of the first congress of

ZAIRE

Education. (1969–70) Primary, pupils 2,822,908, teachers 66,709; secondary, pupils 175,481, teachers 5,804; vocational, pupils 33,985, teachers 3,515; teacher training, students 34,532, teachers 2,643; higher, students 10,165, teaching staff 1,294.

Finance. Monetary unit: zaire, with (Sept. 18, 1972) an official exchange rate of 0.50 zaire to U.S. $1 (free rate of 1.22 zaires = £1 sterling). Gold, SDRs, and foreign exchange, central bank: (May 1972) U.S. $102,120,000; (May 1971) U.S. $165,320,000. Budget: revenue (1970 est.) 215 million zaires; expenditure (1971 est.) 285 million zaires. Money supply: (May 1972) 202,470,000 zaires; (May 1971) 191,220,000 zaires. Cost of living (Kinshasa; 1963 = 100): (March 1972) 447; (March 1971) 383.

Foreign Trade. (1970) Imports 266.5 million zaires; exports 367.7 million zaires. Import sources: Belgium-Luxembourg 24%; U.S. 11%; West Germany 10%; France 8%; U.K. 7%; Japan 7%; Italy 5%. Export destinations: Belgium-Luxembourg 43%; Italy 11%; U.K. 7%; France 7%. Main exports: copper 67%; diamonds 6%; coffee 5%.

Transport and Communications. Roads (1970) 140,000 km. Motor vehicles in use (1970): passenger 70,000; commercial 27,500. Railways (1970): 5,795 km.; traffic 657 million passenger-km., freight 1,927,000,000 net ton-km. Air traffic (1971): 595.3 million passenger-km.; freight 17,977,000 net ton-km. Shipping (1971): merchant vessels 100 gross tons and over 7; gross tonnage 39,317. Inland waterways (including Congo River; 1969) *c.* 13,700 km. Telephones (Dec. 1970) 37,000. Radio receivers (Dec. 1970) 63,000. Television receivers (Dec. 1970) *c.* 7,000.

Agriculture. Production (in 000; metric tons; 1971; 1970 in parentheses): rice *c.* 140 (*c.* 140); corn *c.* 350 (*c.* 350); sweet potatoes and yams (1970) *c.* 350, (1969) 350; cassava (1970) *c.* 10,000, (1969) 10,000; peanuts *c.* 200 (200); palm oil *c.* 200 (180); palm kernels *c.* 130 (*c.* 130); coffee *c.* 67 (*c.* 72); sugar, raw value (1970–72) *c.* 52, (1970–71) 43; rubber (exports) *c.* 35 (32); cotton, lint *c.* 17 (17); timber (cu.m.; 1970) 11,600, (1969) 11,600. Livestock (in 000; Dec. 1970): cattle 930; sheep *c.* 575; goats *c.* 1,650; pigs *c.* 450.

Industry. Production (in 000; metric tons; 1970): coal 102; copper 252; zinc 64; tin 1.4; manganese ore (metal content) 156; gold (troy oz.) 177; silver (troy oz.) 1,707; diamonds (metric carats) 14,086; electricity (kw-hr.) 3,194,000.

Yiddish Literature:
see Literature

Mobutu's Mouvement Populaire de la Révolution (MPR) was attended by seven heads of state and 50 delegations from other countries, in addition to more than 1,000 delegates from Zaire itself. The congress followed a period of gradual withdrawal from the Common Organization of Africa, Malagasy, and Mauritius (OCAM), partly arising from rivalry between some of the more senior heads of state involved and partly from an effort to avoid the continuing influence of France. The emergence of a new regional grouping was suggested by the presence at the congress of the presidents of Chad, Gabon, and Upper Volta, and also of Pres. Kenneth Kaunda of Zambia, who agreed to the creation of closer ties between Zaire and his country. Tanzania was represented at the congress by its second vice-president, Rashidi Kawawa, but, like Nigeria, it had been disturbed by another manifestation of Mobutu's authenticity campaign, the expulsion of non-Zairean Africans in the closing months of 1971. Speaking of Zaire's relations with South Africa, Mobutu told the congress that he did not wish to criticize the policies of other states but that Zaire would not become involved in any negotiations with the South African government. Critics noted, however, that Zaire continued to trade with South Africa. In early October Mobutu visited Pres. Idi Amin in Kampala, Uganda, but failed in his attempt to mediate on behalf of the Ugandan Asians whom Amin was expelling from his country.

The hydroelectric project at Inga, financed mainly by Zaire itself, with loans from Italy, the EEC, and the World Bank, was officially inaugurated on November 24, the seventh anniversary of Mobutu's accession to power. On the same day full diplomatic relations with China were established. (KENNETH INGHAM)

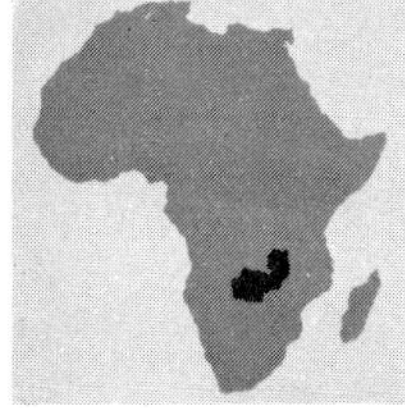

Zambia

A republic and a member of the Commonwealth of Nations, Zambia is bounded by Tanzania, Malawi, Mozambique, Rhodesia, South West Africa, Angola, and Zaire. Area: 290,586 sq.mi. (752,614 sq.km.). Pop. (1972 est.): 4,515,000, of whom about 99% are Africans. Cap.: Lusaka (pop., 1972 est., 347,900). Language: English and Bantu. Religion: predominantly animist. President in 1972, Kenneth Kaunda.

Eleven by-elections for Zambia's National Assembly held in December 1971 produced results that were too indecisive to satisfy any of the political parties involved. Simon Kapwepwe, leader of the recently founded United Progressive Party (UPP), was himself elected with a modest majority, but his other candidates were unsuccessful. The governing United National Independence Party (UNIP) gained two seats at the expense of the main opposition party, the African National Congress (ANC), but the latter held three seats in the south to demonstrate its continuing hold on the Tonga people. On Feb. 4, 1972, President Kaunda banned the UPP and placed its leaders under restriction for having allegedly attempted to isolate the Bemba of the northern province from the rest of the country. Shortly afterward the president appointed a commission to recommend ways of introducing a one-party state, and after the report was received a bill banning all opposition parties was published on October 30. The bill also proposed to give the Zambian armed forces direct representation in Parliament, along with members of the church, the traditional chiefs, and the University of Zambia. Although the bill was bitterly opposed by opposition leader Harry Nkumbula of the ANC, who warned that it could lead to civil war, it was passed by the National Assembly, where UNIP held 85 of the 110 seats, and signed by the president on December 13. At the end of the year Kapwepwe and the other UPP leaders were released.

On May 26 a bomb in a parcel addressed to President Kaunda exploded when opened by a girl secretary; she was blinded and lost an arm. The incident was not officially regarded as part of any conspiracy, and no roundup of political opponents followed.

In the economic sphere 1972 began unfavourably for the government. Low prices for copper, as well as a decline in copper production, had produced a record balance of payments deficit of 202 million kwachas, while agriculture's contribution to the country's prosperity had fallen well below the hoped-for level. This situation had led to the devaluation of the currency by 8% in December 1971, and early in 1972 President Kaunda outlined a five-year plan (1972–76) to combat the difficulties facing the country. Inevitably, recovery would depend largely on developing the copper resources, and an increase in output of 39.5% over 1971 was looked for in the next five years. Manufacturing was also expected to show considerable growth, while marked increases in agricultural output were demanded.

Prospects of improvement received a setback with the publication in May of the auditor-general's report for 1970. This revealed numerous examples of the misappropriation of public funds, a situation difficult to remedy because of the frequent changes of government ministers. In addition, the large number of vacancies in the public service suggested a serious shortage of trained manpower. (KENNETH INGHAM)

ZAMBIA

Education. (1970) Primary, pupils 694,670, teachers 14,852; secondary, pupils 52,472, teachers 2,465; vocational, pupils 948; teacher training, students 2,146, teachers 182; higher, students 1,466, teaching staff 189.

Finance. Monetary unit: kwacha, with (Sept. 18, 1972) a par value of 0.71 kwacha to U.S. $1 (free rate of 1.75 kwachas = £1 sterling). Gold and foreign exchange, official: (June 1972): U.S. $153.5 million; (June 1971) U.S. $361.4 million. Budget (1971 est.): revenue 421 million kwachas; expenditure 329 million kwachas. Gross domestic product: (1970) 1,146,000,000 kwachas; (1969) 1,240,000,000 kwachas. Cost of living (1963 = 100): (June 1972) 168; (June 1971) 160.

Foreign Trade. (1971) Imports 392.5 million kwachas; exports 480.2 million kwachas. Import sources (1970): U.K. 23%; South Africa 17%; U.S. 9%; Rhodesia 6%; Japan 6%; West Germany 5%. Export destinations (1970): Japan 23%; U.K. 22%; West Germany 12%. Main export copper 94%.

Transport and Communications. Roads (1969) 34,653 km. Motor vehicles in use: passenger (1968) 48,200; commercial (including buses; 1970) 30,600. Railways (1968) 1,365 km. Construction of a *c.* 1,800-km. railway linking Kapini Mposh in Zambia with Dar es Salaam in Tanzania began in 1970; completion was planned for 1976. Air traffic (1970): 228,014,000 passenger-km.; freight 5,530,000 net ton-km. Telephones (Dec. 1970) 56,000. Radio receivers (Dec. 1970) 75,000. Television receivers (Dec. 1969) 20,000.

Agriculture. Production (in 000; metric tons; 1971; 1970 in parentheses): corn *c.* 750 (*c.* 550); peanuts *c.* 103 (*c.* 42); cassava (1970) *c.* 143, (1969) *c.* 145; millet and sorghum *c.* 250 (*c.* 250); sugar, raw value (1971–72) *c.* 41, (1970–71) *c.* 41; tobacco 6.5 (5.1). Livestock (in 000; 1970–71): cattle *c.* 1,600; sheep *c.* 28; goats *c.* 185; pigs *c.* 105; chickens *c.* 6,900.

Industry. Production (in 000; metric tons; 1971): copper 535; zinc 57; lead 28; coal (1970) 623; electricity (kw-hr.) 1,167,000.

Zanzibar: *see* Tanzania
Zinc: *see* Mining
Zoology: *see* Life Sciences

United States Statistical Supplement

Developments in the states in 1972

A historic breakthrough in federal-state relations, federal revenue-sharing provided the highlight event for state governments in 1972. The development came as state expenditures for welfare, education and other services mounted rapidly while legislatures were under strong voter pressure to avoid increased taxes.

Controversy continued over methods of financing educational systems. Trends toward legalized abortions and liberalized gambling laws also continued, and many legislatures approved new laws safeguarding the environment. The year also saw financial scandals and criminal indictments of state officials, both past and present.

Thirty-nine states held regular legislative sessions, and 10 had special sessions. In addition, 24 states staged presidential primary elections, 44 held state legislative ballots, and 44 conducted statewide referenda over a wide range of issues.

Party Strengths. Twenty-eight governors were Democrats in 1972; twenty-one Republicans; and one (Minnesota) Democratic Farmer Labor Party. The November elections produced a one-statehouse gain for the Democrats to make the prospective 1973 majority 29 to 20. Republicans gained governorships in Missouri and North Carolina, but Democrats more than offset their losses by turning out Republican administrations in Illinois, Delaware, and Vermont. The results left Democrats with the advantage in all major regions of the country except the Northeast, where the prospective 1973 gubernatorial lineup includes five Republicans and four Democrats.

Despite a Republican landslide at the presidential level, the November election also produced Democratic gains in state legislative alignments. During 1972, Democrats held majorities in both legislative chambers of 23 states, while Republicans had two-house majorities in 16. But the elections saw the GOP gain control of only the Connecticut legislature, while Democrats wrested full sway over Oregon, Montana, Nevada, Minnesota, and Washington for the first time. As a result, Republicans will control 17 legislatures in 1973 while Democrats will dominate a minimum of 25.

Federal-State Relations. Representatives of the nation's states and cities achieved a signal victory Sept. 15 when a House-Senate conference committee approved a compromise revenue-sharing bill. The State and Local Fiscal Assistance Act of 1972, signed into law by President Nixon on Oct. 20, will provide a total of $30.2 billion in federal funds to state and local governments over a five-year period. The first allocations, totaling $2.7 billion, were distributed in December.

Lobbyists for the bill hailed the breakthrough as the opportunity for states and localities to demonstrate that, given sufficient resources, smaller units of government can be more responsive to the needs and priorities of the people than can the distant federal government.

Under the new bill, two-thirds of the grants will be distributed to local general purpose governmental units (counties, townships and incorporated municipalities) and one-third to state governments. No strings were attached to the state grants, except that they could not be used to match federal funds in other programs, and the program would not be used as an excuse to reduce state aid already underway to cities.

The funds to local governments must be spent on any of seven "high-priority" categories: public safety, environmental protection, public transportation, health and recreation, social services for poor and aged, financial administration and libraries. Cities were not to spend the funds on operating costs of education or for general administration needs.

The *Wall Street Journal* commented that the "major significance of the disbursal is that it may well mark the turning point in who benefits from federal funds—away from the 'have-not' minorities and toward the general 'have' population." Charls E. Walker, deputy secretary of the treasury, agreed that the main beneficiaries of revenue-sharing would be different from those benefiting from most ongoing Great Society welfare programs.

While signing the bill Oct. 20, Nixon said he hoped the funds would be used to "stop the alarming escalation" of state and local taxes, as well as to improve public services and to move toward a goal of "better government" rather than "bigger government."

Although the idea of revenue-sharing is nearly as old as the Republic itself, the current effort for revenue-sharing began building in the 1960s, with the National Governors' Conference and the National Legislative Conference among the organizational leaders. Nixon endorsed the concept in his 1972 State of the Union message, and a congressional logjam over the proposal was broken in March, 1972, when Rep. Wilbur Mills (D-Ark.), chairman of the powerful House Ways and Means Committee, reversed his previous opposition to revenue-sharing. The House passed a version June 22 that formulated aid on the basis of population, urbanized population and population inversely weighted for per capita income.

A revenue-sharing bill was approved by the Senate Sept. 12, but it would have distributed the funds on the basis of population, state and local tax effort, and inverse per capita income (the so-called poverty factor), a formula that generally favored smaller states over larger ones. House and Senate conferees solved the impasse Sept. 12 by allowing states to select the formula that benefited them most, but reducing each state's projected allocation by 9.1 percent to reach the first-year target of $5.3 billion. The conference committee decision was accepted on Oct. 12 by the House, 265 to 110, and on Oct. 13 by the Senate, 59 to 19.

For the third consecutive year, federal takeover of most state welfare expenditures foundered in the Senate. The Senate Finance Committee, chaired by Russell Long (D-La.), stripped a national minimum-income plan from the session's welfare bill before reporting it back to the full Senate, substituting a work requirement for parents of school-age children. Sen. Long said the minimum-income idea, if enacted, "would destroy this country."

A three-way battle ensued on the Senate floor. Fiscal conservatives, led by Long, faced welfare liberals led by Sen. Abraham Ribicoff (D-Conn.), while the administration position was unclear. In 1969, Nixon had proposed a family assistance plan including a guaranteed minimum income, and he had since called welfare reform his "number one domestic priority." But when, late in the session, Ribicoff and others introduced a compromise plan similar to Nixon's program, the administration lobbied against it.

As a result, virtually no significant alterations in the welfare system were enacted in the final bill passed by Congress shortly before adjournment Oct. 18, although it did provide for complete federal takeover of aid to aged, blind, and disabled by 1974. Ribicoff, shortly before the compromise plan was defeated, 50 to 35 on Oct. 4, charged Nixon with attempting to kill welfare reform in order to create a campaign issue over Congress' inability to reform the welfare system. Nonetheless, Nixon promised to resubmit his original family assistance proposal to Congress in 1973.

Finance. State legislatures showed a distinct reluctance to raise taxes or impose new ones during 1972. Although state budgets again reached record highs, the increases were fewer in both numbers and dollar amounts than in recent years: by mid-November only 14 legislatures had approved new taxing laws in 1972 for an estimated increase of $875 million, compared with 30 states imposing new or higher taxes of about $5 billion in 1971. The 1972 tax increases were the second-lowest total enacted by state legislatures since 1966.

No state imposed new sales, personal income or corporate income taxes. Only Connecticut raised its general sales tax rate, from 6½ to 7 percent, the highest in the nation. Two states, New York and Virginia, increased personal income taxes for some taxpayers, while some modifications and reforms in personal income levies were approved by legislatures in Idaho, Michigan, Missouri, and Vermont. Corporate income taxes were increased in Idaho, Nebraska, New Jersey, and Virginia, and modifications, usually enlarging corporate tax burdens, were approved in Connecticut, Kansas, Kentucky, Michigan, and Missouri.

More popular were tax increases through higher rates on existing excise and business levies. Motor fuel excise taxes were increased in Idaho, Kentucky, Maryland, Virginia, Missouri, Mississippi, New Jersey, New York, and South Carolina. Six states hiked assessments on cigarettes and/or tobacco products: Idaho, Kansas, Mississippi, New Jersey, New York, and Oregon. Excise taxes on alcoholic beverages were boosted in Florida, Maryland, Michigan, Nebraska, New Jersey, New York, South Carolina, South Dakota, and Virginia.

Among states providing significant tax relief for individuals, Kentucky removed grocery store food from sales-tax coverage, New Mexico provided a variable series of state-local tax credits against the state personal-income levy, and Illinois enacted a $5,000 deduction on assessed valuation for the personal property tax, thus virtually eliminating the levy for most individuals. In addition, 13 states either initiated or increased property tax relief for elderly and/or disabled persons: Colorado, Delaware, Georgia, Kansas, Illinois, Missouri, Nebraska, Oregon, South Carolina, South Dakota, Washington, West Virginia, and Wisconsin.

State tax collections in the 1972 fiscal year totaled $59.8 billion, up 16.1 percent from the 1971 figure. Of the new total, $17.6 billion was from general sales and gross receipts taxes; $15.6 billion from selective sales taxes; $13.0 billion from individual income taxes; $4.4 billion from corporation income taxes; and $5.3 billion from motor vehicle and other licenses.

Figures accumulated in 1972 showed that state revenue from all sources totaled $97.2 billion in fiscal 1971, an increase of 9.3 percent from the preceding year. General revenue (excluding state liquor and state insurance trust revenue) was $85.1 billion, up 9.4 percent. Total state expenditures were $98.8 billion, an increase of 16.2 percent, creating a deficit for the year of $1.6 billion. General expenditures, not including outlays of the liquor stores and insurance trust systems, amounted to $89.1 billion, up 15.8 percent for the year. Of general revenue, 60.6 percent came from state taxes; 11.5 percent from charges and miscellaneous revenue, including education charges; and 26.7 percent ($22.8 billion) from the federal government.

The largest state outlay was $35.1 billion for education, of which $19.3 billion went to local public schools and $12.4 billion for state colleges and universities. Other major outlays were $16.3 billion for public welfare (a 23.2 percent increase over fiscal 1970), $14.8 billion for highways, and $4.6 billion for hospitals.

Administrative Structures, Powers. Consolidation and reorganization plans for state governmental executive agencies were approved by several state legislatures, including those of Maine, Idaho, Arizona, South Dakota, and Ohio. The new organizational orders typically provided greater centralized control, either in the governor's office or in central administrative offices.

Montana voters approved a new state constitution on June 6, but North Dakota's proposed new constitution lost. A large number of states adopted measures reforming court structures and procedures, including Alabama, Indiana, Iowa, Georgia, Kansas, Minnesota, Nebraska, North Carolina, South Carolina, South Dakota, and Wyoming. Legislative concern over court systems was further demonstrated by invitations issued the chief justices of four states—Alaska, Maryland, Oklahoma, and Kansas—to deliver "state of the judiciary" messages to joint legislative sessions in 1972. Colorado and Michigan had pioneered the judicial addresses in 1971.

Legislative Systems. As the 1972 elections approached, 43 states redrew their legislative boundary lines to reflect population changes in the 1970 census. In most cases, the legislatures were able to reapportion themselves, but courts were forced to draw the details in at least seven states, and special masters or commissions were pressed into service in nine others.

Montana and Minnesota voters authorized annual legislative sessions, bringing to 35 the number of states where legislatures meet every year.

Ethics. During 1972, two states historically plagued with corruption problems, Texas and New Jersey, again furnished top news stories. In March, a state jury in Abilene, Texas, convicted Gus Mutscher, speaker of the Texas House of Representatives, another state representative, and a Mutscher aide on felony charges arising from a stock fraud scheme. The three were given five-year suspended prison terms for conspiring to accept a bribe; prosecutors charged they accepted unsecured bank loans from Houston financier Frank Sharp in return for passing legislation Sharp desired.

Other Texas officials, past and present, also were in the news. Former Atty.-Gen. Waggoner Carr and former state insurance commissioner John Oasrio were indicted by a federal grand jury in July for conspiring to defraud an insurance company. A former state senator was convicted in October of stealing a state treasury warrant, and other officials were charged with stealing state postage and unlawfully putting relatives on state payrolls.

In New Jersey, former Secretary of State Robert Burkhardt pleaded guilty May 12 to charges of bribery and extortion of a construction firm seeking a bridge contract. Another New Jersey political leader, John V. Kenny, was fined $30,000 on six counts of income tax evasion later in May. And in November, the incumbent New Jersey secretary of state, Paul J. Sherwin, was convicted by a federal jury, again for extorting money from a construction firm.

The Kentucky and New Jersey legislatures adopted new ethics codes, but Texas Atty.-Gen. Crawford Martin declared a 1971 ethics bill to be unconstitutional because financial disclosure requirements were too broad. Massachusetts approved a new election law limiting campaign spending by candidates, and Colorado and Nebraska voters approved new ethics referendums covering state officials.

Two Washington state officials and San Francisco Mayor Joseph Alioto were cleared in March of civil charges stemming from their splitting of $2.3 million in legal fees. The three also were acquitted in June of federal bribery, conspiracy, and mail fraud charges originating from the same incident.

Equal Rights. Although the U.S. Supreme Court had ruled that the equal protection clause of the 14th Amendment prohibited at least some forms of discrimination against women, most states had statutes on the books that either granted concessions or imposed restrictions on women solely on account of their gender. On March 22, the U.S. Senate approved an equal rights amendment to the U.S. Constitution and sent it to the states for ratification (the House had approved the amendment in 1971).

As of mid-November, 22 of the 38 states required had ratified the proposed 27th Amendment. The amendment would theoretically give women all rights accorded men; attempts by some senators to exempt women legally from the draft, to forbid their assignment to combat units, and to preserve laws that "extend protections or exemptions to women" were defeated decisively.

When states put the matter to a public vote, either as a state constitutional amendment or as an advisory ballot, the equal rights for women forces invariably won. Among states holding such elections in November were Colorado, Hawaii, Maryland, New Mexico, Texas, and Washington.

Education. Financing of the nation's primary and secondary schools, including nonpublic and parochial schools, continued to receive major attention in the states. The controversy over the local property tax as a major source of financing public education, first brought to national attention by a 1971 California Supreme Court decision, expanded in several directions. But by year's end neither the federal government nor any state had resolved the school financing dilemma.

Courts in two additional states, New Jersey and Kansas, ruled that the local property tax system violated the constitutional right to equal protection under the law because rich communities could more easily raise educational funds than could poorer school districts. Previously, courts in California, Minnesota, and Texas had issued similar rulings.

The issue reached the U.S. Supreme Court in October through the Texas case, which arose in San Antonio. The plaintiffs asked the high court to require Texas to equalize tax assessment power between rich and poor school districts by imposing a varying state aid formula; attorneys for the state replied that the plaintiff's plan would "impose a straitjacket" on state educational systems by limiting the amount parents could constitutionally pay for their children's education. The case had nationwide implications, but the high court had not announced its decision by the end of the year.

Efforts by states to devise a constitutional method to aid parochial and private schools received additional setbacks in the nation's courts. The U.S. Supreme Court ruled Oct. 10, without hearing arguments, that an Ohio plan to reimburse parents of children in such schools with tuition grants was unconstitutional. The 8–1 decision cast gloomy shadows over similar programs in Maryland, Connecticut, and Illinois, and left church leaders and state and federal officials still searching for a legal method of aiding the nation's hard-pressed nonpublic schools. A Census Bureau study released in March revealed that enrollment at Roman Catholic primary and secondary schools dropped by 30 percent to 3.9 million students between 1965 and 1971; most of the missing students enrolled in public schools, increasing state educational costs.

The year also found the first court decisions ordering busing across established school district lines to eliminate patterns of school segregation. Judges in Richmond, Va., and Detroit, Mich. ordered the cross-district transfers. However, the orders were later rendered ineffective, at least temporarily, by other courts, and were being appealed to the U.S. Supreme Court at the end of the year.

In the meantime, the high court heard another case with great potential impact for northern cities. Most previous court integration orders had their origin in the segregated school systems set up by law in post-Civil War southern states. But in October, the court heard a school desegregation case from Denver, Colo., where racial imbalance in city schools had grown up because of segregated housing patterns within the city. The trial court had ruled that these housing patterns were sanctioned by the city, and that the city thus had a duty to undo their effects. A Supreme Court opinion supporting the trial court would have profound impact upon northern school systems. A study released by the U.S. Department of Health, Education, and Welfare showed that for the first time in 1971–72, a greater percentage of black students in 32 northern and western states (11.2 percent) attended all-black schools than did black students in the 11 southern states (9.2 percent).

Although public opinion polls indicated widespread opposition to busing as a means of integrating public school systems, it was not until 1972 that the first public referenda on the issue were held. As expected, voters in Florida, Tennessee, and California overwhelmingly voiced their opposition to busing, although the elections had no binding effect. Congress passed an anti-busing bill in July over administration protests that it was too weak and ineffectual. By November, Supreme Court justices had four times ruled that the bill's moratorium on new busing orders designed to achieve racial balance did not apply to court orders written to correct unlawful segregation.

Welfare. Welfare expenditures by the states resumed their upward rise in 1972, reversing a brief leveling trend in the relief rolls of the previous year. On Jan. 24, the U.S. Supreme Court voided one-year residency requirements for welfare eligibility in New York and Connecticut; those states, along with Hawaii, Illinois, and Rhode Island, had approved the one-year standard in hopes of discouraging the influx of migrant poor and easing the mounting burden on state treasuries. A number of states, including New York, California, Ohio, and Hawaii, adopted some form of work requirement for able-bodied welfare recipients.

On two occasions, the federal government moved to cut back on intergovernmental welfare assistance to those states, usually in the North, that provide highest monthly welfare allowances. One attempt, an announced ceiling on payments under the federal food stamp program, was abandoned in January in the face of protests from northern officials. As part of the revenue-sharing bill approved by Congress in October, a limit of $2.5 billion in federal aid to states for various social service programs was imposed. The limit was a severe blow to larger states such as New York, which had expected to receive more than three times the $223 million it was allocated under the new bill.

Mental Health. A federal court in Alabama declared in March that inmates of mental hospitals have a constitutional right to medical treatment, and wrote 76 detailed guidelines for treatment at the state's three institutions for the mentally ill. The court had previously declared that patients had a constitutional right to psychiatric treatment and not merely custodial care. But the new ruling ordered the state to provide more staff, a reduction in patient population, control of use of behaviour-modifying drugs, and correction of health and fire hazards at a state hospital. At year's end, the order was being appealed.

On Nov. 29, a federal court jury in Tallahassee, Fla., awarded $38,500 in damages to a former mental patient who charged he was locked up in a state mental hospital for 15 years without psychiatric treatment. The suit was expected to spur more states into improving mental health care services.

Law and Justice. Three U.S. Supreme Court opinions issued in spring, 1972, sent ripples through the judicial systems of most states. One found the death penalty as administered in the U.S. to be unconstitutional; another dramatically broadened the right to free legal counsel for persons accused of misdemeanors; and the third held that state laws allowing less-than-unanimous jury verdicts were unconstitutional.

The death penalty decision was significant even though states had ceased executing prisoners in 1967 while awaiting the Supreme Court ruling. When the 5 to 4 verdict was announced at the end of June, 35 states had accumulated 631 prisoners on death row. At year's end, it appeared that all prisoners then under death sentence would have their proposed punishments voided. None could be executed under new laws, either, because such statutes could not be made retroactive. California voters were first to voice endorsement of such a law, declaring in a November referendum by a 2 to 1 margin that capital punishment should be revived. The Florida legislature approved a new capital punishment law in December. But arguments still raged over whether any death penalty statute could pass Supreme Court muster, and in the meantime, at least 17 states closed down their death row facilities and began integrating condemned prisoners with the general penal population.

A unanimous court determined in *Argersinger* v. *Hamlin* that no defendant can be jailed for any offense, no matter how minor, unless he had been represented by a lawyer at trial. An estimated 4 to 5 million misdemeanor defendants are brought annually into state courts, and court experts estimated that lawyers will now be required for about one million charged with the most serious crimes.

A 5 to 4 decision in *Apodaca* v. *Oregon* upheld laws that allow juries in state prosecutions to convict defendants by as close as a 9 to 3 vote. A previous court decision allowed six-man juries in some trials. Only four states had laws allowing less-than-unanimous juries in 1972, and no new laws were approved in the wake of the Supreme Court decision. However, voters in November referenda in Connecticut, Arizona, and Oregon approved measures allowing six-man juries.

In other legal developments, the California electorate rejected, by 2 to 1, a constitutional amendment that would have legalized the private use (but not the sale) of marijuana. Backers of the defeated referendum expressed satisfaction, however, because it received more than one million votes.

Abortion. The controversy over state anti-abortion laws continued, and at year's end it appeared that the U.S. Supreme Court was preparing to issue nationwide guidelines on a woman's right to abort an unwanted pregnancy.

Vermont's abortion law, enacted in 1846, was declared unconstitutional by the Vermont Supreme Court Jan. 14. Federal courts in Connecticut and New Jersey later voided strict abortion laws in those states, but the effective dates of the orders were stayed pending a decision on similar questions by the U.S. Supreme Court. Florida enacted a liberalized abortion law in April, permitting the procedure when a mother's health is threatened, and New York Gov. Nelson

Rockefeller vetoed a legislative repeal of the state's 1970 statute. The New York law, most liberal in the nation, allows a woman to have abortion on demand through the 24th week of pregnancy.

The U.S. Supreme Court had heard oral arguments on abortion cases from Texas and Georgia in December, 1971, while only seven justices were seated. The ruling on the case was expected in June, but instead, the court announced it would rehear the cases in October with a full nine-man court in attendance. The cases were again argued Oct. 10 but by the end of the year the court had not announced its verdict on the constitutionality of state abortion laws.

Legal Gambling. The trend toward liberalizing gambling restrictions accelerated during 1972, with six states taking affirmative action on lotteries, off-track betting, and other forms of gambling. In most cases, the moves were designed both to raise revenue and to cut into illicit gambling profits.

Pennsylvania, Massachusetts, and Connecticut initiated statewide, government-run lotteries in 1972, joining similar systems already in effect in New Hampshire, New Jersey, and New York. (A private nonprofit group conducts a legal lottery in South Dakota.) Michigan, Maryland, Iowa, and Colorado approved lottery referenda during 1972, and officials moved to start lottery systems there before mid-1973.

Montana's new constitution provided for legalized gambling; the forms are to be determined by the state legislature in future sessions. New York's legislature gave preliminary approval to casino-style gambling, but the measure must pass a final legislative vote and gain statewide voter endorsement in 1973 before it would become effective. As the lotteries proved themselves, officials began eyeing off-track betting (Schenectady, N.Y. in July joined New York City in establishing an off-track wager system) and the individually-selected numbers game as possible avenues to government-run gambling expansion. New Jersey initiated a daily lottery in November.

Drugs. State efforts to solve drug-abuse problems received a major boost from the federal government in January with the creation of the Office of Drug Abuse Law Enforcement. The new agency quickly supervised creation of a nationwide network of special prosecutors, investigators, and grand juries to help state and local law enforcement personnel in combating drug dealers.

New surveys indicated the drug problem continued to increase. A February Gallup poll revealed that 51 percent of college students had tried marijuana at least once, and 18 percent had experimented with "mind-expanding" drugs. The federal government estimated in June that the nation's heroin addict population stood at 560,000, more than double the estimate of 1969.

The trend toward reducing penalties for marijuana possession, increasing them for drug pushing, and tightening anti-heroin laws continued in 1972. New Mexico, Maine, Michigan, Hawaii, and Mississippi were among states adopting similar legislation during the year.

Environment. Nearly 30 states approved new measures dealing with environmental problems, a marked increase from 1971. Land use received the most attention, with a wide array of new controls over subdivisions, natural areas, wetlands, and strip mining, but significant new legislation was also adopted covering air and water pollution, dredging, protection of endangered species, noise, and solid wastes.

Montana's new constitution and amendments approved by Massachusetts and North Carolina established life in a clean environment as a basic constitutional right of all citizens. Colorado and New Mexico passed new laws to limit subdivision development, and Florida and Virginia moved to protect areas threatened by commercial and residential growth. Connecticut, Virginia, and Michigan approved laws to preserve wetlands and primitive tracts in their natural state. Maryland banned strip mining on state-owned land; additional controls over strip mining were imposed in Ohio, Tennessee, and West Virginia.

Michigan, New Hampshire, and Pennsylvania tightened air pollution laws, while Alabama, Mississippi, Florida, Missouri, Wisconsin, Oklahoma, and Hawaii gave extra teeth to both air and water pollution regulations. New environmental protection departments were established in Kentucky, Ohio, and Iowa, and environmental advisory councils were established or given additional power in several other states, including Louisiana, Virginia, Missouri, Indiana, and West Virginia.

New Jersey set up new standards for noise pollution control. Virginia adopted two measures designed to limit population growth by facilitating voluntary sterilization and encouraging birth control, and Colorado established a population advisory commission to consider long-term growth policy. Hawaii created a novel commission to recommend annual limits on automobile populations on each state island.

Oregon's law banning metal pull-top caps and requiring deposits on beer and soft-drink containers went into effect in October despite loud protests from bottlers and brewers. The Vermont legislature passed a similar law providing for a tax on nonreturnable containers until July 1, 1973, when nonreturnables will be prohibited.

A controversial initiative measure in California, which would have regulated vehicle fuel, industrial pollution, pesticides, banned most off-shore oil and gas drilling, and placed a five-year ban on nuclear power plant construction, was defeated 2 to 1 by voters in June. But in November, the California electorate approved an ambitious coastal protection measure over strong opposition from oil and real estate groups; the new act will impose strict zoning on coastal property as far as five miles inland and set up a new commission with authority to veto all new development within 1,000 yards of the entire 1,087-mile California coastline.

Environmentalists also won a major victory in Colorado when voters in November banned use of state and Denver city funds for the 1976 Winter Olympic games. Nearly $2 million had been spent on the games before a combination of the killings at the 1972 Munich Summer Olympics, the threat of unwanted development in mountain areas, plus the heavy financial expense, caused voters to reject the games.

New York voters approved $1.15 billion in new bonding authority for pollution control, including $650 million for water quality projects, $150 million for cleaner air, and $350 million for land preservation. Florida voters allocated up to $240 million in new bonds to acquire endangered natural lands and turn them into parks. Washington approved $265 million in new environmental and anti-pollution bonds.

Maryland decreed that littering from automobiles be a "moving violation" on a driver's record, possibly contributing to higher insurance rates. Illinois and South Carolina banned sale of products made from endangered species; Wisconsin authorized state officials to outlaw killing of endangered local species.

The first joint meeting between top federal and state environmental officials was held in Washington Mar. 15–18, sponsored by the Council of State Governments and the President's Council on Environmental Quality. More than 300 state government and 50 federal environmental leaders attended the National Symposium on State Environmental Legislation to draw up model bills for future legislative consideration.

Consumer Protection. Spurred by largely-favorable results from Massachusetts, which in 1971 became the first state to inaugurate a full-fledged system, no-fault automobile insurance continued to make headway in the states. By the end of the year, legislatures in Connecticut, Maryland, New Jersey, and South Dakota had approved some form of no-fault; five other states had previously adopted a no-fault legislation version.

The Massachusetts experiment, started in January, 1971, seemed to please virtually everyone except some accident victims and their trial attorneys. Insurance premiums for personal injury liability dropped by 42.6 percent for 1972 compared with 1970; without no-fault, estimates were that premiums would have jumped 25–30 percent in the same period. The number of bodily injury claims fell 48 percent, and insurance companies continued to make adequate profits.

The U.S. Senate considered imposing mandatory federal no-fault insurance standards upon the states before shelving the proposal for the year Aug. 8 in a 49–46 vote. The Senate bill, sponsored by Sens. Philip Hart (D-Mich.) and Warren Magnuson (D-Wash.) would have required states to enact minimum no-fault auto insurance legislation or else be subjected to federal no-fault guidelines. None of the state plans enacted through 1972 would have satisfied the bill's minimum standards.

Other consumer legislation continued to make progress in state legislatures. Twelve states approved new laws covering a variety of consumer frauds and deceptive practices. Ohio, Kentucky, and Wisconsin enacted "cooling-off periods" for buyers from door-to-door salesmen; the new laws allow cancellation of purchases within a few days without penalty.

David Cameron Beckwith

Area and Population

Area and population of the states

State	AREA in sq. mi. Total	Inland water*	POPULATION (000) July 1, 1970	July 1, 1971†	Percent change 1970–71
Alabama	51,609	549	3,451	3,479	0.8
Alaska	586,400	15,335	305	313	2.7
Arizona	113,909	334	1,792	1,849	3.1
Arkansas	53,104	605	1,926	1,944	0.9
California	158,693	2,120	19,994	20,223	1.1
Colorado	104,247	363	2,225	2,283	2.6
Connecticut	5,009	110	3,039	3,081	1.4
Delaware	2,057	79	550	558	1.3
Dist. of Columbia	69	8	753	741	−1.5
Florida	58,560	4,308	6,845	7,041	2.8
Georgia	58,876	602	4,602	4,664	1.4
Hawaii	6,424	9	774	789	2.0
Idaho	83,557	849	717	732	2.1
Illinois	56,400	470	11,137	11,196	0.5
Indiana	36,291	106	5,208	5,274	1.3
Iowa	56,290	258	2,830	2,852	0.8
Kansas	82,264	216	2,248	2,258	0.4
Kentucky	40,395	532	3,224	3,282	1.8
Louisiana	48,523	3,417	3,644	3,681	1.0
Maine	33,215	2,203	995	1,003	0.7
Maryland	10,577	703	3,937	4,000	1.6
Massachusetts	8,257	390	5,699	5,758	1.0
Michigan	58,216	1,197	8,901	8,997	1.1
Minnesota	84,068	4,059	3,822	3,881	1.5
Mississippi	47,716	493	2,216	2,226	0.5
Missouri	69,686	548	4,693	4,749	1.2
Montana	147,138	1,402	697	708	1.6
Nebraska	77,227	615	1,490	1,512	1.5
Nevada	110,540	752	493	507	2.8
New Hampshire	9,304	290	742	762	2.8
New Jersey	7,836	315	7,195	7,300	1.4
New Mexico	121,666	156	1,018	1,030	1.2
New York	49,576	1,637	18,260	18,391	0.7
North Carolina	52,712	3,645	5,091	5,146	1.1
North Dakota	70,665	1,208	618	625	1.0
Ohio	41,222	250	10,688	10,778	0.8
Oklahoma	69,919	1,032	2,572	2,610	1.5
Oregon	96,981	733	2,102	2,158	2.7
Pennsylvania	45,333	326	11,817	11,879	0.5
Rhode Island	1,214	156	951	960	0.9
South Carolina	31,055	783	2,596	2,627	1.2
South Dakota	77,047	669	666	670	0.6
Tennessee	42,244	482	3,932	3,990	1.5
Texas	267,338	4,499	11,254	11,460	1.8
Utah	84,916	2,577	1,069	1,099	2.9
Vermont	9,609	333	447	458	2.5
Virginia	40,815	977	4,653	4,714	1.3
Washington	68,192	1,483	3,414	3,449	1.0
West Virginia	24,181	102	1,746	1,752	0.3
Wisconsin	56,154	1,449	4,433	4,476	1.0
Wyoming	97,914	503	334	340	1.9
TOTAL U.S.	3,615,210	66,237	203,805	206,256	1.2

*Excludes the Great Lakes and coastal waters.
†Preliminary.
Source: U.S. Department of Commerce, Bureau of the Census, *Statistical Abstract of the United States.*

Population change

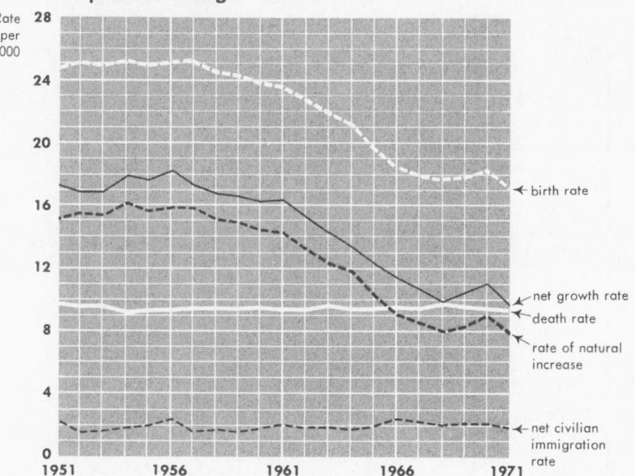

Source: U.S. Department of Commerce, Bureau of the Census, *Current Population Reports.*

Marriage and divorce rates

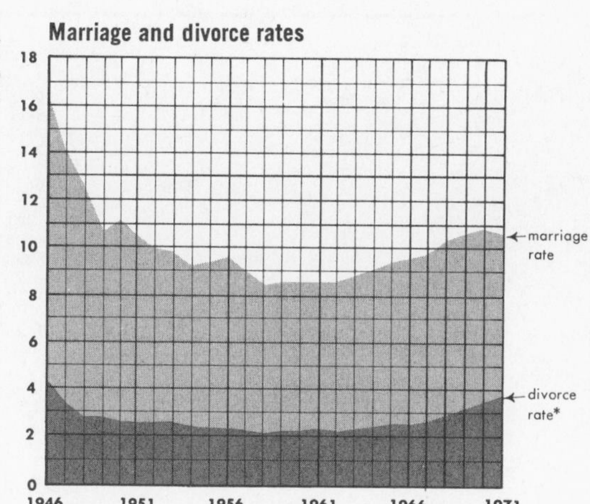

All rates are based on population excluding Armed Forces abroad, except 1946 divorce rate which includes Armed Forces abroad.
*Includes annulments.
Source: U.S. Department of Health, Education, and Welfare, Public Health Service, *Monthly Vital Statistics Report.*

State population characteristics, 1970

percent distribution

State	1970 census population	SEX Male	Female	RACE White	Nonwhite	RESIDENCE Urban	Rural
Alabama	3,444,165	48.25	51.75	73.6	26.4	58.4	41.6
Alaska	300,382	54.35	45.65	78.8	21.2	48.4	51.6
Arizona	1,770,900	49.18	50.82	90.6	9.4	79.6	20.4
Arkansas	1,923,295	48.47	51.53	81.4	18.6	50.0	50.0
California	19,953,134	49.20	50.80	89.0	11.0	90.9	9.1
Colorado	2,207,259	49.35	50.65	95.7	4.3	78.5	21.5
Connecticut	3,031,709	48.50	51.50	93.5	6.5	77.4	22.6
Delaware	548,104	48.77	51.23	85.1	14.9	72.2	27.8
Dist. of Columbia	756,510	46.46	53.54	27.7	72.3	100.0	—
Florida	6,789,443	48.25	51.75	84.2	15.8	80.5	19.5
Georgia	4,589,575	48.60	51.40	73.9	26.1	60.3	39.7
Hawaii	768,561	51.94	48.06	38.8	61.2	83.1	16.9
Idaho	712,567	49.93	50.07	98.1	1.9	54.1	45.9
Illinois	11,113,976	48.51	51.49	86.4	13.6	83.0	17.0
Indiana	5,193,669	48.74	51.26	92.8	7.2	64.9	35.1
Iowa	2,824,376	48.61	51.39	98.5	1.5	57.2	42.8
Kansas	2,246,578	49.03	50.97	94.5	5.5	66.1	33.9
Kentucky	3,218,706	49.06	50.94	92.6	7.4	52.3	47.7
Louisiana	3,641,306	48.65	51.35	69.8	30.2	66.1	33.9
Maine	992,048	48.67	51.33	99.3	0.7	50.8	49.2
Maryland	3,922,399	48.86	51.14	81.5	18.5	76.6	23.4
Massachusetts	5,689,170	47.80	52.20	96.3	3.7	84.6	15.4
Michigan	8,875,083	49.00	51.00	88.3	11.7	73.8	26.2
Minnesota	3,804,971	48.98	51.02	98.2	1.8	66.4	33.6
Mississippi	2,216,912	48.46	51.54	62.8	37.2	44.5	55.5
Missouri	4,676,501	48.24	51.76	89.3	10.7	70.1	29.9
Montana	694,409	49.97	50.03	95.5	4.5	53.4	46.6
Nebraska	1,483,493	48.83	51.17	96.6	3.4	61.5	38.5
Nevada	488,738	50.70	49.30	91.7	8.3	80.9	19.1
New Hampshire	737,681	48.89	51.11	99.4	0.6	56.4	43.6
New Jersey	7,168,164	48.37	51.63	88.6	11.4	88.9	11.1
New Mexico	1,016,000	49.29	50.71	90.1	9.9	69.8	30.2
New York	18,236,967	47.79	52.21	86.8	13.2	85.6	14.4
North Carolina	5,082,059	48.96	51.04	76.8	23.2	45.0	55.0
North Dakota	617,761	50.44	49.56	97.0	3.0	44.3	55.7
Ohio	10,652,017	48.47	51.53	90.6	9.4	75.3	24.7
Oklahoma	2,559,229	48.70	51.30	89.1	10.9	68.0	32.0
Oregon	2,091,385	48.96	51.04	97.2	2.8	67.1	32.9
Pennsylvania	11,793,909	48.04	51.96	91.0	9.0	71.5	28.5
Rhode Island	946,725	49.04	50.96	96.6	3.4	87.1	12.9
South Carolina	2,590,516	49.11	50.89	69.3	30.7	47.6	52.4
South Dakota	665,507	49.59	50.41	94.7	5.3	44.6	55.4
Tennessee	3,923,687	48.36	51.64	83.9	16.1	58.8	41.2
Texas	11,196,730	48.95	51.05	86.8	13.2	79.7	20.3
Utah	1,059,273	49.40	50.60	97.4	2.6	80.4	19.6
Vermont	444,330	48.87	51.13	99.6	0.4	32.2	67.8
Virginia	4,648,494	49.42	50.58	80.9	19.1	63.1	36.9
Washington	3,409,169	49.68	50.32	95.4	4.6	72.6	27.4
West Virginia	1,744,237	48.43	51.57	95.9	4.1	39.0	61.0
Wisconsin	4,417,731	49.06	50.94	96.4	3.6	65.9	34.1
Wyoming	332,416	50.17	49.83	97.2	2.8	60.5	39.5
TOTAL U.S.	203,211,926	48.67	51.33	87.5	12.5	73.5	26.5

Source: U.S. Department of Commerce, Bureau of the Census, *1970 Census of Population.*

Characteristics of family heads, 1971

percent distribution, by age of head

Characteristics	under 25	25–34	35–44	45–54	55–64	65 and over
All families	7.2	20.5	20.9	21.3	16.3	13.8
White head						
male, married, wife present	89.2	91.1	89.6	87.7	88.5	82.5
wife in paid labor force	47.9	37.5	41.0	46.0	38.5	15.6
female	8.9	7.6	8.7	9.8	9.0	13.4
Negro head						
male, married, wife present	54.7	64.1	64.5	67.2	71.3	69.3
wife in paid labor force	51.1	59.4	63.4	57.7	50.2	26.0
female	41.8	34.5	31.7	28.0	24.7	23.9
Family size						
Two persons	44.9	13.9		40.5		79.6
Three persons	34.7	18.7		22.9		12.8
Four persons or more	20.4	67.4		36.6		7.6
Education completed*						
Elementary		20.4	24.9	30.1	36.8	40.0
High school		57.4	49.1	45.5	34.7	19.9
College		18.1	17.3	13.1	10.4	7.9

*Limited to families with head 25 years old and over.
Source: U.S. Department of Commerce, Bureau of the Census, *Current Population Reports.*

Largest cities

City	Population 1970 census	Land area in sq. mi.	Population per sq. mi.	% nonwhite population 1960	% nonwhite population 1970
New York, New York	7,894,862	299.7	26,343	14.7	23.4
Chicago, Illinois	3,366,957	222.6	15,126	23.6	34.4
Los Angeles, California	2,816,061	463.7	6,073	16.8	22.8
Philadelphia, Pennsylvania	1,948,609	128.5	15,164	26.7	34.4
Detroit, Michigan	1,511,482	138.0	10,953	29.2	44.5
Houston, Texas	1,232,802	433.9	2,842	23.2	26.6
Baltimore, Maryland	905,759	78.3	11,568	35.0	47.0
Dallas, Texas	844,401	265.6	3,179	19.3	25.8
Washington, Dist. of Columbia	756,510	61.4	12,321	54.8	72.3
Cleveland, Ohio	750,903	75.9	9,893	28.9	39.0
Indianapolis, Indiana	744,624	383.9	1,940	20.7	18.4
Milwaukee, Wisconsin	717,099	95.0	7,548	8.9	15.6
San Francisco, California	715,674	45.4	15,764	18.4	28.6
San Diego, California	696,769	316.9	2,199	7.8	11.1
San Antonio, Texas	654,153	184.0	3,555	7.4	8.6
Boston, Massachusetts	641,071	46.0	13,936	9.8	18.2
Memphis, Tennessee	623,530	217.4	2,868	37.1	39.2
St. Louis, Missouri	622,236	61.2	10,167	28.8	41.3
New Orleans, Louisiana	593,471	197.1	3,011	37.4	45.5
Phoenix, Arizona	581,562	247.9	2,346	5.8	6.7
Columbus, Ohio	539,677	134.6	4,009	16.6	19.0
Seattle, Washington	530,831	83.6	6,350	8.4	12.6
Jacksonville, Florida	528,865	765.7	691	41.2	22.9
Pittsburgh, Pennsylvania	520,117	55.2	9,422	16.8	20.7
Denver, Colorado	514,678	95.2	5,406	7.1	11.0
Kansas City, Missouri	507,087	316.3	1,603	17.7	22.8
Atlanta, Georgia	496,973	131.5	3,779	38.3	51.6
Buffalo, New York	462,768	41.3	11,205	13.8	21.3
Cincinnati, Ohio	452,524	78.1	5,794	21.8	28.1
San Jose, California	445,779	136.2	3,273	3.3	6.4
Minneapolis, Minnesota	434,400	53.4	8,135	3.2	6.4

Source: U.S. Department of Commerce, Bureau of the Census, *1970 Census of Population.*

Church membership

Religious body	Total clergy	Inclusive membership
Adventists, Seventh-day	3,365	433,906
Baptist Bodies		
American Baptist Association	3,368	869,000
American Baptist Churches in the U.S.A.	8,222	1,562,636
Baptist General Conference	1,032	108,474
Baptist Missionary Association of America	1,800	193,439
Conservative Baptist Association of America	...	300,000
Free Will Baptists	3,374	210,000
General Baptists (General Association of)	1,115	65,000
National Baptist Convention of America	28,574	2,668,799
National Baptist Convention, U.S.A., Inc.	27,500	5,500,000
National Baptist Evangelical Life and Soul Saving Assembly of U.S.A.	137	57,674
National Primitive Baptist Convention, Inc.	601	1,645,000
North American Baptist General Conference	423	54,441
Primitive Baptists	...	72,000
Progressive National Baptist Convention, Inc.	863	521,692
Regular Baptist Churches, General Association of	...	204,357
Southern Baptist Convention	...	11,824,676
United Free Will Baptist Church	784	100,000
Brethren (German Baptists)		
Church of the Brethren	2,011	181,183
Buddhist Churches of America	101	100,000
Christian and Missionary Alliance	1,227	127,353
Christian Church (Disciples of Christ)	6,886	1,386,374
Christian Churches and Churches of Christ	7,314	1,036,288
Christian Congregation	267	51,310
Church of God (Anderson, Ind.)	3,352	152,787
Church of the Nazarene	6,774	394,197
Churches of Christ	6,200	2,400,000
Congregational Christian Churches, National Association of	391	85,000
Eastern Churches		
Albanian Orthodox Archdiocese in America	23	62,000
American Carpatho-Russian Orthodox Greek Catholic Church	67	108,000
Antiochian Orthodox Christian Archdiocese of New York and all North America	110	100,000
Armenian Apostolic Church of America	34	125,000
Armenian Church of North America, Diocese of the (including Diocese of California)	71	300,000
Bulgarian Eastern Orthodox Church	11	86,000
Greek Orthodox Archdiocese of North and South America	675	1,950,000
Orthodox Church in America	448	1,000,000
Romanian Orthodox Episcopate of America	50	50,000
Russian Orthodox Church in the U.S.A., Patriarchal Parishes of the	98	152,973
Russian Orthodox Church Outside Russia	168	55,000
Serbian Eastern Orthodox Church for the U.S.A. and Canada	64	65,000
Ukrainian Orthodox Church in America	131	87,475
Episcopal Church	11,108	3,217,365
Evangelical Covenant Church of America	671	68,428
Evangelical Free Church of America	...	70,490
Friends United Meeting	554	68,773
Independent Fundamental Churches of America	1,231	139,932
Jehovah's Witnesses	None	416,789
Jewish Congregations	6,400	6,060,000
Latter Day Saints		
Church of Jesus Christ of Latter-day Saints	17,272	2,133,072
Reorganized Church of Jesus Christ of Latter Day Saints	14,634	154,481
Lutherans		
American Lutheran Church	6,169	2,521,930
Lutheran Church in America	7,377	3,069,679
Lutheran Church—Missouri Synod	7,041	2,788,110
Wisconsin Evangelical Lutheran Synod	967	383,263
Mennonites		
Mennonite Church	2,335	88,947
Old Order (Wisler) Mennonite Church	101	81,000
Methodists		
African Methodist Episcopal Church	7,089	1,166,301
African Methodist Episcopal Zion Church	5,500	940,000
Christian Methodist Episcopal Church	2,259	466,718
Free Methodist Church of North America	1,740	65,040
United Methodist Church	34,822	10,509,198
Moravian Church in America	217	57,339
North American Old Roman Catholic Church	112	60,098
Old Roman Catholic Church (English Rite)	201	65,128
Pentecostal Assemblies		
Apostolic Overcoming Holy Church of God	350	75,000
Assemblies of God	12,037	1,078,332
Church of God	2,737	75,890
Church of God (Cleveland, Tenn.)	4,095	287,099
Church of God in Christ	4,500	425,000
Church of God in Christ, International	1,041	501,000
Church of God of Prophecy	...	51,527
International Church of the Foursquare Gospel	2,690	89,215
Pentecostal Church of God of America, Inc.	1,375	115,000
Pentecostal Holiness Church, Inc.	2,422	72,696
United Pentecostal Church	...	250,000
Polish National Catholic Church of America	144	282,411
Presbyterians		
Cumberland Presbyterian Church	633	90,368
Presbyterian Church in the U.S.	4,858	949,857
United Presbyterian Church in the U.S.A.	13,451	3,013,808
Reformed Bodies		
Christian Reformed Church	999	286,094
Reformed Church in America	1,277	369,951
Roman Catholic Church	57,778	48,390,990
Salvation Army	5,180	335,684
Spiritualists, International General Assembly	...	164,072
Triumph the Church and Kingdom of God in Christ	1,375	54,307
Unitarian Universalist Association	868	265,408
United Church of Christ	9,378	1,928,674
Wesleyan Church	2,925	84,499

Table includes churches reporting a membership of 50,000 or more and represents the latest information available.
Source: National Council of Churches, *Yearbook of American Churches, 1973.*

(CONSTANT H. JACQUET)

The Economy

Farms and farm income

State	Number of farms 1972*	Land in farms 1972* in 000 acres	CASH INCOME, 1971, IN $000: Farm marketings			Realized net income per farm 1971
			Crops	Livestock and products	Government payments	
Alabama	81,000	14,300	284,570	525,785	$ 60,901	$ 3,459
Alaska	310†	1,835†	1,532	2,952	117	2,861
Arizona	5,700	43,100	309,595	420,087	45,804	34,616
Arkansas	74,000	18,100	653,062	586,900	79,935	6,305
California	56,000	36,400	3,040,996	1,883,319	113,010	20,803
Colorado	29,500	39,000	285,281	1,063,681	53,180	7,827
Connecticut	4,300	560	66,999	98,637	493	10,722
Delaware	3,600	690	50,812	92,223	1,328	11,809
Florida	34,000	16,200	1,011,102	410,806	15,000	15,991
Georgia	75,000	16,800	557,426	701,423	63,813	5,876
Hawaii	4,100	2,340	177,552	43,125	10,414	19,208
Idaho	27,900	15,500	389,014	321,175	45,106	8,412
Illinois	123,000	29,200	1,624,279	1,174,238	176,786	6,662
Indiana	98,000	17,600	844,240	795,158	92,304	5,484
Iowa	137,000	34,400	1,295,091	2,729,789	203,510	7,452
Kansas	85,000	49,900	763,930	1,491,977	217,741	7,797
Kentucky	121,000	16,700	945,627	536,912	24,194	3,210
Louisiana	51,000	12,200	423,323	274,470	49,785	6,047
Maine	9,400	2,250	88,987	154,665	1,055	6,023
Maryland	17,500	3,150	129,841	266,696	6,307	6,062
Massachusetts	5,900	690	82,190	82,535	491	7,506
Michigan	83,000	12,900	457,273	514,042	52,532	3,022
Minnesota	119,000	31,800	829,633	1,453,565	112,414	5,766
Mississippi	91,000	17,300	491,667	524,759	124,413	5,253
Missouri	139,000	32,900	615,919	1,086,725	111,889	3,939
Montana	25,400	66,900	225,243	408,585	77,789	8,807
Nebraska	71,000	48,100	718,701	1,524,108	$171,040	$ 7,726
Nevada	2,000	9,000	13,353	75,217	1,461	10,993
New Hampshire	34,000	710	14,179	41,211	389	2,978
New Jersey	8,400	990	151,448	88,666	2,661	4,947
New Mexico	12,900	47,900	107,145	374,482	53,180	10,437
New York	56,000	11,400	315,858	807,328	16,619	5,295
North Carolina	151,000	15,800	924,976	601,504	40,998	4,176
North Dakota	41,000	42,000	554,376	299,625	140,517	7,187
Ohio	110,000	17,300	647,958	767,447	71,191	3,357
Oklahoma	89,000	37,100	269,044	858,443	112.067	3,045
Oregon	37,500	20,900	311,505	276,021	21,020	3,578
Pennsylvania	71,000	10,450	275,748	793,194	18,101	4,130
Rhode Island	800	83	10,652	9,280	57	4,602
South Carolina	49,000	7,900	287,904	178,594	44,071	3,295
South Dakota	44,500	45,500	247,705	866,735	77,824	8,013
Tennessee	123,000	15,300	327,401	419,172	49,465	1,968
Texas	184,000	144,800	1,132,267	2,121,595	468,552	5,595
Utah	13,500	13,000	43,956	179,379	10,301	4,303
Vermont	6,800	2,150	14,919	155,416	821	8,125
Virginia	69,000	11,300	266,699	351,836	14,400	2,576
Washington	44,000	17,900	558,154	291,141	54,276	5,712
West Virginia	27,000	4,900	24,978	81,723	2,645	334
Wisconsin	108,000	20,000	240,358	1,425,027	36,857	4,651
Wyoming	8,000	37,000	41,205	222,800	14,949	7,171
Total U.S.	2,831,410	1,114,198	22,608,761	30,454,173	3,144,655	5,581

*Preliminary. †Exclusive of grazing land leased from the U.S. Government, Alaska farmland totals about 70,000 acres.
Source: U.S. Department of Agriculture, Economics Research Service.

Principal crops

of the United States, 1971

State	Corn, grain (bu.)		Hay (tons)		Soybeans for beans (bu.)		Wheat (bu.)		Tobacco (lbs.)		Cotton lint (bales)		Sorghum grain (bu.)		Potatoes (cwt.)	
	Amount produced in 000	Value in $000	Amount produced in 000	Value in $000	Amount produced in 000	Value in $000	Amount produced in 000	Value in $000	Amount produced in 000	Value in $000	Amount produced in 000	Value in $000	Amount produced in 000	Value in $000	Amount produced in 000	Value in $000
Ala.	25,746	29,608	851	23,828	17,543	50,875	3,480	5,150	1,035	756	630	86,184	2,520	2,470	1,810	5,604
Alaska	...	...	...	...	...	...	...	...	...	...	...	...	...	...	...	...
Ariz.	448	578	1,272	40,704	...	...	11,764	20,234	...	...	505	74,856	12,702	16,767	2,828	7,749
Ark.	1,517	1,896	1,263	32,207	91,719	275,157	9,639	13,880	...	...	1,220	161,040	12,032	12,032	91	382
Calif.	24,816	36,728	8,271	256,401	...	...	19,965	31,832	...	...	1,121	169,536	28,755	38,532	26,400	57,513
Colo.	34,916	40,153	3,228	91,998	...	...	70,920	84,409	...	...	...	...	10,624	10,624	10,330	18,059
Conn.	...	...	226	10,170	...	...	...	...	7,644	23,845	...	...	...	...	1,081	3,027
Del.	10,800	12,744	68	2,584	4,256	12,555	975	1,404	...	...	...	...	...	...	1,400	3,570
Fla.	17,297	18,508	343	11,319	5,796	17,098	2,010	2,915	24,946	26,359	11	1,503	...	...	4,862	19,438
Ga.	85,792	98,661	973	30,650	16,193	46,960	8,170	11,847	115,119	91,054	360	48,384	2,760	2,318	...	...
Hawaii	...	...	...	...	...	...	...	...	...	...	...	...	...	...	...	...
Ida.	2,407	3,201	3,804	98,904	...	...	50,623	67,119	...	...	...	...	...	...	75,850	135,569
Ill.	1,037,340	1,099,580	3,277	83,564	235,950	707,850	43,252	60,553	...	...	1	100	12,750	11,730	310	713
Ind.	534,373	539,717	2,228	55,700	113,130	333,734	33,075	43,990	13,230	10,584	...	...	5,400	5,616	1,756	4,325
Iowa	1,180,140	1,215,544	6,941	142,291	174,080	513,536	1,332	1,772	...	...	...	...	8,500	7,650	656	1,181
Kan.	120,612	133,879	5,255	126,120	17,856	51,782	312,605	406,387	...	...	...	...	233,550	217,202	124	279
Ky.	94,402	102,898	3,241	95,610	21,889	64,573	7,600	11,096	380,278	288,604	5	620	2,470	1,902	168	680
La.	4,320	5,530	553	13,825	37,812	113,436	1,035	1,584	170	139	575	78,660	3,360	3,192	189	491
Me.	...	...	478	16,730	...	...	...	...	...	...	...	...	...	...	37,700	69,745
Md.	36,000	42,120	688	24,424	6,510	19,205	4,400	6,424	29,680	23,328	...	...	...	...	375	879
Mass.	...	...	240	10,080	...	...	...	...	2,560	8,463	...	...	...	...	966	2,463
Mich.	115,600	115,600	2,835	75,128	11,070	33,210	20,520	27,702	...	...	...	...	...	...	8,241	20,870
Minn.	475,175	465,672	8,336	158,384	65,573	193,440	57,014	78,581	...	...	...	...	...	...	16,725	23,860
Miss.	10,608	13,154	1,231	30,775	54,257	162,771	5,130	7,695	...	...	1,675	225,120	6,900	6,348	170	510
Mo.	272,096	296,585	5,299	129,826	97,335	287,138	34,344	48,082	5,460	4,313	405	52,488	47,700	47,700	84	252
Mont.	532	692	3,928	98,200	...	...	112,011	136,700	...	...	...	...	...	...	1,326	4,243
Neb.	455,260	500,786	7,046	147,966	16,000	46,400	107,436	134,295	...	...	...	...	125,160	111,392	2,171	2,520
Nev.	...	...	919	26,192	...	...	625	936	...	...	2	230	...	...	...	...
N.H.	...	...	209	8,987	...	...	...	...	...	...	...	...	...	...	175	490
N.J.	5,200	6,188	316	12,798	1,428	3,998	1,551	2,202	...	...	...	...	...	...	2,750	6,738
N.M.	935	1,234	1,092	37,674	...	...	4,000	5,600	...	...	145	22,104	24,131	26,303	480	1,320
N.Y.	24,648	27,852	5,729	166,141	147	404	5,200	6,968	...	...	...	...	...	...	15,180	39,279
N.C.	86,640	98,770	592	20,720	22,464	64,022	11,610	16,951	728,790	565,126	130	18,096	6,000	6,060	2,060	4,843
N.D.	9,976	10,076	4,435	70,960	2,912	8,299	285,231	359,639	...	...	...	...	...	...	18,445	26,376
Ohio	313,814	326,367	3,180	79,500	76,067	228,201	42,674	57,610	20,325	14,845	...	...	...	...	2,858	8,429
Okla.	5,166	6,354	3,189	89,292	3,150	8,820	69,500	98,690	...	...	180	23,760	27,000	28,620	...	...
Ore.	960	1,344	2,388	72,834	...	...	34,500	48,621	...	...	...	...	...	...	13,998	26,477
Penn.	77,700	99,456	4,351	130,530	928	2,691	10,296	15,341	31,025	11,169	...	...	...	...	8,165	22,046
R.I.	...	...	23	1,104	...	...	...	...	...	...	...	...	...	...	1,344	3,360
S.C.	24,516	29,419	364	11,466	22,511	65,282	5,040	7,308	132,300	100,283	270	37,584	1,209	1,185	...	...
S.D.	123,234	128,163	5,691	96,747	5,040	14,868	68,768	90,769	...	...	...	...	12,985	11,297	1,053	1,790
Tenn.	37,125	43,436	2,038	59,102	33,852	98,171	8,750	12,863	113,160	84,462	530	69,960	3,869	3,134	390	1,619
Tex.	43,056	57,695	4,114	123,420	2,781	8,065	31,416	45,867	...	...	2,782	356,866	303,004	351,485	3,779	12,601
Utah	...	...	1,546	44,061	...	...	6,278	8,690	...	...	...	...	...	...	928	2,042
Vt.	...	...	964	37,596	...	...	...	...	...	...	...	...	...	...	264	713
Va.	31,348	38,245	1,766	64,459	8,296	24,058	8,360	11,871	121,570	92,812	2	255	1,968	1,811	4,318	11,073
Wash.	6,864	9,266	2,385	67,973	...	...	118,921	162,922	...	...	...	...	...	...	30,110	42,252
W. Va.	3,599	4,355	924	30,492	...	...	429	669	2,960	2,353	...	...	...	...	287	1,062
Wis.	203,603	225,999	10,950	224,475	2,816	8,307	1,685	2,141	21,060	10,762	...	...	...	...	13,183	28,682
Wyo.	1,672	2,240	1,914	48,807	...	...	7,382	8,402	...	...	...	...	...	...	703	1,336
TOTAL U.S.	5,540,253	5,890,293	130,954	3,332,718	1,169,361	3,464,906	1,639,516	2,167,711	1,751,312	1,359,257	10,548	1,427,346	895,349	925,370	316,083	626,450

Source: U.S. Department of Agriculture, Statistical Reporting Service, Crop Reporting Board, *Crop Production and Crop Values*.

Principal manufactures, 1970

monetary figures in millions of dollars

Industry	LABOR Employees (000)	Labor costs	Cost of materials	Value added by manufacture	Value of industry shipments
Food and tobacco manufactures: meat products	317.3	$2,635.7	$20,620.8	$4,372.3	$25,038.9
Dairy products	204.4	1,657.9	10,016.4	3,744.1	13,733.5
Beverages	229.6	2,098.4	6,260.8	5,926.6	12,152.7
Canned, cured, frozen foods	267.8	1,659.8	6,734.3	4,250.1	10,968.2
Grain mill products	112.7	1,015.8	7,440.8	3,340.7	10,759.6
Bakery products	255.1	2,143.8	3,172.0	3,987.6	7,152.8
Cigars, cigarettes	54.3	419.7	1,619.4	2,259.7	3,878.7
Confectionery, sugar	135.5	855.3	3,606.4	2,382.8	6,960.4
Textiles and apparel: textile mill products	921.6	5,579.9	13,034.6	9,251.0	22,338.7
Women's, children's wear	600.9	2,986.4	5,039.1	5,177.9	10,131.1
Knitting mills	254.9	1,390.2	3,244.6	2,346.5	5,586.0
Men's, boys' furnishings	333.2	1,599.9	2,840.4	2,685.8	5,509.6
Yarn, thread mills	127.4	706.6	1,999.8	1,183.0	3,183.0
Floor covering mills	53.0	360.7	1,531.4	824.1	2,357.3
Textile finishing, except wool	75.0	526.2	1,119.6	823.6	1,960.9
Lumber and wood products	358.5	2,490.5	5,050.9	3,808.9	8,823.7
Furniture and fixtures	350.6	2,304.8	3,369.6	3,775.6	7,121.1
Paper and allied products: paperboard containers, boxes	224.4	1,873.6	3,786.0	3,096.8	6,878.8
Papermills, except building paper	137.8	1,484.4	3,047.4	2,651.9	5,674.0
Paperboard mills	67.0	730.0	1,754.8	1,648.8	3,388.6
Printing and publishing: commercial printing	357.7	3,220.9	3,129.0	4,929.2	8,046.2
Newspapers	350.6	3,047.4	1,773.6	5,213.6	6,990.9
Books	102.7	927.3	1,138.8	2,321.5	3,376.6
Periodicals	76.9	762.4	1,210.6	1,930.6	3,157.9
Petro-chemicals and allied products: petroleum refining	108.5	1,340.3	18,226.1	4,561.0	22,737.9
Industrial chemicals	252.2	2,862.4	7,372.1	8,621.1	15,895.2
Plastic materials, synthetics	187.4	1,868.5	4,239.2	4,630.0	8,785.7
Soap, cleaners, toiletries	109.0	1,013.9	3,191.0	5,092.7	8,183.5
Drugs	130.7	1,470.3	1,659.5	5,203.9	6,792.8
Tires, inner tubes	103.2	1,161.8	2,276.1	2,364.6	4,587.2
Paints, allied products	70.1	652.6	1,837.5	1,611.7	3,407.8
Agricultural chemicals	40.7	334.7	1,608.2	1,006.3	2,615.8
Leather and leather goods	226.6	1,247.9	1,845.8	2,077.8	3,941.4
Nonmetallic mineral products: concrete, gypsum, plaster products	185.4	1,536.3	2,963.3	2,994.0	5,911.3
Glass, glassware	119.4	1,034.7	959.6	1,979.5	2,915.9
Primary metal manufactures: blast furnace, basic steel products	604.1	6,860.5	14,661.2	10,721.1	25,031.7
Nonferrous rolling, drawing	192.9	1,897.2	8,172.2	3,445.0	11,566.8
Primary nonferrous metals	65.5	703.2	4,358.5	1,864.8	6,055.8
Iron, steel foundries	225.0	2,138.5	1,854.3	2,844.5	4,694.4
Nonferrous foundries	85.6	735.9	914.4	1,092.5	1,998.1
Fabricated metal products: fabricated structural metal products	387.4	3,261.8	6,034.1	5,677.7	11,684.3
Metal stampings	215.0	2,273.8	3,111.4	3,356.7	6,453.5
Cutlery, handtools, hardware	154.9	1,357.4	1,544.3	2,515.5	3,988.9
Metal cans	71.0	763.1	2,362.7	1,638.9	3,912.7
Screw machine products, bolts, etc.	107.8	1,000.3	1,091.6	1,618.6	2,694.4
Valves, pipe fittings	97.1	912.2	1,153.4	1,587.8	2,678.7
Plumbing, heating, nonelectric	69.4	594.7	1,074.1	1,053.8	2,091.3
Machinery, except electrical: construction, related machinery	281.4	2,823.1	4,602.7	4,929.7	9,367.6
General industrial machinery	278.4	2,721.1	3,144.4	4,551.0	7,590.3
Office, computing machines	225.3	2,324.6	3,248.7	4,373.2	7,518.0
Metalworking machinery	311.3	3,328.1	2,527.1	4,914.9	7,505.5
Service industry machines	160.5	1,436.3	3,123.7	2,701.0	5,718.0
Special industry machinery	202.6	1,949.3	2,287.8	3,137.8	5,371.1
Engines, turbines	116.2	1,316.9	2,297.1	2,307.7	4,464.7
Farm machinery	124.6	1,143.5	2,352.3	2,038.4	4,367.3
Electrical equipment and supplies: communication equipment	545.3	5,650.6	4,999.4	8,286.5	13,287.1
Electronic components, accessories	354.9	2,940.0	2,970.8	4,401.1	7,224.2
Household appliances	174.3	1,501.3	3,140.0	3,044.7	6,052.9
Electrical industrial apparatus	198.3	1,793.8	2,019.3	2,986.3	4,931.4
Electrical lighting, wiring equipment	171.5	1,364.3	2,005.1	2,720.4	4,665.8
Electric test, distributing equipment	176.7	1,567.1	1,855.0	2,811.6	4,592.7
Radio, TV receiving equipment	108.7	818.5	2,324.7	1,671.6	4,032.3
Transportation equipment: motor vehicles, equipment	720.2	8,255.5	28,171.0	14,523.8	42,536.9
Aircraft, parts	644.9	7,763.3	8,904.4	10,303.2	19,992.8
Ship, boat building	160.8	1,493.5	1,313.0	1,904.9	3,207.6
Railroad equipment	54 0	559.4	1,307.1	833.3	2,159.6
Instruments and related products: photographic equipment, supplies	92.7	1,081.9	1,268.3	3,147.6	4,372.5
Mechanical measuring, control devices	103.6	930.5	735.0	1,556.3	2,249.6
Medical instruments, supplies	77.9	644.7	778.4	1,345.6	2,114.0
Miscellaneous manufactures	171.8	1,111.9	1,715.5	2,191.3	3,881.5

Source: U.S. Department of Commerce, Bureau of the Census, *Annual Survey of Manufactures.*

Commercial fishing

principal species caught

Species	QUANTITY in 000 lb. 1960	1965	1971
TOTAL	4,942,229	4,776,766	4,969,400
Menhaden	2,018,263	1,726,089	2,190,073
Salmon	235,447	326,871	312,071
Tuna	298,203	318,895	348,040
Shrimps	249,452	243,645	387,932
Crabs	221,681	335,407	276,374
Flounder	127,048	180,121	156,550
Herring, sea	239,018	110,293	87,437
Whitings	111,602	82,574	33,201
Ocean perch	150,275	111,960	70,695
Haddock	118,697	133,892	21,599
Clams	49,572	70,849	82,659
Cod	45,753	46,201	59,296
Jack mackerel	75,137	66,856	59,099
Oysters	60,010	54,688	54,585
Lobsters, Northern	31,168	30,246	33,347
Mullet	40,839	41,392	28,787
Halibut	51,202	40,825	28,651
Scup	49,229	35,870	8,938

Source: U.S. Department of Commerce, National Marine Fisheries Service, *Fisheries of the United States.*

Lumber production

in millions of board feet

Kind of wood	1965	1967	1970*
Hardwoods	7,306	7,430	7,120
Ash	141	149	148
Basswood	87	77	60
Beech	182	163	187
Birch	109	99	113
Cottonwood and aspen	198	202	229
Elm	206	200	153
Maple	786	715	735
Oak	3,356	3,424	3,270
Sweet (red and sap) gum	387	385	613
Tupelo and black gum	385	344	309
Yellow poplar	681	666	613
Other hardwoods†	788	1,006	942

Kind of wood	1965	1967	1970*
Softwoods	29,295	27,311	27,297
Cedar	633	586	633
Douglas fir	8,783	7,822	7,727
Hemlock	2,576	2,257	1,988
Ponderosa pine	3,776	3,583	3,429
Redwood	1,087	939	1,078
Southern yellow pine	6,628	6,511	6,806
Spruce	641	686	814
Sugar pine	464	495	459
White fir	2,422	2,116	2,063
White pine	1,151	1,085	1,025
Other softwoods	1,134	1,231	1,275
TOTAL	36,601	34,741	34,417

*Preliminary. †Includes estimate for western hardwoods not specified. Source: U.S. Department of Commerce, Bureau of the Census, *Current Industrial Reports;* and U.S. Department of Agriculture, Forest Service.

Principal minerals produced

in the United States and each state

Mineral (unit of production)	1970 Quantity	1970 Value in $000	1971 Quantity	1971 Value in $000
UNITED STATES		29,088,717		
Mineral fuels		20,151,703		21,258,480
Petroleum, crude (000 42-gal. bbl.)	3,371,751	10,426,680	3,453,914	11,692,998
Coal (000 short tons)				
Bituminous and lignite*	602,932	3,772,622	552,192	3,901,496
Pennsylvania anthracite	9,729	105,341	8,727	103,469
Natural gas (000,000 cu.ft.)	21,920,642	3,745,680	22,493,012	4,096,550
Natural-gas liquids (000 gal.)				
Natural gasoline and cycle products	8,664,810	603,024	8,407,602	616,657
Liquefied petroleum gases	16,783,662	672,088	17,540,628	769,397
Nonmetallic minerals, except fuels		5,711,000		6,068,020
Stone† (000 short tons)	874,512	1,474,917	875,716	1,601,391
Cement				
Portland (000 376-lb. bbl.)	381,001	1,268,718	403,621	1,421,388
Masonry (000 280-lb. bbl.)	21,275	67,537	23,860	84,556
Natural and slag (000 376-lb. bbl.)	‡	‡	‡	‡
Sand and gravel (000 short tons)	943,941	1,115,705	919,593	1,148,969
Salt (000 short tons)	45,896	304,759	44,077	303,687
Lime (000 short tons)	19,747	286,155	19,591	308,100
Clays (000 short tons)	54,853	267,912	56,666	274,431
Phosphate rock (000 long tons)	38,739	203,218	38,886	203,828
Sulfur, Frasch-process (000 long tons)	6,419	151,779	6,756	118,245
Potassium salts, K_2O equivalent (000 short tons)	2,729	98,123	2,587	100,527
Boron minerals (000 short tons)	1,041	86,827	1,047	89,856
Metals		3,914,309		
Copper, recoverable (000 short tons)	1,720	1,984,484	1,522	1,583
Iron ore, usable (000 long tons)	87,176	941,739	77,106	891,002
Molybdenum, content of concentrate (000 lb.)	110,381	190,077	97,882	164,917
Lead, recoverable (000 short tons)	572	178,609	579	159,679
Zinc, recoverable (000 short tons)	534	163,650	491	158,234
Uranium (recoverable U_3O_8) (000 lb.)	24,682	149,464	24,520	152,029
Silver, recoverable (000 troy oz.)	45,006	79,697	41,564	64,258
Gold (troy oz.)	1,743,322	63,439	1,495,108	61,673
Alabama [23]		323,245		291,492
Coal, bituminous (000 short tons)	20,560	166,308	17,499	146,180
Cement†§ (000 376-lb. bbl.)	17,841	58,715	13,996	50,938
Stone (000 short tons)	19,982	37,166	17,773	34,413
Petroleum, crude (000 42-gal. bbl.)	7,263	20,627	7,832	23,496
Lime (000 short tons)	749	10,286	761	11,454
Clays† (000 short tons)	2,748	8,213	2,915	6,913
Sand and gravel (000 short tons)	6,725	8,144	6,674	7,513
Iron ore, usable (000 long tons)	‡	‡	415	2,773
Alaska [21]		338,271		333,923
Petroleum, crude (000 42-gal. bbl.)	83,616	251,684	79,494	257,562
Sand and gravel (000 short tons)	25,825	41,092	23,617	32,806
Natural gas (000,000 cu.ft.)	111,576	27,448	121,618	28,945
Arizona [8]		1,166,767		981,020
Copper, recoverable (000 short tons)	918	1,059,277	820	852,978
Molybdenum (000 lb.)	15,672	26,700	22,684	39,872
Sand and gravel (000 short tons)	17,822	19,804	19,791	24,391
Silver, recoverable (000 troy oz.)	7,330	12,981	6,170	9,538
Stone (000 short tons)	3,511	7,094	2,873	5,848
Petroleum, crude (000 42-gal. bbl.)	1,784	5,281	1,236	3,918
Arkansas [27]		225,625		253,219
Petroleum, crude (000 42-gal. bbl.)	18,035	51,760	18,263	56,805
Natural gas (000,000 cu.ft.)	181,351	29,560	172,154	29,426
Bauxite (000 long tons)	1,869	26,293	1,781	24,979
Stone (000 short tons)	15,284	22,786	17,116	35,677
Sand and gravel (000 short tons)	13,301	16,036	11,630	15,603
California [3]		1,899,682		1,920,648
Petroleum, crude (000 42-gal. bbl.)	372,191	945,365	358,484	975,076
Natural gas (000,000 cu.ft.)	649,117	208,367	612,629	199,717
Sand and gravel (000 short tons)	140,259	174,221	115,468	157,683
Cement (000 376-lb. bbl.)	49,499	173,126	48,493	169,921
Boron minerals (000 short tons)	1,041	86,827	1,047	89,856
Stone (000 short tons)	46,399	66,950	43,336	86,255
Natural-gas liquids§ (000 gal.)	799,848	54,484	747,600	52,027
Salt, common (000 short tons)	1,656	15,053	1,887	21,142
Lime (000 short tons)	572	9,911	630	10,846
Magnesium compounds (000 short tons) MgO. equiv.	74	7,489	153	16,836
Mercury (76-lb. flasks)	18,593	7,582	18,233	3,869
Asbestos (short tons)	78,966	6,332	87,144	7,806
Colorado [18]		389,824		392,721
Molybdenum (000 lb.)	‡	‡	‡	‡
Petroleum, crude (000 42-gal. bbl.)	24,723	78,619	27,391	92,855
Coal, bituminous (000 short tons)	6,025	35,243	6,337	33,813
Sand and gravel (000 short tons)	22,261	24,190	27,000	30,155
Zinc, recoverable (000 short tons)	57	17,370	61	19,700
Uranium (recoverable U_3O_8) (000 lb.)	2,727	15,832	2,536	15,725
Natural gas (000,000 cu.ft.)	105,804	15,553	108,537	16,932
Connecticut [46]		28,383		27,961
Stone (000 short tons)	8,338	16,915	7,193	15,649
Sand and gravel (000 short tons)	6,765	9,202	6,921	10,262
Delaware [50]		1,615		2,241
Sand and gravel (000 short tons)	1,565	1,603	2,205	2,231
Florida [20]		300,042		343,731
Phosphate rock (000 long tons)	‡	‡	‡	‡
Stone† (000 short tons)	43,089	61,302	42,816	64,332
Clays (000 short tons)	872	12,661	993†	12,834†
Sand and gravel (000 short tons)	12,482	12,254	23,228	18,836
Titanium concentrate (000 short tons)	‡	‡	‡	‡
Georgia [29]		203,225		229,397
Clays (000 short tons)	5,684	110,149	5,791†	119,096†
Stone (000 short tons)	26,635	59,200	30,669	69,897
Cement§ (000 376-lb. bbl.)	‡	‡	6,791	23,940
Sand and gravel (000 short tons)	3,667	4,437	3,697	5,310
Hawaii [45]		28,965		28,107
Stone (000 short tons)	6,332	15,538	6,056	14,357
Cement (000 376-lb. bbl.)	2,162	10,334	2,051	10,627
Idaho [33]		119,759		112,280
Silver, recoverable (000 troy oz.)	19,115	33,849	19,140	29,590
Lead, recoverable (000 short tons)	61	19,121	67	18,384
Zinc, recoverable (000 short tons)	41	12,578	45	14,515
Phosphate rock (000 long tons)	‡	‡	‡	‡
Sand and gravel (000 short tons)	12,953	10,022	11,279	11,437
Illinois [11]		688,697		700,819
Coal, bituminous (000 short tons)	65,119	320,705	58,402	318,878
Petroleum, crude (000 42-gal. bbl.)	43,747	141,994	39,084	135,621
Stone (000 short tons)	55,776	86,502	61,991	106,084
Sand and gravel (000 short tons)	43,926	60,155	45,364	59,397
Cement§ (000 376-lb. bbl.)	8,324	27,126	7,966	28,311
Natural-gas liquids (000 gal.)	‡	‡	‡	‡
Fluorspar (000 short tons)	148	8,637	138	9,883
Indiana [25]		255,786		281,565
Coal, bituminous (000 short tons)	22,263	102,371	21,896	110,796
Stone (000 short tons)	25,818	45,215	26,233	48,218
Cement, portland† (000 376-lb. bbl.)	12,432	41,810	‡	‡
Sand and gravel (000 short tons)	23,476	25,796	24,982	29,094
Petroleum, crude (000 42-gal. bbl.)	7,487	23,958	6,658	22,770
Iowa [31]		120,822		—
Cement§ (000 376-lb. bbl.)	13,232	47,190	13,078	49,644
Coal, bituminous (000 short tons)	987	4,059	989	4,609
Stone (000 short tons)	25,305	41,119	25,389	44,977
Sand and gravel (000 short tons)	21,058	20,642	18,279	20,530
Gypsum (000 short tons)	1,136	4,223	1,154	4,460
Kansas [15]		583,989		589,444
Petroleum, crude (000 42-gal. bbl.)	84,853	277,469	78,532	276,433
Natural gas (000,000 cu.ft.)	899,955	125,994	885,144	127,267
Natural-gas liquids§ (000 gal.)	1,149,246	45,214	1,201,074	51,254
Helium§ (000,000 cu.ft.)	2,904	38,737	2,852	37,302
Cement§ (000 376-lb. bbl.)	9,441	29,206	9,472	31,193
Stone (000 short tons)	15,161	22,406	14,908	23,697
Salt (000 short tons)	1,230	18,206	1,240	18,712
Kentucky [9]		847,465		925,885
Coal, bituminous (000 short tons)	125,305	711,163	119,389	774,735
Stone (000 short tons)	29,310	45,208	32,514	52,296
Petroleum, crude (000 42-gal. bbl.)	11,575	36,461	10,692	35,925
Sand and gravel (000 short tons)	8,760	10,474	8,202	11,061
Natural gas (000,000 cu.ft.)	77,892	19,161	72,723	18,253
Louisiana [2]		5,102,321		5,553,009
Petroleum, crude (000 42-gal. bbl.)	906,907	3,061,558	935,243	3,359,710
Natural gas (000,000 cu.ft.)	7,788,276	1,503,137	8,081,907	1,632,545
Natural-gas liquids				
Natural gasoline (000 gal.)	2,374,092	174,637	2,285,808	173,425
Petroleum gases, liquefied (000 gal.)	3,376,170	138,262	3,791,382	166,099
Sulfur, Frasch-process (000 long tons)	3,618	89,489	3,681	‡
Salt (000 short tons)	13,584	64,854	13,352	67,950
Sand and gravel (000 short tons)	18,155	22,363	19,228	24,492
Maine [47]		23,780		21,898
Sand and gravel (000 short tons)	12,971	6,888	8,292	5,881
Stone (000 short tons)	1,041	3,682	1,133	2,913
Copper (000 short tons)	3	3,120	3	2,610
Maryland [35]		88,216		99,429
Stone (000 short tons)	16,051	32,783	15,912	34,770
Sand and gravel (000 short tons)	12,951	20,434	12,842	23,201
Coal, bituminous (000 short tons)	1,615	8,083	1,644	10,274
Massachusetts [43]		50,360		50,199
Stone (000 short tons)	8,136	24,349	7,816	23,582
Sand and gravel (000 short tons)	17,925	22,244	17,343	23,058
Michigan [13]		670,729		640,636
Iron ore, usable (000 long tons)	13,100	168,958	11,833	159,854
Cement§ (000 376-lb. bbl.)	30,944	106,272	33,758	110,537
Copper, recoverable (000 short tons)	68	77,945	56	58,245
Sand and gravel (000 short tons)	53,092	54,646	56,613	62,898
Salt (000 short tons)	4,899	49,963	4,458	49,007
Stone (000 short tons)	41,687	49,501	40,705	49,240
Magnesium compounds, MgO equivalent (000 short tons)	412	38,050	273	27,777
Petroleum, crude (000 42-gal. bbl.)	11,693	36,246	11,893	38,859
Lime (000 short tons)	1,538	21,355	1,444	20,549
Minnesota [14]		633,006		608,775
Iron ore, usable (000 long tons)	54,791	571,488	49,054	547,607
Sand and gravel (000 short tons)	46,851	38,802	44,916	37,645
Stone (000 short tons)	4,579	12,311	5,838	14,346
Manganiferous ore (000 short tons)	321	‡	170	‡
Mississippi [26]		249,973		262,393
Petroleum, crude (000 42-gal. bbl.)	65,119	194,706	64,066	201,808
Natural gas (000,000 cu.ft.)	126,031	23,190	118,805	24,830
Sand and gravel (000 short tons)	10,859	11,950	11,289	13,526
Missouri [17]		392,996		400,089
Lead, recoverable (000 short tons)	422	131,751	430	118,579
Cement§ (000 376-lb. bbl.)	21,523	65,495	24,403	79,197
Stone (000 short tons)	39,726	57,285	41,099	64,772
Iron ore, usable (000 long tons)	2,612	38,100	2,727	‡
Coal, bituminous (000 short tons)	4,447	19,526	4,036	19,670
Zinc, recoverable (000 short tons)	51	15,540	48	15,525
Sand and gravel (000 short tons)	12,446	15,379	10,327	15,109
Montana [24]		313,016		285,073
Copper, recoverable (000 short tons)	120	138,955	89	92,125
Petroleum, crude (000 42-gal. bbl.)	37,879	105,403	34,599	104,128
Sand and gravel (000 short tons)	19,275	20,249	15,781	25,207
Silver, recoverable (000 troy oz.)	4,304	7,622	2,748	4,248

Principal minerals produced (continued)

Mineral (unit of production)	1970 Quantity	1970 Value in $000	1971 Quantity	1971 Value in $000
Montana (continued)				
Stone (000 short tons)	6,501	6,896	‡	‡
Coal, bituminous & lignite (short tons)	3,447	6,394	7,064	12,817
Nebraska [40]		72,657		74,079
Petroleum, crude (000 42-gal. bbl.)	11,451	35,384	10,062	34,010
Sand and gravel (000 short tons)	12,232	12,974	13,224	13,626
Stone (000 short tons)	4,265	7,378	4,174	7,892
Natural gas (000,000 cu. ft.)	5,991	1,024	3,496	612
Nevada [30]		186,349		164,774
Copper, recoverable (000 short tons)	107	123,118	97	100,806
Gold (troy oz.)	408,144	17,472	374,878	15,464
Sand and gravel (000 short tons)	8,574	9,819	9,379	12,225
Stone (000 short tons)	1,860	2,722	2,531	3,800
Mercury (76-lb. flasks)	4,909	2,001	1,589	465
Gypsum (000 short tons)	451	1,457	695	2,372
Barite (000 short tons)	192	1,455	192	1,490
New Hampshire [48]		8,730		10,284
Sand and gravel (000 short tons)	6,529	4,753	8,404	6,777
Stone (000 short tons)	397	3,924	429	3,433
New Jersey [37]		89,281		93,575
Stone (000 short tons)	15,160	40,567	13,469	36,057
Sand and gravel (000 short tons)	16,732	31,571	18,511	38,279
Zinc, recoverable (000 short tons)	29	8,788	30	9,653
Clays (000 short tons)	262	990	201	864
New Mexico [7]		1,060,358		1,046,284
Petroleum, crude (000 42-gal. bbl.)	128,184	410,320	118,412	402,602
Copper, recoverable (000 short tons)	166	191,885	157,419	163,715
Natural gas (000,000 cu.ft.)	1,138,980	162,874	1,167,577	175,137
Potash, K_2O equivalent (000 short tons)	2,390	85,877	2,291	86,689
Uranium (U_3O_8) (000 lb.)	11,574	69,970	10,567	65,517
Natural-gas liquids§ (000 gal.)	1,495,410	62,727	1,555,428	71,796
Coal, bituminous (000 short tons)	7,361	21,249	8,175	26,657
New York [22]		299,564		298,835
Stone (000 short tons)	37,616	68,118	37,778	73,418
Salt (000 short tons)	5,990	47,254	5,303	43,601
Sand and gravel (000 short tons)	35,537	38,839	23,221	28,328
Zinc, recoverable (000 short tons)	59	17,947	63	20,421
North Carolina [32]		98,365		112,451
Stone (000 short tons)	30,363	54,121	30,917	58,026
Sand and gravel (000 short tons)	12,772	13,277	14,240	14,690
Feldspar (000 long tons)	345	5,173	352	4,681
Clays† (000 short tons)	3,318	3,102	3,503	3,802
Mica, scrap (000 short tons)	64	1,457	67	1,770
North Dakota [34]		96,047		99,901
Petroleum, crude (000 42-gal. bbl.)	21,998	67,107	21,653	70,805
Coal, lignite (000 short tons)	5,639	11,009	6,075	11,580
Sand and gravel (000 short tons)	8,090	6,336	8,196	6,210
Natural gas (000,000 cu.ft.)	34,889	5,722	33,864	5,655
Natural-gas liquids§ (000 gal.)	98,448	4,320	‡	‡
Ohio [12]		612,166		652,151
Coal, bituminous (000 short tons)	55,351	262,390	51,431	269,601
Stone (000 short tons)	47,244	81,506	46,891	88,372
Lime (000 short tons)	3,951	61,197	4,007	65,258
Sand and gravel (000 short tons)	42,069	57,506	40,797	54,044
Salt (000 short tons)	5,329	47,498	5,709	46,651
Cement§ (000 376-lb. bbl.)	12,398	43,113	16,168	58,149
Petroleum, crude (000 42-gal. bbl.)	9,864	32,914	8,286	29,801
Natural gas (000,000 cu.ft.)	52,113	14,123	79,903	27,007
Clays (000 short tons)	3,920	10,100	3,973	11,380
Oklahoma [5]		1,138,272		1,189,516
Petroleum, crude (000 42-gal. bbl.)	223,574	712,419	213,313	725,611
Natural gas (000,000 cu.ft.)	1,594,943	248,811	1,684,260	273,945
Natural-gas liquids				
Natural gasoline (000 gal.)	622,146	39,933	596,274	40,856
Petroleum gases, liquefied (000 gal.)	1,177,218	52,975	1,156,680	56,732
Stone (000 short tons)	18,177	23,701	19,449	27,125
Coal, bituminous (000 short tons)	2,427	15,211	2,234	15,004
Oregon [39]		68,081		77,885
Sand and gravel (000 short tons)	17,532	25,978	20,230	28,707
Stone (000 short tons)	13,439	20,948	13,794	26,708
Nickel, content of ore (000 short tons)	16	‡	17	‡
Lime (000 short tons)	96	1,777	106	1,989
Pennsylvania [6]		1,095,743		1,149,107
Coal				
Bituminous (000 short tons)	80,491	585,057	72,835	620,196
Anthracite (000 short tons)	9,729	105,341	8,727	103,469
Cement§ (000 376-lb. bbl.)	40,910	129,424	43,983	151,707
Stone (000 short tons)	66,119	120,187	64,467	118,469
Sand and gravel (000 short tons)	18,504	33,915	19,668	36,162

Mineral (unit of production)	1970 Quantity	1970 Value in $000	1971 Quantity	1971 Value in $000
Pennsylvania (continued)				
Lime (000 short tons)	1,887	29,279	1,760	30,008
Natural gas (000,000 cu.ft.)	76,841	21,439	76,451	20,770
Petroleum, crude (000 42-gal. bbl.)	4,093	18,500	3,798	17,699
Rhode Island [49]		4,386		4,299
Sand and gravel (000 short tons)	2,387	2,913	2,252	3,052
Stone (000 short tons)	‡	‡	3	422
South Carolina [41]		56,365		66,888
Stone (000 short tons)	9,710	14,734	11,047	17,852
Clays (000 short tons)	1,974	9,878	2,049†	10,201†
Sand and gravel (000 short tons)	5,864	7,766	6,438	9,119
South Dakota [42]		61,576		62,988
Gold (troy oz.)	578,716	21,059	513,427	21,179
Sand and gravel (000 short tons)	16,556	16,656	16,727	18,392
Stone (000 short tons)	1,979	13,375	2,199	8,874
Tennessee [28]		220,465		236,076
Stone† (000 short tons)	35,374	50,013	32,369	48,665
Coal, bituminous (000 short tons)	8,237	40,372	9,271	59,368
Zinc, recoverable (000 short tons)	118	36,233	108	34,827
Cement§ (000 376-lb. bbl.)	9,600	32,581	9,955	37,382
Copper, recoverable (000 short tons)	16	17,928	14	14,473
Phosphate rock (000 short tons)	3,073	15,005	2,571	12,151
Sand and gravel (000 short tons)	6,715	10,639	8,018	11,845
Texas [1]		6,401,999		6,807,955
Petroleum, crude (000 42-gal. bbl.)	1,249,697	4,104,005	1,222,926	4,261,775
Natural gas (000,000 cu.ft.)	8,357,716	1,203,511	8,550,705	1,376,664
Natural-gas liquids				
Natural gasoline (000 gal.)	4,095,462	284,871	4,043,886	299,981
Petroleum gases, liquefied (000 gal.)	8,575,434	334,850	8,838,270	380,887
Cement§ (000 376-lb. bbl.)	34,717	126,729	39,187	144,720
Stone (000 short tons)	45,557	64,422	41,168	62,144
Sulfur, Frasch-process (000 long tons)	2,801	62,290	3,075	‡
Sand and gravel (000 short tons)	31,438	46,362	32,788	51,814
Salt (000 short tons)	10,184	45,000	9,217	40,838
Lime (000 short tons)	1,673	24,427	1,612	24,583
Helium§ (000 cu.ft.)	1,239	16,124	1,258	16,246
Utah [16]		602,551		525,700
Copper, recoverable (000 short tons)	296	341,282	263	273,989
Petroleum, crude (000 42-gal. bbl.)	23,370	65,603	23,630	71,886
Coal, bituminous (000 short tons)	4,733	34,472	4,626	34,082
Gold (troy oz.)	408,029	14,848	368,996	15,221
Lead, recoverable (000 short tons)	45	14,175	38	10,562
Iron ore, usable (000 long tons)	1,990	13,837	1,681	11,886
Silver, recoverable (000 troy ounces)	6,030	10,678	5,294	8,185
Sand and gravel (000 short tons)	12,010	10,439	10,505	10,190
Vermont [44]		27,843		36,284
Stone (000 short tons)	1,514	19,088	2,498	28,135
Sand and gravel (000 short tons)	4,046	4,122	3,761	3,518
Virginia [19]		374,321		385,161
Coal, bituminous (000 short tons)	35,016	246,181	30,628	254,870
Stone (000 short tons)	35,415	60,477	34,643	63,482
Sand and gravel (000 short tons)	11,126	15,229	12,796	20,201
Lime (000 short tons)	1,046	14,090	759	11,049
Zinc, recoverable (000 short tons)	18	5,534	17	5,419
Washington [36]		90,922		94,601
Sand and gravel (000 short tons)	25,089	27,902	22,702	26,658
Cement§ (000 376-lb. bbl.)	6,526	24,990	‡	‡
Stone (000 short tons)	13,701	19,100	12,436	20,489
Zinc, recoverable (000 short tons)	12	3,663	6	1,862
Lead, recoverable (000 short tons)	7	2,119	5	1,429
Coal, bituminous (000 short tons)	37	470	1,134	7,614
West Virginia [4]		1,285,364		1,273,960
Coal (000 short tons)	144,072	1,142,245	118,258	1,128,282
Natural gas (000,000 cu.ft.)	242,452	61,583	234,027	60,613
Natural-gas liquids (000 gal.)	‡	‡	‡	‡
Stone† (000 short tons)	9,470	16,722	9,880	18,066
Petroleum, crude (000 42-gal. bbl.)	3,124	11,871	2,969	11,609
Sand and gravel (000 short tons)	4,396	11,473	7,107	16,756
Wisconsin [38]		87,670		84,036
Sand and gravel (000 short tons)	41,103	35,107	38,561	32,748
Stone (000 short tons)	17,577	25,167	15,568	25,105
Zinc, recoverable (000 short tons)	21	6,322	11	3,428
Wyoming [10]		705,533		717,937
Petroleum, crude (000 42-gal. bbl.)	160,345	469,811	148,114	459,079
Natural gas (000,000 cu.ft.)	338,520	49,762	380,105	58,156
Uranium (U_3O_8) (000 lb.)	6,346	38,768	6,986	43,311
Coal, bituminous (000 short tons)	7,222	24,423	8,052	27,335
Clays (000 short tons)	1,950	18,829	1,798	17,378
Natural-gas liquids§ (000 gal.)	300,426	14,557	335,496	17,542

Figure in brackets is the rank of the states by value of 1971 mineral production. Boldface type indicates the state that leads in value of production for that mineral.

Production is measured by mine shipments, sales, or marketable production (including consumption by producers).

*Includes small quantity of anthracite mined in states other than Pennsylvania.
†Excludes certain varieties. ‡Figure withheld to avoid disclosing confidential data. §For cement, portland and masonry figures combined; for helium, grade A and crude figures combined; for natural-gas liquids, natural gasoline, cycle products, and liquefied petroleum gases figures combined.
Source: U.S. Department of the Interior, Bureau of Mines.

(FRANK H. SKELDING)

National income

by type of income, in billion dollars

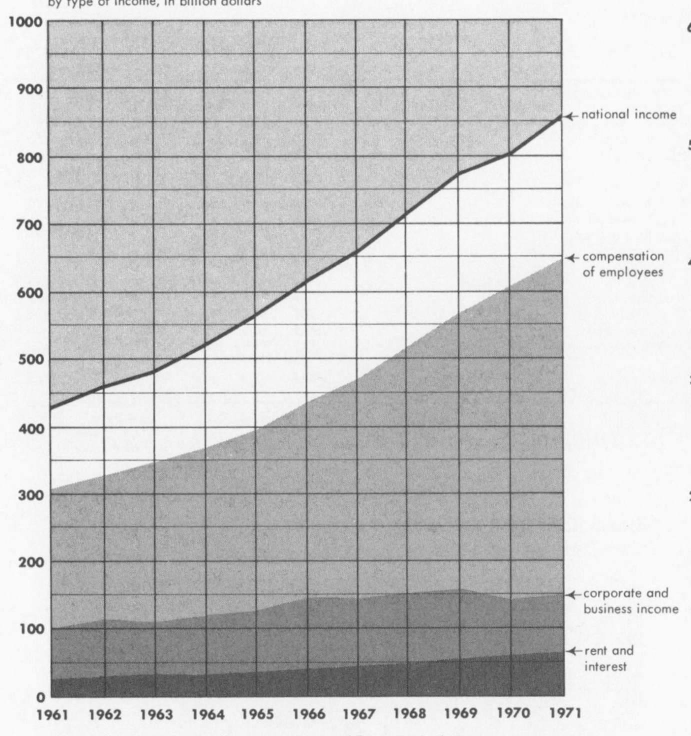

Source: U.S. Department of Commerce, Bureau of Economic Analysis, *Survey of Current Business.*

New building construction

constant values, in billion dollars

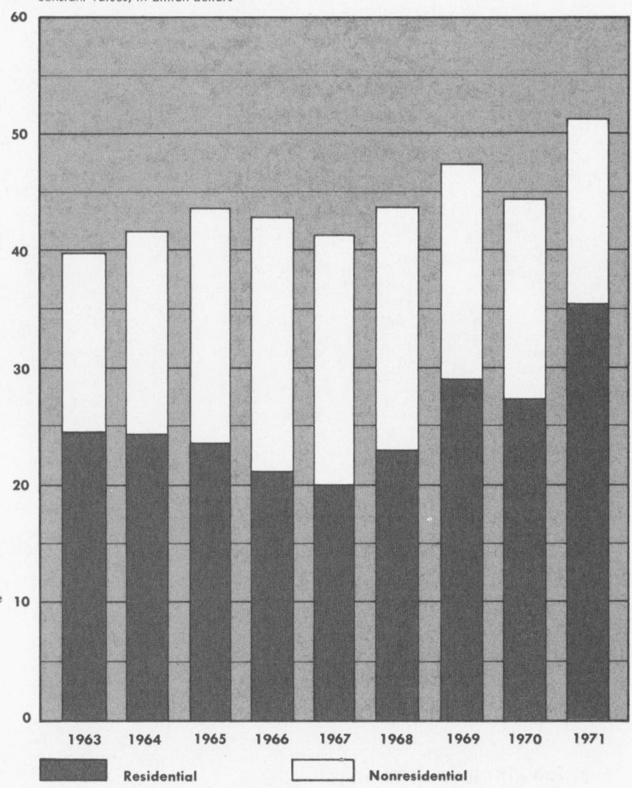

Data are for new private construction only.

Source: U.S. Department of Commerce, Bureau of Domestic Commerce, *Construction Review.*

Personal income per capita

State	1956	1961	1966	1971
Alabama	$1,304	$1,508	$2,066	$3,050
Alaska	2,446	2,704	3,421	4,749
Arizona	1,767	2,070	2,544	3,871
Arkansas	1,194	1,486	2,010	3,036
California	2,419	2,777	3,457	4,677
Colorado	1,887	2,343	2,916	4,057
Connecticut	2,603	2,892	3,690	5,032
Delaware	2,755	2,759	3,529	4,570
District of Columbia	2,660	3,065	3,948	6,000
Florida	1,723	1,970	2,614	3,848
Georgia	1,446	1,678	2,379	3,547
Hawaii	1,900	2,488	3,124	4,797
Idaho	1,667	1,913	2,445	3,402
Illinois	2,416	2,720	3,532	4,772
Indiana	1,991	2,222	3,076	3,973
Iowa	1,694	2,081	2,992	3,876
Kansas	1,795	2,210	2,862	4,090
Kentucky	1,417	1,668	2,246	3,288
Louisiana	1,500	1,687	2,277	3,248
Maine	1,635	1,829	2,477	3,419
Maryland	2,126	2,464	3,204	4,514
Massachusetts	2,146	2,553	3,271	4,586
Michigan	2,214	2,299	3,269	4,317
Minnesota	1,783	2,193	2,904	3,974
Mississippi	1,026	1,268	1,777	2,766
Missouri	1,884	2,166	2,817	3,877
Montana	1,892	1,973	2,623	3,479
Nebraska	1,628	2,114	2,905	3,998
Nevada	2,500	2,928	3,497	4,895
New Hampshire	1,829	2,205	2,808	3,708
New Jersey	2,443	2,765	3,445	4,832
New Mexico	1,593	1,953	2,385	3,394
New York	2,396	2,796	3,497	5,021
North Carolina	1,377	1,626	2,277	3,387
North Dakota	1,437	1,504	2,384	3,383
Ohio	2,171	2,328	3,056	4,154
Oklahoma	1,580	1,910	2,462	3,506
Oregon	2,015	2,275	2,908	3,920
Pennsylvania	2,032	2,257	2,968	4,127
Rhode Island	1,993	2,280	3,047	4,077
South Carolina	1,210	1,429	2,052	3,162
South Dakota	1,364	1,771	2,420	3,446
Tennessee	1,368	1,620	2,227	3,325
Texas	1,752	1,984	2,542	3,682
Utah	1,707	2,039	2,485	3,395
Vermont	1,586	1,877	2,595	3,610
Virginia	1,635	1,898	2,605	3,866
Washington	2,093	2,455	3,222	4,135
West Virginia	1,491	1,634	2,176	3,228
Wisconsin	1,927	2,227	2,973	3,880
Wyoming	1,939	2,303	2,739	3,753
United States	1,975	2,264	2,963	4,138

Source: U.S. Department of Commerce, Bureau of Economic Analysis, *Survey of Current Business.*

Personal consumption expenditures

in billions of dollars

Type of expenditure	1966	1967	1968	1969	1970	1971
Food, beverages, tobacco	115.4	117.7	125.1	132.6	142.9	148.1
Clothing, accessories, personal care	56.6	59.6	64.5	69.5	72.4	77.5
Housing	67.1	71.8	77.3	84.0	91.2	99.2
Household operation	66.7	70.5	76.2	81.6	85.6	93.6
Medical care expenses	31.3	34.5	37.8	42.4	47.3	51.4
Personal business	24.0	26.2	29.5	33.3	35.5	37.1
Transportation	59.6	62.6	72.0	78.0	77.9	90.1
Recreation	28.7	30.8	33.6	36.3	39.0	42.5
Private education and research	6.7	7.6	8.7	9.6	10.4	11.1
Religious and welfare activities	6.5	6.9	7.6	8.1	8.8	9.1
Foreign travel and other, net	3.4	3.9	3.8	4.2	4.8	5.2
TOTAL	466.0	492.1	536.1	579.6	615.8	664.9

Source: U.S. Department of Commerce, Bureau of Economic Analysis, *Survey of Current Business.*

Individual income levels

persons 14 years old and over

March 1972 income level	MALE				FEMALE			
	Nonfarm	Farm	White	Negro	Nonfarm	Farm	White	Negro
Number of persons, (000)	68,603	3,866	64,611	7,041	75,961	3,604	70,293	8,428
Number of income earners, (000)	62,926	3,560	59,729	6,024	50,656	1,947	45,941	6,151
Percent under $1,000	9.4	19.0	9.4	15.0	24.3	41.9	25.0	25.1
$ 1,000 to $ 1,499	3.7	6.1	3.5	6.6	10.4	11.7	10.2	12.6
$ 1,500 to $ 1,999	3.7	5.0	3.6	5.6	8.8	7.0	8.6	9.7
$ 2,000 to $ 2,499	4.0	6.0	3.9	5.8	7.2	5.8	6.9	8.9
$ 2,500 to $ 2,999	3.0	4.8	3.0	4.5	5.2	4.2	5.0	6.2
$ 3,000 to $ 3,499	3.5	4.6	3.4	5.1	5.7	5.2	5.6	6.3
$ 3,500 to $ 3,999	3.0	3.7	2.9	4.3	4.6	3.1	4.6	4.4
$ 4,000 to $ 4,499	3.4	4.4	3.2	5.7	5.0	3.7	4.9	4.9
$ 4,500 to $ 4,999	3.0	3.3	2.9	4.2	3.8	2.7	3.9	3.2
$ 5,000 to $ 5,999	6.3	7.2	6.1	8.9	7.3	4.6	7.3	5.9
$ 6,000 to $ 6,999	6.4	6.3	6.3	7.1	5.5	3.0	5.5	4.4
$ 7,000 to $ 7,999	7.3	5.9	7.2	7.9	3.9	2.1	4.0	2.9
$ 8,000 to $ 9,999	12.8	7.4	12.9	9.3	4.4	2.9	4.5	3.1
$10,000 to $14,999	19.5	10.9	20.1	8.4	3.1	1.7	3.1	2.1
$15,000 to $24,999	8.3	3.9	8.7	1.4	0.6	0.2	0.6	0.1
$25,000 to $49,999	2.1	1.5	2.3	0.2	0.1	—	0.1	*
$50,000 and over	0.4	0.1	0.5	0.1	*	—	*	*
Median income dollars	7,068	4,092	7,237	4,274	2,449	1,344	2,448	2,145

—Represents zero.
*Less than 0.05%.
Percentages do not add to 100 because of rounding.
Source: U.S. Department of Commerce, Bureau of the Census, *Current Population Reports.*

Retail food prices

in cents per pound, except as indicated

Commodity and unit	1965	1968	1971	1972*
Cereals and bakery products				
Flour, wheat	11.6	11.7	12.0	11.9
Corn flakes (12 oz.)	28.9	31.3	33.4	31.4
Bread, white	20.9	22.4	25.0	24.7
Meats, poultry, and fish				
Steak, round	108.4	114.3	136.1	147.4
Hamburger	50.8	56.1	68.1	73.8
Pork chops, center cut	97.3	102.9	108.1	116.8
Bacon, sliced	81.3	81.4	80.0	92.5
Frying chickens	39.0	39.8	41.0	40.9
Ocean perch, fillet, frozen	52.7	54.3	72.5	73.1
Dairy products				
Milk, fresh (grocery, ½ gal.)	47.3	53.7	58.9	60.1
Butter	75.4	83.6	87.6	87.4
Cheese, Am. process (½ lb.)	37.7	44.4	52.8	54.1
Fruits and vegetables				
Apples	17.8	23.8	23.5	23.1
Oranges, size 200 (doz.)	77.8	96.6	94.3	88.2
Potatoes	9.4	7.6	8.6	8.3
Tomatoes	34.3	40.2	46.6	46.1
Peas, green, No. 303 can	23.7	24.9	26.3	26.6
Other				
Eggs, Grade A, large (doz.)	52.7	52.9	52.9	50.0
Margarine	27.9	27.9	32.7	33.3
Sugar	11.8	12.2	13.6	13.9
Coffee, instant (6 oz.)	95.2	89.4	109.3	110.1

*April, 1972.
Source: U.S. Department of Commerce, Bureau of the Census, *Statistical Abstract of the United States*. Data compiled by the U.S. Department of Labor, Bureau of Labor Statistics, *Retail Food Prices by Cities* and *Estimated Retail Food Prices by Cities*.

Average employee earnings

June figures

Industry	AVERAGE WEEKLY EARNINGS 1970	AVERAGE WEEKLY EARNINGS 1972	AVERAGE HOURLY EARNINGS 1970	AVERAGE HOURLY EARNINGS 1972
MANUFACTURING				
Durable goods	$144.94	$168.06	$3.57	$4.04
Ordnance and accessories	146.11	172.60	3.59	4.09
Lumber and wood products	119.50	138.78	2.98	3.32
Furniture and fixtures	107.92	125.36	2.76	3.05
Stone, clay, and glass products	141.10	165.39	3.40	3.91
Primary metal industries	159.54	193.53	3.92	4.63
Fabricated metal products	145.49	165.17	3.54	3.98
Nonelectrical machinery	155.32	179.35	3.77	4.26
Electrical equipment and supplies	130.68	149.37	3.30	3.67
Transportation equipment	170.56	199.13	4.10	4.73
Instruments and related products	133.39	151.40	3.31	3.72
Nondurable goods	119.95	137.66	3.06	3.45
Food and kindred products	127.58	145.71	3.15	3.58
Tobacco manufactures	115.14	122.50	3.03	3.52
Textile mill products	97.93	113.42	2.43	2.72
Apparel and related products	84.25	93.60	2.38	2.60
Paper and allied products	142.61	168.99	3.42	3.93
Printing and publishing	147.03	169.03	3.90	4.46
Chemicals and allied products	152.72	176.40	3.68	4.67
Petroleum and coal products	181.04	209.88	4.23	4.95
Rubber and plastics products	127.26	148.57	3.15	3.58
Leather and leather products	94.87	105.84	2.49	2.70
NONMANUFACTURING	166.45	184.36	3.88	4.40
Metal mining	182.34	214.35	4.48	5.19
Coal mining	152.01	171.07	3.56	3.96
Oil and gas extraction	196.99	224.47	5.13	5.97
Contract construction				
Local and suburban trans-	143.31	161.59	3.38	3.82
portation	132.38	163.55	3.36	4.13
Telephone communication				
Electric, gas, and sanitary	169.74	198.37	4.11	4.78
services	136.80	154.00	3.42	3.85
Wholesale trade	82.86	91.73	2.43	2.69
Retail trade				
Hotels, tourist courts, and motels*	67.57	75.94	1.97	2.24

*Excludes tips.
Source: U.S. Department of Labor, Bureau of Labor Statistics, *Employment and Earnings*.

Consumer prices by commodity groups

1967=100

Commodity	1962	1964	1966	1968	1970	1972*
Food	89.9	92.4	99.1	103.6	114.9	124.2
Food away from home	85.4	88.9	95.1	105.2	119.9	131.3
Food at home	91.0	93.2	100.3	103.2	113.7	122.4
Housing	91.7	93.8	97.2	104.2	118.9	129.5
Rent	94.0	95.9	98.2	102.4	110.1	119.0
Home ownership	87.9	90.8	96.3	105.7	128.5	140.7
Fuel and utilities	97.3	98.4	98.8	101.3	107.6	120.2
Household furnishings and operation	93.8	95.0	97.0	104.4	113.4	121.1
Apparel and upkeep	90.9	92.7	96.1	105.4	116.1	121.1
Transportation	92.5	94.3	97.2	103.2	112.7	120.3
Private	93.0	94.7	97.5	103.0	111.1	117.8
Public	87.4	90.1	95.2	104.6	128.5	143.3
Health and recreation	88.4	91.8	96.1	105.0	116.2	126.3
Medical care	83.5	87.3	93.4	106.1	120.6	132.7
Personal care	92.2	94.5	97.1	104.2	113.2	120.0
Reading and recreation	91.3	95.0	97.5	104.7	113.4	123.0
All items	90.6	92.9	97.2	104.2	116.3	125.5

*July 1972.
Source: U.S. Department of Labor, Bureau of Labor Statistics, *Monthly Labor Review*.

Unemployment trends

quarterly averages, seasonally adjusted

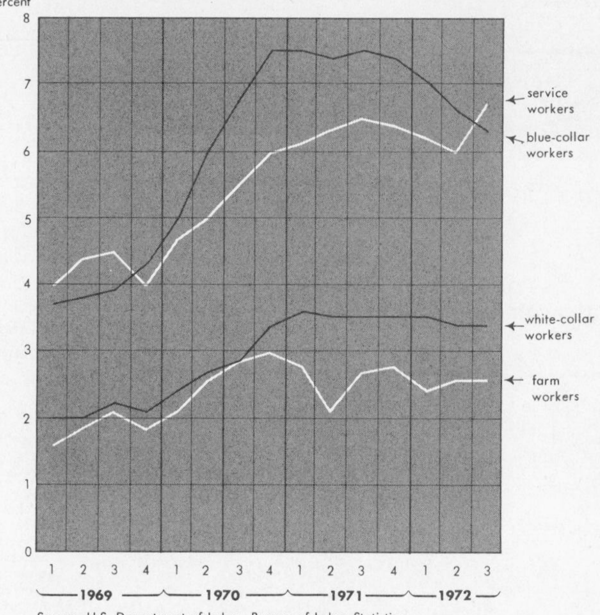

Source: U.S. Department of Labor, Bureau of Labor Statistics, *Monthly Labor Review*.

Consumer prices in selected cities, 1971

1967=100

Standard Metropolitan Statistical Area	Food	Housing	Apparel and upkeep	Medical care	Transportation	All items
Average*	118.4	124.3	119.8	128.4	118.6	121.3
Atlanta	118.1	127.0	116.0	136.1	115.2	121.7
Baltimore	121.0	126.9	123.4	135.9	117.5	123.4
Boston	118.5	126.8	121.8	130.4	120.7	122.8
Chicago	118.5	120.3	117.4	128.4	125.4	120.8
Cincinnati	118.4	121.2	122.3	131.8	120.0	120.7
Cleveland	118.9	122.4	121.6	140.0	124.4	122.8
Detroit	117.3	128.3	115.5	134.1	114.6	121.7
Honolulu	118.1	120.3	117.6	124.7	120.2	118.9
Houston	118.8	124.6	122.0	130.1	113.1	120.9
Kansas City	118.6	121.7	124.4	124.4	118.4	120.5
Los Angeles–Long Beach	114.9	122.8	118.0	125.7	114.9	118.5
Milwaukee	115.7	122.6	124.2	126.1	117.1	120.1
Minneapolis–St. Paul	119.2	126.4	118.1	123.8	115.5	121.7
New York	123.1	128.7	120.5	135.8	129.0	125.9
Philadelphia	120.1	125.8	119.2	137.4	123.1	123.5
Pittsburgh	118.9	125.5	119.6	122.6	120.0	121.5
St. Louis	118.0	119.5	119.1	123.5	119.3	119.6
San Diego	117.3	127.5	117.8	121.0	113.8	119.9
San Francisco–Oakland	116.1	125.3	119.0	123.1	118.0	120.2
Seattle	115.9	119.1	116.0	122.9	107.0	116.4
Washington, D.C.	120.2	122.6	123.0	136.5	123.4	122.7

*1971; 56 areas.
Source: U.S. Department of Commerce, Bureau of the Census, *Statistical Abstract of the United States*. Data compiled by U.S. Department of Labor, Bureau of Labor Statistics, *Monthly Labor Review*.

Stock market prices

1941-43 = 100

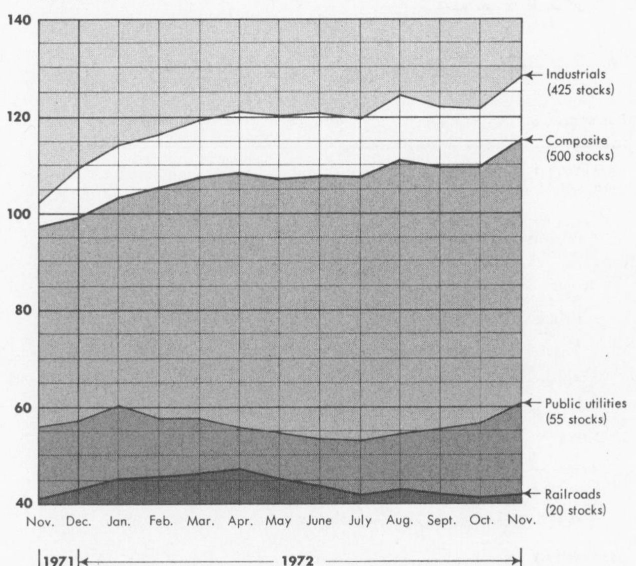

Source: U.S. Department of Commerce, Bureau of Economic Analysis, *Survey of Current Business*. Data compiled by Standard & Poor's Corporation.

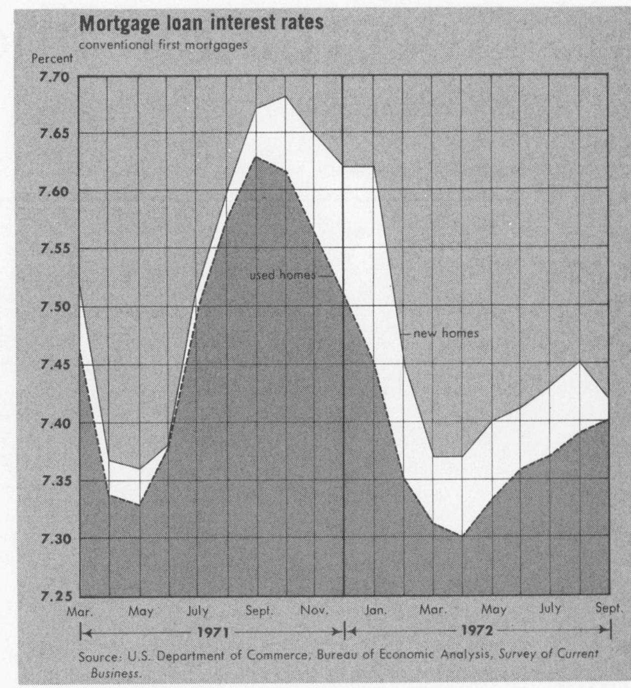

Residential rents

1967=100

Standard Metropolitan Statistical Area	1960	1965	1968	1970	1971
Atlanta, Ga.	94.2	96.9	102.5	109.9	113.8
Baltimore, Md.	93.1	97.6	101.7	106.9	110.2
Boston, Mass.	86.0	96.3	102.7	115.4	122.7
Chicago, Ill.-Northwestern Ind.	94.5	97.5	101.8	107.6	110.4
Cincinnati, Ohio	97.6	99.0	100.6	105.7	108.1
Cleveland, Ohio-Ky.	98.5	98.2	101.7	107.5	111.4
Dallas, Tex.	...	98.5	102.6	110.1	111.6
Detroit, Mich.	95.7	94.5	103.3	111.5	116.4
Honolulu, Hawaii	...	95.8	103.3	118.1	124.0
Houston, Tex.	97.7	97.7	102.2	106.9	109.8
Kansas City, Mo.-Kans.	96.5	98.8	101.1	106.3	109.0
Los Angeles-Long Beach, Calif.	90.9	97.8	102.0	111.9	116.3
Minneapolis-St. Paul, Minn.	93.1	97.9	102.9	114.2	118.6
New York, N.Y.-Northeastern N.J.	87.1	96.5	102.6	110.9	119.3
Philadelphia, Pa.-N.J.	91.3	96.9	102.1	112.5	119.1
Pittsburgh, Pa.	93.8	97.	101.8	109.0	114.2
St. Louis, Mo.-Ill.	95.7	98.1	101.6	105.6	107.6
San Diego, Calif.	...	97.8	105.8	123.6	130.5
San Francisco-Oakland, Calif.	82.5	94.7	105.2	119.3	125.4
Seattle, Wash.	88.9	92.8	104.7	109.1	106.9
Washington, D.C.-Md.-Va.	88.6	96.9	101.9	109.4	114.5

Source: U.S. Department of Commerce, Bureau of the Census, *Statistical Abstract of the United States*. Data compiled by the U.S. Department of Labor, Bureau of Labor Statistics, *The Consumer Price Index*.

Homes with selected electrical appliances

number of wired homes in millions

Appliance	1965 Number	1965 Percent	1970 Number	1970 Percent	1971 Number	1971 Percent
Total number of wired homes	57.6	100.0	64.0	100.0	65.6	100.0
Air conditioners, room	13.9	24.2	26.0	40.6	29.2	44.5
Bed coverings	20.0	34.7	31.7	49.5	33.5	51.1
Blenders	7.5	13.0	23.4	36.5	26.2	40.0
Can openers	14.2	24.7	29.1	45.5	31.5	48.1
Coffee makers	41.3	71.7	56.7	88.6	59.7	91.0
Dishwashers	7.8	13.5	17.0	26.5	19.4	29.6
Dryers, clothes*	15.2	26.4	28.6	44.6	31.2	47.6
Food waste disposers	7.9	13.6	16.3	25.5	18.6	28.4
Freezers	15.7	27.2	20.0	31.2	21.4	32.7
Frypans	28.3	49.2	36.0	56.2	38.0	58.0
Irons	57.1	99.1	63.8	99.7	65.4	99.8
Mixers	41.9	72.8	52.8	82.4	55.3	84.4
Radios†	58.2	99.3	63.9	99.8	65.4	99.8
Ranges						
Free-standing	18.5	32.1	25.9	40.5	27.9	42.6
Built-in	5.9	10.3	9.6	15.0	10.3	15.7
Refrigerators	57.3	99.5	63.9	99.8	65.4	99.8
Television						
Black and white	55.9	97.1	63.2	98.7	65.4	99.8
Color	5.5	9.5	27.2	42.5	33.5	51.1
Toasters	48.1	83.6	59.3	92.6	61.7	94.2
Vacuum cleaners	48.1	83.5	58.9	92.0	61.9	94.4
Washers, clothes	50.3	87.4	59.0	92.1	61.8	94.3

Data as of December 31. *Includes gas dryers. †1965 data based on total homes.
Source: U.S. Department of Commerce, Bureau of the Census, *Statistical Abstract of the United States*. Data from Billboard Publications, Inc., *Merchandising Week*.

Medical care price indexes

1967=100

Year	Total medical care	Hospital daily service charges	Drugs and prescriptions	PROFESSIONAL SERVICES: Physicians' fees	Obstetrical case	Tonsillectomy and adenoidectomy	Dentists' fees	Optometric examination and eye glasses
1950	53.7	28.9	88.5	55.2	51.2	60.7	63.9	73.5
1955	64.8	41.5	94.7	65.4	68.6	69.0	73.0	77.0
1960	79.1	56.3	104.5	77.0	79.4	80.3	82.1	85.1
1965	89.5	76.6	100.2	88.3	89.0	91.0	92.2	92.8
1966	93.4	84.0	100.5	93.4	93.0	94.9	95.2	95.3
1967	100.0	100.0	100.0	100.0	100.0	100.0	100.0	100.0
1968	106.1	113.2	100.2	105.6	105.2	104.9	105.5	103.2
1969	113.4	127.9	101.3	112.9	113.5	110.3	112.9	107.6
1970	120.6	143.9	103.6	121.4	121.8	117.1	119.4	113.5
1971	128.4	160.8	105.4	129.8	129.0	125.2	127.0	120.3

Prior to 1965, data excludes Alaska and Hawaii. Source: U.S. Department of Commerce, Bureau of the Census, *Statistical Abstract of the United States*. Data compiled by the U.S. Department of Labor, Bureau of Labor Statistics, *Price Indexes for Selected Items and Groups, Annual Averages*.

Government and Politics

The national executive

November 15, 1972

Department, bureau, or office	Executive officer and official title
PRESIDENT OF THE UNITED STATES	Richard M. Nixon
Vice President	Spiro T. Agnew
EXECUTIVE OFFICE OF THE PRESIDENT	
Counsellor to the President	Robert H. Finch
Assistant, National Security	Henry A. Kissinger
Assistant, Domestic Affairs	John D. Ehrlichman
Management and Budget	Caspar W. Weinberger, director
Science and Technology	Edward E. David, Jr., director
Environmental Quality	Russell E. Train, chairman
Council of Economic Advisers	Herbert Stein, chairman
Office of Econ. Opportunity	Phillip V. Sanchez, director
Office of Consumer Affairs	Virginia H. Knauer, director
Drug Abuse Prevention	Jerome H. Jaffe, director
DEPARTMENT OF STATE	William P. Rogers, secretary
	John N. Irwin II, undersecretary
Political Affairs	U. Alexis Johnson, undersecretary
Economic Affairs	Willis C. Armstrong, asst. secretary
Educational and Cultural Affairs	John Richardson, Jr., asst. secretary
African Affairs	David D. Newsom, asst. secretary
Inter-American Affairs	Charles A. Meyer, asst. secretary
European Affairs	Walter J. Stroessel, Jr., asst. secy.-designate
East Asian and Pacific Affairs	Marshall Green, asst. secretary
Near Eastern, South Asian Affairs	Joseph J. Sisco, asst. secretary
International Organization Affairs	Samuel DePalma, asst. secretary
DEPARTMENT OF THE TREASURY	George P. Shultz, secretary
	Edwin S. Cohen, undersecretary
Monetary Affairs	Paul A. Volcker, undersecretary
Bureau of Customs	Vernon D. Acree, commissioner
Bureau of Engraving and Printing	James A. Conlon, director
Bureau of the Mint	Mary T. Brooks, director
Internal Revenue Service	Johnnie M. Walters, commissioner
U.S. Savings Bonds Division	Jesse L. Adams, Jr., acting national director
U.S. Secret Service	James J. Rowley, director
Office of the Treasurer	Romana Acosta Banuelos, treasurer
DEPARTMENT OF DEFENSE	Melvin R. Laird, secretary
	Kenneth Rush, deputy secretary
Joint Chiefs of Staff	Adm. Thomas H. Moorer, chairman
Chief of Staff, U.S. Army	Gen. Bruce Palmer, Jr.
Chief of Naval Operations	Adm. Elmo R. Zumwalt
Chief of Staff, U.S. Air Force	Gen. John D. Ryan
Commandant, Marine Corps	Gen. Robert E. Cushman, Jr.
Department of the Army	Robert F. Froehlke, secretary
	Kenneth E. BeLieu, undersecretary
Department of the Navy	John W. Warner, secretary
	Frank P. Sanders, undersecretary
Department of the Air Force	Robert C. Seamans, Jr., secretary
	John L. McLucas, undersecretary
DEPARTMENT OF JUSTICE	R. G. Kleindienst, attorney general
	Ralph Erickson, deputy atty. gen.
Solicitor General	Erwin N. Griswold
Federal Bureau of Investigation	L. Patrick Gray III, acting director
Bureau of Prisons	Norman A. Carlson, director
Narcotics, Dangerous Drugs	John E. Ingersoll, director
Immigration and Naturalization	Raymond F. Farrell, commissioner
U.S. Marshals	Wayne B. Colburn, director
DEPARTMENT OF THE INTERIOR	Rogers C. B. Morton, secretary
Fish and Wildlife, and Parks	Nathaniel P. Reed, asst. secretary
National Park Service	George B. Hartzog, Jr., director
Mineral Resources	Hollis Dole, asst. secretary
Bureau of Mines	Elburt F. Osborn, director
Geological Survey	Vincent E. McKelvey, director
Public Land Management	Harrison Loesch, asst. secretary
Indian Affairs	Louis R. Bruce, commissioner
Program Policy	John W. Larson, asst. secretary
Bureau of Outdoor Recreation	James G. Watt, director
Water and Power Resources	James R. Smith, asst. secretary
Bureau of Reclamation	Ellis L. Armstrong, commissioner
DEPARTMENT OF AGRICULTURE	Earl L. Butz, secretary
	J. Phil Campbell, undersecretary
Rural Development, Conservation	Thomas K. Cowden, asst. secretary
Farmer Co-op Service	Eric Thor, administrator
Forest Service	John R. McGuire, chief
Rural Electrification	David A. Hamil, administrator
Soil Conservation Service	Kenneth E. Grant, administrator
Marketing, Consumer Services	Richard Lyng, asst. secretary
International Affairs	Carroll G. Brunthaver, asst. secretary
DEPARTMENT OF COMMERCE	Peter G. Peterson, secretary
	James T. Lynn, undersecretary
Economic Development	Robert A. Podesta, asst. secretary
Domestic, Internat'l Business	Andrew E. Gibson, asst. secretary
Science and Technology	James H. Wakelin, Jr., asst. secretary
Patent Office	Robert Gottschalk, commissioner
Economic Affairs	Harold C. Passer, asst. secretary
Tourism	J. L. Hamilton, acting asst. secy.
Maritime Affairs	Robert Blackwell, asst. secretary
DEPARTMENT OF LABOR	James D. Hodgson, secretary
	Laurence H. Silberman, undersecretary
Manpower	Malcolm R. Lovell, Jr., asst. secretary
Labor-Management Relations	W. J. Usery, Jr., asst. secretary
Employment Standards	Richard Grunewald, asst. secretary
Women's Bureau	Elizabeth D. Koontz, director
Occupational Safety, Health	George C. Guenther, asst. secretary
Labor Statistics	Geoffrey H. Moore, commissioner

Department, bureau, or office	Executive officer and official title
DEPARTMENT OF HEALTH, EDUCATION, AND WELFARE	Elliot L. Richardson, secretary
	John G. Veneman, undersecretary
Office for Civil Rights	J. Stanley Pottinger, director
Community and Field Services	Patricia Reilly Hitt, asst. secretary
Planning and Evaluation	Lawrence H. Lynn, Jr., assistant secy.
Health	Merlin K. Duval, asst. secretary
Surgeon General	Jesse L. Steinfeld, M.D.
Food and Drug Administration	Charles C. Edwards, commissioner
Health Service, Mental Health	Vernon E. Wilson, administrator
National Institutes of Health	Robert Q. Marston, director
Social, Rehabilitation Service	John D. Twiname, administrator
Social Security Administration	Robert M. Ball, commissioner
Office of Education	Sidney P. Marland, Jr., commissioner
DEPARTMENT OF HOUSING AND URBAN DEVELOPMENT	George Romney, secretary
	Richard C. Van Dusen, undersecretary
Community Planning, Management	Samuel C. Jackson, asst. secretary
Housing Production	Eugene A. Gulledge, asst. secretary
Community Development	Floyd H. Hyde, asst. secretary
Research and Technology	Harold B. Finger, asst. secretary
DEPARTMENT OF TRANSPORTATION	John A. Volpe, secretary
	James M. Beggs, undersecretary
U.S. Coast Guard	Adm. Chester R. Bender, commandant
Federal Aviation Administration	John H. Shaffer, administrator
Federal Highway Administration	R. R. Bartelsmeyer, acting admin.
Federal Railroad Administration	John W. Ingram, administrator
Urban Mass Transportation	Carlos C. Villarreal, administrator
St. Lawrence Seaway	David W. Oberlin, administrator
National Highway Traffic Safety	Douglas W. Toms, administrator
INDEPENDENT OFFICES AND ESTABLISHMENTS	
Atomic Energy Commission	James R. Schlesinger, chairman
Civil Aeronautics Board	Secor D. Browne, chairman
District of Columbia	Walter E. Washington, commissioner
Environmental Protection Agency	William D. Ruckelshaus, admin.
Export-Import Bank of the U.S.	Henry Kearns, pres. and chairman
Farm Credit Administration	Millard F. Dailey, chairman
Federal Communications Comm.	Dean Burch, chairman
Federal Deposit Insurance Corp.	Frank Wille, chairman
Federal Maritime Commission	Helen Delich Bentley, chairman
Federal Power Commission	John N. Nassikas, chairman
Federal Reserve System	Arthur F. Burns, chairman
Federal Trade Commission	Miles W. Kirkpatrick, chairman
Indian Claims Commission	Jerome K. Kuykendall, chairman
Interstate Commerce Commission	George M. Stafford, chairman
National Aero. and Space Adm.	James C. Fletcher, administrator
National Labor Relations Board	Edward B. Miller, chairman
National Science Foundation	H. Guyford Stever, director
Securities and Exchange Comm.	William J. Casey, chairman
Selective Service System	Byron V. Pepitone, acting director
Small Business Administration	Thomas S. Kleppe, administrator
U.S. Civil Service Commission	Robert E. Hampton, chairman
U.S. Information Agency	Frank Shakespeare, director
U.S. Postal Service	E. T. Klassen, postmaster general
U.S. Tariff Commission	Catherine Bedell, commissioner
Veterans Administration	Donald E. Johnson, administrator

During November and December 1972, President Nixon nominated the following, pending Senate confirmation:

Counsellor to the President	Anne Armstrong
Assistant, Domestic Affairs	Kenneth R. Cole, Jr.
Assistant, Management and Budget	Roy L. Ash
DEPT. OF STATE	Kenneth Rush, undersecretary
Political Affairs	William J. Porter, undersecretary
Economic Affairs	William J. Casey, undersecretary
DEPT. OF DEFENSE	Elliot L. Richardson, secretary
	William P. Clements, deputy secy.
DEPT. OF JUSTICE	Joseph T. Sneed, deputy atty. gen.
Solicitor General	Robert H. Bork
DEPT. OF THE INTERIOR	John C. Whitaker, undersecretary
National Park Service	Ronald H. Walker, director
DEPT. OF COMMERCE	Frederick B. Dent, secretary
DEPT. OF LABOR	Peter J. Brennan, secretary
DEPT. OF HEALTH, EDUCATION, AND WELFARE	Caspar W. Weinberger, secretary
DEPT. OF HOUSING AND URBAN DEVELOPMENT	James T. Lynn, secretary
DEPT. OF TRANSPORTATION	Claude S. Brinegar, secretary
	Emil Krogh, undersecretary
Urban Mass Transportation	Frank C. Herringer, administrator
U.S. Information Agency	James Keogh, director

Supreme Court

Chief Justice of the United States:
Warren Earl Burger

Associate Justices:
William O. Douglas
William J. Brennan, Jr.
Potter Stewart
Byron R. White
Thurgood Marshall
Harry A. Blackmun
Lewis F. Powell, Jr.
William H. Rehnquist

House of Representatives

membership in 1972, and
winners in November 1972 elections

State, district, name, and party

Ala.—1. Edwards, W. J. (R)
2. Dickinson, W. L. (R)
3. Andrews, Elizabeth (D)*§
Nichols, William (D)
4. Nichols, William (D)*
Bevill, Tom (D)
5. Flowers, W. W. (D)*
Jones, Robert E. Jr. (D)
6. Buchanan, John H. Jr. (R)
7. Bevill, Tom (D)*
Flowers, W. W. (D)
8. Jones, Robert E. Jr. (D)†
Alaska—Begich, Nick J. (D)‖
Ariz.—1. Rhodes, John J. (R)
2. Udall, Morris K. (D)
3. Steiger, Sam (R)
4. Conlan, J. B. (R)‡
Ark.—1. Alexander, Bill (D)
2. Mills, Wilbur D. (D)
3. Hammerschmidt, J. P. (R)
4. Pryor, David (D)*
Thornton, Ray (D)
Calif.—1. Clausen, Don H. (R)
2. Johnson, Harold T. (D)
3. Moss, John E. (D)
4. Leggett, Robert L. (D)
5. Burton, Phillip (D)
6. Mailliard, William S. (R)
7. Dellums, R. V. (D)
8. Miller, George P. (D)*
Stark, F. H. (D)
9. Edwards, W. Donlon (D)
10. Gubser, Charles S. (R)
11. McCloskey, Paul N. Jr. (R)*
Ryan, Leo J. (D)
12. Talcott, Burt L. (R)
13. Teague, Charles M. (R)
14. Waldie, Jerome R. (D)
15. McFall, John J. (D)
16. Sisk, B. F. (D)
17. Anderson, Glenn M. (D)*
McCloskey, Paul N. Jr. (R)
18. Mathias, Robert B. (R)
19. Holifield, Chet (D)
20. Smith, H. Allen (R)*
Moorhead, C. J. (R)
21. Hawkins, Augustus F. (D)
22. Corman, James C. (D)
23. Clawson, Del M. (R)
24. Rousselot, John H. (R)
25. Wiggins, Charles (R)
26. Rees, Thomas (D)
27. Goldwater, Barry, Jr. (R)
28. Bell, Alphonzo (R)
29. Danielson, George E. (D)
30. Roybal, Edward R. (D)
31. Wilson, Charles H. (D)
32. Hosmer, Craig (R)
33. Pettis, Jerry (R)
34. Hanna, Richard T. (D)
35. Schmitz, John G. (R)*
Anderson, Glenn M. (D)
36. Wilson, Bob (R)*
Ketchum, W. M. (R)
37. Van Deerlin, Lionel (D)*
Burke, Y. B. (D)
38. Veysey, Victor V. (R)*
Brown, G. E. Jr. (D)
39. Hinshaw, A. J. (R)‡
40. Wilson, Bob (R)‡
41. Van Deerlin, Lionel (D)‡
42. Burgener, C. W. (R)‡
43. Veysey, Victor V. (R)‡
Colo.—1. McKevitt, James D. (R)*
Schroeder, P. (D)
2. Brotzman, D. G. (R)
3. Evans, Frank (D)
4. Aspinall, Wayne N. (D)*
Johnson, J. T. (R)
5. Armstrong, W. L. (R)‡
Conn.—1. Cotter, William R. (D)
2. Steele, Robert H. (R)
3. Giaimo, Robert N. (D)
4. McKinney, Stewart B. (R)
5. Monagan, John S. (D)*
Sarasin, A. (R)
6. Grasso, Ella T. (D)
Del.—duPont, Pierre S., IV (R)
Fla.—1. Sikes, Robert L. F. (D)
2. Fuqua, Don (D)
3. Bennett, Charles E. (D)
4. Chappell, William, Jr. (D)
5. Frey, Louis, Jr. (R)*
Gunter, W. D. Jr. (D)
6. Gibbons, Sam (D)*
Young, C. William (R)
7. Haley, James A. (D)*
Gibbons, Sam (D)
8. Young, C. William (R)*
Haley, James A. (D)
9. Rogers, Paul G. (D)*
Frey, Louis Jr. (R)
10. Burke, J. Herbert (R)*
Bafalis, L. A. (R)
11. Pepper, Claude (D)*
Rogers, Paul G. (D)
12. Fascell, Dante B. (D)*
Burke, J. Herbert (R)
13. Lehman, William (D)‡
14. Pepper, Claude (D)‡
15. Fascell, Dante B. (D)‡
Ga.—1. Hagan, G. Elliott (D)*
Ginn, R. B. (D)
2. Mathis, Dawson (D)
3. Brinkley, Jack (D)
4. Blackburn, B. B. (R)
5. Thompson, S. F. (R)*
Young, Andrew (D)
6. Flynt, J. J., Jr. (D)
7. Davis, John W. (D)
8. Stuckey, W. S., Jr. (D)
9. Landrum, Phil M. (D)
10. Stephens, Robert G., Jr. (D)
Hawaii—1. Matsunaga, Spark M. (D)
2. Mink, Patsy (D)
Ida.—1. McClure, James A. (R)*
Symms, S. D. (R)
2. Hansen, Orval (R)
Ill.—1. Metcalfe, Ralph (D)
2. Mikva, Abner (D)*
Murphy, Morgan (D)
3. Murphy, Morgan (D)*
Hanrahan, R. P. (R)
4. Derwinski, Edward J. (R)
5. Kluczynski, John C. (D)
6. Vacancy¶
Collier, H. R. (R)
7. Annunzio, Frank (D)*
Vacancy¶
8. Rostenkowski, Dan (D)
9. Yates, Sidney R. (D)
10. Collier, H. R. (R)*
Young, S. H. (R)
11. Pucinski, Roman C. (R)*
Annunzio, Frank (D)
12. McClory, Robert (R)*
Crane, Philip M. (R)
13. Crane, Philip M. (R)*
McClory, Robert (R)
14. Erlenborn, J. N. (R)
15. Carlson, Clifford (R)*♀
Arends, Leslie C. (R)
16. Anderson, John B. (R)
17. Arends, Leslie C. (R)*
O'Brien, G. M. (R)
18. Michel, Robert H. (R)
19. Railsback, Thomas F. (R)
20. Findley, Paul (R)
21. Gray, Kenneth J. (D)*
Madigan, E. R. (R)
22. Springer, William L. (R)*
Shipley, George E. (D)
23. Shipley, George E. (D)*
Price, Melvin (D)
24. Price, Melvin (D)*
Gray, Kenneth J. (D)
Ind.—1. Madden, Ray J. (D)
2. Landgrebe, Earl F. (R)
3. Brademas, John (D)
4. Roush, J. Edward (D)
5. Hillis, Elwood H. (R)
6. Bray, William G. (R)
7. Myers, John (R)
8. Zion, Roger (R)
9. Hamilton, L. H. (D)
10. Dennis, David (R)
11. Jacobs, A. Jr. (D)*
Hudnut, W. H. III (R)
Iowa—1. Schwengel, Fred (R)*
Mezvinsky, E. (D)
2. Culver, J. C. (D)
3. Gross, H. R. (R)
4. Kyl, John H. (R)*
Smith, Neal (D)
5. Smith, Neal (D)*
Scherle, W. J. (R)
6. Mayne, Wiley (R)
7. Scherle, W. J. (R)†
Kan.—1. Sebelius, Keith G. (R)
2. Roy, William R. (D)
3. Winn, Larry, Jr. (R)
4. Shriver, Garner E. (R)
5. Skubitz, Joseph (R)
Ky.—1. Stubblefield, Frank A. (D)
2. Natcher, William H. (D)
3. Mazzoli, Romano L. (D)
4. Snyder, Gene (R)
5. Carter, Tim L. (R)
6. Curlin, William F. Jr. (D)*
Breckinridge, J. B. (D)
7. Perkins, Carl D. (D)
La.—1. Hébert, F. Edward (D)
2. Boggs, Hale (D)‖
3. Caffery, Patrick (D)*
Treen, David C. (R)
4. Waggonner, Joe D., Jr. (D)
5. Passman, Otto E. (D)
6. Rarick, John R. (D)
7. Breaux, John B. (D)♂
8. Long, Speedy O. (D)*
Long, Gillis W. (D)
Me.—1. Kyros, Peter (D)
2. Hathaway, W. D. (D)*
Cohen, W. S. (R)
Md.—1. Mills, William O. (R)
2. Long, Clarence D. (D)
3. Garmatz, Edward A. (D)*
Sarbanes, Paul S. (D)
4. Sarbanes, Paul S. (D)*
Holt, M. S. (R)
5. Hogan, Lawrence J. (R)
6. Byron, Goodloe E. (D)
7. Mitchell, Parren J. (D)
8. Gude, Gilbert (R)
Mass.—1. Conte, Silvio O. (R)
2. Boland, Edward P. (D)
3. Drinan, Robert F. (D)*
Donohue, Harold D. (D)
4. Donohue, Harold D (D)*
Drinan, Robert F. (D)
5. Vacancy□
Cronin, Paul W. (R)
6. Harrington, M. J. (D)
7. Macdonald, Torbert H. (D)
8. O'Neill, Thomas P., Jr. (D)
9. Hicks, Louise Day (D)*
Moakley, J. J. (I)
10. Heckler, Margaret (R)
11. Burke, James A. (D)
12. Keith, Hastings (R)*
Studds, Gerry E. (D)
Mich.—1. Conyers, John, Jr. (D)
2. Esch, Marvin (R)
3. Brown, Garry E. (R)
4. Hutchinson, Edward (R)
5. Ford, Gerald R., Jr. (R)
6. Chamberlain, Charles E. (R)
7. Riegle, D. W., Jr. (R)
8. Harvey, James (R)
9. Vander Jagt, Guy (R)
10. Cederberg, Elford A. (R)
11. Ruppe, Philip (R)
12. O'Hara, James G. (D)
13. Diggs, Charles C., Jr. (D)
14. Nedzi, Lucien N. (D)
15. Ford, W. D. (D)
16. Dingell, John D. (D)
17. Griffiths, Martha W. (D)
18. Broomfield, William S. (R)*
Huber, R. J. (R)
19. McDonald, J. H. (R)*
Broomfield, William S. (R)
Minn.—1. Quie, Albert H. (R)
2. Nelsen, Ancher (R)
3. Frenzel, William (R)
4. Karth, Joseph E. (D)
5. Fraser, Donald M. (D)
6. Zwach, John M. (R)
7. Bergland, Bob S. (D)
8. Blatnik, John A. (D)
Miss.—1. Abernethy, Thomas G. (D)*
Whitten, Jamie L. (D)
2. Whitten, Jamie L. (D)*
Bowen, D. R. (D)
3. Griffin, Charles (D)*
Montgomery, G. V. (D)
4. Montgomery, G. V. (D)*
Cochran, Thad (R)
5. Colmer, William M. (D)*
Lott, Trent (R)
Mo.—1. Clay, William (D)
2. Symington, James W. (D)
3. Sullivan, Leonor K. (D)
4. Randall, William J. (D)
5. Bolling, Richard (D)
6. Hull, W. R. Jr. (D)*
Litton, Jerry (D)
7. Hall, Durward G. (R)*
Taylor, Gene (R)
8. Ichord, Richard H. (D)
9. Hungate, W. L. (D)
10. Burlison, Bill D. (D)
Mont.—1. Shoup, Richard G. (R)
2. Melcher, John (D)
Neb.—1. Thone, Charles (R)
2. McCollister, John Y. (R)
3. Martin, David (R)
Nev.—Baring, Walter S. (D)*
Towell, David (R)
N.H.—1. Wyman, Louis C. (R)
2. Cleveland, James C. (R)
N.J.—1. Hunt, John E. (R)
2. Sandman, Charles W., Jr. (R)
3. Howard, J. J. (D)
4. Thompson, Frank, Jr. (D)
5. Frelinghuysen, Peter, Jr. (R)
6. Forsythe, Edwin B. (R)
7. Widnall, William B. (R)
8. Roe, Robert A. (D)
9. Helstoski, Henry (D)
10. Rodino, Peter W., Jr. (D)
11. Minish, Joseph G. (D)
12. Dwyer, Florence P. (R)*
Rinaldo, M. J. (R)
13. Gallagher, Cornelius E. (D)*
Maraziti, J. J. (R)
14. Daniels, Dominick V. (D)
15. Patten, Edward J. (D)
N.M.—1. Lujan, Manuel, Jr. (R)
2. Runnels, Harold L. (D)

Senate

membership in 1972, and
winners in November 1972 elections

State, name, and party	Term expires
Ala.—Allen, James B. (D)	1975
Sparkman, John (D)	1979
Alaska—Gravel, Mike (D)	1975
Stevens, Theodore F (R)	1979
Ariz.—Goldwater, Barry (R)	1975
Fannin, Paul J. (R)	1977
Ark.—Fulbright, J. W. (D)	1975
McClellan, John (D)	1979
Calif.—Cranston, Alan (D)	1975
Tunney, John V. (D)	1977
Colo.—Dominick, Peter (R)	1975
Allott, Gordon (R)*	1973
Haskell, F. K. (D)	1979
Conn.—Ribicoff, Abraham (D)	1975
Weicker, Lowell P., Jr. (R)	1977
Del.—Boggs, J. Caleb (R)*	1973
Biden, J. R. (D)	1979
Roth, William V., Jr. (R)	1977
Fla.—Gurney, Edward (R)	1975
Chiles, Lawton (D)	1977
Ga.—Talmadge, Herman (D)	1975
Gambrell, David H. (D)*	1972
Nunn, Sam (D)	1979
Hawaii—Inouye, Daniel K. (D)	1975
Fong, Hiram L. (R)	1977
Ida.—Church, Frank (D)	1975
Jordan, Len B. (R)*	1973
McClure, J. A. (R)	1979
Ill.—Stevenson, Adlai, III (D)	1975
Percy, Charles H. (R)	1979
Ind.—Bayh, Birch E., Jr. (D)	1975
Hartke, Vance (D)	1977
Ia.—Hughes, Harold (D)	1975
Miller, Jack R. (R)*	1973
Clark, Richard (D)	1979
Kan.—Dole, Robert (R)	1975
Pearson, James B. (R)	1979
Ky.—Cook, Marlow W. (R)	1975
Cooper, John S. (R)*	1973
Huddleston, Walter (D)	1979
La.—Long, Russell (D)	1975
Ellender, Allen J. (D)*	1973
Johnston, J. B. (D)	1979
Me.—Muskie, Edmund S. (D)	1977
Smith, Margaret Chase (R)*	1973
Hathaway, W. D. (D)	1979
Md.—Mathias, C. M., Jr. (R)	1975
Beall, J. Glenn, Jr. (R)	1977
Mass.—Kennedy, Edward M. (D)	1977
Brooke, Edward W. (R)	1979
Mich.—Hart, Philip A. (D)	1977
Griffin, Robert P. (R)	1979
Minn.—Humphrey, Hubert H. (D)	1977
Mondale, Walter F. (D)	1979
Miss.—Stennis, John (D)	1977
Eastland, James (D)	1979
Mo.—Eagleton, T. F. (D)	1975
Symington, Stuart (D)	1977
Mont.—Mansfield, Mike (D)	1977
Metcalf, Lee (D)	1979
Neb.—Hruska, Roman L. (R)	1977
Curtis, Carl T. (R)	1979
Nev.—Bible, Alan (D)	1975
Cannon, Howard W. (D)	1977
N.H.—Cotton, Norris (R)	1975
McIntyre, Thomas J. (D)	1979
N.J.—Williams, Harrison, Jr. (D)	1977
Case, Clifford P. (R)	1979
N.M.—Anderson, Clinton (D)*	1973
Domenici, P. V. (R)	1979
Montoya, Joseph M. (D)	1977
N.Y.—Javits, Jacob K. (R)	1975
Buckley, James L. (C)	1977
N.C.—Ervin, Sam J., Jr. (D)	1975
Jordan, B. Everett (D)*	1973
Helms, Jesse A. (R)	1979
N.D.—Young, Milton R. (R)	1975
Burdick, Quentin N. (D)	1977
Ohio—Saxbe, William (R)	1975
Taft, Robert, Jr. (R)	1977
Okla.—Bellmon, Henry (R)	1975
Harris, Fred R. (D)*	1973
Bartlett, D. F. (R)	1979
Ore.—Packwood, Robert (R)	1975
Hatfield, Mark O. (R)	1979
Penn.—Schweiker, R. S. (R)	1975
Scott, Hugh (R)	1977
R. I.—Pastore, John O. (D)	1977
Pell, Claiborne (D)	1979
S.C.—Hollings, Ernest F. (D)	1975
Thurmond, Strom (R)	1979
S.D.—McGovern, George (D)	1975
Mundt, Karl E. (R)*	1973
Abourezk, James (D)	1979
Tenn.—Brock, William E., III (R)	1977
Baker, Howard, Jr. (R)	1979
Tex.—Bentsen, Lloyd M., Jr. (D)	1977
Tower, John G. (R)	1979
Utah—Bennett, Wallace (R)	1975
Moss, Frank E. (D)	1977
Vt.—Aiken, George D. (R)	1975
Stafford, Robert T. (R)	1977
Va.—Byrd, Harry F., Jr. (D)	1977
Spong, William, Jr. (D)*	1973
Scott, W. L. (R)	1979
Wash.—Magnuson, Warren (D)	1975
Jackson, Henry M. (D)	1977
W.Va.—Byrd, Robert C. (D)	1977
Randolph, Jennings (D)	1979
Wis.—Nelson, Gaylord (D)	1975
Proxmire, William (D)	1977
Wyo.—McGee, Gale W. (D)	1977
Hansen, Clifford P. (R)	1979

*Incumbent replaced by member listed immediately below.

House of Representatives (continued)

State, district, name, and party

N.Y.—1. Pike, Otis G. (D)
2. Grover, James R., Jr. (R)
3. Wolff, L. L. (D)*
Roncallo, A. D. (R)
4. Wydler, John W. (R)*
Lent, Norman F. (R)
5. Lent, Norman F. (R)*
Wydler, John W. (R)
6. Halpern, Seymour (R)*
Wolff, L. L. (D)
7. Addabbo, Joseph P. (D)
8. Rosenthal, Benjamin S. (D)
9. Delaney, James J. (D)
10. Celler, Emanuel (D)*
Biaggi, Mario (D)
11. Brasco, Frank J. (D)
12. Chisholm, Shirley (D)
13. Podell, B. L. (D)
14. Rooney, John J. (D)
15. Carey, Hugh L. (D)
16. Murphy, John M. (D)*
Holtzman, E. (D)
17. Koch, Edward I. (D)*
Murphy, John M. (D)
18. Rangel, Charles B. (D)*
Koch, Edward I (D)
19. Abzug, Bella (D)*
Rangel, Charles B. (D)
20. Vacancy◊
Abzug, Bella (D)
21. Badillo, Herman (D)
22. Schener, James (D)*
Bingham, J. B. (D)
23. Bingham, J. B. (D)*
Peyser, Peter A. (R)
24. Biaggi, Mario (D)*
Reid, Ogden R. (R)
25. Peyser, Peter A. (R)*
Fish, Hamilton, Jr. (R)
26. Reid, Ogden R. (R)*▲
Gilman, B. A. (R)
27. Dow, John G. (D)*
Robison, Howard W. (R)
28. Fish, Hamilton, Jr. (R)*
Stratton, Samuel S. (D)
29. Stratton, Samuel S. (D)*
King, Carleton J. (R)
30. King, Carleton J. (R)*
McEwen, Robert (R)
31. McEwen, Robert (R)*
Mitchell, D. J. (R)
32. Pirnie, Alexander (R)*
Hanley, James M. (D)
33. Robison, Howard W. (R)*
Walsh, W. F. (R)
34. Terry, John H. (R)*
Horton, Frank J. (R)
35. Hanley, James M. (D)*
Conable, B., Jr. (R)
36. Horton, Frank J. (R)*
Smith, H. P. III (R)
37. Conable, B., Jr. (R)*
Dulski, Thaddeus J. (D)
38. Hastings, James F. (R)*
Kemp, Jack F. (R)
39. Kemp, Jack F. (R)*
Hastings, James F. (R)
40. Smith, H. P. III (R)†
41. Dulski, Thaddeus J. (D)†
N.C.—1. Jones, Walter B. (D)
2. Fountain, L. H. (D)
3. Henderson, David N. (D)
4. Galifianakis, Nick (D)*
Andrews, Ike F. (D)
5. Mizell, Wilmer (R)
6. Preyer, L. R. (D)
7. Lennon, Alton (D)*
Rose, C. G. III (D)
8. Ruth, Earl B. (R)
9. Jonas, Charles Raper (R)*
Martin, J. G. (R)
10. Broyhill, James T. (R)
11. Taylor, Roy A. (D)
N.D.—1. Andrews, Mark (R)
2. Link, Arthur A. (D)†
Ohio—1. Keating, William J. (R)
2. Clancy, Donald D. (R)
3. Whalen, Charles W., Jr. (R)
4. McCulloch, William M. (R)*
Guyer, Tennyson (R)
5. Latta, Delbert L. (R)
6. Harsha, William H., Jr. (R)
7. Brown, Clarence J., Jr. (R)
8. Betts, Jackson E. (R)*
Powell, Walter E. (R)
9. Ashley, Thomas L. (D)
10. Miller, Clarence E. (R)
11. Stanton, John W. (R)
12. Devine, Samuel L. (R)
13. Mosher, Charles A. (R)
14. Seiberling, John F., Jr. (D)
15. Wylie, Chalmers P. (R)
16. Bow, Frank T. (R)*
Regula, R. S. (R)
17. Ashbrook, John M. (R)
18. Hays, Wayne L. (D)
19. Carney, Charles J. (D)
20. Stanton, James V. (D)
21. Stokes, Louis (D)
22. Vanik, Charles A. (D)
23. Minshall, William E. (R)
24. Powell, Walter E. (R)†
Okla.—1. Belcher, Page (R)*
Jones, James R. (D)
2. Edmondson, Ed (D)*
McSpadden, C. R. (D)
3. Albert, Carl (D)
4. Steed, Tom (D)
5. Jarman, John (D)
6. Camp, J. N. H. (R)
Ore.—1. Wyatt, Wendell (R)
2. Ullman, Al (D)
3. Green, Edith (D)
4. Dellenback, John R. (R)
Penn.—1. Barrett, William A. (D)
2. Nix, Robert N. C. (D)
3. Byrne, James A. (D)*
Green, William J., III (D)
4. Eilberg, Joshua (D)
5. Green, William J., III (D)*
Ware, John H., III (R)
6. Yatron, Gus (D)
7. Williams, L. G. (R)
8. Biester, E. G., Jr. (R)
9. Ware, John H., III (R)*
Shuster, E. G. (R)
10. McDade, Joseph M. (R)
11. Flood, Daniel J. (D)
12. Whalley, J. Irving (R)*
Saylor, John P. (R)
13. Coughlin, R. L. (R)
14. Moorhead, William S. (D)
15. Rooney, Fred B. (D)
16. Eshleman, Edwin D. (R)
17. Schneebeli, Herman T. (R)
18. H. John Heinz III (R)
19. Goodling, George A. (R)
20. Gaydos, Joseph (D)
21. Dent, John H. (D)
22. Saylor, John P. (R)*
Morgan, Thomas E. (D)
23. Johnson, Albert W. (R)
24. Vigorito, J. P. (D)
25. Clark, Frank M. (D)
26. Morgan, Thomas E. (D)†
27. Conover, W.S. II†
R.I.—1. St. Germain, Fernand J. (D)
2. Tiernan, Robert O. (D)
S.C.—1. Davis, Mendel (D)
2. Spence, Floyd D. (R)
3. Dorn, W. J. Bryan (D)
4. Mann, James R. (D)
5. Gettys, Thomas S. (D)
6. McMillan, John L. (D)*
Young, E. L. (R)
S.D.—1. Denholm, Frank E. (D)
2. Abourezk, James (D)*
Abdnor, James (R)
Tenn.—1. Quillen, James H. (R)
2. Duncan, John J. (R)
3. Baker, LaMar E. (R)
4. Evins, Joseph L. (D)
5. Fulton, Richard (D)
6. Anderson, W. R. (D)*
Beard, R. L. Jr. (R)
7. Blanton, Ray (D)*
Jones, Edward (D)
8. Jones, Edward (D)*
Kuykendall, Dan (R)
9. Kuykendall, Dan (R)†
Tex.—1. Patman, Wright (D)
2. Dowdy, John (D)*
Wilson, Charles (D)
3. Collins, James M. (R)
4. Roberts, Ray (D)
5. Cabell, Earle (D)*
Steelman, Alan (R)
6. Teague, Olin E. (D)
7. Archer, William R. (R)
8. Eckhardt, Robert C. (D)
9. Brooks, Jack (D)
10. Pickle, J. J. (D)
11. Poage, W. R. (D)
12. Wright, James C., Jr. (D)
13. Purcell, Graham (D)*
Price, Robert (R)
14. Young, John (D)
15. de la Garza, E. (D)
16. White, Richard C. (D)
17. Burleson, Omar (D)
18. Price, Robert (R)*
Jordan, B. C. (D)
19. Mahon, George (D)
20. Gonzalez, Henry B. (D)
21. Fisher, O. C. (D)
22. Casey, Robert R. (D)
23. Kazen, Abraham, Jr. (D)
24. Milford, Dale (D)‡
Utah—1. McKay, Koln G. (D)
2. Lloyd, Sherman P. (R)*
Owens, Wayne (D)
Vt.—Mallary, R. W. (R)+
Va.—1. Downing, Thomas N. (D)
2. Whitehurst, G. W. (R)
3. Satterfield, D. E., III (D)
4. Abbitt, Watkins M. (D)*
Daniel, R. W. (R)
5. Daniel, W. C. (D)
6. Vacancy⊕
Butler, M. C. (R)
7. Robinson, James K. (R)
8. Scott, William L. (R)*
Parris, S. E. (R)
9. Wampler, William C. (R)
10. Broyhill, Joel T. (R)
Wash.—1. Pelly, Thomas M. (R)*
Hempelmann, J. (D)
2. Meeds, Lloyd (D)
3. Hansen, Julia Butler (D)
4. McCormack, Mike (D)
5. Foley, Thomas S. (D)
6. Hicks, Floyd V. (D)
7. Adams, B. (D)
W.Va.—1. Mollohan, R. H. (D)
2. Staggers, Harley O. (D)
3. Slack, John M., Jr. (D)
4. Hechler, Ken (D)
5. Kee, James (D)†
Wis.—1. Aspin, Leslie (D)
2. Kastenmeier, Robert W. (D)
3. Thomson, Vernon W. (R)
4. Zablocki, Clement J. (D)
5. Reuss, Henry S. (D)
6. Steiger, William A. (R)
7. Obey, David R. (D)
8. Byrnes, John W. (R)*
Froehlich, H. V. (R)
9. Davis, Glenn R. (R)
10. O'Konski, Alvin E. (R)†
Wyo.—Roncalio, Teno (D)

*Incumbent replaced by member listed immediately below.
†District eliminated in 1972.
‡New district.
§Sworn in April 10, 1972 to succeed George W. Andrews (deceased).
||Reps. Begich and Boggs disappeared on a plane flight in Alaska, Oct. 16, 1972.
¶Vacancies created by death of George W. Collins, Dec. 8, 1972.
♀Sworn in April 11, 1972 to succeed Charlotte T. Reid (resigned).
♂Sworn in Oct. 12, 1972 to succeed Edwin Edwards (resigned).
□Vacancy created by resignation of F. Bradford Morse, May 1, 1971.
◊Vacancy created by death of William Ryan, Sept. 17, 1972.
▲Changed party affiliation from R to D, March 27, 1972.
+Sworn in Jan. 18, 1972 to succeed Robert T. Stafford (resigned).
⊕Vacancy created by resignation of Richard Poff, Aug. 29, 1972.

Major legislation passed by Congress, 1972

Act	House vote	Senate vote	Date of enactment
Campaign Spending (S382)—Placed limits on spending for advertising in all media by candidates for federal office, and tightened requirements for reporting sources and expenditures of campaign funds.	334–20 Jan. 19, 1972 Yeas: D. 197, R. 137 Nays: D. 9, R. 11	Passed by voice vote Dec. 14, 1971	Signed Feb. 7, 1972 PL 92-225
Drugs (S2097)—Approved the creation of the Special Action Office for Drug Abuse Prevention in the Executive Office of the President to co-ordinate all federal drug programs; and authorized $1 billion for state and local drug programs through fiscal 1975.	366–0 March 16, 1972 Yeas: D. 212, R. 154 Nays: D. 0, R. 0	63–0 March 17, 1972 Yeas: D. 32, R. 31 Nays: D. 0, R. 0	Signed March 21, 1972 PL 92-255
Higher Education (S659)—Authorized $19 billion for higher education programs through fiscal 1975, and $2 billion for school desegregation aid through fiscal 1974; established new program of direct federal aid to needy students; and postponed implementation of court desegregation orders requiring busing of school children.	218–180 June 8, 1972 Yeas: D. 129, R. 89 Nays: D. 104, R. 76	63–15 May 24, 1972 Yeas: D. 33, R. 30 Nays: D. 10, R. 5	Signed June 23, 1972 PL 92-318
Social Security (HR 15390)—Approved a 20% increase in Social Security benefits; provided for automatic increases for rises in the Consumer Price Index beginning with 1975; raised the taxable wage base to $10,800 in 1973, and to $12,000 in 1974.	302–35 June 30, 1972 Yeas: D. 194, R. 108 Nays: D. 7, R. 28	78–3 June 30, 1972 Yeas: D. 42, R. 36 Nays: D. 2, R. 1	Signed July 1, 1972 PL 92-336
Secret Pacts (S596)—Required the Secretary of State to submit to Congress within 60 days the text of any agreement (other than a treaty) with another nation.	Passed by voice vote Aug. 14, 1972	81–0 Feb. 16, 1972 Yeas: D. 42, R 39 Nays: D. 0, R. 0	Signed Aug. 22, 1972 PL 92-403
Water Pollution (S2770)—Authorized $24.7 billion over a 3-yr. period, including $18 billion in grants to states for construction of sewage treatment plants, to provide a comprehensive program to clean up the nation's waters by eliminating all pollutant discharges by 1985, and making the waters safe for fish, wildlife, and recreation by 1983.	366–11 Oct. 4, 1972 Yeas: D. 223, R. 143 Nays: D. 2, R. 9	74–0 Oct. 4, 1972 Yeas: D. 42, R. 32 Nays: D. 0, R. 0	Vetoed Oct. 17, 1972 Overrode by Congress House: 274–23, Senate: 52–12 Oct. 18, 1972 PL 92-500
Revenue Sharing (HR 14370)—Created a State and Local Government Fiscal Assistance Trust Fund for a 5-yr. program to share $30.2 billion in federal revenues with state and local governments, retroactive to Jan. 1, 1972, at an initial annual level of $5.3 billion, to run until Dec. 31, 1976.	265–110 Oct. 12, 1972 Yeas: D. 139, R. 126 Nays: D. 77, R. 33	59–19 Yeas: D. 30, R. 29 Nays: D. 14, R. 5	Signed Oct. 20, 1972 PL 92-512
Pesticides (HR 10729)—Approved broad powers for the Environmental Protection Agency to regulate the uses and sale of pesticides, and provided for compensation to manufacturers whose products were banned by the EPA.	198–99 Oct. 12, 1972 Yeas: D. 86, R. 112 Nays: D. 84, R. 15	Passed by voice vote Oct. 5, 1972	Signed Oct. 21, 1972 PL 92-516
Product Safety (S3419)—Established an independent 5-member commission to protect consumers from unreasonable product hazards.	Passed by voice vote Oct. 13, 1972	Passed by voice vote Oct. 14, 1972	Signed Oct. 28, 1972 PL 92-573
Welfare-Social Security (HR 1)—Provided $5.3 billion in increased benefits for the aged, blind, and disabled, and medicine for the disabled; provided for an increase in Social Security taxes as of 1973.	305–1 Oct. 17, 1972 Yeas: D. 176, R. 129 Nays: D. 1, R. 0	61–0 Oct. 17, 1972 Yeas: D. 37, R. 24 Nays: D. 0, R. 0	Signed Oct. 30, 1972 PL 92-603
Women's Rights (HJ Res. 208)—Sent to the states for ratification a constitutional amendment prohibiting discrimination based on sex.	354–24 Oct. 12, 1971 Yeas: D. 217, R. 137 Nays: D. 12, R. 12	84–8 March 22, 1972 Yeas: D. 47, R. 37 Nays: D. 2, R. 6	Signed March 22, 1972 Ratified by 22 states as of Dec. 31 (38 states needed)

State executive officials

incumbents and winners in 1972 elections

State	Governor	Secretary of State
Alabama	George Wallace(D)	Mabel Amos(D)
Alaska	William Egan(D)	—
Arizona	Jack Williams(R)	Wesley Bolin(D)
Arkansas	*Dale Bumpers(D)	*Kelly Bryant(D)
California	Ronald Reagan(R)	Edmund Brown, Jr.(D)
Colorado	John Love(R)	Byron Anderson(R)
Connecticut	Thomas Meskill(R)	Gloria Schaffer(D)
Delaware	Russell Peterson(R)	Eugene Bunting(R)
	†S. W. Tribbitt(D)	
Florida	Reubin Askew(D)	Richard Stone(D)
Georgia	James Earl Carter(D)	Ben Fortson, Jr.(D)
Hawaii	John Burns(D)	—
Idaho	Cecil Andrus(D)	Pete Cenarrusa(R)
Illinois	Richard Ogilvie(R)	John Lewis(R)
	†Daniel Walker(D)	†Michael J. Howlett(D)
Indiana	Edgar Whitcomb(R)	Larry Conrad(D)
	†Otis R. Bowen(R)	
Iowa	*Robert Ray(R)	*Melvin Synhorst(R)
Kansas	*Robert Docking(D)	*Elwill Shanahan(R)
Kentucky	Wendell Ford(D)	Thelma Stovall(D)
Louisiana	John McKeithen(D)	Wade Martin, Jr.(D)
	†Edwin Edwards(D)	
Maine	Kenneth Curtis(D)	Joseph Edgar(R)
Maryland	Marvin Mandel(D)	Fred Wineland(D)
Massachusetts	Francis Sargent(R)	John Davoren(D)
Michigan	William Milliken(R)	Richard Austin(D)
Minnesota	Wendell Anderson(DFL)	Arlen Erdahl(R)
Mississippi	W. L. Waller(D)	Heber Ladner(D)
Missouri	Warren Hearnes(D)	*James Kirkpatrick(D)
	†C. S. Bond(R)	
Montana	Forrest Anderson(D)	*Frank Murray(D)
	†T. L. Judge(D)	
Nebraska	J. James Exon(D)	Allen Beermann(R)
Nevada	Mike O'Callaghan(D)	John Koontz(D)
New Hampshire	Walter Peterson(R)	Robert Stark(R)
	†M. Thomson, Jr.(R)	
New Jersey	William Cahill(R)	Paul Sherwin(R)
New Mexico	Bruce King(D)	Betty Fiorina(D)
New York	Nelson Rockefeller(R)	John Lomenzo(R)
North Carolina	Robert Scott(D)	*Thad Eure(D)
	†J. Holshouser, Jr.(R)	
North Dakota	William Guy(D)	*Ben Meier(R)
	†Arthur A. Link(D)	
Ohio	John Gilligan(D)	Ted Brown(R)
Oklahoma	David Hall(D)	John Rogers(D)
Oregon	Tom McCall(R)	*Clay Meyers(R)
Pennsylvania	Milton Shapp(D)	C. DeLores Tucker(D)
Rhode Island	Frank Licht(D)	August LaFrance(D)
	†Philip W. Noel(D)	†Robert F. Burns(D)
South Carolina	John West(D)	O. Frank Thornton(D)
South Dakota	*Richard Kneip(D)	Alma Larson(R)
		†Lorna Herseth(D)
Tennessee	Winfield Dunn(R)	Joe Carr(D)
Texas	Preston Smith(D)	Martin Dies, Jr.(D)
	†Dolph Briscoe(D)	
Utah	*Calvin Rampton(D)	*Clyde Miller(D)
Vermont	Deane Davis(R)	*Richard Thomas(R)
	†Thomas Salmon(D)	
Virginia	A. Linwood Holton(R)	Cynthia Newman(R)
Washington	*Daniel Evans(R)	*A. Ludlow Kramer(R)
West Virginia	*Arch Moore, Jr.(R)	John D. Rockefeller IV(D)
		†Edgar F. Heiskell III(R)
Wisconsin	Patrick Lucey(D)	Robert Zimmerman(R)
Wyoming	Stanley Hathaway(R)	Thyra Thomson(R)

*Incumbent reelected. †Winner, replacing official immediately above.

Source: Council of State Governments.

Apportionment of presidential electoral votes, 1972

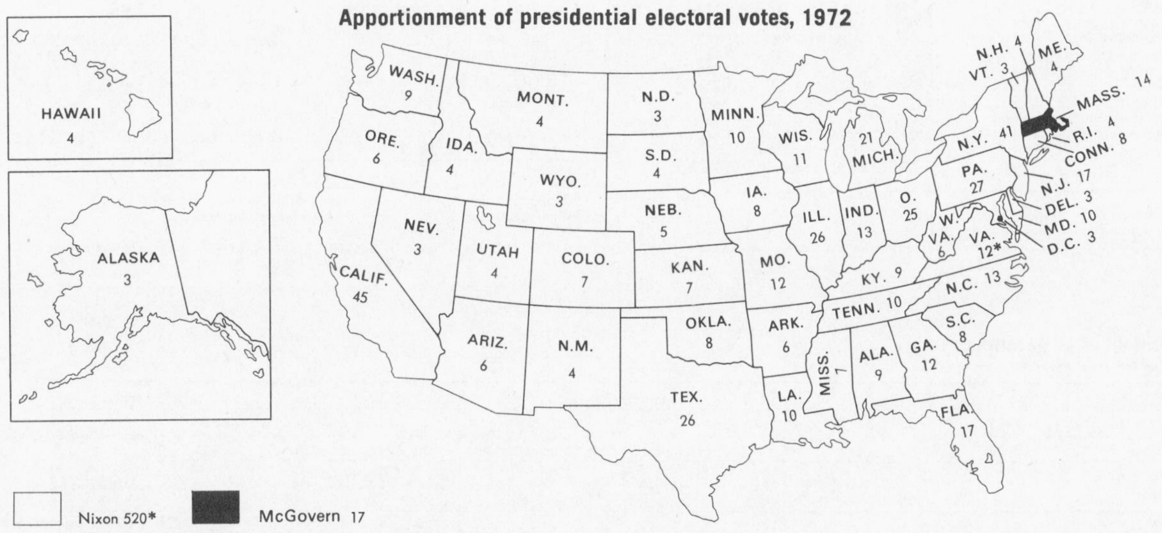

*One Virginia elector cast his vote for John Hospers, a noncandidate.

Electoral votes in past presidential elections

Year	Winning candidate	Party	TOTAL ELECTORAL VOTES CAST: For winner	TOTAL ELECTORAL VOTES CAST: Others
1789*	G. Washington	†	69	69
1792*	G. Washington	Federalist	132	132
1796*	J. Adams	Federalist	71	205
1800*	T. Jefferson	Democratic-Republican	73‡	203
1804	T. Jefferson	Democratic-Republican	162	14
1808	J. Madison	Democratic-Republican	122	53
1812	J. Madison	Democratic-Republican	128	89
1816	J. Monroe	Republican	183	34
1820	J. Monroe	Republican	231	1
1824	J.Q. Adams	§	84‖	177‖
1828	A. Jackson	Democratic	178	83
1832	A. Jackson	Democratic	219	67
1836	M. Van Buren	Democratic	170	124
1840	W.H. Harrison	Whig	234	60
1844	J.K. Polk	Democratic	170	105
1848	Z. Taylor	Whig	163	127
1852	F. Pierce	Democratic	254	42
1856	J. Buchanan	Democratic	174	122
1860	A. Lincoln	Republican	180	123
1864	A. Lincoln	Unionist	212	21
1868	U.S. Grant	Republican	214	80
1872	U.S. Grant	Republican	286	63
1876	R.B. Hayes	Republican	185	184
1880	J.A. Garfield	Republican	214	155
1884	G. Cleveland	Democratic	219	182
1888	B. Harrison	Republican	233	168
1892	G. Cleveland	Democratic	277	167
1896	W. McKinley	Republican	271	176
1900	W. McKinley	Republican	292	155
1904	T. Roosevelt	Republican	336	140
1908	W.H. Taft	Republican	321	162
1912	W. Wilson	Democratic	435	96
1916	W. Wilson	Democratic	277	254
1920	W.G. Harding	Republican	404	127
1924	C. Coolidge	Republican	382	149
1928	H.C. Hoover	Republican	444	87
1932	F.D. Roosevelt	Democratic	472	59
1936	F.D. Roosevelt	Democratic	523	8
1940	F.D. Roosevelt	Democratic	449	82
1944	F.D. Roosevelt	Democratic	432	99
1948	H.S. Truman	Democratic	303	228
1952	D.D. Eisenhower	Republican	442	89
1956	D.D. Eisenhower	Republican	457	74
1960	J.F. Kennedy	Democratic	303	234
1964	L.B. Johnson	Democratic	486	52
1968	R.M. Nixon	Republican	301	237
1972	R.M. Nixon	Republican	520	18

*In these elections, each elector voted for two men without indicating which was to be president and which vice-president. Thus, the winner need only have 25% +1 vote. †No formally organized parties. ‡As both Jefferson and Burr received the same number of electoral votes the decision was referred to the House of Representatives. §No distinct party designations. ‖As no candidate received a majority of the electoral votes the decision was made by the House of Representatives. Source: *Encyclopaedia Britannica*.

V. WALKER

Federal moneys to state and local governments

in million dollars

Purpose	1963	1964	1965	1966	1967	1968	1969	1970	1971	1972 (estimate)
Public welfare	2,811	3,031	3,133	3,726	3,945	5,582	6,534	8,525	11,292	15,208
Highways	3,023	3,644	4,018	4,010	4,028	4,196	4,162	4,333	4,664	4,742
Education	465	481	610	1,525	2,298	2,721	2,612	2,981	3,331	3,496
Economic opportunity and manpower	441	573	567	921	1,190	1,789	1,805	2,026	2,899	3,890
Urban affairs	400	452	576	934	1,273	1,394	1,670	2,432	2,854	3,229
Health	546	584	635	766	1,234	1,218	1,244	1,483	1,937	2,020
Others	948	1,376	1,367	1,080	1,277	1,699	2,228	2,235	2,867	6,495
Total	8,634	10,141	10,906	12,962	15,245	18,599	20,255	24,015	29,844	39,080

Years ending June 30. Source: U.S. Department of Commerce, Bureau of the Census, *Statistical Abstract of the United States.*

Expenditures of all governments

Fiscal year 1971; million dollars

Function	Total	Federal	State	Local
Intergovernmental expenditure	*	27,500	32,640	601
Direct expenditure	369,423	198,657	66,200	104,566
General expenditure	301,096	150,422	56,478	94,196
National defense and international relations	80,910	80,910	—	—
Postal service	8,683	8,683	—	—
Space research and technology	3,334	3,334	—	—
Education	64,042	4,629	15,800	43,613
Highways	18,396	301	12,304	5,792
Public welfare	20,446	2,220	10,518	7,708
Health and hospitals	14,835	3,630	5,400	5,806
Police and fire protection	8,009	478	797	6,733
Sewerage and sanitation	4,087	—	—	4,087
Natural resources	13,740	10,658	2,484	597
Housing and urban renewal	4,467	1,913	32	2,522
Air transportation	3,176	2,115	148	913
Water transport and terminals	2,150	1,646	161	343
Social insurance administration	2,031	1,086	942	3
Financial administration	3,612	1,341	1,131	1,141
Interest on general debt	21,688	16,599	1,761	3,328
Other	27,490	10,879	5,001	11,611
Utility expenditure	8,675	—	—	8,675
Liquor stores expenditure	1,625	—	1,395	230
Insurance trust expenditure	58,028	48,235	8,327	1,466
Total expenditure	369,423*	226,157	98,840	105,167*

Detail may not add to totals because of rounding.
*Duplicative transactions between levels of government are excluded.
Source: U.S. Department of Commerce, Bureau of the Census, *Governmental Finances.*

Revenue of all governments

Fiscal year 1971; million dollars

Source	Total	Federal	State	Local
Intergovernmental revenue	*	—	23,809	34,473
Revenue from own sources	342,489	202,544	73,424	66,521
General revenue from own sources	275,669	156,887	61,290	57,491
Taxes	232,252	137,277	51,541	43,434
Property	37,852	—	1,126	36,726
Individual income	98,130	86,230	10,153	1,747
Corporation income	30,209	26,785	3,424	†
Sales and gross receipts	52,660	19,427	29,570	3,662
Customs duties	2,591	2,591	—	—
General sales, gross receipts	17,812	—	15,473	2,339
Motor fuel	10,588	3,918	6,628	42
Alcoholic beverages	6,370	4,781	1,527	63
Tobacco products	4,883	2,207	2,536	140
Public utilities	3,844	2,096	1,012	735
Other	6,571	3,834	2,394	343
Motor vehicle, operators license	3,140	—	2,953	186
Death and gift	4,839	3,735	1,104	‡
All other	5,423	1,100	3,211	1,112
Charges, miscellaneous revenue	43,417	19,610	9,749	14,058
Utility revenue	7,276	—	—	7,276
Liquor stores revenue	2,083	—	1,814	269
Insurance trust revenue	57,461	45,657	10,320	1,484
Total revenue	342,489*	202,544	97,233	100,993*

Detail may not add to totals because of rounding.
*Duplicative transactions between levels of government are excluded.
†Minor amount included in individual income tax figures.
‡Minor amount included in "All other" taxes.
Source: U.S. Department of Commerce, Bureau of the Census, *Governmental Finances.*

Gross debt of all government

In billion dollars; at end of fiscal years

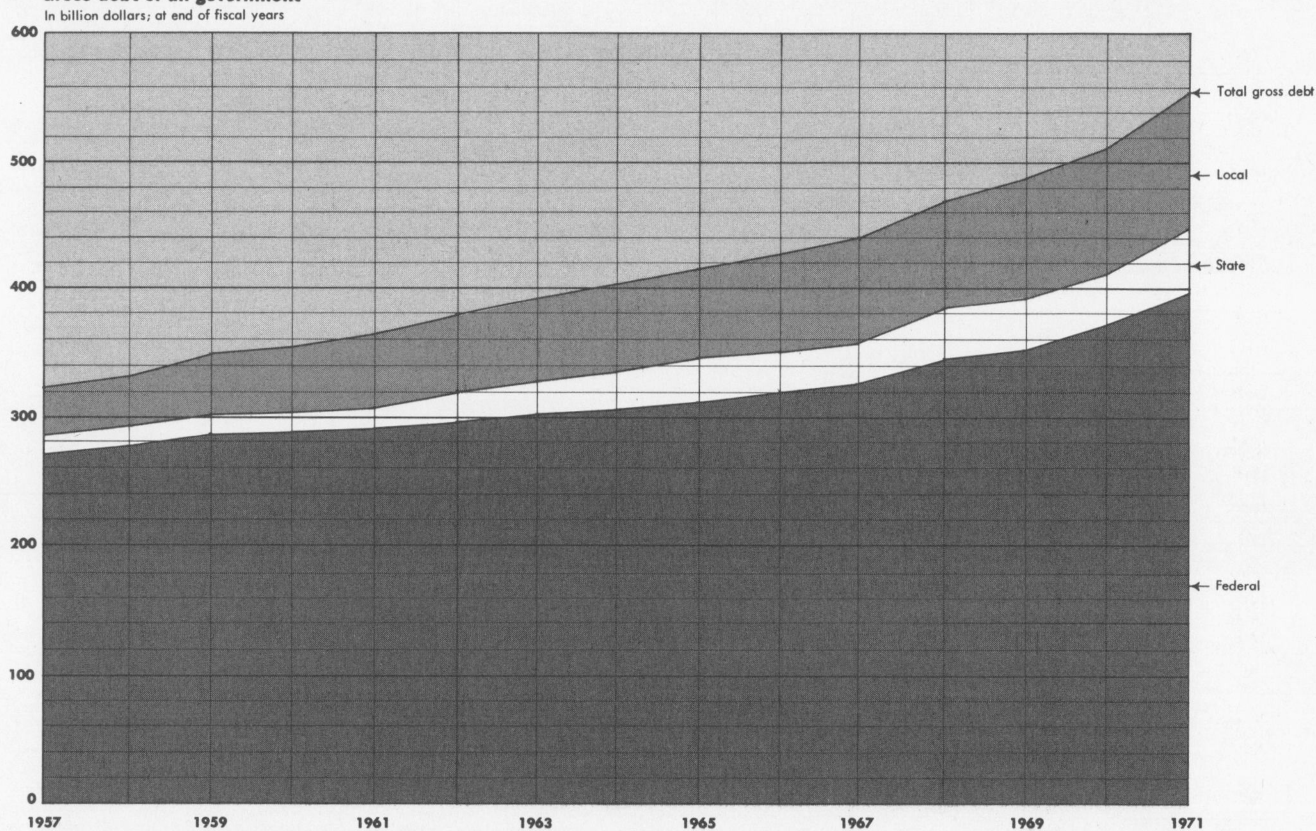

Source: U.S. Department of Commerce, Bureau of the Census; and Treasury Department. Data compiled by Tax Foundation, Inc.

Education

Federal funds supporting education

in thousand dollars

Funds	1966	1968	1970	1972*
Supporting education in educational institutions	6,779,578	7,804,454	9,237,410	11,720,848
Grants, total	6,167,878	7,201,173	8,631,114	11,417,956
Elementary-secondary education	2,480,078	2,967,004	3,212,418	4,083,489
Higher education	2,830,400	3,262,988	3,829,603	4,804,840
Vocational-technical and continuing education (not classifiable by level)	857,400	971,181	1,589,093	2,529,627
Loans, total	611,700	603,281	606,296	302,892
Student loan program, National Defense Education Act	235,900	226,303	295,173	223,005
College facilities loans	375,800	376,978	311,123	79,887
Other funds for education and related activities	3,903,859	3,605,629	3,426,074	4,128,291
Applied research and development	1,026,600	1,142,350	1,234,099	1,444,000
School lunch and milk programs	421,900	543,845	676,196	927,547
Training of federal personnel	1,706,700	1,138,333	691,694	727,118
Library services	86,300	136,099	170,135	184,871
International education	232,658	272,008	193,464	246,872
Other	429,701	372,994	460,486	597,883

*Estimated data.
Source: U.S. Department of Health, Education, and Welfare, Office of Education, *Digest of Educational Statistics*.

Vocational education

Type of program	NUMBER OF STUDENTS 1964–65	1967–68	1970–71
Agriculture	887,529	851,158	845,085
Distributive occupations	333,342	574,785	578,075
Home economics	2,098,520	2,283,338	3,129,804
Trades and industry	1,087,807	1,628,542	2,075,166
Health occupations	66,772	140,987	269,546
Technical education	225,737	269,882	313,860
Office occupations	730,904	1,735,997	2,226,854
Special programs	—	49,297	1,087,270
Total	5,430,611	7,533,986*	10,495,411

Data refer to vocational programs receiving federal aid. Details do not add to total because some students are enrolled in more than one program.
Source: U.S. Department of Health, Education, and Welfare, Office of Education, annual reports on vocational and technical education, and unpublished data.

Cost of attending college

in current dollars

Expenditure	1962–63 Public	1962–63 Private	1967–68 Public	1967–68 Private	1972–73 Public	1972–73 Private
Tuition and required fees						
Universities	268	1,149	366	1,534	520	2,266
Other 4-year institutions	192	869	268	1,238	394	1,881
2-year institutions	97	600	144	893	242	1,401
Board rates						
Universities	456	507	496	556	618	691
Other 4-year institutions	403	462	437	501	555	622
2-year institutions	361	427	403	504	528	667
Charges for dormitory rooms						
Universities	262	366	337	454	483	629
Other 4-year institutions	219	277	292	365	441	519
2-year institutions	157	244	243	366	398	568

Data are for the entire academic year and are average charges per full-time resident degree-credit student.
Source: U.S. Department of Health, Education, and Welfare, Office of Education, *Digest of Educational Statistics*.

Level of school completed

25 years old and over, by color

Level of school completed	April 1940	April 1950	April 1960	March 1970
Less than 5 years elementary school, percent:				
White	10.9	8.7	6.7	4.2
Nonwhite	41.8	31.4	23.5	14.7
4 years of high school or more, percent:				
White	26.1	35.5	43.2	57.4
Nonwhite	7.7	13.4	21.7	36.1
4 or more years of college, percent:				
White	4.9	6.4	8.1	11.6
Nonwhite	1.3	2.2	3.5	6.1
Median school years completed, percent:				
White	8.7	9.7	10.8	12.2
Nonwhite	5.7	6.9	8.2	10.1

Source: U.S. Department of Health, Education and Welfare, Office of Education, *Digest of Educational Statistics*. Data compiled by U.S. Department of Commerce, Bureau of the Census.

Universities and colleges

state statistics

State	NUMBER OF INSTITUTIONS fall, 1971 Total	Public	Enrollment fall, 1971	EARNED DEGREES CONFERRED 1970–1971 Bachelor's and first professional	Master's, except first professional	Doctor's
Alabama	49	29	111,305	13,425	2,561	265
Alaska	3	1	12,342	369	231	12
Arizona	18	14	118,434	8,473	3,155	396
Arkansas	20	9	53,724	7,490	1,185	116
California	207	113	1,304,134	77,737	21,097	3,349
Colorado	29	20	128,160	12,903	3,571	656
Connecticut	46	19	129,505	11,948	4,352	519
Delaware	7	3	27,704	1,602	472	75
District of Columbia	19	3	80,452	7,541	4,632	576
Florida	62	34	251,861	21,599	5,069	702
Georgia	61	28	136,232	15,886	4,541	456
Hawaii	12	7	40,466	3,051	1,104	78
Idaho	10	6	35,591	2,778	462	57
Illinois	136	49	473,410	44,322	13,767	2,086
Indiana	45	6	203,481	24,508	8,632	1,355
Iowa	53	17	111,109	15,382	2,666	702
Kansas	52	27	106,495	12,747	2,849	387
Kentucky	36	8	104,798	13,303	2,765	190
Louisiana	23	12	129,995	14,871	3,343	391
Maine	18	3	32,897	4,540	746	25
Maryland	48	24	158,892	13,226	3,244	552
Massachusetts	120	30	315,349	32,743	11,236	1,791
Michigan	88	42	405,817	38,273	13,261	1,793
Minnesota	55	25	158,830	19,412	2,781	613
Mississippi	41	24	77,284	9,011	1,656	225
Missouri	70	22	188,335	20,938	6,009	645
Montana	12	9	29,421	4,026	682	76
Nebraska	27	13	66,663	10,278	1,374	223
Nevada	6	5	15,065	1,253	260	19
New Hampshire	19	4	30,064	4,328	598	54
New Jersey	58	25	233,214	20,373	5,694	551
New Mexico	11	8	48,538	4,409	1,301	182
New York	221	77	835,411	76,430	29,971	3,370
North Carolina	98	54	184,519	20,584	3,443	723
North Dakota	12	9	30,642	4,051	665	118
Ohio	97	29	387,299	46,055	9,762	1,419
Oklahoma	39	25	119,089	12,740	2,898	467
Oregon	40	20	122,189	10,558	3,251	494
Pennsylvania	142	30	426,391	52,460	12,434	1,636
Rhode Island	13	3	48,354	5,107	1,304	207
South Carolina	46	22	76,708	8,317	1,092	125
South Dakota	16	6	31,191	4,854	866	52
Tennessee	59	18	142,061	17,443	3,236	484
Texas	125	72	463,261	45,441	9,603	1,358
Utah	13	9	83,228	9,552	2,016	394
Vermont	19	5	24,353	3,091	704	28
Virginia	65	32	163,554	15,570	3,174	372
Washington	43	31	186,783	16,943	3,427	574
West Virginia	24	13	65,475	8,085	1,265	102
Wisconsin	57	27	213,654	23,314	4,815	960
Wyoming	8	8	17,257	1,349	329	88
Total U. S.	2,598	1,129	8,940,986	868,079	228,574	32,082

All totals exclude data for service academies.
Source: U.S. Department of Health, Education, and Welfare, Office of Education.

Public elementary and secondary schools

Fall 1971 estimates

State	ENROLLMENT Elementary	ENROLLMENT Secondary	INSTRUCTIONAL STAFF Total*	Principals and supervisors	Teachers, elementary	Teachers, secondary	TEACHERS' AVERAGE ANNUAL SALARIES Elementary	Secondary	STUDENT-TEACHER RATIO Elementary	Secondary	Expenditure per pupil†
Alabama	427,696	378,619	34,785	1,613	16,087	17,085	$ 7,659	$ 7,812	26.6	22.2	$ 511
Alaska	61,411	22,387	4,533	249	2,591	1,513	14,154	14,086	23.7	14.8	1,346
Arizona	316,498	138,014	21,885	842	14,185	5,971	9,450	10,450	22.3	23.1	787
Arkansas	248,586	212,766	21,700	761	9,899	10,406	6,899	7,137	25.1	20.4	571
California	2,934,735	1,776,881	205,610	12,025	111,303	74,266	11,021	12,095	26.4	23.9	786
Colorado	309,602	254,900	28,403	1,276	12,016	12,458	9,020	9,155	25.8	20.5	847
Connecticut	483,836	183,031	39,358	1,987	19,689	14,220	9,995	10,700	24.6	12.9	1,039
Delaware	73,887	61,126	7,040	380	3,110	3,140	10,025	10,397	23.8	19.5	1,023
District of Columbia	87,629	55,204	8,276	617	3,765	2,750	—	—	23.3	20.1	1,172
Florida	780,189	649,763	73,690	3,535	33,148	31,002	8,884	9,159	23.5	21.0	792
Georgia	701,000	393,000	51,837	2,909	29,301	19,627	7,422	8,143	23.9	20.0	722
Hawaii	102,106	80,357	9,637	720	4,774	3,339	10,665	10,750	21.4	24.1	960
Idaho	93,148	91,966	9,273	775	3,777	4,232	7,275	7,450	24.7	21.7	...
Illinois	1,489,500	878,000	122,912	5,022	67,050	45,440	10,320	11,200	22.2	19.3	960
Indiana	672,447	558,343	58,787	3,530	26,501	25,781	9,315	9,820	25.4	21.7	792
Iowa	465,122	195,301	39,795	2,207	17,223	15,905	9,198	10,067	27.0	12.3	923
Kansas	291,455	214,179	28,800	1,431	13,066	12,818	8,120	8,385	22.3	16.7	811
Kentucky	455,500	263,900	33,858	1,675	18,168	11,725	7,250	7,631	25.1	22.5	611
Louisiana	517,821	339,497	41,662	2,282	21,884	17,496	8,699	9,036	23.7	19.4	800
Maine	178,500	69,200	12,171	590	7,369	3,962	8,287	8,925	24.2	17.5	756
Maryland	529,060	401,930	47,884	2,894	21,903	20,647	10,204	10,737	24.2	19.5	1,071
Massachusetts	685,000	490,000	59,024	4,000	26,959	25,465	9,779	10,029	25.4	19.2	836
Michigan	1,199,257	1,009,852	103,470	5,500	41,200	55,270	11,291	11,866	29.1	18.3	...
Minnesota	492,115	439,950	48,600	2,500	21,300	22,500	9,500	10,900	23.1	19.6	891
Mississippi	307,631	221,735	25,665	1,593	12,612	10,237	6,395	6,670	24.4	21.7	599
Missouri	778,184	300,015	50,798	3,100	30,491	15,007	8,707	9,006	25.5	20.0	768
Montana	105,711	68,046	9,841	375	5,362	3,604	8,229	9,187	19.7	18.9	854
Nebraska	188,500	142,500	18,400	740	8,935	7,950	7,945	9,027	21.1	17.9	682
Nevada	75,920	55,475	6,000	320	2,875	2,450	10,100	10,300	26.4	22.6	847
New Hampshire	97,345	66,757	8,594	436	4,097	3,353	8,536	8,871	23.8	19.9	795
New Jersey	1,003,556	516,983	89,163	5,261	44,560	30,331	10,600	11,025	22.5	17.0	1,160
New Mexico	154,295	131,379	13,520	900	6,110	5,750	8,000	8,100	25.2	22.8	747
New York	1,921,000	1,596,000	215,600	14,189	92,600	94,900	11,100	11,700	20.7	16.8	1,322
North Carolina	821,511	358,473	54,925	2,527	32,726	16,321	8,041	8,408	25.1	22.0	654
North Dakota	97,557	46,862	7,678	319	4,430	2,645	6,960	8,100	22.0	17.7	713
Ohio	1,686,650	736,400	114,000	5,400	55,480	49,820	8,798	9,341	30.4	14.8	812
Oklahoma	353,436	280,424	31,268	1,600	15,195	13,563	7,530	8,300	23.3	20.7	586
Oregon	278,685	201,805	26,000	1,560	11,870	9,988	9,309	9,679	23.5	20.2	917
Pennsylvania	1,244,400	1,128,100	121,100	5,000	56,300	53,600	9,800	10,000	22.1	21.0	1,007
Rhode Island	106,914	83,782	10,423	563	4,668	4,558	9,961	10,040	22.9	18.4	960
South Carolina	387,035	242,291	32,100	1,350	15,950	12,050	7,115	7,545	24.3	20.1	666
South Dakota	111,340	52,117	9,135	410	5,335	2,934	7,480	8,263	20.9	17.8	747
Tennessee	570,724	326,189	40,104	1,930	21,500	14,589	7,720	8,390	26.5	22.4	623
Texas	2,000,299	777,893	139,610	7,005	67,363	59,737	8,376	8,376	29.7	13.0	646
Utah	164,363	141,383	13,296	756	5,828	5,570	8,457	8,615	28.2	25.4	657
Vermont	67,236	48,784	7,224	450	3,186	3,118	8,142	8,846	21.1	15.6	1,148
Virginia	672,257	401,816	55,000	3,600	29,450	21,950	8,800	9,500	22.8	18.3	823
Washington	427,401	377,648	38,830	3,000	17,249	16,231	9,824	10,570	24.8	23.3	...
West Virginia	225,210	177,906	18,946	1,630	8,860	7,888	7,795	8,180	25.4	22.6	669
Wisconsin	580,296	419,625	52,886	2,353	26,806	23,727	10,028	10,758	21.6	17.7	1,017
Wyoming	45,855	40,575	5,189	313	2,312	2,316	9,046	9,421	19.8	17.5	898
Total U.S.	28,069,411	18,099,129	2,328,285	126,000	1,138,418	951,205	9,420	10,015	24.7	19.0	867

Kindergartens are included in the elementary schools; junior high schools, in the secondary schools.
All dollar amounts for Alaska should be reduced by about 30% to make purchasing power generally more comparable to data reported for other areas.
*Includes librarians, guidance and psychological personnel, and related instructional workers.
†Based on average daily membership.
Source: National Education Association, Research Division, *Estimates of School Statistics, 1971–72* (Copyright 1971. All rights reserved. Used by permission).

Private elementary and secondary day schools

Fall 1972 estimates

State	Enrollment Elementary	Enrollment Secondary	Total Classroom teachers*
Alabama	41,000	13,300	2,370
Alaska	300	300	60
Arizona	22,700	7,000	1,270
Arkansas	8,800	3,300	530
California	265,100	71,100	14,060
Colorado	26,300	8,900	1,700
Connecticut	68,400	39,500	5,200
Delaware	13,300	5,200	870
District of Columbia	13,500	9,200	1,200
Florida	80,700	31,100	5,010
Georgia	21,400	11,300	1,740
Hawaii	15,200	6,500	910
Idaho	4,500	1,600	250
Illinois	335,400	106,200	16,520
Indiana	84,000	22,700	4,320
Iowa	51,000	19,900	3,110
Kansas	26,600	8,100	1,490
Kentucky	46,100	16,500	2,720
Louisiana	105,000	35,600	5,490
Maine	11,400	8,200	1,060
Maryland	85,600	30,100	4,910
Massachusetts	134,700	63,600	9,000
Michigan	194,700	70,300	10,120
Minnesota	92,500	24,300	5,270
Mississippi	41,300	26,200	3,000
Missouri	92,000	12,200	4,210
Montana	7,500	3,400	510
Nebraska	31,300	13,200	1,960
Nevada	2,100	800	90
New Hampshire	18,700	8,900	1,380
New Jersey	201,000	59,200	10,040
New Mexico	10,500	3,200	680
New York	555,200	187,600	29,060
North Carolina	22,600	5,800	1,470
North Dakota	8,400	3,600	530
Ohio	237,400	81,600	11,810
Oklahoma	9,000	3,500	710
Oregon	19,500	6,200	1,170
Pennsylvania	368,600	129,700	18,430
Rhode Island	27,200	9,600	1,580
South Carolina	25,100	5,500	1,590
South Dakota	9,100	3,000	620
Tennessee	22,400	12,400	1,920
Texas	93,700	28,400	6,000
Utah	3,300	1,400	200
Vermont	6,200	6,100	750
Virginia	44,300	21,300	3,740
Washington	33,400	12,500	2,150
West Virginia	7,800	3,900	530
Wisconsin	152,200	36,800	7,580
Wyoming	2,000	200	110
Total U. S.	3,800,000	1,300,000	211,000

Data exclude subcollegiate departments of institutions of higher education and residential schools for exceptional children.
*Part-time teachers are included in full-time equivalents.
Source: U. S. Department of Health, Education, and Welfare, Office of Education, *Digest of Educational Statistics.*

Universities and colleges, 1971-72

Selected list of four-year schools

Institution	Location	Year founded	Total students	Faculty	Bound library volumes	Endowment fund
ALABAMA						
Alabama A. & M.	Normal	1875	2,286	155	97,000	—
Alabama State U.	Montgomery	1874	2,704	111	125,000	—
Auburn U.	Auburn	1856	14,503	850	760,000	$10,105,175
Birmingham-Southern	Birmingham	1856	1,031	86	100,000	6,169,119
Florence State U.	Florence	1873	3,425	145	110,000	—
Jacksonville State U.	Jacksonville	1883	5,749	253	310,000	—
Livingston U.	Livingston	1835	1,641	81	60,000	—
Miles	Birmingham	1905	1,139	72	. . .	—
Samford U.	Birmingham	1842	2,973	165	249,599	3,480,851
Troy State U.	Troy	1887	6,075	190	115,000	355,000
Tuskegee Inst.	Tuskegee Inst.	1881	3,073	253	195,000	17,467
U. of Alabama	University	1831	13,055	717	1,092,082	12,974,000
U. of Montevallo	Montevallo	1896	3,000	130	115,000	684,000
U. of South Alabama	Mobile	1963	5,440	266	180,000	504,067
ALASKA						
Alaska Methodist U.	Anchorage	1957	1,086	51	300,000	—
U. of Alaska	Fairbanks	1917	2,958	194	305,000	2,000,666
ARIZONA						
Arizona State U.	Tempe	1885	26,564	1,268	1,175,000	940,000
Northern Arizona U.	Flagstaff	1899	9,883	440	290,000	3,000,000
U. of Arizona	Tucson	1885	26,558	1,831	1,672,040	4,112,476
ARKANSAS						
Arkansas Polytech.	Russellville	1909	2,525	110	65,856	—
Arkansas State U.	State University	1909	6,605	299	293,000	—
Harding	Searcy	1924	2,060	108	105,000	12,670,000
Henderson State	Arkadelphia	1929	3,300	150	140,000	—
Ouachita Baptist U.	Arkadelphia	1886	1,322	86	84,244	1,842,000
Southern State	Magnolia	1909	2,052	103	70,000	—
State Col. of Arkansas	Conway	1907	4,386	190	120,000	—
U. of Arkansas	Fayetteville	1871	12,131	800	600,000	—
U. of A. at Little Rock	Little Rock	1927	4,460	160	110,000	6,000,000
U. of A. at Monticello	Monticello	1909	1,958	102	56,650	—
CALIFORNIA						
Art Center Col. of Design	Los Angeles	1930	1,067	70	9,500	1,547,488
Biola	La Mirada	1908	1,628	87	95,000	—
California Arts & Crafts	Oakland	1907	1,562	84	20,000	87,000
California Inst. of Tech.	Pasadena	1891	1,533	671	238,379	112,116,000
California Lutheran	Thousand Oaks	1959	1,449	74	68,000	152,000
Cal. State, Bakersfield	Bakersfield	1965	1,770	113	93,000	—
Dominguez Hills	Dominguez Hills	1962	3,832	160	111,000	—
Hayward	Hayward	1959	12,520	558	380,000	—
Long Beach	Long Beach	1949	28,450	1,150	546,000	—
San Bernardino	San Bernardino	1967	2,557	132	157,000	—
Cal. St. Polytech. U.	Pomona	1956	9,893	450	172,000	—
Cal. Polytech. State U.	San Luis Obispo	1901	12,107	655	360,000	—
Cal. St. U., Chico	Chico	1887	10,651	561	325,000	1,555,000
Fresno	Fresno	1911	14,688	744	342,529	—
Fullerton	Fullerton	1959	15,694	612	389,000	—
Los Angeles	Los Angeles	1947	23,252	850	531,000	—
Northridge	Northridge	1958	24,450	1,425	500,000	—
Sacramento	Sacramento	1947	17,386	765	396,000	—
San Diego	San Diego	1897	25,886	1,128	700,000	—
San Francisco	San Francisco	1899	18,778	823	456,000	104,778
Chapman	Orange	1861	3,600	270	80,000	2,300,000
Col. of Notre Dame	Belmont	1851	1,484	59	68,500	—
Golden Gate	San Francisco	1901	5,000	200	90,000	860,000
Humboldt State	Arcata	1913	5,918	350	149,754	—
La Verne	La Verne	1891	1,142	60	70,000	791,028
Loma Linda U.	Riverside	1905	3,574	1,200	255,000	3,178,000
Loyola U.	Los Angeles	1911	3,928	185	290,000	4,258,000
‡Mt. St. Mary's	Los Angeles	1925	1,267	81	106,377	451,889
Naval Postgraduate Sch.	Monterey	1909	1,700	300	282,000	—
Northrop Inst. of Tech.	Inglewood	1942	1,982	106	126,000	370,000
Occidental	Los Angeles	1887	1,879	120	255,000	14,705,480
Pacific Union	Angwin	1882	1,977	150	90,097	—
Pasadena	Pasadena	1902	1,330	61	114,000	—
Pepperdine U.	Los Angeles	1937	2,802	141	105,000	2,500,000
Saint Mary's	Moraga	1863	1,226	95	101,000	1,010,000
San Diego City	San Diego	1914	2,750	145	52,000	—
San Jose State	San Jose	1857	25,982	1,150	547,000	450,000
Sonoma State	Rohnert Park	1960	5,000	285	145,000	—
Stanford U.	Stanford	1885	12,479	1,297	3,584,000	279,700,000
Stanislaus State	Turlock	1960	2,689	181	104,051	—
U. of California	Berkeley	1868	109,104	7,407	11,500,000	254,590,000
U. of C., Berkeley	Berkeley	1868	27,712	1,668	4,000,000	9,243,000
U. of C., Davis	Davis	1905	13,362	825	992,000	—
U. of C., Irvine	Irvine	1964	6,207	293	450,688	1,221,834
U. of C., Los Angeles	Los Angeles	1919	29,093	1,824	3,000,000	—
U. of C., Riverside	Riverside	1868	5,717	490	643,941	—
U. of C., San Diego	La Jolla	1912	6,167	465	900,000	—
U. of C., Santa Barbara	Santa Barbara	1944	12,916	707	900,000	—
U. of C., Santa Cruz	Santa Cruz	1965	3,772	324	325,000	—
U. of Pacific	Stockton	1851	5,689	388	278,000	5,018,000
U. of Redlands	Redlands	1907	2,005	136	177,000	15,500,000
U. of San Francisco	San Francisco	1855	6,831	320	312,000	3,160,000
U. of Santa Clara	Santa Clara	1851	6,085	306	295,000	6,796,155
U. of Southern California	Los Angeles	1880	18,884	2,000	1,452,590	39,953,281
West Coast U.	Los Angeles	1909	1,135	76	7,000	—
Whittier	Whittier	1901	2,006	107	102,000	5,035,000
Woodbury	Los Angeles	1884	2,296	82	18,000	—
COLORADO						
Adams State	Alamosa	1921	2,854	129	132,000	—
Colorado	Colorado Sprgs.	1874	1,820	146	320,032	10,352,854
Colorado Sch. of Mines	Golden	1874	1,699	136	136,000	420,000
Colorado State U.	Fort Collins	1870	17,608	920	808,000	—
Fort Lewis	Durango	1911	2,078	100	85,000	90,000
Metropolitan State	Denver	1965	8,201	320	120,000	—
Regis	Denver	1877	1,414	92	65,000	$ 750,000
Southern Colorado State	Pueblo	1933	6,621	278	125,000	—
†U.S. Air Force Academy	USAF Academy	1954	4,201	638	320,000	—
U. of Colorado	Boulder	1876	31,712	1,627	1,503,187	8,152,000
U. of Denver	Denver	1864	9,119	598	714,000	15,872,000
U. of Northern Colorado	Greeley	1890	10,756	493	323,000	180,000
Western State	Gunnison	1901	3,194	133	110,000	—
CONNECTICUT						
Central Connecticut State	New Britain	1849	11,486	435	201,764	—
Eastern Connecticut State	Willimantic	1889	2,309	125	74,000	—
Fairfield U.	Fairfield	1942	3,762	240	115,000	—
Quinnipiac	Hamden	1929	2,975	150	80,000	—
Sacred Heart U.	Bridgeport	1963	2,042	61	74,000	—
Southern Connecticut St.	New Haven	1893	12,727	531	267,000	—
Trinity	Hartford	1823	1,994	132	480,000	19,699,000
†U.S. Coast Guard Acad.	New London	1876	1,100	121	90,000	—
U. of Bridgeport	Bridgeport	1927	8,318	398	211,000	4,700,000
U. of Connecticut	Storrs	1881	24,203	1,200	1,073,000	1,713,000
U. of Hartford	West Hartford	1877	9,214	357	180,000	4,238,316
U. of New Haven	West Haven	1920	4,713	264	65,000	100,000
Wesleyan U.	Middletown	1831	1,881	206	673,000	158,807,000
Western Connecticut S t.	Danbury	1903	4,351	233	104,452	—
Yale U.	New Haven	1701	9,231	2,000	5,800,000	534,379,000
DELAWARE						
Delaware State	Dover	1891	1,921	105	75,162	104,000
U. of Delaware	Newark	1833	16,722	652	950,000	62,413,310
DISTRICT OF COLUMBIA						
American U.	Washington	1893	14,508	499	431,274	4,446,731
Catholic U.	Washington	1887	6,161	492	789,000	7,743,000
D.C. Teachers	Washington	1851	2,856	121	96,000	—
George Washington U.	Washington	1821	15,190	987	546,236	11,352,005
Georgetown U.	Washington	1789	8,855	848	720,000	34,000,000
Howard U.	Washington	1867	10,315	1,027	665,659	9,410,765
FLORIDA						
‡Barry	Miami	1940	1,294	81	82,195	109,000
Bethune-Cookman	Daytona Bch.	1872	1,200	58	60,000	1,485,000
Eckerd	St. Petersburg	1958	1,108	76	92,454	1,609,144
Florida A. & M. U.	Tallahassee	1887	4,490	267	211,476	—
Florida Atlantic U.	Boca Raton	1961	5,732	341	300,000	1,322,000
Florida Inst. of Tech.	Melbourne	1958	2,119	105	60,000	18,890
Florida Southern	Lakeland	1885	1,480	107	125,500	7,955,707
Florida State U.	Tallahassee	1857	15,513	1,150	872,000	84,000
Florida Tech. U.	Orlando	1968	6,137	309	122,000	—
Jacksonville U.	Jacksonville	1934	3,016	150	150,000	1,600,000
Rollins	Winter Park	1885	2,867	135	162,180	8,700,000
Stetson U.	DeLand	1883	2,804	119	207,797	5,763,754
U. of Florida	Gainesville	1853	23,031	2,495	1,500,000	4,305,000
U. of Miami	Coral Gables	1925	18,241	1,033	1,000,000	27,295,113
U. of South Florida	Tampa	1960	18,496	961	325,000	219,000
U. of Tampa	Tampa	1931	2,319	98	120,000	1,000,000
U. of West Florida	Pensacola	1963	3,206	222	277,000	—
GEORGIA						
Albany State	Albany	1903	1,926	125	80,000	—
Armstrong State	Savannah	1935	2,712	112	86,957	—
Atlanta U.	Atlanta	1865	1,048	113	241,000	12,835,376
Augusta	Augusta	1925	2,973	153	91,000	—
Clark	Atlanta	1869	1,118	94	45,327	—
Columbus	Columbus	1958	3,814	135	66,052	42,062
Emory U.	Atlanta	1836	5,435	746	966,459	85,437,825
Fort Valley State	Fort Valley	1895	2,247	105	91,000	85,442
Georgia	Milledgeville	1889	1,923	110	100,000	—
Georgia Inst. of Tech.	Atlanta	1885	7,113	469	560,000	2,329,000
Georgia Southern	Statesboro	1906	6,156	304	161,017	—
Georgia Southwestern	Americus	1926	2,383	137	61,000	—
Georgia State U.	Atlanta	1913	16,044	776	344,680	18,681
Mercer U.	Macon	1833	1,929	110	180,000	9,900,000
†Morehouse	Atlanta	1867	1,227	75	297,296	4,623,569
North Georgia	Dahlonega	1873	1,300	68	93,000	—
Oglethorpe	Atlanta	1835	1,050	44	44,500	3,500,000
Savannah State	Savannah	1890	3,003	131	75,000	—
‡Spelman	Atlanta	1881	1,118	96	30,819	6,770,000
U. of Georgia	Athens	1785	21,298	1,600	1,300,000	4,800,000
Valdosta State	Valdosta	1906	2,888	153	97,000	—
West Georgia	Carrollton	1933	6,114	285	125,000	—
GUAM						
U. of Guam	Agana	1952	3,068	199	112,000	—
HAWAII						
Church Col. of Hawaii	Laie	1955	1,299	70	80,000	100,000
U. of Hawaii	Honolulu	1907	22,061	1,389	1,116,932	795,974
IDAHO						
Boise State	Boise	1932	8,300	304	137,000	—
Idaho State U.	Pocatello	1901	6,190	290	200,000	47,136
Lewis-Clark State	Lewiston	1955	1,247	100	58,000	197,000
Northwest Nazarene	Nampa	1913	1,114	68	65,800	150,000
U. of Idaho	Moscow	1889	6,999	506	727,000	14,540,000
ILLINOIS						
Augustana	Rock Island	1860	2,261	114	154,000	4,003,760
Aurora	Aurora	1893	1,094	51	76,000	290,700
Bradley U.	Peoria	1897	5,703	366	209,000	5,061,000
Chicago State U.	Chicago	1869	5,806	320	159,000	—
Concordia Teachers	River Forest	1864	1,367	100	100,110	450,000
De Paul U.	Chicago	1898	9,404	420	309,189	2,294,810

†Men's schools, ‡women's schools; the others are coeducational.

Universities and colleges (continued)

Institution	Location	Year founded	Total students	Faculty	Bound library volumes	Endowment fund
Eastern Illinois U.	Charleston	1895	8,790	489	255,662	—
Elmhurst	Elmhurst	1871	1,550	125	89,000	$ 1,000,000
Illinois Inst. of Tech.	Chicago	1892	7,067	531	1,100,000	13,717,000
Illinois State U.	Normal	1857	17,930	1,153	500,000	—
Illinois Wesleyan U.	Bloomington	1850	1,728	132	110,000	6,500,000
Knox	Galesburg	1837	1,437	91	146,903	11,934,000
Lake Forest	Lake Forest	1857	1,224	97	125,000	7,265,000
Lewis	Lockport	1930	2,119	115	52,000	—
Loyola U.	Chicago	1870	14,469	920	550,000	17,871,000
Millikin U.	Decatur	1901	1,505	120	121,000	2,264,000
Monmouth	Monmouth	1853	1,175	71	127,000	2,300,000
‡Mundelein	Chicago	1930	1,362	69	98,000	392,934
National Col. of Ed.	Evanston	1886	3,088	82	68,000	692,000
Northeastern Illinois St.	Chicago	1869	8,409	420	170,295	—
Northern Illinois U.	DeKalb	1895	22,817	1,408	489,000	—
North Park	Chicago	1891	1,294	81	127,000	1,633,000
Northwestern U.	Evanston	1851	15,006	1,360	2,374,913	195,868,000
Olivet Nazarene	Kankakee	1907	1,805	99	85,000	72,000
Quincy	Quincy	1860	2,164	142	150,000	845,298
Rockford	Rockford	1847	1,433	120	74,000	3,100,000
Roosevelt U.	Chicago	1945	7,143	241	260,000	1,402,000
Rosary	River Forest	1901	1,297	89	140,000	700,000
Schools of the Art Inst.	Chicago	1866	1,500	84	91,000	3,425,000
Southern Illinois U.	Carbondale	1869	35,238	3,146	1,400,000	—
at Edwardsville	Edwardsville	1869	12,856	558	474,041	—
U. of Chicago	Chicago	1892	8,962	1,133	3,077,000	276,384,000
U. of Illinois	Urbana	1868	32,296	4,243	4,609,000	18,616,394
Chicago Circle	Chicago	1965	18,996	1,457	368,032	—
Western Illinois U.	Macomb	1899	13,711	880	319,000	—
Wheaton	Wheaton	1860	2,079	144	155,000	10,662,558
INDIANA						
Anderson	Anderson	1917	1,764	106	117,000	564,000
Ball State U.	Muncie	1918	17,933	760	556,000	—
Butler U.	Indianapolis	1855	4,363	170	217,000	26,500,000
De Pauw U.	Greencastle	1837	2,274	158	300,354	15,781,000
Earlham	Richmond	1847	1,162	78	180,000	7,417,842
Goshen	Goshen	1894	1,258	75	109,000	292,000
Hanover	Hanover	1827	1,034	73	160,000	7,592,000
Indiana Central	Indianapolis	1902	2,469	93	67,000	1,172,043
Indiana State U.	Terre Haute	1865	13,508	828	499,500	759,580
Indiana U.	Bloomington	1820	67,448	3,303	3,064,788	11,500,000
Manchester	N. Manchester	1889	1,410	83	113,000	1,671,000
Purdue U.	Lafayette	1869	35,864	2,272	1,100,000	22,650,000
†Rose Polytech. Inst.	Terre Haute	1874	1,059	69	40,000	17,923,712
St. Francis	Fort Wayne	1890	2,008	74	69,000	—
St. Joseph	Rensselaer	1889	1,197	90	152,000	1,050,000
‡St. Mary's	Notre Dame	1844	1,790	105	127,000	892,000
Taylor U.	Upland	1846	1,420	79	94,000	795,000
Tri-State	Angola	1884	1,605	93	75,000	849,815
U. of Evansville	Evansville	1854	5,393	230	140,000	3,383,000
U. of Notre Dame	Notre Dame	1842	8,237	728	1,016,000	65,000,000
Valparaiso U.	Valparaiso	1859	4,703	259	227,000	4,199,000
IOWA						
Briar Cliff	Sioux City	1930	1,096	55	65,975	131,246
Central U. of Iowa	Pella	1853	1,253	80	84,000	1,321,618
Coe	Cedar Rapids	1851	1,164	72	127,018	8,118,000
Drake U.	Des Moines	1881	7,749	326	327,418	4,983,763
Graceland	Lamoni	1895	1,350	80	70,000	527,000
Grinnell	Grinnell	1846	1,304	114	201,000	11,011,000
Iowa State U.	Ames	1858	19,642	1,166	887,000	3,692,000
Loras	Dubuque	1839	1,427	96	180,000	—
Luther	Decorah	1861	2,025	122	188,000	2,101,000
Marycrest	Davenport	1939	1,025	63	82,000	338,000
Morningside	Sioux City	1894	1,398	75	105,000	2,513,633
Parsons	Fairfield	1875	1,270	64	131,000	653,000
St. Ambrose	Davenport	1882	1,336	85	86,200	1,500,000
U. of Dubuque	Dubuque	1852	1,113	63	118,000	2,458,417
U. of Iowa	Iowa City	1847	20,387	1,563	1,672,927	4,708,012
U. of Northern Iowa	Cedar Falls	1876	10,234	502	350,000	—
Wartburg	Waverly	1852	1,361	84	90,440	329,000
KANSAS						
Fort Hays Kansas State	Hays	1902	5,246	228	235,000	671,698
Kansas State	Pittsburg	1903	5,706	317	340,000	534,000
Kansas State Teachers	Emporia	1863	7,112	292	320,000	1,000,000
Kansas State U.	Manhattan	1863	14,789	780	625,000	6,207,325
U. of Kansas	Lawrence	1866	20,043	1,099	1,568,000	36,620,000
Washburn U.	Topeka	1865	5,195	176	115,000	490,000
Wichita State U.	Wichita	1895	13,034	495	384,000	5,650,000
KENTUCKY						
Asbury	Wilmore	1890	1,091	66	69,000	5,400,000
Bellarmine	Louisville	1950	1,655	71	62,000	—
Berea	Berea	1855	1,449	110	180,000	45,596,000
Cumberland	Williamsburg	1889	1,807	88	60,000	1,400,000
Eastern Kentucky U.	Richmond	1906	10,170	571	346,000	—
Georgetown	Georgetown	1829	1,225	90	100,000	1,604,156
Kentucky State	Frankfort	1886	1,970	115	90,000	—
Morehead State U.	Morehead	1922	6,255	325	275,000	—
Murray State U.	Murray	1922	7,071	375	260,000	—
Spalding	Louisville	1814	1,067	85	108,000	121,000
Thomas More	Ft. Mitchell	1921	1,812	89	74,000	64,000
U. of Kentucky	Lexington	1865	16,201	1,330	1,000,000	639,000
U. of Louisville	Louisville	1798	10,468	800	640,000	11,692,000
Western Kentucky U.	Bowling Green	1906	11,345	555	461,000	664,569
LOUISIANA						
Grambling	Grambling	1901	3,674	198	84,285	201,160
Louisiana S. U. System	Baton Rouge	1860	37,779	2,306	1,830,409	956,000
L.S.U. in Baton Rouge	Baton Rouge	1860	20,536	1,125	1,348,290	956,000
L.S.U. in New Orleans	New Orleans	1958	12,985	330	350,000	—
Louisiana Tech U.	Ruston	1894	8,133	393	179,734	—
Loyola U.	New Orleans	1912	4,904	250	251,000	$ 4,608,098
McNeese State	Lake Charles	1939	5,067	274	113,000	—
Nicholls State U.	Thibodaux	1948	5,411	178	117,260	—
Northeast Louisiana U.	Monroe	1931	8,810	351	180,000	—
Northwestern State U.	Natchitoches	1884	6,188	320	180,000	—
Southeastern La. U.	Hammond	1925	5,790	229	136,000	—
Southern U.	Baton Rouge	1880	8,315	405	276,318	—
Tulane U.	New Orleans	1834	8,732	956	1,071,638	62,262,601
U. of Southwestern La.	Lafayette	1898	10,654	500	371,587	—
Xavier U.	New Orleans	1925	1,207	87	98,000	—
MAINE						
Bates	Lewiston	1864	1,240	90	154,716	10,725,440
Bowdoin	Brunswick	1794	1,034	100	450,000	33,200,000
Colby	Waterville	1813	1,572	119	315,000	19,225,643
U. of Maine						
Farmington	Farmington	1864	1,344	95	55,000	268,000
Orano	Orano	1865	8,315	658	450,000	6,501,000
Portland-Gorham	Portland	1957	7,700	215	238,000	—
MARYLAND						
Bowie State	Bowie	1867	2,658	121	63,000	—
Columbia Union	Takoma Park	1904	1,130	90	80,000	—
Coppin State	Baltimore	1900	1,205	83	55,000	—
Frostburg State	Frostburg	1898	2,316	130	80,000	—
‡Goucher	Baltimore	1885	1,050	90	151,177	9,197,058
Johns Hopkins U.	Baltimore	1876	9,564	994	2,059,342	94,105,699
Loyola	Baltimore	1852	3,400	121	89,000	2,973,000
Maryland Inst. of Art	Baltimore	. . .	1,050	69	27,000	1,200,000
Morgan State	Baltimore	1867	5,743	240	152,000	—
Mt. St. Mary's	Emmitsburg	1808	1,140	83	83,000	591,000
Salisbury State	Salisbury	1925	1,984	93	98,000	—
Towson State	Baltimore	1866	8,577	402	150,000	—
†U.S. Naval Academy	Annapolis	1845	4,200	550	325,000	—
U. of Maryland	College Park	1807	54,129	4,784	1,191,218	10,407,000
Western Maryland	Westminster	1867	2,327	96	95,000	3,128,000
MASSACHUSETTS						
American International	Springfield	1885	1,738	103	95,000	1,021,000
Amherst	Amherst	1821	1,221	141	438,000	72,000,000
Assumption	Worcester	1904	1,575	80	110,000	—
Babson	Babson Park	1919	1,767	47	54,300	5,000,000
Bentley	Waltham	1917	3,331	83	62,000	—
Boston	Chestnut Hill	1863	11,111	750	848,000	5,121,036
Boston State	Boston	1852	7,953	418	88,000	—
Boston U.	Boston	1869	24,568	2,700	755,500	20,000,000
Brandeis U.	Waltham	1947	2,286	340	416,000	19,859,000
Bridgewater State	Bridgewater	1840	3,514	238	100,000	—
Clark U.	Worcester	1887	3,461	264	300,000	12,070,000
Emerson	Boston	1880	1,879	145	50,000	295,000
‡Emmanuel	Boston	1919	1,449	110	86,217	—
Fitchburg State	Fitchburg	1894	2,502	186	78,000	—
Framingham State	Framingham	1839	4,429	172	90,000	—
Harvard U.	Cambridge	1636	15,832	8,423	8,451,000	756,048,000
‡Radcliffe	Cambridge	1879	1,420			23,708,000
Holy Cross	Worcester	1843	2,488	180	299,555	6,435,548
Lowell State	Lowell	1894	2,434	155	80,000	—
Lowell Tech. Inst.	Lowell	1895	6,544	230	125,000	159,000
Mass. Inst. of Tech.	Cambridge	1861	7,799	982	1,221,000	158,515,000
Merrimack	North Andover	1947	2,128	125	69,000	564,000
‡Mt. Holyoke	South Hadley	1837	1,919	11	332,000	24,298,000
North Adams State	North Adams	1894	1,500	75	73,000	—
Northeastern U.	Boston	1898	35,542	1,158	295,000	24,682
Salem State	Salem	1854	5,989	212	71,000	—
‡Simmons	Boston	1899	2,585	186	161,000	10,086,000
Smith	Northampton	1871	2,542	240	770,000	50,050,800
Southeastern Mass. U.	N. Dartmouth	1895	3,515	225	120,000	115,000
Springfield	Springfield	1885	2,692	121	100,000	5,531,813
Stonehill	North Easton	1948	1,909	85	73,000	—
Suffolk U.	Boston	1906	5,235	148	122,031	3,655,000
Tufts U.	Medford	1852	5,660	1,824	480,000	22,016,000
U. of Massachusetts	Amherst	1863	19,118	1,195	967,000	1,259,000
‡Wellesley	Wellesley	1870	1,872	187	500,000	77,063,000
Western New England	Springfield	1919	3,457	130	62,000	182,000
Westfield State	Westfield	1839	3,647	150	65,000	—
‡Wheaton	Norton	1834	1,217	99	152,000	6,644,000
Williams	Williamstown	1793	1,592	165	375,000	68,857,000
Worcester Polytech. Inst.	Worcester	1865	2,513	170	100,000	24,900,000
Worcester State	Worcester	1874	3,919	180	95,000	—
MICHIGAN						
Adrian	Adrian	1859	1,447	93	91,200	2,750,000
Albion	Albion	1835	1,809	126	175,000	11,804,000
Alma	Alma	1886	1,393	78	85,000	2,800,000
Andrews U.	Berrien Sprgs.	1874	2,191	184	238,041	565,000
Aquinas	Grand Rapids	1923	1,422	80	83,500	—
Calvin	Grand Rapids	1876	3,306	180	240,000	—
Central Michigan U.	Mt. Pleasant	1892	14,741	712	365,000	213,000
Detroit Inst. of Tech.	Detroit	1891	1,139	50	41,000	99,500
Eastern Michigan U.	Ypsilanti	1849	19,627	774	351,000	497,000
Ferris State	Big Rapids	1884	9,161	420	198,785	—
General Motors Inst.	Flint	1919	3,075	218	50,000	—
Grand Valley State	Allendale	1960	4,174	183	150,000	670,603
Hillsdale	Hillsdale	1844	1,148	69	55,000	4,357,000
Hope	Holland	1866	2,101	136	137,000	2,207,000
Kalamazoo	Kalamazoo	1833	1,365	80	165,000	14,000,000
Lake Superior State	Sault Ste. Marie	1946	1,712	97	57,199	—
Lawrence Inst. of Tech.	Southfield	1932	4,107	110	44,000	—
Marygrove	Detroit	1910	1,102	62	150,094	826,000
Mercy	Detroit	1941	1,620	100	68,000	—
Michigan State U.	East Lansing	1855	41,649	2,493	1,750,000	10,875,000
Michigan Tech. U.	Houghton	1885	5,002	300	266,000	713,000
Northern Michigan U.	Marquette	1899	8,167	343	187,342	—
Oakland U.	Rochester	1957	7,069	311	196,000	1,031,000
Saginaw Valley	University Ctr.	1964	2,124	81	62,000	418,000
U. of Detroit	Detroit	1877	9,597	. . .	407,000	3,530,000

Institution	Location	Year founded	Total students	Faculty	Bound library volumes	Endowment fund
U. of Michigan	Ann Arbor	1817	39,986	3,069	4,396,525	$66,102,000
Wayne State U.	Detroit	1868	36,765	1,650	1,368,000	3,443,930
Western Michigan U.	Kalamazoo	1903	21,846	1,173	713,644	49,400

MINNESOTA

Institution	Location	Year founded	Total students	Faculty	Bound library volumes	Endowment fund
Augsburg	Minneapolis	1869	1,616	90	126,500	564,000
Bemidji State	Bemidji	1913	4,865	278	184,000	—
Bethel	St. Paul	1871	1,044	68	75,000	462,891
Carleton	Northfield	1866	1,591	127	187,582	28,639,539
Concordia	Moorhead	1891	2,402	161	153,225	1,189,502
Gustavus Adolphus	St. Peter	1862	1,918	129	127,000	1,496,000
Hamline U.	St. Paul	1854	1,283	90	120,000	11,500,000
Macalester	St. Paul	1885	2,097	153	204,636	28,840,121
Mankato State	Mankato	1867	12,600	685	350,000	—
Moorhead State	Moorhead	1887	5,254	340	150,000	—
‡St. Catherine	St. Paul	1905	1,344	104	185,000	1,416,000
St. Cloud State	St. Cloud	1869	9,509	526	325,808	11,500
†St. John's U.	Collegeville	1857	1,724	130	350,000	6,684,000
St. Mary's	Winona	1912	1,052	62	101,000	100,000
St. Olaf	Northfield	1874	2,650	202	254,000	3,589,000
†St. Thomas	St. Paul	1885	2,490	137	160,000	6,850,000
U. of Minnesota	Minneapolis	1851	71,962	3,000	3,000,000	81,627,373
Winona State	Winona	1858	4,263	228	126,000	—

MISSISSIPPI

Institution	Location	Year founded	Total students	Faculty	Bound library volumes	Endowment fund
Alcorn A. & M.	Lorman	1871	2,677	120	67,000	—
Delta State	Cleveland	1924	2,535	117	75,000	—
Jackson State	Jackson	1877	5,058	254	124,000	—
Mississippi	Clinton	1826	2,414	108	131,000	2,259,000
‡Mississippi State	Columbus	1884	2,591	147	172,000	—
Mississippi State U.	State College	1878	9,509	595	373,000	1,470,699
Mississippi Valley State	Itta Bena	1946	2,410	132	72,000	—
U. of Mississippi	University	1848	7,823	450	500,000	1,543,415
U. of Southern Mississippi	Hattiesburg	1910	8,625	565	300,000	—

MISSOURI

Institution	Location	Year founded	Total students	Faculty	Bound library volumes	Endowment fund
Central Missouri State	Warrensburg	1871	12,635	540	280,000	—
Drury	Springfield	1873	2,469	170	120,000	3,732,000
Evangel	Springfield	1955	1,228	67	66,000	—
Harris Teachers	St. Louis	1857	1,156	62	44,000	—
Lincoln U.	Jefferson City	1866	2,411	134	91,000	—
Missouri Southern	Joplin	1949	3,158	120	72,000	—
Missouri Western	St. Joseph	1915	3,151	150	46,000	—
Northeast Missouri State	Kirksville	1867	6,273	245	160,000	—
Northwest Missouri St. U.	Maryville	1905	5,632	290	140,000	—
Rockhurst	Kansas City	1910	2,415	142	90,000	1,430,082
St. Louis U.	St. Louis	1818	10,490	1,237	843,450	28,371,397
School of the Ozarks	Point Lookout	1906	1,151	65	75,000	—
Southeast Missouri St.	Cape Girardeau	1873	7,554	356	193,000	—
Southwest Baptist	Bolivar	1878	1,145	55	72,000	90,000
Southwest Missouri St.	Springfield	1906	9,478	394	200,000	—
‡Stephens	Columbia	1833	2,095	160	98,000	3,100,000
U. of Missouri—						
Columbia	Columbia	1839	21,942	2,496	1,589,115	7,104,000
U. of M.—Kansas City	Kansas City	1929	9,894	646	490,786	5,500,000
U. of M.—Rolla	Rolla	1870	5,422	402	200,000	658,000
U. of M.—St. Louis	St. Louis	1963	10,188	441	335,000	2,000
Washington U.	St. Louis	1853	11,221	1,166	1,421,349	126,726,000
Webster	St. Louis	1915	1,665	80	30,000	—
‡William Woods	Fulton	1870	1,224	58	106,000	850,000

MONTANA

Institution	Location	Year founded	Total students	Faculty	Bound library volumes	Endowment fund
Carroll	Helena	1909	1,034	75	50,000	550,000
Eastern Montana	Billings	1927	3,466	160	124,000	—
Great Falls	Great Falls	1932	1,031	46	48,000	428,900
Montana State U.	Bozeman	1893	8,113	403	582,000	3,375,660
Northern Montana	Havre	1929	1,330	85	50,000	—
U. of Montana	Missoula	1893	8,800	490	781,169	1,865,109
Western Montana	Dillon	1883	1,072	49	42,000	—

NEBRASKA

Institution	Location	Year founded	Total students	Faculty	Bound library volumes	Endowment fund
Chadron State	Chadron	1911	2,428	96	95,953	—
Concordia Teachers	Seward	1894	1,737	115	85,000	116,000
Creighton U.	Omaha	1878	4,172	373	297,851	6,789,702
Kearney State	Kearney	1905	5,783	241	153,000	250,000
Nebraska Wesleyan U.	Lincoln	1887	1,177	94	108,000	4,100,000
Peru State	Peru	1867	1,001	46	90,000	85,000
U. of Nebraska	Lincoln	1869	20,810	1,020	1,000,000	10,386,000
U. of N. at Omaha	Omaha	1908	13,185	374	261,000	—
Wayne State	Wayne	1891	2,668	137	110,000	—

NEVADA

Institution	Location	Year founded	Total students	Faculty	Bound library volumes	Endowment fund
U. of Nevada—Las Vegas	Las Vegas	1964	5,782	202	214,661	—
U. of Nevada—Reno	Reno	1874	10,142	385	420,000	4,718,000

NEW HAMPSHIRE

Institution	Location	Year founded	Total students	Faculty	Bound library volumes	Endowment fund
Dartmouth	Hanover	1769	3,279	302	1,050,000	154,350,096
Franklin Pierce	Rindge	1962	1,077	76	36,000	66,000
Keene State	Keene	1909	2,014	125	80,000	—
New England	Henniker	1946	1,393	107	62,000	151,000
Plymouth State	Plymouth	1870	2,262	131	110,000	—
†St. Anselm's	Manchester	1889	1,674	137	90,000	—
U. of New Hampshire	Durham	1866	8,984	553	610,439	5,093,547

NEW JERSEY

Institution	Location	Year founded	Total students	Faculty	Bound library volumes	Endowment fund
Bloomfield	Bloomfield	1868	1,698	74	66,000	1,300,000
Drew U.	Madison	1866	1,558	123	326,000	11,684,000
Fairleigh Dickinson U.	Rutherford	1941	20,130	894	392,000	6,759,777
Glassboro State	Glassboro	1923	11,335	450	151,360	—
Jersey City State	Jersey City	1927	9,957	450	100,000	—
Monmouth	W. Long Branch	1933	5,758	237	138,000	$ 1,370,353
Montclair State	Upper Montclair	1908	11,178	427	158,000	168,000
Newark Engineering	Newark	1881	5,775	280	82,950	207,000
Newark State	Union	1855	12,059	353	177,000	—
Princeton U.	Princeton	1746	5,327	732	2,726,000	292,160,908
Rider	Trenton	1865	5,665	205	200,000	3,229,735
Rutgers U.	New Brunswick	1766	36,869	2,590	1,916,036	35,740,700
St. Peter's	Jersey City	1872	4,561	150	140,000	500,000
Seton Hall U.	South Orange	1856	9,469	605	300,593	3,923,000
Stevens Inst. of Tech.	Hoboken	1870	2,340	193	91,000	46,000,000
Trenton State	Trenton	1855	11,500	410	230,000	—
Upsala	East Orange	1893	1,963	97	123,116	1,345,000
William Patterson	Wayne	1855	7,525	358	200,000	—

NEW MEXICO

Institution	Location	Year founded	Total students	Faculty	Bound library volumes	Endowment fund
Eastern New Mexico U.	Portales	1934	4,015	161	143,000	—
N.M. Highlands U.	Las Vegas	1893	2,657	106	100,000	—
New Mexico State U.	Las Cruces	1889	9,075	342	309,382	2,210,000
Santa Fe	Santa Fe	1947	1,271	63	65,000	—
U. of Albuquerque	Albuquerque	1940	2,919	90	60,000	—
U. of New Mexico	Albuquerque	1889	18,061	561	759,000	11,126,000
Western New Mexico U.	Silver City	1893	1,505	65	75,000	—

NEW YORK

Institution	Location	Year founded	Total students	Faculty	Bound library volumes	Endowment fund
Adelphi U.	Garden City	1896	7,877	410	208,000	2,244,000
Alfred U.	Alfred	1857	2,364	174	175,000	5,742,000
Canisius	Buffalo	1870	4,162	280	171,000	—
City U. of New York	New York	1847	197,664	8,641	2,900,000	14,400,000
Bernard M. Baruch	New York	1968	12,251	459	85,000	—
Brooklyn	Brooklyn	1930	29,315	1,221	541,000	315,907
City	New York	1847	20,092	1,216	866,135	2,270,000
Herbert H. Lehman	Bronx	1931	13,083	835	242,401	—
Hunter	New York	1870	23,110	1,036	345,000	1,216,968
Queens	Flushing	1937	26,664	1,294	392,000	64,000
Richmond	Staten Island	1965	3,388	174	140,000	—
York	Jamaica	1966	2,707	186	60,000	—
Clarkson Tech.	Potsdam	1895	2,608	169	101,000	3,843,000
Colgate U.	Hamilton	1819	2,290	172	270,000	28,393,627
Columbia U.	New York	1754	15,315	2,485	4,241,130	254,000,000
‡Barnard	New York	1889	1,932	143	125,000	19,590,000
Teachers	New York	1887	5,487	280	380,000	22,800,000
Cooper Union	New York	1859	1,011	175	88,272	30,562,458
Cornell U.	Ithaca	1865	16,812	1,800	3,780,000	224,083,399
‡D'Youville	Buffalo	1908	1,174	97	95,000	236,000
Elmira	Elmira	1855	3,266	85	112,000	3,300,000
Fordham U.	Bronx	1841	12,591	560	886,674	5,062,000
Hartwick	Oneonta	1928	1,687	120	102,000	4,841,000
Hobart & William Smith	Geneva	1822	1,665	103	141,000	3,999,000
Hofstra U.	Hempstead	1935	12,616	528	520,000	7,248,194
Houghton	Houghton	1883	1,210	78	88,000	785,824
Iona	New Rochelle	1940	3,198	180	92,000	515,000
Ithaca	Ithaca	1892	4,189	274	180,000	542,000
Juilliard	New York	1905	1,121	110	50,000	—
Le Moyne	Syracuse	1946	1,646	110	100,893	1,402,963
Long Island U.	Greenvale	1926	20,838	922	437,000	3,235,000
†Manhattan	Bronx	1853	4,598	258	140,000	1,839,386
Manhattanville	Purchase	1841	1,518	102	185,000	2,477,000
Marist	Poughkeepsie	1929	1,692	72	73,000	270,000
‡Marymount	Tarrytown	1918	1,007	79	86,000	—
Mercy	Dobbs Ferry	1950	1,605	98	64,000	713,000
‡Molloy	Rockville Ctr.	1955	1,125	84	55,000	37,000
‡Nazareth	Rochester	1924	1,616	86	125,000	3,563,943
‡New Rochelle	New Rochelle	1904	1,400	91	105,000	1,100,000
New School	New York	1919	15,500	480	75,000	—
New York Inst. of Tech.	Old Westbury	1955	4,909	337	110,000	—
New York U.	New York	1831	40,126	3,560	2,270,000	100,000,000
Niagara U.	Niagara Univ.	1856	3,336	192	136,781	571,000
Pace	New York	1906	10,137	375	232,000	3,087,769
Polytechnic Inst.	Brooklyn	1854	3,852	252	218,000	6,600,000
Pratt Inst.	Brooklyn	1887	4,552	266	242,000	15,015,000
Rensselaer Polytech.	Troy	1824	4,737	436	194,000	76,303,181
Rochester Inst. of Tech.	Rochester	1829	12,042	557	120,000	23,203,782
Rosary Hill	Buffalo	1948	1,249	90	72,925	16,100
Russell Sage	Troy	1916	1,418	100	106,000	6,000,000
St. Bonaventure U.	St. Bonaventure	1859	2,637	160	166,208	410,000
St. Francis	Brooklyn	1884	2,580	94	83,000	145,000
St. John Fisher	Rochester	1948	1,385	80	80,000	688,650
St. John's U.	Jamaica	1870	13,207	565	448,000	1,031,000
St. Lawrence U.	Canton	1856	2,464	157	224,000	10,293,000
St. Rose	Albany	1920	1,512	89	87,000	400,630
Siena	Loudonville	1937	1,605	100	136,500	795,932
Skidmore	Saratoga Springs	1911	1,887	171	171,000	3,200,000
State U. of New York	Albany	1948	141,010	8,118	6,675,160	—
SUNY at Albany	Albany	1844	13,905	794	611,478	—
SUNY at Binghamton	Binghamton	1946	7,604	449	371,701	—
SUNY at Buffalo	Buffalo	1846	24,386	1,462	1,575,872	—
SUNY at Stony Brook	Stony Brook	1957	11,815	770	632,292	—
State U. Colleges						
Brockport	Brockport	1867	10,023	491	228,504	—
Buffalo	Buffalo	1867	10,895	513	263,103	—
Cortland	Cortland	1868	5,565	305	179,035	—
Fredonia	Fredonia	1867	5,129	283	206,454	—
Geneseo	Geneseo	1871	5,905	315	196,293	—
New Paltz	New Paltz	1885	7,880	396	231,795	—
Oneonta	Oneonta	1887	5,893	339	247,546	—
Oswego	Oswego	1861	8,528	441	274,892	—
Plattsburgh	Plattsburgh	1889	5,754	286	195,358	—
Potsdam	Potsdam	1867	4,844	255	199,434	—
Syracuse U.	Syracuse	1870	23,000	1,007	1,451,000	55,000,000
Union Col. & U.	Schenectady	1795	1,894	149	283,800	31,353,551
†U.S. Merchant Marine Acad.	Kings Point	1938	1,016	91	68,000	—
†U.S. Military Acad.	West Point	1802	4,078	554	345,000	—
U. of Rochester	Rochester	1850	8,679	1,744	1,200,000	85,500,000

Institution	Location	Year founded	Total students	Faculty	Bound library volumes	Endowment fund
Vassar	Poughkeepsie	1861	2,130	213	416,338	$51,912,260
Wagner	Staten Island	1883	3,298	145	190,000	1,615,071
Yeshiva U.	New York	1886	3,475	1,654	568,000	3,560,000

NORTH CAROLINA

Institution	Location	Year founded	Total students	Faculty	Bound library volumes	Endowment fund
Appalachian State U.	Boone	1903	7,668	372	242,000	672,000
Atlantic Christian	Wilson	1902	1,794	87	88,000	985,980
Campbell	Buie's Creek	1887	2,407	118	102,000	1,350,000
Catawba	Salisbury	1851	1,133	80	93,000	5,075,000
†Davidson	Davidson	1837	1,087	95	183,000	16,561,468
Duke U.	Durham	1838	8,682	1,100	2,231,519	80,258,000
East Carolina U.	Greenville	1907	10,106	589	432,000	114,000
Elizabeth City State U.	Elizabeth City	1891	1,011	72	62,000	—
Elon	Elon College	1889	1,715	97	76,520	1,546,000
Fayetteville State U.	Fayetteville	1877	1,798	99	78,660	—
Guilford	Greensboro	1837	1,741	101	147,000	4,062,898
High Point	High Point	1924	1,060	64	81,000	2,967,000
Johnson C. Smith U.	Charlotte	1867	1,117	63	72,777	667,428
Lenoir Rhyne	Hickory	1891	1,395	97	78,600	2,223,085
Mars Hill	Mars Hill	1856	1,467	94	70,000	750,000
‡Meredith	Raleigh	1891	1,206	71	58,116	1,500,000
N. Carolina A.&T. St. U.	Greensboro	1891	4,445	267	306,000	—
N. Carolina Central U.	Durham	1910	3,723	285	...	—
Pembroke State U.	Pembroke	1887	2,077	119	63,446	—
St. Augustine's	Raleigh	1867	1,041	76	25,000	479,000
Shaw U.	Raleigh	1865	1,334	74	42,634	527,000
U. of North Carolina	Chapel Hill	1795	47,452	4,672	3,010,647	19,719,886
N. Carolina St. U., Raleigh	Raleigh	1887	13,483	866	570,000	1,700,000
U. of N.C.						
Chapel Hill	Chapel Hill	1789	19,160	1,762	1,722,768	20,994,000
Charlotte	Charlotte	1965	4,676	256	137,059	294,649
Greensboro	Greensboro	1891	6,983	451	600,000	—
Wilmington	Wilmington	1947	1,930	112	82,000	—
Wake Forest U.	Winston-Salem	1834	3,238	432	450,150	37,000,000
Western Carolina U.	Cullowhee	1889	5,330	326	158,000	217,000
Winston-Salem State U.	Winston-Salem	1892	1,623	112	85,892	284,381

NORTH DAKOTA

Institution	Location	Year founded	Total students	Faculty	Bound library volumes	Endowment fund
Dickinson State	Dickinson	1916	1,430	90	60,000	—
Minot State	Minot	1913	3,200	140	125,000	—
North Dakota State U.	Fargo	1890	6,696	328	345,000	2,905,000
U. of North Dakota	Grand Forks	1883	8,395	504	380,000	1,420,000
Valley City State	Valley City	1889	1,200	68	75,500	900,000

OHIO

Institution	Location	Year founded	Total students	Faculty	Bound library volumes	Endowment fund
Antioch	Yellow Springs	1852	2,280	117	200,000	5,598,980
Ashland	Ashland	1878	2,841	262	162,000	1,570,960
Baldwin-Wallace	Berea	1845	2,982	184	160,000	6,473,000
Bowling Green State U.	Bowling Green	1910	16,874	759	650,000	—
Capital U.	Columbus	1850	2,276	135	130,693	2,087,400
Case Western Reserve U.	Cleveland	1826	9,174	1,163	1,184,210	83,000,000
Central State U.	Wilberforce	1887	2,525	139	97,000	—
Cleveland State U.	Cleveland	1964	15,201	539	312,268	—
Defiance	Defiance	1850	1,049	74	69,000	1,367,000
Denison U.	Granville	1831	2,132	157	200,000	14,926,310
Findlay	Findlay	1882	1,175	63	60,000	775,000
Heidelberg	Tiffin	1850	1,240	102	110,077	4,307,512
Hiram	Hiram	1850	1,286	86	115,000	6,555,000
John Carroll U.	Cleveland	1886	3,964	212	209,744	5,600,000
Kent State U.	Kent	1910	29,112	1,365	870,000	—
Kenyon	Gambier	1824	1,138	97	182,000	8,000,000
Marietta	Marietta	1835	1,987	130	180,388	5,000,000
Miami U.	Oxford	1809	13,131	544	600,000	2,391,413
Mt. Union	Alliance	1846	1,325	98	145,000	6,000,000
Muskingum	New Concord	1837	1,301	107	125,000	7,141,000
Oberlin	Oberlin	1833	2,710	228	696,000	79,673,000
Ohio Northern U.	Ada	1871	2,450	161	97,000	3,805,342
Ohio State U.	Columbus	1870	50,804	5,105	2,600,000	29,201,345
Ohio U.	Athens	1804	20,317	802	1,234,597	534,000
Ohio Wesleyan U.	Delaware	1842	2,543	169	341,895	10,184,090
Otterbein	Westerville	1847	1,346	91	93,000	2,609,204
Steubenville	Steubenville	1946	1,304	70	85,000	—
U. of Akron	Akron	1870	19,674	575	490,000	2,803,000
U. of Cincinnati	Cincinnati	1819	34,676	1,956	1,156,971	48,065,898
U. of Dayton	Dayton	1850	8,713	444	330,000	4,845,000
U. of Toledo	Toledo	1872	14,903	784	900,000	676,000
Wilberforce U.	Wilberforce	1856	1,328	46	43,000	100,000
Wittenberg U.	Springfield	1845	3,386	173	235,000	14,172,667
Wooster	Wooster	1866	1,806	150	199,000	14,000,000
Wright State U.	Dayton	1967	11,020	300	210,000	8,921
Xavier U.	Cincinnati	1831	5,964	202	179,494	3,129,000
Youngstown State U.	Youngstown	1908	14,588	601	277,000	—

OKLAHOMA

Institution	Location	Year founded	Total students	Faculty	Bound library volumes	Endowment fund
Bethany Nazarene	Bethany	1899	1,667	92	80,000	—
Cameron	Lawton	1909	4,323	145	100,000	—
Central State U.	Edmond	1890	10,678	386	250,000	—
East Central State	Ada	1909	3,017	125	143,000	—
Langston U.	Langston	1897	1,110	63	110,000	—
Northeastern State	Tahlequah	1846	5,520	229	156,000	—
Northwestern State	Alva	1897	2,258	95	142,000	—
Oklahoma Baptist U.	Shawnee	1911	1,587	105	95,000	9,180,000
Oklahoma Christian	Oklahoma City	1950	1,149	35	70,000	1,312,000
Oklahoma City U.	Oklahoma City	1904	2,471	94	129,000	2,500,000
Oklahoma Liberal Arts	Chickasha	1908	1,015	54	75,000	—
Oklahoma Panhandle St.	Goodwell	1909	1,268	63	57,580	—
Oklahoma State U.	Stillwater	1890	18,670	940	1,006	11,027
Oral Roberts U.	Tulsa	1963	1,334	82	113,000	1,006,000
Phillips U.	Enid	1906	1,361	97	170,000	3,857,000
Southeastern State	Durant	1909	3,740	130	110,000	—
Southwestern State	Weatherford	1901	5,482	243	300,000	—
U. of Oklahoma	Norman	1890	22,020	971	1,158,596	$29,859,876
U. of Tulsa	Tulsa	1894	6,567	318	350,000	9,000,000

OREGON

Institution	Location	Year founded	Total students	Faculty	Bound library volumes	Endowment fund
Eastern Oregon	La Grande	1929	1,628	115	78,467	—
Lewis and Clark	Portland	1867	2,443	135	136,186	3,430,000
Linfield	McMinnville	1849	1,085	70	70,000	2,600,000
Oregon Col. of Ed.	Monmouth	1856	3,975	221	101,000	—
Oregon State U.	Corvallis	1868	15,542	936	650,000	—
Oregon Technical Inst.	Klamath Falls	1947	1,598	136	35,000	—
Pacific U.	Forest Grove	1849	1,236	94	91,000	5,974,113
Portland State U.	Portland	1955	14,701	665	360,000	—
Reed	Portland	1908	1,323	91	220,000	6,112,009
Southern Oregon	Ashland	1926	4,766	280	130,000	—
U. of Oregon	Eugene	1872	15,249	894	1,287,087	4,409,609
U. of Portland	Portland	1901	1,945	118	145,000	1,756,000
Williamette U.	Salem	1842	1,707	112	155,000	10,662,394

PENNSYLVANIA

Institution	Location	Year founded	Total students	Faculty	Bound library volumes	Endowment fund
Albright	Reading	1856	1,593	104	129,000	3,083,666
Allegheny	Meadville	1815	1,794	122	207,331	8,561,000
Bloomsburg State	Bloomsburg	1839	4,956	292	346,000	—
‡Bryn Mawr	Bryn Mawr	1885	1,421	161	363,957	26,178,000
Bucknell U.	Lewisburg	1846	2,962	220	374,800	24,000,000
California State	California	1852	6,485	390	135,000	—
‡Carlow	Pittsburgh	1929	1,045	61	79,697	193,435
Carnegie-Mellon U.	Pittsburgh	1967	4,540	536	377,508	113,296,544
‡Chestnut Hill	Philadelphia	1924	1,128	61	85,877	621,960
Cheyney State	Cheyney	1837	2,350	220	100,000	—
Clarion State	Clarion	1867	4,372	290	210,000	—
Delaware Valley	Doylestown	1896	1,265	74	61,050	2,592,479
Dickinson	Carlisle	1773	1,621	107	206,000	11,891,000
Drexel U.	Philadelphia	1891	9,195	543	330,000	11,981,000
Duquesne U.	Pittsburgh	1878	8,427	400	315,600	—
East Stroudsburg State	E. Stroudsburg	1893	3,400	220	205,000	—
Edinboro State	Edinboro	1857	7,154	471	221,000	575,000
Elizabethtown	Elizabethtown	1899	1,670	125	97,000	—
Franklin and Marshall	Lancaster	1787	2,609	145	215,000	11,299,000
Gannon	Erie	1944	3,568	203	98,000	735,000
Geneva	Beaver Falls	1848	1,605	87	94,000	3,901,146
Gettysburg	Gettysburg	1832	1,909	145	193,000	3,438,000
Grove City	Grove City	1876	2,117	123	120,000	4,867,000
Gwynedd-Mercy	Gwynedd Valley	1948	1,057	79	37,000	—
‡Immaculata	Immaculata	1920	1,473	74	95,000	255,000
Indiana U.	Indiana	1875	10,532	619	402,000	—
Juniata	Huntingdon	1876	1,222	90	125,000	4,259,000
King's	Wilkes-Barre	1946	2,669	130	120,000	590,000
Kutztown State	Kutztown	1866	4,918	273	160,000	—
Lafayette	Easton	1826	2,212	146	267,000	29,400,000
La Salle	Philadelphia	1863	7,000	190	185,000	3,200,000
Lebanon Valley	Annville	1866	1,017	74	93,000	2,754,000
Lehigh U.	Bethlehem	1865	5,440	388	562,286	38,396,219
Lincoln U.	Lincoln Univ.	1854	1,079	91	108,537	1,480
Lock Haven State	Lock Haven	1870	2,387	187	207,741	—
Lycoming	Williamsport	1812	1,635	90	96,850	1,711,000
Mansfield State	Mansfield	1857	2,625	203	86,000	—
‡Marywood	Scranton	1915	2,214	125	106,834	310,353
Millersville State	Millersville	1855	5,900	330	180,000	—
Moravian	Bethlehem	1807	1,345	77	119,000	5,535,000
Muhlenberg	Allentown	1848	1,605	104	150,000	5,100,000
Pennsylvania State U.	University Park	1855	51,303	3,467	1,667,000	—
Philadelphia Col. of Art	Philadelphia	1876	1,616	88	33,000	985,000
Phila. Col. of Tex. & Sci.	Philadelphia	1884	1,511	74	30,000	2,184,000
Point Park	Pittsburgh	1960	2,523	125	105,000	610,000
Robert Morris	Pittsburgh	1921	4,176	111	57,000	581,322
St. Francis	Loretto	1847	1,635	105	114,000	—
St. Joseph's	Philadelphia	1851	6,738	178	128,000	657,000
†St. Vincent	Latrobe	1846	1,027	57	254,164	666,000
Shippensburg State	Shippensburg	1871	3,708	300	225,000	—
Slippery Rock State	Slippery Rock	1889	5,968	364	259,000	—
Susquehanna U.	Selinsgrove	1858	1,404	96	1,649,400	91,200
Swarthmore	Swarthmore	1864	1,170	139	365,000	37,027,265
Temple U.	Philadelphia	1884	29,754	2,242	1,056,000	6,955,000
Thiel	Greenville	1866	1,354	79	85,000	1,130,000
U. of Pennsylvania	Philadelphia	1740	19,577	2,175	2,271,000	158,847,000
U. of Pittsburgh	Pittsburgh	1787	26,167	1,930	1,456,573	81,762,780
U. of Scranton	Scranton	1888	3,258	142	131,538	2,325,000
Ursinus	Collegeville	1869	1,926	98	99,000	6,537,000
Villanova U.	Villanova	1842	9,993	516	444,147	445,000
Washington & Jefferson	Washington	1781	1,094	90	152,000	7,955,000
Waynesburg	Waynesburg	1849	1,081	65	92,000	2,278,995
West Chester State	West Chester	1812	6,503	483	250,000	—
Westminster	New Wilmington	1852	1,992	117	120,000	3,750,000
Widener College	Chester	1821	3,037	150	91,000	865,016
Wilkes	Wilkes-Barre	1933	3,089	196	119,020	3,750,000
York	York	1941	2,514	83	70,000	1,161,517

PUERTO RICO

Institution	Location	Year founded	Total students	Faculty	Bound library volumes	Endowment fund
Catholic U.	Ponce	1948	6,564	365	140,000	428,402
Inter American U.	San German	1912	8,010	336	182,745	970,000
U. of Puerto Rico	Rio Piedras	1903	25,448	1,397	1,088,831	—

RHODE ISLAND

Institution	Location	Year founded	Total students	Faculty	Bound library volumes	Endowment fund
Brown U.	Providence	1764	5,789	912	1,382,293	96,579,059
Bryant	Smithfield	1863	3,457	90	60,000	—
Providence	Providence	1917	3,732	176	151,000	1,576,067
Rhode Island	Providence	1854	4,969	344	135,000	—
R.I. Sch. of Design	Providence	1877	1,223	109	44,344	14,432,972
U. of Rhode Island	Kingston	1892	8,011	860	435,000	67,740

SOUTH CAROLINA

Institution	Location	Year found-ed	Total stu-dents	Faculty	Bound library volumes	Endowment fund
Baptist	Charleston	...	1,918	85	71,000	—
Benedict	Columbia	1870	1,340	79	50,000	$ 451,112
†The Citadel	Charleston	1842	2,666	162	114,000	—
Clemson U.	Clemson	1889	8,890	580	475,000	742,000
Furman U.	Greenville	1826	2,075	135	190,000	10,602,000
South Carolina State	Orangeburg	1896	2,191	120	103,420	1,000,000
U. of South Carolina	Columbia	1801	15,724	865	1,060,820	2,275,764
Winthrop	Rock Hill	1886	3,954	202	203,620	—
Wofford	Spartanburg	1854	1,014	63	120,000	2,681,736

SOUTH DAKOTA

Institution	Location	Year found-ed	Total stu-dents	Faculty	Bound library volumes	Endowment fund
Augustana	Sioux Falls	1860	2,078	140	100,000	1,290,000
Black Hills State	Spearfish	1883	2,245	114	67,000	650,000
Dakota State	Madison	1881	1,208	68	50,000	—
Northern State	Aberdeen	1901	3,082	152	150,000	—
S. Dakota Mines & Tech.	Rapid City	1885	1,605	133	100,000	525,000
South Dakota State U.	Brookings	1883	6,519	330	240,000	3,582,000
U. of South Dakota	Vermillion	1882	5,623	290	254,000	—

TENNESSEE

Institution	Location	Year found-ed	Total stu-dents	Faculty	Bound library volumes	Endowment fund
Austin Peay State U.	Clarksville	1929	3,822	155	130,000	—
Carson-Newman	Jefferson City	1851	1,726	105	103,000	1,833,000
David Lipscomb	Nashville	1891	2,196	99	93,703	3,333,724
East Tennessee State U.	Johnson City	1911	9,545	506	328,000	—
Fisk U.	Nashville	1867	1,326	101	169,896	8,988,500
George Peabody	Nashville	1875	2,000	200	1,300,000	13,000,000
Knoxville	Knoxville	1875	1,039	78	57,500	1,309,000
Lee	Cleveland	1918	1,093	56	51,000	798,000
Memphis State U.	Memphis	1909	19,700	697	442,420	1,464,000
Middle Tennessee St. U.	Murfreesboro	1911	8,630	423	218,000	310,000
Southern Missionary	Collegedale	1892	1,414	110	60,000	—
Southwestern	Memphis	1848	1,022	90	140,000	7,080,000
Tennessee State U.	Nashville	1909	4,543	276	120,000	36,450,270
Tennessee Tech. U.	Cookeville	1915	6,438	296	368,000	—
U. of Tennessee	Knoxville	1794	41,129	2,384	1,546,152	8,390,603
Vanderbilt U.	Nashville	1872	6,756	1,358	1,301,391	80,667,871

TEXAS

Institution	Location	Year found-ed	Total stu-dents	Faculty	Bound library volumes	Endowment fund
Abilene Christian	Abilene	1906	3,311	144	178,000	7,563,000
Angelo State U.	San Angelo	1928	3,892	148	88,703	—
Austin	Sherman	1849	1,145	89	119,000	7,200,000
Baylor U.	Waco	1845	6,613	348	600,000	26,500,000
Bishop	Dallas	1881	1,968	143	77,000	614,000
Dallas Baptist	Dallas	1898	1,452	75	60,000	350,000
East Texas State U.	Commerce	1889	8,805	418	530,300	—
Hardin-Simmons U.	Abilene	1891	1,610	92	200,000	5,179,361
Houston Baptist	Houston	1960	1,047	73	60,000	—
Howard Payne	Brownwood	1889	1,407	75	89,000	3,091,000
Incarnate Word	San Antonio	1881	1,321	117	85,981	1,004,651
Lamar U.	Beaumont	1923	10,440	336	230,007	—
McMurry	Abilene	1922	1,600	88	100,560	3,325,000
Midwestern U.	Wichita Falls	1922	4,100	150	140,000	—
North Texas State U.	Denton	1890	15,015	911	720,000	—
Our Lady of the Lake	San Antonio	1911	2,018	122	78,234	1,448,117
Pan American U.	Edinburg	1927	6,217	183	110,000	62,000
Prairie View A. & M.	Prairie View	1876	4,115	220	130,000	1,170,000
Rice U.	Houston	1891	3,163	450	550,000	—
St. Edward's U.	Austin	1871	1,210	84	50,000	—
St. Mary's U.	San Antonio	1852	4,211	127	170,000	833,184
Sam Houston State U.	Huntsville	1879	10,642	345	390,000	—
Southern Methodist U.	Dallas	1911	10,016	650	1,165,000	34,097,858
Southwest Texas State U.	San Marcos	1899	11,280	460	304,081	38,000
Stephen F. Austin St. U.	Nacogdoches	1923	9,976	420	390,000	—
Sul Ross State U.	Alpine	1920	2,800	125	155,000	—
Tarleton State	Stephenville	1899	3,181	133	110,000	—
Texas A. & M. U.	College Station	1876	14,775	1,214	700,000	5,301,000
Texas A&I U.	Kingsville	1925	7,682	325	294,000	—
Texas Christian U.	Fort Worth	1873	6,537	374	750,000	26,398,000
Texas Southern U.	Houston	1947	6,175	261	212,000	64,000
Texas Tech. U.	Lubbock	1923	21,313	1,009	770,000	2,538,167
Texas Wesleyan	Fort Worth	1891	1,874	78	88,000	—
‡Texas Woman's U.	Denton	1901	5,800	310	447,589	500,000
Trinity U.	San Antonio	1869	3,008	203	390,000	44,000,000
U. of Dallas	Irving	1956	1,403	73	87,200	8,500,000
U. of Houston	Houston	1927	26,475	796	665,000	6,224,000
U. of St. Thomas	Houston	1947	1,511	107	57,000	—
U. of Texas System	Austin	1883	67,535	3,877	3,650,800	646,247,926
at Arlington	Arlington	1895	13,569	475	500,000	290,000
at Austin	Austin	1881	39,503	1,935	2,427,000	25,058,761
at El Paso	El Paso	1913	11,348	400	300,000	3,700,000
West Texas State U.	Canyon	1910	6,888	352	125,000	—

UTAH

Institution	Location	Year found-ed	Total stu-dents	Faculty	Bound library volumes	Endowment fund
Brigham Young U.	Provo	1875	25,116	1,119	1,039,000	—
Southern Utah State	Cedar City	1897	1,786	98	58,000	—
U. of Utah	Salt Lake City	1850	23,111	975	1,157,529	12,833,108
Utah State U.	Logan	1888	8,842	472	415,330	574,000
Weber State	Ogden	1889	9,772	382	176,910	74,000

VERMONT

Institution	Location	Year found-ed	Total stu-dents	Faculty	Bound library volumes	Endowment fund
Castleton State	Castleton	1867	1,534	82	46,000	$ 8,500
Goddard	Plainfield	1938	1,527	76	50,000	—
Middlebury	Middlebury	1800	1,891	114	209,568	19,114,902
†Norwich U.	Northfield	1819	1,041	107	105,000	7,240,000
St. Michael's	Winooski	1903	1,269	85	65,767	310,703
U. of Vermont	Burlington	1791	9,064	910	630,000	13,600,000

VIRGINIA

Institution	Location	Year found-ed	Total stu-dents	Faculty	Bound library volumes	Endowment fund
Eastern Mennonite	Harrisburg	1917	1,005	86	62,092	450,444
George Mason	Fairfax	1957	3,110	160	78,500	—
Hampton Inst.	Hampton	1868	2,770	202	132,000	35,642,332
‡Hollins	Hollins College	1842	1,149	81	125,000	6,050,000
Longwood	Farmville	1839	2,373	148	123,534	—
Lynchburg	Lynchburg	1903	2,047	106	76,000	2,300,000
Madison	Harrisonburg	1908	4,574	302	173,253	—
Mary Washington	Fredericksburg	1908	2,111	145	219,864	81,000
Old Dominion U.	Norfolk	1930	9,903	468	230,000	—
‡Radford	Radford	1910	3,500	246	120,000	—
Roanoke	Salem	1842	1,399	77	85,000	1,839,620
U. of Richmond	Richmond	1830	5,376	253	201,000	52,968,000
U. of Virginia	Charlottesville	1819	12,351	1,167	1,699,151	73,308,419
Va. Commonwealth U.	Richmond	1838	15,045	1,110	292,146	8,097,770
†Virginia Military Inst.	Lexington	1839	1,193	128	191,000	8,554,000
Virginia Polytech. Inst.	Blacksburg	1872	9,427	934	485,000	875,000
Virginia State	Petersburg	1882	3,267	237	143,735	183,314
Virginia Union U.	Petersburg	1865	1,280	79	67,000	1,490,000
†Washington & Lee U.	Lexington	1749	1,610	143	303,000	15,869,000
William & Mary	Williamsburg	1693	4,351	390	559,637	5,600,356

WASHINGTON

Institution	Location	Year found-ed	Total stu-dents	Faculty	Bound library volumes	Endowment fund
Central Washington St.	Ellensburg	1891	7,425	433	182,000	—
Eastern Washington St.	Cheney	1890	6,618	348	209,681	2,000,000
Gonzaga U.	Spokane	1887	2,873	193	332,000	—
Pacific Lutheran U.	Tacoma	1890	3,038	178	142,621	791,122
Seattle Pacific	Seattle	1891	1,984	124	81,000	92,000
Seattle U.	Seattle	1891	3,170	172	150,000	—
U. of Puget Sound	Tacoma	1888	4,107	192	168,000	6,230,000
U. of Washington	Seattle	1861	33,478	2,321	1,900,000	54,669,355
Walla Walla	College Place	1892	1,853	119	120,000	—
Washington State U.	Pullman	1890	14,463	716	900,000	46,076,000
Western Washington St.	Bellingham	1899	9,864	510	255,000	75,000
Whitman	Walla Walla	1859	1,072	81	161,424	16,670,400
Whitworth	Spokane	1890	1,654	74	63,000	—

WEST VIRGINIA

Institution	Location	Year found-ed	Total stu-dents	Faculty	Bound library volumes	Endowment fund
Alderson-Broaddus	Philippi	1871	1,024	61	50,000	850,000
Bethany	Bethany	1840	1,138	70	107,000	8,371,000
Bluefield State	Bluefield	1895	1,177	73	57,000	—
Concord	Athens	1872	2,019	109	122,000	—
Fairmont State	Fairmont	1867	3,680	181	120,000	—
Glenville State	Glenville	1872	1,450	83	90,000	—
Marshall U.	Huntington	1837	9,476	399	190,000	—
Morris Harvey	Charleston	1888	3,095	101	65,000	2,510,000
Salem	Salem	1888	1,449	71	68,000	1,500,000
Shepherd	Shepherdstown	1871	2,054	93	73,000	—
West Liberty State	West Liberty	1837	3,953	181	122,000	—
W. Virginia Inst. of Tech.	Montgomery	1895	2,452	146	75,000	—
West Virginia State	Institute	1891	3,590	154	109,000	—
West Virginia U.	Morgantown	1867	16,038	1,435	1,277,987	139,200
West Virginia Wesleyan	Buckhannon	1890	1,675	108	99,000	2,231,000

WISCONSIN

Institution	Location	Year found-ed	Total stu-dents	Faculty	Bound library volumes	Endowment fund
Beloit	Beloit	1846	1,783	132	230,000	8,730,000
Carroll	Waukesha	1846	1,260	84	112,690	2,737,490
Carthage	Kenosha	1847	1,807	94	80,000	3,451,000
Lawrence U.	Appleton	1847	1,380	121	180,000	25,300,000
Marquette U.	Milwaukee	1864	10,235	744	550,000	7,372,000
Ripon	Ripon	1850	1,048	87	90,000	2,350,000
St. Norbert	West De Pere	1898	1,659	104	100,119	1,400,000
U. of W.—Eau Claire	Eau Claire	1916	8,288	509	180,000	—
U. of W.—Green Bay	Green Bay	...	4,579	206	145,796	—
U. of W.—La Crosse	La Crosse	1909	7,009	434	280,000	—
U. of W.—Madison	Madison	1848	33,943	2,102	2,417,024	48,630,275
U. of W.—Milwaukee	Milwaukee	1956	22,277	681	663,974	133,536
U. of W.—Oshkosh	Oshkosh	1871	11,811	675	300,000	—
U. of W.—Parkside	Parkside	...	4,343	142	159,113	8,588
U. of W.—Platteville	Platteville	1866	4,708	300	175,000	—
U. of W.—River Falls	River Falls	1874	4,256	270	170,000	—
U. of W.—Stevens Point	Stevens Point	1894	9,130	505	215,000	—
U. of W.—Stout	Menomonie	1893	5,231	360	120,000	110,000
U. of W.—Superior	Superior	1896	3,004	223	168,000	400,000
U. of W.—Whitewater	Whitewater	1868	8,868	546	346,000	—

WYOMING

Institution	Location	Year found-ed	Total stu-dents	Faculty	Bound library volumes	Endowment fund
Casper	Casper	1945	2,994	104	39,000	316,000
U. of Wyoming	Laramie	1886	8,495	587	477,000	13,400,120

Health and Welfare

Health personnel and facilities

State	Physicians* December 31, 1971	Dentists* December, 1970	Nurses* 1966	Hospital facilities December 1, 1970: Hospitals	Beds	Nursing homes, 1971: Facilities	Beds
Alabama	3,143	1,180	5,912	119	14,217	200	13,745
Alaska	231	114	590	13	546	8	653
Arizona	2,814	865	5,862	56	6,553	85	5,359
Arkansas	1,845	655	2,609	89	7,906	223	15,501
California	39,435	13,489	58,694	527	72,699	4,395	149,672
Colorado	3,981	1,344	8,312	70	9,222	218	17,212
Connecticut	6,015	2,032	15,438	35	10,051	384	22,150
Delaware	770	240	2,098	6	1,878	35	1,944
Dist. of Columbia	3,070	737	3,662	13	5,253	74	2,786
Florida	11,216	3,731	21,760	162	27,870	381	36,712
Georgia	5,141	1,577	6,956	137	16,134	287	23,168
Hawaii	1,220	509	2,334	20	2,267	135	2,303
Idaho	705	358	1,954	47	2,873	67	4,262
Illinois	15,809	6,395	35,552	248	51,274	1,060	67,809
Indiana	5,408	2,321	12,829	110	20,597	537	33,622
Iowa	2,967	1,526	9,981	132	15,437	759	34,278
Kansas	2,649	1,084	6,895	145	11,826	484	22,128
Kentucky	3,353	1,274	6,297	106	12,386	349	18,894
Louisiana	4,478	1,457	6,758	131	15,003	217	15,049
Maine	1,180	447	4,051	47	4,213	298	7,772
Maryland	7,557	1,888	10,005	46	12,044	203	15,507
Massachusetts	12,199	4,094	28,743	129	25,008	980	50,915
Michigan	11,454	4,734	23,441	195	33,052	570	44,147
Minnesota	5,863	2,671	14,441	180	23,120	609	42,041
Mississippi	1,838	647	3,670	96	8,946	137	7,245
Missouri	6,165	2,405	11,291	117	20,947	501	32,486
Montana	752	375	2,483	55	3,834	104	4,473
Nebraska	1,775	966	4,730	96	8,788	255	15,172
Nevada	577	254	1,060	17	1,980	44	1,459
New Hampshire	1,072	363	3,521	29	3,088	143	5,670
New Jersey	10,878	4,554	24,942	98	25,020	567	31,798
New Mexico	1,211	364	2,511	39	3,323	61	3,339
New York	43,969	14,925	74,280	334	82,973	1,133	85,312
North Carolina	5,694	1,710	12,126	134	18,725	862	19,479
North Dakota	592	283	2,114	55	4,057	110	6,215
Ohio	14,499	5,240	32,649	187	41,256	1,223	61,425
Oklahoma	2,277	1,028	4,650	115	10,680	424	27,771
Oregon	3,162	1,636	6,814	82	8,799	322	18,038
Pennsylvania	18,348	6,739	45,809	228	52,654	767	58,680
Rhode Island	1,542	493	3,673	15	3,871	194	6,736
South Carolina	2,468	782	5,625	70	9,258	120	7,669
South Dakota	536	301	2,089	54	3,552	155	7,153
Tennessee	4,833	1,737	6,755	129	17,573	241	14,763
Texas	13,462	4,700	20,167	477	45,683	976	73,360
Utah	1,560	661	2,347	32	3,607	143	4,782
Vermont	847	217	1,836	19	2,019	102	3,045
Virginia	5,850	1,966	11,511	98	16,223	342	16,105
Washington	5,085	2,318	11,361	104	11,028	405	30,270
West Virginia	1,911	692	4,707	73	9,259	125	3,902
Wisconsin	5,563	2,634	14,084	152	22,366	510	39,732
Wyoming	339	167	1,209	27	1,812	34	1,697
TOTAL U.S.	309,685	112,879	613,188	5,695	842,750	22,558	1,235,405

*Excluding those in government service not allocated by state. Sources: American Medical Association, *Distribution of Physicians in the United States;* American Dental Association; American Nurses' Association; U.S. Department of Health, Education, and Welfare, Public Health Service.

Social insurance beneficiaries and benefits

State	OLD-AGE AND SURVIVORS INSURANCE: Benefi-ciaries Jan. 1, 1971	Benefits for year ending Jan. 1 1971 (in 000)	DISABILITY INSURANCE: Benefi-ciaries Jan. 1, 1971	Benefits for year ending Jan. 1 1971 (in 000)	Medicare* enrollment July 1, 1970	UNEMPLOYMENT INSURANCE STATE PROGRAMS: Benefi-ciaries† June 1971	Benefits for year ending June 30 1971 (in 000)
Alabama	399,364	$ 404,192	68,251	$ 69,330	329,343	16,839	$ 38,761
Alaska	11,136	13,183	1,218	1,365	6,662	4,524	13,779
Arizona	196,797	239,003	25,547	30,468	159,158	7,525	21,342
Arkansas	278,344	268,337	46,953	45,275	239,025	9,812	23,458
California	2,031,457	2,587,057	250,743	322,375	1,801,491	263,626	783,740
Colorado	212,792	254,279	21,557	24,932	190,032	4,236	14,748
Connecticut	321,731	456,897	24,929	33,515	288,852	79,818	199,453
Delaware	54,177	69,371	5,878	7,084	45,157	3,951	12,759
District of Columbia	69,881	80,516	8,039	9,106	68,827	6,257	16,028
Florida	1,066,649	1,293,270	104,168	121,840	936,595	24,177	47,282
Georgia	443,921	456,017	82,382	82,279	369,655	14,538	37,738
Hawaii	59,967	70,026	6,521	7,567	45,232	9,139	21,753
Idaho	84,019	98,583	9,043	10,450	69,309	3,608	10,771
Illinois	1,220,569	1,627,293	101,817	131,869	1,100,271	80,467	222,798
Indiana	584,949	749,684	55,615	68,461	495,653	27,495	73,492
Iowa	389,138	470,600	28,129	32,929	355,257	11,832	36,461
Kansas	290,739	348,922	21,323	25,091	268,794	12,597	41,443
Kentucky	401,770	417,552	70,025	67,930	342,878	14,692	38,815
Louisiana	358,801	372,836	70,601	67,267	306,687	25,006	60,264
Maine	136,035	160,090	13,680	14,892	120,640	9,723	24,403
Maryland	343,685	429,292	33,301	41,418	294,980	23,717	63,689
Massachusetts	673,597	906,349	53,891	67,035	635,927	89,052	240,438
Michigan	947,593	1,249,142	101,924	130,871	767,435	83,643	332,483
Minnesota	464,160	546,773	31,152	36,429	414,905	21,127	70,085
Mississippi	274,263	243,939	49,297	44,500	226,016	6,368	13,907
Missouri	614,821	730,871	64,442	72,838	562,274	29,232	83,583
Montana	83,600	$ 100,221	9,333	$ 10,523	69,994	3,037	$ 8,234
Nebraska	199,619	235,574	13,302	15,090	184,743	4,323	13,345
Nevada	38,369	50,557	4,481	5,883	31,722	6,100	15,547
New Hampshire	92,177	119,384	7,240	8,763	81,996	4,901	11,943
New Jersey	789,106	1,095,684	71,161	94,294	695,773	114,909	309,300
New Mexico	94,177	99,442	17,055	16,005	73,625	4,865	13,249
New York	2,177,388	3,034,061	200,486	260,892	1,970,332	212,241	635,978
North Carolina	540,788	555,729	82,706	84,281	418,374	28,527	57,099
North Dakota	80,504	88,667	6,407	6,314	67,981	1,647	5,864
Ohio	1,142,354	1,470,929	116,319	144,033	1,001,102	65,537	177,803
Oklahoma	323,508	362,169	43,953	47,100	298,769	14,040	26,439
Oregon	267,896	335,906	28,003	35,207	227,102	19,720	52,713
Pennsylvania	1,449,127	1,893,642	140,960	183,164	1,278,387	110,981	262,753
Rhode Island	115,939	152,919	11,541	14,233	105,197	13,987	39,813
South Carolina	257,194	259,313	49,578	49,720	194,732	14,432	31,787
South Dakota	94,066	103,953	7,231	7,476	81,559	770	2,859
Tennessee	459,550	471,675	69,083	70,070	389,454	24,090	57,714
Texas	1,142,942	1,259,553	134,035	142,112	993,761	37,610	80,423
Utah	93,202	115,879	8,814	10,416	77,616	5,294	14,175
Vermont	55,536	66,944	5,687	6,319	49,870	4,562	12,310
Virginia	443,965	486,931	66,731	71,317	367,890	9,502	22,500
Washington	377,204	481,652	35,106	44,713	324,636	66,217	236,900
West Virginia	245,116	274,624	56,384	62,087	199,791	8,594	17,123
Wisconsin	554,741	695,413	45,730	55,884	478,279	29,216	105,893
Wyoming	36,042	43,690	3,313	3,903	31,095	714	2,602
Total U.S.‡	23,563,634	28,796,378	2,664,995	3,067,002	20,490,908	1,688,817	4,757,839

*Includes hospital and/or medical insurance.
†Weekly average.
‡Includes data for American Samoa, Guam, Puerto Rico, Virgin Islands and for beneficiaries or enrollees living abroad for all categories except unemployment insurance state programs.
Source: U.S. Department of Health, Education, and Welfare, Social Security Administration.

Public assistance

June 1972

State	Number of recipients: Old-age assistance	Number of recipients: Aid to dependent children*	Number of recipients: Aid to the permanently and totally disabled	Number of recipients: Aid to the blind	Number of recipients: General assistance	Average money payments: Old-age assistance	Average money payments: Aid to dependent children, per recipient	Average money payments: Aid to the permanently and totally disabled	Average money payments: Aid to the blind	Average money payments: General assistance
Alabama	113,134	151,986	18,148	1,923	140	$ 78.80	$19.86	$ 76.77	$107.20	$ 12.50
Alaska	2,007	11,678	1,310	90	412	128.71	72.90	168.58	170.64	38.09
Arizona	13,591	69,477	10,229	460	6,627	82.66	35.32	88.19	88.51	35.24
Arkansas	58,163	77,896	12,315	1,680	816	65.39	26.78	75.95	82.89	5.83
California	308,190	1,496,582	198,710	14,060	45,740	107.02	62.97	139.01	158.25	77.31
Colorado	31,194	102,350	12,858	313	4,213	77.08	51.31	80.60	77.54	86.97
Connecticut	8,259	110,992	9,176	239	20,766	108.54	66.02	133.89	115.62	49.47
Delaware	2,943	30,591	1,834	337	5,025	91.01	34.12	115.69	125.55	30.00
Dist. of Columbia	4,447	91,885	10,033	238	3,507	94.35	56.14	106.07	115.07	105.28
Florida	63,760	318,638	23,293	2,302	20,700†	64.30	24.67	78.24	79.15	—
Georgia	91,519	323,200	40,990	3,234	2,979	54.86	29.50	62.43	67.75	25.14
Hawaii	2,940	40,947	2,224	86	15,505	104.61	78.51	143.49	124.72	66.50
Idaho	3,353	23,269	3,404	104	—	74.63	59.98	98.22	94.33	—
Illinois	34,206	715,598	81,301	1,729	55,322	64.74	58.46	102.43	101.80	84.29
Indiana	15,984	168,608	9,493	1,279	—	58.88	41.05	66.85	81.32	—
Iowa	21,715	84,108	3,541	1,237	8,300	129.94	54.42	157.15	123.83	—
Kansas	10,270	71,261	6,482	424	9,003	64.10	57.44	76.29	77.20	65.23
Kentucky	57,279	144,909	18,060	2,069	—	59.63	33.58	80.45	78.83	—
Louisiana	114,306	248,587	22,928	2,260	9,077	73.71	23.26	56.55	77.65	50.55
Maine	10,943	64,385	4,863	256	11,432	63.94	39.95	98.04	96.53	17.90
Maryland	9,834	200,741	17,737	393	15,511	66.79	44.20	90.08	102.36	86.77
Massachusetts	58,027	286,590	23,093	2,998	41,532	103.30	97.85	143 35	152.77	68.97
Michigan	42,477	558,543	43,712	1,644	67,402	81.05	67.13	113.70	112.70	81.43
Minnesota	16,973	123,311	14,538	867	14,763	77.30	74.22	99.13	110.75	52.88
Mississippi	82,626	162,955	26,213	2,165	1,398	57.79	14.72	67.09	67.42	14.47
Missouri	93,444	221,414	22,625	4,127	14,789	75.89	31.03	78.23	101.16	61.93
Montana	3,009	20,716	2,853	175	1,731	56.15	41.53	83.16	76.80	22.12
Nebraska	7,252	41,021	5,892	299	—	58.03	43.23	87.98	101.57	—
Nevada	2,861	14,844	—	128	—	75.34	35.15	—	93.75	—
New Hampshire	4,672	20,672	1,160	245	2,766	167.32	68.36	163.38	154.57	31.29
New Jersey	20,329	387,514	18,423	999	13,285	84.12	70.91	111.27	99.43	134.11
New Mexico	8,463	57,177	9,435	364	—	54.08	32.26	73.76	75.88	—
New York	115,123	1,290,163	156,143	4,285	230,333	101.19	70.54	108.14	114.63	68.15
North Carolina	35,443	171,940	32,982	4,800	3,220	73.65	32.25	82.41	90.73	15.03
North Dakota	3,637	14,710	2,554	77	642	91.24	61.32	105.02	109.14	17.00
Ohio	50,461	467,805	43,317	2,647	77,250	62.21	44.41	80.68	79.09	50.86
Oklahoma	66,519	110,459	24,076	1,206	3,541	68.01	39.63	100.31	106.53	9.20
Oregon	7,385	86,764	8,676	703	2,862	62.04	50.17	80.30	105.85	52.86
Pennsylvania	50,263	660,372	34,026	7,231	112,254	117.12	61.24	104.83	135.40	97.27
Rhode Island	3,975	50,984	4,451	127	13,360	61.28	64.09	102.15	99.19	39.90
South Carolina	17,353	99,504	12,354	1,878	326	48.99	19.85	57.12	67.19	31.56
South Dakota	3,670	21,311	1,707	114	901	63.83	50.80	74.66	92.55	14.68
Tennessee	48,951	186,315	28,362	1,675	4,094	49.83	30.20	66.64	69.32	12.54
Texas	207,703	445,735	26,308	3,778	...	54.35	30.54	64.08	75.16	—
Utah	2,830	44,987	5,140	169	1,303	67.10	58.63	84.64	107.60	64.28
Vermont	4,107	19,027	2,445	91	—	76.61	65.50	114.45	105.65	—
Virginia	14,618	155,798	11,919	1,294	9,622	71.38	47.95	89.49	94.55	65.11
Washington	19,245	146,271	25,354	435	4,710	70.73	62.90	108.89	101.24	71.04
West Virginia	12,889	78,643	11,681	544	2,950	98.45	29.49	88.26	93.53	11.41
Wisconsin	20,219	138,783	8,686	734	14,518	143.79	72.67	133.98	98.20	59.27
Wyoming	1,353	7,022	955	33	301	56.07	43.95	66.89	—	23.12
Total U.S.	2,003,914	10,639,038	1,119,009	80,545	895,606‡	$ 78.12§	$52.16§	$ 99.85§	$108.04§	$ 67.42

*Includes children and parents or caretaker relatives in families in which these adults were included in determining amount of assistance. †Estimated.
‡Excludes Idaho, Indiana, Kentucky, Nebraska, Nevada, New Mexico, and Vermont. §Includes Guam, Puerto Rico, and the Virgin Islands.
Source: U.S. Department of Health, Education, and Welfare, Social Security Administration, *Social Security Bulletin*.

Vocational rehabilitation

year ending June 30, 1972

State	Disabled persons: Number rehabilitated	Disabled persons: Number in process of rehabilitation June 30	Total federal and state funds	State	Disabled persons: Number rehabilitated	Disabled persons: Number in process of rehabilitation June 30	Total federal and state funds
Alabama	7,770	16,583	$19,688,511	Montana	1,265	5,021	$ 3,054,565
Alaska	390	1,357	1,250,000	Nebraska	1,917	5,242	5,326,775
Arizona	1,932	4,164	7,332,720	Nevada	738	1,338	1,269,460
Arkansas	5,850	10,860	11,512,188	New Hampshire	765	1,967	2,693,073
California	12,990	30,686	46,397,025	New Jersey	9,900	15,454*	16,561,489
Colorado	3,287	7,137	7,875,873	New Mexico	1,498	2,992	5,070,675
Connecticut	2,438	5,800	5,595,070	New York	13,717	34,885	39,022,652
Delaware	734	2,541	1,490,276	North Carolina	14,605	28,593	25,356,885
Dist. of Columbia	3,638	4,746	5,728,226	North Dakota	1,363	3,564	3,013,398
Florida	13,253	26,560	25,835,039	Ohio	10,092	20,417	29,987,884
Georgia	12,592	21,129	21,736,736	Oklahoma	7,560	20,720	11,672,346
Hawaii	873	2,496	2,330,156	Oregon	2,297	5,341	7,398,223
Idaho	1,030	3,143	3,458,764	Pennsylvania	21,145	45,914	40,224,540
Illinois	14,315	23,108	25,880,604	Rhode Island	1,622	4,723	2,831,864
Indiana	3,140	9,570	9,000,000	South Carolina	11,002	21,205	14,568,555
Iowa	4,143	12,520	10,195,567	South Dakota	913	3,668	3,111,725
Kansas	2,305	3,467	6,035,993	Tennessee	7,265	16,069	15,345,000
Kentucky	10,534	12,413	15,701,075	Texas	24,735	46,552	47,096,331
Louisiana	5,737	20,593	18,467,716	Utah	2,486	8,487	5,014,745
Maine	829	2,060	3,347,473	Vermont	655	1,416	1,775,249
Maryland	8,788	14,655	11,202,728	Virginia	12,782	20,181	18,964,399
Massachusetts	5,148	10,240	14,495,246	Washington	3,460	9,944	10,010,164
Michigan	10,642	21,438	25,391,326	West Virginia	7,279	9,231	9,683,741
Minnesota	6,072	17,999	13,341,370	Wisconsin	9,896	19,423	15,387,102
Mississippi	6,353	10,979	14,400,081	Wyoming	573	1,382	1,333,863
Missouri	7,299	10,162	17,464,392	Total U. S.	321,612	660,135	680,928,858

*Estimated.
Source: U. S. Department of Health, Education, and Welfare, Social and Rehabilitation Service.

Defense

Vietnam

U.S. armed forces and casualties

	1961	1962	1963	1964	1965	1966	1967	1968	1969	1970	1971	1972*
Military forces	3,200	11,300	16,300	23,300	184,300	385,300	485,600	536,100	475,200	334,600	156,800	32,200
Army	2,100	7,900	10,100	14,700	116,800	239,400	319,500	359,800	331,100	249,600	119,700	18,900
Navy†	100	500	800	1,100	8,400	23,300	31,700	36,100	30,200	16,700	7,600	1,800
Marine Corps	—	500	800	900	38,200	69,200	78,000	81,400	55,100	25,100	600	1,300
Air Force	1,000	2,400	4,600	6,600	20,600	52,900	55,900	58,400	58,400	43,100	28,800	10,100
Coast Guard	—	—	—	—	300	500	500	400	400	100	100	100
Casualties‡												
Battle deaths	11	31	78	147	1,369	5,008	9,378	14,592	9,414	4,221	1,380	281
Killed	1	19	53	112	1,130	4,179	7,482	12,588	8,119	3,483	1,087	177
Died of wounds	—	1	5	6	87	517	981	1,636	1,170	556	160	22
Died while missing	10	11	20	28	151	309	911	367	120	180	132	81
Died while captured	—	—	—	1	1	3	4	1	5	2	1	1
Wounded, nonfatal												
Hospital care required	2	41	218	522	3,308	16,526	32,371	46,799	32,940	15,211	4,767	513
Hospital care not required	1	37	193	517	2,806	13,567	29,654	46,021	37,276	15,432	4,169	60

Data are for December 31 of years reported, except as indicated. *As of October 31. †Excludes personnel on ships off Vietnam shores.
‡Represents casualties from enemy action. Deaths exclude servicemen who died in accidents or from disease.
Source: U.S. Department of Defense.

National defense expenditures

in million dollars

Function	1962	1963	1964	1965	1966	1967	1968	1969	1970	1971	1972*
Department of defense—Military:											
Military personnel (including retired)	13,032	13,000	14,195	14,771	16,753	19,787	21,954	23,818	25,158	24,104	26,528
Operation and maintenance	11,594	11,874	11,932	12,349	14,710	19,000	20,578	22,227	21,500	19,650	20,500
Procurement	14,532	16,632	15,351	11,839	14,339	19,012	23,283	23,988	21,550	18,799	17,944
Research and development	6,319	6,376	7,021	6,236	6,259	7,160	7,747	7,457	7,300	7,382	7,780
Military construction and other	1,602	513	1,236	928	2,279	2,636	3,975	525	1,139	1,421	1,594
Allowances	—	—	—	—	—	—	—	—	—	—	800
Deductions for offsetting receipts	−163	−251	−159	−150	−160	−138	−164	−135	−140	−163	−146
Subtotal, Dept. of defense—Military	46,916	48,144	49,576	45,973	54,180	67,457	77,373	77,880	76,505	71,193	75,000
Atomic energy	2,806	2,758	2,764	2,625	2,403	2,264	2,466	2,450	2,461	2,411	2,358
Military assistance	1,337	1,406	1,209	1,125	1,003	858	654	789	495	600	800
Defense-related activities	92	24	172	136	− 62	− 17	139	260	119	− 51	90
Deductions for offsetting receipts	− 53	− 74	−130	−281	−738	−481	−116	−138	−150	−572	−218
Total national defense	51,098	52,258	53,591	49,578	56,786	70,081	80,516	81,241	79,432	73,581	78,030

Source: Executive Office of the President, Bureau of the Budget, *The Budget in Brief.*

Armed forces personnel

as of June 30, 1972

Branch of service	Personnel on active duty*		Reserve personnel†		Total military personnel
	Officers	Enlisted men	Officers	Enlisted men	
Army	121,290	689,670	80,834	590,190	1,481,984
Navy	73,155	514,888	23,329	104,065	715,437
Air Force	121,674	604,164	23,737	114,944	864,519
Marine Corps	19,843	178,395	3,753	37,731	239,722
Coast Guard	6,912	30,996	1,584	10,244	49,736
Total	342,874	2,018,113	133,237	857,174	3,351,398

*Includes cadets and officer candidates.
†Paid status only; excludes personnel on inactive reserve.
Sources: U.S. Department of Defense and U.S. Department of Transportation, United States Coast Guard.

Status of selective service draftees examined

Status	1950–1971*		Number in thousands, 1971			Percent, 1971		
	Number (000)	Percent	Total	White	Non-white	Total	White	Non-white
Examined	15,841	100.0	596	528	68	100.0	100.0	100.0
Found acceptable	9,347	59.0	301	271	30	50.5	51.4	43.2
Disqualified	6,494	41.0	295	257	38	49.5	48.6	56.8
Medically disqualified only	3,740	1.2	242	227	15	40.4	42.9	22.5
Failed mental requirements only	2,190	13.8	31	15	16	5.4	2.9	24.0
Failed mental test only†	1,725	10.9	25	12	13	4.3	2.3	19.6
Trainability limited‡	465	2.9	6	6	6	1.1	0.6	4.4
Failed mental test and medically disqualified	379	2.4	13	8	5	2.2	1.4	7.9
Administratively disqualified	185	23.6	9	7	2	1.5	1.4	2.4

Based on results of preinduction examinations.
*1950 data are for July through December only.
†Examinees who failed minimum requirement on Armed Forces Qualification Test.
‡Examinees classified as mental group IV on basis of AFQT but who failed to meet additional aptitude area requirements.
Source: U.S. Department of Commerce, Bureau of the Census, *Statistical Abstract of the United States.* Data compiled by the Department of the Army, Office of the Surgeon General.

Law Enforcement

Public expenditures and employment for law enforcement

Expenditures in million dollars	1962	1965	1969	1970
All governments	3,800	4,573	7,340	8,571
Police protection	2,326	2,792	4,430	5,080
Judicial	628	748	1,449	1,734
Correction*	846	1,033	1,462	1,706
Federal government				
Police protection	196	243	492	589
Judicial	57	75	238	287
Correction*	51	59	71	83
State governments				
Police protection	276	348	621	689
Judicial	118	155	314	374
Correction*	508	632	914	1,051
Local governments				
Police protection	1,854	2,201	3,317	3,803
Judicial	453	518	898	1,073
Correction*	287	343	477	572
Employees (in 000)				
Police protection				
Federal	22	23	36	40
State	36	41	54	57
Local	322	357	432	451
Correction				
Federal	6	3	5	6
State	61	71	86	92
Local	36	43	51	55

Expenditures are for fiscal years ending June 30. Employees as of October.
*Includes capital outlay.
Source: U.S. Department of Commerce, Bureau of the Census, *Statistical Abstract of the United States.*

Arrests, 1971

Offense charged	UNDER 18 Persons arrested	UNDER 18 Percent change from 1970	18 AND OVER Persons arrested	18 AND OVER Percent change from 1970	ALL AGES Persons arrested	ALL AGES Percent change from 1970
Murder and nonnegligent manslaughter	1,415	+ 9.3	12,157	+10.7	13,572	+10.5
Negligent manslaughter	228	+ 0.4	2,301	−10.5	2,529	− 9.6
Forcible rape	3,181	+ 5.0	12,074	+ 6.5	15,255	+ 6.2
Robbery	31,653	+10.8	65,752	+17.1	97,405	+15.0
Aggravated assault	23,052	+15.9	104,698	+ 6.6	127,750	+ 8.2
Other assaults	54,239	+ 8.2	226,630	+ 1.6	280,869	+ 2.8
Burglary—breaking or entering	145,685	+ 4.5	140,880	+10.0	286,565	+ 7.1
Larceny—theft	314,913	+ 6.5	305,968	+ 7.8	620,881	+ 7.2
Auto theft	64,352	− 5.3	57,198	+ 8.2	121,550	+ 0.6
Arson	5,573	+ 5.8	4,553	+28.7	10,126	+15.0
Forgery, counterfeiting	3,811	−12.9	37,179	+ 1.5	40,990	*
Fraud	3,481	+16.3	80,584	+16.4	84,065	+16.4
Embezzlement	328	+11.9	6,321	−13.6	6,649	−12.6
Stolen property; buying, receiving, possessing	20,704	+15.5	48,286	+16.6	68,990	+16.2
Vandalism	78,487	+ 4.5	31,174	+ 7.2	109,661	+ 5.3
Weapons; carrying, possessing, etc.	16,408	+ 0.1	89,641	+ 8.7	106,049	+ 7.2
Prostitution, commercialized vice	1,316	+14.3	50,212	+ 5.2	51,528	+ 5.4
Sex offenses (except forcible rape and prostitution)	9,732	− 1.7	36,564	+ 1.4	46,296	+ 0.7
Narcotic drug laws	80,657	+ 8.3	288,078	+11.6	368,735	+10.9
Gambling	1,948	+21.2	80,831	*	82,779	+ 0.4
Offenses against family and children	761	+ 0.3	47,387	− 8.0	48,148	− 7.9
Driving while intoxicated	4,758	+ 7.4	432,352	+11.8	437,110	+11.8
Liquor law violations	72,473	+ 5.9	132,639	− 0.5	205,112	+ 1.7
Drunkenness	40,077	+ 5.4	1,331,176	− 4.4	1,371,253	− 4.2
Disorderly conduct	124,683	+ 6.1	448,763	+ 3.5	573,446	+ 4.0
Vagrancy	9,993	−24.9	65,760	−24.1	75,753	−24.2
All other offenses, except traffic	238,316	+ 7.0	552,154	+ 5.3	790,470	+ 5.8
Suspicion	17,087	− 9.8	33,263	−26.7	50,350	−21.7
Curfew and loitering law violations	94,715	− 4.3	—	—	94,715	− 4.3
Runaways	182,796	+ 9.7	—	—	182,796	+ 9.7
Total arrests†	1,629,735	+ 5.4	4,691,312	+ 2.7	6,321,047	+ 3.4

Data are from 4,483 agencies reporting on 1971 population of 139,239,000.
*Change is less than a tenth of a percent.
†Excludes arrests for suspicion.
Source: U.S. Department of Justice, Federal Bureau of Investigation, *Uniform Crime Reports.*

Disposition of persons formally charged, 1971

Offense	Charged (held for prosecution)	Guilty: As charged	Guilty: Lesser Offense	Acquitted or dismissed	Referred to juvenile court
Total	2,251,647	60.7%	4.0%	16.8%	18.5%
Murder, nonnegligent manslaughter	2,956	38.5	19.7	28.9	12.8
Manslaughter by negligence	790	33.7	14.2	43.0	9.1
Forcible rape	4,291	27.0	13.3	36.1	23.5
Robbery	21,549	20.2	11.3	25.4	43.1
Aggravated assault	36,807	34.7	13.9	31.4	20.1
Burglary: breaking, entering	93,627	22.8	7.9	13.5	55.8
Larceny: theft	207,737	49.8	4.5	16.2	29.4
Auto theft	39,682	16.9	5.4	14.0	63.7
Other assaults	117,723	43.6	3.9	39.5	12.9
Arson	2,871	16.7	5.5	16.3	61.6
Forgery and counterfeiting	11,682	53.6	11.3	22.9	12.1
Fraud	28,323	62.0	4.0	31.1	3.0
Embezzlement	1,805	61.7	7.9	23.6	6.9
Stolen property; buying, receiving, possessing	21,713	35.0	7.1	23.7	34.3
Vandalism	34,618	22.8	1.9	20.4	55.0
Weapons; carrying, possessing, etc.	33,518	54.4	7.9	23.8	13.9
Prostitution, commercialized vice	10,941	64.7	2.3	30.5	2.4
Sex offenses (except forcible rape, prostitution)	15,903	48.5	8.2	23.2	20.0
Narcotic drug laws	100,526	41.6	5.5	26.4	26.5
Gambling	22,988	67.1	2.2	29.5	1.2
Offenses against family, children	18,528	51.5	3.8	31.7	13.1
Driving while intoxicated	174,923	73.7	17.8	7.7	0.9
Liquor laws	105,427	64.5	1.2	11.6	22.7
Drunkenness	639,724	90.1	0.3	7.8	1.8
Disorderly conduct	153,165	50.8	1.6	28.5	19.1
Vagrancy	24,562	68.0	1.1	24.6	6.4
All other offenses	325,268	47.9	1.7	16.9	33.4

Data are from 2,990 cities with a 1971 population of 63,269,000. Source: U.S. Department of Justice, Federal Bureau of Investigation, *Uniform Crime Reports.*

Crime rates per 100,000 population

Metropolitan area	MURDER* 1966	MURDER* 1971	FORCIBLE RAPE 1966	FORCIBLE RAPE 1971	ROBBERY 1966	ROBBERY 1971	AGGRAVATED ASSAULT 1966	AGGRAVATED ASSAULT 1971	BURGLARY 1966	BURGLARY 1971	LARCENY† 1966	LARCENY† 1971	AUTO THEFT 1966	AUTO THEFT 1971
Baltimore	10.5	17.3	21.1	34.2	199.7	497.3	**259.7**	380.6	852.5	1,414.5	760.2	1,193.6	586.3	640.2
Boston	2.6	4.8	6.9	12.8	57.4	186.4	62.4	120.9	614.6	1,252.9	378.0	877.9	**677.2**	1,119.9
Chicago	9.0	13.1	21.6	27.4	271.8	373.6	215.9	236.0	642.5	921.6	439.0	669.2	572.4	650.5
Cleveland	7.7	14.8	10.6	24.8	150.9	319.5	78.1	134.6	497.8	903.6	176.0	579.4	430.7	**1,233.8**
Detroit	6.8	16.3	31.8	31.7	**281.6**	605.3	160.7	234.7	1,240.0	2,062.2	691.1	1,495.7	531.3	825.4
Houston	**14.4**	**18.1**	15.7	31.9	147.3	264.0	211.6	196.6	1,178.9	1,555.0	480.7	768.7	397.4	684.7
Los Angeles–Long Beach	5.8	10.7	**34.9**	**51.3**	189.5	348.5	245.9	**384.3**	**1,653.8**	2,209.0	1,003.9	1,427.2	646.4	1,012.6
Minneapolis–St. Paul	3.3	3.5	13.4	20.5	101.6	152.3	77.8	107.5	948.6	1,293.9	598.3	1,267.3	431.3	598.0
Newark	5.1	10.4	13.2	23.3	116.9	414.2	160.9	207.1	1,038.5	1,529.6	529.8	972.4	428.5	681.3
New York	6.4	13.6	16.5	22.3	213.5	**790.4**	214.3	307.6	1,210.5	1,820.5	**1,091.9**	1,400.4	455.0	952.1
Philadelphia	5.3	10.9	16.3	17.7	73.2	241.1	113.3	149.0	514.2	958.9	270.9	556.3	274.6	615.4
Pittsburgh	2.7	4.1	12.4	17.7	86.7	148.4	56.9	118.3	500.9	814.4	296.1	537.8	355.3	441.9
St. Louis	7.2	12.7	20.8	31.2	140.4	266.1	139.3	203.5	917.7	1,494.7	362.7	748.8	398.9	765.9
San Francisco–Oakland	4.9	9.4	18.4	39.7	162.1	403.4	165.1	235.6	1,265.1	**2,247.6**	647.3	**1,642.5**	554.3	936.0
Washington, D.C.	7.7	12.3	13.5	36.5	189.4	510.1	198.5	237.1	985.8	1,335.0	530.2	1,144.9	487.1	698.1

Boldface type indicates highest rate for that crime among the listed metropolitan areas.
*Includes nonnegligent manslaughter. †$50 and over.
Source: U.S. Department of Justice, Federal Bureau of Investigation, *Uniform Crime Reports.*

Transport, Power, and Communication

Mineral fuels and electricity production

in trillion British thermal units

Year	MINERAL FUELS: Total production	MINERAL FUELS: Bituminous coal and lignite	MINERAL FUELS: Anthracite	MINERAL FUELS: Crude petroleum	MINERAL FUELS: Natural gas, wet (unprocessed)	ELECTRICITY*: Hydropower	ELECTRICITY*: Nuclear power
1965	49,467	13,417	378	15,930	17,652	2,051	39
1966	51,741†	13,507†	329	16,925	18,894	2,029†	57†
1967	58,265†	11,982†	274†	25,335†	18,250†	2,344†	80
1968	61,763†	12,481†	258†	27,052†	19,580†	2,342†	130
1969	64,979†	12,509†	224†	28,421†	21,020†	2,659†	146
1970†	67,221	12,488	210	29,614	22,029	2,651	229
1971‡	68,790	11,887	186	30,649	22,819	2,845	404

Represents outputs of hydropower and nuclear power converted to theoretical energy inputs calculated from national average heat rates for fossil-fueled steam-electric plants provided by the Federal Power Commission using 10,432 Btu per net kilowatt-hour in 1967; 10,398 Btu in 1968; 10,447 Btu in 1969; 10,494 Btu in 1970; and 10,494 Btu in 1971 for hydropower. Energy input for nuclear power in 1971 is converted at an average heat rate of 10,660 Btu per net kilowatt-hour based on information from the Atomic Energy Commission.

*Includes installations owned by manufacturing plants and mines, as well as government owned and public utilities. †Revised. ‡Preliminary.

Source: U.S. Department of Interior, Bureau of Mines. (FRANK H. SKELDING)

Railroads

years ending December 31

Item		1965	1967	1970
Number of operating companies*		372	370	351
Miles of road owned, first track†		211,384	209,292	205,782
Total miles operated		370,636	368,030	360,240
Number of locomotives in service		30,061	29,874	29,122
Number of passenger-train cars in service‡		20,022	17,822	11,378
Operating revenues	($000,000)	10,425	10,582	12,209
Operating expenses	($000,000)	8,003	8,359	9,806
Net income§	($000,000)	866	368‖	126‖
Passenger revenue	($000,000)	556	489	423
Passengers carried	(000,000)	306	304	289
Passenger-miles	(000,000)	17,454	15,264	10,786
Revenue per passenger-mile	(cents)	3.185	3.201	3.924
Average journey per passenger	(miles)	57.07	50.21	37.26
Freight revenue	($000,000)	9,037	9,329	11,124
Freight revenue-tons originated	(000,000)	1,479	1,498	1,572
Tons carried one mile	(000,000)	705,705	727,075	771,012
Revenue ton-miles per mile of road	(000)	3,121	3,238	3,468
Revenue per ton-mile	(cents)	1.281	1.283	1.443
Haul per ton				
U.S. as a system	(miles)	477.15	485.21	490.41
Individual railroad	(miles)	257.40	262.49	275.53
Revenue per ton				
U.S. as a system	(dollars)	6.11	6.23	7.08
Individual railroad	(dollars)	3.30	3.37	3.98
Average number of employees	(000)	655	624	577
Compensation of employees	($000,000)	4,887	5,026	5,646

All data are for Classes I and II.
*Includes unofficial companies.
†Includes lessors, proprietary and unofficial companies.
‡Includes switching and terminal companies.
§Includes lessors.
‖After extraordinary and prior period items.
Source: Interstate Commerce Commission.

Transportation

State	ROAD AND STREET MILEAGE Jan. 1, 1972: Total*	Municipal mileage	Rural mileage: State controlled	Rural mileage: Locally controlled	AUTOMOBILES, TRUCKS, AND BUSES registrations, in 000, 1971: Total	Private, commercial: Automobiles	Private, commercial: Trucks and buses	Publicly owned†	RAILROAD MILEAGE OWNED Jan. 1, 1971: Total	Class 1	AIRPORTS‡ Jan. 1, 1972: Total	Private	CIVIL AIRCRAFT Jan. 1, 1972: Total	Active
Alabama	79,036	11,462	19,938§	47,361	2,093	1,650	413	30	4,566	3,887	130	40	2,182	1,697
Alaska	7,817	862	4,611	1,713	151	100	45	6	20	—	762	225	3,341	2,697
Arizona	47,085	6,166	5,464	19,034	1,185	885	277	22	2,053	1,879	209	105	3,186	2,405
Arkansas	78,680	9,231	12,948	54,659	1,075	747	314	15	3,582	3,316	151	78	2,095	1,686
California	165,990	45,997	13,953	71,490	12,324	10,160	1,978	186	7,432	6,622	746	469	21,909	17,442
Colorado	81,870	7,581	8,350	65,888	1,548	1,170	351	27	3,576	3,459	217	143	2,812	2,307
Connecticut	18,531	13,168	1,517	3,846	1,791	1,619	149	23	664	609	86	72	1,366	1,080
Delaware	5,104	766	4,338§	—	317	261	50	5	287	—	25	23	460	382
District of Columbia	1,087	1,087	—	—	260	232	17	11	31	12	7	2	27	12
Florida	93,310	22,275	17,041	52,942	4,534	3,899	572	64	4,274	3,797	323	209	7,345	5,794
Georgia	100,214	15,028	15,576	68,512	2,753	2,188	530	35	5,435	3,807	218	111	3,744	3,042
Hawaii	3,591	998	824	1,678	426	372	47	7	—	—	58	35	362	266
Idaho	57,144	2,963	4,747	26,304	509	351	145	14	2,668	2,478	169	47	1,459	1,163
Illinois	130,187	27,753	13,324	89,110	5,383	4,646	680	57	10,831	9,055	652	570	7,035	5,666
Indiana	90,908	15,507	10,261	65,140	2,903	2,333	543	27	6,416	3,424	199	134	4,021	3,346
Iowa	112,831	13,663	9,066	90,101	1,842	1,417	392	33	8,058	7,797	241	132	3,056	2,550
Kansas	134,182	11,088	9,966	113,128	1,599	1,149	425	26	7,779	7,755	295	176	3,494	2,795
Kentucky	69,123	5,852	23,837§	38,998	1,860	1,440	396	24	3,513	3,092	73	26	1,246	1,054
Louisiana	53,340	10,993	14,202‖	27,859	1,832	1,426	382	25	3,752	3,444	240	170	2,652	2,144
Maine	21,424	2,449	10,962‖	7,851	537	430	100	7	1,678	1,522	148	106	846	684
Maryland	26,522	4,146	4,988	17,243	2,003	1,724	257	22	1,110	564	91	71	2,294	1,852
Massachusetts	29,355	21,858	1,242	6,206	2,700	2,421	245	34	1,441	1,237	116	90	2,394	2,018
Michigan	115,064	20,115	7,977	86,970	4,740	4,029	641	70	6,183	4,109	376	247	6,625	5,511
Minnesota	127,744	17,201	11,375	97,330	2,293	1,808	454	32	7,738	7,617	266	127	4,211	3,400
Mississippi	66,766	6,599	9,713	49,924	1,176	864	294	19	3,653	3,170	130	59	1,820	1,440
Missouri	115,544	15,386	30,050	69,419	2,498	1,944	530	25	6,351	5,722	313	211	3,715	2,977
Montana	77,920	2,333	12,129	53,315	511	326	175	10	5,030	4,965	180	63	1,578	1,286
Nebraska	98,765	6,681	9,581	81,966	1,033	743	274	16	5,498	5,498	276	186	2,041	1,657
Nevada	49,702	1,919	6,167§	41,616	373	275	85	13	1,574	1,413	104	52	1,174	906
New Hampshire	14,926	4,816	3,041	6,949	375	312	56	7	817	680	54	38	675	531
New Jersey	32,237	17,512	1,722	12,998	3,737	3,337	334	66	1,764	915	189	162	3,644	2,983
New Mexico	68,371	4,836	11,711	45,746	661	460	186	15	2,120	2,046	129	64	1,509	1,225
New York	106,490	40,618	12,830	53,007	6,891	6,130	659	102	5,624	4,704	444	376	6,419	5,172
North Carolina	86,478	13,885	70,776§	—	3,002	2,345	577	80	4,154	2,951	231	170	3,193	2,597
North Dakota	106,530	3,130	6,617	95,490	444	276	159	9	5,098	5,098	191	101	1,253	979
Ohio	109,240	23,563	16,902	68,775	6,043	5,328	657	58	7,845	4,549	491	389	7,155	5,783
Oklahoma	107,870	14,246	11,473	82,123	1,789	1,261	501	28	5,399	5,307	265	150	4,177	3,292
Oregon	97,453	6,348	9,152	35,217	1,432	1,156	245	31	3,070	2,523	255	157	3,088	2,442
Pennsylvania	115,658	24,171	44,166	46,599	6,011	5,195	751	66	8,371	5,572	511	443	5,640	4,526
Rhode Island	5,461	4,444	493	524	509	449	54	6	146	103	14	7	247	206
South Carolina	59,629	6,838	31,665	20,673	1,383	1,114	245	25	3,092	2,111	116	57	1,412	1,109
South Dakota	84,078	2,973	8,707	70,733	442	298	133	11	3,571	3,571	114	44	1,085	887
Tennessee	80,290	11,926	8,283	58,875	2,136	1,696	407	32	3,242	2,851	113	44	2,212	1,827
Texas	248,340	49,476	61,425	136,441	6,984	5,308	1,569	110	13,616	12,920	1,128	862	12,694	9,889
Utah	40,981	4,412	4,779	22,190	711	509	188	14	1,760	1,696	85	31	966	792
Vermont	14,512	1,004	2,541	10,795	237	193	40	4	769	324	45	32	324	259
Virginia	61,508	8,636	49,921§	853	2,410	1,992	369	49	3,880	3,255	192	140	2,299	1,883
Washington	80,219	9,965	14,023	39,546	2,163	1,643	476	44	4,931	4,438	256	151	4,443	3,488
West Virginia	35,941	3,612	31,742§	—	826	619	193	14	3,553	3,162	46	23	824	684
Wisconsin	103,352	14,222	10,803	78,259	2,230	1,864	333	34	5,955	5,914	274	174	3,257	2,615
Wyoming	40,540	1,287	5,866	20,875	260	232	88	7	1,812	1,805	84	43	739	627
Total U.S.	3,758,942	593,047	712,785	2,256,271	112,922	92,255	18,977	1,691	205,782	176,745	12,070	7,652	166,784	133,870

*Includes federally controlled rural roads. †Excludes vehicles owned by military services. ‡Includes seaplane bases, heliports, and military fields having joint civil-military use.
§Includes mileage of state-controlled county roads. ‖Includes mileage designated as farm-to-market. ¶Includes the state-aid system.
Sources: Interstate Commerce Commission; U.S. Department of Transportation, Federal Aviation Administration; Federal Highway Administration, Bureau of Public Roads.

Commerce of selected ports

1971 in thousands of short tons (cargo)

Port	FOREIGN Imports	FOREIGN Exports	DOMESTIC Receipts	DOMESTIC Shipments
COASTAL PORTS				
Atlantic coast				
Portland, Me.	26,375	9	3,938	905
Salem, Mass.	805	—	240	3
Boston, Mass.	7,141	639	14,752	1,822
Providence, R.I.	1,864	213	5,936	448
New Haven, Conn.	3,280	189	6,557	1,585
Bridgeport, Conn.	1,658	39	1,530	279
Norwalk, Conn.	—	—	918	—
New York, N.Y. and N.J.	48,356	5,590	37,198	20,625
Hempstead, N.Y.	—	—	2,166	2,161
Port Jefferson, N.Y.	868	—	3,077	302
Albany, N.Y.	2,236	164	2,671	5
Delaware River ports*	52,079	3,300	34,404	9,023
Baltimore, Md.	18,282	6,475	5,468	1,512
Norfolk, Va.	7,003	27,645	2,479	197
Newport News, Va.	731	8,594	4	2
Wilmington, N.C.	2,458	161	2,255	163
Charleston, S.C.	2,706	733	2,949	233
Savannah, Ga.	3,158	1,302	1,844	288
Jacksonville, Fla.	4,435	1,752	3,962	590
Port Everglades, Fla.	3,002	134	6,016	814
Pacific coast				
Long Beach, Calif.	6,351	4,720	5,711	3,285
Los Angeles, Calif.	7,123	3,622	5,970	5,559
San Francisco Bay area, Calif.	9,186	5,368	15,508	10,311
Stockton, Calif.	116	554	264	40
Portland, Ore.	1,307	2,737	4,382	261
Longview, Wash.	346	2,217	453	71
Tacoma, Wash.	2,003	2,091	374	96
Seattle, Wash.	2,927	1,321	2,021	1,079
Honolulu, Hawaii	1,419	106	3,404	2,455
Gulf coast				
Tampa, Fla.	2,870	11,374	12,976	6,403
Mobile, Ala.	8,527	2,325	15	1,774
New Orleans, La.	8,796	21,608	2,310	27,496
Baton Rouge, La.	7,715	5,967	720	8,347
Lake Charles, La.†	359	1,362	43	4,777
Galveston, Tex.	673	2,063	205	495
Texas City, Tex.	406	409	305	5,642
Houston, Tex.	6,000	13,804	2,236	20,703
Corpus Christi, Tex.	5,185	2,279	132	9,678
Harbor Island, Tex.	—	—	—	4,181
Freeport, Tex.	69	1,306	125	1,101
Brazos Island, Tex.	1,535	485	89	1,255
Beaumont, Tex.	578	2,774	457	15,407
Port Arthur, Tex.	346	2,180	4,087	10,081

GREAT LAKES PORTS	ALL COMMERCE‡ Receipts	ALL COMMERCE‡ Shipments
Ashtabula, Ohio	5,745	5,507
Buffalo, N.Y.	10,198	556
Chicago, Ill.	15,090	10,467
Cleveland, Ohio	19,743	732
Conneaut, Ohio	7,947	7,904
Detroit, Mich.	28,204	1,339
Duluth-Superior, Minn. and Wis.	2,971	34,079
Indiana Harbor, Ind.	9,656	5,158
Lorain, Ohio	4,698	2,439
Milwaukee, Wis.	4,239	1,418
Sandusky, Ohio	56	4,792
Toledo, Ohio	6,390	20,555

Data exclude purely local port traffic and commerce with ports on internal rivers and canals.
*Includes tributaries. †Includes Calcasieu River and Pass.
‡Includes both foreign and domestic shipping.
Source: U.S. Department of the Army, Corps of Engineers, *Waterborne Commerce of the United States.*

Communication facilities

State	Post offices July 1, 1972	RADIO STATIONS January 1, 1971 AM	RADIO STATIONS January 1, 1971 FM	TV STATIONS March 1, 1971 Commercial	TV STATIONS March 1, 1971 Educational	TELEPHONES January 1, 1972‡ Total	TELEPHONES January 1, 1972‡ Residence	NEWSPAPERS Daily Number Feb. 1, 1972	NEWSPAPERS Daily Circulation Sept. 30, 1971	NEWSPAPERS Weekly April 1, 1971 Number	NEWSPAPERS Weekly April 1, 1971 Circulation	NEWSPAPERS Sunday Number Feb. 1, 1972	NEWSPAPERS Sunday Circulation Sept. 30, 1971
Alabama	668	136	53	16	9	1,650.0	1,237.9	23	725,891	106	388,146	15	640,918
Alaska	199	16	3	7	—	...	...	6	74,224	6	9,540	1	17,631
Arizona	216	59	17	11	2	1,055.3	738.5	12	456,568	56	141,453	4	376,848
Arkansas	699	84	35	6	1	919.6	686.1	35	426,219	124	271,499	11	356,294
California	1,162	231	153	48	9	13,750.8	9,733.6	128	5,748,915	433	5,092,540	38	4,685,675
Colorado	424	66	28	11	2	1,468.4	1,024.3	26	727,210	124	247,881	9	774,993
Connecticut	250	38	20	5	3	2,122.6	1,561.1	27	952,329	49	290,194	7	625,128
Delaware	57	10	5	—	1	387.4	285.5	3	157,414	11	55,963	1	26,242
Dist. of Columbia	1	6	7	6	1	914.1	471.4	3	1,021,845	...	...	2	996,581
Florida	471	194	95	23	9	4,546.1	3,269.3	51	2,131,899	133	511,034	29	1,820,123
Georgia	660	169	59	16	10	2,586.8	1,873.4	33	1,007,182	182	530,618	11	945,887
Hawaii	79	25	4	10	2	...	...	5	237,512	2	17,127	2	191,828
Idaho	275	43	7	7	1	380.4	275.1	15	184,902	57	104,611	5	146,307
Illinois	1,293	121	101	23	5	7,342.8	5,311.6	91	3,973,238	556	2,772,558	20	2,821,222
Indiana	768	84	75	18	5	3,044.6	2,308.6	80	1,676,804	194	466,634	19	1,151,501
Iowa	969	72	38	13	2	1,685.5	1,291.3	42	977,181	360	701,033	9	835,057
Kansas	715	58	25	12	2	1,347.5	1,017.0	50	651,283	246	453,578	15	448,734
Kentucky	1,348	103	61	10	14	1,518.3	1,136.3	27	768,851	138	456,363	13	574,417
Louisiana	547	90	43	16	1	1,857.5	1,390.8	25	803,547	90	256,897	12	704,662
Maine	511	36	14	7	4	520.9	391.8	9	265,887	35	137,681	1	109,357
Maryland	429	52	33	6	1	2,591.1	1,888.6	12	719,651	66	534,327	4	690,017
Massachusetts	451	63	40	10	2	3,638.2	2,538.2	46	2,231,531	145	851,495	9	1,579,364
Michigan	882	125	78	20	4	5,344.6	4,012.2	55	2,446,738	295	1,421,973	13	2,186,927
Minnesota	884	84	40	13	4	2,356.8	1,766.2	30	1,098,983	321	674,766	7	989,204
Mississippi	482	100	38	9	1	955.2	728.8	21	338,484	99	236,514	8	237,143
Missouri	1,009	104	45	23	2	2,857.1	2,107.1	54	1,789,303	281	642,344	14	1,481,866
Montana	392	41	7	12	—	376.1	273.3	14	191,256	73	127,912	9	186,419
Nebraska	562	48	15	14	9	926.4	689.9	19	486,671	199	426,761	4	353,880
Nevada	99	21	8	7	1	362.4	230.1	7	147,687	16	33,547	4	135,184
New Hampshire	253	27	12	1	5	452.3	340.9	9	168,662	33	101,937	1	56,626
New Jersey	521	34	27	1	—	4,971.6	3,691.0	30	1,850,875	213	1,175,659	7	1,002,755
New Mexico	346	54	19	7	1	530.6	355.9	20	224,377	25	60,609	13	193,853
New York	1,649	159	95	30	8	12,341.8	8,409.4	80	7,404,768	405	1,722,368	18	6,460,278
North Carolina	792	200	73	17	6	2,528.0	1,889.5	48	1,281,218	135	467,331	19	938,460
North Dakota	479	27	10	12	1	336.5	253.0	10	190,598	91	163,635	3	106,621
Ohio	1,090	117	109	27	8	6,378.3	4,765.6	95	3,494,437	263	1,414,318	19	2,323,602
Oklahoma	658	66	37	10	3	1,554.5	1,127.4	52	847,396	211	369,185	42	807,184
Oregon	368	80	20	13	2	1,260.0	910.2	22	663,000	93	309,737	5	537,822
Pennsylvania	1,845	170	114	24	8	7,715.4	5,845.9	107	4,066,831	229	1,273,045	10	2,987,058
Rhode Island	59	15	7	3	1	552.4	404.5	7	311,596	13	91,468	2	207,803
South Carolina	401	102	39	11	5	1,247.7	930.0	17	568,315	77	235,752	7	446,436
South Dakota	438	30	7	10	4	350.5	265.2	13	174,967	146	200,680	4	122,223
Tennessee	605	146	67	16	5	2,068.1	1,538.6	33	1,138,798	123	384,371	14	940,142
Texas	1,568	286	126	50	6	6,680.3	4,780.9	112	3,300,039	490	1,179,733	83	3,245,034
Utah	231	32	10	3	4	635.2	461.1	5	258,651	50	109,222	4	254,656
Vermont	296	18	4	2	4	249.8	178.6	9	117,355	13	26,778	—	—
Virginia	963	126	56	13	5	2,652.3	1,898.1	32	1,008,895	109	484,257	13	727,169
Washington	497	97	42	15	6	2,048.0	1,484.6	23	1,011,676	143	833,512	12	936,100
West Virginia	1,071	58	24	9	3	792.7	600.4	30	497,180	81	233,982	9	397,789
Wisconsin	797	98	76	17	3	2,479.0	1,813.4	37	1,212,418	241	667,644	6	832,654
Wyoming	180	29	1	3	—	205.8	144.2	9	77,066	29	62,275	3	50,969
TOTAL U.S.	31,609	4,250	2,122	673	195	124,536.9	90,326.4	1,749*	62,231,258*	7,610†	29,422,487†	590*	49,664,643*

*Total has been adjusted to account for double listings of Covington, Ky. edition of an Ohio newspaper. †Excludes District of Columbia. ‡In thousands.
Sources: U.S. Postal Service. Federal Communications Commission. Television Digest, Inc., *Television Factbook* (Copyright 1971. All rights reserved. Used by permission.) American Telephone and Telegraph Co. The Editor & Publisher Co., Inc., *International Year Book* (Copyright 1972. All rights reserved. Used by permission.) American Newspaper Representatives, Inc.

Foreign Trade and Affairs

Major recipients of foreign assistance

in million dollars; fiscal years

Program and country	1962	1965	1968	1971
Total	7,311	5,668	8,065	9,247
By program				
Economic assistance programs	4,749	4,486	4,865	4,811
Agency for International Development	2,618	2,187	2,176	1,861
Loans	1,342	1,217	1,084	718
Grants	1,276	970	1,092	1,143
Food for Peace	1,402	1,369	1,349	1,237
Export-Import Bank long-term loans	277	358	743	1,362
Other economic programs	452	572	597	351
Military assistance programs	2,562	1,182	3,200	4,436
By country				
Africa				
Algeria	10	15	—	13
Ethiopia	30	30	21	35
Ghana	104	3	37	22
Guinea	10	22	5	13
Kenya*	10	9	5	14
Liberia	13	43	9	12
Morocco	54	45	74	71
Nigeria	25	36	26	42
Tunisia	52	51	52	53
Zaire	85	31	29	44
Asia				
Cambodia	45	†	†	260
Ceylon	6	4	24	21
India	752	727	677	463
Indonesia	46	7	107	213
Iran	133	123	164	209
Israel	93	65	101	69‡
Japan	167	55	49	120
Korea, South	500	298	849	875
Laos	73	91	145	205
Pakistan	476	360	357	120
Philippines	59	52	53	112
Taiwan	254	112	132	114
Thailand	119	68	107	137
Turkey	450	290	179	201
Vietnam, South	360	546	1,592	2,433
Canada	—	—	10	64
Europe				
France	67	†	—	128
Germany, West	2	—	9	71
Greece	164	97	39	46
Italy	164	7	88	83
Norway	61	34	—	49
Spain	98	67	33	40
Yugoslavia	116	88	12	31
Latin America				
Argentina	61	42	55	56
Bolivia	40	21	21	13
Brazil	255	288	368	209
Chile	188	140	105	14
Colombia	87	42	110	110
Dominican Republic	36	77	68	30
Ecuador	42	27	16	25
Guatemala	12	15	19	26
Jamaica	2	10	9	28
Mexico	48	98	80	46
Nicaragua	15	25	32	16
Panama	26	24	21	15
Peru	98	48	20	20
Venezuela	72	53	67	30
Oceania				
Australia	20	10	156	145
New Zealand	†	—	56	43
Trust Territory of the Pacific Islands	6	18	39	54

Obligations and loan authorizations for economic assistance are on a gross basis; military assistance on a program basis.
*Excludes share of east Africa regional aid. †Less than $50,000.
‡Economic assistance only; military assistance data classified. Excludes reimbursement by the Department of Defense for grants of $30.6 million in 1968 and $64.7 million in 1971.
Source: U.S. Department of State, Agency for International Development.

International investment position

in millions of dollars

Item	1960	1965	1970	1971*
U.S. assets abroad	85,589	120,374	166,574	180,626
Nonliquid	66,230	103,156	149,714	164,432
Private	49,310	79,760	117,517	130,238
Long-term	44,497	71,375	104,693	115,554
Direct investments	31,865	49,474	78,090	86,001
Portfolio	12,632	21,901	26,603	29,559
Short-term	4,813	8,385	12,824	14,684
U.S. government	16,920	23,396	32,197	34,194
Long-term credits	14,028	20,200	29,699	31,792
Foreign currencies and other claims	2,892	3,196	2,498	2,402
Liquid	19,359	17,218	16,860	16,194
Private	—	1,768	2,373	4,027
U.S. monetary reserve assets	19,359	15,450	14,487	12,167
Gold	17,804	13,806	11,072	10,206
Special drawing rights	—	—	851	1,100
Convertible currencies	—	781	629	276
IMF gold tranche position	1,555	863	1,935	585
U.S. liabilities to foreigners	40,859	58,797	97,507	122,775
Nonliquid	19,830	29,224	50,466	54,917
Private	19,037	27,280	48,496	53,394
Long-term	18,418	26,315	44,758	49,583
Direct investments	6,910	8,797	13,209	13,704
Portfolio	11,508	17,518	31,549	35,879
Short-term	619	965	3,738	3,811
U.S. government	793	1,944	1,970	1,523
Liquid	21,029	29,573	47,041	67,858
To private foreigners	9,139	12,909	22,645	16,614
To foreign official agencies	11,890	16,664	24,396	51,244
Net international investment position	44,730	61,577	69,067	57,851

Estimates for end of year. *Preliminary.
Source: U.S. Department of Commerce, Bureau of Economic Analysis, *Survey of Current Business*.

Major commodities traded, 1971

in millions of dollars

Item	Total*	Canada	American Republics	Western Europe†	Far East‡
Total exports	44,137	10,366	5,667	14,190	8,103
Agricultural commodities					
Grains and preparations§	2,447	120	249	705	936
Fruits, nuts, and vegetables§	613	251	44	211	76
Tobacco, unmanufactured	463	3	7	324	88
Soybeans	1,325	115	24	751	382
Cotton, excluding linters, waste	584	45	5	90	418
Nonagricultural commodities					
Ores and scrap, metal	486	75	37	203	167
Coal, coke, and briquettes	951	226	72	290	355
Petroleum products	473	59	98	152	101
Chemicals	3,837	593	746	1,392	624
Machinery	11,797	2,916	1,858	3,686	1,764
Agricultural machines, tractors, parts	875	326	181	149	86
Other nonelectrical	7,855	1,861	1,182	2,577	1,108
Electrical apparatus	3,068	730	496	960	570
Road motor vehicles‖	3,815	2,699	482	213	140
Automotive parts, nonmilitary	1,852	1,416	205	94	40
Aircraft, civilian, and parts for all aircraft	2,756	181	169	1,294	516
Pulp, paper, and manufactures	1,070	145	183	456	150
Metals and manufactures	2,183	680	338	606	323
Iron and steelmill products¶	760	262	133	127	148
Textile yarn, fabrics, and made-up articles	632	172	78	187	81
Other exports	10,705	2,086	1,277	3,630	1,982
Total imports	45,602	12,762	4,882	12,623	11,203
Agricultural commodities					
Meat and preparations	1,050	76	259	234	4
Fruits, nuts, and vegetables	747	32	404	117	144
Coffee	1,168	—	758	♀	53
Sugar	764	—	418	2	249
Nonagricultural commodities					
Alcoholic beverages	766	184	6	567	4
Pulp, paper, and manufactures	1,649	1,512	9	88	30
Ores and scrap, metal	1,044	447	260	34	22
Petroleum, crude and partly refined	1,879	764	504	8	73
Petroleum products	1,445	51	597	110	13
Chemicals	1,612	397	69	708	214
Machinery	6,059	1,434	201	2,261	2,124
Transport equipment‖	7,844	3,989	20	2,243	1,585
Automobiles, new	5,134	2,396	♀	1,808	929
Iron and steelmill products¶	2,615	208	71	1,194	1,106
Nonferrous base metals	1,432	667	179	272	206
Textile yarn, fabrics, and made-up articles	1,392	33	51	554	697
Fish, including shellfish	879	206	189	165	170
Other imports	13,256	2,762	887	4,066	4,509

*Includes areas not shown separately. †Includes Greece and Turkey. ‡Asia, excluding Near East. §Includes shipments for relief by individuals and private agencies. ‖Excludes parts for tractors. ¶Excludes pig iron. ♀Less than $500,000. Source: U.S. Department of Commerce, Bureau of the Census, *Statistical Abstract of the United States*. Data compiled by the U.S. Department of Commerce, Bureau of International Commerce.

CONTRIBUTORS

Names of contributors to the Britannica Book of the Year *with the articles written by them. The arrangement is alphabetical by last name.*

AARSDAL, STENER. Economic Editor, *Borsen.* Press Officer, Chamber of Commerce, Copenhagen.
Biography (*in part*); Denmark

ACCARDO, JOSEPH J(OHN). Washington Columnist.
Fuel and Power (*in part*)

AGRELLA, JOSEPH C. Turf Editor, *Chicago Sun-Times.* Author of *Ten Commandments for Professional Handicapping.*
Horse Racing (*in part*)

AGUS, JACOB B(ERNARD). Visiting Professor of Modern Jewish Philosophy, Dropsie University, Philadelphia, Pa. Author of *The Evolution of Jewish Thought; Dialogue and Tradition.*
Religion (*in part*)

ALLAN, J(OHN) A(NTHONY). Lecturer in Geography, School of Oriental and African Studies, University of London.
Libya

ALLEN, V(ICTOR) L(EONARD). Reader in Industrial Relations, University of Leeds, Eng. Author of *Power in Trade Unions; Trade Union Leadership; Trade Unions and the Government; Militant Trade Unionism; International Bibliography of Trade Unionism.*
Labour Unions

ALSTON, (ARTHUR) REX. Broadcaster and Journalist. Author of *Taking the Air; Over to Rex Alston; Test Commentary; Watching Cricket.*
Cricket

ANTONINI, GUSTAVO ARTHUR. Associate Professor, Center for Latin American Studies, University of Florida.
Dominican Republic

ANTRIM, HARRY T(HOMAS). Associate Professor of English and Assistant Dean, College of Arts and Sciences, Florida International University. Author of *T. S. Eliot's Concept of Language.*
Literature (*in part*)

ARCHIBALD, JOHN J. Writer, *St. Louis Post-Dispatch.* Author of *Bowling for Boys and Girls.*
Bowling and Lawn Bowls (*in part*)

ARMSTRONG, A(LAN) G(ORDON). Lecturer, Department of Economics, University of Bristol, Eng.
Investment, International; Trade, International

ARNOLD, BRUCE. Free-lance Journalist and Writer, Dublin.
Biography (*in part*); Ireland

ARRINGTON, LEONARD JAMES. Church Historian, Church of Jesus Christ of Latter-day Saints. Author of *Great Basin Kingdom: An Economic History of the Latter-day Saints.*
Religion (*in part*)

ASTROM, ERIC A(RTHUR). Executive Assistant to the Vice-President, Ontario Jockey Club; Director, National Association of Canadian Race Tracks.
Horse Racing (*in part*)

AYTON, CYRIL J. Editor, *Motorcycle Sport,* London.
Motor Sports (*in part*)

BAILY, MICHAEL. Shipping and Transport Correspondent, *The Times,* London.
Transportation (*in part*)

BARROS, SALVADOR. Literary Critic, *Visión; El Día.* Lecturer in Latin American Literature, University of Mexico.
Literature (*in part*)

BASS, HOWARD. Journalist and Broadcaster. Editor, *Winter Sports* annuals; Winter Sports Correspondent, *Daily Telegraph,* London; *Christian Science Monitor,* Boston; *Ski Racing,* Denver; *World Sports,* London. Author of *The Magic of Skiing; Winter Sports; International Encyclopaedia of Winter Sports.*
Biography (*in part*); Hockey (*in part*); Ice Skating; Skiing

BATEMAN, LESLIE C(HARLES). Manager, Tariffs and Trade Regulations Section, International Department, British Steel Corporation, London.
Industrial Review (*in part*)

BEATTY, J. R. Senior Research Associate, B. F. Goodrich Research Center, Brecksville, O.
Rubber

BECKWITH, DAVID CAMERON. Correspondent, *Time* magazine, Washington, D.C.
United States Statistical Supplement: *Developments in the states in 1972*

BEDDOES, R(ICHARD) H(ERBERT). Sports Columnist, *Toronto Globe and Mail.*
Hockey (*in part*)

BEEMAN, WILLIAM J(OSEPH). Senior Economist, Board of Governors of the U.S. Federal Reserve System.
Government Finance (*in part*)

BELTRÁN, WILLIAM. Economic Research Officer, Lloyds and Bolsa International Bank Ltd., London.
Argentina

BENTLEY, JOHN (BERESFORD). Editor, *Air-Cushion Vehicles.* Publisher, *Hoverfoil News.*
Industrial Review (*in part*); Transportation (*in part*)

BERÈS, PIERRE. Managing Director, Hermann Publishing Company, Paris. Founder and Editor in Chief, *Sciences.* Expert in rare books.
Art Sales (*in part*)

BERGERRE, MAX. Correspondent ANSA for Vatican Affairs, Rome.
Vatican City State

BERGSTEIN, STANLEY F. Executive Secretary, Harness Tracks of America Inc.; Vice-President, United States Trotting Association.
Horse Racing (*in part*)

BICKELHAUPT, DAVID L(YNN). Professor of Insurance, College of Administrative Science, Ohio State University. Author of *Transition to Multiple-Line Insurance Companies.* Co-author of *General Insurance.*
Insurance (*in part*)

BILEFIELD, LIONEL. Technical Journalist.
Industrial Review (*in part*)

BLYTH, ALAN (GEOFFREY). Music Critic, London.
Biography (*in part*); Music (*in part*)

BOBBITT, JOHN T(EAL). Writer and Producer of Encyclopædia Britannica Films: *The Bill of Rights of the United States; The Congress; The Constitution of the United States; The Declaration of Independence by the Colonies; The Supreme Court.*
Motion Pictures (*in part*)

BODDY, WILLIAM C(HARLES). Editor, *Motor Sport.* Full Member, Guild of Motoring Writers. Author of *The Story of Brooklands; The 200 Mile Race; The World's Land Speed Record; Continental Sports Cars; The Sports Car Pocketbook; The Bugatti Story.*
Motor Sports (*in part*)

BOONSTRA, DICK. Member of the staff, Department of Political Science, Free University, Amsterdam.
Netherlands

BOOTH, JOHN NICHOLLS. Unitarian Universalist clergyman. Co-founder Japan Free Religious Association. Author of *The Quest for Preaching Power; Introducing Unitarian Universalism.*
Religion (*in part*)

BOSWALL, JEFFERY (HUGH). Producer of Sound and Television Programs, British Broadcasting Corporation Natural History Unit, Bristol, Eng.
Life Sciences (*in part*)

BOYD, MARY (BEATRICE). Senior Lecturer in History, Victoria University of Wellington, N.Z.
Fiji; Tonga; Western Samoa

BOYLE, C(HARLES) L(EOFRIC). Lieutenant Colonel, R.A. (retd.). Chairman, Survival Service Commission, International Union for Conservation of Nature and Natural Resources, 1958–63; Secretary, Fauna Preservation Society, London, 1950–63.
Environment (*in part*)

BRACKMAN, ARNOLD C. Author of *Indonesian Communism: A History; Southeast Asia's Second Front: The Power Struggle in the Malay Archipelago; The Communist Collapse in Indonesia.*
Indonesia

BRAIDWOOD, ROBERT J. Professor of Old World Prehistory, the Oriental Institute and the Department of Anthropology, the University of Chicago.
Archaeology (*in part*)

BRAZEE, RUTLAGE J. Senior Seismologist, Solid Earth Data Services Division, D62, NOAA, Boulder, Colo.
Seismology

BRICKHOUSE, JACK. Vice-President and Manager of Sports, WGN Continental Broadcasting Company.
Baseball (*in part*)

BRIERRE, ANNIE. Literary Critic, *Les Nouvelles Littéraires; La Revue des Deux Mondes; France—U.S.A.* Author of *Ninon de Lenclos.*
Literature (*in part*)

BRONNER, EDWIN (BLAINE). Professor of History and Curator of the Quaker Collection, Haverford (Pa.) College. Author of *William Penn's Holy Experiment.* Editor, *American Quakers Today; An English View of American Quakerism.*
Religion (*in part*)

BURKE, DONALD P. Senior Editor, *Chemical Week.*
Industrial Review (*in part*)

BURKS, ARDATH W(ALTER). Professor and Director, International Programs, Rutgers University, New Brunswick, N.J. Author of *The Government of Japan; East Asia: China, Korea, Japan.*
Japan

BUSHONG, ALLEN D. Associate Professor of Geography, University of South Carolina.
El Salvador; Honduras

BUTLER, FRANK. Sports Editor, *News of the World,* London.
Boxing

BYRNE, DON. Washington correspondent, *Electronic Design and Microwaves.*
Telecommunications *(in part)*

CALASCIONE, JOHN. Press and Publications Officer, International Organization of Consumers Unions, The Hague, Neth.
Consumer Affairs *(in part)*

CAMPBELL, H(ENRY) C(UMMINGS). Chief Librarian, Toronto Public Library, Toronto.
Literature *(in part)*

CARSANIGA, GIOVANNI. Reader in Italian, University of Sussex, Eng.
Literature *(in part)*

CHALMEY, LUCIEN. Adviser, Union Internationale des Producteurs et Distributeurs d'Énergie Électrique, Paris.
Fuel and Power *(in part)*

CHAPMAN, KENNETH F(RANCIS). Editor, *Stamp Collecting;* Philatelic Correspondent, *The Times,* London. Author of *Good Stamp Collecting; Commonwealth Stamp Collecting.*
Philately and Numismatics *(in part)*

CHAPMAN, ROBIN. Economic Research Officer, Lloyds and Bolsa International Bank Ltd., London.
Cuba; Haiti; Portugal

CHAPPELL, DUNCAN. Associate Professor of Criminal Justice. State University of New York at Albany. Author of *The Police and the Public in Australia and New Zealand.*
Crime *(in part)*

CHAUSSIN, ROBERT. Government Civil Engineer, SETRA (Service d'études Techniques des Routes et Autoroutes), Bagneux, France.
Engineering Projects *(in part)*

CHU, HUNG-TI. Expert in Far Eastern Affairs. UN Area Specialist and Chief of Asia-Africa Section and Trusteeship Council Section, 1946–67; Professor of Government, Texas Tech University, Lubbock, 1968–69.
China; Taiwan

CLEARY, BARBARA W(HITNEY). Production Coordinator, *Great Ideas Today.*
Biography *(in part)*

CLIFTON, DONALD F(REDERIC). Professor of Metallurgy, University of Idaho.
Metallurgy

COGLE, T(HOMAS) C(HARLES) J(OHN). Technical Editor, *Electrical Review,* London.
Industrial Review *(in part)*

COHEN, STANLEY E(DWARD). Washington Editor, *Advertising Age.*
Consumer Affairs *(in part)*

COLLINS, L(ESLIE) J(OHN) D(UDLEY). Lecturer in Bulgarian History, School of Slavonic and East European Studies, University of London.
Cyprus

COOK, JESS, JR. Correspondent, *Time* magazine, Washington, D.C.
Biography *(in part)*

COPELAND, JAMES C(LINTON). Associate Professor, Department of Microbiology, Ohio State University.
Life Sciences *(in part)*

COSTIN, STANLEY H(ARRY). London Correspondent, *Nykytekstiili* (Finland), *Textil Branschen* (Sweden).
Fashion and Dress *(in part)*

CRATER, RUFUS W(ILLIAM). Chief Correspondent, *Broadcasting,* New York City.
Television and Radio *(in part)*

CROSSLAND, NORMAN. Bonn Correspondent, the *Guardian,* London.
Biography *(in part)*; **Germany** *(in part)*

CUMPER, GLORIA C(LARE). Chairman, Council of Voluntary Social Services; Member, Judicial Services Commission, Kingston, Jamaica.
Jamaica

CVIIC, K(RSTO) F(RANJO). Leader Writer and East European Specialist, *The Economist,* London.
Yugoslavia

DAIFUKU, HIROSHI. Chief, Section for the Development of the Cultural Heritage, UNESCO, Paris.
Historic Buildings

DAVID, TUDOR. Managing Editor, *Education,* London.
Education *(in part)*

DAVIES, ERNEST (ALBERT JOHN). Editor, *Traffic Engineering and Control* (monthly); *Roads and Their Traffic; Traffic Engineering Practice.*
Transportation *(in part)*

DAWBER, ALFRED. Textile consultant in all aspects of textile production. Specialized writer on textile, engineering, and electrical subjects.
Industrial Review *(in part)*

DEANE, RALPH. Economic Research Officer, Lloyds and Bolsa International Bank Ltd., London.
Biography *(in part)*; **Spain**

d'ECA, RAUL. Formerly Fulbright Visiting Lecturer on American History, University of Minas Gerais, Belo Horizonte, Braz. Co-author of *Latin American History.*
Brazil

DECRAENE, PHILIPPE. Member of editorial staff, *Le Monde,* Paris. Editor in Chief, *Revue française d'Études politiques africaines.* Author of *Le Panafricanisme; Tableau des Partis Politiques Africains.*
Cameroon; Central African Republic; Chad; Congo, People's Republic of the; Dahomey; Gabon; Guinea; Ivory Coast; Malagasy Republic; Mali; Mauritania; Niger; Senegal; Togo; Tunisia; Upper Volta

de la BARRE, KENNETH. Director, Montreal Office, Arctic Institute of North America.
Arctic Regions

DEMPSEY, GEOFFREY. Manager, Overseas Department, J. Walter Thompson Co. Ltd., London.
Advertising *(in part)*

DENNERSTEIN, R. J. M. Associate Editor, *Encyclopædia Britannica,* London.
Bhutan; Biography *(in part)*; **Crime** *(in part)*; **Equatorial Guinea; Laos; Trinidad and Tobago**

DE PUY, NORMAN R(OBERT). Director, Print Media Division of Communication, American Baptist Convention, Valley Forge, Pa. Author of *The Bible Alive.*
Religion *(in part)*

DILLARD, DUDLEY. Professor and Head, Department of Economics, University of Maryland. Author of *The Economics of John Maynard Keynes; Economic Development of the North Atlantic Community.*
Economics

DIRNBACHER, ELFRIEDE. Austrian Civil Servant.
Austria

EDGERTON, ROBERT B(RECKENRIDGE). Professor, Departments of Psychiatry and Anthropology (in residence), University of California at Los Angeles. Author of *The Cloak of Competence; The Individual in Cultural Adaptation.*
Anthropology

EDLIN, H(ERBERT) L(EESON). Publications Officer, Forestry Commission of Great Britain. Author of *Trees, Woods and Man; Wayside and Woodland Trees; Man and Plants; What Wood Is That?; Guide to Tree Planting and Cultivation.*
Environment *(in part)*

EDWARDS, JOHN (ROBIN). Research Fellow, Southampton (Eng.) University. Author of *Social Patterns in Birmingham.*
Housing

EISENBERG, WARREN W(OLFF). Administrative Assistant to Rep. H. John Heinz III, Washington, D.C.
Populations and Areas

EISLER, KIM (ISAAC). Editorial Assistant, *Time* magazine. Student at George Washington University.
Biography *(in part)*

ELDERS, W(ILFRED) A. Associate Professor of Geology, University of California at Riverside.
Geology

ENGELS, JAN R(OBERT). Editor, *Vooruitgang* (Quarterly of the Belgian Party for Freedom and Progress).
Belgium

EWART, W(ILLIAM) D(UNLOP). Editor and Director, *Fairplay International Shipping Journal.* Author of *Marine Engines; Atomic Submarines; Hydrofoils and Hovercraft; Building a Ship.*
Industrial Review *(in part)*

FARR, D(AVID) M. L. Professor of History, Carleton University, Ottawa. Author of *The Colonial Office and Canada, 1867–1887; Two Democracies; The Canadian Experience.*
Canada

FENDELL, ROBERT J(OSEPH). New York Editor, *Automotive News.* Automobile Columnist for *Action.* President, International Motor Press Association. Co-author, *Encyclopedia of Motor Racing Personalities.*
Motor Sports *(in part)*

FERRIER, R(ONALD) W(HITAKER). Company Historian, British Petroleum.
Fuel and Power *(in part)*

FOWELL, R(OBERT) J(OHN). Lecturer, Department of Mining Engineering, University of Newcastle upon Tyne, Eng.
Fuel and Power *(in part)*

FRANKLIN, HAROLD. Editor, *English Bridge Quarterly.* Bridge Correspondent, *Yorkshire Post; Yorkshire Evening Post.* Broadcaster. Author of *Best of Bridge on the Air.*
Contract Bridge

FREDRICKSON, DAVID A. Associate Professor of Anthropology, Sonoma State College, Rohnert Park, Calif.
Archaeology *(in part)*

FREEMAN, KENNETH C(HARLES). Fellow, Department of Astronomy, Australian National University (Mt. Stromlo and Siding Spring Observatory), Australia.
Astronomy

FRIDOVICH, IRWIN. Professor of Biochemistry, Duke University Medical Center, Durham, N.C.
Life Sciences *(in part)*

FRIEDLY, ROBERT L(OUIS). Director, Office of Communication, Christian Church (Disciples of Christ), Indianapolis, Ind.
Religion *(in part)*

FRIEDMAN, IRVING S. Economic Adviser to the President of the International Bank for Reconstruction and Development, 1964–70. Author of *Exchange Controls and the International Monetary System; U.S. Foreign Economic Policy.*
Development, Economic

FROST, DAVID (BROUGH JAMES). Rugby Union Correspondent, the *Guardian,* London.
Football *(in part)*

FULLER, M(ICHAEL) F(REDERICK). Lecturer in Economic and Social Statistics, Darwin College, University of Kent at Canterbury, Eng.
Income, National

GADDUM, PETER W(ILLIAM). Chairman, H. T. Gaddum and Company Ltd., Silk Merchants, Macclesfield, Cheshire, Eng. President, International Silk Association. Author of *Silk—How and Where It is Produced.*
Industrial Review *(in part)*

GALVANO, FABIO. London Correspondent, *Epoca,* Milan.
Biography (*in part*); Italy

GANADO, ALBERT. Lawyer, Malta.
Malta

GEHRET, KENNETH G. Education Editor, the *Christian Science Monitor.*
Education (*in part*)

GEORGE, T(HAYIL) J(ACOB) S(ONY). Assistant Editor, *Far Eastern Economic Review,* Hong Kong. Author of *Krishna Menon: A Biography.*
Biography (*in part*); Cambodia; Korea; Southeast Asia; Thailand; Vietnam (*in part*)

GIFFORD, NELLIE L. Administrative Editor/Yearbooks, Encyclopædia Britannica, Inc.
Biography (*in part*)

GLIKSON, PAUL. Secretary, Division of Jewish Demography and Statistics, Institute of Contemporary Jewry, the Hebrew University of Jerusalem, Israel.
Religion (*in part*)

GODWIN, MORGAN W(ESLEY). Assistant Secretary, American Radio Relay League, Newington, Conn.
Television and Radio (*in part*)

GOLLAND, B(RIAN) L(LEWELLYN). General Secretary, the General Assembly of Unitarian and Free Christian Churches, London.
Religion (*in part*)

GOLOMBEK, HARRY. British Chess Champion, 1947, 1949, and 1955. Chess Correspondent, *The Times* and *Observer,* London. Author of *Penguin Handbook on the Game of Chess; Modern Opening Chess Strategy.*
Chess

GOODWIN, R(OBERT) M(ARSHALL). Assistant Editor, *Encyclopædia Britannica,* London.
Horse Racing (*in part*)

GORALSKI, ROBERT. NBC News Pentagon Correspondent.
Vietnam (*in part*)

GOULD, LAURENCE M. Professor of Geology, University of Arizona. Chairman, Committee on Polar Research, National Academy of Sciences. Author of *Cold: The Record of an Antarctic Sledge Journey.*
Antarctica

GOULDING, ROY. Director, Poisons Reference Service, Guy's Hospital, London. Co-editor, *Modern Trends in Toxicology.* Contributor to *Modern Trends in Forensic Medicine.*
Drugs and Narcotics (*in part*)

GRAHAM, JARLATH JOHN. Editor, *Advertising Age.*
Advertising (*in part*)

GREEN, BENNY. Jazz Critic, *Observer,* London; Record Reviewer, British Broadcasting Corporation. Author of *The Reluctant Art; Blame It on My Youth; 58 Minutes to London; Jazz Decade.* Contributor to *Encyclopedia of Jazz.*
Music (*in part*)

GREENOUGH, RICHARD D. A. Chief English writer, Press Division, UNESCO, Paris. Author of *Africa Prospect; Children's Progress; Africa Calls.*
United Nations (*in part*)

GRIFFITHS, A(NTHONY) R(OYSTON) G(RANT). Lecturer in History, Flinders University of South Australia.
Australia; Nauru

GROVE, ROBERT D. Former Director, Division of Vital Statistics, U.S. Public Health Service. Author of *Vital Statistics Rates in the United States, 1900–1940; Vital Statistics Rates in the United States, 1940–1960.*
Vital Statistics

HACHTEN, WILLIAM A. Professor, School of Journalism and Mass Communication, University of Wisconsin.
Publishing (*in part*)

HADDEN, JEFFREY K. Professor of Sociology, Department of Sociology and Anthropology, University of Virginia. Author of *The Gathering Storm in the Churches; American Cities: Their Social Characteristics.*
Sociology

HAIGH, CLIFFORD. Editor, *The Friend,* London.
Religion (*in part*)

HARRIES, DAVID A(LEXANDER). Director and Chief Engineer, the Mitchell Construction Kinnear Moodie Group Ltd., London.
Engineering Projects (*in part*)

HARRIS, LEONARD R(ICHARD). Executive Vice-President and Publisher, World Publishing Company.
Publishing (*in part*)

HASEGAWA, RYUSAKU. Editor, TBS-Britannica Ltd., Tokyo.
Baseball (*in part*)

HATELY, DAVID. Associate Editor, *Encyclopædia Britannica,* London.
Biography (*in part*)

HATHAWAY, RICHARD O. Teaching Faculty, History and International Studies, Goddard College, Plainfield, Vt. Member, Board of Editors, *Current.*
Peace Movements

HAUSER, PHILIP M(ORRIS). Professor of Sociology and Director, Population Research Center, the University of Chicago. Editor of *Urbanization in Latin America.*
Cities and Urban Affairs (*in part*)

HAWKLAND, WILLIAM D. Professor of Law, University of Illinois. Author of *Sales Under Uniform Commercial Code; Cases on Bills and Notes; Commercial Paper; Transactional Guide of the Uniform Commercial Code; Cases on Sales and Security.*
Law (*in part*)

HAWLEY, H(ENRY) B(ERNARD). Consultant, Human Nutrition and Food Science, Sherborne, Eng.
Food (*in part*)

HAZO, SAMUEL. Director, International Poetry Forum, and Professor, Duquesne University, Pittsburgh, Pa. Author of *Once for the Last Bandit; Seascript; Blood Rights; My Sons in God; The Quiet Wars.*
Literature (*in part*)

HEBBLETHWAITE, THE REV. PETER, S.J. Editor, *The Month.* Author of *Bernanos; The Council Fathers and Atheism; Understanding the Synod.* Editor of *Faith in Question; Talking with Unbelievers; The Documents of Vatican II.*
Religion (*in part*)

HENDERSHOTT, MYRL C(HALMERS). Assistant Professor of Oceanography, Scripps Institution of Oceanography, La Jolla, Calif.
Oceanography

HOCKLEY, G(RAHAM) C(HARLES). Lecturer, Department of Economics, University College, Cardiff, Wales. Author of *Monetary Policy and Public Finance.* Co-author of *The Wealth of the Nation: The Balance Sheet of the United Kingdom, 1957–61.*
Merchandising (*in part*); Taxation (*in part*)

HODGSON, ROBERT D(AVID). Geographer, U.S. Department of State, Washington, D.C. Author of *The Changing Map of Africa.*
Andorra; Liechtenstein; Luxembourg; Monaco; San Marino

HOLLANDS, R(ICHARD) L(YNTON). Hockey Correspondent, the *Daily Telegraph,* London. Co-author of *Hockey.*
Hockey (*in part*)

HORN, PATRICE DAILY. Managing Editor, *Behavior Today.*
Psychology

HOTZ, LOUIS. Former editorial writer, the *Johannesburg* (S.Af.) *Star.* Co-author and contributor to *The Jews in South Africa: A History.*
South Africa

HUNNINGS, NEVILLE MARCH. Senior Research Officer, British Institute of International and Comparative Law, London. Author of *Film Censors and the Law.*
Law (*in part*)

HURTIG, SERGE. Director of Studies and Research, Fondation Nationale des Sciences Politiques; Professor, Paris Institute of Political Studies. Former Secretary-General, International Political Science Association.
Political Science

INGHAM, KENNETH. Professor of History, University of Bristol, Eng. Author of *Reformers in India; A History of East Africa.*
Dependent States (*in part*); Kenya; Malawi; Rhodesia; Tanzania; Uganda; Zaire; Zambia

INTERNATIONAL TELECOMMUNICATION UNION, Geneva.
Telecommunications (*in part*)

IULA. Research staff, International Union of Local Authorities, The Hague, Neth.
Cities and Urban Affairs (*in part*)

JACKSON, D(UDLEY) A(NTHONY) S(TEPHENSON). Research Officer, Department of Applied Economics, University of Cambridge; Fellow of St. Catharine's College, Cambridge.
Employment, Wages, and Hours

JACQUET, CONSTANT H(ERBERT), JR. Director of Research Library and Research Associate, National Council of Churches. Editor, *Yearbook of American and Canadian Churches.*
United States Statistical Supplement: *Church Membership Table*

JAMES, DAVID R. Editor, *Toys International,* London.
Toys and Games

JARDINE, ADRIAN. Company Director and Public Relations Consultant. Secretary, Guild of Yachting Writers.
Sailing

JASPERT, W. PINCUS. Technical editorial consultant. European Editor, North American Publishing Company, Philadelphia, Pa. Member, Society of Photographic Scientists and Engineers. Editor of *Encyclopaedia of Type Faces.*
Industrial Review (*in part*)

JOHN, LAURIE (LAURENCE HENRY). Producer, Science Unit, British Broadcasting Corporation (radio).
Telecommunications (*in part*)

JONES, C(LARENCE) M(EDLYCOTT). Editor, *World Bowls; Lawn Tennis.* Author of *Winning Bowls; The Watney Book of Bowls; Bowls; How to Become a Champion.* Co-author of *Tackle Bowls My Way; Bryant on Bowls.*
Bowling and Lawn Bowls (*in part*)

JONES, W(ALTON) GLYN. Reader in Danish, University College, London. Author of *Johannes Jørgensens modne år; Johannes Jörgensen; Denmark.*
Literature (*in part*)

JOSEPH, LOU. Assistant Director, Bureau of Public Information, American Dental Association. Author of *Allergy—Facts and Fallacies.*
Medicine (*in part*)

JUNZ, HELLA B. Senior Economist, Board of Governors of the Federal Reserve System, U.S.
Government Finance (*in part*)

KAAN, FREDERIK H(ERMAN). Secretary of the Department of Cooperation and Witness, World Alliance of Reformed Churches (Presbyterian and Congregational), Geneva.
Religion (*in part*)

KAPLANSKY, IRVING. George Herbert Mead Distinguished Service Professor, Department of Mathematics, the University of Chicago.
Mathematics

KATZ, BERNARD S(OLOMON). Public Information Specialist with the U.S. Department of Defense.
Biography (*in part*)

KATZ, WILLIAM A. Professor, School of Library Science, State University of New York. Author of *Magazines for Libraries; Introduction to Reference Work.*
Publishing (*in part*)

KELLEHER, JOHN A(RNOLD). Editor, *The Dominion,* Wellington, N.Z.
New Zealand

KENT, LOTTE. Editor, *Cooperative News Service,* International Cooperative Alliance, London.
Cooperatives

KERR, J(AMES) A(LISTAIR). Lecturer, University of Birmingham, Eng.
Chemistry (*in part*)

KERRIGAN, (THOMAS) ANTHONY. Editor and translator of *Selected Works* of Miguel de Unamuno (10 vol.). Author of *At the Front Door of the Atlantic.* Co-translator of *Selected Poems* of Pablo Neruda.
Literature (*in part*)

KILLIN, ORLAND B(ENJAMIN). Associate Professor of Industrial Education and Technology, Eastern Washington State College.
Industrial Review (*in part*)

KILNER, PETER. Editor, *Arab Report and Record.*
Algeria; Morocco; Sudan

KIMCHE, JON. Expert on Middle East Affairs, *Evening Standard,* London. Author of *The Second Arab Awakening: The Middle East, 1914–1969.*
Israel

KIND, JOSHUA B. Associate Professor of Art History, Northern Illinois University. Author of *Rouault; Titian.*
Museums and Galleries (*in part*)

KITAGAWA, JOSEPH M. Professor of History of Religions and Dean of the Divinity School, the University of Chicago. Author of *Religions of the East; Religion in Japanese History.*
Religion (*in part*)

KLARE, HUGH J(OHN). Member of Parole Board for England and Wales; Member of the Council, International Penal and Penitentiary Foundations. Secretary, Howard League for Penal Reform 1950–71. Author of *People in Prison.*
Prisons and Penology

KLAUSLER, ALFRED P(AUL). Executive Secretary, Associated Church Press; Religion Editor, Westinghouse Broadcasting Company. Author of *Censorship, Obscenity and Sex; Growth in Worship.*
Religion (*in part*)

KNECHT, JEAN (MARCEL). Assistant Foreign Editor, *Le Monde,* Paris. Former Permanent Correspondent in Washington and Vice-President of the Association de la Presse Diplomatique Française.
France

KNEESHAW, JOHN. Economist, Bank for International Settlements, Basel, Switz.
Money and Banking

KNORR, N(ATHAN) H(OMER). President, Watch Tower Bible and Tract Society of Pennsylvania.
Religion (*in part*)

KNUDSEN, OLE F(ERDINAND). Editor, *Norway Exports,* Oslo.
Norway

KOPPER, PHILIP. Free-lance Writer, Washington, D.C.
Biography (*in part*); Nobel Prizes; Publishing (*in part*)

KOVAN, RICHARD W(ALTER). Features Editor, *Nuclear Engineering International,* London.
Industrial Review (*in part*)

KRADER, BARBARA. President, Society for Ethnomusicology; Executive Secretary, International Folk Music Council, Kingston, Ont., 1965–66.
Music (*in part*)

KRISTINSSON, VALDIMAR. Editor of *Fjarmalatidindi,* Reykjavik.
Iceland

KRIZ, MIROSLAV A. Vice-President, First National City Bank, New York City, 1965–73. Author of *The Price of Gold; Gold in World Monetary Affairs Today; Gold: Barbarous Relic or Useful Instrument?*
Economy, World; Payments and Reserves, International

KUBITSCHEK, H(ERBERT) E. Senior Biophysicist, Division of Biological and Medical Research, Argonne National Laboratory. Author of *Introduction to Research with Continuous Cultures.*
Life Sciences (*in part*)

LAST, G(EOFFREY) C(HARLES). Adviser, Imperial Ethiopian Ministry of Education and Fine Arts, Addis Ababa. Author of *A Regional Survey of Africa; A Geography of Ethiopia.* Co-author of *A History of Ethiopia in Pictures.*
Ethiopia

LAWS, WILMA. Journalist, London. Member, International Association of Art Critics.
Art Sales (*in part*)

LEGUM, COLIN. Commonwealth Correspondent, *Observer,* London. Author of *Must We Lose Africa?; Bandung, Cairo and Accra; Congo Disaster; Pan-Africanism—A Short Political Guide.* Co-author of *Attitude to Africa; South Africa; Crisis for the West; The Bitter Choice.* Editor of *Africa—A Handbook to the Continent.*
Biography (*in part*)

LEWRY, R(AYMOND) B(ASIL). Senior Research Officer, Lloyds and Bolsa International Bank Ltd., London.
Colombia; Ecuador

LINFORD, AARON. Editor of *Redemption Tidings,* weekly official organ of Assemblies of God in Great Britain and Ireland. Author of *Will the Church Go Through the Tribulation?; A Course of Study in Spiritual Gifts; The Baptism in the Holy Spirit; Living like Angels; Fabulously Rich.*
Religion (*in part*)

LITTELL, FRANKLIN H(AMLIN). Professor, Department of Religion, Temple University, Philadelphia, Pa. Co-editor of *Weltkirchenlexikon.*
Religion (*in part*)

LULING, VIRGINIA R. Social Anthropologist.
Somalia

MacDONALD, M(ALCOLM) C(HARLES). Director Econtel Research Ltd., London. Editor, *World Series; Business Cycle Series.*
Agriculture (*in part*); Transportation (*in part*); *statistical sections of articles on the various countries*

McMURRIN, STERLING M. Ericksen Distinguished Professor and Dean of the Graduate School, University of Utah. Co-author of *A History of Philosophy.*
Philosophy

McWHIRTER, NORRIS and ROSS. Television commentators, British Broadcasting Corporation, London. Co-compilers of *Guinness Book of Records.*
Track and Field Sports (*in part*)

MADER, WILLIAM. Diplomatic Correspondent, *Time* magazine.
Biography (*in part*)

MAHONEY, J(OHN) W(ILLIAM). Director, Society of Friends of Wine, London. Director, Wine and Spirit Education Trust, London. Author of *A Guide to Good Wine* (Introduction); *Wines; Spirits and Liquers; The Labelling of Wines and Spirits.*
Alcoholic Beverages (*in part*)

MALLETT, H(UGH) M(ICHAEL) F(INER). Editor, *Weekly Wool Chart,* Bradford, Eng.
Industrial Review (*in part*)

MANGO, ANDREW (JAMES ALEXANDER). Orientalist and Broadcaster.
Biography (*in part*); Turkey

MANSFIELD, PETER (JOHN). Formerly Middle East Correspondent, *Sunday Times,* London. Free-lance Writer on Middle East affairs.
Bahrain; Biography (*in part*); Egypt; Iraq; Jordan; Kuwait; Lebanon; Middle East; Oman; Qatar; Saudi Arabia; Syria; United Arab Emirates; Yemen, People's Democratic Republic of; Yemen Arab Republic

MARCELLO, ALDO. Civil Engineer.
Engineering Projects (*in part*)

MARCUS, IRVING H. Publisher, *Wine Publications;* Columnist, *Wines and Vines.* Author of *Dictionary of Wine Terms; Lines About Wines; How to Test and Improve Your Wine Judging Ability.*
Alcoholic Beverages (*in part*)

MARSHALL, J(OHN) G(RAHAM) SCOTT. Horticultural Consultant.
Gardening (*in part*)

MARTENHOFF, J(AMES) E(DWARD). Boating Editor, *Miami* (Fla.) *Herald.* Author of *How to Buy a Better Boat; Handbook of Skin and Scuba Diving.*
Motor Sports (*in part*)

MAUDE, N(EVILLE) F(REDERIC). Consultant Editor, *British Journal of Photography; Photo News Weekly.* Editor, *Photographic Processor.* Author of *Take Better Photos; Choosing a Camera.*
Photography

MAZIE, DAVID M(ICHAEL). Associate of Carl T. Rowan, syndicated columnist. Free-lance Writer.
Social Services (*in part*)

MERMEL, T. W. Assistant to Commissioner for Research and Chief, General Engineering Division, Bureau of Reclamation, U.S. Department of the Interior, Washington, D.C. Chairman, Committee on World Register of Dams, International Commission on Large Dams. Author of *Register of Dams in the United States.*
Engineering Projects (*in part*)

MEYENDORFF, JOHN. Professor of Church History and Patristics, St. Vladimir's Seminary; Professor of History, Fordham University, New York City; Adjunct-Professor of Religion, Columbia University.
Religion (*in part*)

MILES, PETER W(ALLACE). Professor of Zoology, University of Zambia, Lusaka.
Life Sciences (*in part*)

MILLARD, R(AYMOND) S(PENCER). Deputy Director, Road Research Laboratory, Department of Environment, Crowthorne, Berkshire, Eng.
Engineering Projects (*in part*)

MILLER, WILLIAM B. Manager, Department of History, United Presbyterian Church, U.S.A.
Religion (*in part*)

MILLIKIN, SANDRA. Architectural Historian.
Architecture; Art Exhibitions

MINNES, GORDON. Secretary, Canadian Pulp and Paper Association.
Industrial Review (*in part*)

MITCHELL, K(EITH) K(IRKMAN). Lecturer, Department of Physical Education, Leeds University. Hon. General Secretary, Amateur Basket Ball Association.
Basketball (*in part*)

MODEAN, ERIK W. Director, News Bureau, Lutheran Council in the U.S.A.
Religion *(in part)*

MODIANO, MARIO. Athens Correspondent, *The Times,* London.
Greece

MORGAN, HAZEL (ROMOLA). Production Assistant (Sleevenotes and Covers), Creative Services Dept., E.M.I. Ltd., London.
Music *(in part)*

MORTIMER, MOLLY. Writer on Commonwealth and International Affairs. Author of *Trusteeship in Practice; Kenya.*
Botswana; Burundi; Commonwealth of Nations; Dependent States *(in part)*; **Gambia, The; Ghana; Lesotho; Maldives; Mauritius; Nigeria; Rwanda; Sierra Leone; Swaziland**

MOSS, JOHN. Barrister-at-Law. Author of *Hadden's Health and Welfare Services Handbook.* Editor of *Local Government Law and Administration.*
Social Services *(in part)*

MOSS, ROBERT V. President, United Church of Christ, New York City; President, American Association of Theological Schools, 1966–68. Author of *The Life of Paul; We Believe; As Paul Sees Christ.*
Religion *(in part)*

MULLINS, STEPHANIE. Historian.
Biography *(in part)*

NATOLI, SALVATORE J(OHN). Educational Affairs Director, Association of American Geographers. Co-author of *Dictionary of Basic Geography.*
Geography

NAYLOR, ERNEST. Professor of Marine Biology, University of Liverpool; Director, Marine Biological Laboratory, Port Erin, Isle of Man. Author of *British Marine Isopods.*
Life Sciences *(in part)*

NEILL, JOHN. Head of Chemical Engineering Department, C. & W. Walker Ltd. Author of Climbers' Club Guides: *Cwm Silyn and Tremadoc, Snowdon South;* Alpine Club Guide: *Selected Climbs in the Pennine Alps.*
Mountaineering

NELSON, BERT. Editor and Publisher, *Track and Field News.*
Track and Field Sports *(in part)*

NELSON, C. EMIL. National Chief Secretary and Colonel, Salvation Army, U.S.A.
Religion *(in part)*

NETSCHERT, BRUCE C(ARLTON). Vice-President, National Economic Research Associates, Inc., Washington, D.C. Author of *The Future Supply of Oil and Gas.* Co-author of *Energy in the American Economy: 1850–1975.*
Fuel and Power *(in part)*

NOEL, H(AROLD) S(TANLEY). Editor, *World Fishing,* London.
Fisheries

NOVALES, RONALD R(ICHARDS). Professor of Biological Sciences, Northwestern University, Evanston, Ill. Member, Editorial Board, *American Zoologist.*
Life Sciences *(in part)*

NOVICK, JULIUS. Associate Professor of Literature, State University of New York at Purchase; Dramaturge, Juilliard Acting Company and Drama Division of the Juilliard School. Dramatic Critic for the *Village Voice* and *The Humanist.* Contributor to *The Nation;* the *New York Times.* Author of *Beyond Broadway: The Quest for Permanent Theatres.*
Theatre *(in part)*

O'LEARY, JEREMIAH A(LOYSIUS). Latin-American Correspondent, *Washington* (D.C.) *Evening Star-News.* Author of *Dominican Action—1965; Panama: Canal Issues and Treaty Talks—1967.*
Biography *(in part)*; **Chile**

OSBORNE, KEITH (LANGFORD). Editor, *Rowing,* 1961–63. Hon. Editor, *British Rowing Almanack,* 1961–.
Rowing

OSTERBIND, CARTER C(LARKE). Director, Bureau of Economic and Business Research, University of Florida. Editor, *Feasible Planning for Social Change in the Field of Aging.*
Engineering Projects *(in part)*; **Industrial Review** *(in part)*

PAKEMAN, SIDNEY A(RNOLD). Historian. Author of *Ceylon.*
Ceylon (Sri Lanka)

PALMER, S(TUART) B(EAUMONT). Lecturer, Department of Applied Physics, University of Hull, Eng.
Physics

PANIĆ, MILIVOJE. Senior Economic Adviser, National Economic Development Office, London.
Prices

PARGAS, RAFAEL. National Geographic Society, Washington, D.C.
Philippines

PARKER, SANDY. Fur Editor, *Women's Wear Daily.*
Furs

PARTINGTON, DOROTHY M. Free-lance Writer, London.
Literature *(in part)*; **Publishing** *(in part)*

PATON, ALEXANDER. Consultant Physician, Birmingham Hospital Group, Eng. Postgraduate Clinical Tutor, University of Birmingham, Eng.
Medicine *(in part)*

PATTEN, GEORGE P(HILLIP). Professor of Geography, Ohio State University.
Nicaragua

PATTERSON, SHEILA (CAFFYN). Research Fellow, Centre for Multi-Racial Studies, University of Sussex, Brighton, Eng. Author of *Colour and Culture in South Africa; The Last Trek; Dark Strangers; Immigrants in Industry.*
Barbados; Dependent States *(in part)*; **Migration, International** *(in part)*; **Race Relations** *(in part)*

PENFOLD, ROBIN CHARLES. Public relations executive, Carl Byoir and Associates Ltd., London. Author of *A Journalist's Guide to Plastics.*
Industrial Review *(in part)*

PETERSON, VIRGIL W. Executive Director, Chicago Crime Commission, 1942–70. Author of *Gambling—Should It Be Legalized?; Barbarians in Our Midst.*
Crime *(in part)*; **Police** *(in part)*

PETHERICK, KARIN (ROSAMUND). Crown Princess Louise Lecturer in Swedish, University College, London.
Literature *(in part)*

PETTIGREW, THOMAS F(RASER). Professor of Social Psychology, Harvard University. Author of *A Profile of the Negro American; Racially Separate or Together?*
Race Relations *(in part)*

PFEFFER, IRVING. Professor of Insurance and Finance, College of Business, Virginia Polytechnic Institute and State University. Author of *Insurance and Economic Theory; The Financing of Small Business.*
Stock Exchanges *(in part)*

PHILLIPS, D(AVID) K(EMSLEY) R(OBIN). Secretary-General, Association of Track and Field Statisticians. Contributor, *World Sports.* Editor, *World Sports Olympic Games Report.* Co-compiler of *Guinness Book of Olympic Records.*
Sporting Record

PICK, OTTO. Visiting Professor of International Relations, University of Surrey, Guildford, Eng. Director, Atlantic Information Centre for Teachers, London.
Czechoslovakia; Union of Soviet Socialist Republics

PITTERA, FREDERICK P. Chairman, International Exposition Consultants Co.; Member, Board of Trustees, New York Institute of Technology; Member, Board of Governors, National Business and Professional Council. Author of *The Art and Science of International Fairs and Exhibitions; The Fairs of the United States and Canada; Fairs of the World.*
Fairs and Shows

PLATT, MAURICE. Consulting Engineer. Former Director of Engineering, Vauxhall Motors, Ltd. Author of *Elements of Automobile Engineering.*
Industrial Review *(in part)*

POLLACK, GERALD A. Senior Economic Adviser, Standard Oil Co. (N.J.). Author of *Perspectives on the U.S. International Financial Position.*
Profits

POTTER, SIMEON. Emeritus Professor of English Language and Philology, University of Liverpool, Eng. Author of *Our Language; Language in the Modern World; Modern Linguistics; Changing English.*
Words and Meanings, New *(in part)*

PRASAD, H(OLENARASIPUR) Y. SHARADA. Director of Information, Prime Minister's Secretariat, New Delhi, India.
Biography *(in part)*; **India**

PREIL, GABRIEL. Writer. Hebrew and Yiddish poet. Author of *Israeli Poetry in Peace and War; Nof Shemesh Ukhfor* ("Landscape of Sun and Frost"); *Ner Mul Kokhavim* ("Candle Against the Stars"); *Mapat Erev* ("Map of Evening"); *Lieder* ("Poems"); *Haesh Vehadmama* ("The Fire and the Silence"); *Shirim* ("Poems").
Literature *(in part)*

PROTIN, RENÉ. Director, International Vine and Wine Office, Paris.
Alcoholic Beverages *(in part)*

PULGAR, MANUEL. Senior Economic Research Officer, Lloyds and Bolsa International Bank Ltd., London.
Mexico

RANDALL, CHARLES EDGAR. Assistant Editor, *Journal of Forestry.* Author of *Famous Trees; Our Forests.*
Timber

RANDHAVA, MAHINDER SINGH. Subeditor, the *Straits Times,* Kuala Lumpur, Malaysia.
Malaysia; Singapore

RANGER, ROBERT J(OHN). Assistant Professor, Department of Political Science, St. Francis Xavier University, Antigonish, Nova Scotia.
Defense

RAVEN, VIVIAN (FOSTER). Editor, *Tobacco,* London.
Tobacco

RAWLINS, RANDOLPH (RICHARD). Journalist and Broadcaster. Tutor, Extramural Department, University of the West Indies, St. Augustine, Trinidad.
Guyana

RAY, G(EORGE) F(RANK). Senior Research Fellow, National Institute of Economic and Social Research, London.
Industrial Review *(in part)*

READ, HARRY. Director, Salvation Army International Information Services, London.
Religion *(in part)*

REICHELDERFER, FRANCIS W. Aeronautical and Marine Meteorology Consultant. Former Chief, Weather Bureau, U.S. Department of Commerce, Washington, D.C.
Meteorology

REID, J(AMES) H(ENDERSON). Lecturer in German, University of Nottingham, Eng. Author of *Critical Strategies; German Fiction in the 20th Century.*
Literature *(in part)*

REYNOLDS, ARTHUR GUY. Registrar and Professor of Church History, Emmanuel College, Toronto.
Religion (*in part*)

RILEY, WALLACE B. Computers Editor, *Electronics* magazine.
Computers

ROBERTS, R(OGER) L(EWIS). Editorial Consultant, *Church Times,* London.
Religion (*in part*)

ROBINSON, DAVID (JULIEN). Film Critic, *The Financial Times.* Author of *Buster Keaton; Hollywood in the Twenties; The Great Funnies—A History of Screen Comedy.*
Biography (*in part*); Motion Pictures (*in part*)

ROSE, JOHN KERR. Senior Specialist in Natural Resources and Conservation, Congressional Research Service, Library of Congress, Washington, D.C.
Agriculture (*in part*)

ROWE, P(HILIP) M(ORTON). Press Officer, British Man-Made Fibres Federation, Manchester.
Industrial Review (*in part*)

RYBCZYNSKI, T(ADEUSZ) M(IECZYSLAW). Economist, Lazard Brothers, London.
Savings and Investment

SALTONSTALL, RICHARD, JR. Author of *Your Environment and What You Can Do About It.* Co-author of *Brown Out and Slow Down.*
Environment (*in part*)

SANDELIN, CARL FREDRIK. Editor in Chief, Finnish News Agency. President, Society of Swedish-Speaking Writers in Finland.
Biography (*in part*); Finland

SANDON, HAROLD. Former Professor of Zoology, University of Khartoum, Sudan. Author of *The Protozoan Fauna of the Soil; The Food of Protozoa; An Illustrated Guide to the Fresh-Water Fishes of the Sudan; Essays on Protozoology.*
Life Sciences (*in part*)

SARAHETE, YRJÖ. Secretary, Fédération Internationale des Quilleurs, Helsinki, Fin.
Bowling and Lawn Bowls (*in part*)

SCHATTMANN, S(TEPHAN) E. Economist, London.
Germany (*in part*)

SCHELLHARDT, TIMOTHY D(ALE). Reporter, the *Wall Street Journal,* Washington, D.C.
Postal Services (*in part*)

SCHMITT, TILMAN. Brewery Engineer. Editor of *Brauwelt; Brauwissenschaft.*
Alcoholic Beverages (*in part*)

SCHOENFIELD, ALBERT. Editor, *Swimming World.*
Swimming

SCHULIAN, JOHN. Reporter, the *Baltimore Evening Sun.*
Basketball (*in part*); Football (*in part*)

SERGEANT, HOWARD. Lecturer and Writer. Editor of *Outposts,* Walton-on Thames, Eng. Author of *The Cumberland Wordsworth; Tradition in the Making of Modern Poetry.*
Literature (*in part*)

SHACKLEFORD, PETER. Research Officer, International Union of Official Travel Organisations (IUOTO), Geneva.
Tourism

SHARPE, MITCHELL R. Science Writer. Author of *Living in Space: The Environment of the Astronaut; Yuri Gagarin, First Man in Space; Satellites and Probes: The Development of Unmanned Space Flight.* Co-author of *Applied Astronautics; Basic Astronautics; Dividends from Space.*
Astronautics

SHAW, T(REVOR) R(OYLE). Commander, Royal Navy. Vice-President, British Speleological Association.
Speleology

SHERMAN, HARVEY R. Environmental Policy Division, Congressional Research Service, Library of Congress.
Agriculture (*in part*); Food (*in part*)

SHIH, CONSTANT CHUNG-TSE. Counsellor, Trade Policy Department, General Agreement on Tariffs and Trade (GATT), Switzerland.
Commercial Policies

SHINODA, HAJIME. Assistant Professor, Tokyo Metropolitan University.
Literature (*in part*)

SILVA, MICHEL. Editor in chief, *Britannica Book of the Year; Britannica Yearbook of Science and the Future; Britannica Roundtable.*
Publishing (*in part*)

SIMPSON, NOEL. Managing Director, Sydney Bloodstock Proprietary Ltd., Sydney, Austr.
Horse Racing (*in part*)

SKELDING, FRANK H. Director, Corporate Planning, Fluor Utah, Inc.
Fuel and Power (*in part*); Mining (*in part*); United States Statistical Supplement: *Principal Minerals table; Mineral Fuels and Electricity Production table.*

SMEDLEY, GLENN B. Governor, American Numismatic Association.
Philately and Numismatics (*in part*)

SMITH, DAN THROOP. Senior Research Fellow, Hoover Institution, Stanford (Calif.) University; Director, Cambridge Research Institute; Former Deputy to Secretary of the Treasury. Author of *Federal Tax Reform; Tax Factors in Business Decisions.*
Taxation (*in part*)

SMITH, DAVID L(AWRENCE). Staff member, Centre for Environmental Studies, London.
Environment (*in part*)

SMITH, M. BERNARD. Free-lance Writer and Reporter.
Fuel and Power (*in part*); Merchandising (*in part*); Publishing (*in part*)

SMITH, R(EUBEN) W(ILLIAM). Assistant Professor of Islamic History, the University of Chicago.
Religion (*in part*)

SMITHCORS, J. F(REDERICK). Editor, American Veterinary Publications, Inc., Santa Barbara, Calif. Author of *Evolution of the Veterinary Art; The American Veterinary Profession.*
Veterinary Medicine

SMOGORZEWSKI, K(AZIMIERZ) M(ACIEJ). Writer on contemporary history. Founder and Editor, *Free Europe,* London. Author of *The United States and Great Britain; Poland's Access to the Sea.*
Albania; Biography (*in part*); Bulgaria; Hungary; Intelligence Operations; Mongolia; Poland; Political Parties; Romania; Soviet Bloc Economies

SOKOLSKY, WALLACE. Associate Professor, History Department, Bronx Community College, the New School for Social Research, New York University, Division of Adult Education. Co-author of *Contemporary Civilization; African Nationalism in the Twentieth Century.*
Africa

SOUSTER, TIM. Music Critic.
Biography (*in part*)

SPENCE, M. J. Economic Research Officer, Lloyds and Bolsa International Bank Ltd., London.
Paraguay; Uruguay

STAERK, MELANIE F. Editor, *UNESCO Press,* Swiss National Commission for UNESCO.
Switzerland

STARKMAN, MOSHE. Essayist in Yiddish and Hebrew; Bibliographer. President, Yiddish P.E.N. Club; New York Editor, *Hemshekh Anthology of American Yiddish Poetry.* Associate Editor, *Lexicon of Yiddish Literature.*
Literature (*in part*)

STEBBINGS, PERCY. Insurance Correspondent of *Investors' Chronicle; Post Magazine,* London.
Insurance (*in part*)

STENT, ROBERT (EDWARD). Economic and Political Research Officer, Lloyds and Bolsa International Bank Ltd., London.
Costa Rica; Guatemala; Venezuela

STEVENSON, TOM. Garden Columnist, *Baltimore News American; Washington Post;* Washington Post-Los Angeles Times News Service. Author of *Pruning Guide for Trees, Shrubs and Vines; Lawn Guide; Gardening for the Beginner.*
Gardening (*in part*)

STOKES, J. BUROUGHS. Manager, Committees on Publication, the First Church of Christ, Scientist, Boston.
Religion (*in part*)

STOLER, PETER. Medical Editor, *Time* magazine, New York.
Medicine (*in part*)

STØVERUD, TORBJØRN. W. P. Ker Senior Lecturer in Norwegian, University College, London.
Literature (*in part*)

SWEETINBURGH, THELMA. Paris Fashion Correspondent for *International Textiles* (Amsterdam) and the British Wool Textile Industry.
Fashion and Dress (*in part*)

SWIFT, RICHARD N. Professor of Politics, New York University, New York City. Author of *International Law: Current and Classic.*
United Nations (*in part*)

SYNAN, (HAROLD) VINSON. Division Chairman, Emmanuel College; Pastor, Hartwell Pentecostal Holiness Church, Georgia. Author of *Emmanuel College—The First Fifty Years; The Holiness-Pentecostal Movement.*
Religion (*in part*)

SZPAKOWSKI, ANDREW. Head, Section of Standards, Research and Museums, UNESCO, Paris.
Museums and Galleries (*in part*)

TAISHOFF, SOL. Chairman and Editor, *Broadcasting,* Washington, D.C.
Television and Radio (*in part*)

TATTERSALL, ARTHUR. Textile Trade Expert and Statistician, Manchester, Eng.
Industrial Review (*in part*)

TAYLOR, WINSTON H(OWARTH). Director, Washington Office, Commission on Public Relations and United Methodist Information. Author of *Angels Don't Need Public Relations; Ending Racial Segregation in the Methodist Church; Toward an Inclusive Church.*
Religion (*in part*)

TERRY, WALTER. Dance Critic, *Saturday Review.* Author of *The Dance in America; The Ballet Companion; Miss Ruth: The "More Living Life" of Ruth St. Denis.*
Dance (*in part*)

THERIO, ADRIEN. Professor of Lettres Françaises, University of Ottawa. Author of *L'Humour au Canada français; Soliloque en hommage à une femme.*
Literature (*in part*)

THOMAS, (WILLIAM) HARFORD. City Editor, the *Guardian,* London and Manchester.
Biography (*in part*); Publishing (*in part*); United Kingdom

THOMPSON, ANTHONY. General Secretary, International Federation of Library Associations, 1962–70. Author of *Vocabularium Bibliothecarii; Library Buildings of Britain and Europe.*
Libraries

THOMSON, R(ONALD) W(ILLIAM). Former Assistant General Secretary, Baptist Union of Great Britain and Ireland. Author of *Heroes of the Baptist Church; William Carey; The Service of Our Lives; A Pocket History of the Baptists.*
Religion (*in part*)

TINGAY, LANCE (LANCELOT OLIVER). Lawn Tennis Correspondent, the *Daily Telegraph,* London
Tennis

TREWHITT, HENRY L(ANE). Chief Diplomatic Correspondent, *Newsweek* magazine. Author of *McNamara: His Ordeal in the Pentagon.*
Propaganda

TRIGG, ROBERT H. Manager, Institutional Research, New York Stock Exchange.
Stock Exchanges (*in part*)

TRILLING, OSSIA. Vice-President, International Association of Theatre Critics. Co-editor and contributor, *International Theatre.* Contributor, *The Times,* London.
Theatre (*in part*)

TUCKER, PAT. Free-lance Journalist.
Biography (*in part*)

TYPE, MICHAEL. Assistant Editor, European Broadcasting Union, Geneva.
Television and Radio (*in part*)

UNHCR. The Office of the United Nations High Commissioner for Refugees, Geneva.
Refugees

UNNY, GOVINDAN. Agence France-Presse Special Correspondent for India, Nepal, and Ceylon.
Bangladesh; Biography (*in part*); Burma; Dependent States (*in part*); Nepal.

URQUHART, NORMAN R(ICHARD). Assistant Vice-President, in charge of Commodity Section, Economics Department, First National City Bank, New York City.
Commodities, Primary

VIANSSON-PONTÉ, PIERRE. Assistant Executive Editor and Senior Editorial Writer, *Le Monde,* Paris. Author of *Les Gaullistes; The King and His Court; Les Politiques; Histoire de la République Gaullienne.*
Biography (*in part*)

WADLEY, J(OHN) B(ORLAND). Writer and Broadcaster on cycling. Author of *Tour de France 1970 and 1971.*
Cycling

WALKER, V(ALERIE) (LANGHAM). Production Editor, *Encyclopædia Britannica;* Free-lance Writer.
United States Statistical Supplement: *Electoral Votes table*

WARD-THOMAS, P(ERCY) A(INSWORTH). Golf Correspondent, the *Guardian,* London.
Golf

WEBB, W(ILLIAM) L(ESLIE). Literary Editor, the *Guardian,* London and Manchester.
Literature (*in part*)

WEBER, GEORGE. Editor in chief, *The Oil and Gas Journal.*
Industrial Review (*in part*)

WEEDEN, CYRIL. Assistant Director, Glass Manufacturers' Federation, London.
Industrial Review (*in part*)

WILE, JULIUS. Senior Vice-President, Julius Wile Sons & Co., Inc., New York City. Vice-President, New England Distillers, Inc., Teterboro, N.J. Chairman, Table Wine Committee, National Association of Alcoholic Beverage Importers, Inc. Lecturer on wines, School of Hotel Administration, Cornell University.
Alcoholic Beverages (*in part*)

WILLIAMS, DAVID L(OUIS). Assistant Professor of Government, Ohio University.
Communist Movement

WILLIAMS, L(AURENCE) F(REDERIC) RUSHBROOK. Fellow of All Souls College, Oxford University, 1914–21; Professor of Modern Indian History, Allahabad, India, 1914–19. Author of *India Under the Company and the Crown; The State of Pakistan; What About India?; Kutch in History and Legend.* Editor of *Handbook to India, Pakistan, Burma, and Ceylon.*
Afghanistan; Iran; Pakistan

WILLIAMS, PETER. Editor, *Dance and Dancers.*
Dance (*in part*)

WILLIAMSON, TREVOR. Sports subeditor, the *Daily Telegraph,* London.
Biography (*in part*); Football (*in part*)

WILLOUGHBY, JEREMY. Economic Research Officer, Lloyds and Bolsa International Bank Ltd., London.
Bolivia; Inter-American Affairs; Peru

WILSON, ALAN (DAVID). Assistant Editor, *Sweden Now.*
Sweden

WOOD, KENNETH H. Editor, *The Advent Review and Sabbath Herald.* Author of *Meditations for Moderns; Relevant Religions.* Co-author of *His Initials Were F. D. N.*
Religion (*in part*)

WOODCOCK, C(HRISTOPHER) L(EONARD) F(RANK). Lecturer on Biology and Associate in Electron Microscopy, Department of Biology, Harvard University.
Life Sciences (*in part*)

WOODWARD, THE REV. MAX W. British Secretary, World Methodist Council.
Religion (*in part*)

WOOLLEY, DAVID (HUMPHREY). Air Transport Editor, *Flight International,* London.
Transportation (*in part*)

WORSNOP, RICHARD L. Writer, Editorial Research Reports, Washington, D.C.
Biography (*in part*); Liberia; United States

WRIGHT, ALMON R(OBERT). Retired Senior Historian, U.S. Department of State.
Panama

YOLLES, STANLEY F., M.D. Professor and Chairman, Department of Psychiatry, School of Medicine, Health Sciences Center, State University of New York at Stony Brook.
Drugs and Narcotics (*in part*)

YOPES, P(AUL) F(REDERICK). Mining Engineer, Bureau of Mines, U.S. Department of the Interior, Washington, D.C.
Mining (*in part*)

YOUNG, J(OHN) C(OLIN). Lecturer in Chemistry, University College of Wales.
Chemistry (*in part*)

YOUNG, M. NORVEL. Chancellor, Pepperdine University, Los Angeles. Editor of *Twentieth Century Christian; Power for Today.* Author of *Churches of Today.*
Religion (*in part*)

ZURCHER, ARNOLD J. Professor of Comparative Politics, Graduate School of Arts and Sciences, New York University.
European Unity

Index

The black type entries are article headings in the *Book of the Year*. These black type article entries do not show page notations because they are to be found in their alphabetical position in the body of the book. They show the dates of the issues of the *Book of the Year* in which the articles appear. For example "Agriculture 73, 72, 71" indicates that the article "Agriculture" is to be found in the 1973, 1972 and 1971 *Book of the Year*.

The light type headings that are indented under black type article headings refer to material elsewhere in the text related to the subject under which they are listed. The light type headings that are not indented refer to information in the text not given a special article. Biographies and obituaries are listed as cross references to the articles "*Biography*" and "*Obituaries*" for the year in which they appear. References to illustrations are preceded by the abbreviation "il."

All headings, whether consisting of a single word or more, are treated for the purpose of alphabetization as single complete headings. Names beginning with "Mc" and "Mac" are alphabetized as "Mac"; "St." is treated as "Saint." All references below show the exact quarter of the page by means of the letters *a, b, c* and *d*, signifying, respectively, the upper and lower halves of the first column and the upper and lower halves of the second column. Exceptions to this rule are tables, illustrations, and references from biographies and the articles "*Fuel and Power*," "*Industrial Review*," and the *States Statistical Supplement*.

A

C

D

H

I

L

M

N

S

U

V

Printed in U.S.A. by R. R. Donnelley & Sons Company